The Descendants of Robert Russell and Mary Marshall of Andover Through Six Generations

Including Male and Female Lines of Descent from Generation One to Generation Six

Compiled by:
Patricia A. Abbott

ISBN-13: 978-1-7351258-1-7 (Patricia A. Abbott)

Dedication: For my millions of Russell cousins everywhere

Introduction

This compilation is an attempt to provide as complete information as possible of the descendants of Robert Russell and Mary Marshall including complete families through five generations and all the children that comprise the sixth generation. This includes coverage of more than 1,000 complete families. Both the male and female lines are included so there are many Holts, Farnums, Abbotts, Ingalls, Osgoods, Johnsons, and many more names.

Within these pages you will find the full range of human behavior: individuals with great accomplishments, those with humble, ordinary lives, and those who faced incredible hardship and tragedy. There are personal struggles including poverty and reliance on almshouses for subsistence, out-of-wedlock children, and persons who wrestled with alcoholism, depression, and other mental illness. There are also Harvard graduates, attorneys, physicians, and clergymen. There are women pioneers persevering in the face of tremendous challenges. There are the first settlers of many communities in Massachusetts, Connecticut, New Hampshire, Maine, Vermont, Pennsylvania, and upstate New York. Moving into the fifth generation who will find more descendants who made their way to Canada and into Ohio and Michigan and the southern states. By the sixth generation, descendants can be found in most of the continental United States.

Although this is a genealogical compilation, I hope that the presentation of the individual families will allow at least some sense of the humanity of these individuals and their contributions to the founding and development of the country.

Why this book?

This is one of the first attempts at a comprehensive compilation of the descendants of Robert Russell and Mary Marshall. George Ely Russell prepared a typed manuscript providing brief coverage of individuals with the name of Russell in 17th century New England. In 1981, Marjorie Russell prepared a volume "Russell Roots and Branches" which focuses on a sixth-generation descendant of Robert Russell, Ira Otis Russell born in 1804. I have been unable to locate this volume which is not in print for purchase and seems to have limited availability in libraries. There is a compilation prepared by John Russell Bartlett of the descendants of John Russell of Woburn, this volume privately printed in 1879. It just seemed it might be time to attempt a consideration of the descendants of Robert Russell and Mary Marshall.

I aimed to verify each piece of information with documents (birth, death, and marriage records; wills and probate records; and land transactions) to the degree that these could be accessed online. Admittedly this is a quite limited record access, but even within these limits, a large amount of information was able to be verified. Vital records present their own problems as what are mostly available are transcriptions of records, not original records. There are doubtless errors that crept into the transcriptions. Undoubtedly, I also made errors entering my data from the transcriptions. There are inconsistencies in records. For example, there are birth records for a single family in which one child is listed as born in April and a second child is recorded as being born in October of the same year. Often, birth records were recorded in more than one location (for example, when a family had their family information recorded in the town records after moving to the town), so it is not possible to *really* know where the person was born unless it can be certainly established where the family was living at the time of the birth. But within the limits of available records, I have done my best to be accurate.

Of course, there are not available records for all events (certainly not yet online), or even any records for some persons. For that, I have relied on previously published and unpublished genealogical material and town and county histories. You will find a complete list of references at the end of the book. Sources are also noted in footnotes. Even in those cases in which previously published work was used, I attempted to verify the information contained in those sources. In several cases, there was information that conflicted with available vital records, wills, or land records and I have noted those discrepancies and how they were resolved.

A note about the spelling of names

There tend not to be many variations of spelling for Russell, although some records may use Russel, but I have chosen to use Russell uniformly. There are other surnames that are less consistent such as Abbot/Abbott, Farnham/Farnum, Goodale/Goodell, Coburn/Colburn, Payn/Paine, and several others that are prominent in this book. Variations of spelling occur among different documents for the same person, and often these variations occur on the same page of a document. As far as possible, I have tried to use the variation used by that family if ii

one spelling was used consistently, but I am sure I have missed some of those. If you are a Farnham rather than a Farnum, and I spelled the name of your ancestor not the way you would spell it, I can only apologize.

How the book is organized

The book is divided into chapters based on generations. When an individual is first introduced, if that person married and had children, you will see a number at the start of the entry that will allow you to know where to look for the next generation for that person. For example, you will see this type of entry when a person is first introduced:

2)   i   MARY RUSSELL, b. at Andover, 14 Jan 1661; d. at Andover, 1 Apr 1717; m. 8 Jan 1679/80, NICHOLAS HOLT, b. at Andover, 1645 son of Nicholas and Elizabeth (Short) Holt; Nicholas d. at Andover, 8 Oct 1715.

The "2)" indicates that you will find follow-up information later in the book. (The "i" indicates that this is the first child in that family.) Of course, there are complications. There are many instances in which descendants of the immigrant Robert Russell married each other. In those cases, I have cross-referenced the information, so you hopefully will be able to find what you are looking for from either side of the couple.

The book is organized by generations. All the second generation, followed by all the third generation, then all the fourth, and then all the fifth. There are some complications with this, for example when a descendant from the second generation married a descendant from the third generation. In those cases, that couple and their children are included in the generation that appears first.

When moving down the generations, you will find in parentheses the track back to Robert Russell. For example, Daniel Holt son of Nicholas and Dorcas (Abbott) Holt married Hannah Holt daughter of Thomas and Hannah (Kimball) Holt. Both Daniel and Hannah were descendants of Robert Russell. When the family is introduced, you will see this.

66)   DANIEL HOLT (*Nicholas Holt³, Mary Russell Holt², Robert¹*), b. at Andover, 10 Feb 1732/3 son of Nicholas and Dorcas (Abbott) Holt; d. at Andover, 15 Feb 1796; m. 29 Nov 1759, his first cousin once removed, HANNAH HOLT, (*Thomas Holt⁴, Thomas Holt³, Mary Russell Holt², Robert¹*), b. 11 Feb 1738/9 daughter of Thomas and Hannah (Kimball) Holt; Hannah d. at Andover, 2 Aug 1831.

When just the first name is given within the parentheses, the last name is Russell. For many individuals, there are several paths of descent from Robert Russell, in some cases as many as five paths. For simplicity, just one path is listed.

Table of Contents

Introduction 1
Generation One.. 1
Generation Two.. 3
Generation Three 11
    Children of Mary Russell and Nicholas Holt...11
    Children of Thomas Russell and Phebe Johnson 16
    Children of James Russell and Priscilla Osgood.. 22
    Children of Sarah Russell and John Ingalls... 24
    Children of Benjamin Russell and Mary Preston 28
    Children of Hannah Russell and Oliver Holt 32
    Children of John Russell and Sarah Chandler 34
    Children of Elizabeth Russell and Moses Holt 38

Generation Four...41
    Grandchildren of Mary Russell and Nicholas Holt 41
    Grandchildren of Thomas Russell and Phebe Johnson 67
    Grandchildren of James Russell and Priscilla Osgood 94
    Grandchildren of Sarah Russell and John Ingalls.. 104
    Grandchildren of Benjamin Russell and Sarah Preston 119
    Grandchildren of Hannah Russell and Oliver Holt 137
    Grandchildren of John Russell and Sarah Chandler 145
    A Few Great-Grandchildren of Thomas Russell 160

Generation Five 163
    Great-Grandchildren of Mary Russell and Nicholas Holt 163
    Great-Grandchildren of Thomas Russell and Phebe Johnson 265
    Great-Grandchildren of James Russell and Priscilla Osgood 372
    Great-Grandchildren of Sarah Russell and John Ingalls 411
    Great-Grandchildren of Benjamin Russell and Sarah Preston...................... 468
    Great-Grandchildren of Hannah Russell and Oliver Holt 546
    Great-Grandchildren of John Russell and Sarah Chandler 571
    A Few Great-Great Grandchildren of Thomas Russell................................... 634

Master List of Families.. 639
References 659
Name Index 679

The Descendants of Robert Russell and Mary Marshall of Andover Through Six Generations

Introduction

Robert Russell of Andover represents one of several Russell lines that immigrated to New England in the early to mid-1600's. John Russell from Ipswich in England arrived in Cambridge on the *Defence* on 3 October 1635 and remained in Cambridge until 1648 or 1649. He then accompanied his son Rev. John Russell to Wethersfield, Connecticut when Rev. Russell was named first pastor there.[1] Another John Russell was a first settler of the new settlement at Woburn in 1640.[2] A third John Russell was John Russell of Dartmouth who was in Marshfield as early as 1642 or 1643 and later settled in Dartmouth.[3] Ralph Russell was early in Taunton associated with the iron works there in the early 1640's.[4] Early New Haven, Connecticut was home to the families of James Russell and William Russell.[5] George Russell was an early inhabitant of Hingham, although there is no clear information on children of George Russell.[6] Other Russell families can be found in records of Barnstable, Hampden, and Lexington. Henry Russell of Weymouth in his 1639 will provided for his wife left his estate to daughter Elizabeth Russell.[7]

Robert Russell and Mary Marshall settled in Andover, but Robert was not one of the first arriving settlers. The first European settlers arrived about 1636 when the area was known as Cochichewick. It was incorporated as Andover in 1646. Andover was one of the first inland settlements of New England. To induce new settlers to come inland from the coast, they were offered three years exemption from taxes and levies. John Woodbridge led a group of settlers from Ipswich and Newbury, a group that included Holt, Osgood, Stevens, Abbott, Parker, Chandler, Barnard, Bradstreet, and other names associated with early Andover.[8]

Generation One

1)   ROBERT RUSSELL, b. in Scotland, about 1630; d. at Andover, 13 Dec 1710;[9] m. at Andover, 6 Jul 1659, MARY MARSHALL, b. at Reading, about 1642 daughter of Thomas and Joanna (-) Marshall; Mary d. at Andover, 14 Jan 1715/6.[10]

By tradition, Robert Russell was native of Scotland born about 1630 and arrived in New England by 1659 when his marriage to Mary Marshall was recorded at Andover.[11] Robert Russell appears on an early military list from about 1659 when the town militia selected John Osgood as sergeant.[12]

Mary Marshall was the eldest daughter of Thomas and Joanna Marshall. Thomas Marshall was a carpenter and resided in Reading, Ipswich, and Andover. It is not known with certainty when the Marshall family arrived from England but was by the mid-1630's.[13] On 31 May 1704, Thomas and Joanna Marshal made their last known land transaction when Thomas and wife Joannah, formerly of Ipswich but now of Andover, conveyed a property in Ipswich to Abiel Marshall for the purpose of settling a property dispute (Abiel Marshall was a grandson of Thomas and Joanna). The transaction was witnessed by Robert Russell, Mary Russell, and James Russell.[14] It seems likely that in their advanced years Thomas and Joanna Marshall were living with their daughter Mary and her family. Thomas and wife Joanna each lived to nearly age 100 years.[15]

---

[1] Russell, *An Account of Some of the Descendants of John Russell, the Emigrant from Ipswich, England*, pp 109-110

[2] Bartlett, *Genealogy of that Branch of the Russell Family which Comprised the Descendants of John Russell, of Woburn*, p 9

[3] Russell, Barret Beard, "The Descendants of John Russell of Dartmouth, Mass.", NEHGR, Oct 1904, vol 58, p 364ff

[4] Hall, J.W.D., *Ancient Iron Works in Taunton*, NEHGR, 1884, vol 38, p 295

[5] Jacobus, *Families of Ancient New Haven*, volume vii, p 1572

[6] Anderson, The Great Migration, volume vi, George Russell, pp 125-133

[7] Massachusetts Wills and Probate, Suffolk County, volume 1, pp 23-24

[8] North Andover Historical Society, Founding Families; https://www.northandoverhistoricalsociety.org/new-page-3. Town of Andover, Andover History; https://andoverma.gov/386/Andover-History

[9] Rob[er]t, Dec. 13, 1710, a. abt. 80y.; Massachusetts: Vital Records, 1620-1850 (Online Database: *AmericanAncestors.org*, New England Historic Genealogical Society, 2001-2016).

[10] Mary, wid. Rob[er]t, Jan. 14, 1715-16, a. abt. 74 y.

[11] Cutter, *Genealogical and Personal Memoirs Relating to the Families of the State of Massachusetts*, volume 4, p 2180

[12] Bailey, *Historical Sketches of Andover*, p 167

[13] Lindberg, "3 Thomas Marshalls", Essex Genealogist, volume 16, 1996, p 158; Anderson, *The Great Migration*, entries for Thomas Marshall

[14] Massachusetts Land Records, Essex County, 15:230

[15] Thomas, Jan. 15, 1708-9, a. near 100 y; Joannah, wid. Thomas, May 16, 1708, a. abt. 100 y.

On 13 April 1691, Robberd Russell was made freeman in Andover.[16] He received a 4-acre house-lot in the town of Andover prior to 1662.[17] On 6 January 1676/7 (recorded 8 August 1716), Robert and wife Mary sold their 4-acre house lot and dwelling house, ten acres of upland, and six acres of meadow to Samuel Martin for £57 and other and diverse good causes.[18]

The main Russell property was south of the Shawsheen River and adjoined the property of Nicholas Holt and family. On 30 April 1684, Robert Russell acquired from Daniel Chace of Newbury 20 acres of upland lying between Robert's current holdings and the land of Samuel and Henry Holt which was part of the great division of Nicholas Holt.[19] The Russell landholdings were known as "Scotland Yard" or the "Scotland District."[20] The Russell homestead was at Rocky Hill and continuing to the east, an area that underwent development in 1984.[21]

Mary *Marshall* Russell was one of the 35 founding members of South parish church in Andover which was legally organized on 17 October 1711.[22] Robert was the first person buried in the South parish burial ground. His burial occurred three days after Rev. Samuel Phillips was called as the first pastor of South parish in December 1710.[23]

Robert Russell wrote his will on 25 August 1707. "I Robert Russell of Andover in the County of Essex in New England through the goodness of God of sound mind and memory, yet through age and infirmityes of body being put in mind of my mortality, have thought meet to make this my last will and testament. I committ my soul into the hands of God and my body to a decent burial. And for the (unreadable) my outward estate which god hath given (unreadable) my will is as follows viz.

1. I give to my dear and loving wife fourty shillings in money yearly & all my household goods during her life, also I give her two cows, and six sheep. Also I give her twelve barrels of corn, the one half in English and the other half in Indian corn, and a good hog, and two barrels of cider, and two bushels of malt all this to be payd her yearly by my two sons James and John or their heirs. Also I give her use of the east room of my house, and the use of a horse when she hath occasion. My will is that the forementioned money and provisions shall be payd to my wife yearly only during her widowhood.

2. I give to my son Thomas thirty acres of plowing and mowing ground adjoyning to my homestead as it is now bounded. And a piece of meadow that he has improved many years according as is already bounded.

3. I give to my son Benjamin the land both upland swampland and meadows which he hath for some years improved according as it hath been formerly bounded.

4. I give to my son James the one half of my homestead both orchards, plowing ground and meadows, except what I have given to my sons Thomas and Benjamin aforesaid. Also I give him a piece of meadow which I bought of Samuel Holt commonly called Bald hill meadow and my will is that when my homestead meadow is equally divided that my son James shall have his choice. (There is here an unreadable section due to damage related to the dwelling house except what is given to his wife and his daughters.) My will is that my son James shall pay to his mother yearly the one half of what I have given her in my will and shall winter a cow and six sheep for his mother.

5. I give to my son John half my homestead both orchards, plowing and mowing ground and half my meadows except what I have given to my other sons and half my stock except what I have otherwise disposed of. And my will is that my son John shall pay to his mother yearly one half of what I have given her by my will, and to winter a cow for her.

6. I give to my daughters Mary, Sarah and Hannah each of them a cow (unreadable) formerly given them according to my (unreadable).

7. I give to my daughter Elizabeth twenty pounds to be payd her out of my household goods after her mother's decease.

8. I give to my grandson Robert Holt a Pair of steers of four years old or two cows which he shall choose, provided he shall live with one of my sons James or John till he is of the age twenty one years, and if he so shall do, my will is that my son that he shall live with shall teach him a trade.

I constitute my son James to be the sole executor of this my last will and testament. And I do hereby revoke and dissannull all and every other former testaments wills by me made ratifying and confirming this to be my last will and testament, In witness whereof I have here unto set my hand and seal this twenty fifth day of August Anno Domini one thousand seven hundred and seven. Robert Russell his mark R." The will was witnessed by John Abbott, John Chandler, and George Abbott.

The will was proved 1 January 1710/11. On 24 January 1715/6, daughter Elizabeth Russell signed that she had received from her brother James her full settlement from the estate. This acknowledgement was one week before her marriage to Moses Holt.[24]

On 4 February 1716/7 (recorded 12 March 1722/3), son-in-law John Ingalls conveyed to Henry Ingalls two parcels, one of which included property that had belonged to Robert Russell and was conveyed in his wife's right through her inheritance (his wife being Sarah).[25] On 11 July 1747 (recorded 30 October 1765), son John Russell of Andover conveyed property that he

---

[16] "List of Freemen", NEHGR, volume 3, 1849, p 351

[17] Greven, *Four Generations*, p 46

[18] Massachusetts Land Records, Essex County, 30:139

[19] Massachusetts Land Records, Essex County, 6:129

[20] Bailey, *Historical Sketches of Andover*, p 119. The reference to the Scotland District in Andover derives from the early property holdings of Robert Russell and the designation of the Scotland district continues. Just one example of this was the Scotland School which served the South parish of Andover until it was lost to fire in 1902; https://preservation.mhl.org/348-south-main-street

[21] Andover Historic Preservation, "28 Rocky Hill Road", https://preservation.mhl.org/28-rocky-hill-rd. The location is now site of a seven-bedroom, million-dollar plus home.

[22] "The Founding of the South Parish of Andover", http://www.southchurch.com/images/EarlySCHistory.pdf

[23] South Church of Andover, *Historical Manual of the South Church in Andover*, p 58

[24] *Essex County, MA: Probate File Papers, 1638-1881*. Online database. *AmericanAncestors.org*. New England Historic Genealogical Society, 2014. Case 24415

[25] Massachusetts Land Records, Essex County, 41:142

inherited from his father Robert Russell to his kinsmen (nephews, sons of his brother James) James Russell and Thomas Russell both of Andover. This property was the share of the inheritance due to John's brother James who died in 1717.[26]

Robert Russell and Mary Marshall were parents of ten children born at Andover.

2) i MARY RUSSELL, b. at Andover, 14 Jan 1661; d. at Andover, 1 Apr 1717; m. 8 Jan 1679/80, NICHOLAS HOLT, b. at Andover, 1645 son of Nicholas and Elizabeth (-) Holt; Nicholas d. at Andover, 8 Oct 1715.

3) ii THOMAS RUSSELL, b. at Andover, 16 Dec 1663; d. at Andover, 30 Aug 1731; m. about 1685, PHEBE JOHNSON, b. at Andover, 3 Jan 1664 daughter of Thomas and Mary (Holt) Johnson; Phebe d. at Andover, 4 Feb 1738.

4) iii JAMES RUSSELL, b. at Andover, 16 Sep 1667; d. at Andover, 7 Mar 1717; m. at Andover, 18 Dec 1707, PRISCILLA OSGOOD, b. at Andover, 1 Apr 1681 daughter of Christopher and Hannah (Barker) Osgood. Priscilla married second John Eaton on 31 Jan 1721/2.

   iv ROBERT RUSSELL, b. about 1669; d. 27 May 1689. "Robert, "att ye great Island" [soldier at Portsmouth. CTR], May 27, 1689."

4a) v JOSEPH RUSSELL, b. 1 Apr 1671; d. at Boston, 9 Nov 1702;[27] m. at Boston, 5 Jun 1693, SUSANNA CHEEVER, b. at Boston, 1660 daughter of Ezekiel and Ellen (Lathrop) Cheever; Susanna d. at Boston, 10 Nov 1744.

5) vi SARAH RUSSELL, b. at Andover, 1674; d. at Abington, CT, 25 May 1764; m. at Andover, 10 Jun 1696, JOHN INGALLS, b. at Andover, 21 May 1661 son of Henry and Mary (Osgood) Ingalls; John d. at Abington, 6 Jan 1743.

6) vii BENJAMIN RUSSELL, b. at Andover, 12 Jun 1677; d. at Eastford, CT, 5 Oct 1754; m. at Andover, 26 Mar 1702, MARY PRESTON, b. at Andover, 5 Jan 1678/9 daughter of Samuel and Susanna (Gutterson) Preston; Mary d. at Eastford, 18 Nov 1753.

7) viii HANNAH RUSSELL, b. at Andover, 28 Jun 1679; d. at Andover, 16 May 1715; m. at Andover, 9 Mar 1697/8, OLIVER HOLT, b. at Andover, 14 Jan 1671/2 son of Henry and Sarah (Ballard) Holt; Oliver d. at Andover, 24 Dec 1747. Oliver m. 2nd at Newbury, 10 Jul 1716, MARY HUSE, b. at Newbury, 23 Mar 1690/1 daughter of Thomas and Mary (Webster) Huse.

8) ix JOHN RUSSELL, b. at Andover, 14 Oct 1682; d. at Andover, 8 Feb 1778; m. at Andover, 20 Oct 1712, SARAH CHANDLER, b. at Andover, 10 Mar 1692/3 daughter of Joseph and Sarah (Abbott) Chandler.

9) x ELIZABETH RUSSELL, b. at Andover, 16 Jul 1687; d. at Andover, 3 Nov 1772; m. at Andover, 31 Jan 1715/6, MOSES HOLT, b. at Andover, 7 Jun 1686 son of John and Sarah (Geary) Holt; Moses d. at Andover, 7 Nov 1730. Elizabeth m. 2nd, 27 Jul 1745, CHARLES FURBUSH, b. 1709 son of Samuel and Abigail (Rice) Furbush;[28] Charles d. at Saratoga in 1756 during the French and Indian War. Charles was first married to Margaret Lovejoy.

Generation Two

2) MARY RUSSELL (*Robert¹*), b. at Andover, 14 Jan 1661 daughter of Robert and Mary (Marshall) Russell; d. at Andover, 1 Apr 1717; m. 8 Jan 1679/80, NICHOLAS HOLT, b. at Andover, 1645 son of Nicholas and Elizabeth (Short) Holt; Nicholas d. at Andover, 8 Oct 1715.

On 16 June 1682, Nicholas Holt received from his father Nicholas a deed in return for providing maintenance for his father and his wife Martha. Nicholas's deed included one third of the homestead farm, parcels of meadows, and the dwelling, well, and orchard.[29] Nicholas and Mary resided on this farm.

On 1 March 1710/11, Nicholas Holt, signed also by Mary his wife, transferred property in Andover for love and affection to his sons Nicholas Holt and Thomas Holt, this land generally to be equally divided although Nicholas was to receive three more acres than Thomas. It was noted that sons Nicholas and Thomas had obliged themselves to do several things for their father. The property granted to the sons included the property where father Nicholas then resided. In a deed recorded 15 June 1715, Nicholas conveyed to his two eldest sons Nicholas and Thomas his rights to all the common land in Andover.[30]

---

[26] Massachusetts Land Records, Essex County, 124:49

[27] Russell, Joseph of Andover; s. Robert & Mary; Boston City Hall Archives, Index to Deaths 1700-1799

[28] In 1761 as Elizabeth Furbush, Elizabeth filed a petition related to the administration of the estate of her grandson Phineas Holt.

[29] Anderson, *The Great Migration*, volume III, pp 398-399

[30] Massachusetts Land Records 1620-1986, Essex County, 23:88; 28:49

Nicholas Holt and Mary Russell were parents of eleven children born at Andover.

10)   i   MARY HOLT, b. at Andover, 13 Feb 1680/1; d. at Andover, 9 Feb 1714/5; m. at Andover, 19 Sep 1705, JOSIAH INGALLS, b. at Andover, 28 Feb 1676 son of Henry and Mary (Osgood) Ingalls. Josiah d. at Andover, 14 Aug 1755. After Mary's death, Josiah married Esther Frye.

11)   ii   NICHOLAS HOLT, b. at Andover, 21 Dec 1683; d. at Andover, 1 Dec 1756; m. 1st, 16 Sep 1708, MARY MANNING; Mary d. at Andover, 3 Mar 1715/6. Nicholas m. 2nd, 12 Apr 1717, DORCAS ABBOTT, b. at Andover, 25 Apr 1698 daughter of Timothy and Hannah (Graves) Abbott; Dorcas d. at Andover, 25 Oct 1758.

12)   iii   THOMAS HOLT, b. at Andover, 16 Aug 1686; d. at Andover, 12 Jan 1767; m. 1st, at Andover, 14 Dec 1708, ALICE PEABODY, b. at Andover, 5 Jan 1685 daughter of Joseph and Bethiah (Bridges) Peabody; Alice d. at Andover, 29 Jul 1726. Thomas m. 2nd, at Boxford, 16 Nov 1727, ABIGAIL POORE (widow of John Fiske), b. at Newbury, 9 Sep 1680 daughter of Henry and Abigail (Hale) Poore; Abigail d. at Andover, 20 Nov 1766.

13)   iv   ABIGAIL HOLT, b. at Andover, 23 Nov 1688; d. at Hampton, 12 Aug 1742; m. at Andover, 10 Jan 1711/2, her first cousin, PAUL HOLT, b. 7 Feb 1684 son of Henry and Sarah (Ballard) Holt; Paul d. at Hampton, 6 May 1742.

    v   SARAH HOLT, b. 10 Mar 1690/1; d. at Andover, 26 Oct 1761. Sarah did not marry.

    vi   JAMES HOLT, b. 23 Jul 1693; d. 12 Dec 1722.

14)   vii   ROBERT HOLT, b. at Andover, 23 Jan 1695/6; d. at Windham, CT, 1768 (probate 4 May 1768); m. 1st, 22 May 1718, REBECCA PRESTON (widow of her cousin Joseph Preston), b. at Andover, 23 Jan 1688/9 daughter of John and Sarah (Gear) Preston; Rebecca d. at Windham, 1 May 1727. Robert m. 2nd, 13 Dec 1727, BETHIAH PEABODY, b. at Boxford, 3 Apr 1681 daughter of Joseph and Bethiah (Bridges) Peabody; Bethiah d. 6 Feb 1742. Robert m. 3rd, at Hampton, 28 Mar 1743, HANNAH ADROSS who has not been identified; Hannah was living in 1767.

15)   viii   ABIEL HOLT, b. at Andover, 28 Jun 1698; d. at Willington, 10 Nov 1772; m. 1st, at Andover, 21 Feb 1721, HANNAH ABBOTT, b. at Andover, 5 Apr 1701 daughter of William and Elizabeth (Geary) Abbott; Hannah d. at Windham, 11 Feb 1751/2. Abiel m. 2nd, at Willington, 19 Dec 1752, SARAH DOWNER, b. about 1699; Sarah d. 15 Apr 1784.

16)   ix   DEBORAH HOLT, b. at Andover, 16 Nov 1700; d. at Willington, 26 Nov 1784; m. at Windham, 5 May 1727, BENJAMIN PRESTON, b. at Andover, 1705 son of Jacob and Sarah (Wilson) Preston; Benjamin d. at Willington, 26 Nov 1784.[31]

17)   x   JOSHUA HOLT, b. at Andover, 1703; d. at Hampton, 26 Jan 1787; m. at Windham, 16 Feb 1724/5, KETURAH HOLT, b. at Andover, 15 Dec 1690 daughter of Henry and Sarah (Ballard) Holt; Keturah d. at Hampton, 2 Oct 1781.

18)   xi   DANIEL HOLT, b. at Andover, 1705; d. at Pomfret, 5 Nov 1773; m. 1st, 31 Mar 1731, ABIGAIL SMITH, b. at Lebanon, CT, 22 Jun 1706 daughter of John and Abigail (-) Smith; Abigail d. at Pomfret, CT, 9 Feb 1752. Daniel m. 2nd, at Pomfret, Dec 1752, KEZIA STRONG (widow of Noah Rust), b. at Northampton, MA, 1 Dec 1709 daughter of Joseph and Sarah (Allen) Strong;[32] Kezia d. at Cherry Valley, NY, 1796.

3)   THOMAS RUSSELL (*Robert¹*), b. at Andover, 16 Dec 1663 son of Robert and Mary (Marshall) Russell; d. at Andover, 30 Aug 1731; m. about 1685, PHEBE JOHNSON, b. at Andover, 3 Jan 1664 daughter of Thomas and Mary (Holt) Johnson; Phebe d. at Andover, 4 Feb 1738.

Thomas was a farmer in Andover and married Phebe Johnson about 1685. Phebe was the daughter of Thomas Johnson who served as lieutenant in the militia. Thomas Johnson was a carpenter by trade and a prominent man in the community serving as constable and selectman.[33]

On 24 February 1726/7 (recorded 31 May 1727), Thomas Russell and his wife Phebe conveyed to their well-beloved son Joseph Russell several parcels of upland in Andover together with the homestead on which Thomas and Phebe then resided. Joseph receives all the movable estate, the stock animals, and money. Thomas and Phebe reserve for themselves use of one-half of the buildings, uplands, orchard, and stock animals during their natural lives.[34]

---

[31] The deaths of Deborah and Benjamin are recorded as occurring on the same day.
[32] Dwight, *History of the Descendants of Elder John Strong*, p 310
[33] Johnson, *Johnson Genealogy*, p 15
[34] Massachusetts Land Records, Essex County, 48:264

       i   THOMAS RUSSELL, b. at Andover, 13 Aug 1687. Nothing definitive is known of Thomas.

19)   ii   MEHITABLE RUSSELL, b. at Andover, about 1688; d. at Andover, 18 Dec 1733; m. at Andover, 10 Jun 1708, JOSEPH CHANDLER, b. at Andover, 17 Jul 1682 son of William and Bridget (Henchman) Chandler; Joseph d. at Andover, 22 Apr 1734.

20)   iii   ROBERT RUSSELL, b. at Andover, about 1690; d. at Reading, 1759 (probate 1759); m. 1st at Andover, 22 Jun 1716, ABIGAIL FLINT; Abigail d. at Andover, 10 May 1723. Robert m. 2nd at Andover, 2 Jan 1727/8, HANNAH HOLT, b. at Andover, 30 Nov 1702 daughter of Samuel and Hannah (Farnum) Holt; Hannah d. at Reading, 3 Apr 1749. Robert m. 3rd at Andover, 23 Dec 1749, widow ELIZABETH MANNING. Robert m. 4th at Andover, 17 Apr 1755, widow MARTHA PARKER.

21)   iv   PHEBE RUSSELL, b. at Andover, 21 Jan 1689/90; d. at Windham, CT, after 1753 (distribution of widow's dower to Phebe Farnum aka Robins 13 Apr 1753 from the estate of Henry Farnum); m. at Andover, 12 Jun 1712, HENRY FARNUM, b. at Andover, 15 Sep 1687 son of Ralph and Sarah (Sterling) Farnum; Henry d. at Windham, 23 Jul 1732. Phebe m. 2nd at Canterbury, 3 Jan 1734, NATHANIEL ROBBINS; Nathaniel d. at Windham, 7 Apr 1753.

22)   v   MARY RUSSELL, b. at Andover, 10 Feb 1692/3; d. at Andover, 1778 (probate 3 Feb 1778); m. at Andover, 10 May 1716, TIMOTHY OSGOOD, b. at Andover, 22 Aug 1693 son of Timothy and Deborah (Poor) Osgood; Timothy d. 1772 (probate 24 Nov 1772).

23)   vi   SARAH RUSSELL, b. at Andover, about 1695; m. at Andover, 9 Sep 1715, JOHN ROSS, b. at Billerica, 18 Jan 1686/7 son of Thomas and Seeth (Holman) Ross.

24)   vii   PETER RUSSELL, b. at Andover, 23 Apr 1700; d. at Litchfield, NH, Nov 1759 (will 3 Nov, proved 28 Nov 1759); m. 31 Mar 1727, DEBORAH CROSBY, b. at Billerica, 13 Jul 1709 daughter of Joseph and Sarah (French) Crosby.

25)   viii   JOSEPH RUSSELL, b. at Andover, Apr 1702; m. 1st at Reading, 26 Nov 1728, HEPSIBAH EATON; Hepsibah d. at Andover, 14 Mar 1742/3. Joseph m 2nd at Andover, 27 Nov 1746, HANNAH PERKINS, b. at Andover, 15 Nov 1720 daughter of Timothy and Hannah (Buxton) Perkins; Hannah d. at Andover, 22 Mar 1775.

26)   ix   JEMIMA RUSSELL, b. at Andover, 18 Jul 1704; d. at Littleton, MA, 20 Sep 1790; m. at Andover, 16 Jul 1724, JOSEPH HUNT, b. at Billerica, 21 Sep 1694 son of Samuel and Mary (-) Hunt; Joseph d. at Andover, 1743 (probate 7 Nov 1743). Jemima m. 2nd, 13 Dec 1743, CHRISTOPHER TEMPLE, b. 1690 and d. at Littleton, 8 May 1782.

27)   x   JAMES RUSSELL, b. at Andover, 15 Jun 1706; m. at Amesbury, 3 Jun 1729, RHODA CHANDLER, b. at Andover, 1705 daughter of Joseph and Sarah (Abbott) Chandler.

4)   JAMES RUSSELL (*Robert¹*), b. at Andover, 16 Sep 1667 son of Robert and Mary (Marshall) Russell; d. at Andover, 7 Mar 1717; m. at Andover, 18 Dec 1707, PRISCILLA OSGOOD, b. at Andover, 1 Apr 1681 daughter of Christopher and Hannah (Barker) Osgood. Priscilla married second John Eaton on 31 Jan 1721/2. Pricilla was living in 1734 when she conveyed property.

    James married Priscilla Osgood in 1707. Priscilla was the daughter of Capt. Christopher Osgood by his second wife Hannah Barker. Christopher Osgood was a millwright and built Frye's mills in Andover.[35]

    James Russell did not leave a will and his estate entered probate 13 May 1717 with widow Priscilla as administratrix. Real estate was valued at £80 and personal estate at £87.[36]

    On 8 March 1733/4 (recorded 29 September 1735), Priscilla Eaton of Andover, widow, "for diverse good causes and considerations but especially for love and affection that I bear towards my two sons James Russell and Thomas Russell both of Andover" conveyed to James and Thomas two parcels of land in Andover that Priscilla purchased of John Farnaum and James Farnaum.[37]

    James and Priscilla were parents of five children born at Andover.

28)   i   JAMES RUSSELL, b. at Andover, Apr 1710; d. at Walpole, NH, 8 Oct 1784; m. at Andover, 15 Jan 1740/1, LUCY FARRAR, b. at Woburn, 8 Oct 1714 daughter of Isaac and Mary (Wolcott) Farrar; Lucy d. at Walpole, 24 Apr 1791.

---

[35] Osgood, *A Genealogy of the Descendants of John, Christopher and William Osgood*, p 259

[36] *Essex County, MA: Probate File Papers, 1638-1881.* Online database. *AmericanAncestors.org.* New England Historic Genealogical Society, 2014. Case 24389

[37] Massachusetts Land Records, Essex County, 70:44

ii   PRISCILLA RUSSELL, b. at Andover, 19 Aug 1712; d. at Reading, about 1732; m. at Andover, 6 Mar 1731, EDWARD HIRKCUM, b. about 1700; Edward d. at Wilmington, MA, 1781 (probate 1781). Priscilla and Edward did not have children. Edward was first married to Hannah Eaton on 21 Jul 1720 and third married to Prudence Wolcott on 6 Dec 1733.

iii   AQUILLA RUSSELL, b. 12 Sep 1712; d. 24 Dec 1718.

29)   iv   THOMAS RUSSELL, b. at Andover, 18 Jun 1714; d. at Andover, 23 Apr 1753; m. at Andover, 15 Apr 1742, ABIGAIL BALLARD, b. at Andover, 17 Aug 1718 daughter of Uriah and Elizabeth (Henshaw) Ballard; Abigail d. at Andover, 15 Jul 1802.

30)   v   MARY RUSSELL, baptized at Andover, 22 Apr 1716; d. at Haverhill, 9 Sep 1803; m. 15 Jun 1743, as his second wife, SAMUEL APPLETON, b. at Ipswich, 20 Mar 1713 son of Oliver and Sarah (-) Appleton; Samuel d. at Haverhill, 20 Oct 1780. Samuel was first married to Mary Stevens.

4a)   JOSEPH RUSSELL (*Robert¹*), b. at Andover, 1 Apr 1671 son of Robert and Mary (Marshall) Russell; d. at Boston, 9 Nov 1702;[38] m. at Boston, 5 Jun 1693, SUSANNA CHEEVER, b. at Boston, 1660 daughter of Ezekiel and Ellen (Lathrop) Cheever; Susanna d. at Boston, 10 Nov 1744.
Joseph Russell and Susanna Cheever were parents of three children born at Boston.

i   EZEKIEL RUSSELL, b. 6 May 1694; d. at Boston, 24 Oct 1708.

ii   JOSEPH RUSSELL, b. 24 Oct 1695; d. at Boston, 20 Sep 1767; m. 1st at Boston, 2 Oct 1718, ABIGAIL VEREIN, b. at Boston, 19 Feb 1697 daughter of Thomas and Hannah (Fitch) Verein; Abigail d. at Boston, 3 Aug 1743. Joseph m. 2nd at Boston, 29 Mar 1744, MARY TILESTON, b. at Dorchester, 9 Dec 1705 daughter of Thomas and Mary (Gardner) Tileston; Mary d. at Boston, 28 Jun 1748. Joseph m. 3rd at Boston, 15 Dec 1748, LYDIA GERRISH who was the widow at probate; Lydia d. at Boston, 1788. Joseph had a total of seven children two of whom were living at the time of his probate. Daughter Mary (likely a daughter with Mary Tileston) married her first cousin Jeremiah Russell (son of Benjamin just below). Son Joseph (likely a son with Lydia Gerrish) married but did not have children.

iii   BENJAMIN RUSSELL, b. 10 Mar 1698; d. at Boston, 29 Jul 1760; m. at Boston, 26 Oct 1727, ELIZABETH BELKNAP, b. at Boston, 17 Jan 1709 daughter of Joseph and Abigail Bultoph Belknap; Elizabeth d. at Boston, 19 Jan 1772. Benjamin and Elizabeth were parents of twelve children three of whom died in childhood. Son Joseph married Mary Willey; Jeremiah married his first cousin Mary Russell; Elizabeth married Joseph Callender, Ezekiel married Sarah Hood; and Nathaniel married Mary Hibbard and Almy Greene. Nathaniel was a Loyalist who migrated to Halifax, Nova Scotia in 1776.

5)   SARAH RUSSELL (*Robert¹*), b. at Andover, 1674 daughter of Robert and Mary (Marshall) Russell; d. at Abington, CT, 25 May 1764; m. at Andover, 10 Jun 1696, JOHN INGALLS, b. at Andover, 21 May 1661 son of Henry and Mary (Osgood) Ingalls; John d. at Abington, 6 Jan 1743.
Sarah and John had their nine children in Andover but were then part of the migration of families from Andover to Connecticut which began about 1720. On 17 March 1724 John Ingalls and his wife Sarah conveyed to the widow Abigail Ingalls a two-acre plot of land for payment of £20.[39]

31)   i   JOHN INGALLS, b. at Andover, 23 Mar 1696/7; d. at Abington, 2 Apr 1783; m. 1st, at Pomfret, 4 Jan 1735, MARY WILLIS who has not been identified. After Mary's death, John married SARAH who was his wife at the time he wrote his will.

ii   SARAH INGALLS, b. at Andover, 25 Nov 1698; d. at Andover, 1764 (probate 1764); m. at Andover, 3 Jun 1724, DANIEL OSGOOD, b. at Andover, 19 Jan 1693 son of John and Hannah (Ayers) Osgood; Daniel d. at Andover, 17 Mar 1754. Sarah and Daniel did not have children. In her will written 26 March 1764, Sarah included bequests to her sisters Elizabeth Stevens the widow of John Stevens late of Charlestown and Martha Goodale the wife of Ebenezer Goodale of Pomfret. There are also bequests to the daughters (Mehitable and Sarah) of her sister Mehitable Allen wife of Benjamin Allen of Pomfret who is deceased and the daughters (Mary Merrill and Sarah Farnum) of her sister Mary Farnum who is deceased. Cousin Benjamin Farnum receives the great bible and John Osgood, Jr. of Andover receives a chair and household

---

[38] Russell, Joseph of Andover; s. Robert & Mary; Boston City Hall Archives, Index to Deaths 1700-1799
[39] Massachusetts Land Records, Essex County, 43:304

items. John Osgood was named executor.[40] The distribution of the estate of Daniel Osgood included his brothers and their heirs as the heirs-at-law.

      iii   ANNA INGALLS, b. at Andover, 22 Jun 1701; nothing further known.[41]

32)   iv   MARY INGALLS, b. at Andover, 27 Mar 1705; m. at Andover, 12 Nov 1728, EPHRAIM FARNUM, b. at Andover, 12 Oct 1700 son of Ephraim and Priscilla (Holt) Farnum; Ephraim d. at Concord, NH, 1775.

33)   v   MEHITABLE INGALLS, b. at Andover, about 1708; d. at Pomfret, about 1756; m. at Pomfret, 20 Dec 1731, BENJAMIN ALLEN, b. at Pomfret, 12 Jan 1708 son of Daniel and Hannah (Davis) Allen; Benjamin d. at Norwich, 23 May 1783. Benjamin married second Rebecca Perkins on 19 Jan 1757.

34)   vi   STEPHEN INGALLS, b. at Andover, 24 Jul 1710; d. at Pomfret, 10 Dec 1771; m. 1st at Pomfret, 16 Jun 1734, REBEKAH GROW, b. at Andover, 21 Apr 1712 daughter of Thomas and Rebekah (Holt) Grow; Rebekah d. at Pomfret, 30 Jan 1762. Stephen m. 2nd, 27 Jan 1763, MARY TRESCOTT who has not been identified.

35)   vii   ELIZABETH INGALLS, b. at Andover, 24 Jul 1710; m. at Andover, 22 Apr 1731, JOHN STEVENS of Charlestown.

36)   viii   MARTHA INGALLS, b. at Andover, 9 Feb 1712/13; m. 1st at Andover, 10 Mar 1729/30, WILLIAM BARKER, b. at Andover, about 1708 son of William and Mary (Barker) Barker; William d. at Rumford, NH, 1 Jan 1741. Martha m. 2nd at Pomfret, 20 Dec 1743, JACOB GOODALE, b. 28 Feb 1708 son of Thomas and Sarah (Horrell) Goodale; Jacob d. about 1756. Martha m. 3rd EBENEZER GOODALE likely the brother of Jacob.

37)   ix   BENJAMIN INGALLS, b. at Andover, 8 Nov 1716; d. at Pomfret, 11 Oct 1800; m. at Pomfret, 4 Feb 1741, MARY LYON, b. at Pomfret, 8 Oct 1717 daughter of Abiel and Judith (Farrington) Lyon; Mary d. at Pomfret, 20 Apr 1784.

6)   BENJAMIN RUSSELL (*Robert[i]*), b. at Andover, 12 Jun 1677 son of Robert and Mary (Marshall) Russell; d. at Eastford, CT, 5 Oct 1754; m. at Andover, 26 Mar 1702, MARY PRESTON, b. at Andover, 5 Jan 1678/9 daughter of Samuel and Susanna (Gutterson) Preston; Mary d. at Eastford, 18 Nov 1753.

    The first five children of the seven children of Benjamin and Mary were born at Andover.[42] The family then moved to Ashford in 1715. On 11 January 1714/15, Benjamin Russell with wife Mary sold to Joseph Chandler property consisting of their current dwelling house and tract of land for £180. This was followed on 13 May 1715 (recorded 16 March 1718) with sale to Henry Holt, Jr. all Benjamin's rights to the common land in Andover for payment of £16.[43]

38)   i   BENJAMIN RUSSELL, b. at Andover, 1702; d. at Ashford, CT, 7 Oct 1754; m. SARAH PERRY, b. 4 Apr 1708 daughter of John and Sarah (Ingoldsby) Perry; Sarah d. at Eastford, 9 Dec 1786.

39)   ii   MARY RUSSELL, b. at Andover, 1705; m. 13 Feb 1724, SAMUEL MARCY, b. at Woodstock, 28 Jul 1704 son of John and Sarah (Hadlock) Marcy; Samuel d. at Union, CT, 31 Jul 1783.[44]

40)   iii   HANNAH RUSSELL, b. at Andover, about 1707; m. at Ashford, 4 Dec 1727, JOHN HUMPHREY, b. 14 Apr 1702 son of Arthur and Rachel (Rice) Humphrey; John d. at Eastford, 28 Mar 1784.

41)   iv   ABIGAIL RUSSELL, b. at Andover, Mar 1710; m. 29 Mar 1726, SETH LYON, b. at Woodstock, 27 Mar 1704 son of Thomas and Abigail (Clark) Lyon.

42)   v   LYDIA RUSSELL, b. at Andover, 15 Dec 1713; *likely* m. 27 Jan 1731, JONATHAN SANGER, b. at Woodstock, 8 Sep 1695 son of Nathaniel and Mary (Cutter) Sanger; Jonathan d. at Willington, 18 May 1767.

43)   vi   JOSEPH RUSSELL, b. at Ashford, 5 Jun 1717; m. at Ashford, 13 May 1742, HANNAH LINKHORN, b. about 1716; Hannah d. at Ashford, 14 Dec 1801.

---

[40] *Essex County, MA: Probate File Papers, 1638-1881.* Online database. *AmericanAncestors.org.* New England Historic Genealogical Society, 2014. Case 20273

[41] It has been speculated that Anna Ingalls married Charles Willis of Boston in 1727. However, Anna Ingalls who married Charles Willis was living in 1764 when Sarah Ingalls wrote her will and Anna and Charles also had children. As neither Anna nor her heirs are mentioned in the 1764 will of Sarah Ingalls, it seems more likely that it was not this Anna Ingalls that married Charles Willis.

[42] The children are as given in Bowen, *The History of Woodstock*, volume 8, p 229

[43] Massachusetts Land Records, Essex County, 28:80; 35:132

[44] Hammond, *The History of Union, Conn.*

44) vii ZERVIAH RUSSELL, baptized at Woodstock, 20 Mar 1719; d. at Ashford, 17 Dec 1743; m. EZRA SMITH; Ezra d. at Ashford, 1798 (will proved 4 Mar 1798). Ezra married second Judah Bosworth on 23 May 1745 and married third Catherine Billings.

7) HANNAH RUSSELL (*Robert¹*), b. at Andover, 28 Jun 1679 daughter of Robert and Mary (Marshall) Russell; d. at Andover, 16 May 1715; m. at Andover, 9 Mar 1697/8, OLIVER HOLT, b. at Andover, 14 Jan 1671/2 son of Henry and Sarah (Ballard) Holt; Oliver d. at Andover, 24 Dec 1747. Oliver m. 2nd at Newbury, 10 Jul 1716, MARY HUSE, b. at Newbury, 23 Mar 1690/1 daughter of Thomas and Mary (Webster) Huse.

  Oliver Holt was a farmer and blacksmith in Andover and lived in what was known as the Scotland district. Oliver and Hannah were members of the South Church. Oliver and Hannah were parents of nine children before Hannah's death at age 35. Oliver then married Mary Huse of Newbury and they had four children.[45]

45) i OLIVER HOLT, b. 26 Dec 1698; d. of smallpox, at Andover, 11 Nov 1760; m. 5 Jul 1722, SUSANNAH WRIGHT, b. at Andover, 24 Jul 1700 daughter of John and Mary (Wardwell) Wright; Susannah d. of smallpox, 1 Dec 1760.

46) ii URIAH HOLT, b. 25 Jun 1701; d. at Lancaster, MA, 24 Aug 1741; m. 28 Sep 1725, SARAH WRIGHT, b. at Andover, 20 Mar 1696 daughter of Walter and Elizabeth (Peters) Wright; Sarah d. at Beverly, 5 Mar 1779.[46] Sarah m. 2nd, at Harvard, 24 Jun 1747, Jonathan Cole (1699-1779).

  iii ZEBADIAH HOLT, b. 30 Dec 1702; d. 17 Mar 1704.

  iv HANNAH HOLT, b. 9 May 1707; d. 1708.

47) v DAVID HOLT, b. 5 Jun 1708; d. at Andover, 21 Aug 1747; m. 14 Sep 1732, his first cousin, SARAH RUSSELL, b. 5 Apr 1713 daughter of John and Sarah (Chandler) Russell; Sarah d. at Andover, 27 Apr 1781.

  vi PRISCILLA HOLT, b. about 1709[47]

48) vii JONATHAN HOLT, b. 29 Aug 1711; d. at Andover, 14 Oct 1791; m. 10 Feb 1734/5, LYDIA BLANCHARD, b. at Andover, 21 Aug 1714 daughter of Thomas and Rose (Holmes) Blanchard; Lydia d. at Andover, 17 Dec 1788.

  viii JOSEPH HOLT, b. 9 Feb 1713; d. 1714.

49) ix JACOB HOLT, b. 30 Mar 1714; d. 25 Dec 1760; m. 1st 29 Dec 1737, MARY OSGOOD, b. 1706 daughter of Stephen and Hannah (Blanchard) Osgood;[48] Mary d. 4 Nov 1745. Jacob m. 2nd 25 May 1747, MARGARET DOLLIVER; Margaret d. 22 Dec 1760.

8) JOHN RUSSELL (*Robert¹*), b. at Andover, 14 Oct 1682 son of Robert and Mary (Marshall) Russell; d. at Andover, 8 Feb 1778;[49] m. at Andover, 20 Oct 1712, SARAH CHANDLER, b. at Andover, 10 Mar 1692/3 daughter of Joseph and Sarah (Abbott) Chandler.

  On 11 July 1747 (recorded 30 October 1765), John Russell conveyed to his kinsmen James Russell and Thomas Russell of Andover a portion of land in Andover that had belonged to John's father Robert who was the grandfather of James

[45] Durrie's Holt Genealogy includes a fifth child, Benjamin, for Oliver and Mary. Charlotte Helen Abbott places Benjamin in the family of Moses and Elizabeth (Russell) Holt. Benjamin Holt married Elizabeth Lovejoy in 1745 and Elizabeth (Lovejoy) Holt died in 1745 (according to records of the South Church of Andover). It is not known what became of Benjamin Holt after that and he is not included here.

[46] ____, wid. Jonathan, small pox, bur. Mar. 5, 1779, a. 85 y. C. R.1.

[47] All published genealogies include a daughter Priscilla for Oliver and Hannah and report that she married Nathan Chandler. It seems more likely that Priscilla was a daughter of Timothy Holt and Rhoda Chandler. There are two reasons for this. First, the 1758 will of Timothy Holt includes a bequest for his daughter Priscilla and notes that she is married (without providing the last names of his married daughters). Previously, Timothy's daughter Priscilla was described as having an unknown outcome, but it can be confirmed that she was married and living in 1758. Second, Benjamin Holt the son of Oliver Holt and Hannah Russell wrote a will (probate 1783) in which he names all his other living siblings and half-siblings and there is no sister Priscilla in his will. The will of Benjamin Holt has bequests to beloved wife Elizabeth; son-in-law James Holt, Jr. (husband of Dorothy Lovejoy who was a daughter of Elizabeth Wilson and her first husband Ezekiel Lovejoy); "my beloved brothers and sisters namely Jonathan Holt, Thomas Holt, Mary Holt, and Judath Batchelder"; son Phineas Lovejoy (a son of Elizabeth and Ezekiel Lovejoy); daughter-in-law Dorothy Hagget; daughter-in-law Elizabeth Brown; six beloved cousins namely Nathaniel Holt, Uriah Holt, Jacob Holt, Timothy Holt, Joseph Holt, and Timothy Russell; and Timothy Gray, Jr. *Essex County, MA: Probate File Papers, 1638-1881.*Online database. *AmericanAncestors.org.* New England Historic Genealogical Society, 2014. Case 13625. This at least suggests that Oliver did not have a sister Priscilla, or not living at that time.

[48] The 1743 will of Stephen Osgood includes a bequest to his daughter Mary Holt.

[49] John, bur. Feb. 10, 1778, a. 96 y. 4 m. C.R.2.

and Thomas. This was property of the estate of Robert Russell that had never been divided among the heirs.[50] James and Thomas were sons of John's brother James who died in 1717.

John and Sarah were parents of nine children born at Andover.

47) i SARAH RUSSELL, b. at Andover, 5 Apr 1713; d. at Andover, 27 Sep 1781; m. at Andover, 14 Sep 1732, her first cousin, DAVID HOLT, b. at Andover, 5 Jun 1708 son of Oliver and Hannah (Russell) Holt; David d. at Andover, 21 Aug 1747.

50) ii PHEBE RUSSELL, baptized at Andover, 10 Jun 1716; m. 1st, 13 Feb 1735, EPHRAIM HOLT, b. May 1713 son of Henry and Martha (Marston) Holt; Ephraim d. at Andover, 31 Dec 1749. Phebe m. 2nd, 5 Dec 1750, ABRAHAM SHELDON, b. at Reading, 4 Jun 1717 son of William and Mary (Robarts) Sheldon; Abraham d. at Reading, 15 May 1790. Abraham Sheldon was first married to Sarah Gowing.

51) iii JOHN RUSSELL, b. at Andover, 8 Jun 1717; d. at Andover, 2 Oct 1788; m. at Andover, 16 Feb 1737/8, HANNAH FOSTER, b. at Andover, 13 Jun 1716 daughter of Abraham and Mary (Johnson) Foster.

52) iv JOSEPH RUSSELL, b. at Andover, 8 Jan 1719/20; d. at Andover, 31 Aug 1783;[51] m. at Andover, 26 Feb 1756, HEPHZIBAH RUSSELL, baptized at Andover, 30 Jun 1734 daughter of Joseph and Hepsibah (Eaton) Russell; Hephzibah was living in 1783.

53) v ROBERT RUSSELL, baptized at Andover, 21 Jan 1722; d. at Andover, 4 Jan 1794; m. at Andover, 5 Dec 1745, ANNE FELT, baptized at Wakefield, 13 Jul 1723 daughter of Joshua and Anne (Walcott) Felt; Anne d. at Andover, 12 Oct 1816.

54) vi ISAAC RUSSELL, b. at Andover, 3 Dec 1724; m. at Andover, 18 Apr 1754, ELIZABETH GILBARD.

55) vii MARY RUSSELL, b. at Andover, 10 Feb 1728/9; m. about 1755, her second cousin once removed, JOSEPH HOLT, b. 14 Feb 1718 son of Timothy and Rhoda (Chandler) Holt; Joseph d. at Wilton, NH, Aug 1789.

56) viii HANNAH RUSSELL, b. at Andover, 28 Dec 1730; m. at Billerica, 8 Apr 1761, JACOB CROSBY, b. at Billerica, 19 Sep 1729 son of Thomas and Anna (Parker) Crosby; Jacob d. at Billerica, 1776 (probate 1776).

57) ix JEMIMA RUSSELL, baptized at Andover, 28 Jan 1733; d. at Boston, 30 Apr 1813; m. at Andover, 8 Sep 1763, as his second wife, JONATHAN STEVENS, b. at Andover, 1726 son of John and Elizabeth (Chandler) Stevens; Jonathan d. about 1771 (will 5 Jun 1771, proved 7 Jan 1772). Jonathan was first married to Lydia Felch.

9) ELIZABETH RUSSELL (*Robert¹*), b. at Andover, 16 Jul 1687 daughter of Robert and Mary (Marshall) Russell; d. at Andover, 3 Nov 1772; m. at Andover, 31 Jan 1715/6, MOSES HOLT, b. at Andover, 7 Jun 1686 son of John and Sarah (Geary) Holt; Moses d. at Andover, 7 Nov 1730. Elizabeth m. 2nd, 27 Jul 1745, CHARLES FURBUSH, b. 1709 son of Samuel and Abigail (Rice) Furbush;[52] Charles d. at Saratoga in 1756 during the French and Indian War. Charles was first married to Margaret Lovejoy.

Moses Holt did not leave a will and his estate entered probate on 14 December 1730 with Nicholas Holt and Timothy Holt as administrators. The final division of the estate occurred 16 November 1743 which was after the death of son Moses. In the division, one-third was set off to the widow and the other two-thirds were divided in four parts. Two-fourths were distributed to the heirs of son Moses deceased and one-fourth each to daughters Mary and Elizabeth.[53]

Moses Holt and Elizabeth Russell were parents of four children.

58) i MOSES HOLT, b. at Andover, 21 Oct 1716; d. at Andover, 6 Jul 1743; m. 9 Jul 1741, his first cousin once removed, PRUDENCE RUSSELL (*Robert³, Thomas², Robert¹*), baptized at Andover, 31 Jul 1720 daughter of Robert and Abigail (Flint) Russell; Prudence d. at Andover, 15 Nov 1745. Prudence Russell m. 2nd, 11 Mar 1744/5, her first cousin, JOHN CHANDLER (*Mehitable Russell Chandler³, Thomas², Robert¹*), b. at Andover, 19 Jan 1722 son of Joseph and Mehitable (Russell) Chandler; John d. at Andover, 11 May 1759. John Chandler m. 2nd, at Andover, 15 Oct 1747, HANNAH PHELPS, b. at Andover, 1709 daughter of Samuel and Hannah (Dane) Phelps; Hannah d. at Andover, 5 Aug 1781.

ii ELIZABETH HOLT, b. at Andover, 12 Mar 1719/20; d. 19 Aug 1744; m. 4 Oct 1743, BENJAMIN BLANCHARD, b. at Andover, 19 Mar 1720/1 son of Benjamin and Mary (Abbott) Blanchard; Benjamin d. at

[50] Essex County Deeds, 124:49
[51] Joseph, Aug. 31, 1783. [a. 64 y. CR2]. The 1783 probate record of Joseph Russell refers to widow Hephzibah.
[52] In 1761 as Elizabeth Furbush, Elizabeth filed a petition related to the administration of the estate of her grandson Phineas Holt.
[53] *Essex County, MA: Probate File Papers, 1638-1881*. Online database. *AmericanAncestors.org*. New England Historic Genealogical Society, 2014. Case 13674

Canterbury, NH, 7 Mar 1791. Benjamin had two further marriages to Keziah Hastings on 27 Dec 1744 and Sarah Burbank on 9 Jul 1778. Elizabeth Holt and Benjamin Blanchard had one son, Benjamin who was born 2 Jul 1744 and died 2 Oct 1744.

iii   MARY HOLT, b. at Andover, 4 Jul 1722; Mary was living in 1744 at the final division of her father's estate. Nothing further in known.

iv   SARAH HOLT, baptized 22 Mar 1724; d. 23 Jan 1737/8.

Generation Three

Children of Mary Russell and Nicholas Holt

10) MARY HOLT (*Mary Russell Holt², Robert¹*), b. at Andover, 13 Feb 1680/1 daughter of Nicholas and Mary (Russell) Holt; d. at Andover, 9 Feb 1714/5; m. at Andover, 19 Sep 1705, JOSIAH INGALLS, b. at Andover, 28 Feb 1676 son of Henry and Mary (Osgood) Ingalls. Josiah d. at Andover, 14 Aug 1755. After Mary's death, Josiah married Esther Frye.

Mary Holt and Josiah Ingalls were parents of five children born at Andover. Josiah had two children with his second wife Esther Frye, a daughter Anne born 6 June 1717 and a son Josiah born 4 August 1719. On 30 December 1743, Josiah Ingalls conveyed to his son Josiah Ingalls, one-half of his property and dwelling house in Andover. On 6 January 1742 (executed 30 December 1743), Josiah conveyed to his son Josiah his full right to grant land known as Rowley Cannada.[54]

	i	Son b. 15 Mar 1706
59)	ii	PHEBE INGALLS, b. at Andover 1708; d. after 1784 perhaps in Poland, ME;[55] m. at Andover, 12 Aug 1731, JAMES PARKER, b. at Andover, 12 Oct 1696 son of John and Hannah (Brown) Parker; James d. at Andover, 1782 (will 1773; probate 1782).
	iii	ABIGAIL INGALLS, b. 1710; nothing further known.
	iv	Child, perhaps Josiah, b. 22 May 1712; died young.
	v	RACHEL INGALLS, b. 3 Sep 1713; nothing further known.

11) NICHOLAS HOLT (*Mary Russell Holt², Robert¹*), b. at Andover, 21 Dec 1683 son of Nicholas and Mary (Russell) Holt; d. at Andover, 1 Dec 1756; m. 1st, 16 Sep 1708, MARY MANNING; Mary d. at Andover, 3 Mar 1715/6. Nicholas m. 2nd, 12 Apr 1717, DORCAS ABBOTT, b. at Andover, 25 Apr 1698 daughter of Timothy and Hannah (Graves) Abbott; Dorcas d. at Andover, 25 Oct 1758.

Nicholas Holt was a yeoman in Andover. In his will, Nicholas Holt makes bequests to the following persons: dearly beloved wife Dorcas, eldest and well-beloved son Benjamin, well-beloved son Stephen, well-beloved son Nicholas, well-beloved son Timothy, well-beloved son James, well-beloved son Nathan, well-beloved son Joshua, well-beloved son Daniel, eldest and well-beloved daughter Mary, and well-beloved daughter Dorcas. Benjamin, Mary, Stephen, and Nicholas are Nicholas's children from his first marriage to Mary Manning.[56]

Nicholas Holt and Mary Manning were parents of four children born at Andover.

60)	i	BENJAMIN HOLT, b. at Andover, 23 Jul 1709; d. at Pembroke, NH, 1774 (probate 26 Oct 1774); m. at Andover, 7 Apr 1737, SARAH FRYE, b. May 1717 daughter of Nathan and Sarah (Bridges) Frye; Sarah d. at Pembroke, 1804.
61)	ii	MARY HOLT, b. at Andover, 1 Aug 1711; m. 1st at Andover, 4 Mar 1735/6, WILLIAM CHANDLER, b. 14 Jul 1704 son of Thomas and Mary (Stevens) Chandler; William d. at Andover, 15 Apr 1741. William Chandler was first married to Elizabeth Blanchard. Mary Holt m. 2nd, about 1745, JEREMIAH OSGOOD, b. at Andover, 1702 son of Christopher and Sarah (Osgood). Jeremiah was first married to Lydia Poor.
62)	iii	STEPHEN HOLT, b. at Andover, 14 Apr 1713; d. at Andover, 25 Apr 1798; m. 12 Jul 1739, MARY FARNUM, b. at Andover, 21 May 1714 daughter of John and Joanna (Barker) Farnum; Mary d. at Andover, 9 Aug 1802.
63)	iv	NICHOLAS HOLT, b. at Andover, 29 Feb 1716; d. at Blue Hill, ME, 16 Mar 1798; m. 1st at Andover, 26 Apr 1739, HANNAH OSGOOD, baptized at Andover 1 Jun 1718 daughter of Ezekiel and Rebecca (Wardwell) Osgood;[57] Rebecca d. at Andover, 1 Sep 1744. Nicholas m. 2nd at Andover, 7 Feb 1750/1, LOIS PHELPS, b. at Reading, about 1720 daughter of Samuel and Elizabeth (Bare) Phelps; Lois d. at Blue Hill, Jan 1814.

Nicholas and Dorcas had six children all born at Andover.

---

[54] Massachusetts Land Records, Essex County, 93:18, 93:19
[55] Phebe was living in November 1784 when she consented to the sale of the dwelling house and land in Andover by her son James Parker, then of Poland, ME. It seems possible that Phebe and her daughter accompanied James to Poland.
[56] *Essex County, MA: Probate File Papers, 1638-1881*. Probate of Nicholas Holt, 27 Dec 1756, Case number 13680.
[57] The 1740 will of Ezekiel Osgood includes a bequest to his daughter Hannah Osgood alias Holt.

64)   i   TIMOTHY HOLT, b. 17 Jan 1720/1; d. at Wilton, NH, Nov 1801; m. 18 Sep 1744, his second cousin, ELIZABETH HOLT, baptized at Andover 8 Jun 1718 daughter of John and Mehitable (Wilson) Holt; Elizabeth d. at Wilton 21 Mar 1776.

65)   ii   JAMES HOLT, b. 13 Jan 1722/3; d. 22 Aug 1812; m. 1st, SARAH ABBOTT, b. 2 Aug 1718 daughter of Benjamin and Elizabeth (Abbott) Abbott; Sarah d. 5 Mar 1778. James m. 2nd, 22 Jun 1779, PHEBE BALLARD, b. at Andover, 25 Jul 1738 daughter of Josiah and Mary (Chandler) Ballard and widow of Abiel Abbot; Phebe d. 9 Jun 1815.

66)   iii   NATHAN HOLT, b. 28 Feb 1725; d. at Danvers, 2 Aug 1792; m. 4 Aug 1757, SARAH ABBOTT, b. 14 Jan 1729/30 daughter of George and Mary (Phillips) Abbott; Sarah d. 29 Dec 1797.

67)   iv   DORCAS HOLT, b. 4 Sep 1727; death unknown but may have been at Wilton, NH; m. 26 Jan 1749, as his second wife, her first cousin, THOMAS HOLT (*Thomas Holt³, Mary Russell Holt², Robert¹*), b. Mar 1711/2 son of Thomas and Alice (Peabody) Holt; Thomas d. at Andover, 21 Nov 1776. Thomas was 1st married 15 Aug 1734 to HANNAH KIMBALL, baptized at Boxford 7 Sep 1712 daughter of John and Elizabeth (Chapman) Kimball; Hannah d. at Andover, 12 Jun 1748.

68)   v   JOSHUA HOLT, b. 30 Jun 1730; d. 24 Jul 1810; m. 2 Dec 1755, PHEBE FARNUM, b. 10 Oct 1731 daughter of Timothy and Dinah (Ingalls) Farnum; Phebe d. 26 Jan 1806.

69)   vi   DANIEL HOLT, b. 10 Feb 1732/3; d. at Andover, 15 Feb 1796; m. 29 Nov 1759, his first cousin once removed, HANNAH HOLT (*Thomas Holt⁴, Thomas Holt³, Mary Russell Holt², Robert¹*), b. 11 Feb 1738/9 daughter of Thomas and Hannah (Kimball) Holt; Hannah d. at Andover, 2 Aug 1831.

12)   THOMAS HOLT (*Mary Russell Holt², Robert¹*), b. at Andover, 16 Aug 1686 son of Nicholas and Mary (Russell) Holt; d. at Andover, 12 Jan 1767; m. 1st, at Andover, 14 Dec 1708, ALICE PEABODY, b. at Andover, 5 Jan 1685 daughter of Joseph and Bethiah (Bridges) Peabody; Alice d. at Andover, 29 Jul 1726. Thomas m. 2nd, at Boxford, 16 Nov 1727, ABIGAIL POORE (widow of John Fiske), b. at Newbury, 9 Sep 1680 daughter of Henry and Abigail (Hale) Poore; Abigail d. at Andover, 20 Nov 1766.

Thomas Holt was a farmer in Andover. He and his wife Alice were received into Andover south church on 7 July 1723.[58]

In his will written 11 February 1766, Thomas Holt makes bequests to the following persons: eldest and well beloved son Thomas, two grandsons Abiel and Joseph Holt who are the sons of his deceased son Joseph, his fourth son William, his fifth and well beloved son Daniel, well beloved daughter Allace, and well beloved daughter Lydia. Clothing is divided among three sons Thomas, William, and Daniel. He also makes son Thomas responsible for the care of his mother-in-law (stepmother Abigail) and after her death to return household items to her two children John Fisk and Phebe Abbott.

Thomas Holt and Alice Peabody were parents of eight children born at Andover.

67)   i   THOMAS HOLT, b. at Andover, Mar 1711/2; d. at Andover, 21 Nov 1776; m. 1st, 15 Oct 1734, his first cousin, HANNAH KIMBALL, baptized at Boxford, 7 Sep 1712 daughter of John and Elizabeth (Chapman) Kimball; Hannah d. at Andover, 12 Jun 1748. Thomas m. 2nd, 26 Jan 1749, DORCAS HOLT (*Nicholas Holt³, Mary Russell Holt², Robert¹*), b. at Andover, 4 Sep 1727 daughter of Nicholas and Dorcas (Abbott) Holt.

70)   ii   LYDIA HOLT, b. at Andover, 2 Jan 1713/4; m. at Andover, 30 Jan 1734/5, her second cousin, BENJAMIN HOLT, b. 1704 son of Henry and Mary (Marston) Holt; Benjamin d. at Andover, 17 Mar 1779.

71)   iii   JOSEPH HOLT, b. at Andover, 28 Feb 1715/6; d. at Lunenburg, 1754; m. 1st 14 Aug 1742, MARY ABBOTT, b. at Andover, 4 Aug 1713 daughter of Stephen and Sarah (Stevens) Abbott; Mary d. at Lunenburg, 5 Aug 1748. Joseph m. 2nd at Lunenburg, 20 May 1749, DORCAS BOYNTON, b. at Groton, MA, 21 Dec 1715 daughter of Benoni and Anna (Mighill) Boynton; Dorcas d. at Lunenburg, 11 Jun 1775. Dorcas Boynton was first married to Thomas Frost.

         iv   ABIEL HOLT, b. 25 Apr 1718; d. 11 Sep 1744.

72)   v   WILLIAM HOLT, b. at Andover, 10 Dec 1720; d. at Hampton, CT, 2 Aug 1793; m. 1st at Hampton, 14 Jul 1742, his first cousin, HANNAH HOLT (*Abiel Holt³, Mary Russell Holt², Robert¹*), b. at Windham, CT, 17 Apr 1723 daughter of Abiel and Hannah (Abbott) Holt; Hannah d. at Windham, 25 Jan 1750/1. William m. 2nd at Windham, 14 May 1752, SYBEL DURKEE, b. at Windham, 10 Jan 1731 daughter of Stephen and Lois (Moulton) Durkee; Sybel d. at Hampton, 11 Jan 1794.

73)   vi   ALICE HOLT, b. at Andover, about 1722; d. at Andover, 1762 (probate 22 Nov 1762); m. 13 Mar 1739/40, as his third wife, JOHN BARNARD, b. at Andover, 16 Apr 1697 son of John and Naomi (Hoyt) Barnard; John

---

58 South Church, *Historical Manual of South Church in Andover*, p 128

d. at Andover, 1752 (probate 15 Jun 1752). John was first married to Sarah Osgood and second married to Mehitable Stiles.

vii   DANIEL HOLT, b. 18 Sep 1723; living in 1767 but nothing further known.

viii   JONATHAN HOLT, b. 18 May 1726; d. 2 Jun 1726.

13)   ABIGAIL HOLT (*Mary Russell Holt², Robert¹*), b. at Andover, 23 Nov 1688 daughter of Nicholas and Mary (Russell) Holt; d. at Hampton, 12 Aug 1742; m. at Andover, 10 Jan 1711/2, her first cousin, PAUL HOLT, b. 7 Feb 1684 son of Henry and Sarah (Ballard) Holt; Paul d. at Hampton, 6 May 1742.

    Paul and Abigail had their two children in Andover and then relocated to Hampton, Connecticut in 1726 along with Paul's brother George.

74) i   ABIGAIL HOLT, b. at Andover, 21 Aug 1716; d. at Hampton, CT, 3 Nov 1749; m. 3 Dec 1736, JONATHAN KINGSBURY, b. 1712 son of Thomas and Margaret (Haines) Kingsbury; Jonathan d. at Hampton, 28 Dec 1770. Jonathan married second Hannah Clark on 9 Jan 1751 and married third Sarah *How* Ballard the widow of John Ballard.

75) ii   PAUL HOLT, b. at Andover, Aug 1720; d. at Hampton, CT, 21 Dec 1804; m. 20 Jan 1742, MEHITABLE CHANDLER, b. 12 Apr 1719 daughter of Philemon and Hannah (Clary) Chandler; Mehitable d. at Hampton, 10 May 1773. Paul m. 2nd, 4 Jan 1774, MARY SPENCER.

14)   ROBERT HOLT (*Mary Russell Holt², Robert¹*), b. at Andover, 23 Jan 1695/6 son of Nicholas and Mary (Russell) Holt; d. at Windham, CT, 1768 (probate 4 May 1768); m. 1st, 22 May 1718, REBECCA PRESTON (widow of her cousin Joseph Preston), b. at Andover, 23 Jan 1688/9 daughter of John and Sarah (Gear) Preston; Rebecca d. at Windham, 1 May 1727. Robert m. 2nd, 13 Dec 1727, BETHIAH PEABODY, b. at Boxford, 3 Apr 1681 daughter of Joseph and Bethiah (Bridges) Peabody; Bethiah d. 6 Feb 1742. Robert m. 3rd, at Hampton, 28 Mar 1743, HANNAH ADROSS who has not been identified; Hannah was living in 1767.

    Robert Holt was part of the migration to Windham. He and Rebecca had their first children in Andover before relocating to Connecticut.

    In his will written 27 February 1767 (proved 4 May 1768), Robert Holt bequeaths to beloved wife Hannah the dwelling house with an acre of land, all the stock animals, and the household furnishings to be hers forever. Son Ezekiel receives five shillings and a fifth part of the wearing apparel. Grandson Robert Lyon receives £4 and one-fourth of the remaining estate not otherwise dispose of. Daughter Abigail Kendall receives a fourth part and daughter Mary Truesdell receives a fourth part. His grandchildren Reuben Richardson, Sarah Richardson, and Stephen Richardson the children of daughter Martha Richardson deceased receive the remining fourth. Friend Mr. Joseph Burnam of Windham was named executor.[59]

    Robert Holt and Rebecca Preston were parents of seven children.

i   ABIGAIL HOLT, b. at Andover, 12 Aug 1719; died young.

ii   SARAH HOLT, b. at Andover, 18 Jan 1720/1; died young.

76) iii   ABIGAIL HOLT, b. at Windham, 20 Feb 1722; m. at Windham, 5 Nov 1741, DAVID KENDALL; David d. at Ashford, 16 Dec 1777.

77) iv   SARAH HOLT, b. at Windham, 20 Feb 1722; d. at Pomfret, 11 Oct 1743; m. at Pomfret, 2 Feb 1741/2, PELETIAH LYON, b. at Pomfret, 20 Sep 1711 son of Abiel and Judith (Farrington) Lyon.

78) v   MARY HOLT, b. at Windham, 7 Feb 1725; m. at Pomfret, 15 Jun 1742, JOSEPH TRUESDELL, b. at Pomfret, 24 Jun 1719 son of Ebenezer and Rachel (Davis) Truesdell; Joseph d. at Havana, 8 Oct 1762.

79) vi   MARTHA HOLT, b. at Windham, 11 Apr 1725; d. at Pomfret, 4 Oct 1759; m. 1 Jan 1754, JOHN RICHARDSON.

vii   EZEKIEL HOLT, b. at Windham, 21 Apr 1727; d. 6 Jan 1807; m. 1st 5 Nov 1746, LUCY DURKEE, b. at Windham, 6 Jan 1728 daughter of William and Rebecca (Gould) Durkee; Lucy d. at Windham, 11 Aug 1747. Ezekiel m. 2nd, 2 May 1748, ABIAH SESSIONS; Abiah d. 23 May 1811. Ezekiel did not have children.

15)   ABIEL HOLT (*Mary Russell Holt², Robert¹*), b. at Andover, 28 Jun 1698 son of Nicholas and Mary (Russell) Holt; d. at Willington, 10 Nov 1772; m. 1st, at Andover, 21 Feb 1721, HANNAH ABBOTT, b. at Andover, 5 Apr 1701 daughter of William

[59] Connecticut. *Probate Court (Windham District)*; Probate Place: *Windham, Connecticut, Probate Records, Vol 7-8, 1764-1775, Folio 394*

and Elizabeth (Geary) Abbott; Hannah d. at Windham, 11 Feb 1751/2. Abiel m. 2nd, at Willington, 19 Dec 1752, SARAH DOWNER, b. about 1699; Sarah d. 15 Apr 1784.

 Hannah and Abiel were part of the migration of several Andover families to Windham. There are records for ten children, all born at Windham, Connecticut. Most of the children in this family relocated to Willington.

72)   i   HANNAH HOLT, b. 17 Apr 1723; d. 25 Jan 1750/1; m. 14 Jul 1742, her first cousin WILLIAM HOLT, b. at Andover 10 Dec 1720 son of Thomas and Alice (Peabody) Holt. William m. 2nd Sybel Durkee; William d. at Hampton 2 Aug 1793.

80)   ii   ELIZABETH HOLT, b. 16 Feb 1724/5; d. about 1753; m. 10 Jun 1746, FRANCIS FENTON, b. at Willington, b. 16 Mar 1718 son of Francis and Ann (Berry) Fenton.[60] Francis m. 2nd Ann Newcomb.

81)   iii   ABIEL HOLT, b. 1 Feb 1726/7; d. 2 Oct 1785; m. 1st 22 Apr 1755, MARY DOWNER whose origins are unknown; Mary d. 28 Jan 1766. Abiel m. 2nd 2 Apr 1767, EUNICE KINGSBURY (widow of John Marshall), b. about 1733; Eunice d. 2 Jun 1784.

82)   iv   CALEB HOLT, b. 6 Mar 1729; d. 18 Aug 1810; m. 29 Jan 1755, MARY MERRICK, b. 6 Dec 1726 daughter of John and Sarah (Parsons) Merrick; Mary d. 4 Jun 1790. Caleb m. 2nd Chloe Hatch.

83)   v   NATHAN HOLT, b. 18 Apr 1733; d. 31 May 1800; m. 1st 19 Jan 1758, ABIGAIL MERRICK, b. 17 Jun 1737 daughter of John and Sarah (Parsons) Merrick; Abigail d. 1 Dec 1765. Nathan m. 2nd 26 Nov 1766, BATHSHEBA WILLIAMS, b. at Lebanon, 22 Mar 1737 daughter of Samuel and Deborah (Throope) Williams; Bathsheba d. 1 Aug 1769. Nathan m. 3rd 6 Jun 1770, LYDIA KINGSBURY, b. at Bolton, 1737 daughter of John and Deborah (Spaulding) Kingsbury; Lydia d. 22 Mar 1776.

84)   vi   ANNA HOLT, b. 14 Jan 1735; d. 10 Oct 1806; m. 29 Jan 1755, JOSEPH MERRICK, b. 17 Oct 1733 son of John and Sarah (Parsons) Merrick; Joseph d. 9 Apr 1787.

85)   vii   ISAAC HOLT, b. 2 Mar 1737/8; d. 14 Oct 1822; m. 26 May 1762, SARAH ORCUTT, b. at Stafford, 7 Nov 1740 daughter of William and Sarah (Leonard) Orcutt; Sarah d. 30 Mar 1816.

86)   viii   TIMOTHY HOLT, b. 2 Dec 1739; d. 7 May 1807; m. 7 May 1761 as her 2nd husband, REBECCA CHAMBERLAIN (widow of Nathaniel Fenton);[61] Rebecca was b. about 1730 probably the daughter of Edmund and Sarah (Furbush) Chamberlain; Rebecca d. 11 Apr 1809.

87)   ix   MARY HOLT, b. 4 May 1742; d. 13 Jan 1823; m. 27 Nov 1760, JOSEPH PERSONS, birth record not found but son of Joseph and Hannah (-) Persons; Joseph d. at Willington, 4 Nov 1812.

88)   x   JAMES HOLT, b. 27 Aug 1746; d. 30 Sep 1818; m. 1st 20 Apr 1769, ESTHER OWENS, b. 20 Feb 1747 son of Eleazer and Jerusha (Russ) Owens; Esther d. 5 Dec 1774. James m. 2nd LUCE SAWINS, b. 28 Sep 1740 daughter of George and Anne (Farrar) Sawins; Luce d. 25 Dec 1824.

16)   DEBORAH HOLT (*Mary Russell Holt², Robert¹*), b. at Andover, 16 Nov 1700 daughter of Nicholas and Mary (Russell) Holt; d. at Willington, 26 Nov 1784; m. at Windham, 5 May 1727, BENJAMIN PRESTON, b. at Andover, 1705 son of Jacob and Sarah (Wilson) Preston; Benjamin d. at Willington, 26 Nov 1784.[62]

 Benjamin traveled with his parents to Connecticut the family arriving about 1723. Benjamin was an early settler in Willington and had a tanning business.[63] Deborah and Benjamin were parents of eight children born at Windham.

89)   i   BENJAMIN PRESTON, b. at Windham, 31 Dec 1727; d. at Ashford, 1 Dec 1798; m. at Ashford, 17 Nov 1763, BATHSHEBA SNOW, b. at Bridgewater, about 1732 daughter of Solomon and Bathsheba (Mahurin) Snow;[64] Bathsheba d. at Ashford, 22 Jan 1813.

90)   ii   DANIEL PRESTON, b. at Windham, 16 Mar 1729; m. at Windham, 4 Mar 1756, his second cousin once removed, DINAH FORD, b. at Windham, 17 Sep 1735 daughter of Nathaniel and Daniel (Holt) Ford.

91)   iii   DARIUS PRESTON, b. at Windham, 3 Mar 1731/2; d. at Willington, 30 May 1821; m. at Willington, 15 Nov 1759, HANNAH FISKE, b. at Willington, 26 Mar 1740 daughter of William and Mary (Blancher) Fiske; Hannah d. at Willington, 12 Jan 1813.

---

[60] William Weaver, *Genealogy of the Fenton Family.* (Willimantic, CT, 1867).

[61] This information is confirmed by the 1809 probate record of Rebecca Holt which includes heirs from her first marriage to Nathaniel Fenton.

[62] The deaths of Deborah and Benjamin are recorded as occurring on the same day.

[63] Preston, *Descendants of Roger Preston*, p 60

[64] *Mayflower Families Fifth Generation Descendants, 1700-1880.* (Online database: *AmericanAncestors.org*, New England Historic Genealogical Society, 2017). John Alden, volume 16, part 3, p 207

  iv MARY PRESTON, b. 2 Apr 1734; d. 31 Aug 1742.

92) v JERUSHA PRESTON, b. at Windham, 29 Jul 1736; m. at Ashford, 25 Aug 1767, as his third wife, JOHN PECK, b. at Uxbridge, MA, 30 Dec 1726 son of Simon and Sarah (-) Peck; John d. in VT, 1805.[65] John was first married to Mary Bowen and second married to Elizabeth Dennerson.

  vi AMOS PRESTON, b. 27 Jan 1738; d. 5 Nov 1756.

93) vii DEBORAH PRESTON, b. at Windham, 10 Dec 1740; d. at Willington, 6 Mar 1822; m. at Willington, 19 Oct 1763, TIMOTHY POOL, b. at Willington, 11 Jun 1739 son of John and Mary (Parker) Pool; Timothy d. at Willington, 16 Jul 1821.

  viii MARY PRESTON, baptized at Hampton 4 Nov 1744. She is *perhaps* the Mary Preston who married Stevens Chandler (*Mary Holt Chandler⁴, Nicholas Holt³, Mary Russell², Robert¹*) as his second wife.

17) JOSHUA HOLT (*Mary Russell Holt², Robert¹*), b. at Andover, 1703 son of Nicholas and Mary (Russell) Holt; d. at Hampton, 26 Jan 1787; m. at Windham, 16 Feb 1724/5, KETURAH HOLT, b. at Andover, 15 Dec 1690 daughter of Henry and Sarah (Ballard) Holt; Keturah d. at Hampton, 2 Oct 1781.
  Keturah and Joshua Holt settled in Windham around the time of their marriage, and their four children were born there.

94) i DINAH HOLT, b. at Windham, 17 Mar 1725/6; d. at Willington, 25 Sep 1805; m. at Windham, 6 Nov 1746, TIMOTHY PEARL, b. at Windham, 24 Oct 1723 son of Timothy and Elizabeth (Stevens) Pearl; Timothy d. at Willington, 19 Oct 1789.

95) ii JOSHUA HOLT, b. at Windham, 19 Mar 1728; d. at Hampton, 5 Jul 1791; m. 1ˢᵗ 28 Jun 1749, MARY ABBOTT, b. at Pomfret, 3 Mar 1728 daughter of Paul and Elizabeth (Gray) Abbott; Mary d. at Windham, 10 Aug 1769. Joshua m. 2ⁿᵈ, 26 Apr 1770, SUSANNA GOODELL, b. at Pomfret, 22 Jan 1728 daughter of Zachariah and Hannah (Cheney) Goodell; Susanna d. at Windham, 28 Jun 1812. Susanna was first married to Samuel Darby.

  iii KETURAH HOLT, b. at Windham, 22 Nov 1729; d. at Willington, 1805; m. at Willington, 17 Jun 1750, JOHN PEARL, b. at Windham, 20 Jan 1725/6 son of Timothy and Elizabeth (Stevens) Pearl. There do not seem to be any children for this couple. There is a probate record for Keturah from 1805. The distributions of the estate of Keturah Holt Pearl are to the following persons: sister Dinah Pearl; sister Phebe Goodale; and heirs of brother Joshua Holt who is deceased.

96) iv PHEBE HOLT, b. at Windham, 16 Aug 1734; d. at South Windsor, CT, 7 Feb 1808; m. at Hampton, 13 Feb 1755, EBENEZER GOODALE, b. at Pomfret, 12 Sep 1729 son of Ebenezer and Experience (Lyon) Goodale; Ebenezer d. at East Windsor, 1794.

18) DANIEL HOLT (*Mary Russell Holt², Robert¹*), b. at Andover, 1705 son of Nicholas and Mary (Russell) Holt; d. at Pomfret, 5 Nov 1773; m. 1ˢᵗ, 31 Mar 1731, ABIGAIL SMITH, b. at Lebanon, CT, 22 Jun 1706 daughter of John and Abigail (-) Smith; Abigail d. at Pomfret, CT, 9 Feb 1752. Daniel m. 2ⁿᵈ, at Pomfret, Dec 1752, KEZIA STRONG (widow of Noah Rust), b. at Northampton, MA, 1 Dec 1709 daughter of Joseph and Sarah (Allen) Strong;[66] Kezia d. at Cherry Valley, NY, 1796.
  Daniel Holt was the youngest of eleven children. He likely traveled to Windham County, Connecticut with his older brothers. He was a farmer in Pomfret.
  In his will written 23 October 1773 (proved 7 December 1773), Daniel Holt bequeathed to beloved wife Kezia use of the north great room, part of the cellar, and other provisions for her support while she is a widow. Son Daniel receives all the real and personal estate in Pomfret. The outlands, particularly those in the Delaware purchase, are to be divided among sons Daniel and Asa and the male heirs of son Silas. Daughters Abigail, Lois, Eunice, and Lucy each receives £1.[67]
  Daniel and Abigail were parents of seven children born (recorded) at Windham and Pomfret.

[65] Peck, *Genealogical History of the Descendants of Joseph Peck*, p 279
[66] Dwight, *History of the Descendants of Elder John Strong*, p 310
[67] *Connecticut. Probate Court (Pomfret District); Probate Place: Windham, Connecticut, Probate Records, Vol 3-4, 1762-1778, volume 3, pp 391-392*

97)   i   DANIEL HOLT, b. at Windham, 5 Apr 1731; d. at Cherry Valley, NY, 21 Jan 1796; m. at Pomfret, 26 Dec 1753, his stepsister, KEZIA RUST, b. at Coventry, 16 Aug 1735 daughter of Noah and Kezia (Strong) Rust;[68] Kezia d. at Cherry Valley, 23 Dec 1825.

98)   ii   ABIGAIL HOLT, b. at Windham, 20 Feb 1732; d. at Abington, 11 Oct 1774; m. RICHARD KIMBALL, b. at Bradford, MA, 18 Jul 1722 son of Samuel and Sarah (Spofford) Kimball; Richard d. at Ames, NY, 30 Apr 1810.

99)   iii   SILAS HOLT, b. at Windham, 29 Dec 1735; d. at Ashford, 23 Oct 1773; m. at Pomfret, 20 Jan 1757, MARY BROOKS, b. at Pomfret, 14 Oct 1735 daughter of John and Phebe (Richardson) Brooks.

100)   iv   LOIS HOLT, b. at Windham, 4 Feb 1739; d. at Ashford, Oct 1792; m. at Pomfret, 26 Sep 1758, MOSES ROGERS, b. at Billerica, 24 Feb 1730/1 son of Nathaniel and Mary (Haggit) Rogers; Moses d. at Ashford, 1797 (probate 1797).

101)   v   EUNICE HOLT, b. at Pomfret, 22 Aug 1741; m. at Pomfret, 28 Nov 1760, JOSIAH WHEELER, b. at Pomfret, 21 Mar 1737/8 son of Josiah and Anna (Grosvenor) Wheeler.

102)   vi   ASA HOLT, b. at Pomfret, 7 Jun 1745; d. at Springfield, VT, 1 Mar 1813; m. at Pomfret, 20 Nov 1766, MARGARET HAMMOND, baptized at Woodstock, 9 Dec 1744 daughter of Jonathan and Katherine (Davis) Hammond; Margaret d. at Springfield, 28 Sep 1834.

103)   vii   LUCY HOLT, b. at Pomfret, 10 Oct 1747; m. at Brooklyn, CT, 27 Nov 1770, JEDEDIAH DANA, b. at Ashford, 9 Aug 1739 son of Jedediah and Elizabeth (Barnard) Dana; Jedediah d. at German Flatts, NY, 1809 (probate 31 Jan 1809).

Children of Thomas Russell and Phebe Johnson

19)   MEHITABLE RUSSELL (*Thomas², Robert¹*), b. at Andover, about 1688 daughter of Thomas and Phebe (Johnson) Russell; d. at Andover, 18 Dec 1733; m. at Andover, 10 Jun 1708, JOSEPH CHANDLER, b. at Andover, 17 Jul 1682 son of William and Bridget (Henchman) Chandler; Joseph d. at Andover, 22 Apr 1734.
     Mehitable and Joseph farmed in Andover where they lived throughout their lives. Joseph was admitted to South Church on 15 May 1720 and Mehitable on 5 June 1720 where they remained members until their deaths.[69]
     In his will written 18 December 1732 (probate 20 May 1734), Joseph Chandler bequeaths to beloved wife Mehitable all the beds and bedding, and the brass, pewter, and iron ware that are household items. Son Thomas Chandler receives all the lands and buildings in Andover particularly the homestead. He also receives the husbandry tools. Son Joseph Chandler receives £20 in the current money of New England to be paid by Thomas. Son John Chandler also receives £20. Daughter Mebitabel Crosby receives five shillings as she received her portion at her marriage. Daughter Mary Chandler receives £20. Daughters Bridget, Phebe, and Hannah each also receives £20. Thomas Chandler is named sole executor.[70]

104)   i   MEHITABLE CHANDLER, b. at Andover, about 1709; d. at Townsend, MA, Jul 1768;[71] m. 1st at Andover, 7 Feb 1731/2, ROBERT CROSBY, b. at Billerica, 20 Jul 1711 son of Joseph and Sarah (French) Crosby; Robert d. at Townsend, 10 Feb 1743. Mehitable m. 2nd 26 Nov 1745, ANDREW SPALDING, b. at Chelmsford, 8 Dec 1701 son of Andrew and Abigail (Waring) Spalding. Andrew was first married to Hannah Wright.

105)   ii   THOMAS CHANDLER, b. at Andover, 22 Apr 1711; d. at Andover, about 1761 (probate 13 Sep 1761); m. at Andover, ELIZABETH WALCOTT, b. about 1718 daughter of Ebenezer and Elizabeth (Wiley) Walcott; Elizabeth d. after 1765 when she sold land from the estate.

106)   iii   MARY CHANDLER, b. at Andover, 4 Mar 1712/3; d. at Andover, 10 Feb 1751; m. at Andover, 22 Oct 1733, JAMES HOLT, b. at Andover, 1707 son of James and Susanna (Preston) Holt; James d. at Andover, 1751 (probate 16 Dec 1751).

        iv   PHEBE CHANDLER, b. about 1717; d. at Andover, 13 May 1737.

---

[68] The distribution of the estate of Noah Russ includes distribution to daughter Keziah Holt. Distribution is 27 December 1753 the day after the wedding of Daniel and Kezia.

[69] South Church of Andover, Historical Manual, p 128

[70] *Essex County, MA: Probate File Papers, 1638-1881.* Online database. *AmericanAncestors.org.* New England Historic Genealogical Society, 2014. Case 4945

[71] Mehetabel Spalding the wife of Andrew Spalding deceast this life July the . . . 1768 (Townsend, MA town records)

107)   v   JOSEPH CHANDLER, b. at Andover; m. 30 Dec 1741, SARAH RICHARDSON, b. at Bradford, MA, 26 Sep 1719 daughter of Joseph and Hannah (Nelson) Richardson.[72]

vi   BRIDGET CHANDLER, b. 19 Sep 1719; d. 20 Aug 1736.

58)   vii   JOHN CHANDLER, b. at Andover, 19 Jan 1721/2; d. at Andover, 11 May 1759; m. 1st at Andover, 11 Mar 1744/5, his first cousin, PRUDENCE RUSSELL, baptized at Andover 11 Jul 1720 daughter of Robert and Abigail (Flint) Russell; Prudence d. 15 Nov 1745. John m. 2nd at Andover, 15 Oct 1757, HANNAH PHELPS, b. at Andover, 1709 daughter of Samuel and Hannah (Dane) Phelps; Hannah d. at Andover, 5 Aug 1781. Hannah was first married to Ephraim Abbott.

108)   viii   HANNAH CHANDLER, baptized at Andover, 2 Feb 1724; m. at Andover, 10 Aug 1741, DAVID ABBOTT, b. at Andover, Dec 1716 son of Jonathan and Zerviah (Holt) Abbott; David d. at Pembroke, NH, 1777 (probate 31 Dec 1777).

ix   Son b. 10 Sep 1726 and d. 16 Sep 1726.

20)   ROBERT RUSSELL (*Thomas², Robert¹*), b. at Andover, about 1690 son of Thomas and Phebe (Johnson) Russell; d. at Reading, 1759 (probate 1759); m. 1st at Andover, 22 Jun 1716, ABIGAIL FLINT; Abigail d. at Andover, 10 May 1723. Robert m. 2nd at Andover, 2 Jan 1727/8, HANNAH HOLT, b. at Andover, 30 Nov 1702 daughter of Samuel and Hannah (Farnum) Holt; Hannah d. at Reading, 3 Apr 1749. Robert m. 3rd at Andover, 23 Dec 1749, widow ELIZABETH MANNING. Robert m. 4th at Andover, 17 Apr 1755, widow MARTHA PARKER.

Robert Russell resided in Reading where he served on a committee to find a suitable place to keep school.[73]

In his will written 8 June 1757 (probate 31 December 1759), Robert Russell bequeathed to beloved wife Martha the income of one-third part of the real estate during her natural life as well house one-third of the household goods. Son Ezekiel receives £3.6.8 which makes his full portion. Son Timothy receives all the lands and buildings in Reading and Andover. Daughter Hannah Peirce receives £3.6.8 and daughters Mary, Eunice, Phebe, and Elizabeth each receives £13.6.8. Granddaughter Abigail Bachelor receives six shillings as does grandson Phineas Holt. Household goods are to be equally divided among his five daughters and clothing divided between his two sons. Son Timothy was named sole executor.[74] Personal estate was valued at £21.8.11. Son Timothy Russell married but did not have children. In his will, he includes small bequests to brother Ezekiel Russell, sister Pierce, sister Mary Levis, sister Eunice Brown, sister Phebe Cheney, and sister Elizabeth Perley.

Robert Russell and Abigail Flint were parents of three children born at Andover.

109)   i   ABIGAIL RUSSELL, b. at Andover, 4 Oct 1717; d. at Reading, 1746 (probate Sep 1746); m. at Reading, 23 Sep 1735, EBENEZER EATON; Ebenezer d. at Reading, 1738 (probate 1738).

58)   ii   PRUDENCE RUSSELL, baptized at Andover, 31 Jul 1720; d. at Andover, 15 Nov 1745; m. 1st 9 Jul 1741, her first cousin once removed, MOSES HOLT, b. at Andover, 21 Oct 1716 son of Moses and Elizabeth (Russell) Holt; Moses d. at Andover, 6 Ju; 1743. Prudence m. 2nd 11 Mar 1744/5, her first cousin, JOHN CHANDLER, b. at Andover, 19 Jan 1721/2 son of Joseph and Mehitable (Russell) Chandler; John d. at Andover, 11 May 1759. John married second Hannah Phelps.

110)   iii   EZEKIEL RUSSELL, b. at Andover, 10 Jun 1722; d. at Wilbraham, MA, 3 Jan 1802; m. TABATHA FLINT, b. at Reading, 18 May 1721 daughter of Ebenezer and Tabitha (Burnap) Flint; Tabitha d. at Wilbraham, 4 Jan 1808.[75]

Robert Russell and Hannah Holt were parents of seven children born at Reading.

i   HANNAH RUSSELL, b. 20 Apr 1730; not mentioned in father's will.

ii   MARY RUSSELL, b. 1731; died young.

iii   TIMOTHY RUSSELL, b. at Reading, 11 Aug 1733; d. at Boxford, 1818 (probate 20 Oct 1818); m. MARGARET who has not been identified. Timothy and Margaret did not have children.

iv   BENJAMIN RUSSELL, b. 1735; not mentioned in father's will.

---

[72] The 1746 will of Joseph Richardson of Bradford includes a bequest to daughter Sarah wife of Joseph Chandler.

[73] Eaton, *Genealogical History of the Town of Reading*, p 146

[74] *Middlesex County, MA: Probate File Papers, 1648-1871.* Online database. *AmericanAncestors.org.* New England Historic Genealogical Society, 2014. Case 19690

[75] Ezekiel and Tabatha are married at the Old Hampden Cemetery in Hampden. Find A Grave 43582031 and 43582032

     v   MARY RUSSELL, b. at Andover, 7 Jun 1740. She perhaps married John Lovis in 1781. If so, she did not have children.

     vi   ASA RUSSELL, b. 28 Sep 1744; not mentioned in father's will.

     vii   EUNICE RUSSELL, b. at Andover, 23 Feb 1746; m. at Reading, 29 Nov 1764, JONATHAN BROWN. No children were identified for Eunice and Jonathan.

Robert and Elizabeth Russell were parents of two children born at Reading.

111)   i   PHEBE RUSSELL, b. 1751; m. at Andover, 19 Nov 1776, DAVID CHENEY, b. at Boxford, 11 Sep 1750 son of Ichabod and Rebekah (Smith) Cheney.

112)   ii   ELIZABETH RUSSELL, b. at Reading, 1752; d. at Boxford, 12 Mar 1840; m. 1st at Danvers, 12 Dec 1776, ELIJAH MOULTON, b. at Danvers, 5 Dec 1748 son of Benjamin and Sarah (Smith) Moulton; Elijah d. at Danvers, 1782 (probate 7 Oct 1782). Elizabeth m. 2nd at Boxford, 10 Jun 1788, JESSE PERLEY, b. at Boxford, 20 Jun 1761 son of Nathaniel and Mehitable (Perley) Perley; Jesse d. at Boxford, 18 Apr 1846.

21)   PHEBE RUSSELL (*Thomas²*, *Robert¹*), b. at Andover, 21 Jan 1689/90 daughter of Thomas and Phebe (Johnson) Russell; d. at Windham, CT, after 1753 (distribution of widow's dower to Phebe Farnum aka Robins 13 Apr 1753 from the estate of Henry Farnum); m. at Andover, 12 Jun 1712, HENRY FARNUM, b. at Andover, 15 Sep 1687 son of Ralph and Sarah (Sterling) Farnum; Henry d. at Windham, 23 Jul 1732. Phebe m. 2nd at Canterbury, 3 Jan 1734, NATHANIEL ROBBINS; Nathaniel d. at Windham, 7 Apr 1753.

     Henry and Phebe began their family in Andover. Henry purchased land in Windham County, Connecticut in 1725 and the family relocated there. Henry committed suicide by hanging.[76] Phebe remarried, and her second husband died in 1753. In 1753, the dower from the estate of Henry Farnum was set off to his widow Phebe Farnum alias Robens.[77]

     Phebe Russell and Henry Farnum were parents of nine children, all but the youngest two children born perhaps at Andover, although most of the births are recorded both at Andover and at Windham.

113)   i   PHEBE FARNUM, b. at Andover, 4 Jul 1713; d. at Windham, 1750 (probate Apr 1750); m. at Windham, 9 May 1735, JOSEPH PRESTON, b. at Andover, 22 Aug 1713 son of Joseph and Rebecca (Preston) Preston; Joseph d. at Windham, 24 Feb 1738.

114)   ii   HENRY FARNUM, b. at Andover, 8 Apr 1715; d. at Sprague, CT, 20 Jun 1799; m. 3 Nov 1741, SARAH READ (widow of Joseph Knight), b. at Norwich, 28 Dec 1711 daughter of William and Ann (Stark) Read; Sarah d. at Sprague, 24 Feb 1781.

115)   iii   MANASSEH FARNUM, b. at Windham, 15 Feb 1717; d. at Ashford, 1768 (probate 1768); m. at Windham, 23 Apr 1739, KEZIAH FORD, b. at Windham, 27 Mar 1721 daughter of Joseph and Elizabeth (Hovey) Ford; Keziah was living in 1768.

     iv   JEMIMA FARNUM, b. at Windham, 6 Feb 1719; m. 7 Feb 1746, NATHANIEL JOHNSON. No children have been located for Jemima and Nathaniel.

116)   v   EPHRAIM FARNUM, b. at Windham, 20 Mar 1721; d. at Norwich, about 1750 (probate 17 Jan 1751); m. 1 Nov 1744, CHENEY ANNE WHITE, b. at Marshfield, MA, 16 Jul 1722 daughter of Ebenezer and Hannah (Doggett) White. Cheney Anne second married John Louden.

117)   vi   JOSHUA FARNUM, b. at Windham, 29 Mar 1723; d. at Scotland, CT, 3 Feb 1797; m. at Hampton, 6 Jun 1748, SARAH FORD, b. at Windham, 20 Dec 1714 daughter of Joseph and Elizabeth (Hovey) Ford; Sarah d. at Scotland, 28 Apr 1789.

118)   vii   ELIPHALET FARNUM, b. at Windham, 21 Mar 1725; m. 1st at Canterbury, 11 Oct 1750, MARY ROGERS, possibly Mary b. at Windham, 6 Oct 1727 daughter of Hope and Esther (Meacham) Rogers; Mary d. at Canterbury, 1 May 1753. Eliphalet m. 2nd at Canterbury, 1 Feb 1757, MARY ADAMS.

     viii   STEPHEN FARNUM, b. at Windham, 27 Mar 1728. He perhaps m. at Pomfret, 2 Mar 1752, JOANNA WARNER. No children were located for Stephen with his possible marriage to Joanna.

---

[76] Farnham, *The New England Descendants of Immigrant Ralph Farnum*, p 91

[77] *Connecticut State Library (Hartford, Connecticut); Probate Place: Hartford, Connecticut, Probate Packets, Durkee, P-Fitch, Eleazer, 1719-1880, Estate of Henry Farnam, Case 1312*

119)   ix   ELIAB FARNUM, b. at Windham, 24 Jul 1731; d. at Otisville, NY, 9 Jun 1806; m. at Preston, 19 Jun 1754, ABIGAIL KILLAM, b. at Norwich, 19 Aug 1736 daughter of John and Abigail (Kimball) Killam; Abigail d. at Otisville, about 1782. Eliab m. 2nd EUNICE NICHOLS, b. about 1739. Eunice had two previous marriages to John Osborne and Samuel Bouton.

22)   MARY RUSSELL (*Thomas², Robert¹*), b. at Andover, 10 Feb 1692/3 daughter of Thomas and Phebe (Johnson) Russell; d. at Andover, 1778 (probate 3 Feb 1778); m. at Andover, 10 May 1716, TIMOTHY OSGOOD, b. at Andover, 22 Aug 1693 son of Timothy and Deborah (Poor) Osgood; Timothy d. 1772 (probate 24 Nov 1772).

In his will written 13 June 1769 (probate 24 November 1772), Timothy Osgood bequeaths to beloved wife Mary all the household goods and one-third of the personal estate to be at her disposal. She also receives the improvement on one-third of the real estate. Son Peter receives the dwelling house and the tanner house on the land where Peter now lives which completes his portion. Son Isaac receives £67 to complete his portion. Grandchildren who are the children of Timothy deceased receive five shillings and no more as Timothy received his full portion. The grandchildren are Timothy, Phebe, Abiah, and Asa. Daughter Deborah wife of Obadiah Wood receives £90. Daughter Phebe wife of Thomas Poor receives forty shillings and daughter Hannah wife of John Adams receives £107. Son Thomas Osgood receives all the real and personal estate in Andover as well as the money and bonds. Thomas is named executor. Real property was valued at £883 and personal estate at £155.[78]

In her will written 30 January 1775 (probate 3 February 1778), Mary Osgood made bequests of six shillings each to her children and the grandchildren of those children who were deceased as named: son Peter Osgood; son Timothy Osgood; son Thomas Osgood; son Isaac Osgood; the children of son Timothy Osgood who are Timothy, Phebe, Abiah, and Asa; granddaughter Susannah Kittredge; grandsons John Adams and Isaac Adams the children of Hannah the late wife of John Adams. Daughters Phebe Poor wife of Thomas Poor and Deborah Wood wife of Obadiah Wood receive all the household goods. Son-in-law Thomas Poor was named executor.[79] Susanna Kittredge named in the will is a daughter of Peter; she married Thomas Kittredge.

Mary Russell and Timothy Osgood were parents of eight children born at Andover.

120)   i   PETER OSGOOD, b. at Andover, 14 Nov 1717; d. at Andover, 17 Nov 1801; m. at Andover, 8 Sep 1743, SARAH JOHNSON, b. at Andover, Nov 1719 daughter of Timothy and Katherine (Sprague) Johnson; Sarah d. at Andover, 1 Aug 1804.

121)   ii   TIMOTHY OSGOOD, b. at Andover, 26 Aug 1719; d. at Andover, 31 Aug 1753; m. 6 Jan 1742, PHEBE FRYE, b. at Andover, 19 Mar 1721 daughter of Nathan and Hannah (Bridges) Frye; Phebe d. at Andover, after 1783 (living at time of daughter's will).

122)   iii   THOMAS OSGOOD, b. at Andover, 2 Nov 1721; d. at Andover, 3 Nov 1798; m. 3 Dec 1747, SARAH HUTCHINSON, b. at Andover, 24 Sep 1719 daughter of John and Sarah (Adams) Hutchinson; Sarah d. 3 Nov 1798.

123)   iv   ISAAC OSGOOD, b. at Andover, 4 Aug 1724; d. at Haverhill, 17 May 1791; m. 18 Jun 1752, ABIGAIL BAILEY, b. at Haverhill, 10 Jan 1730 daughter of Joshua and Elizabeth (Johnson) Bailey; Abigail d. at Haverhill, 25 Jan 1801 of black jaundice.

       v   MARY OSGOOD, b. 21 Feb 1726; likely died young.

124)   vi   DEBORAH OSGOOD, b. at Andover, 28 Apr 1730; d. about 1793; m. 2 Jan 1759, OBADIAH WOOD, b. about 1734 likely the son of Nathaniel and Elizabeth (Powell) Wood; Obadiah d. at Andover, 23 Oct 1810. Obadiah m. 2nd 8 May 1794 widow Lydia Blanchard.

125)   vii   PHEBE OSGOOD, b. at Andover, 26 May 1733; d. at Methuen, 2 Mar 1797; m. about 1757, THOMAS POOR, b. at Andover 19 Jul 1732 son of Thomas and Mary (Adams) Poor; Thomas d. at Methuen, 23 Sep 1804. Thomas married second Miriam Sargent.

126)   viii   HANNAH OSGOOD, b. at Andover, 31 Jul 1735; d. at Andover, 22 Oct 1771; m. at Andover, 23 Nov 1758, JOHN ADAMS, b. at Andover, 3 Jul 1735 son of Israel and Tabitha (Farnum) Adams; John d. at Andover, 27 Jun 1813. John married second Hannah Thurston. John m. 3rd, 21 May 1776, MARY HOLT (*Stephen Holt⁴, Nicholas Holt³, Mary Russell Holt², Robert¹*), b. at Andover, 15 Dec 1741 daughter of Stephen and Mary (Farnum) Holt; Mary d. at Andover, 9 Nov 1829.

---

[78] *Essex County, MA: Probate File Papers, 1638-1881.* Online database. *AmericanAncestors.org.* New England Historic Genealogical Society, 2014. Case 20285

[79] *Essex County, MA: Probate File Papers, 1638-1881.* Online database. *AmericanAncestors.org.* New England Historic Genealogical Society, 2014. Case 20245

23)   SARAH RUSSELL (*Thomas², Robert¹*), b. at Andover, about 1695 daughter of Thomas and Phebe (Johnson) Russell; m. at Andover, 9 Sep 1715, JOHN ROSS, b. at Billerica, 18 Jan 1686/7 son of Thomas and Seeth (Holman) Ross.
          Births of three children are recorded for Sarah and John. It is not known what became of this family.

          i   JOHN ROSS, b. at Billerica, 23 Dec 1716

          ii   THOMAS ROSS, b. at Andover, 5 Oct 1718; d. 19 Dec 1719.

          iii   SARAH ROSS, b. at Andover, 3 Nov 1720

24)   PETER RUSSELL (*Thomas², Robert¹*), b. at Andover, 23 Apr 1700 son of Thomas and Phebe (Johnson) Russell; d. at Litchfield, NH, Nov 1759 (will 3 Nov, proved 28 Nov 1759); m. 31 Mar 1727, DEBORAH CROSBY, b. at Billerica, 13 Jul 1709 daughter of Joseph and Sarah (French) Crosby.
          Peter and Deborah had their first four children in Andover and then settled in Litchfield, New Hampshire.
          In his will written 3 November 1759 (proved 28 November 1759), Peter Russell bequeaths to beloved wife Deborah the income from one-third of the real estate and one-half of the house. The heirs of son Peletiah who is deceased receive five shillings and daughter Rachel also receives five shillings which completed her portion. There are bequests to other daughters Rebackah (three pounds five shillings), Phebe (four pounds), Deborah (five shillings), Hannah (four pounds), and Sarah (four pounds). His four sons will divide the rest of the estate and these are Peter, Joseph, James, and Thomas.[80]
          Peter Russell and Deborah Crosby were parents of eleven children.

  127)   i   PELETIAH RUSSELL, b. at Andover, 27 Dec 1727; d. in Nova Scotia in 1757 during the French and Indian War; m. about 1752, OLIVE MOORE, b. at Westford, 27 Dec 1729 daughter of Samuel and Deborah (Butterfield) Moore; Olive d. at Bath, NH, 11 Oct 1807. Olive m. 2nd Timothy Barron.

  128)   ii   RACHEL RUSSELL, b. at Andover, 1 Nov 1730; d. 28 Nov 1802; m. about 1747; TIMOTHY UNDERWOOD, b. about 1725 son of Joseph and Susannah (Parker) Underwood; Timothy d. at Putney, VT, about 1804.

          iii   REBECCA RUSSELL, b. at Andover, 29 Aug 1734; living in 1759 but nothing further certain known.

  129)   iv   PHEBE RUSSELL, b. at Andover, 16 May 1736; d. at Goffstown, NH, Nov 1836; m. 1st about 1752, JOHN BUTTERFIELD, b. at Chelmsford, 20 Feb 1731 son of John and Anne (Hildreth) Butterfield; John d. at Goffstown, 1765. Phebe m. 2nd, 774, SAMUEL ROBIE, b. at Hampton, NH, 17 Oct 1717 son of Ichabod and Sarah (Cass) Robie; Samuel d. at Goffstown, 18 Oct 1793.

  130)   v   PETER RUSSELL, b. at Litchfield, NH, 6 Aug 1738; d. at Peeling (later Woodstock), NH, 20 Aug 1815; m. about 1760, MEHITABLE STILES, b. at Middleton, MA, 10 Jun 1739 daughter of Caleb and Sarah (Walton) Stiles; Mehitable d. at Peeling, NH, 27 May 1811.

  131)   vi   DEBORAH RUSSELL, b. at Litchfield, NH, 3 Jun 1740; d. at Merrimack, NH, 9 Sep 1820; m. about 1758, JONATHAN CUMMINGS, b. at Dunstable, 5 Jun 1729 son of Jonathan and Elizabeth (Blanchard) Cummings; Jonathan d. at Merrimack, 10 Jul 1787.

          vii   HANNAH RUSSELL, b. at Litchfield, about 1742; living in 1759; nothing further known.

          viii   SARAH RUSSELL, b. about 1743; living in 1759; nothing further known.

          ix   JOSEPH RUSSELL, b. at Litchfield, about 1744; d. at Litchfield, 23 Jun 1762.

  132)   x   JAMES RUSSELL, b. at Litchfield, 31 May 1746; d. at Belpre, OH, 1821; m. 1st about 1774, MARY FRENCH, b. at Dunstable, NH, 18 Oct 1755 daughter of Benjamin and Mary (Lovewell) French; Mary d. at Woodstock, VT, about 1790. James m. 2nd at Ross, OH, 9 Aug 1814 the widow JUDAH O'NEAL.

          xi   THOMAS RUSSELL, b. at Litchfield, 13 Dec 1749; living in 1759; nothing further known.

25)   JOSEPH RUSSELL (*Thomas², Robert¹*), b. at Andover, Apr 1702 son of Thomas and Phebe (Johnson) Russell; m. 1st at Reading, 26 Nov 1728, HEPSIBAH EATON; Hepsibah d. at Andover, 14 Mar 1742/3. Joseph m 2nd at Andover, 27 Nov 1746, HANNAH PERKINS, b. at Andover, 15 Nov 1720 daughter of Timothy and Hannah (Buxton) Perkins; Hannah d. at Andover, 22 Mar 1775.
          Joseph Russell and Hepsibah Eaton were parents of five children born at Andover.

---

[80] Ancestry.com. *New Hampshire, Wills and Probate Records, 1643-1982* [database on-line]. Otis G. Hammond, New Hampshire Wills, volumes 35-38, pp 488-489

   i JOSEPH RUSSELL, b. 9 Jan 1729/30; d. at Andover, 1758 (probate 4 Dec 1758). Joseph did not marry. In his will, he left his entire estate to his brother Thomas "for the love, good will and affection I bear for him above the rest of my friends and relations."

133) ii THOMAS RUSSELL, b. at Andover, 5 Jun 1732; d. at Wilton, 30 Mar 1818; m. at Andover, 15 May 1760, his second cousin, BETHIAH HOLT (*Phebe Russell Holt³, John², Robert¹*), b. at Andover, 20 Mar 1743 daughter of Ephraim and Phebe (Russell) Holt; Bethiah d. at Wilton, 20 Aug 1817.

52) iii HEPHZIBAH RUSSELL, baptized at Andover, 30 Jun 1734; m. at Andover, 26 Feb 1756, her first cousin once removed, JOSEPH RUSSELL (*John², Robert¹*), b. at Andover, 8 Jan 1719/20 son of John and Sarah (Chandler) Russell; Joseph d. at Andover, 31 Aug 1783.

   iv HANNAH RUSSELL, b. 11 Jan 1739/40; likely died young.

   v DANIEL RUSSELL, baptized 17 Oct 1742; d. 3 Feb 1743.

Joseph Russell and Hannah Perkins were parents of eight children born at Andover.

   i PERKINS RUSSELL, b. 7 May 1748; *perhaps* d. at Middleton, 23 Aug 1765.

134) ii JONATHAN RUSSELL, b. 14 Oct 1749; d. after 1820 when he was living in Pamelia, NY; m. at Middleton, 17 Jan 1771, RUTH HUTCHINSON, baptized 16 Sep 1750 daughter of Josiah and Sarah (Dean) Hutchinson; Ruth d. after 1820.

135) iii SARAH RUSSELL, b. 29 Oct 1750; d. at Middleton, MA, 2 Jan 1844; m. at Middleton, 12 Aug 1772, NEHEMIAH WILKINS, b. at Middleton, 14 Aug 1752 son of Ichabod and Mary (Clark) Wilkins; Nehemiah d. at Middleton, 17 Jun 1811.

136) iv JAMES RUSSELL, b. at Andover, 7 Jan 1753; d. at Boxford, 24 Apr 1830; m. about 1782, REBECCA PEABODY, b. at Middleton, 24 Mar 1763 daughter of Joseph and Mary (·) Peabody; Rebecca d. at Middleton, 11 Oct 1844.

   v DANIEL RUSSELL, b. 21 Aug 1754

   vi ELIJAH RUSSELL, b. 8 Mar 1756

137) vii RACHEL RUSSELL, b. at Andover, 23 Feb 1757; d. after 1830 when she as living at Hillsborough; m. at Middleton, 29 Jan 1784, JONATHAN DWINELLS, b. at Lynn, 4 May 1759 son of David and Keziah (Ramsdell) Dunnel; Jonathan d. after 1830.

138) viii HANNAH RUSSELL, b. at Andover, 11 Oct 1760; d. at Newburyport, 24 Aug 1840; m. at Middleton, 10 May 1784, CALEB PUTNAM, b. at Danvers, 24 Nov 1763 son of Archelaus and Abigail (Goodrich) Putnam; Caleb d. at Newburyport, 6 Mar 1826.

26) JEMIMA RUSSELL (*Thomas², Robert¹*), b. at Andover, 18 Jul 1704 daughter of Thomas and Phebe (Johnson) Russell; d. at Littleton, MA, 20 Sep 1790;[81] m. at Andover, 16 Jul 1724, JOSEPH HUNT, b. at Billerica, 21 Sep 1694 son of Samuel and Mary (·) Hunt; Joseph d. at Andover, 1743 (probate 7 Nov 1743). Jemima m. 2nd, 13 Dec 1743, CHRISTOPHER TEMPLE, b. 1690 and d. at Littleton, 8 May 1782.

  Joseph Hunt did not leave a will and his estate entered probate 7 November 1743 with widow Jemima as administratrix and Joseph Russell and Robert Russell as sureties.[82] Personal estate was valued at £10.10.7.

  Jemima and Joseph were parents of five children born at Billerica.

139) i SARAH HUNT, b. at Billerica, 23 Dec 1725; m. at Westford, 7 Mar 1750, JOSIAH JOHNSON, b. at Lancaster, 5 Jun 1726 son of Josiah and Annis (Chandler) Johnson.

   ii JOSEPH HUNT, b. 11 May 1728; nothing further known.

   iii AMOS HUNT, b. 25 Nov 1729; nothing further known.

140) iv ROBERT HUNT, b. at Billerica, 20 Jan 1731/2; m. at Canaan, CT, 26 Dec 1753, REBEKAH PECK, b. at Litchfield, 15 Dec 1736 daughter of Isaac and Ruth (Tomlinson) Peck; Rebekah d. at Salisbury, CT, 1812.

---

[81] 1790 20 September was buried Jemima Widow aged 88 a member of this Church.

[82] *Essex County, MA: Probate File Papers, 1638-1881.* Online database. *AmericanAncestors.org.* New England Historic Genealogical Society, 2014. Case 14255.

141)   v   RUSSELL HUNT, b. at Billerica, about 1733; d. at Canaan, CT, 18 Oct 1806; m. at Canaan, 3 May 1758, LYDIA PECK, b. about 1738 likely the daughter of Isaac and Ruth (Tomlinson) Peck; Lydia d. at Canaan, 18 Feb 1818.

27)   JAMES RUSSELL (*Thomas², Robert¹*), b. at Andover, 15 Jun 1706 son of Thomas and Phebe (Johnson) Russell; m. at Amesbury, 3 Jun 1729, RHODA CHANDLER, b. at Andover, 1705 daughter of Joseph and Sarah (Abbott) Chandler.

     Although James and Rhoda likely had more than the three children listed, that cannot be confirmed yet. Sons James Russell and Thomas Chandler Russell are confirmed with birth records[83] and Joseph is a likely son of this family.

142)   i   JAMES RUSSELL, b. at North Yarmouth, ME, 7 Aug 1737; m. at North Yarmouth, 5 Jun 1760, LYDIA MITCHELL.

143)   ii   THOMAS CHANDLER RUSSELL, b. at Cumberland, 9 Oct 1740; m. about 1767, SARAH GOOCH, b. 17 Oct 1751 daughter of John and Elizabeth (Boothbay) Gooch.

144)   iii   JOSEPH RUSSELL, b. about 1742 and baptized at Yarmouth, 20 Feb 1743; d. 1775; m. at Cumberland, 22 Oct 1765, MIRIAM BROWN, b. at Cumberland, 10 Jun 1746 daughter of Jacob and Lydia (Weare) Brown.

Children of James Russell and Priscilla Osgood

28)   JAMES RUSSELL (*James², Robert¹*), b. at Andover, Apr 1710 son of James and Priscilla (Osgood) Russell; d. at Walpole, NH, 8 Oct 1784; m. at Andover, 15 Jan 1740/1, LUCY FARRAR, b. at Woburn, 8 Oct 1714 daughter of Isaac and Mary (Wolcott) Farrar; Lucy d. at Walpole, 24 Apr 1791.

     James resided in Andover until about 1750. While resident of Andover, he received property from his mother Priscilla Eaton on 8 March 1733/4 and from his uncle John Russell on 11 July 1747.[84] The property from uncle John was related to the estate division of James's grandfather Robert Russell. On 25 June 1741 (recorded 2 November 1754), James and his brother Thomas conveyed a small piece of land in Bearmeadow Swamp to Josiah Holt of Andover for payment of £4.10.[85] On 3 November 1748 (recorded 30 October 1765), James Russell of Andover conveyed to his brother Thomas of Andover for payment of £2,300 all his lands both upland meadow and swamp lying in the township of Andover including his homestead.[86]

     James and Lucy were in Andover, then Willington, Connecticut, and finally in Walpole, New Hampshire. They arrived in Walpole by 1770 where they were members of the church of Rev. Thomas Fessenden. The homestead James established was held in the family until 1879.[87] On 13 June 1773, James Russell of Walpole conveyed 25 acres of his property in Walpole to his sone Aquilla.[88]

     James Russell and Lucy Farrar were parents of nine children.

     i   JAMES RUSSELL, b. at Andover, 11 Jan 1741/2; d. at Willington, 19 Nov 1752.

     ii   PRISCILLA RUSSELL, b. at Andover, 5 Jul 1743; d. at Willington, 12 Nov 1752.

145)   iii   JEDUTHAN RUSSELL, b. at Andover, 31 Jan 1745; d. at Walpole, NH, 13 May 1813; m. 28 Nov 1772, SUSANNAH GLAZIER, b. at Willington, 24 Feb 1756 daughter of William and Freelove (Reed) Glazier; Susannah d. 8 Sep 1799.

     iv   LUCY RUSSELL, b. at Andover, Sep 1746; m. JOHN FLETCHER, b. 1748; John d. at Westmoreland, 6 Dec 1828. There are no children known for Lucy and John. In 1800, they were living in Westmoreland with one male age 10-15 in the home with them, but that child has not been identified.

146)   v   AQUILLA RUSSELL, b. at Andover, 1 May 1748; d. at Rochester, VT, 4 Dec 1823; m. 3 May 1780, ABIGAIL GLAZIER, b. about 1762 daughter of William and Freelove (Reed) Glazier; Abigail d. at Rochester, 15 Sep 1835.

---

[83] Bennett, Thomas C., Vital Records of Cumberland, Maine 1701-1892, 2014; http://digitalmaine.com/cumberland_books/1
[84] Essex County Deeds, 70:44; 124:79
[85] Essex County Deed, 100:211
[86] Essex County Deeds, 124:50
[87] Aldrich, *Walpole As It Was*, p 349
[88] New Hampshire, Cheshire County Deeds, Book 5, page 78

147) vi THOMAS RUSSELL, b. at Willington, 10 Apr 1751; d. at Walpole, NH, 28 Nov 1845; m. at Walpole, 25 Jan 1785, EUNICE ALEXANDER, b. 8 Sep 1769 daughter of Richard and Jerusha (Wyman) Alexander; Eunice d. at Walpole, 11 Jan 1859.

148) vii PRISCILLA RUSSELL, b. at Willington, 20 Feb 1753; d. at Rockingham, VT, 12 Jun 1816; m. at Walpole, 15 Oct 1778, DAVID PULSIPHER, b. 28 Sep 1757 son of David and Elizabeth (-) Pulsipher;[89] David d. at Rockingham, VT, 14 Jun 1835.

149) viii HANNAH RUSSELL, b. at Willington, 15 Nov 1754; d. at Stockholm, NY, 18 May 1840; m. LUKE FLETCHER, b. at Lancaster, MA, 24 Oct 1759 son of Robert and Rebecca (Edmunds) Fletcher; Luke d. at Stockholm, 14 Jan 1841.

ix JAMES RUSSELL, b. at Willington, 14 Feb 1757; d. 26 Mar 1759.

29) THOMAS RUSSELL (*James²*, *Robert¹*), b. at Andover, 18 Jun 1714 son of James and Priscilla (Osgood) Russell; d. at Andover, 23 Apr 1753; m. at Andover, 15 Apr 1742, ABIGAIL BALLARD, b. at Andover, 17 Aug 1718 daughter of Uriah and Elizabeth (Henshaw) Ballard; Abigail d. at Andover, 15 Jul 1802.

Thomas Russell did not leave a will and his estate entered probate 7 May 1753 with Abigail as administratrix. The homestead containing about 90 acres with buildings was valued at £376 and other small acreages totaled £182.[90]

Abigail and Thomas were parents of six children born at Andover.

150) i URIAH RUSSELL, b. at Andover, 14 May 1743; d. at Andover, 9 Nov 1822; m. at Andover, 15 Aug 1771, LYDIA ABBOTT, b. at Andover, 7 Mar 1744/5 daughter of Barachias and Hannah (Holt) Abbott; Lydia d. at Andover, 11 Jul 1829.

151) ii ELIZABETH RUSSELL, baptized at Andover, 24 Jan 1745; d. at Andover, 15 Sep 1820; m. at Andover, 3 Mar 1768, GIDEON FOSTER, b. at Andover, 21 Aug 1739 son of John and Mary (Osgood) Foster; Gideon d. at Andover, 9 Aug 1817.

152) iii THOMAS RUSSELL, b. at Andover, 12 Feb 1746/7; d. at Conway, NH, 15 Jul 1823; m. about 1767, SARAH EASTMAN b. 6 May 1749 daughter of Richard and Mary (Lovejoy) Eastman; Sarah d. at Conway, 29 Dec 1836.

iv JAMES RUSSELL, b. 7 May 1749; d. 22 Jun 1749.

153) v ABIGAIL RUSSELL, b. at Andover, 12 May 1750; d. at Salem, 4 May 1822; m. 1 Nov 1770 (intention) HENRY WILLIAMS, baptized at Salem, 22 Jul 1744 son of Henry and Mary (Waters) Williams; Henry d. at Salem, 17 Aug 1814.

vi PRISCILLA RUSSELL, b. at Andover, 2 Aug 1753; d. at Andover, 28 Mar 1842. Priscilla was a nurse known for her good works. She did not marry.

30) MARY RUSSELL (*James²*, *Robert¹*), baptized at Andover, 22 Apr 1716 daughter of James and Priscilla (Osgood) Russell; d. at Haverhill, 9 Sep 1803; m. 15 Jun 1743, as his second wife, SAMUEL APPLETON, b. at Ipswich, 20 Mar 1713 son of Oliver and Sarah (-) Appleton; Samuel d. at Haverhill, 20 Oct 1780. Samuel had other marriages to Mary Phillips and Mary Stevens.

Samuel was a hatter in Haverhill. He also served as town clerk and was a member of the Fire Society.[91]

In his will written 1 August 1780 (probate 7 November 1780), Samuel Appleton bequeathed to beloved wife Mary use of one-half of the dwelling house except one room reserved for daughter Hannah until she marries. Mary also receives use of one-half of the house lot and one-half of the pew in the meeting house along with specific provisions to be provided by the executor. Son Samuel receives a fifth part of all the money after the other sons have been made equal to what Samuel has received and the portion received by Hannah is equal to that of Mary. Son Thomas also receives a fifth part of the money with the same provisions as the bequest to Samuel. Son Daniel receives one-half of the dwelling house and house lot and will receive the other half after the death of his mother. Daniel also receives the hatter shop and tools and some other parcels of land. He also receives the other half of the pew. Son William receives a fifth part of the money. Daughter Mary Gale receives a tenth part of the money as does daughter Hannah. Son Daniel was named executor.[92] An addendum to the will leaves the great bible to wife Mary and wearing apparel to son-in-law Moses Gale. Real estate was valued at £368.6.8. Hard money on hand totaled

[89] Hayes, *History of the Town of Rockingham*, p 732

[90] Essex County, MA: Probate File Papers, 1638-1881.Online database. AmericanAncestors.org. New England Historic Genealogical Society, 2014. Case 24429

[91] Chase, *History of Haverhill*

[92] *Essex County, MA: Probate File Papers, 1638-1881.*Online database. *AmericanAncestors.org.* New England Historic Genealogical Society, 2014.

£156.19.8. The inventory also included many notes that Samuel held totaling more than £3300. Son Samuel mentioned in the will is his son from his marriage to Mary Stevens.

Mary Russell and Samuel Appleton were parents of six children born at Haverhill.

154) i   THOMAS APPLETON, b. at Haverhill, 15 Mar 1743/4; d. at Boston, 1 Dec 1803; m. at Boston, 15 Dec 1766, MARTHA BARNARD, baptized at Boston 7 Dec 1746 daughter of Benjamin and Lydia (Danforth) Barnard; Martha d. at Boston, 30 Jan 1829.

155) ii   MARY APPLETON, b. at Haverhill, 5 Jun 1746; d. at Haverhill, 29 Mar 1830; m. at Haverhill, 12 Oct 1769, MOSES GALE, b. at Haverhill, 21 Mar 1745/6 son of Benjamin and Hannah (Clement) Gale; Moses d. at Haverhill, 20 Jun 1827.

      iii HANNAH APPLETON, b. 13 Sep 1748; d. 22 Jul 1750.

156) iv   DANIEL APPLETON, b. at Haverhill, 16 Mar 1750/1; d. at Haverhill, 15 May 1828; m. at Haverhill, 26 Oct 1775, LYDIA ELA, b. at Haverhill, 30 Mar 1747 daughter of Jacob and Ednah (Little) Ela;[93] Lydia d. at Haverhill, 17 May 1826.

157) v   WILLIAM APPLETON, b. at Haverhill, 6 Apr 1754; d. at Boston, about 1799 (probate Feb 1800); m. 17 Dec 1782, HANNAH CLARK, b. about 1763 daughter of Samuel Clark. Hannah married second Amasa Delano in 1803. Hannah seems to have died before the probate of the estate of Amasa Delano in 1823.

158) vi   HANNAH APPLETON, b. at Haverhill, 19 Nov 1756; d. at Haverhill, 24 Oct 1824; m. at Haverhill, 20 Nov 1785, Dr. EDWARD WOODBURY, b. 1761; Edward d. at Haverhill, 29 Jan 1793.

Children of Sarah Russell and John Ingalls

31)   JOHN INGALLS (*Sarah Russell Ingalls², Robert¹*), b. at Andover, 23 Mar 1696/7 son of John and Sarah (Russell) Ingalls; d. at Abington, 2 Apr 1783; m. 1st, at Pomfret, 4 Jan 1735, MARY WILLIS who has not been identified. After Mary's death, John married SARAH who was his wife at the time he wrote his will.

In his will written 5 January 1769 (probate 1783), John Ingalls bequeathed to beloved wife Sarah one-half of the indoor movables to dispose of as she pleases. Son John is to provide her with whatever is necessary. Only daughter Mary Fisk, in addition to what she has received, receives a tract of land on the east part of his farm. Only son John receives all the real estate, lands, and buildings.[94]

159) i   MARY INGALLS, b. at Pomfret, 13 Nov 1735; m. at Pomfret, 9 Jan 1755, JOHN FISK, b. at Lexington, MA, 18 Nov 1731 son of Robert and Mary (Stimpson) Fisk; John d. at Pomfret, 6 Aug 1790.

      ii   JOHN INGALLS, b. at Pomfret, 13 Dec 1737; d. at Abington, 5 May 1818. John does not seem to have married

32)   MARY INGALLS (*Sarah Russell Ingalls², Robert¹*), b. at Andover, 27 Mar 1705 daughter of John and Sarah (Russell) Ingalls; m. at Andover, 12 Nov 1728, EPHRAIM FARNUM, b. at Andover, 12 Oct 1700 son of Ephraim and Priscilla (Holt) Farnum; Ephraim d. at Concord, NH, 1775.

Ephraim and Mary had their first child in Andover, but then relocated to Concord (Rumford) where Ephraim and four of his brothers were first settlers.[95] Ephraim and Mary were parents of six children.

      i   MARY FARNUM, b. at Andover, 16 Sep 1729; d. at Concord, 13 Jun 1736.

160) ii   EPHRAIM FARNUM, b. at Rumford, 21 Sep 1733; d. at Concord, 12 May 1827; m. at Bradford, MA, 23 Mar 1758, JUDITH HALL, b. at Bradford, 12 Apr 1739 daughter of David and Naomi (Gage) Hall; Judith d. at Concord, 13 Jul 1809.

[93] Ela, *Genealogy of the Ela Family*, p 8

[94] *Connecticut State Library (Hartford, Connecticut)*; Probate Place: *Hartford, Connecticut, Probate Packets, Humphrey, M-Johnson, H, 1752-1880, Estate of John Ingalls, Case 2278.*

[95] Bouton, *History of Concord*, p 655

161)   iii   MARY FARNUM, b. at Rumford, 8 Aug 1737; d. at Sanbornton, NH, 14 Feb 1805; m. about 1760, JONATHAN MERRILL, b. at Rumford, 10 Feb 1733 son of John and Lydia (Haynes) Merrill; Jonathan d. at New Chester, NH, 1795 (probate 21 Feb 1795).

162)   iv   BENJAMIN FARNUM, b. at Rumford, 21 Mar 1739; d. at Concord, 18 Mar 1812; m. ANNA MERRILL, b. at Rumford, 20 Dec 1743 daughter of John and Lydia (Haynes) Merrill;[96] Anna d. at Concord, 7 Mar 1803.

       v   JOHN FARNUM, b. at Rumford, 1 May 1743; d. 4 Sep 1746.

163)   vi   SARAH FARNUM, b. at Concord, 26 Jul 1747; d. at Fryeburg, ME, Mar 1829; m. WILLIAM EATON, b. at Hampstead, NH, 21 Apr 1743 son of Jeremiah and Hannah (Osgood) Eaton; William d. about 1780.

33)   MEHITABLE INGALLS (*Sarah Russell Ingalls², Robert¹*), b. at Andover, about 1708 daughter of John and Sarah (Russell) Ingalls; d. at Pomfret, about 1756; m. at Pomfret, 20 Dec 1731, BENJAMIN ALLEN, b. at Pomfret, 12 Jan 1708 son of Daniel and Hannah (Davis) Allen; Benjamin d. at Norwich, 23 May 1783. Benjamin married second Rebecca Perkins on 19 Jan 1757.

       Mehitable and Benjamin resided in Pomfret where they were admitted to the full communion of the church on 9 May 1756.[97] Mehitable likely died soon after as Benjamin remarried in January 1757.

       In his will written 17 May 1782 (proved 5 August 1783), Benjamin bequeathed to loving wife Rebecca one third of the personal to be hers forever and the use of one-third of the real estate during her natural life. The wearing apparel is to be divided equally among his sons Benjamin and Joseph and grandson Sluman son of Isaac deceased. Daughter Mehitabel wife of Simeon Case receives twenty shillings and daughter Hannah Allen receives fifteen pounds. The two daughter of son Isaac, Zipporah and Sarah, each receives twenty shillings. Daughter Mary Allen receives twenty-five pounds. All the real estate goes to son John who is responsible to pay the legacies. John is also named executor. Real estate was valued at £281.4.0 and the total estate value was £416.3.7.[98] Mary and John mentioned in the will are children from Benjamin's second marriage.[99]

164)   i   MEHITABLE ALLEN, b. at Pomfret, 9 Dec 1732; d. at Norwich, 4 Nov 1788; m. at Pomfret, 13 Mar 1759, SIMEON CASE, baptized at Norwich, 8 Apr 1733 son of John and Hannah (Ormsby) Case; Simeon d. at Norwich, 7 Jun 1785.

165)   ii   BENJAMIN ALLEN, b. at Pomfret, 9 Aug 1734; m. 1st at Pomfret, 24 Nov 1760, HANNAH CASE, baptized at Norwich, 18 Nov 1737 daughter of John and Hannah (Ormsby) Case; Hannah d. at Pomfret, 6 Nov 1780. Benjamin m. 2nd at Pomfret, 4 Dec 1782, SABRA HOSMER (widow of Edward Cleveland), baptized at Woodstock, 24 Sep 1732 daughter of Ephraim and Dorcas (Carpenter) Hosmer.

166)   iii   ISAAC ALLEN, b. at Pomfret, 12 Mar 1735; d. at Pomfret, 5 Apr 1765; m. at Norwich, 30 Jan 1760, SARAH FRENCH, baptized at Norwich, 1 Sep 1728 daughter of Abner and Sarah (Sluman) French.

167)   iv   JOSEPH ALLEN, b. at Pomfret, 2 Apr 1738; d. at Groton, NY, 4 Dec 1815; m. at Pomfret, 13 Oct 1761, ELIZABETH WARNER, baptized at Ipswich, MA, 10 Feb 1738/9 daughter of Daniel and Sarah (Warner) Warner; Elizabeth d. at Groton, 2 Dec 1815.

       v   SARAH ALLEN, b. 25 May 1740; d. 21 Feb 1761.

       vi   HANNAH ALLEN, b. at Pomfret, 23 Jun 1742. Hannah was unmarried when her father wrote his will in 1782.

       vii   SETH ALLEN, b. 20 Feb 1749; nothing further known, and he is not in father's will. It may be that this birth transcription is an error and it represent the death of Seth. There is a death of Seth recorded as 17 Oct 1748, and perhaps the two dates are just reversed.

34)   STEPHEN INGALLS (*Sarah Russell Ingalls², Robert¹*), b. at Andover, 24 Jul 1710 son of John and Sarah (Russell) Ingalls; d. at Pomfret, 10 Dec 1771; m. 1st at Pomfret, 16 Jun 1734, REBEKAH GROW, b. at Andover, 21 Apr 1712 daughter of Thomas and Rebekah (Holt) Grow; Rebekah d. at Pomfret, 30 Jan 1762. Stephen m. 2nd, 27 Jan 1763, MARY TRESCOTT who has not been identified.

       At the settlement of Stephen Ingalls's estate, the widow Mary Ingalls and the four surviving children reach an amicable agreement of the division of the estate. The children listed and agreeing to the division are sons Thomas Ingalls and

---

[96] The 1773 will of John Merrill includes a bequest to his daughter Ann Farnham.

[97] Connecticut Church Record Abstracts, volume 090, Pomfret, p 3

[98] Connecticut Wills and Probate, Norwich District, Estate of Benjamin Allen, Case 161

[99] Daughter Molly Allen has a birth date of 17 Jan 1761, and although she is recorded as daughter of Benjamin and Mehitable, she was born four years after Benjamin's second marriage. Son John was baptized at Norwich on 2 May 1762.

Samuel Ingalls, daughter Sarah Copeland wife of James Copeland, and daughter Ruth Ingalls.[100] Real estate was valued at £167.15.0.

Rebekah and Stephen were parents of five children born at Pomfret. Son Stephen died one week before his father.

168)   i   SARAH INGALLS, b. at Pomfret, 7 Nov 1735; m. at Pomfret, 26 Feb 1756, JAMES COPELAND, b. at Braintree, MA, 19 Mar 1724 son of William and Mary (Thayer) Copeland.[101]

        ii   STEPHEN INGALLS, b. 13 Dec 1737; d. at Pomfret, 2 Dec 1771.[102]

        iii   RUTH INGALLS, b. at Pomfret, 27 Jan 1739/40; d. at Pomfret, 1 Sep 1819. Ruth did not marry.

169)   iv   THOMAS INGALLS, b. at Pomfret, 9 Dec 1742; d. at Abington, CT, 10 Jan 1816; m. 1st at Pomfret, 26 Jun 1777, SARAH BOWEN, b. about 1749; Sarah d. at Pomfret, 6 Oct 1777. Thomas m. 2nd 8 Nov 1786, RUTH WOODWORTH; Ruth d. at Pomfret, 12 Apr 1827.

170)   v   SAMUEL INGALLS, b. at Pomfret, 22 Apr 1746; m. at Brooklyn, CT, 9 Nov 1769, DEBORAH MEACHAM, b. at Windham, 3 Nov 1749 daughter of Daniel and Lydia (Lillie) Meacham.

35)   ELIZABETH INGALLS (*Sarah Russell Ingalls², Robert¹*), b. at Andover, 24 Jul 1710 daughter of John and Sarah (Russell) Ingalls; m. at Andover, 22 Apr 1731, JOHN STEVENS of Charlestown.

        Little definitive information could be found for this family. From the will of Elizabeth's sister Sarah, it is known that John was deceased before 1763 and Elizabeth was living in 1763. The Charlestown records have just one birth as recorded as the child of John and Elizabeth (Mary born in 1750), but seven other birth records listing just father John might be assumed to be of this family. There were two other John Stevens in Charlestown having children around the same time, but one of these (John Stevens and Abigail Wyer) were married in 1722 and having children earlier and the other (John Stevens and Lydia Soley) were married in 1746. There are no probate or other records that would help settle on marriages for any of the children.

        i   JOHN STEVENS, b. 1733

        ii   WILLIAM STEVENS, b. Dec 1734

        iii   EBENEZER STEVENS, b. 1737

        iv   SAMUEL STEVENS, b. about 1740 (date blank but listed on the page with 1739 and 1740 births)

        v   SARAH STEVENS, b. Dec 1742

        vi   ANNA STEVENS, b. Feb 1744

        vii   MARY STEVENS, b. Apr 1747

        viii MARY STEVENS, b. 1 Dec 1750

36)   MARTHA INGALLS (*Sarah Russell Ingalls², Robert¹*), b. at Andover, 9 Feb 1712/13 daughter of John and Sarah (Russell) Ingalls; m. 1st at Andover, 10 Mar 1729/30, WILLIAM BARKER, b. at Andover, about 1708 son of William and Mary (Barker) Barker; William d. at Rumford, NH, 1 Jan 1741. Martha m. 2nd at Pomfret, 20 Dec 1743, JACOB GOODALE, b. 28 Feb 1708 son of Thomas and Sarah (Horrell) Goodale; Jacob d. about 1756. Martha m. 3rd EBENEZER GOODALE likely the brother of Jacob.

        Martha and her first husband William Barker resided in Rumford. After William's death, Mrs. Martha Barker of Rumford married Jacob Goodale of Pomfret on 20 Dec 1743. Jacob Goodale was first married to Peggy Atwell with whom he had six children.[103]

        Martha Ingalls and William Barker were parents of seven children.

171)   i   EPHRAIM BARKER, b. at Andover, 23 May 1730; m. 1st at Pomfret, 27 Feb 1752, HANNAH GROW, b. at Andover, 8 Nov 1723 daughter of Thomas and Rebekah (holt) Grow; Hannah d. at Windham, 29 Jul 1765. Ephraim m. 2nd at Norwich, 21 Dec 1767, widow MARY BURNHAM.

---

[100] *Connecticut State Library (Hartford, Connecticut); Probate Place: Hartford, Connecticut, Probate Packets, Humphrey, M-Johnson, H, 1752-1880,*
[101] Copeland, *The Copeland Family*, p 34
[102] Stephen is not known to have married. The Ingalls genealogy suggests he might have had a wife Rebecca and lists several children of a Rebecca who died at Pomfret. However, in each case the children listed in the Ingalls book are listed as the children of Ephraim and Mary Ingalls in the Barbour Collection.
[103] Williams, *A Genealogy of the Descendants of Robert Goodale*, p 30

172) ii WILLIAM BARKER, b. at Rumford, NH, 28 Jan 1731; d. at Worcester, MA, 1804 (probate Apr 1804); m. at Pomfret, 22 Sep 1765, SARAH FOSTER; b. about 1745; Sarah d. after 1804.

iii JOHN BARKER, b. at Rumford, 28 Nov 1733; living in 1748;[104] nothing further known.

173) iv MARY BARKER, b. at Rumford, 23 Nov 1735; m. at Pomfret, 29 Apr 1756, ISAAC ABBOTT, b. at Pomfret, 29 Aug 1732 son of Paul and Elizabeth (Gray) Abbott; Isaac d. at Milford, NH, about 1800.

v MARTHA BARKER, b. at Rumford, 22 Oct 1737; d. at Pomfret, about 1765; m. at Pomfret, 2 Apr 1765, THOMAS HOWARD, b. at Ipswich, 5 Sep 1742 son of Hezekiah and Sarah (Newman) Howard; Thomas d. at Tolland, 18 Oct 1805. Martha likely died soon after her marriage as Thomas married Priscilla Grow on 25 Nov 1765.

174) vi DEBORAH BARKER, b. at Rumford, 20 Sep 1739; d. at Royalton, VT, 13 Jul 1820; m. at Pomfret, 12 Jul 1763, JONATHAN COY, b. at Grafton, MA (as Jonathan MacCoye), 30 Oct 1730 son of William and Mary (Clark) MacCoye; Jonathan d. at Royalton, 7 Sep 1815.

175) vii STEPHEN BARKER, b. at Rumford, 21 Jan 1741; d. at Heath, MA, 15 Aug 1834; m. at Concord, MA, 8 Jun 1772, REBEKAH GIBSON, b. at Stow, MA 31 Mar 1754 daughter of Stephen and Sarah (Goss) Gibson; Rebekah d. at Heath, 15 Mar 1824.

Martha Ingalls and Jacob Goodale were parents of seven children born at Pomfret.

176) i REUBEN GOODELL, b. at Pomfret, 16 Aug 1744; d. at New Haven, 11 Feb 1822; m. at Pomfret, 27 May 1772, ABIGAIL SHARPE, b. at Pomfret, 14 May 1744 daughter of John and Dorcas (Davis) Sharpe;[105] Abigail d. at New Haven, 19 Mar 1819.

177) ii SIMEON GOODELL, b. at Pomfret, 13 Feb 1746; d. at Cherry Valley, NY, 2 Jul 1837; m. 8 Jun 1775, MARTHA WILLIAMS, b. at Pomfret, 25 Apr 1755 daughter of William and Martha (Williams) Williams;[106] Martha d. at Cherry Valley, 3 May 1786.

178) iii SILAS GOODELL, b. at Pomfret, 16 Aug 1747; d. at Norwich, 20 Mar 1825; m. at Norwich, 24 Jun 1784, SARAH MARSHALL, b. at Norwich, 20 Sep 1757 daughter of Thomas and Ann (Manwaring) Marshall; Sarah d. 11 Dec 1822.

179) iv PEGGY GOODALE, b. at Pomfret, 1 Sep 1749; d. at Brimfield, MA, 7 Jan 1826; m. about 1771, RICHARD BISHOP, b. at Manchester, MA, 9 Aug 1732 son of John and Elizabeth (Hooper) Bishop; Richard d. at Brimfield, 30 Apr 1806. Richard was first married to Sarah King.

v SARAH GOODALE, b. at Pomfret, 24 Jun 1751; m. at Pomfret, 17 Sep 1771, WILLIAM CLARK, b. at Pomfret, 1 Nov 1751 son of Nathaniel and Mary (Cummings) Clark. Further clear information was not found for this family. They may be the William and Sarah Clark settled in Dudley, MA but that is not certain.

180) vi BENJAMIN GOODALE, b. at Pomfret, 27 Jun 1753; d. at Sturbridge, MA, 19 Feb 1801; m. at Pomfret, 4 Mar 1779, ABIGAIL KIMBALL, b. about 1761 whose parents are not identified.

vii ESTHER GOODALE, b. 24 Feb 1756; d. 11 Sep 1764.

37) BENJAMIN INGALLS (*Sarah Russell Ingalls², Robert¹*), b. at Andover, 8 Nov 1716 son of John and Sarah (Russell) Ingalls; d. at Pomfret, 11 Oct 1800; m. at Pomfret, 4 Feb 1741, MARY LYON, b. at Pomfret, 8 Oct 1717 daughter of Abiel and Judith (Farrington) Lyon; Mary d. at Pomfret, 20 Apr 1784.

Benjamin Ingalls and Mary Lyon were parents of eight children born at Pomfret.[107]

i ALLIS INGALLS, b. 17 Oct 1742; d. 7 Feb 1744.

---

[104] Perley, Essex Antiquarian, volume 6, p 66

[105] The 1779 will of John Sharpe includes a bequest to his daughter Abigail Goodell

[106] Williams, *A Genealogy of the Descendants of Robert Goodale*, p 63. The 1810 will of Martha Williams relict of William Williams includes a bequest to the children of her daughter Martha Goodell.

[107] The Ingalls genealogy (Burleigh, *Genealogy and History of the Ingalls Family*, p 37) reports that Benjamin married Mary Stebbins and had children Caleb, Daniel, and Benjamin, but that is not supported by the records. The Ingalls genealogy also reports that son Daniel married Eunice, but it was son Benjamin that married Eunice Woodworth.

          ii   MARY INGALLS, b. 19 Feb 1743; d. 3 Apr 1744.

181)   iii   BENJAMIN INGALLS, b. at Pomfret, 25 Jul 1746; d. at Pomfret, 8 Oct 1825; m. at Pomfret, 6 Jul 1769, EUNICE WOODWORTH, likely the Eunice b. at Groton, 24 Jan 1748 daughter of Asa and Sarah (Lester) Woodworth; Eunice d. at Pomfret, 10 Aug 1819.

182)   iv   DAVID INGALLS, b. at Pomfret, 2 Aug 1747; d. at Pomfret, 10 May 1814; m. 1 Apr 1772, MARY MAY whose parents have not been identified.

183)   v   MARY INGALLS, b. at Pomfret, 13 Jun 1749; m. at Pomfret, 1 Jun 1769, DIER HASTINGS likely the son of Joseph and Zerviah (Crocker) Hastings.

          vi   DANIEL INGALLS, b. 3 Oct 1751; d. 5 Oct 1755.

          vii   PELETIAH INGALLS, b. 11 Dec 1753; d. 11 Nov 1776.

          viii ALLIS INGALLS, b. 13 Sep 1756; d. 21 Jan 1758.

Children of Benjamin Russell and Mary Preston

38)   BENJAMIN RUSSELL (*Benjamin², Robert¹*), b. at Andover, 1702 son of Benjamin and Mary (Preston) Russell; d. at Ashford, CT, 7 Oct 1754; m. SARAH PERRY, b. 4 Apr 1708 daughter of John and Sarah (Ingoldsby) Perry; Sarah d. at Eastford, 9 Dec 1786.

      Benjamin Russell did not leave a will and his estate entered probate 5 November 1754 with Benjamin Russell as administrator.[108] Real estate was valued at £1,000 and personal estate of £822. The dower was set-off to widow Sarah. John Russell signed receipt acknowledging payment to him for his portion of the estate. Receipt of payment from the estate was also signed by Ingoldsby Work and Mary Work. There is also a statement from Constant Hart acknowledging receipt and holding harmless Benjamin Russell for any matters related to his administration of the estate, and that if neither of the heirs Josiah Hart or John Hart lives to age twenty-one, their inheritance from the estate will revert to the estate.

      Benjamin Russell and Sarah Perry were parents of six children born at Ashford.

          i   EZEKIEL RUSSELL, b. 24 Jan 1724; d. 3 Feb 1724.

          ii   HANNAH RUSSELL, b. and d. 24 Mar 1725/6.

184)   iii   SARAH RUSSELL, b. at Ashford, 26 Feb 1726; d. at Eastford, 12 Mar 1752; m. by 1748, CONSTANT HART, baptized at Little Compton, RI, 14 Jul 1728 son of Nathaniel and Elizabeth (Perkins) Hart; Constant d. at Charlestown, NH, 1792 (probate 1792).

185)   iv   BENJAMIN RUSSELL, b. at Ashford, 26 Jan 1728; d. at Burlington, VT, 27 Jan 1808; m. 1st at Ashford, 11 Oct 1750, ELIZABETH REED; Elizabeth d. at Ashford, 6 Dec 1756. Benjamin m. 2nd at Ashford, 28 Feb 1757, PHEBE SMITH, b. 1735; Phebe d. at Burlington, 8 Sep 1823.

186)   v   JOHN RUSSELL, b. at Ashford, 11 Oct 1730; m. at Ashford, 10 Jul 1750, ALICE LYON, likely his first cousin b. about 1731 daughter of Seth and Abigail (Russell) Lyon; Alice d. at Springfield, VT, 2 Nov 1794.

187)   vi   MARY RUSSELL, b. at Ashford, 8 Jul 1733; d. at Ashford, 25 Mar 1771; m. 8 Aug 1750, INGOLDSBY WORK, b. at Ashford, 17 Feb 1726 son of Joseph and Elizabeth (Ingoldsby) Work; Ingoldsby d. at Ashford, 22 Mar 1813. After Mary's death, Ingoldsby married Esther Bugbee on 11 Jul 1771.

39)   MARY RUSSELL (*Benjamin², Robert¹*), b. at Andover, 1705 daughter of Benjamin and Mary (Preston) Russell; m. 13 Feb 1724, SAMUEL MARCY, b. at Woodstock, 28 Jul 1704 son of John and Sarah (Hadlock) Marcy; Samuel d. at Union, CT, 31 Jul 1783.[109]

      Mary and Samuel were in Ashford and Woodstock. Samuel purchased property in Union in 1753.[110] Mary Russell and Samuel Marcy were parents of eight children.

---

[108] *Connecticut State Library (Hartford, Connecticut);* Probate Place: *Hartford, Connecticut, Probate Packets, Randall, Jonathan-Russell, Smith, 1752-1880, Estate of Benjamin Russell, Case 3484.*

[109] Hammond, *The History of Union, Conn.*

[110] Hammond, *The History of Union, Conn.*, p 408

188) i JOHN MARCY, b. at Ashford, 23 Jul 1724; d. at Windsor, VT, 23 Nov 1797; m. at Middletown, 5 Mar 1751, HANNAH SHARPE, b. about 1724; Hannah d. at Windsor, 11 Apr 1801.[111]

189) ii DORCAS MARCY, b. at Ashford, 24 May 1727; d. at Mansfield, CT, 13 Dec 1766; m. at Woodstock, 12 Sep 1751, NATHANIEL CARY, b. at Windham, 23 Oct 1729 son of Jabez and Hannah (Handee) Cary; Nathaniel d. at Willington, 26 Jan 1818. Nathaniel married second Sarah Sargent and third Tabitha Root.

190) iii WILLIAM MARCY, b. at Woodstock, 17 Mar 1729/30; d. at Hartland, VT, Apr 1813; m. 1st at Union, 2 May 1756, LUCY BUGBEE, b. at Woodstock, 1740 daughter of Jesse and Elizabeth (Peake) Bugbee; Lucy d. about 1792. William m. 2nd before 1797, ROSANNA TUCKER, b. about 1754; Rosanna d. at Morristown, VT, 11 Oct 1830. Rosanna married second Thomas Hoadley.

191) iv ZEBADIAH MARCY, b. at Woodstock, 23 Aug 1732; d. at Willington, 1 Dec 1806; m. 21 Aug 1754, PRISCILLA MORRIS, b. 28 Apr 1737 daughter of Edward and Bethiah (Peake) Morris; Priscilla d. 30 Jul 1785.

192) v SAMUEL MARCY, b. at Woodstock, 19 Oct 1739; d. at Windsor, VT, 5 Feb 1820; m. at Union, 10 Apr 1763, LOIS PEAKE, b. at Union, about 1743 daughter of Christopher and Rebekah (Bugbee) Peake.

193) vi TABITHA MARCY, b. at Woodstock, 12 Sep 1742; d. at Union, 22 Jul 1807; m. about 1762, JOSEPH FAIRBANKS, b. at Holliston, MA, 3 Jun 1741 son of Jabez and Susannah (Corning) Fairbanks; Joseph d. at Union, 4 Jan 1817.

194) vii SIBBEL MARCY, b. at Woodstock, 13 Mar 1744/5; m. at Union, 28 Feb 1763, MOSES PEAKE, b. at Killingly, 10 Aug 1736 son of Christopher and Rebekah (Bugbee) Peake.

      viii ZERVIAH MARCY, b. at Woodstock, 30 Nov 1747; m. at Union, 28 Dec 1767, JAMES PAUL, b. at Union, 1742 son of Matthew and Sara (-) Paul. According to Hammond's History of Union, Conn., this family settled in Walpole, NH and James Paul is listed as head of household there in the 1790 census. No further certain record was found, and no children were identified.

40)   HANNAH RUSSELL (*Benjamin², Robert¹*), b. at Andover, about 1707 daughter of Benjamin and Mary (Preston) Russell; m. at Ashford, 4 Dec 1727, JOHN HUMPHREY, b. 14 Apr 1702 son of Arthur and Rachel (Rice) Humphrey; John d. at Eastford, 28 Mar 1784.
      Hannah Russell and John Humphrey were parents of ten children born at Ashford.

195) i HANNAH HUMPHREY, b. at Ashford, 11 Sep 1728; d. at Ashford, 1752; m. at Ashford, 6 Dec 1749, JONATHAN AVERY, b. at Dedham, 13 Sep 1722 son of Jonathan and Lydia (Healy) Avery; Jonathan d. at Ashford, 15 Jan 1749/50.

196) ii DOROTHY HUMPHREY, b. 25 Jun 1730. Dorothy had an out-of-wedlock child with JAMES DANIELSON. Dorothy m. 1st about 1752, JOHN GAGGILL who d. about 1758. Dorothy m. 2nd at Ashford, 1 Mar 1759, SAMUEL EASTMAN, b. at Ashford, 17 May 1716 son of Philip and Sarah (Parker) Eastman; Samuel d. at Rockingham, VT, 26 Jun 1789. Samuel was first married to Thankful Reed.

197) iii RACHEL HUMPHREY, b. 2 Apr 1732; m. at Ashford, 10 Jan 1754, JOHN PITTS, b. at Ashford, 25 Aug 1733 son of John and Susannah (Preston) Pitts.

198) iv MARY HUMPHREY, b. 5 Jul 1734; d. at Sherburne, NY, 20 Apr 1816; m. at Woodstock, 10 May 1753, EBENEZER EATON, b. at Tolland, 16 Feb 1734 son of Thomas and Elizabeth (Parker) Eaton; Ebenezer d. at Sherburne, 9 Jun 1815.

199) v SARAH HUMPHREY, b. 17 Jun 1737; d. at Westminster, VT, 1 Dec 1812; m. about 1756, JOSHUA STODDARD, likely Joshua b. at Newton, MA, 3 Apr 1732 son of Eleazer and Susannah (Hall) Stoddard; Joshua d. at Westminster, 6 Dec 1816.

      vi NATHAN HUMPHREY, b. 8 Oct 1739; d. 1 May 1740.

200) vii ZERVIAH HUMPHREY, b. 7 Dec 1743; d. at Eastford, 14 Aug 1827; m. at Ashford, 5 Mar 1771, NOAH PAINE, b. at Pomfret, 1 Apr 1742 son of Noah and Mehitable (Storrs) Paine; Noah d. at Eastford, 11 Mar 1826.

---

[111] There is another John Marcy born in Woodstock 27 Feb 1726/7 son of John and Experience Marcy who has been proposed as the husband of Hannah Sharpe. However, John the husband of Hannah died in 1797 at age 73 and the source that suggests he was the son of John and Experience gives his birth date as 1724 (the birth year of John son of Samuel) and their son John was born in 1727.

viii　BENJAMIN HUMPHREY, b. 5 May 1746; d. 23 Sep 1748.

ix　JOHN HUMPHREY, (birth record torn); d. 16 Sep 1748

x　ABIGAIL HUMPHREY, b. at d. 7 Mar 1749.

41)　ABIGAIL RUSSELL (*Benjamin², Robert¹*), b. at Andover, Mar 1710 daughter of Benjamin and Mary (Preston) Russell; m. 29 Mar 1726, SETH LYON, b. at Woodstock, 27 Mar 1704 son of Thomas and Abigail (Clark) Lyon.
　　There are records of five children of Seth and Abigail born at Ashford and Alice Lyon who married John Russell is likely a child in this family. There may be other children.

201)　i　MEHITABLE LYON, b. at Ashford, 6 Jan 1727; m. 1st at Ashford, 10 Apr 1749, JOSEPH CHUBB, b. at Ashford, 28 Dec 1719 son of Joseph and Mehitable (Presson) Chubb; Joseph d. at Ashford, 24 May 1755. Mehitable m. 2nd at Ashford, 1 Feb 1757, WILLIAM CHENEY, b. at Cambridge, about 1717; death not clear.[112] William Cheney was first married to Ruth Eastman. William and Ruth (Eastman) Cheney were the parents of Ebenezer who married Mehitable's sister Priscilla (see below).

ii　MARY LYON, b. 16 Jun 1728; nothing further known.

186)　iii　ALICE LYON, b. about 1731; d. at Springfield, VT, 2 Nov 1794; m. at Ashford, 10 Jul 1750, her first cousin, JOHN RUSSELL (*Benjamin³, Benjamin², Robert¹*), b. at Ashford, 11 Oct 1730 son of Benjamin and Sarah (Perry) Russell.

iv　SETH LYON, b. 24 Jul 1734; nothing further known.

202)　v　PRISCILLA LYON, b. at Ashford, 22 Mar 1741; d. at Fly Creek, NY, 26 Feb 1813; m. at Ashford, 2 Mar 1760, EBENEZER CHENEY, b. at Ashford, 23 May 1740 son of William and Ruth (Eastman) Cheney; Ebenezer d. at Fly Creek, 21 Sep 1800.

vi　ABIGAIL LYON, birth not known; d. at Ashford, 19 Aug 1760.

42)　LYDIA RUSSELL (*Benjamin², Robert¹*), b. at Andover, 15 Dec 1713 daughter of Benjamin and Mary (Preston) Russell; *likely* m. 27 Jan 1731, JONATHAN SANGER, b. at Woodstock, 8 Sep 1695 son of Nathaniel and Mary (Cutter) Sanger;[113] Jonathan d. at Willington, 18 May 1767.
　　Jonathan Sanger and Lydia Russell resided in Woodstock and Ashford.
　　Daughter Chloe married but did not have children. In her will written 26 September 1814, Chloe Holt made bequests to the heirs of her brother Azariah Sanger deceased, sister Lydia Wadkins, heirs of brother Noadiah Sanger deceased, heirs of sister Zuriah Convers deceased (Roxy Fuller, Charles Convers, and Stephen Convers), sister Mary Sanger, the heirs of brother Nathaniel Sanger, and brother Jonathan Sanger. There are bequests to Anson Law (no relationship given) and to Molly Weston wife of John Weston (no relationship given but likely Molly who was the daughter of Zerviah). The remainder of the estate is to be divided among her siblings and their heirs.[114]
　　Lydia Russell and Jonathan Sanger were parents of eleven children.

203)　i　AZARIAH SANGER, b. at Woodstock, 24 Jan 1732; d. at East Windsor, 1801 (probate 14 Dec 1801); m. at Willington, 22 Apr 1760, ELIZABETH ABBE, b. at Willington, 29 Aug 1734 daughter of Obadiah and Elizabeth (Bushnell) Abbe.

ii　DINAH SANGER, b. at Woodstock, 20 Sep 1734

iii　LYDIA SANGER, b. at Woodstock, 11 Jan 1736/7; likely m. at Ashford, 1757, THADDEUS WATKINS, b. at Ashford, 19 Nov 1729 son of Thaddeus and Anne (Humphrey) Watkins. There are records of four children of Lydia and Thaddeus at Ashford, but each of the records were torn and the first names of children were not readable (Barbour collection). From portions of the names, it may be the names were Edward, Thaddeus, Lydia, and Hannah but no further reliable information was found.

204)　iv　NOADIAH SANGER, b. at Woodstock, 12 Dec 1738; d. at Willington, 7 Aug 1808; m. at Willington, 14 Apr 1766, PRISCILLA RUSS, b. at Ashford, 23 Feb 1742/3 daughter of Abraham and Hannah (-) Russ; Priscilla d. about 1807.

v　JEDEDIAH SANGER, b. at Woodstock, 17 Apr 1741; d. during the Havana Expedition, 12 Nov 1762.

---

[112] There was a William Cheney of Connecticut killed at the Battle of Bunker Hill, but it is not clear that is was this William.
[113] Bowen, *The History of Woodstock*, volume 8, p 245
[114] Connecticut Wills and Probate, Stafford, Probate District, Town of Willington, estate of Chloe Holt, 1815, No. 1061

205) vi ZERUIAH SANGER, b. at Ashford, 31 Mar 1744; d. at Stafford, CT, 27 Apr 1777; m. 17 Nov 1768, STEPHEN CONVERS, b. at Killingly, 5 Aug 1745 son of Pain and Mary (Halford) Convers; Stephen d. at Stafford, 9 Oct 1823. Stephen married second Sarah Kimball on 12 Oct 1778.

vii MARY SANGER, b. at Ashford, 15 Dec 1745; Mary was living and unmarried when her sister Chloe wrote her will.

viii CHLOE SANGER, b. at Ashford, 2 Aug 1748; d. at Willington, 21 Feb 1815; m. 1st 18 Dec 1771, JUSTUS HATCH, b. at Tolland, 1 Nov 1751 son of Justus and Abigail (Case) Hatch; Justus d. at Willington, 14 Jun 1790. Chloe m. 2nd 17 May 1791, as his second wife, CALEB HOLT, b. at Windham, 6 Mar 1729 son of Abiel and Hannah (Abbott) Holt; Caleb d. at Willington, 18 Aug 1810. Chloe did not have children. Caleb Holt was fist married to Mary Merrick. In his will, Justus Hatch made bequests to his wife Chloe and to his brothers and sisters.[115]

ix HANNAH SANGER, baptized 23 May 1750

206) x NATHANIEL SANGER, b. at Ashford, 17 Jul 1754; d. at East Windsor, 11 Jan 1803; m. 28 Aug 1783, OLIVE CHAFFEE, b. at Woodstock, 24 Mar 1756 daughter of Ebenezer and Sarah (Adams) Chaffee.

207) xi JONATHAN SANGER, baptized 24 Aug 1755; d. at Canandaigua, NY, 21 Aug 1819; m. at Pomfret, 24 May 1781, LUCY SAWYER, b. at Petersham, 28 May 1759 daughter of John and Prudence (-) Sawyer; Lucy d. at Canandaigua, 31 May 1846.

43) JOSEPH RUSSELL (*Benjamin², Robert¹*), b. at Ashford, 5 Jun 1717 son of Benjamin and Mary (Preston) Russell; m. at Ashford, 13 May 1742, HANNAH LINKHORN, b. about 1716; Hannah d. at Ashford, 14 Dec 1801.
Little information was located for this family. There are records for eight children born at Ashford.

208) i JOHN RUSSELL, b. at Ashford, 16 Oct 1742; d. at Willington, 23 Jan 1811; m. at Ashford, 1 May 1766 REBEKAH WILSON, b. about 1740; Rebekah d. at Ashford, 19 Feb 1824.

ii MARY RUSSELL, b. 3 Oct 1744

209) iii ELISHA RUSSELL, b. at Ashford, 29 Sep 1746; d. at New Hartford, CT, 14 Feb 1791; m. at Middletown, 8 Nov 1772, ANNE WINSHIP, b. at Middletown, 26 Apr 1746 daughter of Timothy and Margaret (Merrick) Winship.

iv HANNAH RUSSELL, b. 8 Jun 1749

v NATHAN RUSSELL, b. 7 Apr 1751

vi BENJAMIN RUSSELL, b. 26 Nov 1753

vii JOSIAH RUSSELL, b. at Ashford, 7 May 1756; d. at Austerlitz, NY, 19 Jun 1820; m. at New Hartford, 4 Sep 1777, MARGARET SMITH, possibly the Margaret baptized at New Hartford, 6 Oct 1757 daughter of Martin and Elizabeth (Seymour) Smith; Margaret d. at Austerlitz, 24 May 1817. After Margaret's death, Josiah married Electa who has not been identified. Josiah and Margaret did not have children (or at least not children who lived to adulthood). In his will, Josiah has bequests to nieces and nephews including to a niece of his "late lamented" wife Margaret.

viii ANNA RUSSELL, b. 7 May 1756

44) ZERVIAH RUSSELL (*Benjamin², Robert¹*), baptized at Woodstock, 20 Mar 1719 of Benjamin and Mary (Preston) Russell; d. at Ashford, 17 Dec 1743; m. EZRA SMITH; Ezra d. at Ashford, 1798 (will proved 4 Mar 1798). Ezra married second Judah Bosworth on 23 May 1745, married third Catherine Billings, and married fourth Alice.
Zerviah was the mother of two children with Ezra Smith.
In his will written 24 August 1784 (probate 4 March 1798), Ezra Smith made bequest to beloved wife Alice, grandson Ezra Smith, granddaughter Judith Walker, daughters Elizabeth Webb and Sarah Walker, and son Simeon Smith. Simeon was named executor.[116]

i EZRA SMITH, b. at Ashford, 1739; d. at Ashford, 19 Nov 1758.

[115] Connecticut Wills and Probate, Stafford Probate District, Town of Willington, Estate of Justus Hatch, Jr., 1790, No. 3290
[116] Connecticut Wills and Probate, Pomfret District, Town of Ashford, Estate of Ezra Smith, 1798, No. 3707

210)   ii   SIMEON SMITH, b. at Ashford, 10 Nov 1741; d. at Ashford, 16 Jan 1799; m. 1st at Ashford, 18 Feb 1766,
                ANNA BYLES, b. at Ashford, 17 May 1749 daughter of Ebenezer and Anne (Bicknell) Byles; Anna d. at
                Ashford, 12 Apr 1791. Simeon m. 2nd about 1792, LUCY LYMAN (widow of John Waldo), b. at Coventry, 16
                Jul 1756 daughter of Elijah and Esther (Clark) Lyman; Lucy d. at Newark Valley, NY, 11 Jul 1826.

Children of Hannah Russell and Oliver Holt

45)   OLIVER HOLT (*Hannah Russell Holt², Robert¹*), b. 26 Dec 1698 son of Oliver and Hannah (Russell) Holt; d. of
smallpox, at Andover, 11 Nov 1760; m. 5 Jul 1722, SUSANNAH WRIGHT, b. at Andover, 24 Jul 1700 daughter of John and
Mary (Wardwell) Wright; Susannah d. of smallpox, 1 Dec 1760.
        Oliver was a blacksmith in Andover. He and Susannah died in a smallpox epidemic.
        In his will written 2 May 1760 (probate 9 March 1761), Oliver Holt bequeaths to beloved wife Susannah the use of the
east end of the house, a lengthy list of provisions, and the household goods. Eldest son Nathaniel receives all the lands and
buildings. Second son Oliver receives £13.6.8. Only surviving daughter Bula receives £6.13.4 when she arrives at age twenty-
one or marries. Nathaniel was named executor. Real estate was valued at £190.8.0.[117]
        Oliver and Susannah were parents of eight children born at Andover.

        i   OLIVER HOLT, b. 1 Jan 1723; d. 15 Apr 1738.

211)   ii   NATHANIEL HOLT, b. at Andover, 23 Nov 1725; d. at Andover, Feb 1806; m. 1 Aug 1751, ELIZABETH
                STEVENS, b. at Andover, 21 Oct 1730 daughter of John and Elizabeth (Chandler) Stevens; Elizabeth d. Dec
                1807.

        iii   HANNAH HOLT, b. at Andover, 29 Aug 1728; d. at Boxford, about 1756; m. 16 Nov 1752, JOHN STILES, b.
                at Boxford, 17 Mar 1724/5 son of John and Eleanor (Pearl) Stiles. John married second Hannah Deney on
                14 Mar 1757. There are no known children of Hannah and John.

        iv   SUSANNAH HOLT, b. 6 Apr 1731; d. 16 Jan 1747/8.

        v   URIAH HOLT, b. 1 Dec 1733; he was not living in 1760.

        vi   ASA HOLT, b. 4 Aug 1736; d. 25 Jan 1737/8.

212)   vii   OLIVER HOLT, b. at Andover, 24 Jan 1739/40; m. at Andover, 8 Oct 1761, EUNICE RAYMOND, b. at
                Beverly, 30 Apr 1744 daughter of Boanerges and Jemima (Meacham) Raymond. Oliver and Eunice lived in
                Wilton, NH.

213)   viii   BEULAH HOLT, b. at Andover, 12 Apr 1744; m. at Andover, 26 Apr 1770, her third cousin (through Holt
                line), JOHN GRAY, b. at Andover, 26 Dec 1745 son of Edward and Sarah (-) Gray.

46)   URIAH HOLT (*Hannah Russell Holt², Robert¹*), b. 25 Jun 1701 son of Oliver and Hannah (Russell) Holt; d. at
Lancaster, MA, 24 Aug 1741; m. 28 Sep 1725, SARAH WRIGHT, b. at Andover, 20 Mar 1696 daughter of Walter and Elizabeth
(Peters) Wright; Sarah d. at Beverly, 5 Mar 1779.[118] Sarah m. 2nd, at Harvard, 24 Jun 1747, Jonathan Cole (1699-1779).
        Uriah Holt was a blacksmith in Lancaster. After Uriah's early death, Sarah and her children relocated to Harvard
where the children married and where Sarah remarried.
        Uriah Holt did not leave a will and his estate entered probate 7 September 1741 with Sarah as administratrix.[119] His
personal estate include blacksmith tools and materials was appraised at £338.
        Uriah and Sarah were parents of seven children born at Lancaster.

        i   URIAH HOLT, b. 10 May 1726; died young.

214)   ii   SARAH HOLT, b. at Lancaster, 18 Mar 1727; d. at Harvard, 29 Oct 1769; m. at Harvard, 27 Nov 1746,
                JONATHAN WHITNEY, b. 1724 son of Jonathan and Alice (Willard) Whitney;[120] Jonathan d. at Harvard,
                20 Jan 1770.

---

[117] *Essex County, MA: Probate File Papers, 1638-1881.*Online database. *AmericanAncestors.org.* New England Historic Genealogical Society, 2014.
Case 13681

[118] ____ , wid. Jonathan, small pox, bur. Mar. 5, 1779, a. 85 y. C. R.1.

[119] *Worcester County, MA: Probate File Papers, 1731-1881.* Online database. AmericanAncestors.org. New England Historic Genealogical Society,
2015. Case 30680

[120] Although there is not a birth record for Jonathan, he can be established as the son of Jonathan and Alice through probate records.

215) iii URIAH HOLT, b. at Lancaster, 7 Feb 1729; d. at Woodstock, VT, 1812; m. at Harvard, 20 Feb 1752, ANNESS WILLARD, b. at Harvard, 20 Jun 1730 daughter of Henry and Abigail (Fairbanks) Willard; Anness d. at Ashburnham, 28 Nov 1779. Uriah m. 2nd, at Ashburnham, 6 Jun 1785, SARAH GOODRIDGE.

iv JOSHUA HOLT, b. 18 May 1733; nothing further known.

v HANNAH HOLT, b. at Lancaster, 6 Oct 1735; m. at Harvard, 22 Feb 1770, as his second wife, WILLIAM FARMER, b. about 1720. William was first married to Ruth Willard. Hannah and William do not seem to have had children.

vi LEMUEL HOLT, b. 10 Feb 1737; nothing further known.

216) vii MARY HOLT, b. at Lancaster, 5 Apr 1740; m. at Harvard, 7 Sep 1764, THOMAS DARBY, b. at Harvard, 22 Sep 1739 son of Simon and Mercy (Wilson) Darby; Thomas d. at Westminster, VT, 7 Dec 1833.[121]

47) DAVID HOLT (*Hannah Russell Holt², Robert¹*), b. at Andover, 5 Jun 1708 son of Oliver and Hannah (Russell) Holt; d. at Andover, 21 Aug 1747; m. 14 Sep 1732, his first cousin, SARAH RUSSELL, b. 5 Apr 1713 daughter of John and Sarah (Chandler) Russell; Sarah d. at Andover, 27 Apr 1781.

David Holt did not leave a will and his estate entered probate 5 October 1747 with widow Sarah as administratrix. Real estate was valued at £158 which included a house and barn with 30 acres and a separate 2-acre parcel.[122]

David Holt and Sarah Russell were parents of six children born at Andover.

217) i SARAH HOLT, b. at Andover, 20 Nov 1733; d. at Andover, 30 Sep 1769; m. 26 May 1757, JAMES BARNARD, b. at Andover, 24 Sep 1727 son of James and Abigail (Wilson) Barnard. James m. 2nd, 11 Mar 1775 widow Mary Barker.

ii DORCAS HOLT, b. 31 Jan 1735/6; d. 8 Sep 1736.

218) iii DORCAS HOLT,[123] baptized at Andover 31 Jul 1737; m. at Andover, 22 Mar 1759, THOMAS PEAVEY, b. at Andover, 14 Nov 1736 son of Peter and Esther (Barker) Peavey.

219) iv DAVID HOLT, b. at Andover, 4 Jul 1740; m. at Andover, 22 Jun 1769, REBECCA OSGOOD, b. at Andover, 6 Feb 1739/40 daughter of Samuel and Dorothy (Wardwell) Osgood; Rebecca d. at Andover, 21 May 1790.

v LOIS HOLT, b. 28 Jun 1743; d. at Andover, 20 Aug 1812. Lois did not marry.

vi EUNICE HOLT, b. 22 May 1747; d. at Andover, 27 Nov 1774. Eunice did not marry.

48) JONATHAN HOLT (*Hannah Russell Holt², Robert¹*), b. at Andover, 29 Aug 1711 son of Oliver and Hannah (Russell) Holt; d. at Andover, 14 Oct 1791; m. 10 Feb 1734/5, LYDIA BLANCHARD, b. at Andover, 21 Aug 1714 daughter of Thomas and Rose (Holmes) Blanchard; Lydia d. at Andover, 17 Dec 1788.

Jonathan is referred to as Lt. Jonathan Holt on his death record. Jonathan and Lydia were parents of six children born at Andover.

i LYDIA HOLT, b. 7 Mar 1735/6; died young.

220) ii JONATHAN HOLT, b. 29 Sep 1738; d. at Albany, ME, 1810 (probate 1810); m. at Andover, 31 Dec 1761, RUTH KIMBALL, baptized 30 Mar 1739 daughter of Josiah and Elizabeth (Bragg) Kimball;[124] Ruth d. at Albany, ME, 5 Mar 1823.

iii LYDIA HOLT, b. 16 Mar 1739/40; d. 20 Mar 1758.

iv ROSE HOLT, b. 5 Jan 1742; d. at Andover, Mar 1784. Rose did not marry.

---

[121] Thomas Darby, age 95, born about 1738, died 7 Dec 1833.

[122] *Essex County, MA: Probate File Papers, 1638-1881.* Online database. *AmericanAncestors.org.* New England Historic Genealogical Society, 2014. Case 13631

[123] Although sources (Durrie's Holt genealogy and Charlotte Helen Abbott's Andover notes) state that Dorcas who married Thomas Peavey was the daughter of Ephraim Holt and Phebe Russell, there is no evidence that Ephraim and Phebe had a daughter Dorcas. The 1759 distribution of the estate of Ephraim Russell has only the following children as heirs: eldest son Ephraim, Phebe Houghton, Bethiah Holt, Asenath Holt, and Mastin Holt. These are also the only children of Ephraim and Phebe for whom there are birth records.

[124] Morrison and Sharples, *History of the Kimball Family*, p 113

      v   MOSES HOLT, b. at Andover, 19 Jan 1743/4; d. at Portland, ME, 26 Jan 1772;[125] m. 1771, MARY COTTON, b. about 1753 daughter of William and Sarah (Fletcher) Cotton; Mary d. at Portland, 27 Jul 1808. Mary married second Stephen Hall on 4 Jul 1778. Moses received the A.M. degree from Harvard in 1767.[126] He was a preacher for a time, then a teacher and involved in business in Portland. He did not have children.

221)   vi   HANNAH HOLT, b. at Andover, 19 Dec 1745; d. at Concord, NH, 1 Dec 1818; m. at Andover, 1763, NATHAN BALLARD, b. at Andover, 1 Nov 1744 son of Timothy and Hannah (Chandler) Ballard; Nathan d. at Concord, 14 Jan 1835.

49)   JACOB HOLT (*Hannah Russell Holt², Robert¹*), b. at Andover, 30 Mar 1714 son of Oliver and Hannah (Russell) Holt; d. at Andover, 25 Dec 1760; m. 1st 29 Dec 1737, MARY OSGOOD, b. 1706 daughter of Stephen and Hannah (Blanchard) Osgood;[127] Mary d. 4 Nov 1745. Jacob m. 2nd 25 May 1747, MARGARET DOLLIVER; Margaret d. 22 Dec 1760.

      Jacob Holt did not leave a will and his estate entered probate 9 March 1761 with son Jacob Holt as administrator. Real estate was valued at £269.10.0 and personal estate at £113.1.9. Debts were £85.13.3. Part of the estate accounting is money for the support of Mary Holt.[128]

      Jacob Holt and Mary Osgood were parents of four children born at Andover.

222)   i   JACOB HOLT, b. at Andover, 29 Mar 1739; d. at Albany, ME, 12 May 1816; m. at Andover, 22 Mar 1764, RHODA ABBOTT, b. at Andover, 22 Jun 1741 daughter of Ephraim and Hannah (Phelps) Holt; Rhoda d. at Albany, ME, 12 Jan 1821.

223)   ii   NEHEMIAH HOLT, b. at Andover, 24 Oct 1740; d. at Salem, 1786 (probate 1786); m. at Salem, 21 Jul 1771, ESTHER VARNUM, b. 2 May 1747; Esther d. at Salem, 12 Feb 1822.

      iii   MARY HOLT, baptized 25 Mar 1744; died young.

      iv   MARY HOLT, baptized 1 Sep 1745; seems to be living in 1760 as part of the accounting of her father's estate includes payments for the support of Mary Holt; nothing further known.

      Jacob Holt and Margaret Dolliver were parents of four children born at Andover.

224)   i   ELIZABETH HOLT, b. at Andover, 24 Jan 1747/8; d. at Chelmsford, 8 Aug 1794; m. at Andover, 28 Feb 1771, FRANCIS BOWERS, baptized at Chelmsford, 22 Jul 1744 son of Jonathan and Mary (Grimes) Bowers.

      ii   DAVID HOLT, b. 13 Jul 1749; d. 18 Dec 1749.

      iii   DAVID HOLT, b. at Andover, 4 Oct 1751; d. at Peterborough, NH, 24 Apr 1835; m. at Topsfield, 13 Dec 1781, RUTH DWINELL, b. at Topsfield, 8 Feb 1751 (baptized 17 Oct 1756) daughter of Jacob and Keziah (Gould) Dwinell;[129] Ruth d. at Peterborough, 24 Jun 1833. No children were identified for David and Ruth.

225)   iv   TABITHA HOLT, b. at Andover, 19 May 1753; d. at Andover, 23 Sep 1778; m. at Andover, 16 Nov 1769, ABIEL STEVENS, b. at Andover, 21 Mar 1749/50 son of John and Lydia (Gray) Stevens. Abiel m. 2nd at Andover, 7 Jan 1779, his second cousin once removed, ELIZABETH HOLT (*Nathaniel Holt⁴, Oliver Holt³, Hannah Russell Holt², Robert¹*), b. at Andover, 14 Nov 1752 daughter of Nathaniel and Elizabeth (Stevens) Holt.

Children of John Russell and Sarah Chandler

50)   PHEBE RUSSELL (*John², Robert¹*), baptized at Andover, 10 Jun 1716 daughter of John and Sarah (Chandler) Russell; m. 1st, 13 Feb 1735, EPHRAIM HOLT, b. May 1713 son of Henry and Martha (Marston) Holt; Ephraim d. at Andover, 31 Dec 1749. Phebe m. 2nd, 5 Dec 1750, ABRAHAM SHELDON, b. at Reading, 4 Jun 1717 son of William and Mary (Robarts) Sheldon; Abraham d. at Reading, 15 May 1790. Abraham Sheldon was first married to Sarah Gowing.

---

[125] Grave Inscription: Here lies buried the Body of Mr. Moses Holt, who departed this life the 26th January, 1772, aged 28 years

[126] Harvard University, *Quinquennial Catalogue,* p 130

[127] The 1743 will of Stephen Osgood includes a bequest to his daughter Mary Holt.

[128] *Essex County, MA: Probate File Papers, 1638-1881.* Online database. *AmericanAncestors.org.* New England Historic Genealogical Society, 2014. Case 13645

[129] The 1784 will of Jacob Dwinell of Topsfield includes a bequest to daughter Ruth Holt.

The estate of Ephraim Holt entered probate 2 April 1750. The real estate distribution on 9 April 1759 included one-third to the widow for her use during her lifetime and the other two-thirds to eldest son Ephraim Holt. Ephraim is to make payments of £19.6.8 to sister Phebe Houghton, sister Bethiah Holt, sister Asenath, and brother Marston Holt.[130]

Phebe Russell and Ephraim Holt were parents of five children born at Andover.[131]

226) i   PHEBE HOLT, b. at Andover, Apr 1735; m. at Andover, 11 Sep 1755, JAMES HOUGHTON, b. at Pomfret, 13 Sep 1728 son of Edward and Abigail (Coy) Houghton.

227) ii   EPHRAIM HOLT, b. at Andover, Jan 1736/7; d. at Holden, MA, 25 May 1816;[132] m. at Boxford, 7 Jan 1762, SARAH BLACK, baptized at Boxford, 24 Jul 1743 daughter of Daniel and Sarah (Symonds) Black.[133]

133) iii   BETHIAH HOLT, b. at Andover, about 1740; d. at Wilton, NH, 20 Aug 1817; m. at Andover, 15 May 1760, her second cousin, THOMAS RUSSELL (*Joseph³, Thomas², Robert¹*), b. at Andover, 5 Jun 1732 son of Joseph and Hepsibah (Eaton) Russell; Thomas d. at Wilton 30 Mar 1818.

228) iv   ASENATH HOLT, b. at Andover, 31 Mar 1743; d. at Reading, 8 Nov 1785; m. at Reading, 7 Jun 1764, EBENEZER FLINT, b. at Reading, 17 Jun 1742 son of Ebenezer and Abigail (Sawyer) Flint; Ebenezer d. at Wilton, 29 Apr 1829. After Asenath's death, Ebenezer married Mary Damon (widow Mrs. Taylor) on 29 Nov 1789.

229) v   MARSTIN HOLT, b. at Andover, 13 Aug 1747; m. at Holden, 13 Feb 1772, ABIGAIL WHEELER, b. at Holden, 20 Sep 1746 daughter of Moses and Abigail (Godin) Wheeler.

Phebe Russell and Abraham Sheldon were parents of four children born at Reading.

230) i   RUSSELL SHELDON, b. at Reading, 14 Jan 1752; d. at Reading, 1816 (probate 3 May 1816); m. at Reading, 6 Aug 1778, SUSANNAH SHELDON, b. at Reading, 5 Jun 1756 daughter of Nathaniel and Anna (Fitch) Sheldon.

231) ii   PHEBE SHELDON, b. at Reading, 1 Mar 1754; d. at Mont Vernon, NH, 2 Feb 1824; m. at Andover, 3 Aug 1786, ISRAEL FARNUM, b. at Andover, 14 Jun 1758 son of Thomas and Lydia (Abbott) Farnum; Israel d. at Mont Vernon, 1842. After Phebe's death, Israel married Susannah Farnum on 17 May 1825.

232) iii   REBEKAH SHELDON, b. at Reading, 23 Jan 1757; d. 10 May 1813; m. 26 Jun 1777, PETER TOWNE, b. at Andover, 10 Aug 1749 son of Nathan and Eunice (-) Towne; Peter d. at Andover, 20 May 1830. Peter was first married to Lydia Abbott daughter of Ebenezer and Lydia (Farrington) Abbott.

233) iv   AMOS SHELDON, b. at Reading, 11 Aug 1759; d. at Fitchburg, 2 Nov 1828; m. at Fitchburg, 12 Jun 1788, SARAH NEEDHAM, b. at Billerica, 12 May 1762 daughter of Benjamin and Rebecca (Jaquith) Needham; Sarah d. at Fitchburg, 8 Jan 1816.

51)   JOHN RUSSELL (*John², Robert¹*), b. at Andover, 8 Jun 1717 son of John and Sarah (Chandler) Russell; d. at Andover, 2 Oct 1788; m. at Andover, 16 Feb 1737/8, HANNAH FOSTER, b. at Andover, 13 Jun 1716 daughter of Abraham and Mary (Johnson) Foster.

John and Hannah were parents of ten children born at Andover.

234) i   BENJAMIN RUSSELL, b. at Andover, 28 Jan 1739; d. at Bethel, ME, 23 Nov 1802; m. 7 Oct 1762, MARY FEAVER, b. at Andover, 1 Mar 1738/9 daughter of Jacob and Hannah (Farrington) Feaver.

ii   SARAH RUSSELL, b. 7 Jul 1742; d. 4 Jun 1743.

iii   WILLIAM RUSSELL, b. 5 Mar 1743/4; nothing further known.

235) iv   JOHN RUSSELL, b. at Andover, 1 Jul 1746; d. at Andover, 12 Aug 1830; m. 1st at Andover, 1 Feb 1774, PHEBE ABBOTT, b. at Andover, 29 Aug 1749 daughter of Barachias and Hannah (Holt) Abbott; Phebe d.

[130] *Essex County, MA: Probate File Papers, 1638-1881.*Online database. *AmericanAncestors.org.* New England Historic Genealogical Society, 2014. Case 13637
[131] Although sources (Charlotte Helen Abbott and Durrie's Holt genealogy) state that Dorcas who married Thomas Peavey is the daughter of Ephraim Holt, Ephraim Holt did not have a daughter Dorcas. This can be established by the 1759 estate distribution of Ephraim Holt with heir eldest son Ephraim who receives two-thirds of the estate and makes payments to his sister Phebe Houghton, sister Bethiah Holt, sister Asenath, and brother Marston.
[132] U.S., Newspaper Extractions from the Northeast, 1704-1930
[133] Perley, *Essex Antiquarian*, volume 9, p 187

at Andover, 17 Apr 1809. John m. 2nd at Middleton, MA, 3 Mar 1811, MARY WILKINS; Mary d. at Andover, 9 Sep 1830.

v   DAVID RUSSELL, b. 8 Feb 1747/8; d. 1776 of disease while in the army.

236)   vi   ABRAHAM RUSSELL, b. at Andover, 7 Nov 1750; d. at Bethel, ME, 9 Dec 1839; m. 1775, SARAH SWAN, b. 9 Feb 1756 daughter of James and Mary (Smith) Swan; Sarah d. at Bethel, 13 Jan 1802.

vii   ISAAC RUSSELL, b. 24 May 1752; d. 11 Jun 1754.

viii   HANNAH RUSSELL, b. 21 Feb 1754; nothing further known.

ix   ISAAC RUSSELL, b. at Andover, 28 Jan 1759; m. at Wilmington, 20 Jan 1785, MARY EAMES. No further definitive information was located for this couple.[134]

237)   x   JACOB RUSSELL, baptized at Andover, 1 Feb 1761; d. at Bethel, ME, 1799; m. at Andover, 26 Feb 1784, DOROTHY SHATTUCK, b. at Andover, 14 Apr 1764 daughter of Zebadiah and Elizabeth (Abbott) Shattuck; Dorothy d. at Bethel, 24 Jan 1852.

52)   JOSEPH RUSSELL (*John²*, *Robert¹*), b. at Andover, 8 Jan 1719/20 son of John and Sarah (Chandler) Russell; d. at Andover, 31 Aug 1783;[135] m. at Andover, 26 Feb 1756, HEPHZIBAH RUSSELL, baptized at Andover, 30 Jun 1734 daughter of Joseph and Hepsibah (Eaton) Russell; Hephzibah was living in 1783.

Joseph Russell did not leave a will and his estate entered probate 4 November 1783 with Hephzibah Russell as administratrix.[136] Personal estate was valued at £97.1.10. No real estate inventory was given in the available records.

Joseph and Hephzibah were parents of seven children born at Andover. Although it is likely that other of the children married, marriages could be confirmed for just two of the children, Lydia and Chandler who settled in Bethel, Maine.

i   HEPHZIBAH RUSSELL, b. 18 Jun 1756

ii   JOSEPH RUSSELL, b. 8 Jul 1758

iii   SIMEON RUSSELL, b. 27 May 1761

iv   HANNAH RUSSELL, b. 27 May 1761

238)   v   LYDIA RUSSELL, b. at Andover, 17 May 1764; d. at Bethel, ME, 12 Sep 1847; m. 7 Jun 1787, JOHN HOLT,[137] b. 12 May 1764 son of Humphrey and Mary (Holton) Holt; John d. at Bethel, 12 Jul 1820.

vi   ELIJAH RUSSELL, b. 1 Nov 1768

239)   vii   CHANDLER RUSSELL, b. at Andover, 20 Sep 1775; d. 8 Jun 1846, m. at Bethel 14 Dec 1803, BETSEY DUSTON, b. 12 Jul 1782 daughter of Jacob and Elizabeth (Swan) Duston.[138]

53)   ROBERT RUSSELL (*John²*, *Robert¹*), baptized at Andover, 21 Jan 1722 son of John and Sarah (Chandler) Russell; d. at Andover, 4 Jan 1794; m. at Andover, 5 Dec 1745, ANNE FELT, baptized at Wakefield, 13 Jul 1723 daughter of Joshua and Anne (Walcott) Felt; Anne d. at Andover, 12 Oct 1816.

Little information was located for this family. Births/baptisms of seven children were recorded at Andover and likely marriages were located for two children.

i   SARAH RUSSELL, b. 13 Sep 1746

ii   PRUDENCE RUSSELL, b. 27 May 1748

iii   NATHANIEL RUSSELL, baptized 3 Feb 1751

240)   iv   JEDEDIAH RUSSELL, baptized at Andover, 26 Nov 1752; d. at Lyndeborough, 17 Feb 1848; m. RHODA PRATT, b. 6 Nov 1762 daughter of Ephraim and Phebe (-) Pratt.

---

[134] There is an Isaac Russell who died at Batavia, NY in 1838 but would be born about 1757 based on age 72 at death. That Isaac was married to Mary Green so seems to not be this Isaac.

[135] Joseph, Aug. 31, 1783. [a. 64 y. CR2]. The 1783 probate record of Joseph Russell refers to widow Hephzibah.

[136] *Essex County, MA: Probate File Papers, 1638-1881.* Online database. *AmericanAncestors.org.* New England Historic Genealogical Society, 2014. Case 24466

[137] Durrie's Holt genealogy reports that Lydia who married John Holt was born in 1772 and was a daughter of Elijah. However, the gravestone gives her age at death as 83 years old meaning she was born in 1764. As Lydia's brother Chandler also settled in Bethel, it is reasonable to assume that it is this Lydia that married John Holt.

[138] Lapham, *History of Bethel*, p 520

v   HEPHZIBAH RUSSELL, baptized 25 May 1755

241)   vi   JONATHAN RUSSELL, baptized at Andover, 30 Apr 1758; d. at Dublin, NH, Apr 1834; m. 19 Jun 1782, RACHEL WHITE, b. 1758; Rachel d. at Dublin, 1 Jun 1821.

vii   PRUDENCE RUSSELL, baptized at Andover, 10 Feb 1760

54)   ISAAC RUSSELL (*John², Robert¹*), b. at Andover, 3 Dec 1724 son of John and Sarah (Chandler) Russell; m. at Andover, 18 Apr 1754, ELIZABETH GILBARD.
       Births of three children are recorded at Andover for Isaac and Elizabeth. Nothing further is known of this family.

i   RHODA RUSSELL, b. 23 Aug 1755

ii   SUSANNA RUSSELL, b. 3 Aug 1757

iii   ISAAC RUSSELL, b. 1 Jul 1759

55)   MARY RUSSELL (*John², Robert¹*), b. at Andover, 10 Feb 1728/9 daughter of John and Sarah (Chandler) Russell; m. about 1755, her second cousin once removed, JOSEPH HOLT, b. 14 Feb 1718 son of Timothy and Rhoda (Chandler) Holt; Joseph d. at Wilton, NH, Aug 1789. Joseph was fist married to Dorothy Johnson.
       Joseph Holt graduated from Harvard in 1739 and was schoolmaster in Andover. He participated in the expedition to Canada in 1758 and kept a journal of his experiences. Joseph and his wife Mary Russell moved to Wilton about 1765 where Joseph was a teacher and owned a mill. He also served as selectman.[139]
       Joseph Holt served in the company of Capt. Ebenezer Jones during the expedition to Canada. His journal recounts details of the expedition including number of miles marched per day and locations on the march. The full journal is published in *The New England Historical and Genealogical Register*.[140]
       Mary Russell and Joseph Holt were parents of eight children. Joseph had five children with his first wife Dorothy Johnson.

242)   i   MARY HOLT, b. at Andover, 24 Nov 1755; d. at Wilton, 24 Oct 1844; m. 18 Nov 1779, EDWARD HERRICK, b. at Methuen, 9 Oct 1754 son of Edward and Mary (Kimball) Herrick; Edward d. 5 Feb 1811.

243)   ii   RHODA HOLT, b. at Andover, 16 Oct 1757; d. at Wilton, 25 Jul 1799, m. 25 Nov 1778, JOHN DALE, b. 26 Jul 1748 son of John and Mary (Ellinwood) Dale; John d. at Wilton, 11 Jul 1809. After Rhoda's death, John married Lydia Lamon.

iii   ESTHER HOLT, b. at Andover, 22 Mar 1760; died young, reported to have drowned.

iv   Twin1 b. and d. 16 Aug 1762.

v   Twin2 b. and d. 16 Aug 1762.

244)   vi   VALENTINE HOLT, b. recorded at Wilton, 25 Dec 1763 and baptized at Andover 1 Jan 1764; d. at Mercer, ME, 6 Dec 1840; m. at Wilton, 13 Sep 1787, ANNA "NANCY" GOODRICH whose parents have not been identified. Nancy likely died before 1810. Valentine married second HANNAH DAY, b. about 1792. Hannah d. after 1860 when she was living with her son in Augusta, Maine.

vii   JOSHUA HOLT, b. at Andover, 5 Nov 1765; nothing further known.

245)   viii ESTHER HOLT, b. at Wilton, 25 Jul 1766; d. at Lyndeborough, 14 Jul 1839; m. about 1791, EBENEZER PEARSON, b. at Reading, MA, 19 Jun 1768 son of Amos and Elizabeth (Nichols) Pearson; Ebenezer d. at Lyndeborough, 22 May 1852.

56)   HANNAH RUSSELL (*John², Robert¹*), b. at Andover, 28 Dec 1730 daughter of John and Sarah (Chandler) Russell; m. at Billerica, 8 Apr 1761, JACOB CROSBY, b. at Billerica, 19 Sep 1729 son of Thomas and Anna (Parker) Crosby; Jacob d. at Billerica, 1776 (probate 1776).

---

[139] Livermore, *History of Wilton*, p 405
[140] "Journals of Joseph Holt, of Wilton, N.H.", NEHGR, volume 10, 1856, pp 307-310

Jacob Crosby did not leave a will and his estate entered probate 27 February 1776 with Asa Spaulding appointed administrator at the request of the widow Hannah.[141] Personal estate was valued at £20.1.8. Real estate of about 31 acres in Billerica was valued at £50. One-third valued at £16.13.4 was set off to the widow.

246)   i   HANNAH CROSBY, b. at Billerica, 28 Dec 1761; d. at Lyndeborough, 13 Jun 1850; m. at Chelmsford, MA, 20 Nov 1785, PHINEHAS KIDDER, b. at Chelmsford, 17 Jul 1756 son of David and Esther (Corey) Kidder;[142] Phinehas d. at Lyndeborough, 20 Jan 1846.

        ii   REUBEN CROSBY, b. at Billerica, 11 Feb 1764. Northing further is known for certain. He may be the Reuben Crosby who married the widow Elizabeth (Pierce) Bundy in 1808 in Vermont, but there is no evidence of any children for them.

247)   iii ZILPAH CROSBY, b. at Billerica, 26 Oct 1767; d. at Billerica, 1825; m. at Billerica, 5 Dec 1787, JOSEPH STEARNS, b. at Billerica, 27 Jun 1763 son of Samuel and Hannah (Trask) Stearns;[143] Joseph d. at Billerica, 1834 (probate 3 Jun 1834); Joseph married second Elizabeth Prentice on 6 Apr 1828.

        iv   JACOB CROSBY, b. 18 Apr 1769; nothing further known.

        v   SAMUEL CROSBY, b. 1 Jun 1773; nothing further known.

57)   JEMIMA RUSSELL (*John², Robert¹*), baptized at Andover, 28 Jan 1733 daughter of John and Sarah (Chandler) Russell; d. at Boston, 30 Apr 1813; m. at Andover, 8 Sep 1763, as his second wife, JONATHAN STEVENS, b. at Andover, 1726 son of John and Elizabeth (Chandler) Stevens; Jonathan d. about 1771 (will 5 Jun 1771, proved 7 Jan 1772). Jonathan was first married to Lydia Felch.

In his will written 5 June 1771 (proved 7 January 1772), Jonathan bequeaths to beloved wife Jemima the use of the dwelling house and the land around it while she is a widow and all the household goods to be at her disposal. Son Jonathan receives £33.6.8 as does daughter Lydia. Jonathan and Lydia also will divide the household goods his first wife (their) mother brought to the marriage. Sons John and William and daughter Jemima receive the remainder of the estate with John and William each receiving two-fifths and Jemima receiving one-fifth. Zebadiah Abbot was named executor. The total estate was valued at £224.7.9 which included dwelling house and one-quarter acre valued at £40 and £162.12.10 in cash and notes.[144]

Jemima Russell and Jonathan Stevens were parents of three children born at Andover.

        i   JOHN STEVENS, b. at Andover, 25 Aug 1764; nothing further known.[145]

        ii   WILLIAM STEVENS, b. at Andover, 12 Jul 1767; nothing further known.

248)   iii JEMIMA STEVENS, baptized at Andover, 8 Jul 1770; d. after 1821; m. at Loudon, NH, 6 Mar 1794, JONAS AMES, b. 1771; Jonas d. at Boston, 27 Dec 1820.

Children of Elizabeth Russell and Moses Holt

58)   MOSES HOLT (*Elizabeth Russell Holt², Robert¹*), b. at Andover, 21 Oct 1716 son of Moses and Elizabeth (Russell) Holt; d. at Andover, 6 Jul 1743; m. 9 Jul 1741, his first cousin once removed, PRUDENCE RUSSELL (*Robert³, Thomas², Robert¹*), baptized at Andover, 31 Jul 1720 daughter of Robert and Abigail (Flint) Russell; Prudence d. at Andover, 15 Nov 1745. Prudence Russell m. 2nd, 11 Mar 1744/5, her first cousin, JOHN CHANDLER (*Mehitable Russell Chandler³, Thomas², Robert¹*), b. at Andover, 19 Jan 1722 son of Joseph and Mehitable (Russell) Chandler; John d. at Andover, 11 May 1759. John Chandler m. 2nd, at Andover, 15 Oct 1747, HANNAH PHELPS, b. at Andover, 1709 daughter of Samuel and Hannah (Dane) Phelps; Hannah d. at Andover, 5 Aug 1781.

Prudence Russell and John Chandler did not have children. Moses Holt and Prudence Russell were parents of one child.

[141] *Middlesex County, MA: Probate File Papers, 1648-1871.* Online database. *AmericanAncestors.org.* New England Historic Genealogical Society, 2014. Case 5344

[142] Stafford, *Genealogy of the Kidder Family*, p 24

[143] Van Wagenen, *Genealogy and Memoirs of Isaac Stearns*, p 203

[144] *Essex County, Massachusetts, Probate Records and Indexes 1638-1916*; Author: *Massachusetts. Court of Insolvency (Essex County), Probate Records, Vol 347-348, Book 46-48, 1771-1772, volume 347, pp 167-169*

[145] In her notes on the Stevens family, Charlotte Helen Abbott wonders if John Stevens married Elizabeth Frye in 1783. But that John Stevens was born about 1753 based on his age at time of death. Elizabeth Frye was born in 1755.

i   PHINEAS HOLT, b. at Andover, 3 Mar 1741/2;[146] d. at Andover, about 1761. In 1756, Phineas made choice of his uncle Joseph Russell for his guardian. In 1761, the estate of Phineas Holt of Andover was in probate with reversion of part of his property to his grandmother Elizabeth Furbush.

John Chandler and Hannah Phelps were parents of three children.

i   JOHN CHANDLER, b. 7 Jul 1748; d. 14 Mar 1749.

249)   ii   JOHN CHANDLER, b. at Andover, 18 Jul 1750; d. at Princeton, MA, 26 Mar 1832; m. 1st at Lancaster, 29 Feb 1776, KATHARINE "KATY" HOLMAN, b. at Sutton, MA, 23 Mar 1753 daughter of Solomon and Sarah (Waite) Holman, Katy d. at Princeton, 18 Feb 1781. John m. 2nd at Westminster, 1 Jan 1782, MARY JACKSON, b. at Westminster, 11 Sep 1755 daughter of Josiah and Mary (Darby) Jackson; Mary d. at Princeton, 26 Jan 1836.

250)   iii   JOSEPH CHANDLER, b. at Andover, 30 Jan 1753; d. at Salem, 27 Nov 1827; m. at Danvers, 12 Nov 1780, DORCAS ABBOTT, b. at Andover, 26 Oct 1755 daughter of Joseph and Anna (Peabody) Abbott; Dorcas d. at Salem, 19 Aug 1821.

---

[146] Phineas, s. Moses and Prudence, Mar. 3, 1741. [Only child. Deposition of wid. Mercy How, midwife, on Sept. 13, 1748.]

Generation Four

Grandchildren of Mary Russell and Nicholas Holt

59)   PHEBE INGALLS (*Mary Holt Ingalls³, Mary Russell Holt², Robert¹*), b. at Andover 1708 daughter of Josiah and Mary (Holt) Ingalls; d after 1784; m. at Andover, 12 Aug 1731, JAMES PARKER, b. at Andover, 12 Oct 1696 son of John and Hannah (Brown) Parker; James d. at Andover, 1782 (will 9 Oct 1773; probate 2 Dec 1782).

James Parker was tailor in Andover and had a farm.

In his will dated 9 October 1773 (probate 2 December 1782), James Parker bequeaths to beloved wife Phebe a lengthy list of yearly provisions to be provided by son James Parker. Phebe also has use and improvement of as much of the dwelling house and cellar as she needs for her natural life. Son James is to meet all the needs of his mother during her life. These provisions are in lieu of her dower. Daughter Anne Bragg receives all the household furniture after her mother's decease and the sum of £3.6.8. Anne also has the use of the east room of the house and use of the cellar and oven. Anne has use of the house while she is a single woman, but the furniture and money are hers forever. Son James receives all the remaining personal and real estate and is named executor. Real estate was valued at £417 and personal estate at £60.16.0.[147]

On 8 July 1784, son James Parker now residing in the new town of Bakerstown (later Poland) in Cumberland County of the Commonwealth of Massachusetts (current day Maine) sold land and dwelling house in Andover to Samuel Johnson for £60. The said James Parker, his mother Phebe Parker, and sister Anne Bragg give their consent to the conveyance.[148]

Phebe Ingalls and James Parker were parents of seven children born at Andover.

i   Stillborn son 27 Jul 1732; "Parker, ——, s. stillborn, James and Phebe, June 27, 1732."

ii   PHEBE PARKER, b. 12 Jul 1734; d. 14 Aug 1737.

iii   ANNE PARKER, b. at Andover, 9 Apr 1736; d. after 1784; m. at Andover, 8 May 1753, JOHN BRAGG who has not been identified. John was a cordwainer, resident of Andover and deed records suggest he was related to Thomas Bragg innholder at Andover. John was living in 1762 when he was involved in three land transactions including the gift of land from James Parker to John and Anne Bragg for "love, good will, and affection."[149] No children were identified for Anne and John.

iv   JESSE PARKER, b. 25 Oct 1738. Jesse was captured during the French and Indian War and taken to prison in Canada and is believed to have died in prison. There were attempts to ransom Jesse and other prisoners.[150]

251)   v   JAMES PARKER, b. at Andover, 30 Aug 1746; d. at Livermore, ME, 26 Apr 1815;[151] m. at New Gloucester, ME, 16 Aug 1783, PHEBE NOYES, b. 13 Apr 1763 daughter of Simon and Elizabeth (Eaton) Noyes; Phebe d. at Livermore, 23 Jul 1848.

vi   PHEBE PARKER, b. 7 Dec 1748; not living in 1773.

vii   MARY PARKER, b. 3 Jul 1751; d. 20 Feb 1752.

60)   BENJAMIN HOLT (*Nicholas Holt³, Mary Russell Holt², Robert¹*), b. at Andover, 23 Jul 1709 son of Nicholas and Mary (Manning) Holt; d. at Pembroke, NH, 1774 (probate 26 Oct 1774); m. at Andover, 7 Apr 1737, SARAH FRYE, b. May 1717 daughter of Nathan and Sarah (Bridges) Frye; Sarah d. at Pembroke, 1804.

Benjamin and Sarah started their family in Andover and settled in Suncook about 1745. They were parents of twelve children.

Benjamin Holt did not leave a will and his estate entered probate 26 October 1774 with widow Sarah Holt as administratrix. Real estate was valued at £145 and Benjamin also held multiple notes owed to him totaling £1051 and debts of

[147] *Essex County, MA: Probate File Papers, 1638-1881.* Online database. *AmericanAncestors.org.* New England Historic Genealogical Society, 2014. Case 20508

[148] Massachusetts Land Records 1620-1986, Essex County, volume 142, p 233, Film #007463322; accessed through familysearch.org. https://www.familysearch.org/ark:/61903/3:1:3QS7-89ZZ-1S6Q?i=519&cc=2106411&cat=209907

[149] Massachusetts Land Records 1620-1986, Essex County, volume 110, p 113, accessed through familysearch.org.

[150] Bailey, Historical Sketches of Andover, p 266

[151] Livermore Vital Records, p 269; accessed through familysearch,org

the estate £104.7.9. Debts of the estate were more than the personal estate and a portion of real estate was sold to settle the debts. The widow's thirds were set off to Sarah 7 March 1775.[152]

252)   i   WILLIAM HOLT, b. at Andover, Oct 1737; m. at Andover, 2 Sep 1769, ELIZABETH "BETSEY" AMES who has not been identified.

253)   ii   SARAH HOLT, b. at Andover, about 1738; m. about 1756, STEPHEN COFFIN, b. at Newbury, 6 Aug 1729 son of Daniel and Lydia (Moulton) Coffin.

254)   iii   NATHAN HOLT, b. at Andover, about 1740; d. at Pembroke, NH, 3 Mar 1818; m. at Pembroke, 1762, SUSANNAH BLANCHARD, b. about 1742; Susannah d. at Pembroke, 28 Aug 1837.

255)   iv   BENJAMIN HOLT, b. at Andover, 28 Feb 1741; d. at Pembroke, 28 Feb 1826; m. 22 Sep 1763, his third cousin, HANNAH ABBOTT (*Hannah Chandler Abbott⁴, Mehitable Russell Chandler³, Thomas², Robert¹*), b. at Pembroke, 7 Sep 1743 daughter of David and Hannah (Chandler) Abbott; Hannah d. at Pembroke, 17 Mar 1813.

256)   v   DANIEL HOLT, b. at Pembroke, 14 Sep 1744; d. at Pembroke, 5 Dec 1813; m. about 1770, ABIGAIL LOVEJOY, b. at Pembroke, 12 Sep 1750 daughter of David and Elizabeth (Chandler) Lovejoy; Abigail d. at Pembroke, 18 Mar 1833.

257)   vi   FRYE HOLT, b. at Pembroke, about 1746; m. about 1770, MARY POOR who has not been identified.

258)   vii   ABIAH HOLT, b. at Pembroke, about 1747; d. about 1790; m. about 1766, RICHARD EASTMAN, b. at Pembroke, 20 Apr 1747; Richard d. at Strafford County, NH, 6 Dec 1826. Richard married second Susannah Runnels.

       viii   PHEBE HOLT, b. at Pembroke, about 1750; d. at Pembroke, 15 Aug 1823; m. 30 Mar 1780, as his second wife, RICHARD BARTLETT, b. 23 Mar 1743 son of Christopher Bartlett; Richard d. at Pembroke, 5 Aug 1805. Richard was first married to Abigail Belknap. Phebe and Richard had one child, Frank, who died as an infant. In his will, Richard left his estate to his wife Phebe and his two children from his first marriage, Caleb and Abigail.

259)   ix   MARY "MOLLY" HOLT, b. at Pembroke, about 1752; m. about 1770, NATHANIEL GILMAN, b. at Exeter, NH, 29 Aug 1748 son of Peter and Abigial (-) Gilman.[153]

260)   x   HANNAH HOLT, b. at Pembroke, 28 Feb 1758; d. 15 Apr 1820; m. NOAH EASTMAN, b. at Pembroke, 20 Mar 1753; Noah d. 28 Aug 1829.

261)   xi   DORCAS HOLT, b. at Pembroke, about 1764; d. at Pembroke, 17 Sep 1850; m. 16 Sep 1787, JOSEPH EMERY, b. 19 Dec 1764 son of Joseph and Hannah (Stickney) Emery; Joseph d. 8 Jun 1830.

       xii   NICHOLAS HOLT, reported as being unmarried in published genealogies.

61)   MARY HOLT (*Nicholas Holt³, Mary Russell Holt², Robert¹*), b. at Andover, 1 Aug 1711 daughter of Nicholas and Mary (Manning) Holt; m. 1st at Andover, 4 Mar 1735/6, WILLIAM CHANDLER, b. 14 Jul 1704 son of Thomas and Mary (Stevens) Chandler; William d. at Andover, 15 Apr 1741. William Chandler was first married to Elizabeth Blanchard. Mary Holt m. 2nd, about 1745, JEREMIAH OSGOOD, b. at Andover, 1702 son of Christopher and Sarah (Osgood). Jeremiah was first married to Lydia Poor.

        William Chandler was a miller in Andover. He did not leave a will and his estate entered probate June 1741. Real estate at inventory was valued at £150. On 30 May 1748, the division of the estate occurred, and it was determined that division of the real estate could not be done without harm to its value. The real estate was settled on eldest son Thomas Chandler with Thomas to pay his brothers and sisters their proportional shares. Thomas was to make payments of £8.5.10 to each of the following brothers and sisters: Rose Chandler, William Chandler, James Chandler, Stevens Chandler, and Mary Chandler.[154] Thomas, Rose, and William were children of William and his first wife Elizabeth Blanchard.

        On 19 April 1742, Mary Chandler was granted guardianship of her three minor children James, Stevens, and Mary. On 28 May 1753, James made choice of his uncle Nicholas Holt of Andover as his guardian and Stevens made choice of his uncle the Rev. James Chandler of Rowley as his guardian.

        Mary Holt was second married to Jeremiah Osgood and they had two children in Andover, but then relocated to Pomfret where Jeremiah purchased a farm of 148 acres in 1748.[155]

[152] *New Hampshire. Probate Court (Rockingham County)*; Probate Place: *Rockingham, New Hampshire, Estate file 4128*

[153] Ames, *The Story of the Gilmans*, p 110

[154] *Essex County, MA: Probate File Papers, 1638-1881.* Online database. *AmericanAncestors.org.* New England Historic Genealogical Society, 2014. Case 4981

[155] Osgood, *A Genealogy of the Descendants of John, Christopher, and William Osgood*, p 262

The three children of Mary Holt that married each married a child of Joseph and Sarah (Cornell) Snow.

i   JAMES CHANDLER, b. 13 Dec 1735; d. between 1753 and 1763.

262) ii   STEVENS CHANDLER, b. at Andover, 15 Dec 1738; d. at Andover, Nov 1814 (buried 10 Nov 1814); m. 1st at Ashford, about 1762, ALICE SNOW, b. at Ashford, 23 Sep 1741 daughter of Joseph and Sarah (Cornell) Snow; Alice d. at Ashford, 17 Jan 1782. Stevens m. 2nd at Ashford, Jun 1784, MARY PRESTON; Mary d. 10 Mar 1787. Stevens m. 3rd at Ashford, 3 Jul 1790, SARAH ROGERS; Sarah d. at Andover, 26 Aug 1817.

263) iii   MARY CHANDLER, b. at Andover, 8 Feb 1740/1; d. at Ashford, 11 Mar 1787; m. at Ashford, 18 Nov 1762, JOSEPH SNOW, b. at Ashford, 15 Nov 1738 son of Joseph and Sarah (Cornell) Snow.

Mary Holt and Jeremiah Osgood were parents of two children.

i   DORCAS OSGOOD, b. 14 Jul 1746; died young.

264) ii   DORCAS OSGOOD, b. at Andover, 11 Aug 1748; d. at Westport, NY, 31 Aug 1811; m. at Ashford, CT, 5 Jul 1764, BENJAMIN SNOW, b. at Ashford, 23 Jan 1743/4 son of Joseph and Sarah (Cornell) Snow.

62) STEPHEN HOLT (*Nicholas Holt³, Mary Russell Holt², Robert¹*), b. at Andover, 14 Apr 1713 son of Nicholas and Mary (Manning) Holt; d. at Andover, 25 Apr 1798; m. 12 Jul 1739, MARY FARNUM, b. at Andover, 21 May 1714 daughter of John and Joanna (Barker) Farnum; Mary d. at Andover, 9 Aug 1802.

Stephen and Mary were in Suncook after their marriage and their children were born there. However, they returned to Andover with their children.

In his will written 9 December 1793 (probate 7 May 1798), Stephen Holt bequeathed to beloved wife Mary all the household goods to be at her disposal except the clock. Mary also has use of all the personal and real estate and is not to want for anything. Daughter Mary wife of John Adams receives the pew in the north meeting house. Daughter Mary also receives the clock and the buildings that Stephen owns that are on the property of John Adams. Grandsons Samuel and Stephen Holt the sons of Jedediah receive two-thirds of the estate that remains after his wife decease. Daughter-in-law Lydia Lary receives twenty shillings. Mr. William Frost is named executor.[156] Real estate was valued at $60 and personal estate at $503.98.

Samuel and Mary were parents of four children born at Suncook.

i   MARY HOLT, b. at Suncook, 15 Dec 1741; m. at Andover, 21 May 1776, Lt. JOHN ADAMS, b. 3 Jul 1735 son of Israel and Tabitha (Farnum) Adams; John d. at Andover, 27 Jun 1813. John was first married to Hannah Osgood and second married to Hannah Thurston. Mary and John did not have children.

ii   STEPHEN HOLT, b. 23 Feb 1743/4; d. at Andover, 8 Mar 1771; m. 21 Jan 1768, LYDIA JOHNSON. Lydia married second Jonathan Larey. Stephen and Lydia did not have children.

265) iii   JEDEDIAH HOLT, b. at Suncook, 23 Feb 1743/4; d. at Andover, 12 Feb 1790; m. at Andover, 19 Jun 1766, PHEBE BARKER, b. at Andover, 2 Jan 1749/50 daughter of Samuel and Sarah (Robinson) Barker.

iv   PETER HOLT, b. 8 Feb 1749/50; d. 3 Mar 1749/50.

63) NICHOLAS HOLT (*Nicholas Holt³, Mary Russell Holt², Robert¹*), b. at Andover, 29 Feb 1716 son of Nicholas and Mary (Manning) Holt; d. at Blue Hill, ME, 16 Mar 1798; m. 1st at Andover, 26 Apr 1739, HANNAH OSGOOD, baptized at Andover 1 Jun 1718 daughter of Ezekiel and Rebecca (Wardwell) Osgood;[157] Rebecca d. at Andover, 1 Sep 1744. Nicholas m. 2nd at Andover, 7 Feb 1750/1, LOIS PHELPS, b. at Reading, about 1720 daughter of Samuel and Elizabeth (Bare) Phelps; Lois d. at Blue Hill, Jan 1814.

Nicholas was in Andover where his children were born. He relocated to Blue Hill Maine about 1765. He was prominent in the town of Blue Hill serving in positions such as justice of the peace, Colonel in the local militia, town clerk, and foreman of the coroner's jury.[158][159]

Nicholas Holt and Hannah Osgood were parents of two children.

i   JEDEDIAH HOLT, b. 19 Apr 1740; d. 8 Sep 1740.

---

[156] *Essex County, MA: Probate File Papers, 1638-1881.* Online database. *AmericanAncestors.org.* New England Historic Genealogical Society, 2014. Case 13696

[157] The 1740 will of Ezekiel Osgood includes a bequest to his daughter Hannah Osgood alias Holt.

[158] Durrie, Holt Genealogy

[159] *Blue Hill, ME: Vital Records, 1766-1809.* (Online database: *AmericanAncestors.org*, New England Historic Genealogical Society, 2012)

266)   ii   HANNAH HOLT, b. at Andover, 16 Nov 1741; m. at Andover, 15 Sep 1763, JONATHAN DARLING,
              baptized at Salem, 11 Jul 1742 son of Jonathan and Sarah (Wardwell) Darling.

        Nicholas Holt and Lois Phelps were parents of three children.

267)   i   PHEBE HOLT, b. at Andover, 29 Jan 1752; d. at Blue Hill, 12 Feb 1831; m. about 1769, ISRAEL WOOD, b.
              at Beverly, MA, 17 Oct 1744 son of Joseph and Ruth (Haskell) Wood; Israel d. at Blue Hill, 13 Nov 1800.

268)   ii   JEDEDIAH HOLT, b. at Andover, 12 Mar 1754; d. at Blue Hill, 17 Aug 1847; m. at Beverly, 24 Feb 1778,
              SARAH THORNDIKE, b. at Beverly, Sep 1751 (baptized 4 Jul 1756) daughter of Hezekiah and Sarah
              (Prince) Thorndike; Sarah d. at Blue Hill, 15 Jan 1836.

269)   iii   NICHOLAS HOLT, b. at Andover, Feb 1756; d. at Blue Hill, about 1838; m. 1st at Reading, 26 Nov 1782,
              PHEBE BATCHELDER, b. at North Reading, 3 Nov 1754 daughter of Jonathan and Phebe (Holt)
              Batchelder; Phebe d. at Blue Hill, about 1790. Nicholas m. 2nd at Blue Hill 13 Apr 1795, MOLLY
              WORMWOOD.

64)   TIMOTHY HOLT (*Nicholas Holt³, Mary Russell Holt², Robert¹*), b. 17 Jan 1720/1 son of Nicholas and Dorcas (Abbott)
Holt; d. at Wilton, NH, Nov 1801; m. 18 Sep 1744, his second cousin, ELIZABETH HOLT, baptized at Andover, 8 Jun 1718
daughter of John and Mehitable (Wilson) Holt; Elizabeth d. at Wilton 21 Mar 1776.
        Timothy Holt and Elizabeth Holt had four children whose births are recorded at Andover. The family relocated to
Wilton.

270)   i   TIMOTHY HOLT, b. 19 May 1746; d. at Weston, VT, 3 May 1836; m. HANNAH JOHNSON, b. at Andover,
              8 Feb 1753 daughter of Obadiah and Dorothy (Ballard) Johnson.[160]

271)   ii   ELIZABETH HOLT, b. 25 Nov 1748; m. 1 Jun 1769, ISAAC FRYE, b. at Andover, 6 Feb 1748 son of Abiel
              and Abigail (Emery) Frye; Isaac d. at Wilton, NH, 3 Nov 1791.

272)   iii   HANNAH HOLT, b. 18 Jan 1754; m. about 1774, as his second wife, RICHARD WHITNEY, b. at Oxford,
              MA, 22 Apr 1743 son of Israel and Hannah (Blodgett) Whitney. Richard was first married to Sarah
              Butterfield who died in 1773. This family lived in Wilton until 1795 but may have relocated to Vermont
              after all the children were born.

273)   iv   SARAH HOLT, b. at Andover, 31 May 1757; m. at Wilton, 30 Mar 1780, her second cousin once removed,
              WILLIAM PIERCE, b. at Ashford, CT, 28 Jun 1759 son of William and Hannah (·) Pierce of Wilton,
              NH.[161][162]

65)   JAMES HOLT (*Nicholas Holt³, Mary Russell Holt², Robert¹*), b. at Andover, 13 Jan 1722/3 son of Nicholas and Dorcas
(Abbott) Holt; d. at Andover, 22 Aug 1812; m. 1st, SARAH ABBOTT, b. 2 Aug 1718 daughter of Benjamin and Elizabeth (Abbott)
Abbott; Sarah d. 5 Mar 1778. James m. 2nd, 22 Jun 1779, PHEBE BALLARD, b. at Andover, 25 Jul 1738 daughter of Josiah and
Mary (Chandler) Ballard and widow of Abiel Abbot; Phebe d. 9 Jun 1815.
        In his will written 24 March 1804, James Holt has bequests to the following persons: well beloved wife Phebe (second
wife), grandson James Abbot (who has lived with him for 10 years), beloved daughter Sarah wife of Barachias Abbott, beloved
daughter Abigail wife of Isaac Chandler, and his two sons-in-law Barachias Abbott and Isaac Chandler. Grandson James Abbot
is named executor.[163]
        James Holt elaborates on his bequest to his grandson: "For special and weighty reasons in my mind, I give to my
beloved grandson, James Abbot, who has lived with me about ten years, and to his heirs and assigns, all my estate, both real
and personal, not herein disposed of." He goes on to list several household items that are to go to him stating these were mostly
items that had belonged to James Abbot's uncle. We can only imagine the nature of these "special and weighty reasons."
        Sarah and James had seven children, all born at Andover.

        i   JAMES HOLT, b. 16 Apr 1749; d. 26 Nov 1800; m. 5 Jun 1778, HANNAH FOSTER, b. 23 Jul 1754 daughter
              of Jacob and Abigail (Frost) Foster; Hannah died from consumption 24 Oct 1794. They do not seem to have

---

[160] There are two Timothy Holts of similar age, one who married Hannah Johnson and one who married Ede Mc'Intire. It is generally accepted in published genealogies that this Timothy married Hannah Johnson.
[161] Livermore, *History of Wilton*, p 470
[162] Littlefield, *Genealogies of the Early Settlers of Weston*
[163] *Essex County, MA: Probate File Papers, 1638-1881. Probate of James Holt, 5 Nov 1812, Case number 13653.*

had any children that lived to adulthood. There is a daughter Hannah baptized in 1777 who is perhaps their child, but there is no further record for her and since she is not mentioned in the wills of either of her grandfathers, she likely died young. James is not mentioned in his father's will. Likewise, Hannah Foster is not mentioned in the will of her father Jacob who died in 1806.

    ii   ELIZABETH HOLT, b. 10 Mar 1750/1; d. 12 Nov 1777; Elizabeth did not marry.

    iii   JOEL HOLT, b. 7 Aug 1753; d. 20 Mar 1755.

    iv   DORCAS HOLT, b. 6 May 1756; d. 16 May 1778; Dorcas did not marry.

274)   v   ABIGAIL HOLT, b. 18 Jun 1758; d. 2 Oct 1824; m. 7 Dec 1780, her fourth cousin, ISAAC CHANDLER, b. 4 Oct 1754 son of William and Rebecca (Lovejoy) Chandler; Isaac d. 12 Jan 1832. After Abigail's death, Isaac married Elizabeth Upton.

275)   vi   SARAH HOLT, b. 7 Mar 1746/7; d. 11 Feb 1808; m. 6 Dec 1770, her third cousin BARACHIAS ABBOTT, b. 22 May 1739 son of Barachias and Hannah (Holt) Abbott; Barachias d. 29 Jan 1812.

    vii   SUSANNA HOLT, b. 27 Oct 1760; d. 26 Nov 1760.

66)   NATHAN HOLT (*Nicholas Holt³, Mary Russell Holt², Robert¹*), b. at Andover, 28 Feb 1725 son of Nicholas and Dorcas (Abbott) Holt; d. at Danvers, 2 Aug 1792; m. 4 Aug 1757, SARAH ABBOTT, b. 14 Jan 1729/30 daughter of George and Mary (Phillips) Abbott; Sarah d. 29 Dec 1797.

    Sarah and Nathan had four children. The births of the three daughters are recorded at Danvers. The son James is attributed to this family in Durrie's Holt genealogy.[164] Nathan did not leave a will. The administrator of the estate was his son-in-law William Frost.

276)   i   SARAH HOLT, b. 29 Oct 1758; d. 17 Sep 1841; m. at Danvers, 2 Dec 1777, WILLIAM FROST, b. at New Castle, NH, 15 Nov 1754 son of William and Elizabeth (Prescott) Frost; William d. at Andover 28 Sep 1836. Sarah and William are second great grandparents of Robert Frost.

277)   ii   MARY HOLT, b. 3 Oct 1761; d. at Beverly, 7 Jan 1850; m. 1 Nov 1781, ROBERT ENDICOTT, b. 29 Oct 1756 son of John and Elizabeth (Jacobs) Endicott; Robert d. at Beverly, 6 Mar 1819.

278)   iii   HANNAH HOLT, b. 11 May 1769; d. at Beverly 26 Jul 1857; m. 23 Jan 1793, her first cousin, PETER HOLT, b. at Andover 12 Jun 1763 son of Joshua and Phebe (Farnum) Holt; Peter d. at Greenfield, NH 25 Apr 1851. Two of the daughters of Hannah and Peter married Samuel Endicott son of Mary Holt and Robert Endicott (Hannah's sister Mary just above).

279)   iv   JAMES HOLT, b. 1772; d. in India, Aug 1807;[165] m. 30 Aug 1796, LUCY WHIPPLE, b. 8 Mar 1778; Lucy d. at Danvers, 6 Mar 1839. Although James's death is reported as August 1807, the probate of his estate was April 1807.

67)   DORCAS HOLT (*Nicholas Holt³, Mary Russell Holt², Robert¹*), b. at Andover, 4 Sep 1727 daughter of Nicholas and Dorcas (Abbott) Holt; death unknown but may have been at Wilton, NH; m. 26 Jan 1749, as his second wife, her first cousin, THOMAS HOLT (*Thomas Holt³, Mary Russell Holt², Robert¹*), b. Mar 1711/2 son of Thomas and Alice (Peabody) Holt; Thomas d. at Andover, 21 Nov 1776. Thomas was 1ˢᵗ married 15 Aug 1734 to HANNAH KIMBALL, baptized at Boxford 7 Sep 1712 daughter of John and Elizabeth (Chapman) Kimball; Hannah d. at Andover, 12 Jun 1748.

    Thomas's first marriage was to Hannah Kimball with whom he had six children. Following her death, Thomas married his cousin Dorcas and they had six children. The story is that Thomas Holt was the largest landholder in Andover at that time. Dorcas was also a horse lover and is supposed to have had the first horse gig in town.[166] After the death of her husband, Dorcas went with one, or perhaps more, of her children to Wilton and she is believed to have died there.

    Thomas wrote his will 8 Oct 1774. Dorcas was named executor of the estate in Thomas's will, but she requested that this duty be assumed by her brother Joshua Holt. In his will, Thomas Holt has bequests for the following persons: dearly beloved wife Dorcas who receives use of the West end of the dwelling house as well as other provisions for her support and son William is charged with seeing to her support and care; well-beloved son Nathan receives a token bequest of six shillings to make up his total portion; well-beloved son Daniel receives £13; well-beloved son Asa, six shillings; well-beloved son Thomas, a tract of land that was purchased from Samuel Ames; well-beloved son William, real and personal estate not otherwise disposed of; well-beloved son Joseph, a tract of land lying south of the land of the widow Rebecca Gray; beloved daughters Hannah and

---

[164] Durrie, *Genealogical History of the Holt Family*, p 44

[165] James, h. Lucy (Whipple), at India, Aug. —, 1807.

[166] Livermore, *History of the Town of Wilton*, p 404

Mehitable receive six shillings each; beloved daughter Dorcas receives a piece of pasture land; beloved daughter Mary, £53; beloved daughter Lois, £53; daughters Lois and Mary also allowed use of a bed and chest in the house where they might stay in times of sickness as long as they are unmarried.[167] Hannah, Mehitable, Nathan, Daniel, and Asa are children from Thomas's first marriage.

There are birth records for six children of Dorcas Holt and Thomas Holt recorded at Andover.

279a) i   THOMAS HOLT, b. 15 Jun 1750; m. 27 Oct 1774, his second cousin, LYDIA FARNUM, b. 10 Nov 1756 daughter of Thomas and Lydia (Abbott) Farnum.

280) ii   DORCAS HOLT, b. 19 Mar 1753; m. 25 Nov 1773, her third cousin, MOSES LOVEJOY, b. 9 Sep 1751 son of Daniel and Mary (Holt) Lovejoy; Moses d. at Wilton 19 Mar 1807.

iii   MARY HOLT, b. 11 Mar 1758. Durrie's Holt genealogy lists Mary as the Mary Holt that married John Adams in 1776 (his third marriage). However, John Adams's Mary died in 1829 at age 89, meaning she was born about 1740 so that is not this Mary. There are several marriages for Mary Holts about the time this Mary would have married, but all those other options are not yet explored.

281) iv   LOIS HOLT, b. 29 Oct 1760; d. at Andover, 17 Apr 1852; m. 4 Jan 1785, MOSES PEARSON, b. at Wilmington, about 1752 son of Nathan and Mary (Wilson) Pearson; Moses d. at Andover 11 Aug 1835.

282) v   WILLIAM HOLT, b. 7 Sep 1763; m. 29 Jul 1784, ELIZABETH JONES daughter of Jacob Jones; Elizabeth d. at Weld, ME, 1829.

283) vi   JOSEPH HOLT, b. 29 Sep 1766; d. at Andover, 8 Jun 1791; m. 27 Nov 1788, his third cousin once removed, ABIGAIL HOLT, b. 19 May 1767 daughter of Samuel and Abigail (Blanchard) Holt; Abigail d. 13 May 1821.

Thomas Holt and Hannah Kimball were parents of six children.

i   NATHAN HOLT, b. at Andover, 17 Jul 1735; d. at Andover, 26 Aug 1785. Nathan did not marry.

69) ii   HANNAH HOLT, b. at Andover, 11 Feb 1738/9; d. at Andover, 2 Aug 1831; m. at Andover, 29 Nov 1759, her first cousin once removed, DANIEL HOLT (*Nicholas Holt³, Mary Russell Holt², Robert¹*), b. at Andover, 10 Feb 1732/3 son of Nicholas and Dorcas (Abbott) Holt; Daniel d. at Andover, 15 Feb 1796.

284) iii   DANIEL HOLT, b. at Andover, 11 Sep 1740; m. at Andover, 3 Dec 1761, his first cousin, ALICE HOLT (*Lydia Holt Holt⁴, Thomas Holt³, Mary Russell Holt², Robert¹*), b. at Andover, 13 Nov 1742 daughter of Benjamin and Lydia (Holt) Holt; Alice d. at Morrisville, NY, 7 Mar 1826.

285) iv   ASA HOLT, b. at Andover, 3 May 1742; d. at Andover, 20 Feb 1793; m. 1st 10 Sep 1765, his third cousin, DINAH HOLT, b. at Andover, 6 Nov 1744 daughter of Samuel and Jemima (Gray) Holt; Dinah d. at Andover, 20 Nov 1780. Asa m. 2nd at Andover, 5 Jul 1781, LYDIA STEVENS, b. at Andover, 15 Nov 1753 daughter of Jonathan and Lydia (Felch) Stevens.

286) v   MEHITABLE HOLT, b. at Andover, 8 Feb 1743/4; d. at Hillsborough, 20 Oct 1816; m. 1st 28 May 1761, SAMUEL LUFKIN son of Samuel Lufkin; Samuel d. 30 Apr 1777. Mehitable m. 2nd at Andover, 14 Jul 1785, ABNER WILKINS, b. 1 Jul 1743; Abner d. at Middleton, 17 Aug 1820. Abner was first married to Eunice Smith.

287) vi   ABIEL HOLT, b. at Andover, 3 Apr 1746; d. at Andover, 17 Nov 1824; m. 23 Jun 1767, his third cousin once removed (through Holt line), LYDIA LOVEJOY, b. at Andover, 21 Jul 1747 daughter of Joshua and Lydea (Abbott) Lovejoy; Lydia d. at Haverhill, 3 Jan 1838.

68)   JOSHUA HOLT (*Nicholas Holt³, Mary Russell Holt², Robert¹*), b. at Andover, 30 Jun 1730 son of Nicholas and Dorcas (Abbott) Holt; d. at Andover, 24 Jul 1810; m. 2 Dec 1755, his second cousin once removed, PHEBE FARNUM, b. 10 Oct 1731 daughter of Timothy and Dinah (Ingalls) Farnum; Phebe d. 26 Jan 1806.

Joshua Holt and Phebe Farnum had as their homestead what is now 111 Reservation Road in Andover, known as the Solomon Holt farm. Joshua is believed to have built this homestead in 1790. His son Solomon, as noted in the will, received the homestead from his father.[168]

Joshua was deacon of the South Parish church in Andover for 34 years. He also served in the Revolutionary War as a member of the 4th Essex County militia.[169]

---

[167] *Essex County, MA: Probate File Papers, 1638-1881. Probate of Thomas Holt, 3 Feb 1777, Case number 13699.*
[168] Andover Historic Preservation. https://preservation.mhl.org/111-reservation-road
[169] Massachusetts Soldiers and Sailors, volume 8, p 193

Joshua Holt revised his will 24 May 1807 in response to "great alterations" that had taken place in his family. Perhaps these "great alterations" related to the death of his wife Phebe in 1806. Four sons, John, Joshua, Timothy, and Stephen, each receive $40. Son Peter receives $110. Each of his daughters receive $33.34. These daughters are Phebe the wife of Joseph Batchelder, Mary the wife of Isaac Foster, Abiah the wife of Deacon Daniel Kimbal, Hannah the wife of Ephraim Holt, and Chloe the wife of Francis Bowers. The daughters also receive all the household goods and furniture. Son Solomon receives all the lands and buildings that Joshua still holds at the time as his death as well as his pew in the meeting house. His six sons will divide his wearing apparel, although Solomon is free to select what items he wants. Solomon is named sole executor.[170]

Solomon was the only child in this family that remained in Andover. All the other children moved to New Hampshire and settled in towns in Hillsborough County.

Joshua Holt and Phebe Farnum had eleven children whose births are recorded at Andover. Some sources (e. g., Durrie's *A Genealogical History of the Holt Family*) also list a child Ruth in this family, but there was another Joshua Holt married to Ruth Burnap who was in Andover at the same time and rearing a family. There were records for two girls named Ruth in Andover, one baptized in January 1756 and the other born 11 May 1758; both these dates conflict with births of other children of Joshua and Phebe, so perhaps Ruth was the daughter of Joshua and Ruth.

288) i PHEBE HOLT, b. 28 Nov 1756; d. at Greenfield, 1849; m. 11 Dec 1778, JOSEPH BATCHELDER, b. 6 Mar 1748 son of Joseph and Judith (Rea) Batchelder; Joseph d. 1826.

289) ii JOSHUA HOLT, b. 17 Jan 1758; d at Greenfield, 14 Mar 1835; m. 1787, HANNAH INGALLS, b. 20 Feb 1759 daughter of David and Priscilla (Howe) Ingalls; Hannah d. 1 Dec 1838.

290) iii MARY HOLT, b. 5 Dec 1759; d. at Greenfield, 9 Jul 1819; m. 26 Aug 1784, ISAAC FOSTER, b. 23 Dec 1751 son of Jacob and Abigail (Frost) Foster.

291) iv ABIAH HOLT, b. 16 Apr 1761; d. at Hancock, NH, 4 May 1841; m. 21 Jun 1791, as his second wife, DANIEL KIMBALL, b. at Ipswich, 20 Oct 1755 son of Daniel and Hephzibah (Howe) Kimball; d. 24 May 1843. Daniel's first wife was Elizabeth Osgood.

278) v PETER HOLT, b. 12 Jun 1763; d. at Greenfield, 25 Apr 1851; m. 23 Jan 1793, his first cousin, HANNAH HOLT, b. at Danvers, 11 May 1769 daughter of Nathan and Sarah (Abbott) Holt; Hannah d. at Beverly, 26 Jul 1857.

292) vi JOHN HOLT, b. 12 Jan 1765; d, at Greenfield, 11 Feb 1835; m. 6 Jan 1792, his third cousin, DORCAS ABBOTT, b. Dec 1766 daughter of George and Hannah (Lovejoy) Abbott; Dorcas d. 15 Mar 1841.

293) vii TIMOTHY HOLT, b. Apr 1767; d. at Peterborough, 1856; m. 7 Nov 1793, his second cousin once removed, LYDIA HOLT, b. 18 Apr 1767 daughter of Joseph and Ruth (Johnson) Holt; Lydia d. 22 Nov 1825.

294) viii SOLOMON HOLT, b. Dec 1768; d. at Andover, 15 Apr 1830; m. 22 May 1798, MARY CUMMINGS, b. about 1775 daughter of Justin and Mary (-) Cummings;[171] Mary d. 8 Oct 1852.

295) ix HANNAH HOLT, b. Jun 1771; d. at Greenfield, 21 Apr 1842; m. 27 Nov 1794, her third cousin once removed, EPHRAIM HOLT (*Jacob Holt⁴, Jacob Holt³, Hannah Russell Holt², Robert¹*), b. 19 Mar 1769 son of Jacob and Rhoda (Abbott) Holt; Ephraim d. 24 Oct 1836.

296) x STEPHEN HOLT, b. May 1773; d. at Greenfield, 26 Mar 1868; m. 1799, FANNY BOWERS, b. at Chelmsford, Jun 1773 daughter of Francis and Elizabeth (Holt) Bowers; Fanny d. 18 Apr 1828. Stephen married in 1831, MARGARET BATCHELDER, b. 1784 and d. 1867.

297) xi CHLOE HOLT, b. Jun 1775; d. at Peterborough, 6 Nov 1849; m. 23 Oct 1798, FRANCIS BOWERS, b. at Chelmsford, 20 May 1775 son of Francis and Elizabeth (Holt) Bowers; Francis d. 15 Oct 1835.

69) DANIEL HOLT (*Nicholas Holt³, Mary Russell Holt², Robert¹*), b. at Andover, 10 Feb 1732/3 son of Nicholas and Dorcas (Abbott) Holt; d. at Andover, 15 Feb 1796; m. 29 Nov 1759, his first cousin once removed, HANNAH HOLT, (*Thomas Holt⁴, Thomas Holt³, Mary Russell Holt², Robert¹*), b. 11 Feb 1738/9 daughter of Thomas and Hannah (Kimball) Holt; Hannah d. at Andover, 2 Aug 1831.

There are births for three children in this family that are recorded at Andover. A probate record was not located, and no other specific information about this couple.

---

[170] *Essex County, MA: Probate File Papers, 1638-1881.* Probate of Joshua Holt, 9 Aug 1810, Case number 13666.
[171] These are the parents given by Durrie's Holt family genealogy. There are no records that support this.

298) i   DANIEL HOLT, b. Dec 1761; d. at Fitchburg, 27 Nov 1830; m. 5 Jan 1790, MARY JONES, b. at Andover, about 1769 daughter of Jacob and Mary (Winn) Jones.[172]

299) ii   ABIEL HOLT, b. 8 Jun 1765; d. at Rindge, NH, 18 Jun 1825; m. 26 Jul 1791, PHEBE PUTNAM, b. at Fitchburg, 20 Sep 1770 daughter of Daniel and Rachel (·) Putnam; Phebe d. at Fitchburg, 12 Nov 1827.

      iii   NATHAN HOLT, b. 13 Jul 1767; d. 1 Sep 1778.

70)   LYDIA HOLT (*Thomas Holt³, Mary Russell Holt², Robert¹*), b. at Andover, 2 Jan 1713/4 daughter of Thomas and Alice (Peabody) Holt.; m. at Andover, 30 Jan 1734/5, her second cousin, BENJAMIN HOLT, b. 1704 son of Henry and Mary (Marston) Holt; Benjamin d. at Andover, 17 Mar 1779.

      Benjamin and Lydia resided in Andover where they kept a farm. On 31 May 1749, Henry Holt of Andover, in consideration of £2,000 in bills of credit, conveyed to his son Benjamin Holt, Jr. husbandman of Andover 35 acres of tillage and woodland in Andover, this being land that Benjamin had been improving for some years.[173]

      On 26 April 1762, Benjamin Holt, Jr. yeoman of Andover, in consideration of £100, conveyed to Joseph Holt, Jr. all his lands lying in Falls meadow containing about 16 acres with half the dwelling house. On 22 February 1765, Benjamin Holt, Jr., yeoman of Andover, in consideration of £113 lawful money, conveyed to his son Joseph Holt, Jr. parcels of land in Andover containing 36 acres, one 6-acre tract and a 30-acre tract (this latter tract described in a manner similar to the property conveyed to Benjamin by his father Henry).[174]

      Benjamin and Lydia were parents of nine children born at Andover.

      i   LYDIA HOLT, b. 18 Dec 1735; d. 18 Dec 1765.

      ii   BENJAMIN HOLT, b. 4 Apr 1737; d. 22 Nov 1741.

300) iii   JOSEPH HOLT, b. at Andover, 20 Aug 1740; d. at Andover, 15 Dec 1801; m. at Andover, 1 Jun 1762, RUTH JOHNSON, b. at Haverhill, 27 Oct 1744 daughter of Cornelius and Eleanor (Currier) Johnson;[175] Ruth d. at Andover, 18 May 1827.

284) iv   ALICE HOLT, b. at Andover, 13 Nov 1742; d. at Morrisville, NY, 7 Mar 1826; m. at Andover, 3 Dec 1761, her first cousin, DANIEL HOLT (*Thomas Holt⁴, Thomas Holt³, Mary Russell Holt², Robert¹*), b. at Andover, 11 Sep 1740 son of Thomas and Hannah (Kimball) Holt.

301) v   BETHIAH HOLT, b. at Andover, 3 Aug 1744; d. at Nelson, NH, 13 Apr 1812; m. at Andover, 20 Oct 1767, her third cousin, SOLOMON WARDWELL,[176] b. at Andover, 14 Jul 1743 son of Thomas and Abigail (Gray) Wardwell; Solomon d. at Packersfield, 20 Sep 1825.

      vi   BENJAMIN HOLT, b. 6 Dec 1746; d. 31 Aug 1748.

      vii   BENJAMIN HOLT, b. May 1749; d. at Andover, 12 Apr 1822. Benjamin likely did not marry.

302) viii   MARY HOLT, b. at Andover, 19 Sep 1751; d. at Lynn, 31 Dec 1819; m. 1st at Andover, 13 Apr 1772, JAMES LARRABEE[177] perhaps the son of Joseph and Elizabeth (Trask) Larrabee; James d. before 1784 and likely before that. Mary m. 2nd at Lynn (intention 12 Dec 1784), EBENEZER TARBOX, b. at Lynn, 10 Sep 1763 son of Benjamin and Annah (Rice) Tarbox; Ebenezer d. at Lynn, 12 Aug 1827.

303) ix   MARTHA HOLT, b. at Andover, 15 Oct 1754; d. at Smithville, NY, 9 Oct 1829; m. at Andover, 23 Nov 1775, JONATHAN FELT, b. at Temple, NH, 8 Apr 1753 son of Aaron and Mary (Wyatt) Felt; Jonathan d. at Packersfield (Nelson), NH, 17 Feb 1807 (probate 1807).

71)   JOSEPH HOLT (*Thomas Holt³, Mary Russell Holt², Robert¹*), b. at Andover, 28 Feb 1715/6 son of Thomas and Alice (Peabody) Holt; d. at Lunenburg, 1754; m. 1st 14 Aug 1742, MARY ABBOTT, b. at Andover, 4 Aug 1713 daughter of Stephen and Sarah (Stevens) Abbott; Mary d. at Lunenburg, 5 Aug 1748. Joseph m. 2nd at Lunenburg, 20 May 1749, DORCAS BOYNTON, b.

---

[172] The will of Jacob Jones includes a bequest to his granddaughter Mary Holt the child of his daughter Mary who is deceased.

[173] Massachusetts Land Records, Essex County, 94:212

[174] Massachusetts Land Records, Essex County, 110:159, 117:62

[175] The 1774 will of Cornelius Johnson of Concord includes a bequest to his daughter Ruth Holt.

[176] There are two Bethiah Holts near in age, one of whom married Solomon Wardwell and one who married Thomas Russell. There do not seem to be any records that clearly establish which was which, and I have chosen this arrangement: Bethiah daughter of Benjamin married Solomon Wardwell and Bethiah daughter of Ephraim Holt and Phebe Russell married Thomas Russell. It could well be the other way around.

[177] Name is also spelled Leatherby

at Groton, MA, 21 Dec 1715 daughter of Benoni and Anna (Mighill) Boynton; Dorcas d. at Lunenburg, 11 Jun 1775. Dorcas Boynton was first married to Thomas Frost.

In his will written 16 February 1754 (probate 26 Apr 1754), Joseph Holt bequeaths to beloved wife Dorcas the use of all the real estate, mansion house, and barn until his youngest son Joseph reaches age seven years four months old. He adds several stipulations related Dorcas keeping the farm and barn in good repair. After son Joseph reaches age seven, Dorcas will have the use of one-third of the estate. Dorcas receives all the husbandry tools, smith tools, and smith shop which are hers forever except that part of the estate that he leaves to his two daughters Mary Holt and Sarah Holt. He bequeaths to Dorcas's daughter Dorcas Frost £3.6.8 for her service while she was with the family. His two sons Abiel and Joseph are to receive two-thirds of the real estate and are to pay to their sister Mary and Sarah £13.6.8 when they reach age twenty-one. He also bequeaths to his two daughters household items that belonged to their mother which are currently in the care of Stephen Abbott in Andover. His four children will equally divide the books. Wife Dorcas and brother Thomas Holt are named executors. Real estate was valued at £200.[178]

Mary Abbott and Joseph Holt had four children all born at Lunenburg.

	i	JOSEPH HOLT, b. 4 Apr 1744; d. in infancy.
304)	ii	MARY HOLT, b. 17 Aug 1745; m. 26 Jun 1766, BENJAMIN DARLING, b. 28 Apr 1728 son of John and Lois (Gowing) Darling; Benjamin d. at Lunenburg, about 1783 based on date of probate.
305)	iii	SARAH HOLT, baptized at Lunenburg 14 Dec 1746; m. at Lunenburg, 1 Feb 1767, BARNABAS WOOD, b. at Lunenburg, 21 May 1746 son of Jonathan and Sarah (Whitney) Wood; Barnabas d. at Windsor, VT, 5 Apr 1822.
306)	iv	ABIEL HOLT, b. 14 Jul 1748; d. at Temple, NH, 7 Jan 1811; m. 25 Nov 1773, his third cousin, SARAH ABBOTT, b. at Suncook, 1751 daughter of Job and Sarah (Abbott) Abbott; Sarah d. 9 Oct 1854 (age at death inscribed as 103 years, 2 months, 25 days on her gravestone).[179]

Joseph Holt and Dorcas Boynton were parents of one child.

307)	i	JOSEPH HOLT, b. at Lunenburg, 18 Dec 1752; d. at Fitchburg, 3 Sep 1803 (suicide by hanging); m. 30 Jan 1777, ELIZABETH STRATTON.

72)   WILLIAM HOLT (*Thomas Holt[3], Mary Russell Holt[2], Robert[1]*), b. at Andover, 10 Dec 1720 son of Thomas and Alice (Peabody) Holt; d. at Hampton, CT, 2 Aug 1793; m. 1st at Hampton, 14 Jul 1742, his first cousin, HANNAH HOLT (*Abiel Holt[3], Mary Russell Holt[2], Robert[1]*), b. at Windham, CT, 17 Apr 1723 daughter of Abiel and Hannah (Abbott) Holt; Hannah d. at Windham, 25 Jan 1750/1. William m. 2nd at Windham, 14 May 1752, SYBEL DURKEE, b. at Windham, 10 Jan 1731 daughter of Stephen and Lois (Moulton) Durkee;[180] Sybel d. at Hampton, 11 Jan 1794.

Hannah Holt and William Holt had four children whose births are recorded at Windham.

308)	i	WILLIAM HOLT, b. 15 Jul 1743; d. at Hampton, 6 Aug 1815;[181] m. 8 Sep 1763, his third cousin, MERCY HOLT, b. 14 Feb 1740/1 daughter of Zebadiah and Sarah (Flint) Holt; Mercy d. 15 Sep 1799.
	ii	HANNAH HOLT, b. 26 Jan 1744/5; d. 30 Aug 1754.
309)	iii	ALICE HOLT, b. 26 Apr 1747; d. at Stockbridge, VT, 28 Nov 1814;[182] m. 13 Nov 1764, her second cousin, ROBERT LYON (*Sarah Holt Lyon[4], Robert Holt[3], Mary Russell Holt[2], Robert[1]*), b. at Pomfret, 30 Sep 1743 son of Peletiah and Sarah (Holt) Lyon; Robert d. 12 Feb 1809.
310)	iv	SARAH HOLT, b. 21 Jun 1748; d. at Hampton, 7 Apr 1777; m. 16 Nov 1769, HENRY DURKEE, b. 29 Sep 1749 son of Henry and Relief (Adams) Durkee. Henry m. 2nd, Sarah Loomis; Henry d. 22 Apr 1820.

William Holt and Sybel Durkee were parents of four children born and Windham.

	i	BETHIAH HOLT, b. and d. 16 Aug 1754

---

[178] *Worcester County, MA: Probate File Papers, 1731-1881*. Online database. AmericanAncestors.org. New England Historic Genealogical Society, 2015. Case 30653
[179] Findagrave.com
[180] The 1766 will of Stephen Durkee of Windham includes a bequest to his daughter Sibbel Holt.
[181] *Connecticut, Deaths and Burials Index, 1650-1934*.
[182] *Vermont, Vital Records, 1720-1908*.

    ii   ABIEL HOLT, b. 8 Jul 1755; m. at Windham, 18 Jul 1776, ABIGAIL DURKEE, b. at Windham, 11 Feb 1756 daughter of Joseph and Elizabeth (Fiske) Durkee. Abiel and Abigail had one son Abiel Holt who was born at Windham on 24 Oct 1790. Nothing further that is certain is known of the son Abiel.

    iii   HANNAH HOLT, b. 25 Apr 1756; d. 10 Sep 1774.

    iv   AMASA HOLT, b. at Windham, 24 May 1759; perhaps the Amasa who d. at Waterford, CT, 23 Jul 1847 at age 88.

73)   ALICE HOLT (*Thomas Holt³, Mary Russell Holt², Robert¹*), b. at Andover, about 1722 daughter of Thomas and Alice (Peabody) Holt; d. at Andover, 1762 (probate 22 Nov 1762); m. 13 Mar 1739/40, as his third wife, JOHN BARNARD, b. at Andover, 16 Apr 1697 son of John and Naomi (Hoyt) Barnard; John d. at Andover, 1752 (probate 15 Jun 1752). John was first married to Sarah Osgood and second married to Mehitable Stiles.

    John Barnard did not leave a will and his estate entered probate 15 Jun 1752 with widow Alice declining administration which was assumed by John Barnard. The dower was set off to widow Alice which was for life. The other real estate was settled on eldest son John who received the double portion and daughter Sarah Kidder who were children from John's first marriage to Sarah Osgood. The children of Alice and Abigail receiving potions in the settlement were Mehitable, Allis, Jacob, Abigail, Lidia, and Rebecca.[183]

    Alice's estate entered probate 22 November 1762.[184] The value of her estate consisting of clothing and household items was £16.4.9.

    Alice Holt and John Barnard were parents of seven children born at Andover.

    i   MEHITABLE BARNARD, b. at Andover, 17 Dec 1740; d. at Andover, 23 Apr 1824. Mehitable did not marry. She did have an out-of-wedlock child Josiah Sawyer born in 1773.

    ii   ALICE BARNARD, b. at Andover, 28 Jul 1742. Alice was living in 1762 at the estate settlement, but no marriage or death record was located.

311)   iii   ABIGAIL BARNARD, b. at Andover, 15 May 1744; m. at Andover, 22 Mar 1764, SAMUEL DOWNING, baptized at Salem, 2 May 1742 son of Richard and Temperance (Derby) Downing; Samuel d. at Minot, ME, 13 Dec 1812.

312)   iv   LYDIA BARNARD, b. at Andover, 23 Jan 1745/6; d. at Sharon, NH, 9 Feb 1829; m. at Andover, 3 Sep 1767, JOSIAH SAWYER, b. at Reading, 17 Sep 1744 son of Josiah and Hannah (Gowing) Sawyer; Josiah d. at Sharon, 3 Oct 1829.

    v   MARY BARNARD, b. 21 Jan and d. 29 Jan 1747/8.

    vi   REBECCA BARNARD, b. at Andover, 21 Jan 1747/8; m. at Wilmington, 27 Jan 1791, as his second wife, THOMAS EVANS, likely b. at Salisbury, 15 Oct 1725 son of Thomas and Dorothy (Stockman) Evans; Thomas d. at Wilmington, 1802 (probate). Thomas was first married to Ruth Ballard. Rebecca did not have children.

    vii   JACOB BARNARD, b. at Andover, 20 Jul 1750. Jacob served in the Revolution in 1775 in Capt. Benjamin Farnum's company.

74)   ABIGAIL HOLT (*Abigail Holt Holt³, Mary Russell Holt², Robert¹*), b. at Andover, 21 Aug 1716 daughter of Paul and Abigail (Holt) Holt; d. at Hampton, CT, 3 Nov 1749; m. 3 Dec 1736, JONATHAN KINGSBURY, b. 1712 son of Thomas and Margaret (Haines) Kingsbury; Jonathan d. at Hampton, 28 Dec 1770. Jonathan married second Hannah Clark on 9 Jan 1751 and married third Sarah *How* Ballard the widow of John Ballard.

    In his will written 12 October 1770 (proved 17 January 1771), Jonathan Kingsbury bequeaths to beloved wife Sarah the household items that she had when they married, £8, other household items, a saddle and bridle, and other provisions for her support including improvements on a portion of the real estate. Beloved daughter Abigail Abbot receives a piece of land with house and barn in Ashford that he holds by deed from William Knowlton. Beloved son Jonathan receives the remainder of the estate real and personal provided he pay the other legacies in the will. These legacies are £200 each to daughters Hannah Kingsbury, Elizabeth Kingsbury, Mary Kingsbury, and Esther Kingsbury when arriving at the age of twenty with provision for

[183] *Essex County, MA: Probate File Papers, 1638-1881.* Online database. *AmericanAncestors.org.* New England Historic Genealogical Society, 2014. Case 1745

[184] *Essex County, MA: Probate File Papers, 1638-1881.* Online database. *AmericanAncestors.org.* New England Historic Genealogical Society, 2014. Case 1732

land valued at £220 each if Jonathan refuses to pay the legacies. Grandsons John Goold and Jonathan Goold each receives £10. Son Jonathan is sole executor. The total value of the estate was £1755.6.4 which included one farm in Ashford with 434 acres and a second farm of 41 acres.[185]

Abigail Holt and Jonathan Kingsbury were parents of two children born at Hampton.

313)   i   ABIGAIL KINGSBURY, b. at Hampton, 17 May 1742; d. at Lima, NY, 1791; m. 1st, at Windham, 13 Nov 1759, JOHN GOULD, b. 1731 son of Henry and Rebecca (Cole) Gould; John d. at Hampton, 29 Oct 1764 (probate Nov 1764). Abigail m. 2nd, at Hampton, 11 Sep 1770, JOHN ABBOTT. On 14 Mar 1791, Abigail filed for divorce from John Abbott on grounds of desertion.[186]

315)   ii   JONATHAN KINGSBURY, b. at Hampton, 25 Apr 1745; d. at Hampton, 25 Sep 1802; m. 1st, 14 Jan 1768, ANNE GEER, b. at Preston, 22 Dec 1745 daughter of Aaron and Mercy (Fisher) Geer;[187] Anne d. 23 Oct 1773. Jonathan m. 2nd, 21 Jun 1775, LODEMA RANSOM, b. at Kent, 8 Mar 1752 daughter of John and Bethia (Lewis) Ransom;[188] Lodema d. 24 Mar 1814.

75)   PAUL HOLT (*Abigail Holt Holt³, Mary Russell Holt², Robert¹*), b. at Andover, Aug 1720 son of Paul and Abigail (Holt) Holt; d. at Hampton, CT, 21 Dec 1804; m. 20 Jan 1742, MEHITABLE CHANDLER, b. 12 Apr 1719 daughter of Philemon and Hannah (Clary) Chandler; Mehitable d. at Hampton, 10 May 1773. Paul m. 2nd, 4 Jan 1774, MARY SPENCER.

Paul was born in Andover but migrated to Hampton with his father. It is reported that Mehitable died while doing her washing at a tub.[189]

Paul Holt did not leave a will and son Paul Holt was named administrator 18 January 1805. The inventory was taken 31 December 1804 with a total value of $2,061.76 including a farm of 104 acres. The widow's dower was set off to Mary Holt. Other heirs receiving distribution from the estate were Paul Holt, Philemon Holt, Ebenezer Holt, Stephen Holt, James Holt, Josiah Holt, and Mahitabel Phelps wife of Jeremiah Phelps.[190]

315)   i   PAUL HOLT, b. at Windham, 4 Jan 1742/3; d. at Hampton, 26 Oct 1827; m. 1st, 20 Aug 1767, SARAH WELCH, b. at Norwich, 6 Jul 1742 daughter of Joseph and Lydia (Rudd) Welch; Sarah d. 26 Dec 1784. Paul m. 2nd, 15 Jan 1789, PHEBE WELCH CADY, b. 1754 daughter of Gideon and Sarah (Hutchins) Cady;[191] Phebe d. at Hampton, 31 May 1800. Paul m. 3rd, 27 Nov 1800, his second cousin, DINAH HOLT (*Joshua Holt⁴, Joshua Holt³, Mary Russell Holt², Robert¹*) (widow of Seth Stowell), b. at Windham, 22 Mar 1750 daughter of Joshua and Mary (Abbott) Holt; Dinah d. 21 Feb 1826.

316)   ii   PHILEMON HOLT, b. at Hampton, 22 Jun 1744; d. at Willington, 31 Jul 1818; m. at Willington, 27 Aug 1771, JEMIMA ELDREDGE, b. at Willington, 28 Mar 1755 daughter of Jesse and Abigail (Smith) Eldredge; Jemima d. at Willington, 3 Oct 1821.

317)   iii   EBENEZER HOLT, b. recorded at Windham, 23 Feb 1745/6; m. at Somers, 29 Aug 1771, MARY COLLINS.

318)   iv   STEPHEN HOLT, b. 12 Mar 1748; d. at Pittsfield, VT, 31 Dec 1838; m. 20 Nov 1774, HANNAH GEER, b. 2 Nov 1755 daughter of Aaron and Mercy (Fisher) Geer;[192] Hannah d. at Chaplin, CT, 1858.

319)   v   JAMES HOLT, b. at Hampton, 21 May 1750; d. at Bristol, CT, 29 Mar 1826; m. 1st, 31 Dec 1769, HULDAH STILES, b. at Hampton, 18 Sep 1736 daughter of Samuel and Huldah (Durkee) Stiles; Huldah d. at Hampton, 12 Jul 1799.[193] James m. 2nd, 29 Jun 1800, CHLOE STILES (niece of Huldah), b. 4 May 1781 daughter of Isaac and Abigail (Case) Stiles. Chloe Holt was living in Bristol in 1850 with her son James.

   vi   THOMAS HOLT, b. 25 Feb 1752; d. 17 Aug 1754.

[185] *Connecticut. Probate Court (Windham District), Probate records volume 8, pp 131-138*

[186] Knox and Ferris, Connecticut Divorces: Superior Court Records for the Counties of Tolland, New London & Windham 1719-1910, p 259; John, Wrentham, MA m. Abigail Gould, Windham, 11 Sep 1770; desertion 14 Mar 1791

[187] The 1797 will of Aaron Geer includes a bequest to the heirs of Anne Kingsbury wife of Jonathan Kingsbury.

[188] The 1791 will of John Ransom of Kent includes a bequest to his daughter Lodema Kingsbury.

[189] Chandler, *The Chandler Family: The Descendants of William and Annis* Chandler, p 99

[190] *Connecticut State Library (Hartford, Connecticut), Probate Packets, Hicks-Hovey, Elisha, 1719-1880, Estate of Paul Holt 1804, number 1952*

[191] The 1799 will of Gideon Cady includes a bequest to his daughter Phebe Holt.

[192] The 1797 will of Aaron Geer includes a bequest to daughter Hannah Holt wife of Stephen Holt.

[193] Huldah the wife of James Holt died at age 63.

      vii   JOSIAH HOLT, b. at Windham, 28 May 1754; d. at Burlington, CT, 14 Jan 1810; m. at Medfield, MA, 28 May 1777, KEZIAH ADAMS, b. at Medfield, 31 Mar 1747 daughter of Henry and Jemima (Morse) Adams;[194] Keziah d. at Bristol, CT, 7 Apr 1811. No children were identified for Josiah Holt and Keziah Adams.

320)   viii MEHITABLE HOLT, b. at Windham, 1 May 1757; d. at Hampton, 27 Oct 1819; m. at Pomfret, 27 Nov 1789, JEREMIAH PHELPS, b. at Hebron, 13 Jul 1729 son of Timothy and Hannah (Calkins) Phelps.[195]

76)   ABIGAIL HOLT (*Robert Holt³, Mary Russell Holt², Robert¹*), b. at Windham, 20 Feb 1722 daughter of Robert and Rebecca (Preston) Holt; m. at Windham, 5 Nov 1741, DAVID KENDALL; David d. at Ashford, 16 Dec 1777.
    There are records of five children of Abigail Holt and David Kendall.

321)   i   ABIGAIL KENDALL, b. at Windham, 21 Oct 1742; d. at Ashford, 8 Nov 1781; m. 28 May 1771, ENOS PRESTON, b. at Windham, 7 Jun 1737 son of John and Sarah (Foster) Preston. Enos married second Hannah Stiles on 12 Nov 1783.

322)   ii DAVID KENDALL, b. at Windham, 13 Nov 1744; m. at Ashford, 23 Feb 1775, MEHITABLE STILES, b. at Windham, 15 Nov 1740 daughter of Samuel and Huldah (Durkee) Stiles; Mehitable d. at Ashford, 27 Jan 1827.

      iii ALICE KENDALL, b. at Windham, 18 Jan 1746; d. at Ashford, 16 Apr 1798.

      iv REBECCA KENDALL, baptized at Hampton, 22 Jan 1749

      v   EZEKIEL KENDALL, baptized at Hampton, 30 Jun 1751

77)   SARAH HOLT (*Robert Holt³, Mary Russell Holt², Robert¹*), b. at Windham, 20 Feb 1722 daughter of Robert and Rebecca (Preston) Holt; d. at Pomfret, 11 Oct 1743; m. at Pomfret, 2 Feb 1741/2, PELETIAH LYON, b. at Pomfret, 20 Sep 1711 son of Abiel and Judith (Farrington) Lyon.
    Sarah Holt and Peletiah Lyon were parents of one child.

309)   i   ROBERT LYON, b. at Pomfret, 30 Sep 1743; d. at Stockbridge, VT, 12 Feb 1809; m. 13 Nov 1764, his second cousin, ALICE HOLT (*William Holt⁴, Thomas Holt³, Mary Russell Holt², Robert¹*), b. at Windham, 26 Apr 1747 daughter of William and Hannah (Holt) Holt; Alice d. at Stockbridge, 28 Nov 1814.

78)   MARY HOLT (*Robert Holt³, Mary Russell Holt², Robert¹*), b. at Windham, 7 Feb 1725 daughter of Robert and Rebecca (Preston) Holt; m. at Pomfret, 15 Jun 1742, JOSEPH TRUESDELL, b. at Pomfret, 24 Jun 1719 son of Ebenezer and Rachel (Davis) Truesdell; Joseph d. at Havana, 8 Oct 1762.
    Joseph Truesdell did not leave a will and his estate entered probate 4 January 1763 with Samuel Craft as administrator. The total value of the estate was £16.6.4 with debts exceeding its value.[196]
    The births of eight children are recorded for Joseph Truesdell and Mary Holt.

      i   JERUSHA TRUESDELL, b. at Pomfret, 4 Apr 1743; d. 30 Jun 177__ in the death transcription. Jerusha did not marry.

      ii ASA TRUESDELL, b. at Pomfret, 16 Aug 1744; d. at Suffield, CT, 1796; perhaps m. in 1778, SYBIL CARRINGTON. No children were identified.

323)   iii SETH TRUESDELL, b. at Pomfret, 23 Mar 1746; d. at Pomfret, 19 Oct 1776; m. at Pomfret, 10 Jan 1771, ESTHER WEST.

324)   iv JEDUTHAN TRUESDELL, b. recorded at Killingly, 21 Jan 1748; d. at Pomfret, 12 Apr 1801; m. at Pomfret, 20 Jan 1774; ABIGAIL WHITE.

      v   RACHEL TRUESDELL, b. 17 Oct 1750; d. 29 Jan 1767.

---

[194] Adams, *A Genealogical History of Henry Adams of Braintree*, p 15
[195] Phelps and Servin, *The Phelps Family in America*, volume 1, p 211
[196] *Connecticut State Library (Hartford, Connecticut)*; Probate Place: *Hartford, Connecticut, Probate Packets, Thayer, E-Tyler, Septimus, 1752-1880*, Estate of Joseph Truesdell, Case 4064

325)   vi   DARIUS TRUESDELL, b. at Pomfret, 16 Jan 1752; d. at Woodstock, 6 May 1808; m. at Woodstock, 10 Oct 1772, RHODA CHAFFEE, b. at Woodstock, 10 May 1751 daughter of Thomas and Dorcas (Abbott) Chaffee; Rhoda d. at Woodstock, 19 Nov 1834.

        vii   SARAH TRUESDELL, b. at Pomfret, 20 Aug 1753; d. at Pomfret, 27 Mar 1787. Sarah did not marry.

       viii   MOLLY TRUESDELL, b. at Pomfret, 9 Jul 1756. Molly is not known to have married but had an out-of-wedlock child, Hannah Abbott b. at Pomfret 12 Oct 1779. It is not known what became of daughter Hannah.

79)   MARTHA HOLT (*Robert Holt³, Mary Russell Holt², Robert¹*), b. at Windham, 11 Apr 1725 daughter of Robert and Rebecca (Preston) Holt; d. at Pomfret, 4 Oct 1759; m. 1 Jan 1754, JOHN RICHARDSON.
          Martha and John had three children in Windham County and Martha died after the birth of her third child. John remarried and took his family to Yarmouth, Nova Scotia where he was by 1761.[197]

326)   i   REUBEN RICHARDSON, b. at Windham, 7 Dec 1754; m. at Yarmouth, 24 Aug 1775, MARY BURGESS daughter of Joshua Burgess.

        ii   SARAH RICHARDSON, b. at Pomfret, 22 Apr 1758

327)   iii   STEPHEN RICHARDSON, b. at Pomfret, 26 Sep 1759; d. at Middletown, VT, 3 Jan 1834;[198] m. at Norwich, CT, 21 Dec 1786, HANNAH RUDD, b. about 1767; Hannah d. at Middletown, about 1848.

80)   ELIZABETH HOLT (*Abiel Holt³, Mary Russell Holt², Robert¹*), b. 16 Feb 1724/5 daughter of Abiel and Hannah (Abbott) Holt; d. about 1753; m. 10 Jun 1746, FRANCIS FENTON, b. at Willington, b. 16 Mar 1718 son of Francis and Ann (Berry) Fenton.[199] Francis m. 2nd Ann Newcomb, 31 Oct 1754. Francis Fenton d. at Willington, 1781 (date of probate).
          Elizabeth Holt and Francis Fenton had two children whose births are recorded at Willington.

328)   i   MARY FENTON, b. 13 Apr 1748; d. at Willington, 14 Apr 1822; m. 1st, 21 May 1770, ISAAC SAWIN, b. 23 Sep 1748 son of George and Anna (Farrar) Sawin; Isaac d. 29 Oct 1776. Mary m. 2nd, 2 Jul 1778, as his second wife, JAMES NILES, b. at Braintree, 2 Apr 1747 son of John and Dorothy (Reynolds) Niles; James d. 18 Jan 1822.

329)   ii   FRANCIS FENTON, b. 13 Feb 1750/1; m. 25 May 1775, CHLOE GOODALE, b. at Pomfret, 28 Dec 1755 daughter of Ebenezer and Phebe (Holt) Goodale; Chloe d. at New Haven, Oct 1833.[200]

81)   ABIEL HOLT (*Abiel Holt³, Mary Russell Holt², Robert¹*), b. 1 Feb 1726/7 son of Abiel and Hannah (Abbott) Holt; d. at Willington, 2 Oct 1785; m. 1st 22 Apr 1755, MARY DOWNER whose origins are unknown, although perhaps the daughter of Andrew Downer and Sarah Lazell; Mary d. 28 Jan 1766. Abiel m. 2nd 2 Apr 1767, EUNICE KINGSBURY (widow of John Marshall), b. about 1733; Eunice d. 2 Jun 1784.
          The distributions from the estate of Abiel Holt were made 19 December 1785 to the following heirs: Hannah Pearl, eldest daughter; Sarah Crocker, second daughter; Mary Needham, third daughter; Abial Holt, eldest son; Bethiah Holt, fourth daughter; Andrew Holt, second son; Abel Holt, third son; and Eunice Holt, youngest daughter. The first five children are from Abiel's marriage to Mary Downer; Eunice Kingsbury is the mother of the three youngest children.[201]
          Abiel Holt and Mary Downer had six children born at Willington.

330)   i   HANNAH HOLT, b. 14 Mar 1756; d. 20 Nov 1832; m. 24 Apr 1782, as his second wife, her second cousin, OLIVER PEARL, b. 9 Oct 1749 son of Timothy and Dinah (Holt) Pearl. Oliver was married first to Mercy Hinkley.

---

[197] Campbell, *A History of the County of Yarmouth, Nova Scotia*
[198] *U.S., Revolutionary War Pension and Bounty-Land Warrant Application Files, 1800-1900* [database on-line].
[199] Weaver, *Genealogy of the Fenton Family*
[200] Connecticut, Deaths and Burials Index, 1650-1934
[201] *Connecticut Wills and Probate, 1609-1999*, Probate of Abial Holt, Hartford, 1785, Case number 1057.

331)   ii   SARAH HOLT, b. 8 Dec 1757; d. at Willington, 1856;[202] m. 24 Oct 1782, ZEBULON CROCKER, b. at
                Willington, 5 Mar 1757 son of Ebenezer and Hannah (Hatch) Crocker; Zebulon d. at Willington, 17 Jan
                1826.

        iii   MARY HOLT, b. 13 Jul 1759; d. 4 Feb 1760.

332)   iv   MARY HOLT, b. 8 Dec 1760; m. at Charlton, MA, 17 Feb 1783,[203] DANIEL NEEDHAM possibly the son of
                Daniel and Hannah (Allen) Needham; Daniel d. at Paxton, MA 1801 (date of probate 6 Oct 1801; will
                written 4 Mar 1801).

333)   v   ABIEL HOLT, b. 12 Jul 1762; d. at Fairfax, VT, 6 Jun 1829; m. by 1787, MARY MOSHER, b. 21 Jul 1762
                daughter of Nathaniel and Elizabeth (Crandall) Mosher; Mary d. 6 Sep 1827.

        vi   BETHIAH HOLT, b. 26 Mar 1764; d. 1833. Bethiah did not marry.

        Abiel Holt and Eunice Kingsbury had three children born at Willington.

        i   ANDREW HOLT, b. 3 May 1768; d. at Hadley, MA, 21 Sep 1853;[204] m. HANNAH SMITH, b. at Hadley, 28
                Aug 1775, daughter of Joseph and Nancy (Day) Smith; Hannah d. 28 Jul 1855. Andrew and Hannah did not
                have children.

334)   ii   ABEL HOLT, b. 1770; m. 1st at Norwich, 17 Nov 1793, ANNA ABEL, b. at Norwich, 8 Jul 1771 daughter of
                Thomas and Zerviah (Hyde) Abel; Anna d. at Sharon, VT 13 Apr 1798. Abel m. 2nd, by 1798, RUTH KING,
                b. at Wilbraham, MA, 13 Feb 1779 daughter of Oliver and Ruth (Cooley) King.

        iii   EUNICE HOLT, b. 5 Mar 1772. She was living at the time of her father's will, but no record found
                following that.

82)   CALEB HOLT (*Abiel Holt³, Mary Russell Holt², Robert¹*), b. 6 Mar 1729 son of Abiel and Hannah (Abbott) Holt; d. at
Willington, 18 Aug 1810; m. 29 Jan 1755, MARY MERRICK, b. 6 Dec 1726 daughter of John and Sarah (Parsons) Merrick; Mary
d. 4 Jun 1790. Caleb m. 2nd Chloe Hatch.
        Caleb wrote a will 11 Apr 1793.[205] There are bequests for wife Chloe, sons Elijah and Caleb, and daughter Elizabeth
Howe(?). He wrote a codicil 4 April 1798, it which he bequeathed to his wife Chloe the whole of a farm that he purchased from
Samuel Dunham so long as she gives up rights to property she brought with her into the marriage. There are no other changes
to heirs. The estate entered probate 29 August 1810. The distribution documents include the division set off to widow Chloe
and an acknowledgment from Elijah and Caleb that they have received their portions. There is not a distribution document
related to Elizabeth. The will is difficult to decipher in terms of Elizabeth's married name (it might be Howe or Hovey or
something else altogether or maybe it is a poorly written Holt). In any event, no marriage record was located for her and no
death record.
        Caleb Holt and Mary Merrick had five children whose births are recorded at Willington.

        i   ELIZABETH HOLT, b. 29 Apr 1756. From her father's will, it seems that Elizabeth married, but the last
                name is unclear. It could be Howe or Hovey or some other name. No marriage record was located that
                would fit with the name in the will. Durrie's Holt genealogy gives her spouse as Abiel Stevens. But Abiel
                Stevens and Elizabeth Holt married at Andover so that does not seem right, and other sources suggest it
                was Elizabeth the daughter of Nathaniel Holt that married Abiel Stevens.

335)   ii   ELIJAH HOLT, b. 24 Oct 1757; d. 4 Jul 1817; m. 5 Nov 1783,[206] MOLLY SIMMONS, b. 1754 possibly the
                daughter of Paul and Mary (Isham) Simmons, but this is not confirmed; Molly d. 6 May 1814. Elijah m. 2nd,
                Lovina *Marcy* Dunton 17 Aug 1815. Lovina Marcy was first married to Samuel Dunton.

---

[202] In the 1850 U.S. Census, 92-year old widow Sarah Crocker was living at the home of her daughter Bethiah Hull. Probate of estate was 1856 with
Joseph Hull as administrator.
[203] *Massachusetts, Compiled Marriages, 1633-1850*. Daniel and Mary Holt of Willington, int. Feb. 17, 1783.
[204] *Massachusetts, Death Records, 1841-1915*, New England Historic Genealogical Society; Boston, Massachusetts; Massachusetts Vital Records,
1840–1911. Parents are listed on the death record as Abiel and Eunice Holt.
[205] *Connecticut Wills and Probate, 1609-1999*, Probate of Caleb Holt, Hartford, 1810, Case number 1059.
[206] "Connecticut Marriages, 1640-1939," database with images, *FamilySearch* (https://familysearch.org/ark:/61903/1:1:F7PB-68K: 11 February
2018), Elijah Holt and Molley Simons, Marriage 05 Nov 1783, Willington Tolland, Connecticut, United States; Connecticut State Library, Hartford;
FHL microfilm 1,376,042.

336)   iii   CALEB HOLT, b. 23 Apr 1759; d. at Willington, 8 Sep 1826; m. 8 Jan 1783, his second cousin, SARAH GOODALE (*Phebe Holt Goodale⁴, Joshua Holt³, Mary Russell Holt², Robert¹*), b. at Pomfret, 10 Jul 1760 daughter of Ebenezer and Phebe (Holt) Goodale; Sally d. 4 Oct 1831.

        iv   JOSHUA HOLT, b. 31 Mar 1763; d. 12 Aug 1790.

        v   JAMES HOLT, 24 Oct 1764; d. 25 Jan 1766.

83)   NATHAN HOLT (*Abiel Holt³, Mary Russell Holt², Robert¹*), b. 18 Apr 1733 son of Abiel and Hannah (Abbott) Holt; d. at Willington, 31 May 1800; m. 1ˢᵗ 19 Jan 1758, ABIGAIL MERRICK, b. 17 Jun 1737 daughter of John and Sarah (Parsons) Merrick; Abigail d. 1 Dec 1765. Nathan m. 2ⁿᵈ 26 Nov 1766, BATHSHEBA WILLIAMS, b. 22 May 1737 daughter of Samuel and Deborah (Throope) Williams; Bathsheba d. 1 Aug 1769. Nathan m. 3ʳᵈ 6 Jun 1770, LYDIA KINGSBURY, b. 1737 daughter of John and Deborah (Spaulding) Kingsbury; Lydia d. 22 Mar 1776.

      In his will written March 1790, Nathan leaves his estate to his two children: Nathan and Abigail. In the will, Nathan is allowed used of one-half of the homestead including use of half the well (as long as he maintains it), a chamber in the house, and privilege to use of part of the cellar. The remainder of the estate is left to his daughter Abigail, both real and personal, and she is to pay her brother Nathan 50 pounds over a three-year period. Nathan and Abigail are the sole executors of the estate.[207] The will is unusual in that the daughter is bequeathed the whole estate and the son receives just use of part of the house.

      Nathan Holt and Abigail Merrick had one child.

337)   i   NATHAN HOLT, b. 29 Aug 1761; d. at Willington, 5 Sep 1820; m. his second cousin, LOIS GOODALE (*Phebe Holt Goodale⁴, Joshua Holt³, Mary Russell Holt², Robert¹*), b. at Pomfret, 31 Jul 1764 daughter of Ebenezer and Phebe (Holt) Goodale; Lois d. 20 May 1842.

      Nathan Holt and Bathsheba Williams had one child born at Willington.

       i   ABIGAIL HOLT, b. 4 Sep 1767; she was living at the time of probate of her father's estate in 1800 as Abigail Holt.

      Nathan Holt and Lydia Kingsbury had two children born at Willington.

       i   BATHSHEBA HOLT, b. 11 Jan 1772; d. 20 Jan 1790.

       ii   JOHN HOLT, b. 11 Apr 1774; d. 11 Mar 1776.

84)   ANNA HOLT (*Abiel Holt³, Mary Russell Holt², Robert¹*), b. 14 Jan 1735 daughter of Abiel and Hannah (Abbott) Holt; d. at Willington, 10 Oct 1806; m. 29 Jan 1755, JOSEPH MERRICK, b. 17 Oct 1733 son of John and Sarah (Parsons) Merrick; Joseph d. 9 Apr 1787.

      Captain Joseph Merrick commanded a militia company during the Revolutionary War.

      Anna Merrick's estate entered probate in 1806.[208] She did not leave a will. The value of the personal property resulted in a value of personal items of $56.67 to each of the heirs. There are distributions to the following heirs: Timothy Merrick, Thomas Merrick, Joseph Merrick, Caleb Merrick, Constant Merrick, Anna Hinkley, Hannah Merrick, and Elizabeth Nye.

      Anna Holt and Joseph Merrick had eight children whose births are recorded at Willington.

338)   i   ANNE MERRICK, b. 19 Sep 1756; d. 2 May 1809; m. 10 Jan 1782, DAVID HINCKLEY, b. 24 Feb 1754 son of John and Susannah (Harris) Hinckley; David d. 24 Jan 1835.

339)   ii   TIMOTHY MERRICK, b. 31 Aug 1760; d. 4 Jan 1810; m. 29 Nov 1787, MEHITABLE ATWOOD, b. 1765 daughter of Thomas and Sarah (Fenton) Atwood; Mehitable d. 14 May 1855.

340)   iii   THOMAS MERRICK, b. 6 Jan 1763; d. at Willington, 8 Sep 1840; m. 10 Jan 1790, JOANNA NOBLE, b. 8 Oct 1769 daughter of Gideon and Christian (Cadwell) Noble; Joanna d. 28 Apr 1860.

341)   iv   JOSEPH MERRICK, b. 22 Feb 1765; death uncertain but about 1814 possibly by drowning; m. 21 Oct 1796, IRENA ALDEN, b. at Bellingham, MA, 24 Feb 1772 daughter of Elisha and Irene (Markham) Alden. Irena m. 2ⁿᵈ, Samuel Churchill; Irena d. at Pleasantville, PA, 13 Nov 1858.

---

[207] *Connecticut Wills and Probate, 1609-1999*, Probate of Nathan Holt, Hartford, 1800, Case number 1066.
[208] *Connecticut Wills and Probate, 1609-1999*, Probate of Anna Merrick, Hartford, 1806, Case number 1476.

342)   v   CALEB MERRICK, b. 17 May 1767; d. at Vernon, CT, Jun 1822; m. 15 Sep 1791, CHARLOTTE NOBLE, b. at Willington, 19 Aug 1771 daughter of Gideon and Christian (Cadwell) Noble; Charlotte d. at Franklin, CT, 21 Nov 1805.

         vi   HANNAH MERRICK, b. 23 Jul 1769; d. 31 May 1842. Hannah did not marry.

343)   vii   CONSTANT MERRICK, b. 14 Jan 1772; d. at Lebanon, NY, 29 Jul 1828; m. at Longmeadow, MA, 22 Sep 1796, EXPERIENCE BURT, b. 8 Aug 1776 daughter of Nathaniel and Experience (Chapin) Burt; Experience d. 1833 at Lebanon, NY, 24 Jul 1833.

344)   viii   ELIZABETH MERRICK, b. 13 Jul 1774; d. at Tolland, 29 Jun 1824; m. 24 Apr 1800, as his second wife, SAMUEL NYE, b. 25 Dec 1773 son of Samuel and Abigail (Benton) Nye. Samuel m. 3rd, Anna Hatch; Samuel's first wife was Elizabeth Brewster; Samuel d. at Tolland 25 Nov 1837.

85)   ISAAC HOLT (*Abiel Holt³, Mary Russell Holt², Robert¹*), b. 2 Mar 1737/8 son of Abiel and Hannah (Abbott) Holt; d. at Willington, 14 Oct 1822; m. 26 May 1762, SARAH ORCUTT, b. at Stafford, 7 Nov 1740 daughter of William and Sarah (Leonard) Orcutt; Sarah d. 30 Mar 1816.

         Isaac and Sarah Holt made their home in Willington where they were admitted to full communion of the Church of Willington 12 July 1767.[209]

         Isaac Holt wrote his will 8 May 1798. In the will, he makes special provision for his son Moses "being sensible that he is unable to provide for himself." The will has bequests for well beloved wife Sarah Holt, son Isaac, daughter Sarah, daughter Hannah, daughter Mary, daughter Elizabeth, son Leonard, daughter Anne, son Oliver, and son Moses. The estate entered probate 18 November 1822. Son Oliver Holt served as administrator.[210]

         Isaac Holt and Sarah Orcutt had nine children whose births are recorded at Willington.

345)   i   ISAAC HOLT, b. 3 Nov 1763; d. at Sharon, VT, 7 Aug 1813; m. at Sharon, 1 Jan 1789,[211] MEHITABLE ORCUTT, b. at Stafford, CT, 17 Jan 1769 daughter of Caleb and Chloe (Parker) Orcutt; Mehitable d. 12 Nov 1851.

         ii   MOSES HOLT, b. 28 Oct 1765; d. 7 Mar 1819.

         iii   SARAH HOLT, b. 22 Feb 1769; d. 13 May 1836. Sarah did not marry.

346)   iv   HANNAH HOLT, b. 19 May 1771; d. likely at Clarksfield, OH before 1850;[212] m. 9 Apr 1795, ELEAZER FELLOWS, b. at Tolland, 2 Apr 1772 son of Verney and Hannah (Lathrop) Fellows; Eleazer d. after 1850 in Ohio.

347)   v   MARY HOLT, b. 1 May 1773; d. at Willington, 6 Jun 1861; m. 27 Nov 1799, WILLIAM CURTIS, b. about 1774; William d. 3 Nov 1860.

348)   vi   OLIVER HOLT, b. 16 Jul 1775; d. 6 Mar 1869; m. 16 May 1799, MARTHA "PATTY" SIBLEY,[213] b. 9 Feb 1776 daughter of Jonathan and Patty (Brooks) Sibley; Martha "Patty" d. 16 Dec 1846.

349)   vii   ELIZABETH HOLT, b. 6 Aug 1777; m. 11 Apr 1799, DANIEL GLAZIER, b. 2 Jun 1776 son of Silas and Suze (Johnson) Glazier; Daniel d. 28 Dec 1852.

350)   viii   LEONARD HOLT, b. 15 Feb 1782; d. 12 Mar 1857; m. 1st, 29 Dec 1809, his first cousin once removed, ASENATH HOLT, b. 26 Jan 1786 daughter of Nathan and Lois (Goodell) Holt; Asenath d. 13 Feb 1813. Leonard m. 2nd, about 1813, JOANNA ALDEN, b. 14 Jul 1782 daughter of Elisha and Irene (Markham) Alden; Joanna d. 30 Sep 1849.

351)   ix   ANNE HOLT, b. 21 Oct 1784; d. 27 Jun 1855; m. SIMON CARPENTER, b. 13 Dec 1783 son of Elijah and Sarah (Younglove) Carpenter; Simon d. 24 Aug 1862.

---

[209] Talcott, Mary, "Records of the Church at Willington, Conn.", *New England Historical and Genealogical Register*, volume 67, 1913, p 217

[210] *Connecticut Wills and Probate, 1609-1999*, Probate of Isaac Holt, Hartford, 1822, Case number 1063.

[211] *Vermont, Vital Records, 1720-1908*.

[212] In the 1850 U.S. Census, Eleazer Fellows, age 78, was living in Clarksfield OH; also in the home are Betsey Haskins age 43 and five children named Haskins. Betsey is the daughter of Eleazer and Hannah. Eleazer and Hannah's son Leonard also relocated to Huron County, Ohio.

[213] Connecticut, Marriage Index, 1620-1926; the handwritten marriage record confirms that the marriage is to Patty and not to her younger sister Polly.

86)   TIMOTHY HOLT (*Abiel Holt³, Mary Russell Holt², Robert¹*), b. 2 Dec 1739 son of Abiel and Hannah (Abbott) Holt; d. 7 May 1807; m. 7 May 1761 as her 2nd husband, REBECCA CHAMBERLAIN (widow of Nathaniel Fenton).[214] Rebecca was b. about 1730 probably the daughter of Edmund and Sarah (Furbush) Chamberlain; Rebecca d. 11 Apr 1809.

The settlement of the estate of Timothy Holt in 1807 included distributions to the following persons: widow Mrs. Rebekah Holt, son Timothy Holt, and daughter Anna Crocker. The probate of the estate of Rebekah Chamberlain Fenton Holt in 1809 included distributions to the following persons: Timothy Holt, Nathaniel Fenton, Anna Crocker, Eleazer Fenton, and Rebecca Knowlton.[215] Nathaniel Fenton, Eleazer Fenton, and Rebecca Knowlton were children of Rebecca and her first husband Nathaniel Fenton.

Timothy Holt and Rebecca Chamberlain had two children whose births are recorded at Willington.

352)   i   ANNA HOLT, b. 12 Feb 1762; m. 17 Nov 1785, STEPHEN CROCKER, b. 14 Dec 1760 son of Ebenezer and Hannah (Hatch) Crocker.

353)   ii   TIMOTHY HOLT, b. 19 May 1765; d. 17 Apr 1850; m. 10 Dec 1789, ESTHER SCRIPTURE, b. 26 Aug 1765 son of John and Esther (Lee) Scripture; Esther d. 1 Aug 1841.

87)   MARY HOLT (*Abiel Holt³, Mary Russell Holt², Robert¹*), b. 4 May 1742 daughter of Abiel and Hannah (Abbott) Holt; d. 13 Jan 1823; m. 27 Nov 1760, JOSEPH PERSONS, birth record not found but son of Joseph and Hannah (-) Persons of Willington; Joseph d. at Willington, 4 Nov 1812.

Joseph and Mary do not seem to have had children. Joseph's will included bequests to his wife Mary and to his siblings and their heirs. In her will, written 10 June 1819 and proved 1 Feb 1823, Mary Parsons left her entire estate to the children of Joseph and Betsy Holt. Joseph and Betsy Holt were deceased at that time; their children who were heirs were Hannah Whitaker, Esther Heath, Alva Holt, Lucy Holt, Joseph P. Holt, and Mary Holt.[216] This is the family of Joseph and Betsy (Parker) Holt. Joseph Holt was a nephew of Mary Holt Persons, the son of Mary's brother James.

This Joseph Persons is often confused (at least in "internet" trees) with Joseph Parsons of Springfield, Massachusetts who married Naomi Hitchcock and had several children in Springfield. Joseph Persons, Jr. and Mary Holt lived in Willington. They were members of the church in Willington, Joseph, Jr. and Mary admitted as members February 1777. They were also listed as members in 1806 and Joseph's death is noted in the church records in 1813.[217] It is during this same time frame that Joseph Parsons and Naomi Hitchcock were married and having children in Springfield. Adding to the confusion is that each of these Josephs had fathers named Joseph and mothers named Hannah, but they are two different people.

88)   JAMES HOLT (*Abiel Holt³, Mary Russell Holt², Robert¹*), b. 27 Aug 1746 son of Abiel and Hannah (Abbott) Holt; d. at Willington, 30 Sep 1818; m. 1st 20 Apr 1769, ESTHER OWENS, b. 20 Feb 1747 son of Eleazer and Jerusha (Russ) Owens; Esther d. 5 Dec 1774. James m. 2nd LUCE SAWINS, b. 28 Sep 1740 daughter of George and Anne (Farrar) Sawins; Luce d. 25 Dec 1824.

James Holt wrote his will 7 February 1814 (proved 19 October 1818) and includes bequests to the following persons: well beloved wife Lucy Holt who receives one half of the personal estate which is to be at her disposal forever; sons James, Joseph, and Solomon each receive $25; daughter Esther Parker, $1; son Abiel Holt, $25; and daughter Lucy Walker, $1. These are token money bequests as the children have previously received their full portions from the estate. The entire remainder of the estate is bequeathed to son John Holt who is also named the executor.[218]

James Holt and Esther Owens had four children whose birth are recorded at Willington, Connecticut.

354)   i   JAMES HOLT, b. 12 Apr 1770; d. at Willington, 16 Jan 1856; m. 4 Dec 1794, MARY POOL, b. at Willington, 14 Aug 1770 daughter of Timothy and Deborah (Presson) Pool; Mary d. 18 Jan 1853.

355)   ii   JOSEPH HOLT (twin of James), b. 12 Apr 1770; d. at Willington, 29 Jan 1816; m. 6 Mar 1794, BETSY PARKER, b. at Willington, 23 Feb 1775 daughter of Jonathan and Betsy (Johnson) Parker; Betsy d. 7 May 1814.

356)   iii   SOLOMON HOLT, b. 14 Apr 1772; d. in Iowa, 4 Jun 1838; m. at Franklin, CT, 7 Apr 1799, ZERVIAH ABELL, b. at Norwich, 26 Aug 1780 daughter of Thomas and Zerviah (Hyde) Abell; Zerviah d. 1845.

---

[214] This information is confirmed by the 1809 probate record of Rebecca Holt which includes heirs from her first marriage to Nathaniel Fenton.
[215] *Connecticut Wills and Probate, 1609-1999*, Probate of Rebekah Holt, Hartford, 1809, Case number 1069.
[216] *Connecticut Wills and Probate, 1609-1999*, Probate of Mary Parsons, Hartford, 1823, Case number 1617.
[217] Ancestry.com, Connecticut, Church Record Abstracts, 1630-1920
[218] *Connecticut Wills and Probate, 1609-1999*, Probate of James Holt, Hartford, 1818, Case number 1064.

357)   iv   ESTHER HOLT, b. 20 Nov 1774; m. 9 Jan 1800, DANIEL PARKER, b. at Willington, 5 Mar 1777 son of
             Jonathan and Betsy (Johnson) Parker.

       James Holt and Luce Sawins had three children whose births are recorded at Willington.

358)   i   JOHN HOLT, b. 11 Apr 1776; d. at Willington, 22 Apr 1841; m. 6 Sep 1804, his second cousin once removed,
             CLARISSA HOLT, b. 1775 (based on age at time of death) daughter of Philemon and Jemima (Eldredge)
             Holt; Clarissa d. at Willington, 25 Feb 1840.

359)   ii   LUCE HOLT, b. 11 Jun 1778; d. 22 Feb 1847;[219] m. at Ashford, 26 Jan 1809, AARON WALKER, b. 21 Jan
             1776 son of Samuel and Alice (Case) Walker; Aaron d. at Ashford, 1 Nov 1815.

360)   iii   ABIEL HOLT, b. 14 Jan 1780; d. at Mansfield, about 1826 (probate of estate in 1826); m. 30 Apr 1805,
             SALLY CONVERSE, b. at Stafford, 9 Mar 1781 daughter of Stephen and Zerviah (Sanger) Converse;[220]
             Sally's date of death is uncertain. She was alive in 1823 when her father wrote his will but there is no
             mention of her in the probate of Abiel's estate.

89)   BENJAMIN PRESTON (*Deborah Holt Preston³, Mary Russell Holt², Robert¹*), b. at Windham, 31 Dec 1727 son of
Benjamin and Deborah (Holt) Preston; d. at Ashford, 1 Dec 1798; m. at Ashford, 17 Nov 1763, BATHSHEBA SNOW, b. at
Bridgewater, about 1732 daughter of Solomon and Bathsheba (Mahurin) Snow;[221] Bathsheba d. at Ashford, 22 Jan 1813.
       There are records of four children of Benjamin and Bathsheba born at Ashford.

        i   AMOS PRESTON, b. 29 Dec 1765; d. 31 Jul 1776.

        ii   OLIVER PRESTON, b. 13 Feb 1768

361)   iii   SOLOMON PRESTON, b. at Ashford, 10 Sep 1770; d. at Ashford, 29 Sep 1851; m. at Ashford, 13 Jun 1799,
             SUSANNAH HAWES, b. at Medway, MA, 29 Oct 1779 daughter of Eli and Susannah (Bigelow) Hawes;
             Susannah d. at Ashford, 9 Sep 1860.[222]

        iv   BENJAMIN PRESTON, b. 26 Jun 1773

90)   DANIEL PRESTON (*Deborah Holt Preston³, Mary Russell Holt², Robert¹*), b. at Windham, 16 Mar 1729 son of
Benjamin and Deborah (Holt) Preston; m. at Windham, 4 Mar 1756, his second cousin once removed (through Holt line), DINAH
FORD, b. at Windham, 17 Sep 1735 daughter of Nathaniel and Daniel (Holt) Ford.
       Daniel Preston and Dinah Ford were parents of six children.

362)   i   DINAH PRESTON, b. at Ashford, 13 Sep 1756; d. at Braintree, VT, 1 Jan 1836; m. at Hampton, 18 Dec
             1777, STEPHEN CLARK, b. at Hampton, 15 Mar 1752 son of Stephen and Hannah (Durkee) Clark;
             Stephen d. at Braintree, 30 Oct 1820.

363)   ii   EUNICE FORD PRESTON, b. at Ashford, 12 Mar 1759; d. at Preston, NY, 31 Oct 1856; m. at Hampton, 15
             Apr 1783, WILLIAM CLARK, b. at Hampton, 7 Feb 1754 son of Stephen and Hannah (Durkee) Clark;
             William d. at Preston, 4 Oct 1840.

364)   iii   CHLOE PRESTON, b. at Ashford, about 1761; d. at Ashford, 28 Nov 1839; m. at Ashford, 15 Nov 1781,
             JAMES BOUTELL, b. at Ashford, 30 Jul 1760 son of Jacob and Eunice (Drew) Boutell; James d. at Ashford,
             13 May 1822.

365)   iv   DANIEL PRESTON, b. at Ashford, 4 May 1763; d. at Fly Creek, NY, 23 Aug 1849; m. at Burlington, NY, 1
             Dec 1791, ESTHER CUMMINGS, b. about 1771; Esther d. at Fly Creek, 27 Nov 1862.

---

[219] Durrie, *A Genealogy of the Holt Family*, p 50
[220] The 1823 will of Stephen Converse includes a bequest to his daughter Sally Holt.
[221] *Mayflower Families Fifth Generation Descendants, 1700-1880*. (Online database: *AmericanAncestors.org*, New England Historic Genealogical
Society, 2017). John Alden, volume 16, part 3, p 207
[222] Although the marriage transcription in the Barbour collection gives her name as Susannah Harris, this seems to be an error. Other information
supports that she is Susannah Hawes, for example the 1825 probate of the estate of Eli Hawes of Ashford which is administered by Solomon
Preston. The "internet" reports she is daughter of Reuben Harris, but that is refuted by the 1825 will of Reuben which clearly states his daughter
Susannah is unmarried.

366)   v   CALVIN PRESTON, b. at Ashford, 7 Sep 1766; m. at Mansfield, 22 Jun 1785, PHILATHETA BIBBENS, b. at Mansfield, 22 Dec 1766 daughter of Hannah Bibbens, single woman.

      vi   Child b. at Stafford, 20 Aug 1768

91)   DARIUS PRESTON (*Deborah Holt Preston³, Mary Russell Holt², Robert¹*), b. at Windham, 3 Mar 1731/2 son of Benjamin and Deborah (Holt) Preston; d. at Willington, 30 May 1821; m. at Willington, 15 Nov 1759, HANNAH FISKE, b. at Willington, 26 Mar 1740 daughter of William and Mary (Blancher) Fiske; Hannah D. at Willington, 12 Jan 1813.
     Darius was a tanner in Willington. He and Hannah were parents of ten children.

      i   HANNAH PRESTON, b. at Willington, 23 Aug 1760; d. at Willington, 23 Jan 1837. Hannah did not marry.

      ii   Infant b. and d. same day

367)   iii   SARAH PRESTON, b. at Willington, 3 Mar 1764; m. at Willington, 3 Jan 1788, TIMOTHY NYE, b. at Willington, 26 Jan 1765 son of Benjamin and Phebe (West) Nye.[223]

368)   iv   DARIUS PRESTON, b. at Willington, 18 Dec 1766; d. at Hanover, PA, 1 Apr 1845; m. 26 Aug 1788, NAOMI HIBBARD b. at Bolton, 1770 daughter of William Bathsheba (Strong) Hibbard; Naomi d. at Wilkes-Barre.

369)   v   JOSHUA PRESTON, b. at Willington, 25 Sep 1768; d. at Willington, 1 Nov 1810; m. 25 Sep 1794, SARAH HOLT who has not been identified.

      vi   JERUSHA PRESTON, b. 18 Jun 1770; d. 13 Jul 1792. Jerusha did not marry.

370)   vii   CHLOE PRESTON, b. at Willington, 11 Feb 1772; d. at Corinth, NY, 9 Jun 1841; m. 10 Sep 1789, LUKE FENTON, b. at Willington, 20 Dec 1769 son of Asa and Jerusha (Hatch) Fenton; Luke d. after 1850 when he was living in Corinth with his son Darius and his family.

371)   viii   EUNICE PRESTON, b. at Willington, 15 Jul 1777; d. at Willington, 16 Oct 1807; m. at Willington, 6 Feb 1800, ELIJAH NYE b. at Willington, 15 Sep 1777 son of Benjamin and Mary (Crocker) Nye;[224] Elijah d. at Willington, 11 Jun 1844. Elijah was the half-brother of Timothy who married Eunice's sister Sarah.

372)   ix   DEBORAH PRESTON, b. at Willington, 30 Apr 1780; d. at Willington, 14 Oct 1857; m. at Willington, 10 Mar 1803, ABEL JOHNSON, b. at Willington, 28 Sep 1781 son of Abel and Eunice (Merrick) Johnson; Abel d. after 1870 when he was living at Willington.

373)   x   AMOS PRESTON, b. at Willington, 8 Feb 1782; d. at Willington, 6 Oct 1864; m. 4 Sep 1804, MARTHA TAYLOR, b. at Willington, 28 Jun 1779 daughter of Thomas and Experience (Freeman) Taylor; Martha d. at Willington, 7 Dec 1860.

92)   JERUSHA PRESTON (*Deborah Holt Preston³, Mary Russell Holt², Robert¹*), b. at Windham, 29 Jul 1736 daughter of Benjamin and Deborah (Holt) Preston; m. at Ashford, 25 Aug 1767, as his third wife, JOHN PECK, b. at Uxbridge, MA, 30 Dec 1726 son of Simon and Sarah (-) Peck; John d. in VT, 1805.[225] John was first married to Mary Bowen and second married to Elizabeth Dennerson.
     John Peck was born in Uxbridge and was first married there. After the death of his first wife, he relocated to Ashford and was married to Elizabeth Dennerson and after Elizabeth's death to Jerusha. There is some disagreement in the published genealogies about which wife was the mother of which children, but the five children given below are given in the Ashford records as children of Jerusha and John. The oldest son of John and Jerusha settled in Vermont and it is thought that John Peck, Sr. died there. Jerusha's death was not found, but a fourth marriage for John to a widow Hollis has been reported.[226]

374)   i   JOHN PECK, b. at Ashford, 8 May 1768; d. at Weston, VT, 21 Sep 1849; m. 1st about 1789, REBECCA BADGER, b. at Ashford, 1 Jan 1768 daughter of Ezekiel and Doratha (Scarborough) Badger; Rebecca d. at Cavendish, VT, about 1810. John m. 2nd about 1811, HANNAH FOSTER (widow of Phineas Austin), b. at Temple, NH, 28 Dec 1771 daughter of James and Hannah (Jewett) Foster; Hannah d. at Weston, 14 Nov 1848.

---

[223] Nye, *A Genealogy of the Nye Family*, p 217

[224] Nye, *A Genealogy of the Nye Family*, volume 2, p 218

[225] Peck, *Genealogical History of the Descendants of Joseph Peck*, p 279

[226] Peck, *A Genealogical History of the Descendants of Joseph Peck*, p 279

375)   ii   ANNA PECK, b. at Ashford, 10 Sep 1769; d. at Rushford, NY, 17 May 1855; m. at Ashford, Jan 1789, ROBERT SNOW,[227] b. at Ashford, 19 Jun 1763 son of Robert and Sarah (Chubb) Snow; Robert d. at Cavendish, VT, 13 Aug 1806.

        iii   EUNICE PECK, b. at Ashford, 25 Sep 1770

        iv   OLIVER PECK, b. at Ashford, 7 Aug 1772

376)   v   ELISHA PECK, b. at Ashford, 25 Mar 1777; d. at Abington, 26 Sep 1866; m. 1st at Ashford, 23 Sep 1802, SARAH BADGER, b. at Ashford, 26 Apr 1771 daughter of Ezekiel and Doratha (Scarborough) Badger; Sarah d. at Pomfret, 6 Mar 1843. Sarah had an out-of-wedlock daughter Myra Ingraham prior to her marriage to Elisha. Elisha m. 2nd 29 Oct 1844, MARY WHITMAN, b. about 1790; Mary d. at Abington, 9 Feb 1860.

93)   **DEBORAH PRESTON** (*Deborah Holt Preston³, Mary Russell Holt², Robert¹*), b. at Windham, 10 Dec 1740 daughter of Benjamin and Deborah (Holt) Preston; d. at Willington, 6 Mar 1822; m. at Willington, 19 Oct 1763, TIMOTHY POOL, b. at Willington, 11 Jun 1739 son of John and Mary (Parker) Pool; Timothy d. at Willington, 16 Jul 1821.
        There are records for nine children of Deborah and Timothy born at Willington.

377)   i   ALICE POOL, b. at Willington, 11 Dec 1765; m. at Willington, 18 Mar 1782, JOSEPH FENTON, b. at Willington, 28 Feb 1760 son of Samuel and Experience (Ingalls) Fenton; Joseph d. at Willington, 12 May 1814.

378)   ii   ANNA POOL, b. at Willington, 8 May 1767; d. at Willington, 12 Oct 1831; m. at Willington, 9 Apr 1795, ERASTUS EDWARDS, b. at Coventry, 1770 son of Erastus and Anna (Porter) Edwards; Erastus d. at Willington, 24 Nov 1850. Erastus was first married to Jerusha Fuller who died in 1794.

        iii   DEBORAH POOL, b. 26 Apr 1769; d. Jul 1771.

354)   iv   MARY POOL, b. at Willington, 14 Aug 1770; d. at Willington, 19 Jan 1853; m. 4 Dec 1794, her second cousin, JAMES HOLT (*James Holt⁴, Abiel Holt³, Mary Russell Holt², Robert¹*), b. at Willington, 12 Apr 1770 son of James and Esther (Owens) Holt; James d. at Willington, 16 Jan 1856.

        v   LOIS POOL, b. 18 Aug 1772; nothing further known.

        vi   TIMOTHY POOL, b. 4 Jul 1774; likely died young.

379)   vii   AMY POOL, b. at Willington, 7 Aug 1775; d. at Willington, about 1817;[228] m. at Willington, 24 Dec 1795, her second cousin once removed, ELIJAH SAWIN (*Mary Fenton Sawin⁵, Elizabeth Holt Fenton⁴, Abiel Holt³, Mary Russell Holt², Robert¹*), b. at Willington, 31 Oct 1774 son of Isaac and Mary (Fenton) Sawin; Elijah d. at Willington, about 1814 (probate 1814).

        viii SARAH POOL, b. 7 Apr 1777; d. 21 May 1777.

        ix   DEBORAH POOL, b. 19 Jul 1781; d. at Willington, 15 Oct 1823. Deborah did not marry.

94)   **DINAH HOLT** (*Joshua Holt³, Mary Russell Holt², Robert¹*), b. at Windham, 17 Mar 1725/6 daughter of Joshua and Keturah (Holt) Holt; d. at Willington, 25 Sep 1805; m. at Windham, 6 Nov 1746, TIMOTHY PEARL, b. at Windham, 24 Oct 1723 son of Timothy and Elizabeth (Stevens) Pearl; Timothy d. at Willington, 19 Oct 1789.
        There are some double-birth records at Windham which have children (Hannah, Phineas) of the same names and birthdates with one attributed to Timothy and Dinah and one attributed to Timothy's father Timothy and his second wife Mary. [Phineas, s. of Timothy and Mary, b. 2 Aug 1753; Phineas, s. of Timothy and Dinah, b. 2 Aug 1753.] These children are all named in the will of the elder Timothy. Also, they are recorded at Windham and Timothy and Dinah were at Willington soon after their marriage. Therefore, they are not included here as it seems more likely they are the children of Timothy and Mary. There are births of nine children recorded for Timothy and Dinah, the oldest at Windham and the rest of the children at Willington.

        i   ALICE PEARL, b. 6 Sep 1747; d. 10 Sep 1747.

---

[227] The marriage transcription gives the name of Abigail Peck as the wife of Robert Snow, but other records (for example the Revolutionary War pension file) establish that Robert married Anna.

[228] Sawin, *Sawin: Summary Notes Concerning John Sawin*, p 38

380) ii ALICE PEARL, b. 6 Jul 1748. The birth transcription says 6 Jul 1743, but this seems an error and Durrie's Holt genealogy says 1748; her age at death in 1826 was 76. Alice d. Dec 1826; m. at Willington, 10 Oct 1767, ELEAZER SCRIPTURE, b. at Willington, 10 May 1742 son of John and Hannah (Wells) Scripture; Eleazer d. at Willington, 1813 (estate inventory 13 Oct 1813).

330) iii OLIVER PEARL, b. 9 Oct 1749; d. 4 Nov 1831; m. 1st, 1 Jan 1772, MERCY HINCKLEY; Mercy d. 15 Nov 1781. Oliver m. 2nd, 24 Apr 1782, his second cousin, HANNAH HOLT, b. 14 Mar 1756 daughter of Abiel and Mary (Downer) Holt; Hannah d. 20 Nov 1832.

381) iv JOSHUA PEARL, b. 15 Sep 1752; d. at Vernon, 11 Oct 1837; m. 14 Jan 1773, DEBORAH MARSHALL, b. at Bolton, 1755 daughter of John and Eunice (Kingsbury) Marshall; Deborah d. at Vernon, 11 May 1818.

382) v LOIS PEARL, b. 21 Apr 1753; d. at Willington, 15 Jul 1788; m. 6 Aug 1771, SAMUEL DUNTON, b. at Wrentham, MA, 10 Nov 1748 son of Samuel and Sarah (Bennet) Dunton; Samuel d. at Willington, 1 May 1813. After Lois's death, Samuel married Lovina Marcy.

383) vi ELIZABETH PEARL, b. 15 Jan 1756; d. 8 Jan 1779; m. 6 Aug 1771, ZOETH ELDRIDGE, b. at Willington, about 1751 son of Jesse and Abigail (Smith) Eldridge; Zoeth d. at Willington, 18 Mar 1828. Zoeth m. 2nd, Bethiah Hinkley.[229]

384) vii SARAH PEARL, b. 16 Nov 1758; d. 11 Oct 1826; m. 17 Nov 1776, SAMUEL JOHNSON, b. 1751 (based on age 92 at time of death); Samuel d. at Willington, 22 Mar 1843. Samuel is likely the son of Daniel and Keziah (Dodge) Johnson born at Lebanon 10 Jun 1751.

385) viii TIMOTHY PEARL, b. 6 Jun 1760; d. at Willington, 2 Jul 1834; m. 9 Jan 1783, LOIS CROCKER, b. 9 Dec 1763 daughter of Joseph and Anne (Fenton) Crocker; Lois d. 24 Sep 1850.

386) ix PHEBE PEARL, b. 27 Nov 1765; d. at Willington, 10 Apr 1816; m. 24 Mar 1785, her third cousin, ZEBADIAH MARCY (*Zebadiah Marcy⁴, Mary Russell Marcy³, Benjamin², Robert¹*), b. at Woodstock, 2 Jul 1761 son of Zebadiah and Priscilla (Morris) Marcy; Zebadiah d. 24 Sep 1851.

---

95) JOSHUA HOLT (*Joshua Holt³, Mary Russell Holt², Robert¹*), b. at Windham, 19 Mar 1728 son of Joshua and Keturah (Holt) Holt; d. at Hampton, 5 Jul 1791; m. 1st 28 Jun 1749, MARY ABBOTT, b. at Pomfret, 3 Mar 1728 daughter of Paul and Elizabeth (Gray) Abbott; Mary d. at Windham, 10 Aug 1769. Joshua m. 2nd, 26 Apr 1770, SUSANNA GOODELL, b. at Pomfret, 22 Jan 1728 daughter of Zachariah and Hannah (Cheney) Goodell; Susanna d. at Windham, 28 Jun 1812. Susanna was first married to Samuel Darby.

In his will written 13 April 1791,[230] Joshua Holt has bequests for the following persons: dear and loving wife Susannah, daughter Dinah Stoel, daughter Mary Fuller, son Uriah, son Lemuel, daughter Keturah Amidown, daughter Sarah Durkee (although there are other last names for Sarah crossed out, one of them Holt), daughter Hannah Carpenter, daughter Dorcas Fuller, daughter Zilphia, and sons Samuel and Oliver who divide equally everything not given to the other children. Zilphia,

Mary Abbott and Joshua Holt had eight children whose births are recorded at Windham.

315) i DINAH HOLT, b. 22 Mar 1750; d. 21 Feb 1826; m. 30 Jun 1778, SETH STOWELL, b. 29 May 1742 son of Nathaniel and Margaret (Trowbridge) Stowell; Seth d. about 1798 (when estate went to probate). Dinah m. 2nd, 27 Nov 1800, PAUL HOLT, b. 1743 and d. 1827. Dinah was Paul Holt's third wife.

387) ii MARY HOLT, b. 11 Jul 1752; d. at Hampton, 23 Oct 1824; m. 7 Nov 1771, JOSEPH FULLER, b. at Ipswich, 1738 son of John and Hannah (Lord) Fuller; Joseph d. 29 Jan 1805.

388) iii URIAH HOLT, b. 23 Mar 1754; d. at West Springfield, MA, 22 Sep 1828; m. at Ashford, 11 Nov 1779, MARGARET MASON, b. at Ashford, 13 Aug 1754 daughter of Ebenezer and Mehitable (Holmes) Mason; Margaret d. 1817.

389) iv LEMUEL HOLT, b. 28 Feb 1756; d. at Lyme, NH, 1 Aug 1836; m. 1778, his first cousin, MARY ABBOTT, b. 20 Jan 1757 daughter of Isaac and Mary (Barker) Abbott; Mary d. 8 Sep 1849.

390) v KETURAH HOLT, b. 21 Aug 1758; d. at Randolph, VT, 25 Jul 1839;[231] m. 29 Jan 1784, JONATHAN AMIDON, b. 7 Feb 1759 son of Henry and Sarah (Doubleday) Amidon; Jonathan d. at Randolph, 15 Apr 1838.

---

[229] Eldredge, *Eldredge Genealogy*, p 8
[230] *Connecticut Wills and Probate, 1609-1999*, Probate of Joshua Holt, Hartford, 1791, Case number 1945.
[231] Ancestry.com, *Vermont, Vital Records, 1720-1908* (Provo, UT, USA: Ancestry.com Operations, Inc., 2013).

391)   vi   SARAH HOLT, b. 26 Oct 1761; d. at Stockbridge, VT, 19 Feb 1813; m. 1783, JOHN DURKEE, b. at
              Windham, 2 Jul 1762 son of Joseph and Elizabeth (Fiske) Durkee; John d. at Stockbridge, 2 May 1838.

392)   vii   HANNAH HOLT, b. 24 May 1764; d. in Vermont, 7 Aug 1855; m. at Clarendon, VT, 21 Jan 1788, AARON
              CARPENTER, b. at Rehoboth, 9 May 1763 son of Jabez and Abigail (Dyer) Carpenter; Aaron d. 26 Sep
              1836.[232]

393)   viii DORCAS HOLT, b. 30 Mar 1767; d. at Middlebury, VT, 1 Jul 1800; m. JOSIAH FULLER, b. 30 Oct 1764
              son of David and Hannah (Fuller) Fuller; Josiah d. Potsdam, NY, 4 Dec 1835.

        Joshua Holt and Susanna Goodell were parents of three children.

394)   i   SAMUEL HOLT, b. at Windham, 16 May 1771; d. at Hampton, 22 Jun 1846; m. at Hampton, 28 Nov 1799,
              HANNAH BENNETT, b. at Windham, 5 Jan 1775 daughter of Isaac and Sarah (Cady) Bennett;[233] Hannah
              d. at Hampton, 5 Oct 1862.

395)   ii   OLIVER HOLT, baptized at Windham, 9 May 1773; d. at Pomfret, CT, 1 Nov 1821; m. at Eastford, 26 May
              1803, SIDNEY BEDOLPH CLAPP, b. 1784 daughter of Seth and Charlotte (Borden) Clapp;[234] Sidney d. at
              Pomfret, 6 Sep 1837

396)   iii   ZILPHA HOLT, b. at Windham, 2 Feb 1776 and baptized at Hampton, 28 Apr 1776; d. at Stockbridge, VT, 8
              Mar 1830; m. at Stockbridge, VT, 17 Mar 1808, as the third of his four wives, JONATHAN WHITNEY, b. at
              Willington, 20 Feb 1766 son of Peter and Marcy (Case) Whitney; Jonathan d. at Tunbridge, VT, 12 Apr
              1853. Jonathan was first married to Eunice Story, second married to Dora Marsh, and third married to
              Betsey Goodell.

96)   PHEBE HOLT (*Joshua Holt³, Mary Russell Holt², Robert¹*), b. at Windham, 16 Aug 1734 daughter of Joshua and
Keturah (Holt) Holt; d. at South Windsor, CT, 7 Feb 1808; m. at Hampton, 13 Feb 1755, EBENEZER GOODALE, b. at Pomfret,
12 Sep 1729 son of Ebenezer and Experience (Lyon) Goodale; Ebenezer d. at East Windsor, 1794.
        Ebenezer Goodale did not leave a will and his estate entered probate 19 December 1794 with Phebe as administratrix
and surety provided by Walter Goodale. Personal estate was valued at £34.10.3.[235]
        Phebe Holt and Ebenezer Goodale were parents of thirteen children.

329)   i   CHLOE GOODALE, b. at Pomfret, 28 Dec 1755; d. at New Haven, Oct 1833; m. at Willington, 25 May 1775,
              her second cousin, FRANCIS FENTON (*Elizabeth Holt Fenton⁴, Abiel Holt³, Mary Russell Holt², Robert¹*),
              b. at Willington, 13 Feb 1750/1 son of Francis and Elizabeth (Holt) Fenton.

397)   ii   RHODA GOODALE, b. at Pomfret, 28 Feb 1758; d. at South Windsor, CT, 17 Nov 1841; m. at Willington,
              JOSEPH ELDREDGE, b. at Willington, 28 Feb 1759 son of Joseph and Abigail (Smith) Eldredge.[236]

        iii   SARAH GOODALE, b. 19 May 1759; d. 20 Jun 1759.

336)   iv   SARAH GOODALE, b. at Pomfret, 10 Jul 1760; d. at Willington, 4 Oct 1831; m. at Willington, 8 Jan 1783,
              her second cousin, CALEB HOLT (*Caleb Holt⁴, Abiel Holt³, Mary Russell Holt², Robert¹*), b. at Willington,
              23 Apr 1759 son of Caleb and Mary (Merrick) Holt; Caleb d. at Willington, 8 Sep 1826.

398)   v   CHESTER GOODALE, b. at Pomfret, 3 Sep 1762; d. at Egremont, MA, 29 Jan 1835; m. at Richmond, MA,
              10 Jul 1790, ASENATH COOK, b. at Goshen, CT, 11 Oct 1769 daughter of Walter and Ruhamah (Collins)
              Cook;[237] Asenath d. at Egremont, 7 May 1858.

337)   vi   LOIS GOODALE, b. at Pomfret, 31 Jul 1764; d. at Willington, 20 May 1842; m. at Willington, 6 Feb 1783,
              her second cousin, NATHAN HOLT (*Nathan Holt⁴, Abiel Holt³, Mary Russell Holt², Robert¹*), b. at
              Windham, 29 Aug 1761 son of Nathan and Abigail (Merrick) Holt; Nathan d. at Willington, 5 Sep 1820.

---

[232] Ancestry.com, Vermont, Vital Records, 1720-1908
[233] The 1817 probate of Isaac Bennett includes a distribution to Hannah Holt and spouse Samuel Holt.
[234] Clapp, *The Clapp Memorial*, p 165
[235] *Connecticut State Library (Hartford, Connecticut),* Estate of Ebenezer Goodale, case 1303
[236] Eldredge, *Eldredge Genealogy*
[237] Hibbard, *A History of the Town of Goshen*, p 450

399) vii WALTER GOODALE, b. at Pomfret, 6 Apr 1766; d. at South Windsor, 20 Jul 1820; m. about 1787, SABRA BISSELL (widow of John Loomis), b. at Windsor, 25 May 1763 daughter of Hezekiah and Sabra (Trumbull) Bissell; Sabra d. at East Windsor, 17 Nov 1834.

400) viii WILLARD GOODALE, b. at Pomfret, 8 Mar 1768; d. at Perry, NY, 11 Nov 1858; m. MARY ANN MCLEAN, b. 1772; Mary Ann d. at Perry, 2 Oct 1752.

ix LUTHER GOODALE, b. at Pomfret, 21 Feb 1770; d. at East Windsor, CT, 1816; m. at East Windsor, 23 Apr 1795, ELIZABETH GRANT b. about 1770 daughter of Samuel Rockwell and Mabel (Loomis) Grant.[238] Luther and Elizabeth may not have had children. At the 1800 census, the household consists of one male 26-44 and one female 26-44.[239] Luther seems to have had a second marriage as the widow on the probate record is Dosha Goodale. No children were identified for Luther Goodale and Elizabeth Grant.

x OLIVER GOODALE, b. 4 Nov 1771; d. 4 Feb 1773.

xi PHEBE GOODALE, b. 4 Nov 1773; d. 7 Jan 1774.

xii OLIVER GOODALE, b. about 1774 (record for birth of second Oliver in the family has an unreadable date); m. at Pomfret, 10 Apr 1796, his second cousin once removed, JERUSHA TRUESDELL (*Seth Truesdell⁵, Mary Holt Truesdell⁴, Robert Holt³, Mary Russell Holt², Robert¹*), b. at Pomfret, 6 Apr 1776 daughter of Seth and Esther (West) Truesdell. Nothing further was found for this couple. No children were identified for Oliver Goodale and Jerusha Truesdell.

401) xiii PHEBE GOODALE, b. at Willington, 29 Aug 1775; d. at South Windsor, 6 Nov 1856; m. as his third wife, GUSTAVUS GRANT, b at East Windsor, 1759 son of Samuel Rockwell and Mabel (Loomis) Grant;[240] Gustavus d. at South Windsor, 11 Mar 1841. Gustavus was first married to Lucina Grant and second married to Electa Goodwin.

97) DANIEL HOLT (*Daniel Holt³, Mary Russell Holt², Robert¹*), b. at Windham, 5 Apr 1731 son of Daniel and Abigail (Smith) Holt; d. at Cherry Valley, NY, 21 Jan 1796; m. at Pomfret, 26 Dec 1753, KEZIA RUST, b. at Coventry, 16 Aug 1735 daughter of Noah and Kezia (Strong) Rust;[241] Kezia d. at Cherry Valley, 23 Dec 1825.

Daniel and Kezia were parents of thirteen children born at Pomfret. The family relocated to Cherry Valley and the children who lived to adulthood settled in New York.

i CHLOE HOLT, b. at Pomfret, 10 Feb 1755

ii DELIA HOLT, b. 1757; d. at Pomfret, 6 May 1775.

iii LESTER HOLT, b. 1759; d. at Pomfret, 17 Sep 1764.

402) iv ABIGAIL HOLT (twin), b. at Pomfret, 29 Mar 1761; d. after 1829; m. about 1783, WILLIAM AVERILL, b. at Windham, 19 Apr 1755 son of Stephen and Sarah (Handee) Averill;[242] William d. at Warren, NY, 1829 (probate 1829).

403) v KEZIAH HOLT (twin), b. at Pomfret, 29 Mar 1761; d. at Buffalo, NY, 13 Jan 1820; m. at Pomfret, 8 Apr 1784, ROWLAND COTTON, b. at Pomfret, 22 Mar 1759 son of Samuel and Mary (Dresser) Cotton; Rowland d. at Attica, NY, 11 Jun 1847.

404) vi ELIJAH HOLT, b. at Pomfret, 6 Jun 1762; d. at Cherry Valley, NY, 25 Sep 1826; m. 1ˢᵗ ELIZABETH WILLIAMS, b. at Pomfret, 2 Apr 1768 daughter of Ebenezer and Jerusha (Porter) Williams; Elizabeth d. 16 Jan 1796. Elijah m. 2ⁿᵈ MARY "POLLY" ADAMS, b. at Windham, 10 Dec 1771 daughter of David and Lucy (Fitch) Adams;[243] Mary d. at Buffalo, 3 Jan 1820.

405) vii LESTER HOLT, b. at Pomfret, 21 Feb 1766; d. at Cherry Valley, NY, 11 Jan 1841; m. about 1789, CATHERINE CLYDE, b. 1769 daughter of Samuel and Catherine (Wasson) Clyde; Catherine d. at Cherry Valley, 16 May 1848.

[238] Grant, *The Grant Family*, p 48
[239] Year: 1800; Census Place: East Windsor, Hartford, Connecticut; Series: M32; Roll: 1; Page: 366; Image: 198; Family History Library Film: 205618
[240] Cutter, *New England Families, Genealogical and Memorial*, volume 3, p 1304
[241] The distribution of the estate of Noah Russ includes distribution to daughter Keziah Holt. Distribution is 27 December 1753 the day after the wedding of Daniel and Kezia.
[242] Avery, *The Averill Family*, p 397
[243] The 1814 will of Lucy Adams widow of David of Pomfret includes a bequest to her daughter Polly Holt wife of Elijah Holt.

406)   viii   OLIVE HOLT, b. at Pomfret, 15 Oct 1768; d. 20 Sep 1792; m. 1787, JOSEPH WHITE, b. at Chatham, CT, 26 Sep 1762 son of Joseph and Ruth (Churchill) White; Joseph d. at Cherry Valley, 3 Jun 1832. Joseph second married Olive's sister Deborah (see below).

        ix   JOSEPH HOLT, b. 28 Apr 1771; d. 6 Mar 1773.

407)   x   MARY HOLT, b. at Pomfret, 28 Apr 1771; d. at Cherry Valley, 19 Mar 1819; m. 1st about 1791, JOSEPH CLARY who has not been identified; Joseph d. about 1800. Mary m. 2nd 4 Feb 1803, JOHN DIELL, b. 1769; John d. at Cherry Valley, 19 May 1813.

408)   xi   MARCIA HOLT, b. at Pomfret, about 1773; m. AUGUSTUS SHARP.

406)   xii   DEBORAH HOLT, b. at Pomfret, 1 Feb 1775; d. at Cherry Valley, 23 Aug 1827; m. about 1793, JOSEPH WHITE who was first married to her sister Olive (see above).

409)   xiii   ADELIA HOLT, b. at Pomfret, 23 Jan 1778; m. CHARLES MUDGE, b. at New London, about 1770 son of Jarvis and Prudence (Treat) Mudge;[244] Charles d. of typhus at Williamsville Hospital, NY, Aug 1814 while serving in the army in the War of 1812.[245]

98)   ABIGAIL HOLT (*Daniel Holt³, Mary Russell Holt², Robert¹*), b. at Windham, 20 Feb 1732 daughter of Daniel and Abigail (Smith) Holt; d. at Abington, 11 Oct 1774; m. RICHARD KIMBALL, b. at Bradford, MA, 18 Jul 1722 son of Samuel and Sarah (Spofford) Kimball; Richard d. at Ames, NY, 30 Apr 1810.
        There are records for six children of Abigail Holt and Richard Kimball.

410)   i   LEBBEUS KIMBALL, b. at Pomfret, 14 Feb 1750/1; d. at Ames, NY, 4 Sep 1839; m. at Pomfret, 7 May 1778, SARAH CRAFT, b. at Pomfret, 29 Apr 1756 daughter of Samuel and Judith (Payson) Craft; Sarah d. at Ames, 3 Aug 1831.

        ii   ABIGAIL KIMBALL, b. at Pomfret, 30 Nov 1754

411)   iii   PERSIS KIMBALL, b. at Pomfret, 5 Nov 1760; d. at Ames, NY, 6 Mar 1845; m. at Pomfret, 18 Jan 1781, GEORGE ELLIOT, b. at Voluntown, 1 Mar 1757 son of Andrew and Hannah (Palmer) Elliot; George d. at Ames, 30 Mar 1817.

412)   iv   CHESTER KIMBALL, b. at Pomfret, 19 Sep 1763; d. at New London, 2 Jan 1824; m. at New London, 8 Nov 1786; LUCIA "LUCY" FOX, b. at Chatham, CT, 19 May 1766 daughter of John and Mary (Waterman) Fox; Lucy d. at New London, 6 Apr 1855.

        v   FLAVEL KIMBALL, b. about 1765 and baptized at Hampton, 29 Apr 1770. Flavel had service during the Revolution. He did not marry.

        vi   BETTY KIMBALL, b. about 1767 and baptized at Hampton, 29 Apr 1770. Nothing further found.

99)   SILAS HOLT (*Daniel Holt³, Mary Russell Holt², Robert¹*), b. at Windham, 29 Dec 1735 son of Daniel and Abigail (Smith) Holt; d. at Ashford, 23 Oct 1773; m. at Pomfret, 20 Jan 1757, MARY BROOKS, b. at Pomfret, 14 Oct 1735 daughter of John and Phebe (Richardson) Brooks. Mary Brooks married second, Nehemiah Howe. Mary Brooks and Nehemiah Howe had one daughter, Almira.
        Silas Holt and Mary Brooks were parents of seven children.

        i   SILAS HOLT, b. at Pomfret, 17 Dec 1757; d. at Abington, 10 Feb 1784.

413)   ii   ROXLANA HOLT, b. at Pomfret, 21 Sep 1760; d. at Ashford, about 1787; m. at Ashford, 13 Jun 1782, EBENEZER SUMNER, b. at Ashford, 3 Aug 1757 son of Ebenezer and Experience (Marsh) Sumner; Ebenezer d. at Eastford, Aug 1806. Ebenezer second married Sarah Perrin on 26 May 1788.

        iii   ALVAH HOLT, b. at Pomfret, 10 Feb 1763; nothing further known.

        iv   MOLLY HOLT, b. at Pomfret, 7 Jul 1765; nothing further known.

        v   PERCY HOLT, b. at Pomfret, 19 Aug 1767; nothing further known.

---

[244] Mudge, *Memorials: A Genealogical Account of the Name Mudge in America*, p 73
[245] U.S. Army, Register of Enlistments, 1798-1914

414)   vi   CLARINA HOLT, b. at Ashford, 6 Nov 1769; d. at Vernon, NY, 14 Nov 1845; m. at Ashford, 12 May 1793, ELIAS FRINK, b. 1770; Elias d. at Vernon, NY, 14 Apr 1854.

415)   vii   LUCINDA HOLT, b. at Ashford, 26 Jul 1773; d. at Ashford, 24 Mar 1847; m. at Ashford, 14 Jan 1799, DYER CLARK, b. 1772; Dyer d. at Ashford, 28 Sep 1846.

100)   LOIS HOLT (*Daniel Holt³, Mary Russell Holt², Robert¹*), b. at Windham, 4 Feb 1739 daughter of Daniel and Abigail (Smith) Holt; d. at Ashford, Oct 1792; m. at Pomfret, 26 Sep 1758, MOSES ROGERS, b. at Billerica, 24 Feb 1730/1 son of Nathaniel and Mary (Haggit) Rogers; Moses d. at Ashford, 1797 (probate 1797).

    Lois and Moses started their family in Pomfret. They were dismissed to the church at Eastford in 1783.

    Moses Rogers did not leave a will and his estate entered probate 2 May 1797 with Abel Dow (his son-in-law) as administrator. The debts of the estate exceeded the value of the personal estate to the degree that all the real estate was sold to settle the debts.[246]

416)   i   OLIVE ROGERS, b. at Pomfret, 7 Mar 1759; d. at Ashford, 2 Mar 1855; m. at Ashford, 28 Sep 1784, ABEL DOW, b. at Ashford, 3 Jul 1757 son of Daniel and Elizabeth (Marsh) Dow; Abel d. at Ashford, 6 Jan 1826.

    ii   CHESTER ROGERS, b. at Pomfret, 10 Oct 1760; nothing further definitive known. He may be one of the Chester Rogers who served from Connecticut during the Revolution. He was not administrator of his father's estate perhaps suggesting he was deceased by that time but that is not known.

    iii   LOIS ROGERS, b. at Pomfret, 16 Dec 1762; nothing further known.

417)   iv   ELISHA ROGERS, b. at Pomfret, 11 Feb 1766; d. at Springfield, VT, 24 Apr 1807;[247] m. at Springfield, 11 Jul 1788, ANNA WARD, b. 1767 daughter of Jabez Ward; Anna d. at Brownville, NY, 14 Jul 1872.[248]

418)   v   ABIGAIL ROGERS, b. at Pomfret, 23 Mar 1769; d. at Sherburne, NY, 29 Mar 1849; m. CYRUS DOW, b. at Ashford, 17 Jun 1764 son of Daniel and Elizabeth (Marsh) Dow; Cyrus d. at Sherburne, 23 Mar 1842 (date of death given at the proving of the will on 21 Mar 1843).

    vi   DANIEL ROGERS, b. 23 Mar 1769; d. 2 Apr 1769.

419)   vii   LUCIA "LUCY" ROGERS, b. at Ashford, 28 May 1771; d. at Springfield, MA, Jan 1823; m. at Ashford, 16 Nov 1797, NATHAN CROCKER, b. about 1772 son of Gershom and Ann (Fisher) Crocker;[249] Nathan d. at Springfield, 26 Jul 1817.

420)   viii   ALVA ROGERS, b. at Ashford, 18 Jun 1776; d. at Sherburne, NY, after 1850; m. at Ashford, 8 Sep 1803, his third cousin, DESIRE EATON, b. at Ashford, 29 May 1778 daughter of Ebenezer and Mary (Humphrey) Eaton; Desire d. at Sherburne, NY, Dec 1859.

101)   EUNICE HOLT (*Daniel Holt³, Mary Russell Holt², Robert¹*), b. at Pomfret, 22 Aug 1741 daughter of Daniel and Abigail (Smith) Holt; m. at Pomfret, 28 Nov 1760, JOSIAH WHEELER, b. at Pomfret, 21 Mar 1737/8 son of Josiah and Anna (Grosvenor) Wheeler.

    There are records for ten children of Eunice and Josiah. Marriages were located for just four of the children.

421)   i   PERTHENE WHEELER, b. at Pomfret, 19 Sep 1762; m. 26 Oct 1783, DANIEL CHAPIN, b. at Salisbury, CT, 2 Feb 1761 son of Charles and Anna (Camp) Chapin;[250] Daniel d. at Buffalo, NY, 16 Nov 1821.

    ii   ESTHER WHEELER, b. at Pomfret, 6 Jan 1763

    iii   PERCEY WHEELER, b. at Pomfret, 9 Dec 1764

422)   iv   ELIJAH WHEELER, b. at Pomfret, 28 Aug 1767; d. at Great Barrington, MA, 20 Apr 1827; m. 1ˢᵗ MARY MATILDA MINER, b. at Woodbury, CT, 11 Apr 1773 daughter of Jehu and Sarah (Canfield) Miner; Mary d.

---

[246] Connecticut State Library (Hartford, Connecticut); Probate Place: *Hartford, Connecticut, Probate Packets, Randall, Jonathan-Russell, Smith, 1752-1880, Case 3467, Estate of Moses Rogers*

[247] The date of give is given in his widow's pension application and the family seems to have still been in Vermont at that time.

[248] All the records available support that Anna did indeed live to 105. In 1838, she gave her age as 71 on a pension application and her age on the 1860 census is given as 94.

[249] Crocker, *Crocker Genealogy*, p 93

[250] Chapin, Orange, *Chapin Genealogy*

at Great Barrington, 11 Oct 1812. Elijah m. 2nd ELIZABETH WHITING, b. 1773 likely daughter of Gamaliel and Anne (Gillette) Whiting; Elizabeth d. at Great Barrington, 21 Feb 1848.

423)   v   PHILADELPHIA "PHILA" WHEELER, b. at Pomfret, 28 Nov 1769; d. at East Bloomfield, NY, after 1855; m. MOSES GAYLORD, b. at West Hartford, about 1768 son of Moses and Susanna (Wells) Gaylord; Moses d. at Bloomfield, NY, 1812.[251]

424)   vi   RESOLVED GROSVENOR WHEELER, b. at Pomfret, 8 Mar 1772; d. at Pembroke, NY, 29 May 1839; m. N. ANNA VANDEVENTER, b. about 1785; Anna d. at Reedsburg, WI, 4 Oct 1863.

        vii SARAH WHEELER, b. at Pomfret, 25 Dec 1774

        viii ANNA WHEELER, b. at Pomfret, 20 Feb 1777

        ix   ABIGAIL WHEELER, b. at Pomfret, 20 Feb 1777

        x   JOSIAH WHEELER, b, at Salisbury, 22 Jan 1779

102)   ASA HOLT (*Daniel Holt³, Mary Russell Holt², Robert¹*), b. at Pomfret, 7 Jun 1745 son of Daniel and Abigail (Smith) Holt; d. at Springfield, VT, 1 Mar 1813; m. at Pomfret, 20 Nov 1766, MARGARET HAMMOND, baptized at Woodstock, 9 Dec 1744 daughter of Jonathan and Katherine (Davis) Hammond; Margaret d. at Springfield, 28 Sep 1834.

Asa and Margaret married at Pomfret and there are records of births of several of their children and Hartford and Winsted, Connecticut. The family was in Springfield, Vermont by 1800.

Daughter Clarissa married twice but did not have children. On 31 January 1872, Almira Tower the only surviving sibling of Clarissa declined administration of the estate and requested John Farnham be appointed. The following heirs-at-law of the estate were provided by John Farnham he having obtained this information from Almira Tower: the children of Smith Holt deceased who are Asa (known to be living) and Orin Holt, Polly Wright, and Lovina Tolcot who were living when last known of; the children of Alfleety Fasset deceased who are Perley Fasset, Abel Fasset, and Anney White; Erastus Holt is deceased many years ago and nothing is known of any family; sister Almira Tower; the children of Polly Rumrill deceased who are Serina Clark, Eliza Spafford, Polly Stone, Harvey Rumrill, Solom Rumrill, and Elmira Young; children of Asa Holt deceased who are Louisa Graves, Charles Holt, Parmely Griffin, Betsey Cleaveland, Clarissa Washburn, Mary Kennedy, Laura Holt, and Harriet Holt.[252]

Asa Holt and Margaret Hammond were parents of nine children.[253]

        i   ELISHA HOLT; reported in the Hammond genealogy, but no records located and has no heirs in sister Clarissa's estate settlement.

        ii   ERASTUS HOLT, b. about 1769; in Clarissa's probate record, he is reported to have died "many years ago" and without family.

425)   iii SMITH HOLT, b. at Hartford, about 1769; d. at Keene, NY, 28 Dec 1814; m. his second cousin once removed LYDIA SNOW (*Dorcas Osgood Snow⁵, Mary Holt Osgood⁴, Nicholas Holt³, Mary Russell Holt², Robert¹*), b. 6 Oct 1769 daughter of Benjamin and Dorcas (Osgood) Snow.

        iv   DANIEL HOLT, b. about 1775; d. at Springfield, VT, 24 Apr 1847; m. LYDIA who is not identified, b. about 1783 and d. at Springfield, 21 Mar 1843. The Hammond genealogy reports Daniel and Lydia had one son who died at age 19. Neither Daniel nor any heirs are mentioned in sister Clarissa's probate.

426)   v   ASA HOLT, b. 12 Dec 1777; d. at Rushford, NY, 1852; m. 1st at Springfield, VT, 26 Mar 1801, ELIZABETH "BETSEY" WOODWARD, b. at Springfield, 25 Oct 1782 daughter of Samuel and Eunice (Bigelow) Woodward; Betsey d. at Springfield, 2 Feb 1814. Asa m. 2nd 7 Oct 1815, POLLY ROGERS (widow of Samuel Tarbell), b. 1784 daughter of Jeremiah and Fannie (Wickes) Rogers; Polly d. at Fillmore, NY, 2 Sep 1874.

427)   vi   ALFREADA HOLT, b. about 1779; d. at Cavendish, VT, about 1814; m. at Springfield, 3 Jun 1799, PEARLY FASSET, b. about 1769 son of Adonijah and Anna (Copeland) Fasset; Pearly d. at Winchester, NH, 23 Feb 1826. Pearly married second Esther Gowing.

[251] *Connecticut, Hale Collection of Cemetery Inscriptions and Newspaper Notices, 1629-1934*
[252] *Vermont. Probate Court (Windsor District), Estate of Clarissa Taylor, 6 February 1872.*
[253] Hammond, *Histories and Genealogies of the Hammond Families in America*, Volume II, Part IV, p 285. The nine children given are those listed in the Hammond genealogy. Seven of these children can be known from the probate record of daughter Clarissa.

428) vii POLLY HOLT, b. 1 Jun 1782; d. at Springfield, VT, 7 Jan 1852; m. at Springfield, 9 Aug 1805, SIMEON RUMRILL, b. at New Ipswich, 12 Jun 1769 son of David and Priscilla (Corey) Rumrill; Simeon d. at Baltimore, VT, 19 Mar 1822.

viii ALMIRA HOLT, b. at Winsted, CT, 4 Apr 1790; d. at Springfield, VT, 7 Oct 1874; m. 30 Apr 1840, ABRAHAM TOWER, b. at Springfield, 11 Apr 1781 son of Isaac and Elizabeth (Stoddard) Tower; Abraham d. at Springfield, 16 Jun 1857. Almira did not have children. In her will, she left her estate to her two stepdaughters.

ix CLARISSA HOLT, b. about 1791; d. at Springfield, 1872 (probate 1872); m. 1st JOHN ADAMS. Clarissa m. 2nd ARTHUR TAYLOR. Clarissa did not have children

103) LUCY HOLT (*Daniel Holt³, Mary Russell Holt², Robert¹*), b. at Pomfret, 10 Oct 1747 daughter of Daniel and Abigail (Smith) Holt; m. at Brooklyn, CT, 27 Nov 1770, JEDEDIAH DANA, b. at Ashford, 9 Aug 1739 son of Jedediah and Elizabeth (Barnard) Dana.

Lucy and Jedediah resided in Ashford for much of their lives and were listed in the census there in 1790. The family relocated to German Flatts after 1790 where Jedediah died.

Jedediah Dana did not leave a will and his estate entered probate 31 January 1809. Widow Lucy declined administration of the estate and this was assumed by Jedediah Dana, Jr. with Silas Dana and Thomas Paine (a son-in-law) acting as sureties for the bond. There is an inventory of the personal estate and no real estate was reported in the inventory. In 1815, a notice was sent to Jedediah Dana, Jr. requiring him to come and show why he had not closed the administration of the estate.[254]

Jedediah Dana and Lucy Holt were parents of nine children born at Ashford.

429) i ELIZABETH DANA, b. at Ashford, 8 Jun 1771; d. at Wilbern, IL, 1840; m. at Mansfield, CT, 1 Jun 1794, AMASA OWEN, b. at Ashford, 12 Aug 1766 son of Timothy and Kezia (-) Owen; Amasa d. at Wilbern, 1842.

ii LUCY DANA, b. 8 Jul 1772

iii CLARISSA DANA, b. 14 Oct 1773

430) iv SILAS DANA, b. at Ashford, 9 Mar 1775; d. at Grove, NY, 14 Feb 1846; m. by 1800, SALLY COWEL, b. 6 Feb 1782; Sally d. at Grove, 23 Jan 1831. Silas m. 2nd, MARY who has not been identified.

431) v SALLY DANA, b. at Ashford, 23 Mar 1777; d. at German Flatts (Paine's Hollow), NY, 1 Jul 1856; m. 10 Oct 1802, THOMAS PAYN, b. at Lebanon, CT, 26 Jan 1778 son of Seth and Jerusha (Swift) Payn; Thomas d. at German Flatts, 26 Sep 1856.[255]

vi JEDEDIAH DANA, b. at Ashford, 8 Nov 1778; m. BETSEY who is not clearly identified. In 1810, Jedediah with a wife and one son under age 10 appear to be living in German Flatts, NY but nothing else definitive has been found.

432) vii MARY "POLLY" DANA, b. at Ashford, 15 Jan 1781; d. at Nunda, NY, 27 Dec 1850; m. JAMES PAYN, b. at Lebanon, CT, 27 Jan 1783 son of Seth and Jerusha (Swift) Payn; James d. at Nunda, 8 Apr 1861.

viii ANNA DANA, b. 16 Sep 1783

ix DANIEL DANA, b. 3 Dec 1785

Grandchildren of Thomas Russell and Phebe Johnson

104) MEHITABLE CHANDLER (*Mehitable Russell Chandler³, Thomas², Robert¹*), b. at Andover, about 1709 daughter of Joseph and Mehitable (Russell) Chandler; d. at Townsend, MA, Jul 1768;[256] m. 1st at Andover, 7 Feb 1731/2, ROBERT CROSBY, b. at Billerica, 20 Jul 1711 son of Joseph and Sarah (French) Crosby; Robert d. at Townsend, 10 Feb 1743. Mehitable m. 2nd 26

[254] New York Probate Records 1629-1971, Herkimer County, Estate Papers 1794-1838 D, Case 01842, Estate of Jedediah Dana, Sr.; accessed through family search.org.
[255] Towne and Jones, Seth Payn and Some of His Descendants, NEHGR, 1943, p 138
[256] Mehetabel Spalding the wife of Andrew Spalding deceast this life July the . . . 1768 (Townsend, MA town records)

Nov 1745, ANDREW SPALDING, b. at Chelmsford, 8 Dec 1701 son of Andrew and Abigail (Waring) Spalding. Andrew was first married to Hannah Wright.

After her first marriage, Mehitable settled in Townsend with her first husband Robert Crosby. After his death, Mehitable married Andrew Spalding. Andrew had been a resident of that part of Chelmsford that was set off as Westford. He also was one of the grantees of the 1750 Masonian charter of New Ipswich.[257] Andrew also intervened by making application to the General Court on behalf of his "son-in-law" Joel Crosby. Joel was taken captive at Halfway Brook near Lake George on 20 June 1758.[258]

Mehitable Chandler and Robert Crosby were parents of six children born at Townsend.

433)   i   ROBERT CROSBY, b. at Townsend, 13 Sep 1732; m. at Dunstable, 5 Mar 1760, SUSANNAH SHERWIN, b. at Boxford, 28 Aug 1734 daughter of Ebenezer and Hephzibah (Cole) Sherwin; Susannah d. at Winslow, ME, 7 May 1807. This family resided in New Ipswich.

434)   ii   JONAH CROSBY, b. about 1736; d. at Albion, ME, 24 Apr 1814; m. 22 Dec 1757, LYDIA CHANDLER, b. 10 Dec 1735 daughter of William and Susanna (Burge) Chandler; Lydia d. at Albion, 18 Dec 1814.

435)   iii   PHEBE CROSBY, baptized 10 Dec 1738; d. at Shirley, MA, 22 Jul 1826; m. at Westford, 7 Jul 1757, JABEZ KEEP, b. at Westford, 13 Dec 1736 son of Jabez and Sarah (Leonard) Keep; Jabez d. at Sheffield, MA, 21 Jan 1821. Phebe and Jabez had one son and five daughters. Phebe took the daughters and joined a Shaker village. Jabez remarried the widow Elizabeth Rogers about 1785.[259]

436)   iv   JOEL CROSBY, baptized 29 Jun 1740; d. at Winslow, ME, 27 Mar 1775; m. at Chelmsford, 30 Mar 1763, HANNAH STEVENS, b. at Chelmsford, 22 Jun 1737 daughter of Samuel and Ruth (Wright) Stevens; Hannah d. at Winslow, 28 Mar 1828. Hannah married second William Richardson.

       v   JOSIAH CROSBY, b. about 1741. He was living in New Ipswich in 1763 but nothing further found.[260]

       vi   MARAH CROSBY, b. unknown; d. at Townsend, 18 Mar 1743.

Mehitable Chandler and Andrew Spalding were parents of five children born at Westford.

       i   RUTH SPALDING, b. 25 Dec 1746; died young.

437)   ii   SOLOMON SPALDING, b. 28 Sep 1748; d. at Westford, 6 Aug 1826; m. 3 May 1780, JEMIMA REED, b. at Westford, 19 Nov 1761 daughter of Thomas and Susanna (Dutton) Reed; Jemima d. 3 Mar 1845.

438)   iii   HENRY SPALDING, b. 5 Jul 1750; d. likely at Clinton, ME where he was living in 1810; m. about 1776, BETSEY TAGART.

439)   iv   RUTH SPALDING, b. 15 May 1752; d. at Temple, NH, 8 May 1790; m. at Westford, 3 Dec 1772, ISAAC BUTTERFIELD, b. 1 Nov 1750;[261] Isaac d. at Wilton, ME, 12 Oct 1812. Isaac married second Ruth Butterfield on 22 Jul 1790.

440)   v   ABIGAIL SPALDING, b. 3 Jun 1754; d. at Dunstable, MA, 19 Jan 1830; m. 1st at Westford, 28 Nov 1774, THOMAS RICHARDSON, b at Westford, 8 Jan 1751 son of Abiel and Sarah (Boynton) Richardson; Thomas d. at Temple, NH, 8 Apr 1786. Abigail m. 2nd 30 Dec 1794, OLIVER TAYLOR, b. 1 May 1746 son of Samuel and Susannah (Perham) Taylor; Oliver d. 13 Oct 1823. Oliver Taylor was first married to Bridget Blodgett.

105)   THOMAS CHANDLER (*Mehitable Russell Chandler³, Thomas², Robert¹*), b. at Andover, 22 Apr 1711 son of Joseph and Mehitable (Russell) Chandler; d. at Andover, about 1761 (probate 13 Sep 1761); m. at Andover, 15 Feb 1739, ELIZABETH WALCOTT perhaps the daughter of Ebenezer and Elizabeth (Wiley) Walcott.[262]

Thomas and Elizabeth owned the property in Andover that is now the site of the historic home at 102 Gould Road. Thomas originally obtained the land from Elizabeth's father Ebenezer. Elizabeth sold the property in 1777 to Joel and Martha Jenkins.[263]

[257] Chandler, *The History of New Ipswich*, p 54
[258] Chandler, The Descendants of William and Annis Chandler, p 112.
[259] Best, *John Keep of Longmeadow, Massachusetts*, p 25, pp 38-39; available on familysearch.org
[260] Chandler, Descendants of William and Annis Chandler, p 112
[261] Maine, Nathan Hale Cemetery Collection, 1780-1980; date of birth is given on the cemetery record
[262] The historic property at 102 Gould Road in Andover is reported as being obtained by Thomas Chandler from Ebenezer Walcott. https://preservation.mhl.org/102-gould-rd
[263] Andover Historic Preservation, 102 Gould Road, https://preservation.mhl.org/102-gould-rd

Thomas Chandler did not leave a will and his estate entered probate 13 April 1761 with Elizabeth as administratrix. The real estate was sold to settle the debts of the estate. There was remaining £128.2.7 for distribution to the children. Eldest son Ebenezer received £32.8 and the other children received £16.4. Those children were Thomas, Elijah, Peter, Joseph, Asa, and Elizabeth.[264]

Thomas Chandler and Elizabeth Walcott were parents of ten children born at Andover.

	i	ELIZABETH CHANDLER, b. 17 Dec 1739; d. 15 Jan 1740.
	ii	ELIZABETH CHANDLER, b. 13 Mar 1741/2
	iii	BRIDGET CHANDLER, b. 2 Apr 1744; d. about 1761.
	iv	EUNICE CHANDLER, b. 12 Feb 1745/6; d. 20 May 1749.
441)	v	EBENEZER CHANDLER, b. 14 May 1749; d. at Wilton, NH, 15 Sep 1823; m. 1st at Reading, MA, 29 Nov 1768, MARY BURNAP, likely b. at Reading, 1744 daughter of John and Ruth (Smith) Burnap; Mary d. at Wilton, 22 Oct 1778. Ebenezer m. 2nd 25 May 1779, SARAH AVERILL (widow of James Hutchinson), b. at Andover, 30 Nov 1751 daughter of Thomas and Sarah (Kneeland) Averill; Sarah d. at Wilton, 19 Jun 1794. Ebenezer m. 3rd REMEMBRANCE FLETCHER (widow of Levi Pierce), b. at Chelmsford, 23 Dec 1752 daughter of Robert and Remembrance (Foster) Fletcher; Remembrance d. at Temple, NH, 30 Nov 1833.
	vi	THOMAS CHANDLER, b. 22 Oct 1751; d. about 1767.
	vii	ELIJAH CHANDLER, b. 6 Aug 1753; d. 1775 reported by the Chandler genealogy as dying at Bunker Hill, but that could not be confirmed.
442)	viii	PETER CHANDLER, b. 25 Mar 1755; d. at Nelson, NH, 14 Jul 1819; m. 6 Mar 1787, MERCY INGALLS, b. at Andover, 29 Apr 1761 daughter of David and Priscilla (Howe) Ingalls; Mercy d. at Wilton, 12 Feb 1842.
	ix	JOSEPH CHANDLER, b. 22 Dec 1756; reported to have died in military service.
443)	x	ASA CHANDLER, b. 25 Apr 1759; d. at Stoddard, NH, 7 Dec 1822 (will 6 Dec 1822); m. 20 Nov 1781, ELINOR RICHARDSON, b. 22 Jul 1753; Elinor d. 6 Dec 1834.[265]

106)   MARY CHANDLER (*Mehitable Russell Chandler³, Thomas², Robert¹*), b. at Andover, 4 Mar 1712/3 daughter of Joseph and Mehitable (Russell) Chandler; d. at Andover, 10 Feb 1751; m. at Andover, 22 Oct 1733, JAMES HOLT, b. at Andover, 1707 son of James and Susanna (Preston) Holt; James d. at Andover, 1751 (probate 16 Dec 1751).

In his will written 21 November 1751, James Holt ordered that all his real estate be sold. Eldest beloved son Zelah Holt receives £20, second son Jesse receives £13, and third son Lemuel receives £17. Daughters Mary and Bridget each receives £8. The personal estate is also to be sold except the books will be divided among the five children. The proceeds from the sale of his shoemaker and carpenter tools is to be divided among his sons. His brother Brazillai Holt of Lancaster was named executor. The value of the farm was £217.5.1, and the total estate value was £236.1.9.[266]

James and Mary were parents of five children born at Andover.

444)	i	MARY HOLT, baptized at Andover, 18 May 1735; m. 1st, 3 Sep 1754, NATHANIEL ANDREWS likely the son of Thomas and Ruth (Bixbee) Andrews; Nathaniel d. at Boxford, 1759 (probate 1759). Mary m. 2nd, 19 Nov 1761, JACOB ANDREWS; Jacob d. at Boxford, 1786 (probate 1786).
445)	ii	BRIDGET HOLT, baptized at Andover, 16 Jan 1737; m. at Boxford, 16 Oct 1757, LEVI ANDREWS, b. at Boxford, 27 Aug 1727 son of Thomas and Ruth (Bixbee) Andrews.
446)	iii	ZELA HOLT, b. at Andover, 29 Dec 1738; d. likely at Bethel, ME; m. at Andover, 16 Nov 1762, his second cousin, PRISCILLA ABBOTT, b. at Andover, 13 Feb 1742/3 daughter of Barachias and Hannah (Holt) Abbott.
447)	iv	JESSE HOLT, b. at Andover, 8 Oct 1739; d. at Tewksbury, Feb 1817; m. at Tewksbury, 30 Aug 1781, MARY CLARK, b. at Tewksbury, 26 May 1745 daughter of Nathaniel and Mary (Wyman) Clark . Mary was first married at Tewksbury, 29 Jun 1769 to MOSES GRAY, baptized at Andover, 11 Jan 1747 son of Robert and Lydia (Peabody) Gray; Moses d. at Tewksbury, 11 Sep 1775.

---

[264] *Essex County, MA: Probate File Papers, 1638-1881.*Online database. *AmericanAncestors.org.* New England Historic Genealogical Society, 2014. Case 4977

[265] Chandler, *Descendants of William and Annis Chandler*

[266] Essex County, MA: Probate File Papers, 1638-1881.Online database. AmericanAncestors.org. New England Historic Genealogical Society, 2014. Case 13649

     v   LEMUEL HOLT, baptized at Andover, 24 Jan 1748; m. at Andover, 19 Oct 1769, MEHITABLE LOVEJOY, b. at Andover, 20 May 1742 daughter of Joseph and Mehitable (Foster) Lovejoy; Lemuel d. at Andover, 1782 (probate 1782). Lemuel and Mehitable did not have children. In his will written 5 Mar 1776, Lemuel made bequests to wife Mehitable, brother Zela, brother Jesse, sister Mary, and sister Bridget.

107)   JOSEPH CHANDLER (*Mehitable Russell Chandler³, Thomas², Robert¹*), b. at Andover, 13 Feb 1716/7 son of Joseph and Mehitable (Russell) Chandler; m. 30 Dec 1741, SARAH RICHARDSON, b. at Bradford, 26 Sep 1719 daughter of Joseph and Hannah (Nelson) Richardson.[267]

     It is not known where Joseph died. The Chandler genealogy reports that he moved to Readsboro, Vermont about 1765 and after that was in either Ware, Massachusetts or Weare, New Hampshire.[268] This family apparently moved frequently as there are records related to their children at Andover, Groton, Ware, Massachusetts and at Willington, Connecticut.

     i   JOSEPH CHANDLER, b. at Andover, 1 Apr 1743; died young

     ii   REUBEN CHANDLER, b. at Andover, 6 Dec 1744; may be the Reuben son of Joseph whose death is recorded at Ashford, CT, 7 May 1751.

448)   iii   THOMAS CHANDLER, b. at Groton, 20 Jan 1746. Thomas married but the name of his wife is not known.

449)   iv   JOHN CHANDLER, b. at Groton, MA, 29 May 1749; d. at Westhampton, MA, about 1824; m. 1st at Sutton, MA, 8 Jun 1775, ELIZABETH ESTY, b. 19 Nov 1755; Elizabeth d. at Lunenburg, 19 Apr 1812. John m. 2nd at Easthampton, 26 May 1815, REBEKAH ALVORD, b. about 1768 daughter of Zebadiah and Rebecca (Searle) Alvord; Rebekah d. at Easthampton, 7 May 1820.

     v   SARAH CHANDLER, b. about 1750; m. JAMES STURTEVANT and resided in Eaton, Québec. Information on children in this family was not found.

     vi   SALMON CHANDLER, b. about 1753; m. at Warren, MA, 27 Jan 1776, EXPERIENCE WALCOTT, possibly Experience b. at Brookfield, 15 Sep 1751 daughter of John and Experience (-) Walcott. Salmon was living in Swanzey, NH in 1790 and in Winchester, NH in 1810. Census records suggest there were children, but that are not yet identified.

     vii   HANNAH CHANDLER, b. about 1754; d. at Willington, 30 Dec 1755.

     viii   JOSEPH CHANDLER, b. at Willington, 3 Apr 1756; d. at Ballston Spa, Saratoga as reported in the Chandler genealogy.

108)   HANNAH CHANDLER (*Mehitable Russell Chandler³, Thomas², Robert¹*), baptized at Andover, 2 Feb 1724 daughter of Joseph and Mehitable (Russell) Chandler; m. at Andover, 10 Aug 1741, DAVID ABBOT, b. at Andover, Dec 1716 son of Jonathan and Zerviah (Holt) Abbott; David d. at Pembroke, NH, 1777 (probate 31 Dec 1777). Hannah's death not known but she was living at the time of her husband's will.

     The will of David Abbot, written 11 June 1771, includes bequests to the following persons: son John Abbot receives a pair of three year old steers, one cow and all his wearing apparel; daughter Hannah Holt receives 5 shillings; daughter Bridget Abbot receives 15 pounds and a yearling heifer; daughter Mehitable also get 15 pounds and a heifer at marriage or the age of 21; son Job Abbot is to be the sole executor; beloved wife Hannah has use of all the household during her widowhood; son Job receives remainder of real and personal estate, although noting that certain tracts of land have been granted to son John by warrantee deed.[269]

     The five children listed in the will are given here. The *History of Pembroke* and other sources list a son Benjamin with this family. However, I believe that Benjamin is the son of David Abbott and Hannah Danforth, and as he is not mentioned/living at the time of the will, he is not included here. Five children were born at Pembroke.

450)   i   JOB ABBOT, b. about 1742; d. at West Barnet, VT, 15 Dec 1815; m. PHEBE FARNUM, likely the daughter of Ebenezer and Phebe (Ingalls) Farnum, b. at Andover, 15 Dec 1750.

255)   ii   HANNAH ABBOT, b. 7 Sep 1743; d. at Pembroke, 17 Mar 1813; m. her third cousin, BENJAMIN HOLT, b. 28 Feb 1741 son of Benjamin and Sarah (Frye) Holt.

---

[267] The 1746 will of Joseph Richardson of Bradford includes a bequest to his daughter Sarah wife of Joseph Chandler.
[268] Chandler, *Descendants of William and Annis Chandler*, p 114
[269] *New Hampshire Wills and Probate Records 1643-1982*, Probate of David Abbott, Rockingham, 31 Dec 1777, Case number 4406.

iii   JOHN ABBOT, b. about 1752 (although he may be the oldest child in this family born in the early 1740's); still living in 1771. There are no records located yet for him. As he was an adult at the time of his father's will having already received land through deed, it is possible that he married although clear evidence not found yet.

451)   iv   BRIDGET ABBOT, b. about 1761; m. 24 Dec 1787, her third cousin, PHINEAS AMES, b. 7 Sep 1764 son of Samuel and Elizabeth (Stevens) Ames; Phineas d. about 1792. Bridget m. 2nd, 17 Dec 1793, STEPHEN HARRIMAN.

v   MEHITABLE ABBOT, b. about 1762; still living in 1771.

109)   ABIGAIL RUSSELL (*Robert³, Thomas², Robert¹*), b. at Andover, 4 Oct 1717 daughter of Robert and Abigail (Flint) Russell; d. at Reading, 1746 (probate Sep 1746); m. at Reading, 23 Sep 1735, EBENEZER EATON; Ebenezer d. at Reading, 1738 (probate 1738).

In his will written 5 February 1738, Ebenezer bequeathed to wife Abigail all the movable estate both outdoors and household goods to be at her disposal. The remainder of the estate goes one-half to Abigail to be for her use and possession and the other half divided between daughters Abigail and Phebe. Robert Russell was named executor.[270]

In her will written 28 May 1740 (probate Sep 1746), Abigail Eaton of Reading relict of Ebenezer bequeathed to brother Ezekiel Russell and Prudence Russell twenty pounds each when they come of age. All the remainder of the estate goes to her two daughters Abigail and Phebe to be equally divided between them. Father Robert Russell was named executor.[271]

Abigail Russell and Ebenezer Eaton were parents of two children born at Reading.

452)   i   ABIGAIL EATON, b. about 1736; d. at Reading, Nov 1817; m. about 1755, as his second wife, JONATHAN BATCHELDER, b. at Reading, 22 Mar 1730 son of Jonathan and Sarah (Lewis) Batchelder; Jonathan d. at Reading, 6 Oct 1817. Jonathan was first married to Phebe Holt.

ii   PHEBE EATON, b. about 1737; she was living when her mother wrote her will in 1740 but not mentioned in her grandfather's 1757 will.

110)   EZEKIEL RUSSELL (*Robert³, Thomas², Robert¹*), b. at Andover, 10 Jun 1722 son of Robert and Abigail (Flint) Russell; d. at Wilbraham, MA, 3 Jan 1802; m. TABATHA FLINT, b. at Reading, 18 May 1721 daughter of Ebenezer and Tabitha (Burnap) Flint; Tabitha d. at Wilbraham, 4 Jan 1808.[272]

Ezekiel and Tabitha began their family in Ashford. The relocated to western Massachusetts about 1759 as on 20 April 1759 (recorded 21 October 1765), Ezekiel Russell of Ashford purchased a tract of land in Springfield, Massachusetts from Abraham Skinner, Jr. of Woodstock. Ezekiel was of Wilbraham when he purchased land on the east side of the Connecticut River from William King on 3 January 1771 and made an additional purchase from the inhabitants of Wilbraham on 20 May 1773.[273] On 3 September 1782, Ezekiel sold to his son Ezekiel, Jr. several lots in Wilbraham (no. 75, 76, 78, 79, and 80) for a payment of £20. Ezekiel sold to his son Robert the homestead farm with buildings for £100.[274]

Ezekiel Russell served in Capt. James Warriner's company of Wilbraham that marched at the alarm in April 1775 for the Battle of Lexington.[275]

Ezekiel Russell and Tabatha Flint were parents of six children.

i   TABITHA RUSSELL, b. at Ashford, CT, 19 Aug 1749; d. at Wilbraham, MA, 9 Jul 1776.

453)   ii   EZEKIEL RUSSELL, b. at Ashford, 22 Jun 1751; d. at Wilbraham, 1798 (probate 1798); m. 1st at Wilbraham, 19 Aug 1775, HEPHZIBAH HILLS, b. at Glastonbury, 10 Aug 1749; Hephzibah d. 24 Feb 1778. Ezekiel m. 2nd at Wilbraham, 2 Oct 1778, HANNAH MEACHAM; Hannah d. at Wilbraham, 27 Jan 1822.

[270] *Middlesex County, MA: Probate File Papers, 1648-1871.*Online database. *AmericanAncestors.org.* New England Historic Genealogical Society, 2014. Case 6728

[271] *Middlesex County, MA: Probate File Papers, 1648-1871.*Online database. *AmericanAncestors.org.* New England Historic Genealogical Society, 2014. Case 6722

[272] Ezekiel and Tabatha are buried at the Old Hampden Cemetery in Hampden. Find A Grave 43582031 and 43582032

[273] Massachusetts Land Records, Hampden County, 6:716; 11:126; 12:343

[274] Massachusetts Land Records, Hampden County, 36:435; 33:444

[275] Peck, *The History of Wilbraham*, p 138

454)   iii   ABIGAIL RUSSELL, b. at Ashford, 19 May 1755; d. at Wilbraham, 16 May 1812; m. at Wilbraham, 1 May 1782, NATHAN STEDMAN, b. 18 Jan 1751 son of Joseph and Abigail (Rockwell) Stedman; Nathan d. at Wilbraham, 27 Nov 1794.

455)   iv   ROBERT RUSSELL, b. at Ashford, 15 May 1757; d. at Hampden, MA, 9 Dec 1836; m. at Wilbraham, 14 Sep 1782, LYDIA BEEBE, b. 1761; Lydia d. at Hampden, 21 Aug 1837.

        v   BENJAMIN RUSSELL, b. at Wilbraham, 1759

        vi   ASA RUSSELL, b. at Wilbraham, 6 Oct 1761; m. at Wilbraham, 25 Nov 1790, THANKFUL ROOT. Asa was living in Longmeadow, MA in 1796 when he sold a piece of land to James Beebe. Another deed in 1796 includes both Asa and Thankful as signers. Nothing else is known of them and no records of children were located.

111)   PHEBE RUSSELL (*Robert³, Thomas², Robert¹*), b. at Reading, 1751 daughter of Robert and Elizabeth (-) Russell; m. at Andover, 19 Nov 1776, DAVID CHENEY, b. at Boxford, 11 Sep 1750 son of Ichabod and Rebekah (Smith) Cheney. Phebe is perhaps the widow Phebe Cheney who married John Perley in Rowley in 1805; if so, she died in 1811.
        There is just one child identified for Phebe Russell and David Cheney.

        i   PHEBE RUSSELL CHENEY, b. about 1782 (as noted on death record); d. at Rowley, 20 Dec 1860; m. at Rowley, 1 Nov 1832, DAVID SAUNDERS, b. at Rowley, 20 May 1766 son of John and Mary (Dresser) Saunders; David d. at Rowley, 1 Dec 1847. David was first married to Priscilla Nelson.

112)   ELIZABETH RUSSELL (*Robert³, Thomas², Robert¹*), b. at Reading, 1752 daughter of Robert and Elizabeth (-) Russell; d. at Boxford, 12 Mar 1840; m. 1ˢᵗ at Danvers, 12 Dec 1776, ELIJAH MOULTON, b. at Danvers, 5 Dec 1748 son of Benjamin and Sarah (Smith) Moulton; Elijah d. at Danvers, 1782 (probate 7 Oct 1782). Elizabeth m. 2ⁿᵈ at Boxford, 10 Jun 1788, JESSE PERLEY, b. at Boxford, 20 Jun 1761 son of Nathaniel and Mehitable (Perley) Perley; Jesse d. at Boxford, 18 Apr 1846.
        Elijah Mouton was a yeoman in Danvers. On 6 July 1778, Elijah and wife Elizabeth sold a tract of land of about 32 acres to John Selman of Marblehead.[276]
        Elijah Moulton's estate entered probate 7 October 1782 with Elizabeth Moulton as administratrix. The total value of the estate including some small acreage was £263.4.0.[277]
        In his will written 26 March 1842 (probate 21 April 1846), Jesse Perley, directs that his estate be sold, except for certain legacies, and the proceeds used to pay debts, funeral charges, and for the erection of appropriate gravestones for him and his late wife Elizabeth. Son Jesse Perley, Jr. receives the income from one-third of the proceeds of the estate and after Jesse, Jr.'s death, this legacy goes to his children (Elizabeth W., Sarah Jane, and Edward Payson Perley). Son Jesse also receives his choice of the stock animals and the best foreplane jointer and smoothing plane. Louisa Perley widow of son Francis received eighty dollars. His grandchildren who are the children of Francis each receives eighty dollars: Osgood Perley, Louisa Hood, Charlotte Wait, Caroline Augusta Perley, John Perley, Nathaniel Perley, and Dean Andrews Perley. Son-in-law Francis Gould receives five dollars, granddaughter Irene Gould receives one hundred-fifty dollars, grandson Francis Gould receives eighty dollars, and grandson Jesse Perley Gould receive one hundred dollars. There are additional legacies to previously named grandchildren and the residue is to be equally divided among his grandchildren. Moses Dorman of Boxford was named executor.[278]
        Elizabeth Russell and Elijah Moulton were parents of two children.

456)   i   SARAH "SALLY" MOULTON, b. likely at Danvers, about 1777; d. at Rowley, MA, 19 May 1852; m. at Boxford, 1800, JONATHAN HARRIMAN, b. 1776 according to gravestone; Jonathan d. at Rowley, 1824.

457)   ii   MARY MOULTON, b. likely at Danvers, 1780; d. at Winthrop, ME, 29 Mar 1839; m. at Boxford, 1 Apr 1799, THOMAS LANCASTER, b. at Rowley, 5 May 1773 son of Paul and Mary (Gage) Lancaster; Thomas d. at Winthrop, 4 May 1864.

        Elizabeth Russell and Jesse Perley were parents of four children born at Boxford.

---

[276] Massachusetts Land Records, Essex County, 136:165

[277] *Essex County, MA: Probate File Papers, 1638-1881.*Online database. *AmericanAncestors.org.* New England Historic Genealogical Society, 2014. Case 19102

[278][278] *Essex County, MA: Probate File Papers, 1638-1881.*Online database. *AmericanAncestors.org.* New England Historic Genealogical Society, 2014. Case 49908

458)   i   FRANCIS PERLEY, b. at Boxford, 19 Oct 1792; d. at Boxford, 1 Sep 1836; m. at Boxford, 18 May 1815, LOUISA GOULD, b. at Topsfield, 25 Jun 1790 daughter of Nathaniel and Hannah (Killam) Gould; Louisa d. at Topsfield, 9 Dec 1843.

459)   ii   JESSE PERLEY, b. at Boxford, 29 Oct 1795; d. at Boxford, 19 Nov 1851; m. at Boxford, 22 May 1824, SALLY GOULD, b. at Topsfield, 26 May 1800 daughter of Simon and Sarah (White) Gould; Sally d. 29 Dec 1857.

     iii   ANCIL PERLEY, b. 3 Jul 1798; d. at Boxford, 28 Dec 1831. Ancil does not seem to have married.

460)   iv   IRENA PERLEY, b. at Boxford, 29 Jan 1801; d. at Boxford, 28 Jul 1837; m. at Boxford, 26 Aug 1822, FRANCIS GOULD, b. at Topsfield, 5 Sep 1798 son of Nathaniel and Betty (Andrews) Gould; Francis d. at Topsfield, 13 Oct 1870. Francis Gould was the half-brother of Louisa Gould who married Irena's brother Francis.

113)   PHEBE FARNUM (*Phebe Russell Farnum³, Thomas², Robert¹*), b. at Andover, 4 Jul 1713 daughter of Henry and Phebe (Russell) Farnum; d. at Windham, 1750 (probate Apr 1750); m. at Windham, 9 May 1735, JOSEPH PRESTON, b. at Andover, 22 Aug 1713 son of Joseph and Rebecca (Preston) Preston; Joseph d. at Windham, 24 Feb 1738.

     Phebe Preston did not leave a will and her estate entered probate 4 April 1750. On 3 March 1757, Henry Preston of Lebanon signed that he as only heir to the estate had received eighty-six pounds six shillings from his guardian Eliphalet Farnum as his full payment from the estate.[279]

     Phebe Farnum and Joseph Preston were parents of one child.

     i   HENRY PRESTON, b. at Canterbury, 12 Feb 1736 and baptized at Hampton, 14 Jun 1736. Henry was living in 1757 but nothing further is known.

114)   HENRY FARNUM (*Phebe Russell Farnum³, Thomas², Robert¹*), b. at Andover, 8 Apr 1715 son of Henry and Phebe (Russell) Farnum; d. at Sprague, CT, 20 Jun 1799; m. 3 Nov 1741, SARAH READ (widow of Joseph Knight), b. at Norwich, 28 Dec 1711 daughter of William and Ann (Stark) Read; Sarah d. at Sprague, 24 Feb 1781.

     There are three known children for Henry Farnum and Sarah Read.

461)   i   HENRY FARNHAM, b. at Norwich, 8 Oct 1742; d. at Lisbon, CT, about 1824 (will 1818; probate 1824); m. at Norwich, 2 Jan 1766, ABIGAIL RUDD, b. about 1746 likely the daughter of Joseph and Sarah (Moseley) Rudd; Sarah d. at Sprague, 11 Dec 1824.

462)   ii   LYDIA FARNUM, b. at Canterbury, 17 Nov 1744; d. at Ashford, 5 Dec 1785; m. 14 Jun 1764, PHINEAS BIRCHARD, baptized at Norwich, 24 Sep 1738 son of John and Jane (Hyde) Birchard; Phineas d. at Ashford, 8 Jun 1811. Phineas had a second wife, Dorcas.

463)   iii   PHEBE FARNUM, b. at Canterbury, 7 Mar 1746; d. at Canterbury, 21 Dec 1808; m. at Canterbury, 16 Dec 1773, DANIEL FROST, b. at Canterbury, 6 Jul 1748 son of Daniel and Elizabeth (Bond) Frost; Daniel d. at Canterbury, 27 Aug 1839. Daniel married second Hannah Stevens on 21 Dec 1809.

115)   MANASSEH FARNUM (*Phebe Russell Farnum³, Thomas², Robert¹*), b. at Windham, 15 Feb 1717 son of Henry and Phebe (Russell) Farnum; d. at Ashford, 1768 (probate 1768); m. at Windham, 23 Apr 1739, KEZIAH FORD, b. at Windham, 27 Mar 1721 daughter of Joseph and Elizabeth (Hovey) Ford; Keziah was living in 1768.

     Manasseh was a farmer in Ashford and the family were members of the church at Scotland.[280]

     In his will written 20 June 1768, Manasseh Farnum bequeaths to dearly beloved wife Kezia the use of the southeast room in the dwelling house while she is a widow, one cow, and a list of provision for her maintenance to be provided by the executor. She also receives the weaving loom and other household items which after her decease will be divided equally among his daughters. Son Manasseh receives ten shillings which with the one pound that Manasseh owes his father and the twenty pounds he has received is his full portion. Daughter Elizabeth Knowlton receives five shillings in addition to the thirteen pounds she received at her marriage. Daughters Kezia, Jemima, Unice, and Hannah each receive thirteen pounds in household goods, these amounts to be paid five, ten, fifteen, and twenty years after Manasseh's decease. Son Joseph receives the whole of

[279] *Connecticut State Library (Hartford, Connecticut)*; Probate Place: *Hartford, Connecticut, Probate Packets, Pettis, James-Richardson, John, 1719-1880, Estate of Phebe Preston, Case 3102*
[280] Farnham, *New England Descendants of Ralph Farnum*, p 177

the buildings, lands, and livestock and is also named executor.[281] Real estate was valued at £81 and personal estate at £79.15.11.

     Manasseh Farnum and Keziah Ford were parents of eight children.

464)   i   MANASSEH FARNHAM, b. at Windham, 29 Jul 1739; d. at Ashford, 16 May 1808; m. 19 Apr 1758, PATIENCE BIBBINS, b. 23 Oct 1733 daughter of Arthur and Abigail (Follett) Bibbins.[282]

       ii   KEZIAH FARNUM, b. 6 Jan 1741; d. 24 Feb 1741.

465)   iii   ELIZABETH FARNUM, b. at Windham, 10 Mar 1742; d. at Ashford, 1 Jun 1786; m. 3 Nov 1763, DANIEL KNOWLTON, b. at Boxford, 23 Dec 1738 son of William and Martha (Pinder) Knowlton; Daniel d. at Ashford, 31 May 1825. Daniel married second Rebeckah Fenton on 24 Apr 1788.

466)   iv   JOSEPH FARNUM, b. at Windham, 28 Nov 1748; d. at Enfield, 1777 (probate 1777); m. 15 Mar 1770, CATHERINE SPRING, b. at Ashford, 3 Mar 1750 daughter of Josiah and Catherine (Bicknell) Spring. Catherine married second HENRY WORK (1752-1832) (*Mary Russell Work⁴, Benjamin³, Benjamin², Robert¹*). Catherine likely died by 1786 as Henry Work remarried in 1787.

467)   v   KEZIAH FARNUM, b. at Windham, 28 Nov 1751; m. about 1770 (first child born 1771), JOSEPH CHAPMAN, b. at Ashford, 9 May 1747 son of Thomas and Mary (Throop) Chapman; Joseph d. at Manlius, NY, 12 Dec 1796.

      vi   JEMIMA FARNUM, baptized at Scotland, CT, 26 May 1754

468)   vii   EUNICE FARNUM, b. at Windham, 1 Feb 1757; d. at Marcellus, NY, after 1810;[283] m. at Ashford, 16 Dec 1782, SILAS SNOW, b. at Ashford 18 Apr 1761 son of Oliver and Elizabeth (Phillips) Snow;[284] Silas d. at Granby, NY, about 1835.

   viii   HANNAH FARNUM, baptized at Scotland, 13 Apr 1762; d. at Marcellus, NY, 2 Feb 1841; m. 13 Nov 1788, JOSHUA CHANDLER, b. at Woodstock, 19 Sep 1763 son of Moses and Frances (Lyon) Chandler; Joshua d. at Marcellus, 19 Aug 1834. Hannah and Joshua did not have children. In his will, Joshua made bequests in the form of trusts to religious organizations.[285]

116)   EPHRAIM FARNUM (*Phebe Russell Farnum³, Thomas², Robert¹*), b. at Windham, 20 Mar 1721 son of Henry and Phebe (Russell) Farnum; d. at Norwich, about 1750 (probate 17 Jan 1751); m. 1 Nov 1744, CHENEY ANNE WHITE, b. at Marshfield, MA, 16 Jul 1722 daughter of Ebenezer and Hannah (Doggett) White. Cheney Anne second married John Louden.

     Ephraim Farnum was a farmer in Norwich. He did not leave a will and his estate entered probate on 24 January 1751 with Channey Anne Farnum as administratrix. In May 1759, John Lowdon and Chenyanna Lowdon petitioned for the sale of the real estate as was necessary to pay debts of the estate of £549.7.8.[286]

     Ephraim Farnum and Cheney Anne White were parents of two children.

469)   i   EPHRAIM FARNUM, b. at Norwich, 7 Aug 1745; m. at Norwich, 7 Jan 1768, SARAH HUNN, b. about 1736 (based on age 69 at time of death); Sarah d. at Boston, 6 Nov 1805.

       ii   EBENEZER FARNUM, b. at Norwich, 4 Dec 1747. He left for Cornwallis, Nova Scotia perhaps arriving there in 1776. He received a land grant of 100 acres in 1783 in Nova Scotia. He did marry and had a family, but the information about that has not been located.[287][288]

---

[281] *Connecticut State Library (Hartford, Connecticut);* Probate Place: *Hartford, Connecticut, Probate Packets, Falshaw, S-Fuller, E, 1752-1880, estate of Manassah Farnam, town of Ashford, case 1672*

[282] The 1758 probate record of Arter Bibbins includes a receipt signed by Manasseh Farnum in 1761 stating that he has received from Mrs. Abigail Bibbins payment from the estate.

[283] Silas and Eunice moved from Ashford to Marcellus in 1808 (according to his pension file) and Eunice appears to be living at the 1810 census but not in 1820. Some genealogies report that Eunice died in Ashford in 1834 but that is the death record of Eunice the wife of Perley Snow.

[284] Silas provides his birth date in his Revolutionary War pension application file as 18 Apr 1761 which leads to the conclusion that his parents are Oliver and Elizabeth Snow. Also in the record is a statement in 1839 from daughter Eunice Snow applying for a payment from the pension board related to the case of her father who was then deceased.

[285] Chandler, *The Chandler Family*, p 586

[286] *Connecticut State Library (Hartford, Connecticut);* Probate Place: *Hartford, Connecticut, Estate of Ephraim Farnam, Town of Norwich, Case 3762*

[287] Nova Scotia Archives; Halifax, Nova Scotia, Canada; Census, Assesment and Poll Tax Records 1767-1827; Reference: Commissioner of Public Records Nova Scotia Archives RG 1 vol. 443 no. 38

[288] Halifax, Nova Scotia, Canada; Nova Scotia Land Petitions (1765-1800); Volume Number: 1

117)   JOSHUA FARNUM (*Phebe Russell Farnum³, Thomas², Robert¹*), b. at Windham, 29 Mar 1723 son of Henry and Phebe (Russell) Farnum; d. at Scotland, CT, 3 Feb 1797; m. at Hampton, 6 Jun 1748, SARAH FORD, b. at Windham, 20 Dec 1714 daughter of Joseph and Elizabeth (Hovey) Ford; Sarah d. at Scotland, 28 Apr 1789.

   Joshua Farnum and Sarah Ford were parents of two children.

   i   SARAH FARNUM, b. at Windham, 27 Mar 1749; d. 26 Aug 1758.

470)   ii   ELIZABETH FARNUM, b. at Windham, 17 Jan 1752; d. 30 Jan 1832; m. at Windham, 7 Apr 1774, ASA BOTTUM,[289] b. at Norwich, 3 Aug 1748 son of David and Lucy (Read) Bottum; Asa d. at Windham, 1812 (probate 1812).

118)   ELIPHALET FARNUM (*Phebe Russell Farnum³, Thomas², Robert¹*), b. at Windham, 21 Mar 1725 son of Henry and Phebe (Russell) Farnum; m. 1st at Canterbury, 11 Oct 1750, MARY ROGERS, possibly Mary b. at Windham, 6 Oct 1727 daughter of Hope and Esther (Meacham) Rogers; Mary d. at Canterbury, 1 May 1753. Eliphalet m. 2nd at Canterbury, 1 Feb 1757, MARY ADAMS.

   Eliphalet Farnum and Mary Rogers were parents of one child.

   i   ELIPHALET FARNUM, b. 14 Sep 1751; d. 8 Nov 1754.

   Eliphalet Farnum and Mary Adams were parents of one child.

471)   i   ELIPHALET FARNUM, b. at Canterbury, 25 Aug 1759; d. at Middlebury, VT, 10 Sep 1833; m. at Gilsum, NH, 16 Oct 1786, HANNAH ADAMS, b. about 1762 daughter of Jonathan and Hannah (Yeamans) Adams;[290] Hannah d. at Middlebury, VT, 14 Apr 1844.

119)   ELIAB FARNUM (*Phebe Russell Farnum³, Thomas², Robert¹*), b. at Windham, 24 Jul 1731 son of Henry and Phebe (Russell) Farnum; d. at Otisville, NY, 9 Jun 1806; m. at Preston, 19 Jun 1754, ABIGAIL KILLAM, b. at Norwich, 19 Aug 1736 daughter of John and Abigail (Kimball) Killam; Abigail d. at Otisville, about 1782. Eliab m. 2nd EUNICE NICHOLS, b. 5 Mar 1739. Eunice had two previous marriages to John Osborne and Samuel Bouton.

   Eliab Farnum served during the French and Indian War as a drummer in the second Connecticut regiment commanded by Col. Nathan Whiting.[291] During the Revolution, Capt. Eliab Farnum commanded the eighth Lackaway company in the 24th regiment of Col. Nathan Denison. This regiment participated in the June 1778 Battle of Wyoming.[292]

   Eliab received property on 20 May 1773 in the Delaware Purchase of what was to become Palmyra Township in Pike County, Pennsylvania.[293]

   In his will written 20 March 1805, Eliab Farnum of Deer Park bequeathed to wife Eunice provisions for her support currently provided by sons Eliab and Joshua to continue after his decease. Son Russell receives one undivided half of property in Lackawack and the other half to be divided among sons George Whitfield, Jeffrey Amherst, Eliab, Stephen, and Joshua. The moveable estate is divided among his five daughters Abigail, Martha, Mary, Sarah, and Marcy.[294]

   Eliab Farnum and Abigail Killam were parents of fourteen children.

472)   i   PHEBE FARNUM, b. at Preston, 10 Sep 1756; m. at Preston, 24 Mar 1774, AMOS PARKE, b. at Preston, 9 Sep 1749 son of Silas and Sarah (Ayer) Parke; Amos d. at Preston, 1 Oct 1825. Amos married second Margaret Moore.

   ii   JOSHUA FARNUM, b. at Preston, 31 Aug 1758; d. in the Wyoming Valley during the Revolution. The Farnum genealogy reports there are reports that Joshua died in the Wyoming massacre which was in July

---

[289] Asa's father was David Longbottom, but the name was shortened to Bottom. Asa's father wrote his will as David Bottom. Asa's birth transcription lists his father as David Longbottom. Asa adopted the spelling Bottum consistently.

[290] Adams, *A Genealogical History of Henry Adams of Braintree, Mass.*, volume 1, p 544

[291] Guertin, Iris, Rose, comp. *Connecticut Soldiers, French and Indian War, 1755-62* [database on-line]. Provo, UT, USA: Ancestry.com Operations Inc, 2000.

[292] Brewster, *History of the Certified Township of Kingston, Pennsylvania*, p 131

[293] Farnham, *New England Descendants of Ralph Farnum*, p 184. A detailed description of Eliab's military and civic service can be found on pp 182-184.

[294] New York Probate Records, 1629-1971, Orange County, Wills 1797-1807, Vol C, pp 349-351.

1778. Miner's History of Wyoming records his death as 28 March 1781 during an attack on Chamber's Mills on the Delaware.[295]

473) iii   ABIGAIL FARNUM, b. at Preston, 2 Sep 1760; m. 1st about 1778, ELEAZER OWEN, b. at Salisbury, CT, 16 Apr 1755 son of Jonathan and Patience (Vallance) Owen; Eleazer died at the Battle of Minisink, 22 Jul 1779. Abigail m. 2nd at Goshen, NY, 2 Feb 1784, ABIEL FRYE, b. at Andover, 8 Nov 1734 son of Abiel and Abigail (Emery) Frye; Abiel d. at Chemung, NY, 2 Oct 1806.

474) iv   MARTHA FARNUM (twin), b. at Preston, 29 Aug 1762; d. likely at Sanford, NY, 2 Nov 1843; m. 1791, NATHAN AUSTIN, b. at Preston, 5 Apr 1764 son of Benjamin and Susanna (Burdick) Austin; Nathan d. 1847.

      v   MARY FARNUM (twin), b. at Preston, 29 Aug 1762; d. at New Castle, NY, 5 Feb 1838;[296] m. an unknown PURDY.[297] Nothing further was located for this family.

475) vi   RUSSELL FARNUM (twin), b. at Preston, 9 Sep 1764; d. at McClure, NY, 23 Feb 1820; m. about 1794, EUNICE VAN DEUZEN, b. about 1773; Eunice d. at McClure, 26 Oct 1834.

      vii   MERCY FARNUM (twin), b. 9 Sep 1764

476) viii SARAH FARNUM, b. 13 Jan 1769; d. at McClure, NY, 10 Mar 1807 in childbirth; m. 26 Feb 1791, WILLIAM MACCLURE,[298] b. at Chester, NH, 1726 son of James and Jean (Andrews) MacClure; William d. at McClure, 14 Dec 1826. William married second Lydia Austin.

477) ix   JEFFREY AMHERST FARNUM (twin), b. at Preston, 17 Oct 1772; d. at Scipio, NY, 12 Nov 1841; m. at Big Flats, NY, Dec 1793, MERCY TRACY, b. at Norwich, 16 Sep 1775 daughter of Benjamin and Olive (Killam) Tracy; Mercy d. at Pittsford, NY, 11 May 1873.

478) x   GEORGE WHITFIELD FARNUM (twin), b. at Preston, 17 Oct 1772; d. after 1838[299] likely at Ledyard, NY; m. about 1800, ANNA ALLEN, b. about 1780 daughter of Gideon and Phebe (Beardsley) Allen; Anna d. after 1838.

479) xi   ELIAB FARNUM, b. at Coventry, CT, 4 Aug 1775; d. at Benton Township, PA, 31 Mar 1855; m. at Deer Park, NY, 1 Jan 1797, HANNAH OSBORNE, b. at South Salem, NY, 24 Apr 1778 daughter of John and Eunice (Nichols) Osborne; Hannah d. 24 Aug 1835. Hannah Osborne was daughter of Eliab's stepmother.

      xii   EPHRAIM FARNUM, b. 9 Nov 1777; perhaps died young

480) xiii STEPHEN FARNUM, b. at Deer Park, NY, 19 Oct 1779; d. at Crawford, NY, 27 Apr 1868; m. about 1810, KETURAH SAYBOTT, b. at Goshen, NY, 6 Sep 1787 daughter of Frederick and Abigail (Reeve) Saybott; Keturah d. at Hopewell, NY, 6 Dec 1872.

      xiv   JOSHUA FARNUM, b. at Deer Park, 8 Dec 1781; m. before 1806 PERSIS who has not been identified. No records of children were located.

120)   PETER OSGOOD (*Mary Russell Osgood³, Thomas², Robert¹*), b. at Andover, 14 Nov 1717 son of Timothy and Mary (Russell) Osgood; d. at Andover, 17 Nov 1801; m. at Andover, 8 Sep 1743, SARAH JOHNSON, b. at Andover, Nov 1719 daughter of Timothy and Katherine (Sprague) Johnson; Sarah d. at Andover, 1 Aug 1804.

Capt. Peter Osgood and Sarah Johnson raised their family in Andover. Peter was a successful merchant and served as magistrate. He also served as representative to the General Court and the state convention for the adoption of the constitution 9 January 1783. Son Samuel Osgood graduated from Harvard in 1770 and served as the first Postmaster General of the United States.[300] Son Isaac was a successful entrepreneur in Andover and his estate included a mill, a homestead of 104 acres valued at $10,000, an additional eight dwelling houses, and a machine shop.[301]

In his will written 15 September 1800 (probate 7 December 1801), Peter Osgood bequeathed to beloved wife Sarah the use of the dwelling house she now possesses and what is necessary for her comfortable maintenance. Son Peter receives a piece

[295] Miner, *History of Wyoming*, p 294

[296] The grave of Mary Purdy in Archer-Sarles Cemetery bears this inscription: In memory of Mary Purdy who died Feb. 5, 1838 aged 75 yrs. 6 mo. & 18 d's; Findagrave: 128537582

[297] Farnham, The Descendants of Ralph Farnum

[298] Transcripts of letters written by William to Sarah during his courtship of her can be seen in Farnham's Farnum genealogy.

[299] When he executed a deed

[300] Osgood, *A Genealogy of the Descendants of John, Christopher, and William Osgood*, pp 85-86

[301] *Essex County, MA: Probate File Papers, 1638-1881.*Online database. *AmericanAncestors.org.* New England Historic Genealogical Society, 2014. Case 48886, Estate of Isaac Osgood, 1847.

of woodland and fifty dollars. Son Samuel receives five dollars which completes his portion. Daughter Susanna receives fifty dollars and half the stock in the Union Bank, and "considering her husband's industry, prudence, and fame in his profession" his income is such that his family is in better circumstances that some of his other children, that will be her full portion. Son Isaac receives five dollars to complete his portion. The remainder of the estate goes to son Timothy.[302] Son Peter named in the will died 5 January 1801 between the time of the will and the time of probate.

Peter Osgood and Sarah Johnson were parents of ten children born at Andover.

	i	ISAAC OSGOOD, b. 27 Jan 1744; d. 17 Oct 1753.
481)	ii	PETER OSGOOD, b. at Andover, 24 Jun 1745; d. at Andover, 5 Jan 1801; m. at Andover, 24 Nov 1788, HANNAH PORTER, b. about 1762 at Boxford (according to her death record); Hannah d. at Andover, 18 Sep 1854. Peter also had a child with Susannah Poor but it is unclear if they were married.
482)	iii	SAMUEL OSGOOD, b. at Andover, 3 Feb 1748; d. at New York, NY, 12 Aug 1813; m. 1st at Cambridge, 4 Jan 1775, MARTHA BRANDON, b. about 1752 likely the daughter of Benjamin and Elizabeth (Foxcroft) Brandon; Martha d. at Andover, 13 Sep 1778. Samuel m. 2nd at New York, 24 May 1786, MARIA BOURNE (widow of Walter Franklin), b. about 1754 daughter of Daniel Bourne;[303] Maria d. at New York, Oct 1814.
	iv	SARAH OSGOOD, b. 11 Feb 1750; d. 24 Oct 1762.
	v	JOSEPH OSGOOD, b. 3 Dec 1751; d. 14 Oct 1753.
483)	vi	SUSANNA OSGOOD, b. at Andover, 23 Oct 1754; d. at Andover, 28 Apr 1840; m. at Andover, 7 Nov 1771, Dr. THOMAS KITTREDGE, b. at Andover, 13 Jul 1746 son of John and Sarah (Merriam) Kittredge; Thomas d. at Andover, 16 Oct 1818.
484)	vii	ISAAC OSGOOD, b. at Andover, 15 Jul 1755; d. at Andover, 30 Sep 1847; m. 1st at Salem, 12 Oct 1790, SALLY PICKMAN, b. at Salem, 7 Jun 1771 daughter of Clarke Gayton and Sarah (Orne) Pickman; Sally d. at Salem 10 Aug 1791. Isaac m. 2nd, Sally's sister, REBECCA TAYLOR PICKMAN, b. at Salem, about 1772; Rebecca d. at Salem, 29 Aug 1801. Isaac m. 3rd at Salem, 28 Jun 1803, MARY PICKMAN, b. at Salem, 20 Sep 1765 daughter of Benjamin and Mary (Toppan) Pickman; Mary d. at North Andover, 7 Sep 1856.
	viii	JOSEPH OSGOOD, b. 30 May 1758; d. 17 Oct 1762.
	ix	LYDIA OSGOOD, b. 22 Mar 1760; d. 22 Feb 1763.
485)	x	TIMOTHY OSGOOD, b. at Andover, 17 Mar 1763; d. at Andover, 13 Dec 1842; m. 13 Nov 1788, his second cousin once removed, SARAH "SALLY" FARNUM, b. at Andover, 10 Mar 1771 daughter of Isaac and Mary (Osgood) Farnum.

121)　　TIMOTHY OSGOOD (*Mary Russell Osgood³, Thomas², Robert¹*), b. at Andover, 26 Aug 1719 son of Timothy and Mary (Russell) Osgood; d. at Andover, 31 Aug 1753; m. 6 Jan 1742, PHEBE FRYE, b. at Andover, 19 Mar 1721 daughter of Nathan and Hannah (Bridges) Frye; Phebe d. at Andover, after 1783 (living at time of daughter's will).

Timothy Osgood was a farmer in Andover. He did not leave a will and his estate entered probate 22 October 1823 with widow Phebe as administratrix. Dower was set off to the widow on 26 April 1756. The value of the estate not set off to the widow was £491.2.6. The division of the estate was made 10 October 1765 with the two-thirds of the real estate not set off as dower going to eldest son Timothy on condition that he pay £35.2.5 each to brother Asa and sisters Phebe and Abiah.[304]

Daughter Phebe did not marry and in her will written 18 February 1783, she left bequests of six shillings each to her mother, brother Timothy Osgood, and brother Asa Osgood. The remainder of her estate was bequeathed to sister Abiah Osgood who was also named executrix.[305]

Timothy Osgood and Phebe Frye were parents of seven children born at Andover, the youngest child born two months after Timothy's death. Timothy and three of the children died in the fall/winter of 1753, Timothy and his son James dying on the same day.

---

[302] *Essex County, MA: Probate File Papers, 1638-1881.* Online database. *AmericanAncestors.org.* New England Historic Genealogical Society, 2014. Case 20256

[303] The will of Walter Franklin of Long Island makes mention of his father-in-law Daniel Bourne. His name is also given in some sources as Daniel Browne.

[304] *Essex County, MA: Probate File Papers, 1638-1881.* Online database. *AmericanAncestors.org.* New England Historic Genealogical Society, 2014. Case 20283

[305305] *Essex County, MA: Probate File Papers, 1638-1881.* Online database. *AmericanAncestors.org.* New England Historic Genealogical Society, 2014. Case 20257

486)   i   TIMOTHY OSGOOD, b. 27 Jul 1743; d. at Andover, 16 Aug 1816; m. at Andover, 13 Mar 1765, his first cousin once removed (through the Bridges line), CHLOE BRIDGES, b. at Andover, 28 Dec 1743 daughter of James and Mary (Abbott) Bridges; Chloe d. at Andover, 5 Dec 1798.

       ii   ASA OSGOOD, b. Oct 1744; d. 1 Dec 1753.

       iii   PHEBE OSGOOD, b. 29 Apr 1746; d. at Andover, 4 Mar 1783. Phebe did not marry.

       iv   ABIAH OSGOOD, b. 13 Dec 1747; d. at Dracut, 17 Sep 1825; m. at Dracut, 24 Nov 1801, PARKER VARNUM, b. about 1746 son of John and Phebe (Parker) Varnum; Parker d. at Dracut, 18 Dec 1824.

       v   JAMES OSGOOD, b. 26 Dec 1749; d. 31 Aug 1753.

       vi   MARY OSGOOD, b. 24 Mar 1752; d. 16 Oct 1753.

487)   vii   ASA OSGOOD, b. 22 Dec 1753; d. at Hiram, ME, 29 Jul 1833; m. 1st 19 Jun 1780, his fourth cousin, DORCAS STEVENS, b. at Andover, 9 Oct 1755 daughter of Asa and Mehitable (Farnum) Stevens; Dorcas d. 1780. Asa m. 2nd at Methuen, 22 May 1784, Mrs. LYDIA HOOD; Lydia d. 1807. Asa m. 3rd 18 Jul 1808, HANNAH POWERS; Hannah d. 25 Dec 1853.

122)   THOMAS OSGOOD (*Mary Russell Osgood³, Thomas², Robert¹*), b. at Andover, 2 Nov 1721 son of Timothy and Mary (Russell) Osgood; d. at Andover, 3 Nov 1798; m. 3 Dec 1747, SARAH HUTCHINSON, b. at Andover, 24 Sep 1719 daughter of John and Sarah (Adams) Hutchinson; Sarah d. 3 Nov 1798.

       In his will dated 5 June 1793 (probate 3 December 1798), Thomas Osgood bequeaths the use of one-third part of his real estate and one-half of stock animals to beloved wife Sarah. After her decease, any remaining goes to his grandchildren children of his deceased daughter Sarah wife of Jonathan Bradley and to his daughter Molly the wife of Joseph Bradley to be equally divided between them. The six children of his daughter Sarah are to receive one-half of the real estate which will be in trust with their father Jonathan Bradley. Son-in-law Jonathan Bradley receives one-quarter part of the stock animals. Daughter Molly Bradley receives the other half of the real estate. His two sons-in-law were named executors.[306]

       Thomas Osgood and Sarah Hutchinson were parents of three children born at Andover.

488)   i   SARAH OSGOOD, b. 3 Dec 1749; d. at Andover, 14 Sep 1790; m. at Haverhill, 11 Feb 1773, JONATHAN BRADLEY, b. at Haverhill, 14 Feb 1744/5 son of William and Mehitable (Emerson) Bradley;[307] Jonathan d. at Andover, 23 Feb 1818. Jonathan m. 2nd at Haverhill, 14 Apr 1791, Sarah Ayer.

       ii   THOMAS OSGOOD, b. 28 Oct 1751; nothing further known, but not living and without heirs at the time of father's will.

489)   iii   MARY "POLLY" OSGOOD, b. at Andover, 1755; d. at Andover, 10 Aug 1840; m. at Haverhill, 28 Mar 1781, JOSEPH BRADLEY, b. at Haverhill, 14 Feb 1744/5 son of William and Mehitable (Emerson) Bradley; Joseph d. at Andover, 21 Mar 1802.

123)   ISAAC OSGOOD (*Mary Russell Osgood³, Thomas², Robert¹*), b. at Andover, 4 Aug 1724 son of Timothy and Mary (Russell) Osgood; d. at Haverhill, 17 May 1791; m. 18 Jun 1752, ABIGAIL BAILEY, b. at Haverhill, 10 Jan 1730 daughter of Joshua and Elizabeth (Johnson) Bailey; Abigail d. at Haverhill, 25 Jan 1801 of black jaundice.

       Isaac Osgood graduated from Harvard College in 1744 and was a merchant in Haverhill. Sons Joshua and Isaac also attended Harvard.

       Isaac Osgood did not leave a will and his estate entered probate 23 July 1791 with widow Abigail declining administration and requesting that son Timothy be named administrator. There were some conflicts in the settlement of the estate related to claims against the estate some of which were disputed. The estate was declared insolvent and some real estate needed to be sold to settle the estate. Real property was valued at £1640.3.3 which included a wharf, brew house, malt house,

---

[306] *Essex County, MA: Probate File Papers, 1638-1881.* Online database. *AmericanAncestors.org.* New England Historic Genealogical Society, 2014. Case 20280

[307] Crane, *Historic Homes and Institutions and Personal Memoirs of Worcester County, Massachusetts*, volume 1, p 367. One oddity in the records is that the twin sons of William and Mehitable Bradley are listed as stillborn on 14 Feb 1744/5 but then they were baptized on 17 Feb 1744/5. The 1780 probate of William Bradley of Haverhill includes a will that has as heirs sons Jonathan and Joseph (among other children).

and a stone and cooper shop. There was other substantial real estate that had been mortgaged for more than it was worth. No distribution was included with the probate documents.[308]

Isaac Osgood and Abigail Bailey were parents of eight children born at Haverhill.

490)   i   JOSHUA BAILEY OSGOOD, b. at Haverhill, 29 Apr 1753; d. at Boston (although resident of Fryeburg), 30 May 1791; m. May 1780, ELIZABETH BROWN, b. at Haverhill, 26 Apr 1757 daughter of Henry Young and Elizabeth (Lovejoy) Brown; Elizabeth d. at Fryeburg, 30 Jun 1790. Joshua graduated from Harvard in 1772. He was a merchant in Fryeburg. He served as a Colonel of a regiment that was part of the Canada expedition.[309]

      ii   ISAAC OSGOOD, b. 29 Sep 1754; d. at Haverhill, 27 Jan 1799. Dr. Isaac Osgood graduated from Harvard in 1775. He spent some years in Madagascar before returning to Haverhill where he died. Isaac did not marry.

      iii   MARY OSGOOD, b. 3 Jul 1756; d. 1 May 1758.

      iv   TIMOTHY OSGOOD, b. 13 Apr 1758; d. 1 Aug 1759.

      v   TIMOTHY OSGOOD, b. at Haverhill, 2 Dec 1759; d. at Portland, 22 Aug 1839; m. at Portland, 24 May 1812, SARAH "SALLY" CODMAN, b. 1765 daughter of Richard and Sarah (Smith) Codman; Sally d. at Portland, 16 Nov 1838. Timothy did not have children.

      vi   WILLIAM OSGOOD, b. 23 May 1761; d. at Haverhill, 16 Jul 1792. William did not marry.

491)   vii   PETER OSGOOD, b. at Haverhill, 5 Aug 1764; d. at Haverhill, 28 Sep 1856; m. at Haverhill, 13 Jul 1796, MARY WILLIS, b. about 1774 daughter of Benjamin and Mary (Ball) Willis; Mary d. at Haverhill, 23 Oct 1825.

      viii   JOSEPH OSGOOD, b. 21 Jun 1767; d. 12 Jul 1767.

124)   DEBORAH OSGOOD (*Mary Russell Osgood³, Thomas², Robert¹*), b. at Andover, 28 Apr 1730 daughter of Timothy and Mary (Russell) Osgood; d. about 1793; m. 2 Jan 1759, OBADIAH WOOD, b. about 1734 likely the son of Nathaniel and Elizabeth (Powell) Wood; Obadiah d. at Andover, 23 Oct 1810. Obadiah m. 2nd 8 May 1794 widow Lydia Blanchard.

Obadiah Wood did not leave a will and his estate entered probate 6 November 1810 with widow Lydia as administratrix. The personal estate was valued at $151.19.[310]

There are just two children known for Deborah Osgood and Obadiah Wood. Neither daughter married. In her will dated 9 February 1824, Susanna Wood single lady of Andover expressed that Mr. Timothy Osgood in whose family she resides should have proper compensation for his attention to her. She bequeaths to sister Deborah the dwelling house in which Deborah now resides. Deborah should also receive $60 per year from the estate. The remainder of the estate goes to Timothy Osgood who is also named executor.[311] It is possible that Timothy Osgood mentioned is her first cousin son of Peter and Sarah (Johnson) Osgood.

      i   SUSANNA WOOD, b. at Andover, 5 Nov 1759; d. at Andover, 13 Feb 1824. Susanna did not marry.

      ii   DEBORAH WOOD, b. about 1772; d. at Andover, 30 Mar 1852. Deborah did not marry.[312]

125)   PHEBE OSGOOD (*Mary Russell Osgood³, Thomas², Robert¹*), b. at Andover, 26 May 1733 daughter of Timothy and Mary (Russell) Osgood; d. at Methuen, 2 Mar 1797; m. about 1757, THOMAS POOR, b. at Andover 19 Jul 1732 son of Thomas and Mary (Adams) Poor; Thomas d. at Methuen, 23 Sep 1804. Thomas married second Miriam Sargent.

[308] *Essex County, MA: Probate File Papers, 1638-1881.*Online database. *AmericanAncestors.org.* New England Historic Genealogical Society, 2014. Case 20205

[309] Osgood, *A Genealogy of the Descendants of John, Christopher and William Osgood*, p 92

[310] *Essex County, MA: Probate File Papers, 1638-1881.*Online database. *AmericanAncestors.org.* New England Historic Genealogical Society, 2014. Case 30303

[311] *Massachusetts, Essex County, Probate Records; Author: Massachusetts. Supreme Judicial Court (Essex County), Probate Records, Wood, N-Wood, S, 1828-1991*

[312] Deborah Wood described as a "single lady" daughter of Obadiah and as born at North Andover.

Thomas Poor was the captain of a company of Minute Men in Col. James Frye's regiment and marched at the alarm 19 April 1775. He received promotion to Major in May 1775. He was commissioned as Colonel on 13 May 1778 and was in command of a regiment raised for service at Peekskill.[313]

In his will written 11 September 1804, Thomas Poor bequeathed to beloved wife Miriam use of part of the house and provisions for her support to be provided annually, and the household furniture that was hers at the time of marriage. Son Stephen received five dollars which completes his full portion. Son Caleb receives one-sixty-eighth part of the land of the original Shelburne grant and a 100-acre lot number fifteen and one undivided half-part of lot twenty-eight and additional parcels. Daughter Polly Lovejoy wife of Abiel Lovejoy receive 100 acres in East Andover. Daughter Hannah Whittier wife of William Whittier receives 100 acres also in East Andover and daughter Phebe Plummer wife of Moses Plummer receives a similar bequest. Daughter Sarah receives use and occupancy of a chamber in the house and other provisions for her support while she is unmarried. Daughter Nancy Frye wife of Robinson Frye receives a 58-acre lot and daughter Suzee Frye wife of Daniel Frye receives a 100-acre lot. The remaining household items is to be equally divided among the daughters. The remaining outlands are to be sold and what is owed him collected and the remainder to be divided among the children except Stephen who has received his full amount. Sons Enoch and Thomas receive the remainder of the estate real and personal to divide equally and they are also named executors. After the sale of the outlands, the total value of the personal estate was $3,294.10.[314]

On 8 July 1806, son Stephen, then of Andover, sold his property in Methuen to his brothers Enoch and Thomas for $400. On 8 June 1815, Enoch and Thomas along with Thomas's wife Prudence sold 48 acres of property to Asa Currier for $400.[315]

Phebe Osgood and Thomas Poor were parents of ten children. Sons Enoch and Caleb settled in North Carolina, although Enoch returned to Massachusetts.

492) i   MARY POOR, b. at Andover, 23 Dec 1757; d. likely at Andover, ME; m. at Andover, 30 Apr 1776, ABIEL LOVEJOY, b. at Andover, 28 Apr 1749 son of Christopher and Anne (Mooar) Lovejoy; Abiel d. at Andover, ME, about 1820.[316]

493) ii   HANNAH POOR, b. at Andover, 4 Dec 1759; d. at Methuen, 11 Mar 1835; m. 19 Mar 1789, as his second wife, WILLIAM WHITTIER, b. at Methuen, 26 Sep 1752 son of Richard and Elizabeth (Bodwell) Whittier; William d. at Methuen, 25 Aug 1812. William was first married to Lydia Haseltine.

494) iii PHEBE POOR, b. at Andover, 3 Jul 1761; m. at Andover, 22 Nov 1796, as his second wife, MOSES PLUMMER, b. at Rowley, 24 Jan 1744/5 son of Thomas and Bethiah (Tenney) Plummer. Moses was first married to Hannah Hale.

495) iv   STEPHEN POOR, b. at Andover, 16 Feb 1763; d. at Newburyport, 17 Jul 1812; m. 1st at Andover, 25 Oct 1795, ELIZABETH DUSTIN, b. at Windham, NH, 8 Sep 1773 daughter of Peter and Betty (Sawyer) Dustin;[317] Elizabeth d. about 1800. Stephen m. 2nd 24 Aug 1801, MARY PLUMMER, b. about 1782 (based on age at time of death); Mary d. at Andover, 2 Dec 1845. Mary married second Joseph Cummings at Andover on 19 Dec 1815.

496) v   ENOCH POOR, b. at Andover, 20 Apr 1765; d. at Methuen, 17 Mar 1834; m. at Rowan County, NC, 1794 (bond 8 Apr 1794), PRUDENCE BREVARD, b. in NC, 4 Jan 1772 daughter of Robert and Sarah (Craig) Brevard; Prudence d. at Methuen, 29 Jul 1850. Enoch and Prudence had five children in North Carolina and then Enoch returned to Methuen.

497) vi   CALEB POOR, b. at Andover, 28 Mar 1767; d. after 1813 (living in Morganton, NC in 1810); m. Jul 1796, POLLY MIRA AVERY, b. at Burke County, NC, 24 Aug 1779 daughter of Waightstill and Leah (Probart) Avery;[318] Polly Mira d. at Henderson County, NC, 20 Feb 1857. Caleb and Polly divorced in 1813.[319] Polly Mira married second Jacob Summey in 1823.

498) vii NANCY POOR, b. about 1771; d. at Methuen, 9 Jan 1855; m. at Methuen, 25 Oct 1797, ROBINSON FRYE, b. at Methuen, 28 May 1771 son of James and Mehitable (Robinson) Frye; Robinson d. at Methuen, 5 Dec 1816.

---

[313] Massachusetts Soldiers and Sailors in the Revolution, volume 12, p 562

[314] *Essex County, MA: Probate File Papers, 1638-1881.* Online database. *AmericanAncestors.org.* New England Historic Genealogical Society, 2014. Case 22391

[315] Massachusetts Land Records, Essex County, 178:280-281; 207:9-10

[316] Poor, "History of Andover, Maine"

[317] The 1825 will of Peter Dustin includes a bequest to his granddaughter Eliza Poor, now Eliza Osborne.

[318] The 1823 will of Waightstill Avery includes a bequest to his daughter Polly Mira Poor.

[319] Insooe, Mountain Masters: Slavery and the Sectional Crisis in Western North Carolina, p 119

viii   SARAH POOR, b. about 1772 (based on age 65 at time of death); d. at Andover, 16 Dec 1837; m. at Andover, 29 Sep 1825, as his third wife, ISAAC MOOAR, b. at Andover, 16 Feb 1759 son of Abraham and Lydia (Abbott) Mooar; Isaac d. at Andover, 12 Jan 1832. Isaac was first married to Sarah Abbott and second married to Lydia Cawley.

ix   THOMAS POOR, baptized at Andover, 27 Mar 1774; d. at Methuen 20 Oct 1815. Thomas does not seem to have married. His estate was administered by Enoch Poor. The accounting of the estate includes costs of Enoch Poor for providing boarding, support, and a nurse for Thomas from 4 Nov 1811 through 25 oct 1815.

x   SUSANNAH POOR, b. at Methuen, 14 Jan 1778; d. at Methuen, 5 Feb 1834; m. at Methuen, 17 Dec 1795, DANIEL FRYE, b. at Methuen, 7 Jun 1773 son of James and Mehitable (Robinson) Frye; Daniel d. at Methuen, 14 Oct 1837. After Susannah's death, Daniel married Phebe Carleton. Susannah and Daniel did not have children of their own, but adopted two children, Daniel Frye and Susan who married Josiah Osgood. In his 1837 will, Daniel makes provision for his wife Phebe and left the bulk of the estate to adopted son Daniel Frye and adopted daughter Susan wife of Josiah Osgood.[320]

126)   HANNAH OSGOOD (*Mary Russell Osgood³, Thomas², Robert¹*), b. at Andover, 31 Jul 1735 daughter of Timothy and Mary (Russell) Osgood; d. at Andover, 22 Oct 1771; [321] m. at Andover, 23 Nov 1758, JOHN ADAMS, b. at Andover, 3 Jul 1735 son of Israel and Tabitha (Farnum) Adams; John d. at Andover, 27 Jun 1813. John m. 2nd at Rowley, 24 Jun 1773, HANNAH THURSTON, b. at Rowley, 25 Dec 1743 daughter of Richard and Mehitable (Jewett) Thurston; Hannah d. at Andover, 22 Jan 1774.. John m. 3rd, 21 May 1776, his first cousin once removed, MARY HOLT (*Stephen Holt⁴, Nicholas Holt³, Mary Russell Holt², Robert¹*), b. at Andover, 15 Dec 1741 daughter of Stephen and Mary (Farnum) Holt; Mary d. at Andover, 9 Nov 1829.

Capt. John Adams served in the French and Indian War and was an officer during the Revolution. He served as deacon of the North Church in Andover.[322]

In his will written 22 March 1813 (probate 6 September 1813), John Adams bequeaths to his beloved wife Mary the use and improved of the northeast room and the back part of the house while she is a widow. Mary also receives the interest on $600 annually and a lengthy list of other provisions for her support to be provided by the executor. Son Isaac Adams receives £40. Son John Adams receives the remainder of the estate real and personal and is named executor.[323]

John Adams and Hannah Osgood were parents of five children born at Andover.

i   HANNAH ADAMS, b. 26 Jul 1760; d. 30 Aug 1763.

ii   SARAH ADAMS, baptized 18 Jul 1762; d. 2 Sep 1763.

iii   HANNAH ADAMS, baptized 3 Jun 1764; likely died young.

499)   iv   JOHN ADAMS, b. at Andover, 26 Feb 1766; d. at Andover, 28 Sep 1839; m. 8 Dec 1789, DORCAS FAULKNER, b. at Andover, 26 Sep 1766 daughter of Joseph and Hannah (Hovey) Faulkner; Dorcas d. at Andover, 23 Sep 1837.

500)   v   ISAAC ADAMS, b. at Andover, 25 Apr 1767; d. after 1850 when he was living in Troy, MI; m. at Newburyport, MA, 7 Jun 1807, SARAH MCHARD, b. at Newburyport, 26 Apr 1777 daughter of William and Mary (-) McHard; Sarah was living in 1850.

127)   PELETIAH RUSSELL (*Peter³, Thomas², Robert¹*), b. at Andover, 27 Dec 1727 son of Peter and Deborah (Crosby) Russell; d. in Nova Scotia in 1757 during the French and Indian War; m. about 1752, OLIVE MOORE, b. at Westford, 27 Dec 1729 daughter of Samuel and Deborah (Butterfield) Moore; Olive d. at Bath, NH, 11 Oct 1807. Olive m. 2nd Timothy Barron.

As a child, Peletiah went with his family to Litchfield, New Hampshire. He and his wife Olive had five children there. From 24 April 1755 to 1 November 1755, he served as a sergeant in Capt. Tash's company of Col. Blanchard's regiment which was stationed at Fort Edward. In 1757 he participated in the Crown Point expedition serving as second lieutenant in Capt. Emery's company. Peletiah was wounded near Lake George and was taking to Nova Scotia where he died of his injuries.[324]

[320] *Essex County, MA: Probate File Papers, 1638-1881.*Online database. *AmericanAncestors.org.* New England Historic Genealogical Society, 2014. Case 10281

[321] The death transcription says 57th year of her age but this seems just an error for 37th year.

[322] Bailey, *Historical Sketches of Andover*, p 160

[323] *Essex County, MA: Probate File Papers, 1638-1881.*Online database. *AmericanAncestors.org.* New England Historic Genealogical Society, 2014. Case 255

[324] Stearns, *Genealogical and Family History of the State of New Hampshire*, volume 2, p 732

      i   REUBEN RUSSELL, b. 1 Nov 1749; d. Nov 1753.

      ii   OLIVE RUSSELL, b. 1751

501)   iii   PELETIAH RUSSELL, b. 1753; d. at Groton, MA, 21 Jan 1831; m. at Groton, 30 May 1780, SARAH DERUMPLE, b. at Groton, 23 Mar 1753 daughter of William and Elizabeth (Shed) Derumple; Sarah d. at Groton, 21 Apr 1795.

502)   iv   JOHN RUSSELL, b. 7 Sep 1753; d. at Richmond, VT, 26 Dec 1814; m. at Haverhill, NH, SARAH HAZELTINE, b. about 1760; Sarah d. at Burlington, VT, 26 Aug 1848.

503)   v   MOOR RUSSELL, b. 30 Oct 1757; d. at Holderness, NH, 29 Aug 1851; m. at Plymouth, NH, 23 Dec 1790, ELIZABETH WEBSTER, b. at Plymouth, NH, 8 Jul 1773 daughter of David and Elizabeth (Clough) Webster;[325] Elizabeth d. at Holderness, 4 Jun 1839.

128)   RACHEL RUSSELL (*Peter³, Thomas², Robert¹*), b. at Andover, 1 Nov 1730 daughter of Peter and Deborah (Crosby) Russell; d. 28 Nov 1802; m. about 1747; TIMOTHY UNDERWOOD, b. about 1725 son of Joseph and Susannah (Parker) Underwood; Timothy d. at Putney, VT, about 1804.

     Timothy Underwood was a captain of a company of minutemen in the regiment of Col. William Prescott which marched at the alarm on 19 April 1775 and had 42 days of service.[326]

     Rachel Russell and Timothy Underwood were parents of eleven children born at Westford. Timothy and Rachel moved their family from Westford to Putney, Vermont in 1776[327] where they purchased a farm in 1778. In addition to farming, Timothy produced bricks.[328]

504)   i   RACHEL UNDERWOOD, b. 21 May 1747; d. at Shrewsbury, 21 Dec 1810; m. at Shrewsbury, 1 Mar 1775, SAMUEL BRIGHAM, b. at Shrewsbury, 1 Jul 1741 son of John and Susannah (Fiske) Brigham; Samuel d. at Shrewsbury, 28 Feb 1836.

      ii   TIMOTHY UNDERWOOD, b. 15 Aug 1749; d. 30 May 1759.

      iii   JOSEPH UNDERWOOD, b. 8 Sep 1751; died young.

505)   iv   DEBORAH UNDERWOOD, b. 19 Sep 1754; d. at Putney, VT, Dec 1840; m. at Shrewsbury, 24 Jun 1773, ABNER MILES, b. at Shrewsbury, 12 Jan 1744/5 son of Joseph and Jemima (Lee) Miles; Abner d. at Putney, 1803.

506)   v   JOSEPH UNDERWOOD, b. 1 Aug 1757; d. at Putney, VT, 30 May 1818; m. at Putney, 4 Oct 1781, ELIZABETH REYNOLDS, b. Dec 1758 daughter of Grindall and Sarah (Searle) Reynolds; Elizabeth d. at Putney, Oct 1817.

507)   vi   TIMOTHY UNDERWOOD, b. 30 Nov 1759; d. at Northborough, MA, 18 Dec 1824; m. at Shrewsbury, 6 Aug 1791, MARY "POLLY" ADAMS, b. at Shrewsbury, 12 Sep 1761 daughter of Jonathan and Hephzibah (Baker) Adams;[329] Mary d. at Northborough, 13 Sep 1805. Timothy m. 2nd at Northborough, MA, 26 Jul 1807, Polly's sister, HEPHZIBAH ADAMS, b. at Shrewsbury, 20 Nov 1768; Hephzibah d. at Northborough, 2 Jan 1814.

      vii   SUSANNA UNDERWOOD, b. 6 May 1762; m. at Putney, 31 Jul 1785, JOHN MOORE. No clear information related to children in this family were found. There were possibly three children (Polly, James, and John) but records for them were not located.

508)   viii   PHINEAS UNDERWOOD, b. 18 Mar 1764; d. at Virginia, IL, 2 Apr 1843; m. SARAH who has not been identified.

509)   ix   RUSSELL UNDERWOOD, b. 16 Aug 1766; d. about 1821; m. at Shrewsbury, 1 Jan 1789, ELIZABETH "BETTY" ALLEN, b. at Shrewsbury, 13 Mar 1765 daughter of Elnathan and Thankful (Hastings) Allen;[330] Elizabeth d. at Kendall, NY, 6 Oct 1854.

---

[325] Stearns, *Genealogical and Family History of the State of New Hampshire*, volume 1, p 26
[326] Massachusetts Soldiers and Sailors in the Revolution, volume 16, p 257
[327] Underwood, *The Underwood Families of America*, volume 1, p 50
[328] De Wolfe, *The History of Putney, Vt.*, p 43, p 56
[329] The 1801 will of Jonathan Adams of Shrewsbury includes a bequest to his daughter Mary Underwood.
[330] The 1800 will of Elnathan Allen of Shrewsbury includes a bequest to his daughter Betty Underwood.

510)   x   MARY "MOLLY" UNDERWOOD, b. 10 Aug 1768; d. at Shrewsbury, 6 Oct 1789; m. 20 Dec 1786, HUMPHREY BIGELOW, b. at Shrewsbury, 4 Sep 1761 son of Samuel and Phebe (Rand) Bigelow; Humphrey d. at Shrewsbury, 2 Oct 1842. Humphrey married second Hannah Whipple.

511)   xi   JAMES UNDERWOOD, b. 7 Mar 1771; d. at Swanzey, NH, 4 Feb 1832; m. at Westmoreland, NH, 25 Apr 1793, HANNAH AMSBURY, b. at Westmoreland, 30 Jun 1775 daughter of Israel and Anna (-) Amsbury; Hannah d. at Rockingham, VT, 22 Jan 1809.

129)   PHEBE RUSSELL (*Peter³, Thomas², Robert¹*), b. at Andover, 16 May 1736 daughter of Peter and Deborah (Crosby) Russell; d. at Goffstown, NH, Nov 1836; m. 1st about 1752, JOHN BUTTERFIELD, b. at Chelmsford, 20 Feb 1731 son of John and Anne (Hildreth) Butterfield; John d. at Goffstown, 1765. Phebe m. 2nd, 774, SAMUEL ROBIE, b. at Hampton, NH, 17 Oct 1717 son of Ichabod and Sarah (Cass) Robie; Samuel d. at Goffstown, 18 Oct 1793. Samuel Robie was first married to Mary Perkins.

    John and Phebe settled in Goffstown, New Hampshire and they were parents of five children. John Butterfield died of wounds he received when accidentally shot at a blacksmith shop.[331] Phebe remarried to Samuel Robie who was a widower. Phebe and Samuel were in Goffstown by 1779. And their homestead was on what became known as Robie Hill. Samuel served as selectman and served on a committee to formulate a plan of government.[332]

    Phebe Russell and John Butterfield were parents of five children.

512)   i   JOHN BUTTERFIELD, b. at Litchfield, 7 Sep 1753; d. at New Boston, NH, 10 Oct 1828, m. about 1772, NAOMI STEVENS, b. at Plaistow, 24 Oct 1751 daughter of Thomas and Prudence (Merrill) Stevens; Naomi d. at Goffstown, 9 Jan 1816.

513)   ii   PETER BUTTERFIELD, b. at Litchfield, 6 Jan 1755; d. at Goffstown, 22 Oct 1838; m. 1st at Goffstown, 1 Oct 1776, HANNAH GAY who died at Goffstown, 1803. Peter m. 2nd 19 Aug 1810, RACHEL RICHARDS (widow of David Greer), b. 1767 daughter of Benjamin and Susannah (Eaton) Richards; Rachel d. at Goffstown, 21 Oct 1851.

514)   iii   SARAH BUTTERFIELD, b. 1758; d. at Goffstown, 2 Sep 1850; m. at Goffstown, 21 Dec 1785, ELIPHALET RICHARDS, b. at Goffstown, 1761 son of Benjamin and Susannah (Eaton) Richards; Eliphalet d. 8 Oct 1846.

515)   iv   PHEBE BUTTERFIELD, b. 1760; d. 1839 at unknown location;[333] m. 9 Dec 1779, NATHANIEL GLIDDEN, b. at Exeter, 1747 son of Nathaniel and Anna (Lord) Glidden; Nathaniel d. at Chester, NH, 26 Apr 1814.

516)   v   DEBORAH BUTTERFIELD, b. at Goffstown, 11 Jan 1762; d. at Goffstown, 11 Sep 1840; m. at Goffstown, 25 Dec 1781, JONATHAN BELL, b. at Pelham, 23 Apr 1755 son of William and Abigail (Kittredge) Bell; Jonathan d. at Goffstown, 10 Jun 1844.

    Phebe Russell and Samuel Robie were parents of three children.

517)   i   SAMUEL ROBIE, b. 1777; d. at Goffstown, 8 Jul 1865; m. about 1796, DEBORAH MOORE, b. 27 Mar 1776 daughter of Abraham and Esther (Walker) Moore; Deborah d. at Manchester, NH, 8 May 1868.

518)   ii   THOMAS R. ROBIE, b. at Goffstown, 1779; d. at Goffstown, 12 Sep 1811; m. at Goffstown, 8 Feb 1803, RACHEL BARRON, b. at Merrimack, NH, 22 Feb 1776 daughter of William and Rebecca (Fassett) Barron; Rachel d. 23 April 1839.

519)   iii   MARY ROBIE, b. at Goffstown, 1782; d. 22 Mar 1829; m. BENJAMIN WALKER PATTEE, b. 9 Jun 1781 son of John and Mary (Hadley) Pattee; Benjamin d. 17 Nov 1849.

130)   PETER RUSSELL (*Peter³, Thomas², Robert¹*), b. at Litchfield, NH, 6 Aug 1738 son of Peter and Deborah (Crosby) Russell; d. at Peeling (later Woodstock), NH, 20 Aug 1815; m. about 1760, MEHITABLE STILES, b. at Middleton, MA, 10 Jun 1739 daughter of Caleb and Sarah (Walton) Stiles; Mehitable d. at Peeling, NH, 27 May 1811.

---

[331] Hadley, *History of the Town of Goffstown*, p 61
[332] Hadley, *History of the Town of Goffstown*, p 433
[333] The Butterfield cemetery monument includes dates for Phebe wife of Nathaniel Glidden as 1760-1839.

Peter and Mehitable settled in Lyndeborough where Mehitable was admitted as a church member in 1780. It is believed that Peter served in the same company as his brother Peletiah Russell during the French and Indian War.[334] He is likely the Peter Russell of Lyndeborough who did "half a turn" of service as sergeant during the Revolution for the Ticonderoga campaign in 1776.[335]

Peter and Mehitable were parents of seven children including an unnamed infant who died soon after birth.[336]

i   PETER RUSSELL, d. about age 24 without marrying

ii   SARAH RUSSELL, b. estimate 1763; *perhaps* the Sally Bickford who d. at Dover, NH, Mar 1850 at age 90;[337] m. at Amherst, 17 Aug 1786, JOSIAH BICKFORD. No records of children were located.

520)   iii   MEHITABLE RUSSELL, b. 20 Jan 1768; d. at Charleston, ME, 4 Feb 1848; m. 1st at Amherst, 27 Nov 1788, STEPHEN KITTREDGE, b. at Tewksbury, 27 Jun 1765 son of Solomon and Tabitha (Ingalls) Kittredge; Stephen d. at Hancock, NH, 16 Oct 1806. Mehitable m. 2nd, 17 Sep 1811, DANIEL BICKFORD, b. 13 Feb 1765 son of Edmond and Elizabeth (Clough) Bickford; Daniel d. at Charleston, ME, 22 Mar 1834.

521)   iv   JOSEPH RUSSELL, b. about 1770; d. by about 1826; m. about 1795, MARY ROBBINS, b. at Plymouth, NH, about 1770 daughter of Jonathan and Mary (Fletcher) Robbins; Mary d. at Woodstock, NH, 17 Mar 1844. Mary married second John Gray on 14 Oct 1827.

522)   v   BETSEY RUSSELL, b. about 1776; d. at Hancock, NH, 21 Nov 1843; m. at Peeling, NH, 7 Feb 1805, ASA SYMONDS, b. at Groton, MA, 5 Apr 1776 son of Joseph and Mehitable (Cummings) Symonds; Asa d. at Hancock, 18 Jul 1858. Asa married Clarissa Newell on 7 May 1845.

523)   vi   MARY "POLLY" RUSSELL; b. estimate 1780; d. about 1835; m. at Woodstock, NH, 9 Mar 1809, Col. JOHN PALMER, b. at Salisbury, NH, 26 Dec 1783 son of Dudley and Rebecca (Pingry) Palmer; John d. at Meredith, NH, 8 Mar 1861.[338] John Palmer married second Betsey *Cate* Batchelder in 1837.

131)   DEBORAH RUSSELL (*Peter³, Thomas², Robert¹*), b. at Litchfield, NH, 3 Jun 1740 daughter of Peter and Deborah (Crosby) Russell; d. at Merrimack, NH, 9 Sep 1820; m. about 1758, JONATHAN CUMMINGS, b. at Dunstable, 5 Jun 1729 son of Jonathan and Elizabeth (Blanchard) Cummings; Jonathan d. at Merrimack, 10 Jul 1787.

Deborah and Jonathan resided in Merrimack, New Hampshire where Jonathan filled numerous civic duties such as fence viewer, field driver, constable, and surveyor of highways.[339]

Deborah Russell and Jonathan Cummings were parents of sixteen children born at Merrimack, New Hampshire.[340]

524)   i   JONATHAN CUMMINGS, b. 4 Mar 1759; m. at Merrimack, 28 Jun 1785, LYDIA HILLS, b. at Merrimack, 13 Jul 1761 daughter of Ebenezer and Elizabeth (-) Hills.

525)   ii   DEBORAH CUMMINGS, b. 14 Jun 1761; m. at Merrimack, 12 Apr 1781, JAMES COOMBS, b. at Merrimack, 5 Jul 1760 son of John and Margaret (Alld) Coombs; James d. at Merrimack, NH, 17 Jan 1827.

526)   iii   SYBIL CUMMINGS, b. 8 May 1763; d. at Merrimack, 17 Apr 1811; m. at Merrimack, 12 Oct 1783, as the second of his three wives, SAMUEL BARRON, b. at Bedford, NH, 26 Feb 1757 son of Moses and Lucy (Parker) Barron; Samuel d. at Merrimack, 3 Oct 1836. Lt. Samuel Barron was first married to Mary Arbuckle and third married to Jenny Moore.

527)   iv   THOMAS CUMMINGS, b. 15 Dec 1764; d. at White Pigeon, MI, 28 Nov 1838; m. 25 Oct 1792, as her second husband, ANNA GIBSON (widow of Samuel May), b. at Lyme, 1769 daughter of Samuel and Elizabeth (Stewart) Gibson;[341] Anna d. at Hinesburg, VT, 3 Sep 1845.

v   REBECCA CUMMINGS, b. 28 Sep 1767; d. 13 Jun 1782.

---

[334] Stearns, *History of Plymouth, New Hampshire*, volume 2, p 594

[335] Donovan, *History of Lyndeborough*, p 199

[336] Stearns, *History of Plymouth, New Hampshire*, volume 2, p 594

[337] New Hampshire State Library; Concord, New Hampshire; U.S. Census Mortality Schedules, New Hampshire, 1850-1880; Archive Roll Number: 3; Census Year: 1850; Census Place: Dover, Strafford, New Hampshire

[338] This is a marriage reported in the History of Plymouth. However, the marriage is in 1809 and that would be a relatively late marriage for Mary. On the other hand, there are only four children in this family all born before 1817. The death records for at least two of the children of John and Mary Palmer give mother's place of birth as Lyndeborough which would fit for Mary in this family.

[339] Merrimack Historical Society, History of Merrimack, New Hampshire, p 226

[340] The three youngest children are given in Mooar's *Cummings Memorial*, pp 58-59.

[341] The 1811 will (probate 1823) of Samuel Gibson of Merrimack includes a bequest to his daughter Anna Cummings.

528)   vi   SUSANNAH CUMMINGS, b. 7 Sep 1768; m. 7 Jan 1793, JOHN STACY.

        vii   JENNE CUMMINGS, b. 30 Sep 1770; d. 6 Sep 1775.

        viii   ELIZABETH CUMMINGS, b. 12 Sep 1772; d. at Waterville, ME, 8 Feb 1858.[342] Elizabeth did not marry. In 1850, she was living with her sister Rebecca and her husband Stephen Benson.

        ix   JOSEPH CUMMINGS, b. 29 Mar 1774; d. 16 May 1774.

        x   BENJAMIN CUMMINGS, b. 29 Mar 1774; d. 24 May 1774.

        xi   RACHEL CUMMINGS, b. 12 May 1775

529)   xii   CYRUS CUMMINGS, b. 21 May 1777; d. at Newport, VT, 11 Feb 1858; m. ABIGAIL DAVIS, b. at Poland, ME, 17 Nov 1780 daughter of Moses and Olive (Bodwell) Davis;[343] Abigail d. at Newport, 9 Feb 1854.

        xiii   MARY CUMMINGS, b. 2 Jun 1779; d. at Merrimack, 3 Mar 1830; m. 26 Mar 1823, Dr. ABEL GOODRICH, b. at Lunenburg, MA, 19 Sep 1761 son of Philip and Jane (Boynton) Goodrich;[344] Abel d. at Merrimack, 12 Jan 1841.

530)   xiv   SARAH CUMMINGS, b. 1781; m. by 1799, JOSIAH HODGMAN, b. at Merrimack, 28 Jan 1778 son of Josiah and Rebecca (Foster) Hodgman.

531)   xv   REBECCA CUMMINGS, b. 6 Apr 1783; d. at Waterville, ME, 14 Dec 1857; m. Dec 1800, STEPHEN BENSON, b. at Middleborough, 8 Jun 1777 son of Ichabod and Abigail (Griffith) Benson;[345] Stephen d. at Waterville, 27 Aug 1852.

        xvi   RUTH W. CUMMINGS, b. 13 Jul 1785

132)   JAMES RUSSELL (*Peter³, Thomas², Robert¹*), b. at Litchfield, 31 May 1746 son of Peter and Deborah (Crosby) Russell; d. at Belpre, OH, 1821; m. 1st about 1774, MARY FRENCH, b. at Dunstable, NH, 18 Oct 1755 daughter of Benjamin and Mary (Lovewell) French; Mary d. at Woodstock, VT, about 1790. James m. 2nd at Ross, OH, 9 Aug 1814 the widow JUDAH O'NEAL.

        James Russell enlisted for military service on 28 April 1775 with the rank of second lieutenant. He later achieved the rank of captain in Colonel Brooks's regiment. After the war, the family moved from Litchfield, New Hampshire to Woodstock, Vermont. Mary died there about 1790. After Mary's death, James went to Ohio where his older sons had settled.[346]

        The children of James and Mary are not well documented. There are three known sons and perhaps a fourth. There were perhaps two daughters in this family, but no certain information has been found for them. The three likely sons are given here. One of the grandsons of James and Mary, Samuel Russell son of James, died in the Civil War serving with Union forces. Another grandson, Daniel R. Russell son of Frederick, was a colonel with Confederate forces.

532)   i   ROBERT RUSSELL, b. likely at Litchfield, 30 Jan 1782; d. at Seneca County, OH, 28 Apr 1860; m. about 1808, MARY ANN KEAN, b. in VA, about 1792; Mary Ann d. at Columbus, 7 Jul 1850.

533)   ii   JAMES RUSSELL, b. about 1785; d. at Ross County, OH, about 1819; m. at Ross County, 27 Apr 1813, as her second husband, SOPHIA PARMENTER, b. 9 Oct 1793 daughter of Artemus and Lucy (Grant) Parmenter; Sophia d. at Ross County, 9 Dec 1845. Sophia was first married to Abiasher Rogers about 1809 and third married to Thomas Bradford on 5 Jul 1820.

534)   iii   FREDERICK AUGUSTUS RUSSELL, b. 13 Mar 1787; d. at Vevay, IN, 30 Apr 1866; m. 1st at Newburyport, MA, 28 Nov 1810, ANNA BARTLETT who died about 1814. Frederick m. 2nd at Washington, DC, 13 May 1815, THEODOSIA GUSTINE, b. at Culpepper, VA, 1792 daughter of Joel Trumbull and Anne (Greene) Gustine; Theodisia d. at Washington, 25 Jul 1828. Frederick m. 3rd 10 Mar 1846, ANTOINETTE DEROLODS, b. in Spain, about 1827. Antoinette d. at Vevay, 1 Sep 1898.

133)   THOMAS RUSSELL (*Joseph³, Thomas², Robert¹*), b. at Andover, 5 Jun 1732 son of Joseph and Hepsibah (Eaton) Russell; d. at Wilton, 30 Mar 1818; m. at Andover, 15 May 1760, his second cousin, BETHIAH HOLT (*Phebe Russell Holt³,*

[342] Maine, Nathan Hale Cemetery Collection, 1780-1980
[343] NEHGR, Early Vital Records of Poland, Maine, 1934, vol 88, p 60
[344] Cunningham, *History of the Town of Lunenburg*, volume E-H, p 313
[345] NEHGR, Early Vital Records of Poland, Maine, 1934, vol 88, p 155
[346] DAR, *Ohio Early State and Local History*, p 180

John², Robert¹), b. at Andover, 20 Mar 1743 daughter of Ephraim and Phebe (Russell) Holt; Bethiah d. at Wilton, 20 Aug 1817.
        Thomas and Bethiah started their family in Andover and relocated to Wilton in 1769. They were parents of eleven
children.

| | i | BETHIAH RUSSELL, b. at Andover, 20 Apr 1761; d. 25 Apr 1761. |

535) ii   BETHIAH RUSSELL, b. at Andover, 7 Jan 1763; d. likely at Dublin, NH, Dec 1821; m. 1st at Wilton, 18 Apr
            1782, DANIEL SIMONDS; Daniel d. at Dublin, about 1805. Bethiah m. 2nd at Dublin, 5 Jan 1809, DRURY
            MORSE, b. at Holliston, MA, 16 Aug 1757 son of Micah and Mary (Faribanks) Morse; Drury d. at Dublin,
            16 Nov 1820. Drury was first married to Mary Adams.

536) iii   THOMAS RUSSELL, b. at Andover, 5 Jun 1765; d. at Temple, ME, 9 Jul 1863; m. 10 Feb 1789, his fourth
            cousin once removed (through Holt lines), LYDIA ABBOTT, b. at Wilton, 1 May 1771 daughter of Jacob and
            Lydia (Stevens) Abbott; Lydia d. at Temple, 20 Jun 1855.

537) iv   HANNAH RUSSELL, b. at Andover, 23 Sep 1767; d. at Weld, ME, Nov 1850; m. at Wilton, 23 Aug 1787, her
            first cousin, JAMES HOUGHTON (*Phebe Holt Houghton⁴, Phebe Russell Holt³, John², Robert¹*), b. at
            Andover, 16 Jun 1756 son of James and Phebe (Holt) Houghton; James d. at Weld, 21 Dec 1835.

539) v   DANIEL RUSSELL, b. at Andover, 7 Nov 1769; d. at Wilton, 3 Jan 1841; m. at Wilton, 25 Nov 1794,
            ELIZABETH DASCOMB, b. at Wilton, 20 Jan 1771 daughter of James and Elizabeth (Farrington)
            Dascomb; Elizabeth d. at Wilton, 18 Oct 1852.

539) vi   PHEBE RUSSELL, b. at Wilton, 13 Sep 1772; d. at Weld, ME, 13 Sep 1852; m. about 1811, DAVID
            BARRETT, b. at Mason, NH, 1782 son of Reuben and Sarah (Fletcher) Barrett; David d. at Weld, 12 Feb
            1864.

      vii   MOLLY RUSSELL, b. at Wilton, 4 Jun 1775; d. at Peterborough, NH, 4 Jun 1864; m. 1st at Wilton, 20 Dec
            1804, THOMAS EATON, b. about 1775; Thomas d. at Wilton, Aug 1812. Molly m. 2nd 4 Feb 1817, as his
            second wife, SAMUEL EDES, b. at Needham, MA, 15 Oct 1753 son of Nathan and Sarah (-) Edes; Samuel d.
            at Peterborough, 10 Jul 1846. The 1810 census for Wilton suggests one son under the age of 10, but names
            of children were not found. Molly did not have children with Samuel Edes.

540) viii ABEL RUSSELL, b. at Wilton, 5 Feb 1778; d. at Weld, ME, 10 Jun 1859; m. at Royalston, MA, 2 Jan 1806,
            NANCY CLEMENT, b. at Petersham, MA, 2 Sep 1780 daughter of Thomas and Mary (Smith) Clement;
            Nancy d. at Weld, 25 Feb 1862.

541) ix   JOSEPH RUSSELL, b. at Wilton, 6 May 1780; d. at Weld, ME, 28 Jun 1858; m. 1st about 1802, HANNAH
            DASCOMB, b. at Wilton, about 1779 daughter of James and Elizabeth (Farrington) Dascomb;[347] Hannah d.
            at Weld, 17 Dec 1806. Joseph m. 2nd 8 Jan 1809, his fourth cousin, SARAH HOLT, b. at Wilton, 21 Sep 1780
            daughter of Simeon and Mary (Dale) Holt; Sarah d. at Weld, 13 Mar 1857.

542) x   EPHRAIM RUSSELL, b. at Wilton, 16 Jul 1783; d. at Readfield, ME, 3 Dec 1875; m. 6 Apr 1809, REBECCA
            IRELAND, b. at Canaan, ME, 1789 daughter of Abraham and Betsey (Wyman) Ireland; Rebecca d. at Weld,
            ME, 2 Apr 1833.

      xi   ASENATH RUSSELL, b. at Wilton, 31 May 1786; d. at Weld, ME, 17 May 1868. Asenath did not marry.

134)   JONATHAN RUSSELL (*Joseph³, Thomas², Robert¹*), b. at Andover, 14 Oct 1749 son of Joseph and Hannah (Perkins)
Russell; d. after 1820 when he was living in Pamelia, NY; m. at Middleton, 17 Jan 1771, RUTH HUTCHINSON, baptized 16
Sep 1750 daughter of Josiah and Sarah (Dean) Hutchinson; Ruth d. after 1820.
        Jonathan and Ruth married and started their family in Middleton where Ruth's family lived. Three children were
born in Middleton, and they then relocated to Wendell where their remaining children were born. Jonathan and Ruth remained
in Wendell until 2 January 1816 when they sold "the farm on which I now live" consisting of about 75 acres to Fester Foster of
Petersham for $450.[348] They were then in Pamelia, Jefferson County, New York where several of their children were also
located. In the 1820 census, Jonathan Russell above age 45 with one female above age 45 were living in Pamelia. Living next to
them was son James and his young family. Nearby were daughter Hannah and her husband Stephen Farr and daughter Rachel
and her husband Curtis Goulding.[349] Daughter Phebe and her husband Reuben Locke also settled in Pamelia.
        Jonathan and Ruth were parents of eleven children.[350]

---

[347] Cunningham, *History of Lunenburg*, volume A-D, p 178
[348] Massachusetts Land Records, 1620-1986, Franklin County, Deed 1815-1816 volume 35, pp 517-519
[349] 1820 U S Census; Census Place: Pamelia, Jefferson, New York; Page: 456; NARA Roll: M33_72; Image: 248
[350] Vital Records of Wendell, 1760-1896, p 33 and p 262; accessed through familysearch.org

543)   i   JOSEPH RUSSELL, b. at Middleton, 19 Jul 1771; d. at Alexandria, NY (burial Orleans Four Corners), 23 Oct 1853; m. at Montague, MA, 1 Apr 1795, POLLY W. BENJAMIN, b. likely at Hardwick, MA, 1775 daughter of Abel and Susannah (Carpenter) Benjamin; Polly d. after 1850 when she and Joseph were living with their daughter and son-in-law in Alexandria.

544)   ii   BETSY RUSSELL (twin), b. at Middleton, 18 Sep 1773; d. after 1870 when she was living (age 97) at the home of her son Lyman in Pamelia; m. at Warren, MA, 1 Dec 1796, ROBERT WHITE, b. at Warren, MA, 26 May 1774 son of William and Janet (Marr) White; Robert d. at Pamelia, 30 Oct 1851.

       iii   RUTH RUSSELL (twin), b. at Middleton, 18 Sep 1773; d. at Wendell, 2 Aug 1790.

       iv   SARAH RUSSELL, b. at Wendell, 7 Feb 1780

545)   v   HANNAH RUSSELL, b. at Wendell, 3 Jan 1782; d. about 1824; m. at Wendell, 18 Feb 1806, STEPHEN FARR, b. 14 Aug 1781 son of Stephen and Lois (Randall) Farr; Stephen d. at Clayton, NY, 1872.

546)   vi   RACHEL RUSSELL, b. at Wendell, 17 Oct 1783; d. at Pamelia, 21 Mar 1871; m. at Wendell, 1805, CURTIS GOULDING, b. at Holliston, MA, 10 Aug 1776 son of Joseph and Kezia (Parker) Goulding; Curtis d. at Pamelia, 10 Jul 1857.

547)   vii   PHEBE RUSSELL, b. at Wendell, 19 Oct 1785; d. at Pamelia, NY, 27 Jan 1856; m. at Wendell, 28 Jan 1805, REUBEN LOCKE, b. at Shutesbury, MA, 6 Apr 1783 son of Ebenezer and Hannah (Randall) Locke; Reuben d. at Pamelia, 30 Oct 1855.

       viii   JONATHAN RUSSELL, b. at Wendell, 12 Sep 1786; d. 30 Jul 1808.

       ix   Son twin b. and d. 30 Nov 1790

       x   Daughter twin b. and d. 30 Nov 1790

548)   xi   JAMES RUSSELL, b. at Wendell, 27 Jul 1793; d. after 1870 when he was living in Pea Ridge, IL at the home of his daughter Harriet and her husband; m. 1st LORA, b. about 1796 and who d. after 1860. James m. 2nd MINERVA, b. about 1797; Minerva d. after 1870 when she was living at Pea Ridge.

135)   SARAH RUSSELL (*Joseph³, Thomas², Robert¹*), b. at Andover, 29 Oct 1750 daughter of Joseph and Hannah (Perkins) Russell; d. at Middleton, MA, 2 Jan 1844; m. at Middleton, 12 Aug 1772, NEHEMIAH WILKINS, b. at Middleton, 14 Aug 1752 son of Ichabod and Mary (Clark) Wilkins; Nehemiah d. at Middleton, 17 Jun 1811.

Nehemiah Wilkins served in the Revolution as a private in the company of Capt. Stephen Wilkins from 1 July 1776 to 7 January 1777. In 1837, Sarah applied for and received a widow's pension.

In September 1776, Nehemiah wrote the following letter to Sarah from Camp Ticonderoga: "Dear wife and parents and all ther friends I take this my opportunity to inform you of my Estate hoping thes Lines will find you and our Children and my parents and all other of my friends well through the Goodness of god. I my Self have been very poorley but I am betor so I leave our fetague is Very Hard so that wee cant Hardly get time to cook. It is very sickly, There was to of men fired on by the Ingines yesterday between ground pint and Ticonderoga but made there Escape with out being hurt there was a party of Ingines seen by the mils and wee espect the Regulers very. Out alowans is very poore sum times half a pund of meat and a pound and a half of bread and sum times a pound of meat and one pound of bread no saus nor no pint only when upon fetague then we have half a glas of rum, Rum is one doler per quart shugar and cheas two shillings per pound. I beg you to write to me so send said to ware receive this. I still remain your Loving Husband till Deth shall part, Nehemiah Wilkins."

On 26 September 1776, Sarah wrote this letter to her husband: "Thes lines comes with my love to you hoping that by the blessing of God that tha will find you in good health as has left me and the children and I shall be glad that you would come home when your time is oute, and your father and mother is well and all your friends so nomore at prissent but I remain your faithful wife, Sary Wilkins." [351]

On 21 February 1803, Nehemiah Wilkins conveyed to Nehemiah Wilkins, Jr., mariner, a tract of land in Middleton consisting of seven and one-half acres for $175.[352] On 15 April 1806, Nehemiah Wilkins, for $480, conveyed to Ephraim Wilkins the farm in Middleton with buildings. For an additional $228.32, Nehemiah sold to Ephraim a lengthy list of household items and tools including four beds, thirteen chairs, kitchen items, axe, and two candlesticks.[353]

Sarah Russell and Nehemiah Wilkins were parents of ten children born at Middleton.

[351] Revolutionary War Pension and Bounty-Land Warrant Application Files, Case W26086. The two letters are included in the pension application file.
[352] Massachusetts Land Records, Essex County, 171:180
[353] Massachusetts Land Records, Essex County, 177:213; 177:214

     i   SARAH WILKINS, b. 18 Mar 1774; d. likely at Danvers, 1816;[354] m. likely 15 Mar 1804, EBENEZER GOODHUE, b. at Bradford, 20 Mar 1783 son of Phineas and Hannah (Parsons) Goodhue; Ebenezer d. at Middleton, 20 Mar 1843. Ebenezer married second Sarah's sister Mary. Sarah and Ebenezer did not have children.

549) ii   LUCY WILKINS, b. 20 Oct 1775; d. at Topsfield, 9 Dec 1868; m. at Middleton, 20 May 1802, MOSES PERKINS, b. at Topsfield, 21 Aug 1775 son of Oliver and Lucy (Gould) Perkins; Moses d. at Topsfield, 18 Oct 1858.

550) iii ABIGAIL WILKINS, b. 7 Sep 1777; d. at Middleton, 8 Apr 1806; m. at Middleton, 13 May 1798, JOSEPH WRIGHT, b. about 1770; Joseph d. at Middleton, 5 Nov 1836.

    iv NEHEMIAH WILKINS, b. 16 Dec 1779; likely the mariner Nehemiah lost at sea, Nov 1803. "Nehemiah, mariner in the schooner Friendship, sailed from Winyan, Nov. —, 1803, lost at sea, ____. P. R. 82."

551) v   EPHRAIM WILKINS, b. 13 Sep 1781; d. at Middleton, 22 Feb 1827; m. at Middleton, 6 Apr 1806, HANNAH DIXEY, baptized at Marblehead, 8 Jul 1787 daughter of Richard and Rebecca (Homan) Dixey; Hannah d. at Middleton, 4 Sep 1831.

    vi MARY WILKINS, b. 31 Oct 1783; d. at Middleton, 7 Mar 1861; m. at Middleton, 28 Sep 1816, EBENEZER GOODHUE (see sister Sarah above). Mary and Ebenezer did not have children.

552) vii JAMES WILKINS, b. 1 Nov 1785; d. at Middleton, 23 Jul 1875; m. 1 May 1817, BETSEY WILKINS, b. at Middleton, 21 Jan 1793 daughter of Samuel and Sarah (Fuller) Wilkins;[355] Betsey d. at Middleton, 21 Jun 1872.

    viii ROBERT CLARK WILKINS, b. 5 Mar 1788; d. at Middleton, 21 Aug 1827. Robert does not seem to have married.

553) ix NANCY WILKINS, b. 18 Mar 1790; d. at Danvers, 26 Aug 1874; m. at Middleton, 22 Oct 1812, WILLIAM GIFFORD, b. at Danvers, 27 Feb 1784 son of William and Lydia (Putnam) Gifford; William d. at Middleton, 2 Jan 1849.

554) x   JESSE WILKINS, b. 8 Mar 1792; d. at Middleton, 27 Jan 1827; m. at Middleton, 10 Oct 1810, PEGGY PEABODY, b. 14 Dec 1791 daughter of Benjamin and Hannah (Black) Peabody; Peggy d. at Middleton, 21 Dec 1840.

136)   JAMES RUSSELL (*Joseph³, Thomas², Robert¹*), b. at Andover, 7 Jan 1753 son of Joseph and Hannah (Perkins) Russell; d. at Boxford, 24 Apr 1830; m. about 1782, REBECCA PEABODY, b. at Middleton, 24 Mar 1763 daughter of Joseph and Mary (-) Peabody; Rebecca d. at Middleton, 11 Oct 1844.

James and Rebecca started their family in Middleton but moved to Boxford in 1784. In 1824, James conveyed the homestead farm to his sons Perkins and Peabody.[356]

James Russell and Rebecca Peabody were parents of eleven children, the oldest child born at Middleton and the remainder at Boxford.

555) i   JOSEPH RUSSELL, b. 14 Mar 1783; d. at Lyndeborough, NH, 14 Mar 1827; m. at Lyndeborough, 13 Jan 1805, NAOMI WILKINS, b. at Amherst, NH, 16 May 1783 daughter of Aaron and Lydia (Smith) Wilkins; Naomi d. at Lyndeborough, 2 Jun 1869.[357]

    ii REBECCA RUSSELL, b. 14 Apr 1785; d. at Londonderry, about 1811 (husband's remarriage); m. at Londonderry, 21 May 1804, ELIJAH DWINELL. Elijah married Emilia Eastman on 7 Mar 1812. Nothing further was found related to Rebecca and Elijah.

556) iii JAMES RUSSELL, b. 4 Oct 1787; d. of cholera at Lowell, 5 Sep 1849; m. at Lyndeborough, 18 Aug 1816, HANNAH PEABODY, b. at Middleton, 6 Feb 1793 daughter of Nathaniel and Ruth (Elliott) Peabody; Hannah d. at Lowell, 12 Feb 1881.

    iv PERKINS RUSSELL (twin), b. 2 Dec 1789; d. at Boxford, 14 Aug 1857; m. at Salem, 27 Aug 1848, ANN PERKINS who has not been identified. Perkins married late in life and did not have children. At the

[354] U.S., Newspaper Extractions from the Northeast, 1704-1930
[355] The names of Betsey's parents are given as Samuel Wilkins and Sarah Fuller on her death record.
[356] Perley, *The Dwellings of Boxford*, p 137
[357] Donovan, *The History of the Town of Lyndeborough*, p 848

probate, widow Ann stated he had no issue and she was the only one entitled to the estate. Although married, Perkins and Ann were not living together in either the 1850 or the 1855 census at which time Perkins was living with other relatives.

557)   v   PEABODY RUSSELL (twin), b. 2 Dec 1789; d. at Boxford, 14 Aug 1846; m. at Middleton, 17 Jan 1817, DOLLY KENNEY, b. at Middleton, 6 Nov 1785 daughter of Archelaus and Elizabeth (·) Kenney; Dolly d. at Boxford, 1 Jul 1845.

558)   vi   MARY "POLLY" RUSSELL, b. 15 Apr 1792; d. at North Reading, 11 Oct 1884; m. at Middleton, 30 Oct 1813, FRANCIS PEABODY, b. at Middleton, 12 Feb 1793 son of Francis and Lucy (Masury) Peabody; Francis d. at Middleton, 16 Feb 1866.

     vii   ALMOODY RUSSELL, b. 25 Apr 1794; nothing further found.

     viii   DANIEL RUSSELL, b. 15 Oct 1796; d. at Boxford, 1819.

559)   ix   SAMUEL RUSSELL, b. 27 May 1799; d. at Salem, 19 Apr 1831; m. at Salem, 26 May 1822, LYDIA BRIDGES PICKETT, b. at Rowley, 14 May 1798 daughter of Benjamin Scudder and Sarah (Bridges) Pickett; Lydia d. at Boston, 18 Apr 1841.

560)   x   IRA RUSSELL, b. 21 Apr 1802; d. at Manchester, NH, 1 Mar 1859; m. at Lowell, 14 Nov 1831, MARY JANE ALLEN, b. 1809; Mary Jane d. at Manchester, 3 Apr 1883.

561)   xi   PETER RUSSELL, b. 3 Oct 1805; d. at Danvers, 14 Apr 1843; m. at Danvers, 20 Dec 1832, MEHITABLE P. DWINELL, b. at Danvers, 22 May 1805 daughter of Stephen and Mehitable (Putnam) Dwinell; Mehitable d. at Danvers, 5 Feb 1880.

137)   RACHEL RUSSELL (*Joseph³, Thomas², Robert¹*), b. at Andover, 23 Feb 1757 daughter of Joseph and Hannah (Perkins) Russell; m. at Middleton, 29 Jan 1784, JONATHAN DWINELLS,[358] b. at Lynn, 4 May 1759 son of David and Keziah (Ramsdell) Dunnel. Rachel and Jonathan were living in Hillsborough, New Hampshire in 1830 (male and female each age 70-79 in the 1830 census).

     Rachel and Jonathan were in Middleton for the first years of their marriage and three children were born there. They were in Hillsborough, New Hampshire in 1790 where two more children were born.[359] They were still living in Hillsborough in 1830, but no record of their deaths was found.

     i   CATHERINE DWINELLS, b. at Middleton, 1 Jan 1786; nothing further found.

562)   ii   LYDIA SYMONDS DWINELLS, b. at Middleton, 28 Sep 1787; d. at Hillsborough, 27 Sep 1874; m. at Hillsborough, 25 Deb 1817, ADAM D. MILLS, b. at Deering, about 1790 son of Robert and Margaret (Dinsmoor) Mills;[360] Adam d. at Deering, 30 Sep 1866.

563)   iii   CHARLOTTE DWINELLS, b. at Middleton, 26 May 1789; d. after 1870 when she was living with her son Hiram at Hinsdale, NY; m. at Hillsborough, 8 Sep 1808, DANIEL WILEY who is not yet identified. Charlotte was a widow at least by 1855 and likely much before.

564)   iv   JONATHAN DWINELLS, b. at Hillsborough, 10 Sep 1795; d. at Yorkshire, NY, 1881 (probate 16 May 1881); m. about 1823, ELIZABETH "BETSEY" ATWOOD, b. about 1795; Betsey d. at Yorkshire, 27 Sep 1880.

565)   v   JAMES DWINELLS, b. at Hillsborough, 28 Jun 1800; d. at West Canaan, NH, 17 Dec 1859; m. at Hillsborough, 22 Feb 1832, LOUISA R. CRAIN, b. at Hillsborough, 24 Mar 1806 daughter of Joshua and Sarah (Giddings) Crain; Louisa d. at West Canaan, 18 Oct 1857. Louisa's father Dr. Joshua Crain was a physician and surgeon in Hillsborough.[361]

138)   HANNAH RUSSELL (*Joseph³, Thomas², Robert¹*), b. at Andover, 11 Oct 1760 daughter of Joseph and Hannah (Perkins) Russell; d. at Newburyport, 24 Aug 1840; m. at Middleton, 10 May 1784, CALEB PUTNAM, b. at Danvers, 24 Nov 1763 son of Archelaus and Abigail (Goodrich) Putnam; Caleb d. at Newburyport, 6 Mar 1826.

---

[358] Jonathan's last name has multiple spellings. On his birth record it is Dunnell, but Dwinell at marriage, but the name seems to settle as Dwinells which is the spelling used by the children, although some use Dwinnells.
[359] Browne, *The History of Hillsborough*, p 186
[360] Adam's death record gives the names of his parents as Robert and Margaret Mills.
[361] Browne, *The History of Hillsborough*, p 154

Hannah Russell and Caleb Putnam were parents of at least seven children. There are perhaps one or two other children who died in childhood, but records are scant. The family seems to have been mostly in Newburyport but were also in Maine and New Hampshire. They were in Topsham, Maine in the 1790 census and in Newburyport in 1820. The two oldest children settled in Mississippi.

566)   i   JAMES RUSSELL PUTNAM, b. at Topsham, ME, 11 Nov 1789; d. at Vicksburg, MS, 1 Apr 1843; m. in Davidson County, TN, 24 May 1822, SOPHIA ANN PERKINS, b. about 1802; Sophia d. at New Orleans, 1851.

567)   ii   CHARLES CALEB PUTNAM, b. about 1790; d. at Canton, MS, 1862; m. at Washington, DC, MARGARET MURDOCH, b. 4 Jul 1805 daughter of John and Ann (Corby) Murdoch;[362] Margaret d. at Orleans, LA, 13 Apr 1886.

568)   iii   ABIGAIL PUTNAM, b. perhaps at Lyme, NH, about 1793; m. at Hallowell, ME, 4 Apr 1813, JOHN KINSMAN GILMAN, b. at Exeter, NH, 14 Aug 1787 son of Samuel and Martha (Kinsman) Gilman.

         iv   HANNAH RUSSELL PUTNAM, b. at Lyme, about 1795; d. at Stoneham, MA (although resident of Newburyport), 12 Sep 1874. Hannah did not marry.

569)   v   DEBORAH PUTNAM, b. at Lyme, about 1797; d. at Newburyport, 1 Sep 1877; m. at Newburyport, 24 May 1825, WILLIAM GREELEY.

570)   vi   BENJAMIN FRANKLIN PUTNAM, b. about 1800; d. at Boston, 5 Jan 1845; m. at Portsmouth, NH, 14 May 1824, NANCY MELCHER, b. at Portsmouth, about 1799 daughter of Nathaniel and Elizabeth (Ward) Melcher;[363] Nancy d. at Boston, 6 Jul 1856.

         vii   JOHN PUTNAM, b. 1802; d. at Newburyport, 20 Sep 1805.

139)   SARAH HUNT (*Jemima Russell Hunt³, Thomas², Robert¹*), b. at Billerica, 23 Dec 1725 daughter of Joseph and Jemima (Russell) Hunt; m. at Westford, 7 Mar 1750, JOSIAH JOHNSON, b. at Lancaster, 5 Jun 1726 son of Josiah and Annis (Chandler) Johnson.
        Records are scant for this family. An account of son Jeremiah Johnson written by Jeremiah's grandson states he had two brothers and three sisters and suggests that one of Jeremiah's sisters married a Kimball and another married a Bingham.[364] The is an additional son Thomas that is identified from the pension record of son Jeremiah.

         i   JOSIAH JOHNSON, b. at Leominster, 20 Jan 1752

         ii   HANNAH JOHNSON, b. at Westford, 1754[365]

         iii   THOMAS JOHNSON, b. about 1756; d. at Moreau, NY, before 1819; m. MARTHA who is known only from the pension record of Thomas's brother Jeremiah. Martha was living in Windsor County, VT in 1819.[366]

571)   iv   JEMIMA JOHNSON, b. at Montague, 2 May 1757; *perhaps* m. at Newton, NH, 5 Apr 1784, ARCHELAUS COLBY, b. at Newton, 24 Mar 1762 son of Moses and Mary (Sargent) Colby; Archelaus d. at Dunbarton, 20 Feb 1827.

572)   v   JOSEPH JOHNSON, b. at Montague, 21 Jan 1761; m. 1st about 1785, MARY HUNT; Mary d. at Charlestown, NH, about 1796. Joseph m. 2nd about 1797, ANNA who has not been identified.

573)   vi   JEREMIAH JOHNSON, b. at Montague, 16 Sep 1763; d. at Reading, VT, 2 Dec 1847; m. 1st at Charlestown, NH, THOMAZIN "FANNY" BLANCHARD, b. at Quincy, MA, 20 Sep 1765 daughter of Nehemiah and Mary (Gibson) Blanchard; Fanny d. at Reading, 10 Dec 1824. Jeremiah m. 2nd about 1826, SYBIL KIMBALL; Sybil d. at Mineral Point, WI, 1852 where she had been living with her son Solon Kimball Johnson.

574)   vii   SARAH JOHNSON, b. at Montague, 24 Apr 1766; m. at Springfield, VT, 19 Dec 1787, HORATIO BINGHAM, b. about 1765. Sarah and Horatio were living in Springfield, VT in 1830.

---

[362] The 1820 will of John Murdoch of Washington, DC gives Margaret's date of birth and the maiden name of her mother.
[363] The names of Nancy's parents are given as Nathaniel and Elizabeth Melcher on her death record.
[364] Johnson, *The Johnson Memorial: Jeremiah Johnson and Thomazin Blanchard Johnson, His Wife*, p 25
[365] Hannah is a possible daughter in this family.
[366] U. S. Revolutionary War Pension and Bounty-Land Warrant Application Files, Jeremiah Johnson, Case S39789

140)   ROBERT HUNT (*Jemima Russell Hunt³, Thomas², Robert¹*), b. at Billerica, 20 Jan 1731/2 son of Joseph and Jemima (Russell) Hunt; m. at Canaan, CT, 26 Dec 1753, REBEKAH PECK, b. at Litchfield, 15 Dec 1736 daughter of Isaac and Ruth (Tomlinson) Peck; Rebekah d. at Salisbury, CT, 1812.

Robert Hunt and Rebekah Peck were parents of twelve children born at Canaan, Connecticut.[367]

	i	AMOS HUNT, b. 14 Jul 1754; d. at Canaan, 8 Jun 1768.
575)	ii	RUSSELL HUNT, b. 11 Mar 1756; d. at Canaan, 26 Aug 1831; m. ESTHER BEEBE,[368] b. 1763 daughter of Asahel and Rebecca (Wright) Beebe;[369] Hester d. at Canaan, 8 Jul 1850.
	iii	CHLOE HUNT, b. 7 Feb 1759; d. at Sherburne, NY, 3 Jan 1822; m. at Canaan, 18 Nov 1777, AARON MILLS, b. at Staatsburg, NY, 1754[370] son of Daniel and Jerusha (Steele) Mills; Aaron d. at Sherburne, 18 Apr 1835. The pension file for Aaron Miles has no mention of children. The 1810 census suggests one child in the family, but no names of children have been located.
576)	iv	SAMPSON ROBERT HUNT, b. 23 Feb 1761; d. at Glastonbury, CT, 30 Jul 1826; m. 1st about 1782, CHARITY DUTCHER, b. at Glastonbury, 30 Jan 1764 daughter of Rufus and Jane (Ashley) Dutcher; Charity d. at Glastonbury, 23 Feb 1807. Samson m. 2nd at Glastonbury, 23 Oct 1807, POLLY BIDWELL, b. at Glastonbury, 4 Apr 1785 daughter of Jonathan and Hannah (Matson) Bidwell.[371]
577)	v	SARAH HUNT, b. 11 Jun 1763; d. at Salisbury, 1 Oct 1832; m. RUFUS LANDON, b. at Salisbury, CT, 4 Feb 1759 son of John and Katherine (-) Landon;[372][373] Rufus d. at Salisbury, 17 Jan 1848. Rufus married second Huldah.
	vi	MILO HUNT, b. 11 Oct 1765; d. at Montague, MA, 16 Mar 1815; m. LYDIA ROWE, b. at Montague, 15 Jan 1770 daughter of Daniel and Lucretia (Austin) Rowe; Lydia d. of typhus, at Montague, 6 Dec 1818. Milo and Lydia do not seem to have had children. In the 1810 census at Montague the household consists of one male 26-44 and one female 26-44.[374]
578)	vii	JOHN HUNT, b. 11 Dec 1767; d. at Glastonbury, 28 Feb 1831; m. at Glastonbury, 18 Feb 1790, ELIZABETH PULSIFER, b. at Glastonbury, 21 Feb 1773 daughter of Sylvester and Huldah (Hollister) Pulsifer; Elizabeth d. at New Haven, 28 Sep 1820.[375]
579)	viii	EMMA HUNT, b. 19 Dec 1769; d. at Great Barrington, MA, 17 Oct 1862; m. 1st EZRA TUPPER, b. at Stafford, CT, 19 Mar 1766 son of Solomon and Abiah (West) Tupper. Emma m. 2nd at Sherburne, NY, 17 Feb 1815, as his second wife, JOHN WOODWARD DEWEY, b. at Lebanon, CT, 31 Dec 1762 son of John and Rhoda (Gillett) Dewey; John d. at Hamilton, Canada West while visiting his daughter, 15 Nov 1839.[376] John W. Dewey was first married to Abigail Rudd.
	ix	FREDERICK HUNT, b. 29 Feb 1772; perhaps m. at Canaan, 27 Feb 1793, JERUSHA LOWREY, b. at Canaan, 21 Feb 1774 daughter of Nathaniel and Jerusha (Newell) Lowrey. Frederick was living in Litchfield, CT in 1800 and census records suggest two children at that time, but records have not been located.
	x	ELIZABETH "BETSEY" HUNT, b. 29 May 1774. Elizabeth is reported as marrying a Beebe who was perhaps Solomon Beebe son of Asahel and Rebecca (Wright) Beebe. Clear records for her marriage and possible children were not located.
	xi	REBECCA HUNT, b. 13 Aug 1778. She is reported in the Hunt genealogy as marrying a Knickerbocker, but no clear information related to that was found. It is remotely possible that she was the wife of Solomon Knickerbocker (1783-1831) whose wife was named Rebecca. However, the youngest child of that Knickerbocker was born in 1829 which seems a stretch in terms of Rebecca Hunt's birth in 1778.

---

[367] Connecticut Births and Christenings, 1649-1906

[368] Name is given as both Esther and Hester in records but is Esther on her gravestone.

[369] The 1806 probate distribution for the estate of Asahel Bugbee includes a distribution to daughter Hester Hunt.

[370] U. S. Revolutionary War Pension and Bounty-Land Application Files, Case S13927

[371] The name of Polly's father as Jonathan is given on the marriage transcription. The 1810 will of Jonathan Hunt of Glastonbury includes a bequest to his daughter Polly Hunt.

[372] Date and place of birth are given in Rufus's Revolutionary War pension application file.

[373] *Salisbury, CT: Vital Records, 1720-1914.* (Online Database, NewEnglandAncestors.org. New England Historic Genealogical Society, 2010.) p 54

[374] Year: 1810; Census Place: Montague, Hampshire, Massachusetts; Roll: 19; Page: 236; Image: 00248; Family History Library Film: 0205627

[375] *U.S., Newspaper Extractions from the Northeast, 1704-1930.*

[376] Dewey, *Life of George Dewey and Dewey Family History*, p 441

xii   AMOS HUNT, b. 17 Jul 1780. Amos is reported in the Hunt genealogy as marrying and having one sone Salmon born in 1823. This possible Salmon Hunt may have married Harriet born about 1823 and was living in Peoria, IL in 1850. This is a family that needs further research.

141)   RUSSELL HUNT (*Jemima Russell Hunt³, Thomas², Robert¹*), b. at Billerica, about 1733 son of Joseph and Jemima (Russell) Hunt; d. at Canaan, CT, 18 Oct 1806; m. at Canaan, 3 May 1758, LYDIA PECK, b. about 1738 likely the daughter of Isaac and Ruth (Tomlinson) Peck; Lydia d. at Canaan, 18 Feb 1818.

Russell Hunt did not leave a will and the estate entered probate 11 November 1806 with Amos Hunt and Salmon Hunt providing the administrative bond. The total value of his estate was $3,043.44 in an inventory made 10 December 1806. The widow's dower was set off to Lydia 11 May 1807.[377]

Russell Hunt and Lydia Peck were parents of eight children born at Canaan.

i   ISAAC HUNT, b. 9 Apr 1759

580)   ii   RUSSELL HUNT, b. 11 Oct 1762; d. at Canaan, 20 Jan 1839; m. 1st about 1785, LUCY SWIFT who has not been identified.

581)   iii   SALMON HUNT, b. 23 Jan 1765; d. at Canaan, 28 Apr 1839; m. REUBY WHITNEY, b. at Canaan, about 1765 daughter of John and Elizabeth (Adams) Whitney;[378] Reuby d. at Canaan, 10 Feb 1837.

582)   iv   DAVID HUNT, b. 22 Apr 1767; d. at Canaan, 22 Feb 1834; m. 1st at Canaan, 1791, HANNAH JOHNSON, b. about 1768; Hannah d. at Canaan, 2 Feb 1806. David m. 2nd 1807, WEALTHY ANN BURRALL, b. 16 Oct 1775 daughter of William and Elizabeth (Morgan) Burrall;[379] Wealthy d. 9 Apr 1840.

v   CYRUS HUNT, b. 25 Sep 1769

583)   vi   LYDIA HUNT, b. 18 Feb 1772; d. at South Danby, NY, 6 Jul 1826; m. WILLIAM HUGG, b. at Canaan, CT, 18 Dec 1764 son of William and Margaret (Johnson) Hugg; William d. at South Danby, 10 Jun 1826.

584)   vii   AMOS HUNT, b. 6 May 1774; d. (buried at South Canaan), 13 Jul 1851; m. MARY LOWRY, b. 1779 daughter of Nathaniel and Jerusha (Newell) Lowry; Mary d. at Canaan, 19 Aug 1863.

585)   viii   JEMIMA HUNT, b. 1777; d. at Cornwall, CT, 7 Apr 1832; m. JOSEPH WILCOX, b. 1769; Joseph d. at Cornwall, 23 Mar 1852.

142)   JAMES RUSSELL (*James³, Thomas², Robert¹*), b. at North Yarmouth, 7 Aug 1737 son of James and Rhoda (Chandler) Russell; m. at North Yarmouth, 5 Jun 1760, LYDIA MITCHELL.

James Russell and Lydia Mitchell were parents of six children born at North Yarmouth.

i   PHEBE RUSSELL, b. 2 Sep 1760

586)   ii   LYDIA RUSSELL, b. 12 Mar 1762; d. after 1820 when she was living at Brokenstraw; m. 13 Aug 1782, SOLOMON JORDAN, b. Sep 1756 *perhaps* son of Elijah and Joanna (Veasey) Jordan; Solomon d. at Brokenstraw, PA, 4 Mar 1846.

587)   iii   TEMPERANCE RUSSELL, b. 27 Apr 1764; d. at South Waterford, ME, 18 Jan 1831; m. about 1783, DAVID JORDAN, b. 1759 son of Elijah and Joanna (Veasey) Jordan; David d. at South Waterford, 30 May 1847.

588)   iv   JANE "JENNY" RUSSELL, baptized 10 Jun 1770; d. at Norway, ME, 1 Mar 1856; m. at New Gloucester, ME, 4 Jun 1791, as his second wife, JAMES LEBARON, b. at Middleborough, MA, 30 Nov 1759 son of James and Hannah (Turner) LeBaron;[380] James d. at Paris, ME, 9 Jun 1836. James was first married to Elizabeth Washburn.

589)   v   EUNICE RUSSELL, b. 1772; d. at New Gloucester, ME, 24 Dec 1825; m. ENOCH MORSE, b. 3 Jul 1772 son of John and Sarah (Sander) Morse; Enoch d. at New Gloucester, 16 Aug 1852.

---

[377] *Connecticut State Library (Hartford, Connecticut);* Probate Place: *Hartford, Connecticut, Probate Packets, Hull-Kilmer, 1755-1880, Russell Hunt, Case 1739*

[378] The 1793 estate of John Whitney of Canaan includes a distribution to Ruby and Salmon Hunt.

[379] Morgan, *Morgan Genealogy: James Morgan of New London, Conn. and His Descendants*

[380] Lapham and Maxim, *History of Paris, Maine*, p 659

590)   vi   NATHANIEL RUSSELL, b. about 1774 (based on age 68 at death); d. at Oxford, ME, 10 Nov 1842; m. SARAH MORSE, b. at Oxford, ME, 26 Sep 1774 daughter of John and Sarah (Sanders) Morse; Sarah d. at Norway, ME, 20 Jul 1861.

143)   THOMAS CHANDLER RUSSELL (*James³, Thomas², Robert¹*), b. at Cumberland, 9 Oct 1740 son of James and Rhoda (Chandler) Russell; m. about 1767, SARAH GOOCH, b. 17 Oct 1751 daughter of John and Elizabeth (Boothbay) Gooch.
        There are records of fifteen children of Thomas C. Russell and Sarah Gooch all born (recorded) at Cumberland, Maine.[381]

591)   i   BETSY RUSSELL, b. at Cumberland, 23 Jun 1768; d. at Hartford, ME, 14 May 1857; m. 1st at North Yarmouth, Dec 1785, DANIEL BROWN, b. at Cumberland, 10 Dec 1756 son of Jacob and Lydia (Weare) Brown; Daniel d. at Yarmouth, Oct 1797. Betsy m. 2nd 11 Mar 1800, her first cousin, JEREMIAH RUSSELL (*Joseph⁴, James³, Thomas², Robert¹*), b. at Yarmouth, 3 Apr 1772 son of Joseph and Miriam (Brown) Russell; Jeremiah d. at Hartford, ME, 30 Nov 1843.[382]

592)   ii   RHODA RUSSELL, b. at Cumberland, 10 Mar 1770; d. at West Boylston, MA, 13 Dec 1852; m. at Cumberland, 1787, SAMUEL LAWRENCE, b. at Cumberland, 6 Jul 1766 son of Joseph and Abigail (Brown) Lawrence; Samuel d. at West Boylston, 31 Mar 1824.

593)   iii   JAMES RUSSELL, b. 3 Dec 1771; d. at North Yarmouth, 5 Jul 1859; m. at Cumberland, 20 Dec 1796, JOANNA TRUE, b. at Cumberland, 22 Aug 1777 daughter of William and Susannah (Brown) True; Joanna d. at North Yarmouth, 27 Feb 1863.

       iv   SARAH RUSSELL, b. 14 Nov 1773; d. after 1850 when she was living in Somersworth, NH with her two daughters; m. at Cumberland, 18 Jun 1795, THOMAS THOMPSON, b. at Scarborough, ME, about 1768; Thomas d. after 1830 when the family was living in Parsonsfield, ME. There is record evidence for two daughters of Sarah and Thomas, Sarah and Susan. Neither daughter married and in her 1865 will daughter Sarah left her entire estate to her sister Susan. Susan's 1884 death record gives the names of her parents as Sarah Russell and Thomas Thompson and father's place of birth as Scarborough.

594)   v   JOSEPH RUSSELL, b. 17 Dec 1775; likely m. at Cumberland, 8 Jan 1801, RACHEL PRATT, b. at Cumberland, 23 Apr 1778 daughter of Sherebiah and Anna (Millett) Pratt.

       vi   MIRIAM RUSSELL, b. 23 May 1777; m. at Cumberland, 1801, JAMES RUSSELL. No further information was found for this family.

595)   vii   JOANNA RUSSELL, b. at Cumberland, 23 Apr 1779; d. at Yarmouth, 20 Jan 1848; m. 28 Jan 1808, ASA S. TRUE, b. at Cumberland, 28 Feb 1780 son of William and Susannah (Brown) True; Asa d. at Yarmouth, 13 Nov 1848.

       viii   JOHN RUSSELL, b. 30 Apr 1781

596)   ix   PHEBE RUSSELL, b. 16 May 1783; d. at Parsonsfield, ME, 29 Jan 1858; m. 1800, JOHN F. HUNTRESS, b. at Newington, NH, 7 Nov 1775 son of Nathan and Susanna (Chick) Huntress; John d. at Parsonsfield, 13 Sep 1852.

597)   x   MARY RUSSELL, b. 14 May 1784; d. at Yarmouth, 4 Jan 1857; m. at Cumberland, 30 Mar 1803, DAVID PRATT, b. at Cumberland, 3 May 1776 son of Sherebiah and Anna (Millett) Pratt; David d. at Yarmouth, 28 Feb 1850.

       xi   HANNAH RUSSELL, b. 15 May 1786

598)   xii   DORCAS RUSSELL, b. 7 May 1789; d. at Hartford, ME, May 1860; m. BENJAMIN THOMAS, b. at Middleborough, MA, 25 Dec 1785 son of Perez and Sarah (Wood) Thomas; Benjamin d. at Hartford, 1867 (probate 1867).

       xiii   RACHEL RUSSELL, b. 29 Nov 1790

599)   xiv   JACOB MITCHELL RUSSELL, b. 18 Aug 1792; d. after 1860 when he was living in Aroostook County, ME; m. by 1828, MARGARET E. who has not been identified, but born about 1805.

[381] Bennett, Vital Records of Cumberland, Maine 1701-1892, https://digitalmaine.com/cumberland_books/1
[382] U. S. Revolutionary War Pension and Bounty-Land Application, Case W22129

600)   xv   DESIRE RUSSELL, b. at Cumberland, 16 May 1794; d. at Melrose, MA, 5 Jun 1882; m. at Hartford, ME, 22 Aug 1813, MARTIN ELLIS, b. 15 Sep 1791 son of Perez and Mary (Hathaway) Ellis; Martin d at Canton, ME, 14 May 1871.

144)   JOSEPH RUSSELL (*James³, Thomas², Robert¹*), b. about 1742 son of James and Rhoda (Chandler) Russell; d. 1775; m. at Cumberland, 22 Oct 1765, MIRIAM BROWN, b. at Cumberland, 10 Jun 1746 daughter of Jacob and Lydia (Weare) Brown. Joseph Russell and Miriam Brown were parents of five children born at Cumberland.

     i   RHODA RUSSELL, b. at Cumberland, 10 Feb 1766

601)   ii   ANDREW RUSSELL, b. at Cumberland, 13 Apr 1768; d. after 1810 when he was living at North Yarmouth; m. about 1793, SARAH who has not been identified.

     iii   JOSEPH RUSSELL, b. at Cumberland, 26 May 1770

591)   iv   JEREMIAH RUSSELL, b. at Cumberland, 3 Apr 1772; d. at Hartford, ME, 30 Nov 1843; m. 11 Mar 1800, his first cousin, BETSY RUSSELL (*Thomas⁴, James³, Thomas², Robert¹*), b. at Cumberland, 23 Jun 1768 daughter of Thomas Chandler and Sarah (Gooch) Russell; Betsy d. at Hartford, ME, 14 May 1857. Betsy was firs married to Daniel Brown.

     v   SARAH RUSSELL, b. at Cumberland, 26 Nov 1773

Grandchildren of James Russell and Priscilla Osgood

145)   JEDUTHAN RUSSELL (*James³, James², Robert¹*), b. at Andover, 31 Jan 1745 son of James and Lucy (Farrar) Russell; d. at Walpole, NH, 13 May 1813; m. 28 Nov 1772, SUSANNAH GLAZIER, b. at Willington, 24 Feb 1756 daughter of William and Freelove (Reed) Glazier; Susannah d. 8 Sep 1799.

     Jeduthan was born in Andover and went with his family to Walpole, New Hampshire. He resided on the homestead farm that had been his father's. Jeduthan was killed at a barn raising when he fell to the ground.[383]

     Jeduthan Russell did not leave a will and Eli Russell was named administrator on 3 June 1813. The homestead farm was valued at $2,010 and personal estate at $265.73. Claims against the estate were $290.73. The personal estate was not sufficient to settle the debts and Eli Russell petitioned to sell the whole of the real estate as selling just a portion of the real estate would be injurious to the value of the remainder. Heirs or representatives required to be notified and then signing that they received notification were Jason and Martha Dudley, John and Lucy Graves, Erasmus and Susannah Wellington, Joseph Russell, Jeduthan Russell, Hannah and Amos Graves, Ezra and Priscilla Hall, and Silas Angier acting as guardian for William Russell and Martin Russell.[384] Eli sold the property to Amos Graves of Walpole.[385]

     Jeduthan Russell and Susannah Glazier were parents of eleven children born at Walpole, New Hampshire.

     i   MARTHA RUSSELL, b. 19 Mar 1773; m. JASON DUDLEY who has not been identified. Martha and Jason may not have had children. At the 1800 census, the household consisted of three adults (2 male and one female) all over age 25.

602)   ii   ELI RUSSELL, b. 13 Mar 1775; d. at Westminster, VT, 11 Dec 1841; m. at Walpole, 5 Jan 1803, HEPSIBAH FLOYD, b. at Walpole, 3 Sep 1779 daughter of Benjamin and Lydia (Bond) Floyd; Hepsibah d. at Westminster, 30 Jul 1840.

603)   iii   LUCY RUSSELL, b. 13 Apr 1777; d. at Walpole, NH, 6 May 1854; m. at Westmoreland, 27 Jan 1803, JOHN GRAVES, b. at Saybrook, CT, about 1775.

604)   iv   LYDIA RUSSELL, b. 18 Dec 1779; d. at Roxbury, VT, 26 May 1866; m. at Westmoreland, 15 Jan 1804, WILLIAM KENDALL, baptized at Lancaster, MA, 27 Jul 1777 son of William and Mary (Knight) Kendall; William d. at Roxbury, 11 Nov 1828.

[383] Aldrich, *Walpole As It Was*, p 352
[384] New Hampshire Wills and Probate, Cheshire County, Estate Files, Case R106
[385] New Hampshire Land Records, Cheshire County, 67:55

605) v HANNAH RUSSELL, b. 6 Aug 1782; d. after 1855 when living at Penfield, NY; m. at Walpole, 27 Oct 1800, AMOS GRAVES, b. about 1779 son of John and Lydia (Clark) Graves; Amos d. after 1855.

606) vi JEDUTHAN RUSSELL, b. 14 Mar 1785; d. at Rockingham, VT, 19 Dec 1857; m. 23 Jul 1807, RHODA HALL, b. at Walpole, 1781 daughter of David and Lydia (Graves) Hall; Rhoda d. at Rockingham, 6 Oct 1822. Jeduthan m. 2nd 1823, LUCY GURNSEY, b. at Westminster, VT, 30 Oct 1791 daughter of Amos and Abigail (Bolles) Gurnsey; Lucy d. at Saxtons River, 6 Jul 1845. Jeduthan m. 3rd, Rhoda's sister REBECCA HALL, b. 19 Jul 1788; Rebecca d. 12 Mar 1863.

607) vii JOSEPH RUSSELL, b. 6 Jul 1787; d. at Alamo, MI, 28 Jul 1867; m. 1st at Walpole, 4 Jan 1810, LUCY ANGIER, b. at Fitzwilliam, NH, 14 May 1792; Lucy d. at Walpole, 30 Mar 1826. Joseph m. 2nd at Keene, 7 Sep 1826, HARRIET ROBINSON, b. at Walpole, 25 Dec 1807 daughter of William and Sarah (Baker) Robinson; Harriet at Nunda, NY, 15 Sep 1850. Joseph m. 3rd MARY ANN LABBELL, b. about 1815. Joseph Russell and Harriet Robinson were parents of artist and photographer Andrew Joseph Russell. Among his other accomplishments, A. J. Russell was the official photographer of the Union Pacific Railroad.[386]

608) viii PRISCILLA RUSSELL, b. 13 May 1790; d. after 1850; m. at Walpole, 9 Jul 1807, EZRA HALL, b. at Walpole, about 1787 son of David and Lydia (Graves) Hall; Ezra d. at Walpole, 20 Aug 1863.

609) ix SUSANNA RUSSELL, b. 11 Jan 1793; d. at Cherry Valley, IL, 20 Sep 1887; m. at Walpole, 20 Jan 1810, ERASMUS WELLINGTON, b. at Sturbridge, MA, 28 Aug 1785 son of Ebenezer and Rebecca (Levens) Wellington; Erasmus d. at Cherry Valley, 7 Apr 1854.

610) x WILLIAM G. RUSSELL, b. 7 Aug 1795; d. at Rochester, NY, Sep 1850; m. about 1822, SARAH A. who has not been identified; Sarah d. at Rochester, 14 May 1885.

611) xi MARTIN RUSSELL, b. 20 Aug 1799; d. at Troy, NY, by 1878 (probate 26 Apr 1878); m. at Lansingburgh, NY, 26 Feb 1821, ELIZA CHOATE, b. at Lansingburgh, 30 Nov 1801 daughter of Jonathan and Lois (Browning) Choate; Eliza d. at Troy, 1877.

146) AQUILLA RUSSELL (*James³, James², Robert¹*), b. at Andover, 1 May 1748 son of James and Lucy (Farrar) Russell; d. at Rochester, VT, 4 Dec 1823; m. 3 May 1780, ABIGAIL GLAZIER, b. about 1762 daughter of William and Freelove (Reed) Glazier; Abigail d. at Rochester, 15 Sep 1835.

Aquilla and Abigail resided in Walpole, New Hampshire. Aquilla was town sexton for several years. They had a family of nine children and adopted two children in addition.[387]

612) i ELIJAH RUSSELL, b. at Walpole, 18 Jan 1781; d. at Rochester, VT, 3 Dec 1844; m. 1st at Walpole, 23 Feb 1808, SALLY GRIFFIN, b. 1787; Sally d. at Rochester, 18 Nov 1832. Elijah m. 2nd 8 Mar 1834, AMITY CHILD (widow of Levi Rodgers), b. at Sharon, VT, 9 Apr 1801 daughter of David and Ruth (Brown) Child; Amity d. 8 Jan 1871.

ii ABNER RUSSELL, b. at Walpole, 20 Nov 1782

613) iii JAMES RUSSELL, b. at Walpole, 27 Jan 1785; d. at West Windsor, VT, 3 Aug 1858; m. at Walpole, 8 Mar 1807, ELIZA P. HOUGHTON, b. 1788; Eliza d. at Quechee, VT, 12 Jun 1830.

iv THOMAS RUSSELL, 21 Jan 1786; died young

614) v LUCY FARRAR RUSSELL, b. at Walpole, 3 Sep 1783; d. after 1850, at Grant County, WI; m. at Troy, NY, 16 Dec 1820, as his second wife, AMOS ROGERS, b. at New Haven, 3 Mar 1783 son of Amos and Sarah (Phillips) Rogers;[388] Amos d. by 1850 when Lucy was head of household in Grant County.

vi THOMAS RUSSELL, b. 15 Feb 1790

615) vii GIDEON G. RUSSELL, b. at Walpole, 28 Sep 1791; d. at Weathersfield, VT, 25 Feb 1833; m. at Weathersfield, VT 29 Jul 1817, SARAH PLANT, b. 25 Jan 1798 daughter of Eli and Sarah (Stent) Plant; Sarah d. at Cornish, NH, 18 Jun 1874.

[386] Smithsonian American Art Museum, "Andrew Joseph Russell", https://americanart.si.edu/artist/andrew-joseph-russell-6741
[387] Aldrich, *Walpole as it Was*, p 349
[388] Rogers, *James Rogers of New London, Ct. and His Descendants*, p 166

616)   viii   RUTH RUSSELL, b. at Walpole, 29 Sep 1793; d. at Pittsfield, IL, 13 Dec 1870; m. 21 Nov 1813, ELIAS B. WILLIAMS, b. 25 May 1791;[389] Elias d. at Pittsfield, 1 Mar 1826.

617)   ix   SARAH GLAZIER RUSSELL, b. at Walpole, 19 Apr 1799; d. at Bloomington, WI, 8 Sep 1869; m. 16 Jun 1822, JOHN HOLLENBECK THOMAS, b. at Hartford, NY, 1795; John d. at Glen Haven, WI, 6 Mar 1885.

147)   THOMAS RUSSELL (*James³, James², Robert¹*), b. at Willington, 10 Apr 1751 son of James and Lucy (Farrar) Russell; d. at Walpole, NH, 28 Nov 1845; m. at Walpole, 25 Jan 1785, EUNICE ALEXANDER, b. 8 Sep 1769 daughter of Richard and Jerusha (Wyman) Alexander; Eunice d. at Walpole, 11 Jan 1859.

Thomas Russell accompanied his parents to Walpole, New Hampshire and lived there the remainder of his long life of ninety-four years.

In his will written 29 September 1843 (probate 2 December 1845), Thomas Russell bequeathed to beloved wife Eunice the use of half his lands and buildings except the half of the dwelling house now belonging to son David. Eunice also has use of all the livestock, farming tools, and household furniture. Son Thomas Russell receives the land and dwelling house where Thomas now lives this being the land Thomas purchased in Walpole for his son. Thomas also receives $25. Son John Russell receives $80 with what he has received completes his portion. Son Richard receives $25 to complete his portion. Son David receives $220 and grandson Ira W. Russell son of Levi deceased receives $80. Daughter-in-law Eliza Russell alias Cheney and the widow of Levi receives $40. Daughter Betsey P. Dickey receives $40. His three grandchildren (Caleb, Henry, and Elizabeth) the children of Henry Foster and Philena Foster deceased receive $90 to be divided. At his decease, one-half of the farm and buildings is to be appraised and son David is to pay one-fifth of that amount each to beloved wife Eunice and daughters Sally Angier widow, Elvira Jennison married woman, and Eunice Frink married woman. Son David will receive the other undivided half. Any residue of the estate is to be divided among children David Russell, Sally Angier, Elvira Jennison, and Eunice Frink. Son David was named executor. The farm was valued at $2000 and the total value of the estate was $2838.28.[390]

Thomas Russell and Eunice Alexander were parents of ten children born at Walpole.

618)   i   THOMAS RUSSELL, b. at Walpole, NH, 3 Sep 1785; d. at Walpole, 28 Mar 1872; m. at Walpole, 9 Oct 1817, as her second husband, HANNAH FLINT, b. at Carlisle, MA, 11 Jan 1782 daughter of Amos and Elizabeth (Ball) Flint; Hannah d. at Walpole, 5 Jan 1866. Hannah was first married to Josiah Willington.

619)   ii   JOHN RUSSELL, b. at Walpole, NH, 8 Jun 1787; d. at Harpersfield, OH, 1 Oct 1845; m. REMEMBRANCE EASTMAN, b. at Canada West, about 1802 daughter of Amos and Mary (Ingalls) Eastman; Remembrance d. after 1880 when she was living in Rolling Green, MN. Remembrance m. 2nd A. B. Hall.

620)   iii   RICHARD RUSSELL, b. at Walpole, NH, 15 Jan 1790; d. at Austinburg, OH, 1866; m. about 1812, TIRZAH HALL, b. at Walpole, 1795 daughter of David and Lydia (Graves) Hall; Tirzah d. at Cherry Valley, OH, 23 Jan 1887.

621)   iv   LEVI RUSSELL, b. at Walpole, NH, about 1795; d. at Keene, 21 Sep 1831; m. about 1824, ELIZABETH "ELIZA" WALDO, b. 23 Aug 1801 daughter of Elijah and Betsey (Angier) Waldo. Eliza married second Ebenezer Cheney.

622)   v   SALLY RUSSELL, b. at Walpole, NH, 30 Aug 1796; d. at Alstead, NH, 1859 (probate 1859); m. 17 Oct 1811, ELISHA ANGIER, b. at Fitzwilliam, NH, 6 Dec 1789 son of Silas and Priscilla (Harris) Angier; Elisha d. at Walpole, 23 Sep 1835.

623)   vi   DAVID RUSSELL, b. at Walpole, NH, 30 Aug 1796; d. at Walpole, 5 Jun 1875; m. 25 Dec 1817, MARY A. WHEELER, b. at Deerfield, MA, about 1796 (1 Jul 1796 in Walpole history) (Deerfield according to death record); Mary d. at Walpole, 30 Oct 1887.

624)   vii   PHYLENA RUSSELL, b. at Walpole, NH, 23 Apr 1803; d. at Walpole, 27 Apr 1839; m. 1823, HENRY PRENTISS FOSTER, b. 10 Oct 1796 son of Henry and Susannah (Hooper) Foster; Henry d. at Walpole, 18 Aug 1861. Henry married second Eliza Marsh.

625)   viii   ELVIRA RUSSELL, b. at Walpole, NH, about 1804; d. at Walpole, 13 Jan 1894; m. JOHN JENNISON, b. at Northfield, MA (per death record), 14 Jun 1807 son of Thomas and Martha (Moore) Jennison; John d. at Walpole, Jul 1880.

---

[389] Elias's date of birth is on his gravestone

[390] *New Hampshire. Probate Court (Cheshire County)*; Probate Place: *Cheshire, New Hampshire, Estate Files, R239-R294, 1840-1850, Estate of Thomas Russell*

626) ix EUNICE RUSSELL, b. at Walpole, NH, 7 Mar 1808; d. at Swanzey, NH, 23 Oct 1852; m. 20 Apr 1830, ORLANDO FRINK, b. at Deerfield, MA, 10 Mar 1810 son of Samuel and Mehitable (Eams) Frink; Orlando d. at Swanzey 16 Apr 1877. Orlando married second Mary A. Willard on 1 Mar 1853.

627) x BETSEY P. RUSSELL, b. at Walpole, NH, 5 May 1812; d. at Walpole, 24 Aug 1903; m. CLEMENT S. DICKEY, b. 12 Mar 1806 son of Matthew and Betsey (Murch) Dickey; Clement d. at Walpole, 11 Jun 1892.

148) PRISCILLA RUSSELL (*James³, James², Robert¹*), b. at Willington, 20 Feb 1753 daughter of James and Lucy (Farrar) Russell; d. at Rockingham, VT, 12 Jun 1816; m. at Walpole, 15 Oct 1778, DAVID PULSIPHER, b. 28 Sep 1757 son of David and Elizabeth (-) Pulsipher;[391] David d. at Rockingham, VT, 14 Jun 1835.

David's father went to Bunker Hill and never returned home, and his fate is unknown. The father David Pulsipher was the first innkeeper in Rockingham.[392]

David and Priscilla resided in Rockingham where David filled duties such as served on a committee to give notice to the pastor of "all public and open breaches and violations of Christian duty."[393]

Priscilla Russell and David Pulsipher were parents of nine children born at Rockingham, Vermont.

i ELIZABETH STOWELL PULSIPHER, b. 21 Dec 1779; d. at Rockingham, 24 Feb 1811. Elizabeth did not marry.

629) ii SAMUEL WOOD PULSIPHER, b. 13 Jan 1782; d. at Rockingham, 14 Jul 1817; m. at Rockingham, 29 Mar 1806, SALLY WEAVER, b. at Rockingham, 13 Mar 1787 daughter of Daniel and Joanna (Preston) Weaver; Sally d. at Rockingham, 17 Jun 1863. Sally married second Isaac Severens.

iii LUCY PULSIPHER, b. 29 Nov 1784; d. at Rockingham, 11 Dec 1830; m. at Rockingham, 4 Jun 1829, as his second wife, EDWARD DARBY. Lucy did not have children.

iv IRENA PULSIPHER, b. 20 Dec 1786; d. at Rockingham, 27 May 1809; m. 4 Dec 1808, ALPHEUS KENDALL, baptized at Westmoreland, NH, 13 Apr 1788 son of William and Mary (Knight) Kendall; Alpheus d. at Brookfield, VT, before 1850. Alpheus married second Lucy Young on 8 Mar 1810. Irena did not have children.

v PHILENA PULSIPHER, b. 28 Aug 1789; d. at Rockingham, 30 Dec 1860. Philena did not marry.

629) vi DAVID PULSIPHER, b. 6 Dec 1791; d. at Brimfield, IL, 14 Dec 1865; m. at Walpole, NH, 15 Mar 1815, REBECCA LANE, b. at Walpole, 7 Apr 1794 daughter of Ephraim and Elizabeth Danforth (Abbott) Lane; Rebecca d. at Rockingham, VT, 5 Feb 1847. David m. 2nd EUNICE HEWITT, b. at Wallingford, about 1794; Eunice d. at Wallingford, 15 Feb 1867.[394]

630) vii ELIAS PULSIPHER, b. 20 Jun 1794; d. at Rockingham, 22 Jun 1858; m. at Walpole, NH, 30 Jan 1820, SUSAN LANE, b. at Walpole, 1 Oct 1796 daughter of Ephraim and Elizabeth Danforth (Abbott) Lane; Susan d. at Rockingham, 7 Jun 1880.

viii PATTY PULSIPHER, b. 5 Sep 1796; d. 19 Feb 1798.

631) ix WILLIAM WILEY PULSIPHER, b. 21 Jul 1800; d. at Rockingham, VT, 26 Sep 1870; m. 5 Jan 1830, ELECTA BARNES, b. at Weathersfield, VT, 25 Jan 1807 daughter of Solomon S. and Zada (Plant) Barnes; Electa d. at Springfield, VT, 26 Jun 1891.

149) HANNAH RUSSELL (*James³, James², Robert¹*), b. at Willington, 15 Nov 1754 daughter of James and Lucy (Farrar) Russell; d. at Stockholm, NY, 18 May 1840; m. LUKE FLETCHER, b. at Lancaster, MA, 24 Oct 1759 son of Robert and Rebecca (Edmunds) Fletcher; Luke d. at Stockholm, 14 Jan 1841.

On 8 May 1818, Luke Fletcher aged fifty-eight and resident of Randolph, Vermont provided a statement related to his application for a pension. He enlisted 1 May 1775 at Cambridge for a term of eight months in the company of Capt. Watkins of Col. Patterson's regiment. Immediately following that enlistment, he enlisted for a term of one year in the company of Capt. William Scott and transferred to the company of Capt. Asa Barns and was at the Battle of Trenton. He had a third enlistment for a term of five months. During his service in addition to the Battle of Trenton, he was at the evacuation of Boston by the British and the retreat from New York and well as other skirmishes. In a statement 3 July 1820 while living in Randolph

[391] Hayes, *History of the Town of Rockingham*, p 732
[392] Hayes, *History of the Town of Rockingham*
[393] Hayes, *History of the Town of Rockingham*, p 134
[394] Vermont, Vital Records, 1720-1908

Vermont age sixty, personal estate reported was as $42.75 with $20 in debts. Household at that time was wife Bethiah[395] age 58 and daughter Sabina age 22. On 5 March 1832 while living in Stockholm, New York, Luke requested transfer of pension to New York. He moved to Stockholm as his children resided there and he wished to be with him. He had no means to support himself except his pension. A letter 6 June 1850 from Ira Haly on behalf of the children of Luke stated that Luke died in January 1843 and wondered if anything further might be due to the children as they had not received bounty land.[396]

There is evidence for four children of Luke Fletcher and Hannah Russell, although there may be others. The children were likely all born in Vermont.

	i	LUCINDA FLETCHER, b. about 1789; d. at Stockholm, NY, 18 May 1875. Lucinda did not marry. In 1850, she lived with her sister Hannah Coon and her daughter Hester.
632)	ii	HANNAH FLETCHER, b. about 1792; d. at Stockholm, NY, 14 Jun 1880; m. WILLIAM COON who was deceased before 1850.
633)	iii	ADOLPHUS FLETCHER, b. 1795; d. at Stockholm, NY, 9 Apr 1851; m. at Walpole, NH, 4 Nov 1817, SALLY WELLINGTON, b. at Walpole, 21 Aug 1799 daughter of Ebenezer and Rebecca (Levens) Wellington; Sally d. at Stockholm, 8 Sep 1872.
	iv	SABINA FLETCHER, b. about 1798; living in 1820 with her parents; nothing further known.

150)   URIAH RUSSELL (*Thomas³, James², Robert¹*), b. at Andover, 14 May 1743 son of Thomas and Abigail (Ballard) Russell; d. at Andover, 9 Nov 1822; m. at Andover, 15 Aug 1771, LYDIA ABBOTT, b. at Andover, 7 Mar 1744/5 daughter of Barachias and Hannah (Holt) Abbott; Lydia d. at Andover, 11 Jul 1829.

Uriah Russell wrote his will 31 March 1818 and his estate entered probate 7 January 1823.[397] His beloved wife Lydia is to have the improvements on all the household furniture during her lifetime, and after her decease, the household items will pass to his two daughters. The executor is to see that she is comfortably provided for. Sons James, Thomas, and Abiel each receives $125. The two daughters, Hannah Abbot the wife of Nathan Abbot and Lydia Faulkner wife of Joseph Faulkner, each receives $15. Son Joel Russell receives all the residue of the estate, both real and personal, and is named executor.

There are records for eleven children born at Andover. There is a daughter Phebe for which there is only a baptismal record. The oldest son died of yellow fever at Curacao.

	i	URIAH RUSSELL, b. Sep 1773; d. of yellow fever at Curacao, 1799.[398]
	ii	THOMAS RUSSELL, b. Dec 1774; d. Sep 1775.
	iii	HANNAH RUSSELL, b. Sep 1775; d. 9 Oct 1776.
634)	iv	JAMES RUSSELL, b. Nov 1777; d. about 1861 in Oxford County, ME;[399] m. at East Andover, ME, 13 Aug 1804, his first cousin once removed, DOLLY RUSSELL (*Jacob⁴, John³, John², Robert¹*), b. about 1784 daughter of Jacob and Dorothy (Shattuck) Russell; Dolly d. at Boxford, MA, 20 Sep 1863.
635)	v	THOMAS RUSSELL, b. Nov 1777 (twin of James); d. at Andover, 18 Jan 1849; m. at Albany, ME, 22 Apr 1806, ABIGAIL BELL, b. likely at Albany about 1786 of not yet verified parents; Abigail d. at Andover 10 Oct 1833.
636)	vi	HANNAH RUSSELL, b. Apr 1780 (based on age at death); d. at Andover, 16 Nov 1832; m. 10 Nov 1801, her third cousin, NATHAN ABBOTT, b. at Andover, 25 Aug 1778 son of Nathan and Sarah (Ballard) Abbott; Nathan d. 13 Feb 1837.
	vii	LYDIA RUSSELL, b. Sep 1782; d. Oct 1782.
637)	viii	JOEL RUSSELL, b. Aug 1783; d. at Andover, 22 Jul 1871; m. 2 Apr 1805, SARAH CURTIS, b. at Middleton, 16 Oct 1782 daughter of Israel and Elizabeth (Wilkins) Curtis; Sarah d. at Andover, 6 Feb 1857.

---

[395] The one discrepancy in this file is reference to wife named Bethiah. Luke and Hannah Fletcher are buried together Sandfordville Cemetery in Saint Lawrence County, New York (findagrave ID: 119357346) Hannah's death given as May 18, 1840 at 85 years. The name in the pension file is perhaps just an error by the person taking the statement. Daughter Lucinda (gravestone inscribed as Lucinda daughter of Luke and Hannah Fletcher) and daughter Hannah (inscribed as Hannah daughter of Luke and Hannah Fletcher and wife of Wm. Coon) are buried in the same cemetery.

[396] U. S. Revolutionary War Pension and Bounty-Land Warrant Application Files, Case S44824

[397] *Essex County, MA: Probate File Papers, 1638-1881. Probate of Uriah Russell, 7 Jan 1823, Case number 24434.*

[398] Uriah, jr., yellow fever, at Curacoa, —— —, 1799. CR2

[399] James Russell was living at the time of the 1860 U.S. Census; his wife was a widow when she died in 1863.

638) ix LYDIA RUSSELL, b. 5 Dec 1785; d. at Andover, 2 Dec 1865; m. 13 Jun 1809, her third cousin once removed (through Abbott line), JOSEPH FAULKNER, b. at Andover, 30 Jul 1783 son of Abiel and Hannah (Abbott) Faulkner; Joseph d. 5 Aug 1831.

x PHEBE RUSSELL, baptized 29 Jan 1786; no further record and likely died young.

639) xi ABIEL RUSSELL, b. Mar 1789; d. at Andover, 14 Jan 1881; m. 17 Jun 1813, his third cousin (through Abbott line), SARAH ABBOTT, b. at Andover, 20 Dec 1792 daughter of Nathan and Sarah (Ballard) Abbott; Sarah d. 20 Sep 1846. Abiel m. 2nd at Andover, 6 May 1848, ELIZA MOOAR, b. at Greenfield, NH, 17 Sep 1807 daughter of Benjamin and Phebe (Chandler) Mooar; Eliza d. at Andover, 20 Jul 1892.

151) ELIZABETH RUSSELL (*Thomas³, James², Robert¹*), baptized at Andover, 24 Jan 1745 daughter of Thomas and Abigail (Ballard) Russell; d. at Andover, 15 Sep 1820; m. at Andover, 3 Mar 1768, GIDEON FOSTER, b. at Andover, 21 Aug 1739 son of John and Mary (Osgood) Foster; Gideon d. at Andover, 9 Aug 1817.

Gideon served as a private in the company of Capt. Joshua Holt's 4th Andover that marched at the alarm to Cambridge on 19 April 1775. He did 1 ½ days service.[400] Gideon was a tenant on Ballard property in Andover.[401] He owned at least one small piece of land of 40 poles (about one-quarter acre) which he sold to Jonathan Gleason on 22 November 1803 for a payment of ten dollars.[402]

Elizabeth Russell and Gideon Foster were parents of five children born at Andover.

640) i ELIZABETH RUSSELL FOSTER, b. 23 Feb 1769; m. at Andover, 13 Jun 1793, SAMUEL CLARK.

641) ii ABIGAIL FOSTER, b. 13 Jan 1771; d. at Andover, 30 Dec 1846; m. at Andover, 17 Nov 1791, WILLIAM SHATTUCK, b. at Andover, 26 Apr 1769 son of Joseph and Anna (Johnson) Shattuck; William d. at Otisfield, ME, 30 Aug 1806.

iii TAMISEN FOSTER, b. 1 May 1773; d. 23 Mar 1776.

642) iv SARAH FOSTER, b. 14 Jun 1775; d. at Andover, 1 Mar 1847; m. at Andover, 19 May 1803, as his second wife, JONATHAN GLEASON, b. at Bedford, MA, about 1771 son of Benjamin and Deborah (Beard) Gleason; Jonathan d. at Andover, 30 Oct 1846.

v PRISCILLA FOSTER, b. 5 Apr 1778; d. at Andover, of dysentery, 23 Aug 1848. Priscilla did not marry.

152) THOMAS RUSSELL (*Thomas³, James², Robert¹*), b. at Andover, 12 Feb 1746/7 son of Thomas and Abigail (Ballard) Russell; d. at Conway, NH, 15 Jul 1823; m. about 1767, SARAH EASTMAN b. 6 May 1749 daughter of Richard and Mary (Lovejoy) Eastman; Sarah d. at Conway, 29 Dec 1836.

Thomas and Sarah married in Andover and their first two children were born there. They were then in Conway, New Hampshire where Thomas was enumerated as one of the men fit to bear arms on 10 June 1775. He signed the association test on 9 June 1776. Sarah and Thomas were members of the First Church of Conway and subscribed to a covenant with the church in August 1778.[403]

Thomas Russell and Sarah Eastman were parents of thirteen children.

643) i THOMAS RUSSELL, b. at Andover, MA, 22 Feb 1768; d. at Bartlett, NH, 1853; m. at Conway, 19 Jul 1798, RUTH HARRIMAN, b. at Concord, 12 Mar 1774 daughter of Philip and Hannah (Eastman) Harriman; Ruth d. 1850.

644) ii SARAH RUSSELL, b. at Andover, 2 Jan 1770; d. at Conway, NH, 4 Dec 1852; m. 17 Nov 1790, LEAVITT HILL, b. 2 Mar 1770 son of Charles and Sarah (Prentice) Hill; Leavitt d. at Conway, 4 Dec 1843.

iii JAMES RUSSELL, b. at Conway, 4 Mar 1772

iv RICHARD RUSSELL, b. at Conway, 2 Feb 1774

645) v ABIGAIL RUSSELL, b. at Conway, 22 Mar 1776; d. at Hanover, NH, 21 Dec 1856; m. at Conway, 12 Oct 1806, as his second wife, ASA CROSBY, b. 15 Jul 1765 son of Josiah and Sarah (Fitch) Crosby; Asa d. at Hanover, 12 Apr 1836. Asa was first married to Betsey Hoit.

[400] Massachusetts Soldiers and Sailors in the Revolutionary War, volume 5, p 901
[401] Pierce, *Foster Genealogy*, Part I, p 196
[402] Massachusetts Land Records, Essex County, 173:83
[403] Merrill, *History of Carroll County, New Hampshire*, p 81, p 822, p 861

646)   vi   JAMES RUSSELL, b. at Conway, 5 May 1778; d. at Albany, NH, 30 Sep 1861; m. SARAH ALLEN, b. in
                ME, about 1788; Sarah d. at Conway, 17 Feb 1859.

647)   vii   ESTHER RUSSELL, b. at Conway, 4 May 1780; d. at Conway, 4 Sep 1807; m. at Conway, 1 May 1800,
                JONATHAN PHILBRICK, b. 5 Aug 1775 son of Jonathan and Hannah (Gilman) Philbrick; Jonathan d.
                after 1850 when he was living at Lawrenceburg, IN. Jonathan was second married to Jane Hardy.

648)   viii   MARY RUSSELL, b. at Conway, 7 Aug 1782; d. at Freehold, NJ, 3 Mar 1859; m. at Hanover, 1 Feb 1809,
                JONATHAN FREEMAN, b. at Hanover, 21 Mar 1783 son of Otis and Ruth (Bicknell) Freeman; Jonathan d.
                at Freehold, 11 Sep 1871.

        ix   ELIZABETH RUSSELL, b. at Conway, 20 May 1785; d. at Conway, 28 Sep 1865. Eliza did not marry.

        x   PRISSILLA RUSSELL, b. at Conway, 25 May 1787

649)   xi   URIAH B. RUSSELL, b. at Conway, 9 Aug 1791; m. 1st, about 1810, ANNA C. FORREST, b. at
                Bridgewater, MA, about 1790 *possibly* daughter of Spencer and Abigail (Wade) Forrest; Anna d. about 1823.
                Uriah m. 2nd BETSEY PALMER, b. at Eaton, NH, about 1797; death not known but *possibly* the Betsey
                Russell who died at Lowell, 13 Nov 1844. Uriah m. 3rd at Lowell, 24 Jul 1845, BETSEY GREENOUGH, b.
                about 1804.

        xii   JONATHAN E. RUSSELL, b. at Conway, 7 Jul 1793

650)   xiii   ALVAH RUSSELL, b. at Conway, 9 Dec 1796; d. at Conway, 15 Jul 1856; m. at Eaton, NH, 28 Mar 1833,
                ASENATH DAVIS, b. at Eaton, NH, 17 Apr 1812 daughter of Nathaniel and Nancy (March) Davis;[404]
                Asenath d. at Laconia, NH, 11 Feb 1893. Asenath married second, James S. Hoit.

153)   ABIGAIL RUSSELL (*Thomas³, James², Robert¹*), b. at Andover, 12 May 1750 daughter of Thomas and Abigail
(Ballard) Russell; d. at Salem, 4 May 1822; m. 1 Nov 1770 (intention) HENRY WILLIAMS, baptized at Salem, 22 Jul 1744 son
of Henry and Mary (Waters) Williams; Henry d. at Salem, 17 Aug 1814. (Henry, Capt., Aug. 17, 1814, a. 70 y. GR1)
        Capt. Henry Williams was a master mariner in Salem.[405] On 21 December 1780, he was commissioned as commander
of the brigantine *Salem*, a privateer during the Revolution.[406]
        There are records of eight children of Henry Williams and Abigail Russell born at Salem.

651)   i   ABIGAIL WILLIAMS, baptized 11 Aug 1771; d. at Beverly, MA, 6 Aug 1828; m. at Salem, 17 Mar 1791,
                JOSIAH GOULD, b. at Salem, 23 Oct 1765[407] (baptized 14 Aug 1768) son of Josiah and Sarah (Sherman)
                Gould; Josiah d. at Beverly, 28 Sep 1822

        ii   HENRY RUSSELL WILLIAMS, baptized 13 Jun 1773

        iii   JOSEPH WARREN WILLIAMS, baptized 9 Nov 1777; d. at Port McCue, 1814;[408] m. 13 Jul 1805, HANNAH
                BYRNE.

652)   iv   CATHARINE "KATY" WILLIAMS, b. 7 Apr 1780; d. after 1865 when she was living at Salem; m. at Salem,
                12 Sep 1799, THOMAS DOWNING, b. at Salem, 23 Sep 1772 son of Thomas and Abigail (Brown) Browning;
                Thomas d. at Salem, 7 Feb 1835.

653)   v   THOMAS RUSSELL WILLIAMS, baptized 30 Mar 1783; d. at Boston, 1827 (probate 26 Feb 1827); m. at
                Salem, 22 Jun 1806, his fourth cousin, RUTH ABBOTT (*Ruth Holt Abbott⁶, Joseph Holt⁵, Lydia Holt Holt⁴,
                Thomas Holt³, Mary Russell Holt², Robert¹*), b. at Andover, Jul 1785 daughter of Abner and Ruth (Holt)
                Abbott; Ruth d. after 1850 when she was living at Boston.

654)   vi   LYDIA WILLIAMS, baptized 23 Oct 1785; d. at Salem, 28 Apr 1861; m. at Salem, 23 Feb 1808, SETH
                RICHARDSON, b. Oct 1786 son of Josiah and Ruth (Brooks) Richardson; Seth d. at Salem, 12 Jan 1809.

---

[404] The names of Asenath's parents are given as Nathaniel Davis and Mary Williams on her death record and as Nathaniel Davis and Nancy March
on the record of her second marriage to James Hoit. The death record of one of Asenath's siblings gives parents as Nathaniel Davis and Nancy
March.
[405] Massachusetts, Mason Membership Cards, 1733-1990
[406] Massachusetts Soldiers and Sailors in the Revolutionary War, volume 17, p 435
[407] Birth date is given in the town records of Beverly, MA
[408] Joseph Warren, Capt., at Port McCue, Rappahanock, a. 36 y. Issue of June 3, 1814. NR9

655)   vii   WILLARD WILLIAMS, baptized 24 Feb 1788; d. at Boston, 2 May 1834; m. at Boston, 22 Dec 1820, ELIZABETH "BETSEY" OSGOOD, b. at Salem, 20 May 1789 son of Christopher and Mary (Shepard) Osgood; Betsey d. at Boston, 22 May 1835.

        viii   JOHN WILLIAMS, baptized at Salem, 30 Sep 1792

154)   THOMAS APPLETON (*Mary Russell Appleton³, James², Robert¹*), b. at Haverhill, 15 Mar 1743/4 son of Samuel and Mary (Russell) Appleton; d. at Boston, 1 Dec 1803; m. at Boston, 15 Dec 1766, MARTHA BARNARD, baptized at Boston 7 Dec 1746 daughter of Benjamin and Lydia (Danforth) Barnard; Martha d. at Boston, 30 Jan 1829.

Thomas Appleton was a housewright in Boston.[409] On 8 May 1771, the selectmen of Boston approved Thomas Appleton as an engine man in the company of Engine No. 7.[410]

In his will written 17 May 1803 (probate 19 December 1803), Thomas Appleton bequeathed to beloved wife Martha the use of all the estate, real and personal, while she continues a widow or for the remainder of her life. At the remarriage or decease of Martha, the estate is to be equally divided in eight shares among his children: Samuel Appleton, Martha Thayer wife of Richard Thayer, Thomas Russell Appleton, John Appleton, Lydia Wells wife of Benjamin Tuttle Wells, Benjamin Barnard Appleton, George Washington Appleton, and Henry Knox Appleton. Wife Martha was named executrix. In a codicil written 31 May 1803, Thomas directs that when the two youngest children come of age, and if Martha sees fit, that the small dwelling house and land with it that is situated in the yard of the mansion house be sold and the proceeds divided in eighths and distributed among the children. Inventory made on 26 March 1804 valued house and land at $7,000 and personal estate at $242.35.[411]

Thomas Appleton and Martha Barnard were parents of eleven children born at Boston, including a set of triplets.

        i   SAMUEL APPLETON, b. 8 May 1768; d. at Boston, 8 Jan 1815. Samuel does not seem to have married.

656)   ii   MARTHA APPLETON, b. 16 Jun 1770; d. at South Boston, 7 Oct 1847; m. at Boston, 13 Mar 1798, RICHARD FRENCH THAYER, b. at Braintree, 21 Mar 1769 son of Richard and Esther (French) Thayer; Richard d. at South Boston, 13 Aug 1845.

657)   iii   THOMAS RUSSELL APPLETON, b. 12 Jun 1772; d. at Haverhill, 6 Apr 1863; m. 1st 31 Dec 1797, ANNA SWETT, b. at Haverhill, 14 Mar 1765 daughter of Abraham and Sarah (*Bradley* Poor) Swett; Anna d. at Haverhill, 9 Aug 1826. Thomas m. 2nd 28 May 1827, his first cousin, HANNAH GALE, baptized at Haverhill, 26 Sep 1779 daughter of Moses and Mary (Appleton) Gale; Hannah d. at Haverhill, 6 Apr 1868.

658)   iv   JOHN APPLETON, b. 2 Dec 1774; d. at Newton, MA, 9 Nov 1868; m. at Boston, 22 Mar 1806, MARY TUTTLE, b. at Salem 1778 daughter of Ebenezer and Hannah (Stone) Tuttle;[412] Maty d. at Boston, 12 Nov 1866.

        v   BENJAMIN APPLETON, b. 24 Sep 1777; d. 15 Mar 1778.

659)   vi   LYDIA APPLETON, b. 17 Feb 1779; d. at Boston, 22 Mar 1872; m. at Boston, Oct 1799, BENJAMIN TUTTLE WELLS, b. at Boston, 17 Mar 1775 son of John and Joanna (Tuttle) Wells; Benjamin d. at Boston, 17 Apr 1822.

660)   vii   BENJAMIN BARNARD APPLETON, B. 8 May 1781; d. at Boston, 23 Apr 1844; m. at Boston, 3 Jul 1814, CATHERINE HOOTON, b. at Boston, 18 Nov 1790 daughter of John and Catharine (Thompson) Hooton; Catherine d. 7 Nov 1875.

        viii   MARY APPLETON, b. 24 Apr 1783; d. 5 Jan 1791.

        ix   JOSEPH WARREN APPLETON (triplet), b. 6 Jun 1786; d. 19 Jan 1787.

661)   x   HENRY KNOX APPLETON (triplet), b. 6 Jun 1786; d. at Boston, 18 Aug 1829; m. at Boston, 29 Mar 1810, MARY OWEN, b. at Boston, about 1786 daughter of William Owen who was from England; Mary d. at Boston, 28 Mar 1861.

---

[409] Boston, MA, Inhabitants and Estates of the Town of Boston (Thwing Collection), p 1767

[410] Boston Registrar, Report of the Record Commissioners, volume 23, p 84; this refers to the Boston fire department which in 1771 contained 16 fire wards.

[411] *Suffolk County, MA: Probate File Papers.* Online database. *AmericanAncestors.org.* New England Historic Genealogical Society, 2017-2019. Case 22019

[412] The names of Mary's parents are given and Eben and Hannah Tuttle on her death record.

662)   xi   GEORGE WASHINGTON APPLETON (triplet), b. 6 Jun 1786; d. at Delavan, IL, 28 Mar 1851; m. at
              Wrentham, MA, 4 Apr 1819, MARY GUILD, b. at Franklin, MA, 31 Oct 1798 daughter of John and Ruth
              (Morse) Guild; Mary d. at Delavan, 4 Feb 1859.

155)   MARY APPLETON (*Mary Russell Appleton³, James², Robert¹*), b. at Haverhill, 5 Jun 1746 daughter of Samuel and
Mary (Russell) Appleton; d. at Haverhill, 29 Mar 1830; m. at Haverhill, 12 Oct 1769, MOSES GALE, b. at Haverhill, 21 Mar
1745/6 son of Benjamin and Hannah (Clement) Gale; Moses d. at Haverhill, 20 Jun 1827.
        Moses Gale was a merchant in Haverhill some of his trade conducted by ship, at least one of those ships constructed at
a shipyard at Haverhill. Moses was member of the Fire Society in Haverhill.[413]
        In his will written 11 November 1818 (probate 26 June 1827), Moses Gale bequeathed to beloved wife Mary Gale, two
hundred dollars in household goods. Her support and maintenance is to be provided by son Samuel Appleton Gale at his own
expense. In order for Samuel to provide for his mother, he will have the use and improvement of the home dwelling and lost and
the twenty-three-acre Hazzen pasture. The residue of the estate, real and personal, and the home lot and Hazzen pasture after
Mary's decease are to be divided as follows: to son Moses Gale, two undivided eighteenth parts; son Samuel Appleton Gale,
seven undivided eighteenth parts; daughter Mary Treat, four undivided eighteenth parts; and daughter Hannah Gale, five
undivided eighteenth parts. Son Samuel was empowered to sell any of the estate necessary to pay any debts and was also
named executor. In a codicil written 10 August 1825, Moses revoked the appointment of son Samuel as executor and named
Isaac R. How as sole executor, the reason being "the infirmities of my said son." Real estate was valued at $7,659 which
included the dwelling house with three acres assessed at $2,500. Personal estate was $512.88.[414]
        Son Moses, who was a merchant in Haverhill, did marry but did not have children. In his will written 27 May 1848
(probate 21 October 1851), he bequeathed all his furniture to wife Sarah R. Gale, three hundred dollars to Charles R. Merrill,
one thousand dollars to Hannah Emery who has been with him from her youth, two hundred dollars to Harriet How wife of
Moses How, and two hundred dollars to brother-in-law Porter Russell. The use and improvement of the remainder of the estate
goes to wife Sarah and after her decease to be divided: nephew Samuel Gale, two hundred dollars; nephew Nathaniel G. Treat,
two hundred dollars; bequests to the Home Missionary Society, American Bible Society, and American Tract Society; and the
remainder divided among Charles R. Merrill, Hannah Emery, and Harriet N. How. Moses How was named executor. Real estate
was valued at $6,055.[415]
        Mary Appleton and Moses Gale were parents of seven children born at Haverhill.

        i   MOSES GALE, baptized 31 Mar 1771; d. at Haverhill, 8 Oct 1851; m. 6 Nov 1802, SARAH "SALLY"
              RUSSELL, baptized at Bradford, 18 Feb 1776 daughter of Peter and Molly (Chadwick) Russell;[416] Sally d. at
              Haverhill, 26 Oct 1849. Moses and Sarah did not have children.

663)   ii   MARY GALE, baptized 27 Dec 1772; d. at Bangor, ME, 20 Feb 1842; m. at Haverhill, 28 Feb 1804, as his
              second wife, ROBERT TREAT, b. 14 Jul 1752 son of Joseph and Mary (-) Treat; Robert d. at Bangor, 27 May
              1824. Robert was first married to Mary Partridge on 28 Nov 1774.

        iii   HANNAH GALE, baptized 4 Dec 1774; d. 17 Nov 1775.

        iv   NATHANIEL GALE, b. 1777; d. of consumption, 13 Jan 1800.

        v   HANNAH GALE, baptized 26 Sep 1779; d. at Haverhill, 6 Apr 1868; m. at Haverhill, 28 May 1827, as his
              second wife, her first cousin, THOMAS RUSSELL APPLETON (*Thomas Appleton⁴, Mary Russell Appleton³,
              James², Robert¹*), b. at Boston, 12 Jun 1772 son of Thomas and Mary (Barnard) Appleton; Thomas d. at
              Haverhill, 6 Apr 1863. Thomas was first married to Anna Swett. Thomas Russell Appleton and Anna Swett
              are Family 642.

664)   vi   SAMUEL APPLETON GALE, baptized 18 Nov 1781; d. at Haverhill, about Jan 1829 (probate 8 Feb 1831);
              m. at Gloucester, 14 May 1807, MARY A. FOSTER, b. about 1780 whose parents are not clearly identified
              but might be Jeremiah and Polly (Tarr) Foster of Gloucester; Mary d. at Haverhill, 31 Dec 1822.

        vii   JOHN GALE, baptized 15 August 1784; d. 19 Jan 1787.

[413] Chase, *The History of Haverhill, Massachusetts*, p 491 and p 428
[414] *Essex County, MA: Probate File Papers, 1638-1881*. Online database. *AmericanAncestors.org*. New England Historic Genealogical Society, 2014.
Case 10554
[415] *Essex County, MA: Probate File Papers, 1638-1881*. Online database. *AmericanAncestors.org*. New England Historic Genealogical Society, 2014.
Case 39961
[416] The 1806 probate of Peter Russell includes Moses Gale signing as an heir.

156)   DANIEL APPLETON (*Mary Russell Appleton³, James², Robert¹*), b. at Haverhill, 16 Mar 1750/1 son of Samuel and Mary (Russell) Appleton; d. at Haverhill, 15 May 1828; m. at Haverhill, 26 Oct 1775, LYDIA ELA, b. at Haverhill, 30 Mar 1747 daughter of Jacob and Ednah (Little) Ela;[417] Lydia d. at Haverhill, 17 May 1826.

Daniel and Lydia lived in Haverhill where Daniel was active in civic duties such as being a member of the Fire Society which served the function of a volunteer fire department. He served as militia captain during the period of the Revolution and on 19 September 1775 led a detachment "to march instantly to Beverly."[418] Daniel was relatively prosperous for the time and this trend continued with his son Daniel and his grandchildren several of whom were notable in their respective fields.

In his will written 20 October 1827 (probate 3 June 1828), Daniel Appleton bequeathed to daughters Lydia and Abigail $2000 each and $600 to daughter Alice Swett. Son William has already received a considerable advancement from the estate, but he is to receive $30 annually during his natural life. This annual payment to William will come from an account of $500 earning interest. After William's death, the principal is to be divided in equal fourths and to be paid to Daniel's three daughters and to the children of his son Daniel. Son Daniel receives $10. The residue of the estate is to be divided among his three daughters and the children of his son Daniel. Son-in-law John Swett was named executor, although John declined this responsibility at the time of probate. Real estate was valued at $6,493 which included a store and part of a distillery house. Personal estate totaled $1,946.75. Debts were $411.93.[419]

Daniel Appleton and Lydia Ela were parents of six children born at Haverhill.

	i	WILLIAM APPLETON, b. 7 Aug 1776; d. (buried) at Fryeburg, ME, 10 Sep 1841.[420] William did not marry.
665)	ii	ALICE APPLETON, b. 11 Dec 1778; d. at Haverhill, 25 Jun 1842; m. at Haverhill, 17 Jun 1806, JOHN SWETT thought to be the son of John and Mary (Folsom) Swett;[421] John d. at New York, NY, 1834 (probate 3 Dec 1834).
	iii	ABIGAIL APPLETON, b. 7 Dec 1780; d. at Haverhill, 21 Apr 1853. Abigail did not marry.
	iv	SAMUEL APPLETON, b. 14 Aug 1783; d. 16 Jun 1787.
666)	v	DANIEL APPLETON, b. 10 Dec 1785; d. at New York, NY, 27 Mar 1849; m. 4 May 1813, his third cousin once removed, HANNAH ADAMS (*John Adams⁵, Hannah Osgood Adams⁴, Mary Russell Osgood³, Thomas², Robert¹*), b. at Andover, 18 Dec 1791 daughter of John and Dorcas (Faulkner) Adams;[422] Hannah d. at New York, 28 May 1859.
	vi	LYDIA APPLETON, b. 8 Dec 1787; d. at Haverhill, 14 Nov 1863. Lydia did not marry.

157)   WILLIAM APPLETON (*Mary Russell Appleton³, James², Robert¹*), b. at Haverhill, 6 Apr 1754 son of Samuel and Mary (Russell) Appleton; d. at Boston, about 1799 (probate Feb 1799); m. 17 Dec 1782, HANNAH CLARK, b. about 1763 daughter of Samuel Clark. Hannah married second Amasa Delano in 1803. Hannah seems to have died before the probate of the estate of Amasa Delano in 1823.

William Appleton was a housewright in Boston. In his will written 13 October 1798 (proved 19 February 1799), William Appleton bequeathed to beloved wife Hannah, for use and improvement of while she is a widow, all the real and personal estate for her comfortable support and maintenance and that of his children (who are not named). At Hannah's death or intermarriage, the estate is to be divided among his children then living in equal portions. William requested that Hannah be guardian of the children and she was named executrix.[423]

Daughter Ann did not marry. Her will written 3 February 1865 includes bequests to Anna Rockwell daughter of Charles W. Rockwell of Sing Sing, New York and to Charles H. Rockwell serving in the United States Army and to John Rockwell residing in La Salle, Illinois. Relatives named in the will are nephew Edward Appleton, niece Ann E. Appleton, Thomas Appleton son of nephew Edward, and cousin Sarah A. Bent. After multiple other bequests, the remainder of the estate goes to nephew Edward Appleton and friend Edward T. Hall to be held in trust and used for the benefit of her brother Thomas Appleton. After Thomas's decease, the property is to go to Thomas's legal heirs.[424]

William Appleton and Hannah Clark were parents of seven children born at Boston.[425]

[417] Ela, *Genealogy of the Ela Family*, p 8

[418] Chase, *The History of Haverhill*, p 487

[419] *Essex County, MA: Probate File Papers, 1638-1881.*Online database. *AmericanAncestors.org.* New England Historic Genealogical Society, 2014. Case 781

[420] Maine, J. Gary Nichols Cemetery Collection, ca. 1780-1999. Mr. William Appleton formerly of Haverhill, Mass, age 65

[421] Stackpole, *Swett Genealogy*, p 44

[422] The will of John Adams includes a bequest to his daughter Hannah wife of Daniel Appleton.

[423] Ancestry.com. *Massachusetts, Wills and Probate Records, 1635-1991* [database on-line]. Suffolk County, Probate Records, Volume 97, pp 148-149

[424] Massachusetts Wills and Probate, Suffolk County, volume 167, pp 1-3

[425] Appleton, *A Genealogy of the Appleton Family*, p 21

| | i | WILLIAM APPLETON, b. 1784; d. at Boston, 17 Aug 1806. |

| 667) | ii | THOMAS APPLETON, b. 26 Dec 1785; d. at Reading, MA, 11 Jul 1872; m. at Templeton, 5 Jul 1812, BEULAH GOODRIDGE, b. at Templeton, MA, 20 Dec 1790 daughter of Ebenezer and Beulah (Childs) Goodridge; Beulah d. at Reading, 21 May 1880. |

| | iii | EDWARD APPLETON, b. about 1787; died young |

| | iv | GEORGE APPLETON, b. 1789; died young |

| | v | HANNAH APPLETON, b. 7 May 1791; d. at Worcester, 3 Mar 1843. Hannah did not marry. |

| | vi | ANN APPLETON, b. 24 Sep 1793; d. at Boston, 18 Dec 1868. Ann did not marry. |

| | vii | GEORGE APPLETON, lost at sea, about 1830 |

158)   HANNAH APPLETON (*Mary Russell Appleton³, James², Robert¹*), b. at Haverhill, 19 Nov 1756 daughter of Samuel and Mary (Russell) Appleton; d. of asthma, at Haverhill, 24 Oct 1824; m. at Haverhill, 20 Nov 1785, Dr. EDWARD WOODBURY, b. 1761; Edward d. at Haverhill, 29 Jan 1793.

Edward was a physician/apothecary in Haverhill. Edward Woodbury did not leave a will and his estate entered probate 4 February 1793 with widow Hannah as administratrix. The inventory included a lengthy list of items in the apothecary such as English saffron, anise oil, diuretic salt, rosemary oil, salt tartar, and corrosive sublimate.[426] The estate was heavily in debt and the value of the real estate after the provisions for the dower was not enough to pay the debts.[427]

Hannah and Edward were parents of five children born at Haverhill, the youngest child born seven months after Edward's death.

| 668) | i | MARY "POLLY" WOODBURY, b. at Haverhill, 23 Aug 1786; d. at Bangor, ME, 13 Sep 1844; m. at Haverhill, 25 Oct 1811, JOSEPH BARTLETT, b. at Newburyport, 22 Mar 1776 son of Thomas and Sarah (Cilley) Bartlett. |

| 669) | ii | HANNAH WOODBURY, b. at Haverhill, 19 Apr 1788; m. at Haverhill, 7 Jun 1807, JAMES BARTLETT, b. at Haverhill, 21 Apr 1785 son of Israel and Tabitha (Walker) Bartlett; James d. at Boston, 18 Sep 1809. |

| 670) | iii | ELIZABETH WOODBURY, b. at Haverhill, 8 Dec 1789; d. at Salem, MA, 6 Apr 1868; m. at Haverhill, 28 Nov 1814, NATHAN BURRILL, b. at Salem, about 1787 son of Ezra and Ann (Breed) Burrill; Nathan d. at Haverhill, 25 Jan 1866. |

| 671) | iv | EDWARD WOODBURY, b. at Haverhill, 29 Oct 1791; d. at sea on passage from New Orleans, 7 Jun 1834;[428] m. JUDITH MOODY JEWETT, b. at Ipswich, MA, 28 Oct 1781 daughter of Epes and Betsey (Hidden) Jewett; Judith d. at Ipswich, 1 Jan 1849. |

| | v | SAMUEL APPLETON WOODBURY, b. at Haverhill, 23 Aug 1793; d. at San Francisco, CA, 15 Nov 1850.[429] |

Grandchildren of Sarah Russell and John Ingalls

159)   MARY INGALLS (*John Ingalls³, Sarah Russell Ingalls², Robert¹*), b. at Pomfret, 13 Nov 1735 daughter of John and Mary (Willis) Ingalls; m. at Pomfret, 9 Jan 1755, JOHN FISK, *likely* b. at Lexington, MA, 18 Nov 1731 son of Robert and Mary (Stimpson) Fisk; John d. at Pomfret, 6 Aug 1790.

John Fisk, known as lieutenant, participated in the French and Indian War. He was a carpenter and housewright.

A summary of the will provided in the Fiske genealogy reports the will included provisions for support of wife Mary, one-half the estate to son Daniel, and the other half divided among his three daughters, Mary, Sarah, and Alice.[430]

Mary and John were parents of five children born at Pomfret.

---

[426] The apothecary inventory goes on for several pages and would be interesting reading for anyone interested in the contents of a well-stocked late 18th century apothecary.

[427] *Essex County, MA: Probate File Papers, 1638-1881.*Online database. *AmericanAncestors.org.* New England Historic Genealogical Society, 2014. Case 30380

[428] Edward, of Newburyport, on passage from New Orleans, June 7, 1834, a. 43 y. G. R. 1.

[429] California State Library Mortuary Records (Northern California), 1849-1900; Sacramento, California; Microfilm Reel #: 13

[430] Pierce, *Fisk and Fiske Family*, p 121

      i   MOLLY FISK, b. at Pomfret, 25 Oct 1755; d. at Otsego County, NY, after 1796 when she was unmarried.[431]

      ii   JOHN WILLYS FISK, b. at Pomfret, 16 Jan 1758; d. at Pomfret, 14 Sep 1776.

672)   iii   SARAH FISK, b. at Pomfret, 3 Apr 1761; m. at Pomfret, 1 Mar 1785, SOLOMON ELDRIDGE son of Lemuel Eldridge.

673)   iv   ALLIS FISK, b. at Pomfret, 15 Apr 1763; d. at Aurora, OH, 1850; m. at Pomfret, 7 Feb 1793, SYLVANUS ELDRIDGE son of Lemuel Eldridge; Sylvanus d. at Aurora, 1812.

      v   DANIEL FISK, b. at Pomfret, 28 Sep 1766; d. after 1830 when he was living at Springfield, NY. Census records suggest that Daniel did marry and had children, but the names of his children were not found.

160)   EPHRAIM FARNUM (*Mary Ingalls Farnum³, Sarah Russell Ingalls², Robert¹*), b. at Rumford, 21 Sep 1733 son of Ephraim and Mary (Ingalls) Farnum; d. at Concord, 12 May 1827; m. at Bradford, MA, 23 Mar 1758, JUDITH HALL, b. at Bradford, 12 Apr 1739 daughter of David and Naomi (Gage) Hall; Judith d. at Concord, 13 Jul 1809.

      Ephraim Farnum was a farmer and Concord. He and his brother Benjamin inherited the family homestead from their father.[432] Ephraim and Judith were parents of seven children born at Concord.

674)   i   NAOMI FARNUM, b. 20 Apr 1760; d. at Boscawen, 20 Mar 1832; m. Mar 1780, JOHN CHANDLER, b. at Concord, 11 Dec 1752 son of John and Mary (Carter) Chandler; John d. at Boscawen, 24 Jan 1825.

      ii   JOHN FARNUM, b. 6 May 1762; d. Feb 1763.

675)   iii   JUDITH FARNUM, b. 13 Jun 1764; d. at Gorham, ME, 21 Feb 1851; m. 3 Jun 1791, JEREMIAH CHANDLER, b. at Concord, 31 Mar 1763 son of John and Mary (Carter) Chandler; Jeremiah d. at Lovell, ME, 12 Feb 1828.

676)   iv   SARAH FARNUM, b. 9 Aug 1767; m. at Boscawen, 21 Nov 1786, NATHAN CARTER, b. at Boscawen, 6 Apr 1761 son of Winthrop and Susannah (Eastman) Carter; Nathan d. at Boscawen, 25 Sep 1840.

677)   v   MOSES FARNUM, b. 20 Oct 1769; d. at Concord, 6 Mar 1840; m. 1st 13 Jun 1792, RHODA CARTER, b. 17 Feb 1771 daughter of Ezra and Phebe (Whittemore) Carter; Rhoda d. Oct 1808. Moses m. 2nd 21 Dec 1809, Rhoda's sister, ESTHER CARTER, b. 21 Feb 1778; Esther d. at Concord, 30 May 1857.

678)   vi   ESTHER FARNUM, b. 25 Oct 1772; d. at Franklin, NH, 1 Oct 1854; m. 30 Nov 1790, EBENEZER EASTMAN, b. at Concord, 19 Oct 1765 son of Moses and Elizabeth (Kimball) Eastman; Ebenezer d. at Salisbury, NH, 16 Apr 1833.

679)   vii SUSANNAH FARNUM, b. 3 Jun 1781; d. at Boscawen, 4 May 1843; m. 29 Jan 1803, MOSES COFFIN, b. at Boscawen, 22 Jul 1779 son of Peter and Rebecca (Haseltine) Coffin; Moses d. at Boscawen, 4 Sep 1854.

161)   MARY FARNUM (*Mary Ingalls Farnum³, Sarah Russell Ingalls², Robert¹*), b. at Rumford, 8 Aug 1737 daughter of Ephraim and Mary (Ingalls) Farnum; d. at Sanbornton, NH, 14 Feb 1805; m. about 1760, JONATHAN MERRILL, b. at Rumford, 10 Feb 1733 son of John and Lydia (Haynes) Merrill; Jonathan d. at New Chester, NH, 1795 (probate 21 Feb 1795).

      Jonathan Merrill was a farmer. He and Mary were first in Concord, were in Alexandria, New Hampshire about 1773, and then in Bristol, New Hampshire.[433]

      In his will written 27 March 1794 (probate 21 February 1795), Jonathan Merrill bequeathed to his beloved wife one-third of the whole of the lands, stock, buildings, and husbandry tools during her natural life. At her decease, these items will be divided among sons John, Jonathan, and Moses. His wife is to have the household furniture which can be at her disposal. Sons John, Jonathan, and Moses receive all the lands, stock, buildings, husbandry utensils, and clothing not otherwise disposed of. Each of the other children receives £15: daughter Mary Goolding, daughter Lydia Merrill, son Stephen Merrill, daughter Sarah Merrill, son Ephraim Merrill, and daughter Abigail Merrill. These amounts were to include interest in relation to when these children had reached age 18. On 4 January 1814, estate executors John, Jonathan, and Moses Merrill exhibited payments that had been made to the heirs (although it is not clear when the payments were made): Windsor and Mary Goolden, $110; Lydia

---

[431] Reported in the Pierce's Fisk genealogy as executing a deed in Jan 1796 and unmarried at that time.

[432] Bouton, *History of Concord*, p 655

[433] Merrill, *A Merrill Memorial*, p 296

Merrill, $173; Stephen Merrill, $100; Wyman and Sally Hardy, $50; Ephraim Merrill, $50; Abigail Merrill, $50; Nathaniel Merrill, $10; Moses Merrill, $1.[434]

Mary Farnum and Jonathan Merrill were parents of thirteen children.

	i	JOHN MERRILL, b. at Concord, 6 Oct 1760; died young.
	ii	JONATHAN MERRILL, b. 23 Dec 1761; d. 16 Mar 1763.
680)	iii	MARY MERRILL, b. at Concord, 31 Dec 1763; d. about 1800;[435] m. about 1785, WINSOR GOOLDEN, baptized at Newbury, MA, 12 Jul 1761 son of Winsor and Jane (Sampson) Goolden; Winsor d. at Madrid, NY, 6 Jan 1840. Winsor was second married to Ruby who survived him.
	iv	SARAH MERRILL, b. 26 Apr 1766; died in childhood.
	v	LYDIA MERRILL, b. at Concord, 23 Nov 1767. Lydia does not seem to have married as probate records for her father refer to her as Lydia Merrill through 1814.
681)	vi	JOHN MERRILL, b. at Concord, 9 Mar 1769; d. at Hill, NH, 13 May 1831; m. 12 Nov 1794, ELIZABETH DARLING, b. 27 Apr 1771 daughter of Benjamin and Hannah (Clark) Darling; Elizabeth d. at Hill, 8 Oct 1834.
	vii	LUCY MERRILL, b. at Concord, 7 Feb 1771; likely died in childhood as she is not in father's will or in the payments from father's estate.
682)	viii	JONATHAN MERRILL, b. at Concord, 6 Sep 1772; d. at Hill, NH, 20 Jan 1820; m. MARY BARNARD, b. at Warner, 20 Dec 1779 daughter of Ezekiel Barnard; Mary d. at Bristol, NH, 1 Oct 1875. Mary married second Ezekiel Moore.
683)	ix	MOSES MERRILL, b. at Concord, 28 Dec 1774; d. at Alexandria, NH, 29 Oct 1841; m. 1st Mar 1810, MIRIAM BARNARD, b. about 1783 daughter of Ezekiel Barnard; Miriam d. at Alexandria, 26 Nov 1815. Moses m. 2nd about 1816, SARAH WORTHING (widow of Sherburn Sanborn), b. at Bridgewater, NH, 11 Mar 1785 daughter of Samuel and Hannah (Ingalls) Worthing; Sarah d. 1863.
684)	x	STEPHEN MERRILL, b. likely at Hill, NH, about 1776; d. at Bristol, NH, 5 Jan 1860; m. 3 Jun 1803, RUTH DARLING, b. 4 Jul 1774 daughter of Benjamin and Hannah (Clark) Darling; Ruth d. 29 Dec 1835.
685)	xi	SARAH MERRILL, b. at Hill, 14 Apr 1778; d. at Sutton, OH, 1831; m. at Hebron, NH, 7 Nov 1803, WYMAN HARDY, b. at Bow, NH, 4 Oct 1777 son of Thomas and Abigail (-) Hardy; Wyman d. at Sutton, after 1820 and before 1829.
686)	xii	EPHRAIM MERRILL, b. at Hill, 24 Nov 1779; d. at Bridgewater, NH, 15 Oct 1844; m. Apr 1808, SALLY DREW, b. at Bridgewater, NH, 28 Sep 1791 daughter of Samuel and Elizabeth (Webber) Drew; Sally d. 21 Sep 1885.
	xiii	ABIGAIL MERRILL, b. at Hill, 13 Mar 1782. Abigail was living and unmarried at the distribution of her father's estate; nothing further known.

162)   BENJAMIN FARNUM (*Mary Ingalls Farnum³, Sarah Russell Ingalls², Robert¹*), b. at Rumford, 21 Mar 1739 son of Ephraim and Mary (Ingalls) Farnum; d. at Concord, 18 Mar 1812; m. ANNA MERRILL, b. at Rumford, 20 Dec 1743 daughter of John and Lydia (Haynes) Merrill;[436] Anna d. at Concord, 7 Mar 1803.

Benjamin and Anna resided in Concord where Benjamin served as a surveyor of highways and hogreeve.[437] A copy of Benjamin's will was not located, but the Farnum genealogy provides a summary of the 23 April 1806 will which lists the following heirs: beloved wife; sons Benjamin, Haines, Nathaniel, Jonathan, Abiel, and Jeremiah who each receives ten dollars; daughters Mary Hall, Lydia Conant, and Ann Wilson each receives ten dollars; daughters Abigail Farnum and Sarah Farnum each receives $110; and son Ephraim receives the residue of the estate.[438]

Benjamin Farnum and Anna Merrill were parents of fifteen children born at Concord.

---

[434] *New Hampshire. Court of Probate (Grafton County). Estate of Jonathan Merrill*
[435] This is based on the pension application file for Winsor Goolden in which his second wife Ruby reports she and Winsor were married in 1801.
[436] The 1773 will of John Merrill includes a bequest to his daughter Ann Farnham.
[437] Bouton, *The History of Concord*
[438] Farnham, *The Descendants of Ralph Farnum*, p 276

687) i   MARY FARNUM, b. 26 Aug 1764; d. at Alfred, ME, 23 Nov 1816; m. about 1785, ABIEL HALL, b. at Rumford, NH, 31 May 1761 son of Ebenezer and Dorcas (Abbott) Hall; Abiel d. at Alfred, Oct 1829. Abiel Hall married second Anna Francis.

688) ii   JOHN FARNUM, b. 2 Jan 1766; m. 1st about 1790, SARAH THOMPSON; Sarah d. about 1812. John m. 2nd at Warren, 3 Sep 1813, POLLY STONE (widow of John Jones), b. about 1776 likely the daughter of Uriah and Hephzibah (Hadley) Stone.

      iii ANNA FARNUM, b. 18 Mar 1767; d. 18 Jun 1778.

689) iv   BENJAMIN FARNUM, b. 10 Sep 1768; d. at Rumford, ME, 1850 (probate 26 Nov 1850); m. at Concord, 3 Jun 1790, SARAH GRAHAM, b. at Concord, 18 Feb 1770 daughter of George and Azubah (-) Graham.

690) v   EPHRAIM FARNUM, b. 5 Apr 1770; d. at Concord, 12 Feb 1836; m. SARAH BROWN, b. 1774; Sarah d. at Concord, 24 Jul 1851.

691) vi   HAINES FARNUM, b. 31 Oct 1771; d. at Plymouth, NH, 23 Dec 1824 (will 14 Dec 1824); m. at Pembroke, 31 Dec 1800, ELIZABETH "BETSY" WHITEHOUSE, b. at Pembroke, 23 May 1777 daughter of Solomon and Mary (Knox) Whitehouse;[439][440] Elizabeth d. at Plymouth, 1834 (will written 21 Jan 1832 and proved 26 Mar 1834).

      vii JONATHAN FARNUM, b. 2 Aug 1773; d. 25 Jun 1778.

692) viii NATHANIEL FARNUM, b. 5 Apr 1775; d. at Alfred, ME, 28 Sep 1861; m. HANNAH SAYWARD, b. 20 Jan 1780 daughter of John and Elizabeth (Trafton) Sayward;[441] Hannah d. at Alfred, 4 Jun 1846.

693) ix   LYDIA FARNUM, b. 26 Dec 1776; d. at Alfred, ME, 28 May 1842; m. at Pembroke, 21 Jan 1796, JOHN CONANT, b. at Beverly, MA, 10 Sep 1771 son of Nathaniel and Abigail (Dodge) Conant; John d. at Alfred, 27 Feb 1850.

694) x   JONATHAN FARNUM, b. 26 Jul 1778; d. at Alfred, ME, 11 Jan 1831; m. ESTHER PERKINS, b. at Kennebunkport, ME, 10 Jun 1787 daughter of Christopher and Esther (-) Perkins;[442] Esther d. at Brewer, MA, 2 Jul 1885.

695) xi   ABIEL FARNUM, b. 24 Apr 1780; d. at Alfred, ME, 29 Apr 1864; m. ADELIA CONANT, b. 1793 daughter of Joshua and Adelia (Gile) Conant; Adelia d. at Alfred, 7 Jun 1846.

696) xii ANNA "NANCY" FARNUM, b. 30 Jan 1783; d. at Franklin, NH, 10 Mar 1854; m. at Concord, 8 Oct 1801, Dr. JOB WILSON, b. at Belmont, NH, 25 Jan 1776 son of Nathaniel and Elizabeth (Barber) Wilson; Job d. at Franklin, 22 Sep 1851 (will proved Oct 1851).

697) xiii ABIGAIL FARNUM, b. 30 Oct 1783; d. at Alfred, ME, 23 Apr 1855; m. at Lyman, ME, 4 Dec 1813, Major ISSACHAR KIMBALL, b. at Lyman, 15 May 1784 son of Ezra and Lucretia (Cousins) Kimball; Issachar d. at Alfred, 3 Apr 1860.

698) xiv JEREMIAH FARNHAM, b. 29 Jul 1785; d. at Rumford, ME, 21 Nov 1869; m. at Concord, 16 Jan 1811, SALLY HALL, b. at Concord, 11 Sep 1788 daughter of Daniel and Deborah (Davis) Hall; Sally d. at Rumford, 26 Sep 1859.

699) xv   SARAH FARNUM, b. 29 Mar 1787; d. at Augusta, ME (burial at Alfred), 15 Oct 1864; m. at Concord, 6 Mar 1810, CHARLES P. GRIFFIN, b. at Concord, 1786; Charles d. at Alfred, 2 Mar 1825.

163)   SARAH FARNUM (*Mary Ingalls Farnum³, Sarah Russell Ingalls², Robert¹*), b. at Concord, 26 Jul 1747 daughter of Ephraim and Mary (Ingalls) Farnum; d. at Fryeburg, ME, Mar 1829; m. about 1765, WILLIAM EATON, b. at Hampstead, NH, 21 Apr 1743 son of Jeremiah and Hannah (Osgood) Eaton; William d. about 1780.

Sarah Farnum and William Eaton were parents of seven children born at Fryeburg, Maine.

---

[439] The 1821 will of Solomon Whitehouse includes a bequest to his daughter Betsy Farnum. Published genealogies give Haine's wife's name as Mary Whitehouse, or as Mary Elizabeth, but that is an error. All the records located (marriage, births of children, deaths of children, probate records of her father and her husband; and Elizabeth's own will) give her name as Elizabeth or Betsy. Solomon Whitehouse also had a daughter Mary who married Jonathan Freeman.

[440] Carter, *History of Pembroke*, p 315

[441] Sayward, *The Sayward Family*, p 100

[442] Esther's place of birth and names of parents are given on her death record.

700) i WILLIAM EATON, b. 3 Mar 1766; d. at Chatham, NH, 27 May 1852; m. at Fryeburg, 26 Nov 1795, NANCY FARRINGTON, b. 1779; Nancy d. likely at Frueburg, 28 Jul 1858.[443]

701) ii OSGOOD EATON, b. 6 Mar 1768; d. at Rumford, ME, 1 Jul 1836; m. at Concord, 10 Sep 1793, BETHIAH VIRGIN, b. at Concord, 23 Feb 1775 daughter of William and Mehitable (Stickney) Virgin; Bethiah d. at Rumford, 18 Dec 1857.

702) iii SARAH EATON, b. 20 Dec 1769; d. (burial at Stow, ME), 2 Oct 1854; m. as his third wife, JOSEPH F. CHASE, b. at Canterbury, NH, 19 Sep 1770 son of Josiah and Mehitable (Frye) Chase; Joseph d. at Conway, 29 Jan 1823. Joseph Chase was first married to Mehitable Day and second married to Joanna Day.

703) iv HANNAH EATON, b. 31 Jan 1772; m. at Concord, 4 Oct 1796, DAVID BLANCHARD, b. at Concord, 4 Dec 1771 son of John and Eleanor (Stevens) Blanchard; David d. at Concord, 1810 (probate 7 Jan 1810).

      v JEREMIAH EATON, b. 8 Mar 1774

704) vi MARY EATON, b. 2 Jul 1776; d. at Waterford, ME, 20 Jun 1849; m. at Eddington, ME, 29 Jan 1795, DAVID WHITCOMB, b. at Bolton, MA, 13 Apr 1764 son of Levi and Sarah (Gates) Whitcomb; David d. at Waterford, 27 Apr 1835.

705) vii SUSANNAH EATON, b. 21 Jan 1778; m. at Concord, 1 Mar 1803, JEREMIAH WARDWELL, baptized at Andover, 22 Jan 1771 son of Joshua and Mary (Saunders) Wardwell. Susannah and Jeremiah were living at Sidney, ME in 1850.

164) MEHITABLE ALLEN (*Mehitable Ingalls Allen³, Sarah Russell Ingalls², Robert¹*), b. at Pomfret, 9 Dec 1732 daughter of Benjamin and Mehitable (Ingalls) Allen; d. at Norwich, 4 Nov 1788; m. at Pomfret, 13 Mar 1759, SIMEON CASE, baptized at Norwich, 8 Apr 1733 son of John and Hannah (Ormsby) Case; Simeon d. at Norwich, 7 Jun 1785.

Simeon Case did not leave a will and his estate entered probate 2 August 1785 with Simeon Case as administrator. The total value of the estate was £154.9.3. The real estate included 21 ½ rods of land, a dwelling house, and an old cooper shop.[444]

Mehitable Allen and Simeon Case were parents of nine children born at Norwich including a set of triplets each of whom died soon after birth.

      i JOHN CASE, b. 18 Jan 1760; d. 27 Oct 1761

      ii SIMEON CASE, b. 24 May 1761; d. at Norwich, 20 Mar 1816. No record of a marriage was found for Simeon. However, in the 1810 census of Norwich the household of Simeon Case included one male over age 45, a female age 26-44, and a female age 16-25.[445] There are records of two children born at Norwich, a son John born to Simeon and Mehitable on 19 Feb 1788 and a daughter Mehitable born to Simeon on 4 Nov 1788. No further information was found for either of these children.

706) iii SAMUEL CASE, b. 29 Dec 1762; d. at Norwich, 8 Jan 1791; m. about 1786, SUSANNAH COWDREY,[446] b. about 1762; Susannah d. at Norwich, 24 May 1848.

      iv JOHN CASE, b. 25 Jul 1764; d. at Norwich, 19 Feb 1788.

      v DANIEL CASE, b. 30 May 1766; d. 10 Jul 1766.

      vi MEHITABLE CASE, b. 21 May 1767; d. at Norwich, 1811. Mehitable did not marry.

      vii ELIZABETH CASE, b. 19 Feb 1769; d. 20 Feb 1769.

      viii WILLIAM CASE, b. and d. 19 Feb 1769

      ix MARY CASE, b. 19 Feb 1769; d. 20 Feb 1769.

165) BENJAMIN ALLEN (*Mehitable Ingalls Allen³, Sarah Russell Ingalls², Robert¹*), b. at Pomfret, 9 Aug 1734 son of Benjamin and Mehitable (Ingalls) Allen; m. 1st at Pomfret, 24 Nov 1760, HANNAH CASE, baptized at Norwich, 18 Nov 1737

---

[443] The dates of death for both William and Nancy are given in pension records. Pension file W3666

[444] *Connecticut State Library (Hartford, Connecticut)*; Probate Place: *Hartford, Connecticut, Probate Packets, Carew, W-Chapman and Norris, 1748-1880, Case 2244*

[445] Year: 1810; Census Place: Norwich, New London, Connecticut; Roll: 3; Page: 194; Image: 00112; Family History Library Film: 0281231

[446] Perkins, *Old Houses of the Ancient Town of Norwich*, p 438

daughter of John and Hannah (Ormsby) Case; Hannah d. at Pomfret, 6 Nov 1780. Benjamin m. 2ⁿᵈ at Pomfret, 4 Dec 1782, SABRA HOSMER (widow of Edward Cleveland), baptized at Woodstock, 24 Sep 1732 daughter of Ephraim and Dorcas (Carpenter) Hosmer.

There are records of six children of Benjamin and Hannah three of whom died in childhood. Marriages were not identified for the other three children. The children were all born at Pomfret.

i	SARAH ALLEN, b. 28 Jan 1762	
ii	HANNAH ALLEN, b. 14 Jun 1764; d. 26 May 1783.	
iii	JERUSHA ALLEN, b. 5 Jun 1767; d. 11 Feb 1783.	
iv	CHLOE ALLEN, b. 9 Aug 1769; d. 16 Aug 1771.	
v	BENJAMIN ALLEN, 6 Jul 1773	
vi	CHLOE ALLEN, b. 17 Aug 1776	

166)   ISAAC ALLEN (*Mehitable Ingalls Allen³, Sarah Russell Ingalls², Robert¹*), b. at Pomfret, 12 Mar 1735 son of Benjamin and Mehitable (Ingalls) Allen; d. at Pomfret, 5 Apr 1765; m. at Norwich, 30 Jan 1760, SARAH FRENCH, baptized at Norwich, 1 Sep 1728 daughter of Abner and Sarah (Sluman) French.

Isaac Allen and Sarah French were parents of three children.

707)   i   SLUMAN ALLEN, b. at Norwich, 24 Oct 1760; d. at Chelsea, VT, 15 Apr 1834; m. at Royalton, VT, 18 Mar 1786, HANNAH STORRS, b. at Lebanon, NH, 18 Feb 1765 son of Huckins and Jerusha (Bicknell) Storrs; Hannah d. at Chelsea, after 1855 (time of statement related to pension).

708)   ii   ZIPPORAH ALLEN, b. at Pomfret, 10 Nov 1762; d. at West Killingly, 28 Aug 1846; m. at Norwich, 26 Mar 1795, DANIEL FITCH, b. in Nova Scotia, about 1762; Daniel d. at West Killingly, 3 Nov 1855.

        iii   SARAH ALLEN, b. at Pomfret, 23 Apr 1765 and baptized 28 Apr 1765

167)   JOSEPH ALLEN (*Mehitable Ingalls Allen³, Sarah Russell Ingalls², Robert¹*), b. at Pomfret, 2 Apr 1738 son of Benjamin and Mehitable (Ingalls) Allen; d. at Groton, NY, 4 Dec 1815 (age 77 on gravestone); m. at Pomfret, 13 Oct 1761, ELIZABETH WARNER, baptized at Ipswich, MA, 10 Feb 1738/9 daughter of Daniel and Sarah (Warner) Warner; Elizabeth d. at Groton, 2 Dec 1815 (age 76 on gravestone).[447]

Joseph Allen and Elizabeth Warner were parents of eleven children.

709)   i   EBENEZER ALLEN, b. at Pomfret, 24 May 1762; d. at Jefferson County, NY, 3 Jul 1824; m. at Dudley, 16 Mar 1786, PHEBE HEALY, b. at Dudley, 6 Dec 1765 daughter of Samuel and Phebe (Curtis) Healy; Phebe d. 4 Nov 1828.

        ii   SETH ALLEN, b. at Pomfret, 24 May 1764; d. 29 Nov 1765.

710)   iii   MARY "POLLY" ALLEN, b. at Pomfret, 1 Apr 1766; d. at Charlton, MA, 13 Aug 1830; m. at Dudley, 26 Jan 1792, NATHANIEL BLOOD, b. at Oxford, MA, 22 Feb 1754 son of Nathaniel and Ruth (Hall) Blood; Nathaniel d. at Charlton, 9 Apr 1838. Nathaniel was first married to Bathsheba Upham.

711)   iv   BETTY ALLEN, b. at Pomfret, 28 Feb 1768; d. at Woodstock, CT, 4 Sep 1810; m. at Dudley, 20 Apr 1786, NATHANIEL MAY, b. at Dudley, 5 Sep 1762 son of Samuel and Abigail (Lyon) May; Nathaniel d. at Oxford, MA, 25 Feb 1837.

        v   JOSEPH ALLEN, b. at Pomfret, 17 Feb 1770

        vi   DAVID ALLEN, b. at Pomfret, 11 Feb 1772

712)   vii   ISAAC ALLEN, b. at Pomfret, 1774; d. at Groton, NY, 3 Mar 1825; m. SUSAN F. SELLEN, b. 18 Feb 1794 daughter of John and Martha (Moseley) Sellen; Susan d. at Groton, 9 Dec 1881.

713)   viii   JOHN ALLEN, b. at Pomfret, 17 Feb 1776; d. at Jefferson County, NY, 24 Apr 1859; m. 1796, POLLY (or Molly) MCDOWELL, b. at Winchester, NH, 11 Apr 1776 daughter of Alexander and Levina (Oak) McDowell; Polly d. at Watertown, NY, 14 Nov 1851.

---

[447] Burial of Joseph and Elizabeth in Stearns Cemetery in Groton; findagrave ID: 47710902

714)   ix   ASAPH ALLEN, b. at Dudley, 25 Jan 1778; d. 25 Oct 1814; m. about 1800, LOIS KING, b. at Wilbraham, 13 Dec 1777 daughter of Oliver and Ruth (Cooley) King; Lois d. at Cuba, NY, 2 Aug 1847.

        x   SARAH ALLEN, b. at Dudley, 23 Feb 1780

        xi   EDITH ALLEN, b. at Dudley, 28 Apr 1782

168)   SARAH INGALLS (*Stephen Ingalls³, Sarah Russell Ingalls², Robert¹*), b. at Pomfret, 7 Nov 1735 daughter of Stephen and Rebekah (Grow) Ingalls; m. at Pomfret, 26 Feb 1756, JAMES COPELAND, b. at Braintree, MA, 19 Mar 1724 son of William and Mary (Thayer) Copeland.[448]

Sarah and James resided in Pomfret for the births of three children and were later in Brooklyn, Connecticut where perhaps an additional eight children were born (baptized).[449]

        i   PHEBE COPELAND, b. 19 Nov 1756

715)   ii   AMASA COPELAND, b. at Pomfret, 22 Apr 1758; d. at Pomfret, CT, 18 Aug 1852; m. at Pomfret, 24 Jan 1788, TRYPHENA LISCOMB, b. at Pomfret, 7 Oct 1759 daughter of Thomas and Sarah (Parkhurst) Liscomb;[450] Tryphena d. at Hampton, 2 Apr 1834.

716)   iii   SARAH COPELAND, b. at Pomfret, 4 May 1760; m. at Pomfret, 9 Nov 1783, RICHARD RINDGE, b. about 1760; Richard d. at Calais, VT, 27 Aug 1843.

        iv   JOSEPH COPELAND, baptized at Brooklyn, 19 Aug 1764.

717)   v   REBECCA COPELAND, baptized at Brooklyn, 28 Sep 1766; d. at Marshall, NY, 2 Oct 1844; m. at Hampton, CT, 27 Oct 1788, her fourth cousin (through Holt line), NATHANIEL FORD, b. at Hampton, 11 Jul 1765 son of Amos and Lydia (Davison) Ford; Nathaniel d. at Marshall, 31 Oct 1849.

        vi   WYLLYS COPELAND, baptized at Brooklyn, 4 Dec 1768; d. after 1850 when he was living in Killingly, CT. Census records suggest that Wyllys did marry and had at least one child, but the name of his wife is not found. In 1850, he was living with a family headed by David Darby.

718)   vii   WILLARD COPELAND, baptized at Brooklyn, 4 Dec 1768; d. at Braintree, VT, 20 Feb 1852;[451] m. 1st about 1795, Alice Lyon *likely* his fourth cousin, ALICE LYON (*Robert Lyon⁵, Sarah Holt Lyon⁴, Robert Holt³, Mary Russell Holt², Robert¹*), b. at Hampton, 14 Jun 1769 daughter of Robert and Alice (Holt) Lyon; Alice d. at Braintree, 1804. Willard m. 2nd at Braintree, 12 Dec 1805, REBECCA WHITE, b. at Braintree, MA, 30 May 1766 daughter of Micah and Susanna (Eager) White; Rebecca d. at Randolph, VT, 1 Aug 1856.[452]

        viii   LYDIA COPELAND, baptized at Brooklyn, 4 Aug 1771

        ix   MOLLY COPELAND, baptized at Brooklyn, 25 Jul 1773

        x   STEPHEN COPELAND, baptized at Brooklyn, 3 Mar 1776. He may be the Stephen Copeland born in CT, living in Conneaut, PA in 1860 with his son Joseph and his family.

        xi   JOHN COPELAND, baptized at Brooklyn, 21 Sep 1778

169)   THOMAS INGALLS (*Stephen Ingalls³, Sarah Russell Ingalls², Robert¹*), b. at Pomfret, 9 Dec 1742 son of Stephen and Rebekah (Grow) Ingalls; d. at Abington, CT, 10 Jan 1816; m. 1st at Pomfret, 26 Jun 1777, SARAH BOWEN, b. about 1749; Sarah d. at Pomfret, 6 Oct 1777. Thomas m. 2nd 8 Nov 1786, RUTH WOODWORTH; Ruth d. at Pomfret, 12 Apr 1827.

Thomas's first wife Sarah died just four months after their marriage. Thomas and Ruth had two daughters born at Pomfret. Both daughters lived single. Daughter Nancy was a spinner and weaver in Abington.

        i   ROXY INGALLS, b. at Pomfret, 19 Nov 1788; d. at Pomfret, 21 Jul 1857.

[448] Copeland, *The Copeland Family*, p 34
[449] Coon, "The Children of James and Sarah (Ingalls) Copeland", *Mayflower Quarterly Magazine*, 2019. This recently published article documents baptisms of seven children not previously identified for this family.
[450] The 1802 probate of Thomas Liscomb of Pomfret includes a distribution to daughter Triphena Copeland.
[451] Bass, *History of Braintree, Vermont*, p 127
[452] Bass, *History of Braintree, Vermont*

ii   NANCY INGALLS, b. at Pomfret, 16 Nov 1790; d. at Abington, 7 Dec 1847. "Nancy, spinner & weaver, of Abington Soc., d. Dec. 7, 1847, age 57."

170)   SAMUEL INGALLS (*Stephen Ingalls³, Sarah Russell Ingalls², Robert¹*), b. at Pomfret, 22 Apr 1746 son of Stephen and Rebekah (Grow) Ingalls; m. at Brooklyn, CT, 9 Nov 1769, DEBORAH MEACHAM, b. at Windham, 3 Nov 1749 daughter of Daniel and Lydia (Lillie) Meacham.

There are records of four children of Samuel and Deborah born at Pomfret.

719)   i   SAMUEL INGALLS (twin), b. at Pomfret, 24 Aug 1770; d. at Dunklee's Grove, IL, Oct 1839; m. at Belchertown, 22 Oct 1802, DIANA DODGE, b. 1778; Diana d. at Pelham, MA, 3 Dec 1833.

720)   ii   LEMUEL INGALLS (twin), b. at Pomfret, 24 Aug 1770; m. at Belchertown, MA, 1 Oct 1802, LOUISA PRENTISS.

        iii   STEPHEN INGALLS, b. 10 Sep 1772

        iv   ALICE INGALLS, b. 21 Feb 1775

171)   EPHRAIM BARKER (*Martha Ingalls Barker Goodale³, Sarah Russell Ingalls², Robert¹*), b. at Andover, 23 May 1730 son of William and Martha (Ingalls) Barker; m. 1st at Pomfret, 27 Feb 1752, HANNAH GROW, b. at Andover, 8 Nov 1723 daughter of Thomas and Rebekah (holt) Grow; Hannah d. at Windham, 29 Jul 1765. Ephraim m. 2nd at Norwich, 21 Dec 1767, widow MARY BURNHAM at Norwich, 21 Dec 1767.

Hannah Grow and Ephraim Barker were parents of six children.

721)   i   WILLIAM BARKER, b. at Pomfret, 18 Nov 1753; d. at Madison, NY, 17 May 1826; m. about 1782, BETSEY ARMSTRONG, baptized at Norwich, 30 May 1762 daughter of Silas and Bathsheba (Worden) Armstrong;[453] Betsey d. at Madison, 29 Aug 1832.[454]

722)   ii   HANNAH BARKER, baptized at Pomfret 29 Aug 1754; d. at Norwich, 1840; m. at Norwich, 20 Jan 1771, ELIJAH PITCHER,[455] b. likely at Stoughton, MA, 4 Nov 1752 son of Elijah and Tabitha (Smith) Pitcher; Elijah d. at Norwich, 14 Jun 1839.

723)   iii   JOHN BARKER, b. at Pomfret, 18 Dec 1755; d. at Stoddard, NH, 15 Mar 1834; m. 1st 1786, ESTHER RICHARDSON, b. at Leominster, 9 Mar 1767 daughter of James and Hannah (House) Richardson; Esther d. at Stoddard, 17 Jul 1806. John m. 2nd 4 Dec 1806, SALLY GUILD (widow of Daniel Warner), b. at Newton, MA, 31 Jul 1775 daughter of Samuel and Sarah (Smith) Guild;[456] Sally d. at Stoddard, 19 Jan 1843.

724)   iv   EPHRAIM BARKER, b. at Pomfret, 28 Feb 1759. He may be the Ephraim Barker who married at Wayland, MA, 27 Mar 1783, RUTH GOODNOW,[457] b. at Wayland, 18 Oct 1757 daughter of Silas and Jerusha (Willis) Goodnow; Ruth d. at Sudbury, 27 Jun 1843.

725)   v   NATHAN BARKER, b. at Pomfret, 8 Jun 1761; d. at Palmer, MA, 10 Oct 1849; m. 11 Dec 1783, LYDIA BARKER, b. 4 Jun 1763; Lydia d. at Palmer, 2 Dec 1849.

        vi   Son b. 19 Mar and d. 20 Mar 1763 at Windham.

172)   WILLIAM BARKER (*Martha Ingalls Barker Goodale³, Sarah Russell Ingalls², Robert¹*), b. at Rumford, NH, 28 Jan 1731 son of William and Martha (Ingalls) Barker; d. at Worcester, MA, 1804 (probate Apr 1804); m. at Pomfret, 22 Sep 1765, SARAH FOSTER; b. about 1745; Sarah d. after 1804.

---

[453] The 1798 will of Silas Armstrong includes a bequest to his daughter Betty wife of William Barker.

[454] Parshall's Barker genealogy provided limited information on William but included that he had married and located in Madison, NY. William and Betsey Barker had all their children in Norwich, so this marriage fits in terms of location. There is also a Revolutionary War pension file for William Barker in Madison, NY that fits this William in terms of age and location at time of enlistment.

[455] This is a supposed marriage for Hannah. The family was living in Norwich at the time of Hannah's marriage and this marriage fits for her in terms of age and location. There were not records located that firmly establish that this Hannah married Elijah Pitcher.

[456] Burleigh, *The History and Genealogy of the Guild Family*, p 45

[457] Parshall, *The Barker Genealogy*, p 7. This Barker genealogy lists a son of this Ephraim, Silas G. Barker, who was the son of Ephraim and Ruth (Goodnow) Barker.

William's mother and sister Mary located in Pomfret, and it seems plausible that William also traveled there where he married Sarah Foster. After the marriage, William and Sarah were in Wayland, Massachusetts where births of four children are recorded. They were for a time in Dudley. They were finally in Worcester where William died in 1804.

On 11 December 1794, a William Barker of Cumberland, Rhode Island sold his pew in the meeting house in Dudley to Aaron Tufts of Dudley for payment of £10.[458] It is not clear if this is William or a son William who made this transaction.

On 21 April 1804, Aaron Tufts was named administrator of the estate of William Barker. This appointment was made at the request of widow Sarah Barker who declined administration and asked the son-in-law Aaron Tufts be appointed. The estate was insolvent, and the settlement of the estate 5 November 1805 had payments of about one-third of the owed amounts to each of the creditors.[459]

There are records of five children of William and Sarah, although there may be other children. Other possible children in this family are William Barker who married Nancy Larned in Dudley in 1791 and Esther Barker who married Ebenezer Kendall in Worcester in 1796.

726)   i   SALLY BARKER, b. 9 Aug 1766;[460] d. at Dudley, 2 Mar 1842; m. at Dudley, 23 May 1790, Dr. AARON TUFTS, b. at Charlestown, MA, 30 Jan 1770 son of Aaron and Mary (Stone) Tufts; Aaron d. at Dudley, 17 Oct 1843.

        ii   POLLY BARKER, b. at Wayland, MA, 9 Jan 1774

        iii   FANNY BARKER, b. at Wayland, 5 Mar 1776

        iv   CHARLOTTE BARKER, b. at Wayland, 19 Dec 1779

727)   v   ALMIRA BARKER, b. at Wayland, MA, 26 Nov 1780; d. at Penobscot, ME, 13 Feb 1859; m. at Worcester, 3 Oct 1802, JOSEPH CARR, b. at Amesbury, MA, 14 Nov 1773 son of Francis and Mary (Elliot) Carr;[461] Joseph d. (burial at Bangor), 2 Oct 1849.

173)   MARY BARKER (*Martha Ingalls Barker Goodale³, Sarah Russell Ingalls², Robert¹*), b. at Rumford, 23 Nov 1735 daughter of William and Martha (Ingalls) Barker; m. at Pomfret, 29 Apr 1756, ISAAC ABBOTT, b. at Pomfret, 29 Aug 1732 son of Paul and Elizabeth (Gray) Abbott; Isaac d. at Milford, NH, about 1800.

Isaac Abbott was a farmer. He was born in Pomfret and there married Mary Barker. Mary had come to Pomfret from Concord, New Hampshire when her mother remarried. The births of their first seven children are recorded at Pomfret, but there is also a recording of these births at Princeton, Massachusetts. The young family left Pomfret by 1769, were for a time in Princeton where they were early settlers recorded there in 1769,[462] and finally settled in Milford, New Hampshire where they were about 1778.[463] Isaac Abbott served as a private in the company of Colonel Stickney during the Revolutionary War.

Isaac Abbott and Mary Barker had twelve children, the oldest seven recorded at Pomfret, the births of four children recorded at Princeton, and the youngest child whose birthplace is unknown. This youngest child died in Milford.

389)   i   MARY ABBOTT, b. at Pomfret, 20 Jan 1757; d. at Lyme, NH, 8 Sep 1849; m. 9 Dec 1778, her first cousin, LEMUEL HOLT, b. at Windham, 28 Feb 1756 son of Joshua and Mary (Abbott) Holt; Lemuel d. 1 Aug 1836.

728)   ii   HANNAH ABBOTT, b. at Pomfret, 2 Aug 1758; d. at Stoddard, NH, 9 Mar 1847; m. at Amherst, NH, 25 May 1781, ISRAEL TOWNE, b. at Stoddard, NH, 17 Jun 1761 son of Israel and Lydia (Hopkins) Towne; Israel d. 2 May 1848.

        iii   CHLOE ABBOTT, b. at Pomfret, 7 Aug 1760; d. at Lyme, 1835. Chloe is reported to have married twice, but the name of her first husband has not been found. She m. 2nd, about 1801, WILLIAM PORTER, b. 1761 son of William and Esther (Carpenter) Porter. William was a widower with several children, his wife Phebe Kingsbury having died in 1800. William d. 3 Mar 1847. Chloe did not have children.

729)   iv   SARAH "SALLY" ABBOTT, b. at Pomfret, 14 Oct 1762; d. at Mason, NH, 1846; m. at Amherst, 25 Oct 1795, JAMES BROWN.

        v   METYLDA ABBOTT, b. at Pomfret, 29 Aug 1764.

---

[458] Massachusetts Land Records, Worcester County, 124:512

[459] *Worcester County, MA: Probate File Papers, 1731-1881*. Online database. AmericanAncestors.org. New England Historic Genealogical Society, 2015. Case 3427

[460] Sally's date of birth is given in the Dudley town records, but this seems related to the family record there rather than her place of birth.

[461] "The Carr Family", Bangor Historical Magazine, volume 1, number 1, 1885, pp 10-11

[462] Blake, *The History of Princeton*, p 81

[463] Ramsdell, *The History of Milford, volume 1*, p 560

730) vi ISAAC ABBOTT, b. at Pomfret, 17 Jul 1766; d. at Milford, NH, 1 Sep 1831; m. 15 Oct 1793, RUTH AMES, b. at Wilmington, MA, 31 Jul 1776 daughter of Caleb and Mary (Harvey) Ames/Eams; Ruth d. at Milford, 29 Jul 1844.

vii ESTHER ABBOTT, b. at Pomfret, 28 Jun 1768.

viii FIDELIA ABBOTT, b. at Princeton, 29 May 1770.

731) ix OLIVE ABBOTT, b. at Princeton, 28 Oct 1772. It is possible that she married Isaac Parker 6 Feb 1794 at Amherst. The Olive Abbott that married Isaac was of Milford and she died 2 Jan 1862 at age 89 which fits for this Olive. Isaac Parker was b. at Monson, NH, 2 Mar 1769 son of Josiah and Hannah (Parkis) Parker.

x DOROTHY ABBOTT, b. at Princeton, 10 Sep 1774; d. at Milford, 16 Aug 1802.

xi DEBORAH ABBOTT, b. at Princeton, 10 Sep 1774; d. at Milford, 22 May 1806.

xii STEPHEN ABBOTT, b. 1778; d. at Milford, 9 Jul 1792.

174) DEBORAH BARKER (*Martha Ingalls Barker Goodale³, Sarah Russell Ingalls², Robert¹*), b. at Rumford, 20 Sep 1739 daughter of William and Martha (Ingalls) Barker; d. at Royalton, VT, 13 Jul 1820; m. at Pomfret, 12 Jul 1763, JONATHAN COY,[464] b. at Grafton, MA (as Jonathan MacCoye), 30 Oct 1730 son of William and Mary (Clark) MacCoye; Jonathan d. at Royalton, 7 Sep 1815.

Deborah and Jonathan resided in Hampden County, Massachusetts until at least 1790 and were later in Royalton, Vermont where they both died. On 10 September 1785, Jonathan Coye of Brimfield for payment of £300 conveyed to Wyllys Coye of Brimfield a parcel in Brimfield containing 78 acres. He conveyed small lots on 20 May 1789 to Aaron Lombard and on 24 September 1790 to Samuel Hale which is the last transaction in Brimfield for Jonathan Coye.[465] On 13 October 1788, Jonathan and Reuben Coy bought property "17 Dutch" in Royalton, Vermont. On 13 November 1796, Mrs. Deborah Coy was admitted as member of the First Congregational Church in Royalton, Vermont.[466]

Jonathan Coy and Deborah Barker were parents of nine children born at Monson, Massachusetts.

732) i WILLIS COY, b. 18 Jun 1764; d. at Amherst, MA, 30 Aug 1848; m. at Brimfield, 28 May 1789, AMY YOUNG, b. at Providence, RI, about 1765; Amy d. at Amherst, 1823.

733) ii PATTY COY, b. 24 Feb 1766; d. at Brimfield, 23 Jun 1861; m. at Brimfield, 24 Jan 1787, PELEG CHENEY JANES, b. at Brimfield, 2 Dec 1760 son of William and Hannah (Cheney) Janes; Cheney d. at Brimfield, 25 Jun 1834.

734) iii JONATHAN COY, b. 11 Jul 1768; d. at Royalton, VT, 30 May 1841; m. 1st 1793, OLIVE PIXLEY, b. at Dighton, MA, 25 Jun 1768 daughter of Robert and Sarah (Trask) Pixley; Olive d. at Royalton, 15 Sep 1795. Jonathan m. 2nd 1803, LUCY BINGHAM, b. at Lebanon, CT, 19 Jul 1770 daughter of Thomas and Mercy (House) Bingham; Lucy d. at Royalton, 8 Jul 1852.

735) iv REUBEN COYE, b. 24 Apr 1770; d. at Northfield, MI, 3 Dec 1843; m. at Tunbridge, VT, 17 Feb 1799, SARAH CHAMBERS, b. in NH, 1780 (census records); Sarah d. at Northfield, 1865.

736) v BEULAH COYE, b. 24 Apr 1770; d. at New Woodstock, NY, 1831; m. at Holland, MA, 20 Aug 1789, CHANDLER WEBBER, b. at Holland, MA, 1763 son of Samuel and Mehitable (Frizell) Webber; Chandler d. at New Woodstock, 13 Jun 1837.

vi JOHN COYE, b. 13 Jan 1773

737) vii SIMEON COYE, b. 24 Jan 1774; d. at Brimfield, 29 Apr 1857; m. RHODA BROWN, b. at Brimfield, 5 Sep 1775 daughter of Issachar and Rhoda (Nichols) Brown; Rhoda d. at Brimfield, 27 Oct 1846.

viii BENJAMIN COYE, b. 3 Nov 1776

738) ix DAVID COYE, b. 26 May 1781; d. at Homer, NY, 23 May 1860; m. 1st, about 1809, DORCAS HANNUM, b. at Southampton, MA, 28 Jul 1786 daughter of Seth and Anna (Searle) Hannum; Dorcas d. at Homer, NY, Jul 1818. David m. 2nd at Homer, 24 May 1820, NANCY CANFIELD, b. at Sandisfield, MA, 18 May 1791 daughter of John and Deborah (Norton) Canfield; Nancy d. at Homer, 7 Jun 1867.

[464] The last name has various spellings. Most of the children in the family used Coye more often as the spelling.
[465] Massachusetts Land Records, Hampden County, 25:339; 29:419; 28: 693
[466] Lovejoy, *History of Royalton, Vermont, Part I and II*, p 219, p 732

175)   STEPHEN BARKER (*Martha Ingalls Barker Goodale³, Sarah Russell Ingalls², Robert¹*), b. at Rumford, 21 Jan 1741 son of William and Martha (Ingalls) Barker; d. at Heath, MA, 15 Aug 1834; m. at Concord, MA, 8 Jun 1772, REBEKAH GIBSON, b. at Stow, MA 31 Mar 1754 daughter of Stephen and Sarah (Goss) Gibson; Rebekah d. at Heath, 15 Mar 1824.

      Stephen Barker was a Baptist minister and had posts in Heath and Whately. Rev. Stephen Barker of Heath was installed as pastor of the Baptist church in Whately in 1807 a position he held until 1820.[467]

      On 5 May 1825 (deed recorded 18 August 1834), Stephen Barker of Heath for payment of $1,000 conveyed to Stephen Gerry of Heath, blacksmith, land in Heath of about 50 acres, one-half of the buildings, and the blacksmith shop. On 5 May 1825 (deed recorded 18 April 1837), Stephen Barker of Heath for payment of $1,000 conveyed to Sarah Barker of Heath a tract of land in Heath with one-half of the buildings except the blacksmith shop.[468]

      On 11 August 1843, Sally Barker of Heath mortgaged a property to David Purrington and William Long for a payment of $79.63. On 12 December 1845, Purrington and Long released and transferred the deed to Rebecca Gerry of Heath for payment of $90.88. On 2 July 1847, Stephen Barker of Franklin Township, Washington County, Indiana for $22.85 quitclaimed to Rebecca Gerry any interest in a tract of land in Heath that was previously owned by Sally Barker now deceased.[469] Rebecca Gerry was the unmarried daughter of Anna Barker and Stephen Gerry.

      There is record evidence for seven children of Stephen and Rebekah.

        i   STEPHEN BARKER, b. at Ashby, 31 Oct 1772. Stephen married and was in Washington County, Indiana in the 1830 and 1840 censuses. In 1830, his household consisted of one male 50-59, one female 50-59, one male 20-29, two females 10-14, and two females, 20-29.[470] The names of his family members have not been found.

739)   ii   JOSEPH BARKER, b. at Ashby, 25 Mar 1774; m. about 1798, ELIZABETH WASHBURN.

740)   iii   REBECCA BARKER, b. at Heath, MA, 26 Jun 1776; d. at Montrose, PA, 29 Jun 1819; m. at Heath, 6 Oct 1799, DANIEL LYONS, b. at Roxbury, MA, 26 May 1778 son of David and Abigail (Draper) Lyons;[471] Daniel d. at Great Bend, PA, 7 Sep 1850.

741)   iv   TIMOTHY BARKER, b. at Heath, 30 Mar 1778; d. at Lottsville, PA, 6 Mar 1869; m. BETSEY who has not been identified, b. in VT, 1787; Betsey d. at Lottsville, 4 May 1872.

742)   v   ANNA BARKER, b. 1780; d. at Heath, MA, 25 Aug 1850; m. at Heath, 21 Oct 1810, STEPHEN GERRY, b. at Hatfield, 22 Aug 1784 son of Nathan and Martha (Waite) Gerry; Stephen d. at Wautoma, WI, 2 Mar 1867.

       vi   SALLY BARKER, b. estimate 1782. Sally did not marry and is likely the Sarah Barker who mortgaged property in Heath in 1843. She was deceased by 1847.

743)   vii   LUCY BARKER, b. at Heath, 1784; d. at Willing, NY, 25 Feb 1847; m. at Heath, 4 Dec 1813, MATTHEW WILSON, b. 1794; Matthew d. at Willing, 14 Jul 1877. Matthew married second Patience Harrington and married third Ruth Eaton.

176)   REUBEN GOODELL (*Martha Ingalls Barker Goodale³, Sarah Russell Ingalls², Robert¹*), b. at Pomfret, 16 Aug 1744 son of Jacob and Martha (Ingalls) Goodale; d. at New Haven, 11 Feb 1822; m. at Pomfret, 27 May 1772, ABIGAIL SHARPE, b. at Pomfret, 14 May 1744 daughter of John and Dorcas (Davis) Sharpe;[472] Abigail d. (burial at New Haven), 19 Mar 1819.

      Son Clement married but did not have children. In his will written 15 December 1825 (probate 18 March 1843), Clement Goodell of New Haven bequeathed to beloved wife Rebecca all the buildings he erected on her land and all the personal estate. He bequeathed all his real estate to his three beloved brothers now living: Reuben, John, and Erastus. Wife Rebecca was named executrix. Real estate was valued at $1,145.[473]

      There are four children known for Reuben and Abigail and there may have been other children who died before adulthood.

744)   i   REUBEN GOODELL, b. likely at New Haven, about 1775; d. at New Haven, 19 Nov 1851; m. about 1802, SARAH who has not been identified; Sarah d. at New Haven, 16 Jan 1849.

[467] Temple, *History of the Town of Whately*, p 119
[468] Massachusetts Land Records, Franklin County, 88:350; 98:105
[469] Massachusetts Land Records, Franklin County, 123:39; 174:5
[470] Year: 1830; Census Place: Washington, Indiana; Series: M19; Roll: 31; Page: 345; Family History Library Film: 0007720
[471] Lyon, *Lyon Memorial*, p 186
[472] The 1779 will of John Sharpe includes a bequest to his daughter Abigail Goodell
[473] Connecticut Wills and Probate, New Haven, Probate Records volume 55, pp 126-127 and New Haven Estate packet number 4346

ii   CLEMENT GOODELL, b. 1779; d. at New Haven, CT, 2 Mar 1853; m. REBECCA OSBORN, b. 1785 daughter of Medad and Rachel (Hotchkiss) Osborn; Rebecca d. at New Haven, 30 Jun 1862. Clement and Rebecca did not have children.

745)   iii   JOHN GOODELL, b. likely at New Haven, 1782; d. after 1855 when he was living at Homer, NY; m. 1st DEBORAH LAFLIN, b. at Charlton, MA, 10 Apr 1780 daughter of Joseph and Martha (Cummins) Laflin; Deborah d. about 1823. John m. 2nd, BETSEY E., b. in CT, about 1793; Betsey d. after 1860 when she was living at Homer.

746)   iv   ERASTUS GOODELL, b. likely at New Haven, about 1785; d. at Homer, 25 Oct 1868; m. at Fairlee, VT, 4 Mar 1812, MARY "POLLY" C. COBURN, b. in MA, about 1785; Mary d. at Homer, 29 Sep 1856.

177)   SIMEON GOODELL (*Martha Ingalls Barker Goodale³, Sarah Russell Ingalls², Robert¹*), b. at Pomfret, 13 Feb 1746 son of Jacob and Martha (Ingalls) Goodale; d. at Cherry Valley, NY, 2 Jul 1837;[474] m. at Brooklyn, CT, 8 Jun 1775, MARTHA WILLIAMS, b. at Pomfret, 25 Apr 1755 daughter of William and Martha (Williams) Williams;[475] Martha d. at Cherry Valley, 3 May 1786.[476]

Simeon and Martha resided in Cherry Valley, New York. In 1800, the household consisted of one male 45 and over, one female 45 and over, two males 16-25, one female under 10, one female 10-15, and one female 16-25.[477] This suggests Simeon remarried after the death of Martha, but the name of his second wife was not found.

There are four children reported in the Goodale genealogy[478] and a fifth child, Joshua, is likely in this family.

i   POLLY GOODELL, b. about 1775

ii   JOSHUA GOODELL, b. 1776; d. at Cherry Valley, NY, 27 Sep 1851. Joshua does not seem to have married.

747)   iii   LUCY GOODELL, b. about 1778; m. Mr. Newbury.

748)   iv   WILLIAM GOODELL, b. 13 Mar 1779; d. at Parma, NY, 28 Jul 1867; m. 9 Feb 1812, SYLVIA DUTCHER, b. 2 Mar 1789 daughter John and Sylvia (Beardsley) Dutcher; Sylvia d. at Parma, 6 Nov 1865.

v   MARGARET GOODELL, b. about 1780; reported has marrying Mr. Knapp who was not identified. Two children, Edwin and Margaret, are reported but information on these children was not located.

178)   SILAS GOODELL[479] (*Martha Ingalls Barker Goodale³, Sarah Russell Ingalls², Robert¹*), b. at Pomfret, 16 Aug 1747 son of Jacob and Martha (Ingalls) Goodale; d. at Norwich, 20 Mar 1825; m. at Norwich, 24 Jun 1784, SARAH MARSHALL, b. at Norwich, 20 Sep 1757 daughter of Thomas and Ann (Manwaring) Marshall; Sarah d. 11 Dec 1822.

Silas served as lieutenant during the Revolution and received the honorary promotion of captain by brevet on 3 February 1784. He received his commission as lieutenant in the 3rd Connecticut regiment on 25 April 1778.[480]

Silas Goodell had an oil mill and was a merchant of products such as linseed oil. He set up a mill near the falls in Norwich in 1786.[481] His probate record includes records of his sales of oil. Silas did not leave a will and Ephaphras Porter of New Haven was appointed administrator 5 April 1825 with William Goodell as surety. The inventory had a value of $2,770.37 with $136.25 of that being the value of one-sixth part of the real estate of Mrs. Sarah Goodell deceased. Two of those signing receipts for receiving payment for their claims against the estate were Lucretia Goodell for $260 and William Goodell for $549.38.[482]

Silas Goodale and Sarah Marshall were parents of seven children born at Norwich. William, Nancy, Lucretia, and Sally did not marry and lived together in Norwich where they were in 1870.[483]

i   CHARLES GOODELL, b. 14 May 1785; d. at Warren, MA, 25 Jan 1867; m. at Brookfield, MA, 2 Apr 1822, CATHERINE F. BEMIS, b. at Paxton, 1798 daughter of John and Mary (Flagg) Bemis; Catherine d. at

[474] U.S., Headstone Applications for Military Veterans, 1925-1963
[475] Williams, *A Genealogy of the Descendants of Robert Goodale*, p 63
[476] Simeon and Martha are buried in Cherry Valley Cemetery, findagrave ID: 46324803
[477] Year: 1800; Census Place: Cherry Valley, Otsego, New York; Series: M32; Roll: 25; Page: 700; Image: 9; Family History Library Film: 193713
[478] Williams, *A Genealogy of the Descendants of Robert Goodale*, p 64
[479] Records have spellings of both Goodell and Goodale for Silas
[480] U. S. Revolutionary War Pension and Bounty-Land Warrant Application Files, S36559
[481] Caulkins, *History of Norwich, Connecticut*, p 606
[482] Connecticut Wills and Probate, Norwich Probate District, Town of Norwich, Estate of Silas Goodell, Case 4524
[483] Year: 1870; Census Place: Norwich, New London, Connecticut; Roll: M593_114; Page: 628A; Family History Library Film: 545613

Warren, 3 May 1878. Charles and Catherine do not seem to have had children, or at least no children that survived childhood.

| | ii | WILLIAM GOODELL, b. 16 Oct 1786; d. by drowning 28 Jun 1790. |

      ii   WILLIAM GOODELL, b. 16 Oct 1786; d. by drowning 28 Jun 1790.

      iii   ANNE "NANCY" GOODELL, b. 23 Dec 1787; d. at Norwich, 6 Sep 1874.

      iv   LUCRETIA GOODELL, b. 1 Nov 1789; d. at Norwich, 6 Dec 1879.

      v   SARAH "SALLY" GOODELL, b. 25 Feb 1793; d. at Norwich, 4 Feb 1879. In her will written 30 Nov 1877, Sally left her estate to her sister Lucretia for her use during her natural life, the estate to then to go to her cousin Mary A. Dean.[484]

      vi   WILLIAM GOODELL, b. 21 May 1795; d. at Norwich, 20 Dec 1871.

749)   vii   OLIVER GOODELL, b. 13 Feb 1797; m. 1st at Norwich, 1823, HARRIET BACKUS, b. at Bozrah, CT, 23 Apr 1799 daughter of Ozias and Elizabeth (Abell) Backus; Harriet d. at Jewett City, 6 Apr 1825. Oliver m. 2nd about 1827, PAULINA SALISBURY, b. about 1804 *perhaps* the daughter of Abraham and Penelope (Arnold) Salisbury; Paulina seems to have died before 1850 when their youngest daughter Phila, then age 8, was living with relatives in Rhode Island.

179)   PEGGY GOODALE (*Martha Ingalls Barker Goodale³, Sarah Russell Ingalls², Robert¹*), b. at Pomfret, 1 Sep 1749 daughter of Jacob and Martha (Ingalls) Goodale; d. at Brimfield, MA, 7 Jan 1826; m. about 1771, as his third wife, RICHARD BISHOP, b. at Manchester, MA, 9 Aug 1732 son of John and Elizabeth (Hooper) Bishop; Richard d. at Brimfield, 30 Apr 1806. Richard was first married to Sarah King and second married to Rachel Lee.

    Richard and Peggy resided in Brimfield where they had a farm. On 13 July 1803, Richard Bishop conveyed to Jacob Bishop, innholder, three tracts of land in Brimfield, the first containing 134 acres, for payment of £500.[485]

    Son Jacob Bishop married but did not have children. In his will written 23 March 1847, he bequeathed to George Bishop son of brother Calvin Bishop, one hundred dollars; to Rufus Bishop his brother of Scipio, Ohio, one hundred dollars; to brother Harrison G. Bishop of Warren in Worcester County, one hundred dollars; and to his other brothers and sisters he thought it not expedient to leave them any legacy. The remainder of the estate goes to his beloved wife Lucy Bishop and she is to have the whole of the estate during her life with the other legacies in the will not paid until after her decease.[486]

    Peggy Goodale and Richard Bishop were parents of ten children born at Brimfield.

      i   JACOB BISHOP, b. at Brimfield, 6 Apr 1773; d. at Brimfield, 12 Nov 1847; m. LUCY WEBB, b. at Huntington, MA, 27 Oct 1780 daughter of Darius and Deborah (Palmer) Webb; Lucy d. at Brimfield, 8 Aug 1863. Jacob and Lucy did not have children.

750)   ABIGAIL BISHOP, b. at Brimfield, 13 Sep 1774; d. at Brimfield, 2 Nov 1833; m. at Brimfield, 14 Jun 1792, SOLOMON HOAR (later HOMER) b. at Brimfield, 17 Mar 1771 son of Joseph and Mary (Hitchcock) Hoar; Solomon d. at Brimfield, 11 Dec 1844.

751)   ii   JOHN BISHOP, b. at Brimfield, 29 Apr 1776; d. at Homer, NY, 6 Dec 1850; m. at Brimfield, 23 Dec 1798, ALFLEDA BLASHFIELD, b. at Brimfield, 30 Mar 1774 daughter of William and Lois (Lumbard) Blashfield; Alfleda d. at Homer, NY, 20 Oct 1855.

752)   iii   GRATIS BISHOP, b. at Brimfield, 15 Nov 1777; d. at Brimfield, 5 Sep 1862; m. at Brimfield, 8 Mar 1798, ISSACHAR BROWN, b. 20 May 1770 son of Issachar and Rhoda (Nicholas) Brown; Issachar d. at Brimfield, 27 Mar 1855.

      iv   RICHARD BISHOP, b. at Brimfield, 19 Mar 1780. There is a marriage intention of Richard Bishop and Sally Blodgett (daughter of Jonas Blodgett and Rhoda Dady) on 4 Jan 1803, but it is noted that the intention was not recorded, and perhaps they did not marry. In any case, no children for the couple were located.

753)   v   CALVIN BISHOP, b. at Brimfield, 4 Jul 1782; d. at Spafford, NY, 3 May 1846; m. about 1809, OLIVE DADY, b. at Southampton, MA, 2 Jul 1789 daughter of Nathaniel and Sarah (Hannum) Dady; Olive d. 1873.

      vi   LUCY BISHOP, b. 4 Jul 1782; Lucy d. at Brimfield, 6 Jun 1824. Lucy did not marry.

---

[484] Connecticut Will and Probate, Norwich Probate District, Estate of Sally Goodell, Case 4523

[485] Massachusetts Land Records, Hamden County, 46:698

[486] Massachusetts Wills and Probate, Hampden County, Estate of Jacob Bishop, 7 Feb 1848

754) vii MATILDE BISHOP, b. at Brimfield, 30 Nov 1785; d. (recorded at Brimfield), 15 Nov 1815; m. 6 Aug 1807, ABNER NUTTING, b. at Brimfield, 9 May 1783 son of Jonathan and Abigail (Bannister) Nutting; Abner d. at Brimfield, 29 Dec 1810.

755) viii RUFUS BISHOP, b. at Brimfield, 15 Jul 1787; d. at Scipio, OH, 19 Sep 1851; m. at Brimfield, 30 May 1810, SUSANNAH WEBB, b. Feb 1785 daughter of Darius and Deborah (Palmer) Webb; Susannah d. at Republic, OH, 8 Mar 1863.

756) ix HARRISON BISHOP, b. at Brimfield, 25 Oct 1789; d. at Warren, MA, 30 May 1856; m. 1812, MARGARET BROWNING, b. at Brimfield, 1793 daughter of Joseph Davis and Margaret (Morgan) Browning; Margaret d. at Warren, MA, 10 Feb 1845.

180) BENJAMIN GOODALE (*Martha Ingalls Barker Goodale³, Sarah Russell Ingalls², Robert¹*), b. at Pomfret, 27 Jun 1753 son of Jacob and Martha (Ingalls) Goodale; d. at Sturbridge, MA, 19 Feb 1801; m. at Pomfret, 4 Mar 1779, ABIGAIL KIMBALL, b. about 1761 whose parents are not identified.

The family was in Pomfret, Norwich, and finally in Sturbridge, Massachusetts by 1791. Benjamin was killed at age 46 while felling a tree.[487] Benjamin Goodell did not leave a will and his estate entered probate 13 March 1801 with Zophaniah Gibbs and Augusta Goodell (later signing as Augusta Briggs) as administrators of the estate as widow Abigail declined administration. Simeon Fiske was named as guardian to minor children: Roxalana, Harriot, and Ward above age fourteen and Ralph and Chester Kimball under age fourteen. The homestead farm was valued at $3,015 and the total estate value was $4,081.63. Debts of the estate were $1,346.40.[488]

Benjamin and Abigail were parents of nine children.

757) i AUGUSTA GOODALE, b. at Pomfret, 29 Jun 1779; d. at Henry County, IL, 18 Dec 1857; m. at Sturbridge, MA, 18 Feb 1802, as his second wife, DANIEL BRIGGS, b. at Taunton, MA, about 1769 son of Daniel and Mehitable (Dean) Briggs; Daniel d. at Henry County, Feb 1840. Daniel was first married to Patty Morris.

758) ii ROXILANA GOODALE, b. at Pomfret, 11 Mar 1781; d. at Buffalo, NY, Mar 1860; m. at Sturbridge, 25 Nov 1802, DANIEL PLIMPTON, b. at Sturbridge, 16 Mar 1781 son of Elijah and Mary (Cheney) Plimpton; Daniel d. at Holland, MA, 21 Sep 1851.

       iii HARRIET GOODALE, b. at Norwich, 21 Jul 1784; d. at Sturbridge, MA, 5 Sep 1842; m. at Sturbridge, 29 Nov 1804, JOSEPH CHENEY PLIMPTON, b. at Sturbridge, 4 Sep 1783 son of Elijah and Mary (Cheney) Plimpton; Joseph d. at Sturbridge, 16 Jul 1831. No children were identified for Harriet and Joseph.

759) iv WARD GOODALE, b. at Norwich, 12 May 1786; d. after 1830 when he was living at Manlius, NY; m. CHAMPANY who has not been identified.

       v RALPH GOODALE, b. at Norwich, 28 Apr 1788

       vi SILAS GOODALE, b. at Norwich, 20 Apr 1790; d. 4 Nov 1790.

       vii BENJAMIN GOODALE, b. at Sturbridge, 8 Jul 1791; d. 8 Jul 1791.

       viii LOUISA GOODALE, b. 12 Oct 1792; d. 15 Dec 1794.

       ix CHESTER KIMBALL GOODALE, b. at Sturbridge, 6 Dec 1794

181) BENJAMIN INGALLS (*Benjamin Ingalls³, Sarah Russell Ingalls², Robert¹*), b. at Pomfret, 25 Jul 1746 son of Benjamin and Mary (Lyon) Ingalls; d. at Pomfret, 8 Oct 1825;[489] m. at Pomfret, 6 Jul 1769, EUNICE WOODWORTH, likely the Eunice b. at Groton, CT, 24 Jan 1748 daughter of Asa and Sarah (Lester) Woodworth; Eunice d. at Pomfret, 10 Aug 1819 in her 71st year.[490]

Benjamin and Eunice were parents of seven children born at Pomfret. In 1800, the household of Benjamin Ingalls of Pomfret included seven persons: one male over 45; one female over 45; two females under 10; two females 16 to 24; and one female 26 to 44.[491]

---

[487] Benjamin, "killed falling a tree," Feb. 19, 1801. [a. 46, G.R.1.]

[488] *Worcester County, MA: Probate File Papers, 1731-1881.* Online database. AmericanAncestors.org. New England Historic Genealogical Society, 2015. Case 24480

[489] Benjamin Ingalls died at age 80; Connecticut Church Record Abstracts, volume 090, Pomfret, p 57

[490] Connecticut Church Record Abstracts, volume 090, Pomfret, p 59

[491] Year: 1800; Census Place: Pomfret, Windham, Connecticut; Series: M32; Roll: 2; Page: 804; Image: 408; Family History Library Film: 205619

760)   i   DANIEL INGALLS, b. 3 May 1770; d. after 1810 and before 1816; m. at Pomfret, 2 Nov 1794, BETHIAH BROWN, b. at Pomfret, 12 Jun 1769 daughter of Samuel and Sarah (Bowman) Brown; Bethiah d. as a widow, at Pomfret, 21 June 1816.

       ii   ASA INGALLS, b. 31 Mar 1772; d. 28 Mar 1776.

       iii   MOLLY INGALLS, b. 27 Sep 1774; d. 8 Mar 1776.

       iv   BENJAMIN INGALLS, b. 27 Sep 1774; d. 24 Sep 1778.

761)   v   CALEB INGALLS, b. 29 Jan 1777; m. at Pomfret, 1 Jul 1804, CLARISSA ANN DOWNER.[492]

       vi   BETSEY INGALLS, b. 22 May 1780; m. at Pomfret, 30 Sep 1804, her third cousin once removed, JOSEPH TRUESDELL (*Jeduthan Truesdell[5], Mary Holt Truesdell[4], Robert Holt[3], Mary Russell Holt[2], Robert[1]*), b. at Pomfret, 27 Aug 1779 son of Jeduthan and Abigail (White) Truesdell. Joseph Truesdell was "of Homer" at the time of the couple's marriage in 1804. Joseph occurs in the 1820 at Homer and there appear to be four children in the home. However, no definitive information has yet been located for this couple.

       vii   HANNAH INGALLS, b. 1 Feb 1784; d. 22 Mar 1816. Hannah did not marry.

182)   DAVID INGALLS (*Benjamin Ingalls[3], Sarah Russell Ingalls[2], Robert[1]*), b. at Pomfret, 2 Aug 1747 son of Benjamin and Mary (Lyon) Ingalls; d. at Pomfret, 10 May 1814; m. 1 Apr 1772, MARY MAY whose parents have not been identified.
       There are records for five children of David Ingalls and Mary May born at Pomfret.

762)   i   THEDA INGALLS, b. at Pomfret, 24 Mar 1773; m. at Pomfret, 25 Dec 1793, JOSHUA PRATT, b. at Plymouth, MA, 20 Jun 1770 son of Daniel and Lydia (Cobb) Pratt;[493] Joshua d. 20 Jan 1834. Joshua married second Phebe Lisseaur.

763)   ii   DORCAS INGALLS, b. at Pomfret, 6 Dec 1774; d. at Woodstock, CT, 15 Mar 1814; m. at Pomfret, 17 Apr 1803, as his second wife, TIMOTHY PERRIN, b. at Woodstock, 25 May 1767 son of Timothy and Mary (Wolly) Perrin; Timothy d. at Woodstock, 23 Mar 1814. Timothy was first married to Lydia Raymond.

764)   iii   LUCY INGALLS, b. at Pomfret, 31 Mar 1777; d. at Dansville, MI, 24 Jun 1849; m. 4 Jul 1811, as his second wife, ZEPHANIAH HICKS, b. at Rehoboth, MA, 21 Nov 1773 son of Israel and Elizabeth (Bowen) Hicks; Zephaniah d. at Dansville, 14 Jun 1864.

       iv   MARY INGALLS, b. at Pomfret, 24 May 1779; may be the Mary Ingalls, housekeeper, who died at Pomfret, 4 Sep 1856, age 77.

       v   ESTHER INGALLS, b. at Pomfret, 20 Mar 1782

183)   MARY INGALLS (*Benjamin Ingalls[3], Sarah Russell Ingalls[2], Robert[1]*), b. at Pomfret, 13 Jun 1749 daughter of Benjamin and Mary (Lyon) Ingalls; m. at Pomfret, 1 Jun 1769, DIER HASTINGS likely the son of Joseph and Zerviah (Crocker) Hastings.
       Mary and Dier were parents of six children born at Norwich.

765)   i   OLIVER HASTINGS, b. at Norwich, 15 Oct 1769; d. at Sprague, CT, 29 Dec 1848; m. 1st at Canterbury, 13 Nov 1796, PHILURA PAINE, b. 1772; Philura d. at Lisbon, CT, 28 Jul 1822. Oliver m. 2nd at Lisbon, 11 May 1823, as her second husband, LEMIRA BUSHNELL (widow of Andrew Lee), b. 1789 daughter of Jason and Hannah (Kirkland) Bushnell; Lemira d. at Springfield, OH, Mar 1860. Lemira married third Josiah Spencer on 22 Nov 1852.

766)   ii   DYER HASTINGS, b. at Norwich, 27 Sep 1771; d. at Maryland, NY, 25 Jul 1843; m. about 1802, ANNA WATTLES, b. 30 Jan 1782 (calculated from age at death of 38 years, 9 months, 4 days); Anna d. at Maryland, NY, 3 Oct 1838.

       iii   MOLLY HASTINGS, b. at Norwich 11 Jul 1773

---

[492] The marriage transcription and the transcriptions of the births of all the children give her name as Clarissa; death records for two of the children gives her name as Ann Downer and Anna Downing.
[493] Pratt, *The Pratt Directory*, 1998 edition, p 562

iv   LYDIA HASTINGS, b. 9 May 1775; d. 28 May 1776

v   CHARLES HASTINGS, b. at Norwich, 5 Apr 1777

vi   LYDIA HASTINGS, b. at Norwich, 10 Apr 1779

Grandchildren of Benjamin Russell and Sarah Preston

184)   SARAH RUSSELL (*Benjamin³, Benjamin², Robert¹*), b. at Ashford, 26 Feb 1726 daughter of Benjamin and Sarah (Perry) Russell; d. at Eastford, 12 Mar 1752; m. by 1748, CONSTANT HART, baptized at Little Compton, RI, 14 Jul 1728 son of Nathaniel and Elizabeth (Perkins) Hart; Constant d. at Charlestown, NH, 1792 (probate 1792).

After the death of his wife, Constant went to Charlestown, New Hampshire arriving there after 1760.[494]

Constant Hart did not leave a will and his estate entered probate 5 July 1792 with Josiah Hart, millwright, allowed as administrator. The estate was reported as insolvent in October 1792. After administration expenses, the estate had a balance of £31 which was ordered to be paid to the creditors.[495]

Sarah Russell and Constant Hart were parents of three children born at Ashford.

767)   i   JOSIAH HART, b. 18 Aug 1748; d. at Charlestown, NH, 1832 (probate 1832); m. 1st about 1773, MEHITABLE who has not been identified; Mehitable d. at Charlestown, NH, 1 Aug 1790. Josiah m. 2nd 19 Dec 1790, SUSANNA PUTNAM, *perhaps* b. at Lunenburg, MA, 16 Sep 1756 daughter of Thomas and Ruth (Weatherbee) Putnam; Susanna d. at Charlestown, 8 Feb 1808. Josiah m. 3rd at Charlestown, 17 Jul 1808, RUTH GROUT.

768)   ii   JOHN HART, b. 23 Apr 1750; m. at Charlestown, NH, 9 Jul 1773, SUBMIT FARNSWORTH, b. at Charlestown, 29 Jun 1750 daughter of Stephen and Eunice (Hastings) Farnsworth.

        iii   BENJAMIN HART, b. and d. 4 Mar 1752

185)   BENJAMIN RUSSELL (*Benjamin³, Benjamin², Robert¹*), b. at Ashford, 26 Jan 1728 son of Benjamin and Sarah (Perry) Russell; d. at Burlington, VT, 27 Jan 1808; m. 1st at Ashford, 11 Oct 1750, ELIZABETH REED; Elizabeth d. at Ashford, 6 Dec 1756. Benjamin m. 2nd at Ashford, 28 Feb 1757, PHEBE SMITH, b. 1735; Phebe d. at Burlington, 8 Sep 1823.

Benjamin Russell and Elizabeth Reed were parents of three children born at Ashford.

        i   ELIZABETH RUSSELL, b. 28 Jul 1751; d. 27 Aug 1754.

        ii   SARAH RUSSELL, b. 17 Jun 1753; d. 8 Oct 1754.

        iii   BENJAMIN RUSSELL, b. at Ashford, 30 Jul 1755

Benjamin Russell and Phebe Smith were parents of eight children born at Ashford.

769)   i   DAVID RUSSELL, b. 10 Jun 1758; d. at Burlington, VT, 3 Oct 1843; m. at Fairfield, CT, 26 Nov 1789, MARTHA PYNCHON, b. at Boston, 22 Jan 1755 daughter of Joseph and Mary (Cotton) Pynchon; Martha d. at Burlington, 23 Jan 1805. David m. 2nd, KEZIAH PLIMPTON (widow of Converse Barrell), b. at Southbridge, MA, 29 Aug 1770 daughter of Gershom and Martha (Marcy) Plimpton; Keziah d. at Burlington, VT, 14 May 1847.

770)   ii   ELEAZER RUSSELL, b. 15 Nov 1761; d. after 1840 when he was living at New Hartford, NY; m. EUNICE SYKES, b. at Suffield, CT, 6 Nov 1770 daughter of Titus and Rhoda (Miller) Sykes;[496] Eunice d. about 1835.

771)   iii   JAMES RUSSELL, b. 1763; d. after 1810 when he was living at Pompey, NY; m. LYDIA BROWN.

772)   iv   STEPHEN RUSSELL, b. 28 Jan 1765; d. at Burlington, VT, 5 Mar 1847; m. at Pomfret, 12 Feb 1800, MARY SHARP, b. at Pomfret, 14 Feb 1776 daughter of Robert and Sarah (Davis) Sharp; Mary d. at Burlington, 18 Dec 1844.

[494] Saunderson, *History of Charlestown*, p 103

[495] New Hampshire Wills and Probate, Cheshire County, Estate of Constant Hart

[496] Suffield Historical Society, Family History of Victory Sikes, http://www.suffieldhistoricalsociety.org/families_sikes

     v   PHEBE RUSSELL, b. 16 Dec 1766

     vi   ELIJAH RUSSELL, b. 5 Oct 1768

773)   vii ANNA RUSSELL, b. 25 Nov 1770; d. at Burlington, VT, 23 Jan 1813; m. at Ashford, 22 Aug 1793, RICHARD WARE, b. at Wrentham, MA, 30 Jun 1766 son of John and Hannah (George) Ware; Richard d. after 1850 when he was living at Potsdam, NY. Richard had a second marriage, but the name of his second wife has not been found.

774)   viii SALLY RUSSELL, b. 28 Feb 1774; d. at Pittsfield, MA, 23 Dec 1833; m. at Hampton, 25 Sep 1794, HENRY DURKEE, b. at Hampton, 25 Aug 1770 son of Henry and Sarah (Holt) Durkee.

186)   JOHN RUSSELL (*Benjamin³, Benjamin², Robert¹*), b. at Ashford, 11 Oct 1730 son of Benjamin and Sarah (Perry) Russell; m. at Ashford, 10 Jul 1750, ALICE LYON, likely his first cousin b. about 1731 daughter of Seth and Abigail (Russell) Lyon; Alice d. at Springfield, VT. 2 Nov 1794.

    John Russell and Alice Lyon were parents of ten children born at Windham, Connecticut. Marriages were confirmed for just two of the children.

     i   MEHITABLE RUSSELL, b. 12 Nov 1751

     ii   ABIGAIL RUSSELL, b. 26 Sep 1753

     iii SARAH RUSSELL, b. 11 Jan 1756

     iv JOHN RUSSELL, b. 3 Apr 1758

     v   ELIZABETH RUSSELL, b. 11 Jan 1760

     vi THOMAS RUSSELL, b. 24 Sep 1761

     vii ABILENE RUSSELL, b. 12 Apr 1764

775)   viii CYNTHIA RUSSELL, b. at Windham, CT, 22 Jan 1771; m. at Springfield, VT, 9 May 1793, ASA HALL.

776)   ix EBENEZER RUSSELL, b. at Windham, CT, 15 Feb 1773; m. at Springfield, VT, 29 Jan 1795, REBECCA HUDSON, b. 1775; Rebecca d. at Brandon, VT, 1850.

     x   LEVI RUSSELL, b. 6 May 1776

187)   MARY RUSSELL (*Benjamin³, Benjamin², Robert¹*), b. at Ashford, 8 Jul 1733 daughter of Benjamin and Sarah (Perry) Russell; d. at Ashford, 25 Mar 1771; m. 8 Aug 1750, INGOLDSBY WORK, b. at Ashford, 17 Feb 1726 son of Joseph and Elizabeth (Ingoldsby) Work; Ingoldsby d. at Ashford, 22 Mar 1813. After Mary's death, Ingoldsby married Esther Bugbee on 11 Jul 1771.

    Ingoldsby Work was a farmer in Ashford (now Eastford).

    In his will written 2 June 1802 (proved 6 April 1813), Ingoldsby Work of Ashford bequeathed to beloved wife Esther use of half of the farm where he now lives, the personal estate to be at her disposal, and the pew in the bottom of the meeting house during her natural life. The children of daughter Sarah Crawford deceased receive one hundred dollars to equally divide. Son Joseph Work receives two dollars; children of Elizabeth Judson deceased, fifty dollars; children of daughter Mary Keyes, fifty dollars; son Henry Work, ten dollars; son Alexander Work, ten dollars; children of daughter Lucy Hayward, twenty dollars; daughter Anna Phillips, fifty dollars; and daughter Esther Trowbridge, twenty dollars. Son Samuel Work receives all the lands of what was originally called the Perry Farm in Ashford, one half of the pine lot, and one-half of the corner pew in the meeting house. Samuel is responsible to pay legacies to the children of Sarah Crawford and to daughter Esther Trowbridge. Son John receives the wearing apparel and one-half of the corner pew. Son Levi receives the remainder of the estate, is responsible to pay the other legacies and is named executor. Real estate consisted of the homestead farm of 150 acres valued at $3,000, the Perry farm of 50 acres valued at $1,000, the pine lot valued at $60, and two pews in the Eastford meeting house valued at $30.[497] Esther and Levi are children from Ingoldsby' second marriage to Esther Bugbee.

    Mary Russell and Ingoldsby Work were parents of nine children born at Ashford.

777)   i   SARAH WORK, b. 20 Feb 1751; d. at Union, CT, 23 May 1793; m. at Danbury, CT, 28 May 1767, SAMUEL CRAWFORD, b. 22 Jul 1748 son of Hugh and Margaret (Campbell) Crawford; Samuel d. 11 May 1824. Samuel was second married to Olive Eddy.

---

[497] Connecticut Wills and Probate, Pomfret Probate District, Town of Ashford, Estate of Ingoldsby Work, Case 4564

466)   ii   HENRY WORK, b. 22 Jan 1752; d. at Eastford, 22 Apr 1832; m. 1st about 1778, CATHERINE SPRING, b. at Ashford, 3 Mar 1750 daughter of Josiah and Catherine (Bicknell) Spring; Catherine d. about 1786. Henry m. 2nd, at Ashford, 11 Jan 1787, HANNAH DEAN, b. at Woodstock, 22 Dec 1766 daughter of Zephaniah and Hannah (Hayward) Dean;[498] Hannah d. at West Woodstock, 26 Oct 1848. Catherine was first married on 15 Mar 1770 to JOSEPH FARNUM (*Manasseh Farnum⁴, Phebe Russell Farnum³, Thomas², Robert¹*), b. at Windham, 28 Nov 1748 son of Manasseh and Keziah (Ford) Farnum.

       iii   BENJAMIN WORK, b. 26 Nov 1754; d. 27 May 1777.

778)   iv   ELIZABETH WORK, b. 1 Feb 1757; d. at Eastford, 14 Jan 1785; m. at Ashford, 7 Jan 1779, Rev. ANDREW JUDSON, b. about 1749; Andrew d. at Eastford, 15 Nov 1804. Andrew was second married to Mary Work on 13 Mar 1785.

779)   v   MARY WORK, b. 1 Jan 1759; d. at Eastford, 9 Mar 1798; m. at Ashford, 16 Jun 1779, EDWARD KEYES, b. at Ashford, 4 Jun 1759 son of Solomon and Sarah (Sumner) Keyes; Edward d. at Ashford, 1 May 1827. Edward married second Sarah Whitmore.

780)   vi   ALEXANDER WORK, b. 8 Mar 1763; d. at Williamstown, VT, 24 Apr 1822; m. at Ashford, 26 Nov 1789, DOROTHY SMITH, b. at Woodstock, CT, 25 Jan 1769 daughter of Asa and Hannah (Bowen) Smith; Dorothy d. at Williamstown, VT, 4 Sep 1828.

781)   vii   LUCY WORK, b. 14 Sep 1765; d. at Eastford, 3 Nov 1801; m. at Eastford, 26 Jun 1788, MANASSEH HOWARD, b. at Ashford, 25 Nov 1763 son of John and Rebecca (Peake) Hayward; Manasseh d. at Eastford, 13 Jun 1836. Manasseh was second married to Dorothy Corbin.

      viii   ARIEL WORK, b. 29 Sep 1767; d. at Eastford, CT, 29 Jan 1788.

782)   ix   ANNA WORK, b. 5 Feb 1771; d. at Fulton, NY, 24 Aug 1848; m. at Ashford, 9 Feb 1792, ASA PHILLIPS, b. at Smithfield, RI, 8 May 1769 son of Elijah and Rhoda (Sayles) Phillips; Asa d. at Fulton, 17 Feb 1813.

188)   JOHN MARCY (*Mary Russell Marcy³, Benjamin², Robert¹*), b. at Ashford, 23 Jul 1724 son of Samuel and Mary (Russell) Marcy; d. at Windsor, VT, 23 Nov 1797; m. at Middletown, 5 Mar 1751, HANNAH SHARPE, b. about 1724; Hannah d. at Windsor, 11 Apr 1801.[499]

     John and Hannah started their family in Middletown, were in Walpole, New Hampshire for a time, and settled finally in Windsor, Vermont. The births/baptisms of six children are recorded in Middletown. The family was in Walpole by 1765 when John was selectman at Walpole.[500] John is in records of town officers in Walpole through 1773 and daughter Hannah married Nathan Hatch in Walpole in 1778.

     Capt. John Marcy did not leave a will and his estate entered probate on 28 November 1797 with Reuben Smith as administrator. Stephen Marcy and Samuel Marcy were sureties for the bond. Total estate was valued at $1,468.82, $921.50 being real estate. Dower was set off to widow Hannah on 18 May 1798. The distribution to the heirs was 18 May 1798: children of Mary Hodgman deceased late wife of Jonathan Hodgman, Jr. (Mary Hodgman and Marshall Hodgman); Stephen Marcy; Hannah Hatch wife of Nathan Hatch of Reading, Vermont; John Marcy of Cambridge, Vermont; Joseph Marcy of Windsor, Vermont; Samuel Marcy of Windsor; and Martha Smith wife of Reuben Smith.[501]

     John Marcy and Hannah Sharpe were parents of nine children.

       i   STEPHEN MARCY, b. at Middletown, 14 Feb 1751/2; d. 8 Oct 1753.

783)   ii   JOHN MARCY, b. at Middletown, 18 Sep 1753; m. LUCY.

784)   iii   HANNAH MARCY, b. at Middletown, 10 Apr 1755; d. at Fort Miller, NY, 15 Oct 1841; m. at Walpole, NH, 12 Aug 1778, NATHAN HATCH, b. at Tolland, 17 Sep 1757 son of Joseph and Sarah (Stearns) Hatch; Nathan d. at Fort Miller, 1 Jun 1841.

785)   iv   STEPHEN MARCY, b. 14 Feb 1757; d. at Gorham, NY, 10 Nov 1843; m. ACHSAH HOWE, b. 1769; Achsah d. 1836.

---

[498] The 1803 will of Zephaniah Dean includes a bequest to daughter Hannah wife of Henry Work.
[499] There is another John Marcy born in Woodstock 27 Feb 1726/7 son of John and Experience Marcy who has been proposed as the husband of Hannah Sharpe. However, John the husband of Hannah died in 1797 at age 73 and the source that suggests he was the son of John and Experience gives his birth date as 1724 (the birth year of John son of Samuel) and their son John was born in 1727.
[500] Aldrich, *Walpole As It Was*, p 160
[501] Vermont Wills and Probate, Windsor County, Probate Estate Files, Estate of Capt. John Marcy, Nov. 28, 1797

786)   v   SAMUEL MARCY, b. at Middletown, Jun 1759; d. at Windsor, VT, 18 Feb 1838; m. at Brookfield, MA, 9 Sep 1787, PRISCILLA DORR, b. at Roxbury, MA, 22 Sep 1764 daughter of Moses and Eleanor (Gerald) Dorr; Priscilla d. at Windsor, 8 Feb 1846.

787)   vi   MARY "POLLY" MARCY, baptized at Middletown, CT, 22 Feb 1761; d. at Windsor, VT, 7 Sep 1797; m. about 1783, JONATHAN HODGMAN, likely b. at Concord, MA, 3 Apr 1753 son of Jonathan and Mercy (Buttrick) Hodgman; Jonathan d. at age 97 at Fairfax, VT, 16 Jun 1847. Jonathan married second Marvil Burdick on 19 January 1799.

        vii MARTHA "PATTY" MARCY, b. at Walpole, NH, about 1764; d. at Windsor, VT, 14 Feb 1831; m. at Windsor, VT, 3 Oct 1782, REUBEN SMITH, baptized. at Farmington, CT, 15 Feb 1761 son of Steele and Lois (Newell) Smith; Reuben d. at Windsor, 12 Jan 1838. Reuben and Martha did not have children. In his will written 19 September 1831, Reuben had bequeathed his wearing apparel to his brothers Russell Smith, Asahel Smith, Samuel Smith, and Hart Smith. All real and personal estate was left to orphan children Martha S. Norton and Sarah Norton children of Rufus Norton deceased.[502]

        viii JOSEPH MARCY, b. estimate 1765; living in Windsor, VT in 1800. In the 1800 census, Joseph appears to be married with two children (one male under 10 and one male 16-25), but the name of his wife was not found.

189)   DORCAS MARCY (*Mary Russell Marcy³, Benjamin², Robert¹*), b. at Ashford, 24 May 1727 daughter of Samuel and Mary (Russell) Marcy; d. at Mansfield, CT, 13 Dec 1766; m. at Woodstock, 12 Sep 1751, NATHANIEL CARY, b. at Windham, 23 Oct 1729 son of Jabez and Hannah (Handee) Cary; Nathaniel d. at Willington, 26 Jan 1818. Nathaniel married second Sarah Sargent and third Tabitha Root.
        Dorcas and Nathaniel were parents of seven children, the first six children all baptized at Mansfield on 13 November 1763.[503] Nathaniel had eight other children by his second and third wives.

788)   i   MARY CARY, b. 16 Jul 1752; d. at Fowler, NY, 16 Mar 1839; *likely* m. before 1781, JEDEDIAH KINGSLEY, b. at Becket, MA, 15 Nov 1753 son of Nathaniel and Sarah (Walden) Kingsley; Jedediah d. at Fowler, 13 Nov 1832.

789)   ii   DELIGHT CARY, b. 6 Sep 1754; m. at Mansfield, CT, 15 Jun 1774, TIMOTHY FULLER.

790)   iii DORCAS CARY, b. 11 Jul 1756; m. at Mansfield, 21 Apr 1779, RUFUS PALMER, b. at Mansfield, 11 Feb 1756 son of Joshua and Ruth (Sargent) Palmer

        iv   NATHANIEL CARY, b. 18 Apr 1758; d. about 1778 while in the service.[504]

        v   LUCRETIA CARY, b. 2 Oct 1760

        vi   SIBBEL CARY, b. 11 Oct 1762

791)   vii SARAH CARY, b. 1 Oct 1764; m. 1st about 1785, EBENEZER BUSH. Sarah m. 2nd about 1792, ZACCHAEUS BARNUM, b. about 1763; Zacchaeus d. at Shoreham, VT, 28 Aug 1840.

190)   WILLIAM MARCY (*Mary Russell Marcy³, Benjamin², Robert¹*), b. at Woodstock, 17 Mar 1729/30 son of Samuel and Mary (Russell) Marcy; d. at Hartland, VT, Apr 1813;[505] m. 1st at Union, 2 May 1756, LUCY BUGBEE, b. at Woodstock, 1740 daughter of Jesse and Elizabeth (Peake) Bugbee; Lucy d. about 1792. William m. 2nd before 1797, ROSANNA TUCKER, b. about 1754; Rosanna d. at Morristown, VT, 11 Oct 1830. Rosanna married second Thomas Hoadley.
        William was born in Woodstock. He is perhaps the William Marcy who in 1758 participated in the French and Indian War in the company of Capt. David Holmes.[506] William started his family in Connecticut, was for a time in Sturbridge before traveling to Hartland, Vermont on oxcart in 1778.[507]
        William Marcy and Lucy Bugbee were parents of seven children.

---

[502] Vermont Wills and Probate, Windsor County, Probate Records volume 15, p 360
[503] Connecticut Church Record Abstracts, volume 065, Mansfield, p 27
[504] Cary, *John Cary the Plymouth Pilgrim*, p 97
[505] Marcy, *Record of the Marcy Family*, p 306
[506] Connecticut Soldiers, French and Indian War, 1755-62
[507] Darling, *History and Anniversary of Hartland, Vermont*, p 233

792)   i   CHESTER MARCY, b. at Woodstock, CT, 6 Nov 1759; d. 25 Oct 1845; m. about 1793, MATILDA KING (widow of Daniel Waldo), b. at Brookfield, MA, 6 Mar 1761 daughter of Jonathan and Abigail (Manning) King.

793)   ii   GARDNER MARCY, b. at Woodstock, 1762; d. at Hartland, VT, 8 Oct 1837; m. 4 Dec 1791, ELIZABETH DANFORTH, b. at Billerica, MA, 1 Apr 1763 daughter of Nicholas and Elizabeth (Jaquith) Danforth; Elizabeth d. at Hancock, 10 May 1857.

794)   iii   OLIVE MARCY, b. about 1763; m. at Hartland, VT, 10 Jan 1782, WILDER WILLARD, b. 1760 son of Oliver and Thankful (Doolittle) Willard; Wilder d. at Hartland, 1791.

795)   iv   WILLARD MARCY, b. at Woodstock, CT, 3 Oct 1764; d. at Hartland, VT, 31 Jan 1849; m. LYDIA PIKE, b. at Sturbridge, 3 Mar 1767 daughter of John and Mehitable (Howard) Pike; Lydia d. at Hartland, 4 Mar 1839.

796)   v   WINTHROP MARCY, b. at Woodstock, CT, 28 Jun 1767; d. at Windsor, VT, 1841 (probate 1 Apr 1841); m. 1st at Hartland, VT, 7 Nov 1793, ABIGAIL SARGENT daughter of Isaac and Ruth (Blaisdell) Sargent. Winthrop m. 2nd at Cornish, NH, 15 Mar 1806, OLIVE AYERS. Winthrop m. 3rd at Hartland, 1 Feb 1827, CATHERINE RAWSON, b. about 1763; Catherine d. at Hartland, 25 Sep 1837. Winthrop m. 4th at Hartland, 13 Apr 1840, SOPHIA KEYES, b. at Reading, VT, 27 Mar 1789 daughter of Solomon and Thankful (-) Keyes; Sophia d. at West Windsor, VT, 15 Aug 1876.

797)   vi   SALOME MARCY, b. at Sturbridge, MA, 1 Apr 1771; d. at Cornish, NH, 22 Jul 1809; m. at Hartland, VT, about 1788, EBENEZER PIKE, b. at Sturbridge, 9 Nov 1764 son of John and Mehitable (Howard) Pike; Ebenezer d. at Northumberland, NH, 12 Aug 1819. Ebenezer married second Lucinda Kimball (widow of Alexander Waters) on 28 Sep 1809.

798)   vii   LEVI MARCY, b. at Sturbridge, MA, 3 Sep 1773; d. at Hartland, VT, 7 Mar 1838; m 1796, RUTH SARGENT, b. 13 Apr 1773 daughter of Isaac and Ruth (Blaisdell) Sargent; Ruth d. at Hartland, 15 May 1847.

William Marcy and Rosanne Tucker were parents of two children.

799)   i   MARY "POLLY" MARCY, b. at Hartland, VT, 20 Nov 1797; d. at St. Albans, VT, 6 Nov 1877; m. at Hartland, 21 Aug 1820, NATHAN PERKINS, b. at Woodstock, VT, 8 Apr 1793 son of Nathan and Hannah (Sturtevant) Perkins; Nathan d. at St. Albans, 6 Apr 1865.

800)   ii   SARAH "SALLY" MARCY, b. at Hartland, VT, 22 Oct 1799; d. at Morristown, VT, 5 Dec 1880; m. DANIEL GILBERT, b. at Hartford, VT, 17 Apr 1796 son of Nathaniel and Rachel (Strong) Gilbert; Daniel d. at Morristown, 18 Mar 1874.

191)   ZEBADIAH MARCY (*Mary Russell Marcy³, Benjamin², Robert¹*), b. at Woodstock, 23 Aug 1732 son of Samuel and Mary (Russell) Marcy; d. at Willington, 1 Dec 1806; m. 21 Aug 1754, PRISCILLA MORRIS, b. 28 Apr 1737 daughter of Edward and Bethiah (Peake) Morris; Priscilla d. 30 Jul 1785. Zebadiah m. 2nd at Willington, 8 March 1787, SARAH KNOX, b. about 1744; Sarah d. at Ashford, 8 Aug 1802.

     Zebadiah was a farmer in Woodstock and Ashford. The estate of Zebadiah Marcy entered probate 23 December 1806 with Zebadiah Marcy as administrator and Daniel Dimmick as surety. The total value of the estate was $4,489.91 and debts were $416.24. Distribution of the estate was made 29 April 1807 each heir receiving value of $538.17. Those heirs were Zebadiah Marcy, Hannah Dimmick wife of Daniel Dimmick, heirs of Dorcas Lamb, Priscilla Converse, Mary Curtis wife of James Curtis, Levine Dunton wife of Samuel Dunton, Martha Marcy, Sylinda Marcy. A final distribution on 5 March 1810 named the separate heirs of daughter Dorcas Lamb: Joseph Lamb, Morris Lamb, Dorcas Billings, Selenda Willard, Lovina Holt, Lydia Lamb, Polly Lamb, and Lucinda Lamb.[508]

     Zebadiah Marcy and Priscilla Morris were parents of twelve children.

   i   Son, b. at Woodstock 15 Feb 1756

   ii   MARY "MOLLY" MARCY, b. at Woodstock, 16 Feb 1757; d. at Woodstock, 6 May 1776

   iii   ADIN MARCY, b. at Woodstock, 17 Apr 1758; d. aboard a prison ship in New York Harbor during the Revolution.

[508] Connecticut Wills and Probate, Hartford, Stafford District, Town of Willington, Estate of Zebadiah Marcy, Case 1463.

801)   iv   PRISCILLA MARCY, b. at Woodstock, 6 Jan 1760; d. at Navarino, NY, 15 Aug 1834; m. about 1778, JEDEDIAH "DYER" CONVERSE, baptized at Thompson, CT, 28 Jul 1754 son of Josiah and Mary (Sabin) Converse; Dyer d. at East Windsor, CT, 11 Sep 1818.

386)   v   ZEBADIAH MARCY, b. at Woodstock, 2 Jul 1761; d. at Willington, 26 Sep 1851; m. 1st at Willington, 24 Mar 1785, his third cousin, PHEBE PEARL (*Dinah Holt Pearl⁴, Joshua Holt³, Mary Russell Holt², Robert¹*), b. at Willington, 27 Nov 1765 daughter of Timothy and Dinah (Holt) Pearl; Phebe d. at Willington, 10 Apr 1816. Zebadiah m. 2nd MARY "POLLY" BRITT, b. about 1780; Mary d. at Willington, 10 Feb 1846.

802)   vi   LOVINA MARCY, b. at Ashford, 27 Jan 1763; d. at Willington, 10 Nov 1840; m. 1st at Willington, 4 Dec 1788, as his second wife, SAMUEL DUNTON, b. at Wrentham, MA, 10 Nov 1748 son of Samuel and Sarah (Bennet) Dunton; Samuel d. at Willington, 1 May 1813. Lovina m. 2nd at Willington, 17 Aug 1815, as his second wife, ELIJAH HOLT, b. at Willington, 24 Oct 1757 son of Caleb and Mary (Merrick) Holt; Elijah d. at Willington, 4 Jul 1817. Elijah was first married to Molly Simmons. Elijah Holt and his first wife Molly Simmons are Family 320.

803)   vii   HANNAH MARCY, b. at Ashford, 1766; d. at Ashford, 6 Aug 1828; m. about 1792, as his second wife, DANIEL DIMOCK, b. at Ashford, 15 Jul 1750 son of Ebenezer and Mary (Keyes) Dimock. Daniel d. at Ashford, 2 Feb 1823.

804)   viii   DORCAS MARCY, b. at Ashford, 15 Mar 1768; d. at Randolph, VT, 1803; m. at Randolph, VT, 1 Feb 1786, JOSEPH LAMB, b. at Hopkinton, RI, 22 May 1763 son of Nathan and Lydia (Plummer) Lamb; Joseph d. at Sheldon, VT, 25 Mar 1848. Joseph married second Clara Willard.

805)   ix   MARTHA MARCY, b. at Ashford, 29 Oct 1769; d. at Willington, 11 Aug 1853; m. at Willington, 26 Nov 1807, THOMAS KNOWLTON, b. at Ashford, 13 Jul 1765 son of Thomas and Anna (Keyes) Knowlton; Thomas d. at Willington, 14 Apr 1858.

        x   THOMAS MARCY, b. at Ashford, 15 Mar 1770; d. about 1772.

806)   xi   MARY "POLLY" MARCY, b. at Willington, about 1779; m. JAMES CURTIS, b. at Ashford, 19 Mar 1779 son of Ransom and Alice (Whitten) Curtis; James d. at Machias, NY, 1863.

807)   xii   CYLINDA MARCY, b. at Stafford, 27 Jun 1780; d. at Willington, 4 Apr 1816; m. at Willington, 19 Apr 1808, as his second wife, DAVID GLAZIER, b. at Willington, 5 Nov 1771 son of Silas and Suze (Johnson) Glazier; David d. at Willington, 2 Sep 1858. David married first Fear Alden, third married Fanny Woodworth Gager, and fourth married Alice Walker.

192)   SAMUEL MARCY (*Mary Russell Marcy³, Benjamin², Robert¹*), b. at Woodstock, 19 Oct 1739 son of Samuel and Mary (Russell) Marcy; d. at Windsor, VT, 5 Feb 1820; m. at Union, 10 Apr 1763, LOIS PEAKE, b. at Union, about 1743 daughter of Christopher and Rebekah (Bugbee) Peake.
        Samuel was born in Woodstock but went with his parents to Union when his father bought land there in 1753.[509] Samuel and Lois relocated to Windsor, Vermont. Samuel Marcy and Lois Peake were parents of twelve children, the oldest ten children given in Hammond's *History of Union*.

808)   i   ESTHER MARCY, b. at Union, CT, 28 Apr 1763; d. at Weathersfield (Ascutney), VT, 24 Mar 1839; m. at Windsor, VT, 3 Oct 1787, ISAAC PARKER, perhaps the Isaac b. at Mansfield, CT, b. at Mansfield, CT, 24 Feb 1755 son of Zachariah and Peace (Ames) Parker; Isaac d. at Weathersfield, 23 Jun 1821.

809)   ii   ALVAN MARCY, b. at Union, 22 Jun 1765; d. at Windsor, VT, 24 Jan 1834; m. at Windsor, 1 Oct 1797, as her second husband, MARY DRAKE (widow of Thomas Bunce), b. 1764 daughter of Samuel and Martha (Pratt) Drake;[510] Mary d. at Windsor, 13 Dec 1841.

        iii   PROSPER MARCY, b. 26 Jul 1767; d. 26 Jan 1770

810)   iv   AVIS MARCY, b. at Union, 5 Sep 1769; d. at Weathersfield, VT, 1820; m. about 1791, as his second wife, BURPEE PROUTY, b. 10 Mar 1763 son of Richard and Esther (Smith) Prouty; Burpee d. at Hartford, VT, 1 Feb 1849. Burpee was first married to Amarillis Tolles and third married to Martha Ballard.

811)   v   PROSPER MARCY, b. 1 Mar 1772; d. at Windsor, VT, 15 May 1855; m. JANE DUTTON, baptized at Rindge, NH 15 Nov 1771 daughter of Silas and Sarah (Whitney) Dutton; Jane d. at Windsor, 26 Mar 1849.

---

[509] Hammond, *The History of Union, Conn.*, p 408
[510] Gay, *Descendants of John Drake of Windsor*, p 62

812) vi ORRIN MARCY, b. 25 Apr 1774; d. at Ashford, CT, 21 Jul 1828; m. 1st at Eastford 14 May 1797, POLLY WORK, b. 1779 daughter of Joseph and Elizabeth (Hayward) Work; Polly d. at Eastford, 9 Jul 1816. Orrin m. 2nd Polly's sister, LUCY WORK, b. about 1791; Lucy d. at Eastford, 12 Mar 1830.

vii JOHN SULLIVAN MARCY, b. 2 Dec 1776. John is reported to have gone to Georgia where he died.[511]

813) viii DORCAS MARCY, b. 18 Jan 1779; d. at Windsor, VT, 29 Nov 1838; m. 1st by 1803, ISAAC PROCTOR who has not been identified but d. before 1810. Dorcas m. 2nd about 1813, as his second wife, SEYMOUR BURNHAM, b. 1777; Seymour d. at Windsor, 30 Sep 1832. Seymour was first married to Mabel Potter.

ix LOIS MARCY, b. 9 Jan 1781; m. DAVID BROWN. No information was located for this family.

814) x SAMUEL MARCY, b. 22 Apr 1783; d. at Windsor County, VT, 10 Dec 1846;[512] m. at Weathersfield, 1 May 1806, RUTH HATCH, b. about 1785; d. at Weathersfield, VT, 17 Mar 1846.

xi STEPHEN MARCY, b. 13 Oct 1785; d. at Weathersfield, 21 Jul 1806.

xii REBECCA MARCY, b. about 1789; m. OTIS PRIM. No information was located for this family.[513]

193)   TABITHA MARCY (*Mary Russell Marcy³, Benjamin², Robert¹*), b. at Woodstock, 12 Sep 1742 daughter of Samuel and Mary (Russell) Marcy; d. at Union, 22 Jul 1807; m. about 1762, JOSEPH FAIRBANK,[514] b. at Holliston, MA, 3 Jun 1741 son of Jabez and Susannah (Corning) Fairbanks; Joseph d. at Union, 4 Jan 1817.

Joseph Fairbank was born in Holliston and located in Union, Connecticut where he married Tabitha Marcy.

Stephen Fairbank was named administrator of his father's estate on 9 January 1817. Debts were $151.92 and the total amount for distribution was $2,054.15 with each heir entitled to $293.54. Those heirs were representatives of Joshua Fairbanks, Molly Fairbanks, Joseph Faribanks, Orrin Fairbanks, Tabitha Sawin, Daniel Fairbanks, and Stephen Fairbanks. Two items on the administrative costs filed by administrator Stephen Fairbank were three pints of gin and two quarts of rum.[515]

Daughter Molly did not marry and wrote her will 24 August 1818 and it was recorded in Stafford district in 1823. The will is damaged, and images are not available. Heirs listed in the will provided in a probate abstract are brother Joshua Fairbanks, sister Tabitha Sawings, brother Joseph Fairbanks, brother Orin Fairbanks, brother Daniel Fairbanks, and brother Stephen Fairbanks. There is also a bequest to Mary Mercy Hammond the daughter of sister Sibbel Fairbanks. William Foster was named executor.[516]

Joseph Fairbanks and Tabitha Marcy were parents of nine children born at Union.

i STEPHEN FAIRBANK, b. 4 Mar 1763; d. at Union, 7 Jul 1783.

815) ii JOSHUA FAIRBANK, b. at Union, 23 Dec 1764; d. at Sheddsville, VT, 9 Dec 1812 (probate 19 Dec 1812); m. ZEULIME SAWIN, baptized at Belchertown, MA, 20 Sep 1766 daughter of Samuel and Hannah (Capen) Sawin; Zeulima d. after 1820 when she was head of household at Bridgewater, VT.

iii MOLLY FAIRBANK, b. 2 Nov 1767; d. at Union, 1823. Molly did not marry.

iv TABITHA FAIRBANK, b. at Union, 14 Oct 1770; d. at Sheddsville, VT, 9 Mar 1846; m. about 1790, JEROHAM SAWIN, baptized at Greenwich, MA, 15 May 1763 son of Samuel and Hannah (Capen) Sawin; Jeroham d. at West Windsor, 23 Jun 1859. No children were identified for Tabitha and Jeroham. Jeroham served three enlistments during the Revolution with total service of 20 months.[517]

816) v JOSEPH FAIRBANK, b. at Union, 13 Jul 1773; d. at Felchville, VT, Feb 1859; m. 1st MARY HUMPHREY, b. 1785 daughter of Daniel and Naomi (Elmore) Humphrey; Mary d. 29 Jun 1812. Joseph m. 2nd HANNAH WILBUR.

817) vi SIBBEL FAIRBANK, b. at Union, 9 Jul 1779; d. at Union, about 1807. Sibbel had an out-of-wedlock child with SHUBAEL HAMMOND, b. at Sturbridge, MA, 28 Feb 1776 son of Job and Jemima (Baker) Hamant; Shubael d. at Union, CT, 25 Jul 1857. Shubael married Polly Paul.

---

[511] Marcy, *Record of the Marcy Family*, p 6
[512] This is the date of death given in the Marcy genealogy. Samuel's wife Ruth wrote a will before this date leaving her estate to her daughter and to her four sons after her daughter's death and she does not mention being married in the will.
[513] Rebecca is a child reported in Marcy's *Record of the Marcy Family*, p 6 for whom no records were found.
[514] Joseph uses last name spelling of Fairbank in most records, but sometimes is given as Fairbanks.
[515] Connecticut Wills and Probate, Stafford District, Town of Union, Probate Packet Estate of Joseph Fairbanks, Case 740
[516] *Connecticut State Library (Hartford, Connecticut); Probate Place: Hartford, Connecticut, Probate Packets, Enos-Foskit, John, 1759-1880, Estate of Molly Fairbanks*
[517] U. S. Revolutionary War Pension and Bounty-Land Warrant Application Files, Case S21465

        vii   DANIEL FAIRBANK, b. 29 Aug 1781

        viii   ORRIN FAIRBANK, b. about 1783

818)   ix   STEPHEN FAIRBANK, b. at Union, 11 Jul 1787; d. at Litchfield, MI, 10 Feb 1847; m. at Union, 10 Apr 1810, MARTHA SABIN, b. at Thompson, CT, 20 Jan 1792 daughter of Peter and Sarah (Allen) Sabin; Martha d. at Albion, MI, 24 Sep 1877.

194)   SIBBEL MARCY (*Mary Russell Marcy³, Benjamin², Robert¹*), b. at Woodstock, 13 Mar 1744/5 daughter of Samuel and Mary (Russell) Marcy; m. at Union, 28 Feb 1763, MOSES PEAKE, b. at Killingly, 10 Aug 1736 son of Christopher and Rebekah (Bugbee) Peake; Moses d. after 1790 when living at Montgomery, NY.[518]

        Moses Peake served in the Revolution in the company of Capt. George Peck in Reed's regiment of militia.[519] This regiment served at Greenwich and Westchester. He was likely part of the militia that was hit by British warship artillery at Kip's Bay on 15 September 1776.[520]

        Sibbel and Moses were parents of seven children.[521]

        i   DORCAS PEAKE, b. at Tolland, 19 Mar 1763

        ii   EBENEZER PEAKE, b. about 1768

        iii   ELEAZER PEAKE, b. about 1770; m. MARY VOORHIS. No information was found for this family.

819)   iv   OLIVER PEAKE, b. 18 Oct 1772; d. at Delhi, NY, 19 Feb 1859; m. 12 Sep 1792, ELIZABETH who has not been identified, b. about 1775; Elizabeth d. at Delhi, 12 Jan 1846.

820)   v   ROSWELL PEAKE, b. 1774; d. at Hamden, NY, 1824; m. 1798, JANE MASON, b. in Ireland, 1782 daughter of James and Anne (Boyd) Mason; Jane d. at Hamden, 1849.

821)   vi   ELIJAH PEAKE, b. 1775; d. at Warren, NY, 26 Oct 1858; m. by 1803 although the name of his wife has not been found.

822)   vii   SYBIL PEAKE, b. about 1780; m. about 1800, EPHRAIM FRISBEE, b. at Ellsworth, CT, 21 May 1778 son of Hezekiah and Susan (Marvin) Frisbee.[522] Ephraim d. at Pittsburgh, PA, 2 Nov 1862. Ephraim had a second marriage to Mary.

195)   HANNAH HUMPHREY (*Hannah Russell Humphrey³, Benjamin², Robert¹*), b. at Ashford, 11 Sep 1728 daughter of John and Hannah (Russell) Humphrey; d. at Ashford, 1752;[523] m. at Ashford, 6 Dec 1749, JONATHAN AVERY, b. at Dedham, 13 Sep 1722 son of Jonathan and Lydia (Healy) Avery; Jonathan d. at Ashford, 15 Jan 1750.[524]

        Jonathan died about six weeks after his marriage to Hannah and their only child was born six months after his death. Inventory of his estate was made on 15 March 1749/50. Estate was valued at £1309.5.6 of which £939.16.0 was notes owed to the estate. The estate was distributed to widow Hannah and only child Jonathan on 16 June 1752.[525] Jonathan's father Jonathan Avery wrote his will 16 January 1754 (probate 1761) includes a bequest to his grandson Jonathan Avery son of his son Jonathan deceased.[526]

823)   i   JONATHAN AVERY, b. at Ashford, 2 Jul 1750; d. at Canajoharie, NY, 24 Feb 1803; (probate 28 Feb 1803) m. at Ashford, 29 Nov 1773, CHLOE WALES, b. 1758 daughter of Elisha and Mary (Abbe) Wales.

---

[518] Year: 1790; Census Place: Mohawk, Montgomery, New York; Series: M637; Roll: 6; Page: 48; Image: 38; Family History Library Film: 0568146

[519] U.S., Revolutionary War Rolls, 1775-1783

[520] DeJulia, "America's Citizen Soldier: Hero or Coward", *Connecticut Nutmegger*, volume 27, 1994, pp 583-584

[521] DeJulia, "America's Citizen Soldier: Hero or Coward", p 583

[522] Frisbee, *Frisbee-Frisbie Genealogy*, p 185

[523] Hannah is interred at Old Ashford Cemetery, Find a Grave 45491287

[524] Town Clerk, Windham County, Ashford, Births, Marriages, and Deaths, FHL Film #007730715, image 81, p 107 of the volume; https://www.familysearch.org/ark:/61903/3:1:3Q9M-C9BT-D9VR-G?i=80&cc=2448940

[525] Connecticut Wills and Probate, Hartford, Windham District, Town of Ashford, Estate of Jonathan Avery, Jr., No. 107

[526] Connecticut Wills and Probate, Windham County, volume 1, p 556

196)   DOROTHY HUMPHREY (*Hannah Russell Humphrey³, Benjamin², Robert¹*), b. at Ashford, 25 Jun 1730 daughter of John and Hannah (Russell) Humphrey. Dorothy had an out-of-wedlock child with JAMES DANIELSON. Dorothy m. 1st about 1752, JOHN GAGGILL who d. about 1758. Dorothy m. 2nd at Ashford, 1 Mar 1759, SAMUEL EASTMAN, b. at Ashford, 17 May 1716 son of Philip and Sarah (Parker) Eastman; Samuel d. at Rockingham, VT, 26 Jun 1789. Samuel was first married to Thankful Reed.

Dorothy had an out-of-wedlock daughter with James Danielson and a daughter with her first husband John Gaggill. Nothing further was found for these children.

Samuel Eastman was a tavern keeper in Ashford in 1762 and moved his family to Rehoboth about 1767[527] where Samuel kept a farm. On 20 November 1766, Samuel Eastman of Ashford purchased the 81-acre homestead of Ebenezer Walker in Rehoboth for payment of £490 along with several smaller lots also purchased of Ebenezer Walker. Samuel purchased further acreage of meadow from Comfort Walker and Oliver Reed in 1773.[528]

On 19 May 1774, Samuel and Dorothy conveyed property in Rehoboth to Caleb Carpenter. On 11 December 1775, Samuel Eastman of Rehoboth and his wife Dorothy conveyed a one-acre parcel in Rehoboth to James French for payment of seven pounds, ten shillings.[529] On 1 November 1776, Samuel conveyed his 80-acre homestead for £520 and his other properties for £80 to Lemuel Bishop of Rehoboth.[530]

The family was then in Walpole, New Hampshire for a time, but in Rockingham, Vermont in 1781. On 7 April 1781, Samuel Eastman of Walpole, New Hampshire purchased 57 acres in Rockingham from Isaac Stoel for payment of £160. On 20 May 1787, Samuel conveyed to Ruth Eastman a parcel of land in Rockingham for payment of six pounds. On 11 February 1788, Samuel conveyed for love and affection to his sons John Eastman and Samuel Eastman, Jr. all the farm Samuel purchased of Isaac Stowel. On 14 July 1800, John Eastman sold his part of the property to Ichabod Eastman for payment of six hundred dollars.[531]

Child of Dorothy Humphrey and James Danielson:

i   MARRIAM HUMPHREY, b. at Ashford, 7 Jan 1749[532]

Child of Dorothy Humphrey and John Gaggill:

i   HANNAH GAGGILL, b. at Ashford, 19 Dec 1753

Dorothy Humphrey and Samuel Eastman were parents of six children.

i   DOROTHY EASTMAN, b. at Ashford, 1 Sep 1761

ii   ABIGAIL EASTMAN, b. at Ashford, 8 Jan 1764

824)   iii   RUTH EASTMAN, b. at Ashford, 20 Mar 1766; d. at Rockingham, VT, 31 Dec 1829; m. at Rockingham, 26 Aug 1789, JOHN BURT STEARNS, b. at Harvard, MA, 7 Sep 1764 son of William and Elizabeth (Burt) Stearns; John d. at Rockingham, 3 Oct 1845.

825)   iv   SAMUEL EASTMAN, b. at Rehoboth, MA, 30 Mar 1768; m. at Rockingham, VT, 24 May 1789, ABIGAIL STOWELL, b. at Willington, 9 Aug 1770 daughter of Samuel and Anna (Russ) Stowell.

826)   v   JOHN EASTMAN, b. at Rehoboth, 6 Sep 1770; d. at Grafton, VT, 24 Jul 1827; m. 18 Dec 1794, ELIZABETH STICKNEY, b. at Billerica, 31 May 1772 daughter of William and Abigail (Walker) Stickney; Elizabeth d. at Grafton, 15 May 1857.

827)   vi   ICHABOD EASTMAN, b. at Rehoboth, 30 Sep 1773; d. at Hancock, VT, 7 Feb 1841; m. at Rockingham, 23 Feb 1804, MABEL WOLF, b. at Rockingham, 14 Sep 1783 daughter of John C. and Rachel (Battles) Wolf; Mabel d. at Hancock, 22 Mar 1841.

[527] Rix, *History and Genealogy of the Eastman Family*, p 79
[528] Massachusetts Land Records, Bristol County, 50:373, 50:374, 56:507, 56:508
[529] Massachusetts Land Records, Bristol County, 58:276, 59:8
[530] Massachusetts Land Records, Bristol County, 59:37, 59:37
[531] Vermont Land Records, Town of Rockingham, 1:108, 1:304, 1:389, 1:390, 2:814
[532] Marriam, d. of Dorithy Humphrey, reputed father James Danielson, "Connecticut Births and Christenings, 1649-1906", database, *FamilySearch* (https://familysearch.org/ark:/61903/1:1:F7WV-SWY : 7 January 2020), Marriam Humphry or Danielson, 1748.

197)   RACHEL HUMPHREY (*Hannah Russell Humphrey³, Benjamin², Robert¹*), b. at Ashford, 2 Apr 1732 daughter of John and Hannah (Russell) Humphrey; m. at Ashford, 10 Jan 1754, JOHN PITTS, b. at Ashford, 25 Aug 1733 son of John and Susannah (Preston) Pitts.

There are records for eight children of Rachel Humphrey and John Pitts born at Ashford.

828)   i   BENJAMIN PITTS, b. at Ashford, 6 Nov 1754; d. at Ashford, by 1794 (guardianship of son); m. at Ashford, 19 Sep 1776, FREELOVE WHIPPLE, b. about 1747; Freelove d. at Providence, RI, 3 Feb 1805.

ii   JOHN PITTS, b. 24 May 1756; d. 4 May 1758.

829)   iii   JEREMIAH PITTS, b. at Ashford, 24 Jan 1758; m. at Ashford, 17 Apr 1780, IRENA YOUNGLOVE, baptized at Thompson, 21 Feb 1758 daughter of Samuel and Sarah (Pitts) Younglove.

iv   LOIS PITTS, b. at Ashford, 6 Jan 1760

v   SAMUEL PITTS, b. 20 Nov 1762

830)   vi   SALOME PITTS, b. at Ashford, 24 Mar 1766; d. at Sauk County, WI, Apr 1860; m. at Ashford, 22 Jun 1790, JOHN GREENSLIT, b. at Hampton, CT, 5 Jun 1767 son of John and Sarah (Burnham) Greenslit; John d. at Sauk County, 1 Apr 1856.

vii   JOHN PITTS, b. 28 Mar 1768

viii   ELIZABETH PITTS, b. 28 Jun 1770

198)   MARY HUMPHREY (*Hannah Russell Humphrey³, Benjamin², Robert¹*), b. at Ashford, 5 Jul 1734 daughter of John and Hannah (Russell) Humphrey; d. at Sherburne, NY, 20 Apr 1816;[533] m. at Woodstock, 10 May 1753, EBENEZER EATON, b. at Tolland, 16 Feb 1734 son of Thomas and Elizabeth (Parker) Eaton; Ebenezer d. at Sherburne, 9 Jun 1815.

Ebenezer is reported to have kept a shoemaker shop and ran a tavern in Ashford.[534] In 1790, he headed a household of nine persons in Ashford: two males 16 and over, two males under 16, and five females.[535] In 1800, the household was five persons: one male 45 and over, one female 45 and over, one female 10 to 15, and two females 16 to 25.[536]

There are records of twelve children of Mary Humphrey and Ebenezer Eaton born at Ashford.[537]

831)   i   NATHAN EATON, b. 29 Aug 1755; d. at Manchester, VT, 2 Jun 1840; m. at Ashford, 16 Dec 1779, PHEBE BROOKS, b. at Ashford, 24 Jul 1757 daughter of John and Abial (Wright) Brooks; Phebe d. 19 Feb 1836.

ii   MARY EATON, b. 13 Feb 1759

832)   iii   EBENEZER EATON, b. 18 Dec 1760; d. at Sherburne, NY, 10 Dec 1839; m. about 1784, MARY "POLLY" BERRY, b. 1763; Polly d. at Sherburne, 24 Nov 1849.

833)   iv   DIADAMA EATON, b. 3 Apr 1763; d. about 1788; m. at Tolland, 4 May 1780, BENJAMIN WEAVER, b. in RI, about 1755 son of John and Mary (Brownell) Weaver; d. after 1820 when living at Palmer MA. Benjamin married second Hannah Thwing.

v   EUNICE EATON, b. 19 Mar 1765

vi   ELIZABETH EATON, b. 6 Jan 1767

834)   vii   MERIAM EATON, b. 17 Feb 1769; m. 1ˢᵗ at Ashford, 16 Jan 1786, EZRA TAYLOR, b. at Montague, MA, 20 Aug 1760 son of Moses and Miriam (Keet) Taylor; Ezra d. at Winhall, VT, 27 Feb 1790. Meriam m. 2ⁿᵈ, 1791, ELISHA WHITNEY, b. at Montague, 27 Aug 1767 son of Ephraim and Rhoda (-) Whitney. Elisha was first married to Esther Clark.

viii   HANNAH EATON, b. 1 Feb 1771

835)   ix   THANKFUL EATON, b. 2 Feb 1773; d. at Tolland, 11 Oct 1799; m. at Tolland, JOSHUA COGSWELL, b. about 1772 son of Benjamin and Zerviah (Thompson) Cogswell; Joshua d. after 1830 when living at Tolland.

---

[533] Mary and Ebenezer are interred at Sherburne Quarter Cemetery in Sherburne; Find a Grave 92835113

[534] Molyneux, *History Genealogical and Biographical of the Eaton Families*, p 159

[535] Year: 1790; Census Place: Ashford, Windham, Connecticut; Series: M637; Roll: 1; Page: 286; Image: 543; Family History Library Film: 0568141

[536] Year: 1800; Census Place: Ashford, Windham, Connecticut; Series: M32; Roll: 2; Page: 848; Image: 386; Family History Library Film: 205619

[537] Molyneux's Eaton genealogy also reports children Samuel and George and possibly Thomas, but records were not located for those possible children, and they are not included here.

836)   x   DILLA EATON, b. 13 Jan 1776; d. at Sherburne, NY, 22 Mar 1855; m. about 1797, NATHANIEL B.
               BROWN, b. 10 Jun 1772 (calculated from age at death); Nathaniel d. at Sherburne, 30 Aug 1852 at age 80
               years, 2 months, 20 days.

        xi   FREELOVE EATON, b. 29 May 1778

420)   xii   DESIRE EATON, b. 29 May 1778; d. at Sherburne, Dec 1859; m. at Ashford, 8 Sep 1803, her third cousin,
               ALVA ROGERS, b. at Ashford, 18 Jun 1776 son of Moses and Lois (Holt) Rogers; Alva d. after 1855 when
               living at Sherburne.

199)   SARAH HUMPHREY (*Hannah Russell Humphrey³, Benjamin², Robert¹*), b. at Ashford, 17 Jun 1737 daughter of John
and Hannah (Russell) Humphrey; d. at Westminster, VT, 1 Dec 1812; m. about 1756, JOSHUA STODDARD, likely Joshua b. at
Newton, MA, 3 Apr 1732 son of Eleazer and Susannah (Hall) Stoddard; Joshua d. at Westminster, 6 Dec 1816.
        Sarah and Joshua were in Connecticut but were likely in Westminster, Vermont by about 1770.
        In his will written 19 October 1807 (probate 20 January 1817), Joshua Stoddard bequeathed to beloved wife Sarah the
use and improvement of one-third of all the estate. It is his intention that son Amasa should maintain the thirds and provide
support to his mother, but if not, the thirds are to be set off to Sarah. Son John receives ten dollars and the share in the
sawmill. Sons Joshua and Ebenezer each receives ten dollars and sons Daniel, Ezra, and Isaac, five dollars. Daughters Lydia
Abbot, Hannah Peck, and Zerviah Washburn each receives five dollars. Daughter Rhoda receives one hundred dollars, two
feather beds, other furniture, and the great bible. The remainder of estate goes to son Amasa.[538]
        Sarah Humphrey and Joshua Stoddard were parents of eleven children.

        i   LYDIA STODDARD, b. at Ashford, 8 Aug 1757; d. at Hartland, VT, 21 Sep 1843; m. 1st thought to Mr.
               Stone who has not been identified. Lydia m. 2nd 3 Dec 1778, as his second wife, SAMUEL ABBOTT, b. at
               Pomfret 4 Mar 1743 son of Caleb and Elizabeth (Paine) Abbott; Samuel d. at Hartland, 25 Sep 1825.
               Samuel was first married to Rachel Ward with whom he had two children. Lydia did not have children.

837)   ii   HANNAH STODDARD, b. about 1759; d. at Westminster, 15 Feb 1842; m. 27 Dec 1785, LEVI PECK, b. at
               Cumberland, RI, 14 Apr 1757 son of Solomon and Mercy (Foster) Peck; Levi d. at Westminster, 17 Sep 1835.

838)   iii   JOHN STODDARD, b. at Pomfret, 19 Nov 1761; d. at Westminster, 13 Aug 1831; m. 14 Sep 1786, MARY
               HENDRICK, b. at Union, CT, 5 Dec 1765 daughter of John and Hannah (Abbott) Hendrick; Mary d. at
               Westminster, 12 Jun 1849.

839)   iv   JOSHUA STODDARD, b. about 1764; d. at Sutton, VT, 23 Dec 1854; m. at Westminster, VT, 19 Dec 1792,
               ABIGAIL LAWRENCE, b. at Westminster, 1776 daughter of Joseph Lawrence (per death record); Abigail d.
               at Sutton, 13 Jan 1859.

840)   v   DANIEL STODDARD, b. 23 Aug 1768; d. at Woodstock, OH, 2 Apr 1854; m. 1st at Westminster, 13 Jan
               1791, ELEANOR SMITH, b. 1775 perhaps daughter of Sylvanus Smith; Eleanor d. at Sutton, VT, 14 Aug
               1805. Daniel m. 2nd 1805, LUCRETIA HARVEY, b. 29 Jan 1787 daughter of William and Jane (Beebe)
               Harvey;[539] Lucretia d. at Woodstock, OH, 7 Aug 1857.

841)   vi   ZERVIAH STODDARD, b. about 1770; d. at East Putney, VT, 1856; m. AMASA WASHBURN, b. at
               Killingly, CT, 3 Sep 1768 son of Joseph and Ruth (Wetmore) Washburn; Amasa d. at East Putney, 21 Oct
               1857.

842)   vii   EZRA STODDARD, b. 21 Jul 1772; d. at Sutton, VT, 25 Jun 1811; m. 16 Nov 1797, JERUSHA GOODELL,
               b. 26 Aug 1776 daughter of Abiel and Margaret (Brown) Goodell; Jerusha d. at Westminster, 19 May 1849.

843)   viii   EBENEZER STODDARD, b. about 1774; d. at Ruiter's Corner, Estrie, Québec, 31 Jan 1847 at age 72 years,
               11 months;[540] m. SUSAN who has not been identified, b. about 1774; Susan d. at Ruiter's Corner, 10 Sep
               1863.

844)   ix   ISAAC STODDARD, b. at Westminster, 22 Oct 1776; d. at Sherbrooke, Québec, 23 Sep 1842; m. at
               Westminster, 23 Aug 1810, MIRIAM PARSONS, b. at Swanzey, NH, 30 Dec 1785 daughter of Benjamin and
               Miriam (Winslow) Parsons;[541] Miriam d. at Quitman, MS, 24 Jul 1855.

---

[538] Vermont Wills and Probate, Windham County, volume E, pp 462-464
[539] Harvey, *Rev. Erastus Harvey and His Descendants*, p 4
[540] Interred at Reuter's Corner Cemetery; Find a Grave 88754644
[541] Winslow, *Winslow Memorial*, p 354

845)   x   AMASA STODDARD, b. 1779; d. at Westminster, 28 Mar 1846; m. at Rockingham, 22 Apr 1810, ANNA
             WILLARD, b. at Westminster, 1786 daughter of Lynde Willard (per death record); Anna d. at Westminster,
             24 Jun 1858.

846)   xi   RHODA STODDARD, b. at Westminster, 2 Apr 1781; d. at Bethel, VT, 24 Oct 1867; m. at Westminster, 12
             Dec 1809, MOSES WEBSTER, b. at Hartland, VT, 4 Mar 1783 son of Moses and Elizabeth (Woods)
             Webster; Moses d. at Bethel, 15 Feb 1872.

200)   ZERVIAH HUMPHREY (*Hannah Russell Humphrey³, Benjamin², Robert¹*), b. at Ashford 7 Dec 1743 daughter of John
and Hannah (Russell) Humphrey; d. at Eastford, 14 Aug 1827; m. at Ashford, 5 Mar 1771, NOAH PAINE, b. at Pomfret, 1 Apr
1742 son of Noah and Mehitable (Storrs) Paine; Noah d. at Eastford, 11 Mar 1826.
        Zerviah and Noah resided in Ashford/Eastford. Noah was part of the crew that built the first road through Pomfret,
Vermont in 1770-1771. Noah was chosen deacon of the Congregational church at Eastford on 1 January 1790.[542]
        In his will written 28 December 1816 (probate 4 April 1826), Noah Paine of Ashford bequeathed to beloved wife Zeviah
the west room of the dwelling house with the cellar under and the chamber above and kitchen privileges. She is to be provided
an ample, good, and full support from the estate. Sons John and Elisha each receives five dollars in addition to what they have
received. Daughters Hannah Work and Percy Hayward also receive five dollars. His grandsons sons of Augustus deceased,
Albert and Mason, receive five dollars to divide. The children and heirs of daughter Lucy Hayward deceased (not named) receive
five dollars. Son Noah receives the remainder of the estate and is named executor.[543] Real estate was 125 acres with buildings
valued at $2,252.90. Heirs signing that they received their legacies from the estate were Percy Howard and Hannah and John
Work. Son John Paine died between the time of the will and the probate of the estate. His widow, signing as Sarah Payne
Tarant (or Parant), verified that she received five dollars from the estate for her two minor daughters.
        Zerviah Humphrey and Noah Paine were parents of nine children born at Ashford.

847)   i   LUCY PAINE, b. 19 Dec 1771; d. at Woodstock, CT, 31 Mar 1814; m. at Ashford, 4 Apr 1798, KING
             HAYWARD, b. at Ashford, 15 Mar 1768 son of Benjamin and Hannah (King) Hayward; King d. at Ashford,
             13 Jan 1829.

848)   ii   HANNAH PAINE, b. 1 Oct 1773; d. at Eastford, 10 Mar 1855; m. at Ashford, 9 May 1798, JOHN WORK, b.
             at Ashford, 17 Nov 1775 son of Ingoldsby and Esther (Bugbee) Work; John d. at Eastford, 25 Mar 1863.

        iii SARAH PAINE, b. 5 Apr 1775; d. 5 Dec 1780.

        iv   ELIAS PAINE, b. 1 Jan 1777; d. 7 Dec 1780.

        v   NOAH PAINE (twin), b. 9 Sep 1778; d. at Eastford, 25 Dec 1847; m. ANNA, b. at Ashford, 1772; Anna d. at
             Eastford, 29 Dec 1847. No children were identified for Noah and Anna.

        vi   JOHN PAINE (twin), b. 9 Sep 1778; d. at Orange, VT, 17 Oct 1817; m. SARAH who has not been identified.
             The probate record of Noah Paine supports that John and wife Sarah had two daughters who were minors
             in 1827. The names of his children were not found.

849)   vii ELISHA PAINE, b. 1780; d. at Pomfret, 27 Dec 1817; m. at Pomfret, 16 Jun 1808, JERUSHA WELCH, b. at
             Windham, 24 Feb 1787 daughter of John and Olive (Fitch) Welch; Jerusha d. at Pomfret, 23 Jul 1835.

850)   viii AUGUSTINE PAINE, b. 1782; d. at Belchertown, MA, 23 Aug 1814; m. at Spencer, MA, 25 Feb 1808,
             ABIGAIL MASON, b. at Spencer, 26 Nov 1787 daughter of Ebenezer and Judith (White) Mason; Abigail d.
             at Spencer, 30 Sep 1823.

851)   ix   PERSIS "PERCY" PAINE, b. 18 Mar 1785; d. at Eastford, 30 Apr 1848; m. at Hartford, 14 May 1807,
             DAVID HOWARD, b. 4 Jul 1780 son of David and Priscilla (Knowlton) Howard; David d. at Eastford, 10
             May 1848.

201)   MEHITABLE LYON (*Abigail Russell Lyon³, Benjamin², Robert¹*), b. at Ashford, 6 Jan 1727 daughter of Seth and
Abigail (Russell) Lyon; m. 1st at Ashford, 10 Apr 1749, JOSEPH CHUBB, b. at Ashford, 28 Dec 1719 son of Joseph and
Mehitable (Presson) Chubb; Joseph d. at Ashford, 24 May 1755. Mehitable m. 2nd at Ashford, 1 Feb 1757, WILLIAM CHENEY,

---

[542] *Early Vermont Settlers, 1700-1784.* (Original Online Database: *AmericanAncestors.org*, New England Historic Genealogical Society, 2015. (By
Scott Andrew Bartley, Lead Genealogist.) Profile of Deacon Noah Paine
[543] Connecticut Wills and Probate, Hartford, Pomfret Probate District, Town of Ashford, Estate of Noah Paine, 1826, No. 3075

b. at Cambridge, about 1717 son of Benjamin and Mary (Harbart) Cheney;[544] death not clear.[545] William Cheney was first married to Ruth Eastman. William and Ruth (Eastman) Cheney were the parents of Ebenezer who married Mehitable's sister Priscilla.

No children were identified for Martha and Joseph Chubb. William Cheney was a farmer in Ashford. His death is unclear, but he was deceased prior to 1778 when his brother's estate was distributed.

The heirs of William Cheney deceased named in the distribution of the estate of Col. Thomas Cheney were Ebenezer Cheney, Benjamin Cheney, Thomas Cheney, William Cheney, Joseph Cheney, and Elizabeth wife of John Babyno.[546] All the named heirs of William except Joseph were William's children with his first wife Ruth Eastman.

Mehitable and William were parents of twins.

852)   i   JOSEPH CHENEY, b. at Ashford, Feb 1759; d. at Auburn, NY, 10 Jan 1831; m. at Brooklyn, CT, 22 Jun 1784, SELAH TYLER, b. 1766; Selah d. at Auburn, 3 Mar 1823.

       ii   Daughter, b. Feb 1859

202)   PRISCILLA LYON (*Abigail Russell Lyon³, Benjamin², Robert¹*), b. at Ashford, 22 Mar 1741 daughter of Seth and Abigail (Russell) Lyon; d. at Fly Creek, NY, 26 Feb 1813; m. at Ashford, 2 Mar 1760, EBENEZER CHENEY,[547] b. at Ashford, 23 May 1740 son of William and Ruth (Eastman) Cheney; Ebenezer d. at Fly Creek, 21 Sep 1800.

Priscilla Lyon and Ebenezer Cheney were parents of eight children born at Ashford.

       i   SILENCE CHENEY, b. and d. 9 Oct 1760

       ii   MARY CHENEY, b. 16 Feb 1762

853)   iii   WILLIAM CHENEY, b. 12 Apr 1765; d. at Colebrook, OH, 13 Jun 1851; m. DELIA SHIPMAN, b. 1770 daughter of David Shipman; Delia d. Hartwick, NY, 24 Jan 1830.

854)   iv   RUTH CHENEY, b. 7 Apr 1767; m. about 1787, OLIVER GARDNER, b. about 1760; Oliver d. at Fly Creek, NY, 1812.

855)   v   EBENEZER CHENEY, b. 6 Aug 1769; d. at Fly Creek, NY, 10 Mar 1803; m. 1796, TABITHA WHIPPLE, b. 1768 daughter of Benajah and Tabitha (Barrett) Whipple; Tabitha d. 1848.

       vi   JOHN CHENEY, b. 11 Aug 1772

856)   vii   JOSEPH CHENEY, b. 11 Oct 1774; d. at Fly Creek, NY, 23 Apr 1852; m. LYDIA ADAMS, b. 1782 daughter of John and Submit (Butts) Adams; Lydia d. at Fly Creek, 30 Mar 1866.

857)   viii   PERSIS CHENEY, b. 10 Nov 1778; d. at Fly Creek, NY, 2 Sep 1853; m. JOHN ADAMS, b. at Canterbury, CT, 20 Jan 1776 son of John and Submit (Butts) Adams; John d. at Fly Creek, 15 Apr 1843.

203)   AZARIAH SANGER (*Lydia Russell Sanger³, Benjamin², Robert¹*), b. at Woodstock, 24 Jan 1732 son of Jonathan and Lydia (Russell) Sanger; d. at East Windsor, 1801 (probate 14 Dec 1801); m. at Willington, 22 Apr 1760, ELIZABETH ABBE, b. at Willington, 29 Aug 1734 daughter of Obadiah and Elizabeth (Bushnell) Abbe.

Daniel Sanger was named administrator of the estate of Azariah Sanger on 14 December 1801. In the distribution from the estate on 4 January 1803, sixth parts (the distribution consistently says sixth parts but names seven heirs) were assigned to the following heirs: Daniel Sanger, Jedediah Sanger, Azariah Sanger, Hannah Harris, Esther Convers, heirs of Elizabeth Wakefield deceased, and Cynthia Melross. Each heirs received $30.98 in value from the personal estate and $134.16 in value from the real estate.[548]

Azariah Sanger and Elizabeth Abbe were parents of seven children born at Willington.

858)   i   DANIEL SANGER, b. 24 Dec 1760; d. at Washington, MA, 26 Sep 1844; m. at Willington, 5 Feb 1784, ALICE WAKEFIELD, b. at Ashford, 12 Feb 1765 daughter of John and Ellis (-) Wakefield; Alice d. at Washington, 3 Jan 1842.

[544] Pope, Cheney Genealogy, p 67
[545] There was a William Cheney of Connecticut killed at the Battle of Bunker Hill, but it is not clear that it was this William.
[546] *Worcester County, MA: Probate File Papers, 1731-1881*. Online database. AmericanAncestors.org. New England Historic Genealogical Society, 2015. Case 11556
[547] Pope, *The Cheney Genealogy*, p 84. The Cheney genealogy reports that Ebenezer married Priscilla daughter of Set and Abigail.
[548] Connecticut Wills and Probate, East Windsor Probate District, Town of East Windsor, Estate of Azariah Sanger, No. 2735

859)   ii   CYNTHIA SANGER, b. 27 Nov 1761; d. 10 May 1842 (pension file); m. at Willington, 29 Nov 1779, WILLIAM MELROSS who has not been identified; William d. at Willington, 11 Mar 1815.

860)   iii   ELIZABETH SANGER, b. 30 Sep 1763; d. before 1801; m. at Stafford, 15 Mar 1787, CHESTER WAKEFIELD, b. at Union, CT, 30 Apr 1760 son of John and Ellis (-) Wakefield.

861)   iv   JEDEDIAH SANGER, b. 12 Aug 1765; d. after 1830 when living at Chardon, OH; m. at Willington, 31 Jul 1794, MEHITABLE FENTON, b. at Mansfield, 18 Jan 1767 daughter of Ebenezer and Lydia (Conant) Fenton; Mehitable d. at Chardon, 3 Mar 1847.

         v   HANNAH SANGER, b. 12 Apr 1768. Hannah is named in the distribution from Azariah's estate as Hannah Harris (or perhaps Harrick) but a marriage consistent with this was not located.

862)   vi   ESTHER SANGER, b. 29 Apr 1770; d. at Ludlow, MA, 11 Mar 1851; m. her first cousin, CHARLES CONVERS, b. at Worthington, MA, 6 Jun 1771 son of Stephen and Zeruiah (Sanger) Convers; Charles d. at Ludlow, 19 Apr 1854.

863)   vii   AZARIAH SANGER, b. 12 Jun 1772; m. at Willington, 16 Apr 1795, DESIRE ROOT, b. at Willington, 30 May 1774 daughter of Nathan and Hannah (Scripture) Root; Desire d. at Ludlow, 29 Mar 1871.

204)   NOADIAH SANGER (*Lydia Russell Sanger³, Benjamin², Robert¹*), b. at Woodstock, 12 Dec 1738 son of Jonathan and Lydia (Russell) Sanger; d. at Willington, 7 Aug 1808; m. at Willington, 14 Apr 1766, PRISCILLA RUSS, b. at Ashford, 23 Feb 1742/3 daughter of Abraham and Hannah (-) Russ; Priscilla d. about 1807.

       Noadiah and Priscilla resided in Willington.

       In his will written 22 December 1806 (probate 7 November 1808), Noadiah bequeathed to wife Priscilla the lease of land and buildings made to him by his son Noadiah date 22 December 1806. His children receive $199 to divide with the sons receiving double shares and the daughter single shares: Adin, Ashbel, Achsah White, Zerviah Knowlton, Asenath, and Priscilla. Son Noadiah receives one dollar to complete his full share.[549]

       Noadiah and Priscilla were parents of eleven children born at Willington.

         i   ACHSAH SANGER, b. 25 Aug 1766; m. Mr. White who was not identified. Nothing further was found.

         ii   LYDIA SANGER, b. 12 Jul 1768

864)   iii   ADEN SANGER, b. 6 Aug 1770; d. at Ontario County, NY, 1 Oct 1828; m. at Willington, 11 Jun 1795, ELIZABETH NILES, b. at Braintree, MA, 13 Apr 1774 daughter of James and Elizabeth (Vinton) Niles; Elizabeth d. at Cedar Creek, IN, 28 May 1855.

         iv   ASHBEL SANGER, b. 27 Mar 1772; d. 20 Aug 1778.

         v   ASENATH SANGER, b. 5 May 1774; d. 18 Oct 1778.

         vi   ADNA SANGER, b. 11 Apr 1776; d. 14 Oct 1778.

865)   vii   ZERVIAH SANGER, b. 26 Jan 1778; d. at Ashford, 16 May 1848; m. at Ashford, 4 Apr 1802, JONATHAN KNOWLTON, b. at Ashford, 27 Jun 1779 son of Thomas and Hepsibah (Peak) Knowlton; Jonathan d. at Ashford, 1 Jul 1848.

866)   viii   ASHBEL SANGER, b. 25 Apr 1780; d. at Perry, NY, 1831; m. 1807, SARAH SOUTHWORTH, b. 1778.

         ix   ASENATH SANGER, b. 25 Apr 1782; living in 1806

867)   x   NOADIAH "NOAH D." SANGER, b. 21 Apr 1785; d. at Bristol, IN, 2 Sep 1842; m. at Willington, 12 Apr 1807, REBECCA BARRETT BACON, b. at Bolton, MA, 1 Jul 1785 daughter of Noah and Mary (Brown) Bacon; Rebecca d. at Ontario, IN, 15 Sep 1861.

868)   xi   PRISCILLA SANGER, b. 3 Sep 1787; d. at Pike, NY (burial at Centerville), 17 Nov 1877; m. 1 Jul 1807, CHESTER KNOWLTON, b. at Ashford, 12 Oct 1787 son of Thomas and Hepsibah (Peak) Knowlton; Chester d. at Centerville, 30 Apr 1871.

205)   ZERUIAH SANGER (*Lydia Russell Sanger³, Benjamin², Robert¹*), b. at Ashford, 31 Mar 1744 daughter of Jonathan and Lydia (Russell) Sanger; d. at Stafford, CT, 27 Apr 1777; m. 17 Nov 1768, STEPHEN CONVERS, b. at Killingly, 5 Aug 1745

---

549 Connecticut Wills and Probate, Stafford District, Town of Willington, Estate of Noadiah Sanger, 1808, No. 1871

son of Pain and Mary (Halford) Convers; Stephen d. at Stafford, 9 Oct 1823. Stephen married second Sarah Kimball on 12 Oct 1778.

Stephen Convers served during the Revolution, and his widow Sarah applied for a pension on 5 April 1777. Stephen Convers enlisted first as first sergeant on 1 December 1776 serving until the middle of March 1777 in the company of Capt. Paine Converse in the regiment of Col. John Ely. His next enlistment was May 1777 for a term of eight months as an orderly sergeant in the company of Col. Roger Ewes. A third enlistment of 2 ½ months began 25 October 1778, again as orderly sergeant, in Capt. Chase's company of Col. Sparhawk's regiment. The first two enlistments were in Connecticut and the third in Massachusetts.[550]

The pension file contains pages apparently from a personal notebook with pages on which sayings are written out over and over: "Education makes the man"; "Understanding gets friends"; "Abundance like want". There are diary entries with one example given here. "Fishkill October 15th day 1777. This day we struck our tents and marched down to the landing and back again and the next day our orders was to march (unreadable) the precipice and we marched three miles up that way and staid that night and pitch out tents and then the 17 instant we marched up to precipice there we stopped and went to cucking. After that we marched about ten miles the same day. The 18 day instant we marched on the Limbeck. . ."

The pension file includes bible pages which provide the following information: Stephen Convers was born August 16th 1745; Zeruiah Sanger was born March 31st 1744; Sarah Kimbol was born November 10th 1756; Stephen Convers and Zeruiah Sanger were married November 17th 1768; Stephen Convers and Sarah Kimbel were married October 12th 1778; Rockse Convers was born July 28th 1769; Charles Convers was born June 6th 1771; Molly Convers was born March 14th 1775; Stephen Convers, Jr. was born April 7th 1775; Rufus Convers was born April 13th 1777; Zeruiah Convers was born March 26th 1779; Salle Convers was born March 9th 1781; Line Convers was born September 10th 1783; Prudy Convers was born November 28th 1785; Arnal Convers was born October 7th 1787; Charlotte Convers was born February 14th 1790; Rossel Convers was born June 18th 1792; Bithiah Convers was born November 6th 1794; Cyrel Convers was born July 2nd 1796; Anna Convers was born February 4th 1799; Zeruiah Convers the wife of Stephen Convers died April 27th 1777 aged 33 years 27 days; Rufus Convers died May 7th 1777 aged 25 days; Line Convers died September 6th 1786 aged 2 years and 17 months and 27 days; Prudy Convers died September 9th 1786 aged 9 months and 11 days; Bithiah Convers died April 17th 1795 aged 5 months; Cyrel Convers died January 8th 1798 aged one year six months and five days; Arnold Convers died January 25th 1804 aged 16 years and 3 months and 25 days; Anne Convers died February 15th 1816 aged 16 years and 12 days.

In his will written 11 June 1821 (probate 25 February 1825), Stephen Convers of Stafford bequeathed twenty-one dollars to his daughter Roxana Fuller. Monetary bequests were made to the following: son Charles, twenty dollars; daughter Molly Weston, fifty-three dollars; son Stephen, Jr., twenty dollars; daughter Zerviah Birt, fifty dollars; daughter Sally Hale, forty-eight dollars; daughter Charlotte Bragg, eight dollars; and grandson Cyril Converse, thirty dollars. His five daughters, Roxie, Molly, Zerviah, Sally, and Charlottte receive the household furniture after the death of his wife Sarah. The wearing apparel is to be divided among his three sons Charles, Stephen, and Roswell. It is his wife's Sarah's will that her apparel be divided among her three daughters Zerviah, Sally, and Charlotte. Daniel Peck was named executor.[551]

Zerviah's sister Chloe in her will written 26 September 1814 made bequests to the children of her sister Zerviah Convers deceased (Roxy Fuller, Charles Convers, and Stephen Convers). There is also a bequest of seventy dollars to Molly Weston wife of John Weston. John Weston was named executor of the will.[552]

Zeruiah Sanger and Stephen Convers were parents of five children.

868a)	i	ROXANA "ROXY" CONVERS, b. at Worthington, MA, 28 Jul 1769; d. at Mount Morris, NY, 23 Jan 1842; m. about 1790, JOSEPH FULLER, b. 16 Nov 1760; Joseph d. at Mount Morris, 7 Nov 1837.
862)	ii	CHARLES CONVERS, b. at Worthington, 6 Jun 1771; d. at Ludlow, MA, 19 Apr 1854; m. his first cousin, ESTHER SANGER, b. at Willington, 29 Apr 1770 daughter of Azariah and Elizabeth (Abbe) Sanger; Esther d. at Ludlow, 11 Mar 1851.
869)	iii	MOLLY CONVERS, b. at Worthington, 14 Mar 1773; d. at Willington, 25 Jun 1856; m. at Willington, 10 May 1792, JOHN WESTON, b. at Willington, 3 Dec 1768 son of James and Anna (Abbe) Weston; John d. at Willington, 29 Dec 1820.
870)	iv	STEPHEN CONVERS, b. at Stafford, CT, 7 Apr 1775; d. at Springfield, MA, 14 Mar 1864; m. NELLIE WHIPPLE, b. 1773; Nellie d. at Belchertown, 1 Oct 1856.
	v	RUFUS CONVERS, b. 13 Apr 1777; d. 7 May 1777.

550 U. S. Revolutionary War Pension and Bounty Land Warrant Application Files, W22847
551 Connecticut Wills and Probate, Tolland County, volume 13, pp 261-263, will of Stephen Converse
552 Connecticut Wills and Probate, Stafford, Probate District, Town of Willington, estate of Chloe Holt, 1815, No. 1061

206)   NATHANIEL SANGER (*Lydia Russell Sanger³, Benjamin², Robert¹*), b. at Ashford, 17 Jul 1754 son of Jonathan and Lydia (Russell) Sanger; d. at East Windsor, 11 Jan 1803; m. 28 Aug 1783, OLIVE CHAFFEE, b. at Woodstock, 24 Mar 1756 daughter of Ebenezer and Sarah (Adams) Chaffee. Olive married second Mr. Adams who was not identified.[553]

Nathaniel and Olive resided in East Windsor.

Nathaniel did not leave a will and his estate entered probate 15 February 1803 with Olive Sanger as administratrix. Estate value was $730.22 with debts and charges of $183.30, $182.11 set to the widow, and $364.81 to the heirs. Four children, James, Ebenezer, Ira, and Sally received distribution from the estate.[554]

Nathaniel Sanger and Olive Chaffee were parents of four children.

870a)   i   JAMES C. SANGER, b. at Ellington, 17 Jun 1786; d. at Bennington, OH, 20 Jul 1832; m. 21 Mar 1807, ACHSA BLODGETT, b. at East Windsor, 4 Feb 1789 daughter of Abner and Rachel (Phelps) Blodgett; Achsa d. at Bennington, 11 Jul 1872. On 9 Jan 1804, Olive Sanger was allowed as guardian to James aged 17 years. On 13 May 1806, Asher Allen was chosen as guardian to James Sanger aged 20 years.[555]

871)   ii   EBENEZER SANGER, b. 1790; d. at Canterbury, CT, 21 Feb 1863; m. 1st OLIVE CHAFFEE, b. at Canterbury, 19 Dec 1782 daughter of Ebenezer and Alice (Fassett) Chaffee; Olive d. at Brooklyn, CT, 31 Jul 1821. Ebenezer m. 2nd at Plainfield, 2 Jun 1824, EUNICE HUTCHINS, b. 1796 daughter of Amasa and Hannah (Leffingwell) Hutchins; Eunice d. at Canterbury, 12 Feb 1857. On 9 Jan 1804, Olive Sanger was appointed guardian to Ebenezer aged 14 years.

        iii   IRA SANGER, b. about 1797; on 9 Jan 1804, Olive Sanger was allowed as guardian to Ira aged 7 years.

        iv   SALLY SANGER, b. about 1799; on 9 Jan 1804, Olive Sanger was allowed as guardian to Sally aged 5 years.

207)   JONATHAN SANGER (*Lydia Russell Sanger³, Benjamin², Robert¹*), baptized 24 Aug 1755 son of Jonathan and Lydia (Russell) Sanger; d. at Canandaigua, NY, 21 Aug 1819; m. at Pomfret, 24 May 1781, LUCY SAWYER, b. at Petersham, 28 May 1759 daughter of John and Prudence (·) Sawyer; Lucy d. at Canandaigua, 31 May 1846.

Jonathan was the youngest of eleven children in his family and his father died when Jonathan was about 12 years old. Abiel Holt was named as his guardian.

In the Revolution, Jonathan was one of those who marched at the alarm from Pomfret and served for twenty days. He served eleven training days in the company of Capt. Zebadiah in June 1775.[556]

Jonathan and Lucy resided in Pomfret and nearby towns of East Windsor and Tolland until about 1794. On 28 March 1794, Jonathan conveyed 180 acres in Pomfret to Ebenezer Ross for £260 to be paid over 15 years. About 1809, the family relocated to Canandaigua where they remained.[557]

On 28 March 1810, Jonathan and his son Benjamin, for payment of $512 to Abner and Mary Barlow, purchased 64 acres in Canandaigua taken from the east part of lot number forty-eight which was east of east street and north of the square.[558]

In his will written 16 December 1818, Jonathan Sanger bequeathed to son Benjamin one hundred dollars in the form of a note held against Prescott Sanger. Son Justus also receives a note held against Prescott. Daughter Phila Hulburt receives $45.50 to come from demands against William Sawyer. Daughters Chloe Brocklebank and Lucy Carr also receive amounts from notes owed by Prescott. William S. Green son of daughter Pamelia receives $86.71. Beloved wife Lucy receives the note held against William Sawyer and also the legacy left to Jonathan by his sister Chloe.[559]

Son Capt. Prescott did not marry. In his will written 11 December 1823 (probate 4 July 1825), Prescott bequeathed four hundred dollars to his nephew Jonathan Hurlbut. The remainder of the estate in equal sixth parts was bequeathed to brother Benjamin, brother Justus H., sister Chloe Brocklebank, sister Lucy Carr, nephew William Green son of William Green, and the heirs of sister Phila Hurlbut (who are named John, Joseph, Lucy N., Mary, and Innocent).[560]

Jonathan Sanger and Lucy Sawyer were parents of seven children.

[553] Bowen, *The History of Woodstock*, volume 8, p 249
[554] Connecticut Wills and Probate, East Windsor District, Town of East Windsor, Estate of Nathaniel Sanger, No. 2740
[555] Connecticut Wills and Probate, East Windsor District, Town of East Windsor, James Sanger, minor, 1804, No. 2739
[556] Hagen and Hagen, *The Sanger Family*, p 10
[557] Hagen and Hagen, *The Sanger Family*, p 10
[558] New York Land Records, Ontario County, 15:23
[559] New York Wills and Probate, Ontario County, Probate Records volume 14, pp 89-90
[560] New York Wills and Probate, Ontario County, Probate Records volume 18, pp 87-89

872) i BENJAMIN SANGER, b. at Pomfret, 13 Aug 1782; d. at Seneca, MI, Feb 1849; m. about 1808, ELIZABETH "BETSEY" WOODWARD, b. 1788 daughter of Seth and Elizabeth (·) Woodard; d. at Canandaigua, NY, 29 Apr 1830.

873) ii PAMELIA SANGER, b. at East Windsor, CT, 18 Nov 1784; d. about 1810; m. about 1807, WILLIAM GREEN, b. 1 Oct 1785 son of Henry and Submit (Clark) Green; William d. at Italy, NY, 3 Aug 1860. William married second Polly Hutchins about 1811.

iii Capt. PRESCOTT S. SANGER, b. about 1786; d. at Canandaigua, NY, 15 Dec 1824. Prescott did not marry. Prescott was named a lieutenant in 1821 of Ontario County militia and was later captain in a company of the 11th infantry.[561]

874) iv PHILA SANGER, b. about 1790; d. about 1822; m. about 1810, JOSEPH HURLBURT, b. about 1787.

875) v JUSTUS HATCH SANGER, b. 16 Oct 1791; d. at DeWitt, IA, 20 Jan 1874; m. 1st at Canandaigua, 30 May 1819, ARAMINTA REID, b. about 1801 daughter of John and Irene (Parrish) Reid;[562] Araminta d. at Canandaigua, 11 Mar 1832. Justus m. 2nd at Canandaigua, 27 Dec 1832, DELILAH WHITMORE, b. a Peru, MA, 29 Aug 1812 daughter of William and Lydia (Daws) Whitmore; Delilah d. at DeWitt, IA, 23 Nov 1885.

876) vi CHLOE SANGER, b. 1796; d. at Canandaigua, 21 Aug 1852; m. about 1819, JOHN B. BROCKLEBANK, b. 1797 son of Samuel and Mary (Harvey) Brocklebank; John d. at Canandaigua, 3 Mar 1874.

877) vii LUCY SANGER, b. 1799; d. at Canandaigua, 15 Nov 1844; m. at Canandaigua, 1818, JOHN CARR, b. at Vershire, VT, 7 Jul 1796 son of John and Mary (Prescott) Carr; d. at Middlesex, NY, 15 Nov 1861. John married second about 1847 Sophronia *Case* Crow.

208) JOHN RUSSELL (*Joseph³, Benjamin², Robert¹*), b. at Ashford, 16 Oct 1742 son of Joseph and Hannah (Linkhorn) Russell; d. at Willington, 23 Jan 1811; m. at Ashford, 1 May 1766 REBEKAH WILSON, b. about 1740 likely daughter of Jonathan and Rebecca (Russell) Wilson; Rebekah d. at Ashford, 19 Feb 1824.

In his will written 12 February 1806 (proved 30 January 1811), John Russell of Willington bequeathed to beloved wife Rebeckah the use of one-half the household furniture during her natural life and one-half of what shall be raised on the farm if she should need it for her support to be delivered to her by son Pearly Russell yearly. Daughter Hannah Williams receives one-third of the beds and bedding left after his wife's decease and $21.40. Son Jonathan Russell receives one dollar. Daughter Cynthia James receives one-third of the beds and one dollar. Son Elisha receives one dollar. The amounts to the two sons and two daughters named are because they have received already their portions of the estate. The remainder of the estate goes to son Pearly and he is to pay the legacies, the debts of the estate, and to erect a decent monument for the graves of John and Rebeckah. Pearly was also named executor. The total value of the estate was $607.56.[563]

John Russell and Rebekah Wilson were parents of five known children. The children were all baptized at Ashford on 11 June 1780.

878) i HANNAH RUSSELL, b. 8 Jun 1768; d. at Sudbury, VT, 3 Jan 1841; m. JOSEPH WILLIAMS, b. 1765; Joseph d. at Sudbury, 5 Feb 1841.

ii JONATHAN RUSSELL, b. 21 May 1770. Jonathan was a silversmith in Geneva and Auburn, New York and was in Auburn at least until 1817.[564] A marriage was not identified for him.

879) iii CYNTHIA RUSSELL, b. 5 Oct 1772; d. at Union, CT, 22 Nov 1833; m. at Ashford, 20 Feb 1794, BENJAMIN JAMES, b. at Ashford, 1771 son of Benjamin and Rhoda (Kenyon) James; Benjamin d. at Union, 2 Jan 1848.

880) iv PARLEY RUSSELL, b. 28 Oct 1777; d. at Ashford, 2 Aug 1841; m.1st at Willington, 28 Sep 1800, ABIGAIL CONE, b. 20 Jan 1778 daughter of Simon and Hannah (Clark) Cone; Abigail d. at Willington, 27 Nov 1820. Pearly m. 2nd at Willington, 27 Jun 1822, LYDIA SNELL, b. 1789 daughter of Joseph and Lydia (Farnum) Snell; Lydia d. at Ashford, 29 Apr 1841.

v ELISHA RUSSELL, baptized 11 Jun 1780.

---

[561] New York, U.S., Military Service Cards, 1816-1979
[562] Araminta's parents' names, John and Irene Reid, are inscribed on her tombstone; Pioneer Cemetery, Canandaigua, Find a Grave 50196232
[563] *Connecticut State Library (Hartford, Connecticut)*; Probate Place: *Hartford, Connecticut, Probate Packets, Rockwell, N-Sessions, O, 1759-1880, Case number 1854*
[564] U.S., Craftperson Files, 1600-1995

209)   ELISHA RUSSELL (*Joseph³, Benjamin², Robert¹*), b. at Ashford, 29 Sep 1746 son of Joseph and Hannah (Linkhorn) Russell; d. at New Hartford, CT, 14 Feb 1791; m. at Middletown, 8 Nov 1772, ANNE WINSHIP, b. at Middletown, 26 Apr 1746 daughter of Timothy and Margaret (Merrick) Winship.

　　　Elisha and Anne were parents of seven children, the birth of the oldest child recorded at Middletown, Connecticut, and the others at New Hartford. A marriage was located for just one of the children.

881)   i   RACHEL RUSSELL, b. at Middletown, CT, 17 Jul 1773; d. at Holland Patent, NY, 12 Feb 1850; m. at New Hartford, 26 Jul 1792, GEORGE HOPKINS, b. 19 Feb 1758 son of Consider and Lydia (Gilbert) Hopkins; George d. at Floyd, NY, 18 Jul 1842.

        ii   JOSIAH RUSSELL, b. 26 Apr 1775

        iii ELISHA RUSSELL, b. 20 Jan 1777

        iv   JOHN RUSSELL, b. 17 Oct 1779

        v   ANNA RUSSELL, b. 15 Nov 1781

        vi   HANNAH HARRINGTON RUSSELL, b. 3 Aug 1784

        vii SALLY WINSHIP RUSSELL, b. 2 Jun 1787

210)   SIMEON SMITH (*Zerviah Russell Smith³, Benjamin², Robert¹*), b. at Ashford, 10 Nov 1741 son of Ezra and Zerviah (Russell) Smith; d. at Ashford, 16 Jan 1799; m. 1st at Ashford, 18 Feb 1766, ANNA BYLES, b. at Ashford, 17 May 1749 daughter of Ebenezer and Anne (Bicknell) Byles; Anna d. at Ashford, 12 Apr 1791. Simeon m. 2nd about 1792, LUCY LYMAN (widow of John Waldo),[565] b. at Coventry, 16 Jul 1756 daughter of Elijah and Esther (Clark) Lyman; Lucy d. at Newark Valley, NY, 11 Jul 1826.

　　　Simeon Smith served as lieutenant in the company of Capt. Thomas Knowlton of the Ashford militia that marched at the alarm in April 1775. He was credited with six days service.[566]

　　　Simeon resided in Ashford where in 1790 he headed a household of thirteen persons: four males 16 and over, two males under 16, and seven females.[567]

　　　In his will written 12 January 1799, Simeon Smith bequeathed to well-beloved wife Lucy the bald-faced mare, two cows, ten sheep, and the household furniture she brought to the marriage. She also receives the bridle and saddle she brought, and these things are hers, forever. Son Ezra Smith receives four dollars which completes his portion. The remainder of the estate is to be divided among his other children: Polly, Zerviah, Anna, Abigail, Simeon, Matilda, Elisha, Hannah, and Lucy. Son-in-law Andrew Huntington was named executor. A distribution from the estate on 16 May 1810 related to release of property that was used for support of Simeon's mother-in-law included the following heirs: Ezra Smith, Mrs. Polly Woodward, Zerviah Huntington, Anna Wing, Abigail, Matilda, Lucy, and Dr. Andrew Huntington who had been assigned the shares of Simeon Smith, Elisha Smith, and Hannah Smith. A further distribution on 14 September 1826 included the following heirs: Zerviah Huntington, Elisha Smith, Simeon Smith, Polly Woodward, Abigail Waldo, Lucy Smith, Hannah Chaffee, Anna Wing, and Matilda Whiton. Nothing was set to Ezra Smith as he had received his full portion.[568]

　　　Simeon Smith and Anna Byles were parents of nine children born at Ashford.

882)   i   EZRA SMITH, b. 20 Dec 1767; d. at Ellington, 18 Dec 1852; m. at Ashford, 22 Nov 1792, ROXANA KENDALL, b. 1771 daughter of Isaac and Mary (Russell) Kendall; Roxana d. at Ellington, 30 Dec 1830.

883)   ii   MARY "POLLY" SMITH, b. 12 Aug 1770; d. before 1839; m. at Ashford, 4 Apr 1793, PERKINS BUSHNELL WOODWARD, b. at Ashford, 17 Aug 1770 son of Joseph and Elizabeth (Perkins) Woodward; Perkins d. at Centerville, NY, 9 Apr 1860.

884)   iii ZERVIAH SMITH, b. 15 Oct 1772; d. at Ashford, 13 May 1837; m. at Ashford, 3 Feb 1790, ANDREW HUNTINGTON, b. at Griswold, 23 Nov 1766 son of Andrew and Lucy (Lamphere) Huntington; Andrew d. at Ashford, 1 Feb 1837.

885)   iv   ANNA SMITH, b. 1 Jan 1774; d. at East Hartford, CT, 29 Jul 1854; m. SYLVANUS WING, b. at Rehoboth, MA, 11 Nov 1770 son of Sylvanus and Elizabeth (Ward) Wing; Sylvanus d. at East Hartford, 23 Apr 1839.

565 Lincoln, *Genealogy of the Waldo Family*, p 246
566 Connecticut General Assembly, *Record of Service of Connecticut Men in the I. War of the Revolution*, p 5
567 Year: 1790; Census Place: Ashford, Windham, Connecticut; Series: M637; Roll: 1; Page: 282; Image: 541; Family History Library Film: 0568141
568 Connecticut Wills and Probate, Pomfret Probate District, Town of Ashford, Estate of Simeon Smith, 1799, No. 3739

886)   v   ABIGAIL SMITH, b. 2 Feb 1777; d. at Portageville, NY, 29 Sep 1862; m. 1799, her stepbrother, LYMAN WALDO, b. at Coventry, 8 Jul 1774 son of John and Lucy (Lyman) Waldo; Lyman d. at Portageville, 23 Jul 1865.

887)   vi   SIMEON SMITH, b. 12 Apr 1779; d. at Granby, MA, 3 Jan 1853; m. at Ashford, 23 Feb 1804, SALLY HAWES, b. at Ashford, 22 Sep 1781 daughter of Eli and Susannah (Bigelow) Hawes; Sally d. at Granby, 19 Jan 1845.

888)   vii   MATILDA SMITH, b. 26 Jun 1781; d. at Ashford, 10 Aug 1861; m. at Ashford, 25 Nov 1802, ELIJAH WHITON, b. at Ashford, 3 Apr 1778 son of Joseph and Johannah (Chaffee) Whiton; Elijah d. at Ashford, 7 Sep 1854.

      viii   ELISHA SMITH, b. 23 Nov 1783

889)   ix   HANNAH SMITH, b. 14 Apr 1789; d. at Ashford, 22 Aug 1873; m. at Ashford, 22 Mar 1822, EBENEZER CHAFFEE, b. at Ashford, 29 Nov 1796 son of Abner and Judith (Walker) Chaffee; Ebenezer d. at Mansfield, CT, 26 Sep 1875.

Simeon Smith and Lucy Lyman were parents of one child.

      i   LUCY SMITH, b. at Ashford, 20 Jul 1794. Lucy was living and unmarried in 1826.

Grandchildren of Hannah Russell and Oliver Holt

211)   NATHANIEL HOLT (*Oliver Holt³, Hannah Russell Holt², Robert¹*), b. at Andover, 23 Nov 1725 son of Oliver and Susannah (Wright) Holt; d. at Andover, Feb 1806; m. 1 Aug 1751, ELIZABETH STEVENS, b. at Andover, 21 Oct 1730 daughter of John and Elizabeth (Chandler) Stevens; Elizabeth d. Dec 1807.
      Nathaniel and Elizabeth resided in Andover where they were admitted to South Church on 7 October 1764 by profession of faith.[569] They were parents of six children born at Andover.

225)   i   ELIZABETH HOLT, b. 14 Nov 1752; m. likely at Andover, 7 Jan 1779, as his second wife, her second cousin once removed (through Holt lines), ABIEL STEVENS,[570] b. at Andover, 24 Mar 1749/50 son of John and Lydia (Gray) Stevens; Abiel d. at Stafford, VT, 1806. Abiel was first married to Tabitha Holt daughter of Jacob and Mary (Dolliver) Holt.

890)   ii   SUSANNAH HOLT, b. 11 May 1755; m. 18 Apr 1776; CARLTON PARKER, baptized at Reading, 1750 son of Timothy and Priscilla (Carleton) Parker; Carlton d. at Andover, 23 Dec 1809.

      iii   URIAH HOLT, b. 13 Sep 1757; d. 13 Feb 1761.

      iv   NATHANIEL HOLT, b. 19 Dec 1759; d. 16 Mar 1761.

891)   v   CHLOE HOLT, baptized 21 Sep 1766; d. at Andover, 11 Apr 1855; m. 1st at Andover, 20 Apr 1789, DAVID WILEY who d. by about 1799. Chloe m. 2nd 25 Feb 1800, her fourth cousin, JOHN HOLT, b. at Andover, 22 Feb 1769 son of David and Hannah (Martin) Holt; John d. at Andover, 21 Oct 1815. Chloe m. 3rd 21 Jul 1821, her fourth cousin, JOHN FRYE, b. at Andover, 16 Aug 1754 son of Ebenezer and Elizabeth (Kimball) Frye; John d. 26 Mar 1843. John Frye was first married to Lydia Batchelder.

892)   vi   NATHANIEL HOLT, b. 6 Apr 1769; d. at Andover, 24 May 1829; m. at Andover, 3 Mar 1791, MEHITABLE FOSTER, b. at Andover, 17 Sep 1772 daughter of Dudley and Rachel (Steel) Foster; Mehitable d. at Andover, 16 Aug 1859.

---

[569] South *Church, Historical Manual*, p 12
[570] Durrie's Holt genealogy gives Elizabeth Holt born in 1756 daughter of Caleb and Mary (Merrick) Holt as the second wife of Abiel Stevens. However, Caleb Holt's will written in 1793 names his daughter as Elizabeth Howe.

212)   OLIVER HOLT (*Oliver Holt³, Hannah Russell Holt², Robert¹*), b. at Andover, 24 Jan 1739/40 son of Oliver and Susannah (Wright) Holt; m. at Andover, 8 Oct 1761, EUNICE RAYMOND, b. at Beverly, 30 Apr 1744 daughter of Boanerges and Jemima (Meacham) Raymond. Oliver and Eunice lived in Wilton, NH.

     Oliver and Eunice lived in Wilton, New Hampshire and were parents of two known children.

893)   i   EUNICE HOLT, b. at Wilton, 25 Jul 1764; d. at Andover, VT, 18 Jun 1798; m. at Wilton, 18 Dec 1794, JOSEPH FULLER, b. at Middleton, MA, 21 Jul 1760 son of Amos and Hannah (Putnam) Fuller. Joseph married second about 1799, Submit.

894)   ii   OLIVER HOLT, b. at Wilton, 13 Feb 1776; d. at Ellenburg, NY, 24 Jun 1837; m. at Andover, VT, 16 Apr 1804, PHEBE HASELTINE, b. about 1786; Phebe d. after 1850 when she was living in Elleburg with her son Raymond and his family.

213)   BEULAH HOLT (*Oliver Holt³, Hannah Russell Holt², Robert¹*), b. at Andover, 12 Apr 1744 daughter of Oliver and Susannah (Wright) Holt; m. at Andover, 26 Apr 1770, JOHN GRAY, b. at Andover, 26 Dec 1745 son of Edward and Sarah (-) Gray.

     Beulah Holt and John Gray were parents of six children who were all baptized in Salem, Massachusetts on 13 May 1787. It is not clear when or where they were each born. The couple married in Andover and then were in Milton, New Hampshire. They moved from Milton to Rindge in February 1773 with their son Eliphalet.[571] John signed the association test at Rindge in 1776 and served in the regiment of Col. Enoch Hale in 1778. When the children were baptized at Salem, they were described as being of Andover. Two of the sons in the family were in Jay, Maine in their adulthood. Marriages were located for just two of the children.

895)   i   ELIPHALET GRAY, b. about 1771 perhaps at Milton, NH and baptized at Salem, MA, 13 May 1787; m. about 1795, MARY COOLIDGE, b. at Watertown, MA, 5 Sep 1767 daughter of Simon and Mary (Jennison) Coolidge.[572] Eliphalet was in Jay, Maine in 1810 but is thought to have gone to Carthage after that.

      ii   JOHN GRAY baptized at Salem 13 May 1787

      iii   SUSANNA WRIGHT GRAY baptized at Salem 13 May 1787

      iv   OLIVE GRAY baptized at Salem 13 May 1787

      v   FREDERICK GRAY baptized at Salem 13 May 1787

896)   vi   URIAH HOLT GRAY, b. about 1784 and baptized 13 May 1787; d. at Jay, ME, after 1840; m. about 1807, ANNA DAVENPORT, b. at Winthrop, ME, 13 Jul 1786 daughter of Ebenezer and Mary (Crane) Davenport;[573] Anna d. at Jay, 1866.

214)   SARAH HOLT (*Uriah Holt³, Hannah Russell Holt², Robert¹*), b. at Lancaster, 18 Mar 1727 daughter of Uriah and Sarah (Wright) Holt; d. at Harvard, 29 Oct 1769; m. at Harvard, 27 Nov 1746, JONATHAN WHITNEY, b. 1724 son of Jonathan and Alice (Willard) Whitney;[574] Jonathan d. at Harvard, 30 Jan 1770.

     Jonathan Whitney did not leave a will and his estate entered probate 30 January 1770. The total value of the estate was £161.5.0. In the estate settlement 20 April 1771, land of about 35 acres was settled on son Phineas and he was to pay to each of his sisters or their guardians or representatives the sum of £26.6.11. Those sisters were Sarah, Relief, Abigail, and Rachel.[575]

     Sarah Holt and Jonathan Whitney were parents of ten children born at Harvard.

897)   i   PHINEHAS WHITNEY, b. 3 Jul 1747; d. at Norway, ME, 21 May 1830; m. at Harvard, 31 Oct 1765, KEZIAH FARNSWORTH, likely b. at Harvard, 1 Jun 1742 daughter of Phineas and Azubah (Burt) Farnsworth; Keziah d. at Norway, 1827.

      ii   JONATHAN WHITNEY, b.1 Jul 1749; d. 27 Oct 1756.

---

[571] Stearns, *History of the Town of Rindge*, p 539
[572] Bond, *Genealogies of the Families and Descendants of the Early Settlers of Watertown*, p 175
[573] Stackpole, *History of Winthrop, Maine*, p 343
[574] Although there is not a birth record for Jonathan, he can be established as the son of Jonathan and Alice through probate records.
[575] *Worcester County, MA: Probate File Papers, 1731-1881*. Online database. AmericanAncestors.org. New England Historic Genealogical Society, 2015. Case 64948

898) iii SARAH WHITNEY, b. 5 Aug 1751; likely m. at Harvard, 26 Aug 1771; JOHN MEAD, b. at Harvard, MA, 29 Jun 1749 son of Samuel and Hannah (Willard) Mead.

iv RELIEF WHITNEY, b. 21 May 1754; d. 15 Aug 1756.

899) v RELIEF WHITNEY, b. 13 Nov 1758; d. at Harvard, 17 Apr 1818; m. at Harvard, 2 Jul 1780, JONAS WHITNEY, b. at Harvard, 3 Mar 1756 son of Jonas and Zebudah (Davis) Whitney; Jonas d. at Harvard, 26 Nov 1803.

vi ANNAS WHITNEY, b. 26 Feb 1761; d. 1 Jun 1761.

900) vii ABIGAIL WHITNEY, b. 29 Jan 1763; m. at Harvard, 17 Nov 1789, BENJAMIN HOAR (later Benjamin Whitney), b. at Leominster, MA, 21 Sep 1757 son of Oliver and Silence (Houghton) Hoar. On 3 March 1815, a special act was passed by the State of New York allowing Benjamin Hoar and each of the members of his family to legally change their name to Whitney. The family included Benjamin, his wife Abigail, and children Theophilus, Abel, Silence, Oliver, Polly, and Abigail. The family were residents of Cambridge, NY at that time.[576]

viii OLIVER WHITNEY, b. 29 Jan 1763; d. 29 Mar 1763.

ix ANNAS WHITNEY, b. 30 Mar 1765; d. 23 Jan 1768.

901) x RACHEL WHITNEY, b. 19 Sep1767; d. at Harvard, Aug 1825; m. at Harvard, 7 Nov 1793, SALMON WILLARD, baptized at Harvard, 15 Jul 1770 son of Benjamin and Hannah (Godfrey) Willard; Salmon d. at Lancaster, MA, 10 Jul 1860. Salmon was second married to Mercy Kelly.

215) URIAH HOLT (*Uriah Holt[3], Hannah Russell Holt[2], Robert[1]*), b. at Lancaster, 7 Feb 1729 son of Uriah and Sarah (Wright) Holt; d. at Woodstock, VT, 1812; m. at Harvard, 20 Feb 1752, ANNESS WILLARD, b. at Harvard, 20 Jun 1730 daughter of Henry and Abigail (Fairbanks) Willard; Anness d. at Ashburnham, 28 Nov 1779. Uriah m. 2nd, at Ashburnham, 6 Jun 1785, SARAH GOODRIDGE.

Uriah and Anness resided in Harvard for about twenty years after their marriage and then were in Ashburnham where Anness died. Uriah continued in Ashburnham for a few more years but was in Woodstock, Vermont by 1790.

There are records for ten children of Uriah and Anness.

i JOSHUA HOLT, b. at Harvard, 23 Jun 1753. Joshua "marched at the alarm" on 19 April 1775 from Ashburnham in the company of Capt. Jonathan Gates.[577]

ii URIAH HOLT, b. at Harvard, 10 May 1755

902) iii ANNESS HOLT, b. at Harvard, 1 Sep 1757; m. at Ashburnham, 30 Oct 1780, JONATHAN BENJAMIN, b. at Ashburnham, 30 Jul 1760 son of William and Sarah (Child) Benjamin; Jonathan d. at Woodstock, VT, 24 Apr 1834.

903) iv JACOB HOLT, b. 23 Jun 1759; d. after 1830 at Woodstock, VT; m. at Ashburnham, 5 Jul 1781, ANNA MELVIN, b.at Ashburnham, 8 Nov 1760 daughter of Nathan and Anna (Foster) Melvin.

v SARAH HOLT, baptized at Harvard, 20 Sep 1761; died young

vi JONATHAN HOLT, baptized at Harvard, 9 Sep 1764; died young

904) vii LEMUEL HOLT, baptized at Harvard, 1 Nov 1767; d. at Hartland, VT, 8 Mar 1848; m. ABIGAIL HODGMAN, b. 1774; Abigail d. at Hartland, 26 Oct 1839.

viii SARAH HOLT, baptized at Harvard, 15 Jul 1770

905) ix JONATHAN HOLT, baptized at Ashburnham, 14 Jun 1772; d. at Berlin Corners, VT, 1 Nov 1843; m. about 1800, SARAH LAKE, b. at Woodstock, VT, 22 Feb 1777 son of George and Sarah (Lovejoy) Lake; Sarah d. at Berlin Corners, 8 Dec 1857.

x OLIVER HOLT, baptized at Ashburnham, 1 Oct 1775; d. 1 Feb 1779.

---

[576] New York State, Laws of the State of New York: Revised and Passed at the Thirty-sixth Session of the Legislature, volume 3, p 60
[577] Stearns, *History of Ashburnham*, p 142

216)   MARY HOLT (*Uriah Holt³, Hannah Russell Holt², Robert¹*), b. at Lancaster, 5 Apr 1740 daughter of Uriah and Sarah (Wright) Holt; m. at Harvard, 7 Sep 1764, THOMAS DARBY, b. at Harvard, 22 Sep 1739 son of Simon and Mercy (Wilson) Darby; Thomas d. at Westminster, VT, 7 Dec 1833.[578]

Thomas and Mary started their family in Harvard, but were in Chesterfield, Vermont about 1771. They disappear from records in Chesterfield in 1804[579] and were after in Westminster, Vermont. There are records of four children in this family although there may well be others.

	i	MOLLY DARBY, b. at Harvard, 10 May 1765
906)	ii	OLIVER DARBY, baptized at Harvard, 24 May 1767; m. 29 Nov 1788, LOVINA STOCKWELL *perhaps* the daughter of Abel and Patience (Thomas) Stockwell. Oliver and Lovina seem to have gone to Essex County, New York before heading west to Washtenaw County, MI where they were living in 1840.
	iii	LYDIA DARBY, b. at Chesterfield, 30 Oct 1776
	iv	ASA DARBY, b. at Chesterfield, 16 Jan 1782

217)   SARAH HOLT (*David Holt³, Hannah Russell Holt², Robert¹*), b. at Andover, 20 Nov 1733 daughter of David and Sarah (Russell) Holt; d. at Andover, 30 Sep 1769; m. 26 May 1757, JAMES BARNARD, b. at Andover, 24 Sep 1727 son of James and Abigail (Wilson) Barnard. James m. 2nd, 11 Mar 1775 widow Mary Barker.

Sarah Holt and James Barnard were parents of five children born at Andover. Daughter Abigail Barnard Downing did not leave a will and her estate entered probate 29 November 1836. The nearest next of kin listed were first cousins.

	i	DAVID BARNARD, b. 18 Nov 1758; nothing further known.
	ii	SARAH BARNARD, baptized 2 Aug 1761; died young.
	iii	SARAH BARNARD, b. 10 Jun 1764; d. 8 Nov 1774.
	iv	ABIGAIL BARNARD, b. 21 Feb 1767; d. at Andover, 18 Nov 1836; m. at Andover, 3 Dec 1805, as his second wife, PALFREY DOWNING, baptized at Andover, 12 Apr 1761 son of Richard and Temperance (Derby) Downing; Palfrey d. at Andover, 28 Sep 1835. Palfrey was first married to Lydia Lovejoy daughter of Isaac and Deborah (Sheldon) Lovejoy. Abigail did not have children. Palfrey Downing had six children with his first wife Lydia Lovejoy.
907)	v	JAMES BARNARD, b. 27 Jun 1769; d. at Andover, 10 Dec 1811; m. at Andover, 6 Sep 1791, HANNAH HAWLEY, baptized at Marblehead, 1 Mar 1772 daughter of Joseph and Hannah (Pearce) Hawley.[580]

218)   DORCAS HOLT (*David Holt³, Hannah Russell Holt², Robert¹*),[581] baptized at Andover 31 Jul 1737 daughter of David and Sarah (Russell) Holt; m. at Andover, 22 Mar 1759, THOMAS PEAVEY, b. at Andover, 14 Nov 1736 son of Peter and Esther (Barker) Peavey.

Dorcas Holt and Thomas Peavey were parents four children born at Andover who are known to have reached adulthood. There may be two or three other children who died in childhood but the records for this are not clear.

908)	i	PETER PEAVEY, b. at Andover, 14 Apr 1762; d. at Greenfield, NH, 28 Jul 1836; m. 8 Apr 1788, LUCY CUMMINGS, b. at Hollis, 9 Jul 1767 daughter of Ebenezer and Elizabeth (Abbott) Cummings; Lucy d. 15 Oct 1854.
909)	ii	THOMAS PEVEY, b. at Andover, about 1765; m. by 1795, LYDIA ABBOTT, b. at Wilton, 22 Oct 1768 daughter of Jeremiah and Cloe (Abbott) Abbott; Lydia d. at Peterborough, NH, 1 Sep 1832.
	iii	HANNAH PEAVEY, b. about 1773; m. at Andover, 10 Sep 1795, PETER JOHNSON who has not been identified. Nothing further is known of this family at this time.

---

[578] Thomas Darby, age 95, born about 1738, died 7 Dec 1833.

[579] Randall, *History of Chesterfield*, p 265

[580] Hawley, *Genealogy of the Hawley Family of Marblehead*, p 5, https://archive.org/details/genealogyofhawle00hawl_0

[581] Although sources (Durrie's Holt genealogy and Charlotte Helen Abbott's Andover notes) state that Dorcas who married Thomas Peavey was the daughter of Ephraim Holt and Phebe Russell, there is no evidence that Ephraim and Phebe had a daughter Dorcas. The 1759 distribution of the estate of Ephraim Russell has only the following children as heirs: eldest son Ephraim, Phebe Houghton, Bethiah Holt, Asenath Holt, and Mastin Holt. These are also the only children of Ephraim and Phebe for whom there are birth records.

iv DORCAS PEAVEY, b. about 1774, d. at Salem, MA, 30 Jun 1855; m. at Andover, 12 Mar 1794, as his second wife, GEORGE SMITH, b. about 1758; George d. at Salem, 12 Sep 1843. George Smith was first married to Mary Greg. Dorcas does not seem to have had children. In her will, she has bequests to several grandchildren, but these are the children of her stepchildren Andrew Smith and Mary Smith Frye.

219) DAVID HOLT (*David Holt³, Hannah Russell Holt², Robert¹*), b. at Andover, 4 Jul 1740 son of David and Sarah (Russell) Holt; m. at Andover, 22 Jun 1769, REBECCA OSGOOD, b. at Andover, 6 Feb 1739/40 daughter of Samuel and Dorothy (Wardwell) Osgood; Rebecca d. at Andover, 21 May 1790.

David Holt and Rebecca Osgood were parents of five children born at Andover.

i REBECCA HOLT, b. 10 Dec 1770; d. 23 Nov 1774.

ii SARAH HOLT, b. 12 Sep 1773; d. 3 Nov 1774.

910) iii REBECCA OSGOOD HOLT, b. 25 Aug 1776; d. at Boscawen, NH, 20 Jan 1805; m. at Andover, 1 Apr 1800, her third cousin once removed, NATHAN KIMBALL HOLT (*Abiel Holt⁵, Thomas Holt⁴, Thomas Holt³, Mary Russell Holt², Robert¹*), baptized at Andover, 30 Aug 1778 son of Abiel and Lydia (Lovejoy) Holt; Nathan d. at Boscawen, NH, 10 Nov 1836.

iv SARAH HOLT, b. 12 Jul 1779

911) v DORCAS HOLT, b. 20 Nov 1781; d. at Andover, 24 Mar 1842; m. 23 Sep 1803, her third cousin (through Holt line), HENRY ABBOTT, b.at Andover, 22 Sep 1778 son of Moses and Elizabeth (Holt) Abbott; Henry d. at Andover, 24 Sep 1845.

220) JONATHAN HOLT (*Jonathan Holt³, Hannah Russell Holt², Robert¹*), b. at Andover, 29 Sep 1738 son of Jonathan and Lydia (Blanchard) Holt; d. at Albany, ME, 1810 (probate 1810); m. at Andover, 31 Dec 1761, RUTH KIMBALL, baptized 30 Mar 1739 daughter of Josiah and Elizabeth (Bragg) Kimball;[582] Ruth d. at Albany, ME, 5 Mar 1823.

Jonathan and Ruth had their children in Andover. They relocated to Albany, Maine in 1803 where Jonathan served as deacon.

Jonathan Holt did not leave a will and his estate entered probate 15 December 1810 with widow Ruth requesting that Uriah Holt of Norway be named administrator. The real estate was ordered to be sold to satisfy the debts of the estate. The dower was set off to widow Ruth on 22 December 1810.[583] Uriah Holt was a cousin of Jonathan.

Jonathan Holt and Ruth Kimball were parents of seven children born at Andover.

i JONATHAN HOLT, b. 29 Jun 1763; d. 22 Mar 1764.

ii BETTY HOLT, b. 25 Aug 1767; d. at Andover, 7 Feb 1827; m. at Andover, 4 Sep 1794, WILLIAM GRIFFIN, b. 1767 son of William and Mary (Howard) Griffin; William d. at Andover, 24 May 1830. Betty and William did not have children. In his will, he left his estate to Betsy Town daughter of Samuel. Betsy was Betty's niece, daughter of Lydia and Samuel Towne.

912) iii LYDIA HOLT, b. 15 May 1770; d. at Albany, ME, 12 Jan 1834; m. at Andover, 22 Nov 1795, SAMUEL TOWNE, b. at Andover, 26 Mar 1769 son of Nathan and Mary (Curtis) Towne; Samuel d. at Albany, 1 Nov 1850. Samuel was first married to Rachel Fish who died in 1793 and married third, Cynthia Frye.

913) iv MOSES HOLT, b. 3 Sep 1773; m. 28 Jun 1796, MARY AUSTIN, b. at Andover, 15 Aug 1771 daughter of Daniel and Eunice (Kimball) Austin.

914) v AMY HOLT, b. 25 Jul 1776; d. at Andover, 29 Sep 1803, of consumption; m. at Andover, 23 Oct 1798, DAVIS FOSTER, b. at Reading, 15 Aug 1771 son of Jonathan and Sarah (Townsend) Foster; Davis d. at Reading, 15 Dec 1855. Davis married second widow Nancy (Johnson) Russell the widow of Stephen Russell and married third Susannah Flint.

vi NANCY HOLT, b. 22 Jul 1779; m. likely at Andover, 21 Oct 1800, CHARLES NEWELL who has not been identified. The family seems to be living in Andover in 1810 with three children, but the names of children or further information was not located.

---

[582] Morrison and Sharples, *History of the Kimball Family*, p 113

[583] *Maine. Probate Court (Oxford County)*; Probate Place: *Oxford, Maine, Estate Files, Timothy Gibson-Daniel Leavitt, Pre 1820, Estate of Jonathan Holt*

vii   RUTH KIMBALL HOLT, b. 18 Apr 1782; d. 11 Apr 1799.

221)   HANNAH HOLT (*Jonathan Holt³, Hannah Russell Holt², Robert¹*), b. at Andover, 19 Dec 1745 daughter of Jonathan and Lydia (Blanchard) Holt; d. at Concord, NH, 1 Dec 1818; m. at Andover, 1763, her third cousin, NATHAN BALLARD, b. at Andover, 1 Nov 1744 son of Timothy and Hannah (Chandler) Ballard; Nathan d. at Concord, 14 Jan 1835.

Nathan and Hannah moved from Andover to Wilton soon after their marriage. Nathan was a farmer there from 1765-1782. He served in the Revolution in Captain Benjamin Taylor's Company in 1775 and in 1777 in the company that marched from Wilton and Amherst to Ticonderoga. He was a selectman of Wilton for several years. After 1782, the family relocated to Concord where they were first settlers at Little Pond at Concord.[584]

Nathan and Hannah Ballard were parents of nine children, the oldest daughter born at Andover and the other children at Wilton.

915)   i   HANNAH BALLARD, b. at Andover, 12 May 1764; d. about 1809; m. at Wilton, 28 Mar 1793, DAVID MCINTIRE, b. about 1762 of undetermined origins; David's death is unknown, but after 1820.

916)   ii   SARAH BALLARD, b. 13 Apr 1766; d. at Wilton, 4 Jan 1856; m. at Wilton, 1 Jun 1797, WILLIAM PETTENGILL, b. at Andover, 23 Aug 1759 son of Samuel and Mary (Holt) Pettengill; William d. at Wilton, 13 Oct 1844.

917)   iii   MARY BALLARD, b. 8 May 1768; d. at Milford, after 1850; m. about 1790, her fourth cousin (through Holt line), AMOS HOLT, b. 20 Oct 1768 son of Amos and Jemima (Ingalls) Holt; Amos d. at Wilton, 13 Dec 1826.

918)   iv   BETSEY BALLARD, b. 19 Aug 1771; d. at Peterborough, 5 Nov 1856; m. at Wilton, 13 May 1794, RICHARD TAYLOR BUSS, b. at Wilton, 7 Sep 1772 son of Stephen and Phebe (Keyes) Buss; Richard d. at Peterborough, 20 Oct 1862.

919)   v   PHEBE BALLARD, b. 30 Apr 1773; d. at Wilton, 15 Nov 1840; m. at Concord, 23 Feb 1794, JOHN GUTTERSON, b. at Andover, 27 Aug 1766 son of Samuel and Lydia (Stevens) Gutterson; John d. at Milford, 13 Dec 1841.

920)   vi   NATHAN BALLARD, b. 21 Feb 1775; d. at Concord, 5 Jul 1856; m. at Wilton, 29 May 1800, HANNAH BUSS, b. at Wilton, 3 Dec 1774 daughter of Stephen and Phebe (Keyes) Buss; Hannah d. 1857.

921)   vii   JOHN BALLARD, b. 22 Feb 1778; d. at Wilton, 28 Sep 1855; m. at Wilton, 20 Jan 1808, RHODA BALES, b. at Wilton, 16 May 1779 daughter of William and Rhoda (Keyes) Bales; Rhoda d. at Wilton, 15 Jan 1839.

        viii   EZRA BALLARD, b. 2 Feb 1780; d. 16 Sep 1781.

        ix   TIMOTHY BALLARD, b. 1 Jan 1782; d. 14 Jan 1782.

222)   JACOB HOLT (*Jacob Holt³, Hannah Russell Holt², Robert¹*), b. at Andover, 29 Mar 1739 son of Jacob and Mary (Osgood) Holt; d. at Albany, ME, 12 May 1816; m. at Andover, 22 Mar 1764, RHODA ABBOTT, b. at Andover, 22 Jun 1741 daughter of Ephraim and Hannah (Phelps) Holt; Rhoda d. at Albany, ME, 12 Jan 1821.

Rhoda Abbott and Jacob Holt had their twelve children in Andover, and then in 1795 went north to the new settlement of Oxford Township in Maine.

922)   i   JACOB HOLT, b. 15 Feb 1765; d. at Charlestown, MA, 22 Sep 1800; m. at Andover, 11 May 1787, his third cousin once removed, ABIGAIL HOLT, b. at Reading, Sep 1765 daughter of Joseph and Abigail (Bean) Holt; Abigail d. at Charlestown, 16 Jun 1851.

923)   ii   NEHEMIAH HOLT, b. 25 Dec 1767; d. at Bethel, ME, 25 Mar 1846; m. 24 Jan 1793, ABIGAIL TWIST, b. about 1771; Abigail d. at Bethel, 31 Jan 1853.

295)   iii   EPHRAIM HOLT, b. 19 Mar 1769; d. at Greenfield, NH, 24 Oct 1836; m. at Andover, 27 Nov 1794, his third cousin, HANNAH HOLT (*Joshua Holt⁴, Nicholas Holt³, Mary Russell Holt², Robert¹*), b. at Andover, Jun 1771 daughter of Joshua and Phebe (Farnum) Holt; Hannah d. at Greenfield, 21 Apr 1842.

924)   iv   STEPHEN HOLT, b. 7 Jun 1771; d. at Norway, ME, 25 Sep 1817; m. at Albany, VT, 1 Jul 1806, MOLLY BRAGG, b. at Andover, 29 Apr 1779 daughter of Ingalls and Molly (Frye) Bragg; Molly d. at Norway, 17 Aug 1823.

---

[584] Livermore, *History of Wilton*, p 304

      v   RHODA HOLT, b. 5 Jul 1772; d. before 1773.

925)   vi   RHODA HOLT, b. 13 Jul 1773; d. 1 Apr 1850 (burial at Albany, ME); m. 1803, JOHN LOVEJOY, b. at Andover, 24 Mar 1773 son of Joseph and Mary (Gorden) Lovejoy; John d. at Albany, ME, 8 Nov 1832.

926)   vii   URIAH HOLT, b. 25 May 1775; d. at Norway, ME, 21 Jun 1849; m. 4 Feb 1808, HANNAH FARNUM, b. at Andover, 27 Oct 1789 daughter of Benjamin and Dolly (Holt) Farnum; Hannah d. 4 Feb 1835.

927)   viii MARY OSGOOD HOLT, b. 21 Apr 1777; d. at Andover, 11 Feb 1856; m. 22 Dec 1802, her second cousin once removed, ZACHARIAH CHICKERING, b. at Andover, 19 May 1764 son of Samuel and Mary (Dane) Chickering; Zachariah d. at Andover, 30 Jun 1841.

928)   ix   TABITHA HOLT, b. 11 Aug 1779; d. likely at Waterford, ME; m. at Waterford, 19 Jun 1798, THOMAS GREENE, b. at Rowley, 17 Mar 1775 son of Thomas and Lydia (Kilburn) Greene; Thomas d. at Waterford, Oct 1809 (probate 12 Dec 1809).

929)   x   HANNAH HOLT, b. 17 Jul 1781; d. at Albany, ME, 23 Dec 1856; m. 1 Oct 1801, PARSONS HASKELL, b. at Falmouth, ME, 27 Oct 1777 son of Benjamin and Lydia (Freeman) Haskell; Parsons d. at Albany, 6 Jul 1829.

930)   xi   DAVID HOLT, b. 21 Aug 1783; d. at Andover, 3 Oct 1836; m. 2 Jul 1820, his second cousin, SARAH ABBOTT (*Ruth Holt Abbott⁶, Joseph Holt⁵, Lydia Holt Holt⁴, Thomas Holt³, Mary Russell Holt², Robert¹*), b. at Andover, 11 Jul 1787 daughter of Abner and Ruth (Holt) Abbott; Sarah d. at Andover, 26 Jul 1874.

931)   xii   SARAH ABBOTT HOLT, b. 19 May 1786; d. at Phillipston, MA, 23 Jun 1845; m. Jun 1817, JOSEPH CHICKERING, b. at Dedham, 30 Apr 1780 son of Jabez and Hannah (Balch) Chickering; Joseph d. at Phillipston, 27 Jan 1844.

223)   NEHEMIAH HOLT (*Jacob Holt³, Hannah Russell Holt², Robert¹*), b. at Andover, 24 Oct 1740 son of Jacob and Mary (Osgood) Holt; d. at Salem, MA, 1786 (probate 1786); m. at Salem, 21 Jul 1771, ESTHER VARNUM, b. 21 May 1747; Esther d. at Salem, 12 Feb 1822.

    Nehemiah Holt did not leave a will and his estate entered probate 12 July 1786 with widow Esther as administratrix. Claims exceeded the assets and the estate was declared insolvent. Esther Holt was named as guardian for the three minor children: Nehemiah age thirteen, Molley age eight, and Esther age four.[585]

    In her will written 14 June 1821 (probate 2 April 1822), Esther Varnum Holt bequeathed to her daughter Esther Andrews one dollar and the remainder of her estate went to her other daughter Mary Proctor who was also named executrix. Real estate was valued at $550 and personal estate at $78.55.[586]

    Nehemiah Holt and Esther Varnum were parents of seven children born at Salem. Son Nehemiah was a mariner and died at Alexandria while on a voyage. Daughter Mary's first husband died while at sea and age 29 and it is possible that her second husband also died at sea.

      i   NEHEMIAH HOLT, baptized at Salem, 6 Dec 1772; d. at Alexandria, 25 Apr 1798.

      ii   HANNAH HOLT, baptized at Salem, 13 Jun 1773; died young.

      iii   ESTHER HOLT, b. 2 Jul 1775; d. 23 Sep 1777.

932)   iv   MARY "MOLLY" HOLT, b. 9 Sep 1777; d. at Salem, 7 Dec 1856; m. 1ˢᵗ at Salem, 22 Jun 1794, JOSHUA FOSTER, b. about 1766; Joshua d. at the West Indies, 6 Dec 1795.[587] Mary m. 2ⁿᵈ at Salem, 17 Oct 1800, DANIEL PROCTOR, b. at Danvers, 12 Jul 1768 son of Benjamin and Keziah (Littlefield) Proctor.

      v   VARNUM HOLT, b. 13 Nov 1779; d. 28 Dec 1783.

933)   vi   ESTHER HOLT, b. 9 Dec 1781; d. at Salem, 31 Mar 1874; m. at Salem, 20 Sep 1807, DANIEL ANDREWS, b. at Salem, 23 Sep 1779 son of Nehemiah and Catherine (Seamore) Andrews; Daniel d. at Salem, 25 Dec 1820.

      vii   JACOB HOLT, b. 24 Aug 1783; d. 3 Feb 1784.

---

[585] *Essex County, MA: Probate File Papers, 1638-1881.* Online database. *AmericanAncestors.org.* New England Historic Genealogical Society, 2014. Case 13678

[586] *Essex County, MA: Probate File Papers, 1638-1881.* Online database. *AmericanAncestors.org.* New England Historic Genealogical Society, 2014. Case 13639

[587] Joshua, native of Ipswich, h.____ (Holt), mate of a vessel, Capt. Patten, at the West Indies, fever, Dec. 6, 1795, a. 29 y. C. R. 4.

224)   ELIZABETH HOLT (*Jacob Holt³, Hannah Russell Holt², Robert¹*), b. at Andover, 24 Jan 1747/8 daughter of Jacob and Margaret (Dolliver) Holt; d. at Chelmsford, 8 Aug 1794; m. at Andover, 28 Feb 1771, FRANCIS BOWERS, baptized at Chelmsford, 22 Jul 1744 son of Jonathan and Mary (Grimes) Bowers. Francis married second Mrs. Rachel Harwood on 6 Dec 1797.

       Francis Bowers was a blacksmith in Chelmsford. After Elizabeth's death Francis sold his property (deed recorded 1 October 1795) in Chelmsford including the dwelling house, about fifty acres of land, and blacksmith shop to Cyrus Baldwin of Billerica for £200. On 13 August 1794 (deed recorded 1803), Francis conveyed one acre of his property to the Middlesex Canal for £6, this property to be used for the building of the canal.[588] Francis's place and date of death were not found, but on 5 January 1800, Rachel Bowers was dismissed from the church in Chelmsford to the church in Greenfield.[589]

       Elizabeth Holt and Francis Bowers were parents of five children born at Chelmsford.

296)   i   FANNY BOWERS, baptized at Chelmsford, 13 Jun 1773; d. at Peterborough, NH, 18 Apr 1828; m. 1799, her third cousin once removed, STEPHEN HOLT (*Joshua Holt⁴, Nicholas Holt³, Mary Russell Holt², Robert¹*), baptized at Andover, 2 May 1773 son of Joshua and Phebe (Farnum) Holt; Stephen d. at Greenfield, NH, 26 Mar 1868. Stephen was second married to Margaret Batchelder.

297)   ii   FRANCIS BOWERS, b. 20 May 1775; d. at Peterborough, NH, 15 Oct 1835; m. at Andover, 23 Oct 1798, his third cousin once removed, CHLOE HOLT (*Joshua Holt⁴, Nicholas Holt³, Mary Russell Holt², Robert¹*), baptized at Andover, 4 Jun 1775 daughter of Joshua and Phebe (Farnum) Holt; Chloe d. at Peterborough, 6 Nov 1849.

          iii   DAVID BOWERS, b. 13 Apr1777

          iv   TABITHA BOWERS, b. 24 Dec 1780; d. 14 Jan 1781.

          v   BENJAMIN BOWERS, b. 8 Mar 1783

225)   TABITHA HOLT (*Jacob Holt³, Hannah Russell Holt², Robert¹*), b. at Andover, 19 May 1753 daughter of Jacob and Margaret (Dolliver) Holt; d. at Andover, 23 Sep 1778; m. at Andover, 16 May 1769, her third cousin (through the Holt line) ABIEL STEVENS, b. at Andover, 24 Mar 1749/50 son of John and Lydia (Gray) Stevens; Abiel d. at Strafford, VT, 1806 (probate 31 Mar 1806). Abiel m. 2nd at Andover, 7 Jan 1779, his second cousin once removed, ELIZABETH HOLT (*Nathaniel Holt⁴, Oliver Holt³, Hannah Russell Holt², Robert¹*), b. at Andover, 14 Nov 1752 daughter of Nathaniel and Elizabeth (Stevens) Holt.

       The estate of Abiel Stevens of Strafford entered probate on 31 March 1806, but the inventory or distribution were not in the available probate records.[590]

       Tabitha Holt and Abiel Stevens were parents of four children born at Andover.

934)   i   ABIEL STEVENS, b. 10 Oct 1770; d. at East Bethany, NY, 7 Sep 1853; m. 1st about 1793, EUNICE who has not been identified; Eunice d. at Strafford, 5 May 1804. Abiel m. 2nd about 1804, MARCY HASKELL, b. 1777 daughter of Job and Isabel (Winship) Haskell; Marcy d. at East Bethany, 27 Jun 1837.

          ii   TABITHA STEVENS, b. 1774; d. 26 Aug 1775.

935)   iii   JACOB STEVENS, b. 12 Mar 1776; d. at East Bethany, NY, 26 Mar 1856; m. at Strafford, VT, 17 Mar 1779, DINAH NORTON (widow of Jonathan Frary), b. about 1773 daughter of Elihu and Dinah (Snow) Norton; Dinah d. at Strafford, 16 Feb 1803.

          iv   NEHEMIAH STEVENS, baptized 3 May 1778

       Abiel Stevens and Elizabeth Holt were parents of three children born at Andover.

936)   i   URIAH HOLT STEVENS, baptized 31 Oct 1779; d. at Strafford, VT, 17 May 1845; m. SALLY ELVINA BLAISDELL, b. about 1785 daughter of Harvey and Elizabeth (Sargent) Blaisdell;[591] Sally d. after 1850 when she was living in Strafford.

---

[588] Massachusetts Land Records. Middlesex County, 120:4; 150:58

[589] Massachusetts, Town and Vital Records, 1620-1988, Chelmsford church records

[590] Ancestry.com. *Vermont, Wills and Probate Records, 1749-1999* [database on-line]. Orange County

[591] The 1826 will of Harvey Blaisdell of Strafford has bequests to daughter Elvina Stevens and daughter Ruth Stevens

937)   ii   DAVID STEVENS, baptized 16 Sep 1781; d. at Clymer, NY, 29 Jun 1842; m. at Strafford, 6 Dec 1804,
                RUTH BLAISDELL, b. 11 Jan 1785 daughter of Harvey and Elizabeth (Sargent) Blaisdell; Ruth d. at
                Clymer, 30 Apr 1837.

        iii   LEONARD STEVENS, baptized 25 Jun 1785

Grandchildren of John Russell and Sarah Chandler

226)   PHEBE HOLT (*Phebe Russell Holt Sheldon³, John², Robert¹*), b. at Andover, Apr 1735 daughter of Ephraim and
Phebe (Russell) Holt; m. at Andover, 11 Sep 1755, JAMES HOUGHTON, b. at Pomfret, 13 Sep 1728 son of Edward and Abigail
(Coy) Houghton.

        Phebe and James started their family in Andover but were soon after in Union, Connecticut where seven of their eight
children were born. The family with one of the sons and the five daughters moved on the Dublin, New Hampshire where they
were by 1781.[592] Son James remained in Connecticut but came to Dublin about five years after his father. Son Silvanus
remained in Connecticut. Two of the children relocated to Bethel, Maine after marriage and some of the children returned to
Connecticut where they married and settled.

537)   i   JAMES HOUGHTON, b. at Andover, MA, 16 Jun 1756; d. at Weld, ME, 21 Dec 1835;[593] m. at Wilton, 23
                Aug 1787, his first cousin, HANNAH RUSSELL (*Thomas⁴, Joseph³, Thomas², Robert¹*), b. at Andover, 23
                Sep 1767 daughter of Thomas and Bethiah (Holt) Russell; Phebe d. at Weld, Nov 1850.

938)   ii   EPHRAIM HOUGHTON, b. at Union, 18 May 1759; d. at Woodstock, CT, 6 May 1840; m 1ˢᵗ at Thompson,
                ABIGAIL "NABBY" HOLBROOK, b. at Woodstock, 26 Apr 1770 daughter of Thomas and Abigail (Adams)
                Holbrook; Nabby d. at Woodstock, 23 Sep 1815. Ephraim m. 2ⁿᵈ Mar 1817,[594] MARY "POLLY" NICHOLS
                (widow of Benjamin Skinner), b. at Thompson, 3 May 1773 daughter of Jonathan and Mary (Sibley) Nichols;
                Polly d. at Woodstock, 4 Aug 1855.

939)   iii   PHEBE HOUGHTON, b. at Union, 11 Aug 1762; d. at Thompson, 25 Feb 1800; m. at Thompson, 6 Jan
                1789, EBENEZER ORMSBY, b. at Killingly, 17 Mar 1764 son of Thomas and Hannah (Carpenter) Ormsbee;
                Ebenezer d. at Thompson, 1806 (probate 1806 with widow Experience). Ebenezer married second Phebe's
                sister Experience (see below).

940)   iv   SILVANUS HOUGHTON, b. at Union, 21 Jun 1765; d. at Thompson, 7 Feb 1816; m. at Thompson, 15 Jan
                1795, BETSEY HOLBROOK, b. at Woodstock, 24 Oct 1774 daughter of Thomas and Abigail (Adams)
                Holbrook; Betsey d. at Thompson, 27 Sep 1820.

941)   v   ORINDA HOUGHTON, b. at Union, 14 Feb 1768; d. at Wilton, ME, 9 May 1843; m. at Dublin, NH, about
                1790, BENJAMIN LEARNED, b. at Dublin, 23 Sep 1767 son of Benjamin and Elizabeth (Wilson) Learned;
                Benjamin d. at Wilton, ME, 16 Sep 1853. After Orinda's death, Benjamin married widow Jane Hardy.

942)   vi   BETHIAH HOUGHTON, b. at Union, 8 Mar 1771; d. at Gilead, ME, 21 Apr 1846; m. at Dublin, 16 Jan
                1789, JOHN MASON, b. at Dublin, 8 May 1769 son of Moses and Lydia (Knapp) Mason; John d. at Gilead,
                19 Sep 1844.

943)   vii   ASENATH HOUGHTON, b. at Union, CT, 29 Nov 1775; d. at Thompson, CT, 30 Dec 1860; m. about 1796,
                WILLIAM JORDAN, b. at Dudley, MA, 5 Dec 1774 son of William and Comfort (Palmer) Jordan; William d.
                at Thompson, 27 Jun 1849 (probate 1849 with widow Asenath).

939)   viii   EXPERIENCE HOUGHTON, b. at Union, 8 Feb 1777; m. about 1801, EBENEZER ORMSBY who was first
                married to her sister Phebe (see above). Experience was living in Thompson in 1810 but nothing is known
                after that.

---
[592] Leonard, *History of Dublin, NH*, p 179 and p 630
[593] Abstract of Graves of Revolutionary Patriots; Volume: 2
[594] U.S., Revolutionary War Pension and Bounty-Land Warrant Application Files, 1800-1900; Case W2550, widow's pension application of Mary
Houghton

227)   EPHRAIM HOLT (*Phebe Russell Holt Sheldon³, John², Robert¹*), b. at Andover, Jan 1736/7 son of Ephraim and Phebe (Russell) Holt; d. at Holden, MA, 25 May 1816;[595] m. at Boxford, 7 Jan 1762, SARAH BLACK, baptized at Boxford, 24 Jul 1743 daughter of Daniel and Sarah (Symonds) Black.[596]

      On 13 May 1799, Ephraim Holt and Sarah his wife in her right, and all the other of Sarah's siblings, quitclaimed to John Black rights in property left by the will of Sarah's father Daniel Black.[597]

      Ephraim and Sarah were parents of eight children born at Holden.

944)   i   EPHRAIM HOLT, b. 3 Dec 1762; d. at Hubbardston, 3 Jun 1844; m. at Middleton, 24 Feb 1795, JERUSHA "RUSHA" KENNEY, b. at Middleton, 5 May 1769 daughter of Simeon and Jerusha (Johnson) Kenney; Jerusha d. at Grafton, MA, 2 Nov 1857.

945)   ii   SARAH HOLT, b. 23 Aug 1764; d. at Holden, Jul 1859; m. at Holden, 29 Mar 1792, ISRAEL DAVIS, b. at Holden, 29 Oct 1766 son of Israel and Rebecca (Hubbard) Davis; Israel d. at Hubbardston, 24 Aug 1848.

      iii   SAMUEL HOLT, b. 2 Oct 1767

      iv   PHEBE HOLT, b. 30 Mar 1770; d. 3 Jun 1773.

      v   DANIEL HOLT, b. 20 Jan 1774; d. 3 Apr 1774.

      vi   DANIEL HOLT, b. 27 Mar 1775

946)   vii   JOHN HOLT, b. 22 Jan 1777; d. at Troy, NH, 1 Apr 1836; m. at Holden, 24 Nov 1803, HANNAH WRIGHT, b. at Holden, 29 Apr 1781 daughter of Judah and Tabitha (Hartwell) Wright; Hannah d. at West Boylston, MA, 8 Jan 1857.

947)   viii   PHEBE HOLT, b. 28 Jun 1779; d. at Keene, NH, 11 Apr 1867; m. at Holden, 20 Jan 1803, ZALMON HOW, b. at Winchendon, MA, 23 Feb 1775 son of Jotham and Dorothy (Smith) How; Zalmon d. at Fitzwilliam, NH, 1855.

228)   ASENATH HOLT (*Phebe Russell Holt Sheldon³, John², Robert¹*), b. at Andover, 31 Mar 1743 daughter of Ephraim and Phebe (Russell) Holt; d. at Reading, 8 Nov 1785; m. at Reading, 7 Jun 1764, EBENEZER FLINT, b. at Reading, 17 Jun 1742 son of Ebenezer and Abigail (Sawyer) Flint; Ebenezer d. at Wilton, 29 Apr 1829. After Asenath's death, Ebenezer married Mary Damon (widow Mrs. Taylor) on 29 Nov 1789.

      Ebenezer Flint, Jr. was a member of the company of Capt. John Flint that marched at the alarm on 19 April 1775. He was also listed on 15 May 1775 in the 3rd Reading company commanded by Capt. Flint.[598]

      Ebenezer Flint and Asenath Holt were parents of nine children born at Reading.

948)   i   EBENEZER FLINT, b. 13 May 1765; d. at Hillsborough, NH, 14 Mar 1833; m. at Andover, 14 Mar 1793, his third cousin once removed, DORCAS LUFKIN (*Mehitable Holt Lufkin⁵, Thomas Holt⁴, Thomas Holt³, Mary Russell Holt², Robert¹*), b. at Andover, 1776 (baptized 23 May 1779) daughter of Samuel and Mehitable (Holt) Lufkin); Dorcas d. at Hillsborough, 26 Apr 1848.

949)   ii   DANIEL FLINT, b. 27 Mar 1767; d. at Hillsborough, 27 Jun 1853; m. at Andover, 28 Jan 1795, his fourth cousin (through Abbott lines) LYDIA SHATTUCK, b. at Andover, 27 Apr 1765 daughter of Joseph and Anna (Johnson) Shattuck; Lydia d. at Hillsborough, 1 Apr 1843.

950)   iii   ASENATH FLINT, b. 4 Mar 1769; d. at Temple, NH, 8 Dec 1817; m. 21 Mar 1792, EDWARD PRATT, b. at Reading, 25 Apr 1765 son of Daniel and Abigail (Humphrey) Pratt; Edward d. at Temple, 17 Nov 1829. Edward married second Hannah Emerson in 1819.

951)   iv   ABIGAIL FLINT, b. 30 Jun 1771; d. 21 May 1798; m. 29 Mar 1795, her second cousin, ABNER HOLT (*Joseph Holt⁵, Lydia Holt Holt⁴, Thomas Holt³, Mary Russell Holt², Robert¹*), b. at Andover, 6 Oct 1771 son of Joseph and Ruth (Johnson) Holt; Abner d. at Albany, ME, 14 Dec 1854. Abner had three further marriages.

952)   v   EPHRAIM FLINT, b. 4 Sep 1773; d. at Albany, ME, 13 Oct 1859; m. 21 Jan 1799, his second cousin, ELEANOR HOLT (*Joseph Holt⁵, Lydia Holt Holt⁴, Thomas Holt³, Mary Russell Holt², Robert¹*), b. at Andover, 3 Nov 1777 daughter of Joseph and Ruth (Johnson) Holt; Eleanor d. at Albany, 23 Jun 1858.

[595] U.S., Newspaper Extractions from the Northeast, 1704-1930

[596] Perley, *Essex Antiquarian*, volume 9, p 187

[597] Massachusetts Land Records, Worcester County, 165:40

[598] Massachusetts Soldiers and Sailors in the Revolution, volume 5, p 792

	vi	JOHN FLINT, b. 4 Apr 1776; d. 4 Sep 1778.
953)	vii	AMOS FLINT, b. 16 Apr 1778; d. at Francestown, 27 Apr 1873; m. 3 Feb 1803, ABIGAIL MORSE, b. at Francestown, 1 Aug 1787 daughter of Timothy and Abigail (Dean) Morse; Abigail d. at Francestown, 1 Mar 1885.
954)	viii	JOHN FLINT, b. 23 Feb 1780; d. at Wilton, NH, 30 May 1847; m. 13 Feb 1803, SARAH FLINT, b. at Reading, 25 Nov 1783 daughter of Levi and Sarah (Parker) Flint; Sarah d. at Wilton, 6 Oct 1863.
	ix	PHEBE FLINT, b. 4 May 1782; d. 30 May 1797.

229)   MARSTIN HOLT (*Phebe Russell Holt Sheldon³, John², Robert¹*), b. at Andover, 13 Aug 1747 son of Ephraim and Phebe (Russell) Holt; m. at Holden, 13 Feb 1772, ABIGAIL WHEELER, b. at Holden, 20 Sep 1746 daughter of Moses and Abigail (Godin) Wheeler.

Marstin and Abigail had three children in Holden, Massachusetts and relocated to Dublin, New Hampshire 2 February 1779[599] where their two youngest children were born. Abigail seems to have died before 1800 as in 1800, Marstin and his two daughters seem to be in Barre, Vermont. Marstin does not appear on the census records after that. Daughter Abigail married in nearby Berlin, Vermont in 1810 and daughter Phebe lived single in Berlin where she was in 1860. Phebe was living alone and head of household in Berlin in 1840. She worked as a washerwoman.

955)	i	MOSES HOLT, b. at Holden, 4 Dec 1772; d. at Boston, 25 Apr 1823; m. 31 Mar 1796, AZUBA HUBBARD, b. at Holden, 13 Aug 1776 daughter of Elisha and Mercy (Hubbard) Hubbard; Azuba d. at Hubbardston, 9 Apr 1857.
956)	ii	AMOS SHELDON HOLT, b. at Holden, 17 Jul 1774; d. at Holden, 7 Apr 1855; m. 1ˢᵗ at Princeton, 29 Dec 1794, SALLY WOOLEY, b. at Princeton, 16 Dec 1774 daughter of David and Sarah (Porter) Wooley; Sally d. at Holden, 14 Dec 1814. Amos m. 2ⁿᵈ at Ashburnham, 4 Oct 1818, SALLY LINDAL, b. at Pepperell, 24 Nov 1794 daughter of James and Abigail (Collins) Lindal; Sally d. at Holden, 1838.
957)	iii	AARON HOLT, b. at Holden, 7 Oct 1776; d. at Troy, NH, 21 Oct 1826; m. at Holden, 28 Nov 1799, DOROTHY HOW, b. at Holden, 13 Sep 1780 daughter of Jotham and Dorothy (Smith) How; Dorothy d. at Holden, 21 Jul 1873. Dorothy married second John Hall on 27 Nov 1849.
958)	iv	ABIGAIL HOLT, b. at Dublin, NH, 2 Nov 1782; m. at Berlin, VT, 14 Jun 1810, MOSES BATCHELDER whose parents have not been identified. Moses d. at Dunham, Québec, Oct 1843.[600]
	v	PHEBE HOLT, b. at Dublin, NH, 13 Feb 1785; d. at Berlin, VT, after 1860. Phebe did not marry.

230)   RUSSELL SHELDON (*Phebe Russell Holt Sheldon³, John², Robert¹*), b. at Reading, 14 Jan 1752 son of Abraham and Phebe (Russell) Sheldon; d. at Reading, 1816 (probate 3 May 1816); m. at Reading, 6 Aug 1778, SUSANNAH SHELDON, b. at Reading, 5 Jun 1756 daughter of Nathaniel and Anna (Fitch) Sheldon.

Russell Sheldon was a farmer in Reading. On 9 October 1805 (recorded 9 May 1826), Russell Sheldon with consent of wife Susannah sold four acres of meadow in Reading to Joseph Batchelder for payment of $250. On 4 April 1808, Russell Sheldon with wife Susannah sold twenty-two acres in Reading to Benjamin Holt for payment of four hundred dollars. [601]

Russell Sheldon did not leave a will and his estate entered probate 3 May 1816 with Benjamin Holt of Reading as administrator at the request of widow Susan Sheldon. The homestead farm of 105 acres was valued at $2,893. Personal estate was valued at $183.12. Claims against the estate were $3,153.44. The personal estate was sold 30 May 1816. Dower was set off to widow Susanna 23 December 1816 and she accepted the dower 4 March 1817. The real estate was sold 4 February 1817 to settle the debts.[602] On 9 May 1817 (recorded 4 February 1824), Benjamin Holt acting as administrator of the estate of Russell Sheldon sold a tract of land of 16 acres with buildings to Ephraim Pratt, Treasurer of the Town of Reading for payment of $195. This is property that Russell mortgaged 31 December 1811 for $166.67.[603]

Russell and Susannah were parents of seven children with four children all baptized on 12 November 1797. The deaths of sons Russell and Daniel are recorded on the same date, 29 June 1843.

---

[599] Leonard, *The History of Dublin*, p 795

[600] Institut Généalogique Drouin; Montreal, Quebec, Canada; Drouin Collection; Author: Gabriel Drouin, comp.

[601] Massachusetts Land Records, Essex County, 267:302, 181:138

[602] *Middlesex County, MA: Probate File Papers, 1648-1871.* Online database. *AmericanAncestors.org.* New England Historic Genealogical Society, 2014. Case 20262

[603] Massachusetts Land Records, Essex County, 252:141

959)   i   HANNAH SHELDON, b. at Reading, 1786; d. at Reading, 9 Jul 1836; m. at Reading, 3 Apr 1804, BENJAMIN HOLT, b. at Reading, 28 Aug 1781 son of Joseph and Mary Eaton (Carter) Holt; Benjamin d. at Reading, 31 Mar 1847.

960)   ii   ABRAHAM SHELDON, b. at Reading 1789; d. at Middleton, 10 Oct 1858; m. at Reading, 9 Apr 1812, HANNAH C. EATON, b. at Reading, 24 Jun 1792 daughter of Nathaniel and Lydia (Holt) Eaton; Hannah d. at Middleton, 26 Aug 1854.

961)   iii   DANIEL SHELDON, b. 1791; d. at Reading, 29 Jun 1843; m. at Reading, 18 May 1817, PHEBE EATON, b. at Reading, 27 Jul 1787 daughter of Nathaniel and Lydia (Holt) Eaton; Phebe d. at North Reading, 1 May 1868.

        iv   MARY JOHNSON SHELDON, baptized 12 Nov 1797

        v   AMOS SHELDON, baptized 12 Nov 1797 (likely not the Amos Sheldon that marries Fanny Brown)

        vi   SUSANNAH SHELDON, baptized 12 Nov 1797

        vii   RUSSELL SHELDON, baptized 12 Nov 1797; d. at Reading, 29 Jun 1843.

231)   PHEBE SHELDON (*Phebe Russell Holt Sheldon³, John², Robert¹*), b. at Reading, 1 Mar 1754 daughter of Abraham and Phebe (Russell) Sheldon; d. at Mont Vernon, NH, 2 Feb 1824; m. at Andover, 3 Aug 1786, ISRAEL FARNUM, b. at Andover, 14 Jun 1758 son of Thomas and Lydia (Abbott) Farnum; Israel d. at Mont Vernon, 1842. After Phebe's death, Israel married Susannah Farnum daughter of Asa and Susannah (Town) Farnum on 17 May 1825. [604]
        Israel Farnum and Phebe Sheldon were parents of three children.

962)   i   PHEBE FARNUM, b. at Andover, 31 Mar 1788; d. at Landgrove, VT, 8 Sep 1863; m. at Mont Vernon, NH, 19 Jul 1810, her fourth cousin, EBENEZER HOLT LAMSON, b. at Amherst, NH, 23 Dec 1784 son of Jonathan and Elizabeth (Holt) Lampson; Ebenezer d. at Landgrove, 10 Apr 1855.

963)   ii   ISRAEL FARNUM, b. at Mont Vernon, 8 Jun 1790; d. at Mont Vernon, 30 Dec 1861; m. 4 Nov 1816, CATHERINE TALBERT, *perhaps* b. 5 Apr 1788 daughter of William and Mary (Andrews) Talbert; Catherine d. at Mont Vernon, 16 May 1875.

        iii   AMOS FARNUM, b. at Mont Vernon, 17 May 1792; d. 17 Oct 1812.

232)   REBEKAH SHELDON (*Phebe Russell Holt Sheldon³, John², Robert¹*), b. at Reading, 23 Jan 1757 daughter of Abraham and Phebe (Russell) Sheldon; d. 10 May 1813; m. 26 Jun 1777, PETER TOWNE, b. at Andover, 10 Aug 1749 son of Nathan and Eunice (-) Towne; Peter d. at Andover, 20 May 1830. Peter was first married to Lydia Abbott daughter of Ebenezer and Lydia (Farrington) Abbott.
        Peter Towne was a yeoman in Andover. In his will (probate 1 June 1830), Peter Towne bequeaths the household furniture to be equally divided among his daughters: Lydia wife of Nathaniel Berry, Sene wife of Caleb Swan of Methuen, Hannah wife of Moses Town, Abiah wife of Amos Carlton, and the children of Fanny. There are monetary bequests: one thousand dollars to Lydia and twelve hundred dollars each to daughters Sene, Hannah, and Abiah. The children of Fanny late wife of Michael Parker receive twelve hundred dollars to divide. Son Peter receives two hundred dollars and sons Amos, Joel, and Daniel each receives five dollars. Residue of the estate is to be divided equally among daughters Lydia, Sene, Hannah, and Abiah and sons Peter, Joel, and Daniel. William Johnson, Esq. was named executor. Real estate was valued at $7,281 which included the 100-acre homestead valued at $1,700. Personal estate was appraised at $2,546.26 which included $1,266 in the form of notes owed to Peter. Claims against the estate were $779, $508 of that claimed by son Peter. A petition to divide the real estate was filed 1 July 1831 at which time daughter Sene was deceased. The real estate division was made 7 September 1831. [605]
        Peter Towne and his first wife Lydia Abbott had one son who died in infancy. Peter Towne and Rebekah Sheldon were parents of ten children born at Andover. The four sons Daniel, Peter, Amos, and Joel all settled in Norway, Maine arriving there between 1802 and 1816. [606]

[604] Smith, *History of Mont Vernon*, p 63

[605] *Essex County, MA: Probate File Papers, 1638-1881.*Online database. *AmericanAncestors.org.* New England Historic Genealogical Society, 2014. Case 27917

[606] Whitman, *A History of Norway*, Maine, p 520

964) i PETER TOWNE, b. at Andover, 18 Nov 1777; d. at Norway, ME, 25 Mar 1854; m. at Andover, 31 May 1804, SALLY KIMBALL, b. 13 May 1786 daughter of John and Hannah (Farrington) Kimball; Sally d. at Norway, 11 Aug 1845.

965) ii AMOS TOWNE, b. at Andover, 28 May 1779; d. at Norway, ME, 8 Jan 1837; m. at Andover, 30 Jan 1806, MARY "MOLLY" FARNUM, b. at Andover, 18 Oct 1780 daughter of Benjamin and Dorothy (Holt) Farnum; Mary d. at Norway, 21 Oct 1847.

966) iii LYDIA TOWNE, b. at Andover, 1 Mar 1781; d. at North Andover, 14 Aug 1868; m. at Andover, 24 Jun 1800, NATHANIEL BERRY, b. at Middleton, MA, 27 Mar 1776 son of Nathaniel and Susannah (Easty) Berry; Nathaniel d. at North Andover, 1 Aug 1862.

iv JOEL TOWNE, b. at Andover, 17 Feb 1783; d. at Norway, ME, 1841 (probate 2 Mar 1841); m. at Andover, 10 Jun 1806, BETSEY KIMBALL, b. about 1785; Betsey was living in 1841. Joel and Betsey did not have children. In the 1820 and 1830 census of Norway, they were living as just two adults in the home.

967) v FANNY TOWNE, b. at Andover, 24 Mar 1785; d. at Andover, 3 Sep 1812; m. at Andover, 11 Dec 1804, MICHAEL PARKER, b. at Andover, 17 Jan 1773 son of Michael and Phebe (Farrington) Parker.

968) vi DANIEL TOWNE, b. at Andover, 8 Jan 1787; d. at Norway, ME, 1 Nov 1855; m. about 1813, SUSAN GURNEY, b. at Minot, ME, 3 Nov 1791 daughter of Jonathan and Susannah (Bryam) Gurney; Susan d. at Norway, 7 Feb 1864.

969) vii ASENATH "SENA" TOWNE, b. at Andover, 16 Feb 1789; d. at Methuen, 18 Feb 1831; m. at Methuen, 19 Jun 1814, CALEB SWAN, b. at Methuen, 20 Mar 1790 son of Caleb and Dorcas (Ingalls) Swan; Caleb d. at Methuen, 4 Dec 1863. Caleb married second Judith Pettengill.

viii HANNAH TOWNE, b. at Andover, 12 Oct 1792; d. at North Andover, 24 Feb 1875; m. at Andover, 11 Mar 1824, MOSES TOWNE, b. at Andover, 30 Sep 1792 son of Nathan and Hannah (Gould) Towne; Moses d. at Middleton, MA, 21 Feb 1886. Hannah and Moses did not have children. In his will, Moses Towne bequeathed to the inhabitants of North Andover $4,000 to be held in trust and used for the benefit of the district schools. There are other substantial bequests (several thousand dollars each) to other relations including the heirs of his deceased brothers and sisters.[607]

ix HARMON TOWNE, b. 14 Jan 1797; d. 29 Dec 1799.

970) x ABIAH TOWNE, b. at Andover, 19 Oct 1800; d. at Middleton, 30 Nov 1874; m. at Andover, Apr 1828, AMOS CARLETON, b. at Andover, 25 Apr 1802 son of Amos and Hannah (Farnum) Carleton; Amos d. at Cutler, ME, 20 Jul 1837.

---

233) AMOS SHELDON (*Phebe Russell Holt Sheldon³, John², Robert¹*), b. at Reading, 11 Aug 1759 son of Abraham and Phebe (Russell) Sheldon; d. at Fitchburg, 2 Nov 1828; m. at Fitchburg, 12 Jun 1788, SARAH NEEDHAM, b. at Billerica, 12 May 1762 daughter of Benjamin and Rebecca (Jaquith) Needham; Sarah d. at Fitchburg, 8 Jan 1816.

Amos Sheldon resided in Fitchburg. From Fitchburg, he enlisted in January 1777 for one year as private in the company of Capt. John Dinkins of the Massachusetts line. Amos received a pension based on his service in 1819.[608]

Amos was a farmer in Fitchburg. On 6 October 1818, Amos Sheldon sold to his son Amos for payment of $200 half of all his real estate which included the homestead farm in Fitchburg and a tract of land in Westminster. At the same time, Amos entered into an indenture agreement with his son on 26 October 1818 in which Amos leased this same property from his son for rent of three cents per year. On 14 April 1827, son Amos and his wife Mary sold this same property back to his father Amos for payment of $1,000.[609]

In his will written 27 November 1827 (proved 6 January 1829), Amos Sheldon of Fitchburg bequeathed to beloved daughters Sally Sheldon and Asenath Sheldon $150 each. Son Amos received $10 as he has already received a large portion of the estate. Sally and Asenath also receive specific furniture items. All the remainder of the estate, real and personal, is to be divided equally among Sally, Asenath, and daughter Rebecca Hilton wife of Clark Hilton. Friend Zachariah Sheldon was named sole executor.[610] Real estate was valued at $3,200 and personal estate was $486.23.[611]

Amos Sheldon and Sarah Needham were parents of four children born at Fitchburg.

[607] Massachusetts Wills and Probate, Essex County, Probate Records volume 441, pp 572-573
[608] U. S. Revolutionary War Pension and Bounty-Land Warrant Application Files, Case S33654
[609] Massachusetts Land Records, Worcester County, 213:216; 213:530; 255:378
[610] *Probate Records (Worcester County, Massachusetts); Index 1731-1881, probate records volume 66, pp 352-353*
[611] *Worcester County, MA: Probate File Papers, 1731-1881.* Online database. AmericanAncestors.org. New England Historic Genealogical Society, 2015. Case 53094

i   SALLY SHELDON, b. 27 Dec 1790; d. at Wendell, 24 Mar 1866. Sally did not marry.

ii   ASENATH SHELDON, b. 12 Aug 1792; d. at Fitchburg, 18 Feb 1837. Asenath did not marry.

971)   iii   AMOS SHELDON, b. 17 Sep 1796; d. 6 Feb 1841 (buried at Fitchburg); m. 20 Jun 1824, MARY E
                WILLARD, b. at Fitchburg, 8 Jul 1801 daughter of Joseph and Mary (Willard) Willard; Mary d. at
                Edgartown, 10 Sep 1879.

972)   iv   REBECCA SHELDON, b. 18 Jul 1799; d. at Fitchburg, 15 May 1871; m. CLARK HILTON, b. at Fitchburg,
                23 Mar 1798 son of Thomas and Sarah (Stratton) Hilton; Clark d. at Fitchburg, 25 Jul 1834.

234)   BENJAMIN RUSSELL (*John³, John², Robert¹*), b. at Andover, 28 Jan 1739 son of John and Hannah (Foster) Russell;
d. at Bethel, ME, 23 Nov 1802; m. 7 Oct 1762, MARY FEAVER, b. at Andover, 1 Mar 1738/9 daughter of Jacob and Hannah
(Farrington) Feaver.
        After the births of their first three children, Benjamin and Mary located in Fryeburg, Maine where Benjamin was a
leading citizen serving as chairman of the selectman. They were first proprietors of Fryeburg.[612] The family made one further
move to Bethel in 1779 where Benjamin served as the first town clerk.[613]
        There are five known children of Benjamin Russell and Mary Feaver.

973)   i   BENJAMIN RUSSELL, b. at Andover, 28 Jul 1763; d. at Newry, ME, 21 Aug 1842; m. at Andover, 20 Sep
                1787, MEHITABLE ABBOTT, b. at Andover, 29 Sep 1764 daughter of Jonathan and Mehitable (Abbott)
                Abbott; Mehitable d. at Newry, 6 Feb 1858.

974)   ii   MARY RUSSELL, b. at Andover, 15 Oct 1764; m. about 1788, NATHANIEL SEGAR, b. at Newton, MA, 28
                Jan 1755 son of Josiah and Thankful (Allen) Segar; Nathaniel d. at Hanover, ME, 10 Sep 1847.

975)   iii   THEODORE RUSSELL, b. at Andover, 6 Dec 1765; d. at Bethel, ME, 4 Jun 1821; m. 1st at Andover, 17 Sep
                1789, ABIGAIL ABBOTT, b. at Andover, 30 Jul 1770 daughter of Jonathan and Mehitable (Abbott) Abbott;
                Abigail d. at Bethel, 2 Jun 1810. Theodore m. 2nd about 1811, TABITHA STRICKLAND, b. 1783; Tabitha d.
                at Bethel, 1855.

976)   iv   WILLIAM RUSSELL, b. about 1770; m. about 1791, MEHITABLE KILGORE, b. about 1773 daughter of
                John and Elizabeth (Brackett) Kilgore.

977)   v   JOHN RUSSELL, b. about 1775; d. at Bethel, 1 Jul 1850; m. about 1798, SUSANNAH TWITCHELL, b. 27
                Nov 1777 daughter of Ezra and Susannah (Rice) Twitchell; Susannah d. at Bethel, 2 Sep 1856.

235)   JOHN RUSSELL (*John³, John², Robert¹*), b. at Andover, 1 Jul 1746 son of John and Hannah (Foster) Russell; d. at
Andover, 12 Aug 1830; m. at Andover, 1 Feb 1774, PHEBE ABBOTT, b. at Andover, 29 Aug 1749 daughter of Barachias and
Hannah (Holt) Abbott; Phebe d. at Andover, 17 Apr 1809. John m. 2nd at Middleton, MA, 3 Mar 1811, MARY WILKINS; Mary d.
at Andover, 9 Sep 1830. Mary Wilkins was first married to Nathaniel Sherman.
        The estate of John Russell entered probate 17 August 1830.[614] The will of John Russell has bequests to the following
persons: beloved wife Mary; grandson John Russell (oldest male heir with the name Russell), daughters Phebe Lovejoy,
Hannah Abbot, Betsy Smith, Sally Loring, the heirs of daughter Dolly Lovejoy who is deceased, and heirs of daughter Nancy
Woodbridge who is deceased; daughter-in-law Phebe Russell (this to be in the hands of a trustee);[615] and grandchildren John
Russell, William Russell, Edward Russell, Phebe Russell, and Joseph Russell. Benjamin Jenkins is named executor and trustee.
        John Russell and Phebe Abbott had eight children born at Andover.

978)   i   JOHN RUSSELL, b. 10 Oct 1774; d. at Andover, May 1818; m. at Andover, 21 Jul 1799, DIANA BRAY, b. at
                Gloucester, Oct 1775 daughter of Edward and Edith (Doane) Bray; Diana d. at Andover, 4 Mar 1858.[616]

---

[612] Barrows, *Fryeburg, Maine*, p 79
[613] Lapham, *History of Bethel*, p 606
[614] Ess*ex County, MA: Probate File Papers, 1638-1881*.Online database. *AmericanAncestors.org.* New England Historic Genealogical Society, 2014.
Case number 24400
[615] It has not been determined who daughter-in-law Phebe Russell is.
[616] Diana's death record confirms Gloucester as her place of birth making Edward and Edith her likely parents.

979)   ii   PHEBE RUSSELL, b. 1776; d. at Andover, 2 Dec 1858; m. 2 Nov 1794, her third cousin, EBENEZER LOVEJOY, b. at Andover, 16 Feb 1773 son of Jeremiah and Dorothy (Ballard) Lovejoy; Ebenezer d. at Andover, 7 Jun 1851.

980)   iii   HANNAH RUSSELL, b. Sep 1778; d. at Andover, 3 Jan 1840; m. 13 Aug 1801, her third cousin, STEPHEN ABBOT, b. at Andover, 30 Dec 1779 son of Jonathan and Dorcas (Abbott) Abbott; Stephen d. at Andover, 1 Oct 1835.

981)   iv   BETTY RUSSELL, b. 1780; d. at Andover, 7 Nov 1866; m. 27 Sep 1804, THOMAS SMITH, b. at Andover, 13 Mar 1781 son of Thomas and Mary (Harris) Smith; Thomas d. at Andover, 18 Sep 1832.

982)   v   SALLY RUSSELL, b. 1783; d. at Andover, 10 Jun 1848; m. at Andover, 23 Oct 1806, THOMAS LORING, born in NH, about 1780 son of John and Sarah (Foster) Loring; Thomas d. at New Orleans, 1826. Thomas was a machinist and he placed the machinery in the first steamboat to go down the Ohio River. He died of spotted fever in New Orleans.[617][618]

983)   vi   DOLLY RUSSELL, b. baptized at Andover, 21 Sep 1788; d. at Andover, 26 Jun 1809; m. 19 May 1808, her third cousin, JOHN LOVEJOY, b. at Andover, 25 Jul 1780 son of Jeremiah and Dorothy (Ballard) Lovejoy; John d. at Andover, 26 Feb 1817. After Dolly's death, John married PERSIS BAILEY, b. at Andover, 25 May 1783 daughter of William and Rebecca (Hildreth) Bailey; Persis d. at Andover, 18 Feb 1816.

       vii   WILLIAM RUSSELL, b. 1785; d. 21 Nov 1788.

984)   viii   NANCY RUSSELL, b. Aug 1790; d. at Arlington, MA, 29 Dec 1818; m. 1812, SAMUEL WOODBRIDGE, b. at Marblehead, 13 Jan 1788 son of Dudley and Sara (Brock) Woodbridge; Dudley d. at Cambridge, 28 Jan 1867. After Nancy's death, Samuel married, 30 Sep 1821, DORCAS RUSSELL (*Benjamin⁵, Benjamin⁴, John³, John², Robert¹*), b. at Bethel, ME, 8 Apr 1796 daughter of Benjamin and Mehitable (Abbott) Russell; Dorcas d. at Boston, 29 Nov 1877.

236)   ABRAHAM RUSSELL (*John³, John², Robert¹*), b. at Andover, 7 Nov 1750 son of John and Hannah (Foster) Russell; d. at Bethel, ME, 9 Dec 1839; m. 1775, SARAH SWAN, b. 9 Feb 1756 daughter of James and Mary (Smith) Swan; Sarah d. at Bethel, 13 Jan 1802.

     Abraham owned property in Fryeburg in addition to property in Bethel, and Abraham and Sarah were in Fryeburg in the early part of their marriage. Abraham and Sarah had their home in Bethel, first living near the Alder River. Their home was lost in the "great freshet" of 1785. They rebuilt near the base of Bethel Hill on Rumford road.[619]

     Abraham Russell and Sarah Swan were parents of nine children.

985)   i   HANNAH RUSSELL, b. at Fryeburg, 19 Sep 1776; d. at Newry, ME, 1848; m. 1794, FREDERICK BALLARD, b. at Middleton, MA, 13 Oct 1762 son of Jonathan and Priscilla (Farnum) Ballard; Frederick d. at Newry, 1851.

986)   ii   SARAH RUSSELL, b. 26 Apr 1779; d. at Portland, ME, 5 Jun 1846; m. 2 Apr 1800, ELIJAH BOND, b. at Watertown, 12 May 1767 son of Jonas and Ruth (Harrington) Bond;[620] Elijah d. at Portland, 31 Dec 1835.

987)   iii   ABIAH RUSSELL, b. (recorded at Conway, NH), 16 Apr 1781; d. at Bethel, ME, 14 Jul 1831; m. about 1800, PETER YORK, b. at Standish, ME, 29 Aug 1779 son of John and Abigail (Bean) York; Peter d. at Bethel, 10 Dec 1862.

       iv   MARY RUSSELL, b. at Bethel, 3 Oct 1784; d. at Bethel, 4 Sep 1856; m. DANIEL GROUT, b. in MA, about 1777; Daniel d. after 1860 when he was living in Portland with his sister-in-law Dorcas Russell and her husband Hiram Allen. There are no children known for Mary and Daniel.

988)   v   APPHIA RUSSELL, b. at Bethel, 6 Apr 1787; d. 24 Apr 1858; m. by 1806, GIDEON POWERS, b. at Bethel, 1790 son of Gideon and Ruth (Packard) Powers; Gideon d. at Bethel, 13 Aug 1879.

       vi   SUSAN RUSSELL, b. at Bethel, 4 Jul 1789; d. at Portland, 6 Sep 1862; m. OTIS HORN who has not been identified. Otis was deceased before 1850. There are no children known.

---

[617] *New Hampshire, Death and Burial Records Index, 1654-1949.*
[618] Charlotte Helen Abbott, The Loring Family
[619] Lapham, History of Bethel, p 610
[620] Lapham, *History of Bethel*, p 493

989)   vii   ESTHER RUSSELL, b. at Bethel, 18 Sep 1792; d. at Bethel, 12 Oct 1876; m. 1819, JOHN OLIVER, b. at Bridgton, ME, 8 May 1795 son of William and Hannah (Fowler) Oliver; John d. at St. Charles, IL, 13 Jan 1875. Esther and John divorced at Oxford County, ME, Oct 1848.[621]

990)   viii   FLETCHER RUSSELL, b. at Bethel, 2 Jul 1795; d. at Canaan, VT, 3 Jun 1853; m. 20 Apr 1823, HANNAH HOWARD, b. at Fryeburg, ME 1796 daughter of William and Lucy (Freeman) Howard;[622] Hannah d. at Canaan, 20 Jun 1879.

991)   ix   DORCAS RUSSELL, b. at Bethel, 10 Mar 1800; d. at Portland, ME, 8 Jul 1860; m. about 1818, HIRAM ALLEN, b. 1795; Hiram d. at Portland, 12 Mar 1873.

237)   JACOB RUSSELL (*John³, John², Robert¹*), baptized at Andover, 1 Feb 1761 son of John and Hannah (Foster) Russell; d. at Bethel, ME, 1799; m. at Andover, 26 Feb 1784, DOROTHY SHATTUCK, b. at Andover, 14 Apr 1764 daughter of Zebadiah and Elizabeth (Abbott) Shattuck; Dorothy d. at Bethel, 24 Jan 1852.

      Dorothy Shattuck and Jacob Russell were married in Andover and perhaps some of the children were born in Andover before the family moved to Bethel, Maine. Birth dates are estimates based on census records and age at death. Four children are known for Dorothy and Jacob.[623]

634)   i   DOLLY RUSSELL, b. perhaps at Andover, 1784; d. at Beverly, MA, 20 Sep 1863; m. at East Andover, ME, 13 Aug 1804, her first cousin once removed, JAMES RUSSELL (*Uriah⁴, Thomas³, James², Robert¹*), b. at Andover, Nov 1777 son of Uriah and Lydia (Abbott) Russell; James d. at Paris, ME, 2 Nov 1861.

992)   ii   ABIGAIL RUSSELL, b. perhaps at Andover, 1786; d. at Potter, NY, Jan 1859; m. at Bethel, 21 Nov 1822, as his second wife, ELI TWITCHELL, b. at Dublin, NH, 26 Jul 1786 son of Ezra and Susanna (Rice) Twitchell; Eli d. at Potter, NY, 1869 (probate 11 Oct 1869). Eli was first married to Betsy Gould 20 Jan 1807 and third married to Betsey's sister Clarissa Gould about 1862.

993)   iii   JACOB RUSSELL, b. likely at Bethel, about 1788; d. at Richland, NY, 20 May 1873 (probate 15 Oct 1873); m. 1ˢᵗ, by 1828, SOPHIA STARK, b. 27 Dec 1794 daughter of Abel and Lydia (Fletcher) Stark;[624] Sophia d. at Richland, 11 Nov 1847. Jacob m. 2ⁿᵈ, about 1848, Susan who has not been identified; Susan d. at Richland, 20 Feb 1871.

      iv   CHARLES RUSSELL, b. at Bethel, about 1793; d. at Bethel, after 1850. Charles lived with his sister Dolly and her husband. He did not marry.

238)   LYDIA RUSSELL (*Joseph³, John², Robert¹*), b. at Andover, 17 May 1764 daughter of Joseph and Hephzibah (Russell) Russell; d. at Bethel, ME, 12 Sep 1847; m. 7 Jun 1787, JOHN HOLT,[625] b. 12 May 1764 son of Humphrey and Mary (Holton) Holt; John d. at Bethel, 12 Jul 1820.

      John Holt went to Bethel where he cleared his property before returning to Andover to marry Lydia Russell and then returning with his bride to Bethel. John served as a Captain in the militia at Bethel and was deacon of the Baptist church. He served for three years during the Revolution.[626]

      John Holt did not leave a will and his estate entered probate October 1830 with son Hiram Holt as administrator at the request of widow Lydia Holt. At the time of his death, John had no real estate and personal estate was valued at $206.79.[627]

      John Holt and Lydia Russell were parents of nine children born at Bethel.

      i   JOHN HOLT, b. 1 Jun 1788; d. 22 Jan 1789.

994)   ii   HARMON HOLT, b. 12 Nov 1789; d. at Medford, ME, May 1861; m. 10 Nov 1810, SALLY DUSTIN, b. about 1790; Sally d. after 1860 (living at 1860 census).

---

[621] Maine, Divorce Records, 1798-1891

[622] Father's name is given as William and mother's name as Lucy Freeman on Hannah's death record.

[623] Lapham, *History of Bethel, Maine*, p 611

[624] Walworth, *Hyde Genealogy*, p 517

[625] Durrie's Holt genealogy reports that Lydia who married John Holt was born in 1772 and was a daughter of Elijah. However, the gravestone gives her age at death as 83 years old meaning she was born in 1764. As Lydia's brother Chandler also settled in Bethel, it is reasonable to assume that it is this Lydia that married John Holt.

[626] Lapham, *History of Bethel*, p 424

[627] Maine. *Probate Court (Oxford County)*; Probate Place: *Oxford, Maine, Estate Files, Drawer H52, Hamlin, Cyrus-Howe, Jacob, 1820-1834, Estate of John Holt*

995) iii WILLIAM HOLT, b. 4 Feb 1792; d. at Bethel, 6 Dec 1868; m. 4 May 1814, MARY STEARNS, b. at Bethel, 18 Apr 1795 daughter of Thomas and Lois (Colby) Stearns; Mary d. at Bethel, 5 Jan 1875.

996) iv JOSEPH R. HOLT, b. at Bethel, 28 Feb 1795; d. at Bethel, 22 Sep 1878; m. 4 Dec 1817, SUSAN STEARNS, b. at Bethel, 30 Dec 1797 daughter of Thomas and Lois (Colby) Stearns; Susan d. at Bethel, 28 Feb 1873.

      v MARY HOLT, b. 20 Jan 1797; d. 20 Oct 1802.

      vi NATHAN HOLT, b. 20 Mar 1799; d. 6 Aug 1802.

      vii HASKELL HOLT, b. 3 Jun 1801; d. 30 Sep 1802.

997) viii HIRAM HOLT, b. at Bethel, 21 Jul 1803; d. likely at Bethel, after 1870; m. 9 Jun 1826, ELOHE VARRIL, b. 6 Nov 1801 daughter of Samuel and Sarah (Prince) Varril; Elohe was living in 1870.

998) ix LYDIA HOLT, b. at Bethel, 17 Nov 1805; d. at Bethel, 1891; m. 9 Jun 1832, HUMPHREY BEAN, b. at Bethel, 22 Jan 1802 son of Amos and Huldah (Kimball) Bean; Humphrey d. at Bethel, 1884.

239) CHANDLER RUSSELL (*Joseph³, John², Robert¹*), b. at Andover, 20 Sep 1775 son of Joseph and Hephzibah (Russell) Russell; d. 8 Jun 1846, m. at Bethel 14 Dec 1803, BETSEY DUSTON, b. 12 Jul 1782 daughter of Jacob and Elizabeth (Swan) Duston.[628]
      Chandler Russell and Betsey Duston were parents of eight children born at Bethel, Maine.[629]

999) i ELIJAH RUSSELL, b. at Bethel, 17 Jun 1804; d. at Hanover, ME, 8 Apr 1888; m. about 1828, ALMIRA BEAN, b. at Bethel, 27 Oct 1802 daughter of John and Hannah (McGill) Bean; Almira d. at Hanover, 22 Sep 1880.

1000) ii MARIA H. RUSSELL, b. at Bethel, 22 Oct 1809; d. at Bethel, about 1855; m. KIMBALL BEAN, b. 26 Apr 1796 son of Timothy and Hannah (Kimball) Bean; Kimball d. at Bethel 5 Apr 1864. Kimball was first married to Lovina Powers and third married to Dolly whom he married in 1856.

1001) iii EZEKIEL DUSTIN RUSSELL, b. at Bethel, 19 Apr 1811; d. at Bethel, 8 Aug 1883; m. at Townsend, MA, 19 Apr 1835, HANNAH ELIZABETH VERDER, b. at Townsend, 14 Sep 1810 daughter of George and Nancy (Tarbox) Verder; Hannah d. at Bethel, 12 Mar 1889.

      iv PEREGRINE RUSSELL, b. 12 Jul 1813; d. 14 Jan 1837.

      v JOSEPH H. RUSSELL, b. at Bethel, 16 May 1814; d. likely at Nashville, TN. Joseph married, but the identity of his wife has not been found.

1002) vi LOVINA D. RUSSELL, b. at Bethel, 17 Sep 1816; d. at Bethel, 1 Sep 1844; m. TIMOTHY BEAN, b. at Bethel, 6 Apr 1813 son of Timothy and Hannah (Kimball) Bean. Timothy married second Betsey E. Swift.

      vii FARNUM D. RUSSELL, b. 12 Jun 1820

      viii JOSHUA R. RUSSELL, b. at Bethel, 27 Mar 1824; m. his second cousin once removed, MELISSA YORK (*Abiah Russell York⁵, Abraham⁴, John³, John², Robert¹*), b. at Bethel, 10 Jul 1821 daughter of Peter and Abiah (Russell) York; Melissa d. at Tioga, IL, 5 Sep 1881. No children were identified for Joseph and Melissa.

240) JEDEDIAH RUSSELL (*Robert³, John², Robert¹*), baptized at Andover, 26 Nov 1752 son of Robert and Anne (Felt) Russell; d. at Lyndeborough, 17 Feb 1848; m. RHODA PRATT, b. 6 Nov 1762 daughter of Ephraim and Phebe (-) Pratt.
      Jedediah and Rhoda were in Reading and then later in Lyndeborough where they were members of the Congregational church. They had a farm in the southwest part of Lyndeborough.[630]
      On 3 June 1818, Jedediah Russell of Lyndeborough then in his sixty-sixth year, provided a statement related to his application for a pension application. He reported enlisting in December 1775 while a resident of Andover and joined his regiment at Cambridge 1 January 1776. He served twelve months in Capt. Vinton's company in Col. Sargent's regiment of the Massachusetts line. He was discharged 1 January 1777 at Peck's Hill (in another place given as Fishkill), New York. He first

---

[628] Lapham, *History of Bethel*, p 520

[629] There is a Chandler Russell who died at Peru, Maine in 1835 leaving a widow Joanna; who this Chandler Russell is has not been determined and *perhaps* he was a child in this family. Maine Wills and Probate, Oxford County Estate Files, Estate of Chandler Russell

[630] Donovan, *History of Lyndeborough*, p 847

served three months in the Massachusetts militia in the Fall of 1775 in Capt. John Abbot's company. He was awarded a pension based on his service.[631]

     Jedediah Russell and Rhoda Pratt were parents of twelve children, the older children born at Reading and the younger children at Lyndeborough, although the recording of the births and baptisms are not entirely consistent.

1003)   i   JEDEDIAH RUSSELL, b. at Reading, 29 Aug 1780; d. at Mayfield, OH, 15 Sep 1863; m. at Amherst, NH, 23 Oct 1803,[632] ABIGAIL WHITING, b. at Amherst, 6 Nov 1780 daughter of John and Elizabeth (-) Whiting; Abigail d. at Mayfield, 1832.

1004)   ii   RHODA RUSSELL, b. (recorded) at Lyndeborough, 9 Feb 1782; d. at Sullivan, NH, 28 Jun 1867; m. at Temple, NH, 1801, EPHRAIM ADAMS HOLT, b. at Temple, 14 Aug 1778 son of Samuel and Lydia (Adams) Holt; Ephraim d. at Sullivan, 31 Jul 1857.

1005)   iii   HEPHZIBAH RUSSELL, b. 28 Oct 1783; m. 1st at Lyndeborough, 17 Mar 1806, HERMAN LADD SARGENT, b. at Methuen, MA, 27 Sep 1782 son of Joshua and Abigail (Ladd) Sargent; Herman d. 1816. Hephzibah m. 2nd at Lyndeborough, 6 May 1819, SAMUEL CHAMBERLAIN, b. at Lyndeborough, 4 May 1779 son of Samuel and Hannah (Abbott) Chamberlain. Samuel was first married to Olive who has not been identified.

1006)   iv   EPHRAIM PRATT RUSSELL, baptized at Reading, 3 Jul 1785; d. after 1855 when he was living at Seneca, NY at the home of his son William; married OLIVE ORDWAY, b. about 1787 *likely* daughter of Enoch and Anne (Fletcher) Ordway; Olive d. after 1855.

           v   JAMES RUSSELL, baptized at Reading, 19 Aug 1787. In 1820, James was living in Phelps, NY next to his older brother Jedediah. The census information suggests he was married with children, but further information on his family has not been found.[633]

           vi   CHLOE RUSSELL, b. 2 Aug 1789; d. 5 Feb 1808.

           vii   WILLIAM RUSSELL, b. 21 Feb 1792; d. 16 Nov 1814.

1007)   viii   EBENEZER RUSSELL, b. 17 Feb 1794; d. at South Merrimack, NH, 25 Apr 1883; m. 1st 7 Jul 1818, ARTIMESIA LYNCH; Artimesia d. at Nashua, NH, 22 Jun 1860. Ebenezer m. 2nd 2 Aug 1863, ELIZABETH STEVENS, b. about 1814 daughter of William and Roxanne (Finch) Stevens. Elizabeth was twice widowed before her marriage to Ebenezer.

1008)   ix   SALLY PRATT RUSSELL, b. 20 Jun 1796; d. after 1860 when she was living at Hanover, NH; m. at Lyndeborough, 27 Jan 1818, ASA CHAMBERLAIN, b. at Lyndeborough, 10 Apr 1793 son of Jonathan and Margaret (Cram) Chamberlain; Asa d. at Hanover, 24 Jul 1858.

           x   SAMUEL RUSSELL, b. 31 Mar 1798; d. 12 Oct 1800.

1009)   xi   SAMUEL RUSSELL, b. 4 Apr 1801; d. after 1850 when living at Meredith, NH; m. 29 Dec 1822, HANNAH DUSTIN, b. about 1801; Hannah d. after 1850.

1010)   xii   ELIAB RUSSELL, b. 9 Mar 1804; d. at Shortsville, NY, 29 May 1874; m. DIANA NICHOLS, b. 1804; Diana d. at Shortsville, 26 Nov 1867.

241)   JONATHAN RUSSELL (*Robert³, John², Robert¹*), baptized at Andover, 30 Apr 1758 son of Robert and Anne (Felt) Russell; d. at Dublin, NH, Apr 1834; m. 19 Jun 1782, RACHEL WHITE, b. 1758; Rachel d. at Dublin, 1 Jun 1821.
     Jonathan Russell and Rachel White were parents of ten children likely all born at Dublin, New Hampshire.[634]

           i   HEPHZIBAH RUSSELL, b. 17 Mar 1783; d. May 1834.

1011)   ii   JONATHAN RUSSELL, b. 26 Jan 1785; d. at Dublin, 10 Sep 1848; m. 2 Jan 1806, MARY LEWIS, b. at Marlborough, NH, 14 Dec 1786 daughter of John and Rebecca (Upham) Lewis.

           iii   ELIAS RUSSELL, b. 8 Mar 1787; likely died young

---

[631] U.S. Revolutionary War Pension and Bounty-Land Warrant Application Files, Case S45127

[632] The marriage transcription gives a year of 1813, but this seems an error given that children were born to this couple by 1806.

[633] 1820 U S Census; Census Place: Phelps, Ontario, New York; Page: 303; NARA Roll: M33_62; Image: 162. James Russell head of household; 1 male 26-44; 1 female 26-44; 2 males under 10; 1 male 10-15; 2 females under 10; and 1 female 16-25

[634] Leonard, *History of Dublin*, p 886

1012) iv SALLY RUSSELL, b. 6 Apr 1788; d. at Marlborough, NH, 22 Nov 1843; m. at Marlborough, 23 Oct 1813, ASA METCALF, b. about 1787 (died at age 34) son of Asa and Mehitable (Upham) Metcalf;[635] Asa d. at Marlborough, 21 Aug 1821.

1013) v ABNER RUSSELL, b. 3 Mar 1791; d. at Marlborough, NH, 24 Mar 1855; m. 1816, BETSEY HERRICK, b. at Marlborough, 2 Sep 1794 daughter of Ebenezer and Lydia (Eaton) Herrick; Betsey d. at Harrisville, NH, 21 Jan 1875.

vi NANCY RUSSELL, b. 9 Apr 1793; d. after 1860 when she was living in Keene at the home of her stepson; m. at Keene, 21 Mar 1839, as his second wife, DAVID HEATON, b. at Keene, 6 Aug 1785 son of Samuel and Sarah (Boynton) Heaton; David d. at Keene, 24 Sep 1846. David was first married to Rebecca Moore. David and Rebecca (Moore) Heaton were parents of Nancy Heaton who married Gilbert Russell son of Abner and Betsey (Herrick) Russell (see just above).

vii HULDAH RUSSELL, b. 3 May 1795; d. at Dublin, 14 Nov 1865. Huldah did not marry.

1014) viii EBENEZER RUSSELL, b. 27 Nov 1797; d. at Keene, 8 Apr 1859; m. at Dublin, 18 Feb 1823, OLIVE NEWELL, b. 30 Mar 1801; Olive d. at Rochester, NY, 4 Apr 1891. After the death of Ebenezer, Olive lived with their son Osgood M. Russell.

1015) ix AMELIA "MILLE" RUSSELL, b. 9 Jan 1800; d. at Westminster, VT, 6 Apr 1873; m. at Westminster, 6 Mar 1833, ALVIN G. KEYES, b. at Putney, 1808 son of Israel and Hannah (Grout) Keyes; Alvin d. at Putney, 11 Jul 1872.

1016) x MARY W. RUSSELL, b. 15 Jun 1806; d. at Putney, VT, 13 Aug 1878; m. 1st at Dublin, 31 Oct 1837, PROCTOR HIRAM KEYES, b. at Putney, 20 Dec 1810 son of Asa and Hannah (Taylor) Keyes; Proctor d. at Putney, 27 May 1840. Mary m. 2nd at Putney, 1 Nov 1843, as his second wife, EPHRAIM BROWN, b. 1790 likely son of Silas and Mary (Nims) Brown; Ephraim d. at Putney, at 22 Sep 1871. Ephraim was first married to Sophia Eddey who died in 1841.

242) MARY HOLT (*Mary Russell Holt³, John², Robert¹*), b. at Andover, 24 Nov 1755 daughter of Joseph and Mary (Russell) Holt; d. at Wilton, 24 Oct 1844; m. 18 Nov 1779, EDWARD HERRICK, b. at Methuen, 9 Oct 1754 son of Edward and Mary (Kimball) Herrick; Edward d. at Wilton, 5 Feb 1811.

Edward and Mary located in Wilton at the time of their marriage, Edward arriving there in 1779. Edward purchased part of the estate of Caleb Putnam and also owned the mills at Barnes's Falls. Edward served as a Sergeant during the Revolution and was afterwards a Lieutenant in the New Hampshire militia.[636]

In his will written 2 February 1811 (proved 9 April 1811), Edward Herrick bequeathed to son Benjamin thirty-eight dollars in addition to what he has received. Daughter Mary wife of John Putnam receives two dollars and thirty-three cents. Son George receives eight dollars. Son Edward receives three dollars and daughter Sarah Herrick, ten dollars. Daughter Anna Herrick receives eighty-eight dollars in one year or at the time of marriage if she marries earlier. Son Israel receives eighty-eight dollars at age twenty-one. Son Larkin receives sixty-eight dollars. To beloved wife Mary, he bequeaths all the real and personal estate to have and to hold to her Mary Herrick and her heirs forever. Mary is responsible to pay the debts and legacies and is named executrix.[637]

Mary Holt and Edward Herrick were parents of nine children born at Wilton.

1017) i BENJAMIN HERRICK, b. 13 Dec 1780; m. at Boston, 22 Jul 1807, ELCY NUGENT, b. at Stonington, CT, about 1781.

1018) ii MARY HERRICK, b. 13 Apr 1782; d. at Dexter, ME, 16 Jun 1882; m. 7 Jul 1803, JOHN PUTNAM, b. at Wilton, 27 Nov 1774 son of Jacob and Abigail (Burnap) Putnam; John d. at Nashua, NH, 16 Mar 1835.

1019) iii GEORGE HERRICK, b. 12 Feb 1784; d. at Wilton, after 1840; m. about 1808, his third cousin once removed (through Holt line), MARY "POLLY" HOLT, b. at Wilton, 17 Apr 1787 daughter of Joel and Mary (Coburn) Holt; Mary d. after 1860 when she was living with her son Daniel H. Herrick in Dayton, NY.

1020) iv EDWARD HERRICK, b. 29 Oct 1785; d. at Wilton, 9 Dec 1873; m. 1st 27 Dec 1810, NANCY BARRETT, b. at Westford, MA, 28 Dec 1790 daughter of Ebenezer and Jane (Reed) Barrett; Nancy d. 27 Nov 1824. Edward

[635] Bemis, *History of the Town of Marlborough*, p 579
[636] Livermore, *History of the Town of Wilton*, p 398
[637] *New Hampshire. Probate Court (Hillsborough County), Probate Records volume 17, pp 210-211*

m. 2nd 22 Nov 1825, his second cousin once removed, MARY ANDREWS, b. at Hillsborough, 1 Jan 1796 daughter of Abraham and Mary (Chandler) Andrews.[638]

1021)   v   SARAH HERRICK, b. 27 Dec 1788; d. at Norridgewock, ME, 17 Mar 1866; m. 8 Sep 1814, JOSIAH PEET, b. at Bethlehem, CT, 21 Jun 1780 son of Benjamin and Elizabeth (Hendee) Peet; Josiah d. at Norridgewock, 17 Feb 1852.

          vi   ANNA HERRICK, b. 6 Dec 1790; d. at Wilton, 7 Oct 1873; m. at Wilton, 6 Oct 1814, ELIJAH STOCKWELL, b. at Westborough, MA, 14 May 1784 son of Daniel and Rebecca (Warren) Stockwell; Elijah d. at Wilton, 26 Jul 1852. Anna and Elijah did not have children. In his will written 31 May 1852, after making provision for his wife Anna, left buildings with land and farming tools to Israel Herrick and Daniel H. Herrick.[639] (Daniel H. Herrick was son of Anna's brother George Herrick.)

1022)   vii ISRAEL HERRICK, b. 9 Jul 1794; d. at Lyndeborough, 18 Feb 1866; m. 1st at Milford, 28 Nov 1822, ELIZA H. BURNS, b. at Milford, 24 Nov 1802 son of Samuel and Abigail (Jones) Burns;[640] Eliza d. at Milford, 28 Nov 1848. Israel m. 2nd 12 Dec 1849, his third cousin once removed (through Holt line), EMELINE GRAY, b. at Wilton, 11 Oct 1811 daughter of Joseph and Chloe (Abbott) Gray; Emeline d. at Lyndeborough, 3 Jun 1891.

          viii DIADAMIA HERRICK, b. 1 Jan 1797; d. 6 Feb 1797.

1023)   ix   LARKIN HERRICK, b. 16 Dec 1799; d. at Wilton, 6 Nov 1866; m. at Wilton, 17 May 1827, SARAH SHELDON, b. at Wilton, 19 Jul 1804 daughter of Samuel and Phebe (Keyes) Sheldon; Sarah d. at Lebanon, NH, 2 May 1891.

243)   RHODA HOLT (*Mary Russell Holt³, John², Robert¹*), b. at Andover, 16 Oct 1757 daughter of Joseph and Mary (Russell) Holt; d. at Wilton, 25 Jul 1799, m. 25 Nov 1778, JOHN DALE, b. 26 Jul 1748 son of John and Mary (Ellinwood) Dale; John d. at Wilton, 11 Jul 1809. After Rhoda's death, John married Lydia Lamon.

John Dale was a farmer in Wilton living on the family homestead. He served during the Revolution at Winter Hill and at White Plains.[641]

In his will written 20 May 1809 (proved 10 August 1809), John Dale bequeathed to beloved wife Lydia a list of annual provisions to be provided by the executor and other specified support which were in lieu of her thirds. Daughter Rhoda wife of Ebenezer Hutchinson receives five dollars. Daughter Abigail wife of Abel Fiske receives $21.75. Daughter Polly receives $200 in five years or earlier if she marries. Daughters Anna, Betsey, and Sally also each receive $200 within a specified number of years or at the time of marriage. Son Lemon received $200 when he arrives at age twenty-one and daughter Lydia receives $130. Sons John and Ebenezer receive all the real and personal estate to be equally divided. They are responsible for the maintenance of Mrs. Dale and their unmarried sisters. John and Ebenezer were named executors.[642] Lamon and Lydia were children from John's second marriage to Lydia Lamon.

Rhoda Holt and John Dale were parents of eleven children born at Wilton.

          i   JOHN DALE, b. 6 Jan 1779; d. 7 Jan 1779.

1024)   ii   RHODA DALE, b. 15 Feb 1780; d. at Weld, ME, 27 Jun 1852; m. 22 Dec 1803, EBENEZER HUTCHINSON, b. at Wilton, 18 Sep 1780 son of Ebenezer and Phebe (Sawtell) Hutchinson; Ebenezer d. at Weld, 23 Jan 1845.

1025)   iii ABIGAIL DALE, b. 7 Nov 1781; d. at Wilton, 26 Jan 1852; m. 12 Apr 1804, ABEL FISKE, b. at Wilton, 24 Jul 1784 son of Abel and Anna (Spaulding) Fiske; Abel d. at Wilton, 25 Sep 1877.

1026)   iv   MARY DALE, b. 10 Sep 1783; d. after 1860 when she was living in Wilton; m. 8 Aug 1811, FREDERICK HUTCHINSON, b. at Wilton 10 Jul 1783 son of Samuel and Mary (Wilkins) Hutchinson; Frederick d. at Wilton, 18 Dec 1850.

1027)   v   JOHN DALE, b. 3 Aug 1785; d. at Wilton, 12 Apr 1843; m. 1st at Sandwich, 3 Oct 1822, NANCY BEEDE, b. at Sandwich, NH, 1796 son of John and Sarah (Sleeper) Beede;[643] Nancy d. at Wilton, 7 Oct 1825. John m.

[638] Chandler, *Descendants and William and Annis Chandler*, p 619
[639] New Hampshire Wills and Probate, Hillsborough County, Probate Records Volume 57, p 282
[640] Ramsdell, *History of Milford*, p 612
[641] Livermore, *History of Wilton*, p 357
[642] *New Hampshire. Probate Court (Hillsborough County), Probate Records volume 16, pp 263-266*
[643] The 1841 will of John Beede of Sandwich includes bequests to his granddaughter Nancy B. Dale child of his deceased daughter and to his daughter Mehitable Dale (who married Ebenezer Dale).

2nd at New Boston, 3 May 1827, MARY ANN COCHRAN, b. at New Boston, about 1805 daughter of James and Jane (Crombie) Cochran;[644] Mary d. at New Boston, 4 Oct 1876.

1028)   vi   EBENEZER DALE, b. 17 Mar 1788; d. at Sandwich, NH, 1 Sep 1862; m. about 1824, MEHITABLE BEEDE, b. at Sandwich, 12 Apr 1800 daughter of John and Sarah (Sleeper) Beede;[645] Mehitable d. at Sandwich, 14 Aug 1861.

         vii   ANNA DALE, b. 20 Nov 1789; d. at Francestown, 16 Sep 1862; m. 22 Jan 1834, as his second wife, ABNER BLANCHARD, b. at Wilton, 31 May 1787 son of Benjamin and Sarah (Griffin) Blanchard; Abel d. 24 Mar 1855. Abner was first married to Hannah Tarbell.

         viii   SALLY DALE, b. 3 Dec 1791; d. 6 Jun 1796.

1029)   ix   BETSEY DALE, b. 10 Jul 1793; d. at Milford, NH, Mar 1852; m. 7 Dec 1815, JESSE RAYMOND, b. at Mont Vernon, 1792 son of Nathaniel and Phebe (Dodge) Raymond;[646] Jesse d. at Milford, 14 Jul 1864. Jesse was second married to Nancy.

         x   SUMNER DALE, b. 20 Jun 1795; d. 25 Jun 1796.

1030)   xi   SARAH DALE, b. 4 Aug 1797; d. at Weld, ME, 17 May 1862; m. 25 Dec 1817, JOHN BURTON, b. at Wilton, 25 Oct 1796 son of Abraham and Elizabeth (Dale) Burton; John d. at Weld, 24 Feb 1873.

---

244)   VALENTINE HOLT (*Mary Russell Holt³, John², Robert¹*), b. at Andover (recorded at Wilton), 25 Dec 1763 and baptized at Andover 1 Jan 1764 son of Joseph and Mary (Russell) Holt; d. at Mercer, ME, 6 Dec 1840; m. at Wilton, 13 Sep 1787, ANNA "NANCY" GOODRICH whose parents have not been identified. Nancy likely died before 1810. Valentine married second HANNAH DAY, b. about 1792. Hannah d. after 1860 when she was living with her son in Augusta, Maine.

     Valentine was born in Andover but went with his family to Wilton. He married and had eight children there with his first wife. It is not known if Anna died before or after the family move to Maine, but Valentine and his family were in Maine about 1803. There Valentine had a second marriage to Hannah Day and there is record evidence for five children from his second marriage.

     On 10 March 1840, Valentine Holt then aged seventy-six of Mercer, Maine (where he had lived for about thirty-seven years), made a statement related to his application for a pension. He enlisted 5 February 1777 in Capt. Benjamin Farnham's company of Col. Tupper's regiment of the Massachusetts line. He served as a waiter for Capt. Farnham who was his brother-in-law.[647] He served more than nine months and was discharged the end of November 1777. He reported being born in Andover 25 December 1763 and then moving with his father's family to Wilton, which is where he resided at his enlistment. His father Joseph had a man with a sleigh carry him from Wilton to Worcester where Valentine met Capt. Farnham. The company went to Danbury for winter quarters and in the spring went to Fishkill, then to Newburgh on the North River, and from there to Saratoga. Capt. Farnham then sent Valentine to Andover and on to Wilton on business where Valentine stayed four or five days. At that time, there was need of militia due to the advance of General Burgoyne and Valentine joined the company of Capt. Goff and was at the Battle of Bennington. He then re-joined with Capt. Farnham and was at Stillwater for five days before being sent to West Point for discharge. In June 1780, he enlisted in the New Hampshire line in the company of Capt. William Barron for three months. He then marched to Hudson, New York. After the desertion of General Arnold, Valentine was sent to West Point where he was discharged October 1780. Valentine went on to say that he sought assistance of Capt. Vose about six years previously to obtain his pension, but Capt. Vose died, and Valentine heard no more about it. The pension application was rejected as the service as a waiter was not provided for unless he had been previously enlisted and detached from the ranks to be a waiter. He was not enlisted and paid as a soldier. His service of three months, sixteen days in 1780 was not long enough to qualify for a pension.[648]

     Children of Valentine Holt and Anna Goodrich:

1031)   i   NANCY HOLT, b. at Wilton, 13 Mar 1788; m. at Charlestown, MA, 31 May 1812, JAMES WHITTIER who is not yet identified.

1032)   ii   AMMI RUHAMA HOLT, b. at Wilton, 8 Jun 1789; d. at Clayton, NY, 1827; m. MARTHA ABBOTT, b. about 1800; Martha d. at Clayton, 28 Jan 1850.

         iii   LYDIA PORTER HOLT, b. 17 Aug 1791; d. 28 Jul 1792.

---

[644] Mary Ann's parents are given as James and Jane Cochran on her death record.

[645] The 1841 will of John Beede of Sandwich includes a bequest to his daughter Mehitable Dale.

[646] Smith, *History of the Town of Mont Vernon*, Genealogies, p 128

[647] Capt. Benjamin Farnum was married to Valentine's half-sister Dolly Holt.

[648] U.S. Revolutionary War Pension and Bounty-Land Application Files, Case R5188

1033)   iv   LYDIA PORTER HOLT, b. at Wilton, 13 May 1793; d. at Barre, VT, 9 Feb 1868; m. at Lyndeborough, 25 May 1815, ROBERT PARKER, b. 1789; Robert d. at Barre, 7 Apr 1831.

1034)   v   HANNAH GOODRICH HOLT, b. at Wilton, 15 May 1795; d. at Charlestown, MA, 24 Jun 1858; m. at Charlestown, MA, 7 Oct 1818, JOHN SYLVESTER, b. about 1788; John d. at Charlestown, 14 Dec 1848.

        vi   SAMUEL GOODRICH HOLT, b. 14 Apr 1797

        vii ISRAEL HOLT, b. 1 Aug 1799

1035)   viii ROBERT GOODRICH HOLT, b. at Wilton, 15 Jan 1802; d. after 1850; m. at Lyndeborough, 10 Sep 1822, LUCY LAKIN, b. at Lyndeborough, about 1802 daughter of Thomas and Lucy (Burton) Lakin; Lucy d. at Lyndeborough, 9 May 1850.

Children of Valentine Holt and Hannah Day:

1036)   i   VALENTINE HOLT, b. 18 Nov 1812; d. at Chelsea, ME, 22 Jan 1899; m. about 1836, MARY ANN MORRILL, b. about 1814; Mary Ann d. at Augusta, ME, after 1870 and before 1880.

1037)   ii   SARAH D. HOLT, b. about 1818;[649] d. at Boston, 28 Feb 1874; m. HENRY D. BROWN, b. in ME, about 1818; Henry d. during the Civil War, enlisted 29 Feb 1864 and did not survive the war.

1038)   iii MARY HARRICK HOLT, b. at Rome, ME, 23 Apr 1818; d. at Chelsea, MA, 1 Jan 1906; m. at Lowell, MA, 1 Aug 1842, SAMUEL ALDEN RICH, b. 25 Aug 1812 son of Ezekiel and Elizabeth (Brown) Rich; Samuel d. at Chelsea, MA, 5 Aug 1890.

1039)   iv   ANNA T. HOLT, b. at Mercer, ME, about 1819; d. at Charlestown, MA, 6 Aug 1873; m. 1st at Hallowell, ME, 4 Jun 1842, HENRY C. SLADE. Anna m. 2nd C. C. FOSTER who is not yet identified.

1040)   v   WESLEY RUSSELL HOLT, b. at Mercer, 10 Aug 1829; d. at South Gardiner, ME, 28 Jan 1902; m. at Somersworth, NH, 4 Apr 1850, ANN WITHAM, b. 1830; Ann d. at Hallowell, ME, 31 Aug 1869. Wesley m. 2nd, 1772, MARY LOUISE BOYD, b. in ME, May 1838; Mary Louise d. 1907.

245)   ESTHER HOLT (*Mary Russell Holt³, John², Robert¹*), b. at Wilton, 25 Jul 1766 daughter of Joseph and Mary (Russell) Holt; d. at Lyndeborough, 14 Jul 1839; m. about 1791, EBENEZER PEARSON, b. at Reading, MA, 19 Jun 1768 son of Amos and Elizabeth (Nichols) Pearson; Ebenezer d. at Lyndeborough, 22 May 1852.

There are four children known for Esther Holt and Ebenezer Pearson with the births recorded at Wilton or Lyndeborough. The family lived in Lyndeborough.

1041)   i   ESTHER PEARSON, b. at Wilton, 11 Nov 1792; d. at Lyndeborough, 12 Mar 1856; m. 8 Feb 1814, EPHRAIM PUTNAM, b. at Lyndeborough, 30 Apr 1785 son of Ephraim and Rachel (Cram) Putnam; Ephraim d. at Lyndeborough, 11 Jun 1862.

1042)   ii   EBENEZER PEARSON, b. at Lyndeborough, 11 Jan 1797; d. at Hancock, NH, 6 Aug 1864; m. 1824, JOANNA KARR, b. at Lyndeborough, 6 Apr 1803 daughter of James and Sarah (Huse) Karr; Joanna d. at Hancock, 5 Aug 1874.

        iii ABIGAIL PEARSON, b. at Wilton, 16 Aug 1800; d. at Lyndeborough, 26 Jun 1879; m. 10 Nov 1844, as his second wife, MARK HADLEY, b. at Lyndeborough, 19 Apr 1793 son of Joshua and Betsey (Giddings) Hadley; Mark d. at Lyndeborough, 26 Mar 1858. Mark was first married to Elizabeth Herrick. Abigail did not have children.

1043)   iv   WILLARD PEARSON, b. at Lyndeborough, 21 May 1806; d. at Woburn, MA, 31 Mar 1841; m. 7 Jul 1833, ANN P. CHILD, b. at Medford, MA, 15 Dec 1810 daughter of Aaron and Catherine (Floyd) Child;[650] Ann d. at Woburn, 21 Nov 1886.

---

[649] Names of parents are given as Valentine Holt and Hannah on her death record.
[650] The names of Ann's parents are given as Aaron and Catharine on her death record.

246)   HANNAH CROSBY (*Hannah Russell Crosby³, John², Robert¹*), b. at Billerica, 28 Dec 1761 daughter of Jacob and Hannah (Russell) Crosby; d. at Lyndeborough, 13 Jun 1850; m. at Chelmsford, MA, 20 Nov 1785, PHINEHAS KIDDER, b. at Chelmsford, 17 Jul 1756 son of David and Esther (Corey) Kidder;[651] Phinehas d. at Lyndeborough, 20 Jan 1846.

Hannah and Phinehas married in Chelmsford but were soon after in Lyndeborough where they raised their four children. The births of the four children are recorded at Lyndeborough, although it is possible the oldest child was born right around the time of the move.

On 30 August 1832, Phinehas Kidder of Lyndeborough then age seventy-six, made a statement related to his application for a pension. He reported a total of 17 months of services: eight months from April 1775 in Capt. Walker's company, three months starting in August 1777 in Capt. Russell's company, and six months beginning in July 1780 in the regiment of Col. Jackson. Phinehas received pension which was continued by his widow Hannah.[652]

1044)   i   SAMUEL KIDDER, b. 13 Mar 1787; d. at Francestown, NH, 6 Mar 1866; m. 12 Oct 1812, HANNAH BROWN, baptized at Ipswich, 9 Jul 1786 daughter of Jeremiah and Lucy (Potter) Brown;[653] Hannah d. at Francestown, 28 Feb 1864.

1045)   ii   PHINEAS KIDDER, b. 5 Dec 1789; d. at Lyndeborough, 20 Jan 1864; m. 1st ANN MANLEY; Ann d. about 1810. Phineas m. 2nd 12 Oct 1812, PATTY ROSE, b. at Scituate, MA, 1 Jul 1794 daughter of Abraham and Desire (Fisher) Rose; Patty d. 30 Apr 1882.

         iii   ANN KIDDER, b. 27 Aug 1791; d. at Lyndeborough, 8 Oct 1863; m. 19 Jan 1828, as his second wife, ELIPHALET ATWOOD, b. 30 Jan 1787 son of Paul and Judith (Stickney) Atwood; Eliphalet d. at Lyndeborough, 4 Dec 1851. Eliphalet was first married to Sarah Gould. Ann did not have children.

         iv   HANNAH KIDDER, b. 30 Jul 1793; d. after 1850 when she was living with her sister Ann and her husband Eliphalet in Lyndeborough; m. at Mont Vernon, NH, Feb 1818, LUKE GIDDINGS, b. about 1779 son of Joseph and Eleanor (Dodge) Giddings; Luke d. at New Boston, NH, 20 Apr 1826. The estate of Luke Giddings entered probate 14 January 1828 with the administration document stating he left a widow "who long since absented herself to parts unknown" and that Luke had no legitimate children.[654]

247)   ZILPAH CROSBY (*Hannah Russell Crosby³, John², Robert¹*), b. at Billerica, 26 Oct 1767 daughter of Jacob and Hannah (Russell) Crosby; d. at Billerica, 1825; m. at Billerica, 5 Dec 1787, JOSEPH STEARNS, b. at Billerica, 27 Jun 1763 son of Samuel and Hannah (Trask) Stearns;[655] Joseph d. at Billerica, 1834 (probate 3 Jun 1834); Joseph married second Elizabeth Prentice on 6 Apr 1828.

Zilpah and Joseph resided in Reading. Joseph Stearns did not leave a will and widow Elizabeth assumed administration of the estate on 3 June 1834. Personal estate was valued at $409.41 and an additional $116 in cash and notes was later identified. Two hundred dollars was allotted to the widow and the personal estate was sold to settle charges against the estate.[656]

Son Joseph married but did not have children. His probate record identifies brother Jerome B. Stearns as only heir-at-law. In his will written 26 March 1883 (probate 17 June 1883), Joseph made bequests to the following persons and organizations: Joseph E. Woods of Hudson, New Hampshire; First Baptist Society of Billerica; Second Baptist Society of Billerica; town of Billerica for benefit of "deserving poor"; to the overseers of the poor of Billerica for the specific support of Harvey Stearns; Esther Woods of Manchester, New Hampshire; L. P. Griffin of Lowell; George Stearns of Manchester; and George P. Woods. Bequests to each of these ranged from $300 to $2,000. The residue of the estate was given to the trustees of Howe school. Dudley Foster was named executor. Real estate was valued at $5,650 and personal estate at $10,527.25, $8,000 of that amount being bank deposits.[657]

Zilpah Crosby and Joseph Stearns were parents of eight children.[658]

         i   SAMUEL STEARNS, b. about 1789. Samuel is reported to have gone West and was never heard from after.[659]

---

[651] Stafford, *Genealogy of the Kidder Family*, p 24

[652] U.S. Revolutionary War Pension and Bounty-Land Applications, Case W26720

[653] The 1828 will of Jeremiah Brown of Lyndeborough includes a bequest to his daughter Hannah Kidder.

[654] *New Hampshire. Probate Court (Hillsborough County), Probate Records, volume 30, p 559*

[655] Van Wagenen, *Genealogy and Memoirs of Isaac Stearns*, p 203

[656] *Middlesex County, MA: Probate File Papers, 1648-1871*.Online database. *AmericanAncestors.org*. New England Historic Genealogical Society, 2014. Case 21276

[657] Massachusetts Wills and Probate, Middlesex County, Probate Packet 15896

[658] Van Wagenen, *Genealogy and Memoirs of Isaac Stearns*, p 203

[659] Van Wagenen, *Genealogy and Memoirs of Isaac Stearns*, p 203

1046)   ii   MARY STEARNS, b. at Billerica, about 1791; m. at Chelmsford, 13 Aug 1815, MARSHALL PIERCE, b. at Chelmsford, 14 Nov 1793 son of Stephen and Hannah (Marshall) Pierce; Marshall d. at Chelmsford, 2 Jun 1839.

1047)   iii   ROYAL STEARNS, b. about 1794; d. at Billerica, 30 May 1825; m. at Lexington, MA, 2 May 1824, ESTHER LAWRENCE, b. 23 Apr 1801 daughter of Jonathan and Polly (Reed) Lawrence. Esther married second Samuel P. Griffin on 13 May 1827.

         iv   JOSEPH STEARNS, b. at Billerica, Jul 1796; d. at Billerica, 17 Jun 1883; m. at Billerica, 29 Dec 1831, his first cousin, HARRIET STEARNS, b. at Billerica, Aug 1801 daughter of Elijah and Esther (Walker) Stearns; Harriet d. at Billerica, 14 Aug 1878. Joseph and Harriet did not have children.

1048)   v   ZILPAH STEARNS, b. about 1803; d. after 1870 when she was living in Manchester, NH; m. at Billerica, 29 Oct 1821, her first cousin, JOHN STEARNS, b. 1797 son of Josiah Stearns; John d. at Manchester, about 1875 (probate 25 Jan 1875).

         vi   HIRAM STEARNS, b. estimated 1804; died young

1049)   vii   MAHALA STEARNS, b. at Bedford, MA, 7 Aug 1809; d. at Billerica, 4 Sep 1882; m. JAMES A. LOVEJOY, b. at Hebron, NH, 16 Jul 1805 son of Samuel Abbott and Elizabeth (Bowers) Lovejoy; James d. at Cambridge, Feb 1883.

1050)   viii   JEROME BONAPARTE STEARNS, b. 1811; d. at Billerica, 8 Apr 1895; m. at Charlestown, MA, 3 Nov 1832, ELIZABETH S. "BETSY" WHICHER, b. about 1808; Betsy d. of consumption, at Charlestown, 5 Mar 1848. Jerome was living at the almshouse in Billerica in 1880 and died as a pauper.

248)   JEMIMA STEVENS (*Jemima Russell Stevens³, John², Robert¹*), baptized at Andover, 8 Jul 1770 daughter of Jonathan and Jemima (Russell) Stevens; d. after 1821; m. at Loudon, NH, 6 Mar 1794, JONAS AMES, b. 1771; Jonas d. at Boston, 27 Dec 1820.

    Jemima's father died when she was two years old and her mother moved to Boston with her three children. Jemima and Jonas married at Loudon and settled in Boston. Jonas and Jemima Ames were admitted as members of New South Church of Boston on 3 May 1800.[660] Jonas Ames was a painter in Boston. He did not leave a will, and widow Jemima assumed administration of his estate on 9 January 1821. Personal was valued at $307.38.[661]

    Little could be found for this family. There is one daughter likely and census records suggests there were perhaps three other children, but information on those children was not located.

         i   HARRIET AMES, baptized at Boston, 6 Sep 1801. (Harriet Ames daughter of ___ presented by Jonas & Jemimah Ames).

A Few Great-Grandchildren of Thomas Russell

249)   JOHN CHANDLER (*John Chandler⁴, Mehitable Russell Chandler³, Thomas², Robert¹*), b. at Andover, 18 Jul 1750 son of John and Hannah (Phelps) Chandler; d. at Princeton, MA, 26 Mar 1832; m. 1st at Lancaster, 29 Feb 1776, KATHARINE "KATY" HOLMAN, b. at Sutton, MA, 23 Mar 1753 daughter of Solomon and Sarah (Waite) Holman, Katy d. at Princeton, 18 Feb 1781. John m. 2nd at Westminster, 1 Jan 1782, MARY JACKSON, b. at Westminster, 11 Sep 1755 daughter of Josiah and Mary (Darby) Jackson; Mary d. at Princeton, 26 Jan 1836.

    John Chandler and Katharine Holman were parents of two children born at Princeton, Massachusetts.

1051)   i   JOHN CHANDLER, b. at Princeton, 22 May 1777; d. at Peru, VT, 6 Feb 1859; m. at Chelsea, MA, 8 Nov 1804, MARY WYMAN, b. at Chelsea, 15 Jul 1782; Mary d. at Peru, 23 Jan 1846.

---

[660] "Boston, MA: Church Records, 1630-1895" The Records of the Churches of Boston. CD_ROM. Boston, Mass.: New England Historic Genealogical Society, 2002. New South Church, p 120

[661] *Suffolk County, MA: Probate File Papers*. Online database. *AmericanAncestors.org*. New England Historic Genealogical Society, 2017-2019. Case 26330

1052) ii JOSEPH CHANDLER, b. at Princeton, 20 Mar 1780; d. at Hartland, VT, 7 Apr 1854; m. at Charlestown, MA, 17 Dec 1809, SARAH "SALLY" BENNETT, b. at Lunenburg, 31 May 1778 daughter of James Bennett; Sally d. at Hartland, 20 Jan 1851.

John Chandler and Mary Jackson were parents of two children.

1053) i EPHRAIM H. CHANDLER, b. at New Braintree, 9 Jun 1783; d. at Princeton, MA, 30 Oct 1856; m. at Princeton, 19 Apr 1810, MARY POWERS, b. 3 Dec 1790 daughter of John Powers; Mary d. at Princeton, 16 Jun 1854.

1054) ii MARY "POLLY" CHANDLER, b. at Princeton, 31 May 1795; d. at Salisbury, VT, 21 Dec 1842; m. at Sterling, 26 Apr 1815, SILAS HOLMAN, b. at Sterling, 17 Apr 1790 possible son of Samuel and Sarah (Davis) Holman;[662] Silas d. at Salisbury, 17 Mar 1839.

250) JOSEPH CHANDLER (*John Chandler⁴, Mehitable Russell Chandler³, Thomas², Robert¹*), b. at Andover, 30 Jan 1753 son of John and Hannah (Phelps) Chandler; d. at Salem, 27 Nov 1827; m. at Danvers, 12 Nov 1780, DORCAS ABBOTT, b. at Andover, 26 Oct 1755 daughter of Joseph and Anna (Peabody) Abbott; Dorcas d. at Salem, 19 Aug 1821.

Joseph worked for Elias Hasket Derby in Salem, one of the wealthiest merchants of the era and a pioneer in trade with China. Joseph later worked for Elias's son John Derby.[663]

In his will dated 28 March 1826, Joseph Chandler named son-in-law Jonathan Kenney as executor. Son Joseph Abbot Chandler had debts to the father totaling $219.34, and the bequest to Joseph Abbot is to include this owed amount. Joseph Abbot Chandler will receive a one-third part of the estate, but this is to be held by Jonathan Kenney and all the profit from this third is to be paid to Joseph's wife Deborah as long as she remains his wife or his widow. After Deborah's decease, that third of the estate is to go to grandson Joseph T. Chandler. The remaining two-thirds of the estate goes to daughter Dorcas Chandler and daughter Hannah Kenney. The real estate was valued at $1,325.00 and the personal estate was $1,939,15 which included about $1,700 in cash, notes, and bank deposits. The heirs-at-law providing their consent to the presentation of the will were Joseph A. Chandler and his wife Deborah Chandler, Dorcas Chandler, and Hannah Kenney.[664]

Daughter Dorcas did not marry. In her will dated 28 January 1843, Dorcas Chandler made bequests to Mrs. Hannah Kenney of one hundred dollars, her niece Dorcas Kenney to receive silver spoons, and her brother Joseph A. Chandler receives fifty dollars. There are several small bequests to what seem other relations and friends. One-half of the remainder of the estate goes to her nephew Joseph T. Chandler who is to hold this in trust and pay to his father Joseph A. Chandler the interest on the estate annually. At the decease of Joseph A. Chandler, that part of the estate is to go to Susan E. Chandler. The other half of the estate is to be equally divided among her nieces and nephews.[665] The value of the real estate was $1,200 for a house and lot and personal estate valued at $828.

Dorcas Abbott and Joseph Chandler had four children born at Danvers.

1055) i HANNAH CHANDLER, b. 15 Dec 1781; d. at Salem, 21 Dec 1856; m. at Salem, 20 Oct 1805, JONATHAN KENNEY, b. at Middleton, 23 Aug 1771 son of Simeon and Jerusha (Johnson) Kenney; Jonathan d. at Salem, 29 Dec 1847.

ii DORCAS CHANDLER, b. 11 Jun 1785; d. at Salem, 1 Feb 1843. Dorcas did not marry.

1056) iii JOSEPH ABBOT CHANDLER, b. 28 Dec 1789; d. at Salem, 25 Nov 1861; m. at Salem, 24 May 1812, DEBORAH SYMONDS, b. at Salem, 1796 daughter of Thorndike and Betsey (Gurley) Symonds; Deborah d. at Salm, 3 Nov 1832.

iv JOHN CHANDLER, b. 21 Jun 1795; d. 27 Sep 1803.

[662] Holman, *The Holmans in America*, p 58. The parentage of Silas is not certain. The Chandler genealogy reports that his father is Stephen, but he might be the grandson of Stephen.
[663] McKey, Richard Haskayne. "Elias Hasket Derby, Merchant of Salem, Massachusetts, 1739-1799." PhD diss., Clark University, 1961.
[664] Essex County, MA: Probate File Papers, 1638-1881.Online database. AmericanAncestors.org. New England Historic Genealogical Society, 2014. Case number 4951, Probate of Joseph Chandler
[665] *Essex County, Massachusetts, Probate Records and Indexes 1638-1916;* Author: *Massachusetts. Probate Court (Essex County);* Probate Place: *Essex, Massachusetts, Probate Records, Vol 412-414, Book 112-114, 1843-1847*

Generation Five

Great-Grandchildren of Mary Russell and Nicholas Holt

251)   JAMES PARKER (*Phebe Ingalls Parker⁴, Mary Holt Ingalls³, Mary Russell Holt², Robert¹*), b. at Andover, 30 Aug 1746 son of James and Phebe (Ingalls) Parker; d. at Livermore, ME, 26 Apr 1815;[666] m. at New Gloucester, ME, 16 Aug 1783, PHEBE NOYES, b. 13 Apr 1763 daughter of Simon and Elizabeth (Eaton) Noyes; Phebe d. at Livermore, 23 Jul 1848.

James's father died in 1782 and the following year, James married Phebe Noyes in New Gloucester, Maine. On 11 February 1784, James Parker then of a new township called Bakerstown[667] in Cumberland County, Commonwealth of Massachusetts, sold to Samuel Johnson for £60 his property in Andover including the dwelling house. This sale was made with consent and approval of his mother Phebe Parker and of his sister Anna Bragg who relinquished their rights as heirs to the property.[668]

James and Phebe had ten children nine births recorded at Poland, Maine, and the youngest child at Livermore. James is listed in the 1800 census at Poland. In 1800, the family relocated to Livermore where James for a time owned the grist mill at Gibbs Mills.[669] James was in Livermore just a few years before his death.[670] He sold his mill interest to Eli Putnam, but the date of the transaction is not given in Washburn's Livermore notes. Phebe is buried at Livermore where her son Alfred resided.

i   JAMES PARKER, b. 23 Apr 1784; d. after 1850 when he was living at Sedgwick, ME; m. about 1830, MARY TAY,[671] b. about 1805; Mary d. after 1870 when she was living at St. George, ME.

ii   PHEBE PARKER, b. 17 Feb 1786

iii   ALFRED PARKER, b. 23 Feb 1788; d. at Livermore, ME, 1876; m. about 1815, RUTH PRAY,[672] b. at Oxford, MA, 23 Mar 1796 daughter of Ebenezer and Deborah (Leonard) Pray; Ruth d. after 1870.

iv   NANCY PARKER, b. 15 Mar 1790

v   SIMON PARKER, b. 26 Jul 1792

vi   SARAH PARKER, b. 5 Feb 1794

vii   ELIZABETH PARKER, b. 11 Jul 1797

viii   BENJAMIN PARKER, b. 13 Jun 1800; m. 1st ANNA, b. about 1800 who has not been identified and who d. likely at Dracut about 1851. Benjamin m. 2nd at Lowell, MA, 25 Nov 1852, EUNICE THURSTON, b. perhaps in Canada (census record), about 1826 daughter of Nathaniel and Martha (·) Thurston.

ix   JESSE PARKER, b. 13 Jun 1800; d. at East Vassalboro, ME, 23 Mar 1885; m. 6 Jun 1826, CLEMENTINE ELDRIDGE CHANDLER, b. at Monmouth, ME, 1 Aug 1805 daughter of Daniel R. and Sally C. (Maloon) Chandler; Clementine d. at Vassalboro, 4 Oct 1860.

x   CHARLES PARKER, b. at Livermore, 21 Aug 1804.[673]

252)   WILLIAM HOLT (*Benjamin Holt⁴, Nicholas Holt³, Mary Russell Holt², Robert¹*), b. at Andover, Oct 1737 son of Benjamin and Sarah (Frye) Holt; d. at Allenstown, NH, 28 Aug 1816; m. at Andover, 2 Sep 1769, ELIZABETH "BETSEY" AMES, perhaps b. at Andover, 13 Jan 1744/5 daughter of Samuel and Elizabeth (Stevens) Ames.

William Holt and Betsey Ames resided in Pembroke and were parents of seven children.[674]

i   WILLIAM HOLT, b. at Pembroke, 1775; d. at Pembroke, 29 Dec 1801.

ii   DORCAS HOLT, b. at Pembroke, about 1776; d. at Bradford, MA, 19 Aug 1853; m. FRANCIS KIMBALL, b. at Bradford, 10 May 1777 son of Francis and Betsey (Head) Kimball; Francis d. at Bradford, 1 Dec 1843.

---

[666] Livermore Vital Records, p 269; accessed through familysearch,org
[667] The Bakerstown Plantation was later to be Poland, Maine.
[668] Massachusetts Land Records, 1620-1986, Essex County, 142:233, accessed through familysearch.org.
[669] Monroe, *History of the Town of Livermore*, p 188
[670] Washburn, *Notes Historical, Descriptive, and Personal of Livermore*, p 45
[671] Mary's maiden name is given as Mary Tay on the death record of her son Marcellus.
[672] Washburn, *Notes Historical, Descriptive, and Personal of Livermore*, p 45
[673] Livermore Vital Records, p 269; accessed through familysearch,org
[674] Carter, *History of Pembroke*, p 148

iii   OLIVE HOLT, b. about 1777

iv   ENOCH HOLT, b. at Pembroke, about 1780; d. at Salem, MA, 5 Dec 1873; m. at Pembroke, 25 Apr 1805, SALLY MORGAN, b. at Pembroke, 31 May 1781 daughter of Jeremiah and Elizabeth (Lovejoy) Morgan; Sally d. at Bow, NH, 15 Mar 1848.

v   BETSEY HOLT, b. 1781; d. 8 Jul 1801.

vi   FANNY HOLT, b. at Allenstown, about 1782; reported in the History of Pembroke to marry a Clark but no records have yet been found.

vii   BENJAMIN HOLT, b. at Allenstown, about 1783; d. after 1870 when he was living at Alexandria, NH; m. about 1805, BETSEY EVANS.

253)   SARAH HOLT (*Benjamin Holt⁴, Nicholas Holt³, Mary Russell Holt², Robert¹*), b. at Andover, about 1738 daughter of Benjamin and Sarah (Frye) Holt; m. about 1756, STEPHEN COFFIN, b. at Newbury, 6 Aug 1729 son of Daniel and Lydia (Moulton) Coffin.
          Stephen Coffin was an early settler in Alfred, Maine following there after his brother Simeon was a first settler.[675] Sarah Holt and Stephen Coffin were likely parents of seven children.[676]

i   SARAH COFFIN, b. 1756; d. at South Berwick, ME, 15 Oct 1836; m. at Berwick, 9 Oct 1773, BENJAMIN KNIGHT, b. 21 Sep 1757 son of John and Olive (Hamilton) Knight; Benjamin d. at South Berwick, 16 Apr 1843.

ii   PETER COFFIN, b. about 1758; d. at Gilead, ME, 1 Nov 1843; m. 1st 7 Feb 1782, SARAH WALKER, b. about 1758 daughter of Timothy and Martha (Colby) Walker; Sarah d. at Conway, NH, 31 Aug 1803. Peter m. 2nd at Carroll, NH, 12 Aug 1804, JANE ORDWAY (widow of John Evens), b. at Goffstown, NH, 8 May 1770 daughter of Joseph and Mehitable (Abbott) Ordway; Jane d. at Stoneham, ME, 6 Dec 1854.

iii   MARY COFFIN, b. at Kittery, ME, 8 May 1763; d. at Knox, ME, 22 Sep 1842; m. 1782, PAUL WENTWORTH, b. 1759 son of Paul and Patience (Abbott) Wentworth; Paul d. at Knox, 4 Sep 1833.

iv   ABIAH COFFIN, b. about 1764; d. after 1840 at Waterboro, ME; m. about 1790, JONATHAN KNIGHT, b. 1762 son of John and Olive (Hamilton) Knight; Jonathan d. at Waterboro, 1848.

v   NICHOLAS COFFIN, b. 5 Apr 1765; d. at Lincoln, ME, 14 Feb 1850; m. 10 Jun 1788, POLLY HEATH.

vi   LYDIA COFFIN, b. about 1768; m. at Conway, NH, 17 Mar 1791, JAMES STERLING, b. 1767 son of Hugh and Isabel (Stark) Sterling.

vii   BENJAMIN COFFIN

254)   NATHAN HOLT (*Benjamin Holt⁴, Nicholas Holt³, Mary Russell Holt², Robert¹*), b. at Andover, about 1740 son of Benjamin and Sarah (Frye) Holt; d. at Pembroke, NH, 3 Mar 1818; m. at Pembroke, 1762, SUSANNAH BLANCHARD, b. about 1742; Susannah d. at Pembroke, 28 Aug 1837.
          Nathan Holt served in the Revolution and was wounded at Bunker Hill by a musket ball passing through his right thigh.[677][678] Nathan enrolled in Capt. Daniel Moore's company of Col. John Stark's regiment on 1 May 1775.[679] He received a pension as an invalid commencing 4 March 1795 related to his service.[680] The allowed payment was a one-fourth pension.
          On 31 January 1846, Phebe Holt, then age sixty-eight and resident of Concord, appeared to give a statement related to the pension and receiving possible payments due. Her deceased mother Susannah Holt had been the widow of Nathan Holt. Her parents were married at Pembroke in 1762 by Rev. Aaron Whittemore. Her father Nathan died 3 March 1818 and her mother died at Pembroke on 28 August 1837. On 19 February 1846, Calvin Ainsworth register of probate for Merrimack County, New Hampshire stated that satisfactory evidence had been presented to support that Susannah Holt died 28 August 1837 and the only surviving children were Stephen Holt of Pembroke, Frye Holt of Concord, Phebe Holt of Concord, Sally Goodwin wife of James Goodwin, and Mary Wheeler widow of Jonas Wheeler.
          Nathan's sister Dorcas Emery provided a statement on 13 February 1846. Dorcas, then age eighty-three and resident of Pembroke, reported she was the youngest of thirteen children in the family. Her brother Nathan married Susannah

[675] Parsons, *Centennial History of Alfred, York County*, Maine, p 8

[676] Appleton, *Gatherings toward a Genealogy of the Coffin Family: Five Generations of Descendants of Tristram Coffin of Newbury and Nantucket*, https://www.ancestry.com/search/collections/16038/

[677] U S. Revolutionary War Pension and Bounty-Land Warrant Application Files, Case W15913

[678] Carter, *History of Pembroke*, volume II, p 147

[679] *U.S., Revolutionary War Rolls, 1775-1783* [database on-line]. Provo, UT, USA: Ancestry.com Operations, Inc., 2007. *Reeds Regiment, 1775 (Folder 136) - Waldron's Regiment, 1776 (Folder 159)*

[680] U.S. Pension Roll of 1835, New Hampshire Pension Roll

Blanchard and they had a family of nine children five of whom were currently living. George W. Dow, town clerk of Pembroke, on 13 February 1846, provided a statement that he examined the town records from 1767 forward and could find no record of the marriage or the births of the children, but noted that the records were irregular and that some of the records of the town had been destroyed by fire.

On 20 September 1847, Arthur Fletcher contacted the pension board regarding possible payment that may be due to surviving children based on the widow's pension of their mother Susan who died in 1836. A payment of arrears was allowed in October 1847 to the "only children": Stephen Holt, Frye Holt, Phebe Holt, Sally Goodwin, and Mary Wheeler.[681]

Nathan and Susannah lived in Pembroke throughout their married lives. Nathan with his son Nathan, Jr. built a grist mill on Great Brook about 1800.[682]

Nathan Holt did not leave a will and his estate entered probate 20 May 1818 with William Holt as administrator. Real estate of about 20 acres in the 7th range was valued at $200 and personal estate was valued at $83.62.[683]

Nathan Holt and Susannah Blanchard were parents of eleven children[684] born at Pembroke.

i   NATHAN HOLT, b. 1762; d. at North Pembroke, 11 Apr 1841; m. at Pembroke, 16 Jul 1783, SARAH BLACK, perhaps b. at Haverhill, MA, 11 Feb 1762 daughter of Edmund and Sarah (Lufkin) Black; Sarah d. at North Pembroke, 9 Apr 1854 at age 92.

ii   ABIAH HOLT, b. 1765; d. at Pembroke, 2 Nov 1835; m. at Pembroke, 5 May 1790, as his second wife, JAMES FIFE, b. 1742 son of John and Jane (Garvin) Fife; James d. at Pembroke, after 1820.

iii ESTHER HOLT, b. about 1766; d. at North Pembroke, 30 Oct 1824; m. 28 Dec 1797, ROBERT FIFE, b. at Pembroke, Feb 1766 son of William and Phebe (White) Fife; Robert d. at North Pembroke, 9 Jun 1854.

iv   SUSANNAH BALLARD HOLT, b. 1771; d. at Pembroke, 16 Jul 1843; m. at Pembroke, 29 Dec 1806, as his second wife, SAMUEL GARVIN, b. at Bow, NH, 15 Sep 1777 son of James and Deborah (-) Garvin; Samuel d. at Pembroke, 22 April 1837. Samuel was first married at Pembroke, 26 Nov 1799 to MEHITABLE LOVEJOY, b. at Pembroke, 11 Feb 1781 daughter of Caleb and Mehitable (Kimball) Lovejoy; Mehitable d. 1804.

v   STEPHEN HOLT, b. 1773; d. at Pembroke, 11 May 1856. Stephen did not marry. In his will proved May 1856, Stephen Holt left his entire estate to his niece Almira Blake wife of Stephen Blake "to her sole and separate use free from the interference and control of her husband" during her natural life. At Almira's decease the estate goes to her children Louisa H. Blake and Henry F. Blake. If Almira's children both die with heirs, then the estate goes to Phillip F. Holt.[685] Almira Holt Blake was a daughter of Frye Holt and his wife Lydia Eastman.

vi   WILLIAM HOLT, b. about 1776; d. at Pembroke, 25 May 1843; m. SARAH FIFE, b. about 1785 daughter of William and Phebe (White) Fife; Sarah d. at Pembroke, 3 Mar 1865.

vii PHEBE HOLT, b. about 1778; d. after 1846 when she was living at Concord and unmarried.

viii FRYE HOLT, b. 15 Sep 1779; d. at North Conway, 8 Apr 1850; m. 26 May 1801, his fourth cousin once removed, LYDIA EASTMAN, b. at Conway, 4 Sep 1779 daughter of Abiathar and Phebe (Merrill) Eastman; Lydia d. at Bartlett, NH, 21 Apr 1872.

ix   MARY "POLLY" HOLT, b. about 1780; d. after 1850; m. about 1798, JONAS WHEELER, b. estimated 1772; Jonas d. before 1847.

x   SARAH "SALLY" HOLT, b. about 1780; d. after 1850 when she was living at Concord; m. 9 Mar 1826, JAMES GOODWIN, b. at Merrimack, 23 Jan 1784 son of Alpheus and Abiah (Heath) Goodwin; James d. after 1850.

xi   OLIVE HOLT, b. about 1785; d. at Pembroke, 6 Jul 1818.

255)   BENJAMIN HOLT (*Benjamin Holt⁴, Nicholas Holt³, Mary Russell Holt², Robert¹*), b. at Andover, 28 Feb 1741 son of Benjamin and Sarah (Frye) Holt; d. at Pembroke, 28 Feb 1826; m. 22 Sep 1763, his third cousin, HANNAH ABBOTT (*Hannah Chandler Abbott⁴, Mehitable Russell Chandler³, Thomas², Robert¹*), b. at Pembroke, 7 Sep 1743 daughter of David and Hannah (Chandler) Abbott; Hannah d. at Pembroke, 17 Mar 1813.

In his will written 7 January 1811 and proved 1 March 1826, Benjamin Holt directs that his executor David Holt pay the legacies in the will. Beloved wife Hannah receives a full one-third part of the real estate and full use of all the household furniture during her natural life. Son Nicolas receives twenty-two dollars which completes his portion. Son David receives all the real and personal estate except Benjamin reserves one yoke of oxen. To complete their full portions daughter Sarah

[681] U. S. Revolutionary War Pension and Bounty-Land Warrant Application Files, Case W15913
[682] Carter, *History of Pembroke*, volume I
[683] *New Hampshire. Probate Court (Rockingham County), Estate Papers, No 9686-9748, 1818, Case 9731*
[684] In the pension file, Nathan's sister Dorcas states that Nathan and Susannah had nine children and perhaps that is a misstatement, or perhaps there is still more to learn about the children in this family.
[685] *New Hampshire. Probate Court (Merrimack County), volume 25, p 652*

Chandler receives twenty-two dollars, daughters Hannah Mason, Molly Russell, Mehitable Shannon, and Phebe Chandler each receive twenty-five dollars, and daughter Dolly Shannon twenty-two dollars. Daughter Betty Holt receives one hundred dollars. Granddaughter Hannah Norris with what she has received is her full share. Daughter Betty Holt and granddaughter Hannah Norris receive use of part of the house as long as they remain unmarried. Hannah and Betty will also share equally in the household furniture after his wife's demise.[686]

Hannah Abbot and Benjamin Holt were parents of eleven children likely all born at Pembroke.

i   SARAH HOLT, b. 23 Jan 1764; d. at Danbury, NH, after 1830; m. at Pembroke, 17 Apr 1787, JOSIAH CHANDLER, b. 1763 of undetermined parents;[687] Josiah d. at Danbury, after 1830. Josiah served as a private in the Revolution and received a pension as an invalid.

ii   NICHOLAS HOLT, b. 4 Aug 1766; d. at Danbury, NH, 24 Jun 1816; m. at Concord, 9 Jun 1790, ACHSAH RUSSELL, b. at Haverhill, MA, 14 Sep 1758 daughter of Edward and Mary (Page) Russell; Achsah d. at Warrensburg, NY, 26 May 1851.

iii HANNAH HOLT, b. 15 Sep 1768; d. at Pembroke, 22 Aug 1831; m. 18 Oct 1789, ISAAC MORRISON, b. at Nottingham, NH, 3 Feb 1760 son of James and Martha (White) Morrison; Isaac d. at Pembroke, 9 Jan 1846.

iv   MOLLY HOLT, b. 7 Apr 1770; m. 3 Mar 1791, JOHN RUSSELL, *perhaps* b. at Haverhill, MA, 16 Jun 1767 son of James and Susannah (Richardson) Russell. Molly and John had seven children born at New London, NH, but have not located clear information on their deaths.

v   PHEBE HOLT, b. 14 Jul 1772; d. at Lovell, ME, 1 Jun 1850; m. 13 Nov 1798, her fourth cousin, TIMOTHY CHANDLER, b. at Andover, Sep 1775 son of Timothy and Mary (Walker) Chandler; Timothy d. at Lovell, 29 Nov 1854. Timothy is a child in Family 446.

vi   DAVID HOLT, b. 12 May 1774; d. at Rumford, ME, 1 Feb 1859; m. 10 Nov 1795, his fourth cousin, CHLOE CHANDLER, b. at Andover, 30 Aug 1771 daughter of Timothy and Mary (Walker) Chandler; Chloe d. at Rumford, 17 Mar 1859. Chloe is a child in Family 446.

vii MEHITABLE HOLT, b. 28 Jul 1776; d. 16 Jan 1778.

viii MEHITABLE HOLT, b. 17 Jul 1778; d. at Cottage, NY, 28 Jan 1855; m. 1st, at Pembroke, NH, Sep 1798, as his second wife, JOHN SHANNON, b. 1 Feb 1769;[688] John d. at Perrysburg, NY, about 1840. Mehitable m. 2nd, about 1842, AZARIAH DARBEE, b. in CT, 1762 son of Jedediah and Lucretia (Cleveland) Darbee; Azariah d. at Dayton, NY, 18 Aug 1851. John Shannon was first married to Ruth Whittemore daughter of Benjamin and Abigail (Abbott) Whittemore. Azariah Darbee was first married to Susannah Phelps.

ix   ELIZABETH HOLT, b. 7 May 1780; d. at Chichester, NH, after 1844; m. at Pembroke, 12 Feb 1835, as his third wife, JONATHAN LEAVITT, b. at Chichester, 17 Nov 1772 son of Jonathan and Anna (Tilton) Leavitt; Jonathan d. at Chichester, 24 Dec 1844. Jonathan was first married to Rebecca Lake and second married to Hannah Perkins.

x   DORCAS HOLT, b. 7 May 1783; d. 27 Feb 1810.

xi   DOLLY HOLT, b. 1 May 1785; d. at Leon, NY, 1851; m. Mar 1802, SAMUEL SHANNON, b. 1774;[689] Samuel d. at Leon, NY, 1 Oct 1849.

256)   DANIEL HOLT (*Benjamin Holt⁴, Nicholas Holt³, Mary Russell Holt², Robert¹*), b. at Pembroke, 14 Sep 1744 son of Benjamin and Sarah (Frye) Holt; d. at Pembroke, 5 Dec 1813; m. about 1770, ABIGAIL LOVEJOY, b. at Pembroke, 12 Sep 1750 daughter of David and Elizabeth (Chandler) Lovejoy; Abigail d. at Pembroke, 18 Mar 1833.

In his will written 18 October 1813, Daniel Holt bequeaths to beloved wife Abigail one-third of the real and personal estate while she is a widow. Children Abigail Little, Jedediah Holt, Benjamin Holt, Stephen Holt, Esther Johnson, and John Holt each receive one dollar exclusive of what they have already received. Sons Richard Holt and Daniel Holt receive all the real and personal estate in Pembroke and elsewhere not otherwise disposed of. Son Richard Holt was named executor.[690]

[686] New Hampshire County Probate Records, 1660-1973, Merrimack, case 282, probate of Benjamin Holt, 1:211, 6:523. Accessed through familysearch.org

[687] There is another Josiah Chandler born 1762 son of David and Mary (Ballard) Chandler who married Margaret Aiken.

[688] John's birth date is from a family bible record.

[689] John Shannon and Samuel Shannon are likely brothers, but they do not seem to be the children of Samuel and Lydia (Leavitt) Shannon. The 1817 probate of Samuel Shannon of Rockingham County, NY (a Revolutionary War pensioner with widow Lydia) includes a statement that Lydia Taber Shannon, Thomas Shannon, and Sarah Shannon are the only children of the deceased.

[690] *New Hampshire. Probate Court (Rockingham County); Probate Place: Rockingham, New Hampshire, Probate Records, Vol 41-42, 1812-1815*, vol 42, p 52, will of Daniel Holt

Abigail Lovejoy and Daniel Holt were parents of eight children all born at Pembroke.[691]

i   ABIGAIL HOLT, b. 14 Apr 1771; m. at unknown date Mr. Little. Nothing else is known.[692]

ii   JEDEDIAH HOLT, b. 12 Aug 1774; d. at Dorchester, NH, 25 Oct 1850; m. at Concord, 1805, MARTHA "PATTY" NOYES, b. at Bow, 28 Mar 1787 daughter of John and Mary (Fowler) Noyes.

iii   BENJAMIN HOLT, b. 4 Dec 1776; d. at Loudon, 15 Jun 1867; m. at Pembroke, 28 Nov 1805, ANNA KNOX, b. at Pembroke, 12 Aug 1782 daughter of William and Elinor (McDaniel) Knox; Anna d. at Loudon, 10 Oct 1867.

iv   STEPHEN HOLT, b. 16 Sep 1779; d. at Pembroke, 28 Jun 1839; m. 6 Mar 1814, POLLY KNOX, b. 15 Aug 1792 daughter of John and Mary Ann (Knox) Knox; Polly d. at Pembroke, 10 Oct 1849.

v   RICHARD HOLT, b. 12 Feb 1782; d. at Pembroke, 18 Aug 1836; m. 2 Mar 1834, MARY ANN KNOX, b. 11 Aug 1796 daughter of Daniel and Rachel (McClintock) Knox; Mary Ann d. at Pembroke, 13 Aug 1865.

vi   JOHN HOLT, b. 14 Feb 1784; d. at Pembroke, 22 Aug 1856; m. 19 Dec 1817, HANNAH AYER, b. at Pembroke, 15 Jul 1791 daughter of John and Abia (-) Ayer; Hannah d. at Pembroke, 22 Apr 1848.

vii   ESTHER HOLT, b. 7 Jun 1787; d. at Allenstown, NH, about 1843; m. 4 Feb 1809, JOHN JOHNSON, b. at Allenstown, about 1786. By 1850, John was apparently married to Mary with whom he had a six-year child.

viii   DANIEL LOVEJOY HOLT, b. 14 Jun 1791; d. at Pembroke, after 1870; m. 23 Apr 1815, SALLY HOLT, b. at Pembroke, 16 Apr 1789 daughter of Nathan and Sarah (Black) Holt; Sally d. at Pembroke, 16 Apr 1841.

257)   FRYE HOLT (*Benjamin Holt⁴, Nicholas Holt³, Mary Russell Holt², Robert¹*), b. at Pembroke, about 1746 son of Benjamin and Sarah (Frye) Holt; m. about 1770, MARY POOR who has not been identified.

    This is a family for which there is little firm information. Both Durrie's Holt genealogy and History of Pembroke list fifteen children but little else in terms of births, deaths, and marriages and little was located in records. Frye is reported to have gone to Hull, Canada late in life.[693] The order of the children is not known.

i   SALLY HOLT, b. about 1773; m. at Pembroke, 25 Jan 1793, her first cousin, NICHOLAS GILMAN (*Mary Holt Gilman⁵, Benjamin Holt⁴, Nicholas Holt³, Mary Russell Holt², Robert¹*), b. at Pembroke, 21 Apr 1773 son of Nathaniel and Mary (Holt) Gilman; Nicholas d. at Dorchester, NH, 29 Mar 1817.

ii   JOSEPH HOLT

iii   ELIZABETH "BETSEY" HOLT, b. about 1782 (age 68 in 1850); d. after 1850; m. at Dorchester, NH, 24 Mar 1801, DAVID HUTCHINS, b. about 1769 son of Hezekiah and Anna (Merrill) Hutchins;[694] David d. after 1850 when he was living in Rumford, ME.

iv   FRYE HOLT, b. estimate 1788 (age 40-49 in 1830); m. at Bristol, NH, 11 Jul 1822, HANNAH DODGE, b. estimate 1802. The family was living in Bristol, NH in 1830 with a total household of five.[695]

v   NANCY HOLT, d. at age 20 years.

vi   ENOCH HOLT

vii   PHEBE HOLT

viii   DOLLY HOLT

ix   DANIEL HOLT; died young

x   CLARISSA HOLT

xi   HARRIET HOLT

xii   ABIGAIL HOLT

xiii   CHARLOTTE HOLT

---

[691] Durrie's Holt genealogy also reports a set of twins, unnamed, who died in early infancy.
[692] The Holt genealogy and History of Pembroke report that Abigail married twice and did not have children. No records related to her marriages have been located.
[693] Carter, *History of Pembroke*, p 149
[694] Lapham, *History of Rumford, Oxford County, Maine*, p 356
[695] 1830; Census Place: Bristol, Grafton, New Hampshire; Series: M19; Roll: 75; Page: 91; Family History Library Film: 0337928; 1 male 40-49, 2 females 20-29, 1 male under 5, and 1 female under 5

xiv   MOSES HOLT

xv   LUCINDA HOLT; d. at age 5 years.

258)   ABIAH HOLT (*Benjamin Holt⁴, Nicholas Holt³, Mary Russell Holt², Robert¹*), b. at Pembroke, about 1747 daughter of
Benjamin and Sarah (Frye) Holt; d. about 1790; m. about 1766, RICHARD EASTMAN, b. at Pembroke, 20 Apr 1747; Richard d.
at Strafford County, NH, 6 Dec 1826. Richard m. 2ⁿᵈ 27 Aug 1791, SUSANNAH RUNNELS (widow of Benjamin Durgin), b.
1765 daughter of Jonathan and Keziah (Carter) Runnels;[696] Susannah d. at North Conway, 29 May 1849.
        Richard Eastman had gone from Pembroke to Conway with his father and they were among first settlers there.
Richard and Abiah's son Jonathan is reported as the first white child born in Conway.[697] Richard built his first house in a low-
lying tract of land but were forced to move to higher ground following spring floods in 1785.[698]
        Richard Eastman and Abiah Holt were parents of eleven children. Richard also had seven children with his second
wife Susannah Runnels.

i   SALLY EASTMAN, b. (recorded) at Conway, 2 Jun 1766; d. at Conway, 19 Feb 1801; m. 24 Apr 1788, her second
           cousin, ABIEL LOVEJOY, b. at Concord, 10 Aug 1763 son of Abiel and Anna (Stickney) Lovejoy; Abiel d. at
           Lancaster, NH, 2 Nov 1837. Abiel married second Betsey White daughter of Nathaniel and Betsy (Martin) White.

ii   JONATHAN EASTMAN, b. at Conway, 18 Jul 1770; d. at North Conway, 11 May 1868; m. 18 Apr 1793, his
           second cousin, PHEBE LOVEJOY, b. at Conway, 26 Jul 1774 daughter of Abiel and Anna (Stickney) Lovejoy;
           Phebe d. at North Conway, 6 May 1852.

iii   POLLY EASTMAN, b. at Conway, 17 Feb 1772; d. at North Conway, 19 Aug 1859; m. 22 Jul 1790, AMOS
           BARNES, b. at Groton, MA, 9 Jan 1757 son of Joseph and Sarah (Melvin) Barnes; Amos d. at North Conway, 6
           Dec 1840.

iv   PHEBE EASTMAN, b. 21 Oct 1773; d. at North Conway, 14 May 1866; m. 5 Jul 1797, her fourth cousin,
           HUMPHREY CRAM, b. at Wales, MA, 1772 son of Jonathan and Abigail (Webber) Cram; Humphrey d. at
           Lancaster, NH, 17 Mar 1813.

v   ABIAH EASTMAN, b. 26 Jan 1776; d. 6 Oct 1776.

vi   HANNAH EASTMAN, b. at Conway, 25 Feb 1778; d. at Conway, 6 Jul 1876; m. 18 Dec 1803, ISAAC MERRILL,
           b. at Fryeburg, ME, 19 Apr 1775 son of Nathaniel and Ann (Walker) Merrill; Isaac d. at Conway, 17 Aug 1843.

vii   RICHARD EASTMAN, b. 18 Apr 1780; d. at Ogden, KS, 13 May 1876; m. 1ˢᵗ ELMIRA MORRILL who has not
           been identified. Richard m. 2ⁿᵈ, LOUISA MORRILL, b. at Falmouth, ME, 31 Jan 1798; Louisa d. at Ogden, 14 Oct
           1874.

viii   ABIAH EASTMAN, b. at Conway, 6 Apr 1782; d. at North Conway, 19 Nov 1840; m. at Conway, 24 Jun 1806,
           WILLIAM CHURCH FORD, b. at Cornwall, CT, 19 Mar 1776 son of Hezekiah and Deborah (Chandler) Ford.

ix   WILLIAM EASTMAN, b. at Conway, 18 Apr 1784; d. at Jackson, NH, 25 Mar 1872; m. 1ˢᵗ ANNA "NANCY"
           LOVEJOY, b. at Conway, 16 Apr 1785 daughter of Abiel and Anna (Stickney) Lovejoy; Anna d. at Conway, 19
           Mar 1827. William m. 2ⁿᵈ, at Adams, NH, 10 Apr 1828, RUTH B. ELKINS (widow of James C. Trickey), b. at
           Jackson, about 1801 daughter of Daniel and Hannah (Gray) Elkins; Ruth d. at Jackson, 2 Mar 1880.

x   DORCAS EASTMAN, b. at Conway, 4 Jun 1786; d. at Conway, 7 Nov 1873; m. SAMUEL MERRILL, b. at
           Fryeburg, ME, 19 Dec 1780 son of Nathaniel and Ann (Walker) Merrill.

xi   MARTHA "PATTY" EASTMAN, b. at Conway, 22 Jun 1788; d. at Brownfield, ME, 20 Feb 1887; m. JONATHAN
           STICKNEY, b. at Conway, 4 Mar 1784 son of John and Mary (Evans) Stickney; Jonathan d. at Brownfield, 11 Feb
           1832.

259)   MARY "MOLLY" HOLT (*Benjamin Holt⁴, Nicholas Holt³, Mary Russell Holt², Robert¹*), b. at Pembroke, about 1752
daughter of Benjamin and Sarah (Frye) Holt; m. about 1770, NATHANIEL GILMAN, b. at Exeter, NH, 29 Aug 1748 son of
Peter and Abigial (-) Gilman.[699]
        Mary and Nathaniel were parents of eight children as reported in *The Story of the Gilmans*. There are records for six
of the children.[700]

---

[696] Runnels, *Genealogy of the Runnels and Reynolds Families in America*, p 131
[697] Rix, *History and Genealogy of the Eastman Family*, p 175
[698] Merrill, *History of Carroll County, New Hampshire*, p 845
[699] Ames, *The Story of the Gilmans*, p 110
[700] New Hampshire Births and Christenings 1714-1904

i   EZEKIEL GILMAN, b. at Pembroke, NH, 27 Apr 1771; d. at Deerfield, NH, 1804 (probate 1804); m. at Candia, NH, 28 Nov 1799, SALLY BEAN, b. likely at Candia, about 1780 daughter of Nathan and Hannah (Buswell) Bean. Sally m. 2nd by about 1809, Woodin Norris (b. 1763). Son of Sally and Woodin Norris, Ezekiel Gilman Norris, was born 1809.

ii   NICHOLAS GILMAN, b. at Pembroke, 21 Apr 1773; d. at Dorchester, NH, 29 Mar 1817; m. at Pembroke, 25 Jan 1798, his first cousin, SALLY HOLT (*Frye Holt5, Benjamin Holt4, Nicholas Holt3, Mary Russell Holt2, Robert1*), b. about 1773 daughter of Frye and Mary (Poor) Holt.

iii   ABIGAIL GILMAN, b. at Groton, 22 Mar 1777; d. at Waterville, VT, 12 Feb 1851; m. STEVENS REDDING, b. at Middleborough, MA, 27 Oct 1780 son of Moses and Priscilla (Rider) Redding; Stevens d. at Bangor, WI, 24 Dec 1868.

iv   SALLY GILMAN, b. at Groton, 25 May 1779

v   JOHN GILMAN, b. at Groton, 7 Feb 1782

vi   PHEBE GILMAN, b. about 1783; d. at Canaan, NH, 26 Oct 1868; m. 14 Jun 1805, JOHN R. DUSTIN, b. about 1784; John d. after 1850 when he was living at Canaan.

vii   POLLY GILMAN

viii   DOLLY GILMAN

260)   HANNAH HOLT (*Benjamin Holt4, Nicholas Holt3, Mary Russell Holt2, Robert1*), b. at Pembroke, 28 Feb 1758 daughter of Benjamin and Sarah (Frye) Holt; d. 15 Apr 1820; m. NOAH EASTMAN, b. at Pembroke, 20 Mar 1753; Noah d. 28 Aug 1829. Noah and Hannah resided in Conway. Noah served as selectman in 1795-1796, 1798, and 1800. He was the miller of North Conway for fifty years.[701]

Noah Eastman and Hannah Holt were parents of thirteen children whose births are recorded at Conway, New Hampshire.[702]

i   BENJAMIN EASTMAN, b. 28 Dec 1775; d. at North Conway, 30 Apr 1846; m. about 1815, APPHIA STEVENS, b. at Norway, ME, 1786 daughter of Joseph and Elizabeth (Hammond) Stevens.[703]

ii   RICHARD EASTMAN, b. 8 Feb 1778; d. at Lancaster, NH, 22 Jan 1852; m. 5 May 1801, his fourth cousin, PERSIS FAULKNER, b. at Sturbridge, MA, 14 Dec 1775 daughter of Peter and Chloe (Cram) Faulkner; Persis d. at St. Johnsbury, VT, 27 Jan 1872.

iii   NOAH EASTMAN, b. 7 May 1780; died young

iv   JOB EASTMAN, b. 3 Jun 1782; d. at Bartlett, NH, 5 Feb 1869; m. at Conway, 11 Feb 1803, LYDIA DURGIN, b. at Conway, 18 Oct 1785 daughter of Benjamin and Susannah (Runnels) Durgin; Lydia d. 13 Oct 1841. Job m. 2nd 19 May 1842, MARY A. LANG; Mary d. at Bartlett, 24 May 1888.

v   NOAH EASTMAN, b. 15 Oct 1784; d. at North Conway, 15 Oct 1857; m. at Conway, 14 Nov 1816, SALLY DOLLOFF, b. at Conway, 16 Jun 1781 daughter of Josiah and Jene (Knox) Dolloff; Sally d. at Somerville, MA, 13 Sep 1855.

vi   SUSANNA "SUKEY" EASTMAN, b. 12 May 1786; d. at Intervale, NH, 29 May 1844; m. at Conway, 8 Oct 1806, JOHN PENDEXTER, b. 29 Jul 1784 son of John and Martha (Jackson) Pendexter;[704] John d. at Intervale, 21 May 1840.

vii   ESTHER EASTMAN, b. 14 Aug 1788; d. at North Conway, 1876; m. 1815, her first cousin, HENRY EASTMAN, b. at Conway, 29 Jul 1786 son of Abiathar and Phebe (Merrill) Eastman; Henry d. at North Conway, 3 Jul 1838.

viii   FRY HOLT EASTMAN, b. 12 Aug 1790; d. at Bartlett, NH, 15 May 1874; m. 25 Aug 1812, HANNAH UPTON HENLEY, b. at Norway, ME, Aug 1795 daughter of John and Sarah (Upton) Henley; Hannah d. recorded at Bartlett, 31 Mar 1878.

[701] Merrill, *History of Carroll County, New Hampshire*, p 840, p 846
[702] New Hampshire, Birth Records, 1659-1900, accessed through ancestry.com
[703] Lapham, *Centennial History of Norway, Oxford County, Maine*, p 603
[704] New Hampshire Historical Society, John Pendexter, https://www.nhhistory.org/object/253007/pendexter-john

ix   DANIEL EASTMAN, b. 6 Sep 1792; d. at Conway, 22 Aug 1885; m. MARTHA LEWIS CHADBOURNE, b. at Conway, 12 May 1793 daughter of William and Martha (McMillan) Chadbourne; Martha d. at Conway, 21 Dec 1879.

x   JOHN EASTMAN, b. 25 Nov 1794; d. at Saco, ME, 1854; m. about 1819 ELIMIRA STEVENS, b. at Norway, ME, 1794 daughter of Joseph and Elizabeth (Hobbs) Stevens; Elmira d. 5 Jan 1863.

xi   HANNAH EASTMAN, b. 22 Jun 1796; d. at Bartlett, 13 Aug 1887; m. 12 Sep 1816, JOHN DINSMORE, b. at Conway, 11 Nov 1792 son of Stephen and Mehitable (Frye) Dinsmore; John d. at Bartlett, 4 Feb 1879.

xii   PHEBE B. EASTMAN, b. 27 Aug 1799; d. at Conway, 1 Jan 1893; m. DEAN CARBY, b. at Lunenburg, VT, about 1807 son of Thaddeus and Sally (Reed) Carby; Dean d. at Conway, 11 Nov 1882.

xiii   POLLY CUMMINGS EASTMAN, b. 7 Dec 1801; d. at Conway, 12 Nov 1855; m. 21 Oct 1822, her third cousin once removed, JEREMIAH CHANDLER, b. at Newmarket, NH, 23 Mar 1794 son of Moses and Sally (Goodwin) Chandler; Jeremiah d. at Conway, 16 May 1864.

261)   DORCAS HOLT (*Benjamin Holt⁴, Nicholas Holt³, Mary Russell Holt², Robert¹*), b. at Pembroke, about 1764 daughter of Benjamin and Sarah (Frye) Holt; d. at Pembroke, 17 Sep 1850; m. 16 Sep 1787, JOSEPH EMERY, b. 19 Dec 1764 son of Joseph and Hannah (Stickney) Emery; Joseph d. 8 Jun 1830.
        Dorcas and Joseph resided in Pembroke where Joseph was selected as constable in 1805. They were members of the south meeting house church in Pembroke.[705]
        Dorcas Holt and Joseph Emery were parents of nine children born at Pembroke.

i   PHEBE EMERY, b. 28 Apr 1788; d. at Pembroke, 18 Oct 1818; m. 11 Dec 1817, CHARLES KING WILLIAMS, b. 1 Sep 1780 son of Jonathan and Elizabeth (King) Williams; Charles d. at Pembroke, 12 Apr 1861. After Phebe's death, Charles married her sister Abigail (see below).

ii   SARAH "SALLY" EMERY, b. 14 Feb 1790; d. after 1855 when she was living in Somerville, MA; m. 8 Aug 1811, JOHN BUSS, b. at Boston, about 1790; John d. at Boston, of intemperance, 8 Sep 1828. Sarah and John had five daughters two of whom died in early childhood.

iii   DORCAS EMERY, b. 28 Sep 1791; d. at Pembroke, Sep 1852; m. at Pembroke, 12 Sep 1826, as his second wife, JOHN PARKER, b. at Andover, MA, 20 May 1783 son of John and Joanna (Bailey) Parker; John d. at Pembroke, 18 Jan 1862. John married first Esther Baker.

iv   JOSEPH EMERY, b. Sep 1793; d. 24 Dec 1796.

v   HANNAH EMERY, b. 5 Jul 1795; d. at Pembroke, 6 May 1883; m. 29 Dec 1824, as his third wife, STEPHEN BATES, b. at Hingham, MA, 4 Sep 1784 son of Stephen and Susanna (Trufont) Bates; Stephen d. at Pembroke, 20 Sep 1872. Stephen was first married to Anne Thurston and second married to Anna Shattuck.

vi   ABIGAIL EMERY, b. 10 Sep 1797; d. at Pembroke, 3 Jan 1859; m. about 1822, as his second wife CHARLES KING WILLIAMS who was first married to Abigail's sister Phebe (see above).

vii   JOSEPH EMERY, b. 13 Sep 1799; d. at Pembroke, 22 Sep 1886; m. 16 Sep 1829, HANNAH MORRILL, b. at Epping, 28 Apr 1809 daughter of Nathaniel and Hannah (Rowell) Morrill; Hannah d. at Pembroke, 2 Aug 1859.

viii   FANNY EMERY, b. 21 Sep 1801; d. 4 Nov 1802.

ix   MELINDA EMERY, b. 18 Jun 1805; d. 10 Jul 1827.

262)   STEVENS CHANDLER (*Mary Holt Chandler Osgood⁴, Nicholas Holt³, Mary Russell Holt², Robert¹*), b. at Andover, 15 Dec 1738 son of William and Mary (Holt) Chandler; d. at Andover, Nov 1814 (buried 10 Nov 1814); m. 1ˢᵗ at Ashford, about 1762, ALICE SNOW, b. at Ashford, 23 Sep 1741 daughter of Joseph and Sarah (Cornell) Snow; Alice d. at Ashford, 17 Jan 1782. Stevens m. 2ⁿᵈ at Ashford, Jun 1784, MARY PRESTON; Mary d. 10 Mar 1787. Stevens m. 3ʳᵈ at Ashford, 3 Jul 1790, SARAH ROGERS; Sarah d. at the almshouse in Andover, 26 Aug 1817.
        Stevens Chandler lived in Connecticut for most of his adult life but returned to Andover by 1814 when he was received into the church at South Andover 15 May 1814. He was a tailor by trade. He was living at the almshouse in Andover at the time of his death.[706] Two of his daughters, Lois and Alice, also died at the almshouse in Andover.[707]
        Stevens Chandler and Alice Snow were parents of six children.

[705] Carter, *History of Pembroke*, p 162, p 252
[706] Chandler, *Descendants of William and Annis Chandler*, p 212
[707] Massachusetts Vital Records Project, Andover

i   JAMES CHANDLER, b. at Ashford, 25 Jul 1763

ii   JOEL CHANDLER, b. at Ashford, 10 Mar 1765

iii   MARY CHANDLER, b. at Willington, 22 Apr 767

iv   WILLIAM CHANDLER, b. at Willington, 14 Jan 1771; d. about 1800; m. MATILDA BURT

v   ELIZABETH CHANDLER, b. at Willington, 9 Apr 1774; d. after 1850 when she was living at the poor house in Dedham; m. at Dedham, MA, 29 Oct 1809, THOMAS COLBURN, b. at Dedham, 28 Feb 1753 son of Samuel and Mercy (Dean) Chandler; Thomas d. at Dedham, 22 Feb 1836.

vi   STEVENS CHANDLER, b. recorded at Ashford, 12 Nov 1781; d. at Cortlandville, NY, Oct 1850; m. POLLY WINCHESTER, b. 6 Jun 1779 daughter of Amariah Winchester;[708] Polly d. at Homer, NY, 14 Jan 1844.

Stevens Chandler and Mary Preston were parents of one child.

i   BENJAMIN CHANDLER, b. at Ashford, 31 May 1785; d. of illness near Fort Niagara, 21 Sep 1813 during the War of 1812; m. CHARITY CARPENTER, b. at Tolland, 27 Oct 1783 daughter of Simeon and Abigail (Cushman) Carpenter.

Stevens Chandler and Sarah Rogers were parents of two children.

i   ALICE CHANDLER, b. at Ashford, 27 Nov 1791; d. at Andover, 11 Oct 1833.

ii   LOIS CHANDLER, b. at Ashford, 18 Oct 1797; d. at Andover, 13 Feb 1811.

263)   MARY CHANDLER (*Mary Holt Chandler Osgood⁴, Nicholas Holt³, Mary Russell Holt², Robert¹*), b. at Andover, 8 Feb 1740/1 daughter of William and Mary (Holt) Chandler; d. at Ashford, 11 Mar 1787; m. at Ashford, 18 Nov 1762, JOSEPH SNOW, b. at Ashford, 15 Nov 1738 son of Joseph and Sarah (Cornell) Snow. Joseph married second Desire Swift on 1 Jan 1788. Joseph d. at Ashford, about 1801 (notice of insolvent estate given 1802).
    Joseph Snow and Mary Chandler were parents of eight children born at Ashford.

i   SIMEON SNOW, b. 1 Sep 1763; m. by 1788, LYDIA BILLINGS

ii   AMOS SNOW, b. 20 Sep 1765; d. at Ashford, 13 Sep 1805; m. at Ashford, 27 Jun 1797, his fourth cousin once removed, EUNICE BURNHAM, b. at Ashford, 25 May 1777 daughter of Joseph and Elizabeth (Durkee) Burnham.

iii   MARY SNOW, b. 18 Mar 1768

iv   JUSTUS SNOW, b. 26 Mar 1769; m. about 1796, his third cousin once removed, SABRA HOLT, b. at Windham, 12 Jan 1768 daughter of Nehemiah and Anna (Farnum) Holt.

v   JOSEPH SNOW, b. 31 Mar 1772

vi   LEMUEL SNOW, b. 22 Jul 1777

vii   CHLOE SNOW, b. 7 Apr 1780

viii ELIPHALET SNOW, b. 7 Jul 1784; d. after 1850 when he was living at Mansfield, CT; m. at Mansfield, 24 May 1807, ANNA ROBINSON, b. about 1788; Anna d. after 1850.

264)   DORCAS OSGOOD (*Mary Holt Chandler Osgood⁴, Nicholas Holt³, Mary Russell Holt², Robert¹*), b. at Andover, 11 Aug 1748 daughter of Jeremiah and Mary (Holt) Osgood; d. at Westport, NY, 31 Aug 1811; m. at Ashford, CT, 5 Jul 1764, BENJAMIN SNOW, b. at Ashford, 23 Jan 1743/4 son of Joseph and Sarah (Cornell) Snow.
    There are records for two children of Dorcas and Benjamin born at Ashford.

i   JESSE SNOW, b. 3 Jan 1765

---

[708] Chandler, *Descendants of William and Annis Chandler*

ii   LYDIA SNOW, b. 6 Oct 1769; d. at Keene, NY, 21 Dec 1853; m. 26 Jan 1792, her second cousin once removed, SMITH HOLT (*Asa Holt⁴, Daniel Holt³, Mary Russell Holt², Robert¹*), b. at Hartford, about 1769 son of Asa and Margaret (Hammond) Holt; Smith d. at Keene, 28 Dec 1814. Lydia Snow and Smith Holt are Family 410.

265)   JEDEDIAH HOLT (*Stephen Holt⁴, Nicholas Holt³, Mary Russell Holt², Robert¹*), b. at Suncook, 23 Feb 1743/4 son of Stephen and Mary (Farnum) Holt; d. at Andover, 12 Feb 1790; m. at Andover, 19 Jun 1766, his second cousin once removed, PHEBE BARKER, b. at Andover, 2 Jan 1749/50 daughter of Samuel and Sarah (Robinson) Barker.

Jedediah Holt did not leave a will and the estate entered probate 7 June 1790. Widow Phebe Holt was named administratrix. The heirs signing their agreement with the plan for inventory of the estate were Phebe Holt also signing as the guardian for Samuel Holt and Stephen Holt, Nathan Barker signing on behalf of his wife, and Phebe Holt. Real estate was valued at £455.12.4 and personal estate at £398.7.10. The children receiving distributions from the estate were Samuel Holt, Stephen Holt, Phebe Holt, and Sarah Barker.[709]

Phebe Barker and Jedediah Holt were parents of five children born at Andover.

i   SARAH HOLT, b. 16 Jan 1768; d. at Boxford, 9 Jul 1843; m. at Andover, 12 Aug 1788, NATHAN BARKER, b. at Andover, 12 Aug 1768 son of Samuel and Susannah (Foster) Barker; Nathan d. at Boxford, 17 Dec 1821.

ii   PHEBE HOLT, b. 18 Feb 1771; d. at Andover, 23 Jan 1844; m. at Andover, 1805, WILLIAM FOSTER, b. about 1772 son of William and Mehitable (Fuller) Foster; William d. at Andover, 14 Nov 1833.

iii   MOLLY HOLT, b. 2 Jul 1773; d. 18 Apr 1784.

iv   SAMUEL HOLT, b. 24 Jan 1778; d. at Winthrop, ME, 1819 (probate 21 Dec 1819); m. at Andover, 10 May 1803, LYDIA FARNUM, b. at Andover, 14 Jul 1780 daughter of Jedediah and Rebecca (Poor) Farnum.

v   STEPHEN HOLT, b. 4 Feb 1786; d. before 1850; m. *likely*, 2 Mar 1809, ABIGAIL DOLE, b. about 1790 daughter of Greenleaf and Mary (Moore) Dole; Abigail d. after 1850.[710]

266)   HANNAH HOLT (*Nicholas Holt⁴, Nicholas Holt³, Mary Russell Holt², Robert¹*), b. at Andover, 16 Nov 1741 daughter of Nicholas and Hannah (Osgood) Holt; d. at Blue Hill, ME, 31 Dec 1826; m. at Andover, 15 Sep 1763, JONATHAN DARLING, baptized at Salem, 11 Jul 1742 son of Jonathan and Sarah (Wardwell) Darling; Jonathan d. at Blue Hill, 26 Feb 1828.

Jonathan participated in the siege of Louisburg in 1759. He came to Blue Hill about 1762-1763 and settled at what became known as Darling's Point. He was involved in civic affairs of the town.[711]

Jonathan Darling kept a diary and an abstract of the diary can be found in Maine Historical Magazine, volume 2, starting on page 76. In the diary, Jonathan notes the death of his father at Louisburg in 1746 and his mother's death in 1755. He recounts some of the details of his participation in the expedition to Louisburg in 1759-1760. The walls at Louisburg were fully blown up on 8 November 1760 for which "the Governor gave us four days pay, and a pint of rum a man for our good behavior." He also recounts his selection of a property in Blue Hill on which to settle. The diary continues through 1773.

Hannah Holt and Jonathan Darling were parents of nine children. The birth of the oldest child is recorded at Andover although the "Families of the Early Settlers of Blue Hill Maine" reports this child as the first while male child born in Blue Hill. It may be that the second child Jonathan was the first white male child born at Blue Hill.

i   JONATHAN DARLING, possibly b. at Blue Hill, 25 Nov 1763; d. 7 Mar 1765.

ii   JONATHAN DARLING, b. at Blue Hill, 17 Oct 1765; d. at Enfield, ME, 17 Dec 1848; m. 28 Dec 1797, MIRIAM GRAY, b. at Sedgwick, ME, 22 May 1777 daughter of John and Hannah (Getchell) Gray; Miriam d. at Enfield, 9 Feb 1858.

iii   HANNAH DARLING, b. Mar 1767; d. 6 Jul 1767.

iv   HANNAH DARLING, b. 12 Jun 1768; d. 13 Dec 1768.

v   SARAH "SALLY" DARLING, b. at Blue Hill, 30 Jun 1770; d. at Blue Hill, 16 Oct 1836; m. 13 Sep 1794, PETER PARKER, b. at Andover, 17 Oct 1769 son of Peter and Phebe (Marble) Parker; Peter d. at Blue Hill, 30 Apr 1855.

---

[709] Essex County, MA: Probate File Papers, 1638-1881.Online database. AmericanAncestors.org. New England Historic Genealogical Society, 2014. Case 13654

[710] Abigail Dole daughter of Greenleaf did marry a Stephen Holt. This is confirmed by the 1829 will of Greenleaf Dole which includes a bequest to daughter Abigail wife of Stephen Holt. The question is whether it is this Stephen Holt. The two other Stephen Holts (born 1782 and 1786) in Andover of an appropriate age can be accounted for as having other spouses. But this marriage should be considered tentative.

[711] "Families and Early Settlers of Blue Hill Maine," The Maine Historical Magazine, volume 5, p 187

vi   MARY DARLING, b. at Blue Hill, 8 Aug 1774; d. at Lowell, ME, 7 Jun 1849; m. 15 Dec 1796, STEPHEN MESSER, b. at Andover, 10 May 1773 son of Stephen and Ann (Barker) Messer; Stephen d. at Lowell, 10 Dec 1833.

vii   PHEBE DARLING, b. at Blue Hill, 26 Feb 1776; d. at Enfield, ME, 3 Oct 1851; m. 5 Mar 1810, ELISHA GUPTILL, b. at Steuben, ME, 1 May 1791 son of William and Jane (Downs) Guptill; Elisha d. at Bradley, ME, 1 Nov 1867.

viii   SAMUEL DARLING, b. at Blue Hill, 28 Jul 1781; d. at Patten, ME, 1859; m. 1st 29 Jul 1805, his second cousin, HANNAH OSGOOD, b. at Andover, May 1786 daughter of Joseph and Hannah (Bailey) Osgood; Hannah d. at Blue Hill, 6 Jun 1806. Samuel m. 2nd MARY "POLLY" JELLISON, b. 1792 daughter of William and Martha (Hopkins) Jellison; Polly d. at Patten, 1871.

ix   JEDEDIAH DARLING, b. at Blue Hill, 24 Jul 1784; d. at Blue Hill, 30 Dec 1862; m. 2 Nov 1807, LYDIA STINSON, b. 4 Apr 1788; Lydia d. at Blue Hill, 27 Feb 1881.

267)   PHEBE HOLT (*Nicholas Holt4, Nicholas Holt3, Mary Russell Holt2, Robert1*), b. at Andover, 29 Jan 1752 daughter of Nicholas and Lois (Phelps) Holt; d. at Blue Hill, 12 Feb 1831; m. about 1769, ISRAEL WOOD, b. at Beverly, MA, 17 Oct 1744 son of Joseph and Ruth (Haskell) Wood; Israel d. at Blue Hill, 13 Nov 1800.

Israel Wood came to Blue Hill, Maine with his father in 1763. He there married Phebe Holt and their nine children were born there. Israel lived in the property established by his father across from the schoolhouse in Blue Hill.[712]

Israel Wood did not leave a will and widow Phebe requested that Phineas Pillsbury be named administrator. The heirs-at-law in addition to wife Phebe were Phebe wife of Phineas Pillsbury, Lois wife of Ezra Parker, Anna single woman, Ruth single woman, Joseph age 16, Hannah age 14, Samuel Holt age 10, and Israel age 19. The dower was set off to widow Phebe. Real estate was valued at $1,075 which include the homestead valued at $365 and 100 acres of land valued at $500. At the time of the estate settlement on 6 May 1802, daughter Phebe was deceased, and her portion was paid to her heirs.[713]

Phebe Holt and Israel Wood were parents of nine children born at Blue Hill.[714]

i   PHEBE WOOD, b. at Blue Hill, 22 Apr 1769; d. at Blue Hill, 14 Sep 1801; m. 21 Oct 1788, PHINEAS PILLSBURY, b. at Bradford, MA (baptized at Newburyport), 18 Feb 1767 son of Parker and Aphhia (Jaques) Pillsbury; Phineas d. at Greene, ME, 4 Nov 1859. Phineas married second Sarah T. Larrabee.

ii   ANNA WOOD, b. 13 Apr 1771; d. 16 Dec 1776.

iii   LOIS WOOD, b. at Blue Hill, 6 Feb 1774; d. at Blue Hill, 31 Dec 1861; m. 17 Dec 1791, EZRA PARKER, b. 15 Jul 1767; Ezra d. 14 Jul 1818.

iv   ANNA WOOD, b. at Blue Hill, 24 Dec 1776; d. at Blue Hill, 11 Mar 1841. Anna did not marry.

v   RUTH WOOD, b. at Blue Hill, 15 Nov 1779; d. at Blue Hill, 28 Nov 1865; m. 7 Mar 1811, JAMES SAVAGE, b. at Sharon, MA, 29 Jun 1781 son of Nathan and Remember (Tupper) Savage;[715] James d. at Blue Hill, 3 Jun 1847.

vi   ISRAEL WOOD, b. at Blue Hill, 20 Jul 1782; d. at Blue Hill, 25 May 1831; m. 1st 15 Dec 1808, JOANNA PARKER, b. at Blue Hill, 7 May 1784 daughter of Peter and Phebe (Marble) Parker; Joanna d. at Blue Hill, 4 Mar 1820. Israel m. 2nd, BETSEY BRIGGS HATCH, b. at Pembroke, MA, 31 Jan 1796 daughter of Briggs and Betsey (Hatch) Hatch. After Israel's death, Betsey married Benjamin Herrick.

vii   JOSEPH WOOD, b. 1 Apr 1785; d. at Blue Hill, 20 Jan 1834; m. 1st 4 Nov 1813, HANNAH JOHNSON, b. at Penobscot, 30 Jul 1787 daughter of Giles and Elizabeth (Brooks) Johnson; Hannah d. at Blue Hill, 17 Apr 1817. Joseph m. 2nd about 1819, JOANNA HINCKLEY, b. at Blue Hill, 6 Mar 1792 daughter of Isaiah and Annie (Horton) Hinckley; Joanna d. at Blue Hill, 27 Aug 1846.

viii   HANNAH WOOD, b. at Blue Hill, 27 Jan 1788; d. at Orland, ME, 30 Oct 1846; m. 21 Dec 1815, as his second wife, ISAAC PERRY, b. about 1775; Isaac d. after 1850 when he was living in Orland. Isaac was first married to Rhoda Burnham.

ix   SAMUEL HOLT WOOD, b. at Blue Hill, 19 Jul 1791; d. at Blue Hill, 2 May 1826.

[712] Candage, *Historical Sketches of Bluehill, Maine*, p 23
[713] *Maine, Wills and Probate Records, 1584-1999, Hancock, Maine, Estate Files, No 484-563, 1790-1915, Estate of Israel Wood*
[714] "Families and Early Settlers of Blue Hill Maine," The Maine Historical Magazine, volume 5
[715] Cochrane, History of Francestown, p 909

268)   JEDEDIAH HOLT (*Nicholas Holt⁴, Nicholas Holt³, Mary Russell Holt², Robert¹*), b. at Andover, 12 Mar 1754 son of Nicholas and Lois (Phelps) Holt; d. at Blue Hill, 17 Aug 1847; m. at Beverly, 24 Feb 1778, SARAH THORNDIKE, b. at Beverly, Sep 1751 (baptized 4 Jul 1756) daughter of Hezekiah and Sarah (Prince) Thorndike; Sarah d. at Blue Hill, 15 Jan 1836.

     Jedediah had gone to Blue Hill with his father. At the outbreak of the Revolution, the British occupied nearby Castine. Citizens of Blue Hill were compelled to sign a loyalty oath to the king. When a second oath was required, Jedediah fled to Beverly where he remained until the end of the war. His two oldest children were born there and after the war, the family returned to Blue Hill.[716]

     Jedediah Holt did not leave a will, and there seemed to be a delay in the probate of the estate as the administrator's bond was signed on 11 April 1849 with son Jonah as administrator. Real estate was valued at $1,333 for the homestead property and $10 for 5 acres of wild sand and personal estate at $43.32.[717]

     Jedediah Holt and Sarah Thorndike were parents of six children.

i   JEDEDIAH HOLT, b. at Beverly, MA, 3 Mar 1779; d. at Blue Hill, ME, 5 Aug 1842; m. 11 Oct 1802, MARY VILES, b. at Orland, ME, 28 Nov 1782 daughter of Joseph and Hannah (Horton) Viles; Mary d. at Blue Hill, 22 Jan 1843.

ii   JEREMIAH THORNDIKE HOLT, b. at Beverly, 12 May 1781; d. at Blue Hill, Apr 1832 (probate 5 Jul 1832); m. Nov 1808, his fourth cousin once removed, ELIZABETH OSGOOD, b. at Andover, Nov 1789 daughter of Joseph and Hannah (Bailey) Osgood; Elizabeth d. at Blue Hill, 4 Feb 1858.

iii   JONAH HOLT, b. at Blue Hill, 4 Nov 1783; d. at Blue Hill, 19 Feb 1860; m. 27 Feb 1811, his fourth cousin once removed, ELIZABETH OSGOOD STEVENS, b. at Blue Hill, 8 Dec 1793 daughter of Theodore and Dorcas (Osgood) Stevens; Elizabeth d. at Blue Hill, 20 Nov 1847. Jonah m. 2nd about 1848, ALMIRA WILCOX, b. about 1821; Almira was living in 1860.

iv   SAMUEL P. HOLT, b. at Blue Hill, 8 Jul 1785; d. at Blue Hill, 29 Sep 1827; m. 4 Nov 1813, LYDIA LOWELL, b. 2 Feb 1789 daughter of Eliphalet and Elizabeth (Haney) Lowell;[718] Lydia d. at Blue Hill, 7 May 1857.

v   STEPHEN HOLT, b. at Blue Hill, 10 May 1788; d. at Blue Hill, 16 May 1830; m. about 1818, EDITH PARKER, b. at Blue Hill, 2 Mar 1795 daughter of Robert and Ruth (Wood) Parker; Edith d. after 1860 when she was living in Rockland, ME.

vi   SALLY P. HOLT, b. at Blue Hill, 3 Jul 1793; d. at Blue Hill, 1 Nov 1803.

269)   NICHOLAS HOLT (*Nicholas Holt⁴, Nicholas Holt³, Mary Russell Holt², Robert¹*), b. at Andover, Feb 1756 son of Nicholas and Lois (Phelps) Holt; d. at Blue Hill, 8 Mar 1833;[719] m. 1st at Reading, 26 Nov 1782, his third cousin once removed, PHEBE BATCHELDER, b. at North Reading, 3 Nov 1754 daughter of Jonathan and Phebe (Holt) Batchelder; Phebe d. at Blue Hill, about 1790. Nicholas m. 2nd at Blue Hill 13 Apr 1795, MOLLY WORMWOOD; Molly d. at Blue Hill, 30 Nov 1831.

     Nicholas Holt served in the Revolution and applied for a pension, but this was rejected as he had not served for the required six-month period for a pension.[720] In his pension application, Nicholas reported enlisting in 1780 from Reading in Capt. Flint's company in Col. Jackson's regiment of the Continental line. He joined the army at West Point. He left the service on 1 January 1781 after serving nine months. In 1852, son Joseph applied for the payment of the pension which had not been drawn by his father.[721]

     Nicholas Holt and Phebe Batchelder were parents of two children born at Blue Hill, Maine.

i   LEVI HOLT, b. at Blue Hill, 16 Aug 1785; d. at Hampden, ME, 5 Mar 1879; m. at Blue Hill, 4 Apr 1809, BETSEY STEVENS, b. at Andover, 14 May 1782 daughter of Benjamin and Hannah (Varnum) Stevens; Betsey d. at Hampden between 1850 and 1860 (in the 1850 census but Levi is widowed in 1860).

ii   JONATHAN HOLT, b. at Blue Hill, 15 Aug 1787; d. at Bangor, ME, 9 Oct 1818; m. CYNTHIA EMERY.

     Nicholas Holt and Molly Wormwood were parents of three children born at Blue Hill.

i   PHEBE BATCHELDER HOLT, b. at Blue Hill, 28 Jan 1796; m. NATHAN FISH.[722]

ii   HANNAH HOLT, b. at Blue Hill, 6 May 1798

---

[716] Durrie, Holt genealogy, p 43
[717] Hancock Maine Estate Files, Estate of Jedediah Holt
[718] Lowell, The Historic Genealogy of the Lowells of America, p 69
[719] The dates of death for Nicholas Holt and Molly Wormwood are those given by son Joseph Holt in the pension application file.
[720] Rejected or Suspended Applications for Revolutionary War Pensions
[721] U.S., Revolutionary War Pension and Bounty-Land Warrant Application Files, 1800-1900, Case R5186
[722] Durrie, Holt genealogy

iii   JOSEPH HOLT, b. at Blue Hill, 21 Jul 1801; d. at Blue Hill, 1885; m. 10 Feb 1825, MARGARET MORSE, b. 31 Oct 1799 daughter of Samuel and Elizabeth (Candage) Morse;[723] Margaret d. at Blue Hill, 30 May 1869.

270)   TIMOTHY HOLT (*Timothy Holt⁴, Nicholas Holt³, Mary Russell Holt², Robert¹*), b. at Andover, 19 May 1746 son of Timothy and Elizabeth (Holt) Holt; d. at Weston, VT, 3 May 1836; m. by 1773, his third cousin, HANNAH JOHNSON, b. at Andover, 8 Feb 1753 daughter of Obadiah and Dorothy (Ballard) Johnson.[724]

     Hannah and Timothy were in Andover, members of South Church admitted on profession of faith on 22 August 1775 and were dismissed to the church at Wilton on 25 June 1780.[725] It is not known how long the family was in Wilton, but they were in Weston, Vermont by 1810.[726] Timothy over age 45 was head of household and Hannah appears to be deceased by 1810.

     There are just three children known for Hannah Johnson and Timothy Holt.

i   HANNAH HOLT, b. at Andover, 29 Jun 1773

ii   ELIZABETH HOLT, baptized at Andover, 24 Sep 1775; d. at Brookline, VT, 24 Nov 1874;[727] m. at Wilton, 27 Nov 1794, her first cousin, ISRAEL WHITNEY (*Hannah Holt Whitney⁵, Timothy Holt⁴, Nicholas Holt³, Mary Russell Holt², Robert¹*), b. at Wilton, 4 Jul 1774 son of Richard and Hannah (Holt) Whitney; Israel d. at Brookline, 14 Dec 1850.

iii   TIMOTHY HOLT, b. at Andover, 7 Sep 1777; d. at Weston, VT, 31 May 1860; m. 16 Oct 1804, HANNAH TYLER, b. at Rindge, NH, 20 Oct 1786 daughter of Parker and Hannah (Flint) Tyler; Hannah d. at Unity, NH, 10 Sep 1874.

271)   ELIZABETH HOLT (*Timothy Holt⁴, Nicholas Holt³, Mary Russell Holt², Robert¹*), b. at Andover, 25 Nov 1748 daughter of Timothy and Elizabeth (Holt) Holt; m. 1 Jun 1769, ISAAC FRYE, b. at Andover, 6 Feb 1748 son of Abiel and Abigail (Emery) Frye; Isaac d. at Wilton, NH, 3 Nov 1791.

     Elizabeth and Isaac were in Wilton soon after their marriage arriving there in 1771 or 1772.

     Isaac Frye distinguished himself in the Revolution. He was quartermaster in the third New Hampshire regiment of Col. James Reed in 1775 and was at the Battle of Bunker Hill. He received his commission as captain on 1 January 1776. Capt. Frye was the muster-master at Amherst in 1782. Following the war, he was breveted with the rank of major on 27 Nov 1783.[728]

     Elizabeth Holt and Isaac Frye were parents of ten children.

i   ISAAC FRYE, baptized at Andover, 17 Dec 1769; d. at Wilton, 14 Sep 1814; m. at Wilton, 19 Jun 1794, HANNAH PHELPS, b. at Andover, 18 Jan 1774 daughter of Joseph and Abigail (Smith) Phelps; Hannah d. at Wilton, 28 Oct 1861.

ii   TIMOTHY FRYE, b. at Wilton, 21 Sep 1773; d. 17 Mar 1776.

iii   ABIEL FRYE, b. at Wilton, 28 Jul 1774; d. at Wilton, about 1820. Abiel did not marry.

iv   JOHN FRYE, b. at Wilton, 23 Aug 1775; d. at Edinboro, PA, 11 Sep 1851; m. LUCY WELLMAN, b. in VT, 1782 daughter of Timothy and Lucy (Skinner) Wellman;[729] Lucy d. at Edinboro, 1867.

v   TIMOTHY HOLT FRYE, b. at Wilton, 27 Oct 1777; d. at Weld, ME, 7 Jan 1830; m. 8 Jan 1809, his fourth cousin, RACHEL HOLT, b. at Wilton, 7 Feb 1783 daughter of Simeon and Mary (Dale) Holt; Rachel d. after 1860 when she was living in Weld.

vi   JOSHUA FRYE, b. at Wilton, 21 Dec 1779; d. at Wilton, 20 Jun 1864; m. 1st about 1805, LOIS FARRINGTON, b. at Hubbardston, MA, 4 Mar 1783 daughter of Elijah and Elizabeth (Sawin) Farrington; Lois d. at Athens, VT, 17 Aug 1815. Joshua m. 2nd 19 May 1831, LUCY JONES, b. at Hillsborough, NH, 27 Apr 1787 daughter of Joel and Mary (Bishop) Jones; Lucy d. at Wilton, 17 Dec 1875.

vii   BETSY FRYE, b. at Wilton, 21 Dec 1781; d. at Wilton, 9 Jun 1862. Betsy did not marry. In 1860, she was living with her brother Joshua and his wife Lucy.

---

[723] "Families and Early Settlers of Blue Hill Maine," *The Maine Historical Magazine*, volume 5, p 200

[724] There are two Timothy Holts of similar age, one who married Hannah Johnson and one who married Ede Mc'Intire. It is generally accepted in published genealogies that this Timothy married Hannah Johnson.

[725] South Church, *Historical Manual of South Church of Andover*

[726] Year: 1810; Census Place: Weston, Windsor, Vermont; Roll: 65; Page: 468; Image: 00335; Family History Library Film: 0218669

[727] Death record gives father as Timothy Holt and age at death as 99 years, 2 months, 7 days

[728] Livermore, *History of the Town of Wilton*, p 106

[729] Wellman, *Descendants of Thomas Wellman*, p 213

viii   HANNAH FRYE, b. at Wilton, 30 May 1785; d. at Wilton, 31 Oct 1863; m. 26 Oct 1813, BENJAMIN
        BLANCHARD, b. at Wilton, 5 Apr 1781, Benjamin and Sarah (Griffin) Blanchard; Benjamin d. 12 Jul 1855.

ix   ALFRED FRYE, b. at Wilton, 28 Feb 1787; d. at Wilton, 25 Sep 1867; m. 1st 19 Aug 1817, LUCY FARRINGTON,
        b. at Hubbardston, MA, 29 Apr 1787 daughter of Elijah and Elizabeth (Sawin) Farrington; Lucy d. at Wilton, 12
        Dec 1835. Alfred m. 2nd about 1836, BETSEY BLANCHARD, b. at Milford, NH, 9 Jul 1801 daughter of Phineas
        and Sarah (Stevens) Blanchard; Betsey d. at Wilton, 11 Feb 1863.

x   SARAH "SALLY" FRYE, b. at Wilton, 20 Sep 1790; d. at Wilton, 18 May 1835. Sally did not marry.

272)   HANNAH HOLT (*Timothy Holt⁴, Nicholas Holt³, Mary Russell Holt², Robert¹*), b. at Andover, 18 Jan 1754 daughter of
Timothy and Elizabeth (Holt) Holt; d. at Brookline, VT, Apr 1833; m. about 1774, as his second wife, RICHARD WHITNEY, b.
at Oxford, MA, 22 Apr 1743 son of Israel and Hannah (Blodgett) Whitney Richard d. at Brookline, 20 Apr 1816. Richard was
first married to Sarah Butterfield who died in 1773.
        Hannah and Richard were in Wilton, New Hampshire where Richard served one term as selectman in 1780.[730] The
family then settled in Brookline, Vermont where they were one of the early families.[731] They settled in area that was known as
Whitney hill.
        Hannah Holt and Richard Whitney were parents of ten children, the first nine children born at Wilton and the
youngest child born perhaps at Brookline, Vermont.

i   ISRAEL WHITNEY, b. 4 Jul 1774; d. at Brookline, VT, 14 Dec 1850; m. at Wilton, 27 Nov 1794, his first cousin,
        ELIZABETH HOLT (*Timothy Holt⁵, Timothy Holt⁴, Nicholas Holt³, Mary Russell Holt², Robert¹*), b. at Andover,
        17 Sep 1775 daughter of Timothy and Hannah (Johnson) Holt;[732] Elizabeth d. at Brookline, 24 Nov 1874.

ii   TIMOTHY HOLT WHITNEY, b. 21 Nov 1776; d. at Athens, VT, 16 Mar 1859; m. 1st 11 Feb 1800, ABIGAIL
        BLANCHARD, b. at Wilton, 11 Jun 1777 daughter of Benjamin and Sarah (Griffin) Blanchard; Abigail d. at
        Athens, 27 Apr 1843. Timothy m. 2nd about 1844, ARATHUSA BARTLETT, b. at Newfane, VT, about 1794
        daughter of William and Arathusa (Gibson) Bartlett; Arathusa d. at Newfane, 1 Oct 1868.

iii   EBENEZER WHITNEY, b. 3 Jul 1778; d. at Brookline, VT, 12 Apr 1869; m. DEBORAH JOY whose parents are
        not identified, b. about 1778; Deborah d. at Brookline, 20 Sep 1850.

iv   ABRAM WHITNEY, b. 8 Jan 1780; d. at Lindley, NY, Mar 1860; m. BETSEY who has not been identified, b. in
        VT, about 1783; Betsey d. after 1865 when she was living in Hornby, NY.

v   ISAAC WHITNEY, b. 21 Jan 1782; d. at Weston, VT, 22 Nov 1860; m. at Chester, VT, Dec 1806, ABIGAIL
        EDSON.

vi   JACOB WHITNEY, b. 15 Jan 1784; d. 9 Jul 1785.

vii   HANNAH WHITNEY, b. 15 Aug 1785; d. at Newfane, VT, 27 Jan 1871; m. 1st about 1810, JAMES CAMPBELL.
        Hannah m. 2nd JOSEPHUS ORVIS, b. 28 Feb 1780 son of Waitstill and Elizabeth (Church) Orvis; Josephus d. at
        South Newfane, 24 Dec 1855.

viii   SARAH BUTTERFIELD WHITNEY, b. 1 Nov 1787; d. at Brookline, VT, 17 Sep 1873; m. JOEL HARWOOD, b.
        about 1786; Joel d. at Brookline, 11 Dec 1849.

ix   SOLOMON WHITNEY, b. 26 Aug 1790; d. at Austinburg, OH, 1862 (probate 1862); m. SARAH, b. in NY, about
        1784; Sarah d. after 1862.

x   CHLOE WHITNEY, b. 22 Nov 1795; d. after 1870 when she was living in Putney, VT; m. DAVID KIDDER, b. at
        Oxford, MA, 11 May 1797 son of David and Sarah (Fressenden) Kidder; David d. after 1870.

273)   SARAH HOLT (*Timothy Holt⁴, Nicholas Holt³, Mary Russell Holt², Robert¹*), b. at Andover, 31 May 1757 daughter of
Timothy and Elizabeth (Holt) Holt; m. at Wilton, 30 Mar 1780, her second cousin once removed, WILLIAM PIERCE, b. at
Ashford, CT, 28 Jun 1759 son of William and Hannah (-) Pierce of Wilton, NH.[733][734]

---

[730] Livermore, *History of the Town of Wilton*, p 50

[731] Stickney, *The Local History of Brookline, Vermont*, p 6

[732] Elizabeth's death record gives her father as Timothy and age at death of 99 years, 2 months, 7 days which corresponds to the birth of Elizabeth
daughter of Timothy and Hannah.

[733] Livermore, *History of Wilton*, p 470

[734] Littlefield, *Genealogies of the Early Settlers of Weston*

Sarah Holt and William Pierce were parents of ten children,[735][736] the older children likely born at Wilton and the younger children at Weston, Vermont.

i   SARAH PIERCE, b. 1782; d. at Weston, VT, 22 Jan 1857; m. at Weston, 2 May 1813, JOHN KIMBALL, b. about 1785; John d. at Weston, after 1820.

ii   HANNAH PIERCE, b. about 1783; d. at Springfield, VT, about 1820; m. at Weston, 23 Aug 1803, CHARLES LOCKWOOD, b. at Springfield, VT, 28 Dec 1780 son of Abraham and Lydia (Pollard) Lockwood. Charles married second Lucy Lewis on 20 Jan 1821.

iii   WILLIAM PIERCE, b. 20 Sep 1785; d. at Salem, NY, 26 May 1867; m. about 1815, MARY MONCRIEF, b. 4 Oct 1786;[737] Mary d. at Salem, 5 Jan 1847.

iv   ASA PIERCE, b. 6 Dec 1788; d. at Weston, 3 Feb 1874; m. at Jamaica, VT, 13 May 1817, HANNAH HIGGINS, b. at Jamaica, 30 Mar 1798 daughter of Ichabod and Elizabeth (Young) Higgins; Hannah d. at Clarendon, VT, 30 Dec 1872.

v   ELIZABETH "BETSEY" PIERCE, b. estimate 1790. Betsey is reported as marrying Mr. Lockwood, but no further information has been located.

vi   LYDIA PIERCE; m. AARON BLANCHARD.[738] There are no clear records for this family. They may be the Aaron and Lydia who died at Norfolk, NY with burial in the Bixby Cemetery. Lydia Blanchard died there 3 Jan 1848.

vii   PHEBE PIERCE, b. 1793; d. at Weston, 4 Nov 1834.

viii   POLLY PIERCE, b. about 1795

ix   CALVIN PIERCE, b. about 1797

x   ROXANA PIERCE, b. 2 Jul 1801; d. at Weston, 17 May 1874; m. 15 Nov 1832, WILLIAM CAMPBELL, b. at Andover, VT, 16 Apr 1811 son of Hezekiah and Betsey (·) Campbell; William d. at Weston, 8 Nov 1859.

274)   ABIGAIL HOLT (*James Holt⁴, Nicholas Holt³, Mary Russell Holt², Robert¹*), b. at Andover, 18 Jun 1758 daughter of James and Sarah (Abbott) Holt; d. 2 Oct 1824; m. 7 Dec 1780, her fourth cousin, ISAAC CHANDLER, b. 4 Oct 1754 son of William and Rebecca (Lovejoy) Chandler; Isaac d. 12 Jan 1832. After Abigail's death, Isaac married Elizabeth Upton.

Isaac Chandler was a farmer and the family lived on the farm that had belonged to Abigail Holt's maternal grandfather Benjamin Abbott.[739] The property owned by Isaac Chandler is the site of 17 Hidden Road in Andover. The house on the property was built by David Hidden, a son-in-law of Isaac and Abigail Chandler.[740] The house was built in 1812 on Isaac's property and half the house was deeded to David Hidden in 1828. The house passed into the hands of the two children of David and Mary (Chandler) Hidden, Mary Elizabeth Hidden and David Isaac Chandler Hidden.

Isaac Chandler wrote his will 9 November 1831. Wife Elizabeth receives a bequest of $300 and is allowed all the household property that she brought to the marriage providing that Elizabeth quit claim and release the estate from her right of dower. Beloved granddaughter Sarah Ann Chandler receives $100 in addition to what she has already received. Beloved daughter Mary Hidden wife of David Hidden receives one-fourth part of the estate. Beloved daughter Abigail Chandler receives the remaining three-fourths of the estate. Captain Timothy Flagg was named sole executor. The real property of the estate was valued at $3,230.00 including the homestead valued at $2,200.00. The personal estate was valued at $96.33.[741]

Isaac and Abigail Chandler had five children born at Andover.

i   ABIGAIL CHANDLER, b. 13 Dec 1781; d. 20 Sep 1788.

ii   ISAAC CHANDLER, b. 11 Jun 1784; d. 28 Sep 1813; m. 7 Nov 1812, SALLY THOMPSON, b. at Wilmington, 18 Jul 1789 daughter of Benjamin and Susanna (Jaquith) Thompson; Sally d. at Wilmington, 19 Sep 1853.

iii   MARY CHANDLER, b. 5 Jun 1786; d. at Andover, 9 Sep 1855; m. 1 Jul 1816, DAVID HIDDEN, b. at Newbury, 21 Sep 1784 son of David and Susanna (Jaquith) Hidden; David d. at Andover, 5 Jun 1861.

---

[735] Pierce, *Pierce Genealogy*, p 104

[736] Littlefield, *Genealogies of the Early Settlers of Weston, p 306*

[737] Pierce, *Pierce Genealogy*, p 180. Mary is perhaps the daughter of Hugh Moncrief of Scotland who was in Salem, NY at this time. William Moncrief was also there, but his daughter Mary was Mary Safford.

[738] Littlefield, *Genealogies of Early Settlers of Weston*, p 306

[739] Chandler, *Descendants of William and Annis Chandler*, p 422

[740] "17 Hidden Road," https://preservation.mhl.org/17-hidden-road

[741] Essex County, MA: Probate File Papers, 1638-1881. Probate of Isaac Chandler, 21 Feb 1832, case number 4934.

iv   ABIGAIL CHANDLER, b. 3 Sep 1794; d. at Andover, 22 Oct 1866. Abigail did not marry. She lived with her sister Mary and her family. Abigail's estate was valued at $2,635.00 which included real estate valued at $485.00 and $2,150.00 in amounts that were due to the estate. In her will, Abigail made bequests of $150 to her niece Sarah Ann Crocker, $300 to niece Mary E. Hidden, and the remainder of the estate to her nephew David I. C. Hidden who was also named executor.

v   HANNAH CHANDLER, b. 10 Jan 1798; d. from fever 1 May 1807.

275)   SARAH HOLT (*James Holt[4], Nicholas Holt[3], Mary Russell Holt[2], Robert[1]*), b. at Andover, 7 Mar 1746/7 daughter of James and Sarah (Abbott) Holt; d. 11 Feb 1808; m. 6 Dec 1770, her third cousin, BARACHIAS ABBOTT, b. 22 May 1739 son of Barachias and Hannah (Holt) Abbott; Barachias d. 29 Jan 1812.
       Barachias and Sarah had their seven children in Andover, but then relocated to Wilton about 1786. Barachias owned property there which he previously cleared and established a farm. Barachias Abbot served as a selectman in Wilton 1791-1792.[742] One of the children died in infancy. The two daughters did not marry and remained in Wilton. Sons Timothy and Joel remained in Wilton, Timothy living with his father. Barachias, the oldest son, moved on to Landgrove, Vermont. Barachias and Sarah perhaps returned to Andover in their later years as both their deaths are recorded there, as well as the death of their son Timothy.

i   BARACHIAS ABBOTT, b. 20 Dec 1771; d. at Landgrove, VT, 23 Mar 1855; m. at Temple, NH, 18 Jan 1798, ANNA COLBURN, b. at Temple, 20 Feb 1777 daughter of Elias and Mehitable (Wheeler) Colburn. Anna d. at Landgrove, 1 May 1856.[743] There are twelve children recorded for this family.

ii   TIMOTHY ABBOTT, b. 30 Mar 1773; death recorded at Andover, 1 Jan 1837; m. at Montague, MA, 22 Sep 1801, MARY "POLLY" BANCROFT, b. about 1778 likely the daughter of Kendall and Susanna (Ewers) Bancroft;[744] Polly's death is recorded at Wilton, 13 Feb 1852. Polly was living with her son Henry in Chelmsford at the 1850 U.S. Census. Timothy and Polly had seven children. Son Henry married Caroline Abbott, Nancy Abbott from whom he was divorced,[745] and Harriet Robinson.

iii   JOEL ABBOTT, b. 29 Apr 1775; d. 7 May 1775

iv   JOEL ABBOTT, b. 10 Oct 1776; d. at Wilton, 26 Mar 1863; m. 24 Mar 1803, his third cousin once removed, JUDITH RAY BATCHELDER, b. 21 Jun 1779 daughter of Daniel and Rebecca (Abbott) Batchelder. Joel and Judith are the parents in Family 1072.

v   SARAH ABBOTT, b. 10 Oct 1779; d. at Wilton, 19 Oct 1858. Sarah did not marry. In the 1850 U.S. Census, Sarah was living in the household next to her brother Joel in Wilton but living on her own.

vi   JAMES ABBOTT, b. 30 Mar 1780; d. at Andover, 4 Oct 1858. m. 31 May 1806, MARY FOSTER, b. at Greenfield, NH, about 1784 perhaps the daughter of Isaac and Mary (Holt) Foster;[746] Mary d. at Andover 20 Feb 1862. Isaac Foster and Mary Holt are Family 868.

vii   ELIZABETH ABBOTT, b. 14 Sep 1784; d. at Wilton, 9 Apr 1854. Elizabeth did not marry.

276)   SARAH HOLT (*Nathan Holt[4], Nicholas Holt[3], Mary Russell Holt[2], Robert[1]*), b. at Danvers, 29 Oct 1758 daughter of Nathan and Sarah (Abbott) Holt; d. 17 Sep 1841; m. at Danvers, 2 Dec 1777, WILLIAM FROST, b. at New Castle, NH, 15 Nov 1754 son of William and Elizabeth (Prescott) Frost; William d. at Andover 28 Sep 1836. Sarah and William are second great grandparents of Robert Frost.
       William Frost served as a lieutenant in the Continental Army during the Revolution.[747] He was also deacon of the Congregational Church.[748]

---

[742] Livermore, *History of Wilton*
[743] The graves of Barachias and Anna are in the Old Landgrove Cemetery in Landgrove, VT; FIndagrave memorial ID 184633891
[744] Kendall Bancroft lived in Montague where he died in 1806. His will includes a daughter Mary, although the will does not give the last names of any of the children. One of the children of Timothy and Polly was named Kendall Bancroft Abbott.
[745] *New Hampshire, Marriage and Divorce Records, 1659-1947*, New England Historical Genealogical Society; New Hampshire Bureau of Vital Records, Concord, New Hampshire; New Hampshire, Marriage and Divorce Records, 1659–1947. Married in 1854 and divorced 1864
[746] There is a possibility that Mary Foster was the daughter of Isaac's first wife Mary Hartwell. All published genealogies say mother is Mary Holt who was the second wife. Isaac Foster married Mary Hartwell in 1779 and she died in 1781, and this may be too early of a birth date for Mary Foster, but there is no birth record for Mary Foster. This is offered as an option as Mary Foster and James Abbott named one of their sons Hartwell Barachias Abbott which would be a name that honored father's father and mother's mother.
[747] Compiled Service Records of Soldiers Who Served in the American Army During the Revolutionary War 1775-1785, accessed through fold3
[748] Frost, *The Nicholas Frost Family*, p 23

Sarah Holt and William Frost had twelve children all born at Andover.

i NATHAN HOLT FROST, b. 4 Sep 1778; d. 9 Jun 1784.

ii SALLY FROST, b. 28 Dec 1779; d. at Newburyport, 3 May 1863; m. at Andover, 16 Nov 1802, SAMUEL DRAKE, b. at Epping, about 1775 son of Simon and Judith (Perkins) Drake; Samuel d. at Newburyport, 27 Jun 1845.

iii BETSEY FROST, b. 21 Aug 1781; d. at Andover, 9 Aug 1819. Betsey did not marry.

iv WILLIAM FROST, b. 28 Mar 1783; d. 12 Apr 1784.

v DOROTHY CLIFFORD FROST, b. 1 Mar 1785; d. at Northwood, NH, 20 Apr 1822; m. at Andover, 7 Oct 1806, DUDLEY LEAVITT, b. about 1772 (based on age at death); Dudley d. at Northwood, 5 Feb 1838. After Dorothy's death, Dudley married her sister Mary.

vi MARY "POLLY" FROST, b. 18 Jan 1787; d. at Northwood, 17 Apr 1846; m. 5 Aug 1823, DUDLEY LEAVITT (see sister Dorothy).

vii NATHAN HOLT FROST, b. Jan 1789; d. at Rutherford County, TN, 19 Mar 1866;[749] m. at Charlotte County, VA, 20 Nov 1817, MARTHA HEWETT JOHNSON,[750] b. in Virginia about 1791; Martha d. at Rutherford County, 24 Oct 1873. Nathan attended Phillips Academy in Andover graduating in 1808.[751] He was a merchant who was in Virginia from about 1810 to 1826 and then relocated to Tennessee.

viii HARRIET HOLT FROST, b. 29 Mar 1791; d. at Andover, 11 Dec 1818; m. at Salem, 29 Aug 1814, ROBERT CROWELL, b. at Salem, 9 Dec 1787 son of Samuel and Lydia (Woodbury) Crowell; Robert d. at Essex, 10 Nov 1855. After Harriet's death, Robert married Hannah Choate.

ix WILLIAM FROST, b. 12 Jun 1793; d. at Andover, 28 Mar 1866; m. 1st, 11 Dec 1823, LUCY FOSTER, b. 17 Nov 1800 daughter of Charles and Lucy (Austin) Foster; Lucy d. 4 Nov 1838. William m. 2nd, 18 Mar 1840, MARY WOMSTEAD MEAD, b. 23 Apr 1804 daughter of Levi and Susannah (Hilton) Mead; Mary d. 11 Dec 1866.

x SAMUEL ABBOTT FROST, b. 11 Jun 1795; d. at Brentwood, NH, 11 Jan 1848; m. at Eden, ME, 10 Oct 1821, MARY "POLLY" BLUNT, b. at New Castle, NH, 28 Jun 1787 daughter of William and Mary (Fernald) Blunt; Mary d. 14 Jan 1875.

xi LUCY FROST, b. 28 Nov 1798; d. at Andover, 26 Feb 1842; m. at Leicester, MA, 23 Feb 1820, JOHN RICHARDSON, b. about 1789; John d. at Andover, 3 Oct 1841.

xii BENJAMIN PRESCOT FROST, b. 17 Nov 1800; d. at Andover, 25 Jun 1827.

277) MARY HOLT (*Nathan Holt⁴, Nicholas Holt³, Mary Russell Holt², Robert¹*), b. at Danvers, 3 Oct 1761 daughter of Nathan and Sarah (Abbott) Holt; d. at Beverly, 7 Jan 1850; m. 1 Nov 1781, ROBERT ENDICOTT, b. 29 Oct 1756 son of John and Elizabeth (Jacobs) Endicott; Robert d. at Beverly, 6 Mar 1819.

  Mary Holt married Robert Endicott a descendant of Governor John Endicott. They settled in Beverly where they had a family of seven children. The Endicott family was instrumental in the shipping industry in Salem and three of the sons of Robert and Mary were mariners.

  Son Robert Endicott went to sea at age 20,[752] and although he did not die at sea, he died at age 28 of "decline." Son Nathan Holt Endicott went to sea at age 16 and was chief mate when he died of fever aboard the ship *Glide* in Calcutta. A son-in-law, John Ellingwood, also died at sea. He was first officer of the ship *Bramin* when he died in the Bay of Bengal.[753]

  Third oldest son, Captain Samuel Endicott, was a shipmaster in command of the ship *George* for several years. The ship *George* was built in Salem in 1814 and was part of a large fleet of merchant vessels owned by Joseph Peabody. This ship made annual trips to Calcutta and the round trip took nearly a year. The average outbound trip was 115 days and the average return took 103 days.[754] After his seafaring days, Samuel was president of the bank in Beverly.

  Youngest son, William, lived to be 99 years 10 months old. He was a successful business owner having a mercantile and drug store at the corner of Cabot and Washington Streets in Beverly.[755]

  Robert and Mary Endicott had seven children born at Beverly.

---

[749] Year: 1860; Census Place: Murfreesboro, Rutherford, Tennessee; Roll: M653_1271; Page: 83; Family History Library Film: 805271
[750] Virginia, Compiled Marriages, 1740-1850
[751] Biographical catalogue of the trustees, teachers, and students of Phillips Academy, Andover, 1778-1830.
[752] Web: US, New England Seamen's Protection Certificate Index, 1796-1871
[753] Ancestry.com, U.S., Newspaper Extractions from the Northeast, 1704-1930
[754] Essex Institute, *Old-Time Ships of Salem*
[755] Hurd, *History of Essex County, Massachusetts*

i   MARY ENDICOTT, b. 29 Jul 1782; d. at Beverly, 8 Jan 1813; m. at Beverly, 18 Oct 1808, JOHN ELLINGWOOD, b. at Beverly, 20 Dec 1783 son of John and Hannah (Glover) Ellingwood; John d. aboard ship in Calcutta, 7 Nov 1816.

ii   ROBERT ENDICOTT, b. 5 May 1785; d. at Beverly, 29 Aug 1813 of "decline." Robert did not marry. He was a mariner.

iii   NATHAN HOLT ENDICOTT, b. 31 Jan 1788; d. aboard ship at the Bay of Bengal, 2 Jul 1816. Nathan did not marry. He died from a fever.

iv   Daughter, b. 7 Jun 1790 and d. 10 Jun 1790

v   SAMUEL ENDICOTT, b. 18 Jul 1793; d. at Beverly, 28 Jan 1872; m. 1st, 11 Jun 1820, his first cousin, HANNAH HOLT (descended from George Abbott by multiple lines; see Family 536), b. at Epping, NH, 4 May 1794 daughter of Peter and Hannah (Holt) Holt; Hannah d. 14 Mar 1825. Samuel m. 2nd, 21 May 1826, SARAH FARNUM HOLT, b. at Epping, 12 Feb 1809 daughter of Peter and Hannah (Holt) Holt; Sarah d. 23 Aug 1847. Samuel m. 3rd, 7 Jun 1852, MARY THORNDIKE LEECH, b. at Beverly, 3 Aug 1803 daughter of William and Ruth (Lee) Leech. Mary T. Leech had first married ship captain John Giddings. Mary d. 20 Dec 1881.

vi   Daughter, b. 7 Sep 1796 and d. 11 Sep 1796

vii   WILLIAM ENDICOTT, b. 11 Mar 1799; d. just two months before his 100th birthday on 8 Jan 1899; m. 26 Sep 1824, JOANNA LOVETT RANTOUL, b. at Beverly, 13 Jan 1803 daughter of Robert and Joanna (Lovett) Rantoul; Joanna d. 26 Jun 1863.[756]

278)   HANNAH HOLT (*Nathan Holt⁴, Nicholas Holt³, Mary Russell Holt², Robert¹*), b. at Danvers, 11 May 1769 daughter of Nathan and Sarah (Abbott) Holt; d. at Beverly 26 Jul 1857; m. 23 Jan 1793, her first cousin, PETER HOLT (*Joshua Holt⁴, Nicholas Holt³, Mary Russell Holt², Robert¹*), b. at Andover 12 Jun 1763 son of Joshua and Phebe (Farnum) Holt; Peter d. at Greenfield, NH, 25 Apr 1851.

        Reverend Peter Holt graduated from Harvard in 1790.[757] He was installed at the Presbyterian Church in Peterborough and Greenfield.[758]

        In his will written 26 November 1847 and proved 6 May 1851, Peter Holt bequeaths to beloved wife Hannah all his household furniture and all the farming tools to be at her own use and disposal. He notes that he has prospects of an inheritance from England, and if that occurs and it is a large amount, then he wishes for a reasonable amount of that sum to be divided among the families of his deceased brothers and the families of his deceased brothers-in-law. He also wishes that something be given to his daughter-in-law Henrietta Adams. The reside of the estate he bequeaths to his wife during her lifetime. Following that, the estate is to be divided equally between his beloved daughter Mary E. W. Holt and his beloved son-in-law Samuel Endicott.[759]

        Peter Holt and Hannah Holt were parents of seven children all born at Epping, New Hampshire.

i   HANNAH HOLT, b. 4 May 1794; d. at Beverly, MA, 14 Mar 1825; m. at Beverly, 11 Jun 1820, her first cousin, SAMUEL ENDICOTT, b. at Beverly, 18 Jul 1793 son of Robert and Mary (Holt) Endicott; Samuel d. at Beverly, 28 Jan 1872.

ii   NATHAN HOLT, b. 16 Aug 1795; d. 23 Jul 1807.

iii   PETER HOLT, b. 20 Feb 1802; d. 16 Jul 1817.

iv   JEREMIAH HOLT, b. 5 Sep 1803; d. 20 Nov 1817.

v   JOSHUA HOLT, b. 9 Mar 1805; married at unknown date, Henrietta about whom nothing else in known at this time. Henrietta is the daughter-in-law Henrietta Adams referred to in Peter Holt's will.

vi   SARAH FARNUM HOLT, b. 12 Feb 1809; d. at Beverly, 23 Aug 1847; m. 21 May 1826, SAMUEL ENDICOTT (refer to sister Hannah above).

vii   MARY E. W. HOLT, b. 27 May 1812; d. at Beverly, 19 Aug 1887. Mary did not marry.

---

[756] Joanna Endicott's death is recorded in the Beverly records but noted as occurring in St. Louis.
[757] Quinquennial Catalogue of the Officers and Graduates of Harvard University
[758] The Quarterly Christian Spectator, volume 1, 1827, p 336
[759] New Hampshire, County Probate Records, 1660-1973, Hillsborough, 57:213, will of Peter Holt

279)   JAMES HOLT (*Nathan Holt⁴, Nicholas Holt³, Mary Russell Holt², Robert¹*), b. at Danvers, 1772 son of Nathan and Sarah (Abbott) Holt; d. in India, Aug 1807;[760] m. 30 Aug 1796, LUCY WHIPPLE, b. 8 Mar 1778; Lucy d. at Danvers, 6 Mar 1839. Although James's death is reported as August 1807, the probate of his estate was April 1807.

James Holt was a seaman who died on a voyage to India leaving a widow with three small children. Lucy Holt was administratrix of his estate which entered probate 20 April 1807. The value of the personal estate was $61.65. After expenses of the estate, the allowance to Lucy was $45.65.[761]

James Holt and Lucy Whipple were parents of four children born at Danvers.

i   JAMES HOLT, b. 25 Feb 1797; d. at Danvers, 12 Nov 1856; m. 6 Apr 1819, MERCY SMITH, b. at Danvers, 9 Oct 1796 daughter of Israel and Margaret (-) Smith (mother was the widow Margaret Standly); Mercy d. at Danvers, 6 Nov 1856.

ii   STEPHEN HOLT, b. 24 Jan 1799; d. 2 Oct 1800.

iii   LUCY ANN HOLT, b. 29 Aug 1801; d. at Danvers, 28 Sep 1829; m. at Danvers, 15 May 1823, GILMAN PARKER, b. at Topsfield, 19 Sep 1802 son of Edmund and Jane (Pingrey) Parker; Gilman d. 3 Jun 1866. After Lucy's death, Gilman married Abigail Welch.

iv   LYDIA HOLT, b. 27 Jan 1804; d. at Danvers, 3 Apr 1889; m. at Danvers, 28 Dec 1824, SAMUEL HARRIS, b. at Ipswich, 3 Apr 1799 son of Daniel and Sarah (Emmons) Harris; Daniel d. at Danvers, 7 Dec 1877.

279a)   THOMAS HOLT (*Dorcas Holt Holt⁴, Nicholas Holt³, Mary Russell Holt², Robert¹*), b. at Andover, 15 Jun 1750 son of Thomas and Dorcas (Holt) Holt; d. after 1794 when living at Lyndeborough; m. 27 Oct 1774, his second cousin, LYDIA FARNUM, b. 10 Nov 1756 daughter of Thomas and Lydia (Abbott) Farnum.

Thomas and Lydia married in Andover and baptisms of three children are recorded there. The family was then in Amherst, New Hampshire. In 1779, Thomas Holt of Andover purchased property in Amherst from Isaac and Hannah Holt of Andover. Thomas and Lydia sold their property in Amherst in 1793 and 1794 and were of Lyndeborough in 1794 when they sold the last of their property in Amherst. They perhaps were next in Greenfield, but that is not known.[762]

Thomas Holt's household was six persons in Amherst in 1790: two males 16 and over, one male under 16, and three females.[763] Three children were identified for Thomas Holt and Lydia Farnum

i   STEPHEN HOLT, baptized at Andover, 27 Apr 1777

ii   LYDIA HOLT, baptized at Andover, 12 Jul 1778; d. at Greenfield, NH, 25 Nov 1869; m. at Lyndeborough, 30 Apr 1793, JOHN SAVAGE, b. at Marblehead, MA, 13 Sep 1771 son of John and Mary (Jackson) Savage; John d. at Greenfield, 5 Oct 1850.

iii   PHEBE HOLT, baptized 11 Jun 1780; *perhaps* m. at Andover, 15 Mar 1805, SAMUEL EATON, b. at Reading, 17 Oct 1782 son of Samuel Phillips and Sarah (Evans) Eaton; Samuel d. at Lynn, 14 Nov 1871.

280)   DORCAS HOLT (*Dorcas Holt Holt⁴, Nicholas Holt³, Mary Russell Holt², Robert¹*), b. at Andover, 19 Mar 1753 daughter of Thomas and Dorcas (Holt) Holt; m. 25 Nov 1773, her third cousin, MOSES LOVEJOY, b. 9 Sep 1751 son of Daniel and Mary (Holt) Lovejoy; Moses d. at Wilton, 19 Mar 1807.

Moses Lovejoy served in the Revolution in Nichols Regiment of militia in New Hampshire. He enlisted 29 September 1777 and was discharged 25 October 1777. This unit joined the northern Continental Army at Saratoga.[764]

Moses and Dorcas were parents of six children born at Wilton.

i   MOSES LOVEJOY, b. Feb 1776; died young

[760] James, h. Lucy (Whipple), at India, Aug. —, 1807.

[761] Essex County, MA: Probate File Papers, 1638-1881.Online database. AmericanAncestors.org. New England Historic Genealogical Society, 2014. Case 13651

[762] New Hampshire Land Records, Hillsborough County, 8:179, 30:450, 30:452, 35:272

[763] Year: 1790; Census Place: Amherst, Hillsborough, New Hampshire; Series: M637; Roll: 5; Page: 227; Image: 144; Family History Library Film: 0568145

[764] Compiled Service Records of Soldiers Who Served in the American Army During the Revolutionary War

ii   MOSES LOVEJOY, b. at Wilton, 29 Mar 1778; d. at Wilton, 13 Nov 1846; m. at Mason, 6 Nov 1807, NANCY
         TARBELL, b. at Mason, NH, 4 Jun 1786 daughter of Samuel and Anne (Heldrick) Tarbell;[765] Nancy d. at Mason,
         NH, 16 Oct 1851.

iii   DORCAS LOVEJOY, b. 30 May 1780; d. at Wilton, 8 Jul 1858. Dorcas did not marry.

iv   HENRY LOVEJOY, b. at Wilton, 14 May 1782; d. at Weston, VT, 15 May 1848; m. 1st, about 1807, BETSEY
         PEASE, b. at Weston, 31 Oct 1788 daughter of Augustus and Tirzah (Hall) Pease; Betsey d. 16 Jan 1819. Henry
         m. 2nd, 2 Dec 1819, SALLY AUSTIN, b. at Weston, 11 Jun 1798 daughter of David and Dorcas (Barker) Austin;
         Sally d. at Weston, 17 Jul 1868.

v   EZEKIEL LOVEJOY, b. at Wilton, 14 Nov 1784; d. at Weston, VT, 30 Jan 1840; m. at Wilton, 15 Feb 1810,
         EUNICE GAGE, b. at Pelham, NH, 7 Apr 1786 daughter of Pierce and Eunice (Eaton) Gage;[766] Eunice d. at
         Weston, 7 Aug 1872.

vi   HANNAH LOVEJOY, b. at Wilton, 22 Jun 1787; d. at Weld, ME, 5 Nov 1843; m. about 1815, STEPHEN HOLT,
         b. at Andover, 11 Apr 1786 son of William and Elizabeth (Jones) Holt; Stephen d. at Weld, 7 Dec 1855. After
         Hannah's death, Stephen married Phebe Douglas.

281)   LOIS HOLT (*Dorcas Holt Holt⁴, Nicholas Holt³, Mary Russell Holt², Robert¹*), b. at Andover, 29 Oct 1760 daughter of
Thomas and Dorcas (Holt) Holt; d. at Andover, 17 Apr 1852; m. 4 Jan 1785, MOSES PEARSON, b. at Wilmington, 6 Nov 1750
son of Nathan and Mary (Wilson) Pearson; Moses d. recorded at Andover 11 Aug 1836 (1835).[767] Moses Pearson was first
married to Hephzibah Jones.
         Moses Pearson served in the Revolution as a private first enlisting in September 1776 in the militia company of
Captain Putnam of Wilton, New Hampshire. In his pension application, Moses reported he was living in Amherst, New
Hampshire at the time of his enlistment. He saw service at White Plains, New York. He had another enlistment for nine months
in 1778 and marched to Fishkill for two months and was later in Hampstead, Connecticut. The total period of service was
credited at twelve months. Moses and later his widow Lois received a pension related to his service.[768]
         Moses and Lois lived in Wilmington (although their deaths are recorded in Andover) and they were parents of nine
children all born at Wilmington.

i   THOMAS PEARSON, b. 28 Oct 1785; d. at Haverhill, 1 Aug 1863; m. at Andover, 24 Nov 1811, LUCY TROW, b.
         at Beverly, 1786 daughter of John and Hannah (Dodge) Trow; Lucy d. at Haverhill, about 1863.

ii   NATHAN PEARSON, b. 20 Aug 1787; d. at Wilmington, 20 Feb 1855; m. LYDIA ANN HOWE.

iii   HEPHZIBAH PEARSON, b. 28 Mar 1790; d. at North Andover, 29 Aug 1880; m. at Wilmington, 30 Nov 1815,
         WILLIAM TUCKER, b. at Wilmington, 10 Aug 1789 son of William and Hannah (Holt) Tucker; William d. 26 Mar
         1861.

iv   JOSEPH J. PEARSON, b. 5 Sep 1792; d. at Andover, 15 Jul 1841; m. at Andover, 23 Oct 1814, SARAH FOSTER,
         b. at Ashby, about 1790; Sarah d. at Andover, 11 Feb 1853.

v   ABIEL PEARSON, b. 8 Jun 1795; d. at Wilmington, 9 Nov 1851; m. at Reading, 18 Apr 1822, JERUSHA
         DAMON, b. about 1804 perhaps the daughter of Edmund and Lucy (Flint) Damon; Lucy d. at Andover, 21 Feb
         1884.

vi   JABEZ PEARSON, b. 1 Aug 1797; d. at Boston, 28 Apr 1850; m. at Andover, 15 Sep 1823, OLIVE P. TUCKER.

vii   JAMES PEARSON, b. 21 Dec 1799. Nothing further certain is known, but it is possible he was the James Pearson
         who married ELIZA ANN BRADLEY in Boston 6 Dec 1827. James's brother Jabez was in Boston. This is
         speculation at this point. If so, James died in Boston in 1836 (probate May 1836) leaving two sons, James Bradley
         Pearson and Joel F. Pearson.

viii   AMOS PEARSON, b. 5 oct 1802; d. at Haverhill, MA, 3 Jul 1866; m. at Boston, 13 Feb 1836, ANNIS TROW, b. at
         Andover, 10 May 1800 daughter of Dudley and Annis (Johnson) Trow; Annis d. at Medford, 20 Apr 1873.

ix   KENDALL PEARSON, b. 30 Jan 1805; d. recorded at Andover, 16 May 1824.

---

[765] The 1824 will of Samuel Tarbell includes a bequest to his daughter Nancy Lovejoy.
[766] Gage, *A Record of Pierce Gage and His Descendants*, p 17
[767] The transcription of the death record says 1835 but the pension application and the gravestone say 1836.
[768] U.S., Revolutionary War Pension and Bounty-Land Warrant Application Files, 1800-1900

282)   WILLIAM HOLT (*Dorcas Holt Holt⁴, Nicholas Holt³, Mary Russell Holt², Robert¹*), b. at Andover, 7 Sep 1763 son of Thomas and Dorcas (Holt) Holt; d. at Wilton, 23 Dec 1810; m. 29 Jul 1784, ELIZABETH JONES, b. at Andover, about 1763 daughter of Jacob and Mary (Winn) Jones;[769][770] Elizabeth d. at Weld, ME, 1829.

William Holt and Elizabeth Jones were parents of eight children, the oldest six at Andover and youngest two at Wilton, New Hampshire.

i   JACOB HOLT, b. 13 Dec 1784; d. by suicide in Boston Harbor, Dec 1817; m. at Beverly, 19 Oct 1806, HANNAH RAYMOND, b. at Beverly, 19 Mar 1781 daughter of David and Hannah (Giles) Raymond. Jacob was a sea captain. He committed suicide by jumping into Boston Harbor.[771]

ii   STEPHEN HOLT, b. 11 Apr 1786; d. at Weld, ME, 7 Dec 1855; m. 1ˢᵗ, about 1815, his first cousin, HANNAH LOVEJOY (*Dorcas Holt Lovejoy⁵, Thomas Holt⁴, Thomas Holt³, Mary Russell Holt², Robert¹*), b. at Wilton 22 Jun 1787 daughter of Moses and Dorcas (Holt) Lovejoy; Hannah d. at Weld, 5 Nov 1843. Stephen m. 2ⁿᵈ, about 1846, PHEBE DOUGLAS. Hannah Lovejoy is a child in Family 862.

iii   WILLIAM HOLT, b. 6 Mar 1788; d. at sea, 22 Oct 1820; m. 28 Nov 1812, LUCY WOODBURY, b. at Beverly, 31 May 1789 daughter of Thomas and Jane (Homan) Woodbury; Lucy d. at Beverly, 19 Aug 1870. William was master of a ship out of Beverly and died while on voyage.

iv   ELIZABETH HOLT, b. 12 Mar 1790; d. Mar 1797.

v   JOSEPH HOLT, b. 28 Jan 1792; d. at Wilton, 20 Jun 1864; m. at Wilton, 31 Jan 1813, BETSEY SMITH, b. at Wilton, 9 Jan 1791 daughter of Uriah and Lydia (Keyes) Smith; Betsey d. at Wilton, 8 Sep 1869.

vi   ASA HOLT, b. 5 May 1794; d. at Weld, ME, 12 Jul 1825; m. at Brattleboro, VT, 24 Jul 1822, SYBIL BUTTERFIELD, b. at Brattleboro, 5 Apr 1792 daughter of Benjamin and Lois (Herrick) Butterfield; Sybil d. at Weld, 22 Dec 1830. After Asa's death Sybil married Joshua Eaton.

vii   ELIZABETH HOLT, b. about 1798; d. at Weld, ME, 23 Mar 1867; m. at Andover, MA, 16 Feb 1818, BENJAMIN HOUGHTON, b. about 1790; Benjamin d. at Weld, 6 Mar 1882.

viii   NATHAN HOLT, b. about 1801; d. at Weld, ME, after 1880; m. Nov 1824, PHEBE SEVERY, b. in ME, 5 Dec 1803 daughter of Aaron and Phebe (Tucker) Severy; Phebe d. 16 Nov 1884.

283)   JOSEPH HOLT (*Dorcas Holt Holt⁴, Nicholas Holt³, Mary Russell Holt², Robert¹*), b. at Andover, 29 Sep 1766 son of Thomas and Dorcas (Holt) Holt; d. at Andover, 8 Jun 1791; m. 27 Nov 1788, his third cousin once removed, ABIGAIL HOLT, b. 19 May 1767 daughter of Samuel and Abigail (Blanchard) Holt; Abigail d. 13 May 1821.

Joseph Holt died at the young age 24 of nervous fever.[772] Joseph and Abigail had two children at Andover, the younger child born after Joseph's death.

i   JOSEPH HOLT, b. 20 Jan 1790; d. at Andover, 4 Jul 1866; m. 18 Oct 1821, ELIZABETH BRADDOCK, b. in ME, 1792 daughter of John Braddock; Elizabeth d. at Andover, 3 Dec 1875.

ii   SAMUEL HOLT, b. 24 Sep 1791; d. 1 Apr 1802.

284)   DANIEL HOLT (*Thomas Holt⁴, Thomas Holt³, Mary Russell Holt², Robert¹*), b. at Andover, 11 Sep 1740 son of Thomas and Hannah (Kimball) Holt; m. at Andover, 3 Dec 1761, his first cousin, ALICE HOLT (*Lydia Holt Holt⁴, Thomas Holt³, Mary Russell Holt², Robert¹*), b. at Andover, 13 Nov 1742 daughter of Benjamin and Lydia (Holt) Holt; Alice d. at Morrisville, NY, 7 Mar 1826.

Daniel and Alice Holt had their six children in Lunenburg, but they were then in Wilton, New Hampshire. Daniel served in the Revolution beginning in 1777 and was present at the Battle of Bennington. He was in a unit from New Hampshire that joined the Continental army in Rhode Island. He had another enlistment from Wilton on 13 July 1779 and was stationed at West Point. He had a further three-year enlistment on 27 February 1781. Following the war, Daniel and Alice moved to Packersfield (Nelson) and were there until about 1809. Their final move was to Madison County, New York.[773]

Alice and Daniel Holt were parents of six children born at Lunenburg.

---

[769] A birth record was not located for Elizabeth, but the will of Jacob Jones includes a bequest to his daughter Betty.

[770] Bartlett, *Hugh Jones of Salem*, p 18

[771] Newspaper Extractions from the Northeast, 1704-1930

[772] Joseph, jr., nervous fever, bur. June 8, 1791, a. 24 y. 9 m. CR2

[773] Nelson Picnic Association, *Celebration of the Town of Nelson*, p 92

i   HANNAH HOLT, b. 15 Feb 1763

ii   THOMAS HOLT, b. 25 Nov 1764; d. at Morrisville, NY, 14 Mar 1847; m. at Westford, MA, 26 Jan 1785; POLLY BEVINS, b. 1762; Polly d. at Morrisville, 2 Oct 1840.

iii   LYDIA HOLT, b. 29 Aug 1767

iv   ENOCH HOLT, b. 15 Aug 1770

v   LOIS HOLT, b. 19 Sep 1772; d. at Morrisville, NY, 28 May 1826; m. at Nelson, NH, 24 Oct 1793, ABIATHAR GATES, b. at Bolton, MA, 20 Aug 1769 son of Cyrus and Ruth (Bruce) Gates.

vi   DORCAS HOLT, baptized 17 Dec 1775; d. at Hanover, NY, 7 May 1850; m. at Andover, MA, 17 Apr 1796, her fourth cousin once removed, DANIEL FARNUM, b. at Andover, 13 Apr 1770 son of Daniel and Lydia (Porter) Farnum; Daniel d. at Hanover, NY, 25 Nov 1847.

285)   ASA HOLT (*Thomas Holt⁴, Thomas Holt³, Mary Russell Holt², Robert¹*), b. at Andover, 3 May 1742 son of Thomas and Hannah (Kimball) Holt; d. at Andover, 20 Feb 1793; m. 1st 10 Sep 1765, his third cousin, DINAH HOLT, b. at Andover, 6 Nov 1744 daughter of Samuel and Jemima (Gray) Holt; Dinah d. at Andover, 20 Nov 1780. Asa m. 2nd at Andover, 5 Jul 1781, LYDIA STEVENS, b. at Andover, 15 Nov 1753 daughter of Jonathan and Lydia (Felch) Stevens.

     Asa Holt did not leave a will and his estate entered probate 12 April 1793 with widow Lydia as administratrix. Real estate was valued at £363.10 and personal estate at £163.7.7. Charges against the estate, including an allowance to the widow, were £125.8.0.[774]

     Son Abiel Holt married but did not have children. In his will written 14 March 1801, he bequeathed to his honored mother-in-law Molly Jones wife of Jacob Jones all the pewter and bedding items that his deceased wife brought to the marriage. He bequeathed to sister Hannah wife of William Tucker all the household stuff and furniture. Brother Asa Holt and brother-in-law William Tucker receive all the real estate and personal estate to equally divide. Brother Stephen Holt receives two hundred and fifty dollars. William Tucker was named executor.[775]

     Son Stephen Holt was a cabinetmaker who relocated to New York in 1808 and opened a boarding house on the corner of Front Street between Fulton Street and the Burling Slip. After some years as the proprietor there, he set about building the six-story Holt's Hotel, later known as United States Hotel, on Fulton Street from Pearl Street to Water Street. The hotel, constructed of white marble, opened 3 January 1833.[776]

     Dinah Holt and Asa Holt were parents of three children.

i   HANNAH HOLT, b. at Andover, 20 Jun 1766; d. at Andover, 3 Mar 1852; m. 23 Oct 1788, WILLIAM TUCKER, b. at Wilmington, MA, 21 Mar 1761 son of David and Martha (Mooar) Tucker; William d. at Andover, 29 Aug 1848.

ii   ASA HOLT, b. at Andover, 26 Mar 1768; m. at Wilmington, 9 Aug 1796, ABIGAIL GRIFFIN, b. at Andover, 7 Oct 1764 daughter of James and Phebe (Abbott) Griffin; Abigail d. at Middleton, 28 Jan 1859.

iii   ABIEL HOLT, b. at Andover, 23 Nov 1773; d. of consumption, at Andover, 11 Apr 1801; m. 25 Aug 1793, PHEBE JONES, b. 1774 daughter of Jacob and Mary (Winn) Jones; Phebe d. at Andover, 20 Feb 1798.

     Asa Holt and Lydia Stevens were parents of one child.

i   STEPHEN HOLT, b. at Andover, 26 May 1782; d. at Manhattan, Sep 1852; m. 20 Mar 1803, MARY POTTER BROWN, b. 1780 daughter of Stephen and Elizabeth (Potter) Brown; Mary d. at Manhattan, 12 Apr 1853.

286)   MEHITABLE HOLT (*Thomas Holt⁴, Thomas Holt³, Mary Russell Holt², Robert¹*), b. at Andover, 8 Feb 1743/4 daughter of Thomas and Hannah (Kimball) Holt; d. at Hillsborough, 20 Oct 1816; m. 1st 28 May 1761, SAMUEL LUFKIN son of Samuel Lufkin; Samuel d. 30 Apr 1777. Mehitable m. 2nd at Andover, 14 Jul 1785, ABNER WILKINS, b. 1 Jul 1743; Abner d. at Middleton, 17 Aug 1820. Abner was first married to Eunice Smith.

     Mehitable Holt and Samuel Lufkin were parents of five children for whom there are records. There may be a sixth child who died before 1779. The birth dates and locations are uncertain. Mehitable had all her children baptized at Andover on 23 May 1779.

---

[774] *Essex County, MA: Probate File Papers, 1638-1881.* Online database. *AmericanAncestors.org.* New England Historic Genealogical Society, 2014. Case 13622

[775] *Essex County, MA: Probate File Papers, 1638-1881.* Online database. *AmericanAncestors.org.* New England Historic Genealogical Society, 2014. Case 13615

[776] Enton, James V., "An Old Street of New York," The American Historical Magazine, volume 3, p 70ff

i   SAMUEL LUFKIN, b. 25 Mar 1762; d. at Acworth, NH, 30 Jul 1838; m. at Billerica, 19 Dec 1786, SARAH LIVINGSTON, b. at Billerica, 18 Feb 1766 daughter of Seth and Mary (Sprague) Livingston; Sarah d. at Acworth, 15 Jul 1849.

ii   MEHITABLE LUFKIN, b. at Chelmsford, 1767; d.at Jaffrey, NH, 24 Feb 1804; m. at Amherst, NH, 16 Jul 1787, JACOB DANFORTH, b. at Billerica, 27 Feb 1766 son of David and Joanna (Shed) Danforth; Jacob d. at Amherst, 15 Nov 1851.

iii   SARAH LUFKIN, b. about 1769; d. at Hillsborough, 26 Jan 1848; m. at Amherst, NH, 31 Aug 1790, GEORGE DASCOMB, b. at Northfield, MA, 16 Oct 1764 son of James and Elizabeth (Farrington) Dascomb; George d. at Hillsborough, 21 Jun 1842.

iv   JONATHAN LUFKIN, b. about 1774; m. Mar 1801, JANE DAVIDSON

v   DORCAS LUFKIN, b. 1776; d. at Hillsborough, 26 Apr 1848; m. at Andover, 14 Mar 1793, her fourth cousin, EBENEZER FLINT (*Asenath Holt Flint⁴, Phebe Russell Holt³, John², Robert¹*), b. at Reading, MA, 13 May 1765 son of Ebenezer and Asenath (Holt) Flint; Ebenezer d. at Hillsborough, 14 Mar 1833. Dorcas Lufkin and Ebenezer Flint are Family 875.

287)   ABIEL HOLT (*Thomas Holt⁴, Thomas Holt³, Mary Russell Holt², Robert¹*), b. at Andover, 3 Apr 1746 son of Thomas and Hannah (Kimball) Holt; d. at Andover, 17 Nov 1824; m. 23 Jun 1767, his third cousin once removed (through Holt line), LYDIA LOVEJOY, b. at Andover, 21 Jul 1747 daughter of Joshua and Lydea (Abbott) Lovejoy; Lydia d. at Haverhill, 3 Jan 1838.

     Abiel Holt served in the Revolution as a private in Colonel Tupper's Regiment of the Massachusetts line. He received a pension related to his service. An inventory of his estate related to his pension conducted in 1820 found that he had no real estate and had personal property valued at $26.59. Abiel was then seventy-six years old and a laborer, although he reported recent palsy rendered him unable to go out. Living in the home was his wife age 73, daughter Hannah age 28, and a grandchild age 6 years, "a sickly feeble race totally unable to support themselves, they have been assisted by the town for the last six years."[777]

     Lydia Lovejoy and Abiel Holt were the parents of nine children all born at Andover.

i   CHLOE HOLT, baptized 10 Apr 1768; d. at Norway, ME, 11 Oct 1849; m. 24 May 1785, DARIUS HOLT, b. at Andover, 6 Mar 1765 son of David and Hannah (Martin) Holt; d. at Norway, 3 Jul 1854.

ii   ABIEL HOLT, baptized 10 Jan 1770; d. at Milford, NH, 11 Feb 1834; m. 1792, his fourth cousin, ELIZABETH HOLT, b. at Wilton, 5 Apr 1772 daughter of Daniel and Mehitable (Putnam) Holt; Elizabeth d. at Milford, 20 Oct 1854.

iii   HANNAH HOLT, baptized 19 Jan 1772; d. 18 Sep 1775.

iv   SIMEON KIMBALL HOLT, b. about 1774; d. 23 Sep 1775.

v   NATHAN KIMBALL HOLT, baptized 30 Aug 1778; d. at Boscawen, NH, 10 Nov 1836; m. at Andover, 1 Apr 1800, his third cousin once removed, REBECCA HOLT, b. at Andover, 25 Aug 1776 daughter of David and Rebecca (Osgood) Holt.

vi   DANIEL HOLT, baptized 30 Sep 1781; d. at Norway, ME, 15 Sep 1851; m. 1802, MARY "POLLY" HALE, b. in MA, about 1783 daughter of Israel and Esther (Taylor) Hale;[778] Polly d. at Norway, 4 Nov 1851.

vii   JONATHAN LOVEJOY HOLT, b. Jul 1784; d. at Haverhill, MA, 12 Apr 1848; m. at Andover, 9 May 1808, JANE KIMBALL, b. at Andover, 25 Jul 1789 daughter of Moses and Jane (Gordon) Kimball; Jane d. at Lowell, 20 Aug 1861.

viii   THOMAS HOLT, b. 15 Jan 1790; d. at Andover, after 1858; m. 1812, RUTH BEARD, b. at Wilmington, MA, about 1789 daughter of Jacob and Anna (Evans) Beard; Ruth d. at Andover, 1 Sep 1858.

ix   HANNAH KIMBALL HOLT, b. 4 Jun 1792; d at Lowell, 2 Apr 1842. Hannah did not marry.

---

[777] Revolutionary War Pension and Bounty-Land Warrant Application Files, 1800-1900
[778] The 1841 will of Israel Hale includes a bequest to his daughter Polly Holt.

288)   PHEBE HOLT (*Joshua Holt⁴, Nicholas Holt³, Mary Russell Holt², Robert¹*), b. at Andover, 28 Nov 1756 daughter of Joshua and Phebe (Farnum) Holt; d. at Greenfield, 1849; m. 11 Dec 1778, JOSEPH BATCHELDER, b. 6 Mar 1748 son of Joseph and Judith (Rea) Batchelder; Joseph d. 1826.

     This family started in Andover, were in Lyndeborough where at least one child was born, and were in Greenfield by about 1786. Joseph was a deacon in Greenfield. Phebe Holt and Joseph Batchelder were parents of ten children.[779]

i   ANNA CARLTON BATCHELDER, b. at Andover, 2 Apr 1781; d. after 1850 when she and Hezekiah were living in Lyndeborough; m. 25 Feb 1813, HEZEKIAH DUNKLEE, b. at Greenfield, 16 Feb 1784 son of Hezekiah and Mehitable (White) Duncklee; Hexekiah d. at Francestown, 16 Nov 1863.

ii   PHEBE BATCHELDER, b. at Lyndeborough, 2 Nov 1782; d. at Mont Vernon, NH, 20 Feb 1866; m. Apr 1820, WILLIAM RICHARDSON, b. at Billerica, MA, 20 Aug 1778 son of Jacob and Sarah (Brown) Richardson; William d. at Mont Vernon, 16 Mar 1863.

iii   FANNY BATCHELDER, b. 30 Aug 1784

iv   JOSEPH BATCHELDER, b. 13 Mar 1786; d. at Peoria, IL, 27 Nov 1849; m. 1ˢᵗ, at Athol, MA, 20 May 1819, MARY TILESTON HUMPHREY, b. at Athol, 5 Jul 1795 daughter of John and Hannah (Brinton) Humphrey; Mary d. at Athol, 20 Aug 1825. Joseph m. 2ⁿᵈ, 5 Jan 1832, RACHEL STONE, b. at Jericho, NY, 26 Sep 1796 daughter of William and Tamson (Graves) Stone;[780] Rachel d. at Peoria, 22 Aug 1842.

v   CHLOE BATCHELDER, b. at Greenfield, 22 Feb 1788; d. at Tioga, NY, after 1870; m. 30 Mar 1817, MOSES CARLETON, b. at Lyndeborough, 7 Sep 1792 son of Jeremiah and Lois (Hoyt) Carleton; Moses d. at Tioga, after 1860.

vi   BETSEY BATCHELDER, b. 29 May 1789; d. at Greenwood, NY, 4 Aug 1856; m. 30 Dec 1813, JOHN JOHNSON HOLT, b. at Wilton, 21 Jul 1787 son of Simeon and Mary (Dale) Holt; John d. at Jasper, NY, after 1870.

vii   JOHN BATCHELDER, b. 7 May 1791; d. 27 May 1792.

viii   PERSIS BATCHELDER, b. 6 May 1793

ix   JUDITH BATCHELDER, b. 19 May 1795

x   LUCY BATCHELDER, b. 3 Jul 1797

289)   JOSHUA HOLT (*Joshua Holt⁴, Nicholas Holt³, Mary Russell Holt², Robert¹*), b. at Andover, 17 Jan 1758 son of Joshua and Phebe (Farnum) Holt; d at Greenfield, 14 Mar 1835; m. 31 Oct 1782,[781] HANNAH INGALLS, b. 20 Feb 1759 daughter of David and Priscilla (Howe) Ingalls; Hannah d. 1 Dec 1838.

     Joshua served in the Revolutionary War. After the war, he settled in New Hampshire in the area later known as Greenfield on land his father had purchased prior to 1780.[782][783] He received a pension of thirty-six dollars per year for his war service.[784]

     In his will dated 13 March 1835, left five dollars each to his children Joshua, Farnum, Hannah Balch, and Mary. His son Herman, who "has been absent for many years," also receives five dollars whenever he returns. All the remainder of the estate is bequeathed to his beloved wife Hannah and it is to be at her entire use and disposal. Executors of the estate are Hannah and Joshua's brother Stephen Holt.[785]

     Hannah Ingalls Holt did not leave a will. Her estate was probated in 1839 when Stephen Holt petitioned to be administrator as her "several children" had not stepped forward to administer the estate. The total value of her estate was $1722 which included real estate valued at $850 being one undivided half of the old Holt farm consisting of 170 acres and buildings.[786]

     Joshua Holt and Hannah Ingalls had six children born at Greenfield.

[779] Pierce, Batchelder Genealogy, p 410
[780] Stone, The Family of John Stone, p 27 (This genealogy was written by William Leete Stone who was Rachel's brother.)
[781] This is the marriage date given by Hannah in her widow's pension application.
[782] Durrie, Holt Genealogy, p 44
[783] Hurd, *History of Hillsborough County, NH*, p 344
[784] Revolutionary War Pension and Bounty-Land Warrant Application Files, fold3
[785] New Hampshire, County Probate Records, 1660-1973, Hillsborough, 41:65, 37:255, 41:116, 41:285, Probate of Joshua Holt
[786] New Hampshire, County Probate Records, 1660-1973, Hillsborough, 44:66, 43:499, 27:385, 46:212, probate of Hannah Holt

i   JOSHUA HOLT, b. 13 Jun 1788; d. at Roseville Park, IA, 21 Jun 1848;[787] m. at Antrim, 11 May 1815, ISABELLA READ NESMITH, b. at Antrim, 16 Oct 1784 daughter of James and Elizabeth (Brewster) Nesmith; Isabella d. at Indianapolis, after 1850. Joshua graduated from Dartmouth in 1814 and was a teacher in Harrisburg, PA and later in Indianapolis.[788] Durrie's Holt genealogy describes him as having superior intellect "but intemperance wrought his ruin."[789]

ii   FARNUM HOLT, b. 15 Apr 1791; d. at Greenfield, 27 Feb 1865; m. 14 Jun 1816, his fourth cousin, LUCY CUMMINGS PEAVEY (*Peter Peavey⁵, Dorcas Holt Peavey⁴, David Holt³, Hannah Russell Holt², Robert¹*), b. at Greenfield, 3 Jul 1792 daughter of Peter and Lucy (Cummings) Peavey; Lucy d. at Milford, 13 Feb 1874. Lucy is a child in Family 1790.

iii   NATHAN HOLT, b. and d. 1792 at age 11 weeks.

iv   HERMAN HOLT, b. 4 Apr 1793. According to the Holt genealogy, he went to Mississippi. No records were located for him and he does not show up in any census records.

v   HANNAH HOLT, b. 3 May 1796; d, at Francestown, 7 Oct 1856; m. about 1832, as his second wife, MASON BALCH, b. at Francestown, 23 Oct 1800 son of Isiah and Elizabeth (Epps) Balch; Mason d. at Greenfield, 21 Jul 1873. Mason was first married to Sabrina Holmes, and after Hannah's death, he married Elizabeth Gould (the widow Elizabeth Stiles).

vi   MARY HOLT, b. 19 Aug 1798; d. at Greenfield, 23 Mar 1856. Mary was a teacher. She did not marry.

290)   MARY HOLT (*Joshua Holt⁴, Nicholas Holt³, Mary Russell Holt², Robert¹*), b. at Andover, 5 Dec 1759 daughter of Joshua and Phebe (Farnum) Holt; d. at Greenfield, 9 Jul 1819; m. at Andover, 26 Aug 1784, ISAAC FOSTER, b. 23 Dec 1751 son of Jacob and Abigail (Frost) Foster. Isaac Foster was first married to Mary Hartwell who died in 1781.

     Isaac Foster had his first marriage in Andover and his wife Mary Hartwell died there; they did not have children. Isaac Foster and Mary Holt married in Andover, although Mary's family was already in Greenfield. Isaac and Mary settled in Greenfield where their nine children were born.

i   MARY FOSTER, b. about 1785; d. at Andover, 20 Feb 1862; m. 31 May 1806, her second cousin, JAMES ABBOTT (*Sarah Holt Abbott⁵, James Holt⁴, Nicholas Holt³, Mary Russell Holt², Robert¹*), b. at Andover, 30 Mar 1780 son of Barachias and Sarah (Holt) Abbott; James d. at Andover, 4 Oct 1858.

ii   DORCAS FOSTER, b. about 1787; d. at Greenfield, 8 May 1879; m. about 1838, JOSIAH TAYLOR, b. at Boxborough, MA, 3 Mar 1778 son of Silas and Mary (Wilkins) Taylor; Josiah d. at Temple, NH, 4 Oct 1850. Josiah Taylor was first married to Elizabeth Sargent.

iii   ISAAC H. FOSTER, b. 1789; d. at Greenfield, 8 Mar 1882; m. about 1847, LUCINDA WOODWARD, b. at Lyndeborough, 1812 daughter of Ephraim and Hannah (Badger) Woodward; Lucinda d. at Bennington, NH, 29 Oct 1887.

iv   TIMOTHY FOSTER, b. 1790; d. at Greenfield, 19 Nov 1863. Timothy did not marry.

v   AMOS FOSTER, b. 31 Jul 1794; d. at Greenfield, 10 Oct 1882; m. 1ˢᵗ, about 1823, BETSEY PRATT, b. at Easthampton, MA, 13 Feb 1800 daughter of Joshua and Sylvia (Smith) Pratt;[790] Betsey d. at Greenfield, 10 Dec 1853. Amos m. 2ⁿᵈ, about 1854, MARY M. DYKE, b. at Greenfield, 1810 daughter of Gideon and Mary (Fuller) Dyke; Mary d. at Peterborough, 29 Dec 1905. Mary Dyke was first married to Samuel Gould.

vi   HANNAH FOSTER, b. 18 Jun 1796; d. at Tilton, NH, 17 Oct 1885; m. at Greenfield, 22 Jun 1829, her fourth cousin once removed, PASCHAL ABBOTT, b. at Andover, 23 Jul 1788 son of Nathan and Sarah (Ballard) Abbott; Paschal d. at Dexter, ME, 30 May 1859. Paschal Abbott was first married to MARY FOSTER ABBOTT (1791-1828) daughter of Job and Anna (Ballard) Abbott.

vii   ABIGAIL FOSTER, b. 1799; d. at Lyndeborough, 7 Mar 1853; m. about 1848 as the third of his five wives, DAVID PUTNAM, b. at Lyndeborough, 19 Jun 1790 son of David and Abigail (Carleton) Putnam; David d. at Lyndeborough, 10 Jun 1870. David Putnam's other marriages were to Tryphena Butler, Sarah Fletcher, Nancy Pierce, and Sarah Brown.

---

[787] Joshua was living in Indianapolis at the time of his death but was on a trip to Iowa when he died.

[788] Chapman, *Sketches of the Alumni of Dartmouth College*, p 172

[789] Durrie, Holt Genealogy, p 94

[790] Pratt, *The Pratt Family*, p 54

viii   PHEBE FOSTER, b. 1802; d. at Andover, 2 May 1886; m. at Brentwood, NH, as his second wife, JOSEPH
         CUMMINGS, b. at Andover, 6 Dec 1792 son of Stephen and Deborah (Peabody) Cummings; Joseph d. at Andover,
         10 Oct 1860. Joseph was first married to Mary Poor.

ix   ANN FOSTER, b. about 1805; d. at Medford, MA, 7 Mar 1869; m. at Medford, 1 Jan 1837, as his second wife,
         THOMAS OLIVER PRATT, b. at Chelsea, 26 Apr 1792 son of Daniel and Abigail (Wilcott) Pratt; Thomas d. at
         Medford, 24 Jun 1870. Thomas was first married to Phebe Hudson.

291)   ABIAH HOLT (*Joshua Holt⁴, Nicholas Holt³, Mary Russell Holt², Robert¹*), b. at Andover, 16 Apr 1761 daughter of
Joshua and Phebe (Farnum) Holt; d. at Hancock, NH, 4 May 1841; m. 21 Jun 1791, as his second wife, DANIEL KIMBALL, b.
at Ipswich, 20 Oct 1755 son of Daniel and Hephzibah (Howe) Kimball; d. 24 May 1843. Daniel's first wife was Elizabeth
Osgood.
         Daniel Kimball and Abiah Holt made their home in Hancock, New Hampshire where Daniel served as a deacon and
selectman. He had served in the Revolution and worked at a powder mill making gunpowder for the Continental army.[791]
         Daniel had three children with his first wife Elizabeth Osgood. Daniel and Abiah Kimball were parents of eight
children all born at Hancock.

i   BETSEY KIMBALL, b. 1 Apr 1793; d. at Unadilla, NY, 6 Mar 1872; m. at Hancock, NH, 30 Jan 1817, EPHRAIM
         SMITH, b. 18 Apr 1789 son of James and Keturah (Putnam) Smith; Ephraim d. at Unadilla, 1 Aug 1862.

ii   PHEBE KIMBALL, b. 28 Mar 1795; d. at Andover, 18 Jan 1836; m. at Andover, 20 Oct 1814, RALPH
         HOLBROOK CHANDLER, b. at Andover, 17 Feb 1791 son of John and Mary (King) Chandler; Ralph d. at
         Andover, Aug 1861. After Phebe's death, Ralph married Phebe's sister Mary (see below).

iii   HANNAH KIMBALL, b. 17 Nov 1796; d. at Hancock, 1881; m. 16 Sep 1818, LUKE BOWERS, b. at Hancock, 25
         Oct 1792 son of John and Elizabeth (Boutelle) Bowers; Luke d. at Hancock, 11 Aug 1834.

iv   ANNA KIMBALL, b. 23 Jul 1798; d. Nov 1800.

v   JOSEPH KIMBALL, b. 6 Dec 1799; d. Nov 1800.

vi   JOSEPH KIMBALL, b. 21 Jan 1801; d. at Somerville, MA, Sep 1864; m. 20 Oct 1831, LUCY BOYD, b. at Antrim,
         6 Oct 1802 daughter of James and Fanny (Baldwin) Boyd; Lucy d. at Antrim, 10 Feb 1879.

vii   BENJAMIN KIMBALL, b. 8 Feb 1803; d. at Hancock, 18 Mar 1877; m. 27 Oct 1829, SALLY MATTHEWS, b. 5
         Jan 1804 daughter of Thomas and Sally (Goodhue) Matthews; Sally d. at Hancock, 31 Mar 1887.

viii   MARY KIMBALL, b. 14 Oct 1805; d. at Andover, 28 Jul 1891; m. at Hancock, 20 Oct 1836, RALPH HOLBROOK
         CHANDLER who was first married to Mary's sister Phebe (see above).

292)   JOHN HOLT (*Joshua Holt⁴, Nicholas Holt³, Mary Russell Holt², Robert¹*), b. at Andover, 12 Jan 1765 son of Joshua
and Phebe (Farnum) Holt; d, at Greenfield, 11 Feb 1835; m. 6 Jan 1792, his third cousin, DORCAS ABBOTT, b. at Andover, Dec
1766 daughter of George and Hannah (Lovejoy) Abbott; Dorcas d. 15 Mar 1841.
         Dorcas Abbott and John Holt married in Andover, but were soon after in Greenfield, New Hampshire where they
reared their family.
         In his will written 17 April 1827, John Holt bequeaths to beloved wife Dorcas use of one-half of the dwelling house
while she remains a widow and all the household furniture not otherwise disposed of the be at her own disposal. There are also
several specific provisions for the continued care and support of Dorcas. This includes provisions for medical care if needed,
annual supplies of staple goods, and $200 in cash. Daughter Dorcas wife of Peter Pevey receives $50; daughter Sarah wife of
Francis Dunkley, $50; daughter Tamesin, $250; daughter Phebe, $250; daughter Martha, $250; and daughter Elizabeth, $250.
He also provides that the four unmarried daughters can remain in the mother's household if they choose to do so. He also wills
that the four daughters, if employed, should pay some moderate amount to continue to live in the home and this is to be paid to
their brother John. His only son John receives all the estate real and personal not otherwise disposed of. The wearing apparel is
to be divided equally between John and his brothers-in-law. John is named sole executor.[792]
         Dorcas Abbott and John Holt were parents of eight children born at Greenfield.

---

[791] Hayward, *History of Hancock*, p 694
[792] *New Hampshire. Probate Court (Hillsborough County); Probate Place: Hillsborough, New Hampshire, Probate Records, Vol 40-41, 1833-1835*, pp
32-34

i   DORCAS HOLT, b. 12 Jan 1793; d. at Greenfield, 4 Jan 1856; m. about 1815, PETER PEAVEY, b. at Wilton, 27 Jul 1788 son of Peter and Lucy (Cummings) Peavey; Peter d. at Greenfield, 26 Oct 1879. After Dorcas's death, Peter married her sister Tamesin (see below).

ii   SARAH HOLT, b. 10 Mar 1795; d. at Francestown, 4 Jun 1885; m. at Greenfield, 28 Feb 1817, FRANCIS DUNCKLEE, b. at Greenfield, 1791 son of Hezekiah and Mehitable (White) Duncklee; Francis d. at Francestown, 14 Feb 1859.

iii   HANNAH HOLT, b. 15 Sep 1797; d. at Greenfield, 10 Nov 1821.

iv   JOHN HOLT, b. 9 Aug 1799; d. at Greenfield, 16 Apr 1869; m. 1st, 1836, his first cousin, PHEBE HOLT (*Ephraim Holt[5], Jacob Holt[4], Jacob Holt[3], Hannah Russell Holt[2], Robert[1]*), b. 9 Jun 1797 daughter of Ephraim and Hannah (Holt) Holt; Phebe d. at Greenfield, 8 May 1862. John m. 2nd, about 1863, MARY R. HOLT, b. 1823 (based on census records) whose parents are not identified; Mary d. at Greenfield, 24 Aug 1868. Phebe Holt is a child in Family 872.

v   TAMESIN HOLT, b. 23 Nov 1803; d. at Greenfield, 4 Jan 1896; m. about 1857, PETER PEAVEY who was first married to her sister Dorcas (see above).

vi   PHEBE FARNUM HOLT, b. 1806; d. at Bennington, NH, 31 Oct 1880; m. 30 Apr 1844, as his second wife, FRANCIS BURNHAM. b. at Greenfield, 13 Jan 1784 son of Nathaniel and Mary (-) Burnham; Francis d. at Greenfield, 27 Mar 1870. Francis was first married to Mary Fletcher.

vii   MARTHA HOLT, b. 24 Apr 1808; d. at Portsmouth, NH, 10 Mar 1895; m. about 1837, as his second wife, ARNOLD B. HUTCHINSON, b. at Lyndeborough, 17 Apr 1808 son of Ebenezer and Thomasin (Griffin) Hutchinson; Arnold d. at Portsmouth, 30 Jul 1888. Arnold was first married to Clarissa Fuller.

viii   ELIZABETH HOLT, b. 2 Apr 1811; d. 20 Jun 1830.

293)   TIMOTHY HOLT (*Joshua Holt[4], Nicholas Holt[3], Mary Russell Holt[2], Robert[1]*), b. at Andover, Apr 1767 son of Joshua and Phebe (Farnum) Holt; d. at Peterborough, 1856; m. 7 Nov 1793, his second cousin once removed, LYDIA HOLT, b. 18 Apr 1767 daughter of Joseph and Ruth (Johnson) Holt; Lydia d. 22 Nov 1825. Timothy m. 2nd, 11 Mar 1830, CHARITY SAVAGE, b. 1779 and d. at Peterborough, 28 Feb 1846.

    Timothy and Lydia Holt located in Peterborough immediately after their marriage. Their farm was at East Mountain on the border of Peterborough and Greenfield. Timothy was deacon at the Congregational Church in Greenfield.[793]

    In his will written 29 April 1847 (proved 5 November 1856), Timothy Holt bequeathed to son Timothy Holt ten dollars. Daughter Chloe Baldwin wife of Ziba Baldwin and Ruth Hovey wife of Timothy Hovey each receive five dollars. Daughters Lydia Holt and Tabitha Holt have the privilege of occupying the southeast chamber, but if the executor disposes of the dwelling, they are to be paid five dollars each. Son Joseph Holt receives all the real estate and all the residue of the personal estate and is named executor.[794]

    Timothy and Lydia were parents of eight children. The births of the three oldest children are recorded at Andover, although the births may have occurred in Peterborough.

i   LYDIA HOLT, b. 19 Apr 1795; d. at Peterborough, 5 Nov 1867. Lydia did not marry.

ii   CHLOE HOLT, b. 30 Mar 1797; d. at Peterborough, 1876; m. 1834, ZIBA BALDWIN, b. at Milford, 1787 son of Jeremiah Baldwin; Ziba d. at Peterborough, 28 Oct 1872. Ziba was first married to Eliza Morse who died in 1831.

iii   TABITHA HOLT, b. 16 Sep 1799; d. at Peterborough, 22 Jan 1855. Tabitha did not marry.

iv   TIMOTHY HOLT, b. 16 Mar 1802; d. at Concord, 22 Apr 1867; m. 1825, MARY JACKMAN, b. at Boscawen, 12 Nov 1802 daughter of Nehemiah and Ruth (Flanders) Jackman; Mary d. at Concord, 12 Mar 1884.

v   JOSEPH HOLT, b. 4 Apr 1804; d. at Peterborough, 13 Dec 1861; m. at Peterborough, 17 Jan 1832, MARY JANE MILLER, b. 1806 daughter of Adams and Ann (Robertson) Miller; Mary Jane d. at Lowell, 16 Jul 1870.

vi   JOSHUA HOLT, b. 17 Mar 1807; d. 6 Jul 1811.

vii   RUTH HOLT, b. 8 Feb 1809; d. 18 Jul 1811.

viii   RUTH HOLT, b. 19 May 1812; d. at Peterborough, 29 Jul 1874; m. at Peterborough, 17 Nov 1836, TIMOTHY L. HOVEY, b. at Peterborough, 9 Aug 1813 son of Richard and Asenath (Baxter) Hovey; Timothy d. at Peterborough,

[793] Smith and Morison, *History of Peterborough: Genealogy and History of Peterborough Families*, p 117
[794] *New Hampshire. Probate Court (Hillsborough County); Probate Place: Hillsborough, New Hampshire, Probate Records, Vol 68, 1856-1869*, p 62

31 Mar 1887. After Ruth's death, Timothy married Myra Parker (widow of Charles Hutchinson) daughter of Jonathan and Alice (Gutterson) Parker.

294)   SOLOMON HOLT (*Joshua Holt⁴, Nicholas Holt³, Mary Russell Holt², Robert¹*), b. at Andover, Dec 1768 son of Joshua and Phebe (Farnum) Holt; d. 15 Apr 1830; m. 22 May 1798, MARY CUMMINGS, b. about 1775 daughter of Justin and Mary (·) Cummings;[795] Mary d. 8 Oct 1852.

     Solomon Holt inherited the homestead from his father Joshua Holt. The historic home is at 111 Reservation Road in Andover. Solomon served as a deacon of the newly formed West Parish church in Andover.[796]

     In his will written 24 Feb 1830, Solomon Holt bequeaths to beloved wife Mary the use and improvement of one-third part of the homestead farm in Andover and several provisions for her support. Son Solomon is to furnish his mother with a horse and chaise. Sons Solomon and Nathan each receive $450. Son Abiathar receives his support including board and tuition to prosecute his studies "till he is fitted to enter college" and his executor is to furnish this support to Abiathar out of the estate. When he enters college, Abiathar will receive $450, and if he does not enter college, he will receive that amount when he is age twenty-one. Son Stephen will also receive $450 at age twenty-one, and until that time he is to labor on the farm for son Solomon, and Solomon will provide his support. Daughters Mary and Phebe C. each receive $200 and the improvements on the northeast chamber as long as they remain single. Mary and Phebe each receive a seat in the pew at the west parish meeting house. His wearing apparel is to be divided among his five sons, the books are to be equally divided among all the children, and his military equipment goes to Solomon. The remainder of the estate goes to Solomon who is also named executor.[797]

     Solomon Holt and Mary Cummings were parents of eight children born at Andover.

i   SOLOMON HOLT, b. 1799; d. at Andover, 3 Apr 1883; m. 25 May 1824, his fourth cousin, PHEBE ABBOTT, b. at Andover, 27 Nov 1798 daughter of Benjamin and Rhoda (Chandler) Abbott; Phebe d. at Andover, 18 Oct 1872. Phebe is a child in Family 845.

ii   MARY HOLT, b. 8 Mar 1801; d. 17 Feb 1803.

iii   JOSHUA HOLT, b. 6 Mar 1804; d. at Haverhill, 24 Sep 1886; m. 1ˢᵗ, 26 Nov 1829, REBECCA BAILEY, b. at Andover, 19 Nov 1804 daughter of William and Rebecca (Gillson) Bailey; Rebecca d. 4 Sep 1834. Joshua m. 2ⁿᵈ, 2 Apr 1836, CHARLOTTE GAGE, b. at Andover, 18 Jun 1806 daughter of Nathaniel and Betsey (Kimball) Gage; Charlotte d. at Bradford, 30 Nov 1846. Joshua m. 3ʳᵈ, 25 Oct 1848, his first cousin once removed, SARAH ABBOTT (*James Abbott⁶, Sarah Holt Abbott⁵, James Holt⁴, Nicholas Holt³, Mary Russell Holt², Robert¹*), b. at Andover, 23 Jul 1814 daughter of James and Mary (Foster) Abbott; Sarah d. at Bradford, 10 Jul 1857. Joshua m. 4ᵗʰ, 7 Apr 1859, MARY A. SARGENT, b. at Walton, NH, about 1811 daughter of William and Susan (Stackpole) Sargent; Mary d. at Lawrence, 26 Sep 1891. Mary Sargent was first married to Charles Gault.

iv   MARY HOLT, b. 20 Feb 1806; d. at Lyndon, VT, 23 Feb 1900; m. at Andover, 6 Jun 1837, as his second wife, SAMUEL READ HALL, b. at Croydon, NH, 27 Oct 1795 son of Samuel Read and Elizabeth (Hall) Hall; Samuel d. at Brownington, VT, 24 Jun 1877. Samuel was first married to Mary Dascomb.

v   NATHAN HOLT, b. 18 Apr 1808; d. at Lawrence, MA, 26 Dec 1891; m. at Andover, 21 Aug 1832, ABIGAIL COCHRAN, b. at Andover, 13 Apr 1812 daughter of Samuel and Mary (Bailey) Cochran; Abigail d. at Lawrence, 5 Sep 1892.

vi   PHEBE CUMMINGS HOLT, b. 30 Apr 1810; d. at Andover, Aug 1858; m. at Andover, 19 Oct 1835, TIMOTHY DWIGHT PORTER STONE, b. at Cornwall, CT, 21 Jul 1811 son of Timothy and Mary (Merwin) Stone; Timothy d. at Andover, 11 Apr 1887. After Phebe's death, Timothy married Susan Margaret Dickinson.

vii   ABIATHER HOLT, b. 31 Jan 1813; d. at Lowell, 18 Aug 1846; m. at Andover, 15 Sep 1836, ELIZABETH PLUNKETT, b. at Belfast, Ireland, 8 Feb 1814 daughter of John and Elizabeth (Keenan) Plunkett; Elizabeth d. at Matagorda, TX, 7 Jan 1887.[798] Elizabeth immigrated with her parents around 1830.[799] Abiather was a manufacturer in Lowell.

viii   STEPHEN P. HOLT, b. 12 Feb 1816; d. at Andover, 17 Nov 1860; m. at Andover, 2 Dec 1847, JEANETTE M. SMITH, b. at Andover, 14 May 1824 daughter of Peter and Rebecca (Bartlett) Smith; Jeanette d. at Andover, 23 May 1872.

---

[795] These are the parents given by Durrie's Holt family genealogy. There are no records that support this.

[796] Andover Historic Preservation, 111 Reservation Road, https://preservation.mhl.org/111-reservation-road

[797] Essex County, MA: Probate File Papers, 1638-1881. Online database. AmericanAncestors.org. New England Historic Genealogical Society, 2014. Case number 13695, probate of Solomon Holt

[798] *Texas, Death Certificates, 1903-1982*, Texas Department of State Health Services; Austin Texas, USA.

[799] "John Plunkett" Veteran Biographies, San Jacinto Museum of History, https://www.sanjacinto-museum.org/Library/Veteran_Bios/Bio_page/?id=677&army=Texian

295)   HANNAH HOLT (*Joshua Holt⁴, Nicholas Holt³, Mary Russell Holt², Robert¹*), b. at Andover, Jun 1771 daughter of Joshua and Phebe (Farnum) Holt; d. at Greenfield, 21 Apr 1842; m. 27 Nov 1794, her third cousin once removed, EPHRAIM HOLT (*Jacob Holt⁴, Jacob Holt³, Hannah Russell Holt², Robert¹*), b. 19 Mar 1769 son of Jacob and Rhoda (Abbott) Holt; Ephraim d. 24 Oct 1836.

Ephraim and Hannah lived in Greenfield where Ephraim was a selectman from 1811 to 1827 and a representative to the General Court from 1829 to 1832.[800]

Ephraim and Hannah Holt were parents of seven children born at Greenfield.

i   HANNAH HOLT, b. 19 Oct 1795; d. at Peterborough, 15 Nov 1879. Hannah did not marry.

ii   PHEBE HOLT, b. 9 Jun 1797; d. at Greenfield, 8 May 1862; m. 1836, her first cousin, JOHN HOLT (*John Holt⁵, Joshua Holt⁴, Nicholas Holt³, Mary Russell Holt², Robert¹*), b. 9 Aug 1799 son of John and Dorcas (Abbott) Holt; John d. at Greenfield, 19 Apr 1869. After Phebe's death, John married Mary R. Holt, b. 1823 and d. at Greenfield, 24 Aug 1868. John Holt is a child in Family 526.

iii   EPHRAIM HOLT, b. 2 Jul 1799; d. 26 Apr 1801.

iv   JACOB HOLT, b. 23 Apr 1801; d. 26 Apr 1811.

v   EPHRAIM HOLT, b. 12 Dec 1803; d. at Greenfield, 26 Aug 1867; m. SELINDA HILL, b. 26 May 1809 daughter of Job and Betsey (Perry) Hill; Selinda d. at Peterborough, 25 Aug 1891.

vi   RHODA HOLT, b. 26 Dec 1809; d. 1 Jul 1811.

vii   RHODA HOLT, b. 7 Aug 1815; d. at Pepperell, MA, 15 Feb 1849; m. 7 Oct 1845, JOHN VARNUM AMES, b. at Pepperell, 16 Jul 1821 son of John and Jane (Varnum) Ames; John d. after 1865. After Rhoda's death, John married Jane M. Wolcott in 1852 and Harriet R. Perry in 1855.

296)   STEPHEN HOLT (*Joshua Holt⁴, Nicholas Holt³, Mary Russell Holt², Robert¹*), b. at Andover, May 1773 son of Joshua and Phebe (Farnum) Holt; d. at Greenfield, 26 Mar 1868; m. 1799, FANNY BOWERS (*Elizabeth Holt Bowers⁴, Jacob Holt³, Hannah Russell Holt², Robert¹*), b. at Chelmsford, Jun 1773 daughter of Francis and Elizabeth (Holt) Bowers; Fanny d. 18 Apr 1828. Stephen married in 1831, MARGARET BATCHELDER, b. Sep 1784 and d. at Greenfield, 17 Aug 1867.

Stephen and Fanny Holt resided in Greenfield, New Hampshire where Stephen was a selectman in 1805 and 1806. Son Stephen Holt, Jr. operated the first steam mill in Greenfield.[801]

In his will dated 2 September 1867, Stephen Holt bequeaths to Jane Bradford wife of Robert Bradford all the household furniture her mother brought at the time of our marriage. The remaining household items, books, and wearing apparel are to be divided among the following heirs: son Stephen Holt, Jr., daughter Mary Jaquith wife of Benjamin Jaquith, daughter Ann Jaquith widow of Ambrose Jaquith, and Benjamin F. Jaquith and Fannie Hardy children of daughter Fannie Jaquith deceased. All the rest and residue of the estate real and personal is to be divided among the same heirs with the addition of the children of daughter Rhoda Dane who is deceased. The children of Rhoda are Maria, Moses, and Dexter. He also directs the erection of gravestones for deceased family members. Ephraim Holt of Greenfield, New Hampshire was named executor.[802]

Stephen Holt and Fanny Bowers were parents of eight children all born at Greenfield.

i   FANNY HOLT, b. 3 Jun 1800; d. at Greenfield, 20 Nov 1834; m. at Lyndeborough, 26 Dec 1826, BENJAMIN JAQUITH, b. at Wilmington, MA, 13 Apr 1798 son of Benjamin and Phebe (Ames) Jaquith; Benjamin d. at Greenfield, 8 Dec 1881. Benjamin married second, Fanny's sister MARY BOWERS HOLT (see below). After Mary's death, Benjamin married Hannah Marshall.

ii   BETSEY HOLT, b. 11 Jun 1802; d. 1816.

iii   STEPHEN HOLT, b. 4 Mar 1804; d. 12 Mar 1804.

iv   MARY BOWERS HOLT, b. 5 Jul 1805; d. at Greenfield, 1870; m. 1835, BENJAMIN JAQUITH (see sister Fanny above).

---

[800] Hurd, *History of Hillsborough County, New Hampshire*
[801] Hurd, *History of Hillsborough County, New Hampshire*
[802] *New Hampshire. Probate Court (Hillsborough County)*; Probate Place: *Hillsborough, New Hampshire, Probate Records, Vol 81-84, 1865-1890*, p 218, will of Stephen Holt

v   RHODA HOLT, b. 11 Sep 1807; d. at Lowell, MA, 2 Apr 1846; m. MOSES DANE, b. about 1800 son of John and Deborah (Bailey) Dane; Moses d. at Cedar, IA, 24 Mar 1888. After Rhoda's death, Moses married Lavina Lane.

vi   STEPHEN HOLT, b. 24 Apr 1810; d. at Francestown, NH, 24 Nov 1879; m. 2 Jun 1839, SARAH A. SPAULDING, b. at Lyndeborough, 2 Jan 1820 daughter of Henry and Lucy (Dunklee) Spaulding; Sarah d. at Francestown, 30 Mar 1890.

vii   ANNA DANDRIDGE HOLT, b. 13 Jul 1812; d. at Peterborough, 17 Jan 1895; m. AMBROSE JAQUITH, b. 1810 son of Benjamin and Phebe (Ames) Jaquith; Ambrose d. at Greenfield, 6 Jan 1864.

viii   BENJAMIN HOLT, b. 25 Nov 1816; d. 19 Apr 1827.

297)   CHLOE HOLT (*Joshua Holt⁴, Nicholas Holt³, Mary Russell Holt², Robert¹*), b. at Andover, Jun 1775 daughter of Joshua and Phebe (Farnum) Holt; d. at Peterborough, 6 Nov 1849; m. 23 Oct 1798, FRANCIS BOWERS (*Elizabeth Holt Bowers⁴, Jacob Holt³, Hannah Russell Holt², Robert¹*), b. at Chelmsford, 20 May 1775 son of Francis and Elizabeth (Holt) Bowers; Francis d. 15 Oct 1835.

        Francis Bowers and Chloe Holt came to Peterborough about 1800. He had a homestead farm, but from about 1820 to 1835 he operated what was known as Holmes' Mills.[803]

        Francis Bowers did not leave a will. His widow declined administration, and this was assumed by Samuel Miller December 1835. On 18 June 1836, an allowance of one hundred-fifty dollars was made to the widow for her support. Real estate was valued at $1,075 and personal estate $1,483.97.[804]

        Francis Bowers and Chloe Holt were parents of eight children born at Peterborough.

i   CHLOE BOWERS, b. 15 Jan 1799; d. at Francestown, 7 Oct 1844; m. JOHN DANE, b. at Andover, 22 Nov 1786 son of John and Deborah (Bailey) Dane; John d. at Francestown, 8 Jul 1850.

ii   RUTH D. BOWERS, b. 20 Jan 1803; d. at Lowell, MA, 10 Dec 1883; m. 1831, SAMUEL MILLER, b. at Peterborough, about 1796 son of Hugh and Jane (Templeton) Miller; Samuel d. at Peterborough, 9 May 1872.

iii   BENJAMIN BOWERS, b. 16 Mar 1807; d. 16 Mar 1811.

iv   PHEBE F. BOWERS, b. 18 Apr 1809; d. 28 Feb 1811.

v   FRANCIS H. BOWERS, b. 24 Feb 1811; d. at Billerica, MA, 5 Feb 1864; m. at Lowell, 16 Jan 1845, MARTHA A. SHERBURN, b. at Epsom, NH, about 1825 daughter of John and Abigail (Page) Sherburn; Martha d. at Somerville, MA, 23 Feb 1904.

vi   HANNAH BOWERS, b. 11 Jun 1812; d. at Carrollton, MN, 11 May 1886; m. 1ˢᵗ, about 1835, EZRA DANE, b. at Greenfield, about 1802 son of John and Deborah (Bailey) Dane; Ezra d. before 1866. Hannah m. 2ⁿᵈ, at Lowell, 5 Aug 1867, LUKE MILLER, b. at Wakefield, NH, 18 Aug 1815 son of Andrew and Jenny (Ames) Miller; Luke d. at Lanesboro, MN, 5 Sep 1881. Luke Miller was first married to Abby D. Lovell.

vii   BETSEY H. BOWERS, b. 28 Nov 1820; d. at Peterborough, 15 Oct 1861. Betsey did not marry. She lived with her sister Ruth and her husband.

viii   PHEBE F. BOWERS, b. 12 Oct 1823; d. at Lowell, 19 Apr 1910; m. at Lowell, 29 Nov 1883, NATHANIEL GAY, b. at Raymond, ME, 22 Apr 1814 son of Luther and Mary (Cash) Gay; Nathaniel d. at Lowell, 30 Jun 1889.

298)   DANIEL HOLT (*Daniel Holt⁴, Nicholas Holt³, Mary Russell Holt², Robert¹*), b. at Andover, Dec 1761 son of Daniel and Hannah (Holt) Holt; d. at Fitchburg, 27 Nov 1830; m. 5 Jan 1790, MARY JONES, b. at Andover, about 1769 daughter of Jacob and Mary (Winn) Jones.[805]

        Daniel and Mary Holt had one daughter and Mary likely died soon after that. Deacon Daniel Holt lived in Fitchburg and does not seem to have remarried.

        Daniel Holt did not leave a will and John Andrews assumed administration of the estate. Debts exceeded the value of the estate, the estate was sold, and creditors received eighty cents on the dollar.[806]

---

[803] Smith and Morison, *History of Peterborough: Genealogy and History of Peterborough Families*, p 21

[804] New Hampshire, County Probate Records, 1660-1973, Hillsborough, 37:272, 41:229, 41:1, 27:308, probate of Francis Bowers, 1835

[805] The 1810 will of Jacob Jones includes a bequest to his granddaughter Mary Holt the child of his daughter Mary who is deceased.

[806] Worcester County, MA: Probate File Papers, 1731-1881. Online database. AmericanAncestors.org. New England Historic Genealogical Society, 2015. Case 30625

i   MARY "POLLY" HOLT, b. at Fitchburg, 14 Mar 1792; d. at Fitchburg, 19 Oct 1818; m. at Fitchburg, 7 Aug 1810, JOHN ANDREWS, b. at Ipswich, about 1786 son of Daniel and Susan (Choate) Andrews; John d. at Fitchburg, 1 Apr 1874. After Mary's death, John married Zoa Lawrence.

299)   ABIEL HOLT (*Daniel Holt⁴, Nicholas Holt³, Mary Russell Holt², Robert¹*), b. at Andover, 8 Jun 1765 son of Daniel and Hannah (Holt) Holt; d. at Rindge, NH, 18 Jun 1825; m. 26 Jul 1791, PHEBE PUTNAM, b. at Fitchburg, 20 Sep 1770 daughter of Daniel and Rachel (-) Putnam; Phebe d. at Fitchburg, 12 Nov 1827.

Abiel and Phebe Holt spent their early married life in Fitchburg where four children were born. They relocated to Rindge, New Hampshire in 1806 where a fifth child was born. Abiel died in Rindge and Phebe seems to have returned to Fitchburg.[807]

Abiel Holt did not leave a will. Widow Phebe Holt declined administration of the estate and requested oldest son Abiel to be named administrator. This document is also signed by Nathan Holt and Edah Holt. On 15 October 1825, widow Phebe Holt was allowed to take $150 from the estate account. A committee was named to set off the dower to widow Phebe.[808]

i   ABIEL HOLT, b. 16 Aug 1791; d. at Winthrop, MA, 10 Jun 1864; m. at Rindge, NH, Nov 1815, EDAH DARLING, b. at Rindge, 14 Apr 1792 daughter of Amos and Ede (Stone) Darling; Edah d. at Ashburnham, 30 Oct 1864.

ii   DANIEL HOLT, b. about 1795. The History of Rindge reports that Daniel went to New York, had a family there, and died 1871. A tentative marriage is being suggested for him. Only one Daniel Holt of the correct age was found in the census records in the state of New York. That Daniel was married in Worcester County, MA which would fit for him. Daniel Holt, m. at Warren, MA, 16 Sep 1820, FRANCES BRIGHAM, b. at Brookfield, 27 Nov 1798 daughter of Tilly and Rachel (Walker) Brigham. Daniel Holt who married Frances was a grocer in New York. He died in New York City, 1866 (probate Sep 1866). Frances d. after 1870. Daniel and Frances Holt had two daughters, Sarah and Maria.

iii   NATHAN HOLT, b. about 1798; d. 25 Oct 1827. Nathan did not marry.

iv   EDAH PUTNAM HOLT, b. at Lunenburg, 29 Sep 1804; d. at Fitchburg, 9 Jul 1861; m. at Fitchburg, 18 Sep 1859, WILLIAM BASCOM PHELPS, b. at Fitchburg, 2 Mar 1811 son of Samuel and Elizabeth (Hartwell) Phelps; William d. at Fitchburg, 2 Apr 1882.

v   LIBERTY HOLT, b. at Rindge, 9 Nov 1813; d. at Ashburnham, 29 Jun 1887; m. 1st, at Westminster, MA, 7 Nov 1837, LUCY WHEELER, b. at Westminster, 5 Oct 1812 daughter of Haman and Sally (Wheeler) Wheeler; Lucy d. at Fitchburg, 18 Jul 1863. Liberty m. 2nd, at Ashburnham, 30 Oct 1864, SARAH WHEELER, b. at Sudbury, about 1813 daughter of Nathan and Dolly (-) Wheeler; Sarah d. at Ayer, MA, 12 Sep 1899. Sarah Wheeler was first married to Elnathan Haynes.

300)   JOSEPH HOLT (*Lydia Holt Holt⁴, Thomas Holt³, Mary Russell Holt², Robert¹*), b. at Andover, 20 Aug 1740 son of Benjamin and Lydia (Holt) Holt; d. at Andover, 15 Dec 1801; m. at Andover, 1 Jun 1762, RUTH JOHNSON, b. at Haverhill, 27 Oct 1744 daughter of Cornelius and Eleanor (Currier) Johnson;[809] Ruth d. at Andover, 18 May 1827.[810] She was living in 1814 when her brother James wrote his will.[811]

Joseph and Ruth resided in Andover. Joseph is called lieutenant on his death record. He is likely the Joseph Holt of Andover who served as Sergeant in the company of Capt. Henry Abbot that marched at the alarm on 19 April 1775.[812]

Joseph received the homestead property of his father Benjamin by deed.[813]

In his will written 9 October 1798 (probate 1 February 1802), Joseph Holt bequeathed to beloved wife Ruth all the "household stuff proper for woman's use" excepting the clock which is Henry's. She also receives two good cows and one good hog to be at her disposal. Ruth also has use of the two east lower rooms, porch, and garret over the rooms. She also has other specified access and use of the property. She also receives the use and improvement of one-third of the lands and barn. Son Henry is to provide his mother with a suitable horse and horseman to take her to meetings and to doctors and nurses while she is widow. Son Henry receives all the real estate in Andover and Wilton. Henry also receives all the personal estate. Son Abner receives one-third of the lands "for quality and quantity" lying in township number five, now called Oxford, in the county of

---

[807] Stearns, *History of the Town of Rindge*, p 556

[808] *New Hampshire. Probate Court (Cheshire County); Probate Place: Cheshire, New Hampshire, Estate Files, H324-H374, 1822-1826*, probate of Abiel Holt

[809] The 1774 will of Cornelius Johnson of Concord includes a bequest to his daughter Ruth Holt.

[810] The transcription of the death record incorrectly gives her as the widow of Henry. However, her probate record establishes she was widow of Joseph.

[811] New Hampshire Probate, Rockingham County, will of James Johnson, volume 42, p 106

[812] Massachusetts Soldiers and Sailors in the Revolutionary War, volume 8, p 193

[813] Massachusetts Land Records, Essex County, 110:159, 117:62

York. Sons Joseph and Paul with have the first choice of their thirds of the lands in Oxford. Joseph also receives $150 and a good pair of three-year-old steer which he will receive at age twenty-one, and he also has the benefit of his own labor after age twenty. Son Paul receives $50 and the benefit of his own labor at age twenty-one. Daughters Ruth and Lydia each receives one dollar which completes their shares. Daughter Elinor and Hannah each receives $133.33 at age twenty-one or on the day of marriage. Son Henry is ordered to take care of Joseph's brother Benjamin "in health and sickness during the term of his natural life."[814] Daughter Hannah is to have the comfortable privilege of living in that portion of the house reserved for Ruth while Hannah is unmarried. Ruth has use of the great bible during her life, and it then goes to Joseph. Joseph receives the firelock, bayonet, and cartridge box and Paul receives the swords. Henry is named executor. Real estate was valued at $5,685.[815]

In her will written 15 November 1822 (probate 5 June 1827), Ruth Holt bequeathed to her grandchildren Henry Holt, Herman Holt, Eliza Holt, and Mary Holt the children of her son Henry the sum of one dollar "by reason of what they received from the estate of their late father Henry Holt deceased do not stand in need of my bounty." She releases her son-in-law Abner Abbot of Albany, Maine from a promissory note for $21.66. One dollar each was bequeathed to the following grandchildren: Ruth Williams wife of Thomas Williams of Boston, Sarah Holt wife of David Holt of Andover, Obed Abbot, Stephen Abbot, and Mary Phillips wife of Edwin Phillips of Boston. Household furniture and wearing apparel was bequeathed to her daughters to equally divide between them: Lydia Holt wife of Timothy Holt of Greenfield, New Hampshire, Eleanor Flint wife of Ephraim Flint of Albany, Maine, and Hannah Faulkner wife of John Faulkner of Andover. One-tenth part of the remainder of the estate was left to son Abner Holt of Albany. Three-tenths part is left to Job Abbot to hold in trust with interest used for the support of son Joseph Holt and his family. A further three-tenths is to be held in trust by Job Abbot for the support of son Paul Holt and his family. The remaining three-tenths was bequeathed to daughter Hannah Faulkner. Job Abbot was named executor.[816]

Joseph Holt and Ruth Johnson were parents of twelve children born at Andover.

i   HENRY HOLT, b. 20 Aug 1763; d. at Andover, 24 Feb 1821; m. 1st 22 Jun 1790, MEHITABLE BLUNT, b. at Andover, 4 Jan 1769 daughter of Isaac and Mary (Kimball) Blunt; Mehitable d. at Andover, 1 Sep 1802. Henry m. 2nd 27 Jan 1803, Mehitable's sister, ANNA BLUNT, b. 9 May 1763; Anna d. at Andover, 13 Jun 1840.

ii   RUTH HOLT, b. 25 Feb 1765; d. at Albany, ME, 17 Nov 1806; m. at Andover, 29 Jan 1784, ABNER ABBOTT, b. at Andover, 29 Jan 1761 son of Stephen and Mary (Abbott) Abbott; Abner d. at Albany, 16 Sep 1833. Abner married second Dorcas J. Jason on 10 Mar 1808.

iii   LYDIA HOLT, b. 18 Apr 1767; d at Peterborough, NH, 22 Nov 1825; m. at Andover, 7 Nov 1793, her second cousin once removed, TIMOTHY HOLT (*Joshua Holt⁴, Nicholas Holt³, Mary Russell Holt², Robert¹*), b. at Andover, Apr 1767 son of Joshua and Phebe (Farnum) Holt; Timothy d. at Peterborough, 22 Oct 1856. Timothy married second on 11 Mar 1830, Charity Savage. Lydia Holt and Timothy Holt are Family 278.

iv   JOSEPH HOLT, b. 16 Apr 1769; d. 8 Sep 1775.

v   ABNER HOLT, b. 6 Oct 1771; d. at Albany, ME, 14 Dec 1854; m. 1st 29 Mar 1795, his second cousin, ABIGAIL FLINT (*Asenath Holt Flint⁴, Phebe Russell Holt³, John², Robert¹*), b. at Reading, 30 Jun 1771 daughter of Ebenezer and Asenath (Holt) Flint; Abigail d. 21 May 1798. Abner m. 2nd 20 Jun 1799, ELIZABETH CHANDLER, b. at Andover, 1 Jun 1777 daughter of William and Elizabeth (Chandler) Chandler; Elizabeth d. at Albany, ME, 1 Nov 1816. Abner m. 3rd 1 Feb 1819, Mrs. DELILAH PIPIN who died at Albany, 16 Jul 1821. Abner m. 4th 12 Jan 1822, ABIGAIL SHEA, b. about 1782; Abigail d. at Albany, 13 May 1856. Abner Holt and Abigail Flint are Family 878.

vi   OBED HOLT, b. 25 Nov 1773; d. 8 Sep 1775.

vii   HANNAH HOLT, b. 28 Sep 1775; d. 7 Jul 1778.

viii   ELEANOR HOLT, b. 3 Nov 1777; d. at Albany, ME, 23 Jun 1858; m. 21 Jan 1799, her second cousin, EPHRAIM FLINT (*Asenath Holt Flint⁴, Phebe Russell Holt³, John², Robert¹*), b. at Reading, 4 Sep 1773 son of Ebenezer and Asenath (Holt) Flint; Ephraim d. at Albany, 13 Oct 1859. Eleanor Holt and Ephraim Flint are Family 879.

ix   JOSEPH HOLT, b. 5 Nov 1780; d. at Andover, 18 Jul 1860; m. 13 Jan 1803, LYDIA JONES, b. at Londonderry, 6 Oct 1780 daughter of Josiah and Rebecca (Jenkins) Jones; Lydia d. at Andover, 14 Jul 1858.

x   PAUL HOLT, b. 11 Jan 1783; d. at Lowell, MA, 15 Oct 1868; m. 12 Apr 1805, ELIZABETH "BETTY" BELL, b. at Tewksbury, 1 Nov 1784 daughter of John and Hannah (Peacock) Bell;[817] Elizabeth d. at Lowell, 1 Oct 1867.

xi   TABITHA HOLT, b. 22 May 1785; d. 12 Nov 1789.

---

[814] Joseph's brother Benjamin had been found *non compos mentis*.

[815] *Essex County, MA: Probate File Papers, 1638-1881.* Online database. *AmericanAncestors.org.* New England Historic Genealogical Society, 2014. Case 13664

[816] *Essex County, MA: Probate File Papers, 1638-1881.* Online database. *AmericanAncestors.org.* New England Historic Genealogical Society, 2014. Case 13686

[817] Elizabeth's parents are given as John and Hannah Bell on her death record.

xii   HANNAH HOLT, b. 7 Apr 1787; d. at Lawrence, MA, 22 Jan 1873; m. at Andover, 14 Jun 1812, JOHN FAULKNER, b. at Andover, 7 Mar 1785 son of Abiel and Hannah (Abbott) Faulkner; John d. at Andover, 27 Jan 1823.

301)   BETHIAH HOLT (*Lydia Holt Holt[4], Thomas Holt[3], Mary Russell Holt[2], Robert[1]*), b. at Andover, 3 Aug 1744 daughter of Benjamin and Lydia (Holt) Holt; d. at Nelson, NH, 13 Apr 1812; m. at Andover, 20 Oct 1767, her third cousin, SOLOMON WARDWELL,[818] b. at Andover, 14 Jul 1743 son of Thomas and Abigail (Gray) Wardwell; Solomon d. at Packersfield, 20 Sep 1825.

      Solomon Wardwell was a cabinetmaker and had a shop in Andover. The family was in Andover until 1777 when Solomon purchased a farm in Hollis, and Solomon was a selectman there in 1783. The family moved on to Packersfield, which was later Nelson, in 1784. Solomon was selectman in Packersfield in 1786 and served as delegate to the Constitutional Convention in 1791.

      Solomon was a member of Capt. Henry Abbot's company of Minute Men in Andover and marched on 19 April 1775, but as news of the day developed including that the British had fallen back, Wardwell and some others turned back at Bedford.[819]

      Bethiah Holt and Solomon Wardwell were parents of nine children.[820][821]

i   SOLOMON WARDWELL, b. at Andover, 3 Feb 1768; d. at Nelson, NH, 19 Feb 1789.

ii   BENJAMIN WARDWELL, b. at Andover, 6 Aug 1769; d. at Salem, 4 Jun 1832; m. at Danvers, 20 Oct 1797, SUSAN "SUKEY" HAMMOND, baptized at Danvers, 26 Nov 1780 daughter of Benjamin and Susanna (Elledge) Hammond. Benjamin Wardwell's estate was administered by his son-in-law Aaron Perkins whose wife Susan was the only heir to the estate.

iii   ABIEL WARDWELL, b. at Andover, 25 Aug 1771; d. Jan 1821 at Charleston, SC (he was a mariner resident in Salem); m. 1st at Salem, 28 Apr 1800, HANNAH ELLEDGE, b. about 1779 daughter of Richard and Hannah (Mullett) Elledge; Hannah d. at Salem, 18 Oct 1805. Abiel m. 2nd at Salem, 20 Jan 1811, his third cousin, ESTHER ANDREWS (*Mary Holt Andrews[5], Mary Chandler Holt[4], Mehitable Russell Chandler[3], Thomas[2], Robert[1]*), b. at Boxford, 16 Dec 1777 daughter of Jacob and Mary (Holt) Andrews; Esther d. at Salem, 5 Jun 1861.

iv   EZRA WARDWELL, b. at Andover, 24 Aug 1773; d. at Sullivan, NH, 3 Jun 1845; m. at Packersfield, 28 Jan 1800, LOIS WHITNEY, b. at Packersfield, 15 Mar 1781 daughter of Josiah and Anna (Scollay) Whitney; Lois d. at Sullivan, 16 Jan 1859.

v   EZEKIEL WARDWELL, b. at Andover, 17 Aug 1777; d. at Baltimore, MD, 1 Jan 1803.[822]

vi   AMOS WARDWELL, b. at Hollis, 25 Jul 1779; d. at Sullivan, NH, 1 Dec 1843; m. 1st at Corinth, VT, 8 Jun 1807, LODICE CORLISS, b. 1781; d. at Sullivan, 17 Oct 1807. Amos m. 2nd at Sullivan, 6 Sep 1808, BETSEY WILDER, b. at Lancaster, MA, 22 Feb 1777 daughter of Phineas and Bridget (Bailey) Wilder; Betsey d. at Sullivan, 31 Mar 1859.

vii   BETHIAH WARDWELL, b. at Hollis, 2 Feb 1782; d. at Andover, 2 Mar 1855. Bethiah did not marry. Her probate lists heirs all of whom are nieces and nephews as she was the last surviving sibling. Those nieces and nephews were Lois Beals, Suzy Buckminster, Ichabod N. Wardwell, Henry Wardwell, Granville Wardwell, Amos Wardwell, George Wardwell, Lodica Wardwell, Betsey Hubbard, William H. Wardwell, Octavia S. Wardwell, Nathaniel A. Wardwell, Harriet Sims, and Susan W. Perkins.[823]

viii   DANIEL WARDWELL, b. at Hollis, 11 Jan 1784; d. at Andover, 14 Apr 1851; m. at Andover, 24 Sep 1816, his fourth cousin, SARAH OSGOOD (*Timothy Osgood[5], Peter Osgood[4], Mary Russell Osgood[3], Thomas[2], Robert[1]*), b. at Andover, 9 Sep 1789 daughter of Timothy and Sarah (Farnum) Osgood; Sarah d. at Andover, 8 Jun 1867. Daniel Osgood was a physician.

---

[818] There are two Bethiah Holts near in age, one of whom married Solomon Wardwell and one who married Thomas Russell. There do not seem to be any records that clearly establish which was which, and I have chosen this arrangement: Bethiah daughter of Benjamin married Solomon Wardwell and Bethiah daughter of Ephraim Holt and Phebe Russell married Thomas Russell. It could well be the other way around.

[819] Nelson Picnic Association, *Celebration of the Town of Nelson*, pp 148-149

[820] Published genealogies give nine children of Bethiah Holt and Solomon Wardwell. There are two areas of conflict in records. First, there is a record for a daughter Anna born 25 July 1779 and in published genealogies this child is given as Amos. This may simply be a transcription error as there are no other records for a daughter Anna. Second, there is the record of a baptism for a daughter Chloe at Andover on 1 September 1771. As there was a son Abiel born on 25 Aug 1771, this may again just be a transcription error. There are no other records related to a daughter Chloe.

[821] Stay, *Wardwell: A Brief Sketch of the Antecedents of Solomon Wardwell*, pp 10-11

[822] This is per Stay's Wardwell genealogy

[823] *Essex County, MA: Probate File Papers, 1638-1881.* Online database. *AmericanAncestors.org.* New England Historic Genealogical Society, 2014. Case 56330

ix   JOEL WARDWELL, b. at Nelson, NH, 29 May 1787; d. at Andover, 8 Jan 1813. Joel was studying to be a physician at the time of his death.

302)   MARY HOLT (*Lydia Holt Holt⁴, Thomas Holt³, Mary Russell Holt², Robert¹*), b. at Andover, 19 Sep 1751; d. at Lynn, 31 Dec 1819; m. 1ˢᵗ at Andover, 13 Apr 1772, JAMES LARRABEE[824] described as "of Lynn" *perhaps* the son of Joseph and Elizabeth (Trask) Larrabee; James d. before 1784 and likely before that. Mary m. 2ⁿᵈ at Lynn (intention 12 Dec 1784), EBENEZER TARBOX, b. at Lynn, 10 Sep 1763 son of Benjamin and Annah (Rice) Tarbox; Ebenezer d. at Lynn, 12 Aug 1827.
       There is one child known for Mary and James.

i   JAMES HOLT LEATHERBEE,[825] b. at Andover, 17 Jul 1772; d. at Boston, 6 May 1821; m. at Boston, 17 Aug 1792, RACHEL WILLIAMS, b. at Medford, 14 Sep 1766 daughter of John and Rachel (Tufts) Williams; Rachel d. at Boston, 14 Apr 1823.

      Mary Holt and Ebenezer Tarbox were parents of seven children born at Lynn.

i   EBENEZER TARBOX, later THORNDIKE, b. 19 Feb 1785; d. at Swampscott, MA, 17 Dec 1877; m. 1ˢᵗ at Weymouth, MARY "POLLY" RICHARDS, b. at Weymouth, 24 Feb 1785 daughter of Nathaniel and Mary (Bayley) Richards; Mary d. at Lynn, 22 Jan 1823. Ebenezer m. 2ⁿᵈ at Boston, 22 May 1823, MARY G. GODSHALL (widow of Thomas Brackett), b. at Salem, 1797 daughter of William and Dorcas (Mansfield) Godshall; Mary d. at Swampscott, 1 Jan 1880 at age 82 years, 9 months, 21 days. On 7 February 1824, Ebenezer Tarbox, Jr. of Charlestown legally changed his name to Ebenezer Thorndike, along with his children Nathaniel, Ebenezer, and Catherine. On 12 June 1824, Mary G. Tarbox was permitted to change her name to Mary G. Thorndike.[826]

ii   BENJAMIN TARBOX, b. 14 Feb 1787; m. at Lynn, 20 Sep 1807, LYDIA RHODES, b. at Lynn, 30 Dec 1786 daughter of Samuel and Hannah (Derby) Rhodes; Lydia d. after 1850 when she was living at the home of her daughter Martha and her husband.[827] On 26 April 1847, two of the sons of Benjamin and Lydia, Samuel Franklin Tarbox and Benjamin Washington Tarbox, were legally permitted to change their last name to Appleton.[828] Lydia's name seems to have been changed about the same time as she is later Appleton in census records.

iii   ELIZABETH "BETSEY" TARBOX, b. 18 Nov 1789; d. at Lynn, 1 Oct 1871; m. 1ˢᵗ at Lynn, 28 Sep 1806, JOSEPH THOMAS of Salem; Joseph d. at Salem, 1812 (probate 3 Mar 1812). Elizabeth m. 2ⁿᵈ at Lynn, 26 Jul 1812, as his fourth Capt. DANIEL GALEUCIA, b. at Norton, 1 Aug 1740 son of Jacob and Martha (Norton) Galeucia; Daniel d. at Lynn, 9 Dec 1825.

iv   JOHN TARBOX, b. 21 Jul 1791; d. at Lynn, 16 Apr 1861. John had a first marriage that was not clearly identified. John m. 2ⁿᵈ at Lynn, 10 May 1851, LUCY ANN ROUSE (widow Lucy Brown), b. at Oxford, Upper Canada, 1819 daughter of George and Ann (-) Rouse; Lucy d. at Lynn, 27 Sep 1875. Lucy married Samuel Goldsmith in 1864. John Tarbox was a teamster. In 1850, John was living in the home of his sister Lucinda and her family. In 1860, John was at the poor house in Lynn with condition given as intemperance.[829]

v   SUSAN "SUKEY" TARBOX, b. 17 Aug 1796; d. at Lynn, 2 Sep 1848; m. at Lynn, 8 Mar 1818, THOMAS PATRON, b. in England, about 1798 son of Francis and Lydia (-) Patron; Thomas d. at Lynn, 23 Jun 1862. Thomas married second, Mary Orr Goodhue of 29 Nov 1848.

vi   LYDIA TARBOX, b. 7 May 1795; d. at Swampscott, 27 Jul 1861; m. at Lynn, 8 Dec 1811, JOHN HEATH, b. at Salem, NH, 1789; John d. at Topsfield, 17 May 1857.

vii   LUCINDA TARBOX, b. 23 Sep 1799 (calculated); d. at Lynn, 17 Dec 1871; m. at Lynn, 7 Aug 1814, ASAPH BISBEE, b. at Plympton, 27 Dec 1788 son of Asaph and Jenney (Douglas) Bisbee; Asaph d. at Lynn, 14 Oct 1825. Lucinda m. 2ⁿᵈ at Lynn, 24 Apr 1827, Asaph's brother, NOAH BISBEE, b. (recorded at Carver), 10 Apr 1803; Noah d. at Lynn, 5 Mar 1880.

---

[824] Name is also spelled Leatherby

[825] The spelling of the last name shifts from Larrabee used by the father to Leatherbee used by the son.

[826] Laws of the Commonwealth of Massachusetts, Sessions of the General Court, Volume IX, Acts and Resolves Passed by the General Court, General Laws May 1822 to March 1825, Chapter LXXII Feb 7, 1824, p 292 and Chapter XXX June 12, 1824, p 452

[827] The National Archives in Washington D.C.; Record Group: Records of the Bureau of the Census; Record Group Number: 29; Series Number: M432; Residence Date: 1850; Home in 1850: Lynn, Essex, Massachusetts; Roll: 311; Page: 358a

[828] Laws of the Commonwealth of Massachusetts, Sessions of the General Court, Acts and Resolves Passed by the General Court, General Laws 1846-1848, Chapter 275, April 26, 1847, p 493

[829] The National Archives in Washington D.C.; Record Group: Records of the Bureau of the Census; Record Group Number: 29; Series Number: M653; Residence Date: 1860; Home in 1860: Lynn Ward 7, Essex, Massachusetts; Roll: M653_495; Page: 967

303)   MARTHA HOLT (*Lydia Holt Holt⁴, Thomas Holt³, Mary Russell Holt², Robert¹*) , b. at Andover, 15 Oct 1754 daughter of Benjamin and Lydia (Holt) Holt; d. at Smithville, NY, 9 Oct 1829; m. at Andover, 23 Nov 1775, JONATHAN FELT, b. at Temple, NH, 8 Apr 1753 son of Aaron and Mary (Wyatt) Felt; Jonathan d. at Packersfield (Nelson), NH, 17 Feb 1807 (probate 1807).

   Martha and Jonathan settled at Packersfield, New Hampshire prior to 1775 and their twelve children were born there.[830] Jonathan was a signer of the Association Test and had one month of service from 28 September to 24 October 1777 in the company of Capt. James Lewis that marched to Saratoga.[831]

   In his will written 4 February 1807, Jonathan Felt notes that he made a deed to son Jonathan on 8 December last, but this was put in the hands of Samuel Griffin for one year. Jonathan wants the deed to be held by Samuel Griffin after his decease and to keep the bond that Jonathan took of Jonathan, Jr. and this is to be used for the support of his wife and his minor children. He has given sons Jonathan and Benjamin each $300 and wills that sons Joseph, Henry, and Amos receive the same when they come of age. Each of his daughters Patty, Mary, and Milla are to be set out with household furniture equal to daughters Lydia and Polly, which he estimates as $150 of value each, at their marriages. The remainder of the estate is to be divided among his sons and daughters, the sons each receive two shares and daughter one share.[832]

i   JONATHAN FELT, b. 6 Nov 1776; d. at Adams, NY, 17 Dec 1862; m. 27 Apr 1802, ABIGAIL HUNTING, b. 5 Aug 1780 daughter of Jonathan and Mary (Sawin) Hunting;[833] Abigail d. at Adams, 21 May 1836.

ii   LYDIA FELT, b. 20 Sep 1778; d. at Nelson, 4 Feb 1827; m. 12 Apr 1796, NOAH ROBBINS, b. at Temple, NH, 23 Apr 1771;[834] Noah d. at Nelson, 1841 (probate 1841).

iii BENJAMIN FELT, b. 31 Jul 1780; d. at Granby, NY, 19 Sep 1827; m. 1ˢᵗ 14 Dec 1802, NANCY PETTS; Nancy d. at Granby, 1821. Benjamin m. 2ⁿᵈ about 1825, as her second husband, SALLY HUTCHINS, b. at Lyndon, 18 Jun 1797 daughter of John and Elizabeth (Russell) Hutchins; Sally d. at Fremont, OH, 23 Dec 1898. Sally Hutchins was first married to John Babcock and was third married to John Allen.

iv   MARTHA "PATTY" FELT, b. 28 Sep 1783; d. at Cleveland, OH, 1 Mar 1863; m. at Rodman, NY, 7 Apr 1807, JOHN SEYMOUR HALE, b. at Leominster, MA, 9 Dec 1779 son of Ephraim and Hannah (Spofford) Hale; John d. at Solon, OH, 10 Feb 1852.

v   POLLY FELT, b. 14 Jul 1785; d. at Newark, OH, 15 Mar 1855; m. at Nelson, NH, 12 Feb 1806, JESSE SMITH, b. 25 Feb 1784 son of Ezra and Phebe (Walcott) Smith; Jesse d. at Peru, IN, 7 Jun 1867.

vi   JOSEPH FELT, b. 14 Jul 1787; d. at Peterborough, NH, 16 Oct 1874; m. at Peterborough, 5 May 1816, BETSEY NAY, b. 21 Jun 1796 daughter of John and Betsey (Puffer) Nay;[835] Betsey d. at Peterborough, 2 Oct 1852. After Betsey's death, Joseph married Nancy who has not been identified.

vii SOLOMON FELT, b. 15 Apr 1789; d. 14 Sep 1801.

viii HENRY FELT, b. 18 Aug 1791; d. at Adams, NY, 29 Feb 1872; m. about 1820, MALINDA MORSE, b. at Adams, NY, 17 Jun 1799 daughter of Alpheus and Melinda (Thompson) Morse; Malinda d. at Lorraine, NY, 31 Oct 1888.

ix   MARCY FELT, b. 6 Jul 1793; d. at Porter, NY, 9 May 1873; m. about 1814, ZIBA HENRY, b. at Stoddard, NH, 14 Mar 1791 son of Ziba and Sarah (·) Henry; Ziba d. at Porter, NY, 11 Sep 1859.

x   MILLY FELT, b. 3 Sep 1795; d. 18 Aug 1814.

xi   BETSY FELT, b. 27 Oct 1797; d. 24 Jan 1798.

xii AMOS FELT, b. 11 May 1799; d. 19 Mar 1812.

304)   MARY HOLT (*Joseph Holt⁴, Thomas Holt³, Mary Russell Holt², Robert¹*), b. 17 Aug 1745 daughter of Joseph and Mary (Abbott) Holt; m. 26 Jun 1766, BENJAMIN DARLING, b. 28 Apr 1728 son of John and Lois (Gowing) Darling; Benjamin d. at Lunenburg, about 1783 based on date of probate.

   In his young adult life, Benjamin was a mariner, but returned home and married Mary Holt. He inherited property in Lunenburg form his father and settled there.[836]

[830] Much of the information on the spouses of the children in this family was taken from Morris, *The Felt Genealogy*.
[831] Nelson Picnic Association, *Celebration of the Town of Nelson*, p 71
[832] *New Hampshire. Probate Court (Cheshire County), wills volume 76, pp 123-124*
[833] Morris, *The Felt Genealogy*, p 113
[834] Morris, *The Felt Genealogy*, p 64
[835] The names of Betsey's parents are given on the marriage record of Betsey and Joseph.
[836] Weeks, *The Darling Family in America*, p 14

Benjamin Darling did not leave a will. The personal estate was insufficient to pay the debts and widow Mary Darling petitioned the Court to be allowed to sell as much of the real estate as was needed to pay his debts.[837]

Mary Abbott and Benjamin Darling were parents of seven children born at Lunenburg.

i PATIENCE DARLING, b. 28 Mar 1767; m. at Lunenburg, 1785, JOHN DARLING, b. at Lunenburg, 13 Aug 1759 son of Timothy and Joanna (Blood) Darling.

ii MOLLY DARLING, b. 11 Jun 1769; d. at Temple, ME; m. at Lunenburg, 22 May 1792, MITCHELL RICHARDS, b. at Lunenburg, 1759 likely the son of Mitchel and Esther (Mitchell) Richards; Mitchell d. at Temple, 2 May 1845.

iii LOIS DARLING, b. 29 Aug 1771; nothing further known.

iv EUNICE DARLING, b. 13 Apr 1774; d. at Jaffrey, NH, 27 Jul 1834; m. at Jaffrey, 25 Nov 1811, RUFUS SAWYER, b. at Lancaster, MA (baptized 20 Jul 1760) son of Bezeleel and Lois (Lawrence) Sawyer; Rufus d. at Jaffrey, 29 Sep 1845.

v BENJAMIN DARLING, b. 11 Dec 1775; d. at Northfield, MA, 4 Nov 1840; m. FANNY AMES, *perhaps* b. at Hollis, 5 Sep 1773 daughter of Jonathan Robbins and Fanny (Powers) Ames; Fanny d. at Northfield, 18 Dec 1859.

vi JAMES DARLING, b. 5 Dec 1779; d. at Northfield, 5 May 1811; m. at Lunenburg, 3 Oct 1801, OLIVE READ, b. at Westford, MA, 30 Jun 1781 daughter of Abel and Rebekah (Farrar) Read.

vii LEVI DARLING, b. 8 May 1782; d. at Northfield, after 1821. Levi may not have married. In 1821, he was being supported by the town of Northfield.[838]

305) SARAH HOLT (*Joseph Holt⁴, Thomas Holt³, Mary Russell Holt², Robert¹*), baptized at Lunenburg 14 Dec 1746 daughter of Joseph and Mary (Abbott) Holt; m. at Lunenburg, 1 Feb 1767, BARNABAS WOOD, b. at Lunenburg, 21 May 1746 son of Jonathan and Sarah (Whitney) Wood; Barnabas d. at Windsor, VT, 5 Apr 1822.

Sarah and Barnabas were first in Lunenburg where their first two children were baptized.[839] They were in Jaffrey, New Hampshire by 1782 where Barnabas was highway surveyor in 1782 and 1785.[840] The family was in Westminster, Vermont for a time before being finally in Windsor, Vermont.

There are four likely children for Sarah and Barnabas, although there may well be other children.

i OLIVE WOOD, baptized at Lunenburg, 25 Jun 1769; d. at Springfield, VT, 21 Jan 1815; m. 1st at Rockingham, VT, 10 May 1791, ISAIAH EDSON; Isaiah d. about 1798. Olive m. 2nd at Springfield, VT, 8 Jul 1799, EBENEZER SHED, b. at Lunenburg, about 1777 son of Solomon and Elizabeth (Boynton) Shed; Ebenezer d. at Springfield, 30 Jul 1860.

ii JONATHAN BRADSTREET WOOD, baptized at Lunenburg, 7 Jan 1771; d. at Springfield, VT, 19 Mar 1805; m. at Rockingham, VT, 6 Dec 1792, RELIEF STICKNEY likely b. at Holden, 13 May 1775 daughter of Moses and Abigail (Hale) Stickney; Relief d. at Springfield, 24 Jan 1842.

iii BAZALEEL WOOD, b. 1780; d. at Springfield, VT, 1849; m. at Chester, VT, 19 Apr 1821, HANNAH LOVELL, b. 1793; Hannah d. at Springfield, 19 Mar 1853.

iv JOHN WOOD, b. at Rockingham, VT, 1788; d. at West Rutland, VT, 3 Feb 1861; m. LUCY PHIPPEN, b. at Westminster, VT, 5 Dec 1786 daughter of Joseph and Lilie (Paul) Phippen; Lucy d. at West Rutland, 27 Sep 1828.

306) ABIEL HOLT (*Joseph Holt⁴, Thomas Holt³, Mary Russell Holt², Robert¹*), b. at Lunenburg, 14 Jul 1748 son of Joseph and Mary (Abbott) Holt; d. at Temple, NH, 7 Jan 1811; m. 25 Nov 1773, his third cousin, SARAH ABBOTT, b. at Suncook, 1751 daughter of Job and Sarah (Abbott) Abbott; Sarah d. 9 Oct 1854 (age at death inscribed as 103 years, 2 months, 25 days on her gravestone).[841]

Abiel Holt was a farmer in Temple. He and Sarah Abbott were parents of five children born at Temple, New Hampshire.

---

[837] Worcester County, MA: Probate File Papers, 1731-1881. Online database. AmericanAncestors.org. New England Historic Genealogical Society, 2015. Case Number 15392

[838] Cunningham, *Cunningham's History of the Town of Lunenburg*, p 178

[839] Cunningham, *Cunningham's History of the Town of Lunenburg*, p 828

[840] Cutter, *History of the Town of Jaffrey*, p 521

[841] Findagrave.com

i ABIEL HOLT, b. 25 Nov 1774; d. at Temple, 11 Mar 1839; m. 31 Jan 1799, ELIZABETH "BETSEY" HOWARD, b. at Temple, NH, 15 May 1776 daughter of Samuel and Elizabeth (Barrett) Howard; Betsey d. at Temple, 30 Dec 1847.

ii ABIGAIL HOLT, b. 22 May 1779; d. at Waterford, ME, about 1806; m. 1799, JONATHAN KIMBALL, b. at Waterford, 1773 son of Isaac and Abigail (Raymond) Kimball. Jonathan Kimball married Elizabeth Bowers 26 Feb 1807.

iii JOSEPH HOLT, b. 23 Feb 1782; d. at Temple, 19 Jul 1835; m. ANNA P.,[842] b. about 1780; Ruth d. at Tempe 12 Feb 1872. Joseph and Anna did not have children.

iv EMELIA HOLT, b. 11 Jun 1784; d. at Temple, 26 Sep 1834. Emelia did not marry.

v NATHAN ABBOT HOLT, b. about 1790; d. at Temple, 25 Mar 1839; m. at Temple, 7 Dec 1815, BETSY PARKHURST, b. at Temple, 10 Oct 1788 daughter of William Parkhurst; Betsy d. at Temple, 29 Dec 1875.

307) JOSEPH HOLT (*Joseph Holt⁴, Thomas Holt³, Mary Russell Holt², Robert¹*), b. at Lunenburg, 18 Dec 1752 son of Joseph and Dorcas (Boynton) Holt; d. at Fitchburg, 3 Sep 1803 (suicide by hanging); m. 30 Jan 1777, ELIZABETH STRATTON.
 Joseph died by suicide on 3 September 1803. The following account was given of his death: "He was found dead hanging with a pair of bridle rains by his neck upon the limb of a small chestnut tree half after ten in the Evening, they had a Jury on the body, & their verdict was that he was insane."[843]
 Joseph Holt did not leave a will and his estate entered probate 22 September 1803 with son Abiel Holt as administrator at the request of widow Elisabeth Holt and eldest son Joseph Holt. The home farm was valued at $850 with a total real estate value of $1,063.33 and personal estate of $363.34.[844] On 23 January 1804, Ephraim Gibson of Fitchburg was named as guardian to represent the interests of the minor children Dolly and Sally. On 10 September 1803, son Joseph then of Lunenburg quitclaimed his right to the property of his honored father Joseph to his brother Abiel Holt.
 Joseph Holt and Elizabeth Stratton were parents of six children born at Fitchburg.[845]

i BETSEY HOLT, b. 23 Sep 1777; d. at Ashby, MA, 9 Jun 1844; m. at Fitchburg, 28 Oct 1797, JACOB BARNARD, b. at Harvard, 16 Apr 1769 son of Jotham and Lucy (Wetherbee) Barnard; Jacob d. at Ashby, 2 Feb 1854. Betsey and Jacob were in Schenectady for several years and later returned to Massachusetts. The 1808 probate of Jacob's father Jotham includes a statement that son Jacob was living out of the Commonwealth. Jacob is on the 1810 census at Schenectady and Betsy and Jacob's daughter Eliza was born there in 1807.

ii JOSEPH HOLT, b. 22 Jul 1779; d. at Chesterfield, NH, 9 Mar 1832; m. at Fitchburg, 9 Feb 1802, BETSEY OSBORN, b. at Fitchburg, 9 Mar 1779 daughter of Ephraim and Sarah (-) Osborn; Betsey d. at Chesterfield, 18 Dec 1838.

iii ABIEL HOLT, b. 29 Aug 1781; d. before 1841 (wife died as a widow); m. at Fitchburg, 21 Jan 1807, CATHERINE GOODRICH, b. at Fitchburg, 7 Sep 1786 daughter of Abijah and Eunice (Martin) Goodrich; Catherine d. at Fitchburg, 18 Feb 1841.

iv SALLY HOLT, b. 10 Sep 1785; d. at Lunenburg, 18 Feb 1847;[846] m. 1st 3 Dec 1807, ZACHARIAH WHITNEY, b. at Lunenburg, 1781 son of Zachariah and Betty (Wetherbee) Whitney; Zachariah d. at Lunenburg, 5 Jul 1812. The 1828 will of Zachariah's father Zachariah includes bequests to his three grandchildren the children of Zachariah deceased: Joseph H. and Josiah B. Whitney and Lavina Eaton widow of John Eaton. Sally Holt m. 2nd 6 Aug 1828, as his second wife, AARON PATCH, b. at Ipswich 1768 son of John Patch; Aaron d. at Holden, 6 Dec 1859.

v DOLLY HOLT, b. 1 Jul 1787

vi DORCAS HOLT, b. 4 Mar 1791; d. at Malden, 24 Sep 1868; m. at Fitchburg, 2 Jun 1814, NATHAN HOLDEN, b. 1786; Nathan d. at Malden, 12 Jan 1829.

308) WILLIAM HOLT (*William Holt⁴, Thomas Holt³, Mary Russell Holt², Robert¹*), b. at Windham, 15 Jul 1743 son of William and Hannah (Holt) Holt; d. at Hampton, 6 Aug 1815;[847] m. 8 Sep 1763, his third cousin, MERCY HOLT, b. 14 Feb 1740/1 daughter of Zebadiah and Sarah (Flint) Holt; Mercy d. at Hampton, 15 Sep 1799.

[842] The will of Joseph Holt includes a bequest to his wife Anna P. Holt.

[843] Davis, *The Old Records of the Town of Fitchburg*, p 345

[844] *Worcester County, MA: Probate File Papers, 1731-1881*. Online database. AmericanAncestors.org. New England Historic Genealogical Society, 2015. Case 30654

[845] Davis, *The Old Records of the Town of Fitchburg*, pp 345-346

[846] Cunningham's History of Lunenburg

[847] *Connecticut, Deaths and Burials Index, 1650-1934*.

William Holt and Mercy Holt were parents of three children born at Hampton.

i   WILLIAM HOLT, b. 22 Nov 1764; d. at Hampton, 8 May 1793; m. at Hampton, 6 Nov 1788, SARAH FULLER, b. at Hampton, 14 Jul 1768 daughter of Samuel and Sarah (Reed) Fuller.

ii   MERCY HOLT, b. 7 Dec 1766; d. at Cooperstown, NY, 14 Sep 1834; m. 1788, JAMES AVERILL, b. at Ashford, 14 Dec 1763 son of James and Mary (Walker) Averill; James d. at St. Johnsville, NY, 17 Dec 1835.

iii   ABIGAIL HOLT, b. 27 Sep 1774

309)   ALICE HOLT (*William Holt⁴, Thomas Holt³, Mary Russell Holt², Robert¹*), b. 26 Apr 1747 at Windham daughter of William and Hannah (Holt) Holt; d. at Stockbridge, VT, 28 Nov 1814;[848] m. 13 Nov 1764, her second cousin, ROBERT LYON (*Sarah Holt Lyon⁴, Robert Holt³, Mary Russell Holt², Robert¹*), b. at Pomfret, 30 Sep 1743 son of Peletiah and Sarah (Holt) Lyon; Robert d. 12 Feb 1809.
        Robert Lyon and Alice Holt were parents of five children born at Hampton, Connecticut. They relocated to Stockbridge, Vermont after the births of their children.

i   ROBERT LYON, b. 23 Dec 1765; d. at Stockbridge, VT, 17 Mar 1844; m. at Stockbridge, 26 Nov 1789, KATHERINE BURNET, b. about 1762; Katherine d. at Stockbridge, 4 Apr 1833.

ii   RUFUS LYON, b. 24 Apr 1767; d. at Stockbridge, 30 Jan 1841; m. at Stockbridge, 5 Oct 1792, LOVINA WILLARD, b. in VT, about 1775; Lovina d. at Stockbridge, Aug 1852.

iii   ALICE LYON, b. 14 Jun 1769; d. at Braintree, VT, 1804; *perhaps* m. about 1795, her fourth cousin, WILLARD COPELAND (*Sarah Ingalls Copeland⁴, Stephen Ingalls³, Sarah Russell Ingalls², Robert¹*), baptized at Brooklyn, CT, 4 Dec 1768 son of James and Sarah (Ingalls) Copeland; Willard d. at Braintree, VT, 20 Feb 1852. Willard married second Rebecca White on 12 Dec 1805. Alice Lyon and Willard Copeland are Family 703.

iv   ROSWELL LYON, b. 2 Oct 1770; d. at Stockbridge, 8 Nov 1814; m. at Stockbridge, 27 Aug 1795, LYDIA ROBERTS, b. 1778; Lydia d. at Stockbridge, 19 Jul 1859.

v   CHESTER LYON, b. 25 May 1772; d. at Braintree, VT, 17 Mar 1812; m. about 1795, THIRZA POOLER, b. at Pomfret, 10 Nov 1772 daughter of Amasa and Hannah (Cady) Pooler; Thirza d. at Braintree, 18 Oct 1843.

310)   SARAH HOLT (*William Holt⁴, Thomas Holt³, Mary Russell Holt², Robert¹*), b. at Windham, 21 Jun 1748 daughter of William and Hannah (Holt) Holt; d. at Hampton, 7 Apr 1777; m. 16 Nov 1769, HENRY DURKEE, b. 29 Sep 1749 son of Henry and Relief (Adams) Durkee. Henry m. 2ⁿᵈ, Sarah Loomis; Henry d. 22 Apr 1820.
        Sarah Holt and Henry Durkee were parents of three children born at Hampton.

i   HENRY DURKEE, b. 25 Aug 1770; m. at Hampton, 25 Sep 1794, SALLY RUSSELL, b. at Ashford, 28 Feb 1774 daughter of Benjamin and Phebe (Smith) Russell; Sally d. at Pittsfield, MA, 23 Dec 1833.

ii   ABIEL DURKEE, b. 14 Mar 1774; d. 8 Feb 1778.

iii   SARAH DURKEE, b. 18 Jan 1777; d. at Hampton, 2 Jan 1806; m. 22 Dec 1796, AZEL GOODWIN, b. at Lebanon, CT, 31 Aug 1769 son of Jonathan and Anna (Clark) Goodwin; Azel d. at Coventry, 14 Apr 1829. Azel married second Clarissa Hunt.

311)   ABIGAIL BARNARD (*Alice Holt Barnard⁴, Thomas Holt³, Mary Russell Holt², Robert¹*), b. at Andover, 15 May 1744 daughter of John and Alice (Holt) Barnard; m. at Andover, 22 Mar 1764, SAMUEL DOWNING, baptized at Salem, 2 May 1742 son of Richard and Temperance (Derby) Downing; Samuel d. at Minot, ME, 13 Dec 1812.
        Abigail and Samuel had their ten children in Andover. After the Revolution, Samuel obtained a land grant in Minot, Maine based on his service.[849] In 1798, Samuel Downing was listed at lot 81 of Auburn (Minot), son Samuel, Jr. at lot 79, and Thomas Downing also on lot 81.[850]

---

[848] *Vermont, Vital Records, 1720-1908.*

[849] Maine, Revolutionary War Land Grants, 1776-1780. Both Samuel and his son Samuel, Jr. had lots of land in Androscoggin County, Maine, and it is not clear if the land bounty is for Samuel or his son. However, the son Samuel's pension file (the application of his widow Lucy) states there was not previously obtained land bounty.

[850] Merrill, History of Androscoggin County, Maine, p 602

i   SAMUEL DOWNING, b. 3 Jan 1765; d. at Minot, 30 Sep 1847; m. at Andover, 25 Aug 1789, ELIZABETH BAILEY, b. at Andover, 6 Jul 1768 daughter of Moses and Elizabeth (Mooar) Bailey; Elizabeth d. at Minot, 1830. Samuel m. 2nd 15 Jun 1833, LUCY MERRILL, b. 6 Apr 1785 daughter of Moses and Mary (True) Merrill; Lucy d. at New Gloucester, ME, 9 May 1862. He may be the Samuel Downing who was paid a bounty by Capt. Benjamin Ames, Chairman of Class No. 13 of the town of Andover to serve in the Continental army for the three-year term.[851]

ii   JOHN DOWNING, b. 1 Feb 1766; d. at Auburn, ME, 12 Sep 1852; m. 14 Nov 1788, RUTH EMERY, b. 29 May 1769 daughter of Moses and Ruth (Bodwell) Emery; Ruth d. at Monmouth, ME, 26 Oct 1864.

iii   ABIGAIL DOWNING, b. 29 Sep 1768; d. at Dracut, 8 Apr 1814; m. at Andover, 26 Nov 1793, JOHN GILCREASE, b. at Dracut, 23 Jun 1770 son of John and Martha (-) Gilcrease; John d. at Dracut, Aug 1826 (probate 26 Sep 1826).

iv   THOMAS DOWNING, b. 24 Jul 1770; d. at Cambridge, ME, 1 Apr 1852; m. at New Gloucester, 27 Apr 1791, ABIGAIL BAYLEY, b. at Newbury, MA, 6 Apr 1772 daughter of Edmund and Abigail (West) Bayley; Abigail d. at Cambridge, ME, 24 Mar 1849.

v   SALLY DOWNING, b. 9 Aug 1772; d. at Andover, 6 Aug 1854; m. at Andover, 12 Jan 1794, THEODORE POOR, b. at Andover, 24 Jan 1766 son of Timothy and Mary (Stevens) Poor; Theodore d. at Andover, 13 May 1851.

vi   MOLLY DOWNING, b. 13 Aug 1774

vii   ALICE DOWNING, b. 8 Jul 1778; d. at Auburn, 4 Sep 1820; m. 1799, REUBEN MERROW, b. at Dover, NH, 24 May 1776 son of Thomas and Hannah (Woodbury) Merrow; Reuben d. at Auburn, 8 Jan 1864. Reuben married second Catherine Verrill.

viii HANNAH DOWNING, b. 20 Aug 1780; d. at Minot, 18 Apr 1867; m. at Minot, 23 Jun 1798, BENJAMIN FRANKLIN LANE, b. 1777; Benjamin d. at Minot, 4 Oct 1846.

ix   AMOS DOWNING, b. 13 Jul 1783; d. at Oxford, ME, 24 Sep 1856; m. RUTH WOLCOTT, b. at Methuen, 7 Nov 1780 daughter of Solomon and Lydia (Bodwell) Wolcott; Ruth d. at Oxford, Mar 1856.

x   RICHARD DERBY DOWNING, b. 31 Mar 1785; d. at Auburn, ME, 2 Nov 1875; m. 1810, ELIZABETH "BETSEY" RICE, b. at Yarmouth, Nova Scotia, 1787 daughter of Jessie and Sarah (Cann) Rice; Betsey d. at Auburn, 4 May 1838.

312)   LYDIA BARNARD (*Alice Holt Barnard⁴, Thomas Holt³, Mary Russell Holt², Robert¹*), b. at Andover, 23 Jan 1745/6 daughter of John and Alice (Holt) Barnard; d. at Sharon, NH, 9 Feb 1829; m. at Andover, 3 Sep 1767, JOSIAH SAWYER, b. at Reading, 17 Sep 1744 son of Josiah and Hannah (Gowing) Sawyer; Josiah d. at Sharon, 3 Oct 1829.
    Josiah Sawyer and Lydia Barnard were parents of eight children. [852]

i   LYDIA SAWYER, baptized at Andover, 21 Feb 1768; d. at Peterborough, 28 Aug 1850; m. WILLIAM NAY, b. Mar 1763 son of William and Betsy (Russell) McNay;[853] William d. at Sharon, NH, 1 Jun 1813 (probate 7 Jun 1813).

ii   JOSIAH SAWYER, baptized at Methuen, 24 Jun 1770; d. at Peterborough, NH, 23 Apr 1800; m. about 1795, MARTHA "PATTY" WYMAN.

iii   HANNAH SAWYER, b. at Methuen, 10 Feb 1772; d. at Lowell, MA, 27 Sep 1860; m. 1st by 1793, SIMEON BASS who has not been identified; Simeon d. by 1808. Hannah m. 2nd at Deering, 3 Nov 1808, PHINEAS EVERETT, b. at Rutland, MA, 22 Apr 1776 son of Phineas and Mary (Clapp) Everett; Phineas d. at Bradford, NH, 30 Jul 1830. Phineas was first married to Lydia Bullard.

iv   MOSES SAWYER, b. 1774; d. at Sharon, NH, 1851; m. 1st by 1797, HEPHZIBAH HARTSHORN, b. 28 Nov 1771 (Sharon town records); Hephzibah d. at Sharon, 25 Jun 1816. Moses m. 2nd SARAH INGALLS, b. at Rindge, NH, 28 Aug 1782 daughter of Josiah and Sarah (Bowers) Ingalls; Sarah d. at Rindge, 16 Nov 1871.

v   JACOB SAWYER, b. 1779; d. at Murray, NY, 2 Jul 1841; m. at Townsend, MA, 18 Jan 1803, ANNA FOSTER, b. at Pepperell, 9 Jul 1781 daughter of Leonard and Lucy (Wetherbee) Foster; Anna d. at Murray, 6 Sep 1858.

vi   ALICE SAWYER, b. at Sharon, 1781; d. at Peterborough, 4 Sep 1849; m. 24 Nov 1801, GEORGE SHEDD, b. at Billerica, 28 Feb 1778 son of Reuben and Sybil (Bullard) Shedd; George d. at Peterborough, 30 Oct 1855.

[851] Massachusetts Soldiers and Sailors in the Revolution, volume 4, p 931
[852] Some children are as given in Smith, *History of the Town of Peterborough*, p 242
[853] Smith, *History of the Town of Peterborough*, p 213

vii   REBECCA SAWYER, b. at Sharon, about 1783; d. at Wilton, 24 Dec 1869; m. at Peterborough, 22 Nov 1810, her fourth cousin once removed, WILLIAM PETTENGILL, b. at Wilton, 12 Nov 1785 son of William and Rhoda (Hagget) Pettengill; William d. at Wilton, 13 Oct 1865.

viii   ABIAL SAWYER, b. 25 Apr 1784; d. at Peterborough, 23 Oct 1870; m. SYBIL BUSS, b. at Sharon, 16 Jan 1787 daughter of Silas and Hannah (Pierce) Buss; Sybil d. at Peterborough, 26 Feb 1866.

313)   ABIGAIL KINGSBURY (*Abigail Holt Kingsbury⁴, Abigail Holt Holt³, Mary Russell Holt², Robert¹*), b. at Hampton, CT, 17 May 1742 daughter of Jonathan and Abigail (Holt) Kingsbury; d. at Lima, NY, 1791; m. 1st, at Windham, 13 Nov 1759, JOHN GOULD, baptized at Ipswich 28 Mar 1731 son of Henry and Rebecca (Cole) Gould; John d. at Hampton, 29 Oct 1764 (probate Nov 1764). Abigail m. 2nd, at Hampton, 11 Sep 1770, JOHN ABBOTT. On 14 Mar 1791, Abigail filed for divorce from John Abbott on grounds of desertion.[854]

     John Gould did not leave a will and his estate entered probate November 1764 with the inventory taken 8 March 1765. Real estate was valued at £111 and personal estate at £59. The settlement on 24 November 1766 included a set-off to widow Abigail Gould, sons John and Jonathan and daughters Abigail and Sally.[855]

     Abigail Kingsbury and John Gould were parents of four children, the youngest child born after John's death. No children were identified for Abigail Kingsbury and John Abbott. After her divorce from John Abbott, Abigail went with her children to Lima, New York but Abigail died soon after arrival.

i   ABIGAIL GOULD, b. at Windham, 14 Feb 1760; d. at Lima, NY, 16 May 1852; m. 3 Jul 1782, JEDEDIAH WATKINS, b. at Ashford, 5 Oct 1739 son of William and Mehitable (Humphrey) Watkins; Jedediah d. at Lima, 19 Aug 1832.

ii   JOHN GOULD, b. at Windham, 12 Oct 1761; living in 1766 but nothing further known that is definite.

iii   JONATHAN GOULD, b. at Windham, 28 Apr 1763; d. at Livonia, NY, 3 Mar 1816; m. 1st at Ashford, 1 Jan 1795, PATIENCE DYER; Patience d. at Lima, NY, 1811. Jonathan m. 2nd RACHEL who has not been identified; Rachel d. at Livonia, 7 Mar 1830.

iv   SALLY GOULD, b. at Windham, 8 Jul 1765; d. at Lima, NY, 19 Oct 1844; m. 1785, PAUL DAVISON, b. at Ashford, 1765; Paul d. at Lima, NY, 19 Feb 1805.

314)   JONATHAN KINGSBURY (*Abigail Holt Kingsbury⁴, Abigail Holt Holt³, Mary Russell Holt², Robert¹*), b. at Hampton, CT, 25 Apr 1745 son of Jonathan and Abigail (Holt) Kingsbury; d. at Hampton, 25 Sep 1802; m. 1st, 14 Jan 1768, ANNE GEER, b. at Preston, 22 Dec 1745 daughter of Aaron and Mercy (Fisher) Geer;[856] Anne d. 23 Oct 1773. Jonathan m. 2nd, 21 Jun 1775, LODEMA RANSOM, b. at Kent, 8 Mar 1752 daughter of John and Bethia (Lewis) Ransom;[857] Lodema d. 24 Mar 1814.

     Jonathan Kingsbury was educated at Yale graduating in 1767. He was a farmer in Hampton and owned considerable property. He represented the town of Hampton in the General Assembly during three sessions 1789-1791.[858]

     In his will written 6 May 1801 (proved 30 November 1802), Jonathan Kingsbury bequeathed to beloved wife Lodema one-third of the household furniture, one-third of the farming tools, and two hundred dollars-worth of neat stock for her own use and disposal forever. She also receives the use and improvement of one-third part of the home farm which consists of about 450 acres but excludes the Holt farm and the so-called Ashford farm. Daughter Anna Rindge receives one-fourteenth part of the estate real and personal. Second daughter Lora Hammond, third daughter Artimesia Wallace, fourth daughter Rhoda Kingsbury, fifth daughter Lodema Kingsbury, and youngest daughter Amie Kingsbury also receive one-fourteenth part each. Sons Lewis, Lester, Ransom, and Jonathan each receives one-seventh of the estate. Grandson Jonathan Rindge receives thirty dollars at age twenty-one. Trusty friend Daniel Dennison was named executor. The total value of the estate was $12,029.96. The home farm of 450 acres was valued at $6,600.[859]

     Jonathan Kingsbury and Anne Geer were parents of three children.

i   ANNA KINGSBURY, b. at Hampton, 21 Nov 1768; d. at Hampton, 15 May 1857; m. at Hampton, 22 Dec 1787, THOMAS RINDGE, b. about 1763; Thomas d. at Hampton, Oct 1819.[860] Thomas served as a private in the Revolution and Anna received a widow's pension based on his service. Thomas Rindge enlisted for one year in

[854] Knox and Ferris, *Connecticut Divorces: Superior Court Records for the Counties of Tolland, New London & Windham 1719-1910*, p 259; John, Wrentham, MA m. Abigail Gould, Windham, 11 Sep 1770; desertion 14 Mar 1791

[855] *Connecticut State Library (Hartford, Connecticut)*; Probate Place: *Hartford, Connecticut, Probate Packets, Geer, J-Gurley, 1719-1880, Estate of John Gould, Case 1644*

[856] The 1797 will of Aaron Geer includes a bequest to the heirs of Anne Kingsbury wife of Jonathan Kingsbury.

[857] The 1791 will of John Ransom of Kent includes a bequest to his daughter Lodema Kingsbury.

[858] Dexter, *Biographical Sketches of the Graduates of Yale College: May 1763-July 1778*, p 234

[859] *Connecticut, Wills and Probate Records, 1609-1999, Windham, Volume 15, pp 39-42*

[860] This is the death date given in the pension application file and the estate was in probate in 1820.

June 1780 and served in the Connecticut line. He enlisted for a second term in April 1782 and was discharged 19 March 1783 at West Point.

ii   LORA KINGSBURY, b. at Windham, 8 Sep 1771; d. at Bolton, CT, 17 Jan 1810; m. LEMUEL HAMMOND, b. at Bolton, 4 Nov 1766 son of Nathaniel and Dorothy (Tucker) Hammond; Lemuel d. at Bolton, 31 Oct 1805.

iii   MERCY KINGSBURY, b. 9 Oct 1773; d. 12 May 1774.

Jonathan Kingsbury and Lodema Ransom were parents of eight children born at Hampton.[861]

i   ARTIMISSA KINGSBURY, b. 15 Jun 1776; d. at Ann Arbor, MI, 9 Dec 1835; m. Mr. Wallace who has not been identified. Their son, Jonathan Kingsbury Wallace, lived in Ann Arbor.

ii   RHODA KINGSBURY, b. 31 Mar 1778; d. at Hampton, 6 Jun 1852; m. at Hampton, 20 Oct 1801, JOHN TWEEDY, b. at Danbury, 16 Mar 1774 son of Samuel and Anna (Smith) Tweedy; John d. at Hampton, 18 Apr 1852.

iii   LODEMA KINGSBURY, b. 24 Feb 1780; d. in West Virginia while traveling to handle affairs related to husband's estate who had died in Kentucky; m. Mr. Nettleton who has not been identified, but is perhaps Henry Nettleton whose brother William Nettleton, of both Connecticut and Kentucky, died in 1837 and left his entire estate to his brother Henry.

iv   AMY KINGSBURY, b. 13 Aug 1783; m. ROBERT DURKEE, b. at Hampton, 23 Feb 1779 son of Andrew and Mary (Benjamin) Durkee; Robert d. at Perry, Feb 1867.

v   LEWIS KINGSBURY, b. 5 Mar 1785; d. at Batavia, MI, about 1846 (probate 1846). Lewis does not seem to have married. No widow or children are mentioned in his probate file. His estate was sold to settle debts of the estate.

vi   LESTER KINGSBURY, b. 28 May 1787; d. at Dansville, NY, 30 Mar 1837; m. 1813, ANNE SPENCER, b. at Litchfield, CT, 1796 son of Samuel and Lucretia (Parsons) Spencer; d. 14 Feb 1877.

vii   RANSOM KINGSBURY, b. 10 Mar 1789; m. 1st at Mansfield, 28 Apr 1813, MARIA FRANCIS, b. 1794; Maria d. at Willington, 24 May 1834. Ransom m. 2nd at Willington, 5 Nov 1834, HANNAH CROCKER (widow of Ira Heath), b. 1794; Hannah d. at Fillmore, NY, Mar 1881.

viii JONATHAN KINGSBURY, b. 15 Apr 1794; d. at Livonia, NY, 5 Nov 1869; m. ARTEMISIA CLARK, b. at Brooklyn, 20 Feb 1794 daughter of Moses and Millicent (Skinner) Clark;[862] d. at Livonia, 1 Oct 1887.

315)   PAUL HOLT (*Paul Holt[4], Abigail Holt Holt[3], Mary Russell Holt[2], Robert[1]*), b. at Windham, 4 Jan 1742/3 son of Paul and Mehitable (Chandler) Holt; d. at Hampton, 26 Oct 1827; m. 1st, 20 Aug 1767, SARAH WELCH, b. at Norwich, 6 Jul 1742 daughter of Joseph and Lydia (Rudd) Welch; Sarah d. 26 Dec 1784. Paul m. 2nd, 15 Jan 1789, PHEBE WELCH CADY, b. 1754 daughter of Gideon and Sarah (Hutchins) Cady;[863] Phebe d. at Hampton, 31 May 1800. Paul m. 3rd, 27 Nov 1800, his second cousin, DINAH HOLT (*Joshua Holt[4], Joshua Holt[3], Mary Russell Holt[2], Robert[1]*) (widow of Seth Stowell), b. at Windham, 22 Mar 1750 daughter of Joshua and Mary (Abbott) Holt; Dinah d. 21 Feb 1826. DINAH HOLT 1st m. 30 Jun 1778, SETH STOWELL, b. 29 May 1742 son of Nathaniel and Margaret (Trowbridge) Stowell; Seth d. about 1798 (when estate went to probate).

Paul Holt served in the Revolution in the Connecticut militia and is reported to have been at the Battle of Bunker Hill.[864]

Paul Holt and Sarah Welch were parents of ten children.

i   THOMAS HOLT, b. at Windham, 3 Sep 1768; d. at Hampton, 13 Sep 1831; m. at Hampton, 12 Jun 1792, EDE MARTIN, b. at Hampton, 30 Sep 1766 daughter of Benjamin and Lucy (Clark) Martin; Ede d. at Hampton, 28 Jan 1844.

ii   VINE HOLT, b. at Windham, 16 Feb 1770; d. at Bristol, CT, 9 Apr 1828; m. at Brooklyn, CT, 28 Oct 1793, SUSAN KNOWLES who has not been identified.

[861] Kingsbury, The Genealogy of the Descendants of Henry Kingsbury, p 173
[862] The 1862 will of Moses Clark of Brooklyn, CT includes a bequest to his daughter Artemisia Kingsbury
[863] The 1799 will of Gideon Cady includes a bequest to his daughter Phebe Holt.
[864] Durrie, *Genealogical History of the Holt Family*, p 89

iii ZIBA HOLT, b. at Windham, 25 Aug 1771; d. at Delphi, IN, 6 May 1860; m. 1st at Gallatin County, KY, 1 Dec 1804, PENELOPE KING, b. 1778; Penelope d. 1811. Ziba m. 2nd at Gallatin County, Oct 1811, LUCINDA WOOD, b. 1793; Lucinda d. 15 Mar 1825.[865]

iv MEHITABLE HOLT, b. at Hampton, 7 Jun 1773; *perhaps* d. at Webster, MA, 5 Nov 1848; m. by 1797, OLIVER RICHMOND, b. at Killingly, 2 May 1765 son of Philip and Abilene (-) Richmond.

v SARAH HOLT, b. at Hampton, 3 Mar 1775; d. at Chaplin, CT, 10 Feb 1833; m. at Hampton, 15 Jan 1797, STEPHEN UTLEY, b. at Windham, 21 Nov 1762 son of Samuel and Hannah (Abbott) Utley; Stephen d. at Chaplin, 1 Mar 1841.

vi CHANDLER HOLT, b. at Hampton, 17 Jan 1777; d. at Paris, NY, 1797.[866]

vii ERASTUS HOLT, b. at Hampton, 8 Sep 1778; d. at Pittsfield, VT, 28 Mar 1875; m. 1 Jun 1800, SARAH PARMENTER, b. at Oakham, MA, about 1782 daughter of Isaiah and Lydia (Hayden) Parmenter; Sarah d. at Pittsfield, 28 Dec 1863.

viii LYDIA HOLT, b. at Hampton, 7 Oct 1780; m. ZACHARIAH YOUNG; Lydia and Zachariah were living in Greenfield, PA in 1840.

ix RUFUS HOLT, b. at Hampton, 1 Feb 1783; d. at Willington, 22 Dec 1852; m. at Willington, 12 Jan 1809, BETSEY HORTON, b. at Ashford, 5 Apr 1785 daughter of Moses and Silence (Wilson) Horton.

x ABIGAIL HOLT, b. at Hampton, 17 Dec 1784. Durrie in his Holt genealogy reports that Abigail did not marry, although I wonder if she is the Abigail that married Benjamin Minor in 1804 at Hampton).

Paul Holt's third wife, Dinah Holt, was first married to Seth Stowell. Seth participated in the Revolution as one of those who helped buy and equip a privateer.[867] Seth did not leave a will and his estate entered probate 5 May 1798 with widow Dinah as administratrix. Heirs of the estate were Olive, Keziah, Artimissa, and Mardin.[868]

Dinah Holt and Seth Stowell were parents of four children.

i OLIVE STOWELL, b. at Pomfret, 2 Apr 1779; d. at New Woodstock, NY, 13 Jun 1829; m. at Woodstock, 6 Feb 1803, LUTHER CORBIN, b. at Woodstock, 18 Feb 1775 son of Silas and Anna (Fisk) Corbin; Luther d. at New Woodstock, 5 Aug 1848.

ii KEZIA STOWELL, b. at Pomfret, 4 Sep 1781; living in 1798 but nothing further known.

iii ARTEMESIA STOWELL, b. at Pomfret, 7 Nov 1784; d. at New Woodstock, NY, 25 Jan 1853; m. at New Woodstock, 1 Jan 1806, ABIEL AINSWORTH, b. at Woodstock, 10 May 1777 son of Nathan and Phebe (Kinsley) Ainsworth; Abiel d. at New Woodstock, 4 Nov 1866.

iv MARVIN CHARLES STOWELL, b. at Union, CT, 15 Mar 1789; d. at Cazenovia, NY; m. at Pomfret, 17 Jan 1813, LUCY HOUGHTON, *likely* the Lucy b. at Woodstock, 20 Jul 1790 daughter of Jonas and Sarah (Abbott) Houghton.

316) PHILEMON HOLT (*Paul Holt⁴, Abigail Holt Holt³, Mary Russell Holt², Robert¹*), b. at Hampton, 22 Jun 1744 son of Paul and Mehitable (Chandler) Holt; d. at Willington, 31 Jul 1818; m. at Willington, 27 Aug 1771, JEMIMA ELDREDGE, b. at Willington, 28 Mar 1755 daughter of Jesse and Abigail (Smith) Eldredge; Jemima d. at Willington, 3 Oct 1821.

The estate of Philemon Holt entered probate 17 October 1818 with Jemima Holt and Amasa Holt as administrators. The distribution of the personal estate included one-third to widow Jemima Holt and the remainder in four equal shares to each of the following heirs: son Jerome Holt, one share to daughter Clarissa Holt wife of John Holt, one share to son Amasa Holt, and one share to representatives of Lucinda Fenton deceased late wife of Abiel Fenton.[869]

There is evidence for five children of Philemon and Jemima likely all born at Windham.[870]

i JEROME HOLT, b. unknown. He is the first child listed in the distribution, but his brother Amasa was administrator of the estate. Nothing else is known of him.

[865] Stewart, *Recollections of the Early Settlement of Carroll County, Indiana*, pp 106-110; this source has a lengthy, colorful biography of Col. Ziba Holt.
[866] Durrie, Holt genealogy
[867] Stowell, *The Stowell Genealogy*, p 107
[868] Connecticut State Library (Hartford, Connecticut); Probate Place: *Hartford, Connecticut, Probate Packets, Spencer, Hulda-Thompson, Calvin, 1759-1880*, case 4169, Seth Stowell
[869] *Connecticut State Library (Hartford, Connecticut)*; Probate Place: *Hartford, Connecticut, Philemon Holt estate*
[870] Durrie's Holt genealogy reports eight children (not named), but evidence was found for just one child beyond the four in the probate.

ii   MATILDA HOLT, b. at Windham, 14 Feb 1773; likely died young.

iii   CLARISSA HOLT, b. about 1775; d. at Willington, 25 Feb 1840; m. at Willington, 6 Sep 1804, her second cousin once removed, JOHN HOLT (*James Holt⁴, Abiel Holt³, Mary Russell Holt², Robert¹*), b. at Willington, 11 Apr 1776 son of James and Luce (Sawins) Holt; John d. at Willington, 22 Apr 1841. Clarissa and John are Family 343.

iv   LUCINDA HOLT, b. at Windham, 30 Apr 1775; d. at Willington, 15 Dec 1816; m. at Willington, 27 Jun 1791, ABIEL FENTON, b. at Willington, 27 May 1767 son of Eleazer and Elizabeth (Davis) Fenton; Abiel d. at Willington, 30 May 1822.

v   AMASA HOLT, b. about 1781; d. at Willington, 22 Jun 1850; m. BETSEY who has not been identified; Betsey was b. about 1777 and d. at Willington, 3 Oct 1851.

317)   EBENEZER HOLT (*Paul Holt⁴, Abigail Holt Holt³, Mary Russell Holt², Robert¹*), b. recorded at Windham, 23 Feb 1745/6 son of Paul and Mehitable (Chandler) Holt; m. at Somers, 29 Aug 1771, MARY COLLINS.

     Ebenezer Holt and Mary Collins were parents of six children born at Hampton, Connecticut. The movements of this family are not clear after the births of their children, but Ebenezer perhaps went to Pittsfield, Vermont with his brother Stephen.

i   EBENEZER HOLT, b. 1772; died young

ii   MOLLY HOLT, b. 29 Jun 1773

iii   CHLOE HOLT, b. 6 Apr 1775; d. 7 Apr 1776

iv   CHLOE HOLT, b. 24 Feb 1777

v   LEVI HOLT, b. 17 Apr 1779; d. at South Wilbraham, MA, 1814 (probate 6 Jun 1814); m. at Somers, CT, 2 Mar 1807, LUCINDA JONES, b. at Somers, 4 Apr 1787 daughter of Issachar and Eleanor (Hunt) Jones. Lucinda married second Maj. David Elliot on 5 Dec 1815.

vi   JUSTIN HOLT, b. about 1781; died young[871]

318)   STEPHEN HOLT (*Paul Holt⁴, Abigail Holt Holt³, Mary Russell Holt², Robert¹*), b. at Hampton, 12 Mar 1748 son of Paul and Mehitable (Chandler) Holt; d. at Pittsfield, VT, 31 Dec 1838; m. 20 Nov 1774, HANNAH GEER, b. 2 Nov 1755 daughter of Aaron and Mercy (Fisher) Geer;[872] Hannah d. at Chaplin, CT, 1858.

     Stephen and Hannah began their family in Windham and moved to Pittsfield, Vermont in 1787 and erected a sawmill in 1797. He was as one of the first selectmen when the town of officially organized in 1793.[873]

     Stephen and Hannah were parents of eight children.

i   STEPHEN HOLT, b. at Windham, 2 Oct 1775; d. 15 Feb 1779.

ii   ELISHA HOLT, b. at Windham, 8 Oct 1778; d. at Worthington, OH, 9 Oct 1857; m. 1st at Pittsfield, 19 Jan 1803, SAREPTA HOSINGTON, b. about 1783; Sarepta d. at Pittsfield, about 1812. Elisha m. 2nd at Pittsfield, 29 May 1815, LOUISA B. HARRISON, b. at Chittenden, VT, about 1785 daughter of Samuel and Rebecca (Keeler) Harrison; Louisa d. at Worthington, OH, 1841. Elisha m. 3rd about 1842, EMILY M. who has not been identified but born in PA about 1812.

iii   HANNAH HOLT, b. at Windham, 13 Nov 1780; d. at Pittsfield, VT, 27 Jan 1868; m. 20 Mar 1800, ROBERT CROSSMAN, b. at Sutton, MA, 29 Sep 1778 son of Jacob and Anne (Claflin) Crossman;[874] Robert d. at Pittsfield, 13 May 1859.

iv   STEPHEN HOLT, b. at Windham, 12 Sep 1783; d. at Pittsfield, VT, 7 Feb 1856; m. at Pittsfield, 23 Mar 1806, REBECCA PARMENTER, b. 1783 daughter of Thomas and Mary (Walker) Parmenter; Rebecca d. at Pittsfield, 15 Sep 1856.

v   JOSIAH HOLT, b. at Windham, 20 May 1786; d. at Stockbridge, VT, 5 Dec 1871; m. at Pittsfield, 28 May 1815, LUCINDA CHASE, b. at Ticonderoga, NY[875] about 1791; Lucinda d. at Stockbridge, 5 Dec 1871.

[871] Durrie, Holt genealogy
[872] The 1797 will of Aaron Geer includes a bequest to daughter Hannah Holt wife of Stephen Holt.
[873] Smith, *History of Rutland County, Vermont*, p 603 and p 720
[874] The names of Robert's parents are given as Jacob and Ann on his death record.
[875] Lucinda's place of birth is given on the death record of one of her children.

vi CLARISSA HOLT, b. likely at Pittsfield, 27 Jul 1789; d. at Pittsfield, 18 Jan 1822; m. at Pittsfield, 28 Feb 1814, MOSES RICE, b. 1787; Moses d. after 1850 when he was living at Leicester, VT. Moses was second married to Edna Hubbard on 24 Feb 1823.

vii AMOS HOLT, b. at Pittsfield, VT, 16 Mar 1795; d. 8 Sep 1796.

viii AMOS HOLT, b. at Pittsfield, 16 Mar 1799; d. at Brandon, VT, 30 Apr 1874; m. about 1825, ANNA E. GAINES, b. at Pittsfield, 1806 daughter of Asa and Annah (Doyle) Gaines; Anna d. at Brandon, 28 Apr 1860.

319) JAMES HOLT (*Paul Holt⁴, Abigail Holt Holt³, Mary Russell Holt², Robert¹*), b. at Hampton, 21 May 1750 son of Paul and Mehitable (Chandler) Holt; d. at Bristol, CT, 29 Mar 1826; m. 1ˢᵗ, 31 Dec 1769, HULDAH STILES, b. at Hampton, 18 Sep 1736 daughter of Samuel and Huldah (Durkee) Stiles; Huldah d. at Hampton, 12 Jul 1799.[876] James m. 2ⁿᵈ, 29 Jun 1800, CHLOE STILES (niece of Huldah), b. 4 May 1781 daughter of Isaac and Abigail (Case) Stiles. Chloe Holt was living in Bristol in 1850 with her son James.
  James Holt and Huldah Stiles were parents of two children.

i LYDIA HOLT, b. at Hampton, 28 Jan 1770; m. at Hampton, 12 Aug 1792, NATHANIEL SWEET NILES, b. at Warwick, RI, 1759 son of Benjamin and Ruth (Niles) Niles; Nathaniel d. likely at Pomfret, 16 Nov 1832.[877]

ii HULDAH HOLT, b. at Hampton, 9 Sep 1772; d. 28 Sep 1775.

  James Holt and Chloe Stiles were parents of one child.

i JAMES HOLT, b. at Willington, 13 Oct 1801; d. at Bristol, CT, 13 Dec 1890. James did not marry. He owned a sawmill in Bristol.

320) MEHITABLE HOLT (*Paul Holt⁴, Abigail Holt Holt³, Mary Russell Holt², Robert¹*), b. at Windham, 1 May 1757 daughter of Paul and Mehitable (Chandler) Holt; d. at Hampton, 27 Oct 1819; m. at Pomfret, 27 Nov 1789, JEREMIAH PHELPS, b. at Hebron, 13 Jul 1729 son of Timothy and Hannah (Calkins) Phelps.[878]
  The estate of Mehitable Phelps entered probate 1 November 1819 with Ziba H. Phelps as administrator. Proceeds of the sale of the personal estate were $368.88 which was not sufficient for the claims against the estate of $597.34 and a portion of the real estate was sold to settle the estate. Heirs were Zibha H. Phelps, Lucy Martin, Josiah H. Phelps and John Phelps.[879]
  Mehitable Holt and Jeremiah Phelps were parents of four children.

i LUCY PHELPS, b. at Pomfret, 27 Jun 1790; likely d. at Hartford, 28 May 1871; m. at Hampton, 19 Jan 1817, ASA U. MARTIN, b. 8 Feb 1792 son of Amasa and Ursula (Utley) Martin.

ii ZIBA HOLT PHELPS, b. at Pomfret, 14 Oct 1793; d. at Hampton, 16 Jan 1878; m. at Hampton, 1 Jan 1818, BETSEY GRIFFIN, b. about 1798 likely daughter of Ebenezer and Mary (Fuller) Griffin; Betsey d. at Hampton, 4 Dec 1866.

iii JOSIAH H. PHELPS, b. at Pomfret, 7 Oct 1795;[880] d. at Manhattan, KS, 30 Jan 1885; m. RUTH, b. at Rochester, VT, 14 May 1801; Ruth d. at Manhattan, KS, 15 May 1865. Josiah m. 2ⁿᵈ at Manhattan, KS, 10 Nov 1878, a woman 55 years his junior, MARY MATILDA PAXTON, b. in NY, about 1851. Josiah attended Yale and was a physician in Rochester, VT and later in Manhattan, KS. In his will written in 1879, he left his entire estate to his wife Mary M. Phelps. No children are mentioned in the will. The Hampton, CT records from the Barbour collection mention a son Peter but without year of birth and without the name of mother.

iv JOHN PHELPS, b. about 1797; d. at Tolland, 26 Sep 1847; m. at Hampton, 30 Nov 1818, BETSEY ROBINSON, b. at Windham, 26 Dec 1793 daughter of Asa and Olive (Huntington) Robinson; Betsey d. at Tolland, 3 Feb 1832.

321) ABIGAIL KENDALL (*Abigail Holt Kendall⁴, Robert Holt³, Mary Russell Holt², Robert¹*), b. at Windham, 21 Oct 1742 daughter of David and Abigail (Holt) Kendall; d. at Ashford, 8 Nov 1781; m. 28 May 1771, ENOS PRESTON, b. at Windham, 7 Jun 1737 son of John and Sarah (Foster) Preston. Enos married second Hannah Stiles on 12 Nov 1783.
  Abigail Kendall and Enos Preston were parents of three children born at Ashford.

---

[876] Huldah the wife of James Holt died at age 63.

[877] U.S., The Pension Roll of 1835

[878] Phelps and Servin, *The Phelps Family in America*, volume 1, p 211

[879] *Connecticut State Library (Hartford, Connecticut)*; Probate Place: *Hartford, Connecticut, Estate of Mehitable Phelps, Case 3023*

[880] Josiah's birthdate, and that of his wife Ruth, is engraved on his tombstone.

i   ABRAHAM PRESTON, b. 5 Aug 1771; d. at Perry, OH, 1860; m. LOVINA HAVENS, b. at Ashford, 27 Jan 1774 daughter of Simon and Elizabeth (Vincent) Havens;[881] Lovina d. at Worthington, OH, 1 Mar 1869. After their marriage, Abraham and Lovina were in Otsego County, NY before moving to Franklin County, OH in 1817.[882]

ii   ALLIS PRESTON, b. 12 Oct 1773

iii   ALVAH PRESTON, b. 9 Mar 1779; d. at Ellington, NY, 30 Mar 1852; m. LYDIA POWERS, b. at Lancaster, MA, 12 Nov 1774 daughter of Oliver and Lydia (Winn) Powers; Lydia d. at Ellington, 20 Feb 1843.

322)   DAVID KENDALL (*Abigail Holt Kendall⁴, Robert Holt³, Mary Russell Holt², Robert¹*), b. at Windham, 13 Nov 1744 son of David and Abigail (Holt) Kendall; d. at Ashford, after 1820; m. at Ashford, 23 Feb 1775, MEHITABLE STILES, b. at Windham, 15 Nov 1740 daughter of Samuel and Huldah (Durkee) Stiles; Mehitable d. at Ashford, 27 Jan 1827.

    David and Mehitable were admitted to the church at Ashford 24 February 1799 and two of their children, Eunice and Daniel, were baptized on 12 May 1799.[883]

    David and Mehitable were parents of four children born at Ashford.

i   SARAH KENDALL, b. 27 Oct 1776

ii   LUCY HOLT KENDALL, b. 26 Mar 1779; d. at Ashford, 11 Jul 1786.

iii   EUNICE KENDALL, b. 19 Jul 1784; d. at Ashford, 4 Feb 1856; m. at Ashford, 28 Jan 1844, as his second wife, BENJAMIN WHEATON, b. at Swansea, 30 Oct 1775 son of James and Sarah (Slade) Wheaton; Benjamin d. at Ashford, 30 Mar 1852. Benjamin was first married to Annah Lyon.

iv   DANIEL KENDALL, b. 29 May 1785 and baptized at Ashford 12 May 1799; nothing further definitive found.

323)   SETH TRUESDELL (*Mary Holt Truesdell⁴, Robert Holt³, Mary Russell Holt², Robert¹*), b. at Pomfret, 23 Mar 1746 son of Joseph and Mary (Holt) Truesdell; d. at Pomfret, 19 Oct 1776; m. at Pomfret, 10 Jan 1771, ESTHER WEST, likely b. at Tolland, 17 Mar 1754 daughter of Solomon and Abigail (Strong) West

    Seth Truesdell and Esther West were parents of four children born at Pomfret.

i   RUTH TRUESDELL, b. 10 Aug 1771

ii   JOSEPH TRUESDELL, b. 20 Dec 1772; d. 1 Sep 1777.

iii   SAMUEL TRUESDELL, b. 22 Sep 1774; d. at Thompson, 30 Jan 1842; m. about 1800, LOIS FAY RICHARDS, b. at Killingly, 21 Sep 1777 daughter of Israel and Lois (Holmes) Richards; Lois d. at Thompson, 10 Mar 1832. Samuel m. 2nd at Thompson, 29 Sep 1833, NANCY NICHOLS (widow of Sylvester Stanley), b. 1782 daughter of Jonathan and Rebecca (Swift) Stanley; Nancy d. at Putnam, CT, 23 Oct 1851.

iv   JERUSHA TRUESDELL, b 6 Apr 1776; m. at Pomfret, 10 Apr 1796, her second cousin once removed, OLIVER GOODALE (*Phebe Holt Goodale⁴, Joshua Holt³, Mary Russell Holt², Robert¹*), b. at Willington, about 1774 son of Ebenezer and Phebe (Holt) Goodale.

324)   JEDUTHAN TRUESDELL (*Mary Holt Truesdell⁴, Robert Holt³, Mary Russell Holt², Robert¹*), b. recorded at Killingly, 21 Jan 1748 son of Joseph and Mary (Holt) Truesdell; d. at Pomfret, 12 Apr 1801; m. at Pomfret, 20 Jan 1774; ABIGAIL WHITE.

    Jeduthun Truesdell and Abigail White were parents of seven children born at Pomfret. Four of the children died in childhood.

i   SILAS TRUESDELL, b. 2 Nov 1774; d. 17 Nov 1774.

ii   SILAS TRUESDELL, b. 27 Mar 1777; d. 7 May 1787.

iii   JOSEPH TRUESDELL, b. 27 Aug 1779; *possibly* m. at Pomfret, 30 Sep 1804, BETSEY INGALLS, b. at Pomfret, 22 May 1780 daughter of Benjamin and Eunice (Woodworth) Ingalls.

---

[881] The 1816 will of Simon Havens of Ashford includes a bequest to his daughter Lovina Preston.

[882] Williams Brothers, History of Franklin and Pickaway Counties, Ohio, p 378

[883] *Connecticut, Church Record Abstracts, 1630-1920, volume 001, Ashford*

iv   ELISHA TRUESDELL, b. 28 Apr 1782; d. at Harpursville, NY, 16 Oct 1849; m. SARAH CARPENTER, b. at Tolland, 11 Nov 1787 daughter of Simeon and Abigail (Cushman) Carpenter; Sarah d. at Harpursville, 1857.

v   HARVEY TRUESDELL, b. 28 Dec 1783; d. 29 Aug 1789.

vi   SARAH TRUESDELL, b. 11 Aug 1787; d. 5 Sep 1789.

vii   JEDUTHUN TRUESDELL, b. 25 Dec 1789

325)   DARIUS TRUESDELL (*Mary Holt Truesdell⁴, Robert Holt³, Mary Russell Holt², Robert¹*), b. at Pomfret, 16 Jan 1752 son of Joseph and Mary (Holt) Truesdell; d. at Woodstock, 6 May 1808; m. at Woodstock, 10 Oct 1772, RHODA CHAFFEE, b. at Woodstock, 10 May 1751 daughter of Thomas and Dorcas (Abbott) Chaffee; Rhoda d. at Woodstock, 19 Nov 1834.
        Rhoda had an out-of-wedlock child, daughter Annice Corbin born at Woodstock, 18 May 1771. Nothing further is known regarding Anice.
        Rhoda Chaffee and Darius Truesdell were parents of nine children born at Woodstock.

i   ASA TRUESDELL, b. 17 Jul 1773; nothing further known.

ii   DARIUS TRUESDELL, b. 1 Aug 1775; d. at Hartford, 16 Mar 1814; m. at Chester, MA, 14 Sep 1794, RACHEL SIZER, b. at Middletown, CT, 12 Mar 1772 daughter of William and Abigail (Wilcox) Sizer; Rachel d. at Fishkill, NY, 16 Dec 1853.

iii   RHODA TRUESDELL, b. 31 Jan 1778; d. at Colrain, MA, 26 Mar 1795. From the Colrain, MA records: "Truesdale, Rhode, drowned while crossing North River on a log. She was on a visit from Connecticut at the house of Ephraim Manning, Mar. 26, 1795."

iv   SILAS CHAFFEE TRUESDELL, b. 14 Jan 1784; nothing further known.

v   CYRUS TRUESDELL, b. about 1785; d. at Woodstock, 6 Jan 1815.

vi   JOHN TRUESDELL, b. 25 Jul 1786; d. at Killingly, CT, 17 May 1860; m. at Sturbridge, MA, 4 Sep 1808, SOPHIA BAYLIS, b. at Taunton, 2 Jul 1784 daughter of Frederick and Hannah (Brown) Baylis; Sophia d. at Putnam, CT, 24 Oct 1833.

vii   THOMAS TRUESDELL, b. 10 Jul 1789; d. at Montclair, NJ, 20 Mar 1874; m. 1ˢᵗ, at Providence, RI, 14 Oct 1811, HARRIET LEE, b. at Providence, 10 Jul 1786 daughter of William and Abigail (Kinnicutt) Lee; Harriet d. at Brooklyn, NY, 30 Jun 1862. Thomas m. 2ⁿᵈ, 1865, JESSIE MARGERY GUNN, b. at Thurso, Caithness, Scotland, 4 Feb 1827; Jessie d. at Caldwell, NJ, 1888.

viii SARAH TRUESDELL, b. 29 Jul 1791; d. at Woodstock, 19 Jan 1815.

ix   POLLY TRUESDELL, b. 5 Feb 1794; d. at Jefferson, OH, after 1850; m. at Woodstock, about 1815, JEREMIAH C. OLNEY, b. 1 Jun 1792 son of Ithamar and Anne (Cady) Olney; Jeremiah d. at Jefferson, OH, 1860.

326)   REUBEN RICHARDSON (*Martha Holt Richardson⁴, Robert Holt³, Mary Russell Holt², Robert¹*), b. at Windham, 7 Dec 1754 son of John and Martha (Holt) Richardson; m. at Yarmouth, 24 Aug 1775, MARY BURGESS daughter of Joshua Burgess. Reuben Richardson and Mary Burgess were parents of five children born at Yarmouth, Nova Scotia.[884]

i   SARAH RICHARDSON, b. 21 Dec 1776; d. at Yarmouth, Oct 1823; m. about 1798, EBENEZER CROSBY, b. 1772 son of Ebenezer Crosby; Ebenezer d. at Yarmouth, 13 Dec 1863.

ii   MARY RICHARDSON, b. 11 Oct 1778; m. LEVI HERSEY, b. at Yarmouth, 30 Dec 1780 son of Levi and Chloe (Day) Hersey.

iii   STEPHEN RICHARDSON, b. 21 Aug 1780

iv   REUBEN RICHARDSON, b. 11 Jul 1782

v   JOHN RICHARDSON, b. 10 Nov 1784

---

[884] Trask, *Early Vital Records of the Township of Yarmouth, Nova Scotia*, p 10

327) STEPHEN RICHARDSON (*Martha Holt Richardson[4], Robert Holt[3], Mary Russell Holt[2], Robert[1]*), b. at Pomfret, 26 Sep 1759 son of John and Martha (Holt) Richardson; d. at Middletown, VT, 3 Jan 1834;[885] m. at Norwich, CT, 21 Dec 1786, HANNAH RUDD, b. about 1767; Hannah d. at Middletown, about 1848.

Stephen Richardson served in the Revolution being drafted from Norwich, Connecticut in 1777. He was in the Battle of Stillwater and the capture of Burgoyne. In 1778, he enlisted and was discharged at the beginning of 1779. He entered the service as a private with a final rank of first sergeant. In his pension application file, Stephen reported he was born 24 September 1759 in Abington and he moved to Vermont around the end of the war and was in Bennington. At the time of his pension application in 1832, he was living in Rutland. Stephen married Hannah Rudd in Connecticut in 1786. In 1842, Hannah Richardson made application for her pension as a widow. Daughter Clarissa Burnum and son Harvey Richardson made statements in support of their mother's application.[886]

The only two children located for this family are the two children identified in the pension file. Very little in the way of records was located.

i CLARISSA RICHARDSON, b. at Middletown, 24 Oct 1795; m. at Middletown, 28 Nov 1816, ORSON BURNUM.

ii HARVEY RICHARDSON, b. at Middletown, about 1801; d. at Middletown Springs, 10 Jan 1885; m. 1st about 1825, MIRIAM AMES[887] who has not been identified. Harvey m. 2nd about 1842, LAURA who is not identified but may be Laura Leonard.[888]

328) MARY FENTON (*Elizabeth Holt Fenton[4], Abiel Holt[3], Mary Russell Holt[2], Robert[1]*), b. at Willington, 13 Apr 1748 daughter of Francis and Elizabeth (Holt) Fenton; d. at Willington, 14 Apr 1822; m. 1st, 21 May 1770, ISAAC SAWIN, b. 23 Sep 1748 son of George and Anna (Farrar) Sawin; Isaac d. 29 Oct 1776. Mary m. 2nd, 2 Jul 1778, as his second wife, JAMES NILES, b. at Braintree, 2 Apr 1747 son of John and Dorothy (Reynolds) Niles; James d. 18 Jan 1822. James Niles was first married to Elizabeth Vinton.

Isaac Sawin did not leave a will. The inventory of his estate was completed 5 February 1777 with a total value of £126 including house and land valued at £80. George Sawin was named guardian for three-year-old Elijah. The distribution of the estate includes a set-off of one-third part for widow Mary and the remaining two-thirds to only child Elijah.[889]

After Isaac's death, Mary married James Niles and had four children. James had three children with his first wife, Elizabeth Vinton. James Niles wrote his will 8 June 1819 and the estate entered probate 1822. In his will, beloved wife Mary receives one cow, four sheep, the use of a west room of the house and a number of provisions to be provided by the executors. Five of the children will divide the household items after their mother's decease (Elizabeth, Phebe, Isaac, Joshua Holt, and Molly). Oldest son James receives $50. There are in-kind money bequests to Elizabeth, Phebe, and Molly. Son Isaac receives the house Isaac is living in and the land it stands upon. Son Joshua Holt receives his father's house. Sons Isaac and Joshua Holt are named executors.[890] Children James, Elizabeth, and Phebe are children from James Nile's marriage to Elizabeth Vinton.

Mary Fenton and Isaac Sawin had two children born at Willington.

i ELIZABETH SAWIN, b. 16 Dec 1770; d. 8 Feb 1771.

ii ELIJAH SAWIN, b. 31 Oct 1774; d. at Willington, 1814 (date of probate); m. at Willington, 24 Dec 1795, his second cousin once removed, AMY POOL (*Deborah Preston Pool[4], Deborah Holt Preston[3], Mary Russell Holt[2], Robert[1]*), b. at Willington, 7 Aug 1775 daughter of Timothy and Deborah (Preston) Pool; d. at Willington, about 1817.[891] Amy Pool and Elijah Sawin are Family 364.

Mary Fenton and James Niles had four children born at Willington.

i JOHN NILES, b. 2 Oct 1779; d. 26 Jun 1803.

ii MOLLY NILES, b. 3 Oct 1782. No birth or death record was located for Molly, but she was living in 1819 at the time of her father's will.

---

[885] *U.S., Revolutionary War Pension and Bounty-Land Warrant Application Files, 1800-1900* [database on-line].

[886] U.S., Revolutionary War Pension and Bounty-Land Warrant Application Files, 1800-1900, Case W26386

[887] Miriam Ames is given as the name of the mother of James Richardson on his death record. He is the one known son of Harvey from his first marriage.

[888] There is not a clear record of the name of Harvey's second wife. The two census records give her name as Laura, the death record of one of the children says her name was Lucy Leonard and one says her name was Smith.

[889] *Connecticut Wills and Probate, 1609-1999*, Probate of Isaac Sawin, Tolland, 1777, Case number 1879.

[890] *Connecticut Wills and Probate, 1609-1999*, Probate of James Niles, Stafford District, 1822, Case number 1554.

[891] Sawin: *Sawin: Summary Notes*, p 38

iii   ISAAC NILES, b. 9 Mar 1786; d. at Tolland, 7 Oct 1858; m. at Willington, 27 Oct 1808, his third cousin, ALLICE SCRIPTURE (*Alice Pearl Scripture⁵, Dinah Holt Pearl⁴, Joshua Holt³, Mary Russell Holt², Robert¹*), b. at Willington, 14 Jul 1790 daughter of Eleazer and Alice (Pearl) Scripture; Allice d. 3 Mar 1863.

iv   JOSHUA HOLT NILES, b. 6 Sep 1790; d. at Willington, 10 Apr 1850; m. at Willington, 3 Dec 1812, SIBYL HUGHES, b. at Ashford, 4 May 1795 daughter of Jonathan and Eunice (Fuller) Hughes; Sibyl d. at Willington, 29 May 1873.

329)   FRANCIS FENTON (*Elizabeth Holt Fenton⁴, Abiel Holt³, Mary Russell Holt², Robert¹*), b. at Willington, 13 Feb 1750/1 son of Francis and Elizabeth (Holt) Fenton; m. 25 May 1775, CHLOE GOODALE, b. at Pomfret, 28 Dec 1755 daughter of Ebenezer and Phebe (Holt) Goodale; Chloe d. at New Haven, Oct 1833.[892]
        Francis Fenton and Chloe Goodale were parents of six children born at Willington.

i   ELIZABETH FENTON, b. 27 Mar 1777

ii   OLIVER FENTON, b. 1 Nov 1778; d. 22 Nov 1781.

iii   CHLOE FENTON, b. 20 May 1780; d. at South Windsor, CT, 19 Feb 1823; m. ELLIOT GRANT, b. at Windsor, CT, 23 Apr 1762 son of Edward and Hannah (Foster) Grant; Elliot d. at East Windsor, 7 Jun 1846.

iv   CHESTER FENTON, b. 11 Mar 1782; d. 5 Mar 1783.

v   PHEBE FENTON, b. 1 Sep 1783

vi   LEISTER FENTON, b. 26 Jun 1786

330)   HANNAH HOLT (*Abiel Holt⁴, Abiel Holt³, Mary Russell Holt², Robert¹*), b. at Willington, 14 Mar 1756 daughter of Abiel and Mary (Downer) Holt; d. 20 Nov 1832; m. 24 Apr 1782, as his second wife, her second cousin, OLIVER PEARL (*Dinah Holt Pearl⁴, Joshua Holt³, Mary Russell Holt², Robert¹*), b. 9 Oct 1749 son of Timothy and Dinah (Holt) Pearl. Oliver was married 1st, 1 Jan 1772 MERCY HINCKLEY, b. 1749 daughter of John and Susanna (Harris) Hinckley;[893] Mercy d. at Willington, 15 Nov 1781.
        Hannah Holt and Oliver Pearl were parents of six children born at Willington.

i   HANNAH PEARL, b. 29 Apr 1783; d. 23 Nov 1786.

ii   MARCY PEARL, b. 18 Aug 1785; m. 1st, at Ashford, 1 Jan 1810, WILLIAM BUFFINGTON, b. at Ashford, 21 Jun 1789 son of William and Candace (Salisbury) Buffington; William d. at Ashford, 20 Jan 1814. Marcy m. 2nd, about 1815, LOREN FULLER.[894]

iii   OLIVER PEARL, b. 10 Nov 1788; d. at Berlin Heights, OH, 26 May 1835; m. about 1811, MARY SEXTON, b. at Ellington, 5 Dec 1795 daughter of William and Docia (Emerson) Sexton; Mary d. at Berlin Heights, 15 May 1884.

iv   WALTER PEARL, b. 15 Sep 1791; m. at Mansfield, CT, 24 Nov 1814, MARIA DAVIS, b. at Mansfield, 9 Jul 1794 daughter of Thomas and Patience (Dennison) Davis.[895]

v   HANNAH PEARL, b. 17 May 1794; d. at Berlin Heights, OH, 26 Oct 1849; m. 1822, PHILIP SEELY BAKER, b. in CT, 22 Jul 1790; Philip d. at Berlin Heights, 12 May 1889. Philip married second the widow Lavinia Decker.

vi   CYREL PEARL, b. 16 Sep 1797; d. at Lounsberry, NY, 20 Jul 1837; m. 29 May 1820, ROSANNAH FARMER, b. 24 Jun 1804 daughter of Thomas and Rosannah (Thompson) Farmer; Rosannah d. at Lounsberry, 17 Jun 1875.

        Oliver Pearl and Mercy Hinckley were parents of five children born at Willington.

i   ALICE PEARL, b. 15 Dec 1772; d. 30 Mar 1773.

ii   OLIVER PEARL, b. 14 Sep 1774; d. 6 Apr 1775.

---

[892] Connecticut, Deaths and Burials Index, 1650-1934

[893] The 1788 Connecticut probate record of John Hinckley (widow Susanna) includes as heirs grandsons Daniel Pearl and Oliver Pearl the children of Mercy who is deceased.

[894] Gay, *Historical Gazetteer of Tioga County, part I*, p 370

[895] Dimock, *Births, Baptisms, Marriages, and Deaths: From the Records of the Town and Churches in Mansfield, Connecticut*, p 59

iii   OLIVER PEARL, b. 15 May 1776; d. 16 Oct 1786.

iv   DANIEL PEARL, b. 1779; d. 14 Jul 1779.

v   DANIEL PEARL, b. 29 May 1780; d. before 1850; m. at Willington, 5 Mar 1806, POLLY HORTON, b. about 1783; Polly d. at Owego, NY, after 1860.

331)   SARAH HOLT (*Abiel Holt[4], Abiel Holt[3], Mary Russell Holt[2], Robert[1]*), b. at Willington, 8 Dec 1757 daughter of Abiel and Mary (Downer) Holt; d. at Willington, 1856;[896] m. 24 Oct 1782, ZEBULON CROCKER, b. at Willington, 5 Mar 1757 son of Ebenezer and Hannah (Hatch) Crocker; Zebulon d. at Willington, 17 Jan 1826.

      The estate of Zebulon Crocker was probated in 1826 with son Zebulon Crocker as administrator. The inventory was completed 27 January 1826 with a total value of $2,081.88. The distribution of the dower was made to widow Sarah Crocker on 4 October 1826. The distribution agreement included the following children as heirs: Candace Crocker, Alpheus Crocker, Bethiah Crocker, Ira Heath and Hannah his wife, and Zebulon Crocker.[897]

      Zebulon and Sarah Crocker had six children born at Willington.

i   ALPHEUS CROCKER, b. 3 Sep 1783; d. 23 May 1784.

ii   CANDACE CROCKER, b. 6 Jun 1785; d. at Willington, 11 Jan 1849. Candace did not marry.

iii   ALPHEUS CROCKER, b. 3 Jul 1787; d. 24 Nov 1873; m. at Willington, 28 Apr 1808, his third cousin, PHEBE MARCY (*Zebadiah Marcy[5], Zebadiah Marcy[4], Mary Russell Marcy[3], Benjamin[2], Robert[1]*), b. at Willington, 12 Oct 1789 daughter of Zebadiah and Phebe (Pearl) Marcy; Phebe d. at Webster, NY, 11 Jun 1871. This family lived in Webster, NY.[898] Phebe Marcy is a child in Family 1165.

iv   BETHIAH CROCKER, b. 1 Jun 1791; d. at Willington, 10 Dec 1860; m. at Willington, 3 Oct 1832, JOSEPH HULL, b. at Willington, 16 Feb 1788 son of Hazard and Abigail (-) Hull; Joseph d. at Willington, 26 Mar 1871.

v   HANNAH CROCKER, b. 9 Apr 1796; m. about 1815, IRA HEATH, b. at Willington, 13 Oct 1793 son of David and Abigail (Scripture) Heath. There have been found just two records for children in this family and it is uncertain what became of Hannah and Ira. One of the sons settled in New York, so perhaps they will be found there, although there is no evidence of them in census records after 1820.

vi   Reverend ZEBULON CROCKER, b. 8 Mar 1802; d. at Middletown, CT, 14 Nov 1847; m. at East Windsor, 11 Oct 1830, ELIZABETH "BETSY" PORTER, b. about 1799 daughter of Daniel and Ann (Allyn) Porter;[899] Betsy d. at Cromwell, 25 Feb 1877. Zebulon and Betsy do not seem to have had any children. Zebulon's will leaves the entire estate to Betsy.

332)   MARY HOLT (*Abiel Holt[4], Abiel Holt[3], Mary Russell Holt[2], Robert[1]*), b. at Willington, 8 Dec 1760 daughter of Abiel and Mary (Downer) Holt; d. at Dracut, 6 Nov 1833;[900] m. at Charlton, MA, 17 Feb 1783,[901] DANIEL NEEDHAM *possibly* the son of Daniel and Hannah (Allen) Needham; Daniel d. at Paxton, MA 1801 (date of probate 6 Oct 1801; will written 4 Mar 1801).

      The will of Daniel Needham written 4 March 1801 includes a bequest of the widow's third to his wife Mary, and the equal division of the remainder of the estate among his four children namely Polly, Parsons, Rachel, and Sally.[902]

      Daniel Needham and Mary Holt were parents of five children the births reported either at Paxton or Charlton.

i   MARY "POLLY" NEEDHAM, b. at Paxton, 31 Mar 1784; m. at Danvers, 30 Sep 1807[903], JOHN NEEDHAM who has not been identified.

ii   JOHN NEEDHAM, baptized at Charlton, 16 Apr 1786; d. before his father's will in 1801.

---

[896] In the 1850 U.S. Census, 92-year old widow Sarah Crocker was living at the home of her daughter Bethiah Hull. Probate of estate was 1856 with Joseph Hull as administrator.

[897] Ancestry.com. *Connecticut, Wills and Probate Records, 1609-1999* [database on-line]. Case number 545, Probate of Zebulon Crocker

[898] Year: 1870; Census Place: Webster, Monroe, New York; Roll: M593_971; Page: 447B; Family History Library Film: 552470

[899] Betsy's parents are confirmed by the 1833 probate of Dr. Daniel Porter that includes a distribution to daughter Betsy Crocker.

[900] Mary, w. Daniel, Nov. 6, 1833, a. 73.

[901] *Massachusetts, Compiled Marriages, 1633-1850*. Daniel and Mary Holt of Willington, int. Feb. 17, 1783.

[902] Worcester County, MA: Probate File Papers, 1731-1881. Online database. AmericanAncestors.org. New England Historic Genealogical Society, 2015.

[903] From Danvers vital records: Needham, Mary, of Charlton, and John Needham, Sept. 30, 1807.

iii   JOSEPH PARSONS NEEDHAM, baptized at Charlton, Jun 1788; d. at Buffalo, NY, after 1865; m. at Medway, MA, 1 Feb 1815, JOANNA WIGHT, b. at Medway, 22 Jan 1794 daughter of Aaron and Jemima (Rutter) Wright; Joanna d. after 1865.

iv   RACHEL NEEDHAM, b. at Paxton, 14 Dec 1791; d. at Perinton, NY, 12 Apr 1887; m. at Salem, JOSEPH BLOOD, b. 24 Jun 1787 perhaps the son of Joseph and Priscilla (French) Blood; Joseph d. 14 Sep 1840.

v   SARAH NEEDHAM, baptized at Charlton, 14 Oct 1798; d. at Dracut, 22 Oct 1880; m. 26 Aug 1821, JOEL FOX, b. at Dracut, 12 Aug 1784 son of Joel and Hannah (Cheever) Fox; Joel d. at Lowell, 21 Dec 1861.

333)   ABIEL HOLT (*Abiel Holt⁴, Abiel Holt³, Mary Russell Holt², Robert¹*), b. at Willington, 12 Jul 1762 son of Abiel and Mary (Downer) Holt; d. at Fairfax, VT, 6 Jun 1829; m. by 1787, MARY MOSHER, b. 21 Jul 1762 daughter of Nathaniel and Elizabeth (Crandall) Mosher; Mary d. at Fairfax, 6 Sep 1827.
       Abiel Holt served in the Revolution as a private in Captain Abner Robinson's company. Abiel Holt and Mary Mosher were parents of eight children.

i   PHEBE HOLT, b. at Fairfax, 14 Oct 1787; d. at Sharon, VT, 11 May 1851; m. at Sharon, 19 Feb 1818, JOSEPH ROICE, b. about 1792; Joseph d. at Sharon, 7 Apr 1827.

ii   LUCINDA HOLT, b. at Fairfax, 14 Oct 1789; d. at Fairfax, 24 Mar 1849; m. at Sharon, 1 Feb 1820, IRA FARNSWORTH, b. at Fairfax, 27 Nov 1799 son of Thomas and Chloe (Balch) Farnsworth; Ira d. at Fairfax, 5 Dec 1860.

iii   ABIEL HOLT, b. at Sharon, 9 Sep 1791; d. at Boston, NY, 9 Dec 1869; m. at Albany, 20 Jan 1817, his third cousin, MARY ABBOTT, b. at Colden, NY, 8 Mar 1798 daughter of Caleb and Hannah (Wheat) Abbott;[904] Mary d. at Colden, NY, 16 Oct 1879. Mary Abbott is a child in Family 713.

iv   ARNOLD HOLT, b. at Sharon, 5 Jul 1794; d. at Moline, IL, about 1869 (probate Jan 1870); m. 1st, 22 Nov 1815, RUEY AUSTIN, b. at Milton, VT, 2 Jul 1797 daughter of David and Judith (Hall) Austin; Ruey d. at Colden, NY, 21 Oct 1841. Arnold m. 2nd, 19 Oct 1842, HANNAH MILLINGTON, b. in VT, 18 Sep 1819 daughter of John and Mary (Gardiner) Millington; Hannah d. at Washington, IA, 27 Sep 1906.

v   ZEBINA HOLT, b. at Sharon, 7 Sep 1797; d. at Salem, MN, 19 Feb 1871; m. about 1820, his third cousin, ORINDA ABBOTT, b. at Colden, 21 Aug 1803 daughter of Caleb and Hannah (Wheat) Abbott; Orinda d. at Salem, MN, 10 Mar 1880. Orinda Abbott is a child in Family 713.

vi   WORSTER HOLT, b. at Sharon, 19 Nov 1799; d. at Salem, MN, 17 Sep 1881; m. NANCY LEWIS, b. in VT, 1814; Nancy d. at Concord, NY, before 1870.

vii   NICHOLAS MOSHER HOLT, b. at Sharon, 16 Mar 1801; d. at Brecksville, OH, 1866; m. at Burlington, VT, 1 Jan 1827, ANN REYNOLDS, b. in MA, 1804; Ann d. at Brecksville, after 1880.

viii   ELIZABETH HOLT, b. at Sharon, 16 Mar 1801; d. at Springville, NY, 2 Aug 1848; m. about 1823, ALVA DUTTON, b. at Fairfax, 29 Jan 1798 son of Reuben and Polly (Farnsworth) Dutton; Alva d. at Springville, 25 Jun 1878. Alva married second Martha Ann Jewett.

334)   ABEL HOLT (*Abiel Holt⁴, Abiel Holt³, Mary Russell Holt², Robert¹*), b. at Willington, 1770 son of Abiel and Eunice (Kingsbury) Holt; m. 1st, at Norwich, 17 Nov 1793, ANNA ABEL, b. at Norwich, 8 Jul 1771 daughter of Thomas and Zerviah (Hyde) Abel;[905] Anna d. at Sharon, 13 Apr 1798. Abel m. 2nd, by 1798, RUTH KING, b. at Wilbraham, MA, 13 Feb 1779 daughter of Oliver and Ruth (Cooley) King.
       Abel Holt and Anna Abel had one child.

i   THOMAS ABEL HOLT, b. at Sharon, VT, 23 Jul 1796; d. at Sharon, 26 Aug 1815.

       Abel Holt and Ruth King were parents of nine children, the first eight children born at Sharon, Vermont and the youngest child at Burlington, Vermont. After the births of their children, the family relocated to Oneida, New York.

[904] Durrie, Holt Genealogy, p 100; Abbot, Genealogical Register, p 62
[905] Walworth, *Hyde Genealogy*, p 136

i   ANNA HOLT, b. 1 Oct 1798; m. at Sharon, 25 Oct 1824, THOMAS MOREHOUSE, b. about 1801; Thomas d. at Sharon, 6 Jun 1825.

ii   RUTH HOLT, b. 22 Sep 1801; d. 11 Jul 1820.

iii   EUNICE HOLT, b. 18 Jan 1804; d. at Sharon, 13 Sep 1819.

iv   SAMUEL KING HOLT, b. 2 May 1806

v   HORACE HOLT, b. 5 May 1808

vi   CHARLES HOLT, b. 9 Aug 1810

vii   ORAMEL HOLT, b. 17 Jan 1813; d. at Whittaker, MI, 5 Nov 1893; m. ELECTA GEER, b. about 1815 daughter of Thomas and Laura (-) Geer; Electa d. at Augusta, MI, 2 Nov 1875.

viii THOMAS ABEL HOLT, b. 10 Aug 1815

ix   EMILY HOLT, b. 16 Feb 1818; d. at Willowvale, NY, 9 Jun 1883; m. 2 Feb 1837, AMOS ROGERS, b. at Laurens, NY, 24 Oct 1815 son of Oliver Glason and Deborah (Lewis) Rogers;[906] Amos d. at New Hartford, NY, 2 Dec 1879.

335)   ELIJAH HOLT (*Caleb Holt⁴, Abiel Holt³, Mary Russell Holt², Robert¹*), b. at Willington, 24 Oct 1757 son of Caleb and Mary (Merrick) Holt; d. 4 Jul 1817; m. 5 Nov 1783,[907] MOLLY SIMMONS, b. 1754 possibly the daughter of Paul and Mary (Isham) Simmons, but this is not confirmed; Molly d. 6 May 1814. Elijah m. 2nd, Lovina *Marcy* Dunton 17 Aug 1815. Lovina Marcy was first married to Samuel Dunton.

     Elijah Holt's estate was probated in 1817. He did not leave a will. The total value of the estate was $4898.49. The distribution of the estate was made equally between Chloe wife of Chester Carpenter and Mary wife of Chester Burnham. Widow Lovina Holt received a distribution of $300 in accordance with the pre-marriage contract.[908] The pre-marriage contract provided that Lovina would retain all the property she brought to the marriage. She had inherited real estate from her father Zebadiah Marcy and her first husband Samuel Dunton.

     Elijah Holt and Molly Simmons had four children born at Willington.

i   CHLOE HOLT, b. 2 Jul 1788; d. at Willington, 24 Oct 1819; m. at Willington, 16 Mar 1815, CHESTER CARPENTER, b. at Ashford, 3 Jul 1780 Jonah and Zerviah (Whittemore) Carpenter; Chester d. 3 Apr 1868. After Chloe's death, Chester married Betsey Kilbourn.

ii   MARY HOLT, b. 14 Sep 1790; d. at Willington, 25 Feb 1851; m. 30 Mar 1813, CHESTER BURNHAM, b. at Ashford, 28 Jun 1788 son of Roswell and Esther (Child) Burnham; Chester d. 25 Oct 1857.

iii   ELIJAH HOLT, b. 23 Apr 1792; d. 8 Mar 1809.

iv   CALEB HOLT, b. 30 Jun 1798; d. 16 Sep 1811.

336)   CALEB HOLT (*Caleb Holt⁴, Abiel Holt³, Mary Russell Holt², Robert¹*), b. at Willington, 23 Apr 1759 son of Caleb and Mary (Merrick) Holt; d. at Willington, 8 Sep 1826; m. 8 Jan 1783, his second cousin, SARAH GOODALE (*Phebe Holt Goodale⁴, Joshua Holt³, Mary Russell Holt², Robert¹*), b. at Pomfret, 10 Jul 1760 daughter of Ebenezer and Phebe (Holt) Goodale; Sally d. at Willington, 4 Oct 1831.

     Caleb Holt was a tanner and currier, and had a large, successful farm in Willington. He owned enough land to be able to give each of his four sons a farm.[909]

     Caleb Holt and Sally Goodale had five children born at Willington.

i   HORACE HOLT, 29 Aug 1784; d. at Norwich, 30 Jan 1863; m. his second cousin, POLLY HOLT (*James Holt⁵, James Holt⁴, Abiel Holt³, Mary Russell Holt², Robert¹*), b. at Willington, 7 Sep 1798 daughter of James and Mary (Pool) Holt; Polly d. at Willington, 24 Jan 1853.

[906] Rogers, *James Rogers of New London, CT*, p 404

[907] "Connecticut Marriages, 1640-1939," database with images, *FamilySearch* (https://familysearch.org/ark:/61903/1:1:F7PB-68K: 11 February 2018), Elijah Holt and Molley Simons, Marriage 05 Nov 1783, Willington Tolland, Connecticut, United States; Connecticut State Library, Hartford; FHL microfilm 1,376,042.

[908] Ancestry.com. *Connecticut, Wills and Probate Records, 1609-1999* [database on-line]. Provo, UT, USA: Ancestry.com Operations, Inc., 2015. Original data: Connecticut County, District and Probate Courts, Stafford Probate District. Probate of Elijah Holt, Case number 1062, 1817

[909] 1903, *Commemorative Biographical Record of Tolland and Windham*, volume I, p 221

ii   ROYAL HOLT, b. 2 Dec 1786; d. at Willington, 20 Feb 1864; m. at Willington, 13 Aug 1809, LOVINA LAMB, b. at Randolph, VT, 17 Jan 1791 daughter of Joseph and Darias (Marcy) Lamb; Lovina d. at Willington, 5 May 1856.

iii   JOSHUA HOLT, b. 17 Apr 1782; d. at Willington, 8 Nov 1834; m. 27 Oct 1831, DALUKA LEONARD, of Ashford, b. about 1806; Daluka d. at Willington, 17 Mar 1885.

iv   RALPH HOLT, b. 10 Oct 1794; d. at Willington, 22 Feb 1873; m. 1819, SALLY RIDER, b. at Willington, 18 Nov 1796 daughter of Joseph and Ruanna (·) Rider; Sally d. at Willington, 26 Jun 1868.

v   JULIANNA HOLT, b. 25 Apr 1796; d. at Willington, 4 Nov 1862; m. 2 Nov 1823, as his second wife, ROBERT SHARP, b. about 1791 likely the son of Solomon and Rebecca (Perkins) Sharp; Robert d. at Willington, 1 Nov 1874. Robert was first married to CELINDA HOLT (*James Holt⁵, James Holt⁴, Abiel Holt³, Mary Russell Holt², Robert¹*), b. at Willington, 16 Jan 1796 daughter of James and Mary (Pool) Holt; Celinda d. at Willington, 20 May 1823. Celinda Holt is a child in Family 699.

337)   NATHAN HOLT (*Nathan Holt⁴, Abiel Holt³, Mary Russell Holt², Robert¹*), b. at Windham, 29 Aug 1761 son of Nathan and Abigail (Merrick) Holt; d. at Willington, 5 Sep 1820; m. his second cousin, LOIS GOODALE (*Phebe Holt Goodale⁴, Joshua Holt³, Mary Russell Holt², Robert¹*), b. at Pomfret, 31 Jul 1764 daughter of Ebenezer and Phebe (Holt) Goodale; Lois d. 20 May 1842.

    Nathan Holt and Lois Goodale were parents of seven children all born at Willington.

i   LOIS HOLT, b. 9 May 1784; d. 20 Feb 1821; m. about 1806, ASA CURTIS, b. 1785 *likely* the son of Ransom and Alice (Whitten) Curtis; Asa was living in Black Hawk, IL in 1860.

ii   ASENATH HOLT, b. 26 Jan 1786; d. at Willington, 13 Feb 1813; m. 29 Dec 1809, her first cousin once removed, LEONARD HOLT (*Isaac Holt⁴, Abiel Holt³, Mary Russell Holt², Robert¹*), b. at Willington, 15 Feb 1782 son of Isaac and Sarah (Orcutt) Holt; Leonard d. at Willington, 12 Mar 1857. Leonard m. 2ⁿᵈ, about 1813, JOANNA ALDEN, b. at Stafford, 14 Jul 1782 daughter of Elisha and Irene (Markham) Alden; Joanna d. at Willington, 30 Sep 1849. Asenath Holt and Leonard Holt are Family 335.

iii   CONSTANT HOLT, b. 11 Dec 1787; d. at Webster, NY, 15 Nov 1835; m. 1ˢᵗ, 9 Apr 1812, SALLY DART, b. at Manchester, CT, 1789 daughter of Joseph and Sybil (Loomis) Dart; Sally d. 8 Oct 1813. Constant m. 2ⁿᵈ, 13 Feb 1815, Sally's sister SYBIL DART, b. 1787; Sybil d. 12 Aug 1822. Constant m. 3ʳᵈ, at Willington, 2 Feb 1823, POLLY SIBLEY, b. at Willington, 26 Mar 1781 daughter of Jonathan and Patty (Brooks) Sibley; Polly d. at Penfield, NY, 17 Dec 1858. Polly Sibley married second David Baker 24 Oct 1841.

iv   BATHSHEBA HOLT, b. 13 Feb 1792; d. at Willington, 25 Sep 1880. Bathsheba did not marry.

v   PHEBE HOLT, b. 12 Aug 1795; d. at Jewett City, 5 Dec 1844; m. 28 Dec 1814, STEPHEN BARROWS, b. 24 Nov 1789 son of Isaac and Rebecca (Turner) Barrows; Stephen d. at Jewett City, 28 Feb 1878. Stephen married second Hannah Hazard.

vi   EBENEZER GOODALE HOLT, b. 24 Jul 1798; d. at Auburn, NY, 17 Oct 1835; m. about 1822, ANN F. WHITE, b. in NY, about 1805 daughter of Jonas White; Anna d. after 1850.

vii   MARILDA HOLT, b. 19 Nov 1802; d. at Willington, 31 Mar 1868; m. at Hartford, 27 Oct 1844, RICHARD SALE, b. about 1800; Richard d. at Willington, 1856 (probate 21 Jun 1856). Richard and Marilda lived in Brooklyn, NY although they seem to have been in Willington at the time of Richard's death as his will and probate are in Connecticut. They did not have children.

338)   ANNE MERRICK (*Anna Holt, Merrick⁴, Abiel Holt³, Mary Russell Holt², Robert¹*), b. at Willington, 19 Sep 1756 daughter of Joseph and Anna (Holt) Merrick; d. 2 May 1809; m. 10 Jan 1782, DAVID HINCKLEY, b. 24 Feb 1754 son of John and Susannah (Harris) Hinckley; David d. 24 Jan 1835.

    In his will written 18 February 1830, David Hinckley left his entire estate, real and personal, to his daughter Joanna Hinckley. But if son Benjamin was living when David died, Benjamin was to have the wearing apparel. After the payment of debts, Joanna at her discretion, might divide what was left between herself and David's other two daughters Hannah Hinckley and Betsey Torrey. Joanna was named executrix of the estate.[910]

    Anne and David Hinckley had six children whose births are recorded at Willington.

---

[910] *Connecticut, Wills and Probate Records, 1609-1999*, Author: Connecticut State Library (Hartford, Connecticut); Probate Place: Hartford, Connecticut.

i   BENJAMIN HINCKLEY, b. 23 Nov 1782; d. at Hiram, OH, 1835 (probate 1835); m. at Willington, 10 Feb 1806, SUSANNA DAVIS, b. about 1782 daughter of Avery and Amy (Lillibridge) Avery;[911] Susanna d. at Hiram, 8 Jan 1873.

ii   HANNAH HINCKLEY, b. 14 Aug 1786. Her death is uncertain, but she was living and unmarried in 1830 when her father wrote his will. It is believed she traveled with her sister Joanna and brother Benjamin to Ohio.

iii   CALEB HINCKLEY, b. 3 Jun 1790; d. 26 Jul 1790.

iv   EBER HINCKLEY, b. 17 Oct 1791; d. 9 May 1796.

v   BETSEY HINCKLEY, b. 28 Jul 1796; d. at Union, IA, 21 Feb 1879; m. at Tolland, 21 Jun 1826, DAVID B. TORREY, b. about 1784 in Connecticut; David d. at Burlington, IA, 3 Dec 1863.

vi   JOANNA HINCKLEY, b. 12 Mar 1799; d. at Windsor, OH, 19 Apr 1857; m. at Portage County, OH, 20 Jun 1840, as his second wife, Rev. RUSSELL DOWNING, b. in New York 20 Nov 1796; Russell d. at Windsor, 8 Apr 1881.[912]

339)   TIMOTHY MERRICK (*Anna Holt, Merrick⁴, Abiel Holt³, Mary Russell Holt², Robert¹*), b. at Willington, 31 Aug 1760 son of Joseph and Anna (Holt) Merrick; d. 4 Jan 1810; m. 29 Nov 1787, MEHITABLE PEARL ATWOOD, b. 1765 daughter of Thomas and Sarah (Fenton) Atwood; Mehitable d. at Wilton, 14 May 1855.

    Timothy was a farmer in Willington. The Merrick genealogy reports he built one of the more pretentious houses in Willington at the time. He was respected in the town, often serving as the moderator of the town meeting.[913]

    Timothy Merrick did not leave a will and the estate entered probate 5 February 1810. The total value of the estate was $2,438 with the 101-acre homestead farm with buildings valued at $1,628.[914]

    There are two children known for Timothy and Mehitable both born at Willington.

i   JOSEPH MERRICK, b. 2 Jul 1789; d. at Willington, 5 Jan 1854; m. 10 Apr 1814, LODICIA DUNTON, b. at Willington, 22 Sep 1794 daughter of Samuel and Lovina (Marcy) Dunton; Lodicia d. at Willington, 1 Sep 1857.

ii   ANNE MERRICK, b. 26 Feb 1791; d. at Willington, 28 Oct 1817; m. CYREL JAMES, b. at Willington, 21 Sep 1791 son of Amos and Christian (Noble) James.

340)   THOMAS MERRICK (*Anna Holt, Merrick⁴, Abiel Holt³, Mary Russell Holt², Robert¹*), b. at Willington, 6 Jan 1763 son of Joseph and Anna (Holt) Merrick; d. at Willington, 8 Sep 1840; m. 10 Jan 1790, JOANNA NOBLE, b. 8 Oct 1769 daughter of Gideon and Christian (Cadwell) Noble; Joanna d. 28 Apr 1860.

    Thomas Merrick was a farmer in Willington. He and his wife Joanna Noble were parents of five children born at Willington.

i   LOVISA MERRICK, b. 22 Mar 1791; d. at Willington, 14 May 1863; m. 14 Nov 1827, ELEAZER ROOT, b. about 1790 *likely* the son of Eleazer Root; Eleazer d. at Willington, Mar 1837 (probate 13 Mar 1837).

ii   GIDEON NOBLE MERRICK, b. Jan 1793; d. at Willington, 24 Jan 1862; m. 16 Apr 1820, POLLY NILES, b. at Willington, 5 Oct 1798 daughter of James and Polly (Woodward) Niles; Polly d. at Willington, 2 Mar 1869.

iii   HARRIET MERRICK, b. 24 Jan 1795; d. at Willington, 9 May 1860; m. at Willington, 22 Sep 1831, JONATHAN CASE WALKER, b. at Ashford, 5 Jan 1799 son of Samuel and Alice (Case) Walker; Jonathan d. at Willington, 2 Nov 1863.

iv   MARILDA MERRICK, b. Mar 1801; d. at Wintonbury, CT, 26 Jul 1872; m. at Willington, 15 Jun 1821, RALPH R. GRIGGS, b. at Tolland, 31 Jan 1798 son of Stephen and Betsey (Lathrop) Griggs; Ralph d. at Wintonbury, 22 Aug 1874.

v   HARVEY MERRICK, b. 2 May 1808; d. at Bristol, CT, 17 Aug 1887; m. at Willington, 23 Apr 1838, his second cousin once removed, ESTHER CHILDS BURNHAM (*Mary Holt Burnham⁶, Elijah Holt⁵, Caleb Holt⁴, Abiel*

---

[911] Susanna's parents are confirmed by the 1836 Connecticut probate record of father Avery Davis and the 1859 will of brother Avery Davis which includes a bequest to sister Susan Hinckley.

[912] Web: Ashtabula County, Ohio, Obituary Index, 1858-2012

[913] Merrick, *Genealogy of the Merrick Family*, p 284

[914] *Connecticut State Library (Hartford, Connecticut)*; Probate Place: *Hartford, Connecticut, Probate Packets, McKinney, H-Nash, S, 1759-1880*, Probate of Timothy Merick, Case 1480

Holt³, Mary Russell Holt², Robert¹), b. at Willington, 13 Feb 1816 daughter of Chester and Mary (Holt) Burnham; Esther d. at Bristol, 7 Feb 1905.

341)   JOSEPH MERRICK (*Anna Holt, Merrick⁴, Abiel Holt³, Mary Russell Holt², Robert¹*), b. at Willington, 22 Feb 1765 son of Joseph and Anna (Holt) Merrick; death uncertain but about 1820 possibly by drowning; m. 21 Oct 1796, IRENA ALDEN, b. at Bellingham, MA, 24 Feb 1772 daughter of Elisha and Irene (Markham) Alden. Irena m. 2ⁿᵈ, Samuel Churchill; Irena d. at Pleasantville, PA, 13 Nov 1858.
        Joseph Merrick and Irene Alden were parents of five children all born at Willington.

i   IRENE MERRICK, b. 21 Aug 1797; d. at Willington, 29 Apr 1814.

ii   LODICA MERRICK, b. 14 Dec 1798; d. at Oil Creek, PA, 1 Aug 1863; m. at Longmeadow, MA, 15 Sep 1821, AMOS HALL, b. 5 Mar 1790;[915] Amos d. at Oil Creek, 9 Mar 1863.

iii   ELISHA ALDEN MERRICK, b. 3 Apr 1800; d. at Belvidere, IL, 13 Aug 1839; m. about 1827, JERUSHA TENANT, b. at Colchester, 21 Aug 1807 daughter of John and Hannah (Atwell) Tenant; Jerusha d. at Huntington, WV, 15 Oct 1904. Jerusha married second James McClintock.

iv   AUSTIN MERRICK, b. 13 Sep 1801; d. at Pleasantville, PA, 6 Aug 1876; m. 1ˢᵗ, 5 Feb 1839, SYLVIA WITCHER, b. at Rochester, VT, 6 May 1808 daughter of Stephen and Esther (Emerson) Witcher; Sylvia d. 1849. Austin m. 2ⁿᵈ, about 1851, ELIZA, b. about 1812 who has not been identified; Eliza d. 1869.

v   LAURA MERRICK, b. 14 Nov 1803; d. at Adams, NE, 2 Sep 1885; m. about 1830, her second cousin, WILLIAM CURTIS (*Mary Holt Curtis⁵, Isaac Holt⁴, Abiel Holt³, Mary Russell Holt², Robert¹*), b. at Willington, 20 May 1802 son of William and Mary (Holt) Curtis; William d. a Adams, 17 Mar 1879..

342)   CALEB MERRICK (*Anna Holt, Merrick⁴, Abiel Holt³, Mary Russell Holt², Robert¹*), b. at Willington, 17 May 1767 son of Joseph and Anna (Holt) Merrick; d. at Vernon, CT, Jun 1822; m. 15 Sep 1791, CHARLOTTE NOBLE, b. at Willington, 19 Aug 1771 daughter of Gideon and Christian (Cadwell) Noble; Charlotte d. at Franklin, CT, 21 Nov 1805.
        Dr. Caleb Merrick had a practice in Willington and Franklin, Connecticut.[916]
        Caleb and Charlotte had five children.

i   WEALTHY MERRICK, b. at Willington, 20 Sep 1792; d. at Ellington, 12 Oct 1861; m. Mar 1818, BUELL NYE, b. at Tolland, 7 Mar 1790 son of Hezekiah and Asenath (Buell) Nye; Buell d. at Springfield, MA, 10 Apr 1833.[917]

ii   MARK MERRICK, b. at Amherst, MA, 14 Nov 1794; d. at Vernon, 18 Apr 1853; m. HANNAH SPARKS, b. at Vernon, 8 May 1794 daughter of Jonas and Olive (Smith) Sparks;[918] Hannah d. after 1870 at Chatham, NJ (living at Chatham at the 1870 Census).

iii   SOPHRONIA MERRICK, b. at Amherst, 1 Apr 1797; d. at Willington, 14 May 1843; m. at Willington, 20 Nov 1814, SPAFFORD BRIGHAM, b. 1782 son od Stephen and Hannah (Field) Brigham;[919] Spafford d. at Ellington, 26 Sep 1866.

iv   LEANDER MERRICK, b. at Tolland, 31 May 1799; d. at Amherst, 24 May 1856; m. 1ˢᵗ, 2 Dec 1824, HARRIET HODGE, b. 1798 daughter of John and Sarah (Dickinson) Hodge; Harriet d. at Amherst, 3 May 1825. Leander m. 2ⁿᵈ, 27 Nov 1827, HARRIET ELVIRA MORTON, b. 3 Feb 1808 daughter of Ebenezer and Hannah (Ingram) Morton; Harriet d. at Amherst, 18 Jun 1882.

v   CHARLOTTE MERRICK, b. at Willington, 29 Jan 1802; d. at Willington, 1818.

343)   CONSTANT MERRICK (*Anna Holt, Merrick⁴, Abiel Holt³, Mary Russell Holt², Robert¹*), b. at Willington, 14 Jan 1772 son of Joseph and Anna (Holt) Merrick; d. at Lebanon, NY, 29 Jul 1828; m. at Longmeadow, MA, 22 Sep 1796, EXPERIENCE BURT, b. 8 Aug 1776 daughter of Nathaniel and Experience (Chapin) Burt; Experience d. 1833 at Lebanon, NY, 24 Jul 1833.

---

[915] Birth date is calculated from age at death of 73 years, 4 days. Bell, *History of Venango County*, 9 734
[916] Merrick, *Genealogy of the Merrick Family*, p 285
[917] Nye, *Genealogy of the Nye Family*, p 354
[918] Hannah's parents are confirmed by the 1823 Connecticut probate of Jonas Sparks which includes a distribution to daughter Hannah Merrick.
[919] Brigham, *History of the Brigham Family*, p 169

Dr. Constant Merrick was a physician, but like many individuals in this era also maintained a farm. After Constant and Experience married, they relocated to Madison County, New York about 1800.[920] The family lived near Billings Hill in Madison County and then settled in the village of Lebanon about 1806 where Dr. Merrick was the second physician in the village.[921]

Constant Merrick and Elizabeth Burt had nine children the oldest born in Longmeadow and the other children at Lebanon, New York.

i   ELIZA MERRICK, b. at Longmeadow, 27 Apr 1797; d. at Lebanon, NY, 9 Jan 1815; m. 17 Apr 1814, JAMES KNAPP BENEDICT, b. 3 Feb 1790 son of Czar and Elizabeth (Knapp) Benedict;[922] James d. at Lebanon, 9 May 1864. After Eliza's death, James married Pamelia Sweet. Eliza did not have children.

ii   LAURA MERRICK, b. 17 Mar 1799; d. at Longmeadow, MA, 7 Sep 1875; m. at Lebanon, 12 Sep 1821, SAMUEL COLTON STEBBINS, b. at Longmeadow, 27 Jun 1796 son of Benjamin and Lucy (Colton) Stebbins; Samuel d. at Longmeadow, 12 Dec 1873.

iii   EXPERIENCE MERRICK, b. 27 Feb 1801; d. 11 Mar 1801.

iv   NATHANIEL BURT MERRICK, b. 5 Mar 1802; d. at Hudson, NY, 18 Jan 1877; m. 12 Jun 1832, LAURA H. HAMILTON, b. about 1810 daughter of Samuel and Mehitable (Bemis) Hamilton; Laura d. 27 Jan 1840. Nathaniel m. 2nd, Mar 1841, MARTHA M. BURCHARD who was "of Rochester;" Martha d. at Rochester, 7 Mar 1897.

v   CONSTANT MERRICK, b. 14 Apr 1804; d. 16 Aug 1805.

vi   EXPERIENCE MERRICK, b. at Lebanon, 28 Jul 1806; d. at Earlville, NY, 1870; m. 10 Jun 1830, DAVID CLARK, b. 1800 in Connecticut of as yet undetermined origins; David d. at Earlville, 1873.

vii   CONSTANT MERRICK, b. at Lebanon, 22 Nov 1808; d. at Lebanon, 3 Apr 1834.

viii   ANNA MERRICK, b. at Lebanon, 1 Sep 1810; d. at Chicago, 21 Jan 1886; m. 10 Jun 1830, GORDON HYDE, b. at Columbus, NY, 10 Feb 1801 son of Ambrose and Phebe (Hyde) Hyde; Gordon d. at Hamilton, NY, 1885.

ix   JERUSHA MERRICK, b. at Lebanon, 8 Jun 1819; d. at Norwich, NY, 1874; m. 2 Sep 1840, ISAAC FOOTE, b. 28 May 1817 son of Isaac and Harriet (Hyde) Foote; Isaac d. at Norwich, 1893.

344)   ELIZABETH MERRICK (*Anna Holt, Merrick⁴, Abiel Holt³, Mary Russell Holt², Robert¹*), b. at Willington, 13 Jul 1774 daughter of Joseph and Anna (Holt) Merrick; d. at Tolland, 29 Jun 1824; m. 24 Apr 1800, as his second wife, SAMUEL NYE, b. 25 Dec 1773 son of Samuel and Abigail (Benton) Nye. Samuel m. 3rd, Anna Hatch; Samuel's first wife was Elizabeth Brewster; Samuel d. at Tolland 25 Nov 1837.

Samuel Nye wrote his will 24 December 1836[923] and entered probate 29 Nov 1837. Beloved wife Ann receives the use and improvement of one-third of the real estate during her natural life. Ann also receives two shares in the Tolland County Bank. He makes other provisions for her support and she also receives the cloak. Daughter Harriet Brigham receives one hundred dollars. Son Horace and daughters Harriet and Anne receiving the wearing apparel except the cloak. The remainder of the personal estate goes to two grandchildren Buey (?) Nye and Samuel Nye. The remainder of the estate goes to son-in-law William Holman who is also named executor. Conspicuously absent from the will is Chester Nye, Samuel's son from his first marriage. Chester was living at the time the will was written. The two grandchildren mentioned are William B. Nye and Samuel Nye who were sons of Horace.

Elizabeth Merrick and Samuel Nye had four children all born at Tolland.

i   HARRIET NYE, b. 15 Aug 1801; d. at Coventry, CT, 21 Mar 1879; m. 29 Nov 1827, URIAH BRIGHAM, b. at Coventry, 26 Aug 1793 son of Cephas and Amelia (Robertson) Brigham; Uriah d. at Coventry, 2 May 1860. Uriah was first married to Emily Wright who died in 1827.

ii   HORACE NYE, b. 22 Aug 1803; death unknown; m. Apr 1827, BETSEY BRIGHAM, b. at Mansfield, CT, about 1805 daughter of Stephen and Huldah (Freeman) Brigham; Betsey d. at Mansfield, 17 Sep 1872.

iii   SUSANNA NYE, b. 16 Feb 1805; d. 7 Feb 1828.

---

[920] Merrick, *Genealogy of the Merrick Family*, p 286

[921] Smith, *Our County and Its People. . .Madison County*, p 371

[922] Benedict, *Genealogy of the Benedicts*, p 270

[923] Connecticut State Library (Hartford, Connecticut); Probate Place: Hartford, Connecticut, Probate Packets, Kimball, N-Warren, H, 1827-1895, Probate of Samuel Nye, case number 700.

iv ANNA NYE, b. 12 Aug 1810; d. at Tolland, 15 Mar 1870; m. 26 Mar 1833, WILLIAM HOLMAN, b. at Ashford, 24 Oct 1811 son of Abraham and Polly (Converse) Holman; William d. at East Hoosuck, MA, 8 Oct 1887.

345) ISAAC HOLT (*Isaac Holt[4], Abiel Holt[3], Mary Russell Holt[2], Robert[1]*), b. at Willington, 3 Nov 1763 son of Isaac and Sarah (Orcutt) Holt; d. at Sharon, VT, 7 Aug 1813; m. at Sharon, 1 Jan 1789,[924] MEHITABLE ORCUTT, b. at Stafford, CT, 17 Jan 1769 daughter of Caleb and Chloe (Parker) Orcutt; Mehitable d. 12 Nov 1851.

  Isaac and Mehitable were married in Connecticut and moved soon after to Sharon, Vermont where their three children were born. Little information has been located for this couple. Probate records were not found.

i FREEMAN HOLT, b. 19 Apr 1790; d. at Sharon, 14 Jun 1865; m. 1st, LUCY PAGE, b. at Sharon, 13 Aug 1797 daughter of Samuel and Elizabeth (Mosher) Page; Lucy d. at Sharon, 10 Oct 1859. Freeman m. 2nd, 9 Jul 1860 at Gloucester, MA, MARY BRADLEY (widow Cressy), b. at Rumney, NH, 11 Feb 1801 daughter of Ebenezer and Sarah (Hall) Bradley; Mary d. at Haverhill, MA, 30 Mar 1885.

ii CALEB HOLT, b. 28 Oct 1791; d. at Sharon, 29 Jan 1880; m. 1st, at Sharon 16 Jan 1822, CLARISSA PARKER, b. at Sharon, 28 Jul 1797 daughter of James and Kezia (Weatherbee) Parker; Clarissa d. 6 Oct 1852. Caleb m. 2nd, at Rumney 20 May 1853, MARY P. HERRICK, b. at Londonderry, 17 May 1808 daughter of Nehemiah and Sarah (Day) Herrick; Mary d. at Sharon, 6 Apr 1874.

iii HANNAH HOLT, b. 11 Sep 1793; d. likely at Bethel, VT after 1850; m. at Sharon, 3 Nov 1833, as his third wife, ELISHA TERRY, b. at Bethel, 22 Nov 1786 son of Ephraim and Lucinda (Bugbee) Terry; Elisha d. at Bethel after 1850. Hannah and Elisha were both living at the 1850 Census but not located after that.

346) HANNAH HOLT (*Isaac Holt[4], Abiel Holt[3], Mary Russell Holt[2], Robert[1]*), b. at Willington, 19 May 1771 daughter of Isaac and Sarah (Orcutt) Holt; d. before 1850;[925] m. 9 Apr 1795, ELEAZER FELLOWS, b. at Tolland, 2 Apr 1772 son of Verney and Hannah (Lathrop) Fellows; Eleazer d. after 1850 in Ohio.

  Hannah and Eleazer had their children in Willington. In 1849, perhaps after the death of Hannah, Eleazer followed his son Eleazer to Clarksfield, Ohio. He bought ten acres of land there and lived with his daughter Betsey and her family.[926]

  Eleazer Fellows and Hannah Holt were parents of three children born at Willington.

i LEONARD FELLOWS, b. 23 Oct 1800; d. at Clarksfield, OH, Aug 1849; m. 24 Nov 1824, ARMINDA JOHNSON, b. at Sweden, NY, 10 Jun 1807;[927] Arminda d. at Marion, MN, 18 Nov 1893.

ii LOTHROP FELLOWS, b. 4 Nov 1803; d. at Lockport, NY, 2 Jan 1845; m. 5 Dec 1827, MELINDA FISKE PARSONS, b. at Lockport, 16 Jun 1809 daughter of Seth and Achsah (Tenney) Parsons;[928] Melinda d. at Milwaukee, 10 Mar 1891.

iii BETSEY PRIOR FELLOWS, b. 13 May 1806; m. about 1831, Mr. HASKINS, not identified but perhaps Jarius Haskins. Their youngest child was born about 1845. *Pioneer History of Clarksfield* reports that Mr. Haskins died, and Betsey married Mr. Lang but continued to use the name Haskins and she is the head of household in census records in Clarksfield. She was living in 1860.

347) MARY HOLT (*Isaac Holt[4], Abiel Holt[3], Mary Russell Holt[2], Robert[1]*), b. at Willington, 1 May 1773 daughter of Isaac and Sarah (Orcutt) Holt; d. at Willington, 6 Jun 1861; m. 27 Nov 1799, WILLIAM CURTIS, b. about 1774 *likely* the son of Ransom and Alice (Whitten) Curtis; William d. 3 Nov 1860.

  In his will written 7 February 1852, William leaves his entire estate to children Sarah H. Curtis and Wilson W. Curtis stating that he has already provided for his other children (who are not named). "The said Wilson W. Curtis and Sara H. Curtis

---

[924] *Vermont, Vital Records, 1720-1908.*
[925] In the 1850 U.S. Census, Eleazer Fellows, age 78, was living in Clarksfield OH; also in the home are Betsey Haskins age 43 and five children named Haskins. Betsey is the daughter of Eleazer and Hannah. Eleazer and Hannah's son Leonard also relocated to Huron County, Ohio.
[926] Weeks, *Pioneer History of Clarksfield*, p 130
[927] Date of birth is on her cemetery record. Dalby, John. *Minnesota Cemetery Inscription Index, Select Counties* [database on-line]. Provo, UT, USA: Ancestry.com Operations Inc, 2003.
[928] Parsons, *Parsons Family: Descendant of Cornet Joseph Parsons*, p 164

shall well and truly provide for support and maintain myself and my wife Mary Curtis during the whole period of each of our natural lives and at the death of each myself and my said wife Mary Curtis to give to each of us a decent christian burial."[929]

Daughter Sarah Holt Curtis did not marry. In her will dated 1 August 1874, Sarah bequeaths twenty-five dollars to her brother Selden; to Chiara Ann wife of George Plimpton and daughter of her brother Oliver H. Curtis she leaves a string of gold beads to be solely her property; to brother Alfred Curtis, twenty dollars; and the remainder of the estate goes to brother Wilson W. Curtis who is also named executor.[930]

Mary and William Curtis had nine children born at Willington. This family illustrates a pattern for this generation: a new wave of migration with children heading to the western territories, western New York, and western Massachusetts.

i SANFORD CURTIS, b. 7 Nov 1800; d. 9 May 1807.

ii WILLIAM CURTIS, b. 20 May 1802; d. at Adams, NE, 17 Mar 1879; m. about 1803, his second cousin, LAURA MERRICK (*Joseph Merrick⁵, Anna Holt Merrick⁴, Abiel Holt³, Mary Russell², Robert¹*), b. at Willington, 14 Nov 1803 daughter of Joseph and Irene (Alden) Merrick; Laura d. at Adams, 2 Sep 1885.

iii HORACE CURTIS, b. 9 Feb 1804; d. at Buchanan, MI, 31 Dec 1887;[931] m. SALLY M. CLARK, b. in Pennsylvania, 3 Dec 1814 daughter of Benjamin and Esther (-) Clark; Sally d. at Buchanan, 24 Mar 1899.

iv SARAH HOLT CURTIS, b. 24 Oct 1805; d. at Willington, 30 Sep 1874. Sarah did not marry.

v ALFRED CURTIS, b. 7 Jun 1809; d. at Westfield, NY, 2 Dec 1878; m. at Willington, 5 Dec 1831, EUNICE RIDER, b. 9 Dec 1812 of undetermined parents;[932] Eunice d. at Westfield, 3 Sep 1892.

vi OLIVER HOLT CURTIS, b. 30 Mar 1811; d. at Amherst, MA, 27 Feb 1899; m. at Tolland, 14 Nov 1837, EMILY HILLS, b. at Ellington, 12 Mar 1811 daughter of Leonard and Mary (Ladd) Hills; Emily d. at Amherst, 27 Mar 1888.

vii WILSON WHITING CURTIS, b. 25 Feb 1813; d. at Willington, 10 Aug 1890; m. at Willington, 12 Feb 1852, SARAH ELDREDGE, b. at Willington, 14 Feb 1813 daughter of Elijah and Sally (Hunt) Eldridge; Sarah d. at Willington, 13 Feb 1887.

viii SELDEN CURTIS, b. 1 Dec 1815; d. at Willington, 18 Feb 1902; m. 1st, 28 Mar 1841, MARY ELIZABETH PARSONS, b. at Somers, CT, 24 Feb 1821 daughter of Rufus and Chloe (Weston) Parsons;[933] Mary d. at Willington, 21 Oct 1852. Selden m. 2nd, at Ashford, 5 Jun 1853, MARTHA AURELIA SKINNER, b. 14 Mar 1822 daughter of Ezekiel and Sarah (Mott) Skinner; Martha d. at Willington, 21 Sep 1892. Martha was first married to Richard Boon.

ix HENRY CURTIS, b. 1 Jun 1818; d. 3 Aug 1846.

348) OLIVER HOLT (*Isaac Holt⁴, Abiel Holt³, Mary Russell Holt², Robert¹*), b. at Willington, 16 Jul 1775 son of Isaac and Sarah (Orcutt) Holt; d. 6 Mar 1869; m. 16 May 1799, MARTHA "PATTY" SIBLEY,[934] b. 9 Feb 1776 daughter of Jonathan and Patty (Brooks) Sibley; Martha "Patty" d. 16 Dec 1846.

There are records for five children of Oliver and Patty Holt all born at Willington.

i MARCIA HOLT, b. 22 Feb 1800; d. 1 Mar 1831. Marcia did not marry.

ii SUSANNAH HOLT, b. 4 Feb 1802; d. at Mansfield, CT, 2 May 1874; m. at Willington, 18 Jun 1827, EBER DUNHAM, b. at Mansfield, 23 Jan 1798 son of Jonathan and Betty (Babcock) Dunham; Eber d. at Mansfield, 21 Oct 1878.

iii MARIAH HOLT, b. 16 Aug 1806; d. at Mansfield, 4 Jun 1867; m. 1 Jan 1846, CHAUNCEY DUNHAM, b. at Mansfield, about 1798 of undetermined parents; Chauncey d. at Mansfield, 11 Jul 1850.

---

[929] *Connecticut State Library (Hartford, Connecticut)*; Probate Place: *Hartford, Connecticut, Probate Packets, Carpenter, Comfort-Kimball, J, 1833-1880*, Case number 222, accessed through ancestry.com

[930] *Connecticut State Library (Hartford, Connecticut)*; Probate Place: *Hartford, Connecticut, Probate Packets, Carpenter, Comfort-Kimball, J, 1833-1880*, Case 221

[931] *Michigan, Death Records, 1867-1950*, Michigan Department of Community Health, Division for Vital Records and Health Statistics; Lansing, Michigan. The death record includes parents as William and Mary and birth place as Connecticut. The death record for Sally Clark includes names of parents as Benjamin and Esther.

[932] Eunice's birth date is on her gravestone; findagrave ID: 87772382

[933] Parsons, *Parsons Family*, volume 2, p 319

[934] Connecticut, Marriage Index, 1620-1926; the handwritten marriage record confirms that the marriage is to Patty and not to her younger sister Polly.

iv   MARTHA SIBLEY HOLT, b. 15 May 1810; d. at Tamaroa, IL, 18 Jul 1864; m. at Willington, 20 Oct 1834, BENAJAH GUERNSEY "B.G." ROOTS, b. at Fabius, NY, 20 Apr 1811 son of Peter and Elizabeth (Keep) Roots; B.G. d. at Tamaroa, 9 May 1888. After Martha's death, B.G. married Elizabeth Reynolds. Benajah Guernsey Roots was an abolitionist and is believed to have been active in the Underground Railroad.[935]

v   ELIZA HOLT, b. 7 Feb 1821; d. at Tamaroa, IL, 7 Dec 1870; m. 13 Sep 1840, her second cousin once removed, NELSON HOLT (*Constant Holt⁶, Nathan Holt⁵, Nathan Holt⁴, Abiel Holt³, Mary Russell Holt², Robert¹*), b. at Penfield, NY, 6 Jan 1816 son of Constant and Sibyl (Dart) Holt;[936] Nelson d. at Tamaroa, 29 Oct 1900.

349)   ELIZABETH HOLT (*Isaac Holt⁴, Abiel Holt³, Mary Russell Holt², Robert¹*), b. at Willington, 6 Aug 1777 daughter of Isaac and Sarah (Orcutt) Holt; m. 11 Apr 1799, DANIEL GLAZIER, b. 2 Jun 1776 son of Silas and Suze (Johnson) Glazier; Daniel d. 28 Dec 1852. After Elizabeth's death, Daniel married Mary G. whose last name is unknown.

Daniel Glazier was the builder and owner of the Daniel Glazier Tavern which is now the home of the Willington Historical Society.[937]

In his will written 10 September 1852, Daniel Glazier bequeaths to beloved wife Mary all the furniture she brought to the marriage, all the furniture obtained since their marriage (except the secretary), $850, and the use of one-third part of the house as long as she remains a widow; grandson Daniel Johnson Glazier, $150 over what he has received; grandson Isaac Glazier receives 10 shares of bank stock; Elizabeth Spalden and Sarah R. Glazier receive all of his furniture (except the secretary) and $4000 to be divided equally between them; grandson Hiram Rider receives a piece of land; and son Orlen Glazier receives the remainder of the estate and is named executor.[938] Elizabeth Spalden and Sarah R. Glazier are daughters of son Isaac. Daniel Johnson Glazier is the son of Isaac. Hiram Rider is the son of daughter Sarah.

There are records for four children of Daniel and Elizabeth Glazier. The Willington Historical Society states there were five children, but records for that child were not found and perhaps there was a fifth child that died before adulthood.

i   SARAH GLAZIER, b. 17 Apr 1800; d. at Willington, 1850; m. at Willington, 3 May 1818, HIRAM RIDER, b. at Willington, 28 Apr 1790 son of Joseph and Jane (Poole) Rider; Hiram d. at Willington, 26 Sep 1851.

ii   ISAAC GLAZIER, b. 19 Jan 1803; d. at Willington, 4 Feb 1835; m. 7 Mar 1824, LUCIA SNOW, b. at Ashford, 23 Nov 1804 daughter of Amos and Eunice (Burnham) Snow; Lucia d. at Willington, 30 Sep 1849.

iii   ORLAN GLAZIER, b. 12 May 1805; d. at Willington, 13 Apr 1857; m. 2 Aug 1836, SOPHRONIA JOHNSON, b. at Willington, 4 Apr 1814 daughter of Abel and Deborah (Preston) Johnson; Sophronia d. at Hartford, 25 Mar 1898.

iv   ELIZA GLAZIER, b. 1814; d. 2 Mar 1815.

350)   LEONARD HOLT (*Isaac Holt⁴, Abiel Holt³, Mary Russell Holt², Robert¹*), b. at Willington, 15 Feb 1782 son of Isaac and Sarah (Orcutt) Holt; d. 12 Mar 1857; m. 1ˢᵗ, 29 Dec 1809, his first cousin once removed, ASENATH HOLT (*Nathan Holt⁵, Nathan Holt⁴, Abiel Holt³, Mary Russell Holt², Robert¹*), b. 26 Jan 1786 daughter of Nathan and Lois (Goodell) Holt; Asenath d. 13 Feb 1813. Leonard m. 2ⁿᵈ, about 1813, JOANNA ALDEN, b. 14 Jul 1782 daughter of Elisha and Irene (Markham) Alden; Joanna d. 30 Sep 1849. Joanna was first married to Josiah Converse.

Leonard Holt and his three children are somewhat of a mystery. His son William married twice, and one child has been identified for William. Leonard's two children by his second wife, Asenath Frances and Oliver A., led lives out of the ordinary. Oliver and Asenath lived with their father until after 1850. Asenath and her father Leonard were excommunicated from the church in Willington 31 December 1852[939] but the reasons for this are not known. After that, Asenath attended Thetford Academy in Vermont[940] and worked as a teacher for the remainder of her life. Oliver A. Holt married Nancy Abbe in 1853 and they had one son Leonard O. Holt who died of croup at age two years. After the birth of Leonard O., Oliver relocated to Tamaroa, IL and that is where his son Leonard O. died. Oliver lived in Tamaroa the remainder of his life, but his wife Nancy lived in Connecticut with her family. They do not seem to have divorced, and after Oliver's death, Nancy listed herself as the widow of Oliver in town registers. Asenath went to Tamaroa and was living with her brother in 1860 and she was there as a

[935] National Park Service. "Network to Freedom." https://www.nps.gov/subjects/ugrr/ntf_member/ntf_member_details.htm?SPFID=4068809&SPFTerritory=NULL&SPFType=NULL&SPFKeywords=NULL

[936] Durrie, *Holt Genealogy*, p 164

[937] Willington Historical Society. "About the Daniel Glazier Tavern." http://www.willingtonhistoricalsocietyct.org/html/DanielGlazierTavern2.html

[938] *Connecticut State Library (Hartford, Connecticut);* Probate Place: *Hartford, Connecticut, Probate Packets, Carpenter, Comfort-Kimball, J, 1833-1880*, probate of Daniel Glazier, case number 354

[939] Connecticut, Church Record Abstracts, 1630-1927, volume 127 Willington

[940] *U.S., High School Student Lists, 1821-1923.* Asenath F. Holt of Willington, CT sponsored by Leonard Holt, Thetford Academy

single head of household in 1880.[941] Asenath spent her later years in Washington, D.C. where she died in 1904, although she was buried in Tamaroa.

Leonard Holt did not leave a will and the only probate document available was the administration bond given by Oliver A. Holt and Eber Dunham.

Leonard Holt and Asenath Holt had one child.

i   WILLIAM HOLT, b. at Willington, 6 May 1811; d. at Willington, 5 Feb 1878; m. 1st, 21 Mar 1836, CAROLINE DELAURA CARPENTER, b. at Waterford, VT, 23 Mar 1811 daughter of Isaiah and Caroline (Bugbee) Carpenter; Caroline d. at Willington, 29 Feb 1864. William m. 2nd, at Waterford, VT, 13 Oct 1864, MARY B. PARKER, b. at New Hampton, NH, 22 Feb 1822 daughter of Ezra and Hannah (Burleigh) Parker; Mary d. at Newbury, VT, 23 Mar 1900.

Leonard and Joanna Holt had two children.

i   OLIVER A. HOLT, b. at Willington about 1817; d. at Tamaroa, IL, 27 Aug 1876; m. 10 Oct 1853, NANCY AMELIA ABBE, b. at Enfield, 16 Oct 1830 daughter of Harvey C. and Mary A. (Gowdy) Abbe; Nancy d. at Bristol, CT, 5 Apr 1917.

ii   ASENATH FRANCES HOLT, b. at Willington, Sep 1820; d. at Washington, D. C., 28 Jun 1904.

351)   ANNE HOLT (*Isaac Holt⁴, Abiel Holt³, Mary Russell Holt², Robert¹*), b. at Willington, 21 Oct 1784 daughter of Isaac and Sarah (Orcutt) Holt; d. 27 Jun 1855; m. SIMON CARPENTER, b. 13 Dec 1783 son of Elijah and Sarah (Younglove) Carpenter; Simon d. 24 Aug 1862.

Simon Carpenter did not leave a will. Lucien H. Carpenter and Elisa A. Carpenter signed the administrator's bond. Anne and Simon had two children neither of whom married. The two children lived together in Willington throughout their lives.

i   LUCIEN HOLT CARPENTER, b. 21 May 1817; d. at Willington, 6 Aug 1889.

ii   ELIZA A. CARPENTER, b. about 1823; d. at Willington, 31 Dec 1880.

352)   ANNA HOLT (*Timothy Holt⁴, Abiel Holt³, Mary Russell Holt², Robert¹*), b. at Willington, 12 Feb 1762 daughter of Timothy and Rebecca (Chamberlain) Holt; m. 17 Nov 1785, STEPHEN CROCKER, b. 14 Dec 1760 son of Ebenezer and Hannah (Hatch) Crocker. This family was in Schoharie County, New York by about 1788.[942]

Anna and Stephen Crocker went to Rhode Island following their marriage where at least one child was born. The family was in Schoharie County by 1788 and settled in Carlisle. Stephen seems to still be living at the time of the 1820 census as the head of household, male over age 45. If so, Anna had died before that as the female in the household was age 26-44 and there are two children under age 10 in the household.

There are just three children identified for Anna and Stephen, although there may well be other children.

i   BERIAH CROCKER, b. 1785; d. at Sloansville, NY, 19 Jan 1874; m. at Reformed Protestant Church, Nassau, NY, 31 Oct 1813,[943] SARAH GARRISON, b. about 1795; Sarah d. at Sloansville, 1 Oct 1868.

ii   HANNAH CROCKER, b. about 1786; m. New London, CT, 8 Jan 1801, JOSEPH WEEKS, b. at New London, 26 May 1771 son of Joseph and Elizabeth (Grant) Weeks; Joseph d. at New London, 31 Jul 1809.

iii   EDEY CROCKER, b. in RI, 1794; d. at Sloansville, NY, 23 Jan 1876; m. JACOB TEEPLE, b. 1791 son of John and Lanah (Vosseller) Teeple; Jacob d. at Sloansville, 1866.

353)   TIMOTHY HOLT (*Timothy Holt⁴, Abiel Holt³, Mary Russell Holt², Robert¹*), b. at Willington, 19 May 1765 son of Timothy and Rebecca (Chamberlain) Holt; d. 17 Apr 1850; m. 10 Dec 1789, ESTHER SCRIPTURE, b. 26 Aug 1765 son of John and Esther (Lee) Scripture; Esther d. 1 Aug 1841.

Timothy and Esther Holt lived in Willington throughout their lives and were parents to three children.

[941] Saints, *1880 United States Federal Census*, Year: 1880; Census Place: Tamaroa, Perry, Illinois; Roll: 241; Page: 8C; Enumeration District: 071.
[942] Roscoe, *History of Schoharie County*, p 316
[943] New York Marriages 1686-1980, familysearch.org

i   NORMAN HOLT, b. 6 Aug 1791; d. 12 Apr 1792.

ii   ORRIN HOLT, b. 13 Mar 1793; d. at Willington, 20 Jun 1855; m. 24 Sep 1819, ELIZA DUNTON, b. at Willington, 12 Apr 1801 daughter of Samuel and Lovina (Marcy) Dunton; Eliza d. at Willington, 8 Apr 1850. Orrin was a member of the Connecticut state legislature and elected to the twenty-fourth U.S. Congress as a Jacksonian. He was re-elected as a Democrat to the twenty-fifth Congress with total period of service in the U.S. Congress 1836-1839. He held positions within the Connecticut state militia up to the rank of Inspector General.[944]

iii   REBECCA HOLT, b. 1 May 1797; d. at Willington, 14 Feb 1857. Rebecca did not marry.

354)   JAMES HOLT (*James Holt⁴, Abiel Holt³, Mary Russell Holt², Robert¹*), b. at Willington, 12 Apr 1770 son of James and Esther (Owens) Holt; d. at Willington, 16 Jan 1856; m. 4 Dec 1794, MARY POOL, b. at Willington, 14 Aug 1770 daughter of Timothy and Deborah (Presson) Pool; Mary d. 18 Jan 1853.

      James Holt and Mary Pool were parents to five children born at Willington.

i   CELINDA HOLT, b. 16 Jan 1796; d. at Willington, 20 May 1823; m. 18 Nov 1816, ROBERT SHARP, b. about 1791 likely the son of Solomon and Rebecca (Perkins) Sharp; Robert d. at Willington, 1 Nov 1874. After Celinda's death, Robert married Julianna Holt (see Family 321).

ii   POLLY HOLT, b. 7 Sep 1798; d. at Willington, 24 Jan 1853; m. her second cousin, HORACE HOLT (*Caleb Holt⁵, Caleb Holt⁴, Abiel Holt³, Mary Russell Holt², Robert¹*), b. at Willington, 29 Aug 1784 son of Caleb and Sarah (Goodale) Holt; Horace d. at Willington, 30 Jan 1863. Horace is a child in Family 681.

iii   TIMOTHY HOLT, b. 12 Jul 1801; d. at Willington, 29 Dec 1864; m. 1st, at Mansfield, CT, 2 Mar 1827, THANKFUL WILSON, b. at Mendon, MA, 8 May 1801 daughter of Reuben and Joanna (Taft) Wilson; Thankful d. at Willington, 6 Dec 1835. Timothy m. 2nd, at Mansfield, 4 Mar 1836, ALMIRA A. PERKINS, b. about 1809 daughter of Ransom and Huldah (Montgomery) Perkins; Almira d. at Willington, 29 Apr 1874.

iv   JAMES HOLT, b. 15 Aug 1804; d. at Webster, MA, 22 Sep 1851; m. at Willington, 5 May 1830, PHILEA WILSON, b. at Mendon, 24 Nov 1803 daughter of John and Leah (Darling) Wilson; Philea d. at Webster, 26 Apr 1858.

v   ALMIRA HOLT, b. 30 Aug 1810; d. 3 Nov 1813.

355)   JOSEPH HOLT (*James Holt⁴, Abiel Holt³, Mary Russell Holt², Robert¹*), b. at Willington, 12 Apr 1770 son of James and Esther (Owens) Holt; d. at Willington, 29 Jan 1816; m. 6 Mar 1794, BETSY PARKER, b. at Willington, 23 Feb 1775 daughter of Jonathan and Betsy (Johnson) Parker; Betsy d. 7 May 1814.

      The probate record for Joseph Holt includes few documents as the documents are damaged and not able to be digitally rendered. There was not a will. The surety bond for the administration was $10,000 suggesting a substantial estate. There are six guardian bonds, although the documents are not available; only folder sheets are available for minors Lucy, Mary, and Alvah.[945] There are birth records for six children which do not include Mary, but there are six minor children at the time of probate, and son Thomas was deceased in 1814.

      There is evidence for seven children of Joseph Holt and Betsy Parker, all born at Willington.

i   HANNAH HOLT, b. 16 Jan 1795, no further record

ii   ESTHER HOLT, b. 27 Jan 1797; no further record

iii   THOMAS HOLT, b. 27 May 1799; d. at Willington, 5 May 1814.

iv   ALVAH HOLT, b. 14 Aug 1801; d. at Hartford, 30 Mar 1876; m. 13 Feb 1823, BETSEY KELSEY, b. at Hartford, 18 Mar 1794 daughter of Levi and Sarah (Burkett) Kelsey;[946] Betsey d. at Hartford, 2 Jun 1869.

v   LUCY HOLT, b. 22 Jan 1804; d. at Willington, 3 Feb 1868; m. 24 Nov 1825, ELI ELDREDGE, b. at Ashford, 18 Apr 1803 son of Elijah and Bethiah (Chapman) Eldredge; Eli d. at Willington, 31 May 1864.

---

944 Biographical Directory of the United States Congress, Orrin Holt, http://bioguide.congress.gov/scripts/biodisplay.pl?index=H000748

945 Connecticut State Library (Hartford, Connecticut); Probate Place: Hartford, Connecticut, Probate Packets, Holt, Clarisa-Hunt, O, 1759-1880, case number 1064

946 Barbour, *Families of Early Hartford, Conn.*, p 354

vi   JOSEPH PARSONS HOLT, b. 19 Jul 1806; d. at Northfield, MN, 8 May 1886; m. 23 Nov 1834, JULIA CUSHMAN, of Stafford, b. about 1817; Julia d. at Northfield, 3 Apr 1892.[947]

vii   MARY HOLT, b. about 1808; only known through guardian record and no further record.

356)   SOLOMON HOLT (*James Holt⁴, Abiel Holt³, Mary Russell Holt², Robert¹*), b. at Willington, 14 Apr 1772 son of James and Esther (Owens) Holt; d. at Iowa City, IA, 4 Jun 1838; m. at Franklin, CT, 7 Apr 1799, ZERVIAH ABELL, b. at Norwich, 26 Aug 1780 daughter of Thomas and Zerviah (Hyde) Abell;[948] Zerviah d. at Johnson County, IA, 1845.
        Solomon and Zerviah were married in Connecticut, but were in Exeter, New York by 1810. After 1830, they relocated to Iowa City, Iowa. Solomon Holt and Zerviah Abell were parents of eight children born at Exeter, New York.[949]

i   ESTHER HOLT, b. 16 Jun 1804; d. at Lebanon, NY, 31 May 1882; m. DANIEL ABBOTT, b. 3 Nov 1805 son of Daniel and Sally (Bellows) Abbott; Daniel d. at Lebanon, 1891. Daniel Abbott is a descendant of George Abbott of Rowley.

ii   AUSTIN HOLT, b. about 1807; d. at Jefferson County, KY, about 1839; m. at Jefferson County, 17 Dec 1833, SUSANNAH WARWIC, b. about 1810. Susannah married second James Hamilton on 13 Sep 1840.

iii   DIODATE HOLT, b. about 1809; d. after 1870 when he was living in Elizabethtown, KY; m. at Jefferson County, KY, 7 Mar 1834, ELIZABETH OWINGS TOY, b. in Maryland, Dec 1811 daughter of Joseph and Sarah (Owings) Toy; Elizabeth d. after 1900 when she was living in Elizabethtown, KY.

iv   HARVEY HOLT, b. about 1813; d. before 1828. He was baptized in 1825 but there seems to be a second son Harvey born by 1828.

v   EUNICE HITCHCOCK HOLT, b. about 1816; d. at Johnson County, IA, 22 Mar 1869; m. 20 Jul 1851, DAVID WRAY, b. at Hamilton County, OH, 15 Oct 1815 son of Richard and Catherine (Buford) Wray; David d. at Johnson County, 27 Sep 1872. David Wray was first married to Maria Alt.[950]

vi   MARY CALISTA HOLT, b. about 1820; m. at Johnson County, IA, 12 Jan 1845, JAMES M. PRICE; James d. before 1850.

vii   JAMES THOMPSON HOLT, b. 22 Nov 1822; d. at Berwick, IA, 2 Mar 1901; m. 1850, PHEBE E. DUNKLE, b. in OH, 5 Nov 1832; Phebe d. at Berwick, 19 Feb 1917.

viii   HARVEY HOLT, b. about 1828; d. after 1850 when he was living in Iowa City, IA with his sisters Eunice Holt and Mary C. Price.

357)   ESTHER HOLT (*James Holt⁴, Abiel Holt³, Mary Russell Holt², Robert¹*), b. at Willington, 20 Nov 1774 daughter of James and Esther (Owens) Holt; d. at Ashtabula County, OH; m. 9 Jan 1800, DANIEL PARKER, b. at Willington, 5 Mar 1777 son of Jonathan and Betsy (Johnson) Parker; Daniel d. at Orwell, OH, 18 Mar 1855.
        Esther Holt and Daniel Parker were parents of seven children born at Willington. They then made the trip west and were in Ashtabula County, Ohio by 1820.

i   JONATHAN PARKER, b. 1 Feb 1801; d. at Madison, OH, after 1850; m. at Ashtabula County, 14 Mar 1827, ABIGAIL DEVAN, b. 1802 daughter of Talcott and Temperance (-) Devan; Abigail d. at Montville, OH, 18 Mar 1838.

ii   KEZIAH PARKER, b. 16 Oct 1802; d. at Geneva, OH, 5 Jul 1833; m. at Ashtabula County, 24 Feb 1820, EZEKIEL ARNOLD, b. at Ontario, NY, 1797; Ezekiel d. at Geneva, 5 Jun 1880.

iii   DANIEL PARKER, b. 2 Mar 1805; d. 7 Apr 1805.

iv   HANNAH PARKER, b. 1 Mar 1806; d. at Sycamore, IL, 15 Jul 1883; m. MARSHALL CALL, b. at Randolph, VT, 24 Feb 1800 son of Rufus and Lydia (Ellis) Call; Marshall d. at Sycamore, 26 May 1873.

[947] Neill, *History of Rice County*
[948] Abell, *The Abell Family in America*, p 80
[949] There are baptism records for children of Solomon and Zerviah Holt at the Congregational Church at Exeter: Austin, Diodate, Harvey, Eunice Hitchcock, Mary Calista, and James Thompson all on 27 March 1825. Presbyterian Historical Society; Philadelphia, Pennsylvania; *U.S., Presbyterian Church Records, 1701-1907*; Book Title: *1825 – 1861*. The names of Esther's parents, Solomon and Zeviah, are engraved on her gravestone. The younger Harvey is listed on the 1850 census as born about 1830. There may be another child born before Esther, but that information is not determined.
[950] Iowa City, *History of Johnson County, Iowa*, p 955

v   NEHEMIAH PARKER, b. 2 Jun 1808; d. at Orwell, OH, 13 Mar 1871; m. 1st, at Ashtabula County, 6 Apr 1836, CHLOE SAMANTHA COOK, b. 1817 daughter of Zera and Chloe (Loomis) Cook; Chloe d. 12 Jun 1847. Nehemiah m. 2nd, 16 Nov 1848, ZILPHA FENTON, b. 1813; Zelpha d. at Orwell, 4 Jan 1898. After Nehemiah's death, Zelpha married Ichabod Clapp 27 May 1880.

vi   ESTHER PARKER, b. 2 Jun 1810. Esther's marriage is uncertain, but most likely m. at Madison, OH, 14 Mar 1826, DAVID MORSE, b. in NY, about 1800 and d. at Thompson, OH, 1851. If this is Esther's marriage, she died at Thompson, OH, 20 May 1883.

vii BETSY PARKER, b. 18 Aug 1812; nothing further known.

358) JOHN HOLT (*James Holt⁴, Abiel Holt³, Mary Russell Holt², Robert¹*), b. at Willington, 11 Apr 1776 son of James and Luce (Sawins) Holt; d. at Willington, 22 Apr 1841; m. 6 Sep 1804, his second cousin once removed, CLARISSA HOLT (*Philemon Holt⁵, Paul Holt⁴, Abigail Holt³, Mary Russell Holt², Robert¹*), b. 1775 (based on age at time of death) daughter of Philemon and Jemima (Eldredge) Holt; Clarissa d. at Willington, 25 Feb 1840.
      There is little information on this family. Three children are known, all born at Willington.

i   MATILDA HOLT, b. 13 Jun 1805; d. at Willington, 26 Jun 1834. Matilda did not marry.

ii   JOHN HOLT, b. 15 Mar 1809; d. at Colchester, CT, 1851 (probate 15 Oct 1851 with widow Waity Holt declining administration); m. at Willington, 29 Aug 1832, WAITY MOORE, b. in Rhode Island about 1812; Waity d. at Willington, 22 Jan 1868. After John's death, Waity married Lester Carew, 29 Mar 1859.

iii LAUNDA HOLT, b. 5 Sep 1813; no further record.

359) LUCE HOLT (*James Holt⁴, Abiel Holt³, Mary Russell Holt², Robert¹*), b. at Willington, 11 Jun 1778 daughter of James and Luce (Sawins) Holt; d. at Ashford, 22 Feb 1847;[951][952] m. at Ashford, 26 Jan 1809, AARON WALKER, b. 21 Jan 1776 son of Samuel and Alice (Case) Walker; Aaron d. at Ashford, 1 Nov 1815.
      Luce did not remarry after Aaron's death and in the 1830 U.S. Census at Ashford, she is listed as Mrs. Lucy Walker with the household consisting of one female age 50-59 and one female 15-19.[953]
      The estate of Aaron Walker entered probate 1815 and the inventory was completed 29 November 1815 with a total value of $2,016.81 which included the value of the home farm and buildings of $1,164. Claims against the estate totaled $755.07. The administration of the estate included a consideration of the part of the estate which was still part of the widow's portion of Aaron's mother Alice Walker Wilson.[954]
      Luce and Aaron had two daughters whose births are recorded at Ashford.

i   MARIA TRUMBULL WALKER, b. 11 Jul 1810; d. 18 May 1812.[955]

ii   LUCY MAIN WALKER, b. 11 Nov 1813; d. at Ashford, 5 May 1881; m. at Willington, 8 Apr 1840, GEORGE WHITON, b. at Ashford, 8 Jun 1816 son of Abner and Amy (Chaffee) Whiton; George d. at Ashford, 22 Sep 1887.

360) ABIEL HOLT (*James Holt⁴, Abiel Holt³, Mary Russell Holt², Robert¹*), b. 14 Jan 1780 son of James and Luce (Sawins) Holt; d. at Mansfield, about 1826 (probate of estate in 1826); m. 30 Apr 1805, SALLY CONVERSE, b. at Stafford, 9 Mar 1781 daughter of Stephen and Zerviah (Sanger) Converse;[956] Sally's date of death is uncertain. She was alive in 1823 when her father wrote his will but there is no mention of her in the probate of Abiel's estate. The probate includes some provisions of the support of the two younger sons (Sanford and Arnold) who were underage at the time.
      Abiel and Sally had three children whose birth are recorded at Ashford.

i   ALFRED CONVERSE HOLT, b. 25 Feb 1806; d. at Hillsdale County, MI, 17 Mar 1852; m. 29 Mar 1830, ADELINE L. HURLBUT, b. at Bozrah, CT, about 1810 daughter of Asa and Salome (Arnold) Hurlbut;[957] Adeline

[951] Durrie, *A Genealogy of the Holt Family*, p 50

[952] Ancestry.com, Connecticut, Deaths and Burials Index, 1650-1934

[953] 1830; Census Place: Ashford, Windham, Connecticut; Series: M19; Roll: 11; Page: 176; Family History Library Film: 0002804

[954] *Connecticut Wills and Probate, 1609-1999*, Probate of Aaron Walker, Hartford, 1815, Case number 4184.

[955] Durrie, *A Genealogy of the Holt Family*, p 103

[956] The 1823 will of Stephen Converse includes a bequest to his daughter Sally Holt.

[957] Hurlbut, *The Hurlbut Genealogy*, p 151

d. at Reading, MI, 24 Aug 1887. After Alfred's death, Adeline married Herman C. Hawse who was first married to Elvira Bacon. At the 1860 U.S. Census for Butler, MI, Adeline and H. C. Hawse are living in a household that includes two Hawse children and 10-year old Amos C. Holt.[958]

ii SANFORD HOLT, b. 5 Feb 1815; d. at Haverhill, MA, 22 Oct 1886; m. at Willington, 30 Aug 1835, FIDELIA STUDLEY, b. 1t Mansfield, 12 Jan 1816 daughter of Ebenezer and Fidelia (Hodges) Studley. Fidelia d. at West Boylston, MA, 15 Nov 1882. After Fidelia's death, Sanford married Lydia P. Sawyer on 28 Nov 1883. Lydia Sawyer was the daughter of Timothy Sawyer and Nancy Porter Pendleton.

iii ARNOLD HOLT, b. 24 Sep 1816; d. at Hartford, 21 Dec 1862; m. at Hartford, 7 May 1838, JULIA CURTISS, b. about 1816 daughter of Lyman Curtiss. Arnold and Julia did not have children.

361) SOLOMON PRESTON (*Benjamin Preston⁴, Deborah Holt Preston³, Mary Russell Holt², Robert¹*), b. at Ashford, 10 Sep 1770; d. at Ashford, 29 Sep 1851 son of Benjamin and Bathsheba (Snow) Preston; m. at Ashford, 13 Jun 1799, SUSANNAH HAWES, b. at Medway, MA, 29 Oct 1779 daughter of Eli and Susannah (Bigelow) Hawes; Susannah d. at Ashford, 9 Sep 1860.[959]

There are three children known for Solomon Preston and Susannah Hawes.

i CLARISSA PRESTON, b. at Ashford, 16 Apr 1800; d. at Ashford, 30 Jul 1853. Clarissa did not marry.

ii ERMINA PRESTON, b, at Ashford, 16 Aug 1801; d. at Ashford, 2 Jul 1886; Ermina m. 1st 27 Mar 1829, ELIPHALET BROWN, b. at Windham, 18 Oct 1801 son of John and Olive (Martin) Brown; Eliphalet d. 5 Oct 1834. Ermina m. 2nd 4 Apr 1854, LUCIUS HORTON, b. at Willington, 15 Dec 1804 son of Moses and Silence (Wilson) Horton; Lucius d. at Ashford, 14 Sep 1884. Lucius Horton was first married to Huldreth Thayer. Ermina and Eliphalet were parents of Theron Brown a noted minister and author of his day.

iii MINERVA PRESTON, b. at Ashford, 5 Aug 1807; d. at Ashford, 3 Nov 1848; m. at Ashford, 24 May 1837, ALFRED CHAFFEE, b. 1811 son of Carpenter and Lois (Lyon) Chaffee;[960] Alfred d. at Ashford, 13 Jul 1866. Alfred was second married to Almira Dean.

362) DINAH PRESTON (*Daniel Preston⁴, Deborah Holt Preston³, Mary Russell Holt², Robert¹*), b. at Ashford, 13 Sep 1756 daughter of Daniel and Dinah (Ford) Preston; d. at Braintree, VT, 1 Jan 1836; m. at Hampton, 18 Dec 1777, STEPHEN CLARK, b. at Hampton, 15 Mar 1752 son of Stephen and Hannah (Durkee) Clark; Stephen d. at Braintree, 30 Oct 1820.

Dinah and Stephen started their family in Hampton and relocated to Braintree, Vermont after 1800. Stephen served as a private in the Revolution in Captain James Stedman's company. He marched from Windham for the relief of Boston in April 1775.[961]

Son Fielder Clark married but did not leave any children. In his will written 18 May 1869 (proved 22 April 1875), he bequeathed his estate to his beloved wife Mary with the exception of two hundred dollars to be used for gravestones. Following his wife's death, his estate is to be divided among the children of or the legal heirs of the children of his brothers and sisters. The brothers and sisters are named as Hosea Clark, Eli Clark, Orilla Spear, Sophia Wiley, Phebe Wiley, and Permelia Fisk. Edson Martin of Williamstown was named executor, or if he is not able, then Myron J. Pratt.[962]

Dinah Preston and Stephen Clark were parents of eleven children. The births of the first six children are recorded at Hampton, and the younger five children may also have been born there.

i ABEL CLARK, b. 10 Jan 1779; d. 11 Sep 1790.

ii PERMELIA CLARK, b. 28 May 1781; d. at Brookfield, VT, 8 Oct 1866; m. CHARLES FISK, b. at Hampton, about 1782 son of John and Eunice (Jennings) Fisk; Charles d. at Brookfield, 1 Dec 1868.

iii ARASTUS CLARK, b. 6 May 1783; d. at Randolph, VT, 7 Feb 1857; m. EUNICE BLODGETT, b. at Randolph, 23 Sep 1793 daughter of Henry and Abigail (Parmalee) Blodgett; Eunice d. at Randolph, 10 Oct 1854. Arastus and Eunice do not seem to have had children.

[958] Year: 1860; Census Place: Butler, Branch, Michigan; Roll: M653_538; Page: 1041; Family History Library Film: 803538
[959] Although the marriage transcription in the Barbour collection gives her name as Susannah Harris, this seems to be an error. Other information supports that she is Susannah Hawes, for example the 1825 probate of the estate of Eli Hawes of Ashford which is administered by Solomon Preston. The "internet" reports she is daughter of Reuben Harris, but that is refuted by the 1825 will of Reuben which clearly states his daughter Susannah is unmarried.
[960] Chaffee, *The Chaffee Genealogy*, p 140
[961] Record of Service of Connecticut Men in the War of the Revolution,
[962] *Vermont. Probate Court (Randolph District), Folder 113, Bugbee, Isaac-Currier, Jacob, 1875-1886, will of Fielder Clark*

iv   PHEBE CLARK, b. 3 Apr 1786; d. at Williamstown, VT, 29 Mar 1854; m. JONATHAN WILEY, b. at Dublin, NH, 6 Feb 1796 son of Benjamin and Abigail (Townsend) Wiley.

v   AUGUSTUS CLARK, b. 20 Mar 1788; d. 10 Nov 1790.

vi   WILLARD CLARK, b. 1790; d. 9 Oct 1790.

vii   FIELDER CLARK, b. 1792; d. at Randolph, VT, 19 Apr 1875; m. MARY "POLLY" SPEAR, b. at Braintree, 15 May 1790 daughter of Elias and Mary (Dyer) Spear; Polly d. at Braintree, 4 Feb 1876.

viii   ELI K. CLARK, b. 1799; d. at Andover, OH, 14 Aug 1868; m. 1st EUNICE BROWN, b. 1799; Eunice d. at Andover, OH, 30 Apr 1852. Eli m. 2nd at Ashtabula, OH, 22 Sep 1853, BETSEY SMITH.

ix   SOPHIA CLARK, b. 1797; d. at Roxbury, VT, 8 Jun 1843; m. JAMES WILEY who has not been identified.

x   ORILLA CLARK, b. 1799; d. at Stowe, VT, 12 Dec 1881; m. at Braintree, 6 Mar 1817, ELIAS SPEAR, b. at Braintree, 28 Jan 1795 son of Elias and Mary (Dyer) Spear.

xi   HOSEA CLARK, b. 25 Apr 1801; d. 24 at Northfield, VT, Dec 1874; m. HULDAH WORTHINGTON, b. at Williamstown, VT, 31 Jul 1801 daughter of Daniel and Mary (Fisk) Worthington; Huldah d. at Northfield, VT, 15 Sep 1874.

363)   EUNICE FORD PRESTON (*Daniel Preston⁴, Deborah Holt Preston³, Mary Russell Holt², Robert¹*), b. at Ashford, 12 Mar 1759 daughter of Daniel and Dinah (Ford) Preston; d. at Preston, NY, 31 Oct 1856; m. at Hampton, 15 Apr 1783, WILLIAM CLARK, b. at Hampton, 7 Feb 1754 son of Stephen and Hannah (Durkee) Clark; William d. at Preston, 4 Oct 1840.

     In his pension application file, William reported that he enlisted for six months in a militia company from Hampton, Connecticut. The regimental commander was Colonel John Chester. The troops were shipped to New York where he participated in the Battle of Long Island. He was also in White Plains and Morristown. In the fall of 1777, he enlisted for another month again in the militia. He reported he was born in Hampton 7 February 1754. After the war, he stayed in Hampton until 1795 and then went to Burlington, New York. He was in Burlington about thirty years before moving to Preston, New York. Following William's death in 1840, Eunice F. Clark made her application for widow's pension. Eunice reported she and William married 15 April 1783. In 1844, children Eunice Nicholson of Preston and Alfred Clark of Preston made depositions in support of their mother's application.

     There are three children known for Eunice F. Preston and William Clark, born at Hampton, Connecticut.

i   ALFRED CLARK, b. 22 May 1784; d. 1 Nov 1787.

ii   EUNICE CLARK, b. 19 Jan 1786; d. at Preston, NY, after 1844; m. WILLIAM NICHOLSON, b. at Preston, CT, 7 Jul 1789 son of William Beard and Marvel (Palmer) Nicholson. William was living in the almshouse in Preston in 1873.

iii   ALFRED CLARK, b. 19 Jun 1789; d. at Preston, NY, 10 Feb 1880; m. SUSAN MINER, b. about 1791; Susan d. at Norwich, NY, 17 Dec 1862.

364)   CHLOE PRESTON (*Daniel Preston⁴, Deborah Holt Preston³, Mary Russell Holt², Robert¹*), b. at Ashford, about 1761 daughter of Daniel and Dinah (Ford) Preston; d. at Ashford, 28 Nov 1839; m. at Ashford, 15 Nov 1781, JAMES BOUTELL, b. at Ashford, 30 Jul 1760 son of Jacob and Eunice (Drew) Boutell; James d. at Ashford, 13 May 1822.

     In 1852, daughter Marcia Robinson, then of Ashford and age fifty-five, made application for pension benefits that may have been due her mother Chloe Boutell deceased. On 25 May 1852, the judge of probate court for Ashford in Windham County stated that sufficient evidence had been presented to support that James Boutell was a Revolutionary soldier enlisting in 1776 in the company of Capt. Reuben Marcy, and at the time of his enlistment he was a minor under age twenty-one. James was the son of Jacob Boutell who was a corporal in the same company. James Boutell married Chloe Preston on 15 November 1781. James died on 13 May 1822 at age sixty-two and Chloe died on 28 November 1839 at age seventy-six. In 1852, there were still living the following children: Jacob Boutell, Marcia Robinson, Sally Boutell, and James Boutell. Niece Mary Franklin, formerly Mary Boutell, also provided a statement in 1852 confirming information about her uncle including the four surviving children. Mary's husband William Franklin also provided a statement. The pension documents include a statement by Benjamin C. Simmons, town clerk of Ashford, reporting records for the marriage of Jacob Boutell and Eunice Drew on 20 June 1759 and the birth of their son James on 30 July 1760. James Boutell and Chloe Preston were joined in marriage 15 November 1781.[963]

     James and Chloe were parents of nine children born at Ashford.

---

[963] U.S. Revolutionary War Pension and Bounty-Land Warrant Application File, Case W20740

i   IRA BOUTELL, b. 20 Jan 1785; d. *perhaps* at Batavia, NY, before 1852;[964] m. about 1810, ELIZABETH BROWN, b. about 1785; Elizabeth d. at Batavia, 7 Oct 1828. Ira m. 2nd about 1829, HARRIET JANE KETCHAM, b. about 1793; Harriet d. at Batavia, 28 Jan 1858.

ii   JOHN BOUTELL, b. 1 Sep 1789

iii   JACOB BOUTELL, b. 17 Oct 1791; d. at Eastford, CT, 15 Jan 1886; m. at Ashford, 24 Oct 1827, SYBIL SNOW, b. about 1795 likely daughter of Araunah and Sarah (Hovey) Snow; Sybil d. at Eastford, 10 Apr 1876.

iv   WILLARD BOUTELL, b. 20 Aug 1794; d. at Logan County, OH, about 1850; m. MARY who is not clearly identified, b. about 1793; Mary d. at Logan County, May 1850.[965]

v   MARCIA BOUTELL (twin), b. 12 Sep 1797; d. at Ashford, 15 Mar 1869; m. at Ashford, 1 Jun 1835, as his second wife, AMASA ROBINSON, b. at Woodstock, 31 Dec 1764 son of Timothy and Keziah (Goodell) Robinson; Amasa d. at Ashford, 28 Sep 1843. Amasa was first married to Hannah Chubb.

vi   LUSHA BOUTELL (twin), b. 12 Sep 1797; d. 7 Sep 1800.

vii   JAMES BOUTELL, b. 25 Feb 1800; d. at Wrentham, MA 16 Aug 1879; m. at Ashford, 22 Mar 1824, JULIA ANN PRESTON, b. at Ashford, 6 Jun 1797 daughter of Zera and Hannah (Smith) Preston; Julia d. at Wrentham, 2 Feb 1878.

viii   LUCIUS BOUTELL, b. 14 May 1805; d. 27 Apr 1817.

ix   SALLY BOUTELL, b. 16 Apr 1807; d. after 1852 when she was living in Wrentham, MA (according to information in the pension file for her father). Sally did not marry.

365)   DANIEL PRESTON (*Daniel Preston⁴, Deborah Holt Preston³, Mary Russell Holt², Robert¹*), b. at Ashford, 4 May 1763 son of Daniel and Dinah (Ford) Preston; d. at Fly Creek, NY, 23 Aug 1849; m. at Burlington, NY, 1 Dec 1791, ESTHER CUMMINGS, b. about 1771; Esther d. at Fly Creek, 27 Nov 1862.

     On 16 October 1832, Daniel Preston, aged seventy years and a resident of Otsego, appeared in the court of common pleas to provide information for his pension application. He reported enlisting from Mansfield, Connecticut in January 1778 for a period of three months in the company of Capt. Benjamin Clark. He marched to Providence where he served mostly garrison duty. He enlisted again in August 1779 and was then at Fort Griswold. He had a third enlistment for a period of six months in June 1780 and marched to West Point and from there to Stoney Point. In the pension file, he also reports his birth as 4 May 1762. He lived in various locations in Connecticut until about forty years ago (about 1792) and then moved to Butternuts in Otsego County where he lived about one year. He then moved on to Burlington where he stayed for four years and was then in the town of Otsego where he currently resided. On 18 October 1849, widow Esther Preston then aged seventy-nine years appeared at court to provide information for the widow's pension. She reported she and Daniel were married on 4 December in 1790 or 1791 in the town of Burlington, New York. She reported that six children were still living the oldest being now fifty-four years old. Others making statements in support of the application were daughter Abigail and her husband Leander Plumb. In a statement on 13 September 1851, Abigail Plumb stated she had a sister living and another sister who if still living would be fifty-five. She has brothers living named Alson, Leander, and Daniel. A statement was made by son Alson on 13 September 1851, then age forty-eight. He reported having two older sisters still living and the eldest was fifty-five. Names of other children given in the pension record were Edward, Marcia, Lavina, and Juliann.[966]

     Daniel and Esther were parents of nine children all born in Otsego County, New York. Birth dates are not known for most of the children and are estimated.

i   RUFUS PRESTON, b. about 1794; d. at Fly Creek, NY, 26 Mar 1837; m. OLIVE HECOX, b. at Otsego County, 1798 daughter of Samuel and Elizabeth (-) Hecox; Olive d. at Fly Creek, 12 Jul 1830.

ii   MARCIA PRESTON, b. about 1795; d. before 1851.

iii   EDWARD PRESTON, b. about 1796; d. before 1851.

iv   ABIGAIL PRESTON, b. about 1798; d. at Fly Creek, NY, 19 Jul 1871; m. LEANDER PLUMB, b. about 1796; Leander d. at Fly Creek, 3 Oct 1876. Three children, Electa, Maria, and Orville, are named in Leander's will.

v   ALSON PRESTON, b. 9 May 1803; d. at Cooperstown, NY, 12 Feb 1877; m. LUCY CARPENTER, b. 1804; Lucy d. at Cooperstown, 30 Aug 1875.

---

[964] Ira's date of death is most often reported as 20 July 1861 and there is an Ira Boutell living in Batavia in 1860, but that is perhaps a different person. There are statements from three family members in the pension file of James Boutell that there were only four children living in 1852: Jacob, Marcia, James, and Sally. It may be that the marriages I have reported are for a different Ira Boutell, but this is yet to be determined.
[965] U.S., Federal Census Mortality Schedules Index, 1850-1880
[966] Revolutionary War Pension and Bounty-Land Warrant Application Files, Case W5581

vi   JULIANN PRESTON, b. estimated 1805; d. before 1851.

vii   DANIEL PRESTON, b. 22 Apr 1810; d. at Fly Creek, 27 Jun 1885; m. LAVINA, b. about 1811 who is not firmly identified but may be Lavina Sherwood; Lavina was living in 1880.

viii   LAVINA PRESTON, b. about 1815; d. after 1865 when she was living in Otsego; m. Mr. Brown who has not been identified. Lavina was apparently widowed before 1850 when she was living with her brother Daniel. There were no children living with her.

ix   LEANDER PRESTON, b. 9 Mar 1818; d. at Dodge, WI, 4 Sep 1901; m. 1843, EUNICE BLOOMFIELD, b. in NY, Feb 1820 daughter of Samuel and Sarah (Wheeler) Bloomfield; Eunice d. at Waupun, WI, 27 Jun 1913.

366)   CALVIN PRESTON (*Daniel Preston⁴, Deborah Holt Preston³, Mary Russell Holt², Robert¹*), b. at Ashford, 7 Sep 1766 son of Daniel and Dinah (Ford) Preston; m. at Mansfield, 22 Jun 1785, PHILATHETA BIBBENS, b. at Mansfield, 22 Dec 1766 daughter of Hannah Bibbens, single woman.
        Calvin and Philatheta were parents of four children born at Mansfield, Connecticut.

i   ZALMON PRESTON, b. 3 Sep 1785; m. by 1808, ANNA BUTRICK, baptized at Windsor, MA, 16 Sep 1787 daughter of Oliver and Patience (Sabin) Butrick.

ii   FIDELIA PRESTON, b. 22 Sep 1786; d. at Caton, NY, 20 Apr 1872; m. 8 Dec 1805, CHRISTOPHER TOBEY, b. at Conway, MA, 20 Nov 1784 son of Zacchaeus and Mary (Gifford) Tobey; Christopher d. at Caton, 8 Nov 1867.

iii   AMELIA PRESTON, b. 4 Mar 1788

iv   CHARLES PRESTON, b. 24 Jul 1789; d. at Corning, NY, 18 Jan 1872; m. about 1812, BETSEY BLANDIN, b. in VT, about 1794.

367)   SARAH PRESTON (*Darius Preston⁴, Deborah Holt Preston³, Mary Russell Holt², Robert¹*), b. at Willington, 3 Mar 1764 daughter of Darius and Hannah (Fiske) Preston; m. at Willington, 3 Jan 1788, TIMOTHY NYE, b. at Willington, 26 Jan 1765 son of Benjamin and Phebe (West) Nye.[967]
        Little information was located for this family. There is a birth record for one child, and it seems that Timothy and Sarah went to Richfield, New York and had other children. However, records related to that are not yet found.

i   CHLOE NYE, b. at Willington, 22 Jan 1792

368)   DARIUS PRESTON (*Darius Preston⁴, Deborah Holt Preston³, Mary Russell Holt², Robert¹*), b. at Willington, 18 Dec 1766 son of Darius and Hannah (Fiske) Preston; d. at Hanover, PA, 1 Apr 1845; m. 26 Aug 1788, NAOMI HIBBARD b. at Bolton, 1770 daughter of William Bathsheba (Strong) Hibbard; Naomi d. at Wilkes-Barre.
        Darius and Naomi moved from Connecticut to Hanover, Pennsylvania prior to 1790 and lived in what was known as Back Road near Ashley.[968]
        Darius Preston and Naomi Hibbard were parents of seven children.[969]

i   HIBBARD PRESTON, b. at Willington, 18 Mar 1790; d. at Wilkes-Barre, PA, 20 Mar 1870; m. MARGARET PEASE, b. 11 Mar 1794 (on gravestone) daughter of Samuel and Lydia (-) Pease; Margaret d. at Wilkes-Barre, 3 Feb 1875.

ii   HANNAH PRESTON, b. about 1792; m. DAVID PEASE son of Samuel and Lydia (-) Pease

iii   JERUSHA PRESTON, b. about 1796; d. at Susquehanna, PA, Apr 1870; m. JACOB RUDOLPH who has not been identified.

iv   ISABELLA PRESTON, b. about 1798; m. HENRY BARKMAN, b. about 1789. Isabella and Henry were living in Wilkes-Barre in 1860.

v   ASENATH PRESTON, b. at Wilkes-Barre, 29 May 1801; d. at New Haven, CT, 3 May 1875; m. DANIEL S. BARNES, b. 1798; Daniel d. at New Haven, 15 Mar 1883.

[967] Nye, *A Genealogy of the Nye Family*, p 217
[968] Plumb, *History of Hanover Township*, p 465
[969] The marriages as are given in Plumb, *History of Hanover Township*, p 465

vi   WILLISTON PRESTON, b. about 1803; d. after 1875; m. RACHEL KREIDLER, b. about 1810; Rachel d. at Wilkes-Barre, 12 Aug 1875.

vii   CYPRIAN PRESTON, b. about 1814; d. at Bellevue, PA, 19 Jul 1877; m. CHRISTIANA WILEY, b. about 1820; Christiana d. at likely at Cranford, NY (burial at Pittsburgh), 1881. Christiana was living in New Jersey with her children in 1880.

369)   JOSHUA PRESTON (*Darius Preston⁴, Deborah Holt Preston³, Mary Russell Holt², Robert¹*), b. at Willington, 25 Sep 1768 son of Darius and Hannah (Fiske) Preston; d. at Willington, 1 Nov 1810; m. 25 Sep 1794, SARAH HOLT who has not been identified.
       Joshua and Sarah were parents of two children born at Willington.

i   FLORINDA PRESTON, b. 26 Aug 1799; d. at Chaplin, CT, 16 Feb 1869; m. 31 Mar 1824, ORRIN WITTER, b. at Brooklyn, CT, 15 Jul 1797 son of Jacob B. and Olive (Brown) Witter. Orrin d. at Chaplin, 2 Feb 1869.

ii   AUSTIN PRESTON, b. 5 Nov 1803; d. at Saugerties, NY, 23 Jan 1886; m. at Hampton, 10 Jan 1825, HARRIET BURNHAM, b. at Hampton, 23 Jun 1806 daughter of Jedediah and Phebe (Martin) Burnham; Harriet d. at Hampton, 15 Apr 1888.

370)   CHLOE PRESTON (*Darius Preston⁴, Deborah Holt Preston³, Mary Russell Holt², Robert¹*), b. at Willington, 11 Feb 1772 daughter of Darius and Hannah (Fiske) Preston; d. at Corinth, NY, 9 Jun 1841; m. 10 Sep 1789, LUKE FENTON, b. at Willington, 20 Dec 1769 son of Asa and Jerusha (Hatch) Fenton; Luke d. after 1850 when he was living in Corinth with his son Darius and his family.[970]
       Chloe and Luke Fenton were parents of twelve children.

i   CHLOE FENTON, b. 17 Feb 1790; d. 29 Oct 1790.

ii   ORRIN FENTON, b. 13 Apr 1791; d. 1 May 1791.

iii   LUKE FENTON, b. 23 Aug 1792; d. at Luzerne, NY, 7 Nov 1848; m. about 1818, ANNA CHURCH, b. about 1800 who has not been identified.

iv   WELTHY FENTON, b. 3 Jan 1795; d. at Moriah, NY, 15 Apr 1887; m. EZRA H. BOARDMAN, b. at Corinth, NY, 31 Aug 1791 son of Daniel and Electa (Hickok) Boardman; Ezra d. at Schroon, NY, 19 Apr 1831.

v   ORRIN FENTON, b. 23 Apr 1797

vi   EUNICE FENTON, b. 21 Aug 1799

vii   DARIUS FENTON, b. 20 Oct 1801; d. at Corinth, NY, 12 Feb 1885; m. SARAH EGGLESTON, b. 10 Mar 1801 daughter of John and Lucinda (Standish) Eggleston; Sarah d. at Corinth, 21 Nov 1877.

viii LYMAN FENTON, b. 3 Mar 1804; d. at Rockford, IL, 1884 (will 28 Apr 1884); m. FANNY ROBERTS, b. about 1810 and d. Dec 1877. Lyman and Fanny seem not to have had children. In his will, Lyman left his estate to his housekeeper (his house, all the furnishings and $5,000) and the residue to any of his brothers and sisters now living who came forward within a year and proved their identity.

ix   LEWIS FENTON, b. 12 Jan 1806

x   LOUISA FENTON, b. 20 Mar 1809; reported in the Fenton genealogy as marrying Mr. Angle who has not been identified but may be Samuel Smith Angle.

xi   HORACE FENTON, b. 12 Mar 1812; d. at Saratoga, NY, 5 Feb 1850; m. about 1839, CAROLINE D. HAMMOND, b. 1819 daughter of George and Nancy (Taber) Hammond;[971] Caroline d. at Saratoga, 22 Mar 1853.

xii   ALMIRA FENTON, b. 27 Mar 1818

371)   EUNICE PRESTON (*Darius Preston⁴, Deborah Holt Preston³, Mary Russell Holt², Robert¹*), b. at Willington, 15 Jul 1777 daughter of Darius and Hannah (Fiske) Preston; d. at Willington, 16 Oct 1807; m. at Willington, 6 Feb 1800, ELIJAH NYE

---

[970] There is a gravestone in Corinth that gives his death as 1848, but he does seem to be the Luke Fenton listed at age 80 in 1850 in the household of Darius Fenton in Corinth.

[971] The 1839 probate of George Hammond includes heir Caroline Fenton wife of Horace Fenton.

b. at Willington, 15 Sep 1777 son of Benjamin and Mary (Crocker) Nye;[972] Elijah d. at Willington, 11 Jun 1844. Elijah was the half-brother of Timothy who married Eunice's sister Sarah.

Eunice Preston and Elijah Nye were parents of four children born at Willington.

i   POLLY NYE, b. 28 Apr 1801; d. at Willington, 13 May 1875. Polly did not marry.

ii   JERUSHA NYE, b. 5 May 1803; d. at Elyria, OH, 19 Oct 1877; m. at Lee, MA, 4 Jul 1825, JOSEPH INGERSOLL, b. at Lee, 25 Dec 1796 son of William and Mercy (Crocker) Ingersoll; Joseph d. at Elyria, 23 Jan 1861.

iii   ELIJAH CROCKER NYE, b. 22 May 1805; d. at Somers, 19 Dec 1848; m. at Ellington, 26 Nov 1843, JULIA ANN MCKINNEY, b. at Ellington, 22 Sep 1817 daughter of John and Sarah (Denison) McKinney; Julia d. at Tolland, 25 Jan 1896. Julia was second married to Mr. Eaton.

iv   PHEBE NYE, b. 10 Apr 1807; d. at Andover, CT, 25 Mar 1879; m. at Willington, 18 Oct 1835, as his second wife, NATHAN BURNAP, b. 1798; Nathan d. at Coventry, CT, 25 Mar 1886.

372)   DEBORAH PRESTON (*Darius Preston⁴, Deborah Holt Preston³, Mary Russell Holt², Robert¹*), b. at Willington, 30 Apr 1780 daughter of Darius and Hannah (Fiske) Preston; d. at Willington, 14 Oct 1857; m. at Willington, 10 Mar 1803, ABEL JOHNSON, b. at Willington, 28 Sep 1781 son of Abel and Eunice (Merrick) Johnson; Abel d. after 1870 when he was living at Willington.

Abel Johnson was a farmer is Willington. Deborah and Abel were parents of eleven children born a Willington.

i   EUNICE JOHNSON, b. 22 Jan 1804; d. 23 Sep 1805.

ii   ELISHA JOHNSON, b. 22 Jul 1805; d. at Hartford, CT, 12 Dec 1873; m. at Tolland, 19 Nov 1832, HANNAH CUSHMAN, b. at Willington, 1 Aug 1813 daughter of Joan and Hannah (Swift) Cushman; Hannah d. at Wethersfield, CT, 2 Feb 1899.

iii   TRUMAN PRESTON, b. 11 Jan 1807; d. at Willington, 11 Feb 1822.

iv   MERRICK JOHNSON, b. 15 Apr 1809; d. at Willimantic, CT, 25 Apr 1895; m. at Willington, 25 Sep 1837, CELINDA GLAZIER, b. at Willington, 25 Jun 1818 daughter of David and Fanny (-) Glazier; Celinda d. at Willimantic, 16 Jan 1896.

v   MARCUS JOHNSON, b. 15 Dec 1811; d. at Willington, 27 Aug 1852; m. at Willington, 13 Sep 1834, BETHIAH B. MARTIN, b. 29 Aug 1812 daughter of Elisha Martin; Bethiah d. at Willington, 12 Feb 1875.

vi   EUNICE JOHNSON, b. 11 Aug 1812; d. at Westfield, MA, 2 Nov 1890; m. at Willington, 28 Sep 1830, SETH DUNHAM GRIGGS, b. at Tolland, 1 May 1809 son of Roswell and Sarah (Dunham) Griggs; Seth d. at Westfield, 1 Nov 1890.

vii   SOPHRONIA JOHNSON, b. 4 Apr 1814; d. at Hartford, CT, 25 Mar 1898; m. at Willington, 2 Aug 1836, her third cousin, ORLAN GLAZIER (*Elizabeth Holt Glazier⁵, Isaac Holt⁴, Abiel Holt³, Mary Russell Holt², Robert¹*), b. at Willington, 12 May 1805 son of Daniel and Elizabeth (Holt) Glazier; Orlan d. at Willington, 13 Apr 1857.

viii   ELIZA JOHNSON, b. 5 Feb 1816; d. 6 Feb 1818.

ix   ELIZA JOHNSON, b. 3 Jan 1818; d. (burial at Willington), 3 Jul 1894; m. at Wethersfield, 15 Oct 1849, JOSEPH WALKER PRATT, b. at Hebron, NH, 29 Mar 1821 son of Joseph S. and Sarah (Walker) Pratt; Joseph d. 25 Apr 1898.

x   ABEL JOHNSON, b. 15 Dec 1819; d. at Willington, 28 Jul 1861; m. at Willington, 25 Apr 1843, his third cousin once removed, SARAH G. HOLT (*Royal Holt⁶, Caleb Holt⁵, Caleb Holt⁴, Abiel Holt³, Mary Russell Holt², Robert¹*), b. 6 Nov 1819 daughter of Royal and Lovina (Lamb) Holt; Sarah d. at Willington, Oct 1890.

xi   TRUMAN JOHNSON, b. 1822; d. at Willington, 30 Nov 1851; m. at Willington, 4 Mar 1844, EMILY FRANCES MERRICK, b. at Willington, 21 Nov 1824 daughter of Gideon N. and Polly (Niles) Merrick; Emily d. at Willington, 21 Apr 1895.

373)   AMOS PRESTON (*Darius Preston⁴, Deborah Holt Preston³, Mary Russell Holt², Robert¹*), b. at Willington, 8 Feb 1782 son of Darius and Hannah (Fiske) Preston; d. at Willington, 6 Oct 1864; m. 4 Sep 1804, MARTHA TAYLOR, b. at Willington, 28 Jun 1779 daughter of Thomas and Experience (Freeman) Taylor; Martha d. at Willington, 7 Dec 1860.

[972] Nye, *A Genealogy of the Nye Family*, volume 2, p 218

Amos Preston was a tanner and lived at Willington Hollow.[973] There are records of eleven children of Amos and Martha.

i ALMIRA PRESTON, b. 6 Aug 1805; d. at Willington, 30 Jul 1869. Almira did not marry.

ii SALINA PRESTON, b. 22 Dec 1806; d. at Willimantic, CT, 17 Dec 1861; m. at Willington, 23 Mar 1829, ORIGEN B. HALL, b. at Mansfield, CT, 4 Dec 1806 son of Nathan and Philomela (Fisk) Hall; Origen d. at Willimantic, 16 Jul 1888. Origen married second Almira Barrows on 22 Jan 1863.

iii SYLVESTER TAYLOR PRESTON, b. 5 Aug 1808; d. at Willington, 15 Mar 1887; m. at Willington, 16 Sep 1833, FEAR GLAZIER, b. at Willington, 25 Nov 1813 daughter of David and Cylinda (Marcy) Glazier; Fear d. at Willington, 23 Mar 1891.

iv FLORINDA PRESTON, b. 19 Feb 1810; d. at Brooklyn, CT, 20 Oct 1880; m. at Willington, 6 Mar 1833, CALEB DAVIS WILLIAMS, b. at Brooklyn, CT, 12 Oct 1802 son of John and Sukey (Farrington) Williams; Caleb d. at Brooklyn, 21 May 1878.

v OLIVIA PRESTON, b. 5 Oct 1811; d. at Stafford, CT, 7 Jun 1865; m. at Willington, 14 May 1832, JOHN FULLER, b. at Willington, 17 May 1803 son of John and Azubah (Vinton) Fuller; John d. at Stafford, 14 May 1871.

vi JOSHUA PRESTON, b. 15 Jul 1813; d. at Hartford, CT, Apr 1900; m. at Willington, 3 Mar 1835, CAROLINE ELDRIDGE, b. at Willington, 6 Feb 1816 daughter of Arial and Betsey (Dimmock) Eldridge; Caroline d. at Chicago, 27 Apr 1882.

vii HARRIET PRESTON, b. 8 Jan 1815; d. at Windham, 24 Feb 1884; m. at Willington, 1 Feb 1837, ANDREW H. FULLER, b. 19 Oct 1811 son of Daniel and Zernah (Hall) Fuller; Andrew d. at Windham, 27 Apr 1891.

viii LUCIUS PRESTON, b. 12 May 1816; d. at Willington, 23 Dec 1899; m. at Willington, 19 Feb 1839, OLIVIA A. DIMOCK, b. at Tolland, 12 Sep 1815 daughter of Otis and Wealthy (Kinney) Dimock; Olivia d. at Willington, 10 Sep 1888.

ix LOUISA PRESTON, b. 13 Feb 1819; d. at Willington, 6 Apr 1896; m. at Willington, 6 Jul 1841, CHARLES FRANCIS MORRISON, b. at Hebron, 15 Aug 1815 son of Jon and Betsey (Palmer) Morrison; Charles d. at Willington, 12 Sep 1882.

x ORREN PRESTON, b. Mar 1821; d. 22 Jul 1821.

xi CHARLES PRESTON, b. 1822; d. at age 6 years 6 months, 10 Feb 1829.

374) JOHN PECK (*Jerusha Preston Peck⁴, Deborah Holt Preston³, Mary Russell Holt², Robert¹*), b. at Ashford, 8 May 1768 son of John and Jerusha (Preston) Peck; d. at Weston, VT, 21 Sep 1849; m. 1ˢᵗ about 1789, REBECCA BADGER, b. at Ashford, 1 Jan 1768 daughter of Ezekiel and Doratha (Scarborough) Badger; Rebecca d. at Cavendish, VT, about 1810. John m. 2ⁿᵈ about 1811, HANNAH FOSTER (widow of Phineas Austin), b. at Temple, NH, 28 Dec 1771 daughter of James and Hannah (Jewett) Foster; Hannah d. at Weston, 14 Nov 1848.

John Peck and Rebecca Badger were parents of eight children.

i OLIVER PECK, b. at Ashford, CT, 13 Sep 1789; died young.

ii OLIVE PECK, b. at Cavendish, VT, about 1791; d. at Proctorsville, VT, 8 Nov 1840; m. 8 Dec 1808, JOSEPH BALDWIN, b. at Cavendish, VT, 22 Feb 1783 son of Joseph and Elizabeth (Danforth) Baldwin; Joseph d. at Proctorsville, 9 Mar 1860.

iii PALMER PECK, b. at Cavendish, 7 Dec 1793; d. 1816.

iv DOLLY PECK, b. at Cavendish, 15 Jan 1794; d. at Weston, 15 Feb 1870; m. 3 Oct 1818, EPHRAIM KILE, b. at Reading, VT, 16 Sep 1789 son of William and Ruth (Sherwin) Kile; Ephraim d. at Weston, 22 Mar 1872.

v OLIVER PECK, b. at Cavendish, 24 Jan 1797; d. at Stockbridge, VT, 20 Dec 1878; m. 31 Mar 1819, his stepsister, LUCY AUSTIN, b. 1801 daughter of Phineas and Hannah (Foster) Austin;[974] Lucy d. at Westminster, 7 Apr 1889.

vi OREN A. PECK, b. at Cavendish, 4 Jul 1799; d. at Weston, 18 Feb 1880; m. 4 Dec 1823, SARAH SHATTUCK, b. 29 Jan 1799 daughter of Parker and Sarah (Spofford) Shattuck; Sarah d. 18 Sep 1884. Sarah married second Lemuel Abbott.

---

[973] Preston, *Descendants of Roger Preston*, p 161
[974] Lucy's parents' names are given as Phineas and Hannah Austin on her death record.

vii   EZEKIEL PECK, b. at Cavendish, 24 Jan 1801; d. at Keene, NH, 28 Apr 1891; m. 3 Mar 1831, SINA FENN, b. at Ludlow, VT, 1 Sep 1805 daughter of Austin and Hannah (Ives) Fenn; Sina d. at Troy, NH, 11 Sep 1885.

viii   RHODA PECK, b. at Cavendish, 1 Jul 1804; d. 1808.

John Peck and Hannah Foster were parents of two children.

i   JAMES FOSTER PECK, b. at Cavendish, 28 Jul 1812; d. at Weston, 31 Jan 1880; m. 1st 29 Apr 1841, PHEBE RHODES, b. 22 Jun 1817 daughter of Amasa and Olive (-) Rhodes; Phebe d. at Weston, 12 Jul 1856. James m. 2nd 16 Oct 1856, MARY BARRETT WINSHIP, b. at Weston, 27 Jun 1828 daughter of John and Sally (Richardson) Winship; Mary d. at Malden, MA, 21 Jun 1895.

ii   DANIEL DENNISON PECK, b. at Cavendish, 14 Feb 1817; d. at Weston, 15 Jan 1852; m. 5 Dec 1842, JANE STEVENS, b. at Cambridge, NY,[975] 28 Feb 1826 daughter of David and Lydia (Fletcher) Stevens; Jane d. at Troy, NH, 20 Apr 1896. Jane married second John H. Condon.

375)   ANNA PECK (*Jerusha Preston Peck⁴, Deborah Holt Preston³, Mary Russell Holt², Robert¹*), b. at Ashford, 10 Sep 1769 daughter of John and Jerusha (Preston) Peck; d. at Rushford, NY, 17 May 1855; m. at Ashford, 29 Jan 1789, ROBERT SNOW,[976] b. at Ashford, 19 Jun 1763 son of Robert and Sarah (Chubb) Snow; Robert d. at Cavendish, VT, 13 Aug 1806.
       On 5 February 1839, Anna Snow of Rushford aged seventy-one appeared before the court of common pleas to provide information related to her application for a widow's pension. She stated that Robert Snow served five years during the Revolution, part of the time with the militia and part of the time in the regular army. One of the enlistments was as substitute for Oliver Utley. He was in two engagements, one of those at White Plains. Anna and Robert married at Ashford 29 January 1789 and soon after moved to Cavendish, Vermont where Robert died on 18 August 1806. For the past seven years (since 1832), Anna resided in Rushford, New York. On 17 March 1855, Anna made application for bounty land to which she might be entitled.[977] Anna did not leave a will and administration of her estate was granted to her son-in-law Samuel White on 16 June 1856.[978]
       Robert Snow did not leave a will and his estate entered probate 5 September 1806 with David Chubb and Anna Snow as administrators. Anna Snow was allowed as guardian to Clary Snow, who was over fourteen, Anna agreeing to pay to Clary what was due from the estate "when she shall arrive at full age." Anna was also named guardian to Alden, Warren, Percy, Nancy, and Sybil on 5 September 1806. Later, Reuben Chapman was allowed as guardian for Alden and Anna continued as guardian to the other children. On 15 June 1809, it was determined that the personal estate was not sufficient to cover the debts and a portion of the real estate needed to be sold. Clary signed a statement that she had no objection to the sale of part of the real estate for the support of the family.[979]
       Robert and Anna were parents of seven children born at Cavendish, Vermont.

i   ALDEN SNOW, b. 1 Feb 1793; d. at Mount Vernon, OH, 26 Mar 1880; m. 1st at Geauga County, OH, 19 Jul 1827, RUTH PARKER who d. at Mount Vernon about 1849. Alden m. 2nd at Knox, OH, 20 May 1851, MATILDA T. CRUTCHLY, b. in MD about 1805; Matilda d. at Mount Vernon, 1889.

ii   WARNER SNOW, b. 10 Apr 1795; d. at Rushford, NY, about 1840; m. about 1828, his third cousin, ALMIRA RUMRILL (*Polly Holt Rumrill⁵, Asa Holt⁴, Daniel Holt³, Mary Russell Holt², Robert¹*), b. about 1808 daughter of Simeon and Polly (Holt) Rumrill; Almira d. at Rushford, 26 Aug 1894. Polly married second Winthrop G. Young.

iii   PERCY SNOW, b. 8 Nov 1798; d. at Rushford, NY, 20 Sep 1875; m. 26 Nov 1818, SAMUEL WHITE, b. at Cavendish, VT, 16 Jan 1795 son of Thomas and Betsey (Lincoln) White; Samuel d. at Rushford, 15 May 1874.

iv   JEFFERSON SNOW, b. 18 Mar 1801; nothing further known. Jefferson was not part of the guardianship case for the other children.

v   NANCY SNOW, b. 18 Apr 1803; d. at Otho, IA, 19 May 1891; m. at Rushford, 18 Aug 1826, BENJAMIN J. CHENEY, b. 3 Apr 1803 son of Benjamin and Eunice (Hubbard) Cheney; Benjamin d. at Otho, 30 Mar 1882.

vi   SYBIL SNOW, b. May 1806

---

[975] Jane's place of birth is given as Cambridge, NY on her death record.

[976] The marriage transcription gives the name of Abigail Peck as the wife of Robert Snow, but other records (for example the Revolutionary War pension file) establish that Robert married Anna.

[977] Revolutionary War Pension and Bounty-Land Warrant Application Files, 1800-1900, Case W25041

[978] *Record of Wills, Other Miscellaneous Surrogate Records, 1807-1930*; Author: *New York. Surrogate's Court (Allegany County)*; Probate Place: *Allegany, New York, Letter of Administration, volume 001, p 125*

[979] *Vermont. Probate Court (Windsor District)*; Probate Place: *Windsor, Vermont, Estate of Robert Snow*

376) ELISHA PECK (*Jerusha Preston Peck⁴, Deborah Holt Preston³, Mary Russell Holt², Robert¹*), b. at Ashford, 25 Mar 1777 son of John and Jerusha (Preston) Peck; d. at Abington, 26 Sep 1866; m. 1ˢᵗ at Ashford, 23 Sep 1802, SARAH BADGER, b. at Ashford, 26 Apr 1771 daughter of Ezekiel and Doratha (Scarborough) Badger; Sarah d. at Pomfret, 6 Mar 1843. Sarah had an out-of-wedlock daughter Myra Ingraham prior to her marriage to Elisha. Elisha m. 2ⁿᵈ 29 Oct 1844, MARY WHITMAN, b. about 1790; Mary d. at Abington, 9 Feb 1860.

Elisha Peck and Sarah Badger were parents of three children.[980]

i   POLLY PECK, b. at Ashford, 29 Jul 1803; d. 2 Apr 1805.

ii   ALANSON PECK, b. at Pomfret, 30 Jun 1805; d. at Ashford, 10 Dec 1886; m. 13 Apr 1829, ABIGAIL CARPENTER, b. 19 Dec 1802 daughter of Joseph Titus and Huldah (Davison) Carpenter; Abigail d. at Ashford, 14 May 1889.

iii MINERVA PECK, b. at Ashford, 19 Apr 1809; d. after 1880 when she was living in Eastford; m. at Pomfret, 2 Apr 1839, CYREL W. KENT, b. in Rhode Island, about 1815 son of James and Betsy (Whittaker) Kent; Cyrel d. at Eastford, about 1900 (probate 1900).

377) ALICE POOL (*Deborah Preston Pool⁴, Deborah Holt Preston³, Mary Russell Holt², Robert¹*), b. at Willington, 11 Dec 1765 daughter of Timothy and Deborah (Preston) Pool; m. at Willington, 18 Mar 1782, JOSEPH FENTON, b. at Willington, 28 Feb 1760 son of Samuel and Experience (Ingalls) Fenton; Joseph d. at Willington, 12 May 1814.

Joseph Fenton did not leave a will and the dower was set off to widow Alice on 11 July 1814. The settlement of Joseph Fenton's estate on 14 July 1817 included distributions to the following heirs: son Nathan Fenton, son Joseph Fenton, son Alva Fenton, son Miner Fenton, daughter Julia King, daughter Amy Fenton, daughter Lois Fenton, daughter Experience Badcock, and daughter Alice Fenton.[981]

Alice Pool and Joseph Fenton were parents of eleven children born at Willington.

i   LOIS FENTON, b. at Willington, 7 Feb 1783; d. at Charleston, PA, after 1860; m. at Willington, 6 Feb 1800, ELIJAH FENTON, b. at Willington, 18 Oct 1778 son of Asa and Jerusha (Hatch) Fenton; Elijah d. at Charleston, after 1850.

ii   EXPERIENCE FENTON, b. at Willington, 17 Nov 1784; d. at Tolland, 6 Jan 1846; m. at Tolland, 24 Nov 1803, CHESTER BABCOCK, b. at Mansfield, CT, 8 Jun 1781 son of Elijah and Ruth (King) Babcock; Chester d. at Tolland, 12 Dec 1864. Chester married second the widow Olive D. Fuller on 20 Sep 1846.

iii DEBORAH FENTON, b. 26 Apr 1769; d. Jul 1771.

iv   MARY "POLLY" FENTON, b. 17 Aug 1790; d. at Willington, 13 Apr 1814.

v   AMY FENTON, b. at Willington, 23 Oct 1792; d. at Homer, NY, 3 Mar 1867; m. 20 Nov 1817, WILLIAM MARTIN HIBBARD, b. at Mansfield, CT, 9 Sep 1795 son of Andrew and Ruth (Loomis) Hibbard; William d. at Homer, 7 Jun 1861.

vi   JULIA FENTON, b. at Willington, 1 Jan 1795; d. at Mansfield, CT, 13 Sep 1850; m. ALVA KING, b. about 1793; Alva d. at Mansfield, 10 Jun 1852.

vii NATHAN FENTON, b. at Willington, 5 May 1797; d. at Hartford, 4 Dec 1873; m. LUCINDA HUGHES, b. 1798; Lucinda d. at Hartford, 1870.

viii JOSEPH FENTON, b. at Willington, 17 Dec 1801. It is possible that he married Mary Parker and relocated to Pennsylvania, but that is not certain.

ix   ALBRAY FENTON, b. 13 Sep 1803; likely died young.

x   ALVA FENTON, b. at Willington, 4 Apr 1806; d. at Windsor, CT, 23 Apr 1891; m. 1830, ELIZABETH B. PORTER, b. 10 Mar 1809 daughter of William and Mary (Burt) Porter.

xi   MINER FENTON, b. at Willington, 22 Nov 1808; d. at Enfield, CT, 18 Oct 1870; m. 1ˢᵗ at Stafford, 8 Dec 1834, EMILY STROUD who died about 1836. Miner m. 2ⁿᵈ at Stafford, 6 Nov 1836, CAROLINA CARPENTER.

[980] Peck's *Genealogical History of the Descendants of Joseph Peck*, p 281, reports daughters Jerusha born in 1795 and Betsey born in 1796, but these births are several years before the marriage of Elisha Peck and Sarah Badger. Perhaps Elisha had an earlier marriage but that would require his marrying before age eighteen which would not be typical for this period.
[981] Connecticut State Library (Hartford, Connecticut); Probate Place: *Hartford, Connecticut, Probate Packets, Enos-Foskit, John, 1759-1880, Estate of Joseph Fenton, Case 768*

378)   ANNA POOL (*Deborah Preston Pool⁴, Deborah Holt Preston³, Mary Russell Holt², Robert¹*), b. at Willington, 8 May 1767 daughter of Timothy and Deborah (Preston) Pool; d. at Willington, 12 Oct 1831; m. at Willington, 9 Apr 1795, ERASTUS EDWARDS, b. at Coventry, 1770 son of Erastus and Anna (Porter) Edwards; Erastus d. at Willington, 24 Nov 1850. Erastus was first married to Jerusha Fuller who died in 1794.

Anna Pool and Erastus Edwards were parents of five children born at Willington.

i   JERUSHA EDWARDS, b. 19 Jul 1796; d. at Willington, 31 Jul 1829. Jerusha did not marry.

ii   ANNA EDWARDS, b. 22 Jul 1798; nothing further known.

iii   ERASTUS EDWARDS, b. 4 Oct 1801; d. at Willington, 4 Nov 1880; m. at Thompson, 27 Feb 1837, MARY ANN CHILDS, b. at Woodstock, 1807 daughter of Cyril and Mary (Bartholomew) Childs; Mary Ann d. at Woodstock, 8 Dec 1883.

iv   AMOS PORTER EDWARDS, b. 3 Sep 1804; d. at Thompson, CT, 13 Aug 1843; m. at Thompson, 8 Dec 1828, CAROLINE CORBIN, b. at Thompson, 5 May 1806 daughter of Alpheus and Lucy (Prince) Corbin;[982] Caroline d. at Worcester, 3 Jun 1893.

v   DEBORAH EDWARDS, b. 19 Apr 1807; d. at Worcester, MA, 30 Sep 1887; m. about 1860, as his second wife, HEZEKIAH ELDREDGE, b. at Ashford, 2 Nov 1796 son of Elijah and Bethiah (Chapman) Eldredge; Hezekiah d. 11 Dec 1881. Hezekiah was first married to Laura Chapman.

379)   AMY POOL (*Deborah Preston Pool⁴, Deborah Holt Preston³, Mary Russell Holt², Robert¹*), b. at Willington, 7 Aug 1775 daughter of Timothy and Deborah (Preston) Pool; d. at Willington, about 1817;[983] m. at Willington, 24 Dec 1795, her second cousin once removed, ELIJAH SAWIN (*Mary Fenton Sawin⁵, Elizabeth Holt Fenton⁴, Abiel Holt³, Mary Russell Holt², Robert¹*), b. at Willington, 31 Oct 1774 son of Isaac and Mary (Fenton) Sawin; Elijah d. at Willington, about 1814 (probate 1814).

Isaac, son of Amy and Elijah, provided some communication for the preparation of Sawin's *Summary Notes Concerning John Sawin.* He reported that his father Elijah was the only child of his father Isaac and was orphaned when his father died in the war. The family lived in Willington. In 1851, son Isaac reported he was the only child still living and that he then resided in North Bergen. His brother operated a tavern in Massachusetts.[984]

Elijah Sawin did not leave a will and Amy Sawin was named administratrix. Real estate included 54 acres with buildings valued at $500 but still incumbered by the dower thirds of Elijah's mother Mary Fenton Sawin Niles. The widow thirds were set off to Amy on 1 November 1815. The remainder of the estate real and personal was equally divided among the children Isaac, Ephraim, Elizabeth, and Lucy with the sons receiving their shares from the real property as far as the estate would allow.[985]

Amy Pool and Elijah Sawin were parents of six children born at Willington.

i   ELIZABETH SAWIN, b. 5 Jun 1797; living in 1815.

ii   ROENA SAWIN, b. 22 Oct 1800; d. 11 Mar 1801.

iii   ISAAC SAWIN, b. at Willington, 2 Mar 1804; d. at Sherwood, MI, 12 May 1898; m. ELEANOR HAMMOND, b. in CT, 11 Feb 1806 daughter of Eli and Olivia (Howard) Hammond; Eleanor d. at Sherwood, 21 Jan 1887. This family was in Bergen, NY before relocating to Michigan.

iv   EPHRAIM SAWIN, b. at Willington, 21 Mar 1806; d. at Ludlow, MA, 22 Jan 1835 (probate 3 Mar 1835); m. at Springfield, MA, 12 Oct 1831, ELIZA HAYDEN. After Ephraim's death, Eliza married David Pease of Ludlow on 9 Apr 1840.

v   MANERVA SAWIN, b. 23 Aug 1808; died young.

vi   LUCY SAWIN, b. at Willington, 11 Oct 1812; d. at Alabama, NY, 20 Jun 1849; m. at Bergen, about 1840, HIRAM HOTCHKISS, b. perhaps at New Haven, 1815 son of Moses and Lucy (Griswold) Hotchkiss;[986] Hiram d. at Alabama, NY, 11 Jan 1848. Lucy had gone to Bergen, NY with her brother Isaac.

380)   ALICE PEARL (*Dinah Holt Pearl⁴, Joshua Holt³, Mary Russell Holt², Robert¹*), b. at Willington, 6 Jul 1748 daughter of Timothy and Dinah (Holt) Pearl. The birth transcription says 6 Jul 1743, but this seems an error and Durrie's Holt genealogy

---

[982] The names of Caroline's parents are given as Alpheus Corbin and Lucy Prince on her death record.
[983] Sawin, *Sawin: Summary Notes Concerning John Sawin*, p 38
[984] Sawin, *Sawin: Summary Notes Concerning John Sawin*, p 38
[985] *Connecticut State Library (Hartford, Connecticut)*; Probate Place: *Hartford, Connecticut, Probate Packets, Rockwell, N-Sessions, O, 1759-1880, Estate of Elijah Sawin, Case 1877*
[986] Beers, *Gazetteer and Biographical Record of Genesee County, NY, 1788-1890*, p 130

says 1748; her age at death in 1826 was 76. Alice d. Dec 1826; m. at Willington, 10 Oct 1767, ELEAZER SCRIPTURE, b. at Willington, 10 May 1742 son of John and Hannah (Wells) Scripture; Eleazer d. at Willington, 1813 (estate inventory 13 Oct 1813).

Eleazer Scripture did not leave a will and his estate entered probate October 1813 with Alpheus Scripture as administrator. The widow's dower was set off to Alice Scripture. The estate was insolvent and sold to pay debts.[987]

Alice Pearl and Eleazer Scripture were parents of ten children born at Willington.

i   ROSWELL SCRIPTURE, b. 18 Apr 1768; d. at Stafford, CT, 8 Feb 1839; m. SOPHIA DANA, b. 1777 daughter of James and Elizabeth (Whittemore) Dana; Sophia d. at Cobleskill, NY, 17 Dec 1861.

ii   HIRAM SCRIPTURE, b. 2 Apr 1772; d. at Westmoreland, NY, 17 Apr 1849; m. ELIZABETH PARKER, b. about 1773; Elizabeth d. at Westmoreland, 23 Aug 1862.

iii   ZEVINAH SCRIPTURE, b. 24 Dec 1774; nothing further known.

iv   ALPHEUS SCRIPTURE, b. 1 Sep 1777; d. at Willington, 23 Oct 1846; m. ELIZABETH, b. 1777; Elizabeth d. at Willington, 21 Sep 1865.

v   IRENE SCRIPTURE, b. 24 Mar 1779; d. at Willington, 31 Aug 1861; m. RUFUS FISK, b. at Willington, 10 Feb 1773 son of Rufus and Dorcas (Gleason) Fisk; Rufus d. at Willington, 22 Sep 1848.

vi   ELIZABETH SCRIPTURE, b. 14 Oct 1781; d. at Rushville, NY, 1 Jan 1864; m. PORTER HINKLEY, b. at Willington, 19 Oct 1781 son of John and Ann (Whipple) Hinkley; Porter d. at Gorham, NY, 6 Jun 1849.

vii   ELEAZER SCRIPTURE, b. 24 Mar 1783. What became of Eleazer is not clear. On 2 September 1805, Eleazer Scripture born in Connecticut was convicted in Oneida County of grand larceny and sentenced to one year in Newgate Prison. Eleazer's older brother Hiram was in Oneida County at this time, so perhaps that is this Eleazer. There is also an Eleazer Scripture from Connecticut who died in Pewaukee, IL, after 1855. That Eleazer was married to Susan Saunders who was born in RI in 1796 daughter of Thomas and Elizabeth (Cross) Saunders.

viii   CYRREL SCRIPTURE, b. 17 Mar 1785; d. at Willington, 15 Feb 1853; m. ABIGAIL HALL, b. 1788; Abigail d. at Willington, 15 Apr 1845.

ix   LOIS SCRIPTURE, b. 11 Sep 1788; d. at Rushville, NY, 17 Sep 1846; m. at Willington, 17 Jul 1808, STEPHEN CARD, b. 1785 who has not been identified.

x   ALLICE SCRIPTURE, b. 14 Jul 1790; d. at Tolland, 3 Mar 1863; m. at Willington, 27 Oct 1808, ISAAC NILES, b. at Willington, 9 Mar 1786 son of James and Mary (Fenton) Niles; Isaac d. at Tolland, 7 Oct 1858.

381)   JOSHUA PEARL (*Dinah Holt Pearl⁴, Joshua Holt³, Mary Russell Holt², Robert¹*), b. at Willington, 15 Sep 1752 son of Timothy and Dinah (Holt) Pearl; d. at Vernon, 11 Oct 1837; m. 14 Jan 1773, DEBORAH MARSHALL, b. at Bolton, 1755 daughter of John and Eunice (Kingsbury) Marshall; Deborah d. at Vernon, 11 May 1818.

Joshua Pearl and Deborah Marshall were parents of eleven children, nine of the births recorded at Bolton, Connecticut and two additional children whose parents are identified on death records.

i   JOHN MARSHALL PEARL, b. at Bolton, 28 Apr 1774; d. at Belchertown, MA, 26 Apr 1853; m. 1797, ACHSAH FENTON, b. at Willington, 10 Aug 1773 daughter of Eleazer and Elizabeth (Davis) Fenton; Achsah d. at Belchertown, 17 Jan 1863.

ii   TIMOTHY PEARL, b. at Bolton, 19 Jul 1776; d. at Belchertown, 10 Dec 1837; m. SALLY PERRY, b. about 1774 daughter of Joseph Perry; Sally d. at Belchertown, 30 Oct 1837.

iii   JOSHUA PEARL, b. at Bolton, 8 Nov 1778; d. at Vernon, CT, 27 Jan 1817; m. 14 May 1801, EUNICE STEDMAN who has not been identified. Eunice was living in Vernon in 1830 as head of household.

iv   ELIZABETH PEARL, b. at Bolton, 24 Oct 1780; no further information.

v   LYDIA PEARL, b. at Bolton, 6 Mar 1783; d. at Vernon, 6 Nov 1841; m. at Vernon, 27 Oct 1808, ELIJAH CHAPMAN, likely the Elijah b. 1783 who d. at Vernon, 31 Aug 1872.

vi   EUNICE PEARL, b. 13 Jan 1786; d. 13 Mar 1797.

vii   WALTER PEARL, b. 6 Mar 1788; d. 16 Feb 1789.

viii   CYRIL PEARL, b. 1790; d. 11 Mar 1797.

---

[987] *Connecticut State Library (Hartford, Connecticut)*; Probate Place: *Hartford, Connecticut, Probate Packets, Rockwell, N-Sessions, O, 1759-1880*, probate of Eleazer Scripture, 1813, case number 1893

ix POLLY PEARL, b. likely at Bolton, 1792; d. at Belchertown, 24 Sep 1857; m. at Vernon, 12 May 1825, as his second wife, ISRAEL COWLES, b. at Belchertown, 5 Nov 1788 son of Josiah and Chloe (Mehuren) Cowles; Israel d. at Belchertown, 11 Feb 1857. Israel was first married to Lois Dunton.

x ACHSAH PEARL, b. at Bolton, 15 May 1795; d. at Vernon, 13 Dec 1857; m. about 1816, ANSON ROGERS, b. likely at Vernon, about 1790; Anson d. at Vernon, 22 Dec 1872.

xi EUNICE PEARL, b. at Vernon, 1798; d. at Belchertown, 4 Jan 1873;[988] m. as his second wife, HORATIO RICE, b. at Belchertown, 5 Feb 1787 son of Timothy and Elizabeth (Howe) Rice; Horatio d. at Belchertown, 9 Mar 1871. Horatio was first married to Elizabeth Allen.

382) LOIS PEARL (*Dinah Holt Pearl⁴, Joshua Holt³, Mary Russell Holt², Robert¹*), b. at Willington, 21 Apr 1753 daughter of Timothy and Dinah (Holt) Pearl; d. at Willington, 15 Jul 1788; m. 6 Aug 1771, SAMUEL DUNTON, b. at Wrentham, MA, 10 Nov 1748 son of Samuel and Sarah (Bennet) Dunton; Samuel d. at Willington, 1 May 1813. After Lois's death, Samuel married Lovina Marcy.

  Samuel Dunton served as a Sergeant during the Revolution in Wadsworth Brigade.[989]

  In his will written 21 February 1810 (probate 6 November 1813), Samuel Dunton notes that his five first children namely Amasa, Josiah, Leonard, Sally, and Lois have received £40 each, except Josiah received £33 10 shillings; Josiah will receive an amount to bring his up to £40. Sons Amasa, Josiah, and Leonard also receive land in Willington. Two oldest daughters, Sally Stewart and Lois Eldridge, each receives $33 to bring their portion to £50 which is their full portion of the estate. His two youngest daughters, Lodicia and Eliza, each receives one dollar and the remainder of the estate both real and personal goes to his beloved wife Lovina. Wife Lovina Dunton was named executrix.[990]

  Lois Pearl and Samuel Dunton were parents of seven children born at Willington. Samuel had three children with his second wife Lovina Marcy.

i AMASA DUNTON, b. 5 Jan 1772; d. at Earlville, NY, 11 Apr 1836; m. at Willington, 9 Apr 1793. MERCY TAYLOR, b. at Mansfield, CT, 21 Jun 1777 daughter of Thomas and Experience (Freeman) Taylor; Mercy d. at Earlville, 5 Mar 1848.

ii LEONARD DUNTON, b. 20 Mar 1774; d. 29 Oct 1775.

iii JOSIAH DUNTON, b. 20 Nov 1777; d. at Cambridge, NY, 24 Nov 1866; m. SARAH CROCKER, b. 4 Mar 1779 daughter of Seth and Mary (Hinckley) Crocker;[991] Sarah d. at Cambridge, NY, 10 May 1863.

iv SARAH "SALLY" DUNTON, b. 8 Dec 1779; b. at Fort Edward, NY, after 1850; m. by 1810, JOSEPH STEWART, b. 14 Mar 1778 son of Joseph and Rosanna (Harmon) Stewart;[992] Joseph d. after 1850.

v LEONARD DUNTON, b. 2 Jul 1782; d. at Rome, NY, Jan 1832; m. at Ellington, CT, 4 Nov 1806, ROSINA MCKINSTRY, b. at Ellington, 25 Jan 1783 daughter of Ezekiel and Rosina (Chapman) McKinstry; Rosina d. at Rome, 1 Sep 1847.

vi LOIS DUNTON, b. 4 Oct 1784; d. likely at Syracuse; m. at Willington, 8 Oct 1804, ZOETH ELDRIDGE, b. 1 Apr 1782 son of Zoeth and Bethiah (Hinkley) Eldridge; Zoeth d. at Syracuse, 1844.

vii SAMUEL DUNTON, b. 13 Dec 1787; d. 2 Jun 1798.

383) ELIZABETH PEARL (*Dinah Holt Pearl⁴, Joshua Holt³, Mary Russell Holt², Robert¹*), b. at Willington, 15 Jan 1756 daughter of Timothy and Dinah (Holt) Pearl; d. 8 Jan 1779; m. 6 Aug 1771, ZOETH ELDRIDGE, b. at Willington, about 1751 son of Jesse and Abigail (Smith) Eldridge; Zoeth d. at Willington, 18 Mar 1828. Zoeth m. 2nd, Bethiah Hinkley.[993]

  Zoeth Eldridge was a farmer in Willington. He served in the Revolution first as part of the Minute Men militia and later in the Second Connecticut Regiment which participated in the siege of Boston.

  Elizabeth Pearl and Zoeth Eldridge were parents of five children born at Willington. Zoeth's son with his second wife Bethiah Hinkley (Zoeth) married Elizabeth's niece Lois Pearl.

i ZOETH ELDRIDGE, b. 29 Jan 1772; d. 6 Sep 1780.

[988] The death record of Eunice Rice gives parents names as Joshua and Deborah.
[989] Eldridge, *Eldridge Genealogy*, p 11
[990] *Connecticut. Probate Court (Stafford District)*; Probate Place: *Tolland, Connecticut, Probate Records, Vol 7-8, 1809-1815*, volume 8, pp 98-100
[991] The 1806 will of Seth Crocker of Cambridge, NY includes a bequest to his daughter Sarah Dunton.
[992] Edson, Stewart Clan Magazine, volume 1, number 3, 1922, p 28, Stewarts of Londonderry, NH
[993] Eldredge, *Eldredge Genealogy*, p 8

ii   TIMOTHY ELDRIDGE, b. 8 Sep 1773; d. 3 Jul 1775.

iii   ERASTUS ELDRIDGE, b. 30 Apr 1775; d. at Springfield, MA, 6 May 1820; m. at Enfield, CT, 1 Nov 1795, RUBY ALLEN, b. at Enfield, 14 May 1778 daughter of Moses and Mary (Adams) Allen; Ruby d. at Whitehall, NY, 15 Sep 1844.

iv   TIMOTHY ELDRIDGE, b. 16 Feb 1777; d. likely in western New York; m. by 1804, CLARISSA HAZEN, b. at Hartford, VT, 9 Nov 1784 daughter of Solomon and Theodore (Pease) Hazen; Clarissa d. at Greenville, IL, about 1857.[994] Timothy and Clarissa were in Hartford, Vermont for about twenty years where they had nine children.

v   ELIJAH ELDRIDGE, b. 26 Dec 1778; d. at sea, 1799. He shipped from Boston on the *Pickering* 15 Feb 1799 and was never heard from again.[995]

384)   SARAH PEARL (*Dinah Holt Pearl⁴, Joshua Holt³, Mary Russell Holt², Robert¹*), b. at Willington, 16 Nov 1758 daughter of Timothy and Dinah (Holt) Pearl; d. at Willington, 11 Oct 1826; m. 17 Nov 1776, SAMUEL JOHNSON, b. 1751 (based on age 92 at time of death); Samuel d. at Willington, 22 Mar 1843. Samuel is likely the son of Daniel and Keziah (Dodge) Johnson born at Lebanon, CT 10 Jun 1751.

      Samuel Johnson and Sarah Pearl were parents of ten children born at Willington. Marriages were identified for just two of the children.

i   DINAH JOHNSON, b. 1 May 1777

ii   DAVID JOHNSON, b. 15 Jan 1779; d. 4 Jun 1785.

iii   KETURAH JOHNSON, b. 8 Jan 1781

iv   JOHN JOHNSON, b. 28 Nov 1782

v   SAMUEL JOHNSON,[996] b. 21 Oct 1784; d. at Medfield, MA, 28 Jan 1840; m. 1st, at Medfield, 31 Mar 1812, BETSEY FISHER; Betsey d. at Medfield, 12 Dec 1814. Samuel m. 2nd, 28 Mar 1816, CATHERINE HARTSHORN, b. at Medfield, 1 Sep 1792 daughter of Moses and Catherine (Clark) Hartshorn; Catherine d. at Medfield, 27 Dec 1860.

vi   DAVID JOHNSON, b. 15 Sep 1786

vii   DANIEL JOHNSON, b. 29 Sep 1788

viii   SARAH JOHNSON, b. 11 Jun 1791

ix   IRA JOHNSON, b. 3 Nov 1794; d. at Willington, 15 Aug 1878; m. 21 Oct 1819, CYNTHIA SWIFT CUSHMAN, b. at Willington, 29 Mar 1797 daughter of Joab and Hannah (Swift) Cushman; Cynthia d. at Willington, 23 Sep 1892.

x   RALPH JOHNSON, b. 27 Jun 1798; d. at Willington, 6 Oct 1826.

385)   TIMOTHY PEARL (*Dinah Holt Pearl⁴, Joshua Holt³, Mary Russell Holt², Robert¹*), b. at Willington, 6 Jun 1760 son of Timothy and Dinah (Holt) Pearl; d. at Willington, 2 Jul 1834; m. 9 Jan 1783, LOIS CROCKER, b. 9 Dec 1763 daughter of Joseph and Anne (Fenton) Crocker; Lois d. 24 Sep 1850.

      Timothy Pearl did not leave a will and his estate entered probate 15 July 1834. There was a $150 surety provided by Austin Pearl as principal and Chloe Pearl both of Willington.[997]

      Timothy Pearl and Lois Crocker were parents of five children born at Willington.

i   ELIJAH CROCKER PEARL,[998] b. 18 Jun 1783; d. at Georgetown, WV, 21 Mar 1864; m. at Willington, 6 Dec 1804, POLLY ELDRIDGE, b. at Willington, 29 Jun 1786 daughter of Zoeth and Bethiah (Hinkley) Eldridge; Polly d. at Amsterdam, NY, 23 Jun 1874.

---

[994] Hazen, *The Hazen Family in America*, p 290

[995] Eldridge, *Eldridge Genealogy*, p 9. The Eldridge genealogy suggests the Pickering was a pirate ship, but it was the USS Pickering and there is no information on the history of that ship that suggests it was a pirate ship.

[996] Tilden, *History of Medfield*, reports that Samuel Johnson was born in 1784 and came from Ashford, CT. He was a stagecoach driver. The death record of one of his children gives Samuel's place of birth as Willington.

[997] *Connecticut State Library (Hartford, Connecticut);* Probate Place: *Hartford, Connecticut, Probate Packets, Kimball, N-Warren, H, 1827-1895*

[998] *Biographical Review: This Volume Contains Biographical Sketches of Leading Citizens of Clinton and Essex Counties, New York, Part 1*, p 479, Biographical Review Publishing Company, 1896; details on Elijah's biography and business ventures can be found at this source.

ii   LOIS PEARL, b. 23 Aug 1785; d. at Willington, 19 Sep 1807.

iii   CHLOE PEARL, b. 24 Jan 1792; d. at Willington, 1 Jun 1835. Chloe did not marry.

iv   ANNA PEARL, b. 24 Apr 1794; d. 1 Jan 1800.

v   AUSTIN PEARL, b. 21 Aug 1798; d. at Willington, 14 Jul 1863; m. at Willington, 24 Oct 1824, SOPHRONIA ELDRIDGE, b. at Willington, 11 Dec 1799 daughter of Zoeth and Bethiah (Hinkley) Eldridge; Sophronia d. at Brookfield, MA, 6 Aug 1882.

386)   PHEBE PEARL (*Dinah Holt Pearl⁴, Joshua Holt³, Mary Russell Holt², Robert¹*), b. at Willington, 27 Nov 1765 daughter of Timothy and Dinah (Holt) Pearl; d. at Willington, 10 Apr 1816; m. 24 Mar 1785, her third cousin, ZEBADIAH MARCY (*Zebadiah Marcy⁴, Mary Russell Marcy³, Benjamin², Robert¹*), b. at Woodstock, 2 Jul 1761 son of Zebadiah and Priscilla (Morris) Marcy; Zebadiah d. at Willington, 24 Sep 1851. Zebadiah m. 2nd MARY "POLLY" BRITT, b. about 1780; Mary d. at Willington, 10 Feb 1846.
         Zebadiah was born at Woodstock but settled at Willington about 1782. Phebe Pearl and Zebadiah Marcy were parents of eleven children born at Willington.

i   PRISCILLA MARCY, b. 29 Nov 1786; d. at Worcester, MA, 4 Aug 1874; m. 1st, about 1808, JESSE OAKLEY. Priscilla m. 2nd, JONAS GREEN, b. in MA, about 1784; Jonas d. at Tolland, 1860.

ii   ELIZABETH MARCY, b. 14 Feb 1788; m. at Willington, 1 Sep 1804, JOHN GIPSON.

iii   PHEBE MARCY, b. 12 Oct 1789; d. at Webster, NY, 11 Jun 1871; m. at Willington, 28 Apr 1808, her third cousin, ALPHEUS CROCKER (*Sarah Holt Crocker⁵, Abiel Holt⁴, Abiel Holt³, Mary Russell Holt², Robert¹*), b. at Willington, 3 Jul 1787 son of Zebulon and Sarah (Holt) Crocker; Alpheus d. at Webster, 24 Nov 1873.

iv   LOIS MARCY, b. 7 Aug 1791; d. at Franklin, IL, 20 Dec 1860; m. PETER STOLP, b. at Claverack, NY, 19 Aug 1791 son of Johannes Pieter and Catrina (Chrysler) Stolp;⁹⁹⁹ Peter d. at Franklin, 17 Oct 1853.

v   LUCY MARCY, b. 21 Apr 1793; d. at Concord, NY, 19 Mar 1859; m. at Skaneateles, NY, 1 Jan 1816, ABIJAH SIBLEY, b. at Willington, 1 Nov 1788 son of Jonathan and Patty (Brooks) Sibley; Abijah d. at Concord, NY, 3 Jun 1856.

vi   HANNAH MARCY, b. 21 Aug 1795

vii   SARAH MARCY, b. 2 Sep 1797

viii   THOMAS J. MARCY, b. 16 Sep 1780; d. at Coventry, CT, 16 Jul 1866; m. at Somers, 9 Dec 1824, AMELIA KIBBE, b. in CT, about 1805; Amelia d. at Coventry, 11 Sep 1866.

ix   TIMOTHY MARCY, b. 6 Aug 1803; d. at Willimantic, CT, 6 Sep 1858; m. ANGELINE GAGER, b. 1805 daughter of Samuel and Fanny (Woodworth) Gager; Angeline d. at Willimantic, 5 Jun 1891.

x   ZEBADIAH MARCY, b. 26 Jan 1806; d. at Riverhead, NY, 1878; m. at Willington, 5 Nov 1827, ABIGAIL STILES, b. at Willington, 7 Feb 1795 daughter of Isaac and Abigail (Case) Stiles.

xi   LUCINDA MARCY, b. 30 Nov 1808; d. at West Haven, CT, 13 Sep 1881; m. at Hartford, 9 Jan 1825, ELIAS H. SNOW, b. in CT, about 1797; Elias d. after 1870 when he was living in New Haven.

         Zebadiah and Polly were parents of three children born at Willington.

i   NEWMAN S. MARCY, b. at Willington, 12 Aug 1817; d. at Willington, 11 Jan 1904; m. at Ashford, 1 Oct 1844, SARAH A. LYON, b. about 1818; Sarah d. at Willington, 12 Aug 1894.

ii   MARY MARCY, b. at Willington, 16 Aug 1821; d. at Willington, 9 Oct 1839; m. at Willington, 29 Dec 1838, NATHAN MORSE, b. at Union, CT, 1 Jan 1816 son of Nathan and Persis (Robbins) Morse; Nathan d. (burial at Willington), 1892.

iii   LOUISA M. MARCY, b. 28 Feb 1825; d. at Willington, 19 Sep 1851.

---
⁹⁹⁹ Peter's date of birth is on his gravestone; findagrave: 7580071

387)   MARY HOLT (*Joshua Holt⁴, Joshua Holt³, Mary Russell Holt², Robert¹*), b. at Windham, 11 Jul 1752 daughter of Joshua and Mary (Abbott) Holt; d. at Hampton, 23 Oct 1824; m. 7 Nov 1771, JOSEPH FULLER, b. at Ipswich, 1738[1000] son of John and Hannah (Lord) Fuller; Joseph d. 29 Jan 1805.

Joseph Fuller and Mary Holt were parents of seven children born at Hampton.

i   MARY "POLLY" FULLER, b. 13 Oct 1772; d. at Middlefield, NY, 29 Oct 1851; m. THOMAS FULLER, b. at Windham, 21 Jul 1765 son of Thomas and Sarah (Griffin) Fuller; Thomas d. at Middlefield, 11 Jul 1837.

ii   CHLOE FULLER, b. 11 Dec 1774; d. at Cooperstown, NY, 24 Aug 1854;[1001] m. 21 Nov 1803, TRUMBULL DORRANCE, b. about 1774 son of George and Alice (Trumbull) Dorrance; Trumbull d. at Dalton, MA, 9 Aug 1824.

iii   ELIJAH FULLER, b. 21 Apr 1777; d. at Chenango County, NY, 30 Apr 1864; m. 5 Dec 1803, RUTH ROBINSON, b. at Tolland, CT, 10 Jan 1781 daughter of Joshua and Sybil (Webb) Robinson; Ruth d. at Chenango County, 12 Feb 1849.

iv   JOSEPH FULLER, b. 6 Jan 1779; m. at Canterbury, Dec 1809, ELIZABETH FISH, b. at Canterbury, 14 Mar 1782 daughter of Darius and Sarah (Howard) Fish.

v   ELISHA FULLER, b. 30 Jan 1782; d. at Hampton, 25 May 1837; m. at Hampton, 29 Oct 1805, PHEBE BURNHAM, b. 24 Apr 1788 daughter of Jedediah and Phebe (Martin) Burnham; Phebe, d. 30 Oct 1820.

vi   HARVEY FULLER, b. 13 Sep 1784; d. at Hampton, 21 Apr 1860; m. 16 Dec 1810, LYDIA DENISON, b. at Hampton, 20 Jul 1789 daughter of Daniel and Lydia (Clark) Denison; Lydia d. 4 Feb 1838.

vii   DANIEL FULLER, b. 14 Feb 1789; d. at Philadelphia, 12 Mar 1856; m. 1821, MARY ANN BIRD, b. at Philadelphia, 1792 daughter of William and Mary (Ross) Bird;[1002] Mary Ann d. at Philadelphia, 23 Dec 1859.

388)   URIAH HOLT (*Joshua Holt⁴, Joshua Holt³, Mary Russell Holt², Robert¹*), b. at Windham, 23 Mar 1754 son of Joshua and Mary (Abbott) Holt; d. at West Springfield, MA, 22 Sep 1828; m. at Ashford, 11 Nov 1779, MARGARET MASON, b. at Ashford, 13 Aug 1754 daughter of Ebenezer and Mehitable (Holmes) Mason; Margaret d. 1817. Uriah m. 2nd, at West Springfield, 15 Oct 1818, EUNICE CHAPIN (widow of Charles Ferry), b. at Springfield, 22 Feb 1769 daughter of Elisha and Eunice (Jones) Chapin; Eunice d. at West Springfield, 1843.

Uriah and Margaret started their family in Ashford and relocated to West Springfield after the births of their first two children.

The estate of Uriah Holt was probated in 1829.[1003] Rodney Holt was administrator of the estate. The value of the estate was $230.85 and debts against the estate totaled $477.83. Widow Eunice requested relief as the value of the estate was not enough to support her in her infirm condition.

Uriah Holt and Margaret Mason were parents of seven children.

i   SALLY HOLT, b. at Ashford, 18 Sep 1780; d. 9 Oct 1848; m. at Northampton, MA, 9 Apr 1803, WILLIAM SHELDON, b. at Northampton, 2 Jun 1768 son of Benjamin and Elizabeth (Hunt) Sheldon.

ii   MARY "POLLY" HOLT, b. at Ashford, 2 Mar 1782; d. 1 Jun 1842; m. at West Springfield, 14 Nov 1805, ALPHEUS STEBBINS, b. at Wilbraham, 28 Jul 1780 son of Eldad and Ann (Badger) Stebbins;[1004] Alpheus d. at Wilbraham, 25 Sep 1857.

iii   CLARISSA HOLT, b. at West Springfield, 11 Mar 1784; d. 4 Feb 1813. Clarissa did not marry.

iv   BETSEY HOLT, b. at West Springfield, 7 May 1786; d. at Kirkland, NY, after 1865; m. 1812, as his second wife, STEPHEN BUSHNELL, b. in Connecticut, 4 Aug 1781;[1005] Stephen d. at Kirkland, 20 Jul 1862. Stephen was first married to Thankful Wilcox.

[1000] Fuller, *Genealogy of Descendants of Captain Matthew Fuller*, p 216

[1001] U.S., Newspaper Extractions from the Northeast, 1704-1930; Mrs. C. Dorrance wid of the late Dr. Trumbull Dorrance of Pittsfield, Mass.

[1002] The 1903 SAR application of William A.M. Fuller, grandson of Daniel Fuller gives the names of his grandparents and names the parents of his grandmother Mary Ann Bird and William Bird and Mary Ross.

[1003] *Probate Records, 1809-1881, Hampden County, Massachusetts*; Author: *Massachusetts. Probate Court (Hampden County)*; Probate Place: *Hampden, Massachusetts*. Probate of Uriah Holt, 1829, Case number 5783.

[1004] Badger, *Giles Badger and His Descendants*, p 28

[1005] Stephen's date of birth is on his gravestone. Findagrave: 69227383

v   RODNEY HOLT, b. at West Springfield, 18 Jun 1788; d. at Springfield, 25 Sep 1862; m. at West Springfield, 18 Apr 1822, CHLOE FOSTER, b. at Barkhamsted, CT, 15 Jan 1799 daughter of Eli and Catherine (Barker) Foster;[1006][1007] Chloe d. at Springfield, 9 Dec 1886.

vi   JOHN HOLT, b. at West Springfield, 5 Dec 1792; d. at West Springfield, 21 Aug 1825; m. 16 May 1821, TAMAR LEONARD, b. at West Springfield, 2 Jan 1795 daughter of Rufus and Betsey (Flower) Leonard; Tamar d. at West Springfield, 1825.

vii   PERLEY HOLT, b. at West Springfield, 21 Apr 1795; d. at New York, NY, after 1868 (listed in the city directory); m. at Simsbury, CT, 1824,[1008] LYDIA E. OWEN, b. in CT, about 1798 daughter of Isaac and Zerviah (Cornish) Owen;[1009] Lydia d. after 1860. Perley was a tobacco merchant in New York.

389)   LEMUEL HOLT (*Joshua Holt⁴, Joshua Holt³, Mary Russell Holt², Robert¹*), b. at Windham, 28 Feb 1756 son of Joshua and Mary (Abbott) Holt; d. at Lyme, NH, 1 Aug 1836; m. 1778, his first cousin, MARY ABBOTT (*Mary Barker Abbott⁴, Martha Ingalls Barker³, Sarah Russell Ingalls², Robert¹*), b. 20 Jan 1757 daughter of Isaac and Mary (Barker) Abbott; Mary d. 8 Sep 1849.

    Lemuel Holt and Mary Abbott were parents of seven children.

i   LESTER HOLT, b. at Windham, CT, 27 Aug 1779; d. at Lyme, 3 May 1869; m. at Hollis, 14 Feb 1809, LYDIA FRENCH, b. at Bedford, NH, 24 May 1784 daughter of David and Lydia (Parker) French; Lydia d. at Lyme, 5 Jan 1852.

ii   DOROTHY "DOLLY" HOLT, b. at Windham, 3 Oct 1781; d. at Lyme, 18 Jun 1861; m. 17 Nov 1808, NATHAN PUSHEE; Nathan, b. at Lunenburg, 5 Aug 1784 son of David and Susanna (Pierce) Pushee; Nathan d. at Lyme, 16 Dec 1810. Dolly m. 2nd, May 1824, FREEMAN JOSSELYN, b. at Pembroke, MA, 25 Aug 1778 son of Joseph and Mercy (Waterman) Josselyn; Freeman d. at Lyme, 15 Dec 1868. Freeman Josselyn was first married to Deborah Turner who died in 1822. When Nathan Pushee died, David Pushee was appointed guardian of Nathan's two daughters, Debby and Dolly.

iii   DEBORAH HOLT, b. at Lyme, 3 Oct 1781; d. at Lyme, 4 May 1866. Deborah did not marry.

iv   HARVEY HOLT, b. at Hanover, 27 Sep 1785; d. at Lyme, 23 Oct 1842; m. 21 Jun 1819, HANNAH CUMMINGS, b. at Cornish, NH, 4 Jun 1789 daughter of Isaac and Abigail (Kimball) Cummings; Hannah d. at Bradford, VT, 5 Mar 1885.

v   ISAAC HOLT, b. at Hanover, 18 Nov 1792; d. at Piermont, NH, 4 Jun 1851; m. 1st, at Thetford, VT, 7 Mar 1822, RACHEL FLETCHER. Isaac m. 2nd, at Corinth, VT, PHEBE PAGE. Isaac m. 3rd, at Orange, VT, 10 Mar 1847, SALLY DINSMOOR.

vi   MARY HOLT, b. at Lyme, 22 Oct 1795; d. at Lyme, 9 Aug 1884. Mary did not marry.

vii   CHLOE HOLT, b. at Lyme, 30 Nov 1797; d. before 1860; m. 27 Nov 1825, ALBERT BALCH, b. at Lyme, 5 Sep 1802 son of Isaac and Elizabeth (Bell) Balch;[1010] Albert d. at Whitewater, WI, 8 Mar 1879. After Chloe's death, Albert went to Wisconsin and married Alice who has not been identified.

390)   KETURAH HOLT (*Joshua Holt⁴, Joshua Holt³, Mary Russell Holt², Robert¹*), b. at Windham, 21 Aug 1758 daughter of Joshua and Mary (Abbott) Holt; d. at Randolph, VT, 25 Jul 1839;[1011] m. 29 Jan 1784, JONATHAN AMIDON, b. 7 Feb 1759 son of Henry and Sarah (Doubleday) Amidon; Jonathan d. at Randolph, 15 Apr 1838.

    Jonathan Amidon served in the Revolutionary War with enlistments in 1777 and 1779 as a private. His war service included the battle of White Marsh and spending the winter at Valley Forge.[1012]

    Jonathan Amidon did not leave a will and his estate entered probate 1 May 1838. J. K. Parish was named administrator at the request of widow Keturah Amidon. The real estate was sold for $566.00 and after the settlement of all the debts, there was $119 to be distributed to the heirs.[1013]

[1006] Chloe's parents are given as Eli and Catherine Foster on her death record.
[1007] Chapin, *Sketches of the Old Inhabitants of Old Springfield*, p 218
[1008] U.S., Newspaper Extractions from the Northeast, 1704-1930
[1009] The 1825 will of Isaac Owen in Connecticut includes a bequest to daughter Lydia wife of Perly Holt.
[1010] Balch, *Genealogy of the Balch Families*, p 138
[1011] Ancestry.com, *Vermont, Vital Records, 1720-1908* (Provo, UT, USA: Ancestry.com Operations, Inc., 2013).
[1012] Best, *Amidon Family*, p 27
[1013] *Vermont. Probate Court (Randolph District)*; Probate Place: *Orange, Vermont, Folder 45, Abbott, Benjamin-Brown, Enoch, 1832-1841*, probate of Jonathan Amidon, 1 May 1838

Jonathan Amidon and Keturah Holt were parents of eight children, the first two children born at Willington and the other children at Randolph, Vermont.

i   HANNAH AMIDON, b. 28 Oct 1784; d. at Randolph, VT, after 1850; m. SAMUEL BRUCE, b. in Massachusetts, 1770 (census records); Samuel d. at Randolph, after 1850.

ii ELIJAH AMIDON, b. 1 Jul 1786; d. at Bernardston, MA, 7 Nov 1863; m. at Randolph, VT, 19 Oct 1809, REBECCA AVERILL, b. about 1793 daughter of Samuel and Molly (Barnes) Averill;[1014] Rebecca D. at Monson, MA, 30 Nov 1870.

iii ALFRED AUGUSTUS AMIDON, b. 16 May 1789; d. at Onondaga County, NY, 8 Dec 1817; m. at Barnard, VT, 1 Dec 1815, BERTHA STEVENS, b. at Barnard, about 1792 daughter of Andrew and Sarah (Clark) Stevens;[1015] Bertha d. at Barnard, 19 Apr 1837.

iv JACOB AMIDON, b. 26 Sep 1791; d. at Northfield, VT, 5 May 1866; m. 1st, 22 Apr 1816, MERCY COLE WHITTEN, b. at Cornish, NH, 31 Mar 1794 daughter of Samuel and Rebecca (·) Whitten; Mercy d. at Northfield, 9 Oct 1833. Jacob m. 2nd, 4 Dec 1834, ARMENIA RICHMOND, b. at Barnard, 4 Apr 1807 daughter of Paul and Fanny (Udall) Richmond;[1016] Armenia d. at Northfield, 22 Oct 1887.

v   DYER AMIDON, b. 7 Mar 1794; d. at Richfield, MI, 26 Aug 1853; m. at Brookfield, VT, 23 Aug 1814, SABRA M. SMITH, b. 1795 daughter of Shubal and Mary (Parish) Smith; Sabra d. at Richfield, 9 Jul 1872.

vi MARY AMIDON, b. 18 Aug 1796; d. at Randolph, 18 Sep 1819.

vii SARAH AMIDON, b. about 1800; d. at Brookfield, VT, 31 Mar 1873; m. 2 Dec 1820, her second cousin, WALTER ABBOTT, b. at Brookfield, 10 Jul 1796 son of Benjamin and Lucy (Flint) Abbott; Walter d. at Brookfield, 2 Jan 1879.

viii LUCINDA AMIDON, b. 1804; d. at Moretown, VT, 3 Nov 1883; m. SOLOMON TUBBS, b. about 1800 son of Ananias Tubbs; Solomon d. at Northfield, 14 Mar 1865.

391)   SARAH HOLT (*Joshua Holt⁴, Joshua Holt³, Mary Russell Holt², Robert¹*), b. at Windham, 26 Oct 1761 daughter of Joshua and Mary (Abbott) Holt; d. at Stockbridge, VT, 19 Feb 1813; m. 1783, JOHN DURKEE, b. at Windham, 2 Jul 1762 son of Joseph and Elizabeth (Fiske) Durkee; John d. at Stockbridge, 2 May 1838. After Sarah's death, John married second Polly Webber and third Jemima Strong.

John Durkee served in the Revolution in from Connecticut in Captain Robbins's company. John and his brother Eben Durkee served in the same company. His widow Jemima was granted 160 acres of bounty land related to this service.[1017]

In his will written 14 March 1838 (probate 4 July 1838), John Durkee bequeathed to beloved wife Jemima one hundred eighty-five dollars payable in one cow and in household furniture she brought to the marriage. Jemima also receives the use of one-half of the farm and buildings in Stockbridge while she is a widow. Eunice Durkee widow of son John Durkee receives five dollars in addition to what John received during his life. Son Oren Durkee receives five dollars in addition to what he has received. Daughters Sally Morgain, Polly Bloss, and Elisa Whitcomb each receive five dollars. Harriet Durkee daughter of Harvy Durkee receives five dollars in addition to what her father received from the estate. Youngest son Fisk Durkee receives one-half of the farm and will receive the whole farm after the decease of Jemima. Justin Morgain was named sole executor.[1018]

Sarah Holt and John Durkee were parents of seven children born at Stockbridge, Vermont.

i   JOHN DURKEE, b. 20 Nov 1784; d. at Stockbridge, 17 Aug 1836; m. about 1807, EUNICE RANNEY, b. at Chester, VT, 12 Dec 1784 daughter of Daniel and Eunice (Gile) Ranney; Eunice d. at Elk Grove, IL, after 1850.

ii OREN DURKEE, b. 5 Nov 1786; d. at Stockbridge, 14 Oct 1862; m. at Bethel, VT, 7 Oct 1813, PHILENA RICH, b. at Bethel, 1 Apr 1791 daughter of Justus and Mary (Tufts) Rich; Philena d. 8 Mar 1849.

iii SALLY DURKEE, b. Jun 1789; d. at Stockbridge, 18 Apr 1879; m. at Rochester, VT, 25 Mar 1814, JUSTIN MORGAN, b. at West Springfield, MA, 15 Mar 1786 son of Justin and Mary (Day) Morgan; Justin d. at Stockbridge, 4 May 1853.

1014 Avery, *The Averell Family*, p 301
1015 The 1839 will of Andrew Stevens of Barnard includes bequests to grandson Alfred Amidon and granddaughter Harriet Rand.
1016 Richmond, *The Richmond Family*, p 150
1017 Revolutionary War Pension and Bounty-Land Warrant Application Files
1018 *Vermont. Probate Court (Hartford District)*; Probate Place: *Windsor, Vermont, Probate Records, Vol 12-13 1835-1840*, vol 13, pp 85-86

iv   MARY DURKEE, b. 29 Mar 1791; d. at Middlesex, VT, 28 Mar 1873; m. 1811, BENJAMIN BLOSS, b. likely at Killingly, 19 Nov 1784 son of Richard and Sarah (Barrett) Bloss;[1019] Benjamin d. 23 Sep 1862.

v   ELIZABETH DURKEE, b. 26 Jun 1794; d. at Claridon, OH, 21 Oct 1872; m. 1st, at Stockbridge, VT, 17 Mar 1836, JAMES WHITCOMB, b. at Hardwick, MA, 1781 son of Lot and Lydia (Nye) Whitcomb; James d. at Burton, OH, 10 Nov 1844. Elizabeth m. 2nd, about 1848, NERI WRIGHT, b. at Westminster, VT, 1 Nov 1785 son of Medad and Mary (Willard) Wright; Meri d. at Claridon, 28 Nov 1864.

vi   HARVEY DURKEE, b. 21 Dec 1797; d. at Pittsfield, 28 Nov 1826; m. 22 May 1825, HARRIET GAY, b. 1804; Harriet d. at Pittsfield, 3 Dec 1835. After Harvey's death, Harriet m. Horace Rice.

vii   FISK DURKEE, b. 7 May 1803; d. at Stockbridge, 13 Feb 1885; m. 20 May 1841, ABBY S. EVERETT, b. at Stockbridge, about 1820 daughter of Ebenezer and Lucy (Kinch) Everett; Abby d. at Stockbridge, 20 Feb 1896.

392)   HANNAH HOLT (*Joshua Holt⁴, Joshua Holt³, Mary Russell Holt², Robert¹*), b. at Windham, 24 May 1764 daughter of Joshua and Mary (Abbott) Holt; d. in Vermont, 7 Aug 1855; m. at Clarendon, VT, 21 Jan 1788, AARON CARPENTER, b. at Rehoboth, 9 May 1763 son of Jabez and Abigail (Dyer) Carpenter; Aaron d. at Milton, 26 Sep 1836.[1020]

Hannah and Aaron resided in Milton, Vermont and were first members of the Congregational church when it was organized 21 September 1804.[1021]

In his will written 4 June 1836, Aaron Carpenter bequeathed to beloved wife Hannah the rents and profits on one-third part of the real estate during her life. She also has use of specified rooms in the house and cooking privileges. Daughters Patty Dorance, Hannah Brigham, and Dorcas Meers and son Harvey Carpenter receive one hundred dollars each. Daughter Sally Collins receives sixty dollars (as she already received forty) and daughters Polly Carpenter and Abigail Carpenter each receive one hundred dollars. Fifty dollars of each legacy is to be paid in cattle and a schedule is set out for the payments. Polly and Abigail will continue to have a room in the house. Son Alfred Carpenter receives the remainder of the estate and is responsible to pay the legacies. Alfred is named executor. Real estate, a 234-acre home farm, was valued at $3,252.50 and personal estate and personal estate at $798.59. Claims against the estate were $121.33.[1022]

Aaron Carpenter and Hannah Holt were parents of eight children born at Milton, Vermont.

i   PATTIE CARPENTER, b. 5 Nov 1788; d. at Irasburg, VT, 4 Mar 1864; m. ELISHA DORRANCE, b. about 1775; Elisha d. at Colchester, 10 Dec 1846.

ii   SALLY CARPENTER, b. 21 Apr 1793; d. at Craftsbury, VT, 1885; m. about 1814, NATHAN COLLINS, b. at Ira, VT, 17 May 1792 son of Nathan and Keziah (Carpenter) Collins; Nathan d. at Craftsbury, 23 Jan 1887.

iii   POLLY CARPENTER, b. 5 Mar 1797; d. at Milton, 12 May 1863. Polly did not marry. In 1850, she was living with her sister Abigail.

iv   HANNAH CARPENTER, b. 1 May 1799; d. at Monroe, OH, 3 Aug 1859; m. 1st, about 1829, HIRAM BRIGHAM, b. at Milton, Nov 1800 son of Leonard and Abigail (Forbush) Brigham; Hiram d. at Croton, OH, 1838. Hannah m. 2nd, at Licking, OH, 6 May 1841, ALLEN WILLIAMS, b. in NJ, about 1803; Allen d. at Robinson, IL, after 1880. Allen was first married to Elizabeth Stadden in 1825 and third married to Emeline.

v   ALFRED CARPENTER, b. 6 Jun 1801; d. at Milton, 29 Mar 1863; m. 1st, 19 Oct 1835, MARY EASTMAN, b. at Westford, VT, 12 Oct 1806 daughter of Caleb and Dorcas (Faxon) Eastman; Mary d. at Milton, 14 Sep 1841. Alfred m. 2nd, 20 Apr 1842, HANNAH FULLINGTON, b. 19 Aug 1802 daughter of Ephraim and Hannah (Patten) Fullington; Hannah d. at Milton, 24 Sep 1866.

vi   HARVEY CARPENTER, b. 6 Feb 1804; d. at Hartford, OH, 31 Aug 1856; m. about 1828, ALTHEA THOMAS, b. at Colchester, VT, 9 Jan 1810; Althea d. at Hartford, OH, 1891. Althea married second David Weaver.

vii   ABIGAIL CARPENTER, b. 29 Jul 1807; d. at Milton, 4 Oct 1866; m. about 1838, WARREN HOLMES, b. at Westford, VT, 1810 son of Manley and Sarah (Howe) Holmes; Warren d. at Westford, 31 Mar 1884. Warren second married Anna Eliza Tucker about 1867.

viii   DORCAS CARPENTER, b. about 1810; d. at Willis, KS, 1 Jan 1892; m. about 1835, TIMOTHY VILLERY MEARS, b. at Milton, 10 Feb 1812 son of Stephen and Hannah (Crittenden) Mears; Timothy d. at Willis, 5 Jan 1892.

[1019] Lovejoy, *History of Royalton*, p 690
[1020] Ancestry.com, Vermont, Vital Records, 1720-1908
[1021] Rann, *History of Chittenden County, Vermont*, p 653
[1022] *Vermont. Probate Court (Chittenden District)*; Probate Place: *Chittenden, Vermont, Estate Files, Box 9, Files #914-941, 1813-1841*

393) DORCAS HOLT (*Joshua Holt⁴, Joshua Holt³, Mary Russell Holt², Robert¹*), b. at Windham, 30 Mar 1767 daughter of Joshua and Mary (Abbott) Holt; d. at Middlebury, VT, 1 Jul 1800; m. JOSIAH FULLER, b. 30 Oct 1764 son of David and Hannah (Fuller) Fuller; Josiah d. Potsdam, NY, 4 Dec 1835. Josiah was first married to Deliverance and third married to Olivia Moore.

Dorcas and Josiah had two children one of whom died in childhood and no further information on the second child.

i   LUDOPHICUS FULLER, b. about 1797; d. at Middlebury, 11 Aug 1802.

ii   MERTIA FULLER, b. at Middlebury, 4 Jul 1799; nothing further known.

394) SAMUEL HOLT (*Joshua Holt⁴, Joshua Holt³, Mary Russell Holt², Robert¹*), b. at Windham, 16 May 1771 son of Joshua and Susanna (Goodell) Holt; d. at Hampton, 22 Jun 1846; m. at Hampton, 28 Nov 1799, HANNAH BENNETT, b. at Windham, 5 Jan 1775 daughter of Isaac and Sarah (Cady) Bennett;[1023] Hannah d. at Hampton, 5 Oct 1862.

In 1860, Hannah Bennett Holt was living in Hampton with her three single daughters Anna, Mary, and Louisa. Hannah died in 1862, and two of the daughters later married. Daughter Louisa married a man about twenty years her junior. In 1870, daughter Mary was living with Louisa and her husband.

Samuel Holt and Hannah Bennett were parents of eleven children all born at Hampton. There are not records of the births for most of the children and year of birth for several children is estimated from census records and death records. Six of the children (Daniel Cady, Susanna, Samuel Bennett, Fidelia, Hannah, and Louisa) were baptized at Hampton on 15 November 1825.

i   SUSANNAH HOLT, b. 22 Sep 1800; d. at Hampton, 25 Dec 1856. Susannah did not marry.

ii   SARAH "SALLY" HOLT, b. 20 Nov 1801; d. at Monson, MA, 16 Nov 1861; m. about 1822, HARVEY HORTON, b. at Willington, 27 Nov 1799 son of Moses and Silence (Wilson) Horton;[1024] Harvey d. at Monson, 27 Apr 1886.

iii   ANNA HOLT, b. 1803; d. at Hampton, 27 Jun 1897; m. about 1861, as his second wife, LEWIS FULLER, b. at Hampton, 20 Oct 1797 son of Benjamin and Joanna (Trowbridge) Fuller; Lewis d. at Hampton, 1 Nov 1883. Lewis was first married on 2 Dec 1819 to ELIZA HOLT, b. at Hampton, 18 Sep 1800 daughter of Jacob and Eleanor (Hammond) Holt; Eliza d. at Hampton, 20 May 1860.

iv   LESTER HOLT, b. 13 Oct 1804; d. at Hampton, 18 Jul 1880; m. 29 Mar 1829, CLARISSA JOHNSON, b. about 1806; Clarissa d. at Hampton, 16 May 1880.

v   MARY HOLT, b. about 1806; d. at Hampton, 2 Nov 1879. Mary did not marry. Her estate was administered by Lester Holt.

vi   SAMUEL BENNETT HOLT, b. about 1807; d. at Hampton, 29 Dec 1844; m. at Hampton, 24 May 1842, ABIGAIL WHITMORE, b. 11 Jul 1815 daughter of John and Anna (Strong) Whitmore; Abigail did not remarry and died at Hamilton, NY, 9 Apr 1907.

vii   ELISHA HOLT, b. 6 Jun 1811; d. at Elba, WI, after 1870; m. about 1838, CORNELIA DUTCHER, b. in NY, about 1816 daughter of James Dutcher; Cornelia d. after 1880 when she was living at Elba.

viii   FIDELIA HOLT, b. 5 May 1812; d. after 1880 when she was living in Milford, WI; m. 8 Jul 1845, ELISHA BENNETT, b. in NY, about 1802; Elisha d. at Milford, after 1870.

ix   HANNAH HOLT, b. 23 Aug 1814; d. at Brooklyn, CT, 4 Feb 1892; m. 11 May 1840, PERRIN SCARBOROUGH, b. at Brooklyn, CT, 12 Sep 1808 son of Samuel and Mary (Cleveland) Scarborough; Perrin d. at Brooklyn, 26 Apr 1874.

x   DANIEL CADY HOLT, b. about 1815; d. at Monson, MA, 23 Dec 1888; m. 1ˢᵗ SARAH GRIFFIN who has not been identified.[1025] Daniel m. 2ⁿᵈ at Hampton, 4 Apr 1847, SOPHIA PARSONS, b. 12 Jan 1826 daughter of Reuben and Lydia (Thurston) Parsons; Sophia d. at Monson, 8 Mar 1914.

xi   LOUISA HOLT, b. about 1821; d. at Hampton, 28 Jan 1879; m. after 1860, OLIVER F. BENNETT, b. about 1837 (per census records).

[1023] The 1817 probate of Isaac Bennett includes a distribution to Hannah Holt and spouse Samuel Holt.
[1024] Harvey's parents are named as Moses and Silence on his death record.
[1025] This is marriage given in Durrie's Holt genealogy; records were not located.

395)   OLIVER HOLT (*Joshua Holt⁴, Joshua Holt³, Mary Russell Holt², Robert¹*), baptized at Windham, 9 May 1773 son of Joshua and Susanna (Goodell) Holt; d. at Pomfret, CT, 1 Nov 1821; m. at Eastford, 26 May 1803, SIDNEY BEDOLPH CLAPP, b. 1784 daughter of Seth and Charlotte (Borden) Clapp;[1026] Sidney d. at Pomfret, 6 Sep 1837.

     Oliver Holt was a blacksmith in Pomfret.

     Oliver Holt did not leave a will and his estate entered probate 28 February with widow Sidney Holt as administratrix. Real estate consisted of a dwelling house with two and three-quarters acres valued at $450 and personal estate of $159.79. Debts were $555.84 and included $180.81 due to Charlotte Clapp secured by mortgage. The estate was declared insolvent. The widow's dower was set off to Sidney which included a portion of the house.[1027]

     Oliver Holt and Sidney Clapp were parents of nine children born at Pomfret.[1028]

i   CHARLES HOLT, b. about 1805; d. at Vineland, NJ, 20 Mar 1874; m. at Pomfret, 28 May 1828, NANCY INGALLS, b. at Pomfret, 23 Nov 1796 daughter of Lemuel and Dorothy (Sumner) Ingalls; Nancy d. at Pomfret, 17 Dec 1840.

ii   LOUISA HOLT, b. about 1806; d. at Stockbridge, WI, 6 Apr 1871; m. at Pomfret, 26 Oct 1835, LEMUEL GOODELL, b. at Pomfret, 27 Nov 1800 son of Richard and Marcy (Parkhurst) Goodell; Lemuel d. at Stockbridge, 9 Apr 1897.

iii   HIRAM HOLT, b. about 1808; d. at Stockbridge, WI, 22 Jun 1856; m. at Hanover, NH, 5 Jan 1835, ELVIRA RICHARDSON, b. in VT, about 1808; Elvira d. at Stockbridge, 23 Mar 1857.

iv   OLIVER HOLT, b. 2 Feb 1809; d. at Hartland, VT, 22 Aug 1883; m. at Woodstock, CT, 16 Mar 1835, ELIZA CLAPP BROWN, b. at Woodstock, 14 Nov 1802 daughter of Azor and Abigail (Clapp) Brown; Eliza d. after 1870.

v   GEORGE W. HOLT, b. at Pomfret, 18 Apr 1811; d. at Scriba, NY, 27 Dec 1877; m. 31 May 1833, ELIZABETH WEST, b. in NY, 10 Oct 1815 daughter of Samuel and Ruth (-) West; Elizabeth d. after 1880.

vi   ALBERT HOLT, b. 1813; d. at Stockbridge, WI, 6 May 1889; m. at Boone, IL, 17 Feb 1841, LAURA STORY, b. in NY, 1819; Laura d. after 1870.

vii   SUSAN HOLT, b. at Pomfret, 7 May 1815; d. at Stockbridge, WI, 21 May 1892; m. 16 Sep 1837, THOMAS CRAFT CLEVELAND, b. at Hartland, VT, 5 Sep 1811 son of Thomas and Anna (Craft) Cleveland; Thomas d. at Stockbridge, Feb 1874.

viii   LEMUEL HOLT, b. about 1817; living in Tehama, CA in 1866. He may have married Clarissa Davis at Jackson, MI, 4 Nov 1844.

ix   JOSEPH W. HOLT, b. about 1819; d. at Saint Charles, MI, 31 Jul 1887; m. CAROLINE C. WOODRUFF, b. in NY, 12 Nov 1830 daughter of Nelson Woodruff; Caroline d. at Saint Charles, 14 Dec 1906.

396)   ZILPHA HOLT (*Joshua Holt⁴, Joshua Holt³, Mary Russell Holt², Robert¹*), b. at Windham, 2 Feb 1776 and baptized at Hampton, 28 Apr 1776 daughter of Joshua and Susanna (Goodell) Holt; d. at Stockbridge, VT, 8 Mar 1830; m. at Stockbridge, VT, 17 Mar 1808, as the third of his four wives, JONATHAN WHITNEY, b. at Willington, 20 Feb 1766 son of Peter and Marcy (Case) Whitney; Jonathan d. at Tunbridge, VT, 12 Apr 1853. Jonathan was first married to Eunice Story, second married to Dora Marsh, and fourth married to Betsey Goodell.

     Zilpha Holt and Jonathan Whitney were parents of five children born at Tunbridge, Vermont.

i   REBECCA WHITNEY, b. 25 Jun 1811

ii   LAURA FISKE WHITNEY, b. 24 Jul 1813; d. after 1880 when she was living at Bloomingdale, IL; m. DANIEL N. BROWN, b. in VT, about 1810; Daniel d. after 1880.

iii   ROSWELL WHITNEY, b. Oct 1815; died young

iv   ALBERT GALLATIN WHITNEY, b. 27 Jul 1817; d. at Tunbridge, 30 Jan 1901; m. 1ˢᵗ at Northfield, VT, 19 May 1844, ADELINE D.M. LEONARD, b. at Berlin, VT, 1823 daughter of John and Eliza (Lougee) Leonard; Adeline d. at Northfield, 19 Aug 1865. Albert m. 2ⁿᵈ at Worcester, VT, WEALTHY CONNOR, b. at Shelburne, 8 Jul 1841 daughter of Milton J. and Mary (Blair) Connor; Wealthy d. at Worcester, VT, 8 Jul 1872.

v   JAMES MONROE WHITNEY, b. 4 Nov 1820; d. at Tunbridge, 18 Oct 1905; m. at Royalton, VT, 21 May 1843, ELIZA COZZENS, b. at Bethel, VT, 1819; Eliza d. at Tunbridge, 10 Mar 1895.

[1026] Clapp, *The Clapp Memorial*, p 165

[1027] *Connecticut State Library (Hartford, Connecticut), Probate Packet, Oliver Holt, Town of Pomfret, Case 2153*

[1028] These are children as given in several published genealogies including Holton's *Winslow Memorial*. Durrie's Holt genealogy does not include son Lemuel.

397)   RHODA GOODALE (*Phebe Holt Goodale⁴, Joshua Holt³, Mary Russell Holt², Robert¹*), b. at Pomfret, 28 Feb 1758 daughter of Ebenezer and Phebe (Holt) Goodale; d. at South Windsor, CT, 17 Nov 1841; m. at Willington, JOSEPH ELDREDGE, b. at Willington, 28 Feb 1759 son of Joseph and Abigail (Smith) Eldredge;[1029] Joseph d. at Willington, 14 Dec 1830.

Rhoda and Joseph resided in Willington, and after Joseph's death, Rhoda lived in South Windsor.

On 25 December 1839, Rhoda Eldridge of East Windsor, then age eighty-two, provided a statement related to her application for a widow's pension. She related that Joseph served in the company of Capt. Jonathan Parker from 20 June 1776 to 1 January 1777. Joseph served a further two months in 1778 when he was drafted to go to New London. The master role of the company of Capt. Jonathan Parker is included in the pension packet. The pension file includes a statement made 5 December 1839 by Abigail Green, age fifty-three of Windsor, in support of the application, given her relationship with the family as "well acquainted."[1030]

Rhoda Goodale and Joseph Eldredge were parents of seven children born at Willington.[1031] A marriage is known for just one of the children.

i   RHODA ELDREDGE, b. 26 Mar 1780; d. 5 Oct 1782.

ii   ELIZABETH ELDREDGE, b. 23 Sep 1781

iii   RHODA ELDREDGE, b. 5 May 1784

iv   ABIGAIL ELDREDGE, b. 19 Sep 1786

v   CALISTA ELDREDGE, b. 22 Nov 1788

vi   CHESTER ELDREDGE, b. 12 Jun 1790

vii   FREEMAN ELDREDGE, b. 10 Nov 1792; d. at Greenville, NY, 6 May 1861; m. at Greenville, 10 Oct 1819, LANA SCHREIBER, b. in NY, about 1800 daughter of Peter E. Schreiber; Lana d. at Greenville, 1881 (probate 2 Jul 1881).

398)   CHESTER GOODALE (*Phebe Holt Goodale⁴, Joshua Holt³, Mary Russell Holt², Robert¹*), b. at Pomfret, 3 Sep 1762 son of Ebenezer and Phebe (Holt) Goodale; d. at Egremont, MA, 29 Jan 1835; m. at Richmond, MA, 10 Jul 1790, ASENATH COOK, b. at Goshen, CT, 11 Oct 1769 daughter of Walter and Ruhamah (Collins) Cook;[1032] Asenath d. at Egremont, 7 May 1858.

On 15 August 1832, Chester Goodale, then age sixty-nine and resident of Egremont, made a statement related to his application for pension. While living in Willington, he enlisted in July 1777 as a substitute for Ebenezer Goodale. He was in the company of Capt. Jedediah Amidown in Col. Root's regiment, and they marched to New London where he was stationed. Later in the same year, he enlisted as a substitute for a Cushman and was stationed at a place called Sandy Beach. He had a further enlistment from 1 April 1780 to 1 January 1781 in the company of Capt. Joshua Bottom. At that enlistment, he was at Peekskill and Horse Neck and was in the battle in November 1780 at Horse Neck. In 1781, he did two months as a substitute for James Holt of Willington. He further stated that he was born in Pomfret in 1762 and that he lived in Willington until he went into service. On 12 January 1839, widow Asenath Goodale made a statement related to her widow's pension. She stated that after their marriage, she and Chester resided at Stockbridge, Becket, Great Barrington, and Egremont. Son Chester Goodale provided a statement on 12 February 1839.[1033]

Son Samuel Goodale graduated from Union College in 1836 and obtained his master's degree in 1839. He also obtained his doctorate from Union Theological Seminary in 1839 giving the commencement address and was a member of Phi Beta Kappa. He was a professor of natural science at Nebraska College and was throughout his career an Episcopal minister. He was chaplain of the Nebraska Senate from 1871-1872. He was a founding member of Psi Upsilon fraternity.[1034]

Chester and Asenath were parents of five children.[1035]

i   CHESTER GOODALE, b. 24 Apr 1791; d. at Egremont, MA, 31 Jan 1884; m. at Sheffield, MA, 9 May 1821, SOPHIA BUSHNELL, b. at Sheffield, 1800 daughter of Samuel and Lucretia (Hubbard) Bushnell; Sophia d. at Egremont, 3 Jun 1871.

[1029] Eldredge, *Eldredge Genealogy*

[1030] U.S. Revolutionary War Pension and Bounty-Land Warrant Application Files, Case W17756

[1031] The births of the children are provided by Rhoda Eldredge in her application for a widow's pension in the form of a page taken from the family bible.

[1032] Hibbard, *A History of the Town of Goshen*, p 450

[1033] U. S. Revolutionary War Pension and Bounty-Land Warrant Application Files, Case W19522

[1034] Psi Upsilon Fraternity, *The Twelfth Annual Catalogue of the Psi Upsilon Fraternity*, p 2

[1035] Daughter Laura completed a sampler with the family births. This sampler was included in the pension application file, but the original sampler has been removed from the file and is now held in the National Archives. A facsimile of the sampler is in the probate packet.

ii   LAURA GOODALE, b. at New Salem, MA, 12 Mar 1793; d. at Egremont, 4 Feb 1855; m. at Richmond, MA, 17 Nov 1811, STEPHEN HADLEY, b. at Gardner, MA, 14 Nov 1785 son of Joseph and Naomi (Pierce) Hadley; Stephen d. at Egremont, 30 Jan 1869.

iii   ASENATH GOODALE, b. 24 May 1795

iv   PHEBE GOODALE, b. at West Stockbridge, MA, 15 Jul 1804; d. at Egremont, MA, 28 Jun 1860; m. ALFORD C. BELL, b. 1808; Alford d. at Ballston, NY, 1 Apr 1851.

v   SAMUEL GOODALE, b. 23 Dec 1813; d. at Columbus, NE, 8 Dec 1898; m. 1st 1843, REBECCA KIMBALL, b. about 1827; Rebecca d. at Kalamazoo, MI, 9 Dec 1850. Samuel m. 2nd at Wilbraham, MA, 6 Aug 1852, ROXANNA STARKWEATHER MERRICK, b. at Wilbraham, 16 Mar 1826 daughter of Samuel F. and Mary (Starkweather) Merrick; Roxanna d. at Columbus, 2 Apr 1918.

399)   WALTER GOODALE (*Phebe Holt Goodale⁴, Joshua Holt³, Mary Russell Holt², Robert¹*), b. at Pomfret, 6 Apr 1766 son of Ebenezer and Phebe (Holt) Goodale; d. at South Windsor, 20 Jul 1820; m. about 1787, SABRA BISSELL (widow of John Loomis), b. at Windsor, 25 May 1763 daughter of Hezekiah and Sabra (Trumbull) Bissell; Sabra d. at East Windsor, 17 Nov 1834.

     Walter Goodale did not leave a will and his estate entered probate 27 October 1820 with Walter Goodale as administrator and John L. Goodale providing surety for the bond. Inventory was made 2 November 1820 with personal estate was valued at $489.99 which included which included $178 in the form of shocks of rye, hay stalks, corn, and flour. Debts were $504.13.[1036]

     There are four children known for Walter Goodale and Sabra Bissell likely born at South Windsor.

i   JOHN L. GOODALE, b. about 1788; d. between 1840 and 1850;[1037] m. 1st at East Hartford, 1 May 1822, BETSEY TREAT, b. about 1798 daughter of Thomas and Jemima (Calkins) Treat; Betsey d. at East Windsor, 1824. John m. second, at East Windsor, 1 Jan 1828, HANNAH LOOMIS, b. 1800 daughter of Gideon and Margaret (Witherhill) Loomis; Hannah d. at South Windsor, 28 May 1867. John does not seem to have had children.

ii   NANCY GOODALE, b. about 1790; d. at Manchester, CT, 20 Jul 1880; m. WHITING RISLEY, baptized at East Hartford, 13 Aug 1786 son of Nehemiah and Mary (Beaumont) Risley; Whiting d. at Manchester, 8 Aug 1853.

iii   WALTER GOODALE, b. about 1794; d. at South Windsor, 7 Oct 1835. No marriage was identified for Walter.

iv   RALPH T. GOODALE, b. about 1802; d. at East Windsor, 29 Apr 1834; m. at East Windsor, 28 Nov 1828, MARY E. SKINNER, b. about 1806; Mary d. at Manchester, CT, 8 Aug 1875. Mary married second Martin Risley on 16 Nov 1836.

400)   WILLARD GOODALE (*Phebe Holt Goodale⁴, Joshua Holt³, Mary Russell Holt², Robert¹*), b. at Pomfret, 8 Mar 1768 son of Ebenezer and Phebe (Holt) Goodale; d. at Perry, NY, 11 Nov 1858; m. MARY ANN MCLEAN, b. 1772; Mary Ann d. at Perry, 2 Oct 1752.

     Willard and Mary Ann were parents of five children.

i   HORACE GOODALE, b. 1800; d. at Perry, NY, about 1837 (probate 9 Jun 1837). Horace does not seem to have married and his father Willard was administrator of his estate.

ii   HECTOR MCLEAN GOODALE, b. 1801; d. of consumption, at Perry, NY, Jan 1850;[1038] m. ELIZA SILVER, b. in VT, 1803; Eliza d. at Perry, 1877.[1039]

iii   LAURA GOODALE, b. Aug 1804; d. at Decatur, IL, 20 Mar 1868; m. Dec 1826, ADMIRAL ROE, b. at Seneca, NY, 25 Nov 1800 son of Thomas Roe;[1040] Admiral d. after 1880 when he was living in Oshkosh, WI.

iv   WILLIAM GOODALE, b. at East Windsor, CT, 16 Sep 1806; d. at Perry, NY, 29 Apr 1843; m. LUCINDA GIBBS, b. at Triangle, NY, 19 Mar 1807. LUCINDA GIBBS, b. 1807; Lucinda d. at Rochester, NY, 7 Sep 1889.[1041]

[1036] *Connecticut State Library (Hartford, Connecticut), East Windsor Probate District, Estate of Walter Goodale of East Windsor, Case 1309*
[1037] John L. Goodale is on the 1840 census at East Windsor with household of one male 40-49 and one female 40-49. His wife is on the 1850 census but not John.
[1038] New York, U.S. Census Mortality Schedule, 1850-1880
[1039] Burial at Prospect Hill Cemetery, Perry Center, findagrave ID: 64554328
[1040] Torrey, *David Roe of Flushing, NY and Some of His Descendants*
[1041] New York Department of Health; Albany, NY; *NY State Death Index, Year 1889*

v   GEORGE WILLARD GOODALE, b. 1808; d. at Perry, NY, 13 Feb 1890; m. SALLY SILVER, b. in VT, about 1816 daughter of Levi and Susannah (Nichols) Silver; Sally d. at Perry, 26 Nov 1897.

401)   PHEBE GOODALE (*Phebe Holt Goodale⁴, Joshua Holt³, Mary Russell Holt², Robert¹*), b. at Willington, 29 Aug 1775 daughter of Ebenezer and Phebe (Holt) Goodale; d. at South Windsor, 6 Nov 1856; m. as his third wife, GUSTAVUS GRANT, b at East Windsor, 1759 son of Samuel Rockwell and Mabel (Loomis) Grant;[1042] Gustavus d. at South Windsor, 11 Mar 1841. Gustavus was first married to Lucina Grant and second married to Electa Goodwin.

Gustavus Grant was a farmer and innkeeper in Windsor. He also served civic duties as selectman, constable, and sheriff.[1043]

In his will written 17 October 1836, Gustavus Grant bequeathed to beloved wife Phebe the use of part of the dwelling house, all the household furniture, and three acres of woodland. After Phebe's decease, the land is to go to son Lucius. Son Marvin receives two plots of land that adjoin Marvin's land. Grandson Sheldon Grant also receives a land bequest as does son Randolph. Sons Frank, William, Willis, and Lucius also receive land bequests. The sons are responsible to pay money legacies to the daughters: Electa Johnson, Marilda Hosmer, Roxey Noble, Lucina, and Phebe Grant. Frank Grant was named executor.

Phebe Goodale and Gustavus Grant were parents of eleven children born at East Windsor. Gustavus also had five children with his wife Lucina Grant.[1044]

i   ELECTA GRANT, b. 28 Feb 1800; d. at South Windsor, 3 Apr 1839; m. at East Windsor, 15 Oct 1820, HENRY JOHNSON, b. 2 Jul 1791 son of John and Olive (Morgan) Johnson;[1045] Henry d. at South Windsor, 27 Nov 1878. Henry was second married to Phebe Barber on 5 Nov 1840.

ii   MARILDA GRANT, b. 16 Mar 1801; d. at Hartford, 29 Mar 1882; m. at East Windsor, 21 Jul 1820, HORACE HOSMER, b. at East Windsor, 8 Sep 1794 son of Joseph and Miriam (Newbury) Hosmer; Horace d. at East Windsor, 12 Sep 1860.

iii   MARVIN GRANT, b. 27 Sep 1802; d. at South Windsor, 2 Sep 1867; m. ABIGAIL BELCHER, b. at East Windsor, 12 Apr 1807 daughter of Elijah Dean and Beersheba (Hosmer) Belcher; Abigail d. at South Windsor, 3 Mar 1889.

iv   FRANK GRANT, b. 19 Jan 1804; d. at South Windsor, Apr 1880; m. 5 Jan 1842, ELECTA MCLEAN, b. at Glastonbury, 12 Dec 1816 daughter of James and Ruth (Hollister) McLean' Electa d. at South Windsor, 1885..

v   GUSTAVUS GRANT, b. 4 Mar 1805; d. at Wapping, CT, 12 Jul 1867. Gustavus did not marry. In 1850, he was living with his mother Phebe.

vi   ROXY GRANT, b. 11 Jan 1807; d. at Pittsfield, MA, 18 Nov 1869; m. at East Windsor, 29 Mar 1834, WILLIAM NOBLE, b. at Washington, MA, 23 Sep 1804 son of William and Mary (Smith) Noble;[1046] William d. at Pittsfield, 18 Aug 1868.

vii   RANDOLPH GRANT, b. 26 Aug 1808; d. at South Windsor, 3 May 1885; m. at East Windsor, 6 Jan 1835, his first cousin once removed, NANCY GRANT (*Chloe Fenton Grant⁶, Francis Fenton⁵, Elizabeth Holt Fenton⁴, Abiel Holt³, Mary Russell Holt², Robert¹*), b. 11 May 1811 daughter of Elliot and Chloe (Fenton) Grant; Nancy d. at Wapping, CT, 28 Mar 1886.

viii   LUCIUS GRANT, b. 18 Sep 1810; d. at South Windsor, 1 Sep 1846; m. at East Windsor, 22 Nov 1838, MARY FOSTER, b. Dec 1816 daughter of Abel and Irena (Olcott) Foster; Mary d. after 1900 when she was living in Hartford.

ix   LUCINA GRANT, b. 11 Jan 1813; d. at South Windsor, 19 Nov 1884; m. at East Windsor, 6 Jan 1835, her first cousin once removed, HORACE GRANT (*Chloe Fenton Grant⁶, Francis Fenton⁵, Elizabeth Holt Fenton⁴, Abiel Holt³, Mary Russell Holt², Robert¹*), b. about 1807 son of Elliot and Chloe (Fenton) Grant; Horace d. at South Windsor, 15 Mar 1851.

x   PHEBE GRANT, b. 16 Jul 1814; m. OTIS BUCKINGHAM of Coventry.[1047] Records were not located for this couple.

[1042] Cutter, *New England Families, Genealogical and Memorial*, volume 3, p 1304

[1043] Grant, *The Grant Family*, p 48

[1044] Stiles, *Families of Ancient Windsor*, p 330

[1045] The names of Henry's parents and his date of birth are given on his death record.

[1046] The names of William's parents are given as William and Mary on his death record. Also, History and Genealogy of the Family of Thomas Noble, p 538

[1047] Stiles, *Families of Ancient Windsor*

xi   WEALTHY GRANT, b. 8 Feb 1816; d. at Hartford, 6 Nov 1899; m. at East Windsor, 21 Jun 1844, WILLIAM SMITH SIMMONS, b. 24 Sep 1813 son of William Smith and Nancy (Sherman) Simmons; William d. at Hartford, 4 Jan 1867.

402)   ABIGAIL HOLT (*Daniel Holt⁴, Daniel Holt³, Mary Russell Holt², Robert¹*), b. at Pomfret, 29 Mar 1761 daughter of Daniel and Kezia (Rust) Holt; d. after 1829; m. about 1783, WILLIAM AVERILL, b. at Windham, 19 Apr 1755 son of Stephen and Sarah (Handee) Averill;[1048] William d. at Warren, NY, 1829 (probate 3 Oct 1829).

William and Abigail started their family in Pomfret but were in Montgomery County, New York by 1790 and later in Warren, New York.[1049]

In his will written 5 May 1828 (proved 3 October 1829), William Averill bequeaths to beloved wife Abigail one-third of the real estate and all the money in his possession at the time of his decease. He also notes that he is due a legacy from his father Stephen's estate, and if that is not received before his death, that legacy is to go to Abigail. If Abigail accepts the legacy from Stephen Averill's estate that is in lieu of her dower. Son Charles receives two hundred dollars in addition to what he has received. Other children receiving two hundred dollars are son Elijah Averill, daughter Arminda wife of Michael Mann, daughter Sophia wife of Robert Henry, and daughter Betsey wife of John Shepherd. These legacies are to be paid is six annual installments. The remainder of the estate goes to daughter Mira wife of Timothy Green and Mira also receives the other one-third of the real estate after the decease of her mother. Mira is responsible for paying the debts and the legacies. Executors named were wife Abigail, Timothy Green, and Muzo White. In a codicil likely 25 April 1829 (although in the will book written as 25 April 1828), William made some adjustments to the legacy providing a lot of land for the benefit of the children of his son Elijah. There were other adjustments made based on payments made or received from his children. Of specific interest was the lot of land which at that time was in the hands of John Shepherd husband of daughter Betsey and there had been agreement that John would place that property in trust, but he had not done so.[1050] Son Elijah was still living at that time and so this may represent that William saw a special need for Elijah's children.

Abigail Holt and William Averill were parents of six children.

i   ARMINDA AVERILL, b. likely at Pomfret, about 1783; d. at Detroit, after 1852; m. MICHAEL D. MANN

ii   CHARLES HOLT AVERILL, b. 7 Oct 1786; d. at Niagara, NY, 28 Jan 1858; m. AGNES B. MARSH, b. 4 Feb 1781; Agnes d. at Niagara, 7 Sep 1858.

iii   ELIJAH AVERILL, b. (recorded) at Pomfret, 2 Jul 1788; d. after 1830 when he was living at Warren, NY; m. 26 Nov 1812, SUSAN SLAYTON, b. at Chester, MA, 27 Jan 1789 daughter of Reuben and Mary (Moore) Slayton; Susan d. after 1875 when she was living at Minden, NY.

iv   SOPHIA AVERILL, b. about 1791; m. ROBERT HENRY

v   BETSEY AVERILL, b. about 1794; m. JOHN SHEPHARD

vi   ALMIRA "MIRA" AVERILL, b. about 1796; d. after 1855 when she was living in Warren, NY; m. TIMOTHY GREEN, b. in NY about1791; Timothy d. after 1855.

403)   KEZIAH HOLT (*Daniel Holt⁴, Daniel Holt³, Mary Russell Holt², Robert¹*), b. at Pomfret, 29 Mar 1761 daughter of Daniel and Kezia (Rust) Holt; d. at Buffalo, NY, 13 Jan 1820; m. at Pomfret, 8 Apr 1784, ROWLAND COTTON, b. at Pomfret, 22 Mar 1759 son of Samuel and Mary (Dresser) Cotton; Rowland d. at Attica, NY, 11 Jun 1847.

Rowland Cotton, through a series of enlistments, served for the entire period of the Revolution in the Continental army increasing in rank from private to first sergeant by the end of the war. He was at the battles of Trenton, Harlem Heights, at the crossing of the Delaware with George Washington, the battles of Princeton, Germantown, and Fort Mifflin, and wintered at Valley Forge. In the War of 1812 beginning 16 December 1813, he served as captain and acting brigade quartermaster under General Timothy S. Hopkins. Rowland was wounded in the knee during the retreat from Black Rock on 30 December 1813 and was discharged 26 January 1814 due to his injury. He was allowed pension with a starting date of 27 January 1814. He was also allowed pension based on his service in the Revolution.

Following the wars, Rowland was in Buffalo in 1817 and had relocated to Attica before 1832. In 1851, inquiry was made by the children regarding possible payments. The children living in 1851 were Lester H. cotton of Milwaukee, Wisconsin; Samuel Cotton of Jackson County, Iowa; Mary Cotton of Wyoming County, New York; Daniel H. Cotton of Erie County, New York, and Elijah H. Cotton of Wyoming County, New York.[1051]

Rowland did not leave a will and Elijah H. Cotton was named administrator on 5 October 1847.[1052] Keziah Holt and Rowland Cotton were parents of five children.

[1048] Avery, *The Averill Family*, p 397

[1049] Avery, *The Averill Family*, p 397

[1050] Ancestry.com. *New York, Wills and Probate Records, 1659-1999* [database on-line]. *Wills, Vol E-F, 1828-1841, volume E, pp 56-58*

[1051] U.S. Revolutionary War Pension and Bounty-Land Warrant Application Files, Case S11170

[1052] New York Wills and Probate Records, Wyoming County, Miscellaneous Records, volume 1, p 169

i   SAMUEL COTTON, b. likely at Cherry Valley, about 1788; d. at Cottonville, IA, 3 Sep 1866; m. about 1820, MARY BEMUS, b. about 1789 daughter of Jotham and Asenath (Andress) Bemus;[1053] Mary d. at Cottonville, 27 Nov 1865.

ii   MARY COTTON, b. about 1790 (based on age 68 at time of death); d. at Attica, NY, 16 Oct 1858. Mary did not marry. She resided with her brother Elijah in 1850. In her will written 23 August 1847, Mary bequeathed to her brother Elijah H. Cotton and Clarissa his wife all her estate in Attica for their use during their natural lives. After their decease, the estate is to be divided among the heirs of Elijah and Clarissa and brothers Lester H., Samuel, and Daniel H. Cotton.[1054]

iii   DANIEL H. COTTON, b. 8 Feb 1794; d. at Cottonville, IA, 5 Jul 1881; m. 13 Jan 1822, CEMANTHA DODGE, b. 7 Mar 1804 daughter of Alvan and Mary (Blount) Dodge; Cemantha d. at Cottonville, 1 Oct 1861.

iv   ELIJAH H. COTTON, b. at Cherry Valley, 21 Jul 1800; d. at Pavilion, NY, 31 Jul 1882; m. at Clarkson, NY, 21 Sep 1825, CLARISSA KENNEDY, b. about 1805; Clarissa d. at Pavilion, 10 May 1886.

v   LESTER HOLT COTTON, b. at Canandaigua, NY, 4 Sep 1804; d. at Detroit, MI, 4 Jan 1878 (probate Wayne County, MI, 1878); m. 1st at Monroe, MI, 3 Jul 1833, MARY ANNA WHITE, b. at Troy, NY, 1814 daughter of Marvin and Abigail (Dexter) White; Mary Anna d. at Milwaukee, WI, 18 Jan 1849. Lester m. 2nd 1850, the widow SARAH L. CULLY, b. in NY, about 1822; Sarah d. at Detroit, 26 Aug 1880.

404)   ELIJAH HOLT (*Daniel Holt⁴, Daniel Holt³, Mary Russell Holt², Robert¹*), b. at Pomfret, 6 Jun 1762 son of Daniel and Kezia (Rust) Holt; d. at Cherry Valley, NY, 25 Sep 1826; m. 1st ELIZABETH WILLIAMS, b. at Pomfret, 2 Apr 1768 daughter of Ebenezer and Jerusha (Porter) Williams; Elizabeth d. 16 Jan 1796. Elijah m. 2nd MARY "POLLY" ADAMS, b. at Windham, 10 Dec 1771 daughter of David and Lucy (Fitch) Adams;[1055] Mary d. at Buffalo, 3 Jan 1820.

     Known as General Elijah Holt, Elijah was active in military affairs of Cherry Valley, New York. He was representative to the General Assembly of New York in 1798 and served as a justice in Cherry Valley.[1056]

     Elijah Holt and Elizabeth Williams were parents of four children.

i   OLIVE HOLT, b. 1787; d. at Buffalo, NY, 13 Apr 1837; m. ELISHA ENSIGN, b. 5 Feb 1785 son of Elisha and Sally (Gay) Ensign; Elisha d. at Buffalo, 12 Sep 1852.

ii   JERUSHA WILLIAMS HOLT, b. at Cherry Valley, 30 Jan 1791; d. at Cherry Valley, 24 Dec 1834; m. at Cherry Valley, 1809, ERASTUS JOHNSON, b. at Middletown, CT, 9 Apr 1786 son of Jesse and Mary (Stevenson) Johnson;[1057] Erastus d. at Cherry Valley, 25 Mar 1837.

iii   ELIZABETH HOLT, b. about 1792; reported to have died accidentally during childhood.[1058]

iv   WILLIAMS HOLT, b. at Cherry Valley, 12 Jul 1795; d. at Winnebago, IL, 18 May 1876; m. LOUISA VIBBARD, b. about 1809 daughter of Leonard and Elizabeth (Klumph) Vibbard;[1059] Louisa d. at Winnebago, 20 Oct 1875.

     Elijah Holt and Mary Adams were parents of seven children likely all born at Cherry Valley.

i   DAVID ADAMS HOLT, b. at Cherry Valley, 6 May 1800; d. at Winnebago, IL, 13 Jul 1839; m. SILVIA HAWKS, b. 20 Nov 1801 daughter of Joseph and Nancy (Alvord) Hawks; Silvia d. at Winnebago, 3 Jan 1889. David Adams and Silvia were in Winnebago County, IL by 1835.[1060]

ii   MARY HOLT; m. (per Durrie's Holt genealogy), Rev. WILLIAM PARSONS. Records were not located for this couple.

iii   ELIZA WILLIAMS HOLT, b. about 1804; d. at Westfield, 10 Mar 1858; m. 1st (according to Durrie) an unknown Mr. Higgins. Eliza m. 2nd 1838, ABRAM DIXON, b. at Manchester, VT, 23 Jul 1787 son of Joseph and Mercy Raymond Dixon; Abram d. at Westfield, 19 Apr 1875. Abram was first married to Caroline Pelton.

[1053] Mary's mother Asenath Bemus was living with Samuel and Mary Cotton in Richland, IA in 1850.
[1054] New York Wills and Probate Records, Wyoming County, Wills volume 3, pp 380-381
[1055] The 1814 will of Lucy Adams widow of David of Pomfret includes a bequest to her daughter Polly Holt wife of Elijah Holt.
[1056] Sawyer, *History of Cherry Valley, New York*, p 51, p 59, and p 63
[1057] Cutter, *Genealogical and Family History of Central New York*, volume 2, p 844
[1058] Durrie, Holt Genealogy
[1059] Klumph, *Klumph Genealogy and Early Klumph History*, p 33
[1060] H.F. Kett, History of Winnebago County, Illinois, p 236

iv   HARRIET HOLT, b. about 1808; d. after 1875 when she was living at Westfield, NY; m. 1st Dr. PETER CANER, b. at Herkimer County, NY, 15 Dec 1800;[1061] Peter d. at Warsaw, NY, 2 Apr 1854. Harriet m. 2nd ELAM CHAFFEE BLISS, b. at Skaneateles, NY, 13 Nov 1802 son of Edward Upham and Mary (Chaffee) Bliss; Elam d. at Westfield, 6 May 1882. Elam Bliss was first married to Mary Harmon. Dr. Peter Caner attended Fairfield Medical College and had a successful practice in Warsaw.

v   HORATIO NELSON HOLT, b. 8 Jan 1811; d. at Brooklyn, NY (buried at Buffalo), 19 May 1894;[1062] m. at Buffalo, 24 Jul 1839, ABBY GOODMAN SEYMOUR, b. 19 Jun 1815 daughter of Henry R. and Elizabeth (Selden) Seymour; Abby d. at Brooklyn, 7 Feb 1865.

vi   GEORGE WASHINGTON HOLT, b. 25 Nov 1813; d. at Westfield, NY, 4 Jan 1889; m. 1863, AMELIA BENTON HARRINGTON, b. at Westfield, 1 Mar 1839 daughter of Jonas and Ruby (Benton) Harrington; Amelia d. at Westfield, 20 May 1904.[1063]

vii   ELIJAH HOLT, b. 1817; d. at Edinboro, PA, 1888; m. about 1843, LAURA CONANT, b. about 1820 daughter of Origen and Mary (Butler) Conant;[1064] Laura d. at Edinboro, 1895.

405)   LESTER HOLT (*Daniel Holt⁴, Daniel Holt³, Mary Russell Holt², Robert¹*), b. at Pomfret, 21 Feb 1766 son of Daniel and Kezia (Rust) Holt; d. at Cherry Valley, NY, 11 Jan 1841; m. about 1789, CATHERINE CLYDE, b. 1769 daughter of Samuel and Catherine (Wasson) Clyde; Catherine d. at Cherry Valley, 16 May 1848.

Major Lester Holt served in the War of 1812.

In his will written 13 Aug 1839 (probate 31 May 1841), Lester Holt of Cherry Valley bequeathed to beloved wife Catherine ten shares of the Central Bank, all the household furnishings, use of the house, and provisions for her support to be provided by Horatio Holt. This bequest is in lieu of her dower. He gives to the executors the lot of land and house in Fort Plain currently occupied by son Daniel. The executors are to use this for the support of Daniel's children and after Daniel's death, the property will go to Daniel's children. Son Daniel also receives $300 in cash which goes to the executors to give to Daniel in small amounts as needed. Daughter Morgiana Danforth wife of Thomas P. Danforth of Middleburgh receives fifteen shares in the Central Bank. Son Lester Holt receives two thousand dollars charged upon the land and property that is being devised to him. Son Horatio receives the property in Cherry Valley where Lester now lives. Son Henry receives property of the west side of Alden Street in Cherry Valley. Henry also receives ten shares of bank stock and the value of a judgment owed to Lester in the amount of $560. Daughter Lucia Marvin wife of Dan Marvin receives fifteen shares of bank stock and $200. Son William Holt receives thirty shares in the Schenectady and Utica railroad. Granddaughter Catherine Jane Magher receives $100. Son Horatio Holt and Horace Lathrop of Cooperstown were named executors.

There are the following heirs noted in the probate: a widow, Horatio Holt of Cherry Valley; William W. Holt of Cherry Valley; Daniel Holt of Fort Plain; Kezia Stewart wife of Alvan Stewart of Utica; Morgiana Danforth wife of Thomas P. Danforth of Middleburgh; Lucia Marvin wife of Dan Marvin of the city of New York; Henry Holt of Fort Brady, Michigan; Lester J. Magher of Michigan City, Indiana, and Catherine J. Magher of unknown location children of Jane Magher deceased; Catherine M. Holt, Martha Holt, Horatio H. Holt, and Chester Holt children of Lester Holt deceased of Mount Hope in Lawrence County, Alabama. Benjamin Davis of Cherry Valley was named special guardian to look after the interests of Lester's children and Peter Magher was special guardian for Jane's children.[1065] Daughter Kezia is not mentioned in the will but is listed as one of the heirs-at-law.

Lester Holt and Catherine Clyde were parents of eleven children likely all born at Cherry Valley, New York.

i   JANE CLYDE HOLT, b. 1790; d. at Cherry Valley, NY, 4 May 1835; m. 25 Nov 1810, PETER MAGHER, b. about 1777; Peter d. at Cooperstown, 16 Jun 1854.

ii   DANIEL HOLT, b. 1 Dec 1792; d. at Fort Plain, NY, 1866; m. 20 Jun 1828, ANN BECKER, b. Oct 1807; Ann d. 7 Apr 1841.

iii   KEZIA HOLT, b. about 1793; d. at New York, NY, 2 Dec 1854; m. 1819, ALVAN STEWART, b. at Granville, NY, 1 Sep 1790 son of Uriel and Anna (Holgate) Stewart; Alvan d. at New York, 14 May 1850.

iv   LESTER HOLT, b. about 1797; d. at Mount Hope, AL, Sep 1840; m. at Lawrence County, AL, 29 Mar 1832, MARY E. CLEERE who has not been firmly identified. Mary married second R. C. Oglesby on 16 Nov 1843. Lester had some type of medical practice in Mount Hope as his estate inventory includes medical supplies. Lester was also postmaster.

1061 Young, *History of the Town of Warsaw, New York*, p 244

1062 New York, New York, Death Index, 1862-1948

1063 The family relationships are confirmed by the DAR application of the daughter of George W. and Amelia Holt, Alice E. Holt.

1064 Conant, *A History and Genealogy of the Conant Family*, p 547

1065 *Wills and Administrations, 1792-1902*; Author: *New York. Surrogate's Court (Otsego County), Wills and Administrations, Book 0005-0007, 1840-1846, pp 61-76*

v   MORGIANNA HOLT, b. about 1800; d. at Middleburgh, NY, 1873 (probate 1873); m. THOMAS P. DANFORTH, b. 20 Jun 1781 son of Jonathan and Judith (Spalding) Danforth; Thomas d. at Middleburgh, 1865. Thomas was a Judge. He was first married to Nancy Wager.

vi   CHARLES HOLT, b. 1802; d. at Fort St. Philip, LA, 24 Sep 1824. Charles graduated from West Point and had rank of 2nd Lieutenant, July 1823.

vii   HORATIO HOLT, b. 12 Apr 1803; d. at Cherry Valley, 30 Jun 1859. Horatio did not marry.

viii   CATHERINE HOLT, b. 1805; d. at Cherry Valley, 29 May 1834 of consumption.

ix   HENRY HOLT, b. about 1810; d. at Washington, DC, after 1881. Henry was an army surgeon stationed at Fort Brady, Michigan and later in Washington, DC. He is likely the Henry C. Holt (a physician) who married at Norfolk, VA, 22 May 1843, SARAH JANE TUCKER (widow of Andrew McD. Jackson), b. in Virginia about 1811. Sarah was living in 1880.

x   WILLIAM W. HOLT, b. 12 May 1812; d. at Middletown, CT (burial at Cherry Valley), 2 Feb 1885; m. MARIA FANNING, b. about 1832 daughter of John and Clarissa (Hoyt) Fanning; Maria d. at Brooklyn, 17 May 1910.

xi   LUCIA L. HOLT, b. 5 Dec 1813; b. at Brooklyn, NY, 29 Nov 1880; m. 25 Feb 1835, DAN MARVIN, b. at Fairfield, NY, 17 Dec 1808 son of Reinold and Mabel (Bushnell) Marvin;[1066] Dan d. 17 Oct 1884.

406)   OLIVE HOLT (*Daniel Holt⁴, Daniel Holt³, Mary Russell Holt², Robert¹*), b. at Pomfret, 15 Oct 1768 daughter of Daniel and Kezia (Rust) Holt; d. 20 Sep 1792; m. 1787, JOSEPH WHITE, b. at Chatham, CT, 26 Sep 1762 son of Joseph and Ruth (Churchill) White; Joseph d, at Cherry Valley, 3 Jun 1832. Joseph second married Olive's sister DEBORAH HOLT, b. at Pomfret, 1 Feb 1775; Deborah d. at Cherry Valley, 23 Aug 1827.

Dr. Joseph White served in the Revolution in Captain Rudd's Company in August and September 1778. He was a physician in Cherry Valley. He served as state senator 1796-1797 and was county judge of Otsego County for twenty-one years beginning in 1800.[1067]

In this will written 30 May 1832 (proved 7 July 1832), Joseph White, M.D. bequeathed to son Delos White, M.D., in addition to what he has received, all the securities that he holds against him including mortgages and notes. He also receives dividends of 100 shares from the Central Bank during his natural life and the shares to revert to grandson Joseph L. White and granddaughter Lavantia White. Delos also receives one thousand dollars. Son Menzo White, M.D. receives all the medical books and instruments, fifty shares in the Central Bank, all the shares of stock in the Albany turnpike, and 209 acres of land known as the Clyde farm. Daughter Lavantia the wife of Jacob Livingston, in addition to the part of the home farm she has received, receives the remainder of the farm to be held in trust for grandson Joseph W. Livingston and granddaughter Lavantia Livingston until they reach age twenty-five. Daughter Lavantia also receives one hundred shares of stock in Central Bank and all the domestic animals and husbandry utensils. Son Joseph White receives $9000 in bonds and mortgages. Son George receives 250 shares in Central Bank and the lands in Cary's patent. The remainder of the estate is to be divided among children Menzo White, Lavintia Livingston, Joseph White, and George White except his gold watch which goes to granddaughter Lavintia Livingston. Joseph White, Jacob Livingston, and Horace Lathrop were named executors.[1068]

Olive Holt and Joseph White were parents of one child.

i   DELOS WHITE, b. at Cherry Valley, about 1790; d. at Cherry Valley, 18 Mar 1835; m. ELIZA OLIVIA LITTLE, b. at Springfield, MA, 9 Nov 1795 daughter of David and Alice (Loomis) Little; Eliza d. at Cherry Valley, 15 Jan 1862.

Deborah Holt and Joseph White were parents of four children.

i   MENZO WHITE, b. at Cherry Valley, 19 Oct 1793; d. at Cherry Valley, 16 Jan 1858. Menzo did not marry.

ii   LEVANTIA WHITE, b. at Cherry Valley, 15 Nov 1795; d. at Cherry Valley, 6 Sep 1889; m. at Cherry Valley, 26 Jun 1821, as his second wife, JACOB LIVINGSTON, b. 1780 son of John and Mary Anne (LeRoy) Livingston; Jacob d. at Cherry Valley, 19 May 1865. Jacob was first married to Catherine De Peyster.

iii   JOSEPH WHITE, b. at Cherry Valley, 26 Nov 1801; d. at Westfield, NY, 22 Sep 1840. Joseph did not marry.

iv   GEORGE WASHINGTON WHITE, b. at Cherry Valley, 9 Aug 1809; d. at Cherry Valley, 1867; m. May 1834, MARY PHELON, b. at Litchfield, CT, 3 Sep 1815 daughter of Joseph and Alcena (Denslow) Phelon; Mary d. at Cherry Valley, 1878.

[1066] Marvin, *Descendants of Reinold and Matthew Marvin*, p 184
[1067] Williams, Descendants of Thomas White of Weymouth
[1068] *New York, Wills and Probate Records, 1659-1999, Otsego County, Wills and Administrations, Book 0001-0002, 1830-1836, pp 176-178*

407)   MARY HOLT (*Daniel Holt⁴, Daniel Holt³, Mary Russell Holt², Robert¹*), b. at Pomfret, 28 Apr 1771 daughter of Daniel and Kezia (Rust) Holt; d. at Cherry Valley, 19 Mar 1819; m. 1ˢᵗ about 1791, JOSEPH CLARY who has not been identified; Joseph d. about 1800. Mary m. 2ⁿᵈ 4 Feb 1803, JOHN DIELL, b. 1769; John d. at Cherry Valley, 19 May 1813.

      Mary and her family resided primarily in Cherry Valley, New York. John Diell was a merchant in Cherry Valley was granted a license to keep a public house and inn in 1800.[1069]

      In his will written 20 August 1812 (proved 7 June 1813), John Diell bequeathed to beloved wife Mary the use and occupation of all the estate, real and personal, during the time she is a widow. This is expressing so that Mary is able to provide for, maintain, and educate their children. Mary also receives the household furniture except the articles that he received by his first wife; those items are to go to his daughter Elisa. He directs that his children be educated in the following manner. Son John is to have a collegiate education and afterward to be educated in such profession as he may choose. Daughters Elisa, Nancy Ann, and their youngest not yet named daughter are to have a good English education, and when they are sufficiently advanced in their school, they are to have the advantage of a year of school abroad. John also directs that his mother is to have a comfortable living out of the estate. He names the following children: daughter Elisa from his former wife; Mary Ann, John, and a young daughter not yet named; and the children of Mary with her former husband, Salena, Joseph, and Betsey.[1070]

      Mary Holt and Joseph Clary were parents of three children. Their oldest child, Joseph, was admitted as an attorney on 14 February 1821 and he became the first law partner of Millard Fillmore in 1830.[1071]

i   JOSEPH CLARY, b. at Paris, NY, 1 Nov 1792; d. at Buffalo, NY, 11 Aug 1842; m. at New York, NY, 1 Feb 1830, MARIA THERESA RATHBUN, b. at Charlemont, MA, 28 Feb 1801 daughter of Samuel and Polly (Turner) Rathbun; Maria d. at Buffalo, 3 Aug 1875. Joseph was an attorney and Millard Filmore's first law partner.

ii   SELENA CLARY, b. at Cherry Valley, about 1794; living in 1812.

iii   BETSEY CLARY, b. at Cherry Valley, about 1796; living in 1812.

      Mary Holt and John Diell were parents of three children.

i   MARY ANN DIELL, b. at Cherry Valley, about 1804; living in 1812.

ii   JOHN DIELL, b. at Cherry Valley, Aug 1808; d. at sea on voyage from Hawaii, 18 Jan 1841; m. at Plattsburgh, NY, 18 Jul 1832, CAROLINE ADRIANCE PLATT, b. at Plattsburgh, 1 Jul 1807 daughter of Isaac and Anne (Tredwell) Platt; Caroline d. at Adriance, VA, 16 Jan 1901. Rev. John Diell was First Chaplain of the American Seaman's Friend Society at Honolulu and served in that position for nine years. He died aboard ship on his voyage home with his wife and children.[1072] John attended Hamilton College in Buffalo and Auburn Theological Seminary in Cherry Valley.

iii   CELINDA DIELL, b. at Cherry Valley, 23 Sep 1811; d. at Cherry Valley, 11 Mar 1890; m. at Cherry Valley, 9 Apr 1829,[1073] EDWIN JUDD, b. at Cherry Valley, 5 Feb 1805 son of Oliver and Elizabeth (Belden) Judd);[1074] Edwin d. at Cherry Valley, 28 Nov 1873.

408)   MARCIA HOLT (*Daniel Holt⁴, Daniel Holt³, Mary Russell Holt², Robert¹*), b. at Pomfret, about 1773 daughter of Daniel and Kezia (Rust) Holt; m. AUGUSTUS SHARP.

      Marcia and Augustus are reported in Durrie's Holt genealogy as settling in Buffalo and having two children. There is an Augustus Sharp in Buffalo in 1820 with a household of male age 26-44, female age 26-44, 2 males under 10, and 1 female under 10. Nothing else was found.

409)   ADELIA HOLT (*Daniel Holt⁴, Daniel Holt³, Mary Russell Holt², Robert¹*), b. at Pomfret, 23 Jan 1778 daughter of Daniel and Kezia (Rust) Holt; m. CHARLES MUDGE, b. at New London, about 1770 son of Jarvis and Prudence (Treat) Mudge;[1075] Charles d. of typhus at Williamsville Hospital, NY, Aug 1814 while serving in the army in the War of 1812.[1076]

[1069] Sawyer, *History of Cherry Valley, New York*, p 52

[1070] New York Probate Records, 1629-1971, Otsego County, Wills and Administrations 1792-1813, volumes A-D, volume D, pp 112-114

[1071] "Sketch of Joseph Clary: Millard Fillmore's First Law Partner", Buffalo Historical Society, Publications of the Buffalo Historical Society, volume 11, pp 98-105. A detailed biography of Joseph Clary can be found in this article.

[1072] Findagrave ID: 35335542

[1073] Marriages from the Cherry Valley Gazette 1818-1834 (provided by New Horizons Genealogy, http://www.newhorizonsgenealogicalservices.com/ny-genealogy/otsego-county/cherry_valley_gazette_marriages.htm)

[1074] Judd, *Thomas Judd and His Descendants*, p 59

[1075] Mudge, *Memorials: A Genealogical Account of the Name Mudge in America*, p 73

[1076] U.S. Army, Register of Enlistments, 1798-1914

Charles Mudge was trader in Cherry Valley and relocated to Buffalo where he built one of the first homes. Adelia and Charles's home was burnt during the War of 1812.[1077] Charles served in the War of 1812 in Capt. Burbank's company of the 21st Regiment of Infantry of Massachusetts.

Adelia Holt and Charles Mudge were parents of three children.

i   HIRAM MUDGE, b. about 1798 and d. about 1812 at age 14.

ii   DEBORAH MUDGE, b. about 1803; d. at Palmyra, NY, 1849; m. at Palmyra, 2 Jan 1821, ERASTUS COLE

iii MARY MUDGE, b. about 1803; m. JOHN JOHNSON

410) LIBBEUS KIMBALL (*Abigail Holt Kimball⁴, Daniel Holt³, Mary Russell Holt², Robert¹*), b. at Pomfret, 14 Feb 1750/1 son of Richard and Abigail (Holt) Kimball; d. at Ames, NY, 4 Sep 1839; m. at Pomfret, 7 May 1778, SARAH CRAFT, b. at Pomfret, 29 Apr 1756 daughter of Samuel and Judith (Payson) Craft; Sarah d. at Ames, 3 Aug 1831.

Libbeus Kimball served as a private during the Revolution and made declaration related to his pension application on 6 August 1832. He was then age eighty-one and resident of Canajoharie. In June 1775, he enlisted from Pomfret and marched seventy miles to Boston and was discharged. In 1776, he enlisted when there was a call for soldiers to go to Lake Champlain and he was then in the company of Capt. Elijah Sharpe. He was in battles at Skenesborough and Fort Anne. He suffered great hardships during these campaigns. He had an additional enlistment in 1781 to go to New London. After the close of the war, he moved to Canajoharie where he still resided.[1078]

Libbeus Kimball and Sarah Craft were parents of three children born at Pomfret.

i   MATILDA KIMBALL, b. at Pomfret, 23 Nov 1780; d. at Ames, NY, 1 Feb 1848; m. at Florida, NY, 5 Aug 1795, RUFUS MORRIS, b. at Scituate, RI, 4 Feb 1772 son of Lemuel and Lydia (Wilkinson) Morris;[1079] Rufus d. 25 Sep 1848.

ii   SYLVESTER KIMBALL, b. at Pomfret, 27 May 1783; d. at Ames, NY, 28 May 1830; m. 26 Feb 1812, LYDIA ATWATER, b. 27 Aug 1792 daughter of Caleb Atwater; Lydia d. at Cherry Valley, NY, 24 May 1881. Lydia married second Waitstill Crumb.

iii CRAFTS PAYSON KIMBALL, b. at Pomfret, 14 Jan 1788; d. at Rutland, NY, 7 Nov 1872; m. 14 Jan 1814, JULIANA PORTER, b. at Clinton, NY, 3 Jun 1796 daughter of Raphael and Mercy (Hamlin) Porter; Juliana d. at Rutland, 21 Apr 1868.

411) PERSIS "PERCY" KIMBALL (*Abigail Holt Kimball⁴, Daniel Holt³, Mary Russell Holt², Robert¹*), b. at Pomfret, 5 Nov 1760 daughter of Richard and Abigail (Holt) Kimball; d. at Ames, NY, 6 Mar 1845; m. at Pomfret, 18 Jan 1781, GEORGE ELLIOT, b. at Voluntown, 1 Mar 1757 son of Andrew and Hannah (Palmer) Elliot; George d. at Canajoharie, 22 Mar 1817.

Rev. George Elliot was a Freewill Baptist minister who served as pastor of the church at Bowman's Creek, New York (later known as Ames). He was ordained 6 February 1794 at Florida, New York.[1080]

George Elliot served in the Revolution and was wounded. On 25 September 1838, Percy Elliot of Canajoharie, then age seventy-eight, appeared to make a statement related to her application for a widow's pension. She reported that she and George were married at Pomfret on 30 January 1781 (although reported by the town clerk as 18 January 1781) at the home of her brother Libeus Kimball. She reported that her husband George died at their residence in Canajoharie on 22 March 1817. Percy further stated that she and George grew up in the same neighborhood. She had known that he served in the Northern campaign during the war. He served for six months at that time and returned in the Fall of the year about the time her brother Libeus returned. George was later drafted into service and went to Rhode Island. At that time, she was under promise of marriage to George. She heard that he was wounded and in the hospital. When he came home, he had a wound over his left eye from being shot and Percy dressed the wound. Percy's brother Libeus also made a statement in support of his sister's application. In 1851, son Elijah Elliot wrote questioning the amount of pension his mother had received, his thought being she was eligible for a larger pension than she had received. In that same letter, Elijah also inquired related to the eligibility of a pension for his sister who was the widow of Charles Morris. His sister married Charles Morris as his second wife on 4 October 1810.[1081]

Persis Kimball and George Elliot were parents of four children.

i   SARAH ELECTA ELLIOT, b. about 1782; d. at Canajoharie, NY, 27 Feb 1861; m. 4 Oct 1810, as his second wife, CHARLES MORRIS, b. at Killingly, 24 Apr 1762 son of Lemuel and Lydia (Wilkinson) Morris; Charles d. at Canajoharie, 7 Jun 1838. Charles was first married to Miriam Nichols.

[1077] Mudge, *Memorials: A Genealogical Account of the Name Mudge in America*, p 97
[1078] U.S. Revolutionary War Pension and Bounty-Land Warrant Application Files, Case S16179
[1079] Morris, *A Genealogical and Historical Register of the Descendants of Edward Morris*, p 188
[1080] Burgess & Ward, *Free Baptist Cyclopaedia*, p 183
[1081] Revolutionary War Pension and Bounty-Land Warrant Application Files, Case 25612

ii   RELECTY ELLIOT, b. 10 Oct 1795; d. at Ames, NY, 15 Feb 1875; m. 1840, as his second wife, JOHN WHITE, b. 1786; John d. after 1875 when he was living in Canajoharie with his daughter. John was first married to Catherine Jones.

iii   ELIJAH ELLIOT, b. 1797; d. at Ames, NY, 9 Jul 1873; m. 1st about 1820, ANN SMITH, b. about 1800; Ann d. at Ames, 12 Feb 1828. Elijah m. 2nd, SALLY who has not been identified and who died at Ames, 3 Jul 1844.

iv   ETHELWINA ELLIOT, b. about 1804; d. at Ames, 23 Jan 1887. Ethelwina did not marry. In 1870, she was living with her brother Elijah who was widowed at that time.

412)   CHESTER KIMBALL (*Abigail Holt Kimball⁴, Daniel Holt³, Mary Russell Holt², Robert¹*), b. at Pomfret, 19 Sep 1763 son of Richard and Abigail (Holt) Kimball; d. at New London, 2 Jan 1824; m. at New London, 8 Nov 1786; LUCIA "LUCY" FOX, b. at Chatham, CT, 19 May 1766 daughter of John and Mary (Waterman) Fox; Lucy d. at New London, 6 Apr 1855.

     Chester resided in New London where he was a dealer in marble and stone.[1082] He also served on the common council for New London from 1810 through 1819.[1083]

     Chester Kimball and Lucy Fox were parents of eleven children born at New London.

i   GURDON KIMBALL, b. 29 Jan 1788; d. at New Haven, 17 May 1871; m. 19 Nov 1809, LUCY WAY HOLT, b. at New Haven, 29 Jun 1793 daughter of Jonathan and Abiah (Dunton) Holt; Lucy d. at New Haven 31 Dec 1865. Lucy Holt is a descendant of William Holt of New Haven.

ii   CHESTER KIMBALL, b. 31 Jan 1790; d. at New London, 15 Jan 1823; m. at New London, 5 Nov 1809, LUCRETIA "LUCY" COIT, b. at New London, 28 Sep 1792 daughter of John and Lucy (Smith) Coit; Lucy d. at New York, NY, 10 Nov 1843.

iii   JOHN KIMBALL, b. 23 Mar 1792; d. 5 Dec 1793.

iv   RICHARD KIMBALL, b. 30 Jan 1794; d. at Savannah, GA, 23 Jan 1818.[1084] Richard was a merchant.

v   LUCY KIMBALL, b. 17 Mar 1796; d. at New London, 15 Jun 1882; m. 1 Dec 1814, GURDON BISHOP, b. at New Haven, 26 Jul 1789 son of Jonathan and Anne (Allen) Bishop; Gurdon d. at Waterford, 28 Apr 1865.

vi   MARY WATERMAN KIMBALL, b. 15 Oct 1798; d. at New London, 9 Dec 1828; m. 14 May 1823, ZEBADIAH C. BAKER, b. 6 May 1802 son of Lemuel and Bethiah (Comstock) Baker; Zebadiah d. 2 Oct 1840. Zebadiah married second Mercy Crandall.

vii   JOHN KIMBALL, b. 4 Nov 1800; d. 2 Nov 1816.

viii   ABIGAIL HOLT KIMBALL, b. 8 Mar 1803; d. at New London, 30 Jun 1835; m. Sep 1822, JAMES BLOYD LYMAN, b. at Lebanon, CT, Nov 1799 son of Elisha and Abigail (Bloyd) Lyman; James d. at Norwich, 3 oct 1865. James married second Abigail's sister Charlotte (see below).

ix   HARRIET KIMBALL, b. 31 Jul 1805; d. at New London, 9 Feb 1834; m. 27 Aug 1829, GURDON TRACY BISHOP, b. at New London, 21 Jul 1804 son of Moses and Elizabeth (Starr) Bishop; Gurdon d. at New London, 1877.

x   EDWIN KIMBALL, b. 4 Nov 1808; d. 22 Jun 1827.

xi   CHARLOTTE ELIZABETH KIMBALL, b. 11 Sep 1810; d. at New London, 9 Jan 1901; m. 2 May 1836, JAMES BLOYD LYMAN who was first married to Charlotte's sister Harriet (see above).

413)   ROXLANA HOLT (*Silas Holt⁴, Daniel Holt³, Mary Russell Holt², Robert¹*), b. at Pomfret, 21 Sep 1760 daughter of Silas and Mary (Brooks) Holt; d. at Ashford, about 1787; m. at Ashford, 13 Jun 1782, EBENEZER SUMNER, b. at Ashford, 3 Aug 1757 son of Ebenezer and Experience (Marsh) Sumner; Ebenezer d. at Eastford, Aug 1806. Ebenezer second married Sarah Perrin on 26 May 1788.

     Roxlana Holt and Ebenezer Sumner were parents of two children.

i   MYRA SUMNER, b. at Ashford, 17 Apr 1783

[1082] Morrison, *History of the Kimball Family*, p 279
[1083] Caulkins, *History of New London*, p 619
[1084] Savannah, Georgia Vital Records, 1803-1966, accessed through ancestry.com

ii   ROXALANA SUMNER, b. about 1785; d. at Burlington, NY, 22 Mar 1873; m. DANIEL BOLTON, b. at Stafford, CT, 15 Nov 1783 son of Daniel and Alice (Leach) Bolton;[1085] Daniel d. at Burlington, 5 Apr 1851.

414)   CLARINA HOLT (*Silas Holt⁴, Daniel Holt³, Mary Russell Holt², Robert¹*), b. at Ashford, 6 Nov 1769 daughter of Silas and Mary (Brooks) Holt; d. at Vernon, NY, 14 Nov 1845; m. at Ashford, 12 May 1793, ELIAS FRINK, b. 1770; Elias d. at Vernon, NY, 14 Apr 1854.

Clarina and Elias were members of the church at West Hartford where Elias served in the post of collector from 1800 to 1811.[1086] The family was later in Vernon, New York. Census records note that Elias was a shoemaker and also deaf, at least in his later years.

There are four children known for Clarina Holt and Elias Frink.

i   LUCIA FRINK, b. about 1795 and baptized at West Hartford, 21 Jul 1803; d. after 1850 when she was living with her father and sister Mary in Vernon, NY. Lucia did not marry.

ii   SILAS HOLT FRINK, b. about 1797 and baptized at West Hartford, 21 Jul 1803; d. at Jackson, MI, 17 Dec 1876; m. SOPHRONIA WILSON, b. in NY 1808; Sophronia d. at Detroit, 12 Nov 1890.

iii   MARY TIFFANY FRINK, b. about 1801 and baptized at West Hartford, 21 Jul 1803; d. at Vernon, NY, 18 Mar 1865. Mary did not marry.

iv   CLARINA FRINK, baptized at West Hartford, 4 Jun 1809; nothing further found.

415)   LUCINDA HOLT (*Silas Holt⁴, Daniel Holt³, Mary Russell Holt², Robert¹*), b. at Ashford, 26 Jul 1773 daughter of Silas and Mary (Brooks) Holt; d. at Ashford, 24 Mar 1847; m. at Ashford, 14 Jan 1799, DYER CLARK, b. 1772; Dyer d. at Ashford, 28 Sep 1846.

Lucinda Holt and Dyer Clark were parents of five children born at Ashford.

i   SABRINA HOWE CLARK, b. 3 Nov 1799; d. at Ashford, 14 Feb 1839; m. at Ashford, 15 Jun 1819, CLARK GRANT, b. at Willington, 28 Feb 1793 son of Miner and Eunice (Swift) Grant; Clark d. at Ashford, 16 Apr 1826.

ii   LUCINDA HOWE CLARK, b. 30 Jul 1802; d. at Ashford, 12 Nov 1860; m. at Ashford, 19 Feb 1829, JOSEPH BURNHAM SIMMONS, b. at Ashford, 12 Oct 1801 son of Alva and Tryphena (Burnham) Simmons; Joseph d. at Ashford, 12 Feb 1835. Lucinda m. 2nd at Ashford, 14 Apr 1841, GEORGE CADY.

iii   NEHEMIAH HOWE CLARK, b. 13 Jun 1805; d. at Ashford, 15 Oct 1812.

iv   ANDREW JUDSON CLARK, b. 11 Apr 1809

v   DYER HOWE CLARK, b. 23 May 1817; d. at Ashford, 13 Dec 1897; m. at West Springfield, MA, 13 Sep 1837, AUGUSTA A. SAUNDERS, b. about 1820 daughter of Ezekiel and Betsey (Potter);[1087] Augusta d. at East Hartford, 18 Sep 1884.

416)   OLIVE ROGERS (*Lois Holt Rogers⁴, Daniel Holt³, Mary Russell Holt², Robert¹*), b. at Pomfret, 7 Mar 1759 daughter of Moses and Lois (Holt) Rogers; d. at Ashford, 2 Mar 1855; m. at Ashford, 28 Sep 1784, ABEL DOW, b. at Ashford, 3 Jul 1757 son of Daniel and Elizabeth (Marsh) Dow; Abel d. at Ashford, 6 Jan 1826.

Olive and Abel lived in Ashford where their four children were born.

In his will written 21 December 1825, Abel Dow bequeathed to wife Olive use of one-third of the real estate during her natural life and one-third of the personal estate to be at her disposal. Grandson Maro Austin, son of Sally and Joseph Austin late of Woodstock deceased, receives twenty dollars. The remainder of the estate, including the dower thirds at the decease of Olive, are to be equally divided between his two daughters Lois H. Carpenter and Laura Hicks. Samuel H. Carpenter and his wife Lois were named executors.[1088]

i   SALLY DOW, b. at Ashford, 28 Nov 1785; d. at Woodstock, 27 Apr 1809; m. JOSEPH AUSTIN who has not been identified. Joseph was second married to Polly.

[1085] Bolton, *Nathaniel Bolton, a Forgotten New England Poet*, p 25

[1086] Connecticut Church Record Abstracts, volume 122, Part I, West Hartford

[1087] Augusta's parents are given in the Connecticut death index as Ezek Saunders and Betsey Potter.

[1088] *Connecticut State Library (Hartford, Connecticut)*; Probate Place: *Hartford, Connecticut, Estate of Abel Dow, Case 1496*

ii   WILLIAM DOW, b. at Ashford, 6 Mar 1788; d. at Ashford, 25 Dec 1816. William did not marry. In his will written 20 August 1814, he bequeathed to uncles Nathan Crocker and Alva Rogers the obligations that William holds against them. There are also bequests to nephew Maro Austin, cousin Horatio Dow, Asaph Smith, his mother, sisters Lois and Laura, and his father.[1089]

iii   LOIS DOW, b. at Ashford, 1 Dec 1790; d. at Ashford, 25 May 1882; m. SAMUEL HAYWARD CARPENTER, b. at Ashford, 26 Jan 1788 son of Comfort and Priscilla (Hayward) Carpenter; Samuel d. at Ashford, 30 Dec 1850.

iv   LAURA DOW, b. at Ashford, 16 Jun 1796; d. at Ashford, 1875; m. 1st 10 Feb 1813, AMOS TROWBRIDGE, b. 16 Oct 1790 son of James and Mary (Kendall) Trowbridge; Amos d. 25 Feb 1822. Laura m. 2nd at Ashford, 30 Sep 1824, ABRA HICKS, b. at Pomfret, 17 Dec 1800 son of Israel and Phebe (Grow) Hicks; Abra d. at Ashford, 1887.

417)   ELISHA ROGERS (*Lois Holt Rogers⁴, Daniel Holt³, Mary Russell Holt², Robert¹*), b. at Pomfret, 11 Feb 1766 son of Moses and Lois (Holt) Rogers; d. perhaps at Springfield, VT, 24 Apr 1807;[1090] m. at Springfield, 11 Jul 1788, ANNA WARD, b. 1767 daughter of Jabez Ward; Anna d. at Brownville, NY, 14 Jul 1872.[1091]
        Elisha Rogers served as a private in the continental army, Connecticut line in the company of Capt. Daniel Allen. Elisha served two three-year enlistments. On 10 September 1838 while living in Lyme, New York, widow Anna Rogers made application for a widow's pension. The probate documents include the date of marriage, the name of Anna's father as Jabez, and the date of Elisha's death. In 1855 while living at Brownville, Anna, then age eighty-eight, made a follow-up statement. In 1855, son Riley Rogers then age sixty-six provide a statement in support of his mother's pension.[1092]
        Elisha Rogers and Anna Ward were parents of four children.

i   RILEY ROGERS, b. at Springfield, VT, 15 Dec 1788; d. at Brownville, NY, 20 Oct 1874; m. LORENA KELLOGG, b. 1792 whose parents have not been identified; Lorena d. at Brownville, 19 May 1858.

ii   NAMAH ROGERS, b. 27 Nov 1790

iii   RALPH H. ROGERS, b. at Springfield, VT, 29 Sep 1792; d. at Lyme, NY, 30 Sep 1866; m. ELIZA HORTON, b. 7 Dec 1799 daughter of Henry and Abigail (Cook) Horton;[1093] Eliza d. at Lyme, 2 Jul 1890.

iv   GEORGE ROGERS, b. at Springfield, 12 Oct 1794; d. at Brownville, NY, 19 Mar 1844; m. ELIZABETH "BETSY" HANCOCK. Elizabeth was living at the time of George's death and in the 1860 census at Brownville with three of her children. Nine children were listed as heirs of the estate. Although Elisha died in 1844 (which is verified in the probate), in 1847 one of the creditors of the estate, Henry W. Hills, was allowed as administrator of the estate.[1094]

418)   ABIGAIL ROGERS (*Lois Holt Rogers⁴, Daniel Holt³, Mary Russell Holt², Robert¹*), b. at Pomfret, 23 Mar 1769 daughter of Moses and Lois (Holt) Rogers; d. at Sherburne, NY, 29 Mar 1849; m. CYRUS DOW, b. at Ashford, 17 Jun 1764 son of Daniel and Elizabeth (Marsh) Dow; Cyrus d. at Sherburne, 23 Mar 1842 (date of death given at the proving of the will on 21 Mar 1843).
        In his will written 24 June 1841 (proved 21 March 1843), Cyrus Dow of Sherburne bequeathed his personal estate to wife Nabby to be at her disposal. She also receives the income from all the real property during her life. After Nabby's decease, all the real property goes to son Cyrus M. Dow on condition that he pay four hundred dollars to daughter Almira Daniels within two years. Cyrus M. Dow was named executor.[1095] At the proving of the will, Cyrus M. Dow gave a statement that the only heirs were widow Nabby Dow, Cyrus M. Dow of Sherburne, and Almira Daniels wife of James Daniels of Columbus, Pennsylvania.
        Two children are known for Abigail Rogers and Cyrus Dow.

i   ALMIRA DOW, b. about 1798 (age 77 at death); d. at Columbus, PA, 8 Jun 1875; m. JAMES DANIELS, b. in CT, about 1796; James d. at Columbus, 14 Feb 1877. James Daniels was a wagon maker.

ii   CYRUS MARSH DOW, b. about 1809; d. at Sherburne, NY, 14 Jan 1873; m. 1st SAMANTHA D. GREEN, b. 1812; Samantha d. at Sherburne, 11 Apr 1842. Cyrus m. 2nd PHILENA, b. about 1818 and d. at Sherburne, 26 Feb

---

[1089] *Connecticut. Probate Court (Pomfret District);* Probate Place: *Windham, Connecticut, volume 12, p 308*

[1090] The date of give is given in his widow's pension application and the family seems to have still been in Vermont at that time.

[1091] All the records available support that Anna did indeed live to 105. In 1838, she gave her age as 71 on a pension application and her age on the 1860 census is given as 94.

[1092] U. S. Revolutionary War Pension and Bounty-Land Warrant Application Files, 1800-1900, Case W22116

[1093] The 1857 will of Henry Horton includes a bequest to his daughter Eliza Rogers.

[1094] *Minutes, Orders and Decrees, 1830-1910;* Author: *New York. Surrogate's Court (Jefferson County), Minutes, Vol B, 1847-1853, pp 41-42*

[1095] *New York. Surrogate's Court (Chenango County);* Probate Place: *Chenango, New York, Wills Volume E 1840-1848, pp 318-319*

1853. Cyrus m. 3rd SUSAN D. SMITH (widow of Thomas Jefferson King), b. about 1810 daughter of Isaac and Susan (Densmore) Smith; Susan d. at Sherburne, Feb 1767. Cyrus m. 4th MARY, b. about 1817.

419)   LUCIA "LUCY" ROGERS (*Lois Holt Rogers⁴, Daniel Holt³, Mary Russell Holt², Robert¹*), b. at Ashford, 28 May 1771 daughter of Moses and Lois (Holt) Rogers; d. at Springfield, MA, Jan 1823; m. at Ashford, 16 Nov 1797, NATHAN CROCKER, b. about 1772 son of Gershom and Ann (Fisher) Crocker;[1096] Nathan d. at Springfield, 26 Jul 1817.
    Lucy Rogers and Nathan Crocker were parents of nine children, the oldest born at Ashford and the other children born at Springfield, Massachusetts.

i   LUCY CROCKER, b. at Ashford, 18 Aug 1798; d. at La Harpe, IL, 1 Dec 1888; m. at Springfield, 13 Nov 1815, HENRY COMSTOCK, b. at Old Saybrook, CT, 11 Jan 1794 son of Josiah and Lucy (Pratt) Comstock; Henry d. at La Harpe, 22 Jan 1879.

ii   FANNY CROCKER, b. at Springfield, 15 Jul 1800; m. at Springfield, 21 Oct 1819, WILLIAM WRIGHT, b. in NY. Fanny and William were in Chatham, NY in 1832 where one of their children was born, but where they were after has not been found.

iii   CLARISSA CROCKER, b. at Springfield, 1 Sep 1802; d. at Union, ME, 1865; m. at Springfield, 1 Sep 1824, JOHN R. POST, b. about 1801; John d. at Union after 1840 and before 1850. There are four known children of Clarissa and John.

iv   WILLIAM DOW CROCKER, b. at Springfield, 31 Mar 1805; m. at Springfield, 23 Nov 1825, MARY STANNARD, b. about 1805; Mary d. at Springfield, 16 Oct 1831.

v   NATHAN F. CROCKER, b. at Springfield, 25 Nov 1807; d. at West Orange, NJ, 8 Jan 1890; m. at Springfield, 20 Sep 1833, LORRAINE KELLOGG, b. in CT, 31 Jul 1805 daughter of Ichabod and Pamelia (Betts) Kellogg; Lorraine d. Feb 1885.

vi   HARVEY CROKER, b. about 1808; d. at Springfield, 30 Sep 1829.

vii   EDWIN CROCKER (twin), b. at Springfield, 24 May 1812

viii   ELIZA CROCKER (twin), b. at Springfield, 24 May 1812

ix   MARY CROCKER, b. at Springfield, 3 Oct 1814

420)   ALVA ROGERS (*Lois Holt Rogers⁴, Daniel Holt³, Mary Russell Holt², Robert¹*), b. at Ashford, 18 Jun 1776 son of Moses and Lois (Holt) Rogers; d. at Sherburne, NY, after 1850; m. at Ashford, 8 Sep 1803, his third cousin, DESIRE EATON, b. at Ashford, 29 May 1778 daughter of Ebenezer and Mary (Humphrey) Eaton; Desire d. at Sherburne, NY, Dec 1859.
    Alva Rogers and Desire Eaton were parents of five children.

i   LEISCTER HOLT ROGERS, b. at Ashford, 4 Jan 1804; d. at Sherburne, NY, 23 Jul 1827.

ii   JARVIS ROGERS, b. at Ashford, 13 Sep 1805; d. at Sherburne, NY, 17 Jul 1857; m. HANNAH, b. about 1807; Hannah living at Sherburne in 1865. Hannah married second Henry A. Poultney.

iii   MARY HUMPHREY ROGERS, b. at Ashford, 10 Sep 1807; d. at Norwich, NY, 1 Feb 1865; m. about 1831, as his second wife, BENJAMIN TALBOT LYON, b. at Foster, RI, 26 Nov 1796 son of Benjamin and Hannah (Talbot) Lyon; Benjamin d. at Norwich, 31 May 1864. Benjamin was first married to Mary Comstock.

iv   HARLOW ROGERS, b. at Sherburne, NY, 20 Apr 1816; d. at Clear Lake, WI, 20 Apr 1908; m. HARRIET M. THAYER, b. at Sherburne, 27 Feb 1818 son of Alanson and Jerusha (Baker) Thayer; Harriet d. at Clear Lake, 15 Feb 1885.

v   ALVA ROGERS, b. at Sherburne, 1820; d. at Clear Lake, WI, 3 Nov 1880; m. ANN ELIZABETH CARR, b. 1822; Ann d. after 1880 when she was living at Clear Lake.

421)   PERTHENE WHEELER (*Eunice Holt Wheeler⁴, Daniel Holt³, Mary Russell Holt², Robert¹*), b. at Pomfret, 19 Sep 1762 daughter of Josiah and Eunice (Holt) Wheeler; m. 26 Oct 1783, DANIEL CHAPIN, b. at Salisbury, CT, 2 Feb 1761 son of Charles and Anna (Camp) Chapin;[1097] Daniel d. at Buffalo, NY, 16 Nov 1821.

[1096] Crocker, *Crocker Genealogy*, p 93
[1097] Chapin, Orange, *Chapin Genealogy*

Dr. Daniel Chapin attended Yale and was a physician in Buffalo from about 1805.[1098] He was also a member of the New York state assembly in 1801-1802.[1099] He served as judge in the court of common pleas in Niagara. The family lived in Bloomfield before setting in Buffalo. Perthene and Daniel were parents of six children. Birth dates of the children, for the most part, are estimates based on age at death, census records, etc.

i   WILLIAM WHITING CHAPIN, b. about 1785; d. at Buffalo, 20 Jun 1857; m. about 1815, MARY NOBLE, b. in CT, about 1785; Mary d. at Buffalo, 13 May 1862.

ii   THOMAS CHAPIN, b. about 1788. The Chapin genealogy reports that Thomas married and had three children, but records related to his family were not located.

iii   ELIZA CHAPIN, b. 11 Jan 1790; d. at Hamburg, NY, 1 Mar 1852; m. at Buffalo, 1 Nov 1812, DAVID BEARD, b. at Derby, CT, 13 Jun 1770 son of James and Ruth (Holbrook) Beard;[1100] David d. at Buffalo, 29 Nov 1838.

iv   JAMES CHAPIN, b. about 1793; d. about 1825. James did not marry.[1101]

v   SOPHIA CHAPIN, b. 1795; d. at Buffalo, 18 Mar 1860; m. about 1820, WALTER NORTON, b. 1786 son of Samuel and Ruth (Kenney) Norton; Walter d. at Buffalo, 21 Feb 1849 (probate 2 Mar 1849).

vi   CLARISSA CHAPIN, b. 1806; d. at St. Catharines, Niagara, Ontario, 2 May 1867; m. about 1825, ELEAZER WILLIAMS STEPHENSON, b. at Springfield, MA, 1798 son of Erastus and Elizabeth (Murphy) Stephenson; Eleazer d. at St, Catharines, 28 Apr 1867. Col. Eleazer Williams Stephenson took his family to St. Catharines about 1825. He had a successful livery stable and established the first Royal mail stage-coach line. He was killed by runaway horses. He was also a promotor of building the Welland canal.[1102] In 1851, Stephenson was elected to the town council and was chosen mayor.[1103]

422)   ELIJAH WHEELER (*Eunice Holt Wheeler⁴, Daniel Holt³, Mary Russell Holt², Robert¹*), b. at Pomfret, 28 Aug 1767 son of Josiah and Eunice (Holt) Wheeler; d. at Great Barrington, MA, 20 Apr 1827; m. 1st MARY MATILDA MINER, b. at Woodbury, CT, 11 Apr 1773 daughter of Jehu and Sarah (Canfield) Miner; Mary d. at Great Barrington, 11 Oct 1812. Elijah m. 2nd ELIZABETH WHITING, b. 1773 likely daughter of Gamaliel and Anne (Gillette) Whiting; Elizabeth d. at Great Barrington, 21 Feb 1848.

Rev. Elijah Wheeler was from Pomfret. He was a physician and practiced medicine in South Britain (Southbury), Connecticut. He later entered the ministry and settled in Great Barrington, Massachusetts in 1805 where he was minister of the congregational church from 1806 to 1823 when he left the position due to failing health.[1104]

In his will (probate 15 August 1827), Elijah Wheeler, who describes himself as minister of the gospel, bequeathed to beloved wife Elizabeth the improvement on one-third of the real estate while she is a widow and all the household furniture as her own property. Beloved son Russel Canfield receives five dollars which completed his portion and son Josiah William receives $420. Any estate remaining after payment of debts is to be divided among his wife and two sons while Elizabeth is a widow and then divided between the two sons. Trusty friend Deacon George Beckwith was named executor.[1105] The probate record specifies that in addition to widow Elizabeth, Russel C. Wheeler of New York City and Josiah W. Wheeler of Albany, New York are the only two heirs.

Elijah Wheeler and Mary Miner were parents of two children. The two sons married sisters who were also their second cousins through the Wheeler line.[1106][1107]

i   RUSSELL CANFIELD WHEELER, b. at Southbury, NY, 1 Dec 1795; d. at Brooklyn, NY, 13 Aug 1847; m. 23 Oct 1833, THEODOSIA MARY DAVENPORT, b. at Stamford, CT, 8 Nov 1810 daughter of John Alfred and Eliza Maria (Wheeler) Davenport; Theodosia d. at New Haven, 14 Sep 1883. Russell graduated from Yale in 1816 and practice law in New York until illness forced his retirement.

[1098] Hill, *Municipality of Buffalo, 1720-1923*, volume 1, p 392

[1099] Daniel Chapin, politicalgraveyard. com

[1100] Beard, *A Genealogy of the Descendants of Widow Martha Beard*, p 22

[1101] Chapin, *The Chapin Book of Genealogical Data*, p 172

[1102] A Cyclopedia of Canadian Biography, volume 1, p 645

[1103] Dictionary of Canadian Biography, volume IX, http://www.biographi.ca/en/bio/stephenson_eleazer_williams_9E.html

[1104] Taylor, *History of Great Barrington*, p 387

[1105] *Probate Records, 1761-1917*; Author: *Massachusetts. Probate Court (Berkshire County), Probate Records, Vol 30-31, 1826-1827, volume 31, pp 231-233*

[1106] Dexter, *Biographical Notices of Graduates of Yale College*

[1107] Davenport, *A History and Genealogy of the Davenport Family*

ii   JOSIAH WILLIAM WHEELER, b. perhaps at Red Hook, NY, 5 Apr 1807; d. at Brooklyn, Mar 1882; m. 15 Oct 1835, MARY BORMAN DAVENPORT, b. at Stamford, 7 Aug 1814 daughter of John Alfred and Eliza Maria (Wheeler) Davenport; Mary d. at Brooklyn, 30 Apr 1896. Josiah graduated from Williams College in 1825.

423)   PHILADELPHIA "PHILA" WHEELER (*Eunice Holt Wheeler⁴, Daniel Holt³, Mary Russell Holt², Robert¹*), b. at Pomfret, 28 Nov 1769 daughter of Josiah and Eunice (Holt) Wheeler; d. at East Bloomfield, NY, after 1855; m. about 1791, MOSES GAYLORD, b. at West Hartford, about 1768 and baptized 17 Jul 1768 son of Moses and Susanna (Wells) Gaylord; Moses d. at Bloomfield, NY, 1812.[1108]

Phila and Moses resided in Bloomfield, New York where Moses was licensed as an inn and tavern keeper.[1109] Moses did not leave a will and his brother Flavel was appointed administrator of his estate on 19 February 1813.[1110]

Names of children have been suggested, but little firm information. Four children in this family can be tracked through cemetery and census records.

i   ELIZA GAYLORD

ii   DELIA GAYLORD

iii   EDWIN GAYLORD

iv   HECTOR GAYLORD, about1798; d. at East Bloomfield, 11 Jan 1848; m. about 1823, HANNAH SMITH, b. in CT, about 1804; Hannah d. after 1850 when she and her children were living with her brother-in-law George in East Bloomfield.

v   HOMER GAYLORD

vi   SARAH E. GAYLORD, b. about 1800; d. at East Bloomfield, 23 May 1843; m. ASAHEL HUNTINGTON, b. at Franklin, CT, 10 Sep 1795 daughter of Azariah and Parnel (Chamption) Huntington; Asahel d. 22 Oct 1822.

vii   GEORGE GAYLORD, b. about 1803; d. after 1875 when he was living in East Bloomfield as a boarder. George did not marry. After the death of his brother Hector, he took in Hector's children for several years.

viii WELLS MOSES GAYLORD, b. about 1804; d. at Rochester, NY, 4 Nov 1846; m. MARY ANN KENDALL, b. in MA, about 1804; Mary d. at Rochester, 23 Sep 1895.[1111]

424)   RESOLVED GROSVENOR WHEELER (*Eunice Holt Wheeler⁴, Daniel Holt³, Mary Russell Holt², Robert¹*), b. at Pomfret, 8 Mar 1772 son of Josiah and Eunice (Holt) Wheeler; d. at Conneaut, PA, 29 May 1839; m. N. ANNA VANDEVENTER, b. about 1785; Anna d. at Reedsburg, WI, 4 Oct 1863.

Resolved G. Wheeler was a wanderer and seems to have been in Lempster, New Hampshire before his marriage, in Clarence, Erie County, New York in 1802,[1112] later in Canada where some of the children were born, in Lempster, New Hampshire in the 1810 and 1820 census, back in New York at Pembroke for the 1830 census, and finally in Conneaut, Pennsylvania. He was named lieutenant in the Genesee County, New York militia in April 1803.[1113]

There are likely eight children in this family.

i   MARY WHEELER, b. 1804; d. 1819.

ii   AMANDA EMELINE WHEELER, b. 20 Aug 1805; d. at Reedsburg, WI, 14 Sep 1886; m. SAMUEL HALL CHASE, b. at East Machias, ME, 1804 son of Eleazer and Alice (Hall) Chase; Samuel d. at Reedsburg, 29 Jan 1890.

iii   CHRISTOPHER VANDEVENTER WHEELER, b. 11 Oct 1807; d. at Bedford, IA, 30 Jul 1882; m. EMILY WEAVER, b. at Willington, CT, 11 Dec 1811 daughter of Thomas and Sarah (Lee) Weaver; Emily d. at Wester, NE, 18 Jun 1902 where she was living at the home of her daughter.

[1108] *Connecticut, Hale Collection of Cemetery Inscriptions and Newspaper Notices, 1629-1934*

[1109] Aldrich, *History of Ontario County, New York*, p 131

[1110] New York Wills and Probate Records, Ontario County, Records of Wills, Volume 0006, pp 132-133

[1111] Presbyterian Historical Society; Philadelphia, Pennsylvania; U.S., Presbyterian Church Records, 1701-1907; Book Title: Church Register 1832-1903; Accession Number: V MI46 R5894r v.2

[1112] White, *Our County and Its People*, volume 1, p 516

[1113] Military Minutes of the Council of Appointment of the State of New York, 1783-1821, volume 1, p 692

iv   ELIJAH G. WHEELER, b. 27 Nov 1812; d. at Yankton, Dakota Territory, 26 Jul 1880; m. 1st about 1833, HARRIET who has not been identified, b. 1816 and d. 1856. Elijah m. 2nd at Allegan County, MI, 15 Jan 1857, HARRIET A. BOGART, b. in PA, 1833; Harriet d. after 1915 when she was living in San Jose, CA.

v   SARAH ANN WHEELER, b. in Canada, 1818; d. after 1885 when she was living in Vinton, IA; m. 1858, as his second wife, WILLIAM P. STEWART, b. in OH, 1814; William d. at Vinton, IA, 7 Jul 1893. William was first married to Isabel Logan and third married to Sarah P. Morton on 19 Jun 1893 shortly before his death. In 1850, Sarah Wheeler and her mother Ann were living in Baraboo, WI.

vi   PETER VANDEVENTER WHEELER, b. in Canada, 18 Aug 1820; d. at Urbana, IA, 9 Jan 1903; m. ELECTA A. WHITFORD, b. in NY, 8 Feb 1827 daughter of Oliver and Phebe (Laampman) Whitford; Electa d. at Vinton, IA, 7 Jul 1916.[1114]

vii   JOHN G. WHEELER, b. in New York, 4 Apr 1822; d. at Milwaukee, WI, 9 May 1913; m. ELLA WAITE, b. in NY 1826; Ella d. at Fairfield, IA, about 1870. John was admitted to the Milwaukee Home for Disabled Volunteer Soldiers in 1896.[1115]

viii   WILLIAM H. WHEELER, b. 8 Feb 1826; d. at Douglas, CO, 6 Apr 1892; m. at DeKalb, IL, 10 Oct 1849, JANE H. KENDALL, b. in NY, 30 May 1830; Jane d. at Glendale, CO, 10 Feb 1918.[1116]

425)   SMITH HOLT (*Asa Holt⁴, Daniel Holt³, Mary Russell Holt², Robert¹*), b. at Hartford, about 1769 son of Asa and Margaret (Hammond) Holt; d. at Keene, NY, 28 Dec 1814; m. 26 Jan 1792, his second cousin once removed LYDIA SNOW (*Dorcas Osgood Snow⁵, Mary Holt Osgood⁴, Nicholas Holt³, Mary Russell Holt², Robert¹*), b. 6 Oct 1769 daughter of Benjamin and Dorcas (Osgood) Snow; Lydia d. at Keene, 21 Dec 1853.

    After the births of their first seven children, Smith and Lydia moved their family to what became Keene, New York along the Ausable River valley arriving there in 1806.[1117]

    Smith Holt and Lydia Snow were parents of ten children, the oldest seven children born in Connecticut, likely at Ashford, and the three youngest in Keene, New York.

i   ALVA SMITH HOLT, b. 1793; d. at Keene, NY, 16 May 1879; m. MARY "POLLY" PEASE, b. 28 Jan 1795 daughter of Augustus and Tirzah (Hall) Pease; Polly d. at Keene, 29 Oct 1872.

ii   ORRIN HOLT, b. 1796; d. at Scotland, Ontario, Canada, 12 Oct 1887, m. at Townsend, Ontario, 7 Feb 1831,[1118] LORETTA DUDBRIDGE, b. in Ontario, about 1813; d. at Townsend, Ontario between 1871 and 1881.

iii   LOIS C. HOLT, b. 1797; d. at Keene, NY, 3 Oct 1876; m. ORRIN DIBBLE, b. in VT, 1795; d. at Keene, NY, 14 Sep 1860.

iv   POLLY HOLT, b. 20 May 1799 (on gravestone); d. at Williston, VT, 28 Aug 1881; m. JOHN WRIGHT, b. at Williston, 8 Oct 1797 son of Elisha and Asenath (Brigham) Wright; John d. at Williston, 28 Oct 1881.

v   LODISA HOLT, b. 1801; d. at Williston, VT, 19 Oct 1887; m. ROSWELL TALCOTT, b. 24 Aug 1798 son of Jonathan and Jerusha (Morton) Talcott; Roswell d. at Williston, 1 Sep 1893.

vi   JAMES SMITH HOLT, b. 1804; d. at Keene, NY, 17 Jul 1878; m. HARRIET SEAMON, b. in NY, about 1807; Harriet d. at Keene, 16 Aug 1874.

vii   JASON HOLT, b. 1805; d. at Sombra, Lambton, Ontario, 26 Apr 1893; m. CHARLOTTE WARD, b. 3 Aug 1810 daughter of Nathan and Charlotte (Beach) Ward;[1119] Charlotte d. at Sombra, 30 Apr 1874. After Charlotte's death, Jason married Ellen (1849-1892) who has not been identified.

viii   HARVEY HOLT, b. at Keene, 4 Mar 1808; d. at Keene, NY, 14 Jan 1893; m. MARIA CHASE, b. 8 Nov 1819 daughter of Ebenezer and Sarah (Cheney) Chase; Maria d. at Keene, 2 Dec 1906.

ix   NEWMAN HOLT, b. 1811; d. at Keene, NY, 1812.

x   LYDIA HOLT, b. at Keene, 1813; d. at Williston, VT, 17 Jan 1841; m. HIRAM MURRAY, b. at Williston, 1807; Hiram d. at Williston, 3 Oct 1864.

[1114] Iowa, Deaths and Burials, 1850-1990. Electa's date of birth and names of her parents are given on her death record.
[1115] U.S. National Homes for Disabled Volunteer Soldiers, 1866-1938, Milwaukee
[1116] The dates of birth for William and Jane are given on their gravestones. Graves are in Fairmount Cemetery, Denver, CO. findagrave ID: 13472092
[1117] Donaldson, *History of the Adirondacks*, p 31
[1118] Witnesses of the marriage were John Dudbridge and Barton Becker.
[1119] Charlotte was baptized in Sombra as an adult in 1868 and names of parents on given as Nathan and C. on the baptism record.

426)   ASA HOLT (*Asa Holt⁴, Daniel Holt³, Mary Russell Holt², Robert¹*), b. likely at Hartford, 12 Dec 1777 son of Asa and Margaret (Hammond) Holt; d. at Rushford, NY, 1852; m. 1st at Springfield, VT, 26 Mar 1801, ELIZABETH "BETSEY" WOODWARD, b. at Springfield, 25 Oct 1782 daughter of Samuel and Eunice (Bigelow) Woodward;[1120] Betsey d. at Springfield, 2 Feb 1814. Asa m. 2nd 7 Oct 1815, POLLY ROGERS (widow of Samuel Tarbell), b. 1784 daughter of Jeremiah and Fannie (Wickes) Rogers; Polly d. at Fillmore, NY, 2 Sep 1874.

Asa settled in Springfield, Vermont where he took the freeman's oath in 1802[1121] shortly after his first marriage. Asa resided in Springfield through the births of his children but was in Rushford, New York in later life.

Asa Holt and Betsey Woodward were parents of six children born at Springfield, Vermont.[1122]

i   LOUISA HOLT, b. 28 Dec 1801; d. at Cuba, NY, 1882; m. at Springfield, VT, 18 Nov 1824, LEWIS GRAVES, b. at Springfield, 26 Jun 1801 son of Selah and Sabra (Graves) Roundy; Lewis d. at Cuba, NY, 1891.

ii   CHARLES HOLT, b. 12 Dec 1803; d. at Springfield, 11 Sep 1888; m. 1st, at Springfield, 30 Jan 1830, BETSEY PARKER, b. at Rockingham, VT, 9 Dec 1800 daughter of Leonard and Abigail (Parker) Parker; Betsey d. at Springfield, 24 Feb 1862.

iii   PERMELIA HOLT, b. 8 Jan 1806; d. at Waterford, NY, 21 Sep 1892; m. about 1827, JASPER GRIFFIN, b. at Jericho, VT, 26 Nov 1806 son of Jasper and Lydia (Lane) Griffin; Jasper d. at Jericho, 1844.

iv   LEWIS M. HOLT (twin), b. 10 Aug 1808; d. at Pampas, IL, 11 Aug 1850; m. about 1832, BETSEY A. CAMPBELL, b. in MA, 1812; d. (buried), at Centerville, WI, 11 Aug 1886. Betsey was second married to James D. Kincaid.

v   MORRIS L. HOLT (twin), b. 10 Aug 1808; d. at Pike, NY, 28 May 1871; m. LUCINDA CAMPBELL, b. 15 Jul 1814 daughter of William and Elizabeth (Pool) Campbell; Lucinda d. at Pike, 21 Feb 1894.

vi   ELIZABETH HOLT, b. 30 Aug 1810; d. at McKean, PA, 22 Jul 1875; m. 1 Jul 1836, as his second wife, PLINNY CLEVELAND, b. at Stockbridge, VT, 7 Jul 1801 son of William Darbee and Phebe (Abbott) Cleveland;[1123] Plinny d. at McKean, 20 Aug 1867. Plinny was first married to Rachel Ketchum.

Asa Holt and Polly Rogers were parents of four children likely all born at Springfield, Vermont.

i   LAURA ANN HOLT, b. 4 Apr 1816; d. at Perry, OH, 3 Nov 1903; m. about 1833, ASAPH W. MORGAN, b. at Springfield, VT, 21 May 1809 son of Isaac and Anna (Wood) Morgan; Asaph d. at Perry, 20 Feb 1898.

ii   CLARISSA HOLT, b. 23 May 1818; d. at Caneadea, NY, 20 Feb 1895; m. 1st SAMUEL MORGAN, b. about 1810; Samuel d. at Almond, NY, 2 Jan 1847. Clarissa m. 2nd about 1848, as his second wife, WILLIS FOX, b. in CT, about 1800; Willis d. at Yorkshire, NY, 1852 (probate 6 Apr 1852). Clarissa m. 3rd ABEL WASHBURN, b. 1817;[1124] Abel d. at Caneadea, 6 Jan 1892.

iii   HARRIET HOLT, b. 2 Feb 1823; d. at Tacoma, WA, 13 Dec 1885; m. before 1850, REUBEN HENRY CRITTENDEN, b. at Savoy, MA, 23 Nov 1823 son of Amos and Mehitable (Thomas) Crittenden; Reuben d. at Tacoma, 20 Sep 1898.

iv   MARY HOLT, b. 1826; d. at Fillmore, NY, 1914; m. NOAH KENNEDY, b. in VT, Aug 1808;[1125] Noah d. at Caneadea, NY, 25 Dec 1881.

427)   ALFREADA HOLT (*Asa Holt⁴, Daniel Holt³, Mary Russell Holt², Robert¹*), b. about 1779 daughter of Asa and Margaret (Hammond) Holt; d. at Cavendish, VT, about 1814; m. at Springfield, 3 Jun 1799, PEARLY FASSET, b. about 1769 son of Adonijah and Anna (Copeland) Fasset; Pearly d. at Winchester, NH, 23 Feb 1826. Pearly married second Esther Gowing.

In his will written 7 February 1826, Pearly Fasset bequeaths one dollar to each of his children: eldest son Perley Fasset, eldest daughter Alfreada Fasset, second daughter Anna Fasset, second son Abel Hammond Fasset, and third son Amos

---

[1120] Hubbard, *History of Springfield, Vermont*, p 511

[1121] Hubbard, *History of Springfield, Vermont*, p 528

[1122] The five oldest children, including twins Morris L. and Lewis M., are recorded together in the Springfield town records kept by S. M. Lewis. Vermont Town Clerk Records, Springfield, volume 3, p 22, https://www.familysearch.org/ark:/61903/3:1:3QS7-L999-24KX?i=16&cc=1987653&cat=693475

[1123] Cleveland, *Genealogy of the Cleveland and Cleaveland Families*, p 705

[1124] In 1870, Polly Holt, then age 87, was living with her daughter Clarissa and her husband Abel Washburn in Caneadea, New York

[1125] Mary's mother Polly Holt was living with Mary and Noah Kennedy in the 1860 census of Genesee Falls, NY, Polly then age 77.

Twitchell Fasset. The remainder of the estate is left to wife Esther Fasset and Esther Fasset and Joseph Gowing are named executors.[1126]

     Alfreada Holt and Pearly Fasset were parents of five children.

i   PEARLY FASSET, b. at Cavendish, 16 Nov 1800; d. at Plymouth, NH, 4 Sep 1884; m. SUSAN L. GREEN, b. at Andover, VT, about 1816 daughter of Thomas and Jerusha (Hardy) Green;[1127] Susan d. at Reading, VT, 28 May 1871.

ii   ALFREADA FASSET, b. about 1803; living in 1826 but nothing further known.

iii   ANNA FASSET, b. at Cavendish, 14 Jul 1804; d. at Springfield, VT, 10 Feb 1873; m. at Springfield, 1 Apr 1829, ABEL PRESCOTT WHITE, b. at Mason, NH, 23 Jul 1804 son of Abel and Ruth (Prescott) White; Abel d. at Springfield, 20 Sep 1893.

iv   ABEL HAMMOND FASSET, b. at Cavendish, 24 Aug 1806; d. at Winchester, NH, 1 Feb 1886; m. at Keene, NH, 4 Mar 1840, EUNICE EVERDEN, b. at Winchester, Aug 1803 daughter of John and Mary (Wright) Everden; Eunice d. at Winchester, 22 Dec 1886.

v   AMOS TWITCHELL FASSET, b. about 1809

428)   POLLY HOLT (*Asa Holt⁴, Daniel Holt³, Mary Russell Holt², Robert¹*), b. 1 Jun 1782 daughter of Asa and Margaret (Hammond) Holt; d. at Springfield, VT, 7 Jan 1852; m. at Springfield, 9 Aug 1805, SIMEON RUMRILL, b. at New Ipswich, 12 Jun 1769 son of David and Priscilla (Corey) Rumrill; Simeon d. at Baltimore, VT, 19 Mar 1822. Simeon was married to Dolly Clark before his marriage to Polly.

     Polly and Simeon live in Weathersfield, Vermont but in a section that was annexed to the school district of Baltimore, Vermont. Simeon bought property in Baltimore from Benjamin Page in 1811.[1128]

     Simeon Rumrill did not leave a will and his estate entered probate 19 April 1822 with Benjamin Page as administrator and the request of widow Polly and son John L. Rumrill (who is a son from Simeon's first marriage). The personal estate was not sufficient to pay the debts and the whole of the farm was sold for $505.[1129]

     Polly and Simeon were parents of ten children.

i   HARVEY H. RUMRILL, b. at Weathersfield, VT, 2 Oct 1806; d. at Midland, MI, 1 May 1883; m. 1st 6 Mar 1831, SARAH MILLER, b. 1811 daughter of Jeremy and Sarah (Hodgeman) Miller; Sarah d. at Midland, about 1849. Harvey m. 2nd about 1850 RUTH ANN MYERS, b. 1816 daughter of Surzardus and Maria (-) Myers; Ruth d. at Midland, 18 Feb 1894. After Harvey's death, Ruth married Ephraim Allen on 7 Jun 1884.

ii   ALMIRA RUMRILL, b. 1808; d. at Rushford, NY, 26 Aug 1894; m. 1st WARNER SNOW who was perhaps her third cousin, Warner b. at Cavendish 10 Apr 1795 son of Robert and Anna (Peck) Snow, but that is not certain. Almira m. 2nd WINTHROP G. YOUNG, b. 1810 son of Jospehus and Esther (Gary) Young; Winthrop d. at Rushford, 30 Mar 1877.

iii   ALVA HOLT RUMRILL, b. 1810; d. at Springfield, VT, 21 Apr 1823

iv   CLARISSA RUMRILL, b. 1811; d. at Springfield, 4 May 1828.

v   HARRIET RUMRILL, b. 1 Jul 1813; d. at Springfield, 17 Jan 1837.

vi   SARINA RUMRILL, b. 8 Aug 1815; d. at Wallingford, VT, 5 Nov 1888; m. WILLIAM CLARK, b. about 1818; William d. at Wallingford, 11 Nov 1889.[1130]

vii   SOLON B. RUMRILL, b. at Springfield, 11 Dec 1817; d. at Sterling Center, MN, 19 Feb 1878; m. at Weathersfield, 11 Mar 1849, ROSINA DE WOLF, b. at Pomfret, VT, 11 Nov 1827 daughter of Daniel Shays and Mary (Hodges) De Wolf; Rosina d. at Spokane, WA, 9 Jul 1909.

viii   ELIZA M. RURMRILL, b. at Baltimore, VT, 20 Feb 1820; d. at Chester, VT, 13 Feb 1884; m. 1 Jan 1837, WILLIAM HULL SPAFFORD, b. at Weathersfield, 13 Sep 1812 son of Abel and Mathilda (Grout) Spafford; William d. at Rutland, 4 Jun 1893.

[1126] *New Hampshire. Probate Court (Cheshire County)*; Probate Place: *Cheshire, New Hampshire, Estate Files, F206-F255, 1826-1836, Estate of Pearly Fasset, Case 208*

[1127] The names of Susan's parents are given as Thomas Green and Jerusha on her death record.

[1128] Pollard, *The History of the Town of Baltimore, Vermont*, p 10 and p 168

[1129] Vermont Wills, Windsor County, Estate Files, Estate of Simeon Rumrill

[1130] On William Clark's death record, the name of his father is given as Mayor Clark.

ix   MARY H. RUMRILL, b. at Baltimore, VT, 11 Mar 1822; d. at Springfield, VT, 16 Oct 1904; m. 1846, CHESTER HUBBARD STONE, b. at Troy, VT, Jul 1822 son of Walter and Nancy (Dexter) Stone; Chester d. at Springfield, 25 Sep 1907.

429)   ELIZABETH DANA (*Lucy Holt Dana⁴, Daniel Holt³, Mary Russell Holt², Robert¹*), b. at Ashford, 8 Jun 1771 daughter of Jedediah and Lucy (Holt) Dana; d. at Wilbern, IL, 1840; m. at Mansfield, CT, 1 Jun 1794, AMASA OWEN, b. at Ashford, 12 Aug 1766 son of Timothy and Kezia (-) Owen; Amasa d. at Wilbern, 1842.

    Elizabeth and Amasa resided in Mansfield, Connecticut until 1819 when they located in Scioto County, Ohio. They later lived in Bureau, Illinois.

    Elizabeth Dana and Amasa Owen were parents of ten children born at Mansfield, Connecticut.

i   WILLIAM DANA OWEN, b. 6 Jan 1795; d. after 1850 when he was living in Randolph, PA; m. SARAH who has not been identified; Sarah b. about 1788 and d. at Guys Mills, PA, 15 Feb 1858.

ii   LUCY OWEN, b. 8 Oct 1796

iii   TIMOTHY OWEN, b. 11 Mar 1799; d. at Lacon, IL, 3 May 1886; m. at Scioto County, OH, 2 Mar 1825, JANE DEVER, b. 1804; Jane d. at Lacon, 5 Mar 1883.

iv   HIRAM OWEN, b. 1 Apr 1801; d. after 1870 when he was living at Hennepin, IL; m. 1ˢᵗ by 1835, MINERVA who has not been identified, but born in NY about 1806 and died after 1850 when the family was living in Washington, PA. Hiram m. 2ⁿᵈ at Woodford, IL, 11 Jul 1858, the widow SARAH A. WATKINS, b. in PA, about 1820.

v   RODERICK OWEN, b. 24 May 1803; d. at Tiskilwa, IL, 19 Apr 1861; m. at Scioto County, OH, 22 Sep 1821, NANCY ADAMS, b. at Elmira, NY, 1806 daughter of Joseph and Abigail (Reike) Adams;[1131] Nancy d. at Tiskilwa, 25 Sep 1849.

vi   JEDEDIAH OWEN, b. 28 May 1805; d. at Lee's Summit, MO, Sep 1881; m. at Tazewell County, IL, 1 May 1831, ELIZABETH SOWARD who died before 1850.

vii   MARIAM ELIZA OWEN, b. 10 Mar 1808; d. at Bolivar, MO, 22 Jan 1873; m. at Scioto County, OH, 15 Jan 1824, SAMUEL HARDIN HADLOCK, b. 1801 likely son of David and Elizabeth (Hardin) Hadlock; Samuel d. at Bolivar, 9 Apr 1886.

viii   LUCY OWEN, b. 1 Oct 1812; d. at Bolivar, MO, 21 Jun 1884; m. at Tazewell County, IL, 1 Jul 1838, CARVER GUNN, b. at Montague, MA, 12 Jul 1799 son of Elisha and Mindwell (Carver) Gunn; Carver d. at Bolivar, 20 Apr 1885.

430)   SILAS DANA (*Lucy Holt Dana⁴, Daniel Holt³, Mary Russell Holt², Robert¹*), b. at Ashford, 9 Mar 1775 son of Jedediah and Lucy (Holt) Dana; d. at Grove, NY, 14 Feb 1846; m. by 1800, SALLY COWEL, b. 6 Feb 1782; Sally d. at Grove, 23 Jan 1831. Silas m. 2ⁿᵈ, MARY who has not been identified.

    In his will written 15 January 1846 (proved 4 March 1846), Silas Dana bequeaths to wife Mary one-third of his real estate, two good cows, one horse worth fifty dollars, one good bed and bedding and bedstead to have and to hold the said real estate during her natural life. Lucy Cowel receives one-third of the real estate to use during her natural life as well as a good bed. Daughter Mary Ann receives the use of the last third of the real estate. The household furniture is to be divided among his wife Mary, Lucy Cowel and daughter Mary Ann. The remainder of the estate is to be divided among his son and daughters. At the decease of his wife, Lucy Cowel, and Mary Ann, the estate is to be sold and divided among his son and daughters (who are not named). Wife Mary and Reuben Ward, Jr. are named executors.[1132] At the proving of the will on 4 March 1846, Reuben Ward presented the will and provided the following list of heirs: widow Mary Dana living in Grove; one son Lester Dana in Bolivia, NY; and four daughters who are Eliza the wife of James White of Grove; Wealthy the wife of Franklin Smith of Castile, Wyoming County; Mary Ann Dana of Grove; Clarissa the wife of William Huffman supposed to reside in the state of Ohio; and the children of Elijah and Lucy White who are James White, Sarah White, Elijah White, Jr., Lucinda White, Joseph White, Albert White, and John White with the last five named children being minors and residing in Grove.[1133] Lucy Cowel is likely a relative, perhaps sister, of Sally Cowel.

    There are six known children of Silas Dana and Sally Cowel perhaps all born at Grove, New York.

[1131] Obituary of Mrs. Nancy Owen, "Western Christian Advocate", Cincinnati, OH, 21 November 1849, p 4

[1132] *Record of Wills, Other Miscellaneous Surrogate Records, 1807-1930*; Author: *New York. Surrogate's Court (Allegany County), Probate of Wills, Vol 0002-0003, 1840-1865, volume 0003, pp 391-392*

[1133] *Record of Wills, Other Miscellaneous Surrogate Records, 1807-1930*; Author: *New York. Surrogate's Court (Allegany County), Orders, Minutes, Decrees, Vol A, E, 1807-1851, p 266*

i   LUCY DANA, b. about 1801; d. at Grove, NY, about 1841; m. at Grove, 1822, ELIJAH WHITE, b. in NY, about 1799; Elijah d. after 1870 when he was living at Grove.

ii   ELIZA DANA, b. about 1803; d. after 1865 when she was living at Bolivar; m. by 1825, JAMES WHITE, b. about 1801; James was living in 1865.

iii   LESTER H. DANA, b. about 1805; d. after 1880 when he was living at East Tawas, MI; m. MARY "POLLY" WHITE.

iv   CLARISSA DANA, b. about 1808; d. after 1860 when she was living at Steuben, IN; m. WILLIAM HUFFMAN, b. in PA, about 1798; William was living at Steuben in 1860.

v   MARY ANN DANA, b. about 1808; d. after 1865 when she was living at Bolivar, NY with her sister Eliza. Mary Ann did not marry.

vi   WEALTHY ANN DANA, b. 6 Sep 1822; d. at Oklahoma City, OK, 8 Jun 1892; m. BENJAMIN FRANKLIN SMITH, b. at Gorham, NY, 16 Apr 1821 son of Isaac Adams and Lydia (Wright) Smith; Benjamin d. at Minco, OK, 4 Feb 1910.

431)   SALLY DANA (*Lucy Holt Dana⁴, Daniel Holt³, Mary Russell Holt², Robert¹*), b. at Ashford, 23 Mar 1777 daughter of Jedediah and Lucy (Holt) Dana; d. at German Flatts (Paine's Hollow), NY, 1 Jul 1856; m. 10 Oct 1802, THOMAS PAYN, b. at Lebanon, CT, 26 Jan 1778 son of Seth and Jerusha (Swift) Payn; Thomas d. at German Flatts, 26 Sep 1856.[1134]
        Sally Dana and Thomas Payn were parents of five children likely all born at Paine's Hollow, New York and all of whom used Paine as spelling for their last name.[1135]

i   THOMAS ALMIREN PAINE, b. 25 Mar 1805; d. at Manistee, MI, 28 Nov 1867; m. 1st about 1828, CAROLINE ALLEN, b. about 1806; Caroline d. at Paine's Hollow, NY, 31 Mar 1832.Thomas m. 2nd, about 1833, MARY GOLDEN, b. in NY, 23 Feb 1810; Mary d. at Manistee, 26 Dec 1892.

ii   WILLIAM DANA PAINE, b. 9 Aug 1809; d. Nunda, NY, 1873; m. SAMANTHA RICE, b. 15 Feb 1815 daughter of Elijah and Anna (Price) Rice; Samantha d. at Nunda, 8 Sep 1903.

iii   CARLOS GRANT PAINE, b. 20 Feb 1811; d. at Nunda, NY, 1882; m. 1st 1835, JERUSHA SWIFT, b. at Mansfield, CT, 25 Jan 1812 daughter of Philip and Fanny (Russ) Swift; Jerusha d. at Nunda, about 1855. Carlos m. 2nd, about 1855, NANCY SWEET (widow of Abraham Burdick), b. 1817; Nancy d. at Nunda, 1901.

iv   PHILANDER ALONZO PAINE, b. 28 Nov 1814; d. (buried at) Richland, IA, 13 Apr 1884;[1136] m. SALLY FILKINS, b. in NY, about 1817; Sally d. 4 Nov 1887 and is also buried at Richland, although living at South Fork, IA in 1885.

v   SALLY AMANDA PAINE, b. 10 Sep 1817; d. at Paine's Hollow, 29 May 1839;[1137] m. at Herkimer County, NY, 19 Aug 1838, DELOS L. FILER, b. 27 Sep 1817 son of Alanson and Polly (Dodge) Filer; Delos d. at Milwaukee, WI, 26 Jul 1879. Delos was second married to Juliet Golden and third married to Mary Pierce.

432)   MARY "POLLY" DANA (*Lucy Holt Dana⁴, Daniel Holt³, Mary Russell Holt², Robert¹*), b. at Ashford, 15 Jan 1781 daughter of Jedediah and Lucy (Holt) Dana; d. at Nunda, NY, 27 Dec 1850; m. JAMES PAYN, b. at Lebanon, CT, 27 Jan 1783 son of Seth and Jerusha (Swift) Payn; James d. at Nunda, 8 Apr 1861.
        James Paine was the first permanent settler (although not the first "pioneer") in Nunda, New York arriving there from Herkimer County on 15 March 1817 with their two oldest sons.[1138] They were parents of four children.

i   EARL JUDSON PAINE, b. at Paine's Hollow, 24 Mar 1807; d. at Nunda, NY, 23 Aug 1881; m. CATHERINE GRIMES, b. 10 Nov 1803 daughter of Richard and Anna (Phillips) Grimes; Catherine d. at Nunda, 25 Feb 1879.

ii   LUCIUS F. PAINE, b. at Paine's Hollow, about 1810; d. at Nunda, 12 Feb 1883; m. EMELINE HOPKINS, b. about 1811 daughter of Charles and Emma (Adams) Hopkins; Emeline d. at Nunda, 23 Apr 1889.

[1134] Towne and Jones, Seth Payn and Some of His Descendants, NEHGR, 1943, p 138

[1135] Towne and Jones, Seth Payn and Some of His Descendants, NEHGR, 1943, p 138

[1136] Philander was living at South Fork, IA in 1880 but burial was in Richland. Iowa, Cemetery Records, 1662-1999

[1137] Sally's only child, Sally Amanda Filer was born 20 May 1839.

[1138] Hand, *Centennial History of the Town of Nunda*, p 120

iii JAMES ALMIRON PAINE, b. at Nunda, 12 Nov 1819; d. at 31 Mar 1899; m. 1st LUCRETIA PUTNAM, b. about 1823. James m. 2nd ESTHER GREENWOOD, b. in England, Aug 1845 daughter of James and Mary (-) Greenwood; Esther d. after 1900 when she was living in Nunda.

iv MARY ALMIRA PAINE, b. at Nunda, 12 Nov 1819; d. at Nunda, 30 Mar 1857; m. Dec 1853, Rev. LYMAN STILSON, b. at Meredith, NY, 29 Jan 1805 son of Cyrenus and Sarah (Baldwin) Stilson; Lyman d. at Jefferson, IA, 23 Mar 1886.

Great-Grandchildren of Thomas Russell and Phebe Johnson

433) ROBERT CROSBY (*Mehitable Chandler Crosby Spalding⁴, Mehitable Russell Chandler³, Thomas², Robert¹*), b. at Townsend, 13 Sep 1732 son of Robert and Mehitable (Chandler) Crosby; m. at Dunstable, 5 Mar 1760, SUSANNAH SHERWIN, b. at Boxford, 28 Aug 1734 daughter of Ebenezer and Hephzibah (Cole) Sherwin; Susannah d. at Winslow, ME, 7 May 1807.
　　Robert and Susannah were in New Ipswich before settling at Winslow, Maine. There are six confirmed children of Robert and Susannah and a possible seventh child is listed. There may be other children born after the family move to Maine who have not been verified.

i ROBERT CROSBY, b. 15 Jan 1761; d. at New Ipswich, 13 Feb 1763.

ii JONATHAN CROSBY, b. at New Ipswich, 5 Feb 1762; d. at Concord, ME, 20 Sep 1840; m. CATHERINE HOUGHTON, b. 1766 daughter of Thomas and Phebe (-) Houghton; Catherine d. at Concord, 24 Mar 1854.

iii ROBERT CROSBY, b. at New Ipswich, 6 Apr 1764; d. at Albion, ME, 29 Mar 1823; m. his first cousin, ABIGAIL CROSBY, b. at Winslow, ME, 8 Feb 1770 daughter of Jonah and Lydia (Chandler) Crosby; Abigail d. at Albion, 31 Mar 1844.

iv ASA CROSBY, b. at New Ipswich, 27 Feb 1766

v SUSANNAH CROSBY, b. at Mason, NH, 9 Oct 1768; d. at Anson, ME, 11 Jun 1805; m. about 1789, THOMAS HOUGHTON, b. 2 Dec 1763 son of Thomas and Phebe (-) Houghton; Thomas d. at Anson, 27 May 1840. Thomas married second Bridget Spaulding (widow of Ephraim Heald).

vi PATTY CROSBY, b. 1770; d. at Madison, ME, 19 Sep 1833; m. NATHAN HOUGHTON, b. 1769 son of Thomas and Phebe (-) Houghton; Nathan d. at Madison, 27 Sep 1853.

vii EBENEZER CROSBY,[1139] b. 1772; d. at Harmony, ME, Mar 1850. Ebenezer may have married Lydia Longley at Norridgewock in 1794.

viii JESSE CROSBY,[1140] b. 23 Apr 1782 (Avon, ME family record for Jesse and his wife Sarah);[1141] d. after 1860 when living at Fairfield, ME; m. at Farmington, ME, 3 Jul 1807, SARAH RIANT, b. likely at Farmington, 2 Apr 1786 daughter of Joseph and Salla (Powers) Riant;[1142] Sarah d. after 1860.

434) JONAH CROSBY (*Mehitable Chandler Crosby Spalding ⁴, Mehitable Russell Chandler³, Thomas², Robert¹*), b. at Townsend, about 1736 son of Robert and Mehitable (Chandler) Crosby; d. at Albion, ME, 24 Apr 1814 (pronate 10 May 1815 with Joseph Cammett as administrator);[1143] m. at Townsend, MA, 22 Dec 1757, LYDIA CHANDLER, b. at Westford, 10 Dec 1735 daughter of William and Susanna (Burge) Chandler; Lydia d. at Albion, 18 Dec 1814.
　　Jonah Crosby resided in Townsend in his early life. He served in the French and Indian War during the expedition to Crown Point in the company of Capt. Benjamin Ballard from 5 April 1755 to 17 December 1755.[1144] He was a delegate to the Massachusetts state Constitutional Convention in 1788 and voted "no".[1145]

[1139] Ebenezer is a possible child in this family.
[1140] Jesse is a possible child in this family. It is possible that Jesse might belong to the family of Robert's brother Jonah. Jesse's parentage is uncertain.
[1141] Avon, Maine Town Records 1802-1827, FHL Film # 007592472, image 39 (p 62 of the record)
[1142] Butler, *History of Farmington, Franklin County, Maine*, p 562
[1143] Maine Wills and Probate, Kennebec County, Executor and Administration Bonds, volume 10, p 50; the estates of Jonah, Sr. and Jonah, Jr. entered probate on the same day.
[1144] *Colonial Soldiers and Officers in New England, 1620-1775.* (Online database: *AmericanAncestors.org*, New England Historic Genealogical Society, 2013). Massachusetts Officers and Soldiers in the French and Indian Wars, 1755-1756, p 49
[1145] A New Nation Votes, American Election Returns, 1788-1825, Massachusetts 1788 Constitutional Convention, https://elections.lib.tufts.edu/catalog/p8418n77q

Jonah and Lydia were in New Ipswich, New Hampshire and later in Albion, Maine. Jonah and his son Jonah died of the black death two days apart in 1814.[1146] Lydia died eight months later.

Jonah Crosby and Lydia Chandler were parents of nine children.[1147]

i   LYDIA CROSBY, b. at New Ipswich, 23 Nov 1758; d. at Sidney, ME, 24 Nov 1821; m. about 1778, FLINT BARTON, b. at Sutton, MA, 3 Dec 1749 son of Edmond and Anna (Flint) Barton; Flint d. at Sidney, 12 May 1833.

ii   JONAH CROSBY, b. at New Ipswich, 4 Dec 1762; d. at Albion, ME, 26 Apr 1814 (probate 10 May 1815 with Joseph Cammett as administrator);[1148] m. 8 Sep 1785, JANE MCKENNEY, b. 15 Apr 1765; Jane d. 29 Mar 1799.

iii   MARIAH CROSBY, b. at New Ipswich, 9 Feb 1763. There is a record for the birth although the date given in the index is just two months after the birth of Jonah.

iv   EZRA CROSBY, b. at New Ipswich, 22 Mar 1765; d. at Winslow, ME, 7 Apr 1814; m. 28 Aug 1788, TERESA SHERWIN, b. 24 Jun 1768 likely daughter of Elnathan and Eunice (Brown) Sherwin; Teresa d. after 1850 when living with her son Cummings Crosby and his family in Plymouth, ME. Teresa married second David Whitmore. Teresa Sherwin was first cousin of Robert Crosby who married Ezra's sister Abigail (see below).

v   MEHITABLE CROSBY, b. at New Ipswich, 16 Sep 1767; d. at Brownville, ME, 26 Aug 1842; m. ICHABOD THOMAS, b. 14 Mar 1758 son of Joseph and Eleanor (Baker) Thomas; Ichabod d. at Brownville, 24 Feb 1845. Ichabod Thomas was a Quaker and entered service in the Revolution after being drafted and served 58 days in 1776. Ichabod and his wife Mehitable Crosby were early settlers of Sidney, Maine. Ichabod was the first town clerk, served five terms as selectman, and was town treasurer. The family moved on from Sydney and finally settled in Brownville.[1149]

vi   ABIGAIL CROSBY, b. at Winslow, ME, 8 Feb 1770; d. at Albion, ME, 31 Mar 1844; m. her first cousin, ROBERT CROSBY, b. at New Ipswich, 6 Apr 1764 son of Robert and Susannah (Sherwin) Crosby; Robert d. at Albion, 29 Mar 1832.

vii   RHODA CROSBY, b. at Winslow, 20 Jan 1772; d. at Albion, 31 Jan 1854; m. DENNIS GETCHELL, b. 8 Feb 1771 son of Dennis Getchell; Dennis d. at Albion, 2 Nov 1852

viii   STEPHEN CROSBY, b. at Winslow, 4 Aug 1774; d. at Winslow, 5 Feb 1834; m. ABIGAIL LEARNED, b. At Auburn, MA, 20 Apr 1779 daughter of Haynes and Mary (Davis) Learned; Abigail d. at Winslow, 8 Sep 1850.

ix   SUSANNA CROSBY, b. at Winslow, 27 Mar 1778; d. at Albion, 13 Oct 1861; m. JOSEPH CAMMETT, b. at Candia, NH, 11 Jun 1774 son of Jonathan and Sarah (-) Cammett; Joseph d. at Albion, 27 Mar 1829.

435)   PHEBE CROSBY (*Mehitable Chandler Crosby Spalding⁴, Mehitable Russell Chandler³, Thomas², Robert¹*), baptized at Townsend, 10 Dec 1738 daughter of Robert and Mehitable (Chandler) Crosby; d. at Shirley, MA, 22 Jul 1826; m. at Westford, 7 Jul 1757, JABEZ KEEP, b. at Westford, 13 Dec 1736 son of Jabez and Sarah (Leonard) Keep; Jabez d. at Sheffield, MA, 21 Jan 1821. Jabez remarried the widow Elizabeth Rogers about 1785.[1150]

Jabez Keep served in the French and Indian War and participated in the campaign at Crown Point. He owned a farm in Harvard and had a trip-hammer forge and bloomery. He served in the Revolution enlisting with rank of sergeant and promoted through rank of captain by the close of the war. He was selectman in Harvard in 1783 and 1784.

Phebe and Jabez had five daughters and one son. Phebe took the five daughters, and they were later at the Shaker Village in Shirley where Phebe and three of the daughters remained.[1151] The youngest daughter left the Shaker community and married.

Jabez did not leave a will and his estate entered probate 8 May 1821 with his son George Keep as administrator. The heirs of the estate were the children form his second marriage: George Keep, Hannah Curtis, and Nancy Callender.[1152]

Jabez Keep and Phebe Crosby were parents of six children born at Harvard. Jabez also had three children with his second wife Elizabeth.

[1146] Early Families of Albion, Maine, http://www.albionme.com/albion_genealogy/getperson.php?personID=I363&tree=1
[1147] New Hampshire, Births and Christenings Index, 1714-1904; FHL Film Number 1000489 for those children born in New Ipswich.
[1148] Maine Wills and Probate, Kennebec County, Executor and Administration Bonds, volume 10, p 51
[1149] Piscataquis County Historical Society, *Historical Collections of Piscataquis County, Maine*, pp 198-199
[1150] Best, *John Keep of Longmeadow, Massachusetts*, p 25, pp 38-39; available on familysearch.org
[1151] Best, *John Keep of Longmeadow*, p 39
[1152] *Berkshire County, MA: Probate File Papers, 1761-1917*. Online database. *AmericanAncestors.org*. New England Historic Genealogical Society, 2017. Case 3916

i   JABEZ KEEP, b. 8 Sep 1759; d. at Pepperell, 22 Jun 1820; m. at Harvard, 1 Jun 1785, LYDIA PARKHURST, b. at Pepperell, 13 Oct 1762 daughter of Silas and Sarah (Atherton) Parkhurst;[1153] Lydia d. at Jay, ME, 14 Apr 1843.

ii   SARAH KEEP, b. 29 Aug 1763; d. at Shirly, MA, 27 Nov 1809.

iii   ELIZABETH KEEP, b. 9 Mar 1769; d. at Shirley, 13 Oct 1796.

iv   RUTH KEEP, b. 21 Mar 1771; d. at Shirley, 13 Apr 1794.

v   MEHITABLE KEEP, b. 8 Nov 1773; d. at Shirley, 3 Mar 1822.

vi   REBECCA KEEP, b. 1782; d. at Harvard by about 1807; m. at Harvard, 14 Dec 1803, BENJAMIN BARNARD, b. at Harvard, 12 Jun 1777 son of Jotham and Lucy (Wetherbee) Barnard; Benjamin d. at Harvard, 1 Jun 1857. Bernard married second about 1808 Jemima Whitcomb (first child born 1809). Rebecca does not seem to have had children.

436)   JOEL CROSBY (*Mehitable Chandler Crosby Spalding⁴, Mehitable Russell Chandler³, Thomas², Robert¹*), baptized at Townsend, 29 Jun 1740 son of Robert and Mehitable (Chandler) Crosby; d. at Winslow, ME, 27 Mar 1775; m. at Chelmsford, 30 Mar 1763, HANNAH STEVENS, b. at Chelmsford, 22 Jun 1737 daughter of Samuel and Ruth (Wright) Stevens; Hannah d. at Winslow, 28 Mar 1828. Hannah married second William Richardson.

     In his will written 13 February 1775 (probate 19 April 1775), Joel Crosby bequeathed to beloved wife Hannah one-half of the real and personal estate after the payment of debts and after the children are brought up to age eighteen. The other half of the estate is to be divided equally among his four daughters: Ruth Right Crosby, Hannah Crosby, Joanna Crosby, and Rebeckah Crosby. Hannah was named executrix.[1154]

     Joel and Hannah were parents of five children born at Winslow, Maine.

i   RUTH WRIGHT CROSBY, b. at New Ipswich, 20 Sep 1764; d. at Albion, ME, 1843 (probate 1843); m. THOMAS SMILEY, b. 1755; Thomas d. at Winslow, 1816 (will 18 May 1816).

ii   HANNAH CROSBY, b. 1767; d. at Unity, ME, 20 Jul 1842; m. 1ˢᵗ about 1784, ELISHA GRANT, b. about 1757; Elisha d. about 1788. Hannah m. 2ⁿᵈ about 1824, THOMAS GILPATRICK, b. 1767 son of Thomas and Hephzibah (Demsey) Gilpatrick; Thomas d. at Unity, 14 May 1845.

iii   JOANNA CROSBY, b. at Winslow, 12 Mar 1770; d. at Hampden, ME, 26 May 1815; m. BENJAMIN WHEELER, b. 1756; Benjamin d. at Hampden, 8 May 1800.

iv   REBECCA CROSBY, b. at Winslow, 18 May 1772; d. (burial at Winslow), 10 Nov 1843; m. at Winslow, 6 Sep 1788, ASHER HINDS, b. at West Boylston, MA, 11 Sep 1759 son of Benjamin and Elizabeth (Temple) Hinds;[1155] Asher d. at Clinton, ME, 19 Apr 1814.

v   SAMUEL CROSBY, b. 1774; d. at Winslow, 21 Jan 1775.

437)   SOLOMON SPAULDING (*Mehitable Chandler Crosby Spalding⁴, Mehitable Russell Chandler³, Thomas², Robert¹*), b. at Westford, 28 Sep 1748 son of Andrew and Mehitable (Chandler) Spalding; d. at Westford, 6 Aug 1826; m. 3 May 1780 by Rev. Matthew Scribner,[1156] JEMIMA REED, b. at Westford, 19 Nov 1761 daughter of Thomas and Susanna (Dutton) Reed; Jemima d. 3 Mar 1845.

     Solomon Spaulding served as sergeant in the company of Capt. Oliver Bates' militia company of Westford that marched at the alarm on 19 April 1775. He had additional service in the company of Capt. Joshua Parker for a 97-day period in 1775. He enlisted in Carpenter's regiment for a term of one year from July 1777.[1157] Solomon was later known as Lieut. Spaulding.

     On 17 June 1806, Solomon Spaulding conveyed 70 acres of property in Westford to Solomon Spaulding, Jr. for payment of $1500.[1158]

     Solomon and Jemima were parents of eleven children born at Westford, Massachusetts.

i   SOLOMON SPAULDING, b. 29 Oct 1780; m. 1ˢᵗ at Charlestown, MA, 29 Oct 1804, POLLY PETERSON, b. (recorded at Lebanon, NH) 19 Apr 1783 daughter of Turner and Polly (Manning) Peterson;[1159] Polly d. at Saratoga

---

[1153] The 1814 will of Silas Parkhurst includes a bequest to daughter Lydia wife of Jabez Keep.

[1154] Maine Genealogical Society, *The Probate Records of Lincoln, Maine 1760-1800*, pp 67-68

[1155] Hinds, *History and Genealogy of the Hinds Family*, p 35

[1156] Hodgman, *History of the Town of Westford*, p 379

[1157] Massachusetts Soldiers and Sailors in the Revolution, volume 14, p 695

[1158] Massachusetts Land Records, Middlesex County, 170:113

[1159] Browne, William Bradford, *The Peterson Family of Duxbury, Mass.*, p 10; reprint from NEHGR, April, July, and October 1916

Springs, NY, 24 Jul 1814. Solomon m. 2nd at Saratoga Springs, 30 Oct 1814, Polly's sister, SALLY PETERSON, b. 28 Feb 1795; Sally d. 4 Oct 1825. Solomon m. 3rd at Boston, 31 May 1827, MARY BOYNTON, b. 9 Jul 1781.

ii   JEMIMA "MARY" SPAULDING,[1160] b. 30 Sep 1782; d. at Randolph, MA, 3 Mar 1861; m. 30 Sep 1804, WILLIAM WORCESTER, b. at Randolph, 8 Nov 1780 son of Samuel and Isabel (Coburn) Worcester; William d. at Randolph, 1 Mar 1857.

iii   JAMES SPAULDING, b. 9 Mar 1785; d. at Dunstable, MA, 8 Jun 1870; m. 10 Mar 1806, ANNA TENNEY, b. at Ashby, 1787 daughter of Samuel and Esther (Parmenter) Tenney; Anna d. at Dunstable, 5 Dec 1869.

iv   ANDREW SPAULDING, b. 5 Feb 1788; d. at Bangor, NY, 26 Mar 1862; m. at Shelburne, VT, 1 Jan 1815, PERMELIA PLACE, b. 1793; Permelia d. at Bangor, 13 Mar 1855.

v   ANNA SPAULDING, b. 7 May 1790; d. 19 May 1790.

vi   THOMAS SPAULDING, b. 11 Jul 1791; d. at Lunenburg, 15 Oct 1844; m. 1st 8 Dec 1818, MARY HILTON, b. at Lunenburg, 4 Jul 1803 daughter of Stephen and Nancy (Braybrooks) Hilton; Mary d. 12 Nov 1839. Thomas m. 2nd 30 Mar 1841, SARAH LORING WHITING, b. at Lunenburg, 8 Sep 1799 daughter of Nathaniel and Lydia (Gardner) Whiting; Sarah d. at Lunenburg, 11 Dec 1886.

vii   MEHITABLE SPAULDING, b. 5 Oct 1793; d. at Westville, NY, 30 Apr 1857; m. 11 Apr 1816, THEODORE WOODWARD, b. at Tyngsboro, 16 Sep 1794 son of John and Esther (Parkhurst) Woodward; Theodore d. at Westville, 23 Dec 1874. After Mehitable's death, Theodore married Rebecca Mansfield on 13 Nov 1863.

viii   GEORGE WASHINGTON SPALDING, b. 8 May 1796; d. at Westford, 1 Jul 1868; m. 6 Dec 1821, RHODA FREDERICK, b. at Tyngsboro, 15 Jan 1799 daughter of George and Rhoda (Read) Frederick; Rhoda d. at Tyngsboro, 8 Dec 1880.

ix   SUSANNA SPALDING, b. 6 Nov 1797; m. at Westford, 30 Jan 1821, JOSEPH SMITH, b. at Westford, 27 Sep 1793 son of Thomas and Molly (Herrick) Smith.

x   ELI SPALDING, b. 4 Aug 1799; m. at Salem, 3 Apr 1825, ABIGAIL WHITING.

xi   ELIZA SPALDING, b. 27 Mar 1805; m. 17 Nov 1827, PARKER WOODWARD, b. at Tyngsboro, 22 Apr 1803 son of John and Mary Parker (Fletcher) Woodward.

438)   HENRY SPALDING (*Mehitable Chandler Crosby Spalding⁴, Mehitable Russell Chandler³, Thomas², Robert¹*), b. at Westford, 5 Jul 1750 son of Andrew and Mehitable (Chandler) Spalding; d. likely at Clinton, ME where he was living in 1810; m. about 1776, BETSEY TAGART.

Henry and Betsey were in Westford, Massachusetts but have relocated to Kennebec County, Maine at least by 1800[1161] and likely before that. The children given here are as given in the *Spalding Memorial*. The locations of the births are not certain.

i   JOHN TAGART SPALDING; died in the West Indies about age 25.[1162]

ii   HENRY SPALDING, b. about 1784; d. about 1811; m. about 1823, MARY "POLLY" REED, b. 10 Apr 1795 daughter of Thomas and Polly (Spalding) Reed. Polly married second Henry's brother Samuel (see below).

iii   ANDREW SPALDING, b. at Westford, 10 Sep 1786; d. at Sebasticook, ME, 10 Dec 1857; m. 19 Aug 1805, RUTH FOSS daughter of Joseph and Hannah (-) Foss.

iv   SAMUEL SPALDING, b. about 1790; d. at Clinton, ME, about 1822; m. 31 Dec 1812, MARY REED who was first married to Samuel's brother Henry (see above).

v   JAMES SPALDING

vi   JOSIAH SPALDING. The *Spalding Memorial* reports he died in infancy.

vii   MARTHA SPALDING, b. at Westford, 1 Dec 1793; d. at Buxton, ME after 1850 and before 1860; m. about 1814, JONATHAN CARLE, b. in York County, ME, 1787 son of Ebenezer and Susannah (Libby) Carle; Jonathan d. at Buxton, after 1870.

[1160] Jemima is Jemima on her birth record and Mary on her death record. Her date of birth of 30 Sep 1782 is on her gravestone. She is Mary in census records.
[1161] Year: 1800; Census Place: Miscellaneous Gores and Settlements, Kennebec, Maine; Series: M32; Roll: 7; Page: 87; Image: 252; Family History Library Film: 218677. Listed in 1800 with a household of nine including 4 boys and 3 girls.
[1162] Spalding, *The Spalding Memorial*, p 104

viii   ELIZABETH SPALDING, b. 1 Dec 1795; m. JOSEPH SMITH.

ix   MEHITABLE CHANDLER SPALDING, b. at Westford, 25 Jul 1797

x   HARRIET SPALDING, b. at Buxton, ME, 11 Aug 1800; d. at Biddeford, ME, 18 Jun 1881; m. 22 Nov 1830, AMOS WOODMAN, b. at Buxton, 16 Jul 1794 son of Moses and Abigail (Leavit) Woodman; Amos d. at Biddeford, 23 Dec 1859.

439)   RUTH SPALDING (*Mehitable Chandler Crosby Spalding⁴, Mehitable Russell Chandler³, Thomas², Robert¹*), b. at Westford, 15 May 1752 daughter of Andrew and Mehitable (Chandler) Spalding; d. at Temple, NH, 8 May 1790; m. at Westford, 3 Dec 1772, ISAAC BUTTERFIELD, b. 1 Nov 1750;[1163] Isaac d. at Wilton, ME, 12 Oct 1812. Isaac married second Ruth Butterfield on 22 Jul 1790.
Ruth and Isaac were parents of seven children born at Wilton, Maine. Isaac also had five children with his second wife Ruth Butterfield.

i   ISAAC BUTTERFIELD, b. 25 Nov 1773; d. at Wilton, 10 May 1816; m. at Farmington, ME, 19 Apr 1799, POLLY PEASE, b. 1776; Polly d. at Wilton, 16 Sep 1829.

ii   SOLOMON BUTTERFIELD, b. 19 Apr 1776; m. at Farmington, ME, 24 Apr 1800, HANNAH BUTTERFIELD.

iii   RUTH BUTTERFIELD, b. 18 Feb 1779; m. at Farmington, 24 Nov 1800, JOSEPH WEBSTER. Joseph and Ruth were parents of seven children born at Wilton, ME.

iv   ABRAHAM BUTTERFIELD, b. 27 Mar 1780; m. at Wilton, 23 Nov 1804, SUSANNAH KNOWLES.

v   JOSEPH BUTTERFIELD, b. 18 Apr 1782; died young

vi   DANIEL BUTTERFIELD, b. 13 Apr 1784; d. at Wilton, ME, 1816 (probate 16 Apr 1816 with widow Susannah); m. at Warren, ME, 26 Sep 1806, SUSANNAH ROLLINS.

vii   MEHITABLE BUTTERFIELD, b. 9 Feb 1788; d. at Wilton, ME, 6 Jan 1867; m. 1811, as his second wife, SAMPSON KEYES, b. at Westford, MA, 22 Nov 1777 son of Issachar and Elizabeth (Richardson) Keyes; Sampson d. at Wilton, ME, 24 Apr 1861. Sampson was first married to Betsey Little.

440)   ABIGAIL SPALDING (*Mehitable Chandler Crosby Spalding⁴, Mehitable Russell Chandler³, Thomas², Robert¹*), b. at Westford, 3 Jun 1754 daughter of Andrew and Mehitable (Chandler) Spalding; d. at Dunstable, MA, 19 Jan 1830;[1164] m. 1st at Westford, 28 Nov 1774, THOMAS RICHARDSON, b at Westford, 8 Jan 1751 son of Abiel and Sarah (Boynton) Richardson; Thomas d. at Temple, NH, 8 Apr 1786. Abigail m. 2nd 30 Dec 1794, OLIVER TAYLOR, b. 1 May 1746 son of Samuel and Susannah (Perham) Taylor; Oliver d. at Dunstable, 13 Oct 1823. Oliver Taylor was first married to Bridget Blodgett.
Abigail and her first husband Thomas Richardson resided in Temple, New Hampshire where they had a farm of about 150 acres. After his death, Abigail married Oliver Taylor who was a widower. They lived in Dunstable and had two children from the second marriage.
In his will written 6 April 1786 (proved 4 May 1786), Thomas Richardson bequeathed to beloved wife Abigail one-third of his stock and movable estate forever and the use of one-third of the real estate during her natural life. She receives the use of the other two-thirds of the estate for a term of ten years in order to bring up their children. She also receives a suit of mourning apparel. Abigail is empowered to give a deed to Daniel Foster for the so-called Borland farm. His two sons Thomas and Abiel receive an equal division of lands when they arrive at twenty-one. If either son dies before twenty-one, that half will be divided among all the children. Each of his four daughters are to receive thirty-seven and one-half Spanish milled dollars at age twenty-one: Abigail, Anna, Sarah, and Edee. Abigail Richardson was named sole executrix.[1165] Real estate was valued at £250.
In his will written 8 April 1819 (probate 11 November 1823), Oliver Taylor bequeathed to beloved wife Abigail, the use of one-third of the real estate during her life and one-half of the money in hand and notes due and one-third of the household furniture to be hers forever. She also receives a cow, four sheep, one swine, and other provisions for her support. Sons James, Oliver, and Josiah receive thirty dollars each. Daughter Rebecca Taylor receives two hundred dollars, one-third of the household furniture, and may live in the home while she is unmarried. Daughter Abigail Parkhurst receives two hundred-fifty dollars and one-third of the furniture. Son Cyrus receives the remainder of the estate and is named executor.[1166] James, Oliver, Josiah, Cyrus, and Rebecca were Oliver's children with his first wife Bridget.
Thomas Richardson and Abigail Spalding were parents of six children born at Temple, New Hampshire.

[1163] Maine, Nathan Hale Cemetery Collection, 1780-1980; date of birth is given on the cemetery record

[1164] Abigail, wid. Oliver, Jan. 19, 1830. [a. 75 y. G. R. 2.]

[1165] New Hampshire Wills and Probate, Hillsborough County, volume 1, pp 480-482

[1166] *Middlesex County, MA: Probate File Papers, 1648-1871.* Online database. *AmericanAncestors.org.* New England Historic Genealogical Society, 2014. Case 22227

i   ABIGAIL RICHARDSON, b. 14 Jun 1775; d. at Dunstable, MA, 9 Sep 1796. "Abigail, d. Thomas and Abigail, Sept. 9, 1796, in her 22d y. GR2" (grave inscription)

ii ANNA RICHARDSON, b. 22 Aug 1777; d. at Wilton, ME, 16 Aug 1846; m. at Dunstable, 8 Jun 1797, LUTHER CHENEY, b.at Groton, MA, 7 Jul 1775 son of John and Susannah (Farwell) Cheney; Luther d. at Wilton, 7 Sep 1851.

iii SARAH "SALLY" RICHARDSON, b. 8 Jul 1779; d. at Dunstable, MA, 14 May 1805; m. at Dunstable, 31 Aug 1797, CALEB READ, b. at Dunstable, 7 Jul 1775 son of Eleazer and Rachel (Cummings) Read; Caleb d. at Dunstable, 25 Nov 1838. Caleb married second Mrs. Caty Blodgett on 5 Dec 1805.

iv THOMAS RICHARDSON, b. 4 May 1781

v   ABIEL RICHARDSON, b. 31 May 1783; d. at Chester, VT, 8 Mar 1864; m. at Dunstable, 12 May 1805, RHODA PARKHURST, b. at Dunstable, MA, 12 Jan 1783 daughter of Joseph and Catherine (Taylor) Parkhurst; Rhoda d. at Chester, 5 Sep 1866.

vi EDEE RICHARDSON, b. 8 Jan 1786; d. at Jay, ME, 27 Sep 1871; m. at Dunstable, 26 Dec 1805, LEVI DAKIN, b. at Hudson, NH, 21 Apr 1782 son of Levi and Sarah (Hamblet) Dakin; Levi d. at Jay, 15 Apr 1874.

Abigail Spalding and Oliver Taylor were parents of two children born at Dunstable.

i   WILLIAM RICHARDSON TAYLOR, b. 13 Jun 1796; d. 28 Mar 1797.

ii ABIGAIL TAYLOR, b. 20 Jan 1798; d. at Dunstable, MA, 6 Sep 1868; m. at Dunstable, 5 Jun 1817, HENRY PARKHURST, b. 17 Jun 1793 son of Leonard and Hannah (Hills) Parkhurst; Henry d. at Dunstable, 4 Sep 1865.

441) EBENEZER CHANDLER (*Thomas Chandler⁴, Mehitable Russell Chandler³, Thomas², Robert¹*), b. at Andover, 14 May 1749 son of Thomas and Elizabeth (Walcott) Chandler; d. at Wilton, NH, 15 Sep 1823; m. 1st at Reading, MA, 29 Nov 1768, MARY BURNAP, likely b. at Reading, 1744 daughter of John and Ruth (Smith) Burnap; Mary d. at Wilton, 22 Oct 1778. Ebenezer m. 2nd 25 May 1779, SARAH AVERILL (widow of James Hutchinson), b. at Andover, 30 Nov 1751 daughter of Thomas and Sarah (Kneeland) Averill; Sarah d. at Wilton, 19 Jun 1794. Ebenezer m. 3rd REMEMBRANCE FLETCHER (widow of Levi Pierce), b. at Chelmsford, 23 Dec 1752 daughter of Robert and Remembrance (Foster) Fletcher; Remembrance d. at Temple, NH, 30 Nov 1833.
    Ebenezer's father died when Ebenezer was 11 years old. Just after his marriage to Mary Burnap, he settled in Wilton on lot eleven of the sixth range. Ebenezer was one of the first members of the Baptist church in Wilton when it was formed in 1817.[1167]
    Ebenezer Chandler and Mary Burnap were parents of five children born at Wilton.

i   MARY CHANDLER, b. 17 Oct 1769; d. at Nelson, NH, 11 Dec 1845; m. at Wilton, 27 Nov 1788, ISAAC JEWETT, b. at Hollis, 5 Jul 1763 son of Ezekiel and Lucy (Townsend) Jewett; Isaac d. at Nelson, 20 Nov 1852.

ii BETSY CHANDLER, b. 7 Feb 1771; d. (burial at Wilton), 3 Nov 1822; m. 1st JOHN PRINCE, b. about 1745 (age 66 at death) possibly the son of James and Hannah (Putnam) Prince born at Danvers; John d. at Wilton, 5 Jun 1811. Betsy m. 2nd at Wilton, Mar 1814, JOSEPH MELENDY, b. at Reading, MA, 12 Mar 1772 son of Richard and Martha (Burnap) Melendy; Joseph d. at Wilton, 12 Aug 1863. Joseph Melendy was first married to Abigail Blanchard (1780-1809).

iii EUNICE CHANDLER, b. 12 Feb 1773; d. at Munsonville, NH, 30 Jan 1840; m. at Wilton, 3 Nov 1800, TIMOTHY RUSSELL BUXTON, b. likely at Wilton, 7 Mar 1773 son of John and Elizabeth (Burnap) Buxton; Timothy d. at Nelson, NH, 10 Apr 1847.

iv RUTH CHANDLER, b. 15 Mar 1775; d. at Wilton, 12 Oct 1849; m. at Dunstable, MA, 12 Sep 1830, as his second wife, SAMUEL DOUGLASS, b. at Hollis, 22 Aug 1767 son of Samuel and Molly (Conant) Douglass; Samuel d. at Wilton, 18 May 1841. Samuel was first married to Sarah Seaver.

v   HANNAH CHANDLER, b. 27 Jul 1778; m. at Wilton, 15 Nov 1798, NATHANIEL BLODGETT, b. 1778 (age 46 at death); Nathaniel d. at Stoddard, NH, 27 Jul 1824.

Ebenezer Chandler and Sarah Averill were parents of nine children born at Wilton.

[1167] Livermore, *History of Wilton*, p 346, p 135

i   EBENEZER CHANDLER, b. 12 Mar 1780; d. 8 May 1781.

ii   EBENEZER CHANDLER, b. 14 May 1781; d. at Wilton, ME, 4 Feb 1859; m. DEMARIES HOWE, b. 1781 daughter of Joel and Mary (Templeton) Howe; Demaries d. at Wilton, ME, 23 Mar 1861.

iii   THOMAS CHANDLER, b. 8 Jan 1783; d. at Temple, ME, 26 Jan 1856; m. 1st 17 Nov 1805, DOROTHY "DOLLY" HOLT, b. at Temple, NH, 27 Jan 1776 daughter of Timothy and Ede (McIntire) Holt; Dolly d. at Temple, ME, 30 Dec 1827. Timothy m. 2nd at Temple, ME, 14 Oct 1828, SALLY AVERILL, b. 31 Dec 1786 daughter of David and Mary (Charlton) Averill;[1168] Sally d. at Solon, IA, 29 Feb 1880. Sally went to live in Iowa with her sister Fanny and her second husband Andrew Meacham by 1870.

iv   SARAH CHANDLER, b. 28 Feb 1785; d. at Wilton, NH, 22 Jan 1861; m. 1st 28 Nov 1820, JACOB CLARK; Jacob d. about 1834. Sarah m. 2nd 19 Feb 1835, EZRA CLARK who d. at Merrimack before 1850.

v   AMY CHANDLER, b. 18 Nov 1787; d. at Putney, VT, 13 Feb 1823; m. at Sullivan, NH, 8 Jun 1814, CHAPIN BOLSTER, b. at Stoddard, NH, 9 Feb 1784 son of Nathan and Chloe (Keith) Chapin; Chapin d. at Winhall, VT, 4 May 1866. Chapin married second Rebecca French.

vi   JOSEPH CHANDLER, b. 28 Jan 1789; d. at Wilton, 27 Aug 1837; m. 1st ASENATH PRATT, b. at Reading, MA, 14 May 1793 daughter of Edward and Asenath (Flint) Pratt; Asenath d. at Wilton, 7 Jan 1836. Joseph m. 2nd 3 Nov 1836, Asenath's sister DORCAS PRATT, b. at Reading 19 Sep 1795; Dorcas d. at Prattville, AL, 19 Apr 1872.

vii   EDNA CHANDLER, b. 6 Jun 1790; d. 21 Jun 1790.

viii   EDNA CHANLDER, B. 6 Sep 1791; d. at Chesterville, ME, 26 Oct 1871; m. at Wilton, 15 Oct 1815, NEHEMIAH BENNETT, b. 20 May 1791 likely son of Elisha and Lucy (Raymond) Bennett; Nehemiah d. at Chesterville, 30 Apr 1872.

ix   JOEL CHANDLER, b. 19 Jun 1794; d. at Weare, NH, 22 Aug 1860; m. 19 Feb 1818, LUCY BURNHAM GRAY, b. at Wilton, 18 Sep 1795 daughter of Timothy and Ruth (Burnham) Gray; Lucy d. at Weare, 22 Jun 1871.

---

442)   PETER CHANDLER (*Thomas Chandler⁴, Mehitable Russell Chandler³, Thomas², Robert¹*), b. at Andover, 25 Mar 1755 son of Thomas and Elizabeth (Walcott) Chandler; d. at Nelson, NH, 14 Jul 1819; m. 6 Mar 1787, MERCY INGALLS, b. at Andover, 29 Apr 1761 daughter of David and Priscilla (Howe) Ingalls; Mercy d. at Wilton, 12 Feb 1842.

Peter Chandler served during the Revolution from 1775 through 1780. Following his marriage to Mercy Ingalls, the family settled in Nelson (Packersfiled), New Hampshire in 1787 residing on Spoonwood pond also known as "Chandler" pond.[1169]

In May 1818, Peter Chandler of Nelson aged sixty-three gave a statement related to his application for pension. He enlisted from Andover, Massachusetts in 1775 in the company of Capt. Ames in the Col. Frye's regiment for a term of eight months. After that service, he enlisted in Capt. Benton's company of the Massachusetts line for a term of one year. His third enlistment was on 4 June 1777 for a term of three years in Capt. Frye's company of Col. Scammel's regiment of the New Hampshire line. Peter received a pension for his service at the rate of eight dollars per month, and his widow Mercy later received a widow's pension. A statement by Ebenezer Chandler relates that Peter was wounded by a musket ball in 1776.[1170]

In his will written 9 July 1819 (proved 11 September 1819), Peter Chandler bequeathed one dollar to each of his children: Moses, Elijah, Hannah Ingalls, and Priscilla. He bequeathed to his beloved wife any money due from his pension and she receives the residue of the estate to be at her use and disposal during her natural life. Brother-in-law Joshua Holt was named executor.[1171]

Son Elijah Chandler married but not happily. He had one daughter (who was born out-of-wedlock or perhaps was an adopted child). In his will written at Pope County, Arkansas 23 March 1860 and proved 28 June 1860, he made the following bequests. After first naming Maj. David West of Pope County the sole executor of his will, Elijah continued. "Second, to my wife Lydia B. Chandler (who married my property but not my self and who by her unkind treatment has driven me from my house and home to seek a shelter in the wide world and having at the time I left her given her the greatest portion of my property there is now nothing her due yet because the law requires it) I give her one dollar." To daughter Abby Ann Chandler, he bequeathed two thousand dollars and to his sister Hannah Ingalls wife of John Ingalls of Newport, New Hampshire, he left three hundred dollars. The remainder of the estate he gave to his daughter Abby Ann Chandler.[1172]

There are records for eight children of Peter and Mercy born at Nelson, New Hampshire.

[1168] Avery, *The Averell Family*, p 308

[1169] Struthers, A History of Nelson, New Hampshire, p 177

[1170] U. S. Revolutionary War Pension and Bounty-Land Warrant Application Files, Case W23783

[1171] New Hampshire Wills and Probate, Cheshire County, Estate Files, C280, will of Peter Chandler

[1172] Arkansas Wills and Probate Records, Pope County, Wills Book B, pp 29-30

i   MOSES CHANDLER, b. 13 Apr 1788; d. at Jackson County, IL, 12 Apr 1850; m. at Vigo County, IN, 25 Feb 1829, MATILDA TRYON (widow of Benjamin Johnson), b. about 1806 daughter of Jeremiah and Mary Ann (-) Tryon;[1173] Matilda d. Oct 1841. Moses m. 2nd at Williamson, IL, 29 Mar 1845, MARY OWENS.

ii   ELIJAH CHANDLER, b. 8 Feb 1790; d. at Dover, AR, 1860 (probate 1860); m. in NH, 9 Feb 1837, LYDIA BURTON (widow of Lubin Rockwood), b. at Wilton, 7 May 1793 daughter of Abraham and Elizabeth (Dale) Burton; Lydia d. at New Ipswich, Oct 1869. Elijah and Lydia separated. Elijah had one child in Arkansas, Abby Ann Chandler, born in Dover, AR on 27 Nov 1850. Elijah was a carpenter. Abby Ann Chandler was raised by Maj. David West.

iii   HANNAH CHANDLER, b. 17 Jul 1792; m. at Packersfield (Nelson), NH, 8 Jan 1811, JOHN INGALLS, b. at Wilton, NH, 16 May 1784 son of David and Anna (Winn) Ingalls. John and Hannah were living in Newport, NH in 1860.

iv   NATHANIEL CHANDLER, b. 19 Apr 1794; d. 11 Sep 1795.

v   PRISCILLA CHANDLER, b. 12 Jun 1796; d. at Nelson, 1830. Priscilla did not marry.

vi   RUTH CHANDLER, b. Jul 1798; d. 23 Jan 1800.

vii   SALLY CHANDLER, b. 15 Apr 1800; d. at Nelson, 1813.

viii NATHANIEL CHANDLER, b. 27 Jun 1802; died before father's will.

443)   ASA CHANDLER (*Thomas Chandler⁴, Mehitable Russell Chandler³, Thomas², Robert¹*), b. at Andover, 25 Apr 1759 son of Thomas and Elizabeth (Walcott) Chandler; d. at Stoddard, NH, 7 Dec 1822 (will 6 Dec 1822); m. 20 Nov 1781, ELINOR RICHARDSON, b. 22 Jul 1753; Eleanor d. 6 Dec 1834.[1174]

       Asa Chandler was a mariner and served as seaman on the sloop *Tyrannicide* commanded by Capt. John Fisk during the Revolution. He served from 2 July 1776 to 30 September 1776 and again from 30 September 1776 to discharge on 1 January 1777. He was wounded 13 July 1776. He perhaps was again wounded at the end of 1776 and was reported as "left on shore" at his discharge.[1175] His wound was reported on his left arm and that he lost two to three inches of the bone in that arm.[1176]

       Asa and Elinor resided in Stoddard, New Hampshire where Asa was a mill owner, his mills known as Chandler's Mills.

       In his will written 6 December 1822 (proved 4 January 1823), Asa bequeathed to wife Elinor the use and occupation of one-half of the real and personal estate during her natural life except that portion bequeathed to son Asa. After Elinor's decease, that half is to be divided equally between daughters Elinor and Achsa. The bequests to his daughters are to be to their use and benefit forever. Son Asa Chandler, Jr. receives the other half of the estate including the mills as well as the fifth lot in the twelfth range in the town of Stoddard. Son Asa was named executor.[1177]

       Asa and Elinor were parents of four children born at Stoddard.

i   ASA CHANDLER, b. at Stoddard, 19 Nov 1782; d. at Keene, NH, 28 Dec 1833; m. at Stoddard, 6 Apr 1819, SARAH BARRETT (widow of Isaac Fisher), b. at Mason, NH, 6 Apr 1780 daughter of Reuben and Mary (-) Barrett;[1178] Sarah d. at Dow City, IA, 27 Sep 1850.

ii   ELINOR CHANDLER, b. 15 Apr 1785; d. at Stoddard, 26 Nov 1851. Elinor did not marry.

iii   LUKE CHANDLER, b. 24 May 1787; d. at Stoddard, 14 Oct 1804.

iv   ACHSAH CHANDLER, b. 12 Sep 1794; d. after 1860 when she was living at Stoddard. Achsah did not marry.

444)   MARY HOLT (*Mary Chandler Holt⁴, Mehitable Russell Chandler³, Thomas², Robert¹*), baptized at Andover, 18 May 1735 daughter of James and Mary (Chandler) Holt; d. after 1811; m. 1st, 3 Sep 1754, NATHANIEL ANDREWS likely the son of Thomas and Ruth (Bixbee) Andrews; Nathaniel d. at Boxford, 1759 (probate 1759). Mary m. 2nd, 19 Nov 1761, JACOB ANDREWS; Jacob d. at Boxford, 1786 (probate 3 Oct 1786).

[1173] Chandler, *Descendants of William and Annis Chandler*, p 219

[1174] Chandler, *Descendants of William and Annis Chandler*

[1175] Massachusetts Soldiers and Sailors in the Revolutionary War, volume 3, p 284.

[1176] Chandler, *Descendants of William and Annis Chandler*, p 220

[1177] New Hampshire Wills and Probate Records, Will volume 76, pp 119-120

[1178] Hill, *History of the Town of Mason*, p 200

Nathaniel Andrews did not leave a will and his estate entered probate 24 September 1759 with widow Mary as administratrix. The dower was not set off to the widow until 1811 after Mary petitioned to the court noting that the dower was never set off to her. This request followed the death of her son Jacob in 1811 and the timing seems related to that.[1179]

Jacob Andrews did not leave a will and his estate entered probate 3 October 1786 with son Jacob as administrator. The total value of the estate was £91.13.4 with the only real estate being 3 acres of upland and 26 acres of pasture. Debts were £148.8.4.[1180]

Mary Holt and Nathaniel Andrews were parents of one child born at Boxford.

i   JOHN ANDREWS, b. 7 Nov 1758

Mary Holt and Jacob Andrews were parents of nine children born at Boxford.

i   JACOB ANDREWS, b. 9 Aug 1762; d. at Boxford 1811[1181] (probate 21 Jan 1811 with widow Jane as administratrix); m. at Topsfield, 1 Apr 1792, JANE GOULD, b. at Topsfield, 30 Jul 1746 daughter of Simon and Jane (Palmer) Gould; Jane d. at Boxford, 24 Feb 1837.

ii   MARY ANDREWS, b. 27 Feb 1764; d. at Boxford, 13 Jan 1810; m. at Boxford, 18 Apr 1794, OLIVER WHITE, baptized at Wenham, 3 Sep 1758 son of Thomas and Lucy (Fiske) White.

iii   NATHANIEL ANDREWS, b. 5 Sep 1765

iv   BETTY ANDREWS, b. 30 Mar 1767; d. at Topsfield, 7 Oct 1851; m. at Topsfield, 3 Mar 1791, NATHANIEL GOULD, b. at Topsfield, 16 Jul 1753 son of Thomas and Mary (Gould) Gould; Nathaniel d. at Topsfield, 3 Jul 1842. Nathaniel was first married to Hannah Killam.

v   HANNAH ANDREWS, b. 15 Jun 1769; d. at Newburyport, 8 Dec 1829; m. at Boxford, 27 Dec 1792, JOHN DORMAN, b. at Boxford, 18 Jun 1763 son of John and Hannah (Jackson) Dorman; John d. at Newburyport, 25 Dec 1857.

vi   DOLLY ANDREWS, b. 25 Dec 1770; d. at Boxford, 1811 (probate Oct 1811 with Seth Saltmarsh as administrator). Dolly did not marry.

vii   ANNA ANDREWS, b. 23 Feb 1774; d. at Cambridge, 11 Apr 1844 (although resident of Salem at time of death); m. at Boxford, 18 Oct 1803, SETH SALTMARSH, b. at Andover, 12 Apr 1778 son of Seth and Ruth (Bowman) Saltmarsh; Seth d. at Salem, 19 Jan 1836.

viii   JOSHUA ANDREWS, b. 30 Nov 1775

ix   ESTHER ANDREWS, b. 16 Dec 1777; d. at Salem, 5 Jun 1861; m. at Salem, 20 Jan 1811, her third cousin, ABIEL WARDWELL (*Bethiah Holt Wardwell⁵, Lydia Holt Holt⁴, Thomas Holt³, Mary Russell Holt², Robert¹*), b. at Andover, 25 Aug 1771 son of Solomon and Bethiah (Holt) Wardwell; Abiel d. of consumption at Charleston, SC, 30 Jan 1821 (probate 3 Apr 1821). Captain Abiel Wardwell was a master mariner and captained the brig *Britannia*.[1182] Other vessels he captained were the *Betsey, Astrea*, and *Eunice*.[1183] Abiel was first married to Hannah Elledge.

445)   BRIDGET HOLT (*Mary Chandler Holt⁴, Mehitable Russell Chandler³, Thomas², Robert¹*), baptized at Andover, 16 Jan 1737 daughter of James and Mary (Chandler) Holt; m. at Boxford, 16 Oct 1757, as his second wife, LEVI ANDREWS, b. at Boxford, 27 Aug 1727 son of Thomas and Ruth (Bixbee) Andrews.   Levi was first married to Sarah Towne.

Bridget and Levi started in Boxford, were in Hudson, New Hampshire for a time before finally settling in Nottingham West before 1775.

Bridget Holt and Levi Andrews were parents of eight children.

i   LYDIA ANDREWS, b. at Boxford, 14 Jan 1758

ii   MARY ANDREWS, baptized at Boxford 15 Nov 1761

iii   LETITIA ANDREWS, b. at Nottingham, 20 Aug 1762; m. EBENEZER CUMMINGS

[1179] *Essex County, MA: Probate File Papers, 1638-1881.* Online database. *AmericanAncestors.org.* New England Historic Genealogical Society, 2014. Case 693

[1180] *Essex County, MA: Probate File Papers, 1638-1881.* Online database. *AmericanAncestors.org.* New England Historic Genealogical Society, 2014. Case 635

[1181] Andrews, Jacob, -, 1811, a. 48 y. P. R. 29.

[1182] Salem and Beverly, Massachusetts, Crew Lists and Shipping Articles, 1797-1934

[1183] Wardwell Family Papers, Phillips Library, Peabody Essex Museum

iv   JOEL ANDREWS, b. at Nottingham, NH, 3 Sep 1764

v   LEVI ANDREWS, b. at Nottingham, 2 Oct 1766; d. at Greenfield, NH, 29 Nov 1825; m. about 1788, BETSEY
          COLBY, b. about 1768.[1184]

vi   JAMES ANDREWS, b. 12 Oct 1768

vii   THOMAS ANDREWS, b. at Nottingham, 2 May 1771; d. at Hudson, NH, 4 Apr 1847; m. about 1795, HANNAH
          MARSHALL, b. at Nottingham, 4 Oct 1774 daughter of John and Susannah (Smith) Marshall; Hannah d. 16 Feb
          1800.

viii   HANNAH ANDREWS, b. at Nottingham, 3 Jan 1780; m. JOHN ESTEY.

446)   ZELA HOLT (*Mary Chandler Holt⁴, Mehitable Russell Chandler³, Thomas², Robert¹*), b. at Andover, 29 Dec 1738 son
of James and Mary (Chandler) Holt; d. likely at Bethel, ME; m. at Andover, 16 Nov 1762, his second cousin, PRISCILLA
ABBOTT, b. at Andover, 13 Feb 1742/3 daughter of Barachias and Hannah (Holt) Abbott.
          Priscilla Abbott and Zela Holt married in Andover, were for a time in Wilton, New Hampshire where some of their
children were born, and finally settled in Bethel, Maine around 1790.[1185][1186] Their six children were likely born in Wilton,
although the birth of one child is recorded in Bethel and the baptism of the youngest child was recorded at Andover.

i   CALVIN HOLT, b. 26 Aug 1763; d. 27 Mar 1795.

ii   JAMES HOLT, b. about 1765; d. perhaps at Bethel; m. at Reading, MA, 28 Feb 1793, MEHITABLE EATON, b. at
          Reading, Jul 1773 daughter of Timothy and Mehitable (Burnup) Eaton.

iii   PRISCILLA HOLT, b. at Wilton, 2 Jan 1768; d. at Bethel, 4 Jan 1848; m. 23 May 1791, JOHN STEARNS, b. Aug
          1762 son of John and Martha (Harrington) Stearns; John d. at Bethel, 14 Dec 1826.

iv   TIMOTHY ABBOT HOLT, b. 15 Aug 1773; d. at Bethel, 1856; m. at Andover, 17 Jan 1799, ANNA STEVENS, b.
          at Andover, 5 Jul 1774 daughter of Peter and Abigail (Johnson) Stevens; Anna d. at Bethel, 1861.

v   MARY HOLT, b. about 1775; d. 18 Feb 1790.

vi   BRIDGET HOLT, baptized Mar 1777; d. at Bethel, after 1850. Bridget did not marry. In 1850, she was living
          with her brother Timothy in Bethel.

447)   JESSE HOLT (*Mary Chandler Holt⁴, Mehitable Russell Chandler³, Thomas², Robert¹*), b. at Andover, 8 Oct 1739 son of
James and Mary (Chandler) Holt; d. of consumption, at Tewksbury, Feb 1817; m. at Tewksbury, 30 Aug 1781, MARY CLARK, b.
at Tewksbury, 26 May 1745 daughter of Nathaniel and Mary (Wyman) Clark. Mary was first married at Tewksbury, 29 Jun
1769 to MOSES GRAY, baptized at Andover, 11 Jan 1747 son of Robert and Lydia (Peabody) Gray; Moses d. at Tewksbury, 11
Sep 1775.
          Jesse married Mary Clark Gray a widow with three children. Mary was first married to Moses Gray. Moses Gray and
Mary Clark were parents of three children born at Tewksbury (these three children are not descendants of Robert Russell).

i   MOSES GRAY, b. 20 Jan 1770; d. at Hancock, NH, 24 May 1847; m. at Tewksbury, 26 Jul 1791, MARY
          SCARLETT, b. at Tewksbury, 26 Aug 1767 daughter of Newman and Betty (Peacock) Scarlett; Mary d. at
          Hancock, 10 Apr 1832.

ii   HENRY GRAY, b. 25 Jul 1772; d. 24 Feb 1810 when crushed by his cartwheel on the road from Boston to
          Tewksbury;[1187] m. at Tewksbury, 20 Oct 1797, SYBIL FARMER, b. at Tewksbury, 3 Dec 1774 daughter of Peter
          and Ednah (Hardy) Farmer; Sybil d. after 1850 when she was living in Tewksbury.

iii   JOHN GRAY, b. 10 Aug 1775; d. at Tewksbury, 3 Nov 1837; m. at Tewksbury, 11 Aug 1796, LUCY FLETCHER.

          Jesse Holt and Mary Clark were parents of one child.

[1184] The family bible of Levi Andrews and Betsey Colby, including three pages of family births, deaths, and marriages, is extant and can be seen at
the following site: https://www.heirloomsreunited.com/2018/06/bible-of-levi-andrews-and-betsey-colby.html
[1185] Lapham, *History of Bethel*, p 563
[1186] Livermore, *History of Wilton*, p 407
[1187] Henry, coming from Boston fell under the wheel of his wagon and was instantly killed, Feb. 24, 1810, a. 35 y. C. R. 1. [a. 34 y. G. R. 2.]

i   MOLLY HOLT, b. at Tewksbury, 29 Sep 1784; m. at Tewksbury, 22 Apr 1810, LOAMMI KITTREDGE, b. at Tewksbury, 14 Jun 1785 son of John and Abigail (Dutton) Kittredge. Loammi and Mary were living in Tewksbury in 1820 with what appear to be three young children. No further record was found for them.

448)   THOMAS CHANDLER (*Joseph Chandler⁴, Mehitable Russell Chandler³, Thomas², Robert¹*), b. at Groton, 20 Jan 1746 son of Joseph and Sarah (Richardson) Chandler. The name of his wife is unknown.

Chandler's genealogy reports that Thomas was a blacksmith and died of spotted fever near Boston about 1800 "leaving a large family" perhaps one a son named Norman.[1188] There is evidence for three children in Northborough, Massachusetts.

i   MARY CHANDLER, b. about 1774; d. at Northborough, 13 Jun 1828; m. at Northborough, 1794, BAXTER RICE, b. at Northborough, 4 May 1772 son of Seth and Ruth (Coolidge) Rice; Baxter d. at Northborough, 1851.

ii   HENRY CHANDLER, baptized at Northborough, 15 Aug 1790

iii   NORMAN CHANDLER, baptized at Northborough, 15 Aug 1790

449)   JOHN CHANDLER (*Joseph Chandler⁴, Mehitable Russell Chandler³, Thomas², Robert¹*), b. at Groton, MA, 29 May 1749 son of Joseph and Sarah (Richardson) Chandler; d. at Westhampton, MA, about 1824; m. 1ˢᵗ at Sutton, MA, 8 Jun 1775, ELIZABETH ESTY, b. 19 Nov 1755; Elizabeth d. at Lunenburg, 19 Apr 1812. John m. 2ⁿᵈ at Easthampton, 26 May 1815, REBEKAH ALVORD, b. about 1768 daughter of Zebadiah and Rebecca (Searle) Alvord; Rebekah d. at Easthampton, 7 May 1820.

John Chandler and Elizabeth Esty were parents of nine children.[1189] The births are recorded in various locations.

i   ABIGAIL CHANDLER, b. at Brimfield, MA, 21 Jun 1778; d. at Lowell, MA, 10 May 1866; m. at Putney, VT, 11 Feb 1799, AARON FISKE, b. at Templeton, MA, 2 Jan 1777 son of Aaron and Tabitha (Metcalf) Fiske; Aaron d. at Guildhall, VT, 30 Sep 1822 (probate 5 Oct 1822).

ii   JOHN CHANDLER, b. at Palmer, MA, 22 Apr 1783; d. at Lunenburg, VT, 16 Jun 1871; m. 1ˢᵗ 28 Jan 1810, SARAH WHIPPLE, b. 11 Apr 1783 daughter of John and Sarah (Chamberlain) Whipple; Sarah d. at Lunenburg, VT, 22 Nov 1822. John m. 2ⁿᵈ 23 Mar 1824, NANCY WHIPPLE, b. 12 Nov 1797 daughter of Jonathan Whipple; Nancy d. at Lunenburg, 13 Feb 1853. John m. 3ʳᵈ 28 Jun 1854, BETSEY E. PORTER, b. in NH, about 1798; Betsey d. at Haverhill, NH, 29 Mar 1882.

iii   WILLIAM CHANDLER, b. at Sturbridge, MA, 15 Jun 1785; d. at Lunenburg, VT, Apr 1813; m. 24 Dec 1807, POLLY BLOSS, b. 19 Mar 1789 daughter of Walter and Hannah (Wilder) Bloss.

iv   HANNAH CHANDLER, b. 24 Aug 1788; d. at Lunenburg, VT, 23 Nov 1863; m. 3 Oct 1808, DANIEL BARNES, b. at Townshend, VT, 28 Nov 1779 daughter of Thomas and Anna (-) Barnes; Daniel d. at Lunenburg, 9 Aug 1838.

v   REUBEN CHANDLER, b. at Westmoreland, NH, 1 Apr 1791; d. at Lunenburg, VT, 9 Apr 1875; m. at Townshend, VT, Jan 1814, FANNY WHIPPLE, b. 22 Jun 1795 daughter of John and Sarah (Chamberlain) Whipple; Fanny d. 19 Apr 1866.

vi   ISAAC CHANDLER, b. at Chesterfield, NH, 30 May 1793

vii   SARAH CHANDLER, b. at Chesterfield, 11 May 1795; m. at Bath, NH, 14 Jan 1819, Dr. OGDEN BUTLER NEWTON, b. at Pomfret, VT, 18 Jul 1791 son of Isaac and Betsey (Quitterfield) Newton; Ogden d. at Franconia, 13 Feb 1836. Sarah was living in Franconia in 1860.

viii   DAVID CHANDLER, b. at Westmoreland, NH, 23 Apr 1797

ix   JOEL CHANDLER, b. at Putney, VT, 29 Mar 1799; d. at Charleston, MI, 16 Dec 1863; m. 24 Jan 1830, REBECCA MORSE, b. at Delhi, NY, 7 Apr 1805;[1190] Rebecca d. at Parsons, KS, 15 Dec 1880.

450)   JOB ABBOT (*Hannah Chandler Abbott⁴, Mehitable Russell Chandler³, Thomas², Robert¹*), b. likely at Pembroke, NH about 1742 son of David and Hannah (Chandler) Abbot; d. at West Barnet, VT, 15 Dec 1815; m. about 1771, PHEBE FARNUM, b. at Andover, 15 Dec 1750 daughter of Ebenezer and Priscilla (Ingalls) Farnum.

[1188] Chandler, *Descendants of William and Annis Chandler*, p 114

[1189] The Chandler genealogy reports information on births of children as coming from the family bible record.

[1190] Chandler, *Descendants of William and Annis Chandler*, p 451

Job Abbot and Phebe Farnum were parents likely of ten children, the oldest six children born at Pembroke, New Hampshire and the youngest four born perhaps at Barnet, Vermont.[1191] Of the six children who married, four of them married children from newly arrived families from Scotland, three of them children of Walter and Janet (Stuart) Brock.

i   SARAH ABBOTT, b. at Pembroke, 21 Mar 1772; d. at Barnet, VT, 14 Sep 1851; m. ALEXANDER STUART, b. in Scotland, 1768 son of Claudius and Janet (McFarlane) Stuart; Alexander d. at Barnet, 2 Mar 1840.

ii   HANNAH ABBOTT, b. at Pembroke, 30 Dec 1773; m. JONATHAN DARLING, b. at Hampstead, NH, 20 Dec 1767 son of John and Phebe (Robards) Darling; Jonathan d. at Groton, VT, 9 Oct 1820.

iii   PHEBE ABBOTT, b. at Pembroke, 28 Feb 1775; d. at Barnet, VT, 5 Oct 1873; m. JOHN BROCK, b. Glasgow, Lanarkshire, Scotland, 31 Oct 1768 son of Walter and Janet (Stuart) Brock;[1192] John d. at Barnet, 5 Nov 1852.

iv   SUSANNA ABBOTT, b. at Pembroke, Dec 1778; d. at Cabot, VT, 24 Sep 1862; m. about 1798, JOSIAH DARLING, b. at Hampstead, NH, 14 Jun 1772 son of John and Phebe (Robards) Darling; Josiah d. at Ryegate about 1830. Susanna m. 2nd, Mr. Lane (or Laird) who has not been identified. Susannah m. 3rd, at Cabot, 16 Apr 1849, ANTHONY PERRY, b. at Cabot, 7 Apr 1774 son of Benjamin and Susannah (Potter) Perry; Anthony d. at Cabot, 1 Dec 1854.

v   JOHN ABBOTT, b. at Pembroke, 27 Aug 1780; d. at Barnet, VT, 5 Sep 1854; m. ANNA BROCK, b. at Barnet, 1 Sep 1780 daughter of Walter and Janet (Stuart) Brock; Anna d. at Barnet, 15 Dec 1870.

vi   MARY ABBOTT, b. at Pembroke, 1782; d. at Peacham, VT, 20 Jul 1864; m. at Barnet, 18 Feb 1805, JAMES BROCK, b. at Barnet, 27 Sep 1783 son of Walter and Janet (Stuart) Brock; James d. at Barnet, 27 Jul 1847.

vii   JEROME JEREMIAH ABBOTT, b. about 1785; d. 1802.

viii   PRISCILLA ABBOTT, b. about 1786; likely died young.

ix   JOB ABBOTT, b. likely at Barnet, about 1788; reported to have "gone West" with no records located.

x   JANET ABBOTT, b. about 1789; likely died young.

451)   BRIDGET ABBOT (*Hannah Chandler Abbott⁴, Mehitable Russell Chandler³, Thomas², Robert¹*), b. in NH, about 1761 daughter of David and Hannah (Chandler) Abbot; d. at Harmony, OH, after 1850; m. 1st, 24 Dec 1787, her third cousin, PHINEAS AMES, b. 7 Sep 1764 son of Samuel and Elizabeth (Stevens) Ames; Phineas d. about 1792. Bridget m. 2nd, 17 Dec 1793, STEPHEN HARRIMAN, b. at Haverhill, MA, 10 Mar 1757 son of Stephen and Sarah (Mascraft) Harriman; Stephen d. at Lisbon, OH, 25 Feb 1828. Stephen Harriman was first married to Lucy Story.

No children were identified for Bridget Abbot and Phineas Ames. Following the death of Phineas, Bridget married Stephen Harriman who was also widowed and had four children from his first marriage. After spending time in Tunbridge, Vermont the family relocated to Clark County, Ohio.

Stephen Harriman did not leave a will and a report on the inventory of the estate was made 22 April 1828 with the final settlement in March 1834. George W. Harriman was administrator. The heirs-at-law, in addition to George W. Harriman, were Bridget Harriman, Noah and Sarah Norton, Isaac and Mary Chamberlain, Stephen Harriman, Ira Harriman, James and Betty Hackett, Thomas Harriman, John and Sophronia Lasky, and Flanders children (Lucy, Charlotte, Walter, James, Stephen, Sarah, William, and Arthur). The real estate was sold to settle the debts of the estate. The sale of the property brought $3,465 and $1,033.97 was paid to creditors.[1193] Sarah Norton, Mary Chamberlain, Stephen Harriman, and the Flanders grandchildren are heirs from Stephen Harriman's first marriage to Lucy Story.

Bridget Abbot and Stephen Harriman had four children who were living at the time of the probate of Stephen's estate in 1828. There are birth records in Tunbridge, Vermont for three of the children. It is possible there were other children who died before adulthood.

i   IRA HARRIMAN, b. 24 Nov 1795; d. at Madison, OH, 7 Jul 1857; m. at Ashtabula, OH, 16 Jan 1823, LOEY BROWN, b. 18 Sep 1803 daughter of Solomon and Lydia (Walton) Brown; Loey d. at Madison, OH, 24 May 1884.

ii   SOPHRONIA HARRIMAN, b. at Tunbridge, 18 Sep 1800; m. 1st, at Clark County, OH, 14 Jun 1829, JOHN LASKY; John d. before 1850. Sophronia m. 2nd, at Kane, IL, 27 May 1850, EDWARD GRAY, b. in Germany, about

---

[1191] The four youngest children are given in the *History of Ryegate*, but not in other sources and there are no other records associated with them. Of these four youngest children, three are reported to died in childhood and the fourth, son Job, is reported to have "gone West."
[1192] *Scotland, Select Births and Baptisms, 1564-1950.*
[1193] Ohio Probate Records, Clark County, Administration Records 1828-1836, pp 62-63; Settlements 1827-1844, volume 1, pp 327-329

1790; Edward d. before 1857. Sophronia m. 3rd, at Houston, MN, 14 Jun 1857, GEORGE HOLLIDAY, b. in England, about 1815.

iii   THOMAS JEFFERSON HARRIMAN, b. at Tunbridge, 25 May 1801; *perhaps* m. at Champaign, OH, 20 May 1830, MARGERY ALEXANDER.

iv   GEORGE WASHINGTON HARRIMAN, b. at Tunbridge, 2 Sep 1803; d. at Garnett, KS, 16 Feb 1875; m. 1st, at Clark County, OH, 22 Nov 1835, ELIZABETH MORRIS, b. likely at Clark County, about 1815 daughter of Joseph and Lavina (Drake) Morris;[1194] Elizabeth d. before 1850. George m. 2nd, 23 Aug 1851, SARAH ANN CAMPBELL, b. in OH, Apr 1835 of undetermined parents; Sarah was still living in 1900 in Indianapolis with her daughter Ida and her husband.

452)   ABIGAIL EATON (*Abigail Russell Eaton⁴, Robert³, Thomas², Robert¹*), b. at Reading, about 1736 daughter of Ebenezer and Abigail (Russell) Eaton; d. at Reading, Nov 1817; m. about 1755, as his second wife, JONATHAN BATCHELDER, b. at Reading, 22 Mar 1730 son of Jonathan and Sarah (Lewis) Batchelder; Jonathan d. at Reading, 6 Oct 1817. Jonathan was first married to PHEBE HOLT, b. at Reading, 22 Jun 1731 daughter of Joseph and Abigail (Rich) Holt; d. at Reading, 3 Nov 1754.

In his will written 2 February 1795 (probate 4 November 1817), Jonathan Batchelder bequeathed to beloved wife Abigail the use of all the household stuff during her natural life, the use of a room in the house and access to the cellar, and a lengthy list of specific provisions to be provided annually by the executor. After Abigail's decease, daughter Sarah is to have one bed and the residue of the household items are to be divided among his three youngest daughters Abigail, Sarah, and Lydia. Wearing apparel is to be divided among his three sons Jonathan, Ebenezer, and John. The executor is to pay within twelve months £4 to daughters Abigail, Sarah, and Lydia and to the children of daughter Phebe deceased. The remainder of the estate goes to son John Batchelder who is also named executor.[1195]

Jonathan Batchelder and Phebe Holt were parents of three children. Phebe died giving birth to twin daughters. The children of Jonathan and Phebe are not Robert Russell descendants.

i   JONATHAN BATCHELDER, b. at Reading, 11 Nov 1752; d. at Mason, NH, 7 Apr 1838 (probate 2 May 1838); m. at Reading, 11 Mar 1784, MARY "POLLY" DIX, b. at Reading, 7 Aug 1758 daughter of John and Mary (-) Dix.[1196]

ii   PHEBE BATCHELDER, b. at North Reading, 3 Nov 1754; d. at Blue Hill, ME, 3 Nov 1790; m. at Reading, 26 Nov 1782, her third cousin once removed, NICHOLAS HOLT (*Nicholas Holt⁴, Nicholas Holt³, Mary Russell Holt², Robert¹*), b. at Andover, Feb 1756 son of Nicholas and Lois (Phelps) Holt; Nicholas d. at Blue Hill, 27 Mar 1838. Nicholas m. 2nd at Blue Hill, 13 Apr 1795, MOLLY WORMWOOD. Phebe Batchelder and Nicholas Holt are Family 254.

iii   HANNAH BATCHELDER, twin of Phebe, b. 3 Nov 1754; likely died young.

Jonathan Batchelder and Abigail Eaton were parents of six children born at Reading.

i   ABIGAIL BATCHELDER, b. 28 Sep 1756; m. at Reading (intention) 5 Mar 1776, DANIEL GOWING, b. at Wilmington, 5 Jul 1764 son of Daniel and Sarah (Burnett) Gowing; Daniel d. at Wilmington, 13 May 1819.

ii   EBENEZER BATCHELDER, b. 27 Jun 1758; m. BETTY DIX, b. at Reading, 12 Jan 1769 son of John and Mary(-) Dix;[1197] Betty d. at Lyndeborough, NH, 11 Oct 1838.

iii   JOHN BATCHELDER, b. 24 Nov 1759; died young.

iv   JOHN BATCHELDER, b. 10 Jan 1762; d. at North Reading, 16 Mar 1840; m. MARY EAMES, b. 29 Apr 1765 daughter of John and Hannah (Cornell) Eames; Mary d. at North Reading, 3 Apr 1845.

v   SARAH BATCHELDER, b. 22 Sep 1764

vi   LYDIA BATCHELDER, b. about 1766; m. TIMOTHY EATON, b. 1767 son of William and Rebecca (Flint) Eaton.

[1194] At the 1850 Census, the three young children of George and Elizabeth Harriman were living with Lavina Morris Murray and her husband George Murray. Lavina Morris is the daughter of Joseph and Lavina (Drake) Morris. It might be assumed that the children went to live with their aunt after mother's death. In 1850, G. W. Harriman was living with his elderly mother Bridget.

[1195] *Middlesex County, MA: Probate File Papers, 1648-1871.* Online database. *AmericanAncestors.org.* New England Historic Genealogical Society, 2014. Case 600

[1196] The 1805 will of John Dix of Reading includes a bequest to his daughter Polly Bacheler.

[1197] The 1806 will of John Dix includes a bequest to his daughter Betty Bachelor.

453)   EZEKIEL RUSSELL (*Ezekiel⁴, Robert³, Thomas², Robert¹*), b. at Ashford, 22 Jun 1751 son of Ezekiel and Tabatha (Flint) Russell; d. at Wilbraham, 1798 (probate 1798); m. 1ˢᵗ at Wilbraham, 19 Aug 1775, HEPHZIBAH HILLS, b. at Glastonbury, 10 Aug 1749; Hephzibah d. 24 Feb 1778. Ezekiel m. 2ⁿᵈ at Wilbraham, 2 Oct 1778, HANNAH MEACHAM; Hannah d. at Wilbraham, 27 Jan 1822.

Ezekiel resided in Wilbraham. He served from Wilbraham in the company of Capt. James Warriner that "marched at the alarm" in April 1775.[1198]

In his will written 17 May 1798 (proved 7 October 1798), Ezekiel bequeathed to beloved wife Hannah the use of one-third of the real estate and she also receives one-third of the personal estate after the payment of debts. He bequeaths to eldest son Benjamin Hills Russell "twice as much" out of the real and personal estate as son Joseph Russell will receive. Daughters Susanna Russell and Submit Russell will receive two-thirds of the amount that son Joseph receives. Dear wife Hannah was named sole executrix. The home farm of about 70 acres was valued at $1,267. He also owned one-eighth of a sawmill valued at $20. Personal estate was valued at $348.92. Jonathan Flynt served as guardian for minor children Submit and Joseph over the age of fourteen in 1803. Division of the personal estate was made 8 November 1803.[1199]

Ezekiel and Hephzibah were parents of one child.

i   Daughter, b. 3 Feb 1777 and d. 17 May 1777

Ezekiel and Hannah were parents of four children born at Wilbraham.

i   BENJAMIN HILLS RUSSELL, b. 24 Jun 1780; d. at Wilbraham, 2 Oct 1848; m. at Wilbraham, 19 Jun 1804, LYDIA TILDEN, b. at Wilbraham, 28 Jun 1780 daughter of William and Mary (Withington) Tilden; Lydia d. at Wilbraham, 15 Jun 1847.

ii   SUSANNA RUSSELL, b. 2 Jun 1786; d. at Palmer, MA, 11 Dec 1824; m. at Wilbraham, 7 Jun 1817, WILLIAM TILDEN, b. at Wilbraham, 2 Jun 1786 son of William and Mary (Withington) Tilden; William d. after 1850 when he was living at Monson.

iii   SUBMIT RUSSELL, b. 15 Jul 1784; living at the time of the estate distribution in 1803.

iv   JOSEPH RUSSELL, b. 1786; d. at Hambden, OH, 26 Aug 1853; m. at Wilbraham, 8 Oct 1812, MARIAM MORGAN, b. at Springfield, MA, 6 Jul 1785 daughter of Ebenezer and Miriam (Kilbourn) Morgan; Mariam d. at Hambden, 27 Aug 1853.

454)   ABIGAIL RUSSELL (*Ezekiel⁴, Robert³, Thomas², Robert¹*), b. at Ashford, 19 May 1755 daughter of Ezekiel and Tabatha (Flint) Russell; d. at Wilbraham, 16 May 1812; m. at Wilbraham, 1 May 1782, NATHAN STEDMAN, b. 18 Jan 1751 son of Joseph and Abigail (Rockwell) Stedman; Nathan d. at Wilbraham, 27 Nov 1794.

Abigail Russell and Nathan Stedman were parents of six children born at Wilbraham. Abigail did not remarry after her husband's early death and raised her children in Wilbraham until her death just as the children were reaching adulthood. Three of the children died in a one-year period of the death of their mother. The three remaining children (Nathan, Erastus, and Achsah) went together to North Brunswick, New Jersey where they were living in 1818 when they sold the last remaining property in Wilbraham to John Work on 22 April 1818.[1200] The three siblings then made their way to Hartford, Connecticut the home of their father's family. Only one of the children married.

Nathan Stedman did not leave a will and on 13 December 1794, Abigail Stedman widow was allowed as guardian to six minor children: Nathan age 11, Beulah age 10, Erastus age 8, Sofia age 6, Achsah age 3, and Abigail age 2 months. The house with 70 acres of land was valued as £210.[1201]

i   NATHAN STEDMAN, b. at Wilbraham, 24 Feb 1783; d. at Hartford, 8 Mar 1832; m. at Wilbraham, 11 Nov 1810, BELINDA STEBBINS, b. at Wilbraham, 22 Aug 1786 daughter of James and Rachel (Wright) Stebbins; Belinda d. at Hartford, 12 Aug 1869.

ii   BEULAH STEDMAN, b. 1784; d. at Wilbraham, 26 Nov 1812.

iii   ERASTUS STEDMAN, b. 1786; d. at Hartford, 29 Dec 1841.

iv   SOFIA STEDMAN, b. 1788; d. at Wilbraham, 18 Mar 1811.

v   ACHSAH STEDMAN, b. 1791; d. at Hartford, 11 Mar 1833.

[1198] Peck, *The History of Wilbraham*, p 138

[1199] *Hampshire County, MA: Probate File Papers, 1660-1889.* Online database. *AmericanAncestors.org.* Box 126, File 2

[1200] Massachusetts Land Records 1620-1986, Hampden County, 47:395

[1201] *Hampshire County, MA: Probate File Papers, 1660-1889.* Online database. *AmericanAncestors.org.* New England Historic Genealogical Society, 2016, 2017. Case 141-54

vi   ABIGAIL STEDMAN, b. 1794; d. at Wilbraham, 16 Jul 1812.

455)   ROBERT RUSSELL (*Ezekiel⁴, Robert³, Thomas², Robert¹*), b. at Ashford, 15 May 1757 son of Ezekiel and Tabatha (Flint) Russell; d. at Hampden, MA, 9 Dec 1836; m. at Wilbraham, 14 Sep 1782, LYDIA BEEBE, b. 1761; Lydia d. at Hampden, 21 Aug 1837.
        Robert Russell and Lydia Beebe were parents of four children born at Wilbraham.

i   HEPHZIBAH RUSSELL, b. 3 Sep 1783; d. at Hampden, MA, 1873; m. at Wilbraham, 28 Nov 1805, SOLOMON WRIGHT, b. about 1779 son of Solomon and Ruth (McCall) Wright; Solomon d. at Wilbraham, 24 Mar 1843.

ii   LYDIA RUSSELL, b. 9 Jul 1785; d. at Ellington, CT, 23 Feb 1855; m. at Wilbraham, 26 Nov 1807, JOSEPH MORRIS, b. at Wilbraham, 27 Feb 1782 son of Darius and Rebecca (Chandler) Morris; Joseph d. at Ellington, 20 Feb 1847.

iii   ROBERT RUSSELL, b. 17 Aug 1787; d. 2 Jan 1788.

iv   ROBERT RUSSELL, b. 8 Aug 1789; d. at Hebron, CT, 10 Feb 1825; m. at Hebron, 8 Nov 1815, ABIGAIL GILBERT BARBER, b. at Hebron, 18 Feb 1797 daughter of Josiah and Abigail (Gilbert) Barber; Abigail d. at Cleveland, OH, 21 May 1864. Abigail did not remarry. Robert graduated from Williams College and was an attorney. Abigail's father was Judge Josiah Barber who was the first mayor of Ohio City, OH.[1202]

456)   SARAH "SALLY" MOULTON (*Elizabeth Russell Moulton Perley⁴, Robert³, Thomas², Robert¹*), b. likely at Danvers, about 1777 daughter of Elijah and Elizabeth (Russell) Moulton; d. at Rowley, MA, 19 May 1852; m. at Boxford, 1800, JONATHAN HARRIMAN, b. 1776 according to gravestone;[1203] Jonathan d. at Rowley, 1824.
        Sally and Jonathan were parents of eight children born at Rowley.

i   ELIZABETH R. HARRIMAN, b. at Rowley, 20 Mar 1801; d. at Georgetown, MA, 9 Feb 1880. Elizabeth did not marry. She worked as a dressmaker.

ii   JESSE PERLEY HARRIMAN, b. at Rowley, 15 Jan 1803; d. at Independence, IA, 9 Apr 1889; m. at Danvers, 21 Aug 1827, ELLEN JOHNSON, b. at Danvers, 12 Oct 1800 daughter of William and Betsey (Buxton) Johnson; Ellen d. at Independence, 25 Aug 1886.

iii   GEORGE HARRIMAN, b. at Rowley, 13 Sep 1805

iv   SARAH HARRIMAN, b. at Rowley, 15 Aug 1807; d. at Georgetown, 14 Jun 1889; m. at Rowley, 19 Mar 1829, her third cousin once removed, CYRUS DORMAN (*Hannah Andrews Dorman⁶, Mary Holt Andrews⁵, Hannah Chandler Holt⁴, Mehitable Russell Chandler³, Thomas², Robert¹*), b. at Boxford, 30 Oct 1799 son of John and Hannah (Andrews) Dorman; Cyrus d. at Georgetown, 14 Mar 1871.

v   MARY HARRIMAN, b. at Rowley, 22 Sep 1809; d. at Haverhill, 19 Feb 1887; m. at Haverhill, 5 Sep 1835, CALEB B. LE BOSQUET, b. at Haverhill, 17 Jan 1808 son of Caleb Brooks and Olive (Lamson) Le Bosquet; Caleb d. at Haverhill, 15 Feb 1880.

vi   IRENE P. HARRIMAN, b. at Rowley, 26 Sep 1812; d. at Georgetown, 12 Feb 1905; m. at Georgetown, 13 Sep 1838, BENJAMIN F. PICKETT, b. at Georgetown, 30 Sep 1812 son of Benjamin Scudder and Sarah (Bridges) Pickett; Benjamin d. at Georgetown, 28 Aug 1897.

vii   MARTHA H. HARRIMAN, b. at Rowley, 7 Sep 1815; d. at Waltham, 6 Nov 1855; m. at Lowell, 3 Apr 1833, GEORGE HASTINGS, b. at Waltham, 9 Oct 1812 son of Eliphalet and Dorothy (Temple) Hastings; George d. at Waltham, 6 Mar 1873.

viii   LYDIA MOULTON HARRIMAN, b. at Rowley, 14 Jul 1820; d. at Georgetown, 6 Jan 1915; m. at Andover, 24 Nov 1847, ORLANDO B. TENNEY, b. at Salem, 18 Oct 1816 son of David B. and Hannah T. (Little) Tenney; Orlando d. at Georgetown, 8 May 1909.

[1202] Orth, *A History of Cleveland, Ohio: Biographical*, volume II, p 31

[1203] There is a Jonathan Harriman born at Rowley in 1780 son of Jonathan and Martha (Plummer) Harriman, and perhaps this is that Jonathan, but that is not clear.

457)   MARY MOULTON (*Elizabeth Russell Moulton Perley⁴, Robert³, Thomas², Robert¹*), b. likely at Danvers, 1780 daughter of Elijah and Elizabeth (Russell) Moulton; d. at Winthrop, ME, 29 Mar 1839; m. at Boxford, 1 Apr 1799, THOMAS LANCASTER, b. at Rowley, 5 May 1773 son of Paul and Mary (Gage) Lancaster; Thomas d. at Winthrop, 4 May 1864.

Thomas and Mary came to Winthrop, Maine just after their marriage arriving in 1800. They lived on Carr Road in East Winthrop. Thomas was a farmer and butcher. He is credited with inventing a type of jug first produced at the Gardiner pottery works.[1204]

Mary and Thomas were parents of eight children born at Winthrop, Maine.

i   ELIJAH MOULTON LANCASTER, b. at Winthrop, ME, 10 Oct 1800; d. at Lewiston, ME, 12 Apr 1891; m. 16 Oct 1825, CLARINDA WING, b. at Winthrop, 1800 daughter of Ichabod and Elizabeth (Prescott) Wing; Clarinda d. at Lewiston, 22 Dec 1892.

ii   THOMAS GAGE LANCASTER, b. at Winthrop, 21 May 1803; d. at California, MO, 2 May 1852; m. at Moniteau County, MO, 6 Feb 1849, MELINDA JANE DUNLAP, b. in TN, about 1830 daughter of William and Martha (Yarnell) Dunlap;[1205] Melinda d. at Versailles, MO, 27 Aug 1883. Melinda married second W. B. Jones.

iii SEWALL LANCASTER, b. at Winthrop, 15 Nov 1805; d. at Augusta, ME, 3 Mar 1885; m. 1st 6 Sep 1835, ADELINE E. SYMONDS, b. at Boxford, 4 Jan 1810 daughter of Joseph and Lucy (Kimball) Symonds; Adeline d. 1843. Sewall m. 2nd 1845, Adeline's sister REBECCA KIMBALL SYMONDS, b. at Boxford, 22 Mar 1803; Rebecca d. 20 Jul 1886. Sewall was an attorney in Augusta.

iv   CHARLES LANCASTER, b. at Winthrop, 29 Mar 1808; d. at Plainfield, NJ, 4 Jul 1903; m. 1st at Augusta, ME, about 1832, MARY JANE NORTH, b. about 1810 daughter of Joseph and Lydia (McKechnie) North; Mary d. at Philadelphia, PA, 3 Nov 1843. Charles m. 2nd at Plainfield, NJ, 24 Oct 1867, MARY LOUISE VERMEULE, b. in NJ, about 1841 daughter of Jethro and Mary (Thompson) Vermeule. Charles was a physician.

v   MARY LANCASTER, b. at Winthrop, 12 Aug 1812; d. at Skowhegan, ME, 2 May 1844; m. 1839, ROBERT STRONG PAINE, b. at Gorham, ME, 22 Mar 1812 son of Thomas and Sarah B. (Hill) Paine; Robert d. at Bridgewater, MA, 21 May 1893.

vi   GEROGE WASHINGTON LANCASTER, b. at Winthrop, 6 Nov 1815; d. at Augusta, 7 Sep 1887; m. 17 Dec 1846, ANN MARIA PERKINS, b. at Augusta, 27 Sep 1821 daughter of Theodore and Abigail (Soule) Perkins; Ann d. at Boston, 17 May 1898.

vii JOSEPH FREDERIC LANCASTER (twin), b. at Winthrop, 25 Nov 1818; d. at Monmouth, ME, 15 Jul 1898; m. 1850, POLLY ANDREWS STANLEY, b. 7 Jan 1830 daughter of Morrill and Charlotte (Gilman) Stanley.

viii BENJAMIN FRANKLIN LANCASTER (twin), at Winthrop, 25 Nov 1818; d. at Monmouth, 28 Oct 1906; m. 1st 25 Jul 1852, AURORA DEBORAH NORCROSS, b. at Dixfield, ME, 16 Jul 1826 daughter of Leonard and Deborah (Nelson) Norcross; Aurora d. at Winthrop, 16 Jun 1867. Benjamin m. 2nd at Monmouth, 31 Aug 1893, LUCY S. LEMTON (widow Lucy Elder), b. in Nova Scotia, 1837 daughter of Charles C. and Mary (Lohnas) Lemton; Lucy d. at Windham, ME, 1932.

458)   FRANCIS PERLEY (*Elizabeth Russell Moulton Perley⁴, Robert³, Thomas², Robert¹*), b. at Boxford, 19 Oct 1792 son of Jesse and Elizabeth (Russell) Perley; d. at Boxford, 1 Sep 1836; m. at Boxford, 18 May 1815, LOUISA GOULD, b. at Topsfield, 25 Jun 1790 daughter of Nathaniel and Hannah (Killam) Gould; Louisa d. at Topsfield, 9 Dec 1843.

Francis and Louisa resided in Boxford where their seven children were born. Francis's father Jesse Perley died in 1846 and his will written 6 March 1842 includes bequests to Francis's widow and children. Those named are widow Louisa Perley, grandson Osgood Perley, granddaughter Louisa Hood, granddaughter Charlotte Waitt, granddaughter Caroline Augusta Perley, grandson John Perley, grandson Nathaniel Perley, and grandson Dean Andrews Perley.[1206]

i   OSGOOD PERLEY, b. at Boxford, 1815; d. at Topsfield, 8 Jan 1886; m. at Topsfield, 7 Apr 1840, ANN MARIE LAKE, b. at Middleton, 25 Oct 1818 daughter of Silas and Phebe (Batchelder) Lake; Ann d. at Topsfield, 12 Aug 1875.

[1204] Stackpole, *History of Winthrop, Maine*, p 475

[1205] Ford, *History of Moniteau County, Missouri*

[1206] *Essex County, MA: Probate File Papers, 1638-1881*. Online database. *AmericanAncestors.org*. New England Historic Genealogical Society, 2014. Case 49908

ii   LOUISA PERLEY,[1207] b. at Boxford, 2 Sep 1818; d. at Danvers, 23 Aug 1902; m. at Boxford, 20 Oct 1836, GEORGE W. HOOD, b. at Boxford, 9 Jan 1808 son of Francis and Hannah (Gould) Hood; George d. at Danvers, 9 Feb 1892.

iii   CHARLOTTE PERLEY, b. at Boxford, 1820; d. at Topsfield, 17 Nov 1843; m. about 1842, WILLIAM WAITT, b. at Topsfield, 21 Sep 1811 son of William and Elizabeth (Wildes) Waitt; William d. at Topsfield, 2 Aug 1888.

iv   CAROLINE AUGUSTA PERLEY, b. at Boxford, 1822; d. at Danvers, 18 Jun 1870; m. at Topsfield, 6 Apr 1844, BURLEY E. ORNE, b. likely at Wolfeboro, NH, about 1825; Burley d. at Wolfeboro, 5 Sep 1855. Burley is likely from the Orne/Horne family prominent in Wolfeboro. In the 1850 census, Burley was living at an inn in Stoneham and Caroline was living with her sister. Caroline and Burley had two children, Cecilia born about 1845 who died in 1925 and a son Lafayette who died in 1850 about age 2.

v   JOHN FRANKLIN PERLEY, b. at Boxford, 1824; d. at Topsfield, 15 Nov 1893; m. at Manchester, MA, 27 Apr 1854, LOUISA A. WHITTAKER, b. at Salem, about 1823 daughter of Robert and Mary Ann (Woodward) Whittaker; Louisa d. at Topsfield, 30 Jul 1881.

vi   NATHANIEL PERLEY, b. at Boxford, 1827; d. at Topsfield, 8 Apr 1864; m. at Windham, NH, 20 Oct 1847, MARY ANN MOORE, b. at Topsfield, 14 Aug 1829 daughter of Thomas and Lois (Peabody) Moore; Mary Ann d. at Topsfield, 20 Oct 1857.

vii   DEAN ANDREWS PERLEY, b. at Boxford, 31 Dec 1830; d. at Danvers, 30 Jan 1911; m. at Topsfield, 8 May 1854, NANCY ADAMS TOWNE, b. at Boxford, 6 Sep 1833 daughter of Samuel and Charlotte (Fletcher) Towne; Nancy d. at Danvers, 18 Mar 1915.

459)   JESSE PERLEY (*Elizabeth Russell Moulton Perley⁴, Robert³, Thomas², Robert¹*), b. at Boxford, 29 Oct 1795 son of Jesse and Elizabeth (Russell) Perley; d. at Boxford, 19 Nov 1851; m. at Boxford, 22 May 1824, SALLY GOULD, b. at Topsfield, 26 May 1800 daughter of Simon and Sarah (White) Gould; Sally d. 29 Dec 1857.

Jesse and Sally lived in Georgetown and Topsfield before returning to Boxford in 1838 where they lived until their deaths. The entire family had smallpox in 1841 but survived. Jesse died at age fifty-six and Sally survived him by six years.[1208]

In his 1842 will, Jesse's father, in addition to his bequests to his son Jesse, included bequests to his grandchildren children of son Jesse: Elizabeth W. Perley, Sarah Jane Perley, and Edward Payson Perley.[1209]

Jesse Perley and Sally Gould were parents of three children.

i   ELIZABETH WHITE PERLEY, b. at Georgetown, 8 Sep 1825; d. at Springfield, MA, 8 Mar 1905; m. at Salem, 4 Jul 1864, GEORGE WOODS, b. at Hollis, NH, about 1822 son of Ephraim and Eunice (White) Woods; George d. at Springfield, 27 Jul 1898.

ii   SARAH JANE PERLEY, b. at Georgetown, 9 Sep 1829; d. at Georgetown, 13 Jun 1909; m. at Georgetown, 10 Mar 1855, GEORGE W. ADAMS, b. at Georgetown, 29 Jan 1816 son of Benjamin and Lois (Perley) Adams; George d. at Georgetown, 3 Jan 1897.

iii   EDWARD PAYSON PERLEY, b. at Topsfield, 10 Nov 1836; d. at Danvers, 2 Jan 1913; m. at Danvers, 12 Jun 1861, MARTHA L. BARKER, b. at South Danvers, 25 Oct 1841 daughter of Charles and Betsey (Wilson) Barker; Martha d. at Danvers, 13 Jul 1925.

460)   IRENA PERLEY (*Elizabeth Russell Moulton Perley⁴, Robert³, Thomas², Robert¹*), b. at Boxford, 29 Jan 1801 daughter of Jesse and Elizabeth (Russell) Perley; d. at Boxford, 28 Jul 1837; m. at Boxford, 26 Aug 1822, FRANCIS GOULD, b. at Topsfield, 5 Sep 1798 son of Nathaniel and Betty (Andrews) Gould; Francis d. at Topsfield, 13 Oct 1870. Francis Gould was the half-brother of Louisa Gould who married Irena's brother Francis.

Irena and Francis resided in Topsfield and four children were born there. In his 1842 will, Irena's father Jesse Perley included bequests to his son-in-law and grandchildren: son-in-law Francis Gould and his children Irene Gould, Franklin Gould, and Jesse Perley Gould.[1210]

[1207] The transcription of Louisa's birth record gives her father as Abraham, but her death record says Francis Perley and Louisa Gould and she is named in grandfather's will as Louisa Waitt daughter of Francis.

[1208] Perley, *The Dwellings of Boxford*, p 117

[1209] *Essex County, MA: Probate File Papers, 1638-1881.* Online database. *AmericanAncestors.org.* New England Historic Genealogical Society, 2014. Case 49908

[1210] *Essex County, MA: Probate File Papers, 1638-1881.* Online database. *AmericanAncestors.org.* New England Historic Genealogical Society, 2014. Case 49908

i   IRENE BELSORA GOULD, b. at Topsfield, 7 Mar 1823; d. at Georgetown, MA, 5 Mar 1892; m. at Boxford, 12 Jun 1850, ALLEN GOULD HOOD, b. at Boxford, 12 Apr 1816 son of Francis and Hannah (Gould) Hood; Allen d. at Georgetown, 22 Apr 1878.

ii   NATHANIEL FRANKLIN GOULD, b. at Topsfield, about 1824; d. at Danvers, 10 Apr 1857; m. 21 Sep 1847, IRENA C. KENT, b. at Beverly, 1823 daughter of Benjamin and Harriet (Conant) Kent; Irena d. at Beverly, 12 Jan 1892.

iii   CATHERIN GOULD, b. 1827; d. at Topsfield, 10 Jan 1833.

iv   JESSE PERLEY GOULD, b. at Topsfield, 1833; d. at Georgetown, 4 Sep 1857. "Gould, Jesse Perley, s. Francis and Irene, b. here, consumption, Sept. 4, 1857, a. 24 y. (Died at Georgetown, body brought into town [Topsfield])"

461)   HENRY FARNHAM (*Henry Farnum⁴, Phebe Russell Farnum³, Thomas², Robert¹*), b. at Norwich, 8 Oct 1742 son of Henry and Sarah (Read) Farnum; d. at Lisbon, CT, about 1824 (will 1818; probate 1824); m. at Norwich, 2 Jan 1766, ABIGAIL RUDD, b. about 1746 likely the daughter of Joseph and Sarah (Moseley) Rudd; Sarah d. at Sprague, 11 Dec 1824.

     Henry and Abigail resided in Lisbon where they had a farm.

     In his will dated 26 October 1818 (proved 6 January 1824), Henry Farnham bequeathed to beloved wife Abigail all the household furniture except the clock, desk, meal chest, and casks. Bequests including a dwelling house and garden were made to Zeruiah Farnham widow of her son Erastus and their heirs: Lewis Farnham, Anna Farnham, Lydia Farnham, Henry Farnham, Jr., and Abigail Farnham. The bequest to Erastus's children included a 33-acre lot to grandson Lewis. Daughter Clarissa wife of Simeon Palmer received ten dollars in addition to what she has received. Daughter Lydia wife of Asa Bushnell receives forty-seven dollars. Daughter Ruby widow of Adonijah Knight receives twenty dollars and privilege to live in the house. Daughter Phebe wife of Samuel Ladd receives fifteen dollars. The heirs of late son Daniel receive three dollars. Son Jared Farnham receives the remainder of the estate including the remaining furniture items, stock, and money and is also named executor.[1211]

     Henry and Abigail were parents of eight children.

i   CLARISSA FARNHAM, b. at Norwich, 1 Dec 1766; m. at Norwich, 1 Dec 1791, SIMEON PALMER, b. 1763; Simeon d. at Le Roy, NY, 15 Jan 1829.[1212]

ii   LYDIA FARNHAM, b. at Norwich, 29 Jun 1768; d. at Lee, NY, 20 Feb 1858; m. at Norwich, 29 May 1785, ASA BUSHNELL, b. at Norwich, 27 Jul 1764 son of Aaron and Irene (Burnham) Bushnell;[1213] Asa d. at Lee, 28 Sep 1856.

iii   ERASTUS FARNHAM, b. at Norwich, 25 Apr 1770; d. at Sprague, CT, 21 May 1813; m. at Hanover, 21 Mar 1793, ZERUIAH KNIGHT, b. at Sprague, 8 Nov 1768 daughter of Phineas and Abigail (Birchard) Knight;

iv   RUBY FARNHAM, b. at Norwich, 11 Mar 1772; d. at Sprague, CT, 24 Dec 1840; m. at Lisbon, 27 Mar 1794, ADONIJAH KNIGHT, b. 1764 son of Phineas and Abigail (Birchard) Knight; Adonijah d. off the coast of Labrador near Green Island, 24 Jun 1807.[1214]

v   PHEBE FARNHAM, b. at Norwich, 29 Jun 1774; m. 1ˢᵗ 1803, JABEZ LADD, b. at Norwich, 4 Apr 1777 son of Ezekiel and Ruth (Hyde) Ladd; Jabez d. at Franklin, CT, 5 Sep 1814. Phebe m. 2ⁿᵈ at Franklin, CT, 21 Nov 1816, as his second wife, SAMUEL LADD, b. 17 Oct 1768 son of Samuel and Hannah (Hyde) Ladd; Samuel d. at Franklin, 23 Sep 1841. Samuel was first married to Abigail Ladd.

vi   DANIEL FARNHAM, b. at Norwich, 13 Apr 1777; d. at Sprague, 9 May 1814; m. about 1810, SARAH "SALLY" GRANT, b. at North Stonington, 11 Nov 1785 daughter of Joshua and Lucy (Green) Grant; Sarah d. at Stonington, 15 May 1851. Sarah married second Dudley Randall.

vii   JOHN FARNHAM, b. at Hanover, CT, 3 Sep 1780; d. 15 May 1781.

viii   JARED FARNHAM, b. at Hanover, 27 Aug 1783; d. at Sprague, CT, 20 Oct 1835; m. at Lisbon, 19 Feb 1817, DYCE LATHROP, b. at Bozrah, CT, 3 Dec 1789 daughter of Andrew and Lucretia (Smith) Lathrop; Dyce d. at Sprague, 20 Sep 1872.

462)   LYDIA FARNUM (*Henry Farnum⁴, Phebe Russell Farnum³, Thomas², Robert¹*), b. at Canterbury, 17 Nov 1744 daughter of Henry and Sarah (Read) Farnum; d. at Ashford, 5 Dec 1785; m. 14 Jun 1764, PHINEAS BIRCHARD, baptized at

[1211] Connecticut Wills and Probate Records, Hartford, Norwich Probate District, Town of Lisbon, Estate of Henry Farnham, Case 3765
[1212] Burial at Jug City Cemetery in Genesee County, New York; findagrave: 17668369
[1213] Walworth, *Hyde Genealogy*, p 1092
[1214] Connecticut, Church Record Abstracts, 1630-1920, volume 108, Sprague

Norwich, 24 Sep 1738 son of John and Jane (Hyde) Birchard; Phineas d. at Ashford, 8 Jun 1811. Phineas had a second wife, Dorcas.

Phineas and Lydia resided in Ashford. In his will written 24 May 1811, Phineas Birchard bequeaths to beloved wife Dorcas the improvement of one-third of the estate both real and personal. Grandson Phineas Birchard Knowlton son of daughter Betsey received $33.34. Grandson Phineas Converse son of daughter Phebe receives $16.67. Granddaughter Lydia Rice daughter of Lois Rice deceased receives fifty dollars at age twenty-one. Grandson Charles Thatcher son of daughter Polly Thatcher deceased receives fifty dollars at age twenty-one. The remainder of the estate is to be divided equally among his children Betsey Knowlton, Phineas Birchard, Gurdon Birchard, Phebe Converse, and Mima McCulloch. Wife Dorcas and son-in-law Daniel Knowlton were named executors. Real estate of about 120 acres of land with buildings was valued at $1,800 and personal estate, much of it in the form of notes owed to him, was $1.098.71.[1215]

Phineas and Lydia were parents of seven children born at Ashford.

i   AMASA BIRCHARD, b. 19 Jan 1765

ii   BETSEY BIRCHARD, b. 11 Oct 1768; m. at Ashford, 4 Apr 1793, her second cousin, DANIEL KNOWLTON (*Elizabeth Farnum Knowlton[5], Manasseh Farnum[4], Phebe Russell Farnum[3], Thomas[2], Robert[1]*), b. at Ashford, 7 Dec 1765 son of Daniel and Elizabeth (Farnum) Knowlton; Daniel d. at Ashford, Feb 1834.

iii   PHINEAS BIRCHARD, b. 22 Nov 1771; d. at Lima, NY, 6 Jan 1817; m. CLARISSA MILES, b. at Deerfield, MA, 1777;[1216] Clarissa d. at Lima, 28 May 1830.

iv   GURDON BIRCHARD, b. 5 Oct 1773; m. at Ashford, 16 Sep 1798, ANNA WALKER.

v   LOIS BIRCHARD, b. 2 May 1776; d. 13 Aug 1799; m. Mr. Rice who has not been identified but described as Dr. Rice in the Birchard genealogy.[1217]

vi   POLLY BIRCHARD, b. a 11 Aug 1777; d. at Tunbridge, VT, 11 Feb 1804; m. about 1798, AMOS THATCHER, b. at Lebanon, CT, 1771 son of Benjamin and Desire (Yarrington) Thatcher; Amos d. at Tunbridge, 3 Dec 1869. Amos married second Amy Tracy.

vii   PHEBE BIRCHARD, b. 16 Apr 1783; m. her fourth cousin, ADIN M. CONVERSE (*Priscilla Marcy Converse[5], Zebadiah Marcy[4], Mary Russell Marcy[3], Benjamin[2], Robert[1]*), b. 1779 son of Jedediah and Priscilla (Marcy) Converse; Adin d. at Navarino, NY, Jul 1816.

463)   PHEBE FARNUM (*Henry Farnum[4], Phebe Russell Farnum[3], Thomas[2], Robert[1]*), b. at Canterbury, 7 Mar 1746 daughter of Henry and Sarah (Read) Farnum; d. at Canterbury, 21 Dec 1808; m. at Canterbury, 16 Dec 1773, DANIEL FROST, b. at Canterbury, 6 Jul 1748 son of Daniel and Elizabeth (Bond) Frost; Daniel d. at Canterbury, 27 Aug 1839. Daniel married second Hannah Stevens on 21 Dec 1809.

There are records of two children of Phebe Farnum and Daniel Frost.

i   HEZEKIAH FROST, b. at Canterbury, 7 Feb 1778; d. of consumption at Portland, ME, 27 May 1827; m. 1st at Plymouth, VT, Jan 1808, ESTHER CLARKE, b. at Brooklyn, CT, 15 Mar 1786 daughter of Daniel and Lydia (Davison) Clarke; Esther d. at Windham, 10 Jun 1819. Hezekiah m. 2nd 17 Jun 1821, HANNAH BROWN who has not been identified. After Hezekiah's death, Hannah married John Harmon. Hezekiah graduated from Yale College and practiced law in Windham, Vermont and Portland, Maine.[1218]

ii   DANIEL FROST, b. at Canterbury, 17 Apr 1787; d. at Canterbury, 18 Jul 1863; m. 1st at Canterbury, 3 Feb 1811, LOUISA CLARKE, b. 5 May 1790 daughter of John and Theresa (Larke) Clarke;[1219] Louisa d. at Canterbury, 9 Mar 1833. Daniel m. 2nd ROXANNA MAYO (widow of George Wheelock), b. at Orange, MA, 21 Jun 1797 daughter of Benjamin and Dorothy (Goddard) Mayo; Roxanna d. of consumption at Orange, 30 Jun 1855.

464)   MANASSEH FARNHAM (*Manasseh Farnum[4], Phebe Russell Farnum[3], Thomas[2], Robert[1]*), b. at Windham, 29 Jul 1739 son of Manasseh and Keziah (Ford) Farnum; d. at Ashford, 16 May 1808; m. 19 Apr 1758, PATIENCE BIBBINS, b. 23 Oct 1733 daughter of Arthur and Abigail (Follett) Bibbins.[1220]

[1215] Connecticut Wills and Probate Records, Hartford District, Town of Ashford, Estate of Phineas Birchard, Case 406, 1811

[1216] Birchard, *The Birchard-Burchard Genealogy*, p 132

[1217] Birchard, *The Birchard-Burchard Genealogy*, p 131

[1218] Dexter, *Biographical Sketches of the Graduates of Yale College* June 1792-Spetember 1805, p 494

[1219] The will of John Clarke of Canterbury written in 1829 includes a bequest to his daughter Louisa Frost.

[1220] The 1758 probate record of Arter Bibbins includes a receipt signed by Manasseh Farnum in 1761 stating that he has received from Mrs. Abigail Bibbins payment from the estate.

Manasseh and Patience resided in Ashford. He served a six-month term in the Revolution from 20 July to 15 December 1776.[1221]

Manasseh Farnham did not leave a will and his estate was administered by Elijah Farnham. The estate was reported as insolvent on 5 July 1808.[1222]

Manasseh and Patience were parents of nine children, the birth of the first child recorded at Windham and the others at Ashford.

i   ARTHUR BENJAMIN FARNUM, b. 7 Jan 1759; d. at Ashford, 5 May 1807; m. at Ashford, 28 Mar 1781, ANN CHUBB, b. at Ashford, 26 Dec 1756 daughter of William and Rachel (Squire) Chubb.

ii EPHRAIM FARNUM, b. 10 Oct 1760; d. 20 Oct 1776.

iii ABIGAIL FARNUM, b. 8 Jan 1763; d. at Eastford, 5 Aug 1847; m. at Ashford, 26 Feb 1789, EPHRAIM HAYWARD, b. at Ashford, 12 Oct 1759 son of John and Rebecca (Peake) Hayward; Ephraim d. at Ashford, 27 Aug 1831.

iv STEPHEN FARNUM, b. 3 Feb 1765; d. at Ashford, 2 Mar 1839; m. ANNA ELDREDGE, b. at Willington, 28 Feb 1759 daughter of Jesse and Abigail (Smith) Eldredge; Anna d. at Ashford, 16 Jun 1833.

v   ISAAC FARNUM, b. 11 Oct 1766; d. at Onondaga, NY, 3 Oct 1813; m. at Ashford, 15 Oct 1792, MEHITABLE SNOW, b. at Ashford, 5 Apr 1767 daughter of Robert and Sarah (Chubb) Snow; Mehitable d. a Onondaga, 22 Apr 1854.

vi ELIJAH FARNHAM, b. 26 Sep 1768; d. at Ashford, 31 Dec 1837; m. at Ashford, 4 Aug 1793, THANKFUL ROBINSON, b. at Willington, 1762 daughter of Elisha and Thankful (-) Robinson; Thankful d. at Ashford, 16 Jan 1846.

vii JOSHUA FARNUM, b. 31 Mar 1771; d. at Italy, NY, 28 Jun 1846; m. 1st at Ashford, 31 Mar 1795, WATY DYER who has not been identified. Joshua m. 2nd HANNAH GREEN.

viii ELIZABETH FARNUM, b. 17 Nov 1773; m. at Windham, 29 May 1796, BELA BIBBINS. Bela was living in Bennington, NY in 1840.

ix AME FARNUM, b. 13 Oct 1776; d. at Ashford, 8 Mar 1813. Ame did not marry.

465)   ELIZABETH FARNUM (*Manasseh Farnum[4], Phebe Russell Farnum[3], Thomas[2], Robert[1]*), b. at Windham, 10 Mar 1742 daughter of Manasseh and Keziah (Ford) Farnum; d. at Ashford, 1 Jun 1786; m. 3 Nov 1763, DANIEL KNOWLTON, b. at Boxford, 23 Dec 1738 son of William and Martha (Pinder) Knowlton; Daniel d. at Ashford, 31 May 1825. Daniel married second Rebeckah Fenton on 24 Apr 1788.

Lieut. Daniel Knowlton first enlisted for service in the French and Indian War at age sixteen and saw service at Crown Point. He had distinguished service during the Revolution serving with his brother Col. Thomas Knowlton in Knowlton's Rangers. Daniel was taken prisoner at Fort Washington and was held for two years. Part of this time was on the prison ship *Jersey*. A detailed account of his military service can be found in Stocking's Knowlton genealogy.[1223]

In his will written 9 March 1824 (probate 7 June 1825), Daniel Knowlton bequeaths to beloved wife Rebekah one-third of the personal estate and the use of one-third of the real estate during her natural life. Son Marvin receives all the real estate provided he pays all the debts, provides a decent burial for Daniel and his wife, and pays the other legacies. These legacies are Daniel Knowlton, Jr., seventy dollars; heirs of Elizabeth Chaffee, eighty dollars; son Nathaniel Knowlton, one hundred and ten dollars; son Manasseh, fifty dollars; son Ephraim Knowlton, ten dollars; daughter Martha Brandon, fifty dollars; daughter Keziah Lyon, sixty dollars; daughter Hannah Knowlton, sixty dollars; and son Erastus P. Knowlton, one hundred and ten dollars. Daniel Knowlton, Jr. and Marvin Knowlton were named executors. Real estate was 53 acres valued at $662.50 and personal estate at $320.48.[1224]

Daniel Knowlton and Elizabeth Farnum were parents of eight children born at Ashford. Daniel also had Erastus and Marvin from his marriage to Rebekah Fenton.

i   DANIEL KNOWLTON, b. 7 Dec 1765; d. at Ashford, Feb 1834; m. 4 Apr 1793, his second cousin, BETSEY BIRCHARD (*Lydia Farnum Birchard[5], Henry Farnum[4], Phebe Russell Farnum[3], Thomas[2], Robert[1]*), b. at Ashford, 11 Oct 1768 daughter of Phineas and Lydia (Farnum) Birchard.[1225]

[1221] Farnham, *New England Descendants of Immigrant Ralph Farnum*, p 322

[1222] Connecticut Wills and Probate, Hartford, Pomfret Probate District, Town of Ashford, Estate of Manasseh Farnham, Case 1673

[1223] Stocking, The History and Genealogy of the Knowltons, volume I, p 83ff

[1224] Connecticut Wills and Probate, Hartford District, Town of Pomfret, Estate of Daniel Knowlton, Case 2488

[1225] The 1811 will of Phineas Birchard includes a bequest to his daughter Betsey Knowlton.

ii   ELIZABETH KNOWLTON, b. 24 Mar 1768; d. at Ashford, 19 Nov 1806; m. 6 Mar 1788, FREDERICK CHAFFEE, b. at Ashford, 6 Mar 1767 son of Josiah and Elizabeth (Dimmock) Chaffee; Frederick d. at West Springfield, MA, 1 Jan 1837. Frederick married second Betsey Shurtliff on 13 Nov 1814.

iii NATHANIEL KNOWLTON (twin), b. 24 Dec 1770; d. at Greenbush, NY, 6 Jul 1850; m. 25 Nov 1798, SARAH LEACH; Sarah d. 7 Feb 1844.

iv   MANASSEH KNOWLTON (twin), b. 24 Dec 1770; d. at East Greenbush, NY, 21 Jan 1841; m. 1st 19 Mar 1793, LYDIA BURTON, b. 19 Mar 1773; Lydia d. at East Greenbush, 15 Jul 1806. Manasseh m. 2nd ELIZABETH CARD, b. 1774; Elizabeth d. at East Greenbush, 5 Aug 1821. Manasseh m. 3rd CLARISSA COGSWELL, b. 1775; Clarissa d. at East Greenbush, 23 Nov 1841.

v   EPHRAIM KNOWLTON, b. 3 Oct 1773; likely d. at Rush, PA, 26 Oct 1838;[1226] m. about 1793, his first cousin, JEMIMA FARNUM (*Joseph Farnum⁵, Manasseh Farnum⁴, Phebe Russell Farnum³, Thomas², Robert¹*), b. 1 Jul 1773 daughter of Joseph and Catherine (Spring) Farnum. Ephraim and Jemima were parents of six children. They then seem to have divorced and both had second marriages. Ephraim's second wife was Sarah who died 4 April 1870 and is buried at Snyder-Rush Cemetery in Lawton, PA.[1227] Jemima Knowlton married Robert A. Johnson at Geauga County, OH on 14 Jan 1829. Jemima age 77 and Robert age 84 were living at Madison, OH in 1850.[1228]

vi   MARTHA KNOWLTON, b. 24 Feb 1777; d. at Joliet, IL, 30 Mar 1855; m. at Ashford, 12 Jun 1796, CHARLES WILLIS BRANDON; Charles d. at Joliet, 25 Sep 1832.

vii KEZIAH KNOWLTON, b. 9 Feb 1781; d. at Eastford, CT, 13 Jan 1852; m. at Ashford, 3 Jan 1805, AMASA LYON, b. at Ashford, 19 Nov 1771 son of Ephraim and Elizabeth (Bennett) Lyon; Amasa d. at Eastford, 1843. General Nathaniel Lyon was son of Amasa and Keziah (Knowlton) Lyon. He was the first Union general killed during the Civil War. Gen. Lyon graduated from West Point in 1841.

viii HANNAH KNOWLTON, b. 19 Apr 1783; d. at Ashford, 24 Dec 1854; m. 24 Nov 1803, DANIEL KNOWLTON, b. at Ashford, 17 Mar 1781 son of Abraham and Molly (Knox) Knowlton; Daniel d. at Ashford, 20 Jul 1852.

466) JOSEPH FARNUM (*Manasseh Farnum⁴, Phebe Russell Farnum³, Thomas², Robert¹*), b. at Windham, 28 Nov 1748 son of Manasseh and Keziah (Ford) Farnum; d. at Enfield, 1777 (probate 1777); m. 15 Mar 1770, CATHERINE SPRING, b. at Ashford, 3 Mar 1750 daughter of Josiah and Catherine (Bicknell) Spring; Catherine d. about 1786. Catherine married second in 1778, as his second wife, HENRY WORK (*Mary Russell Work⁴, Benjamin³, Benjamin², Robert¹*), b. at Ashford, 22 Jan 1752 son of Ingoldsby and Mary (Russell) Work; Henry d. at Eastford, 22 Apr 1832. Henry Work was second married to HANNAH DEAN, b. at Woodstock, 22 Dec 1766 daughter of Zephaniah and Hannah (Hayward) Dean; Hannah d. at West Woodstock, 26 Oct 1848.

Joseph was a farmer in Enfield and married Catherine Spring with whom he had two children. Joseph Farnum did not leave a will and his estate entered probate 4 February 1777 with widow Catherine of Enfield as administratrix and Samuel Spring of Ashford as surety for the bond. The inventory included a piece of land in Ashford valued at £37.10.0 and stock animals valued at £26.9.0. Total valued of the estate was £113.16.8. On 6 April 1778, Nathan Pease of Enfield provided a statement to the probate court at the request of Henry Work husband of Catherine widow of Joseph Farnum that there were no debts of the estate.[1229]

i   SALLY FARNUM, b. at Ashford, 11 Feb 1771; d. at Bristol, OH, 11 Feb 1848; m. at Ashford, 26 Nov 1789, JONATHAN CHAFFEE, b. at Ashford, 11 Feb 1765 son of William and Anna (Bibbins) Chaffee;[1230] Jonathan d. at Bristol, 23 Jun 1848.

ii   JEMIMA FARNUM, b. 1 Jul 1773; m. about 1793, her first cousin, EPHRAIM KNOWLTON (*Elizabeth Farnum Knowlton⁵, Manasseh Farnum⁴, Phebe Russell Farnum³, Thomas², Robert¹*), b. at Ashford, 3 Oct 1773 son of Daniel and Elizabeth (Farnum) Knowlton. Jemima m. 2nd at Geauga County, OH, 14 Jan 1829, ROBERT A. JOHNSON, b. in MA about 1766 (per 1850 census); Robert d. at Madison, 31 Aug 1855.

After Joseph's death, Catherine married Henry Work. Catherine and Henry did not have children, and Henry married second Hannah Dean. Henry and Hannah were parents of nine children born at Woodstock.

In his will written 8 September 1826 (probate 1 May 1832), Henry Work bequeathed to loving wife Hannah the use of one0third of the real estate during her life, one-third of the provisions on hand, and all the household furnishings to be at her disposal. Sons Henry and Ezra each receives one hundred dollars which completes their portions. Son Benjamin is to receive

---

[1226] Findagrave ID: 43195755; Snyder-Rush Cemetery

[1227] Findagrave ID: 101768729

[1228] Year: 1850; Census Place: Madison, Lake, Ohio; Roll: 701; Page: 123A

[1229] Connecticut Wills and Probate, Hartford District, Town of Enfield, Estate of Joseph Farnam, Case 1938, 1777

[1230] Chaffee, *The Chaffee Genealogy*, p 146

twenty-five dollars at age twenty-one and immediately after the decease of Henry, he is to be decently clothed to go learn a trade that he chooses. Son Alonzo is also to receive twenty-five dollars at age twenty-one, and Alonzo is to live with son John who is to school and clothe him until age nineteen. Daughter Polly wife of Stephen Bradford receives one good cow and five dollars to complete her portion. Daughter Hannah is to receive one good cow and five dollars at age twenty-one or marriage and is to live with her mother until of age. She is to have equal in value to what is given daughters Polly and Emily in household furniture. Sons Ingoldsby and John receive the residue of the estate to equally divide, are responsible to pay the debts and legacies and are named executors. On 12 July 1830, Henry made a codicil to his will in which he added one cow and the use of a horse and carriage to his bequest to wife Hannah and adjusted the bequest to son Alonzo to one hundred dollars. The inventory included buildings and about 170 acres of land valued at $3,740 and personal estate valued at $904.50.[1231]

i   INGOLDSBY WORK, b. 2 Dec 1788; d. at Eastford, CT, 23 Sep 1872; m. at Ashford, 1819, BETSEY MUMFORD, b. at Ashford, 8 Sep 1794 daughter of Jeremiah and Betsey (Manning) Mumford; Betsey d. at Eastford, 23 Nov 1872.

ii   HENRY WORK, b. 25 Oct 1791; d. at Boston, 14 May 1877; m. at Ashford, 23 Apr 1817, MARCIA BOLLES, b. at Ashford, 3 May 1800 daughter of David and Elizabeth (Dow) Bolles; Marcia d. at Plainfield, CT, 22 Sep 1856.

iii   JOHN WORK, b. 18 Feb 1796; d. at Woodstock, 30 Sep 1862; m. 1st at Woodstock, 7 Nov 1826, MATILDA DARROW MASCRAFT, b. at Woodstock, 4 Oct 1800 daughter of Daniel and Phebe (Trowbridge) Mascraft;[1232] Matilda d. at Woodstock, 3 May 1852. John m. 2nd 5 Jan 1855, EUNICE CHAPIN DEWING (widow of Larned Haskell), b. at Woodstock, 5 Feb 1808 daughter of Ebenezer and Catherine (Chapin) Dewing; Eunice d. 18 Feb 1892.

iv   POLLY WORK, b. 7 Jan 1799; d. at Woodstock, 3 Aug 1863; m. about 1824, STEPHEN M. BRADFORD, b. at Woodstock, 1798 son of Carpenter and Rebecca (Marcy) Bradford; Stephen d. at Woodstock, Mar 1870 (probate 1870).

v   EZRA D. WORK, b. 3 May 1801; d. at Woodstock, 4 Jan 1842; m. at Dudley, MA, 7 Apr 1825, PRUDENCE H. WHITE, b. at Uxbridge, Jan 1803 (calculated from death age of 49 years 9 months); Prudence d. at Lawrence, MA, 8 Oct 1852.

vi   EMILY WORK, b. 6 Jun 1805; d. at Thompson, CT, 7 May 1884; m. 1827, CHARLES CHILDS, b. 15 Oct 1802 (as engraved on gravestone); Charles d. at Thompson, 15 Mar 1869.

vii   BENJAMIN WORK, b. 31 Oct 1807; d. at Woodstock, 11 Mar 1880; m. 1st 24 Apr 1831, SUSAN CHURCH, b. at Woodstock, 22 Aug 1811 daughter of Jeremiah and Susan (Burdick) Church; Susan d. at Woodstock, 9 Oct 1856. Benjamin m. 2nd, BETSEY who has not been identified, b. in VT, about 1811 (census records); Betsey d. at Woodstock, 2 Sep 1872.

viii ALONZO WORK, b. 3 Jan 1810; d. at Woodstock, 1878; m. MARY N. PHILLIPS (maiden name on cemetery record), b. in CT, 1814; Mary d. at Woodstock, 1898.

ix   HANNAH DEAN WORK, b. 1814; d. at Union, CT, 8 Dec 1896; m. at Woodstock, 4 May 1836, SAMUEL A. WHIPPLE, b. at Pownal, VT, 1813 son of Samuel and Mary (Chaffee) Whipple; Samuel d. at Union, 8 Sep 1886.

467)   KEZIAH FARNUM (*Manasseh Farnum⁴, Phebe Russell Farnum³, Thomas², Robert¹*), b. at Windham, 28 Nov 1751 daughter of Manasseh and Keziah (Ford) Farnum; m. about 1770 (first child born 1771), JOSEPH CHAPMAN, b. at Ashford, 9 May 1747 son of Thomas and Mary (Throop) Chapman; Joseph d. at Manlius, NY, 12 Dec 1796.

    The births of five children of Keziah and Joseph are recorded at Ashford. It is possible there were additional children born after the family move to Marcellus.

i   JOSEPH CHAPMAN, b. 26 May 1771; d. at Marcellus, NY, 1847; m. ELSIE SNOW, b. in CT, about 1790 likely daughter of Silas and Eunice (Farnum) Snow (and Joseph's first cousin); Elsie d. at Colon, MI, 12 Jan 1868.[1233]

ii   KEZIAH FORD CHAPMAN, b. 23 Apr 1774

[1231] Connecticut Wills and Probate, Woodstock Probate District, Estate of Henry Work, Case 1630, 1832

[1232] Bowen, *The History of Woodstock, Connecticut*, volume 7, p 396

[1233] The death index for Elsie gives parents as Silas and Hannah Snow. However, it seems more likely that she is the daughter of Silas Snow and Eunice Farnum and that the Hannah in the index is an error. Consider that Joseph and Elsie named one of their sons Manasseh Farnum Chapman and that Manasseh Farnum was Eunice Farnum's father.

iii   SARAH CHAPMAN, b. 10 May 1776; d. at Marcellus, NY, 25 Nov 1814; m. 10 Mar 1800, ELIJAH CODY, b. 27 Dec 1775 (on gravestone) son of Joseph and Mary (Parmenter) Cody; Elijah d. at Centreville, Ontario. 21 Sep 1828.[1234] Elijah was second married to Philena Staples.

iv   EUNICE CHAPMAN, b. 2 Jun 1780; d. at Navarino, NY, 11 Jul 1831; m. DAVID CHAFFEE, b. at Ashford, 25 Jul 1772 son of David and Prescilla (Robbins) Chaffee;[1235] David d. at Navarino, 18 Sep 1847.

v   HANNAH CHAPMAN, b. 20 Oct 1791; d. (burial at Navarino),19 Oct 1835;[1236] m. at Marcellus, 1 Jan 1813, JOSEPH CHAFFEE, b. at Woodstock, CT, 12 Jan 1795 son of Joseph and Clarissa (Griggs) Chaffee;[1237] Joseph d. at Three Rivers, MI, 2 Aug 1883.[1238] Joseph served in the War of 1812.[1239] Joseph was second married to Phebe Enos.

468)   EUNICE FARNUM (*Manasseh Farnum⁴, Phebe Russell Farnum³, Thomas², Robert¹*), b. at Windham, 1 Feb 1757 daughter of Manasseh and Keziah (Ford) Farnum; d. at Marcellus, NY, after 1810;[1240] m. at Ashford, 16 Dec 1782, SILAS SNOW, b. at Ashford 18 Apr 1761 son of Oliver and Elizabeth (Phillips) Snow;[1241] Silas d. at Granby, NY, about 1835.

     In a statement for his pension application dated 12 September 1832, Silas reported he was born in Ashford on 18 April 1761 and he resided there until 1808 when he relocated to Marcellus, New York. In 1826, he moved to Granby where he was living in 1832. He enlisted in May 1777 in the company of Capt. John Keyes and regiment of Col. Ely. He was a Fort Griswold until the beginning of autumn when they went to Rhode Island and then back to Fort Griswold. The troops were involved in skirmishes. He was discharged from that enlistment in January 1778 and on 1 May 1778, he enlisted for a term of one year in the company of Capt. Squire Hill in the regiment of Col. McClellan. Silas had a third enlistment in June 1779 for a term of three months under Capt. Whittemore. His fourth enlistment was in 1780 as a substitute for Samuel Walker and his fifth enlistment in 1781 was as a substitute for Solomon Snow. On 13 February 1839, daughter Eunice Snow, through her attorney, requested payment of arrears of the pension.[1242]

     There are records of six children of Eunice and Silas born at Ashford and there is likely a seventh child.[1243] Clear outcomes were identified for just one child.

i   LUCENA SNOW, b. 17 Mar 1783

ii   EUNICE SNOW, b. 4 Sep 1784; d. after 1839 when she was unmarried.

iii   DIEDAMIA SNOW, b. 16 Sep 1787

iv   ELI SNOW, b. 15 Apr 1789

v   ELSIE SNOW, b. about 1790; d. at Colon, MI, 12 Jan 1868; m. her first cousin, JOSEPH CHAPMAN, b. at Ashford, 26 May 1771 son of Joseph and Keziah (Farnum) Chapman; Joseph d. at Marcellus, NY, 1847.

vi   SILAS SNOW, b. 26 Jun 1791

vii   HANNAH SNOW, b. 15 Feb 1793

469)   EPHRAIM FARNUM (*Ephraim Farnum⁴, Phebe Russell Farnum³, Thomas², Robert¹*), b. at Norwich, 7 Aug 1745 son of Ephraim and Cheney Ann (White) Farnum; m. at Norwich, 7 Jan 1768, SARAH HUNN, b. about 1736 (based on age 69 at time of death); Sarah d. at Boston, 6 Nov 1805.

     Ephraim and Sarah's son Henry was a successful silversmith in Boston and established his business in Boston in 1800.[1244]

     There are records for two children of Ephraim and Sarah born at Norwich, Connecticut.

[1234] Findagrave ID: 77807081

[1235] Chaffee, *The Chaffee Genealogy*, p 162

[1236] Findagrave ID: 34064705

[1237] Chaffee, *The Chaffe Genealogy*, p 318

[1238] Michigan, Deaths and Burials Index, 1867-1995; father's name as Joseph Chaffee is given on the death index.

[1239] War of 1812 Pension Application Files Index, 1812-1815

[1240] Silas and Eunice moved from Ashford to Marcellus in 1808 (according to his pension file) and Eunice appears to be living at the 1810 census but not in 1820. Some genealogies report that Eunice died in Ashford in 1834 but that is the death record of Eunice the wife of Perley Snow.

[1241] Silas provides his birth date in his Revolutionary War pension application file as 18 Apr 1761 which leads to the conclusion that his parents are Oliver and Elizabeth Snow. Also, in the record is a statement in 1839 from daughter Eunice Snow applying for a payment from the pension board related to the case of her father who was then deceased.

[1242] U. S. Revolutionary War Pension and Bounty-Land Warrant Application Files, Case S14544

[1243] Elsie Snow who married Joseph Chapman is a likely child in this family. It might also be considered that the record transcription recorded as Eli is really a record for Elsie as the date of birth would match closely the age of Elsie, but Eli and Elsie are listed separately here.

[1244] New Hampshire Historical Society, https://www.nhhistory.org/object/973259/farnam-henry-1773-1852

i   EPHRAIM FARNUM, 13 Oct 1769

ii   HNERY FARNAM, b. 10 Oct 1773; d. at Boston, 22 May 1852; m. in RI, 28 Jan 1802, NANCY NEWELL, b. 1781
         daughter of Andrew and Olive (-) Newell; Nancy d. at Roxbury, 8 May 1840.

470)   ELIZABETH FARNUM (*Joshua Farnum⁴, Phebe Russell Farnum³, Thomas², Robert¹*), b. at Windham, 17 Jan 1752
daughter of Joshua and Sarah (Ford) Farnum; d. 30 Jan 1832;[1245] m. at Windham, 7 Apr 1774, ASA BOTTUM,[1246] b. at Norwich,
3 Aug 1748 son of David and Lucy (Read) Bottom; Asa d. at Windham, 1812 (probate 1812).
         Asa Bottom was a cooper by trade.[1247] The family lived in Norwich early in their marriage and were then in Windham.
Asa Bottom did not leave a will and his estate entered probate 28 April 1812 with Walter Bottum as administrator and Joshua
Bottum providing surety for the bond. Personal estate was valued at $162.73. Debts were $353.43 and the personal estate was
sold. Elizabeth Bottum was allowed as guardian for minor child Septa Bottum on 23 May 1812. On 13 April 1812, Jacob Burnett
provided bond for the guardianship of Septa noting that Septa was anxious to go live with his brother.[1248]
         Elizabeth Farnum and Asa Bottom were parents of nine children born at Windham.

i   CHARLES BOTTUM, b. 2 Jan 1775; d. at Genoa, NY, 31 Mar 1813; m. 18 Jan 1803, MARY BASSETT who has
         not been identified.

ii   SARAH BOTTUM, b. 18 Nov 1776; m. at Windham, 1 Oct 1801, JEREMIAH WHITE, b. at Hebron, CT, 8 Jun
         1780 son of Asa and Mary (Bingham) White. Jeremiah had three further marriages including to Sarah's sister
         Elizabeth (see below).

iii   JAIRUS BOTTUM, b. 2 Jan 1779; d. 27 Jun 1828 perhaps as Rhinebeck, NY where he was taxed in 1803; m. 10
         Dec 1807, 10 Dec 1807, SARAH DECKER, b. at Linlithgo, NY, 24 Nov 1790 daughter of Jan Jacobson and Lois
         (Stephens) Decker.

iv   WALTER BOTTUM, b. 29 Oct 1781; d. at Elkland, PA, 2 Jul 1857; m. 30 Jan 1802, DOLLY CLARK, b. 6 Mar
         1779; Dolly d. at Elkland, 14 Aug 1854.

v   DAVID BOTTUM, b. 12 Feb 1784; d. at Ridgeway, NY, about 1829; m. 1ˢᵗ at Norwich, 2 May 1813, LUCY
         ATWATER, b. 18 Feb 1790; Lucy d. 14 Feb 1817. Joshua m. 2ⁿᵈ about 1818, LUCINDA BAKER, b. at Windham, 9
         Oct 1786 daughter of Elijah and Olive (Kasson) Baker; Lucinda d. at Amboy, IL, 22 Oct 1878.

vi   JOSHUA BOTTUM, b. 9 Sep 1786; d. at Mansfield, 18 Sep 1855; m. at Norwich, 1812, PHEBE ADAMS, b 1787
         whose parents were not identified; Phebe d. at Mansfield, 3 Nov 1876.

vii   ELIZABETH BOTTUM, b. 5 Sep 1788; m. about 1818, as his second wife, JEREMIAH WHITE who was first
         married to Elizabeth's sister Sarah. Jeremiah was third married to Alice Utley about 1824 and fourth married to
         Anna Parkhurst about 1832.

viii   ASA BOTTUM, b. 2 Nov 1791; d. 9 Apr 1831.[1249]

ix   SEPTA BOTTUM, b. 17 Jan 1795; d. at St. John's, MI, 17 Feb 1873; m. 1ˢᵗ 12 Jan 1817, THANKFUL DUNHAM,
         b. 1799; Thankful d. at Moravia, 25 Dec 1831. Septa m. 2ⁿᵈ 30 Jan 1833, ELEIZABETH CARR, b. in NY, about
         1802; Elizabeth d. after 1870.

471)   ELIPHALET FARNUM (*Eliphalet Farnum⁴, Phebe Russell Farnum³, Thomas², Robert¹*), b. at Canterbury, 25 Aug
1759 son of Eliphalet and Mary (Rogers) Farnum; d. at Middlebury, VT, 10 Sep 1833; m. at Gilsum, NH, 16 Oct 1786, HANNAH
ADAMS, b. about 1762 daughter of Jonathan and Hannah (Yeamans) Adams;[1250] Hannah d. at Middlebury, VT, 14 Apr 1844.
         On 24 July 1832, Eliphalet Farnum, then aged seventy-three of Kingston, Vermont, gave a statement related to his
pension application. He first enlisted in August 1776 from Canterbury in the Connecticut militia company of Capt. William
Hebard in the regiment of Col. John Douglas. His company was in Westchester, New York and was in the Battle of White
Plains. Following this enlistment, he enlisted in the winter of 1776-1777 on the privateer *American Revenue* under command of
Capt. Samuel Champlain.[1251] After picking up additional crew at Stonington and Martha's Vineyard, they were out to sea and

---

[1245] This is date of death given in the Bottum (Longbottom) genealogy.

[1246] Asa's father was David Longbottom, but the name was shortened to Bottum. Asa's father wrote his will as David Bottum. Asa's birth transcription lists his father as David Longbottom. Asa used the spelling Bottum

[1247] Oliver, *The Bottum (Longbottom) Family Album*, p 175

[1248] Connecticut Wills and Probate, Hartford, Windham Probate District, Town of Windham, Estate of Asa Bottum, Case 428

[1249] Oliver, *The Bottum (Longbottom) Family Album*, p 175

[1250] Adams, *A Genealogical History of Henry Adams of Braintree, Mass.*, volume 1, p 544

[1251] After the time Eliphalet was on the *American Revenue*, it was captured by the British frigate *Greyhound* on 19 July 1779.
https://threedecks.org/index.php?display_type=show_ship&id=19808

captured the British *Lovely Lass* which they took to Boston. The ship was then in Martinique and on the return trip the crew was taken sick and one crew member died before getting to New Bedford. He served about five months. He was then in the militia company of Capt. John Johnson for two months before again serving on the privateer sloop *Hancock* of 12 guns. They were sailing in the company of the *American Revenue* and had a narrow escape from British ships. Back on land, in July 1779, Eliphalet had a nine-month enlistment in the company of Capt. Joseph Durkee from Canterbury. He was then back at sea again on the *Hancock* for a period of four months before another five-month enlisted with ground forces. He had a near continual four years of services.

Eliphalet reported his birth as 15 August 1758 at Canterbury. After the war, he remained in Canterbury until his was about forty years old and then went to Windsor County, Vermont. He remined there about one year before buying land in Addison County where he stayed for three of four years. He was then in Kingston until 1808 before locating in Avery's Gore an unorganized area near Kingston. He received a pension based on his service and following his decease his widow Hannah received a pension.[1252]

There are records for seven children of Eliphalet and Hannah, the oldest child at Canterbury and the others at Kingston, Vermont. Kingston was renamed Granville in 1833.

Son Amasa married Polly Thompson. They resided for a time in upstate New York and were then in Vermont from 1817 to 1831. Amasa, Polly, and their children then made the trip to Ohio via team, canal, and lake to Sandusky. They were later in Hardin County, Ohio where they both died.[1253]

i   MARY FARNUM, b. at Canterbury, CT, 18 Dec 1787; reported to be living in Ohio in 1841.

ii   AMASA FARNUM, b. at Kingston, VT, 17 Jul 1789; d. at Dudley, OH, 27 Sep 1839; m. at Surry, NH, 1 Jan 1810, MARY "POLLY" THOMPSON, b. at Gilsum, NH, 16 Jun 1790 daughter of David and Molly (Bliss) Thompson;[1254] Polly d. at Dudley, 14 Oct 1835.

iii   RUSSELL FARNHAM, b. at Kingston, 24 May 1791; d. after 1860 when living at Middlebury, VT; m. SARAH who has not been identified, b. in CT, about 1792 and d. after 1860.

iv   JOSHUA FARNUM, b. at Kingston, 12 Feb 1793

v   ELIPHALET FARNUM, b. at Kingston, 24 Dec 1794; d. at Acton, ME, 2 Mar 1870. Eliphalet did not marry.

vi   HANNAH FARNUM, b. at Kingston, 18 Feb 1797

vii   JONATHAN FARNUM, b. at Kingston, 12 Sep 1798

472)   PHEBE FARNUM (*Eliab Farnum⁴, Phebe Russell Farnum³, Thomas², Robert¹*), b. at Preston, 10 Sep 1756 son of Eliab and Abigail (Killum) Farnum; m. at Preston, 24 Mar 1774, AMOS PARKE,[1255] b. at Preston, 9 Sep 1749 son of Silas and Sarah (Ayer) Parke; Amos d. at Preston, 1 Oct 1825. Amos married second Margaret Moore.

Amos Parke was a physician in Preston. Phebe and Amos were parents of five children born at Preston. Amos had twelve children with his second wife Margaret Moore.[1256]

i   ELISHA PARK, b. about 1776 and d. about 1797 (reported as dying about age twenty).

ii   SHUBAEL PARK, b. 13 Feb 1777; d. 13 Feb 1826; m. 29 Nov 1801, HULDAH SKINNER, b. 5 Oct 1782; Huldah d. 4 Jul 1864.

iii   ERASTUS PARK, b. 1779; d. at Walworth, NY, 4 Apr 1861; m. at Salina, NY, 19 Jul 1812, LUCRETIA VAN VLECK, b. at Kinderhook, NY, 1788 daughter of Isaac and Bata (Goes) Van Vleck; Lucretia d. at Adrian, MI, Apr 1858.

iv   JOSHUA PARK

v   PHEBE PARK

473)   ABIGAIL FARNUM (*Eliab Farnum⁴, Phebe Russell Farnum³, Thomas², Robert¹*), b. at Preston, 2 Sep 1760 daughter of Eliab and Abigail (Killum) Farnum; m. 1st about 1778, ELEAZER OWEN, b. at Salisbury, CT, 16 Apr 1755 son of Jonathan and Patience (Vallance) Owen; Eleazer died at the Battle of Minisink, 22 Jul 1779. Abigail m. 2nd at Goshen, NY, 2 Feb 1784, ABIEL FRY, b. at Andover, 8 Nov 1734 son of Abiel and Abigail (Emery) Frye; Abiel d. at Chemung, NY, 2 Oct 1806.

[1252] U. S. Revolutionary War Pension and Bounty-Land Warrant Application Files, Case W24175
[1253] Perrin, *History of Summit County*, p 707
[1254] Hayward, *History of the Town of Gilsum*, p 400
[1255] The spellings of Parke and Park are both used. The children use Park.
[1256] Children are as reported in Parks, *Genealogy of the Parke Families*, p 90 who report the children were given by a list made by Charles T. Park.

A story reported by Charlotte Helen Abbott in her notes on the Frye family was that Abiel was on Washington's staff in the Revolution. While in Pennsylvania, he courted Abigail in Connecticut, but she married Eleazer Owen. When Abiel learned she widowed, he followed the family while they were moving to the Mohawk Valley and proposed to Abigail.[1257]

Abiel Fry did not leave a will and Elijah Buck, Esq. and Charles F. Fry assumed administration of the estate on 10 December 1806.[1258]

Abigail and Eleazer were parents of one child.

i   ELEAZER OWEN, b. 1 Jan 1780; d. at Big Flats, NY, 20 Dec 1859; m. 1805, MARGARET BUCK, b. 10 Jan 1779 daughter of Elijah and Margaret (Foster) Buck;[1259] Margaret d. at Big Flats, 14 Nov 1843.

Abigail Farnum and Abiel Frye were parents of ten children born at Chemung, New York.

i   CHARLES FREDERICK FRY, b. 20 Nov 1784; d. at Morgan County, IL, 10 Oct 1845; m. 8 Jan 1809, MATILDA BUCK daughter of Elijah and Margaret (Foster) Buck; Matilda d. 5 Aug 1846.

ii   HENRY LAURENS FRY, b. 5 Jul 1786; d. at Osceola, MI, 31 May 1860; m. 25 Dec 1812, ELIZABETH WELLS, b. 10 May 1792; Elizabeth d. at Osceola, 15 Jan 1883.

iii   ALFRED FRY, b. 6 Sep 1788; d. at Chemung, 1848 (probate 10 Oct 1848); m. 2 Dec 1819, HARRIET WYNKOOP, b. at Chemung, 19 May 1797 daughter of Benjamin and Hannah (Wynkoop) Wynkoop.[1260]

iv   ABIGAIL FRY, b. 20 Oct 1790; m. JACOB SMITH.[1261]

v   PHEBE RUSSELL FRY, b. 16 Dec 1792; d. at Chemung, NY, 23 Dec 1838; m. 4 Jul 1811, ASAHEL BUCK, b. at Chemung, 1 May 1792 son of Elijah and Margaret (Foster) Buck; Asahel d. at Chemung, 15 May 1863.

vi   Triplet 1, b. 11 Feb 1795; d. 11 Feb 1795.

vii   Triplet 2, b. 11 Feb 1795; d. 20 Feb 1795.

viii   Triplet 3, b. 11 Feb 1795; d. 17 Feb 1795.

ix   SARAH FRY, b. 5 Apr 1797; d. at Lodi, NY, 1866; m. 1 Mar 1843, JOHN I. HAGAMAN, b. 21 Mar 1792; d. at Lodi, 1853 (probate 1853).

x   CLARISSA FRY, b. 27 Aug 1799; d. 1842; m. ASA HIBBARD, b. at Leyden, MA, 1 Feb 1792 son of Asa and Abigail (Armstrong) Hibbard;[1262] Asa d. at Whitewater, IN, 3 Aug 1821.

474)   MARTHA FARNUM (*Eliab Farnum⁴, Phebe Russell Farnum³, Thomas², Robert¹*), b. at Preston, 29 Aug 1762 daughter of Eliab and Abigail (Killum) Farnum; d. likely at Sanford, NY, 2 Nov 1843; m. about 1791, NATHAN AUSTIN, b. at Preston, 5 Apr 1764 son of Benjamin and Susanna (Burdick) Austin; Nathan d. 1847.

Martha and Nathan resided primarily in Sanford, New York during the time they were rearing their children. They were members of the Methodist church in Sanford.[1263]

On 12 May 1839, Nathan Austin od Sanford, New York who would be age seventy-five on April 5 next provided a statement related to his application for a pension. He was born in Preston on 5 April 1764. On 1 June 1779, he enlisted from Preston at age fifteen years and two months with recruiting sergeant Amos Gallup in the artillery company of Capt. Latham. That same day, they marched to Fort Griswold where he served garrison duty. Following that enlistment, he was next drafted in July 1780 for three months in the company of Capt. Elijah Palmer in the regiment of Col. Richards. He had a third term when he enlisted in May 1781 in a company of "minute men" under Capt. David Green. After the war, he resided in Preston until 1785. He was then in Shawangunk in New York until 1787 and then was in Cherry Ridge which is now in Warren County, Pennsylvania. He was there seven years before moving to Sanford. Nathan's sister Susan Love of Bridgewater, New York provided a statement in support of his application.[1264]

The Farnum genealogy reports five children in this family, but one of the children (Edward Lewis Austin) reported was born in 1815 which seems not possible for Martha.[1265]

[1257] Abbott, *Early Records of the Frye Family of Andover*, https://www.mhl.org/sites/default/files/files/Abbott/Frye%20Family.pdf
[1258] New York Wills and Probate, Tioga County, Will Book A-B, volume 002, p 129. Elijah Buck, Esq. was father-in-law of Charles F. Fry.
[1259] Buck, *Buck History and Genealogy*, p 89
[1260] Wynkoop, *Wynkoop Genealogy*, p 110
[1261] Barker, *Frye Genealogy*, p 64
[1262] Hibbard, *Genealogy of the Hibbard Family*, p 98
[1263] Farnham, *New England Descendants of Ralph Farnum*, p 332
[1264] U. S. Revolutionary War Pension and Bounty-Land Warrant Application Files, Case S14932
[1265] Farnham, *New England Descendants of Ralph Farnum*, p 333

i   ELIAB AUSTIN, b. at Cherry Ridge, 1792; d. at Broome County, NY, 1817 (probate 28 Jul 1817); m. BETSEY UNDERWOOD, b. 3 Aug 1793; Betsey daughter of Jonas and Sarah (Pine) Underwood; d. at Deposit, NY, 24 Oct 1856. Betsey married second Jedediah Alexander.

ii   BENJAMIN AUSTIN, b. at Sanford, NY, 1794; d. at Sanford, 13 Jun 1871; m. 1st BETSEY who has not been identified but perhaps Betsey Pine, b. about 1804 and d. at Sanford, 21 Dec 1844.Benjamin m. 2nd the widow MIVERVA RAY, b. 1805; Minerva d. at Sanford, 1 Apr 1875.

iii   MARY ANN AUSTIN, b. 1796

iv   ABIGAIL AUSTIN, b. 1798; d. 1847; reported as marrying Mr. Corwin who has not been identified (Farnum genealogy).

475)   RUSSELL FARNUM (*Eliab Farnum4, Phebe Russell Farnum3, Thomas2, Robert1*), b. at Preston, 9 Sep 1764 son of Eliab and Abigail (Killum) Farnum; d. at McClure, NY, 23 Feb 1820; m. about 1794, EUNICE VAN DEUZEN, b. about 1773; Eunice d. at McClure, 26 Oct 1834.

Russell was the sixth child and eldest son of Eliab and Abigail Farnum. He was born in Preston. He may be the Russell Farnum who served as a private in Beatty's First American Regiment for a total of thirteen months in 1789-1790.[1266]

Russell and Eunice settled in Broome County, New York where they were first settlers of the area that became Sanford on 2 April 1821. The settlement of this area was begum by Russell's brother-in-law William MacClure.[1267]

There are two known children of Russell and Eunice,[1268] although the 1820 census for Windsor. Broome County, New York with Eunice as head of household suggests a larger family of perhaps as many as ten children. The household consists of one female 45 and over; two males under 10; one male 10-15; one male 16-18; three males 16-25; two female 10-15; and two females 16-25.[1269]

i   PHEBE FARNUM, b. 1795; d. at Deposit, NY, about 1868;[1270] m. 1817, JABEZ PEMBER who is not clearly identified but may be the Jabez b. at Norwich, CT, 1780 son of Jacob and Lydia (Fillmore) Pember.[1271] If so, Jabez was first married to Rebecca Sellick in Middlebury, VT on 17 Jan 1809. Phebe was living in Tompkins, NY in 1865 with her daughter Adelia and her husband Thomas W. Powell. Phebe was head of household in Tompkins, NY in 1830 with two females under age 14 in the household with her.[1272]

ii   MOSES H. FARNUM, b. 3 Oct 1797; d. at Sanford, NY, 2 May 1869; m. about 1819, SUSAN BIDWELL, b. 19 May 1801 daughter of Amos and Abigail (Tomkin) Bidwell; Susan d. 11 Apr 1868.

476)   SARAH FARNUM (*Eliab Farnum4, Phebe Russell Farnum3, Thomas2, Robert1*), b. at Preston, 13 Jan 1769 daughter of Eliab and Abigail (Killum) Farnum; d. at McClure, NY, 10 Mar 1807 in childbirth; m. 26 Feb 1791, WILLIAM MACCLURE,[1273] b. at Chester, NH, 1726 son of James and Jean (Andrews) MacClure; William d. at McClure, 14 Dec 1826. William married second Lydia Austin.

The first settlement in the area that became Sanford, New York was begum by William MacClure in 1787. He was trained as a surveyor and had done this work in Dutchess and Orange counties in New York. He was sent to survey this new area for Robert Harpur owner of large tracts of property in that area. William MacClure kept a detailed journal which included transcripts of many letters that he wrote.[1274]

William married later in life to the much younger Sarah Farnum whose family were also early settlers of this area of Broome County. William courted Sarah in a series of letters written from his colorfully named "Castle William."[1275] William and Sarah were parents of nine children, Sarah dying two days after the birth of their ninth child.

Thomas MacClure and Henry MacClure were administrators of the estate. On 12 October 1827, the probate court issued an order allowing sale of some of the real estate as the personal estate was insufficient to pay debts.[1276]

[1266] U. S. Compiled Service Records, Post-Revolutionary War Soldiers, Roll 01-02, First U. S. Regiment (Harmar), Card 43210322
[1267] French, *Gazetteer of the State of New York*, p 183, and p 183 footnote 6
[1268] Farnham, *The New England Descendants of Ralph Farnum*, p 334
[1269] 1820 U S Census; Census Place: Windsor, Broome, New York; Page: 13; NARA Roll: M33_65; Image: 25
[1270] Phebe is buried at Pine Grove Cemetery in Deposit, age at death of 72; findagrave ID: 94626744
[1271] Hazen, *John Pember*, p 100
[1272] Year: 1830; Census Place: Tompkins, Delaware, New York; Series: M19; Roll: 89; Page: 206; Family History Library Film: 0017149
[1273] Transcripts of letters written by William to Sarah during his courtship of her can be seen in Farnham's Farnum genealogy, pp 334-339
[1274] Transcripts of some letters and other diary entries can be found in Smith's *History of Broome County* starting on page 299
[1275] Much information on William MacClure, his early survey work and courtship of Sarah is documented in previously published sources included the History of Broome County and the Farnum genealogy and the reader is referred to those sources.
[1276] New York Wills and Probate, Broome County, Wills, Letters, volume B, pp 2-3

i   WILLIAM MACCLURE, b. Dec 1791; d. at Deposit, NY, 2 Mar 1874; m. MARY ALLEN, b. in CT, about 1790; Mary d. at Deposit, 12 Oct 1869.

ii   DAVID C. MACCLURE, b. 2 Mar 1793; d. at McClure, NY, 29 Jan 1870; m. 1812, HANNAH SPRINGSTEEN, b. at Windsor, 16 Oct 1790 daughter of John and Deanna (Rector) Springsteen.

iii   HENRY MACCLURE, b. 16 Sep 1794; d. at McClure, NY, 24 Sep 1870; m. LAURINDA BIDWELL, b. 23 May 1799 daughter of Amos and Abigail (Tomkin) Bidwell; Laurinda d. 23 Aug 1881.

iv   WALTER MACCLURE, b. 4 Sep 1798; d. at Sanford, NY, 26 Feb 1866; m. MARGARET WHITAKER, b. 1801 daughter and Benjamin and Eunice (Hine) Whitaker; Margaret d. 12 Dec 1869.

v   SALLY MACCLURE, b. 18 Dec 1800; d. at Woodstock, IL, 15 Apr 1882; m. CYRUS DOOLITTLE, b. at Windsor, 24 Nov 1797 son of Abel and Deborah (Fancher) Doolittle; Cyrus d. at Conklin, NY, 8 Jun 1856.

vi   THOMAS MACCLURE, b. 25 May 1802; d. at McClure, 12 Aug 1855; m. LURANA JENNINGS, b. 1812; Lurana d. (burial at McClure), 28 Feb 1888.

vii   FRANCES "FANNY" MACCLURE, b. 9 Dec 1803; d. at McClure, NY, 12 May 1846; m. about 1832, CHARLES HEWITT, b. 24 Dec 1807 son of Charles and Susanna (Pine) Hewitt; Charles d. at McClure, 3 Nov 1868. Charles Hewitt (although uncertain if this Charles or his son) was the first postmaster of the McClure settlement when the post office was established there in 1865.[1277]

viii   ALEXANDER HAMILTON MACCLURE, b. 18 Apr 1805; d. at Barrington, IL, 14 Mar 1887; m. at Broome County, NY, Nov 1834, ELIZABETH LUSCOMB, b. about 1819, Elizabeth d. at Pontiac, MI, 29 Jun 1891. Alexander and Elizabeth divorced about 1844 and Elizabeth was later married to O. Charles Allen,

ix   PRUDENCE MACCLURE, b. 8 Mar 1807; d. at McClure, NY, 1876; m. 1834, NICHOLAS HEMPSTEAD, b. at Hempstead, Long Island, 1809 son of David and Eunice (Murray) Hempstead; Nicholas d. at McClure, 1863.

477)   JEFFREY AMHERST FARNUM (*Eliab Farnum⁴, Phebe Russell Farnum³, Thomas², Robert¹*), b. at Preston, 17 Oct 1772 son of Eliab and Abigail (Killum) Farnum; d. at Scipio, NY, 12 Nov 1841; m. at Big Flats, NY, Dec 1793, MERCY TRACY, b. at Norwich, 16 Sep 1775 daughter of Benjamin and Olive (Killam) Tracy; Mercy d. at Pittsford, NY, 11 May 1873.

    Jeffrey was an early settler of Scipio having a property near the Square of "No. 1".[1278]

    The Farnum genealogy reports on probate records (not located) that identified the following heirs to Jeffrey's estate: Marshall Hurd and Jeffrey A. Farnam of Scipio; Benjamin F. Farnam and Alfred Farnam of Somerset; Eliab Farnum of Whitesfield; Avery F. Farnam and Phebe Parks wife of Phil Parks of Victor; Stephen Farnam of Eaton, Michigan; Lucinda Gaylord wife of John Gaylord of Kirtland, Ohio; Fena A. Hurd of Marshall, Michigan; Joseph Johnson of Attica, New York; Henry Farnam of New Haven, Connecticut; and Newton Hurd of Albion.[1279]

    Jeffrey and Mercy were parents of eleven children, the oldest child born at Big Flats and the other children at Scipio, New York.

i   LUCINDA FARNUM, b. Mar 1795; d. at Lyons, WI, 25 May 1856; m. at Scipio, NY, 1812, JOHN GAYLORD, b. 27 Jul 1790 son of John and Charlotte (Hitchcock) Gaylord; John d. at Plano, IL, 4 Sep 1866.

ii   ELIAB FARNUM, b. 3 Dec 1796; d. at Ellington, WI, Jun 1873; m. at Scipio, 1821, SALLY PECK, b. in CT about 1799; Sally d. at Ellington, 15 Mar 1873.

iii   ABIGAIL FARNUM, b. 9 Jun 1799; d. at Attica, NY, 19 Jun 1827; m. 1st 1817, MARSHALL HURD, b. at Arlington, VT, 4 Mar 1794 son of Tyrus and Contents (Newton) Hurd. Abigail m. 2nd, 1826, JOSEPH JOHNSON.

iv   BENJAMIN FRANKLIN FARNUM, b. 17 Sep 1801; d. at Hillsdale, MI, 17 Oct 1885; m. at Royalton, NY, 2 Oct 1825, SALLY JULINA BRYANT, b. 1805 daughter of James Bryant; Sally d. at Hillsdale, 15 Mar 1881.

v   GEORGE WASHINGTON FARNUM, b. 17 Sep 1801; d. at Pittsford, NY, 23 Feb 1881; m. 1st at Ledyard, NY, 1820, ELIZABETH AMELIA HOYT, b. at Norwalk, CT, 6 Mar 1802 daughter of Thomas and Betsey (Netheway) Hoyt; Elizabeth d. at Cayuga County, NY, 12 Feb 1852. George m. 2nd 20 Oct 1853, THEODOCIA BOUGHTON (widow of John Powell), b. 8 Jun 1806 daughter of Eleazer and Deborah (Benedict) Boughton; Theodocia d. 13 Sep 1880.

[1277] Smith, *History of Broome County*, p 323
[1278] Storke, *History of Cayuga County, New York*, p 424
[1279] Farnham, *The New England Descendants of Ralph Farnum*, p 342

vi   HENRY FARNUM, b. 9 Nov 1803; d. at New Haven, CT, 4 Oct 1883; m. at Farmington, CT, 1 Dec 1839, ANNE SOPHIA WHITMAN, b. at Farmington, 15 Sep 1816 daughter of William and Elizabeth (-) Whitman; Anne d. at New Haven, 6 Mar 1904.

vii   STEPHEN FARNUM, b. 2 Feb 1805; d. at Eaton Rapids, MI, 2 Mar 1889; m. at Scipio, 15 Sep 1830, ELIZABETH SHERMAN, b. in NY, 1804 (on gravestone); Elizabeth d. at Eaton Rapids, 6 Jul 1886.

viii   ALFRED T. FARNUM, b. 15 Aug 1808; d. at Cassville, MO, 10 Jan 1886. Alfred did not marry. He may be the Alfred who was in Mud Springs, CA in 1850 during the Gold Rush.

ix   AVERY TRACY FARNUM, b. 5 Feb 1811; d. at Sheffield, IL, 16 Aug 1889; m. at Perinton, NY, 12 Nov 1840, DORCAS BREWER, b. in England, about 1818 daughter of Thomas and Mary (-) Brewer.

x   PHEBE FARNUM, b. 6 May 1814; d. at Grinnell, IL, 25 Jan 1894; m. at Scipio, 10 Nov 1836, PHILO PARKS, b. at Victor, NY, 25 Jul 1812 son of Simeon and Abigail (Tracy) Parks; Philo d. at Poweshiek County, IA, 1862.

xi   JEFFREY AMHERST FARNUM, b. 27 Oct 1817; d. at Wausau, WI, 5 May 1883; m. 1st at Wausau, 12 Sep 1864, EMILY SANBORN (widow of Henry White Johnston), b. at Wheelock, VT, 4 Nov 1826 (date is on gravestone) daughter of William and Mary (Page) Sanborn;[1280] Emily d. at Wausau, 2 Apr 1881. Jefferey m. 2nd 11 Apr 1882, MARY BUTTERFIELD (widow of Daniel Franklin Newcomb), b. at Washington County, NY, 12 Sep 1831 daughter of John and Sarah Ann (Jacques) Butterfield; Mary d. at Madison, WI, 26 Jul 1923.

478)   GEORGE WHITFIELD FARNUM (*Eliab Farnum⁴, Phebe Russell Farnum³, Thomas², Robert¹*), b. at Preston, 17 Oct 1772 son of Eliab and Abigail (Killum) Farnum; d. after 1838[1281] likely at Ledyard, NY; m. about 1800, ANNA ALLEN, b. about 1780 daughter of Gideon and Phebe (Beardsley) Allen; Anna d. after 1838.

George and Anna resided in Scipio where in 1820 they lived next door to Jeffrey A. Farnham. In 1820, the household consisted of on male over 45; one female 26-44; one male under 10; two males 10-15; and two females under 10.[1282] There are a possible six children of George and Anna.[1283]

i   SARAH FARNUM, b. 1804

ii   FANNY FARNUM, b. at Ledyard, NY, 1808

iii   CHARLES FARNUM, b. at Ledyard, 27 Jan 1810; d. at Hamlin, NY, 6 Jun 1887; m. about 1841, LUCY M. KIRTLAND, b. at Albany County, NY, 1817; Lucy d. at Kendall, NY, 1879.

iv   ALLAN FARNUM, b. at Ledyard, 1811

v   GEORGE WHITFIELD FARNUM, b. at Ledyard, 1815; d. at Cayuga County, NY, 15 Mar 1852; m. 1st by 1837, SARAH who has not been identified and who d. by 1840. George m. 2nd 31 Oct 1840, ANNA ELIZA WAGER, b. at Tompkins County, NY, 1 Apr 1813 daughter of Peter D. and Phebe (Norris) Wager; Ann d. at Elmira, NY, 13 Apr 1872.

vi   HENRY FARNUM, b. at Ledyard, 22 Jun 1826; d. at Niles, NY, 15 Feb 1906; m. at Scipio, 4 Dec 1845, CORNELIA ADELINE DARROW, b. at Scipio, 19 Apr 1825, daughter of John and Nancy E. (Newell) Darrow; Cornelia d. at Niles, 25 May 1901.

479)   ELIAB FARNUM (*Eliab Farnum⁴, Phebe Russell Farnum³, Thomas², Robert¹*), b. at Coventry, CT, 4 Aug 1775 son of Eliab and Abigail (Killum) Farnum; d. at Benton Township, PA, 31 Mar 1855; m. at Deer Park, NY, 1 Jan 1797, HANNAH OSBORNE, b. at South Salem, NY, 24 Apr 1778 daughter of John and Eunice (Nichols) Osborne; Hannah d. 24 Aug 1835.

Eliab and Hannah resided in Deer Park, New York in the early part of their marriage and resided there until about 1813 when they obtained property in Luzerne County, Pennsylvania[1284] where they resided in Nicholson and Benton Township. In 1850, Eliab was listed as head of household in Benton Township with son Daniel O. Farnum and his family. Real property was valued at $1,600 on census records.[1285]

Eliab and Hannah were parents of eleven children, the older children born at Deer Park and the younger children likely in Luzerne County, Pennsylvania.

[1280] The 1876 probate of William Sanborn of Jefferson County, WI includes a petition by J. A. Farnham, Alden Sanborn, and W. P. Forsyth the named executors of the will.
[1281] When he executed a deed; Farnham, *New England Descendants of Ralph Farnum*, p 340
[1282] 1820 U S Census; Census Place: Scipio, Cayuga, New York; Page: 121; NARA Roll: M33_68; Image: 135
[1283] Farnham, *New England Descendants of Ralph Farnum*, pp 340-341
[1284] Farnham, *New England Descendants of Ralph Farnum*, pp 348-349
[1285] Year: 1850; Census Place: Benton, Luzerne, Pennsylvania; Roll: 793; Page: 217b

i   ELISHA PARKE FARNUM, b. 22 Oct 1797; d. at Lenox, PA, 10 Nov 1871; m. at Lenoxville, PA, 1 Jan 1816, CATHERINE ANN QUICK (widow of John Decker), b. about 1788 daughter of Jacob and Rachel (Wood) Quick;[1286] Catherine d. at Lemon, PA, 1 Jun 1881.

ii   MARIAH FARNUM, b. 24 Jul 1799; d. at Marshbrook, Pa, 9 Oct 1814.

iii   ABIGAIL FARNUM, b. at Orange County, NY, 29 May 1801; d. at Scott, PA, 27 Feb 1890; m. at Abington, PA, 1 Jan 1825, as his second wife, HARVEY VAIL, b. at Orange County, NY, 18 Jan 1800 son of Micah and Esther (Slawson) Vail; Harvey d. at Scott, 1885 (probate 1885). Harvey was first married to Miranda Jerusha Orvis.

iv   ROXY FARNUM, b. 14 Jun 1803; d. at Benton, PA, 27 Jul 1876; m. at Benton, 14 Sep 1818, MILTON HAYDEN, b. at Roxbury, MA, 15 Dec 1798 son of Isaac and Sarah (Jillson) Hayden; Milton d. at Benton, 7 Feb 1862.

v   STEPHEN NICHOLS FARNUM, b. perhaps at Marshbrook, PA, 8 Jun 1805; d. at Dinsmore, PA, 21 Dec 1879; m. 1st at Benton, 21 Aug 1828, ELIZA MATILDA BAKER, b. 1810 daughter of Isaac and Louisa (Barnes) Baker; Eliza d. at Benton, 23 Mar 1847. Stephen m. 2nd about 1847, ABIGAIL ANN FITZGERALD, b. at Amenia, NY, 15 Oct 1815; Abigail d. at Blakely, PA, 3 May 1888.

vi   DANIEL OSBORN FARNUM, b. 31 May 1807; d. at Nicholson, PA, 3 Apr 1886; m. about 1829, DEMILAH HASKINS, b. 1810; Demilah b. at Lenox, 26 Jul 1883.

vii   PHEBE FARNUM, b. 16 Dec 1809; d. at Benton, PA, 11 Jan 1888; m. at Abington, PA, 17 Oct 1827, JAMES BRUNDAGE, b. at Eagle Rock, NJ, 10 Aug 1805 son of Parmalias and Lillis (Brundage) Brundage; James d. at Benton, 27 Feb 1888.

viii   SALLY ANN FARNHAM, b. 14 Jan 1812; d. at Clifford, PA, 17 Aug 1897; m. 12 Jan 1832, NELSON PHILLIPS, b. at Orange County, NY, 21 Aug 1805 son of Thomas Phillips; Nelson d. at Clifford, 21 Jan 1881.

ix   MALINDA FARNUM, b. 22 Apr 1814; d. after 1880 when she was living at Benton; m. about 1860, as at least his second wife, ABRAM WRIGLEY, b. in England, about 1787; Abram d. at Abington, PA, 20 Aug 1862. In his 1859 will, Abram Wrigley includes bequests to daughter and grandchildren and nieces. In a codicil written in 1861, he adds a bequest to his wife Melinda of $30 per year as well as any of the household items she chooses. Malinda was unmarried and living with her father in 1850.

x   MAHALA FARNUM, b. 12 Jul 1816; d. at Benton, PA, 17 Mar 1861; m. at Nicholson, PA, 15 Mar 1838, JAMES HARTLEY, b. 3 May 1810; James d. at Benton, 27 Apr 1871. James married second Polly.

xi   JULIA FARNHAM, b. 6 Apr 1819; d. at Benton, PA, 16 Jan 1881; m. about 1858, as his second wife, RILEY ELLIOTT PHILLIPS, b. 1810; Riley d. at Benton, 2 Feb 1882. Riley was first married to Mary Ann Robinson. Julia and Riley had one son. In her will written 15 January 1881 (filed 11 February 1882), Julia Phillips of Benton wife of Riley Phillips left her entire estate to her only son Riley Ellsworth Phillips.[1287]

480)   STEPHEN FARNUM (*Eliab Farnum⁴, Phebe Russell Farnum³, Thomas², Robert¹*), b. at Deer Park, NY, 19 Oct 1779 son of Eliab and Abigail (Killum) Farnum; d. at Crawford, NY, 27 Apr 1868; m. about 1810, KETURAH SAYBOTT, b. at Goshen, NY, 6 Sep 1787 daughter of Frederick and Abigail (Reeve) Saybott; Keturah d. at Hopewell, NY, 6 Dec 1872.

Stephen Farnum was a farmer in Orange County, New York residing in Mount Hope, likely Deer Park, and lastly in Crawford, New York. He was trustee of the Farmers Library at Mt. Hope in 1807, town clerk in 1809, and town supervisor in 1822.[1288]

On 6 June 1868, widow Keturah Farnum provided the following lists of heirs-at-law of the estate of Stephen Farnam who died on 27 April 1868 without leaving a will: the petitioner widow of Crawford; Abigail Corwin wife of Archibald Corwin of Mountainville; Mary Sherwood wife of Henry L. Sherwood of Florida; Harriet Crawford widow of Albert Crawford of Crawford; Matilda Sloat wife of Alexander Sloat residing in Wallkill (all these first listed in Orange County); and George Farnam residing in La Crosse, Wisconsin.[1289]

Stephen and Keturah were parents of seven children born at Mount Hope, New York.

i   ABIGAIL FARNUM, b. 4 Feb 1815; d. at Otisville, NY, 14 Jul 1894; m. 1834, ARCHIBALD CORWIN, b. 1809 son of John and Julia (Vail) Corwin;[1290] Archibald d. at Otisville, 30 Jul 1878.

1286 Quick, *Genealogy of the Quick Family in America*, p 165

1287 Pennsylvania Wills and Probate, Lackawanna County, Estate of Julia Phillips, Case 366

1288 Farnham, *The New England Descendants of Ralph Farnum*, p 352

1289 New York Wills and Probate, Orange County, Estate Files, Petitions for Administrations, Canister 481, 1865-1869; accessed through ancestry.com

1290 Corwin, *The Corwin Genealogy*, p 121

ii   MARY FARNUM, b. 16 Sep 1816; d. at La Crosse, WI, 4 May 1877; m. 1ˢᵗ about 1835, JAMES MANNING FINCH, b. 11 Apr 1811 son of James and Sarah Tooker (Manning) Finch;[1291] James d. of typhus fever at Hopewell, NY, 4 Feb 1844. Mary m. 2ⁿᵈ at Pomona, NY, 9 Feb 1846, HENRY L. SHERWOOD, b. 18 Oct 1810 son of Levi and Mariah (Estler) Sherwood; Henry d. at Lodi, NY, 19 Aug 1886 (probate Dec 1886). Henry was first married to Leah Ann Traphagen and third married to Sophia. Mary and James Finch had one child, Mary Frances Finch.

iii   HARRIET FARNUM, b. 1820; d. at Montgomery, NY, 17 Sep 1907; m. about 1841, ALBERT CRAWFORD, b. 1814 likely son of Robert and Deborah (Dickerson) Crawford;[1292] Albert d. at Newburgh, NY, 22 Sep 1853.

iv   MATILDA FARNUM, b. 20 Oct 1822; d. at Walden, NY, 15 Apr 1901; m. at Hopewell, 7 Feb 1850, ALEXANDER C. SLOAT, b. at Crawford, NY, Oct 1822 son of Cornelius and Charity (Cummins) Sloat; Alexander d. at Scotchtown, NY, 11 Aug 1900.

v   GEORGE FARNUM, b. 24 Feb 1825; d. at La Crosse, WI, 12 Sep 1891; m. 1ˢᵗ at Johnson County, IA, 8 Mar 1852, ANN M. STOVER, b. in PA, 1831 daughter of Jacob H. and Rebecca (Hess) Stover; Ann d. at La Crosse, 13 Oct 1867. George m. 2ⁿᵈ at Sparta, WI, 1 Dec 1870, SARAH MONTGOMERY, b. in OH 1838 daughter of Abel and Sarah (Burgett) Montgomery; Sarah d. at La Crosse, 13 Sep 1897.

vi   EMILY FARNUM, b. 10 Jan 1828; d. at Orange County, NY, 14 Jul 1861.

vii   SARAH FARNUM, b. 10 Dec 1830; d. 27 Apr 1844.

481)   PETER OSGOOD (*Peter Osgood⁴, Mary Russell Osgood³, Thomas², Robert¹*), b. at Andover, 24 Jun 1745 son of Peter and Sarah (Johnson) Osgood; d. at Andover, 5 Jan 1801; m. at Andover, 24 Nov 1788, HANNAH PORTER, b. about 1762 at Boxford (according to her death record); Hannah d. at Andover, 18 Sep 1854. Peter also had a child with Susannah Poor, but it is unclear if they were married, and it seems more likely this was an out-of-wedlock child.

    Peter Osgood was a merchant in Andover. He did not leave a will and his estate entered probate 3 February 1801 with widow Hannah as administratrix. Personal estate was valued at $674.36 and real estate at $2670.77.[1293]

    Peter Osgood and Susannah Poor had one child.

i   CHARLES GRANDISON OSGOOD, b. at Andover, 4 Jun 1785 (Charles Grandison, s. Peter and Susanna Poor, June 4, 1785) and baptized at Andover 20 Sep 1789 as the son of Peter and Hannah (Charles Grandison, s. Capt. Peter, Jr. and Hannah, bp. Sept. 20, 1789). Likely he is the Charles G. Osgood living in Danvers in 1865. On 28 September 1801, Charles G. Osgood, then age sixteen, made choice of Isaac Osgood, Esq. of Andover who was the brother of his father Peter to be his guardian.[1294] Charles did not marry. He was a tanner. He may be the Charles Osgood who died at the almshouse in Peabody, age 82, on 7 Apr 1868.

    Peter Osgood and Hannah Porter were parents of four children born at Andover. Son Peter Osgood entered Harvard in 1810 and graduated in 1814. He immediately followed with theological studies as a member of the first class of Harvard Divinity School. He was ordained 30 June 1819 and took up his post as minister in Sterling, Massachusetts.[1295] He served as minister at Sterling for more than twenty years. Peter did not marry, and his will written 19 December 1849 (probate 14 November 1865) includes bequests to his nieces and nephews the children of his brother Samuel W. Osgood and sister Harriot Putnam. There are other bequests to individuals who had been of assistance to him and to the church at Sterling. The residue of the estate goes to his sister Hannah and his niece Mary Augusta.[1296]

i   SAMUEL W. OSGOOD, baptized at Andover, 20 Sep 1789; d. at New York, NY, Jul 1832; m. at New York, NY, 30 Jul 1814, his first cousin, JULIA ANN OSGOOD, b. at New York, 14 Aug 1788 daughter of Samuel and Maria (Bourne) Osgood; Julia d. at Marlborough, MA, 10 Feb 1871. Julia married second Israel Warburton Putnam who was first married to Samuel's sister Harriot (see below). Samuel was an attorney in New York.

[1291] Thummel, *The Descendants of John Finch of Connecticut*, p 212 and p 397

[1292] Genealogical Society of Bergen County, Family Files, p 241, https://www.njgsbc.org/files/familyfiles/p241.htm#i4468

[1293] *Essex County, MA: Probate File Papers, 1638-1881.* Online database. *AmericanAncestors.org.* New England Historic Genealogical Society, 2014. Case 20255

[1294] *Essex County, MA: Probate File Papers, 1638-1881.* Online database. *AmericanAncestors.org.* New England Historic Genealogical Society, 2014. Case 20177

[1295] Allen, *The Worcester Association and Its Antecedents*, pp 329-330

[1296] *Essex County, MA: Probate File Papers, 1638-1881.* Online database. *AmericanAncestors.org.* New England Historic Genealogical Society, 2014. Case 48921

ii   HARRIOT OSGOOD, b. 28 Mar 1791; d. at Portsmouth, NH, 10 Jun 1832; m. at Andover, 2 Dec 1815, ISRAEL WARBURTON PUTNAM, b. at Danvers, 24 Nov 1786 son of Eleazer and Sarah (Fuller) Putnam; Israel d. at Middleborough, MA, 3 May 1868. Israel married second Julia Ann Osgood on 29 Apr 1833.

iii   PETER OSGOOD, b. 4 Feb 1793; d. at North Andover, 27 Aug 1865. Rev. Peter Osgood did not marry.

iv   HANNAH P. OSGOOD, b. 23 Dec 1794; d. at Andover, 5 Jun 1888. Hannah did not marry.

482)   SAMUEL OSGOOD (*Peter Osgood⁴, Mary Russell Osgood³, Thomas², Robert¹*), b. at Andover, 3 Feb 1748 son of Peter and Sarah (Johnson) Osgood; d. at New York, NY, 12 Aug 1813; m. 1st at Cambridge, 4 Jan 1775, MARTHA BRANDON, b. about 1752 likely the daughter of Benjamin and Elizabeth (Foxcroft) Brandon; Martha d. at Andover, 13 Sep 1778. Samuel m. 2nd at New York, 24 May 1786, MARIA BOURNE (widow of Walter Franklin), b. about 1754 daughter of Daniel Bourne;[1297] Maria d. at New York, Oct 1814.

     Samuel Osgood obtained a bachelor's degree from Harvard in 1770 and later completed the A.M. degree.[1298] Although he studied theology at Harvard, Samuel was involved in mercantile trade. He served as Brigade Major was at the Battle of Bunker Hill. He was named Aide-de-camp to Maj. Gen. Ward.[1299] He left the service with rank of colonel and assistant quartermaster. He was member of the Continental Congress and member of state house of representatives.[1300]

     Samuel Osgood was the first Postmaster General of the newly formed United States, appointed by George Washington on 26 September 1789. There were three earlier postmaster generals appointed in the period of the Continental Congress.[1301] On 9 December 1789, Osgood wrote to George Washington outlining what he saw as necessary and an overall assessment of postal services in the new nation. This document addressed issues such as who might be permitted to carry mail, identifying crimes and frauds related to mail delivery, and defining the duties of the office of postmaster general.[1302]

     Samuel Osgood wrote his will 8 February 1792 (proved 2 September 1813), twenty-one years before his death. He requested to be buried in a decent and inexpensive manner. He appointed his dear wife Maria as guardian to his children: Martha Brandon Osgood, Julianna Osgood, and Walter Franklin Osgood, and of any future children he might have. He leaves his entire estate to wife Maria for the support and education of his children and she will distribute the estate as she sees fit. Maria was named executrix.[1303]

     Samuel Osgood and Maria Bourne were parents of six children.

i   MARTHA BRANDON OSGOOD, b. 6 Feb 1787; d. at New York, 24 Jan 1853; m. at New York, 31 Jul 1814, as his second wife, EDMOND CHARLES GENET, b. at Versailles, France, 8 Jan 1763 son of Edmond Jacques Genêt; Edmond d. at Schodack Center, NY, 14 Jul 1834. Edmond was first married to Cornelia Tappen Clinton. Edmond was known as Citizen Genêt and was the French revolutionary era diplomat who was the center of the "Genêt Affair."

ii   JULIA ANN OSGOOD, b. 14 Aug 1788; d. at Middleborough, MA, 10 Feb 1871; m. 1st at New York, NY, 30 Jul 1814, SAMUEL W. OSGOOD (*Peter Osgood⁵, Peter Osgood⁴, Mary Russell Osgood³, Thomas², Robert¹*), baptized at Andover, MA, 20 Sep 1789 son of Peter and Hannah (Porter) Osgood; Samuel d. at New York, Jul 1832. Julia m. 2nd at New York, 29 Apr 1833, as his second wife, ISRAEL WARBURTON PUTNAM, b. at Danvers, 24 Nov 1786 son of Eleazer and Sarah (Fuller) Putnam; Israel d. at Middleborough, 3 May 1868. Israel was first married to Harriet Osgood.

iii   WALTER FRANKLIN OSGOOD, b. 26 Mar 1791; d. at New York, 1836; m. ELLEN who is not identified with whom he had one son, Samuel, born about 1810. Walter graduated from Columbia in 1809. Son Samuel died during the Civil War at New Bern, NC, 2 Dec 1862.

iv   ELIZA OSGOOD, b. 1793; d. 1800.

v   SUSANNA KITTREDGE OSGOOD, b. 12 Apr 1795; d. at New York, May 1834; m. at New York, 18 May 1821, MOSES FIELD, b. 4 Oct 1779 son of John and Lydia (Hazard) Field;[1304] Moses d. at New York, 18 Oct 1833.

vi   CAROLINE M. OSGOOD, b. 27 Feb 1799; d. 1800.

[1297] The will of Walter Franklin of Long Island makes mention of his father-in-law Daniel Bourne. His name is also given in some sources as Daniel Browne.

[1298] Harvard University, Quinquennial Catalogue, p 146

[1299] *Massachusetts Soldiers and Sailors in the Revolution*, volume 11, p 707

[1300] Biographical Directory of the United States Congress, Samuel Osgood (1748-1813), https://bioguideretro.congress.gov/Home/MemberDetails?memIndex=O000116

[1301] "U. S. Postmasters General", Smithsonian National Postal Museum; https://postalmuseum.si.edu/topics/us-postmasters-general

[1302] National Archives, Founders Online, "To George Washington from Samuel Osgood, 9 December 1789", https://founders.archives.gov/documents/Washington/05-04-02-0272

[1303] New York Wills and Probate, New York County, Wills, volume 051, pp 53-54

[1304] Pierce, *Field Genealogy*, volume 1, p 268

483)   SUSANNA OSGOOD (*Peter Osgood⁴, Mary Russell Osgood³, Thomas², Robert¹*), b. at Andover, 23 Oct 1754 daughter of Peter and Sarah (Johnson) Osgood; d. at Andover, 28 Apr 1840; m. at Andover, 7 Nov 1771, Dr. THOMAS KITTREDGE, b. at Andover, 13 Jul 1746 son of John and Sarah (Merriam) Kittredge; Thomas d. at Andover, 16 Oct 1818.[1305]

Dr. Thomas Kittredge studied medicine in Newburyport and then settled in Andover. He was surgeon to Col. James Frye's regiment during the Revolution and was at the Battle of Bunker Hill. He served in the Massachusetts legislature and was an early member of the Massachusetts medical society.[1306]

Susanna and Thomas's sons John and Joseph followed in the medical tradition of the family. Granddaughter Maria Susanna Cummins (daughter of Maria and David Cummins) was author of *The Lamplighter* published in 1854, a best-selling novel of the era.

Thomas Kittredge did not leave a will and on 4 December 1818, the following heirs petitioned requesting that William Johnson be named administrator: widow Susannah, John Kittredge, Lemuel LeBarron, D. Cummins, and Joseph Kittredge. Those signing as witnesses to this document were Susan Kittredge, Martha LeBarron, Catherine Cummins, and Maria F. Kittredge. William Johnson was named administrator 5 January 1819. Thomas had an extensive estate with real estate valued at $16,208. This included the main house with outbuildings on 20 acres valued at $6,500, tavern house on five acres valued at $3,000, the "old house" at $850, a mill house with nine acres at $650, and several other lots of land. There was $4,650 in bank stock. Numerous notes were due the estate and the total value of the personal estate was $17,221.35 for a total estate value of $33,429.35.[1307]

Susanna Kittredge did not leave a will and on 5 May 1840, the following heirs-at-law requested that Francis Cummins be named administrator: D. Cummins, Thomas Kittredge, William LeBaron, and Joseph W. Kittredge. Susanna had no real estate and personal estate was valued at $7,112.51, all but a cow valued at $25 in the form of bank notes, cash, and notes due the estate.[1308]

Susanna and Thomas were parents of seven children born at Andover.

i   SUSANNA KITTREDGE, b. 10 Aug 1772; d. 19 May 1829. Susanna did not marry.

ii   JOHN KITTREDGE, b. 15 Dec 1775; d. at Gloucester, MA, 31 Aug 1822; m. at Gloucester, 21 May 1806, MARY PLUMMER, b. at Milton, 1783 daughter of David and Mary (Card) Plummer; Mary d. at Milton, 8 May 1865. Mary married second Gen. Moses Whitney on 16 Nov 1825.

iii MARTHA OSGOOD KITTREDGE, b. 31 Oct 1778; d. at Andover, 6 Nov 1839; m. at Andover, 29 Nov 1809, LEMUEL LEBARRON, b. at Rochester, MA, 10 Jan 1780 son of Lemuel and Elizabeth (Allen) LeBarron; Lemuel d. at Bergen, NY, 5 Dec 1843.

iv   SARAH KITTREDGE, b. 27 Apr 1781; d. 12 Feb 1796.

v   JOSEPH KITTREDGE, b. 25 Oct 1783; d. at Andover, 4 Sep 1847; m. at Salem, 19 Dec 1819, HANNAH HODGES, b. at Salem, 10 Oct 1793 daughter of George and Lydia (Gale) Hodges; Hannah d. at North Andover, 1 Jul 1877.

vi   CATHERINE KITTREDGE, b. 15 Nov 1788; d. at Salem, 17 Jul 1824; m. at Andover, 17 Aug 1815, as his second wife, DAVID CUMMINS, b. at Topsfield, 13 Aug 1785 son of David and Mehitable (Cave) Cummins; David d. at Dorchester, MA, 3 Apr 1855. David was first married to Sally Porter and third married to Catherine's sister Maria (see below).

vii MARIA FRANKLIN KITTREDGE, b. 26 Dec 1792; d. at Boston, 31 Jan 1873; m. at Andover, 17 Oct 1825, as his third wife, DAVID CUMMINS (see sister Catherine just above).

484)   ISAAC OSGOOD (*Peter Osgood⁴, Mary Russell Osgood³, Thomas², Robert¹*), b. at Andover, 15 Jul 1755 son of Peter and Sarah (Johnson) Osgood; d. at Andover, 30 Sep 1847; m. 1ˢᵗ at Salem, 12 Oct 1790, SALLY PICKMAN, b. at Salem, 7 Jun 1771 daughter of Clarke Gayton and Sarah (Orne) Pickman; Sally d. at Salem 10 Aug 1791. Isaac m. 2ⁿᵈ, Sally's sister, REBECCA TAYLOR PICKMAN, b. at Salem, about 1772; Rebecca d. at Salem, 29 Aug 1801. Isaac m. 3ʳᵈ at Salem, 28 Jun 1803, MARY PICKMAN, b. at Salem, 20 Sep 1765 daughter of Benjamin and Mary (Toppan) Pickman;[1309] Mary d. at North Andover, 7 Sep 1856.

[1305] Thomas, Dr., M. D., an eminent Physician and Surgeon, a firm supporter of Civil and Religious Liberty, - for many years a Representative of the town in the General Court" [apoplexy, C.R.1.], Oct. 16, 1818, a. 72 y.

[1306] "Thomas Kittredge", Appleton's Cyclopedia of American Biography 1600-1889, volume III, p 559

[1307] *Essex County, MA: Probate File Papers, 1638-1881.* Online database. *AmericanAncestors.org.* New England Historic Genealogical Society, 2014. Case 15891

[1308] *Essex County, MA: Probate File Papers, 1638-1881.* Online database. *AmericanAncestors.org.* New England Historic Genealogical Society, 2014. Case 15890

[1309] Names of Mary's parents are given as Benjamin and Mary Pickman on her death record; New England Historic Genealogical Society; Boston, Massachusetts; Massachusetts Vital Records, 1840–1911

Isaac Osgood was a prosperous farmer and mill owner in Andover. In his will written 10 July 1845 (proved 19 October 1847), Isaac Osgood bequeathed to beloved wife Mary bank shares from multiple banks, insurance company shares, and railroad stock shares. Mary also receives all the plate, household goods and furniture, best horse and chaise, and occupation of the mansion house and farm so long as she chooses. Son Gayton P. Osgood "in consideration of his services in the management and care of my affairs" receives the farm and mansion house after Mary ceases to occupy it. He also receives the lot of land with buildings opposite the mansion house. The remainder of the estate goes one-third to Gayton, one-third to grandchildren who are children of Sally P. Loring (George B. Loring, Isaac O. Loring, Gayton P. Loring, and John A. Loring), and one-third to be held in trust by Gayton P. Osgood and son-in-law Rev. Bailey Loring for the benefit of the children of late son Isaac Osgood, Jr. (Rebecca P. Osgood, Isaac F. Osgood, John A. Osgood, Francis G. Osgood, and Charlotte E. Osgood). Gayton P. Osgood and Bailey Loring were named executors.[1310] Isaac had extensive real estate holdings valued at $49,270 which included home farm with 104 acres worth $10,000 and $30,000 value for machine shop, mills, water power, and eight dwelling houses. Total estate value was $66,303.76.[1311]

Isaac Osgood and Rebecca T. Pickman were parents of four children born at Salem. Son Gayton Pickman Osgood was an attorney and a member of the U.S. House of Representatives for one term fron 1833-1835.

i   SARAH PICKMAN OSGOOD, b. 12 Apr 1796; d. at Andover, 18 Jul 1835; m. at Andover, 20 Feb 1816, BAILEY LORING, b. at Duxbury 1786 and baptized at Pembroke, MA, 24 Sep 1786 son of William and Alithea (Alden) Loring; Bailey d. at North Andover, 15 Apr 1860.

ii   GAYTON PICKMAN OSGOOD, baptized 9 Jul 1797; d. at North Andover, 26 Jun 1861; m. at Andover, 24 Mar 1859, his third cousin once removed, MARY FARNHAM, b. at Andover, 7 May 1812 daughter of Isaac and Persis (Stevens) Farnham; Mary d. at North Andover, 22 Mar 1864.

iii   ISAAC OSGOOD, baptized 9 Jun 1799; d. at sea, 2 Sep 1834 ("Isaac, died while in command of the ship *Henry Tuke*,[1312] on her passage from Java to Boston, Sept. 2, 1834, a. 35 y. 3 m. 9 d."); m. at Andover, 7 Aug 1821, his second cousin, CHARLOTTE ADAMS (*John Adams⁵, Hannah Osgood Adams⁴, Mary Russell Osgood³, Thomas², Robert¹*), b. at Andover, 29 May 1796 daughter of John and Dorcas (Faulkner) Adams; Charlotte d. at North Andover, 27 Jul 1871.

iv   REBECCA PICKMAN OSGOOD, baptized 31 Aug 1801; likely died young.

485)   TIMOTHY OSGOOD (*Peter Osgood⁴, Mary Russell Osgood³, Thomas², Robert¹*), b. at Andover, 17 Mar 1763 son of Peter and Sarah (Johnson) Osgood; d. at Andover, 13 Dec 1842; m. 13 Nov 1788, his second cousin once removed, SARAH "SALLY" FARNUM, b. at Andover, 10 Mar 1771 daughter of Isaac and Mary (Osgood) Farnum.

Timothy was a tanner and farmer. He was captain of a horse company in which capacity he provided escort for George Washington in September 1789 from Bradford to Wilmington.[1313]

Timothy Osgood did not leave a will and his estate entered probate 17 January 1843 with Henry Osgood as administrator at the request of widow Sarah. Heirs agreeing to the appointment of Henry were Susan Osgood, Mary L. Osgood, Peter Osgood, and Sarah Wardwell. Real estate was valued at $11,104 including a 40-acre homestead property with tanyard valued at $4,100. Eighty-three acres adjoining Great Pond were valued at $3,500. Personal estate was valued at $1,974.[1314]

Son Henry Osgood did not marry, and sister Susan Osgood was executrix of his will. The following heirs-at-law were identified by executrix Susan Osgood on 6 March 1865: brother Isaac Osgood of Flushing, New York; brother J. Granville Osgood of New Orleans, Louisiana; sister Mrs. Wardwell of North Andover; sister Mary L. Osgood of North Andover; Miss Susan Osgood of North Andover, and the children of brother Peter Osgood. Real estate was valued at $2,309.17 and personal estate at $2,047.06.[1315]

Timothy Osgood and Sally Farnum were parents of ten children born at Andover.

i   SARAH OSGOOD, b. 9 Sep 1789; d. at North Andover, 8 Jun 1867; m. at Andover, 24 Sep 1816, DANIEL WARDWELL, b. at Hollis, NH, 11 Jan 1784 son of Solomon and Bethiah (Holt) Wardwell; Daniel d. at Andover, 14 Apr 1851.

ii   HENRY OSGOOD, b. 14 Aug 1791; d. at North Andover, 4 Feb 1865. Henry did not marry. He was a selectman and town clerk of Andover.

[1310] Massachusetts Wills and Probate, Essex County, volume 114, pp 220-223

[1311] *Essex County, MA: Probate File Papers, 1638-1881.*Online database. *AmericanAncestors.org.* New England Historic Genealogical Society, 2014. Case 48886

[1312] The *Henry Tuke* was a 365-ton ship built at Medford, MA in 1824; Essex Institute Historical Collections, volume 40, p 228

[1313] Osgood, *Genealogy of the Descendants of John, Christopher, and William Osgood*, p 89

[1314] *Essex County, MA: Probate File Papers, 1638-1881.*Online database. *AmericanAncestors.org.* New England Historic Genealogical Society, 2014. Case 48939

[1315] *Essex County, MA: Probate File Papers, 1638-1881.*Online database. *AmericanAncestors.org.* New England Historic Genealogical Society, 2014. Case 48885

iii   ISAAC OSGOOD, b. 20 Apr 1793; d. at New Orleans, LA, 1 May 1873; m. 1st at St. George's Church in NY, 16 Jun 1828, JANE REBECCA HALL, b. 19 Feb 1803 daughter of Benjamin and Cathrine (Benjamin) Hall; Jane d. likely at New Orleans, 23 May 1841. Isaac m. 2nd 19 Jun 1845, Jane's sister, ELIZA LUCRETIA HALL, b. 20 Apr 1805; Eliza d. at Flushing, NY, 26 Dec 1877.

iv   SUSAN OSGOOD, b. 17 Feb 1795; d. at North Andover, 17 Nov 1878. Susan did not marry.

v   WILLIAM OSGOOD, b. 9 Apr 1798. William did not marry. He was a merchant and reported in the Osgood genealogy as dying in Washington, DC.[1316]

vi   TIMOTHY OSGOOD, b. 26 Apr 1800; d. at Canton, AL, 26 Aug 1823. Timothy did not marry.

vii   PETER OSGOOD, b. 6 Aug 1802; d. at Andover, 31 Aug 1849; m. 1st at Methuen, 14 Apr 1829, SARAH TIBBETS,[1317] b. at Salem, NH, 10 Jul 1798 daughter of Joseph and Ruth (Seacomb) Tibbets; Sarah d. at Andover, 16 Jan 1835. Peter m. 2nd at Andover, 27 Apr 1839, REBECCA M. RUSSELL, b. in Gray, ME, 1809 whose parents have not been identified; Rebecca d. at Lawrence, MA, 30 Jan 1893.

viii   MARY LOUISA OSGOOD, b. 14 Oct 1804; d. at North Andover, 30 Mar 1879. Mary did not marry. She was blind much of her life.

ix   CHARLOTTE F. OSGOOD, b. 26 Feb 1809; d. at Andover, 5 Jul 1838.[1318] Charlotte did not marry.

x   JOSEPH GRANVILLE OSGOOD, b. 25 Oct 1811; d. at Jefferson Parish, LA, 27 Mar 1878; m. about 1852, ESTHER PEARSALL LAWRENCE (widow of William T. Post), b. at Flushing, NY, 25 Apr 1815 daughter of Henry and Amy (Pearsall) Lawrence;[1319] Esther d. at Flushing, 10 Aug 1885.

486)   TIMOTHY OSGOOD (*Timothy Osgood⁴, Mary Russell Osgood³, Thomas², Robert¹*), b. at Andover, 27 Jul 1743 son of Timothy and Phebe (Frye) Osgood; d. at Andover, 16 Aug 1816; m. at Andover, 13 Mar 1765, his first cousin once removed (through the Bridges line), CHLOE BRIDGES, b. at Andover, 28 Dec 1743 daughter of James and Mary (Abbott) Bridges; Chloe d. at Andover, 5 Dec 1798.

Chloe and Chloe resided in Andover where Timothy was a carpenter by trade and was a "gentleman".

In his will written 9 December 1807 (probate 3 September 1816), Timothy Osgood bequeathed to son Timothy, two hundred dollars; to son James, one hundred dollars adding that what he has already done for James that this is his equal portion of the estate; to son John Osgood, two hundred dollars; to daughter Chloe Osgood, two hundred dollars; to daughter Mary wife of Enoch Farnham, two hundred dollars and one cow; and to daughter Hannah Osgood, two hundred dollars. He makes separate provision for the support of Chloe while she is unmarried "considering the great services my daughter Chloe has done for me since the decease of her mother in superintending the affairs of my family." There are also provisions for support of unmarried daughter Hannah, his two unmarried daughters are to have use and improvement of the west lower room, kitchen, and well, and annual provisions to be delivered annually by the executor. Chloe and Hannah also receive one-half of the household furniture. Granddaughter Sarah Frye Farnum daughter of Mary receives one cow. His unmarried children have privilege of a seat in pew 111 of the North meeting house in Andover. The residue of the estate goes to son Samuel who is also named executor.[1320]

Timothy Osgood and Chloe Bridges were parents of eight children born at Andover.

i   CHLOE OSGOOD, b. 1 Mar 1766; d. at Andover, 16 Aug 1846. Chloe did not marry.[1321]

ii   TIMOTHY OSGOOD, b. 7 Jul 1767; d. at Newburyport, 17 Jan 1824; m. 1st at Andover, 11 Feb 1797,[1322] ANNA BRIDGES, likely Anna b. at Andover, 26 Aug 1765 daughter of John and Mary (Spaulding) Bridges;[1323] Anna d. at Newburyport, 15 Dec 1806. Timothy m. 2nd 21 Oct 1807 SALLY PATCH MARSHALL, b. at Tewksbury, 12 Feb 1780 daughter of Joel and Anne (Mooar) Marshall; Sally d. 23 May 1817. Timothy m. 3rd at Newburyport, 26 Jul 1819, SALLY GAGE.

iii   JAMES OSGOOD, b. 28 Nov 1768; d. at Andover, 21 Nov 1809; m. at Boston, 2 Sep 1808, SALLY BEELS who has not been identified. James did not have children.

[1316] Osgood, *Genealogy of the Descendants of John, Christopher, and William Osgood*, p 90

[1317] The name is also spelled Tippets

[1318] Charlotte, d. Timothy and Sally [scarlet fever. CR1], July 5, 1838, a. 29 y. [a. 30 y. CR1].

[1319] Hinshaw, *Encyclopedia of American Quaker Genealogy*, volume III, p 381, Flushing Monthly Meeting

[1320] *Essex County, MA: Probate File Papers, 1638-1881*.Online database. *AmericanAncestors.org*. New England Historic Genealogical Society, 2014. Case 20286

[1321] Chloe, unm., d. Timothy and Chloe, old age [consumption. CR1], Aug. 18, 1846, a. 80 y.

[1322] The marriage is also recorded at Wilton, NH as on 11 Sep 1797

[1323] John and Mary Bridges went to Wilton in 1777 which would explain why the marriage record is also given at Wilton. Anna's age at death was 42 which fits with the 1765 birth date.

iv   ISAAC OSGOOD, b. 8 Dec 1771; d. 17 Dec 1796. Isaac did not marry.

v   JOHN OSGOOD, b. 25 Oct 1773; d. at Andover, 3 Apr 1828; m. at Roxbury, 21 Nov 1810, ELIZABETH FULLER, b. at West Roxbury, 1775 (based on age 62 at death); Elizabeth d. at Andover, 13 Feb 1837.

vi   MARY OSGOOD, b. 6 Aug 1776; d. at Andover, 16 Jan 1848; m. at Andover, 1 May 1806, her second cousin once removed, ENOCH FARNUM, b. at Andover, 2 Aug 1766 son of John and Sarah (Frye) Farnum; Enoch d. at Andover, 13 May 1815.

vii   SAMUEL OSGOOD, b. 2 Nov 1779; d. at Andover, 8 Jul 1859. Samuel did not marry.

viii   HANNAH OSGOOD, baptized 28 Oct 1781; Hannah d. at Newburyport, 18 Dec 1855. Hannah did not marry.

487)   ASA OSGOOD (*Timothy Osgood⁴, Mary Russell Osgood³, Thomas², Robert¹*), b. at Andover, 22 Dec 1753 son of Timothy and Phebe (Frye) Osgood; d. at Hiram, ME, 29 Jul 1833; m. 1st at Andover, 19 Jun 1780, his fourth cousin, DORCAS STEVENS, b. at Andover, 9 Oct 1755 daughter of Asa and Mehitable (Farnum) Stevens; Dorcas d. 1780. Asa m. 2nd at Methuen, 22 May 1784, Mrs. LYDIA HOOD; Lydia d. 1807. Asa m. 3rd at Hiram, ME, 18 Jul 1808, HANNAH POWERS; Hannah d. 25 Dec 1853.

     Asa was the youngest child of Timothy and Phebe Osgood, born five months after his father's death. Asa served in the Revolution for the duration of the war achieving rank of Sergeant Major by the end of the war. He remained in Andover for a time after the war before moving to Maine, likely first to Brownfield by 1787[1324] before settling in Hiram, Maine.

     In his pension application, Asa reported he first enlisted from Andover in the spring of 1775 and served eight months in the company of Capt. Thomas Poor. He then served one year in the Rhode Island regiment of Col. Varnum. His third enlistment was February or March 1777 when he served as corporal, then sergeant, and then sergeant major in Col. Marshall's and Col. Tupper's Massachusetts regiments. He served for the remainder of the war and was discharged June 1783. On 25 July 1820, Asa gave an inventory of his property as one cow, one heifer, one calf, one hog, six sheep, six lambs, farming utensils, and household furniture. He owed 50 dollars. His household at that time was given as wife Hannah age 42 who was unhealthy, son Stephen age 11, daughter Phebe age 6, and daughter Abigail, age 3 (this seems an error for daughter Abiah).[1325]

     Several pages from the probate record are included within the pension file. The probate records relate to pension arrears that might be due the surviving children. A document dated 7 March 1854 by the register of probate related to administration of Asa's estate following the death of widow Hannah Osgood noted evidence had been presented that the only surviving children of Hannah Osgood deceased were Asa Osgood, Abiah A. Rogers, and Phebe A. Trafton. But this specific statement seems an error as on 6 February 1855, James Osgood, Jr., son of James Osgood and grandson of Asa, of Portland provided the following information. James, Jr. recalled the following members of the family: James Osgood, Asa Osgood, Phebe F. Trafton, Abiah F. Osgood, and Stephen Osgood. Stephen Osgood about eighteen years previously (about 1837) leaving a wife in the town of Windham, Maine. The last word of Stephen was about six months after he left and was believed to be deceased. The only current surviving children of Asa Osgood were James Osgood, Asa Osgood, Phebe F. Trafton, and Abiah F. Rogers. James, Jr. also corrects a statement elsewhere in the pension file that there was an Abigail in the family as there was no Abigail in the family (which perhaps was a miswriting of Abiah in the record). On 16 July 1855, a statement was provided to the court by Zebulon Harmon administrator of the estate. Asa Osgood was a pensioner in 1818 at rate of $96 per year but was struck from the pension rolls in 1820 and reinstated in 1832 and received a pension until his death on 10 August 1833. Asa's widow Hannah Osgood applied for widow's pension which she received from the act passed 3 February 1853 until her death on 24 December 1853. Mr. Harmon understood that Asa Osgood left son James by a former wife and his current surviving children were James Osgood, Asa Osgood, Abiah F. Osgood, and Phebe F. Trafton.[1326] Zebulon Harmon was named administrator of the estate of Asa Osgood related to pension arears on 5 January 1855 at request of children James Osgood, Abiah F. Osgood, and Phebe F. Trafton.[1327]

     Asa Osgood and Dorcas Stevens were parents of one child.

i   ASA OSGOOD, baptized at Andover, 5 Nov 1780; died young.

     Asa Osgood and Lydia Hood were parents of six children and there may be two unnamed children who died near time of birth.[1328]

i   ASA OSGOOD, b. about 1787; d. at Hiram, about 1822; m. at Hiram, 19 Mar 1821, HANNAH WENTWORTH, b. 1802; Hannah d. at Hiram, 1839. Hannah married second John Bucknell. On 10 June 1836, Asa Osgood of Hiram age fourteen, son of Asa Osgood, Jr., made choice of Ephraim Kendall of Hiram as his guardian.[1329]

[1324] Maine Early Census Index, 1787, Brownfield, Maine
[1325] U. S. Revolutionary War Pension and Bounty-Land Warrant Application Files, Case W27894
[1326] U. S. Revolutionary War Pension and Bounty-Land Warrant Application Files, Case W27894
[1327] Maine Wills and Probate, Oxford County, volume 16, p 186
[1328] Osgood, *A Genealogy of the Descendants of John, Christopher, and William Osgood*, p 91
[1329] Maine Wills and Probate, Oxford County, volume 8, p 70

ii   ISAAC OSGOOD, est. 1788; died young

iii   ISAAC OSGOOD, b. estimate 1790; d. at Hiram, ME, 4 Jul 1824; m. at Hiram, 20 Nov 1817, CATHERINE BURBANK. Catherine married second Isaac's brother Timothy (see below).

iv   TIMOTHY OSGOOD, b. about 1798; d. Dec 1847; m. at Hiram, 26 Jan 1825, CATHERINE BURBANK who was first married to Timothy's brother Isaac (see above).

v   JAMES OSGOOD, b. 15 Mar 1800; d. at Hiram, 29 Jan 1879; m. 1st at Chatham, NH, 16 Jun 1822, BETSEY MCDONALD, b. 1799 likely daughter of Samuel M. and Anna (Whitten) McDonald; Betsey d. at Hiram, 26 Jun 1862. James m. 2nd 1863, MARY O. COLE, b. at Hiram, 6 Sep 1833 daughter of Tobias and Lydia (Gray) Cole; Mary d. at Hiram, 8 Feb 1903. Mary married second Francis H. Tibbetts.

vi   PHEBE F. OSGOOD; died young

       Asa Osgood and Hannah Powers were parents of six children.

i   STEPHEN OSGOOD, b. 1 Aug 1809; d. about 1837 after leaving his home. Reported in the Osgood book as dying of cholera at Mobile, AL about 1835. Stephen m. 1833, ANNA MAYBERRY, b. about 1810 who was living in Windham, ME in 1850.[1330]

ii   PHEBE OSGOOD, b. 1811; d. 1813.

iii   PHEBE F. OSGOOD, b. 17 Jul 1814; d. at Alfred, ME, 27 Mar 1885; m. 1 Dec 1836, as his second wife, EBENEZER TRAFTON, b. 20 Aug 1803 son of John and Mercy (Sayward) Trafton; Ebenezer d. at Alfred, 16 Feb 1875. Ebenezer was first married to Asenath Getchell.

iv   ABIAH OSGOOD, b. 23 Mar 1817; d. at Windham, ME, 3 May 1880; m. 1 Nov 1835, JOHN ROGERS, b. at Windham, ME, 11 Mar 1804 son of John and Lorana (Riggs) Rogers; John d. at Windham, 20 Feb 1873.

v   JOSEPH OSGOOD, b. about 1820

vi   ASA OSGOOD, b. 16 Jun 1822; d. 1857. Asa did not marry.[1331]

488)   SARAH OSGOOD (*Thomas Osgood⁴, Mary Russell Osgood³, Thomas², Robert¹*), b. at Andover, 3 Dec 1749 daughter of Thomas and Sarah (Hutchinson) Osgood; d. at Andover, 14 Sep 1790; m. at Haverhill, 11 Feb 1773, JONATHAN BRADLEY, b. at Haverhill, 14 Feb 1744/5 son of William and Mehitable (Emerson) Bradley;[1332] Jonathan d. at Andover, 23 Feb 1818. Jonathan m. 2nd at Haverhill, 14 Apr 1791, Sarah Ayer.
       Jonathan was a farmer in Andover. Jonathan Bradley did not leave a will and Charles White was named estate administrator on 31 March 1818 as widow Sarah declined administration. On 28 April 1818, widow Sarah requested assistance from the court noting that she was in destitute circumstances with a family of two children. Real estate was valued at $3,532 and personal estate at $1,390.67. The heirs of the estate identified April 1823 were Thomas O. Bradley deceased who left two children, Sarah McFarland deceased who left children, Mary Poor wife of Joseph Poor, Elizabeth McFarland wife of Moses McFarland, Jonathan Bradley, William Bradley, Charles Bradley, Harrison Bradley, James Bradley, Ann White wife of L. White, and Susanna Bradley.[1333] The children Charles, Harrison, James, Ann, and Susanna were children with Jonathan's second wife Sally Ayer.
       Sarah Osgood and Thomas Bradley were parents of seven children born at Andover. Jonathan also had five children with his second wife Sally Ayer.

i   THOMAS OSGOOD BRADLEY, b. at Haverhill, 28 Sep 1774; d. at Andover, 12 Oct 1821; m. at Bradford, 2 Jun 1796, MEHITABLE CARLTON, b. at Bradford, 1775;[1334] Mehitable d. at Worcester, 5 Sep 1849.

ii   SARAH BRADLEY, b. at Haverhill, 10 Aug 1776; d. at Marietta, OH, 10 Aug 1807; m. at Haverhill, 6 Aug 1797, MOSES MCFARLAND, b. at Haverhill, 19 Jun 1775 son of Moses and Eunice (Clark) McFarland; Moses d. at Marietta, 1854 (probate 25 Apr 1854). Moses married second Sarah's sister Elizabeth (see below).

[1330] Year: 1850; Census Place: Windham, Cumberland, Maine; Roll: 251; Page: 154b

[1331] Osgood, *A Genealogy of the Descendants of John, Christopher, and William Osgood*, p 91

[1332] Crane, *Historic Homes and Institutions and Personal Memoirs of Worcester County, Massachusetts*, volume 1, p 367. One oddity in the records is that the twin sons of William and Mehitable Bradley are listed as stillborn on 14 Feb 1744/5 but then they were baptized on 17 Feb 1744/5. The 1780 probate of William Bradley of Haverhill includes a will that has as heirs sons Jonathan and Joseph (among other children).

[1333] *Essex County, MA: Probate File Papers, 1638-1881.* Online database. *AmericanAncestors.org.* New England Historic Genealogical Society, 2014. Case 3036

[1334] The name of Mehitable's father is given as John on her death record, but the names of her parents are undetermined.

iii   MARY BRADLEY, b. at Andover, 3 May 1779; d. at Lexington, MA, 20 May 1859; m. 16 Apr 1801, JOSEPH POOR, b. at Andover, 19 Sep 1776 son of Abraham and Elizabeth (Barker) Poor; Joseph d. at Andover, 25 Nov 1842.

iv   WILLIAM BRADLEY, b. 7 Jan 1782; d. 12 Jul 1784.

v   ELIZABETH "BETSEY" BRADLEY, b. at Andover, 10 Jun 1784; Betsey d. after 1860 when she was living at Marietta, OH; m. 1st at Andover, 15 Jul 1802, ELIPHALET PAYSON, b. at Bradford, MA, 22 Aug 1776 son of Eliot and Mary (Haseltine) Payson; Eliphalet d. at Wiscasset, ME, 1 Jul 1807. Betsey m. 2nd about 1808, MOSES MCFARLAND who was first married to Betsey's sister Sarah.

vi   JONATHAN BRADLEY, b. at Andover, 19 Oct 1786; d. at Andover, 28 Apr 1867; m. at Andover, 25 Jan 1814, SALLY WEBSTER, b. at Haverhill, 14 Jul 1791 daughter of Joshua and Susannah (Bailey) Webster; Sally d. at North Andover, 6 Aug 1861.

vii   WILLIAM BRADLEY, b. at Andover, 16 Jan 1789; m. at Wiscasset, ME, 1 Mar 1811, MARTHA "PATTY" LUMMAS. William was living in Wiscasset in 1820.

489)   MARY "POLLY" OSGOOD (*Thomas Osgood⁴, Mary Russell Osgood³, Thomas², Robert¹*), b. at Andover, 1755 daughter of Thomas and Sarah (Hutchinson) Osgood; d. at Andover, 10 Aug 1840; m. at Haverhill, 28 Mar 1781, JOSEPH BRADLEY, b. at Haverhill, 14 Feb 1744/5 son of William and Mehitable (Emerson) Bradley; Joseph d. at Andover, 21 Mar 1802.

Mary married Joseph Bradley who was the twin of Jonathan Bradley who married Mary's sister Sarah. Joseph was a farmer in Andover. He did not leave a will and his widow Mary was named administratrix of his estate on 3 May 1802. Personal estate was valued at $143.13.[1335]

Joseph Bradley and Mary Osgood were parents of nine children the oldest eight born at Haverhill and the youngest child at North Andover.

i   JOSEPH BRADLEY, b. 10 Mar 1782; d. 1 Apr 1782.

ii   POLLY OSGOOD BRADLEY, b. and d. 11 Jun 1783.

iii   JOSEPH BRADLEY, b. 13 Aug 1784; d. at Andover, 6 Apr 1842; m. 2 Jul 1811, CHARLOTTE BARKER, b. at Andover, 11 Mar 1788 daughter of John and Phebe (Wood) Barker; Charlotte d. at North Andover, 7 Mar 1865.

iv   MARY "POLLY" OSGOOD BRADLEY, b. 13 Nov 1786; d. at Andover, 20 Feb 1829; m. 28 Dec 1804, JOHN POOR, b. at Andover, 3 Aug 1777 son of John and Chloe (Lovejoy) Poor; John d. at Medford, MA, 24 Oct 1844.

v   JOHN BRADLEY, b. 10 Feb 1789; d. at Haverhill, 30 Nov 1830; m. at Methuen, 31 Dec 1811, FANNY SWAN, b. at Methuen, 8 Jul 1792 daughter of Caleb and Dorcas (Ingalls) Swan; Fanny d. at Philadelphia, PA, 8 Nov 1862.

vi   THOMAS OSGOOD BRADLEY, b. 10 Oct 1792; d. at Haverhill, 18 Oct 1798.

vii   WILLIAM BRADLEY, b. 20 Aug 1795; d. at Andover, 19 Aug 1838; m. May 1826, HARRIET SHATTUCK, b. 10 Dec 1805 daughter of Peter and Susanna (Clark) Shattuck; Harriet d. at Andover, 16 Sep 1880. Harriet married second Alfred Putnam.

viii   THOMAS OSGOOD BRADLEY, b. 12 Aug 1798; d. at Buenos Aries, Argentina, 26 Apr 1859;[1336] m. at Boston, 3 Aug 1827, LUCY ANN SUTTON, b. at Portland, ME, 1804 daughter of Richard and Lucy (Lord) Sutton; Lucy d. at Buenos Aries, 6 Dec 1888. Thomas was a dry goods merchant who resided part of the time in Buenos Aires.[1337]

ix   GEORGE BRADLEY, b. at North Andover, 4 Dec 1800; d. at North Andover, 8 Jan 1872; m. 1st 20 Jun 1825, LOUISA ADAMS, b. at Andover, 30 Dec 1804 daughter of John and Susanna (Cutler) Adams; Louisa d. at Andover, 3 Mar 1839. George m. 2nd at Andover, 20 Oct 1839, SUSAN SHATTUCK, b. 1 Oct 1803 daughter of Peter and Susanna (Clark) Shattuck; Susan d. at Andover, 18 Sep 1884.

[1335] *Essex County, MA: Probate File Papers, 1638-1881.* Online database. *AmericanAncestors.org.* New England Historic Genealogical Society, 2014. Case 3042

[1336] Source provided by bradleyfoundation.org; British Cemetery Records, Chacarita, Buenos Aires, Argentina, Book 4, Fº 43, Line 1, Thomas Osgood Bradley Foundation. "Grave Section 1E, № 23. Number 379. 26 April 1859. Thos. O. Bradley. Æ 63. Birth Place: Haverhill, Mass. Trade: Merchant. Cause of Death: Old age. Abode: Buenos Aires. Ceremony performed by: W. Goodf ellow, Pastor, Meth. E. ch."

[1337] Hawthorne, Manning, "A Glimpse of Hawthorne's Boyhood", Essex Institute Historical Collections, volume 83, 1947, p 178-179. Lucy Ann Sutton was a relation of Nathaniel Hawthorne and had written an article for the New York Observer related to family recollections of Hawthorne. That information is reviewed in the Essex Institute article.

490)   JOSHUA BAILEY OSGOOD (*Isaac Osgood⁴, Mary Russell Osgood³, Thomas², Robert¹*), b. at Haverhill, 29 Apr 1753 son of Isaac and Abigail (Bailey) Osgood; d. at Boston (although resident of Fryeburg), 30 May 1791; m. May 1780, ELIZABETH BROWN, b. at Haverhill, 26 Apr 1757 daughter of Henry Young and Elizabeth (Lovejoy) Brown; Elizabeth d. at Fryeburg, 30 Jun 1790.

Joshua and Elizabeth resided in Maine on what was then known as Brownfield Plantation and later incorporated as Brownfield, Maine. Joshua graduated from Harvard in 1772[1338] and was a merchant in Fryeburg. He served as a Colonel of a regiment that was part of the Canada expedition.[1339]

Joshua Bailey Osgood was colonel of the 5th regiment of Maine militia in the 6th division. He also served as Justice of the Peace for the county of York. He was buried with military honors at Biddeford.[1340]

In his will written 19 May 1791 (proved 27 June 1791), Joshua B. Osgood of Brownfield Plantation bequeathed to his dear children all his estate, real and personal, to be equally divided: Henry Young Brown Osgood, Joshua Bailey Osgood, Mary Sherburne Osgood, and Eliza Lovejoy Osgood. Good friend William Fessenden was named executor. The greatest part of the real estate was mortgaged. Estate was valued at £205.19.9.[1341] Henry Young Brown was allowed as guardian for the minor children Henry Young Brown Osgood, Joshua Bailey Osgood, Polly Sherburne Osgood, and Eliza Lovejoy Osgood.[1342]

Joshua and Elizabeth Osgood were parents of four children. Each of the children married an Osgood cousin who were all children of James and Abigail (Evans) Osgood.

i   JOSHUA BAILEY OSGOOD, b. 30 Oct 1782; d. at Portland, ME, 24 Oct 1861; m. 1st 31 Oct 1815, ANN OSGOOD, b. at Fryeburg, 17 Aug 1794 daughter of James and Abigail (Evans) Osgood; Ann d. at Denmark, ME, 20 Jun 1821. Joshua m. 2nd Oct 1832, SALLY W. STICKNEY, b. 17 Jan 1788 daughter of John and Mary (Evans) Stickney; Sally d. at Brownfield, ME, 3 Feb 1882.

ii   HENRY YOUNG BROWN OSGOOD, b. 14 Apr 1784; d. at Fryeburg, May 1831; m. about 1810, SUSAN OSGOOD, b. at Fryeburg, 25 Apr 1790 daughter of James and Abigail (Evans) Osgood; Susan d. at Fryeburg, 23 Apr 1832.

iii   MARY SHERBURNE OSGOOD, b. 1786; d. at Worcester, MA, 30 Jun 1871; m. at Springfield, MA, 15 Apr 1809, SAMUEL OSGOOD, b. at Fryeburg, 3 Sep 1784 son of James and Abigail (Evans) Osgood; Samuel d. at Springfield, 8 Dec 1863.

iv   ELIZA LOVEJOY BROWN OSGOOD, b. 1789; d. at Fryeburg, 22 Dec 1837; m. 26 Dec 1810, JAMES OSGOOD, b. at Fryeburg, 9 May 1788 son of James and Abigail (Evans) Osgood; James d. at Fryeburg, 9 Jun 1856.

491)   PETER OSGOOD (*Isaac Osgood⁴, Mary Russell Osgood³, Thomas², Robert¹*), b. at Haverhill, 5 Aug 1764 son of Isaac and Abigail (Bailey) Osgood; d. at Haverhill, 28 Sep 1856; m. at Haverhill, 13 Jul 1796, MARY WILLIS, b. about 1774 daughter of Benjamin and Mary (Ball) Willis; Mary d. at Haverhill, 23 Oct 1825.

Peter Osgood was a physician and druggist in Haverhill. His father Isaac was a storekeeper in Haverhill and Peter took up his father's business after his death.[1343]

In his will written 8 May 1856 (proved 21 October 1856), Peter Osgood bequeathed to his daughters Mary Willis, Caroline, and Ann the silverware, portraits, plate, time pieces, jewelry, books, and all the household furniture. Daughter Abigail B. Nichols wife of Moses Nichols receives $2,000. The remainder of the personal estate and all the real estate is to be divided equally among four daughters Mary Willis, Caroline, Ann, and Harriet and sons William and Willis. There is a provision that Harriet's share is to be held by her without the intervention of a trustee for her sole and separate use free from the interference or control of her husband. Robert B. Willis of Haverhill was named executor. Real estate was valued at $33,500 and personal estate at $4,094.72.[1344]

Peter Osgood and Mary Willis were parents of eight children born at Haverhill. Only two of the children married. Caroline, Ann, and William resided together in Haverhill in 1860.[1345]

i   MARY WILLIS OSGOOD, b. 7 Jan 1797; d. at Haverhill, 22 Nov 1857. Mary did not marry. In her will, Mary W. Osgood had bequests for sisters Caroline and Ann, sister Abigail B. Nichols, and brother William A.[1346]

[1338] Harvard University, Quinquennial Catalogue 1636-1905, p 133

[1339] Osgood, *A Genealogy of the Descendants of John, Christopher and William Osgood*, p 92

[1340] Cumberland Gazette, Portland Maine, June 2, 1791, p 3

[1341] Maine, York County Probate Estate Files, Estate of Joshua B. Osgood, Case 14352

[1342] Maine, York County Probate Estate Files, Estate of Joshua B. Osgood, Case 14350

[1343] Chase, The History of Haverhill, Massachusetts, pp 452-453

[1344] *Essex County, MA: Probate File Papers, 1638-1881*.Online database. *AmericanAncestors.org.* New England Historic Genealogical Society, 2014. Case 48918

[1345] Year: 1860; Census Place: Haverhill, Essex, Massachusetts; Page: 983; Family History Library Film: 803500

[1346] *Essex County, MA: Probate File Papers, 1638-1881*.Online database. *AmericanAncestors.org.* New England Historic Genealogical Society, 2014. Case 48911

ii   ABIGAIL BAILEY OSGOOD, b. 30 Mar 1798; d. at Haverhill, 8 May 1884; m. at Haverhill, 11 Nov 1824, MOSES NICHOLS, b. at Amesbury, 10 May 1799 son of Stephen and Martha (Robinson) Nichols; Moses d. at Haverhill, 15 Sep 1893.

iii   ISAAC OSGOOD, b. 31 Oct 1799; d. at Haverhill, 19 Aug 1850.

iv   CAROLINE OSGOOD, b. 22 Mar 1801; d. at Haverhill, 10 Oct 1886. Caroline did not marry.

v   ANN OSGOOD, b. 3 Nov 1802; d. at Haverhill, 19 Feb 1895. Ann did not marry.

vi   HARRIET M. OSGOOD, b. 13 Aug 1804; d. at Yonkers, NY, 17 Dec 1860; m. at Haverhill, 31 Mar 1830, as his second wife, AROET MELVIN "A.M." HATCH, b. 30 Jan 1792 son of Joseph and Phebe Lewis (Tilden) Hatch; Aroet d. at Yonkers, 10 Jun 1876.[1347] Aroet was first married to Susan Prescott Spofford who died in 1829. Harriet and A.M. had one daughter, Harriet Melvin Hatch. A.M. had several children with his first wife.

vii   WILLIAM AUGUSTUS OSGOOD, b. 14 Dec 1806; d. at Haverhill, 16 Jan 1885. William did not marry.

viii   WILLIS OSGOOD, b. 22 Aug 1808; d. at Haverhill, 9 Apr 1887. Willis did not marry. In his will, Willis left his estate to sisters Caroline and Ann and brother William A. Osgood.[1348]

492)   MARY POOR (*Phebe Osgood Poor⁴, Mary Russell Osgood³, Thomas², Robert¹*), b. at Andover, 23 Dec 1757 daughter of Thomas and Phebe (Osgood) Poor; d. likely at Andover, ME; m. at Andover, 30 Apr 1776, ABIEL LOVEJOY, b. at Andover, 28 Apr 1749 son of Christopher and Anne (Mooar) Lovejoy; Abiel d. at Andover, ME, about 1820.[1349]

Abiel Lovejoy was a first settler of Andover, Maine being one of those signing to purchase the township lands that would become Andover, Maine. Mary's father Thomas Poor along with Enoch Adams had traveled to this area from Andover, Massachusetts in 1787 seeking a new area to settle.[1350] Abiel's property was lot 12 on the east side of the settlement. His farm was later divided among his sons Stephen, Abiel, and Benjamin.[1351]

Mary Poor and Abiel Lovejoy were parents of six children born at Andover, Massachusetts.

i   BENJAMIN LOVEJOY, b. 15 Sep 1776; d at Andover, ME, 26 Oct 1842; m. at Andover, ME, 1 Dec 1808, BATHANY (also given as Barthania) STRICKLAND, b. Feb 1780 daughter of Rev. John and Patty (Stone) Strickland; Bathany d. at Andover, ME, 16 Aug 1855.

ii   JOHN LOVEJOY, b. 25 Jun 1779; d. at Rockland, ME, 17 Oct 1843; m. at Newburyport, 20 Oct 1807, ELIZA LITTLE, b. 10 Feb 1787 daughter of Micajah and Sarah (Noyes) Little;[1352] Eliza d. at Camden, ME (burial at Rockland), 20 Oct 1875.

iii   ENOCH LOVEJOY, b. 11 Sep 1781; d. at East Thomaston, ME, 17 Nov 1848; m. 1ˢᵗ 23 Mar 1812, MARTHA TILLSON, b. 1792 daughter of William and Anna (Haskell) Tillson; Martha d. at Rockland, 18 Jun 1834[1353]. Enoch m. 2ⁿᵈ 6 Nov 1837 Mrs. MARGARET PORTERFIELD who has not been identified. Enoch Lovejoy was a physician.

iv   ABIEL LOVEJOY, b. 3 Aug 1784; d. at Andover, ME, 28 Sep 1858; m. LUCRETIA SEAVEY, b. 1793; Lucretia d. at Andover, ME, 13 Jul 1883.[1354]

v   STEPHEN LOVEJOY, b. 10 Jul 1787; d. after 1860 when he was living at Andover, ME; m. 8 Nov 1812, PAMELA BRAGG, b. at Andover, MA, 31 Oct 1791 daughter of Ingalls and Molly (Frye) Bragg; Pamela d. at Andover, ME, 28 Jan 1878.

vi   POLLY LOVEJOY, b. 29 Jul 1791 and baptized 31 Jul 1791; d. at Andover, ME, 19 Mar 1816.

493)   HANNAH POOR (*Phebe Osgood Poor⁴, Mary Russell Osgood³, Thomas², Robert¹*), b. at Andover, 4 Dec 1759 daughter of Thomas and Phebe (Osgood) Poor; d. at Methuen, 11 Mar 1835; m. 19 Mar 1789, as his second wife, WILLIAM WHITTIER, b. at Methuen, 26 Sep 1752 son of Richard and Elizabeth (Bodwell) Whittier; William d. at Methuen, 25 Aug 1812. William was first married to Lydia Haseltine.

[1347] Presbyterian Historical Society; Philadelphia, Pennsylvania; U.S., Presbyterian Church Records, 1701-1907; Book Title: Church Register 1852-1877; Accession Number: V MI46 Y8r

[1348] Massachusetts Wills and Probate, Essex County, Volume 451, p 255

[1349] Poor, "History of Andover, Maine"

[1350] Poor, "History of Andover, Maine", p 3

[1351] Poor, "History of Andover, Maine", pp 7-8

[1352] Eaton, *History of Rockland, Thomaston, and South Thomaston*, volume 2, p 310

[1353] Maine, Nathan Hale Cemetery Collection, 1780-1980

[1354] Maine, Nathan Hale Cemetery Collection, 1780-1980

In his will written 16 July 1810 (probate 8 September 1812), William Whittier, yeoman, bequeathed to beloved wife Hannah to use of and improvement of one-third of the real estate, as well as the use of the sleigh, chaise, and horse. Hannah and the unmarried daughters will have use of the pew on the lower floor of the meeting house. Daughter Betsey wife of Seth Johnson is to have one-seventh part of two-thirds of the real estate. Seventh parts of the real estate go to the other children: Lydia wife of Francis Frye, Samuel Whittier, Hannah P. Whittier, Nancy Whittier, and Abiah Whittier. William Whittier receives the remainder and will also receive the one-third set off as the dower after the decease of Hannah. There are several other provisions including the gallery pew going to Samuel. There are also deductions from the bequests to the three oldest children (Betsey, Lydia, and Samuel) and these deductions are to be divided equally among the four youngest daughters. Real estate was valued at $4,729 and personal estate at $1,319.44.[1355] The distribution of the real estate on 1 May 1813, in addition to the dower to widow Hannah, included lots set off to Betsey Johnson wife of Seth Johnson, to Lydia Frye wife of Francis Frye, to Samuel Whittier, to Hannah Whittier, to Nancy Whittier, to Abiah Whittier, to Sukey Whittier, and to William Whittier. Children Lydia, Betsey, and Samuel are from William's first marriage to Lydia Haseltine.

Hannah Poor and William Whittier were parents of six children born at Methuen. William had four children with his first wife Lydia Haseltine.

i   HANNAH POOR WHITTIER, b. 4 Aug 1791; d. at Methuen, 4 Oct 1824; m. at Methuen, 4 May 1818, SAMUEL RICHARDSON, b. at Methuen, 4 Jul 1781 son of Samuel and Lucy (Parker) Richardson; Samuel d. at Methuen, 13 Jan 1869. Hannah and Samuel did not have children. At the probate of his estate, the only heirs of Samuel were a brother Aaron and sister Betsey.

ii   NANCY WHITTIER, b. 5 Apr 1793; d. at Methuen, 2 Nov 1856; m. at Methuen, 18 Oct 1816, GEORGE BARKER, b. at Methuen, 30 Jul 1788 son of Thomas and Hannah (Whittemore) Barker; George d. at Methuen, 13 Feb 1820.

iii   WILLIAM WHITTIER, b. 4 Apr 1795; d. at Methuen, 1 Apr 1836; m. 1st at Methuen, 1 Feb 1816, MARY WEBSTER, b. 1799; Mary d. at Methuen, 5 Mar 1825. William m. 2nd at Methuen, 19 Jan 1826, his first cousin, MEHITABLE WHITTIER, b. at Methuen, 6 Jul 1802 daughter of Nathaniel and Anna (Carleton) Whittier; Mehitable d. at Methuen, 26 Jan 1850.

iv   DANIEL BODWELL WHITTIER, b. 24 Jan 1797; d. 7 Mar 1797.

v   ABIAH WHITTIER, b. 1 Apr 1798; d. at Methuen, 20 Jul 1878; m. at Methuen, 1 May 1817, WILLIAM RICHARDSON, b. at Methuen, 26 Apr 1794 son of Samuel and Lucy (Parker) Richardson; William d. at Methuen, 2 Aug 1836.

vi   SUSAN FRYE WHITTIER, b. 26 Sep 1803; d. at Methuen, 31 Mar 1857; m. at Methuen, 13 Mar 1830, as his second wife, DAVID CROSS, b. at Methuen, 13 Nov 1795 son of Abijah and Elizabeth (Parker) Cross; David d. at Methuen, 27 Dec 1833. David was first married to Mary Frye.

494)   PHEBE POOR (*Phebe Osgood Poor⁴, Mary Russell Osgood³, Thomas², Robert¹*), b. at Andover, 3 Jul 1761 daughter of Thomas and Phebe (Osgood) Poor; m. at Andover, 22 Nov 1796, as his second wife, MOSES PLUMMER, b. at Rowley, 24 Jan 1744/5 son of Thomas and Bethiah (Tenney) Plummer. Moses was first married to Hannah Hale.

Moses Plummer was a wheelwright and resided in Rowley, Andover, Londonderry, and Methuen.[1356] Phebe Poor and Moses Plummer were parents of three children. Moses had three children with his first wife Hannah Hale.

i   DAVID PLUMMER, b. 23 Mar 1798 (recorded in Methuen town records with family record);[1357] m. at Dracut, 15 Sep 1821, RHODA HARRIS, b. at Dracut, 26 Dec 1797 daughter of Peter and Rachel (Parker) Harris; Rhoda d. at Methuen, 28 Oct 1829.

ii   PHEBE OSGOOD PLUMMER, b. at Londonderry, NH, 14 Jul 1799; d. at Brighton, MA, 4 May 1873. Phebe did not marry. Phebe lived with her brother Enoch in Brighton.

iii   ENOCH PLUMMER, b. at Londonderry, 9 Oct 1801; d. at Lynn, MA, 25 Jan 1880; m. 25 Dec 1826, ELIZABETH "BETSEY" JOHNSTON, b. at Groveland, 1803 daughter of Thomas and Rhoda (Atwood) Johnston; Elizabeth d. at Newburyport, 13 Aug 1898 of senile debility. At least for a time, Elizabeth's brother Thomas Johnston lived with Enoch and Elizabeth at Brighton.

495)   STEPHEN POOR (*Phebe Osgood Poor⁴, Mary Russell Osgood³, Thomas², Robert¹*), b. at Andover, 16 Feb 1763 son of Thomas and Phebe (Osgood) Poor; d. at Newburyport, 17 Jul 1812; m. 1st at Andover, 25 Oct 1795, ELIZABETH DUSTIN, b. at

[1355] *Essex County, MA: Probate File Papers, 1638-1881.* Online database. *AmericanAncestors.org.* New England Historic Genealogical Society, 2014. Case 29750
[1356] Perley, *The Plumer Genealogy*, p 134
[1357] Ancestry.com, Massachusetts Town and Vital Records 1620-1988, Methuen, p 188 of Methuen Vital Records 1770-1857

Windham, NH, 8 Sep 1773 daughter of Peter and Betty (Sawyer) Dustin;[1358] Elizabeth d. about 1800. Stephen m. 2nd 24 Aug 1801, MARY PLUMMER, b. about 1782 (based on age at time of death); Mary d. at Andover, 2 Dec 1845. Mary married second Joseph Cummings at Andover on 19 Dec 1815.

Stephen was a teamster who resided in Andover but moved to Newburyport prior to his death. On 8 Jul 1806, Stephen Poor then of Andover, sold his land in Methuen to Enoch Poor and Thomas Poor.[1359] Stephen did not leave a will and his estate entered probate 10 September 1812 with Levi Mills as administrator at request of widow Mary. His estate was valued at $206.55 which included $40 value of a fishing place on the "Shaysin river" (Shawsheen River) in Andover which was the only real estate. Debts were $385.08.[1360]

Stephen Poor and Elizabeth Dustin were parents of two children.

i   GEORGE POOR, b. at Andover, 24 Nov 1796; d. at Danvers, 13 Feb 1825. George did not marry. In his will written 5 February 1825, George left his estate to his sister Eliza Osborn wife of Miles Osborn "as a memorial of her brother's love for her."[1361]

ii   ELIZABETH "ELIZA" POOR, b. at Andover, 23 May 1798; d. at Danvers, 20 Dec 1835; m. at Danvers, 17 Dec 1820, MILES OSBORN, b. at Danvers, 6 Mar 1795 son of John and Lydia (Southwick) Osborn; Miles d. at Peabody, 30 Jan 1873. Miles married second Sally Brown on 25 Dec 1836.

Stephen Poor and Mary Plummer were parents of three children.

i   STEPHEN POOR, b. at Andover, 14 Nov 1803. Stephen was living in Andover in 1825 when he signed consent to the will of his half-brother George Poor. Nothing further is known.

ii   MARY "POLLY" POOR, b. at Andover, 22 Oct 1807; d. at Holyoke, MA, 13 Oct 1888; m. at Andover, 30 Apr 1827, her fourth cousin, JOEL RUSSELL (*Joel⁵, Uriah⁴, Thomas³, James², Robert¹*), b. at Andover, 10 Oct 1808 son of Joel and Sally (Curtis) Russell; Joel d. at Holyoke, 30 Oct 1883.

iii   SARAH BOND POOR, b. at Andover, 14 Mar 1810; d. at Epping, NH, 13 Nov 1902; m. at Andover, 9 Mar 1835, STEPHEN W. BUTMAN, b. at New Ipswich, about 1810 son of John and Betsey (Wheeler) Butman;[1362] Stephen d. at Epping, 25 Jan 1885.

496)   ENOCH POOR (*Phebe Osgood Poor⁴, Mary Russell Osgood³, Thomas², Robert¹*), b. at Andover, 20 Apr 1765 son of Thomas and Phebe (Osgood) Poor; d. at Methuen, 17 Mar 1834; m. at Rowan County, NC, 1794 (bond 8 Apr 1794), PRUDENCE BREVARD, b. in NC, 4 Jan 1772 daughter of Robert and Sarah (Craig) Brevard;[1363] Prudence d. at Methuen, 29 Jul 1850.

Enoch and Prudence had five children in North Carolina and then Enoch returned to Methuen. In 1800, the family was in Salisbury, Iredell County, North Carolina with a household of sixteen which include nine slaves.[1364] After Enoch's death, Prudence and daughters Adeline and Cecilia lived with daughter Harriet, who was widowed, in Lawrence.[1365]

Enoch Poor did not leave a will and the estate entered probate 1 October 1834 with widow Prudence declining administration and requesting that Joshua Buswell, Jr. fill this role. Real estate was valued at $3,595 and personal estate at $1,201.77. The dower was set off to widow Prudence.[1366] The debts of the estate required that $1,530 worth of the real estate be sold to settle the debts. On 18 September 1835, Joshua Buswell sold parcels from the estate as needed to settle debts.[1367]

On 26 October 1845 (recorded 10 April 1850), the heirs of the estate for payment of twenty-five dollars by the Essex Company quitclaimed fishing privilege on the northern side of the Merrimack River in Methuen at Bodwell's Falls. Those signing the quitclaim were Thomas O. Poor yeoman, Cecilia P. Poor, Adaline Poor, and Caroline B. Poor singlewomen, Joshua Buswell gentleman and Harriet P. Buswell his wife, all of Methuen; Enoch A. Poor of Amesbury, manufacturer; Caleb F. Poor of Andover, Maine; and Alfred J. Poor, printer and Joel W. Poor, machinist of New York City.[1368]

[1358] The 1825 will of Peter Dustin includes a bequest to his granddaughter Eliza Poor, now Eliza Osborne.

[1359] Massachusetts Land Records, Essex County, 177:133

[1360] *Essex County, MA: Probate File Papers, 1638-1881.*Online database. *AmericanAncestors.org.* New England Historic Genealogical Society, 2014. Case 22385

[1361] *Essex County, MA: Probate File Papers, 1638-1881.*Online database. *AmericanAncestors.org.* New England Historic Genealogical Society, 2014. Case 22346

[1362] The names of Stephen's parents are given as John Butman and Betsey Wheeler on his death record.

[1363] The wills of both Robert Brevard (1797) and Sarah Brevard (1801) of Iredell County, North Carolina name daughter Prudence, although neither will provides the last names of the daughters named in the wills. The bible records for this family are transcribed and in the archives of the Charles A. Cannon Memorial Library in Concord, North Carolina.

[1364] Year: 1800; Census Place: Salisbury, Iredell, North Carolina; Series: M32; Roll: 29; Page: 663; Image: 341; Family History Library Film: 337905

[1365] Year: 1850; Census Place: Lawrence, Essex, Massachusetts; Roll: 314; Page: 233a

[1366] *Essex County, MA: Probate File Papers, 1638-1881.*Online database. *AmericanAncestors.org.* New England Historic Genealogical Society, 2014. Case 22344

[1367] Massachusetts Land Records, Essex County, 289:294; 289:295

[1368] Massachusetts Land Records, Essex County, 426:136

Son Alfred J. Poor was a printer in Lawrence. He did not marry, and his sister Cecilia was administratrix of his estate. On 9 July 1864, Cecilia provided the following list of heirs-at-law in addition to herself: Caleb Franklin Poor brother of Andover, Maine; Joel W. Poor brother of New York City; Harriet P. Buswell sister of Philadelphia; Adeline Poor sister of Lawrence; and the representatives of brother Enoch Poor. Estate was valued at $600 all of it in personal estate.[1369]

Enoch Poor and Prudence Brevard were parents of ten children.[1370]

i   THOMAS OSGOOD POOR, b. in Rowan County, NC, 9 Mar 1795; d. at Methuen, 4 May 1856. Thomas did not marry. In his will, Thomas O. Poor left his brothers and sisters his best wishes and directed that the estate be sold, and proceeds be used by ministerial services in Methuen to create a fund for the poor. The total value of the estate was $169.50.[1371]

ii ROBERT BREVARD POOR, b. at Rowan County, NC, 12 Mar 1798; d. at Smithfield, NC, 1820. Robert attended Phillips Academy and graduated from Harvard in 1819. He taught in Smithfield for a few months after his graduation until his early death.[1372]

iii ENOCH ADAMS POOR, b. in Rowan County, NC, 4 Dec 1799; d. at Amesbury, MA, 1 Mar 1847; m. at Amesbury, 26 Oct 1833, MARY BLAISDELL, b. 15 Nov 1813 daughter of John and Dorothy (Bagley) Blaisdell; Mary d. at Amesbury, 16 Apr 1891.

iv CALEB FRANKLIN POOR, b. in Rowan County, 10 Apr 1802; d. at Andover, ME, 15 Sep 1880; m. 1st about 1835, MARY FRYE MERRILL, b. 1811 daughter of Moses and Dorothy (Bragg) Merrill; Mary d. at Andover, 16 Jul 1851. Caleb m. 2nd ELIZA CLARK BARKER, b. 1813 daughter of David G. and Deborah (Joslyn) Barker;[1373] Eliza d. at Andover, 25 Dec 1896.

v   ALFRED JONES POOR, b. in Iredell County, NC, 17 Jan 1804; d. at Lawrence, MA, 18 Jun 1864. Alfred did not marry.

vi PRUDENCE CECILIA POOR, b. at Methuen, 16 Feb 1806; d. at Lawrence, MA, 24 May 1868. Cecilia did not marry. In her will written 2 November 1767, Cecilia left her estate to sister Adeline, her nephew, and her five nieces.[1374]

vii JOEL W. POOR, b. at Methuen, about 1808; d. at New York, NY, 9 Mar 1885; m. at Lowell, 30 Oct 1831, MARY JANE BAILEY, b. in NH about 1810; Mary d. after 1886 when she was living in Brooklyn. Joel was a piano manufacturer.

viii HARRIET POOR, b. at Methuen, 1810; d. at Springfield, MA, 31 May 1901; m. at Methuen, 13 Jan 1833, JOSHUA BUSWELL, b. at Methuen, 10 Feb 1804 son of Joshua and Polly (Gage) Buswell; Joshua d. at Methuen, 10 Nov 1846.

ix ADELINE POOR, b. at Methuen, 1812; d. at Lawrence, MA, 12 Aug 1870. Adeline did not marry. In her will written 6 March 1868, Adeline left her estate to sister Cecilia P. Poor, brother Franklin Poor, five nieces, and one nephew.[1375]

x   CAROLINE B. POOR, b. at Methuen, 1817; d. at Methuen, 12 Apr 1850. Caroline did not marry.

497)   CALEB POOR (*Phebe Osgood Poor⁴, Mary Russell Osgood³, Thomas², Robert¹*), b. at Andover, 28 Mar 1767 son of Thomas and Phebe (Osgood) Poor; d. after 1813 (living in Morganton, NC in 1810); m. Jul 1796, POLLY MIRA AVERY, b. at Burke County, NC, 24 Aug 1779 daughter of Waightstill and Leah (Probart) Avery;[1376] Polly Mira d. at Henderson County, NC, 20 Feb 1857. Caleb and Polly divorced in 1813.[1377] Polly Mira married second Jacob Summey in 1823.

[1369] Massachusetts Wills and Probate, Essex County, Estate of Alfred J. Poor, Case 50548
[1370] The births of six of the children are noted in the Methuen records but five are recorded as occurring in NC (Alfred, Caleb, Enoch, Robert, and Thomas); Massachusetts Vital Records Project; https://ma-vitalrecords.org/MA/Essex/Methuen/aBirthsP.shtml
[1371] *Essex County, MA: Probate File Papers, 1638-1881.*Online database. *AmericanAncestors.org.* New England Historic Genealogical Society, 2014. Case 50617
[1372] Carpenter, *Biographical Catalogue of the Trustees, Teachers and Students of Phillips Academy*, p 73
[1373] The names of Eliza's parents are given as David G. Barker and Deborah Joslyn on her death record.
[1374] Massachusetts Wills and Probate, Essex County, Probate Records Poll, L – Poor, E; will of Cecilia P. Poor
[1375] *Essex County, MA: Probate File Papers, 1638-1881.*Online database. *AmericanAncestors.org.* New England Historic Genealogical Society, 2014. Case 50546
[1376] The 1823 will of Waightstill Avery includes a bequest to his daughter Polly Mira Poor.
[1377] Insooe, *Mountain Masters: Slavery and the Sectional Crisis in Western North Carolina*, p 119

Defying her parents' wishes, Polly Mira Avery married Caleb Poor in 1796. Her father denied her a dowry, although Caleb and Polly were allowed to live on one of the family's plantations in Burke County. Caleb worked in a tannery. The marriage ended in a bitter divorce in 1813.[1378] It is not known where Caleb wound up after the divorce.

Caleb Poor and Polly Mira Avery were parents of seven children born in Burke County, North Carolina.[1379]

i   EDWIN POOR, b. 1797; d. at Morganton, NC, 17 Nov 1830.

ii POLLY OSGOOD POOR, b. 29 Apr 1799; d. at Horse Shoe, NC, 31 Jan 1881; m. 1818, JOHN MCCLAIN, b. 18 Feb 1792 son of John McClain; John d. at Horse Shoe, NC, 31 Dec 1879 (probate 1880).

iii LEAH CAROLINE POOR, b. 1800; d. after 1850 when the family is listed living "North of the Yallobusha River, Yalobusha, Mississippi"; m. about 1822, JOHN SPANN, b. about 1797 who has not been identified. Leah and John were parents of at least seven children.

iv PHEBE POOR, b. 1803; d. at Morganton, 1833.

v   WILLIAM PROBART POOR, b. 1806; d. at Davidson River, NC, 18 Jul 1889; m. 1st about 1831, ELIZABETH EMELINE MCCARSON, b. about 1811; Elizabeth d. at Horse Shoe, NC, 29 Jun 1850. William m. 2nd at Henderson County, NC, 12 Jun 1856, SARAH ANN WILSON, b. at Buncombe County, NC, 29 Feb 1832 daughter of William and Ruth (Clayton) Wilson; Sarah d. at Davidson River, 3 Apr 1909.

vi ISAAC THOMAS POOR, b. 1808; d. at Horse Shoe, NC, 24 Mar 1842.

vii MILTON POOR, b. 1812; d. at Morganton, 4 Jul 1828.

498)   NANCY POOR (*Phebe Osgood Poor⁴, Mary Russell Osgood³, Thomas², Robert¹*), b. about 1771 daughter of Thomas and Phebe (Osgood) Poor; d. at Methuen, 9 Jan 1855; m. at Methuen, 25 Oct 1797, ROBINSON FRYE, b. at Methuen, 28 May 1771 son of James and Mehitable (Robinson) Frye; Robinson d. at Methuen, 5 Dec 1816.

Nancy Poor and Robinson Frye were parents of seven children born at Methuen. Guardian was appointed for minor children of Robinson Frye on 15 April 1817. Francis Frye of Methuen was named guardian for John Frye aged nineteen, Robinson Frye aged twelve, Daniel Frye aged ten, James Frye aged seven, and Caleb Frye aged three.[1380] Guardianship cases for the daughters were not located.

i   JOHN FRYE, b. 27 Jan 1798; d. at Methuen, 9 Jul 1878. John did not marry.

ii NANCY FRYE, b. 15 Sep 1799; d. 12 Sep 1809.

iii SUSANNAH FRYE, b. 8 Mar 1803; d. at Chicopee, MA, 18 Feb 1868; m. at Methuen, 15 Oct 1826, JOSIAH OSGOOD, b. at Methuen, 31 Dec 1801 son of Benjamin and Mary (Wilson) Osgood; Josiah d. at Chicopee, 19 Jan 1868.

iv ROBINSON FRYE, b. 7 Apr 1805; d. about 1818.

v   DANIEL FRYE, b. 10 Jul 1807; d. at Bradford, MA, 18 Aug 1864; m. at Methuen, 16 Aug 1846, JOANNA D. "ANNA" KIMBALL, b. at Bradford, 22 Feb 1804 daughter of Nathan and Betsey (Day) Kimball; Joanna d. at Bradford, 27 Feb 1879.

vi JAMES FRYE, b. 14 Jul 1810; d. at Methuen, 28 Jan 1859; m. at Haverhill, 14 Sep 1845, LYDIA HERSEY, b. at Hingham, 18 Jul 1819 daughter of Eben and Elizabeth (Franks) Hersey; Lydia d. at Hingham, 19 Apr 1894. Lydia married second Levi Thaxter.

vii CALEB FRYE, b. 27 Aug 1813; d. 1819.

499)   JOHN ADAMS (*Hannah Osgood Adams⁴, Mary Russell Osgood³, Thomas², Robert¹*), b. at Andover, 26 Feb 1766 son of John and Hannah (Osgood) Adams; d. at Andover, 28 Sep 1839; m. 8 Dec 1789, DORCAS FAULKNER, b. at Andover, 26 Sep 1766 daughter of Joseph and Hannah (Hovey) Faulkner; Dorcas d. at Andover, 23 Sep 1837.

John Adams was a farmer in Andover. He was commissioned as captain in 1793 and was later Brigade Major in the State militia.[1381]

In his will written 30 November 1838 (probate 15 October 1839), John Adams bequeathed $200 to each of his daughters: Hannah Appleton wife of Mr. Daniel Appleton, Charlotte A. Osgood widow of the late Isaac Osgood, Jr., Martha

[1378] Insooe, *Mountain Masters: Slavery and the Sectional Crisis in Western North Carolina*, p 119
[1379] Avery, *The Groton Avery Clan*, pp 365-366
[1380] *Essex County, MA: Probate File Papers, 1638-1881*. Online database. *AmericanAncestors.org*. New England Historic Genealogical Society, 2014. Case 10306
[1381] Adams, *Genealogical History of Robert Adams*, p 73

Clancy wife of the Rev. John Clancy, Louisa Leavitt wife of Mr. Jonathan Leavitt, and Sarah Ann Smith wife of the Rev. Asa D. Smith. Daughter Mary H. Lord wife of Nathaniel Lord receives $250. All the rest of the estate goes to son Joseph H. Adams of Boston to be held in trust for the use and benefit of his children: Joseph H. Adams, Jr., Caroline M. Adams, Sarah F. Adams, John Adams, Frederick S. Adams, and Julia M. Adams, plus any child yet to be born. The estate is to be managed by a trustee during the lifetime of Joseph H. Adams, and at his decease to be equally divided among Joseph's children. Joseph H. Adams was named executor. Real estate was valued at $5,025 and personal estate at $1,001.31.[1382]

John Adams and Dorcas Faulkner were parents of ten children born at Andover. John Adams was also ward to Sarah who was baptized at Andover 4 September 1825.[1383]

i   JOSEPH H. ADAMS, b. 21 Mar 1790; d. at North Andover, 26 Jun 1861; m. at Haverhill, 12 Oct 1816, SARAH BROWN WHITE, b. at Haverhill, 29 Sep 1793 daughter of Samuel and Lydia (Ayer) White; Sarah d. at Boston, 26 Jul 1859. Joseph and Sarah lived in Boston where Joseph was president of Ocean Insurance Company and president of New England Mutual Marine Insurance. He also served as Lt. Col. in the Independent Corps of Cadets.[1384]

ii   HANNAH ADAMS, b. 18 Dec 1791; d. 28 May 1859; m. 4 May 1813, her third cousin once removed, DANIEL APPLETON (*Daniel Appleton⁴, Mary Russell Appleton³, James², Robert¹*), b. 10 Dec 1785 son of Daniel and Lydia (Ela) Appleton; Daniel d. at New York, NY, 27 Mar 1849. Daniel and his brother-in-law Jonathan Leavitt (Louisa's husband) were in the publishing business together. Hannah Adams and Daniel Appleton are Family 651.

iii MARY HOLT ADAMS, b. 4 Nov 1793; d. at Schenectady, NY, 23 Jan 1869; m. at Andover, 6 Sep 1838, as his second wife, NATHANIEL LORD, b. at Ipswich, 25 Sep 1780 son of Isaac and Susanna (Lord) Lord; Nathaniel d. at Ipswich, 16 Oct 1852. Nathaniel was first married to Eunice Kimball (1778-1837). Nathaniel graduated Harvard in 1798 and was the Register of Probate for Essex County from 1815-1851.[1385]

iv   CHARLOTTE ADAMS, b. 29 May 1796; d. at Andover, 27 Jul 1871; m. at Andover, 7 Aug 1821, ISAAC OSGOOD, baptized at Salem, 9 Jun 1799 son of Isaac and Rebecca Taylor (Pickman) Osgood; Isaac d. while at sea, 2 Sep 1834. "Isaac, died while in command of the ship Henry Tuke, on her passage from Java to Boston, Sept. 2, 1834, a. 35 y. 3 m. 9 d. PR92"

v   ISAAC ADAMS, b. 27 Oct 1798; d. 27 Oct 1801.

vi   MARTHA ADAMS, b. at Andover, 28 May 1801; d. at Schenectady, 25 Jul 1875; m. at Andover, 30 Sep 1829, JOHN CLANCY, b. at Johnstown, NY, 23 Mar 1793 son of William and Lydia (Allen) Clancy; John d. at Schenectady, 9 Sep 1876. John Clancy graduated from Middlebury College and Andover Theological Seminary and was ordained in 1822. He was missionary pastor in Virginia 1822-1823, followed by positions as pastor in Freehold, NY, Belchertown, MA, and several locations in NY, his final post at Schenectady.[1386]

vii LOUISA ADAMS[1387], b. 28 Dec 1803; d. at New York, NY, 1842; m. at Andover, 7 Dec 1825, as his second wife, JONATHAN LEAVITT, b. 20 Jan 1797 son of Simeon and Elizabeth (Tuck) Leavitt; Jonathan d. at Manhattan, 6 May 1852. Jonathan was first married to Joan Ayer who died 7 Nov 1824. Jonathan was third married to Angelica Patterson. Jonathan was a bookbinder and later founder of the publishing house Leavitt, Trow, and Company.

viii SARAH ANN ADAMS, b. 24 Sep 1806; d. at Hanover, NH, 24 Sep 1882; m. at Andover, 9 Nov 1836, ASA DODGE SMITH, b. at Amherst, NH, 21 Sep 1809 son of Rogers and Sarah (Dodge) Smith; Asa d. at Hanover, 16 Aug 1877. Asa was a graduate of Dartmouth College, was pastor of the 14th Street Presbyterian church in New York and was president of Dartmouth College from 1863-1877.[1388]

ix   EMELINE OSGOOD ADAMS, b. 31 Jan 1808; d. 21 Mar 1810.

x   JOHN OSGOOD ADAMS, b. 3 Sep 1811; d. in NY, 1 Jan 1832. "John O[sgood. CR1], s. Maj. John and Dorcas [he was residing in NY, pursuing the study of medicine, died of inflammation of the bowels. CR1], Jan. 1, 1832, a. 20 y."

[1382] *Essex County, MA: Probate File Papers, 1638-1881.* Online database. *AmericanAncestors.org.* New England Historic Genealogical Society, 2014. Case 259
[1383] Sarah, ward of Maj. John, bp. Sept. 4, 1825. CR1
[1384] Adams, *A Genealogical History of Robert Adams*, p 151
[1385] Metropolitan Publishing, *Biographical Encyclopedia of Massachusetts in the Nineteenth Century*, p 61
[1386] Middlebury College, *Catalogue of Officers and Student of Middlebury College 1800-1900*, p 59
[1387] A portrait of Louisa Adams Leavitt can be seen at https://andoverhistorical.org/andover-stories/louisa-adams-leavitt
[1388] Dartmouth College, "The Wheelock Succession of Dartmouth Presidents", https://www.dartmouth.edu/president/succession/smith.html

500)   ISAAC ADAMS (*Hannah Osgood Adams⁴, Mary Russell Osgood³, Thomas², Robert¹*), b. at Andover, 25 Apr 1767 son of John and Hannah (Osgood) Adams; d. after 1850 when he was living in Troy, MI; m. at Newburyport, MA, 7 Jun 1807, SARAH MCHARD, b. at Newburyport, 26 Apr 1777 daughter of William and Mary (-) McHard; Sarah was living in 1850.

Isaac Adams attended Harvard but did not graduate. He was a physician in Newburyport. He also served as a ship master and made several foreign voyages.[1389] Isaac and Sarah were parents of six children born at Newburyport. In 1850, Isaac Adams, physician, age 82 and his wife Sarah age 70 (as on the census records) were in Troy.

Daughter Sarah married Sheldon McKnight, a printer and publisher who printed the first daily paper in Michigan, the Free Press, in 1835. He was postmaster of Detroit from 1836 to 1841. He was a member of the Michigan governor's military staff and held the rank of colonel. President Polk appointed him Miner Agent for the Lake Superior Region.[1390]

Son Charles married Mary Sibley. Mary's father Solomon Sibley was the first Mayor of Detroit. Among his many civic accomplishments, Solomon Sibley was appointed by President Monroe to serve as Chief Justice of the Supreme Court of the Michigan Territory, a post he held from 1823 to 1837.[1391]

Isaac and Sarah were parents of seven children born at Newburyport.

i   SARAH MCHARD ADAMS, baptized at Newburyport, 22 May 1808; d. after 1867 when living in New York, NY; m. in Detroit, about 1833, SHELDON MCKNIGHT, b. at Herkimer County, NY, 30 Aug 1810 son of Alexander and Amanda (Sheldon) McKnight; Sheldon d. at Washington, DC, 21 Jul 1860 (probate in Michigan).

ii   ISAAC OSGOOD ADAMS, b. 30 Jan 1810; d. at Chicago, 21 Jan 1894; m. at Cook County, IL, 4 Jul 1857, MARY ADDIE FOOT, b. in NY, about 1828 daughter of William and Clarinda (-) Foot.

iii   WILLIAM HENRY ADAMS, b. 18 Sep 1811; m. at Detroit, 16 Nov 1836, ISABELLA S. BACKUS, b. 1816 daughter of Andrew and Elizabeth (Rodman) Backus.

iv   CHARLES SIDNEY ADAMS, b. 26 Apr 1813; d. at Los Angeles, CA, 26 Jul 1859; m. MARY SIBLEY, b. 1820 daughter of Solomon and Sarah Whipple (Sproat) Sibley; Mary d. at Detroit, MI, 1852.

v   GEROGE KENDALL ADAMS, b. 21 Dec 1815. He may be the George Kendall Adams who obtained a land grant at Tehama, CA on 1 Dec 1860.[1392]

vi   MARY MORSE ADAMS, b. 23 Apr 1818; m. at Detroit, 21 Feb 1837, WILLIAM E. BOARDMAN.

vii   AUGUSTIN WASHINGTON ADAMS, b. 4 Mar 1820

501)   PELETIAH RUSSELL (*Peletiah⁴, Peter³, Thomas², Robert¹*), b. at Litchfield, NH, 1753 son of Peletiah and Olive (Moore) Russell; d. at Groton, MA, 21 Jan 1831; m. at Groton, 30 May 1780, SARAH DERUMPLE, b. at Groton, 23 Mar 1753 daughter of William and Elizabeth (Shed) Derumple; Sarah d. at Groton, 21 Apr 1795. Peletiah m. 2ⁿᵈ at Groton on 29 May 1796, MARY BROWN; Mary d. at Groton, 26 Mar 1822.

On 31 March 1818, Peletiah Russell of Groton made application for pension based on his service in the Revolution. His first term of service was as a private for eight months starting in 1775. In February 1776 he had the rank of sergeant in the company of Capt. Joseph Moore. Peletiah was promoted to lieutenant the following June then in the regiment of Col. Jonathan Brewer. He continued in service until June 1777 at which time he had served nineteen months. He was awarded a pension of $20 per month. In June 1820, Peletiah provided additional information related to his pension. He reported personal estate value of $62.35. He was a carpenter by occupation but unable to perform his usual work due to age and infirmity.[1393]

The estate of Peletiah Russell entered probate 5 February 1831, it being noted that he had not wife and left just one daughter the wife of Phineas Gould who were indigent persons and unable to assume administration of the estate. Administration was granted to Samuel Dana of Groton. His daughter is described as the only "lineal descendant." Estate was valued at $111.15. Claims against the estate were $133.50.[1394]

Peletiah Russell and Sarah Derumple were parents of two children.

i   SARAH "SALLY" RUSSELL, b. at Groton, 24 Feb 1787; d. at Groton, 11 Sep 1877; m. 18 Dec 1803, PHINEAS FARWELL GOULD, b. at Lunenburg, 25 Oct 1778 son of Samuel and Elizabeth (Farwell) Gould; Phineas d. at Groton, 21 Nov 1857.

ii   JOHN RUSSELL, b. at Groton, 4 Aug 1793; death unknown but before 1831 and without heirs

[1389] Bailey, *Historical Sketches of Andover*, p 160

[1390] Michigan Legislative Biography, Library of Michigan, "Colonel Sheldon McKnight"; https://mdoe.state.mi.us/legislators/Legislator/LegislatorDetail/4799

[1391] Detroit Historical Society, Encyclopedia of Detroit, "Solomon Sibley"; https://detroithistorical.org/learn/encyclopedia-of-detroit/sibley-solomon

[1392] Bureau of Land Management, General Land Office Records; Washington D.C., USA; Federal Land Patents, State Volumes

[1393] U. S. Revolutionary War Pension and Bounty-Land Warrant Application Files, Case S33619

[1394] *Middlesex County, MA: Probate File Papers, 1648-1871.*Online database. *AmericanAncestors.org.* New England Historic Genealogical Society, 2014. Case 19682

502)   JOHN RUSSELL (*Peletiah⁴, Peter³, Thomas², Robert¹*), b. at Litchfield, NH, 7 Sep 1753 son of Peletiah and Olive (Moore) Russell; d. at Richmond, VT, 26 Dec 1814; m. at Haverhill, NH, SARAH HAZELTINE, b. about 1760; Sarah d. at Burlington, VT, 26 Aug 1848.

John Russell was a farmer in Richmond, Vermont. John Russell did not leave a will and Peletiah Russell was named administrator. The homestead farm consisting of 166 acres with buildings was valued at $3,500 and other lots totaling 334 acres were valued at $664 with total estate value was $5,501.88. Debts of the estate were $1,073.45. Dower was set off to the widow on 15 July 1816. On 22 May 1849, Robert Russell petitioned for the final division of the estate after the reversion of the dower. It was noted that two of the heirs-at-law (not named) were minor children requiring a guardian.[1395]

In her will written 25 January 1845, Sarah Russell of Richmond, Vermont bequeathed all the household furniture to granddaughter Hannah Russell. Her wearing apparel was divided among her three daughters: Sally Bronson widow of Thomas Bronson, Phebe Smith wife of Abram Smith, and Hannah Hodges wife of Henry Hodges. The remainder of the estate was left to son Robert Russell who was also named executor.[1396]

Son Heman Russell did not marry. On 15 August 1835, the following heirs petitioned for division of the estate: Robert Russell, Henry and Hannah Hodges, Sally Russell, John Russell, Abner and Phebe Smith, Peletiah Russell, Sally Brownson, and Catherine B. Prime.[1397]

John and Sarah were parents of ten children. Their grandson Henry C. Russell, son of Peletiah, was killed at the Battle of Gettysburg on 3 July 1863. Henry served with the 13th infantry and enlisted at Richmond, VT mustering on 10 September 1862.[1398]

i   PELETIAH RUSSELL, b. 1781; d. at Richmond, VT, 1 Sep 1839; m. about 1820, SALLY PROCTOR, b. about 1800.

ii   ROBERT RUSSELL, b. 1784; d. at Richmond, VT, 1 Aug 1868; m. 1st about 1813, HANNAH FARNSWORTH (widow of Jabez Jones), b. 9 Oct 1777 daughter of John and Hannah (White) Farnsworth; Hannah d. at Richmond, 25 Oct 1828. Robert m. 2nd CYNTHIA BRIGGS, b. 1783 daughter of Benjamin and Naomi (Wells) Briggs; Cynthia d. at Richmond, 23 Feb 1867.

iii   SALLY RUSSELL, b. 1785; d. at Oberlin, OH, 22 Feb 1868; m. 3 Sep 1809, THOMAS BROWNSON, b. at Richmond, VT, 12 Feb 1780 son of Asa and Polly (Harkins) Brownson;[1399] Thomas d. at Richmond, 23 Apr 1824.

iv   MOOR RUSSELL, b. 1788; d. at Minneapolis, MN, 10 Nov 1868; m. 1st LUCY, b. 1789; Lucy d. at Burlington, 21 Jul 1828. Moor m. 2nd at Burlington, VT, 3 Jan 1836, DELPHINE FISKE, b. at Williamston, VT, 21 Sep 1808 daughter of Benjamin and Hannah (Herrick) Fiske; Delphine d. at Burlington, 7 Aug 1839.

v   BETSEY RUSSELL, b. 1793; d. at Richmond, VT, 17 Feb 1815; m. about 1813, LAMSON PRIME.

vi   JOHN RUSSELL, b. estimate 1794; living in 1835; nothing further found.

vii   PHEBE RUSSELL, b. 1796; d. at Richmond, 5 Mar 1888; m. ABRAM SMITH, b. 1796; Abram d. at Richmond, 3 Mar 1869.

viii   HANNAH RUSSELL, b. 26 Aug 1798; d. at Richmond, VT, 8 Oct 1886; m. 2 May 1819, as his second wife, HENRY HODGES, b. at Richmond, 20 Feb 1787 son of Leonard and Sarah (Spafford) Hodges;[1400] Henry d. at Richmond, 27 Jun 1876. Henry was first married to Lucinda Rhodes.

ix   LYMAN K. RUSSELL, b. 1801; d. at Richmond, 12 Mar 1824 (probate 1824).

x   HEMAN RUSSELL, b. 1805; d. at Richmond, 31 Mar 1831. Heman did not marry. The heirs-at-law of his estate are his brothers and sisters.

503)   MOOR RUSSELL (*Peletiah⁴, Peter³, Thomas², Robert¹*), b. at Litchfield, NH, 30 Oct 1757 son of Peletiah and Olive (Moore) Russell; d. at Holderness, NH, 29 Aug 1851; m. at Plymouth, NH, 23 Dec 1790, ELIZABETH WEBSTER, b. at Plymouth, NH, 8 Jul 1773 daughter of David and Elizabeth (Clough) Webster;[1401] Elizabeth d. at Holderness, 4 Jun 1839.

Moor Russel was a surveyor by occupation and was first in Haverhill, New Hampshire where he filled positions such as town moderator in 1801, selectman in 1800, and representative in 1799 and 1800. He was one of the founders of Haverhill

[1395] Vermont Wills and Probate, Chittenden County, Estate Files Box 5, Estate of John Russell, Case 391

[1396] Vermont Wills and Probate, Chittenden County, Estate Files Box 13, will of Sarah Russell

[1397] Vermont Wills and Probate, Chittenden County, Estate Files Box 7, Estate of Heman Russell, Case 762

[1398] U.S., Civil War Soldier Records and Profiles, 1861-1865

[1399] Brownson, Ernest R., One Branch of the Brownson, Bronson, and Brunson, 1951, unpublished manuscript; Ancestry.com. *Genealogy of one branch of the Richard Brownson family, 1631-1951* [database on-line].

[1400] The names of Henry's parents are given as Leonard Hodges and Sally Spafford on his death record.

[1401] Stearns, *Genealogical and Family History of the State of New Hampshire*, volume 1, p 26

Academy. After his move to Plymouth in 1801, he was State senator 1801-1803 and again from 1810 to 1812. He was a successful merchant and farmer.[1402]

On 17 October 1832, Moor Russell of Plymouth aged seventy-four gave a statement related to his pension application. On 13 April 1778, he enlisted from Plymouth in the company of Capt. Timothy Barron for a term of one year. Much of that time was spent in the frontier near the Connecticut River and further north in what is now Vermont. He reported being born in Litchfield on 30 November 1757. After the war, he resided in Haverhill until 1801 and then relocated to Plymouth.[1403]

Son Walter did not marry. In his will written 20 November 1872 (probate 23 September 1878), W. W. Russell of Gainesville, Alabama bequeathed to nephew Walter W. Russell son of brother Charles James Russell his gold watch and chain, books, and all his wearing apparel. Brother Charles James Russell receives one-fourth of all property real and personal. Sister Catherine W. Edwards receives $5,000 which in case of Catherine's decease is to be divided between her two daughters Ann Farnsworth and Katie Webster. Nieces Mary Jane Kidder and Charlotte R. Tucker each receives $1,000 and niece Mary Long Bracker receives $2,500. The residue of the estate is to be divided among his five named nieces. Nephew David M. Russell and business partner Hamilton P. Snow were named executors.[1404]

In his will written 20 September 1863, David M. Russell of Gainesville, Alabama bequeathed to beloved wife Mary F. Russell, twenty thousand dollars, the household furniture, and "also my house servants Tim, Rose, Sally, & Caroline; said slaves to be at her service, but not to be disposed of by her, either at public or private sale, but otherwise to do with said slaves as she may think proper." Sons Edward Russell and David M. Russell each receives thirty thousand dollars. Brother Charles J. Russell of Cambridge, Massachusetts receives five thousand dollars deducting from that amount what Charles owes David. Brother-in-law John Rogers and his wife "my sister" are to have use of the Ward farm in Plymouth, New Hampshire. Wife Mary F. Russell was named executrix.[1405]

Moor Russell and Elizabeth Webster were parents of eleven children, most of the births in the records of Plymouth, New Hampshire and two in the records of Haverhill, New Hampshire.

i   NANCY RUSSELL, b. at Plymouth, NH, 20 Jul 1793; d. at the home of her daughter in NY (burial at Holderness), 28 Jan 1876; m. 31 Jan 1819, JOHN ROGERS, b. at Plymouth, NH, 1 May 1790 son of John and Betsey (Mullikan) Rogers; John d. at Plymouth, 17 Dec 1864.

ii   DAVID MOOR RUSSELL, b. at Plymouth, 6 Jul 1795; d. at Gainesville, AL, 21 Sep 1863; m. at Boxford, MA, 3 Apr 1832, MARY FLINT, b. at Reading, MA, 1 Mar 1793 daughter of David and Priscilla (Sawyer) Flint; Mary d. at Gainesville, 6 Jun 1876. David was a merchant in Plymouth before relocating to Gainesville in 1833. He was a trustee of Holmes Plymouth Academy.[1406]

iii   CATHERINE RUSSELL, b. at Haverhill, 28 May 1797; d. at Plymouth, NH, 24 Sep 1880; m. 5 May 1816, SAMUEL CUMMINGS WEBSTER, b. 28 Jun 1788 son of David and Lydia (Cummings) Webster; Samuel d. at Haverhill, NH, 21 Jul 1835.

iv   ELIZA RUSSELL, b. at Haverhill, NH, 23 Aug 1799; d. at Brooklyn, NY, 26 Jan 1899; m. at Plymouth, NH, BENJAMIN G. EDMONDS, b. at Lynn, MA, 2 Mar 1794 son of Joseph and Nancy (Shepherd) Edmonds; Benjamin d. at Brooklyn, 10 Jan 1875.

v   WILLIAM WALLACE RUSSELL, b. at Plymouth, 15 May 1801; d. at Plymouth, 3 Sep 1872; m. at Plymouth, 9 Nov 1826, SUSAN CARLETON WEBSTER, b. at Salisbury, NH, 3 Jun 1804 daughter of Humphrey and Phebe (Pettengill) Webster; Susan d. 15 Sept 1875. William started as a clerk in his father's business, was a partner with brother David until his move to Alabama, and later ran the business as a sole proprietor.[1407]

vi   MARY RUSSELL, b. at Plymouth, 26 Jan 1804; d. at Barnet, VT, 18 Oct 1832; m. 1828, ELIJAH MAYNOR DAVIS, b. at Lunenburg, VT, 25 Apr 1803 son of Elijah and Temperance (Ladd) Davis. Elijah was postmaster in Barnet.

vii   WALTER WEBSTER RUSSELL, b. at Plymouth, 5 Mar 1806; d. at Gainesville, AL, 17 Jun 1878. Walter did not marry.

viii   JANE AUGUSTA RUSSELL, b. at Plymouth, 9 Aug 1808; d. at Milwaukee, WI, 25 Apr 1889; m. 12 Sep 1838, MILO PARKER JEWETT, b. at St. Johnsbury, VT, 27 Apr 1808 son of Calvin and Sally (Parker) Jewett; Milo d. at Milwaukee, 9 Jun 1882. Milo Parker Jewett was the first president of Vassar College.[1408]

ix   JULIA ANN RUSSELL, b. 13 Aug 1810; d. 23 Nov 1815.

[1402] Stearns, *History of Plymouth, New Hampshire*, volume II, p 594
[1403] U. S. Revolutionary War Pension and Bounty-Land Warrant Application Files, Case S11332
[1404] Alabama Wills and Probate, Sumter County, Wills Volume 3, pp 69-70
[1405] Alabama Wills and Probate, Sumter County, Wills Volume 2, pp 285-287
[1406] Stearns, *History of Plymouth*, volume II, p 596
[1407] Stearns, *History of Plymouth*, volume II, p 597
[1408] Vassar Encyclopedia, "Milo P. Jewett", http://vcencyclopedia.vassar.edu/presidents/milo-p-jewett.html

x   CHARLES JAMES RUSSELL, b. at Plymouth, 16 Jan 1813; d. at Milwaukee, WI, 4 Feb 1893; m. 4 Jan 1844, CATHERINE WEBSTER MERRILL, b. 22 Feb 1819 daughter of Stevens and Mehitable W. (Wells) Merrill; Catherine d. at Milwaukee, 28 Feb 1901.

xi   JULIA ANN RUSSELL, b. at Plymouth, 27 Sep 1815; d. at Thornton, NH, 15 Apr 1850; m. 15 Sep 1835, SAMUEL LONG, b. at Hopkinton, 4 Oct 1803 son of Samuel and Mary (Clement) Long; Samuel d. at Holderness, 28 Nov 1857. Samuel married second Sarah Ann Joy. Samuel was a graduate of Dartmouth Medical College.

504)   RACHEL UNDERWOOD (*Rachel Russell Underwood⁴, Peter³, Thomas², Robert¹*), b. at Westford, MA, 21 May 1747 daughter of Timothy and Rachel (Russell) Underwood; d. at Shrewsbury, 21 Dec 1810; m. at Shrewsbury, 1 Mar 1775, SAMUEL BRIGHAM, b. at Shrewsbury, 1 Jul 1741 son of John and Susannah (Fiske) Brigham; Samuel d. at Shrewsbury, 28 Feb 1836.
      Rachel Underwood and Samuel Brigham were parents of one child.

i   JOHN BRIGHAM b. at Shrewsbury, 22 Mar 1788; d. at Shrewsbury, 1 May 1853; m. 14 Aug 1808, SARAH FAY, b. at Northborough, MA, 15 Oct 1786 daughter of Abraham and Abigail (Martin) Fay; Sarah d. at Shrewsbury, 25 Mar 1869.

505)   DEBORAH UNDERWOOD (*Rachel Russell Underwood⁴, Peter³, Thomas², Robert¹*), b. at Westford, MA, 19 Sep 1754 daughter of Timothy and Rachel (Russell) Underwood; d. at Putney, VT, Dec 1840; m. at Shrewsbury, 24 Jun 1773, ABNER MILES, b. at Shrewsbury, 12 Jan 1744/5 son of Joseph and Jemima (Lee) Miles; Abner d. at Putney, 1803.
      There are records for six children of Deborah Underwood and Abner Miles.[1409]

i   JOEL MILES, b. at Shrewsbury, MA, 3 Jul 1774; d. at Putney, VT, 8 Sep 1814; m. 25 Oct 1795, BETSEY ABBOTT, b. 19 Aug 1773, Kneeland and Betsey (Stanley) Abbott; Betsey d. at Putney, 5 Apr 1860.

ii   SALLY MILES, b. at Shrewsbury, 5 Nov 1775

iii   RACHEL MILES, b. at Shrewsbury, 17 Apr 1777; m. NATHAN HARRINGTON.

iv   JEMIMA MILES, b. at Putney, VT, 5 Apr 1779; m. at Putney, 27 Oct 1796, JOSEPH GLENNE

v   DEBORAH MILES, b. at Putney, 3 Aug 1781; d. at Shrewsbury, MA, 22 Mar 1854; m. JOSEPH CUSHING, b. at Putney, 1 Aug 1785 son of Joseph and Hannah (Sabin) Cushing; Joseph d. at Saxtons River, VT, 2 Nov 1868. Joseph married second Clarissa Cobb.

vi   EZEKIEL MILES, b. at Putney, 5 Apr 1791; d. at New York, NY, 27 Dec 1844; m. 1ˢᵗ about 1812, ROSETTA LE BRETON, b. at Martinique, 1795 daughter of Etienne and Felicite (Luchere) Le Breton;[1410] Rosetta d. at New York, about 1828. Ezekiel m, 2ⁿᵈ at New York, 18 Oct 1829,[1411] SARAH P. STICKNEY (widow of John Robinson), b. about 1800 daughter of Benjamin and Mary (Peck) Stickney.[1412]

506)   JOSEPH UNDERWOOD (*Rachel Russell Underwood⁴, Peter³, Thomas², Robert¹*), b. at Westford, MA, 1 Aug 1757 son of Timothy and Rachel (Russell) Underwood; d. at Putney, VT, 30 May 1818; m. at Putney, 4 Oct 1781, ELIZABETH REYNOLDS, b. Dec 1758 daughter of Grindall and Sarah (Searle) Reynolds; Elizabeth d. at Putney, Oct 1817.
      Joseph was born in Westford, but the family moved to Putney and Joseph resided there. He purchased the farm that had been his father's.[1413]
      On 1 April 1818, Joseph Underwood made application for a pension based on his service in the Revolution. He enlisted in the Continental army in June 1777 in the company of Capt. William Ballard in Col. Alden's regiment of the Massachusetts line. Col. Alden was killed at Cherry Valley and the regiment was then commanded by Col. Brooks. He was honorably discharged June 1780. Joseph died soon after his application and a four-month payment was made.[1414]
      Joseph and Elizabeth were parents of eight children, several of the births recorded at Athens, Vermont although the family was living in Putney.

[1409] The Miles genealogy reports a daughter Nancy and has as questionable children Abner, William, and Frank, but no records were located related to these children and they are not included here. Miles, *Miles Genealogy*, p 8

[1410] Miles, *Miles Genealogy*, p 17

[1411] The Archives of the Reformed Church in America; New Brunswick, New Jersey; Greenwich Church, Records, 1804-1866

[1412] Stickney, *The Stickney Family*, p 212

[1413] Underwood, *The Underwood Families in America*, p 51

[1414] U. S. Revolutionary War Pension and Bounty-Land Warrant Application Files, Case S41278

i   TIMOTHY UNDERWOOD, b. 27 Mar 1782; d. at Putney, 4 Sep 1849; m. about 1807, LUCY HUBBARD, b. at
         Alstead, NH, 1 Apr 1786 daughter of Abel and Lucy (Tainer) Hubbard; Lucy d. at Putney, 8 Jul 1849.

ii   SALLY UNDERWOOD, b. (recorded at Athens, VT), 30 Apr 1784; d. (buried at Putney), 23 Jun 1853; m. at
         Putney, 21 Jun 1817, MOSES JOHNSON who has not been identified.

iii   JOSEPH UNDERWOOD, b. at Athens, VT, 2 Oct 1786; died young

iv   JOSEPH UNDERWOOD, b. at Athens, 17 Jul 1788; d. at Troy, NY, 4 Dec 1854; m. 1st at Putney, 3 Oct 1820,
         SALLY HUBBARD; Sally d. about 1826. Joseph m. 2nd at Putney, 30 Jan 1827, ELIZA FLETCHER, b. in VT
         about 1803; Eliza d. at Brooklyn (burial at Troy), 19 Jan 1882.

v   PHINEAS UNDERWOOD, b. at Athens, 9 Apr 1790; d. at Putney, 27 May 1856; m. at Putney, 23 Mar 1829,
         FANNY B. REED, b. at Putney, 27 Apr 1801 daughter of Timothy and Rebecca (Wilder) Reed; Fanny d. at
         Putney, 6 Jan 1846.

vi   ELIZABETH UNDERWOOD, b. estimate 1792; d. likely in NY, about 1825; m. by 1824, Mr. Baldwin (perhaps
         Elakim Baldwin which is father's name given on the death record of Elizbeth's daughter). Elizabeth had one
         daughter, Mary Elizabeth Baldwin, who married Joseph Jones about 1845. Mary Elizabeth was reared by her
         Aunt Polly (see just below).[1415]

vii   MARY "POLLY" UNDERWOOD, b. about 1793; d. at Putney, 9 Nov 1866. Polly did not marry. In her will written
         29 Jul 1862, Mary Underwood of Putney left her entire estate to Mary Elizabeth Jones wife of Joseph Jones or to
         her children/heirs if Mary Elizabeth pre-deceased her.[1416]

viii   JAMES UNDERWOOD, b. about 1796; d. at New York, NY, 1828 (probate 13 Jul 1828 with brother Joseph as
         administrator). James does not seem to have married.

507)   TIMOTHY UNDERWOOD (*Rachel Russell Underwood⁴, Peter³, Thomas², Robert¹*), b. at Westford, MA, 30 Nov 1759
son of Timothy and Rachel (Russell) Underwood; d. at Northborough, MA, 18 Dec 1824; m. at Shrewsbury, 6 Aug 1791, MARY
"POLLY" ADAMS, b. at Shrewsbury, 12 Sep 1761 daughter of Jonathan and Hephzibah (Baker) Adams;[1417] Mary d. at
Northborough, 13 Sep 1805. Timothy m. 2nd at Northborough, MA, 26 Jul 1807, Polly's sister, HEPHZIBAH ADAMS, b. at
Shrewsbury, 20 Nov 1768; Hephzibah d. at Northborough, 2 Jan 1814.
         Timothy likely served in the Revolution, although it is difficult to determine which of the several Timothy
Underwood's who served represent his service. He was in Putney, Vermont in 1788[1418] but settled in Shrewsbury,
Massachusetts and finally in Northborough. On 9 April 1800, Timothy Underwood then of Shrewsbury purchased the farm of
Joel Rice of Northborough for $2,500. On 4 June 1802, Jonathan Adams of Shrewsbury for payment of $890 by Timothy
Underwood of Shrewsbury quitclaimed all his rights to the real estate that was left to him in the will of his father Jonathan
Adams.[1419]
         Timothy Underwood's estate was administered by brother James Underwood of Swanzey, New Hampshire with bond
given on 23 December 1824. Heirs agreeing to James as administrator were Betsey N. Underwood, Persis B. Marble, and
Hannah Underwood. The homestead farm of 204 acres was valued at $3,978 with total real estate of $5,446 and personal estate
of $2,236.69. There was also property in Vermont and New Hampshire included in the estate accounting. There were also rents
and notes owed to the estate.[1420] On 28 April 1828, Joseph Davis was named as guardian to represent the interests of minor
children Eunice Underwood and Harriet Underwood, Polly Adams Marble, Sarah Putnam Marble, and Elizabeth March
Marble.[1421]
         Timothy and Mary were parents of six children.

i   PERSIS BAKER UNDERWOOD, b. at Shrewsbury, 27 Oct 1793; d. at Northborough, MA, 15 Sep 1825; m. at
         Northborough, 21 Nov 1815, MARCH CHASE MARBLE, b. at Cornish, NH, 4 Nov 1793 son of Antipas and Sarah
         (Putnam) Marble; March d. (burial at Cheshire), 26 Aug 1822.

[1415] Underwood, *The Underwood Families in America*, p 51
[1416] *Vermont. Probate Court (Westminster District), Folder 12, Wrp8-90746, Bundle 11, 1866-1867, will of Mary Underwood*
[1417] The 1801 will of Jonathan Adams of Shrewsbury includes a bequest to his daughter Mary Underwood.
[1418] Underwood, *The Underwood Families in America*, p 56
[1419] Massachusetts Land Records, Worcester County, 141:90; 148:96
[1420] *Worcester County, MA: Probate File Papers, 1731-1881.* Online database. AmericanAncestors.org. New England Historic Genealogical Society,
2015. Case 60528
[1421] *Worcester County, MA: Probate File Papers, 1731-1881.* Online database. AmericanAncestors.org. New England Historic Genealogical Society,
2015. Case 60494

ii   BETSEY NOYES UNDERWOOD, b. at Shrewsbury, 1 Jun 1792; d. at Northborough, 10 Aug 1840; m. at Northborough, 23 Oct 1825, WILLIAM MAYNARD,[1422] b. at Shrewsbury, 20 Sep 1781 son of John and Martha (Brigham) Maynard; William d. at Shrewsbury, 29 Jul 1852.

iii   MARY BUCKLEY UNDERWOOD, b. 5 Dec 1795; d. at Potsdam, NY, 4 Jan 1837; m. at Northborough, 31 Jan 1824, JOHN C. PUTNAM, b. likely in Cornish, NH, 1796 son of Isaac and Mary (Chamberlain) Putnam; John d. at Potsdam, 19 Mar 1877. John married second, Mary's half-sister, Eunice (see below).

iv   HANNAH UNDERWOOD, b. at Shrewsbury, 30 Apr 1797; d. 10 May 1798.

v   HANNAH UNDERWOOD, b. at Shrewsbury, 20 Feb 1799; d. (burial at Shrewsbury), 22 Aug 1836; m. at Northborough, 5 Jan 1825, WAREHAM DODGE RAND, b. at Shrewsbury, 22 Jun 1796 son of Jasper and Mary (Knowlton) Rand. Wareham married second Mary A. R. Snow on 23 Jan 1837.

vi   SALLY UNDERWOOD, baptized at Northborough, 25 Jan 1801; d. at Chester, VT, 14 Jan 1871; m. at Northborough, 21 Oct 1824, HERSCHEL DAVIS, b. at Springfield, VT, 1 May 1798 son of John Davis; Herschel d. at Springfield, VT, 2 Oct 1886.

Timothy and Hephzibah were parents of two children.

i   EUNICE UNDERWOOD, baptized at Northborough, 7 Oct 1810; m. about 1838, JOHN C. PUTNAM who was first married to Eunice's half-sister Mary Buckley Underwood (see above).

ii   HARRIET UNDERWOOD, baptized at Northborough, 7 Oct 1810

508)   PHINEAS UNDERWOOD (*Rachel Russell Underwood⁴, Peter³, Thomas², Robert¹*), b. at Westford, MA, 18 Mar 1764 son of Timothy and Rachel (Russell) Underwood; d. at Virginia, IL, 2 Apr 1843; m. by 1792, SARAH who has not been identified.

     Phineas and Sarah resided early in Putney, Vermont but were in New York City by 1801 where their son Phineas was baptized. Phineas was a dairyman.[1423] His wife Sarah died at unknown date but before 1833. The family lived in New York until 1833 when they moved to Morgan County, Illinois. While living in New York, they were members of the Methodist church. Phineas and his son Phineas were members of the First Methodist Episcopal Church of New York City listed in 1819 records.[1424] Daughter Rachel married in the same church, and her husband Peter Webb was also a member.

     Phineas enlisted in the service from Putney, Vermont in March 1781 in the company of Capt. Isaac Fisk, for which service he received a pension in 1832. Phineas experienced mental decline and in 1833, his son Phineas, Jr. was named conservator for his father. Phineas, Jr. provided the following information on 16 May 1833 while the family was living in New York City. His father had lost his memory over the past six years, "he appears to have forgotten many of his acquaintances whom he well knew many years and calls them by wrong names and often times forgets the names of his children and calls them by wrong names." Phineas, Jr. also stated that Phineas's wife was deceased and there were two living children, Phineas, Jr. and Rachel. A statement was provided on 16 July 1833 by Joseph Underwood of New York (relationship not given) confirming the loss of mental capabilities. On 12 June 1834, Phineas, Jr. provided an additional statement related to the pension, the family then living in Morgan County, Illinois, and Phineas about age seventy-one. Phineas was reported as living in Putney, Vermont, then in New York City where the family lived for "many years" before going to Morgan County, Illinois in 1833.[1425]

     There are two children known for Phineas and Sarah Underwood.

i   RACHEL UNDERWOOD, b. about 1792; *likely* m. at New York, NY, 22 Jul 1812,[1426] PETER L. WEBB who has not been identified. One son of Rachel and Peter was identified, Timothy Underwood Webb born in New York 17 Jun 1813 and baptized 1 Nov 1813.[1427] Peter was member of the same Methodist church where the Underwood family were members, and the marriage is recorded at that church.

ii   PHINEAS UNDERWOOD, baptized at New York, NY, 28 Mar 1801; d. at Virginia, IL, 2 Jun 1884 when he was struck by a train; m. at New York, NY, 16 May 1825, SARAH ANN APPLETON, b. in MA, 1803; Sarah d. at Cass County, IL, 18 Jul 1859. Phineas was a "prominent farmer" in Virginia. He was struck and killed by a

[1422] One marriage transcription gives the marriage as Polly Underwood and William Maynard, but it is Betsey N. who is buried with William Maynard and the births of their children all give parents as William and Betsey.

[1423] Underwood, *The Underwood Families in America*, p 56

[1424] New York and Vicinity, United Methodist Church Records, 1775-1949, volume 75, taken 1819, p 295

[1425] U. S. Revolutionary War Pension and Bounty-:and Warrant Application Files, Case S32562

[1426] New York and Vicinity, United Methodist Church Records, 1775-1949

[1427] New York and Vicinity, United Methodist Church Records, 1775-1949, volume 234, p 240

southbound passenger train while he was walking on the track.[1428] He was at one time assessor and treasurer in Virginia, IL. At the time of his death, Phineas was the oldest Free Mason in the county.[1429]

509)   RUSSELL UNDERWOOD (*Rachel Russell Underwood⁴, Peter³, Thomas², Robert¹*), b. at Westford, MA, 16 Aug 1766 son of Timothy and Rachel (Russell) Underwood; d. about 1821; m. at Shrewsbury, 1 Jan 1789, ELIZABETH "BETTY" ALLEN, b. at Shrewsbury, 13 Mar 1765 daughter of Elnathan and Thankful (Hastings) Allen;[1430] Elizabeth d. at Kendall, NY, 6 Oct 1854.

    Russell and Betty lived in Putney, Vermont but relocated to New York City, perhaps shortly after Russell's brother Phineas made the move to New York. The family were members of the Methodist church in New York, although Russell was dropped from the church rolls in 1815.[1431] Betty Underwood was living with her daughter Elizabeth and her husband at Kendall in 1850.[1432]

    Russell is recorded in the 1790 census at Putney in 1790, his household then one adult male and one adult female.[1433] He may be the Russell Underwood recorded in Granville, New York in 1810 with a household of eight persons which suggests six children in the family. Three children have been identified.

i   ELIZABETH UNDERWOOD, b. at Putney, VT, 1795; d. at Kendall, NY, 17 May 1860; m. about 1820, ALANSON SWEET, b. likely in Granville, NY, 1788 son of Jonathan and Ruth (Nichols) Sweet;[1434] Alanson d. after 1875 when he was living at Troy, NY in the home of one of his children.

ii   RUSSELL UNDERWOOD, b. at Putney, about 1797; d. at New York, NY, 3 Feb 1828.[1435]

iii   LUTHER ALLEN UNDERWOOD, b. at Putney, 23 Nov 1802; d. at New York, NY, 22 Nov 1839; m. at New York, NY, 26 Dec 1830, SUSANNA BABBITT, b. at Albany, NY, 19 Sep 1807 daughter of Ira and Sabra (Vincent) Babbitt;[1436] Susanna d. at New York, NY, 23 Sep 1845.

510)   MARY "MOLLY" UNDERWOOD (*Rachel Russell Underwood⁴, Peter³, Thomas², Robert¹*), b. at Westford, MA, 10 Aug 1768 daughter of Timothy and Rachel (Russell) Underwood; d. at Shrewsbury, 6 Oct 1789; m. 20 Dec 1786, HUMPHREY BIGELOW, b. at Shrewsbury, 4 Sep 1761 son of Samuel and Phebe (Rand) Bigelow; Humphrey d. at Shrewsbury, 2 Oct 1842. Humphrey married second Hannah Whipple.

    Molly Underwood and Humphrey Bigelow were parents of two children born at Shrewsbury.

i   JOHN BIGELOW, b. 12 Aug 1787; d. at Bangor, ME, 6 Sep 1808; m. 15 Nov 1806, MARY JONES, b. at Charlton, MA, 9 Dec 1780 daughter of Seth and Mary (Daggett) Jones; Mary d. at Worcester, 30 Oct 1831. Mary (as Mrs. Mary Bigelow) married second Peter Slater 12 Jun 1820.

ii   SAMUEL BIGELOW, b. 1 Aug 1789; d. Oct 1789.

511)   JAMES UNDERWOOD (*Rachel Russell Underwood⁴, Peter³, Thomas², Robert¹*), b. at Westford, MA, 7 Mar 1771 son of Timothy and Rachel (Russell) Underwood; d. at Swanzey, NH, 4 Feb 1832; m. 1ˢᵗ at Westmoreland, NH, 25 Apr 1793, HANNAH AMSBURY, b. at Westmoreland, 30 Jun 1775 daughter of Israel and Anna (-) Amsbury; Hannah d. at Rockingham, VT, 22 Jan 1809. James m/ 2ⁿᵈ widow EUNICE SEBASTIAN who is perhaps the Mrs. Eunice Underwood who died at Keene, NH, 9 Jun 1841 at age 77.

    James Underwood was in Vermont after his marriage and it is likely his children were born there. He settled in Swanzey, New Hampshire, taxed there for the first time in 1815, and was tavern keeper of what was known as Underwood Tavern. The tavern had been purchased by James's brother Timothy in 1816 from Joshua Graves and Timothy sold the property to James on 11 May 1816. James served as town representative from 1821 to 1823.[1437]

    On 7 February 1832, Elijah Carpenter was named administrator of the estate of James Underwood as widow Eunice Underwood and "only sons" Israel Underwood, Timothy Underwood, and Hiram Underwood declined administration. Claims

[1428] St. Louis Dispatch (St. Louis, Missouri), 03 June 1884, Tuesday, p 5

[1429] St. Louis Globe Democrat (St. Louis, Missouri), 03 June 1884, Tuesday, p 4

[1430] The 1800 will of Elnathan Allen of Shrewsbury includes a bequest to his daughter Betty Underwood.

[1431] New York and Vicinity, United Methodist Church Records, 1775-1949, volume 243, p 8

[1432] Year: 1850; Census Place: Kendall, Orleans, New York; Roll: 575; Page: 64B

[1433] Year: 1790; Census Place: Putney, Windham, Vermont; Series: M637; Roll: 12; Page: 110; Image: 108; Family History Library Film: 0568152

[1434] The 1806 will of Jonathan Sweet of Granville, NY includes a bequest to his son Alanson.

[1435] U.S., Newspaper Extractions from the Northeast, 1704-1930, death notice in New York Evening Post, Russell Underwood, age 31

[1436] Browne, *The Babbitt Family History*, p 101

[1437] Read, The History of Swanzey, p 86, p 232, p 208

against the estate exceeded the value of the personal estate and real estate was sold to settle the debts. Real estate was sold for $3,264.48. Dower was set off to widow Eunice.[1438]

James Underwood and Hannah Amsbury were parents of seven children.[1439]

i   ANNA UNDERWOOD, b. 1793; d. at Warren Center, PA, 10 Feb 1874; m. 1st at Springfield, VT, 23 Apr 1809, JOHN MOORE who has not been identified; John d. about 1814. Anna m. 2nd at Swanzey, NH, 25 Feb 1815, JOHN MARCH CURRIER, b. at Salisbury, MA, 25 May 1789 son of David and Mary (March) Currier; John d. at Warren Center, 6 Mar 1862.

ii   ISRAEL UNDERWOOD, b. about 1794; d. after 1860 when he was living at the poor farm in Swanzey; m. at Littleton, NH, 5 Feb 1824, NANCY CARTER, b. at Littleton, 28 Apr 1797 daughter of Eliphalet and Abigail (Wiggins) Carter; Nancy d. at Littleton, 6 Nov 1832. Israel may have had a second marriage to Sally Dexter on 14 Nov 1833. If so, Sally likely died before 1850 when Israel was living in Swanzey with his widowed sister Rachel and her two children. Israel does not seem to have had children.

iii   HARRIET UNDERWOOD, b. about 1798; d. at Swanzey, 23 Mar 1836; m. 31 Dec 1818, CHAUNCEY BRYANT, b. 1795 son of Daniel Chandler and Susanna (Byum) Bryant; Chauncey d. at Keene, NY, 15 Jan 1863. Chauncey had a second marriage to Samantha who has not been identified.

iv   RACHEL UNDERWOOD, b. about 1801; d. after 1850 when she was living at Swanzey; m. 31 Dec 1827, WILLIAM WRIGHT, b. at Swanzey, about 1800 son of Calvin and Elizabeth (Capron) Wright;[1440] William d. at Swanzey, 17 Jun 1843.

v   TIMOTHY UNDERWOOD, b. at Springfield, VT, 30 Apr 1803 (date of gravestone);[1441] d. at Fitchburg, MA, 30 Sep 1863; m. RUTH BURGESS, b. at Foster, RI (per death record) 18 Jan 1805 daughter of Asel and Alice (Hopkins) Burgess;[1442] Ruth d. at Fitchburg, 13 May 1869.

vi   HIRAM UNDERWOOD, b. 25 Sep 1805; d. at Swanzey, 13 Mar 1876; m. 1st 6 Feb 1825, MARILLA WRIGHT, b. at Swanzey, 1807 daughter of Calvin and Elizabeth (Capron) Wright; Marilla d. 21 Oct 1845. Hiram m. 2nd at Brattleboro, VT, 15 Sep 1846, MARGARET SPRAKER, b. at Spraker's Basin, NY, 30 Jun 1820 and baptized at Stone Arabia, NY, 13 Aug 1820 daughter of George and Mary (Loucks) Spraker;[1443] Margaret d. at Swanzey, 30 Mar 1907.

vii   JAMES UNDERWOOD, b. 1807; d. 4 Apr 1819.

512)   JOHN BUTTERFIELD (*Phebe Russell Butterfield Robie⁴, Peter³, Thomas², Robert¹*), b. at Litchfield, 7 Sep 1753 son of John and Phebe (Russell) Butterfield; d. at New Boston, NH, 10 Oct 1828, m. about 1772, NAOMI STEVENS, b. at Plaistow, 24 Oct 1751 daughter of Thomas and Prudence (Merrill) Stevens; Naomi d. at Goffstown, 9 Jan 1816.

John and Naomi had their property in Goffstown on the road leading from the village to the Uncanoonuc Mountains,[1444] two small peaks with elevation of about 1,300 feet. John served in the Revolution as a sergeant in Moore's regiment in 1776, as a sergeant in Gilman's regiment also in 1776, and as a sergeant in Kelly's regiment of volunteers in 1778.[1445]

John and Naomi were parents of fifteen children born at Goffstown.

i   JOHN BUTTERFIELD, b. 27 Aug 1772; likely died before adulthood.[1446]

ii   LYDIA BUTTERFIELD, b. 8 Jul 1774; d. at Goffstown, 22 Feb 1795; m. at Goffstown, 22 Aug 1791, JOB DOW, b. at Goffstown, 23 Jun 1770 son of Job and Hannah (Pattee) Dow. Job married second Elizabeth Colony.

[1438] New Hampshire Wills and Probate, Cheshire County, Estate Files, U5, Estate of James Underwood, Swanzey

[1439] There is also a woman, Lucy Underwood, who was born in Vermont in 1793 and died at Colrain, MA, 26 April 1869 (and who did not marry). The names of her parents are given as James and Hannah Underwood on her death record, but that is perhaps a different James and Hannah Underwood, although this James and Hannah were living in Vermont when this Lucy was born.

[1440] Benjamin, *The History of Swanzey*, p 504

[1441] Findagrave ID: 126053262; burial at Laurel Hill Cemetery in Fitchburg

[1442] Burgess, *Burgess Genealogy*, p 49

[1443] U.S., Selected States Dutch Reformed Church Membership Records, 1701-1995. The names of Margaret's parents are given as George Spraker and Mary Roucks on her death record; New Hampshire, Death and Burial Records Index, 1654-1949

[1444] Hadley, *History of the Town of Goffstown*, p 61

[1445] Ancestry.com. *U.S., Revolutionary War Rolls, 1775-1783* [database on-line].

[1446] The family gravestone that includes the parents also notes the burial of four children: sons John and William, daughter Lydia Dow who died soon after marriage, and an unnamed infant born in 1790. Butterfield Monument, Hillside Cemetery, Goffstown, NH; findagrave ID: 58804461

iii   REBECCA BUTTERFIELD, b. 10 Sep 1775; d. at Goffstown (burial at New Boston), 7 Sep 1833; m. 21 Nov 1793, DAVID WILSON, b. at New Boston, 29 Mar 1768 son of Thomas and Mary (-) Wilson; David d. at New Boston, 2 Apr 1818.

iv   PHEBE BUTTERFIELD, b. 9 Dec 1776; d. at Goffstown, 8 Jul 1854; m. 15 Nov 1792, ENOCH DOW, b. at Goffstown, 20 Sep 1773 son of Job and Hannah (Pattee) Dow. Enoch is said to have "gone west" where he died, but Phebe remained in Goffstown.[1447] Enoch and Phebe were parents of eleven children.

v   NAOMI BUTTERFIELD, b. 23 May 1778; d. at Deering, NH, 21 May 1841 (probate 7 Jul 1841 of widow Naomi Forsaith); m. JONATHAN FORSAITH, b. at Deering, NH, 9 Jun 1772 son of William and Jane (Wilson) Forsaith; Jonathan d. by Jan 1821 (widow Naomi declines administration of the estate on 8 Jan 1821. In 1830, Naomi was head of household in Deering.

vi   JONATHAN BUTTERFIELD, b. 1 Oct 1779; d. at Goffstown, 30 Jul 1839; m. 27 Nov 1806, JANE FORSAITH, b. at Deering, 23 Aug 1782 daughter of William and Jane (Wilson) Forsaith; Jane d. at Pine Rock, IL, 3 Oct 1871.

vii   PRUDENCE BUTTERFIELD, b. 13 Mar 1781; d. at New Boston, 18 Sep 1818; m. about 1800, ROBERT WARREN, b. at New Boston, 22 Dec 1772 son of Josiah and Jane (Livingstone) Warren; Robert d. at New Boston, 26 Mar 1857.

viii   BENJAMIN BUTTERFIELD, b. 29 Mar 1782; d. at Goffstown, 31 Mar 1871; m. 1st 20 Dec 1804, DOLLY BARRON, b. at Goffstown, 14 Jun 1785 daughter of William and Rebecca (Fassett) Barron; Dolly d. at Goffstown, 5 Feb 1827. Benjamin m. 2nd BETSEY JONES daughter of Joshua and Sarah (Burns) Jones of New Boston.[1448]

ix   OLIVE BUTTERFIELD, b. 6 Dec 1783; d. at Bedford, NH, 31 Mar 1871; m. at Goffstown, 22 Sep 1803, ROBERT DUNLAP, b. at Bedford, 21 Nov 1779 son of John and Martha (Gilmore) Dunlap; Robert d. at Bedford, 16 Nov 1865. Robert was a cabinetmaker in Bedford. Members of the Dunlap family were well-known for cabinetmaking.[1449]

x   DANIEL BUTTERFIELD, b. 7 Jul 1785; d. at Deering, 19 Apr 1877; m. about 1810, SARAH WARREN, b. at New Boston, 4 Sep 1787 daughter of Josiah and Jane (Livingstone) Warren; Sarah d. at New Boston, 17 May 1846.

xi   WILLIAM BUTTERFIELD, b. 12 Jul 1787; likely died before adulthood.

xii   JAMES BUTTERFIELD, b. 30 Aug 1788; d. at Lincoln, VT, 20 Aug 1840; m. at Goffstown, 26 Jan 1808, LYDIA BARNES, b. 24 Jun 1786 daughter of Thomas and Rachel (Barrett) Barnes; Lydia d. at Lincoln, 1865.

xiii   Infant, b. and d. 1790

xiv   MARY BUTTERFIELD, b. 27 May 1791; d. at Manchester, NH, 24 May 1856; m. 1st at Goffstown, 23 Nov 1809, THOMAS WILSON. Mary m. 2nd at Goffstown, 27 Jun 1813, BENJAMIN W. RICHARDS, b. at Goffstown, 28 Jan 1794 son of James and Hannah (Walker) Richards; Benjamin d. at Goffstown, 16 May 1844. After Benjamin's death, Mary lived with her daughter Mary and her husband Daniel Chaplin in Manchester.

xv   SAMUEL BUTTERFIELD, b. 1 Jan 1793; d. at Concord, NH, 4 Jul 1860; m. 1st at Francestown, 18 Nov 1810, NANCY VOSE, b. at Litchfield, NH, about 1793 daughter of Josiah and Judith (Coffin) Vose. Samuel m. 2nd about 1835, MARY B. WARE, b. 13 Sep 1800 daughter of Jonathan and Betsey (Dana) Ware; Mary d. (burial at Pomfret, VT), 3 Jan 1849. Samuel m. 3rd and Charlestown, MA, 6 Mar 1855, ANNA M. ABBOTT, b. at Charlestown about 1821 daughter of Samuel and Lucretia (Fowle) Abbott.

513)   PETER BUTTERFIELD (*Phebe Russell Butterfield Robie⁴, Peter³, Thomas², Robert¹*), b. at Litchfield, 6 Jan 1755 son of John and Phebe (Russell) Butterfield; d. at Goffstown, 22 Oct 1838; m. 1st at Goffstown, 1 Oct 1776, HANNAH GAY who died at Goffstown, 1803. Peter m. 2nd 19 Aug 1810, RACHEL RICHARDS (widow of David Greer), b. 1767 daughter of Benjamin and Susannah (Eaton) Richards; Rachel d. at Goffstown, 21 Oct 1851.

Peter resided in Goffstown on what had been his father's homestead. He served in the Revolution and was later captain of the militia in Goffstown.[1450]

On 27 August 1832, Peter Butterfield then aged seventy-seven and resident of Goffstown, provided a statement related to his pension application. In April 1775, the day after news of the Battle of Lexington reached Goffstown, he and several others took their guns and went to Mystic near Charlestown and enlisted in the company of Capt. Samuel Richards with Lieut. Moses Little and Ens. Jesse Carr who were all of Goffstown. They were in Col. John Stark's regiment. His term expired at the end of December, and has he elected not to reenlist at that time, his good gun was taken from him and given to Nathaniel

[1447] Hadley, *History of Goffstown*, p 128

[1448] Cogswell, *History of New Boston, New Hampshire*, p 444

[1449] Zea and Dunlap, *The Dunlap Cabinetmakers: A Tradition in Craftmanship*

[1450] Hadley, *History of the Town of Goffstown*, p 64

Stevens. In July or August 1778, he reenlisted and went to Rhode Island in the company of Capt. Nichols; that term lasted about two months. He also reported he was born in Litchfield 6 January 1755, that he lived in Goffstown at the time of his enlistment and lived in Goffstown after the war. He was awarded pension of $31.88 based on 8 months 23 days of service.[1451]

Peter Butterfield and Hannah Guy were parents of ten children born at Goffstown.

i PETER BUTTERFIELD, b. 1 Jul 1777; d. at Goffstown, 5 Apr 1844; m. at Goffstown, 28 Feb 1804, HANNAH BARRON, b. Sep 1781 daughter of William and Rebecca (Fassett) Barron; Hannah d. at Goffstown, 24 Mar 1849.

ii SALLY BUTTERFIELD, b. 19 Jul 1779; d. (burial at Goffstown), Feb 1852; m. at Goffstown, 9 Jun 1803, ROBERT GILMORE, b. at Bedford, NH, 5 Apr 1780 son of James and Mary (-) Gilmore

iii JOHN BUTTERFIELD, b. 8 Jun 1781; d. at Hartland, ME, 16 Jun 1857; m. MARGARET MOOR, b. 28 May 1783 daughter of Abraham and Esther (Walker) Moor;[1452] Margaret d. at Hartland, 23 May 1848.

iv HANNAH BUTTERFIELD, b. 30 Nov 1783; m. 1st 5 Jun 1803, DANIEL MCKINNEY. Hannah m. 2nd GEORGE LITTLE, b. at Hampstead, 17 Aug 1762 son of Moses and Mary (Stevens) Little;[1453] George d. at Grafton, NH, 7 May 1850. George was first married to Sarah Kelly and married second Martha Richards. The son of George Little and Sarah Kelly, Elbridge Gerry Little, married the daughter of Hannah and Daniel, Nancy McKinney. George Little served as lieutenant during the Revolution. After the war, he worked as a blacksmith in Goffstown and kept a tavern.

v JONATHAN CUMMINGS BUTTERFIELD, b. about 1785; d. at Loudon, NH, 24 Apr 1871; m. at Goffstown, 3 Oct 1821, CANDACE CENTER, b. at Londonderry, 1796 daughter of Parker and Abigail (Dudley) Senter;[1454] Candace d. at Concord, NH, 16 Sep 1883.

vi BETSEY BUTTERFIELD, b. 1790; d. at Lyme, NY, 20 Sep 1860; m. at Goffstown, 1 May 1810, HUGH MCPHERSON, b. at Deering, 4 Jan 1787 son of William and Mary (Gregg) McPherson; Hugh d. at Lyme, 11 Apr 1875.

vii JOSEPH BUTTERFIELD, b. 13 Nov 1792; d. at Bedford, NH, 20 Jun 1855; m. at Goffstown, 19 Jan 1817, SALLY ROBERTSON, b. 1793; Sally d. at Bedford, 24 Apr 1880.

viii STEPHEN BUTTERFIELD, b. 11 Jan 1794; m. at New Boston, 12 Jan 1819, MARY "POLLY" CLOGSTON, b. at Goffstown, 14 Jan 1796 daughter of Matthew L. and Dorothy (Sargent) Clogston; Mary d. at Nashua, NH, 16 Feb 1855. After his wife's death, Stephen moved to Wisconsin (according to *History of Goffstown*).

ix LYDIA BUTTERFIELD, b. about 1797; m. at Bedford, NH, 30 Dec 1817, JOHN MOOR.

x RELIEF BUTTERFIELD, b. about 1798; d. at Manchester, NH, 26 Aug 1853; m. about 1825, AUSTIN GEORGE, b. 1798; Austin d. at Deerfield, NH, 19 May 1863.

514) SARAH BUTTERFIELD (*Phebe Russell Butterfield Robie⁴, Peter³, Thomas², Robert¹*), b. 1758 daughter of John and Phebe (Russell) Butterfield; d. at Goffstown, 2 Sep 1850; m. at Goffstown, 21 Dec 1785, ELIPHALET RICHARDS, b. at Goffstown, 1761 son of Benjamin and Susannah (Eaton) Richards; Eliphalet d. 8 Oct 1846.

Sarah and Eliphalet resided in Goffstown. Eliphalet served in the Revolution and was at the Battle of Bennington with Gen. Stark. Eliphalet did not receive a pension related to his service but provided a statement for the pension application of his brother Amos which recounts some of his service noting that Amos was at the Battle of Bennington where Eliphalet also served. They also served together in Rhode Island.[1455]

In his will written 17 December 1840 (proved 3 November 1846), Eliphalet bequeathed to beloved wife Sally all the household furniture, annual provisions, and privilege to live on the homestead. Son James E. Richards receives a tract of land in Goffstown on the north side of the Piscataquog River, which is the same land he purchased on Daniel Richards and contains about ten acres. Daughter Phebe Poor wife of George Poor receive $200. Son Eliphalet Richards receives two tracts of land in Goffstown. Son Eliphalet is to pay son John $150. Son Eliphalet also receives the pew in the west meeting house. Daughter Sally Caldwell wife of Isaac J. Caldwell receives fifty dollars. Son Perry receives a tract of land in New Boston on the north side of the north branch of the Piscataquog River. Son Isaiah receives a tract of land in Goffstown, an undivided half-part of the farm on which Isaiah resides, and a second tract of land. Son John receives a tract of land in New Boston. Son Luther Richards and daughter Syrene Little wife of Ira Little receive the homestead farm situated on the north side of the Piscataquog River containing about 190 acres. Luther and Syrene are charged with the maintenance of their mother. Luther and Syrene receive a

[1451] U. S. Revolutionary War Pension and Bounty-Land Warrant Application Files, Case S12365
[1452] Hadley, *History of the Town of Goffstown*, p 344
[1453] Hadley, *History of the Town of Goffstown*, p 284
[1454] The names of Candace's parents are given as Parker Center and Abigail Dudley on her death record. The family used the name Senter and the switch to Center seems to have occurred with Candace.
[1455] U. S. Revolutionary War Pension and Bounty-Land Warrant Application Files, Case W15954

second tract of land, the farming utensils, and one of the pews in the west meeting house. Grandson Calvin Richards, son of Calvin deceased, receives $250. Grandsons George Richards, Noyes Richards, and David Richards, sons of Benaiah deceased, each receives $100. His grandsons named Eliphalet receive twenty-five dollars: Eliphalet Poor son of George Poor, Eliphalet Richards son of Isaiah Richards, Eliphalet Caldwell son of Isaac J. Caldwell, and Eliphalet Richards son of John Richards. The residue of the estate is to be divided equally among his children. James E. Richards, Jesse Carr, Esq. of Goffstown, and George Poor were named executors.[1456]

Sarah Butterfield and Eliphalet Richards were parents of eleven children born at Goffstown.

i　JAMES EATON RICHARDS, b. 17 Jun 1785; d. at Goffstown, 19 Jan 1855; m. 29 Sep 1808, SARAH E. STORY, b. at Dunbarton, 14 Apr 1781 daughter of David and Thankful (Burnham) Story;[1457] Sarah d. at Goffstown, 4 Jan 1867.

ii　PHEBE RUSSELL RICHARDS, b. 9 May 1787; d. at Goffstown, 18 Mar 1864; m. 30 Feb 1812, GEORGE POOR, b. at Goffstown, 10 Jan 1789 son of George and Mary (Little) Poor; George d. 26 May 1870.

iii　ELIPHALET RICHARDS, b. 3 Apr 1790; d. at Goffstown, 30 Mar 1859; m. at Londonderry, 25 Jan 1816, SARAH G. MCQUESTEN, b. about 1792 daughter of William and Sarah (Potter) McQuesten;[1458] Sarah d. at Goffstown, 30 Jul 1858.

iv　SALLY RICHARDS, b. 12 Sep 1792; d. at Lincoln, VT, 6 Sep 1862; m. 25 Jun 1812, ISAAC JACOB CALDWELL, b. at New Boston, 22 Feb 1782 son of James and Martha (McKenney) Caldwell; Isaac d. at Lincoln, 2 Apr 1863.

v　PERRY RICHARDS, b. 30 May 1794; d. at New Boston, 30 Jul 1875; m. 22 Jul 1828, CLARISSA SIMONS, b. at Weare, 2 Jan 1807 daughter of Christopher and Nancy (Locke) Simons; Clarissa d. at New Boston, 16 Mar 1900.

vi　ISAIAH RICHARDS, b. Jun 1796; d. at Goffstown, 6 Aug 1862; m. 27 Dec 1819, MARY TRACY THOMPSON, b. about 1800; Mary d. at Goffstown, 7 Jul 1853.

vii　BENAIAH RICHARDS, b. 12 Jun 1798; d. at Goffstown, 26 Aug 1840; m. at New Boston, 29 Oct 1823, his first cousin once removed, REBECCA WILSON (*Rebecca Butterfield Wilson⁶, John Butterfield⁵, Phebe Russell Butterfield⁴, Peter³, Thomas², Robert¹*), b. at Goffstown, 16 May 1802 daughter of David and Rebecca (Butterfield) Wilson; Rebecca d. at Goffstown, 12 Feb 1860.

viii　JOHN RICHARDS, b. 1800; d. at Goffstown, 14 Mar 1848; m. at Goffstown, 1827, MARTHA GILCHRIST, b. 1794 daughter of Robert and Mary (Shirley) Gilchrist;[1459] Martha d. at Goffstown, 7 Feb 1850.

ix　CALVIN RICHARDS, b. 30 May 1802; d. 23 Mar 1836; m. about 1828, BETSEY M. BURNHAM, b. at Dunbarton, 10 May 1808 daughter of Jabez and Martha (Burnham) Burnham;[1460] Betsey d. at Worcester, MA, 18 Aug 1895. Martha married second Daniel Kidder on 17 May 1842.

x　LUTHER RICHARDS, b. 4 Sep 1804; d. at Goffstown, 2 Aug 1872; m. at New Boston, 10 Oct 1832, his first cousin once removed, MARY JANE WILSON (*Rebecca Butterfield Wilson⁶, John Butterfield⁵, Phebe Russell Butterfield⁴, Peter³, Thomas², Robert¹*), b. at New Boston, 10 Feb 1811 daughter of David and Rebecca (Butterfield) Wilson; Mary Jane d. at Goffstown, 6 Jan 1886.

xi　SYRENE RICHARDS, b. 1806; m. at Goffstown, 1827, IRA LITTLE, b. at Goffstown, 9 Mar 1802 son of Thomas Stevens and Molly (Kelley) Little.

515)　PHEBE BUTTERFIELD (*Phebe Russell Butterfield Robie⁴, Peter³, Thomas², Robert¹*), b. 1760 daughter of John and Phebe (Russell) Butterfield; d. 1839 at unknown location;[1461] m. 9 Dec 1779, NATHANIEL GLIDDEN, b. at Exeter, 1747 son of Nathaniel and Anna (Lord) Glidden; Nathaniel d. at Chester, NH, 26 Apr 1814.

Nathaniel Glidden was from Exeter and relocated to Chester where he was a cabinetmaker. The family lived directly below the burying ground in Chester.[1462]

There is just one child known for Phebe Butterfield and Nathaniel Glidden. The 1800 census for Chester lists the household of Nathaniel Glidden as one male 16-25, one male 45 and over, and one female 45 and over.[1463] In the 1810 census, the household was one male 26-44, one male 45 and over, and one female 45 and over.

[1456] New Hampshire Wills and Probate, Hillsborough County, volume 55, pp 37-42

[1457] The 1833 will of David Story of Dunbarton includes a bequest to his daughter Sally Richards wife of James E. Richards.

[1458] The 1847 will of William McQuesten includes a bequest to his daughter Sarah G. Richards.

[1459] Hadley, *History of Goffstown*, p 414

[1460] The names of Betsey's parents are given as Jabez and Martha Burnham on her death record.

[1461] The Butterfield cemetery monument includes dates for Phebe wife of Nathaniel Glidden as 1760-1839.

[1462] U.S., Craftsperson Files, 1600-1995

[1463] Year: 1800; Census Place: Chester, Rockingham, New Hampshire; Series: M32; Roll: 20; Page: 491; Image: 428; Family History Library Film: 218679

Son John L. Glidden wrote his will 20 November 1827 (probate 17 June 1837) which left his estate to his wife Mary and a bequest of fifty dollars to his mother Phebe Glidden. The estate was insolvent at the time of probate.[1464]

i   JOHN LORD GLIDDEN, b. 8 Feb 1782; d. at Chester 1837 (probate 14 Jun 1837); m. 26 Nov 1816, MARY SIMONDS (widow of Nathan Webster), b. about 1780; Mary d. at Chester, 19 Dec 1863. John and Mary did not have children.

516)   DEBORAH BUTTERFIELD (*Phebe Russell Butterfield Robie⁴, Peter³, Thomas², Robert¹*), b. at Goffstown, 11 Jan 1762 daughter of John and Phebe (Russell) Butterfield; d. at Goffstown, 11 Sep 1840; m. at Goffstown, 25 Dec 1781, JONATHAN BELL, b. at Pelham, 23 Apr 1755 son of William and Abigail (Kittredge) Bell; Jonathan d. at Goffstown, 10 Jun 1844.

Jonathan and Deborah had their homestead farm in Goffstown. Jonathan was at the Battle of Bunker Hill and attended the dedication ceremony for the Bunker Hill monument on 17 June 1843.[1465]

On 27 August 1832, Jonathan Bell provided a statement related to his pension application. In April 1775, he enlisted in the company of Capt. Samuel Richards of Goffstown with Moses Little as lieutenant. The company went to Mystic near Boston where they joined the regiment of Col. John Stark. He was at the Battle of Bunker Hill and later removed with the company to Winter Hill where he remained until the last of December ending his eight-month enlistment. He returned to Goffstown. In August 1776, he enlisted for two months in the company of Capt. Minard, marched to Roxbury, and returned to Goffstown at the end of October. In July or August 1778, he responded to the call of Gen. Sullivan for militia and enrolled in the company of James Aiken of Bedford. He served two months and was discharged in October. He further added that he was born in Tewksbury 23 April 1755 and that he resided in Goffstown since the time of the war. He received pension of $36.44 per annum.[1466]

Deborah Butterfield and Jonathan Bell were parents of eleven children likely all born at Goffstown. Sons James, Rodney, John, Samuel, and Joseph settled in Rushford, New York.

i   JAMES RUSSELL BELL, b. 1782; d. at New Hudson, NY, 1859; m. at Goffstown, 27 Dec 1808, ABIGAIL DAVIDSON, b. at Hancock, NH, 5 Feb 1786 daughter of Nathaniel and Lydia (Eaton) Davidson; Abigail d. at New Hudson, 1861.

ii   JONATHAN BELL, b. 26 Aug 1784; d. at Goffstown, 14 Oct 1858; m. at Goffstown, 17 Sep 1812, LYDIA DOW, b. at Goffstown, 4 Jan 1794 daughter of John and Hannah (Pattee) Dow; Lydia d. 9 Jan 1852.

iii   JOHN BELL, b. 1786; d. likely at Rushford, NY (burial at Goffstown), 15 Sep 1851.

iv   DEBORAH BELL, b. 1 Jun 1789; d. after 1870 when living at Goffstown; m. at Goffstown, 21 Jun 1816, DAVID FERSON, b. at Francestown, 14 Aug 1793 son of James and Mary (Starrett) Ferson; David d. at Goffstown, 24 Jun 1847.

v   SALLY BELL, b. Mar 1792; d. at Goffstown, 9 Apr 1868. Sally did not marry.

vi   SAMUEL BELL, b. about 1795; m. PEGGY MCFARLAND FORSAITH, b. at Deering, NH, 26 Apr 1797 daughter of Mathew and Jenne (McClure) Forsaith.

vii   PHEBE BELL, b. 1797; d. at New Hudson, NH, 25 Apr 1869; m. at Goffstown, 27 Dec 1849, STEPHEN BARNARD, b. at Hollis, 10 Aug 1794 son of Stephen and Martha (Marshall) Barnard; Stephen d. at New Hudson, 16 Oct 1881. Stephen was first married to Anna Foster.

viii   PETER BELL, b. 1800; d. after 1865 when a guardian was appointed for him at North Andover, MA due to insanity;[1467] m. at Methuen, 25 Dec 1822, MARY ROBERTSON BODWELL, b. at Methuen, 30 Nov 1795 daughter of Henry and Sarah (Lowell) Bodwell; Mary d. at North Andover, 27 Aug 1863.

ix   RODNEY BELL, b. 1802; d. at Hornellsville, NY, 23 Apr 1892; m. 1st, about 1828, ALMIRA NOYES, b. 20 Apr 1810 (on gravestone); Almira d. at Bellville, NY, 22 Jan 1867. Rodney m. 2nd at Tilton, NH, 19 Oct 1869, LETITIA M. RICHARDS (widow Letitia Durkham), b. at Goffstown, 26 mar 1804 daughter of Benjamin and Margaret (Moore) Richards; Letitia d. 1 Dec 1882.

x   ROXANA BELL, b. 1803; d. at Goffstown, 2 Mar 1877; m. 6 Jun 1826, SAMUEL S. WESTON, b. at Goffstown, 17 Jan 1805 son of Matthew L. and Dorothy (Sargent) Clogston; Samuel d. at Goffstown, 19 Jan 1871. On 2 July 1847, a law was approved by the Senate and House of Representatives of the General Court allowing the following persons to be called and known by the following names: Samuel S. Clogston of Goffstown may take the

[1464] *New Hampshire. Probate Court (Rockingham County); Estate Papers, No 13304-13381, 1837, Estate of John L. Glidden, case 13345.*
[1465] Hadley, *History of the Town of Goffstown*, volume 2, p 39
[1466] U. S. Revolutionary War Pension and Bounty-Land Warrant Application Files, Case S12172
[1467] *Essex County, MA: Probate File Papers, 1638-1881.*Online database. *AmericanAncestors.org.* New England Historic Genealogical Society, 2014. Case 32543

name Samuel S. Weston; Roxana Clogston, Roxana Weston; Deborah B. Clogston, Deborah B. Weston; Alonzo H. Clogston, Alonzo H. Weston; Frederick A. Clogston, Frederick A. Stone; Joseph A. Clogston, Joseph R. Weston; Samuel Clogston, Samuel Weston.[1468]

xi   JOSEPH BELL, b. about 1805; d. at Geneseo, NY, 1883; m. 1st about 1830, LYDIA DUNHAM; Lydia d. at Rushford, 22 Mar 1849. Joseph m. 2nd MATILDA M. COBURN, b. in NY, Dec 1815; Matilda d. (memorial marker at Rushford), 1903. In 1900, Matilda was living in Otsego, MI with her daughter Mary and her husband Frank Dickey and that is perhaps where Matilda died.

517)   SAMUEL ROBIE (*Phebe Russell Butterfield Robie⁴, Peter³, Thomas², Robert¹*), b. at Goffstown, 1777; d. at Goffstown, 8 Jul 1865 son of Samuel and Phebe (Russell) Robie; m. about 1796, DEBORAH MOORE, b. 27 Mar 1776 daughter of Abraham and Esther (Walker) Moore; Deborah d. at Manchester, NH, 8 May 1868.

Samuel and Deborah resided in Goffstown and had property southwest of the Uncanoonuc Mountains.[1469]

In his will written 6 December 1860 (proved 25 July 1865), Samuel Robie bequeathed to son Albert G. Robie all the landed property situated in Goffstown and Bedford. Albert also receives the farming tools and blacksmith tools. The remaining property of the estate is to be sold and equally divided among four children or their heirs: Lewis Henry Robie of San Francisco, California; James C. Robie of Perryville, New York; Sophromia French wife of Phineas C. French of Oshkosh, Wisconsin, and Samantha Sias wife of John Sias of Milton, Massachusetts. Their other children and their heirs have already received their full portions: Moors Robie, Russell Robie, and Phebe Kennedy.[1470]

Samuel Robie and Deborah Moore were parents of eight children. Some of the children were born in Goffstown, but census records indicate that more that one of the children were born in Maine.

i   THOMAS RUSSELL ROBIE, b. about 1796; m. at Knox County, OH, 24 Dec 1840, SARAH MARIAH NEWCOMB, b. in Livingston County, NY, 8 Aug 1819 daughter of Cromwell and Esther (Lewis) Newcomb;[1471] Sarah d. at Mount Vernon, OH, 3 Jan 1851. Dr. Thomas R. Robie was a physician and was practicing in Morris, OH in 1850. It is not known when he died. He likely had a first wife whose identity is not known as Thomas R. Russell was living in Alexander, NY in 1840 with several children in the household. In 1840, his occupation was in the "learned professional" category.

ii   MOORES ROBIE, b. likely at Goffstown, 22 Mar 1798; d. at Goffstown, 1 Jan 1859 in an accident while sawing shingles; m. 30 Mar 1825, MARY DURANT, b. at Dracut, 17 Sep 1794 daughter of Samuel and Merab (Coburn) Durant; Mary d. at Boston, 8 Jan 1870. Moores and Mary were parents of four children: Sarah Ann, Samuel Moores, John B., and Merab Frances.

iii   PHEBE ROBIE, b. about 1802; d. at Goffstown, 15 Sep 1855; m. Jun 1823, JAMES W. KENNEDY, b. at Goffstown, 12 Jul 1796 son of James J. and Ruth (Buswell) Kennedy; James d. at Lower Lake, CA, 11 Dec 1885.

iv   ALBERT G. ROBIE, b. about 1806; d. at Manchester, NH, 27 Jul 1886; m. at Manchester, 31 Dec 1833, LOUISA B. STARK, b. at Manchester, 12 Oct 1809 daughter of John and Polly (Huse) Stark; Louisa d. at Manchester, 7 Sep 1906.

v   SOPHRONIA ROBIE, b. about 1810; d. (burial at Beaver Dam, WI), 11 Dec 1884; m. at Goffstown, 23 Apr 1833, PHINEAS COBURN FRENCH, b. at Bedford, NH, 19 Aug 1805 son of Ebenezer and Rhoda (Coburn) French; Phineas d. at Oshkosh, WI, 14 Sep 1870.

vi   SAMANTHA ROBIE, b. 1812; d. at Brooklyn, NY, 16 Mar 1900; m. at Goffstown, 28 Feb 1837, JOHN SIAS, b. 1814 son of Samuel and Betsey (Jackson) Sias;[1472] John d. at Milton, 21 Jul 1880.

vii   JAMES C. ROBIE, b. Oct 1815; d. at Sullivan, NY, 1905; m. 1851, ATALANTA CASE, b. in NY, 1833; Atalanta d. at Syracuse, 8 Nov 1905.

viii   LEWIS HENRY ROBIE, b. about 1818; d. at San Francisco, CA, 8 Oct 1869; m. at Boston, 11 Nov 1845, CAROLINE SHERWIN, b. in MA, about 1828; Caroline d. at San Francisco, 30 May 1870.

518)   THOMAS R. ROBIE (*Phebe Russell Butterfield Robie⁴, Peter³, Thomas², Robert¹*), b. at Goffstown, 1779 son of Samuel and Phebe (Russell) Robie; d. at Goffstown, 12 Sep 1811; m. at Goffstown, 8 Feb 1803, RACHEL BARRON, b. at Merrimack, NH, 22 Feb 1776 daughter of William and Rebecca (Fassett) Barron; Rachel d. 23 April 1839.

[1468] As reported in the Farmer's Cabinet (Amherst, New Hampshire), 12 August 1847

[1469] Hadley, *History of the Town of Goffstown*, p 434

[1470] *New Hampshire. Probate Court (Hillsborough County), Probate Records*, volume 76, pp 307-308

[1471] Newcomb, *Andrew Newcomb and his Descendants*, volume 1, p 249

[1472] The names of John's parents are given as Samuel and Betsey J. on his death record.

Thomas resided on the family homestead in Goffstown. He served as a lieutenant in the militia. He died of typhus fever at age 32.[1473] Thomas Robie and Rachel Baron were parents of three children born at Goffstown.

i   PHEBE RUSSELL ROBIE, b. 29 May 1803; d. at Manchester, NH, 28 Mar 1876; m. at Goffstown, 1 Mar 1824, DANIEL MCCURDY WORTHLEY, b. at Goffstown, 17 Jan 1798 son of Stephen and Catherine (-) Worthley; Daniel d. at Manchester, 15 Apr 1878.

ii   SAMUEL ROBIE, b. 1804; d. 13 Sep 1807.

iii   JOHN ARBUCLE ROBIE, b. 24 Mar 1810

519)   MARY ROBIE (*Phebe Russell Butterfield Robie⁴, Peter³, Thomas², Robert¹*), b. at Goffstown, 1782 daughter of Samuel and Phebe (Russell) Robie; d. 22 Mar 1829; m. BENJAMIN WALKER PATTEE, b. 9 Jun 1781 son of John and Mary (Hadley) Pattee; Benjamin d. at Goffstown, 17 Nov 1849.
         Mary and Benjamin resided in Goffstown Village on North Mast Street.[1474] There are two children known for Mary Robie and Benjamin Pattee.

i   DAVID PATTEE, b. 1803; d. 12 Feb 1816.

ii   BENJAMIN FRANKLIN PATTEE, b. 4 Sep 1809; d. at Westphalia, KS, 20 Dec 1861; m. at Pulaski, AR, 22 Apr 1834, REBECCA EMILY HINKSON, b. 1820; Rebecca d. at Arnett, KS, 16 May 1899.

520)   MEHITABLE RUSSELL (*Peter⁴, Peter³, Thomas², Robert¹*), b. 20 Jan 1768 daughter of Peter and Mehitable (Stiles) Russell; d. at Charleston, ME, 4 Feb 1848; m. 1ˢᵗ at Amherst, 27 Nov 1788, STEPHEN KITTREDGE, b. at Tewksbury, 27 Jun 1765 son of Solomon and Tabitha (Ingalls) Kittredge; Stephen d. at Hancock, NH, 16 Oct 1806. Mehitable m. 2ⁿᵈ, 17 Sep 1811, DANIEL BICKFORD, b. 13 Feb 1765 son of Edmond and Elizabeth (Clough) Bickford; Daniel d. at Charleston, ME, 22 Mar 1834.
         Immediately following their marriage, Mehitable and Stephen were in Francestown and then left for Hancock in October 1790 where they settled. They joined the Congregational church in Hancock on 2 May 1802 where Stephen served as deacon until his death. Stephen was the first physician to practice medicine in Hancock.[1475] Stephen was a highly regarded physician and citizen of the town.[1476]
         Mehitable remained in Hancock for five years after the death of Stephen. She then married Daniel Bickford and went with him to Sedgwick, Maine.
         Mehitable Russell and Stephen Kittredge were parents of ten children, the youngest child born after Stephen's death.

i   STEPHEN KITTREDGE, b. at Francestown, 31 May 1789; d. after 1827. Stephen is reported as going to Augusta, Georgia where he had a saddle and harness business, and he was later in Ohio. Nothing is known of him after 1827.[1477] No records were located related to him.

ii   GRATIA KITTREDGE, b. 29 Dec 1790; d. at Milford, NH, 3 Mar 1869; m. at Hancock, 29 Sep 1808, Dr. PETER TUTTLE, b. at Princeton, MA, 15 Apr 1782 son of Joseph and Lucy (Brewer) Tuttle; Peter d. at Hancock, 13 Mar 1828.

iii   RUSSELL KITTREDGE, b. 11 Nov 1792; d. 30 Apr 1799.

iv   PRENTICE KITTREDGE, b. 27 Dec 1794; d. 3 Jan 1820.

v   MARCUS KITTREDGE, b. 22 Oct 1796; d. at Milo, ME, 3 Dec 1869; m. 14 Jan 1823, NANCY TILTON, of Charleston, ME who has not been identified; Nancy d. at Milo, 21 Jun 1886.

vi   CHARLES KITTREDGE, b. 22 Dec 1798; d. after 1880 when he was living at Bangor; m. at Sterling, MA, 24 Sep 1823, MARY NEWHALL, b. in MA, 1803; Mary d. at Bangor, ME, 6 May 1887.

vii   RUSSELL KITTREDGE, b. 14 Jan 1801; d. at Milo, ME, 22 Mar 1875; m. 23 Mar 1826, LUCY R. HART, b. at Atkinson, ME, 26 Sep 1805 daughter of John and Elizabeth (Stover) Hart;[1478] Lucy d. at Milo, ME, 7 Sep 1876.

viii   BETSEY KITTREDGE, b. 12 Nov 1802; d. at Blue Hill, ME, 25 Nov 1823; m. 8 Sep 1819, OLIVER SARGENT.

[1473] Hadley, *History of Goffstown*, p 435
[1474] Hadley, *History of the Town of Goffstown*, p 380
[1475] Cutter, *Genealogical and Personal Memoirs Relating to the Families of Boston*, p 1260
[1476] Hayward, *History of Hancock*, p 698
[1477] Cutter, *Genealogical and Personal Memoirs Relating to the Families of Boston*, p 1260
[1478] The 1838 will (probate Jan 1842) of John Hart of Atkinson, ME includes a bequest to his daughter Lucy Kittredge.

ix   RODNEY KITTREDGE, b. 3 Dec 1804; d. at Charleston, ME, 1 May 1832.

x   JAMES CARTER KITTREDGE, b. 21 Mar 1807; d. at Clinton, MA, 21 Feb 1855; m. at Sterling, MA, 22 Oct 1829, AMANDA MELVINA KENDALL, b. at Sterling, 9 Apr 1810 Heman and Submit (Tuttle) Kendall; Amanda d. at Blackstone, 16 Oct 1857.

Mehitable Russell and Daniel Bickford were parents of two children.

i   CALVIN BICKFORD, b. 1813; d. at Warren, ME, 1883; m. MARY W. FULLER, b. at Warren, 16 May 1822 daughter of Peter and Phebe (Dunbar) Fuller; Mary d. at Warren, 19 Feb 1904. Calvin was preceptor of Warren Academy in Warren, ME.[1479]

ii   MARTIN LUTHER BICKFORD, b. 18 Aug 1814; d. at Elyria, OH, 9 Apr 1876; m. at Dedham, MA, 25 Nov 1841, CELIA A. COLBURN, b. at Dedham, 24 Jul 1819 daughter of Ellis and Celia (Baker) Colburn; Celia d. at Waltham, 1 Jul 1856. Rev. Bickford was a Baptist minister and teacher who established a private school in Hanover County, Virginia in the 1840's. His wife Celia was head of the school in Walpole Corner, MA at the time of her marriage to Marin.[1480] While he lived in Virginia, Martin owned two slaves.[1481]

521)   JOSEPH RUSSELL (*Peter⁴, Peter³, Thomas², Robert¹*), b. about 1770 son of Peter and Mehitable (Stiles) Russell; d. by about 1826; m. about 1795, MARY ROBBINS, b. at Plymouth, NH, about 1770 daughter of Jonathan and Mary (Fletcher) Robbins; Mary d. at Woodstock, NH, 17 Mar 1844. Mary married second John Gray on 14 Oct 1827.

     Joseph and Mary settled in Woodstock, New Hampshire. Joseph served as captain of the local militia. He was well-regarded in the town, but not successful in his business. The *History of Plymouth* reports that Joseph went to Baldwinsville, New York while his family remained in Woodstock.[1482]

     Joseph Russell and Mary Robbins were parents of nine children.

i   JOSEPH RUSSELL, b. 28 Aug 1796; d. at Woodstock, NH, 21 May 1876; m. 27 Apr 1820, ABIGAIL PINKHAM, b. at Durham, NH, 13 Jul 1799 daughter of Abijah and Sarah (Spencer) Pinkham; Abigail d. at Woodstock, 1 Feb 1890.

ii   MARY F. RUSSELL, b. 27 Apr 1799; d. at Salem, VT, 12 Jan 1881; m. at Deering, NH, 14 May 1816, ELIPHALET BLAKE, b. at Thornton, NH, 11 Nov 1794 son of Isaac and Miriam (Carter) Blake; Eliphalet d. at Salem, VT, 30 Apr 1877.

iii   JOHN MOONEY RUSSELL, b. at Woodstock, NH, 15 May 1800; d. at Concord, VT, 4 May 1874; m. at Peeling, NH, 21 May 1818, SARAH FOSS, b. at Thornton, NH, 28 Aug 1795 daughter of Stephen and Keziah (Stearns) Foss; Sarah d. at Concord, VT, 20 Sep 1886. John Mooney Russell was a Free Baptist minister ordained in 1840 and was minister in Concord, VT for 34 years.[1483]

iv   GEORGE WASHINGTON RUSSELL, b. at Woodstock, 1802; d. at North Woodstock, NH, 10 Aug 1886; m. 1ˢᵗ 24 Oct 1822, MARGERY PINKHAM, b. 19 Apr 1796 daughter of Abijah and Sarah (Spencer) Pinkham. Margery d. at Woodstock, 19 Nov 1825. George m. 2ⁿᵈ at Peeling (Woodstock), NH, 1 Jun 1826, SARAH MILLS, b. at Weare, NH, 26 Nov 1801 daughter of Caleb and Sarah (-) Mills; Sarah d. at Woodstock, 22 Aug 1876. George m. 3ʳᵈ at Woodstock, 27 Nov 1879, MARY DARLING, b. at Thornton, NH, 1812 daughter of Jonathan B. and Nathan (Boyce) Darling; Mary d. at Woodstock, 17 Apr 1887. Like his older brother John, George was a Free Baptist minister who preached in Woodstock and Lincoln. He was instrumental in building a church at Woodstock in 1851.

v   LUCINDA RUSSELL, b. at Woodstock, 22 Jun 1804; d. at Franconia, NH, 27 Oct 1852; m. 9 Oct 1823, GEORGE FARRAR WELLS, b. at Plymouth, NH, 8 Sep 1803 son of Samuel and Priscilla (Dolbear) Wells; George d. at Weathersfield, VT, 8 Apr 1883. George married second the widow Rebecca Hadley.

vi   PETER RUSSELL, b. at Woodstock, 31 Oct 1806; d. at Woodstock, 22 Jul 1880; m. 20 May 1833, PAMELIA PINKHAM, b. at Durham, NH, 6 Sep 1805 daughter of Abijah and Sarah (Spencer) Pinkham; Pamelia d. at Woodstock, 20 Jul 1877.

[1479] Cutter, *Genealogical and Personal Memoirs Relating to the Families of Boston*, p 1260

[1480] Slafter, *A Record of Education: The Schools and Teachers of Dedham, Massachusetts*, p 153

[1481] 1850 U.S. Federal Census - Slave Schedules; The National Archive in Washington DC; Washington, DC; NARA Microform Publication: M432; Title: Seventh Census Of The United States, 1850; Record Group: Records of the Bureau of the Census; Record Group Number: 29

[1482] Stearns, *History of Plymouth, New Hampshire*, volume 2, p 565

[1483] Stearns, *History of Plymouth*, volume 2, p 599

vii   JONATHAN ROBBINS RUSSELL, b. at Woodstock, 25 Oct 1808; d. at Middleville, MI, 30 Jan 1899; m. 18 Aug 1828, EUNICE CLIFFORD, b. 12 Mar 1800 (as engraved on gravestone); Eunice d. at Comstock, MI, 16 Dec 1881.

viii   MEHITABLE RUSSELL, b. 1810; d. May 1817.

ix   PELATIAH RUSSELL, b. at Woodstock, 12 Oct 1813; d. at Plymouth, NH, 12 Feb 1892; m. at Peeling, NH, 12 Oct 1834, MARY ANN WOODMAN, b. at Woodstock, 1 May 1816 daughter of Isaac and Mary E. (Locke) Woodman; Mary d. at Tilton, NH, 27 May 1908.

522)   BETSEY RUSSELL (*Peter⁴, Peter³, Thomas², Robert¹*), b. about 1776 daughter of Peter and Mehitable (Stiles) Russell; d. at Hancock, NH, 21 Nov 1843; m. at Peeling, NH, 7 Feb 1805, ASA SYMONDS, b. at Groton, MA, 5 Apr 1776 son of Joseph and Mehitable (Cummings) Symonds; Asa d. at Hancock, 18 Jul 1858. Asa married Clarissa Newell on 7 May 1845.

Asa Symonds was born in Groton, and his family moved to Hancock, New Hampshire in 1779. Asa had a gristmill on Moose brook. Betsey and Asa were members of the Congregational church and Asa served as deacon. He was member of the board of selectmen in 1822 and 1823.[1484]

Betsey and Asa were parents of five children born at Hancock, New Hampshire.

i   BETSY SIMONDS, b. 1806; d. at Hancock, 28 Oct 1825.

ii   ASA SIMONDS, b. 17 May 1809; d. at Hancock, 25 Nov 1888; m. 1st 12 Jan 1837, PRISCILLA GOODHUE, b. 1809 daughter of Ebenezer and Mehitable (Knight) Goodhue; Priscilla d. at Hancock, 28 Oct 1839. Asa m. 2nd 24 Sep 1840, EMILY KNIGHT, b. 1811 daughter of Benjamin and Lucy (Baker) Knight; Emily d. at Hancock, 10 Jul 1854. Asa m. 3rd 2 Sep 1857, LYDIA LAWRENCE DOW, b. at Hancock, 19 Jul 1821 daughter of Nathaniel and Mary (Ames) Dow; Lydia d. at Keene, 18 Jul 1892.

iii   PAMELIA SIMONDS, b. 17 Jul 1813; d. at Hancock, 21 Jan 1828.

iv   RICHARD BAXTER SIMONDS, b. 1 Dec 1816; d. at Hancock, 4 Apr 1869; m. 1st 23 Dec 1847, ELIZABETH A. AMES, b. about 1829 daughter of Gilman and Ann (Bacon) Ames. Richard and Elizabeth divorced Jun 1859. Richard m. 2nd 13 Mar 1869 the AMANDA M. STURTEVANT (widow of Charles Bullard), b. at Sumner, ME, about 1818 daughter of Isaac Sturtevant.

v   MARIAH MEHITABLE SIMONDS, b. 12 Dec 1819; d. at Hancock, 17 Sep 1840.

523)   MARY "POLLY" RUSSELL (*Peter⁴, Peter³, Thomas², Robert¹*); b. estimate 1780 daughter of Peter and Mehitable (Stiles) Russell; d. about 1835; m. at Woodstock, NH, 9 Mar 1809, Col. JOHN PALMER, b. at Salisbury, NH, 26 Dec 1783 son of Dudley and Rebecca (Pingry) Palmer;[1485] John d. at Meredith, NH, 8 Mar 1861.[1486] John Palmer married second Betsey *Cate* Batchelder in 1837.

Mary and John resided in Woodstock, New Hampshire where John was a farmer. They were parents of four children. After Mary's death and his remarriage, John resided in Meredith where he died.

In his will written 4 July 1860 (proved third Tuesday of March 1861), John Palmer of Meredith bequeathed to beloved wife Betsey all the real estate to be hers, her heirs, and assigns, forever. Betsey also receives all the household furniture except the large bible and the writing desk. She also receives the stoves, the clock, two cows, one hog, the hay, and all the provisions on hand at the time of his death. Daughter Louisa Huggins receives the bible and desk and forty dollars. Son John Palmer receives twenty dollars. The remainder of the estate is to be equally divided among his four children: John P. Palmer, Dudley R. Palmer, Louisa Huggins, and Mary Baker. Bradbury C. Tuttle was named executor.[1487]

i   DUDLEY RUSSELL PALMER, b. 1809; d. at Swampscott, MA, 10 Aug 1887; m. at Boston, 19 Oct 1842, ANN E GIBBS, b. in Virginia, 1821 daughter of Walter J. and Charlotte (Curtis) Gibbs;[1488] Ann d. at Boston, 19 May 1867.

ii   LOUISA PALMER, b. about 1812; d. at Boston, 9 Jan 1880; m. at Boston, 20 Apr 1840, CHARLES PICKNEY HUGGINS, b. at Cornish, NH, 24 Nov 1808 son of Nathaniel and Sarah A. (Stone) Huggins;[1489] Charles d. at Cornish, 7 Jun 1893.

[1484] Hayward, *History of Hancock*, p 69, p 83, p 184, 891

[1485] New Hampshire, Births and Christenings Index, 1714-1904

[1486] This is a marriage reported in the History of Plymouth. However, the marriage is in 1809 and that would be a relatively late marriage for Mary. On the other hand, there are only four children in this family all born before 1817. The death records for at least two of the children of John and Mary Palmer give mother's place of birth as Lyndeborough which would fit for Mary in this family.

[1487] New Hampshire Wills and Probate, Belknap County, Probate Records, volume 3, pp 422-423

[1488] The names of Ann's parents are given was Walter J. and Charlotte on her death record.

[1489] Bartlett, *Gregory Stone Genealogy*, p 225

iii   MARY PALMER, b. about 1815; d. at Boston, 27 Apr 1888; m. 15 Oct 1837, WARREN MERRILL BAKER, b. at Holderness, NH, 3 Apr 1813 son of Stephen and Nancy (Chandler) Baker; Warren d. at Boston, 3 Sep 1886.

iv   JOHN P. PALMER, b. about 1817; d. at Swampscott, 18 Dec 1883; m. at Lynn, MA, 18 Feb 1850, MARTHA PHILLIPS, b. at Lynn, 25 Jul 1822 daughter of James and Mary (Burrill) Phillips; Martha d. at Swampscott, 31 Dec 1883.

524)   JONATHAN CUMMINGS (*Deborah Russell Cummings⁴, Peter³, Thomas², Robert¹*), b. at Merrimack, NH, 4 Mar 1759 son of Jonathan and Deborah (Russell) Cummings; m. at Merrimack, 28 Jun 1785, LYDIA HILLS, b. at Merrimack, 13 Jul 1761 daughter of Ebenezer and Elizabeth (-) Hills.

There are records of four children of Jonathan and Lydia born at Merrimack, New Hampshire.

i   ELIZABETH CUMMINGS, b. 21 Aug 1786

ii   LYDIA CUMMINGS, b. 5 Oct 1788

iii   JONATHAN CUMMINGS, b. 1 Sep 1790; d. 12 Apr 1794.

iv   ACHSAH CUMMINGS, b. 26 May 1793; d. at Shirley, MA, 30 May 1863; m. at Hillsborough, 13 Jan 1817, EDWARD HARRINGTON, b. at Watertown, MA, 5 Mar 1781 son of Edward and Susanna (Wellington) Harrington; Edward d. at Shirley, 1 Aug 1855.

525)   DEBORAH CUMMINGS (*Deborah Russell Cummings⁴, Peter³, Thomas², Robert¹*), b. at Merrimack, NH, 14 Jun 1761 daughter of Jonathan and Deborah (Russell) Cummings; m. at Merrimack, 12 Apr 1781, JAMES COOMBS,[1490] b. at Merrimack, 5 Jul 1760 son of John and Margaret (Alld) Coombs; James d. at Merrimack, NH, 17 Jan 1827.

Deborah and James were parents of thirteen children born at Merrimack, New Hampshire.[1491] In 1820, there were five members of the household: one male over 45, one female over 45, one male 16 to 25, one female 10 to 15, and one female 16 to 25.[1492]

i   JAMES COOMBS, b. 1 Jul 1781; d. 28 Jun 1782.

ii   JAMES COOMBS, b. 28 Dec 1782; m. at Pelham, NH, 20 Feb 1806, JANNET "JANE" CALDWELL, b. at Hudson, NH, 11 Dec 1779 daughter of Samuel and Susanna (McCoy) Caldwell; Jane d. at Silvis, IL, 1856 where she was living with her daughter Clarinda.

iii   SIMEON COOMBS, b. 2 Sep 1784; d. at Hudson, NH, 1 Aug 1855; m. at Tyngsboro, MA, 11 Oct 1807, HANNAH CALDWELL, b. at Hudson, NH, 9 Sep 1787 daughter of Samuel and Susanna (McCoy) Caldwell; Hannah d. at Hudson, 21 Nov 1855.

iv   JONATHAN COOMBS, b. 7 Aug 1786; d. at Merrimack, NH, 1844; m. JOANNA HILLS, b. at Merrimack, 28 Aug 1786 daughter of Stephen and Beulah (Coburn) Hills; Joanna d. after 1860 when she was living at Lowell, MA.

v   SUSANNA COOMBS, b. 20 Apr 1788; d. at Merrimack, 14 Nov 1814.

vi   CHARLOTTE G. COOMBS, b. 25 May 1790; d. at Merrimack, 27 Oct 1829; m. 1814, JONATHAN BARRON, b. at Merrimack, 5 Nov 1785 son of Samuel and Sybil (Cummings) Barron; Jonathan d. at Nashua, NH, 30 Aug 1860. Jonathan married second Sally Taggart whom he divorced and married third Hannah Eayrs.

vii   REBECCA COOMBS, b. 19 Feb 1792; d. at Lowell, MA, 4 Jan 1866; m. at Amherst, NH, Nov 1822, AMOS PEARSON, b. in NH, 1797; Amos d. at Dracut, MA, 17 Jul 1851.

viii   DAVID COOMBS, b. 29 Oct 1793

ix   RACHEL COOMBS, b. 10 Dec 1795; d. at Lowell, 21 Sep 1867. Rachel did not marry.

x   HERBERT COOMBS, b. 27 Oct 1797

xi   SOLOMON COOMBS, b. 27 Aug 1799

xii   ELIZABETH COOMBS, b. 1802; d. at Lowell, MA, 19 Aug 1874. Elizabeth did not marry.

xiii   MARY COOMBS, b. 1805; d. at Lowell, 5 Dec 1880. Mary did not marry.

[1490] Name is also spelled Combs
[1491] New Hampshire, Births and Christenings Index, 1714-1904, ancestry.com
[1492] 1820 U S Census; Census Place: Merrimack, Hillsborough, New Hampshire; Page: 865; NARA Roll: M33_61; Image: 199

526)   SYBIL CUMMINGS (*Deborah Russell Cummings⁴, Peter³, Thomas², Robert¹*), b. at Merrimack, NH, 8 May 1763 daughter of Jonathan and Deborah (Russell) Cummings; d. at Merrimack, 17 Apr 1811; m. at Merrimack, 12 Oct 1783, as the second of his three wives, SAMUEL BARRON, b. at Bedford, NH, 26 Feb 1757 son of Moses and Lucy (Parker) Barron; Samuel d. at Merrimack, 3 Oct 1836. Lt. Samuel Barron was first married to Mary Arbuckle and third married to Jenny Moore.

In his pension application of 20 May 1818, Samuel reported enlisting in May 1775 as a private for eight months in the company of Capt. John Moors in the regiment of Col. John Starks of the New Hampshire line. Immediately following his discharge, he enlisted in January 1776 in the company of Capt. Butters of the Massachusetts line for a term of one year. He stayed two months past his enlistment at the request of his officers until replacements arrived. Immediately following, he had a three-year enlistment in the company of Capt. Emerson in the 1ˢᵗ regiment of the New Hampshire line commanded by Col. Joseph Cilley. He was honorably discharged at West Point on 20 May 1780, the discharge signed by Col. Cilley. He was present at the battles of Bunker Hill, Harlem Heights, White Plains, Trenton, Princeton, Monmouth, and Shemung (sic) and Newtown among the Indians. He was also in several smaller engagements. He requested a pension as he was no longer able to labor due to rheumatism. "I cannot say that I am the object of charity and pitty or that I shall call on Town for my support while I have affectionate children setting aside the affections of my friends. I need and claim the assistance of my country to help support me the few remaining days I have to live." Samuel initially received a pension but was struck from the roll in May 1820 due to the amount of his property. He reapplied for pension in July 1832 and received a pension of $80 per annum.¹⁴⁹³

In his will written 28 April 1834 (proved 4 November 1836), Samuel Barron of Merrimack bequeathed to loving wife Jenny all the personal estate except the farming tools. Sons Samuel and Jonathan receive one dollar as does daughter Sibel Gage. Daughter Mary Moor receives ten dollars. Son Moses Lafayette Barron receives all the real estate and the residue of the estate. Wife Jenny was named executrix.¹⁴⁹⁴

Sybil Cummings and Samuel Barron were parents of five children born at Merrimack, New Hampshire. Samuel Barron's third wife Jenny Moor was the sister of two of the spouses of Sybil and Samuel's children.

i   SAMUEL BARRON, b. 31 Aug 1784; d. at Merrimack, 6 Apr 1865; m. 1ˢᵗ 1813, ANN MOOR, b. at Bedford, NH, 12 Jun 1785 daughter of John and Annis (Wallace) Moor; Ann d. at Merrimack, 18 Dec 1841. Samuel m. 2ⁿᵈ 1849, REBEKAH P. EAYRS daughter of William and Hannah (Foster) Eayrs, b. 24 Sep 1806; Rebekah d. at Merrimack, 18 Jun 1863.

ii   JONATHAN BARRON, b. 5 Nov 1785; d. at Nashua, NH, 30 Aug 1860; m. 1ˢᵗ 1814, his first cousin, CHARLOTTE G. COOMBS, b. at Merrimack, 25 May 1790 daughter of James and Deborah (Cummings) Coombs; Charlotte d. 27 Oct 1829. Jonathan m. 2ⁿᵈ 1830, SALLY TAGGERT, b. at Goffstown, 27 Sep 1784 daughter of John and Elizabeth (Jameson) Taggert; Jonathan and Sally divorced at York, ME, Apr 1847;¹⁴⁹⁵ Sally d. at Goffstown, 6 Mar 1860. Jonathan m. 3ʳᵈ at Nashville, NH, 16 Nov 1848, HANNAH EAYRS, b. at Merrimack, 24 Nov 1809 daughter of William and Hannah (Foster) Eayrs; Hannah d. at Nashua, NH, 14 Dec 1891.

iii   SIBYL BARRON, b. 1787; d. at Bedford, NH, 7 Dec 1841; m. MOSES GAGE, b. at Merrimack, 5 Feb 1791 son of Moses and Ruth (Fuller) Gage; Moses d. at Bedford, 5 Dec 1877. Moses married second Sophia Tinker.

iv   SOLOMON BARRON, b. 29 Apr 1789; d. 19 Apr 1798.

v   MARY BARRON, b. 26 Apr 1791; d. at Bedford, 27 Sep 1847; m. 1817, Capt. ROBERT MOORE, b. at Bedford, 18 Jul 1787 son of John and Annis (Wallace) Moor; Robert d. at Bedford, 17 Feb 1858.

Samuel Barron and Jenny Moor were parents of one child.

i   MOSES LAFAYETTE BARRON, b. at Merrimack, 27 Jun 1824; d. at Hannibal, MO, 1856.¹⁴⁹⁶

527)   THOMAS CUMMINGS (*Deborah Russell Cummings⁴, Peter³, Thomas², Robert¹*), b. at Merrimack, NH, 15 Dec 1764 son of Jonathan and Deborah (Russell) Cummings; d. at White Pigeon, MI, 28 Nov 1838;¹⁴⁹⁷ m. 25 Oct 1792, as her second husband, ANNA GIBSON (widow of Samuel May), b. at Lyme, 1769 daughter of Samuel and Elizabeth (Stewart) Gibson;¹⁴⁹⁸ Anna d. at Hinesburg, VT, 3 Sep 1845.

Thomas and Anna were parents of eleven children. Anna had two children with her first husband Samuel May.

¹⁴⁹³ U. S. Revolutionary War Pension and Bounty-Land Warrant Application Files, Case S22101
¹⁴⁹⁴ New Hampshire Wills and Probate, Hillsborough County, volume 41, pp 412-413
¹⁴⁹⁵ Maine, Divorce Records, 1798-1891
¹⁴⁹⁶ Merrimack Historical Society, *History of Merrimack*, volume 1, p 202
¹⁴⁹⁷ Mooar, *The Cummings Memorial*, p 127
¹⁴⁹⁸ The 1811 will (probate 1823) of Samuel Gibson of Merrimack includes a bequest to his daughter Anna Cummings.

i   MARTHA "PATTY" CUMMINGS, b. at Merrimack, NH, 12 Jun 1793; d. after 1870 when she was living at Jefferson, WI listed as a pauper; m. at Concord, VT, 25 Mar 1813, WILLIAM WRIGHT, b. about 1790; William d. after 1870 when living at Jefferson.

ii   JONATHAN CUMMINGS, b. 7 Jul 1794; d. at Mt. Carroll, IL, 27 Jan 1879; m. at Littleton, NH, 24 Jun 1819, CLARISSA GOULD, b. in NH, 1798; Clarissa d. at Mt. Carroll, IL, 1883.

iii   REBECCA CUMMINGS, b. 6 Apr 1796; d. at Mt. Carroll, IL, 1869; m. JAMES FELLOWS. Rebecca was living with her brother Jonathan before her death.

iv   ELIZABETH CUMMINGS, b. 14 May 1797; d. at Wessington Springs, SD, 8 Feb 1890; m. JAMES DUNCAN of Erie, PA.

v   ANDERSON CUMMINGS, b. 23 May 1801; d. of cholera at Québec, 5 Oct 1832.[1499]

vi   LEONARD CUMMINGS, b. 26 Mar 1802; d. at Crown Point, NY, 22 Feb 1859; m. MARY LAMSON, b. 1805; Mary d. at Crown Point, 29 Sep 1834.

vii   RUSSELL CUMMINGS, b. 29 Aug 1804; d. 15 Sep 1808.

viii SIMEON CUMMINGS, b. 13 Aug 1806; d. at Crown Point, 4 Mar 1820.

ix   PELATIAH RUSSELL CUMMINGS, b. recorded at Franconia, NH, 5 Jul 1809; d. at Pekin, IL, 1888; m. 25 Oct 1833, JUDEY INGALLS, b. 1808; Judy d. (burial at Morley, NY), 23 Sep 1848.[1500]

x   HIRAM CUMMINGS, b at Concord, VT, 16 Sep 1810; d. at San Francisco, CA, 10 Dec 1887; m. at Duxbury, 14 Jun 1835, LAVINA SOULE, b. at Duxbury, MA. 28 Dec 1809 daughter of Thomas and Sally (McCarter) Soule; Lavina d. at San Francisco, 9 Sep 1889.

xi   DANIEL GIBSON CUMMINGS, b. at Concord, VT, 5 Mar 1812; d. at San Francisco, CA, 14 Aug 1889; m. 1st at Boston, 9 Sep 1838, MARIA LOUISA FORBES, b. at Roxbury, 11 Nov 1818 daughter of Elisha and Nancy (Burrell) Forces; Louisa d. 9 Jul 1846. Daniel m. 2nd at Nashville, NH, 17 Nov 1848, AMELIA MELVINA WALLACE, b. at Canaan, NH, 14 Dec 1820 daughter of James and Mary (Flint) Wallace; Amelia d. at San Francisco, 18 Mar 1868.[1501]

528)   SUSANNAH CUMMINGS (*Deborah Russell Cummings⁴, Peter³, Thomas², Robert¹*), b. at Merrimack, NH, 7 Sep 1768 daughter of Jonathan and Deborah (Russell) Cummings; m. 7 Jan 1793, JOHN STACY.
     There are records for births of two children of Susannah and John born at Poland, Maine. Their son John settled in Minot, Maine.

i   JOHN STACY, b. at Poland, ME, 10 Jun 1794; m. at Minot, ME, 6 Sep 1816, POLLY SAWTELL who has not been identified. Two children were identified for John and Polly.

ii   SUSANNAH STACY, b. at Poland, 16 May 1796

529)   CYRUS CUMMINGS (*Deborah Russell Cummings⁴, Peter³, Thomas², Robert¹*), b. at Merrimack, NH, 21 May 1777 son of Jonathan and Deborah (Russell) Cummings; d. at Newport, VT, 11 Feb 1858; m. ABIGAIL DAVIS, b. at Poland, ME, 17 Nov 1780 daughter of Moses and Olive (Bodwell) Davis;[1502] Abigail d. at Newport, 9 Feb 1854.
     Cyrus and Abigail were parents of ten children, the birth of the eldest child recorded at Poland, Maine and the others at Lyman, New Hampshire.

i   ABIGAIL CUMMINGS, b. 7 Apr 1801; d. (burial at Woodward, IA), 7 Apr 1866; m. MERRILL PIKE, b. 1798; Merrill d. at Boone County, IA, 16 Aug 1855.

ii   CYRUS CUMMINGS, b. 9 Oct 1803; d. after 1880 when he was living in Lawrence, MA with his daughter Chloe; m. 1st, 1 Oct 1828, CHLOE PROUTY, b. 1806 daughter of Samuel and Mary (King) Prouty; Chloe d. at Waterford, VT, 23 Oct 1830. Cyrus m. 2nd at Barnet, VT, 8 Nov 1832, RUTH ANN PRATT, b. 3 Apr 1808 daughter of Isaiah and Mary (Fellows) Pratt; Ruth d. 17 May 1843. Cyrus m. 3rd, 6 Mar 1844, IRENE PARKER, b. at Lyman, NH, 17 Apr 1815 daughter of John and Mary (·) Parker; Irene d. at Northfield, VT, 4 Oct 1878.

[1499] As reported in Mooar, *Cummings Memorial*, 127
[1500] Findagrave ID: 25627972
[1501] California Department of Public Health, courtesy of www.vitalsearch-worldwide.com. Digital Images.
[1502] NEHGR, Early Vital Records of Poland, Maine, 1934, vol 88, p 60

iii   MOSES CUMMINGS, b. 10 Mar 1806; d. at Dedham, MA, 21 May 1880; m. 30 Dec 1827, SALLY MERRILL, b. at Peacham, VT, 15 Jul 1802 daughter of Moses and Isabella (Hogg) Merrill;[1503] d. at Vineyard Haven (Tisbury), MA, 25 Jul 1892.

iv   RUSSELL CUMMINGS, b. 10 Mar 1809; d. at Newport, VT, 19 Jul 1871; m. at Newport, VT, 30 Oct 1836, LUCY SHERBURNE WOOD, b. 30 May 1808; Lucy d. at Newport, 1 Sep 1883.

v   LORENZO CUMMINGS, b. 15 Jul 1811; d. at Newport, VT, 20 Aug 1899; m. 1st at Waterford, VT, 15 Jan 1839, SERAPHINA SYLVESTER, b. 11 Mar 1816; d. (burial at Newport, VT), 1 Oct 1876. Lorenzo m. 2nd 25 Jan 1882, ESTHER A. WILLIAMS, b. at Derby, VT, 28 Feb 1828 daughter of Henry and Cylinda (Greenleaf) Williams; Esther d. at Burlington, VT, 14 Jan 1916.

vi   OLIVE CUMMINGS, b. 22 Nov 1813; d. at Mt. Carroll, IL, 17 Nov 1899; m. at Derby, VT, 17 May 1843, DENNISON FREDERICK HOLMES, b. at Derby, VT, 10 Apr 1817 son of Frederick and Abigail (Pettice) Holmes; Dennison d. at Mt. Carroll, 3 Jun 1893.

vii   BENJAMIN CUMMINGS, b. 11 Mar 1816

viii   JONATHAN CUMMINGS, b. 29 Apr 1817; m. at Newport, VT, 3 Oct 1836, ABIGAIL E. QUIMBY, b. at Pittsburgh, NH, 7 Mar 1818; Abigail d. at Chico, CA, 5 Jan 1895.

ix   MARY JANE CUMMINGS, b. 23 Aug 1819

x   LOVISA DAVIS CUMMINGS, b. 6 Aug 1822; d. at Derby, VT, 3 Aug 1865; m. ASA B. MOORE, b. at Rupert, VT, 21 Dec 1801 son of Grove and Mary (Buel) Moore; Asa d. at Dorset, VT, 18 Mar 1870. Asa married second Mary Stevens at Dorset, VT on 17 Dec 1865.

530)   SARAH CUMMINGS (*Deborah Russell Cummings⁴, Peter³, Thomas², Robert¹*), b. at Merrimack, NH, 1781 daughter of Jonathan and Deborah (Russell) Cummings; m. by 1799, JOSIAH HODGMAN, b. at Merrimack, 28 Jan 1778 son of Josiah and Rebecca (Foster) Hodgman.

      There are possibly nine children in this family[1504] born at Merrimack, New Hampshire, but there is little in the way of records for several of the proposed children.

i   JOSIAH HODGMAN, b. 13 Feb 1799; d. at Carlisle, MA, 14 Jan 1852; m. at Carlisle, 5 Nov 1818, LUCY SPAULDING, b. at Carlisle, 3 Dec 1792 daughter of William and Lucy (Spaulding) Spaulding;[1505] Lucy d. 25 Jan 1874.

ii   OSWYN HODGMAN, b. 13 Oct 1800; d. about 1817

iii   SARAH CROSBY HODGMAN, b. 26 Jul 1803; d. at Lowell, 24 Sep 1831; m. at Dracut, MA, 2 Sep 1827, NATHANIEL CARTER, b. at Wilmington, MA, 13 Feb 1800[1506] son of Ebenezer and Lydia (Butters) Carter. Nathaniel married second Sarah Burbank and married third Edith Evans.

iv   BENJAMIN HODGMAN (twin), b. 30 May 1805; d. at Lawrence, MA, 17 Sep 1875; m. at Dracut, 26 Oct 1839, BETSEY ANN COBURN, b. 20 Jul 1812 daughter of Willard and Sarah (Sherburn) Coburn; Betsey d. at Lawrence, 26 Aug 1884.

v   JOSEPH HODGMAN (twin), b. 30 May 1805; d. about 1815

vi   STEPHEN BENSON HODGMAN, b. about 1808; d. at Carlisle, MA, 18 Feb 1884; m. at Carlisle, 5 Mar 1842, AMANDA M. BOWERS, b. at Merrimack, 1819 daughter of Timothy and Lucy (Barrett) Bowers; Amanda d. at Carlisle, 28 Feb 1869.

vii   JONATHAN HODGMAN, perhaps the Jonathan who died at Fairfax, VT, 16 Jun 1847 at age 37.

viii   FRANCIS HODGMAN; reported in the Hodgman genealogy as dying young

ix   MARY HODGMAN

[1503] Merrill, *Merrill Memorial: Descendants of Nathaniel Merrill*, p 449

[1504] Hodgman, *Josiah Hodgman Family*, p 10

[1505] Town and City Clerks of Massachusetts. *Massachusetts Vital and Town Records*. Provo, UT: Holbrook Research Institute (Jay and Delene Holbrook). Lucy's parents' names are given as William Spalding and Lucy Spalding on her death record. *Massachusetts: Vital Records, 1841-1910.* (From original records held by the Massachusetts Archives. Online database: *AmericanAncestors.org*, New England Historic Genealogical Society, 2004.)

[1506] Massachusetts: Vital Records, 1620-1850

531)   REBECCA CUMMINGS (*Deborah Russell Cummings⁴, Peter³, Thomas², Robert¹*), b. at Merrimack, NH, 6 Apr 1783 daughter of Jonathan and Deborah (Russell) Cummings; d. at Waterville, ME, 14 Dec 1857; m. Dec 1800, STEPHEN BENSON, b. at Middleborough, 8 Jun 1777 son of Ichabod and Abigail (Griffith) Benson;[1507] Stephen d. at Waterville, 27 Aug 1852.

Stephen Benson was a farmer and blacksmith, and in his ironwork made nails and plows.[1508]

Stephen Benson did not leave a will and son Benjamin C. Benson was named administrator on the second Monday of October 1852. Inventory was taken 15 October 1856 with real estate valued at $1,046.66 and personal estate at $325.39. On 11 February 1853, widow Rebekah Benson requested allowance from the estate for her support. Real estate was sold to settle the debts of the estate.[1509]

Stephen and Rebecca were parents of eight children.[1510]

i   SETH ELLIS BENSON, b. at Otisfield, ME, 30 Nov 1801; d. at Bangor, ME, 23 Nov 1870; m. at Boston, 25 Oct 1826, ELEANOR DEANE, b. at Portland, ME, 27 Mar 1804 daughter of Jonathan and Elizabeth (Bumstead) Deane; Eleanor d. at Bangor, 21 Jul 1889.

ii   REBECCA BENSON, b. 29 Oct 1803; d. at Turner, ME, 6 Oct 1894; m. at Turner, 22 Mar 1829, ISAAC TEAGUE, b. Jul 1802 son of Judah and Eleanor (Knight) Teague; Isaac d. at Turner, 14 Jan 1883.

iii   SEWELL BENSON, b. 19 Nov 1806; d. at San Francisco, 7 Oct 1868; m. at Turner, 30 Mar 1830, LYDIA CUSHING, b. 27 Jul 1807 daughter of Francis and Elizabeth (Harris) Cushing;[1511] Lydia d. at San Francisco, 5 Mar 1862.

iv   BENJAMIN CHANDLER BENSON, b. at Poland, ME, 17 Feb 1809; d. at Oakland, ME, 7 Oct 1894; m. 1837, LUCY D. HITCHINGS, b. at Waterville, 9 Jun 1815 daughter of Samuel and Margaret (Ward) Hitchings;[1512] Lucy d. at Waterville, 23 Mar 1879. Benjamin was raised in the household of his uncle Dr. Benjamin Chandler who was married to the sister of Stephen Benson. [1513]

v   RUSSELL CUMMINGS BENSON, b. 21 Dec 1811; d. at Oakland, ME, 10 Aug 1887; m. at Sharon, MA, 1 Dec 1836, ABIGAIL S. DUNBAR, b. 25 Sep 1814[1514] daughter of Amasa and Abigail (Pond) Dunbar; Abigail d. at Oakland, 16 Dec 1888.

vi   MARY BENSON, b. and d. 27 Sep 1816

vii   ALBERT BENSON, b. 30 Oct 1817; d. at Haverhill, MA, 13 Oct 1847; m. at Haverhill, 21 Mar 1847, ANN LEONARD WHITE, b. at Haverhill, 7 May 1824 daughter of Leonard D. and Ann (Bradley) White; Ann d. at Haverhill, 31 Jan 1911. Ann married second Moses D. George. Albert and Ann had a daughter born after Albert's death: Mary Dalton Benson born at Andover on 28 Apr 1848.

viii   GEORGE B. BENSON, b. 26 May 1824; d. at Oakland, ME, 16 Jun 1900; m. 1850, ELVIRA M. CORNFORTH, b. Oct 1826 daughter of Robinson and Melinda (Hussey) Cornforth;[1515] Elvira d. at Lewiston, 19 Jan 1915.

532)   ROBERT RUSSELL (*James⁴, Peter³, Thomas², Robert¹*), b. likely at Litchfield, NH, 30 Jan 1782 son of James and Mary (French) Russell; d. at Seneca County, OH, 28 Apr 1860; m. about 1808, MARY ANN KEAN, b. in VA, about 1792; Mary Ann d. at Columbus, 7 Jul 1850.

Robert was born in New Hampshire but traveled as a boy with his father to Ohio.

In his will dated 9 January 1860 (proved 14 May 1860), Robert Russell of Seneca County directed that several properties be sold to go toward any debts. These included property in Kenton, Ohio obtained from Alford Russell and Robert Russell by deed and a property in Michigan. If this is not sufficient to pay the debts, he allows for part of the homestead farm to be sold but only as necessary as he desires for his daughter Lucinda Dresbach to have that for her family. He acknowledges a debt to Lucinda of two thousand dollars and bequeaths to her all his estate. He also wishes that five hundred dollars remain in the hands of Lucinda for the support of his son Alfred whom he wishes to remain with his daughter Lucinda.[1516]

There are two known children of Robert Russell and Mary Ann McKean.

[1507] NEHGR, *Early Vital Records of Poland, Maine*, 1934, vol 88, p 155

[1508] Kingsbury, *Illustrated History of Kennebec County, Maine*, p 1079

[1509] Maine, Kennebec County Probate Estate Files, Estate of Stephen Benson, B-16 R; accessed through familysearch.org

[1510] Cummings, *Cummings Memorial*, p 57ff

[1511] Cushing, *The Genealogy of the Cushing Family*, p 455

[1512] The 1840 probate of Samuel Hitchings of Waterville includes the payment of legacy to Lucy Benson.

[1513] Kingsbury and Deyo, *Illustrated History of Kennebec County, Maine*, p 1079

[1514] This is the date of birth recorded in the family entry of the Hanover, MA town records; most other sources give date as 30 Jan 1815.

[1515] The names of Elvira's parents are given as Robinson and Melinda on her death record.

[1516] Ohio Wills and Probate Records, Seneca County, Wills Volume 2, pp 434-435

i   ALFRED RUSSELL, b. about 1809; d. after 1870 when he was living with his sister Lucinda in Tiffin, OH.

ii   LUCINDA RUSSELL, b. about 1815; d. at Tiffin, OH, 15 Nov 1882; m. at Franklin County, OH, 10 Sep 1835, CHARLES FREDERICK DRESBACH, b. at Pickaway County, OH, 12 Mar 1806 son of Daniel and Catharine (-) Dresbach; Charles d. at Tiffin, 8 Nov 1847.

533)   JAMES RUSSELL (*James⁴, Peter³, Thomas², Robert¹*), b. likely at Litchfield, NH, about 1785 son of James and Mary (French) Russell; d. at Ross County, OH, about 1819; m. at Ross County, 27 Apr 1813, as her second husband, SOPHIA PARMENTER, b. 9 Oct 1793 daughter of Artemus and Lucy (Grant) Parmenter; Sophia d. at Ross County, 9 Dec 1845. Sophia was first married to Abiasher Rogers about 1809 and third married to Thomas Bradford on 5 Jul 1820.
    James and Sophia were parents of one child.

i   SAMUEL RUSSELL, b. at Ross County, OH, about 1812; d. of disease at Londonderry, OH, 7 Aug 1862 while serving with Company B of the 63rd Ohio Regiment during the Civil War.[1517] Samuel m. at Ross County, 20 Jan 1842, NANCY SHROPSHIRE, b. about 1824; Nancy d. after 1880 when she was living in Harrison, OH. Nancy second married James White of 23 Oct 1866. Samuel and Nancy were parents of six children including one daughter born after Samuel's death.

534)   FREDERICK AUGUSTUS RUSSELL (*James⁴, Peter³, Thomas², Robert¹*), b. 13 Mar 1787 son of James and Mary (French) Russell; d. at Vevay, IN, 30 Apr 1866; m. 1st at Newburyport, MA, 28 Nov 1810, ANNA BARTLETT who died about 1814. Frederick m. 2nd at Washington, DC, 13 May 1815, THEODOSIA GUSTINE, b. at Culpepper, VA, 1792 daughter of Joel Trumbull and Anne (Greene) Gustine; Theodisia d. at Washington, 25 Jul 1828. Frederick m. 3rd 10 Mar 1846, ANTOINETTE DEROLODS, b. in Spain, about 1827. Antoinette d. at Vevay, 1 Sep 1898.
    Frederick A. Russell was a carriage and floorcloth manufacturer in Georgetown.[1518] The family was in Washington when is was captured by the British in 1814.[1519] Frederick remained in Washington where he continued as a coachmaker until at least 1850.[1520] He was in Switzerland County, Indiana at the later part of his life.
    Frederick Russell and Anna Bartlett were parents of one child

i   MARY ANN RUSSELL, b. at Newburyport, MA, 8 Sep 1811; d. at Washington, DC, 12 Oct 1823.

Frederick Russell and Theodosia Gustine were parents of seven children born at Washington, DC.

i   NANCY GREENE RUSSELL, b. 24 Apr 1816; d. 20 Jun 1817.

ii   FREDERICK AUGUSTS TRUMBULL RUSSELL, b. 22 Jan 1818; d. 10 Jul 1818.

iii ROBERT GREENE GUSTINE RUSSELL, b. 18 Jun 1819; d. at Columbus, OH, 25 Jan 1895; m. at Hardin County, OH, 4 Oct 1852, CATHARINE A. MUSSER, b. about 1828 (census records) who likely died about 1862. Robert appears to have had a second wife CATHARINE C., b. at Canton, OH Mar 1837 (census records) who died at Washington, DC, 19 Sep 1914.[1521]

iv   DANIEL RENOUARD RUSSELL, b. at Washington, DC, 1821; d. at Carrollton, MS, 6 Jan 1870; m. 1st about 1844, JULIA HALL who died in Mississippi about 1846. Daniel m. 2nd MARY ELLA BOOTH, b. at Claiborne County, MS, 1829; Mary d. at Carrollton, 1894.

v   TRUMBULL GUSTINE RUSSELL, b. 7 Apr 1823; d. at Springfield, MO, 26 May 1901; m. 20 Dec 1853, JULIA A. B. RUSSELL, of Virginia b. 16 Oct 1827 daughter of Joseph and Lucy (Bent) Russell; Julia d. at St. Louis, 16 Feb 1901.

vi   THEODOSIA GUSTINE TRUMBULL RUSSELL, b. 17 Apr 1825; d. at Los Angeles, CA, 2 Nov 1895; m. at Hamilton County, OH, 25 Mar 1849, JOHN H. ARMSTRONG, b. in IN, 1820.

vii MARY BALL RUSSELL, b. 1828; d. 1829.

Frederick Russell and Antoinette DeRolods were parents of one child.

[1517] U.S., Civil War Soldier Records and Profiles, 1861-1865

[1518] Russell, *The Moore Scott Family*, p 102

[1519] Hyde and Conrad, *Encyclopedia of the History of St. Louis*, volume 4, p 1942

[1520] Year: 1850; Census Place: Washington Ward 7, Washington, District of Columbia; Roll: 57; Page: 93B

[1521] Obituary notice, The Washington Times (Washington, DC), 20 Sep 1914, Sun

i   ISABELLA ANTOINETTE RUSSELL, b. at Washington, DC, 5 Sep 1849; d. at Indianapolis, IN, 7 Jun 1946; m. about 1875, JOHN GEORGE LONG, b. Jefferson, IN, 1843 son of James S. and Jane (Porter) Long; John d. a Vevay, 1897.

535)   BETHIAH RUSSELL (*Thomas⁴, Joseph³, Thomas², Robert¹*), b. at Andover, 7 Jan 1763 daughter of Thomas and Bethiah (Holt) Russell; d. likely at Dublin, NH, Dec 1821; m. 1ˢᵗ at Wilton, 18 Apr 1782, DANIEL SIMONDS; Daniel d. at Dublin, about 1805. Bethiah m. 2ⁿᵈ at Dublin, 5 Jan 1809, DRURY MORSE, b. at Holliston, MA, 16 Aug 1757 son of Micah and Mary (Fairbanks) Morse; Drury d. at Dublin, 16 Nov 1820. Drury was first married to Mary Adams.
         There is one child known for Bethiah Russell and Daniel Simonds.

i   DANIEL SIMONDS, b. at Dublin, NH, 5 Oct 1782; d. at Fitzwilliam, NH, 13 Aug 1859; m. 4 Jul 1809, NANCY STONE, b. at Fitzwilliam, 10 Apr 1791 daughter of Hezekiah and Elizabeth (Ballard) Stone; Nancy d. at Fitzwilliam, 27 Apr 1840.

536)   THOMAS RUSSEL (*Thomas⁴, Joseph³, Thomas², Robert¹*), b. at Andover, 5 Jun 1765 of Thomas and Bethiah (Holt) Russell; d. at Temple, ME, 9 Jul 1863; m. 10 Feb 1789, his fourth cousin once removed (through Holt lines), LYDIA ABBOTT, b. at Wilton, 1 May 1771 daughter of Jacob and Lydia (Stevens) Abbott; Lydia d. at Temple, 20 Jun 1855.
         Thomas Russell along with his father-in-law Jacob Abbott, William Phillips, John Phillips, and Benjamin Ames purchased five townships in what would become Temple, Maine on 15 February 1794. By 1800, this group was referred to as "Jacob Abbott and Associates." The Phillips brothers were merchants in Boston and Benjamin Ames was a tavern keeper in Andover so not likely to be themselves settlers on the land. Thomas Russell did settle there on the township that he purchased and in 1802 he was occupying the township land purchased by William Phillips.[1522] Thomas and Lydia had married in Wilton and their older children were born there before relocating to the new settlement at Temple.
         Lydia Abbott and Thomas Russell were parents of twelve children, the older children born at Wilton, New Hampshire and the younger children at Temple, Maine.

i   THOMAS RUSSELL, b. 7 Aug 1791; d. 26 Aug 1791.

ii   THOMAS RUSSELL, b. 3 Sep 1792; d. at Temple, ME, 22 Oct 1840; m. 18 Aug 1813, MARTHA TRUE, b. at Farmington, ME, 14 Jan 1799 daughter of Zebulon and Martha (Kennedy) True; Martha d. at Millbury, MA, 25 Feb 1873.

iii   HANNAH ABBOTT RUSSELL, b. at Wilton, 3 May 1794; d. at Temple, 16 Mar 1838; m. about 1813, WILLIAM TRUE, b. at Farmington, 12 Apr 1789 daughter of Zebulon and Martha (Kennedy) True; William d. at Temple, 9 May 1865.

iv   JACOB ABBOTT RUSSELL, b. at Wilton, 25 Jul 1795; d. at Temple, May 1866; m. 1ˢᵗ, 28 Dec 1820, APHIA STAPLES, b. at Temple, 29 May 1803 daughter of George and Phebe (Kennison) Staples; Aphia d. at Temple, 25 Nov 1836. Jacob m. 2ⁿᵈ, 4 Dec 1839, MARY TUFTS, b. likely at Farmington, ME, 24 May 1819 daughter of Samuel and Mary (Baker) Tufts.

v   LYDIA RUSSELL, b. at Wilton, 27 Feb 1797; d. at Temple, 24 Nov 1874; m. 27 Nov 1817, SAMUEL STAPLES, b. at Temple, 10 Jul 1795 son of George and Phebe (Kennison) Staples; Samuel d. at Temple, 22 Oct 1840.

vi   POLLY RUSSELL, b. 10 Aug 1799; d. at Farmington, ME, 10 May 1894; m. 5 Jan 1828, AARON DRESSER, b. 23 Apr 1801; Aaron d. at Farmington, 31 Oct 1890.

vii   JOHN RUSSELL, b. at Temple, 24 May 1801; d. at Weld, ME, 21 Feb 1851; m. 20 Oct 1822, ELEANOR BURNHAM, b. at Farmington, 7 Mar 1804; Eleanor d. at Weld, 5 Dec 1859. After John's death, Eleanor married Samuel Stowers 20 Aug 1852.

viii   JOSEPH RUSSELL, b. 23 Feb 1803; d. 27 Aug 1804.

ix   SAMUEL P. RUSSELL, b. at Temple, 17 Feb 1805; d. at Springfield, MA, 19 Jan 1880; m. at Princeton, MA, 6 Oct 1829, CAROLINE WILDER, b. at Princeton, 26 Nov 1805 daughter of Nahum and Hannah (Woods) Wilder; Caroline d. after 1870.

x   BENJAMIN W. RUSSELL, b. at Temple, 22 Jan 1807; d. at Temple, 23 Sep 1883; m. 7 Apr 1840, HANNAH B. EDES, b. at Temple, 27 Jun 1813 daughter of Joseph and Hannah (Baker) Edes; Hannah d. at Temple, 1 Aug 1888.

[1522] Pierce, *A History of Temple, Maine*, pp 10-11

xi   JOSEPH RUSSELL, b. at Temple, 18 Feb 1809; d. at Temple, after 1850; m. 28 Feb 1832, ALICE ABBOTT, b. 23 Apr 1811 daughter of Jeremiah Abbott; Alice d. at Douglas, MA, 3 Nov 1880.

xii   FISK RUSSELL, b. at Temple, 12 Nov 1810; d. at Cambridge, MA, 3 Apr 1892; m. 26 Mar 1837, ELIZABETH MOORS BATCHELDER, b. at Wilton, 15 Aug 1813 daughter of Daniel and Persis (Maynard) Batchelder; Elizabeth d. at Boston, 29 May 1848.

537)   HANNAH RUSSELL (*Thomas⁴, Joseph³, Thomas², Robert¹*), b. at Andover, 23 Sep 1767 daughter of Thomas and Bethiah (Holt) Russell; d. at Weld, ME, Nov 1850; m. at Wilton, 23 Aug 1787, her first cousin, JAMES HOUGHTON (*Phebe Holt Houghton⁴, Phebe Russell Holt³, John², Robert¹*), b. at Andover, 16 Jun 1756 son of James and Phebe (Holt) Houghton; James d. at Weld, 21 Dec 1835.

    Hannah and James married at Wilton and were first in Dublin, New Hampshire. In Spring 1803, James purchased land in Weld, Maine and began preparations for his family to come. The following spring, James, Hannah, and their children arrived to settle, although the house was not yet completed. Hannah's brothers Abel and Joseph also settled in Weld.[1523]

    Hannah and James were parents of eleven children.

i   EPHRAIM HOUGHTON, b. at Dublin, NH, 25 Oct 1787; d. at Weld, ME, 30 Jan 1867; m. SARAH SPRAGUE MASTERMAN, b. at Deering, NH, 7 Mar 1792 daughter of James and Hannah (Dows) Masterman; Sarah d. at Weld, 20 Mar 1851.

ii   BENJAMIN HOUGHTON, b. at Dublin, 1789; d. at Weld, 6 Mar 1882; m. at Andover, MA, 16 Feb 1818, his fourth cousin once removed, ELIZABETH HOLT (*William Holt⁵, Thomas Holt⁴, Thomas Holt³, Mary Russell Holt², Robert¹*), b. at Wilton, NH, about 1798 daughter of William and Elizabeth (Jones) Holt; Elizabeth d. at Weld, 23 Mar 1867.

iii   JAMES HOUGHTON, b. at Dublin, 1791; d. at West Boylston, MA, of scrofula, 15 Nov 1846; m. about 1819, REBECCA KEYES, b. in Lunenburg (son's death record) perhaps daughter of Simon Keyes; Rebecca d. before 1846.

iv   HANNAH HOUGHTON, b. at Dublin, 26 Mar 1794; d. at Weld, ME, 23 Aug 1853; m. 20 Mar 1814, IRA PARLIN, b. at Sumner, ME, 20 Dec 1790 son of Simon and Elizabeth (Robinson) Parlin; Ira d. at Weld, 29 Mar 1846.

v   ABEL HOUGHTON, b. at Dublin, 15 Aug 1796; d. (burial at Weld), 28 Oct 1890; m. about 1824, ELIZABETH PARLIN, b. at Sumner, ME, 13 Jun 1803 daughter of Simon and Elizabeth (Robinson) Parlin; Elizabeth d. at Weld, 6 May 1881.

vi   PHEBE HOUGHTON, b. at Dublin, 29 Mar 1799; d. at Wilton, ME, 24 Jan 1868; m. 29 Nov 1820, SAMUEL BASS, b. at Wilton, NH, 3 May 1790 son of Jeriah and Lucretia (Savil) Bass; Samuel d. at Weld, 14 Jan 1873.

vii   JOSEPH HOUGHTON, b. at Dublin, 1 Sep 1801; d. at Weld, 29 Jan 1869; m. his first cousin, ORINDA LEARNED, b. at Dublin, 17 Jan 1806 daughter of Benjamin and Orinda (Houghton) learned; Orinda d. after 1880 when she was living with her daughter at Turner, ME.

viii   HARVEY HOUGHTON, b. at Weld, 27 Sep 1804; d. at Loyalton, CA, 16 Aug 1893; m. CATHERINE BARNES, b. 11 Oct 1810; Catherine d. at Loyalton, 12 Dec 1893.

ix   BETHIAH HOUGHTON, b. at Weld, 23 Apr 1807; d. at Milford, ME, 1887; m. ELIJAH PIERCE, b. 1802; Elijah d. at Milford, 1875.

x   SEWELL HOUGHTON, b. at Weld, 25 Aug 1809; d. at Weld, 4 May 1889; m. 1838, MARIA JONES, b. at Andover, 11 Feb 1811 daughter of Jacob and Hannah (Jenkins) Jones; Maria d. at Weld, 11 Feb 1886.

xi   DANIEL HOUGHTON, b. at Weld, 3 Jan 1812; d. at Weld, 17 Jun 1856; m. 1st SARAH PRATT RICHARDSON, b. at Phillips, ME, 2 Dec 1814 daughter of Thaddeus and Sarah (Blethen) Richardson;[1524] Susan d. at Weld, 1 Oct 1848.[1525] Daniel m. 2nd 12 Apr 1849, SOPHIA ELIZABETH PARLIN, b. at Rumford, 23 Mar 1830 daughter of Simon and Sophia (Abbott) Parlin; Sophia d. at Weld, 30 Jun 1909. Sophia married second Vincent Gould Parlin who was the son of Ira and Hannah (Houghton) Parlin (see Daniel's sister Hannah above).

[1523] Foster, *Early Settlers of Weld*, p 172
[1524] Vinton, *Richardson Memorial*, p 289
[1525] Maine, Nathan Hale Cemetery Collection, 1780-1980

538)   DANIEL RUSSELL (*Thomas⁴, Joseph³, Thomas², Robert¹*), b. at Andover, 7 Nov 1769 son of Thomas and Bethiah (Holt) Russell; d. at Wilton, 3 Jan 1841; m. at Wilton, 25 Nov 1794, ELIZABETH DASCOMB, b. at Wilton, 20 Jan 1771 daughter of James and Elizabeth (Farrington) Dascomb; Elizabeth d. at Wilton, 18 Oct 1852.

     Daniel was born in Andover and went with his parents to Wilton where Daniel remained. He settled on the family homestead of his father.[1526]

     Daniel Russell and Elizabeth Dascomb were parents of eleven children born at Wilton.

i   DANIEL RUSSELL, b. 12 May 1795; d. at Milford, NH, 9 Sep 1873; m. 1 Sep 1830, MARY RAMSDELL, b. at Milford, 1 Apr 1805 daughter of William and Mary (Southward) Ramsdell; Mary d. 13 Oct 1891.

ii   BETSEY RUSSELL, b. 4 May 1797; d. about 1844; m. 23 Feb 1819, ASAPH SAWYER, b. at Wilton, 15 Jul 1793 son of Nathaniel and Prudence (Abbott) Sawyer; Asaph d. at Cooper, ME, 1 Aug 1875. Asaph married second Alice Crane Allan about 1845.

iii   JAMES RUSSELL, b. 5 Dec 1798; d. at Boston, 24 Apr 1826. James was a carpenter. He spent three years in Georgia before returning to New England.

iv   HANNAH RUSSELL, b. 11 Aug 1800; d. at Wilton, 14 Mar 1857; m. 27 Jul 1823, ELIPHALET PUTNAM, b. at Wilton, 26 Oct 1799 son of Eliphalet and Dorcas (Abbott) Putnam; Eliphalet d. at Wilton, 16 Oct 1862.

v   JOHN FARRINGTON RUSSELL, b. 16 Dec 1802; d. at Wilton, 15 Aug 1878; m. at Welton, 4 Jul 1831, MARY ABBOTT, b. at Wilton, 21 Jun 1805 daughter of Zebediah and Elizabeth (Hale) Abbott.

vi   THERON RUSSELL, b. 4 Sep 1804; d. 26 Feb 1806.

vii   MARY RUSSELL, b. 15 Feb 1807; d. 30 Jun 1835; m. 29 Sep 1829, ABRAM PUTNAM, b. at Andover, VT, 13 Apr 1802 son of Jacob and Mary (Burton) Putnam; Abram d. at Manchester, 9 Apr 1876. Abram married second Clarissa Greeley.

viii   THERON RUSSELL, b. 20 Jun 1809; d. at Wilton, 29 Jan 1875; m. 4 Sep 1834, ELIZABETH WILSON, b. at Sharon, MA, 6 Nov 1813 daughter of David and Elizabeth (Barker) Wilson; Elizabeth d. at Wilton, 24 Oct 1903.

ix   HARRIET RUSSELL, b. 20 May 1811; d. at Lyndeborough, 29 Jan 1887; m. 29 Sep 1829, LUTHER DASCOMB, b. at Wilton, 20 Dec 1801 son of Jacob and Rachel (Dale) Dascomb; Luther d. at Wilton, 1 Jun 1885.

x   EMILY ADALINE RUSSELL, b. 10 Mar 1814; d. at Wilton, 17 Mar 1885; m. 4 Jun 1834, JOSEPH DASCOMB, b. at Wilton, 5 Feb 1810 son of James and Mary (Lovejoy) Dascomb; Joseph d. at Wilton, 6 Feb 1890.

xi   SARAH D. RUSSELL, b. 25 Jan 1816; d. at Wilton, 6 Aug 1843; m. 10 Mar 1835, WILLIAM SHELDON, b. at Wilton, 9 May 1810 son of Samuel and Phebe (Keyes) Sheldon; William d. at Wilton, 14 Nov 1891. William married second Dorcas Peavey (widow of Edward Pratt).

539)   PHEBE RUSSELL (*Thomas⁴, Joseph³, Thomas², Robert¹*), b. at Wilton, 13 Sep 1772 daughter of Thomas and Bethiah (Holt) Russell; d. at Weld, ME, 13 Sep 1852; m. about 1811, DAVID BARRETT, b. at Mason, NH, 1782 son of Reuben and Sarah (Fletcher) Barrett; David d. at Weld, 12 Feb 1864.

     David Barrett was from Mason but settled in Weld about the time of the outbreak of the War of 1812.[1527] Phebe Russell and David Barrett were parents of two children.

i   ALONSO BARRETT, b. at Weld, 25 Feb 1812; d. of typhoid fever at the regimental hospital (buried on Ship Island, MS), 27 May 1862;[1528] m. by 1850, ALMIRA, b. about 1820; Almira d. at Weld, 23 Apr 1858. Alonso and Almira had three children who were adopted into different families. In 1860, Alonso lived with Joseph Russell and his family in Weld. Alonso was listed as a pauper.[1529] Alonso, then age 49, enlisted as a private on 10 Dec 1861 in Company E of the Maine 13th Infantry.

ii   RIMMON BARRETT, b. at Weld, 6 Dec 1815; d. at Weld, 20 Oct 1895; m. his first cousin, EMMA BARRETT, b. 1 Jul 1818 daughter of Isaac and Polly (Dodge) Barrett; Emma d. at Weld, 1 Oct 1891.

540)   ABEL RUSSELL (*Thomas⁴, Joseph³, Thomas², Robert¹*), b. at Wilton, 5 Feb 1778 son of Thomas and Bethiah (Holt) Russell; d. at Weld, ME, 10 Jun 1859; m. at Royalston, MA, 2 Jan 1806, NANCY CLEMENT, b. at Petersham, MA, 2 Sep 1780 daughter of Thomas and Mary (Smith) Clement; Nancy d. at Weld, 25 Feb 1862.

[1526] Livermore, *History of the Town of Wilton*, p 493
[1527] Foster, *Early Settlers of Weld*, p 182
[1528] U.S., Registers of Deaths of Volunteers, 1861-1865
[1529] Year: 1860; Census Place: Weld, Franklin, Maine; Page: 771; Family History Library Film: 803435

Abel and Nancy settled in Weld along with several of Abel's siblings. Abel served on the school committee.[1530] Abel and brother Joseph originally thought of joining their brother in the new settlement at temple, Maine but ultimately settled in Weld. There are records of four children of Abel Russell and Nancy Clement, all born at Weld.

i   ABEL RUSSELL, b. 1 Aug 1807; d. 15 Sep 1811.

ii   CHARLES RUSSELL, b. 21 Jun 1809; d. at Weld, 13 Oct 1855; m. about 1835, HANNAH DASCOMB, b. 9 Jan 1809 daughter of Brooks and Sarah (Brown) Dascomb; Hannah d. at Weld, May 1874.

iii   NANCY RUSSELL, b. 27 Aug 1811; d. at Wilton, ME, 15 Jul 1883; m. SETH BASS, b. 25 Jul 1803 son of Jeriah and Lucretia (Savil) Bass; Seth d. at Wilton, 26 May 1883.

iv   MARY ANN RUSSELL, b. 11 Oct 1813; d. at Island Falls, ME, 11 Apr 1903; m. JAMES BROWN, b. at Wilton, ME, 24 Jun 1807 son of Ebenezer and Hannah (Billings) Brown; James d. at Patten, ME, 30 May 1872.

541)   JOSEPH RUSSELL (*Thomas⁴, Joseph³, Thomas², Robert¹*), b. at Wilton, 6 May 1780 son of Thomas and Bethiah (Holt) Russell; d. at Weld, ME, 28 Jun 1858; m. 1ˢᵗ about 1802, HANNAH DASCOMB, b. at Wilton, about 1779 daughter of James and Elizabeth (Farrington) Dascomb;[1531] Hannah d. at Weld, 17 Dec 1806. Joseph m. 2ⁿᵈ 8 Jan 1809, his fourth cousin, SARAH HOLT, b. at Wilton, 21 Sep 1780 daughter of Simeon and Mary (Dale) Holt; Sarah d. at Weld, 13 Mar 1857.

Joseph and his brother Abel settled together in Weld. The story is that they were intending to settle on the township land purchased in Temple by their brother Thomas but became a little off course while traveling to Temple. They camped overnight in a meadow and the next morning decided they liked the area. Joseph purchased two lots of the meadow that later became his homestead. Joseph, Abel, and their wives arrived the following spring. Joseph was active in the new town of Weld, for example serving on the committee to establish the school.[1532]

Joseph's first wife Hannah died the month after the birth of their daughter Hannah. Joseph next married Sarah Holt who was also from Wilton. In about 1825, Sarah's parents Simeon and Mary Holt came to live with their daughter and son-in-law.[1533]

Joseph and Hannah were parents of one child.

i   HANNAH DASCOMB RUSSELL, b. at Weld, ME, 18 Nov 1806; d. at Brunswick, ME, 7 Mar 1860; m. Jun 1832, CHARLES WILLARD MORSE, b. at Sutton, MA, 27 Dec 1805 son of Moses Leland and Huldah (Sibley) Morse; Charles d. at Evanston, IL, 30 Mar 1888.

Joseph and Sarah were parents of six children born at Weld, Maine.

i   MARY H. RUSSELL, b. 6 Dec 1809; d. (burial at Weld), 2 Dec 1839; m. about 1835, GEORGE GOODWIN, b. at Hallowell, ME, 7 May 1807 son of Andrew and Martha (Estes) Goodwin; George d. at Farmington, ME, 27 Dec 1893. George married second Elizabeth Harvey.

ii   JOSEPH RUSSELL, b. 2 Oct 1811; d. at Weld, 10 Dec 1887; m. 1ˢᵗ about 1843, MARY HOLT HOUGHTON, b. 2 Feb 1824 daughter of Benjamin and Elizabeth (Holt) Houghton; Mary d. at Weld, 19 Mar 1855. Joseph m. 2ⁿᵈ about 1856, DORCAS HOUGHTON, b. 1820 daughter of James and Rebecca (Keyes) Houghton; Dorcas d. at Weld, 6 Aug 1892.

iii   ABIAH RUSSELL, b. 2 Apr 1813; d. (burial at Weld), 7 Jan 1847; m. about 1836, ELIAB JONES, b. at Andover, MA, 17 Mar 1809 son of Jacob and Hannah (Jenkins) Jones. Eliab married second Susan who has not been identified.

iv   ABEL RUSSELL, b. 26 Mar 1815; d. at Wilton, ME, 6 Jun 1890; m. at Brooklyn, NY, 22 Nov 1849, ELIZABETH JANE MILLER, b. at New York, NY, 1832 daughter of Joseph and Susan (Blondell) Miller; Elizabeth d. at Boston, 24 Sep 1909.

v   JACOB RUSSELL, b. 29 Jun 1817; d. (burial at Weld), 10 Aug 1854; m. BETSEY, b. 1827; Betsey d. at Weld, 28 Mar 1858.

vi   BROOKS DASCOMB RUSSELL, b. 3 Jan 1822; d. at Wilton, ME, 13 Dec 1905; m. at West Boylston, MA, 4 Apr 1847, MARY M. HASTINGS, b. 27 Aug 1828 daughter of Nahum and Anna (Powers) Hastings; Mary d. at Wilton, 25 Mar 1921.

[1530] Foster, *Early Settlers of Weld*, p 181
[1531] Cunningham, *History of Lunenburg*, volume A-D, p 178
[1532] Foster, *Early Settlers of Weld*, pp 122-123, p 99
[1533] Foster, *Early Settlers of Weld*, p 123

542)   EPHRAIM RUSSELL (*Thomas⁴, Joseph³, Thomas², Robert¹*), b. at Wilton, 16 Jul 1783 son of Thomas and Bethiah (Holt) Russell; d. at Readfield, ME, 3 Dec 1875; m. 6 Apr 1809, REBECCA IRELAND, b. at Canaan, ME, 1789 daughter of Abraham and Betsey (Wyman) Ireland; Rebecca d. at Weld, ME, 2 Apr 1833.

Ephraim followed his brother and sisters to Weld arriving there in 1807. He purchased a farm in Weld and was there until 1850 before retiring to Redfield.[1534]

Ephraim and Rebecca were parents of seven children born at Weld, Maine.[1535] Ephraim and Rebecca also adopted a daughter Mary A. Coffran.[1536]

i   REBEKAH RUSSELL, b. 6 Dec 1809; d. at Freeman, ME, 25 Apr 1897; m. before 1835, FREEMAN THOMAS, b. at Strong, ME, 1 Jul 1803 son of Nelson and Sarah (Burnham) Thomas; Freeman d. at Strong, ME, 29 Dec 1884.

ii   EPHRAIM RUSSELL, b. 1 Oct 1811; d. at Minneapolis, MN, 7 Aug 1885; m. at Weld, 10 May 1837, ARMINA CUTTING MASTERMAN, b. at Weld, 19 Jul 1819 daughter of Marmaduke and Hannah (Howe) Masterman; Armina d. at Minneapolis, 7 Nov 1883.

iii   BETSEY RUSSELL, b. 19 Nov 1813; d. at Weld, ME, 7 Oct 1859; m. about 1837, GEORGE W. BUTTERFIELD, b. 1809; George d. at Weld, 27 Oct 1887. George married second Mary Atkins by 1860.

iv   REUBEN RUSSELL, b. 14 Feb 1817; d. at Readfield, ME, 20 Feb 1910; m. at Weld, 8 Jul 1841, ANNA MASTERMAN, b. at Weld, 13 Jul 1824 daughter of Marmaduke and Hannah (Howe) Masterman; Anna d. at Readfield, 25 Oct 1910.

v   PERKINS RUSSELL, b. 15 Jul 1819; d. at Seattle, WA, 13 Mar 1895; m. HARRIET MORRILL, b. 1827; Harriet d. at Livingston, MT, 1 Jan 1905.

vi   NANCY RUSSELL, b. 17 Feb 1821; d. at Northborough, MA, 18 Mar 1886; m. at Wayland, MA, 31 Dec 1846, EPHRAIM EAGER, b. at Sterling, MA, 26 Nov 1812 son of Uriah and Nancy (Fairbank) Eager; Ephraim d. at West Boylston, 27 Oct 1866.

vii   JAMES RUSSELL, b. 5 Feb 1828; d. at Shelburne, MA, 17 Sep 1902; m. at Charlemont, 9 May 1854, ALMIRA D. LUNT, b. at Westbrook, ME, 24 Oct 1832 daughter of Joshua and Polly (Hicks) Lunt;[1537] Almira d. at Easthampton, MA, 5 Apr 1917.

543)   JOSEPH RUSSELL (*Jonathan⁴, Joseph³, Thomas², Robert¹*), b. at Middleton, 19 Jul 1771 son of Jonathan and Ruth (Hutchinson) Russell; d. at Alexandria, NY (burial Orleans Four Corners), 23 Oct 1853; m. at Montague, MA, 1 Apr 1795, POLLY W. BENJAMIN, b. likely at Hardwick, MA, 1775 daughter of Abel and Susannah (Carpenter) Benjamin; Polly d. after 1850 when she and Joseph were living with their daughter and son-in-law in Alexandria.

The births of the first six children in this family are recorded at Wendell, Massachusetts,[1538] although the census records for some of these children state they were born in Vermont. The family was in Wendell for a time, but were in Le Ray in Jefferson County, New York by 1820. In 1820, the household consisted of one male over 45, one female over 45, two males under 10, one male 16 to 25, and one female under 10.[1539] In 1850, Joseph and Polly were living in Alexandria, New York with daughter Susanna and her husband and children also in the home.[1540] There are thought to be three children in addition to the six for whom there are birth records born after the move to New York.[1541] The two youngest children given here are known to be brother and sister to each other (Ruth Russell Pierce is buried in Cottonwood Cemetery next to her brother Rev. Russell according to her obituary), although there is a question whether they are members of this family and their inclusion in this family is speculative.

i   SUSANNA CARPENTER RUSSELL, b. at Wendell, 3 Sep 1795; d. at Alexandria, NY, 3 Feb 1854; m. about 1817, ASAHEL HOUGH, b. at Roxbury, CT, 12 Aug 1792 son of Buel and Elizabeth (Torrance) Hough; Asahel d. at Alexandria, 9 Sep 1874.

ii   POLLY RUSSELL, b. at Wendell, 3 Nov 1797; d. at Ashburnham, 8 May 1868; m. JACOB MCINTIRE, b. at Fitchburg, MA, 1791 son of Daniel and Jane (Hutchinson) McIntire; Jacob d. at Ashburnham, 9 Aug 1863.

[1534] Foster, *Early Settlers of Weld*, volume 2, p 40

[1535] Weld Vital Records, FHL Film # 007599977, image 107 and image 120

[1536] Mary's gravestone includes the inscription that she was the adopted daughter of Ephraim; findagrave ID: 155823407

[1537] The names of Almira's parents are given as Joshua Lunt and Polly Hicks on her death record, which also include date and place of birth. On the marriage register for her marriage to James Russell, parents' names are given as John and A. Lunt.

[1538] Massachusetts Town and Vital Records, Wendell Births, Marriages, and Deaths; accessed through ancestry.com

[1539] 1820 U S Census; Census Place: Le Ray, Jefferson, New York; Page: 435; NARA Roll: M33_72; Image: 237

[1540] Year: 1850; Census Place: Alexandria, Jefferson, New York; Roll: M432_515; Page: 16B; Image: 40

[1541] Jefferson County, New York Pioneers; http://jefferson.nygenweb.net/russelj.htm

iii   JOSEPH HUTCHINSON RUSSELL, b. at Wendell, 5 Apr 1800; d. at Grove, NH, 23 Aug 1871; m. by 1827, SARAH DEAN, b. 15 Sep 1807 daughter of Mial and Sarah (Stafford) Dean; Sarah d. at Battle Creek, MI (burial in Dalton, NY), 17 Mar 1894.

iv   ALDEN RUSSELL, b. 3 Oct 1802; d. at Sparta, WI, about 1857; m. by 1840, AMANDA BENNETT, b. in NY, about 1809; Amanda d. at Storm Lake, IA, 21 Jan 1882 where she lived with her son Jay.

v   SALLY RUSSELL, b. 25 Jul 1805; d. after 1870 when living at Hannibal, MO; m. by 1828, GEORGE W. LANGDON, b. in VT, about 1804; George was living in 1870.

vi   ROXANA RUSSELL, b. 16 Jan 1808

vii   ALFRED W. RUSSELL, b. 24 Jul 1818; d. at Lake City, IA, 5 Jun 1881; m. 1st at McDonough County, IL, 1 Dec 1845, CAROLINE HARRIS, b. at Onondaga County, NY, 27 Jun 1819 daughter of James and Prudence (Harris) Harris; Caroline d. at Table Grove, IL, 26 Nov 1847. Alfred m. 2nd at Fulton County, IL, 15 Feb 1849, MARY FLACK, b. in TN, about 1828; Mary d. 1856. Alfred m. 3rd MARTHA E., b. in KY about 1830; Martha d. Jun 1866. Alfred m. 4th at Sac City, IA, 3 Jun 1867, OLIVE HUTCHINSON (widow of James Reynolds), b. 4 Jan 1838 daughter of Jesses and Abigail (Rudd) Hutchinson; Olive d. at Des Moines, IA, 10 Oct 1916. Rev. A. W. Russell was a Baptist minister in Winterset and other locations in Iowa.[1542]

viii   RUTH ANN RUSSELL, b. 4 Feb 1821; d. at Lake City, IA while visiting her nephew, 6 Aug 1890; m. likely at Jefferson County, NY, about 1842, ALEXANDER C. PIERCE, b. in MA, about 1796; Alexander was living in 1865, but likely died in Hannibal, MO, about 1870. Alexander was first married to Cynthia Frick.

544)   BETSY RUSSELL (*Jonathan⁴, Joseph³, Thomas², Robert¹*) (twin), b. at Middleton, 18 Sep 1773 daughter of Jonathan and Ruth (Hutchinson) Russell; d. after 1870 when she was living (age 97) at the home of her son Lyman in Pamelia; m. at Warren, MA, 1 Dec 1796, ROBERT WHITE, b. at Warren, MA, 26 May 1774 son of William and Janet (Marr) White; Robert d. at Pamelia, 30 Oct 1851.

     Betsy and Roberts were parents of six, and perhaps a seventh child, Betsey.

i   LYMAN WHITE, b. about 1798; d. at Pamelia, NY, 7 Apr 1894; m. 1st HANNAH WILSON, b. 1794; Hannah d. at Pamelia, 1846. Lyman m. 2nd SARAH GOODRICH, b. 1806 and d. 1856. Lyman m. 3rd MARCIA TOWNE, b. 1827 and d. 1903.

ii   RUTH E. WHITE, b. 1799; d. (burial at Wendell, MA), 1 May 1816.

iii   JUSTUS WHITE, b. 27 Oct 1800; d. at Pamelia, NY, 11 Feb 1874; m. ELIZA BANISTER, b. at Watertown, NY, 19 Apr 1811 daughter of Osmond and Charlotte (Wilson) Banister;[1543] Eliza d. at Pamelia, 12 Nov 1883.

iv   JOSEPH WHITE,[1544] b. 30 May 1801; d. at Salt Lake City, UT, 18 Aug 1851; m. 1827, RUBY ELNORA STEARNS, b. at Leyden, MA, 18 Mar 1802 daughter of Charles and Sarah (Norris) Stearns; Ruby d. at Farmington, UT, 1875.

v   WILLIAM WHITE, b. at Boston, 24 May 1813; d. at Farmington, IA, 17 Oct 1845; m. SARAH ANN FASSETT, b. 7 Feb 1813 (on gravestone); Sarah d. at Harrison, IA, 21 Nov 1886. Sarah married second Peter Russell of South Carolina.

vi   BARTON WHITE, b. 1814; d. at Hounsfield, NY, May 1870; m. RACHEL MISNER, b. in NY, 1818 daughter of John and Elizabeth (-) Misner; Rachel d. at Watertown, NY, 18 Apr 1898.

545)   HANNAH RUSSELL (*Jonathan⁴, Joseph³, Thomas², Robert¹*), b. at Wendell, 3 Jan 1782 daughter of Jonathan and Ruth (Hutchinson) Russell; d. about 1824; m. at Wendell, 18 Feb 1806, STEPHEN FARR, b. 14 Aug 1781 son of Stephen and Lois (Randall) Farr; Stephen d. at Clayton, NY, 1872.[1545] Stephen married second Airess Towne about 1825.

     Hannah and Stephen resided in New York and were in Pamelia, New York with a household of nine at the 1820 census: one male 26 to 44; one female 26 to 44; three males under 10; one male 10 to 15; two females under 10; and one female 16 to 25.[1546] Stephen later lived in Clayton.

[1542] Mitchell, *Historical Sketches of Iowa Baptists*, p 167
[1543] Ely, *Records of the Descendants of Nathaniel Ely*, p 288
[1544] Joseph is a possible child in this family. There is a Utah death registration that names parents as Robert and Betsey White, but it is not entirely clear that it is this Robert and Betsey. The birth date of 30 May 1801 is given in the death register.
[1545] Stephen and his second wife Airess are buried together at Brownville Cemetery; findagrave ID: 70607142
[1546] 1820 U S Census; Census Place: Pamelia, Jefferson, New York; Page: 456; NARA Roll: M33_72; Image: 248

Stephen served in the War of 1812 in the New York militia company of Capt. Goodrich from 6 March 1813 to 22 March 1813 and in the militia company of Capt. Thomas Loomis from 10 October to 9 November 1814.[1547]

In his will written 14 April 1870, Stephen Farr left his entire estate, real and personal, to son Lafayette Farr who was also named executor. The following list of heirs to the estate were provided at a probate filing on 23 March 1874: Lafayette Farr; Clarissa Crosby and Alma Steel of Clayton, New York; Francis M. Farr of Potsdam; Anna Shephard of Jordanville, New York; Sally Rappale of Watertown, New York; Ephraim Farr of Cass City, Michigan; Stephen Farr of Des Moines, Iowa; Elias Farr of Hartland, Iowa; Foster Farr of New Hampton, Iowa; and Nancy Baker and Dexter Farr of Wisconsin who are all children of the deceased. Other children who are heirs were Freeman Farr and Joel Farr residing in Iowa at unknown location. Grandchildren named as heirs were Francis Farr and Dempster Farr children of Dempster deceased residing with their mother Frances A. Farr in Watertown, New York; Parly, Lyman, Albert, and Elizabeth Farr the children of James Farr deceased residing with mother Amanda in Watertown; and Madison MacCombs and Cynthia Patcher children of Lucinda MacCombs deceased.[1548]

Hannah and Stephen were parents of seven children who lived to adulthood likely all born in Jefferson County, New York. Stephen had at least eleven children with his second wife.

i   SALLY FARR, b. about 1808; d. at Watertown, NY, 3 Dec 1889; m. about 1831, HENRY RAPPELE, b. about 1808; Henry d. at Watertown after 1875.

ii   FREEMAN FARR, b. at Pamelia, 4 Jun 1810; d. at Fond Du Lac, WI, 13 Feb 1891; m. LOUISA REEVES, b. 20 Aug 1819 (on gravestone); Louisa d. at Fond Du Lac, 28 Oct 1904.

iii   JAMES FARR, b. 1816; d. at Watertown, NY, 1859; m. about 1842, AMANDA VAN HOOSER, b. in NY, about 1821; Amanda d. at Carthage, NY, 18 May 1895.

iv   LUCINDA FARR, b. 15 Apr 1818; d. at Cape Vincent, NY, 24 Apr 1848; m. about 1837, GEORGE MASON MCCOMBS, b. at Frankfort, NY, 6 Mar 1812 son of John Andrew and Magdalena (Frank) McCombs; George d. at Camp Vincent, 16 Apr 1868. George married second Jane Eseltine.

v   JOEL FARR, b. about 1821; d. at Iron Ridge, WI, 28 Apr 1864; m. at Rubicon, WI, 25 Dec 1850, LAURAIN YENDES, b. in NY about 1830.

vi   NANCY FARR, b. about 1822; d. after 1880 when she was living at Des Moines, IA; m. about 1854, GARDNER C. BAKER, b. in NY, about 1832 son of Gardner and Esther (Bronson) Baker;[1549] Gardner d. after 1910 when he was living at Long Creek, IA.

vii   JONATHAN DEXTER FARR, b. about 1824;[1550] d. at West Salem, WI, 30 Dec 1903;[1551] m. ELIZA who has not been identified, but b. in NY, Apr 1834 (census records); Eliza d. 1902. Dexter and Eliza do not seem to have had children. A notice appeared in a Janesville, WI paper in 1903 titled "Did Dexter Farr Leave Any Heirs" posted by a Washington, DC law firm and requesting information to verify his death.[1552]

546)   RACHEL RUSSELL (*Jonathan⁴, Joseph³, Thomas², Robert¹*), b. at Wendell, 17 Oct 1783 daughter of Jonathan and Ruth (Hutchinson) Russell; d. at Pamelia, 21 Mar 1871; m. at Wendell, 1805, CURTIS GOULDING, b. at Holliston, MA, 10 Aug 1776 son of Joseph and Kezia (Parker) Goulding; Curtis d. at Pamelia, 10 Jul 1857.

Rachel and Curtis resided in Pamelia, New York where Curtis was a farmer. The family settled in Pamelia Four Corners about 1812. When the Methodist church was formed at Pamelia Four Corners on 28 February 1847, Curtis Goulding and Rachel Goulding were two of the seven founding members.[1553]

Son Russell did not marry. In his will written 25 March 1866 (probate 11 April 1866), he made bequests to brother Madison Goulding, mother Rachel Goulding, sister-in-law Lucena Goulding, brother Amos Goulding, brother Curtis Goulding, sister Cynthia Wyeth, and sister Elizabeth M. Baum.[1554]

Son Amos married and had two children who pre-deceased him and without marrying. In his will written 7 March 1852, he left his entire estate to wife Polly Goulding, otherwise known as Mary A. Goulding, who was also named executrix. Amos never updated his will, and it was presented to probate on 1 January 1892 by widow Mary Goulding. The following other family members were identified at the probate filing: Curtis Goulding of Port Huron, Michigan; Madison Goulding of Pamelia

[1547] War of 1812 Pension Application Files Index, 1812-1815; New York, War of 1812 Payroll Abstracts for New York State Militia, 1812-1815
[1548] New York Wills and Probate Records, Jefferson County, volume 015, pp 550-553
[1549] The 1877 probate of Gardner Baker of Watertown, NY includes heir Gardner C. Baker of Des Moines, IA.
[1550] 1824 is the year of birth given on Dexter's gravestone (findagrave ID 145927366 in Randolph Cemetery in Randolph, Wisconsin), but census records fluctuate from 1825 to 1830 in terms of estimated birth year. If Dexter was born in 1824, he is the likely child of Hannah. If he was born after, he is likely from Stephen's second marriage.
[1551] Wisconsin, Death Index, 1820-1907
[1552] Janesville Daily Gazette (Janesville, Wisconsin), 03 Jun 1903, Wed, p 7
[1553] L. H. Everts, *History of Jefferson County, New York*, p 463, p 467
[1554] New York Wills and Probate Records, Jefferson County, wills volume 0011, pp 14-15

Four Corner, New York; and Elizabeth Baum of Watertown, Wisconsin. Also identified were Emma Timmerman of Minnesota and George S. Goulding of Denver, Colorado children of Orvis Goulding deceased.[1555]

   Rachel and Curtis were parents of seven children, the older children born in Massachusetts before the move to Pamelia.

i   CYNTHIA GOULDING, b. 7 Jun 1806; d. at Denmark, NY, 21 Mar 1871; m. about 1852, as his second wife, JOSEPH WYETH, b. in MA about 1797; Joseph d. at Denmark, 1872.

ii   RUSSELL GOULDING, b. 1809; d. at Pamelia, NY, 1866. Russell did not marry.

iii   ORVIS GOULDING, b. about 1810; d. at Pamelia, 1858; m. LUCENA who has not been identified, b, in NY, Nov 1818; Lucena d. after 1900 when she was living in Denver, CO with her son George and his family.

iv   AMOS GOULDING, b. 1816; d. at Watertown, NY, 13 Dec 1891; m. by 1844, MARY STEWART, b. Oct 1820 daughter of William and Lucy (Cole) Stewart;[1556] Mary d. at Watertown, 1909.

v   CURTIS GOULDING, b. 16 Feb 1820; d. at Port Huron, MI, 29 May 1902; m. by 1851, MARY JANE WARD, b. in NY, 1826 daughter of James and Lovina (Barber) Ward;[1557] Mary Jane d. at Port Huron, 4 Oct 1892.

vi   MADISON GOULDING, b. at Pamelia, 1826; d. at Pamelia, 27 Dec 1896; m. 20 Feb 1855, ELIZA P. HUNTINGTON, b. 3 Nov 1829 daughter of Cyrus T. and China (Graves) Huntington;[1558] Eliza d. at Watertown, 19 Oct 1907.

vii   MARY ELIZABETH GOULDING, b. at Pamelia, 5 Jan 1829; d. at Watertown, WI, 25 Feb 1905; m. about 1850, AMOS BAUM, b. in NY, 1826; Amos d. at Watertown, 26 May 1902.

547)   PHEBE RUSSELL (*Jonathan⁴, Joseph³, Thomas², Robert¹*), b. at Wendell, 19 Oct 1785 daughter of Jonathan and Ruth (Hutchinson) Russell; d. at Pamelia, NY, 27 Jan 1856; m. at Wendell, 28 Jan 1805, REUBEN LOCKE, b. at Shutesbury, MA, 6 Apr 1783 son of Ebenezer and Hannah (Randall) Locke; Reuben d. at Pamelia, 30 Oct 1855.

   Phebe and Reuben resided in Pamelia. New York. The Locke genealogy reports fourteen children in this family, four of whom died in childhood.[1559] Ten children were identified for Phebe and Reuben.

i   CLARISSA LOCKE, b. Aug 1805; d. at Antioch, IL, 24 Dec 1890; perhaps m. THEODORE FRAZIER, b. in MA, about 1799; Theodore d. at Antioch, 30 Jan 1884.

ii   DAVID LOCKE, b. 1806; d. at Conquest, NY, 24 Jul 1874; m. HARRIET LADD, b. 11 Jan 1809 daughter of Bodwell and Martha (Lewis) Ladd;[1560] Harriet d. after 1875 when she was living with her son in Conquest.

iii   J. RUSSELL LOCKE, b. 3 Jul 1810; d. at Odessa, MI, 7 Aug 1894; m. MARY M. GOODWIN, b. at Oneida, 16 Nov 1821 daughter of Chauncey and Sarah (Hubbard) Goodwin;[1561] Mary d. at Belding, MI, 26 Jul 1854.

iv   REUBEN LOCKE, b. 1812; d. at Pamelia, NY, 4 Jul 1845; m. about 1838, SOPHIA LYON, b. 1 Jan 1814; Sophia d. Evans Mills, NY, 19 Nov 1889.

v   BEZELEEL LOCKE, b. 20 Nov 1814; d. at Ionia, MI, 1892; m. ELIZA CANOUTS, b. Jul 1818 daughter of John F. and Lydia (Jones) Canouts;[1562] Eliza d. at North Shade, MI, 2 Feb 1906.

vi   LYDIA LOCKE

vii   WILBER LOCKE, b. about 1820; d. 5 Mar 1900 at Volney, NY; m. MARTHA ANN TIMMERMAN, b. Apr 1826 daughter of John J. and Mary (Baum) Timmerman;[1563] Martha d. at Fulton, NY, 10 Apr 1905.

viii   ALFRED LOCKE, b. 1823; d. at Ossining, NY, 1896 (probate 20 Sep 1896); m. ELIZA, b. in NY, Nov 1823; Eliza d. at Ossining, 20 Dec 1910.

[1555] New York Wills and Probate Records, Jefferson County, wills volume 030, pp 541-543
[1556] Mary's mother Lucy Stewart lived with the family from 1855 and Lucy was still living at age 97 in 1900 living with her daughter Mary.
[1557] The names of Mary Jane's parents are given as James and Lovina Ward on her death record; Michigan Department of Community Health, Division for Vital Records and Health Statistics; Lansing, Michigan; Death Records
[1558] Huntington, *Genealogical Memoir of the Huntington Family*, p 317
[1559] Locke, *Book of Lockes*, p 156
[1560] Ladd, *The Ladd Family*, p 89
[1561] The 1863 will of Chauncey Goodwin, Sr. of Ronald Township, Michigan includes bequests to Mary Locke and Minersa Locke daughters of Russell Locke of Ionia Township, Michigan.
[1562] The names of Eliza's parents are given as John Canouts and Lydia Johns on her death record.
[1563] The 1835 probate of John J. Timmerman of Herkimer County, NY includes the assignment of a guardian to minor daughter Martha Ann.

ix   PHILANDER LOCKE, b. about 1826; d. at Fulton, NY, 20 Aug 1899; m. 1st about 1848, IRENE WALRATH, b. about 1829; Irene d. at Pamelia, 1862. Philander m. 2nd MERCY PERMELIA PHILLIPS, b. in "English Canada" (on 1910 census), 17 Oct 1841; Mercy d. at Fulton, 13 Nov 1925.

x   MARY LOCKE, b. about 1827; m. about 1846, RICHARD WALTS, b. about 1823. The oldest child of Mary and Richard was born about 1846. Richard and Mary lived in Jefferson County, New York early in their marriage, were in Wisconsin for a time, and were in Fargo, Dakota Territory in 1880.

548)   JAMES RUSSELL (*Jonathan⁴, Joseph³, Thomas², Robert¹*), b. at Wendell, 27 Jul 1793 son of Jonathan and Ruth (Hutchinson) Russell; d. after 1870 when he was living in Pea Ridge, IL at the home of his daughter Harriet and her husband; m. 1st LORA, b. about 1796 and who d. after 1860. James m. 2nd MINERVA, b. about 1797; Minerva d. after 1870 when she was living at Pea Ridge.

James Russell was residing in Pamelia, New York in 1820 with a household of one male 26-44, one female 16-25, and one female under 10.[1564] In 1850, the family was in Le Boeuf, Pennsylvania with household of James age 57 born in Massachusetts, Lora age 54 born in Massachusetts, Jane age 20 born in New York, Jonathan age 18 born in New York, and Trueman, age 13 born in New York. Living next door was Henry Cole age 31 and his wife Cynthia age 29.[1565] In 1870, James Russell, age 77 and born in Massachusetts, and wife Minerva were living with Harriet and Edwin Easton in Pea Ridge, Illinois.[1566] In 1850, Harriet Easton, born in New York in 1819, and her husband Edwin were living in Franklin, Erie County, Pennsylvania.[1567]

There are five likely children of James and Lora born at Jefferson County, New York.

i   HARRIET M. RUSSELL, b. 1819; d. at Pea Ridge, IL, 23 Sep 1888; m. about 1841, EDWIN N. EASTON, b. 1821 son of David and Sarah (Preston) Easton; Edwin d. at Timewell, IL, 16 Dec 1913.

ii   CYNTHIA RUSSELL, b. 1822; d. at Waterford, PA, 1884; m. about 1841, HENRY COLE, b. 1818; Henry d. at Waterford, 30 Nov 1900.

iii   JANE RUSSELL, b. 28 Jun 1830; d. at Erie, PA, 9 Nov 1922; m. GEORGE W. GRAY, b. in PA, 25 Nov 1825;[1568] George d. at Erie, 29 Aug 1893.

iv   JONATHAN RUSSELL, b. 1832

v   TRUEMAN RUSSELL, b. 1837; d. of fever at the regimental hospital at Alexandria, VA, 27 Jun 1864;[1569] m. MATILDA HAMILTON, b. 1840; Matilda d. 1917. Matilda married second Ashley Judd. Trueman served with the 76th regiment of Pennsylvania infantry.

549)   LUCY WILKINS (*Sarah Russell Wilkins⁴, Joseph³, Thomas², Robert¹*), b. at Middleton, MA, 20 Oct 1775 daughter of Nehemiah and Sarah (Russell) Wilkins; d. at Topsfield, 9 Dec 1868;[1570] m. at Middleton, 20 May 1802, MOSES PERKINS, b. at Topsfield, 21 Aug 1775 son of Oliver and Lucy (Gould) Perkins; Moses d. at Topsfield, 18 Oct 1858.

Lucy and Moses resided in Danvers where Moses was a shoemaker. Moses Perkins and Lucy Wilkins were parents of four children born at Danvers.

i   CYNTHIA PERKINS, b. 11 Nov 1804; d. at Middleton, 24 Aug 1830. Cynthia did not marry.

ii   JESSE PERKINS, b. 28 Mar 1808; d. at Middleton, 26 Feb 1843; m. at Danvers, 9 May 1839, CHARLOTTE A. TOWNE, b. at Topsfield, 28 Apr 1819 daughter of Joseph and Hannah (Perkins) Towne; Charlotte d. at Middleton, 29 Jan 1898. Charlotte married second George P. Wilkins on 13 Jan 1849.

iii   LOIS LOUIZA PERKINS, b. 18 Mar 1809; d. at Topsfield, 25 Jun 1875; m. at Danvers, 25 Dec 1838, LORENZO PERKINS TOWNE, b. at Topsfield, 24 Mar 1811 son of Joseph and Hannah (Perkins) Towne; Lorenzo d. at Topsfield, 31 Jan 1877.

[1564] 1820 U S Census; Census Place: Pamelia, Jefferson, New York; Page: 456; NARA Roll: M33_72; Image: 248

[1565] Year: 1850; Census Place: Le Boeuf, Erie, Pennsylvania; Roll: 777; Page: 59A

[1566] Year: 1870; Census Place: Pea Ridge, Brown, Illinois; Roll: M593_189; Page: 121A; Family History Library Film: 545688

[1567] Year: 1850; Census Place: Franklin, Erie, Pennsylvania; Roll: 778; Page: 346A

[1568] George's date of birth is given his veteran burial card; Pennsylvania Historical and Museum Commission; Harrisburg, Pennsylvania; Pennsylvania Veterans Burial Cards, 1929-1990; Series Number: Series 1

[1569] U.S., Registers of Deaths of Volunteers, 1861-1865

[1570] Lucy, wid. Moses, who d. in Danvers, in Nov., 1858, d. Nehemiah and Sarah (Russell) Wilkins, b. Middleton, old age, Dec. 9, 1868, a. 93 y. 1 m. 10 d. (Interred at Middleton.); Massachusetts: Vital Records, 1620-1850 (Online Database: *AmericanAncestors.org*, New England Historic Genealogical Society, 2001-2016).

iv   AMELIA PERKINS, b. 14 Jan 1816; d, at Danvers, 16 Dec 1856; m. at Danvers, 20 Oct 1836, MARK HOWE, b. at Middleton, 25 Dec 1803 son of Asa and Hephzibah (Peabody) Howe; Mark d. at Danvers, 17 Dec 1861.

550)   ABIGAIL WILKINS (*Sarah Russell Wilkins⁴, Joseph³, Thomas², Robert¹*), b. at Middleton, MA, 7 Sep 1777 daughter of Nehemiah and Sarah (Russell) Wilkins; d. at Middleton, 8 Apr 1806; m. at Middleton, 13 May 1798, JOSEPH WRIGHT, b. about 1770; Joseph d. at Middleton, 5 Nov 1836.
     Abigail Wright and Joseph Wilkins were parents of five children born at Middleton.

i   MELANTHA WRIGHT, b. 22 Sep 1798; d. at Danvers, 25 Mar 1826; m. at Middleton, 10 May 1821, WILLIAM GOODHUE, b. at Bradford, 4 Jul 1797 son of Phineas and Hannah (Parsons) Goodhue; William d. at North Andover, 11 Oct 1882. William married second Sally *Upton* Ingalls in 1828.

ii   SALLY R. WRIGHT, b. 30 Jan 1800; d. at Middleton, 23 Feb 1874; m. at Middleton, 25 Nov 1824, JONATHAN BERRY, b. at Middleton, 4 Jan 1803 son of Jonathan and Rebecca (Dale) Berry; Jonathan d. at Middleton, 28 Jun 1880.

iii   HIRAM WRIGHT, b. 29 Apr 1801; d. at Wakefield, MA, 17 Feb 1871; m. at Middleton, 28 May 1829, LYDIA WHITE, b. at Middleton, 9 Oct 1808 daughter of Samuel and Hannah (Hutchinson) White; Lydia d. at Stoneham, 18 Apr 1873.

iv   FRANKLIN WRIGHT, b. 15 Mar 1803; d. at Danvers, 15 Sep 1889; m. 1ˢᵗ at Lowell, 13 Oct 1835, CAROLINE A DURANT, b. at Amherst, NH, about 1813 daughter of Nathan J. and Sarah (Haseltine) Durant; Caroline d. at Bedford, NH, 15 May 1862. Franklin m. 2ⁿᵈ at Danvers, 21 Mar 1868, MARY M. WRIGHT (widow of Daniel Berry), b. at Charlestown, NH, 27 Dec 1819 daughter of Jacob and Dorcas (Walker) Wright;[1571] Mary d. at Danvers, 6 Aug 1900. Franklin lived much of his adult life in Bedford, NH, but returned to Danvers before his death.

v   WILLIAM WRIGHT, b. 2 Sep 1804. William, age 20 of Middleton, obtained his seaman's protection certificate at Salem on 18 October 1824.[1572]

551)   EPHRAIM WILKINS (*Sarah Russell Wilkins⁴, Joseph³, Thomas², Robert¹*), b. at Middleton, MA, 13 Sep 1781 son of Nehemiah and Sarah (Russell) Wilkins; d. at Middleton, 22 Feb 1827; m. at Middleton, 6 Apr 1806, HANNAH DIXEY, baptized at Marblehead, 8 Jul 1787 daughter of Richard and Rebecca (Homan) Dixey; Hannah d. at Middleton, 4 Sep 1831.
     Ephraim Wilkins did not leave a will and his estate entered probate 6 March 1827 with Ezra Nichols as administrator. On 3 April 1827, widow Hannah requested allowance from the court for necessities for herself and her six children under the age of seven.[1573] Real estate was valued at $1363 and personal estate at $620.71. Debts were $1109.06 and the real estate was sold at auction to settle the estate.[1574]
     In her will written 5 August 1831 (probate 27 Sep 1831), Hannah Wilkins bequeathed to daughter Eliza A. Richardson a gown and shoes. Daughter Rebecca H. Wilkins received the best bed and bedding, six silver teaspoons, the great bible, spectacles, and the rocking chair. Daughter Polly Wilkins received the third bed and bedding, a large silver spoon, and other listed items. Daughter Martha R. Wilkins receives the second bed, a large silver spoon, and the desk. Son James and son Dixey each receive one dollar. The rest of the personal estate and the real estate which consists of an undivided one-sixth part of the Dixey farm in Middleton were to be sold, this to be used to pay any debts and the residue to be equally divided among her children named previously. Benjamin Jenkins, Jr. was named executor.[1575]
     Ephraim Wilkins and Hannah Dixey were parents of eight children born at Middleton.

i   ELIZA ANN WILKINS, b. 15 Sep 1806; d. at Middleton, 30 Aug 1846; m. at Middleton, 25 Dec 1827, EZRA RICHARDSON, b. at Middleton, 20 Mar 1795 son of Jonathan and Mary (Peters) Richardson; Ezra d. at Middleton, 30 Jul 1873.

[1571] The names of Mary's parents are given as Jacob Wright and Dorcas Walker on both her marriage record to Franklin Wright and her death record.

[1572] Web: US, New England Seamen's Protection Certificate Index, 1796-1871

[1573] Although the probate states the six children were under seven, there were just six children living at that time, all of whom were minors.

[1574] *Essex County, MA: Probate File Papers, 1638-1881.*Online database. *AmericanAncestors.org.* New England Historic Genealogical Society, 2014. Case 29889

[1575] *Essex County, MA: Probate File Papers, 1638-1881.*Online database. *AmericanAncestors.org.* New England Historic Genealogical Society, 2014. Case 29891

ii   JAMES WILKINS, b. 4 Sep 1808; d. at Gloucester, 24 May 1880; m. at Nashville, NH, 9 May 1844, SARAH W. HASKELL, b. at Gloucester, 1820 daughter of Asa and Caroline (Rust) Haskell; Sarah d. at Gloucester, 14 Jul 1880.

iii RICHARD DIXEY WILKINS, b. 9 Jan 1811; d. at Reading, 8 Apr 1884; m. at Reading, 1 Jun 1848, HARRIET NICHOLS (widow of Andrew F. Curtis), b. at Andover, 4 May 1820 daughter of John and Mary (Davis) Nichols; Harriet d. at Reading, 17 Jun 1904.

iv   REBECCA HOMAN NICHOLS, b. 24 Jan 1813; d. at Middleton, 25 Sep 1871. Rebecca did not marry.

v   POLLY DIXEY WILKINS, b. 6 Feb 1814; d. 8 Jun 1814.

vi   EPHRAIM WALSTON WILKINS, b. 30 May 1816; d. 5 Feb 1817.

vii POLLY DIXEY WILKINS, b. 11 Dec 1817; d. at Middleton, 30 Apr 1842. Polly did not marry.

viii MARTHA READ WILKINS, b. 9 Mar 1819; d. at Middleton, 9 May 1839.

552) JAMES WILKINS (*Sarah Russell Wilkins⁴, Joseph³, Thomas², Robert¹*), b. at Middleton, MA, 1 Nov 1785 son of Nehemiah and Sarah (Russell) Wilkins; d. at Middleton, 23 Jul 1875; m. 1 May 1817, BETSEY WILKINS, b. at Middleton, 21 Jan 1793 daughter of Samuel and Sarah (Fuller) Wilkins;[1576] Betsey d. at Middleton, 21 Jun 1872.

James Wilkins was a farmer in Middleton. In the 1860 census, the value of his real estate was given as $3,300.[1577] On 16 December 1870, James and wife Betsey deeded five parcels in Middleton to Edward W. Wilkins.[1578] James and Betsey Wilkins were parents of thirteen children born at Middleton.

i   BETSEY WILKINS, b. 14 May 1818; d. at Danvers, 11 Mar 1898; m. at Danvers, 4 Jul 1843, JEREMIAH FLINT PEABODY, b. at Middleton, 9 Aug 1812 son of Joseph and Anna (Flint) Peabody; Jeremiah d. at Danvers, 21 Nov 1887.

ii   JAMES WILDER WILKINS, b. 7 Oct 1819; d. at Peabody, MA, 5 Apr 1897; m. 26 Sep 1844, JULIE ANN GOULD, b. at Middleton, 21 Feb 1823 daughter of Henry and Lydia (Howe) Gould; Julie d. at Peabody, 6 May 1904.

iii CYRUS KINGSBURY WILKINS, b. 20 Sep 1821; d. at Minneapolis, MN, 6 Oct 1892; m. at Middleton, 12 May 1847, CAROLINE ELIZABETH GOULD, b. at Middleton, 3 Sep 1825 daughter of Henry and Lydia (Howe) Gould; Caroline d. at Minneapolis, MN, 13 Apr 1906. Cyrus and Caroline lived in Middleton until 1880 and were in Minneapolis in 1885 where they both died.

iv   SARAH SMITH WILKINS, b. 19 Apr 1823; d. at Beverly, MA, 13 Jun 1882; m. at Middleton, 5 Nov 1851, JOHN GIRDLER, b. at Manchester, MA, 11 Nov 1814 son of William and Peggy (Hilton) Girdler; John d. at Beverly, 26 Feb 1915. John Girdler was a coal manufacturer of the Girdler Coal Company in Beverly.

v   WILLIAM WALLACE WILKINS, b. 27 May 1824; d. at Bolinas, CA, 21 Mar 1910; m. 12 Feb 1876, MARY BUTLER MORSE, b. at Manchester, MA, 17 Oct 1846 daughter of Joseph H. and Mary E. (Girdler) Morse; Mary d. at Bolinas, 9 Dec 1929. William went to California via ship in 1849. He had hired on to fit out the ship and was in the boat business in California until about 1852. He then got into mining. Later he was involved in lumber cutting for railroad ties.[1579]

vi   LUCY JANE WILKINS, b. 24 Oct 1825; d. at Princeton, MA, 1922; m. At Middleton, 9 Jun 1859, GEORGE ELLIS PRATT, b. 30 Jan 1827 son of Moses and Elizabeth (Ellis) Pratt; George d. at Princeton, 28 May 1894.

vii MARY ANN WILKINS, b. 5 Mar 1827; d. at Tewksbury, 2 Sep 1867; m. at Newburyport, 2 May 1854, JACOB COGGIN, b. at Tewksbury, about 1812 son of Jacob and Mary (Symmes) Coggin; Jacob d. at Tewksbury, 9 Feb 1890.

viii JESSE A. WILKINS, b. 10 Sep 1828; d. at Woodstock, CT, 26 Dec 1902. Jesse was a clergyman and a farmer who lived in Woodstock. He did not marry. He is buried in the family plot in Middleton.

ix   ESTHER MARIA WILKINS, b. 14 Apr 1830; d. 16 Oct 1842.

x   ADRIAN WHITFIELD WILKINS, b. 4 Dec 1832; d. at Clinton, IA, 14 Feb 1896; m. at Middleton, 7 Apr 1863, MARY FRANCES PUTNAM, b. at Danvers, 5 Jun 1838 daughter of Adrian and Fanny (Flint) Putnam; Mary d.

[1576] The names of Betsey's parents are given as Samuel Wilkins and Sarah Fuller on her death record.
[1577] Year: 1860; Census Place: Middleton, Essex, Massachusetts; Page: 879; Family History Library Film: 803498
[1578] Massachusetts Land Records, Essex County; 812:262, 812:263
[1579] "Death of an Old Pioneer" Marin Journal, Thursday, March 24, 1910, p 1

at Prairie Creek, OR, 28 Feb 1926. Mary went to live with one of her son William Putnam Wilkins after the death of her husband.

xi HARRIET AMELIA WILKINS, b. 12 Mar 1834; d. at Sacramento, CA, 6 Apr 1913; m. ALVIN ELIJAH HUTCHINSON, b. at Middleton, 22 Jan 1826 son of Levi and Betsey (Russell) Hutchinson; Alvin d. at Sacramento, 28 Feb 1883.

xii CHARLES AUGUSTUS WILKINS, b. 25 Jan 1838; d. 20 Dec 1844.

xiii EDWARD WILBERFORCE WILKINS, b. 1 Nov 1839; d. at Middleton, 1922. Edward did not marry.

553) NANCY WILKINS (*Sarah Russell Wilkins⁴, Joseph³, Thomas², Robert¹*), b. at Middleton, MA, 18 Mar 1790 daughter of Nehemiah and Sarah (Russell) Wilkins; d. at Danvers, 26 Aug 1874; m. at Middleton, 22 Oct 1812, WILLIAM GIFFORD, b. at Danvers, 27 Feb 1784 son of William and Lydia (Putnam) Gifford; William d. at Middleton, 2 Jan 1849.
   William Gifford was a farmer in Danvers. There are records of eight children of Nancy Wilkins and William Gifford born at Danvers.

i WILLIAM RUSSELL GIFFORD, b. 2 Dec 1816; d. after 1880 when he was living in Detroit; m. 1st about 1840, MEHITABLE RUTH BRADSTREET, b. at Topsfield, MA, 1820 daughter of Samuel and Mehitable (Gould) Bradstreet; Mehitable d. at Rochester, NY, Apr 1849. William m. 2nd MARTHA MILLER, b. at Rochester, NY, about 1834; Martha d. after 1880. William was a railroad depot master and in 1874 was living in Windsor, Ontario.

ii NANCY PUTNAM GIFFORD, b. 30 Oct 1818; d. at Danvers, 17 Apr 1899; m. at Danvers, 17 Sep 1839, JAREB PRESTON CROSS, b. at Danvers, 13 Jul 1817 son of Peter and Hannah (Preston) Cross; Jareb d. at Danvers, 13 May 1858.

iii JAMES EDWARD GIFFORD, b. 3 Dec 1821; d. at Danvers, 4 Dec 1892; m. at Danvers, 24 May 1851, LYDIA A. PETTENGILL, b. at Danvers, 23 Sep 1828 daughter of Moses and Lydia (Hall) Pettengill; Lydia d. at Danvers, 10 Nov 1903.

iv THOMAS SEAL GIFFORD, b. 26 Nov 1823; d. at Rochester, NY,18 May 1858; m. 13 Sep 1850, HARRIET SMITH NORTON, b. at Strafford, VT, 15 Mar 1831 daughter of Seymour and Fanny (Stevens) Norton; Harriet d. after 1905 when she was living in Buffalo. Harriet married second William Ring in Nov 1863.

v SARAH JANE GIFFORD, b. 25 Dec 1825; d. at Rochester, NY, May 1852.

vi JESSE WILKINS GIFFORD, b. 28 Oct 1827; d. at Rochester, NY, Nov 1889; m. MARTHA CHEQUER BILLINGHURST, b. at Washington, DC, 27 Sep 1837 daughter of William and Mary (Richardson) Billinghurst; Martha d. at Rochester, 6 Aug 1912. William Billinghurst was a gunsmith inventor of a rapid-fire gun used in the Civil War.

vii MALANTHA WRIGHT GIFFORD, b. 26 Jul 1829; d. at Danvers, 18 Jul 1897. Malantha did not marry. She lived for a time in Rochester with her brother William. She worked in a shoe factory.

viii FRANKLIN WALSTIN GIFFORD, b. 31 Oct 1831; d. at Dover, ME, 25 Mar 1905; m. 1873, ELLEN SAWYER, b. at Dover, ME, Jul 1834 daughter of George W. and Elizabeth (Walker) Sawyer; Ellen d. at Dover, 25 Jan 1909.

554) JESSE WILKINS (*Sarah Russell Wilkins⁴, Joseph³, Thomas², Robert¹*), b. at Middleton, MA, 8 Mar 1792 son of Nehemiah and Sarah (Russell) Wilkins; d. at Middleton, 27 Jan 1827; m. at Middleton, 10 Oct 1810, PEGGY PEABODY, b. 14 Dec 1791 daughter of Benjamin and Hannah (Black) Peabody; Peggy d. at Middleton, 21 Dec 1840.
   Jesse was a cordwainer in Middleton. Jesse Wilkins did not leave a will and his estate entered probate 3 April 1827 with widow Peggy as administratrix. Peggy petitions for her wearing apparel and other necessities as she has six children all minors who are depending on her for support. Only real estate was 54 rods of peet meadow valued at five dollars. Personal estate was $201.88.[1580]
   In her will written 30 November 1840 (probate 5 January 1841), Peggy Wilkins bequeathed to son Nehemiah, twenty dollars. Daughter Caroline Wilkins receives the furniture, beds and bedding, silver spoons, great bible, and one hundred dollars. Caroline's board is also to be paid from the estate for the time that Caroline was caring for her mother during her sickness. Grandson Jesse Walston "son of my son Nehemiah above named, on condition his father now absent shall not return to his family during the minority of the said Jesse Walston." Grandson Jesse also receives the small bible. Scott's bible with explanatory notes and practical observations goes to her four beloved daughters "not to be divided but kept by them as a family

[1580] *Essex County, MA: Probate File Papers, 1638-1881.*Online database. *AmericanAncestors.org.* New England Historic Genealogical Society, 2014. Case 29897

to be read in there several families, also for the use and benefit of their children." These four daughters are Sarah Russell Emerson, Abigail Tyler, Nancy Fish, and Caroline Wilkins. The remainder of the estate is divided among her four daughters. James Wilkins, Sr. of Middleton was named executor.[1581]

Jesse Wilkins and Peggy Peabody were parents of eight children born at Middleton.

i   NEHEMIAH WILKINS, b. 7 Nov 1810; d. about 1842 when widow Ruth petitioned to be guardian of son Jess W. Wilkins; m. at Danvers, 17 Dec 1831, RUTH PARKER, b. at Greenwich, MA, 10 May 1809 daughter of Thomas and Esther (Fuller) Parker;[1582] Ruth d. at Danvers 23 Feb 1904. Ruth married second Benjamin R. Sanborn on 29 Nov 1843.

ii   SARAH RUSSELL WILKINS, b. 12 Jun 1813; d. at Middleton, 20 May 1887; m. at Middleton, 23 Feb 1832, STEPHEN EMERSON, b. at Topsfield, 1811 son of Stephen and Hannah (Thomas) Emerson; Stephen d. at Middleton, 6 Jul 1885.

iii NANCY WILKINS, b. 1816; d. 11 Oct 1819.

iv   ABIGAIL WILKINS, b. 8 Feb 1818; d. at Middleton, 17 Mar 1891; m. at Middleton, 19 Apr 1836, ADDISON TYLER, b. at Bradford, MA, 10 Aug 1813 son of Samuel and Fanny (Hardy) Tyler; Addison d. at Middleton, 8 Nov 1884.

v   NANCY WILKINS, b. 6 Apr 1820; d. at Salem, 9 Jun 1903; m. at Middleton, 26 Jan 1837, LEVI FISH, b. at Danvers, 5 Aug 1811 son of Levi and Betsey (Putnam) Fish; Levi d. at Danvers, 20 May 1876.

vi   CAROLINE WILKINS, b. 26 Jan 1822; d. at Stoneham, 23 Nov 1855; m. at Middleton, 23 Nov 1846, STEPHEN LYNDE, b. at Melrose, 25 Mar 1825 son of Stephen and Polly (Bucknam) Lynde; Stephen d. at Billerica, 16 Nov 1899.

vii FRANKLIN W. WILKINS, b. 25 Aug 1824; d. 24 Dec 1828.

viii JESSE WILKINS, b. 31 Jan 1826; d. 27 May 1826.

555) JOSEPH RUSSELL (*James⁴, Joseph³, Thomas², Robert¹*), b. at Middleton, MA, 14 Mar 1783 son of James and Rebecca (Peabody) Russell; d. at Lyndeborough, NH, 14 Mar 1827; m. at Lyndeborough, 13 Jan 1805, NAOMI WILKINS, b. at Amherst, NH, 16 May 1783 daughter of Aaron and Lydia (Smith) Wilkins; Naomi d. at Lyndeborough, 2 Jun 1869.[1583]

Joseph Russell had a farm at Johnson's Corner in Lyndeborough.[1584] Joseph Russell and Naomi Wilkins were parents of six children born at Lyndeborough.

i   BURNAM RUSSELL, b. 21 Oct 1805; d. at Lyndeborough, 22 Jun 1874; m. 29 Jan 1833, ELIZA KIDDER, b. at Lyndeborough, 14 Mar 1814 daughter of Ephraim and Betsey (Bofee) Kidder; Eliza d. at Lyndeborough, 27 Dec 1894.

ii   JAMES RUSSELL, b. 9 Nov 1806; d. at Amherst, NH, 30 Dec 1872; m. about 1835, MARY ANN SUTHERLAND, b. at London, England, 1805 daughter of Robert and Hannah (Wilson) Sutherland;[1585] Mary Ann d. at Amherst, 6 Dec 1888.

iii MARY RUSSELL, b. 9 Dec 1807; d. at Wilton, NH, 22 Oct 1879; m. at New Boston, NH, 17 Apr 1834, JOHN BOFEE KIDDER, b. at Lyndeborough, 16 Aug 1811 son of Ephraim and Betsey (Bofee) Kidder; John d. at Milford, NH, 2 Mar 1892.

iv   ORRIN S. RUSSELL, b. 19 Oct 1810; d. at Fitchburg, MA, 11 Jun 1880. Orrin did not marry.

v   AARON W. RUSSELL, b. 11 Feb 1815; d. at Quincy, MA, 6 Feb 1883; m. at Dedham, MA, 13 May 1840, ELSA O. PRESBY, b. at Bradford, NH, 12 Dec 1820 daughter of William B. and Sally (Watson) Presby; Elsa d. at Quincy, 12 Jan 1894.

vi   CLARA S. RUSSELL, b. 22 Nov 1822; d. 6 Sep 1824.

[1581] *Essex County, MA: Probate File Papers, 1638-1881.* Online database. *AmericanAncestors.org.* New England Historic Genealogical Society, 2014. Case 57218

[1582] The names of Ruth's parents are given as Thomas Parker and Esther Fuller on her death record.

[1583] Donovan, *The History of the Town of Lyndeborough,* p 848

[1584] Donovan, *The History of the Town of Lyndeborough,* p 848

[1585] Names of parents are as given on her death record, Robert Sutherland and Hannah Wilson.

556)   JAMES RUSSELL (*James⁴, Joseph³, Thomas², Robert¹*), b. at Boxford, MA, 4 Oct 1787 son of James and Rebecca (Peabody) Russell; d. of cholera at Lowell, 5 Sep 1849; m. at Lyndeborough, 18 Aug 1816, HANNAH PEABODY, b. at Middleton, 6 Feb 1793 daughter of Nathaniel and Ruth (Elliott) Peabody; Hannah d. at Lowell, 12 Feb 1881.

      Capt. James Russell did not leave a will and Cyril French, Esq. was named administrator on 14 September 1849 at the request of the widow and all the heirs-at-law who were age twenty-one above and these were widow Hannah Russell, William H. Hardy and Mary J. Hardy, Charles Going and Hannah Going, and William Berry and Ruth P. Berry.[1586] Minor children James, Harriet M., and Merriam above fourteen selected Sewell G. Mack trader of Lowell as guardian. Hannah Russell requested that Sewell Mack be named guardian for daughter Senaith A. who was under fourteen.[1587] Personal estate was valued at $4,342.09 much of it in the form of notes owed the estate. Real estate was 1900 feet of land with buildings on the corner of Lowell and Cabbot (sic) Streets in Lowell valued at $9,000, 2300 feet of land on Merrimack street valued at $500 and saltmarsh in Cambridgeport valued at $1,000. Debts of the estate were $12,046.57 and real estate was sold to settle the debts.

      James and Hannah were parents of nine children.

i   MARY JANE RUSSELL, b. at Lyndeborough, 5 Dec 1816; d. at Lowell, 22 Nov 1855; m. at Lowell, 27 Apr 1845, WILLIAM H. HARDY, b. at Lyman, NH, 14 Jul 1820 son of Theodore and Nancy Jane (Davis) Hardy; William d. at Wayland, MA, 24 Mar 1889. William married Wilhelmina Burpee on 25 Aug 1862.

ii   RUTH P. RUSSELL, b. at Lyndeborough, 19 Dec 1818; d. 14 Feb 1820.

iii   RUTH PEABODY RUSSELL, b. 12 Feb 1821; d. at Middleton, MA, 20 Nov 1911; m. 1st at Georgetown, MA, 11 May 1839, WILLIAM BERRY. Ruth m. 2nd at Lawrence, 2 Dec 1858, HIRAM ABBOTT STILES, b. at Middleton, 10 May 1822 son of David and Nancy (Farnum) Stiles; Hiram d. at Middleton, 10 Dec 1907. Hiram was first married to Emeline Russell.

iv   HANNAH RUSSELL, b. at Lyndeborough, 30 Dec 1823; d. at Lowell, 21 Nov 1883; m. CHARLES GOING, b. in ME, 16 Feb 1819 (date on gravestone) son of James and Abigail (-) Going; Charles d. at Lowell, 7 Apr 1879.

v   ELIZA ANN RUSSELL, b. at Lowell, 20 Jun 1826; d. at Lowell, 31 Oct 1854; m. at Lowell, 19 Dec 1851, HENRY H. SMITH, b. at New Ipswich, NH, about 1830 son of George W. and Lydia (-) Smith;[1588] Henry d. at Lowell, 7 Jan 1890.

vi   JAMES RUSSELL, b. at Lowell, 2 Jun 1829; d. at Lowell, 30 Sep 1862. James is listed as married on his death record, but the name of his wife was not found. James served as a wagoner with the 26th Infantry during the Civil War and was discharged at New Orleans 12 Aug 1862 due to disability.[1589]

vii   HARRIET MARIA RUSSELL, b. at Lowell, 1 Jan 1832; d. at Lowell, 27 Nov 1879. Harriet did not marry.

viii   MERRIAM IRENE RUSSELL, b. at Lowell, 13 Feb 1834; d. at Middleton, MA, 25 Jan 1903. Merriam did not marry.

ix   ASENATH AUGUSTA RUSSELL, b. at Lowell, 6 Oct 1836; d. at Lowell, 13 Jun 1892; m. at Lowell, 9 Oct 1854, SYLVESTER A. JONES, b. at North Adams, 13 Oct 1835 son of Dexter and Lucretia (-) Jones; Sylvester d. at Lowell, 14 Feb 1913.

557)   PEABODY RUSSELL (*James⁴, Joseph³, Thomas², Robert¹*), b. at Boxford, MA, 2 Dec 1789 son of James and Rebecca (Peabody) Russell; d. at Boxford, 14 Aug 1846; m. at Middleton, 17 Jan 1817, DOLLY KENNEY, b. at Middleton, 6 Nov 1785 daughter of Archelaus and Elizabeth (-) Kenney; Dolly d. at Boxford, 1 Jul 1845.

      Peabody Russell's estate entered probate 1 September 1846 with Daniel Russell as administrator. In his petition for administration, Daniel stated there was no widow, he was the only son, and there was one daughter. Real estate was valued at $1,870, $1,720 for the homestead and buildings and $150 for Gould meadows. Personal estate was $834.41.[1590]

      Peabody and Dolly were parents of two children.

i   ELIZABETH STEARNS RUSSELL, b. at Boxford, 4 Dec 1817; d. at Beverly, MA, 24 Oct 1890; m. at Boxford, 28 May 1840, ANDREW PEABODY AVERILL, b. at Middleton, 5 Jun 1815 son of Benjamin and Hannah (Peabody) Averill; Andrew d. at Middleton, 19 Dec 1889.

[1586] *Middlesex County, MA: Probate File Papers, 1648-1871.*Online database. *AmericanAncestors.org.* New England Historic Genealogical Society, 2014. Case 40917

[1587] *Middlesex County, MA: Probate File Papers, 1648-1871.*Online database. *AmericanAncestors.org.* New England Historic Genealogical Society, 2014. Case 40918

[1588] Names of Henry's parents are given as George W. and Lydia on the marriage register.

[1589] U.S., Civil War Soldier Records and Profiles, 1861-1865

[1590] *Essex County, MA: Probate File Papers, 1638-1881.*Online database. *AmericanAncestors.org.* New England Historic Genealogical Society, 2014. Case 52338

ii   DANIEL RUSSELL, b. at Boxford, 25 Jun 1820; d. at Boxford, 2 Dec 1878; m. at Boxford, 19 Jan 1843, HARRIET W. FOSTER, b. at Mansfield, MA, 19 Jan 1823 daughter of Perez and Harriet (Williams) Foster; Harriet d. at Danvers, 10 Jul 1889.

558)   MARY "POLLY" RUSSELL (*James⁴, Joseph³, Thomas², Robert¹*), b. at Boxford, 15 Apr 1792 daughter of James and Rebecca (Russell) Peabody; d. at North Reading, 11 Oct 1884; m. at Middleton, 30 Oct 1813, FRANCIS PEABODY, b. at Middleton, 12 Feb 1793 son of Francis and Lucy (Masury) Peabody; Francis d. at Middleton, 16 Feb 1866.

Francis Peabody was a shoemaker in Middleton. In 1860, Francis and Mary were living in the household of their daughter Sally Goodwin who was widowed at that time.[1591]

Polly Russell and Francis Peabody were parents of ten children.

i   FRANCIS PEABODY, b. at Boxford, 16 Jan 1814; d. at North Reading, 9 Nov 1905; m. 31 Dec 1858, ROXANA L. LITTLEFIELD (widow of John Trask), b. at Sanford, ME, 20 Feb 1822 daughter of Ambrose and Susan (Roberts) Littlefield; Roxana d. at North Reading, 13 Dec 1894.

ii   JAMES PEABODY, b. at Boxford, 11 Aug 1815; d. at North Reading, 13 Sep 1891; m. at Reading, 14 Dec 1837, his fourth cousin, SUSAN AUGUSTA SHELDON (*Daniel Sheldon⁵, Russell Sheldon⁴, Phebe Russell Sheldon³, John², Robert¹*), b. at Boston, 1820 daughter of Daniel and Phebe (Eaton) Sheldon; Susan d. at North Reading, 16 May 1894.

iii   DANIEL PEABODY, b. at Middleton, 27 Sep 1817; d. at Alton, NH, 1 Jul 1903; m. 1st 6 Feb 1844, SARAH S. CLARKE, b. at Danvers, 10 Apr 1815 daughter of Samuel and Nancy P. (Cross) Clarke; Sarah d. at Middleton, 24 Apr 1858. Daniel m. 2nd at Newburyport, 21 Mar 1859, his second cousin, MARTHA ENDICOTT GILMAN (*Abigail Putnam Gilman⁵, Hannah Russell Putnam⁴, Joseph³, Thomas², Robert¹*), b. at Hallowell, ME, 10 Apr 1817 daughter of John K. and Abigail (Putnam) Gilman; Martha d. at Stoneham, MA, 19 Mar 1889.

iv   OSGOOD PEABODY, b. at Danvers, 7 Jun 1819; d. at Stow, MA, 6 Nov 1880; m. 1st at Walpole, MA, 7 Aug 1841, FANNY M. RHODES, b. at Sharon, MA, 6 Nov 1817 daughter of Nathaniel and Fanny (Bishop) Rhodes; Fanny d. at Marquette, MI, 7 Jun 1861. Osgood m. 2nd, at Salem, 12 Apr 1871, LUCY R. FARNHAM (his fifth cousin through Holt lines), b. at Salem, MA, 2 Feb 1826 daughter of Jonathan and Mary (Grove) Farnham; Lucy d. at Hudson, MA, 13 Mar 1888.

v   MARY ANN PEABODY, b. at Salem, 12 Jun 1821; d. at Danvers, 14 Jun 1866; m. at Middleton, 29 Dec 1842, JOSIAH ROSS, b. at Ipswich, 7 May 1820 son of Thomas and Abigail (Goodhue) Ross; Josiah d. at Danvers, 16 Jul 1882.

vi   OREN EDWARD PEABODY, b. at Salem, 25 Jan 1824; d. at Danvers, 25 Oct 1897; m. 1st at Newmarket, NH, 4 Jul 1847, OLIVE E. HOWARD, b. at Newmarket, about 1823; Olive d. at Newmarket, 19 Jun 1875. Oren m. 2nd 25 Dec 1877, ANN CATHERINE PERKINS, b. at Middleton, 19 Feb 1845 daughter of Joseph and Martha (Elliot) Perkins; Catherine d. at Beverly, 1921.

vii   SARAH P. PEABODY, b. at Middleton, 10 Jun 1827; d. at Salem, 31 Mar 1921 where she had been living with her daughter Sarah; m. at Middleton, 26 Nov 1846, JOHN R. GOODWIN, b. at Milton, NH, about 1827 son of James and Mary (Wakeham) Goodwin.[1592] Sarah m. 2nd at North Andover, 25 Aug 1860, JOHN GARDNER JOHNSON, b. at Andover, 23 Dec 1818 son of Stephen and Sarah (Foster) Johnson; John d. at Lawrence, 16 Nov 1902.

viii   REBECCA RUSSELL PEABODY, b. 5 Aug 1830; d. 22 Mar 1832.

ix   REBECCA RUSSELL PEABODY, b. 17 Jan 1832; d. at Danvers, 4 Oct 1914; m. 1st at Middleton, 10 Dec 1852, JAMES KELLY, b. at Dracut, about 1831 son of Samuel and Judith (Kelly) Kelly; James d. at North Reading, 26 Aug 1861. Rebecca m. 2nd at Boston, 13 May 1867, EDWARD AUGUSTUS MCINTIRE, b. about 1825 son of Edward and Joanna (-) McIntire.[1593] Rebecca m. 3rd at Middleton, 24 Dec 1874, JOHN E. LOCKE, b. at Wilmot, Nova Scotia, 25 Jun 1843[1594] son of James E. and Mercy (Marshall) Locke; John d. at North Reading, 13 Jan 1910.

x   JANE ALLEN PEABODY, b. 16 Jul 1836; d. 29 Jul 1845.

[1591] Year: 1860; Census Place: Middleton, Essex, Massachusetts; Page: 878; Family History Library Film: 803498

[1592] It is not clear when John Goodwin died. In 1850, Sarah and her two oldest children were living in Middleton with her parents Francis and Mary Peabody. In 1860, she was with her parents but then with three Goodwin children the youngest of whom was born in 1850.

[1593] Names of parents are given as Edward and Joanna on his marriage record.

[1594] This is the date of birth given on his naturalization petition; National Archives at Boston; Waltham, Massachusetts; ARC Title: Copies of Petitions and Records of Naturalization in New England Courts, 1939 - ca. 1942; NAI Number: 4752894; Record Group Title: Records of the Immigration and Naturalization Service, 1787-2

559)   SAMUEL RUSSELL (*James⁴, Joseph³, Thomas², Robert¹*), b. at Boxford, MA, 27 May 1799 son of James and Rebecca (Peabody) Russell; d. at Salem, 19 Apr 1831; m. at Salem, 26 May 1822, LYDIA BRIDGES PICKETT, b. at Rowley, 14 May 1798 daughter of Benjamin Scudder and Sarah (Bridges) Pickett;[1595] Lydia d. at Boston, 18 Apr 1841.

Samuel Russell was a laborer in Salem. Jonathan Kenny was named administrator of his estate on 17 May 1831. A distribution of the balance of the estate was made on 14 August 1832 with payment of $181 to each of the heirs: Lydia P. Russell, widow and children Samuel P. Russell and Harriet M. Russell. Lydia was named as guardian to her two children.[1596]

i   SAMUEL P. RUSSELL, b. at Salem, 1822; d. at Billerica, 17 Feb 1879; m. at Boxford, 25 Jun 1845, ELIZABETH MARIAH WELLS, b. at Danvers, 19 Nov 1825 daughter of Daniel and Elizabeth C. (Smith) Wells;[1597] Elizabeth d. at Lowell, 31 Oct 1849.

ii   HARRIET M. RUSSELL, b. 27 Sep 1826; d. at Denver, CO, 6 Feb 1908; m. at Ipswich, 6 Apr 1845, PHINEAS WARREN BARNES, b. at Boxford, 4 Apr 1822 son of Phineas and Sally (Spofford) Barnes;[1598] Phineas d. at Denver, 20 Mar 1900.

560)   IRA RUSSELL (*James⁴, Joseph³, Thomas², Robert¹*), b. at Boxford, MA, 21 Apr 1802 son of James and Rebecca (Peabody) Russell; d. at Manchester, NH, 1 Mar 1859; m. at Lowell, 14 Nov 1831, MARY JANE ALLEN, b. in NH, 1809; Mary Jane d. at Manchester, 3 Apr 1883.

Ira Russell and Mary Jane Allen were parents of five children.

i   IRA WARREN RUSSELL, b. at Lowell, 14 Feb 1834; d. 16 Apr 1837.

ii   GEORGE WASHINGTON RUSSELL, b. at Lowell, 27 Oct 1835; d. at Manchester, NH, 1838.

iii   MARY JANE RUSSELL, b. at Manchester, NH, 4 Feb 1839; d. at Hartford, CT, 2 Nov 1901; m. at Manchester, 24 Nov 1859, DAVID TILTON, b. at Meredith, NH, 29 Nov 1834 son of Newell and Alice (Clough) Tilton; David d. at Hartford, 26 Apr 1914. David Tilton was an inventor noted for development of a method for making screws. He was superintendent of Atlantic Screw Works in Hartford.[1599]

iv   IRA WARREN RUSSELL, b. at Manchester, 1840; d. at Concord, NH, 9 Feb 1878; m. about 1868, SUE E. BEAL, b. at Sanford, ME, 3 Jun 1839 daughter of Benjamin and Eunice (Hobbs) Beal;[1600] Sue d. at Sanford, ME, 30 Jul 1917. Sue married second Preston C. Lord in 1882. I. Warren served in the Civil War in Company D of the 7th New Hampshire infantry.[1601] He worked as a photographer.

v   GEORGE WASHINGTON RUSSELL, b. 1844; d. at Manchester, 4 Jul 1846.

561)   PETER RUSSELL (*James⁴, Joseph³, Thomas², Robert¹*), b. at Boxford, MA, 3 Oct 1805 son of James and Rebecca (Peabody) Russell; d. at Danvers, 14 Apr 1843; m. at Danvers, 20 Dec 1832, MEHITABLE P. DWINELL, b. at Danvers, 22 May 1805 daughter of Stephen and Mehitable (Putnam) Dwinell; Mehitable d. at Danvers, 5 Feb 1880.

Peter Russell was a laborer in Danvers. At the probate of his estate (2 May 1843), widow Mehitable requested that Joseph Shed be named administrator. She noted she had the care of two minor children. He had no real estate and personal estate was valued at $74.37.[1602]

The estate of Mehitable Russell entered probate 26 March 1880 with Mary E. Mudge requesting that her husband A. H. Mudge be named as administrator of her mother's estate. Mary was the only heir to the estate. House and land on Centre Street were valued at $700 and personal estate included $433.16 in Salem Bank and household furniture valued at $50.[1603]

[1595] The 1853 will (probate 1857) of Benjamin Scudder Pickett includes a bequest to the heirs of his daughter Lydia Russell deceased.
[1596] *Essex County, MA: Probate File Papers, 1638-1881.* Online database. *AmericanAncestors.org.* New England Historic Genealogical Society, 2014. Case 24420
[1597] The names of Elizabeth's parents are given on her death record.
[1598] Spofford, *Descendants of John Spofford and Elizabeth Scott, p 269*
[1599] "Inventors and Manufacturers in Hartford", *The Connecticut Magazine*, volume 9, 1905, p 915
[1600] The names of Sue's parents are given as Benjamin Beal and Eunice Lord on her death record; Maine State Archives; Cultural Building, 84 State House Station, Augusta, ME 04333-0084; 1908-1922 Vital Records; Roll Number: 34. The giving of mother's name as Lord may be a confusion with the name of Sue's second husband Samuel Lord.
[1601] Index to Compiled Service Records of Volunteer Union Soldiers Who Served in Organizations from the State of New Hampshire
[1602] *Essex County, MA: Probate File Papers, 1638-1881.* Online database. *AmericanAncestors.org.* New England Historic Genealogical Society, 2014. Case 52340
[1603] *Essex County, MA: Probate File Papers, 1638-1881.* Online database. *AmericanAncestors.org.* New England Historic Genealogical Society, 2014. Case 52336

Peter Russell and Mehitable Dwinell were parents of four children, the youngest child born seven months after Peter's death.

i   GEORGE HENRY RUSSELL, b. at Lowell; d. at Danvers, 8 Feb 1837

ii   SARAH JANE RUSSELL, b. at Danvers, 20 Jun 1839; d. 23 Mar 1855.

iii   MARY ELIZA RUSSELL, b. at Danvers, 21 Aug 1841; d. at Danvers, 13 Jan 1909; m. at Danvers, 6 Dec 1865, ALBERT HORACE MUDGE, b. at Danvers 20 Jun 1841 son of Josiah and Eliza A. F. (Skinner) Mudge; Albert d. at Danvers, 28 Feb 1911.

iv   ELIZABETH CHAMBERLAIN RUSSELL, b. at Danvers, 14 Nov 1843; d. 29 Aug 1847.

562)   LYDIA SYMONDS DWINELLS (*Rachel Russell Dwinells[4], Joseph[3], Thomas[2], Robert[1]*), b. at Middleton, MA, 28 Sep 1787 daughter of Jonathan and Rachel (Russell) Dwinnels; d. at Hillsborough, 27 Sep 1874; m. at Hillsborough, 25 Deb 1817, ADAM D. MILLS, b. at Deering, about 1790 son of Robert and Margaret (Dinsmoor) Mills;[1604] Adam d. at Deering, 30 Sep 1866. Lydia and Adam had five children who died in infancy[1605] and two children who lived to adulthood who are given here.

i   GAWN W. MILLS, b. at Deering, 30 Dec 1826; d. at Hillsborough (burial at Deering), 2 Nov 1899; m. about 1852, CLARA WILSON DICKEY, b. at Deering, 18 Mar 1826[1606] daughter of William and Mary (Wilson) Dickey; Clara d. at Peabody, MA (burial at Deering), 15 Sep 1915.

ii   ROBERT MILLS, b. at Deering, about 1829; d. at Dracut, 22 Nov 1903; m. at Dracut, 13 Apr 1856, FANNY W. COBURN, b. at Dracut, 27 Jul 1823 daughter of Peter and Mary (Varnum) Coburn; Fanny d. at Dracut, 22 Jul 1901.

563)   CHARLOTTE DWINELLS (*Rachel Russell Dwinells[4], Joseph[3], Thomas[2], Robert[1]*), b. at Middleton, 26 May 1789 daughter of Jonathan and Rachel (Russell) Dwinnels; d. after 1870 when she was living with her son Hiram at Hinsdale, NY; m. at Hillsborough, 8 Sep 1808, DANIEL WILEY who is not yet identified. Charlotte was a widow at least by 1855 and likely much before.

There is one child known for Charlotte Dwinells and Daniel Wiley.

i   HIRAM WILEY, b. at Hillsborough, 1809; d. at Somerville, MA, 11 Mar 1878; m. 1st, about 1830, HANNAH H. WRIGHT, b. in NY, about 1810; Hannah d. at Grand Detour, IL, about 1857. Hiram m. 2nd at Portsmouth, NH, 27 Nov 1858, FIDELIA BARTON, b. at Andover, VT, about 1809 daughter of Jeremiah and Diadama (Blood) Barton; Fidelia d. at Boston, 8 Sep 1894.

564)   JONATHAN DWINELLS (*Rachel Russell Dwinells[4], Joseph[3], Thomas[2], Robert[1]*), b. at Hillsborough, 10 Sep 1795 son of Jonathan and Rachel (Russell) Dwinnels; d. at Yorkshire, NY, 1881 (probate 16 May 1881); m. about 1823, ELIZABETH "BETSEY" ATWOOD, b. about 1795; Betsey d. at Yorkshire, 27 Sep 1880.

Jonathan and Betsey resided in Yorkshire, New York where Jonathan was a farmer. In 1850, the household consisted of Jonathan and Elizabeth and children Caroline age 26, Charlotte age 14, and Chandler age 14.[1607] In 1870, Jonathan and Betsey were living with son Chandler and his wife Lucy.[1608]

The family experienced tragedy when daughter Charlotte Ann, who was pregnant, was murdered by her husband and father-in-law on 29 July 1860. "On Sunday, July 29, in Yorkshire, Cattaraugus county, the wife of James Wheat was found dead. Her husband was declared guilty of murder by the Coroner's jury. Wednesday he was conveyed to jail in Ellicottville, and yesterday he disclosed to the neighbors who visited him, the fact that his father and mother assisted him, the father strangling the victim with a handkerchief. The deceased was enceinte. Great excitement prevails."[1609] James Wheat was sentenced to life in prison for second degree murder and was imprisoned at Auburn Prison. He was released after serving 20 years.[1610]

In his will written 13 October 1875 (probate 16 May 1881), Jonathan Dwinels, of Yorkshire age 80, bequeathed to granddaughter Grace Clark the featherbed that had been her mother's. Son C. S. Dwinels receives his razor. Daughter Sally Barus (or Barnes) receives one dollar. The remainder of the estate is to be divided between his two daughters Emma Jane

---

[1604] Adam's death record gives the names of his parents as Robert and Margaret Mills.

[1605] Hurd, *History of Hillsborough County, New Hampshire*, p 387

[1606] Date of birth is engraved on gravestone.

[1607] Year: 1850; Census Place: Yorkshire, Cattaraugus, New York; Roll: M432_480; Page: 469B; Image: 309

[1608] Year: 1870; Census Place: Yorkshire, Cattaraugus, New York; Roll: M593_909; Page: 576A; Family History Library Film: 552408

[1609] "Wife Murder in Yorkshire, N.Y.", *New York Herald* (New York, NY), August 8, 1860, p 1

[1610] New York, Governor's Registers of Commitments to Prisons, 1842-1908, volume 2, Auburn Prison

Bosworth and Caroline Rose. George H. Whiting of Yorkshire was named executor.[1611] The accounting of George H. Whiting on 23 May 1883 showed a residue of the estate of $47.06 with $23.53 each distributed to Emma Jane Bosworth and Caroline Rose.[1612]

There is evidence of seven children of Jonathan and Betsey Dwinells.

i   EMMA JANE DWINELLS, b. about 1822; d. after 1880 when living at Carrollton, NY; m. AMASA BOSWORTH, b. in NY, about 1821; Amsaa d. at Carrollton, 31 Jan 1875.

ii   CAROLINE DWINELLS, b. 1824; d. at Rushford, NY, about 1891; m. about 1852, NELSON ROSE, b. in NY, about 1812; Nelson d. at Rushford, 15 Dec 1896. Nelson was first married to Mary Ann Richardson.

iii   PARKER K. DWINELLS, b. 1827; d. at Delevan, NY, 6 Jul 1854.[1613]

iv   KATE DWINELLS, b. 1829; d. (burial at Delevan, NY), 15 Oct 1860; m. ENOS CLARK, b. in NY, Nov 1820; Enos d. after 1910 when he was living with his daughter from his second marriage. In 1908, he was at the almshouse/poorhouse in Genesee County, NY.[1614] Kate is the assumed mother of Grace Clark mentioned in the will of Jonathan Dwinells. Kate Clark wife of Enos (on gravestone), age at death of 31, is buried in McKinstry Cemetery with other members of the Dwinells family. Buried with her is an 11-week old daughter.[1615] Kate married to Enos Clark was living in Oakfield, NY in 1860 (census 22 June 1860) with daughter Grace age 1 and daughter Meda age one month.[1616] Enos had a second marriage to Ella Johnson. Daughter Grace Clark married Jeremiah Card and died at Yorkshire, NY 1 Jun 1925.

v   SALLY DWINELLS, b. about 1830; m. Mr. Barus. No clear information was found for Sally.

vi   CHARLOTTE ANN DWINELLS, b. 13 May 1836; d. at Machias, NY, 29 Jul 1860 murdered by her husband; m. about 1860, JAMES WHEAT, b. at Hartford, OH, 6 Sep 1838 son of Salmon and Rosanna (Hills) Wheat; James d. at Preston, NY, 25 Aug 1912. James had a second marriage in 1879 to Nancy M. Clupper.

vii   CHANDLER S. DWINELLS, b. at Yorkshire, NY, 4 Sep 1840; d. at Allegany, NY, 1904; m. 1868, LUCY EMMALINE CARD, b. Feb 1846 daughter of Ray and Amy (·) Card; Lucy d. at Allegany, NY, 5 May 1902. C. S. Dwinells was a farmer, then a teacher, and was later a druggist in Yorkshire. He then studied law and was admitted to the bar in 1883.[1617]

565)   JAMES DWINELLS (*Rachel Russell Dwinells⁴, Joseph³, Thomas², Robert¹*), b. at Hillsborough, 28 Jun 1800 son of Jonathan and Rachel (Russell) Dwinnels; d. at West Canaan, NH, 17 Dec 1859; m. at Hillsborough, 22 Feb 1832, LOUISA R. CRAIN, b. at Hillsborough, 24 Mar 1806 daughter of Joshua and Sarah (Giddings) Crain; Louisa d. at West Canaan, 18 Oct 1857. Louisa's father Dr. Joshua Crain was a physician and surgeon in Hillsborough.[1618]

i   JULIANNA C. DWINELLS, b. at Hillsborough, 23 Feb 1833; d. at Canaan, NH, 14 Nov 1913; m. 1859, MOSES ELIAS WITHINGTON, b. at Hanover, NH, 28 Jan 1828 son of Francis and Joanna (Fitz) Withington;[1619] Moses d. at Hanover, 14 Jun 1900.

ii   CHARLES W. DWINELLS, b. at Hillsborough, 25 Aug 1834; d. at Canaan, NH, 3 Apr 1912; m. 1st about 1865, ALBINA L. RICHARDSON, b. about 1844; Albina d. at Canaan, 1874. Charles m. 2nd at Canaan, 3 Apr 1876, JULIA A. MORRILL (widow of George H. Richardson), b. in OH, Oct 1837 daughter of Samuel and Lucy (Greely) Morrill; Julia d. 1902.

iii   GEORGE DWINELLS, b. 18 Oct 1835; d. 25 Feb 1841.

iv   SARAH C. DWINELLS, b. at Hillsborough, 23 Mar 1837; d. at Canaan, 28 Jun 1868; m. at Enfield, 5 Feb 1868, STEPHEN HADLEY, b. at Canaan, 17 Oct 1835 son of Luther and Sarah (Marshall) Hadley; Stephen d. at Reading, MA, 16 Oct 1912. Stephen married Mira Bithrow on 3 Jul 1870.

v   CHARLOTTE C. DWINELLS, b. 27 Jun 1839; d. 23 Feb 1841.

[1611] New York Probate Records, Cattaraugus County, volume 7, pp 753-756; accessed through familysearch.org

[1612] New York Wills and Probate, Cattaraugus County, minutes volume 0014, pp 226-227

[1613] Findagrave ID: 25821082, McKinstry Cemetery, Delevan, NY

[1614] New York State Archives; Albany, New York; Census of Inmates in Almshouses and Poorhouses, 1875-1921; Series: A1978; Reel: A1978:38; Record Number: 743

[1615] Findagrave ID: 25821051, McKinstry Cemetery

[1616] Year: 1860; Census Place: Oakfield, Genesee, New York; Page: 748; Family History Library Film: 803756

[1617] Adams, *Historical Gazetteer of and Biographical Memorial of Cattaraugus County*, p 406

[1618] Browne, *The History of Hillsborough*, p 154

[1619] The names of Moses's parents are given as Francis Withington and Joanna Fitz on his death record.

566)   JAMES RUSSELL PUTNAM (*Hannah Russell Putnam⁴, Joseph³, Thomas², Robert¹*), b. at Topsham, ME, 11 Nov 1789 son of Caleb and Hannah (Russell) Putnam; d. at Vicksburg, MS, 1 Apr 1843;[1620] m. in Davidson County, TN, 24 May 1822, SOPHIA ANN PERKINS, b. about 1802; Sophia d. at New Orleans, 1851.
      Dr. James R. Russell was a dentist and inventor of dental instruments. The family resided in New Orleans, although James died while he was in Vicksburg. In the 1840 census at New Orleans, the household of J. R. Russell consisted of seven persons: one male 40-49, one female 30-39, one male 5 to 9, one male 15 to 19, and two females 5 to 9.[1621]
      There are two confirmed children of James and Sophia although there are likely others.

i   JAMES MERCIER PUTNAM, b. 1823; d. at New Orleans, LA, 27 Jul 1887; m. about 1845, MARY SPEARING, b. at New Orleans, 6 May 1824 daughter of Henry and Mary (Farmer) Spearing; Mary d. at Hot Springs, AR, 12 Feb 1908.

ii   EMMETT PUTNAM, b. at New Orleans, 6 Dec 1834; d. at New Orleans, 8 Dec 1871; m. about 1858, AMELIA MUMFORD PALFREY, b. at New Orleans, Jan 1838 daughter of Robert Jenkins and Camilla (Davis) Palfrey; Amelia d. at New Orleans, 16 Jul 1907. Emmett served with Confederate forces in the 5th company of Washington Battalion, Louisiana Artillery. He entered the service with rank of corporal and was discharged with rank of sergeant.[1622]

567)   CHARLES CALEB PUTNAM (*Hannah Russell Putnam⁴, Joseph³, Thomas², Robert¹*), b. about 1790 son of Caleb and Hannah (Russell) Putnam; d. at Canton, MS, 1862; m. at Washington, DC, MARGARET MURDOCH, b. 4 Jul 1805 daughter of John and Ann (Corby) Murdoch;[1623] Margaret d. at Orleans, LA, 13 Apr 1886.
      Charles Putnam was an attorney who practice in Washington, DC and later in Tennessee and Mississippi. Charles and Margaret were parents of likely seven children.

i   JOHN MURDOCH PUTNAM, b. at Washington, DC, Nov 1821; d. at Pass Christian, MS, 15 Sep 1908; m. at Madison County, AL, 7 Apr 1847, SOPHRONIA LEE FEARN, b. at Huntsville, AL, 1 Sep 1827 daughter of George R. and Elizabeth (Burrus) Fearn; Sophronia d. at Memphis, 12 Jun 1922.

ii   HANNAH PUTNAM, b. at Washington, DC, 1823; d. at Bold Spring, TN, 1922; m. at Grainger County, TN, 21 Nov 1838, WILLIAM ROBERT KLINE, b. in TN, about 1816.

iii   JAMES RUSSELL PUTNAM, b. in TN 1825; d. 1864; m. 1st 24 Nov 1853, ELIZABETH M. BURRELL who d. 31 Aug 1856 (burial at Vicksburg, MS). James m. 2nd about 1862, MARGARET E. CLEMENT, b. 1844; Margaret d. at St. Helena, LA, 5 Jul 1917. Margaret married second Francis Brewer Watkins.

iv   OSCAR PUTNAM, b. about 1827; d. at Washington, DC, 1865.

v   SAMUEL PUTNAM, b. Oct 1831; d. at Vicksburg, MS, about 1920; m. at Warren, MS, 21 Nov 1854, MARGARET MOORE, b. in MS, Aug 1835; Margaret d. at Vicksburg, 1910.

vi   BRUCE PUTNAM, b. about 1834; d. after 1880 when living at Point Coupee, LA; m. about 1880, KATIE WOOD, b. in England, about 1864 (according to the 1880 census). He may be the Bruce Putnam who served as 2nd Lieutenant and later Adjutant of the 1st Special Battalion of Louisiana Infantry during the Civil War.[1624]

vii   WILLIAM MYNATT PUTNAM, b. about 1836; d. at Madison, MS, 1880; m. at Mobile, AL, 12 Feb 1866, ANNIE T. PHILLIPS, b. at Mobile, AL, 1845 likely daughter of James and Susan (-) Phillips. William was a railroad conductor as listed in the 1860 census when he was living with his parents in Canton, MS.[1625]

568)   ABIGAIL PUTNAM (*Hannah Russell Putnam⁴, Joseph³, Thomas², Robert¹*), b. perhaps at Lyme, NH, about 1793 daughter of Caleb and Hannah (Russell) Putnam; m. at Hallowell, ME, 4 Apr 1813, JOHN KINSMAN GILMAN, b. at Exeter, NH, 14 Aug 1787 son of Samuel and Martha (Kinsman) Gilman.
      There are records of four children of Abigail and John.

[1620] U.S., Newspaper Extractions from the Northeast, 1704-1930; Dr. James R. Putnam, death in Vicksburg, reported in New York Evening Post, 14 April 1843
[1621] Year: 1840; Census Place: New Orleans Ward 1, Orleans, Louisiana; Roll: 132; Page: 14; Family History Library Film: 0009691
[1622] National Park Service, U.S. Civil War Soldiers, 1861-1865
[1623] The 1820 will of John Murdoch of Washington, DC gives Margaret's date of birth and the maiden name of her mother.
[1624] U.S. Civil War Soldiers, 1861-1865
[1625] Year: 1860; Census Place: Canton, Madison, Mississippi; Page: 789; Family History Library Film: 803586

i   MARTHA ENDICOTT GILMAN, b. at Hallowell, 3 Dec 1815; died young

ii   MARTHA ENDICOTT GILMAN, b. at Hallowell, 10 Apr 1817; d. at Stoneham, MA, 19 Mar 1889; m. at Newburyport, 21 Mar 1859, as his second wife, her second cousin, DANIEL PEABODY (*Mary Russell Peabody⁵, James⁴, Joseph³, Thomas², Robert¹*), b. at Middleton, MA, 27 Sep 1817 son of Francis and Mary (Russell) Peabody; Daniel d. at Alton, NH, 1 Jul 1903. Daniel was first married to Sarah S. Clarke.

iii   SAMUEL K. GILMAN, b. at Portsmouth, NH, 22 Sep 1818; d. at Newburyport, MA, 8 Dec 1884; m. at Newburyport, 11 May 1848, LUCY ANN MORRISON WILSON, b. at Derry, NH, Dec 1817 daughter of James and Betsey (Warner) Morrison;[1626] Lucy d. at Newburyport, 26 Mar 1905. Lucy's father was a ship captain lost at sea in a gale off the coast of Cape Cod in Dec 1820.[1627] Her mother remarried to Albert Wilson, and Lucy took the last name of her stepfather.

iv   ABBY MARGARET MURDOCH GILMAN, b. at Newburyport, MA, 30 Nov 1820; d. at Hallowell, 28 Jan 1829.

569)   DEBORAH PUTNAM (*Hannah Russell Putnam⁴, Joseph³, Thomas², Robert¹*), b. at Lyme, about 1797 daughter of Caleb and Hannah (Russell) Putnam; d. at Newburyport, 1 Sep 1877; m. at Newburyport, 24 May 1825, WILLIAM GREELEY.
     In 1850, Deborah Putnam was head of household in Newburyport with children George age 22 and James P. age 17 living with her.[1628] In 1860, she was living with her sister Hannah Putnam in Newburyport.[1629] The identity of William Greeley is not certain, but he may be the William Greeley who was a debtor and at the poor farm in Haverhill in 1865 and 1870.[1630] William is listed as married on the poor farm census.[1631] If this records are for this William Greeley, he was born at Haverhill, 1800 son of Clement and Hannah (Moody) Greeley and died at the poor farm in Haverhill, 18 September 1870.
     There are two children known for Deborah and William.

i   GEORGE ENDICOTT GREELEY, b. in NH, about 1828; d. at Newburyport, MA, 23 Jun 1909; m. 1ˢᵗ at Boston, 7 May 1853, ELIZA J. SMALL, b. at Newburyport, 1834 daughter of James and Hannah (Lunt) Small; Eliza d. at Newburyport, 30 Jun 1864. George m. 2ⁿᵈ 1865, SUSANNA M. PERKINS, b. at Newbury, 21 Aug 1831 daughter of William and Sarah (Harris) Perkins; Susanna d. at Newbury, 12 Aug 1866. George m. 3ʳᵈ, at Middleton, MA, 30 Mar 1867, CARRIE MARION PEABODY, b. at Bangor, about 1842 daughter of Samuel and Marion (-) Peabody; Carrie d. at Newburyport, 12 Jun 1898.

ii   JAMES PUTNAM GREELEY, b. at East Haverhill, MA, 29 Dec 1832; d. at Newbury, MA, 21 Apr 1909; m. 1ˢᵗ at Newbury, 22 Oct 1856, ELLEN JANE TILTON, b. at Newbury, 30 Nov 1839 daughter of Parker and Tamson (Peavey) Tilton; Ellen d. at Newbury, 6 Apr 1914. Ellen and James divorced about 1868, Ellen resumed the use of her maiden name, and her name was legally changed from Ellen J. Greeley to Ellen J. Tilton.[1632] Ellen later married George C. Martin. James m. 2ⁿᵈ at Newbury, 26 May 1879, GEORGIANNA MARIA RUSSELL, b. at Newbury, 4 Sep 1835 daughter of Samuel Perkins and Nancy (Knight) Russell; Georgianna d. at Newburyport, 19 Feb 1915.

570)   BENJAMIN FRANKLIN PUTNAM (*Hannah Russell Putnam⁴, Joseph³, Thomas², Robert¹*), b. about 1800 son of Caleb and Hannah (Russell) Putnam; d. at Boston, 5 Jan 1845; m. at Portsmouth, NH, 14 May 1824, NANCY MELCHER, b. at Portsmouth, about 1799 daughter of Nathaniel and Elizabeth (Ward) Melcher;[1633] Nancy d. at Boston, 6 Jul 1856.
     Benjamin and Nancy seem to have moved frequently. They married in Portsmouth, were in Saco and Portland, Maine, Benjamin died in Boston in 1845, Nancy and her children were in Portsmouth in 1850,[1634] but then returned to Boston. Benjamin and Nancy were parents of seven known children.

i   JAMES RUSSELL PUTNAM, b. 2 Apr 1825; d. at Boston, 10 Jun 1905; m. at Boston, 21 Oct 1849, MARY JANE MULLEN, b. at Dipper Harbor, New Brunswick, Feb 1828 daughter of George and Ann (Dawson) Mullen;[1635] Mary Jane d. at Boston, 15 Nov 1903.

[1626] Adams, *The Descendants of James and William Adams of Londonderry*, p 77

[1627] Adams, *The Descendants of James and William Adams of Londonderry*, p 77

[1628] Year: 1850; Census Place: Newburyport, Essex, Massachusetts; Roll: M432_313; Page: 403A; Image: 318

[1629] Year: 1860; Census Place: Newburyport Ward 2, Essex, Massachusetts; Page: 316; Family History Library Film: 803496

[1630] Year: 1870; Census Place: Haverhill Ward 4, Essex, Massachusetts; Roll: M593_608; Page: 711B; Family History Library Film: 552107

[1631] Massachusetts, State Census, 1865

[1632] Massachusetts, Name Changes, 1780-1892; ancestry.com

[1633] The names of Nancy's parents are given as Nathaniel and Elizabeth Melcher on her death record.

[1634] Year: 1850; Census Place: Portsmouth, Rockingham, New Hampshire; Roll: 437; Page: 23b

[1635] The names of Mary Jane's parents are given as George Mullin and Ann Dawson on her death record which also provides place of birth.

ii   ANN PUTNAM, b. at Saco, 1827; d. at Portland, 1831.

iii   ABBY M. PUTNAM, b. at Saco, 1829; d. at Boston, MA, 28 Jun 1860; m. at Boston, MA, 9 Apr 1848, HENRY N. PHELPS, b. in CT or NY (census records), about 1821; Henry d. at Boston, 22 Sep 1857. Henry Phelps was a carpenter.

iv   HANNAH PUTNAM, b. in ME, 1832; d. at Newton, MA, 6 Mar 1900; m. at Boston, 4 Jul 1869, as his second wife, SAMUEL FRANKLIN, b. at Needham, 1815 son of Samuel and Phebe (-) Franklin; Samuel d. at Newton, 2 Aug 1897. Samuel was first married to Charlotte Lowe.

v   MARY E. PUTNAM, b. at Portland, ME, 1834; d. at Reading, MA, 15 Mar 1886; m. at Boston, 29 Jul 1855, CHARLES E. DAME, b. at Portsmouth, NH, about 1828 son of Nathaniel B. and Mary (Mitchell) Dame; Charles d. at Boston, 27 Sep 1899.

vi   ANN E. PUTNAM, b. at Portsmouth, NH, 1836; d. at Boston, 19 Feb 1861. Ann did not marry.

vii   BENJAMIN PUTNAM, b. 1839; d. at Boston, 22 Sep 1858.

viii   NATHANIEL MELCHER PUTNAM, b. at Hampton, NH, 28 Apr 1841; d. at Hyde Park, MA, 5 Sep 1891; m. at Boston, 28 Aug 1864, HARRIET E. MEANS, b. at Blue Hill, ME, about 1842 daughter of Otis W. and Elsie F. (Berry) Means; Harriet d. at Boston, 20 Jul 1892.

571)   JEMIMA JOHNSON (*Sarah Hunt Johnson⁴, Jemima Russell Hunt³, Thomas², Robert¹*), b. at Montague, 2 May 1757 daughter of Josiah and Sarah (Hunt) Johnson; *perhaps* m. at Newton, NH, 5 Apr 1784, ARCHELAUS COLBY, b. at Newton, 24 Mar 1762 son of Moses and Mary (Sargent) Colby; Archelaus d. at Dunbarton, 20 Feb 1827.
        Jemima and Archelaus resided in Dunbarton. Archelaus was one of about 45 residents who in 1796 protested the assessment of a minister's tax for the salary of Rev. Mr. Harris as they were not members of the same religion as Mr. Harris.
        Both Jemima and Archelaus suffered accidental deaths. Archelaus died when he fell through the ice on Kimball's pond and drowned. Jemima wandered from home "while insane" and died in the woods. Here skeletal remains were found by hunters near Goffstown several months after she went missing.[1636]
        Jemima and Archelaus were parents of four children born at Dunbarton. There were likely one or two other children.

i   SALLY COLBY, b. 11 Oct 1784

ii   MARTH "PATTY" COLBY, b. 1786; d. at Dunbarton, 31 Mar 1861; m. at Goffstown, 13 Feb 1806, TIMOTHY MCINTIRE, b. 1773 son of Timothy and Mehitable (Wells) McIntire; Timothy d. at Dunbarton, 1844.

iii   JOHNSON COLBY, b. 1791; d. at Boston, 1856; m. 1ˢᵗ at Boston, 30 Jun 1822, ANN THOMPSON, b. about 1793; Ann d. at Boston, 1826. Johnson m. 2ⁿᵈ at Boston, 16 May 1828, ELIZABETH HOWE, b. at Ipswich, 1797 daughter of Joseph and Mehitable (Stickney) Howe; Elizabeth d. at Boston, 7 Sep 1870.

iv   NATHANIEL COLBY, b. 28 Jul 1798; d. at Dunbarton, 22 Mar 1872; m. at Dunbarton, 2 Aug 1827, HEPHZIBAH WOODBURY, b. 13 Oct 1804 daughter of Hasadiah and Hephzibah (Colby) Woodbury; Hephzibah d. at Dunbarton, 6 Aug 1874. Nathaniel was selectman in Dunbarton.

572)   JOSEPH JOHNSON (*Sarah Hunt Johnson⁴, Jemima Russell Hunt³, Thomas², Robert¹*), b. at Montague, 21 Jan 1761 son of Josiah and Sarah (Hunt) Johnson; m. 1ˢᵗ about 1785, MARY HUNT; Mary d. at Charlestown, NH, about 1796. Joseph m. 2ⁿᵈ about 1797, ANNA who has not been identified.
        Joseph and Mary were parents of six children born at Charlestown, New Hampshire.[1637]

i   SETH JOHNSON, b. 23 Apr 1786; d. (burial at Antrim, MI), 16 Deb 1856 at age 69 years, 10 months;[1638] m. by 1809, HANNAH who may be Hannah Collins, b. in Vermont in 1788 daughter of Solomon and Lucy (-) Collins.

ii   BULKLEY JOHNSON, b. 17 Feb 1788

iii   JOSIAH JOHNSON, b. 6 Oct 1789

iv   JOSEPH HUNT JOHNSON, b. 15 Jul 1791

v   EMMA JOHNSON, b. 13 Jul 1793

vi   MARY JOHNSON, b. 7 Jun 1795

[1636] Stark, *History of the Town of Dunbarton*, p 24, p 162
[1637] New Hampshire, Birth Records, 1659-1900; ancestry.com
[1638] Findagrave ID: 48686563

Joseph and Anna were parents of one child.

i   POLLY JOHNSON, b. 23 Aug 1797

573)   JEREMIAH JOHNSON (*Sarah Hunt Johnson⁴, Jemima Russell Hunt³, Thomas², Robert¹*), b. at Montague, 16 Sep 1763[1639] son of Josiah and Sarah (Hunt) Johnson; d. at Reading, VT, 2 Dec 1847; m. 1st at Charlestown, NH, THOMAZIN "FANNY" BLANCHARD, b. at Quincy, MA, 20 Sep 1765 daughter of Nehemiah and Mary (Gibson) Blanchard; Fanny d. at Reading, 10 Dec 1824. Jeremiah m. 2nd about 1826, SYBIL KIMBALL; Sybil d. at Mineral Point, WI, 1852 where she had been living with her son Solon Kimball Johnson.[1640]

Jeremiah and his wife Thomazin were in Charlestown, New Hampshire after their marriage and in Windsor County, Vermont about 1791. The family was in Springfield, Vermont in 1810 with a household of six: one male over 45, one female over 45, two males under 10, one male 10 to 15, and one female 10 to 15.[1641]

Jeremiah served in the Revolution and the War of 1812. On 24 April 1818, Jeremiah Johnson age fifty-four and resident of Reading, Vermont provided a statement related to his application for pension. About 1 March 1781 from the town of Keene, he enlisted in the company of Capt. Moody Dustin in the 1st regiment of the New Hampshire line. A statement by Martha Johnson, widow of Jeremiah's brother Thomas, notes that Jeremiah enlisted as a substitute for his brother Thomas. Jeremiah served until the last of May or first of June 1782 when he was discharged at Saratoga. He was awarded a pension of $96 per annum. On 1 August 1820, he provided additional information on his circumstances. He had no property except the clothing he and his wife wore. For the past five years, he had been totally dependent on his son-in-law Robert White who was a pensioner who lost both his arms when struck by a cannon ball at Lake Erie on 17 August 1814. Jeremiah further reported that he enlisted in January 1813 and served through 8 November 1814 and served in the hospital department. He became ill from fever which he believed had debilitated him to the extent he was no longer able to work. His household in 1820 was wife Thomasan G. Johnson age 55 who for more than five years has been "in a state of mental derangement wholly uncapable of taking care of herself or doing anything for the support of the family." His children Susannah aged 16, Lorenzo aged 14, and Thomas aged 12 had been put out to other families. He had debts of about $67. The file also includes a statement that son-in-law Robert White was pensioned by special act of 22 February 1816 at $40 per month.[1642]

In his will written 29 January 1846 (proved 25 January 1848), Jeremiah Johnson left his entire estate to wife Sybil who was named executrix.[1643]

Jeremiah and Thomazin were parents of nine children.

i   MARY DUESBURY JOHNSON, b. at Charlestown, NH, 17 Feb 1789; m. 1st at Springfield, VT, 23 Jan 1812, ABEL SANDERSON, b. (recorded at Springfield), 15 Aug 1791 son of Eli Sanderson; Abel was killed at Fort Erie by cannon fire on 15 Aug 1814. Mary m. 2nd 31 Jul 1815, ROBERT WHITE, b. 15 Apr 1795; Robert d. at Mount Pleasant, IL, 28 Aug 1870. Rev. Robert White lost both his arms in battle in the War of 1812. He developed a method a writing by holding a pen in his mouth.[1644]

ii   THOMASIN JOHNSON, b. at Charlestown, NH, 25 Jan 1790; d. about 1795.

iii   SARAH JOHNSON, b. likely at Reading, VT, 1794; d. at Ontario County, NY, about 1820; m. at Springfield, VT, 25 Sep 1813, JAMES BEMIS.

iv   ANNA JOHNSON, b. at Reading, VT, 4 Dec 1796; m. at Cavendish, VT, EDMUND DAVIS, b. 18 Sep 1786; Anna d. at Cavendish, 12 Jul 1833.

v   THOMASIN JOHNSON, b. at Reading, VT, 3 Oct 1797; d. at East Charleston, VT, 11 Apr 1871; m. CALVIN GRANDY, b. at Reading, VT, 17 Mar 1792 son of Robert and Lydia (Butterfield) Grandy; Calvin d. at Fayston, VT, 26 Apr 1859.

vi   JAMES GIBSON JOHSNON, b. at Reading, VT, 29 Sep 1799; d. at Royal Oak, MI, 16 Apr 1872; m. at Reading 13 Sep 1826, SUSANNAH BOWEN, b. at Reading, 1 Sep 1799 daughter of Daniel and Mehitable (Packard) Bowen; Susannah d. at Bloomfield, MI, 10 May 1879.

[1639] The parentage of the Jeremiah Johnson who married Thomazin Johnson is most often suggested as uncertain (even grandson James Bowen Johnson in his volume states his parentage is uncertain), but the date of birth reported for the husband of Thomazin is 16 Sep 1763 and that is the recorded birth date in the Montague records for Jeremiah son of Josiah and Sarah. The husband of Thomazin was born in 1763 which can be verified by his pension record and other sources.

[1640] The reader is referred to a volume written by a grandson James Bowen Johnson which is a detailed memoir of his grandparents; *The Johnson Memorial: Jeremiah Johnson and Thomazin Blanchard Johnson, His Wife*. The focus of this volume is the lineage of Thomazin Blanchard.

[1641] Year: 1810; Census Place: Springfield, Windsor, Vermont; Roll: 65; Page: 429; Image: 00316; Family History Library Film: 0218669

[1642] U. S. Revolutionary War Pension and Bounty-Land Warrant Application Files, Case S39789

[1643] Vermont Wills and Probate, Windsor County, volume 19, p 601

[1644] "Mouth Writing", The Rutland Herald (Rutland, Vermont), 23 May 1837, Tuesday, p 1

vii   SUSAN JOHNSON, b. at Reading, 29 Sep 1803; d. at West Elkton, OH, 15 Nov 1862; m. LINAS THAYER, b. at Warren, VT, 1805; Linas d. at West Elkton, 2 Nov 1858.

viii   LORENZO DOW JOHNSON, b. at Reading, 21 Aug 1805; d. at Pocasset, MA, 8 Jan 1867; m. MARY BURGES, b. at Rochester, MA, 9 Mar 1810 daughter of Abraham and Rhoda (Caswell) Burges; Mary d. at Rutland, VT, 22 Dec 1887. Lorenzo D. Johnson was a minister of the gospel and the author of *Chaplains of the Government* and *The Churches and Pastors of Washington, D.C.* He was active in the temperance movement.

ix   THOMAS SKEILS JOHNSON, b. at Weathersfield, VT, 6 Dec 1807; d. after 1870 and before 1880 at Lemon, OH; m. at Sandwich, MA, 20 Mar 1836, ANNA PARKER EWER, b. at Sandwich, MA, 5 May 1816 daughter of Lemuel and Abigail (Percival) Ewer; Anna d. after 1880 when she was living at Middletown, OH.

        Jeremiah and Sybil were parents of one child.

i   SOLON KIMBALL JOHNSON, b. at Reading, VT, 28 Mar 1828; d. at Doniphan, NE, 23 Apr 1889; m. at Iowa, WI, 18 Feb 1853, ELLEN RICHARDS, b. in IL, about 1836 daughter of Elisha and Amanda (Swinnerton) Richards. Ellen was living in 1880.

574)   SARAH JOHNSON (*Sarah Hunt Johnson⁴, Jemima Russell Hunt³, Thomas², Robert¹*), b. at Montague, 24 Apr 1766 daughter of Josiah and Sarah (Hunt) Johnson; m. at Springfield, VT, 19 Dec 1787, HORATIO BINGHAM, b. about 1765.
        Horatio Bingham was born in Nova Scotia (according to the death record of one of his children). The family resided in Springfield, Vermont where they were living in 1830.[1645] The household in 1830 consisted of one male 60-69, one female 60-69, one male 15-19, one female 20-29, and one female 30-39.
        There are records of nine children of Horatio Bingham born at Springfield, Vermont.

i   RALPH BINGHAM, b. 3 Jun 1788; severely wounded in battle at Fort Erie and d. at Buffalo, NY, 27 Aug 1814; m. at Springfield, 30 Dec 1810, DORCAS OLNEY, b. at Springfield, 14 Apr 1789 daughter of William and Ruth (Phillips) Olney. Dorcas married second Samuel Newell Chamberlain on 2 Feb 1815. Ralph left two children: Louisa Ann Bingham and Leonard P. Bingham.[1646] Ralph enlisted for the duration of the war on 18 Jan 1813. He was promoted to corporal on 7 Jul 1814.[1647]

ii   NANCY BINGHAM, b. 18 May 1791

iii   CAROLINE BINGHAM, b. 28 Aug 1793; m. at Springfield, 4 Oct 1819, as his second wife, JASPER LELAND, b. 1792 son of Thomas and Lydia (Sherman) Leland. Jasper was first married to Cynthia Lockwood.

iv   REUBEN BINGHAM, b. 16 Jul 1795; d. 4 Mar 1797.

v   JAMES BINGHAM, b. 1 Jun 1798; d. at Stow, MA, 27 Jun 1879; m. at Stow, 21 Apr 1845, BETSEY HAWES (widow of Levi Weatherbee), b. at Weymouth, about 1800 daughter of John Hawes (per death record); Betsey d. at Taunton, 20 Jan 1881.

vi   ERASTUS BINGHAM, b. 21 Jun 1800; d. at Monkton, VT, 21 Apr 1883; m. 1ˢᵗ SARAH LEWIS, b. at Weathersfield, 1796 daughter of Samuel and Sarah (Stiles) Lewis (as given on death record); Sarah d. at Monkton, 10 Mar 1868. Erastus m. 2ⁿᵈ at Monkton, 26 Jul 1874, as her third husband, MARY PEMBERTON, b. at Middlebury, VT, Jan 1815 daughter of William and Elizabeth (-) Pemberton (per marriage record); Mary d. at Monkton, 22 May 1901. Mary's first married to Isaiah Page and second married to Jotham Whitney.

vii   MARY BINGHAM, b. 26 Dec 1803; d. at Lancaster, NH, 23 Mar 1863; m. at Springfield, 4 Jul 1830, FIELDING SMITH, b. in NH, 19 Aug 1807 (calculated from age at death); Fielding d. at Lancaster, 2 Dec 1879.

viii   HARRIET BINGHAM, b. 3 Sep 1809; d. at Fort Atkinson, WI, 29 Jan 1892; m. at Claremont, NH, 25 Dec 1841, GILMAN SARGENT, b. in VT, 4 Oct 1815 son of Elijah and Hannah (Huggins) Sargent;[1648] Gilman d. at Fort Atkinson, 2 Sep 1882.

ix   BETSEY ANN BINGHAM, b. 31 Mar 1811

[1645] 1830; Census Place: Springfield, Windsor, Vermont; Series: M19; Roll: 187; Page: 129; Family History Library Film: 0027453
[1646] U.S., The Pension Roll of 1835
[1647] U.S. Army, Register of Enlistments, 1798-1914
[1648] Sargent, *Sargent Record*, p 58

575)   RUSSELL HUNT (*Robert Hunt⁴, Jemima Russell Hunt³, Thomas², Robert¹*), b. at Canaan, CT, 11 Mar 1756 son of Robert and Rebekah (Peck) Hunt; d. at Canaan, 26 Aug 1831; m. ESTHER BEEBE,[1649] b. 1763 daughter of Asahel and Rebecca (Wright) Beebe;[1650] Hester d. at Canaan, 8 Jul 1850.

The Hunt genealogy suggests seven children in this family (Lucretia, Whiting, Milo, Betsey, John, Russell, and Julia), but clear information was found for just three of the children and that information is given here.[1651] John Hunt of Canaan was named administrator of the estate of Hester Hunt on 23 January 1851.[1652]

i   WHITING HUNT, b. 1782; d. 28 Oct 1782.

ii   JOHN HUNT, b. 23 Sep 1796; d. at Canaan, 31 Mar 1886; m. his first cousin once removed, MARY WILLIAMS, b. 16 Dec 1806 daughter of William and Lucretia (Landon) Williams; Mary d. at Canaan, 9 Jun 1890.

iii   JULIA A. A. HUNT, b. 1802; d. at Canaan, 2 Jan 1880. Julia did not marry. In her will written 1 August 1879, she left her entire estate to her brother John Hunt.[1653]

576)   SAMPSON ROBERT HUNT (*Robert Hunt⁴, Jemima Russell Hunt³, Thomas², Robert¹*), b. at Canaan, CT, 23 Feb 1761 son of Robert and Rebekah (Peck) Hunt; d. at Glastonbury, CT, 30 Jul 1826;[1654] m. 1st about 1782, CHARITY DUTCHER, b. at Glastonbury, 30 Jan 1764 daughter of Rufus and Jane (Ashley) Dutcher; Charity d. at Glastonbury, 23 Feb 1807. Samson m. 2nd at Glastonbury, 23 Oct 1807, POLLY BIDWELL, b. at Glastonbury, 4 Apr 1785 daughter of Jonathan and Hannah (Matson) Bidwell.[1655]

On 3 April 1818 while living in Glastonbury, Sampson R. Hunt gave a statement related to his application for pension. He enlisted in May 1777 for a three-year term in the company of Capt. Titus Watson in the regiment of Col. Swift of the Connecticut line and was honorably discharged in May 1780. He served as a fifer. On 1 August 1820, he provided additional information on his circumstances. He estimated the value of his property as two dollars and had debts of $470. He was a laborer by occupation but was able to work about one-fourth of the time. He had two children to support, Horace Hunt age 10 who has been a cripple since infancy due to a fever sore on his leg and a girl age 8 partially able to support herself. Sampson reported being deaf in one ear due to mortar explosions at Stony Point.[1656]

Sampson did not leave a will and his estate entered probate 2 August 1826 with Alexander Hollister of Glastonbury as administrator. Estate was valued at $25.66 and had a due pension payment of $38.70. Debts were $30.80.[1657]

Sampson and Charity were parents of nine children born at Glastonbury.

i   LOUISE HUNT, b. 27 Dec 1783

ii   GEORGE WASHINGTON DUTCHER HUNT, b. 9 Oct 1785; d. at Pompey, NY, 1825.

iii   CLEMENTINA HUNT, b. 18 Mar 1788; d. at Matanzas, Cuba, Jul 1821. Clementina did not marry.

iv   WALTER ROABND HUNT, b. 28 Jan 1792

v   NORMAN SAMSON HUNT, b. 13 Nov 1794

vi   RODNEY RUSSELL HUNT, b. 8 Oct 1797; d. at Lenox, MA, 16 Nov 1854; m. CLARISSA CLARK.

vii   CHARITY DUTCHER HUNT, b. 12 Oct 1799; d. 23 Feb 1824. Charity did not marry.

viii   WILLIAM BOOL HUNT, b. 17 May 1802; d. at Cuyahoga Falls, OH, 26 Nov 1846; m. at Portage County, OH, 2 Jul 1833, MARIAH MOORE.

ix   JANE LORRAINE HUNT, b. 23 Mar 1806; d. 27 Dec 1814.

Sampson and Polly were parents of three children born at Glastonbury.

i   HENRY HUNT, b. 17 May 1808

[1649] Name is given as both Esther and Hester in records but is Esther on her gravestone.

[1650] The 1806 probate distribution for the estate of Asahel Bugbee includes a distribution to daughter Hester Hunt.

[1651] Wyman, *Genealogy of the Name of Hunt*, p 81

[1652] Connecticut Wills and Probate, Canaan Probate District, Town of Canaan, Estate of Hester Hunt, No. 306

[1653] Connecticut Wills and Probate, Canaan Probate District, Town of Canaan, Estate of Julia A. Hunt, No. 307

[1654] He is referred to as Major Sampson R. Hunt on the cemetery record; Connecticut, Hale Collection of Cemetery Inscriptions and Newspaper Notices, 1629-1934

[1655] The name of Polly's father as Jonathan is given on the marriage transcription. The 1810 will of Jonathan Hunt of Glastonbury includes a bequest to his daughter Polly Hunt.

[1656] U. S. Revolutionary War Pension and Bounty-Land Warrant Application Files, Case S37125

[1657] Connecticut Wills and Probate, Hartford, Probate Packets Humphrey, L – Hurlburt, C. Estate of Sampson R. Hunt of Glastonbury

ii   HORACE HUNT, b. 20 Feb 1810

iii   MARIA HUNT, b. 6 Mar 1813

577)   SARAH HUNT (*Robert Hunt⁴, Jemima Russell Hunt³, Thomas², Robert¹*), b. at Canaan, CT, 11 Jun 1763 daughter of Robert and Rebekah (Peck) Hunt; d. at Salisbury, 1 Oct 1832; m. RUFUS LANDON, b. at Salisbury, CT, 4 Feb 1759 son of John and Katherine (-) Landon;[1658][1659] Rufus d. at Salisbury, 17 Jan 1848. Rufus married second Huldah.

Rufus and Sarah resided in Salisbury, Connecticut throughout their married life.

On 23 July 1832 while resident of Salisbury, Rufus Landon provided a statement related to the reinstatement of his pension. He was born at Salisbury on 4 February 1759. He enlisted in January 1776 in the artillery company of Capt. Bigelow of Hartford and was discharged at the end of his year. He next enlisted on 1 April 1777 in the company of Capt. Pettibone and marched to Peeks Kill at the time the stores and provisions belonging to the United States were burned by the British. Rufus was then in Danbury about the time it was burned but after the British had retreated. He was later in Fish Kill attending on soldiers with smallpox as he had previously had smallpox. He marched several times to Peeks Kill as a guard or reconnoitering. He was discharged in October 1777. In the Spring of 1778, his brother James Landon was drafted, and Rufus took his place as a substitute and returned to the Hudson River. He was discharged after five months but drafted again in 1779 in a militia company and discharged after two weeks. He received a pension certificate dated 26 January 1819 but was dropped from the rolls due to the amount of property.[1660]

In his will written 17 January 1844 (proved 12 February 1848), Rufus Landon bequeaths to beloved wife Huldah all the household items and furniture she brought to the marriage, and she is to receive thirty dollars per year for her natural life. This is in lieu of her right of dower. Daughter Sally Nott receives use of a room lately built as an addition to the house, the use of part of the cellar, and one cow which is to be kept and taken care of by son Robert. Sally also receives one-fourth of the furniture and one-eighth part of the remainder of the estate after the payment of debts and legacies. That part of Sally's legacy is to be held in trust during the life of her husband Hiram Nott, and after the death of Hiram, that portion can go to Sally. Son Robert receives during his natural life the dwelling house which will then go to the heirs of Robert. If Robert dies without heirs of his body, then that legacy goes to the other children except for son Milo Landon and daughter Chloe Hoyt. Robert also receives an eighth part of the estate remainder. Son Milo receives twenty-five dollars as does daughter Chloe Hoyt. Son Luther receives one-eighth part of the estate during his life to go to his heirs after his decease, and son John receives the same. Children of late daughter Lucretia Williams receive money bequests of five or ten dollars. Son Milo receives one-eighth of the estate except the ten dollars Milo owes his father is to be deducted and also the money Milo owes John if Milo has not paid it. Sons Nelson and Elisha and daughter Catherine Abbott each receives an eighth part of the estate. Son Elisha Landon and William M. Burrell were named executors.[1661]

Sarah and Rufus were parents of eleven children born at Salisbury, Connecticut.

i   LUCRETIA LANDON, b. 11 Jun 1780; d. at Salisbury, 29 Jan 1829; m. WILLIAM WILLIAMS, b. 1777; William d. at Salisbury, 7 Apr 1830.

ii   CHLOE LANDON, b. 10 Mar 1782; d. at New Haven, VT, 10 Aug 1857; m. JONATHAN HOYT, b. at Norwalk, CT, 7 May 1775 son of Jonathan and Hannah (-) Hoyt; Jonathan d. at New Haven, 5 Apr 1867.

iii   MILO LANDON, b. 13 Jan 1785; died young

iv   LUTHER LANDON, b. 2 Feb 1787; d. at Salisbury, 18 Aug 1862; m. MARTHA HALLETT, b. 1784; Martha d. at Salisbury, 18 Nov 1871.

v   SARAH LANDON, b. 5 Mar 1791; d. at Salisbury, 3 Dec 1877; m. HIRAM NOTT

vi   MILO LANDON, b. 14 Apr 1793; d. at Salisbury, 28 Oct 1869; m. ELEANOR E. DOOLITTLE; Eleanor d. 1889.

vii   CATHERINE LANDON, b. 6 Sep 1795; d. at Cook County, IL, 3 Oct 1885; m. SEWELL WHITNEY ABBOTT, b. in NY, 1795; Sewell d. at Bloomington, IL, Jun 1874.

viii   JOHN LANDON, b. 7 Mar 1798; d. at Eaton, NY, 10 Jul 1874; m. NANCY MARSH; Nancy d. 1882.

ix   ELISHA H. LANDON, b. 1 Oct 1800; d. at New Haven, VT, 6 Jun 1890; m. 1825, CHARLOTTE HOYT, b. 13 Sep 1805 daughter of Ezra and Jerusha (Phelps) Hoyt; Charlotte d. at New Haven, 7 Mar 1864.

x   ROBERT LANDON, b. 25 Sep 1802; d. at Salisbury, 1 Jan 1874. Robert did not marry. In his will, he left his estate to his niece Delia H. Nott.

xi   NELSON LANDON, b. 26 Jan 1810; d. at Zion, IL, 17 Jun 1884; m. 1ˢᵗ PHEBE PHELPS, b. 1814; Phebe d. at Zion, 28 May 1869. Nelson m. 2ⁿᵈ LOUISE, b. 1834 and d. 1895.

[1658] Date and place of birth are given in Rufus's Revolutionary War pension application file.

[1659] *Salisbury, CT: Vital Records, 1720-1914.* (Online Database, NewEnglandAncestors.org. New England Historic Genealogical Society, 2010.) p 54

[1660] U. S. Revolutionary War Pension and Bounty-Land Warrant Application Files, Case S13682

[1661] Connecticut Wills and Probate, Litchfield, volume 1 1847-1856, pp 31-33

578)   JOHN HUNT (*Robert Hunt⁴, Jemima Russell Hunt³, Thomas², Robert¹*), b. at Canaan, CT, 11 Dec 1767 son of Robert and Rebekah (Peck) Hunt; d. at Glastonbury, 28 Feb 1831; m. at Glastonbury, 18 Feb 1790, ELIZABETH PULSIFER, b. at Glastonbury, 21 Feb 1773 daughter of Sylvester and Huldah (Hollister) Pulsifer; Elizabeth d. at New Haven, 28 Sep 1820.[1662]
     John and Elizabeth were parents of at least ten children born at Glastonbury. In 1810, thirteen persons were enumerated in the family: one male 26 to 44; one female 26 to 44; three males under 10; one male 10 to 15; one male 16 to 25; two females under 10; one female 10 to 15; and one female 16 to 25.[1663]

i   ELIZABETH HUNT, b. 28 Jan 1791; d. at Ottawa, IL, 19 Jun 1835; m. 23 Aug 1807, JOHN BASCOM, b. 20 Jan 1783 son of John and Sarah (Burleigh) Bascom; John d. at Granby, CT, 20 Nov 1817.

ii   MINERVA HUNT, b. 24 Mar 1793; d. at Owego, NY, 1879; m. at Glastonbury, 4 Oct 1812, HORACE TAYLOR, b. in CT, about 1790; Horace d. at Owego, 14 Oct 1885.

iii   ROBERT HUNT, b. 24 Jul 1795; d. at Guilford, CT, 4 Apr 1870; m. at Rocky Hill, CT, 31 Mar 1819, KETURAH "KATY" SHIPMAN, b. 1785 daughter of John and Keturah (Morrell) Shipman; Katy d. at Guilford, 8 Sep 1858.

iv   EMMA HUNT, b. 21 Sep 1798; *perhaps* m. 25 Oct 1818, LEONARD TAYLOR, b. about 1795.

v   JOHN HUNT, b. 11 Nov 1800; d. after 1850 when living at Glastonbury; m. at Glastonbury, 2 Aug 1831, MARY BIDWELL, b. about 1798 daughter of Thomas and Elizabeth (Brooks) Bidwell; Mary d. 15 Jun 1863.

vi   NELSON HUNT, b. 23 Mar 1802; d. at Ellenville, NY, 1 Aug 1849; m. at Middletown, CT, 4 Feb 1827, JULIA SHIPMAN, b. at Glastonbury, 1795 daughter of John and Keturah (Morrell) Shipman; Julia d. at Ellenville, NY, 27 Apr 1890.

vii   HARRIET HUNT, b. 18 Mar 1805; d. at Ogden, UT, 1895; m. 17 Oct 1827, JAMES WHEAT, b. at Hartford, CT, 17 Jun 1806 son of James and Lovisa (Hollister) Wheat; James d. at Sandusky, OH, 20 Aug 1854.

viii   LEONARD HUNT, b. 20 Aug 1807; d. at Danbury, CT, 29 Mar 1884; m. at New York, NY, 7 Oct 1831, HARRIET LYON, b. in NY, about 1817.

ix   MARY ANN HUNT, b. 23 Feb 1810; d. at Sandusky, OH, Nov 1898; m. 12 Mar 1835, ELORY TAYLOR, b. at Glastonbury, 21 Feb 1808 son of Jesse and Julia (House) Taylor; Elory d. at Perkins, OH, 17 Mar 1898.

x   REBECCA HUNT, b. 1 Mar 1813; d. at Owego, NY, 6 Jun 1897; m. WILLIAM HASTINGS, b. 22 Jun 1794 (on gravestone); William d. at Owego, 28 Sep 1859.

579)   EMMA HUNT (*Robert Hunt⁴, Jemima Russell Hunt³, Thomas², Robert¹*), b. at Canaan, CT, 19 Dec 1769 daughter of Robert and Rebekah (Peck) Hunt; d. at Great Barrington, MA, 17 Oct 1862; m. 1ˢᵗ EZRA TUPPER, b. at Stafford, CT, 19 Mar 1766 son of Solomon and Abiah (West) Tupper. Emma m. 2ⁿᵈ at Sherburne, NY, 17 Feb 1815, as his second wife, JOHN WOODWARD DEWEY, b. at Lebanon, CT, 31 Dec 1762 son of John and Rhoda (Gillett) Dewey; John d. at Hamilton, Canada West while visiting his daughter, 15 Nov 1839.[1664] John W. Dewey was first married to Abigail Rudd.
     Ezra Tupper and family were living in Canaan, Connecticut in 1800 with a household of eight persons: one male 26 to 44; one female 26 to 44; one male under 10; one male 10 to 15; three females under 10; and one female over 45.[1665] The date of Ezra's death is not known but by 1815 when Emma remarried.
     Emma applied for widow's pension related to the service of her second husband John Woodward Dewey. On 6 October 1832, John Woodward Dewey age 71 and resident of Romulus, New York. He reported enlisting on 9 June 1781 but did not recall the name of the captain, but the brigade was under command of Gen. La Fayette. His company was in Rhode Island, Connecticut, New York, and Maryland and he was present at the surrender of Gen. Cornwallis. He was discharged on 1 January 1782 and then drafted in the spring or summer that same year. He was in the company of Capt. John Huntington, the company was in New London, Connecticut and then at Fort Trumbull. John stated he was born in 1761 in Lebanon, Connecticut where he lived until 1809, was then in Sherburn, New York, later in Romulus, then Scipio, and returned to Romulus. On 17 August 1834, John requested a transfer of his pension to Pennsylvania where he planned to live with his sons. On 8 February 1854, Emma Dewey aged eighty-four and resident of Great Barrington provided a statement. Her name was Emma Tupper at the time of her marriage to John Dewey. John died on or about the seventeenth day of February eighteen hundred and thirty-six "as she was then informed at a place called St. David's in Canada while there on a visit." She further stated that due to her husband's reduced circumstances and mental infirmity that they had broken up housekeeping some years before he received his pension and that he went to live with his children. A statement by John's son from his first marriage, Jonathan Rudd Dewey, stated his father died on 15 November 1839 while visiting his daughter Maria in Canada West. Jonathan also noted he had

[1662] *U.S., Newspaper Extractions from the Northeast, 1704-1930.*
[1663] Year: 1810; Census Place: Glastonbury, Hartford, Connecticut; Roll: 1; Page: 605; Image: 00604; Family History Library Film: 0281229
[1664] Dewey, *Life of George Dewey and Dewey Family History*, p 441
[1665] Year: 1800; Census Place: Canaan, Litchfield, Connecticut; Series: M32; Roll: 2; Page: 664; Image: 35; Family History Library Film: 205619

forwarded information related to his father's pension and the date of his death to his stepmother. A statement was also provided by Emma's daughter from her first marriage, Emma *Tupper* Peck.[1666]

     Census records suggest as many as five children in this family, but information was located for just two of the children.

i   MINERVA TUPPER, b. at Salisbury, CT, 1796; d. at Great Barrington, MA, 3 May 1874; m. NATHAN PECK, b. 1774; Nathan d. at Great Barrington; 6 Feb 1862.

ii   FREDERICK TUPPER, b. in NY, 1805 (census records); d. at Schenectady, NY, 20 Feb 1880; m. about 1830, GERTRUDE VAN PATTEN, b. in NY, about 1808; Gertrude d. at Schenectady, 18 Apr 1889.

580)   RUSSELL HUNT (*Russell Hunt⁴, Jemima Russell Hunt³, Thomas², Robert¹*), b. at Canaan, CT, 11 Oct 1762 son of Russell and Lydia (Peck) Hunt; d. at Canaan, 20 Jan 1839; m. about 1785, LUCY SWIFT who has not been identified.
     Russell Hunt and Lucy Swift were parents of one child.

i   MARY LUCY HUNT, b. at Canaan, 21 Jul 1800; d. at Cornwall, CT, 4 Oct 1869; m. at Canaan, 22 Oct 1822, ALBERT SEDGWICK, b. a Cornwall, 20 May 1801 son of John A. and Nancy (Buel) Sedgwick; Albert d. at Cornwall, 14 May 1878.

581)   SALMON HUNT (*Russell Hunt⁴, Jemima Russell Hunt³, Thomas², Robert¹*), b. at Canaan, CT, 23 Jan 1765 son of Russell and Lydia (Peck) Hunt; d. at Canaan, 28 Apr 1839;[1667] m. by 1787, REUBY WHITNEY, b. at Canaan, about 1765 daughter of John and Elizabeth (Adams) Whitney;[1668] Reuby d. at Canaan, 10 Feb 1837.
     Salmon and Reuby resided in Canaan where in 1810 they were a household of nine: one male 26 to 44; one female 26 to 44; one male 10 to 15; two males 16 to 25; two females under 10; one female 10 to 15; and one female 16 to 25.[1669]
     Salmon and Reuby were parents of seven children born at Canaan.[1670]

i   CYRUS D. HUNT, b. 28 Aug 1787; reported in the Hunt genealogy as going to New York.

ii   REUBEN WHITNEY HUNT, b. 27 Apr 1788; d. at Bristol, IL, 5 Feb 1872; m. about 1820, his first cousin, EMELINE HUNT, b. 28 Feb 1800 daughter of Amos and Mary (Lowry) Hunt; Emeline d. at Plano, IL, 9 Apr 1883.

iii   BETSEY HUNT, b. 7 Mar 1791

iv   HIRAM HUNT, b. 28 May 1795; reported in the Hunt genealogy as being a counsellor in New York.

v   SALMON HUNT, b. 7 Aug 1796; d. at Bridgeport, CT, 16 Dec 1873; m. at Torrington, CT, 1 Jan 1823, CLARISSA BRADLEY, b. at Torrington, 1806 daughter of Samuel and Chloe (Rossiter) Bradley;[1671] Clarissa d. at Bridgeport, 3 May 1875.

vi   POLLY HUNT, b. 2 Oct 1799; m. at Canaan, 23 Oct 1822, AMOS BIRD HOLABIRD, b. at Canaan, 24 Mar 1787 son of William and Dorcas (Bird) Holabird;[1672] Amos d. at Cincinnati, 18 Sep 1852.

vii   MINERVA HUNT, b. 6 May 1803; may have married Mr. Stevens who has not been identified.[1673]

582)   DAVID HUNT (*Russell Hunt⁴, Jemima Russell Hunt³, Thomas², Robert¹*), b. at Canaan, CT, 22 Apr 1767 son of Russell and Lydia (Peck) Hunt; d. at Canaan, 22 Feb 1834; m. 1ˢᵗ at Canaan, 1791, HANNAH JOHNSON, b. about 1768; Hannah d. at Canaan, 2 Feb 1806. David m. 2ⁿᵈ 1807, WEALTHY ANN BURRALL, b. 16 Oct 1775 daughter of William and Elizabeth (Morgan) Burrall;[1674] Wealthy d. 9 Apr 1840.
     David Hunt resided in Canaan, Connecticut.
     Son David Morgan Hunt did not marry, and his estate entered probate 5 October 1864 with Edward P. Hunt and Wealthy A. Hunt as administrators and Catharine Hunt and Harriet Hunt as sureties. The heirs-at-law agreed to a partial

[1666] U. S. Revolutionary War Pension and Bounty-Land Warrant Application Files, Case W25530

[1667] Connecticut, Deaths and Burials Index, 1650-1934

[1668] The 1793 estate of John Whitney of Canaan includes a distribution to Ruby and Salmon Hunt.

[1669] Year: 1810; Census Place: Canaan, Litchfield, Connecticut; Roll: 2; Page: 171; Image: 00174; Family History Library Film: 0281230

[1670] Connecticut Town Birth Records, pre-1870 (Barbour Collection)

[1671] Orcutt, *History of Torrington, Connecticut*, p 656

[1672] Hurlburt Genealogy, p 515

[1673] Wyman, *Genealogy of the Name and Family of Hunt*, p 82

[1674] Morgan, *Morgan Genealogy: James Morgan of New London, Conn. and His Descendants*

distribution of the estate with an undivided third part ($30,285) paid to Wealthy Ann Hunt and undivided third parts to Catharine E. Hunt and Harriet A. Hunt. The personal property was to remain in the hands of Wealthy A. Hunt for their mutual use. With this agreement, Edward P. Hunt was relieved of further responsibility. The total value of the estate was $111,770.29. This included the dwelling house, a separate farm, 400 acres of land in Iowa, a large stock portfolio, and $3,500 in notes owed by Edward P. Hunt.[1675]

In her will written 18 August 1890, daughter Catharine E. Hunt of Bridgeport bequeathed $500 to half-sister Maria Adam. Minnie Rorabach wife of A. F. Rorabach received $5,000; $4,000 of that that amount was for her children, $2,000 to Catherine Hunt Rorabach and $2,000 to be divided among the other children. Bridgeport Hospital received $2,500. Harriet E. Belden receive $1,000. Elizabeth P. Burrall of Springfield, Massachusetts daughter of the late William P. Burrall received $5,000. There are several other bequests to Barralls: Mary Dickinson Burrall of Richmond, Virginia, Porter S. Burrall of Lime Rock, Connecticut, and William H. Burrall of Springfield. There is a lengthy list of additional bequests in amounts ranging from $1,000 to $5,000.[1676]

David Hunt and Hannah Johnson were parents of three children.

i   LUCY HUNT, b. about 1794; d. at Beloit, WI, Apr 1861; m. 26 Apr 1814, Maj. EDWARD BURRALL, b. at Canaan, 2 May 1786 son of Ovid and Lucy (Wells) Burrall; Edward d. at Beloit, Oct 1872. Lucy and Edward lived in Stockbridge, MA until about 1850.

ii   HANNAH MARIAH HUNT, b. at Canaan, 16 Aug 1797; d. at Canaan, 28 Dec 1891; m. at Stockbridge, MA, 24 Dec 1834, as his second wife, JOHN ADAM, b. at Canaan, 22 Jun 1785 son of John and Abigail (Forbes) Adam; John d. at Falls Village, CT, 3 Nov 1871. John was first married to Amy Brown.

iii   EDWARD P. HUNT, b. at Canaan, 23 Nov 1804; d. at North Canaan, 30 May 1875; m. 1st at Canaan, 24 Sep 1833, CAROLINE BINGHAM, b. at Salisbury, CT, 17 Oct 1810 daughter of Shubael and Elizabeth (Brewster) Bingham;[1677] Caroline d. at Canaan, 3 Dec 1853. Edward m. 2nd 25 Apr 1854, MARY E. PEET, b. 30 Dec 1818 daughter of Samuel S. and Lydia (Nichols) Peet; Mary d. at Canaan, 23 Apr 1876.

David and Wealthy were parents of five children born at Canaan none of whom married.

i   WEALTHY A. HUNT, b. 27 May 1808; d. at Canaan, 16 Dec 1868.

ii   CATHARINE E. HUNT, b. 10 May 1810; d. at Bridgeport, CT, 21 Jun 1891. Catharine did not marry.

iii   DAVID B. HUNT, b. 3 Jul 1812; d. 13 Feb 1814.

iv   HARRIET A. HUNT, b. 13 Feb 1814; d. at Canaan, 1 Sep 1879.

v   DAVID MORGAN HUNT, b. 21 Aug 1816; d. at Huntsville, CT, 12 Sep 1864.

583)   LYDIA HUNT (*Russell Hunt⁴, Jemima Russell Hunt³, Thomas², Robert¹*), b. at Canaan, CT, 18 Feb 1772 daughter of Russell and Lydia (Peck) Hunt; d. at South Danby, NY, 6 Jul 1826; m. WILLIAM HUGG, b. at Canaan, CT, 18 Dec 1764 son of William and Margaret (Johnson) Hugg;[1678] William d. at South Danby, 10 Jun 1826.

Lydia and William married likely in Connecticut but settled in Spencer, New York in 1799.[1679] William's brothers Isaac and Daniel also settled in the area which became informally known as "Hugg Town".[1680] After a few years, the family moved to West Danby where Lydia and William died both in 1826.[1681] In the 1820 census of Danby, William Hugg was head of household of ten persons: one male over 45; one female over 45; two males 10 to 15; three females under 10; one female 10 to 15; and one female 16 to 25.[1682]

Lydia and William were parents of likely eight children and there are perhaps one or two other children.

i   NANCY HUGG, b. likely at Canaan, 22 Aug 1788; d. after 1860 when living at Van Etten, NY; m. about 1807 (first child Jan 1808), LEVI ENGLISH, b. in NY, 18 Aug 1784 son of John and Phebe (Kent) English; Levi d. after 1860.

[1675] Connecticut Wills and Probate, Canaan Probate District, Town of Canaan, Estate of David M. Hunt, Case 305
[1676] Connecticut Will and Probate, Fairfield County, volume 53, pp 190-193
[1677] Jones, *The Brewster Genealogy*, volume I, p 227
[1678] Connecticut Town Birth Records, pre-1870 (Barbour Collection)
[1679] Kingman, *Our County and Its People: Memorial History of Tioga County, New York*, p 709
[1680] Kingman, *Our County and Its People: Memorial History of Tioga County*, p 370
[1681] Lydia and William are interred at Methodist Episcopal Church Cemetery in West Danby; findagrave ID: 41737161
[1682] 1820 U S Census; Census Place: Danby, Tioga, New York; Page: 155; NARA Roll: M33_79; Image: 446

ii   MILTON HUGG, b. May 1790; d. at North Spencer, NY, 19 Jun 1878; m. at Darby, NY, 11 Oct 1818, ESTHER CASE, b. Jan 1800 daughter of Reuben and Experience (Nichols) Case;[1683] Esther d. at North Spencer, 6 Nov 1878.

iii   LYDIA HUGG, b. 1800

iv   DANIEL HUGG, b. 1801; d. at Spencer, 27 Apr 1861.[1684]

v   STATIRA HUGG, b. 6 Mar 1802; d. at Troy, PA, 19 Dec 1896; m. about 1825, REUBEN CASE, b. 30 May 1802 son of Reuben and Experience (Nichols) Case; Reuben d. at Troy, 7 Aug 1882.

vi   RUSSELL HUGG, b. 1804

vii   JEMIMA HUGG, b. at Spencer, NY, 4 Jun 1813; d. at Campbell, NY, 16 Apr 1902; m. at Troy, PA, 1832, ROYAL SARGENT ALVORD, b. in VT, 16 Oct 1806 son of Nathan and Rebecca (Deming) Alvord;[1685] Royal d. at East Smithfield, PA, 10 Sep 1868.

viii   ACHSAH HUGG, b. 26 Apr 1815; d. at Tioga County, PA, 24 Aug 1891; m. about 1838, as his second wife, AVERY KENNEDY,[1686] b. at Halifax, VT, 5 Aug 1800 son of Alexander and Catherine (Brown) Kennedy; Avery d. at Tioga County, PA, 12 Jan 1870. Avery was first married to Julianna Wilcox whom he divorced in 1837.

584)   AMOS HUNT (*Russell Hunt⁴, Jemima Russell Hunt³, Thomas², Robert¹*), b. at Canaan, CT, 6 May 1774 son of Russell and Lydia (Peck) Hunt; d. (buried at South Canaan), 13 Jul 1851; m. MARY LOWRY, b. 1779 daughter of Nathaniel and Jerusha (Newell) Lowry; Mary d. at Canaan, 19 Aug 1863.
        Amos and Mary resided in Canaan, Connecticut in the Huntsville area. Amos was an iron manufacturer. He served as representative in 1809 and 1812.[1687] Amos was known as Col. Amos Hunt.
        Amos and Mary were parents of nine children born at Canaan, Connecticut.

i   Son, b. 5 Feb 1798

ii   EMELINE HUNT, b. 28 Feb 1800; d. at Plano, IL, 9 Apr 1883; m. about 1820, her first cousin, REUBEN WHITNEY HUNT, b. at Canaan, 27 Apr 1788 son of Salmon and Reuby (Whitney) Hunt; Reuben d. at Bristol, IL, 5 Feb 1872.

iii   CAROLINE HUNT, b. 18 Mar 1801; d. at Cincinnati, OH, 1 Jul 1849; m. at Canaan, 2 Dec 1822, HARLOW C. HOLABIRD, b. 24 Sep 1798 son of William and Dorcas (Bird) Holabird; Harlow d. at Cincinnati, 11 Dec 1859. Caroline and her husband Harlow lived in Connecticut until 1833 when they moved to Cincinnati.[1688]

iv   CHARLES HUNT, b. 19 Aug 1803; d. (burial at Canaan), 15 Jan 1869; m. 1st about 1830, LUCY BEEBE, b. at Canaan, 29 Jan 1813 daughter of Asahel and Betsey (Hunt) Beebe; Lucy d. at Great Barrington, MA, Dec 1839. Charles m. 2nd at Canaan, 29 Apr 1841, PAMELA BATES, b. about 1823 daughter of Jonathan and Pamela (Sedgwick) Bates;[1689] Pamela d. at Canaan, 10 Aug 1842. Charles m. 3rd 4 Oct 1849, CHARLOTTE RUSSELL, b. in NY, 7 Aug 1829 daughter of Ely Russell. Charlotte d. at Canaan, 27 Dec 1896. Charles was involved in textile manufacturing and was president of Housatonic Railroad for fifteen years.[1690]

v   WILLIAM HUNT, b. 29 May 1806; d. at Auburn, MA, 27 May 1883; m. by 1832, JOANNA HAWLEY (or Holly), b. in CT 17 Feb 1810 (calculated from death age of 61 years, 3 months, 7 days) daughter of Joseph and Olive (Gibbs) Hawley;[1691] Joanna d. at Worcester, 24 May 1871. William was a mechanic. In 1870, William and Joanna were living with son Frank and his family in Naugatuck, CT. Frank then moved to Auburn in Worcester County and his parents went with him. William, a widower, was living with Frank in 1880.

vi   CHAUNCEY L. HUNT, b. 24 Aug 1808; d. at Canaan, 28 Jun 1881; m. 30 Jun 1841, RUTHEDA L. PECK, b. likely at Canaan, 22 Apr 1823 daughter of Curtis and Olive (Johnson) Peck; Rutheda d. at Lenox, MA, 18 Dec 1913.

vii   ISAAC HUNT, b. 11 Apr 1811; d. 12 Mar 1838.

[1683] Kingman, *Our County and Its People: Memorial History of Tioga County*, p 709

[1684] Burial at Evergreen Cemetery, Spencer, New York, findagrave ID: 109905480; age 59 years, 6 months

[1685] Alvord, *Genealogy of the Descendants of Alexander Alvord*, p 116

[1686] Name is also spelled Cannady

[1687] J. W. Lewis, *History of Litchfield, Connecticut*, Part I, p 271, p 268

[1688] Lake County Publishing Company, *Portrait and Biographical Record of Iroquois County, Illinois*, p 361

[1689] Sedgwick, *A Sedgwick Genealogy*, p 89

[1690] J. W. Lewis, *History of Litchfield, Connecticut*, Part I, p 271

[1691] The names of Joanna's parents are given as Joseph and Olive Holly on her death record.

viii	LUCIUS P. HUNT (twin), b. 2 Apr 1815; d. at Tyngsboro, MA, 30 Oct 1896; m. 1st about 1841, CATHERINE MARY GROS-CLAUDE, b. at Toulon, France, about 1820; Catherine d. before 1860. Lucius m. 2nd at Hudson, NH, 18 Feb 1871, AMANDA MALVINA KENDALL, b. at Tyngsboro, MA, 19 Jul 1830 daughter of Jeremiah and Sarah (Butman) Kendall; Amanda d. at Tyngsboro, 3 Aug 1901.

ix	JUNIUS B. HUNT (twin), b. 2 Apr 1815; d. at Manlius, NY, 9 Aug 1838.

585)	JEMIMA HUNT (*Russell Hunt⁴, Jemima Russell Hunt³, Thomas², Robert¹*), b. at Canaan, CT, 1777 daughter of Russell and Lydia (Peck) Hunt; d. at Cornwall, CT, 7 Apr 1832; m. JOSEPH WILCOX, b. 1769; Joseph d. at Cornwall, 23 Mar 1852.

Jemima and Joseph were parents of ten children likely all born at Canaan.[1692] There were thirteen members of the household in 1820: one male over 45, one female 26 to 44, one male 10 to 15, one male 16 to 18, three males 16 to 25, three females under 10, two females 10 to 15, and two females 16 to 25.[1693] In the 1830 census at Canaan, the household of Joseph Wilcox consisted of nine persons: one male 60-69, one female 50-59, one male 5 to 9, two males 20 to 29, one male 30 to 39, two females 10 to 14, and one female 15 to 19.[1694]

i	AMANDA WILCOX, b. 16 Dec 1797; d. at West Allis, WI, 21 Jun 1881; m. JEREMIAH NOBLE, b. in MA, about 1794 son of William and Lavinia (Gunn) Noble;[1695] Jeremiah d. at West Allis, 13 Jun 1887.

ii	PHEBE WILCOX, b. 1799; d. at Great Barrington, MA, 8 May 1881;[1696] m. MILLER TURNER, b. at Waterford, NY, about 1801 son of Jonathan and Sarah (-) Turner (per death record); Miller d. at Great Barrington, 20 Dec 1876.

iii	RUSSELL HUNT WILCOX, b. 1800; d. after 1880 when he was living at Black Hawk, IA; m. at Cornwall, CT, 27 May 1834, FANNY M. WILCOX, b. 1810 daughter of Reuben and Olive (Cowles) Wilcox; Fanny d. at Cornwall, 18 Apr 1872. After he was widowed, Russell went to live with his son Russel in Iowa.

iv	JEANETTE E. WILCOX, b. at Cornwall, 30 Jul 1803; d. at Great Barrington, MA, 5 Jan 1867; m. at Great Barrington, 26 Nov 1829, her fourth cousin, JOHN CONE RUSSELL (*Pearly⁵, John⁴, Joseph³, Benjamin², Robert¹*), b. at Willington, CT, 21 Jan 1804 son of Pearly and Abigail (Cone) Russell; John d. at Great Barrington, 21 Oct 1873.

v	JOSEPH NELSON WILCOX, b. 1806; d. after 1880 when he was living at Canaan. Joseph is listed as a widower in the 1880 census, but no wife or children were located.

vi	LUCY ANN WILCOX, b. 1808; d. at Great Barrington, 23 Nov 1881; m. at Great Barrington, 16 Jan 1834, BENJAMIN FRANKLIN DURANT, b. in NY, 1800 son of Allen and Parthenia (Holdredge) Durant; Benjamin d. at Great Barrington, 11 Feb 1875.

vii	LYDIA WILCOX, b. about 1813; d. at Chicago, IL, 2 Jan 1881; m. before 1838, HENRY SMITH BEEBE, b. at Canaan, 4 Sep 1811 son of Asahel and Betsey (Hunt) Beebe;[1697] Henry d. at Chicago, 9 Jul 1893. Henry and Lydia were in Peru, La Salle County, Illinois by 1838 and later settled in Chicago.[1698]

viii	CAROLINA WILCOX, b. 1815; d. at Canaan, 25 Feb 1880; m. 30 Dec 1845, HENRY YALE, b. 11 Dec 1821 son of Frederick and Lucretia (Sedgwick) Yale;[1699] Henry d. at Canaan, 11 Apr 1900. Henry married second Mrs. Julie Preston.

ix	RHODA WILCOX, b. 1816; d. at Canaan, 19 Jan 1867. Rhoda did not marry.

x	HELEN WILCOX, b. 1821; d. at Great Barrington, 1 Feb 1854; m. at Great Barrington, 8 Apr 1846, EGBERT HOLLISTER, b. at Salisbury, CT, 1818 son of Julius and Thankful (Spencer) Hollister; Egbert d. at Great Barrington, 7 Aug 1889. Egbert married second Electa M. Hitchcock on 21 Oct 1863.

[1692] Wyman, *Genealogy of the Name and Family of Hunt*, p 132 identifies nine children, but a tenth child can be identified from the records at Great Barrington.
[1693] 1820 U S Census; Census Place: Canaan, Litchfield, Connecticut; Page: 368; NARA Roll: M33_1; Image: 300
[1694] Year: 1830; Census Place: Canaan, Litchfield, Connecticut; Series: M19; Roll: 11; Page: 434; Family History Library Film: 0002804
[1695] Boltwood, *History and Genealogy of the Family of Thomas Noble*, p 384
[1696] Massachusetts, Town and Vital Records, 1620-1988
[1697] Connecticut Town Birth Records, pre-1870 (Barbour Collection)
[1698] Hoffman, *History of La Salle County, Illinois*, p 183
[1699] Sedgwick, *A Sedgwick Genealogy*, p 87

586)   LYDIA RUSSELL (*James⁴, James³, Thomas², Robert¹*), b. at North Yarmouth, ME, 12 Mar 1762 daughter of James and Lydia (Mitchell) Russell; d. after 1820 when she was living at Brokenstraw; m. 13 Aug 1782, SOLOMON JORDAN, b. Sep 1756 *perhaps* son of Elijah and Joanna (Veasey) Jordan; Solomon d. at Brokenstraw, PA, 4 Mar 1846.

On 27 April 1818, Solomon Jordan resident in Lyons, New York made application for a pension based on his service in the Revolutionary War. He reported first enlisting on 1 January 1776 at Dorchester, Massachusetts in the company of Capt. Cranston. He served a one-year term and then had a second enlistment from Portland (now Maine) on 4 March 1777 in the company of Capt. Paul Ellis. He was at the battle of Saratoga and the surrender of Burgoyne. In December 1820, while living in Broken Straw Township, Pennsylvania, he reported being sixty-four years old as of "last September" and that the only family in his household was his wife Lydia aged sixty-one.[1700]

Three children are confirmed for Lydia and Solomon, although it is likely there were other children.

i   SOLOMON JORDAN, b. 16 Aug 1784; d. at Algansee, MI, 19 Jun 1854; m. at Mount Vernon, ME, 22 Mar 1810, SARAH LEIGHTON, b. at Rome, ME, 28 Oct 1789 daughter of Moses and Margaret (Kearil or Carle) Leighton; Sarah d. at Algansee, 2 Apr 1882.

ii   ELIJAH JORDAN, b. 1793; d. at Pittsfield, MI, 16 Feb 1865; m. at Rome, ME, 14 Jul 1813, ELIZABETH LEIGHTON, b. at Rome, 18 Sep 1793 daughter of Moses and Margaret (Kearil or Carle) Leighton; Elizabeth d. Sep 1879.[1701]

iii   PHEBE JORDAN, b. 1795; d. at Fountain Green, IL, 1854; m. 1ˢᵗ about 1810, NATHANIEL HUTCHINSON, b. at Fayette, ME, 23 Dec 1786 son of Ebenezer and Hannah (Littlehale) Hutchinson; Nathaniel d. at Deputy, IN, Oct 1826. Phebe m. 2ⁿᵈ at Jefferson County, IN, 14 May 1837, CORNELIUS T. HUMPHREYS, b. at Louisa County, VA, 12 May 1775 son of William and Sally (Stratham) Humphreys; Cornelius d. at Fountain Green/La Harpe, 26 Sep 1853. Cornelius was first married to Elizabeth Brooks, a marriage that ended in divorce.

587)   TEMPERANCE RUSSELL (*James⁴, James³, Thomas², Robert¹*), b. at North Yarmouth, ME, 27 Apr 1764 daughter of James and Lydia (Mitchell) Russell; d. at South Waterford, ME, 18 Jan 1831; m. about 1783, DAVID JORDAN, b. 1759 son of Elijah and Joanna (Veasey) Jordan; David d. at South Waterford, 30 May 1847.[1702]

In a statement made 8 April 1818, David Jordan reported that while resident of Albany in Oxford County, he enlisted 23 March 1777 for a term of three years in the company of Capt. Paul Ellis in the regiment of Col. Timothy Bigelow. Capt. Ellis was killed at the battle in Monmouth and afterwards David was in the company of Capt. Houdang in the brigade of Gen. John Glover. David was awarded a pension of $96 per annum. On 28 June 1820, David provided additional information about his family and circumstances. He reported having 30 acres of land in Albany township on which he owed $100 which he was paying with his pension. He had two cows, one swine, and a horse, and $3 to $4 worth of utensils. His household at that time included wife Temperance age 57 who was able to do housework and children Jefferson age 16, Buckman age 14, and Phebe age 11 who were able to contribute some to their support.[1703]

Temperance Russell and David Jordan were parents of at least twelve children. Three of the sons married daughters of Josiah and Deborah (Tuttle) Proctor.[1704]

i   DAVID JORDAN, b. 1784

ii   CALVIN JORDAN, b. 1786; d. at Portland, ME, 20 Dec 1859; m. 20 Jan 1811, ELIZABETH WEEKS, perhaps b. 18 Oct 1787 daughter of Joshua and Sarah (Morse) Weeks;[1705] Elizabeth d. at Portland, 23 Dec 1871.

iii   RUTH JORDAN, b. at Gray, ME, 1793;[1706] d. at Albany, ME, 28 Nov 1865; m. at Albany, ME, 27 Jun 1813, a fifth cousin, OBED ABBOTT (*Ruth Holt Abbott⁶, Joseph Holt⁵, Lydia Holt Holt⁴, Thomas Holt³, Mary Russell Holt², Robert¹*), b. at Andover, MA, 14 Sep 1789 son of Abner and Ruth (Holt) Abbott; Obed d. at Albany, 3 Jan 1855.

iv   TEMPERANCE RUSSELL JORDAN, b. at Gray, 1794; d. at Andover, MA, 9 Oct 1842; m. at Albany, ME, 13 Jan 1820, STEPHEN ABBOTT (*Ruth Holt Abbott⁶, Joseph Holt⁵, Lydia Holt Holt⁴, Thomas Holt³, Mary Russell Holt², Robert¹*), b. at Andover, Dec 1794 son of Abner and Ruth (Holt) Abbott; Stephen d. at Andover, 29 Sep 1869.

v   WALES JORDAN, b. Dec 1795; d. at Albany, ME, 30 Jul 1877; m. at Waterford, ME, 26 Dec 1819, MARY NUTTING PROCTOR, b. 1792 daughter of Josiah and Deborah (Tuttle) Proctor; Mary d. at Albany, 11 Jan 1874.

[1700] U. S. Revolutionary War Pension and Bounty-Land Warrant Application Files, Case S39.788

[1701] The Revolution pension file of Elijah's father Solomon contains within it a summary of the 1812 pension application of Elijah which documents information on his marriage and the name of his wife's father. Elijah's file also contains information on his death.

[1702] Maine, J. Gary Nichols Cemetery Collection, ca. 1780-1999

[1703] U. S. Revolutionary War Pension and Bounty-Land Warrant Application Files, Case S35479

[1704] The 1848 probate of Josiah Proctor includes heirs Lydia Jordan, Mary Jordan, and Sarah Jordan. Maine Wills and Probate, Oxford County Estate Files, Drawer 84, Estate of Josiah Proctor

[1705] Morse, *Morse Genealogy*, p 613

[1706] Names of parents are given as David and Temperance Jordan on her death record; Maine, Death Records, 1761-1922

vi   SAMUEL F. JORDAN,[1707] b. about 1797; d. at Palmer, MA, 28 Mar 1875; m. 1st at Albany, ME, 2 Oct 1817, EUNICE CHANDLER, b. at Albany, 22 Oct 1795 daughter of William and Eunice (Howard) Chandler; Eunice d. at Millbury, MA, 5 Apr 1845. Samuel m. 2nd at Royalston, MA, 6 Feb 1853, ANN M. FOSTER, b. in NH, about 1815.

vii   LYDIA JORDAN, b. at Gray, 1798; d. at Harrison, ME, 8 Jan 1855; m. 30 Sep 1819, her first cousin, RUSSELL LEBARON (*Jane Russell LeBaron⁵, James⁴, James³, Thomas², Robert¹*), b. 13 Aug 1797 son of James and Jane "Jenny" (Russell) LeBaron; Russell d. at Harrison, 26 Jun 1873.

viii   JAMES R. JORDAN, b. 1800; d. at Chicago, IL, 7 Oct 1882; m. 1820, SARAH G. PROCTOR, b. 1799 daughter of Josiah and Deborah (Tuttle) Proctor; Sarah d. at Chicago, 23 Aug 1893.

ix   JOANNA JORDAN, b. 1801; d. at Lovell, ME, 18 Sep 1856; m. at Albany, ME, 16 Aug 1819, her first cousin, WILLIAM LEBARON (*Jane Russell LeBaron⁵, James⁴, James³, Thomas², Robert¹*), b. Jul 1795 son of James and Jane (Russell) LeBaron; William d. at Lovell, 10 Aug 1863.

x   THOMAS JEFFERSON JORDAN, b. at Waterford, 9 Oct 1803; d. at Albany, ME, 12 Jun 1881; m. LYDIA PERLEY PROCTOR, b. at Waterford, 13 Aug 1800 daughter of Josiah and Deborah (Tuttle) Proctor; Lydia d. at Albany, 16 Jun 1893.

xi   RUSSELL BUCKMAN JORDAN, b. 1806; d. at North Andover, MA, 5 Dec 1875; m. at Andover, 29 Sep 1831, MARIA STEVENS, b. at Andover, 8 Jul 1809 daughter of Jonathan and Martha (Mooar) Stevens;[1708] Maria d. at North Andover, 25 Nov 1895.

xii   PHEBE JORDAN, b. 1809; d. at Biddeford, ME, 26 Jun 1876; m. NATHANIEL RAND who d. after 1840 and before 1850.

588)   JANE "JENNY" RUSSELL (*James⁴, James³, Thomas², Robert¹*), baptized at North Yarmouth, ME, 10 Jun 1770 daughter of James and Lydia (Mitchell) Russell; d. at Norway, ME, 1 Mar 1856; m. at New Gloucester, ME, 4 Jun 1791, as his second wife, JAMES LEBARON, b. at Middleborough, MA, 30 Nov 1759 son of James and Hannah (Turner) LeBaron;[1709] James d. at Paris, ME, 9 Jun 1836. James was first married to Elizabeth Washburn.

James LeBaron was from Middleborough but settled in Hebron, Maine with his first wife Elizabeth Washburn. Later he moved to South Paris village where James died. After, James's death, Jane lived with her daughter Sarah.[1710]

Jane Russell and James LeBaron were parents of five children born at Paris, Maine. James also had two children with his first wife.

i   NATHANIEL LEBARON, b. June 1793; d. in the spring of 1816 two weeks after killing what might have been a rabid fox.

ii   WILLIAM LEBARON, b. Jul 1795; d. at Lovell, ME, 10 Aug 1863; m. at Albany, ME, 16 Aug 1819, his first cousin, JOANNA JORDAN (*Temperance Russell Jordan⁵, James⁴, James³, Thomas², Robert¹*), b. at Gray, ME, 1801 daughter of David and Temperance (Russell) Jordan; Joanna d. at Lovell, 18 Sep 1856.

iii   RUSSELL LEBARON, b. 13 Aug 1797; d. at Harrison, ME, 26 Jun 1873; m. 30 Sep 1819, his first cousin, LYDIA JORDAN (*Temperance Russell Jordan⁵, James⁴, James³, Thomas², Robert¹*), b. at Gray, 1798 daughter of David and Temperance (Russell) Jordan; Lydia d. at Harrison, 8 Jan 1855.

iv   ELIZABETH "BETSEY" LEBARON, b. 22 May 1806; m. DANIEL HENRY KILPATRICK and reported as settling in Hiram, ME.

v   SARAH LEBARON, b. 24 Aug 1808; d. at Paris, ME, 26 Jul 1894; m. WILLIAM KNIGHT, b. at Norway, ME, about 1816 son of Daniel and Sarah (Tubbs) Knight; William d. at Norway, 17 Mar 1887.

vi   SYLVESTER LEBARON, b. 21 May 1815; d. at sea, 22 Feb 1854; m. at Wolfeboro, NH, 5 Dec 1839, ABIGAIL MCINTIRE, b. 1814 daughter of Joshua and Martha (Earl) McIntire;[1711] Abigail d. at Salem, MA, 17 Aug 1892. Sylvester and Abigail's brother Timothy McIntire died in the same shipping accident.[1712]

[1707] The names of Samuel's parents are given as David and Temperance on his marriage record to Ann M. Foster.
[1708] The names of Maria's parents are given as Jonathan Stevens and Martha Moore on her death record. New England Historic Genealogical Society; Boston, Massachusetts; Massachusetts Vital Records, 1841-1911
[1709] Lapham and Maxim, *History of Paris, Maine*, p 659
[1710] Lapham and Maxim, *History of Paris, Maine*, p 659
[1711] McIntire, *Descendants of Micum McIntire*, p 44
[1712] Massachusetts Town and Vital Records, Gloucester

589)   EUNICE RUSSELL (*James⁴, James³, Thomas², Robert¹*), b. at North Yarmouth, ME, 1772 daughter of James and Lydia (Mitchell) Russell; d. at New Gloucester, ME, 24 Dec 1825; m. ENOCH MORSE, b. 3 Jul 1772 son of John and Sarah (Sander) Morse;[1713] Enoch d. at New Gloucester, 16 Aug 1852. Enoch married second Eleanor *Bradbury* Caswell on 27 May 1826.

Enoch was a farmer and blacksmith in New Gloucester. The family resided in New Gloucester throughout their lives. Enoch and Eunice were parents of ten children born at New Gloucester, Maine.[1714]

i   MARK MORSE, b. 13 Oct 1795

ii   ENOCH MORSE, b. 18 Mar 1799; d. at North Yarmouth, ME, 25 Aug 1862; m. 1st about 1832, SARAH MORSE PORTER (widow of John Hayes), b. 1 Nov 1801 daughter of Benjamin and Hannah (Sylvester) Porter; Sarah d. at North Yarmouth, 3 Jun 1852.

iii   STEPHEN MORSE, b. 15 Jan 1803; d. at New Gloucester, 1886; m. 1st at New Gloucester, 13 Oct 1832, JOANNA MERRILL, b. 1809; Joanna d. at New Gloucester, 1857. Stephen m. 2nd 3 Jun 1858, ORINTHA ADDITON (widow of Stephen Bleffin), b. 1822 daughter of John and Hannah (Robbins) Additon; Orintha d. at New Gloucester, 4 Jul 1889.

iv   SUSAN MORSE, b. 13 May 1804; *perhaps* m. about 1830, SIMEON MARSTON, b. about 1802; Simeon d. at Gray, ME, 1847.

v   MARY MORSE, b. 2 Aug 1806; *perhaps* m. at New Gloucester, 20 Oct 1822, JAMES WALKER.

vi   HAPPIAH MORSE, b. 17 Jan 1808; d. at Gray, 30 Sep 1853; m. at New Gloucester, 1831, EDWARD ALLEN, b. at Cumberland, 12 Jun 1805 son of Edward and Esther (Hall) Allen; Edward d. at Gray, 20 Jul 1844.

vii   BENJAMIN MORSE, b. 18 Dec 1809; d. at New Gloucester, 20 Jan 1890; m. 1st at New Gloucester, 27 May 1837, SALLY ALLEN who d. before 1850. Benjamin m. 2nd by 1850, SARAH BENNETT, b. about 1806.

viii   CYNTHIA MORSE, b. 29 Jun 1811; d. (burial at Cumberland), 4 Sep 1878; m. at New Gloucester, 27 May 1832, ROBERT LEIGHTON, b. 28 Mar 1808 son of Andrew and Mary (Weymouth) Leighton; Robert d. 3 Oct 1861.

ix   HANNAH MORSE, b. 17 Apr 1815; d. at New Gloucester, ME, 12 Mar 1892; m. at New Gloucester, 19 Feb 1836, JAMES HULIT, b. at New Gloucester, 14 Jun 1810; James d. at New Gloucester, 29 Sep 1887.

x   MARGARET MORSE, b. 18 Sep 1820; d. after 1860 when living at Lewiston, ME with her two sons; m. at New Gloucester, 20 May 1838, ALFRED ALLEN, b. about 1818; Alfred d. after 1850 and before 1860. Her son Edward R. Allen was wounded at Chancellorsville, VA on 3 May 1863.[1715]

590)   NATHANIEL RUSSELL (*James⁴, James³, Thomas², Robert¹*), b. at North Yarmouth, about 1774 (based on age 68 at death) son of James and Lydia (Mitchell) Russell; d. at Oxford, ME, 10 Nov 1842; m. SARAH MORSE, b. at Oxford, ME, 26 Sep 1774 daughter of John and Sarah (Sanders) Morse; Sarah d. at Norway, ME, 20 Jul 1861.

Nathaniel and Sarah resided in Oxford, Maine and may have had as many as six children, but just one child was identified.

i   LEONICY RUSSELL, b. at Bethel, ME, Jun 1809; d. at Oxford, ME, 22 Mar 1893; m. at Oxford, 8 Dec 1838, SAMUEL SWIFT, b. 1791; d. at Oxford, ME, 30 Dec 1870.

591)   BETSY RUSSELL (*Thomas⁴, James³, Thomas², Robert¹*), b. at Cumberland, 23 Jun 1768 daughter of Thomas Chandler and Sarah (Gooch) Russell; d. at Hartford, ME, 14 May 1857; m. 1st at North Yarmouth, Dec 1785, DANIEL BROWN, b. at Cumberland, 10 Dec 1756 son of Jacob and Lydia (Weare) Brown; Daniel d. at Yarmouth, Oct 1797. Betsy m. 2nd 11 Mar 1800, her first cousin, JEREMIAH RUSSELL (*Joseph⁴, James³, Thomas², Robert¹*), b. at Yarmouth, 3 Apr 1772 son of Joseph and Miriam (Brown) Russell; Jeremiah d. at Hartford, ME, 30 Nov 1843.[1716]

Daniel Brown of North Yarmouth served in the Continental army from 25 March 1777 to 31 December 1779. He served in companies of Capt. Edward Russell and Capt. Robert Davis. He served at Providence and was taken prisoner of war.[1717]

There is one child known for Betsy Russell and Daniel Brown.

[1713] Lord, *Memorial of the Family of Morse*, p 234
[1714] Maine, Birth Records, 1715-1922; Maine State Archives; Cultural Building, 84 State House Station, Augusta, ME 04333-0084; Pre 1892 Delayed Returns; Roll Number: 78; accessed through ancestry.com
[1715] U.S., Civil War Soldier Records and Profiles, 1861-1865
[1716] U. S. Revolutionary War Pension and Bounty-Land Application, Case W22129
[1717] Massachusetts Soldiers and Sailors of the Revolutionary War, volume 2, p 611

i   RUSSELL BROWN, b. at North Yarmouth, ME, about 1788; d. at Lawrence, MA, 11 Jun 1869; m. by 1825, SUSAN TUTTLE, b. at Yarmouth, about 1799 daughter of Zebulon and Jane (Young) Tuttle;[1718] Susan d. at Lawrence, 14 Apr 1895.

Betsy and Jeremiah Russell were parents of six children born at Hartford, Maine.

i   THOMAS CHANDLER RUSSELL, b. 25 Jan 1801; d. at Hartford, ME, 28 Sep 1884; m. about 1830, EUNICE STANDISH, b. at Windham, ME, 12 Jan 1810 daughter of Ellis and Mary (Bradford) Standish; Eunice d. at Hartford, 27 Jul 1882.

ii   SYLVANUS DRINKWATER RUSSELL, b. 25 Mar 1802; d. at Rockport, ME, 1887; m. at Rockport, 18 Sep 1836, DORCAS M. BARRETT, b. at Rockport, 31 Dec 1801 daughter of Daniel and Margaret (Grose) Barrett;[1719] Dorcas d. at Rockport, 17 Mar 1872.

iii   ANDREW RUSSELL, b. 14 Nov 1803; d. at Hartford, 26 Jul 1887; m. 1st SUSAN LEACH, b. 1801; Susan d. at Hartford, 16 Feb 1844. Andrew m. 2nd SARAH W. BURGESS, b. 1827 daughter of Ebenezer and Celia (Atkins) Burgess;[1720] Sarah d. at Mechanic Falls, ME, 6 Feb 1899.

iv   JOHN RUSSELL, b. 3 Aug 1805; d. at Sumner, ME, 19 Sep 1889; m. 1st at Dexter, ME, 4 Jan 1827, DORCAS L. HUTCHINS, b. 1807; Dorcas d. (burial at East Sumner), 29 Aug 1845. John m. 2nd SALLY H. who has not been identified but born about 1799 and died about 1873. John m. 3rd, DIANA, b. Jan 1812 and d. at East Sumner, 7 Apr 1904.

v   DORCAS RUSSELL, b. 12 May 1808; d. at Canton, ME, 14 Jan 1862; m. about 1829, WILBUR LEACH, b. 13 Feb 1802 son of Isaac and Susan (Wilbur) Leach; Wilbur d. at Hartford, 1858.

vi   JEREMIAH RUSSELL, b. 13 Jul 1810

592)   RHODA RUSSELL (*Thomas⁴, James³, Thomas², Robert¹*), b. at Cumberland, 10 Mar 1770 daughter of Thomas Chandler and Sarah (Gooch) Russell; d. at West Boylston, MA, 13 Dec 1852; m. at Cumberland, 1787, SAMUEL LAWRENCE, b. at Cumberland, 6 Jul 1766 son of Joseph and Abigail (Brown) Lawrence; Samuel d. at West Boylston, 31 Mar 1824.
    Rhoda and Samuel resided at Temple, Maine. In the 1804 census taken in the newly incorporated town of Temple, parents and eight children (Joseph, Chandler, Sallie, Abigail, Betty, Nancy, Samuel, and Seneh) were listed. The family was in North Yarmouth just prior to their move to Temple.[1721] The family was in Temple by 1803 and were there until 1820.[1722] Samuel and Rhoda both died at West Boylston, Massachusetts. Samuel still had property in Temple at the time of his death and his estate in Maine was administered by Joseph Lawrence. The estate was insolvent.[1723]
    Rhoda Russell and Samuel Lawrence were parents of fourteen children, the births recorded at Temple, Maine, although at least the older children where likely born at North Yarmouth where the family was living in 1790.

i   JOSEPH LAWRENCE, b. 30 Mar 1788; d. at West Boylston, MA, 28 Apr 1854; m. at Temple, ME, 15 Nov 1810, BETHIAH HOSMER, b. 1792 daughter of Daniel and Hannah (baker) Hosmer; Bethiah d. at Sterling, MA, 27 Aug 1857.

ii   THOMAS CHANDLER LAWRENCE, b. 27 Dec 1789; d. at Grafton, MA, 1 Sep 1877; m. about 1815, MARY HALL, b. 1793; Mary d. at West Boylston, MA, 16 Sep 1838. Thomas m. 2nd at West Boylston, 17 Feb 1839, ABIGAIL MARSHALL (widow of Thomas Blake), b. at Northumberland, NH 1794 daughter of Antipas and Sarah (Low) Marshall; Abigail d. at Uxbridge, MA, 15 Dec 1873. Thomas C. Russell was a housewright and built the Congregational meeting house in Temple, ME.[1724]

iii   SALLY LAWRENCE, b. 4 Jan 1792; d. at Tempe, 1822; m. at Temple, 23 Jul 1809, DAVID OAKES, b. about 1790 son of John and Patience 9Mason) Oakes; David d. at Old Town, ME, 1861.

[1718] The names of Susan's parents are as given on her death record.
[1719] Robinson, *History of Camden and Rockport, Maine*, p 294
[1720] The names of Sarah's parents are given as Ebenezer and Celia Burgess on her death record.
[1721] Pierce, *A History of Temple, Maine*, p 22, p 26
[1722] 1820 U S Census; Census Place: Temple, Kennebec, Maine; Page: 425; NARA Roll: M33_35; Image: 36
[1723] Maine Wills and Probate, Kennebec County, volume 20, Orders of Notice, p 79; Estate files, Samuel Lawrence L-2
[1724] Pierce, *A History of Temple, Maine*, p 52

iv   ABIGAIL LAWRENCE, b. 7 Jul 1795; d. at Temple, 1821; m. at Temple, 3 Oct 1811, likely his second wife, AMOS HOSMER, b. at Concord, MA, 1775 son of Daniel and Hannah (Baker) Hosmer. After Abigail's death, Amos married Sarah Johnson.

v   BETSEY LAWRENCE, b. 12 Mar 1796; m. at Temple, 9 Jul 1812, JEREMIAH ABBOTT, perhaps the Jeremiah b. at Ashby MA, 15 Feb 1792 son of Jeremiah and Patty (Jaquith) Abbott.

vi   NANCY LAWRENCE, b. 22 Nov 1799; d. at Adams County, WI, 11 Dec 1877; m. at Temple, 16 Jan 1817, EDWARD OAKES, b. at Temple, Aug 1792 son of John and Patience (Mason) Oakes; Edward d. at Adams County, WI, 12 Mar 1863.

vii   SAMUEL LAWRENCE, b. 29 Oct 1800; d. at West Boylston, MA, 27 Jul 1862; m. 1st at West Boylston, 21 Oct 1824, EUNICE BEAMAN NEWTON, b. at West Boylston, 1 Feb 1806 daughter of Silas and Eunice (Prescott) Newton; Eunice d. at West Boylston, 1 Sep 1846. Samuel m. 2nd at West Boylston, 16 May 1847, MARTHA B. HOWE (widow of Levi Bigelow), b. 1808 daughter of Winslow and Dolly (Hayden) Howe.

viii   SENAH LAWRENCE, b. 19 Aug 1802; d. at Grafton, MI, 10 Oct 1874; m. at Temple, 16 Mar 1822, BENJAMIN MCLAUGHLIN, b. at Weld, ME, 9 Nov 1801 son of John and Bethiah (Wilkins) McLaughlin; Benjamin d. at Grafton, MI, 31 Mar 1858.

ix   JOHN B. LAWRENCE, b. 19 Apr 1804; d. at Worcester, MA, 19 Jun 1883; m. at West Boylston, 5 Mar 1831, LUCRETIA BULLARD NEWTON, b. 6 Sep 1811 daughter of Silas and Eunice (Prescott) Newton; Lucretia d. at West Boylston, 29 Jun 1903.

x   WILLIAM LAWRENCE, b. 6 Apr 1806; d. 6 Oct 1812.

xi   SOPHRONIA LAWRENCE, b. 11 Mar 1808; m. at Temple, 20 Nov 1831, JOHN PRATT.

xii   JAMES RUSSELL LAWRENCE, b. 1 Aug 1811; d. at West Boylston, 7 Nov 1846, m. at Temple, 30 Sep 1832, BETSEY WAITE, b. about 1817 daughter of David and Polly (Newton) Waite;[1725] Betsey d. at West Boylston, 2 Oct 1858.

xiii   BENJAMIN LAWRENCE, b. 11 Mar 1813; d. at Greenwood, MN, 1883; m. 1st at Temple, 9 Sep 1834, HANNAH CRANE who d. at Temple, 21 Oct 1835. Benjamin m. 2nd at Temple, 10 Apr 1836, ELMIRA HILLMAN, b. 1816; Elmira d. at Readfield, ME, 31 Jul 1851. Benjamin m. 3rd NANCY PRESTON

xiv   RHODA RUSSELL LAWRENCE, b. 22 Feb 1815; d. at Weld, ME, 6 Jun 1856; m. 1835, JAMES MCLAUGHLIN, b. at Weld, 12 Jun 1805 son of John and Bethiah (Wilkins) McLaughlin; James d. 12 Jul 1884.

593)   JAMES RUSSELL (*Thomas⁴, James³, Thomas², Robert¹*), b. at Cumberland, 3 Dec 1771 son of Thomas Chandler and Sarah (Gooch) Russell; d. at North Yarmouth, 5 Jul 1859; m. at Cumberland, 20 Dec 1796, JOANNA TRUE, b. at Cumberland, 22 Aug 1777 daughter of William and Susannah (Brown) True; Joanna d. at North Yarmouth, 27 Feb 1863.

      James Russell was a farmer in North Yarmouth. There are records for fourteen children of James Russell and Joanna True.[1726] In 1830, James Russell headed a household of twelve persons at Yarmouth: one male 50 to 59, one female 50 to 59, one male 5 to 9, two males, 10 to 14, two males 15 to 19, two males 20 to 29, one female 15 to 19, one female 20 to 29, and one female 30 to 39.[1727] In 1850, James and Joanna were in Yarmouth with their daughter Sarah Heath and grandson James A. Heath with them.[1728]

i   WILLIAM RUSSELL, baptized at North Yarmouth, 22 Sep 1797; d. at Yarmouth, 3 Oct 1877; m. 1st DOLLY TRUE HUMPHREY, b. 28 Feb 1800 daughter of Joshua and Phebe (Loring) Humphrey; Dolly d. 16 Mar 1836. William m. 2nd HANNAH S., b. 1800 and d. at Yarmouth, 1854. William m. 3rd MATILDA BATCHELDER, b. at Cumberland, 16 Nov 1816 daughter of James and Susan (Marston) Batchelder; Matilda d. at North Yarmouth, 14 Apr 1890.

ii   SARAH RUSSELL, baptized at North Yarmouth, 27 Sep 1799; d. at Oakland, CA, 7 Jan 1877.[1729] In 1870, Sarah was living at San Jose, CA with her son James A. Heath and his wife.[1730] Sarah married Mr. Heath who has not

---

[1725] The names of Betsey's parents are given as David and Polly Waite on her death record.

[1726] Maine Births and Christenings, 1739-1900

[1727] Year: 1830; Census Place: North Yarmouth, Cumberland, Maine; Series: M19; Roll: 46; Page: 342; Family History Library Film: 0009700

[1728] Year: 1850; Census Place: Yarmouth, Cumberland, Maine; Roll: 249; Page: 248b

[1729] "California, Oakland, Mountain View Cemetery Records, 1857-1973," database, *FamilySearch* (https://familysearch.org/ark:/61903/1:1:W7BR-1YT2 : 16 September 2019), Sarah R Heath, 7 Jan 1877; citing Burial, California, United States, Mountain View Cemetery, Oakland; FHL microfilm 008266227.

[1730] Year: 1870; Census Place: San Jose, Santa Clara, California; Roll: M593_88; Page: 278A; Family History Library Film: 545587

been identified. In 1850, Sarah Heath and her son James were living with James and Joanna Russell in Yarmouth.[1731] Sarah with her son James were in Roxbury, MA in the 1860 and 1865 census.

iii   RALPH RUSSELL, baptized at Cumberland, 13 Mar 1801

iv   THOMAS G. RUSSELL, baptized at North Yarmouth, 6 Oct 1802; d. at Yarmouth, 10 Apr 1867; m. HANNAH T. who has not been identified, b. 1802; Hannah d. at Yarmouth, 1886.

v   HULDAH GREEN RUSSELL, baptized at North Yarmouth, 15 Aug 1804; d. at Minneapolis, MN, 3 Jun 1872; m. WILLIAM HOYT, b. at North Yarmouth, 13 Sep 1799 son of William and Mehitable (Titcomb) Hoyt;[1732] William d. at Minneapolis, 8 Jun 1888.

vi   JOHN RUSSELL, b. at Cumberland, 25 May 1806; d. 25 Feb 1807.

vii   SUSANNA RUSSELL, baptized at Cumberland, 19 Jan 1808

viii   JOHN JAMES RUSSELL, baptized at Cumberland, 3 Oct 1809; d. at Baring, ME, 14 Apr 1866; m. by 1839, MARY SARGENT, b. at Yarmouth, 20 Mar 1810 daughter of John and Mary (Riggs) Sargent; Mary d. at Baring, 27 Jun 1897.

ix   MOSES RUSSELL, baptized at Cumberland, 25 Sep 1811; d. at Portland, ME, 9 Nov 1871; m. 1st about 1839, NANCY HOYT, b. at North Yarmouth, 24 Oct 1813 daughter of William and Mehitable (Titcomb) Hoyt;[1733] Nancy d. at Portland, 23 Nov 1851. Moses m. 2nd at Somersworth, NH, 3 Nov 1855, MARTHA A. HOOPER (widow Martha Ward), b. in NH, May 1815; Martha d. at Portland, 20 May 1909.

x   TRUE RUSSELL, baptized at Cumberland, 3 oct 1813; d. at Hyde Park, MA, 3 Oct 1888; m. 1st at Roxbury, 1 Jan 1849, SUSAN PRATT, b. at Yarmouth, ME, 1826 daughter of Levi H. and Lois (Thompson) Pratt; Susan d. at Roxbury, 4 Jul 1866. True m. 2nd 16 Sep 1869, PRUDENCE WHITWELL, b. at Boston, 8 Feb 1815 daughter of Jacob P. and Mary A. (Richards) Whitwell; Prudence d. at Hyde Park, 15 Feb 1895.

xi   NANCY JUDSON RUSSELL, b. at Cumberland, Aug 1815

xii   ADONIRAM JUDSON RUSSELL, b. at Cumberland, 28 Jul 1817; d. at North Yarmouth, 1 Aug 1839.

xiii   STEPHEN CHAPIN RUSSELL, b. at Cumberland, 25 Sep 1819; d. at New Orleans, LA, 11 Jun 1902; m. about 1869, MARTHA WHITNEY, b. in ME, 1836; Martha d. at New Orleans, Feb 1905.

xiv   RALPH COLMAN RUSSELL, baptized at Cumberland, 25 Aug 1821; d. after 1894 when he was living at San Diego; m. at Portland, ME, 9 Sep 1849, MATILDA SMITH, b. in ME, Jan 1828; Matilda d. after 1900 when she was living at San Diego.

594)   JOSEPH RUSSELL (*Thomas⁴, James³, Thomas², Robert¹*), b. at Cumberland, 17 Dec 1775 son of Thomas Chandler and Sarah (Gooch) Russell; likely m. at Cumberland, 8 Jan 1801, RACHEL PRATT, b. at Cumberland, 23 Apr 1778 daughter of Sherebiah and Anna (Millett) Pratt.

    Joseph and Rachel were parents of seven children born at Cumberland, Maine.[1734]

i   EUNICE RUSSELL, b. 16 Sep 1801

ii   SALOME RUSSELL, b. 18 Apr 1803; d. at Yarmouth, 1869. Salome did not marry.

iii   SAMUEL G. RUSSELL, b. 10 Jun 1805; m. at Durham, ME, 29 Mar 1843, MARY F. HOYT, b. at Durham, 1814 daughter of John and Mary (Gerrish) Hoyt. Samuel and Mary were living in Yarmouth in 1860.

iv   JANE RUSSELL, b. 31 Mar 1807; d. at Yarmouth, 1836.

v   BENJAMIN P. RUSSELL, b. 15 Jul 1810; d. at Freedom, NH, 28 Jul 1874; m. Sep 1838, BELINDA SAYWARD, b. at Parsonsfield, 30 Jul 1808 daughter of James and Lydia (Witherell) Sayward; Belinda d. at Freedom, 27 May 1873.

vi   HANNAH RUSSELL, b. 9 Apr 1813; d. at Yarmouth, 1832.

vii   RACHEL PRATT RUSSELL, b. 17 Aug 1815; d. at Yarmouth, 1863; m. CHARLES BYLES SMALL, b. 28 Nov 1815 son of Daniel and Joanna (Soule) Small; Charles d. at Yarmouth, 10 Sep 1875.

[1731] Year: 1850; Census Place: Yarmouth, Cumberland, Maine; Roll: 249; Page: 248b

[1732] Hoyt, *Genealogical History of the Hoyt Family*, p 197

[1733] Hoyt, *Genealogical History of the Hoyt Family*, p 197

[1734] "Maine Births and Christenings, 1739-1900", database, *FamilySearch*

595)   JOANNA RUSSELL (*Thomas⁴, James³, Thomas², Robert¹*), b. at Cumberland, 23 Apr 1779 daughter of Thomas Chandler and Sarah (Gooch) Russell; d. at Yarmouth, 20 Jan 1848; m. 28 Jan 1808, ASA S. TRUE, b. at Cumberland, 28 Feb 1780 son of William and Susannah (Brown) True; Asa d. at Yarmouth, 13 Nov 1848.
          One child was identified for Joanna and Asa True.

i   SARAH RUSSELL TRUE, b. at Cumberland, ME, 5 Aug 1820

596)   PHEBE RUSSELL (*Thomas⁴, James³, Thomas², Robert¹*), b. at Cumberland, 16 May 1783 daughter of Thomas Chandler and Sarah (Gooch) Russell; d. at Parsonsfield, ME, 29 Jan 1858; m. 1800, JOHN F. HUNTRESS, b. at Newington, NH, 7 Nov 1775 son of Nathan and Susanna (Chick) Huntress; John d. at Parsonsfield, 13 Sep 1852.
          John Huntress was a shoemaker. In 1850, they resided in Parsonsfield with children Thomas and Sarah still in the home.[1735] They were parents of ten children.

i   ROBERT H. HUNTRESS, b. 1802; d. at Effingham, NH, 22 Mar 1872; m. 22 Dec 1829, BETSEY W. SAYWARD, b. 22 May 1806 daughter of James and Lydia (Witherell) Sayward.

ii   JOHN R. HUNTRESS, b. 1803. In 1860, John Huntress was a farm hand living in Parsonsfield and apparently unmarried.[1736]

iii   FREDERICK C. HUNTRESS, b. 1805; d. at sea 23 Dec 1839; m. at Portland, ME, 26 Feb 1834, ABIGAIL CURTIS

iv   JAMES RUSSELL HUNTRESS, b. 11 Nov 1806; d. at Parsonsfield, 23 Apr 1858; m. 1ˢᵗ at Portland, 30 Apr 1836, ELIA ANN SMITH, b. 1816; Eliza d. at Parsonsfield, 13 Jul 1844. James m. 2ⁿᵈ MARY SWETT, b. at Parsonsfield, 1808 daughter of Stephen and Rachel (Colcord) Swett; Mary d. at Parsonsfield, 23 May 1853.

v   NATHAN HUNTRESS, b. 1808; d. about 1839; m. at Morgan, VA (current WVA), 20 Mar 1833, CHARLOTTE FOUTZ.

vi   THOMAS CHANDLER HUNTRESS, b. 13 Mar 1811; d. at Parsonsfield, 5 Mar 1901; m. about 1853, ANNIE HURN, b. at Freedom, NH, 19 Aug 1822; Annie d. at Parsonsfield, 15 Jul 1889.

vii   SILAS B. HUNTRESS, b. at Parsonsfield, 23 Jul 1813; d. at Portland, ME, 30 Sep 1874; m. at Portland, SARAH JANE DAVIS, b. at Portland, 29 Dec 1814 daughter of James W. and Rhoda (Tukey) Davis; Sarah d. at Portland, 17 Oct 1890.

viii   SARAH ANN HUNTRESS, b. 1816; d. at Freedom, NH, 13 Feb 1880; m. 5 Jan 1852, as his second wife, JOHN BROOKS, b. at Effingham, NH, 18 Mar 1797 son of Daniel and Susan (Dunn) Brooks; John d. at Freedom, 27 Dec 1874. John was first married to Elizabeth Cummings.

ix   MARY M. HUNTRESS, b. 1822; d. at Boston, 17 Apr 1887; m. by 1845, ELIAS W. HARMON, b. at Freedom, NH, 1820 son of Phineas and Ruth (-) Harmon; Elias d. at Boston, 8 Mar 1881.

x   ELIZA JANE HUNTRESS, b. 1825; d. at Haverhill, MA, 27 Jul 1885; m. about 1845, JAMES FOSS, b. at Freedom, NH, 1820 son of Peletiah and Jane (Harmon) Foss;[1737] James d. at Freedom, 22 Mar 1860.

597)   MARY RUSSELL (*Thomas⁴, James³, Thomas², Robert¹*), b. at Cumberland, 14 May 1784 daughter of Thomas Chandler and Sarah (Gooch) Russell; d. at Yarmouth, 4 Jan 1857; m. at Cumberland, 30 Mar 1803, DAVID PRATT, b. at Cumberland, 3 May 1776 son of Sherebiah and Anna (Millett) Pratt; David d. at Yarmouth, 28 Feb 1850.
          David Prat was born in North Yarmouth and resided in Cumberland County, Maine throughout his life. He was a farmer and lumberman and was successful in his endeavors. Son Jacob R. Pratt took over part of the homestead farm in 1839.[1738]
          In the 1830 census for North Yarmouth, there were eleven members of the household: one male 50 to 59, one female 40 to 49, one male 5 to 9, one male 10 to 14, one male 15 to 19, one male 20 to 29, one female under 5, two females 10 to 14, and one female 15 to 19.[1739]

[1735] Year: 1850; Census Place: Parsonsfield, York, Maine; Roll: M432_276; Page: 367A; Image: 503

[1736] Year: 1860; Census Place: Parsonsfield, York, Maine; Page: 620; Family History Library Film: 803451

[1737] Names of parents as Peletiah and Jane are given on the death record.

[1738] Biographical Review, Cumberland County, Maine, pp 215-216

[1739] Year: 1830; Census Place: North Yarmouth, Cumberland, Maine; Series: M19; Roll: 46; Page: 349; Family History Library Film: 0009700

In the 1850 census taken 15 August 1850, Eunice Pratt age 35 and Hannah Y. Pratt age 25 were living in Yarmouth with Mary Pratt age 68 who was head of household.[1740] Daughter Eunice did not marry. In her will written 22 August 1871 (probate November 1876), Eunice Pratt of Yarmouth left her entire estate to her sister Hannah Y. Tibbets who was also named executrix.[1741]

Mary and David were parents of fourteen children likely all born at North Yarmouth although some of the births are recorded at Cumberland.[1742]

i STEPHEN PRATT, b. at Cumberland, 16 Oct 1803; d. after 1880 when living at Yarmouth; m. LOUISA SARGENT, b. about 1803; Louisa d. after 1870.

ii EBENEZER PRATT, b. at Cumberland, 7 Jan 1805; m. 1st SARAH who has not been identified and likely d. about 1840.

iii JOANNA PRATT, b. 15 Aug 1806; d. 8 Jul 1824.

iv ASA PRATT, b. 6 Nov 1807

v THOMAS PRATT, b. at Cumberland, 7 Nov 1809; d. at Yarmouth, 2 Feb 1877; m. about 1839, MARY BUCKNAM, b. about 1816 daughter of Samuel and Phebe (Chandler) Bucknam;[1743] Mary d. at Yarmouth, 4 Aug 1892.

vi LEVI PRATT, b. at Cumberland, 6 Jul 1811; d. at Parsonsfield, 30 Sep 1883; m. about 1840, MARY EDGECOMB, b. Sep 1819 daughter of James and Elizabeth (Lougee) Edgecomb;[1744] Mary d. at Newfield, ME, 28 Feb 1907

vii EUNICE PRATT, b. at Cumberland, 16 May 1813; d. at Yarmouth, 18 Jan 1876. Eunice did not marry.

viii BETSEY PRATT, b. 3 Jul 1815

ix JACOB RUSSELL PRATT, b. at Cumberland, 16 Sep 1817; d. after 1900 when living at Yarmouth; m. 1st SARAH A. BARBOUR, b. 1820; Sarah d. 20 Mar 1848. Jacob m. 2nd CLARINDA S. SPARROW, b. at Hartford, ME, 1820 daughter of William Sparrow.

x SARAH PRATT, b. 7 Jul 1819

xi OTIS BRIGGS PRATT, b. at Cumberland, 9 May 1821; d. after 1860 when living at Yarmouth and before 1870; m. about 1847, ELIZABETH LUFKIN, b. in ME 1825 daughter of Nehemiah and Bethiah (Maxfield) Lufkin; Elizabeth d. after 1870.

xii HANNAH Y. PRATT, b. Apr 1823; d. at Auburn, ME, 29 Jul 1884; m. JOHN E. TIBBETTS, b. about 1825; John d. at Auburn, 1 Feb 1895.

xiii DAVID PRATT, b. at North Yarmouth, Dec 1824

xiv MARY ANN PRATT, b. 1825; d. at Yarmouth, 27 Aug 1836.

598) DORCAS RUSSELL (*Thomas⁴, James³, Thomas², Robert¹*), b. at Cumberland, 7 May 1789 daughter of Thomas Chandler and Sarah (Gooch) Russell; d. at Hartford, ME, May 1860; m. BENJAMIN THOMAS, b. at Middleborough, MA, 25 Dec 1785 son of Perez and Sarah (Wood) Thomas; Benjamin d. at Hartford, 1867 (probate 1867).

In his will written 22 February 1867 (probate July 1867), Benjamin Thomas bequeaths to son Perez Thomas, one hundred dollars. The heirs of son Benjamin, late of Mexico in said county, receive five hundred dollars to divide equally (currently being five in number). Two daughters Sarah J. Goding and Betsey R. Stetson receive all the household furniture. Son William Thomas receives five dollars. The wearing apparel is to be divided equally among Perez, William, and the heirs of Benjamin Thomas, Jr. The remainder of the estate, after payment of debts and erection of a suitable monument over his remains, is to be equally divided among the heirs. Personal estate was valued at $3,179.89.[1745]

Dorcas Russell and Benjamin Thomas were parents of five children born at Hartford, Maine.

i PEREZ THOMAS, b. 6 Apr 1810; d. at Caribou, ME, 21 Feb 1886; m. about 1835, MARY SAMPSON, b. at Hartford, ME, 4 Apr 1813 daughter of Moses and Polly (Thomas) Sampson; Mary d. at Caribou, 3 Aug 1882.

[1740] Year: 1850; Census Place: Yarmouth, Cumberland, Maine; Roll: 249; Page: 248b

[1741] Maine Wills and Probate, Androscoggin County, Estate of Eunice Pratt, Case 1260

[1742] As for example, "Maine Births and Christenings, 1739-1900", database, *FamilySearch* (https://familysearch.org/ark:/61903/1:1:F4CW-X5Z : 14 January 2020), Stephen Pratt, 1803, is recorded as Cumberland, Cumberland County, Maine

[1743] The names of Mary's parents are given as Samuel and Phebe Bucknam on her death record.

[1744] The names of Mary's parents are given as James and Elizabeth Edgecomb on her death record.

[1745] Maine Wills and Probate, Oxford County, Estate of Benjamin Thomas, case 108

ii   SARAH J. THOMAS, b. 14 May 1813; d. at Peru, ME, 18 Dec 1894; m. 1 Mar 1840, THOMAS ADAM GODING, b. 14 May 1813 son of Jonathan and Mary (Coolidge) Goding;[1746] Thomas d. at Peru, 29 Jul 1876.

iii   BETSEY RUSSELL THOMAS, b. 29 Sep 1816; d. at Hartford, 16 Oct 1893; m. SOLOMON M. STETSON, b. 25 Oct 1817 son of Hezekiah and Rebecca (Gowell) Stetson; Solomon d. at Sumner, ME, 6 Jan 1890.

iv   BENJAMIN THOMAS, b. 9 Oct 1819; d. at Mexico, ME, 19 Sep 1864; m. 1st about 1847, LOVINA THOMAS, b. at Hartford, 18 Apr 1818 daughter of Nathaniel and Sarah (Thomas) Thomas; Lovina d. at Mexico, ME, 28 Jul 1856. Benjamin m. 2nd at Mexico, 20 May 1858, NANCY JANE SMITH, b. at Mexico, 1834 daughter of Samuel and Mary (Emerson) Smith.

v   WILLIAM THOMAS, b. 15 Sep 1821; d. after 1880 when living at Pine, ME; m. at Hartford, ME, 25 Jan 1846, MARY ELIZABETH GOWELL, b. 1828 daughter of Hezekiah and Agness (Skillings) Gowell; Mary d. after 1880.

599)   JACOB MITCHELL RUSSELL (*Thomas⁴, James³, Thomas², Robert¹*), b. at Cumberland, 18 Aug 1792 son of Thomas Chandler and Sarah (Gooch) Russell; d. after 1860 when he was living in Aroostook County, ME; m. by 1828, MARGARET E. who has not been identified, but born at New Brunswick, about 1805.

       In 1850, Jacob M. Russell and wife Margaret were living at Number 11, Aroostook, Maine with eight children.[1747] Those eights children are given here.

i   SARAH RUSSELL, b. 1829

ii   BENJAMIN RUSSELL, b. 1835

iii   SAMUEL GEORGE RUSSELL, b. 14 Sep 1836; d. at Somerville, MA, 8 Aug 1911; m. ADA T. BENNETT, b. in ME, 1838 daughter of George and Sarah (Allen) Bennett; Ada d. at Hudson, NH, 12 Nov 1924.

iv   ISRAEL RUSSELL, b. 1837; d. at Washington, DC, 10 Sep 1862 while serving with the 1st Cavalry during the Civil War.

v   DESIRE JANE RUSSELL, b. 1839; d. at Amity, ME, about 1869; m. at Houlton, 27 Apr 1858, THOMAS TRACY, b. 1832 son of Asa and Elizabeth (Nason) Tracy; Thomas d. at Amity, 18 May 1913. Thomas married second Keziah Wilcox.

vi   MARGARET E. RUSSELL, b. 1843; m. at Houlton, ME, 7 Jul 1866, JAMES RUGAN, b. at New Brunswick, 1841 son of Patrick and Ann (-) Rugan. Margaret and James divorced Feb 1872.[1748]

vii   THOMAS C. RUSSELL, b. 1846

viii   MARY RUSSELL, b. 1849

600)   DESIRE RUSSELL (*Thomas⁴, James³, Thomas², Robert¹*), b. at Cumberland, 16 May 1794 daughter of Thomas Chandler and Sarah (Gooch) Russell; d. at Melrose, MA, 5 Jun 1882; m. at Hartford, ME, 22 Aug 1813, MARTIN ELLIS, b. 15 Sep 1791 son of Perez and Mary (Hathaway) Ellis; Martin d at Canton, ME, 14 May 1871.

       Martin was a farmer in Canton, Maine. He served briefly in the War of 1812 from 14 September to 24 September 1814 in the Massachusetts militia company of Capt. Paget.[1749]

       In the 1850 census, the value of his real estate was given as $1,000 and the household was Martin age 58, Desire age 57, Elizabeth age 23, Jacob age 16, Walter B. age 14, and Hannah age 9.[1750]

       Desire and Martin were parents of eleven children likely all born at Canton, Maine.

i   PEREZ RUSSELL ELLIS, b. at Canton, ME, 1 Apr 1814; d. at Melrose, MA, 13 Nov 1882; m. 1st 1838, BETSEY ALLEN, b. 1817; Betsey d. at Malden, 18 Apr 1849. Perez m. 2nd 1849, ELIZA L. GURNEY, b. at Minot, ME, 12 Jan 1817 daughter of Thomas and Ruby (Chandler0 Gurney; Eliza d. at Melrose, 15 Jun 1855. Perez m. 3rd at Medford, 9 Apr 1856, MARY D. LANE, b. at New Gloucester, ME, 23 Dec 1808 daughter of Josiah and Abigail (Cleaves) Lane; Mary d. at Melrose, 3 Jan 1898.

[1746] Goding, *Genealogy of the Goding Family*, p 40

[1747] Year: 1850; Census Place: Number 11, Aroostook, Maine; Roll: M432_248; Page: 26A; Image: 56

[1748] Maine, Divorce Records, 1798-1891; James Rugan, plaintiff

[1749] War of 1812 Pension Application Files Index, 1812-1815; application of widow Desire Russell Ellis

[1750] Year: 1850; Census Place: Canton, Oxford, Maine; Roll: 263; Page: 123A

ii   SARAH G. ELLIS, b. at Canton, ME, 1816; d. at Bedford, MA, 16 Oct 1863; m. at Stoneham, MA, 1842, JAMES BARRETT, b. at Malden, MA, 1 May 1817 son of Jonathan and Fanny (Lynde) Barrett; James d. at Melrose, 27 Dec 1872.

iii   MARTIN ELLIS, b. at Canton, ME, 1818; d. at Woburn, MA, 21 Oct 1895; m. 1st at Wakefield, MA, 8 May 1844, LYDIA L. BARTLETT, b. at Peru, ME, 21 Apr 1821 daughter of John and Fanny (Tilson) Bartlett;[1751] Lydia d. at Melrose, MA, 25 Oct 1858. Martin m. 2nd at Stoneham, MA, 16 Oct 1864, LUCINDA KNOWLES DOANE (widow of Ira Eaton), b. at Eastham, MA, 1829 daughter of Knowles and Lucinda (Cobb) Doane; Lucinda d. at Woburn, 29 Jan 1882.

iv   MARY JANE ELLIS, b. at Canton, about 1820; d. at Canton, 15 Nov 1863; m. THOMAS CHANDLER GURNEY, b. 1813 son of Thomas and Ruby (Chandler) Gurney; Thomas d. at Canton, 5 Feb 1894.

v   DAVID H. ELLIS, b. at Canton, Dec 1820; d. at Hill County, TX, 11 Oct 1918; m. 1st at South Kingston, NH, 8 Sep 1845, SARAH WEBSTER, b. 1819; Sarah d. at Jackson Township, IN, 8 Nov 1885. David and Sarah seemed to have divorced. David m. 2nd at McLennan, TX, 28 Jul 1878, NANCY ANN HICKSON (widow of James Upchurch), b. at Lowndes, AL, 26 Nov 1842 daughter of William and Harriet (Cole) Hickson; Nancy d. at Arlington, TX, 5 Dec 1924.

vi   ELIZABETH W. ELLIS, b. 1825; d. at Canton, ME, 7 Apr 1862; m. at Reading, MA, 15 Sep 1852, MOSES SIMS, b. at Dorchester, MA, 16 Dec 1825 son of Samuel and Abigail (Woods) Sims; Moses d. at Wilmington, NC, 7 Mar 1865. Moses served in the 2nd Maine Cavalry and was taken prisoner at the battle of Marianna, FL on 27 Sep 1864.[1752] Moses was married second to Jane.

vii   THOMAS CHANDLER ELLIS, b. 3 Mar 1827; d. 25 Apr 1838.

viii   DEZIAH RUSSELL ELLIS, b. 15 Sep 1830; d. at Compton, Québec, 31 Dec 1907; m. at Boston, 23 May 1850, AMOS ADAMS MERRILL, b. at Compton, 19 May 1826 son of Amos and Lydia (Reynolds) Merrill; Amos d. at Compton, 2 Dec 1898.

ix   JACOB MITCHELL ELLIS, b. at Canton, 1 Nov 1834; d. at Woburn, MA, 10 Jul 1908; m. 1st at Melrose, 17 Jun 1854, BETSEY JANE PACKARD, b. at Brookfield, MA, 1831 daughter of Moses and Betsey (Robinson) Packard; Betsey d. at Melrose, 16 Mar 1861. Jacob m. 2nd 1867, MARGARET CLINTON, b. at New Orleans, LA, Nov 1839 daughter of William Clinton; Margaret d. at Woburn, 5 Dec 1904.

x   WALTER BYRON ELLIS, b. at Canton, 11 Mar 1836; d. at Melrose, 15 May 1911; m. 1861, MARTHA JANE CHILD, b. in ME, Apr 1841 daughter of Marshall and Olive (Stetson) Child; Martha d. at Melrose, 19 Apr 1909.

xi   HANNAH MARIE ELLIS, b. at Canton, 1840; d. at Woburn, 23 Jan 1881; m. HIRAM CHILD, b. at Livermore, ME, 18 Aug 1835 son of Marshall and Olive (Stetson) Child; Hiram d. at Malden, 3 Dec 1915.

601)   ANDREW RUSSELL (*Joseph⁴, James³, Thomas², Robert¹*), b. at Cumberland, 13 Apr 1768 son of Joseph and Miriam (Brown) Russell; d. after 1810 when he was living at North Yarmouth; m. about 1793, SARAH who has not been identified. Although census records suggest four children in this family, records for just two children were located.

i   JOSEPH RUSSELL, b. at Hartford, ME, 22 Nov 1794

ii   WATSON GRAY RUSSELL, b. at Hartford, ME, 25 Jan 1799; d. at Granville, Nova Scotia, 30 Jan 1869; m. 1st about 1829, ELIZABETH CHURCHILL HALFYARD, b. at Granville, 25 Nov 1809 daughter of Richard and Mary (Woster) Halfyard; Elizabeth d. at Dartmouth, Nova Scotia, 26 Oct 1849. Watson m. 2nd about 1850, CATHERINE BURKE, b. at New Brunswick, 1827.

[1751] Tilson, *The Tilson Genealogy*, p 115
[1752] U.S., Registers of Deaths of Volunteers, 1861-1865

Great-Grandchildren of James Russell and Priscilla Osgood

602)   ELI RUSSELL (*Jeduthan⁴, James³, James², Robert¹*), b. at Walpole, NH, 13 Mar 1775 son of Jeduthan and Susannah (Glazier) Russell; d. at Westminster, VT, 11 Dec 1841; m. at Walpole, 5 Jan 1803, HEPSIBAH FLOYD, b. at Walpole, 3 Sep 1779 daughter of Benjamin and Lydia (Bond) Floyd; Hepsibah d. at Westminster, 30 Jul 1840.

    Eli and Hepsibah married in Walpole and may have been in Keene briefly where the birth of their second child is recorded. They were then in Westminster, Vermont where their four youngest children were born. Sons George Dana Russell and Joseph Martin Russell were music publishers and music dealers in Boston. Son Warren Edmund Russel was an insurance agent.

    Eli Russell and Hepsibah Floyd were parents of six children.

i   Child, b. 1806; d. at Walpole, NH, 4 Aug 1810.

ii   WARREN EDMUND RUSSELL, b. at Keene, NH, 1814; d. at Lexington, MA, 27 Nov 1874; m. about 1839, SARAH ANN RICHARDS, b. at Westminster, VT, 16 Jun 1820 daughter of Luther and Mary (Page) Richards; Sarah d. at Lexington, 25 Nov 1895.

iii   ELI B. RUSSELL, b. at Westminster, VT, 1816; d. at New York, NY, Nov 1885 (burial 20 Nov); m. 1ˢᵗ at Waltham, MA, 12 Mar 1845, MARIA ROXANA GARFIELD, b. at Waltham, 28 May 1824 daughter of Alvis and Susanna (Maynard) Garfield; Maria d. at Waltham, 28 May 1848. After Marias' death, Eli went to sea receiving his seaman's certificate at New York Harbor on 11 Oct 1849. Eli m. 2ⁿᵈ at New Hamburg, NY, 31 Dec 1850, EMMA J. LAWSON, b. in NY about 1834; Emma d. after 1905 when she was living in Manhattan with her sons Harry and Clinton.

iv   JOSEPH MARTIN RUSSELL, b. at Westminster, 24 Nov 1819; d. at Malden, MA, 2 Oct 1893; m. at Boston, 24 Mar 1846, his fourth cousin twice removed, EMMA D. HOLT (*Sylvester Holt⁷, Asa Holt⁶, Asa Holt⁵, Thomas Holt⁴, Thomas Holt³, Mary Russell Holt², Robert¹*), b. at Boston, 1825 daughter of Sylvester and Sarah (Glazier) Holt; Emma d. at Malden, 9 Oct 1900.

v   GEORGE DANA RUSSELL, b. at Westminster, Mar 1822; d. at Boston, 3 Feb 1910; m. at Boston, 31 May 1851, CATHERINE E. CHASE, b. at Portland, ME, 27 Sep 1831 daughter of Thomas and Elizabeth (Perry) Chase;[1753] Catherine, d. at Boston, 9 Jan 1919.

vi   LAURA RUSSELL, b. at Westminster, 11 Jan 1825; d. at Clinton, MA, 11 Oct 1905; m. 29 Sep 1846, CHARLES GODFREY STEVENS, b. at Claremont, NH, 16 Sep 1821 daughter of Godfrey and Hannah (Poole) Stevens; Charles d. at Clinton, MA, 13 Jun 1897.

603)   LUCY RUSSELL (*Jeduthan⁴, James³, James², Robert¹*), b. at Walpole, NH, 13 Apr 1777 daughter of Jeduthan and Susannah (Glazier) Russell; d. at Walpole, NH, 6 May 1854; m. at Westmoreland, 27 Jan 1803, JOHN GRAVES, b. at Saybrook, CT, about 1775 son of Eliphas Graves; John d. at Walpole, 31 Jan 1860.[1754]

    John Graves was a farmer in Walpole and resided on the homestead of his father.[1755] Lydia Russell and John Graves were parents of six children born at Walpole, New Hampshire. In 1850, Lucy and John and three of their children, George W. and his wife Stella, Martha, and Mary, were living on the homestead farm in Walpole. Real estate value reported on the census was $3,000.[1756]

    Daughter Mary did not marry and in her will written 7 September 1881 (probate 1 March 1883) she left her entire estate to her sister Martha.[1757] Daughter Martha did not marry. Her estate was valued at $3,234.05, $3,023.30 of that in stocks and bonds. She left her estate (probate 16 February 1894) to John W. Graves, Russell G. Graves, and Mrs. Frances H. Farr all of Walpole.[1758]

i   HARRIET GRAVES, b. 24 Jan 1804; d. at Walpole, 22 May 1889; m. at Walpole, 19 Jan 1826, LEVI HOOPER, b. at Walpole, 7 Apr 1801 son of Salmon and Rebecca (Foster) Hooper;[1759] Levi d. at Walpole, 25 Apr 1876.

ii   MARTHA GRAVES, b. 1806; d. at Walpole, 21 Jan 1894. Martha did not marry.

[1753] The names of Catherine's parents and her date and place of birth are given on her death record.

[1754] Aldrich, *Walpole As It Was*, p 267

[1755] Aldrich, *Walpole As It Was*, p 267

[1756] Year: 1850; Census Place: Walpole, Cheshire, New Hampshire; Roll: 428; Page: 355B

[1757] New Hampshire Wills and Probate, Cheshire County, Probate Estate Files; Estate of Mary L. Graves

[1758] New Hampshire Wills and Probate, Cheshire County, Probate Estate Files, Estate of Martha Graves, Case 611

[1759] Pope and Hooper, *Hooper Genealogy*, p 43

iii   JOHN HUBBARD GRAVES, b. 1808; d. at Rochester, NY, 1894 (probate 6 Apr 1894); m. 31 Oct 1836, LYDIA ANN SMITH, b. 20 Mar 1816 daughter of Samuel and Sarah (Minor) Smith;[1760] Lydia d. at Rochester, 24 Feb 1906.

iv   GEORGE WEBB GRAVES, b. 1811; d. at Walpole, 5 Apr 1892; m. at Keene, NH, 31 Aug 1847, ESTELLA WATKINS, b. at Walpole, 22 Nov 1822 daughter of Ruggles and Sarah (Nichols) Watkins;[1761] Estella d. at Walpole, 22 Apr 1887.

v   WILLIAM E. GRAVES, b. about 1814; d. at Boston, 15 Jul 1879; m. at Dunstable, 22 Jan 1837, HANNAH L. PIERCE, b. at Nashua, NH, 1815 daughter of Joshua and Dolly (Hutchins) Pierce; Hannah d. at Boston, 1 May 1884.

vi   MARY L. GRAVES, b. 1820; d. at Walpole, 28 Jan 1883. Mary did not marry.

604)   LYDIA RUSSELL (*Jeduthan⁴, James³, James², Robert¹*), b. at Walpole, NH, 18 Dec 1779 daughter of Jeduthan and Susannah (Glazier) Russell; d. at Roxbury, VT, 26 May 1866; m. at Westmoreland, 15 Jan 1804, WILLIAM KENDALL, baptized at Lancaster, MA, 27 Jul 1777 son of William and Mary (Knight) Kendall; William d. at Roxbury, 11 Nov 1828.
    Lydia and William were parents of six children born at Roxbury, Vermont.

i   SUSANNA KENDALL, b. 9 Nov 1804; d. at Walden, VT, 1886; m. ANDREW PHILIPS WALCOTT, b. at Williamstown, VT, 21 Dec 1802 son of Eleazer and Sarah (Phillips) Walcott; Andrew d. at Stannard, VT, 1878.

ii   ERVILLA KENDALL, b. 27 Dec 1806; d. after 1880 when she was living at Roxbury, VT; m. at Roxbury, 20 Dec 1827, ISRAEL STEELE, b. at Warren, VT, 2 Aug 1806 son of James and Anne (Cram) Steele; Israel d. at Roxbury, 1871.

iii   ATLANTEE KENDALL, b. 10 Jul 1808; d. at Roxbury, 3 Sep 1828.

iv   MARTIN RUSSELL KENDALL, b. 4 Dec 1810; d. 3 Jul 1811.

v   MARY N. KENDALL, b. 29 Jul 1812

vi   WILLIAM MARTIN KENDALL, b. 27 Jul 1815; d. at Lebanon, NH, 31 Oct 1904; m. at Hartland, VT, 22 Jan 1845, ROXANA BABCOCK, b. at Hartland, 23 Feb 1818 daughter of Josiah and Hannah (Hodges) Babcock;[1762] Roxana d.at Lebanon, NH, 27 Aug 1891.

605)   HANNAH RUSSELL (*Jeduthan⁴, James³, James², Robert¹*), b. at Walpole, NH, 6 Aug 1782 daughter of Jeduthan and Susannah (Glazier) Russell; d. after 1855 when living at Penfield, NY; m. at Walpole, 27 Oct 1800, AMOS GRAVES, b. about 1779 son of John and Lydia (Clark) Graves;[1763] Amos d. after 1855.
    One certain child was identified for Hannah and Amos, although census records suggest their may have been four children in the family.[1764] In 1850, Amos Graves age 71 born in New Hampshire was head of household in Brighton, NY with wife Hannah age 68 born in New Hampshire and with Martin A. Graves with an apparent wife Lucetta and two young children in the home.[1765]

i   MARTIN A. GRAVES, b. at Walpole, NH, 28 Jan 1814; d. at Antioch, CA, 21 Mar 1874; m. LUSETTA who has not been identified, b. in NY, about 1821; Lusetta d. at Antioch, 22 May 1898.

ii   LETHYS GRAVES, b. about 1822, living with Hannah and Amos in Penfield, NY in 1855. Lethys is listed as a child on the census, but it is also possible (and perhaps more likely) that this is Martin's wife (named as Lusetta above) as there is also in the home a grandchild Amos who was the son of Martin and Lucetta.

[1760] Smith, *A Genealogical History of the Descendants of the Rev. Nehemiah Smith*, p 212

[1761] The names of Stella's parents are given on her death record.

[1762] Hodges, *Genealogical Record of the Hodges Family*, p 210. The names of Hannah's parents are also given on her death record as Josiah Babcock and Hannah Hodges.

[1763] Aldrich, *Walpole As It Was*, p 266

[1764] In the 1810 census of Walpole, NH, there were two males under 10, one female under 10, and one female 10-15 who all may have been children of Hannah and Amos. Year: 1810; Census Place: Walpole, Cheshire, New Hampshire; Roll: 23; Page: 248; Image: 00193; Family History Library Film: 0218684

[1765] Year: 1850; Census Place: Brighton, Monroe, New York; Roll: 528; Page: 339B

606) JEDUTHAN RUSSELL (*Jeduthan⁴, James³, James², Robert¹*), b. at Walpole, NH, 14 Mar 1785 son of Jeduthan and Susannah (Glazier) Russell; d. at Rockingham, VT, 19 Dec 1857; m. 23 Jul 1807, RHODA HALL, b. at Walpole, 1781 daughter of David and Lydia (Graves) Hall; Rhoda d. at Rockingham, 6 Oct 1822. Jeduthan m. 2ⁿᵈ 1823, LUCY GURNSEY, b. at Westminster, VT, 30 Oct 1791 daughter of Amos and Abigail (Bolles) Gurnsey; Lucy d. at Saxtons River, 6 Jul 1845. Jeduthan m. 3ʳᵈ, Rhoda's sister REBECCA HALL, b. 19 Jul 1788; Rebecca d. 12 Mar 1863.

Jeduthan and Rhoda were in Walpole after their marriage but relocated to Rockingham, Vermont in 1814. Jeduthan and his wife Rhoda, then of Rockingham, sold property in Walpole to Samuel Martin on 7 September 1815.[1766] Jeduthan purchased a grist mill in Rockingham which he later sold to his son-in-law Amos Graves.[1767]

Jeduthan Russell did not leave a will and his estate entered probate 11 January 1858 with John A. Farnsworth as administrator. The following heirs signed consent to the administration: Rebecca H. Russell, Harriet Russell, Stephen Childs and Abby Childs, William Marvin and Eliza Marvin, Amos Holmes and Irena A. Holmes, A. W. Russell, and R. F. Hodgkins.[1768] Real estate at the time of his death included the homestead with four acres, a woodlot of 30 acres, the so-called Mott farm of 43 acres in Rockingham plus six undivided seventh parts of the Gurnsey farm in Westminster containing about 118 acres. The dower was set off to widow Rebecca H. Russell. The personal estate was not sufficient to settle the debts and the administrator petitioned to sell all the real estate as the real estate could not be divided without prejudice to its value.

Jeduthan Russell and Rhoda Hall were parents of six children, the three oldest children born at Walpole and the younger children at Rockingham, Vermont.

i   Child, b. 1808; d. at Walpole, 20 Jul 1810

ii   RHODA RUSSELL, b. at Walpole, 14 Sep 1810; d. at Rockingham, VT, 10 Jul 1902; m. at Rockingham, 29 Mar 1836, LEONARD WAIT BLAKE, b. at Rockingham, 27 Aug 1807 son of Bela and Polly (Wait) Blake; Leonard d. at Westminster, 1848 (probate 30 Aug 1848).

iii   HIRAM K. RUSSELL, b. 13 Sep 1812; d. at Rockingham, VT, 25 Apr 1848; m. 1837, SOPHIA ESTERBROOK, b. 1821; Sophia d. at Pleasanton, CA, 10 Jan 1898. Sophia married second George M. Cole.

iv   SOPHIA RUSSELL, b. 21 Feb 1815; d. at Walpole, 1 Dec 1894; m. at Rockingham, 11 Oct 1836, ASA TITUS, b. at Walpole, 1810 son of Asa and Rebecca (Graves) Titus; Asa d. at Walpole, 29 Jun 1874.

v   ALBERT W. RUSSELL, b. 1 Jun 1817; d. at Goffstown, 10 Mar 1892; m. at Rockingham, 29 Mar 1843, REBECCA OBER, b. at Rockingham, 1824 daughter of Isaac and Lydia (Wilkins) Ober; Rebecca d. at Goffstown, 28 Sep 1908.

vi   IRENA A. RUSSELL, b. 7 Sep 1819; d. at Rockingham, VT, 3 Oct 1908; m. about 1844, AMOS HOLMES, b. at Grafton, VT, 13 Jul 1815 son of Given and Lucy (Palmer) Holmes; Amos d. at Rockingham, 19 Nov 1892.

Jeduthan and Lucy were parents of four children.

i   ABIGAIL RUSSELL, b. 30 Dec 1824; d. at Rockingham, VT, 19 Jul 1907; m. at Rockingham, 21 Jan 1847, STEPHEN CHILDS, b. at Bridport, VT, 1820 son of Stephen and Mary (-) Childs (per death record); Stephen d. of typhoid fever at Rockingham, 29 Sep 1887.

ii   HARRIET RUSSELL, b. 2 Jul 1826; d. at Rockingham, 5 Jan 1861. Harriet did not marry.

iii   ELIZA M. RUSSELL, b. 2 Mar 1828; d. at Rockingham, 20 Mar 1899; m. 1ˢᵗ 6 Feb 1850, WILLIAM MARVIN, b. about 1824; William d. at Rockingham, 14 Mar 1858. Eliza m. 2ⁿᵈ ADONIRAM J. SEARLES, b. at Westfield, MA, 1830 son of James and Betsey (Pierce) Searles; Adoniram d. at Rockingham, 5 Dec 1895.

iv   MERAB RUSSELL, b. 17 Nov 1829; d. after 1913 when she was living at Bellows Falls, VT; m. ROSWELL F. HODGKINS, b. at Rockingham, 1823 son of Roswell and Lucretia (Walker) Hodgkins;[1769] Roswell d. at Rockingham, 27 Oct 1889.

607) JOSEPH RUSSELL (*Jeduthan⁴, James³, James², Robert¹*), b. at Walpole, NH, 6 Jul 1787 son of Jeduthan and Susannah (Glazier) Russell; d. at Alamo, MI, 28 Jul 1867; m. 1ˢᵗ at Walpole, 4 Jan 1810, LUCY ANGIER, b. at Fitzwilliam, NH, 14 May 1792; Lucy d. at Walpole, 30 Mar 1826. Joseph m. 2ⁿᵈ at Keene, 7 Sep 1826, HARRIET ROBINSON, b. at Walpole, 25 Dec 1807 daughter of William and Sarah (Baker) Robinson; Harriet at Nunda, NY, 15 Sep 1850. Joseph m. 3ʳᵈ MARY ANN LABBELL, b. about 1815.

[1766] New Hampshire Land Records, Cheshire County, 68:310

[1767] Hayes, *History of Rockingham*, p 745

[1768] Vermont Wills and Probate, Windham County, Estate of Jeduthan Russell

[1769] The names of Roswell's parents are given on his death record as Roswell Hodgkins and Lucretia Walker.

Joseph Russell reached adulthood in Walpole and his first seven children were likely born in Walpole. He moved his family to Oakland, New York (an area near Nunda) about 1825 and on to Nunda about 1838.[1770]

Son Andrew Joseph Russell was an artist and photographer. He began his career as a landscape artist but transitioned to photography. During the Civil War, he was the Army's first official photographer. After the war, he photographed the construction of the Union Pacific, the eastern half of the trans-continental railroad. His photographs of the construction of the railroad were published in The Great West Illustrated in a Series of Photographic Views.[1771]

In his will written 5 June 1867 (probate 7 September 1867), Joseph Russell of Alamo, Michigan bequeathed to wife Mary Ann the farm lying in the town of Alamo to be used, occupied, and enjoyed during her natural life. Mary Ann also receives the personal estate. One-dollar bequests were made to the following persons: daughter Priscilla Brittan, son Charles P. Russell, daughter Louisa Martin, son Andrew Russell, and son George H. Russell. Grandsons William Osgodby, George Osgodby, James Rose, and Henry Rose receive one dollar to equally divide. These bequests are to be paid after the decease of his wife and when his son Warren E. Russell reaches age twenty-one. The remainder of the estate, real and personal, goes to son Warren E. Russell.[1772]

Joseph Russell and Lucy Angier were parents of six children born at Walpole, New Hampshire.

i   PRISCILLA PLATTS RUSSELL, b. about 1810; d. at Cleveland, 1884; m. SURRANUS BRITTON, b. 1806; Surranus d. at Cleveland, 1898.

ii   ALMIRA H. RUSSELL, b. 4 Mar 1813; d. at Nunda, NY, 18 Sep 1836; m. about 1833, JACOB H. OSGOODBY, b. at Lincolnshire, England, 26 Dec 1812 son of Harrison and Ann (-) Osgoodby; Jacob d. at Nunda, 1 Aug 1883. Jacob married second Lucinda Bennett. Jacob traveled with his family from England arriving in New York in 1828.[1773]

iii   CHARLES P. RUSSELL, b. 1816; d. at Kalamazoo, MI, 13 Oct 1889; m. about 1841, MARY ROSETTA ROBINSON, b. at Walpole, NH, 29 Nov 1818 daughter of William and Phebe (-) Robinson; Mary d. at Kalamazoo, 27 May 1894.

iv   WILLIAM G. RUSSELL, b. 1817; d. at Alamo, MI, 1873; m. about 1848, MATILDA C. SHERWOOD, b. in NJ, about 1826 daughter of Granville and Maria (Ament) Sherwood;[1774] Matilda d. at Otsego, MI, 31 Oct 1911.

v   SARAH LOUISA RUSSELL, b. about 1820; d. at Castile, NY, 20 Sep 1896; m. about 1841, WILLIAM H. MARTIN, b. in NY, about 1809; William d. at Angelica, NY, Jul 1869. After William's death, Sarah lived with her daughter Susan and her husband Charles Nye who lived in Castile.

vi   ELIZA JANE RUSSELL, b. 1822; d. at Nunda, 1849; m. at Portage, NY, 3 Jan 1842, CYRUS ROSE, b. in CT, 3 Mar 1807; Cyrus d. at Nunda, 29 Jan 1898.

Joseph Russell and Harriet Robinson were parents of four children, the oldest born at Walpole and the younger children likely born at Livingston County, New York.

i   ANDREW JOSEPH RUSSELL, b. at Walpole, NH, 20 Mar 1829; d. at Brooklyn, NY, 20 Sep 1902; m. about 1850, CATHERINE ADLEIA DURYEA, b. 9 Nov 1830 daughter of William R. and Melinda (Rathbune) Duryea; Catherine d. at St. Cloud, MN, 27 Sep 1903.

ii   GEORGE H. RUSSELL, b. 1830; d. at Buffalo, NY, 1874 (probate 25 Jun 1874); m. about 1852, MARTHA M. DECAMP, b. 23 Feb 1829 (on gravestone) daughter of John C. and Sarah (Miller) DeCamp; Martha d. (burial at Mount Morris, NY), 23 Jan 1855.[1775] George was second married to FRANCES who has not been identified but was his widow at probate; Frances was born in OH about 1838 according to census record. Frances was living in Ohio in 1890 when she applied for a Civil War widow's pension.

iii   EZRA RUSSELL, b. 1832; d. at Portage, NY, 2 Jan 1867. Ezra likely did not marry as no heirs of his are named in father's will.

iv   HARRIET RUSSELL, b. about 1836; not mentioned in father's will.[1776]

One child of Joseph Russell and Mary Ann Labbell:

[1770] Hand, *Centennial History of the Town of Nunda*, pp 287-288

[1771] Construction of the Union Pacific Railroad, Photographs of the Construction of the Union Pacific Railroad by Andrew J. Russell, Beinecke Rare Book & Manuscript Library, https://beinecke.library.yale.edu/collections/highlights/construction-union-pacific-railroad

[1772] Michigan Wills and Probate, Kalamazoo County, volume 11, pp 70-72

[1773] New York, Alien Depositions of Intent to Become U.S. Citizens, 1825-1871

[1774] The names of Matilda's parents are given as Granville Sherwood and Maria Ament on her death record.

[1775] Martha is buried at Mount Morris City Cemetery; findagrave ID: 76549769

[1776] Harriet is reported in the *History of Nunda* as dying without marrying.

i   WARREN E. RUSSELL, b. at Nunda, 1854; m. at Elgin, Ontario, 23 Dec 1875,[1777] FRANCES E. BARNES, b. Culloden, Ontario, 1857 daughter of William Griffin and Charlotte (Dale) Barnes; Frances d. at Chicago, 6 May 1901. Warren was living in Chicago in 1900.

608)   PRISCILLA RUSSELL (*Jeduthan[4], James[3], James[2], Robert[1]*), b. at Walpole, NH, 13 May 1790 daughter of Jeduthan and Susannah (Glazier) Russell; d. after 1850; m. at Walpole, 9 Jul 1807, EZRA HALL, b. at Walpole, about 1787 son of David and Lydia (Graves) Hall; Ezra d. at Walpole, 20 Aug 1863.
        Priscilla and Ezra resided in Walpole where they were parents of seven children. Their son Gardner was a conductor for the Cheshire, later merged with the Fitchburg Railroad.[1778] Son Armstrong went to California and was later in Yale, Idaho where he was living in 1900 with his son Edwin.[1779]
        In his will written 4 October 1761 (filed 1 September 1863), Ezra Hall bequeathed to son Gardner E. Hall all the home farm in Walpole on condition that Gardner pay into the estate $3,000 to be used for the other legacies. Gardner also received the stock of cattle, horses, swine, sheep and all the farming tools. Son Oren receives the other farm in Walpole, that being the farm previously owned by Ezra's father. Son Armstrong receives $1,000. Daughter Almira Batchelder receives $200 and granddaughter Frances Batchelder receives $700. Son Gardner also receives $1,000 to be held in trust for the use and benefit of son Martin Hall. All the household furniture is to be equally divided among the children. The remainder of the estate, after the erection of appropriate gravestone for Ezra's grave, goes to Gardner who is also named executor.[1780]

i   ALMIRA HALL, b. 1808; d. at Walpole, 28 Jan 1813.

ii   GARDNER E. HALL, b. 1810; d. at Walpole, 28 Jun 1878; m. 1st 4 Mar 1835, EMILY DUNSHEE, b. 1809; Emily d. at Walpole, 4 Jun 1867. Gardner m. 2nd at Windsor, VT, 15 Feb 1871, ARABELLA SHATTUCK (widow Arabella Simonds), b. at Windsor, VT, 1828 daughter of Edmund and Lois (Proctor) Shattuck; Arabella d. at Newport, NH, 11 Feb 1900.

iii   ORIN R. HALL, b. 1813; d. at Northfield, VT, 2 Nov 1882; m. about 1853, HULDAH MEROA WAKEFIELD, b. at Newport, NH, 22 Jan 1817 daughter of Silas and Mary (McGregor) Wakefield; Huldah d. at Boston, 5 Jan 1873.

iv   MARTIN G. HALL, b. 1818; d. at Walpole, 24 Jun 1892; m. at Walpole, 3 Jun 1840, MARIA NICHOLS, b. at Walpole, b. 1815 daughter of Thomas and Prudence (Thompson) Nichols; Maria d. at Nashua, NH, 31 Dec 1899.

v   ARMSTRONG HALL, b. Sep 1820; d. after 1900 when living at Yale, ID; m. AMY ANN NICHOLS, b. Dec 1821 daughter of Thomas and Prudence (Thompson) Nichols; Amy d. after 1900.

vi   ALMIRA M. HALL, b. 1823; d. at Franklin, MA, 5 Aug 1905; m. at Brattleboro, VT, 20 Feb 1851, JOSIAH WARREN BATCHELDER, b. a Sutton, MA, 1821 son of Josiah and Polly (Stratton) Batchelder; Josiah d. at Franklin, 22 Dec 1902.

vii   ISAAC H. HALL, b. 1826; d. 1827.

609)   SUSANNA RUSSELL (*Jeduthan[4], James[3], James[2], Robert[1]*), b. at Walpole, NH, 11 Jan 1793 daughter of Jeduthan and Susannah (Glazier) Russell; d. at Cherry Valley, IL, 20 Sep 1887; m. at Walpole, 20 Jan 1810, ERASMUS WELLINGTON, b. at Sturbridge, MA, 28 Aug 1785 son of Ebenezer and Rebecca (Levens) Wellington; Erasmus d. at Cherry Valley, 7 Apr 1854.
        Erasmus and Susanna resided on a farm in the southwest part of town before relocating to Cherry Valley, Illinois later in life.[1781] Susanna Russell and Erasmus Wellington were parents of three children born at Westmoreland.

i   EMILY H. WELLINGTON, b. 2 Dec 1815; d. at Belvidere, IL, 28 Aug 1889; m. at Westmoreland, 4 May 1836, ALEXANDER HAMILTON WHEELER, b. at Westmoreland, 7 Dec 1810 son of Aaron and Dolly (Gleason) Wheeler; Alexander d. at Belvidere, 16 Mar 1877.

ii   ELI R. WELLINGTON, b. 19 Dec 1819; d. at Westmoreland, 30 Apr 1887; m. at Westmoreland, 14 Nov 1843, PERSIS L. ALBEE, b. at Westmoreland, 14 Jul 1825 daughter of John and Elcee (Wild) Albee; Persis d. at Westmoreland, 20 Aug 1895.

[1777] (Brampton, *Ontario, Canada, Marriages, 1826-1938*, Archives of Ontario; Toronto, Ontario, Canada; Registrations of Marriages, 1869-1928; Reel: 20.
[1778] Hall, *The Halls of New England*, p 698
[1779] Year: 1900; Census Place: Yale, Cassia, Idaho; Page: 3; Enumeration District: 0037; FHL microfilm: 1240232
[1780] New Hampshire Wills and Probate Records, Cheshire County, Estate Files, Estate of Ezra Hall, Case 309
[1781] Westmoreland Historical Committee, *History of Westmoreland*, p 571

iii   ELIZA JANE WELLINGTON, b. 6 Aug 1823; d. at Rock Falls, IL, 3 Mar 1887; m. at Westmoreland, 1 Jun 1843, ALMON WHEELER, b. at Westmoreland, 10 Aug 1813 son of Aaron and Dolly (Gleason) Wheeler; Almon d. at Rock Falls, 28 Jun 1892.

610)   WILLIAM G. RUSSELL (*Jeduthan⁴, James³, James², Robert¹*), b. at Walpole, NH, 7 Aug 1795; d. at Rochester, NY, Sep 1850; m. about 1822, SARAH A. who has not been identified, b. about 1803; Sarah d. at Rochester, 14 May 1885.

     In his will written 7 September 1850 (proved 14 October 1850), William G. Russell left his entire estate, real and personal, to his beloved wife Sally Russell who was also named executrix.[1782]

     Daughter Martha Jane did not marry. In her will written 6 May 1889, she bequeathed her house and lot to sister Clara Taylor Bishop of Rochester, New York. The remainder of the estate is to be sold, divided into four equal parts, and distributed to the following: heirs of sister Mary E. Whitney late of Attica, New York; sister Sarah Maria James of Baltimore, Maryland; brother William W. Russell of Rochester, New York; and sister Susan J. Odell of Rochester, New York.[1783]

     William and Sarah Russell were parents of eight children born at Rochester, New York.

i   MARY E. RUSSELL, b. 1822; d. after 1880 when living at Attica, NY and before 1889 when sister write her will; m. by 1847, JOHN O. WHITNEY, b. about 1818; John d. at Attica, 28 Oct 1892 (probate 12 Nov 1892).

ii   MARTHA JANE RUSSELL, b. 1826; d. at Rochester, 8 Apr 1891. Martha did not marry.

iii   WILLIAM W. RUSSELL, b. 1828; d. after 1905 when living at Rochester, NY; m. about 1858, LOUISA E., b. about 1838.

iv   SARAH MARIA RUSSELL, b. 1831; d. at Fairlee, MD, 10 Sep 1909; m. RICHARD H. JAMES, baptized at Blakeney, Gloucester, England, 4 Jul 1827 son of Joseph and Susanna (Hannum) James;[1784] Richard d. at Baltimore, 1904.

v   JACOB M. RUSSELL, b. 1832; Jacob is an apparent child in the family in the 1850 census.[1785]

vi   HARRIET A. RUSSELL, b. 1834; d. at Rochester, 1855.

vii   SUSAN J. RUSSELL, b. 1840; d. at Ogden, NY, 15 Oct 1938; m. WILLIAM ODELL, b. about 1833; William d. after 1880.

viii   CLARA TAYLOR RUSSELL, b. Mar 1842; d. at Rochester, 9 Feb 1919; m. about 1869, WILBUR L. BISHOP, b. in NY, 1845 son of William LeRoy and Juline (Ward) Bishop; Wilbur d. at Rochester, Nov 1877.

611)   MARTIN RUSSELL (*Jeduthan⁴, James³, James², Robert¹*), b. at Waltham, NH, 20 Aug 1799 daughter of Jeduthan and Susannah (Glazier) Russell; d. at Troy, NY, by 1878 (probate 26 Apr 1878); m. at Lansingburgh, NY, 26 Feb 1821, ELIZA CHOATE, b. at Lansingburgh, 30 Nov 1801 daughter of Jonathan and Lois (Browning) Choate; Eliza d. at Troy, 1777.

     Martin and Eliza resided in Troy, New where they raised seven children.[1786] Martin did not leave a will and letters of administration were granted to son Martin Russell on 26 April 1878.[1787]

i   JOHN D. RUSSELL, b. 22 Apr 1822; d. 3 Aug 1882;[1788] m. 1 Apr 1861, SARAH DOLAN who has not been identified. Sarah apparently died within a few years of the marriage as John was living again with his parents in 1870.

ii   EMILY RUSSELL, b. 27 Jan 1824; d. 6 Apr 1869; m. 21 Jul 1857, HENRY STUNBERG.[1789]

iii   LOIS RUSSELL, b. and d. 14 Mar 1829

iv   MARTIN RUSSELL, b. 4 Jan 1831; d. after 1900 when living at Manhattan; m. 1st about 1865, MAGGIE HICKS who d. about 1870. Martin m. 2nd about 1872, SARAH LIVINGSTONE, b. about 1852.

v   GEORGE RUSSELL, b. 29 May 1834; d. 6 Aug 1839.

vi   ELIZA FRANCES RUSSELL, b. 30 Jul 1837; d. 19 Jan 1839.

[1782] New York Wills and Probate, Monroe County, Will Book 004, p 472, will of William G. Russell

[1783] New York Wills and Probate, Monroe County, Will Book 049, p 185, will of Martha Jane Russell

[1784] England, Select Births and Christenings, 1538-1975; Richard was living in Rochester in 1850 with apparent parents Joseph and Susanna James.

[1785] Year: 1850; Census Place: Rochester Ward 7, Monroe, New York; Roll: M432_531; Page: 325B; Image: 205

[1786] Jameson, *The Choates in America*, p 230

[1787] New York Wills and Probate, Rensselaer County, volume 081, p 724

[1788] Jameson, *The Choates in America*, p 230

[1789] Jameson, *The Choates in America*, p 230

vii   JULIA F. RUSSELL, b. 14 Jun 1843; d. after 1900 when living at Camden, NJ; m. 1st 20 Jul 1862, WILLIAM E.
          S. GOSS, b. 1839 son of Ephraim and Elizabeth B. (Stevens) Goss; William d. at Troy, 22 Nov 1878. Julia m. 2nd
          19 Sep 1883, as his second wife, ERSKINE CROSBY SHULTS, b. in NY, Jan 1845 son of Casper and Nancy
          (Ockempaugh) Shults; Erskine d. after 1905.Erskine was first married to Mary Nixon,

612)   ELIJAH RUSSELL (*Aquilla⁴, James³, James², Robert¹*), b. at Walpole, NH, 18 Jan 1781 son of Aquilla and Abigail
(Glazier) Russell; d. at Rochester, VT, 3 Dec 1844;[1790] m. 1st at Walpole, 23 Feb 1808, SALLY GRIFFIN, b. 1787; Sally d. at
Rochester, 18 Nov 1832. Elijah m. 2nd 8 Mar 1834, AMITY CHILD (widow of Levi Rodgers), b. at Sharon, VT, 9 Apr 1801
daughter of David and Ruth (Brown) Child;[1791] Amity d. 8 Jan 1871.
          Elijah was a farmer in Rochester. In the 1840 census of Rochester, Vermont, Elijah Russell headed a household of
eight persons: one male 50 to 59, one female 30 to 30, one male under 5, one male 5 to 9, one male 15 to 19, one female under 5,
and one female 15 to 19.[1792] Elijah Russell and Sally Griffin were parents of six children born at Rochester, Vermont.

i   CHARLES RUSSELL, b. 1809; d. at Rochester, 30 Nov 1816.

ii   HOSEA RUSSELL, b. 30 Nov 1811

iii   ALONZO WATTS RUSSELL, b. 1 Mar 1814; d. at Rochester, 12 Aug 1848; m. ELECTA LEONARD, b. at
          Rochester, about 1818 daughter of Rowland and Mary (Childs) Leonard; Electa d. at Rochester, 17 May 1903.

iv   ANDREW WALES RUSSELL, b. 6 Aug 1817; d. (burial at Albany, NY), 31 Jul 1871; m. ELIZABETH LENOX, b.
          at Bethlehem, NY, 1820; Elizabeth d. at Brooklyn, 11 Feb 1892.[1793] Dr. Andrew W. Russell wrote his will while
          resident of Albany, NY, but his will was proved at Clay County, IA on 16 Oct 1871.[1794] The will is also filed in
          Albany, NY.

v   DAVID RUSSELL, b. 1818; d. 11 Oct 1820.

vi   HORACE RUSSELL, b. 1825; d. at Greenbush, NY, 29 May 1889; m. ABIGAIL SALOMA WORCESTER, b. at
          Rochester, VT, 10 Mar 1821 daughter of Eusebius and Unity (Jackman) Worcester;[1795] Abigail d. at Greenbush, 6
          Jan 1899.

          Elijah Russell and Amity Child were parents of two children.

i   SARAH E. RUSSELL, b. 1835; d. at Granville, VT, 3 Dec 1893; m. 9 Jun 1855, AUGUSTUS VINTON, b. at
          Granville, 1829 son of John and Charlotte (Lamb) Vinton; Augustus d. at Granville, 14 Nov 1897.

ii   LEVI RUSSELL, b. 2 Oct 1838; d. after 1900 when he was living at Fall River, MA with brother-in-law Ralph
          Kay; m. 1887, MARY A. KAY, b. in England, Aug 1842 daughter of Richard and Nancy (Roberson) Kay;[1796] Mary
          d. at Fall River, 17 Sep 1900. Levi was a musician.

613)   JAMES RUSSELL (*Aquilla⁴, James³, James², Robert¹*), b. at Walpole, 27 Jan 1785 son of Aquilla and Abigail (Glazier)
Russell; d. at West Windsor, VT, 3 Aug 1858; m. at Walpole, 8 Mar 1807, ELIZA P. HOUGHTON, b. 1788; Eliza d. at Quechee,
VT, 12 Jun 1830.
          James Russell was a shoemaker in Weathersfield.[1797] James did not leave a will and Thomas F. Hammond was named
administrator of the estate on 5 October 1858. Personal estate was valued at $33.32. The debts of the estate exceeded its value
and creditors received a fraction of what was owed.[1798]
          There are records of four children of James and Eliza born at Weathersfield, Vermont.

i   HENRY HUBBARD RUSSELL, b. 8 Mar 1810; m. at Weathersfield, 14 Oct 1833, OLIVE WHITE

ii   GIDEON GRANGIER RUSSELL, b. 6 Feb 1816; d. at Williston, VT, 26 Feb 1862; m. ALZINA F. ELLISON, b.
          1820 daughter of John and Jemima (Barnes) Ellison.

[1790] Vermont, Vital Records, 1720-1908
[1791] Child, *Genealogy of the Child Families*, p 446
[1792] Year: 1840; Census Place: Rochester, Windsor, Vermont; Roll: 548; Page: 395; Family History Library Film: 0027442
[1793] New York City Department of Records & Information Services; New York City, New York; New York City Death Certificates; Year: 1892
[1794] Iowa Wills and Probate, Clay, volume 2, p 241
[1795] Worcester, *The Worcester Family*, p 43
[1796] Names of Mary's parents are as given on her death record.
[1797] Butterfield, *The Early History of Weathersfield*, Vermont, p 22
[1798] Vermont Wills and Probate, Windsor County, Estate of James Russell

iii   ELIZABETH CARPENTER RUSSELL, b. 26 May 1820; d. at Rochester, VT, 20 Jun 1851; m. EDWIN OSCAR PEASE, b. at Rochester, 21 Aug 1812 son of Chester and Keziah (Griffin) Pease; Edwin d. at Fayston, VT, 8 Nov 1886.

iv   JAMES HOUGHTON RUSSELL, b. 19 Jan 1822; m. at Windsor, VT, 19 Jul 1844, LUCY MCCOLLISTER

614)   LUCY FARRAR RUSSELL (*Aquilla⁴, James³, James², Robert¹*), b. at Walpole, 3 Sep 1783 daughter of Aquilla and Abigail (Glazier) Russell; d. after 1850, at Grant County, WI; m. at Troy, NY, 16 Dec 1820, as his second wife, AMOS ROGERS, b. at New Haven, 3 Mar 1783 son of Amos and Sarah (Phillips) Rogers;[1799] Amos d. by 1850 when Lucy was head of household in Grant County. Amos was first married to Sarah Rogers daughter of Stevens and Abigail (Powers) Rogers.
     Lucy and Amos had five children born at Troy, New York. Amos had six children with his first wife Sarah Rogers. In 1850, Lucy was in Grant County, Wisconsin as head of household and what seem three of her children living with her: Mary M. Rogers, Lucy J. Rogers, and Moses A. Rogers.[1800]

i   MARTHA SUSAN ROGERS, b. at Troy, 24 Mar 1824; d. at Berea, KY, 21 Oct 1906; m. 1ˢᵗ at Pike County, IL, 17 May 1846, DEWITT CLINTON PETRIE, likely b. at Hartland, VT, 6 Jul 1808 son of James and Abigail (Grow) Petrie; Clinton d. at Griggsville, IL, 26 Jul 1851. Martha m. 2ⁿᵈ 30 Oct 1856, SAMUEL LAMSON, b. at Mount Washington, MA, 16 Mar 1820 son of Origen and Eliza (Patterson) Lamson;[1801] Samuel d. at Harvey, IL, 19 Oct 1894.

ii   MARY M. ROGERS, b. about 1827; living in 1850 with her mother in Grant County, WI; nothing further found.

iii WILLIAM EDWARD ROGERS, b. Jan 1829; d. at Lancaster, WI, 23 Feb 1901; m. at Grant County, 3 Jun 1855, LOUISA EDWARDS, b. at Grant County, 8 Apr 1826 daughter of Matthew and Anne (Vivian) Edwards; Louisa d. at Lancaster, 1 Sep 1924.

iv   LUCY JANE ROGERS, b. 9 Nov 1830; d. (burial at Bent County, CO), 1910; m. 14 Mat 1854, GOODPELL LAMSON, b. at Mount Washington, MA, 23 Jan 1817 son of Origen and Eliza (Patterson) Lamson;[1802] Goodpell d. at Lamar, CO, 1896. Goodpell was first married to Sarah Jane Francis.

v   MOSES AQUILA ROGERS, b. Apr 1833; d. after 1900 when living at Elizabethtown, NM; m. at Walla Walla, WA, 10 Jun 1873; MARY ELIZABETH FULLER who has not been identified. Moses and Mary do not seem to have stayed together long as Moses was living on his own in 1880 in Whipple Barracks, AZ and lists himself as divorced at the 1900 census.

615)   GIDEON G. RUSSELL (*Aquilla⁴, James³, James², Robert¹*), b. at Walpole, 28 Sep 1791 son of Aquilla and Abigail (Glazier) Russell; d. at Weathersfield, VT, 25 Feb 1833; m. at Weathersfield, VT 29 Jul 1817, SARAH PLANT, b. 25 Jan 1798 daughter of Eli and Sarah (Stent) Plant; Sarah d. at Cornish, NH, 18 Jun 1874.
     Gideon and Sarah resided in Weathersfield, Vermont. Sarah later lived with her daughter Lucy and her husband in Grantham, New Hampshire.
     Gideon Russell did not leave a will and his estate entered probate 1 April 1833 with widow Sarah Russell and Truman Plant as administrators. Real estate was valued at $153 and personal estate at $64.77. Debts were $287.08. Dower was set off to widow Sarah on 12 May 1834. Truman Plant was named guardian for Lovina A. and Lucy F. Russell and Sarah Russell was guardian for Truman P., Nancy H., and Zada I. Russell.[1803]
     There are six children known for Gideon and Sarah likely all born at Weathersfield, Vermont.

i   LOVINA A. RUSSELL, b. 1818; d. at Cornish, NH, 26 Jan 1899; m. at Rockingham, VT, 3 Jul 1842, JAMES L. LOCKE, b. at Rockingham, 26 Oct 1819 son of Cyrus and Randilla (Thayer) Locke;[1804] James d. after 1870.

ii   LUCY FARRAR RUSSELL, b. 1819; d. at Claremont, NH, 20 Mar 1901; m. about 1839, CHARLES TYLER, b. at Claremont, NH, 1816 son of Ephraim and Sarah (Gookins) Tyler;[1805] Charles d. at Cornish, NH, 31 Dec 1894.

iii TRUMAN PLANT RUSSELL, b. 1822; d. at Grantham, NH, 17 Feb 1850.

[1799] Rogers, *James Rogers of New London, Ct. and His Descendants*, p 166
[1800] Year: 1850; Census Place: District 24, Grant, Wisconsin; Roll: 998; Page: 76B
[1801] Lamson, *Memorial of Elder Ebenezer Lamson*, p 63
[1802] Lamson, *Memorial of Elder Ebenezer Lamson*, p 62
[1803] Vermont Wills and Probate Records, Windsor County, Estate of Gideon G. Russell
[1804] Hayes, *History of the Town of Rockingham*, p 700
[1805] The names of Charles's parents are as given on his death record.

iv   NANCY H. RUSSELL, b. estimate 1826; she is named in the probate of father's estate in 1834; nothing further found.

v   ZADA A. RUSSELL, b. Aug 1827; d. 23 Apr 1828.

vi   ZADA "SARAH" ISABEL RUSSELL, b. 1829; d. at Cornish, NH, 22 Aug 1861; m. at Grantham, NH, 3 May 1851, TRUMAN L. HEATH, b. at Woodbury, VT, 5 Dec 1830 son of Libbeus and Lucinda (Rickard) Heath; Truman d. at Newport, NH, 13 Jul 1892. Truman married second Frances Lavinia Young.

616)   RUTH RUSSELL (*Aquilla⁴, James³, James², Robert¹*), b. at Walpole, 29 Sep 1793 daughter of Aquilla and Abigail (Glazier) Russell; d. at Pittsfield, IL, 13 Dec 1870; m. 21 Nov 1813, ELIAS B. WILLIAMS, b. 25 May 1791;[1806] Elias d. at Pittsfield, 1 Mar 1826.
        Ruth and Elias were parents of two children born at Weathersfield. Neither child married and both were living with their mother in 1870.[1807] In her will written 10 October 1893 (proved 20 November 1893), daughter Lucy made money bequests ranging in amounts of $200 to $1,000 to the following persons whose relationship to her is not given: Josephine S. Gordon of Bloomington, WI, Harriet A. Newcomb of Waitsfield, VT, Lucy J. Sampson of Lamar, CO, Charles P. Thomas of Pasadena, CA, Anson H. Thomas of Glen Haven, WI, Mrs. Urban P. Williams of Salem MA, Mrs. Lucy H. Walker of Lathrop, MO, Lucy's children Charles P. and Ruth Walker, and several more individuals. There are also bequests to organizations and charities including University of Bloomington, Freedman's Old Society, and the Deacon's Home in Chicago. The bequests total $17,800.[1808] As Lydia has no occupation listed on census records, it seems that her estate was inherited from her parents or her brother.

i   CHARLES RUSSELL WILLIAMS, b. 19 Aug 1814; d. at Pittsfield, IL, 20 Mar 1874. Charles was a farmer.

ii   LUCY A. WILLIAMS, b. 19 Mar 1816; d. at Pittsfield, IL, 13 Nov 1893.

617)   SARAH GLAZIER RUSSELL (*Aquilla⁴, James³, James², Robert¹*), b. at Walpole, 19 Apr 1799 daughter of Aquilla and Abigail (Glazier) Russell; d. at Bloomington, WI, 8 Sep 1869; m. at Troy, NY by Rev. Griffin on 16 Jun 1822, JOHN HOLLENBECK THOMAS,[1809] b. at Hartford, NY, 1795; John d. at Glen Haven, WI, 6 Mar 1885.
        Sarah and John were parents of five known children, the older children born likely at Troy, but the younger children at Pike County, Illinois. The names of the children are identified from the 1850 census when the family was living in District 24, Grant County, Wisconsin.[1810] John was a farmer and Sarah was a schoolteacher. The family was in Pike County, Illinois before relocating to Wisconsin in 1843.[1811]

i   ANSON HENRY THOMAS, b. Mar 1823; d. at Bloomington, WI, 26 Apr 1901; m. 1st at Grant County, WI, 12 Feb 1852, MARY JANE SNODGRASS, b. in IN, about 1833; Mary d. at Patch Grove, WI, 31 Jan 1853. Anson m. 2nd at Grant County, 20 Mar 1854, MARTHA COOLEY, b. in NY, Feb 1832 daughter of Moses and Betsey (Bidwell) Cooley; Martha d. at Bloomington, WI, 7 Apr 1869.

ii   JOSEPHINE LOUISA THOMAS, b. Dec 1829; d. at Bloomington, WI, 26 Jun 1909; m. at Grant County, WI, 12 Feb 1852, JAMES REDMON GORDON, b. in IN, 1829 son of John H. and Sarah (-) Gordon; James d. of tuberculosis at Los Angeles, CA, 20 Nov 1897.[1812]

iii   JOHN NELSON THOMAS, b. 18 Jul 1834; d. at Beloit, KS, 12 Sep 1917; m. at Patch Grove, WI, 24 Nov 1859, SARAH DICKINSON, b. at Rockville, WI, 1 Jul 1841 daughter of Justus Marshall and Amanda P. (Hamilton) Dickinson; Sarah d. at Beloit, 6 Nov 1912.

iv   WARREN COLLAMAR THOMAS, b. 1836; d. after 1885; m. by 1873, IDA M. DAVIS,[1813] b. in MI, about 1856. Warren, Ida, and children Archie and Gertrude were living in Bridgeport, OR in 1880. They were living in Seattle, WA in 1885 with a third child, Rolla E., in the home.

[1806] Elias's date of birth is on his gravestone
[1807] Year: 1870; Census Place: Pittsfield, Pike, Illinois; Roll: M593_269; Page: 322A; Family History Library Film: 545768
[1808] Illinois Wills and Probate, Pike County, Book 3, pp 39-40
[1809] Genealogical Publishing Co.; Baltimore, Maryland; 10,000 Vital Records of Eastern New York, 1777-1834
[1810] Year: 1850; Census Place: District 24, Grant, Wisconsin; Roll: 998; Page: 68A
[1811] Butterfield, *History of Grant County, Wisconsin*, p 953
[1812] California, County Birth, Marriage, and Death Records, 1849-1980; California Department of Public Health, courtesy of www.vitalsearch-worldwide.com. Digital Images.
[1813] Ida Davis is the maiden name of mother given on the death record of Warren's son Archie E. Thomas and son Rolla E. Thomas.

v   CHARLES RUSSELL THOMAS, b. at Pike County, IL, 4 Aug 1838; d. at Lenox, CA, 9 Jul 1923; m. at Grant County, WI, 27 Sep 1864, LYDIA ANN HUEY, b. in WI, 1 May 1848 daughter of Joseph and Rachel (Parsons) Huey; Lydia d. at Los Angeles, 28 Mar 1906.

618)   THOMAS RUSSELL (*Thomas⁴, James³, James², Robert¹*), b. at Walpole, NH, 3 Sep 1785 son of Thomas and Eunice (Alexander) Russell; d. at Walpole, 28 Mar 1872; m. at Walpole, 9 Oct 1817, as her second husband, HANNAH FLINT, b. at Carlisle, MA, 11 Jan 1782 daughter of Amos and Elizabeth (Ball) Flint; Hannah d. at Walpole, 5 Jan 1866. Hannah was first married to Josiah Willington.
        Thomas resided in Walpole throughout his life where he farmed.
        Daughter Sarah married James Phelps and had one daughter who married but died within one year of her marriage. In her will written 5 July 1794, Sarah Phelps of Rockingham expressed her will that she be buried next to her husband in Walpole with the erection of suitable headstones. The bequests in her will are to niece Amelia R. Fisher of Brattleboro, niece Elmira S. Russell of Brattleboro, niece Georgianna R. Stewart, niece Frankie F. Russell of Lansing, Michigan, niece Mamie R. Welch of Rockingham, her husband's sister Lucy R. Pratt, nephew Wilbur Phelps of New Ipswich, Harriet Goodhue of Alstead, Nellie Linker of Alstead, brother Franklin F. Russell of Lansing, Michigan, and her brother's wife Mrs. Ellen Russell of Springfield, Vermont.[1814] The remainder of the estate to be divided between Amelia and Elmira.[1815]
        Thomas and Hannah were parents of five children born at Walpole, New Hampshire.

i   AMOS RUSSELL, b. 11 Sep 1818; d. at Boston, MA, 24 Feb 1882; m. at Concord, MA, 7 Mar 1843, ELIZABETH ANN CLARK, b. at Concord, MA, 17 Feb 1814 daughter of John Brooks and Lydia (Flint) Clark

ii   FRANKLIN FLINT RUSSELL, b. 6 May 1820; d. at Lansing, MI, 24 Jan 1900; m. 1st 19 Jan 1845, ELLEN HYNE, b. in NY, 1828; Ellen d. about 1875. Franklin m. 2nd at Lansing, Dec 1875, SOPHRONIA "SOPHIA" KETCHUM (widow of Robert Knott), b. at Riley, OH, 3 Nov 1833 daughter of Isaac and Anna (Hurd) Ketchum; Sophia d. at Lansing, 30 Dec 1910.

iii   LEVI ALEXANDER RUSSELL, b. 18 Apr 1823; d. at Walpole, 29 Jun 1894. Levi did not marry.

iv   SARAH AMANDA RUSSELL, b. 10 Jul 1825; d, at Rockingham, VT, 1896 (probate 1896); m. 2 May 1848, JAMES H. PHELPS, b. at Sutton, MA, 31 Oct 1822 son of Simeon and Levina (Putnam) Phelps; James d. at Rockingham, VT, 1878 (probate 12 Nov 1878).

v   JOSIAH QUINCY RUSSELL, b. 19 Oct 1830; d. at Walpole, 10 Mar 1889; m. 22 Nov 1864, ELLA ABBY MURPHY, b. 18 Mar 1830 daughter of James and Betsy (McArthur) Murphy; Ella d. at Rockingham, 25 May 1920.

619)   JOHN RUSSELL (*Thomas⁴, James³, James², Robert¹*), b. at Walpole, NH, 8 Jun 1787 son of Thomas and Eunice (Alexander) Russell; d. at Harpersfield, OH, 1 Oct 1845; m. by 1823, REMEMBRANCE EASTMAN, b. at Canada West, about 1802 daughter of Amos and Mary (Ingalls) Eastman; Remembrance d. after 1880 when she was living in Rolling Green, MN. Remembrance m. 2nd A. Burnam Hall.
        John was born in Walpole but traveled to Ohio where he married and raised a family of at least nine children, although there may be one or two other children not identified. In the 1840 census for Harpersfield, Ohio, John's household was ten persons (one male under 5; one male 5-9; one male 15-19; one male 50-59; two females under 5; one female 10-14; one female 15-19; and one female 30-39).[1816] After John's death, Remembrance married Burnam Hall and in 1850 she and four of her children (Fidelia, John, Amelia, and Ruth) were with Burnam in Wayne, Wisconsin.[1817]
        John Russell were parents of at least nine children born in Ashtabula County, Ohio.

i   SARAH A. RUSSELL, b. 16 Mar 1823 (calculated from death age of 65 years, 1 month, 20 days); d. at Waterville, MN, 6 May 1888;[1818] m. at Ashtabula County, OH, 5 Oct 1845, LYMAN HOPKINS, b. in NY, 12 Nov 1817 (date on gravestone); Lyman d. at Waterville, 4 Mar 1888.[1819]

[1814] Mrs. Ellen Russell of Springfield likely refers to Josiah's widow Ella who was living in Springfield, Vermont in 1880.

[1815] Vermont Wills and Probates, Windham County, Probates File #38l will of Sarah A. Phelps.

[1816] Year: 1840; Census Place: Harpersfield, Ashtabula, Ohio; Roll: 376; Page: 281; Family History Library Film: 0020158

[1817] Year: 1850; Census Place: Wayne, Lafayette, Wisconsin; Roll: 1001; Page: 333A

[1818] Minnesota Cemetery Inscription Index; ancestry.com

[1819] Sakatah Cemetery, findagrave ID: 72499385

ii   ELISHA RUSSELL, b. 5 Aug 1824; d. at Cherry Grove, MN, 3 Dec 1884; m. at Boone County, IL, 26 Jan 1848, URETTA V. PIERCE, b. in NY, 19 Dec 1827 daughter of Paul and Emeline (Mead) Pierce;[1820] Uretta d. at Wilkinson, MN, 27 Jun 1916.

iii   LODEMA D. RUSSELL, b. 1828; d. at Portland, OR, 7 Feb 1912; m. about 1849, BERRY W. DUNN, b. in KY, 1823;[1821] Berry d. at Lafayette, OR, 9 Oct 1898. Lodema and Berry were parents of twelve children. They traveled by ox team to Oregon in 1852.[1822]

iv   AMOS EASTMAN RUSSELL, b. 1831; d. (burial at Moro, OR), 26 Nov 1910.[1823] Amos is listed as single in the 1910 census at Cedar Creek, WA.[1824]

v   EUNICE RUSSELL, b. 10 Jul 1833; d. at Juneau County, WI, 1903;[1825] m. at Lafayette County, WI, 15 Mar 1854, WILLIAM NELSON TAFT, b. in IL, Jan 1835; Wilson d. at Finley, WI, 12 Sep 1923. After Eunice's death, Wilson married Nellie.

vi   FIDELIA RUSSELL, b. about 1836. Fidelia is living in the 1850 census, but further record was not located.

vii   JOHN FOSTER RUSSELL, b. 4 Aug 1838; d. at David City, NE, 14 Jan 1912; m. at Lafayette County, WI, 24 Aug 1864, ABIGAIL Z. "ABBIE" PINNEY, b. at Wayne, WI, 15 Dec 1847 daughter of Albert and Lucy (Jones) Pinney; Abbie d. at David City, NE, 16 Nov 1920. John served 3rd Wisconsin cavalry during the Civil War. [1826]

viii   AMELIA RUSSELL, b. 27 Aug 1841; d. at Etna, WA, 4 Oct 1926; m. 1st, 1858, CHRISTOPHER TAYLOR EMERICK, b. at Sangamon, IL, 25 Feb 1833 son of Christian Emerick; Christopher d. at La Center, OR, 9 Jul 1867.[1827] Amelia m. 2nd at Hillsboro, OR, 24 Jan 1868, JOHN D. RICHARDSON, b. at Monroe County, OH, 10 May 1821; John d. at Washington County, OR, 6 Mar 1874.[1828] Amelia m. 3rd at Hillsboro, OR, 15 Feb 1880, LEWIS O. BACKSTROM, b. in Sweden 1841; this marriage seems to have ended in divorce. Amelia m. 4th, 27 Dec 1889, as his third wife, ADAM CROCO REID, b. at Etna Green, IN, 1 Aug 1847 son of Robert and Rebecca (Croco) Reid; Adam d. at Etna, 8 Jul 1926. Adam Reid was first married to Jane James and second married to Melinda Newkirk.

ix   RUTH A. RUSSELL, b. about 1842; d. at Goodhue County, MN, 19 Jul 1894;[1829] m. 1st about 1863, GEORGE BLAISDELL, b. in NH, about 1839; George d. at Lafayette County, WI, 11 Jun 1873. Ruth m. 2nd at Goodhue, MN, 5 Nov 1876, GEORGE BUGBY, b. in NY, about 1839. Ruth m. 3rd at Dodge County, MN, 17 Jul 1889, FRANK L. WYMAN, b. China, ME, about 1848 son of Jefferson and Maria (Ward) Wyman; Frank d. at Pine Grove, MN, 1933. George Bugby served in company B of the 32nd Wisconsin infantry during the Civil War for which his minor child Ruth A. Bugby received pension payments with widow Ruth A. Wyman as guardian.[1830]

620)   RICHARD RUSSELL (*Thomas⁴, James³, James², Robert¹*), b. at Walpole, NH, 15 Jan 1790 son of Thomas and Eunice (Alexander) Russell; d. at Austinburg, OH, 1866; m. about 1812, TIRZAH HALL, b. at Walpole, 1795 daughter of David and Lydia (Graves) Hall; Tirzah d. at Cherry Valley, OH, 23 Jan 1887.
          Richard and Tirzah were first in Walpole where their two oldest children were born, were in New York for a time, and in Ashtabula County, Ohio by about 1835. They were parents of eight children.[1831]

i   THOMAS RUSSELL, b. at Walpole, NH, 24 Dec 1813; d. at Cherry Valley, OH, 1900; m. at Ashtabula County, OH, 2 Oct 1845, PAMELIA K. LEONARD, b. in MA, Oct 1819; Pamelia d. at Cherry Valley, 1902.

[1820] The SAR application of Donovan Dirk grandson of Elisha and Uretta identifies the names of Uretta's parents. The names of her parents are given as Franklin and Emeline on the death record (per the death index); "Minnesota Deaths and Burials, 1835-1990", database, *FamilySearch* (https://familysearch.org/ark:/61903/1:1:FDSZ-SH2 : 16 January 2020), Uretta Russell, 1916. However, his name is Paul on the 1850 census; there is a son Franklin Pierce in the family of Paul and Emeline which is perhaps the confusion on the death index.

[1821] Ancestry.com. *Oregon, U.S., Early Oregonians Index, 1800-1860* [database on-line]. Provo, UT, USA: Ancestry.com Operations, Inc., 2014.

[1822] Lodema Dunn, obituary, "The Oregon Daily Journal" (Portland, Oregon), 09 Feb 1912, Fri, page 9

[1823] Moro Cemetery, findagrave ID: 43287277

[1824] Year: 1910; Census Place: Cedar Creek, Clark, Washington; Roll: T624_1655; Page: 5B; Enumeration District: 0056; FHL microfilm: 1375668

[1825] "Wisconsin, Death Records, 1867-1907," database, *FamilySearch* (https://familysearch.org/ark:/61903/1:1:XLFB-YVF : 10 March 2018), Eunice Russell Taft, 1903; citing Death, Juneau, Wisconsin, Wisconsin State Historical Society, Madison; FHL microfilm 1,310,189.

[1826] "Passing of John F. Russell", Butler County Press (David City, Nebraska), 18 Jan 1912, Thu, p 1. The obituary contains the details of birth date, name of spouse, marriage, and military service.

[1827] Oregon, Early Oregonians Index, 1800-1860

[1828] Oregon, Early Oregonians Index, 1800-1860

[1829] Minnesota Department of Health; St Paul, Minnesota, USA; Minnesota, Death Index, 1908-2017

[1830] U.S., Civil War Pension Index: General Index to Pension Files, 1861-1934

[1831] Aldrich, *Walpole as it Was*, p 350

ii ALMINA RUSSELL, b. at Walpole, NH, 15 Oct 1815; d. after 1885 when she was living in Austinburg, OH; m. 3 Nov 1834, ORESTES H. WILLIAMS, b. in OH, about 1808 son of Davison and Jane (Newell) Williams; Orestes d. at Austinburg, 1885 (probate 15 May 1885)

iii SOPHIA RUSSELL, b. in NY, 17 Mar 1817; d. after 1900 when living at Austinburg, OH; m. 23 Dec 1836, ALFRED I. BUCK, b. in OH, about 1817; Alfred d. at Eagleville, OH, 20 Oct 1890.

iv LYDIA H. RUSSELL, b. 29 Dec 1820; d. at Cherry Valley, OH, 1898; m. 1st at Ashtabula County, OH, 29 Feb 1844, ISAAC BARTHOLOMEW, b. in OH, about 1819. Isaac d. about 1863. Lydia m. 2nd 30 Jul 1867, GEORGE HOLMES, b. about 1805; George d. 1898.

v LEVI F. RUSSELL, b. 5 Nov 1823; d. at Ashtabula, OH, after 1870; m. 14 Feb 1853, ELIZA M. COTTON, b. about 1828 daughter of Jacob Cotton; Eliza d. after 1900.

vi RHODA RUSSELL, b. 23 Nov 1825

vii HENRY RUSSELL, b. 25 Apr 1830; d. at Cherry Valley, OH, 1912; m. 12 Feb 1857, ABIGAIL C. BAKER, b. in OH, Jul 1830; Abigail d. at Cherry Valley, 1901.

viii MARY J. RUSSELL, b. in OH, 19 May 1836; d. at Cherry Valley, OH, 1923; m. at Ashtabula County, OH, 23 Jun 1855, JOSEPH R. PIPER, b. at Lenox, OH, Mar 1837 son of William H. and Lucy L. (Walling) Piper; Jospeh d. at Cherry Valley, 4 Mar 1902.

621) LEVI RUSSELL (*Thomas⁴, James³, James², Robert¹*), b. at Walpole, NH, about 1795 son of Thomas and Eunice (Alexander) Russell; d. at Keene, 21 Sep 1831; m. about 1824, ELIZABETH "ELIZA" WALDO, b. 23 Aug 1801 daughter of Elijah and Betsey (Angier) Waldo. Eliza married second Ebenezer Cheney.

 In his will written 3 August 1831, Levi bequeathed to beloved wife Elizabeth the use of all the estate during her natural life or until she remarries. At Elizabeth's decease or remarriage, the estate is to be divided among his children Ira, Emeline, and an infant not yet named.[1832]

 Levi and Eliza were parents of three children born at Keene, New Hampshire.

i IRA WALDO RUSSELL, b. at Keene, 17 May 1825; d. at Swanzey, NH, 19 Jul 1910; m. at Richmond, NH, 3 Sep 1850, HARRIET ANNE BALLOU, b. at Richmond, 4 Nov 1830 daughter of James and Polly (Handy) Ballou; Harriet d. at Keene, 27 Sep 1905. Ira and Harriet divorced Oct 1898. Ira was a dentist. He was the mayor of Keene in 1881.[1833]

ii ELIZA EMELINE RUSSELL, b. 1827; d. at Keene, 16 Nov 1832.

iii MARY FOSTER WILLIAM RUSSELL, b. Jun 1831; d. at Keene, 29 Jan 1832.

622) SALLY RUSSELL (*Thomas⁴, James³, James², Robert¹*), b. at Walpole, NH, 30 Aug 1796 daughter of Thomas and Eunice (Alexander) Russell; d. at Alstead, NH, 1859 (probate 1859); m. 17 Oct 1811, ELISHA ANGIER, b. at Fitzwilliam, NH, 6 Dec 1789 son of Silas and Priscilla (Harris) Angier; Elisha d. at Walpole, 23 Sep 1835.

 Sally and Elisha resided in Walpole, New Hampshire. Elisha was accidentally killed when his two-horse wagon with load went off a bridge at Cold River. Elisha had been on his way home from Keene where he had participated in a regimental muster.[1834]

 Sally Russell Angier did not leave a will and her son Silas was named administrator of the estate on 5 July 1859. After payment of debts and expenses, there was $75.29 available for distribution. Silas was to pay to himself $8.36 and the same to each of the other heirs: Amanda Fay, John Angier, Emily Webb, George Angier, Harriet Titus, Andrew J. Angier, Mary Lane, and Sophia Angier.[1835]

 Sally Russell and Elisha Angier were parents of ten children born at Walpole. Son Andrew Jackson Angier and son-in-law Sala Post Webb died in the Civil War.

i SILAS ANGIER, b. 30 Apr 1812; d. at Alstead, NH, 14 Dec 1874; m. 1st 8 Nov 1838, CAROLINE F. EMERSON, b. at Walpole, 14 Jul 1820 daughter of Jonathan and Lydia (Crosby) Emerson; Caroline d. about 1858. Silas m. 2nd 23 Oct 1859, MARY JANE MARSHALL (widow of Samuel Long), b. at Walpole, about 1829 daughter of John and Hannah (March) Marshall; Mary Jane d. at Walpole, 6 Dec 1886.

[1832] New Hampshire Wills and Probate Records, Cheshire County, Wills volume 78, pp 29-30

[1833] Griffin, *History of the Town of Keene*, p 685

[1834] Aldrich, *Walpole As It Was*, p 104

[1835] *New Hampshire. Probate Court (Cheshire County)*; Probate Place: *Cheshire, New Hampshire, Estate File A254, Sally Angier*

ii   AMANDA ANGIER, b. 3 Apr 1814; d. at Northfield, MA, 13 Aug 1877; m. 6 Apr 1837, STEPHEN FAY, b. at Walpole, 23 Nov 1809 son of Levi and Mary (Prentice) Fay; Stephen d. at Walpole, 20 Jan 1862 (probate 4 Feb 1862).

iii   JOHN ANGIER, b. 18 Dec 1815; d. at Nunda, NY, 20 Mar 1896; m. MARY ROCKAFELLOW, b. in PA, 1819 daughter of Samuel and Elizabeth (Trout) Rockafellow;[1836] Mary d. at Nunda, 16 Nov 1892. John Angier had gone to Nunda with his grandfather Silas and they obtained the farm of Samuel Rockafellow. Grandfather Silas died at Nunda in 1817.[1837]

iv   EMILY SARAH ANGIER,[1838] b. 12 Mar 1819; d. at Watertown, WI, 2 May 1900; m. at Walpole, 1 Jan 1850, SALA POST WEBB, b. in CT, 1825 son of Samuel and Lucy (Post) Webb; Sala d. at a regimental hospital near Arlington, VA, 22 Oct 1861. Emily and Sala were in Blandford, MA just after their marriage, but were in Watertown, WI by 1860 where Sala was listed as an attorney. Sala enlisted in the 6th Regiment of Wisconsin Infantry as a corporal.[1839]

v   MARY PHILENA ANGIER, b. 20 Nov 1820; d. at Keene, 12 Nov 1891; m. at Walpole, 20 Oct 1841, LEWIS LANE, b. at Walpole, 22 Apr 1813 son of Ephraim and Elizabeth Danforth (Abbott) Lane; Lewis d. at Keene, 17 Mar 1886.

vi   SOPHIA E. ANGIER, b. 5 Feb 1825; d. at Marlborough, MA (burial at Walpole, NH, but living at Keene in 1880), 17 Oct 1888. Sophia did not marry. She was a seamstress.

vii   SARAH ANGIER, b. 15 Aug 1829; deceased before 1859.

viii HARRIET M. ANGIER (twin), b. 31 Aug 1831; d. at Keene, 10 Sep 1907; m. 1st, 1858, as his second wife, SYLVANUS TITUS, b. in NH, 1809; Sylvanus d. at Keene, 11 Oct 1873. Sylvanus was first married to Lydia C. Martin. Harriet m. 2nd at Westminster, VT, 28 Aug 1899, MOSES HENRY SMITH (widower of Elsie Gale), b. at Alstead, 20 Mar 1833 son of Ralph and Bia (Hale) Smith. Harriet and Moses went to Nebraska after their marriage and were living there in the 1900 census. Moses d. in Sherman County, NE, 14 Mar 1902. Harriet returned to Keene where she died. Harriet did not have children.

ix   GEORGE H. ANGIER (twin), b. 31 Aug 1831; d. at Walpole 3 Aug 1910; m. at Westmoreland, NH, 26 Nov 1863, ADELINE SMITH, b. at Westmoreland, 4 Jun 1837 daughter of Hiram and Olive (Arnold) Smith; Adeline d. at Walpole, 11 Apr 1889.

x   ANDREW JACKSON ANGIER, b. 18 Apr 1834; d. of wounds suffered at the Battle of Perryville, 3 Nov 1862.[1840] Andrew had gone to Nunda with his brother John, but then to Wisconsin with his sister Emily and her husband Sala Webb. Andrew served with the 10th Regiment of Wisconsin Infantry.[1841]

623)   DAVID RUSSELL (*Thomas⁴, James³, James², Robert¹*), b. at Walpole, NH, 30 Aug 1796 son of Thomas and Eunice (Alexander) Russell; d. at Walpole, 5 Jun 1875; m. 25 Dec 1817, MARY A. WHEELER, b. at Deerfield, MA, about 1796 (1 Jul 1796 in Walpole history) (Deerfield according to death record); Mary d. at Walpole, 30 Oct 1887.
        David and Mary resided in Walpole where their five children were born, four of whom lived to adulthood. Three of the children remained in Walpole throughout their lives.
        In his will written 18 March 1867, David Russell bequeathed to beloved wife Mary three hundred dollars, all the household furniture, and the use and improvement of all the real estate, except the pasture of the Fay farm, during her natural life. Daughter Mary E. Wilder receives seventy-five dollars and four shares of the Cheshire Rail Road Company. Daughter Martha P. Derby receives seventy-five dollars. Grandson John Edward Russell son of John B. Russell receives three hundred dollars. The remainder of the estate, real and personal, is to be equally divided among his four children: David A. Russell, John B. Russell, Mary E. Wilder, and Martha P. Derby. Son John B. Russell was named executor. In a codicil written 7 August 1873, David increased his bequest to his daughter Mary E. Wilder to $475 and she will also receive the home place at the decease of her mother, provided that Mary pay $700 to each of her siblings. The estate was valued at $10,374.[1842]
        David Russell and Mary Wheeler were parents of five children born at Walpole.

i   DAVID ALLEN RUSSELL, b. 16 Aug 1818; d. at Belmont, MA, 13 Oct 1888; m. 1st about 1846, NANCY BURNHAM, b. at Walpole, 13 Jan 1825 daughter of Jacob B. and Elizabeth (Dickey) Burnham; Nancy d. 6 Jun

[1836] Hand, *Centennial History of the Town of Nunda*, p 220
[1837] Hand, *Centennial History of the Town of Nunda*, p 171 and p 219
[1838] Emily Sarah is listed as Emily S. on the marriage record, but later used Sarah E.
[1839] National Park Service, U.S. Civil War Soldiers, 1861-1865
[1840] U.S., Registers of Deaths of Volunteers, 1861-1865, Wisconsin, A-G, p 5
[1841] National Park Service, U.S. Civil War Soldiers, 1861-1865
[1842] *New Hampshire. Probate Court (Cheshire County)*; Probate Place: *Cheshire, New Hampshire, Estate of David Russell, R469*

1860. David m. 2nd at Walpole, 19 Sep 1865, HELEN LOUISA KITTREDGE, b. at Walpole, 7 Aug 1837 daughter of Jeremiah and Mary B. (Stone) Kittredge; Helen d. at Mendon, MA, 10 Oct 1921.

ii   JOHN BENJAMIN RUSSELL, b. 22 Mar 1820; d. at Walpole, 5 Aug 1892; m. 26 May 1842, LUCY HOOPER, b. at Walpole, 17 Sep 1820 daughter of Elisha and Jemima (Ormsby) Hooper; Lucy d. at Walpole, 17 Sep 1891.

iii   GEORGE H. RUSSELL, b. 14 Nov 1824; d. 16 Sep 1828.

iv   MARY ELVIRA RUSSELL, b. 26 Sep 1828; d. at Walpole, 16 Dec 1904; m. at Walpole, 1 Jul 1862, GEORGE SANGER WILDER, b. at Keene, NH, 30 Jun 1826 son of Abijah and Rhoda J. (Sanger) Wilder; George d. at Walpole, 1 Jun 1897.

v   MARTHA P. RUSSELL, b. 18 May 1831; d. in hospital at Boston, 24 Sep 1891 from surgical complications; m. at Rockingham, VT, 1 Jan 1856, ALBERT DERBY, b. at Walpole, Jul 1830 son of Ephraim and Betsey (Whitney) Derby; Albert d. at Bellows Falls, VT, 17 Jan 1914. Martha and Albert resided at Bellows Falls.

624)   PHYLENA RUSSELL (*Thomas⁴, James³, James², Robert¹*), b. at Walpole, NH, 23 Apr 1803 daughter of Thomas and Eunice (Alexander) Russell; d. at Walpole, 27 Apr 1839; m. 1823, HENRY PRENTISS FOSTER, b. 10 Oct 1796 son of Henry and Susannah (Hooper) Foster; Henry d. at Walpole, 18 Aug 1861. Henry married second Eliza Marsh.

Henry P. Foster did not leave a will. The final settlement of his estate occurred January 1863 with the dispersal of $4,448.10 to the heirs. The administrator of the estate at that time was Caleb Foster. Payments were made by Caleb to widow Eliza, Henry T. Foster, Elizabeth P. Huntoon, and to the guardian of Charles M. Foster and Cate J. Foster. Eliza received $1,482.70 and each of the children received $593.08.[1843]

Phylena Russell and Henry P. Foster were parents of three children born at Walpole. Henry also had two children with his second wife Eliza Marsh.

i   CALEB FOSTER, b. 22 Mar 1825; d. at Walpole, 8 Apr 1901; m. at Walpole, 11 Nov 1851, ISABELLA ELIZA MARSH, b. at Walpole, 10 Sep 1826 daughter of Edmund E. and Isabella (Hosmer) Marsh; Isabella d. at Walpole, 14 May 1892.

ii   HENRY THOMAS FOSTER, b. 15 Oct 1826; d. at Walpole, 17 Apr 1879; m. at Westmoreland, 29 Apr 1855, HANNAH M. FULLER, b. at Westmoreland, 10 Aug 1834 daughter of Christopher and Elsie (Clement) Fuller; Hannah d. at Keene, 27 Jul 1897.

iii   ELIZABETH PHILENA FOSTER, b. 1 Nov 1828; d. at Topeka, KS, 1 Apr 1891; m. at Walpole, 22 Nov 1854, ANDREW JACKSON HUNTOON, b. at Unity, NH, 29 Feb 1832 son of Lemuel and Sibyl (Palmer) Huntoon; Andrew d. at Topeka, 27 May 1902.[1844] Dr. Andrew Huntoon served as an army surgeon.

625)   ELVIRA RUSSELL (*Thomas⁴, James³, James², Robert¹*), b. at Walpole, NH, about 1804 daughter of Thomas and Eunice (Alexander) Russell; d. at Walpole, 13 Jan 1894; m. JOHN JENNISON, b. at Northfield, MA (per death record), 14 Jun 1807 son of Thomas and Martha (Moore) Jennison; John d. at Walpole, Jul 1880.

John Jennison was a farmer in Walpole. In his will written 14 May 1880, John Jennison bequeathed to son George R. Jennison the homestead place on Main Street in Walpole Village and all the household goods, implements, and furniture. This bequest is on condition that George move to the homestead as soon as possible after John's decease and provide support for his mother Elvira for her natural life. George also receives $500 to be held in trust and the interest paid to his mother annually. After Elvira's decease, the principal sum is to be divided equally among the other children: Daniel A. Jennison of Ware, Massachusetts; Charles H. Jennison of Winchendon, Massachusetts; Warren Jennison of Walpole, New Hampshire; Mary E. George wife of Frank George of Bellows Falls, Vermont; and Frank R. Jennison of Ithaca, Ohio. Any residue of the estate except one hundred dollars is to be equally divided among all the children. The one hundred dollars goes in equal shares to his grandchildren children of his son John: Arthur, Allice, Lilla, and John. George R. Jennison was named executor.[1845]

Elvira Russell and John Jennison were parents of eight children born at Walpole.

i   GEORGE RUSSELL JENNISON, b. 13 Jan 1834; d. at Walpole, 15 Oct 1901; m. at Ware, MA, 6 Nov 1861, EMILY AUGUSTA SPARHAWK, b. at Lebanon, NH, 14 May 1830 daughter of George and Eliza Parker (Hammond) Sparhawk; Emily d. at Walpole, 19 Jan 1917.

ii   WILLIAM W. JENNISON, b. 31 Aug 1835; died young.

[1843] New Hampshire Wills and Probate, Cheshire County, Estate of Henry P. Foster, Case 435

[1844] Andrew J. Huntoon was a member of SAR and his application packet contains the details on his birth and parents.

[1845] *New Hampshire. Probate Court (Cheshire County);* Probate Place: *Cheshire, New Hampshire, Estate of John Jennison, Case J209*

iii   JOHN JENNISON, b. 4 Oct 1837; d. at Walpole, 30 Nov 1875; m. about 1865, MARY ELIZA. GROUT, b. at Westminster, VT, 12 May 1834 daughter of Sylvester and Cassandra (Hunt) Grout; Mary d. at Pepperell, MA, 29 Nov 1918.

iv   DAVID ALLEN JENNISON, b. 28 Jan 1838; d. at West Brookfield, MA, 7 Nov 1913; m. at Ware, 6 Feb 1862, LOUISA MARY BROCKWAY, b. 20 Dec 1838 daughter of Jesse and Mary (Pratt) Brockway; Louisa d. at West Brookfield, 27 Oct 1933.

v   CHARLES H. JENNISON, b. 28 Aug 1839; d. at Chicago, IL, 7 Jul 1910; m. at Cook County, IL, 3 May 1867, ANNA A. OWEN, b. in NY, Jul 1843 (per 1900 census, although other records suggest 1838); Anna d. at Chicago, 5 May 1910.

vi   MARY E. JENNISON, b. 3 Mar 1842; d. at Bellows Falls, VT, 4 Mar 1918; m. at Walpole, 8 Oct 1867, FRANKLIN A. GEORGE, b. at Acworth, NH, 9 Dec 1835 son of Nathan and Lucy (Mather) George; Frank d. at Bellows Falls, 25 Jul 1922.

vii   FRANK R. JENNISON, b. 31 Dec 1847; d. at Chicago, IL, 21 Oct 1917; m. 1870, LYDIA MILLS, b. in OH, 23 May 1847 daughter of Louis and Mary Ann (Mullen) Mills;[1846] Lydia d. at Oak Park, IL, 6 Apr 1930.

viii   WARREN HENRY JENNISON, b. 28 Mar 1848; d. at Petersham, MA, 23 Jan 1912. Warren did not marry. In census records, he is described as a laborer and hired man and occupation on his death record in carpenter.

626)   EUNICE RUSSELL (*Thomas⁴, James³, James², Robert¹*), b. at Walpole, NH, 7 Mar 1808 daughter of Thomas and Eunice (Alexander) Russell; d. at Swanzey, NH, 23 Oct 1852; m. 20 Apr 1830, ORLANDO FRINK, b. at Deerfield, MA, 10 Mar 1810 son of Samuel and Mehitable (Eams) Frink; Orlando d. at Swanzey 16 Apr 1877. Orlando married second Mary A. Willard on 1 Mar 1853.
        Orlando Frisk was a shoemaker. Eunice and Orlando were parents of three children born at Swanzey. Orlando also had three children with his second wife.

i   MARY E. FRINK, b. 23 Jul 1831; d. at Berlin, MA, 25 Feb 1897; m. 1st 13 Nov 1849, ADONIRAM JUDSON READ, b. at Swanzey, 19 Oct 1827 son of David and Matilda (Cross) Read; Judson d. at Swanzey, 15 Jan 1856. Mary m. 2nd at Berlin, MA, 1 Jun 1868, IRA JONES, b. at Berlin, MA, 2 Sep 1815 son of Peletiah and Persis (Priest) Jones; Ira d. at Berlin, 24 Nov 1891.

ii   HENRY ORLANDO FRINK, b. 18 Mar 1836; d. at Chicago, IL, 15 Jul 1915; m. 1864, ELIZABETH ARBELLE LUCE, b. in NY, Sep 1839 daughter of William and Julia Ann (-) Luce; Elizabeth d. after 1900.

iii   SARAH ELLEN "NELLIE" FRINK, b. Apr 1846; d. at Berlin, MA, 24 Mar 1909; b. 24 Nov 1870, CHARLES BIGELOW MAYNARD, b. at Berlin, MA, 24 Nov 1846 son of George W. and Sophia (Bigelow) Maynard; Charles d. at Berlin, 14 Mar 1914.

627)   BETSEY P. RUSSELL (*Thomas⁴, James³, James², Robert¹*), b. at Walpole, NH, 5 May 1812 daughter of Thomas and Eunice (Alexander) Russell; d. at Walpole, 24 Aug 1903; m. CLEMENT S. DICKEY, b. 12 Mar 1806 son of Matthew and Betsey (Murch) Dickey; Clement d. at Walpole, 11 Jun 1892.
        Betsey and Clement resided in Walpole where Clement was a farmer. Clement did not leave a will and his estate entered probate 28 July 1892 with widow Betsey and next-of-kin son Albert C. Dickey who was named administrator.[1847]
        Betsey Russell and Clement Dickey were parents of two children born at Walpole.

i   JOSEPHINE HELEN DICKEY, b. 26 Jul 1842; d. 3 Feb 1877. Josephine did not marry.

ii   ALBERT CLEMENT DICKEY, b. Dec 1849; d. at Walpole, 4 Aug 1941; m. at Keene, 20 Jun 1912, as her second husband, EDITH MARGARET ROY, b. at Walpole, 12 Nov 1877 daughter of William E. and Mary A. (Watkins) Roy; Edith d. at Bellows Falls, VT, 30 Aug 1960. Edith was first married to Mr. Landon whom she had divorced.

628)   SAMUEL WOOD PULSIPHER (*Priscilla Russell Pulsipher⁴, James³, James², Robert¹*), b. at Rockingham, VT, 13 Jan 1782 son of David and Priscilla (Russell) Pulsipher; d. at Rockingham, 14 Jul 1817; m. at Rockingham, 29 Mar 1806, SALLY WEAVER, b. at Rockingham, 13 Mar 1787 daughter of Daniel and Joanna (Preston) Weaver; Sally d. at Rockingham, 17 Jun 1863. Sally married second Isaac Severens.

[1846] The names of Lydia's parents and her date and place of birth are as given on her death record.
[1847] New Hampshire Wills and Probate, Cheshire County, Estate Files, Clement S. Dickey of Walpole, Case 597

Samuel and Sally lived in Rockingham, Vermont where Samuel served as selectman from 1811-1814. He drowned while attempting to repair the dam for his mill.[1848]

Samuel Wood Pulsipher and Sally Weaver were parents of seven children, the youngest child born after Samuel's death.

i   GEORGE HENRY PULSIPHER, b. 29 Sep 1806; d. at Southport, IL, 11 Feb 1861; m. at Peoria, IL, 24 Nov 1842, ABIGAIL BOSWORTH, b. in NY, 17 Jun 1818 daughter of Ichabod T. and Lydia (Fitch) Bosworth; Abigail d. at Elmwood, IL, 15 May 1903.

ii   CHARLES WEAVER PULSIPHER, b. 15 Sep 1808; d. at Springfield, VT, 9 Apr 1888; m. 10 Oct 1837, LUCY WILSON, b. at Chester, VT, 20 May 1819 daughter of Solomon and Phila (Earl) Wilson;[1849] Lucy d. at Rockingham, 29 Mar 1907.

iii   IRENA KENDAL PULSIPHER, b. 27 Dec 1810

iv   ELIZABETH STOEL PULSIPHER, b. 5 Mar 1813

v   LAURA PULSIPHER, b. 1 Jul 1815; d. at Rockingham, 25 May 1887; m. 29 Mar 1842, RODNEY WILEY, b. at Peterborough, 20 Mar 1815 son of John and Mary (Barry) Wiley;[1850] Rodney d. at Rockingham, 28 Mar 1904.

vi   ELIZABETH PULSIPHER, b. 15 Mar 1816; d. at Rockingham, 28 Sep 1875; m. about 1834, her step-brother, FRANKLIN SEVERENS, b. at Derby, VT, Oct 1811 son of Isaac and Abigail (Dean) Severens; Franklin d. at Clyde, MI, 3 Mar 1897.

vii   SAMUEL PULSIPHER, b. 11 Oct 1817; d. at Brimfield, IL, 19 Feb 1897; m. 6 Apr 1842, ANGELINE ELIZABETH WALKER, b. at Covington, PA, 4 Jul 1825 daughter of Asahel and Anna (Harkness) Walker;[1851] Angeline d. at Brimfield, IL, 9 Nov 1889.

629)   DAVID PULSIPHER (*Priscilla Russell Pulsipher⁴, James³, James², Robert¹*), b. at Rockingham, VT, 6 Dec 1791 son of David and Priscilla (Russell) Pulsipher; d. at Brimfield, IL, 14 Dec 1865; m. at Walpole, NH, 15 Mar 1815, REBECCA LANE, b. at Walpole, 7 Apr 1794 daughter of Ephraim and Elizabeth Danforth (Abbott) Lane; Rebecca d. at Rockingham, VT, 5 Feb 1847. David m. 2nd EUNICE HEWITT, b. at Wallingford, about 1794; Eunice d. at Wallingford, 15 Feb 1867.[1852]

David resided in Rockingham where he had a farm and was a drover taking cattle and sheep from New Hampshire and Vermont to Boston. After the institution of rail service, he used the rails to transport cattle. In the early 1850's, he was seriously injured when crushed by cattle as he was loading them in a rail car. In later life, he moved to Illinois where he was living with his daughter at the time of his death.[1853]

David Pulsipher and Rebecca Lane were parents of nine children born at Rockingham.

i   ELVIRA PULSIPHER, b. 7 Mar 1816; d. at Walpole, NH, 16 Jun 1881; m. 18 Jan 1843, WILLIAM HOOPER, b. at Walpole, 21 Feb 1812 son of James and Eleanor (Wellington) Hooper; William d. at Walpole, 26 Jan 1903.

ii   LEWIS PULSIPHER, b. 3 Apr 1817; d. 24 Jun 1825.

iii   DANA PULSIPHER, b. 9 Sep 1818; d. at Elmwood, IL, 21 Nov 1878; m. at Wallingford, VT, 29 Jan 1848, MARTHA JANE LAW, b. 12 May 1826 (engraved on gravestone);[1854] Martha d. at Peoria, IL, 16 Aug 1896.

iv   MARY PULSIPHER, b. 30 Apr 1820; d. 15 Jul 1821.

v   MARY PULSIPHER, b. 13 Nov 1821; d. 24 Sep 1822.

vi   SOPHIA PULSIPHER, b. 18 Feb 1823; d. at Rockingham, 15 Jun 1876. Sophia did not marry.

vii   GEORGE PULSIPHER, b. 9 Jul 1824. George attended Black River Academy. He did not marry.

viii   ELIZABETH PULSIPHER, b. 26 Jul 1826; d. at Rockingham, 29 Nov 1874; m. 2 Jun 1847, ROBERT W. WILEY, b. at Rockingham, 12 Dec 1825 son of John and Randilla (Weaver) Wiley; Robert d. at Brimfield, IL, 27 Aug 1897. Robert married second Sarah Brewer on 15 Feb 1877.

[1848] Hayes, *History of the Town of Rockingham*, p 734

[1849] Westmoreland Historical Committee, *History of Westmoreland*, p 588

[1850] The names of Rodney's parents are given as John Wiley and Mary Barry on his death record.

[1851] Chandler, *History of the Town of Shirley*, p 656

[1852] Vermont, Vital Records, 1720-1908

[1853] Hayes, *History of the Town of Rockingham*, p 735

[1854] Brimfield Township Cemetery, Brimfield, IL, findagrave ID: 50143651

ix   LEWIS PULSIPHER, b. 5 Oct 1828; d. at Fairbury, IL, 1875; m. 18 Nov 1855, CHLOE CHILSON, b. 15 Jul 1839 daughter of Anson and Maranda (White) Chilson; Chloe d. at Fairbury, IL, 24 Feb 1923. Lewis attended Springfield Wesleyan Seminary.

630)   ELIAS PULSIPHER (*Priscilla Russell Pulsipher⁴, James³, James², Robert¹*), b. at Rockingham, VT, 20 Jun 1794 son of David and Priscilla (Russell) Pulsipher; d. at Rockingham, 22 Jun 1858; m. at Walpole, NH, 30 Jan 1820, SUSAN LANE, b. at Walpole, 1 Oct 1796 daughter of Ephraim and Elizabeth Danforth (Abbott) Lane; Susan d. at Rockingham, 7 Jun 1880.
        Elias and Susan lived in Rockingham on property next to Elias's brother David, the area known as "Pulsipher Hollow." Elias sold the farm about 1850 and moved to South Rockingham.[1855]
        Elias Pulsipher and Susan Lane were parents of three children born at Rockingham.

i   GEORGE F. PULSIPHER, b. and d. 1821

ii   MARTHA A. PULSIPHER, b. 1823; d. at Troy, NY, 28 May 1859; m. 1842, OTHNIEL W. EDSON, b. at Chester, VT, 1818 son of Ophir and Sophia (Williams) Edson; Othniel d. at Albany, NY, 5 Mar 1861. Othniel married second Elizabeth Louisa Andrews in 1860.

iii   IRA A. PULSIPHER, b. 1826; d. at Rockingham, 19 Nov 1865; m. at Ludlow, VT, 4 Dec 1861, RUTH BROWN POLLARD, b. at Plymouth, VT, 12 Jul 1833 daughter of Moses and Abigail (Brown) Pollard; Ruth d. at Concordia, KS, 4 Feb 1899. Ruth Brown Pollard was for many years the principal of Vermont Academy. She had been educated in Georgetown, Kentucky. Ira and Ruth married later than typical, and Ira died just four years after their marriage. They had one sone Park B. Pulsipher with whom Ruth lived just prior to her death.[1856]

631)   WILLIAM WILEY PULSIPHER (*Priscilla Russell Pulsipher⁴, James³, James², Robert¹*), b. at Rockingham, VT, 21 Jul 1800 son of David and Priscilla (Russell) Pulsipher; d. at Rockingham, VT, 26 Sep 1870; m. 5 Jan 1830, ELECTA BARNES, b. at Weathersfield, VT, 25 Jan 1807 daughter of Solomon S. and Zada (Plant) Barnes; Electa d. at Springfield, VT, 26 Jun 1891.
        William resided on the homestead farm in Rockingham. This property was the site of the first inn in Rockingham run by his grandfather David Pusipher.[1857]
        William W. Pulsipher and Electa Barnes were parents of four children born at Rockingham.

i   ZADA P. PULSIPHER, b. 29 May 1831; d. 31 Jul 1833.

ii   LUCY ANN PULSIPHER, b. 23 Nov 1824; d. at Springfield, VT, 17 Jul 1893. Lucy did not marry.

iii   ELI P. B. PULSIPHER, b. 18 Jan 1839; d. at Springfield, VT, 22 Nov 1918; m. 1st at Rockingham, 2 Sep 1873, EMMA SMALLEY (widow of Ira M. Divoll), b. at Grafton, VT, 1844 daughter of Charles and Delania (Davis) Smalley; Emma d. at Springfield, 11 May 1885. Eli m. 2nd, 25 May 1890, NANCY WHITE (widow of Orin Beard), b. at Rockingham, 7 Jun 1844 daughter of Bartlett E. and Mary Adaline (Smalley) White; Nancy d. at Springfield, 29 Nov 1918.

iv   SARAH REBECCA PULSIPHER, b. 4 Apr 1848; d. at Springfield, VT, 16 Mar 1916; m. at Springfield, VT, 26 May 1874, WILLIAM HENRY HARRISON PUTNAM, b. at Grafton, VT, 14 Sep 1840 son of John and Roxana (Howard) Putnam; William d. at Birmingham, AL, 29 Nov 1923.

632)   HANNAH FLETCHER (*Hannah Russell Fletcher⁴, James³, James², Robert¹*), b. about 1792 daughter of Luke and Hannah (Russell) Fletcher; d. at Stockholm, NY, 14 Jun 1880; m. WILLIAM COON who was deceased before 1850.
        There is one child known for Hannah Fletcher and William Coon.

i   HESTER ANN COON, b. about 1828; d. at Stockholm, NY, 1894; m. 5 Feb 1850, CHARLES EMERY, b. 1827 son of Jonathan and Fanny (Dunshee) Emery;[1858] Charles d. at Stockholm, 1900. Charles and Hester were parents of six children.

[1855] Hayes, *History of the Town of Rockingham, Vermont*, p 736
[1856] "Death of Mrs. Ruth B. Pulsipher", Vermont Phoenix, Brattleboro, February 10, 1899
[1857] Hayes, *History of the Town of Rockingham*, p 737
[1858] Emery, *Genealogical Records of Descendants of John and Anthony Emery*, p 478

633) ADOLPHUS FLETCHER (*Hannah Russell Fletcher⁴, James³, James², Robert¹*), b. 1795 son of Luke and Hannah (Russell) Fletcher; d. at Stockholm, NY, 9 Apr 1851; m. at Walpole, NH, 4 Nov 1817, SALLY WELLINGTON, b. at Walpole, 21 Aug 1799 daughter of Ebenezer and Rebecca (Levens) Wellington; Sally d. at Stockholm, 8 Sep 1872.

Adolphus and Sally were parents of eleven children. The older children were likely born at Walpole and the family was in Stockholm, New York by 1830. Children Sarah, Rebecca, and Ira did not marry and in 1900 were living together in Potsdam, New York.[1859] Son Jesse was wounded at Petersburgh during the Civil War but survived.

In his will written 13 July 1850, Adolphus Fletcher bequeathed to beloved wife Sally all the real estate in the town of Stockholm except for 30 acres which is bequeathed to son Gilbert M. L. Fletcher. She also receives all the personal estate except that specifically given to the children in the will. It is Adolphus's intent that the family remain together on the property until the children come of age. His three eldest sons, William W. Fletcher, Charles E. Fletcher, and Jesse L. Fletcher, each receives one dollar as they have received their full portions from the estate. Son Gilbert M. L. Fletcher receives 30 acres as well as a pair of oxen, three cows, and the crops currently growing on the land. Fifth son George W. Fletcher receives two cows, a four-year-old colt, pair of steers, and all the stock in the Northern Rail Road Company. He will also receive $300 at age twenty-one provide he continue to live with his mother and works for her until that time. Sixth son Ira Fletcher receives one cow and $200 at age twenty-one. Seventh son Ebenezer receives a heifer and $200 at age twenty-one. Eldest daughter Almira Grandy wife of Levi Grandy receives one dollar as she has received her portion. Second daughter Rebecca Fletcher receives her support during her natural life, and if she marries $100. His two youngest daughters, Mary and Sarah, receive support until they arrive at lawful age and then will receive $100. Wife Sally was named executrix. In a codicil written apparently immediately after the will, he adds that if his wife remarries and his minor children are deprived of a home, the minor children shall have a lien on the property in order to provide their support.[1860]

i   WILLIAM WELLINGTON FLETCHER, b. likely at Walpole, 1818; d. at Stockholm, NY, 11 Jul 1877; m. FIDELIA L. GRANDY, b. about 1826 daughter of John and Fidelia (Gilson) Grandy; Fidelia d. at Stockholm, 11 Apr 1880.

ii   CHARLES E. FLETCHER, b. about 1820; d. at Yankton, SD, 18 Mar 1893; m. about 1848, MARGERY ANGENETTE LAWRENCE, b. about 1826 daughter of William and Olive (Beals) Lawrence;[1861] Margery d. at Yankton, 18 Aug 1891.

iii   JESSE LYMAN FLETCHER, b. at Walpole, NH, 21 Dec 1822; d. at Mankato, MN, 1900; m. before 1861, MARGARET who has not been identified. It is not known if Jesse and Margaret had children. He was living alone in Mankato in 1875.[1862] He served in the Civil War and was wounded at Petersburgh but survived his wounds and was mustered out 7 January 1865.[1863]

iv   ALMIRA M. FLETCHER, b. about 1826; d. at Stockholm, NY, 1 Jan 1892; m. about 1849, LEVI B. GRANDY, b. about 1828 son of John and Fidelia (Gilson) Grandy; Levi d. at Stockholm, 21 Apr 1887.

v   REBECCA FLETCHER, b. Jan 1829; d. at Norwood, NY, 13 Jun 1908. Rebecca did not marry.

vi   LAFAYETTE GILBERT MORTIMER FLETCHER, b. at Stockholm, NY, 13 Feb 1830; d. at Mankato, MN, 21 Jan 1910; m. 1st 1858, LUCINA BACON (widow of Henry Foote), b. 18 Mar 1830 daughter of Asher and Lydia (Bailey) Bacon; Lucina d. at Mankato, 17 Sep 1870. Lafayette m. 2nd at New Sharon, ME, 15 May 1879, SUSIE M. DYER, b. at New Sharon, ME, 17 Feb 1845 daughter of John W. and Rosanna (Bean) Dyer; Susie d. at Mankato, 27 May 1941.

vii   GEORGE WASHINGTON FLETCHER, b. Mar 1832; d. at Mankato, MN, 1912; m. 1864, MARY E. HOUSER, b. in IL, Oct 1847 daughter of Jonathan and Malinda (Plunkett) Houser; Mary d. at Mankato, 29 Feb 1904.

viii   IRA JOHN FLETCHER, b. Mar 1834; d. at Potsdam, 1915. Ira did not marry. In the 1870 census, he was listed as a farmer, and described as a capitalist at the 1900 census.

ix   EBENEZER E. FLETCHER, b. 1837; d. at Belgrade, MN, 1923; m. at Blue Earth, MN, 27 May 1868, MARY ELIZABETH MEACHAM, b. in IL, Oct 1845; Mary d. at Belgrade, 1938.

x   MARY FLETCHER, b. about 1839; d. at Stockholm, 11 May 1861. Mary did not marry.

xi   SARAH FLETCHER, b. Aug 1841; d. at Potsdam, 1916. Sarah did not marry.

[1859] Year: 1900; Census Place: Potsdam, Saint Lawrence, New York; Page: 8; Enumeration District: 0134; FHL microfilm: 1241158

[1860] New York Wills and Probate Records, St. Lawrence, Will Book 0004, pp 1-3

[1861] Margery's mother Olive Lawrence was living in Yankton with Charles and Margery A. Fletcher in 1880. Year: 1880; Census Place: Yankton, Yankton, Dakota Territory; Roll: 115; Page: 445C; Enumeration District: 105

[1862] Minnesota, Territorial and State Censuses, 1849-1905, 1875, Mankato, Blue Earth, Minnesota

[1863] New York State Archives; Albany, New York; Town Clerks' Registers of Men Who Served in the Civil War, ca 1861-1865; Collection Number: (N-Ar)13774; Box Number: 52; Roll Number: 28

634) JAMES RUSSELL (*Uriah⁴, Thomas³, James², Robert¹*), b. at Andover, Nov 1777 son of Uriah and Lydia (Abbott) Russell; d. about 1861 in Oxford County, ME;[1864] m. at East Andover, ME, 13 Aug 1804, his first cousin once removed, DOLLY RUSSELL (*Jacob⁴, John³, John², Robert¹*), b. about 1784 daughter of Jacob and Dorothy (Shattuck) Russell; Dolly d. at Boxford, MA, 20 Sep 1863.

James and Dolly lived in Albany and then Waterford, Maine and were parents of eleven children. Sons Jacob and Charles were physicians. Son Jacob struck out on his own about age sixteen and settled in Kentucky where he first taught school and later studied medicine in Louisville, Kentucky.[1865]

i   DOLLY RUSSELL, b. at Albany, ME, 1 Nov 1804; died young

ii   JAMES RUSSELL, b. at Albany, 8 Oct 1807

iii   LYDIA ABBOT RUSSELL, b. at Albany, 1 Dec 1808; d. at Boxford, MA, 1 Jan 1893; m. 1st at Baltimore, MD, 17 Sep 1832, MOSES GOULD, b. at Boxford, 27 May 1800 son of Moses and Anna (Mecum) Gould; Moses d. 30 Jun 1843 (recorded at Boxford but described as "of Baltimore"). Lydia m. 2nd at Boxford, 12 Jun 1866, as his second wife, LEONARD GROVER, b. at Bethel, ME, 9 May 1799 son of Eli and Mehitable (Austin) Grover; Leonard d. at Bethel, 25 Feb 1884. Leonard was first married to TABITHA GREENE (*Tabitha Holt Greene⁵, Jacob Holt⁴, Jacob Holt³, Hannah Russell Holt², Robert¹*), b. at Waterford, 1801 daughter of Thomas and Tabitha (Holt) Greene; Tabitha d. at Bethel, 2 Mar 1864.

iv   DOLLY RUSSELL, b. 14 Apr 1811

v   DANIEL GAGE RUSSELL, b. at Albany, 26 Oct 1813; d. at Baltimore, MD, 21 Jan 1845.

vi   JACOB RUSSELL, b. at Albany, 10 Feb 1816; d. after 1860 when living at Scott County, KY; m. before 1850, NANCY MCELWAIN, b. in KY, about 1825 daughter of William and Nancy (Cross) McElwain.[1866]

vii   HENRY JEWETT RUSSELL, b. at Waterford, ME, 7 Jun 1818; d. at Baltimore, MD, 1898; m. at Baltimore, 23 Dec 1842, MARGARET UPPERMAN, b. in MD, 1823; Margaret d. at Baltimore, 1908. Henry was an upholsterer.

viii   CHARLES RUSSELL, b. at Waterford, 19 Jul 1820; d. (burial at West Paris, ME), 4 Jul 1888; m. 15 Oct 1848, ASENATH HOWARD WILLIS, b. at Bethel, 17 May 1825 daughter of Adam and Mary (Adams) Willis; Asenath d. 26 May 1906.

ix   JOEL RUSSELL, b. at Waterford, 16 Jul 1822; d. at Hayward, CA, 1888; m. at Alameda County, CA, 3 Aug 1856,[1867] CAROLINE "CARRIE" BARTLETT, b. at Old Town, ME, Jun 1830; Carrie d. at Honolulu, HI, 5 Jan 1903.[1868]

x   WARREN FAULKNER RUSSELL, b. at Waterford, 15 Aug 1825; d. after 1880 when living at Friendship, ME; m. at North Waldoboro, 22 Feb 1859, AUGUSTA GEYER, b. at West Rockport, ME, 7 Mar 1841 daughter of Robert and Sarah (Weymouth) Geyer; Augusta d. at Rockport, 13 May 1918. Warren and Augusta divorced at Know County, ME, Dec 1875.[1869]

xi   AMANDA MELVINA RUSSELL, b. at Waterford, 6 Jun 1828; d. 17 Mar 1832.

635) THOMAS RUSSELL (*Uriah⁴, Thomas³, James², Robert¹*), b. at Andover, Nov 1777 (twin of James) son of Uriah and Lydia (Abbott) Russell; d. at Andover, 18 Jan 1849;[1870] m. at Albany, ME, 22 Apr 1806, ABIGAIL BELL, b. likely at Albany about 1786 of not yet verified parents; Abigail d. at Andover 10 Oct 1833.

Thomas was a laborer. He and Abigail were in Albany, Maine in the early period of their marriage, but returned to Andover, Massachusetts. They were parents of nine children.

Daughter Priscilla married Thomas Gee as his second wife and Priscilla did not have children. In her will written 20 December 1898, she left her entire estate to her sister Elizabeth K. Morse.[1871]

i   THOMAS RUSSELL, b. at Albany, ME, 10 Aug 1806

ii   ABIEL RUSSELL, b. at Albany, ME, 11 May 1808; d. at Andover (burial at Ludlow, VT), 7 Aug 1885; m. at Albany, 27 Nov 1842, ALVIRA PRINCE, b. at Gray, ME, about 1816; Alvira d. at Ludlow, 24 Nov 1882.

[1864] James Russell was living at the time of the 1860 U.S. Census; his wife was a widow when she died in 1863.
[1865] Perrin, *Kentucky, A History of the State*, p 848
[1866] Perrin, *Kentucky, A History of the State*, p 848
[1867] California, Marriage Records from Select Counties, 1850-1941
[1868] Hawaii, Death Certificates and Indexes, 1841-1942. Carrie's place of birth is given on the death register but no names of parents.
[1869] Maine, Divorce Records, 1798-1891, ancestry.com
[1870] Thomas, widr., laborer, s. Uriah and Lydia, dysuria, Jan. 18, 1849, a. 71 y.
[1871] Massachusetts Wills and Probate, Essex County, , volume 549, p 45

iii   ABIGAIL B. RUSSELL, b. at Andover, 6 Dec 1812; d. at Johnson, VT, 16 Dec 1879; m. at Andover, 14 Oct 1830, JOSEPH BAKER, b. 20 Jun 1803 son of Thomas and Hannah (Balch) Baker;[1872] Joseph d. after 1880 when he was living at Johnson, VT.

iv   WILLARD RUSSELL, b. at Andover, 20 Jul 1814; d. at Westminster, VT, 21 Apr 1900; m. at Ludlow, VT, 6 Apr 1837, ALVINA DAWLEY, b. at Mount Holly, VT, about 1816 daughter of Perry and Martha (Sparhawk) Dawley; Alvina d. at Ludlow, 24 Sep 1880.

v   GARDNER SPRING RUSSELL, b. at Andover, 29 Dec 1815

vi   ELIZABETH RUSSELL, b. 22 Feb 1818; d. 12 Apr 1818.

vii   ELIZABETH KNIGHTS RUSSELL, b. at Andover, 9 Feb 1819; d. at Methuen, 11 Sep 1914; m. 18 Aug 1853, WILLIAM BARTLETT MORSE, b. at Methuen, 13 Nov 1818 son of Jonathan and Hannah (Merrill) Morse; William d. at Boston, 11 Apr 1886.

viii   LYDIA ABBOTT RUSSELL, b. at Andover, 2 Feb 1821; d. at Boston, 5 Apr 1889. Lydia did not marry. Administration of her estate was assigned to her nephew William R. Morse.

ix   PRISCILLA JANE RUSSELL, b. at Andover, about 1824; d. at Andover, 10 Dec 1899; m. at Andover, 5 Dec 1885, as his second wife, THOMAS GEE, b. at Devon, England, 5 Aug 1821 son of Phineas and Mary (Wyett) Gee;[1873] Thomas d. at Andover, 8 Nov 1897.

636)   HANNAH RUSSELL (*Uriah⁴, Thomas³, James², Robert¹*), b. at Andover, Apr 1780 (based on age at death) daughter of Uriah and Lydia (Abbott) Russell; d. at Andover, 16 Nov 1832; m. 10 Nov 1801, her third cousin, NATHAN ABBOTT, b. at Andover, 25 Aug 1778 son of Nathan and Sarah (Ballard) Abbott; Nathan d. at Andover, 13 Feb 1837.

     Nathan Abbott and Hannah Russell were parents of seven children born at Andover.

i   Child b. 13 Jul 1803

ii   Son b. 22 Nov 1804 and d. 26 Nov 1804

iii   Child b. 17 Dec 1805 and d. 25 Jan 1806

iv   HANNAH ABBOTT, b. 9 Sep 1807; d. at Norwood, MA, 4 Apr 1889; m. at Andover, 25 Dec 1828, SAMUEL MORRILL, b. at Salisbury, 14 Apr 1804 son of Samuel and Anna (Noyes) Morrill; Samuel d. at Norwood, 25 Aug 1878.

v   NATHAN ABBOTT, b. 17 Jul 1809; d. at Charlestown, MA, 29 Jul 1863; m. at Andover, 4 Oct 1832, his fourth cousin, MARY ELIZABETH CUMMINGS, b. at Andover, 8 Mar 1814 daughter of Samuel and Lucy (Abbott) Cummings; Mary d. at Charlestown, 27 Nov 1872.

vi   PASCHAL ABBOTT, b. 13 Apr 1812;[1874] d. at Lawrence, MA, 4 Jun 1874; m. 1ˢᵗ at Andover, 14 Oct 1835, his second cousin, PHEBE ABBOT SMITH (*Betty Russell Smith⁵, John⁴, John³, John², Robert¹*), b. at Andover, 27 Oct 1811 daughter of Thomas and Betty (Russell) Smith; Phebe d. at Lawrence, 27 Jun 1866. Paschal m. 2ⁿᵈ at Newburyport, 28 Jun 1868, MARGARET MCNAUGHTON, baptized at Southend, Argyll, Scotland, 15 Mar 1830 daughter of Duncan and Helen (Ralston) McNaughton;[1875] Margaret d. at Newburyport, 30 May 1900.

vii   HENRY RUSSELL ABBOTT, b. 19 Apr 1815; d. at Andover, 9 Oct 1896; m. 1ˢᵗ at Andover, 19 Aug 1843, LYDIA LUSCOMB, b. at Andover, 6 Oct 1821 daughter of Richard and Rhoda (Noyes) Luscomb; Lydia d. at Andover, 12 Feb 1853. Henry m. 2ⁿᵈ 1 Feb 1854, MARY AGNES HAYWARD, b. at Bradford, MA, 12 Nov 1818 daughter of Benjamin and Eliza Jane (Harding) Hayward; Mary d. at Andover, 23 Dec 1877. Henry and Lydia were the parents of Andover schoolteacher and genealogist Charlotte Helen Abbott. Mary Agnes Hayward was first married to Robert Simpson.

[1872] Balch, *Genealogy of the Balch Families in America*, p 146

[1873] The names of Thomas's parents are given Phineas Gee and Mary Wyett on his marriage record to Priscilla J. Russell. Ancestry.com. *Massachusetts, Marriage Records, 1840-1915* [database on-line].

[1874] Although Paschal has an 1819 birth year in the birth transcription, all other records give birth as around 1812 which seems more accurate. The Abbot genealogical record gives 13 Apr 1812 as the date.

[1875] Ancestry.com, Scotland, Select Births and Baptisms, 1564-1950. The names of Margaret's parents are given on her death record. Mother's name is also given on her marriage record to Paschal Abbott.

637)   JOEL RUSSELL (*Uriah⁴, Thomas³, James², Robert¹*), b. at Andover, Aug 1783; d. at Andover, 22 Jul 1871 son of Uriah and Lydia (Abbott) Russell; m. 2 Apr 1805, SARAH CURTIS, b. at Middleton, 16 Oct 1782 daughter of Israel and Elizabeth (Wilkins) Curtis; Sarah d. at Andover, 6 Feb 1857.

Joel was a farmer in Andover and resided in the historic Russell homestead at 28 Rocky Hill Road. On 30 July 1856, Joel Russell, with wife Sally relinquishing right of dower, sold to Ammon Russel the easterly half of the dwelling with the land of same for payment of $1,050. There are three land parcels described with the sale. On the same date, Joel Russell conveyed to John Chandler the westerly half of the dwelling house with land for payment of $250. The transaction with John Chandler was a mortgage and could be reversed by payment of $250 with interest to John Chandler either by Joel or his heirs. On 5 October 1857, also in the form of a mortgage, Joel Russell conveyed to John Chandler acting as guardian for Israel Russell three tracts of land in Andover for payment of $725.[1876]

Daughter Elizabeth did not marry and a statement in her probate dated 13 June 1865 names the following heirs: Joel Russell of Andover, father; Joel Russell of Holyoke, brother; Sally Jenkins of Andover, sister; Ammon Russell of Andover, brother; Levi Russell of Saco, Maine, brother; Phebe Chandler of Andover, sister; Samuel Russell of Groton, brother; Amos Russell of West Springfield, brother; Warren Russell of California, brother; and Uriah Russell of Groton, Connecticut, brother. John B. Abbott was named administrator of the estate at the request of father Joel Russell. There was no real estate and personal estate was $800.[1877]

Joel and Sally were parents of fifteen children (although see below the possible discrepancy of two sons named Henry Warren).

i   URIAH RUSSELL, b. 16 Jul 1805; d. at Andover, 26 Dec 1830; m. at Andover, 10 May 1829, MARIA PLAISTED.

ii   SALLY RUSSELL, b. 13 Dec 1806; d. at Andover, 12 Aug 1896; m. at Andover, 18 Sep 1828, EBENEZER JENKINS, b. at Andover, 28 Apr 1807 son of Samuel and Lydia (Damon) Jenkins; Ebenezer d. at Andover, 22 Dec 1883.

iii   JOEL RUSSELL, b. 10 Oct 1808; d. at Holyoke, MA, 30 Oct 1883; m. at Andover, 30 Apr 1827, MARY "POLLY" POOR, b. at Andover, 22 Oct 1807 daughter of Stephen and Mary (Plummer) Poor; Mary d. at Holyoke, 13 Oct 1888.

iv   AMMON RUSSELL, b. 20 Oct 1810; d. at Andover, 9 Apr 1894; m. ABIGAIL SPEAR, b. at Boston, 13 Dec 1813 daughter of John and Lucy (Bemis) Spear; Abigail d. at Andover, 25 May 1883.

v   LEVI RUSSELL, b. 23 Jun 1812; d. after 1865 when he was living in Saco, ME; m. at Amesbury, 23 Jul 1835, ZORA BAILEY, b. at Amesbury, 8 Jun 1817 daughter of Stephen and Mary (-) Bailey; Zora d. at Saco, 6 Jan 1864.

vi   ISRAEL C. RUSSELL, b. 17 May 1814; d. of consumption at Andover, 30 Nov 1850; m. 19 oct 1839, ISABEL EMERY, b. 1 Jul 1820, of Biddeford, ME daughter of Thomas and Mary (Gray) Emery;[1878] Isabel d. at Biddeford, 14 Jun 1848.

vii   ELIZABETH P. RUSSELL, b. 16 Dec 1815; d. at Andover, 1865 (probate 20 Jun 1865). Elizabeth did not marry.

viii   PHEBE RUSSELL, b. 26 Aug 1818; d. at Boston, 21 May 1905; m. at Andover, 11 Apr 1839, JOHN CHANDLER, b. 27 Dec 1812 son of Ezra and Dolly (Chandler) Chandler; John d. at Andover, 4 Oct 1897.

ix   SAMUEL RUSSELL, b. 8 Aug 1820; d. at Bradford, MA, 10 Feb 1893; m. 1ˢᵗ at Andover, 26 Sep 1844, his fourth cousin twice removed, LYDIA S. HOLT (*Moses Holt⁶, Moses Holt⁵, Marstin Holt⁴, Phebe Russell Holt³, John², Robert¹*), b. 1823 daughter of Moses W. and Lydia (Holt) Holt; Lydia d. at Andover, 19 Nov 1852. Samuel m. 2ⁿᵈ at Groton, 12 Jun 1856, SUSAN ANN WOOLEY, b. at Lexington, 26 Jul 1835 daughter of Charles and Catherine (Colburn) Woolley; Susan d. at Waltham, 30 Aug 1888.

x   JAMES RUSSELL, b. 26 Apr 1822; d. at Andover, 1 Sep 1845.[1879] James did not marry.

xi   AMOS RUSSELL, b. 9 Oct 1824; d. at West Springfield, 23 Apr 1912; m. at Unity, NH, 22 Aug 1847, SARAH A. MOODY, b. at Unity, NH, 15 Apr 1826; Sarah d. at West Springfield, 20 Jul 1876.

xii   Daughter, b. 16 Jul 1827; no name given and assumed to die in infancy

xiii   HENRY WARREN RUSSELL, d. 20 Oct 1828. This is a child in the Andover records reported as being born 20 Oct 1820 and dying 20 Oct 1828. There is another child born 8 Aug 1820 which means there is some error. It may just be that this is a confusion of the birth record of Henry Warren Russell noted just below.

[1876] Massachusetts Land Records, Essex County, 536:165, 536:166, 561:149

[1877] *Essex County, MA: Probate File Papers, 1638-1881.* Online database. *AmericanAncestors.org.* New England Historic Genealogical Society, 2014. Case 52298

[1878] Emery, *Genealogical Record of the Descendants of John and Anthony Emery,* p 368

[1879] This death transcription likely refers to son James although mother says Phebe: "James, unm., machinist, s. Joel and Phebe, typhus fever, Sept. 1, [15. G.R.2.], 1845, a. 23 y."

xiv   HENRY WARREN RUSSELL, b. at Andover, 20 Oct 1829; d. at Garden Valley, CA, 2 Nov 1891; m. at Elk Grove, CA, 25 Dec 1869, AMANDA EUPHEMIA TREAT, b. at Silver Creek, MI, 16 May 1844 daughter of Timothy and Lovisa (Bentley) Treat;[1880] Amanda d. at Stanislaus, CA, 5 Dec 1915.

xv   URIAH RUSSELL, b. 29 Mar 1831; d. at Bristol, CT, 21 Sep 1891; m. JANE E. BARTHOLOMEW, b. at Bristol, CT, Mar 1840 daughter of George W. and Angeline (Ives) Bartholomew; Jane d. at Bristol, 1910.

638)   LYDIA RUSSELL (*Uriah⁴, Thomas³, James², Robert¹*), b. at Andover, 5 Dec 1785 daughter of Uriah and Lydia (Abbott) Russell; d. at Andover, 2 Dec 1865; m. 13 Jun 1809, her third cousin once removed (through Abbott line), JOSEPH FAULKNER, b. at Andover, 30 Jul 1783 son of Abiel and Hannah (Abbott) Faulkner; Joseph d. 5 Aug 1831.

      Joseph Faulkner was a machinist and had a machine-shop business with Warren Richardson and John Smith.[1881] Joseph later developed mental health problems and he died at the psychiatric hospital in Worcester.

      In his will written 7 October 1830 (probate 16 August 1831), Joseph Faulkner bequeathed to son Joseph Warren Faulkner the sum of $4,000 to be paid when he arrives at age twenty-one. Daughters Lydia Abbot Faulkner and Mary Poor Faulkner each receives $2,000. There were bequests to the Church of Christ of Andover and to the sabbath school library, the bible society, and the west parish of Andover. There are other bequests to nephew John S. A. Faulkner, brother-in-law Joel Russell, brother-in-law Nathan Kelley, sister Hannah Fulton, sister-in-law Hannah Faulkner, nieces Hannah Faulkner, Louisa Faulkner, and Julian Faulkner, and his aunt Priscilla Russell. To beloved wife Lydia, he leaves the income on the legacies of the children until they come of age to provide for their support and education. The remainder of the estate, real and personal, goes to beloved wife Lydia to be hers forever. Lydia is also named executrix.[1882]

      In her will, Lydia Faulkner left her entire estate to daughters Lydia Abbot Faulkner and Mary Poor Faulkner to be divided in equal shares. She also requested that daughter Lydia be named guardian for son Joseph Warren Faulkner. Daughter Lydia A. Faulkner was named executrix, although at probate Lydia A. requested that administration of the estate be assumed by E. Francis Holt. Real estate was valued at $3,000 and personal estate at $5,600. Of the three children who were heirs, daughter Lydia A. Faulkner resided in Andover and son Joseph Warren Faulkner and daughter Mary P. Faulkner were described as insane and resident at the "state lunatic hospital" at Worcester.[1883]

      Lydia Russell and Joseph Faulkner were parents of five children born at Andover.

i   LYDIA ABBOT FAULKNER, b. 22 Mar 1810; d. at the "state lunatic asylum" at Northampton, 22 Jun 1881. In her will written 11 October 1871, Lydia left the bulk of her estate to her brother and sister specifying that the guardians for her brother and her sister use the estate for their care and support. Apparently, Lydia was hospitalized late in her life.

ii   JOSEPH WARREN FAULKNER, b. 27 Oct 1812; d. at the hospital in Worcester, 12 Oct 1871. Joseph's condition was given as mania and epilepsy. Joseph had graduated from Yale in 1835 and was described as developing a religious mania.[1884]

iii   Child b. and d. 21 Jan 1815

iv   MARY POOR FAULKNER, b. 10 Jul 1817; d. at Middletown, CT (recorded at Andover), of "general debility" on 10 Dec 1892. Although she had been hospitalized when younger, Mary was released by the time of her sister's probate in 1881. She lived for some time with her cousin Charles Russell in Fayette, ME. In her will written at Middletown in 1890, Mary left the bulk of her estate in the form of a $3,600 bequest to Lillian M. Russell the daughter of her cousin Charles.[1885]

v   Child b. and d. 2 Dec 1824

639)   ABIEL RUSSELL (*Uriah⁴, Thomas³, James², Robert¹*), b. at Andover, Mar 1789 son of Uriah and Lydia (Abbott) Russell; d. at Andover, 14 Jan 1881; m. 17 Jun 1813, his third cousin (through Abbott line), SARAH ABBOTT, b. at Andover, 20 Dec 1792 daughter of Nathan and Sarah (Ballard) Abbott; Sarah d. 20 Sep 1846. Abiel m. 2ⁿᵈ at Andover, 6 May 1848, ELIZA MOOAR, b. at Greenfield, NH, 17 Sep 1807 daughter of Benjamin and Phebe (Chandler) Mooar; Eliza d. at Andover, 20 Jul 1892.

      Abiel was a carpenter in Andover. He and Sarah Abbott were parents of five children born at Andover.

[1880] Andrews, *The Hamlin Family*, p 415

[1881] Abbott, Charlotte Helen, Faulkner Family of Andover

[1882] *Essex County, MA: Probate File Papers, 1638-1881.*Online database. *AmericanAncestors.org.* New England Historic Genealogical Society, 2014. Case 9315

[1883] *Essex County, MA: Probate File Papers, 1638-1881.*Online database. *AmericanAncestors.org.* New England Historic Genealogical Society, 2014. Case 38814

[1884] Abbott, Charlotte Helen, Faulkner Family of Andover

[1885] *Connecticut. Probate Court (Middletown District), Probate Records volume 40, p 539*

i   SARAH BALLARD RUSSELL, b. 24 Dec 1816; d. at Hooksett, NH, 2 Aug 1851; m. at Andover, 25 Sec 1840, STEPHEN BALLARD, b. at Andover, 9 Sep 1815 son of Joshua and Phebe (Abbott) Ballard; Stephen d. at New York, NY, 11 Aug 1901. Stephen married second, at Nashville, NH, Abigail Dodge on 18 Oct 1852. Stephen Ballard and his wives Sarah and Abigail are buried at Andover.

ii   LYDIA ABBOT RUSSELL, b. 2 Jun 1818; d. at Andover, 14 Feb 1878. Lydia did not marry.

iii   ABIEL EDWIN RUSSELL, b. 27 Feb 1821 d. at Andover, 22 Aug 1861; m. 19 Dec 1846, HANNAH DODGE TUCK, b. at Andover, 8 Jan 1820 daughter of John and Elizabeth A. (Ames) Tuck; Hannah d. at Chelmsford, 15 Dec 1867.

iv   MOSES ABBOT RUSSELL, b. 4 Aug 1824; d. of typhus fever at Andover, 31 Oct 1834.

v   JOB ABBOTT RUSSELL, b. 18 Mar 1830; d. 12 Nov 1830.

640)   ELIZABETH RUSSELL FOSTER (*Elizabeth Russell Foster⁴, Thomas³, James², Robert¹*), b. at Andover, 23 Feb 1769 daughter of Gideon and Elizabeth (Russell) Foster; m. at Andover, 13 Jun 1793, SAMUEL CLARK.
        This is a family for which there is little clear information. In her notes on the Clark family of Andover, Charlotte Helen Abbott reports eight children in this family before the family left Andover for Bedford and later to Westchester County, New York. Record of a death of one of the children was found.[1886]

i   SAMUEL CLARK, about 1794

ii   GIDEON FOSTER CLARK, b. 29 Jan 1797; d. at New York, NY, 25 Aug 1831.

iii   THOMAS RUSSELL CLARK, about 1798

iv   ELIZABETH CLARK, about 1800

v   PAMELA CLARK

vi   JOHN T. CLARK

vii   WAAREN CLARK

viii   HANNAH CLARK

641)   ABIGAIL FOSTER (*Elizabeth Russell Foster⁴, Thomas³, James², Robert¹*), b. at Andover, 13 Jan 1771 daughter of Gideon and Elizabeth (Russell) Foster; d. at Andover, 30 Dec 1846; m. at Andover, 17 Nov 1791, WILLIAM SHATTUCK, b. at Andover, 26 Apr 1769 son of Joseph and Anna (Johnson) Shattuck; William d. at Otisfield, ME, 30 Aug 1806.
        William was a farmer and a shoemaker. The family resided first in Hillsborough and then in Otisfield. William was accidentally killed by a falling tree.[1887] He was active in the affairs of Otisfield and known as Capt. William Shattuck as he was captain of the Company of Troopers that was organized in Otisfield in 1802.[1888] Abigail returned to Andover after her husband's death.
        Daughter Elizabeth did not marry. In her will written 9 October 1874 (probate 10 May 1875), Elizabeth Shattuck of Andover made bequests of $100 each to Boston's Seamans' Friend Society, Massachusetts Home Missionary Society, and American Board of Commissioners for Foreign Missions. Elizabeth Hunt receives her pew in the West meeting house in Andover. Her sewing machine goes to Nancy A. Swallow and her clothing to be divided among her sisters Sarah Shattuck, Mary Shattuck, and her nieces. Mary and Sarah receive the furniture. The remainder of the estate, real and personal, is to be divided in fifth parts, one-fifth each to the following: sister Sarah Shattuck, sister Mary Shattuck, Nancy J. Swallow, the children of brother William Shattuck, and the grandchildren of sister Tamison Gleason. Joseph Shattuck was named executor. The heirs-at-law named at probate were sisters Mary and Sarah and brother William. Personal estate was valued at $3,235.85, $2,070 of that being a note she held from William Hardy. Amount owed from the estate was $1,181.30, $605.50 of that a board bill owed to Elizabeth Hunt.[1889]
        Abigail Foster and William Shattuck were parents of nine children including twin daughters born after William's death.

[1886] Abbott, Notes on the Clark family, p 6, https://www.mhl.org/sites/default/files/files/Abbott/Clark%20Family.pdf

[1887] Shattuck, *Memorials of the Descendants of William Shattuck*, p 222

[1888] Spurr, *History of Otisfield*, p 573

[1889] *Essex County, MA: Probate File Papers, 1638-1881.* Online database. *AmericanAncestors.org.* New England Historic Genealogical Society, 2014. Case 52990

i WILLIAM SHATTUCK, b. at Hillsborough, NH, 25 Apr 1792; d. at Acton, MA, 21 Feb 1878; m. at Boston, 5 May 1821, ELIZABETH MARY HILL, b. at Maidstone, Kent, England, 13 Aug 1800 daughter of John and Judith (Porter) Hill;[1890] Elizabeth d. at Acton, 29 Apr 1871.

ii ABIGAIL SHATTUCK, b. at Hillsborough, NH, 20 Mar 1794; d. at Nashua, NH, 9 Mar 1868; m. at Andover, 30 Apr 1815, ISAAC LOVEJOY, b. at Andover, 5 May 1793 son of Isaac and Ruth (Davis) Lovejoy. Isaac was deceased before 1850.

iii TAMISON SHATTUCK, b. at Hillsborough, NH, 22 Jan 1796; d. at Andover, 4 Apr 1831; m. at Andover 22 Feb 1816, JOHN GLEASON, b. at Bedford, MA, about 1785 son of Benjamin and Deborah (Beard) Gleason; John d. at Andover, 29 Dec 1849.

iv SARAH SHATTUCK, b. at Otisfield, ME, 18 Jul 1798; d. at Boston, 19 Nov 1894. Sarah did not marry.

v ANNA SHATTUCK, b. at Otisfield, ME, 9 Sep 1800; d. at Andover, 22 Jan 1869; m. at Andover, 3 Dec 1818, AMOS WARDWELL, b. at Andover, 25 Jul 1796 son of Ezekiel and Damaris (Faulkner) Wardwell. Anna had two daughters who died before marrying.

vi ELIZABETH SHATTUCK, b. at Otisfield, ME, 22 Aug 1802; d. at Andover, 12 Feb 1875. Elizabeth did not marry.

vii JOSEPH SHATTUCK, b. at Otisfield, ME, 4 Sep 1804; d. at St. Bartholomew's Parish, SC, May 1831;[1891] m. in SC, about 1828, ELIZABETH FLOWERS, b. about 1810. Elizabeth may be the Eliza Shadduck who married Ethland Colson about 1835 in Colleton County, SC. Joseph and Elizabeth are reported to have had two daughters, but no further record was found of them.

viii PAMELIA SHATTUCK (twin), b. likely at Andover, 11 Dec 1806; d. at Andover, 28 Apr 1836. Pamelia did not marry.

ix MARY SHATTUCK (twin), b. 11 Dec 1806; d. at Boston, 11 Aug 1875. Mary did not marry.

642) SARAH FOSTER (*Elizabeth Russell Foster⁴, Thomas³, James², Robert¹*), b. at Andover, 14 Jun 1775 daughter of Gideon and Elizabeth (Russell) Foster; d. of consumption, at Andover, 1 Mar 1847; m. at Andover, 19 May 1803, as his second wife, JONATHAN GLEASON, b. at Bedford, MA, about 1771 son of Benjamin and Deborah (Beard) Gleason; Jonathan d. of consumption, at Andover, 30 Oct 1846.

Sarah Foster and Jonathan Gleason were parents of six children born at Andover. Son-in-law Nathan Frye was builder of the historic property at 166 North Main Street in Andover. After she was widowed, Sarah lived at this home with her daughter and son-in-law.[1892]

i SARAH GLEASON, b. 8 Dec 1805; d. at Andover, 10 Mar 1893; m. at Edgartown, MA, 5 Mar 1860, as his second wife, JOHN SMITH, b. at Brechin, Angus, Scotland, 19 May 1796 son of Peter and Janette (Middleton) Smith;[1893] John d. at Andover, 25 Feb 1886. John was first married to Agnes E. Ferguson.

ii AMANDA GLEASON, b. 14 Oct 1807; d. at Andover, 15 Jul 1892; m. at Andover, 4 Apr 1833, NATHAN FRYE, b. at Andover, 27 Dec 1808 son of Amos and Hannah (Durant) Frye; Nathan d. at Andover, 12 Aug 1884.

iii HORATIO GLEASON, b. 10 Jan 1810; m. at Andover, 15 May 1834, SARAH D. FRENCH, b. at Andover, 18 Jul 1812 daughter of Peter and Elizabeth (Jaquith) French; Sarah d. at Andover, 16 Jul 1840. Horatio and Sarah had two children who were adopted after Sarah's death, a son adopted by Horatio's brother Justin and a daughter by Benjamin Punchard.[1894] Benjamin Punchard was a wealthy businessman in Andover who left $50,000 to the town of Andover to build a free school. It is not clear where Horatio died. He seems to be living in New York City in the 1850 census.

iv JUSTIN GLEASON, b. 29 Jul 1812; d. at Lawrence, MA, 31 Aug 1887; m. at Lawrence, 4 Nov 1860, ELIZABETH MCNAUGHTON, b. at Southend, Argyll, Scotland, 14 Nov 1831 daughter of Duncan and Helen (Ralston) McNaughton;[1895] Elizabeth d. at Newburyport, 13 Feb 1917.

v FOSTER GLEASON, b. 28 Apr 1816; d. 3 Oct 1819.

[1890] England, Select Births and Christenings, 1538-1975 (ancestry.com). Elizabeth's parents' names are given as John and Judith on her death record. John Hill and Judith Porter were married at Bearsted, Kent 17 Jun 1798.

[1891] Shattuck, *Memorials of the Descendants of William Shattuck*, p 222

[1892] Andover Historic Preservation; https://preservation.mhl.org/166-north-main-street

[1893] Ancestry.com. *Scotland, Select Births and Baptisms, 1564-1950* [database on-line].

[1894] Abbott, Charlotte Helen, notes on Gleason family of Andover, https://www.mhl.org/sites/default/files/files/Abbott/Gleason%20Family.pdf

[1895] Scotland, Select Births and Baptisms, 1564-1950. The names of Elizabeth's parents are also given on her marriage record and her death record.

vi   GORDON GLEASON, b. 6 Sep 1818; d. 11 Oct 1819.

643)   THOMAS RUSSELL (*Thomas⁴, Thomas³, James², Robert¹*), b. at Andover, MA, 22 Feb 1768 son of Thomas and Sarah (Eastman) Russell; d. at Bartlett, NH, 1853; m. at Conway, 19 Jul 1798, RUTH HARRIMAN, b. at Concord, 12 Mar 1774 daughter of Philip and Hannah (Eastman) Harriman; Ruth d. 1850.
       Thomas and Ruth were parents of three known children born at Bartlett, New Hampshire, although there may be others.

i   IRA OTIS RUSSELL, b. 13 Jan 1804; d. at Wells, MN, 22 Oct 1888; m. 1ˢᵗ at Jackson, NH, 18 Jul 1830, BETSEY B. DEERING, b. at Conway, NH, 11 Jan 1811 daughter of Clement and Anna (Bickford) Deering; Betsey d. at Lemont, IL, 5 Oct 1852. Ira m. 2ⁿᵈ EUNICE J. LEE, b. at Ripley, NY, 20 Nov 1836 daughter of Stephen and Martha Ann (Bailey) Lee; d. at Hewitt, MN, 8 Mar 1928.

ii   AMZI RUSSELL, b. 1810; d. at Albany, NH, 1878 (probate 29 Jul 1878); m. at Conway, NH, 3 Dec 1834, ELIZA M. GEORGE, b. at Conway, 3 Dec 1814 daughter of Daniel and Eliza (Morse) George; Eliza d. at Albany, NH, 21 Feb 1905.

iii   THOMAS RUSSELL, b. 3 Jun 1812; d. after 1900 when living at San Jose, CA with his daughter Emma and her husband Charles H. Perkins; m. EMILY ZANETTE TASKER, b. at Bartlett, NH, 24 Oct 1815 daughter of Jonathan and Belinda (Bassett) Tasker; Emily d. at San Jose, 1896.

644)   SARAH RUSSELL (*Thomas⁴, Thomas³, James², Robert¹*), b. at Andover, 2 Jan 1770 daughter of Thomas and Sarah (Eastman) Russell; d. at Conway, NH, 4 Dec 1852; m. 17 Nov 1790, LEAVITT HILL, b. 2 Mar 1770 son of Charles and Sarah (Prentice) Hill; Leavitt d. at Conway, 4 Dec 1843.
       Capt. Leavitt Hill and his wife Sally resided in Conway where they had their farm of the west side of the Saco River. In addition to his farm, Leavitt ran a tavern in Conway.[1896]
       Sarah and Leavitt were parents of nine children born at Conway, New Hampshire.

i   JOHN HILL, b. 27 Apr 1791; d. at Conway, NH, 24 Apr 1870; m. 6 Dec 1821, ELIZABETH "BETSEY" EASTMAN, b. at Conway, 11 May 1795 daughter of Richard and Susannah (Runnels) Eastman; Betsey d. at Conway, 9 Nov 1891.

ii   SALLY E. HILL, b. 13 Jan 1793; d. at Ossipee, NH, after 1850 and before 1860; m. at Conway, 15 Oct 1816, ASAHEL L. ADAMS, b. at Moultonborough, NH, 1792 son of John and Hannah (Paine) Adams; Asahel d. May 1870. Asahel married second Lucy Straw on 2 May 1866.

iii   ABIGAIL R. HILL, b. 14 Feb 1795; d. at Conway, 10 Apr 1837; m. 12 Jun 1823, HENRY AMBROSE MERRILL, b. 13 Jun 1795 son of Enoch and Mary (Ambrose) Merrill; Henry d. at Granville, OH, 25 Sep 1872. Henry married second Abigail Garland on 6 Nov 1838.

iv   EUNICE HILL, b. 19 Apr 1797; d. at North Conway, 24 Jan 1862; m. 18 Apr 1816, THOMAS EASTMAN, b. at Conway, 18 Jul 1788 son of Abiathar and Phebe (Merrill) Eastman; Thomas d. at North Conway, 7 Aug 1846.

v   THOMAS R. HILL, b. 3 Jan 1799; d. at Champlin, MN, 3 Nov 1878; m. 1ˢᵗ at Conway, 28 Oct 1818, SUSANNA MCMILLEN; Susanna d. before 1850. Thomas m. 2ⁿᵈ at Brooklyn, MN, 5 Mar 1861, NAOMI COLBURN, b. in ME, 1812; Naomi d. at Champlin, 1879.

vi   AMOS ADAMS HILL, b. 10 Mar 1804; d. at Conway, 30 Sep 1818.

vii   MARY R. HILL, b. 6 Dec 1805; d. at Conway, 19 Feb 1889; m. at Conway, 13 Sep 1849, as his second wife, JONATHAN R. THOMPSON, b. at Conway, 21 Jan 1799 son of John and Sarah (Runnels) Thompson; Jonathan d. at Conway, 12 Dec 1869. Jonathan was first married to Abigail Hill Eastman.

viii   CHARLES HILL, b. 10 Feb 1807; d. at Conway, 14 Dec 1877; m. NANCY D. RUSSELL, b. in NH 1803; Nancy d. at Conway, 12 May 1860.

ix   LEAVITT HILL, b. 5 May 1813; d. at Conway, 1846 (probate 1846); m. at Conway, 4 Dec 1839, his first cousin, ABIGAIL CROSBY RUSSELL (*Uriah⁵, Thomas⁴, Thomas³, James², Robert¹*), b. at Albany, NH, 7 Dec 1815 daughter of Uriah B. and Anna C. (Forrest) Russell; Abigail d. at Conway, 14 Jul 1898.

[1896] Merrill, History of Carroll County, New Hampshire, pp 851-852

645) ABIGAIL RUSSELL (*Thomas⁴, Thomas³, James², Robert¹*), b. at Conway, 22 Mar 1776 daughter of Thomas and Sarah (Eastman) Russell; d. at Hanover, NH, 21 Dec 1856; m. at Conway, 12 Oct 1806, as his second wife, ASA CROSBY, b. 15 Jul 1765 son of Josiah and Sarah (Fitch) Crosby; Asa d. at Hanover, 12 Apr 1836. Asa was first married to Betsey Hoit.

Asa Crosby and his first wife Betsey Hoit were parents of ten children, and their youngest son Nathan Hoit Crosby authored a genealogy of the Crosby family and provides a detailed account of his father and his family.[1897]

Dr. Asa Crosby was a physician. As a child, he is described as somewhat invalid which led to his being educated early on owing to his perceived physical weakness. Later in life, he was described as robust. Although his early education was somewhat limited, he is reported as teaching school in Salem, Massachusetts at age 15. He studied medicine with Dr. Ebenezer Rockwood of Wilton, New Hampshire. He may have first practiced in Moultonborough, New Hampshire in 1788, but in 1789 contracted a fever and went to Jaffrey to the home of his brother Alpheus to recover. Perhaps owing to his illness and the fear of the town representatives that he would become a charge of the town, Asa was "warned out" in October 1789. Asa left and started a practice in Moultonborough and about left there and went to Sandwich, New Hampshire where he purchased a farm. He kept a large orchard and a cider mill. He made several moves over the years before selling out his mills and settling in Hanover toward the end of his life. He was awarded an honorary M. D. degree by Dartmouth College in 1811.

Abigail Russell and Asa Crosby were parents of seven children, two of whom lived to adulthood. Asa had ten children with his first wife Betsey Hoit.

i   PRISCILLA CROSBY, b. at Sandwich, NH, 9 Sep 1807; d. 10 Feb 1808.

ii   RUSSELL CROSBY, b. at Sandwich, 8 Oct 1808; d. at Gilmanton, 16 Jun 1816.

iii   ALPHEUS CROSBY, b. at Sandwich, 13 Oct 1810; d. at Salem, MA, 17 Apr 1874; m. 1ˢᵗ at Essex, MA, 1834, ABIGAIL GRANT JONES CUTLER, b. 27 Aug 1809 daughter of Joseph Grant and Abigail (Jones) Cutler; Abigail d. at Paris, France, 25 Mar 1837.[1898] Alpheus m. 2ⁿᵈ at West Bridgewater, 12 Feb 1861, MARTHA KINGMAN, b. at West Bridgewater, 9 Mar 1833 daughter of Joseph and Elizabeth (Howard) Kingman; Martha d. at West Bridgewater, 12 Nov 1915.

iv   CHARLES LITTLE CROSBY, b. 18 Feb 1813; d. 21 Mar 1814.

v   CHARLES CROSBY, b. 27 Jan 1815; d. 23 Feb 1815.

vi   THOMAS R. CROSBY, b. at Gilmanton, 20 Oct 1816; d. at Hanover, NH, 1 Mar 1872; m. LOUISA PARTRIDGE BURTON, b. at West Point, NY, 1821 daughter of Oliver and Almira (Partridge) Burton;[1899] Louisa d. at Norwich, VT, 19 Aug 1903.

vii   STEPHEN MOODY CROSBY, b. at Gilmanton, 22 Sep 1818; d. 2 Mar 1826.

646) JAMES RUSSELL (*Thomas⁴, Thomas³, James², Robert¹*), b. at Conway, 5 May 1778 son of Thomas and Sarah (Eastman) Russell; d. at Albany, NH, 30 Sep 1861; m. SARAH ALLEN, b. in ME, about 1788; Sarah d. at Conway, 17 Feb 1859.

Three children were identified for James and Sarah likely born at Conway, New Hampshire. In 1830, the household of James Russell of Conway consisted of five persons: one male 50 to 59, one female 40 to 49, one male 5 to 9, one female 5 to 9, and one female 10 to 14.[1900] In the 1850 census, James and Sarah Russell which included Alvah Russell age 20 and Hannah, Charles Fifield age 27 and 24 respectively, and Frances Fifield age three months.[1901]

i   SUSAN RUSSELL, b. 1817; d. at Madison, NH, 30 Sep 1904;[1902] m. at Conway, 2 Sep 1838, JOSEPH P. GREENLEAF, b. 27 Jul 1815 son of Joseph and Sally (Stevens) Greenleaf; Joseph d. at Conway, 10 Apr 1893.

ii   ALVAH RUSSELL, b. 1821; d. at Conway, NH, 30 Sep 1885; m. at Conway, 7 Feb 1859, DATY STRATTON, b. 26 Mar 1826 (calculated from death age of 41 years, 6 months, 4 days); Daty d. at Conway, 30 Sep 1867. Daty apparently inherited property as she left a will in which she left her 80 acres of property to her husband Alvah Russell.

iii   HANNAH A. RUSSELL, b. 1 Apr 1823; d. at Conway, NH, 9 Jan 1906; m. at Conway, 17 Sep 1848, CHARLES F. FIFIELD, b. at Fryeburg, ME, 3 Oct 1826 son of Simon Frye and Mary (Morse) Fifield; Charles d. at Somerville, MA, 24 Sep 1863.

[1897] Crosby, *A Crosby Family*, p 57ff, the reader is referred to this volume for a detailed account of the life of Asa Crosby.

[1898] Abig[ai]l G. J., w. Prof. Alpheus, of Dartmouth College, and d. Joseph Cutler, Esq., at Paris, bur. May 15, 1837, a. 28 y. C. R. 2.

[1899] Louisa's place of birth and the names of her parents are given on her death record.

[1900] Year: 1830; Census Place: Conway, Strafford, New Hampshire; Series: M19; Roll: 78; Page: 164; Family History Library Film: 0337931

[1901] Year: 1850; Census Place: Conway, Carroll, New Hampshire; Roll: 426; Page: 25A

[1902] Susan's death records names her parents as James Russell and Sarah Allen; New Hampshire, Death and Disinterment Records, 1754-1947

647)   ESTHER RUSSELL (*Thomas⁴, Thomas³, James², Robert¹*), b. at Conway, 4 May 1780 daughter of Thomas and Sarah (Eastman) Russell; d. at Conway, 4 Sep 1807; m. at Conway, 1 May 1800, JONATHAN PHILBRICK, b. 5 Aug 1775 son of Jonathan and Hannah (Gilman) Philbrick; Jonathan d. after 1850 when he was living at Lawrenceburg, IN.[1903] Jonathan was second married to Jane Hardy.

There are records for two children of Esther and Jonathan. The Philbrook genealogy names three other children (John, Priscilla, and Gordon) but no records were found for these children.[1904]

i   ESTHER PHILBRICK, b. at Conway, NH, 22 May 1801; d. at Paris, ME, 30 Oct 1876; m. 5 Jun 1823, her second cousin, JEREMIAH L. EASTMAN (*Jonathan Eastman⁶, Abiah Holt Eastman⁵, Benjamin Holt⁴, Nicholas Holt³, Mary Russell Holt², Robert¹*), b. at Conway, 15 Sep 1795 son of Jonathan and Phebe (Lovejoy) Eastman; Jeremiah d. at Conway, NH, 21 Oct 1854.

ii   THOMAS PHILBRICK, b. at Conway, 27 Feb 1804; d. at Guildhall, VT, 22 Mar 1886; m. at Portland, ME, 29 Jan 1832, SUSAN M. BOSTON, b. 6 May 1810 (on gravestone) likely daughter of Royal and Sarah (Merrill) Boston; Susan d. at Guildhall, 2 May 1875.

648)   MARY RUSSELL (*Thomas⁴, Thomas³, James², Robert¹*), b. at Conway, 7 Aug 1782 daughter of Thomas and Sarah (Eastman) Russell; d. at Freehold, NJ, 3 Mar 1859; m. at Hanover, 1 Feb 1809, JONATHAN FREEMAN, b. at Hanover, 21 Mar 1783 son of Otis and Ruth (Bicknell) Freeman; Jonathan d. at Freehold, 11 Sep 1871.

Mary and Jonathan resided in Hanover, New Hampshire where they were prominent members of the community. The Freeman family were early settlers in New Hampshire, Jonathan's grandfather being one of the original grantees of Hanover.[1905] Jonathan was town clerk and magistrate in Hanover.[1906] The family was in Hanover through the births of their children and relocated to New Jersey by 1850.

Daughters Martha and Sarah were educators and started one of the first private schools in Berwyn, Pennsylvania, the Spring Cottage Seminary which they started about 1877. The sisters taught, French, Latin, mathematics, and English. Later, Martha's husband James T. Doran who was a gifted mathematician took over direction of the school. The school moved from Berwyn to Malvern 1 April 1888 and was known as Doran's Private School.[1907]

Son Dr. Otis Russell Freeman read medicine at Dartmouth College where he was awarded the M. D. degree. He has a practice in Charlestown, New Hampshire and later in Springfield, Vermont.[1908] He was commissioned surgeon of the 10th Regiment of New Jersey Volunteers on 14 April 1862, He served in Washington, D. C. and Suffolk, Virginia. He was chief medical officer in Philadelphia during the enforcement of the draft. He participated in the Antietam campaign as surgeon-in-chief in the brigade commanded by General Geary. In March 1864, he remustered and was sent to the front with the First Brigade, First Division of the Sixth Army. In was in the field and the battles of Wilderness and Petersburg. He remained on duty until Lee's surrender and mustered out on 1 July 1865.[1909]

Mary and Jonathan were parents of eight children born at Hanover, New Hampshire.

i   OTIS RUSSELL FREEMAN, b. 30 Dec 1809; d. at Freehold, NJ, 8 Jun 1902; m. 11 Sep 1835, ABIGAIL WILLARD ALDEN, b. at Hanover, 28 Oct 1809 daughter of Samuel and Abigail (Willard) Alden; Abigail d. at Freehold, 10 Nov 1854.

ii   CHARLES WHITE FREEMAN, b. 28 Aug 1812; d. 2 Jun 1813.

iii   MARY RUSSELL FREEMAN, b. 4 Aug 1814; d. at Freehold, NJ, 19 Oct 1891. Mary did not marry.

iv   RUTH FREEMAN, b. 1 Jul 1816; d. at Freehold, NJ, 20 Feb 1901; m. at Hanover, 26 Aug 1840, AMOS RICHARDSON, b. at Springfield, NH, 28 Jul 1812 son of Moses D. and Sarah (Collins) Richardson; Amos d. at Freehold, 17 Oct 1882.

v   ELIZA RUSSELL FREEMAN, b. 21 Mar 1819; d. at Freehold, NJ, 19 Jul 1877. Eliza did not marry.

vi   SARAH EASTMAN FREEMAN, b. 13 Jan 1821; Sarah d. after 1880 when she was living at Easttown, PA with her sister Martha and her husband. Sarah was a teacher.

[1903] Year: 1850; Census Place: Miller, Dearborn, Indiana; Roll: M432_141; Page: 294A; Image: 162
[1904] Chapman, *A Genealogy of the Philbrick and Philbrook Families*, p 92. There was a different Jonathan Philbrook married to Esther Dow who also resided in New Hampshire and was having children at the same time as Jonathan Philbrook and Esther Russell.
[1905] Lord, *A History of the Town of Hanover*
[1906] Freeman, *Freeman Genealogy*, p 213
[1907] Fry, C. Herbert, "Private Schools in Easttown Township", Tredyffrin Easttown Historical Society, *History Quarterly* Digital Archives, Spring 2006, volume 43, number 2, pp 43-52; https://tehistory.org/hqda/html/v43/v43n2p043.html#top
[1908] Cogswell, *The New Hampshire Repository*, volume 2, p 80
[1909] Redington, *Military Record of the Sons of Dartmouth in the Union Army and Navy, 1861-1865*, pp 20-21

vii   MARTHA FREEMAN, b. 10 Mar 1823; d. at Freehold, NJ, 1914; m. at Millstone, NJ, 26 Oct 1850, JAMES T. DORAN, b. at Easton, PA, 10 Feb 1828; d. at Malvern, PA, 2 Jul 1900. James graduated from Lafayette College in 1848 (valedictorian) and was a teacher in Malvern and in Freehold.[1910]

viii   SUSAN FREEMAN, b. 12 Jun 1826; d. 4 Jul 1826.

649)   URIAH B. RUSSELL (*Thomas⁴, Thomas³, James², Robert¹*), b. at Conway, 9 Aug 1791 son of Thomas and Sarah (Eastman) Russell; d. by 1852 (remarriage of third wife); m. 1ˢᵗ, about 1810, ANNA C. FORREST,[1911] b. at Bridgewater, MA, about 1790 *possibly* daughter of Spencer and Abigail (Wade) Forrest; Anna d. about 1823. Uriah m. 2ⁿᵈ BETSEY PALMER, b. at Eaton, NH, about 1797; death not known but *possibly* the Betsey Russell who died at Lowell, 13 Nov 1844. Uriah m. 3ʳᵈ at Lowell, 24 Jul 1845, BETSEY GREENOUGH, b. at Salisbury, NH about 1804 daughter of Robert and Hannah (-) Greenough. Betsey Greenough Russell married Trueworthy Gilman at Lowell on 4 May 1852.

     Uriah lived primary in Conway, New Hampshire but was in Lowell, Massachusetts in his later life. At Conway in the 1830 census, Uriah had five members of his household: one male 30 to 39, one female 30 to 39, one male under 5, one male 5 to 9, and one female under 5.[1912] In 1840, he was in Conway as head of household of a family of six persons: one male 40 t0 49, one female 30 to 39, one male 15 to 19, one female under 5, one female 5 to 9, and one female 10 to 14.[1913] In 1850, Uriah was living in Clinton, Massachusetts where he ran a boarding house.[1914]

     Uriah Russell and Anna Forrest were parents of at least two children.

i   ABIGAIL CROSBY RUSSELL, b. at Albany, NH, 7 Dec 1815; d. at Conway, NH, 14 Jul 1898; m. at Conway, 4 Dec 1839, her first cousin, LEAVITT HILL (*Sarah Russell Hill⁵, Thomas⁴, Thomas³, James², Robert¹*), b. at Conway, 5 May 1813 son of Leavitt and Sarah (Russell) Hill; Leavitt d. at Conway, 1846 (probate 1846).

ii   JONATHAN EASTMAN RUSSELL, b. 1818; d. at Effingham, NH, 20 Oct 1856.

     Uriah Russell and Betsey Palmer were parents of at least five children likely all born at Conway, New Hampshire.[1915]

i   URIAH BALLARD RUSSELL, b. 1821; d. after 1863 when living at Somersworth, NH;[1916] m. at Rochester, NH, 23 Jan 1849, MARY ELIZABETH GRANT.

ii   THOMAS RUSSELL, b. 1824; d. 1826.

iii   ADDIE R. RUSSELL, b. about Oct 1826; d. at Worcester, MA, 2 Jul 1901; m. about 1850, DEXTER BUCK. Addie and Dexter divorced,[1917] and Addie resumed the use of Russell as her last name.

iv   ALPHEUS CROSBY RUSSELL, b. 1829; d. 1832.

v   AUGUSTA ELLEN RUSSELL, b. about 1839; d. at Boston, 10 Mar 1888; m. at Boston, 3 Sep 1863, FREDERICK KIMBALL, b. at Bradford, MA, 15 Jul 1840 son of Jacob and Huldah 9Greenough) Kimball; Frederick d. at Rochester, NY, 25 May 1908. Frederick married second Mary E. Tyler Davis on 20 Mar 1889.

650)   ALVAH RUSSELL (*Thomas⁴, Thomas³, James², Robert¹*), b. at Conway, 9 Dec 1796 son of Thomas and Sarah (Eastman) Russell; d. at Conway, 15 Jul 1856; m. at Eaton, NH, 28 Mar 1833, ASENATH DAVIS, b. at Eaton, NH, 17 Apr 1812

[1910] Coffin, *The Men of Lafayette 1826-1893*, p 164

[1911] The death record of daughter Abigail Crosby Russell gives mother's name as Anna Forrest; New Hampshire, Death and Burial Records Index, 1654-1949

[1912] Year: 1830; Census Place: Conway, Strafford, New Hampshire; Series: M19; Roll: 78; Page: 164; Family History Library Film: 0337931

[1913] Year: 1840; Census Place: Conway, Strafford, New Hampshire; Roll: 245; Page: 261; Family History Library Film: 0014934

[1914] Year: 1850; Census Place: Clinton, Worcester, Massachusetts; Roll: 343; Page: 95b

[1915] A possible sixth child is Mary D. Russell born 19 Jul 1831 (19 Jul 1832 on her death record) who married Henry F. Day and died at Worcester 13 Jul 1918. The death record gives names of parents as Uriah B. Russell and Cynthia Parmenter. Mary Russell Day lived in Mansfield, MA and Worcester, MA which were locations where Addie R. Russell Buck lived. No records related to a Uriah B. Russell and a Cynthia Parmenter were found other than this death record. It is possible that the informant for the death record gave incorrect information for the name of mother. Further investigation is needed.

[1916] U.S., Civil War Draft Registrations Records, 1863-1865

[1917] Addies's death record lists her as the divorced wife of Dexter Buck. Her age at death is given as 74 years, 8 months, 12 days and place of birth as "Pammath" NH; parents are given as Uriah Russell and Betsy Palmer; *Massachusetts: Vital Records, 1841-1910*. (From original records held by the Massachusetts Archives. Online database: *AmericanAncestors.org*, volume 518, p 537

daughter of Nathaniel and Nancy (March) Davis;[1918] Asenath d. at Laconia, NH, 11 Feb 1893. Asenath married second, James S. Hoit.

        Alvah was a farmer in Conway, New Hampshire. In the 1850 census, the value of real property was $600.[1919] Alvah and Asenath were parents of five children born at Conway.

i   MARY FREEMAN RUSSELL, b. 8 Jan 1834; d. at Malden, MA, 28 Jan 1915; m. 1854, ALMON CURTS LEAVITT, b. at Washington, VT, 21 Jan 1831 son of Almon B. and Eunice (Kelly) Leavitt; Almon d. at Laconia, NH, 28 Mar 1913.

ii   NANCY A. RUSSELL, b. 1836; d. at Madison, NH, 18 Jul 1863; m. about 1858, FREEMAN MOULTON, b. at Albany, NH, 1828 son of John and Mehitable (Glidden) Moulton; Freeman d. at Effingham, NH, 15 May 1913.

iii   SARAH EASTMAN RUSSELL, b. 31 Aug 1837; d. at Madison, NH, 6 Jun 1872; m. about 1859, WILLIAM KENNETT, b. at Eaton, NH, 6 Nov 1837 son of John F. and Lydia (Guile) Kennett;[1920] William d. at Conway, 16 Aug 1902. William married second Augusta Long on 25 Dec 1873.

iv   NATHANIEL D. RUSSELL, b. 3 Oct 1841; d. (burial at Laconia, NH), 9 Oct 1895; m. at Lynn, MA, 5 Feb 1873, HENRIETTA "ETTA" DAVIS, b. at Eaton, NH, 1843 daughter of Bradbury and Margaret F. (Horton) Davis;[1921] Etta d. at Plymouth, NH, 4 Mar 1911.

v   ELIZABETH RUSSELL, b. 1 Oct 1844; d. 13 Oct 1861.

651)   ABIGAIL WILLIAMS (*Abigail Russell Williams⁴, Thomas³, James², Robert¹*), baptized at Salem 11 Aug 1771 daughter of Henry and Abigail (Russell) Williams; d. at Beverly, MA, 6 Aug 1828; m. at Salem, 17 Mar 1791, JOSIAH GOULD, b. at Salem, 23 Oct 1765[1922] (baptized 14 Aug 1768) son of Josiah and Sarah (Sherman) Gould; Josiah d. at Beverly, 28 Sep 1822.

        Josiah Gould's estate entered probate 5 November 1822 with Josiah Gould as administrator at the request of widow Abigail. Credits of the estate were $6,854.89 and debts were $1,202.16 with net owed the estate of $5,652.13. In addition, real estate was valued at $7,770 and personal estate at $7,874.25. On 30 April 1825, the following heirs signed they were satisfied with the accounting of the estate: Warren Gould, James Gould, Abigail Gould signing for herself and as guardian of Lydia Gould, and Caroline Gould.[1923]

        Abigail Williams and Josiah Gould were parents of nine children born at Beverly.

i   SALLY GOULD, baptized at Beverly, 23 Dec 1792; d. at Beverly, 23 Jan 1809.[1924]

ii   JOSIAH GOULD, baptized at Beverly, 8 Sep 1793; d. of typhoid fever at sea, 21 Nov 1836;[1925] m. at Beverly, 25 Nov 1824, EUNICE ADELINE ABBOTT, b. at Haverhill, MA, 17 Aug 1797 daughter of Abiel and Eunice (Wales) Abbott; Eunice d. at Beverly, 8 Dec 1828.

iii   JAMES GOULD, baptized at Beverly, 5 Apr 1795; James d. at Boston, 15 Jan 1874. James was a jeweler in Boston and Baltimore.[1926] His will proved 16 February 1874 includes bequests to brother-in-law George F. Weld of West Roxbury, sister Catherine Hyde, nephew Warren G. Hyde, and sister Lydia Weld.[1927] In is not clear if James married. He may be the James Gould of Baltimore who married Eliza Leech at Beverly in 1817.

iv   HENRY GOULD, baptized at Beverly, 26 Nov 1797; d. at sea, 25 Dec 1823.[1928]

v   EDWARD GOULD, baptized 10 Nov 1799; d. 23 Jun 1803.

vi   WARREN GOULD, baptized at Beverly, 4 Oct 1801; d. at Boston, 5 May 1845. Warren does not seem to have married.

[1918] The names of Asenath's parents are given as Nathaniel Davis and Mary Williams on her death record and as Nathaniel Davis and Nancy March on the record of her second marriage to James Hoit. The death record of one of Asenath's siblings gives parents as Nathaniel Davis and Nancy March.

[1919] Year: 1850; Census Place: Conway, Carroll, New Hampshire; Roll: M432_426; Page: 26A; Image: 53

[1920] The names of William's parents are given as John Kennett and Lydia Guile on the record of his second marriage.

[1921] Etta's parents are given as Bradbury and Margaret on her marriage record; the death records of two of her siblings give mother's name as Margaret Horton.

[1922] Birth date is given in the town records of Beverly, MA

[1923] *Essex County, MA: Probate File Papers, 1638-1881.*Online database. *AmericanAncestors.org.* New England Historic Genealogical Society, 2014. Case 11404

[1924] Sally [d. Josiah and Nabby. G. R. 4; consumption, occasioned by whooping cough, C.R.1.], Jan. 28, 1809. [a. 17 y. 6 m. G. R. 4.]

[1925] Josiah, s. Josiah and Abigail, at sea, Nov. 21, 1836, a. 43 y. 3m. G. R. 4.

[1926] U.S., Craftperson Files, 1600-1995

[1927] Massachusetts Probate Records, Suffolk County, 468:7, will of James Gould

[1928] Henry, s. Josiah and Abigail, at sea, Dec. 25, 1823, a. 26 y. 1 m. G. R. 4.

vii   CATHERINE GOULD, b. about 1803; m. at Charlestown, 25 Jan 1829, THOMAS HYDE who has not been identified. Catherine was living in 1874.

viii   LYDIA GOULD, baptized at Beverly, 17 Nov 1805; d. at Boston, 27 Apr 1888; m. at Beverly, 1 Sep 1828, GEROGE FRANCIS WELD, b. at Roxbury, 1800 son of Jacob and Sarah (McClelland) Weld; George d. at Boston, 19 Oct 1875.

ix   LOUISA GOULD, baptized 21 Feb 1808; d. at Beverly, 28 Aug 1820.

652)   CATHARINE "KATY" WILLIAMS (*Abigail Russell Williams⁴, Thomas³, James², Robert¹*), b. at Salem 7 Apr 1780 daughter of Henry and Abigail (Russell) Williams; d. after 1865 when she was living at Salem; m. at Salem, 12 Sep 1799, THOMAS DOWNING, b. at Salem, 23 Sep 1772 son of Thomas and Abigail (Brown) Browning; Thomas d. of consumption, at Salem, 7 Feb 1835.

     Capt. Thomas Downing was a master mariner whose routes included South America. For example, he commanded the ship *Thomas Wilson* of Portsmouth during an 1826 trip.[1929]

     Thomas Downing and Katy Williams were parents of eight children born at Salem.

i   THOMAS DOWNING, b. 20 Aug 1800; d. at Salem, 27 Jan 1859; m. at Salem, 30 Oct 1823, NANCY BROWN, b. at Salem, 1799 daughter of Nathaniel and Mary (Pickering) Brown; Nancy d. at Salem, 2 May 1865.

ii   CATHERINE DOWNING, b. 6 Jun 1804; d. 17 Mar 1812.

iii   JOHN WILLIAMS DOWNING, b. 14 Oct 1808; d. at Salem, 20 Feb 1858; m. at Salem, 25 Jan 1836, SARAH R. POMROY, b. at Salem, 20 Aug 1814 daughter of Arad and Sally (Ropes) Pomroy; Sarah d. at Salem, 1 May 1882.

iv   WILLARD WILLIAMS DOWNING, b. 25 Sep 1811; d. 7 Oct 1812.

v   CATHERINE DOWNING, b. 15 Feb 1814; m. at Salem, 24 Apr 1835, JAMES B. FERGUSON, b. at Salem, 1810 son of John and Hannah (Bott) Ferguson; James d. at Salem, 8 Mar 1867. Catherine was living in 1867.

vi   WILLARD WILLIAMS DOWNING, b. 26 May 1816; d. at Everett, MA, 7 Jul 1880; m. at Boston, 23 May 1848, MARIA E. BUCKMAN, b. at Claremont, NH, 1821 daughter of George and Abigail (Rogers) Buckman; Maria d. at Lowell, 20 Jun 1898.

vii   HENRY WARREN DOWINING, b. 26 Jul 1819; d. at sea, 12 Jul 1837.[1930]

viii   NANCY BROWN DOWNING, b. 26 Jun 1821

653)   THOMAS RUSSELL WILLIAMS (*Abigail Russell Williams⁴, Thomas³, James², Robert¹*), baptized at Salem 30 Mar 1783 son of Henry and Abigail (Russell) Williams; d. at Boston, 1827 (probate 26 Feb 1827); m. at Salem, 22 Jun 1806, his fourth cousin, RUTH ABBOTT (*Ruth Holt Abbott⁶, Joseph Holt⁵, Lydia Holt Holt⁴, Thomas Holt³, Mary Russell Holt², Robert¹*), b. at Andover, Jul 1785 daughter of Abner and Ruth (Holt) Abbott; Ruth d. after 1850 when she was living at Boston.

     Thomas was a cabinetmaker in Boston. Thomas did not leave a will and widow Ruth was named administratrix of the estate 26 February 1827. Personal estate was $92.19.[1931]

     Thomas Russell Williams and Ruth Abbott were parents of nine children born at Boston.

i   HENRY RUSSELL WILLIAMS, b. 1806; d. at Boston, 27 Oct 1840; m. at Boston, 8 Jul 1830, ABIGAIL H. ADAMS, b. at Boston, about 1810 daughter of Philip and Joanna (Pearson) Adams;[1932] Abigail d. at Boston, 19 Mar 1883. Henry was a merchant tailor in Boston. In his will, Henry left his entire estate to his wife Abigail.

ii   THOMAS ABBOTT WILLIAMS, b. 1809; d. at Chelsea, MA, 22 Aug 1869; m. at Boston, 9 Mar 1837, MARY P. ADAMS, b. at Boston, 1817 daughter of Philip and Joanna (Pearson) Adams; Mary d. at Woburn, 20 Jul 1898.

iii   RUTH ANN WILLIAMS, b. 1811; d. at Malden, MA, 25 Aug 1868; m. at Boston, 27 Sep 1832, JOSPEH W. RIPLEY, b. at Brewster, MA, 13 Apr 1806 son of Nathaniel and Polly (Hopkins) Ripley; Joseph d. at Malden, 18 Aug 1891.

[1929] Massachusetts, Passenger and Crew Lists, 1820-1963; The National Archives at Washington, D.C.; Washington, D.C.; Series Title: Passenger Lists of Vessels Arriving at Boston, Massachusetts, 1820-1891; Record Group Title: Records of the U.S. Customs Service; Record Group Number: 36; Series Number: M277; NARA

[1930] Henry W., s. Capt. Thomas, deceased, on board the Carthage, July 12, 1837, a. 18 y. G. R. 9.

[1931] *Suffolk County, MA: Probate File Papers.* Online database. *AmericanAncestors.org.* New England Historic Genealogical Society, 2017-2019. Case 28224

[1932] The names of Abigail's parents are given as Philip and Joanna Adams on her death record.

iv WILLARD WILLIAMS, b. 1813; d. at Lowell, 21 Mar 1881; m. at Concord, NH, 7 May 1840, SARAH ANN PERKINS, b. at Northwood, NH, 21 Aug 1821 daughter of John and Nancy (Sanborn) Perkins; Sarah d. at Lowell, 8 Nov 1894.

v SARAH ABBOT WILLIAMS, b. 1815; d. at Boston, 3 Jul 1822.

vi CATHARINE DOWNING WILLIAMS, b. 1817. In 1850, Catherine was unmarried and living with her sister Ruth and her husband in Boston.

vii MARY PHILLIPS WILLIAMS, b. 1819; d. at Boston, 25 Nov 1819.

viii ELIZA P. WILLIAMS, b. 7 Feb 1821; d. at Andover, MA, 25 May 1873; m. at Boston, 30 Sep 1845, WILLIAM CORSE, b. in Scotland, 5 Apr 1806 (calculated from death age of 81 years, 4 months, 7 days); William d. at Malden, MA, 12 Aug 1887.[1933]

ix GEORGE GORHAM WILLIAMS, b. 1823; d. at Manchester, NH, 5 Dec 1889; m. MARGARET A. NEALLEY, b. at Northwood, NH, 18 Jul 1824 daughter of John and Nancy (Sanborn) Nealley; Margaret d. at Manchester, NH, 20 Jan 1910. Margaret Nealley was the half-sister of Sarah Perkins who married George's brother Willard.

654) LYDIA WILLIAMS (*Abigail Russell Williams⁴, Thomas³, James², Robert¹*), baptized at Salem 23 Oct 1785 daughter of Henry and Abigail (Russell) Williams; d. at Salem, 28 Apr 1861; m. at Salem, 23 Feb 1808, SETH RICHARDSON, b. Oct 1786 son of Josiah and Ruth (Brooks) Richardson; Seth d. at Salem, 12 Jan 1809.
  On 1 May 1826, Lydia Richardson, signing on behalf of her daughter, joined the other heirs-at-law of the estate of Josiah Richardson in requesting Benjamin Merrill be named administrator.[1934] Josiah Richardson was Seth's father. Lydia Williams and Seth Richardson were parents of one child. Lydia did not remarry after Seth's death.

i ELIZA RICHARDSON, b. at Salem, 1808; d. at Salem, 10 Dec 1857; m. at Salem, 13 Jun 1830, THOMAS GRIFFITH, b. at Newburyport, 14 May 1803 son of William and Elizabeth (Towers) Griffith; Thomas d. at Newburyport, 28 Jan 1883. Thomas married second Rachel P. Bartlett.

655) WILLARD WILLIAMS (*Abigail Russell Williams⁴, Thomas³, James², Robert¹*), baptized at Salem 24 Feb 1788; d. at Boston, 2 May 1834; m. at Boston, 22 Dec 1820, ELIZABETH "BETSEY" OSGOOD, b. at Salem, 20 May 1789 son of Christopher and Mary (Shepard) Osgood; Betsey d. at Boston, 22 May 1835.
  Daughters Abigail Osgood Williams and Mary Elizabeth Williams were artists and authors. The sisters traveled extensively and are most known for landscape oils.[1935] Son Henry Willard Williams was a renowned physician and was the first American physician to focus his practice solely on ophthalmology. He was the first ophthalmic surgeon at Boston City Hospital.[1936]
  In his will written 1 April 1827 (probate 28 July 1834), Willard Williams bequeathed five dollars each to his children Henry Willard, Abigail Osgood, and Mary Elizabeth "considering that my property will be but small after my debts are cancelled." The rest of the estate was left to wife Betsey Osgood Williams enabling her to bring up and educate the children. If Betsey remarries, one-half of the estate is to be divided among the children and the other half to be secured to Betsey before her marriage. Real estate was a house on Elliot Street in Boston valued at $4,500 and personal estate was $651.50.[1937]
  Willard Williams and Elizabeth Osgood were parents of four children born at Boston.

i HENRY WILLARD WILLIAMS, b. 11 Dec 1821; d. at Boston, 13 Jun 1895; m. at Roxbury, 5 Sep 1860, ELIZABETH A. LOW, b. at Boston, 1831 daughter of John James and Adeline (Ford) Low; Elizabeth d. at Boston, 7 Mar 1898.

ii ABIGAIL OSGOOD WILLIAMS, b. 4 Oct 1823; d. at Salem, 26 Apr 1913.

iii MARY ELIZABETH WILLIAMS, b. 12 Jan 1825; d. at Salem, 15 Sep 1902.

iv SUSAN BAKER WILLIAMS, b. 1827; d. Sep 1828.

[1933] William, who was a shoemaker, may be the William Corse, cordwainer, who arrived on the ship *John* at Portland, Maine on 1 May 1831. On his naturalization petition at Boston in 1847, he gave his date of birth as 14 Mar 1808 at Rosa one of the Orkney Islands.

[1934] *Essex County, MA: Probate File Papers, 1638-1881.* Online database. *AmericanAncestors.org.* New England Historic Genealogical Society, 2014. Case 23628

[1935] Personal papers and correspondence of Abigail and Mary Elizabeth are available through the Phillips Library collections; https://pem.as.atlas-sys.com/repositories/2/resources/644

[1936] Harvard University, Department of Ophthalmology, "Henry Willard Williams"; https://eye.hms.harvard.edu/henrywillardwilliams

[1937] *Suffolk County, MA: Probate File Papers.* Online database. *AmericanAncestors.org.* New England Historic Genealogical Society, 2017-2019. Case 30621

656)   MARTHA APPLETON (*Thomas Appleton⁴, Mary Russell Appleton³, James², Robert¹*), b. at Boston 16 Jun 1770 daughter of Thomas and Martha (Barnard) Appleton; d. at South Boston, 7 Oct 1847; m. at Boston, 13 Mar 1798, RICHARD FRENCH THAYER, b. at Braintree, 21 Mar 1769 son of Richard and Esther (French) Thayer;[1938] Richard d. at South Boston, 13 Aug 1845.

In her will written 26 August 1839, Martha left the house she owned on Acton Street in Boston to husband Richard Thayer for the income of and living in during his natural life. At Richard's decease, the house, land, and furniture go to daughters Mary Ann Hay and Lydia W. Thayer. Mary Ann and Lydia are to pay one dollar to each of their brothers: Thomas A. Thayer, Richard F. Thayer, George H. Thayer, and Charles E. Thayer.[1939]

Martha Appleton and Richard Thayer were parents of seven children born at Boston.

i   THOMAS APPLETON THAYER, b. 1 Mar 1799; d. at Boston, 7 Jun 1870; m. at Boston, 18 Oct 1826, ELIZABETH WALES, b. at Braintree, 6 Feb 1795 daughter of Benjamin and Susannah (Ludden) Wales; Elizabeth d. at Boston, 27 Dec 1869.

ii   MARTHA ANN THAYER, b. 9 Mar 1801; d. at Boston, 24 Apr 1838. Martha did not marry.

iii   RICHARD FRENCH THAYER, b. 19 Mar 1803; d. at the Togus home for disabled volunteers at Chelsea, ME, 17 Sep 1890. Richard was resident in the Togus facility from 1873. He served in the 30th regiment of Massachusetts infantry during the Civil War.[1940] He is buried at Togus National Cemetery.

iv   MARY ANN THAYER, b. 5 Sep 1805; d. after 1880 when she was living at Bloomfield, NJ; m. at Boston, 3 Jan 1831, SAMUEL LUCAS HAY, b. at South Reading, MA, 1809 son of John and Sarah (Lucas) Hay; Samuel d. at Medford, MA, 18 Feb 1864. In 1880, Mary was living in Bloomfield with her daughter Mary and her husband John Bancroft.

v   GEORGE HENRY THAYER, b. 6 Aug 1807. Henry was a mariner and was living in 1847 when George Henry Thayer, born at Boston about 1810, obtained a replacement seaman's certificate at Philadelphia stating he previously received a certificate at Providence.[1941]

vi   LYDIA WELLS THAYER, b. 9 Aug 1809; d. after 1900 when she was living at Bloomfield, NJ. Lydia did not marry. In 1900, she was living with her niece Mary and her husband John Bancroft.

vii   CHARLES EDWARD THAYER, b. 28 May 1812; d. at Wakefield, MA, 9 Apr 1875; m. at Boston, 4 Oct 1838, NANCY HOMAN, b. at Marblehead, MA, 1814 daughter of John and Nancy (Verte) Homan; Nancy d. at Wakefield, 4 Oct 1902.

657)   THOMAS RUSSELL APPLETON (*Thomas Appleton⁴, Mary Russell Appleton³, James², Robert¹*), b. at Boston 12 Jun 1772 son of Thomas and Martha (Barnard) Appleton; d. at Haverhill, 6 Apr 1863; m. 1st 31 Dec 1797, ANNA SWETT, b. at Haverhill, 14 Mar 1765 daughter of Abraham and Sarah (*Bradley* Poor) Swett; Anna d. at Haverhill, 9 Aug 1826. Thomas m. 2nd 28 May 1827, his first cousin, HANNAH GALE, baptized at Haverhill, 26 Sep 1779 daughter of Moses and Mary (Appleton) Gale; Hannah d. at Haverhill, 6 Apr 1868.

Thomas R. Appleton was a merchant in Haverhill with a store nearly opposite the Haverhill bridge. He advertised English and Indian goods, shoemaker tools and carpenter tools, and "most articles useful in families."[1942] He also served as treasurer of the First Congregational Society of Haverhill.[1943]

In his will written 25 November 1856 (probate 21 April 1863), Thomas R. Appleton bequeathed to wife Hannah the use and improvement of all the dwelling house and land where he now resides, during her natural life and all the household furniture. She also receives $500. Son Thomas H. Appleton receives $650 and the interest thereon, but this will be held in trust. There are bequests to sister Lydia Wells, brother John Appleton, and to each of his grandchildren the children of his sons Thomas H., John A., and George Appleton. The remainder of the estate is to be equally divided between his sons John A. Appleton and George Appleton who are also named co-executors. Real estate was valued at $2,500 and personal estate at $17,500.[1944]

Thomas Russell Appleton and Anna Swett were parents of five children born at Haverhill.

[1938] Thayer, *Family Memorial: Genealogy of Fourteen Families*, p 63
[1939] Massachusetts Wills and Probate, Suffolk County, Probate Records volume 145, p 197, will of Martha Thayer, Case 35354
[1940] National Park Service, U.S. Civil War Soldiers, 1861-1865
[1941] The National Archives and Records Administration; Washington, D.C.; Proofs of Citizenship Used to Apply for Seamen's Certificates for the Port of Philadelphia, Pennsylvania, 1792-1905
[1942] Advertisement in the Merrimack Intelligencer, January 14, 1809, p 4
[1943] Haverhill Gazette, August 23, 1823, p 3
[1944] *Essex County, MA: Probate File Papers, 1638-1881.*Online database. *AmericanAncestors.org.* New England Historic Genealogical Society, 2014. Case 31472

i   HARRIET APPLETON, b. 8 Mar 1799; d. 21 Mar 1799.

ii   ANN APPLETON, b. 3 Aug 1800; d. 24 Apr 1803.

iii   THOMAS HENRY APPLETON, b. 3 May 1803; d. at Haverhill, 31 Dec 1886; m. at Andover, 31 Aug 1825, FIDELIA TROW, b. at Andover, 20 Sep 1801 daughter of John and Martha (Swan) Trow; Fidelia d. 24 Aug 1868 likely at the state hospital at Concord where she was hospitalized in 1860 diagnosed with epilepsy.[1945]

iv   JOHN ADAMS APPLETON, b. 11 Dec 1805; d. at Haverhill, 15 Dec 1882; m. at Boston, 8 Sep 1831, his first cousin, MARTHA A. WELLS (*Lydia Appleton Wells⁵, Thomas Appleton⁴, Mary Russell Appleton³, James², Robert¹*), b. at Boston, 1804 daughter of Benjamin Tuttle and Lydia (Appleton) Wells; Martha d. at Haverhill, 29 Dec 1894.

v   GEORGE APPLETON, b. 12 Mar 1808; d. at Haverhill, 23 Jul 1882; m. 8 Jun 1841, TAMEYSON GREENOUGH KIMBALL, b. at Bradford, MA, 2 Oct 1814 daughter of Daniel and Hannah (Parker) Kimball; Tameyson d. at Haverhill, 25 Feb 1907.

658)   JOHN APPLETON (*Thomas Appleton⁴, Mary Russell Appleton³, James², Robert¹*), b. at Boston 2 Dec 1774 son of Thomas and Martha (Barnard) Appleton; d. at Newton, MA, 9 Nov 1868; m. at Boston, 22 Mar 1806, MARY TUTTLE, b. at Salem 1778 daughter of Ebenezer and Hannah (Stone) Tuttle;[1946] Mary d. at Boston, 12 Nov 1866.
        John Appleton was a mason by trade.[1947] In the 1860 census, real property was valued at $3,500.[1948] John Appleton and Mary Tuttle were parents of six children born at Boston.

i   JOHN APPLETON, b. 1 Feb 1807; d. at Boston, 1 Jul 1826.

ii   MARY TUTTLE APPLETON, b. 8 Dec 1808; d. at Boston, 10 Dec 1823.

iii   FRANCES ANN APPLETON, b. 11 Aug 1811; d. at Newton, MA, 27 Sep 1855; m. at Boston, 18 Jun 1845, Rev. JOHN PAULSON, b. in Québec, 24 Dec 1820[1949] son of William and Catherine (-) Paulson;[1950] John d. at Fort Scott, KS, 4 Mar 1893. John married second the widow Bina Strinson Boultenhouse on 18 Aug 1856. John Paulson was an elder of the Fort Scott Methodist Episcopal Church. He served as captain in the 8th Kansas infantry during the Civil War. Frances and John had one daughter, Mary Catherine Paulson. She was raised by her maternal grandparents after the death of her mother. She did not marry and died after 1920 when she was living in Quincy.

iv   WILLIAM HENRY APPLETON, b. 26 Jun 1813; d. at Boston 30 Apr 1837.

v   HARRIET APPLETON, b. 12 Aug 1815; d. at Boston, 1 Apr 1859. Harriet did not marry.

vi   CATHERINE KIMBALL APPLETON, b. 1 Nov 1817; d. at Haverhill, 29 Oct 1899; m. at Boston, 1 May 1845, HORACE SMITH SIMMONS, b. at Leicester, MA, 6 Feb 1817 son of William and Harriet (Smith) Simmons;[1951] Horace d. at Haverhill, 13 Aug 1896.

659)   LYDIA APPLETON (*Thomas Appleton⁴, Mary Russell Appleton³, James², Robert¹*), b. at Boston 17 Feb 1779 daughter of Thomas and Martha (Barnard) Appleton; d. at Boston, 22 Mar 1872; m. at Boston, Oct 1799, BENJAMIN TUTTLE WELLS, b. at Boston, 17 Mar 1775 son of John and Joanna (Tuttle) Wells; Benjamin d. at Boston, 17 Apr 1822.
        Benjamin T. Wells was a coppersmith in Boston. He was in business with his brother in the firm John and Benjamin T. Wells. The estate inventory included one-half value of the coppersmith business contents of materials and tools valued at $1,613.12. Real estate was dwelling house and land value at $2,000. Personal estate in terms of household furnishings and goods was $457, a pew was valued at $60, and stock shares were $875. In his will written 16 March 1822 (probate 22 April 1822), Benjamin T. Wells of Boston left his entire estate to his beloved wife Lydia for the support of herself and their children with "full liberty to use, sell, or dispose of" the property. Lydia was named executrix.[1952]

[1945] Year: 1860; Census Place: Concord Ward 6, Merrimack, New Hampshire; Page: 920; Family History Library Film: 803675

[1946] The names of Mary's parents are given and Eben and Hannah Tuttle on her death record.

[1947] Year: 1850; Census Place: Boston Ward 10, Suffolk, Massachusetts; Roll: 337; Page: 358a

[1948] Year: 1860; Census Place: Boston Ward 9, Suffolk, Massachusetts; Page: 899; Family History Library Film: 803522

[1949] National Archives at Boston; Waltham, Massachusetts; ARC Title: Copies of Petitions and Records of Naturalization in New England Courts, 1939 - ca. 1942; NAI Number: 4752894; Record Group Title: Records of the Immigration and Naturalization Service, 1787-2

[1950] The names of John's parents are given as William and Catherine on the record for his second marriage.

[1951] The names of Horace's parents are given as William Simmons and Harriet Smith on his death record.

[1952] *Suffolk County, MA: Probate File Papers*. Online database. *AmericanAncestors.org*. New England Historic Genealogical Society, 2017-2019. Case 26666

In her will written 10 May 1854 (proved 22 April 1872), Lydia Wells of Boston named son John T. Wells and son-in-law Andrew T. Hall trustees and bequeathed $1,400 to that trust (which was money that John T. owed to Lydia) and that trust fund was to be used for the benefit of daughters Mary Ann Ferguson and Emily Francis Wells. At her decease, any of her children living in her house, will have the right to stay there for two years, then they must vacate the premises and the property sold to be divided among the children. The amount of the estate going to Mary Ann and Emily is to remain in the trust. John T. Hall and Andrew T. Wells were named executors. In a first codicil date 18 May 1855, Lydia noted that daughter Emily had died so they need for her daughters to stay in the house no longer existed so they property could be sold at her decease. She also stipulated that the inheritance going to daughter Caroline wife of James Morgan should be placed in the trust. In a codicil 25 August 1869, she adjusted the amount to be paid to the trust to half the original amount. She also noted she had loaned son-in-law Thomas Capen $200 and that amount was to be collected and used for the benefit of granddaughter Cordelia R. Capen.[1953]

Lydia and Benjamin were parents of eleven children born at Boston.

i LYDIA YOUNG WELLS, b. 20 Dec 1800; d. at Boston, 29 Aug 1880; m. at Boston, 11 Nov 1823, ANDREW TOWNSEND HALL, b. at Cambridge, MA, 30 Aug 1798 son of Edward and Abigail (Townsend) Hall; Andrew d. at Boston, 22 Nov 1875.

ii MARY ANN WELLS, b. 1802; d. at Boston, 1 Aug 1885; m. at Boston, 14 Apr 1836, JOHN FERGUSON who has not been identified. In 1850, Mary Ann was living with her mother in Boston. It is not known what became of John.

iii MARTHA A. WELLS, b. 1804; d. at Haverhill, 29 Dec 1894; m. at Boston, 8 Sep 1831, her first cousin, JOHN ADAMS APPLETON (*Thomas R. Appleton⁵, Thomas Appleton⁴, Mary Russell Appleton³, James², Robert¹*), b. at Haverhill, 11 Dec 1805 son of Thomas Russell and Anna (Swett) Appleton; John d. at Haverhill, 15 Dec 1882.

iv BENJAMIN T. WELLS, b. 1806; d. 1834 perhaps at New Orleans; m. about 1831, MARY ANN PITMAN, b. at Portsmouth, NH, about 1811 daughter of Daniel and Mary (Shortridge) Pitman; Mary Ann d. at Newton, MA, 16 Nov 1891. Mary married second William Hardwick.

v JOANNA WELLS, b. 1809; d. at Boston, 1 May 1864; m. at Boston, 24 Dec 1829, FRANKLIN J. SMITH, b. at Boston, 6 Nov 1807 son of Martin and Margaret (Rush) Smith; Franklin d. at Jaffrey, NH, 17 Apr 1869. Franklin married second at Boston, 6 Jul 1865, Anastasia Noonan.

vi CAROLINE AUGUSTA WELLS, b. 1810; d. at Boston, 29 Jun 1889; m. at Boston, 6 Nov 1839, JAMES H. MORGAN, b. at Eastport, ME, about 1816 son of James and Hannah (-) Morgan; James d. at Boston, 4 Jan 1871.

vii JOHN THOMAS WELLS, b. 18 Mar 1812; d. at Newton Centre, 28 Sep 1904; m. at Boston, 4 Sep 1839, SARAH BARTLETT, b. at Boston, 6 Oct 1819 daughter of Henry and Elizabeth (Atkins) Bartlett; Sarah d. at Newton, 24 Jun 1893.

viii FRANCIS P. WELLS, b. 1815; d. at Beverly, MA, 23 Dec 1873; m. at Boston, 12 Oct 1846, MARY ANN F. SMITH, b. about 1818 daughter of Martin and Sarah (Hersey) Smith;[1954] Mary Ann d. at Beverly, 19 Aug 1891.

ix CORDELIA R. WELLS, b. 19 Jul 1817; d. at Dorchester, MA, 5 Sep 1864; m. at Dorchester, 25 Nov 1840, THOMAS WILLIAMS CAPEN, b. at Dorchester, 14 Dec 1815 son of Joseph and Elizabeth B. (Williams) Capen; Thomas d. at Boston, 29 Nov 1880.

x CHARLES G. WELLS, b. 1818; d. at Boston, 24 Jun 1887; m. about 1855, JANE C. WOODSIDE, b. at Portland, ME, 6 Feb 1828 daughter of Samuel O. and Fidelia F. (Harford) Woodside; Jane d. at Boston, 30 Nov 1895.

xi EMILY FRANCES WELLS, b. 1820; d. at Boston, 19 Mar 1855. Emily did not marry.

660) BENJAMIN BARNARD APPLETON (*Thomas Appleton⁴, Mary Russell Appleton³, James², Robert¹*), b. at Boston 8 May 1781 son of Thomas and Martha (Barnard) Appleton; d. at Boston, 23 Apr 1844; m. at Boston, 3 Jul 1814, CATHERINE HOOTON, b. at Boston, 18 Nov 1790 daughter of John and Catharine (Thompson) Hooton; Catherine d. 7 Nov 1875.

Benjamin was a hardware goods merchant at 26 Union Street in Boston.[1955] He was elected inspector in Boston's first ward in 1827.[1956]

Benjamin B. Appleton did not leave a will and his estate entered probate 6 May 1844 with Joseph W. Ward merchant and Benjamin B. Appleton physician named administrators. The request for administrators of her son and son-in-law was made by widow Catherine Appleton. Charles H. Appleton concurred with this request. Catherine was named as guardian of Louisa Maria Appleton. Real estate was valued at $65,500 which included four houses and the main estate. Personal estate was valued at $11,259.85. Debts were $5,364.62 and the administrators petitioned to sell a portion of the real estate. The widow was

[1953] Massachusetts Wills and Probate, Suffolk County, volume 456, pp 132-134
[1954] The names of Mary's parents are given as Martin Smith and Sarah Hersey on her death record.
[1955] New England Palladium, June 27, 1809, p 4, advertisement of Benjamin B. Appleton
[1956] Boston Commercial Gazette, December 18, 1826, p 4, "Ward Officers for 1827"

allowed $1,100 from the personal estate for the care of her family. The division of the personal estate was to heirs Benjamin B. Appleton, Charles H. Appleton, Joseph W. Ward, and Louisa M. Appleton.[1957]

Benjamin and Catherine were parents of seven children born at Boston.

i   BENJAMIN BARNARD APPLETON, b. 4 May 1815; d. at Cambridge, 17 Jul 1878; m. 1st at Boston, 23 May 1844, KATHERINE EMMA THOMPSON, b. at Boston, about 1815; Katherine d. in Rome, Italy while traveling, 17 Jan 1863. Benjamin m. 2nd at Boston, 29 Jun 1869, JANE WILLIAMS BROOKS widow of his brother Charles (see just below).

ii   CHARLES HENRY APPLETON, b. 14 Jul 1817; d. at Charlestown, MA, 13 Jun 1866; m. 29 Oct 1860, JANE WILLIAMS BROOKS, b. at Boston, 1 Sep 1832 daughter of Charles and Nancy (Dicks) Brooks; Jane d. at Cambridge, 22 Aug 1881.

iii   JAMES AUGUSTUS APPLETON, b. 25 Oct 1821; d. 30 Oct 1823.

iv   CATHERINE MAY APPLETON, b. 6 May 1824; d. at Oakland, CA, 12 Jul 1898; m. at Boston, 22 Jun 1841, JOSEPH WALTER WARD, b. at Shrewsbury, 22 Jul 1814 son of Andrew H. and Sarah (Henshaw) Ward; Joseph d. at Oakland, 13 Jun 1888.

v   LOUISA MARIA APPLETON, b. 1830; d. 26 Mar 1831.

vi   JAMES AUGUSTUS APPLETON, b. 22 Nov 1832; d. 17 Feb 1833.

vii   LOUISA MARIA APPLETON, b. 3 Jan 1836, d. at Intervale, NH, 4 Jul 1903; m. at Boston, 10 Oct 1859, DEXTER N. RICHARDS, b. at Enfield, MA,[1958] 18 May 1822 son of Ephraim and Susan (Cheney) Richards; Dexter d. at Brookline, MA, 28 Mar 1900.

661)   HENRY KNOX APPLETON (*Thomas Appleton⁴, Mary Russell Appleton³, James², Robert¹*), b. at Boston 6 Jun 1786 son of Thomas and Martha (Barnard) Appleton; d. at Boston, 18 Aug 1829; m. at Boston, 29 Mar 1810, MARY OWEN, b. at Boston, about 1786 daughter of William Owen who was from England; Mary d. at Boston, 28 Mar 1861.

Henry and Mary were parents of five children born at Boston.

i   HENRY KNOX APPLETON, b. 20 Apr 1811; d. at Boston, 23 Apr 1894; m. at Boston, 24 Jun 1838, EMELINE C. LORKIN, b. at Boston, 26 Jun 1812 daughter of Thomas and Mary (Batterman) Lorkin; Emeline d. at Boston, 20 Jul 1901.

ii   JOSEPH WARREN APPLETON, b. 17 Jan 1813; d. at Boston, 27 Apr 1892; m. at Boston, 13 Oct 1833, REBECCA SAMUELS, b. at Boston, 1 Dec 1818 daughter of Isaac and Ruth (-) Samuels; Rebecca d. at Boston, 18 Apr 1889.

iii   GEORGE WASHINGTON APPLETON, b. 14 Jun 1815; d. at Newton, MA, 11 May 1895; m. 1st at Boston, 27 Sep 1840, ANN WALES, b. at Milton, 26 Aug 1814 daughter of Samuel and Phebe (Whitcomb) Wales; Ann d. at Roxbury, 28 Jun 1862. George m. 2nd at Roxbury, 14 Jun 1864, ELIZABETH J. REED, b. at Freeport, ME, 1825 daughter of Jacob and Cecilia (Stockbridge) Reed; Elizabeth d. at Roxbury, 4 Jan 1865. George m. 3rd at Roxbury, 26 Nov 1866, MARY L. MORTON, b. at Aylesford, Nova Scotia, about 1822 daughter of William and Mary (Walkinson) Morton

iv   MARIA CARLYLE APPLETON, b. 26 Sep 1817; d. at Boston, 30 Oct 1886; m. at Boston, 9 Apr 1835, JOHN P. COUTHOUY, b. at Boston 1811 son of Joseph and Susannah (-) Couthouy;[1959] John d. at Charlestown, 30 Dec 1852. John was a mariner.

v   CHARLES THOMAS PRATT APPLETON, b. 26 Aug 1820; d. at Newton, MA, 2 Sep 1901; m. in NY, 5 Sep 1849, SARAH JANE MERRILL, b. at Kennebunkport, ME, about 1821 daughter of John and Elizabeth (Rickard) Merrill;[1960] Sarah d. at Cambridge, 2 Apr 1898.

662)   GEORGE WASHINGTON APPLETON (*Thomas Appleton⁴, Mary Russell Appleton³, James², Robert¹*), b. at Boston 6 Jun 1786 son of Thomas and Martha (Barnard) Appleton; d. at Delavan, IL, 28 Mar 1851; m. at Wrentham, MA, 4 Apr 1819, MARY GUILD, b. at Franklin, MA, 31 Oct 1798 daughter of John and Ruth (Morse) Guild; Mary d. at Delavan, 4 Feb 1859.

[1957] *Suffolk County, MA: Probate File Papers.* Online database. *AmericanAncestors.org.* New England Historic Genealogical Society, 2017-2019. Case 33983

[1958] Enfield, MA was one of the towns flooded out of existence in the creation of the Quabbin Reservoir.

[1959] The names of John's parents are given as Joseph and Susannah on his death record.

[1960] The names of Sarah's parents are given as John Merrill and Elizabeth Ricard on her death record.

Rev. George Washington Appleton received the Bachelor of Arts degree from Harvard in 1794 and A.M. degree in 1808.[1961] The family was in Lyme and then Sterling, Connecticut where their children were born, and later in Tazewell County, Illinois. Although he was ordained, his occupation in listed as cabinetmaker on the 1850 census.[1962] His son Joseph Clay Appleton was an early proponent for the incorporation of Delavan, which was first incorporated in 1858, but the organization of the town was not competed until 1865. Joseph C. Appleton was on the first board of trustees of Delavan.[1963]

George Appleton and Mary Guild were parents of three children.

i   ANN JUDSON APPLETON, b. at Lyme, CT, 21 Feb 1820; d. at Delavan, IL, 22 Feb 1885; m. at Wrentham, MA, 5 Mar 1846, as his second wife, DANIEL CHEEVER, b. 23 Jul 1802 son of Daniel and Joanna (Cheever) Titus; Daniel d. at Delavan, 27 Dec 1877. Daniel was first married to Alice Henry.

ii   MARTHA ELIZABETH APPLETON, b. at Sterling, CT, 8 Dec 1823; d. at Bellingham, WA, 16 Feb 1911; m. at Providence, RI, 12 Oct 1847, HORACE LUCIUS FISHER, b. at Dedham, 1819 son of Abijah and Fanny (Field) Fisher; Horace d. at Normal, IL, 12 Mar 1885.

iii   JOSEPH CLAY APPLETON, b. at Sterling, CT, 18 May 1825; d. at Providence, RI, 26 May 1901; m. at Blackstone, MA, 22 Mar 1852, FRANCES F. BACON, b. at Providence, RI, about 1824 (given as Oct 1829 in one census record) daughter of William Bacon (per marriage record); Frances d. at Providence, 30 Oct 1905.

663)   MARY GALE (*Mary Appleton Gale⁴, Mary Russell Appleton³, James², Robert¹*), baptized at Haverhill, MA, 27 Dec 1772 daughter of Moses and Mary (Appleton) Gale; d. at Bangor, ME, 20 Feb 1842; m. at Haverhill, 28 Feb 1804, as his second wife, ROBERT TREAT, b. 14 Jul 1752 son of Joseph and Mary (-) Treat; Robert d. at Bangor, 27 May 1824. Robert was first married to Mary Partridge on 28 Nov 1774.

Robert Treat went to Fort Pownall, Maine with his half-brother in 1769 and was in Bangor by 1773. He was a trader and own the first vessel built in Bangor which was built by William Boyd. In 1785, he was named Major of the First Regiment in the Second Brigade of the Eighth Division of Massachusetts Militia. He had a wide-ranging business being a merchant in Boston and owning a lumber wharf in Lynn.[1964]

Mary and Robert were parents of three children born at Bangor. Robert also had nine children with his first wife.

i   NATHANIEL GALE TREAT, b. 13 Mar 1807; d. at Bangor, 24 Nov 1880; m. 22 May 1842, LUCY JOSEPHINE MCGRATH, b. 1822; Lucy d. at Bangor, 27 Oct 1864.

ii   MARY HANNAH TREAT, b. 23 Apr 1809; d. at Bangor, 20 Mar 1844; m. at Bangor, 8 Sep 1827, ZEBEDIAH ROGERS, b. at Billerica, MA, 2 Apr 1796 son of Josiah and Rhoda (Wooster) Rogers; Zebediah d. at Pitt River Valley, CA, Jan 1857.

iii   ELIZABETH HOLYOKE TREAT, b. 19 Jan 1813; d. at Bangor, 2 Apr 1860; m. 7 Oct 1847, NATHAN JEWELL, b. at Waterford, ME, 5 Mar 1809 son of Nathan and Betsey (Pollard) Jewell; Nathan d. at Easton, ME, 22 Apr 1876.

664)   SAMUEL APPLETON GALE (*Mary Appleton Gale⁴, Mary Russell Appleton³, James², Robert¹*), baptized at Haverhill, MA, 18 Nov 1781 son of Moses and Mary (Appleton) Gale; d. at Haverhill, about Jan 1829[1965] (probate 8 Feb 1831); m. at Gloucester, 14 May 1807, MARY A. FOSTER, b. about 1780 whose parents are not clearly identified but might be Jeremiah and Polly (Tarr) Foster of Gloucester; Mary d. at Haverhill, 31 Dec 1822.

Samuel A. Gale did not leave a will and his estate entered probate 8 February 1831 with Gilman Parker as administrator at the request of heirs Mary A. Gale and Thomas Appleton guardian for Nancy Gale. Real estate was valued at $1133.22 and personal estate at $286.23. Debts were $41.64.[1966]

Samuel's sister Hannah *Gale* Appleton married but did not have children. Her will written 20 July 1864 (probate 21 April 1868) includes bequests to nieces and nephews who were children of her brother Samuel: Samuel Gale of Elizabeth, New Jersey, niece Mary Hardy wife of Abner Hardy of Groveland, niece Sarah Rollins wife of Charles P. Rollins of West Newbury, and niece Nancy Hoagland wife of George T. Hoagland of St. Joseph's, Missouri.[1967]

Samuel and Mary were parents of seven children.

[1961] Harvard University, *Quinquennial Catalogue*, p 144

[1962] Year: 1850; Census Place: Tazewell, Illinois; Roll: M432_129; Page: 99A; Image: 588

[1963] Charles C. Chapman Publishers, *History of Tazewell County, Illinois*, p 436

[1964] "Major Robert Treat of Bangor", *Bangor Historical Magazine*, November 1886, Vol. II, No. V, pp 85-86

[1965] This is the date of death given in the probate record.

[1966] *Essex County, MA: Probate File Papers, 1638-1881.*Online database. *AmericanAncestors.org.* New England Historic Genealogical Society, 2014. Case 10565

[1967] *Essex County, MA: Probate File Papers, 1638-1881.*Online database. *AmericanAncestors.org.* New England Historic Genealogical Society, 2014. Case 31460. Hannah's will also includes a bequest to her nephew Nathaniel Treat who was the son of Hannah's sister Mary *Gale* Treat.

i　　MARY A. GALE, b. at Gloucester, MA, 1808; d. at Groveland, MA, 30 May 1879; m. at Bradford, MA, 8 Feb 1832, ABNER HARDY, b. at Bradford, 20 Feb 1804 son of Silvanus and Mary (Boynton) Hardy; Abner d. at Groveland, 26 Nov 1887.

ii　　SARAH R. GALE, b. at Gloucester, MA, about 1812; d. at West Newbury, MA, 23 Feb 1892; m. at Bradford, MA, 7 Jun 1842, CHARLES PEARSON ROLLINS, b. at Bradford, MA, 28 May 1809 son of Joseph and Rachel (*Parker* Latham) Rollins; Charles d. at West Newbury, 16 Oct 1891.

iii　　SAMUEL A. GALE, b. at Gloucester, MA, about 1814; d. after 1880 when living at Elizabeth, NJ; m. at Essex, NJ, 23 Nov 1837, SARAH HAMILTON, b. in NJ, about 1817; Sarah was living in 1880.

iv　　ELIZA GALE, b about 1815 and baptized at Haverhill, 6 Apr 1817

v　　NANCY GALE, b. 29 Mar 1816; d. at St. Joseph, MO, 3 Jan 1908; m. at Elizabeth, NJ, 2 Feb 1842, GEORGE TUNIS HOAGLAND, b. at Elizabeth, NJ, 7 Feb 1814 (date of gravestone) son of Cornelius Hatfield and Catharine (Brown) Hoagland;[1968] George d. at St. Joseph, 30 Oct 1903.

vi　　MOSES GALE, b. at Haverhill, MA, Jun 1818; d. 30 Sep 1821.

vii　　HARRIET NEWELL GALE, b. at Haverhill, 6 Jun 1821; d. at Haverhill, 12 Aug 1856; m. at Haverhill, 11 Dec 1842, MOSES HOWE,[1969] b. at Methuen, 24 Jun 1819 son of Thomas and Phebe (Howe) Howe; Moses d. at Haverhill, 12 Jan 1896.

665)　　ALICE APPLETON (*Daniel Appleton⁴, Mary Russell Appleton³, James², Robert¹*), b. at Haverhill, MA, 11 Dec 1778 daughter of Daniel and Lydia (Ela) Appleton; d. at Haverhill, 25 Jun 1842; m. at Haverhill, 17 Jun 1806, JOHN SWETT thought to be the son of John and Mary (Folsom) Swett;[1970] John d. at New York, NY, 1834 (probate 3 Dec 1834).

John Swett was a merchant, and although a resident of Dorchester, Massachusetts, his will was filed in New York County, New York. In his will written 17 July 1833 (proved 28 November 1834), he specifies if personal estate is not sufficient to pay the debts, that his property in Dracut be sold. The income, interests, and proceeds of his estate are to be invested and used for the maintenance of his wife Alice A. Swett during her natural life. The exception is that a portion of the estate be used for the maintenance of his adopted daughter Caroline Swett, daughter of his oldest brother Josiah, until Caroline is married. After the decease of his wife, the total estate is to be divided and one-third to son John and one-third to son Charles. The remaining third is for the sole and separate use of Caroline during her natural life. After the decease of Caroline, this third will go to his heirs-at-law.[1971]

Son John Appleton Swett was a renowned physician. He graduated from Harvard in 1828 and received his medical degree there in 1831. He continued his studies in Paris. From 1842 until his death, he was a physician and lecturer at New York hospital. In 1853, he was appointed professor of the theory and practice of medicine at the "University of the city of New York." His lectures were published in the *Lancet*.[1972]

Alice and John were parents of two children.

i　　JOHN APPLETON SWETT, b. at Boston, 3 Dec 1808; d. at New York, NY, 18 Sep 1854; m. at Boston, 1 Aug 1849, MARTHA DALE, baptized at Andover, 7 Dec 1817 daughter of Dr. Ebenezer and Serena Parker (Johnson) Dale;[1973] Martha d. at New York, NY (burial at Gloucester, MA), 10 May 1888. John and Martha did not have children. In her will, Martha Dale Swett left her estate to her siblings, other friends and relations, and charitable causes.[1974]

ii　　CHARLES JAMES SWETT, b. at Boston, 1813; d. before 1870 when Adeline was head of household in Brooklyn; m. at New York, NY, 15 Sep 1855, ADELINE WILLIAMSON, b. at NY, about 1832. Adeline was living in 1892 at the probate of her son's estate named as Adeline W. Peinaing of Brooklyn. Adeline married second Henry Peinaing of Germany. Charles and Adeline were parents of two sons.

[1968] Carpenter, *History and Genealogy of the Hoagland Family*, p 224

[1969] Harriet's uncle Moses Gale did not have children; in his 1848 will, he left much of his estate to his niece Harriet N. How with Moses How named as executor. *Essex County, MA: Probate File Papers, 1638-1881.* Online database. *AmericanAncestors.org.* New England Historic Genealogical Society, 2014. Case 39961

[1970] Stackpole, *Swett Genealogy*, p 44

[1971] New York Wills and Probate, New York County, Record of Wills 1796-1879, volume 073, pp 210-212

[1972] Appleton's Cyclopedia of American Biography, 1600-1889, Volume VI, p 9

[1973] The 1869 probate of Serena P. Dale (Essex County, MA Case 36863) includes as an heir daughter Martha D. Swett widow of John A. Appleton of Boston.

[1974] Massachusetts Wills and Probate, Essex County, volume 457, pp 376-377

666)   DANIEL APPLETON (*Daniel Appleton⁴, Mary Russell Appleton³, James², Robert¹*), b. at Haverhill, MA, 10 Dec 1785 son of Daniel and Lydia (Ela) Appleton; d. at New York, NY, 27 Mar 1849; m. 4 May 1813, his third cousin once removed, HANNAH ADAMS (*John Adams⁵, Hannah Osgood Adams⁴, Mary Russell Osgood³, Thomas², Robert¹*), b. at Andover, 18 Dec 1791 daughter of John and Dorcas (Faulkner) Adams;[1975] Hannah d. at New York, 28 May 1859.

Daniel Appleton began his work life as a dry goods merchant and trader in Haverhill. He had a dry good business in Boston before moving to New York in 1825. He made the transition to book publishing his company known as D. Appleton & Co. Among the publications of his company was *The New American Cyclopaedia*.

In his will written 2 March 1849 (proved 13 April 1849), Daniel Appleton of New York directed that a family vault be purchased at Greenwood Cemetery. He confirmed the grant of real estate previously made to his wife. His wife also receives thirty thousand dollars for her sole use. She also receives the pew in Grace Church in New York and all the household furniture. Son William H. Appleton receives ten thousand dollars as due to his independent circumstances he requires less than the other children. The sum of fifteen thousand dollars is to be held in trust for the benefit of Louisa Maria wife of James E. Cooley and upon her decease, the sum to be equally divided among her children. Son John A. receives fifteen thousand dollars, son George S. receives ten thousand as he has already received five thousand dollars, and son Daniel Sydney receives fifteen thousand as does son Samuel Francis. Fifteen thousand dollars is to be held in trust for the benefit of daughter Sarah Emeline during her life, and at her decease to be divided among any children she may have. The residue of the estate goes to his wife to be at her disposal. The will further addresses the dissolution of the firm D. Appleton & Co. which occurred on 1 January 1849 with a total value of that company of $167,533.50. A new firm has been formed agreeably to his desire to which sons William and John have associated themselves. Sons Daniel Sydney and Samuel Francis have the opportunity to become members of the new firm by Daniel selling to them a part of his interest in the late firm. In order for son George to be on an equal footing with his brothers, in case George desires it for the successful prosecution of his business, George may receive a loan equal in amount to the loan given to Daniel and Samuel. If the estate is not sufficient to pay the legacies, the legacy to his wife is to be paid first. Sons William H. and Daniel Sydney Appleton were named executors.[1976]

Daniel Appleton and Hannah Adams were parents of eight children.

i   WILLIAM HENRY APPLETON, b. at Haverhill, MA, 27 May 1814; d. at Bronx, NY, 19 Oct 1899; m. at Lowell, 16 Apr 1844, MARY MOODY WORTHEN, b. 7 Apr 1824 daughter of Ezra and Mary (Currier) Worthen; Mary d. at Bronx, 28 Jan 1884.

ii   LOUISA MARIA APPLETON, b. at Haverhill, 31 Mar 1815; d. at Bad Homburg, Deutschland (burial in Florence Italy with her husband), 2 Jul 1887;[1977] m. in England, 23 Sep 1838, JAMES EWING COOLEY, b. at Greenwich, MA, 10 Nov 1802 son of Azariah and Mercy (Belden) Cooley; James d. at Lucca, Italy, 19 Aug 1882.[1978]

iii   JOHN ADAMS APPLETON, baptized at Andover, 11 May 1817; d. at Brooklyn, NY, 15 Jul 1881; m. at Gloucester, 18 Sep 1848, SERENA PARKER DALE, b. at Gloucester, MA, about 1825 daughter of Ebenezer and Serena Parker (Johnson) Dale; Serena d. at Brooklyn, 8 Jan 1902.

iv   CHARLES HORATIO APPLETON, b. at Andover, 5 Jul 1819; d. 1820.

v   GEORGE SWETT APPLETON, b. at Andover, 1 Oct 1821; d. at New York, NY, 8 Jul 1878; m. 27 Mar 1847, CAROLINE ARCHER OSGOOD, b. in Baltimore, MD, about 1827 daughter of Robert Hawkins and Sally (Archer) Osgood; Caroline d. 1893 (probate New York County, Sep 1893).

vi   DANIEL SYDNEY APPLETON, b. at Boston, 9 Apr 1824; d. at New York, NY, 13 Nov 1890; m. 1st 25 Mar 1858, MELVINA W. MARSHALL, b. a New York, NY, 1831 daughter of Charles Henry and Fidelia (Wellman) Marshall; Melvina d. at Dobbs Ferry, NY, 30 Nov 1873. Daniel m. 2nd at Providence, RI, 8 Sep 1875, SOPHIA WELLMAN LINCOLN, b. at Portland, ME, 1838 daughter of Thomas Oliver and Malvina (Wellman) Lincoln; Sophia d. at Brooklyn, 17 Dec 1889.

vii   SAMUEL FRANCIS APPLETON, b. at Boston, 24 Sep 1826; d. at Pleasantville, NY, 24 Oct 1883; m. at Lynn, MA, 10 Nov 1849, HANNAH AUGUSTA NASON, b. at Lynn, 23 Dec 1831 daughter of Thomas and Hannah G. (Griffin) Nason; Hannah d. at Lynn, 7 Dec 1905.

viii   SARAH EMELINE APPLETON, b. in NY, 27 Jul 1829; d. at Paris, France, 5 Feb 1861; m. at New York, 26 Apr 1859, LEOPOLD BOSSANGE, b. in Paris, 17 Aug 1821.

667)   THOMAS APPLETON (*William Appleton⁴, Mary Russell Appleton³, James², Robert¹*), b. at Boston 26 Dec 1785 son of William and Hannah (Clark) Appleton; d. at Reading, MA, 11 Jul 1872; m. at Templeton, 5 Jul 1812, BEULAH

[1975] The will of John Adams includes a bequest to his daughter Hannah wife of Daniel Appleton.
[1976] *New York, Wills and Probate Records, 1659-1999* [database on-line], New York County, District and Probate Courts, volume 97, pp 465-467
[1977] Hesse, Germany, Deaths, 1851-1958, Personenstandsregister Sterberegister; Bestand: 908; Laufende Nummer: 1540
[1978] U.S., Newspaper Extractions from the Northeast, 1704-1930

GOODRIDGE,[1979] b. at Templeton, MA, 20 Dec 1790 daughter of Ebenezer and Beulah (Childs) Goodridge; Beulah d. at Reading, 21 May 1880.

Thomas Appleton was an organ builder in Boston. His organs are particularly noted for their joinery and carving. He apprenticed with cabinetmaker Elisha Larned before being hired by the prominent organ builder William Goodrich (who was his brother-in-law). Thomas opened his own shop in 1820. He was awarded a gold medal by the Massachusetts Charitable Mechanic Association in 1839.[1980]

Thomas Appleton and Beulah Goodridge were parents of seven children born at Boston.

i   WILLIAM APPLETON, b. 26 Jul 1813; d. 28 Aug 1815.

ii   EDWARD APPLETON, b. 25 Jan 1816; d. at Reading, 30 Jul 1898; m. at Dover, NH, 29 Sep 1842, FRANCES ANNE ATKINSON, b. at Dover, 18 Feb 1817 daughter of Theodore and Anna Louisa (Tufts) Atkinson; Frances d. at Reading, 30 Jul 1880. Edward attended Harvard and was a civil engineer.

iii   EMELINE APPLETON, b. 1 Nov 1819; d. 23 Jun 1820.

iv   EMILY APPLETON, b. 9 Nov 1821; d. at Cambridge, 14 Oct 1844.

v   ANNE ELIZABETH APPLETON, b. 22 Jul 1824; d. at Reading, 27 Sep 1918. Anne did not marry.

vi   WILLIAM GEORGE APPLETON, b. 22 Aug 1826; d. (buried) 5 Apr 1829.

vii   SARAH THOMAS APPLETON, b. 15 Feb 1830; d. at Reading, 18 Dec 1859.

668)   MARY "POLLY" WOODBURY (*Hannah Appleton Woodbury⁴, Mary Russell Appleton³, James², Robert¹*), b. at Haverhill, 23 Aug 1786 daughter of Edward and Hannah (Appleton) Woodbury; d. at Bangor, ME, 13 Sep 1844; m. at Haverhill, 25 Oct 1811, JOSEPH BARTLETT, b. at Newburyport, 22 Mar 1776 son of Thomas and Sarah (Cilley) Bartlett.

There is a record for one child of Mary and Joseph Bartlett born at Bangor.

i   HANNAH WOODBURY BARTLETT, b. at Bangor, 27 Nov 1819

669)   HANNAH WOODBURY (*Hannah Appleton Woodbury⁴, Mary Russell Appleton³, James², Robert¹*), b. at Haverhill, 19 Apr 1788 daughter of Edward and Hannah (Appleton) Woodbury; m. at Haverhill, 7 Jun 1807, JAMES BARTLETT, b. at Haverhill, 21 Apr 1785 son of Israel and Tabitha (Walker) Bartlett; James d. at Boston, 18 Sep 1809.

James Bartlett did not leave a will and his estate entered probate 23 October 1809 with father Israel Bartlett requesting that his son Enoch be named to administer the estate. Widow Hannah also requested that Enoch be named administrator. The estate was valued at $349.75.[1981]

Hannah and James were parents of one child.

i   MARY ODIORNE BARTLETT, b. 1808; d. at Bangor, ME, 12 Sep 1888; m. at Boston, 1 Jan 1829, DANIEL WOOD PARKER, b. 1803 son of William and Nancy (Myrick) Wood; Daniel d. at Bangor, 18 Nov 1878.

670)   ELIZABETH WOODBURY (*Hannah Appleton Woodbury⁴, Mary Russell Appleton³, James², Robert¹*), b. at Haverhill, 8 Dec 1789 daughter of Edward and Hannah (Appleton) Woodbury; d. at Salem, MA, 6 Apr 1868; m. at Haverhill, 28 Nov 1814, NATHAN BURRILL, b. at Salem, about 1787 son of Ezra and Ann (Breed) Burrill; Nathan d. at Haverhill, 25 Jan 1866.

Nathan Burrill did not leave a will and his estate entered probate 17 April 1866 with Joseph Stanwood as administrator. No real estate was in the inventory and personal estate was valued at $1200. Nathan left a widow Eliza and one daughter Elizabeth B. Mansfield.[1982]

i   ELIZABETH BURRILL, b. at Haverhill, 18 Jul 1817; d. at Salem, 19 Nov 1886; m. at Haverhill, 11 Jun 1851, as his second wife, NATHANIEL B. MANSFIELD, b. at Salem, 4 Oct 1796 son of Benjamin and Mary (Brookhouse) Mansfield; Nathaniel d. at Salem, 24 Sep 1863. Nathaniel was first married to Harriet Fabens.

[1979] A portrait of Beulah Goodridge Appleton painted by her sister Sarah Goodridge is in the Museum of Fine Arts, Boston; https://collections.mfa.org/objects/33379

[1980] His organs are still in use. One of Thomas Appleton's organs is in the collection of the Metropolitan Museum of Art; https://www.metmuseum.org/art/collection/search/503670

[1981] *Suffolk County, MA: Probate File Papers*. Online database. *AmericanAncestors.org.* New England Historic Genealogical Society, 2017-2019. Case 23420

[1982] *Essex County, MA: Probate File Papers, 1638-1881.*Online database. *AmericanAncestors.org.* New England Historic Genealogical Society, 2014. Case 34236

671)   EDWARD WOODBURY (*Hannah Appleton Woodbury⁴, Mary Russell Appleton³, James², Robert¹*), b. at Haverhill, 29 Oct 1791 son of Edward and Hannah (Appleton) Woodbury; d. at sea on passage from New Orleans, 7 Jun 1834;[1983] m. JUDITH MOODY JEWETT, b. at Ipswich, MA, 28 Oct 1781 daughter of Epes and Betsey (Hidden) Jewett; Judith d. at Ipswich, 1 Jan 1849.

Edward Woodbury was a merchant. In his will written 11 October 1830 (probate 1 July 1834), Edward Woodbury bequeathed his entire estate to his wife Judith who was also named executrix. Real estate was valued at $2540 which included the $40 value of the pew of the first Presbyterian church. Personal estate was valued at $1339.45, $941 of that being cash. Debts were $4553.04.[1984]

In her will written 5 October 1834 (probate 27 March 1849), Judith Woodbury left her entire estate to her adopted daughter Lucy Woodbury Jewet.[1985]

i   EDWARD NEWELL WOODBURY, b. and d. at Ipswich, 2 Jul 1817.

Great-Grandchildren of Sarah Russell and John Ingalls

672)   SARAH FISK (*Mary Ingalls Fisk⁴, John Ingalls³, Sarah Russell Ingalls², Robert¹*), b. at Pomfret, 3 Apr 1761 daughter of John and Mary (Ingalls) Fisk; m. at Pomfret, 1 Mar 1785, SOLOMON ELDRIDGE son of Lemuel Eldridge.

Sarah and Solomon married in Pomfret and their oldest three children were likely born in Connecticut. The youngest five of their eight children were born in Springfield, New York where the family located by early 1792.[1986]

Son Willis did not marry. In his will writer 24 September 1853 (proved 3 April 1854), Willis made bequests to his sister Mary Norton of Hastings, Michigan and sister Sally Crandall wife of Bailey Crandall of De Ruyter. There are also bequests to niece Mary Barnes of Medina County, Ohio and nephews Hiram Barnes and Willis Barnes of Olivet, Michigan. There is a complicated explanation of how the bequest to sister Mary is to be paid involving contracts for sale of land to his nephew Seldon Norton of Hastings and his nephew Orville Barnes of Olivet. Bailey Crandall was named executor.[1987] The heirs-at-law given notification of the will were Sarah Ann McGraw, Sally Crandall, H. Louise Randall, Hiram Sears, Mary Norton, Mary Barns, Orville Barns, Harvey Eldridge, and Niles H. Gardiner acting as guardian for Hiram Barns and Willis Barns. H. Louise Randall listed as an heir-at-law was Harriet Louise Eldridge the only child of Evander. Harriet Louise married Paul King Randall.

i   ROSENA ELDRIDGE, b. about 1786; d. about 1812; m. about 1808, SELDON RATHBONE. After the death of Rosena, Seldon went to Michigan.

ii   SARAH ELDRIDGE, b. 13 Nov 1787; d. at Cazenovia, NY, 18 Apr 1857; m. 14 Dec 1806, BAILEY CRANDALL, b. 5 Feb 1784 son of Bailey and Desire (Safford) Crandall;[1988] Bailey d. at De Ruyter, NY, 16 Dec 1861.

iii   WILLIS ELDRIDGE, b. about 1790; d. at De Ruyter, NY, Oct 1854. Willis did not marry.

iv   HARVEY ELDRIDGE, b. 1792; d. at Findlay, OH, 21 Mar 1865; m. SARAH WAY, b. 22 Feb 1795 daughter of Samuel and Sarah (Vibber) Way; Sarah d. at Findlay, 13 Jun 1844.

v   MARY ELDRIDGE, b. about 1792; d. after 1860 when living at Hastings, MI; m. SHELDON NORTON; Sheldon perhaps died about 1837 when he last appears on tax rolls at Andover, OH.

vi   EVANDER ELDRIDGE, b. at Springfield, NY, 10 Nov 1798; d. at Hudson, OH, 29 Nov 1827; m. about 1822, BETSEY OLIVIA WAY, b. at Springfield, NY, 8 Jun 1801 daughter of Samuel and Sarah (Vibber) Way; Betsey d. at Springfield, NY, 28 Aug 1829.

vii   AMELIA ELDRIDGE, b. at Springfield, NY, about 1802; m. at Portage County, OH, 20 Sep 1820, JOHN BIRD BARNES, b. 23 Feb 1795 son of Daniel G. and Sarah (Webster) Barnes; John d. at Olivet, MI, 25 Dec 1856.

[1983] Edward, of Newburyport, on passage from New Orleans, June 7, 1834, a. 43 y. G. R. 1.

[1984] *Essex County, MA: Probate File Papers, 1638-1881.*Online database. *AmericanAncestors.org.* New England Historic Genealogical Society, 2014. Case 30381

[1985] *Essex County, MA: Probate File Papers, 1638-1881.*Online database. *AmericanAncestors.org.* New England Historic Genealogical Society, 2014. Case 57735

[1986] Pierce, *Fiske and Fisk Family*, p 122

[1987] New York Wills and Probate Records, Madison County, Wills Book D, pp 379-380

[1988] Crandall, *Elder John Crandall*, p 42

viii   CELESTIA ELDRIDGE, b. at Springfield, NY, Apr 1805; d. at De Ruyter, NY, 23 Aug 1829; m. STEPHEN G. SEARS, b. at Southeast, NY, 1798 son of Eleazer H. and Betsey (Marvin) Sears; Stephen d. at De Ruyter, 4 Aug 1868. Stephen married second Susan Mitchell.

673)   ALLIS FISK[1989] (*Mary Ingalls Fisk[4], John Ingalls[3], Sarah Russell Ingalls[2], Robert[1]*), b. at Pomfret, 15 Apr 1763 daughter of John and Mary (Ingalls) Fisk; d. at Aurora, OH, 1850;[1990] m. at Pomfret, 7 Feb 1793, SYLVANUS ELDRIDGE son of Lemuel Eldridge; Sylvanus d. at Aurora (or on the way to Aurora), 1812.

        Allis and Sylvanus married in Pomfret and along with Sylvanus's brother Solomon and Allis's sister Sarah settled in Springfield, New York.[1991] After the births of their five children, Allis and Sylvanus left for Ohio, and it is thought that Sylvanus died on the way, although when and where that occurred is not clear. Allis and her children were in Aurora, Ohio around 1814.[1992]

        Allis and Sylvanus were parents of five children.[1993]

i   BETSEY ELDRIDGE, b. 1796; d. at Twinsburg, OH, 27 Oct 1881; m. about 1824, APOLLOS WHITE, b. at Pomfret, CT, 9 Sep 1794 son of Jonathan and Bathsheba (Webster) White; Apollos d. at Cresco, IA, 30 Mar 1868.

ii   JOHN I. ELDRIDGE, b. 1797; d. at Aurora, OH, 1866; m. at Geauga County, OH, 20 Jun 1828, MARIETTA COOK, b. at Wallingford, CT, 4 Mar 1802 daughter of Ephraim and Susan (Ives) Cook;[1994] Marietta d. at Aurora, OH, 11 Jan 1870.

iii   DANIEL D. ELDRIDGE, b. about 1801; d. at Streetsboro, OH, 25 Sep 1878; m. at Portage County, OH, 10 Sep 1840, MARY ANN MASON (possibly a widow), b. in NH, about 1811 (census record); Mary Ann d. at Streetsboro, 25 Oct 1896.

iv   ANNA ELDRIDGE, b. 2 Oct 1802 (on gravestone); d. at Aurora, OH, 7 Jan 1891; m. 1st at Portage County, OH, 1 Oct 1822, CHESTER CARVER, b. about 1803; Chester d. at Aurora, 31 Aug 1827. Anna m. 2nd, 1829, as his second wife, OLIVER SPENCER, b. at Middlefield, MA, 25 Aug 1801 son of Samuel W. and Lucy (Fisk) Spencer; Oliver d. at Aurora, 26 Dec 1891. Oliver was first married to Sally Little.

v   CAROLINE ELDRIDGE, b. 1805; d. at Rockford, IL, 6 Aug 1885; m. at Portage County, OH, 4 Dec 1834, GEORGE COCHRAN, b. at Hudson, OH, 18 Oct 1805 (on death record); George d. at Rockford, IL, 25 Jul 1887.

674)   NAOMI FARNUM (*Ephraim Farnum[4], Mary Ingalls Farnum[3], Sarah Russell Ingalls[2], Robert[1]*), b. at Concord, NH, 20 Apr 1760 daughter of Ephraim and Judith (Hall) Farnum; d. at Boscawen, 20 Mar 1832; m. Mar 1780, JOHN CHANDLER, b. at Concord, 11 Dec 1752 son of John and Mary (Carter) Chandler; John d. at Boscawen, 24 Jan 1825.

        Captain John Chandler was the builder of the Bonney Tavern in Boscawen. The tavern built in 1787 remained at its original site on the corner of North Main and Eel Streets in Boscawen until 1937.[1995]

        John Chandler did not leave a will and son John Chandler was administrator of the estate. The real estate was valued at $1,780 including an $800 value on the homestead farm which was one undivided half of a 70-acre farm. The personal estate was valued at $632.03. Claims against the estate exceeded its value and the estate was declared insolvent 6 September 1825.[1996]

        John and Naomi Chandler were parents of seven children all born at Boscawen.

i   JOHN CHANDLER, b. 25 Oct 1780; d. at Manchester, NH, 6 Mar 1859; m. 28 Sep 1806, PRISCILLA KIMBALL, b. at Boscawen, 7 Aug 1781 daughter of Peter and Elizabeth (Thurston) Kimball; Priscilla d. at Manchester, 24 Mar 1868.

ii   NATHAN CHANDLER, b. 14 Apr 1782; d. at Concord, Apr 1835; m. at Concord, 17 Apr 1805, JANE ROLFE, b. at Concord, 21 Jan 1783 daughter of Nathaniel and Judith (Walker) Rolfe; Jane d. at Concord, 5 Jun 1863.

[1989] Her name has various spellings: Allis, Alice, and Allice; it is Alice on her gravestone

[1990] Alice Eldridge is buried at the Aurora Cemetery; findagrave ID: 92662706

[1991] Sylvanus was taxed in Springfield, New York in 1802; New York, Tax Assessment Rolls of Real and Personal Estates, 1799-1804

[1992] Wickham, *Memorial to the Pioneer Women of the Western Reserve*, Part One, p 443

[1993] A. W. Bowen, *A Portrait and Biographical Record of Portage and Summit Counties, Ohio*, p 713

[1994] Davis, *History of Wallingford, Connecticut*, p 690

[1995] Boscawen Historical Society. http://www.boscawenhistoricalsociety.org/online-resources/links/

[1996] New Hampshire, County Probate Records, 1660-1973, Merrimack County, probate of John Chandler, 3:52, 2:173, 6:127, 7:6, 2:279, 6:228, 1:320, 7:278

iii EPHRAIM CHANDLER, b. 4 Sep 1784; d. at Boscawen, 12 Mar 1837; m. about 1815, TABITHA CURRIER, b. at Warner, NH, 9 Feb 1793 daughter of Theophilus and Sarah (Hacket) Currier; Tabitha d. at Boscawen, 16 Jul 1877.

iv MARY CHANDLER, b. 3 Sep 1786; d. at Concord, 27 Feb 1872; m. at Boscawen, 9 Aug 1804, JONATHAN EASTMAN, b. at Concord, 14 Nov 1781 son of Jonathan and Esther (Johnson) Eastman; Jonathan d. at Concord, 23 Mar 1867.

v SUSANNA FARNUM CHANDLER, b. 7 Dec 1788; d. at Boscawen, 6 Feb 1870; m. 8 Feb 1806, RICHARD GAGE, b. at Methuen, 11 Dec 1776 son of Thaddeus and Abigail (Merrill) Gage; Richard d. at Boscawen, 18 May 1855.

vi JUDITH HALL CHANDLER, b. 19 Mar 1793; d. at Boscawen, 2 Nov 1843; m. 16 Apr 1812, her fourth cousin, REUBEN JOHNSON, b. at Concord, 12 Jan 1792 son of Jonathan and Rhoda (Abbott) Johnson; Reuben d. at Boscawen, 16 Mar 1852. Reuben Johnson is a child in Family 572.

vii RHODA CARTER CHANDLER, b. 10 Jul 1799; d. at Brodhead, WI, about 1881; m. 29 Oct 1829, her first cousin, JOSEPHUS CHANDLER, b. at Fryeburg, ME, 20 Aug 1796 son of Joseph and Hannah L. (Farrington) Chandler; Josephus d. at Primrose, WI, 11 Feb 1859. Josephus first married SARAH COLBY, b. 22 Mar 1802 daughter of Joseph and Elizabeth (Evans) Colby; Sarah d. at Fryeburg, 9 Jul 1828. Josephus Chandler is a child in Family 1080.

675) JUDITH FARNUM (*Ephraim Farnum⁴, Mary Ingalls Farnum³, Sarah Russell Ingalls², Robert¹*), b. at Concord, NH, 13 Jun 1764 daughter of Ephraim and Judith (Hall) Farnum; d. at Gorham, ME, 21 Feb 1851; m. 3 Jun 1791, JEREMIAH CHANDLER, b. at Concord, 31 Mar 1763 son of John and Mary (Carter) Chandler; Jeremiah d. at Lovell, ME, 12 Feb 1828.

Jeremiah was a farmer in Boscawen and later relocated to Lovell, Maine. Jeremiah and Judith had just three children, one who died as a young infant.

i Infant b. and d. 1793

ii JOHN CARTER CHANDLER, b. at Concord, 28 Jul 1794; d. at Lovell, ME, 1866; m. MEHITABLE HAZELTINE, b. about 1795 daughter of Abraham and Polly (-) Hazeltine; Mehitable d. at Lovell, 8 Mar 1846.

iii MARY KIMBALL CHANDLER, b. at Concord, 10 Oct 1796; d. at Washington, DC, 6 Sep 1855; m. about 1818, her fourth cousin, PHILIP CARRIGAN JOHNSON, b. at Concord, 7 Mar 1795 son of Jonathan and Rhoda (Abbott) Johnson; Philip d. at Washington, 10 Aug 1859. Philip Carrigan Johnson was Secretary of State for Maine in 1840 and appointed by President Polk as Chief Clerk in the Bureau of Construction, Equipment, and Repair of the Navy Department.

676) SARAH FARNUM (*Ephraim Farnum⁴, Mary Ingalls Farnum³, Sarah Russell Ingalls², Robert¹*), b. at Concord, NH, 9 Aug 1767 daughter of Ephraim and Judith (Hall) Farnum; d. after 1843 when she was living at Canterbury; m. at Boscawen, 21 Nov 1786, NATHAN CARTER, b. at Boscawen, 6 Apr 1761 son of Winthrop and Susannah (Eastman) Carter; Nathan d. at Boscawen, 25 Sep 1840.

Nathan Carter kept a tavern in Boscawen. He served as a private during the Revolution, the town of Boscawen paying the expenses for his enlistment for two months of service in the company of Capt. Kimball.[1997]

On 29 August 1832, Nathan made application for a pension based on his service. He reported a first enlistment in August 1779 from Boscawen, that his company was in Portsmouth, and he was discharged in August of that year. In 1781, he had a second enlistment for a term of four months in the company of Capt. Head in the regiment of Col. Runnels. The official records showed the 1781 enlistment as a period from 11 September 1781 to 25 November 1781. Nathan was allowed a pension of $20 per annum. However, on 20 April 1843, Nathan's widow Sarah then living in Canterbury, made application for a widow's pension, but the claim was ultimately rejected due to Nathan's service not meeting the six-month requirement.[1998] One of those providing a statement in support of the Sarah's application was John Carter of Canterbury.

Sarah Farnum and Nathan Carter were parents of five children born at Boscawen.

i JUDITH CARTER, b. 5 Dec 1787; d. at Boscawen, 13 Jan 1871; m. at Boscawen, 27 Dec 1807, JOHN FRENCH, b. at Merrimack, NH, 27 May 1783 son of Nicholas and Rachel (Farmer) French; John d. at Boscawen, 11 Aug 1861.

ii MOSES CARTER, b. 6 Aug 1790; d. at Canterbury, NH, 30 May 1851. Moses did not marry.

[1997] Coffin, *History of Boscawen*, p 120, p 255, and p 483
[1998] U.S. Revolutionary War Rejected Pensions, Case R1754

iii   JOHN CARTER,[1999] b. 10 Dec 1797; d. at Canterbury, 12 Aug 1871; m. at Boscawen, 1 Feb 1824, LYDIA GILL, b. at Hopkinton, about 1800 daughter of Bradbury and Rebecca (Straw) Gill; Lydia d. at Canterbury, 2 Feb 1890.

iv   JEREMIAH CARTER, b. 20 Feb 1803; d. at Newburyport, MA, 19 Nov 1871; m. 1st at Newbury, MA, 26 Oct 1827, SARAH WOODMAN, b. at Newburyport, 6 Jun 1803 daughter of David and Sally (Farnum) Woodman; Sarah d. at Newburyport, 18 Aug 1838. Jeremiah m. 2nd at Newburyport, 17 Mar 1839, MARY NORTON (widow of Joseph Young), b. at Northwood, NH, 1802 daughter of Thomas and Elizabeth (-) Norton; Mary d. at Newburyport, 24 Nov 1875.

v   NATHAN CARTER, b. 4 Feb 1807; d. at Newburyport, 18 Feb 1875; m. at Newburyport, 16 Apr 1832, MARY ANN PEARSON, b. at Newburyport, 20 Apr 1809 daughter of Theodore and Sally (Coffin) Pearson; Mary d. at Newburyport, 17 Sep 1884.

677)   MOSES FARNUM (*Ephraim Farnum⁴, Mary Ingalls Farnum³, Sarah Russell Ingalls², Robert¹*), b. at Concord, NH, 20 Oct 1769 son of Ephraim and Judith (Hall) Farnum; d. at Concord, 6 Mar 1840; m. 1st 13 Jun 1792, RHODA CARTER, b. 17 Feb 1771 daughter of Ezra and Phebe (Whittemore) Carter; Rhoda d. Oct 1808. Moses m. 2nd 21 Dec 1809, Rhoda's sister, ESTHER CARTER, b. 21 Feb 1778; Esther d. at Concord, 30 May 1857.

    Moses resided in Concord and his wives Rhoda and Esther were members of the First Congregational Church of Concord, Rhoda from 1800 until her death in 1808 and Esther from 1810 until 1833.[2000] Moses performed civic duties such as surveyor of highways and hogreeve.[2001]

    Moses Farnum and Rhoda Carter were parents of three children born at Concord.

i   HANNAH CARTER FARNUM, b. 7 Sep 1793; d. after 1870 when she was living at Salisbury, NH; m. at Concord, 28 Jul 1815, JOHN ROGERS, b. at Billerica, 31 Jan 1790 son of John and Rhoda (Shed) Rogers;[2002] John d. at Salisbury, 22 Oct 1875.

ii   EMILY FARNUM, b. 15 Jul 1802; d. at Concord, 26 Aug 1888; m. at Concord, 23 Sep 1833, her second cousin, BENJAMIN FARNUM (*Ephraim Farnum⁵, Benjamin Farnum⁴, Mary Ingalls Farnum³, Sarah Russell Ingalls², Robert¹*), b. at Concord, 1 Jun 1804 son of Ephraim and Sarah (Brown) Farnum; Benjamin d. at Concord, 14 Jan 1892.

iii   SAMUEL FARNUM, b. 1805; d. at Concord, 3 Mar 1893. Samuel did not marry. At the probate of his estate, brother Moses H. Farnum and two nephews (Charles Farnum and Walter Lougee) declined administration and requested that Charles C. Rogers of Salisbury be named administrator.

    Moses Farnum and Esther Carter were parents of three children born at Concord.

i   MOSES HALL FARNUM, b. 3 Feb 1811; d. at Concord, 15 Dec 1908; m. 1st at Concord, 20 Jun 1844, JUDITH A. KILBURN, b. at Boscawen, 1815 daughter of Enoch and Betsey (Moore) Kilburn; Judith d. at Concord, 28 Feb 1868. Moses m. 2nd about 1870, ANN HALE (widow of Asa L. Peveare), b. at Franklin, NH, 9 Jan 1829 daughter of Isaac and Betsey (Pearson) Hale;[2003] Ann d. at Concord, 22 Dec 1902.

ii   LAVINA FARNUM, b. 22 May 1813; m. at Concord, 18 Jun 1834, ASA PARKER EASTMAN, b. at Chatham, NH, 8 Mar 1810 son of Asa and Molly (Kimball) Eastman; Asa d. at Chatham, 23 Jun 1869. Lavina was living in Chatham in 1870.

iii   JENNETT W. FARNUM, baptized 28 Apr 1816; m. at Concord, 28 Jul 1838, JAMES W. LOUGEE, b. at Loudon, NH, 1817 likely son of John and Lucy (Wells) Lougee.[2004] It is not clear what became of Jennett and James. There are records of three children who lived to adulthood, and in 1850 census records the two older children were living with other relatives. James may be the James William Lougee of New Hampshire who died in San Francisco in 1869. Known children are Barry H. (ca 1838-1901), Ellen (1838-1904), and Walter (1846-1918).

[1999] The death record of John Carter gives his father's name as Winthrop Carter, but that may be an error. Winthrop Carter would likely be his grandfather.

[2000] Manual of the First Congregational Church of Concord, 1888, p 38

[2001] Bouton, *The History of Concord*, p 317 and p 334

[2002] The names of John's parents are given as John Rogers and Rhoda Shed on his death record.

[2003] The names of Ann's parents are given as Isaac Hale and Betsey Pearson on her death record.

[2004] A daughter of Jannett and James, Barry H., was living with John and Lucy Lougee in 1860 in Somersworth.

678)   ESTHER FARNUM (*Ephraim Farnum⁴, Mary Ingalls Farnum³, Sarah Russell Ingalls², Robert¹*), b. at Concord, NH, 25 Oct 1772 daughter of Ephraim and Judith (Hall) Farnum; d. at Franklin, NH, 1 Oct 1854; m. 30 Nov 1790, EBENEZER EASTMAN, b. at Concord, 19 Oct 1765 son of Moses and Elizabeth (Kimball) Eastman; Ebenezer d. at Salisbury, NH, 16 Apr 1833. After Ebenezer's death, Esther married Mr. Lyford who has not been identified.

Esther and Ebenezer resided in Salisbury, New Hampshire where Ebenezer was a prominent citizen. He was involved in petitioning for the formation of a new town of Franklin to be taken from parts of Salisbury, Sanbornton, and Andover. In 1816, he donated land to Salisbury for "educational purposes" where the school was erected. He also donated the land used for the cemetery of the First Congregational Church. He also ran a tavern.[2005]

In her will written 13 September 1851, Esther Lyford made several donations to charitable religious organizations in the form of money to be held in trust. Other bequests were to nephew Carter Chandler, one hundred dollars; son Benjamin F. Eastman, ten dollars; and niece Adaline Eastman, two hundred. There were also bequests of ten dollars to each of the following grandchildren: Hanabel Merrill, Eben E. Merrill, Comela Dow, Mary Esther George, Charlotte Barritt, Sarah Ester Eastman, and Mary Ann Eastman. George W. Nesmith and Dudley Ladd were named executors. In a codicil written 7 December 1853, she rescinded one bequest to a religious organization. "I devised a certain legacy to the American Colonization Society,[2006] meaning for the aid and support of African Negroes at Liberia, or elsewhere, now, upon mature reflection I hereby revoke my will so far as it relates to said legacy."[2007]

Ebenezer and Esther were parents of four children.

i   JUDITH EASTMAN, b. at Concord, 4 Oct 1793; d. at Franklin, NH, 30 Apr 1848; m. at Salisbury, NH, 31 Dec 1815, CALEB MERRILL, b. at Warren, NH, 1 Jun 1795 son of Joseph and Sarah (Copp) Eastman; Caleb d. at Franklin, 27 Apr 1863. Caleb married second Adeline Eastman.

ii   CHARLOTTE EASTMAN, b. 1798; d. at Franklin, NH, 30 Jan 1826; m. 21 May 1823, DUDLEY LADD, b. at Concord, NH, 19 Aug 1789 son of Dudley and Bertha (Hutchins) Ladd; Dudley d. at Franklin, 20 Mar 1875. Dudley married second Amanda Palmer.

iii   BENJAMIN FRANKLIN EASTMAN, b. at Franklin, about 1802; d. at Arlington, MA, 3 May 1878; m. at Sanbornton, NH, 29 Dec 1836, MARY MORRISON, b. at Sanbornton, 16 Feb 1798 daughter of David and Sarah (Dustin) Morrison;[2008] Mary d. 18 Nov 1861.

iv   MARY A. EASTMAN, b. 8 Feb 1809; d. 12 Jun 1834; m. Dr. JOHN L. PERLEY, b. at Meredith, NH, 10 Jun 1805 son of Stephen and Mehitable (Ladd) Perley; John d. at Laconia, NH, 18 Sep 1888. John married second Dorothy Randlet.

679)   SUSANNAH FARNUM (*Ephraim Farnum⁴, Mary Ingalls Farnum³, Sarah Russell Ingalls², Robert¹*), b. at Concord, NH, 3 Jun 1781 daughter of Ephraim and Judith (Hall) Farnum; d. at Boscawen, 4 May 1843; m. 29 Jan 1803, MOSES COFFIN, b. at Boscawen, 22 Jul 1779 son of Peter and Rebecca (Haseltine) Coffin; Moses d. at Boscawen, 4 Sep 1854.

Susannah and Moses lived in Boscawen. Moses erected the house in which the family lived on Water Street in Boscawen. They were members of the Congregational church.[2009]

Daughter Judith did not marry and her will dated 21 December 1850 she made the following bequests: honored and beloved father Moses Coffin, my large bible; two brothers Peter Coffin and Farnum Coffin, five dollars each; brother Nehemiah Cogswell Coffin, twenty dollars; nephew George Henry Peach, five dollars; and to the American Board of Commissioners of Foreign Missions, five dollars. The remained of the estate is to be divided among her sisters Rebecca Sanborn, Lucy J. Allen, and Susannah C. Morrill. Enoch L. Morrill was named executor.[2010]

Susannah and Moses were parents of eight children born at Boscawen.

i   REBECCA COFFIN, b. 13 Mar 1804; d. at Webster, NH, 23 Nov 1870; m. at Boscawen, 30 Jun 1825, JOHN ABIDEN SANBORN, b. at Boscawen, 26 Jul 1799 son of Tristram and Abigail (Knight) Sanborn; John d. at Webster, 30 Aug 1887.

ii   LUCY JANE COFFIN, b. 9 Jul 1805; d. at Reading, MA, 1 Dec 1879; m. at Reading, 24 Sep 1837, SAMUEL R. ALLEN, b. at Gloucester, MA, 1810 son of Jeremiah and Lucy (Farmer) Allen; Samuel d. at Reading, 13 Nov 1853

[2005] Dearborn, The History of Salisbury, p 203, p 793

[2006] The American Colonization Society was an organization mainly concerned with reducing the number of free black persons living in the United States; it was vehemently opposed by abilitionists.

[2007] New Hampshire Wills and Probate, Merrimack County, Probate Records volume 25, pp 501-503

[2008] Runnels, *History of Sanbornton*, p 503

[2009] Coffin, *The History of Boscawen*, p 493

[2010] New Hampshire Wills and Probate, Merrimack County, Probate Records volume 25, p 305

iii   PETER COFFIN, b. 26 Mar 1808; d. at Boscawen, 27 Jan 1892; m.at Boscawen, 3 Oct 1833, EUNICE TOPPAN COUCH, b. at Boscawen, 4 Jul 1810 daughter of Joseph and Sarah (Pillsbury) Couch; Eunice d. (burial at Webster), 4 Dec 1888

iv   JUDITH HALL COFFIN, b. 7 Mar 1810; d. at Boscawen, 25 Jun 1852. Judith did not marry.

v   EPHRAIM FARNUM COFFIN, b. 16 Mar 1813; d. at Boscawen, 21 Sep 1856; m. at Canterbury, NH, 24 Nov 1842, JUDITH GERRISH, b. at Canterbury, 21 May 1824 daughter of Joseph and Sarah (Church) Gerrish; Judith d. at Boscawen, 24 May 1913.

vi   NEHEMIAH COGSWELL COFFIN, b. 24 Mar 1815; d. at Marblehead, OH, 9 Jan 1868; m. 5 Dec 1842, SUSAN JANE RUST, b. at Wolfeboro, NH, 5 Jan 1825 daughter of Thomas and Phebe (Clark) Rust; Susan d. at Marblehead, 5 Sep 1893. Rev. Nehemiah Coffin graduated from Dartmouth in 1836 and attended Andover Theological Seminary and Lane Theological Seminary.

vii   SUSANNAH C. COFFIN, b. 24 Nov 1818; d. at Franklin, NH, 15 Sep 1880; m. at Boscawen, 24 Nov 1842, ENOCH LUNT MORRILL, b. at Boscawen, 9 Oct 1820 son of Joseph and Lydia (Lunt) Morrill; Enoch d. at Boscawen, 21 Dec 1874.

viii   ESTHER EASTMAN COFFIN, b. 6 May 1821; d. at Boscawen, 28 Oct 1843; m. at Boscawen, 16 Apr 1840, HENRY GERRISH PEACH, b. at Boscawen, 5 Dec 1816 son of Thomas and Sukey (Gerrish) Peach; Henry d. at Lowell, IN, 1858. Henry married second Betsey C. Watson.

680)   MARY MERRILL (*Mary Farnum Merrill⁴, Mary Ingalls Farnum³, Sarah Russell Ingalls², Robert¹*), b. at Concord, 31 Dec 1763 daughter of Jonathan and Mary (Farnum) Merrill; d. about 1800;[2011] m. about 1785, WINSOR GOOLDEN,[2012] baptized at Newbury, MA, 12 Jul 1761 son of Winsor and Jane (Sampson) Goolden; Winsor d. at Madrid, NY, 6 Jan 1840. Winsor was second married to Ruby who survived him.

On 6 April 1818 while living in St. Lawrence County, New York, Windsor Golden may application for a pension based on his service in the Revolution. He enlisted from Beverly, Massachusetts in December 1780 in the 3rd regiment of the Massachusetts line commanded by Col. Hull and he served until his discharge at West Point in December 1783. In a statement given 6 June 1820, Winsor reported his family consisted of his wife who was in ill health and a son who was crippled from rickets. Winsor was granted a pension and his widow Ruby later received a pension. At the time she received a pension, Ruby was living in Vermont[2013]

Mary and Winsor were parents of four children likely all born at Charlotte, Vermont.

i   JONATHAN SAMPSON GOOLDEN, b. 1785; d. at Lisbon, NY, 1835; m. about 1810, CHARLOTTE LAWRENCE.

ii   MARY GOULDEN, b. 1788; d. at Madrid, NY, 13 May 1857; m. 1824, NEWELL FOOTE, b. at Charlotte, VT, 29 Sep 1784 son of Isaac and Anna (Hurlburt) Foote;[2014] Newell d. at Madrid, NY, 17 Apr 1871. Newell was first married to Clarissa Hill.

iii   THOMAS GOOLDEN, b. 1791; d. at Madrid, NY, 16 Apr 1817; m. at Cornwall, VT, 24 Feb 1824, ELINORA COOK, b. 1794; Elinora d. at Madrid, 15 Jun 1872.

iv   FARNUM GOOLDEN, b. 9 Aug 1794; d. at Hopkinton, NY, 27 Apr 1883; m. Mar 1835, OLIVIA FOOTE, b. at Charlotte, VT, 13 Oct 1814 daughter of Johnson and Cynthia (Sherman) Foote; Olivia d. at Hopkinton, 23 Oct 1887.

681)   JOHN MERRILL (*Mary Farnum Merrill⁴, Mary Ingalls Farnum³, Sarah Russell Ingalls², Robert¹*), b. at Concord, 9 Mar 1769 son of Jonathan and Mary (Farnum) Merrill; d. at Hill, NH, 13 May 1831; m. 12 Nov 1794, ELIZABETH DARLING, b. 27 Apr 1771 daughter of Benjamin and Hannah (Clark) Darling; Elizabeth d. at Hill, 8 Oct 1834.

John Merrill was a tanner and shoemaker. His tanyard was below Profile Falls in Bristol, New Hampshire.[2015]

John and Elizabeth's son John was something of an eccentric known as the "philosopher of the pond." He held the belief that the earth was open at the poles and that ships were able to enter through the poles and travel inside an earth that was essentially hollow.[2016]

[2011] This is based on the pension application file for Winsor Goolden in which his second wife Ruby reports she and Winsor were married in 1801.
[2012] The spelling of the name is seen as Goolden, Golden, or Goulden
[2013] U. S. Revolutionary War Pension and Bounty-Land Warrant Application Files, Case W1167
[2014] Foote, *Foote Family*, volume 1, p 140
[2015] Merrill, *A Merrill Memorial*, part 2, p 424
[2016] "Searching for the North Pole", Steuben Republican (Angola, Indiana), 28 Jun 1871, Wed, p 1

Daughter Mary married later in life and did not have children. In her will dated 15 October 1872, Mary M. Chadwick bequeathed one dollar each to brother Clark Merrill, brother John Merrill, and Anna Maria Merrill daughter of Morris Merrill deceased. The remainder of the estate was bequeathed to Mrs. Elizabeth C. Merrill wife of brother Clark Merrill.[2017]

John Merrill and Betsey Darling were parents of six children whose births are recorded at Hill, New Hampshire (New Chester).

i   JONATHAN MERRILL, b. at Hill, NH, 5 Dec 1795; d. at Bristol, NH, 19 Feb 1868; m. 11 Nov 1824, his first cousin, ANNA S. MERRILL, b. 15 Apr 1804 daughter of Stephen and Ruth (Darling) Merrill; Anna d. at Bristol, 20 Nov 1862.

ii   SUSAN MERRILL, b. at Hill, 24 Dec 1797; d. at Bristol, 25 Mar 1869. Susan did not marry. In her will, Susan left her entire estate to her sister Mary M. Chadwick.[2018]

iii   MARY MERRILL, b. at Hill, 23 Jan 1800; d. at Bristol, 19 Jan 1874; m. 20 Apr 1851, as his third wife, JOSEPH CHADWICK, b. at Boscawen, 19 Jul 1787 son of Edmund and Susanna (Atkinson) Chadwick; Joseph d. at Boscawen, 16 Jan 1868. Joseph was first married to Judith Morrill and second married to Eunice Bliss.

iv   JOHN MERRILL, b. at Hill, 10 Apr 1802; d. at Pardeeville, WI, 20 Sep 1892; m. at Andover, NH, 13 Sep 1824, RHODA P. CILLEY, b. at Andover, NH, 28 Jul 1803 daughter of Samuel and Elizabeth (Eastman) Cilley;[2019] Rhoda d. at Pardeeville, 10 Jan 1885.

v   CLARK MERRILL, b. at Hill, 16 Dec 1804; d. at Hill, 2 Apr 1887; m. at Bristol, 26 Mar 1827, ELIZABETH C. COVELL, b. 1808; Elizabeth d. at Alexandria, NH, 26 Mar 1893.

vi   MOSES MERRILL, b. at Hill, 13 Apr 1807; d. at Bristol, 4 Mar 1868; m. 16 Apr 1838, SALLY BENNETT, b. at New Hampton, NH, 23 Apr 1811 daughter of William and Olive (Merrick) Bennett; Sally d. at Bristol, 15 Dec 1881. In his will, Moses left his entire estate to his wife Sally.

682)   JONATHAN MERRILL (*Mary Farnum Merrill⁴, Mary Ingalls Farnum³, Sarah Russell Ingalls², Robert¹*), b. at Concord, 6 Sep 1772 son of Jonathan and Mary (Farnum) Merrill; d. at Hill, NH, 20 Jan 1820; m. MARY BARNARD, b. at Warner, 20 Dec 1779 daughter of Ezekiel Barnard; Mary d. at Bristol, NH, 1 Oct 1875. Mary married second Ezekiel Moore.

Jonathan lived on his father's farm near Profile Falls in Bristol, New Hampshire.[2020] In his will written 16 October 1819 (approved 16 March 1820), Jonathan Merrill bequeathed to beloved wife Polly one-half of the real and personal estate to be hers forever and at her disposal as long as she lives. At Polly's decease, this is to go to daughter Rosanna. The remaining half of the estate goes to daughter Rosanna Merrill at her marriage or at eighteen years. Moses Merrill and Ephraim Merrill were appointed as guardians to Rosanna.[2021]

Jonathan and Polly were parents of two children born at Bristol.

i   ROSANNA MERRILL, b. at Bristol, 6 Dec 1812; d. at Campton, NH, 29 Jan 1834; m. at Plymouth, NH, 13 Nov 1832, ELEAZER WOOSTER, likely to Eleazer b. 2 Oct 1811 (on gravestone); Eleazer d. at Poestenkill, NY, 11 Jan 1879. Rosanna and Eleazer had one son, George Merrill Wooster.

ii   CHAUNCEY MERRILL, b. 1816; d. 11 May 1818.

683)   MOSES MERRILL (*Mary Farnum Merrill⁴, Mary Ingalls Farnum³, Sarah Russell Ingalls², Robert¹*), b. at Concord, 28 Dec 1774 son of Jonathan and Mary (Farnum) Merrill; d. at Alexandria, NH, 29 Oct 1841; m. 1ˢᵗ Mar 1810, MIRIAM BARNARD, b. about 1783 daughter of Ezekiel Barnard; Miriam d. at Alexandria, 26 Nov 1815. Moses m. 2ⁿᵈ about 1816, SARAH WORTHING (widow of Sherburn Sanborn), b. at Bridgewater, NH, 11 Mar 1785 daughter of Samuel and Hannah (Ingalls) Worthing; Sarah d. 1863.

Moses was a farmer in Alexandria, New Hampshire. Moses Merrill and Miriam Barnard were parents of one child.

i   HARUM MERRILL, b. at Alexandria, NH, 3 Feb 1811; d. at Boston, MA, 29 Oct 1890; m. at Boston, 17 Oct 1835, DIANA FRENCH, b. at Concord, MA, 18 Sep 1813 daughter of Nathaniel and Susanna (Brown) French; Diana d. at Chicago, 31 May 1891. Harum was a ticket agent for the Milwaukee and Mississippi Railroad and the family lived primarily in Milwaukee.[2022]

[2017] New Hampshire Wills and Probate, Merrimack County, volume 55, p 57

[2018] New Hampshire Wills and Probate Records, Grafton County, wills volume 47, p 275

[2019] Eastman, *History of the Town of Andover, New Hampshire*, volume II, p 82

[2020] Merrill, *A Merrill Memorial*, part II, p 424

[2021] New Hampshire Wills and Probate, Grafton County, Estate of Jonathan Merrill, 16 March 1820

[2022] Musgrove, *History of the Town of Bristol*, vol II, p 306

Moses Merrill and Sarah Worthing were parents of five children born at Alexandria, New Hampshire.

i   SHERBURN SANBORN MERRILL, b. 28 Jul 1818; d. at Milwaukee, WI, 8 Feb 1885; m. 1st 14 Nov 1847, SARAH DIX KIDDER, b. at Andover, MA, 1 Jul 1825 daughter of Francis and Nancy (Hartwell) Kidder; Sarah d. at Milwaukee, 26 Mar 1855. Sherburn m. 2nd 6 May 1858, MARY ELLEN FREEMAN, b. at Knox, NY, 31 Mar 1831 daughter of John Salter and Lois (Denison) Freeman; Mary d. at Milwaukee, 12 Dec 1927.

ii   MARIAM MERRILL, b. 9 Oct 1820; d. 17 Apr 1822.

iii NARCISSA R. MERRILL, b. 8 Aug 1822; d. at Newton, MA, 3 Jan 1900; m. at Boston, 28 Mar 1852, GALUTIA HEATH, b. at Franklin, NH, Apr 1818 son of Joshua and Mary (Williams) Heath; Galutia d. at Newton, 20 Jul 1900.

iv   CHASTINA MERRILL, b. 18 Jun 1827; d. at Newton, MA, 28 May 1900; m. about 1848, BRADLEY WALKER, b. at Hebron, NH, 19 Jun 1821 son of Daniel Carter and Hannah (Hazelton) Walker; Bradley d. at Boston, 1857 (probate 1857).

v   MOSES WORTHING MERRILL, b. 6 Jan 1829; d. at Newton, MA, 23 Dec 1919; m. at Boston, 12 Nov 1854, ANN ELIZABETH BLACKMORE, b. at Philadelphia, 28 Nov 1832 daughter of William and Letitia (Buckler) Blackmore; Ann d. at Newton, 19 Oct 1904.

684) STEPHEN MERRILL (*Mary Farnum Merrill⁴, Mary Ingalls Farnum³, Sarah Russell Ingalls², Robert¹*), b. likely at Hill, NH, about 1776 son of Jonathan and Mary (Farnum) Merrill; d. at Bristol, NH, 5 Jan 1860; m. 3 Jun 1803, RUTH DARLING, b. 4 Jul 1774 daughter of Benjamin and Hannah (Clark) Darling; Ruth d. 29 Dec 1835.
      Stephen Merrill was a tanner, currier, and shoemaker.[2023] Stephen and Ruth were parents of six children.

i   ANNA S. MERRILL, b. 15 Apr 1804; d. at Bristol, 20 Nov 1862; m. 11 Nov 1824, her first cousin, JONATHAN MERRILL, b. at Hill, NH, 5 Dec 1795 son of John and Betsey (Darling) Merrill; Jonathan d. at Bristol, 19 Feb 1868.

ii   FARNHAM MERRILL, b. at Sanbornton, 25 Mar 1806; d. at Lowell, MA, 27 Mar 1871; m. 1st at Lowell, 9 Oct 1836, ELIZABETH W. REMINGTON, b. in NH, about 1814 daughter of Henry and Elizabeth W. (-) Remington; Elizabeth d. at Lowell, 29 Jun 1862. Farnham m. 2nd at Lowell, 28 Feb 1866, MARY R. HULL (widow of Henry C. Currier), b. at Cambridge, VT, 1826 daughter of Amos and Betsey (Cook) Hull; Mary d. after 1870.

iii ABIGAIL MERRILL, b. at Sanbornton, 29 Aug 1811; d. at Tilton, NH, 17 Jan 1900; m. at Boston, 3 Nov 1842, SAMUEL CONDON, b. at Boston, 15 Dec 1795 son of Philip and Lucretia (Johnson) Condon; Samuel d. at Boston, 24 May 1881.

iv   MARY ANN MERRILL, b. at Sanbornton, 8 Jul 1814; d. at Boston, 30 Mar 1871. Mary did not marry.

v   STEPHEN MERRILL, b. at Sanbornton, 20 Feb 1817; d. at Newton, MA, 28 Mar 1900; m. at Cambridge, 29 Aug 1857, JOSEPHINE SHERLOCK, b. at Bucksport, ME, 1816 and baptized at Lynn, MA, 20 Sep 1818 daughter of John and Eunice (Marston) Sherlock; Josephine d. at Lynn, 13 Mar 1904.

vi   JONATHAN MERRILL, b. 1 Jan 1820; d. 30 Sep 1826.

685) SARAH MERRILL (*Mary Farnum Merrill⁴, Mary Ingalls Farnum³, Sarah Russell Ingalls², Robert¹*), b. at Hill, 14 Apr 1778 daughter of Jonathan and Mary (Farnum) Merrill; d. at Sutton, OH, 1831; m. at Hebron, NH, 7 Nov 1803, WYMAN HARDY, b. at Bow, NH, 4 Oct 1777 son of Thomas and Abigail (-) Hardy; Wyman d. at Sutton, after 1820 and before 1829.
      Sarah and Wyman started their family in Hebron, New Hampshire, were then in Windsor, Vermont where four children were born before making the move to Ohio where they settled in Sutton.[2024] The family made the trip west about 1813, part of the journey by raft down the Allegany and Ohio Rivers. The family rented a farm near Marietta for five years.[2025]
      Sarah and Wyman were parents of eight children.

i   POLLY HARDY, b. at Hebron, NH, 24 Aug 1804

ii   FARNUM HARDY, b. at Hebron, 24 Dec 1805

2023 Merrill, *A Merrill Memorial*, p 426
2024 Larkin, *The Pioneer History of Meigs County*, p 20
2025 Field, *Worthies and Worker*, p 282, biographical information on Otis Hardy

iii   THIRZA HARDY, b. at Hebron, 30 Apr 1807

iv   MERRILL C. HARDY, b. at Windsor, about 1808; d. at New Albany, IN, Jan 1877; m. at Clermont County, OH, 29 Oct 1829, ELIZA JENNINGS, b. in OH, about 1812; Eliza d. after 1887 when she was living at Louisville, KY.

v   RUSSELL HARDY, b. at Windsor, about 1808; d. at Joliet, IL, 23 Jun 1894; m. 1st at Clermont County, 13 Jan 1838, ELIZABETH SMITH, b. in VT, about 1816; d. about 1853. Russell m. 2nd, at Will County, IL, 9 Nov 1854, ELIZABETH SPAULDING (widow of Elisha Jucket), b. 1827; Elizabeth d. at Joliet, IL, 28 Dec 1895.

vi   OTIS HARDY, b. at Windsor, 23 Sep 1810; d. at Joliet, IL, 7 Nov 1889; m. at Will County, IL, 14 Oct 1838, ANGELIA HOPKINS, b. at Swanton, VT, 13 Oct 1811 daughter of Heman and Hannah (Robinson) Hopkins; Angelia d. at Joliet, 4 May 1897.

vii   ELIZA HARDY, b. perhaps in OH, about 1815

viii   EMILY HARDY, b. in OH, 1817; d. at Albany, OH, 13 Jan 1881; m. at Meigs County, OH, 31 Mar 1836, JOSEPHUS PETTIBONE BOSWORTH, b. at West Haven, VT, 21 Jan 1815 son of Hezekiah and Huldah (Pierce) Bosworth; Josephus d. at Salem, OH, 22 Feb 1893.

686)   EPHRAIM MERRILL (*Mary Farnum Merrill⁴, Mary Ingalls Farnum³, Sarah Russell Ingalls², Robert¹*), b. at Hill, 24 Nov 1779 son of Jonathan and Mary (Farnum) Merrill; d. at Bridgewater, NH, 15 Oct 1844; m. Apr 1808, SALLY DREW, b. at Bridgewater, NH, 28 Sep 1791 daughter of Samuel and Elizabeth (Webber) Drew; Sally d. 21 Sep 1885.
    Ephraim farmed and did work as a tanner.[2026] The family resided in Bristol where their ten children were born.

i   RUFUS MERRILL, b. 27 Apr 1809; d. at Lowell, 16 Jan 1850; m. at Lowell, 4 Jul 1839, BETSEY JANE BARTLETT who has not been identified.

ii   CALVIN CLARK MERRILL, b. 24 Jun 1814; d. at Cambridge, MA, 3 Dec 1861; m. Oct 1845, ELIZA B. PARKER, b. at Dedham, 1821 daughter of Abijah and Sally (Kilburn) Parker; Eliza d. at Dedham, 21 Apr 1886. Eliza married second Walter Colburn on 15 Nov 1868.

iii   ELIZA WEBBER MERRILL, b. 22 Jun 1816; d. at Lawrence, 2 Dec 1896; m. 10 Apr 1838, DUDLEY LEAVITT STOKES, b. at Northwood, NH, 13 Mar 1812 son of Jeremiah and Polly (Durgin) Leavitt; Dudley d. at Haverhill, MA, 15 Mar 1863.

iv   DAVID MASON MERRILL, b. 21 Nov 1819; d. at Ashland, NH, 20 May 1901; m. 17 Dec 1845, CLARISSA CASS, b. at Bridgewater, NH, 16 Jan 1827 daughter of John and Semina (Flagg) Cass; Clarissa d. at Bristol, 4 Aug 1870.

v   SARAH HARDY MERRILL, b. 10 Jan 1821; d. at Lawrence, MA, 28 Jul 1874; m. at Holliston, MA, 12 Feb 1843, LEVI J. GILBERT, b. at Leeds, ME, 5 Sep 1817 son of Hersey and Mehitable (Morse) Gilbert; Levi d. at Lawrence, 11 Sep 1879.

vi   JUDITH CROSS MERRILL, b. 11 Sep 1823; d. at Leeds, ME, 24 May 1864; m. Mar 1848, LEVI BATES OWEN, b. at Leeds, 22 Sep 1826 son of Thomas and Betsy (Bates) Owen; Levi d. after 1900 when he was living at Monmouth, ME. Levi married second Amanda Turner Curtis in 1865 and married third Catherine in 1868.

vii   MARY LUCIA MERRILL, b. 21 Jul 1825; d. at Leeds, ME, 24 Apr 1892; m. Apr 1843, TIMOTHY FOSTER, b. at Leeds, 28 Dec 1821 son of John and Priscilla (Gilbert) Foster; Timothy d. at Winthrop, ME, 16 Nov 1902.

viii   ALMIRA E. MERRILL, b. 27 Nov 1827; d. at Otisfield, ME, 28 Jan 1859; m. at Lawrence, MA, 25 Dec 1851, SAMUEL EDGERLY, b. at Woodstock, ME, 1823 son of Josiah and Jane (-) Edgerly.

ix   JOHN FARNHAM MERRILL, b. 19 Dec 1829; d. Dec 1844.

x   STEPHEN M. MERRILL, b. 5 Sep 1831; d. Sep 1836.

687)   MARY FARNUM (*Benjamin Farnum⁴, Mary Ingalls Farnum³, Sarah Russell Ingalls², Robert¹*), b. at Concord, 26 Aug 1764 daughter of Benjamin and Anna (Merrill) Farnum; d. at Alfred, ME, 23 Nov 1816; m. about 1785, ABIEL HALL, b. at Rumford, NH, 31 May 1761 son of Ebenezer and Dorcas (Abbott) Hall; Abiel d. at Alfred, Oct 1829. Abiel Hall married second Anna Francis.
    Dr. Abiel Hall was the first resident physician of Sanford, Maine. He settled in what is now Alfred, Maine in 1780. He served in Capt. Ebenezer Webster's company during the Revolution.[2027]

[2026] Merrill, *A Merrill Memorial*, p 427
[2027] Emery, *The History of Sanford, Maine*, pp 464-465

In his will written 2 October 1829 (presented and approved 2 November 1829), Abiel Hall bequeaths to beloved wife Anna the use of one-third of the real estate while she is a widow and use of one-half of the dwelling house in common with son Porter. Son Abiel Hall, Jr. receives as many acres of land on the west side of the road adjoining the land of Morgan Lewis that he wills to son David. Abiel also receives the land on which his office stands and his father's part of the office. Son David receives a tract of land on the northern part of the homestead. David also receives as much of the store as he hereinafter gives to his son Porter and son-in-law Nathan D. Appleton. Son Ivory receives all the farm he bought of Ebenezer Hall and is the farm on which Ivory resides. Letitia Hall widow of his late son John Hall receives use during her lifetime of all the farm that John had occupied. Son Porter receives the residue of the land. Nathan D. Appleton receives the two rooms in the store that he now occupies, and he and wife Julia receive one acre of land on the east side of road that adjoins Nathan's land. Rufus Sayward and Mary his wife receive one acre of land. The remaining part of the homestead on the east side of the road he gives to his wife and children which the executor is authorized to distribute. Daughters Mary Sayward and Julia Appleton receive the rest of the beds and beddings except what belongs to his wife. Son Abiel Hall is named sole executor. Real estate was valued at $6,725, personal estate at $1,104.83, and cash and notes on hand were $1,693.06. The division of the real estate was made 21 July 1831.[2028]

There are records for seven children of Abiel and Mary born at Alfred, Maine.[2029]

i   ABIEL HALL, b. 16 Sep 1787; d. at Alfred, 11 Dec 1869; m. 16 Nov 1815, ELIZABETH FROST, b. at Sanford, 1795 daughter of William and Betsey (Goodwin) Frost; Elizabeth d. at Alfred, 24 Mar 1863.

ii   JOHN HALL, b. about 1789; d. before 1850 at Alfred; m. 1817, LETITIA LITTLEFIELD, b. 1796 daughter of Aaron and Lydia (Taylor) Littlefield; Letitia d. after 1850 when she was living at Alfred.

iii   DAVID HALL, b. 8 Oct 1791; d. at Portland, ME, 12 Mar 1863; m. 10 Dec 1818, NANCY MERRILL CONANT, b. at Alfred, 27 Dec 1796 daughter of John and Lydia (Farnum) Conant; Nancy d. at Portland, Nov 1865.

iv   IVORY HALL, b. 22 Oct 1796; d. at Alfred, 5 Apr 1873; m. 12 Jun 1820, CHARLOTTE APPLETON KENT, b. at Scituate, MA, 12 Jan 1800 daughter of Samuel and Hannah (Brooks) Kent; Charlotte d. at Alfred, 3 Jan 1885.

v   MARY HALL, b. 21 May 1798; d. at Alfred, 16 Nov 1872; m. 2 Feb 1819, RUFUS SAYWARD, b. 19 May 1789 son of John and Elizabeth (Trafton) Sayward; Rufus d. at Alfred, 11 Apr 1839.

vi   JULIA HALL, b. 13 Jan 1804; d. at Portland, ME, 17 Jul 1880; m. 1826, NATHAN DANE APPLETON, b. at Ipswich, MA, 20 May 1794 son of Samuel and Mary (White) Appleton; Nathan d. at Alfred, 12 Nov 1861.

vii   PORTER HALL, b. 12 Mar 1807; d. at Kennebunk, ME, 18 Jun 1853; m. 1st about 1830, MARY DANE, b. at Kennebunk, 14 Nov 1810 daughter of Joseph and Mary (Clark) Dane; Mary d. at Kennebunk, 14 Apr 1843. Porter m. 2nd about 1844, MARIA PERKINS, b. 18 Jul 1825 (on cemetery record); Maria d. at Kennebunk, Dec 1894. After Porter's death, Maria kept a boarding house in Kennebunk.

688)   JOHN FARNUM (*Benjamin Farnum4, Mary Ingalls Farnum3, Sarah Russell Ingalls2, Robert1*), b. at Concord, 2 Jan 1766 son of Benjamin and Anna (Merrill) Farnum; m. 1st about 1790, SARAH THOMPSON; Sarah d. about 1812. John m. 2nd at Warren, 3 Sep 1813,[2030] POLLY STONE (widow of John Jones), b. about 1776 likely the daughter of Uriah and Hephzibah (Hadley) Stone.

Little is known of this family. John was the father of perhaps nine children. He had two marriages, and it is possible there was a third wife between the marriage to Sarah Thompson and Polly Stone, but that is not clear. What is given here is speculative based on available information from few records and the two Farnum genealogies.[2031]

In 1810, John Farnam was head of household in Warren, New Hampshire with a household of ten persons: one male 26 to 44; one female 26 to 44; one male under 10; one male 10 to 15; two males 16 to 25; three females under 10; and one female 10 to 15.[2032]

John had perhaps eight children with his first wife Sarah Thompson.

i   ROSWELL FARNUM, b. at Plymouth, NH, Oct 1792; d. at Bradford, VT, 20 Dec 1860; m. 1st 14 Sep 1817, RUTH BIXBY, b. at Piermont, 20 Oct 1797 daughter of David and Nancy (Pecker) Bixby; Ruth d. 27 Mar 1819. Roswell m. 2nd 29 Apr 1821, Ruth's sister, NANCY BIXBY, b. at Piermont, NH, 1 May 1795; Nancy d. at Bradford, 30 Jan 1860.

ii   JOHN FARNUM, b. 1794; d. 9 Oct 1840; m. about 1816, MIRIAM B. KIMBALL, b. about 1797 daughter of Isaac and Dorcas (Hubbard) Kimball.

[2028] Maine, York County Probate Estate Files, Estate of Abiel Hall, Case 8099
[2029] There may be an eighth child, a first son Ivory, who was born and died in 1785.
[2030] New Hampshire, Marriage and Divorce Records, 1659-1947
[2031] Farnham, The New England Descendants of Ralph Farnum, pp 488-489; Farnham, *Genealogy of the Farnham Family*, p 18
[2032] Year: 1810; Census Place: Warren, Grafton, New Hampshire; Roll: 24; Page: 481; Image: 00327; Family History Library Film: 0218685

iii   BETSEY FARNUM, b. 1796; m. at Warren, NH, 30 Sep 1813, SAMUEL FLANDERS

iv   CORNELIA FARNUM, b. 1799; Cornelia did not marry.

v   RUFUS G. FARNUM, b. at Plymouth, NH, 1801; m. 1st at Boston, 29 Mar 1827, LYDIA N. DAVIS, b. at
          Hampstead, NH, 1806; Lydia d. at Lowell, 19 Mar 1849. Rufus m. 2nd 11 Dec 1849, ELIZABETH F. FRENCH, b.
          at Salisbury, NH, 1815.

vi   MARY H. FARNUM, b. 1803; Mary did not marry.

vii   THOMPSON FARNUM, b. 1805; Thompson did not marry.

viii   ABIGAIL FARNUM, b. 1807

          John Farnum and Polly Stone were parents of one child.

i   GEORGE FARNUM, b. 1813; reported as having a widow and son who lived in Charlestown, VT in 1880.[2033]

689)   BENJAMIN FARNUM (*Benjamin Farnum⁴, Mary Ingalls Farnum³, Sarah Russell Ingalls², Robert¹*), b. at Concord, 10
Sep 1768 son of Benjamin and Anna (Merrill) Farnum; d. at Rumford, ME, 1850 (probate 26 Nov 1850); m. at Concord, 3 Jun
1790, SARAH GRAHAM, b. at Concord, 18 Feb 1770 daughter of George and Azubah (-) Graham' Sarah was living in 1852.
          Benjamin was a farmer in Rumford, Maine. The Farnum property was on the south side of the river where his father
owned 400 acres. Benjamin and Sarah were members of the Congregational church where their children were baptized.[2034]
          In his will written 17 April 1843 (proved 26 November 1850), Benjamin Farnum bequeathed to son Merrill all the
farming tools. Granddaughter Alvina Virgin daughter of Aaron and Polly Virgin receives two cows and all the household
furniture. Daughter Polly Virgin receives two silver spoons marked B.F. Grandson Alvin B. Farnum receives all the wearing
apparel. Daughters Mahala Dublin (?) wife of M. Dublin and Sally Virgin wife of Ebenezer Virgin each receives one dollar.
Azuba Poor receives all his wife's wearing apparel after the decease of his beloved wife. Alvin B. Farnum one-half of lot twelve
in the second division. Grandson Manly Farnum receives a horse wagon. The residue of the estate goes to Merrill Farnum and
friend Peter Virgin is named executor. At the time of probate, Peter Virgin was unable to fulfill duties of executor and Lyman
Rawson was named administrator. On 27 May 1851, the court issued an order for Merrill Farnum to appear and give statement
under oath as Lyman Rawson alleged that Merrill Farnum had concealed, embezzled, of conveyed away certain personal
property belonging to the estate. In August 1852, widow Sarah requested additional allowance from the personal estate for her
needs. At the time of the estate inventory, the only real estate left in Benjamin's name was the one-half lot that was willed to
grandson Alvin valued at $45. Personal estate was $226.12.[2035]
          Benjamin and Sarah were parents of nine children born at Rumford, Maine.

i   POLLY FARNUM, b. 25 Aug 1791; d. at Rumford, 31 Oct 1862; m. at Rumford, 10 Feb 1813, AARON VIRGIN, b.
          at Concord, NH, 28 Apr 1787 son of Jonathan and Sarah (Austin) Virgin; Aaron d. at Rumford, 29 Dec 1869.

ii   NANCY FARNUM, b. 3 Jan 1793; d. 25 Aug 1800.

iii   MERRILL FARNUM, b. 29 Sep 1794; d. at Rumford, 14 Sep 1871; m. 1st at Concord, 1 Jan 1818, SARAH
          VIRGIN, b. 1796; Sarah d. at Rumford, 31 May 1824. Merrill m. 2nd 26 Dec 1824, LOUISA HOWE, b. at Rumford,
          19 Dec 1805 daughter of Phineas and Dorcas (Abbott) Howe; Louisa d. at Rumford, 21 Aug 1862. Merrill m. 3rd 2
          Jan 1863, SALLY WHITE BUNKER (widow of Daniel G. Taylor and George Gale), b. 13 Jun 1795 daughter of
          John and Sarah (Elliot) Bunker; Sally d. 8 Nov 1882. Merrill had first intended to marry Sally White Bunker in
          1815, but the marriage was called off due to parental objections.[2036]

iv   SALLY FARNUM, b. 3 Apr 1796; d. 5 Aug 1800.

v   AZUBAH FARNUM, b. 17 Nov 1797; d. at Andover, ME, 1873; m. at Rumford, 5 Mar 1817, EDWARD LISTER
          POOR, b. 10 Sep 1795 son of Ebenezer and Betsy (Stevens) Poor; Edward d. at Andover, 1870.

vi   HANNAH FARNUM, b. 22 Aug 1799; d. 12 Aug 1800.

vii   SALLY FARNUM, b. 3 Jun 1801; d. after 1870; m. at Rumford, 16 Nov 1820, EBENEZER "EBEN" VIRGIN, b.
          1793 son of Daniel and Mary (Wheeler) Virgin; Eben d. at Rumford, 26 Mar 1876.

[2033] Farnham, *The New England Descendants of Ralph Farnum*, p 489
[2034] Lapham, *History of Rumford, Oxford County, Maine*, p 51, p 52, p 135
[2035] Maine Wills and Probate, Oxford County, Estate Files, Drawer F41, Estate of Benjamin Farnum
[2036] Moran, *Bunker Genealogy: Descendants of James Bunker*, p 55

viii   MAHALA FARNUM, b. 27 Mar 1803; m. at Rumford, 26 Mar 1828, DANIEL THOMPSON of Westbrook, ME. Mahala appears to have a second marriage to Mr. Dublin (or Devlin) as named in her father's will, but the identity of her second husband has not been found.

ix   ABIEL FARNUM, b. 7 Jan 1808; d. at Rumford, 12 Jun 1836; m. 4 Feb 1830, JENNET BURNHAM, b. 3 Nov 1810 daughter of Enoch and Judith (Virgin) Wardwell; Jennet d. at Rumford, 12 Jun 1886. Jennet married second Jeremiah Wardwell (1810-1887).

690)   EPHRAIM FARNUM (*Benjamin Farnum⁴, Mary Ingalls Farnum³, Sarah Russell Ingalls², Robert¹*), b. at Concord, 5 Apr 1770 son of Benjamin and Anna (Merrill) Farnum; d. at Concord, 12 Feb 1836; m. about 1794, SARAH BROWN, b. 1774; Sarah d. at Concord, 24 Jul 1851.

     Ephraim and Sarah resided in Concord where they were members of the First Congregational Church.[2037]

     In his will written 20 January 1836 (proved fourth Tuesday of March 1836), Ephraim Farnum bequeathed to beloved wife Sarah one-third of the homestead farm and all other real estate in Concord for her use while she is a widow. Sarah also receives the household furniture and one-third of the personal estate. In addition to what she has received, daughter Nancy receives $800, bed and bedding, and privilege of living in the house while she is unmarried. He bequeaths to son Joseph one-half of the farm on which he (Joseph) now lives in Warren provided he pays $400 to son Luther. He places $700 in trust of Samuel Fletcher of Concord to be used for the benefit of daughter Susan Moore wife of Henry E. Moore and her children. Fletcher also receives the household furniture in trust for the use of Susan, and if in the future Susan is in need of a good and comfortable home, his executor is to provide this for Susan in Ephraim's dwelling house. Son Luther receives clothing and expenses until he graduates from college and a further payment of $500 in five years, in addition to the $400 previously mentioned. Niece Mary Farnum daughter of his brother John Farnum receives fifty dollars. The remained to the estate goes to son Benjamin who is named executor.[2038]

     Ephraim and Sarah were parents of nine children born at Concord.

i   NANCY FARNUM, b. 9 Jan 1795; d. at Concord, 20 Mar 1871. Nancy did not marry. In her will written 3 May 1857 (proved May 1871), Nancy left one hundred dollars to four siblings: sister Mrs. Susan D. Moore and brothers Joseph, Benjamin, and Luther. The residue was left to the American Sunday School Union. But in a codicil written 30 January 1871, she revoked the clause related to the residue of the estate and left the residue of the estate to her niece Mrs. S. Francis M. Fellows and to her nephews, the sons of her brother Benjamin, who were Charles Henry, Cyrus Rogers, Harris Calvin, and George Edwin Farnham.[2039]

ii   JOSEPH BROWN FARNUM, b. 15 Apr 1797; d. at Warren, NH, 1887 (probate 8 Nov 1887); m. at Warren, 31 Jan 1828, BETSEY MERRILL, b. at Warren, 9 Jun 1794 daughter of Abel and Tamar (Kimball) Merrill; Betsey d. at Warren, 11 Oct 1873.

iii   SUSAN D. FARNUM, b. 16 Nov 1801; d. at Manchester, NH, 6 Jun 1880; m. at Concord, 1 Nov 1825, HENRY EATON MOORE, b. at Andover, NH, 31 Jul 1803 son of Jacob Bailey and Molly (Eaton) Moore; Henry d. at Cambridge, 25 Oct 1841. Henry Eaton Moore established and edited the *Grafton Journal* in Plymouth, NH from 1824 to 1826. He taught music in Concord, NH and Cambridge, MA and, was a music composer, and published a weekly music journal.[2040]

iv   BENJAMIN FARNUM, b. 1 Jun 1804; d. at Concord, 14 Jan 1892; m. at Concord, 23 Sep 1833, his second cousin, EMILY FARNUM (*Moses Farnum⁵, Ephraim Farnum⁴, Mary Ingalls Farnum³, Sarah Russell Ingalls², Robert¹*), b. at Concord, 15 Jul 1802 daughter of Moses and Rhoda (Carter) Farnum; Emily d. at Concord, 26 Aug 1888.

v   LYDIA FARNUM, b. 23 Jun 1806; d. at Concord, 25 Apr 1834.

vi   LUTHER FARNUM, b. 1809; d. Jun 1813.

vii   HARRIET FARNUM, b. 1811; d. 1815.

viii   GEORGE FARNUM, b. unknown; d. at Concord, 1812.

ix   LUTHER FARNHAM, b. 1816; d. at Boston, 15 Mar 1897; m. at Northfield, MA, 23 Jun 1845, EUGENIA FAY (widow of Francis Alexander), b. at Winchester, NH, about 1817 daughter of Levi and Lucretia C. (Scott) Fay; Eugenia d. at West Springfield, MA, 22 May 1892. Luther was a clergyman.

[2037] First Congregational Church, Manual of the First Congregational Church, Concord, N. H. 1888, p 38

[2038] New Hampshire Wills and Probate, Merrimack County, volume 8, pp 359-361

[2039] New Hampshire Wills and Probate, Merrimack County, volume 48, pp 190-191

[2040] Herringshaw, Thomas William. *Herringshaw's Encyclopedia of American Biography of the Nineteenth Century*. Chicago, IL: American Publishers Association, 1902. Henry Eaton Moore, p 669

691)   HAINES FARNUM (*Benjamin Farnum⁴, Mary Ingalls Farnum³, Sarah Russell Ingalls², Robert¹*), b. at Concord, 31 Oct 1771 son of Benjamin and Anna (Merrill) Farnum; d. at Plymouth, NH, 23 Dec 1824 (will 14 Dec 1824); m. at Pembroke, 31 Dec 1800, ELIZABETH "BETSY" WHITEHOUSE, b. at Pembroke, 23 May 1777 daughter of Solomon and Mary (Knox) Whitehouse;[2041][2042] Elizabeth d. at Plymouth, 1834 (will written 21 Jan 1832 and proved 26 Mar 1834).

Haines and Elizabeth were in Concord where the births of four children are recorded and the births of the younger children are recorded in Pembroke. The family located in Plymouth in 1817 where both Haines and Elizabeth died.[2043]

In his will written 14 December 1824 (proved 12 January 1825), Hanes Farnum of Plymouth bequeathed one hundred dollars to beloved wife Elizabeth. Daughter Mary W. Farnum receives one hundred-fifty dollars and son Charles Farnum, three hundred dollars. Other bequests to his children are son Solomon W. Farnum, two hundred dollars; daughter Eliza and son Hiram, one hundred dollars apiece; son George, seventy-five dollars; and sons Aaron and Moses, fifty dollars each. The remainder of the estate goes to wife Elizabeth during her natural life, and at her decease, to be equally divided among the children. Son Charles Farnum was named executor. The minor children at the time of probate were Hiram, Eliza, George, Moses, Aaron, and Solomon. The homestead farm of 175 acres was valued at $2,500. Total value of personal estate including notes owed to the estate was $1,199.48.[2044]

In her will written 21 January 1832 (proved 26 March 1834), Elizabeth made bequests to children Charles, Hiram, Eliza, George, Moses, and Aaron. There is also a bequest of gold necklace to granddaughter Synthia Jane who is the daughter of Charles.[2045]

Haines and Elizabeth were parents of eight children.

i   MARY WHITEHOUSE FARNUM, b. at Concord, 18 Mar 1802; d. at Plymouth, NH, 19 Sep 1831. Mary did not marry. In her will written 16 September 1831, Mary left her real estate to brother Hiram. There is a bequest to sister Eliza Farnum. The remainder of the estate goes to individuals in Plymouth (who seem friends such as two members of the Association of Ladies) and to charitable purposes.[2046]

ii   CHARLES FARNUM, b. at Concord, 5 Oct 1803; d. at Pittsfield, ME, 1888; m. at Hebron, NH, 3 Oct 1827, CYNTHIA JOHNSON, b. at Hebron, 1808; Cynthia d. at Pittsfield, 19 Jan 1876.

iii   SOLOMON FARNUM, b. at Concord, 25 Oct 1805; d. at Plymouth, 25 Nov 1826.

iv   HIRAM FARNUM, b. at Concord, 10 Oct 1807; d. at Plymouth, NH, 25 May 1872; m. at Campton, NH, 27 Mar 1834, HANNAH C. STRAW, b. at Ellsworth, NH, 1816 daughter of Dudley and Mary (Avery) Straw; Hannah d. 18 Nov 1848.

v   ELIZA FARNUM, b. at Pembroke, NH, 25 Nov 1809; d. at Newbury, VT, 18 Mar 1880; m. 1 Nov 1835, WALTER BLAIR, b. at Holderness, NH, 1 Oct 1796 son of Samuel Livermore and Sarah (Cox) Blair; Water d. at Plymouth, NH, 6 Jun 1849.

vi   GEORGE FARNUM, b. at Pembroke, 7 Nov 1812; d. at Groton, NH, 4 Jan 1890; m. 2 Apr 1834, EMMA HARDY, b. 8 Oct 1814 daughter of David and Emma (Bartlett) Hardy; Emma d. at Groton, 13 Apr 1882.

vii   MOSES FARNUM (twin), b. at Pembroke, 5 Nov 1814; d. at Rumney, NH, 30 Dec 1847; m. 31 Dec 1837, MARY FLETCHER, b. 1813; Mary d. 10 Apr 1849.

viii   AARON FARNUM (twin), b. at Pembroke, 5 Nov 1814; d. at Plymouth, NH, 17 Jul 1839; m. 30 Mar 1836, ELIZA JANE PRESTON, b. at Rumney, 20 Nov 1810 daughter of Benjamin and Ann (Williams) Preston; Eliza d. at Plymouth, 6 Nov 1867.

692)   NATHANIEL FARNUM (*Benjamin Farnum⁴, Mary Ingalls Farnum³, Sarah Russell Ingalls², Robert¹*), b. at Concord, 5 Apr 1775 son of Benjamin and Anna (Merrill) Farnum; d. at Alfred, ME, 28 Sep 1861; m. HANNAH SAYWARD, b. 20 Jan 1780 daughter of John and Elizabeth (Trafton) Sayward;[2047] Hannah d. at Alfred, 4 Jun 1846.

Nathaniel was a cordwainer and tanner in Alfred, Maine.[2048] He also had a homestead farm. In the 1830 census of Alfred, Nathaniel headed a family of ten persons: one male 50 to 59; one female 40 to 49; two males 10 to 14; one male 15 to 19;

[2041] The 1821 will of Solomon Whitehouse includes a bequest to his daughter Betsy Farnum. Published genealogies give Haine's wife's name as Mary Whitehouse, or as Mary Elizabeth, but that is an error. All the records located (marriage, births of children, deaths of children, probate records of her father and her husband; and Elizabeth's own will) give her name as Elizabeth or Betsy. Solomon Whitehouse also had a daughter Mary who married Jonathan Freeman.
[2042] Carter, *History of Pembroke*, p 315
[2043] Stearns, *History of Plymouth*, volume II, p 257
[2044] New Hampshire Wills and Probate, Grafton County, Probate Estate Files, Estate of Haines Farnum, 1825
[2045] New Hampshire Wills and Probate, Grafton County, volume 15, p 59
[2046] New Hampshire Wills and Probate, Grafton County, volume 13, pp 184-185
[2047] Sayward, *The Sayward Family*, p 100
[2048] Farnham, New England Descendants of Ralph Farnum, pp 495-497

two males 20 to 29; one female 5 to 9; one female 15 to 19; and one female 20 to 29.[2049] In 1850, the value of his real property was given as $3,500. At that time, children Rufus and Elizabeth were in the home with him.[2050]

Nathaniel and Hannah were parents of eight children.

i　ROSWELL FARNUM, b. Feb 1803; d. at New Gloucester, ME, 24 Dec 1883; m. 4 Sep 1830, BETSEY MACE CUSHMAN, b. at New Gloucester, 24 Jan 1813 daughter of Samuel and Betsey (Rich) Cushman;[2051] Betsey d. at New Gloucester, 17 Jun 1856.

ii　JOHN SAYWARD FARNUM, b. at Alfred, about 1806; d. at Brockton, MA, 19 Sep 1884; m. at Bartlett, NH, 12 Jan 1837, SUSAN PENDEXTER, b. at Conway, NH, 1816 daughter of John and Susan (Eastman) Pendexter;[2052] Susan d. at Brockton, 13 Mar 1892.

iii　ABIEL FARNUM, b. at Alfred, 15 Feb 1808; d. at Mansfield, CT, 4 Jun 1876. Abiel seems to have had a first wife whose name is unknown with whom he had a son James born in 1834. Abiel m. 2nd at Mansfield, 20 Mar 1859, SUSAN POTTER, b. likely at Mansfield, 18 Oct 1842 daughter of James and Sybil (Brayman) Potter; Susan d. at Mansfield, 4 Jan 1879.

iv　MARY SAYWARD FARNUM, b. 1810; d. at Bucksport, ME, 25 Feb 1892; m. 28 Jun 1834, Rev. WILLIAM H. PILSBURY, b. 24 Aug 1806 son of Moody and Abigail (Mouton) Pillsbury; William d. at Bucksport, 25 Apr 1888.

v　NATHANIEL FARNUM, b. 14 Oct 1813; d. at La Crosse, WI, 14 May 1905; m. 1st about 1845, his first cousin, MARTHA ANN KIMBALL (*Abigail Farnum Kimball⁵, Benjamin Farnum⁴, Mary Ingalls Farnum³, Sarah Russell Ingalls², Robert¹*), b. 1816 daughter of Issachar and Abigail (Farnum) Kimball; Martha d. at Alfred, 11 May 1858. Nathaniel m. 2nd 4 Nov 1866, THEOLINE M. GOODYEAR, b. in NY, 11 Feb 1827 daughter of Merritt and Fannie (Smith) Goodyear; Theoline d. at Ventura, CA, 19 May 1907.

vi　RUFUS FARNUM, b. 27 Apr 1816; d. at Alfred, ME, 3 Jan 1886. Rufus did not marry. In his will, Rufus left his estate to Lucia H. Farnum wife of Henry Farnum of Boston.[2053]

vii　HENRY FARNUM, b. at Alfred, 1820; d. at Boston, 23 Feb 1893; m. at Lincoln, MA, 14 May 1846, LUCIA HAGAR, b. at Lincoln, 23 Apr 1823 daughter of Elisha and Priscilla (Fiske) Hagar; Lucia d. at Boston, 10 Jan 1884.

viii　ELIZABETH FARNUM, b. Aug 1822; d. at Alfred, 16 Nov 1875. Elizabeth did not marry.

693)　LYDIA FARNUM (*Benjamin Farnum⁴, Mary Ingalls Farnum³, Sarah Russell Ingalls², Robert¹*), b. at Concord, 26 Dec 1776 daughter of Benjamin and Anna (Merrill) Farnum; d. at Alfred, ME, 28 May 1842; m. at Pembroke, 21 Jan 1796, JOHN CONANT, b. at Beverly, MA, 10 Sep 1771 son of Nathaniel and Abigail (Dodge) Conant; John d. at Alfred, 27 Feb 1850.

John Conant owned a mill and store in Alfred, Maine which he inherited from his father. The mills were known as Conant's Mills and were later Littlefield's Mills.[2054]

In his will written 29 January 1846 (probate 1 April 1850), John Conant bequeathed to son Alvah one undivided half of a lot of land in Westborough in York County containing about sixty-two acres. Alvah also receives one undivided half of a lot of land in Alfred. In addition, he receives one-seventh part of the estate residue after the payment of the legacies. Son Cyrus receives the farm on which he (Cyrus) now lives in Alfred and two other lots, and Cyrus is to pay $2,230 to the estate executor which sum will be considered part of the estate residue. Cyrus receives one-seventh of the residue. The dwelling house and the two remaining halves of the lots given to Alvah go to Alvah to hold in trust for the benefit of son George and George is to have the income from this property as long as he lives. One-seventh of the estate residue is also held in trust for George. His daughters each receives one-seventh part of the estate residue: Nancy M. Hall, Caroline G. Sumner, Lucy M. Lewis, and Lydia H. Drew. The sums the children owe the father are to be deducted from their seventh parts. Alvah was named executor. In a codicil on 14 April 1847, John made an adjustment in the bequest to Cyrus which seems to adjust the way Cyrus's payment into the estate is made. The personal estate included $1,000 in shares of Atlantic and St. Lawrence Rail Road and $13,842.45 in notes owed to the estate. Real estate was valued at $3,980.[2055]

John and Lydia were parents of nine children born at Alfred, Maine.

[2049] Year: 1830; Census Place: Alfred, York, Maine; Series: M19; Roll: 52; Page: 322; Family History Library Film: 0497948

[2050] Year: 1850; Census Place: Alfred, York, Maine; Roll: 276; Page: 200b

[2051] Maine, Birth Records, 1715-1922

[2052] The names of Susan's parents are given as John Pendexter and Susan Eastman on her death record.

[2053] Farnham, *New England Descendants of Ralph Farnum*, p 842

[2054] Conant, *History and Genealogy of the Conant Family*, p 275

[2055] Maine, York County, Probate Estate Files, Estate of John Conant, Case 3495

i   NANCY MERRILL CONANT, b. 27 Dec 1796; d. at Portland, Nov 1865; m. 10 Dec 1818, her first cousin, DAVID HALL (*Mary Farnum Hall⁵, Benjamin Farnum⁴, Mary Ingalls Farnum³, Sarah Russell Ingalls², Robert¹*), b. at Alfred, 8 Oct 1791 son of Abiel and Mary (Farnum) Hall; David d. at Portland, 12 Mar 1863.

ii   CYRUS CONANT, b. 17 May 1799; d. 19 Jan 1803.

iii   ALVAH CONANT, b. 7 Dec 1800; d. at Portland, ME, 2 Oct 1876; m. 1ˢᵗ at Conway, NH, 30 Oct 1826, ALMIRA ODELL, b. at Conway, 3 Apr 1803 daughter of Richard and Molly (Eastman) Odell; Almira d. at Portland, 23 Jan 1841. Alvah m. 2ⁿᵈ 27 Apr 1843, JUDITH OSBORNE, b. at Danvers, 21 Oct 1801 daughter of Joseph and Judith (Francis) Osborne; Judith d. 3 Feb 1857. Alvah m. 3ʳᵈ at Portland, 8 Jul 1858, Rebecca P. Cook, b. 1815; Rebecca d. at Portland, 17 Jan 1863. Alvah m. 4ᵗʰ at Manchester, CT, 5 Sep 1866, MARY SUMNER (widow Mary Woodbridge), b. 20 Sep 1816 daughter of Reuben and Anna (Perrin) Sumner; Mary d. 20 Mar 1883.

iv   CYRUS KING CONANT, b. 1 Jan 1803; d. at Watertown, MA, 10 Apr 1871; m. at Alfred, 27 Dec 1825, ABIGAIL GILE, b. at Alfred, 14 Jan 1803 daughter of Thomas and Joanna (Smith) Gile; Abigail d. at Watertown, 2 May 1887.

v   LUCINDA CONANT, b. 19 Nov 1804; d. 2 Jan 1808.

vi   CAROLINE CONANT, b. 16 Apr 1809; d. at Brooklyn, NY, 28 Feb 1883; m. at Alfred, 22 Sep 1830, HIRAM FREDERICK SUMNER, b. at Hebron, CT, 14 Feb 1800 son of Reuben and Anna (Perrin) Sumner; Hiram d. at Hartford, CT, 3 Mar 1874.

vii   GEORGE DOW CONANT, b. 2 Feb 1811; d. at Alfred, 29 Dec 1880. George did not marry.

viii   LUCY MARIA CONANT, b. 7 Dec 1812; d. at Southampton, NY (burial at Alfred, ME), 4 Jun 1883; m. at Boston, 17 Dec 1844, DANIEL LEWIS, b. at Alfred, ME, 3 Mar 1803 son of Daniel and Abigail (Parsons) Lewis; Daniel d. at Boston, 26 Jan 1868.

ix   LYDIA HAYNES CONANT, b. 25 Apr 1816; d. at Boston, 18 Oct 1854; m. 20 Oct 1841, ELIJAH CHESLEY DREW, b. at Newfield, ME, 1818 son of Winborn and Martha (Ayer) Drew; Elijah d. at Boston, 26 Jan 1877. Elijah married second Hannah Haynes.

694)   JONATHAN FARNUM (*Benjamin Farnum⁴, Mary Ingalls Farnum³, Sarah Russell Ingalls², Robert¹*), b. at Concord, 26 Jul 1778 son of Benjamin and Anna (Merrill) Farnum; d. at Alfred, ME, 11 Jan 1831; m. by 1814, ESTHER PERKINS, b. at Kennebunkport, ME, 10 Jun 1787 daughter of Christopher and Esther (·) Perkins;²⁰⁵⁶ Esther d. at Brewer, MA, 2 Jul 1885.

    Jonathan Farnum did not leave a will. On 18 May 1832, Nathan A. Appleton and Alvah Conant were named as guardians of the following minor children: Benjamin Farnum, Thomas P. Farnum, James D. Farnum, Frances Farnum, Clement M. Farnum, Lucretia H. Farnum, Lorenzo E. Farnum, and Oliver Farnum. On 9 June 1832, there was notice of guardian's sale of the real estate interests of the minor children of Jonathan Farnum: Benjamin, Thomas P., John D., Frances, Clement M., Lucretia H., Lorenzo E., and Oliver Farnum. An estate inventory to identify distribution amounts for the minor children was made 3 January 1834 with then six children identified as minors: Thomas, James, Frances, Clement, Lucretia, and Oliver each of these to receive one-sixth part of the total inventory of $4,639.38. On 10 March 1838, James Dorrance Farnum trader of Alfred acknowledged final receipt of his settlement from the estate and discharged his guardian. Other children signing discharges were Thomas P. Farnum and Oliver Farnum. ²⁰⁵⁷

    Jonathan and Esther were parents of eight children born at Alfred, Maine.

i   THOMAS PERKINS FARNUM, b. 1814; d. at Chelsea, MA, 18 Dec 1898; m. at Mansfield, MA, 24 Jan 1847, CATHERINE DIXON, b. at Dedham, MA, Jul 1811 daughter of Richard and Lydia (Monk) Dixon; Catherine d. at Chelsea, 29 Aug 1906.

ii   FRANCES FARNUM, b. 1819; d. at Watertown, MA, 21 Apr 1904; m. 1ˢᵗ 8 Nov 1838, Dr. BOOTH CULLEN MULVEY, b. in Ireland,²⁰⁵⁸ about 1800; Booth d. at Saco, ME, 18 Jul 1858. Frances m. 2ⁿᵈ at Lawrence, 7 Mar 1861, SAMUEL P. MORSE, b. at New Boston, NH, 25 Aug 1806 son of Samuel Perley and Rebecca (Hazen) Morse; Samuel d. at Lawrence, 21 Dec 1864. Samuel was first married to Catherine Emerson and second married to Sophia Folsom.

iii   JAMES DORRACNE FARNUM, b. 1819; d. at Medford, MA, 18 Nov 1892; m. at Boston, 14 Mar 1850, LOUISA HUDSON TAFT, b. at Boston, 24 Jun 1826 daughter of Read and Mary (Shurtleff) Taft; Louisa d. at Medford, 1 Dec 1905.

²⁰⁵⁶ Esther's place of birth and names of parents are given on her death record.
²⁰⁵⁷ Maine, York County Estate Files, Estate of Jonathan Farnum, Case 5549
²⁰⁵⁸ Booth came to the U. S. Oct 1823 arriving at Eastport, ME. National Archives and Records Administration (NARA); Washington, D.C.; Index to New England Naturalization Petitions, 1791-1906 (M1299); Microfilm Serial: M1299; Microfilm Roll: 92

iv   BENJAMIN FARNUM, b. about 1820 and baptized 13 Jul 1820; living in 1832 but not included in the 1834 estate distribution.

v   CLEMENT MERRILL FARNUM, b. 1822 and baptized 24 Nov 1822; d. at Chelsea, MA, 18 Dec 1843.

vi   LUCRETIA HOVEY FARNUM, b. 1824; d. at Watertown, MA, 13 Jan 1899; m. at Lawrence, MA, 9 Dec 1860, REUBEN MAYNARD, b. at Sudbury, 1818 son of Warren and Nancy (Holden) Maynard; Reuben d. at Chelsea, 2 Sep 1873.

vii   LORENZO EMERSON FARNUM, b. 1826 and baptized 17 Dec 1826; d. at Alfred, 31 Oct 1832.

viii   OLIVER FARNUM, b. 1828 and baptized 5 Oct 1828

695)   ABIEL FARNUM (*Benjamin Farnum⁴, Mary Ingalls Farnum³, Sarah Russell Ingalls², Robert¹*), b. at Concord, 24 Apr 1780 son of Benjamin and Anna (Merrill) Farnum; d. at Alfred, ME, 29 Apr 1864; m. ADELIA CONANT, b. 1793 daughter of Joshua and Adelia (Gile) Conant; Adelia d. at Alfred, 7 Jun 1846.
           Abiel and Adelia resided in Alfred, Maine. They were parents of five children born at Alfred.[2059] In 1850, Abiel was living in Alfred with young women Harriet M. Farnham age 21 and Lucy H. Farnham age 18 living with him along with William W. Simpson age 15.[2060] In 1860, Abiel was living in Alfred as head of household with his son George B. Farnum and his family living with him.[2061]

i   CHARLES FARNUM, b. about 1814; m. at Lyman, ME, 25 May 1835, SALLY COUSENS. He may be the Charles Farnum age 47 living at Alfred, ME in 1860. At that time, he is listed as a day laborer and living in the household of Jacob Pillsbury.[2062]

ii   GEORGE B. FARNUM, b. 10 Jan 1818; d. at Alfred, 5 Feb 1896; m. at Boston, 26 Sep 1854, SARAH E. COLBY, b. 30 Dec 1820 daughter of Moses and Betsey (Wilkins) Colby;[2063] Sarah d. at Alfred, 7 Sep 1891.

iii   ADELIA FARNUM, b. 1823; d. (burial at Alfred, ME) 11 Apr 1858; m. at Boston, 26 May 1850, BENJAMIN D. SIMPSON, b. about 1821 son of Benjamin Simpson.[2064]

iv   WILLIAM G. FARNUM, b. 1825; d. at Boston, 29 Dec 1892; m. at Boston, 11 Mar 1869, ELIZA KEENE, b. in England, 1825 daughter of Robert and Elizabeth (-) Keene;[2065] Eliza d. at Boston, 28 Jul 1897.

v   HARRIET M. FARNUM, b. about 1828

vi   LUCY H. FARNUM, b. 1832

696)   ANNA "NANCY" FARNUM (*Benjamin Farnum⁴, Mary Ingalls Farnum³, Sarah Russell Ingalls², Robert¹*), b. at Concord, 30 Jan 1783 daughter of Benjamin and Anna (Merrill) Farnum; d. at Franklin, NH, 10 Mar 1854; m. at Concord, 8 Oct 1801, Dr. JOB WILSON, b. at Belmont, NH, 25 Jan 1776 son of Nathaniel and Elizabeth (Barber) Wilson; Job d. at Franklin, 22 Sep 1851 (will proved Oct 1851).
           Job Wilson was a physician. He obtained an M. B. degree from Dartmouth College in 1804 and completed the M. D. degree in 1823. He practiced first in Boscawen but settled in Salisbury, New Hampshire in 1814. He was president of the New Hampshire Medical Society in 1825-1826. He contributed articles to the Boston Medical and Surgical Journal.[2066]
           Medicine was the family business and three sons in this family were physicians. Son Thomas W. Wilson also attended Dartmouth and practiced in Salisbury with his father. Son Jeremiah W. Wilson obtained his medical degree from Castleton Medical College which was the first medical college in Vermont. Dr. Jeremiah had his practice in the village of Contoocook (Hancock), New Hampshire.[2067] Son Ephraim Farnum Wilson also attended Castleton Medical College and first practiced in Sanbornton before settling in Rockville, Connecticut.[2068]
           In his will written 28 May 1847 (proved fourth Tuesday of October 1851), Job Wilson bequeathed to his wife Nancy one-third of the real estate of the Baker farm in Franklin except for forty acres that he has given sons Ephraim F. and George

[2059] Burleigh's Genealogy of the Guild family p 230
[2060] Year: 1850; Census Place: Alfred, York, Maine; Roll: 276; Page: 198b
[2061] Year: 1860; Census Place: Alfred, York, Maine; Page: 771; Family History Library Film: 803449
[2062] Year: 1860; Census Place: Alfred, York, Maine; Page: 753; Family History Library Film: 803449
[2063] Gould and Beals, *Early Families of Bradford*, p 97
[2064] Father's name is given as Benjamin on his marriage record to Adelia; Massachusetts, Town and Vital Records, 1620-1988, marriage at Boston 26 May 1850
[2065] The names of Eliza's parents are given as Robert and Elizabeth Keene on her marriage record.
[2066] Dearborn, *The History of Salisbury, New Hampshire*, p 400
[2067] The Atlantic Medical Weekly, volumes 5-6, May 16, 1896, p 317, obituary of Dr. Jeremiah W. Wilson
[2068] Hurd, *History of Merrimack and Belknap Counties*, p 623

W. Wilson. The following bequest is made to his eldest son: "To my eldest son Benjamin F. Wilson one half of the land I own in Michigan viz. the Prairie lot town 4 Range 11 West ½ N.E. ¼ Sec 29 and the undivided half of one forty acre lot S.E. ¼ N.W. ¼ Sec 26 Town Range 12 west. The above named lands in the State of Michigan I do give and bequeath to the above named Benjamin F. Wilson. But should the embarrassments of the said Benjamin F. Wilson make the bequest improper Thomas W. Wilson should be entitled to the same by paying to Benjamin F. Wilson the full income of said land yearly." There are land bequests to Job P., Jeremiah W., and George W. Wilson. To his beloved daughters Lucinda Eastman and Lydia Stevens he plans to make donations to them from time to time as his circumstances permit. Son George Whitfield Wilson is to par each of his sisters twenty dollars within six months of Job's decease.[2069]

There are records for nine children of Job and Nancy born at Salisbury, New Hampshire.[2070]

i   BENJAMIN FARNUM WILSON, b. 3 May 1804; Benjamin was living in 1847 but further information was not located.

ii   THOMAS W. WILSON, b. 14 Feb 1806; d. at Salisbury, 13 Apr 1861; m. 1831, AMANDA MALVINA SAWYER, b. at Salisbury, 21 Feb 1809 daughter of Isaac F. and Rebecca (Pettengill) Sawyer; Amanda d. at Ohio, MO, 19 Feb 1882.

iii   LUCINDA CONANT WILSON, b. 25 Jul 1808; d. at Concord, after 1880; m. about 1840, THOMAS EASTMAN, b. at Concord, 1805 son of William and Phebe (Elliot) Eastman; Thomas d. at Concord, 25 May 1893.

iv   JOB PEARSON WILSON, b. 25 May 1810; d. at Rumney, NH, after 1870; m. at Plymouth, NH, 10 Oct 1838, LAURA R. STEVENS, b. at Plymouth, NH, 1823 daughter of Samuel and Sarah (Draper) Stevens; Laura d. at Plymouth, 5 Oct 1901. Laura married second Walter Webster.

v   ABIGAIL SANBORN WILSON, b. 25 Jan 1812

vi   LYDIA JOHNSON WILSON, b. 2 Feb 1814; d. at Haverhill, NH, 5 Apr 1872; m. about 1840, GROVE S. STEVENS, b. at Piermont, NH, 25 Oct 1813 son of John and Elizabeth (Fifield) Stevens; Grove d. at Haverhill, 20 Dec 1905.

vii   JEREMIAH W. WILSON, b. 11 Jan 1816; d. at Hopkinton, NH, 30 Apr 1896; m. at Boscawen, 31 Mar 1847, ELIZABETH GERRISH, b. at Boscawen, 5 Sep 1820 daughter of Thomas and Elizabeth (Patrick) Gerrish; Elizabeth d. at Hopkinton, 8 Nov 1882.

viii   EPHRAIM FARNUM WILSON, b. 30 Oct 1817; d. at Vernon, CT, 30 Apr 1883; m. 1st at Hopkinton, NH, 29 Apr 1847, RHODA C. BARNARD, b. at Hopkinton, 1827; Rhoda d. (burial at Hopkinton), 4 Aug 1852. Ephraim m. 2nd ELEANOR EASTMAN, b. Dec 1819; Eleanor d. at Vernon, 5 Mar 1907.

ix   GEORGE WHITEFIELD WILSON, b. 12 Jul 1824; d. at Franklin, NH, 27 Nov 1897; m. about 1854, ELLEN MALVINA SAWYER, b. at Charlestown, MA, 28 Aug 1835 daughter of Stephen and Merinda (Hale) Sawyer; Ellen d. at Franklin, 28 May 1912.

697)   ABIGAIL FARNUM (*Benjamin Farnum⁴, Mary Ingalls Farnum³, Sarah Russell Ingalls², Robert¹*), b. at Concord, 30 Oct 1783 daughter of Benjamin and Anna (Merrill) Farnum; d. at Alfred, ME, 23 Apr 1855; m. at Lyman, ME, 4 Dec 1813, Major ISSACHAR KIMBALL, b. at Lyman, 15 May 1784 son of Ezra and Lucretia (Cousins) Kimball; Issachar d. at Alfred, 3 Apr 1860.

Abigail and Issachar resided in Lyman, Maine until at least 1830[2071] and were in Alfred, Maine by 1840[2072] where they remained. Issachar was deacon of the Congregational church in Alfred.[2073]

In his will written 3 February 1858 (proved first Tuesday of August 1860), Issachar Kimball bequeathed to eldest daughter Martha Ann Farnum one hundred dollars; to second daughter Abigail F. Gile, one hundred dollars; and to third daughter Mary Kimball, two hundred-fifty dollars and one room in the house while she is single. Household furniture is to be equally divided among his three daughters. Only son Alden B. Kimball receives the residue of the estate and is named executor.[2074]

Issachar and Abigail were parents of four children likely born at Lyman, Maine.

i   MARTHA ANN KIMBALL, b. 1816; d. at Alfred, ME, 11 May 1858; m. by 1846, her first cousin, NATHANIEL FARNUM (*Nathaniel Farnum⁵, Benjamin Farnum⁴, Mary Ingalls Farnum³, Sarah Russell Ingalls², Robert¹*), b. in

---

[2069] New Hampshire Wills and Probate, Merrimack County, volume 16, pp 423-424

[2070] There may also be an infant born in 1802 who died young.

[2071] Year: 1830; Census Place: Lyman, York, Maine; Series: M19; Roll: 52; Page: 183; Family History Library Film: 0497948

[2072] Year: 1840; Census Place: Alfred, York, Maine; Roll: 155; Page: 315; Family History Library Film: 0009710

[2073] Issachar is buried in Parish Congregational Church Cemetery in Alfred, the cemetery records noting his as deacon; findagrave ID: 34884280

[2074] Maine, York County, Probate Estate Files, Estate of Issachar Kimball, Case 10906

ME, 1Oct 1813 son of Nathaniel and Hannah (Sayward) Farnum; Nathaniel d. at La Crosse, WI, 1905. Nathaniel married second Theoline Goodyear in 1867. Martha and Thomas had two children: Charles and Martha.

ii   ALDEN BRADFORD KIMBALL, b. 11 Oct 1817; d. at Alfred, ME, 12 Oct 1893; m. about 1856, CAROLINE CLARK, b. at Sanford, ME, Feb 1826 daughter of Abner and Betsy (Wakefield) Clark; Caroline d. at Alfred, 25 Jan 1911.

iii   ABIGAIL F. KIMBALL, b. 17 Mar 1820; d. at Alfred, 21 Oct 1883; m. JEREMIAH R. GILE, b. 17 Dec 1817 son of John and Hannah (Robarts) Gile; Jeremiah d. at Alfred, 6 Apr 1893.

iv   MARY HALL KIMBALL, b. 4 Nov 1822; d. at Alfred, 22 Jul 1882. Mary did not marry.

698)   JEREMIAH FARNHAM[2075] (*Benjamin Farnum[4], Mary Ingalls Farnum[3], Sarah Russell Ingalls[2], Robert[1]*), b. at Concord, 29 Jul 1785 son of Benjamin and Anna (Merrill) Farnum; d. at Rumford, ME, 21 Nov 1869; m. at Concord, 16 Jan 1811, SALLY HALL, b. at Concord, 11 Sep 1788 daughter of Daniel and Deborah (Davis) Hall; Sally d. at Rumford, 26 Sep 1859.

     Jeremiah and Sally resided in Rumford where they had a farm. In 1850, the household consisted of Jeremiah and Sally and children Emily H. age 33 and Walter H. age 28.[2076] After the death of Sally, Jeremiah lived with his son John C. Farnham and his family.[2077]

     Jeremiah Farnham and Sally Hall were parents of ten children born at Rumford.[2078]

i   MILTON FARNHAM, b. 3 Dec 1812; d. at Boston after 1870 (living in 1870 and Emily a widow in 1880); m. 4 Jul 1843, EMILY WARD, b. in ME, 1816 daughter of Thomas and Deborah (Doe) Ward;[2079] Emily d. at Lynn, MA, 31 Mar 1893.

ii   IVORY H. FARNUM, b. 16 Apr 1813; d. 26 Sep 1828.

iii   EMILY H. FARNUM, b. 28 Dec 1814; d. at Rumford, 24 Nov 1856; m. 11 Nov 1855. ALBERT GALLATON GLINES, b. at Rumford, ME, 5 Jan 1803 son of Chandler and Betsey (Davis) Glines; Albert d. at Rumford, 13 Feb 1878.

iv   ALFRED FARNUM, b. 16 Aug 1817; d. at Rumford, 6 Jan 1848; m. at Boston, 15 Sep 1844, CAROLINE SWEETSER of Scarborough, ME who has not been identified.

v   CALVIN H. FARNUM, b. 15 Jul 1819; d. 4 Dec 1819.

vi   JOHN C. FARNHAM, b. 29 Nov 1820; d. at North Rumford, 27 Jan 1892; m. 1 Jun 1845, MARY RAULSTONE BASS, b. at Weld, 12 Mar 1822 daughter of Charles and Susanna (Lane) Bass;[2080] Mary d. at Rumford, 1 Nov 1908.

vii   WALTER H. FARNUM, b. 15 Jan 1823. Walter was living with his parents in Rumford in 1850. It is possible that he is the Walter Harris Farnum, born in Maine about 1824, who was in Alameda County, California in 1866.

viii   SARAH D. FARNUM, b. 28 Feb 1825; d. 11 Aug 1826.

ix   REBECCA E. FARNUM, b. 29 Aug 1827

x   DEBORAH D. FARNUM, b. 27 Feb 1830; d. 26 Sep 1833.

699)   SARAH FARNUM (*Benjamin Farnum[4], Mary Ingalls Farnum[3], Sarah Russell Ingalls[2], Robert[1]*), b. at Concord, 29 Mar 1787 daughter of Benjamin and Anna (Merrill) Farnum; d. at Augusta, ME (burial at Alfred), 15 Oct 1864; m. at Concord, 6 Mar 1810, CHARLES P. GRIFFIN, b. at Concord, 1786; Charles d. at Alfred, 2 Mar 1825.

     Charles was a blacksmith in Alfred, Maine. Charles Griffin did not leave a will and widow Sarah Griffin was named administratrix of the estate on 21 March 1825. The inventory of Charles's estate included a brick dwelling house with land, large stable with shed and had scale valued at $3,000, a second house previously occupied by the deceased with land and blacksmith shop valued at $900 and two smaller lots of land valued at $340. He also owned part of a sawmill privilege, the whole of an old sawmill, carding and picking machine, tools and materials related to the blacksmith business with a total value of personal estate of $1,390.74. There were $1,825 in notes owed to the estate. The dower was set off to the widow. Abiel Hall

[2075] Records for Jeremiah primarily use the spelling Farnham.

[2076] Year: 1850; Census Place: Rumford, Oxford, Maine; Roll: 262; Page: 219b

[2077] Year: 1860; Census Place: Rumford, Oxford, Maine; Page: 366; Family History Library Film: 803444

[2078] Abbot, *Genealogical Register of the Descendants of George Abbot of Andover*, pp 96-97

[2079] The names of Emily's parents are given as Thomas Ward and Deborah Doe on her death records; parents Thomas and Deborah are engraved on her gravestone.

[2080] Roser, *Mayflower Births and Deaths*, volume 1, p 52

and Nathan D. Appleton were named as guardians to the minor children: Henry H. Griffin, William P. Griffin, Mary Ann Griffin, and Sarah Jane Griffin. In April 1832, Hall and Appleton were allowed to sell a portion of the real estate related to settling the estate.[2081]

Later in her life, Sarah developed mental health problems and was confined to the asylum for the insane in Augusta. Selectman of Alfred petitioned on 20 December 1856 for a guardian to be named to manage her affairs. Her son William P. Griffin was named trustee. Augustus O. Clarke was allowed as administrator of Sarah's estate on 6 June 1865 after her decease, the appointment noting that Sarah died in 1864.[2082]

There is evidence of seven children of Charles Griffin and Sarah Farnum born at Alfred, Maine.

i   WILLIAM GRIFFIN, b. 1814; d. at Alfred, ME, 1 Jan 1816.

ii   HENRY H. GRIFFIN, b. about 1815; living in 1832. He may be the Henry H. Griffin whose marriage intention is recorded in Alfred, Maine as well as Leominster, Massachusetts who was of Ann Arbor Michigan when he married Chloe Fletcher of Leominster on 8 Oct 1836.[2083]

iii WILLIAM PORTER GRIFFIN, b. 1817; d. at Everett, MA, 22 Nov 1875; m. at Exeter, NH, 30 Oct 1843, SUSAN EMERSON, b. about 1824. Susan was listed in the Boston city directory in 1895 as widow of William P. Griffin. Son-in-law Thomas Dunham was named administrator of William's estate in York County, Maine.[2084]

iv   MARY ANN GRIFFIN, b. 1818; d. at Alfred, 4 Oct 1835.

v   SARAH JANE GRIFFIN, baptized at Alfred, 9 Dec 1821; d. in ME, about 1860.[2085] Sarah did not marry.

vi   CHARLES GRIFFIN, b. 1823; d. 7 May 1824.

vii ISABELLA GRIFFIN, b. Nov 1824; d. 22 Apr 1825.

700) WILLIAM EATON (*Sarah Farnum Eaton⁴, Mary Ingalls Farnum³, Sarah Russell Ingalls², Robert¹*), b. at Fryeburg, 3 Mar 1766 son of William and Sarah (Farnum) Eaton; d. at Chatham, NH, 27 May 1852; m. at Fryeburg, 26 Nov 1795, NANCY FARRINGTON, b. 1779; Nancy d. likely at Fryeburg, 28 Jul 1858.[2086]

William and Nancy resided in Fryeburg where they were until 1820, but relocated to Chatham, New Hampshire by the time of the 1830 census. In 1850, William and Nancy were living in Chatham and daughter Nancy and her husband Jesse Thomas and their two children were living with them.[2087]

On 16 April 1818, William Eaton of Fryeburg, Maine then age fifty-two provided a statement related to his application for pension. On 10 April 1782, he enlisted for three years in the company of Capt. Hollister of the 1st Massachusetts regiment commanded by Col. Vose in the brigade of Gen. Patterson. He served until December 1783 when he was transferred to the American Regiment until he was discharged on 13 June 1784 at West Point by Gen. Henry Jackson. William was granted a pension of $8 per month. On 20 July 1820, William provided additional information on his family and circumstances. In his household were his mother Sarah age 74, wife Nancy age 41 described as "a very weakly woman", daughter Sarah age 22, daughter Mary age 20, son William age 17 described as an invalid, son Jeremiah age 15, son James age 12, daughter Nancy age 9, daughter Hannah age 7, daughter Betsey age 5, and son Joseph age 3. The value of his property was reported as $98.60. On 6 September 1852, widow Nancy Eaton then age seventy-three and residing in Chatham made application for the widow's pension. On 12 April 1855, Nancy was living in Fryeburg.[2088]

William and Nancy were parents of twelve children born at Fryeburg, Maine.

i   PHILIP FARRINGTON EATON, b. 1 Apr 1796; d. at Bethlehem, NH, 1 Feb 1877; m. about 1822, PHEBE EASTMAN, b. at Fryeburg, 23 Oct 1800 daughter of Jeremiah and Phebe (Powers) Eastman;[2089] Phebe d. at Bethlehem, 9 Mar 1877.

ii   SARAH EATON, b. 1798; d. at Chatham, NH, 27 Mar 1889; m. at Chatham, 27 Oct 1825, CHARLES DREW, b. at Roxbury, MA, 1800; Charles d. at Chatham, 13 Jun 1890.

[2081] Maine York County Probate Estate Files, Case 7852 for the Estate of Charles Griffin; Case 7854 for the guardian file
[2082] Maine York County Probate Estate Files, Case 7861
[2083] "Maine Marriages, 1771-1907", database, *FamilySearch* (https://familysearch.org/ark:/61903/1:1:F46V-52N : 14 January 2020), Henry H. Griffin, 1836. Massachusetts, Town and Vital Records, 1620-1988
[2084] Maine York County Probate Estate Files, Case 7862
[2085] The probate file of Sarah Jane's mother Sarah includes a statement from the estate administrator Augustus O. Clarke that Sarah Jane died about 1860 leaving no estate whatsoever; York County Estate File 7861
[2086] The dates of death for both William and Nancy are given in pension records and William's place of death is given as Chatham, New Hampshire in the pension record. Pension file W3666
[2087] Year: 1850; Census Place: Chatham, Carroll, New Hampshire; Roll: 426; Page: 11a
[2088] U. S. Revolutionary War Pension and Bounty-Land Warrant Application Files, Case W3666
[2089] Rix, *History and Genealogy of the Eastman Family*, p 209

iii   MARY EATON, b. 1800; d. at Stroudsburg, PA, 1883; m. about 1820, JOHN L. THOMAS, b. in ME about 1806 son of Elisha and Hannah (Lombard) Thomas.

iv   WILLIAM EATON, b. 1802; d. at Stow 1880; m. at Chatham, NH, 3 Jul 1828, ABIGIAL THOMAS (widow of James Jack), b. about 1809 daughter of Elisha and Hannah (Lombard) Thomas.

v   JEREMIAH EATON, b. 1805; d. at New London, WI, 1882; m. NANCY, b. in ME, 1803; Nancy d. after 1880.

vi   JAMES FARNHAM EATON, b. 26 Mar 1808; d. at Stow, ME, 17 Jan 1841; m. by 1838, his first cousin, SARAH EATON CHASE, b. 1814 daughter of Joseph F. and Sarah (Eaton) Chase; Sarah d. at Stow, 7 Sep 1852.

vii   NANCY EATON, b. 1809; d. at North Chatham, NH, 21 Oct 1902; m. at Chatham, 18 Jan 1835, JESSE THOMAS, b. at Brookfield, ME 1810 son of Elisha and Hannah (Lombard) Thomas; Jesse d. at Chatham, 10 Nov 1896.

viii   HANNAH EATON, b. 1811; d. at Fryeburg, 4 Dec 1821.

ix   BETSEY PERHAM EATON, b. 2 Jan 1815; d. at Stow, ME, 11 Oct 1879; m. at Chatham, NH, 1 Jan 1848, ALBION PARIS COBB, b. at Limington, ME, 14 Jun 1815 son of Nathan and Mary (Sawyer) Cobb; d. at Brandy Station, VA, 2 Dec 1863 from wounds suffered at the Battle of Mine Run.

x   JOSEPH EATON, b. 1817; d. at Whitefield, NH, 16 Jul 1886; m. EVELYN WENTWORTH, b. at Lancaster, NH, 28 Nov 1827 daughter of Joseph and Joanna (Hayes) Wentworth; Evelyn d. at Whitefield, 3 Jun 1910.

xi   ALFRED EATON, b. 13 Oct 1820; d. at Fryeburg, 8 Aug 1903; m. MEHITABLE CLAY, b. at Chatham, NH, 7 Sep 1823 daughter of James and Olive (Elwell) Clay; Mehitable d. at Conway, NH, 23 Mar 1907.

xii   DOROTHY GORDON EATON, b. 1823; d. 1824.

701)   OSGOOD EATON (*Sarah Farnum Eaton⁴, Mary Ingalls Farnum³, Sarah Russell Ingalls², Robert¹*), b. at Fryeburg, 6 Mar 1768 son of William and Sarah (Farnum) Eaton; d. at Rumford, ME, 1 Jul 1836; m. at Concord, 10 Sep 1793, BETHIAH VIRGIN, b. at Concord, 23 Feb 1775 daughter of William and Mehitable (Stickney) Virgin; Bethiah d. at Rumford, 18 Dec 1857.
        Osgood Eaton was an early settled in Rumford, Maine and live on Eaton Hill. He served civic roles such as surveyor of highways and surveyor of lumber.[2090]
        Osgood and Bethiah were parents of eight children all but the oldest born at Rumford, Maine.

i   JEREMIAH EATON, b. at Concord, 1 Jan 1794

ii   BETSY EATON, b. 23 May 1796; d. at Rumford, ME, 2 Feb 1876; m. at Rumford, 21 Nov 1816, WAID MOORE, b. at Bethel, 7 Sep 1787 son of Aaron and Salome (Goss) Moore; Waid d. at Rumford, 20 Feb 1878.

iii   MEHITABLE S. EATON, b. 21 Jul 1798; d. at Rumford, 15 Jun 1869. Mehitable did not marry.

iv   CLIMENA EATON, b. 15 Apr 1800; d. 18 Oct 1800.

v   WILLIAM EATON, b. 30 Jan 1802

vi   ABIAL EATON, b. 25 Nov 1803; d. at Canterbury, NH, 1873; m. at Belmont, NH, 14 Jan 1835, RHODA G. BURLEIGH, b. at Gilmanton, 4 Sep 1802 daughter of Stevens and Abigail (Taylor) Burleigh;[2091] Rhoda d. at Belmont, 23 Nov 1881.

vii   SYLVESTER EATON, b. about 1808

viii   OSGOOD EATON, b. about 1810; d. of disease at Brashear City, LA, 11 May 1863;[2092] m. 1st 5 Feb 1833, MARIA L. GALE; Maria d. at Rumford, 5 Aug 1842. Osgood m. 2nd at Rumford, 26 Jan 1843, BETSEY PUTNAM, b. at Rumford, 21 Jul 1816 daughter of Samuel and Betsey (Cobb) Putnam; Betsey d. at Rumford, 5 Jul 1907. Osgood served as private in the 12th infantry.[2093]

702)   SARAH EATON (*Sarah Farnum Eaton⁴, Mary Ingalls Farnum³, Sarah Russell Ingalls², Robert¹*), b. at Fryeburg, 20 Dec 1769 daughter of William and Sarah (Farnum) Eaton; d. (burial at Stow, ME), 2 Oct 1854;[2094] m. as his third wife, JOSEPH

[2090] Lapham, *History of Rumford*, p 318, p 59, p 68
[2091] Burleigh, *Genealogy of the Burley Family*, p 22
[2092] U.S., Registers of Deaths of Volunteers, 1861-1865, Maine A-K, p 94
[2093] U.S., Civil War Soldier Records and Profiles, 1861-1865
[2094] Maine, Nathan Hale Cemetery Collection, 1780-1980

F. CHASE, b. at Canterbury, NH, 19 Sep 1770 son of Josiah and Mehitable (Frye) Chase Joseph d. at Conway, 29 Jan 1823.[2095] Joseph Chase was first married to Mehitable Day and second married to Joanna Day.

Sarah is likely the Sarah Eaton who gave birth to an out-of-wedlock child with Isaac Abbott (1762-1861), Enoch Eaton Abbott (b. 1785).[2096]

Sarah had one child with Isaac Abbott who was the son of Isaac and Susannah (Farnum) Abbott.

i   ENOCH EATON ABBOTT, b. at Fryeburg, 30 Jan 1785; d. at Conway, NH, 22 Apr 1862; m. at Conway, 4 Jun 1818, FANNY DINSMORE, b. in NH, about 1794; Fanny d. at Chatham, NH, Apr 1860.

Sarah Eaton and Joseph F. Chase were parents of five children born at Conway. In 1850, Sarah was living in Stow with her daughter Ann and her husband Solomon Eastman.[2097]

i   ANN S. CHASE, b. 23 Mar 1804; d. at Stow, ME, 27 Nov 1865; m. at Conway, 29 Oct 1847, as his third wife, SOLOMON EASTMAN, b. at Lovell, ME, 6 Dec 1792 son of Daniel and Sarah (Whiting) Eastman; Solomon d. at Stow, 19 May 1866. Solomon was first married to Pamelia Dresser and second married to Betsey.

ii   ELIZABETH B. CHASE, b. 1806; d. at Fryeburg, ME, 23 Aug 1879; m. ANSEL PAGE, b. at Conway, 12 Feb 1808 son of Thomas and Elizabeth Farrington (Charles) Page; Ansel d. at Fryeburg, 1 Nov 1882.

iii   JOSEPH F. CHASE, b. 1808; d. at Lovell, ME, 23 Oct 1858; m. LYDIA K. LORD, b. 1813 daughter of Jeremiah and Mary (Lassell) Lord; Lydia d. at River Falls, WI, 7 Apr 1898.

iv   WILLIAM E. CHASE, b. at Conway, 1812; d. at Conway, 4 Aug 1895; m. at Conway, 24 Jan 1839, EMILY WALKER EASTMAN, b. at Conway, 11 Jan 1820 daughter of Stephen and Hannah (Walker) Eastman; Emily d. at Conway, 4 Feb 1887.

v   SARAH EATON CHASE, b. 1814; d. at Stow, ME, 7 Sep 1852; m. by 1838, her first cousin, JAMES FARNHAM EATON, b. 26 Mar 1808 son of William and Nancy (Farrington) Eaton; James d. at Stow, 17 Jan 1841.

703)   HANNAH EATON (*Sarah Farnum Eaton⁴, Mary Ingalls Farnum³, Sarah Russell Ingalls², Robert¹*), b. at Fryeburg, 31 Jan 1772 daughter of William and Sarah (Farnum) Eaton; m. at Concord, 4 Oct 1796, DAVID BLANCHARD, b. at Concord, 4 Dec 1771 son of John and Eleanor (Stevens) Blanchard; David d. at Concord, 1810 (probate 7 January 1810).

David Blanchard did not leave a will and widow Hannah was named as administratrix on 15 January 1810. On 6 September 1810, Hannah was named as guardian to four minor children under age fourteen: Herman Blanchard, Matilda Blanchard, William Blanchard, and Susannah Blanchard. Real estate of about eighty acres was valued at $900.[2098]

Hannah Eaton and David Blanchard were parents of four children born at Concord.

i   HERMAN BLANCHARD, b. 12 Feb 1797; d. at Cooper, MI, 4 May 1882; m. 1ˢᵗ 23 Nov 1824, BETSEY MARIA TAYLOR, b. 30 Jan 1803 daughter of Stephen and Ruth (Lovejoy) Taylor; Betsey d. at Persia, NY, 6 Jun 1838. Herman m. 2ⁿᵈ at Wales, NY, 3 Jan 1839, LAURA WEED,[2099] b. at Saratoga County, NY, 11 Mar 1810 daughter of John D. and Betsey (Wood) Weed; Laura d. at Cooper, 24 Jan 1886.

ii   MATILDA BLANCHARD, b. 5 Nov 1798; d. at Dakota, WI, 8 Feb 1852; m. at Brownville, NY, 18 Jan 1822, GEORGE THORNGATE, b. at Marlborough, Wiltshire, England, 30 Apr 1798 son of William and Hannah (-) Thorngate;[2100] George d. at North Loup, NE, 29 Nov 1881. George married second Betsey Langworthy and third the widow Lucretia *Stevenson* Dickinson. George was a British soldier who came to Canada in 1812, but after leaving the British army, settled first in New York.[2101]

iii   WILLIAM BLANCHARD, b. about 1801

iv   SUSANNAH BLANCHARD, b. about 1804; d. at Bethel, ME, 30 Nov 1892; m. about 1828, SILAS GROVER, b. at Bethel, 21 May 1801 son of Jedediah and Hannah (Wheeler) Grover; Silas d. at Bethel, 19 Jun 1855.

[2095] Chase, *Seven Generations of Descendants of Aquila and Thomas Chase*, p 230

[2096] It is not completely certain whether it was Sarah or her widowed mother Sarah Farnum Eaton who was the mother of Isaac's son.

[2097] Year: 1850; Census Place: Stow, Oxford, Maine; Roll: 262; Page: 139B

[2098] New Hampshire Wills and Probate, Rockingham, Estate Papers, David Blanchard of Concord, Case 8205

[2099] *War of 1812 Pension Application Files Index, 1812-1815*

[2100] England, Select Births and Christenings, 1538-1975

[2101] Obituary of George Thorngate, "The Sabbath Recorder" volume 37 (52), December 29, 1881, p 5

704) MARY EATON (*Sarah Farnum Eaton⁴, Mary Ingalls Farnum³, Sarah Russell Ingalls², Robert¹*), b. at Fryeburg, 2 Jul 1776 daughter of William and Sarah (Farnum) Eaton; d. at Waterford, ME, 20 Jun 1849; m. at Eddington, ME, 29 Jan 1795, DAVID WHITCOMB, b. at Bolton, MA, 13 Apr 1764 son of Levi and Sarah (Gates) Whitcomb; David d. at Waterford, 27 Apr 1835.

David was a farmer and worked at Hall's sawmill in Waterford, Maine where he died in an accident 27 April 1835.[2102] In 1797, David was chosen constable and collector of Waterford and was also surveyor of highways.[2103]

Daughter Mary married but did not have children. In her will written 15 December 1865 (probate 1883), she bequeathed all her money to be equally among brother William Whitcomb, sister Elizabeth Cummings, sister Mercy Whitcomb, sister Rebecca Mabray, and the two children of her deceased brother Ephraim. Sisters Elizabeth Mercy, and Rebecca receive the wearing apparel.

Mary and David were parents of ten children born at Waterford, Maine.

i   ELIZABETH WHITCOMB (twin), b. 17 Sep 1795; d. 1798.

ii   SARAH WHITCOMB (twin), b. 17 Sep 1795; d. 24 Oct 1820.

iii MARY ANN WHITCOMB, b. 28 Feb 1797; d. at Waterford, ME, 6 Jan 1883; m. about 1844, as his third wife, DARIUS WILKINS, b. at Middleton, MA, 26 Feb 1774 son of Abner and Eunice (Smith) Wilkins; Darius d. at Norway, ME, 23 Nov 1858. Darius married first Abigail Merrill and married second Amelia Wetherbee.

iv   ELIZABETH "BETSEY" WHITCOMB, b. 1 Mar 1798; d. at Hancock, WI, 11 Feb 1874; m. 1ˢᵗ at Waterford, 18 Aug 1833, FREDERICK SHARRATT who has not been identified. Betsey m. 2ⁿᵈ 1841, as his second wife, GEORGE WILLIAMS CUMMINGS, b. at Paris, ME, 22 Nov 1788 son of Isaac and Elizabeth (Bryant) Cummings; George d. at Oasis, WI, 16 Mar 1872. George was first married to Lucy Pratt.

v   DAVID WHITCOMB, b. 3 Jul 1800; d. at Lawrence, MA, 27 Mar 1857; m. at Portland, ME, 24 Mar 1832, LAVINIA PIPER who has not been identified.

vi   EPHRAIM WHITCOMB, b. 6 Aug 1803; d. at Paris, ME, 27 Jul 1854; m. ELIZA MERRILLL, b. 27 Jan 1809 daughter of Edmund and Betsey (Bancroft) Merrill; Eliza d. at Portland (burial at Norway, ME), 5 Dec 1893.

vii MERCY WHITCOMB, b. 31 Oct 1806; d. at Boston, 31 Jul 1898. Mercy did not marry.

viii WILLIAM WHITCOMB, b. 6 May 1810; d. at Holden, ME, 14 Mar 1903. William did not marry.

ix   REBECCA WHITCOMB, b. 1 Jul 1812; d. at Medway, ME, 22 Oct 1882; m. 1ˢᵗ 24 May 1832, ANDREW MAYBERRY, b. at Windham, ME, 12 Mar 1807 son of Josiah and Eunice (Miller) Mayberry; Andrew d. at Bangor, 4 Nov 1861. Rebecca m. 2ⁿᵈ 8 Jan 1870, ISAAC BENNETT WHARFF, b. 1789 son of Joseph and Susannah (Bennett) Wharff; Isaac d. Guilford, ME, 30 Jun 1878 (probate Oct 1878).

x   LEVI WHITCOMB, b. 15 Dec 1816; d. 1 May 1817.

705) SUSANNAH EATON (*Sarah Farnum Eaton⁴, Mary Ingalls Farnum³, Sarah Russell Ingalls², Robert¹*), b. at Fryeburg, 21 Jan 1778 daughter of William and Sarah (Farnum) Eaton; m. at Concord, 1 Mar 1803, JEREMIAH WARDWELL, baptized at Andover, 22 Jan 1771 son of Joshua and Mary (Saunders) Wardwell. Susannah and Jeremiah were living at Sidney, ME in 1850.

Susannah and Jeremiah resided in Andover, Maine and later in Sidney, Maine. They were parents of three known children.

In her will written 26 March 1896, daughter Susan O. Barnard bequeathed fifty dollars to George Wardwell and the remainder of the estate to deacons of the West Parish Church to be used for the improvement of the grounds of the West Parish Cemetery. Her furniture is left to Mrs. and Mrs. J. W. Barnard and to George Wardwell and Frank Wardwell.[2104]

i   THOMAS JEFFERSON WARDWELL, b. likely at Andover, ME, 26 Dec 1804; d. at North Andover, MA, 24 Oct 1862; m. about 1845, MARY ANN SWAN, b. at Andover, 12 May 1812 daughter of Joseph and Mary Kimball (Allen) Swan; Mary d. at North Andover, 22 Feb 1871.

ii   JEREMIAH WARDWELL, b. at Andover, ME, 11 Apr 1810; d. at Rumford, ME, 6 Aug 1887; m. JEANETTE BURNHAM, b. 3 Nov 1810 daughter of Enoch and Judith (Virgin) Burnham; Jeanette d. at Rumford, 12 Jun 1886.

[2102] Whitman, *A History of Norway, Maine*, p 529

[2103] Warren, *The History of Waterford, Oxford County, Maine*, p 78

[2104] Massachusetts Wills and Probate, Essex County, volume 424, pp 90-91

iii   SUSAN O. WARDWELL, b. at Andover, ME, 19 Jun 1814; d. at North Andover, MA, 15 Dec 1896; m. at Marblehead, 27 Oct 1858, JACOB BARNARD, b. at Andover, 9 Jul 1791 son of John and Lydia (Mooar) Barnard; Jacob d. at Andover, 13 Aug 1878. Jacob was first married to Hannah Goldsmith.

706)   SAMUEL CASE (*Mehitable Allen Case⁴, Mehitable Ingalls Allen³, Sarah Russell Ingalls², Robert¹*), b. at Norwich, 29 Dec 1762 son of Simeon and Mehitable (Allen) Case; d. at Norwich, 8 Jan 1791; m. about 1786, SUSANNAH COWDREY,[2105] b. about 1762; Susannah d. at Norwich, 24 May 1848.

Samuel Case was a carpenter/joiner in Norwich.[2106] He did not leave a will and his estate entered probate 14 February 1791. His estate was valued at £54.1.10 which included lumber, planks, clapboard, lathe, and vise.[2107]

Samuel and Susannah were parents of three children born at Norwich.

i   SUSANNAH CASE, b. 18 Oct 1786; d. at Norwich, 29 Apr 1820. Susannah did not marry.

ii   JOHN CASE, b. 4 Nov 1788; d. at Norwich, 30 Apr 1849; m. 1812, DIANA CONGDON, b. 1793 daughter of Elisha and Abigail (Miner) Congdon; Diana d. at Norwich, 17 Aug 1841.

iii   SAMUEL CASE, b. 16 Jan 1791; d. at Norwich, 29 Aug 1884; m. 1812, SALLY BAILEY, b. at Preston, CT, 1 Sep 1793 daughter of Samuel and Cynthia (*Story* Meech) Bailey; Sally d. at Norwich, 29 Oct 1892.

707)   SLUMAN ALLEN (*Isaac Allen⁴, Mehitable Ingalls Allen³, Sarah Russell Ingalls², Robert¹*), b. at Norwich, CT, 24 Oct 1760 son of Isaac and Sarah (French) Allen; d. at Chelsea, VT, 15 Apr 1834; m. at Royalton, VT, 18 Mar 1786, HANNAH STORRS, b. at Lebanon, NH, 18 Feb 1765 son of Huckins and Jerusha (Bicknell) Storrs; Hannah d. at Chelsea, after 1855 (time of statement related to pension).

Sluman and Hannah resided in Vermont and were settled in Chelsea before 1791 when Sluman purchased two mills in Chelsea.[2108]

On 21 August 1832, Sluman Allen of Chelsea, Vermont, aged seventy-two, provided a statement related to his pension. In May 1776, he enlisted as a militia man and was out for one month. In Fall 1777, he served another month in the militia under Capt. Seth Grosvenor and had further terms in the militia in 1778 and 1779. In Spring 1780, he enlisted in the Continental service for a term of eight months in Col. Durkee's regiment. He was transferred into the light infantry company of Capt. Buel. He reported he was born in 1760, lived for a time in Pomfret and then Royalton and Chelsea. Sluman's widow Hannah received a widow's pension. On 3 July 1855, Hannah Allen then age ninety provided a statement related to her petition for bounty lands.[2109]

In his will written 2 Apr 1834 (probate 7 May 1834), Sluman Allen bequeathed to beloved wife Hannah all his real and personal estate being the farm in Chelsea on which he lives, two other lots, and all the farming tools and stock animals. At Hannah's decease the property is to be divided between daughters Hannah Allen and Lauretta Allen to be theirs and their heirs forever. John W. Smith of Chelsea was named executor.[2110]

Sluman and Hannah were parents of eleven children, the older children born at Royalton and the younger children at Chelsea. In the 1850 census for Chelsea, Vermont, Hannah was head of household with her two unmarried daughters Hannah and Lauretta living with her.[2111]

i   SALLY ALLEN, b. 1786; d. at Chelsea, 1833. Sally did not marry.

ii   DANIEL ALLEN, b. and d. 1788

iii   ABIGAIL ALLEN, b. 1789; d. at Chelsea, 26 Apr 1820. Abigail did not marry.

iv   POLLY ALLEN, b. 1792; d. at Chelsea, 10 Jan 1826. Polly did not marry.

v   HANNAH ALLEN, b. 1794; died young

vi   ARATHUSA ALLEN, b. 1795; d. at Chelsea, 1821 (husband remarried 1822); m. at Chelsea, 6 Feb 1820, HARRY TRACY. Harry married second Catherine Reynolds on 11 Jul 1822. Harry and Catherine named their first child Almeria Arathusa Tracy.

vii   HANNAH ALLEN, b. 1797; d. at Chelsea, 1864. Hannah did not marry.

[2105] Perkins, *Old Houses of the Ancient Town of Norwich*, p 438
[2106] U.S., Craftperson Files, 1600-1995
[2107] *Connecticut State Library (Hartford, Connecticut)*; Probate Place: *Hartford, Connecticut, Probate Packets, Carew, W-Chapman and Norris, 1748-1880, case 2242*
[2108] Chelsea Historical Society, *History of Chelsea, Vermont* 1784-1984, p 9
[2109] U. S. Revolutionary War Pension and Bounty-Land Warrant Application Files, Case W20576
[2110] *Vermont. Probate Court (Randolph District)*; Probate Place: *Orange, Vermont, Folder 45*
[2111] Year: 1850; Census Place: Chelsea, Orange, Vermont; Roll: 926; Page: 300A

viii   LAURETTA ALLEN, b. 1799; d. at Chelsea, 1873, Lauretta did not marry.

ix   JOHN ALLEN, b. 29 Mar 1801; d. at Petersburg, IL, Apr 1864; m. at Cass County, IL, 6 Mar 1840, EMILY CHANDLER, b. 7 Mar 1811 daughter of John and Huldah (Howard) Chandler;[2112] Emily d. at Petersburg, IL, 26 Mar 1874. John Allen was a physician.

x   HARRIET ALLEN, b. 1803; d. 1804.

xi   HIRAM STORRS ALLEN, b. 18 Sep 1806; d. at Chippewa Falls, WI, 6 Mar 1886; m. Sep 1838, MARY DE MARIE, b. 1822 daughter of Louis and Angeline (Collins) De Marie;[2113] Mary d. at Chippewa Falls, 6 May 1894. Hiram was the first permanent settler of Chippewa County, WI.[2114]

708)   ZIPPORAH ALLEN (*Isaac Allen[4], Mehitable Ingalls Allen[3], Sarah Russell Ingalls[2], Robert[1]*), b. at Pomfret, 10 Nov 1762 daughter of Isaac and Sarah (French) Allen; d. at West Killingly, 28 Aug 1846; m. at Norwich, 26 Mar 1795, DANIEL FITCH, b. in Nova Scotia, about 1762; Daniel d. at West Killingly, 3 Nov 1855. Daniel was first married to Mehitable Bushnel on 4 May 1784; Mehitable died 7 Apr 1793.

      Daniel Fitch first made application for pension on 6 April 1818. He enlisted for the duration of the war on 7 June 1777 from Connecticut in the company of Capt. Abner Bacon in regiment of Col. John Durkee. Later, he was in the company of Capt. John Durkee, Jr. in the same regiment. He was discharged at West Point in June 1783. On 28 June 1820, he provided a statement that he was a cooper by occupation but no longer able to perform his work. His household at that time was wife Zipporah aged 58 who was unable to perform much work and was almost continually confined to her bed and son Charles Fitch aged 15. He gave the value of his estate as $68.53 and debts as $206. On 23 August 1839 was living in Newark, Essex County, New Jersey with his son Charles and requested transfer of pension from Connecticut to New Jersey. He later returned to Connecticut making application for pension transfer on 10 July 1841.[2115]

      Elisha Carpenter was named administrator of David Fitch's estate on 1 December 1855. Estate value was $93 which included $16 of pension not collected.[2116]

      Zipporah Allen and Daniel Fitch were parents of five children. All the children were baptized at Sprague.[2117]

      Son Rev. Charles Fitch prepared for the ministry and entered Brown University in 1824, but due to his poverty needed to withdraw before completing. He completed his theological studies under Rev. C. B. Everett and was ordained at Abington on 30 April 1828. Rev. Fitch had a series of appointments ranging from one to years in length at Abington, Western (Warren) in Massachusetts, Hartford, Boston, and Newark, New Jersey. He was evangelical in his preaching.[2118]

i   LOT FITCH, b. at Sprague, 17 Dec 1795; d. 19 Dec 1795.

ii   DANIEL ALLEN FITCH, b. 27 Dec 1796; d. at Center, WI, 2 Aug 1886; m. at Trumbull County, OH, 2 Oct 1826, NANCY FITCH, b. at Norwalk, 17 Jan 1809 daughter of Thomas and Nancy (Carver) Fitch; Nancy d. at Center, 3 Mar 1888.

iii   CALVIN A. FITCH, b. at Sprague, 30 Jul 1799; d. after 1870 when he was living at Cannon, MI; m. at Lisbon, CT, 17 Feb 1824, MARY ANN ROBINSON, of Lisbon, b. about 1805; Mary Ann d. after 1870.

iv   CATHERINE LORENA FITCH, b. 29 Mar 1802; d. at Plainfield, CT, 21 Jan 1881; m. 1st 18 Dec 1825, DANIEL GREENE, b. 11 Dec 1801 (record at Pomfret and at Warwick, RI) son of Christopher and Catherine (Greene) Greene); Daniel d. at Orwell, PA, 4 Nov 1837. Catherine m. 2nd 6 Jan 1842, GEORGE BLISS who has not been identified, but who seems to have died before 1850 when Catherine was living with her father in Killingly.

v   CHARLES FITCH, b. 27 Dec 1804; d. at Buffalo, NY, 14 Oct 1844; m. at Boston, 30 May 1828, ZERVIAH ROATH, of Brooklyn, CT, b. about 1805; Zerviah d. at Cleveland, OH, Jul 1875.

709)   EBENEZER ALLEN (*Joseph Allen[4], Mehitable Ingalls Allen[3], Sarah Russell Ingalls[2], Robert[1]*), b. at Pomfret, 24 May 1762 son of Joseph and Elizabeth (Warner) Allen; d. at Jefferson County, NY, 3 Jul 1824; m. at Dudley, 16 Mar 1786, PHEBE HEALY, b. at Dudley, 6 Dec 1765 daughter of Samuel and Phebe (Curtis) Healy; Phebe d. 4 Nov 1828.

      Ebenezer and Phebe settled in Hartland, Vermont after their marriage and ten children were born there. They relocated to Hounsfield, Jefferson County, New York in March 1808 where they built a log home on lot 38. The property was

[2112] Chandler, *The Descendants of William and Annis Chandler*, p 488

[2113] Western Historical Company, *History of Northern Wisconsin*, p 193

[2114] American Biographical Publishing Company, *The United Stated Biographical Dictionary*, Wisconsin volume I, p 267

[2115] U. S. Revolutionary War Pension and Bounty-Land Warrant Application Files, Case S37922

[2116] Connecticut Wills and Probate, Hartford, Killingly Probate District, Town of Killingly, Estate of Daniel Fitch, Case 734.

[2117] Connecticut Church Record Abstracts, volume 108, Sprague, p 69

[2118] Learned, "Congregational Churches and Ministers in Windham County, CT.", p 14

originally purchased from Col. Elisha Camp who was agent for Hounsfield. The farm owned by Ebenezer was later occupied by his grandson Lebbeus son of Leonard. Maj. Ebenezer Allen served five years during the Revolution attaining the rank of major by the time of discharge.[2119]

Ebenezer Allen and Phebe Healy were parents of ten children whose births are recorded at Hartland, Vermont.[2120]

i   EBENEZER ALLEN, b. 17 Mar 1788; d. at Hounsfield, NY, 10 Dec 1859; m. LAURA HINMAN, b. 11 Jan 1789 daughter of Thomas and Rhoda (Curtis) Hinman; Laura d. at Hounsfield, 11 Apr 1858.

ii   SETH ALLEN, b. 27 May 1790. In 1820, Seth was head of household in Hounsfield with a family of one male 26-44, one female 16-25, one male under 10 and one female 10-15. The name of his wife has not been found.

iii   PHEBE ALLEN, b. 25 Dec 1791; d. at Sackets Harbor, NY, 1 Apr 1861; m. Maj. SAMUEL FIELD, b. at Woodstock, VT, 17 Jan 1793 son of Elijah and Tamesin (Crain) Field;[2121] Samuel d. at Sackets Harbor, 20 Apr 1843.

iv   ETHAN ALLEN, b. 11 Jun 1793; d. at Hounsfield, NY, 8 Feb 1822.

v   LEONARD ALLEN, b. 21 Apr 1795; d. at Brownville, NY, 5 Dec 1883; m. 1818, EUNICE KNOWLTON, b. at Brownville, NY, 19 Jun 1800 daughter of Jonathan and Dolly (Prouty) Knowlton; Eunice d. at Brownville, 4 Oct 1886.

vi   WARNER ALLEN, b. 26 Nov 1797; d. at Hounsfield, NY, 29 Jul 1820.

vii   LUCY ALLEN, b. 16 May 1800; d. at Lockport, NY, 11 Apr 1874; m. DEMAS PERRY, b. at Woodstock, VT, 1 Jan 1784 (date given in obituary); Demas d. at Lockport, 11 Mar 1880.

viii   MARY "POLLY" ALLEN, b. 11 May 1802

ix   ELIZA ALLEN, b. 24 Oct 1804; d. at Watertown, NY, 31 Mar 1884; m. CHARLES AYERS, b. in VT, 29 May 1798 (engraved on gravestone); Charles d. at Watertown, 8 Jun 1852.

x   CHARLES ALLEN, b. 21 Apr 1807; d. at Brownville, NY, 20 Feb 1882; m. ALVIRA ALLEN, b. in NY, 1810; Alvira d. at Brownville, 17 Nov 1883.

710)   MARY "POLLY" ALLEN (*Joseph Allen⁴, Mehitable Ingalls Allen³, Sarah Russell Ingalls², Robert¹*), b. at Pomfret, 1 Apr 1766 daughter of Joseph and Elizabeth (Warner) Allen; d. at Charlton, MA, 13 Aug 1830; m. at Dudley, 26 Jan 1792, NATHANIEL BLOOD, b. at Oxford, MA, 22 Feb 1754 son of Nathaniel and Ruth (Hall) Blood; Nathaniel d. at Charlton, 9 Apr 1838. Nathaniel was first married to Bathsheba Upham.

Mary Allen and Nathaniel Blood were parents of seven children born at Charlton.

Daughter Polly married but did not have children. In her will written 8 May 1875 (probate 1880), Polly Upham bequeathed all her property to her niece Mary E. Harrington wife of Charles C. Harrington. Mary was also named executrix. The heirs-at-law given in the probate were John Blood of Worcester, Lawson Blood of Springfield, the heirs of Otis Blood of Worcester, and the heirs of Nathaniel Blood who last dwelt in St. Louis.[2122]

i   DANIEL BLOOD, b. 23 Mar 1793. He seems to be the Daniel who married at Charlton, 25 Aug 1816, POLLY EDDY, b. at Charlton,.27 Jul 1796 daughter of Edmond and Phebe (Nichols) Eddy. Daniel and Polly went to Ohio and were living in Franklin, OH in 1830. This marriage is tentative as Daniel and Polly Blood had children who were living in 1875 when Daniel's sister Polly wrote her will, but heirs of David are not given as heirs-at-law in the probate of sister Polly's estate.

ii   HERVA BLOOD, b. 24 Dec 1794

iii   POLLY BLOOD, b. 10 Mar 1797; d. at Sturbridge, 6 Feb 1880; m. at Charlton, 1 Jun 1843, ELIHU L. UPHAM, b. at Dudley, 28 Dec 1783 son of Simeon and Miriam (Larned) Upham; Elihu d. at Upham, 11 May 1868. Elihu was first married to Zoradah Dalrimple.

iv   NATHANIEL BLOOD, b. 25 Feb 1799; d. at St. Louis, MO, 25 Aug 1873; m. at Southbridge, MA, 11 Sep 1831, CLARISSA COOMBS, b. at Dunstable, 30 Jul 1806 daughter of James and Jane (Caldwell) Coombs; Clarinda d. at St. Louis, 21 Mar 1865.

[2119] Everts, *History of Jefferson County, New York*, p 393; Haddock, *Growth of a Century as Illustrated in the History of Jefferson County, New York*, p 616

[2120] Vermont, Vital Records, 1720-1908

[2121] Pierce, *Field Genealogy*, volume 1, p 434

[2122] *Worcester County, MA: Probate File Papers, 1731-1881*. Online database. AmericanAncestors.org. New England Historic Genealogical Society, 2015. Case 60650

v   JOHN BLOOD, b. 9 Jun 1802; d. at Worcester, 27 Mar 1880; m. at Charlton, 17 Apr 1851, CHARLOTTE BLOOD (widow of Joel Adams), b. at Charlton, 1811 daughter of Eli and Patty (Merritt) Blood; Charlotte d. of consumption, at Charlton, 10 Jan 1870. John did not have children.

vi   OTIS BLOOD, b. 19 Sep 1807; d. at Worcester, 30 Jan 1875; m. at Sturbridge, 21 Aug 1830, MARTHA HAMANT, b. 1797 daughter of Job and Sarah (Stow) Hamant; Martha d. at Worcester, 23 Mar 1871.

vii   LAWSON BLOOD, b. 1808; d. at Springfield, MA, 3 Jul 1881; m. 1st at Charlton, 16 Apr 1832, SALLY ELIZABETH TOWNE, b. 1816; Sally d. at Sturbridge, 3 Mar 1837. Lawson m. 2nd at Sturbridge, 17 Sep 1838, SUSANNAH PAMELIA BENNETT, b. about 1812; Pamelia d. at Sturbridge, 17 Jan 1857. Lawson m. 3rd at Charlton, 15 Mar 1862, ADELINE LOMBARD DARLING, b. 29 Aug 1822 daughter of Cyrus and Sophia (Thayer) Darling; Adeline d. at Woonsocket, RI, 8 Feb 1912. Adeline was first married to William F. Roberts.

711)   BETTY ALLEN (*Joseph Allen⁴, Mehitable Ingalls Allen³, Sarah Russell Ingalls², Robert¹*), b. at Pomfret, 28 Feb 1768 daughter of Joseph and Elizabeth (Warner) Allen; d. at Woodstock, CT, 4 Sep 1810; m. at Dudley, 20 Apr 1786, NATHANIEL MAY, b. at Dudley, 5 Sep 1762 son of Samuel and Abigail (Lyon) May; Nathaniel d. at Oxford, MA, 25 Feb 1837. Nathaniel married second Betsey Lawrence on 15 Jan 1817 at Wrentham, MA.

Betty and Nathaniel first resided in Sturbridge and were later in Woodstock where the youngest children were born, and Betty died. Nathaniel was later in Wrentham, Massachusetts, spent some time in Hampton, Connecticut with one of his daughters,[2123] and was finally in Oxford, Massachusetts where he died.

On 1 January 1780, Nathaniel May enlisted for a three-year term in the 9th regiment of the Massachusetts line commanded by Col. Henry Jackson. He was transferred to Capt. Ebenezer Smith's company in the 2nd regiment commanded by Col. Ebenezer Sproat. He was discharged at West Point with the rank of corporal on 27 October 1783 by Gen. Knox. He made application for a pension based on his service on 1 April 1818. On 17 July 1820 while living in Wrentham, he provided additional information reporting the value of his personal property as $33.80. He was a laborer by occupation but unable to work due to infirmity. His household at that time was wife age 51 who was sick and unable to support herself and nine-year old daughter Ruth Billay who was not of sufficient ability to support herself. Following Nathaniel's death, his widow Betsey received a pension. She stated she was Betsey Lawrence prior to the marriage and she and Nathaniel were married on 15 January 1817 and that Nathaniel died at Oxford on 25 February 1837.[2124]

There are records for nine children of Betty and Nathaniel.

i   HOLLOWAY MAY, b. at Dudley, 4 Nov 1786

ii   ALLEN MAY, b. at Dudley, 11 Aug 1788

iii   PRUDA MAY, b. at Dudley, 22 Aug 1790

iv   BETSEY MAY, b. at Dudley, 4 May 1792

v   BURNICE A. MAY (twin), b. at Dudley, 27 Aug 1795; d. at Tewksbury, 30 Dec 1873. Burnice did not marry. In 1850, she lived with her sister Phebe in Cumberland, RI[2125] and in 1870 was living with her nephew Addison Knight in New Haven.[2126]

vi   BARRIS MAY (twin), b. at Dudley, 27 Aug 1795

vii   PHEBE H. MAY, b. 1803; d. at Attleboro, MA, 8 Apr 1866; m. 1st about 1823, WILLIAM CORTTIS, b. at Thompson, CT, about 1798 son of Japheth and Mary (Upham) Corttis; William d. at Thompson, 26 Dec 1823 (probate 10 Jan 1824). Phebe m. 2nd at Charlton, MA, 31 Oct 1838, ADDISON KNIGHT, b. at Leicester, MA, 28 Aug 1803 son of Jonathan and Polly (Sprague) Knight; Addison d. at Cumberland, RI, 15 Jun 1847.

viii   ANGELINE MAY, b. at Sturbridge, 7 Dec 1807

ix   RUTH B. MAY, b. at Woodstock, CT, 30 Aug 1810; d. at Dudley, MA, 12 Oct 1855; m. at Thompson, CT, 2 Jan 1843, HAMILTON BALLARD, b. at Dudley, 17 May 1806 son of Lynde and Polly (Bates) Ballard; Hamilton d. at Putnam, CT, 3 Feb 1895. Hamilton's other marriages were to Julia Prince and to Sarah B. Austin.

712)   ISAAC ALLEN (*Joseph Allen⁴, Mehitable Ingalls Allen³, Sarah Russell Ingalls², Robert¹*), b. at Pomfret, 1774 son of Joseph and Elizabeth (Warner) Allen; d. at Groton, NY, 3 Mar 1825; m. SUSAN F. SELLEN, b. 18 Feb 1794 daughter of John and Martha (Moseley) Sellen; Susan d. at Groton, 9 Dec 1881. Susan married second Jacob Thompson in 1825.[2127]

[2123] The information on his living with a daughter in Hampton is provided in the pension application file.
[2124] U. S. Revolutionary War Pension and Bounty-Land Warrant Application Files, Cas W6775
[2125] Year: 1850; Census Place: Cumberland, Providence, Rhode Island; Roll: 843; Page: 123A
[2126] Year: 1870; Census Place: New Haven Ward 6, New Haven, Connecticut; Roll: M593_110; Page: 574B; Family History Library Film: 545609
[2127] Selkreg, *Landmarks of Tompkins County, New York*, Part III, Family Sketches, p 16

Isaac Allen was one of the founders of West Groton, New York. He came to Tompkins County from Vermont in 1804, built a log cabin, and later the first store in 1823. Isaac's father Joseph and other family came to Groton after Isaac settled there. Isaac farmed in Groton but was also a bridge builder involved in the construction of a bridge over the Potomac River at Washington and the first bridge over Cayuga Lake. At the time of his death he owned 315 acres in Groton.[2128] Susan Allen was named administratrix of his estate on 9 March 1825.[2129]

Isaac and Susan were parents of five children born at Groton.

i AMANDA ALLEN, b. 1816; d. at Groton, NY, 1889; m. at Groton, 3 Mar 1839, Rev. JOSEPH WILCOTT STEARNS, b. at Westhampton, MA, 21 Feb 1808 son of Nathaniel Stockwell and Seviah (Wilcott) Stearns; Joseph d. at Groton, Apr 1888.

ii LOUISA ALLEN, b. and d. 1816

iii PERRY W. ALLEN, b. 10 Feb 1818; d. at Groton, 24 Oct 1900; m. at Groton, 14 Mar 1848, CHARLOTTE E. CLEMENT, b. May 1828 daughter of Daniel R. and Betsy (Watson) Clement; Charlotte d. at West Groton, 6 Jul 1908.

iv MARILLA ALLEN, b. Feb 1819; d. 7 Jul 1821.

v NAPOLEON W. ALLEN, b. 24 Nov 1823; d. at Groton, 20 Jul 1885. Napoleon did not marry. He lived with his mother.

713) JOHN ALLEN (*Joseph Allen⁴, Mehitable Ingalls Allen³, Sarah Russell Ingalls², Robert¹*), b. at Pomfret, 17 Feb 1776 son of Joseph and Elizabeth (Warner) Allen; d. at Jefferson County, NY, 24 Apr 1859; m. 1796, POLLY (or Molly) MCDOWELL, b. at Winchester, NH, 11 Apr 1776 daughter of Alexander and Levina (Oak) McDowell; Polly d. at Watertown, NY, 14 Nov 1851.

John Allen was a farmer. In 1850, John and Mary were living with their daughter Emeline and her husband James V. Warren in Brownville, New York.[2130] He is likely the John Allen in Hounsfield, New York in 1830 then with a household of four: one male 50 to 59; one female 50 to 59; one male 10 to 14; and one female 10 to 14.[2131] The family was first in Strafford, Vermont where in 1800 there were six family members: one male 26 to 44; one female, 16 to 25; two males under 5; one male 10 to 15; and one female under 10.[2132] There are death records of two young children in Strafford, Vermont and daughter Emeline is clearly identified in census records. There are other possible children in this family (Andrew 2ⁿᵈ, Lovina, Sarah, and Mary), but clear information on these possible children was not located.

i ISAAC ALLEN, b. 1797; d. at Strafford, VT, 18 Aug 1801

ii ANDREW ALLEN, b. 1798; d. at Strafford, 11 Aug 1801

iii EMELINE ALLEN, b. about 1813; d. at Fairview, PA, 1887; m. about 1836 JAMES VALENTINE WARREN, b. at Hampstead, New Brunswick, 1812 son of Nathaniel V. and Lavinia (Watrous) Warren; James d. at Fairview, PA, 1896 (probate 18 Apr 1896). James Valentine traveled with his siblings and their father Nathaniel arriving in New York in 1827.[2133] Emeline and James (who sometimes went by Valentine and sometimes V. James and sometimes James V.) were in New York, then Ohio, and finally in Fairview, PA where they ran a hotel.

714) ASAPH ALLEN (*Joseph Allen⁴, Mehitable Ingalls Allen³, Sarah Russell Ingalls², Robert¹*), b. at Dudley, 25 Jan 1778 son of Joseph and Elizabeth (Warner) Allen; d. 25 Oct 1814;[2134] m. about 1800, LOIS KING, b. at Wilbraham, 13 Dec 1777 daughter of Oliver and Ruth (Cooley) King; Lois d. at Cuba, NY, 2 Aug 1847.

Asaph served as sergeant in the 1ˢᵗ regiment of New York militia during the War of 1812.[2135]

Asaph and Lois were parents of eight children, the oldest three children likely born at Chelsea, Vermont (census records of the oldest three children give place of birth as Vermont) and the younger children after the family move to Eaton, New York.

[2128] Selkreg, *Landmarks of Tompkins County, New York*, Part III, Family Sketches, p 4

[2129] New York Wills and Probate, Tompkins County, Letters of Administration, Volume 0035, p 78

[2130] Year: 1850; Census Place: Brownville, Jefferson, New York; Roll: 514; Page: 192A

[2131] Year: 1830; Census Place: Hounsfield, Jefferson, New York; Series: M19; Roll: 92; Page: 179; Family History Library Film: 0017152

[2132] Year: 1800; Census Place: Strafford, Orange, Vermont; Series: M32; Roll: 51; Page: 565; Image: 314; Family History Library Film: 218688

[2133] New York, Passenger and Crew Lists (including Castle Garden and Ellis Island), 1820-1957; Year: 1827; Arrival: New York, New York, USA; Microfilm Serial: M237, 1820-1897; Line: 8; List Number: 363

[2134] It is reported that Asaph served during the War of 1812 and died while returning home on furlough; Biographical Review, Biographical Review of Dane County, Wisconsin, p 527. Date of death is as given on a memorial monument in Cuba Cemetery where his wife is buried; findagrave ID: 169177009

[2135] U.S., War of 1812 Service Records, 1812-1815

i   ASAPH K. ALLEN, b. 1801; d. at Lawrence, KS, 4 May 1871; m. 1st about 1825, MELINDA ELMORE, b. about
         1805; Melinda d. likely at Groton, NY, about 1830. Asaph m. 2nd about 1831, ISABEL S. FRARY, b. 3 Jan 1811;
         Isabel d. at Bellville, NY, 18 Mar 1850. Asaph m. 3rd about 1855, MARIETTA INGALLS (widow of John Prine), b.
         12 May 1812 daughter of James and Margaret (Baxter) Ingalls; Marietta d. at San Francisco, 1890.

ii   ADELINE ALLEN, b. 14 Dec 1802; d. at Middleton, WI, 30 Jun 1876; m. by 1827, JUSTIN F. WILLIAMS, b. at
         Charlemont, MA, 4 May 1804 son of Ebenezer and Elizabeth (Beckwith) Williams; Justin d. at Middleton, 10 Mar
         1883.[2136]

iii   ISAAC ALLEN, b. 1804; d. at Hudson, SD, 19 Apr 1883; m. about 1838, SARAH BLAISDELL, b. 1812 possibly
         daughter of Stephen and Bathsheba (Aldrich) Blaisdell; Sarah d. at Exeter, WI, 31 Jan 1862. Isaac and Sarah
         married in New York, went to Kendall County, Illinois about 1853, and after a few years moved on to Wisconsin.
         Sarah died in Wisconsin and after Isaac was in Iowa before finally settling in South Dakota.[2137]

iv   OLIVER ALLEN, b. 1806; d. at Bath, NY, 1866 (probate 31 Dec 1866); m. 1827, SOPHRONIA INGALLS, b. 27
         Aug 1810 daughter of James and Margaret (Baxter) Ingalls;[2138] Sophronia d. at Horseheads, NY, 27 Nov 1898.

v   LYMAN ALLEN, b. 1808; d. at Wilton, IA, 28 Feb 1888; m. 1st at South Strafford, VT, 5 Jan 1803, SARAH
         BROWN, b. in VT about 1808; Sarah d. about 1855. Lyman m. 2nd at Johnson County, IA, 31 Dec 1856, HEPSEY
         S. BALDWIN, b. in MA, 1812; Hepsey d. at Wilton, 6 May 1895.

vi   HENRY R. ALLEN, b. 1810; d. at Union, WI, 25 Apr 1881; m. about 1830, ELECTA CARPENTER, b. 1811
         daughter of Sylvanus J. and Rhoda (Hathaway) Carpenter;[2139] Electa d. at Utica, NE, 27 Dec 1897.

vii   WILLIAM ALLEN, b. 1812; d. at Groton, NY, 24 Feb 1866; *perhaps* m. about 1848, SARAH JANE WILSON, b.
         1822; Sarah d. at Groton, 29 May 1879.

viii   HARRIET ALLEN, b. 20 Oct 1814; d. at Rushford, NY, 26 Mar 1883; m. about 1832, NATHANIEL JEWELL, b.
         20 Oct 1811 son of Joseph and Asenath (Cross) Jewell;[2140] Nathaniel d. at Rushford, 1883.

715)   AMASA COPELAND (*Sarah Ingalls Copeland⁴, Stephen Ingalls³, Sarah Russell Ingalls², Robert¹*), b. at Pomfret, 22
Apr 1758 son of James and Sarah (Ingalls) Copeland; d. at Pomfret, CT, 18 Aug 1852; m. at Pomfret, 24 Jan 1788, TRYPHENA
LISCOMB, b. at Pomfret, 7 Oct 1759 daughter of Thomas and Sarah (Parkhurst) Liscomb;[2141] Tryphena d. at Hampton, 2 Apr
1834.
         Amasa served as a private in the Connecticut line of the Continental army for a term of three years in the regiment of
Col. Sherburne for which service he received a pension of $96 per year. On 8 April 1818, he provided a statement related to his
pension application. He enlisted in May 1777 for a term of three years in the company of Capt. Amos Stanton. In a statement on
20 June 1820, Amasa reported he was a farmer by occupation but was unable to perform work due to rheumatism. His
household at that time was himself and his wife age sixty-one. On 17 June 1853, E. W. Sessions acting on behalf of the heirs
inquired regarding a retroactive increase in the pension based on evidence of increased rank in Amasa's war service.[2142] Amasa
is reported as the last surviving member of the corps that attended Major André to the gallows.[2143]
         In his will dated 7 January 1839 (proved 20 August 1852), Amasa Copeland bequeathed seventy-five cents to each of
his dutiful children: Sarah Ford, Phebe Grayson, Eliza Choller, Lucy Tucker, Lora Armstrong, Sophia Copeland, and Thomas L.
Copeland. He bequeathed to daughter Sophia Copeland "in consideration of her filial care and attention to her parents in their
declining age, all the rest residue and remainder of my estate, of what name and nature soever, to her, her heirs or assigns
forever." Sophia was named sole executrix. Personal estate was $272.76.[2144]
         Amasa Copeland and Tryphena Liscomb were parents of eight children born at Pomfret.

i   SARAH COPELAND, b. 14 Mar 1789; d. at East Otto, NY, 8 Aug 1880; m. her first cousin, NATHANIEL FORD
         (*Rebecca Copeland Ford⁵, Sarah Ingalls Copeland⁴, Stephen Ingalls³, Sarah Russell Ingalls², Robert¹*), b. 5 Apr
         1795 son of Nathaniel and Rebecca (Copeland) Ford; Nathaniel d. after 1880.

ii   PHEBE COPELAND, b. 23 Oct 1790; d. at Brooklyn, CT, 25 Jun 1888; m. 1st BENJAMIN PRATT who has not
         been identified, but d. about 1833. Phebe m. 2nd at Pomfret, 23 Dec 1833, RICHARD GRAYSON of Rhode Island.

[2136] Biographical Review, Biographical Review of Dane County, Wisconsin, p 527
[2137] Union Publishing Company, History of Butler County, Iowa, p 699
[2138] Burleigh, *History and Genealogy of the Ingalls Family*, p 158
[2139] The 1852 probate of Sylvanus J. Carpenter of Groton, New York names Electa wife of Henry Allen of Cuba, New York as an heir.
[2140] Jewell, *The Jewell Register*, p 46
[2141] The 1802 probate of Thomas Liscomb of Pomfret includes a distribution to daughter Triphena Copeland.
[2142] U. S. Revolutionary War Pension and Bounty-Land Warrant Application Files, Case S36464
[2143] Copeland, *The Copeland Family*, p 75
[2144] Connecticut Wills and Probate, Pomfret Probate District, Town of Pomfret, Estate of Amasa Compeland, Case 1239

The marriage of Phebe and Richard seems to have ended in divorce as Richard seems to have married the widow Mary Atwood on 14 Nov 1840. By 1850 Phebe had returned to using the name Phebe Pratt and was living with her father and sister Sophia in Pomfret.[2145] Benjamin and Phebe Pratt were members of the church at Pomfret.[2146]

iii   ELIZA COPELAND, b. 19 Dec 1792; d. at Pomfret, 14 May 1854; m. SAMUEL CHOLLAR, b. in CT, about 1793; Samuel d. after 1870 when he was living in Pomfret.

iv   LUCY COPELAND, b. 4 Mar 1795; d. at Chester, MA, 30 Apr 1888; m. 1st PASCAL C. TUCKER, b. at Windsor, MA, 16 Sep 1794 son of Ephraim and Sarah (Dresser) Tucker; Pascal d. at about 1848. Lucy m. 2nd at Windsor, 31 Oct 1849, JETSON STETSON, b. at Abington, MA, 7 Jan 1789 son of Levi and Elizabeth (Pratt) Stetson; Jetson d. at Chester,

v   LORA COPELAND, b. 17 Oct 1797; d. at East Otto, NY, 13 Mar 1891; m. JEDEDIAH ARMSTRONG, b. in NY, about 1798; Jedediah d. at East Otto, 19 Nov 1865.

vi   SOPHIA COPELAND, b. 20 Feb 1800; d. at Pomfret, 7 Mar 1883. Sophia did not marry.

vii   THOMAS LISCOMB COPELAND, b. 29 Dec 1801; d. at Pomfret (buried at Abington), 3 Apr 1882; m. at Hampton, 10 Mar 1830, ELIZABETH DAVIS, b. about 1804; Elizabeth d. at Pomfret, 30 Jun 1844. A son of Thomas and Elizabeth, Henry Copeland, died near Richmond on 7 Jul 1862.

viii   JOSEPH COPELAND, b. 21 Aug 1804; d. 10 Nov 1808.

716)   SARAH COPELAND (*Sarah Ingalls Copeland⁴, Stephen Ingalls³, Sarah Russell Ingalls², Robert¹*), b. at Pomfret, 4 May 1760 daughter of James and Sarah (Ingalls) Copeland; m. at Pomfret, 9 Nov 1783, RICHARD RINDGE, b. about 1760; Richard d. at Calais, VT, 27 Aug 1843.

Richard Rindge served for periods spanning seven years of the Revolution. He made declaration for his pension on 6 April 1818 when he was then fifty-eight years old and resident of Randolph, Vermont. While living in Ipswich, he first enlisted on 1 January 1776 for one year in the Massachusetts line in the company of Capt. John Baker in the regiment of Col. Little. After his discharge, he re-enlisted on 11 February 1777 in the company of Capt. Laws and regiment of Col. Jeduthan Baldwin and served until November. During that enlistment he was present at the capture of Burgoyne. He next enlisted as a mariner on the brig Clifton under Capt. Benjamin Lovett and sailed from Beverly on 5 March 1778. He was taken prisoner in June or July and transported to St. Johns in Antigua but was able to escape and arrived in Boston in January 1779. In May 1780, he enlisted for another year in the Massachusetts line in the company of Capt. Peter Pages in regiment of Col. Wigglesworth. His final enlistment was August 1782 in the company of Capt. Benjamin Durkee in the Connecticut line and served until the end of the war.

On 30 June 1820 while resident of Glover, Vermont, he provided additional information on his status. He reported no real property, one yoke of steers, one heifer, three sheep, and one colt. He was farmer by occupation but crippled due to the loss of his left leg thirty-three years previously and confined to crutches ever since. In his household was daughter Polly age 20 who was crippled since birth.[2147]

There are records for eight children of Sarah and Richard born at Hampton, Connecticut and the family lived there in 1800.[2148] Nothing further was found for the children in this family.

i   JOHN RINDGE, b. 24 Jan 1784

ii   SARAH RINDGE, b. 8 Nov 1785

iii   ANNA RINDGE, b. 2 Feb 1788

iv   LUCY RINDGE, b. 2 Jun 1790

v   JOSEPH RINDGE, b. 22 Jul 1792

vi   NATHAN RINDGE, b. 27 May 1795; d. 11 Aug 1795

vii   NATHAN RINDGE, b. 21 Sep 1796

viii   POLLY RINDGE, b. 19 Dec 1799

[2145] Year: 1850; Census Place: Pomfret, Windham, Connecticut; Roll: 51; Page: 394A

[2146] Connecticut Church Record Abstracts, Volume 090, Pomfret, p 82

[2147] U. S. Revolutionary War Pension and Bounty-Land Warrant Application Files, Case S41983

[2148] Year: 1800; Census Place: Hampton, Windham, Connecticut; Series: M32; Roll: 2; Page: 832; Image: 394; Family History Library Film: 205619

717)   REBECCA COPELAND (*Sarah Ingalls Copeland⁴, Stephen Ingalls³, Sarah Russell Ingalls², Robertⁱ*), baptized at Brooklyn, 28 Sep 1766 daughter of James and Sarah (Ingalls) Copeland; d. at Marshall, NY, 2 Oct 1844; m. at Hampton, CT, 27 Oct 1788, her fourth cousin (through Holt line), NATHANIEL FORD, b. at Hampton, 11 Jul 1765 son of Amos and Lydia (Davison) Ford; Nathaniel d. at Marshall, 31 Oct 1849.

On 11 September 1832, Nathaniel Ford of Marshall aged sixty-seven made declaration related to his pension application. He was born at Hampton, Connecticut on 11 July 1765. In May 1782, the "spring after New Haven was burnt", he enlisted as a private as a substitute for Amos Clark in the company of Capt. Benjamin Durkee. He was at Fort Trumbull for the purpose of guarding the fort and the prison ship that was there at that time. He served for six months. For about the past forty years he resided in different parts of New York, twenty-seven years in Paris and later in Marshall. He received pension of $20 per annum.[2149]

In his will written 26 December 1844, Nathaniel Ford of Marshall directed that his property be divided in nine equal parts and distributed to his children who are not named in the will. Daniel L. Barton was named executor.[2150] A statement provided on 7 January 1851 by David L. Barton executor of the will named the following heirs-at-law who were six sons and three daughters: Nathaniel Ford of Mansfield, New York; Stephen Ford of Harmony, New York; Silas Ford of Brownsville, New York; Ebenezer Ford of Michigan whose place of residence was unknown; William Ford of Salt Lake, Upper California; Amos Ford of Beloit, Wisconsin; Asena Mayo wife of Nathaniel Mayo of Clinton, New York; Lydia Andrews wife of Warren Andrews of Corning, New York; and Betsey Phinney wife of Daniel Y. Phinney of Marshall, New York.

Nathaniel Ford and Rebecca Copeland were parents of nine children.

i   EBENEZER FORD, b. at Hampton, 16 Jan 1789; d. likely at Davison, MI where he was living in 1850; m. LUCRETIA PAGE, b. in NY, about 1790.

ii   WILLIAM FORD, b. at Hampton, 9 Aug 1790; d. at Nauvoo, IL, after 1850; m. HANNAH LUCILLE MAYO, b. 25 Nov 1795 daughter of Nathaniel and Lucy (Mays) Mayo; Hannah d. at Council Bluffs, IA, 28 Sep 1857.

iii   NATHANIEL FORD, b. at Paris, NY, 5 Apr 1795; d. after 1880 when living at Otto, NY; m. his first cousin, SARAH COPELAND (*Amasa Copeland⁵, Sarah Ingalls Copeland⁴, Stephen Ingalls³, Sarah Russell Ingalls², Robertⁱ*), b. at Pomfret, 14 Mar 1789 daughter of Amasa and Tryphena (Liscomb) Copeland; Sarah d. at East Otto, 8 Aug 1880.

iv   BETSEY FORD, b. about 1797; d. at Marshall, NY, May 1880; m. DANIEL Y. PHINNEY, b. in CT, 1793 son of Benjamin and Hannah (Yeomans) Phinney; Daniel d. at Marshall, May 1880.

v   STEPHEN FORD, b. 4 Sep 1799; d. at Sherman, NY, 31 Dec 1873; m. ELIZABETH WING, b. 11 Jun 1803 daughter of Ichabod and Mandana (Henderson) Wing; Elizabeth d. 30 Aug 1880.

vi   SILAS FORD, b. 1802; d. at Sherman, NY, 22 Dec 1855; m. about 1843, as her second husband, FANNY REED, b. at Chester, VT, 7 Sep 1800 daughter of Isaac and Mary (White) Reed; Fanny d. at Brownville, NY, 10 Sep 1862. Fanny was first married to Horace Earl.

vii   LYDIA FORD, b. about 1804; d. after 1850 when she was living at Painted Post, NY; m. WARREN ANDREWS, b. about 1804; Warren d. after 1850.

viii   ASENA FORD, b. about 1804; d. after 1860 when living at Oneida, NY; m. NATHANIEL MAYO, b. about 1803 son of Nathaniel and Lucy (Mays) Mayo; Nathaniel d. after 1860.

ix   AMOS FORD, b. at Paris, NY, about 1808; d. after 1880 when living at Arena, Wisconsin. Amos seems to have married three times and the records for two of the marriages provide the names of his parents as Nathaniel and Rebecca Ford. However, the dates of the marriages do not align with who is listed as wife in the census records. Amos was likely first married to ELIZA who is not identified but born in NY about 1812 and died likely at Dane County, WI about 1860. Amos Ford (parents given as Nathaniel and Rebecca Ford on the marriage transcription) married at Black Earth, WI on 24 Jul 1861,[2151] MARGRAM HARRIS (widow Margram Cooper with names of parents given as Solomon and Hannah Harris) who was born at Louth, Lincolnshire, about 1833 daughter of Solomon and Hannah (Tyson) Harris. There is record of a third marriage to MARY A. HARRIS (also daughter of Solomon and Hannah with Amos's parents given as Nathaniel and Rebecca) on 17 Mar 1883 at Black Earth.[2152] However, Amos's wife in the 1870 census seems to be Mary (with a gap in the children allowing for the death of Margram and marriage to Mary between 1865 and 1868). Solomon Harris and Hannah Tyson were married in Lincolnshire in 1832 and arrived in the U.S. at New Orleans in 1850. Amos had at least nine children with his

---

[2149] U. S. Revolutionary War Pension and Bounty-Land Warrant Application Files, Case S13049

[2150] New York Wills and Probate, Oneida County, Wills volume 0009, p 212; administration volume 3, p 143

[2151] "Wisconsin Marriages, 1836-1930", database, *FamilySearch* (https://familysearch.org/ark:/61903/1:1:XRL6-BDB : 30 January 2020), Amos Ford, 1861.

[2152] "Wisconsin Marriages, 1836-1930", database, *FamilySearch* (https://familysearch.org/ark:/61903/1:1:XRTS-QN2 : 30 January 2020), Amos Ford, 1883.

three wives. There may be an error in the marriage transcriptions and needs further investigation. In the 1850 census, Amos Ford age 41 and born in NY was living at Albany, WI with wife Eliza and children Ann, Ellen, Warren, John, and Charles (age 3).[2153] In 1860, Amos Ford age 50 born in NY was living at Black Earth with son Charles age 14.[2154] In 1870, Amos Ford born in NY and age 62 was living at Mazomanie, WI with wife Mary A. Ford and children Edward age 5, and twins Frank and Minnie age 7 months.[2155]

718)   WILLARD COPELAND (*Sarah Ingalls Copeland⁴, Stephen Ingalls³, Sarah Russell Ingalls², Robert¹*), baptized at Brooklyn, 4 Dec 1768 son of James and Sarah (Ingalls) Copeland; d. at Braintree, VT, 20 Feb 1852;[2156] m. 1ˢᵗ about 1795, Alice Lyon *likely* his fourth cousin, ALICE LYON (*Robert Lyon⁵, Sarah Holt Lyon⁴, Robert Holt³, Mary Russell Holt², Robert¹*), b. at Hampton, 14 Jun 1769 daughter of Robert and Alice (Holt) Lyon; Alice d. at Braintree, 1804. Willard m. 2ⁿᵈ at Braintree, 12 Dec 1805, REBECCA WHITE, b. at Braintree, MA, 30 May 1766 daughter of Micah and Susanna (Eager) White; Rebecca d. at Randolph, VT, 1 Aug 1856.[2157]

Willard was in Brooklyn, Connecticut and relocated to Braintree, Vermont about 1803. Willard had three children, two with his first wife Alice Lyon and one with Rebecca White. None of his children married, although they all lived long lives, son James dying at age 94.

In 1850, Willard, age 82, was living in Braintree in the home of Jonathan Sumner, age 25, and wife Hannah, age 21. Willard is lister as a pauper.[2158]

Willard Copeland and Alice Lyon were parents of two children for whom there are records.

i   JAMES COPELAND, b. at Mansfield, CT, 25 Jun 1799; d. at Braintree, VT, 17 Oct 1893. James did not marry.

ii   CLARISSA ALICE COPELAND, b. at Brooklyn, CT, 6 Feb 1802; d. at Braintree, VT, 1888. Clarissa did not marry.

Willard Copeland and Rebecca White were parents of one child.

i   ABEL WYLLYS COPELAND, b. at Braintree, VT, 13 Nov 1809; d. at Braintree, 17 Mar 1867. Abel did not marry.

719)   SAMUEL INGALLS (*Samuel Ingalls⁴, Stephen Ingalls³, Sarah Russell Ingalls², Robert¹*), b. at Pomfret, 24 Aug 1770 son of Samuel and Deborah (Meacham) Ingalls; d. at Dunklee's Grove, IL, Oct 1839; m. at Belchertown, 22 Oct 1802, DIANA DODGE, b. 1778; Diana d. at Pelham, MA, 3 Dec 1833.

Samuel was a farmer in Belchertown.[2159] After the death of his wife, he moved to Illinois where his son Augustus settled.

There are records of three children of Samuel and Diana born at Belchertown.[2160]

i   CLARISSA INGALLS, b. at Belchertown, 26 Dec 1802; d. at Ludlow, MA, 5 Mar 1885; m. at Granby, 7 Nov 1837, DERRICK OBEDIAH CARVER, b. 27 Oct 1804 son of Jonathan and Elizabeth (Horsford) Carver; Derrick d. at Granby, 29 Nov 1850.

ii   JUSTUS D. INGALLS (twin), b. at Belchertown, 12 Mar 1805; d. at Northampton, MI, about 1859. Justus did not marry and was living alone at Northampton in 1850.[2161]

iii   AUGUSTUS G. INGALLS (twin), b. at Belchertown, 12 Mar 1805; d. at Bloomington, IL, 1 Jun 1889; m. 1ˢᵗ at Charlestown, MA, 28 Apr 1833, NANCY S. DUNKLEE, b. 8 May 1806 daughter of Hezekiah and Betsey (Farley) Dunklee; Nancy d. at Dunklee's Grove, IL, 10 Aug 1845. Augustus m. 2ⁿᵈ 6 May 1847, LUCY H. ROLLINS, b. at Mendon, VT, 8 Aug 1817; Lucy d. at Bloomingdale, IL, 16 Apr 1915.

720)   LEMUEL INGALLS (*Samuel Ingalls⁴, Stephen Ingalls³, Sarah Russell Ingalls², Robert¹*), b. at Pomfret, 24 Aug 1770 son of Samuel and Deborah (Meacham) Ingalls; m. at Belchertown, MA, 1 Oct 1802, LOUISA PRENTISS.

[2153] Year: 1850; Census Place: Albany, Green, Wisconsin; Roll: 999; Page: 260b

[2154] Year: 1860; Census Place: Black Earth, Dane, Wisconsin; Page: 78; Family History Library Film: 805403

[2155] Year: 1870; Census Place: Mazomanie, Dane, Wisconsin; Roll: M593_1709; Page: 373A; Family History Library Film: 553208

[2156] Bass, *History of Braintree, Vermont*, p 127

[2157] Bass, *History of Braintree, Vermont*

[2158] Year: 1850; Census Place: Braintree, Orange, Vermont; Roll: M432_926; Page: 313B; Image: 621

[2159] Ingalls, *The Genealogy and History of the Ingalls Family*, p 118

[2160] Massachusetts Town and Vital Records, Belchertown 1765-1893, compiled by Jay Mack Holbrook

[2161] U. S. Census, 1850, Michigan, Saginaw, Northampton; Justice Ingalls, male age 40, born in Massachusetts, farmer, property value $180

Lemuel and Louisa resided in Belchertown and were there until at least 1820.[2162] The Ingalls genealogy reports that Lemuel went to Cortland, New York.[2163]

Lemuel and Louisa were parents of nine children born at Belchertown.[2164]

i   CHESTER INGALLS, b. 26 May 1803; d. at Ann Arbor, MI, 23 Aug 1871; m. SARAH who has not been identified but b. in NY about 1809 and d. at Ann Arbor, 1873.

ii   LEMUEL P. INGALLS, b. 8 Jan 1805; d. after 1880 when he was living at Chicopee; m. at Northampton, 18 Oct 1862, MARY C. BUFFUM, b. at Westmoreland, NH, about 1824 daughter of Erasmus and Hephzibah (Thayer) Buffum; Mary d. at Holyoke, MA, 16 Apr 1865. Lemuel married late in life. He and his wife Mary had one daughter, and his wife died two weeks after her birth. Daughter Nellie married Warren Chase and died in Fresno, CA 23 Mar 1953.

iii   SOLOMON E. INGALLS, b. 13 Aug 1807

iv   SARAH ANN INGALLS, b. 20 Jan 1810; d. at Chicopee, MA, 7 Oct 1895; m. at Stafford, CT, 19 Mar 1829, CALEB STRONG CHAPIN, b. at Springfield, 19 Jun 1807 son of Oliver and Alice (Bush) Chapin; Oliver d. at Chicopee, 31 Jul 1865.

v   LOUISA A. INGALLS, b. 9 Jun 1812; d. at Chicopee, 5 Jun 1837.

vi   BETSEY FIDELIA INGALLS, b. 15 Jul 1815; d. at Ann Arbor, MI, 31 Dec 1890; m. at Washtenaw County, MI, 27 Mar 1838, ORSON S. GILES, b. 20 Sep 1803 son of Robert and Diana (-) Giles;[2165] Orson d. at Ann Arbor, of typhoid fever, on 2 Aug 1880.

vii   RUA DIANA INGALLS, b. 14 Feb 1818; d. at Chicopee, MA, 1 Aug 1902; m. at Stafford, CT, 14 Mar 1847, ALSOP WELLES, b. at Glastonbury, CT, 8 Sep 1806 son of Gordon and Polly (Nickelson) Welles; Alsop d. at Cincinnati, 30 Jan 1898. Diana returned to western Massachusetts after her husband's death but is buried with him in Cincinnati.

viii   MOSES INGALLS, b. 14 Oct 1820; d. at Jefferson, IN, 10 Dec 1881; m. 14 Mar 1856, NANCY TERRELL, b. 11 Dec 1828 (per gravestone, but census records suggest 1834); Nancy d. 16 Dec 1889.

ix   ABIGAIL INGALLS, b. about 1822; d. at Chicopee, 8 Oct 1904; m. 1st at Springfield, MA, LOWELL HATFIELD, b. at South Hadley, about 1824 son of Horace and Almira (Kellogg) Hatfield; Lowell d. unknown but before 1860 and likely about 1855. Abigail m. 2nd by 1860, WILLIAM M. ADAMS, b. at Stafford, CT, 1820 son of Chauncey and Sarah (Conress) Adams (per death record; William d. at Chicopee, 16 Dec 1893.

721)   WILLIAM BARKER (*Ephraim Barker⁴, Martha Ingalls Barker Goodale³, Sarah Russell Ingalls², Robert¹*), b. at Pomfret, 18 Nov 1753 son of Ephraim and Hannah (Grow) Barker; d. at Madison, NY, 17 May 1826; m. about 1782, BETSEY ARMSTRONG, baptized at Norwich, 30 May 1762 daughter of Silas and Bathsheba (Worden) Armstrong;[2166] Betsey d. at Madison, 29 Aug 1832.[2167]

William and Betsey had their children in Norwich and were in Madison, New York by 1818. On 9 June 1818, William Barker of Madison, New York aged sixty-six made a statement related to his pension application. William enlisted on 1 May 1775 from the town of Norwich in the company of Capt. William Gale of Killingworth. He served a term of eight months and immediately following enlisted for one year in the company of Capt. Gill in the regiment of Col. Samuel Pearson of the Connecticut line. He served until 1 January 1777 and was discharged at Peekskill, New York. He was at the Battle of Long Island, was part of the "great retreat" to New York, and at the Battle of White Plains. In a statement on 17 June 1820, he reported household as himself and wife Betsey aged fifty-eight. His personal estate did not exceed fifty dollars in value.[2168]

William Barker and Betsey Armstrong were parents of eight children born at Norwich.[2169]

i   HANNAH BARKER, b. 8 Feb 1783

[2162] 1820 U S Census; Census Place: Belchertown, Hampshire, Massachusetts; Page: 182; NARA Roll: M33_50; Image: 193

[2163] Burleigh, *The History and Genealogy of the Ingalls Family in America*, p 59

[2164] Jay Mack Holbrook, Massachusetts Vital Records, Belchertown 1765-1893

[2165] Names of Orson's parents are given as Robert and Diana on his death record.

[2166] The 1798 will of Silas Armstrong includes a bequest to his daughter Betty wife of William Barker.

[2167] Parshall's Barker genealogy provided limited information on William but included that he had married and located in Madison, NY. William and Betsey Barker had all their children in Norwich, so this marriage fits in terms of location. There is also a Revolutionary War pension file for William Barker in Madison, NY that fits this William in terms of age and location at time of enlistment.

[2168] U. S. Revolutionary War Pension and Bounty-Land Warrant Application Files, Case S45223

[2169] Connecticut Vital Records Prior to 1850, Norwich, accessed through familysearch.org; Connecticut, Church Record Abstracts, 1630-1920, Norwich

ii   SILAS BARKER, b. 28 Nov 1784; d. at Caneadea, NY, 17 Jan 1868; m. at Madison, NY, 18 Sep 1811, HARRIET HALL, b. in CT, 1784; Harriet d. after 1875 when living at Grove, NY.

iii   ASA BARKER, b. about 1786 and baptized 10 Oct 1788

iv   MARTIN BARKER, b. about 1788 and baptized 10 Oct 1788

v   JOSEPH BARKER, b. 25 May 1790

vi   LYDIA BARKER, b. 11 Jul 1794

vii   LUCRETIA BARKER, b. 16 Jun 1797; d. at Koshkonong, WI, 15 Sep 1896; m. 1819, JOHN CHADWICK, b. 28 Dec 1793 (on gravestone); John d. at Koshkonong, 17 Feb 1858.

viii   JOHN BARKER, b. 28 Jun 1799

722)   HANNAH BARKER (*Ephraim Barker⁴, Martha Ingalls Barker Goodale³, Sarah Russell Ingalls², Robert¹*), baptized at Pomfret 29 Aug 1754 daughter of Ephraim and Hannah (Grow) Barker; d. at Norwich, 1840; m. at Norwich, 20 Jan 1771, ELIJAH PITCHER,[2170] b. likely at Stoughton, MA, 4 Nov 1752 son of Elijah and Tabitha (Smith) Pitcher; Elijah d. at Norwich, 14 Jun 1839.

Hannah Barker and Elijah Pitcher were parents of ten children born at Norwich.

i   ELIJAH PITCHER, b. 25 Jul 1771; d. at Norwich, 26 Apr 1843; m. at Norwich, 24 Jun 1798, HANNAH LATHROP, b. at Norwich, 22 Sep 1772 daughter of Zephaniah and Hannah (Lathrop) Lathrop; Hannah d. at Norwich, 24 Dec 1813.

ii   ELISHA PITCHER, b. 2 May 1773; d. at Mexico, NY, 18 Nov 1850; m. at Preston, CT, 16 Mar 1794, JANE COOMBS, b. at Preston, 1774 daughter of Thomas and Abigail (Sealey) Coombs; Jane d. at Mexico, 1843.

iii   WILLIAM PITCHER, b. 26 Aug 1775; d. at Norwich, 18 Jul 1835; m. 1797, LUCY DARBY, b. at Norwich, 1769 daughter of Blanchard and Priscilla (Longbottom) Darby; Lucy d. at Norwich, 1813.

iv   DAVID PITCHER, b. 6 Nov 1777; d. at Norwich, 10 Mar 1857; m. 1st at Norwich, 20 Jun 1802, MARY GIBBONS, b. 1781; Mary d. at Norwich, 8 May 1834. David m. 2nd at Norwich, 11 Apr 1835, MARY HURLBURT, b. 3 Nov 1794 daughter of Asa and Betsey (Kelley) Hurlburt; Mary d. at Lebanon, CT, 7 Feb 1859.

v   EPHRAIM PITCHER, b. 22 Feb 1780; d. at Johnston, OH, 25 Feb 1858; m. 1st at Norwich, 28 May 1805, DESIRE BROWN, b. 1786; Desire d. at Norwich, 30 Jan 1822. Ephraim m. 2nd at Lisbon, CT, 9 May 1822, CHARLOTTE W. CROCKER, b. at Bozrah, 27 Sep 1791 daughter of Asa and Lois (Crocker) Crocker; Charlotte d. at Johnston, 29 Jun 1860.

vi   DANIEL PITCHER, b. 28 Nov 1782; d. at Norwich, 12 Oct 1822; m. 1803, BETSEY ELLIS, b. at Norwich, 13 May 1785 daughter of William and Ann (Edgerton) Ellis; Betsey d. at Warren, PA, 19 Sep 1874. Betsey m. 2nd Parley Coburn.

vii   GURDON PITCHER, b. 15 May 1785; d. at New York, NY, about 1843 (wife remarried 1844); m. 1st about 1805, REBECCA HARRIS, b. 1782; Rebecca d. at Avon, CT, 4 Dec 1825. Gurdon m. 2nd at Harlem, 1826,[2171] CHARLOTTE BIGELOW, b. at Hartford, CT, Sep 1798 daughter of James and Anne (Spencer) Bigelow. Charlotte married second Samuel H. Ames on 14 Jul 1844.

viii   ASHER PITCHER, b. Sep 1788; d. at Norwich, 6 May 1870; m. at Norwich, 27 Feb 1814, BETHIAH ELLIS, b. at Franklin, CT, 15 Mar 1790 daughter of William and Ann (Edgerton) Ellis; Bethiah d. at Norwich, 19 Feb 1863.

ix   HANNAH PITCHER, b. Jun 1791; d. 12 Feb 1796.

x   JERUSHA PITCHER, b. 11 Oct 1797; d. at Norwich, 29 Aug 1884; m. at Norwich, 9 Oct 1825, ERASTUS WATERS, b. 1798 son of Levi and Hannah (Bottom) Waters; Erastus d. at Norwich, 10 May 1848.

723)   JOHN BARKER (*Ephraim Barker⁴, Martha Ingalls Barker Goodale³, Sarah Russell Ingalls², Robert¹*), b. at Pomfret, 18 Dec 1755 son of Ephraim and Hannah (Grow) Barker; d. at Stoddard, NH, 15 Mar 1834; m. 1st 1786, ESTHER RICHARDSON, b. at Leominster, 9 Mar 1767 daughter of James and Hannah (House) Richardson; Esther d. at Stoddard, 17

[2170] This is a supposed marriage for Hannah. The family was living in Norwich at the time of Hannah's marriage and this marriage fits for her in terms of age and location. There were not records located that firmly establish that this Hannah married Elijah Pitcher.
[2171] New York City, Marriages, 1600s-1800s

Jul 1806. John m. 2nd 4 Dec 1806, SALLY GUILD (widow of Daniel Warner), b. at Newton, MA, 31 Jul 1775 daughter of Samuel and Sarah (Smith) Guild;[2172] Sally d. at Stoddard, 19 Jan 1843.

Known as Capt. John Barker in later life, he served as a sergeant during the term of the Revolution. On 20 November 1776, John Barker enlisted from Sudbury, Massachusetts as a sergeant in the company of Capt. Robert Allen in the 7th regiment of the Continental army commanded by Lt. Col. John Brooks. He was discharged in 1783.[2173] In his pension application file, John reported participating in five battles, although they were not named, and that he participated in Sullivan's campaign against the Indians.

In an inventory provided on 4 July 1820 as part of his pension application, real estate consisted of eighty acres in Stoddard with buildings valued at $650, 106 acres of land in Gilsum valued at $275, and pew in the meeting house valued at $10. Personal estate totaled $472 and debts were $400. John reported he was a farmer by trade but no longer able to pursue this work due to a rupture. Living with him in 1820 were his wife Sally age 44, daughter Loinca age 21, son Ephraim age 19 in declining health, son Franklin age 17, Almira age 15, son Samuel G. age 12, Luman age 10, Mary age 8, and Harriet Newell age one. He also noted he had eighteen children, fifteen of whom were living. John was allowed a pension on 14 April 1819.[2174]

John married Esther Richardson on 9 July 1786 and the family resided in Leominster before relocating to Stoddard. John Barker lived in what was known as "Leominster Corner" of Stoddard, New Hampshire, this area being settled by families from Leominster.[2175]

In his will written 4 April 1825 (probate 7 June 1834), John Barker bequeathed fifty dollars to daughter Loency and twenty dollars to son Albemarle. Son Ephraim receives sixty dollars and daughter Almira, seventy dollars. Sons Cephas, Cicero, and Franklin and daughter Sally each receives one dollar. Daughter Betsey receives six dollars. Sons John and William receive the money owed by Franklin to his father. Wife Sally Barker receives the remainder of the estate after payments of the debts to be distributed among her children: Samuel Guile, Lumman, Mary, and Harriet. Wife Sally was named executrix.[2176]

John Barker and Esther Richardson were parents of fourteen children.

i   JOHN BARKER, b. at Leominster, 24 Jan 1787; d. at Stoddard, 14 Jul 1829; m. at Leominster, 24 Jan 1813, SUSAN BIGELOW, b. at Leominster, 17 Sep 1792 daughter of Nathaniel and Anne (Rider) Bigelow; Susan d. at Stoddard, 18 May 1860.

ii   WILLIAM BARKER, b. at Leominster, 20 Oct 1788; d. at Syracuse, NY, 30 Apr 1854; m. 1st 1813, PHEBE ROSE, b. 1797 daughter of William and Mary (DeWitt) Rose; Phebe d. at Syracuse, 14 Jan 1819. William m. 2nd 1819, ESTHER RIGGS ORTON, b. 6 Dec 1796 daughter of Arunah and Lois (Gibbs) Orton; Esther d. at Syracuse, 1 Feb 1881. William was a contractor involved in the building of the Erie Canal.[2177]

iii FRANKLIN BARKER, b. at Leominster, 12 Jul 1790; d. at Stoddard, 12 Apr 1799.

iv   SALLY BARKER, b. at Leominster, 15 Jul 1792; d. at Leominster, 29 Apr 1859; m. at Leominster, 8 Feb 1820, HORACE RICE, b. at Leominster, 1796 son of John and Anne (Bigelow) Leominster; Horace d. at Leominster, 21 Sep 1877.

v   CEPHAS BARKER (twin), b. at Leominster, 15 Dec 1793; d. at Berkshire, NY, 10 Aug 1857; m. 1821, MARY JEWETT, b. 8 Apr 1802 daughter of Ezekiel and Sarah (Blackman) Jewett; Mary d. at Berkshire, 16 Feb 1864.

vi   CICERO BARKER (twin), b. at Leominster, 15 Dec 1793; d. at Onondaga, NY, 22 Jun 1870; m. MARY SATTERLY, b. at Windsor, NY, 20 Feb 1790 daughter of Samuel and Hannah (Woodhull) Satterly; Mary d. at Onondaga, 16 Sep 1881.

vii BETSEY BARKER, b. at Stoddard, 4 Jul 1795; d. at Dalton, MA, 30 May 1877; m. at Leominster, 9 Dec 1819, MOODY TYLER, b. at Leominster, 24 Feb 1789 son of Phineas and Tabitha (Hartwell) Tyler; Moody d. at Dalton, 3 Jul 1870.

viii ALBEMARLE BARKER, b. at Stoddard, 11 Jun 1797; d. at Newton, MA, 22 Apr 1848; m. at Lexington, MA, 20 Jun 1824, ABIGAIL A. FRANCIS, b. at Marblehead, MA, about 1800 daughter of Richard and Elizabeth (Adams) Francis;[2178] Abigail d. at Lowell, 5 May 1891.

ix   LOUISE BARKER (twin), b. and d. 16 Jan 1799.

x   LOENCY BARKER (twin), b. 16 Jan 1799; d. at Newton, MA, 20 Jul 1845. Loency did not marry.

[2172] Burleigh, *The History and Genealogy of the Guild Family*, p 45
[2173] Massachusetts Soldiers and Sailors in the Revolution, volume 1, p 614
[2174] U.S. Revolutionary War Pension and bounty-Land Warrant Application Files, Case S45514
[2175] Gould, *History of Stoddard*, p 98
[2176] New Hampshire Wills and Probate Records, Cheshire County, wills volume 77, 513-514
[2177] Barker, *Barker Genealogy*, p 333
[2178] The names of Abigail's parents are given as Richard and Elizabeth on her death record.

xi   EPHRAIM BARKER, b. at Stoddard, 10 Feb 1801; d. at Walpole, NH, 6 Sep 1876; m. at Amherst, MA, 26 Sep 1825, LYDIA VINTON, b. at Granby, MA, 27 Aug 1804 daughter of Simeon and Roxanna (Church) Vinton;[2179] Lydia d. at Walpole, 1871.

xii   FRANKLIN BARKER, b. at Stoddard, 11 Apr 1803; d. at Syracuse, NY, 1859; m. at Stoddard, 13 Apr 1826, BETSEY BLOOD, b. at Gilsum, NH, 16 Nov 1808 daughter of Levi and Polly (Whipple) Blood; Betsey d. at Clinton, IA, 23 Feb 1894.

xiii   ALMIRA BARKER, b. at Stoddard, 8 Dec 1804; d. at Falmouth, MA, 3 Feb 1885; m. at Leominster, 23 May 1834, DANIEL RUSSELL, b. at Boston, 1803 son of John and Sarah (Stedman) Russell;[2180] Daniel d. at Newton, MA, 10 Oct 1856.

xiv   NATHAN BARKER, b. 25 Jun 1806; d. 21 Jul 1806.

John Barker and Sarah Guild were parents of four children.

i   SAMUEL GUILE BARKER, b. at Stoddard, 6 Oct 1807; d. at Syracuse, NY, 8 Jan 1892; m. 1st at Stoddard, 18 May 1837, SARAH TOWNE, b. at Marlowe, NH, 4 Jan 1803 daughter of Andrew and Sarah (Spaulding) Towne; Sarah d. at Syracuse, 9 Jun 1864. Samuel m. 2nd about 1865, PHEBE MYERS (widow of Waterman Sears), b. 19 Jun 1812 daughter of John N. and Rachel (Smith) Myers; Phebe d. at Syracuse, 28 Jul 1882.

ii   LUMAN BARKER, b. at Stoddard, 8 Jul 1809; m. about 1840, MARY ANN POWERS, b. about 1821; Mary Ann d. after 1870 when she was living at Beaver, IA.[2181] It is unclear how long they stayed together as in 1850 Luman appears to be living in Clayton, NY without his family with him. Mary Ann married John C. Jerome at Muscatine County, IA on 2 Dec 1856. In the 1860 census, Mary Ann and John Jerome were living in Butler with five Barker children.

iii   MARY BARKER, b. at Stoddard, 2 Dec 1811; d. after 1880 when she was living in Brunswick, ME with one of her children; m. at Stoddard, 18 Apr 1837, ELIPHALET FOX, b. 10 Feb 1802 son of Samuel and Sarah (Duncan) Fox, Eliphalet d. at Antrim, NH, 11 Oct 1862.

iv   HARRIET NEWELL BARKER, b. at Stoddard, 7 Jun 1819; d. at Marlborough, NH, 3 Sep 1889; m. at Stoddard, 16 Jun 1842, CHARLES WORCESTER, b. at Stoddard, 1813 son of Nathaniel and Lucy (Fay) Worcester; Charles d. at Keene, 10 May 1903.

724)   EPHRAIM BARKER (*Ephraim Barker⁴, Martha Ingalls Barker Goodale³, Sarah Russell Ingalls², Robert¹*), b. at Pomfret, 28 Feb 1759 son of Ephraim and Hannah (Grow) Barker. He may be the Ephraim Barker who married at Wayland, MA, 27 Mar 1783, RUTH GOODNOW,[2182] b. at Wayland, 18 Oct 1757 daughter of Silas and Jerusha (Willis) Goodnow; Ruth d. at Sudbury, 27 Jan 1843.

    Ephraim abandoned his family sometime between 1800 and 1805 described as "absconded to parts unknown" in a probate file for Ruth's aunt Mary Willis. Ruth Barker was listed as the head of household from 1810 on. Ruth inherited her aunt Mary's estate and beginning in 1813 sold off portions of the land every few years listing herself as a "free agent" in the deeds.

    Ephraim Barker and Ruth Goodnow were parents of seven children born at Sudbury.

i   SILAS GOODNOW BARKER, b. 15 Nov 1784; d. at Chester, VT, 1858 (probate 30 Sep 1858); m. at Dorchester, MA, 19 Nov 1808, POLLY MARSHALL, b. about 1781; Polly d. at Chester, 8 Sep 1856.

ii   EPHRAIM BARKER, b. 23 Aug 1786; d. at Halifax, MA, 16 Sep 1830; m. at Boston, 5 Nov 1809, LUCY S. WATERMAN, b. at Halifax, 6 May 1788 daughter of Isaac and Lucy (Samson) Waterman; Lucy d. at Halifax, 14 May 1877.

iii   LEWIS BARKER, b. 13 Jul 1788; d. at Baton Rouge, LA, 19 Dec 1820. Lewis Barker of Sudbury enlisted at Boston 3 Feb 1820. He was appointed corporal 17 Apr 1820.[2183]

iv   SEWEL BARKER, b. 27 Sep 1791

[2179] Ephraim Barker, then of Granby, was one of the sureties for the administrative bond for the 1827 probate of the estate if Simeon Vinton late of Granby.

[2180] The names of Daniel's parents are given as John and Sarah Russell on his death record.

[2181] The death certificate of one known child of Luman, Harriet Augusta Barker Tyler, gives the names of parents as Luman Barker and Mary Ann Powers.

[2182] Parshall, *The Barker Genealogy*, p 7. This Barker genealogy lists a son of this Ephraim, Silas G. Barker, who was the son of Ephraim and Ruth (Goodnow) Barker.

[2183] U.S. Army, Register of Enlistments, 1798-1914

v   NATHAN BARKER, b. 25 Nov 1792; d. at Medford, 11 Apr 1852; m. at Malden, 19 Aug 1815, HANNAH WAIT TOWNSEND, b. at Malden, 9 Sep 1793 daughter of John and Nancy (Ramsdell) Townsend; Hannah d. at Medford, 28 Apr 1881.

vi   GEORGE W. BARKER, b. 23 Sep 1794; d. at Sudbury, 13 Oct 1860; m. at Medford, 13 Sep 1818, REBECCA LYMAN, b. 1798 daughter of John and Dorothy (-) Lyman;[2184] Rebecca d. at Somerville, 4 Jan 1892.

vii   MARY W. BARKER, b. 4 Mar 1797; d. at Sudbury, 6 Oct 1889; m. at Sudbury, 16 Dec 1817, CYRUS TAYLOR, b. at Sudbury, 1797 son of John and Mary (Conant) Taylor; Cyrus d. at Sudbury, 16 Jan 1872.

725)   NATHAN BARKER (*Ephraim Barker⁴, Martha Ingalls Barker Goodale³, Sarah Russell Ingalls², Robert¹*), b. at Pomfret, 8 Jun 1761 son of Ephraim and Hannah (Grow) Barker; d. at Palmer, MA, 10 Oct 1849; m. 11 Dec 1783, LYDIA BARKER, b. 4 Jun 1763; Lydia d. at Palmer, 2 Dec 1849.

    Nathan and Lydia settled in Palmer. In a series of land transactions, Nathan transferred much of his property to his children. On 19 April 1824, Nathan Barker and Gilbert Barker (likely his son) with Lydia Barker signing her agreement to relinquish right of dower, sold two tracts of land in Wilbraham and Palmer to Calvin Barker for payment of fourteen hundred dollars. On 26 April 1837, Nathan with Lydia in agreement, sold a tract of land in Wilbraham to William S. Barker for payment of six hundred dollars. On 24 June 1837, described then as of Wilbraham, Nathan and Lydia conveyed a tract of land in Palmer to Gilbert Barker. On 2 December 1837, Nathan and Lydia of Wilbraham conveyed to Cyrus G. Barker of Greene, New York a farm in Palmer for payment of four thousand five hundred dollars. On 7 July 1838, Nathan and Lydia Barker of Wilbraham and Cyrus G. and Elisa Barker of Palmer conveyed a small piece of land in Palmer to William S. Barker for dive dollars. On 5 August 1850, Nathan with Lydia's agreement, then of Palmer, conveyed property to Roxana Rindge wife of Royal Rindge a tract of land in Palmer for three hundred dollars.[2185]

    Nathan and Lydia Barker were parents of eleven children. The births are recorded at Ashford, Connecticut, Lenox, Massachusetts, at Tolland, and again at Ashford.

i   JAMES BARKER, b. 5 Mar 1785; d. 6 May 1788.

ii   ELISHA BARKER, b. at Ashford, 13 Dec 1786; d. at Wilbraham, 23 Jul 1870. Elisha did not marry. He lived with his sister Lydia from 1850 until his death.

iii   CALVIN BARKER, b. at Lenox, 24 Jan 1789; d. at Millbury, MA, 30 Dec 1852; m. 1st 28 Nov 1825, LUCY WASHBURN WOODWARD, b. at Millbury, 8 Sep 1801 daughter of Josiah and Lois Chapin (Legg) Woodward; Lucy d. at Millbury, 6 Nov 1833. Calvin m. 2nd at Millbury, 12 Mar 1836, LUCY BLISS, b. at Springfield, MA, 10 Apr 1803 daughter of Gaius and Temperance (Leonard) Bliss; Lucy d. at Millbury, 3 Mar 1888.

iv   DOLLY BARKER, b. 3 Dec 1790; d. at Ashford, 29 Mar 1812.

v   ROXANA BARKER, b. at Ashford, 26 Dec 1792; d. at Wilbraham, MA, 17 Jun 1884; m. at Palmer, MA, 8 May 1820, ROYAL RINDGE, b. at Wilbraham, 10 Apr 1795 son of William and Hannah (Utley) Rindge; Royal d. at Wilbraham, 12 Feb 1878.

vi   NATHAN BARKER, b. 14 Apr 1795; d. at Cortland, NY, 18 Nov 1865; m. at Wilbraham, 18 Jul 1818, EUNICE AUSTIN, b. 1800 daughter of Daniel and Eunice (Allen) Austin; Eunice d. at Cortland, 18 May 1865.

vii   SITNAH BARKER, b. at Tolland, 25 Feb 1797; d. at Springfield, MA, 8 Jul 1870; m. 1st at Palmer, 23 Nov 1823, ALANSON BURR, b. at Wilbraham, 22 Sep 1794 son of Timothy and Naomi (Walden) Burr; Alanson d. at Wilbraham, 25 Dec 1823. Sitnah m. 2nd at Wilbraham, 7 Oct 1824, Alanson's brother, ELISHA BURR, b. 11 Aug 1782; Elisha d. at Wilbraham, 16 Jan 1863. Elisha was first married to Hannah Learned.

viii   GILBERT BARKER, b. 13 Mar 1799; d. at Palmer, 2 Oct 1883; m. at Palmer, 23 Oct 1824, PERSIS KING, b. at Palmer, 23 Feb 1805 son of John and Betsey (Shearer) King; Persis d. at Palmer, 30 Jun 1887.

ix   CYRUS GROW BARKER, b. 13 May 1801; d. at Clinton, WI, 27 Sep 1870; m. at Palmer, 13 Jan 1826, ELIZA KING, b. at Palmer, 8 Jun 1802 daughter of John and Betsey (Shearer) King; Eliza d. at Clinton, 28 Mar 1887.

x   LYDIA BARKER, b. at Ashford, 2 May 1803; d. at Wilbraham, 23 May 1884; m. at Palmer, 28 Aug 1828, SYLVESTER HILLS, b. 1800 son of Elijah and Olive (Rider) Hills; Sylvester d. at Palmer, 26 May 1830.

xi   WILLIAM SEDGWICK BARKER, b. 29 Jun 1807; d. at Springfield, MA, 6 Apr 1855; m. at Palmer, 3 Feb 1831, HERSEY KNOWLTON, b. 6 Jun 1804 son of Nathan and Lydia (Leonard) Knowlton; Hersey d. at Springfield, 2 Oct 1867.

[2184] The names of Rebecca's parents are given as John and Dorothy on her death record.
[2185] Massachusetts Land Records, Hampden County, 71:364; 102:230; 108:93; 19:445; 111-64; 117-148

726)   SALLY BARKER (*William Barker⁴, Martha Ingalls Barker Goodale³, Sarah Russell Ingalls², Robert¹*), b. 9 Aug 1766 daughter of William and Sarah (Foster) Barker;[2186] d. at Dudley, 2 Mar 1842; m. at Dudley, 23 May 1790, Dr. AARON TUFTS, b. at Charlestown, MA, 30 Jan 1770 son of Aaron and Mary (Stone) Tufts; Aaron d. at Dudley, 17 Oct 1843.

Dr. Aaron Tufts also known as Judge Tufts studied medicine with Dr. John Eliot Eaton and later practiced medicine in Dudley for about five years. Following that, he engaged in manufacturing and was prosperous. Tufts Factory Village in Dudley was his undertaking. He represented the town of Dudley in the General Court from 1810 to 1825. He was appointed Justice of the Court of Sessions in 1819. A main enterprise was the woolen mill in Dudley known as Tufts Factory of Rams Horn. The mill was erected in 1816 and Mr. Jewett was principal manager of the mill. The only child of Aaron and Sarah was George Aaron Tufts. George A. Tufts graduated from Harvard in 1818. He studied law with Josiah Fiske and practiced law until his death from consumption in 1835. George was elected to the Massachusetts senate just before his death.[2187]

In his will (proved November 1843), Aaron Tufts bequeathed to David N. Fales and Henry S. Wheaton twenty-five thousand dollars from his factor property to be held in trust. Twenty thousand dollars of the trust is to be for the sole use and behalf of beloved granddaughter Sarah B. T. Wheaton during her natural life. If Sarah dies leaving issue, then the trust is to go to her heirs. If she dies without issue, the trust reverts to the estate. Five thousand dollars is to be for the use of Elvira F. Fales. Mary E. Barker is to have a comfortable support during her natural life. After some smaller bequests, the remainder of the estate is left to Henry S. Wheaton and wife, my granddaughter them, and to their heirs and assigns. David N. Fales, Henry S. Wheaton, and John Jewett were named executors. In a codicil written 12 October 1843, he specifies that the trust money for Elvira will continue only as long as Elvira continues to live with his granddaughter. [2188]

i   GEORGE AARON TUFTS, b. at Dudley, 22 Feb 1797; d. of consumption at Dudley, 25 Aug 1835; m. at Wrentham, 2 Oct 1822, AZUBAH BOYDEN FALES, b. at Wrentham, 18 Aug 1795 daughter of David and Abigail (Farrington) Fales; Azubah d. at Boston, 27 Nov 1835.

727)   ALMIRA BARKER (*William Barker⁴, Martha Ingalls Barker Goodale³, Sarah Russell Ingalls², Robert¹*), b. at Wayland, MA, 26 Nov 1780 daughter of William and Sarah (Foster) Barker; d. at Penobscot, ME, 13 Feb 1859; m. at Worcester, 3 Oct 1802, JOSEPH CARR, b. at Amesbury, MA, 14 Nov 1773 son of Francis and Mary (Elliot) Carr; Joseph d. (burial at Bangor although death was in New York), 2 Oct 1849.[2189]

Joseph Carr was a merchant in business with his father and brother James in Orrington (now Brewer), Maine. He was later in Bangor where he was prominent in civic affairs. He was representative to the General Court from both Orrington and Bangor. He was named inspector of revenue for the port of Bangor in 1816. Joseph and Almira were members of First Church in Bangor.[2190]

In his will written 5 July 1848, Joseph Carr of Bangor bequeathed to be beloved wife Almira all the estate, real and personal, during her natural life with some exceptions such as his gold watch. In the income from the estate is not sufficient, she may sell any of the real estate. At the decease of his wife, the estate is to be divided among his children. Son Joseph or his heirs will receive three-quarters of the estate. Joseph also receives the gold watch, spectacles, and the portrait of his brother William. Daughter Sarah wife of Francis H. Upton receives one-quarter of the estate. Sarah also receives the portrait of her sister Charlotte and the portrait of herself. He bequeaths to son William one good suit and five dollars. He is confident that his son Joseph will not allow his unfortunate brother William to suffer. To daughter Esther wife of his son Joseph, "as a token of my regard", he bequeaths the mahogany French bedstead. Granddaughter Ann Thornton McGaw is to receive three hundred dollars after the death of Almira. Ann also receives the portrait of her mother. Wife Almira was named executrix. In a codicil written 23 December 1848, Joseph made an adjustment to the bequest of daughter Sarah related to Joseph's partial funding of a real estate transaction of Sarah and her husband.[2191]

Almira Barker and Joseph Carr were parents of eight children born at Bangor, Maine.

i   CHARLOTTE CARR, b. 3 Mar 1804; d. 27 Apr 1807.

ii   ANN FRANCES CARR, b. 19 Oct 1805; d. at Cambridge, MA, 12 Feb 1847; m. 19 Oct 1826, THORNTON MCGAW, b. at Newburyport, MA, 24 Jul 1799 son of John and Hannah (Thornton) McGaw. Thornton married second Esther Hathorne on 23 Apr 1855.

iii   JOSEPH CARR, b. 20 Sep 1807; d. at Bangor, 30 Jan 1889; m. ESTHER JACKSON HAMMATT, b. 12 Jan 1816 daughter of William and Esther (Parsons) Hammatt; Esther d. at Bangor, 1 May 1885. Joseph was an attorney in Bangor.

[2186] Sally's date of birth is given in the Dudley town records, but this seems related to the family record there rather than her place of birth.

[2187] Ammidown, *Historical Collections*, pp 453-455, p 436

[2188] *Worcester County, MA: Probate File Papers, 1731-1881*. Online database. AmericanAncestors.org. New England Historic Genealogical Society, 2015. Case 60118

[2189] *Maine, Faylene Hutton Cemetery Collection, 1780-1990*

[2190] Porter (Ed.), "The Carr Family", *Maine Historical Magazine (Bangor Historical Magazine)*, volume I, number 1, July 1885, p 10

[2191] Maine Wills and Probate, Penobscot County, Wills Volume 16, pp 565-568

iv   CHARLOTTE CARR, b. 1 Oct 1809; Charlotte d. at Bangor, 7 Feb 1848. Charlotte did not marry.

v   WILLIAM CARR, b. 5 Apr 1811; d. 17 Nov 1813.

vi   SARAH FOSTER CARR, b. 26 Dec 1812; d. 1880 (obituary 12 Oct 1880) likely in New York, NY as she was living
       there with her son in 1880; m. at Bangor, 1836, FRANCIS HENRY UPTON, b. at Boston, 23 May 1814 son of
       Samuel and Rebecca (Pierce) Upton; Francis d. (burial at Washington, DC), Jun 1876. Francis graduated from
       Harvard Law and was an attorney who specialized in trade law. He was author of "The Law of Nations Affecting
       Commerce During War" published in 1861 and "A Treatise of the Law of Trademarks" published in 1860.

vii   WILLIAM BARKER CARR, b. 20 Mar 1814; d. in CA, 1850.[2192] William does not seem to have married. In the
       1846 city directory for Bangor, he is listed as boarding with Joseph Carr.

viii   MARY TUFTS CARR, b. 20 Feb 1818; d. at Bangor, 3 Jan 1823.

728)   HANNAH ABBOTT (*Mary Barker Abbott[4], Martha Ingalls Barker Goodale[3], Sarah Russell Ingalls[2], Robert[1]*), b. at
Pomfret, 2 Aug 1758 daughter of Isaac and Mary (Barker) Abbott; d. at Stoddard, NH, 9 Mar 1847; m. at Amherst, NH, 25 May
1781, ISRAEL TOWNE, b. at Stoddard, NH, 17 Jun 1761 son of Israel and Lydia (Hopkins) Towne; Israel d. 2 May 1848.
       Hannah and Israel Towne resided in Stoddard. Israel served as the town clerk in 1785 and 1789 and served as
selectman five of the years from 1783 through 1790.
       Hannah Abbott and Israel Towne were parents of nine children all born at Stoddard.

i   LYDIA TOWNE, b. 17 Sep 1781; d. at Stoddard, 28 Jun 1878; m. at Stoddard, 6 Jun 1805, OLIVER HODGMAN,
       b. about 1782 likely the son of Oliver and Submit (Locke) Hodgman; Oliver d. at Stoddard, after 1860.

ii   ARCHELAUS TOWNE, b. 29 Nov 1782; d. at Langdon, 5 May 1875; m. 1st, 14 Dec 1813, CLARISSA GEROULD,
       b. at Stoddard, 15 Aug 1788 daughter of Samuel and Azubah (Thompson) Gerould; Clarissa d. at Stoddard, 25
       May 1816. Archelaus m. 2nd, 22 Jan 1818, RUTH KENNEY, b. at Stoddard, 2 Dec 1783 daughter of Isaac and
       Anna (Adams) Kenney; Ruth d. at Langdon, 9 Sep 1877.

iii   ISRAEL TOWNE, b. 22 Nov 1784; d. at Amherst, NH, 25 Oct 1858; m. 1st, at Boston, 14 Jun 1812, CLARISSA
       WELD, b. 3 Dec 1795 of undetermined parents; Clarissa d. at Boston, 13 Jan 1815. Israel m. 2nd, 23 Jul 1815,
       SARAH L. BRAZIER, b. 11 Jun 1796[2193] of undetermined parents; Sarah d. at Nashua, 22 May 1874.

iv   HANNAH TOWNE, b. 9 Oct 1786; d. at Stoddard, 28 Jul 1864; m. at Stoddard, 2 Apr 1809, ASA COPELAND, b.
       at Stoddard, 9 Jun 1787 son of Jacob and Experience (Niles) Copeland; Asa d. at Stoddard, 13 Jul 1869.

v   ESTHER TOWNE, b. 23 Jun 1788; d. at Sullivan, 23 Aug 1871; m. 5 Oct 1809, ISAAC HOWE, b. at Milford, 2 Jul
       1781 son of Stephen and Hannah (Duncklee) Howe; Isaac d. at Stoddard, 26 Feb 1858.

vi   GRACE TOWNE, b. 24 Mar 1790; d. at Stoddard 1806 or 1807 when she was killed by a falling tree limb while
       trying to get to a bird's nest.[2194]

vii   GARDNER TOWNE, b. 16 Feb 1792; d. at Marlow, NH, 17 Feb 1872; m. 1st, at Stoddard, 23 Dec 1819, MIRIAM
       FLINT, b. at Stoddard, 19 Jul 1798 daughter of Joel and Silence (-) Flint; Miriam d. at Marlow, 16 Aug 1856.
       Gardner m. 2nd, SARAH CRAM (widow of Gilman Tenney), b. at Stoddard, 3 Jul 1806 daughter of Andrew and
       Sally (Towne) Cram; Sarah d. at Marlow, 7 Apr 1875.

viii   EBENEZER TOWNE, b. 31 Aug 1795; d. at Stoddard, 10 Jan 1892; m. 1823, TRYPHENA COREY, b. at
       Stoddard, 29 May 1800 daughter of Willard and Poll (-) Cory; Tryphena d. at Stoddard, 16 Jan 1863.

ix   LUCY TOWNE, b. 16 Aug 1797; d. at Stoddard, 11 Feb 1888; m. at Stoddard, 13 Feb 1816, SAMUEL UPTON, b.
       1793 parents undetermined; Samuel d. at Stoddard, 23 Dec 1862.

729)   SARAH "SALLY" ABBOTT (*Mary Barker Abbott[4], Martha Ingalls Barker Goodale[3], Sarah Russell Ingalls[2], Robert[1]*),
b. at Pomfret, 14 Oct 1762 daughter of Isaac and Mary (Barker) Abbott; d. at Mason, NH, 16 Mar 1846; m. at Amherst, 25 Oct
1795, JAMES BROWN, b. about 1770 (based on age 84 at death); James d. at Mason, 11 Mar 1854.
       Sarah Abbott and James Brown were parents of four children born at Mason.

[2192] The Maine Faylene Hutton Cemetery Collection notes place of death as California; there is a recording of the burial at Bangor.
[2193] Towne, *Descendants of William Towne*, p 157
[2194] Gould, *History of Stoddard*, p 44

i   CHLOE BROWN, b. 14 Aug 1798; d. at Wilton, 27 Jun 1876; m. at Mason, 20 Nov 1826, JOHN BOYNTON, b. at Mason, 1 Aug 1797 son of Nathaniel and Anna (Barrett) Boynton; John d. at Mason, 27 Jun 1858.

ii   SALLY BROWN, b. 13 Jul 1796; d. at Mason, 28 Oct 1831. Sally did not marry.

iii   MARTHA "PATTY" BROWN, b. 4 Mar 1800; d. at Mason, 7 Feb 1883. Patty did not marry.

iv   ISAAC ABBOTT BROWN, b. 6 Apr 1802; d. at Mason, 15 Aug 1878; m. 1834, LYDIA BOYNTON, b. at Mason, 14 Dec 1802 daughter of Nathaniel and Anna (Barrett) Boynton; Lydia d. at Mason, 20 Dec 1891.

730)   ISAAC ABBOTT (*Mary Barker Abbott⁴, Martha Ingalls Barker Goodale³, Sarah Russell Ingalls², Robert¹*), b. at Pomfret, 17 Jul 1766 son of Isaac and Mary (Barker) Abbott; d. at Milford, NH, 1 Sep 1831; m. 15 Oct 1793, RUTH AMES, b. at Wilmington, MA, 31 Jul 1776 daughter of Caleb and Mary (Harvey) Ames/Eams; Ruth d. at Milford, 29 Jul 1844.
    Isaac was a farmer on the homestead inherited from his father in Milford. Isaac and Ruth (Ames) Abbott had eleven children all born at Milford.[2195]

i   MARY ABBOTT, b. 26 Sep 1794; d. at Portland, ME, 7 Jan 1884; m. at Boston, 20 Feb 1823, HENRY NOWELL, b. at Dracut, 19 Feb 1797 son of Moses and Patty (French) Nowell; Henry d. at Portland, 13 May 1869.

ii   STEPHEN ABBOTT, b. 22 Nov 1797; d. at Hillsboro, IL, 30 Dec 1876;[2196] m. MARTHA GUTTERSON, b. at Andover, NH, 6 Nov 1805 daughter of Abiel and Sarah (Frye) Gutterson; Martha d. at Hillsboro, IL, 7 Jul 1861.

iii   REBECCA ABBOTT, b. 22 Jan 1799; d. at Hollis, 11 Nov 1860; m. about 1816, JOHN MOOAR, b. at Hollis, 11 Aug 1796 son of Jacob and Dorcas (Hood) Mooar; John d. at Hollis, 13 Mar 1869. After Rebecca's death, John married her sister Deborah.

iv   HARVEY ABBOTT, b. 1 Apr 1801; d. at Milford, 31 Mar 1864; m. 8 Nov 1831, ALMIRA J. LANCASTER, b. at Newburyport, about 1810 daughter of Joseph and Mary (Gutterson) Lancaster;[2197] Almira d. at Milford, 22 Mar 1861.

v   WALTER ABBOTT, b. 16 Jul 1803; d. at Boston, 20 Dec 1877; m. 1ˢᵗ, about 1830 SARAH AVERY about whom nothing is known at this time; Sarah d. about 1840. Walter m. 2ⁿᵈ, at Lowell, 1 Sep 1842, ELCY PARKS EAMS, b. at Wilmington, MA, 3 Aug 1820 daughter of Caleb and Betsey (Locke) Eams; Elcy d. Wellesley, 1902.

vi   DEBORAH ABBOTT, b. 15 Aug 1805; d. at Nashua, NH, 1 Jul 1872; m. 1862, JOHN MOOAR the husband of her sister Rebecca. In 1860, Deborah Abbott was living with her sister Harriet and Harriet's second husband John Morrill. In her will, Deborah Mooar left her entire estate to John Morrill.[2198]

vii   FRANKLIN ABBOTT, b. 20 Aug 1807, d. at Amherst, NH, 3 May 1889; m. 1ˢᵗ, about 1831, INDIANNA PROCTOR, b. at Hollis, 26 Dec 1803 daughter of Nathaniel and Olive (Goddard) Proctor; Indianna d. at Milford in 1879. Franklin m. 2ⁿᵈ, 2 Dec 1879 at Milford, MARY PATCH, b. about 1834 daughter of Timothy and Mary (Proctor) Patch; Mary d. at Amherst, 15 Sep 1908. It is likely that Indianna Proctor and Mary Patch were related through the Proctor connection, but I have not investigated that.

viii   WILLIAM B. ABBOTT, b. 7 Sep 1811; d. at St; Louis, MO, 1851.[2199] William did not marry. He was a physician. The probate of his estate included that there was no property belonging to the estate. The only thing of value was a possible patent for a sulfur bath, but it was discovered that this had already been patented by someone else.

ix   ROBERT B. ABBOTT, b. 20 Jan 1814; d. at Boston, 16 Apr 1881; m. at Boston, 24 Aug 1845, ARZELIA AVERILL, b. at Alna, ME, about 1812 daughter of Ebenezer and Mary (Lord) Averill;[2200] Arzelia d. at Alna, 3 Nov 1882.

x   DOROTHY ABBOTT, b. 1 Aug 1816; d. at Milford, 22 Mar 1843; m. about 1840, JAMES KNIGHT about whom nothing is known at this time. There is one child known from this marriage a daughter Harriet who died 30 Nov 1842.

[2195] Ramsdell & Colburn, *History of Milford*, p 560-561
[2196] Stephen's gravestone includes his date and place of birth (Milford, NH, 22 Nov 1797); findagrave memorial 66635215
[2197] The names of Almira's parents are given on her death record as Joseph and Mary G. *New Hampshire, Death and Disinterment Records, 1754-1947.*
[2198] *New Hampshire, Wills and Probate Records, 1643-1982*
[2199] The probate record of William B. Abbott includes a statement that Stephen Abbott of Hillsboro, Illinois is his brother and three brothers were living in Massachusetts. Probate Case Files, 1802-1876; Author: Missouri. Probate Court (St. Louis County); Probate Place: St Louis, Missouri
[2200] Avery, *The Averell Family*, volume 1, p 452

xi   HARRIET ABBOTT, b. 20 Dec 1819; d. at Nashua, 1873; m. 1ˢᵗ, about 1837, WILLIAM GUTTERSON, b. at Milford, 30 May 1809 son of Abiel and Sarah (Frye) Gutterson; William d. at Milford, 30 Jun 1838. Harriet m. 2ⁿᵈ, about 1845, JOHN MORRILL, b. at Chichester, NH, 25 Jun 1823 son of Micajah and Sally (Shaw) Morrill;[2201] John d. at Nashua, 6 Dec 1895. After Harriet's death, John Morrill married Helen Kendall 7 Nov 1874. There is one child known for Harriet and William Gutterson, a daughter Harriet who was born and died in 1838. There are four known children for Harriet and John Morrill, three who died in early infancy and John Perley Morrill born 4 May 1856 and died 3 May 1951.

731)   OLIVE ABBOTT (*Mary Barker Abbott⁴, Martha Ingalls Barker Goodale³, Sarah Russell Ingalls², Robert¹*), b. at Princeton, 28 Oct 1772 daughter of Isaac and Mary (Barker) Abbott. It is possible she is the Olive Abbott that married ISAAC PARKER 6 Feb 1794 at Amherst. The Olive Abbott that married Isaac was of Milford and she died 2 Jan 1862 at age 89 which fits for this Olive. Isaac Parker was b. at Monson, NH, 2 Mar 1769 son of Josiah and Hannah (Parkis) Parker; Isaac d. at Hollis, 22 Dec 1857.

      Isaac Parker was a large landowner and successful farmer in Hollis. He was Captain of an infantry company in Hollis in 1804.[2202]

      Olive Abbott and Isaac Parker were parents of five children all born at Hollis.

i   OLIVE PARKER, b. 27 Jun 1795; d. at Hollis, 4 Jan 1825; m. 18 Apr 1816, JEREMIAH KIDDER NEEDHAM, b. at Milford, 20 Sep 1792 son of Stearns and Hannah (Bailey) Needham; Jeremiah d. at Hollis, 9 Apr 1862. After Olive's death, Jeremiah married second Ruhamah Whitney, third Betsey Swallow, and fourth Elizabeth Stevens.

ii   HANNAH PARKER, b. 29 May 1797; d. at Hollis, 2 Nov 1816.

iii   ACHSAH PARKER, b. 24 Jun 1799; d. at Exeter, ME, 6 May 1831; m. at Hollis, 10 Aug 1829, JOHN BOYNTON HILL, b. at Mason, 25 Nov 1796 son of Ebenezer and Rebecca (Bancroft) Hill; John d. at Temple, 2 May 1886.

iv   ISAAC PARKER, b. 12 Apr 1801; d. 20 Aug 1813.

v   JOHN PARKER, b. 30 Jul 1803; d. at Hollis, after 1870; m. 17 Apr 1828, MARY ANN GOULD, b. at Hollis, 1802 daughter of Ambrose and Susan (Farley) Gould; Mary Ann d. at Stoneham, MA, 19 Apr 1877.

732)   WILLIS COY (*Deborah Barker, Coy⁴, Martha Ingalls Barker Goodale³, Sarah Russell Ingalls², Robert¹*), b. at Monson, MA, 18 Jun 1764 son of Jonathan and Deborah (Barker) Coy; d. at Amherst, MA, 30 Aug 1848; m. at Brimfield, 28 May 1789, AMY YOUNG, b. at Providence, RI, about 1765; Amy d. at Amherst, 1823.

      Willis Coy was a farmer in Amherst, Massachusetts. In his will written 4 March 1847 (probate October 1848), Willis Coy of Amherst bequeathed to daughter Sophia Eastman, wife of Isaiah F. Eastman, one dollar. Son Erastus Coy also receives one dollar. The rest of the estate goes to daughter Deborah B. Coy. Enos Dickinson of Amherst was named executor.[2203]

      Willis Coy and Amy Young were parents of four children likely all born at Amherst, Massachusetts.

i   DEBORAH B. COY, b. about 1792; d. at Chicago, IL, 1862 (probate 1862). Deborah did not marry. In her will written 4 Apr 1862 (probate of estate in Massachusetts and Illinois), Deborah B. Coy of Chicago left her entire estate to nephew Erastus Coy, Jr. which included a 5-acre parcel in Amherst that she inherited from her father.[2204]

ii   SOPHIA COY, b. about 1798; d. at Pittsfield, MA, 25 Jul 1886; m. ISAIAH F. EASTMAN, b. in CT, about 1794 son of Asahel and Mary (Fuller) Eastman; Isaiah d. at Pittsfield, 11 Apr 1866.

iii   MARTHA COY, b. about 1799; d. at Amherst, MA, 5 Feb 1840. Martha did not marry. In a will written on the day of her death, Martha has bequests to father Willis Coy, sister Sophia Eastman wife of Isaiah Eastman, brother Erastus Coy, and sister Deborah Coy.[2205]

[2201] The names of John's parents are given on his death record as Micajah Morrill and Sally Shaw.

[2202] Spaulding, *An Account of Some Early Settlers of West Dunstable, Monson and Hollis*, N.H., p 113

[2203] Massachusetts Wills and Probate, Hampshire County, volume 46, pp 661-662

[2204] Massachusetts Wills and Probate, Hampshire County, volume 56, p 149

[2205] *Massachusetts. Probate Court (Hampshire County)*, probate records volume 42, p 470

iv   ERASTUS COY, b. 1801; d. at Amherst, 8 May 1867; m. 1st at Belchertown, 10 Nov 1827, MARY THAYER, b. about 1808 of undetermined parents;[2206] Mary d. at Amherst, 31 May 1836. Erastus m. 2nd, CAROLINE WILSON, b. at Belchertown, 1820 daughter of Sylvester and Lucinda (Whitney) Wilson; Caroline d. at Amherst, 14 Apr 1863.

733)   PATTY COY (*Deborah Barker, Coy⁴, Martha Ingalls Barker Goodale³, Sarah Russell Ingalls², Robert¹*), b. at Monson, MA, 24 Feb 1766 daughter of Jonathan and Deborah (Barker) Coy; d. at Brimfield, 23 Jun 1861; m. at Brimfield, 24 Jan 1787, PELEG CHENEY JANES, b. at Brimfield, 2 Dec 1760 son of William and Hannah (Cheney) Janes;[2207] Cheney d. at Brimfield, 25 Jun 1834.

     Peleg Cheney Janes had mill rights in east Brimfield that he obtained from his father who had a sawmill and gristmill. Cheney operated a gristmill there until 1814. On 20 February 1815, Cheney in connection with Israel Trask, Elias Carter, Augustus Janes, and Elijah Abbot formed the Brimfield Cotton and Woolen Manufacturing Company. Cheney contributed the dam and water rights to the enterprise. The business was bankrupt in three years.[2208]

     On 6 April 1816, Peleg C. Janes and Augustus Janes with consent of Patty Janes conveyed to the Brimfield Cotton and Woolen Manufacturing Company a gristmill, carding machine, and building over it, plus the land they stand on, the dam and water privileges for payment of fifteen hundred dollars. On 16 June 1823, Peleg C. Cheney and Augustus Cheney conveyed a tract of sixteen acres near the Monson and Brimfield Manufacturing Company to the company for payment of one hundred dollars.[2209]

     On 23 January 1816, for payment of one thousand dollars, Peleg C. Janes conveyed to Thomas Janes a tract of land in Brimfield containing about twenty acres lying on the west side of the road leading to Holland. On 9 April 1825, Peleg conveyed to Augustus a tract of land of about twenty-two acres for five hundred dollars.[2210]

     Peleg Janes and Patty Coy were parents of seven children born at Brimfield.

i   AUGUSTUS JANES, b. 12 May 1787; d. at Brimfield, 28 Jun 1846; m. BETSEY BINGHAM, b. at Royalton, VT, 1789 daughter of Thomas and Mercy (House) Bingham; Betsey d. at Brimfield, 16 May 1870.

ii   CYNTHIA JANES, b. 19 Feb 1789; d. at Brimfield, 1 Mar 1822; m. at Brimfield, 26 Apr 1810, ORLANDO GRIGGS, b. 1789 son of Joseph and Penelope (Goodell) Griggs; Orlando d. at Wales, 14 Feb 1869.

iii   TIMOTHY JANES, b. 28 Apr 1791; d. at Warren, MA, 17 Feb 1877; m. at Warren, 1 Nov 1818, LYDIA TYLER, b. 6 Feb 1799 daughter of Isaac and Bethiah (Cutler) Tyler; Lydia d. at Warren, 12 Jul 1875.

iv   FLAVILLA JANES, b. 15 Par 1793; d. at Brimfield, 31 Oct 1885; m. JULIUS WARD, b. at Brimfield, 4 May 1788 son of Christopher and Sarah (Morgan) Ward; Julius d. at Brimfield, 4 Nov 1828.

v   ADOTIA JANES, b. 18 Mar 1795; d. 22 Jan 1797.

vi   CLEMENTINE JANES, b. 24 Jul 1802; d. at Kent, OH, 14 Apr 1892; m. at Brimfield, 1 Jan 1828, EDWARD PARSONS, b. at Northampton, 14 Mar 1797 son of Moses and Esther (Kingsley) Parsons; Edward d. at Franklin, OH, 6 Apr 1874.

vii   WILLIAM C. JANES, b. 5 Jul 1805; d. at New Haven, CT, 12 Apr 1873; m. at Brimfield, 4 Jun 1834, ADELPHIA FULLER, b. about 1811 daughter of Joseph and Lucena (Loring) Fuller; Adelphia d. at New Haven, 1 Apr 1881.

734)   JONATHAN COY (*Deborah Barker, Coy⁴, Martha Ingalls Barker Goodale³, Sarah Russell Ingalls², Robert¹*), b. at Monson, MA, 11 Jul 1768 son of Jonathan and Deborah (Barker) Coy; d. at Royalton, VT, 30 May 1841; m. 1st 1793, OLIVE PIXLEY, b. at Dighton, MA, 25 Jun 1768 daughter of Robert and Sarah (Trask) Pixley; Olive d. at Royalton, 15 Sep 1795. Jonathan m. 2nd 1803, LUCY BINGHAM, b. at Lebanon, CT, 19 Jul 1770 daughter of Thomas and Mercy (House) Bingham; Lucy d. at Royalton, 8 Jul 1852.

     Jonathan's father and his uncle Reuben were early settlers of Royalton arriving there by 1791. Jonathan, Jr. was a farmer with substantial land holdings.[2211]

     Jonathan Coy and Olive Pixley were parents of one child.

[2206] Thayer's *Memorial of the Thayer Name*, p 169, gives parents as John and Mary Thayer. However, the date of birth given for Mary in that same volume is the date of birth for Mary Thayer daughter of Oliver and Hannah Thayer. No records that would assist with the differentiation were located.

[2207] Janes, *The Janes Family*, p 118

[2208] Brimfield, *Historical Celebration of the Town of Brimfield*, p 154

[2209] Massachusetts Land Records, Hampden County, 52:321; 67:592

[2210] Massachusetts Land Records, Hampden County, 52:301 ½; 92:473

[2211] Lovejoy, *History of Royalton*, p 733

i JOHN COY, b. at Royalton, VT, 11 Jul 1794; d. at Royalton, 11 Oct 1870; m. MATILDA THOMPSON, b. at Tunbridge, VT, 5 May 1804 daughter of Richard and Susannah (Peabody) Thompson; Matilda d. at Royalton, 20 Nov 1867.

Jonathan Coy and Lucy Bingham were parents of one child.

i SIMON BINGHAM COY, b. at Royalton, 21 Jan 1807; d. 3 Aug 1814.

735) REUBEN COYE (*Deborah Barker, Coy⁴, Martha Ingalls Barker Goodale³, Sarah Russell Ingalls², Robert¹*), b. at Monson, MA, 24 Apr 1770 son of Jonathan and Deborah (Barker) Coy; d. at Northfield, MI, 3 Dec 1843; m. at Tunbridge, VT, 17 Feb 1799, SARAH CHAMBERS, b. in NH, 1780 (census records); Sarah d. at Northfield, 1865.
    Reuben and Sarah were in Tunbridge, Vermont, then in Livonia, New York, before obtaining property in Michigan. The family was in Tunbridge in 1800 and in Livonia, New York in 1820. On 4 September 1832, Reuben Coye of Monroe County, New York purchased from the United States land office in Detroit eighty acres situated in the east half of the northwest quarter of section eleven in township two south of range six east of Michigan Territory (Michigan-Toledo strip).[2212]
    Reuben Coye and Sarah Chambers were parents of nine children.

i LADOTIA COY, b. at Tunbridge, VT, 9 Feb 1800

ii DELILA COY, b. at Tunbridge, 19 Apr 1802; d. at Duplain, MI, after 1860 and before 1870; m. at Washtenaw County, MI, 11 Jan 1835, JAMES TUCKER, b. in NH, about 1809; James d. after 1870.

iii ALMIRA COY, b. at Tunbridge, 1804; d. at Mount Morris, NY, after 1865; m. PHILANDER GRIFFIN ELDRIDGE, b. about 1809 son of Seth and Rebecca (Reed) Eldridge; Philander d. at Rochester, NY, 21 May 1881.

iv BEMJAMIN CHAMBERS COY, b. at Tunbridge, 31 Aug 1806; d. at Livonia, NY, 6 Apr 1897; m. 1ˢᵗ Feb 1829, CHARLOTTE PRATT, b. 1810 daughter of George and Charlotte (Risdon) Pratt; Charlotte d. at Livonia, 10 Oct 1832. Benjamin m. 2ⁿᵈ 27 Mar 1833, CAROLINE REED, b. at Richmond, NY, 14 Oct 1811 daughter of Wheller and Olive (Risdon) Reed; Caroline d. at Livonia, 22 Apr 1899.

v ROYAL BARKER COY, b. at Tunbridge, 26 Oct 1808; d. at Ann Arbor, MI, before 1850; m. at Plymouth, MI, 2 Mar 1843, LAURA ALLENA BIBBINS, b. in NY, about 1823; Laura d. at Leslie, MI, 13 Feb 1875.

vi HORCE COY, b. 1810; d. at Northfield, MI, 19 Jun 1887; m. at Washtenaw County, MI, 25 Jun 1839, HANNAH SMITH (widow of Weed Worden), b. in NY, about 1805; Hannah d. at Northfield, 21 Oct 1889.

vii LOREN COY, b. at Livonia, NY, 1812; d. at Mount Morris, NY, 1 Dec 1882; m. HARRIET N., b. in NY, about 1821; Harriet d. at Mount Morris, 5 Dec 1893.

viii CHANDLER W. COY, b. 1814; d. at Saint Johns, MI, 12 Nov 1849; m. at Washtenaw County, MI, 21 Dec 1837, LOUISA WILKINSON.

ix EMILY COY, b. 1816; d. at Emmett, MI, 11 Feb 1860; m. about 1834, JOSEPH AVERY MAIN, b. in CT, 1808 son of Joseph and Mary (Avery) Main; Joseph d. at Emmett, 31 Jan 1899. Joseph married second Rachel Phillips.

736) BEULAH COYE (*Deborah Barker, Coy⁴, Martha Ingalls Barker Goodale³, Sarah Russell Ingalls², Robert¹*), b. at Monson, MA, 24 Apr 1770 daughter of Jonathan and Deborah (Barker) Coy; d. at New Woodstock, NY, 1831; m. at Holland, MA, 20 Aug 1789, CHANDLER WEBBER, b. at Holland, MA, 1763 son of Samuel and Mehitable (Frizell) Webber; Chandler d. at New Woodstock, 13 Jun 1837.[2213]
    Beulah and Chandler were in Holland, Massachusetts just after their marriage and their older children were likely born there. In the 1810 census, there were seven members of the household living at Cazenovia: one male over 45, one female 26 to 44, two males under ten, one male 10 to 15, one female 10 to 15, and one female 16 to 25.[2214] On 7 August 1820, Chandler Webber was head of household in Cazenovia, New York with household of one male 45 and over, one female over 45, one male under 10, two males 10 to 15, one female 10 to 15, and one female 16 to 25.[2215]
    Six children were identified for Beulah and Chandler although there is likely one older daughter in the family who has not been identified.

[2212] U. S. General Land Office Records, Michigan, Washtenaw, Certificate 5846
[2213] Several family members are interred at New Woodstock Cemetery; findagrave ID: 12712274
[2214] Year: 1810; Census Place: Cazenovia, Madison, New York; Roll: 28; Page: 746; Image: 00147; Family History Library Film: 0181382
[2215] 820 U S Census; Census Place: Cazenovia, Madison, New York; Page: 33; NARA Roll: M33_73; Image: 45

i ERASTUS WEBBER, b. 11 Feb 1794; d. at Cazenovia, NY, May 1876; m. ROWENA STOWELL, b. at Newtown, CT, 20 May 1791 the adopted daughter of Calvin and Sarah (Kinney) Stowell;[2216]

ii SEMIRA WEBBER, b. 1799; d. at New Woodstock, NY, 1859; m. JAMES LEARY, b. 1793; d. at New Woodstock, 1834 (probate 21 Nov 1834).[2217]

iii EZRA WEBBER, b. 1805; d. at New Woodstock, 5 Oct 1887; m. MARY R. GLEASON, b. 1805; Mary d. at New Woodstock, 1866.

iv CHANDLER WEBBER, b. 1810; d. after 1880 when he was living at Cazenovia;[2218] m. ELSIE who has not been identified, b. in NY about 1814; Elsie d. after 1880.

v HUDSON WEBBER, b. about 1811; d. at Sangamon County, IL, 11 Jul 1856 (probate 1856);[2219] m. SARAH who has not been identified, b. in NY about 1812 and living in 1856.

vi WINTHROP WEBBER, b. 1814; d. at New Woodstock, 1891; m. 1st 1836, LOUISA WEBSTER TUCKER, b. 1811 daughter of Thomas and Hannah (Webster) Tucker; Louisa d. at New Woodstock, 1866. Winthrop m. 2nd CHARLOTTE HOLMES (widow of Lucius Corbin), b. 1818 daughter of Isaac and Elizabeth (Gardner) Holmes; Charlotte d. at New Woodstock, 22 Dec 1893.

737) SIMEON COYE (*Deborah Barker, Coy⁴, Martha Ingalls Barker Goodale³, Sarah Russell Ingalls², Robert¹*), b. at Monson, MA, 24 Jan 1774 son of Jonathan and Deborah (Barker) Coy; d. at Brimfield, 29 Apr 1857; m. RHODA BROWN, b. at Brimfield, 5 Sep 1775 daughter of Issachar and Rhoda (Nichols) Brown; Rhoda d. of cancer, at Brimfield, 27 Oct 1846.[2220]

Simeon and Rhoda resided in Brimfield where Simeon was a farmer. On 19 March 1849, Simeon Coye conveyed to Samuel N. Coye certain parcels of land in Brimfield beginning at his dwelling house for a payment of $750. On 7 March 1863, Samuel sold part of this land to his sister Adaline.[2221]

In his will, Simeon Coye bequeathed $750 to his daughter Adaline B. Tyler wife of John Tyler and $750 to the children of his daughter Mary B. Sumner deceased. The remainder of the estate is to be equally divided among son Samuel N. Coye, daughter Adaline, and his three grandchildren children of Mary. Son-in-law John Tyler was named executor. Distribution from the estate on in 1857 and 1858 included $750 to Adaline B. Tyler and a total of $750 in payments to Cheney Sumner as guardian of Gamaliel Sumner, to Mary E. Sumner, and to Charles E. Sumner. The total value of the estate was $3,226.83.[2222]

Simeon Coye and Rhoda Barker were parents of four children born at Brimfield. The three oldest children were all baptized on 4 Sep 1814.

i SAMUEL NICHOLS COYE, b. 28 Aug 1808; d. at Zion, IL, 10 Jun 1874; m. at Brimfield, 24 Dec 1834, LAURA FERRY, b. at Brimfield, 15 Mar 1816 daughter of Oliver and Phila (*Fuller* Hale) Ferry; Laura d. at Zion, 1 Mar 1874. Samuel and Laura were in Brimfield until 1855 and then headed west with their children.

ii MARY BARKER COYE, b. 21 Nov 1809; d. at Spencer, MA, of consumption on 16 Apr 1848; m. at Brimfield, 9 May 1833, CHENEY SUMNER, b. at Spencer, 17 Feb 1795 son of John and Abigail (Pease) Sumner; John d. at Spencer, 10 Sep 1867.

iii ADALINE BROWN COYE, b. 25 Feb 1811; d. at Warren, MA, 27 Apr 1898; m. at Brimfield, 3 Jan 1834, JOHN TYLER, b. at Warren, 4 Dec 1803 son of Daniel and Abigail (Cutter) Tyler;[2223][2224] John d. at Warren, 9 Jul 1886.

iv WILLIAM PORTER COYE, b. Feb 1817; d. at Brimfield, 12 Nov 1847. William did not marry.

738) DAVID COYE (*Deborah Barker, Coy⁴, Martha Ingalls Barker Goodale³, Sarah Russell Ingalls², Robert¹*), b. at Monson, MA, 26 May 1781 son of Jonathan and Deborah (Barker) Coy; d. at Homer, NY, 23 May 1860; m. 1st, about 1809, DORCAS HANNUM, b. at Southampton, MA, 28 Jul 1786 daughter of Seth and Anna (Searle) Hannum; Dorcas d. at Homer, NY, Jul 1818. David m. 2nd at Homer, 24 May 1820, NANCY CANFIELD, b. at Sandisfield, MA, 18 May 1791 daughter of John and Deborah (Norton) Canfield; Nancy d. at Homer, 7 Jun 1867.

[2216] Stowell, *The Stowell Genealogy*, p 217
[2217] On 21 Nov 1834, executrix Semira Leary presented the will of James Leary to probate court in Madison County; New York Wills and Probate, Madison County, Book A, p 161. James Leary is interred at the New Woodstock Cemetery, findagrave ID: 120954113
[2218] Year: 1880; Census Place: Cazenovia, Madison, New York; Roll: 859; Page: 46D; Enumeration District: 049
[2219] Sangamon County, Illinois wills, conservatorships, guardianships, appraisements, 1821-1982; Author: Illinois. Probate Court (Sangamon County); Probate Place: Sangamon, Illinois
[2220] Rhoda, b. B., w. Simeon, cancer, Oct. 27, 1846, a. 71
[2221] Massachusetts Land Records, Hampden County, 149:196; 225:267
[2222] Massachusetts Wills and Probate, Hampden County, Estate of Simeon Coye, 1857, Case 3124
[2223] Names of parents are given as Daniel and Nabby of John's death record.
[2224] Brigham, *Descendants of Job Tyler*, p 228

Col. David Coye is reported as coming to Homer from Royalton, Vermont in 1806. His skilled trade was as a joiner and he also had a 100-acre property. He served various official functions in the town including postmaster and was elected sheriff in 1822.[2225] He was one of the original trustees of Cortland Academy where his sons and daughters were educated.

In his will written 2 September 1850 (probate 6 August 1860), David Coye bequeaths to beloved wife Nancy, in lieu of the dower, the whole of the real and personal estate during her natural life with the expectation that the estate will provide support and maintenance for his children in the manner that is hereinafter expected. Children John Coye and Mary Jane Coye receive a home at the homestead and education until age twenty-one. Their education is to be the same as provided for the children who are over twenty-one. The estate is to be kept and managed by the executor. After the decease of Nancy and the rearing of the two youngest children, if any property is left, it is to be divided equally among all the children then living. Any advance a child has received is to be deducted from that child's portion. The guardianship of children John and Mary Jane is committed to the executors who are Nancy Coye and son Schuyler Coye. In a codicil written 20 January 1860, David added Caleb H. Sherman of Homer as a third executor.[2226] On 29 May 1860, George J. J. Barber of Homer was named as special guardian to Frank C. DeLong a minor who was an heir to the estate.[2227]

The history of Cortland County mentions that David Coye had eleven children,[2228] but nine children have been identified. Two children have been identified for David Coye and Dorcas Hannum.

i   LEWIS H. COYE, b. about 1814; m. ANNA MARIA, b. about 1814 who has not been identified. Lewis and Anna were living in Linn Creek, MO in 1860 where Lewis was appointed postmaster in 1859.[2229] In 1850, they were living in Homer, NY. Lewis and Anna had a son Edward H. Coye born in 1847 who died in 1861 while he was a student at the Hall Family School for Boys in Ellington, CT.[2230]

ii   DORCAS ANN COYE, b. at Homer, 27 Jun 1818; d. at Lockport, NY, 12 Oct 1847; m. 1842, as his second wife, FRANCIS DELONG, b. at Cornwall, VT, 10 Jan 1808 son of Aaron and Sylvia (Bingham) DeLong; Francis d. at Novato, CA, 11 Feb 1885. Francis was first married to Elizabeth M. Gale (1810-1835). Dorcas and Francis had one child, Frank C. DeLong.

Seven children have been identified for David Coye and Nancy Canfield all born at Homer, New York.

i   CAROLINE COYE, b. Sep 1821; d. at Homer, 2 Mar 1910; m. 1853, CALEB H. SHERMAN, b. Sep 1817 likely son of Eli and Flavia (Bliss) Sherman; Caleb d. at Homer, 12 Jun 1904.

ii   OSCAR COYE, b. 1824 and d. 1825.

iii SCHUYLER COYE, b. 3 Dec 1825; d. at Buffalo, NY, 9 Jun 1885; m. about 1854, CATHERINE M. who has not been identified, b. 19 Sep 1830 (per gravestone); Catherine d. at Buffalo, 13 May 1891. Schuyler and Catherine had two sons who died in childhood, Frank DeLong Coye and Schuyler Coye.

iv   GEORGE C. COYE, b. about 1828. The last record found for George in his 1863 Civil War draft registration while living in Campbell, MO. He and his brother John were in Missouri in 1860 and were traders/merchants.

v   HIRAM LANSING COYE, b. Aug 1829; d. after 1901 when he was living in San Francisco. He was married twice, first to SARAH E., b. about 1840 and second in 1890 to SARAH, b. Dec 1849. On census records, Hiram is described as a capitalist and in 1900 he was the president of Nevada Salt and Borax Company.

vi   JOHN COYE, b. about 1832. Last record of John is living in Linn Creek, MO in 1860.

vii MARY JANE COYE, b. 1835; d. at Homer, 1913. Mary Jane did not marry.

739) JOSEPH BARKER (*Stephen Barker⁴, Martha Ingalls Barker Goodale³, Sarah Russell Ingalls², Robert¹*), b. at Ashby, 25 Mar 1774 son of Stephen and Rebekah (Gibson) Barker; m. about 1798, ELIZABETH WASHBURN.

Joseph Barker and Elizabeth Washburn resided in Heath at least until 1806. On 8 November 1806, Joseph Barker and wife Betsey and Daniel Lyon and wife Rebecca conveyed a 70-acre parcel of land in Heath to Rufus and Luther Thompson for payment of six hundred dollars.[2231] Just two children were identified.

[2225] Smith, *History of Cortland County, NY*
[2226] New York Wills and Probate, Cortland County, Wills Volume D, 1856-1863, pp 524-528
[2227] New York Wills and Probate, Cortland County, Minutes, Orders, Decrees, volume E, I, p 544
[2228] Smith, *History of Cortland County, NY*, p 196
[2229] U.S., Appointments of U. S. Postmasters, 1832-1971
[2230] Connecticut, Hale Collection of Cemetery Inscriptions and Newspaper Notices, 1629-1934
[2231] Massachusetts Land Records, Franklin County, 23:469

i   PELHAM BARKER, b. 1801; d. at Harmony, NY, 18 Feb 1853; m. PERMELIA TILLOTSON, b. at Sherburne, NY, 23 Apr 1806 daughter of Asa and Hannah (Chapman) Tillotson; Permelia d. at Harmony, 8 May 1866.[2232]

ii   ELIZABETH BARKER, b. 22 May 1803; d. at Trempealeau, WI, 11 Oct 1859; m. DANIEL TROWBRIDGE, b. at Cairo, NY, 21 Oct 1794 son of Abel and Anna (Mosier) Trowbridge; Daniel d. at Trempealeau, 5 Dec 1863.

740)   REBECCA BARKER (*Stephen Barker⁴, Martha Ingalls Barker Goodale³, Sarah Russell Ingalls², Robert¹*), b. at Heath, MA, 26 Jun 1776 daughter of Stephen and Rebekah (Gibson) Barker; d. at Montrose, PA, 29 Jun 1819; m. at Heath, 6 Oct 1799, DANIEL LYONS, b. at Roxbury, MA, 26 May 1778 son of David and Abigail (Draper) Lyons;[2233] Daniel d. at Great Bend, PA, 7 Sep 1850.

     Rebecca and Daniel were married at the home of Rebecca's father by Rev. Strong. The family resided in Colerain, Massachusetts until 1813 when they relocated to Great Bend, Pennsylvania. Deacon Daniel Lyons was a Baptist and built the meeting house in Great Bend for the church that was organized there 27 October 1825. It is said that he had a prejudice against singing.[2234]

     Rebecca and Daniel were parents of ten children born at Colrain, Massachusetts. Daniel also had eight children with his second wife Anna B. Smith.

i   NATHANIEL LYONS, b. 6 Oct 1800; d. 9 Jun 1816.

ii   ABIGAIL DRAPER LYONS, b. 10 Mar 1802; d. at Great Bend. PA, 8 Feb 1820.

iii   DAVID LYONS, b. 22 Oct 1804; d. at Lanesboro, PA, 9 Oct 1894; m. 1 Mar 1824, AMANDA SMITH, b. 28 Jun 1804 daughter of Joshua and Sabra (Bill) Smith; Amanda d. 12 Aug 1872. David married the sister of his stepmother.

iv   SAMUEL LYONS, b. and d. 10 Apr 1806.

v   SOPHRONIA LYONS, b. 11 May 1807; d. 12 May 1807.

vi   ANNA LYONS, b. 16 Jun 1808; d. 16 Jun 1812.

vii   JOHN LYONS, b. 16 Oct 1810; d. at Union, PA, 1905; m. at Wayne, PA, 6 Feb 1834, NANCY SMITH, b. Oct 1811 daughter of Samuel and Jane (Dickey) Smith; Nancy d. 1909.

viii   JESSE LYONS, b. 1 Jul 1814; d. at Beaver Dam, PA, 2 Nov 1866; m. 23 Mar 1837, JANE KINCAIDE, b. 7 Jun 1818 daughter of John and Elizabeth (Smith) Kincaid; Jane d. at Beaver Dam, 23 Nov 1866. Jane's mother Elizabeth Smith was the sister of John Lyons's wife Nancy Smith.

ix   BETSEY LYONS, b. 2 Nov 1815; d. at Chattanooga, TN, 8 Sep 1891; m. at Deposit, NY, 1 Oct 1835, CONFUCIUS FITCH LOOMIS, b. at East Windsor, CT, 8 Oct 1809 son of Gershom and Clarissa (Stoughton) Loomis; Confucius d. at Hallstead, PA, 9 Feb 1885.

x   DANIEL LYONS, b. 6 May 1817; d. 7 Jun 1817.

741)   TIMOTHY BARKER (*Stephen Barker⁴, Martha Ingalls Barker Goodale³, Sarah Russell Ingalls², Robert¹*), b. at Heath, 30 Mar 1778 son of Stephen and Rebekah (Gibson) Barker; d. at Lottsville, PA, 6 Mar 1869; m. BETSEY who has not been identified, b. in VT, 13 Mar 1787 (on gravestone); Betsey d. at Lottsville, 4 May 1872.[2235]

     Timothy was a farmer but was also involved in the lumber business and he and son Thomas had a lumber mill in Warren County, Pennsylvania.[2236] In 1850, Timothy and Betsey Barker were living in Columbus, Pennsylvania with three apparent children: Mary age 31, Thomas F. age 28, and Sally age 26.[2237] In 1860, Timothy and Betsey were living with son Thomas F. and his wife Eliza in Columbus Township, Pennsylvania.[2238]

     Three children are identified although the 1830 census suggests as many as seven children in the family (one male under 5; one female under 5; two females 5-9; and three females 10-14).[2239]

[2232] Pelham, Permelia, and one of their sons are interred at the Tillotson Cemetery in New Harmony, New York; https://chautauqua.nygenweb.net/CEMETERY/Till_cem.htm

[2233] Lyon, *Lyon Memorial*, p 186

[2234] Blackman, *History of Susquehanna County, Pennsylvania*, p 82

[2235] Timothy, Betsey, and son Thomas F. and his wife Eliza are buried in a Barker plot in Pine Valley Cemetery in Lottsville, PA; findagrave ID: 12944731

[2236] Schenck, *History of Warren County*, p 488

[2237] Year: 1850; Census Place: Columbus, Warren, Pennsylvania; Roll: 832; Page: 302B

[2238] Year: 1860; Census Place: Columbus, Warren, Pennsylvania; Page: 700; Family History Library Film: 805190

[2239] Year: 1830; Census Place: Columbus, Warren, Pennsylvania; Series: M19; Roll: 165; Page: 28; Family History Library Film: 0020639

i   MARY BARKER, b. in NY, 1819; living with parents and unmarried in 1850.

ii   THOMAS F. BARKER, b. 2 Jan 1821; d. at Bear Lake, PA, 24 Jul 1909; m. ELIZA BARTON, b. in NY, 9 Aug 1832 (on gravestone) daughter of Zenas and Bathsheba (Beals) Barton; Eliza d. at Lottsville, PA, 4 Nov 1896.

iii   SALLY BARKER, b. in PA, 1824; living with parents and unmarried in 1850.

742) ANNA BARKER (*Stephen Barker⁴, Martha Ingalls Barker Goodale³, Sarah Russell Ingalls², Robert¹*), b. at Heath, 1780 daughter of Stephen and Rebekah (Gibson) Barker; d. at Heath, MA, 25 Aug 1850; m. at Heath, 21 Oct 1810, STEPHEN GERRY, b. at Hatfield, 22 Aug 1784 son of Nathan and Martha (Waite) Gerry; Stephen d. at Wautoma, WI, 2 Mar 1867.[2240]
     Stephen and Anna resided in Heath until Anna's death. Stephen then went to Wisconsin where he obtained a homestead patent on 15 December 1856.[2241]
     Anna Barker and Stephen Gerry were parents of seven children.

i   ANNA LYONS GERRY, b. at Heath, 13 Nov 1811; d. at Blue Earth County, MN, 19 May 1865; m. at Whitingham, VT, 11 May 1834, ANTHONY CASE, b. about 1803; Anthony d. after 1880 when he was living with his daughter Anna and her family in Loreno, MN. Anthony was a minister of the gospel.

ii   REBECCA GERRY, b. at Whately, 24 Mar 1813; d. after 1850 when she was living in Heath with her parents.

iii   STEPHEN BARKER GERRY, b. at Whately, 27 Oct 1814; d. at Wautoma, WI, 17 Apr 1856.

iv   EDSON GERRY, b. at Whately, 27 May 1816; d. at Marietta, WA, 7 Mar 1904; m. at Brattleboro, VT, 21 Mar 1842, SARAH B. HARRIS, b. at Brattleboro, VT, 15 Dec 1821; Sarah d. at Garden City, MN, Jan 1918.

v   ELBRIDGE GERRY, b. at Whately, 13 Apr 1818; d. after 1870 when living in Cleveland, OH; m. at Rowe, MA, 29 Sep 1840, MARY ANN BALDWIN, b. at Heath, 19 May 1819 daughter of Phineas and Mary (-) Baldwin.

vi   JAMES GERRY, b. at Heath, 15 Apr 1820; d. 11 Sep 1832.

vii SARAH ANGELINE GERRY, b. at Heath, 25 Nov 1821; d. at Berlin, WI, 9 Dec 1863. Sarah Angeline did not marry.

743) LUCY BARKER (*Stephen Barker⁴, Martha Ingalls Barker Goodale³, Sarah Russell Ingalls², Robert¹*), b. at Heath, 1784 daughter of Stephen and Rebekah (Gibson) Barker; d. at Willing, NY, 25 Feb 1847; m. at Heath, 4 Dec 1813, MATTHEW WILSON, b. 1794; Matthew d. at Willing, 14 Jul 1877. Matthew married second Patience Harrington and married third Ruth Eaton.
     One child was identified for Lucy Barker and Matthew Wilson.

i   REBECCA WILSON, b. at Allegany County, NY, Aug 1823; d. at Liberty, PA, 10 Feb 1906; m. 1840, DENNISON WOODCOCK, b. at Swanzey, NH, 15 Jan 1817 son of Nathan and Abigail (Crossett) Woodcock; Dennison d. at Liberty, 18 Oct 1912.[2242]

744) REUBEN GOODELL (*Reuben Goodell⁴, Martha Ingalls Barker Goodale³, Sarah Russell Ingalls², Robert¹*), b. likely at New Haven, about 1775 son of Reuben and Abigail (Sharpe) Goodell; d. at New Haven, 19 Nov 1851;[2243] m. about 1802, SARAH "Sally" who has not been identified; Sarah d. at New Haven, 16 Jan 1849.
     Reuben and Sarah were parents of six children, births of second, third, and fourth children recorded at Preston, Connecticut[2244] and the younger children perhaps born at New Haven.
     Daughter Rebecca did not marry. Her estate (probate 13 May 1895) was administered by Wilford Ford and the following heirs-at-law were identified: Mary Ella Goodell at 371 Crown Street, niece; Cornelia Goodell of West Haven, niece; Alice Comstock of Ivoryton, sister; Sarah J. Benedict of 371 Crown Street, niece; and Martha Goodell at 12 Hotchkiss, niece.[2245] Mary Ella Goodell and Sarah Benedict were the daughters of Henry Goodell, Cornelia Goodell was daughter of William, and Martha Goodell was daughter of Joseph.

[2240] Stephen is interred at Wautoma Union Cemetery; findagrave ID: 110665703

[2241] Wisconsin, Homestead and Cash Entry Patents, Pre-1908; land description 1 SENE 4TH PM - 1831 MINNESOTA/WISCONSIN No 19 N 10 E 27; issued 15 Dec 1856

[2242] Pennsylvania, Death Certificates, 1906-1964; Pennsylvania Historic and Museum Commission; Harrisburg, Pennsylvania; Pennsylvania (State). Death certificates, 1906–1967; Certificate Number Range: 092841-096230

[2243] Connecticut State Library; Hartford, Connecticut; Reuben Goodell, age 76

[2244] Connecticut Births and Christenings, 1649-1906; accessed through familysearch.org; parents listed as Reuben and Sally

[2245] Connecticut Wills and Probate, New Haven District, Town of New Haven, Estate of Rebecca Goodale, Case 18,499.

i   JOSEPH GOODELL, b. 1802; d. at New Haven, 1 Dec 1854; m. MARTHA, b. 1807; Martha d. at New Haven, 15 Jun 1891.

ii   ABIGIAL GOODELL, b. at Preston, 5 Aug 1806. No heirs of Abigail are listed in sister Rebecca's probate.

iii   WILLIAM GOODELL, b. at Preston, 5 Apr 1808; d. at New Haven, 3 Apr 1890; m. HANNAH M., b. 1810; Hannah d. at New Haven, 15 Feb 1873.

iv   HENRY GOODELL, b. at Preston, 26 Jul 1810; d. at Glastonbury, CT, 1890 (probate 1890); m. by 1840, MARY ELIZABETH CHITTENDEN, b. Jul 1819 daughter of Augustus and Polly (Hotchkiss) Chittenden;[2246] Mary d. at Glastonbury, 1895 (probate 1895).

v   REBECCA GOODELL, b. 1818; d. at New Haven, 5 May 1895. Rebecca did not marry.

vi   ALICE GOODELL, b. 1820; d. at Essex, CT, 19 Jun 1901; m. at Orange, CT, 29 Jul 1845, WILLIAM ARNOLD COMSTOCK, b. at Saybrook, 1824 son of Elisha M. and Sarah (Lane) Comstock;[2247] William d. at Essex, 23 Oct 1851.

745)   JOHN GOODELL (*Reuben Goodell⁴, Martha Ingalls Barker Goodale³, Sarah Russell Ingalls², Robert¹*), b. likely at New Haven, 1782 son of Reuben and Abigail (Sharpe) Goodell; d. after 1855 when he was living at Homer, NY; m. 1ˢᵗ DEBORAH LAFLIN, b. at Charlton, MA, 10 Apr 1780 daughter of Joseph and Martha (Cummins) Laflin; Deborah d. about 1823. John m. 2ⁿᵈ, BETSEY E., b. in CT, about 1793; Betsey d. after 1860 when she was living at Homer.

     John and Deborah were parents of three children.

i   CLEMENT GOODELL, b. at Sturbridge, MA, 22 Jan 1812

ii   JONATHAN RAWSON GOODELL, b. at Sturbridge, 11 May 1814; living in Homer, NY in 1855; m. by 1840, MINERVA A. MAYNARD, b. about 1819; Minerva d. at Homer, May 1856.

iii   SILAS GOODELL, b at Sturbridge, 11 Jul 1817; d. at Ottawa, IL, 1913; m. 1ˢᵗ about 1842, PRISCILLA HUBBARD, b. 1821 daughter of John and Sally (·) Hubbard (on gravestone); Priscilla d. at Homer, 2 Aug 1862. Silas m. 2ⁿᵈ SARAH STRICKLAND, b. in NY about 1824. Silas m. 3ʳᵈ 1891, widow VIOLETTA HARRIS, b. in NY, Oct 1825; Violetta was living in 1900.

     John and Betsey were parents of two children.

i   FREDERICK H. GOODELL, b. about 1832; d. at Homer, NY, 1874 (probate 22 Oct 1874); m. ANNE TRUESDELL, b. at Homer, NY, 1829; Anne d. at Holyoke, MA, 10 Dec 1903.

ii   ELLEN E. GOODELL, b. about 1837; d. at Homer, 1895; m. about 1866, EDMOND D. BUTLER, b. about 1840 son of Edmond C. and Nancy (·) Butler; Edmond d. at Homer, 1931.

746)   ERASTUS GOODELL (*Reuben Goodell⁴, Martha Ingalls Barker Goodale³, Sarah Russell Ingalls², Robert¹*), b. likely at New Haven, about 1785 son of Reuben and Abigail (Sharpe) Goodell; d. at Homer, 25 Oct 1868; m. at Fairlee, VT, 4 Mar 1812, MARY "POLLY" C. COBURN, b. in MA, about 1785; Mary d. at Homer, 29 Sep 1856.

     Erastus and Polly were in Sturbridge for the births of their first two children, and then settled on lot 7 in Homer in 1816. Erastus was a prominent farmer in Homer.[2248] They were parents of five children.

i   CHARLES BENJAMIN GOODELL, baptized at Sturbridge, MA, 8 Dec 1812; d. at Homer, NY, 1887; m. 1ˢᵗ 1840, URETTA N. HOBART, b. about 1816; Uretta d. at Homer, 1843. Charles m. 2ⁿᵈ 1845, MARY LAKE, b. about 1816; Mary d. at Homer, 6 Aug 1899.

ii   AUSTIN GOODELL, baptized at Sturbridge, 20 Aug 1815; d. after 1880 when he was living at Jackson, TN; m. at Madison County, TN, 21 Jun 1855, MARY ANN NEWSOM, b. in TN, about 1839 daughter of Balsam and Mary M. (Herrin) Newsom;[2249] Mary d. before 1880.

[2246] Talcott, *Chittenden Family*, p 114

[2247] Comstock, *A Comstock Genealogy*, p 133

[2248] Smith, *History of Cortland County*, p 197

[2249] Mary Ann Newsom was living in Madison, TN in 1850 with parents Balsam and Mary Newson; Austin Goodell was administrator of the 1872 probate of Balsam Newsom.

iii   LORENZO D. GOODELL, b. at Homer, NY, 30 Aug 1817; d. at Jackson, TN, 14 Dec 1875; m. about 1848, LAURA O. CLARK, b. in TN, 1830 daughter of John Jonas and Ann (Johnston) Clark; Laura d. at Jackson, TN, 1869.

iv   ERASTUS GOODELL, b. at Homer, Jan 1824; d. at Homer, 3 Aug 1901; m. 1849, WATY JANE WADSWORTH, b. at Homer, Nov 1827 daughter of Archibald and Eunice (Main) Wadsworth; Waty d. at Homer, 10 May 1905.

v   MARY ELIZA GOODELL, b. at Homer, Jul 1828; d. at Homer, 1 Mar 1910; m. at Madison County, TN, 27 Jun 1876, as his second wife, JOEL TRAVIS RUSHING, b. in TN, 10 Jul 1810 son of Thomas A. and Sarah J. (Herris) Rushing; Joel d. at Cotton Grove, TN, 29 Jun 1892. Joel was first married to Emily Herron.

747)   LUCY GOODELL (*Simeon Goodell⁴, Martha Ingalls Barker Goodale³, Sarah Russell Ingalls², Robert¹*), b. about 1778 daughter of Simeon and Martha (Williams) Goodell; m. Mr. Newbury.
         The Goodale genealogy reports one child for Lucy and Mr. Newbury.[2250]

i   DOROTHY NEWBURY, b. about 1820; d. at Webster, NY after 1875 and before 1880; m. by 1842, JOEL BLISS, b. Jan 1816 son of Samuel and Nancy (Smith) Bliss;[2251] Joel d. after 1900 when living at Rochester, New York.

748)   WILLIAM GOODELL (*Simeon Goodell⁴, Martha Ingalls Barker Goodale³, Sarah Russell Ingalls², Robert¹*), b. 13 Mar 1779 son of Simeon and Martha (Williams) Goodell; d. at Parma, NY, 28 Jul 1867; m. 9 Feb 1812, SYLVIA DUTCHER, b. 2 Mar 1789 daughter John and Sylvia (Beardsley) Dutcher; Sylvia d. at Parma, 6 Nov 1865.
         William and Sylvia resided in Parma where they kept a farm. William and Sylvia were parents of eight children likely all born at Cherry Valley, New York.[2252]
         In his will written 10 October 1855 (filed 2 September 1867), William Goodel of Parma bequeaths to beloved wife Sylvia all the household furniture and household goods and the use of all the real estate he dies possessed of during her natural life. Son Elijah receives the home farm and the other real estate subject to the life estate of Sylvia. Son John receives seven hundred dollars to be paid by Elijah. Son Pacifer receives six hundred dollars to be paid by Elijah. Daughters Jerusha Wilder wife of Alamander Wilder and Mary Wilder wife of Ira Wilder each receives one hundred dollars. The residue of the estate goes to Elijah and Sylvia and Elijah are named executors.[2253]

i   SIMEON GOODELL, b. 9 Oct 1812; d. 18 Mar 1813.

ii   JERUSHA GOODELL, b. 31 Aug 1813; d. likely at Greece, NY (burial at Riverside Cemetery in Rochester), 12 Mar 1882; m. ALAMANDER WILDER, b. in VT, 1806 son of Richard and Rhoda (Fields) Wilder; Alamander d. at Greece, NY, 14 Apr 1875.

iii   JOHN GOODELL, b. 9 Nov 1815; d. at Paris, MI, 6 Feb 1898; m. 22 Oct 1840, EMELINE EVERTON, b. 14 Apr 1812; Emeline d. at Parma, NY, 24 Sep 1857.

iv   MARY GOODELL, b. 21 Dec 1817; d. at Charlotte, NY, 1 Jan 1892; m. about 1836, IRA WILDER, b. 9 Dec 1811 son of Richard and Rhoda (Fields) Wilder; Ira d. at Charlotte, 18 Feb 1883.

v   KEZIAH GOODELL (twin), b. and d. 24 Apr 1822.

vi   MARIA GOODELL (twin), b. and d. 24 Apr 1822.

vii   PARCEFOR GOODELL, b. 31 Aug 1826; d. at Hilton, NY, 2 Jul 1901 (probate 30 Jul 1901); m. 1854, CATHARINE MARTHA BENNETT,[2254] b. at Parma, Sep 1828 daughter of John and Amy (Buell) Bennett; Catharine was living in 1900.

viii   ELIJAH GOODELL, b. 29 Oct 1828; d. at Parma, NY, 13 Feb 1901; m. 26 Jan 1852, MARTHA HAZEN, b. at Richmond, NY, 12 Mar 1834 daughter of Jonathan and Hannah (Chatfield) Hazen; Martha d. at Hilton, NY, 23 Apr 1915.

749)   OLIVER GOODELL (*Silas Goodale⁴, Martha Ingalls Barker Goodale³, Sarah Russell Ingalls², Robert¹*), b. at Norwich, 13 Feb 1797 son of Silas and Sarah (Marshall) Goodale; m. 1ˢᵗ at Norwich, 1823, HARRIET BACKUS, b. at Bozrah, CT, 23 Apr 1799 daughter of Ozias and Elizabeth (Abell) Backus; Harriet d. at Jewett City, 6 Apr 1825. Oliver m. 2ⁿᵈ about 1827, PAULINA

[2250] Williams, *The Descendants of Robert Goodale*, p 116
[2251] Bliss, *Genealogy of the Bliss Family*, p 237
[2252] Williams, *The Descendants of Robert Goodale*, p 116
[2253] New York Wills and Probate, Monroe County, Wills volume 013, pp 125-126
[2254] Catharine Martha is referred to in census records as Catharine, Martha, and Catharine M. She is named as Catharine M. is her husband's will.

SALISBURY, b. about 1804 *perhaps* the daughter of Abraham and Penelope (Arnold) Salisbury; Paulina seems to have died before 1850 when their youngest daughter Phila, then age 8, was living with relatives in Rhode Island.

Oliver and Paulina were parents of at least three children.

i   HARRIET BAUCKUS GOODELL, b. 1829; d. at Chester, PA, Dec 1894;[2255] m. at Thompson, CT, 3 May 1846, ANGELO HOWLAND, b. 29 Jun 1829 son of Crawford and Mary (Lucas) Howland;[2256] Angelo d. at Chester, 8 Jan 1911. After Harriet's death, Angelo married Catherine Schlauka on 8 Jan 1911.

ii   WILLIAM GOODELL, b. 1831; d. at Killingly, CT, 29 Jul 1915; m. 1852, PHEBE SHAW, b. in RI, 16 May 1833 daughter of Samuel and Barbara (Bates) Shaw;[2257] Phebe d. at Killingly, 4 Nov 1909.

iii PHILA ANNIE GOODELL, b. Mar 1843; d. at Providence, RI, 2 Aug 1924;[2258] m. EDWARD HAYES, b. about 1847; Edward d. at Derby, CT, 6 Jan 1908.

750)   ABIGAIL BISHOP (*Peggy Goodale Bishop⁴, Martha Ingalls Barker Goodale³, Sarah Russell Ingalls², Robert¹*), b. at Brimfield, 13 Sep 1774 daughter of Richard and Peggy (Goodale) Bishop; d. at Brimfield, 2 Nov 1833; m. at Brimfield, 14 Jun 1792, SOLOMON HOAR (later HOMER) b. at Brimfield, 17 Mar 1771 son of Joseph and Mary (Hitchcock) Hoar; Solomon d. at Brimfield, 11 Dec 1844.

Solomon Homer was active in the military, commissioned cornet in a cavalry company on 15 September 1802 rising to the rank of colonel on 12 July 1816.[2259] He also served as deacon and was a farmer.[2260]

About 1830, some members of the Hoar family who settled in Homer, New York took the name Homer as their last name, and the remaining family in Brimfield also made the name change to Homer.[2261]

Abigail and Solomon were parents of seven children born at Brimfield.

i   AMANDA HOAR/HOMER, b. 10 Sep 1792; d. at Goshen, MA, 9 May 1855; m. at Brimfield, 28 Sep 1820, as his second wife, ELIJAH CHAPIN FERRY, b. at Granby, 30 Jun 1790 son of Charles and Mary (Moody) Ferry; Elijah d. at Granby, Jul 1856. Elijah was first married to Speedy Taylor.

ii   LUCIA HOAR/HOMER, b. 4 May 1794; d. at Marion, IL, 16 Oct 1882; m. at Brimfield, 13 Nov 1854, DAUPHIN BROWN, b. at Brimfield, 9 Nov 1791 son of Bartholomew and Lucy (Chubb) Brown; Dauphin d. at Marion, 15 Nov 1871. Dauphin Brown was first married to Sila Patrick on 1 Dec 1814.

iii ALURED HOAR/HOMER, b. 29 Jan 1796; d. at Brimfield, 5 Aug 1870; m. 28 Nov 1822, RUTH BLISS, b. at Brimfield, 1 Sep 1802 daughter of Ichabod and Thirza (McCall) Bliss; Ruth d. at Brimfield, 14 Sep 1889.

iv   BETSEY HOAR, b. 30 Dec 1799; d. at Brimfield, 1 Jul 1816.

v   SOLOMON HOAR/HOMER, b. 1 Oct 1804; d. at Brimfield, 2 Jan 1879; m. 1ˢᵗ at Brimfield, 24 Nov 1831, ELEANOR CONVERSE, b. at Palmer, 1806 daughter of Jacob and Eleanor (Robinson) Converse; Eleanor d. at Brimfield, 4 Aug 1853. Solomon m. 2ⁿᵈ at Brimfield, 28 Feb 1855, MARIONETTE BURCHARD, b. at New London, CT, 1820 daughter of Ariel and Lydia (Warner) Burchard; Marionette d. at Brimfield, 28 Apr 1877.

vi   JACOB GOODELL HOAR, b. 19 Dec 1808; d. 12 May 1809.

vii ABIGAIL GOODELL HOAR/HOMER, b. 13 Dec 1812; d. at Monson, 1 Sep 1888; m. at Brimfield, 16 May 1839, her first cousin, Dr. ALVAN SMITH, b. at Palmer, about 1807 son of Robert and Hannah (Hoar) Smith;[2262] Alvan d. at Monson, 6 Aug 1882.

751)   JOHN BISHOP (*Peggy Goodale Bishop⁴, Martha Ingalls Barker Goodale³, Sarah Russell Ingalls², Robert¹*), b. at Brimfield, 29 Apr 1776 son of Richard and Peggy (Goodale) Bishop; d. at Homer, NY, 6 Dec 1850; m. at Brimfield, 23 Dec 1798, ALFLEDA BLASHFIELD, b. at Brimfield, 30 Mar 1774 daughter of William and Lois (Lumbard) Blashfield;[2263] Alfleda d. at Homer, NY, 20 Oct 1855.

[2255] Historical Society of Pennsylvania; Philadelphia, Pennsylvania; Historic Pennsylvania Church and Town Records; Reel: 1005
[2256] Howland, *A Brief Genealogical and Biographical History of Arthur, Henry, and John Howland*, p 244
[2257] Barbara Shaw was living with her daughter Phebe and her husband William Goodell in 1860 at Killingly. Year: 1860; Census Place: Killingly, Windham, Connecticut; Page: 549; Family History Library Film: 803092
[2258] Rhode Island, Deaths, 1630-1930
[2259] Brimfield (Town), *Historical Celebration of the Town of Brimfield*, p 417
[2260] Massachusetts Vital Records, 1620-1850; Solomon, farmer, d. B., disease of the heart, Dec. 11 [1844], a. 74, in B. [Dea. Solomon, Dec. 11 [dup. Dec. 13], 1844, C.R. Dea. Solomon, Dec. 11, 1844, [on stone beside that of Abigail, see Abigail Hoar] G.R.1. Dea. Solomon, Dec. 11, 1844, P.R.19.]
[2261] Brimfield (Town), *Historical Celebration of the Town of Brimfield*, p 415
[2262] Names of Alvan's parents are given as Robert and Hannah on his death record.
[2263] New England Historic Genealogical Society; Boston, Massachusetts; Vital Records of Brimfield, Massachusetts to the End of the Year 1850

In his will written 25 January 1847, John Bishop bequeathed to wife Alfleda the sum on one thousand dollars to be accepted in lieu of the dower. Son Jacob G. Bishop receives fifty dollars and son Thomas receives one hundred-fifty dollars. Son John N. Bishop receives two hundred dollars. The remainder of the estate is left to his grandchildren who are not all separately named. The legacies to the grandchildren are to be paid within one year and without interest, except the legacies to Sarah Maria Smith and Margaret B. Smith which are to be paid with interest. Wife Alfleda and son Thomas were named executors. On 6 December 1850, the estate entered probate and executor Thomas Bishop identified the following other heirs-at-law: widow Alfleda of Homer; sons Hiram Bishop and John N. Bishop of Homer; Sarah Maria Smith and Margaret B. Smith, minors, children of daughter Maria Smith deceased late wife of William Smith who live in Homer; and son Jacob G. Bishop of Pontiac, Michigan. The grandchildren named are as follows: Julia Taft of Niles, Michigan; Jacob M. Bishop of Detroit; minors Adelaide Eliza Bishop and Sarah Bishop of Pontiac; Thomas Bishop of Greene, New York; and John Bishop of Homer.[2264]

John and Alfleda were parents of six children.

i   HIRAM BISHOP, b. at Brimfield, MA, 10 Nov 1799; d. after 1860 when he was living in Homer, NY where he was an innkeeper; m. ELIZA A. who has not been identified, b. about 1808 and living in 1860. Hiram and Eliza had one son John J. Bishop.

ii   PEGGY BISHOP, b. 1803; d. at Homer, 1809.

iii JACOB GOODEL BISHOP, b. 1806; d. at Pontiac, MI, 26 Apr 1866; m. about 1826, his third cousin, ANNA GROW, b. at Cortland County, NY, 17 Aug 1808 daughter of Elisha and Lois (Palmer) Grow; Anna d. at Pontiac, 9 Sep 1896. Anna married second Uziel F. Phillips.

iv   THOMAS BISHOP, b. about 1810; d. at Greene, NY, 11 Mar 1867; m. ELIZA A. INGERSOLL, b. Apr 1820 daughter of Lambert and Mary (Pier) Ingersoll;[2265] Eliza d. at Greene, 7 Jan 1905.

v   MARIA BISHOP, b. about 1812; d. at Homer, NY by 1850; m. by 1842, WILLIAM H. SMITH, b. about 1813 who has not been identified. Maria was living at the time of the 1850 census but deceased by the time of the probate of father's estate on 6 Dec 1850.

vi   JOHN N. BISHOP, b. about 1815. In 1850, John was living in Homer where he was a carpenter. He was not married in 1850.

752)   GRATIS BISHOP (*Peggy Goodale Bishop⁴, Martha Ingalls Barker Goodale³, Sarah Russell Ingalls², Robert¹*), b. at Brimfield, 15 Nov 1777 daughter of Richard and Peggy (Goodale) Bishop; d. at Brimfield, 5 Sep 1862; m. at Brimfield, 8 Mar 1798, ISSACHAR BROWN, b. 20 May 1770 son of Issachar and Rhoda (Nicholas) Brown; Issachar d. at Brimfield, 27 Mar 1855.

Gratis and Issachar resided in Brimfield. Issachar served a town treasurer for five of the years from 1818 to 1825.[2266]

In his will written 20 March 1850, Issachar bequeathed to wife Gratis all the personal estate after the payment of the debts, and it is understood that this bequest does not affect the right of dower. The rest of the estate is bequeathed to his four daughters to be equally divided: Betsey W. Griggs widow of Lyman Griggs, Lucy Allen wife of Parsons Allen, Eunice Hitchcock widow of Eaton Hitchcock, and Eliza H. Noyes wife of Gilman Noyes. Only son Calvin B. Brown has received his portion, and Calvin is named executor of the estate.[2267] The farm with buildings was appraised at $1,800 and personal estate at $999.37.[2268]

Gratis Bishop and Issachar Brown were parents of six children born at Brimfield.

i   BETSEY MARIA BROWN, b. 9 Jul 1798; d. at Brimfield, 15 Feb 1878; m. at Brimfield, 29 Dec 1825, LYMAN GRIGGS, b, at Union, CT, 30 Mar 1797 son of Albigence and Lydia (Fletcher) Griggs; Lyman d. at Brimfield, 4 Nov 1842.

ii   LUCY BROWN, b. 18 Jan 1800; d. at Brimfield, 6 Jul 1871; m. at Brimfield, 18 Nov 1829, PARSONS ALLEN, b. at Brimfield, 16 Feb 1802 son of Alfred and Lucebia (Ballard) Allen; Parsons d. at Brimfield, 10 Sep 1878.

iii EUNICE BROWN, b. 14 Dec 1802; d. at Brimfield, 13 Feb 1871; m. at Brimfield, 27 Mar 1823, EATON HITCHCOCK, b. about 1795 (age 42 at death); Eaton d. at Brimfield, 25 Feb 1837.

iv   JOHN BROWN, b. 17 Oct 1806; d. at Brimfield, Mar 1828.

v   ELIZA HOOPER BROWN, b. 2 Nov 1811; d. at Brimfield, 13 Feb 1883; m. at Brimfield, 19 Nov 1883, Rev. GILMAN NOYES, b. at Atkinson, NH, 3 May 1804 son of James and Hannah (Hutchinson) Noyes; Gilman d. at Brimfield, 18 Oct 1863.

[2264] New York Wills and Probate, Cortland County, Wills Volume C, pp 175-181
[2265] Avery, *A Genealogy of the Ingersoll Family*, p 157
[2266] Brimfield (Town), *Historical Celebration of the Town of Brimfield*, p 362
[2267] *Probate Records of Hampden County and City of Springfield, 1806-1919 [Massachusetts], volume 23, 287-288*
[2268] Massachusetts Wills and Probate, Hamden County, Estate of Issachar Brown, Case 360

vi   CALVIN BISHOP BROWN, b. 14 Apr 1814; d. at Hyde Park, IL, 27 Sep 1883; m. at Warren, MA, Sep 1835, ATTOSSA AURELIA CUTLER, b. at Warren, 4 Jun 1817 daughter of Thomas and Attossa (Lilly) Cutler;[2269] Aurelia d. at Hyde Park, 23 Jan 1882.

753)   CALVIN BISHOP (*Peggy Goodale Bishop⁴, Martha Ingalls Barker Goodale³, Sarah Russell Ingalls², Robert¹*), b. at Brimfield, 4 Jul 1782 son of Richard and Peggy (Goodale) Bishop; d. at Spafford, NY, 3 May 1846; m. about 1809, OLIVE DADY, b. at Southampton, MA, 2 Jul 1789 daughter of Nathaniel and Sarah (Hannum) Dady; Olive d. 1873.[2270]

    Calvin and Olive settled in Henderson, New York likely early after their marriage. Calvin was a first trustee of the Methodist society formed in Henderson on 29 July 1830.[2271] Calvin was head of a household of ten persons in the 1820 census of Henderson. In 1830, the family was in Henderson, New York with a family of ten children: one male 40 to 49; one female 30 to 39; one male 10 to 14; one male 15 to 19; one male 20 to 29; two females under 5; one female 5 to 9; one female 10 to 14; and one female 20 to 29.[2272]

    In 1850, Olive lived in Alexandria, New York with her son Oscar and his wife Sally. Also in the home was 13-year-old Emelia who is a presumed daughter of Calvin and Olive.[2273] In 1865, Olive lived in Wilna, New York listed as mother in a household headed by William Self of England and his wife Lucy and two of their children Sarah Jane and George. In that census record, Olive is listed as mother of eleven children.[2274]

    It is likely that Calvin and Olive were parents of eleven children, although at this point six are identified as likely belonging to this family.

i   ALONZO BISHOP, b. 11 Oct 1811; d. at Omro, WI, 25 Oct 1868;[2275] m. 1st 1835, CATHERINE "CATY" JEROME SWETT, b. at Pompey, NY, 10 Jun 1810 daughter of James and Elizabeth (Jerome) Swett; Caty d. at Omro, WI, 29 Sep 1856. Alonzo m. 2nd 1861, Caty's half-sister, NANCY MARIE STEARNS, b. at Antwerp, NY, 8 Feb 1830 daughter of Zebina and Elizabeth (Jerome) Stearns; Nancy d. at Omro, 25 Apr 1898.

ii   GEORGE BISHOP, b. at Homer, 1814; d. at Springfield, MA, 3 Apr 1893; m. 1st at Palmer, MA, 26 Oct 1844, ELIZABETH A. BILLINGS, b. 13 Nov 1819 daughter of Daniel and Charlotte (-) Billings;[2276] Elizabeth d. at Springfield, 3 Aug 1863. George m. 2nd at Longmeadow, 14 Apr 1868, ALMINA CRANE, b. at Longmeadow, 9 Aug 1819 daughter of Ziba and Mercy (Kibbee) Crane; Almina d. at Springfield, 7 Nov 1883. Almina was first married to Michael Indicott.

iii   LUCY BISHOP,[2277] b. about 1817; d. after 1881 when living at Wilna, NY; m. by 1842 (first child born 1843), WILLIAM SELF, b. in England, about 1805; William d. at Wilna, 1881 (probate 5 Sep 1881).[2278]

iv   WILLIAM BISHOP, b. 1819; d. at Redwood, NY, 22 Jul 1875; m. about 1843, BETSEY JEROME STEARNS, b. 1825 daughter of Zebina and Elizabeth (Jerome) Stearns; Betsey d. at Redwood, 22 Feb 1884.

v   OSCAR BISHOP, b. 1824; d. at Denmark, NY, 24 Jan 1884; m. SARAH HILDRETH, b. Sep 1829 (census record); Sarah d. at Watertown, NY, 2 Apr 1905.

vi   EMELIA BISHOP, b. about 1835

754)   MATILDE BISHOP (*Peggy Goodale Bishop⁴, Martha Ingalls Barker Goodale³, Sarah Russell Ingalls², Robert¹*), b. at Brimfield, 30 Nov 1785 daughter of Richard and Peggy (Goodale) Bishop; d. (recorded at Brimfield), 15 Nov 1815; m. 6 Aug 1807, ABNER NUTTING, b. at Brimfield, 9 May 1783 son of Jonathan and Abigail (Bannister) Nutting; Abner d. at Brimfield, 29 Dec 1810.

    Abner Nutting was a farmer in Brimfield. He did not leave a will and his estate entered probate 14 February 1811 with widow Matilda declining administration and requesting that this be assumed by Jacob Bishop of Brimfield. Matilda also requested that Jacob Bishop be named guardian for her three children the oldest of whom was five years old. Solomon Hoar was named as guardian with Jacob Bishop as one of the sureties for the guardian bond 0n 14 January 1812. The minor children

[2269] The 1853 probate with will of Thomas Cutler of Warren includes a bequest to his daughter Atossa Aurelia Brown wife of Calvin B. Brown.
[2270] This is the death year given in the SAR application of Clark W. Bishop who was great-grandson of Calvin and Olive, but this was not separately verified.
[2271] L. H. Everts, *History of Jefferson County, New York*, p 385
[2272] Year: 1830; Census Place: Henderson, Jefferson, New York; Series: M19; Roll: 92; Page: 109; Family History Library Film: 0017152
[2273] Year: 1850; Census Place: Alexandria, Jefferson, New York; Roll: 515; Page: 10a
[2274] New York, State Census, 1865
[2275] Findagrave ID: 133308666, Omro Cemetery
[2276] Names of parents are given as Daniel and Charlotte on the death record.
[2277] The death record of Lucy's daughter Sarah Jane Self Gerry gives mother's maiden name as Lucy Bishop.
[2278] New York Wills and Probate, Jefferson County, Wills volume 020, 257

were Elvira, Peggy, and Abigail. The value of the 75-acre homestead was $1,150 but this was an undivided property held in common with Asa Nutting and Abner's share was $575.[2279]

Matilde and Abner were parents of three children born at Brimfield. Matilde was a member of the church in Homer, New York when she had two of her daughters baptized at Brimfield after Abner's death.[2280]

i ELVIRA WHEELER NUTTING, b. 30 Jan 1808; d. at Warren, PA, 4 Nov 1852; m. 1st about 1832, WILLIAM P. MCDOWELL who has not been identified; William d. at Warren, 20 Apr 1839.[2281] Elvira m. 2nd 1842, LEWIS FINDLAY WATSON, b. at Titusville, PA, 14 Apr 1819 son of John and Rebecca (Bradley) Watson; Lewis d. at Washington, DC, 25 Aug 1890. Lewis married second Caroline Eldred. Lewis Findlay Watson served in the U.S. House of Representatives.

ii MARGARET "PEGGY" INGALLS NUTTING, b. 1 Oct 1809; d. at Southport, NY, 11 Mar 1846; m. at Kalamazoo, MI, 6 Mar 1838, Dr. FORDYCE SYLVESTER RHOADES, b. 5 Dec 1811 son of Samuel and Lucy (Porter) Rhoads; Fordyce d. at Seneca, NY, 12 Jun 1888. Fordyce married second Martha Ann Knapp.

iii ABBY BANISTER NUTTING, b. 7 Dec 1810; d. at Brimfield, 6 Dec 1888; m. at Brimfield, 18 Sep 1831, DAUPHIN BROWN, b. 18 Dec 1808 son of Samuel and Mary (Hoar) Brown; Dauphin d. at Brimfield, 28 May 1889.

755) RUFUS BISHOP (*Peggy Goodale Bishop⁴, Martha Ingalls Barker Goodale³, Sarah Russell Ingalls², Robert¹*), b. at Brimfield, 15 Jul 1787 son of Richard and Peggy (Goodale) Bishop; d. at Scipio, OH, 19 Sep 1851; m. at Brimfield, 30 May 1810, SUSANNAH WEBB, b. Feb 1785 daughter of Darius and Deborah (Palmer) Webb; Susannah d. at Republic, OH, 8 Mar 1863.

Rufus and Susannah married in Brimfield but were soon after in Genoa and then Homer, New York. The family was in Seneca, Ohio by 1840.[2282]

In his will 11 September 1851 (proved 19 November 1851), Rufus Bishop left to beloved wife Susannah all the real and personal estate to do with and dispose of as she sees fit.[2283]

There are six known children for Rufus and Susannah, although there may be others.

i SAMUEL AUSTIN BISHOP, b. 13 Mar 1811; d. at Wright, MI, 8 Feb 1882; m. at Huron County, OH, 12 Apr 1835, HARRIET ROE, b. in OH, 28 Nov 1812 daughter of John Sayre and Margaret (Carr) Roe; Harriet d. at Polkton, MI, 21 Jun 1883.

ii MARY P. BISHOP, b.24 Jan 1814; d. at Mulberry, MO, 11 Sep 1892; m. about 1834, LYMAN E. HALL, b. about 1813; Lyman d. at Mulberry, 1 May 1877. The eldest child of Mary and Lyman was named Rufus Bishop Hall.

iii CHARLES GOODELL BISHOP, b. about 1820; d. at Chester, MI, 12 Dec 1879;[2284] m. at Huron County, OH, 22 Jun 1846, LYDIA E. DAVIS, b. in NY, 1823 daughter of James David; Lydia d. at Conklin, MI, 12 Jun 1885.

iv ELIZABETH S. BISHOP, b. 19 Jan 1823; d. at Grand Rapids, MI, 2 Jan 1900;[2285] m. STEPHEN D. MAYNARD, b. in OH, about 1825 son of Stephen and Anna (Phillips) Maynard; Stephen d. at Spokane, WA, 10 Nov 1908.

v LEWIS PORTER BISHOP, b. May 1825; d. at Mount Vernon, OH, 17 Feb 1901; m. at Seneca County, OH, 1 Apr 1849, MARCIA KETTLER, b. in NY, about 1828; Marcia d. at Mount Vernon, 1 Feb 1900.

vi HENRY K. BISHOP, b. about 1828; d. at Bronson, OH, 28 May 1874; m. EMELINE HERRICK, b. at Huron County, OH, 1832 daughter of Ephraim W. and Electa (Webb) Herrick; Emeline d. at Bronson, 29 Mar 1866.

756) HARRISON BISHOP (*Peggy Goodale Bishop⁴, Martha Ingalls Barker Goodale³, Sarah Russell Ingalls², Robert¹*), b. at Brimfield, 25 Oct 1789 son of Richard and Peggy (Goodale) Bishop; d. at Warren, MA, 30 May 1856; m. 1812, MARGARET BROWNING, b. at Brimfield, 1793 daughter of Joseph Davis and Margaret (Morgan) Browning; Margaret d. at Warren, MA, 10 Feb 1845.

[2279] *Hampshire County, MA: Probate File Papers, 1660-1889.* Online database. *AmericanAncestors.org.* New England Historic Genealogical Society, 2016, 2017. Case 106-39

[2280] Elvira Wheeler (Nutting), d. Metilda ("a member of the ch. in Homer, NY"), bp. May 1, 1814. CR; Peggy Ingals (Nutting), d. Metilda ("a member of the ch. in Homer, NY"), bp. May 1, 1814. CR

[2281] Genealogical Publishing Co.; Baltimore, Maryland; 10,000 Vital Records of Western New York, 1809-1850

[2282] Year: 1840; Census Place: Seneca, Ohio; Roll: 426; Page: 212; Family History Library Film: 0020176

[2283] Ohio Wills and Probate, Seneca County, volume 2, p 60

[2284] Michigan Department of Community Health, Division for Vital Records and Health Statistics; Lansing, Michigan; Death Records; Charles G. Bishop son of Rufus and Susan Bishop.

[2285] Michigan Department of Community Health, Division for Vital Records and Health Statistics; Lansing, Michigan; Death Records; Elizabeth Maynard daughter of Rufus Bishop and Susan Webb.

Harrison and Margaret lived in Homer[2286] where they six children were likely born. About 1826, they relocated to Warren, Massachusetts.[2287]

i   MARGARET MORGAN BISHOP, b. 1815; d. at Warren, MA, 29 Dec 1841. Margaret did not marry.

ii   MARY ANN BISHOP, b. 1818; d. at Warren, MA, 8 Mar 1898; m. at Warren, MA, 22 Dec 1847, SHEPARD BLAIR, b. at Brookfield, MA, 1 Jul 1800 son of Reuben and Susannah (Shepard) Blair; Shepard d. at Warren, 6 Nov 1883.

iii   SOPHIA BISHOP, b. 1820; d. at Warren, MA, 26 May 1850; m. at Warren, 28 Apr 1844, WILLIAM A. PATRICK, b. at Warren, 20 Jan 1820 son of Isaac and Mary (Watson) Patrick; William d. at Warren, 6 Jan 1892. William married second Jane Blodget.

iv   LUCIA BISHOP, died young

v   WILLIAM HARRISON BISHOP, b. 5 Mar 1822; d. at Warren, MA, 21 Oct 1910; m. 1st at Brookfield, 17 Feb 1848, OLIVE RANGER, b. at Brookfield, 1826 daughter of Isaac and Olive (Derby) Worcester; Olive d. at Warren, 3 May 1863. William m. 2nd at Warren, 12 Feb 1865, MARTHA A. DAVIS, b. at Chester, MA, 23 Jan 1836 daughter of James T. and Dolly W. (Abbott) Davis; Martha d. at Warren, 7 Oct 1897.

vi   DAVIS BROWNING BISHOP, b. 7 Feb 1824; d. at Palmer, MA, 16 Oct 1884; m. 14 Jan 1849, AUGUSTA BOWEN, b. at Royalton, VT, 7 Apr 1828 daughter of Thomas and Mary (McCormick) Bowen; Augusta d. at Palmer, 15 Feb 1899.

757)   AUGUSTA GOODALE (*Benjamin Goodale⁴, Martha Ingalls Barker Goodale³, Sarah Russell Ingalls², Robert¹*), b. at Pomfret, 29 Jun 1779 daughter of Benjamin and Abigail (Kimball) Goodale; d. at Henry County, IL, 18 Dec 1857;[2288] m. at Sturbridge, MA, 18 Feb 1802, as his second wife, DANIEL BRIGGS, b. at Taunton, MA, about 1769 son of Daniel and Mehitable (Dean) Briggs; Daniel d. at Henry County, Feb 1840. Daniel was first married to Patty Morris.

August and Daniel were in Sturbridge, then in New York, and arrived in Oxford, Illinois (later named Alpha) in 1837 settling in the southwest corner of Henry County. Daniel had a nursery that supplied fruit trees.[2289]

Augusta Goodale and Daniel Briggs were parents of six children, the five oldest recorded at Sturbridge and the youngest child born in New York.

i   MARTHA "PATTY" BRIGGS, b. at Sturbridge, 6 Feb 1803; d. at Hamilton, NY, 26 Aug 1872;[2290] m. by 1833, JOSEPH BALL, b. 1800; Joseph d. at Hamilton, 1877.

ii   AUGUSTA BRIGGS, b. at Sturbridge, 22 Nov 1804; d. at Alpha, IL, 6 Aug 1877; m. by 1832, AMOS B. COLE, b. at Chenango County, NY, 13 Apr 1806 son of Amos and Dinah (Crofoot) Cole; Amos d. at Alpha, 8 Feb 1897.

iii   DANIEL BRIGGS, b. at Sturbridge, 27 Aug 1806; d. at Oxford, IL, 20 Aug 1863; m. at Henry County, IL, 20 Oct 1842, PENIA CALKINS, b. in NY, 3 Dec 1817 daughter of Stephen and Anna (Smith) Calkins;[2291] Penia d. at Oneida, IL, 1906.

iv   MARY BRIGGS, b. at Sturbridge, 4 Mar 1811; d. at Henry County, IL, 22 Apr 1848; m. at Henry County, 25 Sep 1844, JOSEPH CRAWFORD.

v   JAMES MADISON BRIGGS, b. at Sturbridge, 20 Dec 1812; d. at Austin, TX, 3 Apr 1893; m. at Henry County, IL, 10 May 1841, MARY WHITCOMB, b. at Albany, NY, 31 Mar 1822 daughter of Luther and Ruth (Beebe) Whitcomb;[2292] Mary d. at Austin, 14 Aug 1893.[2293]

vi   GEORGE WASHINGTON BRIGGS, b. in NY, 1820; d. at Oxford, IL, 14 Jan 1885; m. at Knox County, IL, 17 Oct 1844, MARY JANE MARKHAM, b. at Green Township, IL, Feb 1827 daughter of Jeptha and Lovina (Vaughan)

[2286] 1820 U S Census; Census Place: Homer, Cortland, New York; Page: 522; NARA Roll: M33_66; Image: 291

[2287] Temple, *History of the Town of Palmer*, p 429

[2288] Augusta and Daniel Briggs are interred at Oxford Cemetery in Henry County, IL; findagrave ID: 43289806

[2289] *Alpha: Century of Progress, 1872-1972*. Alpha, IL, Centennial Book Committee, 1972, p 2

[2290] Burial at Madison Street Cemetery; findagrave ID 87166210

[2291] Fitch, Alta Winchester, "Some Descendants of Stephen Calkins and Elder Brewster", NYGBR, volume 49, 1918, p 19

[2292] Whitcomb, *The Whitcomb Family in America*, p 87

[2293] James and Mary have grave markers that give dates of birth and death; Walnut Creek Baptist Church Cemetery, Austin, Texas; findagrave ID 59383433

Markham;[2294] Mary Jane d. after 1900 when she was living in Rivoli, IL with a grandson and granddaughter living with her.

758)   ROXILANA GOODALE (*Benjamin Goodale⁴, Martha Ingalls Barker Goodale³, Sarah Russell Ingalls², Robert¹*), b. at Pomfret, 11 Mar 1781 daughter of Benjamin and Abigail (Kimball) Goodale; d. at Buffalo, NY, Mar 1860;[2295] m. at Sturbridge, 25 Nov 1802, DANIEL PLIMPTON, b. at Sturbridge, 16 Mar 1781 son of Elijah and Mary (Cheney) Plimpton; Daniel d. at Holland, MA, 21 Sep 1851.

Daniel Plimpton was a straw manufacturer and had a store in Sturbridge. He also served as deacon of the Congregational church.[2296] On 19 May 1824 (recorded 7 May 1854), Daniel and Roxilana for ten dollars sold a lot of land to the Sturbridge school district for the schoolhouse.[2297]

It is possible that Roxilana and Daniel separated as Daniel was living alone in Sturbridge in 1840 and living in the household of John C. Miller in Holland in 1850.[2298] Roxilana lived with her son Luman in Buffalo prior to her death.[2299]

Roxilana and Daniel were parents of four children born at Sturbridge.

i   OTIS PLIMPTON, b. 18 Apr 1804; d. 27 Nov 1806.

ii   LAURETTA PLIMPTON, b. 29 Jun 1806

iii   LUMAN KIMBALL PLIMPTON, b. 4 Sep 1809; d. at Buffalo, NY, 17 Dec 1869; m. at Sturbridge, 13 Sep 1838, MARY STEARNS DAVIS, b. at Sturbridge, 26 Aug 1818 daughter of George and Sophia (Hitchcock) Davis); Mary d. at Buffalo, 15 Aug 1891.

iv   DANIEL WARREN PLIMPTON, b. 22 Mar 1815; d. 22 Aug 1816.

759)   WARD GOODALE (*Benjamin Goodale⁴, Martha Ingalls Barker Goodale³, Sarah Russell Ingalls², Robert¹*), b. at Norwich, 12 May 1786 son of Benjamin and Abigail (Kimball) Goodale; d. after 1830 when he was living at Manlius, NY; m. CHAMPANY[2300] who has not been identified.

Ward and Champany lived in Onondaga County, New York. Census records suggest at least four children in the family. In the 1820 census at Cicero, the household consisted of one male 26-44, one female 26-44, one male under 10, and three females under 10.[2301] Just one child was identified.

i   CHARLES GOODALE, b. at Onondaga County, NY, 29 May 1821; d. at Ashippun, WI, 12 Aug 1901; m. 1st at Dodge County, WI, 14 Oct 1849, SARAH ANN DODGE, b. about 1831; Sarah d. at Ashippun, Sep 1850. Charles m. 2nd about 1851, HANNAH MIELS, b. in England, 26 Mar 1833 daughter of William and Rachel (-) Miels;[2302] Hannah d. at Ashippun, 2 Sep 1903.

760)   DANIEL INGALLS (*Benjamin Ingalls⁴, Benjamin Ingalls³, Sarah Russell Ingalls², Robert¹*), b. at Pomfret, 3 May 1770 son of Benjamin and Eunice (Woodworth) Ingalls; d. after 1810 and before 1816; m. at Pomfret, 2 Nov 1794, BETHIAH BROWN, b. at Pomfret, 12 Jun 1769 daughter of Samuel and Sarah (Bowman) Brown; Bethiah d. as a widow, at Pomfret, 21 June 1816.

There are records for four children of Daniel and Bethiah, all baptized at Pomfret on 3 Sep 1809.

i   HARRIOTT INGALLS, b. 1806; d. at Pomfret, 14 Sep 1818

[2294] Consent to the marriage of George Briggs and Mary J. Markham was given by Jeptha Markham: "I do hereby Certify that I give my willing consent that my daughter Mary J. Markham & George Briggs Shall be united in the holy bonds of matrimony. Jeptha Markham." Knox County, Illinois Marriage Records

[2295] U.S. Federal Census Mortality Schedules, 1850-1885; New York State Education Department, Office of Cultural Education; Albany, New York; U.S. Census Mortality Schedules, New York, 1850-1880; Archive Roll Number: M3; Census Year: 1860; Census Place: Buffalo Ward 9, Erie, New York

[2296] Chase, *A Genealogy and Historical Notices of the Family of Plimpton*, p 114

[2297] Massachusetts Land Records, Worcester County, 528:212

[2298] Year: 1850; Census Place: Holland, Hampden, Massachusetts; Roll: 318; Page: 107a

[2299] New York, State Census, 1855

[2300] Champany Goodell is the name of mother given on the death record of son Charles; Wisconsin, Death Records, 1867-1907

[2301] 1820 U S Census; Census Place: Cicero, Onondaga, New York; Page: 175; NARA Roll: M33_67; Image: 191

[2302] In 1850, Hannah was living in East Troy, Wisconsin with parents William and Rachel; Year: 1850; Census Place: East Troy, Walworth, Wisconsin; Roll: 1007; Page: 166A

ii   OLIVER INGALLS, b. 27 Sep 1806; d. at Hunter, NY, 8 Mar 1862; m. by 1834, SARAH BENJAMIN, b. 1809 daughter of Augustus and Catherine (Groat) Benjamin; Sarah d. at Hunter, 7 Mar 1897.

iii   SARAH INGALLS, baptized 3 Sep 1809

iv   MARY INGALLS, baptized 3 Sep 1809

761)   CALEB INGALLS (*Benjamin Ingalls⁴, Benjamin Ingalls³, Sarah Russell Ingalls², Robert¹*), b. at Pomfret, 29 Jan 1777 son of Benjamin and Eunice (Woodworth) Ingalls; m. at Pomfret, 1 Jul 1804, CLARISSA ANN DOWNER.[2303]
     Caleb and Clarissa resided in Pomfret. In Ingalls genealogy reports that Clarissa, as a widow, moved to Rhode Island in 1824.[2304]

i   ELIZA ANN INGALLS, b. at Pomfret, 8 Feb 1806; d. at North Kingstown, RI, 12 Nov 1829; m. at Kent County, RI, 19 Nov 1826, JOHN B. JACOY, b. at North Kingstown, 4 Aug 1806 son of Elisha and Mary(Brown) Jerket;[2305] John d. at North Kingstown, 14 May 1876.

ii   ARDELIA H. INGALLS, b. at Pomfret, 18 Apr 1809; d. at Norton, MA, 2 May 1893; m. JAMES ADAMS, b. in MA, 1802.

iii   LUCRETIA B. INGALLS, b. at Pomfret, 23 Jul 1811; d. at Brockton, MA, 19 Feb 1883; m. about 1835, DARIUS C. PLACE, b. at Raynham, MA, 1 Dec 1806 son of James and Mary (·) Place; Darius d. at Middleborough, MA, 5 Jun 1871.

iv   HANNAH WOODWORTH INGALLS, b. at Pomfret, 18 Dec 1815

v   DAVID INGALLS[2306]

vi   THOMAS INGALLS

vii   DANIEL INGALLS

762)   THEDA INGALLS (*David Ingalls⁴, Benjamin Ingalls³, Sarah Russell Ingalls², Robert¹*), b. at Pomfret, 24 Mar 1773 daughter of David and Mary (May) Ingalls; m. at Pomfret, 25 Dec 1793, JOSHUA PRATT, b. at Plymouth, MA, 20 Jun 1770 son of Daniel and Lydia (Cobb) Pratt;[2307] Joshua d. at Truxton, NY, 20 Jan 1834. Joshua married second Phebe Lisseaur.
     Joshua Pratt was a farmer in Pomfret before relocating to Truxton, New York.[2308] In the 1820 census for Truxton, Joshua headed a household of eight persons: one male over 45; one female 26 to 44; one male under 10; one male 10 to 15; and four females under 10.[2309] Joshua apparently had financial struggles after locating in Cortland County as a piece of his property was seized by the sheriff and notice was given on 13 February 1829 to sell 100 acres of his land at public auction.[2310]
     Joshua Pratt was father of ten children as identified in his probate record.[2311] It is likely that five of these children are the children of Theda and Joshua.[2312] The heirs identified in the probate on 25 July 1834 are widow Phebe, David Pratt, Walter Pratt, William Pratt, Chester, Pratt, Eliza Pratt, Theda Farley and Benjamin Farley, Lydia Pratt, Hannah Pratt, Nancy Pratt, and Joshua Pratt. Little information was located regarding the children in this family. The older children were likely born at Pomfret.

i   WILLIAM PRATT, b. 24 Sep 1794

ii   DAVID PRATT, b. 1796; d. at Homer, NY, 26 Sep 1864; m. ELECTA ALEXANDER, b. at Dover, VT, 14 Nov 1800 daughter of Daniel and Hannah (Nelson) Alexander;[2313] Electa d. at Homer, 5 Apr 1866.[2314]

[2303] The marriage transcription and the transcriptions of the births of all the children give her name as Clarissa; each of the death records for the children gives her name as Ann.
[2304] Burleigh, *The Genealogy and History of the Ingalls Family*, p 37
[2305] The spelling of the last name is inconsistent and seems to have transitioned from Jerket to Jacoy.
[2306] These last three children are listed in Burleigh's Ingalls genealogy, p 37, but records were not located related to these children.
[2307] Lovelace, *The Pratt Directory*, 1998 edition, p 562
[2308] Cutter, *Genealogical and Family History of Central New York*, volume 3, p 1358
[2309] 1820 U S Census; Census Place: Truxton, Cortland, New York; Page: 609; NARA Roll: M33_66; Image: 335
[2310] Cortland Observer (Homer Village, Cortland County, New York), March 6, 1829 (Fri), p 1
[2311] New York Wills and Probate, Cortland County, Estate of Joshua Pratt
[2312] Lovelace, *The Pratt Directory*, 1998 Edition, p 562
[2313] Vermont, Vital Records, 1720-1908
[2314] Family Name File of Cortland Historical Society, Card for David Pratt and Family, FHL film 1276164

iii   WALTER PRATT, b. about 1801; d. at Homer, NY, 1862.[2315] In 1840, Walter was resident of Scott, NY where he headed a household of five persons: one male 30 to 39; one female 30 to 39; one female 40 to 49; one male 5 to 9; and one female 15 to 19.[2316]

iv   CHESTER PRATT, b. 1803

v   THEDA PRATT, b. 1806; d. at Lockport, IL, 15 Apr 1846;[2317] m. BENJAMIN FARLEY; Benjamin d. at Lockport, 4 Jul 1847 (probate 15 Sep 1847). Theda and Benjamin were in Solon, NY and relocated to Lockport where they died. Benjamin was a carpenter.[2318]

763)   DORCAS INGALLS (*David Ingalls⁴, Benjamin Ingalls³, Sarah Russell Ingalls², Robert¹*), b. at Pomfret, 6 Dec 1774 daughter of David and Mary (May) Ingalls; d. at Woodstock, CT, 15 Mar 1814; m. at Pomfret, 17 Apr 1803, as his second wife, TIMOTHY PERRIN, b. at Woodstock, 25 May 1767 son of Timothy and Mary (Wolly) Perrin; Timothy d. at Woodstock, 23 Mar 1814. Timothy was first married to Lydia Raymond.

Timothy Perrin did not leave a will and his estate entered probate 5 April 1814 with Joseph Raymond as administrator. Real estate included 56 acres of land with house and barn valued at $1,500. Debts exceeded the value of the personal estate and a portion of the real estate was sold to settle the estate. Six surviving children were identified on 24 April 1819: Lydia Cowles, Calvin Perrin, John Perrin, Lucy Perrin, Raimond Perrin, and Gordon Perrin (Polly having died since her father).[2319] The children named were children of Timothy and his first wife Lydia Raymond. Dorcas and Timothy had one child who died young.

i   ALMOND PERRIN, b. at Woodstock, CT, 26 May 1806

764)   LUCY INGALLS (*David Ingalls⁴, Benjamin Ingalls³, Sarah Russell Ingalls², Robert¹*), b. at Pomfret, 31 Mar 1777 daughter of David and Mary (May) Ingalls; d. at Dansville, MI, 24 Jun 1849; m. at Pomfret, 4 Jul 1811, as his second wife, ZEPHANIAH HICKS, b. at Rehoboth, MA, 21 Nov 1773 son of Israel and Elizabeth (Bowen) Hicks; Zephaniah d. at Dansville, 14 Jun 1864. Zephaniah was first married to Polly Preston.

Lucy and Zephaniah resided in Homer but relocated to Ingham County, Michigan where Zephaniah obtained a homestead patent on 7 August 1837.[2320]

There are three known children of Lucy and Zephaniah born at Homer, New York.

i   ELIZA MARY HICKS, b. 25 Feb 1814; d. at Homer, NY, 11 Mar 1846 (a week following the birth of fourth child); m. about 1838, JOHN MILTON DRESSER, b. at Pomfret, 15 Aug 1807 son of Jonathan and Olive (Hunt) Dresser; John d. at Mason, MI, 22 Oct 1879. John married second Susan Ann Pierce.

ii   MARSHALL ZEPHANIAH HICKS, b. 31 Aug 1816; d. at Dansville, MI, 31 Jan 1882; m. at Ingham County, MI, 24 Dec 1846, LOIS ELLEN REYNOLDS, b. in NY, 7 Dec 1823 daughter of Lewis and Laura (Van Orman) Reynolds;[2321] Lois d. at Stockbridge, MI, 21 Mar 1901.

iii   LUCY ANN HICKS, b. 23 Aug 1818; d. at Mason, MI, 18 Nov 1853; m. at Ingham County, MI, 2 Jun 1841, HENRY A. HAWLEY, b. at Winfield, NY, 19 Nov 1815 son of Stephen and Olive (Warner) Hawley;[2322] Henry d. at Mason, 12 Jun 1881.

765)   OLIVER HASTINGS (*Mary Ingalls Hastings⁴, Benjamin Ingalls³, Sarah Russell Ingalls², Robert¹*), b. at Norwich, 15 Oct 1769 son of Dier and Mary (Ingalls) Hastings; d. at Sprague, CT, 29 Dec 1848; m. 1ˢᵗ at Canterbury, 13 Nov 1796, PHILURA PAINE, b. 1772; Philura d. at Lisbon, CT, 28 Jul 1822. Oliver m. 2ⁿᵈ at Lisbon, 11 May 1823, as her second husband, LEMIRA BUSHNELL (widow of Andrew Lee), b. 1789 daughter of Jason and Hannah (Kirkland) Bushnell; Lemira d. at Springfield, OH, Mar 1860. Lemira married third Josiah Spencer on 22 Nov 1852.

Oliver Hastings and Philura Paine were parents of eight children.

[2315] As reported in the Pratt Directory, 1998 edition

[2316] Year: 1840; Census Place: Scott, Cortland, New York; Roll: 275; Page: 156; Family History Library Film: 0017184

[2317] Theda and Benjamin Farley are interred in Lockport Cemetery, findagrave ID: 87451447

[2318] Stevens, *Past and Present of Will County, Illinois*, p 827

[2319] Connecticut Wills and Probate, Pomfret Probate District, Town of Woodstock, Estate of Timothy Perrin, Jr., Case 3225

[2320] Michigan, Homestead and Cash Entry Patents, Pre-1908; 1 E½NW MICHIGAN-TOLEDO STRIP No 2 N 1 E 36; 2 SWNW MICHIGAN-TOLEDO STRIP No 2 N 1 E 36

[2321] Lois's date of birth and names of parents are as given on her death record.

[2322] Warner and Nichols, *The Descendants of Andrew Warner*, p 373

i   PAINE HASTINGS, b. at Canterbury, 13 Nov 1797; d. at Middlefield, NY, 15 Dec 1847; m. before 1827, SARAH who has not been identified. Paine and Sarah were parents of four children.

ii   JULIANA MARIAH HASTINGS, b. at Canterbury, 3 Jan 1800; d. at Springfield, OH, 12 Oct 1886; m. at Lisbon, CT, 31 Dec 1820, JOHN FULLER, b. at Sprague, CT, 17 Nov 1787 son of John and Wealthy (Kazer) Fuller;[2323] John d. at Lisbon, CT, 5 Feb 1850. There are no children known for John and Julianna.

iii   CAROLINE HASTINGS, b. at Canterbury, 17 Dec 1802; d. at Cincinnati, OH, 22 Aug 1887; m. 19 Jun 1832, HORACE BUSHNELL, b. at Lisbon, CT, 20 Nov 1802 son of Jason and Hannah (Kirkland) Bicknell; Horace d. at Cincinnati, 3 Apr 1883.

iv   GEORGE TRUXTON HASTINGS, b. at Canterbury, 28 Jan 1804; d. at Cherry Valley, NY, 1825.[2324] George did not marry.

v   EDMON HASTINGS, b. at Lisbon, 30 Mar 1806

vi   SALLY S. HASTINGS, b. at Lisbon, 12 Feb 1810

vii   HARRIET B. HASTINGS, b. at Lisbon, 12 Mar 1812; d. at Springfield, OH, 1881; m. 1st at Sprague, CT, 13 Apr 1834, EZRA WITTER BUSHNELL, baptized at Sprague, 15 Jun 1800 son of Ephraim and Temperance (Willes) Bushnell; Ezra d. at Sprague, 13 Nov 1842. Harriet m. 2nd about 1863, as his second wife, FREDERICK HOLFORD, b. in Oxfordshire, England, about 1813; Frederick d. at Springfield, 1890. Frederick was first married to Louisa Weisman.

viii   HENRY E. HASTINGS, b. at Lisbon, 7 Aug 1816; d. at Cincinnati, OH, 28 May 1900; m. at Richfield, MI, 6 Aug 1845, ESTHER O. PHILLIPS, b. at Pontiac, MI, 19 Dec 1826 daughter of William and Olivia (Tennant) Phillips; Esther d. at Cincinnati, 9 Mar 1894.

     Oliver Hastings and Lemira Bushnell were parents of three children.

i   LEMIRA LEE HASTINGS, b. at Lisbon, 18 May 1824; d. at Springfield, OH, 1855; m. at Sprague, CT, 31 Jul 1846, ARTHUR O. HOWELL, b. in OH, about 1818. Arthur married second Rebecca Barnes on 26 Feb 1856.

ii   GEORGE WILLIAM HASTINGS, b. at Lisbon, 13 Jan 1827; d. at Springfield, OH, Apr 1916; m. at Lorain County, OH, 10 Oct 1848, CANDACE L. WHITE, b. in NY, Jul 1827; Candace d. at Springfield, OH, 22 Feb 1915.

iii   JOHN HASTINGS, b. 28 Nov 1828; d. 21 Jul 1830.

766)   DYER HASTINGS (*Mary Ingalls Hastings⁴, Benjamin Ingalls³, Sarah Russell Ingalls², Robert¹*), b. at Norwich, 27 Sep 1771 son of Dier and Mary (Ingalls) Hastings; d. at Maryland, NY, 25 Jul 1843; m. about 1802, ANNA WATTLES, b. 30 Jan 1782 (calculated from age at death of 38 years, 9 months, 4 days); Anna d. at Maryland, NY, 3 Oct 1838.
     Dyer and Anna resided in Maryland, New York where they were parents of seven children. Just one of the children married. In her petition of 9 September 1843 to present the will to probate court, executrix Caroline Hastings identified the following heirs to the estate in addition to herself: Eliza Ann Hastings, Mary Soffronia Hastings, George W. Hastings all residing in Maryland, Otsego County, and Joseph Hastings residing in Canajoharie, Montgomery County.[2325]

i   CAROLINE HASTINGS, b. 19 Jan 1803; d. 2 Sep 1803.

ii   OLIVER WATTLES HASTINGS, b. 21 Jul 1804; d. at Cherry Valley, NY, 16 Feb 1843.

iii   JOSEPH HASTINGS, b. about 1808; d. at Canajoharie, NY, 10 Jun 1876; m. ALMIRA COLEMAN, b. in CT, about 1811; Almira d. at Sprout Book, NY, 13 Jul 1892. Joseph and Almira adopted one daughter, Almira C. Hastings who married Arnold V. Sasher.

iv   CAROLINE HASTINGS, baptized 13 Oct 1811; d. at Canajoharie, NY, 1886.

v   ELIZA ANN HASTINGS, b. 11 May 1812; d. 2 Mar 1844.

vi   GEORGE W. HASTINGS, baptized, 5 Aug 1817; d. at Maryland, NY, 1855.

vii   MARY SOPHORNIA HASTINGS, baptized 19 Jul 1818; d. at Maryland, NY, 1857 (probate 1857).

[2323] Fuller, *Genealogy of Some Descendants of Captain Matthew Fuller*, p 233
[2324] Connecticut, Hale Collection of Cemetery Inscriptions and Newspaper Notices, 1629-1934; George son of Oliver of Lisbon, age 21
[2325] New York Wills and Probate Records, Otsego County, Petitions, Box 7, 1841-1844, Estate of Dyer Hastings

Great-Grandchildren of Benjamin Russell and Sarah Preston

767)   JOSIAH HART (*Sarah Russell Hart⁴, Benjamin³, Benjamin², Robert¹*), b. at Ashford, 18 Aug 1748 son of Constant and Sarah (Russell) Hart; d. at Charlestown, NH, 1832 (probate 1832); m. 1ˢᵗ about 1773, MEHITABLE who has not been identified; Mehitable d. at Charlestown, NH, 1 Aug 1790. Josiah m. 2ⁿᵈ 19 Dec 1790, SUSANNA PUTNAM, *perhaps* b. at Lunenburg, MA, 16 Sep 1756 daughter of Thomas and Ruth (Weatherbee) Putnam; Susanna d. at Charlestown, 8 Feb 1808. Josiah m. 3ʳᵈ at Charlestown, 17 Jul 1808, RUTH GROUT.

    Josiah Hart resided in Charlestown, New Hampshire. He received eight shillings for going to Ticonderoga in 1778 with the regiment of Col. Walker. In 1803, he received a payment of $1,600 from the town on contract related to building a new meeting house in the town.[2326]

    In his will dated 8 April 1827 (proved 17 August 1832), Josiah Hart bequeathed one dollar each to children Cynthia Houghton, Naomi Fling, Josiah Hart, Jr., Esther Hunt, and Seth Hart. He bequeathed to wife Ruth Hart one-third of the real estate, the furniture in the house, the young horse, the cow, and the wagon to be of her use and for her heirs forever. The remainder of the estate goes to daughters Susan Hart and Polly Hart to be equally divided between them. Henry Hubbard was named sole executor.[2327] At the time of probate, Henry Hubbard declined to be executor and James Larabee was named administrator.

    Josiah and Mehitable Hart were parents of three children born at Charlestown, New Hampshire.

i   CYNTHIA HART, b. 16 Nov 1773; d. at Columbus, WI, 26 Jul 1849; m. at Springfield, VT, 29 Oct 1797, DANIEL HOUGHTON, b. at Springfield, VT, 2 Jul 1775 son of Abel Houghton; Daniel d. at Columbus, 30 Mar 1855.

ii   NAOMI HART, b. 21 Aug 1775; m. at Charlestown, 31 Aug 1794, as his second wife, LESTER FLING, Lester was first married to POLLY RUSSELL on 19 Dec 1790.

iii   JOSIAH HART, b. 28 Aug 1779; m. about 1803, SUSANNA who is not clearly identified, but b. about 1782; Susanna d. at Enfield, NH, 28 May 1851. Josiah and Susanna were parents of ten children born at Charlestown, NH.

    Josiah Hart and Susanna Putnam were parents of four children born at Charlestown.

i   ESTHER HART, b. 27 Sep 1791; m. about 1812, HENRY HUNT who was from England.

ii   SETH HART, b. 25 Jul 1793; d. at Deposit, NY, 4 Dec 1866; m. 1ˢᵗ at Charlestown, 21 Jul 1816, ALMA LOOMIS, b. at Amherst, NH, 21 Nov 1793 daughter of Porter and Susannah (Ashley) Loomis; Alma d. at Deposit, 2 Jun 1824. Seth m. 2ⁿᵈ, about 1824, ROXANA EDICK, b. at Deposit, 23 Sep 1803 daughter of Conrad and Elizabeth (Sneeden) Edick;[2328] Roxana d. at Cannonsville, NY, 22 Jan 1893.[2329]

iii   SUSAN HART, b. 20 Nov 1795; d. at Cannonsville, NY, 29 Apr 1881; m. 26 May 1831, BENJAMIN LANE, b. at Newport, NH, 25 Jan 1789 son of Jesse and Hester (Wright) Lane;[2330] Benjamin d. at Cannonsville, 20 Oct 1879.

iv   POLLY HART, b. 17 Feb 1798; d. at Cannonsville, NY, 1880. Polly did not marry. She lived with her sister Susan.

768)   JOHN HART (*Sarah Russell Hart⁴, Benjamin³, Benjamin², Robert¹*), b. at Ashford, 23 Apr 1750 son of Constant and Sarah (Russell) Hart; m. at Charlestown, NH, 9 Jul 1773, SUBMIT FARNSWORTH, b. at Charlestown, 29 Jun 1750 daughter of Stephen and Eunice (Hastings) Farnsworth.

    John and Submit resided in Charlestown, New Hampshire. John served as a private in the company of Capt. Abel Walker from 21 July to 23 September 1777, enlisting from Charlestown.[2331] There are records of five children of John Hart and Submit Farnsworth born at Charlestown, but no further record was located for this family.

i   THOMAS HART, b. 5 Dec 1773

ii   HASTINGS HART, b. 11 Mar 1776; d. 28 Jul 1777.

iii   EUNICE HART, b. 11 Mar 1776; d. 19 Aug 1777.

[2326] Saunderson, *History of Charlestown*, p 270, p 589
[2327] *New Hampshire. Probate Court (Sullivan County), Wills volume J, p 94*
[2328] Biographical Review, Leading Citizens of Delaware County, New York, p 638
[2329] New York, Death Index, 1880-1956
[2330] Fitts, *Lane Genealogies*, volume II, p 179
[2331] Compiled Service Records of Soldiers Who Served in the American Army During the Revolutionary War

iv   BENJAMIN HART, b. 4 May 1778

v   JOHN HART, b. 1 May 1790

769)   DAVID RUSSELL (*Benjamin⁴, Benjamin³, Benjamin², Robert¹*), b. at Ashford, 10 Jun 1758 son of Benjamin and Phebe (Smith) Russell; d. at Burlington, VT, 3 Oct 1843; m. at Fairfield, CT, 26 Nov 1789, MARTHA PYNCHON, b. at Boston, 22 Jan 1755 daughter of Joseph and Mary (Cotton) Pynchon; Martha d. at Burlington, 23 Jan 1805. David m. 2nd, KEZIAH PLIMPTON (widow of Converse Barrell), b. at Southbridge, MA, 29 Aug 1770 daughter of Gershom and Martha (Marcy) Plimpton; Keziah d. at Burlington, VT, 14 May 1847.

David Russell resided in Burlington, Vermont. Along with Anthony Haswell, he established the Vermont Gazette in 1784.[2332] David was an active member of the Masons.[2333]

On 17 August 1832, David Russell of Burlington then aged seventy-four, made application for a pension based on his service during the Revolution. He enlisted for a period of six months from Ashford, Connecticut for the first campaign in 1775 in the company of Capt. Sumner. In the spring of 1776, he enlisted for a year in the company of Capt. Daniel Allen and participated in the battles of White Plains and Trenton. During this enlisted he achieved the rank of sergeant. In 1778, he enlisted as a private under Sergeant Scarborough part of the time in the company of Capt. Philips. He was part of the failed attempt to remove the British from Newport. David first applied for and was granted a pension in 1818 but in 1820 it was determined that the value of his property exceeded guidelines.[2334]

In his will written 21 September 1841, David Russell bequeathed to beloved wife Keziah, the use of the entire property and buildings of north side of Main Street in Burlington during her natural life. She also receives the use of all household furniture during her life. Respected brother Stephen Russell receives his overcoat and cloak. Beloved daughter Martha Mary Pierce and respected niece Olivia Wear will receive the household furniture to equally divide, subject to the previous provision for Keziah's use of the furniture, except the silver coffee urn. Much respected daughter-in-law Mary Ann Barrell Adams[2335] receives the coffee urn. Son Joseph P. Russell will receive two quarter-acre lots with buildings after Keziah's use of them. Sons Dwight P. Russell and Harris E. Russell receive the right of land consisting of 320 acres in Craftsbury. Son Harris receives the silver watches and son Joseph P. receives the library of books. Friend Nathan B. Haswell of Burlington was named executor.[2336]

David Russell and Martha Pynchon were parents of four children likely all born at Burlington, Vermont.

i   JOSEPH PYNCHON RUSSELL, b. 18 Aug 1790; d. at Brooklyn, NY, 19 Sep 1849; m. at Brownville, NY, about 1838, KATHERINE KIRBY, b. at Litchfield, CT, 11 Oct 1802 daughter of Ephraim and Ruth (Marvin) Kirby; Katherine d. at Palatka, FL, 6 Jan 1882. Joseph graduated from University of Vermont, class of 1810, received the M.D. degree, and was a surgeon in New York.[2337] He served in the War of 1812.

ii   MARTHA MARY RUSSELL, b. 27 Nov 1791; d. at Outremont, Montreal Region, Québec, Canada, 21 Mar 1874; m. at Burlington, VT, 29 Jan 1824, HIRAM PIERCE, b. 1796; Hiram d. at Outremont, 24 Oct 1862.

iii   DAVID RUSSELL, b. 1794; d. at Burlington, 2 Dec 1794.

iv   DAVID SMITH RUSSELL, b. 1795; d. at Mobile, AL, 9 Oct 1827.[2338]

David Russell and Keziah Plimpton were parents of three children born at Burlington, Vermont.

i   CAROLINE P. RUSSELL, b. 1807; d. at Burlington, 22 Feb 1809.

ii   DWIGHT PLIMPTON RUSSELL, b. 9 May 1810; d. at Brooklyn, NY, 28 Apr 1879; m. 1st at Richmond County, GA, 1 Sep 1836, SARAH A. CLARKE, b. in GA, about 1815; Sarah d. at Brooklyn, about 1861. Dwight m. 2nd about 1865, ELLEN L. GRANGE (widow of Merrick Osborne), b. in NY, Feb 1819 daughter of John Grange; Ellen d. at Brooklyn, 2 Feb 1905. Dwight was an applicant to West Point.[2339]

iii   HARRISON EMERSON RUSSELL, b. 29 Dec 1811; d. unknown but before 1871; m. at New York, NY, 21 Jul 1842, GRACE MCQUEEN, b. at Trois-Rivières, Québec, Canada, 25 Jul 1809 and baptized 23 Sep 1809 daughter of Alexander and Grace (Fraser) McQueen;[2340] Grace d. at Brockville, Leeds-Grenville, Ontario, 5 Sep 1871.

[2332] Library of Congress, Eighteenth Century American Newspapers
[2333] Rann, *History of Chittenden County, Vermont*
[2334] U. S. Revolutionary War Pension and Bounty-Land Application Files, Case S19572
[2335] Mary Ann Barrell Adams was a stepdaughter; she married Charles Adams at Burlington in 1833.
[2336] Vermont Probate Files, Chittenden County, David Russell (1843, Box 12 File 1199); accessed through familysearch.org
[2337] General catalogue of the University of Vermont and State Agricultural College, Burlington, Vermont, 1791-1900, p 40
[2338] As noted in the death notice of the Burlington Weekly Free Press (Burlington, Vermont) November 16, 1827: "Died At Mobile, Alabama, on the 1st of October last, of malignant fever, David S. Russell, aged 31, son of David Russell Esq. of this town."
[2339] National Archives and Records Administration (NARA); Washington, D.C.; Series Number: M2037
[2340] Institut Généalogique Drouin; Montreal, Quebec, Canada; Drouin Collection; Author: Gabriel Drouin, comp.

770)   ELEAZER RUSSELL (*Benjamin⁴, Benjamin³, Benjamin², Robert¹*), b. at Ashford, 15 Nov 1761 son of Benjamin and Phebe (Smith) Russell; d. after 1840 when he was living at New Hartford, NY; m. EUNICE SYKES, b. at Suffield, CT, 6 Nov 1770 daughter of Titus and Rhoda (miller) Sykes; Eunice d. about 1835.

Eleazer Russell served in the Connecticut line of the Continental army for more than six years from 1776 to 1783. He enlisted as a private in June 1776 in the company of Capt. David Allen for a period of one year, but on 18 February 1777 enlisted in the company of Capt. Elias Stillwell for the duration of the war. He served in the 1ˢᵗ regiment of Col. Wyllys of the 1ˢᵗ brigade of the Connecticut line. White resident in Oneida County, New York and "upwards of fifty-five" years of age, he made application for a pension based on his service on 30 March 1818 and was awarded a pension. While living in Whitestown, New York, an inventory of property taken 8 September 1820 as part of the pension review calculated value of the personal estate as $52.20. At that time, his family consisted of wife Eunice aged fifty, daughter Olivia aged twenty, and son Eleazer aged fourteen. From the pension file, it is found that Eleazer was in New Hartford, New York in 1831 and then relocated to Vermont by 1835. On 25 April 1840, Eleazer requested a transfer of his pension from Vermont to New York. He related that he had lost his wife and his family was residing in New Hartford, New York and he removed to New York to be near his family and to remain there.[2341]

Three children have been identified for Eleazer Russell and Eunice Sykes. Two children are given in the pension record. Benjamin is a presumed child based on daughter Olivia living with him after Benjamin was widowed.

i   OLIVIA RUSSELL, b. in VT, about 1800; d. at Clinton, NY, 21 Oct 1886. Olivia did not marry. She lived with her brother Benjamin.

ii   BENJAMIN F. RUSSELL, b. in NY, about 1802; d. at Clinton, NY, 8 Jan 1877; m. MARY A. HUNT, b. about 1809. Mary d. at Clinton, 23 Jan 1841.[2342]

iii ELEAZER RUSSELL, b. in NY, about 1806; d. at Utica, NY, 8 Mar 1875; m. CYNTHIA GOODENOUGH, b. in VT, 10 Feb 1813 daughter of Luke and Elsie (-) Goodenough; Cynthia d. at Utica, 14 Apr 1879.

771)   JAMES RUSSELL (*Benjamin⁴, Benjamin³, Benjamin², Robert¹*), b. at Ashford, 1763 son of Benjamin and Phebe (Smith) Russell; d. after 1810 when he was living at Pompey, NY; m. by 1786, LYDIA BROWN.

James Russell of Woodstock served in the Revolution from 16 July 1779 to 15 January 1780 in the in the 4ᵗʰ regiment commanded by Col. John Durkee.[2343]

James and Lydia made several moves during their marriage. They were in Windham County, Connecticut where births of two children are recorded, the births of two children are recorded at Tyringham, Massashuetts, and later they were in Pompey, New York. He seems to be the James Russell living in Pompey in 1810 with a household of seven: one male over 45, one female over 45, two males under 10, two males 10 to 15, and one female under 10.[2344]

The children of James and Lydia are speculative. There are birth records for just four children. A list of ten children is provided in the SAR application of one of the great-grandsons of Obadiah Brown Russell and those children are given here but must be considered speculative.[2345]

i   SMITH RUSSELL, b. at Ashford, 14 Nov 1786; in 1810, Smith Russell headed a household two houses away from James Russell with family of one male 16 to 25, one female 16 to 25, and two females under 10.[2346]

ii   ELECTA RUSSELL, b. at Woodstock, 30 Nov 1788; d. at Berlin, WI, 1863; m. 1806 FREDERICK WOOD, b. about 1780 son of Ebenezer and Mary (Hutchins) Wood; Frederick d. at Delaware County, OH, 17 Jan 1828.

iii STEPHEN RUSSELL, b. 1790

iv   SAMUEL RUSSELL, b. 1793

v   LYDIA RUSSELL, b. about 1796; d. at Greeley, IA, 1862; m. about 1817, JOHN TROWBRIDGE, b at Williston, VT, 31 Jul 1790 son of Seth and Lucretia (Spoor) Trowbridge;[2347] John d. at Morganville, KS, 19 Nov 1885.

[2341] U. S. Revolutionary War Pension and Bounty-Land Warrant Application Files, Case S42223
[2342] Mary wife of Benjamin Russell, age 32 yrs is buried in Old Clinton Burying Ground; findagrave ID: 20578667. Benjamin F. Russell and Olivia Russell are also buried here.
[2343] Collections of the Connecticut Historical Society, volume VIII, p 66, "Short Term Levies"
[2344] Year: 1810; Census Place: Pompey, Onondaga, New York; Roll: 34; Page: 23; Image: 00019; Family History Library Film: 0181388
[2345] Sons of the American Revolution Membership Applications; application of William Russell Howard who was born in 1904.
[2346] Year: 1810; Census Place: Pompey, Onondaga, New York; Roll: 34; Page: 23; Image: 00019; Family History Library Film: 0181388
[2347] Trowbridge, *The Trowbridge Genealogy*, p 208

vi   JAMES RUSSELL, b. at Tyringham, MA, 13 Nov 1796; d. likely at Perry, OH, 1868; m. at Muskingum County, OH, 6 Nov 1823, CHARLOTTE BALDWIN, b. in VA about 1807 daughter of Samuel B. and Hannah (·) Baldwin;[2348] Charlotte d. Oct 1883 (on gravestone)[2349] likely at Washington, OH where she was living in 1880.

vii   SYLVESTER RUSSELL, b. 1797

viii   CYRIL RUSSELL, b. at Tyringham, 20 May 1799; d. at Bowling Green, OH, 18 Jun 1857; m. RELIEF DOOLITTLE, b. 1806; Relief d. 10 Dec 1889.

ix   ANNA RUSSELL, b. 1802

x   OBADIAH BROWN RUSSELL, b. at Pompey, NY, 16 Jan 1804; d. at Salamanca, NY, 25 Mar 1877; m. 16 May 1824, ABIGAIL FAY, b. 10 Aug 1806 daughter of Nehemiah and Achsah (Stratton) Fay; Abigail d. at Salamanca, 15 Sep 1871.

772)   STEPHEN RUSSELL (*Benjamin⁴, Benjamin³, Benjamin², Robert¹*), b. at Ashford, 28 Jan 1765 son of Benjamin and Phebe (Smith) Russell; d. at Burlington, VT, 5 Mar 1847; m. at Pomfret, 12 Feb 1800, MARY SHARP, b. at Pomfret, 14 Feb 1776 daughter of Robert and Sarah (Davis) Sharp;[2350] Mary d. at Burlington, 18 Dec 1844.

    Stephen and Mary's son G. T. Russell of Bluffville, Illinois contributed a biography of his father to the *Vermont Historical Magazine*.[2351] G. T. related that at age fifteen, his father was determined to enlist in the war and his brother locked him up to prevent that. Stephen nevertheless managed to enlist and served three years. After marrying Mary Sharpe of 12 February 1800, Stephen and Mary went to Burlington, Vermont where they were first settlers. Stephen held town offices such as tax collector and constable. The family lived in the village of Burlington for a time until locating on a farm about one and one-half miles from the Court House Square. He kept the farm about twenty years before selling part of the farm and building a new house just north of the farm. "His treasures were not in this world, but that which is to come. It is not known as he had an enemy in the world."

    Stephen provided at statement for application for a pension on 15 April 1818. He enlisted in June 1781 in the company of Capt. John. K. Smith in the 6th Massachusetts regiment and served a term of three years. He was discharged when peace was declared in 1783 after serving twenty-one months. He received pension 27 October 1819 but was stricken from the pension rolls under the act of 1 May 1820 because of the amount of his property. On 26 June 1820, Stephen, aged fifty-five and resident of Burlington, provided a statement related to his pension. He valued his personal estate at $240. He reported owing $250 and that he had no real estate. He worked on a farm. In 1820, his household consisted of himself, his wife aged 45, and five children who were dependent on him for support. The children were Davis aged 17 who was crippled in both legs, Eliza aged 11, George aged 7, Sarah aged 4, and Stephen aged 2. His pension was later reinstated, and he received payment of $71.21 per annum.[2352]

    There are records of seven children born/recorded at Burlington, Vermont,[2353] the birth of the oldest child recorded as two months before the marriage. An eighth child (George T.) can be confirmed due to his authorship of an article about his father. A ninth child (Sarah) is identified from pension records.

i   SOPHIA RUSSELL, b. 13 Dec 1799; d. at Claremont, NH, 24 Dec 1876;[2354] m. JAMES HENRY PLATT, b. at Salem, NY, 19 Aug 1799;[2355] James d. at Hartford, VT, 7 Apr 1876.

ii   DAVIS SMITH RUSSELL, b. 26 Jan 1802; d. at Springfield, MA, 4 Nov 1874; m. at Burlington, VT, 19 Jan 1832, MARY E. POWERS, b. in Canada, about 1809 daughter of Robert Powers; Mary d. at Springfield, 20 Feb 1878.

iii   CHARLES SHARP RUSSELL, b. 2 Mar 1805; d. 31 Jan 1807.

iv   MARY ELIZA RUSSELL, b. 25 Apr 1807

v   CHARLES S. RUSSELL, b. 1808; d. 28 Jan 1808.

vi   SARAH M. RUSSELL, b. 1811; d. 28 Jul 1811.

vii   GEORGE T. RUSSELL, b. about 1812; d. at Whiteside County, IL, about 1875 (probate Oct 1878 but wife had remarried before this date); m. 1st at Charlotte, VT, 28 Oct 1852, ELIZA RICH, b. at Charlotte, about 1825

[2348] Charlotte is buried in the same cemetery plot as her parents.

[2349] Burial in Salt Creek Cemetery, Smith Mill, Ohio; findagrave ID: 9792646

[2350] Davis, *Samuel Davis of Oxford, Mass.*, p 142

[2351] Russell, G. T., "Stephen Russell, Esq." in Hemenway, *Vermont Historical Gazetteer*, p 592

[2352] U. S. Revolutionary War Pension and Bounty-Land Application Files, Case S18583

[2353] Vermont, Vital Records, 1720-1908

[2354] New Hampshire, Death and Burial Records Index, 1654-1949; Sophia's place of birth as Burlington, VT and parents as Stephen and Mary Russell are given on her death record.

[2355] James's date of birth is on his gravestone and place of birth on death record. Findagrave ID: 79097749

daughter of Everett and Lydia (Chase) Rich;[2356] Eliza d. at Charlotte, 1856. George m. 2nd at Carroll County, IL, 16 Mar 1858, ELIZABETH KENT (widow of Henry Cosner), b. in NJ, about 1812 possible daughter of Jacob and Nancy (Blackford) Kent; Elizabeth d. after 1880 when living at Morrison, IL. Elizabeth Kent married third Hiel Chamberlain before 1878 when Elizabeth and Hiel were administrators of George T. Russell's estate. George Russell and Eliza Rich had one daughter Maria born at Charlotte, VT in 1856. Maria lived with her grandmother Lydia after the death of her mother.

viii   SARAH RUSSELL, b. about 1816

ix   STEPHEN H. RUSSELL, b. 11 Apr 1820; d. at Burlington, 2 Sep 1876; m. at Burlington, 14 Nov 1849, MARIA WARNER, b. at Burlington, 23 Jan 1820 daughter of Isaac Warner; Maria d. at Burlington, 9 Jan 1893.

773)   ANNA RUSSELL (*Benjamin⁴, Benjamin³, Benjamin², Robert¹*), b. at Ashford, 25 Nov 1770 daughter of Benjamin and Phebe (Smith) Russell; d. at Burlington, VT, 23 Jan 1813; m. at Ashford, 22 Aug 1793, RICHARD WARE, b. at Wrentham, MA, 30 Jun 1766 son of John and Hannah (George) Ware; Richard d. after 1850 when he was living at Potsdam, NY. Richard had a second marriage, but the name of his second wife has not been found.[2357]

    Richard and Anna married in Ashford and the oldest two children were likely born in Dalton, Connecticut. They were then in Burlington, Vermont where the other children were likely born and where Anna died. Richard is thought to have remarried. He was living in Potsdam in 1850 with his son Oliver and his family. His son Harvey was also living there.

    Daughter Olivia did not marry. In her will written 24 May 1864 (probate 1870), Olivia Ware of Burlington, Vermont left her estate to various religious charitable organizations. Henry Loomis was named executor.[2358]

    Anna Russell and Richard Ware were parents of six children. Richard also had three children with his second wife.

i   HARVEY WARE, b. about 1794; d. after 1850 when he was living in Potsdam, NY in the home of his brother Oliver with father Richard also in the home. Harvey is described as "idiotic" on the census record.

ii   NANCY D. WARE, b. 12 Dec 1797; d. at Richmond, VT (burial at Potsdam), 20 May 1882; m. 3 Sep 1825, FRANCIS FAULKNER WHITE, b. at Woodstock, VT, Mar 1800 son of Francis and Anna (Tuttle) White; Francis d. at Potsdam, 24 Jun 1882.

iii   CLARISSA WARE, b. estimate 1800. It is not certain what became of Clarissa. She may be the Clarissa, born in Vermont, who lived with the family of Rev. William Paddock first in New Hartford, New York and then in Pennsylvania. That Clarissa did not marry and died at Philadelphia, 25 Jun 1877.

iv   OLIVIA WARE (twin), b. 1802; d. at Burlington, VT, 1870 (probate 1870). Olivia did not marry.

v   OLIVER WARE (twin), b. 1802; d. at Potsdam, NY, 19 Dec 1886; m. 1st date unknown but before 1850, ZERUIAH PERRIN, b. in VT, 1808 daughter of Asa and Zeruiah (Bloss) Perrin; Zruiah d. at Potsdam, 10 May 1874. Oliver m. 2nd, about 1875, HARRIET G. BLOSS (widow of Henry N. Lee), b. at Royalton, VT, 9 Dec 1827 daughter of Benjamin and Mary (Durkee) Bloss; Harriet d. at Burlington, VT, 16 Dec 1914. Harriet was third married to Harvey Collins. Oliver did not have children.

vi   HARRIET P. WARE, b. about 1811; d. at Hardwick, MA, 27 Jan 1887. Harriet did not marry.

774)   SALLY RUSSELL (*Benjamin⁴, Benjamin³, Benjamin², Robert¹*), b. at Ashford, 28 Feb 1774 daughter of Benjamin and Phebe (Smith) Russell; d. at Pittsfield, MA, 23 Dec 1833; m. at Hampton, 25 Sep 1794, HENRY DURKEE, b. at Hampton, 25 Aug 1770 son of Henry and Sarah (Holt) Durkee.

    Sally and Henry were parents of likely three children. There are records for the two sons, and the 1810 census indicates a daughter under age 10.[2359]

i   HENRY DURKEE, b. at Hampton, CT, 28 Apr 1795; perhaps the Henry Durkee who d. at Lowell, NY at age 43, 19 Nov 1838;[2360] m. CLARISSA who has not been identified, b. 1796; Clarissa d. at Lowell, 9 Aug 1840.

ii   AMASA DURKEE, b. at Dalton, MA, 19 Mar 1798; d. at 1870 when living at Monson, MA; m. about 1822, MARIANNA LESTER, b. at Becket, MA, 18 Mar 1798 daughter of Stewart and Abigail (Lester) Lester; Marianna d. at Pittsfield, MA, 1837.

[2356] The will of Everett Rich of Charlotte, VT written 24 Feb 1857 includes a bequest to his granddaughter Maria Russell daughter of Eliza who is deceased.

[2357] Ware, *Ware Genealogy*, p 140

[2358] Vermont Wills and Probate, Chittenden County Estate Files, Estate of Olivia Ware, Case 3478

[2359] Year: 1810; Census Place: Dalton, Berkshire, Massachusetts; Roll: 17; Image: 00094; Family History Library Film: 0205625

[2360] Findagrave ID: 22232389; Lowell Cemetery

iii   Daughter, b. 1803

775)   CYNTHIA RUSSELL (*John⁴, Benjamin³, Benjamin², Robert¹*), b. at Windham, CT, 22 Jan 1771 daughter of John and Alice (Lyon) Russell; m. at Springfield, VT, 9 May 1793, ASA HALL.

        There is a record of one child for Cynthia and Asa. Nothing further was found.

i   JOHN HALL, b. at Springfield, VT, 22 Jan 1771

776)   EBENEZER RUSSELL (*John⁴, Benjamin³, Benjamin², Robert¹*), b. at Windham, CT, 15 Feb 1773 son of John and Alice (Lyon) Russell; d. after 1830 when living at Springfield, VT; m. at Springfield, VT, 29 Jan 1795, REBECCA HUDSON, b. 1775; Rebecca d. at Brandon, VT, 1850.

        Ebenezer and Rebecca resided in Springfield, Vermont and there are records of births of two sons there. There is a likely third child, daughter Rachel, in this family. In 1830, Ebenezer was head of household in Springfield consisting of one male 50-59, one female 50-59, and one female 10-14.[2361] Rebecca Russell age 76 was living in Brandon, Vermont in 1850 in the household of Frederick and Rachel Rockwell.[2362]

i   RILEY RUSSELL, b. at Springfield, VT, 24 Jun 1795

ii   LEWIS RUSSELL, b. at Springfield, about 1814; d. at Middlebury, VT, 7 Mar 1903; m. at Brandon, VT, 1 Sep 1836, MARIA LOUISA WALKER, b. at New Salem, MA, 25 Apr 1815; Maria d. at Middlebury, 4 Mar 1900.[2363]

iii   RACHEL RUSSELL, b. 1817; d. at Brandon, VT, 29 Jun 1858; m. FREDERICK ROCKWELL, b. at Brandon, 1814; Frederick d. at Brandon, 4 Jun 1874.

777)   SARAH WORK (*Mary Russell Work⁴, Benjamin³, Benjamin², Robert¹*), b. at Ashford, 20 Feb 1751 daughter of Ingoldsby and Mary (Russell) Work; d. at Union, CT, 23 May 1793; m. at Danbury, CT, 28 May 1767, SAMUEL CRAWFORD, b. 22 Jul 1748 son of Hugh and Margaret (Campbell) Crawford; Samuel d. at Sturbridge, MA,[2364] 11 May 1824. Samuel was second married to Olive Eddy.

        Deacon Samuel Crawford was a farmer in Union. He was prominent in the town and a major landowner with over 1,000 at one time. He was selectman of Union for seventeen of the years from 1782 to 1804. He was member of the state legislature from 1788 to 1809. His land holdings were such that he was able to give each of his children of farm when they married. He was deacon of the Baptist church in West Woodstock. In 1776, he served for eleven months during the Revolution but was sent home when he became sick with fever.[2365]

        Samuel Crawford did not leave a will and Ingoldsby W. Crawford was named administrator 23 June 1824. The probate documents are tattered and cannot be viewed. There is an incomplete summary of the contents which lists the following possible heirs in two distributions 15 Jul 1824 and 18 January 1826: widow Olive, son Luther, son Samuel, son Ingoldsby W., _lly wife to Benjamin, heirs of Anna Phillips, and Polly Preston wife of Nathan. The summary page notes "see over" at the bottom but the other side is not present.[2366] Polly Preston is a daughter from Samuel's second marriage to Olive Eddy.

        Sarah Work and Samuel Crawford were parents of ten children born at Union, Connecticut. Samuel had three children from his second marriage to Olive Eddy.

i   LUTHER CRAWFORD, b. 22 Feb 1772; d. at Cleveland, OH, 20 Feb 1853; m. 14 Jun 1792, ELIZABETH WILBUR, b. in RI, 1773 daughter of William Wilbur; Elizabeth d. at Cleveland, 30 Mar 1855.

ii   CALVIN CRAWFORD, b. 21 Dec 1773; d. 13 Aug 1776.

iii   LAVINA CRAWFORD, b. 26 Aug 1775; d. at Union, 4 Feb 1796; m. at Union, 24 Sep 1795, JOSEPH PERRIN CORBIN, b. at Woodstock, 2 Oct 1773 son of William and Dorothy (Perris) Corbin; Joseph d. at Mount Clemens, MI, 24 Sep 1848. Joseph married second Mary Howard. Lavina and Joseph had one daughter, Lavina.

[2361] 1830; Census Place: Springfield, Windsor, Vermont; Series: M19; Roll: 187; Page: 140; Family History Library Film: 0027453

[2362] Year: 1850; Census Place: Brandon, Rutland, Vermont; Roll: 927; Page: 96b

[2363] Obituary of Louisa Walker Russell, Middlebury Register (Middlebury, Vermont), 09 March 1900, Friday, p 5; the obituary gives date and place of birth and date and place of marriage.

[2364] Was resident of Union, but died at Sturbridge where he had gone to look at a farm; Hammond, *History of Union*, p 323

[2365] Hammond, The History of Union, p 134, pp 152-154

[2366] Connecticut Wills and Probate, Strafford Probate District, Town of Union, Estate of Samuel Crawford, Case 536

iv   JOHN CRAWFORD, b. 17 Apr 1777; d. at Union, 17 Mar 1863; m. at Union, 24 May 1800, SUSANNAH HAYWARD, b. at Ashford, 11 Dec 1778 daughter of Jonathan and Lydia (Davison) Hayward; Susannah d. at Union, 10 Feb 1854.

v   SAMUEL CRAWFORD, b. 4 Jul 1779; d. at Union, 21 Jun 1858; m. 20 Aug 1801, LYDIA HAYWARD, b. at Ashford, 26 Aug 1781 daughter of Jonathan and Lydia (Davison) Hayward; Lydia d. 22 Aug 1851.

vi   BENJAMIN CRAWFORD, b. 18 Oct 1781; d. 13 May 1789.

vii   WALTER CRAWFORD, b. 30 Jan 1784; d. 10 Mar 1785.

viii   INGOLDSBY WORK CRAWFORD, b. 7 Aug 1786; d. at Union, 24 Nov 1867; m. 29 May 1810, RHODA TAFT, b. at Mendon, MA, 23 Mar 1793 daughter of Daniel and Mary (Sibley) Taft; Rhoda d. 6 Apr 1864.

ix   SARAH CRAWFORD, b. 15 Sep 1788; d. at Woodstock, CT, 9 Sep 1826; m. at Woodstock, 4 Mar 1811, BENJAMIN CHAMBERLAIN, b. at Woodstock, 4 Sep 1787 son of Elisha and Margret (Ledoyt) Chamberlain; Benjamin d. at Woodstock, 19 May 1864. Benjamin married second Almira Bugbee and married third Amanda Crawford.

x   ANNA CRAWFORD, b. 29 Mar 1791; d. at Woodstock, 8 Sep 1820; m. about 1812, WHEELER PHILLIPS, b. at West Woodstock, 2 Feb 1783 son of William and Phebe (Wheeler) Phillips; Wheeler d. at Woodstock, 22 Sep 1863.

778)   ELIZABETH WORK (*Mary Russell Work⁴, Benjamin³, Benjamin², Robert¹*), b. at Ashford, 1 Feb 1757 daughter of Ingoldsby and Mary (Russell) Work; d. at Eastford, 14 Jan 1785; m. at Ashford, 7 Jan 1779, Rev. ANDREW JUDSON, b. about 1749; Andrew d. at Eastford, 15 Nov 1804. Andrew was second married to Mary Work on 13 Mar 1785.

Rev. Andrew Judson was minister of the Congregational church at Eastford from 1778 to his death in 1804. He received a salary of £70 per year.[2367]

Son Andrew Thompson Judson studied law and was admitted to the bar in Windham County, Connecticut in 1806. He had a law practice in Canterbury and was named States Attorney for Windham County in 1819. He held political positions including serving in the U. S. House of Representatives in 1835-1836. He was president of the temperance union in Windham County. He was the trial judge that decided the Amistad case and directed that the United States was responsible to return the enslaved persons to Africa. This may not have been due to any empathy for the slaves, however, as he also was instrumental in the conviction of Prudence Crandall for operating a school for black girls in Canterbury. Prudence Crandall was a neighbor of Andrew Judson and he strongly opposed the school. He made the legal argument that the school violated Connecticut's "Black Law" which prohibited the education of black persons from out of the state of Connecticut unless approved by local officials.[2368] Judson was a proponent of "colonization" or sending freed slaves to Africa.[2369]

Andrew Judson did not leave a will and his estate entered probate 20 November 1804 with John Work Judson as administrator and Andrew Thompson Judson and Samuel Sumner as sureties for the bond. Real estate was valued at $774 and personal estate at $666.31. The widow's thirds were set off to Mary Judson. The distribution from the estate was 13 November 1805. A tract of land of eight acres was set out to Jose Judson, John W, Judson, and Andrew T. Judson as co-tenants. Other heirs receiving distributions were Elizabeth Mary Judson, Sylvester Gilbert Judson, Zuinghus Judson, and Meanathon Judson. The four last named children, who are children from Andrew's second marriage to Mary Work, also have equal rights to use of the east cellar, well, and oven.[2370]

Elizabeth Work and Andrew Judson were parents of three children born at Ashford.

i   JOSE JUDSON, b. 6 Feb 1780; d. at Ashford, 13 Feb 1806. Jose did not marry.

ii   JOHN WORK JUDSON, b. 8 Jul 1782; d. at Eastford, 16 Apr 1811; m. at Ashford, 5 Jan 1808, ALMIRA HOWE, b. at Ashford, 26 Jul 1781 daughter of Nehemiah and Mary (*Brooks* Holt) Howe;[2371] Almira did not remarry and d. at Oswego, NY, 29 Jul 1846.

iii   ANDREW THOMPSON JUDSON, b. 29 Nov 1784; d. at Canterbury, 17 Mar 1853; m. at Mansfield, CT, 20 Mar 1816, REBECCA WARREN, b. at Windham, 2 Mar 1795 daughter of Timothy and Nancy (Poole) Warren;[2372] Rebecca d. 24 Oct 1861.

[2367] Bayles, *History of Windham County, Connecticut*, p 1035

[2368] CT.gov; Andrew Thompson Judson; Andrew Thompson Judson; https://portal.ct.gov/-/media/DECD/Historic-Preservation/04_State_Museums/Prudence-Crandall-Museum/Andrew-Thompson-Judson.pdf?la=en

[2369] Samuel J. May, *Some recollections of our antislavery conflict*. Boston: Fields, Osgood & Co., 1869, p 39-72

[2370] Ancestry.com. *Connecticut, Wills and Probate Records, 1609-1999* [database on-line]. Probate place, Hartford, Connecticut, *Probate Packets, Johnson, I-Kendall, Sabin, 1752-1880, Andrew Judson, Case 2402*

[2371] The 1817 will of Nehemiah Howe includes a bequest to his daughter Almira Judson.

[2372] The 1817 will (probate 1829) of Timothy Warren includes a bequest to daughter Rebecca wife of Andrew T. Judson, Esq.

779)   MARY WORK (*Mary Russell Work⁴, Benjamin³, Benjamin², Robert¹*), b. at Ashford, 1 Jan 1759 daughter of Ingoldsby and Mary (Russell) Work; d. at Eastford, 9 Mar 1798; m. at Ashford, 16 Jun 1779, EDWARD KEYES, b. at Ashford, 4 Jun 1759 son of Solomon and Sarah (Sumner) Keyes; Edward d. at Ashford, 1 May 1827. Edward married second Sarah Whitmore.

Edward Keyes, also known as Ned, was a businessman in the village of Eastford.[2373] Edward and Mary's son Justus was a physician in Brimfield, Massachusetts. Justus's son was Gen. Erasmus D. Keyes (1810-1895) who commanded the IV Corps of the Union Army of the Potomac. Edward and Mary's daughter Sarah married William Upham who served as U.S. senator from Vermont (Whig party) from 4 December 1843 until his death from smallpox on 14 January 1853.[2374]

In his will written 28 December 1825 (proved 14 May 1827), Edward Keyes bequeathed to beloved wife Sarah the use and improvement of one-half of the home farm during her natural life. Grandson Elias Keyes Smith receives $500 at age twenty-one, which is over and above what Edward has given to Elias's mother Esther Smith. The remainder of the estate is to be divided among his ten living children, the sons receiving one and one-half shares and the daughters one share. The children are Roxey Keyes, Justus Keyes, Danforth Keyes, Polly Woodward, Edward Keyes, Sarah Upham, Ann Smith, Giddings W. Keyes, Joseph F Keyes, and David Keyes. Danforth Keyes and Joseph F. Keyes were named executors. The total value of the estate was $16,259.29.[2375] Giddings, Joseph, and David were children from Edward's second marriage. Although daughter Roxy is named as Roxy Keyes in the will, she is named as Roxy Brooks in the estate distribution.

Mary Work and Edward Keyes were parents of ten children born at Ashford. Edward Keyes had three children with his second wife Sarah Whitmore.

i   ROXANA KEYES, b. 1779; d. at Montpelier, VT, 11 Aug 1842; m. about 1801, THOMAS BROOKS, b. at Ashford, 19 Apr 1775 son of Abijah and Lucy (Knowlton) Keyes; Thomas d. at Lockport, NY, 18 Oct 1826.

ii   JUSTUS KEYES, b. 9 Nov 1780; d. at Brimfield, MA, 21 Sep 1835; m. at Sturbridge, MA, 11 May 1806, ELIZABETH "BETSY" COREY, b. at Sturbridge, 26 Feb 1781 daughter of Jacob and Matilda (Walker) Corey; Betsy d. at Brimfield, 3 Mar 1826.

iii   ELIAS KEYES, b. 1781; d. at Eastford, 23 Jun 1801.

iv   ELIZABETH KEYES, b. 1785; d. at Ashford, 13 May 1803.

v   DANFORTH KEYES, b. 24 Apr 1787; d. at Eastford, CT, 6 Nov 1849; m. 22 Sep 1811, OLIVE CHAPMAN, b. 20 Jan 1790 (record in Wales, MA family records but may have occurred in CT) daughter of Elijah and Jemima (Chaffee) Chapman; Olive d. at Clinton, MI, 28 Apr 1870. After the death of her husband, Olive went to Michigan with her son Danforth.

vi   MARY "POLLY" KEYES, b. 9 Nov 1788; d. at Hartford, CT, 29 Aug 1869; m. at Ashford, 31 Dec 1809, HORATIO WOODWARD, b. 29 Jun 1785 son of Jason and Sarah (Sumner) Woodward; Horatio d. at Ashford, 28 Apr 1856.

vii   ESTHER KEYES, b. 23 Jan 1791; d. about 1816; m. about 1814, BARAK SMITH, b. at Dover, MA, 16 Sep 1791 son of Barach and Abigail (Battelle) Smith; Barak d. at Eastford, 27 May 1874. Barak was second married to Esther's sister Anna (see below).

viii   EDWARD KEYES, b. 29 Jan 1793; d. at Galena, IL, 3 Jul 1835; m. at Posey County, IN, 17 Oct 1822, MARY "POLLY" HUGHES, b. in VT, 21 Sep 1802 daughter of Parly and Esther (Ormsby) Hughes;[2376] Polly d. at Rutland, IL, 9 Nov 1890. Polly was second married to Alonzo Walbridge.

ix   SARAH KEYES, b. 10 Oct 1795; d. at Montpelier, VT, 8 May 1856; m. 1814, WILLIAM UPHAM, b. at Leicester, MA, 5 Aug 1792 son of Samuel and Patty (Livermore) Upham; William d. at Washington, DC, 14 Jan 1853. William Upham was an attorney. The family lived in Montpelier, but William died while in Washington.

x   ANNA KEYES, b. 1798; d. at Eastford, 13 Jul 1828; m. at Hartford, 5 May 1818, BARAK SMITH who was first married to Anna's sister Esther (see above).

780)   ALEXANDER WORK (*Mary Russell Work⁴, Benjamin³, Benjamin², Robert¹*), b. at Ashford, 8 Mar 1763 son of Ingoldsby and Mary (Russell) Work; d. at Williamstown, VT, 24 Apr 1822; m. at Ashford, 26 Nov 1789, DOROTHY SMITH, b. at Woodstock, CT, 25 Jan 1769 daughter of Asa and Hannah (Bowen) Smith;[2377] Dorothy d. at Williamstown, VT, 4 Sep 1828.

Alexander and Dorothy started their family in Ashford but were in Williamston, Vermont by 1800. In 1810, there were ten members of the household: one male 45 and over; one female 26-44; two males under 10; two males 10-15; one male 16-25; two females under 10; and one slave.[2378]

[2373] Keyes, *Genealogy of Robert Keyes of Watertown*, p 110

[2374] Appleton's Cyclopedia of American Biography 1600-1889, volume VI, p 213

[2375] Ancestry.com. *Connecticut, Wills and Probate Records, 1609-1999* [database on-line]. Probate place, Hartford, *Probate Packets, Kendall, Septimus-Larned, Daniel, 1752-1880, Edward Keyes, Case 2459*

[2376] Lewis Publishing Company, *Biographical and Genealogical Record of La Salle and Grundy Counties, Illinois*, p 280; entry for Alonzo Walbridge.

[2377] Hamilton, *Work Family History*, p 563

[2378] Year: 1810; Census Place: Williamstown, Orange, Vermont; Roll: 64; Page: 400; Image: 00713; Family History Library Film: 0218668

Alexander Work did not leave a will and on 17 May 1822 widow Dorothy requested that Abial Smith be named administrator of the estate.[2379]

Alexander Work and Dorothy Smith were parents of ten children.

i   ARIEL WORK, b. at Ashford, CT, 4 Jun 1792; d. at Billerica, MA, 23 Nov 1874; m. at Billerica, 30 Aug 1830, SARAH BOWERS PARKER, b. at Billerica, 8 Jun 1806 daughter of Samuel and Sally (Warren) Parker; Sarah d. at Billerica, 19 Oct 1876.

ii   ASA SMITH WORK, b. at Ashford, 9 Feb 1795; d. 24 Jul 1803.

iii   ELIAS WORK (twin), b. at Ashford, 15 Mar 1797; d. at Williamstown, VT, 6 Jul 1846; m. at Williamstown, 21 Feb 1821, SARAH TUFTS, b. at Ashford, 28 Nov 1796 daughter of Aaron and Harmony (Hayward) Tufts; Sarah d. 12 Sep 1847.

iv   LYMAN WORK (twin), b. at Ashford, 15 Mar 1797; d. at Stockbridge, VT, 26 Jul 1803.

v   ALANSON WORK, b. at Ashford, 30 Aug 1799; d. at Hartford, CT, 6 Jul 1879; m. at Middletown, CT, 3 Aug 1825, AMELIA A. FORBES, b. 3 Aug 1803 (on cemetery record); Amelia d. at Hartford, 14 Feb 1891.

vi   JOHN WORK, b. at Williamstown, 22 Jul 1802; d. at Essex, VT, 25 Oct 1862; m. 1st ELECTA BALDWIN, b. at Monkton, VT, 13 May 1794 daughter of Nathan Gaylord and Abigail (Chamberlain) Baldwin. John m. 2nd JULIET who has not been identified, b. in VT, 1818; Juliet d. at Huntington, VT, 1868. John Work was a physician in Huntington and Essex, Vermont.[2380]

vii   HANNAH WORK, b. at Williamstown, VT, 29 Nov 1804; d. 1840.[2381]

viii   JOSE JUDSON WORK, b. at Williamstown, 19 Aug 1807; d. 16 Jul 1822.

ix   MARY WORK, b. at Williamstown, 29 Jul 1810

x   PERLEY WORK, b. at Williamstown, 11 Sep 1813; d. after 1870 when he was living in Ripon, WI and before 1880; m. by 1844, H. OLIVIA MCKNIGHT, b. at Truxton, NY, about 1820 daughter of Thomas and Harriet (Clapp) McKnight; Olivia d. at Ripon, 1897. Perley was a minister.

781)   LUCY WORK (*Mary Russell Work⁴, Benjamin³, Benjamin², Robert¹*), b. at Ashford, 14 Sep 1765 daughter of Ingoldsby and Mary (Russell) Work; d. at Eastford, 3 Nov 1801; m. at Eastford, 26 Jun 1788, MANASSEH HOWARD, b. at Ashford, 25 Nov 1763 son of John and Rebecca (Peake) Hayward;[2382] Manasseh d. at Eastford, 13 Jun 1836. Manasseh was second married to Dorothy Corbin.

Manasseh Howard was a farmer with property in the southeast part of Union.[2383]

Manasseh Howard did not leave a will; John Howard and Reuben Preston were named administrators 21 June 1836. Total value of the estate was $5,260.78; personal estate, $1,954.65; home farm of 264 acres, $2,112; Shelburne lot of 85 acres, $769.50; and Allen lot of 30 acres, $424.63. Dower was set off to widow Dorothy. A portion of the personal estate up to $450 was sold to settle debts. The distribution of the estate included the one-third dower to Dorothy and twelve children: Ezra Howard, Esther Wood wife of Elijah, Eleazer Howard, Lucy Preston wife of Reuben, legal representatives of Polly Marcy deceased late wife of Joseph W. Marcy, Sally Walker wife of Parley, Anna Howard, John Howard, Augustus Howard, Louisa Howard, William C. Howard, and Clinton Howard.[2384]

Lucy and Manasseh were parents of seven children born at Union, Connecticut. Manasseh had five children with his second wife Dorothy Corbin.

i   EZRA HOWARD, b. 4 Mar 1789; d. at Rochester, NY, 3 May 1864; m. by 1824, PERMELIA HERRICK, b. in NY, 1798; Permelia d. at Irondequoit, NY, 28 Jan 1880. Ezra Howard settled in Henrietta, New York where he had large land holdings and made farming implements.[2385]

ii   ESTHER HOWARD, b. 1790; d. at Mansfield, CT, 25 Sep 1849; m. at Mansfield, 24 Dec 1812, ELIJAH WOOD, b. at Mansfield, 28 Sep 1787 son of Gideon and Kezia (Owen) Wood; Elijah d. at Mansfield, 28 Jul 1853.

[2379] Vermont Wills and Probate, Orange County, Folder 35, Miscellaneous Files, Alexander Work

[2380] John Work listed as a physician in the 1850 and 1860 census; Year: 1850; Census Place: Huntington, Chittenden, Vermont; Roll: 923; Page: 223a

[2381] Hamilton, *Work Family History*, p 564 reports this date of death, but no record was found; accessed through ancestry.com

[2382] Connecticut Town Birth Records, pre-1870 (Barbour Collection)

[2383] Hammond, *History of Union*, p 352

[2384] Connecticut Wills and Probate, Stafford Probate District, Town of Union, Estate of Manasseh Howard, Case 1095

[2385] Peck, *Landmarks of Monroe County, New York*, Part I, p 24

iii   ELEAZER HOWARD, b. 21 Aug 1793; d. at LeRoy, IL, 17 Mar 1872; m. MATILDA WOOD, b. at Mansfield, 7 Aug 1792 daughter of Gideon and Kezia (Owen) Wood; Matilda d. after 1870.

iv   LUCY HOWARD, b. 15 Oct 1795; d. at Eastford, CT, 15 Oct 1878; m. REUBEN PRESTON, b. at Ashford, 26 Aug 1792 son of Zephaniah and Mary (Bishop) Preston; Reuben d. at Eastford, 24 Jun 1884.

v   POLLY HOWARD, b. 5 Sep 1798; d. at Eastford, 11 Nov 1831; m. about 1820, her third cousin, JOSEPH WORK MARCY (*Orrin Marcy⁵, Samuel Marcy⁴, Mary Russell Marcy³, Benjamin², Robert¹*), b. at Ashford, 20 Nov 1797 son of Orrin and Polly (Work) Marcy; Joseph d. at Eastford, 2 May 1842. Joseph married second Lois Bugbee.

vi   ANNA HOWARD (twin), b. 24 Sep 1801; d. at Sherman, NY, 16 Oct 1876; m. about 1838, EZRA REED SHELDON, b. in VT, 23 Jun 1813 son of Joel and Sarah (Edgerton) Sheldon;[2386] Ezra d. at Sherman, 9 May 1868.

vii   SARAH "SALLY" HOWARD (twin), b. 24 Sep 1801; d. at Eastford, 1 Feb 1888; m. PARLEY WALKER, b. at Union, CT, 28 Aug 1796 son of Pearly and Rebecca (Broughton) Walker; Parley d. at Eastford, 16 Jan 1871.

782)   ANNA WORK (*Mary Russell Work⁴, Benjamin³, Benjamin², Robert¹*), b. at Ashford, 5 Feb 1771 daughter of Ingoldsby and Mary (Russell) Work; d. at Fulton, NY, 24 Aug 1848; m. at Ashford, 9 Feb 1792, ASA PHILLIPS, b. at Smithfield, RI, 8 May 1769 son of Elijah and Rhoda (Sayles) Phillips; Asa d. at Fulton, 17 Feb 1813.

     Rev. Asa Phillips and his wife Anna Work started their family in Ashford but purchased a farm in Marcellus Hills, New York about 1797.[2387] Asa died at age 44. Anna and Asa were parents of at least eight children.

i   MICHAEL C. PHILLIPS, b. at Ashford, 1 Aug 1792; m. RACHEL JACKSON DIER.

ii   ASA PHILLIPS, b. at Ashford, 12 Jan 1794; d. at Fulton, NY, 2 Nov 1865; m. Jan 1815, POLLY BARNES, b. 1794; Polly d. at Granby, NY, 29 Sep 1865. Asa was a leading citizen of Oswego County with diverse enterprises including a salt-works, blacksmith shop, sawmills, and a large hotel. After his father's death, he bought most of the shares of his siblings in their father's estate.[2388]

iii   ELIJAH PHILLIPS, b. 28 Dec 1795; d. at Oswego County, NY, 5 Jul 1874; m. LUCY EASTMAN, b. 1795; Lucy d. 25 Mar 1861

iv   JOHN W. PHILLIPS, b. about 1798; John d. at Fulton, NY, 20 Jul 1852.

v   GEORGE W. PHILLIPS, b. 9 Sep 1801; d. at Syracuse, NY, 26 Feb 1873; m. MARIA H. WARD, b. at Manlius, NY, 17 Dec 1803 daughter of William and Luthera (Cobb) Ward;[2389] Maria d. at Syracuse, 16 Nov 1888.

vi   MARY PHILLIPS, b. 1804; d. at Syracuse, 1877; m. ANSON TERRY, b. about 1805; Anson d. at Fulton, NY, 1855 (probate 1 Aug 1855).

vii   CYRUS PETER PHILLIPS, b.1807; d. at Fulton, NY, 6 Jul 1879; m. 1ˢᵗ ANN BURT, b. 1806 daughter of Calvin Bradner and Mehitable (Baker) Burt;[2390] Ann d. at Fulton, 26 Apr 1853.

viii   RHODA SAYLES PHILLIPS, b. about 1813; d. at Syracuse, NY, 17 Sep 1893; m. by 1842, Dr. ISAAC MORRELL, b. at Newfield, ME, about 1808; Isaac d. at Elmira, NY, 8 Sep 1887. Isaac was a graduate of Bowdoin College.

783)   JOHN MARCY (*John Marcy⁴, Mary Russell Marcy³, Benjamin², Robert¹*), b. at Middletown, 18 Sep 1753 son of John and Hannah (Sharpe) Marcy; m. LUCY.

     John was living in Cambridge, Vermont in 1820 in a household with one male over 45, one female over 45, one male 16-25, one female 26-44, two males under 10, and one female under 10.[2391] Just one child has been identified.

i   REUBEN MARCY, b. at Cambridge, VT, 23 May 1798; d. at Jericho, VT, 1843 (probate 7 Jun 1843); m. LEONORA DIXON, b. at Underhill, VT, 11 Nov 1801 daughter of Luther and Nancy (Mills) Dixon; Leonora d. at Westford, VT, 20 May 1875. Leonora remarried on 20 Mar 1845 to Artemus Allen.

[2386] Young, *History of Chautauqua County*, p 552
[2387] Johnson, *History of Oswego County, New York*, Part I, p 400
[2388] Johnson, *History of Oswego County, New York*, Part I, p 400
[2389] The 1861 will of William Ward of Syracuse includes a bequest to daughter Maria H. Philips.
[2390] The 1871 will of Calvin Bradner Burt includes bequests to his Phillips grandchildren who are children of his daughter Anna deceased.
[2391] 1820 U S Census; Census Place: Cambridge, Franklin, Vermont; Page: 34; NARA Roll: M33_127; Image: 185

784)   HANNAH MARCY (*John Marcy⁴, Mary Russell Marcy³, Benjamin², Robert¹*), b. at Middletown, 10 Apr 1755 daughter of John and Hannah (Sharpe) Marcy; d. at Fort Miller, NY, 15 Oct 1841; m. at Walpole, NH, 12 Aug 1778, NATHAN HATCH, b. at Tolland, 17 Sep 1757 son of Joseph and Sarah (Stearns) Hatch; Nathan d. at Fort Miller, 1 Jun 1841.

        On 6 August 1832, Nathan Hatch age seventy-four of Cavendish, Vermont made application for pension based on his service in the Revolution. In June 1775, he enlisted from Tolland in the company of Capt. Abraham Tyler and regiment of Col. Huntington for a term of five months. The company was at New London, Stonington, and Roxbury before being dismissed at the end of five months. In the summer of 1776 from Alstead, New Hampshire, he enlisted in the company of Capt. Jason Wetherbee of Charlestown for five months. Immediately after, he and six or seven others who had not had smallpox were ordered to remain in Charlestown and be inoculated with the smallpox which they did, and as soon as they were well of the smallpox, they marched to Mount Independence. His third enlistment was in the summer of 1777 from Walpole, New Hampshire for two months in the company of Capt. Christopher Webber in Col. Hibbard's regiment of Gen. Stark's brigade. They marched to Bennington where he participated in the battle of Bennington where Lieut. Waldo of his company was wounded, and Sgt. Eastman was shot in the chest and died three days later. After Bennington, they marched to Bemis Heights, New York but about the time they arrived, his two-month enlistment was expired, and he was dismissed. Nathan further reported he was born at Tolland on 17 September 1757 and resided in Tolland until his first enlistment. He was then in Alstead where his father had moved two or three years before. When his father went to Alstead, Nathan was left in Tolland with his older brother. In April 1777, Nathan went from Alstead to Walpole and from Walpole to Windsor, Vermont where he resided five years. He remained in Reading about twenty-five years before moving to Cavendish three years previously. On 18 March 1834, Nathan requested transfer of his pension from Vermont to Washington County, New York where he planned to remain.[2392]

        Daughter Fanny did not marry. In her will dated 2 May 1858 (probate 26 November 1861), she left her entire estate to her sister Hannah Seaver wife of Samuel Seaver of Cavendish and her brother Hart Hatch.[2393]

        There are records for nine children of Hannah and Nathan born at Reading, Vermont.[2394]

i   JOSEPH HATCH, b. 24 May 1780; m. likely in Reading, VT, before 1815, MARTHA who has not been clearly identified. A son of Joseph and Martha, Francis Hanson Hatch, was born in Reading 27 Jan 1815 and died at Orleans Parish, LA, 19 Jul 1884.[2395]

ii   FANNY HATCH, b. 2 May 1782; d. at Cavendish, VT, 13 Sep 1861. Fanny did not marry.

iii   SARAH HATCH, b. 19 Apr 1784; d. at Windsor, VT, 10 Jul 1840; m. at Windsor, 27 Apr 1804, DAVID BARLOW, b. 1783; David d. at Windsor, 31 Mar 1867. David married second Betsey Bradley on 13 Dec 1840.

iv   ALVIN HATCH, b. 3 Sep 1786; d. at Woodstock, VT, 27 Dec 1873; m. at Reading, 4 Mar 1810, NANCY RICE, b. about 1788; Nancy d. at Reading, 29 Apr 1843.

v   REUBEN HATCH, b. 12 Aug 1788; d. at Fort Miller, NY, 14 Aug 1837.[2396]

vi   PHINEHAS HATCH, b. 5 Aug 1790; d. at Fort Edward, NY, 7 Jan 1838 (probate 1838); m. LAURA who is the widow named in probate. Wife Laura receives use of one-third of the estate during her life and, after her decease, the estate is to be divided among his heirs-at-law who are not named.[2397]

vii   HANNAH HATCH, b. 6 Mar 1793; d. at Cavendish, VT, 21 Aug 1869; m. SAMUEL SEAVER, b. at Phillipston, MA, 11 Mar 1795 son of Joseph and Abial (Rich) Seaver; Samuel d. at Cavendish, 18 Jan 1874.

viii   HART HATCH, b. 9 Mar 1795; d. at Cavendish, 12 Mar 1875. Hart did not marry.

ix   POLLY HATCH, b. 27 Dec 1799; d. at Ridgefield, CT, 5 Apr 1875; m. ALSON BATES, b. 24 Jan 1802 son of Nathan and Ruth (Taylor) Bates; Alson d. at Ridgefield, 9 Jun 1882.

785)   STEPHEN MARCY (*John Marcy⁴, Mary Russell Marcy³, Benjamin², Robert¹*), b. at Middletown, 14 Feb 1757 son of John and Hannah (Sharpe) Marcy; d. at Gorham, NY, 10 Nov 1843; m. ACHSAH HOWE, b. 1769; Achsah d. at Gorham, 1836.

        Stephen served about ten and one-half months during the Revolution. On 8 August 1832, while living in Gorham, New York at age 75, he provided a statement related to his application for pension. On 1 July 1777 while living in Walpole, New Hampshire he was called out in the company of Capt. Christopher Webber in the regiment of Col. Benjamin Bellows. They marched to Clarendon on Otter Creek, then to Fort Independence, and from there over a floating bridge to Fort Ticonderoga then commanded by Gen. St. Clair. The troops helped to build a brass works and returned home after one and one-half months. In February 1781, while living in Windsor, he enlisted for a term of nine months in the company of Capt. Jesse Stafford, served the whole term and was discharged at Bethel. During the term, he was at Pittsford and helped build Picket Fort and then at

[2392] U. S. Revolutionary War Pension and Bounty-Land Warrant Application Files, Case S13278

[2393] Vermont Wills and Probate, Windsor County, Estate of Fanny Hatch, recorded in volume 26, p 655

[2394] Vermont, Vital Records, 1720-1908

[2395] Louisiana, Statewide Death Index, 1819-1964

[2396] Findagrave ID: 119258065, Riverside Cemetery, Fort Miller, New York

[2397] New York Wills and Probate, Washington County, Wills Book A2, pp 228-229

Bethel on the White River to build another fort. While he was in that area, Royalton was burned. Stephen was not in any battles.

In his statement, Stephen provided information on his movements. He was born in Middletown, Connecticut on 14 February 1757, moved to Walpole when very young, and was in Walpole at his first enlistment. He was later in Windsor, Vermont, then in Stillwater in Saratoga County, then back to Windsor where he remained eleven years, then to Scipio in New York where he lived twenty years, and lastly in Gorham where he resided for the past three years.[2398]

Five children were confirmed for Stephen and Achsah and they were likely parents of other children born before 1800, but that information is so far not confirmed.

i NAHUM S. MARCY, b. 1800; d. at Perry, NY, 1888. In the 1880 census, Nahum was living in Perry with his brother John. Nahum is listed as a widower, but the name of his wife has not been found. In the 1865 census, he was living with his sister Emily and he did not have wife or children with him at that time.

ii JOHN W. MARCY, b. likely at Windsor, VT, 1805; d. at Perry, NY, 2 Jan 1888; m. about 1831, PRUDENCE TURNER FOX, b. at Waterford, CT, 29 Mar 1813 daughter of Samuel and Lucretia (Palmer) Fox;[2399] Prudence d. at Perry, 28 Apr 1896.

iii ALANSON MARCY, b. 16 Oct 1807 (on gravestone); d. at Ingersoll, MI, 15 Jan 1895; m. 1st about 1835, MARY A. BOWEN, b. at Henrietta, NY, 2 Jan 1815 daughter of Darius and Almira (Torrance) Bowen; Mary d. at Hadley, MI, 21 Jun 1852. Alanson m. 2nd at Oakland County, MI, 2 Sep 1853, MARY ANN UPTON, b. 6 Jan 1825 daughter of William and Phebe (Harriman) Upton;[2400] Mary Ann d. at Ingersoll, MI, 11 Sep 1887. Alanson was wounded during the Civil War and was discharged as disabled on 9 Jul 1762. He served with 10th Michigan Infantry.[2401] Alanson resided in Ingersoll and Midland Counites in Michigan. He had six children with wife Mary Bowen and eight children with Mary Upton.[2402]

iv EMILY MARCY, b. 1810; d. at Reading Center, NY, about 1880; m. about 1836, WILLIAM H. HURLEY, b. in NY, likely 13 Jun 1809 son of William and Mary (Mapes) Hurley; William d. after 1870 when living at Reading Center.

v STEPHEN B. MARCY, b. 27 Aug 1813; d. at Omaha, NE, 29 Dec 1899. Stephen seems to have been married three times. His first marriage was to MARTHA who was mother of his son Lyman W. (1844-1872). Stephen married second CHARITY W. who died at Adrian, MI, 1870. Stephen married third, at Omaha, 10 Jan 1871, widow CATHERINE TAYLOR JOHNSON, b. in OH, about 1816; Catherine d. at Omaha, Oct 1895. Son Lyman W. Marcy served with the 4th Michigan Infantry and received a disability discharge on 14 Sep 1864.[2403]

786) SAMUEL MARCY (*John Marcy⁴, Mary Russell Marcy³, Benjamin², Robert¹*), b. at Middletown, Jun 1759 son of John and Hannah (Sharpe) Marcy; d. at Windsor, VT, 18 Feb 1838; m. at Brookfield, MA, 9 Sep 1787, PRISCILLA DORR, b. at Roxbury, MA, 22 Sep 1764 daughter of Moses and Eleanor (Gerald) Dorr; Priscilla d. at Windsor, 8 Feb 1846.

Samuel and Priscilla had a small property in Windsor, Vermont.

In his will dated 6 December 1837 (probate 7 April 1838), Samuel Marcy left his estate, real and personal, to beloved wife Priscilla and to her heirs and assigns forever. Elam Alden of Windsor was named executor. Real estate was three-fourths of an acre and fourteen rods of land with a house and barn.[2404]

In her will written 26 June 1839 (probate 28 March 1846), Priscilla Marcy bequeathed to daughter Sally Gale a bed, the wearing apparel, and twenty dollars. Granddaughter Anna Gale receives bed and bedding. The balance of the personal property is to be divided between daughter Sally Gale and son George Marcy. Son George receives the real estate. George Marcy of Plymouth, New Hampshire was named executor. In a codicil written 24 November 1845, Priscilla revoked the bequest of twenty dollars to daughter Sally. The estate was valued at $407.37 which included the homestead valued at $350 which Priscilla received from her husband in his will.[2405]

There are two known children of Samuel and Priscilla, both likely born at Windsor.

i GEROGE MARCY, b. about 1790; d. at Plainfield, NH, 7 Jun 1862; m. about 1825, CLARA P. REED, b. in NH about 1804; Clara d. at Plainfield, 21 Jul 1875.

[2398] U. S. Revolutionary War Pension and Bounty-Land Warrant Application Files, Case S23784
[2399] Connecticut Town Birth Records, pre-1870 (Barbour Collection)
[2400] Upton, *Upton Family Records*, p 305
[2401] National Park Service. *U.S. Civil War Soldiers, 1861-1865* [database on-line]. Provo, UT, USA: Ancestry.com Operations Inc, 2007.
[2402] Chapman, Brothers, *Midland County, Mich.: Portraits and Biographical Sketches*, Chicago, IL, 1894, p 207
[2403] U.S., Civil War Pension Index: General Index to Pension Files, 1861-1934
[2404] Vermont Wills and Probate, Windsor County, Estate of Samuel Marcy, 1838
[2405] Vermont Wills and Probate, Windsor County, volume 19, pp 60-62

ii   SARAH MARCY, b. about 1792; d. at Lowell, MA, 27 Feb 1876;[2406] m. at Windsor, VT, 20 Oct 1822, SENECA
            GALE, b. at Franconia, NH, 11 Sep 1791 son of Henry and Lucy (Knight) Gale;[2407] Seneca d. at Lowell, 27 Oct
            1877.

787)   MARY "POLLY" MARCY (*John Marcy⁴, Mary Russell Marcy³, Benjamin², Robert¹*), baptized at Middletown, CT, 22
Feb 1761 daughter of John and Hannah (Sharpe) Marcy; d. at Windsor, VT, 7 Sep 1797; m. about 1783, JONATHAN
HODGMAN, likely b. at Concord, MA, 3 Apr 1753 son of Jonathan and Mercy (Buttrick) Hodgman;[2408] Jonathan d. at age 97 at
Fairfax, VT, 16 Jun 1847. Jonathan married second Marvil Burdick on 19 January 1799.
         Jonathan and Polly resided in Windsor. Jonathan was a member of a militia company raised in January 1776 that
marched to Skenesborough (Whitehall).[2409] He is likely the Jonathan Hodgman enrolled in the company of Capt. John Marcy
from Windsor County on 16 October 1780.[2410]
         Three likely children of Mary and Jonathan were identified although there may be others. In 1830, Jonathan headed a
household of five persons at Franklin, Vermont: one male 70 to 79; one male 15 to 19; one male 20 to 29; one female 15 to 19;
and one female 20 to 29.[2411]

i   MARY "POLLY" HODGMAN, b. about 1788

ii   MARSHALL HODGMAN, b. at Windsor, VT, about 1790; m. at Windsor, 14 Dec 1812, LUCY HALL, b. at
            Windsor, 18 Oct 1786 daughter of Jonathan and Mercy (Cady) Hall.[2412]

iii   BENJAMIN HODGMAN, b. about 1790; d. after 1850 when living at Bristol, VT;[2413] m. at Eaton, Québec, 1 Aug
            1819, BETSEY COLBY,[2414] b. about 1800; Betsey d. at New Haven, VT, 9 Jul 1856.

788)   MARY CARY (*Dorcas Marcy Cary⁴, Mary Russell Marcy³, Benjamin², Robert¹*), b. at Mansfield, CT, 16 Jul 1752
daughter of Nathaniel and Dorcas (Marcy) Cary; d. at Fowler, NY, 16 Mar 1839; *likely* m. before 1781, JEDEDIAH KINGSLEY,
b. at Becket, MA, 15 Nov 1753 son of Nathaniel and Sarah (Walden) Kingsley; Jedediah d. at Fowler, 13 Nov 1832.
         Mary and Jedediah resided in Berkshire County, Massachusetts through 1800 and were in Fowler, New York in 1820.
In 1820, Jedediah headed a household of seven in Fowler: one male over 45, one female over 45, two males 26 to 44, one male
under 10, one female under 10, and one female 16 to 25.[2415]
         Jedediah Kingsley enlisted in the company of Capt. Peter Porter in Col. Brown's Berkshire County regiment on 10
July 1777 and was credited with 15 days service. He had a further 16 days of service from 23 September 10 8 October 1777 to
escort prisoners to Springfield. He was sergeant in the company of Capt. Samuel Goodrich from 18 Jul 1779 to 28 August
1779.[2416]
         There are records of seven children for Mary and Jedediah.

i   JEDEDIAH KINGSLEY, b. at Becket, MA, 30 Mar 1781

ii   MARY KINGSLEY, b. at Becket, 10 Nov 1782; d. after 1860 when living at Oconomowoc, WI; m. at Peru, MA, 26
            Nov 1807, ASA WOOD, b. at Upton, MA, 7 Nov 1785 son of Asa and Mary (Goodale) Wood; Asa d. after 1870.

iii   ELEAZER CARY KINGLSEY, b. at Becket, 19 Sep 1785; d. after 1850 when he was living at Oconomowoc, WI.
            Eleazer does not seem to have married.

iv   HORACE KINGSLEY, b. at Becket, 3 Oct 1786

v   IRA D. KINGSLEY, b. at Becket, 15 Apr 1788; d. at Watertown, MN, 12 Sep 1866; m. at Fowler, NY, about 1818,
            PHILENA COLE, b. 1795; Philena d. at St. Louis, MO, 1835. Ira was a physician and an early resident of St.
            Anthony, Minnesota where he was the first town treasurer.[2417]

[2406] Sarah's death record includes parents' names of Samuel and Priscilla Marcy.
[2407] The names of Seneca's parents are given as Henry and Lucy on his death record.
[2408] Massachusetts, Town Birth Records, 1620-1850
[2409] Aldrich, *History of Windsor County, Vermont*, p 294
[2410] U.S., Revolutionary War Rolls, 1775-1783
[2411] 1830; Census Place: Fairfax, Franklin, Vermont; Series: M19; Roll: 183; Page: 5; Family History Library Film: 0027449
[2412] Vermont, Vital Records, 1720-1908
[2413] Year: 1850; Census Place: Bristol, Addison, Vermont; Roll: 920; Page: 325b
[2414] Institut Généalogique Drouin; Montreal, Quebec, Canada; Drouin Collection; Author: Gabriel Drouin, comp.
[2415] 1820 U S Census; Census Place: Fowler, Saint Lawrence, New York; Page: 13; NARA Roll: M33_79; Image: 150
[2416] Massachusetts Soldiers and Sailors of the Revolutionary War, volume 9, p 299
[2417] Holcombe, *Compendium of History and Biography of Minneapolis and Hennepin County, Minnesota*, p 125, p 150

vi   SARAH KINGSLEY, b. at Peru, MA, 26 Feb 1792; d. at Fowler, NY, 10 May 1877; m. about 1817, IRA COLE, b. at Cornwall, CT, 28 Apr 1792 son of James and Annah (Stillson) Cole; Ira d. at Fowler, 24 Nov 1871.

vii   HANNAH KINGSLEY, b. at Peru, 19 Feb 1796

789)   DELIGHT CARY (*Dorcas Marcy Cary⁴, Mary Russell Marcy³, Benjamin², Robert¹*), b. at Mansfield, CT, 6 Sep 1754 daughter of Nathaniel and Dorcas (Marcy) Cary; m. at Mansfield, CT, 15 Jun 1774, TIMOTHY FULLER.
There are records for two children of Delight and Timothy born at Mansfield, Connecticut.[2418]

i   CLARISSA FULLER, b. at Mansfield, CT, 20 Jan 1775; d. 6 Sep 1834; m. at Monson, MA, 29 Nov 1801, ELIJAH RIDDLE, b. at Monson, MA, 27 Jan 1772 son of Thomas and Rebecca (Moulton) Ridel;[2419] Elijah d. at Howell, MI, 10 Oct 1842.

ii   DORCAS FULLER, b. at Mansfield, CT, 20 Aug 1777; d. at Mansfield, 7 Jul 1869; m. at Mansfield, 26 Nov 1795, ROSWELL EATON, b. at Ashford, 9 Mar 1773 son of Samuel and Chloe (Stedman) Eaton; Roswell d. at Mansfield, 27 Aug 1829.

790)   DORCAS CARY (*Dorcas Marcy Cary⁴, Mary Russell Marcy³, Benjamin², Robert¹*), b. at Mansfield, CT, 11 Jul 1756 daughter of Nathaniel and Dorcas (Marcy) Cary; m. at Mansfield, 21 Apr 1779, RUFUS PALMER, b. at Mansfield, 11 Feb 1756 son of Joshua and Ruth (Sargent) Palmer.
Rufus served in the Revolution in the company of Capt. Experience Storrs of Mansfield from 6 May 1775 to 10 December 1775.[2420]
There is record for just one child of Dorcas and Rufus.[2421]
i   ASHER PALMER, b. at Mansfield, CT, 30 Aug 1779; d. at St. Stephens, New Brunswick, 1826; m. about 1813, MARY ANN FULMER, b. in ME, 1790 daughter of George and Nancy (McKenzie) Fulmer; Mary Ann d. at Oakland, CA, 13 Apr 1875.

791)   SARAH CARY (*Dorcas Marcy Cary⁴, Mary Russell Marcy³, Benjamin², Robert¹*), b. at Mansfield, CT, 1 Oct 1764 daughter of Nathaniel and Dorcas (Marcy) Cary; m. 1st about 1785, EBENEZER BUSH. Sarah m. 2nd about 1792, ZACCHAEUS BARNUM, b. about 1763; Zacchaeus d. at Shoreham, VT, 28 Aug 1840.
There are no children known for Sarah and Ebenezer. Zacchaeus and Sarah were parents of four children born at Shoreham, Vermont.

i   ERASTUS WALCOTT BARNUM, b. 18 Sep 1793; d. at Nevada City, CA, 7 Nov 1875; m. at Shoreham, 18 Oct 1815, SARAH JULIA HAND, b. 20 Jun 1786 daughter of Nathan and Anna (Barnes) Hand; Sarah d. at Shoreham, 14 Feb 1855.

ii   JASPER BARNUM, b. 25 Sep 1797; d. (burial at Shoreham, VT), 21 Nov 1859;[2422] m. AMANDA ROE, b. 9 Jun 1800 daughter of Elisha and Electa (Hill) Roe; Amanda d. at Caledonia, WI, 26 Nov 1870 (probate 19 Dec 1870, Racine County, WI with William H. Roe as administrator). Jasper and Amanda did not have children.

iii   OLIVER BARNUM, b. 11 May 1800; d. at Shoreham, 13 Mar 1869; m. ADELINE JONES, b. at Shoreham, 16 Jul 1803 daughter of William Jones; Adeline d. at Shoreham, 5 Apr 1877.

iv   LOYAL C. BARNUM, b. 27 Oct 1805; d. at Bristol, VT, 26 Apr 1863. Loyal was in California with his brother but returned to Vermont. He does not seem to have married.

792)   CHESTER MARCY (*William Marcy⁴, Mary Russell Marcy³, Benjamin², Robert¹*), b. at Woodstock, CT, 6 Nov 1759 son of William and Lucy (Bugbee) Marcy; d. at Hartland, VT, 25 Oct 1845; m. about 1793, MATILDA KING (widow of Daniel Waldo), b. at Brookfield, MA, 6 Mar 1761 daughter of Jonathan and Abigail (Manning) King.
Chester and Matilda resided in Hartland where Chester was town clerk from 1828 to 1830.[2423]

[2418] Dimock, *Births, Baptisms, Marriages and Deaths . . .Mansfield*, p 85
[2419] Rildon, *History of the Ancient Ryedales*, p 278
[2420] Record of Service of Connecticut Men in the War of the Revolution
[2421] Dimock, *Births, Baptisms, Marriages and Deaths . . .Mansfield*, p 135
[2422] Findagrave ID: 42990892
[2423] Darling, *History and Anniversary of Hartland, Vermont*, p 227

In a statement made on 25 January 1833, Chester reported that he first enlisted from Brimfield in January 1776 as a substitute for Mr. Blanchard. He served under Lieut. Gardner in Col. Robinson's regiment. He was discharged after three months and returned to Sturbridge where his father lived with him. In 1777, he moved to Hartland, Vermont and in 1780 enlisted as a substitute for William Ashley and was in the company of Capt. John Benjamin. He was at Newbury, Vermont and discharged after three months. He did not participate in any battles. He reported he was born at Woodstock, Connecticut on 1 November 1759. His brother Gardner Marcy of Hartland made a statement in support of the application.[2424]

Chester and Matilda were parents of six children born at Hartland, Vermont.

i   RUFUS KING MARCY, b. 4 Oct 1797; d. at Plattsburg, 11 Sep 1814.

ii   CHESTER MARCY, b. 16 Mar 1799; d. after 1870 when he was living at Lansing, MI; m. ABIGAIL, b. in NY, about 1814. Abigail d. after 1870.

iii   WILLIAM L. MARCY, b. 2 Jul 1800; d. after 1850 when he was living at Benton, MI; m. LUCY J., b. in NY, about 1806; Lucy was living in Benton in 1850.

iv   HENRY K. MARCY, b. 4 Jan 1802; d. after 1850 likely in Michigan; m. at Bath, NY, 1828,[2425] RUTH ANN SPALDING, b. in PA, 8 May 1806 daughter of William W. and Rebecca (Spalding) Spalding;[2426] Ruth d. at Flint, MI, 24 Apr 1875.

v   MANNING MARCY, b. 20 Nov 1803; d. 25 Jan 1806.

vi   SALLY MARCY

793)   GARDNER MARCY (*William Marcy⁴, Mary Russell Marcy³, Benjamin², Robert¹*), b. at Woodstock, 1762 son of William and Lucy (Bugbee) Marcy; d. at Hartland, VT, 8 Oct 1837; m. 4 Dec 1791, ELIZABETH DANFORTH, b. at Billerica, MA, 1 Apr 1763 daughter of Nicholas and Elizabeth (Jaquith) Danforth; Elizabeth d. at Hancock, 10 May 1857.

On 25 July 1832, Gardner Marcy of Hartland, Vermont, then age seventy, made a statement related to his application for a pension. He enlisted from Wheatly (probably Whately), Massachusetts in the company of Capt. Josiah Smith in the 10th Massachusetts regiment of the Massachusetts line. He served nine months and was discharged at West Point in June 1780. Gardner received a pension, and his widow Elizabeth received a pension following his death. On 19 January 1857, Elizabeth then age ninety-three and resident of Hancock, Vermont made application for bounty land. She was allowed 160 acres of bounty land on warrant number 57753.[2427]

Gardner Marcy and Elizabeth Danforth were parents of five children born at Hartland, Vermont.

i   SULLIVAN MARCY, b. 20 Nov 1792; d. at Windsor, VT, 5 Nov 1871; m. at Hartland, 1 Jan 1818, SARAH WALDRON, b. at Hartland, 14 Oct 1793 daughter of Nathaniel and Lydia (Salisbury) Waldron; Sarah d. at Hartland, 11 Nov 1876.

ii   GARDNER MARCY, b. 5 Nov 1794; d. at Windsor, 23 Dec 1848; m. at Hartland, 20 Mar 1821, MATILDA WALKER, b. 13 Feb 1798 daughter of James and Jane (Morrison) Walker; Matilda d. (buried) at Hartland, 29 Nov 1856.

iii   BETSEY MARCY, b. 28 Oct 1797; d. at Randolph, WI, 1877; m. at Hartland, 4 Jul 1816, ZENAS HOPKINS, b. 1790; Zenas d. at Randolph, 1875.

iv   LUCINDA MARCY, b. 27 Jun 1800; d. at Hartland, 13 Feb 1812.

v   SQUIRE MARCY, b. 12 Mar 1803; d. at Hartland, 23 Jan 1881; m. ELIZA BRADSTREET, b. 5 Jan 1807 daughter of William and Elizabeth (Killam) Bradstreet;[2428] Eliza d. at Hartland, 2 Feb 1881.

794)   OLIVE MARCY (*William Marcy⁴, Mary Russell Marcy³, Benjamin², Robert¹*), b. at Woodstock, CT, about 1763 daughter of William and Lucy (Bugbee) Marcy; m. at Hartland, VT, 10 Jan 1782, WILDER WILLARD, b. 1760 son of Oliver and Thankful (Doolittle) Willard; Wilder d. at Hartland, 1791.

Wilder Willard went to Hartland, Vermont with his father Oliver who was an early settler and prominent member of the town serving as moderator of the first town meeting.[2429]

Olive Marcy and Wilder Willard were parents of three children born at Hartland.

[2424] U. S. Revolutionary War Pension and Bounty-Land Warrant Application Files, Case S21874

[2425] Genealogical Publishing Co.; Baltimore, Maryland; 10,000 Vital Records of Western New York, 1809-1850

[2426] Spalding, *The Spalding Memorial*, p 262

[2427] U. S. Revolutionary War Pension and Bounty-Land Warrant Application Files, Case W18467

[2428] "Descendants of Gov. Bradstreet", NEHGR, Apr 1855, volume 9, p 120

[2429] Darling, *History and Anniversary of Hartland, Vermont*, p 223

i   LUCY WILLARD, b. 12 Jan 1783; m. at Hartland, 29 Dec 1802, JOSIAH JAQUITH, b. at Wilmington, MA, 22 Apr 1778 son of William and Rebecca (Rogers) Jaquith; Josiah d. at Medina County, OH, 1843 (probate 12 Oct 1843). It is not clear when Lucy died, but Josiah had one and perhaps two other wives after Lucy's death. His widow at probate was Marinda (Campbell).

ii   SYBIL WILLARD, b. 12 May 1785; d. at Orange, VT, 11 Mar 1837; m. EBENEZER MELENDY, b. at Sutton, MA, 10 Aug 1781 son of Ebenezer and Azubah (Sibley) Melendy; Ebenezer d. at Orange, 28 Jun 1871.

iii   SCHUYLER WILLARD, b. 6 Jun 1789; d. at Royalton, NY, May 1850; m. about 1822, CLARISSA STONE (widow of Benjamin Montgomery), b. at Royalton, VT, 11 Jul 1794 daughter of Nathan and Clarissa (Smith) Stone; Clarissa d. at Royalton, NY, before 1830 (there was no adult female in the home in the 1830 census). Schuyler m. 2nd HANNAH who has not been identified but was his widow at probate (21 May 1850).

795)   WILLARD MARCY (*William Marcy⁴, Mary Russell Marcy³, Benjamin², Robert¹*), b. at Woodstock, CT, 3 Oct 1764 son of William and Lucy (Bugbee) Marcy; d. at Hartland, VT, 31 Jan 1849; m. LYDIA PIKE, b. at Sturbridge, 3 Mar 1767 daughter of John and Mehitable (Howard) Pike; Lydia d. at Hartland, 4 Mar 1839.
    Willard and Lydia resided in Hartland, Vermont where they were parents of ten children.

i   WILLARD MARCY, b. at Cornish, NH, 28 Aug 1788; d. at Hartland, VT, 19 Aug 1872; m. ASENATH PHELPS, b. at Lyme, CT, 10 Aug 1789 daughter of Thaddeus and Mehitable (Leete) Phelps;[2430] Asenath d. at Hartland, 27 Feb 1871.

ii   MEHITABLE MARCY, b. at Grantham, NH, 11 May 1790; d. at Hartland, VT, 11 Feb 1864; m. 1817, as his second wife, ELIAS BRIMMER HOADLEY, baptized at Brookline, MA, 19 Aug 1770 son of Thomas and Mercy (Stone) Hoadley; Elias d. at Hartland, 29 Mar 1843. Elias was first married to Sarah French.

iii   CLINTON MARCY, b. at Grantham, NH, 24 Dec 1791; d. at Magnolia, NY, 10 Jan 1859; m. 1st at Hartland, 29 Jan 1817, CYNTHIA BLANCHARD, b. at Bradford, NH, 3 Mar 1797 daughter of Jacob and Elizabeth (Crawford) Blanchard; Cynthia d. at Harmony, NY, 27 Jan 1832. Clinton m. 2nd CHARLOTTE HURLBURT, b. in CT, 1805; Charlotte d. 12 Sep 1874.

iv   ADOLPHUS MARCY, b. at Hartland, VT, 13 Jun 1793; d. at Conneaut, OH; m. 1814, BETSEY KENDALL, b. 1795; Betsey d. at Conneaut, 24 Aug 1879. Betsey married second Henry Ball.

v   HIRAM MARCY, b. about 1794; d. at Conneaut, 1856; m. at Woodstock, VT, 15 May 1831, PARTHANA "BATHANA" BLACKWELL, b. in VT, 1812; Parthana d. at Springfield, PA, 1878.

vi   BUCKLEY MARCY, b. at Hartland, 14 Sep 1796; d. at Hartland, 21 Feb 1876; m. 1st about 1821, MARY HADLOCK, b. 1797; Mary d. at Hartland, 29 Dec 1834. Buckley m. 2nd at Windsor, 4 Feb 1836, AMARILLA DUTTON, b. at Waterford, VT, 25 Jan 1799 daughter of Zachariah and Sarah Amarilla (Taylor) Dutton; Amarilla d. at Hartland, 27 Sep 1888.

vii   LUCINDA MARCY, b. at Hartland, 20 Aug 1801; d. at Hartland, 14 Dec 1843; m. at Hartland, 5 Sep 1836, ISRAEL GILBERT, b. at Plainfield, NH, 1801 son of Nathaniel and Rachel (Strong) Gilbert; Israel d. at Randolph, VT, 13 May 1868.

viii   HARRIET MARCY, b. at Hartland, 1804; d. at Hartland, 19 Jun 1879; m. at Hartland, 1 May 1850, JOHN VAUGHN, b. in VT, 1800; John d. at Hartland, 31 Oct 1886. In her will written 13 May 1878, Harriet left her estate to her husband John, and if she survived John, the estate to go to the heirs or representatives of Jabez Vaughan, Elan Vaughan, and Jonah Vaughan.[2431]

ix   MARY MARCY, b. about 1807; d. at Hartland, 12 Apr 1844; m. at Hartland, 25 Mar 1827, ASAHEL BAGLEY, b. 1799 likely son of Thomas J. and Olive (Perkins) Bagley; Asahel d. at Hartland, 11 Jul 1849.

x   JAMES M. MARCY, b. at Hartland, 8 Aug 1808; d. at Pierpont, OH, 13 Apr 1876; m. ANNER D. SHERMAN, b. in NY, 1813; Anner d. at Pierpont, 26 Dec 1878.

796)   WINTHROP MARCY (*William Marcy⁴, Mary Russell Marcy³, Benjamin², Robert¹*), b. at Woodstock, CT, 28 Jun 1767 son of William and Lucy (Bugbee) Marcy; d. at Windsor, VT, 1841 (probate 1 Apr 1841); m. 1st at Hartland, VT, 7 Nov 1793, ABIGAIL SARGENT daughter of Isaac and Ruth (Blaisdell) Sargent. Winthrop m. 2nd at Cornish, NH, 15 Mar 1806, OLIVE

2430 Phelps and Servin, *The Phelps Family in America*, volume I, p 284
2431 Vermont Wills and Probate, Windsor County, volume 36, p 258

AYERS. Winthrop m. 3rd at Hartland, 1 Feb 1827, CATHERINE RAWSON, b. about 1763; Catherine d. at Hartland, 25 Sep 1837. Winthrop m. 4th at Hartland, 13 Apr 1840, SOPHIA KEYES, b. at Reading, VT, 27 Mar 1789 daughter of Solomon and Thankful (·) Keyes; Sophia d. at West Windsor, VT, 15 Aug 1876.

The estate of Winthrop Marcy entered probate 1 April 1841 with Winthrop Marcy, Jr. as administrator. The record contains only a personal estate inventory of $131.35.[2432]

Winthrop Marcy and Abigail Sargent were parents of five children born (recorded) at Hartland, Vermont.

i   OLIVE MARCY, b. 12 May 1794; d. at Hartland, 9 Oct 1877; m. ELIJAH HOISINGTON, b. at Windsor, VT, 29 Aug 1783 son of Elias and Mary (Stowell) Hoisington;[2433] Elijah d. at Hartland, 24 Dec 1847.

ii   RUTH MARCY, b. 17 Apr 1796; d. at Hartland, 8 Feb 1878; m. ELIJAH GROW, b. at Hartland, 11 Aug 1796 son of John Marshall and Polly (Stowell) Grow;[2434] Elijah d. at Hartland, 28 Sep 1863.

iii   ISAAC MARCY, b. 15 Nov 1798; may have died young

iv   GEORGE WASHINGTON MARCY, b. 24 Feb 1801; d. after 1850 when living at Montgomery, VT; m. at Bridgewater, VT, 29 Mar 1829, EMILY HOISINGTON, b. in VT about 1808; Emily was living in 1850.

v   LEVI MARCY, b. about 1803; d. at Hartland, 2 Dec 1862; m. about 1831, MARY ANN KENDALL, b. at Woodstock, VT, 1811 daughter of Amaziah and Lydia (Waldron) Kendall; Mary Ann d. at Lebanon, NH, 17 Mar 1892. After Levi's death, Mary Ann married Moses G. Kelley on 23 Apr 1865.

Winthrop Marcy and Olive Ayers were parents of two children.

i   WINTHROP MARCY, b. about 1806; d. at Windsor, VT, 17 Apr 1880; m. PHILYNIA MARIA STONE, b. at Plainfield, NH, 15 Nov 1816 daughter of Abel and Patience (Goldthwait) Stone;[2435] Maria d. at Woodstock, VT, 4 Apr 1895.

ii   ITHAMAR MARCY, b. 1809; d. at Hartland, 27 Aug 1887; m. at Cornish, NH, 3 Apr 1837, MARY L. SMITH, b. at Cornish, 25 Jun 1819 daughter of Benjamin and Mary (Ayers) Smith;[2436] Mary d. at Hartland, 18 Jul 1901.

797)   SALOME MARCY (*William Marcy⁴, Mary Russell Marcy³, Benjamin², Robert¹*), b. at Sturbridge, MA, 1 Apr 1771 daughter of William and Lucy (Bugbee) Marcy; d. at Cornish, NH, 22 Jul 1809; m. at Hartland, VT, about 1788, EBENEZER PIKE, b. at Sturbridge, 9 Nov 1764 son of John and Mehitable (Howard) Pike; Ebenezer d. at Northumberland, NH, 12 Aug 1819. Ebenezer married second Lucinda Kimball (widow of Alexander Waters) on 28 Sep 1809.

Ebenezer Pike as a young man settled in Cornish, New Hampshire where he was a farmer. He also had a mill on "Blow-Me-Down" brook. After the death of his second wife, Ebenezer moved to Northumberland, New Hampshire.[2437]

Salome Marcy and Ebenezer Pike were parents of four children. Ebenezer also had two children with his second wife Lucinda *Kimball* Waters.

i   EBENEZER PIKE, b. 1789; d. at Cornish, NH, 21 Nov 1861; m. 1st 14 Feb 1827, SARAH CHASE BRYANT, b. at Cornish, 20 Dec 1798 daughter of Sylvanus and Judith (Chase) Bryant; Sarah d. at Cornish, 5 Mar 1831. Ebenezer m. 2nd 16 Apr 1835, MARY HYDE, b. at Chelsea, VT, 2 Jan 1811 daughter of Elihu and Mary (Hatch) Hyde; Mary d. at Chelsea (buried at Cornish), 15 Oct 1892.

ii   PLINY PIKE, b. Jan 1793; d. at Cornish, NH, 26 Dec 1872. Pliny did not marry.

iii   CHESTER PIKE. Reported as living in Northumberland, NH where he died at age 26 without marrying.[2438]

iv   LUCY M. PIKE, b. at Windsor, VT, 1799; d. at Lawrence, MA, 22 Dec 1868; m. 3 Jan 1825, JOHN COLE, b. at Plainfield, NH, 4 Jul 1797 son of Daniel and Edith (Wilbur) Cole; John d. at Lawrence, 24 Jan 1880.

798)   LEVI MARCY (*William Marcy⁴, Mary Russell Marcy³, Benjamin², Robert¹*), b. at Sturbridge, MA, 3 Sep 1773 son of William and Lucy (Bugbee) Marcy; d. at Hartland, VT, 7 Mar 1838; m 1796, RUTH SARGENT, b. 13 Apr 1773 daughter of Isaac and Ruth (Blaisdell) Sargent; Ruth d. at Hartland, 15 May 1847.

[2432] Vermont Wills and Probate, Windsor County, Estate of Winthrop Marcy, recorded in volume 16, p 375

[2433] Vermont, Vital Records, 1720-1908; names of Elias Hoisington and Mary Stowell are given on birth record.

[2434] Stowell, *Stowell Genealogy*, p 104

[2435] Names of parents are given as Abel Stone and Patience Goldthwait on her death record.

[2436] Names of parents are given as Benjamin Smith and Mary Ayers on her death record.

[2437] Child, History of the Town of Cornish, p 284

[2438] Child, *History of the Town of Cornish*, volume II, p 285

Levi Marcy had a tannery in Fieldsville a neighborhood of Hartland. He also had a farm and traded goods in Boston. Before the introduction of trains, he took goods of tanned leather, cheese, apples, and beans on double-sleigh.[2439]

Levi and Ruth were parents of five children born at Hartland, Vermont.

i SALOME MARCY, b. 27 Apr 1798; d. at Windsor, VT, 10 Sep 1885; m. HENRY WILLARD MOORE, b. 1799;[2440] Willard d. at Windsor, 1853.

ii NANCY MARCY, b. 13 Mar 1800; d. at Woodstock, VT, 9 May 1862; m. 25 Mar 1822, JASON DARLING, b. at Woodstock, VT, 19 Apr 1796 son of Seth and Chloe (Marsh) Darling; Jason d. at Woodstock, VT, 7 Feb 1864.

iii ABIEL B. MARCY, b. 19 Sep 1802; d. at Claremont, NH, 27 Jul 1887; m. at Woodstock, VT, 17 Dec 1826, PAMELIA BURNHAM BAILEY, b. at Pomfret, VT, 19 May 1804 daughter of Elisha and Pamelia (Burnham) Bailey;[2441] Pamelia d. at Claremont, 17 Oct 1895.

iv LUCY MARCY, b. 7 Sep 1807; d. at Hartland, 17 May 1887; m. JAMES ADDISON GATES, b. at Hartland, 2 Apr 1803 son of Zelotes and Margaret (Rawson) Gates; James Addison d. at Hartland, 1 Aug 1888.

v HANNAH SARGENT MARCY, b. about 1807; d. at Woodstock, VT, Oct 1887;[2442] m. about 1826 (oldest child born about 1826), IRA MOWER,[2443] b. at Waitsfield, VT, about 1800; Ira d. at Woodstock, 18 Oct 1869.

799) MARY "POLLY" MARCY (*William Marcy⁴, Mary Russell Marcy³, Benjamin², Robert¹*), b. at Hartland, VT, 20 Nov 1797 daughter of William and Roseanne (Tucker) Marcy; d. at St. Albans, VT, 6 Nov 1877; m. at Hartland, 21 Aug 1820, NATHAN PERKINS, b. at Woodstock, VT, 8 Apr 1793 son of Nathan and Hannah (Sturtevant) Perkins; Nathan d. at St. Albans, 6 Apr 1865.

Mary and Nathan resided primarily in the village of Morrisville, Vermont where Nathan had a trade in woolen manufacture. Mary and Nathan located in St. Albans later in life where they both died.

Eldest son Charles worked with his father for a time, but then studied law with Judge Luke Poland. Charles ultimately settled in Galesville, Wisconsin where he served in several local offices including town clerk and was admitted to the bar in 1882.[2444]

In his will dated 11 March 1865 (proved 13 May 1865), Nathan Perkins of St. Albans bequeathed all his personal estate to his beloved wife Mary to be hers, forever. There were no claims against the estate.[2445]

Mary and Nathan were parents of six children.

i CHARLES EDGAR PERKINS, b. about 1822; d. at Arcadia, WI, 11 Feb 1899; m. at Johnson, VT, 2 Apr 1848, MARY B. STEARNS, b. at Lebanon, NH, 17 Jan 1825 daughter of John and Mehitable (Leonard) Stearns; Mary d. after 1910 when she was living at Galesville, WI.

ii MARY MELVINA PERKINS, b. about 1824; d. at Morristown, 1896; m. about 1858, as his second wife, Dr. ALMERIN TINKER, b. at Worthington, MA, 18 Sep 1799 son of John and Cynthia (Jones) Tinker; Almerin d. at Morristown, 1880. Almerin was first married to Caroline Vilas.

iii SARAH JANE PERKINS, b. at Pittsford, VT, about 1826; d. at Waterbury, VT, 28 Nov 1880; m. 1ˢᵗ about 1852, MARVIN GATES FORMAN, b. in Canada, about 1829; Marvin d. about 1870. Sarah m. 2ⁿᵈ at St. Albans, VT, GIDEON D. WILLIAMS, b. about 1824 son of Samuel and V. C. (Simmons) Williams.[2446] At the probate of her estate, children Henry M. Forman and Florence E. Forman and husband G. D. Williams requested that Henry M. Forman be named administrator of her estate.[2447]

iv LAURA ANN PERKINS, b. 1829; d. at Morristown, VT, 15 Aug 1831.

v NATHAN HENRY PERKINS, b. at Morristown, VT, May 1831; d. after 1876 when he was in Oregon. Nathan was an adventurer. He obtained his passport 6 Dec 1852[2448] and departed for Australia and arrived at Port Phillip

[2439] Darling, *History and Anniversary of Hartland, Vermont*, p 244
[2440] Gravestone gives age as 65 which would give birth in 1788, but 1850 census gives age as 51.
[2441] Parmelia's father's name is given as Elisha on her death record.
[2442] Death record of Hannah S. Mower gives her maiden name as Marcy and gives father's name as Levi Marcy and place of birth as Hartland, Vermont.
[2443] Some published genealogies give the name of Hannah's husband as Ira Wood, but that does not seem to be the case.
[2444] Lewis Publishing Company, *Biographical History of La Crosse, Trempealeau, and Buffalo Counties, Wisconsin*, pp 755-756
[2445] Vermont Wills and Probate, Franklin County, Estate of Nathan Perkins, St. Albans, No. 96
[2446] The names of Gideon's parents are given on the marriage record.
[2447] Vermont Wills and Probate, Washington County, volume 2, p 390
[2448] U.S. Passport Applications, 1795-1925; National Archives and Records Administration (NARA); Washington D.C.; Roll #: 40; Volume #: Roll 040 - 01 Aug 1852-31 Dec 1852

Bay, Australia on 21 April 1853.[2449] He left Australia in Mar 1861[2450] and was in Oregon in 1870. It is not known if he married.

vi   GEORGE EDWIN PERKINS, b. about 1836; d. at Butte, MT, 21 Nov 1914; m. at Virginia City, NV, 5 Jan 1878, ROSINA BENJAMIN, b. in England about 1841; Rose d. after 1890. George and Rosina had a daughter Mamie Laura Perkins who married Henry Swanson. George was a merchant.

800)   SARAH "SALLY" MARCY (*William Marcy⁴, Mary Russell Marcy³, Benjamin², Robert¹*), b. at Hartland, VT, 22 Oct 1799 daughter of William and Roseanne (Tucker) Marcy; d. at Morristown, VT, 5 Dec 1880; m. DANIEL GILBERT, b. at Hartford, VT, 17 Apr 1796 son of Nathaniel and Rachel (Strong) Gilbert; Daniel d. at Morristown, 18 Mar 1874.
         Daniel and Sally resided in Morrisville Village of Morristown, Vermont. Daniel was a cabinetmaker and had a furniture store on lower Main Street in Morrisville. He became postmaster of Morristown on 1 December 1841, an office he held for most of the next twenty years.[2451]
         There are six children known for Sarah Marcy and Daniel Gilbert born at Morrisville, Vermont.

i   SARAH LOUISE GILBERT, b. Dec 1821; d. at Morrisville, 17 Mar 1907; m. SIDNEY R. RUTHERFORD, b. 1824 son of Major and Thirza (Wheaton) Rutherford;[2452] Sydney d. at Morrisville, 15 Jun 1880.

ii   DANIEL M. GILBERT, b. about 1825

iii   DANIEL A. GILBERT, b. 1829; d. at Morristown, 10 Nov 1890; m. at Morristown, 2 Jan 1860, KATHERINE ADELINE CLEMENT, b. at West Rutland, VT, 14 Aug 1838 daughter of William R. and Eliza A. (Perry) Clement; Katherine d. at Morristown, 5 Jul 1921.

iv   NATHANIEL GILBERT, b. 1832; d. at Morrisville, 13 Jan 1842.

v   WILLIAM E. GILBERT, b. 1838; d. at Morrisville, 7 Sep 1841.

vi   Daughter, b. 1842 and d. 15 Aug 1842.

801)   PRISCILLA MARCY (*Zebadiah Marcy⁴, Mary Russell Marcy³, Benjamin², Robert¹*), b. at Woodstock, 6 Jan 1760 daughter of Zebadiah and Priscilla (Morris) Marcy; d. at Navarino, NY, 15 Aug 1834; m. about 1778, JEDEDIAH "DYER" CONVERSE, baptized at Thompson, CT, 28 Jul 1754 son of Josiah and Mary (Sabin) Converse; Dyer d. at East Windsor, CT, 11 Sep 1818.
         Priscilla and Dyer were parents of five children likely born at Willington, Connecticut.

i   ADIN M. CONVERSE, b. 1779; d. at Navarino, NY, Jul 1816; m. his fourth cousin, PHEBE BIRCHARD (*Lydia Farnum Birchard⁵, Henry Farnum⁴, Phebe Russell Farnum³, Thomas², Robert¹*), b. at Ashford, 16 Apr 1783 daughter of Phineas and Lydia (Farnum) Birchard.

ii   EDWARD MORRIS CONVERSE, b. at Willington, 8 Apr 1788; d. at Lodi, NY, 8 Jan 1879; m. at Southington, CT, 4 Dec 1811, PHILA PECK, b. 31 Aug 1787 daughter of David and Huldah (Cogswell) Peck; Phila d. at Southington, CT, 24 Nov 1873.

iii   NANCY CONVERSE, b. about 1793; d. at Marcellus, NY, 19 Feb 1877; m. at Ashford, 12 Dec 1812, SAMUEL LAMB, b. 1789 son of Nathan and Abiah (Preston) Lamb; Samuel d. at Marcellus, 20 Jan 1854.

iv   DEBORAH CONVERSE, b. 1795; d. at Sunfield, MI, 21 Aug 1842; m. about 1811, WILLIAM AUGUSTUS WELLS, b. in England (according to death records of one of their children).

v   ORRIN CONVERSE, d. at Willington, 16 Nov 1810

802)   LOVINA MARCY (*Zebadiah Marcy⁴, Mary Russell Marcy³, Benjamin², Robert¹*), b. at Ashford, 27 Jan 1763 daughter of Zebadiah and Priscilla (Morris) Marcy; d. at Willington, 10 Nov 1840; m. 1ˢᵗ at Willington, 4 Dec 1788, as his second wife, SAMUEL DUNTON, b. at Wrentham, MA, 10 Nov 1748 son of Samuel and Sarah (Bennet) Dunton; Samuel d. at Willington, 1

[2449] Victoria, Australia, Assisted and Unassisted Passenger Lists, 1839-1923; Series: VPRS 7667; Series Title: Inward Overseas Passenger Lists (Foreign Ports) [Microfiche Copy of VPRS 947]

[2450] Web: Victoria, Australia, Outward Passenger Index, 1852-1915; Public Record Office of Victoria; North Melbourne, Victoria, Australia; Series Number: VPRS 948

[2451] Mower, *History of Morristown*, pp 240-241

[2452] The names of Sidney's parent are given as Major Rutherford and Thirza on his death record.

May 1813. Lovina m. 2nd at Willington, 17 Aug 1815, as his second wife, ELIJAH HOLT, b. at Willington, 24 Oct 1757 son of Caleb and Mary (Merrick) Holt; Elijah d. at Willington, 4 Jul 1817. Elijah was first married to Molly Simmons.

Samuel Dunton served as a sergeant during the Revolution in Wadsworth Brigade.[2453]

In his will written 21 February 1810 (probate 6 November 1813), Samuel Dunton notes that his five first children namely Amasa, Josiah, Leonard, Sally, and Lois have received £40 each, except Josiah received £33 10 shillings; Josiah will receive an amount to bring his up to £40. Sons Amasa, Josiah, and Leonard also receive land in Willington. Two oldest daughters, Sally Stewart and Lois Eldridge, each receives $33 to bring their portion to £50 which is their full portion of the estate. His two youngest daughters, Lodicia and Eliza, each receives one dollar and the remainder of the estate both real and personal goes to his beloved wife Lovina. Wife Lovina Dunton was named executrix.[2454]

Samuel Dunton and his first wife Lois Pearl were parents of seven children. Lovina Marcy and Samuel Dunton were parents of three children born at Willington.

i   RALPH DUNTON, b. 19 Nov 1792; d. 14 Jan 1793.

ii   LODICIA DUNTON, b. 22 Sep 1794; d. at Willington, 1 Sep 1857; m. 10 Apr 1814, JOSEPH MERRICK, b. at Willington, 2 Jul 1789 son of Timothy and Mehitable (Atwood) Merrick; Joseph d. at Willington, 5 Jan 1854.

iii   ELIZA DUNTON, b. 12 Apr 1801; d. at Willington, 8 Apr 1850; m. at Willington, 24 Sep 1819, ORRIN HOLT, b. at Willington, 13 Mar 1793 son of Timothy and Esther (Scripture) Holt; Orrin d. at Willington, 20 Jun 1855.

803)   HANNAH MARCY (*Zebadiah Marcy[4], Mary Russell Marcy[3], Benjamin[2], Robert[1]*), b. at Ashford, 1766 daughter of Zebadiah and Priscilla (Morris) Marcy; d. at Ashford, 6 Aug 1828; m. about 1792, as his second wife, DANIEL DIMOCK, b. at Ashford, 15 Jul 1750 son of Ebenezer and Mary (Keyes) Dimock. Daniel d. at Ashford, 2 Feb 1823.

In his will written 6 August 1821 (proved 12 March 1823), Daniel Dimick bequeathed to beloved wife Hannah the use of all his lands and buildings so long as she lives. She also receives one-half of the household furniture. Daughters Sally Farnham, Betsey Dimick, and Tirzah Harris each receives fifty dollars. Son Daniel Dimick receive one hundred dollars and son Timothy Dimock receives the wearing apparel and a comfortable support in sickness and in health. Grandson Philip Pearl receives fifty dollars. The remainder of the estate goes to son Origin Dimick who is also named executor.[2455]

Daniel Dimock had seven children with his first wife Zilpha Simmons. Hannah and Daniel were parents of one child.

i   ORIGEN DIMOCK, b. at Willington, 19 Dec 1796; d. at Moline, IL, 17 Sep 1871; m. 1818, ELIZA LYON, b. at Aurelius, NY, 1798;[2456] Eliza d. at Moline, 29 Jul 1875.

804)   DORCAS MARCY (*Zebadiah Marcy[4], Mary Russell Marcy[3], Benjamin[2], Robert[1]*), b. at Ashford, 15 Mar 1768 daughter of Zebadiah and Priscilla (Morris) Marcy; d. at Randolph, VT, 1803; m. at Randolph, VT, 1 Feb 1786, JOSEPH LAMB, b. at Hopkinton, RI, 22 May 1763 son of Nathan and Lydia (Plummer) Lamb; Joseph d. at Sheldon, VT, 25 Mar 1848. Joseph married second Clara Willard on 22 Jan 1804.

Dorcas and Joseph settled in Randolph, Vermont where their ten children were born. After Dorcas's death, Joseph remarried and moved on to Sheldon, Vermont.

The distribution of the estate of Dorcas's father Zebadiah Marcy made on 29 April 1807 included the heirs of daughter Dorcas Lamb: Joseph Lamb, Morris Lamb, Dorcas Billings, Selenda Willard, Lovina Holt, Lydia Lamb, Polly Lamb, and Lucinda Lamb.[2457]

On 29 March 1818, Joseph Lamb appeared to make application for pension. He enlisted from Ashford in July 1779 in the company of Capt. Dana in Col. Wills regiment for a term of eight months. In July 1780, he enlisted in the company of Capt. Shumway for six months. In January 1781, he enlisted for a three-year term from Pelham, Massachusetts in the company of Capt. Wade in Col. Jackson's 8th Massachusetts regiment of the Continental army, and he was discharged 23 December 1783. He was discharged at West Point by Maj. Gen. Henry Knox. He was in "several skirmishes but no important battles." On 12 July 1820, Joseph then resident of Sheldon, Vermont age fifty-six provided an additional statement related to his pension. At that time, he had 75 acres of property that was mortgaged, and he is unable to pay. Due to his inability to pay and other debts, he was confined to jail. His household consisted of his wife aged 44 and four sons and one daughter under his care, the oldest age 15. Joseph's widow Clara later received a widow's pension. Among the statements in support of Clara's pension were those made 2 May 1853 by Joseph Lamb, Jr. aged fifty-seven of Boston, Ohio and Mrs. Silenda Willard aged sixty-five of Cleveland, Ohio.[2458]

[2453] Eldridge, *Eldridge Genealogy*, p 11

[2454] *Connecticut. Probate Court (Stafford District)*; Probate Place: *Tolland, Connecticut, Probate Records, Vol 7-8, 1809-1815*, volume 8, pp 98-100

[2455] Connecticut Wills and Probate, Tolland, Probate Records volume 13, pp 296-298

[2456] Eliza's place of birth is on her gravestone; findagrave ID: 33650125

[2457] Connecticut Wills and Probate, Hartford, Stafford District, Town of Willington, Estate of Zebadiah Marcy, Case 1463.

[2458] U. S. Revolutionary War Pension and Bounty-Land Warrant Application Files, Case W9105

The youngest son of Dorcas and Joseph, Charles Morris Lamb, attended Claremont and Randolph Academies in Vermont and later studied law. He was admitted to the Orange County Bar in 1850 and practiced law in Tunbridge, Vermont.[2459]

Dorcas Marcy and Joseph Lamb were parents of ten children. Joseph also had children with his second wife Clara Willard.

i   DORCAS MARCY LAMB, b. 1787; d. at Hartland, VT, 16 Dec 1825; m. at Hartland, 4 Jun 1806, WILLARD BILLINGS, b. at Hartland, VT 1782 son of Nathan and Myra (Willard) Billings; Willard d. at Hartland, 22 Dec 1855.

ii   SELINDA LAMB, b. 21 Oct 1788; d. at Cleveland, 18 Jan 1865; m. at Hartland, 20 Mar 1808, JOHN OLIVER WILLARD, b. at Windsor, VT, 19 Jan 1789 son of Eli and Polly (Cady) Willard; d. at Cleveland, 19 Mar 1832. Selinda lived with her son Elliott S. Willard prior to her death.

iii   LOVINA LAMB, b. at Randolph, VT, 17 Jan 1791; d. at Willington, CT, 5 May 1856; m. at Willington, 13 Aug 1809, her fourth cousin, ROYAL HOLT (*Caleb Holt⁵, Caleb Holt⁴, Abiel Holt³, Mary Russell Holt², Robert¹*), b. at Willington, 2 Dec 1786 son of Caleb and Sarah (Goodale) Holt; Royal d. at Willington, 20 Feb 1864.

iv   LYDIA LAMB, b. at Randolph, VT, 28 Mar 1792; d. at Mantua, IA, 13 Jan 1884; m. 1 Jan 1814, STEPHEN MILLER, b. 1787 son of William and Dorcas (Trescott) Miller; Stephen d. at Portage County, OH, 16 Jul 1852.

v   THOMAS LAMB, b. at Randolph, 25 Oct 1794; d. 1803.

vi   JOSEPH LAMB, b. at Randolph, 19 Sep 1795; d. at Boston Heights, OH, 10 Oct 1875; m. at Portage County, OH, 17 Apr 1828, MALINDA OZMUN, b. in NY, about 1810 likely daughter of Isaac and Maria (Neuman) Ozmun; Malinda d. at Hudson, OH, 17 Apr 1884.

vii   MARY "POLLY" LAMB, b. at Randolph, 30 May 1797; Polly was living in 1807.

viii   LUCINDA LAMB, b. 1798; d. at Richford, VT, 26 Aug 1864; m. at Hartland, 19 Jan 1817, PORTER BLISS, b. at Hartland, 1795 son of David and Polly (Elmore) Bliss; Porter d. at Richford, 17 Feb 1873.

ix   EBENEZER LAMB, b. 21 Aug 1801; d. 1802.

x   CHARLES MORRIS LAMB, b. 6 Apr 1803; d. at Royalton, VT, 20 May 1891; m. 12 Jan 1832, LOUISA MARIA HUTCHINSON, b. at Tunbridge, 1 Oct 1808 daughter of Amos and Jerusha (Rix) Hutchinson; Louisa d. at South Royalton, 6 Oct 1895.

805)   MARTHA MARCY (*Zebadiah Marcy⁴, Mary Russell Marcy³, Benjamin², Robert¹*), b. at Ashford, 29 Oct 1769 daughter of Zebadiah and Priscilla (Morris) Marcy; d.at Willington, 11 Aug 1853; m. at Willington, 26 Nov 1807, THOMAS KNOWLTON, b. at Ashford, 13 Jul 1765 son of Thomas and Anna (Keyes) Knowlton; Thomas d. at Willington, 14 Apr 1858.

On 18 August 1832, Thomas Knowlton aged sixty-seven of Willington made application for a pension related to his service in the Revolution. He enlisted 9 August 1782 under Lieut. Daniel Knowlton in the company of Capt. Benjamin Durkee. Daniel Knowlton was brother of his father Thomas Knowlton who was killed at Harlem Heights at the time the British took possession of New York. He served at the forts at New London and Groton. He was discharged 1 March 1784. He lived at Ashford at the time of his enlistment, was in Andover, Vermont after the war, then in Hartford, Connecticut, and lived in Willington for the past 24 years.[2460]

In his will written 10 April 1855 (proved 18 May 1858), Thomas Knowlton bequeathed to his daughter Martha E. Marcy an annual payment of $240 to be paid in semi-annual payments of $120 made by his grandchildren. The American Baptist Missionary Union receives the dividends and income from ten shares of the New York and Erie Railroad Company for the purpose of promulgating the gospel among the North American Indians. The Baptist Church of Willington receives the income from twenty shares of the railroad stock, half to be used for poor persons in Willington although no one family is to receive more than six dollars in one year. The remainder of the estate goes to his grandchildren. Martha E. Marcy is named executrix.[2461]

Martha Marcy and Thomas Knowlton were parents of two children born at Willington.

i   THOMAS M. KNOWLTON, b. 10 Sep 1808; d. 5 Jul 1810.

ii   MARTHA E. KNOWLTON, b. 14 Dec 1811; d. at Willington, 8 Sep 1884; m. at Willington, 18 Apr 1832, WILLIAM WATSON MARCY, b. at Willington, 16 Nov 1805 son of Reuben and Hannah (Sumner) Marcy; William d. at Willington, 3 May 1854.

[2459] Aldrich and Holmes, *History of Windsor County, Vermont*, p 980
[2460] U. S. Revolutionary War Pension and Bounty-Land Warrant Application Files, Case S31803
[2461] Connecticut Wills and Probate, Tolland, wills volume 5, 99 167-169, will of Thomas Knowlton

806)   MARY "POLLY" MARCY (*Zebadiah Marcy⁴, Mary Russell Marcy³, Benjamin², Robert¹*), b. at Willington, about 1779 daughter of Zebadiah and Priscilla (Morris) Marcy; m. by 1806, JAMES CURTIS, b. at Ashford, 19 Mar 1779 son of Ransom and Alice (Whitten) Curtis; James d. at Machias, NY, 1863.

James was a carpenter and joiner. James and Mary were in Onondaga County, New York and the family moved to Concord, New York in 1832.[2462] They were parents of four children likely all born in Onondaga County.

i   ZEBADIAH CURTIS, b. about 1806; d. at Concord, NY, about 1840; m. LOVICE HALL.

ii   NANCY MARIA CURTIS, b. 1808; d. at Concord, NY, 14 Feb 1852; m. ERASTUS MAYO, b. at Oxford, MA, 7 Feb 1808 son of Jonathan and Lois (Kingsbury) Mayo; Erastus d. at Concord, 3 Oct 1901.

iii   WILLIAM T. CURTIS, b. 1811; d. at Aurora, NY, 21 Aug 1882; m. 1st, CHARLOTTE M. WILLIAMS, b. about 1817; Charlotte d. at East Aurora, 22 May 1844. William m. 2nd, ANGELINE WILLIAMS, b. about 1810; Angeline d. at East Aurora, Feb 1885.

iv   ORIGIN D. CURTIS, b. 27 Jun 1818; d. after 1881 at Polk County, MN; m. 1839, LUCY MAYO, b. about 1815 daughter of Jonathan and Lois (Kingsbury) Mayo. Origin lived in Concord, NY until 1881 when he moved to Polk County.[2463]

807)   CYLINDA MARCY (*Zebadiah Marcy⁴, Mary Russell Marcy³, Benjamin², Robert¹*), b. at Stafford, 27 Jun 1780 daughter of Zebadiah and Priscilla (Morris) Marcy; d. at Willington, 4 Apr 1816; m. at Willington, 19 Apr 1808, as his second wife, DAVID GLAZIER, b. at Willington, 5 Nov 1771 son of Silas and Suze (Johnson) Glazier; David d. at Willington, 2 Sep 1858. David was first married to Fear Alden, married third Fanny Woodworth Gager, and married fourth Alice Walker.

Cylinda and David resided in Willington. In his will written 1 April 1856 (probate 6 September 1858), David Glazier bequeathed to beloved wife Alice two hundred dollars, the furniture she brought to that marriage, and the parlor and kitchen stoves. Son C. (likely Carlos) Glazier receives the house and land to be held in trust for the support of Alice. The furniture owned by David at the time of his marriage to Alice is to be divided among his three daughters Caroline, Fear, and Cellinda, although he later changes this in a correction to two daughters Fear and Caroline. The remainder of the estate is to be divided in fifty-two shares and distributed as follows: son Charles, twenty shares; son Jasper, ten shares; son Jennison, five shares; son Ira, five shares; son Alden, one share; widow of son Silvester, one share; daughter Caroline, five shares; and daughter Fear, five shares. Son Carlos Glazier and Sylvester T. Preston were named executors.[2464] Charles, Jennison, Ira, Alden, and Silvester were children from David's first marriage to Fear Alden. Cellinda was a daughter from his third marriage to Fanny Gager.

David and Cylinda were parents of four children born at Willington.

i   JASPER MARCY GLAZIER, b. 26 Jul 1809; d. at Hartford, CT, 1875 (probate 21 Sep 1875); m. 1st at Tolland, 3 Apr 1834, MARIVA CASWELL, b. about 1812; Mariva d. at Hartford, 3 May 1847. Jasper m. 2nd at Windham, 11 Dec 1848, ABIGAIL C. WOLCOTT, b. at Windham, about 1830 daughter of George W. and Mary (Kinne) Walcott; Abigail was living in 1875.

ii   CARLOS GLAZIER (twin), b. 25 Oct 1811; d. at Hartford, 1885; m. at Stonington, CT, 23 May 1837, PHEBE E. WALKER, b. 1813 daughter of Levi and Phebe (Burroughs) Walker; Phebe d. at Hartford, 27 Apr 1903.

iii   CAROLINE F. GLAZIER (twin), b. 25 Oct 1811; d. at Willington, 19 Mar 1868; m. at Willington, 1 Dec 1839, CHARLES HENRY AMES, b. at Bridgewater, MA, 26 Aug 1812 son of Bezer and Rebecca (Josselyn) Ames; Charles, serving with the 1st Connecticut Cavalry company L, was killed in action at Ream's Station, VA, 29 Jun 1864.[2465] Charles was first married to Adeline Wilson.

iv   FEAR GLAZIER, b. 25 Nov 1813; d. at Willington, 23 Mar 1891; m. at Willington, 16 Sep 1833, SYLVESTER TAYLOR PRESTON, b. at Germantown, NY, 5 Aug 1808 son of Amos and Martha (Taylor) Preston; Sylvester d. at Willington, 15 Apr 1887.

808)   ESTHER MARCY (*Samuel Marcy⁴, Mary Russell Marcy³, Benjamin², Robert¹*), b. at Union, CT, 28 Apr 1763 daughter of Samuel and Lois (Peake) Marcy; d. at Weathersfield (Ascutney), VT, 24 Mar 1839; m. at Windsor, VT (recorded in the records at Weathersfield), 3 Oct 1787, ISAAC PARKER, perhaps the Isaac b. at Mansfield, CT, b. at Mansfield, CT, 24 Feb 1755 son of Zachariah and Peace (Ames) Parker; Isaac d. at Weathersfield, 23 Jun 1821.

[2462] Briggs, *History of the Original Town of Concord*, p 330

[2463] Briggs, *History of the Original Town of Concord*, p 331

[2464] Connecticut Wills and Probate, Hartford, Tolland Probate District, Town of Willington, Estate of David Glazier, Case 355

[2465] U.S., Civil War Pension Index: General Index to Pension Files, 1861-1934; Connecticut, Hale Collection of Cemetery Inscriptions and Newspaper Notices, 1629-1934. The memorial gravestone in Willington gives date of death as 20 June 1862, but the first battle of Ream's Station was 29 June 1864 and if he was killed at Ream's Station it would be on that date.

Esther and Isaac married in Windsor County, Vermont and settled on a farm in Weathersfield.

Esther Parker provided a statement related to her application for a widow's pension on 11 January 1839. She had no direct evidence of Isaac's service as she met him after the war. He was from Mansfield, Connecticut, and he spoke about enlisting after the Battle of Lexington. He reported being at the Battle of Bunker Hill. She reported being married to Isaac at Windsor, Vermont on 23 October 1787 by Bryant Brown, Justice of the Peace. John Dexter of Pomfret, Vermont provided a statement on 20 February 1839 in which he related that he had known Isaac since childhood, and they grew up together in Mansfield. Immediately after the Battle of Lexington, he and Isaac went to Cambridge to enlist, and they were together in the company of Lieut. James Dana and regiment of Col. Experience Stores. They served eight months and returned to Mansfield in the winter of 1776. They again enlisted in the company of Capt. Gershom Barrows in the regiment of Col. Chester, this service in New York and they were part of the retreat from New York. They were then in New Jersey and after the expiration of the six-month term, they returned to Mansfield. After the war, Isaac went to Windsor, Vermont where he married Esther and they later settled on a farm in Weathersfield. In a statement related to his mother's pension application made 6 February 1839, son Samuel Parker reported he was one of nine children with seven older siblings two of who were deceased. Eldest son John Parker also provided a statement.[2466]

In his will written 2 June 1821 (proved 1 August 1821), Isaac Parker bequeathed to beloved wife Esther one thousand dollars. Son John Parker receives two hundred dollars, but that legacy includes a $150 note that son John owes his father. Son Alvan receives two hundred dollars, but the $150 note that John holds from Alvan is to be reckoned into the legacy. Son Oren also has a legacy of two hundred dollars but owes his father $134. Sons Dexter, Samuel, and Zenos each receives two hundred dollars. Daughter Wealthy Stowell receives two hundred dollars but owes her father $150. The remainder of the estate is to be equally divided among his children. Amos Hulett was named executor.[2467]

Esther's estate entered probate 2 May 1839 with Samuel Parker as administrator. The amount of the estate after claims were paid was $481.08.[2468]

Isaac and Esther were parents of nine children born at Weathersfield, Vermont.

i　JOHN PARKER, b. 27 Jul 1788; m. LAVINA MATHEWS, b. at Weathersfield, 21 Dec 1794 daughter of Amos Mathews. John and Lavina and two of their children were living in Weathersfield in 1850.

ii　WELTHA PARKER, b. 22 Apr 1790; d. at Concord, PA, 21 Aug 1867; m. OLIVER STOWELL, b. at Windsor, VT, 5 Oct 1792 son of Joel and Hannah (Holden) Stowell; Oliver d. at Concord, PA, 6 Oct 1836.

iii　IRA PARKER (twin), b. 24 May 1792; d. 23 Jun 1794.

iv　ALVAN PARKER (twin), b. 24 May 1792; d. at Windsor, VT, 21 Sep 1843; m. at Windsor, 3 Dec 1818, LUCY HUABBRD, b. 1788; Lucy d. at Windsor, 20 May 1839.

v　OTIS PARKER, b. 1795; d. 31 Dec 1795.

vi　OREN PARKER, b. 1797

vii　DEXTER PARKER, b. 29 May 1799; d. at Rutland, WI, 23 May 1853; m. 21 Jan 1824, ESTHER PIPER, b. at Weston, VT, 6 Aug 1797 daughter of Amasa and Mary (Piper) Piper; Esther d. at Rutland, 16 Nov 1888.

viii　SAMUEL PARKER, b. 1802; d. at Windsor, VT, 28 Nov 1882; m. MARCIA ELY, b. at West Windsor, VT, 1 Dec 1812 daughter of Phineas L. and Ann (Woodruff) Ely; Marcia d. at West Windsor, 21 Sep 1860.

ix　ZENOS PARKER, b. 15 Dec 1805; d. at Newcomb, NY, 9 Jun 1896; m. about 1843, RACHEL DORNBURG, b. in NY, 11 Feb 1824 (on gravestone) daughter of John and Sarah (-) Dornburg; Rachel d. at Newcomb, 9 Apr 1901.

809)　ALVAN MARCY (*Samuel Marcy⁴, Mary Russell Marcy³, Benjamin², Robert¹*), b. at Union, 22 Jun 1765 son of Samuel and Lois (Peake) Marcy; d. at Windsor, VT, 24 Jan 1834; m. at Windsor, 1 Oct 1797, as her second husband, MARY DRAKE (widow of Thomas Bunce), b. 1764 daughter of Samuel and Martha (Pratt) Drake;[2469] Mary d. at Windsor, 13 Dec 1841.

Alvan was reared in Connecticut, but went to Windsor, Vermont soon after the Revolution where he remained.

On 4 August 1832, Alvan Marcy made a statement related to his pension application. He was born in Union, Connecticut 22 June 1765. He enlisted in the spring of 1776 for eight or nine months as a waiter for his father Samuel Marcy who was a lieutenant in the company of Capt. Reuben Marcy. After enlistment, they went by ship to New York and were on Long Island until the Battle of Flatbush. At that time, his father sent him away to the fort and he went with Capt. Bacon's waiter whose name was Joseph Merritt. He became separated from Joseph and Joseph was taken by the British, but Alvin made it safely to the fort. They were then in New York until that was taken by the British and were then in Westchester where they built barracks. He was discharged Peekskill on 1 January 1777. His father continued south from there with the army. Alvan again enlisted in 1778 or 1779 in the company of Capt. Norris in the regiment of Col. Wyllis. They marched near New London eventually to Groton Point collecting materials along the way for the construction of Fort Griswold. He had a third

[2466] U. S. Revolutionary War Pension and Bounty-Land Warrant Application Files, Case W19967

[2467] Vermont Wills and Probate Records, Windsor County, volume 9, p 166

[2468] Vermont Wills and Probate, Windsor County, Estate of Esther Parker

[2469] Gay, *Descendants of John Drake of Windsor*, p 62

enlistment in 1780 or 1781 in the company of Capt. Moulton in Maj. Shipman's battalion of the Connecticut state troops. He served a year and built a fort near Coscob. At the close of the war, he lived in Enfield. Soon after, he moved to Windsor, Vermont where he remained until 25 June 1829 when he moved to Woodstock, Vermont. Alvan's sister Esther Parker provided a statement in support of Alvan's application. Esther adds that the waiter captured by the British later escaped by swimming a creek. Esther also states that during the war, she went to live in Partirdgefield (perhaps current Hinsdale), Massachusetts for a year and a half. Brother Prosper Marcy also provided a statement. Alvan was awarded a pension of $80 per year.[2470]

Alvan Marcy and Mary Drake were parents of four children born at Windsor, Vermont. Mary also had eight children with her first husband Thomas Bunce.

i JOHN SULLIVAN MARCY, b. 7 Mar 1799; d. at Ballston, NY, 2 May 1882; m. at Walpole, NH, 27 Oct 1831, REBECCA HUBBARD VOSE, b. at Walpole, NH, 26 Sep 1804 daughter of Roger and Rebecca (Bellows) Vose; Rebecca d. at Royalston, VT, 7 Feb 1866.

ii MARTHA DRAKE MARCY, b. 4 Nov 1800; d. at Lowell, MA, 8 Sep 1885; m. at Windsor, Nov 1829, LEWIS CHAUNCEY STOWELL, b. at Windsor, 27 Mar 1797 son of Jacob and Betsey (Stowell) Stowell;[2471] Lewis d. at Massena, NY, Oct 1841. Lewis was first married to Sophronia Kimball.

iii THOMAS BRUCE MARCY, b. 14 Sep 1802; d. at Everett, MA, 19 Nov 1877; m. CLARA WILDER, b. at Woodstock, VT, 28 Sep 1814 daughter of Jacob and Mary (Wakefield) Wilder;[2472] Clara d. at Everett, 3 Nov 1888.

iv FRANCES "FANNY" WEBSTER MARCY, b. 13 Nov 1804; d. at Windsor, 4 Sep 1835; m. 6 May 1827, TRUMAN IDE, b. 1802 son of Lemuel and Sarah (Stone) Ide; Truman d. at Windsor, 11 Jun 1830.

810) AVIS MARCY (*Samuel Marcy⁴, Mary Russell Marcy³, Benjamin², Robert¹*), b. at Union, 5 Sep 1769 daughter of Samuel and Lois (Peake) Marcy; d. at Weathersfield, VT, 1820; m. about 1791, as his second wife, BURPEE PROUTY, b. 10 Mar 1763 son of Richard and Esther (Smith) Prouty; Burpee d. at Hartford, VT, 1 Feb 1849. Burpee was first married to Amarillis Tolles and third married to Martha Ballard in 1827.

Avis and Burpee resided in Weathersfield where Burpee was a farmer. Later in life, Burpee was in Hartford, Vermont where he served as deacon in West Hartford.[2473]

On 8 April 1818, Burpee Prouty, aged fifty-four and resident of Weathersfield, Vermont, made application for a Revolutionary War pension. About the last day of December 1779, he enlisted as a private under Lieut. Clay in the 6th Massachusetts regiment. He served three years, five months, and twenty days and was honorably discharged on 9 June 1783. On 2 August 1820, he provided additional information on his property and family. He reported real estate of $300, personal estate of $185.76 and debts of $595.79. His household at that time was wife Avis aged fifty and of poor health and children Esther aged 16, Sophia aged 13, Lydia aged 11, and Luke aged 9. Burpee reported his own health was poor and his was little able to perform his work as a farmer. Burpee received pension of $96 per annum. After his death, his widow Martha received the widow's pension.[2474]

Avis and Burpee were parents of ten children born at Weathersfield, Vermont.[2475]

i AMARILLIS PROUTY, b. 13 Aug 1792; d. at Hartford, VT, 21 May 1867; m. at Weathersfield, 27 Feb 1817, SQUIRE ALLEN BALLARD, b. at Hartland, VT, 15 Mar 1784 son of Sherebiah and Sarah (Emerson) Ballard; Squire d. at Stratford, VT, 1 Apr 1864.

ii AVIS PROUTY, b. 29 Jan 1794; d. at Hartford, VT, 1823.

iii LUCY PROUTY, b. 6 Dec 1796; d. at Richland, IA, 4 Apr 1863; m. at Weathersfield, 5 Oct 1817, DAVID WHITCOMB, b. at Hartford, VT, 6 Jun 1795 son of David and Orra (Richardson) Whitcomb; David d. at Ottumwa, IA, 6 Sep 1876. David returned to New Hampshire for his second wife Avis M. *Ballard* Harvey whom he married on 28 Nov 1864. Avis was the daughter of Amarillis Prouty and Squire Ballard (see above).

iv IRA OTIS PROUTY, b. 21 Feb 1798; m. 1st at Pomfret, VT, 19 Feb 1827, MARY THOMAS. Ira m. 2nd at Middlebury, VT, 21 Jul 1831, MARY NIXON.

v MARY "POLLY" PROUTY, b. 6 Nov 1800; d. after 1880 when she was living at Jericho, VT; m. HORACE PEASE, b. at Jericho, VT, 15 Jan 1799 son of Gaius and Abigail (Baird) Pease; Horace d. at Jericho, 12 Sep 1862.

vi MARCIA PROUTY, b. 22 Oct 1801

[2470] U. S. Revolutionary War Pension and Bounty-Land Warrant Application Files, Case S13860
[2471] Stowell, *The Stowell Genealogy*, p 487
[2472] The names of Mary's parents are given as Jacob and Mary on her death record.
[2473] Tucker, *History of Hartford, Vermont*, p 24
[2474] U. S. Revolutionary War Pension and Bounty-Land Warrant Application Files, Case W2665
[2475] Vermont, Vital Records, 1720-1908

vii   ESTHER PROUTY, b. 1803

viii   SOPHIA C. PROUTY, b. 1807; d. at Randolph, VT, 27 Aug 1840; m. at Hartford, VT, 19 Nov 1833, HIRAM PARKHURST, b. at Sharon, VT, 17 Sep 1807 son of Elisha and Hannah (Huntington) Parkhurst; Hiram d. at Dows, IA while visiting his son, 1885 (burial at Danvers, IL). Hiram married second Lois Ingraham.

ix   LYDIA MELINDA PROUTY, b. 12 Mar 1809; d. after 1880 when living at Grafton, OH; m. about 1831, JOHN RILEY JONES, b. at Tyringham, MA, 26 Jun 1808 son of Eliphalet and Polly (·) Jones; Riley d. after 1880.

x   LUKE PROUTY, b. 4 Apr 1811

---

811)   PROSPER MARCY (*Samuel Marcy⁴, Mary Russell Marcy³, Benjamin², Robert¹*), b. 1 Mar 1772 son of Samuel and Lois (Peake) Marcy; d. at Windsor, VT, 15 May 1855; m. JANE DUTTON, baptized at Rindge, NH 15 Nov 1771 daughter of Silas and Sarah (Whitney) Dutton; Jane d. at Windsor, 26 Mar 1849.

      There are two children known for Prosper and Jane, although there may be others. The family lived in Windsor, Vermont.

i   JOHN S. MARCY, b. 1798; d. at Cornish, NH, 28 Sep 1838 (burial and probate in Windsor, VT). John does not seem to have married. His estate consisted primarily of property he held in Windsor, the estate was insolvent, and his property was sold.[2476] Reuben Davis was named administrator 27 October 1838.

ii   SARAH MARCY, b. 1805; d. at Janesville, WI, 16 Jul 1873; m. at Windsor, VT, 9 Mar 1832, HOLMES HAMMOND, b. at Windsor, 17 Jan 1807 son of Jabez H. and Mary (Rowe) Hammond;[2477] Holmes d. at Clinton, WI, 25 Jan 1892. Holmes married second Caroline Winkler on 21 Jul 1874.

---

812)   ORRIN MARCY (*Samuel Marcy⁴, Mary Russell Marcy³, Benjamin², Robert¹*), b. 25 Apr 1774 son of Samuel and Lois (Peake) Marcy; d. at Ashford, CT, 21 Jul 1828; m. 1st at Eastford 14 May 1797, POLLY WORK, b. 1779 daughter of Joseph and Elizabeth (Hayward) Work; Polly d. at Eastford, 9 Jul 1816. Orrin m. 2nd Polly's sister, LUCY WORK, b. about 1791; Lucy d. at Eastford, 12 Mar 1830.

      Orrin lived in Ashford where he had six children with Polly Work and two children with Lucy.

i   JOSEPH WORK MARCY, b. at Ashford, 20 Nov 1797; d. at Eastford, 2 May 1842; m. 1st about 1820, his third cousin, POLLY HOWARD (*Lucy Work Howard⁵, Mary Russell Work⁴, Benjamin³, Benjamin², Robert¹*), b. at Union, CT, 5 Sep 1798 daughter of Manasseh and Lucy (Work) Howard; Lucy d. at Eastford 11 Nov 1831. Joseph m. 2nd at Ashford, 22 Apr 1832, LOIS BUGBEE, b. at Ashford, 13 Mar 1802 daughter of Jesse and Chloe (Hayward) Bugbee;[2478] Lois d. at West Hartford, 5 Apr 1871.

ii   JOHN SULLIVAN MARCY, b. 25 Mar 1800; d. at Woodstock, CT, 7 Jun 1856; m. 1st at Hampton, 4 Dec 1823, MARY LOOMIS, b. at Hampton, about 1803 and baptized at Hampton, 20 Sep 1807[2479] daughter of Jonathan and Elizabeth (Bennett) Loomis;[2480] Mary d. at Eastford, 8 Jul 1845.

iii   MARY MARCY, b. 17 Jul 1806; d. at Eastford, 5 Mar 1850; m. at Ashford, 10 Jan 1826, THOMAS JEFFERSON OLNEY, b. at Ashford, 18 Aug 1804 son of Jeremiah and Abigail (Cheney) Olney; Thomas d. at Eastford, 4 Jul 1854. After Mary's death, Thomas married Almira Peirce on 9 Oct 1850.

iv   OLIVE MARCY, b. 30 Dec 1808; d. after 1870 when living at Eastford and before 1880; m. at Ashford, 1 Jan 1826, HENRY PACKER, b. likely at Abington, CT, 1798 son of David and Lucy (·) Packer;[2481] Henry d. at Worcester, MA, 9 Jan 1885.

v   STEPHEN H. MARCY, b. 22 Jan 1813; d. at New Haven, CT between 1875 and 1878 (when wife is widow); m. at Hartford, 26 Nov 1834, ANN GILLILAND, b. about 1815; Ann d. after 1897 when she was living in New Haven. Stephen was a butcher. After his marriage, he was in Chicago for a time and enlisted there in the Union forces. The family returned to New Haven after the war.

vi   DANFORTH S. MARCY, b. 21 May 1816; d. at Quasqueton, IA, 20 Jun 1884; m. 1st at McHenry County, IL, 24 Apr 1842, ELIZABETH METCALF, b. in NY about 1814; Elizabeth d. at Quasqueton, about 1872. Danforth m. 2nd

---

[2476] Vermont Wills, Windsor County, Estate of John S. Marcy

[2477] Hammond, *History and Genealogy of the Descendants of William Hammond*, p 147

[2478] Hammond, *The History of Union, Conn.*, p 288

[2479] All the children of Jonathan and Elizabeth were baptized on 20 Sep 1807.

[2480] Mary's father is given as Jonathan Loomis on her death record.

[2481] Henry's parents are named as David and Lucy on his death record.

at Buchanan County, IA, 2 Aug 1873, CYNTHIA H. GRIFFITH (widow of Nathaniel Loomis), b. in OH, 1826; Cynthia d. at Quasqueton, 4 Jul 1886.

Orrin Marcy and Lucy Work were parents of two children

i   HANNAH H. MARCY, b. 28 Feb 1821; d. at Eastford, 17 Jan 1898; m. at Ashford, 5 May 1839, HIRAM B. BURNHAM, b. in NY, 1812; Hiram d. at Eastford, 22 Sep 1884.

ii   ESTHER MARCY, b. 1826; d. at Eastford, 13 Sep 1829.

813)   DORCAS MARCY (*Samuel Marcy⁴, Mary Russell Marcy³, Benjamin², Robert¹*), b. 18 Jan 1779 daughter of Samuel and Lois (Peake) Marcy; d. at Windsor, VT, 29 Nov 1838; m. 1ˢᵗ by 1803, ISAAC PROCTOR who has not been identified but d. before 1810. Dorcas m. 2ⁿᵈ about 1813, as his second wife, SEYMOUR BURNHAM, b. 1777; Seymour d. at Windsor, 30 Sep 1832. Seymour was first married to Mabel Potter.
    Dorcas Marcy and Isaac Proctor were parents of two children.

i   CHARLES PROCTOR, b. about 1804; d. at Windsor, VT, 8 Oct 1836. Charles does not seem to have married.

ii   ADALINE PROCTOR, b. at Windsor, 28 Apr 1806; d. at Waltham, MA, 20 Jun 1888; m. at Windsor, 25 Aug 1834, THOMAS ENSWORTH, b. at Norwich, VT, 30 Nov 1806 son of Hezekiah and Erepta (Pike) Ensworth; Thomas d. at Windsor, 30 Jan 1868. Thomas was a cabinetmaker and painter.[2482]

Dorcas and her second husband lived in Windsor. Seymour did not leave a will and his estate entered probate 4 November 1832 with Dorcas as administratrix. The widow was allowed $91.75 in value from the personal estate. The debts exceeded the value of the personal estate. No real estate was reported.[2483]
    Dorcas Marcy and Seymour Burnham were parents of two children.

i   MINERVA BURNHAM, b. at Windsor, 15 Apr 1813; d. at Watervliet, MI, 5 Sep 1873; m. at Windsor, 1 Jan 1833, EBENEZER SIDNEY "EBEN" WOODWARD, b. in VT, 3 Feb 1811 son of Daniel and Betsey (Williams) Woodward;[2484] Eben d. at Watervliet, 25 Nov 1893.

ii   JULIA ANNE BURNHAM, b. at Windsor, 16 Nov 1819; d. after 1850; m. at Windsor, 19 Dec 1837, REUBEN M. PARKER, b. at Woodstock, VT, 24 Aug 1816 son of Joseph and Hannah (Muzzy) Parker; Reuben d. at Woodstock, 11 Nov 1881. Reuben married second Eliza J. Davis about 1855.

814)   SAMUEL MARCY (*Samuel Marcy⁴, Mary Russell Marcy³, Benjamin², Robert¹*), b. 22 Apr 1783 son of Samuel and Lois (Peake) Marcy; d. at Windsor County, VT, 10 Dec 1846;[2485] m. at Weathersfield, 1 May 1806, RUTH HATCH, b. about 1785; d. at Weathersfield, VT, 17 Mar 1846.
    In her will written 3 February 1846 (proved 8 April 1846), Ruth Marcy of Weathersfield, Vermont bequeathed all her estate, real and personal, to daughter Almira Marcy for her support during her natural life. Following the decease of Almira, the estate is to be divided equally among her sons Stephen Marcy, John H. Marcy, Leonard Marcy, and Edward Marcy. Almira was named executrix.[2486] Son Leonard did not marry, and his will written 26 April 1848 has bequests to his three brothers Stephen, John, and Edward and sister Almira.[2487]
    Samuel and Ruth were parents of five children likely all born at Weathersfield.

i   STEPHEN MARCY, b. 5 Jul 1806; d. at Springfield, VT, 3 Jan 1865; m. about 1835, MALINDA MASON, b. 23 Jun 1809 daughter of Russell and Louisa (Holton) Mason; Malinda d. at Springfield, 10 Aug 1866.

ii   JOHN HATCH MARCY, b. about 1810; d. at Weathersfield, VT, 1865 (probate 1 Feb 1865); m. about 1835, ANN LOCKWOOD, b. at Springfield, VT, about 1811; Ann d. at Reading, VT, 6 Mar 1896. John and Ann had one son, George Lockwood Marcy.

[2482] U.S., Craftperson Files, 1600-1995
[2483] Vermont Wills and Probate, Windsor County, Estate of Seymour Burnham
[2484] The names of Sidney's parents are given as Daniel and Betsy on his death record. Most records give his name as Sidney, but Ebenezer is also used. His gravestone says Eben.
[2485] This is the date of death given in the Marcy genealogy. Samuel's wife Ruth wrote a will before this date leaving her estate to her daughter and to her four sons after her daughter's death and she does not mention being married in the will.
[2486] Vermont Wills and Probate, Windsor County, volume 19, p 76
[2487] Vermont Wills and Probate, Windsor County, volume 20, p 85

iii   ALMIRA MARCY, b. about 1816; d. at Weathersfield, 2 Feb 1889. Almira did not marry. She lived with her brother Edward.

iv   LEONARD MARCY, b. about 1820; d. at Weathersfield, 10 Jun 1848.

v   EDWARD WILSON MARCY, b. 27 Mar 1825; d. at Weathersfield, VT, 10 Nov 1892; m. at Weathersfield, 20 Oct 1851, MARY CHASTINA LAZELL, b. at Barnard, VT, 18 Sep 1829 daughter of Rufus and Clarissa (Sherburne) Lazell; Mary d. at Weathersfield, 28 May 1902.

815) JOSHUA FAIRBANK (*Tabitha Marcy Fairbank⁴, Mary Russell Marcy³, Benjamin², Robert¹*), b. at Union, 23 Dec 1764 son of Joseph and Tabitha (Marcy) Fairbank; d. at Sheddsville, VT, 9 Dec 1812 (probate 19 Dec 1812); m. ZEULIME SAWIN, baptized at Belchertown, MA, 20 Sep 1766 daughter of Samuel and Hannah (Capen) Sawin; Zeulima d. after 1820 when she was head of household at Bridgewater, VT.

  The estate of Joshua Fairbank entered probate 19 December 1812 with Joab Lull as administrator. Total value of the estate was $1,076.74 with claims against the estate of $687.46. The real property was mortgaged, and the estate was insolvent. A warrant to sell the whole of the real estate to avoid injury to the value was requested 22 March 1813. A statement was made on 16 July 1813 that the citation related to the sell of the estate had been read in the presence of heirs Sally Fairbank, Tabitha Fairbank, Mary Fairbank, and widow Zulima Fairbank. Dower was ordered set off to widow Zulima on 27 April 1813. On 22 March 1813, Joseph Fairbank chose Nathan Boynton as guardian. Nathan Boynton was named guardian for Sybil Fairbank.[2488]

  Joshua and Zeulime were parents of nine children born at Windsor, Vermont.[2489]

i   ZEULIME FAIRBANK, b. 23 Dec 1788[2490]

ii   TABITHA FAIRBANK, b. 29 Mar 1789; d. after 1850 when living at Bridgewater, VT; m. at Bridgewater, 4 Jan 1821, NATHAN DIMICK; Nathan d. before 1850.

iii   SALLY FAIRBANK, b. 25 Jul 1792; perhaps m. at Windsor, 24 Oct 1813, WILLIAM BURBANK.

iv   MOLLY FAIRBANK, b. 4 Feb 1794

v   JOSEPH FAIRBANK, b. 25 May 1796

vi   OREN FAIRBANK, b. 5 Aug 1798; d. after 1850 and before 1860 at DeWitt, MI; m. about 1829, EUNICE RALPH, b. in VT, 1809; Eunice d. after 1870.

vii   SYBIL FAIRBANK, b. 25 Mar 1800

viii   OSHEA FAIRBANK, b. 22 Feb 1802; d. at Hermon, NY, before 1840 when wife Mehitable was head of household; m. by 1824, MEHITABLE POWERS, b. 1803; Mehitable d. at Hermon, 13 Aug 1882.

ix   DANIEL FAIRBANK, b. 14 Mar 1806; d. at Hermon, NY, 11 Aug 1878. Daniel did not marry.

816) JOSEPH FAIRBANK (*Tabitha Marcy Fairbank⁴, Mary Russell Marcy³, Benjamin², Robert¹*), b. at Union, 13 Jul 1773 son of Joseph and Tabitha (Marcy) Fairbank; d. at Felchville, VT, Feb 1859; m. 1st MARY HUMPHREY, b. 1785 daughter of Daniel and Naomi (Elmore) Humphrey;[2491] Mary d. 29 Jun 1812. Joseph m. 2nd[2492] or 3rd HANNAH WILBUR[2493] who d. at Springfield, VT, 1839.

  Rev. Joseph Fairbank was a Methodist minister admitted to the Methodist conference in 1805[2494] who had postings in Magog (1805), Danville (1806), Athens (1808), and Weathersfield, Vermont before settling on a farm in Felchville (a village in Reading, Vermont).[2495] He was also for a time in North Adams, Massachusetts where he married Hannah Wilbur and where his first daughter was born.

  Joseph Fairbank and Hannah Wilbur were parents of two children.

i   MARY DIAN FAIRBANK, b. at North Adams, MA, 13 Dec 1817; d. at Worcester, MA, 21 Mar 1900; m. at Sturbridge, 2 Apr 1843, ALLEN B. PRICE, b. at Providence, RI, 1820 son of Oliver and Sarah (Field) Pierce; Allen d. at Worcester, 26 Jan 1894.

[2488] Vermont Wills and Probate, Windsor County, Probate Files, Estate of Joshua Fairbank, 19 December 1812
[2489] Vermont, Vital Records, 1720-1908
[2490] The date recorded may be an error as the next child born is recorded in March 1789.
[2491] Humphreys, *The Humphreys Family in America*, volume I, p 298
[2492] The Fairbanks genealogy reports that Joseph had a second marriage, but the name of his second wife is not known.
[2493] Hannah is reported in the Fairbanks genealogy as having two earlier marriages, one of them to a Russell.
[2494] Methodist Episcopal Church, *Minutes of the Annual Conferences of the Methodist Episcopal Church*, volume I, 1773-1828, p 122
[2495] Fairbanks, *Genealogy of the Fairbanks Family*, p 337; Humphreys, *The Humphreys Family in America*, volume I, p 298

ii   EUNICE FAIRBANK, b. at Reading, VT, 14 Feb 1821; d. at Reading, 10 May 1859; m. at Sturbridge, 1 May 1845, PEREZ BRADFORD WOLCOTT, b. at Roxbury, MA, 19 Apr 1814 son of Perez B. and Isabella (Foster) Wolcott; Perez d. at Gardner, MA, 12 Feb 1906. Perez was a widower at the time of his marriage to Eunice, but the named of his first wife was not found.

817)   SIBBEL FAIRBANK (*Tabitha Marcy Fairbank⁴, Mary Russell Marcy³, Benjamin², Robert¹*), b. at Union, 9 Jul 1779 daughter of Joseph and Tabitha (Marcy) Fairbank; d. at Union, about 1807. Sibbel had an out-of-wedlock child with SHUBAEL HAMMOND, b. at Sturbridge, MA, 28 Feb 1776 son of Job and Jemima (Baker) Hamant; Shubael d. at Union, CT, 25 Jul 1857. Shubael married Polly Paul.

Sibbel had an out-of-wedlock child with Shubael Hammond.[2496] Shubael Hammond was a physician who settled in Union where he started his medical practice in 1800. He married Polly Paul in 1812 and had six children with his wife.[2497]

i   MARY MERCY HAMMOND, b. at Union, CT, 9 Apr 1807; d. at Southbridge, MA, 20 Jul 1885; m. at Union, 7 Dec 1826, JOSEPH AMMIDOWN, b. at Sturbridge, MA, 4 Apr 1801 son of Cyrus and Mercy (Perry) Ammidown; Joseph d. at Southbridge, MA, 10 Jun 1863.

818)   STEPHEN FAIRBANK (*Tabitha Marcy Fairbank⁴, Mary Russell Marcy³, Benjamin², Robert¹*), b. at Union, 11 Jul 1787 son of Joseph and Tabitha (Marcy) Fairbank; d. at Litchfield, MI, 10 Feb 1847; m. at Union, 10 Apr 1810, MARTHA SABIN, b. at Thompson, CT, 20 Jan 1792 daughter of Peter and Sarah (Allen) Sabin; Martha d. at Albion, MI, 24 Sep 1877.

Stephen Fairbank was a Methodist minister.[2498] The family was in Union, Connecticut until about 1839 when they relocated to Litchfield, Michigan. Stephen purchased 160 acres in section 17 of Hillsdale County[2499] and he and Martha raised their seven children there. The births of the six oldest children are recorded at Union, Connecticut.

i   SARAH ANN FAIRBANK, b. at Union, CT, 31 Dec 1816; d. at Litchfield, MI, 6 Jul 1897; m. at Union, 25 Jul 1838, ISAAC AGARD, b. at Stafford, CT, 15 Feb 1812 son of Nathan and Hannah (Hall) Agard; Isaac d. at Litchfield, 26 Oct 1848.

ii   TABITHA MARCY FAIRBANK, b. at Union, 8 May 1818; d. at Albion, MI, 30 Apr 1899; m. by 1845, JOHN HAGER, b. in NY, about 1811 son of Henry Hager; John d. at Albion, 17 Apr 1876.

iii   SABIN STEPHEN FAIRBANK, b. at Union, 18 Oct 1822; d. at Litchfield, MI, 25 Apr 1902; m. 1st 21 Apr 1853, LUCRETIA C. ALLEN, b. about 1836 daughter of Ira and Rebecca (Calkins) Allen; Lucretia d. at Litchfield, 6 Jul 1887. Sabin m. 2nd at Tekonsha, MI, 23 Apr 1891, PHEBE STRAY (widow of William Wallace Howard), b. in NY 20 Sep 1835 daughter of George W. and Chloe (Allen) Stray; Phebe d. at Tekonsha, 22 May 1921.

iv   PETER FLETCHER FAIRBANK, b. at Union, 8 Mar 1824; d. at Litchfield, MI, 10 Dec 1845.

v   JOSEPH NEWTON FAIRBANK, b. at Union, 2 Nov 1826; d. at Litchfield, MI, 8 Mar 1916; m. 1st MARY JANE SHIPMAN, b. in NY, 6 May 1830 (on gravestone) daughter of Harlow Shipman; Mary Jane d. at Litchfield, 17 Feb 1895. Joseph m. 2nd at Hillsdale, MI, 17 Oct 1898, CATHERINE "KATIE" HAGER (widow of John Rowley), b. in NY, 9 May 1844, daughter of Jacob and Lorraine (Barr) Hager (as given on death record); Catherine d. at Litchfield, 18 Apr 1925.

vi   ORIN MILTON FAIRBANK, b. at Union, 4 Sep 1829; d. at Ithaca, MI, 3 Oct 1913; m. 4 Jul 1855, ARVILLA HERENDEEN, b. at Litchfield, MI, 15 Apr 1839 daughter of Nathan and Emily (Gilmore) Herendeen; Arvilla d. at Ithaca, 1 Dec 1931.

vii   MARTHA ANN FAIRBANK, b. likely at Litchfield, MI, 1839; d. at Litchfield, MI, 21 Oct 1851.

819)   OLIVER PEAKE (*Sibbel Marcy Peake⁴, Mary Russell Marcy³, Benjamin², Robert¹*), b. 18 Oct 1772 son of Moses and Sibbel (Marcy) Peake; d. at Delhi, NY, 19 Feb 1859; m. 12 Sep 1792, ELIZABETH who has not been identified,[2500] b. about 1775; Elizabeth d. at Delhi, 12 Jan 1846.

[2496] The 1818 will (Probate 1823) of Sibbel's sister Molly Fairbank includes a bequest to Mary Mercy Hammond the daughter of her sister Sibbel Fairbanks. The death record of Mary Mercy Hammond Ammidown gives father's name as Dr. Shubael Hammond and mother's name as Sybil Fairbanks. Sibbel is buried as Sibel Fairbank and there is no record of a marriage.

[2497] Hammond, *History of the Town of Union*, p 350

[2498] Fairbanks, *Genealogy of the Fairbanks Family*, p 357

[2499] Everts and Abbott, *History of Hillsdale County, Michigan*, p 167

[2500] Elizabeth may be Elizabeth Clark.

Oliver Peake settled in Delhi, New York in 1795 and had his property at the mouth of creek now known as Peake Creek. He built and operated a sawmill.[2501]

On 22 February 1859, son Elijah Peake declined administration of his father's estate and requested M. T. Peake and William Stoutenburgh as administrators.[2502] On 15 April 1861, William Stoutenburgh provided his accounting of the estate and the distribution of $504.89 remaining in the estate. Portions of $50.48 were distributed to the sons and daughters or their heirs: Elijah Peake, Mrs. Caroline Stoutenburgh, Mrs. Jane Landon, Oliver Peake, Catherine Ward, Marcus F. Peake, Lucinda Peake, Homer Peake, the heirs of William C. Peake, and the heirs of Frederick F. Peake. The heirs of William C. Peake were widow Ann D. Peake, Ebenezer S. Peake, Susan E. Beldon, Josephine Worthington, Ester Ann Peake, Frederick W. Peake, G. Prindle Peake, Charles H. Peake, Jane Peake, and Alvah Peake. The heirs of Frederick F. Peake were widow Sarah H. Peake, William Creighton Peake, Mary D. Peake, Frederick F. Peake, Octavia Peake, Helen E. Peake, and Ann Peake.[2503]

Sons Frederick Foote Peake and Charles Foote Peake were ministers, Frederick of General Theological Seminary and Charles a graduate of Brown University. Sons Marcus and William were physicians who both practiced in Gloversville for a time. Dr. William C. Peake later resided in Johnstown, New York.[2504]

Oliver and Elizabeth Peake were parents of eleven children likely all born in Delhi, New York.

i   JANE PEAKE, b. 1793; d. after 1865 when living at Delhi, NY; m. JOHN M. LANDON, b. 1789 son of Thomas and Elizabeth (Commer) Landon; John d. at Delhi, 2 Dec 1851.

ii   ELIJAH PEAKE, b. 1795; d. after 1865 when living at Delhi with his sister Jane. Elijah did not marry.

iii   WILLIAM CLARKE PEAKE, b. 17 Nov 1797; d. at Johnstown, NY, 27 Sep 1856; m. 1828, DINAH MERWIN, b. 15 Jan 1806 daughter of Asher and Susannah (Knapp) Merwin; Dinah d. 27 Feb 1887.

iv   LUCINDA PEAKE, b. 1799; d. at Delhi, 1875. Lucinda did not marry.

v   OLIVER PEAKE, b. about 1800; d. after 1865 when living at Hinsdale, NY; m. 1st about 1830, MIRANDA STRONG, b. about 1806 daughter of Josiah and Mary (Reed) Strong;[2505] Miranda d. about 1841. Oliver m. 2nd HULDAH, b. about 1804; Huldah was not in the home in the 1855 census and assumed to be deceased.

vi   CATHARINE PEAKE, b. 1805; d. after 1880 when living at Gloversville, NY; m. JENNISON G. WARD, b. 14 Oct 1805 son of William and Zerviah (Murdock) Ward; Jennison d. after 1865.

vii   MARCUS TULLY PEAKE, b. 24 Jan 1805; d. at Johnstown, NY, 1866 (Sophia named guardian of two children 7 Jun 1866); m. SOPHIA L. BASSETT, b. 1817 daughter of Asahel and Prudence (Weston) Bassett; Sophia d. at Gloversville, NY, 15 Dec 1892.

viii   FREDERICK FOOTE PEAKE, b. 1809; d. at Pensacola, FL, 27 Nov 1846; m. SARAH HAGERTY DENNIS, b. in NJ about 1812 daughter of Isaac and Huldah (Shaw) Dennis;[2506] Sarah d. at Newark, NJ, 9 Jun 1890. Rev. Frederick Peake graduated from General Theological Seminary of New York in 1836. After ordination, he was a missionary in Missouri and was later minister at Christ Church in Pensacola, FL.[2507]

ix   CAROLINE PEAKE, b. 1813; d. at Delhi, NY, 9 Aug 1883; m. WILLIAM STOUTENBURG, b. at Dutchess County, NY, 12 Mar 1811 son of Peter and Lydia (Borden) Stoutenburg; William d. at Delhi, 30 Jan 1901.[2508]

x   HOMER R. PEAKE, b. 10 Jun 1815; d. at Le Roy, MI, 8 Oct 1884. At the time of Homer's death, the only heir identified was nephew Charles Peake of Rose Lake, MI (who was a son of Homer's brother Oliver).[2509] Little else is known of Homer. He may be the Homer Peake who was an innkeeper at Honesdale, PA in 1850. If so, he did have a wife and one daughter, but the wife and daughter disappear from census records after 1850. Homer served in the Civil War as a farrier in G company of the 8th regiment of Pennsylvania cavalry.[2510] He obtained a cash entry land patent in Ionia, MI for 125 acres in 1875.[2511]

[2501] W. W. Munsell, *History of Delaware County, New York*, p 150

[2502] New York Wills and Probate, Delaware County, Minutes volume 0008, p 351

[2503] New York Probate Records, 1629-1971, Delaware County, volume B, p 285-287; accessed through familysearch.org

[2504] Jeffers, Robert L., "History of Gloversville: With Reminiscences of Residents of Stump City and Sodom," The Daily Leader (Gloversville, NY), October 28, 1899, pp 9-13; accessed through New York State Library, https://nyshistoricnewspapers.org/lccn/sn88074616/1899-10-28/ed-1/seq-9/

[2505] The 1833 will of Josiah Strong includes a bequest to daughter Miranda G. Peak.

[2506] The 1864 probate of Isaac Dennis at Warren County NJ includes payment to Sarah H. Peak.

[2507] New York Historical Society Museum and Library, Reverend Frederick Foote Peake (1809-1846); https://emuseum.nyhistory.org/objects/615/reverend-frederick-foote-peake-18091846;jsessionid=AB3E7A60FA7AB7C1D50FBE3754D7AD5A

[2508] Delaware Gazette, February 06, 1901, p 3, obituary of William Stoutenburg

[2509] Michigan Wills and Probate, Osceola County, Packets 211-259, Estate of Homer R. Peake

[2510] National Park Service. *U.S. Civil War Soldiers, 1861-1865* [database on-line]. Provo, UT, USA: Ancestry.com Operations Inc, 2007.

[2511] Bureau of Land Management, General Land Office Records; Washington D.C., USA; Federal Land Patents, State Volumes

xi   CHARLES FOOTE PEAKE, b. 1818; d. at Tuscaloosa, AL, 21 Jul 1849. Rev. Charles Foote Peake attended Brown University and was a minister in Pensacola, FL in 1844[2512] and then in Tuscaloosa, AL where he died.[2513] He did not marry.

820)   ROSWELL PEAKE (*Sibbel Marcy Peake⁴, Mary Russell Marcy³, Benjamin², Robert¹*), b. 1774 son of Moses and Sibbel (Marcy) Peake; d. at Hamden, NY, 1824; m. 1798, JANE MASON, b. in Ireland, 1782 daughter of James and Anne (Boyd) Mason;[2514] Jane d. at Hamden, 1849.

As his brother Oliver had, Roswell settled in Delaware County, New York having his property in Hamden. Roswell was a carpenter by trade and farmed.[2515] In the 1800 census, the household was three members: one male 26 to 44; one female 16 to 25, and one male under 10.[2516] The 1820 census shows a household of thirteen including six males (three under 10, one 10 to 15, one 16 to 18) who are likely children and six females (four under 10 and two 10 to 15) who are likely children.[2517]

Roswell and Jane were parents of thirteen children born at Hamden, New York.[2518]

i   MATILDA PEAKE, b. 22 Aug 1799; d. at Hamden, 24 Dec 1827; m. about 1820, DANIEL PATTERSON. Matilda is reported in *Leading Citizens of Delaware County* as leaving two children.

ii   SARISSA PEAKE, b. about 1801; d. after 1855 when living at Geneseo, NY; m. before 1830, CALEB CHADWICK, b. in MA about 1801 (census records); Caleb d. between 1850 and 1855. Sarissa and Caleb were parents of three children: Caleb, Cornelia, and Walter.

iii   WALTER C. PEAKE, b. 14 Feb 1803; d. at Hamden, 21 Dec 1866; m. about 1827, HANNAH TIFFANY, b. 1804 daughter of Samuel and Mary (Sackett) Tiffany;[2519] Hannah d. at Hamden, 10 Sep 1860.

iv   MARIA PEAKE, b. 1804; d. at Hamden, 29 Jun 1859; m. ANDREW ANDREWS, b. about 1802; Andrew d. at Hamden, 23 May 1894.

v   IRA R. PEAKE, b. 19 Mar 1806; d. at Hamden, NY, 11 Feb 1885; m. 1ˢᵗ about 1826, CELINDA TIFFANY, b. about 1807 daughter of Samuel and Mary (Sackett) Tiffany; Celinda d. 1866. Ira m. 2ⁿᵈ ABIGIAL LAW, b. about 1840 daughter of Samuel A. and Paulina (Holmes) Law. Ira m. 3ʳᵈ 1875, Abigail's sister, HARRIET PAULINA LAW, b. about 1856.[2520]

vi   ELIZA ANN PEAKE, b. 1808; d. after 1865 when living at Colchester, NY; m. at Hamden, 7 Mar 1827, GEORGE SACKETT, b. about 1800 son of Menardus and Fanny (Nimocks) Sackett;[2521] George d. after 1865.

vii   EMELINE PEAKE, b. 1809; d. at Rock Island, IL, 12 Oct 1868; m. 16 Aug 1830, HENRY BRADDOCK DART, b. at New London, CT, 1807 son of Joshua and Frances (Mallory) Dart;[2522] Henry d. at Santa Clara, CA, 12 Sep 1889.

viii   CYRUS PEAKE, b. 9 Oct 1811; d. at Hancock, NY, 8 Mar 1889; m. MARIA LOUISA WARDWELL, b. 1813; Maria d. after 1880.

ix   AUGUSTUS J. PEAKE, b. 1813; d. at Philadelphia, PA, 22 Dec 1847; m. about 1841, MARY ANN CHASE, b. 1819 daughter of Walter and Mary (Walmsley) Chase;[2523] Mary d. at Hamden, 19 Aug 1880. Mary married second Abram Covert.

x   WARREN L. PEAKE, b. 1816; d. at Hamden, after 1860; m. AMY CHASE, b. 1818; Amy was living in 1880 at the home of her daughter Matilda in Stuyvesant, NY.

[2512] U.S., College Student Lists, 1763-1924
[2513] U.S., Newspaper Extractions from the Northeast, 1704-1930
[2514] W. W. Munsell, *History of Delaware County, New York*, p 196
[2515] W. W. Munsell, *History of Delaware County, New York*, p 200
[2516] Year: 1800; Census Place: Delhi, Delaware, New York; Series: M32; Roll: 22; Page: 1326; Image: 385; Family History Library Film: 193710
[2517] 1820 U S Census; Census Place: Delhi, Delaware, New York; Page: 51; NARA Roll: M33_65; Image: 63
[2518] A biography of grandson Albert D. Peake gives the names of the twelve children in this family and their spouses. Biographical Review, *Leading Citizens of Delaware County, New York*, p 404
[2519] Tiffany, *The Tiffanys in America*, p 163
[2520] In the 1865 census of Hamden, Abigail Law and Paulina H. Law were living with their parents Samuel A. and Paulina Law. New York, State Census, 1865
[2521] Weygant, *The Sacketts of America*, p 150
[2522] A son of Emeline and Henry, James Stuart Dart, includes information on his parents and grandparents in his SAR application. Application of James Stuart Dart to the Illinois chapter of SAR approved 17 Sep 1925.
[2523] The 1851 will (probate 1852) of Walter Chase of Hamden includes a bequest to daughter Mary Ann Peak; New York Wills and Probate, Delaware County, volume E, pp 243-244

xi   JULIA PEAKE, b. about 1818; d. at Hartford, PA, 1891; m. ALVIN STEARNS, b. in PA, 18 Jan 1819 son of Ira and Maria (Plumb) Stearns;[2524] Alvin d. at Hartford, 21 Apr 1900.

xii   SYBIL PEAKE, b. 11 Jul 1819;[2525] d. at Chicago, IL, 4 Jun 1899; m. ALBERT DART, b. at Newburgh, NY, 29 Oct 1810 son of Joshua and Frances (Mallory) Dart; Albert d. at Chicago, 22 Apr 1889.

xiii   ELEAZER HOMER PEAKE, b. 15 Oct 1821; d. at Franklin, NY, 1 Sep 1873; m. about 1848, MARY MILLER HOLMES, b. about 1826.

821)   ELIJAH PEAKE (*Sibbel Marcy Peake⁴, Mary Russell Marcy³, Benjamin², Robert¹*), b. 1775 son of Moses and Sibbel (Marcy) Peake; d. at Warren, NY, 26 Oct 1858; m. by 1803 although the name of his wife has not been found.

Elijah resided in Warren, New York. Elijah Peak did leave a will, but the will is not in the available probate file. William Kinne was executor of the will. Probate documents filed by William Kinne on 4 November 1858 identify the following heirs to the estate of Elijah Peak: Polly Peak of Warren; Alanson L. Peak of Medina, Ohio; Uriah A. Peak of Green Bay, Wisconsin; and Powers grandchildren (Lansing Powers, Catherine Powers or McDonals, Perlina Powers, and Ransom Powers). A trust was established for the care of daughter Polly Peak.[2526]

There are four known children of Elijah Peake.[2527]

i   URIAH H. PEAK, b. about 1804; d. after 1870 when living at Fort Howard, WI; m. at Medina County, OH, 22 Nov 1832, SOPHIA SIMMONS, b. in NY, about 1813; Sophia d. after 1870.

ii   PERLINA PEAK, b. about 1807; d. at Granger, OH, after 1850 and before 1858; m. ISAAC POWERS, b. in NY, about 1807; Isaac d. after 1850.

iii   ALANSON LIVINGSTON PEAK, b. 1808; d. at Medina, OH, Apr 1873; m. at Medina County, OH, 19 Dec 1837, HARRIET NEWELL WINSLOW, b. 1820 daughter of John and Mary (Covell) Winslow; Harriet d. at Medina, 3 Dec 1910.

iv   POLLY PEAK, b. 1812; d. after 1875 when living at German Flatts, NY with a cousin. Polly did not marry. In the 1840 census for father Elijah, there is a daughter listed who is disabled and perhaps that refers to Polly.[2528]

822)   SYBIL PEAKE (*Sibbel Marcy Peake⁴, Mary Russell Marcy³, Benjamin², Robert¹*), b. about 1780 daughter of Moses and Sibbel (Marcy) Peake; m. about 1800, EPHRAIM FRISBEE, b. at Ellsworth, CT, 21 May 1778 son of Hezekiah and Susan (Marvin) Frisbee.[2529] Ephraim d. at Pittsburgh, PA, 2 Nov 1862. Ephraim had a second marriage to Mary who was his wife in the 1850 census.

Sybil and Ephraim were first in Schenectady after their marriage but arrived in the Pittsburgh area in 1808. Ephraim was a ship's carpenter by trade working first for Robert Fulton building steam packets,[2530] and about 1808, Ephraim started the first boatyard at the Point in Pittsburgh.[2531]

In 1850, Ephraim and wife Mary, age 66, were living in Pittsburgh. Ephraim's daughter Elizabeth Dilworth and granddaughter Mary Emma Dilworth were living with him. He gave his occupation as spring maker.[2532] In 1860, Ephraim gave his occupation as carpenter, and added to the family then was granddaughter Mary Emma's husband Thomas McLelland and two great-grandchildren.[2533]

In his will written 1 April 1859, Ephraim Firsbee of Pittsburgh bequeathed to son Roswell R. Frisbee three hundred dollars and his wife Catherine, two hundred dollars. The following bequests were made to his five daughters: Elizabeth widow of John Dilworth, three hundred dollars; Jane wife of Abraham Hains, one hundred dollars; Mary wife of William B. Scaife, two hundred dollars; and Syble wife of John Wilson, Sr., one hundred dollars, and Ann wife of Lewis Reno having received her full portion is purposely omitted from the will. The children of deceased son Amos D. Frisbee receive one hundred-fifty dollars to

[2524] Van Wagenen, *Stearns Genealogy and Memoirs*, Volume I, p 236

[2525] This is the birthdate given by her grandson Curtiss Melvin Dart in his SAR application; U.S., Sons of the American Revolution Membership Applications, 1889-1970

[2526] New York Probate Records, Herkimer County, Estate Papers 1857-1863 P, number 5906, Estate of Elijah Peake; accessed through familysearch.org. The settlement of the estate took several years and was marked by controversy among the heirs with copious correspondence in the estate file.

[2527] Although Elijah seemed to use the spelling Peake more often, the children seem to use the spelling Peak.

[2528] Year: 1840; Census Place: Warren, Herkimer, New York; Roll: 290; Page: 208; Family History Library Film: 0017190

[2529] Frisbee, *Frisbee-Frisbie Genealogy*, p 185

[2530] Frisbie, Nora, "The Wonderful Adventures of Roswell Riley Frisbee", *Firsbie-Frisbee Family Bulletin*, volume 51, number 1, 2001; published by Frisbie-Frisbee Family Association of America

[2531] Cushing, *A Genealogical and Biographical History of Allegheny County*, p 397

[2532] Year: 1850; Census Place: Pittsburgh Ward 1, Allegheny, Pennsylvania; Roll: 745; Page: 4B

[2533] Year: 1860; Census Place: Pittsburgh Ward 1, Allegheny, Pennsylvania; Page: 1; Family History Library Film: 805058

equally divide. Stepdaughter Eliza wife of John Bishop receives fifty dollars. William B. Scaife was named executor. In a codicil written 5 May 1861, Ephraim notes that his stepdaughter Eliza Bishop is deceased, and that legacy was revoked.[2534]

Sybil and Ephraim were parents of eight children, the older children born at Schenectady and the younger children at Pittsburgh.

i ROSWELL RILEY FRISBEE, b. at Schenectady, NY, 1 Jan 1802; d. at Pittsburgh, PA, 1880 (probate 31 Jul 1880; m. in Pittsburgh, 1830, CATHERINE JANE JONES, b. in NH, 1813 daughter of Silas and Catherine (Rolfe) Jones; Catherine d. at Pittsburgh, 4 Aug 1884.

ii AMOS DUNHAM FRISBEE, b. 1803; d. at Pittsburgh, 1857; m. 1830, ELEANOR JOHNSON, b. in PA, about 1811; Eleanor d. at Pittsburgh, 1856.

iii ANNA E. FRISBEE, b. 1806; d. at Pittsburgh, 2 May 1869; m. LEWIS H. RENO, b. 22 Nov 1798 son of Zachariah and Martha (McMichael) Reno; Lewis d. at Pittsburgh, 11 Jun 1877.

iv JANE FRISBEE, b. at Pittsburgh, 1808; m. ABRAHAM HAINES.

v ELIZABETH ADELINE FRISBEE, b. 1810; d. at Pittsburgh, 19 Sep 1886; m. 1834, JOHN DILWORTH, b. 1798 and died 1838 (age 40).[2535]

vi SYBIL FRISBEE; m. JOHN WILSON

vii SUSAN FRISBEE[2536]

viii MARY FRISBEE, b. at Pittsburgh, 1815; d. at Pittsburgh, 15 May 1905;[2537] m. WILLIAM BORRETT SCAIFE, b. at Pittsburgh, 5 Sep 1812 son of Jeffrey and Lydia (Borrett) Scaife; William d. at Pittsburgh, 2 Apr 1876.

823) JONATHAN AVERY (*Hannah Humphrey Avery⁴, Hannah Russell Humphrey³, Benjamin², Robert¹*), b. at Ashford, 2 Jul 1750 son of Jonathan and Hannah (Humphrey) Avery; d. at Canajoharie, NY, 24 Feb 1803; (probate 28 Feb 1803) m. at Ashford, 29 Nov 1773, CHLOE WALES, b. 1758 daughter of Elisha and Mary (Abbe) Wales.

Jonathan and Chloe were in Ashford, Connecticut, were for a time in Chester, Vermont where the birth of their fourth child was records, were likely then in Adams, Massachusetts before settling in Canajoharie, New York. In 1790, Jonathan Avery headed a household of eleven persons at Adams, Massachusetts: two male 16 and over, four males under 16, and five females.[2538]

Letters of administration of Jonathan Avery of Canajoharie were granted to his widow Chloe on 28 February 1803.[2539]

Jonathan Avery and Chloe Wells are likely parents of thirteen children, not all of whom have clear records.

i ELISHA AVERY, b. at Ashford, 5 Nov 1774; m. at Charlemont, MA, 1802, BETHIA THOMSON, b. at Charlemont, 4 Aug 1775 daughter of Peter and Bethia (Thayer) Thomson.

ii HANNAH AVERY, b. at Ashford, 22 Feb 1777; perhaps m. at Adams, MA, 27 Oct 1797, DAVID W. HOPKINS who was not identified.

iii POLLY AVERY, b at Ashford, 21 Feb 1779; d. at Clarksburg, MA, 22 May 1830;[2540] m. at Adams, MA, 1 Mar 1797, SAMUEL CLARK, b. at Clarksburg, 20 Dec 1773 son of Nicholas and Esther (Grover) Clark; Samuel d. at North Adams, 5 Apr 1830. Polly was of Bullock's Grant at the time of her marriage.

iv JONATHAN AVERY, b. at Chester, VT, 24 Jul 1781; d. at Prattsburgh, NY, 4 Apr 1849; m. about 1808, MARY SPENCER, b. 11 Oct 1780 daughter of Obadiah Spencer;[2541] Mary d. at Prattsburgh, 25 Apr 1857.

v JOHN AVERY, b. 1783; d. at Prattsburgh, NY, 20 Dec 1857; m. about 1808, RUBY SPENCER, b. at Somers, CT, 1787 daughter of Obadiah Spencer; Ruby d. after 1870 when living at Prattsburgh.[2542]

[2534] Pennsylvania Wills and Probate, Allegheny County, Will Books, volume 10, pp 350-351

[2535] The cemetery records report that John Dilworth died at age 40. He was interred in the Frisbee vault on 12 May 1854. Three of the young children of Elizabeth and John were interred at the same time. The lot record can be seen at findagrave ID: 122292242

[2536] Susan is a child given in the Frisbee genealogy, p 185 who is not in her father's will.

[2537] "Pennsylvania Deaths and Burials, 1720-1999", database, *FamilySearch* (https://www.familysearch.org/ark:/61903/1:1:H541-HGN2 : 9 July 2020), Mary Frisbee Scaife, 1905.

[2538] Year: 1790; Census Place: Adams, Berkshire, Massachusetts; Series: M637; Roll: 4; Page: 23; Image: 40; Family History Library Film: 0568144

[2539] New York Wills and Probate, Montgomery County, Letters of Administration, volume 0001, p 96

[2540] Polly's gravestone includes her date of birth of 21 Feb 1779; Clark Cemetery, Clarksburg, Find a Grave 165420275

[2541] The will of Obadiah Spencer names his daughters Polly and Ruby, but the will was written in 1806 prior to their marriages; New York Wills and Probate, Chenango County, Wills Volume A, p 61

[2542] Year: 1870; Census Place: Prattsburg, Steuben, New York; Roll: M593_1096; Page: 384A

vi   CHLOE AVERY, b. 1785

vii   SILAS AVERY, b. 1788; d. at Otselic, NY, 12 May 1843; m. about 1810, LOVINA PHILLIPS, b. 1795; Lovina d. at Freetown, NY, 9 Jan 1863.

viii   AMELIA AVERY, b. 1790

ix   WALES AVERY, b. 1791; d. at Otselic, NY, 2 Mar 1854; m. about 1815, LUCINDA MORLEY, b. about 1793 likely daughter of Dimick and Ruth (Weston) Morley; Lucinda d. at Otselic, 9 Mar 1854.

x   DANIEL AVERY, b. 1793; d. 1808.

xi   ALPHEUS AVERY, b. 1796; d. at Smyrna, NY, 1824. In the 1820 census for Smyrna, Alpheus appears to have a wife and one child, but the name of his wife was not found.[2543]

xii   ALMIRA K. AVERY, b. 18 Mar 1798; d. at Hinckley, IL, 21 Dec 1890; m. at Halifax, VT, 26 Nov 1818, CYRUS CHASE NICHOLS, b. at Halifax, VT, 4 Mar 1798 son of Samuel and Rhoda (Carpenter) Nichols; Cyrus d. at Hinckley, 31 Jul 1872.

xiii   SALLY AVERY, b. 1801; d. 1802.

824)   RUTH EASTMAN (*Dorothy Humphrey Eastman⁴, Hannah Russell Humphrey³, Benjamin², Robert¹*), b. at Ashford, 20 Mar 1766 daughter of Samuel and Dorothy (Humphrey) Eastman; d. at Rockingham, VT, 31 Dec 1829; m. at Rockingham, 26 Aug 1789, JOHN BURT STEARNS, b. at Harvard, MA, 7 Sep 1764 son of William and Elizabeth (Burt) Stearns; John d. at Rockingham, 3 Oct 1845.

         John Burt Stearns served in the War of 1812. He was a farmer is Rockingham.[2544]
         Ruth Eastman and John Burt Stearns were parents of seven children born at Rockingham, Vermont.

i   ELIZABETH "BETSEY" BURT STEARNS, b. 14 Feb 1790; d. at Rockingham, 25 Nov 1871; m. about 1812, DAVID DAVIS, b. at Rockingham, 30 Oct 1788 son of Henry and Mary (Tuttle) Davis; David d. at Rockingham, 20 Sep 1871.

ii   JOHN EASTMAN STEARNS, b. 13 Mar 1792; m. at Chester, VT, 4 Jan 1816, JANE TARBELL, b. at Chester, 10 Aug 1792 daughter of Jonathan and Jane (Gleason) Tarbell.

iii   OTIS STEARNS, b. 19 May 1794; d. at Chester, VT, 1 Nov 1860; m. at Chester, VT, 4 May 1820, MARTHA "PATTY" OLCOTT, b. at Chester, 17 Dec 1798 daughter of Thomas C. and Betsey (Mann) Olcott; Martha d. at Chester, 3 Feb 1842.

iv   JABEZ STEARNS, b. 9 Oct 1796; d. at Peterborough, NH, 6 Oct 1854; m. at Fitzwilliam, 4 Jan 1829, CLARISSA BUSS, b. at Jaffrey, 20 Apr 1805 daughter of Samuel and Lucy (Emery) Buss; Clarissa d. at East Jaffrey, 14 May 1887. Jabez was a carpenter and cabinetmaker.

v   MARIA STEARNS, b. 9 Jan 1801; d. at Fillmore, NY, 6 Apr 1875; m. at Rockingham, 19 Sep 1832, as his second wife, GEORGE MINARD, b. at Rockingham, 31 May 1802 son of Isaac and Lucy (Waite) Minard; George m. at Fillmore, 1 Apr 1853. George was first married to Irene who died in 1832 at age 24.

vi   WILLIAM BURT STEARNS, b. 18 Dec 1803; d. at Rockingham, 26 Apr 1865; m. SOPHIA MASON, b. Nov 1807 daughter of Aaron and Esther (Plank) Mason; Sophia d. at Chester, 22 Jun 1895.

vii   SAMUEL EASTMAN STEARNS, b. 3 Aug 1806; d. after 1870 when living at Lincoln, IA; m. 1833, RHODA BLANCHARD, b. at Rockingham, 3 Apr 1812 daughter of Jonathan and Mary (Lovell) Blanchard; Rhoda d. at Paxton, IL, 23 Jan 1896.

825)   SAMUEL EASTMAN (*Dorothy Humphrey Eastman⁴, Hannah Russell Humphrey³, Benjamin², Robert¹*), b. at Rehoboth, MA, 30 Mar 1768 son of Samuel and Dorothy (Humphrey) Eastman; m. at Rockingham, VT, 24 May 1789, ABIGAIL STOWELL, b. at Willington, 9 Aug 1770 daughter of Samuel and Anna (Russ) Stowell.[2545]

         Samuel served nine months in the Continental army during the Revolution.[2546]

[2543] 1820 U S Census; Census Place: Smyrna, Chenango, New York; Page: 335; NARA Roll: M33_66; Image: 189

[2544] Van Wagenen, *Genealogy and Memoirs of Isaac Stearns*, p 249

[2545] Stowell, *The Stowell Genealogy*, p 84

[2546] Rix, *History and Genealogy of the Eastman Family*, p 168

Samuel and Abigail were in Rockingham, Vermont where the births of their children are recorded. In 1810, Samuel headed a household of fifteen at Rockingham, Vermont: one male 26 to 44, three females 26 to 44, three males under 10, one male 10 to 15, one male 16 to 25, three females under 10, and three females 10 to 15.[2547]

On 24 April 1816, Samuel Eastman of Rockingham, in consideration of eighteen hundred dollars, sold to Gates Perry, Daniel Kellogg, and John Campbell "all the land I own in Rockingham."[2548]

The family was next in Shrewsbury, Vermont where in 1820, Samuel headed a household of nine persons: one male 45 and over, one female 45 and over, two males 10 to 15, two males 16 to 25, one female under 10, one female 10 to 15, and one female 16 to 25.[2549]

The family may have been next in Mendon, Vermont in 1830 with a household of six persons: one male 60 to 69, one female 60 to 69, one male 20 to 29, one male 30 to 39, one female 5 to 9, and one female 15 to 19.[2550] Samuel also appears in the 1840 census at Mendon with a household of one male 70 to 79 and one female 60 to 69.[2551]

Samuel Eastman and Abigail Stowell were parents of twelve children born at Rockingham, Vermont.

i   RISPAH EASTMAN, b. 23 Jan 1790; d. 9 May 1790.

ii   UMPHIRA EASTMAN, b. 10 Mar 1791; d. 23 Feb 1792.

iii SAMUEL EASTMAN, b. 4 Sep 1792; d. at Anna, IL, 19 Feb 1858; m. 4 Jul 1818, ELIZABETH TANNER, b. at Clarendon, VT, 20 May 1800 daughter of Josias and Hannah (Cheney) Tanner; Elizabeth d. at Pontiac, MI, 4 Sep 1826.

iv   ABIGAIL EASTMAN, b. 8 May 1794; m. at Shrewsbury, VT, 9 Aug 1818, JOHN CHENEY, b. at Clarendon, VT, 4 Oct 1782 son of Ephraim and Bathsheba (Segar) Cheney

v   CAROLINE EASTMAN, b. 16 Aug 1796; d. after 1875 when living at Canaan, NY in the Shaker community;[2552] m. at Shrewsbury, VT, 4 Mar 1823, CONSTANT WEBBER, b. at Shrewsbury, 26 Jul 1791 son of William and Hannah (Barney) Webber; Constant d. at Shrewsbury, 5 Nov 1873. It is assumed that Caroline and Constant divorced, although the record was not located. Constant married second Meriba Aldrich. Caroline is recorded in census records at the Shaker Community in Canaan, NY beginning in 1855.[2553]

vi   SEBA EASTMAN, b. 18 Jul 1798; d. at Peru, OH, 4 Jul 1850; m. at Grafton, VT, 19 Dec 1830, KEZIAH EDSON, b. 8 Dec 1801 daughter of Ebenezer and Keziah (Caldwell) Edson;[2554] Keziah d. at Peru, 3 May 1877.

vii LAURA EASTMAN, b. 11 Jun 1800; d. after 1860 when living at Union, IA; m. at Shrewsbury, VT, 21 Mar 1822. JOHN BULLARD, b. at Shrewsbury, 1800 son of John and Lucy (Buxton) Bullard; John d. after 1850 when living at Le Roy, IL.

viii CHARLES EASTMAN, b. 18 May 1802; d. at Crawford County, OH, 18 Dec 1844.

ix   WALTER EASTMAN, b. 22 Oct 1804; d. after 1865 when living at Hume, NY. Walter was twice married. The named of his first wife was not found, but she was deceased before 1850. Walter m. 2nd about 1851, widow SARAH WILLY, b. about 1822; Sarah d. after 1870 when living at Hume.

x   NANCY EASTMAN, b. 3 May 1806; d. after 1870 when living at Galien, MI; m. HARLEY WATERHOUSE, b. in VT, about 1801; Harley d. after 1880 when living at Lake, MI.

xi   JARVIS CHASE EASTMAN, b. 9 May 1810; d. at Marengo, IL, 6 Apr 1844; m. at McHenry County, IL, 4 Jul 1843, SARAH ANN SPONKNABLE, b. in OH about 1822 daughter of Christopher Sponknable;[2555] Sarah Ann d. Marengo, OH, 1908. Sarah married second Elijah Lyons. Jarvis and Sarah had one daughter Philura.

xii PHILURA EASTMAN, b. 20 Feb 1815; m. JOHN BROWN.[2556]

[2547] Year: 1810; Census Place: Rockingham, Windham, Vermont; Roll: 65; Page: 334; Image: 00241; Family History Library Film: 0218669
[2548] Vermont Land Records, Town of Rockingham, 5:524
[2549] 1820 U S Census; Census Place: Shrewsbury, Rutland, Vermont; Page: 509; NARA Roll: M33_126; Image: 239
[2550] Year: 1830; Census Place: Mendon, Rutland, Vermont; Series: M19; Roll: 188; Page: 118; Family History Library Film: 0027454
[2551] Year: 1840; Census Place: Mendon, Rutland, Vermont; Roll: 545; Page: 82; Family History Library Film: 0027441
[2552] New York, U.S., State Census, 1875
[2553] New York, U.S., State Census, 1855
[2554] Edson, *Edson Family History*, p 591
[2555] The 1854 probate of Christopher Sponknale of McHenry County, Illinois includes a distribution to Sarah Ann Lyon wife of Elijah Lyon (Elijah was Sarah's second husband); Illinois Wills and Probate, McHenry County, Estate of Chris Sponknable, Nov 25 1854
[2556] This is a marriage reported in the Eastman genealogy for which records were not located; Rix, *History and Genealogy of the Eastman Family*, p

826)   JOHN EASTMAN (*Dorothy Humphrey Eastman⁴, Hannah Russell Humphrey³, Benjamin², Robert¹*), b. at Rehoboth, MA, 6 Sep 1770 son of Samuel and Dorothy (Humphrey) Eastman; d. at Grafton, VT, 24 Jul 1827 at age 57 years; m. at Grafton, VT, 18 Dec 1794, ELIZABETH STICKNEY, b. at Billerica, 31 May 1772 daughter of William and Abigail (Walker) Stickney;[2557] Elizabeth d. at Grafton, 15 May 1857.

John had gone with his family to Rockingham, Vermont. On 11 February 1788, Samuel conveyed to his son John half-interest in his farm in Rockingham.[2558]

John married Elizabeth Stickney of Grafton, Vermont and they were in Rockingham immediately after their marriage. They settled in Grafton in 1800 where they kept a farm. On 14 July 1800, John Eastman sold his part of the property to Ichabod Eastman for payment of six hundred dollars.[2559] On 14 July 1800, John Eastman of Rockingham purchased the south half of a lot in the ninth range at Grafton from Ebenezer Burditt for payment of $600. On 9 May 1816, John Eastman of Grafton purchased 250 acres from Simeon Eams and Benjamin Thrasher for payment of $2,100.[2560]

On 3 November 1822, John Eastman conveyed to John Eastman, Jr. several lots in Grafton for payment of $112. The parcels were lot fifteen in the fourth range and lot fifteen in the fourth range. John conveyed additional property to John, Jr. on 14 March 1827.[2561]

On 26 April 1836, Hyman Eastman of Grafton, for payment of $50, conveyed to John Eastman all his interest in the estate of John Eastman deceased. The property was lots three and four of the ninth range. In May 1839, John Eastman quitclaimed his interest in a portion of the estate of John Eastman to Elizabeth Eastman, Nancy Eastman, Horace Eastman, and Hyman Eastman. At the same time, Elizabeth Eastman, Nancy Eastman, and Betsey Eastman quitclaimed interest in other of the properties to Horace and Hyman. On 17 July 1839, Hubbard Eastman, then of Rindge, New Hampshire, quitclaimed his interest in a 250-acre parcel to Horace and Hyman. On 19 February 1840, Elizabeth, Betsey, and Nancy quitclaimed their interest in this 250-acre parcel to Hyman. On 16 July 1840, Hubbard quitclaimed a further interest in the property to Hyman and at the same time quitclaimed part of his interest to Elizabeth and other of his interest in the property to Nancy Eastman.[2562]

In 1850, Elizabeth Eastman was living with her daughter Betsey and her husband John Wyman and their daughter Martha. Also in the home was Nancy Eastman aged 48 who was the daughter of John and Elizabeth.[2563]

In his will, son Hyman Eastman bequeathed to his beloved wife Mary Jane all the household furniture and the second-best gold watch and chain. He notes his obligation to care for his honored mother Elizabeth Eastman and his executor is to provide her a comfortable support. The remainder of the estate goes to his wife and any remaining at her decease is to go to his son Horace Alonzo Eastman. If his son pre-deceases his wife, then the estate is to be divided between the children of his brother John Eastman and his sister Betsey Wyman wife of John Wyman.[2564]

John Eastman and Elizabeth Stickney were parents of eight children the two eldest children likely born at Rockingham, Vermont, and the others at Grafton. The children can be established through deed and probate information.

i   JOHN EASTMAN, b. about 1797; d. at Grafton, VT, 14 Mar 1885; m. MARTHA "PATTY" DAVIS, b. at Grafton, 20 Mar 1804 daughter of Oliver and Patty (Page) Davis; Martha d. at Grafton, 27 Mar 1885.

ii   HORACE EASTMAN, b. about 1798; d. at Grafton, 28 Aug 1839.[2565]

iii   BETSEY EASTMAN, b. about 1800; d. at Rockingham, VT, 29 Sep 1886; m. about 1842, JOHN WYMAN, b. at Walpole, NH, 3 Oct 1804 son of Uzziah and Lydia (Nutting) Wyman; John d. at Grafton, 14 Sep 1883. John and Betsey had an infant that died near birth and a daughter Mary Elizabeth.

iv   NANCY EATMAN, b. 1803; d. at Grafton, 7 Feb 1893. Nancy did not marry.

v   ISAAC EASTMAN, b. 1808; d. at Grafton, 24 Sep 1829.[2566]

vi   Rev. HUBBARD EASTMAN, b. 22 Jan 1809; d. at Jacksonville, VT, 4 May 1891; d. at Jacksonville, VT, 4 May 1891; m. 1ˢᵗ 16 Mar 1836, SARAH CHAMBERLAIN BALCH, b. at Athens, VT, 15 Jan 1810 daughter of Nathaniel and Sarah (Bennett) Balch; Sarah d. (burial at Athens), 26 Nov 1841. Hubbard m. 2ⁿᵈ at Whitingham, VT, 28 Sep 1867, LUCY MELINDA CHASE (widow of Samuel Newell), b. at Whitingham, 6 Oct 1831 daughter of Moses and Anna (Briggs) Chase; Lucy d. at Dublin, NH, 30 Nov 1919.

vii   HYMAN EASTMAN, b. Feb 1811; d. at Grafton, 10 Oct 1814.

[2557] The names of Elizabeth's parents are given as William and Abigail Stickney on her death record; Vermont, Vital Records, 1720-1908

[2558] Vermont Land Records, Town of Rockingham, 1:389

[2559] Vermont Land Records, Town of Rockingham, 2:814

[2560] Vermont Land Records, Town of Grafton, 4:34, 5:272

[2561] Vermont Land Records, Town of Grafton, 6:197, 6:540

[2562] Vermont Land Records, Town of Grafton, 7:379, 8:49, 8:53, 8:65, 8:91, 8:114, 8:115, 8:116

[2563] Year: 1850; Census Place: Grafton, Windham, Vermont; Roll: 929; Page: 306b

[2564] Vermont Wills and Probate, Windham County, Folder 4, Wrp6-90744, Bundle 6-7, Hyman Eastman, Case W423

[2565] Horace is interred at Burgess Cemetery in Grafton; Find a Grave 182771573

[2566] Isaac in interred at Burgess Cemetery in Grafton; Find a Grave 182771586

viii   HYMAN EASTMAN, b. about 1815; d. at Rockingham, 3 Mar 1855; m. at Epping, NH, 20 Oct 1839, MARY JANE LADD, b. at Epping, 31 Mar 1818 daughter of Nathaniel and Mary (Gordon) Ladd; Mary Jane d. at Tilton, NH, 27 Jul 1901.

827)   ICHABOD EASTMAN (*Dorothy Humphrey Eastman⁴, Hannah Russell Humphrey³, Benjamin², Robert¹*), b. at Rehoboth, MA, 30 Sep 1773 son of Samuel and Dorothy (Humphrey) Eastman; d. at Hancock, VT, 7 Feb 1841; m. at Rockingham, 23 Feb 1804, MABEL WOLF, b. at Rockingham, 14 Sep 1783 daughter of John C. and Rachel (Battles) Wolf;[2567] Mabel d. at Hancock, 22 Mar 1841.

Ichabod accompanied his father to Rockingham, Vermont. In 1800, his brother John conveyed his interest in the family homestead to Ichabod.[2568] Ichabod married at Rockingham and remained there until 1817 when the family moved to Hancock, Vermont. On 4 February 1817, Ichabod sold his property in Rockingham to Benjamin Smith for payment of twelve hundred dollars.[2569] On 11 March 1817, Ichabod Eastman of Rockingham purchased lot number two and half (50 acres) of lot number five in Hancock from Benjamin Smith for payment of eight hundred dollars.[2570]

In 1830, Ichabod's household was five persons in Hancock: one male 50 to 59, one female 40 to 49, one male 5 to 9, one female 10 to 14, and one female 15 to 19.[2571] In 1840, Ichabod headed a household of four persons in Hancock: one male 60 to 69, one female 50 to 59, one male 15 to 19, and one female 20 to 29.[2572]

On 11 July 1840, Ichabod Eastman conveyed all his real property in Hancock including his pew in the meeting house to Joseph Phillips (his son-in-law) in exchange for an agreement from Joseph Phillips to maintain Ichabod and his wife Mabel for the remainder of their natural lives.[2573]

There are records for six children of Ichabod Eastman and Mabel Wolf.

i   LUCY EASTMAN, b. at Rockingham, 5 May 1805; d. at Hancock, VT, 21 Aug 1822.

ii   ELECTA EASTMAN, b. at Rockingham, 5 Apr 1807; d. at Leicester, VT, 21 Sep 1881; m. 18 Oct 1829, SILAS WHITNEY STANLEY, b. at Leicester, 27 Nov 1797 son of Jonathan P. and Mary (Whitney) Stanley; Silas d. at Leicester, 9 Par 1879.

iii   DOROTHY HUMPHREY EASTMAN, b. at Rockingham, 5 Oct 1812; d. at Starksboro, VT, 18 Feb 1852; m. 1ˢᵗ at Kingston, VT, 1 Dec 1831, ELIJAH LEE, b. at Kingston, VT, 14 Jan 1806 son of William and Electa (-) Lee; Elijah d. at Hancock, 27 Sep 1835. Dorothy m. 2ⁿᵈ JOSEPH W. PHILLIPS, b. at Starksboro, 23 May 1816 son of Solomon and Susannah (Wilson) Phillips; Joseph d. at Mulvane, KS, 26 Apr 1895. Joseph married second Melissa Chaffee.

iv   MABEL CATHERINE EASTMAN, b. at Rockingham, 9 Aug 1816; d. at Haverhill, MA, 28 Jan 1906; m. 29 Jul 1841, CHARLES WHITE BOARDMAN, b. at Newburyport, 22 Feb 1812 son of Benjamin G. and Susanna (White) Boardman; Charles d. at Haverhill, 23 Sep 1885.

v   JAMES WILLARD EASTMAN, b. 17 Aug 1820; d. 26 Aug 1822.

vi   WILLARD V. EASTMAN, b. at Hancock, 1 Feb 1823; d. at Royalton, VT, 27 Mar 1912; m. at Pomfret, VT, 20 Mar 1845, SARAH P. CULVER, b. at Pomfret, VT, 24 Apr 1824 daughter of John and Martha (Pratt) Culver; Sarah d. at Royalton, 7 May 1910. Willard and Sarah did not have children. In his will written 10 October 1906, Willard left his estate to his wife Sarah during her life, and afterwards to go to Herbert W. Culver of Charlton, Massachusetts.[2574]

828)   BENJAMIN PITTS (*Rachel Humphrey Pitts⁴, Hannah Russell Humphrey³, Benjamin², Robert¹*), b. at Ashford, 6 Nov 1754 son of John and Rachel (Humphrey) Pitts; d. at Ashford, by 1794 (guardianship of son); m. at Ashford, 19 Sep 1776, FREELOVE WHIPPLE, b. about 1747; Freelove d. at Providence, RI, 3 Feb 1805.

Two children of Benjamin and Freelove were born at Ashford. On 26 December 1794, son James selected Comfort Carpenter as his guardian. James's estate was administered by Comfort Carpenter in 1801.[2575]

i   JAMES PITTS, b. 5 Dec 1780; d. at Ashford, 17 Sep 1801.

[2567] Rix, *History and Genealogy of the Eastman Family*, p 169

[2568] Vermont Land Records, Town of Rockingham, 2:814

[2569] Vermont Land Records, Town of Rockingham, 7:83

[2570] Vermont Land Records, Town of Hancock, 2:245

[2571] Year: 1830; Census Place: Hancock, Addison, Vermont; Series: M19; Roll: 184; Page: 277; Family History Library Film: 0027450

[2572] Year: 1840; Census Place: Addison, Vermont; Roll: 538; Page: 66; Family History Library Film: 0027438

[2573] Vermont Land Records, Town of Hancock, 4:281, 4:282

[2574] Vermont Wills and Probate, Windsor County, volume 69, p 562

[2575] Connecticut Wills and Probate, Pomfret District, Town of Ashford, Estate of James Pitts, 1801, No. 3282

ii   MARCY WHIPPLE PITTS, b. 14 Dec 1783

829)   JEREMIAH PITTS (*Rachel Humphrey Pitts⁴, Hannah Russell Humphrey³, Benjamin², Robert¹*), b. at Ashford, 24 Jan 1758 son of John and Rachel (Humphrey) Pitts; m. at Ashford, 17 Apr 1780, IRENA YOUNGLOVE, baptized at Thompson, 21 Feb 1758 daughter of Samuel and Sarah (Pitts) Younglove.
        Jeremiah and Irena were in Ashford and seem to have been in Monson. It is possible that they were later in Cavendish, Vermont.
        In 1800, Jeremiah Pitts headed a household of five persons in Monson: one male 26 to 44, one female 26 to 44, one female under 10, one female 10 to 15, and one female 16 to 25.[2576]
        There are records of five children of Jeremiah and Irena born at Ashford.

i   SALLY PITTS, b. 1 Feb 1781

ii   RACHEL PITTS, b. 25 Nov 1783; m. at Cavendish, VT, 10 Apr 1804, JOSEPH WILKINS, b. 16 Aug 1769 son of
            Joseph and Phebe (-) Wilkins; Joseph d. at Cavendish, 26 Jun 1846.

iii   SAMUEL PITTS, b. 13 Mar 1785; m. at Pawlet, VT, 3 Dec 1809, ELIZABETH HAMILTON.

iv   PERSIS PITTS, b. 6 Sep 1787

v   PERLEY PITTS, b. 20 Sep 1791

830)   SALOME PITTS (*Rachel Humphrey Pitts⁴, Hannah Russell Humphrey³, Benjamin², Robert¹*), b. at Ashford, 24 Mar 1766 daughter of John and Rachel (Humphrey) Pitts; d. at Dellona, WI, Apr 1860; m. at Ashford, 22 Jun 1790 by Benjamin Sumner, Esq., JOHN GREENSLIT, b. at Hampton, CT, 5 Jun 1767 son of John and Sarah (Burnham) Greenslit; John d. at Dellona, 1 Apr 1856.
        On 7 August 1832, John Greenslit, aged 65 years of Warren, Vermont, provided a statement related to his application for pension. He 1 September 1782 for a term of one year in the Connecticut state troops under Capt. Henry Durkee in Col. McClarie's regiment. He was stationed six months at Fort Trumbull in New London and then three at Fort Griswold. He served one year and was discharged 1 September 1783 at Fort Griswold. Lieut. Thomas Hodgkins provided an affidavit of his service. He further reported he was born in Hampton, Windham County in June 1767 and was living at Hampton when he enlisted. He resided at Pomfret and Ashford until 1810 when he moved to Monson, Massachusetts. In 1817, he went to Brookfield, Randolph, and then Warren, Vermont where he had been for the last eleven years. He was granted a pension based on his service. He provided a follow-up statement on 14 April 1855, then aged 87 years and living in Warren, this declaration being made for the purpose of obtaining bounty land.
        On 29 August 1857, widow Salome Greenslit, aged ninety-one years of Dellona, Wisconsin, provided a statement for the widow's pension. She married John Greenslit at Ashford on 20 June 1790 and her maiden name was Salome Pitts. Her husband died on 1 April 1856. On 18 June 1856, Salome made a statement related to receiving bounty land.[2577] Saloem received a bounty for 160 acres in Dodge County, Wisconsin which she assigned to her son Stephen who later reassigned the property.
        John Greenslit was the only Revolutionary War veteran interred in Sauk county, Wisconsin, and on 4 July 1975, a grave-marking ceremony was held. In preparation for this, the Wisconsin State Old Cemetery Society contacted descendants and prepared a booklet on John's life.
        Salome Pitts and John Greenslit were parents of eight children.[2578]

i   PAMELIA GREENSLIT, b. at Ashford, 13 Nov 1790; d. 13 Dec 1791.

ii   AUGUSTINE GREENSLIT, b. at Ashford, 11 Aug 1792; m. at Waitsfield, VT, 25 May 1820, JUDITH NUTTING,
            b. about 1799 perhaps daughter of David and Rebecca (Butterfield) Nutting. Augustine was living at Warren, VT
            in 1840 heading a household of four persons.[2579]

iii   CHESTER GREENSLIT, b. at Ashford, 22 Jul 1794

iv   BETSEY GREENSLIT, b. at Ashford, 16 Jun 1796; *perhaps* m. at Warren, VT, 13 Dec 1838, HIRAM DANA.

v   MARCENIA EDWARD GREENSLIT, b. at Hampton, CT, 8 Jul 1798; d. at Warren, VT, 23 May 1873; m. at
            Brookfield, VT, 24 Feb 1821, SOPHIA BAGLEY, b. 1799; Sophia d. at Warren, 10 Jan 1840.

[2576] Year: 1800; Census Place: Monson, Hampshire, Massachusetts; Series: M32; Roll: 15; Page: 1082; Image: 266; Family History Library Film: 205614

[2577] U. S. Revolutionary War Pension and Bounty-Land Warrant Application Files, case W9465

[2578] Wisconsin State Old Cemetery Society, *Pvt. John Greenslit, Revolutionary War Soldier*, p 23

[2579] Year: 1840; Census Place: Warren, Washington, Vermont; Roll: 546; Page: 278; Family History Library Film: 0027441

vi   JOHN R. GREENSLIT, b. at Hampton, 8 Jul 1798; d. after 1850 when living at Seneca, IL. John likely had a first wife whose name was not found. John m. 2nd at Bridport, VT, 4 Nov 1832, SAREPTA ELIZA SHAW, b. at Craftsbury, VT, 20 Dec 1816 daughter of Seth T. and Clarinda (Mason) Shaw; Sarepta d. by 1860. Sarepta married second Jacob Harder on 9 Feb 1853.

vii   STEPHEN GREENSLIT, b. at Brookfield, VT, 9 Jul 1800; d. at Marshall, MN, 8 Jan 1880; m. at Bridport, 25 Dec 1827, ZURIAH SHAW, b. 20 Feb 1800 daughter of Richard and Eliza (Pitts) Shaw; Zuriah d. at Marshall, 1888.

viii   HENRY GREENSLIT, b. likely at Brookfield, VT, 8 Jun 1804; d. at Mitchell, SD, 9 Oct 1892; m. 1st at New Haven, VT, 11 Nov 1826, AURELIA CRANE, b. 21 Jun 1806 daughter of Martin and Rachel (Thompson) Crane; Aurelia d. at Fairfield, WI, 18 Jan 1874. Henry m. 2nd 24 Apr 1876, RHODA DENNIS.

831)   NATHAN EATON (*Mary Humphrey Eaton⁴, Hannah Russell Humphrey³, Benjamin², Robert¹*), b. at Ashford, 29 Aug 1755 son of Ebenezer and Mary (Humphrey) Eaton; d. at Manchester, VT, 2 Jun 1840; m. at Ashford, 16 Dec 1779, PHEBE BROOKS, b. at Ashford, 24 Jul 1757 daughter of John and Abial (Wright) Brooks; Phebe d. at Manchester, 19 Feb 1836.

Nathan and Phebe started their family in Ashford, Connecticut, were then in Winhall, Vermont and lastly in Manchester.

Nathan headed a household of eight persons at Winhall, Vermont in 1790: one male sixteen and over, two males under 16 and five females.[2580] Six persons are given in the 1810 census at Manchester: one male 45 and over, one female 45 and over, one male under 10, one male 16 to 25, one female 10 to 15, and one female 16 to 25.[2581]

On 7 August 1832, Nathan Eaton, aged seventy-six years of Manchester, Vermont, provided a statement related to his application for a pension. He was born at Ashford on 29 August 1755 and resided there until March 1785. On 25 June 1776, he enlisted at Ashford for six months in the company of Capt. Reuben Marcy in the regiment of Col. John Chester. The troops went to New York and were on Long Island for eight days until driven off with Gen. Sullivan. From there he was a White Plains where the enemy were engaged. He was next at Kingsbridge and Valentine Hill. His enlistment ended on 25 December 1776. He next enlisted in February or 1 March 1777 in the company of Capt. Morley and marched to Providence. In this enlistment, he was a guard. He was drafted on 1 April 1780 from Ashford and was in New London and served six weeks. After the war, Nathan was in Ashford until about 1785 when he went to Winhall, Vermont and in 1799 removed to Manchester. Nathan's brother Ebenezer provided a statement in support of his application.[2582]

Nathan did not leave a will. Gurden Eaton was named estate administrator on 21 September 1840.[2583]

Nathan and Phebe were likely parents of eight children.[2584]

i   MALINDA EATON, b. at Ashford, CT, 4 Jul 1780; d. at Perry, OH, 16 Oct 1865; m. at Manchester, VT, 4 May 1800, WILLIAM WYMAN, b. at Northfield, MA, 16 Jun 1765 son of William and Margaret (Holmes) Wyman; William d. at Perry, 6 Mar 1842.

ii   D'ESTAING EATON, b. 8 Jun 1782; d. at Brookfield, VT, 10 Jan 1847; m. at Manchester, VT, 1 May 1803, EUNICE PEARSON, b. at Manchester, 13 Oct 1784 daughter of Ephraim and Phebe (Cleveland) Pearson;[2585] Eunice d. at New Berlin, NY, 22 Aug 1866.

iii   CLARA EATON, b. 1785

iv   LORINDA EATON, b. 1787

v   GURDEN EATON, b. at Winhall, VT, 1793; d. at Manchester, VT, 23 Sep 1868; m. at Manchester, VT, 20 Dec 1813, ROXANNA DARLING, b. at Leyden, MA, 26 Nov 1795 daughter of Ehud and Martha (Tyler) Darling (parents named as Ehud and Martha on death record); Roxanna d. at Manchester 11 Oct 1880.

vi   SABRINA EATON, b. 12 Nov 1795; m. about 1816, AMOS EASTMAN, b. at Rupert, VT, 6 Sep 1790 son of Stephen and Jerusha (Jones) Eastman;[2586] Amos d. at Manchester, VT, 1845.

vii   AMELIA EATON, b. 1797; d. at Adams, MA, about 1823; m. about 1815, JOHN CAIN, b. at Taunton, 24 May 1790 son of John and Annah (Barrows) Cain.

viii   ORVILLE EATON, b. 1801; d. at Allendale, MI, 8 Jul 1885; m. DIANAH FRANKLIN, b. in NY 1818; Dianah d. at Almont, MI, 10 Apr 1874. Orville and Dianah seem to have divorced. Orville m. 2nd CANDACE L. BOWEN, b. in NY, about 1836.

[2580] Year: 1790; Census Place: Winhall, Bennington, Vermont; Series: M637; Roll: 12; Page: 24; Image: 39; Family History Library Film: 0568152

[2581] Year: 1810; Census Place: Manchester, Bennington, Vermont; Roll: 64; Page: 97A; Image: 00188; Family History Library Film: 0218668

[2582] U. S. Revolutionary War Pension and Bounty-Land Warrant Application Files, Case S15821

[2583] Vermont Wills and Probate, Bennington County, Nathan Eaton, 1840

[2584] The children have varying degrees of support; those in need of additional evidence are Clara and Lorinda.

[2585] Cleveland, *The Genealogy of the Cleveland Family*, p 280

[2586] Rix, *History and Genealogy of the Eastman Family*, p 262

832)   EBENEZER EATON (*Mary Humphrey Eaton⁴, Hannah Russell Humphrey³, Benjamin², Robert¹*), b. at Ashford, 18 Dec 1760 son of Ebenezer and Mary (Humphrey) Eaton; d. at Sherburne, NY, 10 Dec 1839; m. about 1784, MARY "POLLY" BERRY, b. 1763; Polly d. at Sherburne, 24 Nov 1849.

Ebenezer was a farmer. The family settled in Sherburne, New York, although census records suggest the three oldest children were born in Vermont.

Ebenezer served five years in the Revolution. On 10 February 1829, Ebenezer Eaton, aged sixty-eight years of Sherburne, provided a statement related to his application for a pension for his service in the Revolution. He first enlisted for a term of fifteen months in the state of Rhode Island in the company of Capt. Malachi Hamet in the regiment commanded by Col. Barton. At the end of fifteen months, he was discharged at Tiverton, Rhode Island. In this term, he participated in the Battle of Newport. He then enlisted for a one-year term in the state of Connecticut in the company of Capt. Hill. He was discharged at New London. In 1780, he enlisted for a three-year term in the 6th regiment of the Massachusetts line commanded by Col. Smith. He served three years and was discharged at Newburgh, New York at the close of the war. He recalled that he made an earlier application in 1819 but did not receive a pension then due to lack of proof of service. He reported his property as being 40 acres of land of poor quality and an old dwelling house and provided a list of his personal property. He reported that three years before he sold 22 acres to Horace Eaton for two hundred dollars. He provided another statement on 6 September 1832 and at that time the pension was allowed in the amount of eighty dollars per annum. Ebenezer's widow Polly received a pension following his death. In her statement, she reported she and Ebenezer married prior to 1 January 1784, and in another place the marriage was reported as 27 January 1783 (crossed out and changed to 1784). On 15 July 1851, daughter Elsy Austin made a statement that she, Berry Eaton, and Horace Eaton were the only surviving children of Ebenezer and Polly.[2587]

On 13 April 1827, Ebenezer Eaton and his wife Polly, for payment of five dollars, conveyed to Berry Eaton all a parcel of land in Sherburne known in the subdivision of said town as Farm No. 1. Also on 13 April 1827, for payment of two hundred and fifty dollars, Ebenezer and Polly conveyed all of Farm No. 2 to Horace Eaton.[2588]

In his will written 5 June 1838 (probate 24 February 1840), Ebenezer Eaton bequeathed the interest and income of all his property, real and personal, to his wife Polly during her natural life. He bequeathed $100 each to granddaughters Melina Hill and Lydia Hill. His other Hill grandchildren each received $25: Alvina (not readable), Horace, Deville, and Diana. Daughter Elsy Austin received $50. The remainder of the estate goes to daughter Susannah Hill. Cyrus M. Dow was named executor.[2589]

Ebenezer Eaton and Polly Berry were parents of four children, place of birth given as Vermont in the census records for the three eldest children and as New York for Susannah.

i   BERRY EATON, b. 1785; d. at Sherburne, NY, 16 Jul 1867; m. by 1807, LYDIA WELCH, b. 1779; Lydia d. at Sherburne, 14 Sep 1846.

ii   HORACE EATON, b. 1790; d. at Sherburn, 13 May 1861; m. 1st about 1815, MARY SCOTT, b. 1795; Mary d. at Sherburne, 6 Jan 1816. Horace m. 2nd about 1817, CLARISSA BERRY, b. 1797; Clarissa d. at Sherburne, 8 Apr 1878.

iii   ELSY EATON, b. 7 Feb 1793 (date given in pension record); d. after 1865 when living at Sweden, NY; m. 1st about 1815, ASA HILL, b. 1787 son of Ebenezer and Luana (Jones) Hill; Asa d. at Sweden, 1827. Elsy m. 2nd about 1835, AVRA O. AUSTIN, b. about 1791. Although Elsy married Avra Austin, she resumed use of the name Elsy Hill by 1855 when she shared a household with her daughter Lydia.[2590]

iv   SUSANNAH EATON, b. 1803; d. at Sweden, NY, 17 Jul 1849; m. EBENEZER B. HILL, b. 1797 son of Ebenezer and Luana (Jones) Hill; Ebeenzer d. at Sweden, 13 May 1847.

833)   DIADAMA EATON (*Mary Humphrey Eaton⁴, Hannah Russell Humphrey³, Benjamin², Robert¹*), b. at Ashford, 3 Apr 1763 daughter of Ebenezer and Mary (Humphrey) Eaton; d. about 1788; m. at Tolland, 4 May 1780, BENJAMIN WEAVER, b. in RI, about 1755 son of John and Mary (Brownell) Weaver;[2591] d. after 1820 when living at Palmer MA. Benjamin married second Hannah Thwing.

Benjamin was a shoemaker by trade and a farmer. After Diadama's death, Benjamin remarried and moved to Wilbraham, Massachusetts, and later Palmer where he was living in 1820.[2592]

Diadama and Benjamin were parents of two children. Benjamin had seven children with his second wife Hannah Thwing.

[2587] U.S. Revolutionary War Pension and Bounty Land Warrant Application Files, Case W7067

[2588] New York Land Records, Chenango County, KK:284, LL:270

[2589] New York Wills and Probate, Chenango County, Wills Volume D, p 316

[2590] New York, U.S., State Census, 1855

[2591] Weaver, *History and Genealogy of a Branch of the Weaver Family*, p 151

[2592] 1820 U S Census; Census Place: Palmer, Hampden, Massachusetts; Page: 379; NARA Roll: M33_48; Image: 233

i   EUNICE WEAVER, b. at Tolland, 13 Jul 1781; likely died young as Benjamin had a daughter Eunice with his second wife.

ii   HUMPHREY WEAVER, b. at Tolland, 26 Mar 1784; d. at New York, NY, 13 Dec 1823; m. at Glastonbury, 6 Apr 1823, LOUISA BOLLES who was not identified.

834)   MERIAM EATON (*Mary Humphrey Eaton[4], Hannah Russell Humphrey[3], Benjamin[2], Robert[1]*), b. at Ashford, 17 Feb 1769 daughter of Ebenezer and Mary (Humphrey) Eaton; m. 1st at Ashford, 16 Jan 1786, EZRA TAYLOR, b. at Montague, MA, 20 Aug 1760 son of Moses and Miriam (Keet) Taylor; Ezra d. at Winhall, VT, 27 Feb 1790. Meriam m. 2nd, 24 Mar 1791, ELISHA WHITNEY, b. at Montague, 27 Aug 1767 son of Ephraim and Rhoda (·) Whitney. Elisha was first married to Esther Clark.

      Meriam Eaton and Ezra Taylor were parents of one child.

i   MARTIN TAYLOR, b. at Winhall, VT, 5 Nov 1786; d. at Wayne County, NY, 16 Jul 1825;[2593] m. at Sherburne, NY, 1807, NANCY FAIRMAN, b. 1786 daughter of Jared and Chloe (Hanchett) Fairman; Nancy d. at Ontario, NY, 18 Apr 1863. Nancy married second Lester Norton.

      Meriam Eaton and Elisha Whitney were parents of two children.

i   ARVY WHITNEY, b. at Sherburne, NY, 10 Mar 1802; d. at Camden, OH, 30 Dec 1884; m. 1st LUCINDA REMINGTON, b. at Sherburne, 10 Mar 1802 daughter of William and Lovina (Hill) Remington;[2594] Lucinda d. at Camden, 21 Mar 1843. Arvy m. 2nd at Lorain County, OH, 6 Mar 1845, CLARISSA CAMPBELL, b. in NY, about 1807; Clarissa d. after 1880 when living at Camden.

ii   MARY A. WHITNEY, b. at Sherburne, 19 Dec 1812; d. at Rockford, IL, 11 Sep 1898; m. at Clarendon, NY, Oct 1831, SIDNEY LOWELL, b. 28 Jul 1810 son of Timothy and Phebe (·) Lowell; Sidney d. at Rockford, 16 Apr 1877.

835)   THANKFUL EATON (*Mary Humphrey Eaton[4], Hannah Russell Humphrey[3], Benjamin[2], Robert[1]*), b. at Ashford, 2 Feb 1773 daughter of Ebenezer and Mary (Humphrey) Eaton; d. at Tolland, 11 Oct 1799; m. at Tolland, JOSHUA COGSWELL, b. about 1772 son of Benjamin and Zerviah (Thompson) Cogswell;[2595] Joshua d. after 1830 when living at Tolland. Joshua married second Anna Smith, married third Lucia Stewart, and married fourth Mrs. Betsey Cross.

      Joshua Cogswell was a carpenter and wheelwright.[2596]

      Thankful Eaton and Joshua Cogswell were parents of three children born at Tolland. Joshua had seven children with his third wife and two children with his fourth wife.

i   IRA COGSWELL, b. 11 Oct 1793; d. at Oswego, NY, 25 May 1879 (1812 pension file index); m. 1st at Somers, CT, 1 Feb 1815, HEPHZIBAH ALLEN, b. at Lebanon, CT, 13 May 1789 daughter of Timothy and Mary (Burnham) Allen. Ira m. 2nd at Sackets Harbor, NY, 22 Sep 1830, MARTHA CONANT (widow of Ezra Smith), b. 1804 daughter of Joshua and Sybil (Adams) Conant;[2597] Martha d. at Chicago, 15 dec 1884. Ira served as a private in the company of Capt. Ezra Adams of the Connecticut militia in the War of 1812. He was at the Battle of Lundy's Lane.[2598]

ii   HENDRICK COGSWELL, b. 25 Jan 1796; d. 28 Feb 1797.

iii   EBENEZER COGSWELL, b. 24 Jan 1798; d. 31 Mar 1799.

836)   DILLA EATON (*Mary Humphrey Eaton[4], Hannah Russell Humphrey[3], Benjamin[2], Robert[1]*), b. at Ashford, 13 Jan 1776 daughter of Ebenezer and Mary (Humphrey) Eaton; d. at Sherburne, NY, 22 Mar 1855 at age 79 years, 2 months, 10 days; m. about 1797, NATHANIEL B. BROWN, b. 10 Jun 1772 (calculated from age at death of 80 years, 2 months, 20 days); Nathaniel d. at Sherburne, 30 Aug 1852 at age 80 years, 2 months, 20 days.[2599]

      Dilla and Nathaniel perhaps started their family in Connecticut but were in Sherburne, New York by 1808 where they remained.

[2593] Martin is interred at Lakeside Cemetery in Wayne County, Find a Grave 60610016

[2594] Williams Brothers, *History of Lorain County, Ohio*, p 343

[2595] Jameson, *The Cogswells in America*, p 264

[2596] Jameson, *The Cogswells in America*, p 264

[2597] Conant, *A History and Genealogy of the Conant Family in America*, p 382

[2598] U.S., War of 1812 Pension Application Files Index, 1812-1815

[2599] Nathaniel is interred at Sherburne Quarter Cemetery, Find a Grave 92835205

On 9 November 1808, Nathaniel B. Brown was of Sherburne when he purchased a parcel in Sherburne in subdivision of lot 47 in Sherburne from John Watts of New York city for payment of $120. On 3 February 1810, Nathaniel for payment of $220 purchased an adjoining property from Ephraim Whitney. On 7 October 1820, Nathaniel purchased 23 acres from John Watts and on 1 June 1825, 25 acres from Elijah Foster. On 24 September 1827, he made a one-acre purchase from Sylvester Scoville and purchased forty acres from Azel Welch on 2 December 1828.[2600]

On 2 June 1819, Nathaniel and Dilla Brown sold part of lot fifty-one to David Smith for $450. Nathaniel B. Brown and his wife Dilla sold thirty acres to David Miller for $360 on 3 February 1830. On 1 April 1840, Nathaniel and Dilla, in consideration of $2,334, conveyed 63 acres from lot forty-seven to Julius Catlin.[2601]

On 12 December 1849, Harvey Brown and his wife Mariah sold property in Sherburne to Nathaniel B. Brown for payment of $600. On 28 December 1850, Nathaniel B. and Dilla Brown and Harvey and Mariah Brown sold property in Sherburne to William R. Brezee.[2602]

In 1810, Nathaniel B. Brown headed a household of seven persons in Sherburne: one male 26 to 44, one female 26 to 44, one male under 10, one male 10 to 15, two females under 10, and one female 10 to 15.[2603] In 1830, the household was four persons: one male 50 to 59, one female 50 to 59, one male 15 to 19, and one female 10 to 14.[2604] In 1850, Nathaniel and Dilly were in Sherburne with Mary Brown (likely the widow of son Titus) and two children Almeda aged 12 years and Harry aged 5 years.[2605]

Nathaniel B. Brown did not leave a will and widow Dilla Brown and Ezra Brown were named as administrators on 22 October 1852. An accounting by Ezra on 27 January 1854 showed personal estate balance of $528.88 of which $394.37 was used to settle the estate. The amount for distribution was $134.49 with $44.83 going to the widow Dilla Brown and $14.94 to each of the six heirs or representatives: Ezra Brown, Harvey Brown, Dilla Wickham, Sally Rowe, Electa Raymond, and William Avery as the representative of minors Almeda Brown and Harvey Brown.[2606]

On 3 April 1854, Harvey Brown and Maria his wife, Ezra Brown and Harriet his wife, Dilla Brown. Lewis Wickham and Dilla his wife all of Sherburne, and Electa Raymond of Columbus, Warren County, Pennsylvania conveyed property from the estate to Seneca Rixford and Joshua Pratt for payment of $416.67. On 1 April 1854, Harvey and Maria sold additional property to Seneca Rixford and Joshua Pratt for $500. On 12 April 1854, William Avery acting as special guardian for Almeda R. and Harvey Brown, minors, conveyed property to Seneca Rixford and Joshua Pratt.[2607]

Dilla Eaton and Nathaniel B. Brown were parents of seven children. The older children may have been born in Connecticut and the younger children at Sherburne, New York.

i   EZRA D. BROWN, b. 1798; d. at Homer, MI, 16 Apr 1874; m. HARRIET ROWE, b. in NY, about 1799; Harriet d. after 1880 when living at Homer.

ii   ELECTA BROWN, b. 7 Nov 1800; d. at Columbus, PA, 3 Aug 1859; m. at Sherburne, Nov 1818, FITCH RAYMOND, b. at Bedford, NY, 25 Jan 1795 son of Joshua and Ruhamah (Raymond) Raymond;[2608] Fitch d. at Columbus, 3 Jun 1852.

iii   HARVEY BROWN, b. about 1802; d. of senile debility at Minneapolis, MN, 23 Apr 1883; m. about 1824, MARIAH EATON, b. 1 Apr 1800 (calculated from age at death) daughter of John and Lydia (-) Eaton (death record); Mariah d. at Brooklyn Township, MN, 26 Mar 1872.

iv   SARAH "SALLY" BROWN, b. about 1807; d. at Sherburne, 9 Apr 1887; m. about 1828, as his second wife, STEPHEN G. ROWE, b. about 1802 who has not been identified; Stephen d. before 1855. Stephen was first married to Polly who died in 1827.

v   TITUS BROWN, b. 1808; d. before 1850; m. 1st RUTH who was not identified, b. about 1808; Ruth d. at Sherburne, 10 Mar 1836.[2609] Titus m. 2nd about 1837, likely MARY DOUGLAS, b. about 1811. Titus and Mary were parents of two children: Almeda R. and Harvey D. Brown.

vi   DAVID BROWN, b. 1813; d. at Sherburne, 13 May 1815.

vii   DILLA BROWN, b. 1816; d. at Sherburne, 23 Dec 1864; m. LEWIS WICKHAM, b. 1815 son of Rensselaer and Permelia (Hinman) Wickham; Lewis d. at Sherburne, 26 Jan 1862.

[2600] New York Land Records, Chenango County, Q:216, Q:217. HH:196. HH:198, LL:264, LL:265

[2601] New York Land Records, Chenango County, NN:618, PP:97, 60:377

[2602] New York Land Records, Chenango County, 81:367, 83:434, 83:435

[2603] Year: 1810; Census Place: Sherburne, Chenango, New York; Roll: 26; Page: 358; Image: 00190; Family History Library Film: 0181380

[2604] Year: 1830; Census Place: Sherburne, Chenango, New York; Series: M19; Roll: 86; Page: 126; Family History Library Film: 0017146

[2605] Year: 1850; Census Place: Sherburne, Chenango, New York; Roll: 487; Page: 241b

[2606] New York Wills and Probate, Chenango County, Orders and Minutes Volume E, p 357; Orders and Minutes, Volume E, p 515

[2607] New York Land Records, Chenango County, 97:97, 97:99, 97:100

[2608] Raymond, *Genealogies of the Raymond Families*, p 28

[2609] Sherburne Quarter Cemetery, Find a Grave 92835290

837)   HANNAH STODDARD (*Sarah Humphrey Stoddard⁴, Hannah Russell Humphrey³, Benjamin², Robert¹*), b. about 1759 daughter of Joshua and Sarah (Humphrey) Stoddard; d. at Westminster, 15 Feb 1842; m. 27 Dec 1785, LEVI PECK, b. at Cumberland, RI, 14 Apr 1757 son of Solomon and Mercy (Foster) Peck;[2610] Levi d. at Westminster, 17 Sep 1835.

Born in Cumberland, Rhode Island, Levi Peck lived in Wrentham, Massachusetts as a boy and served from there in the Revolution. He was in Rhode Island for a time and came to Vermont before the time of his marriage to Hannah Stoddard. Levi taught school in Brattleboro, Windsor, and Weathersfield.[2611]

In 1800, Levi Peck headed a household of six persons at Westminster: one male 26 to 44, one female 26 to 44, one male under 10, two males 10 to 15, and one female under 10.[2612] In 1830, Hannah and Levi were a household of three in Westminster: one male 70 to 79, one female 70 to 79, and one female 20 to 29.

On 9 August 1832, Levi Peck, aged seventy-five and resident of Westminster, provided a statement related to his application for a pension. He was born at Providence Plantation in Cumberland, Rhode Island on 14 April 1757. At about age twelve years, he went with his parents to Wrentham. In April 1775, he belonged to the militia company of Capt. Cowele and marched when the alarm was received on the 20ᵗʰ or 21ˢᵗ of April. He was at Roxbury and there about twenty days. In August 1776, he entered service on a privateer commanded by Capt. James and sailed from Providence. He returned home after eight weeks. In December 1776, he again entered service, this time as a substitute for Ebenezer Bacon of Attleboro (who, by the way, retained his back pay) in the company commanded by Capt. Clapp. He was at Newport during the winter as part of Col. Daggett's regiment. He remained in service until March 1777 and returned home. In April 1777, he entered a militia company in Cumberland, Rhode Island and served in rotation three weeks at a time. In June 1777, he entered a company of Rhode Island state troops under Capt. Reuben Ballow. He was stationed at Bristol until the last of October of first of November 1777. He then fired Josiah Allen of Attleborough as a substitute. Levi went directly from Bristol to Westminster, Vermont. The pension application was ultimately rejected due to difficulty documenting his service. On 3 September 1838, widow Hannah Peck sought a pension based on her husband's service which application was also rejected.[2613]

Hannah Stoddard and Levi Peck were parents of five children whose births are recorded at Westminster, Vermont.

i   ARA PECK, b. 2 Aug 1787; d. at Salina, NY, 31 Aug 1862; m. 1ˢᵗ at Westmoreland, NH, 23 Nov 1812, PHEBE MITCHELL, b. 1784 *perhaps* daughter of John and Phebe (Lynde) Mitchell; Phebe d. at Westmoreland, 26 Jan 1815. Ara m. 2ⁿᵈ at Westmoreland, 10 Aug 1820, MARY FRANCES PIERCE, b. at Westmoreland, 12 Mar 1788 daughter of John and Sally (Farnsworth) Pierce;[2614] Mary d. at Salina, 17 Nov 1854.

ii   URI PECK, b. 21 Sep 1789; d. at Westminster, 24 Jul 1864; m. at Westminster, 6 Dec 1812, ASENATH POWERS, b. at Chesterfield, NH, 1793; Asenath d. at Westminster, 10 Sep 1869.

iii   SHUBAEL PECK, b. 21 Apr 1794; d. at Westminster, 1 Feb 1872; m. at Westminster, 18 Dec 1821, THIRZA WHEELER, b. at Hinsdale, NH, 10 May 1799 (calculated from age at death) daughter of Jonathan and Betsey (Brooks) Wheeler (names as given on death record);[2615] Thirza d. at Westminster, 25 oct 1867.

iv   RHODA PECK, b. 27 Mar 1798; d. at Hinsdale, NH, 4 Feb 1874; m. at Westminster, 26 Nov 1829, DANIEL FISHER, b. 1796 son of Daniel and Betsey (Wheeler) Fisher; Daniel d. at Hinsdale, 20 Feb 1844.

v   MIRA PECK, b. 29 Dec 1801; d. at Westminster, 7 Nov 1879. Mira did not marry.

838)   JOHN STODDARD (*Sarah Humphrey Stoddard⁴, Hannah Russell Humphrey³, Benjamin², Robert¹*), b. at Pomfret, 19 Nov 1761 son of Joshua and Sarah (Humphrey) Stoddard; d. at Westminster, 13 Aug 1831; m. 14 Sep 1786, MARY HENDRICK, b. at Union, CT, 5 Dec 1765 daughter of John and Hannah (Abbott) Hendrick;[2616] Mary d. at Westminster, 12 Jun 1849.

John accompanied his father to Westminster, Vermont and settled there. On 1 November 1794, John Stoddard conveyed to Joshua Stoddard, Jr. (likely his brother) lot number thirteen of the first range in Westminster for payment of sixty pounds.[2617]

John and Mary kept a farm in Westminster. In 1820, John headed a household of nine persons in Westminster: one male 45 and over, one female 45 and over, one male 10 to 15, one male 16 to 18, two males 16 to 25, and three females 16 to 25.[2618] On 20 June 1814, John Stoddard conveyed to Reuben Stoddard thirty acres in Westminster for payment of $179.50.[2619]

John Stoddard's estate entered probate 31 August 1831. The 75-acre homestead in Westminster was valued at $1,110.63. Personal estate was $410.08.[2620]

[2610] Peck, *Genealogical History of the Descendants of Joseph Peck*, p 47

[2611] Child, Gazetteer and Business Directory of Windham County, Vermont, p 304

[2612] Year: 1800; Census Place: Westminster, Windham, Vermont; Series: M32; Roll: 52; Page: 653; Image: 634; Family History Library Film: 218689

[2613] U. S. Revolutionary War Pension and Bounty Land Warrant Application Files, Case R8056

[2614] Westmoreland History Committee, *History of Westmoreland*, p 512

[2615] The Peck genealogy states Thirza's father was Jonas, but her death record says Jonathan.

[2616] Hendrick, *The Hendrick Genealogy*, p 93

[2617] Westminster, Vermont Deeds, G:201

[2618] 1820 U S Census; Census Place: Westminster, Windham, Vermont; Page: 274; NARA Roll: M33_128; Image: 155

[2619] Westminster, Vermont Deeds, K:156

[2620] Vermont Wills and Probate, Windham County, Estate of John Stoddard, Folder 5, Wrp1-90739, Bundel 13, 1831

On 6 February 1839, Mary Stoddard conveyed all her interest in the real estate of her late husband John Stoddard to John H. Stoddard for payment of $400. On 2 May 1832, Reuben Stoddard conveyed property to John H. Stoddard. On 13 February 1836 and 15 February 1836, Reuben Stoddard and Melinda Stoddard conveyed their interest in their father's estate and their interest in the future reversion of the dower of the estate to John H. Stoddard.[2621]

Mary and John Stoddard had seven children born at Westminster, Vermont.

i   REUBEN STODDARD, b. 10 Apr 1788; d. at Gouverneur, NY, 1 Apr 1872; m. Oct 1817, ABIGAIL FOSTER, b. at Putney, 25 Feb 1789 daughter of David and Anne (Sessions) Foster;[2622] Abigail d. at Gouverneur, 7 Feb 1876.

ii   LYDIA STODDARD, b. 9 Aug 1790; d. at Westminster, 3 Sep 1832. Lydia did not marry.

iii   MELINDA STODDARD, b. 5 Mar 1794; d. at Westminster, 11 Feb 1877. Melinda did not marry.

iv   JOHN HUMPHREY STODDARD, b. 21 Feb 1796; d. at Avon IL, 25 Sep 1881; m. 31 Dec 1823, SARAH PIERCE, b. at Westmoreland, NH, 8 Sep 1800 daughter of John and Hannah (Warner) Pierce; Sarah d. after 1880 (still living at the 1880 U.S. Census).

v   SAREPTA STODDARD, b. 12 Jun 1800; d. at Grafton, 26 Jul 1855; m. 2 Nov 1835, as his second wife, HENRY HOLMES, b. at Grafton, about 1806 son of Given and Lucy (Palmer) Holmes;[2623] Henry d. at Grafton, 22 Sep 1871. Henry was first married to Rhoda who died in 1835.

vi   SALINA STODDARD, b. 19 Nov 1802; d. at Westminster, 20 Mar 1849; m. at Westminster, 22 Oct 1828, RODNEY RANDAL BUXTON, b. at Walpole, NH, 26 Aug 1805 son of Jonathan and Margaret (-) Buxton; Rodney d. at Westminster 29 Dec 1880. After Salina's death, Rodney married Meranda Wheelock.

vii   PROSPER FRANKLIN STODDARD, b. 30 Aug 1806; d. at Westminster, 2 Aug 1852; m. 15 Mar 1828, NANCY MADISON BURR, b. at Putney, 9 Jul 1809 daughter of Ephraim and Freelove (Wheeler) Burr;[2624][2625] Nancy d. at Westminster, 14 Dec 1890. After Prosper's death, Nancy married Edward Glover.

839)   JOSHUA STODDARD (*Sarah Humphrey Stoddard⁴, Hannah Russell Humphrey³, Benjamin², Robert¹*), b. about 1764 son of Joshua and Sarah (Humphrey) Stoddard; d. at Sutton, VT, 23 Dec 1854; m. at Westminster, VT, 19 Dec 1792, ABIGAIL LAWRENCE, b. at Westminster, 1776 daughter of Joseph Lawrence (per death record); Abigail d. at Sutton, 13 Jan 1859.

Joshua and Abigail resided in Sutton, Vermont and are reported as having thirteen children (although names of just eleven children were identified).[2626]

The household was ten persons in 1810 enumerated at Billymead (the original name of Sutton): one male 45 and over, one female 26 to 44, one male under 10, one male 10 to 15, four females under 10, and two females 10 to 15.[2627] In 1820, Joshua headed a household of twelve persons at Stoddard: one male 45 and over, one female 26 to 44, two males under 10, one male 16 to 18, two males 16 to 25 (which includes the one male 16 to 18), three females under 10, one female 10 to 15, and two females 16 to 25.[2628]

In 1850, Joshua and Abigail were in Sutton with the next two households being sons Fred W. and Phineas Stoddard. Real property value was given as $1,800.[2629]

Eleven children were identified for Joshua and Abigail, although there may be two other daughters whose identities were not confirmed.

i   JERUSHA STODDARD, b. 1794; d. at Barton, VT, 24 Sep 1868; m. at Sutton, VT, 7 Dec 1815, PEARSON RICHARDSON TRUE, b. about 1793 son of Enoch and Abigail (Richardson) True; Pearson d. at Barton, 26 Nov 1861.

ii   GRATIA STODDARD, b. 1796; d. at Burke, VT, 27 Jul 1888; m. at Sutton, 30 Jun 1831, WILLIAM THOMPSON, b. in MA about 1785 son of William and Elizabeth (-) Thompson (death record); William d. at Burke, 29 Jun 1870.

[2621] Westminster, Vermont Deeds, O:155, N:114, N:480, N:481

[2622] The 1848 will of Anna Foster (probate 1861) includes a bequest to her daughter Abigail wife of Reuben Stoddard.

[2623] Ancestry.com, Vermont, Vital Records, 1720-1908. Names of parents on death record of Henry Holmes are Given Holmes and Lucy Palmer.

[2624] *Vermont Births, Marriages and Deaths to 2008.* (From microfilmed records. Online database: *AmericanAncestors.org*, New England Historic Genealogical Society, 2013.) Birth of Nancy Madison Burr, parents Ephraim Burr and Freelove Wheeler.

[2625] Ancestry.com, Vermont, Vital Records, 1720-1908. Names of Nancy's parents are listed on her marriage to Edward Glover as Ephraim Burr and Freelove Wheeler. Nancy's death record gives the parents' names as John and "Frila."

[2626] Child, *Gazetteer of Caledonia and Essex Counties, Vt.*, p 254

[2627] Year: 1810; Census Place: Billymead, Caledonia, Vermont; Roll: 64; Page: 333; Image: 00273; Family History Library Film: 0218668

[2628] 1820 U S Census; Census Place: Sutton, Caledonia, Vermont; Page: 444; NARA Roll: M33_127; Image: 87

[2629] Year: 1850; Census Place: Sutton, Caledonia, Vermont; Roll: 922; Page: 189a

iii   JOSEPH L. STODDARD, b. at Durham, Québec, about 1800; d. at Charleston, VT, 24 Sep 1892 (father's name Joshua is given on death record); m. at Sutton, VT, 23 May 1825, BETSEY W. BARTLETT, b. at Hingham, MA, 2 May 1808 daughter of Daniel and Polly (Jacobs) Bartlett (given on death record); Betsey d. at Charleston, 8 Dec 1900.

iv   JOSHUA STODDARD, b. 1801; d. at Westminster, VT, 1802.

v   PHINEAS STODDARD, b. 1803; d. at Burke, VT, 3 Nov 1874; m. ARMELA ANN PARKER,[2630] b. at Lyndon, VT, 1809 daughter of Caleb and Sarah (Watkins) Parker (names given on death record); Armela d. at Lyndon, 22 Apr 1891.

vi   PRISCILLA "SILA" STODDARD, b. at Sutton, 1807; d. at Chicago, IL, 24 Apr 1893; m. at Sutton, 12 Apr 1830, NATHAN L. DENISON, b. at Burke, 2 Apr 1809 son of Isaac and Electra (Newell) Denison; Nathan d. at Mendota, IL, 30 Apr 1854.

vii   JULIA STODDARD, b. at Sutton, 1810; d. at Northfield, VT, 2 Oct 1885; m. at Sutton, 7 Nov 1853, as his third wife, STEPHEN WATKINS, b. at Wendell, MA, 15 Apr 1806 son of Stephen and Eunice (Crane) Watkins; Stephen d. at Northfield, 16 Aug 1882. Stephen was first married to Jerusha Meader and second married to Sarah Sheldon.

viii   JOSHUA STODDARD, b. 1812; d. at Sutton, 13 May 1844.

ix   FREDERICK W. STODDARD, b. at Sutton, 4 Dec 1814; d. at Westminster, 7 Jan 1892; m. at Lyndon, 24 Jan 1843, DOROTHY BURLEIGH QUIMBY, b. at Lyndon, VT, 24 Nov 1824 daughter of Thomas and Delia (Gilman) Quimby (on death record an in obituary); Dorothy d. at Lyndon, 4 Dec 1906.

x   CECILIA STODDARD, b. 1816; d. at Sutton, 25 May 1881; m. at Sutton, 3 Dec 1840, WELCOME ALLARD, b. at Sutton, 1806 son of Caleb and Henrietta (Runnells) Allard; Welcome d. at Newark, VT, 19 Nov 1877.

xi   SUSAN STODDARD, b. at Sutton, Jun 1820; d. at Lyndon, 8 Oct 1906; m. at Sutton, 5 Jan 1843, EPHRAIM HUBBARD RUGGLES, b. at Lyndon, 4 Jul 1815 son of William and Rebekah (Hubbard) Ruggles; Ephraim d. at Lyndon, 25 May 1903.

840)   DANIEL STODDARD (*Sarah Humphrey Stoddard⁴, Hannah Russell Humphrey³, Benjamin², Robert¹*), b. 23 Aug 1768 son of Joshua and Sarah (Humphrey) Stoddard; d. at Woodstock, OH, 2 Apr 1854;[2631] m. 1st at Westminster, 13 Jan 1791, ELEANOR SMITH, b. 1775 perhaps daughter of Sylvanus Smith; Eleanor d. at Sutton, VT, 14 Aug 1805. Daniel m. 2nd 1805, LUCRETIA HARVEY, b. 29 Jan 1787 daughter of William and Jane (Beebe) Harvey; Lucretia d. at Woodstock, OH, 7 Aug 1857.

    Daniel Stoddard resided in Hartland, Vermont and likely all his children were born there.

    In 1820, Daniel Stoddard headed a household of twelve persons at Hartland, Vermont: one male 45 and over, one female 26 to 44, three males under 10, one male 16 to 18, two males 16 to 25 (which includes the one male 16 to 18), two females under 10, two females 10 to 15, and one female 16 to 25.[2632]

    Daniel and his family were in Champaign County, Ohio by 1837. On 16 October 1837, Daniel Stoddard of Champaign County, Ohio, for payment of $1,000, purchased 106 acres on the waters of Darby Creek from Benjamin and Abigail Marks.[2633]

    At Rush, Ohio in 1840, Daniel headed a household of four persons: one male 70 to 79, one female 50 to 59, one male under 5, and one male 15 to 19. Cyrus Stoddard was head of the adjacent household.[2634] In 1850, Daniel and Lucretia were living Rush, Ohio in a household headed by son Sylvanus and his second wife Mary.[2635]

    Daniel Stoddard and Eleanor Smith were parents of eight children (although there may be one or two other children not identified).

i   SARAH STODDARD, b. 1791; d. at Essex, VT, 27 Sep 1853; m. at Stowe, VT, 12 Feb 1815, OLIVER MOODY, b. about 1786. Sarah, Oliver, their son Oliver and his wife Ladona, and their daughter Huldah were living in Essex, Vermont in 1850.[2636]

ii   SOPHIA STODDARD, b. 1792; d. at Woodstock, OH, 28 Dec 1856; m. at Hartland, VT, 6 Dec 1812, DAVID HARVARD HALL, b. at Windsor, VT, 2 Feb 1791 son of David and Olive (Smead) Hall; David d. at Rush, OH, 19 Aug 1875. David married second Aurilla who was the widow of Sophia's brother Cyrus.

[2630] Name is given as Armela on gravestone but is Amelia in other records.

[2631] Daniel is interred at Woodstock Cemetery in Woodstock, Ohio; Find a Grave 34032917

[2632] 1820 U S Census; Census Place: Hartland, Windsor, Vermont; Page: 313; NARA Roll: M33_128; Image: 180

[2633] Ohio Land Records, Champaign County, O:20

[2634] Year: 1840; Census Place: Rush, Champaign, Ohio; Roll: 382; Page: 355; Family History Library Film: 0020160

[2635] Year: 1850; Census Place: Rush, Champaign, Ohio; Roll: 665; Page: 251a

[2636] Year: 1850; Census Place: Essex, Chittenden, Vermont; Roll: 923; Page: 151a

iii   CYRUS STODDARD, b. at Hartland, VT, 2 Jul 1794; d. at Woodstock, OH, 2 Mar 1841; m. about 1822, AURILLA who was not clearly identified, b. about 1797; Aurilla d. at Woodstock, OH, 3 Aug 1872. Aurilla married second David Harvard Hall (see Sophia Stoddard just above).

iv   CELECTA STODDARD, b. 1796; d. at Switzerland County, IN, 13 May 1865; m. WILLIAM B. LINELL, b. in England, about 1802; William d. at Muncie, IN, 6 Sep 1867.

v   HULDAH STODDARD, b. 1798; d. at Glenwood, IA, 19 Jan 1864; m. at Champaign County, OH, 30 Jul 1835, as his second wife, WILLIAM SNUFFIN, b. in NJ, about 1797; William d. after 1880 when living at Weld County, CO with his daughter Esther from his first marriage.[2637]

vi   DANIEL STODDARD, b. 1799; d. at Metamora, IL, 24 Dec 1865; m. at Stowe, VT, 10 Oct 1831, SABRINA DARLING, b. at Pomfret, VT, 20 May 1799 daughter of Joseph and Eleanor (Sanderson) Darling.

vii   CLARISSA STODDARD, b. 1800; d. after 1860 when living next to her brother Sylvanus at Cazenovia, IL; m. at Hartland, VT, 20 Jul 1817, REUBEN CHAPMAN who was not identified.

viii   SYLVANUS S. STODDARD, b. at Hartland, 16 Dec 1803; d. at Woodford County, IL, 21 Apr 1864; m. 1st at Champaign County, OH, 16 Mar 1837, REBECCA SWIFT, b. 8 Aug 1809 (calculated from age at death); Rebecca d. at Champaign County, 24 Nov 1845. Sylvanus married second Mary *Brake* Coffman, b. 1813; Mary d. at Woodford County, 22 Oct 1864.

Daniel Stoddard and Lucretia Harvey were parents of ten children including a set of triplets.

i   ELEANOR STODDARD, b. 11 Oct 1806; d. at Allen, OH, 21 Jun 1871; m. at Champaign County, OH, 8 Nov 1838, JOHN EPPS, b. in VA, about 1809; John d. after 1870 when living at Allen.[2638]

ii   MARTHA STODDARD, b. 1809

iii   DIANA STODDARD, b. 16 Aug 1813; d. at Dayton, OH, Feb 1891; m. 1st at Champaign County, OH, 9 Apr 1836, CHARLES W. SABINE, b. 1811; Charles d. at Fletcher, OH, 1842 (probate 8 Mar 1842). Diana m. 2nd at Champaign County, 6 Sep 1859, BENJAMIN FRANKLIN KELSEY, b. at Stowe, VT, 20 Jul 1809 son of Nathan and Eunice (Churchill) Kelsey; Benjamin d. at Perry County, IL, 7 Jan 1874. Benjamin was first married to Marietta Kimball.

iv   NANCY MARIE STODDARD, b. 12 Aug 1815; d. at East Liberty, OH, 19 Mar 1898; m. 1st at Champaign County, OH, 6 Apr 1840, SAMUEL EVERETT; Samuel d. about 1844. Nancy m. 2nd at Champaign County, 7 Jan 1845, IVORY PROSPER PUGLSEY, b. in OH, 11 Jul 1822 son of Francis and Elizabeth (Green) Pugsley; Ivory d. at East Liberty, 30 Jul 1882.

v   REUBEN H. STODDARD (twin), b. 23 Aug 1818; d. at Colfax, IL, 22 Dec 1898; m. at Champaign County, OH, 13 May 1847, MARGARET RINAKER, b. at Luray, VA, 4 Oct 1822 daughter of Abram Rinaker;[2639] Margaret d. at Chicago, 19 May 1914.

vi   RUFUS H. STODDARD (twin), b. 23 Aug 1818; d. at Woodstock, OH, 22 Sep 1840.

vii   CASENDANA L. STODDARD (triplet), b. at Hartland, 5 Jan 1823;[2640] d. at De Land, IL, 29 Aug 1890; m. 1st 11 May 1852, JOSHUA L. BORTON, b. at Burlington, NJ, 21 Apr 1812 son of Daniel and Tabitha (Rodman) Borton; Joshua d. 9 Jul 1874. Joshua was first married to Mary Johnston. Casendana m. 2nd at De Witt County, IL, 1 Sep 1881, RUFUS C. BENEDICT, b. 1816; Rufus d. at the home of his son in Topeka, KS, 1897.

viii   CARLOS STODDARD (triplet), b. 5 Jan 1823; d. at Iola, KS, 27 May 1908; m. at De Witt County, IL, 14 Oct 1850, NANCY S. RATHBUN, b. in OH, Dec 1826; Nancy d. at Iola, 3 Jul 1905.

ix   CASSANDRA LOUISE STODDARD (triplet), b. 5 Jan 1823; d. at Muncie, IN, 21 May 1892; m. at Warren County, OH, 21 Dec 1848, JOHN ARTHUR HUSTED, b. in IN, 10 Mar 1823 son of John and Abigail (DuBois) Husted; John d. at Muncie, 29 Dec 1881. Cassandra and John were parents of author and journalist Ida Husted Harper.

x   WILLIAM E. STODDARD, b. 1828; d. at Champaign County, OH, 28 Jul 1837.

[2637] Year: 1880; Census Place: Weld, Colorado; Roll: 93; Page: 483A; Enumeration District: 110

[2638] 1870 United States Federal Census

[2639] Cook County, Illinois, U.S., Deaths Index, 1878-1922

[2640] The births of the triplets made the news, the report noting that Daniel then had been father of 20 children 19 of whom were still living. "New Year's Productions", *The Woodstock Observer and Windsor and Orange County Gazette, Woodstock, Vermont*, 07 Jan 1823, Tue, p 2

841)   ZERVIAH STODDARD (*Sarah Humphrey Stoddard⁴, Hannah Russell Humphrey³, Benjamin², Robert¹*), b. about 1770 daughter of Joshua and Sarah (Humphrey) Stoddard; d. at East Putney, VT, 1856; m. AMASA WASHBURN, b. at Killingly, CT, 3 Sep 1768 son of Joseph and Ruth (Wetmore) Washburn; Amasa d. at East Putney, 21 Oct 1857.

Zerviah and Amasa resided in Putney, Vermont where they kept a farm. In 1810, the household was eight persons: one male 26 to 44, one female 26 to 44, one male under 10, one male 16 to 25, one female under 10, and three females 10 to 15.[2641] In 1830, the household was seven persons: one male 60 to 69, two females 60 to 69, one male 20 to 29, one female 5 to 9, one female 20 to 29, and one female 30 to 39.[2642] Amasa, Zerviah, and daughter Minerva were living together in 1850.[2643]

On 10 February 1845, Amasa Washburn entered an agreement with Joseph A. Deming (likely his grandson son of daughter Thirza) in which Joseph would occupy and work the farm and provide one third of the produce from the farm for a period of three years and to pay two-thirds of the taxes. Joseph is also to keep one cow and ten sheep for Amasa during this period. On 12 February 1845, Amasa mortgaged a piece of property in Putney to Minerva Washburn for payment of $86, the deed becoming void with repayment of the $86 with interest. On the same date, Amasa entered a similar agreement with Sarah S. Washburn with repayment to be made on $72 with interest.[2644]

On 11 September 1833, Amasa Washburn, in consideration of $1,1000, sold approximately 102 acres in Putney to Minerva Washburn and Sarah S. Washburn. On 8 July 1847, Minerva and Sarah sold this property to Joseph A. Deming (likely their nephew) for payment of $1,100. On the same date Joseph "sold" the property to Minerva and Sarah this being part of an agreement allowing Sarah and Minerva use of the property during their natural lives.[2645]

There are five confirmed children of Zerviah Stoddard and Amasa Washburn.

i   MINERVA WASHBURN, b. 1795; d. at East Putney, 30 Nov 1876. Minerva did not marry.

ii   RUTH EMILY WASHBURN, b. 1791; d. at Putney, 11 Mar 1813.

iii   THIRZA WASHBURN, b. at Westminster, about 1799; d. at Putney, 10 Jan 1878; m. at Putney, 12 Nov 1821, HERBERT C. DEMING, b. at Berlin, CT, 17 Jul 1796 son of Moses and Sarah (Norton) Deming; Herbert d. at Putney, 25 May 1871.

iv   SARAH S. WASHBURN, b. 1802; d. at Northampton, MA, 22 Oct 1882. Sarah did not marry. In her will written 28 December 1881, Sarah left her estate to her niece Mary Susan Cushing and nephew Arthur Miles Cushing. The only heir-at-law identified in the probate was brother Amasa C. Washburn.[2646] It is not clear how the Cushings mentioned are niece and nephew. Sarah's nephew Joseph A. Deming married a Cushing, but the specific relationship of Mary Susan Cushing and Arthur Miles Cushing was not found. They were children of Abner and Roxana (Gates) Cushing.

v   AMASA CORNWALL WASHBURN, b. 1807; d. at Carbondale, IL, 1890; m. at Tazewell County, IL, 30 Apr 1835, ANN PACKARD who was not identified, but born in Massachusetts, about 1809; Ann d. at Carbondale, 1889.

842)   EZRA STODDARD (*Sarah Humphrey Stoddard⁴, Hannah Russell Humphrey³, Benjamin², Robert¹*), b. 21 Jul 1772 son of Joshua and Sarah (Humphrey) Stoddard; d. at Sutton, VT, 25 Jun 1811; m. 16 Nov 1797, JERUSHA GOODELL, b. 26 Aug 1776 daughter of Abiel and Margaret (Brown) Goodell; Jerusha d. at Westminster, 19 May 1849.

Ezra and Jerusha resided at Sutton, Vermont enumerated at Billymead (later Sutton) with a household of eight persons in 1810: one male 26 to 44, one female 26 to 44, three males under 10, one male 10 to 15, one female under 10, and one female 10 to 15.[2647]

Ezra Stoddard and Jerusha Goodell were parents of seven children likely all born at Sutton, but the family registration of births is at Westminster where Jerusha lived after Ezra's death (the births are registered in the Westminster records as children of widow Mrs. Jerusha Stoddard).

i   MARILLA STODDARD, b. 12 Sep 1798; d. at Grafton, VT, 4 Mar 1867; m. 1ˢᵗ at Westminster, 2 Nov 1820, JAMES WYMAN, b. 1788; James d. at Grafton, 11 Apr 1847. Marilla m. 2ⁿᵈ at Grafton, 5 Jan 1850, GARDNER UPHAM, b. 2 May 1798 son of Jonathan and Polly (Whitney) Upham; Gardner d. at Windham, VT, 20 Sep 1899 at age 101. Gardner was first married to Eunice Emory.

²⁶⁴¹ Year: 1810; Census Place: Putney, Windham, Vermont; Roll: 65; Page: 321; Image: 00233; Family History Library Film: 0218669
²⁶⁴² Year: 1830; Census Place: Putney, Windham, Vermont; Series: M19; Roll: 186; Page: 130; Family History Library Film: 0027452
²⁶⁴³ Year: 1850; Census Place: Putney, Windham, Vermont; Roll: 929; Page: 56b
²⁶⁴⁴ Vermont Land Records, Town of Putney, 9:421, 9:423, 9:424
²⁶⁴⁵ Vermont Land Records, Town of Putney, 9:148, 10:93, 10:94
²⁶⁴⁶ *Hampshire County, MA: Probate File Papers, 1660-1889*. Online database. *AmericanAncestors.org.* New England Historic Genealogical Society, 2016, 2017. (From records supplied by the Massachusetts Supreme Judicial Court Archives and the Hampshire County Court. Digitized images provided by FamilySearch.org) Case 261-49
²⁶⁴⁷ Year: 1810; Census Place: Billymead, Caledonia, Vermont; Roll: 64; Page: 333; Image: 00273; Family History Library Film: 0218668

ii   HARVEY STODDARD, b. 27 Jul 1800; d. at Grafton, VT, 8 Mar 1873; m. 1st HARRIET HOLMES, b. at Grafton, 10 Apr 1802 daughter of Given and Siley (Heath) Holmes; Harriet d. at Grafton, 20 Aug 1850. Harvey m. 2nd 1852, ALTHINE STEDMAN (widow of Lucius Holland), b. 21 Sep 1810 daughter of William and Milla (Allen) Stedman; Althine d. at Grafton, 12 May 1868.

iii   ABIEL STODDARD, b. 11 Apr 1802; d. at Saratoga Springs, NY, 4 Aug 1895; m. 1st MELISSA ROBBINS, b. 7 Apr 1805; Melissa d. at Saratoga Springs, 8 Dec 1862. Abiel m. 2nd at Townshend, VT, 23 Sep 1867, MARY R. MORGAN (widow Mary Elmore), b. at New York, NY, 1820; Mary d. at Saratoga Springs, 1911.

iv   SYLVESTER SAGE STODDARD, b. 24 Feb 1804; d. at Westminster, 26 Oct 1882; m. 1st at Westminster, 19 Mar 1829, MARY HOLTON, b. at Westminster, 13 Sep 1806 daughter of Worthington and Phebe (Phelps) Holton; Mary d. at Westminster, 22 Feb 1859. Sylvester m. 2nd ANN JENETTE HOLTON, b. 12 Jul 1820 daughter of Zoeth and Amanda (Loomis) Holton; Ann d. at Westminster, 20 Dec 1899.

v   ABIGAIL STODDARD, b. 9 Dec 1805; d. at Townshend, VT, 18 Nov 1889; m. 1833, HIRAM HOLMES, b. at Grafton, 25 Jul 1800 son of Given and Siley (Heath) Holmes; Hiram d. at Townshend, 12 May 1867.

vi   EZRA STODDARD, b. 3 Jun 1808; d. at Grafton, 19 Jun 1821.

vii   ABISHAI STODDARD, b. 1 Feb 1811; d. at Westminster, 12 Oct 1893; m. at Windham, 30 Jun 1840, HARRIET EARLE STEVENS, b. 19 Jan 1814 daughter of Martin and Lydia (Earle) Stevens;[2648] Harriet d. at Townshend, 18 Dec 1881.

843)   EBENEZER STODDARD (*Sarah Humphrey Stoddard4, Hannah Russell Humphrey3, Benjamin2, Robert1*), b. about 1774 son of Joshua and Sarah (Humphrey) Stoddard; d. at Ruiter's Corner, Estrie, Québec, 31 Jan 1847 at age 72 years, 11 months;[2649] m. SUSAN who has not been identified, b. about 1774; Susan d. at Ruiter's Corner, 10 Sep 1863.
          In the 1825 census at Stanstead, Ebenezer headed a household of three persons: one person above 6 years to 14 years, one male 60 and upwards, and one female 45 and upwards.[2650]
          One child was identified for Ebenezer and Susan.

i   EBENEZER STODDARD, b. about 1815; d. at Reuter's Corner, Québec, 7 Oct 1874; m. at Stanstead, 6 Feb 1838, SUSAN M. POOL, b. about 1820 daughter of Theodore C. and Betsey E. (Lee) Pool; Susan d. at Ruiter's Corner, 1 Sep 1858. Susan was a minor at the time of marriage requiring consent of a parent; the marriage entry is signed by Theodore C. Pool.[2651] Theodore C. Pool was a near neighbor of the Stoddard family in the 1825 census.

844)   ISAAC STODDARD (*Sarah Humphrey Stoddard4, Hannah Russell Humphrey3, Benjamin2, Robert1*), b. at Westminster, 22 Oct 1776 son of Joshua and Sarah (Humphrey) Stoddard; d. at Sherbrooke, Québec, 23 Sep 1842;[2652] m. at Westminster, 23 Aug 1810, MIRIAM PARSONS, b. at Swanzey, NH, 30 Dec 1785 daughter of Benjamin and Miriam (Winslow) Parsons;[2653] Miriam d. at Quitman, MS, 24 Jul 1855.
          Isaac and Miriam married in Westminster, Vermont and their first four children were born in Vermont before relocating to Québec. The family were members of the Methodist church.[2654]
          Isaac Stoddard and Miriam Parsons were parents of six children.[2655]

i   ADELIA PARSONS STODDARD, b. at Westminster, VT, 14 Sep 1811; d. at Sacramento, CA, 3 Mar 1897; m. at Burlington, VT, 10 Oct 1831, CHARLES HEMAN SWIFT, b. at Fairfax, VT, 24 May 1807 son of Charles and Eunice (Young) Swift; Charles d. at San Francisco, 15 Jul 1885.

ii   RUTH EMILY STODDARD, b. at Westminster, 30 Apr 1813; d. 14 Feb 1814.

iii   CHARLES RUGGLES STODDARD, b. at Westminster, 9 Dec 1814; d. at Montréal, Québec, 1 Apr 1819.

[2648] The names of Harriet's parents are given as Martin and Lydia Stephens on her death record; "Vermont Vital Records, 1760-1954", database with images, *FamilySearch* (https://familysearch.org/ark:/61903/1:1:XFXS-MZT : 19 February 2021), Martin Stephens in entry for Harriet E. S. Stoddard, 1881.
[2649] Interred at Reuter's Corner Cemetery; Find a Grave 88754644
[2650] 1825 Census of Lower Canada
[2651] Quebec, Canada, Vital and Church Records (Drouin Collection), 1621-1968
[2652] Quebec, Canada, Vital and Church Records (Drouin Collection), 1621-1968
[2653] Holton, *Winslow Memorial*, p 354
[2654] Quebec, Canada, Vital and Church Records (Drouin Collection), 1621-1968
[2655] Children are as given in Holton, *Winslow Memorial*, p 354

iv JOHN BURNELL STODDARD, b. at Woodstock, VT, 10 Jun 1816; d. at Chester, IL, 7 Dec 1844; m. at Essex, NY, 14 Dec 1841, MARIA F. PARKHILL, b. at Essex, NY, 19 Jun 1816 daughter of Col. Ezra and Mary Ann (Collins) Parkhill; Maria d. at Chester, 21 Feb 1845.

v JAMES MONROE STODDARD, b. at Montréal, 6 Dec 1818; d. after 1880 when living at DeSoto, LA;[2656] m. at Camden, AL, 6 Feb 1845, CHRISTIANA PERKINS BLAKENEY, b. at Jackson, MS, 1 Oct 1822 daughter of Alfred and Margaret (McIntosh) Blakeney; Christiana d. at Appleby, TX, 5 Nov 1898. James M. Stoddard served as sergeant in the 27th Infantry of Confederate forces during the Civil War.[2657]

vi JANE MIRIAM STODDARD, b. at Montréal, 2 Jun 1821; d. at Sacramento, CA, 24 Aug 1906; m. at Allenton, AL, 26 Apr 1844, FRANCIS WYMAN PAGE, b. at St. Louis, MO, Nov 1820 son of Daniel Dearborn and Deborah (Young) Page; Francis d. at St. Paul, MN, 13 Sep 1883.

845)   AMASA STODDARD (*Sarah Humphrey Stoddard⁴, Hannah Russell Humphrey³, Benjamin², Robert¹*), b. 1779 son of Joshua and Sarah (Humphrey) Stoddard; d. at Westminster, 28 Mar 1846; m. at Rockingham, 22 Apr 1810, ANNA WILLARD, b. at Westminster, 1786 daughter of Lynde Willard (per death record); Anna d. at Westminster, 24 Jun 1858.

Amasa and Anna resided in Westminster, Vermont where in 1820 there were six members of the household: one male 26 to 44, one female 26 to 44, two males under 10, and two females under 10.[2658] In 1830, Amasa Stoddard headed a household of six persons at Westminster, Vermont: one male 40 to 49, one female 40 to 49, one male 5 to 9, one female under 5, one female 5 to 9, and one female 10 to 14.[2659]

On 1 April 1811, Amasa Stoddard of Westminster sold to John Stoddard of Westminster (likely his brother) his interest in lot thirty-five in Westminster known as the lower meadow. On 5 January 1817 entered into a mortgage agreement with James Titcomb involving about 64 acres. On 7 December 1825, Amasa sold his pew in the meeting house which was left to him in the will of Joshua Stoddard to Joel Holton for payment of twenty dollars.[2660]

Amasa and Anna were parents of six likely children born at Westminster, Vermont.[2661]

i   EZRA L. STODDARD, b. 18 Jul 1814; d. at Westminster, 19 May 1890; m. 1 Jun 1840, MARY HENDRICK, b. at Hartland, VT, 22 Jul 1815 daughter of Caleb and Sarah (Abbott) Hendrick; Mary d. at Hartland, 30 oct 1887.

ii   SAREPTA STODDARD, b. 1819; d. at Westminster, 26 Jun 1879; m. at Westminster, VT, 9 Oct 1844, HORACE HUNT, b. at Albany, VT, about 1819; Horace d. at Westminster, 1 Jan 1899. Sarepta and Horace had one son James.

iii   SIMON G. STODDARD, b. 1823; d. at Westminster, 12 Apr 1853; m. at Newfane, VT, 31 May 1849, STELLA SOPHIA HALL, b. at Newfane, 30 Oct 1825 daughter of Jonathan and Olive (Kenny) Hall; Stella d. at Westminster, 21 Apr 1853.

iv   EMILY R. STODDARD, b. 1824; d. at Westminster, 31 Dec 1858; m. at Rockingham, VT, 22 Oct 1846, HENRY WELLS SABIN, b. at Rockingham, 15 Dec 1818 son of William and Rachel (Wolfe) Sabin; Henry d. at Westminster, 27 May 1904. Henry married second Eleanor Willard.

v   PERSIS STODDARD, b. 18 Aug 1826; d. at Central Falls, RI, 28 Jul 1897; m. at Westminster, 17 May 1854, ALONZO E. BURT, b. at Rockingham, VT, 11 Nov 1829 son of David and Mary (Orr) Burt; Alonzo d. at Central Falls, 30 Par 1907.

vi   ROMANZO B. STODDARD, b. about 1828; m. at Westminster, 12 Sep 1847, PHILOMELA BARNES.

846)   RHODA STODDARD (*Sarah Humphrey Stoddard⁴, Hannah Russell Humphrey³, Benjamin², Robert¹*), b. at Westminster, 2 Apr 1781 daughter of Joshua and Sarah (Humphrey) Stoddard; d. at Bethel, VT, 24 Oct 1867; m. at Westminster, 12 Dec 1809, MOSES WEBSTER, b. at Hartland, VT, 4 Mar 1783 son of Moses and Elizabeth (Woods) Webster;[2662] Moses d. at Bethel, 15 Feb 1872.

Moses and Rhoda were in Hartland, Vermont until 1821 when they settled in Bethel. Moses purchased a farm in Bethel in 1806 which was occupied by his brother.[2663]

[2656] Year: 1880; Census Place: 7th Ward, De Soto, Louisiana; Roll: 452; Page: 261B; Enumeration District: 024

[2657] U.S., Confederate Soldiers Compiled Service Records, 1861-1865

[2658] 1820 U S Census; Census Place: Westminster, Windham, Vermont; Page: 273; NARA Roll: M33_128; Image: 155

[2659] Year: 1830; Census Place: Westminster, Windham, Vermont; Series: M19; Roll: 186; Page: 138; Family History Library Film: 0027452

[2660] Vermont Land Records, Town of Westminster, K:25, K:334, M:169

[2661] There were perhaps one or two other children not clearly identified.

[2662] Lapham and Webster, *Genealogy of Some of the Descendants of John Webster*, p 4

[2663] Cox, *The Illustrated Historical Souvenir History of Bethel, Vermont*, p 59

In 1820, Moses Webster, Jr. headed a household of six persons in Hartland: one male 26 to 44, one female 26 to 44, two males under 10, and two females under 10.[2664] In 1830, the family was six persons at Bethel: one male 40 to 49, one female 40 to 49, one male 10 to 14, one male 15 to 19, one female 10 to 14, and one female 15 to 19.[2665]

Rhoda and Moses were parents of four children born at Hartland, Vermont.

i   CHARLES P. WEBSTER, b. at Hartland, 20 Nov 1811; d. at Bethel, 9 May 1902; m. at Bethel, 2 Jan 1839, ISABELLE S. WELLINGTON, b. 16 Jun 1819 daughter of Abel and Elizabeth (Spear) Wellington;[2666] Isabelle d. at Bethel, 16 Mar 1891.

ii SARAH ELIZABETH WEBSTER, b. at Hartland, 26 Apr 1813; d. at Bethel, 15 Feb 1846; m. at Bethel, 21 Oct 1834, LEWIS TURNER, b. about 1807; Lewis d. at Bethel, 1 Apr 1841.

iii SIMEON ALTON WEBSTER, b. at Hartland, 4 Oct 1815; d. at Bethel, 19 Jan 1898; m. at Bethel, 29 Jan 1845, NANCY STEVENS BROOKS, b. at Bethel, 3 Nay 1816 daughter of Asa and Lucy (Stevens) Brooks; Nancy d. at Tunbridge (burial at Bethel), 12 Oct 1902.

iv ROSAMOND R. WEBSTER, b. at Hartland, 18 Jan 1820; d. at Arvada, CO, 17 Feb 1891; m. Dr. HENRY S. GOODELL, b. in VT, about 1821; Henry d. at Arvada, 16 Mar 1894.

847)   LUCY PAINE (*Zerviah Humphrey Paine⁴, Hannah Russell Humphrey³, Benjamin², Robert¹*), b. at Ashford, 19 Dec 1771 daughter of Noah and Zerviah (Humphrey) Paine; d. at Woodstock, CT, 31 Mar 1814; m. at Ashford, 4 Apr 1798, KING HAYWARD, b. at Ashford, 15 Mar 1768 son of Benjamin and Hannah (King) Hayward; King d. at Ashford, 13 Jan 1829.

Lucy Paine and King Hayward resided in Woodstock, Connecticut. In 1800, their household was four persons: one male 26 to 44, one female 26 to 44, one male under 10, and one female under 10.[2667] By 1820, the household had grown to ten persons: one male 45 and over, one female 45 and over,[2668] two males 10 to 15, one male 16 to 18, three males 16 to 25 (which includes the one male 16 to 18), one female 10 to 15, and two females 16 to 25.[2669]

Lucy Paine and King Hayward were parents of eight children.[2670] Sons Pliny and Andrew J. Hayward were corn merchants and active in local politics in McHenry County, Illinois.[2671]

i   GEORGE KING HAYWARD, b. at Woodstock, 15 Feb 1799; d. 18 Sep 1849.[2672]

ii LUCY PAINE HAYWARD, b. at Woodstock, 13 Jul 1800; d. at Norwich, 1 May 1884; m. at Woodstock, 10 Mar 1830, ELIJAH ARNOLD, b. 1803; Elijah d. at Norwich, 27 Apr 1876.

iii NOAH PAINE HAYWARD, b. at Woodstock, 30 Dec 1801; d. at Hartford, 1875 (probate); m. at Hartford, 10 Jan 1828, LYDIA PORTER, b. about 1800; Lydia was living in 1873 when Noah wrote his will.

iv AUGUSTUS STORRS HAYWARD, b. 24 Nov 1803; d. at Worcester, MA, 26 Jul 1859; m. at Millbury, MA, 7 Apr 1827, MARY GREENWOOD BIXBY, b. at Millbury, 6 Jun 1805 daughter of Simon and Hannah (Barton) Bixby; Mary d. at Worcester, 12 Feb 1881.

v   ALMIRA HAYWARD, b. at Woodstock, 9 Apr 1805; d. at Hartford, 1897 (probate); m. at Hartford, 24 Sep 1849, as his second wife, Deacon ISAAC KENDALL, b. at Ashford, 27 Dec 1787 son of Isaac and Rachel (Marcy) Kendall; Isaac was first married to Nancy Smith who died in 1848. Almira did not have children. In her will written 9 October 1883 (probate 1897), she has bequests to Mrs. Lucy Arnold who received fifty dollars with the rest of the estate going to nephew Andrew J. Hayward.[2673]

vi NANCY S. HAYWARD, b. 28 Jul 1806; d. at Norwich, 15 Apr 1844 at age 37 years, 9 months. Nancy did not marry.

vii PLINY HAYWARD, b. at Woodstock, 18 May 1808; d. at Chicago, IL (burial at Woodstock, IL), 6 Apr 1879; m. at Woodstock, CT, 15 Dec 1829, LUCY BLANCHARD, b. at Calais, VT, 8 Jul 1808 daughter of Moses and Lucy

[2664] 1820 U S Census; Census Place: Hartland, Windsor, Vermont; Page: 308; NARA Roll: M33_128; Image: 175

[2665] Year: 1830; Census Place: Bethel, Windsor, Vermont; Series: M19; Roll: 187; Page: 200; Family History Library Film: 0027453

[2666] Cox, *The Illustrated Historical Souvenir History of Bethel, Vermont*, p 69

[2667] Year: 1800; Census Place: Woodstock, Windham, Connecticut; Series: M32; Roll: 2; Page: 788; Image: 416; Family History Library Film: 205619

[2668] A record for King remarrying after Lucy's death was not found, although the census raises the possibility that he did remarry.

[2669] 1820 U S Census; Census Place: Woodstock, Windham, Connecticut; Page: 375; NARA Roll: M33_3; Image: 282

[2670] Birth records were located for the first seven children and the birthdate of Andrew Jackson is given in Hayward, *William Hayward of Mendon*, p 34

[2671] Inter-State Publishing Company, *History of McHenry County, Illinois*

[2672] Hayward, *William Hayward of Mendon*, p 34

[2673] Connecticut Wills and Probate, Eastford Probate District, Town of Eastford, Estate of Almira H. Kendall, 1897, No. 193

(Bacon) Blanchard; Lucy d. at Chicago (burial at Woodstock, IL), 20 Aug 1880.[2674] Pliny Hayward and Andrew J. Hayward were corn merchants in Chicago.[2675]

viii ANDREW JACKSON HAYWARD, b. 10 Jul 1810; d. likely at Chicago (burial at Woodstock, IL), 8 Jun 1872; m. 1st at Hartford, 24 Jul 1834, ELIZABETH JUDD, b. at Chester, MA, 26 Jun 1813 daughter of Salathiel and Irena (Day) Judd;[2676] Elizabeth d. at Hartland, IL, 12 Jan 1842. Andrew m. 2nd about 1851, EMILY DWIGHT (maiden name as given on daughter's death record),[2677] b. in MA, about 1832 (census); Emily d. after 1890 when she was living in Chicago.

848) HANNAH PAINE (*Zerviah Humphrey Paine⁴, Hannah Russell Humphrey³, Benjamin², Robert¹*), b. at Ashford, 1 Oct 1773 daughter of Noah and Zerviah (Humphrey) Paine; d. at Eastford, 10 Mar 1855; m. at Ashford, 9 May 1798, JOHN WORK, b. at Ashford, 17 Nov 1775 son of Ingoldsby and Esther (Bugbee) Work; John d. at Eastford, 25 Mar 1863.

In 1850, John headed a household at Woodstock that included his wife Hannah, Catherine and Erastus Bicknell, two Bicknell children, and two laborers from Ireland. The value given to the farm was $2,900.[2678]

Two children were identified for Hannah and John.

i HANNAH WORK, b. at Eastford, 13 Feb 1799; d. at Eastford, 14 May 1884 at age 79 years, 3 months, 1 day;[2679] m. at Ashford, 29 Apr 1818, EPHRAIM TROWBRIDGE, b. at Pomfret, 4 Aug 1788 son of James and Mary (Kendall) Trowbridge; Ephraim d. at Eastford, 4 Aug 1852.

ii CATHERINE WORK, b. 1804; d. at Woodstock, 8 Oct 1892; m. at Ashford, 3 Jun 1835, ERASTUS BICKNELL, b. at Ashford, 9 Dec 1804 son of Samuel and Sarah (Marcy) Bicknell; Erastus d. at Woodstock, 23 Jul 1870.

849) ELISHA PAINE (*Zerviah Humphrey Paine⁴, Hannah Russell Humphrey³, Benjamin², Robert¹*), b. at Ashford, 1780 son of Noah and Zerviah (Humphrey) Paine; d. at Pomfret, 27 Dec 1817; m. at Pomfret, 16 Jun 1808, JERUSHA WELCH, b. at Windham, 24 Feb 1787 daughter of John and Olive (Fitch) Welch; Jerusha d. at Pomfret, 23 Jul 1835.

Elisha and Jerusha resided in Pomfret. Elisha was head of a household of five persons in 1810: one male 26 to 44, one female 26 to 44, one male under 10, one male 10 to 15, and one female 16 to 25.[2680] Jerusha head a household of five persons in 1820: one female 26 to 44, one male 45 and over, one female under 10, and two females 16 to 25.[2681]

In his will written 30 October 1817, Elisha left his estate to his beloved wife Jerusha trusting that she will have "the best interest of my children much upon her heart & that she will faithfully discharge the duty of a parent."[2682]

There are records of two children of Elisha and Jerusha.

i FRANCIS JAMES PAINE, b. at Pomfret, 3 Aug 1809; d. at Lake Mills, WI, 25 Jan 1856; m. 1st at Windham, 25 May 1835, FRANCES ANN ABBE, b. 1815 daughter of Lucius and Martha (Johnson) Abbe; Frances d. at Aztalan, WI, 19 May 1841. James m. 2nd at Windham, 22 Sep 1845, ABBY L. BURNHAM, b. 1814; Abby d. at Lake Mills, 23 Jan 1847. James m. 3rd at Beaver Dam, WI, 25 Dec 1851, EMELINE R. WOOLEY, b. 1827; Emeline d. at Lake Mills, 10 Apr 1854.

ii OLIVE FITCH PAINE, b. at Pomfret, 21 Sep 1814; d. at Brooklyn, CT, 8 Jun 1835; m. at Pomfret, 8 Apr 1834, CHARLES MATHEWSON, b. at Brooklyn, CT, 24 Mar 1812 son of Darius and Mary (Smith) Mathewson; Charles d. at Norfolk, NE, 10 Ma 1880. Charles married second Mary Gray Grosvenor. Charles served as colonel of the 11th Connecticut regiment during the Civil War.[2683]

850) AUGUSTINE PAINE (*Zerviah Humphrey Paine⁴, Hannah Russell Humphrey³, Benjamin², Robert¹*), b. at Ashford, 1782 son of Noah and Zerviah (Humphrey) Paine; d. at Belchertown, MA, 23 Aug 1814; m. at Spencer, MA, 25 Feb 1808,

[2674] Lucy, Pliny, and Andrew J. Hayward are all interred at Oakland Cemetery in Woodstock, IL; Find a Grave 67623681; 67623607
[2675] U.S., City Directories, 1822-1995, Chicago, 1861
[2676] Dwight, *History of Descendants of Elder John Strong*, p 280
[2677] Death record for daughter Emma Louise *Hayward* Stanwood; "Illinois Deaths and Stillbirths, 1916-1947," database, *FamilySearch* (https://familysearch.org/ark:/61903/1:1:NQDV-YQ8 : 8 March 2018), Andrew J. Hayward in entry for Emma Louise Stanwood, 22 Feb 1925; Public Board of Health, Archives, Springfield; FHL microfilm 1,487,770.
[2678] Year: 1850; Census Place: Woodstock, Windham, Connecticut; Roll: 51; Page: 250b
[2679] "Connecticut Deaths and Burials, 1772-1934", database, *FamilySearch* (https://familysearch.org/ark:/61903/1:1:QLM4-ZX97 : 22 July 2021), Hannah Work Trowbridge, 1884.
[2680] Year: 1810; Census Place: Pomfret, Windham, Connecticut; Roll: 3; Page: 463; Image: 00256; Family History Library Film: 0281231
[2681] 1820 U S Census; Census Place: Pomfret, Windham, Connecticut; Page: 469; NARA Roll: M33_3; Image: 367
[2682] Connecticut Wills and Probate, Pomfret District, Town of Pomfret, Estate of Elisha Paine, No. 3060
[2683] Nebraska, U.S., Grand Army of the Republic, Burial Records, 1861-1948

ABIGAIL MASON, b. at Spencer, 26 Nov 1787 daughter of Ebenezer and Judith (White) Mason; Abigail d. at Spencer, 30 Sep 1823.

Augustine Paine was a physician in Belchertown.

The estate of Dr. Augustine Paine was administered by Mark Doolittle of Belchertown who was appointed on 12 September 1814 at the request of widow Abigail. Total estate value was $1,917.52 after the sale of the real estate. The dower was set to the widow. The debts of the estate exceeded the remaining value and was paid to the creditors. Abigail Payne was allowed as guardian to minor children Albert Augustine Payne and Ebenezer Mason Payne.[2684]

The estate of Abigail Paine entered probate 6 October 1823 with Ebenezer Mason and Josiah Mason requesting that Moses Hall of Spencer be named administrator. The estate was valued at $150.48. After payment of debts and costs, there remained value of $44.77 which was paid to the two children.[2685]

i   ALBERT AUGUSTINE PAINE, b. at Granby, 13 May 1809; d. at Worcester (last resident at Portsmouth, NH), 22 Oct 1889; m. 1st at Grafton, MA, 9 Apr 1835, MARY ELIZABETH PUTNAM, b. at Grafton, MA, 26 Sep 1814 daughter of John and Anna (Wheeler) Putnam; Mary d. at Portsmouth, NH, 19 Jan 1877. Albert m. 2nd at Portsmouth, 13 May 1880, SUSAN C. COLLINS (widow of Alonzo Chadwick), b. about 1826 daughter of Stephen and Sarah (Gunnerson) Collins; Susan d. at Portsmouth, 12 May 1885.

ii   EBENEZER MASON PAINE, b. at Granby, 5 Feb 1811. Ebenezer was living in 1823. Further information was not found.

851)   PERSIS "PERCY" PAINE (*Zerviah Humphrey Paine⁴, Hannah Russell Humphrey³, Benjamin², Robert¹*), b. at Ashford, 18 Mar 1785 daughter of Noah and Zerviah (Humphrey) Paine; d. at Eastford, 30 Apr 1848; m. at Hartford, 14 May 1807, DAVID HOWARD, b. 4 Jul 1780 son of David and Priscilla (Knowlton) Howard; David d. at Eastford, 10 May 1848.

Prior to his marriage, David Howard went to sea obtaining his seaman's certificate at New London 16 May 1805.[2686] Persis and David resided at Ashford, although the birth of the youngest daughter is recorded at Hartford. In 1820, David headed a household of five children at Ashford: one male 26 to 44; one female 26 to 44; and three females under 10.[2687]

There are records of three children of Persis and David.

i   MARTHA LOUISA HOWARD, b. at Ashford, 18 Apr 1811; d. after 1850 when she was living with her sister Jane and her family in Racine, WI.[2688]

ii   LUCY PAINE HOWARD, b. at Ashford, 10 Apr 1815; d. at Eastford (also recorded at Union), 1897; m. at Ashford, 27 Jun 1836, DANIEL BARTLETT, b. 19 Feb 1812 son of William and Betsey (Crocker) Bartlett; Daniel d. at Eastford (also recorded at Union), 1898.

iii   JANE ADELAIDE HOWARD, b. at Hartford, 4 Jul 1818; d. at Benicia, CA, 25 Nov 1903; m. at Ashford, 18 Nov 1844, NATHAN HAMMOND GARRETSON, b. at Bradford County, PA, 26 Aug 1811 son of William and Sarah (Wilson) Garretson;[2689] Nathan d. at Benicia, 4 Jul 1896.

852)   JOSEPH CHENEY (*Mehitable Lyon Chubb Cheney⁴, Abigail Russell Lyon³, Benjamin², Robert¹*), b. at Ashford, Feb 1759 son of William and Mehitable (Lyon) Cheney; d. at Auburn, NY, 10 Jan 1831; m. at Brooklyn, CT, 22 Jun 1784, SELAH TYLER, b. 1766; Selah d. at Auburn, 3 Mar 1823.

In April 1818, while living in the village of Auburn in Cayuga County, Joseph Cheney made application for pension. In March 1781, he enlisted in the 7th company of the 3rd Connecticut regiment, was with that company about two years, and was then transferred to the company of Capt. Riley in Col. Nichols's regiment. He served with that company until his discharged at Fort Constitution in New York "after the arrival of the news of peace." He was present at the capture of Cornwallis. At the time of his application, he provided an inventory that consisted of a village lot in Auburn of 66-feet frontage which was mortgaged and personal estate of $61.65. On 6 July 1820, he reported he was a laborer by trade but as a consequence of "wounds and breaches" he was unable to perform his usual work. His household at that time was wife Seelah age 54 who was weakly, daughter Rocksey age 27 who had her three children with her (twins Willis and Willard age 7 and daughter Minerva age 2), son Jarvis age 16, and daughter Emeline aged 10. Joseph was allowed pension for his service.[2690]

[2684] *Hampshire County, MA: Probate File Papers, 1660-1889.* Online database. *AmericanAncestors.org.* New England Historic Genealogical Society, 2016, 2017. Box 111-23. The estate file of Augustine Paine is filed in the guardianship file of son Ebenezer.

[2685] *Worcester County, MA: Probate File Papers, 1731-1881.* Online database. AmericanAncestors.org. New England Historic Genealogical Society, 2015. Case 44744

[2686] US, New England Seamen's Protection Certificate Index, 1796-1871

[2687] 1820 U S Census; Census Place: Ashford, Windham, Connecticut; Page: 425; NARA Roll: M33_3; Image: 330

[2688] Year: 1850; Census Place: Racine, Racine, Wisconsin; Roll: 1004; Page: 41b

[2689] California, U.S., Pioneer and Immigrant Files, 1790-1950; California State Library; Sacramento, California; Sacramento County, California; Pioneer Index File (1906-1934), A-Z; California History Room: MICROFILM 734; Roll Number: 43

[2690] U. S. Revolutionary War Pension and Bounty-Land Warrant Application Files, Case S44754

Joseph and Selah were likely parents of twelve children.

i   RUBY E. CHENEY, b. 1786; m. about 1810, HOSEA BRONSON, b. 1786; Hosea d. at Brighton, NY, 1827 (probate 4 Jan 1828).

ii JOSEPH CHENEY, b. 7 Aug 1788 (on gravestone);[2691] d. at Penfield, NY, 23 Jun 1865; m. RHODA BAKER, b. 23 Feb 1792 daughter of Elias and Irany (Root) Baker;[2692] Rhoda d. at Penfield, 19 Apr 1847.

iii CHESTER CHENEY, b. 28 Aug 1789; d. at Rome, NY, 28 Jun 1868; m. MARIAH LAW, b. 9 Apr 1796 daughter of Consider and Sarah (Grummon) Law; Mariah d. at Rome, 16 Aug 1861. Chester m. 2nd at Westmoreland, NY, 9 Oct 1862, DEBORAH who has not been identified but was the recipient of a widow's pension related to Chester's service in the War of 1812.[2693]

iv MARY CHENEY, b. 28 Sep 1791; d. at Oakwood, MI, 31 Oct 1858; m. HOMER PELTON, b. 1 Oct 1793 son of Jonathan and Elizabeth (Baker) Pelton;[2694] Homer d. at Lapeer, MI, 26 Mar 1868.

v   ROCKSANA CHENEY, b. 1793 and living in 1820. Rocksana married and had three children (per father's pension record), but the name of her husband has not been found.

vi WILLIAM CHENEY, b. at Williamstown, VT, 17 Nov 1795[2695]

vii PASCHAL P. CHENEY, b. at Williamstown, VT, 27 Jul 1797 (27 Jul 1795 on gravestone); d. at Penfield, NY, 1 Jul 1859; m. ABIGAIL CULVER, b. 10 Sep 1795; Abigail d. at Penfield, 23 Aug 1853.

viii CALVIN R. CHENEY, b. 1798; d. at Dearborn, MI, 8 Aug 1878; m. CHARLOTTE MANN, b. in NJ, 1797 (census records); Charlotte d. at Dearborn Heights, 12 Jul 1888.[2696]

ix WARREN W. CHENEY, b. 10 Sep 1801; d. at Atlas, MI, 28 Apr 1877; m. LUCY MARIA PELTON, b. 1804 daughter of Jonathan and Elizabeth (Baker) Pelton; Lucy d. at Hadley, MI, 22 Sep 1891.

x   ELIZABETH CHENEY, b. 1802; d. 1820.

xi JERVIS CHENEY, b. 5 Dec 1804; d. at Adrian, MI, 16 Jun 1863;[2697] m. SARAH SMITH, b. in NY, 26 Sep 1806; Sarah d. 22 Jan 1888.

xii EMELINE CHENEY, b. 25 Feb 1810; d. at Fairfield, MI, 1 Aug 1847; m. EDWARD PIERCE, b. 17 Oct 1809 son of John S. and Deborah (Field) Pierce; Edward d. at Fairfield, 28 Dec 1894.

---

853)   WILLIAM CHENEY (*Priscilla Lyon Cheney⁴, Abigail Russell Lyon³, Benjamin², Robert¹*), b. at Ashford, 12 Apr 1765 son of Ebenezer and Priscilla (Lyon) Cheney; d. at Colebrook, OH, 13 Jun 1851;[2698] m. DELIA SHIPMAN, b. 1770 daughter of David Shipman; Delia d. Hartwick, NY, 24 Jan 1830. William *perhaps* m. 2nd SARAH CRAYTON in Oct 1844.

William Cheney resided in Otsego County, New York for much of his adult life. Just prior to his death, he lived with his daughter Patience in Colebrook, Ohio.

On 28 August 1832, William Cheney age 66 and residing in Canandaigua, New York, made application for pension. He reported enlisting as a private in the spring of 1781 as a substitute in the company of Capt. Dana in the brigade of General Waterbury. He served about one year. He was allowed pension for his service of $40 per annum. He reported his date of birth as 22 April 1776 and place of birth as Ashford. Following his death, his widow Sarah, living in Pine Grove, Pennsylvania, made application for arrears of the pension and for a widow's pension. She reported marrying William in October 1844, but it seems that sufficient evidence of the marriage was not provided. On 28 September 1839, William Cheney appeared in Hampshire County, Massachusetts stating that he planned to remain there. He reported he made the move for a better livelihood and that his profession was herb doctor. On 6 March 1843, William was in Collins, New York and reported he intended to stay there and reside with his children.[2699]

The pension file provides a glimpse of the unsettled nature of William's life. A letter dated 19 September 1839 from Samuel Hinckley of Northampton describes William as an itinerant herb doctor with no permanent residence who was residing in Northampton for a few weeks. Mr. Hinckley had obtained power or attorney related to William's pension. On 14 September 1842, Samuel Hinckley reported that William left his pension certificate with him for safe keeping but that he now learned that William had returned to Canandaigua. On 29 July 1843, Benjamin Dole of Buffalo, New York wrote to the pension department

[2691] Smith Cemetery, Penfield, NY, findagrave ID: 83535525

[2692] The 1830 will of Elias Baker of Penfield includes a bequest to daughter Rhoda Cheney.

[2693] War of 1812 Pension Application Files Index, 1812-1815

[2694] Pelton, *Genealogy of the Pelton Family*, p 215

[2695] Vermont Vital Records 1760-1954, FHL Film 004543213, image 3283

[2696] Charlotte is interred at Wallaceville Historical Cemetery, Dearborn Heights; findagrave ID: 32512634

[2697] Jervis and Sarah are interred at Oakwood Cemetery in Adrian, MI; findagrave ID: 41986263

[2698] Burial is reported at Colebrook South Cemetery; findagrave ID: 49609758

[2699] U. S. Revolutionary War Pension and Bounty-Land Warrant Application Files, Case R1905

reporting that William had given him power of attorney related to his pension and authorized Mr. Dole to receive the payments. Mr. Dole advanced William $30 but then no pension payments arrived. Mr. Dole had assumed William was dead but later learned he was alive, living in Massachusetts and had a new pension certificate. And in fact, on 16 February 1837 while living in Canandaigua, William requested a substitute pension certificate as he lost his original certificate.

William may be the William Cheney, age 84 and born in Connecticut, living at the poorhouse in Middlefield, New York in 1850.[2700]

William and Delia were parents of eight children.

i   ALVA CHENEY, b. at Fly Creek, 3 May 1790; d. at Fly Creek, 9 Feb 1851; m. at Cooperstown, NY, 26 Feb 1812, ANNA WELCH, b. 1798; Anna d. at Fly Creek, 1 May 1872.

ii   PERCY CHENEY, b. at Fly Creek, 22 Jan 1795; d. at Markesan, WI, 16 Mar 1875; m. 1 Jan 1816, STEPHEN H. WHITE, b. at Petersham, MA, 12 Aug 1792 son of Stephen and Abigail (Hudson) White; Stephen d. at Markesan, 10 Aug 1851.

iii   PATIENCE CHENEY, b. 1799; d. at Troy, KS, after 1880; m. 1818, AMOS PERRY, b. 1795 son of Jonas and Susannah (Damon) Perry; Amos d. at Troy, 1885.

iv   WILLIAM CHENEY, b. at Fly Creek, 18 Apr 1801; d. at Mount Vision, NY, 20 Dec 1889; m. MARIA, b. 23 Nov 1815 (on gravestone); Maria d. at Mount Vision, 20 Mar 1875.

v   EBENEZER CHENEY, b. 9 Feb 1803; d. at Lima Center, WI, 13 Sep 1874; m. PHILIPENIA E. CROMWELL, b. 1805; Philipenia d. at Lima Center, 31 Jan 1845.

vi   JOSEPH CHENEY, b. 3 May 1805; d. at Perrysburg, NY, 30 Jan 1848; m. CAROLINE, b. 11 Jul 1807; Caroline d. at Perrysburg, 3 Jan 1885.

vii   RUTH CHENEY, b. at Cooperstown, NY, 3 Apr 1807; d. at Conway, MI, 21 Oct 1885; m. CAREY C. DAWLEY, b. 11 Nov 1799 son of Job and Bernice (Clark) Dawley; Carey d. at Perrysburg, 6 Jan 1847.

viii   HANNAH CHENEY, b. 29 Oct 1812; d. at Whitewater, WI, 4 Jan 1886; m. LESTER HULSE, b. 24 Apr 1813 son of Elisha Hulse; Lester d. at Whitewater, 15 Dec 1893.

854)   RUTH CHENEY (*Priscilla Lyon Cheney⁴, Abigail Russell Lyon³, Benjamin², Robert¹*), b. at Ashford, 7 Apr 1767 daughter of Ebenezer and Priscilla (Lyon) Cheney; m. about 1787, OLIVER GARDNER, b. about 1760; Oliver d. at Fly Creek, NY, 1812.

The estate of Oliver Gardner entered probate 5 March 1812 with Ruth Gardner as administratrix and William Gardner and Benjamin Wight as sureties.[2701]

One child was identified for Ruth Cheney and Oliver Gardner.

i   WILLIAM GARDNER, b. 22 Mar 1790; d. at Ogdensburg, NY, 5 Jul 1877; m. at Fly Creek, 28 Mar 1813, DEBORAH CARTER, b. at Fly Creek, 10 May 1793 daughter of John and Susannah (Bliss) Carter;[2702] William d. at Ogdensburg, 5 Jul 1877.

855)   EBENEZER CHENEY (*Priscilla Lyon Cheney⁴, Abigail Russell Lyon³, Benjamin², Robert¹*), b. at Ashford, 6 Aug 1769 son of Ebenezer and Priscilla (Lyon) Cheney; d. at Fly Creek, NY, 10 Mar 1803; m. 1796, TABITHA WHIPPLE, b. 1768 daughter of Benajah and Tabitha (Barrett) Whipple; Tabitha d. 1848.

One child was identified for Ebenezer and Tabitha.

i   LUCY CHENEY, b. 1802; d. at New Haven, NY, 16 Feb 1872; m. 1821, DANIEL D. LANDERS, b. 1799; Daniel d. at New Haven, 6 Jun 1873.

856)   JOSEPH CHENEY (*Priscilla Lyon Cheney⁴, Abigail Russell Lyon³, Benjamin², Robert¹*), b. at Ashford, 11 Oct 1774 son of Ebenezer and Priscilla (Lyon) Cheney; d. at Fly Creek, NY, 23 Apr 1852; m. LYDIA ADAMS, b. 1782 daughter of John and Submit (Butts) Adams; Lydia d. at Fly Creek, 30 Mar 1866.

[2700] United States Census, 1850, New York, Otsego, Middlefield, 17 Sep 1850, p 212

[2701] New York Wills and Probate, Otsego County, Book C, pp 154-155; Will Book 9, p 275, FHL Film # 005116505, Image 337

[2702] Carter, Howard, *Carter, A Genealogy of the Descendants of Thomas Carter*, p 56

Joseph settled in Fly Creek with his father Ebenezer and his brothers William and Ebenezer, Jr. Joseph had a farm and built a frame house that he used as an inn after the turnpike through Otsego County opened. It is reported in the History of Otsego County that the turnpike was sited to accommodate Joseph and his inn.[2703]

In his will written 1 March 1848 (proved 28 May 1852), Joseph Cheney bequeathed to his beloved wife one cow, one bed, two sheep, two "chares", and one tea kettle besides what the law gives her as widow. Eldest son Samuel W. Cheney receives five dollars besides the seven hundred dollars "I gave him a long time since." Daughter Celia Ann Cheney receives the little carriage, sixty dollars in personal property in sheep and cows "if she would rather have them" in addition to the land she received by deed. Son Ebenezer W. Cheney receives fifty dollars in real or personal property in addition to the six hundred dollars he received. Son Joseph A. Cheney receives fifty dollars in addition to what he received by deed. Son Stephen Cheney receives fifty dollars in addition to what he has received. Daughter Mitta C. Parmelee receives two dollars in addition to what she received. Daughter Mary M. Cheney has received deed of land and receives five dollars. E. Matilda Cheney receives five dollars in addition to half of the east farm. Granddaughter Mary R. Parmelee receives $214. Any remaining property after the payment of debts is to be equally divided among Celia Ann Cheney, Joseph A. Cheney, Mary M. Cheney, and Eliza Matilda Cheney. Joseph A. Cheney and Mary M. Cheney were named executors. At the proving of the will, the following heirs-at-law were listed: Lydia Cheney, Samuel W. Cheney, Celia A. Cheney, Joseph A, Cheney, Mary M. Cheney, Eliza M. Cheney, and Stephen P. Cheney all residing in Otsego County and Mitta C. Parmelee and Ebenezer W. Cheney residing in Chenango County.[2704]

Joseph Cheney and Lydia Adams were parents of nine children born at Fly Creek, New York.[2705]

i   SAMUEL W. CHENEY, b. 31 Aug 1801; d. at Fly Creek, 8 Dec 1870; m. by 1834, LUCINDA MAY, b. 2 Aug 1805; Lucinda d. at Fly Creek, 30 Oct 1866.

ii   CELIA ANN CHENEY, b. 20 Aug 1803; d. at Fly Creek, 24 Aug 1877. Celia did not marry.

iii   EBENZER W. CHENEY, b. 8 Mar 1805; d. at Norwich, NY, 1 Oct 1893; m. by 1834, MARINDA MAY, b. 17 Aug 1811; Marinda d. at Norwich, 8 Oct 1870.

iv   JOSEPH A. CHENEY, b. 28 Feb 1807; d. at Fly Creek, 1 Jan 1884. Joseph did not marry. In his will, Col. Joseph A. Cheney left the bulk of his estate to Edmund Cheney Parmelee and other bequests to Mitta Parmelee and Joseph F. Parmelee and some provision for the care of Ann W. Parmelee.[2706]

v   MITTA CHENEY, b. 16 Oct 1811; d. at Fly Creek, 16 Sep 1897; m. by 1839, EDWARD HARVEY PARMELEE, b. at Killingworth, CT, 10 Sep 1807 son of Ishi and Esther (Buell) Parmelee; Edward d. at Fly Creek, 2 May 1860.

vi   STEPHEN P. CHENEY, b. 1814; d. at Fly Creek, 24 Feb 1900; m. 1st by 1840, EMERLINE WHEELER, b. 1813 daughter of William Wheeler;[2707] Emerline d. at Fly Creek, 24 Oct 1866. Stephen m. 2nd LUCINDA E. WELCH, b. at Otsego, 1833 daughter of Stephen R. and Polly (·) Welch; Lucinda d. at Fly Creek, 1912.

vii   MARY M. CHENEY, b. 9 Dec 1816; d. at Oneonta, NY, 11 Mar 1912; m. 1859, ALFRED BURNHAM, b. at Arkwright, NY, 23 Jul 1836 son of Stephen J. and Phebe (Clinton) Burnham; Alfred d. at Sparland, IL, 3 Jul 1897. Mary and Alfred lived in Sparland for most of their married life, and Mary returned to Otsego County after Alfred's death and resided with niece Rosa P. Steere at the time of her death.[2708]

viii   ISAAC R. CHENEY, b. 27 Jun 1819; d. at Fly Creek, 23 Feb 1839.

ix   ELIZA MATHILDA CHENEY, b. 28 Feb 1822; d. at Fly Creek, 28 Dec 1866. Mathilda did not marry. In her will written 18 June 1866 (proved 25 February 1867), E. Matilda Cheney of Otsego bequeathed to sister Celia Ann Cheney an undivided half part of the farm that Matilda and her brother Joseph A. Cheney received by deed from father Joseph Cheney. After the decease of Celia, this property is to be divided in two equal parts. One-half goes to Edward C. Parmelee and Carrie W. Gattsee as tenants in common to be held in trusts by their several mothers until they arrive at age twenty-one. The other half is to be divided among Samuel W. Cheney, Ebenezer W. Cheney, Mitta C. Parmelee, and Stephen P. Cheney. The undivided third part of the property that she, her sister Celia, and brother Joseph A. purchased of sister Mary M. C. Burnam is to go to brother Joseph A. Cheney. Bed and bedding goes to niece Rosa P. Gattsee. Wilson S. Cheney was named executor. The probate record notes that Rosa P. Gattsee was resident of Mississippi.[2709]

[2703] Hurd, *History of Otsego County, New York*, p 249

[2704] New York Wills and Probate, Otsego County, Petitions Box 10, Joseph Cheney, petitions related to proving the will

[2705] Most members of this family are buried in the Fly Creek Village Cemetery and their gravestones, for the most part, include dates of birth.

[2706] New York Wills and Probate, Otsego County, Wills 0031, p 134

[2707] Father-in-law William Wheeler was living with Stephen and Emerline at the 1855 census.

[2708] Obituary of Mary M. Cheney Burnham, "The Otsego Farmer & Republican" (Cooperstown, NY), Fri., Mar. 15, 1912

[2709] New York Wills and Probate, Otsego County, Wills volume 0013, pp 429-431

857)   PERSIS CHENEY (*Priscilla Lyon Cheney⁴, Abigail Russell Lyon³, Benjamin², Robert¹*), b. at Ashford, 10 Nov 1778 daughter of Ebenezer and Priscilla (Lyon) Cheney; d. at Fly Creek, NY, 2 Sep 1853; m. JOHN ADAMS, b. at Canterbury, CT, 20 Jan 1776 son of John and Submit (Butts) Adams; John d. at Fly Creek, 15 Apr 1843.

Persis and John resided in Fly Creek, New York where they were pioneers, John having settled there about 1790 with his family.[2710] On 23 April 1843, William B. Adams and Joseph A. Cheney were named administrators of his estate.[2711]

John and Persis were parents of eleven children born at Fly Creek, New York.[2712]

i   ADIN ADAMS, b. 15 Sep 1800; d. at Cooperstown, NY, 3 Mar 1879; m. 19 Apr 1819, SALLY WILLIAMS, b. 19 Apr 1802; Sally d. at Cooperstown, Mar 1869.

ii   NANCY ADAMS, b. 6 Mar 1802; d. at Masonville, NY, 15 Jan 1877; m. at Otsego, NY, 17 Apr 1825, WILLIAM RUTENBER, b. 28 Nov 1804 son of William and Dorothy (Peck) Rutenber; William d. at Masonville, 10 Dec 1870.

iii   DOLLY ADAMS, b. 29 Feb 1804; d. at Lodi (burial at Hartwick), 1 Oct 1841; m. FREDERICK A. ELWELL, b. in CT, 1807 son of Samuel and Jerusha (Smith) Elwell; Frederick d. at Roseboom, NY, 4 Nov 1892. Frederick married 2nd Ann.

iv   PRISCILLA ADAMS, b. 16 Feb 1806; d. at Malden, IL, 27 Jul 1894; m. 13 Dec 1829, WILLIAM B. ADAMS, b. at Fly Creek, 11 Feb 1806 son of William and Abigail (Mallory) Adams;[2713] William d. at Malden, 18 Aug 1869.

v   JOHN J. ADAMS, b. 16 Apr 1808; d. at Avoca, WI, 16 Mar 1885; m. 1st 28 Mar 1831, BETSEY DAY, b. about 1809; Betsey d. 14 Apr 1835. John m. 2nd at Erie County, NY, 1836, HARRIET BACON, b. about 1815. John m. 3rd SARAH ANN HALL, b. about 1823.

vi   PERSIS ADAMS, b. 29 Mar 1810; d. at Middleville, NY, 4 Apr 1852; m. WILLIAM EWELL, b. in CT, 6 Apr 1804 son of Samuel and Jerusha (Smith) Elwell; William d. at Davenport, NY, 27 Jul 1887. William married 2nd Rebecca Krine and married 3rd Polly Kellogg.

vii   ELIZA ADAMS, b. 10 Jan 1812; d. likely at Hector, PA, 29 Jun 1861; m. 1st about 1841, STEPHEN WHEELER, b. in MA, about 1814; Stephen d. after 1850. Eliza m. 2nd by 1860, JOHN TARBELL, b. in NY, about 1827.

viii   EBENEZER CHENEY ADAMS, b. Sep 1814; d. at Painted Post, NY, 14 May 1888; m. 30 Oct 1844, NANCY OWENS, b. 1816; Nancy d. at Painted Post, 1890.

ix   WALTER ADAMS, b. 28 Aug 1816; d. at South Corning, NY, 31 Aug 1897; m. Sep 1838, CEPHRONIA ROBISNON, b. 4 Feb 1818; Cephronia d. at South Corning, 10 Jun 1901. Cephronia's mother was Hephzibah.

x   SUSANNAH ADAMS, b. Jul 1818; d. (burial at Hartwick, NY), 12 Jul 1819.

xi   SAMUEL WILSON ADAMS, b. 17 Aug 1820; d. at Erwin, NY, 1898; m. 21 Jan 1840, MARIA COVENHOVEN, b. 2 Mar 1820; Maria d. at Erwin, 1895.

858)   DANIEL SANGER (*Azariah Sanger⁴, Lydia Russell Sanger³, Benjamin², Robert¹*), b. at Willington, 24 Dec 1760 son of Azariah and Elizabeth (Abbe) Sanger; d. at Washington, MA, 26 Sep 1844; m. at Willington, 5 Feb 1784, ALICE WAKEFIELD, b. at Ashford, 12 Feb 1765 daughter of John and Ellis (-) Wakefield; Alice d. at Washington, 3 Jan 1842.

Daniel and Alice resided in Willington and Ellington, Connecticut and then in Peru and Washington, Massachusetts.

In 1810, Daniel headed a household of eleven persons at Ellington: two males 45 and over, one female 45 and over, one male under 10, one male 10 to 15, three males 16 to 25, one female 10 to 15, one female 16 to 25, and one female 26 to 44.[2714] In 1820, the household was six persons at Washington, Massachusetts: one male 45 and over, one female 45 and over, two males 16 to 25, one female 16 to 25, and one female 26 to 44.[2715]

On 10 November 1832, Daniel Sanger, then aged seventy-two and residing in Washington, Massachusetts, provided a statement related to his application for a pension. He served with the Connecticut state troops for two months in 1776 and two months in 1777. In 1778, he served for six months as a substitute in the Connecticut line in the company of Capt. Barnard and regiment of Col. Willis. On 1 April 1781, he enlisted and served a term of nine months in the company of Capt. Dana.

He reported being born in Willington on 24 September 1760[2716] and residing there until after the war. In 1787, he removed to Ellington where he remained until 1809 or 1810 when he removed to Peru in Berkshire County, Massachusetts. He was in Peru until April of 1816 or 1817, when he moved to Washington, Massachusetts.

[2710] Hurd, *History of Otsego County, New York*, p 250

[2711] New York Wills and Probate, Otsego County, volume 0001, p 110

[2712] Adams, *Genealogical History of Henry Adams*, p 164 identifies ten children and an eleventh child is identified in cemetery records. Find a Grave ID: 77722743l Susanna d/o John & Persis

[2713] W. W. Munsell, *History of Delaware County, N. Y.*, 1880, p 351

[2714] Year: 1810; Census Place: Ellington, Tolland, Connecticut; Roll: 3; Page: 337; Image: 00189; Family History Library Film: 0281231

[2715] 1820 U S Census; Census Place: Washington, Berkshire, Massachusetts; Page: 185; NARA Roll: M33_48; Image: 132

[2716] The date is given as 24 December 1760 in the Barbour collection transcriptions.

Daniel's sister Cynthia Routh living in Willington provided a statement in support of Daniel's application on 27 September 1832.[2717] On 28 March 1854, Chauncey Davis (who was the spouse of Daniel's niece Jane Melross) inquired whether surviving children of a pensioner were eligible for payments.[2718]

Daughter Selinda did not marry, and her estate entered probate 26 May 1851 with Edward Wright as administrator. The heirs-at-law identified were Arthur Sanger, Chester Sanger, Zebina Sanger, Azariah Sanger, Mrs. Allice Balch, and Matilda Gere. Personal estate was valued at $449.09 of which $340.34 was available for distribution after administrative costs and debts were paid. Equal distributions were made to each of the six heirs.[2719]

Daniel Sanger and Alice Wakefield were parents of nine children.

i   ELLIS "ALICE" SANGER, b. at Willington, 3 Apr 1785; d. at Chemung, NY, 26 Apr 1860; m. JOSEPH BALCH, b. 1787; Joseph d. at Chemung, 25 Mar 1877.

ii   DANIEL SANGER, b. at Willington, 22 Feb 1787; d. at Ellington, 13 Aug 1813.

iii   SELINDA SANGER, b. at Ellington, 15 Aug 1789; d. at Washington, MA, 1 Apr 1851. Selinda did not marry.

iv   ARTHUR SANGER, b. 5 Jul 1791; died young

v   ARTHUR SANGER, b. at Ellington, 9 Jun 1793; d. at Lee, MA, 11 Aug 1855; m. before 1826, AFFIA CHAPEL, b. at Washington, MA, 28 Nov 1797 daughter of Ebenezer and Asenath (Miller) Chapel; Affia d. at Pittsfield, MA, 18 Dec 1871.

vi   CHESTER SANGER, b. at Ellington, 1 Dec 1795; d. at Springfield, MA, 9 Jun 1852; m. BETSEY E. SPRAGUE, b. at Worthington, MA, 26 Jul 1799 daughter of Daniel and Ruth (Bates) Sprague; Betsey d. at Springfield, 17 Jul 1887.

vii   MATILDA SANGER, b. about 1797; d. at Lyndon, NY, 1860;[2720] m. by about 1825, JOSEPH GERE, b. about 1798 who was not identified; Joseph d. at Lyndon, 1865.

viii   ZEBINA SANGER, b. 1799; d. at Chatham, NY, 13 Dec 1866; m. CLARISSA HARLOW CHAPEL, b. at Washington, MA, 22 May 1801 daughter of Ebenezer and Asenath (Miller) Chapel; Clarissa d. 4 Nov 1864.

ix   AZARIAH SANGER, b. at Ellington, 1803; d. at Washington, MA, 7 Sep 1853; m. at Washington, 18 Jun 1825, MATILDA PORTER, b. about 1797 daughter of Ebenezer and Tilly (Codding) Porter;[2721] Matilda d. at Washington, 12 Apr 1851.

859)   CYNTHIA SANGER (*Azariah Sanger⁴, Lydia Russell Sanger³, Benjamin², Robert¹*), b. at Willington, 27 Nov 1761 daughter of Azariah and Elizabeth (Abbe) Sanger; d. likely at Ludlow, 10 May 1842 (pension record); m. at Willington, 29 Nov 1779, WILLIAM MELROSS who has not been identified; William d. at Willington, 11 Mar 1815.

Cynthia and William resided at Willington, and after William's death Cynthia was in Ludlow, Massachusetts.

On 15 April 1837, Cynthia Melross of Ludlow aged seventy-six gave a statement related to her application for a widow's pension based on the Revolutionary war service of her husband William Melross. She recalled that William served a nine-month term in 1781 and served again for six months in 1782. He had a third enlistment for three months at the end of 1782. He was in an engagement at Frogs Point. She further declared that she married William Melross on 29 November 1779, and he died at Willington in March 1815. Cynthia's brother Daniel Sanger and her sister Esther Converse provided statements in support of the application. On 17 February 1854, Charles Convers provided a statement related to the application noting that his wife and William's wife were sisters. Charles reported that part of William's service was as a substitute for Cynthia's uncle Noadiah Sanger. For providing this substitute service, William received a 30 to 40-acre tract of land in Willington. Charles reported that Cynthia died on 10 May 1842. Charles noted that daughter Jane wife of Chauncey Davis of Ludlow was the only surviving child of William and Cynthia. The pension application was rejected due to lack of documentation of his service.[2722]

There are records of five children of Cynthia Sanger and William Melross.

i   ALENA MELROSS, b. at Willington, 23 Apr 1780

[2717] Although Cynthia gives her name as Cynthia Routh in 1832, in her own application for a widow's pension (see family of Cynthia Sanger and William Melorss just below), Cynthia stated that she did not remarry after she was widowed.

[2718] U. S. Revolutionary War Pension and Bounty-Land Warrant Application Files, Case S30081

[2719] *Berkshire County, MA: Probate File Papers, 1761-1917.* Online database. *AmericanAncestors.org.* New England Historic Genealogical Society, 2017. Estate of Sylinda Sanger, Case 7580

[2720] Matilda and Joseph are interred at Rawson Cemetery in Cattaraugus County, NY; Find a Grave 119943892

[2721] The names of Matilda's parents are given as Ebenezer and Tilly Porter on her death record; *Massachusetts: Vital Records, 1841-1910.* (From original records held by the Massachusetts Archives. Online database: *AmericanAncestors.org*, New England Historic Genealogical Society, 2004.) volume 57, p 49

[2722] U. S. Revolutionary War Pension and Bounty-Land Warrant Application Files, Case R7111

ii　　　CYNTHIA MELROSS, b. at Willington, 17 May 1783

iii　　GEORGE MELROSS, b. at Willington, 26 Feb 1785

iv　　HANNAH MELROSS, b. at Stafford, 26 Jun 1787

v　　　JANE ROSS,[2723] b. 1804; d. at Ludlow, MA, 12 Oct 1888; m. at Ludlow, MA. 28 May 1829, CHAUNCEY DAVIS, b. at Somers, CT, 23 Jan 1796 son of Job and Sarah (Johnson) Davis;[2724] Chauncey d. at Ludlow, 6 Apr 1854.

860)　　ELIZABETH SANGER (*Azariah Sanger⁴, Lydia Russell Sanger³, Benjamin², Robert¹*), b. at Willington, 30 Sep 1763 daughter of Azariah and Elizabeth (Abbe) Sanger; d. before 1801; m. at Stafford, 15 Mar 1787, CHESTER WAKEFIELD, b. at Union, CT, 30 Apr 1760 son of John and Ellis (·) Wakefield.

In 1800, Chester Wakefield headed a household of five persons at Ellington: one male 26 to 44, one male under 10, one female under 10, and two females 10 to 14.[2725] This suggests that Elizabeth was deceased by 1800.

Elizabeth Sanger and Chester Wakefield were likely parents of four children.

i　　　ELIZABETH WAKEFIELD, b. at Stafford, 13 Dec 1787

ii　　ESTHER WAKEFIELD, b. at Stafford, 24 Feb 1789; d. at Chicopee, MA, 6 Mar 1875; m. at Somers, 29 Sep 1819, HARVEY PARSONS, b. at Somers, 3 Sep 1795 son of Samuel and Sarah (Buck) Parsons; Harvey d. at Somers, 28 Mar 1861.

iii　　RELIEF WAKEFIELD, b. 1790; d. at Somers, 2 Feb 1866; m. at Somers (while resident of Stafford), 21 Jan 1813, JOSIAH PEASE, b. at Somers, 9 Sep 1783 son of James and Sarah (Colton) Pease; Josiah d. at Somers, 26 Sep 1860.

iv　　CHESTER WAKEFIELD, b. about 1800. He may be the Chester Wakefield who married first Amanda Parson and second Huldah Parsons and who died at Springfield, PA on 19 Jul 1842, but that is not certain.

861)　　JEDEDIAH SANGER (*Azariah Sanger⁴, Lydia Russell Sanger³, Benjamin², Robert¹*), b. at Willington, 12 Aug 1765 son of Azariah and Elizabeth (Abbe) Sanger; d. after 1830 when living at Chardon, OH and before 1846; m. at Willington, 31 Jul 1794, MEHITABLE FENTON, b. at Mansfield, 18 Jan 1767 daughter of Ebenezer and Lydia (Conant) Fenton; Mehitable d. at Chardon, 3 Mar 1847.

Jedediah and Mehitable were in Willington after their marriage, were for a time in Springfield, Massachusetts, and settled in Chardon, Ohio about 1814. In 1810, Jedediah's household was six persons at Springfield: one male 26 to 44, one female 26 to 44, one male under 10, one male 10 to 15, and two females 10 to 15.[2726]

The family was then in Geauga County, Ohio where on 10 December 1814, Jedediah Sanger of Hamden in Geauga County, for payment of $841, purchased from Gaius and Philena Pease of Enfield, Connecticut all the parcel of great lot number three in township nine in the eighth range of the Connecticut western reserve.[2727]

In 1820, Jedediah Sanger headed a household of three persons in Chardon, Ohio: one male 45 and over, one female 45 and over, and one male 10 to 15.[2728] In 1830, the household was one male 60 to 69, one female 60 to 69, and one male 20 to 29.[2729]

On 14 May 1824, Jedediah sold the 116 acres of the property he purchased in 1814, lot number three of township nine in the eighth range, to Amasa Sanger for payment of $1,000. Earlier, on 18 June 1822, Amasa purchased parts of lots 12 and 13 of township nine in the eight range from John and Philenda Hunt.[2730]

On 13 May 1836, Nathaniel Sanger of Chardon, in consideration of one dollar, conveyed his interest in lot number 159 in tract three in township nine of the eighth range to Amasa Sanger. On 19 March 1846, Amasa and Laura Sanger together with Mehitable Sanger, for payment of $600, conveyed to Lorenzo Stansell lot number 159 in tract three in township number nine of the eighth range containing 52 acres.[2731]

Three children were identified and a second son, Nathaniel, seems likely from census and land records.

[2723] Jane's name is given as Jane Ross at the time of her marriage.

[2724] Noon, *The History of Ludlow, Massachusetts*, p 389

[2725] Year: 1800; Census Place: Ellington, Tolland, Connecticut; Series: M32; Roll: 2; Page: 649; Image: 342; Family History Library Film: 205619

[2726] Year: 1810; Census Place: Springfield, Hampshire, Massachusetts; Roll: 19; Page: 21; Image: 00029; Family History Library Film: 0205627

[2727] Ohio Land Records, Geauga County, 6:19

[2728] 1820 U S Census; Census Place: Chardon, Geauga, Ohio; Page: 103; NARA Roll: M33_91; Image: 118

[2729] Year: 1830; Census Place: Chardon, Geauga, Ohio; Series: M19; Roll: 131; Page: 251; Family History Library Film: 0337942

[2730] Ohio Land Records, Geauga County, 9:455, 8:358

[2731] Ohio Land Records, Geauga County, 21:465, 8:358

i AMASA SANGER, b. at Willington, 4 Nov 1794; d. at Hambden, OH, 5 Dec 1857; m. at Geauga County, OH, 23 Mar 1823, LAURA PIKE, b. in NY about 1805; Laura d. after 1860 when she was living at Hambden.[2732]

ii PHEBE SANGER, b. at Willington, 1 Jul 1796; d. at Fredericksburg, IA, 21 Feb 1888; m. at Geauga County, OH, by Hosea King, Esq., 24 Oct 1815, MARTIN LANGDON, b. 18 Oct 1792 son of John and Abigail (Chapin) Langdon; Martin d. at Dresden Township, IA, 29 Sep 1880. Phebe and Martin were the first couple married in Chardon.[2733]

iii MARIA SANGER, b. about 1798; d. at Chardon, OH, about 1844; m. at Geauga County, 10 Jun 1819, CHESTER CLOUGH, b. at Belchertown, MA, 1 Jan 1797 son of Amasa and Tryphena (Cowles) Clough; Chester d. at Cortland, OH, 31 Aug 1878. Chester married second Amy Gates on 3 Apr 1845.

iv NATHANIEL SANGER, b. likely at Springfield, MA, about 1800. Nathaniel appears on the tax assessment at Geauga County through 1842 and then disappears from records.

862) ESTHER SANGER (*Azariah Sanger⁴, Lydia Russell Sanger³, Benjamin², Robert¹*), b. at Willington, 29 Apr 1770 daughter of Azariah and Elizabeth (Abbe) Sanger; d. at Ludlow, MA, 11 Mar 1851; m. by about 1797, her first cousin, CHARLES CONVERS (*Zeruiah Sanger Convers⁴, Lydia Russell Sanger³, Benjamin², Robert¹*), b. at Worthington, MA, 6 Jun 1771 son of Stephen and Zeruiah (Sanger) Convers; Charles d. at Ludlow, 19 Apr 1854.

Esther and Charles were in Stafford, Connecticut after their marriage but relocated to Ludlow, Massachusetts by 1810. In 1800, the household was four persons at Stafford: one male 26 to 44, one female 26 to 44, and two males under 10.[2734] In 1810, there were seven members in the household at Ludlow: one male 26 to 44, one female 26 to 44, one male under 10, one male 10 to 15, and three females under 10.[2735]

In his will written 7 August 1852 (probate April 1854), Charles Convers bequeathed to son Rodolphus, five dollars in money, all the farming utensils, and all the wearing apparel. Daughters Clarissa and Roxanna each receives a feather bed. The remainder of the estate is to be divided among three daughters Esther, Clarissa, and Roxanna. If Clarissa does not live three years after Charles's decease, then her portion is to go to Clarissa's son Henry W. Convers. Loren Dutton of Ludlow was named executor. Total estate value was $1,614.07 of which $1,151.56 was notes owed to the estate. Real estate was a 5-acre wood lot valued at $375.[2736]

On 25 August 1854, Aaron M. Cooley and Esther Cooley in her right, of Springfield, Massachusetts, William Bragg and Roxanna Bragg in her right, of New Cumberland, Ohio, and Clarissa Converse of Ludlow, Massachusetts, in consideration of $425, conveyed to Elisha A. Fuller of Springfield a lot of land on Beebe Hill of about five acres, this being the same property conveyed to Charles Converse by Simeon Pease in a deed dated 5 January 1814.[2737]

Esther and Charles were parents of five known children, but there may have been other children who died young.

i CHARLES CONVERS, b. at Stafford, CT, 9 Apr 1798

ii ESTHER CONVERS, b. at Stafford, about 1802; d. at Springfield, MA, 28 Sep 1870; m. at Ludlow, MA, 31 Mar 1827, AARON M. COOLEY, b. at Chester, MA, about 1800 son of Timothy and Rebecca (Smith) Cooley (per death record); Aaron d. at Springfield, 22 Aug 1866.

iii CLARISSA CONVERS, b. about 1804; d. at Ludlow, MA, 16 Mar 1880; m. at Ludlow, 11 Nov 1833, CYREL CONVERS.

iv RODOLPHUS CONVERS, b. about 1807; d. at Ludlow, 27 Feb 1868; m. 1ˢᵗ about 1835, RUTH ELIZABETH MOORS, b. 17 Jul 1811 daughter of George and Ruth (Olds) Moors;[2738] Ruth d. 13 Feb 1845. Rodolphus m. 2ⁿᵈ at Ludlow, 22 Sep 1856, his first cousin once removed, MARIAH CLARK (*Zurviah Weston Clark⁶, Molly Convers Weston⁵, Zeruiah Sanger Convers⁴, Lydia Russell Sanger³, Benjamin², Robert¹*), b. at Belchertown, 11 Oct 1811 daughter of Elijah and Zurviah (Weston) Clark; Mariah d. at Ludlow, 14 May 1896.

v ROXANNA CONVERS, b. about 1810; d. at Lima, OH, 31 Oct 1896;[2739] m. at Ludlow (intention 14 Nov 1835), WILLIAM BRAGG, b. in CT, about 1810; William d. at Lima, 9 Nov 1868.

[2732] Year: 1860; Census Place: Hambden, Geauga, Ohio; Page: 675

[2733] Historical Society of Geauga County, *Pioneer and General History of Geauga County*, p 290

[2734] Year: 1800; Census Place: Stafford, Tolland, Connecticut; Series: M32; Roll: 2; Page: 645; Image: 340; Family History Library Film: 205619

[2735] Year: 1810; Census Place: Ludlow, Hampshire, Massachusetts; Roll: 19; Page: 69; Image: 00077; Family History Library Film: 0205627

[2736] Massachusetts Wills and Probate, Hamden County, Estate of Charles Convers, 1854, No. 2882

[2737] Massachusetts Land Records, Hamden County, 173:17

[2738] Olds, *The Olds Family in America*, p 66

[2739] "Another Pioneer Gone", The Times Democrat, Lima, Ohio, 31 Oct 1896 (Sat.), p 8. "Mrs. Roxanna Bragg, one of the oldest pioneer ladies of this city and county, died at 9:30 o'clock this morning, at the home of her daughter, Mrs. E. D. Randall."

863)   AZARIAH SANGER (*Azariah Sanger⁴, Lydia Russell Sanger³, Benjamin², Robert¹*), b. at Willington, 12 Jun 1772 son of Azariah and Elizabeth (Abbe) Sanger; m. at Willington, 16 Apr 1795, DESIRE ROOT, b. at Willington, 30 May 1774 daughter of Nathan and Hannah (Scripture) Root; Desire d. at Ludlow, MA, 29 Mar 1871.

There is evidence of Azariah and Desire being in Connecticut, Westmoreland, New York, Bridgewater, Vermont, and Ludlow, Massachusetts.

In 1820, Azariah headed a household of ten persons at Bridgewater, Vermont: one male 45 and over, one female 45 and over, three males under 10, one male 16 to 18, one female under 10, two females 10 to 15, and one female 16 to 25.[2740] In 1830, Azariah headed a household of four persons at Ludlow, Massachusetts: listed as one male 40 to 49 (perhaps a mismarking), one female 50 to 59, one male 10 to 14, and one female 30 to 30.[2741]

In 1855, Desire, then aged 82 years, was living with her daughter Lois and her family in Ludlow.[2742] Living next door was Horatio and wife Sarah A. Sanger. Desire, aged 98 years, is listed in the household of her daughter Lois Jenks in 1870.[2743]

There is record evidence for seven children of Azariah Sanger and Desire Root. It is possible there are other sons in the family who were not identified.

i   HANNAH SANGER, b. at Willington, 18 Aug 1795

ii   LURA SANGER, b. at Willington, 4 Apr 1797

iii   ETHEL SANGER, b. at Ashford, 4 Jul 1799; d. at Willington, 30 Oct 1800.

iv   ELIZABETH SANGER, b. at Tolland, 15 Jul 1801

v   HORATIO SANGER, b. at Bridgewater, VT, 1809; d. at Ludlow, MA, 28 Jun 1880; m. SARAH A. BENNETT, b. about 1820 daughter of Benjamin A. and Sally (Cadwell) Bennett (death record); Sarah d. at Springfield, MA, 10 Feb 1901. Horatio and Sarah do not seem to have had children.

vi   LOIS R. SANGER, b. (reported as Westmoreland, NY on death record), about 1810; d. at Ludlow, MA, 2 Dec 1876; m. at Ludlow, 28 Apr 1832, HENRY POWERS JENKS, b. at Central Falls, RI, 27 Jan 1812 son of Arnold and Mary (Healy) Jenks; Henry d. at Ludlow, 4 May 1850.

vii   HANNAH SANGER, b. (reported as Bridgewater, VT on death record), 14 Jan 1814; d. at Springfield, MA, 3 Feb 1903; m. 1834, HENRY J. JOHNSON, b. at Granby, MA, Jul 1810 son of Joseph and Mary (-) Johnson; Henry d. at Springfield, MA, 19 Dec 1850.

864)   ADEN SANGER (*Noahdiah Sanger⁴, Lydia Russell Sanger³, Benjamin², Robert¹*), b. at Willington, 6 Aug 1770 son of Noahdiah and Priscilla (Russ) Sanger; d. at Ontario County, NY, 1 Oct 1828; m. at Willington, 11 Jun 1795, ELIZABETH NILES, b. at Braintree, MA, 13 Apr 1774 daughter of James and Elizabeth (Vinton) Niles; Elizabeth d. at Cedar Creek, IN, 28 May 1855.

Aden Sanger was a tinsmith and coppersmith by trade. Aden and Elizabeth married in Connecticut and were there until about 1800 when they relocated to Cambridge, New York. The family remained there until about 1824 when they move on to Ontario County when Aden purchased a farm.[2744] Aden was the town collector in Cambridge in 1810.[2745]

In 1800, Aden Sanger headed a household of six persons at Cambridge, New York: one male 26 to 44, one female 26 to 44, one male under 10, one male 16 to 25 (who is perhaps one of Aden's younger brothers), and two females under 10.[2746] In 1810, his household was ten persons at Cambridge: one male 26 to 44, one female 26 to 44, four males under 10, one male 10 to 15, one female under 10, and two females 10 to 15.[2747]

Aden Sanger and Elizabeth Niles were parents of nine children.[2748]

i   ADNA SANGER, b. at Willington, 6 Apr 1796; d. 1818.[2749]

ii   LAURA SANGER, b. at Willington, 27 Jul 1797. It is possible that Laura married John G. Somers as his first wife and that she died at Munson, OH in 1831.

[2740] 1820 U S Census; Census Place: Bridgewater, Windsor, Vermont; Page: 325; NARA Roll: M33_128; Image: 192
[2741] Year: 1830; Census Place: Ludlow, Hampden, Massachusetts; Series: M19; Roll: 63; Page: 153; Family History Library Film: 0337921
[2742] Massachusetts, U.S., State Census, 1855
[2743] Year: 1870; Census Place: Ludlow, Hampden, Massachusetts; Roll: M593_617; Page: 385B
[2744] Goodspeed and Blanchard, *Counties of Porter and Lake, Indiana*, p 657
[2745] Johnson, *History of Washington County, New York*, p 256
[2746] Year: 1800; Census Place: Cambridge, Washington, New York; Series: M32; Roll: 26; Page: 188; Image: 184; Family History Library Film: 193714
[2747] Year: 1810; Census Place: Cambridge, Washington, New York; Roll: 30; Page: 478; Image: 00361; Family History Library Film: 0181384
[2748] Vinton, *The Vinton Memorial*, p 168 gives the names of the nine children and their years of birth
[2749] Vinton, *The Vinton Memorial*, p 168

iii   ELIZABETH SANGER, b. at Willington, 1 Apr 1799; d. at Lake County, IN, 13 Apr 1890; m. JOSEPH VAN BUSKIRK, b. 1793; Joseph d. at Lake County, 11 Mar 1866 at age 72 years, 8 months.

iv   ALMIRA SANGER, b. at Cambridge, NY, 8 Dec 1801; d. at Crown Point, IN, 25 Apr 1872; m. at Naples. NY, 8 Nov 1827, EPHRAIM CLEVELAND, b. at Naples, NY, 24 Aug 1805 son of Ephraim and Martha (Bushnell) Cleveland; Ephraim d. at Cedar Creek, IN. 13 Jul 1845.

v   JOHN NILES SANGER, b. at Cambridge, NY, 3 Jan 1804; d. at Lowell, IN, 29 Oct 1895; m. at Naples, NY, 10 Sep 1828, CLARISSA CLEVELAND, b. at Naples, 12 Aug 1810 daughter of Ephraim and Martha (Bushnell) Cleveland; Clarissa d. at Lowell, 1 Apr 1865.

vi   ADIN SANGER, b. 1806; d. likely at Naples, NY, 9 Aug 1837. In the 1830 census, Adin appears to be married with a daughter under age 5, but the name of his wife was not found.[2750]

vii   JAMES HENRY SANGER, b. at Cambridge, NY, 12 Jun 1808; d. at Lowell, IN, 31 Jul 1882; m. at Naples, NY, 28 Feb 1832, MARTHA BRACE CLEVELAND, b. at Naples, 13 Feb 1813 daughter of Ephraim and Martha (Bushnell) Cleveland; Martha d. at Lowell, 29 Dec 1880.

viii   LEANDER W. SANGER, b. at Cambridge, 29 Jun 1810; d. at Burrell, IA, 12 Nov 1881; m. at Lake County, IN, 7 Apr 1848, ESTHER MARIA THOMAS, b. at Monroe County, NY, 11 Dec 1819 daughter of James and Catherine (Moore) Thomas; Esther d. at Center, IA, 12 Aug 1911.[2751]

ix   HARVEY C. SANGER, b. at Cambridge, 22 May 1815; d. at Lowell, IN, 7 Jan 1889; m. 1st at Lake County, IN, 20 Apr 1841, SARAH ANN BRYANT, b. at Washington County, PA, 25 Oct 1820 daughter of Samuel D. and Mary (Ross) Bryant;[2752] Sarah d. at Lowell, IN, 29 May 1855. Harvey m. 2nd at Porter County, IN, 26 Jun 1856, NANCY BROOKS (widow of Peter L. Swaney), b. at Decatur County, IN, 1828 daughter of Cooper and Harriet (Griffin) Brooks; Nancy d. likely at Cedar Lake, IN, 1898 (interred at Hebron with her first husband Peter).

865)   ZERVIAH SANGER (*Noahdiah Sanger⁴, Lydia Russell Sanger³, Benjamin², Robert¹*), b. at Willington, 26 Jan 1778 daughter of Noahdiah and Priscilla (Russ) Sanger; d. at Ashford, 16 May 1848; m. at Ashford, 4 Apr 1802, JONATHAN KNOWLTON, b. at Ashford, 27 Jun 1779 son of Thomas and Hepsibah (Peak) Knowlton; Jonathan d. at Ashford, 1 Jul 1848.
    Zerviah and Jonathan resided in Ashford, Connecticut where they were parents of five children.

i   JONATHAN KNOWLTON, b. 21 Jan 1803; d. 29 Oct 1805.

ii   ARMINDA KNOWLTON, b. 1805; d. at Mansfield, CT, 14 Feb 1886; m. at Ashford, 27 Mar 1825, DANIEL BARDINE READ, b. at Ashford, 6 Feb 1801 son of Daniel and Augusta (Fenton) Read; Daniel d. at Mansfield, 8 Jun 1882.

iii   PALMER KNOWLTON, b. at Ashford, 29 Dec 1807; d. at Mansfield, 29 Dec 1844; m. at Mansfield, 1 Jan 1833, HARRIET ELIZABETH CONANT, b. at North Haven, 20 Feb 1812 daughter of David and Elizabeth (Royce) Conant; Harriet d. at Gurleyville (Mansfield), 9 May 1892. Harriet married second Theodore Conant.

iv   ALMENA KNOWLTON, b. at Ashford, 7 Sep 1811; d. at Ashford, 6 Sep 1895; m. estimate 1872, as his second wife, LEANDER P. ROWLEY, b. 15 Feb 1822 son of Simeon and Elizabeth (Griswold) Rowley; Leander d. at Farmington, CT, 18 Jun 1887. Leander was first married to Philena Buck who died in 1868. Leander was a disabled Civil War veteran discharged as disabled on 12 March 1862. His rank was listed as musician.[2753]

v   JONATHAN WIGHTMAN KNOWLTON, b. at Ashford, 1 Nov 1817; d. at Ashford, 18 Jul 1898; m. at Mansfield, 3 Apr 1842, HARRIET M. BOTTOM, b. 1817 daughter of Joshua and Phebe (Adams) Bottom; Harriet d. at Ashford, 29 Sep 1880.

866)   ASHBEL SANGER (*Noahdiah Sanger⁴, Lydia Russell Sanger³, Benjamin², Robert¹*), b. at Willington, 25 Apr 1780 son of Noahdiah and Priscilla (Russ) Sanger; d. at Perry, NY, 1831; m. 1807, SARAH SOUTHWORTH, likely b. at Ashford, 1 Mar 1778 daughter of John and Levina (Dana) Southworth.

[2750] Year: 1830; Census Place: Naples, Ontario, New York; Series: M19; Roll: 101; Page: 247; Family History Library Film: 0017161
[2751] Date and place of birth and names of parents are given in Esther's obituary; "Death of Mrs. Sanger", The Leon Journal Reporter, Leon Iowa, 29 April 1911 (Thursday), p 10
[2752] Braiden, *Bryant Family History*, p 66
[2753] U.S., Civil War Soldier Records and Profiles, 1861-1865; Civil War Pension Index: General Index to Pension Files, 1861-1934

Ashbel was living in Perry, New York in 1820 with a household of seven: one male 26 to 44, one female 26 to 44, two males under 10, two females under 10, and one female 10 to 15.[2754] Although census records suggest five children, just one child was identified.

i   MARY ANN SANGER, b. 1808; d. at Castile, NY, 1853; m. about 1831, SOLOMON SQUIERS, b. in NY, about 1797 son of Solomon and Deliah (·) Squiers (on death record); Solomon d. at Lansing, MI, 11 Nov 1876. Solomon was first married to Hannah Brown who died in 1830.

867)   NOADIAH "NOAH D." SANGER (*Noahdiah Sanger⁴, Lydia Russell Sanger³, Benjamin², Robert¹*), b. at Willington, 21 Apr 1785 son of Noahdiah and Priscilla (Russ) Sanger; d. at Bristol, IN, 2 Sep 1842;[2755] m. at Willington, 12 Apr 1807, REBECCA BARRETT BACON, b. at Bolton, MA, 1 Jul 1785 daughter of Noah and Mary (Brown) Bacon; Rebecca d. at Ontario, IN, 15 Sep 1861.

Noah D. and Rebecca were in Willington after their marriage and their oldest children were born there.

The family was in Perry, New York by 1818. Noah D. was of Perry on 9 January 1818 when he joined John D. Landon and Charles Leonard in the purchase of property in Perry from Samuel Blakeslee and Horatio Parsons for payment of $700. Noah was involved in multiple land transactions in Perry including the following. On 4 June 1822, Noah D. Sanger and Rebecca B. his wife of Perry sold sixty-six acres in Perry to Benjamin Sanger (likely his first cousin) of Canandaigua for payment of $600. On 1 March 1825, Noah D. purchased sixty-six acres of lot number six of the William Shepard subdivision of the Ogden Tract from Benjamin and Betsey Sanger, then of Perry, for payment of $700. Noah D. and Rebecca B. Sanger sold this same property to John Walker on 15 September 1826 for payment of $715.[2756]

In 1820, Noah D. Sanger headed a household of nine persons at Perry, New York: one male 26 to 44, one female 26 to 44, one male under 10, two males 10 to 15, three females under 10, and one female 16 to 25.[2757]

The family may have been in Centerville for a time with N. D. Sanger enumerated there in 1830 heading a household of eight persons: one male 40 to 49, one female 40 to 49, one male 10 to 14, two males 20 to 29, one female 5 to 9, one female 10 to 14, and one female 30 to 39.[2758]

Noah D. and Rebecca are thought to have gone to Bristol, Indiana by 1840 where they both died. Their son Lucas, then of Allegany County in New York, obtained a land grant in Elkhart County, Indiana on 5 June 1837.[2759] Their eldest son Marcus and the other children in the family also were in Elkhart County, Indiana during this time.

After Noah D.'s death, Rebecca lived were her daughter Celia and her husband Charles Doolittle in LaGrange County, Indiana.[2760]

Noah D. Sanger and Rebecca Bacon were parents of eleven children.

i   MARCUS LYON SANGER, b. at Willington, CT, 2 Jan 1808; d. at Bristol, IN, 10 Feb 1886; m. Dec 1845, LYDIA CROWFOOT, b. at Black Rock, CT, 15 May 1799;[2761] Lydia d. at Bristol, 4 Dec 1878.

ii   LUCAS MARVIN SANGER, b. 1809; d. at Bristol, IN, 15 Jul 1895; m. about 1845, MARTHA LOUISE MORTON, b. 1819 daughter of Calvin and Cynthia (Sylvester) Morton; Martha d. at York Township, IN, 12 Apr 1890.

iii   LUCIEN PARMALLE SANGER, b. 1810; d. 1811.

iv   OLIVIA VILLARS SANGER, b. 1811; d. at Bristol, IN, 1892; d. at Cass County, MI, 29 Dec 1845, ARRINGTON GIBSON, b. about 1812; Arrington d. at Washington, IN, 1862.

v   Son, b. and d. 12 Feb 1814

vi   CELIA SANGER, b. at Batavia, NY, 28 Apr 1815; d. at Ontario, IN, 7 Aug 1888; m. at Elkhart, IN, 1 Jul 1840, CHARLES DOOLITTLE, b. at Madison County, NY, 16 Feb 1813 son of Willard and Pianna (Roberts) Doolittle; Charles d. at Bethlehem, PA, 6 Mar 1889.

vii   LUCIA CELESTA SANGER, b. 1817; d. at Los Angeles, CA, 11 Aug 1896; m. at St. Joseph County, MI, 8 Oct 1844, PETER COOK, b. in NY, about 1802; Peter d. at Elkhart, IN, 19 Aug 1870.

[2754] 1820 U S Census; Census Place: Perry, Genesee, New York; Page: 239; NARA Roll: M33_72; Image: 134

[2755] Noah D. is interred ay Bonneyville Cemetery in Bristol; Find a Grave 21121324

[2756] New York Land Records, Genesee County, 11:220, 15:554, 18:247, 20:372

[2757] 1820 U S Census; Census Place: Perry, Genesee, New York; Page: 234; NARA Roll: M33_72; Image: 131

[2758] Year: 1830; Census Place: Centerville, Allegany, New York; Series: M19; Roll: 84; Page: 64; Family History Library Film: 0017144

[2759] U.S. General Land Office Records, 1776-2015

[2760] Year: 1850; Census Place: East Lima, LaGrange, Indiana; Roll: 157; Page: 97a

[2761] Obituary, Lydia Sanger, Bristol Banner, Bristol, Indiana, 13 December 1878, Friday, p 3

viii RILEY ANSON SANGER, b. 1820; d. at Elkhart, IN, 15 Nov 1890; m. at Elkhart, 28 Jan 1841, OLIVE TAYLOR, b. at Niagara County, NY, 20 Apr 1822 daughter of Elisha and Lydia (Carwell) Taylor;[2762] Olive d. at Newfield, MI, 28 Jan 1900.

ix ELAM HALE SANGER, b. 13 Mar 1823; d. 13 Jul 1823.

x MERCY EUPHRASIA SANGER, b. at Genesee County, NY, 17 Sep 1824; d. at Ontario, IN, 15 Dec 1888. Mercy did not marry. She lived with her sister Celia and her family.[2763]

xi GILBERT LAFAYETTE SANGER, b. 1832; d. 1846.

868) PRISCILLA SANGER (*Noahdiah Sanger⁴, Lydia Russell Sanger³, Benjamin², Robert¹*), b. at Willington, 3 Sep 1787 daughter of Noahdiah and Priscilla (Russ) Sanger; d. at Pike, NY (burial at Centerville), 17 Nov 1877; m. 1 Jul 1807, CHESTER KNOWLTON, b. at Ashford, 12 Oct 1787 son of Thomas and Hepsibah (Peak) Knowlton; Chester d. at Centerville, 30 Apr 1871.
     Priscilla and Chester resided in Centerville, New York and were parents of nine children.[2764] The family was first in Perry, New York where Chester headed a household of ten in 1830: one male 40 to 49, one female 40 to 49, one male 5 to 9, two females under 5, one female 5 to 9, one female 10 to 14, two females 15 to 19, and one female 20 to 29.[2765] In 1850, Chester and Priscilla were in Centerville with daughter Elizabeth and son James and his wife Clarinda.[2766]

i PHILENA M. KNOWLTON, b. in CT, 25 Sep 1808; d. at Logan, NE, about 1886; m. 16 Mar 1835, WILLIAM A. LOCKE, b. in CT, about 1810 son of Ayers and Lydia (Blodgett) Locke; William d. after 1855 when living at Bloomfield, WI.

ii MINERVA ASENATH KNOWLTON, b. 17 Jan 1811; d. after 1885 when living at Logan, NE; m. 29 Nov 1834, HENRY B. LOCKE, b. 29 Apr 1802 son of Ayers and Lydia (Blodgett) Locke; Henry d. at Delavan, WI, 18 Feb 1883.

iii SOPHRONIA KNOWLTON, b. in NY, 29 May 1813; d. at Arcade, NY, 9 Mar 1871; m. 15 Mar 1839, JOHN C. LAMBERSON, b. in NY, about 1812; John d. after 1870 when living at Arcade.[2767]

iv ALVINA KNOWLTON, b. 17 Nov 1815

v ORISSA KNOWLTON, b. 7 Jun 1818; d. at Arcade, NY, 26 Oct 1889; m. 5 Jun 1844, CHARLES TORREY, b. 1818 son of Ira A. Torrey;[2768] Charles d. at Arcade, 19 Feb 1885.

vi JAMES KNOWLTON (twin), b. 19 Apr 1821; d. at Pike, NY, 1878; m. 11 Mar 1845, CLARINDA WHEAT, b. 24 Mar 1824 daughter of Salmon and Chloe (Sanford) Wheat;[2769] Clarinda d. after 1880 when living at Pike.[2770]

vii JANE KNOWLTON (twin), b. 19 Apr 1821; d. at Janesville, CA, 18 Jan 1892; m. 3 May 1845, DERASTUS TORREY, b. 11 Jan 1820 son of Ira A. Torrey; Derastus d. at Janesville, 20 Dec 1896.

viii ADELIA KNOWLTON, b. 10 Dec 1826; m. 3 Jun 1848, ISAAC TORREY.

ix ELIZABETH KNOWLTON, b. 21 Jun 1829; d. at Edgar, NE, 16 Feb 1914; m. 17 May 1862, WILLIAM HENRY ASHLEY, b. 25 Dec 1834 son of James and Julia Ann (Morehouse) Ashley; William d. at Edgar, 5 Jul 1919.

868a) ROXANA "ROXY" CONVERS (*Zeruiah Sanger Convers⁴, Lydia Russell Sanger³, Benjamin², Robert¹*), b. at Worthington, MA, 28 Jul 1769 daughter of Stephen and Zeruiah (Sanger) Convers; d. at Mount Morris, NY, 23 Jan 1842;[2771] m. about 1790, JOSEPH FULLER, b. 16 Nov 1760; Joseph d. at Mount Morris, 7 Nov 1837.
     Roxana and Joseph Fuller were living at Mount Morris, New York in 1830 where Joseph headed a household of six persons: one male 60 to 69, one female 60 to 69, one male 20 to 29, one female 15 to 19, and two females 20 to 29.[2772]
     On 25 November 1830, Moses Fuller and his wife Laura of Mount Morris sold to Joseph Fuller 39 acres in Mount Morris for payment of $405.

[2762] Names of parents are as given on death record; Michigan, U.S., Death Records, 1867-1952
[2763] Year: 1880; Census Place: Ontario, LaGrange, Indiana; Roll: 290; Page: 319A; Enumeration District: 014
[2764] Stocking, *The History and Genealogies of the Knowltons*, p 102
[2765] Year: 1830; Census Place: Perry, Genesee, New York; Series: M19; Roll: 90; Page: 257; Family History Library Film: 0017150
[2766] Year: 1850; Census Place: Centerville, Allegany, New York; Roll: 476; Page: 285b
[2767] Year: 1870; Census Place: Arcade, Wyoming, New York; Roll: M593_1119; Page: 7B
[2768] Torrey, *The Torrey Families and Their Children in America*, volume 1, p 260
[2769] Wheat, *Wheat Genealogy*, p 103
[2770] Year: 1880; Census Place: Pike, Wyoming, New York; Roll: 948; Page: 256D; Enumeration District: 209
[2771] Roxana is interred at Riverview Cemetery at Mount Morris; Find a Grave 57000091
[2772] Year: 1830; Census Place: Mount Morris, Livingston, New York; Series: M19; Roll: 93; Page: 151; Family History Library Film: 0017153

In his will written 1 October 1837 (probate 30 April 1838), Joseph Fuller of Mount Morris bequeathed use of all his estate, real and personal, to his beloved wife Rocksey on condition that she provide a home for daughter Rcoksey who is insane. She is also to provide a home for children Joseph and Sarah as long as they choose to remain with their mother. His intent is to keep his estate whole for the support of his wife Rocksey and his children Rocksey, Sarah, and Joseph. After the decease of his wife Rocksey and his daughter Rocksey, the estate is to be divided among his heirs: son Moses, ten dollars to buy a set of silver spoons; son Joseph Fuller, one hundred dollars; daughter Rhoda Akers, fifty dollars; daughter Persis Cranston, ten dollars to but a set of silver spoons; the heirs of daughter Mary Van Eps deceased, ten dollars to buy a set of silver spoons; and the remainder of the estate to daughter Sarah Fuller. Executors named were William C. Dunning, Benjamin Hoaglan, William B. Munson, and daughter Sarah Fuller.[2773]

Roxana Convers and Joseph Fuller were likely parents of seven children.

i   JOSEPH FULLER, b. estimate 1794. Joseph was living and unmarried in 1837.

ii   MOSES FULLER, b. estimate 1794; m. LAURA who was not identified.

iii   PERSIS FULLER, b. 27 Dec 1796;[2774] d. at Livonia, MI, 22 Dec 1876; m. 21 Jan 1816, SAMUEL CRANSON, b. 1797 perhaps son of Asa and Zillah (Fuller) Cranson; Samuel d. at Livonia, 11 Jan 1859.

iv   MARY FULLER, b. estimate 1798; d. before 1837; m. Mr. Van Eps who was not identified.

v   SARAH FULLER, b. estimate 1802; living and unmarried in 1837.

vi   ROXANA FULLER, b. estimate 1804; living and unmarried in 1837. Roxana is described as insane in father's will.

vii   RHODA FULLER, b. estimate 1808; m. JOSEPH AKERS, b. estimate 1806 likely son of Richard and Hannah (Keeler) Akers. Richard Akers and Hannah Keeler were natives of New Jersey who came to Mount Morris about 1825.[2775] On 14 May 1831, Joseph and Rhoda Akers joined Richard Akers and Hannah his wife and Ralph Akers all of Mount Morris in the conveyance of property to David Howell.[2776]

869)   MOLLY CONVERS (*Zeruiah Sanger Convers⁴, Lydia Russell Sanger³, Benjamin², Robert¹*), b. at Worthington, MA, 14 Mar 1773 daughter of Stephen and Zeruiah (Sanger) Convers; d. at Willington, 25 Jun 1856;[2777] m. at Willington, 10 May 1792, JOHN WESTON, b. at Willington, 3 Dec 1768 son of James and Anna (Abbe) Weston; John d. at Willington, 29 Dec 1820.

Deacon John Weston and Molly Converse resided in Willington.

In 1820, John Weston headed a household of eleven persons at Willington: two males 45 and over, one female 45 and over, two males under 10, one male 10 to 15, one male 16 to 18, two females under 10, one female 10 to 15, and one female 16 to 25.[2778] Molly Weston was head of household of a family of seven at Willington in 1830: one female 50 to 59, one male under 5, two males 15 to 19, one female 10 to 14, and two females 20 to 29.[2779] In 1850, Molly was living in the home of her grandson William S. Parsons. Also in the home were John and Molly's daughter Chloe and her husband Rufus Parsons.[2780]

There are records for twelve children of Molly Convers and John Weston born at Willington.

i   ZURVIAH WESTON, b. 28 Apr 1793; d. by about 1847; m. at Belchertown, MA, 29 Nov 1810, ELIJAH CLARK, b. at Belchertown, 8 Jul 1788 son of Enos and Jenet (Clark) Clark; Elijah d. at Belchertown, 18 Jan 1873. Elijah married second Sarah Goodell on 21 Jun 1848.

ii   POLLY WESTON, b. 12 Feb 1795; m. about 1818, OTIS JOHNSON of Rehoboth.

iii   JAMES WESTON, b. 4 Dec 1797; d. at Orwell, NY, 17 Sep 1865; m. RENA RIDER, b. at Willington, 22 Nov 1798 daughter of Joseph and Ruanna (·) Rider; Rena d. after 1860.

iv   CHLOE WESTON, b. 17 Jul 1799; d. at Worcester, MA, 20 Mar 1875; m. at Willington, 21 Nov 1819, RUFUS PARSONS, b. at Ellington, 20 Feb 1794 son of Rufus and Nancy (Grinman) Parsons;[2781] Rufus d. at Worcester, 7 Jan 1874.

v   ANNA WESTON, b. 17 Dec 1801

[2773] New York Wills and Probate, Livingston County, Wills Volume 0002, p 64

[2774] The date of birth is given in the cemetery records of Clarenceville Cemetery in Wayne County, Michigan, records compiled by the Western Wayne County Genealogical Society and edited by Margaret Najarian; document accessed through https://livonia.gov/1807/Resources

[2775] Smith, *History of Livingston County, New York*, p 321

[2776] New York Land Records, Livingston County, 9:247

[2777] Molly and John are interred at Old Willington Hill Cemetery, Find a Grave 10312772

[2778] 1820 U S Census; Census Place: Willington, Tolland, Connecticut; Page: 1012; NARA Roll: M33_2; Image: 993

[2779] Year: 1830; Census Place: Willington, Tolland, Connecticut; Series: M19; Roll: 8; Page: 242; Family History Library Film: 0002801

[2780] Year: 1850; Census Place: Willington, Tolland, Connecticut; Roll: 50; Page: 258a

[2781] Parsons, Parsons Family, volume 2, p 319

vi   JOHN WESTON, b. 4 Sep 1803; d. at Somers, 11 Mar 1845; m. at Somers, 24 Nov 1825, ANNA BILLINGS, b. at Somers, 5 May 1806 daughter of Alpheus and Abigail (Meacham) Billings. The estate of John Weston was insolvent and real estate was sold to settle the estate. Widow Anna Weston and Alpheus Billings signed agreement for the administration.[2782]

vii   STEPHEN CONVERSE WESTON, b. 13 Nov 1805; d. after 1880 when living at Racine, MN; m. 1st at Brooklyn, CT, 25 Dec 1828, MARY W. FRANKLIN, b. 1810; Mary d. at Worcester, MA, 29 Aug 1837. Stephen m. 2nd, 1838, FANNY ADAMS, b. at Brookfield, MA, 19 Dec 1808 daughter of William and Sarah (Howe) Adams; Fanny d. at Oswego, NY, 1 Oct 1850. Stephen m. 3rd at Oswego, 1851, MARY CARRIER, b. in NY, about 1827; Mary d. at Sioux Falls, SD, 18 Jan 1897.

viii   ROZILLA WESTON, b. 15 Jan 1808; d. at Willimantic, CT, 15 Oct 1851; m. 3 May 1829, GEORGE W. FULLER, b. 12 Dec 1804 (per death record); George d. (burial at Willimantic), 17 Aug 1877.

ix   ELMINA WESTON,[2783] b. 22 May 1810; d. at Osage, IL, 20 Nov 1871; m. at Willington, 12 Mar 1832, GEORGE W. DRESSER, b. at Tolland, 29 Nov 1806 son of John and Delight (Gilbert) Dresser; George d. after 1880 when living at Groveland, IL.

x   ORIGIN WESTON, b. 5 Jan 1813; d. at Willington, 14 Jul 1859; m. at Stafford, CT, 12 Feb 1844, SUSAN PADDLEFORD, b. about 1815; Susan d. at Willington, 15 Apr 1864.

xi   RUFUS WESTON, b. 16 Jun 1815; d. at Stafford, CT, 8 Oct 1883; m. 1st about 1842, HARRIET MURPHY, b. 1823 daughter of Timothy and Lucina (Osborn) Murphy; Harriet d. at Somersville, CT, 17 Apr 1861. Rufus m. 2nd at Stafford, 31 Mar 1862, ELLEN HARVEY, b. at Stafford, 16 Jun 1839 daughter of Amos and Laurinda (Kibbe) Harvey; Ellen d. at Stafford, 29 Mar 1904.

xii   LOUISA WESTON, b. 22 Nov 1816; d. at Orwell, NY, 23 May 1852; m. at Willington, 20 Feb 1839, FIELDER HEATH, b. at Willington, 9 Feb 1816 son of Ira and Hannah (Crocker) Heath; Fielder d. at Olean, NY, 10 Jul 1895. Fielder married second Lavancha Partridge.

870)   STEPHEN CONVERS (*Zeruiah Sanger Convers⁴, Lydia Russell Sanger³, Benjamin², Robert¹*), b. at Stafford, CT, 7 Apr 1775 son of Stephen and Zeruiah (Sanger) Convers; d. at Springfield, MA, 14 Mar 1864; m. about 1798, NELLIE WHIPPLE, b. 1773; Nellie d. at Belchertown, 1 Oct 1856.

        Stephen and Nellie were in Willington and Stafford, Connecticut before being in Belchertown and settling in Ludlow, Massachusetts. In 1810, Stephen headed a household of six persons in Stafford: one male 26 to 44, one female 26 to 44, one male under 10, one male 10 to 15, and two females under 10.[2784] The family is enumerated in Belchertown, Massachusetts in 1820 with a household of eight persons: one male 45 and over, one female 45 and over, one male 10 to 15, one male 16 to 25, two females under 10, one female 10 to 15, and one female 16 to 25.[2785] From 1850, Stephen and Nellie, and Stephen after Nellie's death, lived with daughter Delina and her husband Luther Collis.[2786]

        On 30 November 1825, Stephen Converse was of Ludlow when he and Sylvester Brainerd sold property in Ludlow to Stephen Converse, Jr. for payment of $145. This property was from the first or north division of the outward commons of Ludlow. On 5 September 1826, Stephen Converse, Jr. with his wife Phebe sold his interest in this same property to his father Stephen Converse, Sr. for payment of five dollars.[2787]

        Stephen Convers and Nellie Whipple were parents of six children.

i   STEPHEN CONVERS, b. at Willington, 8 Aug 1799; m. at Ludlow, MA, 28 Oct 1825, PHEBE HAYDEN, b. at Ludlow, about 1805 daughter of Moses and Mary (Buxton) Hayden; Phebe d. at Ludlow, 16 Sep 1875. In 1855, Phebe was head of household in Ludlow with daughter Sarah with her.[2788]

ii   POLLY CONVERS, b. at Willington, 22 Aug 1802; d. at Belchertown, MA, 28 Feb 1856; m. at Belchertown, 5 Aug 1822, BUTLER BARRETT, b. 24 Aug 1801 son of Daniel and Sarah (Convers) Barrett; Butler d. at Belchertown, 18 Aug 1885. Butler married second Harriet Moore.

iii   LEONARD CONVERS, b. at Stafford, CT, 8 Jan 1805; d. at Springfield, MA, 22 Feb 1888; m. at Springfield, 25 Apr 1832, BETSEY P. WEBSTER, b. at Ludlow, MA, 1811 daughter of Ira and Susannah (Russell) Webster; Betsey d. at Springfield, 27 Dec 1891.

[2782] Connecticut Wills and Probate, Hartford, Estate of John Weston

[2783] The transcription of the birth record says Eunice, but other evidence supports the name Elmina.

[2784] Year: 1810; Census Place: Stafford, Tolland, Connecticut; Roll: 3; Page: 385; Image: 00215; Family History Library Film: 0281231

[2785] 1820 U S Census; Census Place: Belchertown, Hampshire, Massachusetts; Page: 183; NARA Roll: M33_50; Image: 194

[2786] Year: 1850; Census Place: Palmer, Hampden, Massachusetts; Roll: 319; Page: 294a

[2787] Massachusetts Land Records, Hampden County, 72:342, 73:638

[2788] Massachusetts, U.S., State Census, 1855

iv   ALMIRA CONVERS, b. at Stafford, 4 Feb 1808; d. at Belchertown, 23 May 1858; m. at Ludlow, 17 Nov 1825, OTIS SEDGWICK, b. at Palmer, 3 Apr 1803 son of Martin and Sally (King) Sedgwick; Otis d. at Belchertown, 10 Dec 1893.

v   DELINA CONVERS, b. at Stafford, 12 Apr 1811; d. at Belchertown, 1860; m. at Belchertown, 14 Mar 1837, LUTHER W. COLLIS, b. at Herkimer, NY, 1811 son of Jonathan and Phebe (Parker) Collis; Luther d. at Palmer, 6 Mar 1896.

vi   JULIANA CONVERS, b. 1817; d. at Palmer, MA, 25 Jun 1887; m. at Palmer, 23 Mar 1839, MARSHALL L. HITCHCOCK, b. at Palmer, 2 Nov 1813 son of Robert and Orra (Lilly) Hitchcock; Marshall d. at Lynn, MA, 29 Nov 1899.

870a)   JAMES C. SANGER (*Nathaniel Sanger⁴, Lydia Russell Sanger³, Benjamin², Robert¹*), b. at Ellington, 17 Jun 1786 son of Nathaniel and Olive (Chaffee) Sanger;[2789] d. at Bennington, OH, 20 Jul 1832; m. 21 Mar 1807, ACHSA BLODGETT, b. at East Windsor, 4 Feb 1789 daughter of Abner and Rachel (Phelps) Blodgett; Achsa d. at Bennington, 11 Jul 1872.

James and Achsa resided in Bennington, Ohio where they were by 1818. In 1820, James headed a household of six persons: one male 26 to 44, one female 26 to 44, two males under 10, one male 10 to 15, and one female 10 to 15.[2790] The household was seven persons in 1830: one male 40 to 49, one female 40 to 49, one male 10 to 14, one male 15 to 19, one male 20 to 29, one female 5 to 9, and one female 20 to 29.[2791] After James's death, son Barton was listed as head of the family household.[2792]

James C. Sanger and Achsa Blodgett were parents of seven children.[2793]

i   OLIVE SANGER, b. 19 May 1808; d. at Bennington, OH, 18 May 1855; m. 3 Apr 1831, JOHN VAN FOSSEN, b. in VA, Sep 1808; John d. at Bennington, 16 Mar 1904.

ii   JAMES SANGER, b. 11 May 1810; d. at Bennington, OH, 27 Jun 1849; m. 2 Feb 1845, ANN MYER, b. 14 Apr 1823 daughter of John and Frances (Brown) Myer; Ann d. at Bennington, 24 Sep 1877.

iii   BARTON SANGER, b. 8 Jul 1812; d. at Bennington, OH, 28 Feb 1889. Barton did not marry.

iv   OLIVER WOLCOTT SANGER, b. 17 Mar 1817; d. at Jefferson, IN, 22 Jul 1904; m. 4 May 1837, CATHERINE ANN SNYDER, b. at Fairfield County, OH, 11 Dec 1817 daughter of Jacob and Margaret (Roberts) Snyder; Catherine d. at Jefferson, 16 Dec 1887.

v   SARAH "SALLY" SANGER, b. 27 Jun 1821; d. at Bennington, OH, 24 Aug 1891; m. at Homer, OH, 12 Sep 1842, LUTHER DANA STONE, b. near Granville, OH, 20 Feb 1816 son of Samuel and Abigail (Stedman) Stone;[2794] Luther d. at Bennington, 30 Sep 1884.

vi   RALPH B. SANGER, b. 16 Apr 1824; d. 6 Mar 1829.

vii   IRA SANGER, b. 27 Dec 1826; d. 26 Nov 1828.

871)   EBENEZER SANGER (*Nathaniel Sanger⁴, Lydia Russell Sanger³, Benjamin², Robert¹*), b. 1790 son of Nathaniel and Olive (Chaffee) Sanger; d. at Canterbury, CT, 21 Feb 1863; m. 1ˢᵗ 1816, OLIVE CHAFFEE, b. at Canterbury, 19 Dec 1782 daughter of Ebenezer and Alice (Fassett) Chaffee; Olive d. at Brooklyn, CT, 31 Jul 1821 at age 38. Ebenezer m. 2ⁿᵈ at Plainfield, 2 Jun 1824, EUNICE HUTCHINS, b. 8 Jan 1796 daughter of Amasa and Hannah (Leffingwell) Hutchins;[2795] Eunice d. at Canterbury, 12 Feb 1857.

Ebenezer resided in Canterbury where he kept a farm. In 1850, Ebenezer headed a household of six persons in Canterbury: Ebenezer aged 62, Eunice aged 55, George aged 25, Marvin aged 23, Hannah aged 19, and Olive aged 17.[2796]

In his will written 8 April 1861 (probate 9 March 1863), Ebenezer Sanger of Canterbury bequeathed twelve hundred dollars to son Ebenezer C. Sanger who is to use the interest from this money for the comfortable support of son Luther during his life, then for the support of Luther's five children born to him by his second wife Hannah Francis Sanger deceased. Son

[2789] Hill, *History of Licking County, Ohio*, p. 756

[2790] 1820 U S Census; Census Place: Bennington, Licking, Ohio; Page: 38A; NARA Roll: M33_94; Image: 52

[2791] Year: 1830; Census Place: Bennington, Licking, Ohio; Series: M19; Roll: 134; Page: 489; Family History Library Film: 0337945

[2792] Year: 1850; Census Place: Bennington, Licking, Ohio; Roll: 702; Page: 244b

[2793] The names and birthdates of the children, the deaths of the children who died in childhood, and the deaths of James and Achsa are given in Hill, *History of Licking County, Ohio*, p. 756, in what appears to be a transcription from a bible record.

[2794] Bartlett, *Gregory Stone Genealogy*, p 600

[2795] Leffingwell, *Leffingwell Record*, p 68

[2796] Year: 1850; Census Place: Canterbury, Windham, Connecticut; Roll: 51; Page: 179a

Marvin H. Sanger receives 55 acres of land in Plainfield. The residue of the estate goes to son George Sanger. Son George was named executor.[2797]

Ebenezer and Olive were parents of two children born at Canterbury.

i   EBENEZER CHAFFEE SANGER, b. 11 Apr 1816; d. at Canterbury, 28 May 1877; m. at Newburyport (also recorded at Taunton), MARTHA ROGERS, b. in MA, about 1823; Martha d. at Canterbury, 13 Sep 1882. Ebenezer and Martha were parents of at least three children.

ii   LUTHER SANGER, b. 21 Apr 1818; m. 1st at Plainfield, 1 Apr 1845, LUCY ANN BETTEY, b. 1825 daughter of Sampson and Abigail (Phillips) Bettey; Lucy d. at Canterbury, 26 Mar 1847. Luther m. 2nd at Canterbury, 7 Jun 1847, HARRIET FRANCIS, b. 2 May 1821 daughter of John and Esther (Palmer) Francis; Harriet d. at Canterbury, 18 Sep 1855.

Ebenezer and Eunice were parents of four children born at Canterbury.

i   GEORGE SANGER, b. 13 May 1825; d. at Canterbury, 19 Aug 1886; m. 24 Mar 1853, MARY HUBBARD JOHNSON, b. at Griswold, CT, 10 Sep 1826 daughter of Nathan and Ruth F. (Meech) Johnson; Mary d. at Canterbury, 3 Jun 1885.

ii   MARVIN HUTCHINS SANGER, b. 12 Apr 1827; d. at Canterbury, 3 Jun 1898; m. 1855, MARY J. BACON, b. 12 Nov 1827 daughter of Benjamin and Joanna (Kinsman) Bacon; Mary d. (burial at Canterbury) 25 Apr 1909.

iii   HANNAH SANGER, b. 12 Dec 1829; d. at Canterbury, 16 Oct 1858. Hannah did not marry.

iv   OLIVE CHAFFE SANGER, b. 17 Aug 1833; d. 4 Jun 1852.

872)   BENJAMIN SANGER (*Jonathan Sanger⁴, Lydia Russell Sanger³, Benjamin², Robert¹*), b. at Pomfret, 13 Aug 1782 son of Jonathan and Lucy (Sawyer) Sanger; d. at Seneca, MI, Feb 1849; m. about 1808, ELIZABETH "BETSEY" WOODWARD, b. 1788 daughter of Seth and Elizabeth (·) Woodard who were of Petersham but later settled in Canandaigua;[2798] Betsey d. at Canandaigua, NY, 29 Apr 1830.

Benjamin was born in Connecticut and as a young man went with his father to Canandaigua. Benjamin served for three months from 24 September 1812 to 28 December 1812 as a sergeant in the company of Capt. Reuben Hart in the New York State Militia.[2799]

Benjamin married Betsey Woodard whose family had nearby property to the Sangers. They were parents of eight children. On 7 August 1820, Benjamin headed a household of nine persons in Canandaigua: one male 26 to 44, one female 26 to 44, two males under 10, four females under 10, and one female 10 to 15.[2800]

After Betsey's death at age forty-two, Benjamin moved with his family to the Michigan territory and settled on 80 acres of government grant land. They traveled via Lake Erie and then overland by wagon.[2801]

In 1840, Benjamin headed a household of four persons in Seneca: one male 50 to 59, one male 15 to 19, one male 20 to 29, and one female 20 to 29.[2802]

Benjamin Sanger and Elizabeth Woodard were parents of eight children, the oldest likely born at Pomfret and the others at Canandaigua.[2803]

i   AMELIA SANGER, b. about 1809; m. at Canandaigua, NY, 25 Feb 1829, WILLIAM EATON.

ii   RHODA WOODARD SANGER, b. 21 Feb 1812 (on gravestone); d. at Grow, MN, 11 Jan 1879; m. 1835, STEPHEN W. POWELL, b. 2 Sep 1813 son of Stephen and Margaret (Norton) Powell; Stephen d. at Grow Township, 9 Jun 1881.

iii   ELIZA C. SANGER, b. about 1814; d. at Seneca, MI, 9 May 1878. Eliza did not marry.

iv   SARAH JANE SANGER, b. 1816; d. at Seneca, MI, 14 Sep 1892; m. about 1839, STEPHEN HAYWARD, b. 22 May 1815 son of Henry and Elizabeth (Willitts) Hayward; Stephen d. at Seneca, 28 Dec 1861.

v   JONATHAN SANGER, b. 1818; d. at Anoka, MN, 21 Jan 1892; m. about 1845, JANE TURNER, b. at Glasgow, Scotland, 5 Apr 1823 daughter of Richard and Martha (Cook) Turner; Jane d. at Brainerd, MN, 1 May 1905.

[2797] Connecticut Wills and Probate, Windham County, volume 3, pp 302-303

[2798] Hagen and Hagen, *The Sanger Family*, p 13

[2799] New York, War of 1812 Payroll Abstracts for New York State Militia, 1812-1815

[2800] 1820 U S Census; Census Place: Canandaigua, Ontario, New York; Page: 219; NARA Roll: M33_62; Image: 120

[2801] Hagen and Hagen, *The Sanger Family*, p 13

[2802] Year: 1840; Census Place: Seneca, Lenawee, Michigan; Roll: 207; Page: 92; Family History Library Film: 0014796

[2803] Names of children are as in Hagen and Hagen, *The Sanger Family*, p 14

vi   HENRY P. SANGER (twin), b. 23 Feb 1820; d. at Seneca, MI, 16 May 1876; m. about 1846, LYDIA GORHAM, b.
        likely at Eldridge, NY, 1822 daughter of Shubael and Mary (Carpenter) Gorham (per death record); Lydia d. at
        Seneca, 30 Nov 1897.

vii   HENRIETTA SANGER (twin), b. 23 Feb 1820; d. at Anoka, MN, 24 Jan 1859; m. about 1840, WAREHAM G.
        RANDOLPH, b. 28 Apr 1816 (on gravestone); Wareham d. at Anoka, 21 Nov 1887. Wareham married second
        widow Mary H. Randolph.

viii   PHILA SANGER, b. 3 Sep 1822; d. at Seneca, MI, 7 Nov 1890; m. 12 May 1839, MICAJAH HAYWARD, b. 1818
        son of Henry and Elizabeth (Willitts) Hayward; Micajah d. at Seneca, 10 Apr 1887.

873)   PAMELIA SANGER (*Jonathan Sanger⁴, Lydia Russell Sanger³, Benjamin², Robert¹*), b. at East Windsor, CT, 18 Nov
1784 daughter of Jonathan and Lucy (Sawyer) Sanger; d. about 1810; m. about 1807, WILLIAM GREEN, b. at Windsor, MA, 1
Oct 1785 son of Henry and Submit (Clark) Green; William d. at Italy, NY, 3 Aug 1860 at age 74 years, 10 months, 3 days.[2804]
William married second Polly Hutchins about 1811.
        William Green resided on lot number seven of the North survey in Italy, New York. He operated the first ashery in
town. He was one of the founding members of the first Baptist church in Italy.[2805]
        Pamelia and William were parents of two children. William had eight children with his second wife Polly Hutchins.

i   WILLIAM SANGER GREEN, b. 1807; d. at Italy, NY, 30 Dec 1877; m. 1ˢᵗ 1829, THEODOSIA KEENEY, b. 1811
        likely daughter of Jeremiah and Lovina (-) Keeney; Theodosia d. at Italy, 3 Apr 1856. William m. 2ⁿᵈ 1857,
        ELMINA COTTON, b. 1815 daughter of Daniel and Sarah (Whitmore) Cotton; Elmina d. at Pecatonica, IL, 21
        Feb 1883.

ii   Infant, b. and d. about 1810.

874)   PHILA SANGER (*Jonathan Sanger⁴, Lydia Russell Sanger³, Benjamin², Robert¹*), b. about 1790 daughter of Jonathan
and Lucy (Sawyer) Sanger; d. about 1822; m. about 1810, JOSEPH HURLBURT, b. about 1787.
        The will of Phila's brother Prescott Sanger included a bequest to the heirs of his sister Phila Hurlbut (who are named
John, Joseph, Lucy N., Mary, and Innocent).[2806] Further records were located for two of the children.

i   JOHN HURLBURT, b. about 1810; d. after 1880 when living at Plainwell, MI; m. 1ˢᵗ about 1835, JULIA BROWN,
        b. 1818 daughter of Ballou and Rhobe (Mason) Brown; Julia d. at Manchester, NY, 7 Feb 1845. John m. 2ⁿᵈ
        MAHALA who has not been identified, born in NY about 1821.

ii   LUCY N. HURLBURT, b. about 1812

iii   MARY HURLBURT, b. estimate 1814

iv   JOSEPH HURLBURT, b. estimate 1815

v   INNOCENT HURLBURT, b. at Canandaigua, 15 Mar 1820; d. at Plainwell, MI, 31 Mar 1910; m. 1837, ORSON
        DAVID DUNHAM, b. 17 Mar 1818 son of David and Sarah (Pierson) Dunham; Orson d. at Benton, MI, 28 Sep
        1902.

875)   JUSTUS HATCH SANGER (*Jonathan Sanger⁴, Lydia Russell Sanger³, Benjamin², Robert¹*), b. 16 Oct 1791 son of
Jonathan and Lucy (Sawyer) Sanger; d. at DeWitt, IA, 20 Jan 1874; m. 1ˢᵗ at Canandaigua, 30 May 1819, ARAMINTA REID, b.
about 1801 daughter of John and Irene (Parrish) Reid;[2807] Araminta d. at Canandaigua, 11 Mar 1832. Justus m. 2ⁿᵈ at
Canandaigua, 27 Dec 1832 (pension record), DELILAH WHITMORE, b. a Peru, MA, 29 Aug 1812 daughter of William and
Lydia (Daws) Whitmore; Delilah d. at DeWitt, IA, 23 Nov 1885.
        Justus was born in Connecticut and went with his father to Canandaigua about 1810. Justus married and raised his
family there until 1857. He was involved in multiple land transactions related to family members including the estate of his
brother Prescott, his brother-in-law- John Carr, and his father-in-law John Reid.[2808]
        In 1840, Justus headed a household of twelve in Canandaigua: one male 40 to 49, two females 20 to 29, one male
under 5, one male 5 to 9, two males 15 to 19, one male 20 to 29, two females under 5, one female 10 to 14, and one female 15 to

2804 William is interred at Italy Valley Cemetery in Italy, New York; Find a Grave 70055197
2805 Cleveland, *History and Directory of Yates County*, volume 1, p 404
2806 New York Wills and Probate, Ontario County, Probate Records volume 18, pp 87-89
2807 Araminta's parents' names, John and Irene Reid, are inscribed on her tombstone; Pioneer Cemetery, Canandaigua, Find a Grave 50196232
2808 New York Land records, Ontario County, 45:631, 51:16, 52:185

19.[2809] In 1850, his household was himself, wife Delilah, and children Russell B., Amanda V., Amarilla S., Justus N., and Lucy.[2810]

On 20 May 1857, Justus with his wife Delilah completed a real estate transaction with Charles Shepard for forty acres in Canandaigua. This was property that Charles Shepard currently occupied and involved Charles assuming the mortgage on the property.[2811]

The family was then in Iowa where they were enumerated at DeWitt in the 1870 census with Justus aged 78, Delila aged 52, and Lucy aged 20.[2812]

Justus H. Sanger served as a private in Capt. Robert Spencer's company of New York militia and was credited with 28 days of service from 12 July to 8 August 1812. Justus made application for a pension related to his service which was rejected due to insufficient service. His widow Delilah pursued efforts to obtain a pension following his death and was ultimately successful in 1878. Justus initially received 40 acres of bounty land but later was determined eligible for an additional 120 acres.[2813] On 10 June 1856, Justus H. Sanger received a land grant in Tama, Iowa for 120 acres.[2814]

The file also includes information on Delilah's pension as mother of Justus N. Sanger who died during the Civil War. As a result, Delilah was illegally receiving payments from two pensions and was found to owe the government $262.66. Delilah responded to this request of her with a letter stating she was unable to pay that amount "nor do I rest easy under the charge of having 'obtained illegally' the money. The facts will not bear you out in making the assertion." She did surrender the pension as a widow of Justus and retained the mother's pension.[2815]

No children were identified for Justus and Araminta, although census records suggest there were perhaps children from the first marriage. Justus Sanger and Delilah Whitmore were parents of five children born at Canandaigua, New York.

i   RUSSELL B. SANGER, b. 1834; d. at Canandaigua, 3 May 1852.

ii   AMANDA VIANNA SANGER, b. about 1835; d. at DeWitt, IA, 25 Aug 1908. Amanda did not marry.

iii   AMARILLA S. SANGER, b. about 1837; d. at Maquoketa, IA, 18 Mar 1917; m. about 1857, ROBERT WILSON HENRY, b. 1835 likely son of Robert Wilson and Lucinda (Crain) Henry; Robert d. at Maquoketa, 12 May 1899.

iv   JUSTUS NELSON SANGER, b. 18 Sep 1838; d. of dysentery on a hospital ship near Young's Point, 13 Feb 1863. Justus did not marry. He enlisted from DeWitt, Iowa on 8 August 1862 in the 26th Regiment of Iowa Infantry.[2816]

v   LUCY L. SANGER, b. 1 Jul 1850 (per death record); d. at Dubuque, IA, 28 Jan 1911. Lucy did not marry.

876)   CHLOE SANGER (*Jonathan Sanger⁴, Lydia Russell Sanger³, Benjamin², Robert¹*), b. 1796 daughter of Jonathan and Lucy (Sawyer) Sanger; d. at Canandaigua, 21 Aug 1852;[2817] m. about 1819, JOHN B. BROCKLEBANK, b. at Canandaigua, 1797 son of Samuel and Mary (Harvey) Brocklebank; John d. at Canandaigua, 3 Mar 1874.

John B. Brocklebank was born in Canandaigua and lived there throughout his life. John's father Samuel was one of the first settlers on Canandaigua. In his 1826 will, Samuel Brocklebank conveyed all his real and personal estate (excepting clothing left to son Samuel) to his son John B. Brocklebank.[2818]

John kept a farm which was later occupied by his son Benjamin.[2819] John also owned property in Bethel, Michigan which he passed on to his son Samuel.

In 1840, John headed a household of nine persons in Canandaigua: one male 40 to 49, one female 30 to 39, one male under 5, one male 5 to 9, two males 10 to 14, one male 20 to 29, and two females 15 to 19.[2820] In 1850, children Walter, John, Benjamin, Levi, and Emily were in the home along with Emily's two-year old daughter Mary Anderson.[2821]

In his will written 9 March 1861 (probate 20 Apr 1874), John B. Brocklebank first addresses a 233-acre property he owns in Bethel, Michigan that involves his brother Levi and provisions allowing his brother and nephew George to occupy the property. Son Samuel S. Brocklebank receives 100 acres of the farm in Michigan. Sons Benjamin S. Brocklebank and Levi Brocklebank each receives one thousand dollars. Daughter Electa wife of Charles Negus receives a bond and mortgage held by John against Charles Negus. Daughter Emily wife of James Anderson receives six hundred dollars. The remainder of the estate is to be divided in equal shares among his seven children: Samuel S. Brocklebank, Levi Brocklebank, Electa Negus, Emily

[2809] Year: 1840; Census Place: Canandaigua, Ontario, New York; Roll: 319; Page: 18; Family History Library Film: 0017201

[2810] Year: 1850; Census Place: Canandaigua, Ontario, New York; Roll: 571; Page: 208b

[2811] New York Land records, Ontario County, 113:263

[2812] Year: 1870; Census Place: De Witt, Clinton, Iowa; Roll: M593_384; Page: 228B

[2813] War of 1812 pension file, 15549, 29206, 20628, Justus H. Sanger

[2814] U.S., General Land Office Records, 1776-2015; https://glorecords.blm.gov/details/patent/default.aspx?accession=0009-455&docClass=MW&sid=34hy44qv.hgf

[2815] War of 1812 pension file, 15549, 29206, 20628, Justus H. Sanger

[2816] U.S., Civil War Soldier Records and Profiles, 1861-1865

[2817] Chloe is interred at Sand Hill Cemetery in Canandaigua, Find a Grave 119962057

[2818] New York Wills and Probate, Ontario County, Probate Records volume 18, p 140

[2819] Aldrich and Conover, *History of Ontario County, New York*, Family Sketches, p 265

[2820] Year: 1840; Census Place: Canandaigua, Ontario, New York; Roll: 319; Page: 17; Family History Library Film: 0017201

[2821] Year: 1850; Census Place: Canandaigua, Ontario, New York; Roll: 571; Page: 208b

Anderson, Walter S. Brocklebank, John Brocklebank, and Benjamin S. Brocklebank. Executors were sons Samuel, Walter, and Benjamin and son-in-law James W. Anderson. In a codicil written 9 November 1871, John amended his will to change the specific property in Michigan to be given to his son Samuel. And on 19 August 1872, he amended the bequest to daughter Emily from six hundred to one thousand dollars.[2822]

Chloe Sanger and John B. Brocklebank were parents of seven children who lived to adulthood.

i　　SAMUEL SANGER BROCKLEBANK, b. 1820; d. at Bethel, MI, 5 Nov 1888; m. 1st about 1845, MARIAH SAGE, b. about 1825; Mariah d. at Bethel, 24 Feb 1870. Samuel m. 2nd at Branch County, MI, 18 Mar 1872, MARY ANN GRISWOLD; Mary Ann d. about 1874. Samuel m. 3rd at Coldwater, MI, 10 Nov 1875, HARRIET RUSSELL (widow Harriet Fairchild), b. in NY, about 1847 daughter of Alonzo and Mary Ann (Card) Russell; Harriet d. at Branch County, MI, 1893. Harriet was Samuel's housekeeper prior to their marriage.

ii　　ELECTA BROCKLEBANK, b. 29 Jul 1821; d. at Adrian, MI, 5 Feb 1905; m. 1844, CHARLES NEGUS, b. at Peru, MA, 8 Sep 1819 son of Moses and Lydia (Daws) Neggis;[2823] Charles d. at Adrian, MI, 12 Aug 1908 at age 89 years, 11 months, 5 days.

iii　　EMILY CARR BROCKLEBANK, b. 1825; d. at Evanston, WY, 5 Jan 1905; m. at Canandaigua, 2 Jul 1845. JAMES WILSON ANDERSON, baptized at St. John's Church, Canandaigua, 10 Jul 1823 son of Hannah Anderson; James d. at Canandaigua, 1 Sep 1884.

iv　　WALTER S. BROCKLEBANK, b. 1827; d. (burial at Canandaigua), 1899; m. about 1856, EVALINA F. BRYANT, b. at Waukegan, IL[2824] Jan 1833 daughter of Hezekiah and Harriet M. (-) Bryant; Evalina d. at Canandaigua, 31 Jan 1911.

v　　JOHN BROCKLEBANK, b. 30 Nov 1830; d. at Battle Creek, MI, 26 Apr 1904; m. JULIA E SAYERS, b. at Emmett, MI, about 1840 daughter of Samuel Sayers; Julia d. at Battle Creek, 11 May 1896.

vi　　BENJAMIN S. BROCKLEBANK, b. 18 Dec 1835; d. at Canandaigua, 18 Aug 1912; m. ELLEN JONES, b. 1838 daughter of John S. and Fanny (Blair) Jones;[2825] Ellen d. at Canandaigua, 1 Jul 1891.

vii　　LEVI C. BROCKLEBANK, b. 1837; d. of a gunshot wound at Finley Hospital in Washington, DC, 10 Jun 1864. Levi served with the 4th New York artillery regiment.[2826] He died of a severe wound to the right shoulder received on 19 May 1864 at Spotsylvania Courthouse, Virginia.[2827]

877)　　LUCY SANGER (*Jonathan Sanger⁴, Lydia Russell Sanger³, Benjamin², Robert¹*), b. 1799 daughter of Jonathan and Lucy (Sawyer) Sanger; d. (burial at Canandaigua), 15 Nov 1844;[2828] m. at Canandaigua, 1818,[2829] JOHN CARR, b. at Vershire, VT, 7 Jul 1796 son of John and Mary (Prescott) Carr;[2830] John d. at Middlesex, NY, 15 Nov 1861. John married second about 1847 Sophronia *Case* Crow (widow of Erastus Crow).

John Carr was born in Vershire and came to Canandaigua about age 19. After their marriage, Lucy and John settled in Middlesex, New York.[2831]

In his will written 16 June 1851 (proved 10 February 1862), John Carr aged fifty-four of Middlesex, New York bequeathed to his sons George G. Carr and Edward Carr all the farm in Middlesex, with Edward to have a two-thousand-dollar greater interest that George. Daughter Mary P. wife of Abijah Otis is to receive the annual interest from five hundred dollars. Second son Edward receives the household furniture and farming utensils, and son George receives the gold watch. Son Edward was named executor.[2832]

Lucy Sanger and John Carr were parents of three children.

[2822] New York Wills and Probate, Ontario County, Record of Wills, volume W, pp 582-585, record of John B. Brocklebank's will

[2823] Names of parents are given as Moses Negus and Lydia Daws on his death record which is consistent with the birth record; Michigan, U.S., Death Records, 1867-1952

[2824] Place of birth is given in her obituary

[2825] Aldrich and Conover, *History of Ontario County, New York*, Family Sketches, p 265

[2826] U.S., Registers of Deaths of Volunteers, 1861-1865; cause of death given as "vulnus sclopet" (which means gunshot wound)

[2827] U.S., Civil War Soldier Records and Profiles, 1861-1865

[2828] Lucy is interred at Pioneer Cemetery in Canandaigua, Find a Grave 50212225

[2829] 10,000 Vital Records of Western New York, 1809-1850

[2830] Carr, *The Carr Family Records*, p 99

[2831] Carr, *The Carr Family Records*, p 166

[2832] New York Probate, Yates County, Wills Book F, p 460

i   MARY P. CARR, b. 3 Feb 1819; d. at Ellenville, NY, 31 May 1864; m. about 1840, Dr. ABIJAH OTIS, b. 31 May 1815 son of Abijah and Eleanor (Austin) Otis; Abijah d. at Ellenville, 26 Sep 1883.[2833] Abijah married second, Jane L. Burnham (1829-1918) daughter of Chester and Mary (Holt) Burnham.

ii   GEORGE G. CARR, b. 1820; d. at Middlesex, NY, 24 Feb 1877; m. 31 Dec 1840, JULIA ANN SMITH, b. 27 Nov 1821 daughter of Northrup and Rebecca (Shepard) Smith (Benham bible record); Julia d. at Middlesex, 27 Nov 1884.

iii   EDWARD CARR, b. 1827; d. at Brown's Grove, KS (burial at Middlesex, NY), 22 Mar 1882;[2834] m. his stepsister, MARIA CROW, b. 1834 daughter of Erastus and Sophronia (Case) Crow; Maria d. at Middlesex, 1878.

878)   HANNAH RUSSELL (*John⁴, Joseph³, Benjamin², Robert¹*), b. at Ashford, 8 Jun 1768 daughter of John and Rebekah (Wilson) Russell; d. at Sudbury, VT, 3 Jan 1841; m. by 1797, JOSEPH WILLIAMS, b. 1765; Joseph d. at Sudbury, 5 Feb 1841.
    There are four children known for Hannah and Joseph. The births of two of the children are noted in the records of Sudbury, Vermont although all but the youngest child may have been born in Connecticut or Essex County, New York.

i   ELIJAH WILLIAMS, b. 25 Aug 1797; d. at Westport, NY, 6 Sep 1872; m. PHEBE GREELEY, b. at Saratoga, NY, 9 Jul 1801 daughter of John and Susan (Marshall) Greeley;[2835] Phebe d. at Westport, 30 Jan 1886.

ii   ORRIN WILLIAMS, b. 21 Mar 1804; d. at Brandon, VT, 20 Mar 1882; m. 1ˢᵗ at Sudbury, VT, 1 Feb 1826, LYDIA LINSLEY, b. in VT, 1804; Lydia d. at Newcomb, NY, after 1855. Orrin m, 2ⁿᵈ ADELIA STEEL, b. in Canada, about 1826 daughter of Abraham and Elizabeth (Newell) Steel;[2836] Adelia d. at Canaan, NH, 5 Jan 1898.

iii   JOSEPHUS WILLIAMS, b. 30 Aug 1807; d. at Castleton, VT, 20 Jun 1878; m. 1ˢᵗ 11 Jul 1838, LUCY S. OLDS, b. at Saratoga, NY, 14 Jun 1814 daughter of William and Nancy J. (Greeley) Olds;[2837] Lucy d. 18 Aug 1847. Josephus m. 2ⁿᵈ 9 Sep 1850, Lucy's sister, ANNA ELIZA OLDS, b. at Saratoga, 17 Sep 1816; Anna d. at Castleton, 8 Apr 1884.

iv   RUSSELL WILLIAMS, b. 19 Dec 1814 (engraved on gravestone); d. (burial at Rochester, MN), 26 Mar 1887; m. at Sudbury, VT, 12 Nov 1840, LOVINA M. GRIFFIN, b. 28 Jan 1815 daughter of Benoni and Martha (Foster) Griffin;[2838] Lovina d. at Cascade, MN, 17 Oct 1898.

879)   CYNTHIA RUSSELL (*John⁴, Joseph³, Benjamin², Robert¹*), b. 5 at Ashford, Oct 1772 daughter of John and Rebekah (Wilson) Russell; d. at Union, CT, 22 Nov 1833; m. at Ashford, 20 Feb 1794, BENJAMIN JAMES, b. at Ashford, 1771 son of Benjamin and Rhoda (Kenyon) James; Benjamin d. at Union, 2 Jan 1848.
    Cynthia and Benjamin were first in Ashford. Benjamin purchased property in Union on 3 March 1795.[2839] They were parents of ten children, the births of the older children recorded at Ashford and the younger children at Union, Connecticut.

i   DIANA JAMES, b. at Ashford, 15 Oct 1794; d. 6 Mar 1796.

ii   BENJAMIN REYNOLDS JAMES, b. 22 Nov 1796; d. at Union, 14 Sep 1819.

iii   JONATHAN JAMES, b. at Ashford, 13 Apr 1799; m. at Union, 24 Nov 1825, PARMELA MOORE, b. at Union, 6 Apr 1797 daughter of William of Bethiah (Weld) Moore

iv   HANNAH DIANA JAMES, b. at Ashford, 10 Jun 1801; d. (burial at North Ashford), 31 Jul 1845; m. at Union, 15 Feb 1827, EPHRAIM LORIN CARPENTER, b. at Ashford, 20 Jan 1799 son of Uriah and Elisphal (Briggs) Carpenter; d. at Eastford, 2 Aug 1845.

v   RHODA JAMES, b. at Ashford, 7 Mar 1803; d. (burial at Ashford), 9 Aug 1875; m. at Union, 25 Dec 1823, DAVID FULLER, b. 1799; David d. 6 Nov 1882.

[2833] Abijah and Mary are interred at Fantinekill Cemetery, Find a Grave 216179727
[2834] Edward died in Kansas, and his remains were returned to New York for burial; Find a Grave 42015869
[2835] Greeley, *Genealogy of the Greely Family*, p 315
[2836] The names of Adelia's parents are given on her death record. In addition, her parents A. G. and Elizabeth Steel were living with Orrin and Adelia at Newcomb, NY in 1865.
[2837] Olds, *The Olds Family in England and America*, p 101
[2838] The names of Lovina's parents are given as Benoni Griffin and Martha Foster on her cemetery record. Dalby, John. *Minnesota Cemetery Inscription Index, Select Counties* [database on-line]. Provo, UT, USA: Ancestry.com Operations Inc, 2003.
[2839] Hammond, *The History of Union*, p 375

vi   REBECCA JAMES, b. at Union, 7 Mar 1805; d. at Union, 1 Jul 1844; m. at Union, 25 Jun 1829, JOSEPH
        WALKER, b. at Ashford, 10 Mar 1803 son of Pearly and Rebecca (Broughton) Walker; Joseph d. at Union, 22 Aug
        1868.

vii   BETSEY JAMES, b. at Union, 30 Mar 1807; d. at Union, 1 Mar 1859. Betsey did not marry. On 10 Apr 1844, a
        conservator was named to manage her affairs as she was deemed to be incompetent.[2840] Betsey owned property of
        a barn and ten acres, plus two other lots of about thirty acres, that had been left to her as a life estate by her
        father Benjamin.

viii   JOSIAH RUSSELL JAMES, b. at Union, 12 Sep 1809; d. at Union, 15 Mar 1900; m. 1st about 1836, ALMEDA C.
        who has not been identified, but b. 1818; Almeda d. at Union, 3 May 1845. Josiah m. at 2nd Union, 12 Oct 1845,
        LUCRETIA WATSON, b. about 1817; Lucretia and Josiah separated by 1860 and he is reported as divorced on
        the 1880 census.

ix   AARON RATHBONE JAMES, b. at Union, 26 Sep 1811; d. at Vernon, CT, 1896; m. 1st at Stafford, 1 Jan 1833,
        JERUSHA BOWEN, b. 1815; Jerusha d. at Middletown, 22 Sep 1866. Aaron m. 2nd CLARISSA B. PARKER
        (widow of Frederick Merten), b. 2 Jan 1826; Clarissa d. 10 Jun 1895.

x   ELISHA BENJAMIN REYNOLDS JAMES, b. at Union, 22 Jun 1814; d. at Vernon, 24 Mar 1876; m. at
        Willington, 21 Mar 1841, MARY ANN THOMAS, b. Apr 1814; Mary d. at Vernon, 1878.

880)   PARLEY RUSSELL (*John⁴, Joseph³, Benjamin², Robert¹*), b. at Ashford, 28 Oct 1777 son of John and Rebekah
(Wilson) Russell; d. at Ashford, 2 Aug 1841; m.1st at Willington, 28 Sep 1800, ABIGAIL CONE, b. 20 Jan 1778 daughter of
Simon and Hannah (Clark) Cone;[2841] Abigail d. at Willington, 27 Nov 1820. Pearly m. 2nd at Willington, 27 Jun 1822, LYDIA
SNELL, b. 1789 daughter of Joseph and Lydia (Farnum) Snell; Lydia d. at Ashford, 29 Apr 1841.
        Parley resided in Willington for much of his adult life. In 1830, he headed a household of six persons: one male 50 to
59, one female 40 to 49, one male under 5, one male 15 to 19, one female 10 to 14, and one female 20 to 29.[2842]
        In his will written 26 July 1841 (proved 4 August 1841), Parley Russell of Willington bequeathed to daughter
Phylancy a list of specific household items and $400. Sons John C. and Asa C. each receives $100 and daughter Rebecca W.
receives bed and bedding and $50. Son Ralph P. Russell receives one dollar. Daughter Abbey H. receives bed and bedding and
$200. The remainder of the estate is to be equally divided among the children except Ralph is to receive just one dollar.[2843]
        Daughter Philancy married but did not have children. The heirs of her estate identified were Asa C. Russell, John C.
Russell, Abby Jewett, Rebecca W. Barker wife of John D. Barker who were brothers and sisters, and the children of Ralph P.
deceased.[2844]
        Parley and Abigail were parents of six children born at Willington. The six "children of Parley" were all baptized at
Ashford on 20 August 1820 on "his wife's account".[2845]

i   PHILANCY FAY RUSSELL, b. 30 Nov 1801; d. at Great Barrington, MA, 28 Aug 1863; m. at Great Barrington,
        12 Nov 1843, WILLIAM DAY, b. at Hartford, 20 Aug 1786 son of Samuel H. and Charity (Pease) Day;[2846] William
        d. at Great Barrington, 23 Arp 1860. William was first married to Mary Pixley.

ii   JOHN CONE RUSSELL, b. 21 Jan 1804; d. at Great Barrington, 21 Oct 1873; m. at Great Barrington, 26 Nov
        1829, his fourth cousin, JENNETTE E. WILCOX (*Jemima Hunt Wilcox⁵, Russell Hunt⁴, Jemima Russell Hunt³,
        Thomas², Robert¹*), b. at Cornwall, CT, 30 Jul 1803 daughter of Joseph and Jemima (Hunt) Wilcox; Jennette d. at
        Great Barrington, 5 Jan 1867.

iii   ASA CHAMPION RUSSELL, b. 6 Apr 1808; d. at Great Barrington, 18 Feb 1876; m. at Bristol, CT, 25 Aug 1840,
        CZARINA ELIZABETH PARDEE, b. at Bristol, CT, 1819 daughter of Jared W. and Ruth (Upson) Pardee;
        Czarina d. at Stockbridge, MA, 30 Aug 1908.

iv   REBECCA WILSON RUSSELL, b. 27 Sep 1810; d. at Villisca, IA, 13 Mar 1880; m. at Willington, 10 Sep 1832,
        JOHN DOW BARKER, b. at Cornville, ME, 3 Apr 1803 (according to his obituary); John d. at Sciola, IA, 8 Dec
        1891.

[2840] Connecticut Wills and Probate Records, Stafford District, Town of Union, Case 1187

[2841] Cone, *Some Account of the Cone Family*, p 323

[2842] Year: 1830; Census Place: Willington, Tolland, Connecticut; Series: M19; Roll: 8; Page: 241; Family History Library Film: 0002801

[2843] Connecticut Wills and Probate, Hartford, Tolland Probate District, Town of Willington, Estate of Parley Russell, Case 814

[2844] *Berkshire County, MA: Probate File Papers, 1761-1917.* Online database. *AmericanAncestors.org.* New England Historic Genealogical Society,
2017. Case 9646, Philancy Day

[2845] Connecticut, Church Record Abstracts, 1630-1920, volume 001, Ashford, p 32

[2846] The names of William's parents are given as Samuel H. and Charity Day on his death record.

v   RALPH PEARLY RUSSELL, b. 26 Feb 1813; d. about 1843 (wife remarried 1844); m. at Woodstock, 3 Mar 1834, LUCY BURNHAM CHILD, b. at Woodstock, 21 Oct 1815 daughter of Aaron and Mary (Spring) Child;[2847] Lucy d. at Brighton, IA, 6 Jan 1902. Lucy married second Charles Wortley in 1844.

vi   HANNAH ABIGAIL "ABBY H." RUSSELL, b. 20 Aug 1816; m. at Willington, 10 Jun 1838, AUGUSTUS B. JEWETT of Great Barrington.

881)   RACHEL RUSSELL (*Elisha⁴, Joseph³, Benjamin², Robert¹*), b. at Middletown, CT, 17 Jul 1773 daughter of Elisha and Anne (Winship) Russell; d. at Holland Patent, NY, 12 Feb 1850; m. at New Hartford, 26 Jul 1792, GEORGE HOPKINS, b. 19 Feb 1758 son of Consider and Lydia (Gilbert) Hopkins; George d. at Floyd, NY, 18 Jul 1842.
        Rachel and George resided in Floyd, New York where George was a farmer.
        On 7 April 1818, while living in Floyd, George Hopkins made application for pension. He enlisted on 1 April 1777 under Capt. James Watson, marched to Weathersfield, and was then in the company of Capt. Whiting to the state of New Jersey. In the summer, they were at Peeks Kill where a regiment was formed under Col. Samuel B. Webb. He was discharged at Morristown, New Jersey on 7 April 1780. He was awarded a pension of $96 per annum. On 8 September 1820, then age 62, he provided information on his family and circumstances. He reported he was a farmer but unable to do much labor. His household was his wife Rachel who was weakly and son Frederick age 14. The value of his property was $178 including a yoke of oxen, sheep, and cows. There was also a note owed to him of $20.26. This put his estate over a $200 limit and George was struck from the pension rolls due to the value of his estate, although reinstated in 1822.
        On 21 September 1842, widow Rachel Hopkins made a statement related to the widow's pension giving the date of her marriage as 26 July 1792 at New Hartford, Connecticut. She reported George's death as 18 July 1842. On 30 March 1843, Frederick M. Hopkins made inquiries for the widow's pension on behalf of his widowed mother Rachel, noting she was receiving just $80 per year and his understanding was that widows would for one year receive the full amount of the pension which was $96.
        The pension file includes two pages of his personal diary. The diary begins on 25 July 1792 and starts with the date of his birth as 19 February 1758 and the birth of wife Rachel Russell as 17 July 1773. The next entries detail sermons he heard over two Sundays, a "remarkable good day" on Saturday 11th after having had rains, thunderstorms, and hail. He received the disagreeable news of the house of Mr. Hopkins being burnt on 7 July 1792, this news coming in a letter from him. On the same day, Uncle Gilbert preached from a text of Jeremiah. On a Saturday night in September, the corn was killed by frost. Other entries noted the death of John Cowls of N. Hartford, his participation in maneuvers of the 25th regiment of Connecticut militia, and hunting squirrels.[2848]
        George and Rachel were parents of six children born at Floyd, New York.[2849]

i   GEORGE HOPKINS, b. 4 Nov 1793; d. at Floyd, 14 Feb 1821.

ii   MARK ANTHONY HOPKINS, b. 19 Oct 1795; d. at Vermillion, OH, 1873. Mark did not marry. He was an abolitionist.[2850] In his will written 7 January 1870, Mark Anthony Hopkins left his estate to brother Grove G. Hopkins and sister Henrietta W. Hopkins to be equally divided.[2851]

iii   JOHN CHESTER HOPKINS, b. 3 Sep 1797; d. at Springfield, MI, 1838; m. 1st at Oneida County, NY, 14 Apr 1824, HARRIET NEWELL AUSTIN, b. 1802 daughter of Enos and Hannah (Whitney) Austin; Harriet d. at Oswego County, NY, 1832. John m. 2nd 1834, CLEORA MITCHELL; Cleora d. at Springfield, MI, 1838.

iv   GROVE GILBERT HOPKINS, b. 14 May 1799; d. at Vermillion, OH, 1879. Grove did not marry.

v   HENRIETTA WINSHIP HOPKINS, b. 13 Mar 1802; d. at Ceylon, OH, 1880. Henrietta did not marry. She was an abolitionist.

vi   FREDERICK MARSH HOPKINS, b. 1 Mar 1806; d. at Brownhelm, OH, Sep 1866; m. at Floyd, 21 Oct 1835, PHILA MARIA BARNES, b. Holland Patent, NY, 19 May 1815 daughter of Amasa and Ruth (White) Barnes; Phila d. at Brownhelm, 2 Sep 1867.

882)   EZRA SMITH (*Simeon Smith⁴, Zerviah Russell Smith³, Benjamin², Robert¹*), b. at Ashford, 20 Dec 1767 son of Simeon and Anna (Byles) Smith; d. at Ellington, 18 Dec 1852; m. at Ashford, 22 Nov 1792, ROXANA KENDALL, b. 1771 daughter of Isaac and Mary (Russell) Kendall; Roxana d. at Ellington, 30 Dec 1830.

[2847] Child, *Genealogy of the Child Families*, p 176
[2848] U. S. Revolutionary War Pension and Bounty-Land Warrant Application Files, Case W18068
[2849] Hopkins, *John Hopkins of Cambridge, Massachusetts and Some of His Descendants*, p 148
[2850] As reported in Hopkins, *John Hopkins of Cambridge, Massachusetts*
[2851] Ohio Wills and Probate, Erie County, Will Record, volume 1, pp 553-554

In 1800, Ezra headed a household of six persons at Ashford: one male 26 to 44, one female 26 to 44, two males under 10, one male 10 to 15, and one female under 10.[2852] Seven persons were enumerated in the household in 1810 including one male under 10, three females under 10, and one female 16 to 25.[2853] In 1830, Ezra headed a household of four persons in Ellington: one male 60 to 69, one female 50 to 59, one female under 5, and one female 5 to 9.[2854]

Three children were identified for Ezra and Roxana, although the 1810 census suggests there were four other children born between 1800 and 1810.

i   CLARISSA SMITH,[2855] b. 1793; d. at Orwell Township, OH, 29 Sep 1878; m. 1st 1811, HENRY AMIDON, b. at Willington, 24 Sep 1788 son of Jedediah and Hannah (Walker) Amidon; Henry d. at Windsor, OH, 5 Sep 1840. Clarissa m. 2nd 1858, REUBEN ROBERTS, b. 1792 son of William and Margaret (Merrill) Roberts; Reuben d. at Gustavus, OH, 10 Nov 1865. Reuben was first married to Sophia Owen.

ii   EZRA SMITH, b. 1795; d. at Ashford, 1 Sep 1800.

iii   ALVA SMITH, b. 1798; d. at Ashford, 17 Sep 1800.

883)   MARY "POLLY" SMITH (*Simeon Smith⁴, Zerviah Russell Smith³, Benjamin², Robert¹*), b. at Ashford, 12 Aug 1770 daughter of Simeon and Anna (Byles) Smith; d. before 1839; m. at Ashford, 4 Apr 1793, PERKINS BUSHNELL WOODWARD, b. at Ashford, 17 Aug 1770 son of Joseph and Elizabeth (Perkins) Woodward;[2856] Perkins d. at Centerville, NY, 9 Apr 1860.[2857]

Mary and Perkins resided in Ashford after their marriage and nine children were born there. The family relocated to Centerville, New York soon after the birth of their last child. They settled about one-half mile north of the village. Perkins was the first person to manufacture brick in the town. He taught the first school in Centerville in the winter of 1813-1814.[2858]

On 7 August 1820, Perkins headed a household of six persons at Centerville: one male 45 and over, one female 45 and over, one male 10 to 15, one male 16 to 18, and two females 10 to 15.[2859] In 1850, Perkins's household was himself aged 79, son Perkins aged 47 and likely his wife Susan aged 32, daughter Christiana aged 38, son Ezra S. aged 45, and what appear to be two grandchildren Elisa aged 9 and Viola aged 3. Also in the home were John H. Roberts aged 20 and Darwin Ellis aged 11.[2860] These same persons were in the household in 1855.[2861]

In his will written 26 December 1839 (probate 18 December 1860), Perkins Bushnell Woodward of Centerville bequeathed to his sons Perkins Bushnell Woodward, Jr. and Ezra Smith Woodward the farm in Centerville and all the real property. Daughters Anna wife of Reuben Ellis, Polly now wife of David Ellis, and Christina each receives one hundred dollars from the personal estate and grandchildren Sally Ellis aged seventeen years and Matthew Clark Ellis aged twelve years each receives fifty dollars. There are also provisions for disposing of the legacies for each of the heirs if they pre-decease Perkins. These include a provision for daughter-in-law Margaret current wife of son Perkins to have use of his legacy while she is a widow. Sons Perkins Bushnell and friend William A. Stacy were named executors.[2862]

Mary Smith and Perkins Woodward were parents of nine children born at Ashford. Three of the children died in a three-day period in August 1800.

i   ANNA WOODWARD, b. 8 Jan 1794; d. at Centerville, NY, 1858; m. REUBEN ELLIS, b. 1790 son of Matthew and Hannah (Clark) Ellis; Reuben d. at Centerville, 29 Jan 1869.

ii   POLLY WOODWARD, b. 20 Aug 1795; d. 18 Aug 1800.

iii   PHINEHAS WOODWARD, b. 6 Aug 1797; d. 16 Aug 1800.

iv   ELIZABETH WOODWARD, b. 19 Jun 1799; d. 18 Aug 1800.

v   ELIZA WOODWARD, b. 22 Mar 1801; d. at Centerville, about 1835; m. about 1820, DAVID ELLIS, b. at Colrain, MA, 3 Aug 1798 son of Matthew and Hannah (Clark) Ellis; David d. at Beaver Dam, WI, 29 Sep 1846. David married second Eliza's sister Polly (see below).

[2852] Year: 1800; Census Place: Ashford, Windham, Connecticut; Series: M32; Roll: 2; Page: 840; Image: 390; Family History Library Film: 205619

[2853] Year: 1810; Census Place: Ashford, Windham, Connecticut; Roll: 3; Page: 559; Image: 00304; Family History Library Film: 0281231

[2854] Year: 1830; Census Place: Ellington, Tolland, Connecticut; Series: M19; Roll: 8; Page: 201; Family History Library Film: 0002801

[2855] Best, *The Amidon Family*, p 44

[2856] Perkins Bushnell Woodward received a one-ninth part of his father Joseph's estate (will 1810; probate 1814 at Ashford); Connecticut Will and Probate, Pomfret District, Town of Ashford, Estate of Joseph Woodward, No. 4559

[2857] "United States, Cemetery Abstracts, 1949-1969", database, *FamilySearch* (https://www.familysearch.org/ark:/61903/1:1:QPTX-126G : 1 July 2021), Perkins Woodard, 1860.

[2858] Minard, *Allegany County and Its People*, p 79, p 781

[2859] 1820 U S Census; Census Place: Centerville, Allegany, New York; Page: 10; NARA Roll: M33_64; Image: 21

[2860] Year: 1850; Census Place: Centerville, Allegany, New York; Roll: 476; Page: 294a

[2861] New York, U.S., State Census, 1855

[2862] New York Probate Records, Allegany County, 4:241 (will)

vi   PERKINS BUSHNELL WOODWARD, b. 11 Sep 1803; d. at Caneadea, NY, 10 Sep 1888; m. 1ˢᵗ MARGARET, b. about 1811; Margaret d. at Centerville, 18 Mar 1844. Perkins m. 2ⁿᵈ SUSAN, b. 1 Jul 1817; Susan d. at Centerville, 8 Jul 1897.

vii   EZRA SMITH WOODWARD, b. 4 Nov 1805; d. at Centerville, NY, 8 Apr 1893. He perhaps married Polly who has not been identified (Polly Woodward living in the household with the family aged 52 which included brother Bushnell and his wife Susan, Christiana, and two children of Bushnell).[2863] No children were identified for Ezra.

viii POLLY WOODWARD, b. 8 Dec 1807; d. after 1880 when living at Caneadea, NY; m. about 1835, DAVID ELLIS who was first married to her sister Eliza (see above).

ix   CHRISTINA WOODWARD, b. 10 Aug 1810; d. after 1860 when she was living in a household with her brothers Bushnell and Ezra.

884)   ZERVIAH SMITH (*Simeon Smith⁴, Zerviah Russell Smith³, Benjamin², Robert¹*), b. at Ashford, 15 Oct 1772 daughter of Simeon and Anna (Byles) Smith; d. at Ashford, 13 May 1837; m. at Ashford, 3 Feb 1790, ANDREW HUNTINGTON, b. at Griswold, 23 Nov 1766 son of Andrew and Lucy (Lamphere) Huntington; Andrew d. at Ashford, 1 Feb 1837.

    Andrew Huntington was a physician in Ashford.[2864] In 1820, Andrew headed a household of eleven persons in Ashford: one male 45 and over, one female 45 and over, one male under 10, three males 10 to 15, one male 16 to 25, one male 26 to 44, one female under 10, one female 10 to 15, and one female 26 to 44.[2865]

    Andrew Huntington and Zerviah Smith were parents of thirteen children born at Ashford.

i   SOPHIA HUNTINGTON, b. 4 May 1791; d. at Ashford, 7 Nov 1849; m. at Ashford, 28 Jan 1813, ELISHA BYLES, b. at Ashford, 28 Jan 1788 son of Josiah and Abigail (Clark) Byles; Elisha d. at Ashford, 23 May 1869. Elisha married second Anna Holt (1791-1883) daughter of Nehemiah and Mary (Lamphear) Holt.

ii   ANNA HUNTINGTON, b. 4 Jun 1792; d. 11 Jan 1795.

iii ELISHA HUNTINGTON, b. 23 May 1793; d. at Mobile, AL, Oct 1853; m. at New York by Rev. Brientnall at Zion's Church, 10 Sep 1823, MARIA ELIZABETH GIVENS, b. about 1793; Maria d. at New York, 22 May 1829.

iv ANDREW HUNTINGTON, b. 1 Aug 1795; d. 18 Aug 1800.

v   HORATIO HUNTINGTON, b. 27 Nov 1797; d. 15 Aug 1800.

vi LUCY HUNTINGTON, b. 28 Aug 1800; d. 12 Jan 1804.

vii ZERUIAH HUNTINGTON, b. 29 Mar 1803; d. 23 May 1804.

viii ENOCH SMITH HUNTINGTON, b. 30 Sep 1804; d. at Danbury, CT, 7 Apr 1862; m. 1ˢᵗ 8 Sep 1836, LUCY COWLES, b. at Amherst, MA, 20 Feb 1815 daughter of Dr. Chester and Sally (Wade) Cowles; Lucy d. at Clinton, CT, 14 Jun 1843. Enoch m. 2ⁿᵈ at Clinton, 29 Oct 1843, ELIZABETH WILCOX (widow of William Talcott), b. 20 Feb 1803 daughter of Edward and Sarane (Taylor) Wilcox; Elizabeth d. at Clinton, 1 Feb 1852. Enoch m. 3ʳᵈ at Fairfield, 13 Apr 1853, ESTHER LYON, b. at Fairfield, 2 Aug 1819 daughter of Burr and Abigail (Burr) Lyon; Esther d. at Fairfield, 8 Aug 1904.

ix DAN HUNTINGTON, b. 19 Feb 1806; d. in Mississippi, Aug 1843.

x   MATILDA HUNTINGTON, b. 26 Dec 1808; d. at Ashford, 10 Oct 1879; m. at Ashford, 22 Mar 1836, as his second wife, FRANCIS P. CLARK, b. 1798; Francis d. at Ashford, 5 Feb 1870. Francis was first married to Jelina Woodward.

xi NATHAN BELCHER HUNTINGTON, b. 23 Feb 1810; d. at Geneseo, IL, 10 Aug 1885; m. 1ˢᵗ at Ashford, 8 May 1833, his first cousin, MATILDA WHITON, b. at Ashford, 15 Feb 1810 daughter of Elijah and Matilda (Smith) Whiton; Matilda d. at Tazewell, IL, 1 Oct 1841. Nathan m. 2ⁿᵈ at Tazewell, 9 Dec 1841, REBECCA WILLARD, b. at Barre, VT, 9 Dec 1809 daughter of Silas and Abigail (Cottle) Willard; Rebecca d. 3 May 1849. Nathan m. 3ʳᵈ at Knox County, IL, 7 Oct 1849, JANE CHAREVOY, b. 2 Jan 1805 daughter of Francis and Elizabeth (West) Charevoy; Jane d. at Knoxville, IL, 4 Apr 1871. Nathan m. 4ᵗʰ at Cook County, IL, 19 Nov 1872, PRISCILLA A. STOUGH (who was widow of Robert Strough), b. 1821; Priscilla d. at Geneseo, 25 Mar 1905.[2866]

xii AMELIA HUNTINGTON, b. 16 Aug 1811; d. at Ashford, 10 Jun 1847.

[2863] Year: 1860; Census Place: Centerville, Allegany, New York; Page: 506
[2864] Huntington, *Genealogical Memoir of the Huntington Family*, p 151, p 225
[2865] 1820 U S Census; Census Place: Ashford, Windham, Connecticut; Page: 434; NARA Roll: M33_3; Image: 339
[2866] Some of this information from Biographical Publishing Company, *Portrait and Biographical Album of Henry County, Illinois*, p 299

xiii   ANDREW HUNTINGTON, b. 7 Dec 1813; d. 4 Jan 1827.

885)   ANNA SMITH (*Simeon Smith⁴, Zerviah Russell Smith³, Benjamin², Robert¹*), b. at Ashford, 1 Jan 1774 daughter of Simeon and Anna (Byles) Smith; d. at East Hartford, CT, 29 Jul 1854; m. SYLVANUS WING, b. at Rehoboth, MA, 11 Nov 1770 son of Sylvanus and Elizabeth (Ward) Wing; Sylvanus d. at East Hartford, 23 Apr 1839.

Anna and Sylvanus resided in Ashford and then East Hartford. In 1810, Sylvanus headed a household of ten persons at East Hartford: one male 26 to 44, one female 26 to 44, one male under 10, five females under 10, one female 10 to 15, and one female 16 to 25.[2867] The household was eleven persons in 1820: one male 45 and over, one female 45 and over, one male under 10, one male 10 to 15, one male 16 to 18, one female under 10, two females 10 to 15, two females 16 to 25, and one female 26 to 44.[2868]

The estate of Sylvanus Wing entered probate 24 June 1839 with Anna Wing and Philetas Woodward as administrators. The value of the personal estate was $460.23 which included inventoried amount of $315.11, debts collected, sale of lumber, and amounts still owed the estate.[2869]

In her will written 15 February 1853 (probate 21 August 1854), Anna Wing bequeathed all her personal estate to her daughter Eliza Deming wife of Timothy Deming. Timothy Deming was named executor.[2870]

Son Sylvanus Wing included some of his siblings in his will. In his will written 7 February 1846 (probate 21 April 1846), Sylvanus Wing of St. Louis willed that two thousand dollars be invested, and the interest used for the support of his mother Ann Wing of Hartford County, Connecticut during his natural life. Five hundred dollars was left to sister Martha C. Wing for her sole use and benefit. Niece Frances J. Kenney receives two hundred dollars. He directs that all his real estate be sold. The ground that is a burial ground on his farm is to be retained as a burial ground and to be used for that purpose for his now family (who are not named), for the family of his brother Andrew H. Wing, and for the family of his brother-in-law Thomas J. Hampstead. Oliver D. Filley was named executor.[2871]

Anna Smith and Sylvanus Wing were parents of nine children.[2872]

i   SABRINA WING, b. at Ashford, 16 Sep 1799; d. at Warrenton, GA, 19 Jan 1832; m. at East Hartford, 17 Sep 1822, ALLEN BRAINARD, b. at Cromwell, CT, 6 Apr 1798 son of Jabez and Abigail (Williams) Brainard.[2873] The family was living in Warrenton on 1830 with a household of thirteen persons which included six slaves.[2874]

ii   ALMIRA WING, b. at Ashford, 21 Jul 1801; d. at Manchester, CT, 30 Mar 1834; m. at East Hartford, 3 May 1818, MARVIN KEENEY, b. 1798; Marvin d. at Manchester, 1876. Marvin married second Diantha Wyllys Warren on 6 Sep 1834.

iii   ELIZA WING, b. at Ashford, 12 Sep 1802; d. at East Hartford, 15 Jul 1886; m. at East Hartford, 22 Nov 1825, TIMOTHY DEMING, b. at East Hartford, 13 Feb 1788 son of David and Anna (Abbe) Deming; Timothy d. at East Hartford, 14 Aug 1879. Timothy was first married to Olive Treat.

iv   SYLVANUS WING, b. likely at East Hartford, 1 Feb 1805; d. at St. Louis, MO, 12 Apr 1846; m. at Bloomfield, CT, 12 Sep 1837, HARRIET NEWBERRY, b. 17 Mar 1812 daughter of James and Sarah (Butler) Newberry; Harriet d. at Bloomfield, 17 Sep 1857. Harriet married second James Larkin Prosser. Sylvanus and Harriet had three children: Julia who died young, Lucy J., and Oliver.

v   MARY ANN WING, b. 4 Dec 1806; d. at St. Louis, MO, 2 May 1855; m. at St. Louis, 3 May 1845, THOMAS J. HEMPSTEAD, b. 1805 son of Joseph and Celinda (Hutchinson) Hempstead. Thomas's mother Celinda was living with him in St. Louis in 1850.[2875] Mary Ann did not have children.

vi   HARRIET WING, b. 19 Jan 1809; d. at Manchester, CT, 27 Jan 1859; m. at East Hartford, 13 Nov 1834, FRANCIS WHITE COWLES, b. at Springfield, VT, 4 Jul 1804 son of Stephen and Patty (Reed) Cowles;[2876] Francis d. at Manchester, 10 Mar 1880.

vii ANNA WING, b. 30 Mar 1811; d. at East Hartford, 1812.

[2867] Year: 1810; Census Place: Hartford, Hartford, Connecticut; Roll: 1; Page: 505; Image: 00505; Family History Library Film: 0281229

[2868] 1820 U S Census; Census Place: East Hartford, Hartford, Connecticut; Page: 209; NARA Roll: M33_2; Image: 213

[2869] Connecticut Wills and Probate, Hartford Probate District, Town of East Hartford, Estate of Sylvanus Wing, 1839

[2870] Connecticut Wills and Probate, Hartford Probate District, Town of East Hartford, Estate of Anna Wing, 1854

[2871] Missouri Wills and Probate, St. Louis, Wills Volume C, pp 229-230

[2872] The births of the eldest three children are in the Ashford records; the specific dates of birth of the youngest six children are from Wing, *A Historical and Genealogical Register of John Wing of Sandwich, Mass.*, p 290

[2873] Brainard, *The Genealogy of the Brainerd-Brainard Family*, p 130

[2874] Year: 1830; Census Place: Warren, Georgia; Series: M19; Roll: 21; Page: 192; Family History Library Film: 0007041

[2875] Year: 1850; Census Place: District 82, St Louis, Missouri; Roll: 414; Page: 518a

[2876] American Historical Society, Encyclopedia of Massachusetts, Biographical-Genealogical, volume 10, p 36

viii ANDREW HUNTINGTON WING, b. 21 Dec 1813, d. at Helena, MT, 15 Dec 1873; m. at East Hartford, 30 Sep 1841, EMELINE R. BURNHAM, b. 1813 daughter of Hezekiah and Sarah B. (Miller) Burnham; Emeline d. at St. Louis, MO, 6 Sep 1864.

ix MARTHA CONANT WING, b. at East Hartford, 4 Aug 1815; d. perhaps at Oak Park, IL (burial at St. Louis), 19 Jan 1895; m. at St. Louis, 5 Nov 1846, Dr. LEANDER HANFORD BAKER, b. at Onondaga, NY, 27 Jun 1814 son of Daniels and Elmina (Hanford) Baker; Leander d. at Oak Park, 4 May 1900. Leander served as a surgeon in the Missouri 24th infantry regiment during the Civil War.[2877]

886) ABIGAIL SMITH (*Simeon Smith⁴, Zerviah Russell Smith³, Benjamin², Robert¹*), b. at Ashford, 2 Feb 1777 daughter of Simeon and Anna (Byles) Smith; d. at Portageville, NY, 29 Sep 1862; m. 1799, her stepbrother, LYMAN WALDO, b. at Coventry, 8 Jul 1774 son of John and Lucy (Lyman) Waldo; Lyman d. at Portageville, 23 Jul 1865.

Abigail and Lyman lived in Edmeston, New York, Berkshire, and finally in Portageville.[2878]

Lyman was of Edmeston on 3 July 1811 when he sold 52 acres from the great lot number seven in Edmeston to Henry Convers for payment of $286. He was still in Edmeston on 14 December 1814 when he sold 26 acres of great lot number two to Eliezer Bass for payment of $800.[2879]

Abigail and Lyman were in Genesee Falls in 1850 living next to their son John L. Waldo. They were enumerated there in 1860.[2880]

Abigail Smith and Lyman Waldo were parents of twelve children.

i ORSON WALDO, b. 26 Dec 1800; d. 29 Dec 1800.

ii LYDIA WALDO, b. at Edmeston, NY, 25 May 1802; d. at Wyalusing, PA, 4 May 1883; m. at Hoopers Valley, NY, 23 Sep 1825, her first cousin, ORSON WALDO, b. at Edmeston, 17 Mar 1802 son of John and Betsey (Clark) Waldo;[2881] Orson d. at Moravia, NY, 24 Dec 1871.

iii CECIL WALDO, b. at Edmeston, 18 Mar 1804; d. at Pulaski, MI, 5 May 1891; m. at Portageville, NY, 12 Feb 1829, CORNELIA SMITH, b. at Pawlet, VT, 15 May 1806 daughter of Whiting and Eunice (Winchester) Smith; Cornelia d. at Litchfield, MI, 24 Apr 1882.

iv HORATIO NELSON WALDO, b. at Edmeston, 21 Feb 1806; d. at Arcade, NY, 18 Sep 1895; m. at Arcade, NY, 8 Oct 1829, EUNICE UPHAM, b. at Rushford, NY, 2 Apr 1815 daughter of Samuel and Polly (Hardy) Upham; Eunice d. at Arcade, 2 Feb 1899. Horatio was a woolen manufacturer known for the development of "Arcade cloth".[2882]

v SIMEON SMITH WALDO, b. at Edmeston, 31 Oct 1807; d. at Saugerties, NY, 17 Oct 1832.

vi EMELINE WALDO, b. 24 Sep 1809; d. 23 Jun 1813.

vii JOHN L. WALDO, b. at Edmeston, 16 Apr 1811; d. at Genesee Falls, NY, 7 Sep 1894; m. at Berkshire, NY, 28 Mar 1837, MARY BALL, b. at Berkshire, 9 Jul 1815 daughter of Josiah and Lucy (Leonard) Ball; Mary d. at Genesee Falls, 13 May 1887.

viii ESTHER WALDO, b. 1 Dec 1812; d. at Attleborough, MA, 4 Sep 1902; m. at West Newark, NY, 14 Feb 1838, HERBERT RICHARDSON, b. at Attleborough, 20 Mar 1810 son of William and Millie (Capron) Richardson; Herbert d. at Newark Valley, NY, 28 Dec 1883.

ix RUTH WALDO, b. 25 Mar 1814; d. 26 Mar 1814.

x LYMAN B. WALDO, b. 9 Apr 1815; d. at West Troy, Ny, 9 Jul 1879; m. 8 Jul 1847, MARY SMITH MCENTEE, b. at Whitestown, NY, 23 Sep 1821 daughter of Philip and Lucy (Douglas) McEntee; Mary d. at Troy, 21 Oct 1891.

xi GEORGE FREDERICK WALDO, b. 17 Apr 1817; d. at Waverly, NY, 21 Apr 1891; m. at Newark Valley, 3 Oct 1838, HANNAH RICHARDSON, b. at Attleborough, 13 Sep 1813 daughter of William and Millie (Capron) Richardson; Hannah d. at Waverly, 6 Apr 1908.

xii ABIGAIL SMITH WALDO, b. at Berkshire, NY, 6 Jul 1820; d. at Warren, PA, 8 Oct 1911; m. 1st at Candor, NY, 4 Mar 1846, WILLIAM AUGUSTUS DELAND, b. at Candor, NY, 20 Aug 1820 son of Levi and Hannah (Brown)

[2877] U.S., Civil War Pension Index: General Index to Pension Files, 1861-1934

[2878] Lincoln, *Genealogy of the Waldo Family*, p 385

[2879] New York Land Records, Otsego County, T:105, S:402

[2880] Year: 1850; Census Place: Genesee Falls, Wyoming, New York; Roll: 617; Page: 246a; Year: 1860; Census Place: Genesee Falls, Wyoming, New York; Page: 403

[2881] Lincoln, *Genealogy of the Waldo Family*, p 596

[2882] Beers, *History of Wyoming County, New York*, p 124

Deland; William d. at Fairport, NY, 17 Nov 1857. Abigail m. 2nd at Maine, NY, 8 Feb 1860, STILES MCCOY, b. at Otsego County, NY, 2 Feb 1820 son of Timothy and Martha (Peck) McCoy; Stiles d. at Newark Valley, 5 May 1897.

887)   SIMEON SMITH (*Simeon Smith⁴, Zerviah Russell Smith³, Benjamin², Robert¹*), b. at Ashford, 12 Apr 1779 son of Simeon and Anna (Byles) Smith; d. at Granby, MA, 3 Jan 1853 at age 74; m. at Ashford, 23 Feb 1804, SARAH "SALLY" HAWES, b. at Ashford, 22 Sep 1781 daughter of Eli and Susannah (Bigelow) Hawes;[2883] Sarah d. at Granby, 19 Jan 1845.

Simeon and Sarah resided in Ashford where Simeon was a farmer. Late in life, Simeon and Sarah were in Granby with their daughter Sarah and her husband Peter Pease, Simeon listed with them in the 1850 census.[2884]

Son Ezra Easton Smith entered the employ of his uncle William Bigelow. After his uncle's death, Ezra and his brother William B. Smith were in the fire insurance business together.[2885]

There are records of five children of Simeon Smith and Sally Hawes born at Ashford.

i   SUSAN SMITH, b. 16 Sep 1804; d. at Stafford, CT, 8 Mar 1842; m. at Monson, MA, 11 Apr 1827, AUSTIN BLISS STEBBINS, b. at Wilbraham, 17 May 1802 son of Augustus and Martha (Bliss) Stebbins;[2886] Austin d. at Stafford, 12 Mar 1852.

ii   ANNA SMITH, b. 20 Aug 1806; d. at Granby, MA, 19 May 1871. Anna did not marry.

iii SARAH "SALLY" SMITH, b. 21 Jul 1809; d. at Granby, 10 Nov 1878; m. at Granby, 7 Sep 1831, PETER PEASE, b. at Longmeadow, MA, 3 Sep 1803 son of John and Nancy (Combs) Pease; Peter d. at Granby, 30 Mar 1872.

iv   WILLIAM B. SMITH, b. 4 Sep 1814; d. at East Hartford, 1886; m. MARY M. RICH, b. Oct 1827 daughter of William and Minerva (Blinn) Rich (per death record); Mary d. at Holyoke, MA (resident of Granby), 21 Dec 1916. In his will, William directed that an appropriate monument be erected for himself and his wife at the burial plot in East Hartford owned by William and his brother Ezra E. Smith. The remainder of the estate is left in trust to his wife Mary M. Smith, brother Ezra E. Smith, and William H. Olmstead with as much of the estate as needed to be used for the comfortable support of his wife. After her decease, any residue of the estate is allotted to the trustees of the Methodist Episcopal Society, brother Ezra E. Smith, niece Jennie Smith wife of Stacy Smith, nephew Ernest E. Smith, Julia Stebbins wife of Andrew Stebbins, Maria Chaffee widow of Philo Chaffee, and nieces Harriet Kellogg and Sarah Dickinson.[2887] Harriet Kellogg and Sarah Dickinson were daughters of William's sister Sally and her husband Peter Pease. Julia Stebbins was Julia Wait the wife of Andrew J. Stebbins son of William's sister Susan Smith and her husband Austin Stebbins. Maria Chafee was widow of William Smith's first cousin Philo Chaffee.

v   EZRA EASTON SMITH, b. 20 Nov 1820; d. at Brookline, MA, 20 Aug 1894; m. at East Hartford, 4 May 1847, MARY ELIZABETH BRYANT, b. at East Hartford, 1825 daughter of Ebenezer and Freelove (Smith) Bryant; Mary d. at Newton, MA, 18 Oct 1905.

888)   MATILDA SMITH (*Simeon Smith⁴, Zerviah Russell Smith³, Benjamin², Robert¹*), b. at Ashford, 26 Jun 1781 daughter of Simeon and Anna (Byles) Smith; d. at Ashford, 10 Aug 1861; m. at Ashford, 25 Nov 1802, ELIJAH WHITON, b. at Ashford, 3 Apr 1778 son of Joseph and Johannah (Chaffee) Whiton; Elijah d. at Ashford, 7 Sep 1854.

Elijah and Matilda resided in Ashford where they kept a farm. In 1820, they were a household of nine in Ashford: one male 26 to 44, one female 26 to 44, one female 45 and over, two males under 10, one male 10 to 15, two females under 10, and one female 16 to 25.[2888] In 1850, Matilda and Elijah were living in Ashford with their daughter Harriet Storrs living with them. Elijah is listed as insane on the census record.[2889]

Matilda Smith and Elijah Whiton were parents of nine children born at Ashford.

i   SOPHRONIA WHITON, b. 6 Mar 1803; d. at East Hartford, 16 Oct 1887; m. at Ashford, 10 Apr 1823, STEPHEN SAUNDERS, b. at Ashford, 1793 son of Esek and Abigail (Angell) Saunders; Stephen d. at East Hartford, 26 Feb 1875.

[2883] The 1825 will/probate of Eli Hawes includes bequests to daughter Sarah Smith and son-in-law Simeon Smith; Connecticut Wills and Probate, Stafford Probate District, Town of Willington, Estate of Eli Hawes, 1825, No. 995
[2884] Year: 1850; Census Place: Granby, Hampshire, Massachusetts; Roll: 321; Page: 294a
[2885] Connecticut Town Birth and Marriage Records, Barbour Collection, East Hartford Vital Records, p 92
[2886] Greenlee and Greenlee, *The Stebbins Genealogy*, p 352
[2887] Connecticut Wills and Probate, Hartford County, volume 117, pp 227-228, will of William B. Smith
[2888] 1820 U S Census; Census Place: Ashford, Windham, Connecticut; Page: 443; NARA Roll: M33_3; Image: 348
[2889] Year: 1850; Census Place: Ashford, Windham, Connecticut; Roll: 51; Page: 222a

ii SIMEON WHITON, b. 13 Apr 1804; d. at Ashford, 1871; m. at Bloomfield, 18 Oct 1832, CORDELIA BIDWELL, b. 24 Jan 1807 and baptized at Bloomfield, 1809 daughter of James and Lovicia (Swetland) Bidwell;[2890] Cordelia d. at New York, NY, 8 Oct 1853.

iii CALISTA WHITON, b. 1806; d. 2 Aug 1808.

iv AUGUSTUS WHITON, b. 25 Aug 1807; d. at Bloomfield, CT, 1 Jul 1885; m. at East Windsor, 1 May 1834, HARRIET FOSTER, b. at East Windsor, 20 Sep 1810 daughter of William and Eunice (Dart) Foster; Harriet d. at Bloomfield, 17 Apr 1886.

v MATILDA WHITON, b. 15 Feb 1810; d. 1 Oct 1841; m. at Ashford, 8 May 1833, NATHAN BELCHER HUNTINGTON (*Zerviah Smith Huntington⁵, Simeon Smith⁴, Zerviah Russell Smith³, Benjamin², Robert¹*), b. at Ashford, 23 Feb 1810 son of Andrew and Zerviah (Smith) Huntington; Nathan d. at Geneseo, IL, 10 Aug 1885. Nathan married second Rebecca Willard and married third Jane Charevoy.

vi MARIA WHITON, b. 13 Mar 1812; d. at South Windsor, 9 Oct 1898; m. at Ashford, 4 Jan 1837, REUBEN GREEN, b. at South Windsor, 1798 son of Asahel and Grace (Grant) Green; Reuben d. at South Windsor, 16 May 1860.

vii ELIJAH WHITON, b. 1814; d. 27 Oct 1815.

viii HENRY WHITON, b. 29 Oct 1817; d. at Hampton, 21 Apr 1839; m. at Hampton, 25 Jan 1839, JERUSHA HODGKINS FULLER, b. at Hampton, 23 Aug 1815 daughter of John and Jerusha (Hodgkins) Fuller; Jerusha d. at Ashford, 24 Jun 1881. Jerusha married second Ashbel Whitton.

ix HARRIET WHITON, b. 26 Feb 1826; d. at Dunsmore, PA, 24 Jan 1893; m. at Ashford, 14 Jun 1850, WILLIAM READ STORRS, b. at Ashford, 28 Dec 1824 son of William and Harriet (Woodward) Storrs; William d. at Scranton, 9 Aug 1905.

889) HANNAH SMITH (*Simeon Smith⁴, Zerviah Russell Smith³, Benjamin², Robert¹*), b. at Ashford, 14 Apr 1789 daughter of Simeon and Anna (Byles) Smith; d. at Ashford, 22 Aug 1873; m. at Ashford, 22 Mar 1822, EBENEZER CHAFFEE, b. at Ashford, 29 Nov 1796 son of Abner and Judith (Walker) Chaffee; Ebenezer d. at Mansfield, CT, 26 Sep 1875.

Ebenezer and Hannah kept a farm in Ashford. In 1830, Ebenezer headed a household of five persons in Ashford: one male 30 to 39, one female 30 to 39, one female 60 to 69 (who was perhaps Ebenezer's mother Judith), one male under 5, and one female 5 to 9.[2891] In 1870, Hannah and Ebenezer were living in Ashford with their daughter Maryette Lyon and granddaughter Jennie Lyon aged 19 years (who was Maryette's adopted daughter) living with them. Real estate was valued at $2,000.[2892]

Ebenezer did not leave a will and his estate was administered by Philo Chaffee. The estate was valued at $2,558.72.[2893]

Hannah and Ebenezer were parents of two children born at Ashford.

i MARYETTE CHAFFEE, b. at Ashford, 9 Dec 1822; d. at Ashford, 19 Mar 1891; m. 1846, WARREN WHITE LYON, b. at Holland, MA, 11 Jul 1817 son of Parley and Phebe (Preston) Lyon; Warren d. at Brooklyn, NY, 9 Nov 1864. In her will, Maryette left her estate to her adopted daughter Jennie E. Clark wife of Dyer H, Clark during her life and the property then to go to Jennie's daughter Maud H. Clark. If Maud pre-deceases her mother, the estate goes to the nieces and nephews of her late husband Warren Lyon.[2894]

ii PHILO CHAFFEE, b. at Ashford, 5 Aug 1826; d. at Mansfield, CT, 28 Jan 1880; m. at Ashford, 10 Sep 1851, MARY A. H. CADY, b. at Hartford, CT, 9 Nov 1832 daughter of Hiram and Miriam (Knowlton) Cady; Mary d. at Mount Hope (Mansfield), 13 Apr 1916. Philo and Mary had three daughters one of whom died in childhood. Philo and Mary divorced, and Mary resumed use of the name Mary A. Cady. Mary petitioned for divorce 19 Dec 1864 on grounds of Philo's adultery with Sarah Reuss.[2895] Philo married second, 1865, SARAH MARIA RUSS, b. at Chaplin, CT, 11 Apr 1843 daughter of John F. and Nancy (Ames) Russ; Sarah d. at Putnam, CT, 23 Jan 1916. Sarah married second Holden H. Lippitt. Philo's will names his two daughters form his marriage to Mary Cady, Eva Elvira and Henrietta, and his wife Sarah Mariah Chaffee.[2896]

[2890] Stiles, *Families of Ancient Windsor*, volume II, p 73

[2891] Year: 1830; Census Place: Ashford, Windham, Connecticut; Series: M19; Roll: 11; Page: 175; Family History Library Film: 0002804

[2892] Year: 1870; Census Place: Ashford, Windham, Connecticut; Roll: M593_116; Page: 288B

[2893] Connecticut Wills and Probate, Mansfield Probate District, Town of Mansfield, Estate of Ebenezer Chaffee, 1875, No. 173

[2894] Connecticut Wills and Probate, Ashford Probate District, Town of Ashford, Estate of Maryette Lyon, 1891, No. 183

[2895] Knox, Grace Louise, *Connecticut Divorces: Superior Court Records for the Counties of New London, Tolland & Windham, 1719-1910*, 1987, Heritage Books, p 284

[2896] Connecticut Wills and Probate, Mansfield Probate District, Town of Mansfield, Estate of Philo Chaffee, 1881, No. 177

Great-Grandchildren of Hannah Russell and Oliver Holt

890)   SUSANNAH HOLT (*Nathaniel Holt⁴, Oliver Holt³, Hannah Russell Holt², Robert¹*), b. at Andover, 11 May 1755 daughter of Nathaniel and Elizabeth (Stevens) Holt; m. 18 Apr 1776; CARLTON PARKER, baptized at Reading, 1750 son of Timothy and Priscilla (Carleton) Parker; Carlton d. at Andover, 23 Dec 1809.

      Susannah and Carlton resided in Andover where Susannah was admitted as a member of South Church on 12 September 1776.[2897] Susanna and Carlton were parents of ten children born at Andover.

i   KENDALL PARKER, baptized 13 Oct 1776; d. at Medford, MA, 28 May 1855; m. at Medford, 20 May 1800, JOANNA FLOYD, b. at Medford, 4 May 1780 daughter of Benjamin and Rebecca (Greenleaf) Floyd; Joanna d. at Medford, 14 Jul 1845.

ii   TIMOTHY PARKER, b. 1779; d. at sea, 1806. "Timothy, s. Carlton, 'at sea of the yellow fever as he was returning from W. Indies,' bur. May 11, 1806, a. 27 y."

iii   CARLTON PARKER, b. 1782; d. at Andover, 24 May 1788.

iv   ANNA PARKER, b. Nov 1784; d. at Andover of "nervous fever", 12 Sep 1799.

v   NATHANIEL PARKER, baptized 28 Sep 1788; d. after 1860 when he was living at Concord, NH; m. at Concord, NH, 8 Apr 1818, BETSEY UNDERHILL, b. at Chester, NH, 1796; Betsey d. after 1860.

vi   ELIZABETH PARKER, baptized 9 Aug 1789

vii CARLTON PARKER, baptized 12 Jun 1791; d. after 1860 when he was living in Concord, NH. In 1850, he was living with his brother Nathaniel and his family; Carlton does not seem to have married.

viii JOSEPH PARKER, baptized 12 May 1793; d. at Andover, 15 Aug 1812.

ix   PRISCILLA PARKER, baptized 31 Dec 1797; d. at Newbury, MA, 26 Apr 1835; m. at Newbury, 11 Nov 1820, JONATHAN MARTIN, b. at Bedford, NH, 7 May 1796 son of Jonathan and Lucy (-) Martin; Jonathan d. at Newbury, 10 Jan 1881. Jonathan married second Abigail Woodbury.

x   CHARLES PARKER, baptized 21 Dec 1800; d. at the almshouse at Andover, 16 Jun 1827.

891)   CHLOE HOLT (*Nathaniel Holt⁴, Oliver Holt³, Hannah Russell Holt², Robert¹*), baptized at Andover, 21 Sep 1766 daughter of Nathaniel and Elizabeth (Stevens) Holt; d. at Andover, 11 Apr 1855; m. 1ˢᵗ at Andover, 20 Apr 1789, DAVID WILEY who d. by about 1799. Chloe m. 2ⁿᵈ 25 Feb 1800, her fourth cousin, JOHN HOLT, b. at Andover, 22 Feb 1769 son of David and Hannah (Martin) Holt; John d. at Andover, 21 Oct 1815. Chloe m. 3ʳᵈ 21 Jul 1821, her fourth cousin, JOHN FRYE, b. at Andover, 16 Aug 1754 son of Ebenezer and Elizabeth (Kimball) Frye; John d. 26 Mar 1843. John Frye was first married to Lydia Batchelder.

      David Wiley and Chloe Holt were parents of two children.

i   JAMES WILEY, baptized at Andover, 28 Feb 1790; d. at Andover, 9 Jan 1850; m. at Boston, 19 Nov 1825, his first cousin, PHEBE FOSTER HOLT (*Nathaniel Holt⁵, Nathaniel Holt⁴, Oliver Holt³, Hannah Russell Holt², Robert¹*), b. at Andover, 27 Jul 1795 daughter of Nathaniel and Mehitable (Foster) Holt; Phebe d. at Millville, MA, 1870.

ii   DAVID WILEY, baptized at Andover, 9 Oct 1791; d. at Ashby, MA, 14 Oct 1864; m. at Reading, 25 May 1815, MARY BUXTON, b. about 1791 daughter of Ebenezer and Susanna (Damon) Buxton;[2898] Mary d. at Ashby, 8 Aug 1865.

      Chloe Holt and John Holt were parents of one child.

i   DEBORAH HOLT, baptized at Andover, 22 Nov 1801; d. at Newburyport, 26 Mar 1860; m. at Andover, 2 Sep 1830, JOHN P. FRYE, b. at Andover, 7 Oct 1805 the out-of-wedlock son of Dolly Frye and Jonathan Perkins Chapman; John d. at Andover, 6 Jan 1883.[2899] John's mother Dolly Frye may be Dolly born in 1786 who was the daughter of Deborah Holt's stepfather John Frye and his first wife Lydia Batchelder.

[2897] South Church, Historical Manual of South Church of Andover
[2898] The names of Mary's parents are given as Ebenezer and Susan on her death record.
[2899] John Frye's death record lists his as illegitimate and the names of parents as Perkins and Dolly Frye.

892)   NATHANIEL HOLT (*Nathaniel Holt⁴, Oliver Holt³, Hannah Russell Holt², Robert¹*), b. at Andover, 6 Apr 1769 son of Nathaniel and Elizabeth (Stevens) Holt; d. at Andover, 24 May 1829; m. at Andover, 3 Mar 1791, his third cousin, MEHITABLE FOSTER, b. at Andover, 17 Sep 1772 daughter of Dudley and Rachel (Steel) Foster; Mehitable d. at Andover, 16 Aug 1859.

Mehitable Foster and Nathaniel Holt were parents of twelve children born at Andover.

i   DUDLEY FOSTER HOLT, b. 6 Dec 1791; d. at Haverhill, 10 Dec 1856; m. 1st, 14 Jun 1813, SALLY BRADLEY who has not been identified; Sally d. by 1821. Dudley m. 2nd, 25 Apr 1822, JUDITH A. CHASE, b. at Haverhill, about 1796 daughter of Josiah and Ruth (Bradley) Chase; Judith d. at Haverhill, 31 Oct 1864.

ii   NATHANIEL HOLT, b. 6 Aug 1793; d. 28 Nov 1813. Nathaniel served in the War of 1812 and died in service: "Nathaniel, jr., d. in the Army, Nov. 28, 1813, a. 21 y."[2900]

iii   PHEBE FOSTER HOLT, b. 27 Jul 1795; d. at Millville, MA, 1870; m. at Boston, 19 Nov 1825, her first cousin, JAMES WILEY, b. at Andover, Feb 1790 son of David and Chloe (Holt) Wiley; James d. at Andover, 9 Jan 1850.

iv   ELIPHALET MARTIN HOLT, b. 15 Jul 1797; d. at Andover, 8 Feb 1868; m. at Haverhill, 31 Mar 1829, MARY ANN COLBY, b. at Haverhill, 1 Sep 1806 daughter of Ephraim and Lydia (Chase) Colby; Mary Ann d. at North Andover, 4 Apr 1872.

v   POLLY HOLT, b. 2 Jun 1799; d. at Andover, 9 Mar 1826. Polly did not marry.

vi   HANNAH HOLT, b. 16 Sep 1801; m. at Boston, 14 Dec 1824, JAMES FRAZER who has not been identified.

vii   ELIZABETH HOLT, b. 7 Jan 1804; d. at Andover, 15 Sep 1832. Elizabeth did not marry. She was deaf and died of consumption. "Elizabeth [deaf and dumb, consumption, C.R.1.], Sept. 15, 1832."

viii   CHARLES HOLT, b. 17 Jun 1806; d. at Exeter, NH, after 1870; m. 1st, about 1834, MELINDA TUCKER, b. at Plaistow, NH, 4 Jul 1812 daughter of Elisha and Mehitable (Davis) Tucker; Melinda d. at Amesbury, 2 Nov 1848. Charles m. 2nd, at Amesbury, 11 May 1849, NANCY SANBORN, b. at Exeter, NH, 1809 daughter of Jesse and Elizabeth (Lovering) Sanborn; Nancy d. at Haverhill, 12 Jan 1892.

ix   SUSANNA HOLT, b. 23 Aug 1808; d. after 1860; m. 9 Sep 1832, WILLIAM FRYE, b. at Andover, 26 Oct 1801 son of Philip and Sarah Smith (Wilkins) Frye; William d. at Andover, 26 Sep 1844.

x   TIMOTHY PARKER HOLT, b. 27 Feb 1811; d. at Andover, 23 Nov 1892; m. at Andover, 27 Nov 1834, MARY H. LOVEJOY, b. at Andover, 24 Sep 1811 daughter of Orlando and Abiah (Gray) Lovejoy; Mary d. at Andover, 4 Feb 1888.

xi   REBECCA HOLT, b. 29 Nov 1813; d. at Stoughton, MA, 19 Jul 1886; m. 1st, 15 Sep 1834, JOSEPH STEVENS, b. at Andover, 20 Feb 1801 son of Joseph and Phebe (Frye) Stevens; Joseph d. at Andover, 13 Jul 1849. Rebecca m. 2nd, at Tisbury, 14 Jun 1853, BENJAMIN MAGOON who was b. at Kingston, NH about 1807.

xii   HARRIET BRADSTREET HOLT, b. 11 Nov 1816; d. 17 Oct 1826.

893)   EUNICE HOLT (*Oliver Holt⁴, Oliver Holt³, Hannah Russell Holt², Robert¹*), b. at Wilton, 25 Jul 1764 daughter of Oliver and Eunice (Raymond) Holt; d. at Andover, VT, 18 Jun 1798; m. at Wilton, 18 Dec 1794, JOSEPH FULLER, b. at Middleton, MA, 21 Jul 1760 son of Amos and Hannah (Putnam) Fuller. Joseph married second about 1799, Submit.

Joseph and Eunice were parents of two children. Joseph also had three children with his second wife Submit.

i   SUSANNA FULLER, b. at Wilton, NH, 25 Feb 1795; d. after 1850 when living at Manchester, VT and before 1860; m. at Andover, VT, 27 Aug 1815, AMOS RIDEOUT, b. in NH, 1793 son of Benjamin and Sarah (Taylor) Rideout; Amos d. after 1860.

ii   EUNICE FULLER, b. at Andover, VT, 15 Apr 1796; d. at South Burlington, VT, 26 May 1868; m. ELEAZER STUART, b. 1786 son of Thaddeus Stuart; Eleazer d. at South Burlington, 4 Sep 1849.

894)   OLIVER HOLT (*Oliver Holt⁴, Oliver Holt³, Hannah Russell Holt², Robert¹*), b. at Wilton, 13 Feb 1776 son of Oliver and Eunice (Raymond) Holt; d. at Ellenburg, NY, 24 Jun 1837; m. at Andover, VT, 16 Apr 1804, PHEBE HASELTINE, b. about 1786; Phebe d. after 1850 when she was living in Elleburg with her son Raymond and his family.

There are records for three children of Oliver and Phebe born at Andover, Vermont.[2901]

[2900] Massachusetts: Vital Records, 1621-1850
[2901] Vermont, Vital Records, 1720-1908

i   JERUSHA HOLT, b. 22 Sep 1804; d. at Ellenburg, NY, 14 Mar 1877; m. at Andover, VT, 8 Jan 1829, CYRUS HESSELTINE, b. at Andover, 17 Oct 1804 son of David and Rachel (McIntire) Haseltine; Cyrus d. at Ellenburg, 17 May 1888.

ii   ISRAEL W. HOLT, b. 28 Feb 1806; d. at Ellenburg, NY, 20 Jun 1869; m. about 1832, ABIGAIL R. EATON, b. at Cavendish, VT, 28 Dec 1803 daughter of Kimball and Mary (Page) Eaton; Abigail d. at Ellenburg, 27 Jan 1899.

iii   BOANERGES RAIMOND "RAYMOND B." HOLT, b. 13 May 1810; d. at Casnovia, MI, 6 Dec 1886; m. RUTH EWING, b. in NH, 1810 daughter of Peter and Judith (Hall) Ewing;[2902] Ruth d. at Sparta, MI, 8 Jan 1892. At age 23, Raymond moved to Ellenburg, New York where he had a farm and mill and raised his family there for 53 years. Toward the end of his life, he went to Casnovia, Michigan with his son Israel and daughter Louisa.[2903]

895)   ELIPHALET GRAY (*Beulah Holt Gray⁴, Oliver Holt³, Hannah Russell Holt², Robert¹*), b. about 1771 perhaps at Milton, NH and baptized at Salem, MA, 13 May 1787 son of John and Beulah (Holt) Gray; m. about 1795, MARY "POLLY" COOLIDGE, b. at Watertown, MA, 5 Sep 1767 daughter of Simon and Mary (Jennison) Coolidge.[2904] Eliphalet was in Jay, Maine in 1810 but is thought to have gone to Carthage after that.

      Eliphalet and Mary had six children born at Jay, Maine.[2905] In the 1810 census of Jay, Eliphalet was head of a household of ten: two males 26 to 44, one female 26 to 44, one female over 45, three males under 10, one male 10 to 15, and two females 10 to 15.[2906]

i   OLIVE GRAY, b. 1796; d. at Carthage, ME, 2 Mar 1848; m. BENJAMIN WINTER, b. at Jay, 28 Aug 1792 son of Joseph and Elizabeth (Carver) Winter;[2907] Benjamin d. at Carthage, 5 Jul 1844.

ii   OLIVER HOLT GRAY, b. 6 Nov 1797

iii   PHEBE GRAY, b. 8 Oct 1799; d. at South Easton, MA, 25 Oct 1853; m. 1st about 1819, JOSEPH WINTER, b. at Jay, 28 May 1794 son of Joseph and Elizabeth (Carver) Winter;[2908] Joseph d. at Carthage, 5 Jun 1845. Phebe m. 2nd at West Bridgewater, MA, 26 Oct 1851, JACOB WILLIAMS, b. at Mansfield, MA, 12 Apr 1791 son of Jacob and Experience (White) Williams; Jacob d. at Middleborough, MA, 20 May 1856.

iv   AARON GRAY, b. 4 Jul 1801

v   JOHN GRAY, b. 1803; d. at Rockland, MA, 4 Feb 1882; m. about 1829, HULDAH REED, b. at Weld, 12 Jul 1807 daughter of Amaziah and Rhoda (Delano) Reed;[2909] Huldah d. at Carthage, ME, 4 Mar 1848.

vi   SAMUEL GRAY, b. 15 Apr 1806

896)   URIAH HOLT GRAY (*Beulah Holt Gray⁴, Oliver Holt³, Hannah Russell Holt², Robert¹*), b. about 1784 and baptized at Salem, MA, 13 May 1787 son of John and Beulah (Holt) Gray; d. at Jay, ME, after 1840; m. about 1807, ANNA DAVENPORT, b. at Winthrop, ME, 13 Jul 1786 daughter of Ebenezer and Mary (Crane) Davenport;[2910] Anna d. at Jay, 1866.

      Uriah Gray and Anna Davenport were parents of ten children born at Jay, Maine.[2911]

i   ELIJAH DAVENPORT GRAY, b. 22 Dec 1808; d. 1831.

ii   HENRY CRANE GRAY, b. 6 Dec 1810; d. at Jay, 3 Mar 1887; m. ANNA MARIA DAVENPORT, b. at Jay, 1815 daughter of Elijah and Mercy (Towne) Davenport;[2912] Anna d. at Jay, 22 Apr 1902.

[2902] Gage, *A Record of Pierce Gage and His Descendants*, p 20. The names of Ruth's parents are given as Peter and Julia Ewing on her death record.

[2903] Israel M. Holt, "The Late Raymond B. Holt" obituary

[2904] Bond, *Genealogies of the Families and Descendants of the Early Settlers of Watertown*, p 175

[2905] "Maine Births and Christenings, 1739-1900", database, *FamilySearch*

[2906] Year: 1810; Census Place: Jay, Oxford, Maine; Roll: 12; Page: 446; Image: 00450; Family History Library Film: 0218683

[2907] "Maine Births and Christenings, 1739-1900", database, *FamilySearch* (https://familysearch.org/ark:/61903/1:1:F44Q-CL4 : 14 January 2020), Benjamin Winter, 1792.

[2908] "Maine Births and Christenings, 1739-1900", database, *FamilySearch* (https://familysearch.org/ark:/61903/1:1:F44Q-8YD : 14 January 2020), Joseph Winter, 1794.

[2909] "Maine Births and Christenings, 1739-1900", database, *FamilySearch* (https://familysearch.org/ark:/61903/1:1:F44C-625 : 14 January 2020), Huldah Reed, 1807. This index lists mother's name as Jedidiah Bumpus who was the second wife of Amaziah Reed, but they did not marry until 1809. Amaziah's first wife Rhoda Delano died following Huldah's birth. This index is taken from the Weld town family records.

[2910] Stackpole, *History of Winthrop, Maine*, p 343

[2911] The youngest child, Vesta M. Gray, is presumed to be a child in this family given that she was in Jay, is of an age to be in this family, there is no other obvious Gray family to which she might belong, and she married the brother of the husband of Ann Gray.

[2912] The names of Anna's parents are given on her death record as Elijah and Mercy.

iii   CHARLOTTE GRAY, b. 20 Feb 1813

iv   ELIAS B. GRAY, b. 22 Jun 1815; d. at Jay, 5 Aug 1882; m. about 1843, ANN C. RICHARDSON, b. 4 Jun 1820 daughter of Jonathan F. and Lucinda (Goding) Richardson;[2913] Ann d. at Jay, 27 Dec 1870.

v   NATHAN GRAY, b. 1817; d. at Jay, 16 Oct 1872; m. about 1838, ANN H. CHILDS, b. at Jay, 19 Sep 1816 daughter of Howland and Achsah (Wing) Childs; Ann d. at Jay, Dec 1861. Nathan m. 2nd ABIGAIL A., b. about 1834 who has not been identified.

vi   DANIEL P. GRAY, b. 1820; d. at Stoughton, MA, 3 Sep 1895; m. FLORA LUDDEN, b. at Canton, ME, about 1823 daughter of Jacob and Lydia (Soule) Ludden;[2914] Flora d. at Stoughton, 19 Sep 1908.

vii   ANN D. GRAY, b. 1823; d. at Norridgewock, ME, 21 Oct 1871; m. SAMUEL W. WALKER, b. about 1824 son of Samuel W. and Elizabeth (Jenkins) Walker; Samuel d. at Norridgewock, 1879.

viii   CHARLES GRAY, b. 1826; d. at Jay, 13 May 1892; m. MARY DAVENPORT, b. Apr 1835 daughter of Samuel W. and Lovina (Cole) Davenport;[2915] d. at Jay, 24 Dec 1912.

ix   MARY M. GRAY, b. 9 Dec 1828; d. at St. Louis, MO, 5 Jan 1896; m. at Turner, ME, 26 Jul 1853, JOHN PHILLIPS, b. in ME, 1827; John d. at St. Louis, 29 Nov 1885.

x   VESTA M. GRAY, b. 31 Mar 1831; d. at Jay, 14 Feb 1870; m. STEPHEN WALKER, b. 5 Feb 1832 son of Samuel W. and Elizabeth (Jenkins) Walker; Stephen d. (burial at Jay), 18 Feb 1871.

897)   PHINEHAS WHITNEY (*Sarah Holt Whitney⁴, Uriah Holt³, Hannah Russell Holt², Robert¹*), b. at Harvard, 3 Jul 1747 son of Jonathan and Sarah (Holt) Whitney; d. at Norway, ME, 21 May 1830; m. at Harvard, 31 Oct 1765, KEZIAH FARNSWORTH, likely b. at Harvard, 1 Jun 1742 daughter of Phineas and Azubah (Burt) Farnsworth; Keziah d. at Norway, 1827.

Phinehas and Keziah resided in Harvard where their children were born and then relocated to Norway, Maine in 1789.[2916]

Phinehas Whitney enlisted in 1776 from Harvard in the company of Capt. Joseph Moore and served one year. He re-enlisted on 1 April 1777 in the company of Capt. Benjamin Brown for three years followed immediately by a three-year enlistment in April 1780 in the company of Capt. Edmund White. He was discharged January 1783. He had rank of corporal. He had one further enlistment (not noted in the pension file) enlisted from Harvard 19 May 1775 in Capt. Joseph Moor's company and served 74 days.[2917] He was allowed pension based on his service effective 11 April 1818.[2918] He was reported as being at the Battle of Bunker Hill.[2919]

Phinehas did not leave a will and James French was named administrator of his estate on 19 October 1830.[2920] Phinehas and Keziah were parents of seven children born at Harvard.[2921]

i   MARY WHITNEY, b. at Harvard, 15 May 1766; d. at Waterford, ME, 6 May 1841; m. at Groton, MA, 16 Apr 1789, RICHARD BRYANT, b. at Kingston, MA, 6 Aug 1766 son of George and Sarah (Lodbell) Bryant;[2922] Richard d. at Waterford, 10 Aug 1815.

ii   ESTHER WHITNEY, baptized 13 Nov 1768; m. at Winslow, ME, 19 Aug 1786 (intention at Harvard, MA, 25 Feb 1786), EDMUND WENTWORTH likely son of Moses and Mindwell (Stone) Wentworth.

iii   SARAH WHITNEY, baptized 8 Jul 1770

iv   JONATHAN WHITNEY, baptized at Harvard, 21 Aug 1774; d. at Morgan County, OH, 15 Dec 1846; m. at Bridgton, ME, 16 Aug 1798, MARY E. GATES, b. at Bridgton, 29 Jul 1775 daughter of Stephen and Mary (Merrick) Gates; Mary d. at Bristol, OH, 1857.

v   RELIEF WHITNEY, baptized 18 Jun 1780

[2913] Vinton, *The Richardson Memorial*, p 168
[2914] The names of Flora's parents are given as Jacob Ludden and Lydia Soule on her death record.
[2915] The names of Mary's parents are given as Samuel W. Davenport and Lovina on her death record.
[2916] Whitman, *A History of Norway, Maine*, p 57
[2917] Massachusetts Solders and Sailors in the Revolution, volume 17, p 242
[2918] U. S. Revolutionary War Pension and Bounty-Land Warrant Application Files; Case S38463
[2919] Pierce, *Whitney: Descendants of John Whitney*, p 188
[2920] Maine Wills and Probate, Oxford County, Estate Files, Box 111, Estate of Phinehas Whitney, 1830
[2921] There is a Phinehas Whitney (1776-1848) of Presque Isle, ME who has been proposed as a child in this family, but his parentage is undetermined. http://wiki.whitneygen.org/wrg/index.php/Family:Whitney,_Phinehas_(1776-1848)
[2922] Smith, D. Alden, "Descendants of Stephen Bryant", NEHGR, volume 155, 2001, p 210

vi   OLIVER WHITNEY, baptized 4 Nov 1781

vii   ANNIS WHITNEY, b. 13 Feb 1785; d. at Norway, ME, 7 Feb 1846; m. JAMES FRENCH, b. 19 Dec 1785.

898)   SARAH WHITNEY (*Sarah Holt Whitney⁴, Uriah Holt³, Hannah Russell Holt², Robert¹*), b. at Harvard, 5 Aug 1751 daughter of Jonathan and Sarah (Holt) Whitney; likely m. at Harvard, 26 Aug 1771; JOHN MEAD, b. at Harvard, MA, 29 Jun 1749 son of Samuel and Hannah (Willard) Mead.

On 13 September 1773 (recorded 20 April 1779), Samuel Mead of Harvard with his wife Hannah conveyed to son John Mead for love, goodwill, and affection and consideration of £80, 40 acres in Harvard on which John then resided and is the property Samuel bought of Timothy Kneeland. On 23 July 1778 (recorded 25 February 1779), John Mead and wife Sally sold this property (matching description of location but described as about 45 acres) for £540 to Cyrus Fairbank.[2923] It seems that Sarah and John might have left Harvard at the time they sold their property, but that is not certain.

There are records for three children of Sarah and John born at Harvard.

i   JONATHAN MEAD, b. 11 Dec 1771

ii   SARAH MEAD, b. 25 Dec 1773; d. at Marlow, NH, 16 Feb 1859; m. at Harvard, 22 May 1794, PHINEHAS STONE, b. at Harvard, 29 Apr 1769 son of James and Deborah (Nutting) Stone; Phinehas d. at Marlow, 7 Oct 1841.

iii   JOHN MEAD, b. 9 Nov 1775; m. at Boston, 6 Oct 1799, MARY "POLLY" WILLIAMS, b. at Brookfield[2924] perhaps the Polly b. at Brookfield, 12 Sep 1778 daughter of Samuel and Eleanor (Wright) Williams.

899)   RELIEF WHITNEY (*Sarah Holt Whitney⁴, Uriah Holt³, Hannah Russell Holt², Robert¹*), b. at Harvard, 13 Nov 1758 daughter of Jonathan and Sarah (Holt) Whitney; d. at Harvard, 17 Apr 1818; m. at Harvard, 2 Jul 1780, JONAS WHITNEY, b. at Harvard, 3 Mar 1756 son of Jonas and Zebudah (Davis) Whitney; Jonas d. at Harvard, 26 Nov 1803.

Jonas and Relief resided in Harvard where Jonas was a blacksmith and had a gristmill. Jonas is reported as building the first aqueduct in Harvard laying wood pipes to carry water from a spring to his house.[2925]

Jonas served during the Revolution mustered from Harvard on 9 July 1778 as a private in the company of Capt. Nathan Fisher in Col. Wade's regiment which was stationed in Rhode Island. He was discharged on 1 January 1779. He is likely also the Jonas who served in Capt. Moore's company of light infantry which was involved in the occupation of Rhode Island.[2926]

Jonas Whitney's estate was administered by Benjamin Kimball at the request of widow Relief. The value of the real estate dower was appraised at $878.67 on 4 May 1805. Those signing agreement to the appraisal were Relief Whitney, Zebudah Whitney, Daniel Willard,[2927] and Francis Farr signing as guardian for minor children Jonas, Nabbe, Rachel, Salley, and Levi. Real estate was valued at $2,391.89 and personal estate at $779.06. The real estate was sold to settle the estate with debts of $2,169.81. Jonas Whitney minor over age fourteen selected Francis Farr as guardian who was also named guardian for Nabby, Sally, Rachel, and Levi.[2928]

The main creditors of the estate were Boston Bank and Thomas Hammond. Jonas had mortgaged a portion of his real property to Boston Bank on 10 July 1803 for a sum of $400 which was to be repaid in one year with interest. On 22 August 1803, Jonas had conveyed property that contained a grist mill, blacksmith part, and part of the dwelling house to Thomas Hammond for $500.[2929]

Relief Whitney did not leave a will and on 22 April 1818, "only son" Levi Whitney of Harvard requested that Francis Farr be named administrator. Personal estate was $76.07.[2930]

There are records of ten children of Relief and Jonas born at Harvard.

i   Infant, b. Aug 1780 and d. 4 Aug 1780.

ii   ZEBUDAH WHITNEY, b. 28 Feb 1782

iii   JONAS WHITNEY, b. 10 Jun 1784; d. at Harvard, 23 Sep 1807.

[2923] Massachusetts Land Records, Worcester County, 80:562; 80:470

[2924] U.S., Newspaper Extractions from the Northeast, 1704-1930

[2925] Pierce, *Whitney: The Descendants of John Whitney*, p 166

[2926] Massachusetts Soldiers and Sailors in the Revolution, volume 17, p 230

[2927] It is not clear who Daniel Willard is or why he would be signing agreement to the appraisal of the dower. Daniel Willard was one of the creditors of the estate, but not one of the major creditors (who were Boston Bank and Thomas Hammond).

[2928] *Worcester County, MA: Probate File Papers, 1731-1881*. Online database. AmericanAncestors.org. New England Historic Genealogical Society, 2015. Case 64936 and Case 64937

[2929] Massachusetts Land Records, Worcester County, 150:611, 151:658

[2930] *Worcester County, MA: Probate File Papers, 1731-1881*. Online database. AmericanAncestors.org. New England Historic Genealogical Society, 2015. Case 65100

iv ABIGAIL WHITNEY, b. 25 Mar 1786

v RACHEL WHITNEY, b. 17 Apr 1788; m. at Boston, 14 Feb 1814, SOLOMON RUSSELL who has not been identified.

vi SALLY WHITNEY, b. 26 Oct 1789. The Whitney genealogy reports that she married John Ellis (and that her Sophronia sister married John Ellis, also). However, Sophronia married Elisha Ellis. There is a record for Elisha Ellis marrying Sarah H. Whitney in Boston in 1829 and perhaps this is Sally's marriage.

vii LEVI WHITNEY, b. 23 Aug 1793; d. at Boston, 9 Aug 1876; m. in NY, 1839, MARY AIKEN, b. at Chester, NH, 20 Jun 1800 daughter of Samuel and Isabella (McDole) Aiken; Mary d. at Derry, NH, 30 Dec 1889.

viii EMILY WHITNEY, b. 23 Jan 1797; d. 6 Nov 1861; m. at Boston, 21 Mar 1818, as his second wife, BILLINGS CLAPP, b. 24 Oct 1790 son of Beriah and Nancy (Wild) Clapp; Billings d. at Enfield, ME, 21 Feb 1873. Billings was first married to Susan Shed and third married to Lorintha Bussell.

ix RELIEF WHITNEY, b. 4 Nov 1799; d. at Waltham, 25 Mar 1870; m. at Boston, 25 Sep 1826, GILLUM BARNES, b. in NH, 1800 (names of parents given as Luther and Ruth on death record); Gillum d. at Waltham, 11 Mar 1884.

x SOPHRONIA WHITNEY, b. 3 Sep 1802; d. at Boston, 23 Nov 1824; m. at Boston, 19 May 1822, ELISHA ELLIS, likely the Elisha b. about 1798 son of Elisha and Esther (-) Ellis; Elisha d. at Boston, 12 Feb 1868.

900) ABIGAIL WHITNEY (*Sarah Holt Whitney⁴, Uriah Holt³, Hannah Russell Holt², Robert¹*), b. at Harvard, 29 Jan 1763 daughter of Jonathan and Sarah (Holt) Whitney; m. at Harvard, 17 Nov 1789, BENJAMIN HOAR (later BENJAMIN WHITNEY), b. at Leominster, MA, 21 Sep 1757 son of Oliver and Silence (Houghton) Hoar.

On 3 March 1815, a special act was passed by the State of New York allowing Benjamin Hoar and each of the members of his family to legally change their name to Whitney. The family included Benjamin, his wife Abigail, and children Theophilus, Abel, Silence, Oliver, Polly, and Abigail. The family were residents of Cambridge, NY at that time.[2931]

On 29 August 1818, Benjamin Whitney, resident of Rush, New York aged fifty-four, made application for pension based on his Revolutionary War service. He enlisted in March 1781 from Pepperell in Massachusetts in an infantry company commanded by Lieut. Foster in the regiment of Col. Michael Jackson of the Massachusetts line. He was discharged October 1782. He was in no important battles. He provided a follow-up statement of 14 September 1821. At that time, he valued his estate at $13.90. His household was his wife age fifty-four and daughters aged 16 and 14. He was a farmer by occupation but was unable to work due to infirmity.[2932]

Abigail and Benjamin were parents of six children.

i THEOPHILUS WHITNEY, b. about 1790; living in 1815. Theophilus may have married ANNA who has not been identified.

ii ABEL WHITNEY, b. at Londonderry, VT, 29 Jun 1793; d. at Huron, NY, Jun 1880; m. 1st about 1820, PERMELIA HOWARD, b. 1799 likely daughter of Abel and Hephzibah (Curtis) Howard; Permelia d. 1849. Abel m. 2nd about 1850, Permelia's sister, ANN MARIE HOWARD, b. at Jackson, NY, 11 Jun 1820; Ann d. at Crab Orchard, NE, 26 Jun 1890.

iii SILENCE WHITNEY, b. at Londonderry, VT, 17 Jun 1795; d. after 1870 when living at Shelbyville, MO. Silence did not marry. She was living with her brother Oliver in 1860.

iv OLIVER WINSHIP FRANCIS WHITNEY, b. at Londonderry, VT, 17 Jun 1799; d. at Republican City, NE, 3 Feb 1877; m. 1830, RACHEL WESTFALL, b. at Knox, NY, 7 Jul 1808 daughter of Solomon and Eva (Warner) Wesphall; Rachel d. at Republican City, 29 Mar 1899.

v MARY "POLLY" WHITNEY, b. 15 Sep 1801; d. at Shelbyville, MO, 31 Jan 1865; m. 10 Feb 1833, EZRA SAYRE, b. at Elizabeth, NJ, 21 Oct 1800 son of Jonathan and Betsey (Pitney) Sayre; Ezra d. at Shelbyville, 18 Jun 1864. Ezra was first married to Sophia Westfall the sister of Oliver's wife (see just above).

vi ABIGAIL WHITNEY, b. 2 May 1804; d. at Bethel, MO, 23 Apr 1870; m. at Shelby County, MO, 23 May 1855, WILLIAM HATFIELD, b. in NC, about 1806; William d. at Bethel, 1880.

901) RACHEL WHITNEY (*Sarah Holt Whitney⁴, Uriah Holt³, Hannah Russell Holt², Robert¹*), b. at Harvard, 19 Sep1767 daughter of Jonathan and Sarah (Holt) Whitney; d. (recorded at Harvard), Aug 1825; m. at Harvard, 7 Nov 1793, SALMON WILLARD, baptized at Harvard, 15 Jul 1770 son of Benjamin and Hannah (Godfrey) Willard; Salmon d. at Lancaster, MA, 10 Jul 1860. Salmon was second married to Mercy Kelly.

[2931] New York State, Laws of the State of New York: Revised and Passed at the Thirty-sixth Session of the Legislature, volume 3, p 60
[2932] U. S. Revolutionary War Pension and Bounty-Land Warrant Application Files, Case S44045

Rachel and Salmon resided at Lancaster, Massachusetts.

On 19 November 1838, Salmon Willard, with wife Mercy relinquishing her right of dower, sold to Abram C. Willard a farm in the northerly part of Lancaster consisting of about 45 acres for payment of four hundred and fifty dollars.[2933]

Salmon did not leave a will and his estate entered probate 2 October 1860 with Rowland Willard of Harvard as administrator as widow Mercy and heir Benjamin Willard declined administration. Real estate of an 80-acre farm in the northerly part of Lancaster was valued at $1,100 and personal estate at $237.78. The administrator petitioned to sell the real estate to settled debts and for administrative costs. Dower was set off to the widow 13 March 1861. James F. Stone was named guardian-ad-litem for Henry W. Willard, a minor, son of Henry Willard and an heir to the estate.[2934]

Rachel Whitney and Salmon Willard were parents of seven children born at Lancaster, Massachusetts.

i   BENJAMIN WILLARD, b. 9 Sep 1794; d. at Harvard, MA, 7 Oct 1866; m. at Cambridge, 29 Sep 1816, ABIGAIL WILDES, b. at Shirley, MA, 1 Oct 1774 daughter of Elijah and Eunice (Safford) Wildes; Abigail d. at Shirley, 12 Oct 1848.[2935] Benjamin and Abigail had one son.

ii   ABRAM CARLETON WILLARD, b. 7 Mar 1796; d. at Ashby, MA, 23 Jul 1863; m. 1st at Lancaster, 18 Apr 1820, SARAH FOLLANSBEE, b. 1792 daughter of Edward and Elizabeth (Taintor) Follansbee;[2936] Sarah d. at Lancaster, 4 Apr 1855. Abraham m. 2nd at Lunenburg, 8 Apr 1858, MARY "POLLY" BARNARD, b. at Lunenburg, 18 Jun 1800 daughter of Jacob and Betsey (Holt) Barnard.

iii   SAMUEL WILLARD, b. 1800; d. at Boston, 27 Jan 1837; m. at Chelmsford, 10 Feb 1825, SALLY INGALLS COBURN, b. at Dracut, 26 Nov 1804 daughter of Hezekiah and Sarah (Butterfield) Coburn; Sally d. at Lowell, 18 Oct 1827. Samuel did not leave a will and on 6 February 1837, his father Salmon and brothers Abram C., Salmon, and Henry declined administration of the estate and Henry Fletcher of Lowell was named.[2937] Samuel was representative to the General Court and died while in Boston for court session.[2938]

iv   SALMON WILLARD, b. 11 Oct 1802; d. at Gardner, MA, 13 Mar 1887; m. 6 May 1824, LAURA COBB who was perhaps a widow, b. about 1797; Laura d. at Gardner, 2 Feb 1888.

v   RACHEL WILLARD, b. 7 Dec 1804. The Willard genealogy reports that Rachel did not marry.

vi   SARAH WILLARD (twin), b. and d. 5 Jul 1810.

vii   HENRY WILLARD (twin), b. 5 Jul 1810; d. at South Reading, 11 Jun 1847; m. at Sterling, 11 Jun 1835, MARY ANN HOUGHTON, b. at Lempster, NH, 27 Jun 1805 daughter of Phinehas and Polly (Whitcomb) Houghton; Mary Ann d. at Lowell, 20 Feb 1847.

902)   ANNESS HOLT (*Uriah Holt⁴, Uriah Holt³, Hannah Russell Holt², Robert¹*), b. at Harvard, 1 Sep 1757 daughter of Uriah and Anness (Willard) Holt; m. at Ashburnham, 30 Oct 1780, JONATHAN BENJAMIN, b. at Ashburnham, 30 Jul 1760 son of William and Sarah (Child) Benjamin; Jonathan d. at Woodstock, VT, 24 Apr 1834.

Anness and Jonathan married after he finished his enlistments during the revolution. They went to Woodstock in 1783 and remained there.

On 25 August 1832, Jonathan Benjamin made a statement related to his application for a pension. In July 1777 while living in Ashburnham, he enlisted, and the troops marched to Vermont for the Battle of Bennington. Afterward, he was at Fort Edward until the surrender of Burgoyne when he was discharged and returned home. In April 1778, he enlisted for one year, went to Worcester, and then to Fishkill where he was in the company of Capt. Smith. Jonathan was taken sick in October and was then in the company of Capt. Cartlow. He was born in Ashburnham on 30 July 1760. In 1783, he went to Woodstock Vermont where he has been ever since. Following Jonathan's death, surviving children were eligible for arrears of the pension, and the following surviving children were named in a document dated 29 July 1848: Lemuel Benjamin, Frederick Benjamin, and Abigail Slayton of Woodstock, Vermont, and Mary Slayton in Hartland.[2939]

Anness and Jonathan were parents of nine children.[2940]

[2933] Massachusetts Land Records, Worcester County, 422:151

[2934] *Worcester County, MA: Probate File Papers, 1731-1881*. Online database. AmericanAncestors.org. New England Historic Genealogical Society, 2015. Case 66052

[2935] Abigail, w. of Benjamin, Oct. 12, 1848, a. 74 y. Dysentery.

[2936] Names of Sarah's parents are given as Edward and Elizabeth on her death record.

[2937] *Middlesex County, MA: Probate File Papers, 1648-1871*. Online database. *AmericanAncestors.org*. New England Historic Genealogical Society, 2014. Case 24953

[2938] Willard, *Willard Genealogy*, p 206

[2939] Daughters Rhoda and Sarah are not listed among the surviving children in 1848, although both appear to be living in 1848 albeit in the west (Ohio and Illinois), so perhaps they were not known to be living. U. S. Revolutionary War Pension and Bounty-Land Warrant Application Files, Case S12134

[2940] Bicha, *The Benjamin Family in America*, pp 140-141

i   JONATHAN BENJAMIN, baptized at Ashburnham, 27 Apr 1782; d. at Sheddsville, VT, 24 Mar 1845; m. HANNAH SWINERTON, b. at Putney, VT, 1785; Hannah d. at Reading, VT, 16 Mar 1866.

ii   ANISE BENJAMIN, baptized at Ashburnham, 26 Jan 1783; d. at South Woodstock, VT, 6 Aug 1846; m. 1st at Woodstock, 27 Dec 1807, EDWARD R. HAYS, b. 1782; Edward d. at South Woodstock, 25 Mar 1813. Anise m. 2nd 1816, DAVID MACK, b. 1784; David d. at Woodstock, 10 Mar 1847.

iii   LEMUEL BENJAMIN, b. at Woodstock, VT, 1 Apr 1784; d. at Woodstock, VT, 29 Jul 1853; m. 1st 10 Mar 1804, ABIGAIL LAKE, b. at Woodstock, 16 Dec 1781 daughter of George and Sarah (Lovejoy) Lake; Abigail d. about 1809. Lemuel m. 2nd 31 Dec 1810, BEULAH FULLERTON, b. 1790; Beulah d. at South Woodstock, 30 Mar 1861.

iv   DANIEL BENJAMIN, b. 1786; d. at Woodstock, VT, 7 Sep 1818; m. 10 Oct 1816, MARTHA WALDRON.

v   SARAH BENJAMIN, b. 3 Sep 1790; d. at Lowell, IL, 21 Feb 1855; m. at Woodstock, 7 Dec 1809, JOHN BAYLEY, b. at Windsor, VT, 2 Jul 1783 son of Joshua and Marcy (Davis) Bayley; John d. at Lowell, 13 Jan 1847.

vi   RHODA BENJAMIN, b. at Woodstock, 1794; d. after 1850 when living with her son at Scipio, OH; m. at Woodstock, 7 Jan 1818, PLINY WATSON, b. about 1794; Pliny d. at Wadsworth, NY, 6 Jul 1832.

vii MARY BENJAMIN, b. 5 Sep 1795; d. at Weathersfield, VT, 5 Aug 1874; m. at Woodstock, ABEL SLAYTON, b. at Woodstock, 4 Nov 1793 son of James and Mary (Bugbee) Slayton; Abel d. at Weathersfield, 30 Jul 1869.

viii ABIGAIL BENJAMIN, b. 20 Oct 1797; d. at Woodstock, 19 Dec 1852; m. at Woodstock, 2 Dec 1819, JEROME C. SLAYTON, b. 1796 son of James and Mary (Bugbee) Slayton; Jerome d. at Mendota, IL, 28 May 1872.

ix   FREDERICK BENJAMIN, b. about 1803; d. at Springfield, VT, Feb 1855 (probate 5 Apr 1855); m. at Woodstock, 7 Apr 1834, LUCY CARLETON, b. 1805; Lucy d. at Creston, IL, 15 Mar 1886. Lucy married second the widower of Frederick's sister Abigail, James C. Slayton.

---

903)   JACOB HOLT (*Uriah Holt⁴, Uriah Holt³, Hannah Russell Holt², Robert¹*), b. at Harvard, 23 Jun 1759 son of Uriah and Anness (Willard) Holt; d. after 1830 at Woodstock, VT; m. at Ashburnham, 5 Jul 1781, ANNA MELVIN, b. at Ashburnham, 8 Nov 1760 daughter of Nathan and Anna (Foster) Melvin.

      Jacob's parents and family went to Woodstock, Vermont, and Jacob remained there throughout his life. In the 1800 census, there were seven persons in his household: one male 26 to 44, one female 26 to 44, one male under 10, one male 10 to 15, one male 16 to 25, one female under 10, and one female 16 to 25.[2941] There are five known children of Jacob and Anna all born at Woodstock.

i   ANNA HOLT, b. at Woodstock, VT, 1781; d. at Hartland, VT, 26 Nov 1865; m. JOSIAH JAQUITH, b. at Billerica, 1777 son of Benjamin and Phebe (Marshall) Jaquith;[2942] Josiah d. at Hartland, 22 Sep 1868.

ii   JACOB HOLT, b. 17 Feb 1783; d. at Woodstock, 10 Apr 1844; m. at Woodstock, 24 Apr 1803, DESIRE SLAYTON, b. at Woodstock, 27 May 1785 daughter of Joshua and Desire (Felton) Slayton;[2943] Desire d. at Woodstock, 20 May 1856.

iii   OLIVER HOLT, b. 1784; m. at Windsor, 15 Feb 1814, HARRIET DELANO, b. 1797 daughter of Jabez and Anna (Stow) Delano;[2944] Harriet d. at Sheddsville, VT, 12 Apr 1836.

iv   NATHAN HOLT, b. at Woodstock, 1787; d. at Hartland, 13 oct 1878; m. about 1816, LUCY LYNDE, b. at Bridgewater, VT, 3 Mar 1786 (on burial record); Lucy d. at Woodstock, 16 Jun 1863.

v   SUSAN HOLT, b. at Woodstock 1792; d. at Woodstock, 30 Mar 1876; m. at Woodstock, 1 Mar 1812, WILLIAM BRIDGE, b. at Fitchburg, MA, 1783 son of Ebenezer and Mehitable (Wood) Bridge;[2945] William d. at Woodstock, 18 Apr 1857.

---

904)   LEMUEL HOLT (*Uriah Holt⁴, Uriah Holt³, Hannah Russell Holt², Robert¹*), baptized at Harvard, 1 Nov 1767 son of Uriah and Anness (Willard) Holt; d. at Hartland, VT, 8 Mar 1848; m. by 1797, ABIGAIL HODGMAN, b. 1774; Abigail d. at Hartland, 26 Oct 1839.

[2941] Year: 1800; Census Place: Woodstock, Windsor, Vermont; Series: M32; Roll: 52; Page: 449; Image: 439; Family History Library Film: 218689

[2942] Josiah's place of birth as Billerica is given on his death records; parents listed as B and P Jaquith. Vermont, Vital Records, 1720-1908

[2943] Vermont, Vital Records, 1720-1908

[2944] Names of Harriet's parents, Jabez and Anna, are on her gravestone.

[2945] The names of Williams' parents are given as Ebenezer and Mehitable Bridge on his death record; Vermont, Vital Records, 1720-1908

Lemuel Holt had gone to Woodstock, Vermont with his parents. Lemuel settled in Hartland in 1796[2946] about the time of his marriage and he remained there. Lemuel and Abigail were parents of seven children recorded at Hartland, Vermont.

i   ABIGAIL HOLT, b. 9 Apr 1797; d. at Pomfret, VT, 1 Sep 1857; m. at Hartland, 7 Jun 1835, as his second wife, STEPHEN RAYMOND, b. at Pomfret, VT, 8 Feb 1792 son of Phineas and Deborah (Vaughn) Raymond; Stephen d. at Pomfret, 12 Sep 1868. Stephen was first married to Emily.

ii   SARAH HOLT, b. 20 Jun 1802; d. at Woodstock, VT, 13 Nov 1843; m. about 1830, AMOS A. MCLAUGHLIN, b. at New Boston, NH, about 1804; Amos d. at Woodstock, 11 Sep 1874. David was second married to Lavinia.

iii   LEMUEL HOLT, b. 3 Jul 1804; d. at Taftsville, VT, 31 Mar 1858; m. at Woodstock, VT, 12 Sep 1831, SUSAN MCKENZIE who has not been identified.

iv   SUSAN HOLT, b. 16 Jan 1807; d. at Hartland, 24 Nov 1835. Susan did not marry.

v   LUCY HOLT, b. 30 Dec 1808; d. at Charlestown, NH, before 1850 (husband's remarriage); m. at Hartland, 1 May 1839, ISAAC MILES, b. at Charlestown, NH, about 1805; d. at Sullivan County, NH almshouse, 18 Dec 1897. Isaac married Sarah M. Hall on 1 Apr 1850.

vi   MARY HOLT, b. 8 Jan 1812

vii   JAMES CONANT HOLT, b. 2 Feb 1816; d. at Hartland, 20 Apr 1887; m. at Hartland, 13 Mar 1843, 13 Mar 1843, ARRIA ELIZABETH SMALL, b. at Goffstown, NH, about 1823 daughter of John and Abigail (Ordway) Small; Arria d. at Hartland, 10 Jul 1910.

905)   JONATHAN HOLT (*Uriah Holt⁴, Uriah Holt³, Hannah Russell Holt², Robert¹*), baptized at Ashburnham, 14 Jun 1772 son of Uriah and Anness (Willard) Holt; d. at Berlin Corners, VT, 1 Nov 1843; m. about 1800, SARAH LAKE, b. at Woodstock, VT, 22 Feb 1777 son of George and Sarah (Lovejoy) Lake; Sarah d. at Berlin Corners, 8 Dec 1857.

Jonathan Holt and Sarah Lake were parents of seven children born at Berlin, Vermont. Four of the children did not marry and lived together in Berlin.

i   CYNTHIA HOLT, b. 14 May 1801; d. at Berlin, 19 Apr 1858. Cynthia did not marry.

ii   WILLARD HOLT, b. 6 Mar 1803; d. at Berlin, 23 May 1863. Willard did not marry.

iii   ABIGAIL HOLT, b. 18 Sep 1804; d. at Berlin, 24 Aug 1871. Abigail di not marry.

iv   HIRAM HOLT, b. 1 Apr 1806; d. at Woodstock, VT, 20 Sep 1886; m. HANNAH STOWE SLAYTON, b. at Woodstock, 1813 daughter of Reuben and Betsey (Tuxbury) Slayton; Hannah d. at Woodstock, 30 Sep 1913.

v   ANNIS HOLT, b. 20 Mar 1808; d. at Morristown, VT, 4 Mar 1882; m. STILLMAN SHERWIN, b. at Reading, VT, 2 Aug 1807 son of Jonathan and Phebe (Merrill) Sherwin; Stillman d. at Morristown, 27 Dec 1869.

vi   MARY "POLLY" HOLT, b. 11 Feb 1810; d. at Berlin, 22 Nov 1872; m. at Berlin, 1 Aug 1833, JOSEPH LECLAIR, b. in Canada, about 1800; Joseph d. at Berlin, 12 Apr 1871.

vii   SARAH "SALLY" HOLT, b. 28 Mar 1813; d. at Berlin, 31 Oct 1865. Sarah did not marry.

906)   OLIVER DARBY (*Mary Holt Darby⁴, Uriah Holt³, Hannah Russell Holt², Robert¹*), baptized at Harvard, 24 May 1767 son of Thomas and Mary (Holt) Darby; m. 29 Nov 1788, LOVINA STOCKWELL *perhaps* the daughter of Abel and Patience (Thomas) Stockwell. Oliver and Lovina seem to have gone to Essex County, New York before heading west to Washtenaw County, MI where they were living in 1840.

Just one daughter Lovina has been located for this family.

i   LOVINA DARBY, b. in NY, 1810; d. at Alaiedon, MI, 19 Sep 1888; m. by 1837, RODOLPHUS TRYON, b. at Deerfield, MA, 20 Oct 1809 son of Zebina and Emily (Hodge) Tryon;[2947] Rodolphus d. at Alaiedon, MI, 13 Nov 1894.

[2946] Child, *Gazetteer and Business Directory of Windham County, Vt. for 1883-1884*, volume 1, p 146
[2947] The names of Rodolphus's parents are given as Zebina and Emily on his death record.

907)   JAMES BARNARD (*Sarah Holt Barnard⁴, David Holt³, Hannah Russell Holt², Robert¹*), b. at Andover, 27 Jun 1769 son of James and Sarah (Holt) Barnard; d. at Andover, 10 Dec 1811; m. at Andover, 6 Sep 1791, HANNAH HAWLEY, baptized at Marblehead, 1 Mar 1772 daughter of Joseph and Hannah (Pearce) Hawley.[2948]

James and Hannah were admitted to South Church 12 July 1796. Hannah was removed from the church records by 1812 suggesting she may have left Andover after the death of her husband.[2949] She was perhaps in Maine as there is some evidence her son James was in Maine for a time. There are records of six children born at Andover.[2950]

i   SARAH BARNARD, b. 22 Sep 1792

ii   DAVID BARNARD, b. 15 May 1794; d. at Andover, 21 Mar 1817.

iii   JAMES BARNARD, b. 26 Jun 1796; d. 2 Mar 1799.

iv   JOSEPH BARNARD, b. 2 oct 1798

v   JAMES BARNARD, b. 4 Jul 1801; d. at Andover, 26 Nov 1832. He may be the James Barnard who married Laura Lord and lived in Maine for a time. There is a Sarah Barnard born in Augusta, ME, 1827 who died at Cambridge, MA 25 Jan 1899. The names of Sarah's parents are given as James Barnard born at Andover and Laura Lord born at Ipswich, MA.

vi   GEORGE BARNARD, b. 20 Jun 1803

908)   PETER PEAVEY (*Dorcas Holt Peavey⁴, David Holt³, Hannah Russell Holt², Robert¹*), b. at Andover, 14 Apr 1762 son of Thomas and Dorcas (Holt) Peavey; d. at Greenfield, NH, 28 Jul 1836; m. 8 Apr 1788, LUCY CUMMINGS, b. at Hollis, 9 Jul 1767 daughter of Ebenezer and Elizabeth (Abbott) Cummings; Lucy d. 15 Oct 1854.

Peter Peavey served in the Revolution and was present at the surrender of Burgoyne. He continued service in the militia following the was achieving the rank of Major. He was a mill owner in Greenfield.[2951]

Lucy Cummings and Peter Peavey were parents of twelve children all born at Greenfield.

i   PETER PEAVEY, b. 27 Jul 1788; d. at Greenfield, 26 Oct 1879; m. 1ˢᵗ, about 1815, his fourth cousin once removed, DORCAS HOLT (*John Holt⁵, Joshua Holt⁴, Nichols Holt³, Mary Russell Holt², Robert¹*), b. at Greenfield, 12 Jan 1793 daughter of John and Dorcas (Abbott) Holt; Dorcas d. at Greenfield, 4 Jan 1856. Peter m. 2ⁿᵈ, about 1857, Dorcas's sister, TAMESIN HOLT, b. 23 Nov 1803; Tamesin d. at Greenfield, 4 Jan 1896. Dorcas and Tamesin Holt are children in Family 526.

ii   SALLY PEAVEY, b. 11 Jul 1790; d. at Greenfield, 18 Sep 1874; m. 2 Jun 1855, as his second wife, WILLIAM WRIGHT, b. about 1790 *perhaps* the son of Jonas and Rebecca (Boynton) Wright; William d. after 1874. William was first married to Nancy Flynn.

iii   LUCY CUMMINGS PEAVEY, b. 3 Jul 1792; d. at Milford, NH, 13 Feb 1874; m. 14 Jun 1816, her fourth cousin, FARNUM HOLT (*Joshua Holt⁵, Joshua Holt⁴, Nichols Holt³, Mary Russell Holt², Robert¹*), b. at Greenfield, 15 Apr 1791 son of Joshua and Hannah (Ingalls) Holt; Farnum d. at Greenfield, 27 Feb 1865. Farnum Holt is a child in Family 867.

iv   BENJAMIN ABBOTT PEAVEY, b. 25 Sep 1794; d. at Boylston, MA, 16 Nov 1864; m. about 1822, CLARISSA WHITTEMORE, b. at Greenfield, 11 Dec 1799 daughter of Amos and Polly (Savage) Whittemore; Clarissa d. at Barre, MA, 19 May 1871.

v   JACOB S. PEAVEY, b. 24 Dec 1797; d. at Londonderry, 5 Mar 1872; m. 1ˢᵗ, at Henniker, 2 Nov 1824, SUSAN CAMPBELL, b. at Henniker, 5 Aug 1805 daughter of Phineas and Susanna (Bowman) Campbell; Susan d. at Henniker, 16 Feb 1838. Jacob m. 2ⁿᵈ, 26 Mar 1840, SARAH MARSH, b. at Henniker, 7 Aug 1802 daughter of Joseph and Mehitable (Harriman) Marsh; Sarah d. at Londonderry, 15 Aug 1884.

vi   ABIEL PEAVEY, b. 27 Mar 1799; d. 29 Nov 1799.

vii   DORCAS PEAVEY, b. 8 Oct 1801; d. at Wilton, 19 Mar 1884; m. 1ˢᵗ, at Lyndeborough, 2 Mar 1824, EDWARD PRATT, b. at Reading, 2 Sep 1797 son of Edward and Asenath (Flint) Pratt; Edward d. at Wilton, 1 Feb 1838.

[2948] Hawley, *Genealogy of the Hawley Family of Marblehead*, p 5, https://archive.org/details/genealogyofhawle00hawl_0
[2949] *Historical Record of the South Church in Andover*, p 149
[2950] Charlotte Helen Abbott suggests a seventh child Nancy in this family. But Nancy is more likely Anna Barnard born 1801 daughter of Theodore and Nancy (Mansur) Barnard. Nancy Barnard Downing Morse lived with Theodore Barnard who was son of Theodore and Nancy. Abbott, Charlotte Helen, *Early Records of the Barnard Family*, p 9, https://mhl.org/sites/default/files/files/Abbott/Barnard%20Family.pdf
[2951] Livermore, *History of Wilton*, p 467

Dorcas m. 2nd, about 1847, WILLIAM SHELDON, b. at Wilton, 9 May 1810 son of Samuel and Phebe (Keyes) Sheldon; William d. at Wilton, 14 Nov 1891.

viii   ELIZABETH PEAVEY, b. 6 Apr 1803; d. 5 Nov 1803.

ix   ELIZABETH PEAVEY, b. 30 Aug 1804; d. at Lowell, MA, 28 Oct 1882; m. 4 Jun 1833, NEHEMIAH LOWE, b. at Greenfield, about 1805 son of Simon and Mary (Burnham) Lowe; Nehemiah d. at Lowell, 1 Nov 1891.

x   ABIEL PEAVEY, b. 17 Jan 1807; d. at Lowell, 14 Sep 1886; m. at Swanzey, NH, 4 Dec 1832, LOUISA STONE, b. at Swanzey, 9 Mar 1813 daughter of Martin and Betsey (Valentine) Stone; Louisa d. at Lowell, 23 Nov 1904.

xi   JOHN MERRILL PEAVEY, b. 30 Nov 1809; d. 2 Dec 1809

xii   MERRILL C. PEAVEY, b. 7 Aug 1812; d. at Lowell, 8 Aug 1873; m. at Swanzey, 3 Jun 1841, ELIZABETH STONE, b. at Swanzey, 24 Feb 1817 daughter of Martin and Betsey (Valentine) Stone; Elizabeth d. at Lowell, 1 Mar 1890.

909)   THOMAS PEVEY (*Dorcas Holt Peavey⁴, David Holt³, Hannah Russell Holt², Robert¹*), b. at Andover, about 1765 son of Thomas and Dorcas (Holt) Peavey; d. after 1840 when resident of Greenfield; m. by 1795, LYDIA ABBOTT, b. at Wilton, 22 Oct 1768 daughter of Jeremiah and Cloe (Abbott) Abbott; Lydia d. (recorded at Peterborough, NH), 1 Sep 1832.

Capt. Thomas Pevey was an early settler of Greenfield, New Hampshire. In 1820, there were eleven household members: one male over 45; two females over 45; one male 10 to 15; four males 16 to 25; one male 26 to 44; one female 10 to 15; and one female 16-25.[2952] In 1840, Thomas's household was one male 70 to 79 and one female 60 to 69.[2953]

Thomas Peavey and Lydia Abbott were parents of nine children born at Greenfield.

i   THOMAS PEVEY, b. 31 Oct 1791; d. 26 Nov 1814.

ii   JEREMIAH PEVEY, b. 4 Nov 1793; d. at Greenfield, after 1840 and before 1850; m. 3 Feb 1824, LOUISA FITCH, b. at Greenfield, about 1801 daughter of Samuel and Eunice (Perry) Fitch; Louisa d. at Greenfield, 23 Nov 1878. Louisa and Jeremiah do not seem to have had children. After Jeremiah's death, Louisa was living with her parents in Greenfield. There were no children in the home in the 1830 census.

iii   ZEBADIAH PEVEY, b. 25 Aug 1795; d. at Greenfield, 27 May 1885; m. 1824, MARY B. PATTERSON, b. at Temple, 6 Jun 1801 daughter of David and Sarah (Betton) Patterson; Mary d. at Greenfield, 21 Dec 1886.

iv   EZRA PEVEY, b. 9 Nov 1797; d. 3 Nov 1800.

v   PETER JOHNSON PEVEY (twin), b. 4 Mar 1800; d. at Peterborough, 1 Jun 1837. Peter does not seem to have married.

vi   GEORGE S. PEVEY (twin), b. 4 Mar 1800; d. 3 Nov 1800.

vii   LYDIA PEVEY, b. 12 Nov 1803; d. at Peterborough, 26 Jan 1856; m. 29 Jun 1826, JOSHUA STEVENS, b. at Peterborough, 5 Dec 1798 son of Ephraim and Jerusha (Chapman) Stevens; Joshua d. at Leominster, MA (burial at Peterborough), 13 Apr 1885. Joshua married second the widow Sarah Dexter Goss on 24 Sep 1868.

viii CHLOE ABBOTT PEVEY, b. 6 Oct 1806; d. 7 Mar 1838; m. at Peterborough, 22 Nov 1831, as his second wife, BROOKS SHATTUCK, b. at Temple, 5 Dec 1805 son of David and Sybil (Brown) Shattuck;[2954] Brooks d. at Lowell, 12 Oct 1872. Brooks was first married to Sophia Searls and third married to Mary Marshall. Brooks was a machinist and factory overseer in Waltham, Taunton, Lawrence, and New Ipswich.[2955]

ix   EZRA PEVEY, b. 14 Aug 1809; d. at Sharon, NH, 14 Aug 1891; m. 1st 14 Apr 1836, LUCINDA LITTLE, b. at Peterborough, 16 Apr 1814 daughter of John and Lucinda (Longley) Little; Lucinda d. at Peterborough, 12 Mar 1847. Ezra m. 2nd at Townsend, MA, 3 Jul 1861, NANCY DIX (widow of George Brown), b. at Townsend, about 1811 daughter of Daniel and Molly (Upton) Dix; Nancy d. at New Ipswich, 9 Mar 1881.

910)   REBECCA OSGOOD HOLT (*David Holt⁴, David Holt³, Hannah Russell Holt², Robert¹*), b. at Andover, 25 Aug 1776 daughter of David and Rebecca (Osgood) Holt; d. at Boscawen, NH, 20 Jan 1805; m. at Andover, 1 Apr 1800, her third cousin

[2952] 1820 U S Census; Census Place: Greenfield, Hillsborough, New Hampshire; Page: 837; NARA Roll: M33_61; Image: 171
[2953] Year: 1840; Census Place: Greenfield, Hillsborough, New Hampshire; Roll: 239; Page: 282; Family History Library Film: 0014932. The identity of the female is not clear as Lydia was deceased in 1832. There was also an older female with the family in 1820 and it is possible that this is Thomas's sister Hannah who was married to Peter Johnson and may have been early widowed. One of Thomas's sons was named for his brother-in-law.
[2954] Shattuck, *Memorials of the Descendants of William Shattuck*, p 347
[2955] Chandler, *The History of New Ipswich*, p 606

once removed, NATHAN KIMBALL HOLT (*Abiel Holt⁵, Thomas Holt⁴, Thomas Holt³, Mary Russell Holt², Robert¹*), baptized at Andover, 30 Aug 1778 son of Abiel and Lydia (Lovejoy) Holt; Nathan d. at Boscawen, NH, 10 Nov 1836.

Rebecca and Nathan were parents of one child.

i   REBECCA OSGOOD HOLT, b. at Boscawen, NH, 12 Aug 1802; d. at Abington, MA, 24 Aug 1826, EMERY BURGESS, b. at Harvard, MA, 22 Jun 1796 son of Loami and Sarah (Whitney) Burgess; Emery d. at Abington, 14 Feb 1872.

911)   DORCAS HOLT (*David Holt⁴, David Holt³, Hannah Russell Holt², Robert¹*), b. at Andover, 20 Nov 1781 daughter of David and Rebecca (Osgood) Holt; d. at Andover, 24 Mar 1842; m. 23 Sep 1803, her third cousin (through Holt line), HENRY ABBOTT, b.at Andover, 22 Sep 1778 son of Moses and Elizabeth (Holt) Abbott; Henry d. of consumption, at Andover, 24 Sep 1845.

Henry Abbott was a farmer in Andover. On 29 May 1840, Henry Abbott, Jr. of Andover conveyed to Ebenezer P. Higgins for a payment of $100 one undivided ninth part of the real estate Henry had inherited from his mother Elizabeth Abbott.[2956]

Dorcas and Henry Abbott were parents of five children born at Andover.

i   ELIZABETH H. ABBOTT, b. 1 Apr 1804; d. at Winchester, MA. 2 Jun 1892; m. at Andover 6 Oct 1829, CHARLES RUSSELL, b. at Plymouth, MA, 11 Dec 1798 son of John and Mary (Jackson) Russell; Charles d. at Winchester, 25 Jun 1851.

ii   REBECCA H. ABBOTT, b. 7 May 1809; d. at Andover, 19 Apr 1871; m. at Andover, 23 Apr 1835, EBEN PARSONS HIGGINS, b. at Framingham, MA, 1 Jun 1811 son of Robert K. and Eunice (Holbrook) Higgins; Eben d. at Andover, 12 Feb 1879.

iii   DORCAS S. ABBOTT, b. 10 Jul 1813; d. at Andover, 14 Jul 1845; m. at Andover, 13 Apr 1837, JOHN COOLIDGE FARNHAM, b. at Andover, 11 Apr 1815 son of Benjamin and Ruth (Saltmarsh) Farnham; John d. at Cambridge, MA, 15 Sep 1877. John married second Sarah Tufts on 7 Apr 1846.

iv   SARAH ANN ABBOTT, b. 16 Aug 1815; d. at Andover, 21 Feb 1905; m. at Andover, 15 Dec 1842, JAMES HARVEY HIGGINS, b. at Framingham, 23 Jan 1816 son of Robert K. and Eunice (Holbrook) Higgins; James d. at Andover (burial at Framingham), 29 Oct 1847. Sarah did not remarry after James's death. She lived in Andover with her two daughters neither of whom married.

v   ABIGAIL B. ABBOTT, b. 22 Sep 1819; d. at Andover, 6 Mar 1834.

912)   LYDIA HOLT (*Jonathan Holt⁴, Jonathan Holt³, Hannah Russell Holt², Robert¹*), b. at Andover, 15 May 1770 daughter of Jonathan and Ruth (Kimball) Holt; d. at Albany, ME, 12 Jan 1834; m. at Andover, 22 Nov 1795, SAMUEL TOWNE, b. at Andover, 26 Mar 1769 son of Nathan and Mary (Curtis) Towne; Samuel d. at Albany, 1 Nov 1850. Samuel was first married to Rachel Fish who died in 1793 and married third, Cynthia Frye.

Samuel and Lydia were parents of four children born at Albany Maine. Samuel also had two children with his first wife Rachel Fish.

i   HERMAN TOWNE, b. 16 Sep 1799 and baptized at Andover 6 October 1799; m. at Albany, ME, 1 May 1822, NIZAULA HUTCHINSON, b. 13 Feb 1801 daughter of Timothy and Nizaula (Rawson) Hutchinson;[2957] Nizaula d. at Portland, ME, 2 Sep 1855. Nizaula divorced Herman in Cumberland County, ME, Nov 1843.[2958] The Towne genealogy reports that Herman later married a Miss Austin, but that marriage was not located.

ii   LYDIA P. C. TOWNE, b. about 1803; d. at Albany, 28 Aug 1857; m. at Albany, 5 Apr 1827, her fourth cousin, EPHRAIM FLINT (*Ephraim Flint⁵, Asenath Holt Flint⁴, Phebe Russell Holt³, John², Robert¹*), b. at Albany, 10 May 1800 son of Ephraim and Eleanor (Holt) Flint; Ephraim d. at Albany, 2 Dec 1865.

iii   BESTEY G. TOWNE, b. 5 Aug 1804; d. at Paris, ME, 11 Jan 1873; m. EZRA HAMMOND, b. at Lincoln, ME, 21 May 1796 son of Benjamin and Rebecca (Smith) Hammond; Ezra d. at Paris, ME, 22 Mar 1863.

iv   MARY TOWNE, b. 14 Feb 1809; d. at Norway, ME, 24 Feb 1898; m. at Albany, 20 Nov 1828, IRA JOHNSON, b. at Waterford, ME, 1796 son of Asa and Hannah (Horr) Johnson;[2959] Ira d. at Norway, 27 Sep 1878.

[2956] Massachusetts Land Records, Essex County, 319:19

[2957] Crane, *The Rawson Family*, p 56

[2958] Maine, Divorce Records, 1798-1891

[2959] Biographical Review, *Biographical Review of Franklin and Oxford Counties, Maine*, p 187

913)   MOSES HOLT (*Jonathan Holt⁴, Jonathan Holt³, Hannah Russell Holt², Robert¹*), b. at Andover, 3 Sep 1773 son of Jonathan and Ruth (Kimball) Holt; m. 28 Jun 1796, MARY AUSTIN, b. at Andover, 15 Aug 1771 daughter of Daniel and Eunice (Kimball) Austin.

Little record information was found for this family. There may be other children but only one child was identified.

i   MOSES HOLT, b. 29 Sep 1796; d. at Aylmer, Ottawa, about 1889 (living in Aylmer at the 1881 census of Canada, age 85); m. ABIGAIL KILBOURN, b. at Kitley, Leeds, Ontario daughter of Samuel and Abigail (Griswold) Kilbourn;[2960] Abigail d. 1844.

914)   AMY HOLT (*Jonathan Holt⁴, Jonathan Holt³, Hannah Russell Holt², Robert¹*), b. at Andover, 25 Jul 1776; daughter of Jonathan and Ruth (Kimball) Holt d. at Andover, 29 Sep 1803, of consumption; m. at Andover, 23 Oct 1798, DAVIS FOSTER, b. at Reading, 15 Aug 1771 son of Jonathan and Sarah (Townsend) Foster; Davis d. at Reading, 15 Dec 1855. Davis married second widow Nancy (Johnson) Russell the widow of Stephen Russell and married third Susannah Flint.

Davis Foster resided in Reading. Amy and David had three children, two of whom likely died in childhood. Their third child, Amy, married but died within fifteen months of marriage and left no children.[2961] Davis had three children with his second wife Nancy *Johnson* Russell.

In his will written 1 June 1845, Davis Foster had bequests of one dollar to son Russell Foster, son Stephen Foster, and daughter Betsey wife of Joel Rogers. The remainder of the estate was left to wife Susannah to be hers, forever.[2962]

i   AMY FOSTER, baptized 6 Oct 1799; d. at Reading, 17 Sep 1823; m. at Reading, 30 Dec 1821, BENJAMIN YOUNG, b. at Reading, 5 Aug 1785 son of Benjamin and Mary (Gould) Young; Benjamin d. at Reading, 20 Jul 1857. Benjamin married second Elizabeth Cook on 29 May 1825. Amy did not have children.

ii   NANCY FOSTER, baptized 4 Jan 1801; not named in father's will

iii   TIRZAH FOSTER, baptized 12 Sep 1802; not named in father's will

915)   HANNAH BALLARD (*Hannah Holt Ballard⁴, Jonathan Holt³, Hannah Russell Holt², Robert¹*), b. at Andover, 12 May 1764 daughter of Nathan and Hannah (Holt) Ballard; d. about 1809; m. at Wilton, 28 Mar 1793, DAVID MCINTIRE, b. about 1762 of undetermined origins; David's death is unknown, but after 1820.

Hannah Ballard and David McIntire were parents of three known children born at Wilton. There may be others.

i   EZRA BALLARD MCINTIRE, b. 4 Sep 1793. Ezra enlisted from Wilton on 12 Feb 1813 for the duration of the war. He was promoted of corporal on 31 Oct 1814 and discharged on 27 May 1815.[2963]

ii   HANNAH BALLARD MCINTIRE, b. 8 Oct 1797; d. at Abington, MA, 8 Jun 1875;[2964] m. at Roxbury, MA, 1 Jan 1827, JAMES H. WEST, b. at East Randolph, MA, 6 Mar 1804 son of John and Relief (Kingman) West;[2965] James d. at Whitman, MA, 6 Jan 1890. James married second Hannah's sister Melinda (see below).

iii   MELINDA MCINTIRE, b. about 1804; d. at South Abington, MA, 8 Sep 1881;[2966] m. 1ˢᵗ at Roxbury, 24 May 1835, LORENZO W. TUCKER son of Seth and Hannah (Fowler) Tucker; Lorenzo d. 20 Sep 1839. Melinda m. 2ⁿᵈ at Roxbury, 11 Apr 1852, DANIEL HERRING, b. at Dedham, 10 Oct 1802 son of Peletiah and Catherine (·) Herring; Daniel d. by suicide at Needham, MA, 8 Oct 1853.[2967] Melinda m. 3ʳᵈ at Holbrook, 15 Jun 1877, JAMES H. WEST (see sister Hannah just above). Daniel Herring was first married to Susan Fowler.

916)   SARAH BALLARD (*Hannah Holt Ballard⁴, Jonathan Holt³, Hannah Russell Holt², Robert¹*), b. at Wilton, NH, 13 Apr 1766 daughter of Nathan and Hannah (Holt) Ballard; d. at Wilton, 4 Jan 1856; m. at Wilton, 1 Jun 1797, WILLIAM

[2960] Kilbourne, *The History and Antiquities of the Name and Family of Kilbourn*, p 266
[2961] Eaton, *Genealogical History of the Town of Reading*, p 402
[2962] *Middlesex County, MA: Probate File Papers, 1648-1871.* Online database. *AmericanAncestors.org*. New England Historic Genealogical Society, 2014. Case 32081
[2963] U.S. Army, Register of Enlistments, 1798-1914
[2964] Massachusetts, Death Records, 1841-1915
[2965] The names of James's parents are given as John and Relief West on his marriage record of his second marriage to Melinda McIntire; *Massachusetts: Vital Records, 1841-1910.* (From original records held by the Massachusetts Archives. Online database: *AmericanAncestors.org*
[2966] *Massachusetts: Vital Records, 1841-1910.* (From original records held by the Massachusetts Archives. Online database: *AmericanAncestors.org*
[2967] *Massachusetts: Vital Records, 1841-1910.* (From original records held by the Massachusetts Archives. Online database: *AmericanAncestors.org*

PETTENGILL, b. at Andover, 23 Aug 1759 son of Samuel and Mary (Holt) Pettengill; William d. at Wilton, 13 Oct 1844. William was first married to Rhoda Hagget.

Sarah and William resided in Wilton. William was active in town affairs serving as selectman for three years. He held the rank of captain in the militia.[2968]

In July 1777, William Pettengill enlisted for three years in the company of Capt. Isaac Frye in the regiment of Col. Alexander Scammel of the New Hampshire line. They marched to Ticonderoga, and he was also at White Plains, Valley Forge, and the taking of Burgoyne. He was discharged in April 1780 at a place called Crump Pond in New York. He received pension on 22 April 1819. In a statement July 1820, he reported real estate of 57 acres with buildings valued at $560 and personal estate of $114.75. His household at that time consisted of his wife Sally age fifty-four with health "as good as that of women in general of her age", his mother Mary Wright age eighty-four, son Herman age twenty-two who works with him as a hired hand, son Leonard age thirteen, son Isaac age eleven who was "out of health", daughter Sally age nineteen who was "out of health" and whose occupation was weaving, and daughter Rhoda age seventeen who was healthy. On 2 October 1848, widow Sally Pettengill made application for the widow's pension.[2969]

In his will written 29 May 1835, William Pettengill bequeathed to beloved wife Sally sixty dollars per year during her natural life. She also has use of all the household furniture and part of the house. Son William Pettengill receives eighty dollars, daughter Lucinda Burton receives twenty-seven dollars to complete her portion, daughter Sarah receives seventy dollars and the use of a room in the house, sons Ballard and Leonard receive ten dollars each, and the other children not mentioned received seventy dollars at the time of their marriages and so have their portions. The remainder of the estate goes to son Hermon who is also named executor.[2970]

Sarah Ballard and William Pettengill were parents of seven children born at Wilton. William had seven children with his first wife Rhoda Hagget (Rhoda, William, Charlotte, Sophia, Betsey, Lucinda, and Phebe).

i   HERMON PETTENGILL, b. 14 Apr 1798; d. at Wilton, 25 Oct 1883; m. 1st 1 Jun 1825, his third cousin, HANNAH FRYE (*Isaac Frye⁶, Elizabeth Holt Frye⁵, Timothy Holt⁴, Nicholas Holt³, Mary Russell Holt², Robert¹*), b. at Wilton, 1802 daughter of Isaac and Hannah (Phelps) Frye; Hannah d. at Wilton, 10 Feb 1850. Hermon m. 2nd at Lyndeborough, 3 Jul 1850, MARY CRAM, b. at Lyndeborough, 25 Nov 1803 daughter of Gideon and Amy (Putnam) Cram; Mary d. at Amherst, NH, 18 Jan 1886.

ii   BALLARD PETTENGILL, b. 16 Sep 1799; d. at Cleveland, OH, 2 Aug 1888; m. at Wilton, 25 Jan 1831, SALLY WASON, b. at Hancock, NH, 22 Feb 1803 daughter of Reuben and Polly (Gardner) Wason;[2971] Sally d. at Cleveland, 18 May 1883.

iii   SALLY PETTENGILL, b. 30 Oct 1801; d. at Wilton, 16 Nov 1875. Sally did not marry.

iv   RHODA PETTENGILL, b. 5 Sep 1803; d. at Wilton, 4 Oct 1893; m. 27 Sep 1825, LEVI TYLER, b. at Wilton, 22 Oct 1800 son of Parker and Hannah (Flint) Tyler; Levi d. at Lyndeborough, 25 May 1870.

v   LEONARD PETTENGILL, b. 4 Mar 1806; d. at Wilton, 28 Sep 1868; m. 22 Dec 1834, HANNAH STEEL, b. at Wilton, 14 Dec 1804 daughter of Benjamin and Judith (Blanchard) Steel; Hannah d. at Wilton, 17 Jul 1882.

vi   ISAAC PETTENGILL, b. 12 Apr 1808; d. 5 Mar 1826.

vii   EZRA PETTENGILL, b. 4 May 1810; d. 1813.

917)   MARY BALLARD (*Hannah Holt Ballard⁴, Jonathan Holt³, Hannah Russell Holt², Robert¹*), b. at Wilton, NH, 8 May 1768 daughter of Nathan and Hannah (Holt) Ballard; d. at Milford, after 1850; m. about 1790, her fourth cousin (through Holt line), AMOS HOLT, b. 20 Oct 1768 son of Amos and Jemima (Ingalls) Holt; Amos d. at Wilton, 13 Dec 1826.

Mary and Amos lived in Wilton on the homestead farm of Amos's father. Amos was a member of the local militia and a selectman.[2972]

On 5 January 1827, Jonathan Barton of Wilton was named administrator of the estate of Amos Holt as his widow and several of the children declined administration. Personal estate was valued at $776.66 and $2,900 for real estate, $2,700 of that for the homestead farm and buildings. Dower was set off to widow Mary Holt. The division of the estate was made on 7 May 1828 to six heirs: Luther Holt, Orville Holt, Calvin Holt, Isaiah Holt, Polly Savory, and Hannah Holt.[2973]

Mary and Amos were parents of seven children born at Wilton.

i   MARY "POLLY" HOLT, b. 13 Jul 1791; m. at Wilton, 22 Nov 1810, WILLIAM SAVORY, b. estimate 1785; d. at Hopkinton, NH, 1826 (probate 20 Mar 1826). Mary was living in 1826.

[2968] Livermore, History of the Town of Wilton, pp 465-466

[2969] U. S. Revolutionary War Pension and Bounty-Land Warrant Application Files, Case W1643

[2970] New Hampshire Wills and Probate, Hillsborough County, volume 48, p 514

[2971] Hayward, *The History of Hancock*, p 979

[2972] Livermore, *History of the Town of Wilton*, p 409

[2973] New Hampshire County Probate, Hillsborough County, 30:483; 35:354; 36:177; 35:519; accessed through familysearch.org

ii   ISAIAH HOLT, b. 14 Mar 1794; died young

iii   LUTHER HOLT, b. 22 Mar 1797; d. at Milford, NH, 31 May 1861; m. 7 Sep 1819, CATHERINE BLANCHARD, b. at Milford, 26 Sep 1793 daughter of Simon and Catherine (Wyman) Blanchard; Catherine d. at Milford, 6 Jul 1871.

iv   CALVIN HOLT, b. 16 May 1801; d. at Wilton, 24 Mar 1863; m. 26 Jun 1825, MARY DALE, b. about 1799; Mary d. at Wilton, 28 Aug 1863.

v   ORVILLE HOLT, b. 16 May 1801; d. at Nashua, NH, Dec 1849; m. REBECCA ABBOTT BLANCHARD, b. at Milford, 12 Jul 1801 daughter of Simon and Catherine (Wyman) Blanchard; Rebecca d. at Nashua, Aug 1875.

vi   HANNAH BALLARD HOLT, b. 22 Jun 1806; d. at Wilton, 9 Jan 1881; m. at Wilton, 4 May 1829, DAVID M. RAY, b. at Henniker, 11 Jul 1806 son of Jonathan and Peggy (-) Ray;[2974] David d. at Wilton, 11 Sep 1881.

vii   ISAIAH HOLT, b. 5 Jun 1812; d. at Nashua, NH, 16 Feb 1878; m. at Dunstable, 1 Mar 1838, ELECTA H. CENTER, b. at Hudson, NH, 7 Apr 1818 daughter of Richard and Catherine (Smith) Center; Electa d. at Manchester, NH, 10 Apr 1905.

918)   BETSEY BALLARD (*Hannah Holt Ballard⁴, Jonathan Holt³, Hannah Russell Holt², Robert¹*), b. at Wilton, NH, 19 Aug 1771 daughter of Nathan and Hannah (Holt) Ballard; d. at Peterborough, 5 Nov 1856; m. at Wilton, 13 May 1794, RICHARD TAYLOR BUSS, b. at Wilton, 7 Sep 1772 son of Stephen and Phebe (Keyes) Buss; Richard d. at Peterborough, 20 Oct 1862.

     Betsey and Richard had a farm in Wilton where their children were born. The family moved to Peterborough about 1814 where Betsey and Richard died.[2975] In 1850, Betsey, Richard, and their unmarried daughter Julia were living in Peterborough with the census estimate of real estate value of $1,000.[2976]

     Betsey Ballard and Richard Taylor Buss were parents of eight children born at Wilton.

i   BETSEY BUSS, b. 26 Jun 1795; d. at New London, NH, 10 Dec 1889; m. at Wilton, 18 Sep 1817, CHARLES CRANE, baptized at Newton, MA, 3 Feb 1793 son of Henry and Elizabeth (Thompson) Crane; Charles d. at Milton, 1824.

ii   ACHSAH BUSS, b. 5 Sep 1797; d. at Peterborough, 24 Jan 1869; m. at Peterborough, 6 Jan 1819, ELIJAH BROWN KIMBALL, b. at Weare, 8 May 1794 son of Joseph and Anna (Brown) Kimball; Elijah d. at Peterborough, 7 May 1877

iii   RICHARD TAYLOR BUSS, b. 27 Jul 1799; d. at Woburn, MA, 13 Dec 1885; m. 1st 27 Mar 1826, ABIGAIL HUNT, b. at Peterborough, 11 Apr 1798 daughter of Timothy and Nancy (Wade) Hunt; Abigail d. at Peterborough, 12 Oct 1838. Richard m. 2nd about 1843, PERSIS HOLMES, b. at Georgetown, NY, 1 Sep 1819 daughter of John and Lettia (McMaster) Holmes; Persis d. at Hartford, CT, 20 Jul 1897. Persis was first married to Hamilton Hill (1809-1841).

iv   ABEL FISKE BUSS, b. 9 Jul 1802; d. at Peterborough, 26 Sep 1838.

v   NATHAN BALLARD BUSS, b. 24 Jul 1804; d. at Peterborough, 12 Feb 1893; m. 8 Jun 1826, ARVILLA NAY, b. at Peterborough, 24 Nov 1804 daughter of William and Lydia (Sawyer) Nay; Arvilla d. at Peterborough, 11 Nov 1844. Nathan m. 2nd 31 Mar 1846, ELIZABETH S. BRACKETT, b. at Peterborough, 16 Feb 1811 daughter of Josiah and Mary (Stuart) Brackett; Elizabeth d. at Peterborough, 12 Sep 1891.

vi   MARIANNE BUSS, b. 2 Oct 1807; d. at Peterborough, 12 Sep 1826.

vii   EUNICE BUSS, b. 2 Oct 1809; d. at Milford, NH, 15 Jan 1897; m. 23 Nov 1837, as his third wife, her first cousin, AMOS GUTTERSON, b. at Milford, 17 Apr 1797 son of John and Phebe (Ballard) Gutterson. Amos was married first to Mary Burns and second to Matilda Gray.

viii   JULIA BUSS, b. 7 Oct 1811; d. at Peterborough, 2 Dec 1861. Julia did not marry.

919)   PHEBE BALLARD (*Hannah Holt Ballard⁴, Jonathan Holt³, Hannah Russell Holt², Robert¹*), b. at Wilton, NH, 30 Apr 1773 daughter of Nathan and Hannah (Holt) Ballard; d. at Wilton, 15 Nov 1840; m. at Concord, 23 Feb 1794, JOHN GUTTERSON, b. at Andover, 27 Aug 1766 son of Samuel and Lydia (Stevens) Gutterson; John d. at Milford, 13 Dec 1841.

2974 Cogswell, *History of the Town of Henniker*, p 704

2975 Livermore, *History of the Town of Wilton*, p 340

2976 Year: 1850; Census Place: Peterborough, Hillsborough, New Hampshire; Roll: 433; Page: 331b

John Gutterson traveled with his parents from Andover to Milford, New Hampshire, and John and Phebe settled there.[2977] Phebe Ballard and John Gutterson were parents of ten children born at Milford, New Hampshire.

i   JOHN GUTTERSON, b. 6 Jan 1795; d. at Milford, 13 Apr 1873; m. at Hollis, 15 Aug 1816, MARTHA SAWTELLE, b. (recorded) at Milford, 6 Oct 1797 daughter of John and Martha (Wallingford) Sawtelle; Martha d. 21 May 1873.

ii   AMOS GUTTERSON, b. 17 Apr 1797; d. at Milford, 12 Nov 1859; m. 1st 22 Jan 1824, MARY BURNS, b. at Milford, 16 May 1801 daughter of Moses and Betty (Bradford) Burns; Mary d. at Milford, 9 Apr 1831. Amos m. 2nd 26 Jan 1832, MATILDA GRAY, b. at Wilton, 24 Jul 1807 daughter of Joseph and Chloe (Abbott) Gray; Matilda d. at Milford, 23 Nov 1835. Amos m. 3rd 23 Nov 1837, his first cousin, EUNICE BUSS, b. at Wilton, 2 Oct 1809 daughter of Richard Taylor and Betsey (Ballard) Buss; Eunice d. at Milford, 15 Jan 1897.

iii   PHEBE GUTTERSON, b. 16 Feb 1799; d. at Alexandria, NH, 12 May 1840; m. at Milford, 5 Jun 1820, MOSES BURNS, b. at Milford, 22 Jan 1796 son of Daniel and Elizabeth (Patterson) Burns; Moses d. at Alexandria, 28 Sep 1864.

iv   NYRHA GUTTERSON, b. 11 Mar 1802; d. at Milford, 19 Mar 1877; m. at Milford, 20 Nov 1823, FRANKLIN HUTCHINSON, b. at Milford, 9 Mar 1796 son of Timothy and Prudence (Elliot) Hutchinson; Franklin d. at Milford, 10 Oct 1878.

v   SAMUEL ADAMS GUTTERSON, b. 23 Aug 1804; d. at Townsend, MA, 1 Jan 1845; m. at Bolton, MA, 17 May 1829, SARAH EATON, b. at Groton, 28 Dec 1809 daughter of Daniel and Anna (Bancroft) Eaton. Sarah married second at Townsend, 2 Mar 1851, Benjamin F. Bancroft.

vi   RODNEY GUTTERSON, b. 22 Jun 1806; d. at Milford, Apr 1836; m. at Bolton, MA, 1 Jul 1834, EUNICE JOHNSON NEWTON, b. at Northborough, MA, 15 Sep 1809 daughter of Martyn and Eunice (Johnson) Newton; Eunice d. at Northborough, 27 Apr 1879.

vii   ELIZA ANN GUTTERSON, b. 5 May 1809; d. 11 Feb 1819.

viii   NATHAN BALLARD GUTTERSON, b. 24 Jun 1811; d. at Milford, 12 Sep 1883; m. 29 Feb 1844, MARY FOSTER, b. at Marblehead, MA, 9 Aug 1816 daughter of Jesse and Mary (Larrabee) Foster; Mary d. at Temple, NH, 24 Jul 1910.

ix   ADELINE GUTTERSON, b. 7 Jul 1813; d. at Milford, 19 Mar 1886; m. 14 Mar 1844, as his second wife, JAMES BEST GRAY, b. at Wilton, 21 Apr 1797 son of Joseph and Chloe (Abbott) Gray; James d. at Milford, 6 Dec 1867. James was first married to Sarah Burns daughter of Moses and Betty (Bradford) Burns.

x   MARY L. GUTTERSON, b. 5 Sep 1816; d. at Milford, 2 Jun 1869. Mary did not marry. She was a seamstress.

920)   NATHAN BALLARD (*Hannah Holt Ballard⁴, Jonathan Holt³, Hannah Russell Holt², Robert¹*), b. at Wilton, NH, 21 Feb 1775 son of Nathan and Hannah (Holt) Ballard; d. at Concord, 5 Jul 1856; m. at Wilton, 29 May 1800, HANNAH BUSS, b. at Wilton, 3 Dec 1774 daughter of Stephen and Phebe (Keyes) Buss; Hannah d. 1857.

Nathan and Hannah resided in Concord. Nathan farmed and taught school in Concord in winter months. In 1799, he was named second assistant chorister of a musical society formed by Asa McFarland. Nathan was named tythingman in 1814 and deacon of First Church in 1818, a position he later resigned.[2978]

Nathan Ballard and Hannah Buss were parents of eleven children born at Concord.

i   WILLIAM BALLARD, b. 3 Mar 1801; d. at Concord, 18 Nov 1819.

ii   EZRA BALLARD, b. 12 May 1802; d. at Concord, 7 May 1872; m. at Concord, 16 Jun 1825, MARY FLANDERS, b. at Concord, 21 Feb 1803 daughter of Richard and Mary (Chandler) Flanders; Mary d. at Concord, 12 Feb 1871.

iii   Infant b. and d. 1804

iv   HANNAH BALLARD, b. 7 Apr 1805; d. at Concord, 6 Aug 1881. Hannah did not marry. She was a teacher in Concord.

v   PHEBE BALLARD, b. 4 Apr 1807; d. at Concord, 3 Jan 1860; m. at Concord, 8 Nov 1832, GEORGE DANIEL ABBOTT, b. at Concord, 14 Aug 1804 son of Samuel and Mary T. (Story) Abbott; George d. at Concord, 29 Sep 1868.

[2977] Ramsdell, *The History of Milford*, volume 2, p 716
[2978] Bouton, *History of Concord*, p 605, p 361, p 532, p 634

vi   MARY ANN BALLARD, b. 8 Mar 1809; d. at Concord, 22 Jul 1880. Mary Ann did not marry. She lived with her sister Hannah in Concord.

vii   CHARLES BALLARD, b. 23 Dec 1810; d. at Amherst, NH, 16 Sep 1872; m. 1st at Andover, MA, 20 Aug 1836, JANE FROST, b. at Tewksbury, 12 Nov 1810 daughter of Aaron and Susanna (Stearns) Frost; Jane d. at Tewksbury, 27 Mar 1850. Charles m. 2nd at Tewksbury, 19 Sep 1852, LYDIA DANE, b. at Andover, 15 Aug 1817 daughter of Benjamin and Lydia (Brown) Dane; Lydia d. at Tewksbury, 6 Oct 1854. Charles m. 3rd at Tewksbury, 26 Nov 1856, MARTHA M. HACKETT (widow of Samuel Steele), b. about 1824 daughter of William and Elizabeth (-) Hackett; Martha d. after 1870.

viii   CLARA BALLARD, b. 3 Jun 1813; d. at Concord, 7 Sep 1850; m. at Washington, DC, 18 Jan 1843, as his second wife, SAMUEL BREWER GODDARD, b. at Brookline, MA, 12 Sep 1782 son of Samuel and Joanna (Brewer) Goddard; Samuel d. at Newburyport, 24 Jun 1851. Samuel was first married to Emily Dawes. The daughter of Samuel Goddard and Emily Dawes married Nathan Ballard (see just below).

ix   NATHAN BALLARD, b. 31 Mar 1816; d. at New York, NY, 2 Dec 1901; m. at Concord, 23 Sep 1851, EMILY J. L. GODDARD, b. at Washington, DC, Mar 1830 daughter of Samuel and Emily (Dawes) Goddard; Emily d. at New York, NY, 31 Dec 1906. Nathan graduated from Dartmouth College in 1837 and was a teacher.[2979]

x   JOHN BALLARD, b. 1 Jan 1818; d. at Concord, 19 Sep 1902; m. 22 May 1845, HANNAH GERRISH ABBOTT, b. at Concord, 9 Jan 1820 daughter of Reuben and Hannah (Abbott) Abbott; Hannah d. at Concord, 6 May 1897.

xi   EUNICE BUSS BALLARD, b. 21 Jan 1820; d. at Brooklyn, NY, 29 Aug 1895; m. at Concord, 16 May 1853, GREENBURY WILLIAM "G.W." WEAVER, b. in MD, 23 Nov 1823 son of George and Mary (Everhart) Weaver; G. W. d. at White Post, VA, 6 Apr 1858. G. W. was named postmaster at White Post in 1855. Eunice was head of household in Manchester, MD in 1860 with her two sons.

921)   JOHN BALLARD (*Hannah Holt Ballard⁴, Jonathan Holt³, Hannah Russell Holt², Robert¹*), b. at Wilton, NH, 22 Feb 1778 son of Nathan and Hannah (Holt) Ballard; d. at Wilton, 28 Sep 1855; m. at Wilton, 20 Jan 1808, RHODA BALES, b. at Wilton, 16 May 1779 daughter of William and Rhoda (Keyes) Bales; Rhoda d. at Wilton, 15 Jan 1839.

      There is evidence for five daughters of John and Rhoda, three of whom lived to adulthood, but none married. The daughters lived with their father and later lived together in Milford. The administration of the estate of daughter Rhoda in 1864 mentions that she has just one sister, Mary Ballard, as an heir.

i   MARY BALLARD, b. 1810; d. at Milford, 14 Apr 1865.

ii   RHODA BALLARD, b. 1813; d. at Milford, 2 Nov 1864.

iii   ABIGAIL BALLARD, b. 1815; d. 3 Jul 1816.

iv   ABIGAIL BALLARD, b. 1817; d. 20 Feb 1818.

v   HANNAH J. BALLARD, b. 1822; d. at Wilton, 3 Aug 1852.

922)   JACOB HOLT (*Jacob Holt⁴, Jacob Holt³, Hannah Russell Holt², Robert¹*), b. at Andover, 15 Feb 1765 son of Jacob and Rhoda (Abbott) Holt; d. at Charlestown, MA, 22 Sep 1800; m. at Andover, 11 May 1787, his third cousin once removed, ABIGAIL HOLT, b. at Reading, Sep 1765 daughter of Joseph and Abigail (Bean) Holt; Abigail d. at Charlestown, 16 Jun 1851.

      Jacob Holt and Abigail Holt were parents of four children born at Charlestown, Massachusetts.

i   VARNUM HOLT, b. 5 Jun 1788; d. at Charlestown, 12 Aug 1818.

ii   BETSEY HOLT, b. 8 Jun 1790; d. at Charlestown, 21 Aug 1808.

iii   ESTHER HOLT, b. about 1794

iv   JACOB HOLT, b. 18 Dec 1797; d. at Charlestown, 29 Jun 1825; m. at Wakefield, 29 Jun 1820, EXPERIENCE CROCKER, b. about 1794 daughter of David and Hannah (-) Crocker;[2980] Experience d. at South Reading, 28 Nov 1851. Experience married second Benjamin Swain on 16 Apr 1833.

[2979] Bouton, *History of Concord*, p 734
[2980] Names of Experience's parents are given as David and Hannah Crocker on her death record.

923)   NEHEMIAH HOLT (*Jacob Holt⁴, Jacob Holt³, Hannah Russell Holt², Robert¹*), b. at Andover, 25 Dec 1767 son of Jacob and Rhoda (Abbott) Holt; d. at Bethel, ME, 26 Mar 1846; m. 24 Jan 1793, ABIGAIL TWIST, b. about 1771; Abigail d. at Bethel, 31 Jan 1853 at age 82.

　　　　Nehemiah Holt and Abigail Twist were parents of fifteen children. The births of the first twelve children are recorded at Albany, Maine which is now an unorganized area of Oxford County. The family was recorded in Bethel 1810 with a household of thirteen including ten children under age 16.[2981] After Nehemiah's death, Abigail lived with her son Daniel and his family.[2982]

i　　　OSGOOD DAMMON HOLT, b. at Albany, ME, 6 May 1794; d. at Andover, MA, 5 Mar 1882; m. 1ˢᵗ ACHSAH COFFIN, b. at Conway, NH, 17 Jan 1793 daughter of Peter and Sarah (Walker) Coffin; Achsah d. (buried at Gilead), 22 Nov 1818. Osgood m. 2ⁿᵈ Jan 1820, CHARLOTTE FIELDS, b. at Bridgewater, MA, May 1793 daughter of Ephraim and Ruby (Brett) Fields; Charlotte d. at Andover, 17 Jul 1878.

ii　　　ABBOT HOLT, b. at Albany, ME, 29 May 1796; d. after 1870 when he was living with his sister Sarah at Greenwood, ME. Abbot did not marry.

iii　　　ABIGAIL HOLT, b. at Albany, ME, 14 May 1797; d. at Bethel, ME, 6 Feb 1842; m. about 1817, JOHN NEEDHAM, b. at Tewksbury, 17 Jan 1792 son of John and Mary (Shed) Needham; John d. at Bethel, 26 Aug 1871.

iv　　　REBECCA HOLT, b. at Albany, 21 Aug 1799

v　　　MARY HOLT, b. at Albany, 22 Oct 1800; d. at Lowell, MA, 9 Mar 1868; m. about 1826, as his second wife, EBENEZER BEAN, b. 25 Mar 1781 son of Daniel and Margaret (Shaw) Bean;[2983] Ebenezer d. at Bethel, 1839. Ebenezer was first married to Eunice Kendall.

vi　　　NEHEMIAH HOLT, b. at Albany, 25 May 1802; d. at Portland, ME, 3 Jul 1844; m. at Portland, 27 Sep 1834, widow SARAH BIGELOW, b. about 1797.

vii　　　ELIZA HOLT, b. at Albany, 31 May 1803; d. at Temple, NH, 5 Aug 1880; m. at Andover, 28 Dec 1828, LEWIS HOWARD, b. at Temple, NH, 14 Nov 1804 son of William and Mary (Hawkins) Howard; Lewis d. at Temple, 19 Mar 1889.

viii　　　STEPHEN HOLT, b. at Albany, 5 Jan 1805; Stephen d. at Bethel, 31 Jul 1875; m. 1ˢᵗ at Andover, MA, 26 Feb 1826, SOPHRONIA AUSTIN, b. at Dracut, 5 Aug 1805 daughter of Henry and Elizabeth (Cross) Austin; Sophronia d. at Andover, 28 Jul 1831. Stephen m. 2ⁿᵈ ARMINDA FOLLANSBEE, b. in NH about 1812; Arminda d. at Bethel, 25 Aug 1888.

ix　　　DAVID HOLT, b. at Albany, 10 Feb 1806; d. at Bethel, 18 May 1891; m. Nov 1830, LAURENA NEEDHAM, b. at Norway, ME, 1811; Laurena d. 10 Feb 1893.

x　　　JACOB HOLT, b. at Albany, 7 Jul 1807; d. at Bethel, 1865; m. 16 Jun 1832, HANNAH W. WATSON, b. at Gorham, ME, 7 Dec 1794 daughter of Daniel and Anna (Maxfield) Watson; Hannah d. 1892.

xi　　　SARAH HOLT, b. at Albany, 7 Jul 1808; d. at Bethel, 27 Jun 1874; m. 29 Nov 1827, WILLIAM F. KENDALL, b. at Bethel, 4 Mar 1804 possible son of Bezaleel and Elizabeth (Spearin) Kendall; William d. at Bethel, 26 Apr 1875.

xii　　　URIAH HOLT, b. at Albany, 19 Jan 1810; d. at Waterford, 1871; m. at Albany, 21 Sep 1837, MARY K. BELL, b. 24 Aug 1814 daughter of John and Elizabeth (Kendall) Bell; Mary d. at Lynn, MA, 1 Dec 1912.

xiii　　　EPHRAIM HOLT, b. at Bethel, about Mar 1811; d. at Bethel, 3 Dec 1841 at age 30 years, 9 months;[2984] m. at Portland, ME, 5 Dec 1835, JULIA ANN KEMP, b. at Gorham, ME, 3 Dec 1820 daughter of David and Anna (Humphrey) Kemp; Julia d. at Gorham, 9 Mar 1852. In his will, Ephraim has bequests to his wife Julia Ann, his two children and one unborn child, and names brother John L. Holt as executor of his will with brother David Holt to assume this duty if brother John L. should die prior to Ephraim's children reaching age twenty-one.[2985] John L. Holt died about six months after Ephraim and brother David served as executor of the estate.

xiv　　　DANIEL G. HOLT, b. 10 Aug 1814; d. at Greenwood, ME, 1 Dec 1895; m. 15 Sep 1839, ABIGAIL CUMMINGS, b. at Albany, ME, 17 Apr 1818 daughter of John and Abigail (Libby) Cummings; Abigail d. 8 Nov 1895.

[2981] Year: 1810; Census Place: Bethel, Oxford, Maine; Roll: 12; Page: 387; Image: 00393; Family History Library Film: 0218683
[2982] Year: 1850; Census Place: Bethel, Oxford, Maine; Roll: 262; Page: 21b
[2983] Lapham, *History of Bethel, Maine*, p 482
[2984] Findagrave ID: 38160285
[2985] Maine Wills and Probate, Oxford County, Estate Files, Drawer H53, Estate of Ephraim Holt

xv   JOHN L. HOLT, b. 26 Jun 1816; d. at Bethel, 2 Jul 1842; m. at Portland, ME, 8 Feb 1840, LUCINDA C. LEACH, b. at Raymond, ME, 20 Dec 1818 daughter of Samuel and Elizabeth (Clark) Leach; Lucinda d. at Salem, MA, 30 Nov 1883.

924)   STEPHEN HOLT (*Jacob Holt⁴, Jacob Holt³, Hannah Russell Holt², Robert¹*), b. at Andover, 7 Jun 1771 son of Jacob and Rhoda (Abbott) Holt; d. at Norway, ME, 25 Sep 1817; m. at Albany, VT, 1 Jul 1806, MOLLY BRAGG, b. at Andover, 29 Apr 1779 daughter of Ingalls and Molly (Frye) Bragg; Molly d. at Norway, 17 Aug 1823.
        Stephen Holt lived in Norway, Maine where assumed duties of captain of the militia and justice of the peace.[2986] Stephen and Molly were parents of four children.

i   STEPHEN MILTON HOLT, b. at Albany, 27 Jun 1807; d. at Lynn, MA, 5 Dec 1833. Stephen did not marry.

ii   MARY ANN HOLT, b. at Albany, 8 Mar 1811; d. 9 Nov 1817.

iii   RHODA ABBOT HOLT, b.at Albany, 31 Mar 1813; d. at Lynn, MA, 18 Nov 1864; m. at Lynn, 1 Jun 1834, AMOS A. BREED, b. at Lynn, 6 Sep 1809 son of Benjamin and Abigail (Alley) Breed; Amos d. at Lynn, 23 Jan 1892. Amos married second Caroline Breed on 13 Dec 1865.

iv   JACOB INGALLS HOLT, b.24 Nov 1815; d. 26 Dec 1815.

925)   RHODA HOLT (*Jacob Holt⁴, Jacob Holt³, Hannah Russell Holt², Robert¹*), b. at Andover, 13 Jul 1773 daughter of Jacob and Rhoda (Abbott) Holt; d. 1 Apr 1850 (burial at Albany, ME); m. 1803, JOHN LOVEJOY, b. at Andover, 24 Mar 1773 son of Joseph and Mary (Gorden) Lovejoy; John d. at Albany, ME, 8 Nov 1832.
        Rhoda and John settled in Oxford County, Maine in the area that would become Norway. John Lovejoy and Rhoda Holt were parents of six children whose births are recorded at Albany, Maine.

i   RHODA LOVEJOY, b.12 Oct 1803; d. at Albany, 1 Jul 1857; m. about 1828, JOHN HUNT, b. about 1802

ii   JOSEPH LOVEJOY, b. 23 Aug 1805; d. at Norway, ME, 1883; m. Nov 1845, EUNICE DANFORTH PRINCE, b. at Albany, 28 Apr 1808 daughter of Grant and Elizabeth (Merrill) Prince; Eunice d. at Oxford, ME, 23 Dec 1877.

iii   HANNAH LOVEJOY, b. 12 Mar 1808; d. 16 Apr 1808.

iv   LOUISA LOVEJOY, b. 31 Jul 1809; d. at Albany, 18 Jan 1869; m. 20 Nov 1838, GEORGE FRENCH, b. at Greenwood, ME, 28 Aug 1809 son of James and Annis (Whitney) French; George d. at Albany, 28 Sep 1883.

v   JACOB HOLT LOVEJOY, b. 26 May 1812; d. at Albany, 24 Oct 1893; m. 16 Oct 1839, HEPHZIBAH GOULD, b. at Bridgton, ME, 29 Mar 1808 daughter of Ezra and Hephzibah (Stevens) Gould; Hephzibah d. at Albany, 2 Nov 1896.

vi   SARAH ABBOT LOVEJOY, b. 15 May 1815; d. at Albany, ME, 17 May 1849; m. May 1843, JOHN ADAMS GREENE, b. at Otisfield, ME, 17 Jan 1818 son of Jedediah and Martha (Lombard) Greene; John d. at Waltham, MA, 29 Dec 1901. John married second Lydia C. Cummings on 22 Sep 1850.

926)   URIAH HOLT (*Jacob Holt⁴, Jacob Holt³, Hannah Russell Holt², Robert¹*), b. at Andover, 25 May 1775 son of Jacob and Rhoda (Abbott) Holt; d. at Norway, ME, 21 Jun 1849; m. 4 Feb 1808, HANNAH FARNUM, b. at Andover, 27 Oct 1789 daughter of Benjamin and Dolly (Holt) Farnum; Hannah d. 4 Feb 1835.
        About 1794, Uriah with his brother Stephen and sister Rhoda went to what would become Oxford County, Maine where they built a log house, raised a barn, and cleated land in preparation for their parents to settle there in 1796. The following year, Uriah attended Phillips Academy in Andover and returned to Maine in 1802. He was clerk of the new town of Albany, Maine for five years and served as selectman. Uriah and Hannah married in 1808 and moved to Norway in 1809. In Norway he was justice of the peace, selectman, and assessor. In addition to his farming interests, he worked as a surveyor.[2987]
        Amos T. Holt assumed administration of his father's estate on 16 October 1849. Personal estate was valued at $90.74.[2988]
        Uriah Holt and Hannah Farnum were parents of ten children born at Norway, Maine.

[2986] Durrie, *Genealogical History of the Holt Family*, p 63
[2987] A detailed biography of Uriah Holt can be found in Durrie's Holt genealogy, pp 63-71
[2988] Maine Wills and Probate, Oxford County, Estate Files Drawer 54, Estate of Uriah Holt

i   DOLLY FARNUM HOLT, b. 26 Oct 1808; d. at Norway, 23 Jul 1887; m. 24 Jul 1831, Dr. JONATHAN SMALL, b. in ME, 1805; Jonathan d. likely at Boston (burial at Harrison, ME), 30 Jan 1854.[2989] Jonathan was a physician with a practice in Boston where the family was living in 1850.[2990] It is assumed he died there, although no record was found. Dolly and Jonathan were parents of five children. Dolly and her children were living in Somerville, MA in 1855 and afterwards Dolly returned to Maine.

ii   RHODA ABBOTT HOLT, b. 8 Feb 1810; d. at Norway, 12 Mar 1878; m. 31 Oct 1831, HIRAM MILLETT, b. at Norway, ME, 27 Apr 1805 son of Solomon and Elizabeth (Dinsmore) Millett; Hiram d. at Norway, 19 Feb 1862.

iii   AMOS TOWN HOLT, b. 21 Oct 1811; d. at Norway, 27 Jan 1887; m. 23 Oct 1838, ELIZABETH M. ROSS, b. in ME, 1816 daughter of Andrew and Betsey (March) Ross. Amos and Elizabeth did not have children of their own but adopted a daughter Emma who was born in 1864.

iv   DAVID OSGOOD HOLT, b. 26 Jul 1814; d. at North Yarmouth, ME, Dec 1879; m. 25 Oct 1838, MARY H. TRICKEY, b. 1818 daughter of David and Mary (Hobbs) Trickey; Mary d. at Portland, 16 Feb 1880.

v   SARAH ABBOTT HOLT, b. 27 Feb 1816; d. at Norway, ME, 9 Jun 1906. Sarah did not marry.

vi   JACOB FARNUM HOLT, b. 13 Dec 1817; d. at Norway, 30 Sep 1890; m. 2 Jun 1853, EMMA JANE FROST, b. at Norway, 29 Jan 1834 daughter of William and Mary (Wheelock) Frost; Emma d. at Norway, 1 May 1920.

vii   STEPHEN ABBOTT HOLT, b. 13 Feb 1820; d. at Boston, 14 Dec 1895; m. 28 May 1850, NANCY WYMAN CUTTER, b. at Woburn, 1 Feb 1830 daughter of Henry and Nancy (Wyman) Cutter; Nancy d. at Cambridge, MA, 13 Jan 1918. Stephen A. Holt graduated from Bowdoin College in 1846 and immediately following entered Bowdoin's theological seminary and graduated in 1849. In early 1850, he was ordained pastor of the Congregational church at Milton, Vermont.[2991]

viii HANNAH FARNUM HOLT, b. 22 Apr 1822; d. Millbury, MA, 5 Apr 1897; m. 15 Dec 1845, Rev. CHARLES PACKARD, b. at Buckfield, ME, 14 Oct 1818 son of Eliphalet and Abigail (Snell) Packard; Charles d. at Windham, NH, 20 Feb 1881.

ix   MARIA PHILLIPS HOLT, b. 9 Apr 1824; d. at Norway, 7 Oct 1842.

x   BENJAMIN GORHAM HOLT, b. 15 Apr 1827; d. at Creighton, NE, 13 Oct 1903; m. 21 Dec 1858, BETSEY ELLEN HOBBS, b. at Norway, 2 Mar 1833 daughter of Robinson and Lavinia (Hall) Hobbs; Betsey d. at Bristow, NE, 5 May 1908. Benjamin and Betsey were parents of eight children, the oldest seven born in Maine. In 1873, the family packed up and went to Nebraska where their youngest child was born. Benjamin served in the 31st and 32nd Maine regiments during the Civil War.[2992]

927)   MARY OSGOOD HOLT (*Jacob Holt⁴, Jacob Holt³, Hannah Russell Holt², Robert¹*), b. at Andover, 21 Apr 1777 daughter of Jacob and Rhoda (Abbott) Holt; d. at Andover, 11 Feb 1856; m. 22 Dec 1802, her second cousin once removed, ZACHARIAH CHICKERING, b. at Andover, 19 May 1764 son of Samuel and Mary (Dane) Chickering; Zachariah d. at Andover, 30 Jun 1841.

    Mary O. Holt and Zachariah Chickering resided in Andover where they were parents of six children.

i   MARY OSGOOD CHICKERING, b. 26 Oct 1804; d. at North Andover, 14 Mar 1888; m. 12 Oct 1831, ALBERT GILBERT REA, b. at Andover, 29 Aug 1802 son of Daniel and Hannah (Gilbert) Rea; Albert d. at North Andover, 24 Jul 1873.

ii   JACOB CHICKERING, b. 2 Aug 1806; d. at Andover, 31 Mar 1887; m. 26 Nov 1835, SARAH JANE MCMURPHY, b. at Londonderry, NH, 7 Aug 1810 daughter of Alexander and Sarah (Duncan) McMurphy;[2993] Sarah d. at Andover, 26 Apr 1893.

iii   SARAH ABBOT CHICKERING, b. 9 Oct 1808; d. at Groton, 14 Jun 1891; m. at Andover, 18 Jun 1834, ISAAC FARNHAM, b. at Andover, 19 Mar 1804 son of Isaac and Persis (Stevens) Farnham; Isaac d. at Groton, 4 Sep 1877.

[2989] Maine, Faylene Hutton Cemetery Collection, 1780-1990
[2990] Annual Report of Harvard University, 1844-1845
[2991] Cleaveland and Packard, *History of Bowdoin College*, p 621
[2992] Historical Data Systems, comp. *U.S., Civil War Soldier Records and Profiles, 1861-1865* [database on-line]. Provo, UT, USA: Ancestry.com Operations Inc, 2009.
[2993] *NEHGS Membership Applications, 1845-1900.* (Online database. *AmericanAncestors.org*, New England Historic Genealogical Society, 2020.) Membership application of Otis Chickering son of Jacob and Sarah Jane Chickering.

iv   WILLIAM CHICKERING, b. 24 Aug 1811; d. at Andover, 5 Jun 1880; m. 6 Oct 1836, FRANCES NOYES, b. at Andover, 13 Oct 1814 daughter of Frederick and Hannah (Varnum) Noyes; Frances d. at Andover, 29 Jul 1887. William Chickering was owner of the historic property at 36 Elm Street in Andover.[2994]

v   CERES CHICKERING, b. 10 Aug 1815; d. 12 Aug 1817.

vi   HANNAH MARIA CHICKERING, b. 15 Sep 1819; d. at Andover, 23 Jan 1870; m. at Andover, 27 Feb 1868, as his fourth or fifth wife, WILLIAM STICKNEY, b. at Norwich, VT, 1817 son of William and Margaret (Forrest) Stickney. William had one further marriage on 1 Aug 1871 to E. Annie Eaton.

928)   TABITHA HOLT (*Jacob Holt⁴, Jacob Holt³, Hannah Russell Holt², Robert¹*), b. at Andover, 11 Aug 1779 daughter of Jacob and Rhoda (Abbott) Holt; d. likely at Waterford, ME; m. at Waterford, 19 Jun 1798, THOMAS GREENE, b. at Rowley, 17 Mar 1775 son of Thomas and Lydia (Kilburn) Greene; Thomas d. at Waterford, Oct 1809 (probate 12 Dec 1809).

     Tabitha and Thomas settled in Waterford, Maine. Thomas was accidentally killed when taking down the frame of a barn.[2995]

     Thomas Greene did not leave a will and Uriah Holt was named estate administrator 12 December 1809. Part of the estate needed to be sold to settle the debts, but it was decided it would be of most benefit to sell the whole of the real estate together. Daniel Green acted as guardian for the minor children. The dower was set off to widow Tabitha.[2996]

     Tabitha Holt and Thomas Greene were parents of six children born at Waterford, Maine.

i   SARAH A. GREENE, b. 1800; d. at Albany, ME, 26 Jul 1823.

ii   TABITHA GREENE, b. 1801; d. at Bethel, ME, 2 Mar 1864; m. LEONARD GROVER, b. at Bethel, 9 May 1799 son of Eli and Mehitable (Austin) Grover; Leonard d. at Bethel, 25 Feb 1884. After Tabitha's death, Leonard married on 12 Jun 1866, LYDIA ABBOT RUSSELL (*James⁵, Uriah⁴, Thomas³, James², Robert¹*) (widow of Moses Gould), b. at Bethel, 1 Dec 1808 daughter of James and Dolly (Russell) Russell; Lydia d. at Boxford, MA, 1 Jan 1893.

iii   JACOB HOLT GREENE, b. 1802; d. at Waterford, ME, 23 Dec 1874; m. SARAH WALKER FRYE, b. at Fryeburg, 20 Feb 1797 daughter of Samuel and Mary (Gordon) Frye; Sarah d. at North Waterford, 22 Sep 1873.

iv   THOMAS GREENE, about 1803; d. at Waterford, 23 May 1805.

v   WILLIAM W. GREENE, b. 1805; d. at North Waterford, 16 Oct 1863; m. RUTH K. CORSER, b. at Boscawen, NH, 18 Dec 1817 daughter of David and Abigail (Kilbourn) Corser; Ruth d. at East Bridgewater, MA, 12 Jan 1901.

vi   THOMAS GREENE, b. 1808; d. at Waterford, 24 Oct 1865; m. ELIZA KIMBALL, b. at Waterford, 1810 daughter of Jonathan and Elizabeth (Bowers) Kimball; Eliza d. at Waterford, Feb 1880.[2997]

929)   HANNAH HOLT (*Jacob Holt⁴, Jacob Holt³, Hannah Russell Holt², Robert¹*), b. at Andover, 17 Jul 1781 daughter of Jacob and Rhoda (Abbott) Holt; d. at Albany, ME, 23 Dec 1856; m. 1 Oct 1801, PARSONS HASKELL, b. at Falmouth, ME, 27 Oct 1777 son of Benjamin and Lydia (Freeman) Haskell; Parsons d. at Albany, 6 Jul 1829.

     Parsons and Hannah resided in Albany, Maine. Parsons Haskell was named administrator of his father's estate on 5 August 1829. On 16 January 1832, John Lovejoy guardian to minor children provided an inventory of the estate of the minor children, their portion totaling $400. Those children were Sarah A. H. Haskell, Lydia P. Haskell, Mary Anne Haskell, and Hannah Haskell. On 5 August 1833, Samuel P. Haskell was named as guardian for the four minor children. Real estate was sold to settle the estate.[2998]

     Parsons and Hannah were parents of nine children born at Albany, Maine.

i   PARSONS HASKELL, b. 27 Jun 1802; d. at Albany, Me, 15 Dec 1857; m. at Waterford, ME, 27 Jun 1829, SUSAN JEWETT, b. at Waterford, 4 Nov 1799 daughter of Ebenezer and Mary (Farrington) Jewett;[2999] Susan d. at Albany, 24 May 1880.

ii   HANNAH HASKELL, b. 11 Feb 1805; d. 1 May 1821.

iii   URIAH HOLT HASKELL, b. 7 Jun 1807; d. 15 Apr 1808.

[2994] Andover Historic Preservation, 36 Elm Street, https://preservation.mhl.org/36-elm-street
[2995] Warren, *History of Waterford, Oxford County, Maine*, p 248
[2996] Maine Wills and Probate, Oxford County, Estate of Thomas Green, Jr., 1809
[2997] Maine State Archives; Augusta, Maine; U.S. Census Mortality Schedules, Maine, 1850-1880; Archive Collection: 4; Census Year: 1880; Census Place: Waterford, Oxford, Maine; Page: 1
[2998] Maine Wills and Probate, Oxford County, 1:326; 6:371; 6:687; 6:201
[2999] Jewett, *History and Genealogy of the Jewetts in America*, p 237

iv   SAMUEL PHILLIP HASKELL, b. 6 Jun 1809; d. at Albany, 16 Jun 1881; m. at Albany, 4 Dec 1862, IRENE CUMMINGS, b. at Albany, 20 Aug 1831 daughter of Stephen and Nancy (Frost) Cummings; Irene d. at Albany, 8 Dec 1870.

v   DAVID HOLT HASKELL, b. 3 Jan 1812; d. at Albany, 21 Mar 1871; m. at Albany, ME, 12 Apr 1843, SOPHIA A. TOWN, b. 1824 daughter of Samuel and Susannah (Crosby) Towne

vi   SARAH ABBOT HOLT HASKELL, b. 11 Sep 1814; d. at Albany, 11 May 1890; m. at Albany, 30 Aug 1846, JOHN MARSHALL, b. about 1814; John d. at Albany, 23 Apr 1879.

vii   LYDIA PARKER HASKELL, b. 3 Aug 1817; d. at Albany, ME, 15 Jul 1859. Lydia did not marry.

viii   MARY ANN HASKELL, b. 20 Mar 1820. Mary Ann did not marry. In 1860, she was living with her brother Samuel in Albany.

ix   HANNAH HASKELL, b. 4 Feb 1823; d. at Albany, 8 Sep 1844.

930)   DAVID HOLT (*Jacob Holt⁴, Jacob Holt³, Hannah Russell Holt², Robert¹*), b. at Andover, 21 Aug 1783 son of Jacob and Rhoda (Abbott) Holt; d. at Andover, 3 Oct 1836; m. 2 Jul 1820, his second cousin, SARAH ABBOTT (*Ruth Holt Abbott⁶, Joseph Holt⁵, Lydia Holt Holt⁴, Thomas Holt³, Mary Russell Holt², Robert¹*), b. at Andover, 11 Jul 1787 daughter of Abner and Ruth (Holt) Abbott; Sarah d. at Andover, 26 Jul 1874.

In his will written 22 September 1836 (probate 18 October 1836), David Holt made the following bequests: Mrs. Rhoda A. Breed wife of Amos Breed and daughter of brother Stephen Holt of Albany, Maine, ten dollars; Mary A. Phillips wife of Mr. Edward Phillips of Taunton and daughter of Abner Abbot, ten dollars; his best suit of clothes bought of Henry R. Williams of Boston to brother Uriah Holt, Esq. of Norway, Maine; nephew David Holt son of Uriah, his pocket pistols; David Holt son of brother Nehemiah of Bethel, Maine, gun and bayonet, knapsack, and cartridge box; brother Nehemiah Holt, hat and boots; nephew Joseph Lovejoy son of sister Mrs. Rhoda Lovejoy widow of John Lovejoy of Albany, Maine, his black vest; nephew Jacob Lovejoy son of Rhoda; Miss Margaret N. Abbot half-sister of his wife Mrs. Sarah A. Holt receives the sheep note that David holds against Mr. Abner Abbot; nephew Samuel Haskell son of sister Hannah Haskell widow of Parsons Haskell, one coat and vest; David Haskell son of Hannah, pantaloons and vest; sister Mrs. Mary Chickering wife of Zachariah Chickering, one pair of white silk stockings; sisters Mrs. Rhoda Lovejoy and Mrs. Hannah Haskell, one pair of black silk stockings each; brother-in-law Mr. Stephen Abbot, the blue great coat; nephew Mr. Joseph Chickering the book "Forsyth on Fruit Trees" which had been given to David by his aunt Sarah Abbot; nephew William Chickering, "Sidney's Discourse on Government"; nephews Samuel Haskell and David Haskell, one pair of stockings each as his wife selects; nephew Benjamin Gorham Holt son of brother Uriah Holt, one cow; wife Sarah A. Holt, the silver watch to hold during her life and after her decease to go to daughter Sarah A. Holt; the remainder of the estate of every kind goes one-third part to daughter Sarah A. Holt and two-thirds to wife Sarah A. Holt. John Flint of Andover, cabinetmaker, was named executor. Real estate was valued at $5,432.50 and personal estate at $471.27.[3000]

David and Sarah were parents of three children born at Andover. Two sons died in infancy and daughter Sarah did not marry.

i   DAVID GORHAM HOLT, b. 21 Jul 1820; d. 15 Jun 1821.

ii   SARAH ABBOT HOLT, b. 17 Oct 1824; d. at Andover, 25 Jan 1851. Sarah did not marry.

iii   Son b. and d. 14 May 1827.

931)   SARAH ABBOTT HOLT (*Jacob Holt⁴, Jacob Holt³, Hannah Russell Holt², Robert¹*), b. at Andover, 19 May 1786 daughter of Jacob and Rhoda (Abbott) Holt; d. at Phillipston, MA, 23 Jun 1845; m. Jun 1817, as his second wife, JOSEPH CHICKERING, b. at Dedham, 30 Apr 1780 son of Jabez and Hannah (Balch) Chickering; Joseph d. at Phillipston, 27 Jan 1844. Joseph Chickering was first married to Betsy White on 1 Sep 1805.

Rev. Joseph Chickering was son of Rev. Jabez Chickering of the South Parish at Dedham. He graduated from Harvard in 1799 and studied theology with Rev. David Tappan. He was ordained 28 March 1804 and was pastor at Woburn for seventeen years. He was minister at Phillipston from 1822 to 1835 before being dismissed for ill health.[3001][3002] The church at Woburn provided Joseph with a salary of $650 per year, 15 cords of good hard wood, and a settlement of $800 to be paid within one year of his hire.[3003]

In his will written 23 October 1833 (probate 14 March 1844), Joseph Chickering of Phillipston bequeathed to his faithful and beloved wife the use and improvement during the natural life the land and buildings which he purchased of Dr. James Stone. She is also to have, at her own disposal, the chaise, household furniture and goods except books, provisions, two

[3000] *Essex County, MA: Probate File Papers, 1638-1881.* Online database. *AmericanAncestors.org.* New England Historic Genealogical Society, 2014. Case 13635

[3001] Rev. Joseph Chickering; Boston Recorder (Boston, Mass.) Feb. 15, 1844

[3002] Barber, *Massachusetts Historical Collections*, p 598

[3003] Sewall, *The History of Woburn*, p 448 and p 461

cows, and the income during her life of ten shares of Amherst Bank. The books are to be divided in seven equal parts among his wife and six children: John W., Joseph, Betsey, Henry, Abbot, and Benjamin. Donations of one hundred dollars each were made to organizations: American Education Society, American Bible Society, American Board of Commissioners for Foreign Missions, and the American Home Missionary Society. The American Temperance Society and Prison Discipline Society received fifty dollars each. The remainder of the estate is to be divided among his six children. Oldest son John W. Chickering was named sole executor, and if he declines, then second son Joseph Chickering. In a codicil 26 April 1835, Joseph changed the bequest of his wife to ten shares of Dedham Bank and added two hundred dollars to the bequest. He also named Oliver Powers, Esq. as executor. At the time of probate of the estate, son Henry Chickering was named administrator. The inventory included real property of $2265, personal estate of $427.03, and 15 bank shares of $1500, and other notes and receipts totaling $1,446.68.[3004] John W. Chickering and James Chickering were children from Joseph's first marriage to Betsy White.

On 3 August 1840, Sarah Chickering petitioned the court for appointment of guardian for her husband Joseph as "she has witnessed with painful emotions the decline of the intellectual facilities of her beloved husband for several years past, until he is reduced to that state of insanity that disqualifies him from taking care of himself, and renders it necessary (in the judgment of your petitioner) that a guardian be appointed for the said Rev. Joseph Chickering." The selectmen of Phillipston signed a statement in support of the petition. Oliver Powers was named as guardian.[3005]

Sarah and Joseph were parents of four children. Joseph also had five children with his first wife Betsey White, three of whom died in childhood.

i   BETSEY CHICKERING, b. at Woburn, 3 May 1818; d. at Pittsfield, MA, 16 Apr 1899. Betsey did not marry.

ii   HENRY CHICKERING, b. at Woburn, 3 Sep 1819; d. at Pittsfield, MA, 5 Mar 1881; m. 1st at Phillipston, 22 Sep 1840, MARTHA NEWTON, b. at Phillipston, 13 Jul 1823 daughter of William W. and Lydia (Rich) Newton; Martha d. at Barre, MA, 10 Feb 1843. Henry m. 2nd at Barre, 20 Sep 1844, ELVIRA PERRY ALLEN, b. at Barre, 27 Jun 1811 daughter of John and Hannah (Robinson) Allen; Elvira d. at Pittsfield, 28 Apr 1893

iii   ABBOT CHICKERING, b. 6 Dec 1821; d. at Phillipston, 11 Jun 1842. "Abbot, June 11, 1842, a. 20 y. 6 m. Employed in a store between 4 & 5 years. Cause of death, enlargement of the heart, which weighed 3-1/16 lbs."

iv   BENJAMIN CHICKERING, b. at Phillipston, Nov 1824; d. at Pittsfield, 3 Aug 1889; m. 1st at Phillipston, 21 May 1846, DEBORAH LOUISA BALDWIN, b. at Phillipston, 11 Jul 1816 daughter of Tilly and Rebecca (Hoar) Baldwin; Deborah d. at Pittsfield, 1 Sep 1863. Benjamin m. 2nd at Reading, 5 Oct 1865, MARY SAFFORD SMITH, baptized at Reading, 14 Aug 1836 daughter of Cyrus and Cecilia (Popkin) Smith; Mary d. at Pittsfield, 24 Jun 1914.

932)   MARY "MOLLY" HOLT (*Nehemiah Holt⁴, Jacob Holt³, Hannah Russell Holt², Robert¹*), b. at Salem, 9 Sep 1777 daughter of Nehemiah and Esther (Varnum) Holt; d. at Salem, 7 Dec 1856; m. 1st at Salem, 22 Jun 1794, JOSHUA FOSTER, b. about 1766; Joshua d. at the West Indies, 6 Dec 1795.[3006] Mary m. 2nd at Salem, 17 Oct 1800, DANIEL PROCTOR, b. at Danvers, 12 Jul 1768 son of Benjamin and Keziah (Littlefield) Proctor; Daniel d. at sea on unknown date (missing in the record transcription: Daniel, s. Benjamin and Kaziah (Littlefield)," at sea".

No children were identified for Joshua Foster and Mary Holt. Molly Foster administered her husband's estate which was valued at $139.82.[3007] Mary Holt and Daniel Proctor were parents of two children born at Salem.

i   DANIEL LITTLEFIELD PROCTOR, b. at Salem, 28 Jan 1802; d. at Salem, 29 Jul 1877; m. at Salem, 5 Oct 1821, OLIVIA RICHARDSON, b. at Salem, 12 Aug 1802 daughter of William and Elizabeth (Townsend) Richardson; Olivia d. at Gloucester, MA, 26 Sep 1882.

ii   NEHEMIAH HOLT PROCTOR, baptized at Salem, 19 Jan 1806; d. at Salem, 16 Sep 1808 of dysentery (age at death given as 1 year 9 months).

933)   ESTHER HOLT (*Nehemiah Holt⁴, Jacob Holt³, Hannah Russell Holt², Robert¹*), b. at Salem, 9 Dec 1781 daughter of Nehemiah and Esther (Varnum) Holt; d. at Salem, 31 Mar 1874; m. at Salem, 20 Sep 1807, DANIEL ANDREWS, b. at Salem, 23 Sep 1779 son of Nehemiah and Catherine (Seamore) Andrews; Daniel d. of consumption, at Salem, 25 Dec 1820.[3008]

[3004] *Worcester County, MA: Probate File Papers, 1731-1881.* Online database. AmericanAncestors.org. New England Historic Genealogical Society, 2015. Case 11593
[3005] *Worcester County, MA: Probate File Papers, 1731-1881.* Online database. AmericanAncestors.org. New England Historic Genealogical Society, 2015. Case 11593
[3006] Joshua, native of Ipswich, h.____ (Holt), mate of a vessel, Capt. Patten, at the West Indies, fever, Dec. 6, 1795, a. 29 y. C. R. 4.
[3007] *Essex County, MA: Probate File Papers, 1638-1881.*Online database. *AmericanAncestors.org.* New England Historic Genealogical Society, 2014. Case 9936
[3008] Daniel [s. Capt. Nehemiah. G. R. 9.], consumption, Dec. 25, 1820, a. 45 y.

Daniel was a master mariner. After the death of her husband, Esther was a schoolteacher in Salem. Esther Holt and Daniel Andrews were parents of five daughters born at Salem. In the 1850 census, Esther and her daughters Esther and Lois lived in Salem next door to daughter Mary and her husband John Mackie.[3009]

i   KATHERINE SEYMOUR ANDREWS, baptized at Salem, 19 Jun 1809.[3010]

ii   ESTHER VARNUM ANDREWS, baptized at Salem, 8 Dec 1812; d. at Taunton, 27 Oct 1883. Esther did not marry.

iii   MARY ELIZABETH ANDREWS, b. at Salem, 21 Jun 1813; d. at Salem, 3 Aug 1872; m. at Salem, 1 Jan 1843, JOHN MACKIE, b. in Scotland, about 1796 son of William and Jane (-) McMarston;[3011] John d. at Salem, 30 Apr 1872. John was an upholsterer.

iv   LOIS BOWDITCH ANDREWS, b. 1816 and baptized at Salem at age 6 on 14 Apr 1822; d. at Salem, 16 Jun 1874. Lois did not marry. Lois was a tailoress in Salem.

v   REBECCA KITTREDGE ANDREWS, b. 1818 and baptized at Salem at age 4 on 14 Apr 1822; d. at Saugus, MA, 26 Jun 1891; m. at Salem, 14 Nov 1839, JOHN INGERSOLL BECKETT, baptized at Salem, 29 Aug 1819 son of David and Elizabeth (Townsend) Beckett; John d. at Saugus, 5 Apr 1887.

934)   ABIEL STEVENS (*Tabitha Holt Stevens⁴, Jacob Holt³, Hannah Russell Holt², Robert¹*), b. at Andover, 10 Oct 1770 son of Abiel and Tabitha (Holt) Stevens; d. at East Bethany, NY, 7 Sep 1853; m. 1st about 1793, EUNICE who has not been identified; Eunice d. at Strafford, VT, 5 May 1804. Abiel m. 2nd about 1804, MARCY HASKELL (widow of Isaac Smith), b. 1777 daughter of Job and Isabel (Winship) Haskell; Marcy d. at East Bethany, 27 Jun 1837.

     Abiel resided in Strafford, Vermont where likely all twelve of his children were born.

     Abiel and Eunice were parents of six children born at Strafford.

i   JOHN STEVENS, b. 13 Oct 1794; m. at Strafford, 6 Mar 1817, SARAH WELLS, b. at Strafford, 30 May 1796 daughter of David and Mary (Roberts) Wells; Sarah d. at Strafford, 21 Mar 1821.

ii   EUNICE STEVENS, b. 2 Mar 1796; m. at Strafford, 1 Jan 1818, CHARLES KENDALL.

iii   JACOB STEVENS, b. 30 Par 1797

iv   ABIEL STEVENS, b. 21 Apr 1799; d. at East Bethany, NY, 19 Apr 1881; m. BETSEY NORTON, b. at Glover, VT, 2 Jul 1805 daughter of Ira and Susannah (Preston) Norton;[3012] Betsey d. at East Bethany, 21 Sep 1892.

v   POLLY STEVENS, b. 21 Apr 1801; d. 9 Jun 1816.

vi   BETSEY STEVENS, b. 1 May 1803

     Abiel and Marcy were parents of six children born at Strafford.

i   FANNY STEVENS, b. 7 Jan 1804; d. at Conesus, NY (burial at Alden), 1888; m. at Strafford, 13 Apr 1828, SEYMOUR MORRISON NORTON, b. at Strafford, 10 May 1802 son of Noah and Margaret (Morrison) Norton; Seymour d. at Alden, 5 Apr 1869.

ii   ALMA STEVENS, b. 29 May 1808; d. at Bethany, NY, 30 Jun 1891; m. her first cousin, LUMAN STEVENS, b. at Strafford, 18 Mar 1800 son of Jacob and Dinah (Frary) Stevens; Luman d. at East Bethany, 15 Apr 1873.

iii   NEHEMIAH JOB STEVENS, b. 29 May 1810; d. at East Bethany, 26 Jan 1897; m. LEMIRA, b. in VT (census records), about 1812; Lemira d. at East Bethany, 10 Mar 1874.

iv   GEORGE WASHINGTON STEVENS, b. 27 Apr 1812; d. at Aurora, IL, 26 May 1885; m. 1st 4 Feb 1836, CAROLINE BETSY HUGGINS, b. 5 Jan 1810 daughter of Nathaniel and Althea (Taylor) Huggins; Caroline d. at Oakfield, NY, 6 Nov 1850. George m. 2nd about 1855, EDNA KENDALL, b. at Strafford, 20 Aug 1824 daughter of Josiah and Lucy (Patterson) Kendall; Edna d. after 1902 when she was living in Aurora.

[3009] Year: 1850; Census Place: Salem Ward 3, Essex, Massachusetts; Roll: 312; Page: 137B

[3010] Katherine Seymour, d. Daniel, bp. June 18, 1809. CR12. There is a death record in Salem in 1836 for Catherine Seymour Andrews, age 27, daughter of Nehemiah. It may be that either the baptismal record or the death record has an error for father's name. No other information was found.

[3011] The names of John's parents are given as William and Jane McMarston on his death record. He seems to have adjusted the spelling of his name.

[3012] The 1866 probate of Ira Norton of Bethany, NY includes daughter Betsey Stevens wife of Abial Stevens.

v   JEDEDIAH H. STEVENS, b. 1 Jul 1815

vi   PEABODY SMITH STEVENS, b. 14 Nov 1818; d. at Buffalo, NY, 1871 (probate 29 Apr 1871); m. about 1854, MARY ANN MITCHELL, b. at Buffalo, Nov 1832 daughter of John P. and Mary (Crocker) Mitchell; Mary Ann d. at Corning, NY, 15 Sep 1908.

935)   JACOB STEVENS (*Tabitha Holt Stevens⁴, Jacob Holt³, Hannah Russell Holt², Robert¹*), b. at Andover, 12 Mar 1776 son of Abiel and Tabitha (Holt) Stevens; d. at East Bethany, NY, 26 Mar 1856; m. at Strafford, VT, 17 Mar 1779, DINAH NORTON (widow of Jonathan Frary), b. about 1773 daughter of Elihu and Dinah (Snow) Norton;[3013] Dinah d. at Strafford, 16 Feb 1803.[3014]

     Jacob and Dinah were parents of two children born at Strafford. After the death of Dinah, Jacob went to Bethany, New York and in the 1820 census there was a household of five: one male 26 to 44; one female 26 to 44; one male under 10; one male 16 to 25; and one female 16 to 25.[3015]

i   SALLY STEVENS (twin), b. at Strafford, 18 Mar 1800

ii   LUMAN STEVENS (twin), b. at Strafford, 18 Mar 1800; d. at East Bethany, NY, 15 Apr 1873; m. his first cousin, ALMA STEVENS, b. at Strafford, 29 May 1808 daughter of Abiel and Marcy (Haskell) Stevens; Alma d. at Bethany, 30 Jun 1891.

     Jacob likely remarried and there is one possible child identified from a second marriage. In 1850, Jacob was living in the household of Sylvester and his wife.[3016] Jacob, Sylvester, and Sylvester's wife Elvira are buried in Maple Lawn cemetery in East Bethany.[3017]

i   SYLVESTER STEVENS, b. at Bethany, NY, 1817; d. at East Bethany, 22 Nov 1880; m. by 1847, ELVIRA SYLVIA NORTON, b. 1823; Elvira d. at Bethany, 22 Nov 1880.

936)   URIAH HOLT STEVENS (*Elizabeth Holt Stevens⁵, Nathaniel Holt⁴, Oliver Holt³, Hannah Russell Holt², Robert¹*), baptized at Andover, 31 Oct 1779 son of Abiel and Elizabeth (Holt) Stevens; d. at Strafford, VT, 17 May 1845; m. SALLY ELVINA BLAISDELL, b. about 1785 daughter of Harvey and Elizabeth (Sargent) Blaisdell;[3018] Sally d. after 1850 when she was living in Strafford.

     Uriah and Sally were parents of eleven children born at Strafford, Vermont.[3019]

i   Rev. AMOS STEVENS, b. 30 Dec 1806; d. at Woodstock, OH, 28 Dec 1843; m. 1827, LUCINDA LAMSON, b. at Randolph, VT, 19 Jul 1801 daughter of Thomas and Anna (Martin) Lamson.

ii   JULIA STEVENS, b. 12 Jan 1809; d. at Schroon, NY, 30 Dec 1888; m. at Burlington, VT, 8 Apr 1833, LEONARD FOSTER, b. at Shrewsbury, VT, 18 Oct 1805 son od Daniel and Susanna (-) Foster;[3020] Leonard d. at Schroon, 1874.

iii   EZRA BLAISDELL STEVENS, b. 1810; d. at Strafford, 6 Jun 1890; m. at Norwich, 6 Mar 1834, AMY BULLARD BABCOCK, b. at Norwich, VT, about 1806; Amy d. at Strafford, 12 Mar 1871. The names of Amy's parents and given as Malastie and Anna Babcock on her death record.

iv   URSULA STEVENS, b. 1 Aug 1812

v   THEODORE STEVENS, b. May 1814; d. at Manchester, MI, 19 Jul 1876; m. JOANNA W. NORRIS, b. at Hardwick, VT, 10 Jul 1803 daughter of David and Hannah (Webber) Norris; Joanna d. at Manchester, 1866.

vi   JACOB BLAISDELL STEVENS, b. 20 Feb 1816; d. at West Fairlee, VT, 5 Mar 1896; m. at Somerset, VT, 22 Jan 1837, LEVINA LILLIE, b. at Woodstock, CT, 14 Mar 1816 daughter of Ezra and Levina (Clark) Lillie; Levina d. (burial at Searsburg, VT), 4 Nov 1890.

vii   SALLY STEVENS, b. 1818; d. at Strafford, 11 Feb 1847.

[3013] Norton, *Norton-Lathrop-Tolles-Doty American Ancestry*, p 17

[3014] Vermont, Vital Records, 1720-1908

[3015] 1820 U S Census; Census Place: Bethany, Genesee, New York; Page: 53; NARA Roll: M33_72; Image: 41

[3016] Year: 1850; Census Place: Bethany, Genesee, New York; Roll: 507; Page: 115B

[3017] Findagrave ID 27602602 and 117691321

[3018] The 1825 will of Harvey Blaisdell of Strafford has bequests to daughter Elvina Stevens and daughter Ruth Stevens

[3019] Vermont, Vital Records, 1720-1908

[3020] The birth records of two of the children in this family give the mother's maiden name as Susannah Foster.

viii   LEONARD STEVENS, b. 1820 (just the year is on the birth record transcription)

ix   MUNROE STEVENS, b. Mar 1822; d. at the National Home for Disabled Volunteer Soldiers in Togus, 4 May 1884. Munroe married LOUISA who was not identified.

x   ADEN N. STEVENS, b. 1824; d. at Woodstock, MI, 8 Dec 1897; m. ROSETTA, b. in VT, about 1826 who has not been identified; Rosetta d. at Woodstock, Dec 1893.

xi   MARY BLAISDELL STEVENS, b. Mar 1829. Mary was living with her mother in Strafford in 1850.

937)   DAVID STEVENS (*Elizabeth Holt Stevens⁵, Nathaniel Holt⁴, Oliver Holt³, Hannah Russell Holt², Robert¹*), baptized at Andover, MA, 16 Sep 1781 son of Abiel and Elizabeth (Holt) Stevens; d. at Clymer, NY, 29 Jun 1842; m. at Strafford, VT, 6 Dec 1804, RUTH BLAISDELL, b. 11 Jan 1785 daughter of Harvey and Elizabeth (Sargent) Blaisdell;[3021] Ruth d. at Clymer, 30 Apr 1837.[3022]

    There are six children known for David Stevens and Ruth Blaisdell. The older children were born at Strafford, the family seems to have been in Bethany, New York before finally settling in Clymer. At Bethany in 1820, the household consisted of seven persons: one male 26 to 44; one female 26 to 44; two males under 10; two males 10 to 15; and one female under 10.[3023] In the 1830 census at Clymer, the family consisted of seven persons: one male 40 to 49, one female 40 to 49, one male 5 to 9, one male 15 to 19, two male 20 to 29, and one female 15 to 19.[3024]

i   ABIEL HARVEY STEVENS, b. at Strafford, VT, 30 Nov 1806; d. at Harmony, WI, 21 Jan 1864;[3025] m. about 1832, BETSY S. REED, b. likely in Orleans County, NY, 11 Feb 1812 daughter of Samuel and Sally (Bates) Reed; Betsy d. at Janesville, WI, 3 Jan 1884. Betsy married second Joel Morrill.

ii   DAVID STEVENS, b. at Strafford, VT, 9 Sep 1808; d. at Norton, KS, 1889; m. ANN ELIZA CROSBY, b. in NY, 1812 daughter of Edmund and Polly (-) Crosby; Ann d. at Norton, 1887.

iii   ELIZABETH STEVENS, b. at Bethany, NY, 18 Mar 1811; d. at Harmony, WI, 5 May 1895; m. by 1835, DAVID LEWIS CROSBY, b. in NY 1807 son of Edmund and Polly (-) Crosby; David d. at Cedar Falls, IA, 14 May 1894.

iv   GEORGE WASHINGTON STEVENS, b. at Bethany, 15 Nov 1814; d. at Cedar Falls, IA, 10 Aug 1891; m. 1st about 1838, SALLY A. GLASS, b. 1818; Sally d. at Janesville, WI, 13 Apr 1848. George m. 2nd, about 1849, RUTH LEAKE, b. in NY, about 1827 daughter of David Z. and Sarah (Eaton) Leake;[3026] Ruth d. at Janesville, 27 Aug 1860.

v   JOHN STEVENS, b. 13 Mar 1817; d. at Bethany, NY, 19 Jul 1823.[3027]

vi   ELHANAN WINCHESTER STEVENS, b. at Bethany, 26 May 1822; d. at Harmony, WI, 10 Dec 1885; m. OLIVE A. TURNEY, b. in CT, Feb 1827 daughter of Seth Downs and Narcissa (Briscoe) Turney; Olive d. at Harmony, 1920.

Great-Grandchildren of John Russell and Sarah Chandler

938)   EPHRAIM HOUGHTON (*Phebe Holt Houghton⁴, Phebe Russell Holt Sheldon³, John², Robert¹*), b. at Union, 18 May 1759 son of James and Phebe (Holt) Houghton; d. at Woodstock, CT, 6 May 1840; m 1st at Thompson, 17 Jan 1788, ABIGAIL "NABBY" HOLBROOK, b. at Woodstock, 26 Apr 1770 daughter of Thomas and Abigail (Adams) Holbrook;[3028] Nabby d. at

---

[3021] The 1825 will (probate 1827) of Harvey Blaisdell of Strafford includes a bequest to daughter Ruth Stevens

[3022] Ruth and David are interred at Clymer Center Cemetery; findagrave ID 42621000 and 42620664

[3023] 1820 U S Census; Census Place: Bethany, Genesee, New York; Page: 53; NARA Roll: M33_72; Image: 41

[3024] Year: 1830; Census Place: Clymer, Chautauqua, New York; Series: M19; Roll: 86; Page: 306; Family History Library Film: 0017146

[3025] Abiel and Betsy are interred at Mount Zion Cemetery in Janesville, Wisconsin; findagrave ID: 13333300

[3026] The 1877 distribution from the estate of David Z. Leake (died 1872) of Rock County, WI includes heir Willis Stevens son of daughter Ruth deceased

[3027] Interred at Maple Lawn Cemetery in East Bethany; age at death of 6 years, 4 months, and 7 days; findagrave ID: 117691288

[3028] The final distribution for the estate of Thomas Holbrook (probate 1796; distribution 1816) includes a distribution to the four children of daughter Nabby Houghton deceased; Connecticut Wills and Probate, Pomfret Probate District, Town of Thompson, Estate of Thomas Holbrook, 1796, No. 2106

Woodstock, 23 Sep 1815. Ephraim m. 2nd Mar 1817,[3029] MARY "POLLY" NICHOLS (widow of Benjamin Skinner), b. at Thompson, 3 May 1773 daughter of Jonathan and Mary (Sibley) Nichols; Polly d. at Woodstock, 4 Aug 1855.

On 18 July 1832, Ephraim Houghton then aged 73 years and resident at Woodstock made statement that on 10 December 1776 he enlisted for three weeks as a private under Lt. Morris. The troops went to Providence, Rhode Island, Stamford, Connecticut, and New Haven. Within a week after his return, he was drafted for two months to Bristol, Rhode Island in the company of Capt. Amos Paine. He then served for two months as a substitute for Manasseh Hosmer in the company of Capt. Ebenezer Crofts of Abington, Connecticut. In July 1779, he enlisted for a nine-month term under Capt. Joseph Durkee. He gave his birth date as May 1759 at Ashford, Connecticut.

On 29 March 1855 (for an update of a statement made 1 August 1853), Mary Houghton, aged 82 years, provided a statement related to her widow's pension. She reported that she and Ephraim were married in March 1817 by Rev. John Nichols and that her name before marriage was Mary Nichols and her first husband was Benjamin Skinner. Her husband Ebenezer Houghton died 6 May 1840.[3030]

In his will written 7 February 1830 (proved 23 May 1840), Ephraim Houghton bequeathed to beloved son James Sibley Houghton his real estate in Woodstock and Thompson except that reserved for the use and improvement of his beloved wife while she is a widow. Beloved wife Mary receives all the household furniture she brought to the marriage to be hers forever. The indoor movables are to be divided equally between Mary and son James Sibley. Mary has use of one-third of the real estate while she is a widow. Mary may also receive the income from the real estate given to son James, if needed, for her support until James reaches age twenty-one. The household furniture that was left at the farmhouse lately sold to Mr. Edward Howard in Thompson is to be divided equally between daughter Lucy Howard and granddaughter Phebe Houghton. Any residue goes to son James Sibley Houghton. Oliver Morse of Woodstock was named executor.[3031]

Ephraim Houghton and Nabby Holbrook were parents of four children born at Thompson.

i   LUCY HOUGHTON, b. 12 Jun 1789; d. at Dudley, MA, Nov 1833; m. at Dudley, 31 Mar 1819, EDWARD HOWARD who has not been identified.

ii   EPHRAIM HOUGHTON, b. 4 Apr 1790 to 4 Apr 1799; the birth record was torn and last number not readable.[3032]

iii   THOMAS HOUGHTON, b. 8 Aug 1791; d. at Thompson, 20 Nov 1827; m. at Lisbon, CT, 17 Sep 1821, ESTHER LOVET STEVENS, b. at Hampton, 18 Oct 1799 daughter of John and Florina (Brewster) Stevens; Esther d. at Woodstock, 17 Dec 1856. Esther married second William Lester. Thomas and Esther had two children, a son who died in infancy and daughter Phebe Elizabeth Houghton.

iv   PHEBE HOUGHTON, b. 15 Aug 1796

Ephraim Houghton and Polly Nichols were parents of one child.

i   JAMES SIBLEY HOUGHTON, b. at Woodstock, 3 Sep 1819; d. at Woodstock, 15 Aug 1845; m. SYLVIA L. CARPENTER, b. at Sutton, MA, 14 Jan 1821 daughter of John and Abigail (Healy) Carpenter; Sylvia d. at Woodstock, 7 Jan 1904. Sylvia did not remarry after James's death.

939)   PHEBE HOUGHTON (*Phebe Holt Houghton4, Phebe Russell Holt Sheldon3, John2, Robert1*), b. at Union, 11 Aug 1762 daughter of James and Phebe (Holt) Houghton; d. at Thompson, 25 Feb 1800; m. at Thompson, 6 Jan 1789, EBENEZER ORMSBY,[3033] b. at Killingly, 17 Mar 1764 son of Thomas and Hannah (Carpenter) Ormsbee; Ebenezer d. at Thompson, 1806 (probate 1806 with widow Experience). Ebenezer married second about 1801, Phebe's sister EXPERIENCE HOUGHTON, b. at Union, 8 Feb 1777; Experience was living in Thompson in 1810 but nothing is known after that.

In his will written 15 September 1806, Ebenezer Ormsby bequeathed to beloved wife Experience use of one-half of the real estate while she is a widow. His four sons receive the remainder of the estate real and personal: Daniel and Ebenezer, Thomas, and James. In addition, son James is to be provided support and maintenance until he reaches age nine years. Other specific provisions are made for the support of Experience. Real estate was valued at $1,070 which consisted of 60 acres with old dwelling house and 17 acres of woodland. Personal estate was valued at $193.75.[3034]

Phebe and Ebenezer were parents of four known children born at Thompson, Connecticut.

[3029] U.S., Revolutionary War Pension and Bounty-Land Warrant Application Files, 1800-1900; Case W2550, widow's pension application of Mary Houghton

[3030] U.S., Revolutionary War Pension and Bounty-Land Warrant Application Files, 1800-1900; Case W2550

[3031] Connecticut Wills, Windham County, Wills, volume 1-2, 1831-1847, images 388-389, accessed through ancestry.com

[3032] Houghton's Houghton genealogy reports that Ephraim had a son Ephraim born in 1822 who went to medical college and practiced in Mobile, AL and died unmarried but this seems as error as there is no Ephraim in father's will.

[3033] The spelling of the last name is given as Ormsbee and Ormsby. The children all seem to use Ormsby.

[3034] Connecticut Wills and Probate, Hartford, Pomfret Probate District, Estate of Ebenezer Ormsby of Thompson, Case 3010

i   DANIEL ORMSBY, b. 1 Nov 1789; d. at Fayette, ME, 25 Feb 1858; m. 18 May 1815, ZERUIAH POWERS, b. at Wilton, ME, 17 Jul 1793 daughter of Gideon and Ruth (Packard) Powers; Zeruiah d. at Fayette, 17 Apr 1885.

ii   EBENEZER ORMSBY, b. 1 Nov 1792

iii   THOMAS ORMSBY, b. about 1796; d. at Thompson, 30 Sep 1832; m. at Thompson, 28 May 1822, MARY ANN G. PHIPPS, b. about 1799 daughter of Jason and Mary (Healy) Phipps; Mary d. (burial at Dudley, MA), 19 Nov 1840.

iv   JAMES ORMSBY, b. about 1799; d. at Thompson, CT, 20 Aug 1871; m. at Thompson, 18 Nov 1824, FIDELIA PHELPS, b. at Sutton, MA, 11 Sep 1803 daughter of Ebenezer and Mary (Russell) Phelps; Fidelia d. at Thompson, 22 Jun 1881.

940)   SILVANUS HOUGHTON (*Phebe Holt Houghton⁴, Phebe Russell Holt Sheldon³, John², Robert¹*), b. at Union, 21 Jun 1765 son of James and Phebe (Holt) Houghton; d. at Thompson, 7 Feb 1816; m. at Thompson, 15 Jan 1795, BETSEY HOLBROOK, b. at Woodstock, 24 Oct 1774 daughter of Thomas and Abigail (Adams) Holbrook; Betsey d. at Thompson, 27 Sep 1820.

Silvanus and Betsey resided in Thompson, Connecticut. Silvanus Houghton did not leave a will and his estate entered probate 29 February 1816 with Betsey Houghton as administratrix. Estate was valued at $649.50. On 17 February 1816, Silvanus Houghton a minor age seventeen made choice of Capt. Theodore Dwight of Thompson as guardian.[3035]

Silvanus and Betsey were parents of eight children born at Thompson, Connecticut, although the children were baptized at Dudley "on account of the Mother."[3036]

i   SILVA HOUGHTON, b 10 Aug 1796

ii   SILVANUS HOUGHTON, b. 5 Dec 1799 and baptized at Dudley, 13 Jul 1800; m. at Sutton, MA, 27 Aug 1819, SALLY PARKER. The Houghton genealogy (p 121) reports that Silvanus went to Cincinnati where he died.

iii   NABBY CARTER HOUGHTON, baptized at Dudley, MA, 13 Jul 1800

iv   HOSEA HOUGHTON, b. 18 Apr 1802; d. in Cuba.[3037] Hosea was a trader based out of Providence, RI where he was living in 1830.[3038]

v   BETSEY CHAPIN HOUGHTON, b. Jan 1806; d. at Thompson, 25 May 1848;[3039] m. at Thompson, 2 Oct 1826, JOHN EDDY DAY, b. at Dudley, 23 Jun 1800 son of Jabez and Sarah (Eddy) Day; John d. at Thompson, 24 Jun 1836.

vi   SAMANTHA ADAMS HOUGHTON, b. 1809 and baptized at Dudley, 30 Jul 1809; d. at Providence, RI, 6 Oct 1838; m. at Providence, 28 Nov 1833, WESTON ADAM FISHER, b. at Wrentham, MA, 12 Sep 1806 son of Cyrus and Hannah (Frost) Fisher; Weston d. at Providence, 15 Feb 1887.

vii   IRENA HOUGHTON, b. 4 Jul 1813; d. 11 Mar 1815.

viii   IRENA HOUGHTON, b. 20 Aug 1815; d. at Thompson, 3 Mar 1849; m. at Providence, RI, 1838, JOEL ELLIS FISHER, b. at Attleboro, MA, 13 Aug 1815 son of William and Polly (Ellis) Fisher; Joel d. at Satilla, GA (burial at Thompson, CT), 15 Oct 1854 from yellow fever. He married second Martha A. Taylor and married third Julia Bryant. Joel was a partner in the cotton mill of William Fisher & Sons. He moved to Georgia after contracting consumption.[3040]

941)   ORINDA HOUGHTON (*Phebe Holt Houghton⁴, Phebe Russell Holt Sheldon³, John², Robert¹*), b. at Union, 14 Feb 1768 daughter of James and Phebe (Holt) Houghton; d. at Wilton, ME, 9 May 1843; m. at Dublin, NH, about 1790, BENJAMIN LEARNED, b. at Dublin, 23 Sep 1767 son of Benjamin and Elizabeth (Wilson) Learned; Benjamin d. at Wilton, ME, 16 Sep 1853. After Orinda's death, Benjamin married widow Jane Hardy.

Benjamin Learned was a farmer. He and Orinda lived in Dublin, New Hampshire prior to relocating in Wilton, Maine by the time of the birth of their youngest child.

In his will written 12 February 1847 (proved 7 November 1853), Benjamin Learned of Wilton bequeathed to beloved wife Jane the use and income of the homestead farm in Wilton while she is a widow. Jane also receives $150 and other provisions for her support. Son Asa Learned receives fifty dollars to be applied to a note of ninety dollars that Benjamin holds

[3035] Connecticut Wills and Probate, Hartford, Pomfret Probate District, Town of Thompson, Estate of Silvanus Houghton, Case 2186
[3036] Massachusetts Vital Records Project, https://ma-vitalrecords.org/MA/Worcester/Dudley/Images/Dudley_B070.shtml
[3037] Houghton, *The Houghton Genealogy*, p 121
[3038] Hosea is listed as a trader in the 1830 city directory for Providence, Rhode Island. Ancestry.com, U.S. City Directories, 1822-1995
[3039] Died at 42 years, 4 months, 23 days; findagrave ID: 55921587
[3040] Fisher, *The Fisher Genealogy*, p 364

against Asa. Bequests of fifty dollars are made to children Benjamin Learned, Asenath Brown, Phebe Reed, Sally Hiscock, Orinda Houghton, and Betsey Allen. Granddaughter Mary Ann Learned[3041] also receives fifty dollars. The payments for the children are to come from notes that Benjamin holds against other persons. George Gage, Esq. of Wilton was named executor. Real estate was valued at $429 and personal estate at $88.47.[3042]

Orinda and Benjamin were parents of nine children.

i   ASA LEARNED, b. at Dublin, NH, 18 May 1791; d. at Farmington, ME, 12 Jul 1867; m. SARAH GREEN, b. 13 Apr 1794 daughter of Abiathar and Zilpha (Jones) Green; Sarah d. at Farmington, 14 Jan 1848.

ii   BENJAMIN LEARNED, b. at Dublin, 7 Apr 1793; d. at Wilton, ME, Dec 1879; m. 1st about 1822, BETSEY POWERS, b. 12 Oct 1798 daughter of Gideon and Ruth (Packard) Powers; Betsey d. at Wilton, 1841. Benjamin m. 2nd ELIZABETH BRIDGES, b. at Wilton, NH, 23 Jul 1800 daughter of Enoch and Elizabeth (Butterfield) Bridges; Elizabeth d. (burial at Wilton), 1886.

iii   ASENATH LEARNED, b. at Dublin, 26 Mar 1795; d. at Wilton, ME, 19 Jul 1882; m. at Wilton, 30 Nov 1815, HAMMON BROWN, b. at Wilton, ME, 22 Sep 1793 son of Isaac and Sarah (Floyd) Brown; Hammon d. at Wilton, 15 Aug 1864.

iv   PHEBE LEARNED, b. at Dublin, 12 Jul 1797; d. at Wilton, ME, 8 Jul 1856; m. ISAAC REED, b. 1797 son of Jacob and Susannah (Chandler) Reed; Isaac d. at Portland, ME, 2 Jun 1864. Isaac Reed was a carpenter and the family lived in Worcester, MA for a time.

v   JOSEPH LEARNED, b. at Dublin, 20 Jun 1799; d. at Wilton, ME, 8 Oct 1829.

vi   GILMAN LEARNED, b. at Dublin, 30 Aug 1801; d. at Jay, ME, 4 May 1827; m. at Jay, 24 Apr 1825, BETSEY B. TOWNSEND, b. 1805 daughter of Bela and Hannah (Burrill) Townsend;[3043] Betsey d. at Farmington, ME, 5 Dec 1887. Betsey was second married to William E. Morse.

vii   POLLY LEARNED, b. at Dublin, 22 Sep 1803; d. at Monson, ME, 5 Jun 1876; m. 1826, SAMUEL HISCOCK, b. 2 Jun 1801 son of Samuel and Elizabeth (Teague) Hiscock; Samuel d. at Monson, 28 Oct 1883.

viii   ORINDA LEARNED, b. at Dublin, 17 Jan 1806; d. after 1880 when living at Turner, ME; m. her first cousin, JOSEPH HOUGHTON (*James Houghton[5], Phebe Holt Houghton[4], Phebe Russell Holt[3], John[2], Robert[1]*), b. at Dublin, 1 Sep 1801 son of James and Hannah (Russell) Houghton; James d. at Weld, 29 Jan 1869.

ix   BETSEY LEARNED, b. at Wilton, ME, 18 Mar 1808; d. at Jay, ME, 1877; m. STEPHEN L. ALLEN, b. 1802 son of Aaron and Huldah (Harris) Allen; Stephen d. at Wilton, 1890.

942)   BETHIAH HOUGHTON (*Phebe Holt Houghton[4], Phebe Russell Holt Sheldon[3], John[2], Robert[1]*), b. at Union, 8 Mar 1771 daughter of James and Phebe (Holt) Houghton; d. at Gilead, ME, 21 Apr 1846; m. at Dublin, 16 Jan 1789, JOHN MASON, b. at Dublin, 8 May 1769 son of Moses and Lydia (Knapp) Mason; John d. at Gilead, 19 Sep 1844.

Bethiah and John married in Dublin but were in Bethel, Maine in 1789 where John's brothers Water and Moses settled. Bethiah and John moved on to Gilead, Maine in 1793.[3044] For time, John Mason had a private school in West Bethel.[3045]

Bethiah Houghton and John Mason were parents of thirteen children, the oldest child born at Dublin, New Hampshire, the second child born at Bethel, and the other children at Gilead, Maine.[3046]

i   JOHN MASON, b. 26 Apr 1789; d. at Bethel, ME, 1877; m. at Gilead, 2 Apr 1811, HANNAH STILES, b. at Gilead, 4 Jul 1792 daughter of Ezra and Hannah (Cutter) Stiles; Hannah d. at Bethel, 1882.

ii   LYDIA MASON, b. 18 Aug 1791; d. at Bethel, 8 Aug 1872; m. 9 Apr 1807, SETH WIGHT, b. at Dublin, NH, 21 May 1783 son of Joel and Elizabeth (Twitchell) Wight; Seth d. at Bethel, 9 Dec 1863.

iii   BETHIAH MASON, b. 2 Aug 1793; d. at Gilead, 1865; m. at Gilead, 7 May 1812, ABRAHAM BENNETT, b. about 1793; Abraham d. at Gilead, 23 Apr 1857.

iv   SYLVANUS MASON, b. 29 Sep 1795; d. at Bethel, 4 Jul 1875; m. at Gilead, 1 Jan 1818, LYDIA SCRIBNER, b. at Harrison, ME, 13 Jul 1798 daughter of Joseph and Annie (Woodsum) Scribner; Lydia d. at West Bethel, 27 Sep 1884.

[3041] Mary Ann Learned is the daughter of Gilman. She was born in 1826 and died 28 May 1848 at Wilton, Maine.

[3042] Maine Wills and Probate Records, Franklin County, File 548, Benjamin Learned

[3043] The 1826 will of Bela Townsend of Wilton includes a bequest to his daughter Betsey B. Learned.

[3044] Lapham, *History of Bethel*, p 586

[3045] Mason, *Descendants of Capt. Hugh Mason*, p 106

[3046] Mason, *Descendants of Capt. Hugh Mason*, p 106. This volume reports that the birth records are taken from an account book kept by Artemas Mason.

v   BETSEY MASON, b. 27 Jul 1797; d. at Bethel, 16 Sep 1869; m. at Gilead, 14 Jul 1817, NATHAN STILES, b. at Gilead, 12 Apr 1787 son of Ezra and Hannah (Cutter) Stiles; Nathan d. at Bethel, 4 Oct 1878.

vi   IRA MASON, b. 16 Jan 1800; d. after 1870 when he was living at Albany; m. at Gilead, 27 Apr 1820, REBECCA SCRIBNER, b. 7 Aug 1801 daughter of Edward and Rebecca (Woodsum) Scribner

vii   PHEBE MASON, b. 7 Feb 1802; d. at Gilead, 29 Aug 1836; m. at Gilead, 13 Mar 1824, WILLIAM WIGHT, b. at Gilead, 26 May 1799 son of Ephraim and Susannah (Patch) Wight; William d. at Gilead, 13 Aug 1870.

viii   LORENZO MASON, b. 8 Feb 1804; d. at Berlin, NH, 29 Apr 1884; m. at Gilead, 24 Oct 1824, MARY CONNER, b. 17 Oct 1802 daughter of Michael and Eunice (·) Conner; Mary d. at Berlin, 11 Jul 1878.

ix   SALOME CHAPMAN MASON, b. 13 Apr 1805; d. at Gilead, 27 Nov 1849. Salome did not marry.

x   MARY C. MASON, b. 23 Apr 1807; d. at Littleton, CO, 31 Jan 1895; m. 21 Jun 1830, JOHN MAREAN BEAN, b. at Bethel, 18 Feb 1805 son of Ebenezer and Eunice (Kendall) Bean; John d. at Gilead, 23 May 1875.

xi   ARTEMAS MASON, b. 12 Aug 1809; d. at Bethel, 24 Aug 1893; m. 1st BETSEY BARTLETT (widow of Hezekiah Grover), b. at Cumberland, ME, 24 Dec 1808 daughter of Thomas Bartlett; Betsey d. at Bethel, 2 Dec 1845. Artemas m. 2nd at Harrison, ME, 3 May 1846, SARAH BRACKETT, b. 11 Apr 1822 daughter of William and Sarah (Hobbs) Brackett; Sarah d. 11 May 1895.

xii   ORINDA LEONARD MASON, b. 12 Apr 1812; d. at Bethel, 19 Sep 1894; m. at Bethel, 12 Dec 1839, JOSEPH ABBOT TWITCHELL, b. at Bethel, 19 May 1817 son of Joseph and Polly (Abbott) Twitchell; Joseph d. at Bethel, 2 May 1890.

xiii   MOSES MASON, b. 22 Feb 1815; d. at Bethel, 6 Aug 1897; m. at Embden, ME, 11 Mar 1838, MARTHA WALKER, b. about 1816 daughter of John and Cynthia (Phillips) Walker; Martha d. at Gilead, 30 Oct 1886.

943)   ASENATH HOUGHTON (*Phebe Holt Houghton⁴, Phebe Russell Holt Sheldon³, John², Robert¹*), b. at Union, CT, 29 Nov 1775 daughter of James and Phebe (Holt) Houghton; d. at Thompson, CT, 30 Dec 1860; m. about 1796, WILLIAM JORDAN, b. at Dudley, MA, 5 Dec 1774 son of William and Comfort (Palmer) Jordan; William d. at Thompson, 27 Jun 1849 (probate 1849 with widow Asenath).

     William Jordan was a farmer in Thomson, Connecticut. He did not leave a will and the estate entered probate 14 July 1849 with Aaron White and Perley Jordan providing the bond for estate administration. In a document signed 20 April 1850, the following persons bound themselves to the administration of the estate: Asenath Jordan, Perley Jordan, William A. Jordan, and Hiram Jordan all of Thompson, Connecticut; David Jordan of Grafton, Massachusetts; Lorenzo Jordan of Attleborough, Massachusetts; and Augustus Ormsbee of Saco, Maine. Real estate was valued at $3.375. The real estate could not be divided without prejudice to its value and was settled on second son Perley Jordan (after the set-off of the dower), the eldest son having refused, and Perley was to pay his siblings a proportional amount of its value. The final settlement of the estate occurred 26 April 1850 with dispersal of $849.31 which was the remainder from the personal estate following the payment of the estate debts: widow Asenath Jordan received $263.11, and $97.70 was paid to David Jordan, Perley Jordan, William A. Jordan, Hiram Jordan, Lorenzo Jordan, and Amanda Omsbee the only known heirs of the deceased.[3047]

     William and Asenath were parents of six children born at Thompson Connecticut. Asenath had all the children baptized at Dudley, Massachusetts (baptized on "mother's account").

i   DAVID JOURDAN, b. 1797 and baptized at Dudley, 25 Jan 1802; d. at Grafton, MA, 11 Aug 1883; m. at Hopkinton, MA, 12 May 1825, SUSANNA ADAMS, b. at Hopkinton, 11 Nov 1798 daughter of Benjamin and Anna (Holmes) Adams; Susanna d. at Grafton, 26 Nov 1877.

ii   PEARLY JORDAN, b. 1799 and baptized at Dudley, 25 Jan 1802; d. at Thompson, 11 Dec 1873; m. at Thompson, 4 Dec 1823, SOPHIA PHELPS, b. at Sutton, MA, 3 Oct 1796 daughter of Ebenezer and Mary (Russell) Phelps; Sophia d. at Thompson, 25 Jan 1885.

iii   WILLIAM AUSTIN JORDAN, b. 1802 and baptized at Dudley, 12 Sep 1802; d. at Thompson, 19 Aug 1872; m. at Thompson, 4 Jan 1824, HEPHZIBAH MCFARLIN, b. at Oxford, MA, 1801 likely daughter of Josiah and Hephzibah (Moffitt) McFarlin; Hephzibah d. at Thompson, 28 Nov 1850.

iv   HIRAM JORDAN, b. 1804 and baptized at Dudley, 3 Jun 1804; d. at Thompson, 1857; m. at Thompson, 1 Jan 1829, NANCY P. CORBIN, b. 1807 daughter of Parley and Dolly (Perrin) Corbin;[3048] Nancy d. at Thompson, 1887.

[3047] Connecticut Wills and Probate, Hartford District, Town of Thompson, Estate of William Jordan, Case 725
[3048] The 1844 probate of Parley Corbin includes a distribution to daughter Nancy Jordan.

v   LORENZO JORDAN, b. 1808 and baptized at Dudley, 9 Oct 1808; d. at Attleboro, MA, 24 Sep 1894; m. at
           Windsor, MA, 23 May 1853, MARY L. DRAPER, b. at Kingston, RI, 1821 (per death record); Mary d. at North
           Attleboro, 16 Mar 1892.

vi   AMANDA MELVINA JORDAN, b. 1811 and baptized at Dudley, 5 May 1811; d. at Thompson, 20 Apr 1882; m. at
           Thompson, 11 May 1832, AUGUSTUS ORMSBEE, b. at Thompson (per death record of children), about 1810;
           Augustus d. at Thompson, 30 Jan 1859. Amanda and Augustus lived in Saco, Maine but returned to Thompson
           before their deaths.

944)   EPHRAIM HOLT (*Ephraim Holt⁴, Phebe Russell Holt Sheldon³, John², Robert¹*), b. at Holden, 3 Dec 1762 son of
Ephraim and Sarah (Black) Holt; d. at Hubbardston, 3 Jun 1844; m. at Middleton, 24 Feb 1795, JERUSHA "RUSHA" KENNEY,
b. at Middleton, 5 May 1769 daughter of Simeon and Jerusha (Johnson) Kenney; Jerusha d. at Grafton, MA, 2 Nov 1857.
           Ephraim was born in Holden but settled in Hubbardston in 1797.[3049] Ephraim served in the Revolution and made
application for a pension on 6 September 1832 based on his service. He enlisted as a private at Holden 1 September 1779 for a
period of six months. His widow Jerusha later received a pension.[3050]
           Ephraim and Jerusha were parents of three children born at Hubbardston.

i   SIMEON K. HOLT, b. 3 Aug 1797; d. at Hubbardston, 28 Feb 1833; m. 7 Jan 1824, SOPHIA MUNDELL, b. at
           Hubbardston, 6 Aug 1802 daughter of Daniel and Phebe (Falis) Mundell; Sophia d. at Hubbardston, 10 Jun 1868.

ii   SALLY D. HOLT, b. 28 Mar 1802; d. at Hubbardston, 22 Mar 1880; m. at Hubbardston, 28 Nov 1827, DAVID
           BAKER, b. at Hubbardston, 7 May 1802 son of Artemas and Sarah (Nichols) Baler; David d. at Hubbardston, 7
           Sep 1864.

iii   BETSEY C. HOLT, b. 21 Aug 1805; d. at Hubbardston, 10 Oct 1857. Betsey did not marry. Her estate was
           administered by Israel Davis at the request of her mother Jerusha Holt and her sister Sally Baker.[3051]

945)   SARAH HOLT (*Ephraim Holt⁴, Phebe Russell Holt Sheldon³, John², Robert¹*), b. at Holden, 23 Aug 1764 daughter of
Ephraim and Sarah (Black) Holt; d. at Holden, Jul 1859; m. at Holden, 29 Mar 1792, ISRAEL DAVIS, b. at Holden, 29 Oct 1766
son of Israel and Rebecca (Hubbard) Davis; Israel d. at Hubbardston, 24 Aug 1848.
           Sarah and Israel resided in Hubbardston where Israel served as selectman for ten years between 1801 and 1822. He
was also assessor in 1804-1805.[3052] Sarah and Israel were parents of five children born at Hubbardston, four of whom died in
early childhood.[3053]

i   SALLY DAVIS, b. 15 Jan 1794; d. 30 Jan 1800.

ii   JOSEPH HUBBARD DAVIS, b. 2 Jul 1797; d. 24 Sep 1799.

iii   Son, d. 8 Jan and d. 26 Jan 1800.

iv   ISRAEL HUBBARD DAVIS, b. 9 Mar 1801; d. 30 Dec 1801.

v   ISRAEL DAVIS, b. 9 Jan 1803; d. at Hubbardston, 24 Oct 1872; m. 1ˢᵗ at Hubbardston, 2 Nov 1824, CHLOE
           WRIGHT WAITE, b. at Hubbardston, 17 Nov 1804 daughter of Jacob and Ruth (Wright) Waite; Chloe d. 21 Oct
           1842. Israel m. 2ⁿᵈ at Hubbardston, 30 May 1848, LOIS STONE (widow of Isaac Williams), b. at Hubbardston, 13
           Aug 1819 daughter of Samson and Dolly (Lamb0 Stone; Lois d. 22 Sep 1875.

946)   JOHN HOLT (*Ephraim Holt⁴, Phebe Russell Holt Sheldon³, John², Robert¹*), b. at Holden, 22 Jan 1777 son of Ephraim
and Sarah (Black) Holt; d. at Troy, NH, 1 Apr 1836; m. at Holden, 24 Nov 1803, HANNAH WRIGHT, b. at Holden, 29 Apr 1781
daughter of Judah and Tabitha (Hartwell) Wright; Hannah d. at West Boylston, MA, 8 Jan 1857.
           John and Hannah were parents of eight children whose births are recorded at Holden, Massachusetts.

[3049] Stowe, *History of the Town of Hubbardston*, p 29

[3050] Revolutionary War Pension and Bounty Land Warrant Application Files, Case W1867

[3051] *Worcester County, MA: Probate File Papers, 1731-1881*. Online database. AmericanAncestors.org. New England Historic Genealogical Society, 2015. Case 30621

[3052] Stowe, *History of the Town of Hubbardston*, pp 210-211

[3053] Massachusetts Town Clerk Records, Hubbardston, Births, Marriages and Deaths 1797-188, p 32;
https://www.familysearch.org/ark:/61903/3:1:3QS7-8979-4LTY?i=27&cc=2061550

i   DORINDA "RENDY" HOLT, b. 2 Mar 1804; d. at Rutland, MA, 14 Feb 1888; m. at Holden, 18 Sep 1826, EPHRAIM CHILDS, baptized at Sturbridge, 13 Jun 1802 son of Ephraim and Catherine (Whitney) Childs; Ephraim d. at Rutland, 6 Jan 1847.

ii   SARAH HOLT, b. 20 May 1806; d. at Millbury, MA, 2 Apr 1874; m. at Springfield, MA, 9 Dec 1829, JOHN J. MUZZY; John d. at Cincinnati, OH, Sep 1833 (widow Sarah named guardian for minor son John J. Muzzy on 7 Oct 1833).

iii   SAMUEL HOLT, b. 30 Oct 1807; d. at Salem, MA, 11 Sep 1893; m. at Millbury, MA, 13 Feb 1832, EMILY BEAMAN DAVENPORT, b. at Boylston, MA, 7 May 1812 daughter of John and Mary (Beaman) Davenport; Emily d. at Salem, 31 Dec 1885.

iv   MARY HOLT, b. 24 Jan 1809; d. at Leicester, MA, 7 May 1880; m. 10 May 1832, JOSIAH Q. LAMB, b. at Spencer, 2 Jan 1803 son of Josiah Q. and Abigail (Muzzy) Lamb; Josiah d. at Leicester, 1 Jun 1850.

v   HANNAH HOLT, b. 14 Oct 1810; d. 1850. Hannah did not marry.

vi   ALONA HOLT, b. 28 Nov 1812; d. at Norwich, CT, 7 Oct 1886; m. at Millbury, MA, 27 May 1831, AUGUSTUS ATWOOD, b. at Sturbridge, MA, 30 Sep 1806 son of Doane and Polly (Allen) Atwood; Augustus d. 24 May 1853.

vii   NANCY HOLT, b. 9 Jan 1817; d. at Mason, NH, 7 Apr 1836.

viii   STEPHEN HOLT, b. 12 Nov 1820; d. at Boylston, 7 Apr 1887; m. 1st 26 Oct 1842, MARY MOORE HASTINGS, b. at Boylston, 19 Apr 1823 daughter of John and Clarimond (Bigelow) Hastings; Mary d. at West Boylston, 23 Mar 1883. Stephen m. 2nd at Sterling, MA, 15 Jan 1885, SARAH ANN POLLARD, b. at Groton, MA, 9 Sep 1828 daughter of Jacob and Mary (Davis) Pollard; Sarah d. at Henniker, NH, 15 Mar 1915.

947)   PHEBE HOLT (*Ephraim Holt⁴, Phebe Russell Holt Sheldon³, John², Robert¹*), b. at Holden, 28 Jun 1779 daughter of Ephraim and Sarah (Black) Holt; d. at Keene, NH, 11 Apr 1867; m. at Holden, 20 Jan 1803, ZALMON HOW, b. at Winchendon, MA, 23 Feb 1775 son of Jotham and Dorothy (Smith) How; Zalmon d. at Fitzwilliam, NH, 1855.

     Zalmon and Phebe married in Holden but were immediately after in Marlborough, New Hampshire in the area now part of Troy.[3054] They were later in Fitzwilliam reported as arriving there in 1837.[3055]

     Phebe and Zalmon were parents of seven children.

i   ASENATH HOW, b. at Marlborough, NH, 12 Aug 1804; d. at Guilford, VT (burial at Brattleboro), 6 Mar 1886; m. at Troy, NH, 4 Dec 1834, JOHN B. SIMONDS, b. at Alstead, NH, 11 Dec 1804 son of Elisha and Mary (Brown) Simonds; John d. at Guilford, 17 Jun 1887.

ii   NELSON HOW, b. at Troy, 7 May 1807; d. at Somerville, MA, 9 Mar 1881; m. 1st at Fitzwilliam, 2 Jan 1832, ELIZA SWEETSER, b. at Fitzwilliam, 14 Mar 1815 daughter of Caleb and Mary (Whittemore) Sweetser; Eliza d. 3 Jun 1850. Nelson m. 2nd at Troy, 3 Dec 1850, MARY ANGELINE PLATT, b. at Millbury, MA, 22 Dec 1831 daughter of David and Elizabeth (Davis) Platt; Mary d. at Somerville, 9 Jul 1879.

iii   SARAH HOW, b. at Marlborough, 10 Aug 1810; d. at Fitzwilliam, about 1847 (husband's remarriage); m. 14 Apr 1831, THOMAS SWEETSER, b. at Fitzwilliam, 14 Feb 1808 son of Caleb and Mary (Whittemore) Sweetser; Thomas d. at Fitzwilliam, 23 Dec 1850. Thomas was second married to Esther.

iv   MARY HOW, b. about 1811; d. at Swanzey, NH, 6 Nov 1879; m. 1st at Troy, 3 Dec 1835, HARVEY BLANDING, b. at Richmond, NH, 1 May 1809 son of Otis and Abigail (Burrus) Blanding; Harvey d. at Troy, 23 Mar 1859. Mary m. 2nd at Keene, 1 Jan 1861, SYLVANUS PERHAM, b. at Spencer, MA, 23 Sep 1807 son of William and Persis (Sargent) Perham; Sylvanus d. at Troy, 1 Feb 1874. Sylvanus was first married to Betsey Damon.

v   MARTHA HOW, b. at Marlborough, 1814; d. at Keene, 11 Feb 1870; m. at Troy, 6 Nov 1834, ASA B. CLARK, b. at Troy, 4 Sep 1814 son of Jonathan and Mary (Brewer) Clark; Asa d. at Marlborough, 3 Feb 1901.

vi   HARRIET N. HOW, b. about 1816; d. after 1870 when she was living at Newfane, VT; m. before 1840, GIDEON GRANGER WILLIS, b. 2 Jan 1812 son of Gideon and Milly (Walkup) Willis; Gideon d. at Northfield, MA, 12 Jun 1869.

vii   JOEL HOW, b. about 1819; d. at Keene, 5 Apr 1867; m. 6 Mar 1844, NANCY RICHARDSON, b. at Royalston, 23 Jan 1829 daughter of George and Sophronia (Nichols) Richardson; Nancy d. at Somersworth, NH, 22 Jan 1912.

[3054] Bemis, *History of the Town of Marlborough*, p 541

[3055] Norton, *History of Fitzwilliam*, p 613

948)   EBENEZER FLINT (*Asenath Holt Flint⁴, Phebe Russell Holt Sheldon³, John², Robert¹*), b. at Reading, 13 May 1765 son of Ebenezer and Asenath (Holt) Flint; d. at Hillsborough, NH, 14 Mar 1833; m. at Andover, 14 Mar 1793, his third cousin once removed, DORCAS LUFKIN (*Mehitable Holt Lufkin⁵, Thomas Holt⁴, Thomas Holt³, Mary Russell Holt², Robert¹*), b. at Andover, 1776 (baptized 23 May 1779) daughter of Samuel and Mehitable (Holt) Lufkin; Dorcas d. at Hillsborough, 26 Apr 1848.

Ebenezer was born in Reading and went with his father and family to Wilton. Ebenezer settled in Hillsborough where he was a farmer.[3056]

Ebenezer Flint and Dorcas Lufkin were parents of eleven children born at Hillsborough.

i   EBENEZER FLINT, b. 1 Dec 1793; d. at Franconia, NH, 22 Jan 1870; m. 16 Nov 1817, SARAH HOWLETT,[3057] b. at Bradford, NH, about 1795 daughter of John and Phebe (Johnson) Howlett; Sarah d. at Alexandria, NH, 9 Oct 1839.

ii   JOHN FLINT, b. 24 Dec 1795

iii   DORCAS FLINT, b. 11 Nov 1797; d. at Andover, NH, 7 Nov 1880; m. at Hillsborough, 29 Sep 1816, IRA WILKINS, b. at Hillsborough, 22 Jun 1793 son of Asaph and Ruth (Curtis) Wilkins; Ira d. at Danbury, NH, 17 Dec 1858.

iv   HENRY FLINT, b. 2 Feb 1801; d. at Woburn, 27 Apr 1847; m. at Boston, 14 Apr 1833, MARY WATSON, b. at Dorchester, 19 Aug 1803 daughter of Jonathan and Sally (Fulton) Watson;[3058] Mary d. at Lynn, MA, 24 Nov 1874.

v   ISAAC FLINT, b. 29 Mar 1803; d. Sep 1804.

vi   ISAAC FLINT, b. 20 Mar 1805; d. Sep 1832.

vii   MARY L. "POLLY" FLINT, b. 31 Jul 1808; d. at Nashua, NH, 26 Apr 1891; m. at Windsor, NH, 3 Jul 1832, JOHN TAYLOR, b. at Milford, 28 Sep 1807 son of Thomas and Susannah (Munroe) Taylor;[3059] John d. at Nashua, NH, 14 Dec 1878.

viii   CHARLES JENKINS FLINT, b. 14 Nov 1810; d. at Bedford, NH, 12 Apr 1841; m. CAROLINE E. GREGG, b. 1814; Caroline d. at Bedford, 1 Jul 1845.

ix   LIZZY DASCOMB FLINT (twin), b. 30 Jan 1812; d. 1815.

x   SARAH BARNS FLINT (twin), b. 30 Jan 1812; d. 1817.

xi   ABIGAIL FLINT, b. 5 Dec 1814; d. at Placerville, CA, 7 Mar 1888; m. at Nashville, NH, 28 Sep 1842, SMITH MORRILL, b. at Henniker, NH, 19 Jun 1816 son of Ephraim and Lucy (Smith) Morrill; Smith d. at Placerville, 12 Apr 1900. Abigail and Smith were early California pioneers.[3060]

949)   DANIEL FLINT (*Asenath Holt Flint⁴, Phebe Russell Holt Sheldon³, John², Robert¹*), b. at Reading, 27 Mar 1767 son of Ebenezer and Asenath (Holt) Flint; d. at Hillsborough, 27 Jun 1853; m. at Andover, 28 Jan 1795, his fourth cousin (through Abbott lines) LYDIA SHATTUCK, b. at Andover, 27 Apr 1765 daughter of Joseph and Anna (Johnson) Shattuck; Lydia d. at Hillsborough, 1 Apr 1843.

Daniel settled in Hillsborough along with his brother Ebenezer. He served as an ensign in the militia and was one of the troops that responded to Shay's rebellion.[3061]

Daniel Flint and Lydia Shattuck were parents of five children born at Hillsborough.

i   LYDIA FLINT, b. 17 Jul 1797; d. at Hillsborough, 6 Oct 1880; m. 27 Dec 1832, DAVID EMERY, b. at Henniker, NH, 14 Aug 1792 son of Daniel and Elizabeth (Straw) Emery; David d. at Hillsborough, 9 Mar 1875.

ii   DANIEL FLINT, b. 17 May 1799; d. 18 Mar 1814.

iii   AMOS FLINT, b. 28 Jun 1801; d. at Campton, NH, 1870 (will 25 Feb 1870 and proved Aug 1870); m. 1st 7 May 1829, MARY STICKNEY, b. 28 Aug 1802 daughter of James and Mary (Baldwin) Stickney; Mary d. 2 Dec 1850.

[3056] Browne, *History of Hillsborough*, p 210
[3057] The marriage record says Polly Howlett, but it seems to be Polly's sister Sarah that married Ebenezer. The death information and records related to son Henry support that it is Sarah. There were sisters Polly and Sarah, Polly reported as marrying Ebenezer Flint and Sarah reported as marrying a Benjamin Flint. Gould and Beals, *Early Families of Bradford, New Hampshire*.
[3058] The names of Mary's parents are given as Jonathan and Sally Watson on her death record. The death is recorded both at Lynn and at Bridgeport, CT, but appears to have occurred at Lynn.
[3059] The names of John's parents are given as Thomas and Susan M. Taylor on his death record.
[3060] Obituary of Smith Morrill, The Mountain Democrat, Placerville, California, April 14, 1900
[3061] Browne, *History of Hillsborough*, p 210

Amos m. 2nd at Boston, 16 Jun 1852, NANCY L. RICHARDSON, b. 23 Apr 1806 daughter of William and Rhoda (Symonds) Howard; Nancy d. at Lancaster, NH, 24 Feb 1891. After Amos's death, Nancy married Gilman Wilder.

iv　　WILLIAM FLINT, b. 2 Apr 1803; d. 13 Sep 1804.

v　　LUTHER FLINT, b. 23 Mar 1807; d. at Hillsborough, 18 Mar 1890; m. 21 Sep 1837, SARAH RICHARDSON, b. at Hillsborough, 7 Mar 1816 daughter of Stephen and Sally (Minot) Richardson; Sarah d. at Hillsborough, 12 Feb 1884.

950)　　ASENATH FLINT (*Asenath Holt Flint⁴, Phebe Russell Holt Sheldon³, John², Robert¹*), b. at Reading, 4 Mar 1769 daughter of Ebenezer and Asenath (Holt) Flint; d. at Temple, NH, 8 Dec 1817; m. 21 Mar 1792, EDWARD PRATT, b. at Reading, 25 Apr 1765 son of Daniel and Abigail (Humphrey) Pratt; Edward d. at Temple, 17 Nov 1829. Edward married second Hannah Emerson in 1819.

Edward and Asenath had a small farm in Temple where they raised their six children. They were members of the Congregational church and recalled by their daughter Eliza as being strict parents. The children in the family attended district school during winter months.[3062]

Son Daniel Pratt was an industrialist about whom much has been written. Among his other accomplishments, he was the founder of Prattville, Alabama where he owned and operated a major cotton gin factory Daniel Pratt Gin Factory.[3063]

Asenath and Edward were parents of six children.

i　　ASENATH PRATT, b. at Reading, MA, 14 May 1793; d. at Wilton, NH, 7 Jan 1836; m. about 1820, her fourth cousin twice removed, JOSEPH CHANDLER (*Ebenezer Chandler⁵, Thomas Chandler⁴, Mehitable Russell Chandler³, Thomas², Robert¹*), b. at Wilton, 28 Jan 1789 son of Ebenezer and Sarah (Averill) Chandler; Joseph d. at Wilton, 27 Aug 1837. Joseph married second Dorcas Pratt (see just below).

ii　　DORCAS PRATT, b. at Reading, 19 Sep 1795; d. at Prattville, AL, 19 Apr 1872; m. 3 Nov 1836, JOSEPH CHANDLER (see sister Asenath above).

iii　　EDWARD PRATT, b. at Reading, 2 Sep 1797; d. at Wilton, 1 Feb 1838; m. at Lyndeborough, 2 Mar 1824, his third cousin, DORCAS PEAVEY (*Peter Peavey⁵, Dorcas Holt Peavey⁴, David Holt³, Hannah Russell Holt², Robert¹*), b. at Greenfield, NH, 8 Oct 1801 daughter of Peter and Lucy (Cummings) Peavey; Dorcas d. at Wilton, 19 Mar 1884. Dorcas married second William Sheldon.

iv　　DANIEL PRATT, b. at Temple, NH, 20 Jul 1799; d. at Prattville, AL, 13 May 1873; m. at Jones County, GA, 6 Sep 1827, ESTHER TICKNOR, b. at Columbia, CT, 23 Jan 1803 daughter of David and Edith (Kingsbury) Ticknor; Esther d. at Prattville, 14 Feb 1875.

v　　ABIGAIL PRATT, b. at Temple, 11 Jun 1804; d. at Temple, 17 Nov 1842; m. ARTEMUS HOWARD, b. at Weston, VT, 27 Nov 1799 son of Joseph and Abigail (Maynard) Howard; Artemus d. at Temple, 5 Apr 1866.

vi　　ELIZA PRATT, b. at Temple, 1808; d. at Prattville, AL, 18 May 1889; m. at Temple, 5 Feb 1833, her fourth cousin, DANIEL HOLT (*Abiel Holt⁶, Abiel Holt⁵, Joseph Holt⁴, Thomas Holt³, Mary Russell Holt², Robert¹*), b. at Temple, 6 Nov 1803 son of Abiel and Elizabeth (Howard) Holt; Daniel d. at Prattville, 19 Dec 1870.

951)　　ABIGAIL FLINT (*Asenath Holt Flint⁴, Phebe Russell Holt Sheldon³, John², Robert¹*), b. at Reading, 30 Jun 1771 daughter of Ebenezer and Asenath (Holt) Flint; d. 21 May 1798; m. 29 Mar 1795, her second cousin, ABNER HOLT (*Joseph Holt⁵, Lydia Holt Holt⁴, Thomas Holt³, Mary Russell Holt², Robert¹*), b. at Andover, 6 Oct 1771 son of Joseph and Ruth (Johnson) Holt; Abner d. at Albany, ME, 14 Dec 1854. Abner m. 2nd 20 Jun 1799, ELIZABETH CHANDLER, b. at Andover, 1 Jun 1777 daughter of William and Elizabeth (Chandler) Chandler; Elizabeth d. at Albany, ME, 1 Nov 1816. Abner m. 3rd 1 Feb 1819, widow DELILAH PIPIN who d. at Albany, 16 Jul 1821. Abner m. 4th 12 Jan 1822, ABIGAIL SHEA, b. in MA, about 1782; Abigail d. at Albany, 13 May 1856.

Abigail Flint and Abner Holt were parents of one child.

i　　TABITHA HOLT, b. at Albany, ME, 26 Jan 1796; d. at Waterford, ME, 8 Apr 1872; m. at Albany, 18 May 1820, WILLIAM BELL, b. at Tewksbury, 18 Jan 1796 son of John and Hannah (Peacock) Bell; William d. at Waterford, 4 Feb 1877.

There are records of six children of Abner Holt and Elizabeth Chandler born at Albany, Maine.

[3062] Tarrant, *Hon. Daniel Pratt*, p 41
[3063] The reader is referred to Tarrant's volume on the Hon. Daniel Pratt for more detailed information; https://archive.org/details/hondanielpratta00mimsgoog/mode/2up

i   ELIZABETH HOLT, b. 13 Jun 1800; d. at Albany, 3 Mar 1872; m. at Albany, 7 Jun 1818, JOSHUA SAUNDERS, b. at Tewksbury, 13 Sep 1791 son of Amos and Dorcas (Frost) Saunders; Joshua d. at Albany, 23 Mar 1856.

ii   ABNER HOLT, b. 1 Jun 1803; d. 7 May 1807.

iii   ABIGAIL HOLT, b. 20 May 1805; d. at Canaan, NH, 23 Jul 1877; m. 13 Nov 1828, EPHRAIM CHAMBERLAIN, b. 24 Aug 1789 son of Ephraim and Persis (Barrett) Chamberlain; Ephraim d. at Sweden, ME, 20 Dec 1845.

iv   ABNER HOLT, b. 14 Oct 1807; d. 16 Sep 1839; m. at Gilead, ME, 17 Apr 1839, BETSEY FRYE WARDWELL, b. at Albany, ME, 26 Jul 1808 daughter of Isaac and Mary (Adley) Wardwell; Betsey d. at Waterford, ME, 22 Jul 1884. Betsey married second Perley French (1815-1892).

v   JOHNSON C. HOLT, b. 8 Mar 1811; d. at Newton, MA, 22 Dec 1889; m. 14 Jan 1832, NANCY DUDLEY, b. at Barnstead, NH, 22 Jun 1809 daughter of Luther and Martha (Wellington) Dudley; Nancy d. at Paris, ME, 3 Apr 1857.

vi   TIMOTHY CARTER HOLT, b. 27 Sep 1815; d. at Poland, ME, 11 Aug 1882; m. 1st about 1835, CATHERINE G. WILLARD, b. at Waterford, ME, 28 Jun 1811 daughter of Lewis and Mary (Plaisted) Willard; Catherine d. 17 Dec 1856. Timothy m. 2nd, 4 Apr 1859, EMERLINE NOBLE, b. at Norway, ME, 9 Jul 1824 daughter of Simeon and Betsey (Flint) Noble; Emerline d. at Poland, 11 Jan 1879.

Child of Abner and Delilah Holt:

i   DELILAH HOLT, b. 7 Jun 1821; d. Sep 1821.

952)   EPHRAIM FLINT (*Asenath Holt Flint4, Phebe Russell Holt Sheldon3, John2, Robert1*), b. at Reading, 4 Sep 1773 son of Ebenezer and Asenath (Holt) Flint; d. at Albany, ME, 13 Oct 1859; m. 21 Jan 1799, his second cousin, ELEANOR HOLT (*Joseph Holt5, Lydia Holt Holt4, Thomas Holt3, Mary Russell Holt2, Robert1*), b. at Andover, 3 Nov 1777 daughter of Joseph and Ruth (Johnson) Holt; Eleanor d. at Albany, 23 Jun 1858.
    Ephraim Flint and Eleanor Holt were parents of eight children born at Albany, Maine.

i   EPHRAIM FLINT, b. 10 May 1800; d. at Albany, ME, 2 Dec 1865; m. at Albany, 5 Apr 1827, LYDIA P. C. TOWNE, b. 1803 daughter of Samuel and Lydia (Holt) Towne; Lydia d. at Albany, 28 Aug 1857.

ii   JOSEPH HOLT FLINT, b. 1 Feb 1802; d. at Albany, 5 Aug 1871; m. 1st 1826, ELIZA JORDAN, b. at Norway, ME, 26 Sep 1803 daughter of Elijah and Elizabeth (Cowan) Jordan; Eliza d. at Albany, 9 Jul 1855. Joseph m. 2nd, 1858, MARY BRIGHAM, b. at Waterford, 1 Aug 1820 daughter of Luther and Rosamond (Jones) Brigham; Mary d. at Albany, 1 Jul 1882.

iii   EBENEZER FLINT, b. 25 Jan 1804; d. 25 May 1820.

iv   DANIEL FLINT, b. 28 Dec 1805; d. at Albany, 1 Jan 1870; m. 1st 26 Nov 1835, SUSANNAH TOWNE, b. 2 Feb 1817 daughter of Samuel and Susannah (Crosby) Towne; Susannah d. 24 Oct 1845. Daniel m. 2nd ANNA EAMES, b. at Norway, 28 Jun 1823 daughter of Samuel and Anna (Foster) Eames; Anna d. at Albany, 1 Sep 1913.

v   ELEANOR FLINT, b. 25 Feb 1808; d. at Waterford, 25 Sep 1875; m. at Albany, 1 Sep 1829, ISAAC C. HORR, b. at Waterford, 1 Jan 1802 son of Isaac and Rebecca (Heald) Horr; Isaac d. at Waterford, 27 May 1861.

vi   AMOS FLINT, b. 20 Dec 1811; d. at Waterford, 21 Mar 1883; m. ELIZA WATSON, b. 1819 daughter of Isaac and Deborah (Sampson) Watson; Eliza d. at Waterford, 15 Dec 1910.

vii   RUTH FLINT, b. 1 May 1814; d. at Lovell, ME, 27 Mar 1906. Ruth did not marry.

viii   LEANDER FLINT, b. 28 Apr 1816; d. 16 Oct 1820.

953)   AMOS FLINT (*Asenath Holt Flint4, Phebe Russell Holt Sheldon3, John2, Robert1*), b. at Reading, 16 Apr 1778 son of Ebenezer and Asenath (Holt) Flint; d. at Francestown, 27 Apr 1873; m. 3 Feb 1803, ABIGAIL MORSE, b. at Francestown, 1 Aug 1787 daughter of Timothy and Abigail (Dean) Morse; Abigail d. at Francestown, 1 Mar 1885.
    Amos was born in Reading, but his parents had gone to Wilton after the children were born. Amos and several of his siblings married in Andover, and Amos and his wife Abigail were there for the births of their first five children. The family settled in Francestown about 1814. Amos was a shoemaker by trade.[3064]
    Amos and Abigail were parents of six children.

[3064] Cochrane, *History of Francestown*, p 706

i   AMOS FLINT, b. at Andover, 9 Nov 1803; d. at Francestown, 4 Nov 1895; m. 3 Jun 1840, as her second husband, HANNAH P. GIBSON (widow of Edward Johnson), b. at Hillsborough, 4 Jul 1803 daughter of John and Serviah (Preston) Gibson; Hannah d. at Woburn, MA, 7 Oct 1892.

ii   ASENATH FLINT, b. at Andover, 10 Apr 1806; d. at Stoneham, MA, 9 Jan 1879; m. at Reading, 7 May 1831, NEWTON NICHOLS, b. at Reading, 19 Sep 1806 son of Amos and Molly (Pratt) Nichols; Newton d. at Stoneham, 14 Sep 1889.

iii   SOPHRONIA W. FLINT, b. at Andover, 15 Sep 1808; d. at Plainville, WI, 13 Nov 1883; m. at Francestown, 21 Nov 1831, TIMOTHY TEMPLE, b. at Reading, 21 Feb 1810 son of John and Elizabeth (Carter) Temple; Timothy d. at Plainville, 30 Sep 1880.

iv   PHEBE B. FLINT, b. at Andover, 7 Nov 1810; d. at Bancroft, NE, 18 May 1903; m. at Francestown, 15 Sep 1836, JOHN MORSE, b. at Bradford, NH, 16 Apr 1806 son of Joseph and Judith (Short) Morse; [3065] John d. at Bancroft, 10 Nov 1892.

v   MAHALA M. FLINT, b. at Andover, 14 Aug 1814; d. at Mutual, OK, 17 Dec 1908; m. at Reading, MA, 19 Jan 1843, ALBERT B. EMERSON, b. 12 Nov 1819 son of David and Salina (Gassett) Emerson; Albert was killed at Battle of the Wilderness, VA, 5 May 1864. Albert served in the 22nd Massachusetts infantry regiment.[3066]

vi   SAMUEL P. FLINT, b. at Francestown, NH, 27 Jul 1817; d. at Reading, MA, 25 Sep 1838.

954)   JOHN FLINT (*Asenath Holt Flint⁴, Phebe Russell Holt Sheldon³, John², Robert¹*), b. at Reading, 23 Feb 1780 son of Ebenezer and Asenath (Holt) Flint; d. at Wilton, NH, 30 May 1847 (probate 4 Jul 1848); m. 13 Feb 1803, SARAH FLINT, b. at Reading, 25 Nov 1783 daughter of Levi and Sarah (Parker) Flint; Sarah d. at Wilton, 6 Oct 1863.

John went with his parents to Wilton, and unlike his older brothers John remained in Wilton until his death. He served in the militia with the rank of captain. He was deacon of the Congregationalist church.[3067]

In his will written 6 May 1846 (proved 4 July 1848), John Flint bequeaths to beloved wife Sarah all the household furniture, the use of one front room and one chamber in the dwelling house, meals and other provisions, medicines when she is ill, and eight dollars annually to be provided by the executor. Granddaughter Sarah W. Burton receives one hundred dollars at age twenty-one. The reminder of the estate goes to son Abiel Flint who is named executor.[3068]

John and Sarah Flint were parents of five children born at Wilton.

i   SARAH FLINT, b. 5 Apr 1804; d. at Wilton, 11 Oct 1836; m. 26 Jun 1828, WARREN BURTON, b. at Wilton, 23 Nov 1800 son of Jonathan and Persis (Warren) Burton; Warren d. at Salem, MA, 6 Jun 1866. Warren married second Mary Merritt on 18 Sep 1845.

ii   JOHN FLINT, b. 30 Jun 1805; d. at Wilton, 25 Dec 1831. John did not marry.

iii   ABIEL FLINT, b. 22 Jan 1809; d. at Wilton, 11 Aug 1889 (probate 13 Sep 1889); m. 26 Sep 1836, HANNAH CARPENTER SHATTUCK, b. at Pembroke, 2 Apr 1810 daughter of Obed and Abigail (Lovejoy) Shattuck; Hannah d. 16 Apr 1879.

iv   ELEANOR FLINT, b. 23 Apr 1812; d. at Wilton, 2 Apr 1836.

v   ABIGAIL H. FLINT, b. 3 Jun 1816; d. at Wilton, 7 Dec 1834.

955)   MOSES HOLT (*Marstin Holt⁴, Phebe Russell Holt Sheldon³, John², Robert¹*), b. at Holden, 4 Dec 1772 son of Marstin and Abigail (Wheeler) Holt; d. at Boston, 25 Apr 1823; m. 31 Mar 1796, AZUBA HUBBARD, b. at Holden, 13 Aug 1776 daughter of Elisha and Mercy (Hubbard) Hubbard; Azuba d. at Hubbardston, 9 Apr 1857.

Moses and Azuba lived in Holden. After the death of her husband, Azuba lived with her son Elias in Hubbardston.[3069] Moses and Azuba were parents of eight children whose births are recorded at Holden.

i   ELIAS HOLT, b. 6 Oct 1796; d. at Hubbardston, MA, 6 Feb 1851; m. 2 Dec 1824, RUTH FROST, b. at Hubbardston, 1 May 1796 daughter of Stephen and Mary (Randall) Frost; Ruth d. at Hubbardston, 9 Aug 1873.

[3065] Gould and Beals, *Early Families of Bradford*
[3066] Massachusetts Army & Navy, 1861-1865; U.S., Civil War Soldier Records and Profiles, 1861-1865
[3067] Livermore, *History of the Town of Wilton*, p 370
[3068] New Hampshire Wills and Probate, Hillsborough County, Probate Records, volume 57, p 22
[3069] Year: 1850; Census Place: Hubbardston, Worcester, Massachusetts; Roll: 342; Page: 352a

ii   ELI HUBBARD HOLT, b. Jul 1798; d. at Abington, MA, 14 Jan 1860; m. at Boston, 29 Feb 1824, MARY B. BATSON who has not been identified; Mary likely died before 1850 as she was not living with the family in the 1850 census.

iii   NANCY HOLT, b. 8 Feb 1800; d. 25 Aug 1801.

iv   MOSES WHEELER HOLT, b. 21 Dec 1801; d. at Andover, 11 Dec 1842; m. at Andover, 4 Sep 1823, his third cousin, LYDIA HOLT, b. at Andover, 27 Oct 1803 daughter of Joseph and Lydia (Jones) Holt; Lydia d. at Andover, 8 Nov 1889.

v   MERCY HUBBARD HOLT, b. 6 May 1803; d. at West Boylston, 7 May 1855; m. at Holden, 18 Oct 1827, WALDO WINTER, b. at Boylston, 2 Aug 1802 son of Calvin and Lucy (Eames) Winter; Waldo d. at Clinton, MA, 28 Feb 1887.

vi   ERASMUS DARWIN HOLT, b. 20 Sep 1805; Durrie's Holt genealogy reports that he died in Illinois in 1840.

vii   HORACE RUSSELL HOLT, b. 14 Aug 1807; d. at Bergen, NY, 28 Jan 1897; m. 17 Apr 1832, MINERVA BREWSTER PARISH, b. at Worthington, MA, 24 Nov 1810 daughter of Eliphalet and Theodosia (Brewster) Parish; Minerva d. at Bergen, 20 Dec 1897.

viii   ABIGAIL BATCHELDER HOLT, b. 16 Feb 1809; d. at Worcester, 12 Aug 1862; m. 1st at West Boylston, 8 Apr 1828, LUTHER WINTER, b. at Northbridge, MA, 29 Jul 1799 son of John and Hephzibah (Cooper) Winter; Luther d. at West Boylston, 13 Mar 1847. Abigail m. 2nd at West Boylston, 5 Oct 1858, MARSON EATON, b. at Amherst, MA, 26 May 1806 son of Marson and Charlotte (Dutton) Eaton; Marson d. at Shrewsbury, 3 Jan 1873. Marson was first married to Betsey Joslin.

956)   AMOS SHELDON HOLT (*Marstin Holt⁴, Phebe Russell Holt Sheldon³, John², Robert¹*), b. at Holden, 17 Jul 1774 son of Marstin and Abigail (Wheeler) Holt; d. at Holden, 7 Apr 1855;[3070] m. 1st at Princeton, 29 Dec 1794, SALLY WOOLEY, b. at Princeton, 16 Dec 1774 daughter of David and Sarah (Porter) Wooley; Sally d. at Holden, 14 Dec 1814. Amos m. 2nd at Ashburnham, 4 Oct 1818, SALLY LINDAL, b. at Pepperell, 24 Nov 1794 daughter of James and Abigail (Collins) Lindal; Sally d. at Holden, 1838.

      Amos was a laborer who resided in Holden. In 1810 he headed a household of six persons: one male 26 to 44; one female 26 to 44; three males under 10; and one female 10 to 15.[3071]

      Amos Holt and Sally Wooley were parents of eight children born at Holden.

i   SALLY HOLT, b. 8 Apr 1795; d. 16 Jul 1828; m. at Southborough, MA, 10 Aug 1816, EDWARD R. PHELPS, b. at Lancaster, MA, 9 Mar 1787 son of Jacob and Prudence (White) Phelps.[3072]

ii   POLLY HOLT, b. 2 Jul 1797; d. 22 Oct 1800.

iii   ABIGAIL HOLT, b. 22 Feb 1799; d. at Holden, 8 Dec 1843; m. at Sterling, 8 Nov 1818, EZRA DARBY, b. at Westminster, 17 Aug 1798 son of Joseph and Lovicea (Calif) Darby; Ezra d. at Westminster, 23 Oct 1835.

iv   AMOS JEFFERSON HOLT, b. 24 Jul 1801; d. at Sterling, MA, 1851 (probate 1851). Amos did not marry; his father administered his estate.

v   JAMES ELDER HOLT, b. 16 May 1803

vi   AARON PORTER HOLT, b. 5 Oct 1808; d. at Lyndon, IL, 6 Mar 1876; m. 1st at Chester, NH, 2 Dec 1829, CLARISSA A. HUSE, b. at Chester, 2 Apr 1808 daughter of Israel and Waity Gray (Emerson) Huse; Clarissa d. at Lyndon, 9 Sep 1854. Aaron m. 2nd at Whiteside, IL, 15 Aug 1855, ROSETTA MITCHELL, b. in Aurora, NY, Mar 1835 daughter of William Wood and Polly (Ward) Mitchell; Rosetta d. at Lyndon, 1910. Dr. Aaron Porter graduate from the Western College of Homeopathy in Cleveland. He practiced in Andover, MA and was later in Lyndon.

vii   MARY ELDER HOLT, b. 22 May 1811; d. at Holden, 16 Oct 1883; m. 1st at Newton, MA, 30 Mar 1836, WILLIAM BROWN BALCH LOWELL, b. at Amesbury, 31 Mar 1813 son of William and Hannah (Balch) Lowell; William d. at Newton, 16 Feb 1850. Mary m. 2nd at Holden, 27 May 1858, JONAS SHEPHERD ROGERS, b. at Holden, 4 Jun 1823 son of John and Sally (Smith) Rogers; Jonas d. at Holden, 9 Jun 1898. It seems that Mary and her second husband separated/divorced as Mary resumed the use of the name Mary Lowell before her death.[3073]

[3070] *Massachusetts: Vital Records, 1841-1910.* (From original records held by the Massachusetts Archives. Online database: AmericanAncestors.org, volume 95, p 125

[3071] Year: 1810; Census Place: Holden, Worcester, Massachusetts; Roll: 22; Page: 792; Image: 00176; Family History Library Film: 0205630

[3072] White, *Genealogy of the Descendants of John White of Wenham*, volume 3, p 221

[3073] Mary's second marriage to Jonas Rogers can be confirmed as the marriage record gives the names of her parents as Amos and Sally Holt. They were separated by 1880.

viii   OLIVE HOLT, b. 30 Oct 1813; d. (burial at Holden), 20 Jan 1848; m. 30 Sep 1832, ELDRIDGE GERRY TURNER, b. at Holden, 6 Aug 1809 son of Samuel and Mary (Gould) Turner; Elbridge d. at Amherst, MA, 4 Mar 1881. Elbridge married second Sarah Ann Cowles on 16 Apr 1850.

Amos Holt and Sally Lindal were parents of seven children born at Holden.

i   SYLVANUS HOUGHTON HOLT, b. 9 Jul 1819. Sylvanus was a whaler. The last record found for him was his departure on the whaling ship Kingfisher II form New Bedford in 1860.[3074]

ii   WILLIAM COLLINS HOLT, b. 17 Nov 1820; died young

iii   ELIZA B. HOLT, b. Sep 1821, d. at Roxbury, MA, 4 Dec 1860; m. at Roxbury, 26 Oct 1845, WILLIAM HARVEY, b. about 1819; William d. after 1855.

iv   JOSEPH AVERY HOLT, b. 23 Aug 1823

v   PHEBE SHELDON HOLT, b. 13 May 1825; d. (burial at Putnam, CT), 14 Jul 1874; m. at Boston, 6 Jul 1850, THOMAS F. HARVEY, b. at Roxbury, 1828 son of William Harvey; Thomas d. 7 Jan 1904.

vi   TABITHA DRYDEN JANE SMITH HOLT, b. 13 Apr 1827; d. at Worcester, 13 Apr 6 Sep 1890; m. at Waltham, 10 Aug 1845, ADAM G. BARNES, b. in NH, 1820 son of William and Sarah (-) Barnes; Adam d. at Worcester, 14 Apr 1868.

vii   WILLIAM COLLINS HOLT, b. at Holden, 19 Mar 1830

957)   AARON HOLT (*Marstin Holt⁴, Phebe Russell Holt Sheldon³, John², Robert¹*), b. at Holden, 7 Oct 1776 son of Marstin and Abigail (Wheeler) Holt; d. at Troy, NH, 21 Oct 1826; m. at Holden, 28 Nov 1799, DOROTHY HOW, b. at Holden, 13 Sep 1780 daughter of Jotham and Dorothy (Smith) How; Dorothy d. at Holden, 21 Jul 1873. Dorothy married second John Hall on 27 Nov 1849.

    Aaron and Dorothy were first in Holden, Massachusetts. In 1806, Aaron purchased a farm in Marlborough, New Hampshire and the family was there for ten years before purchasing another property in Troy. Aaron was killed when he attempted to assist a neighbor with an unruly horse and Aaron was kicked in the stomach by the horse and died the next day.[3075]

    Aaron Holt and Dorothy How were parents of eleven children.[3076]

i   AARON HOLT, b. at Holden, 25 Jan 1801; d. 6 Jan 1818.

ii   JOEL HOLT, b. at Holden, 30 Mar 1803; d. at Troy, NH, 1873;[3077] m. 1st 20 Nov 1828, THIRZA BAKER, b. at Marlborough, 7 Dec 1804 daughter of Bezaleel and Abigail (Wood) Baker;[3078] Thirza d. at Troy, 17 May 1861. Joel m. 2nd at Marlborough, 24 Oct 1861, BATHSHEBA MOORE, b. at Wayland, 8 Nov 1807 daughter of John and Sally (Gibbs) Moore; Bathsheba d. at Wayland, MA, 10 Apr 1893.

iii   JOTHAM HOW HOLT, b. at Holden, 22 Feb 1805; d. at Troy, NH, 2 Jul 1881; m. at Berlin, MA, 19 Apr 1831, MIRIAM BARTLETT, b. at Berlin, 26 Nov 1804 daughter of Adam and Persis (Babcock) Bartlett; Miriam d. at Troy, 10 May 1898.

iv   DOROTHY HOLT, b. at Holden, 8 Sep 1807; d. 13 Nov 1812.

v   MOSES WHEELER HOLT, b. at Marlborough, NH, 6 Jul 1810; d. 21 Sep 1813.

vi   WILLIAM HOLT, b. at Marlborough, 19 Oct 1812; d. at Newport, KY, 10 Aug 1877; m. at Hamilton County, OH, 1 Sep 1837,[3079] MARY VAN WINKLE, b. in DE, 1816; Mary d. at Newport, 6 Dec 1881.

vii   AMOS HOLT, b. at Marlborough, 20 Dec 1814; d. at Cincinnati, OH, May 1895; m. at Pulaski County, KY, 5 Sep 1844, REBECCA ADELINE GRUBB, b. in KY, about 1822; Rebecca d. at Cincinnati, 1884.

[3074] New Bedford, Massachusetts, Whaling Crew Lists Index, 1809-1927; ancestry.com
[3075] Caverly, *Historical Sketch of Troy*, pp 111-112
[3076] Durrie;s Holt genealogy, p 133 includes a twelfth child Horace noted as living in Oakland, OH. Records were not located, and he is not given as one of the children in the family in Caverly, *An Historical Sketch of Troy*, p 112
[3077] New Hampshire, Death and Disinterment Records, 1754-1947
[3078] The names of Thirza's parents are give as Bazaleel and Abigail Baker on her death record; New Hampshire, Death and Disinterment Records, 1754-1947
[3079] Ohio, County Marriages, 1774-1993

viii   DOROTHY HOLT, b. at Troy, 28 Feb 1817; d. at Jaffrey, 19 Apr 1840; m. 1839, as the second of his four wives, JOHN WARD POOLE, b. at Jaffrey, 13 Aug 1812 son of Ebenezer and Olive (Ward) Poole;[3080] John d. at Jaffrey, 7 Jan 1875. John was first married to Edith Cutter, third married to Sybil Cutter, and fourth married to Nancy Witt.

ix   BETSEY F. HOLT, b. at Troy, 16 Mar 1819; d. at Troy, 8 Aug 1847; m. 2 Sep 1844, ERI JONATHAN SPAULDING, b. at Jaffrey, NH, 17 Oct 1821 son of Abel and Lucy (Pierce) Spaulding; Eri d. at Troy, 17 Jan 1886. Eri married second Lucy Ann Jones and married third Maria Ruth Ellis.

x   AARON HOLT, b. at Troy, 15 Jul 1821; d. at Somerset, KY, 16 Aug 1890; m. at Pulaski County, KY, 23 Feb 1846,[3081] MIRIAM ESBEL BUCKNER, b. in TN, 1831 daughter of Daniel and Mary (Hampton) Buckner;[3082] Miriam d. at Dallas, TX, 1918. Aaron Holt was a teacher. One of the children of Aaron and Miriam, Adoniram Judson Holt, wrote a memoir of his family life titled *Pioneering in the Southwest* which is available through online sources.

xi   LYDIA HOLT, b. at Troy, 16 Nov 1825; d. at Holden, MA, 13 Apr 1883; m. at Fitchburg, MA, 24 Apr 1849, as his second wife, HENRY MAYNARD, b. at Shrewsbury, 15 Nov 1813 son of Daniel and Malinda (Allen) Maynard; Henry d. at Holden, 29 Jan 1882. Henry was first married to Cornelia Johnson.

958)   ABIGAIL HOLT (*Marstin Holt[4], Phebe Russell Holt Sheldon[3], John[2], Robert[1]*), b. at Dublin, NH, 2 Nov 1782 daughter of Marstin and Abigail (Wheeler) Holt; m. at Berlin, VT, 14 Jun 1810, MOSES BATCHELDER of Dunham, Québec whose parents have not been identified. Moses d. at Dunham, Québec, Oct 1843.[3083]
        In the 1825 census for Dunham in Lower Canada, Moses Batchelder was head of a household of twelve persons: three females under 6; three females 6 to 14; one male 18 to 25; two single males 26 to 40; one married male 40 to 60; one single female 14 to 45; and one married female 14 to 45.[3084] Although it seems that Abigail and Moses had a large family, the name of just one child has been found.

i   ABIGAIL BATCHELDER, b. at Dunham, Québec, about 1828; d. at Detroit, MI, 24 Dec 1887; m. at Dunham, 1849, WELLINGTON HARRISON RICHMOND, b. at Barnard, VT, 23 Apr 1817 son of Benjamin and Electa (Walker) Richmond. Wellington was living in Dunham in 1857. He was a publisher of legal forms.

959)   HANNAH SHELDON (*Russell Sheldon[4], Phebe Russell Holt Sheldon[3], John[2], Robert[1]*), b. at Reading, MA, 1786 daughter of Russell and Susannah (Sheldon) Sheldon; d. at Reading, 9 Jul 1836; m. at Reading, 3 Apr 1804, BENJAMIN HOLT, b. at Reading, 28 Aug 1781 son of Joseph and Mary Eaton (Carter) Holt; Benjamin d. at Reading, 31 Mar 1847.
        Benjamin Holt was a farmer in Reading. He served on the school committee for North Reading in 1821, 1822, and 1825.[3085]
        In his will written 19 October 1846 (proved 7 April 1847), Benjamin Holt bequeathed to son Benjamin three lots of land containing about three acres and one thousand dollars. Son Charles Holt receives the residue of the so-called Morey farm that was not included in the deed to him. Son Joseph W. Holt receives a lot of land in Reading containing about 25 acres. Son Varnum Holt receives a lot of about twenty acres and eight hundred dollars. Son Lyman Holt receives five hundred dollars. Granddaughter Jane Damon daughter of Ingalls Damon receives one dollar. Daughter Susan Carter wife of Henry A. Carter receives two hundred dollars as does daughter Mary Smith wife of Levi Smith. Daughter Sarah B. Holt receives three hundred dollars and the right to occupy the southwesterly chamber of the dwelling house while she is unmarried. Sons Harmon A. Holt and Joseph E. Holt the residue of the real estate. They are also to provide provision for Sarah B. There are other provisions related to the disposal of the estate if either Harmon A. or Joseph E. died before age twenty-one or without children. The residue of the estate is to be equally divided among the sons. Son Charles was named executor. In a codicil written 11 November 1846, Benjamin revoked the bequest to son Lyman and gave this bequest to Charles and revoked the land bequest to Joseph W. Holt and gave this land to son Charles.[3086]
        Hannah Sheldon and Benjamin Holt were parents of eleven children born at Reading. Two of the sons were named Joseph: Joseph Warren Holt and Joseph Elbridge Holt. Six of the children went to Iowa.

[3080] The names of John's parents are given as Ebenezer and Olive on his death record; New Hampshire, Death and Disinterment Records, 1754-1947
[3081] Kentucky, County Marriages, 1783-1965
[3082] Crozier, *The Buckners of Virginia and Allied Families*, p 297
[3083] Institut Généalogique Drouin; Montreal, Quebec, Canada; Drouin Collection; Author: Gabriel Drouin, comp.
[3084] 1825 Census of Lower Canada; Dunham, Bedford, Quebec, Canada; MG 31 C1; FHL Film Number 2443957; p 841
[3085] Eaton, *Genealogical History of the Town of Reading*, p 271
[3086] *Middlesex County, MA: Probate File Papers, 1648-1871.* Online database. *AmericanAncestors.org.* New England Historic Genealogical Society, 2014. Case 34473

i   BENJAMIN HOLT, b. 12 Apr 1805; d. at Adel, IA, 1856; m. (intention) 16 Mar 1829, his first cousin, MARY KILLAM, b. at Boxford, 19 Oct 1809 daughter of Samuel and Lois (Holt) Killam; Mary d. at Adams, IA, 1886.

ii   HANNAH HOLT, b. 12 Jan 1807; d. at North Reading, Jan 1833; m. at Reading, 14 Apr 1830, INGALLS DAMON, b at Reading, 26 Aug 1795 son of Amos and Phebe (Gray) Damon; Ingalls d. at North Reading, 13 Feb 1867.

iii   SUSAN HOLT, b. 28 Feb 1809; d. at Delaware County, IA, 1851; m. at Reading, 26 Nov 1832, HENRY ADAMS CARTER, b. at North Reading, 7 Dec 1806 son of Elijah and Hannah (Bragg) Carter; Henry d. at Hopkinton, IA, 31 Mar 1883. Henry married second Mary Jackson Nash.

iv   CHARLES HOLT, b. 1 May 1811; d. at Lawrence, MA, 29 Nov 1884; m. at Reading, 29 Jun 1837, SYLVANIA BATCHELDER, b. at Reading, 13 Jan 1820 daughter of Amos and Myra (Nichols) Batchelder; Sylvania d. at North Reading, 23 Apr 1863.

v   JOSEPH WARREN HOLT, b. 8 Aug 1813; d. at Fort Scott, KS, 28 Jan 1897; m. at Dubuque, IA, 11 Jan 1841, MIRANDA N. SHATTUCK, b. at Marlborough, MA, 25 Jan 1818 daughter of Stephen and Hannah (Carter) Shattuck; Miranda d. at Fort Scott, 1909.

vi   VARNUM HOLT, b. 10 Aug 1815; d. at North Reading, 16 Apr 1863; m. at Reading, 19 Jun 1839, SARAH F. UPTON, b. at Reading, 15 Aug 1820 daughter of Amos and Hannah P. (Flint) Upton; Sarah d. at North Reading, 3 Jun 1908.

vii   LYMAN HOLT, b. 5 Apr 1818; d. at Johnson County, IA, about 1849; m. at Johnson County, 16 Jun 1844, as hher second husband, MARTHA PICKETT FISHBECK, b. at Clermont County, OH, 22 Oct 1820 daughter of Owen Thomas and Caroline (Huber) Fishbeck;[3087] Martha d. at Batavia, OH, 11 Jan 1870. Martha was first married to James Hawkins on 20 Feb 1839 and third married to Henry Talley on 30 Jan 1850. Martha's first husband James Hawkins was the postmaster of Iowa City. At his death, there was a move by citizens to have Martha appointed particularly as she had a young child to support. However, there was political plotting and Martha was denied the post. She supported herself teaching music. She was described as "the most handsome woman who ever resided in the city."[3088]

viii   ALBERT HARMAN HOLT, b. 6 May 1820; d. at North Reading, 24 Feb 1890; m. at Reading, 6 May 1847, REBECCA BATCHELDER, b. at Reading, 14 Jun 1827 daughter of George and Rebecca (Evens) Batchelder; Rebecca d. at North Reading, 23 Dec 1906.

ix   MARY HOLT, b. about 1820; m. at Reading, 2 Feb 1841, LEVI SMITH, b. at Lynnfield, 30 Sep 1819 son of William B. and Lois (Parker) Smith. Levi and Mary resided in Iowa City, IA.

x   SARAH BROWN HOLT, b. about 1825; d. at Muscatine, IA, 30 Jun 1859; m. at Reading, 20 Aug 1848, JOHN LEMP, b. at Bern, Switzerland, 2 Feb 1820 son of John and Elizabeth (·) Lemp;[3089] John d. at Chicago, 18 Aug 1905. John Lemp emigrated with his parents as a young child. In the 1840's he went to Muscatine, IA where he opened a store. He was also a director of Garretson Bank. The last 25 years of his life were spent in Chicago.[3090]

xi   JOSEPH ELDRIDGE HOLT, b. about 1828; d. at North Reading, 23 Aug 1882; m. at Andover, 27 Dec 1849, FRANCES ANN CHEEVER, b. at Andover, 15 Aug 1830 daughter of James and Henrietta (Wilkins) Cheever; Frances d. at Andover, 27 Nov 1916.

960)   ABRAHAM SHELDON (*Russell Sheldon⁴, Phebe Russell Holt Sheldon³, John², Robert¹*), b. at Reading 1789 son of Russell and Susannah (Sheldon) Sheldon; d. at Middleton, 10 Oct 1858; m. at Reading, 9 Apr 1812, HANNAH C. EATON, b. at Reading, 24 Jun 1792 daughter of Nathaniel and Lydia (Holt) Eaton; Hannah d. at Middleton, 26 Aug 1854.
    There are records of five children of Abraham and Hannah born either at Middleton or Reading.[3091]

i   HANNAH C. SHELDON, b. 6 Nov 1812; d. at Middleton, MA, 3 Apr 1892; m. at Middleton, 1 Oct 1831, CHARLES MCINTIRE, b. at Middleton, 7 Mar 1806 son of Eliab and Marcy (Johnson) McIntire; Charles d. at Middleton, 9 Apr 1882.

[3087] Nevada Community Historical Society, Martha Pickett Fishbeck, http://iagenweb.org/story//NCHS/f14079.htm#P33131

[3088] Irish, Gil R., "The Beginning of Iowa City", The Iowa City Citizen (Muscatine, Iowa), September 6, 1910, Tuesday, p 3. Further in this same article it is reported that the Crumey House bell was rung so violently to celebrate the marriage of Martha and Lyman that the bell cracked.

[3089] The names of John's parents are given as John and Elizabeth Lemp on his marriage record; date of birth is on his cemetery record.

[3090] "John Lemp, A Pioneer Business Man, Passes Away", Muscatine News-Tribune (Muscatine, Iowa), 22 Aug 1905, Tue, p 7

[3091] Children are identified from marriage and death records; there are no transcriptions of birth records for these children.

ii   HARMON T. SHELDON, b. 1814; d. at Middleton, 27 May 1897; m. at Reading, 30 Jun 1836, ANGELINA
        RICHARDSON, b. at Middleton, 4 Apr 1814 daughter of David and Sally (Richardson) Richardson; Angelina d. at
        Middleton, 20 Nov 1895.

iii   HARRIET N. SHELDON, b. 1818; d. at Middleton, 5 Apr 1860; m. at Middleton, 11 May 1833. ELBRIDGE
        STILES, b. at Middleton, 24 Nov 1806 son of John and Rebecca (Kenney) Stiles; Elbridge d. at Middleton, 25 Apr
        1872.

iv   BENJAMIN HIRAM SHELDON, b. 17 Aug 1822; d. after 1880 when he was living at Derry, NH; m. at
        Middleton, 10 Dec 1844, REBECCA STEVENS, b. at Danvers, 18 Oct 1825 daughter of Benjamin and Ruth
        (Buxton) Stevens; Rebecca d. after 1880.

v   HENRIETTA MARIA SHELDON, b. about 1824; d. at Andover, MA, 9 Jul 1892; m. at Middleton, Dec 1844,
        WILLARD SYMONDS, b. at Andover, 25 Oct 1818 son of Jonas and Martha (Kimball) Symonds; Willard d. at
        North Andover, 10 Sep 1887.

961)   DANIEL SHELDON (*Russell Sheldon⁴, Phebe Russell Holt Sheldon³, John², Robert¹*), b. at Reading, 1791 son of
Russell and Susannah (Sheldon) Sheldon; d. at Reading, 29 Jun 1843; m. at Reading, 18 May 1817, PHEBE EATON, b. at
Reading, 27 Jul 1787 daughter of Nathaniel and Lydia (Holt) Eaton; Phebe d. at North Reading, 1 May 1868.
        There are two children known for Daniel Sheldon and Phebe Eaton.

i   MARY ANN SHELDON, b. at Boston, 1818; d. at Reading, MA, 24 Jan 1908; m. 1st at Reading, 28 Jul 1859, as
        his second wife, PHINEAS GREEN, b. at Melrose, 20 Aug 1803 son of Phineas and Mehitable (Hart) Green;
        Phineas d. at Reading, 30 Apr 1883. Mary Ann m. 2nd at Reading, 7 Jul 1903, as his second wife, THOMAS
        PEARS, b. at Liverpool, Lancashire, England, 1837 son of Thomas and Mary (Ashworth) Pears; Thomas d. at
        Stoneham, MA, 30 Jan 1911. Thomas was first married to Jane Charlesworth, also born in England. Thomas and
        Jane arrived in Boston on 8 Jun 1870.

ii   SUSAN AUGUSTA SHELDON, b. at Boston, 1820; d. at North Reading, 16 May 1894; m. at Reading, 14 Dec
        1837, her fourth cousin, JAMES PEABODY (*Mary Russell Peabody⁵, James⁴, Joseph³, Thomas², Robert¹*), b. at
        Boxford, 11 Aug 1815 son of Francis and Mary (Russell) Peabody; James d. at North Reading, 13 Sep 1891.

962)   PHEBE FARNUM (*Phebe Sheldon Farnum⁴, Phebe Russell Holt Sheldon³, John², Robert¹*), b. at Andover, 31 Mar
1788 daughter of Israel and Phebe (Sheldon) Farnum; d. at Landgrove, VT, 8 Sep 1863; m. at Mont Vernon, NH, 19 Jul 1810,
her fourth cousin, EBENEZER HOLT LAMSON, b. at Amherst, NH, 23 Dec 1784 son of Jonathan and Elizabeth (Holt)
Lampson; Ebenezer d. at Landgrove, 10 Apr 1855.
        This family lived in Mont Vernon, New Hampshire where they were in 1810,[3092] in Weston, Vermont in 1830,[3093] and
Peru, Vermont in 1840 and 1850. In the 1850 census, Ebenezer and Phebe were living in a household headed by son Reuben.
The household consisted of Reuben Lampson age 30, Maranda Lampson age 25, Charles P. Lampson age 12, Ebenezer age 65,
Phebe age 63, and Lucy Pease age 22.[3094]
        Seven children of Ebenezer and Phebe Lamson are reported in the Lamson genealogy.[3095]

i   REBECCA LAMSON, b. at Peru, VT, about 1811; d. at Mount Holly, VT, 1 Nov 1885; m. 1st at Weston, VT, 2 May
        1830, her second cousin once removed, STEPHEN TUTTLE, b. at Peru, VT, 28 Aug 1801 son of Stephen and
        Sarah (Holt) Tuttle; Stephen d. at Landgrove, VT, 5 Oct 1856. Rebecca m. 2nd at Weston, 25 Mar 1858, HIRAM
        BRIDGE, b. about 1803.

ii   REUBEN LAMSON, b. at Mont Vernon, NH, 8 Feb 1816; d. at Peru, VT, 27 Feb 1888; m. 1st 25 May 1845,
        MIRANDA WOODWARD, b. at Landgrove, VT, 5 Jul 1822 daughter of Elijah and Rhoda (Austin) Woodward;
        Miranda d. at Landgrove, 31 May 1863. Reuben m. 2nd at Weston, 9 Jan 1866 DIANTHA COOK (widow of Edson
        Whitney), b. at Granville, NY, 1831 daughter of Seth and Catherine (Richardson) Cook; Diantha was living in
        1880.

[3092] Year: 1810; Census Place: Mont Vernon, Hillsborough, New Hampshire; Roll: 24; Page: 625; Image: 00138; Family History Library Film:
0218685; Eben H. Lampson with one male 26 to 44 and one female 26 to 44
[3093] Year: 1830; Census Place: Weston, Windsor, Vermont; Series: M19; Roll: 187; Page: 163; Family History Library Film: 0027453; Ebenezer H.
Lampson with household of six: one male 40 to 49; one female 40 to 49; one male 5 to 9; two females under 5; and one female 5 to 9
[3094] Year: 1850; Census Place: Peru, Bennington, Vermont; Roll: 921; Page: 97A
[3095] Lamson, *Descendants of William Lamson*, pp 240-241

iii   LUCY P. LAMSON, b. 14 Sep 1817;[3096] d. at Brownville Junction, ME, 13 Nov 1893;[3097] m. at Landgrove, VT, 19 Sep 1841, ALADEN LOVEJOY, b. 9 Oct 1815; Aladen d. at Brownville Junction, 18 Jan 1884.

iv   JANE LAMSON; nothing located

v   ISRAEL LAMSON, b. 1820; d. at Londonderry, VT, 5 May 1902; m. 1st at Mount Tabor, VT, ELECTA BRITTON, b. 1816; Electa d. at Mount Tabor, 17 Jun 1866. Israel m. 2nd, estimate 1882, MARY A. DAVIS (widow of Joseph Utley), b. at Londonderry, VT, Mar 1824 daughter of William and Mary (Sargent) Davis; Mary d. at Landgrove, 10 Oct 1904.

vi   HANNAH MARIA LAMSON, b. at Brattleboro, VT, about 1824; d. at Medford, ME, 1903; m. at Lowell, MA, 2 May 1852, as his second wife, NATHANIEL I. WOODARD, b. at Halifax, VT, 1820 son of Israel and Persis (-) Woodard; Nathaniel d. at Brownville, ME, 1866. Nathaniel was first married to Emily Grant. Hannah m. 2nd STEPHEN PRESCOTT, b. 1806.

vii   LEVI S. LAMSON, b. about 1826; d. at Rensselaer, NY, 3 Mar 1901;[3098] m. about 1858, LOIS STILSON, b. at Sunderland, VT, 8 Apr 1831 daughter of Russell and Amanda (Landon) Stilson; Lois d. at Greenwich, NY, 20 Nov 1916.

963)   ISRAEL FARNUM (*Phebe Sheldon Farnum⁴, Phebe Russell Holt Sheldon³, John², Robert¹*), b. at Mont Vernon, 8 Jun 1790 son of Israel and Phebe (Sheldon) Farnum; d. at Mont Vernon, 30 Dec 1861; m. 4 Nov 1816, CATHERINE TALBERT, *perhaps* b. 5 Apr 1788 daughter of William and Mary (Andrews) Talbert;[3099] Catherine d. at Mont Vernon, 16 May 1875.

     Israel Farnum was a farmer in Mont Vernon, New Hampshire. There are two children known for Israel and Catherine.[3100]

i   AMOS FARNUM, b. at Mont Vernon, 14 Apr 1816. Amos did marry and had one son George H. Farnum born on 22 Dec 1839. The name of Amos's wife is not known. In 1850, then 10-year-old George was living with his grandparents Israel and Catherine in Mont Vernon. George served in the Civil War and was wounded at the Battle of Fredericksburg on 13 Dec 1862. George's enlistment rank was given as musician.[3101]

ii   SARAH J. FARNUM, b. at Mont Vernon, 25 Dec 1818; d. at Mont Vernon, 28 Jan 1879; m. 27 Oct 1842, JOSIAH SWINNINGTON, b. at Mont Vernon, 4 Dec 1819 son of Elisha and Betsey (French) Swinnington;[3102] Josiah d. at Mont Vernon, 21 Apr 1902.

964)   PETER TOWNE (*Rebekah Sheldon Towne⁴, Phebe Russell Holt Sheldon³, John², Robert¹*), b. at Andover, 18 Nov 1777 son of Peter and Rebekah (Sheldon) Towne; d. at Norway, ME, 25 Mar 1854; m. at Andover, 31 May 1804, SALLY KIMBALL, b. 13 May 1786 daughter of John and Hannah (Farrington) Kimball; Sally d. at Norway, 11 Aug 1845.

     Peter and Sally started their family in Andover and the births of their first five children are recorded there. Peter and his brothers Daniel, Peter, and Amos settled in Norway between 1802 and 1816.[3103] On 20 June 1810, Peter Towne, Jr. with agreement of wife Sally sold nineteen acres of meadow to Nathaniel Berry for $621. Two further lots with buildings were sold to William Foster on 12 April 1814 for payment of $1,900. Other lots were sold to Phineas Foster on 14 March 1814 and to Nathaniel Berry on 12 September 1814.[3104]

     There are records for ten children of Peter and Sally.[3105]

i   ALBERT TOWNE, b. at Andover, 28 Sep 1804; d. at Brighton, MA, 26 Sep 1855; m. at Brighton, 22 Jul 1835, MARY ANN HASTINGS, b. at Brighton, 26 May 1811 daughter of Reuben and Deborah (Park) Hastings; Mary Ann d. at Boston, 27 Jun 1880.

[3096] Lucy's date of birth is on her cemetery record; Maine, Nathan Hale Cemetery Collection, 1780-1980

[3097] Lucy's death record gives her parents as E. Lampson and Phebe Farnham; Maine, Death Records, 1761-1922; Maine State Archives; Cultural Building, 84 State House Station, Augusta, ME 04333-0084; 1892-1907 Vital Records; Roll Number: 35

[3098] Menands, New York, Albany Rural Cemetery Burial Cards, 1791-2011

[3099] Catherine's parents are not certain.

[3100] Smith, *History of the Town of Mont Vernon*, p 64; Farnham, *New England Descendants of Ralph Farnum*, p 478

[3101] U.S., Civil War Soldier Records and Profiles, 1861-1865

[3102] The names of Josiah's parents are given as Elisha Swinnington and Betsey French on his death record. Elisha Swinnington married Betsey French in Sep 1819. Smith's *History of Mont Vernon* gives parents as Elisha Swimmington and Betsey Temple.

[3103] Whitman, *History of Norway Maine*, p 420

[3104] Massachusetts Land Records, Essex County, 190:90; 203:139; 203:259; 203:279

[3105] Towne's *Descendants of William Towne*, p 107 adds an eleventh child, Hannah, but not information was located for Hannah.

ii   MYRANDA TOWNE, b. at Andover, 14 Aug 1806; d. at Cambridge, MA, 16 Nov 1847; m. LEVI LOVEJOY, b. at Norway, ME, about 1805 son of Frye and Lucinda (Poole) Lovejoy;[3106] Levi d. at San Francisco, CA, Oct 1882 (burial 22 Oct).[3107]

iii   ANSEL TOWNE, b. at Andover, 20 May 1808; d. at Norway, ME, 30 Oct 1893; m. about 1833, JULIA A. HOBBS, b. at Norway, 8 Dec 1811 daughter of Jeremiah and Anna (Frost) Hobbs;[3108] Julia d. at Norway, 1 Dec 1883.

iv   KENDALL TOWNE, b. at Andover, 20 Mar 1810; d. after 1870 when living at Oyster Bay, NY; m. about 1846, ANN POWELL, b. in NY, 17 Oct 1818 daughter of Richard and Amy (Saxton) Powell;[3109] Ann d. at Amityville, NY, 20 Jul 1904.

v   SARAH TOWNE, b. at Andover, 16 May 1812; d. at Paris, ME, 12 Jun 1877; m. REUBEN FAVOR, b. at Yarmouth, ME, Jun 1806 son of Reuben and Mary (York) Favor;[3110] Reuben d. at Paris, 30 Nov 1862.

vi   REBECCA SHELDON TOWNE, b. at Andover, 21 Jun 1814; d. at Newburgh, NY, 1882; m. at Boston, 9 Sep 1842, WILLIAM STOCKER, b. at Portsmouth, NH, about 1812 son of William Stocker; William d. at Newburgh, 27 Jun 1887. William Stocker was a contractor who assisted with building the Boston, Hartford & Erie Railroad later known as the New York & New England Railroad.[3111]

vii   HARRIET TOWNE, b. at Norway, ME, 1816; m. at Chelsea, MA, 15 Jun 1857, THOMAS LING, b. at Middleborough, MA, 14 Jan 1797 son of Sylvanus and Jane (Cushman) Ling

viii   AMOS TOWNE, b. at Norway, 25 Jun 1821; d. at Scituate, MA, 12 Jun 1898; m. MARY ELIZABETH DANA, b. at Brighton, MA, about 1829 daughter of Charles and Esther (Deming) Dana; Mary d. at Dedham, MA, 16 Apr 1900.

ix   BETSEY K. TOWNE, b. at Norway, 1824; d. at Bethel, ME, 12 Apr 1906; m. at Boston, 20 Oct 1845, NEWTON SWIFT, b. 1823 son of Jonathan and Olive (Wilkins) Swift;[3112] Newton d. at Bethel, 17 Feb 1865.

x   PETER TOWNE, b. at Norway, 24 Dec 1831; d. at Santa Clara, CA, 24 Jun 1909; m. 26 Mar 1867, EMILY JANE "JENNIE" LEE, b. in PA, Jan 1843 daughter of Hugh and Amy (Williamson) Lee;[3113] Jennie d. at Redwood City, CA, 1925.

965)   AMOS TOWN (*Rebekah Sheldon Towne⁴, Phebe Russell Holt Sheldon³, John², Robert¹*), b. at Andover, 28 May 1779 son of Peter and Rebekah (Sheldon) Towne; d. at Norway, ME, 8 Jan 1837; m. at Andover, 30 Jan 1806, MARY "MOLLY" FARNUM, b. at Andover, 18 Oct 1780 daughter of Benjamin and Dorothy (Holt) Farnum; Mary d. at Norway, 21 Oct 1847.
        Amos and Molly resided in Norway, Maine. Amos was active in the militia with a rank of ensign in 1807 and later promoted to colonel.[3114]
        Amos Town did not leave a will and widow Mary Town request that Lieut. Daniel Town be named administrator which was allowed on 4 March 1837. The estate was insolvent, and creditors received about 4% of the amount owed to them.[3115]
        Amos Towne and Mary Farnum were parents of five children born at Norway, Maine.

i   MARY FARNUM TOWNE, b. 8 Jun 1812; d. at Hype Park, MA (burial at Norway), 14 Jan 1892; m. at Norway, 1 May 1839, as his second wife, WILLIAM HALL, b. at Norway, 4 oct 1802 son of Elijah and Lois (Thompson) Hall; William d. at Norway, 24 Nov 1858. William was first married to Almira Pike.

ii   PETER TOWNE, b. and d. 26 Apr 1814.

iii   PETER FARNUM TOWNE, b. 8 Feb 1816; d. at Boston, 25 Feb 1849; m. at Boston, 5 Jul 1846, HARRIET W. MOODY.

[3106] Lovejoy, *The Lovejoy Genealogy*, p 127
[3107] San Francisco Area, California, Funeral Home Records, 1850-1931
[3108] Whitman, *History of Norway, Maine*, p 441
[3109] Bunker, *Long Island Genealogies*, p 46
[3110] Lapham, *Centennial History of Norway, Oxford County, Maine*, p 501
[3111] Chapman Publishing Company, *Portrait and Biographical Record of Orange County, New York*, Part I, p 146
[3112] In 1858, the administration of the estate of Jonathan Swift of Norway, ME was granted to Newton Swift of Bethel at the request of widow Olive.
[3113] Jennie was living in Watsonville, CA with her father Hugh Lee prior to her marriage.
[3114] Whitman, *History of Norway*, p 548
[3115] Maine Wills and Probate, Oxford County, volume 8, p 129; volume 9, p 86

iv   HARMON TOWNE, b. 18 Feb 1817; d. at Boston, 19 May 1872; m. at Boston, 3 Mar 1847, REBECCA SARGENT, b. at Bucksport, ME, 1821 daughter of Daniel and Rebecca (Stanhope) Sargent;[3116] Rebecca d. at Lake Village, NH, 29 May 1891.

v   BENJAMIN TOWNE, b. 5 Jun 1818; d. before 1860, reported as in California; m. at Boston, 15 Feb 1840, CAROLINE F. HASTINGS, b. at Nashua, NH, about 1818 daughter of William and Betsey (McCallery) Hastings;[3117] Caroline d. at Boston, 11 Jan 1898.

966)   LYDIA TOWNE (*Rebekah Sheldon Towne⁴, Phebe Russell Holt Sheldon³, John², Robert¹*), b. at Andover, 1 Mar 1781 daughter of Peter and Rebekah (Sheldon) Towne; d. at North Andover, 14 Aug 1868; m. at Andover, 24 Jun 1800, NATHANIEL BERRY, b. at Middleton, MA, 27 Mar 1776 son of Nathaniel and Susannah (Easty) Berry; Nathaniel d. at North Andover, 1 Aug 1862.

     Nathaniel Berry did not leave a will and his estate entered probate 9 September 1862 with Moses Dorman as administrator. The heirs of the estate were his widow Lydia Berry, and children Maria Greenbank wife of Thomas Greenbank of Gaysville Vermont, Lydia A. Fuller wife of Dean Fuller of Middleton, Rebecca Chickering wife of D. Osgood Chickering of Boston, Harriet Foster wife of Nathan Foster of Andover, Amos Berry of Boxford, Hannah Montgomery of Brooklyn New York, Mary A. Berry of North Andover, and Hermon Berry of North Andover (later the estate of Hermon deceased). Real estate was valued at $4,415 including the dwelling house with 12 acres appraised at $1,800. Personal estate was $3,008 much of that in the form of notes owed to Nathaniel.[3118]

     Lydia Towne and Nathaniel Berry were parents of ten children born at Andover.

i   LYDIA ABBOT BERRY, b. 31 Aug 1801; d. at North Andover, 20 Mar 1878; m. at Andover, 19 Dec 1822, DEAN FULLER, b. at Middleton, 19 Apr 1791 son of Simeon and Rebecca (berry) Fuller; Dean d. at Middleton, 17 Mar 1864.

ii   HERMON BERRY, b. 18 Jan 1804; d. at North Andover, 24 Jan 1863; m. 1st at Lowell, 11 Dec 1831, MARY ANN PEABODY, b. at Middleton, 9 Jun 1813 daughter of Nathaniel and Ruth (Elliott) Peabody; Mary d. at Andover, 18 Jul 1834. Herman m. 2nd at Londonderry, NH, 15 Mar 1848, MARY B. TWISS, b. about 1815 and who was his widow at probate.

iii   AMOS BERRY, b. 14 Aug 1805; d. at Boxford, 28 Aug 1890; m. at Boxford, 8 Sep 1836, REBECCA C. TOWNE, b. at Boxford, 1 May 1810 daughter of Samuel and Charlotte (Fletcher) Towne; Rebecca d. at Boxford, 14 Apr 1859.

iv   HARRIET BERRY, b. 31 Dec 1806; d. at Andover, 10 Mar 1878; m. at Andover, 25 Dec 1832, NATHAN FOSTER, b. at Andover, 4 Sep 1798 son of Nathan and Susannah (Barker) Foster; Nathan d. at North Andover, 24 Nov 1877.

v   REBECCA BERRY, b. 4 Nov 1808; d. at Lawrence, MA, 20 May 1882; m. by 1845 (oldest known child born 1845), DANIEL OSGOOD CHICKERING, b. at Andover, 1 Aug 1811 son of Daniel and Susanna (Stevens) Chickering; Daniel d. at Boston, 14 Dec 1874.

vi   MARIA FANNY BERRY, b. 24 Apr 1810; d. at Salem, NH, 26 Dec 1891; m. at Andover, 30 Aug 1845, THOMAS GREENBANK, b. at Addingham, Yorkshire, England, 13 Apr 1809 son of George and Susanna (Hudson) Greenbank;[3119] Thomas d. at Salem, NH, 5 Nov 1885. Thomas arrived in Boston in 1830.

vii   HANNAH OSGOOD BERRY, b. 12 Jul 1812; d. 1 Oct 1812.

viii   HANNAH BERRY, b. 15 Sep 1813; d. at Springfield, MA, 4 Jun 1908; m. at Andover, 29 Sep 1835, JOHN PORTER MONTGOMERY, b. at Andover, 26 Dec 1812 son of Alexander and Sarah (Porter) Montgomery; John d. at Newburyport, 9 Dec 1861.

ix   WILLIAM BERRY, b. 23 Jul 1817; d. at Andover, 22 Mar 1851.

x   MARY ANN BERRY, b. 4 Mar 1823; d. at Salem, NH, 13 Feb 1913. Mary did not marry.

967)   FANNY TOWNE (*Rebekah Sheldon Towne⁴, Phebe Russell Holt Sheldon³, John², Robert¹*), b. at Andover, 24 Mar 1785 daughter of Peter and Rebekah (Sheldon) Towne; d. at Andover, 3 Sep 1812; m. at Andover, 11 Dec 1804, MICHAEL PARKER,

---

[3116] The names of Rebecca's parents are given as Daniel Sargent and Rebecca Stanhope on her death record.

[3117] The names of Caroline's parents are given as William and Betsey on her death record.

[3118] *Essex County, MA: Probate File Papers, 1638-1881.* Online database. *AmericanAncestors.org.* New England Historic Genealogical Society, 2014. Case 32646

[3119] England Select Births and Christenings; U. S. Immigration and Naturalization Records. The names of Thomas's parents are given on his death record.

b. at Andover, 17 Jan 1773 son of Michael and Phebe (Farrington) Parker. Michael married second Mehitable Fox on 30 Sep 1815. In 1850, Michael was living in Bradford with his daughter Rosina and her family.

Fanny Towne and Michael Parker were parents of five children born at Andover.

i   FANNY TOWN PARKER, b. 27 Jan 1806; m. at Andover, 5 Aug 1826, WILLIAM JONES of Frankfort, NY.

ii   PETER PARKER, b. 10 Apr 1807; d. at Andover, 6 Sep 1832; m. at Andover, 17 Oct 1831, SALLY KIMBALL LOVEJOY, b. at Andover, 26 Jul 1810 daughter of Bodwell and Sally (Poor) Lovejoy; Sally d. at Boston, 24 Jul 1849. Sally married second John H. Grush.

iii   ROSINA PARKER, b. 17 Mar 1809; d. at Andover, 3 Mar 1898; m. at Andover, 19 Mar 1831, SETH KIMBALL, likely b. at Blue Hill, ME, 2 Nov 1807 son of Seth and Molly (Peters) Kimball; Seth d. at Bradford, MA, 9 Jan 1872. Seth was a trader in Bradford.

iv   NATHAN PARKER, b. 5 Oct 1810; d. at Andover, 20 May 1848; m. 18 Sep 1836, MARY PARKER, b. at Methuen, 1817 daughter of Winthrop and Lydia (Hall) Parker.[3120] After Nathan's death, Mary married Lafayette Hall on 23 Nov 1849.[3121] She was living in Newmarket, NH in 1880.

v   ELBRIDGE PARKER, b. 3 Sep 1812; d. 19 Oct 1812.

968)   DANIEL TOWNE (*Rebekah Sheldon Towne4, Phebe Russell Holt Sheldon3, John2, Robert1*), b. at Andover, 8 Jan 1787 son of Peter and Rebekah (Sheldon) Towne; d. at Norway, ME, 1 Nov 1855; m. about 1813, SUSAN GURNEY, b. at Minot, ME, 3 Nov 1791 daughter of Jonathan and Susannah (Bryam) Gurney; Susan d. at Norway, 7 Feb 1864.

Daniel Towne and three of his brothers (Peter, Amos, and Joel) arrived in Norway, Maine between 1802 and 1816. Daniel was a blacksmith and settled at Fuller's Corner in Norway.[3122]

Daniel Towne and Susan Gurney were parents of eight children born at Norway, Maine.

i   DANIEL G. TOWNE, b. 15 Jun 1814; d. at Andover, ME, 16 May 1868; m. 1st about 1840, FANNY D. ABBOTT, b. 1817 daughter of John and Fanny (Dustin) Abbott; Fanny d. at Andover, ME, 26 Aug 1848. Daniel m. 2nd about 1850, Fanny's sister, LOUISA PRESTON ABBOTT, b. at Andover, ME, 1 Nov 1819; Louisa d. at Union, ME, 21 Dec 1890.

ii   FANNY P. TOWNE, b. 17 Mar 1816; d. at Oxford, ME, 8 Feb 1903; m. about 1837, PERRY D. JUDKINS, b. at Greenwood, ME, 30 Sep 1811 son of Moses and Apphia (Perry) Judkins; Perry d. at Cambridge, MA, 18 Dec 1867.

iii   ABIAH TOWNE, b. 19 Aug 1818; d. at Lowell, MA, 13 Apr 1916; m. by 1848, LEWIS FROST, b. in ME, about 1819 son of Joel and Susanna (Fowler) Frost;[3123] Lewis d. at Lowell, 11 Apr 1886.

iv   HONOR P. TOWNE, b. 16 Sep 1820; d. after 1860 when she was living at Waterford, ME; m. JOEL WHITMORE CHADBOURNE, b. 1819 son of James and Mary (Scribner) Chadbourne;

v   JONATHAN G. TOWNE, b. 2 Jun 1822; d. at Paris, ME, 31 May 1848; m. 1846, ABIGAIL D. CROCKETT, b. 29 Apr 1824 daughter of James and Martha (Crockett) Crockett; Abigail d. at Paris, ME, 31 Mar 1895. Abigail married second Isaac Hicks.

vi   ESHBAN P. TOWNE, b. 16 Sep 1825; m. 1st at Portland, ME, 17 Jan 1849, CAROLINE DRESSER. Eshban m. 2nd at Taylor, WV, 2 Jan 1869, NOVVISSA SPRINGER.

vii   ROLLIN TOWNE, b. 17 Feb 1829; d. at Norway, 14 Nov 1906; m. 26 Sep 1852, NANCY J. HAYES, b. 7 May 1831 daughter of Isaac and Martha J. (Swett) Hayes; Nancy d. at Norway, 9 Feb 1898.

viii   ANDREW J. TOWNE, b. 9 Sep 1832; d. at Norway, 24 Nov 1842.

969)   ASENATH "SENA" TOWNE (*Rebekah Sheldon Towne4, Phebe Russell Holt Sheldon3, John2, Robert1*), b. at Andover, 16 Feb 1789 daughter of Peter and Rebekah (Sheldon) Towne; d. at Methuen, 18 Feb 1831; m. at Methuen, 19 Jun 1814, CALEB SWAN, b. at Methuen, 20 Mar 1790 son of Caleb and Dorcas (Ingalls) Swan; Caleb d. at Methuen, 4 Dec 1863. Caleb married second Judith Pettengill.

Caleb and Sena resided in Methuen. Caleb's father Caleb Swan served several enlistments during the Revolutionary War beginning as a Corporal in Captain Archelaus Towne's Company which saw action in the early phases of the war including

[3120] The names of Mary's parents are given as Winthrop and Lydia on the marriage record of her second marriage to Lafayette Hall.
[3121] In 1850, Mary P. Hall and Lafayette Hall were living in Brighton, ME with two of Mary's children with Nathan, Riley H. Parker and Julia F. Parker.
[3122] Whitman, *A History of Norway, Maine*, p 520
[3123] The names of Joel's parents are given as Joel and Susanna on his death record.

the siege of Boston. In 1777, he held the rank of Sergeant in the Continental troops. By 1781, he held the rank of Captain of a company in the 4th Regiment of Essex militia.[3124]

On 19 April 1831, Caleb Swan was named as guardian to the following minor children: Rebekah S. Swan aged 14, Ruth aged 10, Maria aged 8, James R. aged 5, Leverett aged 3, and Horace aged 2.[3125] This guardianship is likely related to the administration of the estate of Asenath's father Peter Towne who died in 1830.

Asenath Towne and Caleb Swan were parents of ten children born at Methuen.

i   CHARLES SWAN, b. 1815; d. 19 Sep 1823.

ii   REBECKAH SHELDON SWAN, b. 24 Feb 1817; d. at Methuen, 12 Apr 1885; m. at Boston, 6 Jun 1844, ADONIRAM JUDSON GUSTIN, b. at Cornish, NH, 1818 son of Thomas and Alice (Vinton) Gustin; Adoniram Judson d. at Methuen, 26 Oct 1880. Rebeckah and Judson were living in Lanids, NJ in 1880 and Judson's will is registered both in the Cumberland County, NJ and Essex County, MA probate courts.

iii   WARD SWAN, b. 27 Jul 1818; d. 22 Feb 1824.

iv   RUSH SWAN, b. 18 Sep 1820; d. at Dracut, 27 Jan 1870; m. at Dracut, 17 Feb 1864, HARRIET E; FOX, b. at Dracut, 1836 daughter of Nathaniel and Fanny (Richardson) Fox; Harriet d. at Haverhill, 20 Aug 1873. After Rush's death, Harriet married William Sawyer.

v   CHARLES W. SWAN, b. 1821; d. 26 Aug 1821.

vi   MARIAH SWAN, b. 30 Dec 1822; d. at San Francisco, 1890; m. at Boston, 9 May 1844, HIRAM PERRY ROGERS, b. in NH, 27 Feb 1820;[3126] Hiram d. at San Francisco, 20 Mar 1864.[3127]

vii   JAMES RODNEY SWAN, b. 30 Sep 1825; d. at Methuen, 16 Apr 1848.

viii   LEVERETT SWAN, b. 28 Mar 1827; d. at New York, NY, 1 Feb 1905;[3128] m. at Methuen, 5 Apr 1865, SARAH ELIZABETH TAYLOR, b. at Methuen, 9 Sep 1835 daughter of Varnum and Charlotte (Currier) Taylor; Sarah d. at Methuen, 23 Nov 1903.

ix   HORACE SWAN, b. 10 Nov 1828

x   ISADORE SWAN, b. and d. 7 Jan 1830.

970)   ABIAH TOWNE (*Rebekah Sheldon Towne⁴, Phebe Russell Holt Sheldon³, John², Robert¹*), b. at Andover, 19 Oct 1800 daughter of Peter and Rebekah (Sheldon) Towne; d. at Middleton, 30 Nov 1874; m. at Andover, Apr 1828, AMOS CARLETON, b. at Andover, 25 Apr 1802 son of Amos and Hannah (Farnum) Carleton; Amos d. at Cutler, ME, 20 Jul 1837.

Although Amos died in Cutler, Maine, he was still a resident of Andover at the time of his death and there are probate records in both Massachusetts and Maine. His estate entered probated in Essex County, Massachusetts 29 August 1837 with Putnam J. Farnham as administrator. Personal estate was valued at $582, $404 of that being a note held against P. J. Farnham. Real estate was described as "none". On 17 November 1846, widow Abiah requested allowance from the estate for the care of herself and her four minor children.[3129]

Abiah Towne and Amos Carleton were parents of four children born at Andover.

i   ABIAH AUGUSTA CARLETON, b. 19 May 1829; d. at Andover, 27 Jan 1849.

ii   AMOS PUTNAM CARLETON, b. 26 Dec 1831; d. at Randolph, MA, 22 Oct 1906; m. at North Andover, 10 Jun 1857, HARRIET ANN BUTTERFIELD, b. at Andover, 10 Jun 1837 daughter of Charles A. and Mary (Bradley) Butterfield; Harriet d. at Andover, 27 Mar 1930.

iii   FREDERICK OSCAR CARLETON, b. 22 Jul 1834; d. at Merrimac, MA, 8 May 1892. Frederick did not marry.

[3124] Fold3.com, Compiled Service Records of Soldiers Who Served in the American Army During the Revolutionary War 1775-1785.

[3125] *Essex County, MA: Probate File Papers, 1638-1881.*Online database. *AmericanAncestors.org.* New England Historic Genealogical Society, 2014. Case 26892

[3126] Date of birth is given in cemetery records

[3127] California, County Birth, Marriage, and Death Records, 1849-1980; California Department of Public Health, courtesy of www.vitalsearch-worldwide.com. Digital Images.

[3128] New York, New York, Index to Death Certificates, 1862-1948; New York City Department of Records & Information Services; New York City, New York; New York City Death Certificates; Borough: Brooklyn; Year: 1905

[3129] *Essex County, MA: Probate File Papers, 1638-1881.*Online database. *AmericanAncestors.org.* New England Historic Genealogical Society, 2014. Case 4610

iv   OSGOOD LORING CARLETON, b. 29 Feb 1836; d. at Danvers, 23 Mar 1915; m. at Middleton, MA, 23 Mar 1870, LUCY DALE BERRY, b. Sep 1837 daughter of Jonathan and Sally R. (Wright) Berry; Lucy d. at Danvers, 6 Dec 1914.

971)   AMOS SHELDON (*Amos Sheldon⁴, Phebe Russell Holt Sheldon³, John², Robert¹*), b. at Fitchburg, 17 Sep 1796 son of Amos and Sarah (Needham) Sheldon; d. 6 Feb 1841 (buried at Fitchburg); m. 20 Jun 1824, MARY E WILLARD, b. at Fitchburg, 8 Jul 1801 daughter of Joseph and Mary (Willard) Willard; Mary d. at Edgartown, 10 Sep 1879.

     There is just one child known for Amos Sheldon and Mary Willard

i   MARY ELIZABETH SHELDON, b. at Fitchburg, 21 Mar 1825; d. at Fitchburg, 24 Jan 1895; m. at Fitchburg, 17 Jul 1856, TRISTRAM C. WALKER, b. at Warner, NH, 1828 son of William B. and Mary (·) Walker; Tristram d. at Fitchburg, 18 Mar 1861.

972)   REBECCA SHELDON (*Amos Sheldon⁴, Phebe Russell Holt Sheldon³, John², Robert¹*), b. at Fitchburg, 18 Jul 1799 daughter of Amos and Sarah (Needham) Sheldon; d. at Fitchburg, 15 May 1871; m. at Fitchburg, 5 Dec 1822, CLARK HILTON, b. at Fitchburg, 23 Mar 1798 son of Thomas and Sarah (Stratton) Hilton; Clark d. at Fitchburg, 25 Jul 1834.

     Clark did not leave a will and widow Rebecca assumed administration of the estate 5 August 1834. William Carleton and Josiah Sheldon were sureties. Real estate was a piece of meadow in the westerly part of Ashburnham valued at $110 and personal estate was $336.22. Claims against the estate were $1,172.19 and creditors received a fraction of what was due to them.[3130]

     Clark and Rebecca were parents of five children born at Fitchburg.

i   ALMER C. HILTON, b. 30 Nov 1823; d. at Fitchburg, 24 Mar 1872; m. at Fitchburg, 23 Apr 1856, MARY HADLEY, b. at Westminster, MA, 1834 daughter of John G. and Jerusha (Babcock) Hadley. Mary married second George D. Foster on 10 Feb 1880.

ii   SARAH ELVIRA HILTON, b. 3 Nov 1825; d. at Fitchburg, 13 Apr 1884. Sarah did not marry.

iii   AMOS S. HILTON, b. 1829; d. at Fitchburg, 6 Jun 1898; m. at Boston, 24 May 1869, as her second husband, SARAH B. GARY (first married to Mr. Hill), b. at Westmoreland, NH, 1834 daughter of Aaron and Brittania (Madison) Gary;[3131] Sarah d. at Jersey City, NJ (burial at Fitchburg), 17 Mar 1878.

iv   JULINA R. HILTON, b. about 1831; d. at Lunenburg, 29 Jul 1908; m. at Fitchburg, 7 Apr 1859, THOMAS SHELDON, b. at Fitchburg, 1827 son of Samuel and Tamer (Pratt) Sheldon; Thomas d. at Fitchburg, 9 Jan 1900.

v   ARIANNA N. HILTON, b. 1835; d. at Fitchburg, 25 Aug 1873. Arianna did not marry.

973)   BENJAMIN RUSSELL (*Benjamin⁴, John³, John², Robert¹*), b. at Andover, 28 Jul 1763 son of Benjamin and Mary (Feaver) Russell; d. at Newry, ME, 21 Aug 1842; m. at Andover, 20 Sep 1787 by Jonathan French pastor of the church of South Parish, MEHITABLE ABBOTT, b. at Andover, 29 Sep 1764 daughter of Jonathan and Mehitable (Abbott) Abbott; Mehitable d. at Newry, 6 Feb 1858.

     Benjamin and Mehitable resided in Bethel where Benjamin was noted for his skills in hunting and trapping.[3132]

     On 17 September 1832, Benjamin Russell, resident of Newry and aged sixty-nine, provided at statement related to his application for pension. In August 1781, he enlisted from Bethel in the company of Capt. John Evans and was sent to guard the frontier from the Canada Indians. The troops also engaged in building a fort at Bethel. He was discharged in January 1782. In June 1782 he enlisted for a term of six months and was again involved in guarding the Canada line and marched three times to the lake at the line and then back to Bethel. He was discharged in December 1782. He was awarded a pension of thirty dollars per annum. Mehitable Russell made application for the widow's pension on 17 July 1844, then living at Mercer, Maine. On 6 June 1849, Mehitable made application for an increase in pension. On 23 April 1855, Mehitable Russell, aged ninety and resident of Newry, made application for bounty land.[3133]

     Benjamin Russell did not leave a will and son Benjamin Russell of Greenwood was named administrator of his estate on 19 September 1842. On 3 November 1842, widow Mehitable was allowed allowance of one hundred-fifty dollars from the personal estate. Personal estate was valued at $203.96.[3134]

[3130] *Worcester County, MA: Probate File Papers, 1731-1881*. Online database. AmericanAncestors.org. New England Historic Genealogical Society, 2015. Case 29565

[3131] The names of Sarah's parents as Aaron and Brittania Gary are given on the marriage registration for her marriage to Amos Hilton, and parents are also named on her death record.

[3132] Lapham, *History of Bethel*, p 607

[3133] U. S. Revolutionary War Pension and Bounty-Land Warrant Application Files, Case W22139

[3134] Maine Wills and Probate, Oxford County, Estate Files, Drawer R90; Estate of Benjamin Rusell

Benjamin Russell and Mehitable Abbott were parents of twelve children born at Bethel, Maine.

i   STEPHEN ABBOT RUSSELL, b. 6 Jul 1788; d. at Bethel, 19 Jun 1860; m. at Andover, MA, 3 Nov 1816, EUNICE MASON, b. 12 Sep 1793 daughter of Moses and Eunice (Ayers) Mason;[3135] Eunice, d. at Bethel, 14 Apr 1868.

ii   SAMUEL RUSSELL, b. 14 Nov 1790; d. at Newry, ME, 20 Nov 1874; m. ABIGAIL BARKER, b. at Newry, 20 Jul 1789 daughter of Jesse and Naamah (Swan) Barker; Abigail d. at Newry, 2 May 1872.

iii   WILLIBE RUSSELL, b. 22 Dec 1791; d. at Newry, ME, 25 Aug 1832; m. by 1825, POLLY H. BARTLETT, b. at Newry, 1802 daughter of Enoch and Anna (Hall) Bartlett; Polly d. at Greenwood, ME, 1868. Polly married second Urban York.

iv   MARY "POLLY" RUSSELL, b. 24 Feb 1794; d. after 1870 when she was living at Newry; m. JAMES EAMES, b. at Needham, MA, 9 Feb 1789 son of James and Ruth (Felch) Eames; James d. at Newry, 24 Oct 1855.

v   DORCAS RUSSELL, b. 8 Apr 1796; d. at Boston, 29 Nov 1877; m. at Andover, MA, 30 Sep 1821, SAMUEL WOODBRIDGE, b. at Marblehead, MA, 13 Jan 1788 son of Dudley and Sarah (Brock) Woodbridge; Samuel d. at Cambridge, 28 Jan 1867. Samuel was first married to NANCY RUSSELL, b. at Andover, Aug 1790 daughter of John and Phebe (Abbott) Russell; Nancy d. 29 Dec 1818. Dorcas and Nancy were first cousins once removed. Samuel Woodbridge, Dorcas Russell, and Nancy Russell are Family 911.

vi   JOHN RUSSELL, b. 22 Jun 1798; d. 28 Jul 1820.

vii   LUKE REILLY RUSSELL, B. 6 Apr 1801; d. at Newry, about 1832 (probate 27 Feb 1832); m. about 1824, ABIGAIL KILGORE, b. 7 Oct 1806 daughter of John and Anna (York) Kilgore; Abigail d. after 1870 when she was living at Woodstock, ME. Abigail married second Silas Billings.

viii BENJAMIN RUSSELL, b. 11 Jan 1803; d. at Texas County, MO, 12 Oct 1871; m. MAHALA WRIGHT, b. in ME, about 1805; Mahala d. at Texas County, MO, Oct 1871. Benjamin and Mahala lived in Greenwood, ME, but in the autumn of 1871, they moved to Texas County, MO with their son Benjamin F. Russell. They both died in October of that year.[3136]

ix   ABIGAIL RUSSELL, b. 3 Jan 1805; d. 20 Jul 1825.

x   MEHITABLE RUSSELL, b. 4 Mar 1807; d. at Lowell, MA, 6 Apr 1880; m. BALLARD HATCH, b. in ME, about 1803 son of Sylvanus and Elizabeth (Ballard) Hatch;[3137] Ballard d. at Lowell, 5 Mar 1866.

xi   MARTHA ABBOTT RUSSELL, b. 23 Dec 1810; d. at Newry, 20 Mar 1894; m. ALONZO FIFIELD, b. at Riley, ME, 26 Apr 1821 son of Orlando Israel and Comfort (Ring) Fifield;[3138] Alonzo d. at Riley Plantation, 2 Feb 1892.

xii   LYDIA RUSSELL, b. 31 Aug 1812; d. at Farmington, ME, 28 Aug 1875; m. IRA KILGORE, b. 19 Oct 1808 son of John and anna (York) Kilgore; Ira d. at Farmington, 28 Oct 1877.

974)   MARY RUSSELL (*Benjamin⁴, John³, John², Robert¹*), b. at Andover, 15 Oct 1764 daughter of Benjamin and Mary (Feaver) Russell; m. about 1788, NATHANIEL SEGAR, b. at Newton, MA, 28 Jan 1755 son of Josiah and Thankful (Allen) Segar; Nathaniel d. at Hanover, ME, 10 Sep 1847.

      Nathaniel Segar was born in Newton, and as a young man went to Sudbury Canada in 1774 where he stayed several months before returning to Newton. After his service in the war, he returned to Bethel where he cleared his farm. It was during this time before his marriage that he was captured during an Indian raid and taken to Canada.[3139]

      On 17 September 1832, Nathaniel Segar aged 77 and resident of Bethel, provided a statement related to his pension application. He had applied for and received a pension in 1818 but was struck from the rolls in 1820 (likely due to the amount of property). He reported that he first enlisted in April 1775 from Newton in the company of Capt. Nathan Fuller of the Massachusetts line. His service at that time was in New York and New Jersey. He had an enlistment on 1 August 1777 in the company of Capt. Joseph Fuller and was then at Bennington, Skenesborough, Stillwater, and Saratoga. He was present at the capture of Burgoyne. He was discharged from that enlistment in December 1777 or January 1778. After his service, he returned to Bethel where, in 1781, he was captured by the Indians and taken to Canada where he was held in captivity for sixteen months.[3140]

[3135] Lapham, *History of Bethel*, p 585

[3136] "Benjamin F. Russell" in *The Bench and Bar of St. Louis, Kansas City, Jefferson County, and Other Missouri Cities: Biographical Sketches*, 1884, p 383

[3137] The names of Ballard's parents are given as Sylvanus and Elizabeth on his death record.

[3138] Wilkins, Martha Fifield, "The Fifields in Ripley Plantation Maine" in *Sunday River Sketches*, 1977

[3139] Lapham, *History of Bethel*, p 41

[3140] U. S. Revolutionary War Pension and Bounty-Land Warrant Application Files, Case S31356

Nathaniel wrote an account of his time in captivity titled *A Brief Narrative of the Captivity and Sufferings of Lt. Nathaniel Segar who was Taken Prisoner by the Indians and Carried to Canada During the Revolutionary War*.[3141] Reference to his captivity is provided elsewhere. Nathaniel was in Bethel when he was captured by members of the Abenakis tribe and taken to St. Francois, Québec. The torments Nathaniel endured included "running the gauntlet".[3142] He was captured by a group of six Indians one of whom he knew. Two members of the Clark family were also taken. Along the trek to Canada, houses were plundered, and a Mr. Poor was scalped. After fourteen days, they arrived at the home camp of their captors and two days later were turned over to English authorities in Montreal. They were held there until after the surrender of Cornwallis when there was a prisoner exchange. On 10 September 1782, the prisoners were placed on a ship to Boston. Nathaniel went from Boston to Newton where he recuperated for several months before returning to Bethel.[3143]

In his will written 10 July 1847, Nathaniel Segar made bequests of two dollars each to the following children: daughter Pamelia Lufkin, son Allan, daughter Apphia Godwin, daughter Lucy Norton, son Edmond, and son John. Daughter Abigail Barker receives a chest of drawers and other furniture listed and son-in-law William Barker received the value of a note, a horse and wagon, and stock animals. William Barker receives the residue of the estate and is named executor. Personal estate was valued at $672.[3144]

Mary Russell and Nathaniel Segar were parents of thirteen children born at Bethel.

i   PAMELIA SEGAR, b. 18 Apr 1798; d. at Rumford, ME, 23 May 1855; m. at Rumford, 28 Nov 1816, SAMUEL LUFKIN, b. at Rumford, 15 Aug 1788 son of Benjamin and Mehitable (Abbott) Lufkin; Samuel d. at Rumford, 4 Apr 1845.

ii   EDMUND SEGAR, b. 1 Apr 1790; d. 18 Sep 1797.

iii   ABIGAIL SEGAR, b. 16 Sep 1791; d. at Hanover, ME, 9 Jul 1888; m. at Rumford, 7 Jul 1816, WILLIAM BARKER, b. at Newry, ME, 22 Nov 1788 son of Jonathan and Nancy (Swan) Barker; William d. at Hanover, ME, 2 Feb 1881.

iv   ALLAN SEGAR, b. 13 May 1793; d. at Erie, IL, 7 Nov 1872; m. 1st at Rumford, 1 Jun 1819, ELIZABETH HOWARD, b. at Rumford, 24 Jun 1800 daughter of Asa and Lydia (Spofford) Howard; Elizabeth d. at Rumford, 1 Aug 1826. Allan m. 2nd ACHSAH HOWARD, b. at Weston, VT, 28 Mar 1800 daughter of William and Mary (Hawkins) Howard; Achsah d. at Erie, 2 Oct 1872.

v   APPHIA SEGAR, b. 8 Nov 1794; d. at Upton, ME, 19 Dec 1861; m. at Rumford, 30 Jul 1814, JAMES GODWIN, b. at Rumford, 1791 son of William and Rachel (Harper) Godwin;[3145] James d. at Upton, 20 Feb 1860.

vi   LUCY SEGAR, b. 21 Jan 1796; d. at Tisbury, MA, 2 Mar 1886; m. about 1820 (first known child born 1822), PETER NORTON,[3146] b. at Edgartown, MA, 30 Mar 1794 son of Eliakim and Hannah (Butler) Norton; Peter d. at Tisbury, 13 Sep 1868.

vii   MARY "POLLY" SEGAR, b. 1 Sep 1797; m. May 1826, DANIEL ESTES, b. at Bethel, 27 Dec 1801 son of Richard and Betsey (Bartlett) Estes; Daniel d. at Bethel, 1 Apr 1867.

viii   EDMUND SEGAR, b. 21 Oct 1798; m. about 1825, BETSEY POWERS, b. 1804 daughter of Arnold and Abigail (Howe) Powers; Betsey d. at Erie, IL, 1888. Edmund and Betsey divorced at Oxford County, ME in Oct 1841.[3147] Betsey lived with her son Edmund Scribner Segar in Erie after his move there.

ix   RUSSELL SEGAR, b. 21 Feb 1800; d. after 1860 when living in Memphis, TN; m. at Campbell County, KY, 9 Jul 1833, LUCY VINTON, b. in MA, about 1795 (census records); Lucy d. after 1850. Russell ran a saloon in Memphis.

x   NATHAN SEGAR, b. 6 Oct 1801. Reported in the History of Bethel as going to Ohio.

xi   JOHN E. SEGAR, b. 4 Mar 1803; d. at Rumford, ME, 30 Oct 1882; m. at Rumford, 26 Aug 1832, LYDIA FARNUM, b. at Rumford, 23 Dec 1803 daughter of Jacob and Betsey (Wheeler) Farnum; Lydia d. at Rumford, 5 Nov 1864.

xii   NATHANIEL SEGAR, b. 4 Sep 1804. Nathaniel is reported in the History of Bethel as "going West".

xiii   SUBMIT SEGAR, b. 28 Feb 1806; d. 28 Nov 1824.

[3141] Unfortunately, I have been unable to locate a copy of this document.
[3142] Barbeau, Marius, "Indian Captivities", Proceedings of the American Philosophical Society, vol. 94, no. 6 (Dec. 22, 1950), pp. 522-548
[3143] Lapham, *History of Bethel*, pp 46-51
[3144] Maine Wills and Probate, Oxford County, volume 13, pp 358-359
[3145] Lapham, *History of Rumford*, p 335
[3146] The *History of Bethel* reports that Lucy married Ichabod Norton, but she was married to Ichabod's brother Peter.
[3147] Ancestry.com. *Maine, Divorce Records, 1798-1891* [database on-line]. Provo, UT, USA: Ancestry.com Operations, Inc., 2011.

975)   THEODORE RUSSELL (*Benjamin⁴, John³, John², Robert¹*), b. at Andover, 6 Dec 1765 son of Benjamin and Mary (Feaver) Russell; d. at Bethel, ME, 4 Jun 1821; m. 1ˢᵗ at Andover, 17 Sep 1789, ABIGAIL ABBOTT, b. at Andover, 30 Jul 1770 daughter of Jonathan and Mehitable (Abbott) Abbott; Abigail d. at Bethel, 2 Jun 1810. Theodore m. 2ⁿᵈ about 1811, TABITHA STRICKLAND (widow Tabitha Twaddle), b. 1783; Tabitha d. at Bethel, 1855.

Theodore and Abigail resided in Bethel on the south side of the Androscoggin River between Bethel Mill and Middle Intervale.[3148]

In his will written 4 June 1821, Theodore Russell bequeathed to beloved wife Tabatha the use, profit, and benefit of one-third of the real estate and the use of all the household furniture that she brought to the marriage and that acquired since during her natural life. After the death of Tabatha, the household furniture is to be divided between two daughters Nabby A. Russell and Zilpha A. Russell. Daughter Lydia A. Cater receives one hundred dollars and son Jonathan Russell receives twelve dollars. Sons Theodore Russell and Leonard M. Russell each receives fifty dollars when they reach age twenty-one. Daughters Nabby and Zipha receive fifty dollars at age eighteen. Son Benjamin Russell receives the homestead farm in Bethel and the residue of the personal estate. Benjamin is to provide support for his brothers and sisters Nabby, Zilpha, Theodore, and Leonard until they are eight years old. Benjamin was named executor.[3149]

Theodore Russell and Abigail Abbott were parents of five children born at Bethel.

i   LYDIA RUSSELL, b. 16 Jul 1790; d. at Bethel, 5 Dec 1844; m. 29 Jun 1818, as his second wife, Dr. TIMOTHY C. CARTER, b. 1768; Timothy d. at Bethel, 5 Mar 1845. Timothy was first married to Fannie Freeland who died in 1815. Lydia and Timothy were parents of five children.

ii   ABIGAIL RUSSELL, b. 8 Jul 1792; d. 22 Jul 1792.

iii   JONATHAN ABBOT RUSSELL, b. 12 Jun 1793; d. at Bethel, 1859;[3150] m. SARAH HALE, b. about 1791 daughter of Oliver and Eunice (Fletcher) Hale; Sarah d. at Bethel, 1864.

iv   BENJAMIN RUSSELL, b. 15 Apr 1795; d. 18 Apr 1795.

v   BENJAMIN RUSSELL, b. 11 Jun 1796; d. at Norway, ME, about 1840; m. 10 Jan 1837, ATHOLINDA CUSHMAN, b. at Bethel, 8 Nov 1809 daughter of Thomas and Rachel (Goud) Cushman; Atholinda d. at Harrison, ME, 23 Apr 1883. Atholinda married second at Bethel, 12 Sep 1842, Micah Allen.

Theodore Russell and Tabitha Strickland were parents of five children born at Bethel.

i   NABBY A. RUSSELL, b. Jul 1812

ii   Infant, b. and d. Jul 1813

iii   ZILPHA RUSSELL, b. 28 Mar 1814

iv   THEODORE RUSSELL, b. 2 Jun 1816; d. at Livermore, 19 Jul 1882; m. at Rumford, 16 Mar 1837, LUCY G. BRAGG, b. Jun 1814 daughter of Ingalls and Elizabeth (Gardner) Bragg, Lucy d. at Rumford, 7 Sep 1901.

v   MARTIN LEONARD RUSSELL, b. 31 Mar 1819

976)   WILLIAM RUSSELL (*Benjamin⁴, John³, John², Robert¹*), b. at Bethel, ME, about 1770 son of Benjamin and Mary (Feaver) Russell; m. about 1791, MEHITABLE KILGORE, b. about 1773 daughter of John and Elizabeth (Brackett) Kilgore.

William lived in Bethel throughout his life. His is reported as being "insane" in his later years.[3151] There are records of eleven children of William and Mehitable born at Bethel, Maine.

i   MEHITABLE RUSSELL, b. 4 Jan 1792; d. at Bethel, 6 Dec 1854; m. SEBRE DUNHAM, b. at Carver, MA, 21 Apr 1796 son of Eleazer and Jane (Bryant) Dunham; Sebre d. at Paris, ME, 30 Nov 1876.

ii   CYNTHIA RUSSELL, b. 20 Dec 1793; d. before 1850; m. about 1825, WILLIAM BENT, b. at Paris, ME, 24 Mar 1798 son of William and Olive Cushman (Bessey) Bent; William d. at Paris, 12 Dec 1878. William married second Hannah before 1850.

iii   ELSIE RUSSELL, b. 8 Mar 1796; died young

iv   WILLIAM RUSSELL, b. 12 Mar 1798

[3148] Lapham, *History of Bethel*, p 607

[3149] *Maine. Probate Court (Oxford County); Probate Place: Oxford, Maine, Estate of Theodore Russell*

[3150] Maine, Faylene Hutton Cemetery Collection, 1780-1990

[3151] Lapham, *History of Bethel*, p 608

v   ELSIE RUSSELL, b. 20 Mar 1800; m. at Rumford, 5 May 1817, WILLIAM BARTLETT, b. at Bethel, 6 Jun 1794 son of Stephen and Dorcas (Barbour) Bartlett.

vi   SAMUEL RUSSELL, b. 9 Mar 1802

vii   HENRY RUSSELL, b. 15 Feb 1804

viii   MARY RUSSELL, b. 13 Jun 1806; d. at Middleton, MA, 27 Nov 1874; m. at Newbury, MA, 5 May 1839, PAUL PEARSON, b. at Newbury, 29 Mar 1814 son of Elihu and Elizabeth (Thurlow) Pearson; Paul d. at Newbury, 24 Jul 1880.

ix   THEODORE RUSSELL, b. 1 Aug 1808; d. at Newbury, 2 Apr 1884; m. at Newbury, 1 Jun 1835, SARAH WOODMAN, b. at Newbury, 3 Oct 1814 daughter of Paul and Judith (Kent) Woodman; Sarah d. at Newbury, 13 May 1875.

x   SOPHIA RUSSELL, b. 8 Aug 1811; d. at Taunton, MA, 10 May 1894; m. at Rumford, ME, 30 Nov 1837, JOSEPH RODENY COLE, m. at Vassalboro, ME, 31 Dec 1805 son of Ezekiel and Mary (Lovejoy) Cole; Rodney d. at Taunton, 3 Nov 1859.

xi   PALMER RUSSELL, b. 1 Aug 1813

977)   JOHN RUSSELL (*Benjamin⁴, John³, John², Robert¹*), b. at Bethel, ME, about 1775 son of Benjamin and Mary (Feaver) Russell; d. at Bethel, 1 Jul 1850; m. about 1798, SUSANNAH TWITCHELL, b. 27 Nov 1777 daughter of Ezra and Susannah (Rice) Twitchell; Susannah d. at Bethel, 2 Sep 1856.
    John Russell was a brick mason and farmer. He lived below Bethel Hill on Middle Intervale Road.[3152] John and Susannah were parents of six children born at Bethel, Maine.

i   PERSIS RUSSELL, b. 13 May 1799; d. at Lyman, ME, 8 Mar 1881; m. about 1822, JEREMIAH VIRGIN who d. before 1830 when Persis was head of household in Bethel.

ii   EZRA TWITCHELL RUSSELL, b. 19 Aug 1803; d. at Bethel, 6 Jan 1839; m. about 1824, PHEBE KIMBALL, b. at Bethel, 21 Feb 1804 daughter of Israel and Phebe (Hazen) Kimball; Phebe d. at Bethel, 26 Nov 1887. Phebe married second Winslow Haywood.

iii   JOHN RUSSELL, b. 17 Jun 1807; d. at Bethel, 14 Sep 1886; m. by 1837, CYNTHIA TWITCHELL, b. at Bethel, 11 Mar 1809 daughter of Ezra and Betsey (Coffin) Twitchell; Cynthia d. at Bethel, 15 Jan 1893.

iv   SUSANNAH RUSSELL, b. 15 Jun 1810

v   ELMIRA RUSSELL, b. 29 Aug 1812

vi   LEANDER GAGE RUSSELL, b. 15 Oct 1816; d. after 1855 when he was living at Haverhill, MA; m. about 1840, SARAH P. WIGHT, b. at Dublin, NH, 1816 daughter of Eli D. and Fanny (Chaplin) Wight; Sarah d. at Haverhill, 26 Apr 1883.

978)   JOHN RUSSELL (*John⁴, John³, John², Robert¹*), b. at Andover, 10 Oct 1774 son of John and Phebe (Abbott) Russell; d. at Andover, May 1818; m. at Andover, 21 Jul 1799, DIANA BRAY, b. at Gloucester, Oct 1775 daughter of Edward and Edith (Doane) Bray; Diana d. at Andover, 4 Mar 1858.[3153]
    John and Diana were parents of five children born at Andover.

i   JOHN RUSSELL, b. 27 May 1800; d. at Reading, 6 Dec 1854; m. 8 Jan 1822, ELIZA HOLT, b. at Dracut, 5 Jul 1804 daughter of Joseph and Elizabeth (Beard) Holt; Eliza d. at Reading, 4 Aug 1892.

ii   WILLIAM RUSSELL, b. 29 Jul 1802

iii   EDWARD RUSSELL, b. 23 Nov 1804; d. at Andover, 15 Oct 1874; m. CAROLINE A. GERRISH, b. at Newfield, ME, 12 Mar 1803 daughter of Nathan and Elinor (·) Gerrish; Caroline d. at Andover, 25 Mar 1882.

iv   PHEBE RUSSELL, b. 30 Mar 1807; d. at Andover, 12 Jun 1896; m. at Andover, 6 May 1827, JOSEPH CONVERSE GOLDSMITH, b. at Andover, 1 Apr 1803 son of Jeremiah and Sarah (Converse) Goldsmith; Joseph d. at Andover, 2 Nov 1854.

[3152] Lapham, *History of Bethel*, p 609
[3153] Diana's death record confirms Gloucester as her place of birth making Edward and Edith her likely parents.

v   JOSEPH RUSSELL, b. 13 Oct 1809; d. after 1880 when he was living at Andover; m. at Andover, 17 Jul 1861, ELIZABETH LEE MCNEIL, b. in England, 1822 daughter of Thomas and Julia (·) McNeil; Elizabeth d. at Andover, 29 Jan 1882.

979)   PHEBE RUSSELL (*John⁴, John³, John², Robert¹*), b. at Andover, 1776 daughter of John and Phebe (Abbott) Russell; d. at Andover, 2 Dec 1858; m. 2 Nov 1794, her third cousin, EBENEZER LOVEJOY, b. at Andover, 16 Feb 1773 son of Jeremiah and Dorothy (Ballard) Lovejoy; Ebenezer d. at Andover, 7 Jun 1851.

Ebenezer Lovejoy had his 60-acre farm on what is now Lovejoy Road in Andover with his house (although now gone) at 108 Lovejoy Road.[3154]

Ebenezer was involved in multiple land transactions, some of them summarized here. On 30 May 1818 and on 8 January 1833, Ebenezer Lovejoy with consent of wife Phebe conveyed to James B. Lovejoy (likely his brother James Ballard Lovejoy) two tracts of land in Andover, the first for payment of three hundred dollars and the second a tract of woodland in Andover for payment of four hundred-fifty dollars. On 8 January 1832, Ebenezer and Phebe sold to William R. Lovejoy of Boston for payment of $3,000 five tracts of land in Andover. This deed mentions that one of the tracts adjoins land that Ebenezer had previously sold to Ebenezer, Jr. On 15 September 1831, Josiah B. and Mercy H. Lovejoy conveyed a tract of land in Andover to Ebenezer Lovejoy, Jr. for $400.[3155]

Phebe Russell and Ebenezer Lovejoy were parents of ten children born at Andover. Five of the children were baptized on 20 November 1814.

i   EBENEZER LOVEJOY, b. 7 Feb 1795; d. at Andover, 7 Dec 1873; m. 1ˢᵗ 9 May 1819, DELINA LYNCH, b. at Greenfield, NH, 4 Jul 1799; Delina d. at Andover, 1 Sep 1856. Ebenezer m. 2ⁿᵈ at Andover, 18 Mar 1857, SARAH WARDWELL (widow of Jere Farnum), b. at Andover, 7 Sep 1803 daughter of John and Sarah (Trussel) Wardwell; Sarah d. at Andover, 18 Aug 1884.

ii   WILLIAM RUSSELL LOVEJOY, b. 26 Sep 1796; d. at Chicago, IL, 25 Sep 1870; m. MARY ANN PERKINS, b. at New Castle, ME, 1804 daughter of Enoch Perkins; Mary Ann d. at Boston, 21 Dec 1886. William and Mary resided in Boston, but William was in Chicago at the time of his death.

iii   GEORGE LOVEJOY, b. 4 Sep 1798; d. at Boston, 18 Mar 1856; m. at Boston, 2 Sep 1821, MARY FITTS (or Fitz), b. at Haverhill, about 1797 daughter of Nathaniel and Phebe (Pike) Pitts; Mary d. at Somerville, MA, 3 May 1882.

iv   JEREMIAH LOVEJOY, b. about 1801 and baptized 20 Nov 1814; d. at Reading, 31 Aug 1867; m. at Reading, 27 Jul 1821, BETSEY PRATT, b. at Reading, 23 Dec 1799 daughter of Benjamin and Mary (Smith) Pratt; Betsey d. at Reading, 19 May 1875.

v   JOSIAH BALLARD LOVEJOY, b. about 1805 and baptized 20 Nov 1814; d. (burial at Bergen, NY), 2 Feb 1844;[3156] m. at Boston, 15 Mar 1826, MERCY HODGES STICKNEY, b. at Duxbury, 2 Nov 1808 daughter of Samuel and Huldah (Hodges) Stickney; Mercy d. at Charlestown, 19 Nov 1868.

vi   SARAH "SALLY" LOVEJOY, b. about 1808 and baptized 20 Nov 1814; d. at Lowell, 5 Apr 1886; m. at Andover, 22 Jul 1828, STEPHEN DINSMORE, b. at Sidney, ME, 1806; Stephen d. at Andover, 10 Feb 1852.

vii   JOHN LOVEJOY, b. about 1810 and baptized 20 Nov 1814; d. at Andover, 11 Jan 1899; m. at Andover, 6 Jun 1833, MARY F. CHICKERING, b. at Andover, 9 Jul 1813 daughter of John and Mary (Carleton) Chickering; Mary d. at Andover, 3 Mar 1880.

viii   PHEBE LOVEJOY, b. 1812 and baptized 20 Nov 1814; d. at Worcester, 9 Jul 1896; m. at Andover, 11 Jun 1835, JOHN INGALLS ABBOTT, b. at Groton, 1810 son of Joseph and Prudence (Phillips) Abbott; Joseph d. at Andover, 16 Dec 1857.

ix   JOSEPH LOVEJOY, b. 25 Jun 1816; d. at Boston, 24 Oct 1874; m. at Boston, 5 Aug 1843, MARGARET G. HOMER, b. at Boston, 11 Dec 1822 daughter of John and Mary (Williams) Homer;[3157] Margaret d. at Brookline, 27 May 1894.

x   JOSHUA LOVEJOY, b. 1818; d. at Andover, 27 Oct 1860; m. at Roxbury, 16 Aug 1853, MATILDA J. DOMETT, b. at Boston, 1822 daughter of George and Harriet (Fracher) Domett;[3158] Matilda d. at Watertown, 9 Sep 1903.

[3154] Andover Historic Preservation, 108 Lovejoy Road, https://preservation.mhl.org/108-lovejoy-road
[3155] Massachusetts Land Records, Essex County, 270:8, 270:9, 266:294, 270:10
[3156] Red Schoolhouse Cemetery, Bergen, NY; findagrave ID: 26673698
[3157] Names of Margaret's parents are given as John Homer and Mary Williams on her death record.
[3158] The names of Matilda's parents are given as George Dommet and Harriet Fracher on her death record.

980)   HANNAH RUSSELL (*John⁴, John³, John², Robert¹*), b. at Andover, Sep 1778 daughter of John and Phebe (Abbott) Russell; d. at Andover, 3 Jan 1840; m. 13 Aug 1801, her third cousin, STEPHEN ABBOT, b. at Andover, 30 Dec 1779 son of Jonathan and Dorcas (Abbott) Abbott; Stephen d. at Andover, 1 Oct 1835.

Stephen Abbot inherited the family homestead at 45 Ballardvale Road from his father Jonathan. Stephen constructed a new home in 1825. The property at 45 Ballardvale was inherited by Stephen's son John B. Abbott and is the historic property at what is now 354 South Main Street in Andover.[3159]

Stephen did not leave a will and his estate entered probate 3 November 1835 with Hannah Abbot as administratrix. The homestead farm of 157 acres with buildings was valued at $6,700. The Russell farm of 104 acres was valued at $3,400. Other real estate parcels totaled $9,029. Personal estate was $13,541.46 for a total estate value of $32,670.46. A distribution from the estate on 16 July 1839 paid $3,378 to Hannah Abbott and $1,126 to each of the other heirs: Stephen D. Abbott, John Abbott, Hannah A. Harding, Martha L. Gray, Mary E. P. Abbott, and Phebe A. Sibley.[3160]

There are records of ten children of Stephen and Hannah born at Andover.

i   HANNAH ABBOTT (twin), b. 4 Oct 1802; d. at Westford, MA, 5 Sep 1870; m. at Andover, 1 Nov 1835, JOHN HARDING, b. at Andover, 27 Jun 1804 son of John and Sarah (Houghton) Harding; John d. at Andover, 18 Aug 1893.

ii   STEPHEN ABBOTT (twin), b. 4 Oct 1802; d. 10 Apr 1822.

iii   MARTHA LOVEJOY ABBOTT, b. at Andover, 9 Sep 1804; d. at Andover, 10 Dec 1856; m. at Andover, 12 Jul 1831, SAMUEL GRAY, b. at Andover, 30 Jan 1803 son of David and Rebecca (Jenkins) Gray; Samuel d. at Andover, 29 Sep 1880.

iv   MARY E. PHILLIPS ABBOTT, b 5 Jan 1807; d. at Andover, 29 Jan 1878; m. 1 Jan 1840, Rev. HENRY SOLOMON GREENE, b. at Boston, 11 Feb 1807 son of John W. and Sophia (Broad) Greene;[3161] Henry d. at Andover (Ballard Vale), 11 Jun 1880. Rev. Henry S. Greene attended Amherst Academy and Amherst College. He then graduated from Andover Theological Seminary and was ordained at Lynnfield on 27 Dec 1837. He was minister at Ballard Vale Union Society.[3162]

v   JONATHAN ABBOTT, baptized 4 Dec 1808; d. at Andover, 1 Oct 1837.

vi   SAMUEL ABBOTT, b. 22 Feb 1811; d. 17 Sep 1834.

vii   PHEBE HUTCHINSON ABBOTT, b. 22 Mar 1813; d. at Worcester, MA, 10 Dec 1884; m. at Andover, 4 Apr 1836, GEORGE VALPEY SIBLEY, b. at Salem, about 1817 son of Joseph and Dorcas (Abbott) Sibley; George d. at Worcester, 5 Sep 1891.

viii STEPHEN DAVID ABBOTT, b. 15 Sep 1817; d. at Andover, 9 Sep 1885; m. 12 Mar 1859, ABIGAIL "ABBY" D. MORTON, b. at Ryegate, VT, 10 Oct 1818 daughter of Josiah and Charity (Downes) Morton; Abby d. at Andover, 14 Dec 1890. Abigail and a 28-year old Rufus Morton were living in Stephen's household in 1850.

ix   JOHN B. ABBOTT, b. about 1818; d. at Andover, 14 Feb 1900; m. at Lynnfield, 28 Jun 1843, his first cousin once removed, CAROLINE DORCAS WOODBRIDGE (*Dorcas Russell Woodbridge⁶, Benjamin⁵, Benjamin⁴, John³, John², Robert¹*), b. at Andover, 1 Aug 1822 daughter of Samuel and Dorcas (Russell) Woodbridge; Caroline d. at Andover, 10 Mar 1898.

x   DORCAS JANE ABBOTT, b. 1820; d. 26 Nov 1822.

981)   BETTY RUSSELL (*John⁴, John³, John², Robert¹*), b. at Andover, 1780 daughter of John and Phebe (Abbott) Russell; d. at Andover, 7 Nov 1866; m. 27 Sep 1804, THOMAS SMITH, b. at Andover, 13 Mar 1781 son of Thomas and Mary (Harris) Smith; Thomas d. at Andover, 18 Sep 1832.

Betty Russell and Thomas Smith were parents of seven children born at Andover.

i   THOMAS SMITH, b. 11 Jan 1805; died young

ii   JOHN RUSSELL SMITH, b. 2 Jul 1807; d. at Andover, 8 May 1870; m. MARY ANN NEVINS, b. at Londonderry, NH, about 1814; Mary Ann d. at Andover, 12 Feb 1886. John and Mary adopted a daughter Mary Ida Smith who was born about 1860. John was a shoemaker in Lowell and Andover.

[3159] Andover, Historic Preservation, "354 South Main Street", https://preservation.mhl.org/354-south-main-street

[3160] *Essex County, MA: Probate File Papers, 1638-1881.* Online database. *AmericanAncestors.org.* New England Historic Genealogical Society, 2014. Case 136

[3161] Biographical Record of the Alumni of Amherst College, 1821-1871, p 115

[3162] Andover Historic Preservation, "1 Church Street", https://preservation.mhl.org/1-church-street

iii   MARY HARRIS SMITH, b. 30 Aug 1809; d. at Andover, 12 Oct 1879; m. at Andover, 3 Nov 1832, RUFUS F. CALDWELL, b. at Hudson, NH, 1808 son of Samuel and Lucinda (Butters) Caldwell;[3163] Rufus d. at Andover, 11 Jan 1890.

iv   PHEBE ABBOT SMITH, b. 27 Oct 1811; d. at Lawrence, MA, 27 Jun 1866; m. at Andover, 14 Oct 1835, her second cousin, PASCHAL ABBOTT (*Hannah Russell Abbott⁵, Uriah⁴, Thomas³, James², Robert¹*), b. at Andover, 13 Apr 1812 son of Nathan and Hannah (Russell) Abbott; Paschal d. at Lawrence, 4 Jun 1874. Paschal married second Margaret McNaughton.

v   ELIZABETH FOSTER SMITH, b. 5 Mar 1815; d. at Andover, 22 Aug 1881. Elizabeth did not marry.

vi   MARGARET WATERHOUSE SMITH, b. 1 Jul 1817; d. at Andover, 20 Jan 1897. Margaret did not marry.

vii   THOMAS SMITH, b. 21 Mar 1820; d. at Andover, 25 Sep 1877; m. at Andover, 4 Feb 1853, LAURA FRANCES RUSSELL, b. at Andover, 4 Jul 1831 daughter of Moody and Frances (Wardwell) Russell; Laura d. at Andover, 12 Jan 1918.

982)   SALLY RUSSELL (*John⁴, John³, John², Robert¹*), b. at Andover, 1783 daughter of John and Phebe (Abbott) Russell; d. of consumption at Andover, 10 Jun 1848;[3164] m. at Andover, 23 Oct 1806, THOMAS LORING, born in NH, about 1780 son of John and Sarah (Foster) Loring; Thomas d. at New Orleans, 1826.

Thomas Loring was a machinist, and he placed the machinery in the first steamboat to go down the Ohio River. He died of spotted fever in New Orleans.[3165] In 1820, the family was living in Cincinnati with a household of five: one male 26 to 44, one female 26 to 44, one male 10 to 15, one female under 10, and one female 10 to 15.[3166]

Thomas Loring and Sally Russell were parents of five children.

i   THOMAS FOSTER LORING, b. at Charlestown, MA 15 Dec 1807; d. after 1870 and before 1880 when he was living in Pease, OH; m. at Jefferson County, OH, 2 Jun 1831, KEZIA MURRAY, b. in OH, about 1811; Kezia d. after 1880 when she was living at Bellaire, OH.

ii   SARAH LORING, b. at Charlestown, 1809; d. after 1880 when she was living at Andover with her sister Mary and her husband; m. 25 Nov 1833, JACOB STICKNEY, b. at Newburyport, 20 Feb 1806; d. in California, 30 Jan 1850. Jacob went to California for the gold rush.

iii   MARY ANN LORING, b. at Andover, 25 Sep 1813; d. at Andover, 26 Oct 1907; m. 1ˢᵗ at Andover, 8 Oct 1835, ANTHONY DAVENPORT CURRIER, b. at Newburyport, 20 Jan 1812 son of Solomon H. and Sarah (Davenport) Currier; Anthony d. 11 Jan 1838 when he drowned in the Merrimac River. Mary Ann m. 2ⁿᵈ at Andover, 6 Dec 1841, ROBERT CALLAHAN, b. at Andover 1809 son of Robert and Dorcas (Pettengill) Callahan; Robert d. at Andover, 22 May 1889.

iv   JOHN RUSSELL LORING, b. estimate 1817; d. at Cincinnati, 1818.

v   JOHN RUSSELL LORING, b. at Cincinnati, 1821; d. at Andover, 3 Dec 1891; m. 1ˢᵗ MARTHA JACOBS, b. at Newburyport, Nov 1828 daughter of Caleb and Mary (Dow) Jacobs; Martha d. at Andover, 4 Mar 1860. John m. 2ⁿᵈ at Reading, 8 Dec 1864, SARAH A. M. BARKER (widow of Asa C. Buck), b. at Tyngsboro, 19 Aug 1837 daughter of Amos R. and Martha (Ames) Barker; Sarah d. at Andover, 1 Jan 1917. Sarah's first husband, Asa C. Buck, died of illness at Baton Rouge while serving in the Civil War. As his father was, John Russell Loring was a machinist employed by the Ballardvale Machine Shop.[3167]

983)   DOLLY RUSSELL (*John⁴, John³, John², Robert¹*), baptized at Andover, 21 Sep 1788 daughter of John and Phebe (Abbott) Russell; d. at Andover, 26 Jun 1809; m. 19 May 1808, her third cousin, JOHN LOVEJOY, b. at Andover, 25 Jul 1780 son of Jeremiah and Dorothy (Ballard) Lovejoy; John d. at Andover, 26 Feb 1817. After Dolly's death, John married PERSIS BAILEY, b. at Andover, 25 May 1783 daughter of William and Rebecca (Hildreth) Bailey; Persis d. at Andover, 18 Feb 1816.

In his will written 7 February 1817 (probate 1 April 1817), John Lovejoy provided that the real estate and the residue of the personal estate after payment of debts be managed for the care of his three daughters, Dolly, Catharine, and Hannah, until they arrive at age eighteen. When the daughters arrive at age eighteen, the estate is to be equally divided among them, except that the portions of the two youngest daughters, Catharine and Hannah, should be twenty dollars more each than the

---

[3163] Names of Rufus's parents are given as Samuel Caldwell and Lucinda Butters on his death record.

[3164] Sarah, wid. Thomas, consumption, June 10,1848, a 65 y. [a. 64 y. C.R.2.]

[3165] *New Hampshire, Death and Burial Records Index, 1654-1949*; Charlotte Helen Abbott, The Loring Family

[3166] 1820 U S Census; Census Place: Cincinnati Ward 2, Hamilton, Ohio; Page: 241; NARA Roll: M33_87; Image: 180

[3167] Lest We Forget, Andover and the Civil War, John Russell Loring, https://www.andoverlestweforget.com/faces-of-andover/loring-poor/john-russell-loring/

portion for Dolly. Brother Ebenezer Lovejoy was named guardian, and Ebenezer was named executor. Real estate was valued at $1,140 and personal estate at $259.48. Debts were $150.76.[3168]

Dolly Russell and John Lovejoy were parents of one child. John also had two children with his second wife Persis Bailey.

i   DOLLY LOVEJOY, b. about 1809; d. at Andover, 17 Nov 1889; m. at Andover, 27 Apr 1854, NATHAN ABBOTT, b. at Andover, 25 Feb 1799 son of Nathan and Hannah (Phelps) Abbott; Nathan d. at Andover, 26 Apr 1872. Although late in life, this was the first marriage for both Dolly and Nathan, and they did not have children.

984)   NANCY RUSSELL (*John⁴, John³, John², Robert¹*), b. at Andover, Aug 1790 daughter of John and Phebe (Abbott) Russell; d. at Arlington, MA, 29 Dec 1818; m. 1812, SAMUEL WOODBRIDGE, b. at Marblehead, 13 Jan 1788 son of Dudley and Sara (Brock) Woodbridge;[3169] Dudley d. at Cambridge, 28 Jan 1867. After Nancy's death, Samuel married, 30 Sep 1821, DORCAS RUSSELL (*Benjamin⁵, Benjamin⁴, John³, John², Robert¹*), b. at Bethel, ME, 8 Apr 1796 daughter of Benjamin and Mehitable (Abbott) Russell; Dorcas d. at Boston, 29 Nov 1877.

Samuel Woodbridge and Nancy Russell were parents of three children.

i   NANCY BROCK WOODBRIDGE, b. at Reading, 26 Apr 1814; d. at Andover, MA, 3 Mar 1880; m. at Andover, 1 Apr 1837, SYLVESTER MERRILL, b. at Lovell, ME, 1812 son of Isaiah and Mary (Trull) Merrill; Sylvester d. at Cambridge, 29 May 1885.

ii   PHEBE R. WOODBRIDGE, b. at Charlestown, 26 Sep 1816; d. at Weston, MA, 9 Sep 1848; m. at Woburn, 20 Oct 1839, WARREN B. PERKINS, b. at Medford, 1817 son of Andrew and Susan (Sweetser) Perkins; Warren d. at Woburn, 13 May 1900. Warren married second Martha Maria Newhall on 18 Oct 1849.

iii   SAMUEL F. WOODBRIDGE, b. at Cambridge, 13 Aug 1818; d. at Cambridge, 21 Nov 1906; m. 5 Apr 1843, HANNAH MUNROE LOCKE, b. at Arlington 14 Mar 1819 daughter of William and Hannah (Porter) Locke; Hannah d. at Cambridge, 25 Jan 1878.

Samuel Woodbridge and Dorcas Russell were parents of eight children.

i   CAROLINE DORCAS WOODBRIDGE, b. at Andover, 1 Aug 1822; d. at Andover, 10 Mar 1898; m. at Lynnfield, 28 Jun 1843, her first cousin once removed, JOHN B. ABBOTT (*Hannah Russell Abbott⁵, John⁴, John³, John², Robert¹*), b. 1818 son of Stephen and Hannah (Russell) Abbott; John d. at Andover, 14 Feb 1900.

ii   ABIGIAL L. WOODBRIDGE, b. at Andover, 26 Nov 1824; d. at Andover, 31 Dec 1901; m. at Cambridge, 28 Sep 1848, JOHN KERSHAW, b. "on the ocean" during his parents' passage, 1822 son of John and Mary (Scott) Kershaw;[3170] John d. at Andover, 20 Dec 1895.

iii   LYDIA JANE WOODBRIDGE, b. at Andover, 15 Jun 1827; d. at Boston, 9 Jul 1898; m. 13 Aug 1850, EZEKIEL G. BYAM, b. at Chelmsford, 19 Aug 1828 son of Ezekiel and Charlotte (Bateman) Byam; Ezekiel d. at Boston, 17 Feb 1896.

iv   JOHN R. WOODBRIDGE, b. 15 Apr 1829; d. at Cambridge, 3 Aug 1879; m. at Andover, 27 Apr 1856, AGNES C. DOHERTY, b. in Scotland, 1835 daughter of John Doherty; Agnes d. at Boston, 23 Apr 1912.

v   STEPHEN A. WOODBRIDGE, b. 29 Nov 1831; d. after 1865 when he was living at Cambridge and unmarried.

vi   HENRY WILLOUGHBY WOODBRIDGE, b. at Medford, 30 Sep 1833; d. of typhoid fever while in Venezuela, 6 Jan 1873; m. at Cambridge, 28 Jun 1863, MARY FRANCES SCHOULER, b. 1836 daughter of Robert and Elizabeth (Dodge) Schouler; Mary d. (burial at Arlington, MA), 26 Feb 1888. Henry worked in the manufacture of foundry facings. The family resided in Bloomfield New Jersey at the time of Henry's death.

vii   ALBERT A. WOODBRIDGE, b. at Medford, 9 May 1835; d. at West Cambridge, 9 May 1859.

viii   GEORGE B. WOODBRIDGE, b. 19 Jan 1840; d. at Cambridge, 9 Aug 1859.

[3168] *Essex County, MA: Probate File Papers, 1638-1881.* Online database. *AmericanAncestors.org.* New England Historic Genealogical Society, 2014. Case 17070
[3169] The names of Samuel's parents are given as Dudley and Sarah Woodbridge on his death record. New England Historic Genealogical Society; Boston, Massachusetts; Massachusetts Vital Records, 1840–1911
[3170] John's place of birth and names of his parents (both born in England) are as reported on his death record.

985)   HANNAH RUSSELL (*Abraham⁴, John³, John², Robert¹*), b. at Fryeburg, 19 Sep 1776 daughter of Abraham and Sarah (Swan) Russell; d. at Newry, ME, 1848; m. 1794, FREDERICK BALLARD, b. at Middleton, MA, 13 Oct 1762 son of Jonathan and Priscilla (Farnum) Ballard; Frederick d. at Newry, 1851.

Hannah and Frederick resided in Wakefield, New Hampshire until relocating to Oxford County, Maine in 1830. Frederick was a hatter by trade.

On 2 August 1825, Frederick Ballard then age sixty-two and resident of Strafford County, New Hampshire provided a statement in application for pension. On 1 June 1778, he enlisted for a term of nine months in Massachusetts in the company of Capt. Benjamin Farnum and the regiment of Col. Tupper in Gen. Patterson's brigade. He was discharged at West Point in March 1779. He had not made application earlier as "I have heretofore been enabled to support myself without any assistance, and was in hopes to have so continued, but being very much embarrassed in my concerns, and in closing then I find myself destitute of property; and old age and infirmities are fast advancing upon me, and having no other resources, I am obliged to apply to my country for assistance." He reported his property as three kitchen chairs, one iron pot, one iron tea kettle (broken), and one old pine table. He reported changes to his property since 1818, primarily selling a property for $400 which he used to pay off a mortgage and pay debts. He also had a horse and a cow which were sold to support his family. He reported his usual occupation as a hatter but unable to perform this work due to a rupture. His wife was age 49 and "does not enjoy very good health." The file contains statements from Ira Fish and Dr. Thomas Lindsey verifying the land transfer and payment of debts. On 18 December 1845, son Joseph W. Ballard of Greenwood, Maine provided a statement that his father had been living with him and on the prior 11th May, Joseph's house burned and along with it the chest containing his father's papers including his pension certificate.[3171]

Deeds contained within the pension file document that on 2 March 1818, Frederick Ballard of Wakefield transferred 62 acres of property to his son Sherebiah Ballard for payment of $400. On 2 March, Sherebiah transferred this property to Ira Fish for $400.

The estate of Frederick Ballard entered probate 23 May 1852. Son-in-law Aaron Smith reported that Frederick lived with him prior to his death, that Frederick died on 28 November 1851, and that he had no personal estate but was a pensioner and there were pension arrears due the estate.[3172]

Hannah Russell and Frederick Ballard were parents of ten children born at Wakefield, New Hampshire.

i   FREDERICK LUCRATUS BALLARD, b. 8 Dec 1796; d. at Jackson, NH, 24 Jan 1869; m. at Wakefield, Apr 1817, MARY FOLSOM, b. at Wakefield, 15 Aug 1794 daughter of James and Sally (Plummer) Folsom; Mary d. at Wakefield, 10 Mar 1891.

ii   JONATHAN BALLARD, b. 20 Aug 1798; d. 1820.

iii   SHEREBIAH BALLARD, b. 25 Jul 1801; d. after 1837 when he was living at Portland, ME; m. at Middleton, NH, 31 Oct 1824, ELSIE TUTTLE.

iv   PUTNAM BALLARD, b. 30 Aug 1803

v   JOHN S. BALLARD, b. 21 Oct 1805

vi   JOSEPH WARREN BALLARD, b. 16 Apr 1808; d. at Dexter, ME, 10 Sep 1905; m. 1st about 1830, MARY CUMMINGS, b. May 1808 (based on age at death); Mary d. 5 Mar 1850; Joseph m. 2nd 8 Mar 1852, DEBORAH WHITTUM, b. 1808; Deborah d. at Upton, ME, 5 Apr 1885.

vii   SARAH BALLARD, b. 6 mar 1810; d. at Newry, ME, 23 Jan 1867; m. AARON SMITH, b. in Maine, 1798, son of Ithiel and Lucy (Littlehale) Smith; Aaron d. at Newry, 31 Mar 1875.

viii   MARY R. BALLARD, b. 9 Jan 1812; d. at Rumford, ME, 29 Jan 1893; m. at Portland, ME, 29 Mar 1832, ISAAC LITTLEHALE, b. at Bethel, 21 Sep 1801 son of Isaac and Betsey (Ripley) Littlehale; Isaac d. at the Isthmus of Panama, 4 Jun 1865. Isaac had gone to California to make his fortune, which he reportedly did, but died on the way home.[3173]

ix   ABRAHAM RUSSELL BALLARD, b. 30 Apr 1814; d. at Greenwood, ME, 19 Apr 1844. Abraham did not marry. In his will, he left his real and personal estate to brother Alpheus Ballard and five dollars to his father Frederick Ballard.[3174]

x   ALPHEUS BALLARD, b. 7 Sep 1816; d. at Upton, ME, 1 Apr 1907; m. REBECCA B. PURRINGTON, b. 1811; Rebecca d. at Upton, 24 Sep 1889.

[3171] U. S. Revolutionary War Pension and Bounty-Land Warrant Application Files, Case S37565
[3172] Maine Wills and Probate, Oxford County, Estate Files, Drawer B10, Estate of Frederick Ballard
[3173] Littlehale, *A Complete History and Genealogy of the Littlehale Family*, p 30
[3174] Maine Will and Probate, Oxford County, Drawer B8, Estate of Abraham R. Ballard.

986)   SARAH RUSSELL (*Abraham⁴, John³, John², Robert¹*), b. 26 Apr 1779 daughter of Abraham and Sarah (Swan) Russell; d. at Portland, ME, 5 Jun 1846; m. 2 Apr 1800, ELIJAH BOND, b. at Watertown, 12 May 1767 son of Jonas and Ruth (Harrington) Bond;[3175] Elijah d. at Portland, 31 Dec 1835.

Elijah was the eighth child in a family of nine children. He was residing in Bethel at the time of his marriage to Sarah. Following their marriage, the couple located in Falmouth (Deering), Maine where they had a farm about one-half mile from Stroudwater Village.[3176]

Sarah and Elijah were parents of seven children, three of whom married.

i   HANNAH BOND, b. 15 Jul 1801; d. at Deering, ME, 31 Dec 1881; m. at Portland, 18 Apr 1824, HENRY CHAPMAN, b. at Parsonsfield, 9 Nov 1794 son of Samuel and Hannah (Quimby) Chapman;[3177] Henry d. at Westbrook, ME, 31 Mar 1873.

ii   SARAH BOND, b. 9 Apr 1803; d. 30 Dec 1881. Sarah did not marry.

iii   JONAS BOND, b. 27 Aug 1805; d. at Portland, 17 Dec 1857. Jonas did not marry. He and his sister Sarah lived in Westbrook.

iv   ELIJAH BOND, b. 10 Sep 1807; d. at Portland, 2 Feb 1851; m. at Westbrook, 12 Mar 1846, ELIZABETH D. ANGEL, b. at South Portland, 15 Jun 1816 daughter of Samuel and Octavia (Dyer) Angel; Elizabeth d. at Portland, 14 Apr 1893.

v   LEONARD BOND, b. at Westbrook, ME, 27 Nov 1809; d. at Boston, 22 Apr 1859, listed as widowed; *perhaps* m. at Boston, 14 Jul 1837, MARY FIFE, b. 1809 and d. at Boston, 25 Aug 1842. Leonard does not seem to have had children.

vi   DENNIS BOND, b. 1812; d. at New Orleans, 26 Oct 1834.[3178]

vii   MARY BOND, b. 1817; d. at Portland, 23 Feb 1884. Mary did not marry.

987)   ABIAH RUSSELL (*Abraham⁴, John³, John², Robert¹*), b. (recorded at Conway, NH), 16 Apr 1781 daughter of Abraham and Sarah (Swan) Russell; d. at Bethel, ME, 14 Jul 1831; m. about 1800, PETER YORK, b. at Standish, ME, 29 Aug 1779 son of John and Abigail (Bean) York; Peter d. at Bethel, 10 Dec 1862.

Abiah and Peter resided in Bethel. Peter was selectman then in 1810, 1811, 1819, and 1822. He held other town offices such as road surveyor in 1815 and constable in 1817. The family resided on the north side of the river. Peter suffered the loss of a leg as result of a falling tree and used a peg leg.[3179]

Peter and Abiah York were parents of eleven children born at Bethel.

i   MARY YORK, b. 28 Apr 1801; d. at Bethel, 6 Apr 1836; m. ASA BARTLETT, b. at Bethel, 4 Dec 1795 son of Reuben and Lydia (Frost) Bartlett; Asa d. at Bethel, 15 Sep 1866. Asa married second Betsey Rowe.

ii   THATCHER YORK, b. 13 Jun 1803; d. at Falmouth, ME, 30 Jan 1873; m. 1ˢᵗ at Bethel, 22 Apr 1824, LARDANA FROST, b. 1802; Lardana d. at Bethel, 12 May 1830. Thatcher m. 2ⁿᵈ LUCY S. POWERS, b. 4 Jul 1809 daughter of Isaac and Mary (Searle) Powers; Lucy d. (burial at Bethel), 5 Dec 1890.

iii   ABRAHAM RUSSELL YORK, b. 20 Jun 1805; d. at Grafton, ME, 6 Feb 1878; m. at Bethel, 27 Feb 1831, APPHIA SMITH, b. about 1807; Apphia d. after 1870 when she was living in Grafton.

iv   AARON MEREON YORK, b. 27 Aug 1807; d. at Santaquin, UT, 13 Nov 1881; m. 1ˢᵗ at Newry, ME, 3 Dec 1830, HANNAH CARTER, b. 28 Jun 1809 daughter of John and Hannah (Libby) Carter; Hannah d. at Provo, 18 Sep 1894. While still married to Hannah, Aaron "married" in 1856, MARY TRUEWORTHY CARTER, b. in Adams County, IA, 23 Sep 1841 daughter of Richard and Hannah (Parker) Carter; Mary d. at Santaquin, UT, 1 Aug 1932. Aaron and his two wives and children were living together in Provo in 1860.

v   DANIEL GROUT YORK, b. 4 Jun 1810; d. at Bethel, 13 Mar 1882; m. about 1835, ELSIE BEAN, b. at Bethel, 9 Sep 1812 daughter of Amos and Huldah (Kimball) Bean; Elsie d. of consumption at Bethel, Jan 1870.

vi   SALLY YORK, b. 25 Aug 1812; d. at Graham County, AZ, 8 Sep 1888; m. 17 Nov 1834, WILLIAM F. CARTER, b. 1 May 1811 son of John and Hannah (Libby) Carter; William d. at Santaquin, UT, 11 Oct 1888. William, who was an elder in the Mormon church, took three other wives during his marriage to Sally.

[3175] Lapham, *History of Bethel*, p 493

[3176] Lapham, *History of Bethel*, p 493

[3177] Chapman, *Edward Chapman of Ipswich, Mass.*, p 55

[3178] Ancestry.com. *U.S., Newspaper Extractions from the Northeast, 1704-1930* [database on-line]

[3179] Lapham, History of Bethel, p 648, p 443, p 170, p 172

vii   MARTHA EAMS YORK, b. 9 Sep 1814; d. at Tioga, IL, 10 Jan 1897; m. at Lowell, MA, 11 Apr 1846, PHILIP LIBBY CARTER, b. 17 Jan 1813 son of John and Hannah (Libby) Carter; Philip d. at Carthage, IL, 27 Jul 1876.

viii   ALBIAN P. YORK, b. 17 Sep 1817; d. 15 Dec 1817.

ix   CHARLOTTE WILLIS YORK, b. 20 Jan 1819; d. at Lowell, MA, 10 Jan 1900; m. NORMAN PEARL, b. at Salem, NY, 10 Dec 1824 son of Elijah Crocker and Polly (Eldredge) Pearl; Norman d. at Plattsburgh, NY, 10 Mar 1896.

x   MELISSA YORK, b. 10 Jun 1821; d. at Tioga, IL, 5 Sep 1881; m. her second cousin once removed, JOSHUA R. RUSSELL (*Chandler⁴, Joseph³, John², Robert¹*), b. at Bethel, 27 Mar 1824 son of Chandler and Betsey (Duston) Russell. No children were identified for Melissa and Joshua.

xi   HESTER ANN YORK, b. 7 Dec 1823; d. at Lowell, MA, 6 May 1920; m. CHARLES AUGUSTUS THISSELL, b. at Dracut, MA, 13 Jan 1825 son of Daniel and Prudence Gale (Varnum) Thissell; Charles d. at Lowell, 23 Apr 1883. Charles was a mechanic and the family lived in Chesapeake, VA for a time.

988)   APPHIA RUSSELL (*Abraham⁴, John³, John², Robert¹*), b. at Bethel, 6 Apr 1787 daughter of Abraham and Sarah (Swan) Russell; d. 24 Apr 1858; m. by 1806, GIDEON POWERS, b. at Bethel, 1790 son of Gideon and Ruth (Packard) Powers; Gideon d. at Bethel, 13 Aug 1879.

     Apphia and Gideon lived in Bethel, Wilton, Carthage, and Augusta, Maine and were last resident in Augusta. Gideon was appointed postmaster of Carthage on 3 February 1834.[3180] Gideon was primarily a farmer but was for a time an agent of the *Maine Farmer* newspaper.[3181]

     Apphia and Gideon were parents of twelve children likely all born at Wilton, Maine.

i   ANNA C. POWERS, b. at Wilton, ME, 25 Nov 1806; d. at Fitchburg, MA, 21 Jun 1885; m. 1st about 1826, JEREMIAH GOULD, *perhaps* b. at Leeds, ME, 4 May 1801 son of Robert and Anna (Parcher) Gould; Jeremiah d. at Carthage, ME, about 1842. Anna m. 2nd about 1843, SAMUEL STONE, b. at Groton, MA, 1 Dec 1798 son of Levi and Lydia (Ward) Stone; Samuel d. at Groton, 16 May 1869. Samuel was first married to Caroline Woods.

ii   SARAH R. POWERS, b. at Wilton, 17 Nov 1808; d. at Paris, ME, 1885; m. 1833, AUSTIN PARTRIDGE, b. 1800 son of Elias and Abigail (Chase) Partridge; Austin d. at Paris, 1889.

iii   ADDISON POWERS, b. at Wilton, 15 Sep 1810; d. at Easton, ME, 18 Sep 1897; m. 1st at Carthage, ME, 30 Oct 1837, HANNAH NEWELL KENNEY, b. at Dixfield, 1816; Hannah d. at Easton, 25 Feb 1867. Addison m. 2nd at Fort Fairfield, ME, 14 Feb 1870, BETSEY BOYNTON (widow of James Madison Curtis), b. 20 May 1819; Betsey d. at Easton, 9 Feb 1886.

iv   RUTH POWERS, b. at Wilton, 14 Mar 1813; d. at Weld, 25 Oct 1832; m. 14 Mar 1831, ISAAC ELLIS, b. 14 Sep 1806 son of Freeman and Lydia (Fuller) Ellis; Isaac d. at Fort Fairfield, 14 Mar 1858. Isaac married second Ruth's sister Susan (see below).

v   APPHIA POWERS, b. at Wilton, 11 Oct 1815; d. at Dixfield, 8 Feb 1905; m. about 1837, AMASA HOLMAN, b. at Dixfield, 16 Apr 1803 son of Jonathan and Polly (Cummings) Holman; Amssa d. at Dixfield, 25 Mar 1892.

vi   SUSAN POWERS, b. 12 Oct 1817; d. at Fort Fairfield, 7 Jun 1877; m. 1st 6 Jan 1834, ISAAC ELLIS who was first married to Susan's sister Ruth (see above). Susan m. 2nd about 1865, EPHRAIM A. ROLLINS, b. 1800 son of James and Sarah (Alley) Rollins;[3182] Ephraim d. at Fort Fairfield, 30 Aug 1889. Ephraim was first married to Lydia Ellis.

vii   RACHEL BUTTERFIELD POWERS, b. at Wilton, 28 May 1820; d. at Fayette, ME, 30 Mar 1855; m. about 1840, DANIEL B. BATCHELDER, b. at Fayette, 3 Nov 1806 son of Nathaniel and Jane L. (Morse) Batchelder; Daniel d. at Chesterville, ME, 15 Jan 1858.

viii   ABRAHAM R. POWERS, b. at Wilton, 1 Apr 1822; d. at Fort Fairfield, 27 Dec 1885; m. about 1845, MARIA DICKEY, b. at Monroe, ME, 18 Feb 1820 daughter of William and Margaret (Curtis) Dickey; Maria d. at Presque Isle, 26 Dec 1903.

ix   LUCY M. POWERS, b. 12 Mar 1824; d. 7 May 1824.

x   HANNAH POWERS, b. 25 Oct 1825; d. 17 May 1852.

[3180] U.S., Appointments of U. S. Postmasters, 1832-1971
[3181] Lapham, *History of Bethel*, p 601
[3182] Rollins, *Records of the Family of the Name of Rawlins*, p 57

xi   LOIS H. POWERS, b. 5 May 1828; d. at Boston, 10 Dec 1847; m. at Boston, 9 May 1847, HENRY BOND, b. at Thetford, VT, 1817 son of Amasa and Harriet (Wood) Bond; Henry d. at Brookline, MA, 17 Oct 1896. Henry married second Mary Ann Cottle on 11 Oct 1849.

xii   ELIZA J. POWERS, b. 29 Mar 1831; d. at Augusta, ME, 29 Nov 1902; m. about 1855, as his second wife, FREDERICK H. TIBBETTS, b. 11 Apr 1819 son of Isaac and Sarah (Hutchins) Tibbetts; Fred d. at Augusta, 22 Feb 1900. Fred was first married to Mary A. White who died in 1854.

989)   ESTHER RUSSELL (*Abraham⁴, John³, John², Robert¹*), b. at Bethel, 18 Sep 1792 daughter of Abraham and Sarah (Swan) Russell; d. at Bethel, 12 Oct 1876; m. 1819, JOHN OLIVER, b. at Bridgton, ME, 8 May 1795 son of William and Hannah (Fowler) Oliver; John d. at St. Charles, IL, 13 Jan 1875. Esther and John divorced at Oxford County, ME, Oct 1848.[3183]
        John Oliver was a hatter and the family was first in Bethel, then Carthage and Portland before returning to Bethel.[3184] John left the family and Esther divorced John in 1848.
        Esther Russell and John Oliver were parents of seven children born at Bethel.

i   JOHN OLIVER, b. 23 Jul 1821; d. 2 Aug 1823.

ii   JOEL FROST OLIVER, b. 6 Apr 1823; d. 12 Aug 1833.

iii   JOHN R. OLIVER, b. 13 Jan 1825; d. at Bethel, 2 Oct 1912; m. at Boston, 12 Feb 1852, ABIGAIL "ABBY" AMES, b. at Charlestown, 16 Apr 1824 daughter of Dean and Nancy (Daniels) Ames;[3185] Abby d. at Somerville, 17 Mar 1890.

iv   MARY OLIVER, b. 30 Nov 1826; d. at Bethel, 2 Nov 1909; m. 1852, HIRAM H. WILSON, b. 12 Jul 1824 son of Evans and Anna (Bray) Wilson;[3186] Hiram d. at Bethel, 2 Feb 1904.

v   ELIZABETH ESTHER OLIVER, b. 16 Feb 1829; m. at Holyoke, MA, 2 Jul 1850, ROBERT HAM, b. in Scotland, about 1829 son of William and Margaret (-) Ham.[3187] There is a record of son Robert born at Holyoke 13 Aug 1852, but further trace of the family was not found.

vi   WILLIAM OLIVER, b. 5 Feb 1832; d. 18 Feb 1848.

vii   AUSTIN PARTRIDGE OLIVER, b. 4 Jun 1834; d. at Saco, ME, 18 Feb 1912; m. 1ˢᵗ about 1858, EMILIE FRANCES ROYAL, b. at Minot, 1834 daughter of Jacob and Rebecca (Campbell) Royal; Emilie d. (burial at Auburn, ME), 24 Sep 1864. Austin m. 2ⁿᵈ JENNIE CONNOR who has not been identified.[3188] Austin and Emilie had a son Oscar who lived with his grandparents Jacob and Rebecca Royal after the death of his mother. He was then with his father in St. Louis and Oscar died there 3 Apr 1877. Austin was an insurance agent who worked primarily in St. Louis.

990)   FLETCHER RUSSELL (*Abraham⁴, John³, John², Robert¹*), b. at Bethel, 2 Jul 1795 son of Abraham and Sarah (Swan) Russell; d. at Canaan, VT, 3 Jun 1853; m. 20 Apr 1823, HANNAH HOWARD, b. at Fryeburg, ME 1796 daughter of William and Lucy (Freeman) Howard;[3189] Hannah d. at Canaan, 20 Jun 1879.
        Fletcher Russell was a blacksmith in Bethel and had his shop on his father's homestead lot.[3190] The family moved to Canaan, Vermont about 1830.
        Fletcher Russell and Hannah Howard were parents of six children.

i   RICHARD H. RUSSELL, b. at Bethel, ME, 17 Dec 1823; d. 14 Aug 1824.

ii   GIDEON POWERS RUSSELL, b. at Bethel, 23 May 1825; d. at Canaan, VT, 3 Dec 1865; m. 1ˢᵗ, about 1848, MARY COOPER, b. in England, about 1830 (per census records); Mary d. at Canaan, about 1860. Gideon married 2ⁿᵈ at Sherbrooke, Québec, 1861, SARAH MALVINA NUTTING,[3191] b. at Danville, Québec, 25 Aug 1837 daughter

[3183] Maine, Divorce Records, 1798-1891

[3184] Lapham, *History of Bethel*, p 596

[3185] The names of Abigail's parents are given as Dean and Nancy Ames on her death record; New England Historic Genealogical Society; Boston, Massachusetts; Massachusetts Vital Records, 1840-1911

[3186] The names of Hiram's parents are given as Evans and Anna Wilson on his death record; Maine State Archives; Cultural Building, 84 State House Station, Augusta, ME 04333-0084; 1892-1907 Vital Records; Roll Number: 61

[3187] Names of parents are as given on his marriage record.

[3188] This second marriage is reported in the History of Bethel but is not yet located in records.

[3189] Father's name is given as William and mother's name as Lucy Freeman on Hannah's death record.

[3190] Lapham, *History of Bethel*, p 610

[3191] *Quebec, Canada, Vital and Church Records (Drouin Collection), 1621-1968*, Institut Généalogique Drouin

of Harry and Abigail (Olney) Nutting; Sarah d. at Canaan, 6 Jun 1907. Sarah Malvina married second, Gideon's brother Horace (see below).

iii   WILLIAM HOWARD RUSSELL, b. at Bethel, 28 Aug 1828; d. at Canaan, VT, 18 Oct 1877; m. about 1860, EMILY THOMPSON, b. about 1834 daughter of William and Almira (Osborne) Thompson;[3192] Emily d. at Canaan, 2 Aug 1904. Emily married second at Lemington, VT, Robert Campbell on 16 Oct 1878.

iv   HORACE FLETCHER RUSSELL, b. 17 Mar 1830; d. at Stewartstown, NH, 15 Feb 1927; m. about 1868, SARAH MALVINA NUTTING who was first married to Horace's brother Gideon (see above).

v   ALONZO BAILEY RUSSELL, b. at Canaan, VT, 31 Aug 1835; killed in action at Savage's Station, VA, 29 Jun 1862;[3193] m. at Clarksville, NH, 21 Mar 1861, MARY A. CORBETT, b. at Stewartstown, 1831 daughter of Jesse and Hannah (Small) Corbett; Mary d. at Colebrook, NH, 6 Dec 1916. Mary married second Hiram Munn on 25 Mar 1863.

vi   SUSAN HILLARD RUSSELL, b. at Canaan, 31 Aug 1835; d. at Wakefield, MA, 11 Feb 1922; m. about 1873, SAMUEL R. ROMNEY of Utica, NY, b. about 1835; Samuel d. 1878. There is one child known for Susan and Samuel, Parepa R. Romney born at Eastport, ME, Dec 1874.

991)   DORCAS RUSSELL (*Abraham⁴, John³, John², Robert¹*), b. at Bethel, 10 Mar 1800 daughter of Abraham and Sarah (Swan) Russell; d. at Portland, ME, 8 Jul 1860; m. about 1818, HIRAM ALLEN, b. at Berwick, 12 Sep 1795; Hiram d. at Portland, 12 Mar 1873.
      Hiram Allen was a carpenter by trade. Hiram and Dorcas had their home in Bethel on the east side of what is now Church Street. The house was later moved to Main Street and became the Methodist parsonage. Hiram sold much of his property in Bethel in 1836 and 1839.[3194] Hiram and Dorcas were living in Portland by 1850 where they both died.[3195]
      Dorcas Russell and Hiram Allen were parents of eight children.

i   LAWSON CARTER ALLEN, b. at Bethel, 12 Jan 1819; d. at sea, Apr 1865.

ii   JUSTUS ALLEN, b. at Bethel, 22 Jan 1821; d. at Portland, ME, 15 Mar 1842.

iii   SAMUEL ABBOT ALLEN, b. at Bethel, 21 Nov 1823; d. at Andover, ME, 2 Feb 1857; m. 14 oct 1854, MARTHA SWAN MERRILL, b. at Andover, ME, 1829 daughter of Ezekiel and Phebe V. (Farrington) Merrill; Martha d. at Andover, 9 Sep 1905. Martha married second Nathan Dresser son of Stephen and Abigail (Kilgore) Dresser. Samuel was a physician in Andover. He did not have children.

iv   JAMES NEAL ALLEN, b. at Bethel, 18 Mar 1829; d. at Portland, 15 Mar 1842.

v   ABIGAIL LEARNED ALLEN, b. at Bethel, 25 Jul 1832; d. at Unity, ME, 27 Nov 1904; m. 1st at Portland, 27 Oct 1851, CHARLES DANFORTH BRIDGES, b. about 1831; Danforth d. about 1865. Abigail m. 2nd at Portland, 10 Oct 1867, ANDREW J. HURD, b. at Unity, ME, 29 Jan 1815 son of Hiram and Parthenia (Pattee) Hurd; Hiram d. at Unity, 10 May 1891. Andrew was first married to Abigail Tripp in 1842.

vi   HORACE WARD ALLEN, b. at Bethel, 28 Nov 1835; d. at Boston, 21 Jan 1882; m. at Boston, 18 Sep 1872, ABBY SARAH MOORE, b. at Whitefield, ME, 1844 daughter of Stetson and Margery (Dunton) Moore.[3196] Abby was first married to Frank Carlton.

vii   ELIZABETH WALKER ALLEN, b. at Portland, 2 Feb 1839; b. at Portland, 21 Oct 1923; m. at Portland, 16 Dec 1866, as his second wife, CHARLES HENRI STARBIRD, b. at Portland, 24 oct 1821 son of George B. and Eliza (Beckett) Starbird; Charles d. at Portland, 20 Jun 1882. Charles was first married to Ellen S. Chase.

viii   SARAH FRANCES ALLEN, b. at Portland, 6 Jun 1841; d. at Portland, 6 Jul 1919; m. at Portland, 10 Dec 1865, EDWARD WARREN PORTER, b. at Lancaster, NH, 20 Mar 1827 son of Warren and Selenda (Cram) Porter; Edward d. at Portland, 23 Jul 1904.

992)   ABIGAIL RUSSELL (*Jacob⁴, John³, John², Robert¹*), b. perhaps at Andover, 1786 daughter of Jacob and Dorothy (Shattuck) Russell; d. at Potter, NY, Jan 1859; m. at Bethel, 21 Nov 1822, as his second wife, ELI TWITCHELL, b. at Dublin,

---

[3192] Emily's death record lists her parents as William Thompson and Mary Osborne, but the record for her second marriage gives parents as William Thompson and Almira Osborne.
[3193] U.S., Registers of Deaths of Volunteers, 1861-1865, Vermont, p 153
[3194] Lapham, *History of Bethel*, p 460
[3195] Year: 1850; Census Place: Portland Ward 7, Cumberland, Maine; Roll: 252; Page: 223a
[3196] The name of Abby's father is given as Stetson Moore on her marriage record.

NH, 26 Jul 1786 son of Ezra and Susanna (Rice) Twitchell; Eli d. at Potter, NY, 1869 (probate 11 Oct 1869). Eli was first married to Betsy Gould 20 Jan 1807 and third married to Betsey's sister Clarissa Gould about 1862.

     Eli was a landlord and trader. The family live in Bethel until 1836 when they relocated to Rushville, New York.[3197]

     In his will dated 5 June 1856 (proved 11 October 1869), Eli Twitchell of Potter, Yates County, New York, age seventy years, bequeaths his personal estate, to be equally divided, to sons William L. Twitchell and George W. Twitchell, and daughter Martha Twitchell. There is nothing else in the will, and although it is signed, it seems incomplete. Nevertheless, the court proved the will although noting that it consisted of just a half sheet of paper.[3198]

     Eli Twitchell and Abigail Russell were parents of five children born at Bethel.[3199] Eli had nine children with his first wife Betsy Gould.

i   PHILOMELA TWITCHELL, b. 15 Oct 1823; d. 26 Aug 1837.

ii   WILLIAM L. TWITCHELL, b. 17 Feb 1825; d. at Alameda, CA, 5 Dec 1886; m. 26 Aug 1853, his first cousin, LYDIA P. RUSSELL (*Jacob⁵, Jacob⁴, John³, John², Robert¹*), b. Aug 1833 daughter of Jacob and Phebe (Stark) Russell; Lydia d. at Alameda, 12 Jan 1921. William attended Bowdoin College and was a physician in Alameda.

iii   BETSEY TWITCHELL, b. 15 Mar 1826; d. 4 Aug 1826.

iv   GEORGE WASHINGTON TWITCHELL, b. 14 Jun 1828; d. at Boxford, MA, 9 May 1909; m. 1st 30 Apr 1851, CAROLINE E. TWITCHELL, b. at Rushville, NY, 21 Aug 1831 daughter of Renfrew and Susanna (French) Twitchell;[3200] Caroline d. at Gorham, NY, 28 Nov 1862. George m. 2nd at Boxford, MA, 21 Jun 1864, his first cousin once removed, ANNIE F. GOULD (*Lydia A. Russell Gould⁶, James⁵, Uriah⁴, Thomas³, James², Robert¹*), b. at Baltimore, MD, 29 Jan 1838 daughter of Moses and Lydia Abbot (Russell) Gould;[3201] Annie d. at Boxford, 1920.

v   MARTHA TWITCHELL, b. 1830; d. at Gorham, NY, 18 Sep 1893; m. about 1861, as his second (or perhaps third) wife, GEORGE W. STEARNS, b. at Bethel, ME, 24 May 1818 son of Theodore and Mary (Besse) Stearns; George d. at Gorham, 22 Apr 1878. George was first married to Nancy Steele and may have had a second marriage to Miranda.

993)   JACOB RUSSELL (*Jacob⁴, John³, John², Robert¹*), b. likely at Bethel, about 1788 son of Jacob and Dorothy (Shattuck) Russell; d. at Richland, NY, 20 May 1873 (probate 15 Oct 1873); m. 1st, by 1828, SOPHIA STARK, b. 27 Dec 1794 daughter of Abel and Lydia (Fletcher) Stark;[3202] Sophia d. at Richland, 11 Nov 1847. Jacob m. 2nd, about 1848, SUSAN who has not been identified; Susan d. at Richland, 20 Feb 1871.

     Jacob resided in Richland where he was a farmer. In his will written 4 May 1868 (probate 15 Oct 1873), Jacob bequeathed to son Charles F. Russell one-fourth of all the real estate. Son William H. Russell receives the remainder of the real estate and is to pay his sister Lydia P. Twitchell, now of California, the sum of four hundred dollars. In exchange for this bequest, William is to care for Jacob and his wife, providing food, clothing, and lodging, for the remainder of their natural lives. Charles F. Russell of Richland was named executor.[3203]

     Jacob and Sophia Russell were parents of three known children.

i   WILLIAM HENRY RUSSELL, b. 3 Feb 1829; d. at Pulaski, NY, 20 Dec 1891; m. about 1864, EMILY ELVIRA SLATER, b. 8 Feb 1839 daughter of Brayton and Philena, (Wescott) Slater; Emily d. at Pulaski, 1897.

ii   CHARLES F. RUSSELL, b. Jul 1830; d. at Richland, NY, 16 Jan 1906; m. Feb 1868, as her second husband, ABIGAIL ANN DWIGHT (widow of Daniel Norton), b. at Oswego, 5 Aug 1841 daughter of Orrin E. and Anne (Wellman) Dwight;[3204] Abigail d. at Richland, 7 Jan 1926.

iii   LYDIA P. RUSSELL, b. Aug 1833; d. at Alameda, CA, 12 Jan 1921; m. about 1855, her first cousin, WILLIAM L. TWITCHELL (*Abigail Russell Twitchell⁵, Jacob⁴, John³, John², Robert¹*), b. at Bethel, ME, 17 Feb 1825 son of Eli and Abigail (Russell) Twitchell; William d. at Alameda, 5 Dec 1886 (probate 31 Jan 1887). William attended Bowdoin College and was a physician in Alameda.

[3197] Twitchell, *Genealogy of the Twitchell Family*, p 122

[3198] *New York. Surrogate's Court (Yates County), Wills, Vol H-I, 1866-1873, Wills, Vol H-I, 1866-1873*, pp 374-375

[3199] The Twitchell genealogy suggests daughter Almira is also a child with Abigail, but Abigail's birth is recorded in 1811, a child from Eli's first marriage to Betsey Gould.

[3200] Twitchell, *Twitchell Genealogy*

[3201] Gould, *The Family of Zaccheus Gould*, p 111

[3202] Walworth, *Hyde Genealogy*, p 517

[3203] Ancestry.com. *New York, Wills and Probate Records, 1659-1999* [database on-line]. Oswego, *Record of Wills, Vol L-M, 1872-1877, Vol L*, pp 484-485

[3204] Wellman, *Descendants of Thomas Wellman*, p 231

994) HARMON HOLT (*Lydia Russell Holt⁴, Joseph³, John², Robert¹*), b. at Bethel, 12 Nov 1789 son of John and Lydia (Russell) Holt; d. at Medford, ME, May 1861; m. 10 Nov 1810, SALLY DUSTIN, b. about 1790; Sally d. after 1860 (living at 1860 census).

In his will 7 May 1860, Harmon Holt of Medford, Maine bequeathed his entire estate to his son William C. Holt of Bangor. At the time of his death, real estate was valued at $5 and personal estate at $213.10.[3205]

Harmon Holt and Sally Dustin were parents of six children born at Bethel.

i   JOHN HOLT, b. Jul 1812 (based on age 51 years, 6 months, 29 days at death); d. at Waterford, ME, 24 Feb 1864; m. 15 Sep 1834, MERCY MUNROE, b. 1816 daughter of William and Achsah (Sawyer) Munroe;[3206] Mercy d. at Waterford, 26 Sep 1895.

ii   SARAH HOLT, b. at Bethel, 5 Sep 1814

iii   MOSES EMERY HOLT, b. 1816; m. by 1845, MARY DUPREE, b. in Maine, about 1813. Moses, Mary and their three children were living in Lowell, Maine in 1860.Two of the children were later in Pennsylvania. Moses disappears from census records after 1860.

iv   SYLVANUS WASHBURN HOLT, b. at Bethel, 15 Dec 1820; d. after 1888 when he was living in San Francisco; m. at Boston, 23 Jan 1858, ANNE E. HUNT, b. at Bangor, about 1823 daughter of Jonathan and Hannah (·) Hunt. Sylvanus and Anne did not stay together long. In 1860, Anne was living in Bangor with other relatives, and by 1866, Sylvanus was in San Francisco. In the 1880 census, his marital status is listed as divorced. Sylvanus was a carpenter.

v   JUSTUS W. HOLT, b. 1825; d. at Medford, ME, 1863;[3207] m. HANNAH E. CAMPBELL, b. in ME, 1828; Hannah d. at Medford, 1868. In 1860, Justus, Hannah, and their four children were living in Medford next to Justus's parents Harmon and Sally. Justus is described as Rev. Justus Holt in census records and his cemetery record.

vi   WILLIAM C. HOLT, b. 13 May 1828; d. at Bangor, 27 Oct 1888; m. by 1855, HARRIET EMMA PERKINS, b. 22 Sep 1830 daughter of John and Harriet (Dorr) Perkins; Harriet Emma d. at Foxborough, MA (buried at Bangor), 31 Jul 1922.

995) WILLIAM HOLT (*Lydia Russell Holt⁴, Joseph³, John², Robert¹*), b. at Bethel, 4 Feb 1792 son of John and Lydia (Russell) Holt; d. at Bethel, 6 Dec 1868; m. 4 May 1814, MARY STEARNS, b. at Bethel, 18 Apr 1795 daughter of Thomas and Lois (Colby) Stearns; Mary d. at Bethel, 5 Jan 1875.

William Holt was a farmer in Bethel. He and Mary Stearns were parents of seven children born at Bethel, Maine.[3208]

i   MARY ANN HOLT, b. 16 Apr 1815; d. at Bethel, 10 Mar 1889; m. at Bethel, 22 Sep 1841, OREN BROWN SWAN, b. at Bethel, 12 Apr 1817 son of Alpheus and Nancy (Brown) Swan; Oren d. at Bethel, 9 Oct 1873.[3209]

ii   HIRAM H. HOLT, b. at Bethel, 27 May 1818; d. at Bethel, 14 May 1895; m. 14 Aug 1846, SARAH WEBBER KIMBALL, b. 22 May 1824 daughter of Israel and Sarah (Webber) Kimball; Sarah d. at Bethel, 7 Feb 1894

iii   GALEN C. HOLT, b. at Bethel, 22 Feb 1821; d. at Bethel, 30 Apr 1876; m. 10 Jun 1848, SYLVIA T. FOSTER, b. 1821; Sylvia d. at Bethel, 5 Jan 1861.

iv   NATHAN WARD HOLT, b. 25 Apr 1827; d. at Boston, 2 Dec 1891; m. at Dorchester, MA, 10 Mar 1855, FLORA C. BROWN, b. at North Turner, ME, Feb 1824 daughter of Aaron and Lydia (Sawtelle) Brown; Flora d. at Boston, 15 Oct 1909.

v   WILLIAM ORMANDO HOLT, b. 1830; d. at Bethel, 1 May 1893; m. 3 Jul 1855, DEBORAH B. YOUNG, b. at Bethel, 13 Jul 1832 daughter of Oliver and Deborah (Haskell) Young; Deborah d. at Bethel, 24 Jul 1917.

vi   MARCIA C. HOLT, b. at Bethel, 25 Sep 1833; d. at Minot, ME, 5 Oct 1869; m. 25 Mar 1858, BENJAMIN FRANKLIN DAVIS, b. at Poland, ME, 21 Apr 1831 son of Benjamin and Sarah (Chandler) Davis; Benjamin d. at Minot, 26 Jul 1900. Benjamin was second married to Alice Elizabeth Thurlow.

[3205] *Maine, Wills and Probate Records, 1584-1999* [database on-line]. *Piscataquis, Maine, Estate Files, Docket No O-384 to O-688, 1857-1862, Estate of Harmon Holt, number 424*

[3206] Names of Mercy's parents are given as William Monroe and Achsah Sawyer on her death record.

[3207] Maine, Nathan Hale Cemetery Collection, 1780-1980

[3208] Durrie, Holt Genealogy, p 146; Bethel, Maine vital records 1801-1923, accessed through familyseaerch.org

[3209] Maine, Faylene Hutton Cemetery Collection, 1780-1990

vii   HUMPHREY B. HOLT, b. at Bethel, 1835; d. at Bethel, 23 Jun 1898; m. CATHERINE MARIA BEAN,[3210] b. 1844 daughter of Zachariah and Emeline B. (Farnum) Bean; Katharine d. at Bethel, 21 Jun 1907.

996)   JOSEPH R. HOLT (*Lydia Russell Holt⁴, Joseph³, John², Robert¹*), b. at Bethel, 28 Feb 1795 son of John and Lydia (Russell) Holt; d. at Bethel, 22 Sep 1878; m. 4 Dec 1817, SUSAN STEARNS, b. at Bethel, 30 Dec 1797 daughter of Thomas and Lois (Colby) Stearns; Susan d. at Bethel, 28 Feb 1873.

Joseph and Susan resided in Bethel where they had a farm and Joseph served as deacon.

In his will written 5 June 1869 (probate 15 November 1878), Joseph Holt of Bethel bequeathed to beloved wife Susan, for her natural life, the homestead in Bethel consisting of about 150 acres, and this is in lieu of her dower. After her decease, son Joseph Holt, Jr. will receive the real estate as described. Daughter Lydia M. Forbes of Hillsborough receives one dollar as she has received her share of the estate. Daughter Sarah M. Estes of Lisbon, Maine also receives one dollar having received her share. Enoch Foster, Jr. was named sole executor. The homestead farm was valued at $1000.[3211]

Joseph R. Holt and Susan Stearns were parents of four children born at Bethel.

i   LYDIA MARIA HOLT, b. 20 Nov 1818; d. at Falls Church, VA, 30 Oct 1906; m. 18 Feb 1845, WELLS FORBES, b. at Hill, NH, 1812 son of Sethus and Ruth (Wells) Forbes; Wells d. at Falls Church, 5 Aug 1880.

ii   JOSEPH HOLT, b. 10 Sep 1823; d. at Fryeburg (buried at Bethel), 12 Jan 1910; m. 1865, FRANCES A. BIRD, b. 28 Sep 1846 daughter of Lyman and Eliza (Young) Bird; Frances d. at Bethel, 9 Jun 1915.

iii   SARAH M. HOLT, b. 30 Oct 1825; m. 28 Jul 1852, SUMNER ESTES, b. at Bethel, 11 Jun 1827 son of Eli and Clarissa (Kimball) Estes; Sumner d. at Sanford, ME, 9 Mar 1903. Rev. Sumner Estes attended Waterville College[3212] and was a Baptist minister. Sarah's death record was not found, but she was living in Sanford in 1880.

iv   Infant, b. and d. 25 Jan 1839

997)   HIRAM HOLT (*Lydia Russell Holt⁴, Joseph³, John², Robert¹*), b. at Bethel, 21 Jul 1803 son of John and Lydia (Russell) Holt; d. likely at Bethel, after 1870; m. 9 Jun 1826, ELOHE VARRIL, b. 6 Nov 1801 daughter of Samuel and Sarah (Prince) Varril; Elohe was living in 1870.

Hiram Holt was the postmaster at East Bethel, Maine appointed 2 April 1845 and held that position until 1849.[3213] Death records were not located for Hiram and Elohe, but they were living in Bethel in 1870.

Hiram and Elohe were parents of two children.

i   LUTHER PRESCOTT HOLT, b. at Bethel, 28 May 1827; d. at Bethel, 29 May 1892; m. 1st CLARISSA ANN DAVIS, b. about 1833 daughter of Benjamin and Sarah (Chandler) Davis; Clarissa d. at Bethel, 20 Mar 1869. Luther m. 2nd DELLA A. KING, b. at Grafton, ME, 17 Apr 1845 daughter of Isaac and Mary (Emery) King; Della d. at Boston, 14 Jan 1901. After Luther's death, Della married John F. Cooledge on 1 Jan 1895.

ii   ARTHUR DRINKWATER HOLT, b. at Bethel, 2 Feb 1830; d. at Hanover, ME, 23 Aug 1893; m. 1st at Hanover, ME, 23 Oct 1859, his second cousin, HELEN ELIZABETH RUSSELL (*Ezekiel D.⁵, Chandler⁴, Joseph³, John², Robert¹*), b. at Bethel, 17 Oct 1842 daughter of Ezekiel Dustin and Hannah Elizabeth (Verder) Russell; Helen d. at Bethel, 12 Nov 1861. Arthur m. 2nd at Hanover, ME, 27 Sep 1862, ROENA BIRD, b. 1843 daughter of Lyman and Eliza (Young) Bird; Roena d. at Waterford, ME, 17 Aug 1912. After Arthur's death, Roena married Henry Sawin on 22 Sep 1895.

998)   LYDIA HOLT (*Lydia Russell Holt⁴, Joseph³, John², Robert¹*), b. at Bethel, 17 Nov 1805 daughter of John and Lydia (Russell) Holt; d. at Bethel, 1891; m. 9 Jun 1832, HUMPHREY BEAN, b. at Bethel, 22 Jan 1802 son of Amos and Huldah (Kimball) Bean; Humphrey d. at Bethel, 1884.

Lydia and Humphrey lived in Bethel at resided on part of the homestead of Humphrey's father.[3214] Lydia Holt and Humphrey Bean were parents of six children born at Bethel.

[3210] Her name is spelled as both Katharine and Catherine in different records but is Catherine on her gravestone.

[3211] *Maine. Probate Court (Oxford County);* Probate Place: *Oxford, Maine, Estate Files, Drawer H58, Heywood, Calvin M-Hutchinson, Lyman, 1873-1879, Estate of Joseph Holt*

[3212] U.S., School Catalogs, 1765-1935, Waterville College, 1854

[3213] U.S., Appointments of U. S. Postmasters, 1832-1971

[3214] Lapham, *History of Bethel*, p 483

i   CHRISTOPHER COLUMBUS BEAN, b. 1 Jan 1833; d. at Bethel, 15 Sep 1900; m. at Lawrence, MA, 7 May 1865, MELINDA L. NEEDHAM, b. at Norway, ME, 17 Jul 1839 daughter of Evi and Maria (Latham) Needham; Melinda d. at Bethel, 6 Dec 1917.

ii   ELOHE VARRILL BEAN, b. 23 May 1835; d. at Errol, NH, 18 Jan 1918; m. 27 Aug 1855, as his second wife, JOTHAM SEWELL LANE, b. at Dexter, ME, 24 May 1831 son of Sylvanus and Submit (Foster) Lane; Jotham d. at Upton, ME, 25 Dec 1903. Jotham was first married to Alvira Carson on 1 Jun 1851.

iii HIRAM HOLT BEAN, b. 27 Feb 1838; d. at Bethel, 1 Oct 1921; m. 1st by 1868, ELLEN M. DAVIS, b. 1841 daughter of Benjamin and Sarah (Chandler) Davis; Ellen d. at Bethel, 1873. Hiram m. 2nd at Portland, ME, 3 Feb 1880, ROSILLA H. HOWE, b. at Rumford, ME, 30 Jun 1849 daughter of Calvin and Thirza (Kimball) Howe; Rosilla d. at Bethel, 21 Apr 1925.

iv   FARMAN L. BEAN, b. 30 Nov 1844; d. 20 Dec 1862.

v   ADESTA FRANCES BEAN, b. 27 May 1848; d. at Hanover, ME, 1928; m. 11 Oct 1876, her second cousin, FRANK JOSHUA RUSSELL (*Ezekiel D.⁵, Chandler⁴, Joseph³, John², Robert¹*), b. 9 May 1847 son of Ezekiel Dustin and Hannah Elizabeth (Verder) Russell; Frank d. at Hanover, 1939.

vi   ALFONSO WELLS BEAN, b. 21 Jan 1852; d. at Bethel, 19 Apr 1934; m. 1878, his first cousin once removed, CLARA FRANCES HOLT (*Justus Holt⁶, Harmon Holt⁵, Lydia Russell Holt⁴, Joseph³, John², Robert¹*) b. at Bethel, 4 Dec 1851 daughter of Justus W. and Hannah E. (Campbell) Holt; Clara d. at Bethel, 28 Jan 1918.

999)   ELIJAH RUSSELL (*Chandler⁴, Joseph³, John², Robert¹*), b. at Bethel, 17 Jun 1804 son of Chandler and Betsey (Duston) Russell; d. at Hanover, ME, 8 Apr 1888; m. about 1828, ALMIRA BEAN, b. at Bethel, 27 Oct 1802 daughter of John and Hannah (McGill) Bean; Almira d. at Hanover, 22 Sep 1880.
    Elijah Russell and Almira Bean were parents of seven children born at Hanover, Maine.

i   JESSE D. RUSSELL, b. 19 Jul 1829; d. at Hanover, 2 Dec 1902; m. 1st at Hanover, 4 Sep 1869, ELSIE JORDAN, b. 1848 daughter of Charles and Alice (Bean) Jordan; Elsie d. at Hanover, 20 Jul 1871. Jesse m. 2nd at Hanover, 25 Jun 1875, BETSEY WHEELER, b. at Hanover, 6 Sep 1841 daughter of Samuel and Elizabeth (Burbank) Wheeler; Betsey d. at Hanover, 22 Oct 1900.

ii   EMILY W. RUSSELL, b. 23 Nov 1830; d. at Hanover, 25 Jun 1851.

iii JOSEPH E. RUSSELL, b. 22 Jan 1832; d. at Hanover, 20 Aug 1906; m. at Lexington, MA, 24 Jan 1868, SARAH M. GOSSOM, b. at Lexington, 14 Dec 1839 daughter of Elijah and Eliza (Harrington) Gossom; Sarah d. at Hanover, 14 May 1906.

iv   FRANCIS M. RUSSELL, b. 28 Jan 1836; d. at Hanover, 15 Sep 1863.

v   WILLIAM B. RUSSELL, b. 27 Oct 1838; d. at Hanover, 8 Dec 1904; m. at Hanover, 29 Oct 1868, VIOLA J. TWITCHELL, b. at Milan, NH, 20 Dec 1851 daughter of Gilman and Lucy (Harris) Twitchell; Viola d. at Gorham, NH, 22 Apr 1939. Viola married second J. Gardner Roberts on 23 Nov 1909.

vi   LYMAN R. RUSSELL, b. 15 May 1842; d. at Hanover, 1 Feb 1864.

vii MARIA E. RUSSELL, b. 24 Oct 1844; d. at Hanover, 8 Feb 1864.

1000)   MARIA H. RUSSELL (*Chandler⁴, Joseph³, John², Robert¹*), b. at Bethel, 22 Oct 1809 daughter of Chandler and Betsey (Duston) Russell; d. at Bethel, about 1855; m. KIMBALL BEAN, b. 26 Apr 1796 son of Timothy and Hannah (Kimball) Bean; Kimball d. at Bethel 5 Apr 1864. Kimball was first married to Lovina Powers and third married to Dolly whom he married in 1856.
    Maria Russell and Kimball Bean were parents of two children. Kimball also had seven children with his first wife Lovina Powers.

i   ELIZA PERRY BEAN, b. at Bethel, 17 Oct 1837; d. at Portland, 26 Ap3 1903; m. 1856, NATHANIEL FIFIELD SWAN, b. 19 Jul 1834 son of John S. and Lydia F. (Holt) Swan; Nathaniel d. at Bethel, 18 Oct 1913.

ii   JOHN DUSTIN BEAN, b. at Bethel, 17 Feb 1839; d. at Bethel, 24 Jul 1918; m. at Charlestown, MA, 31 Oct 1866, LOUISA MCKENZIE, b. at Bar Harbor, ME, about 1837 daughter of William F. and Delia (Moore) McKenzie;[3215] Louisa d. at Somerville, MA, 18 Mar 1900.

1001)   EZEKIEL DUSTIN RUSSELL (*Chandler⁴, Joseph³, John², Robert¹*), b. at Bethel, 19 Apr 1811 son of Chandler and Betsey (Duston) Russell; d. at Bethel, 8 Aug 1883; m. at Townsend, MA, 19 Apr 1835, HANNAH ELIZABETH VERDER, b. at Townsend, 14 Sep 1810 daughter of George and Nancy (Tarbox) Verder; Hannah d. at Bethel, 12 Mar 1889.
          Ezekiel was born in Bethel, perhaps was in Ipswich, New Hampshire for a time, but was then in Bethel where he and his wife both died.[3216] Ezekiel was a carpenter/joiner by trade. In the 1870 census, his real estate value was listed as $800 and personal estate at $382.[3217]
          Ezekiel and Hannah were parents of six children.

i   LORENZO DOW RUSSELL, b. 7 May 1837; d. at Butte, MT, 13 Dec 1901; m. at Hanover, ME, 14 Jan 1868, LETITIA COBURN, b. at Newry, ME, 26 Jan 1843 daughter of Moses and Hannah (Barker) Coburn;[3218] Letitia d. at Butte, 22 Jan 1913.

ii   ORLANDO PERRY RUSSELL, b. 18 Jan 1840; d. at Hanover, ME, 19 Nov 1906; m. at Andover, ME, 11 Jan 1880, ANNIE M. ABBOTT, b. at Cambridge, MA, 7 Oct 1857 daughter of Thomas Parker and Maria (Newton) Abbott; Annie d. at Hanover, 19 Aug 1917.

iii   HELEN ELIZABETH RUSSELL, b. 17 Oct 1842; d. at Bethel, 12 Nov 1861; m. at Hanover, 23 Oct 1859, ARTHUR DRINKWATER HOLT, b. at Bethel, 2 Feb 1830 son of Hiram and Elohe (Varril) Holt; Arthur d. at Hanover, 23 Aug 1893.

iv   FRANK JOSHUA RUSSELL (twin), b. 9 May 1847; d. at Hanover, 1939; m. 11 Oct 1876, ADESTA FRANCES BEAN, b. 27 May 1848 daughter of Humphrey and Lydia (Holt) Bean; Adesta d. at Hanover, 1928.

v   ROSCOE FARNUM RUSSELL (twin), b. 9 May 1847; d. 1 Jun 1849.

vi   OLIVE MAY RUSSELL, b. 30 Apr 1849; d. at Hanover, ME, 28 Dec 1883. Olive May did not marry. She was a dressmaker in Hanover.

1002)   LOVINA D. RUSSELL (*Chandler⁴, Joseph³, John², Robert¹*), b. at Bethel, 17 Sep 1816 daughter of Chandler and Betsey (Duston) Russell; d. at Bethel, 1 Sep 1844; m. by 1839, TIMOTHY BEAN, b. at Bethel, 6 Apr 1813 son of Timothy and Hannah (Kimball) Bean; Timothy d. at Pendleton, OR, 7 Apr 1899. Timothy married second Elizabeth E. Swift.
          Lovina and Timothy were parents of two children born at Bethel. Timothy stayed in Bethel with his second wife, with whom he had at least two children, until 1860, but in 1870 was in Oregon having left his family behind in Maine. He was living alone in Weston, Oregon in 1870 with his occupation listed as shepherd.[3219]

i   TIMOTHY M. BEAN, b. 10 Aug 1839; d. at Greenwood, ME, 7 Apr 1915; m. LYDIA E. POLLARD, b. about 1850 daughter of Kendall and Betsey (Jackson) Pollard; Lydia d. at Greenwood, 27 Dec 1895.

ii   JOHN ELMON BEAN, b. 2 Feb 1843; d. at Pendleton, OR, 13 Jan 1927; m. at Umatilla County, OR, 1871, SOPHIA BISHOP, b. in Washington Territory, 18 Aug 1853 daughter of Bolivar and Luna (Palmer) Bishop;[3220] Sophia d. at Pendleton, OR, 20 Sep 1908.

1003)   JEDEDIAH RUSSELL (*Jedediah⁴, Robert³, John², Robert¹*), b. at Reading, 29 Aug 1780 son of Jedediah and Rhoda (Pratt) Russell; d. at Mayfield, OH, 15 Sep 1863; m. at Amherst, NH, 23 Oct 1803,[3221] ABIGAIL WHITING, b. at Amherst, 6 Nov 1780 daughter of John and Elizabeth (-) Whiting; Abigail d. at Mayfield, 1832.

[3215] The names of Louisa's parents are given as William and Delia on her marriage record and as William McKenzie and Delia Moore on her death record.
[3216] Lapham, *History of Bethel.*, p 657
[3217] Year: 1870; Census Place: Bethel, Oxford, Maine; Roll: M593_550; Page: 29A; Family History Library Film: 552049
[3218] Letitia was a DAR member and provider information on her birth and parents in her application; DAR Lineage Book, volume 098, 1913, p 258
[3219] Year: 1870; Census Place: Weston, Umatilla, Oregon; Roll: M593_1288; Page: 364A; Family History Library Film: 552787
[3220] Year: 1860; Census Place: Tiah, Wasco, Oregon; Page: 610; Family History Library Film: 805056; Sophia living with parents B.B. Bishop and Luna.
[3221] The marriage transcription gives a year of 1813, but this seems an error given that children were born to this couple by 1806.

Jedediah and Abigail started their family in New Hampshire, were for a time in Phelps, New York, and arrived in Mayfield, Ohio about 1830. Abigail died soon after arrival in Ohio. They were parents of four children. In his older years, Jedediah lives with his son William and his family.[3222]

i   CALEB B. RUSSELL, b. in NH, 1807; d. at Saybrook, OH, 22 Dec 1886 (probate 29 Dec 1886); m. 1st about 1830, CAROLINE SANFORD, b. in NY, 1811; Caroline d. at Willoughby Hills, OH, 12 May 1870. Caleb m. 2nd at Lake County, OH, 19 Oct 1870, FLAVIA DOWD (widow of Ira M. Jewell), b. 1814; Flavia d. at Saybrook, 22 Dec 1886. Caleb, Flavia, and Caleb's son John W. Russell died in a house fire.[3223]

ii   CHLOE RUSSELL, b. in NH, 1810; d. at Ann Arbor, MI, 29 Apr 1900; m. by 1830, ELI HART, b. in NY, about 1807 son of Ichabod and Lydia (Delano) Hart;[3224] Eli d. at Plainwell, MI, 21 Apr 1891.

iii   JEDEDIAH RUSSELL, b. in NH, 1812; d. at Penn, IN, 3 Jun 1888; m. 1st an unknown woman who was mother of daughter Olive born in 1837. Jedediah m. 2nd about 1848, BETSEY HARRIS, b. in NY, 27 Aug 1825 daughter of Stephen A. and Susann (-) Harris; Betsey d. at Penn, 4 Feb 1873. Jedediah m. 3rd at South Bend, IN, 8 Aug 1873, Betsey's sister, PHEBE J. HARRIS (widow of Lafayette Osgood), b. 1827; Phebe d. (burial at Indianapolis), 1877.

iv   WILLIAM RUSSELL, b. in NY, 1815; d. at Wakeshma, MI, 24 Sep 1887; m. at Cuyahoga County, OH, 10 Apr 1839, MARY ANN SKIDMORE, b. in VT, 23 Feb 1823 daughter of Sherman and Fanny (Billings) Skidmore; Mary Ann d. at Wakeshma, 23 Apr 1903.

1004)   RHODA RUSSELL (*Jedediah⁴, Robert³, John², Robert¹*), b. (recorded) at Lyndeborough, 9 Feb 1782 daughter of Jedediah and Rhoda (Pratt) Russell; d. at Sullivan, NH, 28 Jun 1867; m. at Temple, NH, 1801, EPHRAIM ADAMS HOLT, b. at Temple, 14 Aug 1778 son of Samuel and Lydia (Adams) Holt; Ephraim d. at Sullivan, 31 Jul 1857.

     Rhoda and Ephraim married at Temple and their first child was born there. They then were in New Ipswich from 1806 until 1811, then in Nelson until 1815 before finally setting in Sullivan where they remained. Ephraim was a farmer.[3225]

     Ephraim Adams Holt wrote his will 18 November 1829, 28 years before his death. He left fifty cents to each of his children: Rachel, Daniel, David, Rhoda, Recta, Rena, Eliud, Elijah, and Jedediah. He bequeathed to beloved wife Rhoda all the real estate in Sullivan and all the personal estate whatsoever. Rhoda was also named executrix.[3226] The will was never updated and was presented by Rhoda on 1 September 1857. Heirs signing that they received the fifty cents bequeathed to them were Rachel P. Tarbox, Daniel Holt, David Holt, Recta Holt, Eliud Holt, Elijah Holt, and Jedediah Holt.[3227]

     Rhoda and Ephraim were parents of twelve children.

i   HENRY HOLT, b. at Temple, NH, 4 Aug 1802; d. 20 Aug 1803.

ii   RACHEL PIERCE HOLT, b. at Temple, 13 Sep 1803; d. at Sullivan, NH, 25 Dec 1891; m. 1st at Nelson, 9 Mar 1849, as his second wife, EBENEZER TARBOX, b. about 1773; Ebenezer d. at Munsonville, NH, 4 Feb 1855. Ebenezer was first married to Mary Blodgett. Rachel m. 2nd 2 Oct 1866, as his second wife, LUTHER RICHARDSON, b. at Stoddard, 4 Sep 1808 son of Nathan and Dorcas (Dodge) Richardson; Luther d. at Sullivan, 2 Oct 1884. Luther was first married to Lucy Tryphena Dunn.

iii   DANIEL HOLT, b. at Temple, 5 Jun 1805; d. at Nelson, 24 Jun 1871; m. 22 Feb 1838, SIBYL BOND BEVERSTOCK, b. at Alstead, 15 Oct 1810 daughter of Daniel and Lucinda (Bingham) Beverstock; Sibyl d. at Sullivan, 21 Jun 1892.

iv   DAVID HOLT, b. at New Ipswich, 28 Feb 1807; d. at Sullivan, 10 Jan 1877; m. 1st 26 Feb 1835, FERLINE ELIZA DUNN, b. at Stoddard, 15 Aug 1812 daughter of Joseph and Sarah (Jenkins) Dunn; Ferline d. at Sullivan, 25 Sep 1863. David m. 2nd at Keene, 17 Mar 1864, LUCY ANN CORSER (widow of Cyrus K. Beal), b. at Derby, VT, 1817 daughter of Friend and Rebecca Joann (Kidder) Corser; Lucy d. at Alstead, 28 Dec 1907.

v   RHODA HOLT, b. at New Ipswich, 28 Dec 1808; d. at Bennington, NH, 16 Oct 1838; m. THOMAS DODGE, b. at Society Land, 22 Mar 1798 son of James and Jane (-) Dodge; Thomas d. after 1860 when he was living at Bennington. Rhoda and Thomas did not have children.

vi   SARAH HOLT, b. at New Ipswich, 3 May 1811; d. at Nelson, 17 Jun 1813.

vii   DIAH HOLT, b. at Nelson, 3 Nov 1812; d. at Sullivan, 17 Apr 1818.

[3222] Year: 1850; Census Place: Mayfield, Cuyahoga, Ohio; Roll: 673; Page: 349b

[3223] "Family Burned to Death", The Dayton Herald (Dayton, Ohio), 23 December 1886, Thu, p 2

[3224] The names of Eli's parents are given as Ichabod and Lydia on his death record; Michigan, Death Records, 1867-1950, ancestry.com

[3225] Seward, *History of the Town of Sullivan*, p 1022

[3226] New Hampshire Wills and Probate, Cheshire County, Wills, volume 79, p 390

[3227] New Hampshire Wills and Probate, Cheshire County, Estate Files, H698, Estate of Ephraim A. Holt.

viii   RECTA HOLT, b. at Sullivan, 2 Jun 1815; d. at Concord, NH, 2 Dec 1889; m. 18 Feb 1847, her first cousin,
        ALBERT HOLT, b. at Temple, 16 Jul 1817 son of Nehemiah and Mary (Wright) Holt; Albert d. at Alstead, 12 Jul
        1893.

ix   RENA HOLT, b. at Sullivan, 21 Jul 1817; d. at Sullivan, 5 Oct 1840. Rena did not marry.

x   ELIUD HOLT, b. at Sullivan, 7 Apr 1822; d. at Stoddard, 30 Oct 1863; m. 1843, MARY MELVINA TARBOX, b. at
        Stoddard, 15 Oct 1820 daughter of Ebenezer and Mary (Blodgett) Tarbox Mary d. at Munsonville, 15 Aug 1872.

xi   ELIJAH HOLT, b. at Sullivan, 22 Oct 1823; d. at Nelson, 13 Nov 1863; 25 Aug 1849, his first cousin once
        removed, LUCY ANN HOLT, b. at Nelson, 29 Apr 1825 daughter of Samuel and Charlotte (Davis) Holt; Lucy d.
        at Nelson, 15 Apr 1911. Lucy married second Samuel Wright Loveland.

xii   JEDEDIAH R. HOLT, b. at Sullivan, 5 Mar 1826; d. at East Sullivan, 26 Feb 1903; m. 18 Apr 1850, CAROLINE
        SANDERS FAY, b. at Mason, NH, 28 Feb 1827 daughter of Taylor and Betsey (Sanders) Fay; Caroline d. at East
        Sullivan, 15 May 1901.

1005)   HEPHZIBAH RUSSELL (*Jedediah⁴, Robert³, John², Robert¹*), b. 28 Oct 1783 daughter of Jedediah and Rhoda (Pratt)
Russell; m. 1st at Lyndeborough, 17 Mar 1806, HERMAN LADD SARGENT, b. at Methuen, MA, 27 Sep 1782 son of Joshua and
Abigail (Ladd) Sargent; Herman d. 1816 in Michigan.[3228] Hephzibah m. 2nd at Lyndeborough, 6 May 1819, SAMUEL
CHAMBERLAIN, b. at Lyndeborough, 4 May 1779 son of Samuel and Hannah (Abbott) Chamberlain. Samuel was first married
to Olive who has not been identified.
        Hephzibah and Herman were parents of three children born at Lyndeborough.

i   LUCINDA SARGENT, b. 29 Oct 1806; d. at Lyndeborough, 7 Nov 1871; m. at Lyndeborough, 20 Jul 1826,
        JOTHAM STEPHENSON, b. at Lyndeborough, 28 Feb 1805 son of John and Mary (Hildreth) Stephenson; Jotham
        d. at Lyndeborough, 14 Oct 1883.

ii   DANIEL E. SARGENT, b. 4 Sep 1808; d. after 1860 when living with his half-brother Samuel in Springfield, MI.
        Daniel does not seem to have married.

iii   JOHN O. SARGENT, b. 13 Sep 1810

        Hephzibah Russell and Samuel Chamberlain were parents of two children.

i   HERMAN SARGENT CHAMBERLAIN, b. at Lyndeborough, 16 Feb 1820; d. at New Haven, MI, 28 Mar 1909; m.
        LUCINDA SAMPSON, b. in NY, 24 Apr 1817 daughter of Newland and Catherine (Hall) Sampson; Lucinda d. at
        Cambria, MI, 12 Nov 1874.

ii   SAMUEL RUSSELL CHAMBERLAIN, b. in NY, 15 Feb 1826; d. at New Haven, MI, 27 Jan 1911; m. at White
        Lake, MI, 24 Jun 1852, HARRIET JANE HOPKINS, b. in NY, 15 Apr 1830 daughter of John Chester and Harriet
        Newell (Austin) Hopkins; Harriet d. at New haven, 19 Dec 1903.

1006)   EPHRAIM PRATT RUSSELL (*Jedediah⁴, Robert³, John², Robert¹*), baptized at Reading, 3 Jul 1785 son of Jedediah
and Rhoda (Pratt) Russell; d. after 1855 when he was living at Seneca, NY at the home of his son William; married OLIVE
ORDWAY, b. about 1787 *likely* daughter of Enoch and Anne (Fletcher) Ordway; Olive d. after 1855.
        There is one known child of Ephraim P. Russell and Olive Ordway.

i   WILLIAM ENOCH RUSSELL, b. about 1810; d. at Mishawaka, IN, 1898 (probate 2 Jun 1898); m. ELIZABETH,
        b. about 1829 who has not been identified. William and Elizabeth were parents of four children: Thomas, Olive,
        Ephraim Pratt, and Matilda.

1007)   EBENEZER RUSSELL (*Jedediah⁴, Robert³, John², Robert¹*), b. 17 Feb 1794 son of Jedediah and Rhoda (Pratt) Russell;
d. at South Merrimack, NH, 25 Apr 1883; m. 1st 7 Jul 1818, ARTIMESIA LYNCH; Artimesia d. at Nashua, NH, 22 Jun 1860.
Ebenezer m. 2nd 2 Aug 1863, ELIZABETH STEVENS, b. Lexington, NY, about 1814 daughter of William and Roxanne (Finch)

3228 Sargent, *Sargent Record*, p 39 reports place of death as Michigan but this was not otherwise confirmed.

Stevens.[3229] Elizabeth was twice widowed (Francis Carlton and Jeremiah K. Needham) before her marriage to Ebenezer. Elizabeth died at Franklin, NH, 10 Jun 1896.

On 16 June 1812, Ebenezer enlisted in the company of Capt. Nathan Wheeler and was stationed at Portsmouth. Ebenezer served as selectman of Lyndeborough in 1832 and 1838.[3230]

Ebenezer Russell and Artimesia Lynch were parents of four children born at Lyndeborough.

i   NANCY RUSSELL, b. 4 Jun 1819; d. at Nashua, NH, 23 Apr 1908; m. 1st at Nashville, NH, 12 Mar 1844, WILLIAM UPTON; William d. at Nashville, 17 Apr 1849 (probate 1 May 1849). Nancy m. 2nd at Nashville, 27 Nov 1851, ASA W. FARMER, b. at North Billerica, MA, 1823 son of Asa and Lydia (Wilson) Farmer;[3231] Asa d. at Nashua, 16 May 1886.

ii ADONIRAM RUSSELL, b. 28 Apr 1822; d. at Lyndeborough, NH, 29 Apr 1891; m. 8 Mar 1849, MARIA E. LAKIN, b. at Hancock, NH, 23 Jul 1828 daughter of Jacob G. and Betsey (Stanley) Lakin;[3232] Maria d. at Peterborough, 17 Dec 1903.

iii SARAH A. RUSSELL, b. 19 Jul 1826; d. at Madison, WI, Apr 1898; m. at Nashville, NH, 2 Sep 1849, ALBERT CHENEY, b. in VT, 26 Apr 1826 (date engraved on tombstone); Albert d. at Madison, 31 Mar 1909.

iv AMANDA M. RUSSELL, b. 10 Feb 1829; d. at Nashua, NH, 18 Oct 1912; m. 1st at Wilton, 16 Jun 1863, JOHN H. GIDDINGS, b. at Medford, MA, 1832 son of John and Eliza (Minchin) Giddings; John d. 6 Aug 1868. Amanda m. 2nd HENRY S. LOWE, b. at Greenfield, NH, 1818 son of Simon and Charlotte (Parker) Lowe; Henry d. at Greenfield, 15 Nov 1895. Henry was first married to Sarah Giddings.

1008)   SALLY PRATT RUSSELL (*Jedediah⁴, Robert³, John², Robert¹*), b. 20 Jun 1796 daughter of Jedediah and Rhoda (Pratt) Russell; d. after 1860 when she was living at Hanover, NH; m. at Lyndeborough, 27 Jan 1818, ASA CHAMBERLAIN, b. at Lyndeborough, 10 Apr 1793 son of Jonathan and Margaret (Cram) Chamberlain; Asa d. at Hanover, 24 Jul 1858.

Sally and Asa were in Norwich, Vermont until about 1830 when they moved to Hanover, New Hampshire. Asa was a farmer. In the 1850 census, he gave the value of his real property at $600.[3233] Asa Chamberlain and Sally Russell were parents of eleven children.

i   RHODA SALINDA CHAMBERLAIN, b. at Norwich, VT, 8 Jan 1819; d. after 1850 when she was living at Hanover, NH and unmarried.

ii   JEDEDIAH RUSSELL CHAMBERLAIN, b. at Norwich, 24 Apr 1820; d. at Edenville, IA, 9 Par 1896; m. JANET ARTHUR, b. in Scotland, about 1821; Janet d. at Edenville, 25 Jun 1899.[3234]

iii SARAH MINERVA CHAMBERLAIN, b. at Norwich, 18 Aug 1821; d. at Rhodes, IA, 1 Apr 1897; m. 1840, BRAINARD SPENCER WEEKS, b. at Warren, NH, 13 Dec 1801 son of John and Esther (Spencer) Weeks; Brainard d. at Rhodes, IA, 16 Jun 1875.

iv   ASA RILEY CHAMBERLAIN, b. at Norwich, 11 Sep 1823; d. at State Center, IA, 18 Feb 1896; m. 30 Dec 1845, LAURA HEAD ABBOTT, b. 23 Jun 1827 daughter of William and Esther (Fowler) Abbott; Laura d. at State Center, 15 Apr 1899.

v   JOHN AUSTIN CHAMBERLAIN, b. at Norwich, VT, 22 Jul 1825

vi   WILLIAM RUSSELL CHAMBERLAIN, b. at Norwich, 17 Jul 1827; d. at Dana, MA, 11 Aug 1880; m. at Clinton, MA, 7 Aug 1855, JANE FRANCES FOSTER, b. at Nashua, NH, 18 Nov 1835 daughter of Moses and Abigail Fuller (Hunting) Foster; Jane d. at Worcester, 22 Feb 1882.

vii ELIZA JANE CHAMBERLAIN, b. at Norwich, 14 Jun 1829; d. at Westminster, VT, 16 Jun 1907; m. JASON GORHAM, b. at Westminster, 25 Mar 1822 son of Isaac and Rebecca (Hall) Gorham; Jason d. at Westminster, 17 Sep 1897.

viii ANN CHLOE CHAMBERLAIN, b. at Hanover, NH, 29 May 1832; d. at Concord, NH, 27 Jan 1895. Ann did not marry.

[3229] The names of Elizabeth parents are given as William Stevens and Roxanie Finch on her marriage record for her marriage to Ebenezer Russell; New Hampshire, Marriage and Divorce Records, 1659-1947, New England Historical Genealogical Society; New Hampshire Bureau of Vital Records, Concord, New Hampshire

[3230] Donovan, The History of the Town of Lyndeborough, p 261, p 230, p 847

[3231] The names of Asa's parents are given as Asa Farmer and Lydia Wilson on his death record.

[3232] The names of Maria's parents are given as Jacob Lakin and Betsey Stanley on her death record.

[3233] Year: 1850; Census Place: Hanover, Grafton, New Hampshire; Roll: M432_430; Page: 50B; Image: 110

[3234] Iowa, Deaths and Burials, 1850-1990; FHL Film 956745, p 35

ix   CATHERINE J. "KATE" CHAMBERLAIN, b. at Hanover, 1835; d. at Hanover, 12 Jun 1868; Catherine did not marry.

x   AUGUSTA CELINA CHAMBERLAIN, b. at Hanover, 3 Oct 1838; d. at Concord, NH, 5 Feb 1918; m. PETER WALKER WEBSTER, b. at Campton, NH, Sep 1834 son of George W. and Ann (Walker) Webster; Peter d. at Concord, 6 Jan 1909.

xi   AUSTIN ELIAB CHAMBERLAIN, b. at Hanover, Mar 1841; d. at Rhodes, IA, 26 Jun 1914; m. his second cousin once removed, MARY EMOGINE RUSSELL (*Ebenezer⁶, Abner⁵, Jonathan⁴, Robert³, John², Robert¹*), b. at Dublin, NH, 7 Aug 1846 daughter of Ebenezer H. and Almira (Mason) Russell.

1009)   SAMUEL RUSSELL (*Jedediah⁴, Robert³, John², Robert¹*), b. 4 Apr 1801 son of Jedediah and Rhoda (Pratt) Russell; d. after 1850 when living at Meredith, NH; m. 29 Dec 1822, HANNAH DUSTIN, b. about 1801; Hannah d. after 1850.
         There are five children living in the family in the 1850 census of Meredith, New Hampshire.[3235] Follow-up information was found for just one child.

i   GALON C. RUSSELL, b. in NH, about 1824

ii   DAVID RUSSELL, b. in MA, 1830

iii   ALMIRA RUSSELL, b. in MA, 1834

iv   ALFRED W. RUSSELL, b. at Boston, 7 Apr 1836; d. at Saint Anne, IL, 12 Aug 1919;[3236] m. about 1870, MARION EUGENIA CUNNINGHAM, b. at Rochester, NY, 16 Aug 1842 daughter of James G. and Anna (Rogers) Cunningham; Marion d. at Laurens, SC, 10 Nov 1930.

v   ALBERT G. RUSSELL, b. in NY, 1839

1010)   ELIAB RUSSELL (*Jedediah⁴, Robert³, John², Robert¹*), b. 9 Mar 1804 son of Jedediah and Rhoda (Pratt) Russell; d. at Shortsville, NY, 29 May 1874; m. DIANA NICHOLS, b. 1804; Diana d. at Shortsville, 26 Nov 1867.
         Eliab Russell was a cooper and resided with his family in Manchester, New York. In 1840, the family was a household of nine in Manchester: one male 40 to 49; one female 30 to 39; two males under 5; three males 10 to 14; one male 30 to 39; and one female 10 to 14.[3237] Children named in the 1850 census of the family were Adelia M. age 20, Wilber age 14, Edgar age 11, Emily age 8, and Duane age 6.[3238]
         Eliab Russell and Diana Nichols were parents of five, and perhaps six, children born at Manchester, New York. The 1840 census suggests six children.[3239]

i   ADELIA M. RUSSELL, b. 1830; d. at Shortsville, NY, 13 Jun 1907. Adelia did not marry.

ii   WILBUR ELIAB RUSSELL, b. 18 Nov 1836; d. at Streator, IL, 20 Jan 1920; m. at Lacon, IL, 25 Nov 1860, TRISSIA A. DAVENPORT, b. at Elkhart, IN, 23 Nov 1841 daughter of Robert and Eveline (Newell) Davenport; Trissia d. at Sidney, NE, 14 Dec 1926.

iii   EDGAR O. RUSSELL, b. 24 Jun 1839; d. at Mendon, NY, 23 Jan 1920; m. 1862, DELIA IRWIN, b. 22 Nov 1836 daughter of John and Maria (Bryan) Irwin; Delia d. at Mendon, Jan 1915.

iv   EMILY RUSSELL, b. about 1842; d. at Shortsville, 7 Jul 1857.

v   DUANE RUSSELL, b. 1845; d. at Mendon, NY, 24 Dec 1882; m. about 1870, EMMA ANGEVINE, b. perhaps in Vermont, about 1846 daughter of Nelson and Sarah (-) Angevine.

1011)   JONATHAN RUSSELL (*Jonathan⁴, Robert³, John², Robert¹*), b. at Dublin, NH, 26 Jan 1785 son of Jonathan and Rachel (White) Russell; d. at Dublin, 10 Sep 1848; m. 2 Jan 1806, MARY LEWIS, b. at Marlborough, NH, 14 Dec 1786 daughter of John and Rebecca (Upham) Lewis.

[3235] Year: 1850; Census Place: Meredith, Belknap, New Hampshire; Roll: 425; Page: 24A

[3236] The names of Alfred's parents are given as Samuel Russell and Hannah Dustin on his death record.

[3237] Year: 1840; Census Place: Manchester, Ontario, New York; Roll: 319; Page: 78; Family History Library Film: 0017201

[3238] Year: 1850; Census Place: Manchester, Ontario, New York; Roll: 572; Page: 320a

[3239] Internet trees suggest that Charles Russell born in Shortsville 1826 and died in Manchester 1911 in a sixth child in this family, but that Charles has an obituary that names his parents as William and Margaret Russell. This might be further investigated.

Jonathan resided in Dublin in Range VIII, lot 22, number 8.[3240] Jonathan Russell and Mary Lewis were parents of two sons born at Dublin.

i   LYMAN RUSSELL, b. at Roxbury, NH, 5 Nov 1808; d. after 1870 when he was living at Dublin; m. about 1848, URSULA MASON, b. at Dublin, 5 Jan 1820 daughter of Samuel and Mary (Willard) Mason; Ursula d. at Harrisville, NH, 2 May 1904.

ii JONATHAN LEWIS RUSSELL, b. at Roxbury, NH, 30 Oct 1814; d. at Marlborough, NH, Apr 1859; m. at Keene, 31 Oct 1849, ANNA PRENTISS MASON, b. at Dublin, 5 Apr 1822 daughter of Samuel and Mary (Willard) Mason; Anna d. at Harrisville, NH, 25 Jan 1892.

1012)   SALLY RUSSELL (*Jonathan⁴, Robert³, John², Robert¹*), b. at Dublin, NH, 6 Apr 1788 daughter of Jonathan and Rachel (White) Russell; d. at Marlborough, NH, 22 Nov 1843; m. at Marlborough, 23 Oct 1813, ASA METCALF, b. about 1787 (died at age 34) son of Asa and Mehitable (Upham) Metcalf;[3241] Asa d. at Marlborough, 21 Aug 1821.
        Sally Russell and Asa Metcalf were parents of three children.

i   ROXANA METCALF, b. about 1815; d. at Boston, 21 Mar 1896; m. about 1835, RICHARD DAVIS who has not been identified; Richard d. about 1850 when Roxana was head of household in Brattleboro, VT with four daughters the youngest 10 months old. The three oldest girls were born at Marlborough, NH and the youngest daughter at Brattleboro.

ii CALVIN METCALF, b. at Marlborough, NH, 17 Aug 1817; d. at Fort Edward, NY, 1904; m. 23 Jan 1838, MARY STOWE MANNING, b. at Whitehall, NY, 25 Nov 1817 daughter of Ziba and Rachel (Polley) Manning; Mary d. at Fort Edward, 1902.

iii ELCENA METCALF, b. at Keene, about 1821; d. at Waltham, MA, 25 Nov 1903; m. AARON B. DARLING, b. at Chesterfield, NH, 1819 son of Aaron and Mercy (Hill) Darling; Aaron d. at Weston, MA, 20 Sep 1867.

1013)   ABNER RUSSELL (*Jonathan⁴, Robert³, John², Robert¹*), b. at Dublin, NH, 3 Mar 1791 son of Jonathan and Rachel (White) Russell; d. at Marlborough, NH, 24 Mar 1855; m. 1816, BETSEY HERRICK, b. at Marlborough, 2 Sep 1794 daughter of Ebenezer and Lydia (Eaton) Herrick; Betsey d. at Harrisville, NH, 21 Jan 1875.
        Abner and Betsey lived in Marlborough, New Hampshire where they had a farm. They were active members of the Methodist church.[3242]
        Abner did not leave a will and his estate entered probate 3 April 1855 with Jeremiah Herrick as administrator at request of Betsey Russell, Ebenezer H. Russell, Gilbert Russell, and William Russell. Ebenezer and William joined in the administration. On 1 November 1856, widow Betsey requested the dower be assigned to her. The homestead farm was valued at $1,025 and 13 acres in Dublin at $50. A portion of the estate was sold to settle debts.[3243]
        Abner and Betsey were parents of eight children born at Marlborough.

i   EBENEZER HERRICK RUSSELL, b. 29 Mar 1817; d. at Marlborough, 19 Apr 1886; m. 28 Nov 1841, ALMIRA MASON, b. at Dublin, NH, 1823 daughter of Samuel and Anna (Kendall) Mason; Almira d. at Marlborough, 17 Oct 1895.

ii GILBERT RUSSELL, b. 28 Feb 1819; d. at Marlborough, 28 Jul 1880; m. 25 Jan 1842, NANCY HEATON, b. at Keene, 9 Mar 1823 daughter of David and Rebecca (Moore) Heaton; Nancy d. at Marlborough, 19 Sep 1890.

iii JONATHAN F. RUSSELL, b. 12 May 1821; died in infancy.

iv MARY ELIZA RUSSELL, b. 27 May 1823; d. at Dublin, 17 Dec 1849; m. 13 Apr 1842, MERRILL MASON, b. at Dublin, 9 Sep 1816 son of Samuel and Mary (Willard) Mason; Merrill d. 13 May 1897. Merrill married second Harriet M. Herrick on 25 Apr 1850. Merrill Mason was the uncle of Nancy Mason who married Mary's brother Ebenezer.

[3240] Leonard, *The History of Dublin*, p 657
[3241] Bemis, *History of the Town of Marlborough*, p 579
[3242] Bemis, *History of the Town of Marlborough*, p 623
[3243] New Hampshire Wills and Probate, Cheshire County, Estate Files, Case R326

v   WILLIAM A. RUSSELL, b. 16 Jul 1825; d. at Keene, NH, 6 Sep 1878; m. at Marlborough, 23 Sep 1849, CAROLINE S. DUDLEY, b. about 1832; Caroline d. after 1884 when she was living in Keene. William and Caroline divorced Apr 1875, William filing on grounds of abandonment.[3244]

vi   EMILY M. RUSSELL (twin), b. Jan 1832; d. 5 Apr 1837.

vii   AMELIA M. RUSSELL (twin), b. Jan 1832; d. 2 May 1837.

viii   JOSEPH MERRILL RUSSELL, b. 7 Jul 1834; d. at Keene, 12 Jul 1893; m. HELEN M. KNOWLTON, b. at Dublin, 10 May 1832 daughter of Elisha and Hannah (Chamberlain) Knowlton; Helen d. at Keene, 20 Mar 1925.

1014)   EBENEZER RUSSELL (*Jonathan⁴, Robert³, John², Robert¹*), b. at Dublin, NH, 27 Nov 1797 son of Jonathan and Rachel (White) Russell; d. at Keene, 8 Apr 1859; m. at Dublin, 18 Feb 1823, OLIVE NEWELL, b. 30 Mar 1801; Olive d. at Rochester, NY, 4 Apr 1891. After the death of Ebenezer, Olive lived with their son Osgood M. Russell.

Ebenezer and Olive married in Dublin, but soon after were in Marlborough where their two oldest children were born. They returned to Dublin where their younger children were born.

i   RACHEL DIANTHA RUSSELL, b. at Marlborough, 27 Nov 1797; d. at Dublin, 19 Mar 1837.

ii   OSGOOD NEWELL RUSSELL, b. at Marlborough, 12 Aug 1827; d. at Rochester, NY, 30 Nov 1882; m. 12 Sep 1847, AMELIA N. SINCLAIR, b. at Ellsworth, ME, 18 Nov 1825 daughter of Joseph and Susan (Noble) Sinclair;[3245] Amelia d. at Rochester, 1 May 1889.

iii   JONATHAN MILAN RUSSELL, b. at Dublin, 16 Jun 1830; d. at Salt Lake City, UT, 2 Sep 1900; m. 1st 25 Apr 1854, ROSILLA DAMON WHITE, b. at Marlborough, 16 Sep 1838 daughter of Noah and Arvilla (Lewis) White; Rosilla d. at Springville, UT, 21 Apr 1919. In 1862, Jonathan left the family and Rosilla remarried to George Harrison on 4 May 1865.[3246] Jonathan m. 2nd 1870, SOPHIA JANE ROMERIL, b. at Grouville, Jersey, Channel Islands, 9 Mar 1848 daughter of Francois and Marie (Belot) Romeril;[3247] Sophia d. at Salt Lake, 1 Oct 1906.

iv   ALLEN K. RUSSELL, b. at Dublin, 7 Jan 1833. Alvin served with the 61st Regiment of New York volunteers and died of rubella 30 Dec 1861 at the regimental hospital in New York.[3248]

v   CHARLES J. RUSSELL, b. at Dublin, 25 Jan 1836; d. at Rochester, NY, 9 Apr 1905; m. Mar 1858, HELEN WAKELY, b. Jul 1837; Helen d. after 1930 when she was living at Le Roy, NY with grandchildren.

1015)   AMELIA "MILLE" RUSSELL (*Jonathan⁴, Robert³, John², Robert¹*), b. at Dublin, NH, 9 Jan 1800 daughter of Jonathan and Rachel (White) Russell; d. at Westminster, VT, 6 Apr 1873; m. at Westminster, 6 Mar 1833, ALVIN G. KEYES, b. at Putney, 1808 son of Israel and Hannah (Grout) Keyes; Alvin d. at Putney, 11 Jul 1872.

Millie and Alvin resided in Putney where Alvin was a farmer.[3249] In 1850, 16-year old Mark and 13-year old Mary were living with their parents. Mille Russell and Alvin Keyes were parents of two children.

i   MARK R. KEYES, b. at Putney, 1834; d. at Putney, Mar 1898; m. at Brattleboro, 2 Dec 1863, ELLA SYBIL F. MORSE, b. at Putney, 19 Apr 1843 daughter of Nelson and Electa (Keyes) Morse; Ella d. at Newfane, 16 Mar 1924. After Mark's death, Ella married George C. Cooley on 11 Sep 1899. Mark and Ella had a daughter Carrie who married Albert L. Davis and a daughter Abbie who married John F. Lewis.

ii   MARY ANN KEYES, b. at Putney, 7 Aug 1836; d. at Newfane, VT, 4 Jul 1874; m. about 1866, as his second wife, CHARLES H. EAGER, b. 1821 son of Benjamin and Eleanor (Perry) Eager; Charles d. at Newfane, 18 Jan 1891. Mary and Charles did not have children. Charles was first married to Louisa Holden. Charles had a third marriage to Maria after Mary Ann's death.

[3244] New Hampshire, Marriage and Divorce Records, 1659-1947; New England Historical Genealogical Society; New Hampshire Bureau of Vital Records, Concord, New Hampshire
[3245] Boltwood, *History and Genealogy of the Family of Thomas Noble*, p 93
[3246] Greenwood, *Greenwood Genealogies*, p 196
[3247] Jersey, Church of England Births and Baptisms, 1813-1915; Jersey Heritage; St Helier, Jersery; Jersey Parish Registers; Reference Number: G/C/06/A2/3. The names of Sophia's parents are also given on her death record as Francois and Mary; Utah, Death and Military Death Certificates, 1904-1961
[3248] U.S., Registers of Deaths of Volunteers, 1861-1865
[3249] Year: 1850; Census Place: Putney, Windham, Vermont; Roll: 929; Page: 57b

1016)   MARY W. RUSSELL (*Jonathan⁴, Robert³, John², Robert¹*), b. at Dublin, NH, 15 Jun 1806 daughter of Jonathan and Rachel (White) Russell; d. at Putney, VT, 13 Aug 1878; m. 1ˢᵗ at Dublin, 31 Oct 1837, PROCTOR HIRAM KEYES, b. at Putney, 20 Dec 1810 son of Asa and Hannah (Taylor) Keyes; Proctor d. at Putney, 27 May 1840. Mary m. 2ⁿᵈ at Putney, 1 Nov 1843, as his second wife, EPHRAIM BROWN, b. 1790 likely son of Silas and Mary (Nims) Brown; Ephraim d. at Putney, at 22 Sep 1871. Ephraim was first married to Sophia Eddey who died in 1841.

Mary W. Russell and Proctor Keyes were parents of two children.

i   ELLEN KEYES, b. at Putney, 1838. Ellen was living in 1850, but nothing further found.

ii   MARY R. KEYES, b. at Putney, 1840; d. after 1910 when she was living at Kansas City, MO; m. at Rockingham, VT, 27 Jul 1863, GEORGE E. COBB, b. at Walpole, NH, 1838 son of Joseph and Jerusha (Waldo) Cobb;[3250] George d. after 1910. Mary and George did not have children. George was a carpenter and a blacksmith.

Mary W. Russell and Ephraim Brown were parents of one child.

i   FLORENCE BROWN, b. at Putney, 1845, Florence was living in 1860, but nothing further found.

1017)   BENJAMIN HERRICK (*Mary Holt Herrick⁴, Mary Russell Holt³, John², Robert¹*), b. at Wilton, 13 Dec 1780 son of Edward and Mary (Holt) Herrick; d. after 1850 when living at Andover, MA; m. at Boston, 22 Jul 1807, ELCY NUGENT, b. at Stonington, CT,[3251] about 1781; d. after 1850.

Benjamin Herrick was a miller. In 1850, he and wife "Alice" and daughter Sarah age 36 were living in Andover.[3252] Benjamin and Elcy were parents of four children born at Salem.

i   BENJAMIN HERRICK, b. at Salem, 1 Jan 1812; d. at Andover, 2 Jan 1892; m. at Leicester, MA, 6 Oct 1845, MARY MARIA HARTWELL, b. at Waltham, 15 Oct 1821 daughter of Levi and Mary (Putnam) Hartwell; Mary d. at Andover, 17 Jun 1891.

ii   GEORGE DODGE HERRICK, b. 1814; d. at Salem, 4 Oct 1814.

iii   SARAH ANN HERRICK, b. at Salem, about 1815; d. at Andover, 22 Dec 1896; m. at Leicester, 14 Dec 1854, EDWARD J. READ, b. in Ireland, about 1813 son of James and Judith (-) Read; Edward d. at Leicester, 23 Jul 1881.

iv   HARRIET HERRICK.[3253] She is *possibly* the Harriet Herrick who married Edwin Farnham at Andover on 12 Oct 1826. If so, she died about 1829. Harriet and Edwin had one daughter Harriet L. Farnham who died at age 3 in 1832. If Harriet was the spouse of Edwin, she would be the oldest child in this family.

1018)   MARY HERRICK (*Mary Holt Herrick⁴, Mary Russell Holt³, John², Robert¹*), b. at Wilton, 13 Apr 1782 daughter of Edward and Mary (Holt) Herrick; d. at Dexter, ME, 16 Jun 1882; m. 7 Jul 1803, JOHN PUTNAM, b. at Wilton, 27 Nov 1774 son of Jacob and Abigail (Burnap) Putnam; John d. at Nashua, NH, 16 Mar 1835.

John was an herbal physician who practiced in Wilton and surrounding communities. Mary died at age 100, the oldest known native of Wilton known at the time the *History of the Town of Wilton* was written.[3254]

John and Mary were parents of twelve children born at Wilton.

i   MARY FARNUM PUTNAM, b. 3 Nov 1803; d. by 1836 (husband's remarriage); m. at Lowell, 29 May 1831, HENCHMAN SYLVESTER, b. about 1788; Henchman d. at Wilton, 7 Mar 1865. Henchman married second Sarah *Sanborn* Avery in Dec 1836. Mary and Henchman had two children who were adopted by Mary's sister Sarah and her husband Samuel Farrar.[3255] The two children went by the name Farrar.

ii   SARAH HERRICK PUTNAM, b. 5 Jun 1805; d. after 1880 when she was living at Dexter, ME with her mother Mary, age 98, also in the home; m. Aug 1831, SAMUEL FARRAR, b. at Portsmouth, NH, 28 Dec 1805 son of Jonathan and Hannah (Cram) Farrar; Samuel d. at Geneva, WI, 8 Dec 1862. Samuel was educated at Bowdoin

[3250] The names of George's parents and place and year of birth are given on the marriage record.

[3251] Elcy's place of birth is given as Stonington on the death record of son Benjamin Herrick.

[3252] Year: 1850; Census Place: Andover, Essex, Massachusetts; Roll: M432_314; Page: 369A; Image: 449

[3253] Harriet is a child listed in the Herrick genealogy for whom records were not found

[3254] Livermore, *History of the Town of Wilton*, p 480

[3255] Livermore, *History of the Town of Wilton*, p 480

Descendants of Robert Russell and Mary Marshall

College (although did not graduate) and was officer of a railway company in Milwaukee. He was also a woolen manufacturer.[3256]

iii   JOHN PUTNAM, b. 8 Jun 1807; d. at Nashua, NH, 24 Aug 1867; m. at Wilton, 12 Sep 1834, ABIGAIL HOLT, b. at Temple, NH, 18 May 1808 daughter of Nathaniel and Sarah (Upham) Holt; Abigail d. at Nashua, 18 Sep 1888.

iv   EPHRAIM ABBOT PUTNAM, b. 3 Apr 1809; d. at Wakefield, MA, 19 Mar 1871; m. at Lynnfield, MA, 4 Apr 1835, RUTH LOUISA BURNHAM, b. at Wakefield, 1818 daughter of Joseph and Ruth (Emerson) Burnham; Ruth d. at Wakefield, 8 Jan 1893.

v   ANN "NANCY" E. PUTNAM, b. 17 Aug 1811; d. at Skowhegan, ME, 22 Sep 1888; m. ALBERT C. THAYER, b. at Fairfield, ME, 3 Mar 1809 son of Stephen and Sophia (Carleton) Thayer; Albert d. at Skowhegan, 28 Dec 1834.

vi   ABBY BURNAP PUTNAM, b. 4 May 1813; d. after 1870 when she was living at Dexter, ME. Abby did not marry.

vii   ADALINE PUTNAM, b. 18 May 1815; d. at Dexter, ME, 9 Aug 1908; m. NATHANIEL BRYANT, likely b. at Pembroke, MA, 4 Oct 1807 son of Nathaniel and Mary (Crooker) Bryant; Nathaniel d. at Dexter, 21 Oct 1883.

viii   LYMAN PUTNAM, b. 29 Jan 1818; d. at Dexter, 23 Feb 1881; m. at Dexter, 19 Jan 1867, AMANDA H. JORDAN, b. at Charleston, ME, 1846 daughter of George W. and Matilda (Joy) Jordan; Amanda d. at Dexter, 13 Feb 1872.

ix   GEORGE PUTNAM, b. 23 May 1820; d. 8 Jun 1820.

x   GEORGE QUINCY HILL PUTNAM, b. 31 May 1821; d. at Dexter, ME, 14 Nov 1895; m. about 1851, SARAH E. STICKNEY, b. at North Anson, ME, Nov 1829 daughter of George W. and Cynthia (French) Stickney; Sarah d. at Brockton, MA, 1 May 1908. After George's death, Sarah lived with their daughter Lucy and her family in Brockton.

xi   FRANKLIN REED PUTNAM, b. 3 Oct 1823; d. at Davenport, IA, 28 Dec 1876; m. at Scott County, IA, 21 Oct 1856, MILDRED ANN MINOR, b. in VA, about 1830; Mildred d. at Topeka, KS, 1895.

xii   CHARLES EDWIN PUTNAM, b. 14 Sep 1826; d. at San Francisco, CA, 4 Feb 1873.[3257] Charles was a stable foreman in San Francisco in 1867. A marriage was not located for Charles.

1019)   GEORGE HERRICK (*Mary Holt Herrick⁴, Mary Russell Holt³, John², Robert¹*), b. at Wilton, 12 Feb 1784 son of Edward and Mary (Holt) Herrick; d. at Wilton, after 1840; m. about 1808, his third cousin once removed (through Holt line), MARY "POLLY" HOLT, b. at Wilton, 17 Apr 1787 daughter of Joel and Mary (Coburn) Holt; Mary d. after 1860 when she was living with her son Daniel H. Herrick in Dayton, NY.

George and Mary lived in Weston, VT just after their marriage and their oldest two children were born there. They then returned to Wilton and George is last noted on the 1840 census.

George and Mary were parents of six children.

i   AMOS HERRICK, b. at Weston, VT, 21 Jul 1810; d. of disease during the Civil War, at New Orleans, 17 Jun 1863;[3258] m. at Lyndeborough, 22 Jan 1835, BETSEY B. LAKIN, b. at Lyndeborough, Feb 1810 daughter of Thomas and Lucy (Burton) Lakin; Betsey d. at Wilton, 15 Feb 1878.

ii   LARKIN HERRICK, b. at Weston, VT, 24 Oct 1812; d. at Wilton, 6 Sep 1831.

iii   MARY HERRICK, b. at Wilton, 8 Mar 1816; d. 13 Apr 1832.

iv   DANIEL H. HERRICK, b. 27 Feb 1818; d. after 1860 when he was living at Dayton, NY; m. at Pepperell, MA, 30 Dec 1847, SARAH A. DUTTON, b. 1822 daughter of Henry Dutton; Sarah d. after 1860.

v   ISRAEL HERRICK, b. 1 Nov 1821; d. perhaps at Milford, NH (burial at Wilton), 17 Apr 1877; m. at Pepperell, 29 Dec 1846, NANCY ELLIOTT, b. at Pepperell, 25 Feb 1821 daughter of David and Nancy (Blood) Elliott; Nancy d. at Brookline, NH, 8 Feb 1890.

vi   GEORGE HERRICK, reported to have married and "gone West." He may be the George Herrick born Aug 1829 in New Hampshire who died at Manitowoc, WI, 6 Apr 1907. George was a laborer and railroad worker. He did not have children but was twice married. His first wife was LUCINDA P., b. in VT, 1825; Lucinda d. at Appleton, WI, 1872. George m. 2nd, 1876, SOPHIA, born in Switzerland (also reported as Germany), Oct 1842; Sophia d. at Manitowoc, 18 Nov 1807.

[3256] Bowdoin College, *General Catalogue of Bowdoin College and the Medical School of Maine: A Biographical Record of Alumni and Officers*, 1795-1950, p 58; published Brunswick, ME, 1950.

[3257] Charles E. Putnam, a native of New Hampshire, died age 46 years. California, County Birth, Marriage, and Death Records, 1849-1980

[3258] U.S., Registers of Deaths of Volunteers, 1861-1865, New Hampshire A-Z, p 80

1020)   EDWARD HERRICK (*Mary Holt Herrick⁴, Mary Russell Holt³, John², Robert¹*), b. at Wilton, 29 Oct 1785 son of Edward and Mary (Holt) Herrick; d. at Wilton, 9 Dec 1873; m. 1ˢᵗ 27 Dec 1810, NANCY BARRETT, b. at Westford, MA, 28 Dec 1790 daughter of Ebenezer and Jane (Reed) Barrett; Nancy d. 27 Nov 1824. Edward m. 2ⁿᵈ 22 Nov 1825, his second cousin once removed, MARY ANDREWS, b. at Hillsborough, 1 Jan 1796 daughter of Abraham and Mary (Chandler) Andrews.[3259]

Edward Herrick and Nancy Barrett were parents of five children.

i   EDWARD BARRETT HERRICK, b. at Wilton, 11 Apr 1812; d. at Lawrence, MA, 9 Nov 1878; m. 1ˢᵗ at Deerfield, NH, 23 Jun 1836, CLYMENA B. SMITH, b. at Deerfield, 6 May 1812; Clymena d. at Lawrence, 20 Feb 1856. Edward m. 2ⁿᵈ at Manchester, NH, 22 Apr 1856, ELIZA M. GOULD, b. at Manchester, 9 Mar 1831 daughter of Oliver and Mary (Upton) Gould; Eliza d. at Lawrence, 2 Apr 1886.

ii   MARY JANE HERRICK, b. at Wilton, 17 Sep 1814; d. at Wilton, 30 May 1878; m. 22 Jan 1835, JOEL HESSELTON, b. at Andover, VT, 9 Oct 1809 son of Nathan and Prudence (Baldwin) Hesselton; Joel d. at Wilton, 14 Dec 1893.

iii   ELIZA ANN HERRICK, b. at Wilton, 2 Jun 1816; d. at Wilton, 31 Mar 1872; m. at Lowell, MA, 14 Jun 1841, OSCAR GILMAN INGALLS, b. at Middleton, MA, 1816 son of Enoch and Sarah (Upton) Ingalls; Oscar d. at Somerville, MA, 11 Sep 1899. Oscar married second Helen F. Hilt on 4 Dec 1876.

iv   CHARLES PRESCOTT HERRICK, b. at Wilton, 27 Apr 1818; d. at Boston, 1 May 1890; m. at Lowell, 24 Nov 1841, CAROLINE MATILDA BAKER, b. at Danville, VT, 23 Dec 1820 daughter of Andrew K. and Elizabeth (Smith) Baker;[3260] Caroline d. at Boston, 11 Jul 1896.

v   NANCY DODGE HERRICK, b. at Lyndeborough, 4 Jul 1820; d. at Wilton, 4 Jun 1894; m. 1ˢᵗ at Wilton, Oct 1841, SILAS BRIDGE WINN, b. at Wilton, 1 Aug 1818 son of Silas and Dorcas (Boynton) Winn; Silas d. at Lowell, MA, 27 Jul 1844. Nancy m. 2ⁿᵈ 27 Nov 1845, as his second wife, PIERCE GAGE, b. at Wilton, 4 Sep 1813 son of Richard and Betsey (Hutchinson) Gage; Pierce d. at Wilton, 4 Sep 1891. Pierce was first married to Mary Lovejoy daughter of David and Rachel (Hutchinson) Lovejoy.

Edward Herrick and Mary Andrews were parents of five children.

i   ALONZO R. HERRICK, b. at Nashua, NH, 9 Dec 1827; d. at Lowell, MA, 19 Jul 1854.

ii   JOHN A. HERRICK, b. at Methuen, 30 Nov 1829; d. at Lowell, 12 Apr 1902; at Lowell, 24 Dec 1854, AGNES G. HUSE, b. at Wilton, ME, Oct 1834 daughter of Jesse and Rhoda (Gould) Huse; Agnes d. at Lowell, 20 Apr 1913.

iii   BETSEY A. HERRICK, b. about 1831. Betsey is listed with the family in the 1850 census at Lowell, age 19. Nothing further was found.

iv   ANDREW J. HERRICK, b. 5 Jun 1834; d. at disease at Suffolk, VA, 1 Dec 1862. Andrew served in company A of the 6ᵗʰ regiment of Massachusetts infantry.[3261]

v   CLIMENA FRANCES HERRICK, b. at Lowell, 5 Apr 1838; d. at New Boston, NH, 11 Jul 1893; m. at Worcester, 18 Oct 1860, JOSEPH L. LASH, b. at Waldoboro, ME, 1832 son of Jacob and Mary (Burnham) Lash; Joseph d. at Temple, NH, 25 Apr 1903.

1021)   SARAH HERRICK (*Mary Holt Herrick⁴, Mary Russell Holt³, John², Robert¹*), b. at Wilton, 27 Dec 1788 daughter of Edward and Mary (Holt) Herrick; d. at Norridgewock, ME, 17 Mar 1866; m. 8 Sep 1814, JOSIAH PEET, b. at Bethlehem, CT, 21 Jun 1780 son of Benjamin and Elizabeth (Hendee) Peet; Josiah d. at Norridgewock, 17 Feb 1852.

Rev. Josiah Peet moved with his parents from Connecticut to West Haven, Vermont at age six. He entered Middlebury College in 1804. He worked as a teacher to support himself through college. He entered the theological seminary at Andover on 24 June 1809. Josiah was licensed to preach by the Haverhill association in 1811. He was ordained and installed as pastor of the Congregational church at Norridgewock on 4 August 1814. Josiah kept a journal from 1806 through most of the rest of his life.[3262]

Josiah and Sarah met while he was in seminary at Andover. Sarah lived in the household of her relative Ephraim Abbott and Josiah boarded there while in seminary.

[3259] Chandler, *Descendants and William and Annis Chandler*, p 619

[3260] The names of Caroline's parents are as given on her death record.

[3261] U.S., Registers of Deaths of Volunteers, 1861-1865, Massachusetts G-N, p 39

[3262] A volume titled *Memoir, with Sermons, of Rev. Josiah Peet* (author David Shepley) contains transcriptions of many of Josiah's journal entries, letters, and sermons. This volume is available online through Google books.

Sarah and Josiah were parents of five children born at Norridgewock.

i   SARAH E. PEET, b. 1815 and d. 20 Aug 1815.

ii   EDWARD JOSIAH PEET, b. 1816; d. at Norridgewock, 1885;[3263] m. MARY FLETCHER, b. 1820 daughter of Amos and Sarah (Ware) Fletcher; Mary d. at Norridgewock, 1892.

iii   SARAH HERRICK PEET, b. 1818; d. at Norridgewock, 30 Apr 1892; m. GEORGE SAWTELLE, b. at Norridgewock, 25 Feb 1815 son of Richard and Sarah (Ware) Sawtelle; George d. at Norridgewock, 16 Oct 1893.

iv   MARY HERRICK PEET, b. 1823; d. at Holland, MA, 1889; m. about 1850, SOLOMON E. BIXBY, b. at Norridgewock, 9 Dec 1821 son of Rufus and Betsey (Weston) Bixby; Solomon d. at Danvers, MA, 28 Apr 1900. Solomon Bixby was a Congregationalist minister who had posts in Kingston, NH, Holland, MA, and Petersham, MA.[3264]

v   WILLIAM HENRY PEET, b. about 1824. William was a merchant in New York and New Orleans. He was living in New Orleans in 1860.[3265] A marriage was not identified for him.

1022)   ISRAEL HERRICK (*Mary Holt Herrick⁴, Mary Russell Holt³, John², Robert¹*), b. at Wilton, 9 Jul 1794 son of Edward and Mary (Holt) Herrick; d. at Lyndeborough, 18 Feb 1866; m. 1st at Milford, 28 Nov 1822, ELIZA H. BURNS, b. at Milford, 24 Nov 1802 son of Samuel and Abigail (Jones) Burns;[3266] Eliza d. at Milford, 28 Nov 1848. Israel m. 2nd 12 Dec 1849, his third cousin once removed (through Holt line), EMELINE GRAY, b. at Wilton, 11 Oct 1811 daughter of Joseph and Chloe (Abbott) Gray; Emeline d. at Lyndeborough, 3 Jun 1891.

     Israel attended the medical school at Dartmouth College and was a homeopathic physician.[3267] In his early manhood he was involved in West India goods trade out of Salem but abandoned this after two years. He began the study of medicine with Dr. John Wallace and after completion of his medical studies settled in Lyndeborough in 1821 and opened a medical practice. Over the years, he switched from traditional medicine to homeopathic methods.[3268]

     In his will written 16 January 1866, Israel Herrick bequeathed to son William J. Herrick two hundred dollars. Son Lafayette received the income from his (Lafayette's) homestead place in Lyndeborough. Son Edward H. Herrick is to have a life maintenance of Israel's homestead in Lyndeborough. Son Benjamin J. Herrick was named guardian to Edward. Beloved wife Emeline received nine hundred dollars and all the household furniture she brought to the marriage. She also has right to live in the household during her life. Son Benjamin G. Herrick receives the residue of the estate.[3269]

     Israel Herrick and Eliza Burns were parents of five children born at Lyndeborough.

i   ELIZA DIADAMIA HERRICK, b. 20 Sep 1823; d. 20 Aug 1825.

ii   LAFAYETTE HERRICK, b. 29 Jan 1825; d. at Lyndeborough, 30 May 1888; m. 1st at Lyndeborough, 3 Feb 1848, SARAH E. JONES, b. at Lyndeborough, 15 Nov 1827 daughter of Francis D. and Mehitable (Haynes) Johnson; Sarah d. by 1854. Lafayette m. 2nd 3 Sep 1854, INDIANA E. WILSON, b. at Pepperell, 19 Apr 1838 daughter of Samuel and Mahali (Elliott) Wilson; Indiana d. at Lyndeborough, 1 Dec 1910.

iii   WILLIAM J. HERRICK, b. 15 Jan 1827; d. (burial) at Plymouth, MO, 5 Jan 1893; m. 1st 30 Apr 1849, CHLOE ANN JONES, b. at Lyndeborough, 27 Feb 1831 daughter of Samuel and Olive (Clark) Jones; Chloe d. at Bates, MO, 21 Nov 1876. William m. 2nd 31 Oct 1878, MARY JANE MATHENA (widow of Henry Mecaskey), b. in KY, 22 Oct 1831 (engraved on gravestone); Mary d. (burial at Utica, MO), 14 Jun 1909.

iv   EDWARD HORATIO HERRICK, b. 11 Oct 1828; d. at Lyndeborough, 24 Jul 1873. Edward did not marry.

v   BENJAMIN GOODWIN HERRICK, b. 1 May 1836; d. at Lyndeborough, 21 Sep 1911; m. 8 Jan 1861, SARAH E. FISH, b. at Greenfield, NH, 13 Jul 1836 daughter of Nathaniel R. and Rebecca (Palmer) Fish; Sarah d. at Lyndeborough, 3 May 1913.

1023)   LARKIN HERRICK (*Mary Holt Herrick⁴, Mary Russell Holt³, John², Robert¹*), b. at Wilton, 16 Dec 1799 son of Edward and Mary (Holt) Herrick; d. at Wilton, 6 Nov 1866; m. at Wilton, 17 May 1827, SARAH SHELDON, b. at Wilton, 19 Jul 1804 daughter of Samuel and Phebe (Keyes) Sheldon; Sarah d. at Lebanon, NH, 2 May 1891.

[3263] Maine, Faylene Hutton Cemetery Collection, 1780-1990

[3264] The Congregational Quarterly; The Congregational Yearbook.

[3265] Year: 1860; Census Place: New Orleans Ward 11, Orleans, Louisiana; Page: 878; Family History Library Film: 803420

[3266] Ramsdell, *History of Milford*, p 612

[3267] Livermore, *History of the Town of Wilton*, p 399

[3268] Donovan, *The History of the Town of Lyndeborough*, pp 765-768. Israel Herrick contributed the information for his biography in the *History of Lyndeborough*.

[3269] New Hampshire Wills and Probate, Hillsborough County, Probate Records volume 82, p 19

Larkin was a carpenter and resided in Wilton. In 1850, Larkin, Sarah, and their younger daughter Harriet resided in Wilton.[3270] Helen M. Lovejoy (daughter) declined administration of the estate on 1 March 1867 and William Wetherbee was named administrator.[3271]

Larkin and Sarah were parents of two known children.

i   HELENA MARIA HERRICK, b. at Nashua, NH, 7 Sep 1829; d. at Bristol, NH, 30 Oct 1919; m. about 1850, JOHN LOVEJOY, b. at Lancaster, NH, 11 Nov 1828 son of Artemas and Mehitable (Wetherbee) Lovejoy; John d. at Bristol, 19 Oct 1907.

ii   HARRIET HERRICK, b. at Wilton, 25 Jun 1840; d. at Bristol, 7 Jun 1927. Harriet did not marry.

1024)   RHODA DALE (*Rhoda Holt Dale⁴, Mary Russell Holt³, John², Robert¹*), b. at Wilton, 15 Feb 1780 daughter of John and Rhoda (Holt) Dale; d. at Weld, ME, 27 Jun 1852; m. 22 Dec 1803, EBENEZER HUTCHINSON, b. at Wilton, 18 Sep 1780 son of Ebenezer and Phebe (Sawtell) Hutchinson; Ebenezer d. at Weld, 23 Jan 1845.

Rhoda and Ebenezer resided in Weld. After her husband's death, Rhoda resided with her daughter Rhoda and her husband in Weld.[3272] Rhoda Dale and Ebenezer Hutchinson were parents of eleven children recorded in the town records of Weld, Maine.[3273]

i   RHODA DALE HUTCHINSON, b. 18 Oct 1804; d. after 1880 when she was living in Weld; m. 1ˢᵗ 20 Oct 1828, JACOB AMES WHITNEY, b. 1802 son of Jeremiah and Lydia (Cole) Whitney; Jacob d. at Carthage, 13 Oct 1852. Rhoda married 2ⁿᵈ about 1855, NATHAN JUDKINS, b. about 1805 son of Philip and Hannah (-) Judkins; Nathan d. at Carthage, 13 Jul 1892. Nathan was first married to Betsey.

ii   EBENEZER HUTCHINSON, b. 8 May 1806; d. at Carthage, ME, 4 Oct 1894; m. 10 Mar 1829, MARY JUDKINS, b. 21 Jan 1809 daughter of Philip and Hannah (-) Judkins; Mary d. at Carthage, 1876.

iii ANNA HUTCHINSON, b. 13 Apr 1808; d. at Carthage, 17 Oct 1881; m. 21 Sep 1826, WILLIAM WINTER, b. at Carthage, 23 Mar 1802; William d. at Carthage, Aug 1883.

iv   ACHSAH HUTCHINSON (twin of Anna), b. 13 Apr 1808; d. at Carthage, 6 Aug 1878; m. 12 Nov 1826, ABIEL HOLT, b. 10 May 1805 son of Abel and Grace (Hubbard) Holt; Abel d. at Carthage, 17 Feb 1850.

v   JOHN H. HUTCHINSON, b. 16 Apr 1810; d. at Carthage, 1887; m. 1ˢᵗ about 1835, HANNAH JUDKINS, b. 4 Mar 1813 daughter of Philip and Hannah (-) Judkins; Hannah d. at Carthage, 26 Oct 1853. John m. 2ⁿᵈ MARTHA S. PHINNEY, b. 2 Aug 1834 daughter of Seth and Sally (Swett) Phinney; Martha d. at Carthage, 1900.

vi   LYDIA HUTCHINSON, b. 22 May 1812; m. 8 Jan 1834, ABNER C. HOLMAN, b. 1801 son of Jonathan and Polly (Cummings) Holman; Abner d. at Lowell, MA, 16 Nov 1865.

vii REUBEN HUTCHINSON, b. 30 May 1814; d. at Carthage, 16 Nov 1904; m. 19 May 1841, ISABEL C. PRATT, b. 19 May 1820 daughter of Seth and Prudence (Judkins) Pratt; Isabel d. at Carthage, 7 Feb 1901.

viii PHEBE HUTCHINSON, b. 18 Dec 1816; d. at Carthage, 16 Jul 1866; m. 26 Nov 1840, REUBEN FRENCH, b. at Lewiston, 11 Jan 1819 son of William and Rachel (Bumpus) French; Reuben d. at East Rochester, NH, 22 Sep 1890.

ix   LUTHER HUTCHINSON, b. 14 Mar 1819; d. at Carthage, 16 Jun 1844; m. LUCY R. BAKER, b. 1813; Lucy d. at Carthage, 19 Apr 1888.

x   BELINDA HUTCHINSON, b. 7 Dec 1821; d. after 1880 when she was living at Dixfield; m. 10 Mar 1846, HEZEKIAH S. TAYLOR, b. 1813 son of Simeon and Mary (Dale) Taylor; Hezekiah d. at Dixfield, 1879.

xi   ELIZA HUTCHINSON, b. 25 Sep 1825; d. at Carthage, 11 Apr 1833.

1025)   ABIGAIL DALE (*Rhoda Holt Dale⁴, Mary Russell Holt³, John², Robert¹*), b. at Wilton, 7 Nov 1781 daughter of John and Rhoda (Holt) Dale; d. at Wilton, 26 Jan 1852; m. 12 Apr 1804, ABEL FISKE, b. at Wilton, 24 Jul 1784 son of Abel and Anna (Spaulding) Fiske; Abel d. at Wilton, 25 Sep 1877.

Abel Fiske attended Phillips Academy at Exeter but was unable to complete due to illness.[3274] Abigail and Abel went to Weld about a year after their marriage and were there until about 1816 when they returned to Wilton. Abel taught school

[3270] Year: 1850; Census Place: Wilton, Hillsborough, New Hampshire; Roll: 433; Page: 325A

[3271] New Hampshire Wills and Probate, Hillsborough County, volume 80, p 199

[3272] Year: 1850; Census Place: Weld, Franklin, Maine; Roll: 253; Page: 12b

[3273] State of Maine, Weld Vital Records, FHL Film # 007599977, image 165

[3274] Pierce, *Fiske and Fisk Family*, p 380

during the winters for twenty-five years. He worked as a painter and paper hanger. He was deacon of the Second Congregational Society in Wilton.[3275]

Abigail and Abel were parents of nine children.

i   ABEL FISKE, b. at Wilton, 10 Oct 1804; d. at Alstead, NH, 15 Oct 1873; m. at Lowell, MA, 24 Nov 1833, MARIA BROWN, b. 1810; Maria d. at Alstead, 18 Jan 1900.

ii   SARAH PUTNAM FISKE, b. at Weld, 12 May 1806; d. at Boston, 16 Dec 1879; m. at Wilton (also recorded at Tewksbury), 4 Feb 1836, JOHN SPAULDING, b. at Tewksbury, 17 Aug 1804 son of John and Mary (Marshall) Spaulding; John d. at Tewksbury, 11 Jul 1842.

iii ANN SPALDING FISKE, b. at Weld, 18 Mar 1808; d. at Boston, 11 Nov 1878; m. about 1849, as his second wife, OTIS R. FISHER, b. about 1811; Otis d. at Framingham, MA, 11 Jan 1878. Otis was first married to Mary Wright. Ann and Otis do not seem to have been together very long. They were living together in Milford, NH in 1850 with all his children from his first marriage. By 1860, Otis was living in Natick with another wife. In 1860, Ann Fisher was living in Wilton in the home of Henry (age 26) and Sophronia (age 28) Fiske

iv   JOHN DALE FISKE, b. at Weld, 17 Dec 1809; d. at Brookfield, MA, 1 Aug 1892; m. at Pepperell, 18 May 1833, ALMIRA SHATTUCK, b. at Pepperell, 20 Nov 1813 daughter of David and Betsy (Chapman) Shattuck; Almira d. at Brookfield, 30 Nov 1892.

v   ACHSAH FARRAR FISKE, b. at Weld, 29 May 1812; d. at Wilton, 4 Mar 1847. Achsah did not marry.

vi   ABBA DALE FISKE, b. at Weld, 3 Jan 1815; d. at Francestown, 23 Jan 1900; m. at Pepperell, 11 Oct 1836, NATHAN R. MARDEN, b. at Mont Vernon, 7 Oct 1812 son of Nathan and Susann (Stevens) Marden; Nathan d. at Francestown, 27 Sep 1904.

vii HARRIET NEWELL FISKE, b. at Wilton, 4 May 1817; d. at Wilton, 3 Jun 1905. Harriet did not marry.

viii ALLETHENIA HOLT FISKE, b. at Wilton, 20 May 1819; d. after 1900 when she was living in Ventura, CA with one of her children; m. at Lyndeborough, 28 Oct 1841, JOHN JONES, b. at Lyndeborough, 8 Sep 1812 son of Joseph and Ann (Richardson) Jones;[3276] John d. at Colorado Springs, CO, 22 Jun 1889. This family was in Illinois before moving on to Colorado.

ix   MARIA ANTOINETTE FISKE, b. at Wilton, 2 Sep 1821; d. at Dunstable, MA, 5 Aug 1888; m. at Dunstable, MA, 30 Sep 1841, LOWELL WHITCOMB, b. at Dunstable, 25 Jul 1816 son of Rhoda Whitcomb; Lowell d. at Dunstable, 27 Aug 1879.

1026)   MARY DALE (*Rhoda Holt Dale⁴, Mary Russell Holt³, John², Robert¹*), b. at Wilton, 10 Sep 1783 daughter of John and Rhoda (Holt) Dale; d. after 1860 when she was living in Wilton; m. 8 Aug 1811, FREDERICK HUTCHINSON, b. at Wilton 10 Jul 1783 son of Samuel and Mary (Wilkins) Hutchinson; Frederick d. at Wilton, 18 Dec 1850.

Frederick Hutchinson and Mary Dale resided in Wilton where their seven children were born.[3277]

i   CHARLES HUTCHINSON, b. 20 Jan 1812; d. at Pepperell, MA, 31 May 1876; m. 30 Nov 1842, THIRZA SHATTUCK, b. at Pepperell, 13 Feb 1804 daughter of David and Betsy (Chapman) Shattuck; Thirza d. at Pepperell, 22 Apr 1893.

ii   MARY D. HUTCHINSON, b. 20 Oct 1813; d. at Wilton, 29 Jan 1880; m. 28 Apr 1840, NATHANIEL HESSELTON, b. at Wilton, 13 Aug 1811 son of Nathan and Prudence (Baldwin) Hesselton; Nathaniel d. at Wilton, 11 Sep 1881.

iii LYDIA HUTCHINSON, b. 5 Feb 1816; d. 1818.

iv   ABEL F. HUTCHINSON, b. 27 Jun 1818; d. at Santa Rosa, CA, 23 Mar 1875; m. about 1838, MARY MOWRY, b. in PA, about 1818; Mary d. after 1880 when she was living at Mechanicsburg, OH. Abel and Mary lived in Mechanicsburg through 1860. Abel then went to California where he died, and Mary remained in Ohio. In his will, he left his entire estate to his wife Mary Hutchinson and son Wilton Hutchinson of Mechanicsburg, OH.[3278]

v   LYMAN HUTCHINSON, b. 20 Oct 1820; d. 19 Mar 1822.

[3275] Livermore, *History of the Town of Wilton*, p 366
[3276] Donovan, The History of Lyndeborough, p 790. John Jones's gravestone in Colorado Springs includes in the engraving that he was born in Lyndeborough in 1812.
[3277] Livermore, *History of the Town of Wilton*, p 417
[3278] California Wills and Probate, Sonoma County, Wills Volume B, p 161

vi LYDIA HUTCHINSON, b. 27 Feb 1823

vii LYMAN F. HUTCHINSON, b. 13 Sep 1827; d. at Milford, NH, 28 Jan 1888; m. 1st 15 May 1852, JOANNA SOPHRONIA HUTCHINSON, b. 6 Aug 1836 daughter of Robert and Eliza Ann (Holt) Hutchinson; Joanna d. at Milford, 16 Apr 1881. Lyman m. 2nd at Milford, 24 Nov 1886, ADALINE S. FARWELL (widow of Rodney Tapley), b. at Milford, 20 Jul 1833 daughter of James B. and Sophia (Hutchinson) Farwell; Adaline d. at Milford, 10 Sep 1909.

1027) JOHN DALE (*Rhoda Holt Dale⁴, Mary Russell Holt³, John², Robert¹*), b. at Wilton, 3 Aug 1785 son of John and Rhoda (Holt) Dale; d. at Wilton, 12 Apr 1843; m. 1st at Sandwich, 3 Oct 1822, NANCY BEEDE, b. at Sandwich, NH, 1796 son of John and Sarah (Sleeper) Beede;[3279] Nancy d. at Wilton, 7 Oct 1825. John m. 2nd at New Boston, 3 May 1827, MARY ANN COCHRAN, b. at New Boston, about 1805 daughter of James and Jane (Crombie) Cochran;[3280] Mary d. at New Boston, 4 Oct 1876.

John and Nancy were parents of one child.

i NANCY BEEDE DALE, b. at Wilton, Aug 1825; d. at Wilton, 24 Jun 1844.

John Dale and Mary Ann Cochran were parents of three children.

i ELIZA J. C. DALE, b. at Wilton, 20 Jan 1828; d. at Keene, 5 Dec 1893; m. 4 Jan 1855, GEORGE GREENWOOD, b. at Dublin, NH, 1822 son of Joshua and Sally (Davis) Greenwood;[3281] George d. at New Boston, 15 Jan 1889.

ii MERCIA A. C. DALE, b. at Wilton, 1833; d. at Concord at the home for the aged, 26 Apr 1916. Mercia did not marry.

iii JOHN FRANKLIN DALE, b. at Wilton, 1 Aug 1835; d. at New Boston, 24 Sep 1854.

1028) EBENEZER DALE (*Rhoda Holt Dale⁴, Mary Russell Holt³, John², Robert¹*), b. at Wilton, 17 Mar 1788 son of John and Rhoda (Holt) Dale; d. at Sandwich, NH, 1 Sep 1862; m. about 1824, MEHITABLE BEEDE, b. at Sandwich, 12 Apr 1800 daughter of John and Sarah (Sleeper) Beede;[3282] Mehitable d. at Sandwich, 14 Aug 1861.

A detailed description of Ebenezer Dale's farming activity is provided by the Sandwich Historical Society. Ebenezer had what was described as a "rich" farm of 100 acres in Sandwich, New Hampshire. Ebenezer kept cattle, sheep, hogs, geese, and turkeys and raised crops of corn, potatoes, wheat, and oats, and grew cherries and apples. They raised melons, cucumbers, and squash in the house garden. Ebenezer was described as an invalid, but the nature of his disability was not described. Ebenezer sold his farm to Charles Atwood.[3283]

Ebenezer and Mehitable were parents of four children born at their house in Sandwich, New Hampshire.

i JOHN B. DALE, b. at Sandwich, about 1833; d. at Belmont, NH, 17 Jan 1887. John did not marry.

ii SARAH E. DALE, b. at Sandwich, about 1837; d. at Sandwich, 15 Feb 1891; m. at Sandwich, 31 Mar 1860, GEORGE GRUDY, b. at Bristol, 24 Mar 1831 son of Jacob and Susan (Doton) Gurdy; George d. at Sandwich, 4 Aug 1898. George married second Emily Ethridge on 1 Apr 1892.

iii EBEN H. DALE, b. 1839; d. at Frederick County, VA, 23 Nov 1864. Eben was wounded at the Third Battle of Winchester on 19 Sep 1864 which resulted in the amputation of his left arm. He died of his wounds on 23 Nov 1864.[3284] Eben had enlisted in the 14th Regiment on 13 Aug 1862.

iv MARY HARRIET DALE, b. at Sandwich, 29 Jul 1842; d. at Hoopeston, IL, 9 Dec 1917; m. at Sandwich, 12 Feb 1865, CHARLES H. SEAVEY, b. at Sandwich, Nov 1837 son of Jesse and Sarah J. (Norris) Seavey; Charles d. at Hoopeston, 31 May 1911.

[3279] The 1841 will of John Beede of Sandwich includes bequests to his granddaughter Nancy B. Dale child of his deceased daughter and to his daughter Mehitable Dale (who married Ebenezer Dale).
[3280] Mary Ann's parents are given as James and Jane Cochran on her death record.
[3281] The names of George's parents are given as Joshua Greenwood and Sally Davis on his death record.
[3282] The 1841 will of John Beede of Sandwich includes a bequest to his daughter Mehitable Dale.
[3283] Sandwich Historical Society, "Twenty-First Annual Excursion of the Sandwich Historical Society", Thursday, August 22, 1940, Covering the Diamond Ledge Section, Sandwich, N.H., pp 39-41
[3284] Longver, *New Hampshire Civil War Death and Burial Locations*

1029) BETSEY DALE (*Rhoda Holt Dale⁴, Mary Russell Holt³, John², Robert¹*), b. at Wilton, 10 Jul 1793 daughter of John and Rhoda (Holt) Dale; d. at Milford, NH, Mar 1852; m. 7 Dec 1815, JESSE RAYMOND, b. at Mont Vernon, 1792 son of Nathaniel and Phebe (Dodge) Raymond;[3285] Jesse d. at Milford, 14 Jul 1864. Jesse was second married to Nancy.

 Jesse Raymond was a blacksmith and farmer. In his will written 7 May 1864 (proved 26 July 1864), Jesse Raymond of Milford bequeathed to beloved wife Nancy $500. Son John G. Raymond received five dollars. The remainder of the estate, real and personal, was bequeathed to his grandchildren, Abby Josephine Raymond and David E. Raymond, the children of John G. Raymond. John Bruce of Milford was named executor.[3286]

i JOHN GOODELL RAYMOND, b. at Mont Vernon, 1816; d. at Milford, NH, 13 Jan 1885; m. 1st at Milford, 1839, ROXANA HUTCHINSON, b. at Milford, 21 Nov 1815 daughter of Alfred and Lydia (Foster) Hutchinson; Roxanna d. at Milford, 1854. John m. 2nd, 20 Mar 1856, ABIGAIL BULLARD, b. 1818 daughter of John and Rosana (Mills) Bullard; Rosana d. 1858. John m. 3rd at Milford, 20 Mar 1877, NANCY J. CILLEY[3287] (widow Mrs. Hill), b. about 1823.

ii DAVID GOODELL RAYMOND, b. 1819; d. at Milford, 7 Sep 1843.

1030) SARAH DALE (*Rhoda Holt Dale⁴, Mary Russell Holt³, John², Robert¹*), b. at Wilton, 4 Aug 1797 daughter of John and Rhoda (Holt) Dale; d. at Weld, ME, 17 May 1862; m. 25 Dec 1817, JOHN BURTON, b. at Wilton, 25 Oct 1796 son of Abraham and Elizabeth (Dale) Burton; John d. at Weld, 24 Feb 1873.

 John Burton was a cabinetmaker and the family lived in Wilton until 1850.[3288] John and Sarah were in Weld, Maine in later life where both are buried.

 John and Sarah were parents of five children born at Wilton, New Hampshire.

i JOHN DALE BURTON, b. 1 Oct 1818; d. after 1865 when living at Boston; m. at Wilton, 4 Apr 1843, MARIA MASON, b. at Wilton, NH, 3 Apr 1822 daughter of Larkin and Hannah (Heald) Mason; Maria d. at Boston, 13 Mar 1866.

ii SARAH BURTON, b. 22 May 1820

iii ABRAHAM BURTON, b. 22 Apr 1822; d. at Manchester, NH, 1870; m. 1st at Nashua, NH, 18 Nov 1847, HARRIET NICHOLS, b. 1827; Harriet d. at Manchester, 24 Apr 1848. Abraham m. 2nd at Nashua, 23 Nov 1848, NANCY CAROLINE GREEN, b. at Hillsborough, NH, 16 Feb 1825 daughter of David and Rachel (Ormsby) Green; Nancy d. at Manchester, 29 Sep 1856; Abraham m. 3rd about 1857, RACHEL ANN PARKHURST, b. at Wilton, NH, 28 Jan 1826 daughter of Jonathan and Betsey (Burton) Parkhurst; Rachel d. at Manchester, 27 Mar 1871.

iv BETSEY DALE BURTON, b. 25 Apr 1824; d. at Auburn, ME, 10 Jun 1886; m. 5 Oct 1853, WILSON DODGE, b. at Franklin, ME, 3 Feb 1829 son of James and Rachel (Curtis) Dodge; Wilson d. at Auburn, 6 Feb 1897.

v CAROLINE L. BURTON, b. 18 Sep 1826; d. at Wilton, ME, 11 Feb 1911; m. about 1847, NATHANIEL L. FLETCHER, b. at Wilton, 20 Jan 1822 son of Abner and Elizabeth (Lyford) Fletcher; Nathaniel d. at Wilton, ME, 28 Jan 1900.

1031) NANCY HOLT (*Valentine Holt⁴, Mary Russell Holt³, John², Robert¹*), b. at Wilton, 13 Mar 1788 daughter of Valentine and Anna (Goodrich) Holt; m. at Charlestown, MA, 31 May 1812, JAMES WHITTIER who is not yet identified.

 The family was living in Charlestown, Third Parish, on 7 August 1820 and the census record suggests as many as four children with one male under 10, two males 16-25, two females under 10, and one female 16-25. Also in the home were two males 26 to 44, one female 26 to 44, and one female over 45.[3289] The four children under age 10 might be children of Nancy and James given their marriage in 1812. Just two children have been identified.

i EMILY WHITTIER, b. at Charlestown, 1813; d. at Quincy, MA, 23 Mar 1897; m. 1st at Boston, 18 Apr 1833, EDMUND PARSONS, b. at Boston, 1811 son of Edmund and Esther (Badger) Parsons; Edmund d. at Boston, 7 Feb 1842. Emily m. 2nd at Quincy, 25 Mar 1846, ISAAC T. NEWCOMB, b. at Quincy, 1818 son of Isaac and Sally

[3285] Smith, *History of the Town of Mont Vernon*, Genealogies, p 128
[3286] *New Hampshire. Probate Court (Hillsborough County), Probate Records, Vol 75-78, 1861-1877, volume 76, pp 185-186*
[3287] Smith, *History of Mont Vernon*, p 128
[3288] Year: 1850; Census Place: Wilton, Hillsborough, New Hampshire; Roll: 433; Page: 321b
[3289] 1820 U S Census; Census Place: Charlestown Third Parish, Middlesex, Massachusetts; Page: 386; NARA Roll: M33_51; Image: 247

(Mead) Newcomb; Isaac d. at Quincy, 1 Apr 1863. Isaac died of illness in Quincy, although he was a Union soldier in the Massachusetts infantry at the time of his death.

ii   ADELINE WHITTIER, b. at Charlestown, 12 Aug 1815; d. at Weymouth, MA, 8 Jul 1888; m. at Weymouth, 12 Mar 1834, JOSHUA PHILLIPS, b. at Weymouth, 20 Mar 1812 son of Isaac and Rhoda (Litchfield) Phillips; Joshua d. at Weymouth, 30 May 1895.

1032)   AMMI RUHAMA HOLT (*Valentine Holt⁴, Mary Russell Holt³, John², Robert¹*), b. at Wilton, 8 Jun 1789 son of Valentine and Anna (Goodrich) Holt; d. at Clayton, NY, 1827;[3290] m. MARTHA ABBOTT, b. about 1800; Martha d. at Clayton, 28 Jan 1850.

     Ammi served in the War of 1812 enlisting from Wilton for the duration of the war on 17 May 1813. He was described as 5'6 ½" with blue eyes and dark hair. He served in companies of Capt. Adams and Capt. Foster and was discharged 30 June 1815.[3291]

     There are three children known for Ammi and Martha.

i   LOUISA HOLT, b. likely at Wilton, NH, 1820; d. at Clayton, NY, 28 Jul 1872; m. about 1840, EBENEZER KNAPP STEELE, b. at Brownville, NY, 13 May 1814 son of George R. and Tamson (Knapp) Steele; Ebenezer d. at Clayton, 26 Nov 1899.

ii   LEANDER A. HOLT, b. 23 Mar 1825 (on gravestone); d. at Potsdam, NY, 3 Aug 1891; m. 1st estimated 1850, NANCY L. SMITH, b. about 1828 daughter of Benjamin Smith; Nancy d. (burial at Potsdam), 3 Jan 1878. Leander m. 2nd about 1856, LAURA A. DART, b. 1838 daughter of Charles J. and Olive (Bailey) Dart;[3292] Laura d. at Potsdam, 18 Feb 1921. Leander's first marriage ended apparently in divorce. Nancy and Leander were together in 1855 in Clayton. Leander Holt was a ship captain.

iii   AMY E. HOLT, b. at Clayton, Jun 1827; d. at Clayton, 1855. Amy did not marry.

1033)   LYDIA PORTER HOLT (*Valentine Holt⁴, Mary Russell Holt³, John², Robert¹*), b. at Wilton, 13 May 1793 daughter of Valentine and Anna (Goodrich) Holt; d. at Barre, VT, 9 Feb 1868; m. at Lyndeborough, 25 May 1815, ROBERT PARKER, b. 1789 likely son of Robert and Rebecca (Carlton) Parker; Robert d. at Barre, 7 Apr 1831.

     There are four children known for Lydia Holt and Robert Parker, the births of the three oldest children recorded at Elmore, Vermont.

i   MARY ANN PARKER, b. 19 Oct 1815; d. at Hyde Park, VT, 4 Feb 1897; m. 1843, ABEL PUTNAM, b. at Bethel, VT, 1806 son of Joshua and Lucy (Lathrop) Putnam; Abel d. at Hyde Park, 8 Sep 1892.

ii   NANCY HOLT PARKER, b. 18 Aug 1821; d. at Barre, VT, 17 Feb 1919; m. at Barre, 16 Dec 1841, BENJAMIN ORRIN WOOD, b. at Barre, 12 Jan 1817 son of Benjamin O. and Jane (Towne) Wood; Benjamin d. at Barre, 25 Oct 1910.

iii   REBECCA C. PARKER, b. 25 Mar 1823; d. at Cambridge, VT, 17 Jan 1912; m. at Barre, 15 Mar 1842, WILLIAM S. NOYES, b. at Barre, 17 Jan 1819 son of William and Mary (Sargent) Noyes; William d. at Cambridge, VT, 15 May 1907.

iv   EDNAH PARKER, b. 1828; d. at Barre, 16 Mar 1830.

1034)   HANNAH GOODRICH HOLT (*Valentine Holt⁴, Mary Russell Holt³, John², Robert¹*), b. at Wilton, 15 May 1795 daughter of Valentine and Anna (Goodrich) Holt; d. at Charlestown, MA, 24 Jun 1858; m. at Charlestown, MA, 7 Oct 1818, JOHN SYLVESTER, b. about 1788; John d. of consumption, at Charlestown, 14 Dec 1848.

     John Sylvester and Hannah Goodrich Holt were parents of six children born at Charlestown, Massachusetts.

i   CAROLINE M. SYLVESTER, b. 20 May 1819; d. at San Francisco, CA, 16 Sep 1907; m. at Charlestown, 22 Oct 1846, FRANCIS SISSON, b. 1812 son of Robert H. and Mary (Calef) Sisson; Francis d. at Boston, 17 Nov 1870.

ii   HELEN AUGUSTA SYLVESTER, b. 5 Jun 1825; d. 1826.[3293]

[3290] Ammi and Martha are buried together at Clayton Village Cemetery, Clayton, New York; findagrave: 101002797

[3291] U.S. Army, Register of Enlistments, 1798-1914

[3292] Leander A. Holt was named administrator of the estate of Charles J. Dart in 1870.

[3293] U.S., Newspaper Extractions from the Northeast, 1704-1930; daughter of John age 1.

iii   HELEN AUGUSTA SYLVESTER, b. about 1828; d. at San Francisco, 22 Feb 1894; m. Charlestown, 7 Jan 1861, JOHN WERNER SCHAEFFER, b. Darmstadt, Germany, 1833 son of John and Amelia (Zimmerman) Schaeffer;[3294] John d. after 1888 when he was listed in the voter register.

iv   FRANCES MARIA SYLVESTER, b. 8 Jun 1831; d. at Los Angeles, 14 Apr 1908; m. 1st at Charlestown, 20 Oct 1853, ASAHEL E. GOULD, b. at Newton, 1831 son of Asahel and Margaret (Whitney) Gould. France m. 2nd at Charlestown, 17 Jul 1863, JOSIAH PRAY, b. at Braintree, 1819 son of George and Sarah (Pratt) Pray; Josiah d. at Weymouth, 27 Jun 1873. Asahel Gould seems to have died at New Haven, CT in 1902 so it may be that Frances and Asahel divorced.

v   SARAH ISABELLA SYLVESTER, b. about 1834; d. at San Francisco, 8 Nov 1918; m. 1st about 1855, THORNTON DAVID SANBORN, b, at Reading, MA, 9 Jan 1826 son of Benjamin C. and Lucinda (Temple) Sanborn; Thornton d. at Reading, 2 Feb 1892. Sarah and Thornton divorced by about 1868 and Thornton, who had been in San Francisco, returned to Massachusetts.[3295] Sarah m. 2nd at San Francisco, 29 Feb 1872, ADOLPHUS SKINNER HUBBARD,[3296] b. at DuPage County, IL, 7 Jul 1838 son of Theodore and Anne Ward (Ballou) Hubbard; Adolphus d. at San Francisco, 29 Jan 1913. Sarah and Thornton had a son William Edgar Sanborn who lived with Sarah and her second husband Adolphus.

vi   JOHN E. SYLVESTER, b. 1837; d. at Charlestown, 14 Jun 1858.

1035)   ROBERT GOODRICH HOLT (*Valentine Holt⁴, Mary Russell Holt³, John², Robert¹*), b. at Wilton, 15 Jan 1802 son of Valentine and Anna (Goodrich) Holt; d. after 1850; m. at Lyndeborough, 10 Sep 1822, LUCY LAKIN, b. at Lyndeborough, about 1802 daughter of Thomas and Lucy (Burton) Lakin; Lucy d. at Lyndeborough, 9 May 1850.
    There is record evidence (from marriage and death records) of five children of Robert Holt and Lucy Lakin. The children may have been born in Lyndeborough.

i   NANCY JANE HOLT, b. about 1825; d. at Andover, MA, about 1859; m. at Andover, 6 Jan 1848, WILLIAM MOODY, b. at Limington, ME, 1821 son of George and Susan (-) Moody (per William's marriage records); William d. at Greensboro, VT, 24 Apr 1899. William married second at Andover widow Sarah Jane Reed (widow of William Peel) on 29 Mar 1860.

ii   THOMAS LAKIN HOLT, b. about 1827; d. at Pawtucket, RI, 1889; m. at Boston, 28 Jul 1852, PHEBE E. MARBLE, b. at Warner, RI, 1829 daughter of Francis and Phebe (Smith) Marble; Phebe d. at Pawtucket, 29 Oct 1914.

iii   JOHN B. HOLT,[3297] b. reported as Claremont, NH, 1831; d. at New Boston, NH, 10 Mar 1892; m. at Dedham, MA, 1 Jan 1863, SARAH E. CROSBY, b. at Dedham, about 1840 daughter of Edmund and Rachel (Newell) Crosby; Sarah d. at Wentworth, NH, 29 Apr 1905.

iv   LUCY ANN HOLT, b. about 1833; d. at Haverhill, MA, 9 Jun 1887; m. at Andover, MA, 16 Nov 1851, STEPHEN T. OSGOOD, b. at Haverhill, 1830 son of James and Sarah (Chase) Osgood; Stephen d. at Haverhill, 14 Feb 1904.

v   ELLEN M. HOLT, b. about 1839; d. at Haverhill, MA, 6 Jan 1854.

1036)   VALENTINE HOLT (*Valentine Holt⁴, Mary Russell Holt³, John², Robert¹*), b. 18 Nov 1812 son of Valentine and Hannah (Day) Holt; d. at Chelsea, ME, 22 Jan 1899; m. about 1836, MARY ANN MORRILL, b. about 1814; Mary Ann d. at Augusta, ME, after 1870 and before 1880.
    In 1860, the family resided in Augusta, Maine with Valentine's occupation listed as laborer. Six children were home at that time from Charles age 19 to 2-year old Ada.[3298]
    Valentine served in the Civil War in company B of the 16th infantry, mustered in on 14 August 1862 and mustered out on 5 June 1865. He was listed as sick and in hospital on 15 June 1863.[3299]

[3294] The names of John's parents and place of birth are given on the marriage record to Helen; Massachusetts, Town and Vital Records, 1620-1988
[3295] Thornton D. Sanborn was living with parents Benjamin C. and Lucinda Sanborn in Medford, MA in 1880; Year: 1880; Census Place: Medford, Middlesex, Massachusetts; Roll: 541; Page: 103A; Enumeration District: 404
[3296] Sons of the American Revolution, Addresses Delivered Before the California Society of the SAR, volume 1, p 105, Biographical sketches by Thomas Allen Perkins, San Francisco, CA, 1913, Published by the society
[3297] John's parents' names are given as Lucy Lakin and Willian G. Holt on his death record, but he likely goes in this family as he was living with Robert G. Holt in Andover in 1850, so likely the death record is just an error of father's first name.
[3298] "United States Census, 1860", database with images, *FamilySearch* (https://familysearch.org/ark:/61903/1:1:MDHG-MV6 : 18 March 2020), Valentine Holt, 1860.
[3299] U.S., Civil War Soldier Records and Profiles, 1861-1865; Historical Data Systems, Inc.; Duxbury, MA 02331; American Civil War Research Database

Valentine and Mary were parents of ten children born at Augusta, Maine.

i   MARY ELIZABETH HOLT, b. 6 Dec 1837; d. at Augusta, 29 Aug 1918; m. 1852, GEORGE F. TAYLOR, b. at Gardiner, ME, 11 Aug 1835 son of Dudley H. and Tabitha W. (Taylor) Taylor; George d. at Farmingdale, ME, 24 Dec 1915.

ii   SUSAN HOLT, b. 20 Jan 1839; m. about 1860, EBEN B. SHOREY, b. at Augusta, ME, about 1819; Eben d. at Augusta after 1870 and before 1880. Susan was living in Augusta in 1882.

iii   CHARLES H. HOLT, b. 20 Apr 1841; m. about 1870, FRANCES A. DAVIS. Charles served in the 1st Maine Calvary during the Civil War, survived the war,[3300] but was at the Togus Home for Disabled Volunteer Soldiers in 1880 for an unspecified "disease of the head."[3301] His widow Frances began receiving a widow's pension in 1893.

iv   ABBIE HOLT, b. 5 Dec 1843; d. after 1920 when living at Vassalboro, ME; m. 1st about 1862, JOHN ROLLINS, b. at Augusta, about 1837 son of Joseph and Mary (Wixon) Rollins; John d. before 1890. Abbie m. 2nd at Boston, 15 Feb 1893, TIMOTHY A. LEIGHTON, b. at Levant, ME, about 1846 son of Hiram and Nancy (Sanborn) Leighton; Timothy d. after 1920.

v   ANNA MARIA HOLT, b. 29 Sep 1845; d. at Boston, 31 Dec 1902; m. at Augusta, 6 Feb 1866, WILSON HAWES, b. about 1845.

vi   JOHN RICHMOND HOLT, b. 17 Jan 1847; d. at Hallowell, ME, 8 Feb 1897; m. at Augusta, 10 Mar 1866, ARVESTA A. HORN, b. 4 May 1845 daughter of Ichabod and Rossa (Howe) Horn; Arvesta d. at Gardiner, ME, 18 Feb 1923.

vii   EMMA JANE HOLT, b. 20 Jul 1850; died young

viii   EMMA JANE HOLT, b. 13 Mar 1852

ix   CALVIN HOLT, b. 11 Mar 1854

x   ADA IDELLA HOLT, b. Sep 1858; d. after 1932 when she was living at Portland; m. 1st at Leeds, ME, 22 Aug 1877, JOSEPH A. TRASK, b. 1858 son of John and Elizabeth (Hinman) Trask; Joseph d. in 1917, but he and Ada divorced by 1895 when Ada remarried. Ada m. 2nd 28 Mar 1895, JOHN S. RAYMOND, b. 1848 son of Hiram and Sarah (Smith) Raymond. The second marriage was short-lived as John married again in 1897. Ada had three children with Joseph Trask.

1037)   SARAH D. HOLT (*Valentine Holt⁴, Mary Russell Holt³, John², Robert¹*), b. about 1818 daughter of Valentine and Hannah (Day) Holt;[3302] d. at Boston, 28 Feb 1874; m. HENRY D. BROWN, b. in ME, about 1818; Henry d. during the Civil War, enlisted 29 Feb 1864 and did not survive the war.[3303]

Sarah and Henry lived in Maine where Henry was a blacksmith. In the 1860 census, the family was living in Bath with seven children in the home ranging in age from 15 to 1.[3304] In 1870, Sarah was living in Jay, Maine with then with four children with her including 8 year old Maria.[3305] The eight children identified from census records are given here.

i   GEORGE F. BROWN, b. at Augusta, ME, 1845; d. at Boston, 22 Dec 1910; m. about 1867, LILLIAN W. WEBBER, b. at Chesterville, ME, Oct 1848 daughter of John C. and Hannah (West) Webber; Lillian d. after 1910 when living at Boston.

ii   CHARLES H. BROWN, b. at Augusta, Oct 1848; d. in an auto accident at Cambridge, MA, 9 Nov 1918; m. at Boston, 7 Oct 1879, CELANIRA "NINA" DAVISON, b. in Nova Scotia, Apr 1858 daughter of Thomas and Sarah (Fletcher) Davison; Celanira d. at Natick, 1933.

iii   VALENTINE HOLT BROWN, b. in ME, 1849; in 1870, he was living in Jay, ME with his mother.

iv   AUGUSTUS C. BROWN, b. in ME, 1853

[3300] U.S., Civil War Soldier Records and Profiles, 1861-1865

[3301] U.S. National Homes for Disabled Volunteer Soldiers, 1866-1938; Charles H. Holt, father Valentine Holt.

[3302] Names of parents are given as Valentine Holt and Hannah on her death record.

[3303] Henry D. Brown enlisted at age 43 while resident of Jay, Maine; enlisted 29 Feb 1864; muster date 29 Feb 1864 in company B of the 29th Infantry; mustered out due to death, 29 Jul 1864; U.S., Civil War Soldier Records and Profiles, 1861-1865

[3304] Year: 1860; Census Place: Bath, Sagadahoc, Maine; Page: 183; Family History Library Film: 803448

[3305] Year: 1870; Census Place: Jay, Franklin, Maine; Roll: M593_543; Page: 106B; Family History Library Film: 552042

v   CLARENCE E. BROWN, b. in ME, 1855; in 1880, was serving as a private in the army stationed at Corpus Christi, TX.[3306]

vi   MARTHA BROWN, b. in ME, 1857; in 1870, she was living with her mother in Jay.

vii   LYDIA A. BROWN, b. in ME, 1859; in 1870, she was living with her mother in Jay.

viii   MARIA A. BROWN, b. in ME, 1862; in 1870, she was living with her mother in Jay.

1038)   MARY HARRICK HOLT (*Valentine Holt⁴, Mary Russell Holt³, John², Robert¹*), b. at Rome, ME, 23 Apr 1818 daughter of Valentine and Hannah (Day) Holt; d. at Chelsea, MA, 1 Jan 1906; m. at Lowell, MA, 1 Aug 1842, SAMUEL ALDEN RICH, b. 25 Aug 1812 son of Ezekiel and Elizabeth (Brown) Rich; Samuel d. at Chelsea, MA, 5 Aug 1890.

Samuel Rich was a sailor and the family lived at Chelsea. In 1850, the family consisted of Samuel, Mary, and three sons William H. age 7, Harris age 5, and George E. age 0 (3/12).[3307] In 1860, the family was living in Boston 3ʳᵈ ward with family of Samuel and Mary and children Harris R. age 15, John R. age 11, Isadore age 5, Mary F. age 3, and Charles age 0. Also in the home was William H. Slade age 13.[3308] William H. Slade was son of Mary's sister Anna and her husband Henry Slade. In 1870 at East Boston, the household consisted of Samuel, Mary, and children Harris R. age 25, John R. age 22, Isadore age 15, Mary age 13, and Charles age 10.[3309]

Mary Harrick Holt and Samuel Alden Rich were parents of seven children.

i   WILLIAM H. RICH, b. at Hallowell, 23 Jun 1843 (death record); d. at Somersworth, NH, 23 Sep 1914.[3310] In 1860, William H. Rich was living with the family of Samuel and Lydia Willett in Somersworth. William served as corporal in the 4ᵗʰ Infantry. He was wounded at Morris Island, SC on 8 Sep 1863 which resulted in the amputation of his left leg. He was mustered out of the service from St. Joseph's Hospital in NY on 1 Jun 1864. He was awarded the Gilmore Medal.[3311] The occupation given on his death record was door keeper at the House of Representatives. William did not marry.

ii   HARRIS R. RICH, b. at Machias, ME, 17 Sep 1845; Harris d. at Chelsea, MA, 11 Jul 1915. Harris did not marry. Harris served as a sailor during the Civil War.

iii   GEORGE E. RICH, b. 1849

iv   JOHN REEVES RICH, b. at Augusta, ME, 23 Mar 1852;[3312] d. at Cambridge, MA, 6 Aug 1928; m. 1ˢᵗ at Chelsea, 25 Jul 1874, ADELAIDE L. HOYT, b. at Charlestown, 3 Sep 1852 daughter of Jason Taylor and Elizabeth B. (Caton) Hoyt. John m. 2ⁿᵈ at Cambridge, 27 May 1908, MINNIE ADELAIDE RICE, b. at Cambridge, 1867 daughter of John S. and Adeline E. (Miller) Rice; Minnie d. at Cambridge, 1928.

v   ISADORE P. RICH, b. in NH, May 1854 (census records); d. after 1940 when she was living in Chelsea with her son; m. at Boston, 8 Oct 1873, FRANK A. JONES, b. at Hyannis, 1847 son of Franklin and Harriet (-) Jones; Frank d. at Chelsea, 31 Jul 1920.

vi   MARY FRANCES RICH, b. at Berwick, ME, 1857; d. at Everett, MA, 2 Dec 1877; m. at East Boston, 18 Oct 1876, ANDREW PHILLIPS, b. at Boston, 1847 son of William W. and Phebe F. (Blackman) Phillips.

vii   CHARLES DIAMOND RICH, b. at Boston, 4 May 1860; d. after 1920 when he was living at Chelsea. Charles did not marry.

1039)   ANNA T. HOLT (*Valentine Holt⁴, Mary Russell Holt³, John², Robert¹*), b. at Mercer, ME, about 1819 daughter of Valentine and Hannah (Day) Holt; d. at Charlestown, MA, 6 Aug 1873;[3313] m. 1ˢᵗ at Hallowell, ME, 4 Jun 1842, HENRY C. SLADE. Anna m. 2ⁿᵈ C. C. FOSTER who is not yet identified.

[3306] Year: 1880; Census Place: Corpus Christi, Nueces, Texas; Roll: 1322; Page: 28C; Enumeration District: 116; Clarence E. Brown, age 25, born in Maine, private in company F of 2ⁿᵈ regiment of U.S. artillery

[3307] Year: 1850; Census Place: Charlestown, Middlesex, Massachusetts; Roll: 322; Page: 153b

[3308] "United States Census, 1860", database with images, *FamilySearch* (https://familysearch.org/ark:/61903/1:1:MZCC-MCJ : 19 March 2020), Saml A Rich, 1860.

[3309] Year: 1870; Census Place: East Boston, Suffolk, Massachusetts; Roll: M593_640; Page: 226B; Family History Library Film: 552139

[3310] William's death index record names parents as Samuel Rich and Mary Hoyt.

[3311] Historical Data Systems, comp. *U.S., Civil War Soldier Records and Profiles, 1861-1865* [database on-line]. Provo, UT, USA: Ancestry.com Operations Inc, 2009.

[3312] This is the date and place of birth given on his Mason membership card.

[3313] Ann T. Foster daughter of Valentine and Hannah Holt died of consumption; Massachusetts, Town and Vital Records, 1620-1988

Three children were identified for Anna Holt and Henry Slade. Ann Slade and her three children were living with her mother Hannah Holt at Hallowell in 1850.[3314]

i   HARRIET F. SLADE, b. at Hallowell, 1842; d. at Boston, 9 Jan 1891; m. at Boston, 14 Nov 1858, CHARLES F. DIMOND, b. about 1835 son of Asa L. and Jane (Garmon) Dimond; Charles d. at Boston, 6 Mar 1914. Charles was a carpet layer. He died by suicide: "an incised wound to the neck".[3315]

ii   WILLIAM H. SLADE, b. at Hallowell, Apr 1844; d. after 1920 when he was living at Chelsea with his cousin Isadore Rich Jones; m. 1st at Charlestown, 25 Oct 1866, GEORGIANNA HOYT, b. at Charlestown, 5 Jun 1850 daughter of Jason Taylor and Elizabeth B. (Caton) Hoyt; Georgianna d. at Lawrence, 27 Jul 1919. William and Georgianna divorced by 1876 when Georgianna married William Henry Oakes. William m. 2nd at Boston, 13 Jul 1881, ELLA AUGUSTA CROSBY, b. at Salem, 21 Sep 1855 daughter of Roswell A. and Mary A. (Richards) Crosby; Ella d. at Chelsea, 9 Nov 1900. William was a cabinetmaker.

iii   JOHN ANDREW SLADE, b. 1849; d. at Boston, 3 Oct 1850.

1040)   WESLEY RUSSELL HOLT (*Valentine Holt⁴, Mary Russell Holt³, John², Robert¹*), b. at Mercer, 10 Aug 1829 son of Valentine and Hannah (Day) Holt; d. at South Gardiner, ME, 28 Jan 1902; m. at Somersworth, NH, 4 Apr 1850, ANN WITHAM, b. 1830; Ann d. at Hallowell, ME, 31 Aug 1869. Wesley m. 2nd, 1772, MARY LOUISE BOYD, b. in ME, May 1838; Mary Louise d. 1907.

Wesley R. Holt, who often went by Russell Holt, was a gardener and laborer in Augusta. Wesley and Ann were parents of eight children born at Augusta, Maine.

i   JACOB WILLIAM HOLT, b. 11 Jan 1851; d. at South Gardiner, 31 Jan 1926; m. 1st at Augusta, 1870, LEONORA V. RICHARDSON, b. at Pittston, ME, 26 Sep 1850 daughter of Ebenezer and Abbie E. A. (Smith) Richardson; Leonora d. 22 May 1873. Jacob m. 2nd, 1874, HONORA ELLA "NORA" HOLBROOK, b. 28 Sep 1857 daughter of Israel W. and Rachel (Taylor) Holbrook; Nora d. at Gardiner, 23 Feb 1939.

ii   VALENTINE HOLT, b. Aug 1853; d. at New Sharon, ME, 1927; m. 1880, ETTA ELMIRA AUSTIN, b. at Phippsburg, 10 May 1856 daughter of Edward and Lydia (French) Austin; Etta d. 7 Jul 1936.

iii   WESLEY R. HOLT, b. 15 Apr 1856; d. at Allentown, PA, 28 Jul 1923; m. at Rockport, MA, 12 Dec 1891, LYDIA J. HAYES (first married to William Ridley), b. at Halifax, Nova Scotia, 11 Jul 1854 daughter of James and Elizabeth M. (Garret) Hayes; Lydia d. at Allentown, 10 Sep 1929.

iv   HANNAH HOLT, b. Nov 1857; d. at Augusta, 3 Dec 1907; m. 1888, JOHN R. WILLIAMS, b. at Gardiner, 2 Sep 1851 son of James and Eliza (Johnson) Williams; John d. at Gardiner, 28 Apr 1917. John married second Georgianna *Lynn* Johnson.

v   JOHN HOLT, b. 1859; d. 1862.

vi   HARRIET ELA HOLT,[3316] b. Aug 1861; d. at South Gardiner, 4 Aug 1928; m. 1887, WILBUR JORDAN, b. at Gardiner, Aug 1864 son of Thomas M. and Martha J. (Pollard) Jordan; Wilbur d. likely at Randolph, ME (burial at South Gardiner) 1943.

vii   MELVINA HOLT, b. 1863

viii JOHN L. HOLT, b. Jul 1866; d. at Oakland, ME, 1942; m. 1885, his first cousin once removed, JULIA F. ROLLINS (*Abbie Holt Rollins⁶, Valentine Holt⁵, Valentine Holt⁴, Mary Russell Holt³, John², Robert¹*), b. at Augusta, ME, Jan 1868 daughter of John and Abbie (Holt) Rollins; Julia d. 3 Dec 1962.

Wesley and Mary Louise were parents of three children born at Augusta. In 1880, Wesley, Mary, and their three children were living on Child Street in Augusta. Children were listed as Florence M. age 8, James P. age 4, and Fred A., age 2. Wesley's occupation is listed as laborer.[3317]

i   FLORENCE M. HOLT, b. 1872; d. at Pomfret, CT, 7 Jul 1955; m. at Boston, 28 Jun 1900, ROSWELL GLEASON HILTON, b. at Jefferson, ME, Aug 1870 son of Leonard A. and Melissa S. (Hatch) Hilton; Roswell d. at New London, 30 Jan 1957.

[3314] Year: 1850; Census Place: Hallowell, Kennebec, Maine; Roll: 256; Page: 187B
[3315] Massachusetts Vital Records, 1911-1915, City of Boston
[3316] Harriet is a presumed child in this family. She was not living with the family in the 1870 census, but she might well have been with other family owing to the recent death of her mother. Harriet was not located in the 1870 census.
[3317] Year: 1880; Census Place: Augusta, Kennebec, Maine; Roll: 481; Page: 35B; Enumeration District: 083

ii   JAMES PRESCOTT HOLT, b. 1875; d. at Augusta, 1954; m. 1st at Burnham, ME, 18 Sep 1898, ADDIE ROSE KIMBALL, b. at Burnham, 8 Nov 1869 daughter of William H. and Mary A. (Wyman) Kimball; Addie d. 1955. James and Addie divorced about 1900. Addie married Elmer Colman on 31 Jan 1903, but they divorced soon after. James and Addie remarried at Boston on 14 Nov 1904. They divorced again and Addie had two further marriages to Clarence Allen in 1914 and Edward Huff in 1930. Addie also had a marriage before her first marriage to James. James married 1913, EVELYN IDA RIGNE, b. at Pittsfield, MA, 19 Nov 1884 daughter of Peter E. and Helen (Sarrisen) Rigne; Evelyn d. at Winthrop, ME, 27 Dec 1975. Evelyn Ida (who mostly used Ida) was first married to Charles S. Murphy.

iii   FRED M. C. HOLT,[3318] b. 1879; m. at Waterville, ME, 17 Aug 1905, CHARLOTTE AUGUSTA FOSS, b. 1879 daughter of Wilson F. and Carrie (Hovey) Foss. Charlotte married second, as Charlotte Foss, Ralph B. Spaulding in 1906 and was third married to Henry Robinson on 11 Apr 1912.

1041)   ESTHER PEARSON (*Esther Holt Pearson⁴, Mary Russell Holt³, John², Robert¹*), b. at Wilton, 11 Nov 1792 daughter of Ebenezer and Esther (Holt) Pearson; d. at Lyndeborough, 12 Mar 1856; m. 8 Feb 1814, EPHRAIM PUTNAM, b. at Lyndeborough, 30 Apr 1785 son of Ephraim and Rachel (Cram) Putnam; Ephraim d. at Lyndeborough, 11 Jun 1862.
    Ephraim and Esther resided in Lyndeborough and were parents of five children.

i   EPHRAIM PUTNAM, b. 17 Nov 1815; d. 4 Aug 1834.

ii   ESTHER PUTNAM, b. 8 Jun 1818; d. at Lyndeborough, 14 Nov 1901; m. at Lyndeborough, 15 Jan 1839, JOEL H. TARBELL, b. at Mason, NH, 6 Feb 1816 son of Joel and Betsey (Shattuck) Tarbell; Joel d. at Lyndeborough, 14 Feb 1891.

iii   WILLARD P. PUTNAM, b. 4 Sep 1820; d. at Lyndeborough, 5 Jun 1856. Willard did not marry.

iv   MARY ANN PUTNAM, b. 18 Apr 1823; d. at Greenfield, NH, 23 May 1853; m. 22 Nov 1850, JOHN FLETCHER, b. at Greenfield, 13 Feb 1819 son of Philip and Penelope (Foster) Fletcher; John d. at Greenfield, 19 May 1911. John married second Amanda Tarbell.

v   EBENEZER PUTNAM, b. 26 Jun 1826; d. 9 Oct 1826.

1042)   EBENEZER PEARSON (*Esther Holt Pearson⁴, Mary Russell Holt³, John², Robert¹*), b. at Lyndeborough, 11 Jan 1797 son of Ebenezer and Esther (Holt) Pearson; d. at Hancock, NH, 6 Aug 1864; m. 1824, JOANNA KARR, b. at Lyndeborough, 6 Apr 1803 daughter of James and Sarah (Huse) Karr; Joanna d. at Hancock, 5 Aug 1874.
    Ebenezer and Joanna had their four children in Lyndeborough, and then relocated to Hancock in 1853 where they resided on Forest Road.[3319]
    Ebenezer Pearson did not leave a will and Joanna K. Pearson was admitted as administratrix on the estate on 26 August 1864.[3320] On 28 August 1874, E. B. Pearson requested administration of his mother's estate and provided the names of her heirs who are the only children: E. B. Pearson eldest son, Joanna A. Carter of Lawrence, Massachusetts, Sarah A. Kent of Lawrence, and James P. Pearson of Hancock.[3321]
    Ebenezer and Joanna were parents of four children born at Lyndeborough.

i   EBENEZER BROOKS PEARSON, b. 23 Jan 1827; d. at Hancock, NH, 8 Jun 1893; m. 7 Mar 1850, CYRENE TOWNE, b. 1827; Cyrene d. at Hancock, 26 Feb 1854.

ii   ADELINE JOANNA PEARSON, b. 15 Oct 1829; d. at Hancock, 23 Sep 1891; m. at Lawrence, MA, 6 May 1849, as his second wife, LEVI HARRISON CARTER, b. at Windham, NH, 17 Jul 1817 son of Samuel and Abigail (Wilson) Carter; Levi d. at Lawrence, 1 Aug 1880. Levi was first married to Martha Batchelder.

iii   SARAH ANN PEARSON, b. 28 Mar 1832; d. at Lawrence, 24 Apr 1894; m. at Hancock, NH, 5 Oct 1859, RICHARD KENT, b. at Orford, NH, 1832 son of Thomas and Ruth (Bailey) Kent; Richard d. at Lawrence, 24 Jul 1873.

iv   JAMES P. PEARSON, b. 21 Jul 1834; d. at Washington, DC, about 1894; m. at Bridgewater, MA, 13 Oct 1866, AMELIA BARSTOW DRAKE, b. at Brockton, MA, 23 Oct 1841 daughter of Aaron Bullock and Jane (Bronsdon) Drake; Amelia d. at Nashua, NH, 10 Aug 1896.

[3318] Although the 1880 Census gives his name as Fred A. Holt, he is Fred M. C. Holt with parents Wesley R. and Mary L. on his marriage records.
[3319] Hayward, *The History of Hancock, New Hampshire*, p 804
[3320] New Hampshire Wills and Probate, Hillsborough County, Probate Records volume 080, p 25
[3321] New Hampshire Wills and Probates, Hillsborough County, Probate Records volume 94, p 201

1043)   WILLARD PEARSON (*Esther Holt Pearson⁴, Mary Russell Holt³, John², Robert¹*), b. at Lyndeborough, 21 May 1806 son of Ebenezer and Esther (Holt) Pearson; d. at Woburn, MA, 31 Mar 1841; m. 7 Jul 1833, ANN P. CHILD, b. at Medford, MA, 15 Dec 1810 daughter of Aaron and Catherine (Floyd) Child;[3322] Ann d. at Woburn, 21 Nov 1886.
    Willard and Ann were parents of four children born at Woburn.

i   JULIA ANN PEARSON, b. 1835; d. at Cambridge, MA, 30 Oct 1902; m. at Woburn, 5 Jun 1862, PHILEMON C. SPAULDING, b. at Ludlow, VT, 1833 son of Owen and Eliza (Wright) Spaulding; Philemon d. at Cambridge, 23 Nov 1896.

ii   ALVA FRANCIS PEARSON, b. 16 Jul 1837; nothing further found

iii   ABBIE F. PEARSON, b. about 1838; d. at Cambridge, 17 Nov 1891; m. at Woburn, 28 Nov 1863, SUMNER S. PUTNAM, b. at Lyndeborough, NH, 4 Aug 1833 son of Israel and Ruth (Sargent) Putnam; d. not found but before 1880 when Abbie was widowed and living with her mother.

iv   MARY M. PEARSON, b. 1841; d. at Painesville, OH, 28 Jun 1883; m. at Woburn, 27 Jan 1864, JESSE RICHARDSON, b. at Woburn, 31 Mar 1840 son of Samuel and Susan B. (Pearson) Richardson; Jesse d. at Painesville, 11 Jan 1922.

1044)   SAMUEL KIDDER (*Hannah Crosby Kidder⁴, Hannah Russell Crosby³, John², Robert¹*), b. at Lyndeborough, 13 Mar 1787 son of Phinehas and Hannah (Crosby) Kidder; d. at Francestown, NH, 6 Mar 1866; m. 12 Oct 1812, HANNAH BROWN, baptized at Ipswich, 9 Jul 1786 daughter of Jeremiah and Lucy (Potter) Brown;[3323] Hannah d. at Francestown, 28 Feb 1864.
    Samuel Kidder was from Lyndeborough and moved to Francestown in 1811 just before the time of his marriage.[3324] Samuel Kidder and Hannah Brown were parents of six children born at Francestown.

i   BETSEY KIDDER, b. 22 May 1815; d. at Ashland, NH, 5 Jun 1897; m. 8 Aug 1839, SYLVANUS SNOW, b. at Brewster, MA, 3 Jan 1817 son of David and Mercy (Lincoln) Snow; Sylvanus d. at Nashua, NH, May 1860.

ii   ANN MARIA KIDDER, b. 3 Nov 1819; d. at Francestown, 15 Aug 1899; m. 4 May 1847, PUTNAM BRADFORD ANDREWS, b. at New Boston, NH, 1822 son of Daniel and Hannah (Dodge) Andrews;[3325] Bradford d. at Francestown, 11 Jul 1891.

iii   HANNAH KIDDER, b. 4 Apr 1821; d. 16 Aug 1840.

iv   JOHN KIDDER, b. 17 Aug 1822; d. at Lowell, MA, 4 Jul 1911; m. at Lawrence, MA, 21 Sep 1850, ELECTA THOMPSON, b. at Bangor, ME, 29 Apr 1827 daughter of Warren and Nancy (Hawthorn) Thompson;[3326] Electa d. at Lowell, 31 Oct 1909.

v   MARTHA KIDDER, b. 2 Mar 1826; d. at Peterborough, 21 Mar 1903; m. at Francestown, 4 Apr 1866, as his second wife, BENJAMIN "FRANK" SMILEY, b. at Peterborough, 21 Apr 1819 son of Francis and Sarah (Ames) Smiley; Frank d. 22 Nov 1876. Frank was first married to Mary Howard.

vi   LEVI KIDDER, b. 7 Nov 1827; d. at Francestown, 29 Dec 1913; m. 15 Jan 1863, ELLEN PARKER, b. at New Boston, NH, 1844 daughter of William and Sarah (Smiley) Parker; Ellen d. at Francestown, 17 Aug 1918.

1045)   PHINEAS KIDDER (*Hannah Crosby Kidder⁴, Hannah Russell Crosby³, John², Robert¹*), b. at Lyndeborough, 5 Dec 1789 son of Phinehas and Hannah (Crosby) Kidder; d. at Lyndeborough, 20 Jan 1864; m. 1st ANN MANLEY; Ann d. about 1810. Phineas m. 2nd 12 Oct 1812, PATTY ROSE, b. at Scituate, MA, 1 Jul 1794 daughter of Abraham and Desire (Fisher) Rose;[3327] Patty d. 30 Apr 1882.
    Phineas resided in Lyndeborough. On 11 October 1805 he was enrolled in the third company of the twenty-sixth regiment of New Hampshire militia.[3328]
    Phineas Kidder and Ann Manley were parents of one child.

[3322] The names of Ann's parents are given as Aaron and Catharine on her death record.
[3323] The 1828 will of Jeremiah Brown of Lyndeborough includes a bequest to his daughter Hannah Kidder.
[3324] Cochrane, *History of Francestown*, p 785
[3325] The names of the parents of Putnam Bradford Andrews are given on his death record.
[3326] Electa's parents are given as Warren Thompson and Nancy Hawthorn on her birth record; on the marriage record, they are listed as Richard and Biddy; her death record gives father's name as Warren.
[3327] Stafford, *A Genealogy of the Kidder Family*, p 100
[3328] Donovan, *History of Lyndeborough*, p 220

i   MANLEY KIDDER, b. at Lyndeborough, 24 Jul 1810; d. at Lyndeborough, 10 Jun 1877; m. 1st at Lyndeborough, 30 Nov 1848, RACHEL P. ABBOTT, b. at Lyndeborough, 11 Dec 1812 daughter of Jonas and Betsey (Parker) Abbott; Rachel d. at Lyndeborough, 27 Oct 1872. Manley m. 2nd at Lyndeborough, 28 Sep 1874, SARAH HOVEY, b. at Peterborough, about 1814 daughter of Daniel and Betsy (Gregg) Hovey; Sarah d. at Lyndeborough, 20 Nov 1879. Rachel Abbott was first married to Moses Buswell. Sarah Hovey was first married to Sylvester Proctor.

Phineas Kidder and Patty Rose were parents of three children born at Lyndeborough.

i   CATHERINE KIDDER, b. 10 Mar 1813; d. at Francestown, 20 Jan 1848; m. 13 Nov 1834, WARNER LINCOLN CLARK, b. at Francestown, 10 Mar 1812 son of Daniel and Irene (Fisher) Clark; Warner d. at Wilton, 6 May 1896. Warren married second widow Sarah Ham.

ii   ANN KIDDER, b. 9 Aug 1815; d. 7 Oct 1815.

iii   PHINEAS CROSBY KIDDER, b. 12 Jan 1817; d. at Francestown, 29 Mar 1892; m. 13 Oct 1842, EMILY HARDY, b. at Greenfield, NH, 3 Apr 1822 daughter of Benjamin and Mehitable (Holt) Hardy; Emily d. at Cambridge, MA, 31 Mar 1899.

1046)   MARY STEARNS (*Zilpah Crosby Stearns⁴, Hannah Russell Crosby³, John², Robert¹*), b. at Billerica, about 1791 daughter of Joseph and Zilpah (Crosby) Stearns; m. at Chelmsford, 13 Aug 1815, MARSHALL PIERCE, b. at Chelmsford, 14 Nov 1793 son of Stephen and Hannah (Marshall) Pierce; Marshall d. at Chelmsford, 2 Jun 1839.
        Mary Stearns and Marshall Pierce were parents of six children likely all born at Chelmsford. In the 1830 census, the household consisted of seven persons: one male 30-39; one female 30-39; one male 10-14; two females under 5; one female 5-9; and one female 10-14.[3329]

i   MARY ANN PIERCE, b. 1816; likely d. at Lowell, 5 May 1843 at age 26. She seems likely the Mary Ann Pierce who m. at Lowell, 14 Apr 1841, JAMES LEWIS HUNTRESS, b. at Portsmouth, NH, 5 May 1818 son of Joseph P. and Sally (Chesley) Huntress; James d. 2 Feb 1883. James married second Harriet P. T. Page on 21 Aug 1844.

ii   SANBORN G. PIERCE, b. at Chelmsford, 6 Dec 1818; d. at Chelmsford, 1 Feb 1874. Sanborn does not seem to have married. He was living on the poor farm in Chelmsford in 1855 and at the almshouse in 1870.

iii   LUCINDA PIERCE, b. 1820; d. at Chelmsford, 2 Oct 1826.

iv   SUSANNA PIERCE, b. at Chelmsford, 22 Aug 1822; d. at Chelmsford, 11 Apr 1875; m. at Thompson, CT, 11 Dec 1845, GEORGE S. WOOD, b. at Chelmsford, Jul 1822 son of Jonathan and Nancy (Stearns) Wood; George d. at Hollis, NH, 9 Aug 1903.

v   LUCINDA PIERCE, b. 1826; d. at Charlestown, MA, 23 Mar 1847; m. at Lowell, 12 Oct 1845, WLLIAM BARRY, b. at Boston, 1818 son of Nowell and Hannah (·) Barry;[3330] William d. at Chelmsford, 9 Aug 1854.

vi   ELIZA PIERCE, b. 1830; d. at Billerica, 14 Oct 1849.[3331]

1047)   ROYAL STEARNS (*Zilpah Crosby Stearns⁴, Hannah Russell Crosby³, John², Robert¹*), b. about 1794 son of Joseph and Zilpah (Crosby) Stearns; d. at Billerica, 30 May 1825; m. at Lexington, MA, 2 May 1824, ESTHER LAWRENCE, b. 23 Apr 1801 daughter of Jonathan and Polly (Reed) Lawrence. Esther married second Samuel P. Griffin on 13 May 1827.
        Royal Stearns was a bricklayer. He died just after the birth of his first child. Widow Esther declined administration of the estate. After the payment of debts, the estate value was $216.96.[3332]

i   SUSANNAH HUNSTABLE STEARNS, b. at Billerica, 7 Apr 1825; d. at Bedford, MA, 25 Jan 1849; m. 1st at Bedford, 3 Jan 1841, JAMES S. COTTING, b. a Marlborough, MA, about 1817; James d. at Bedford, 24 Nov 1843. Susanna m. 2nd at Bedford, 5 Sep 1847, LORENZO PHELPS, b. at Wilton, NH, 14 Aug 1816 son of Joseph and Anna (Stevens) Phelps; Lorenzo d. at Lowell, 23 Apr 1901.

[3329] 1830; Census Place: Chelmsford, Middlesex, Massachusetts; Series: M19; Roll: 67; Page: 227; Family History Library Film: 0337925
[3330] The names of William's parents and given as Nowell and Hannah Barry on the marriage transcription.
[3331] Death record lists parents as Marshall and Mary.
[3332] *Middlesex County, MA: Probate File Papers, 1648-1871.* Online database. *AmericanAncestors.org.* New England Historic Genealogical Society, 2014. Case 21322

1048)   ZILPAH STEARNS (*Zilpah Crosby Stearns⁴, Hannah Russell Crosby³, John², Robert¹*), b. about 1803 daughter of Joseph and Zilpah (Crosby) Stearns; d. after 1870 when she was living in Manchester, NH; m. at Billerica, 29 Oct 1821, her first cousin, JOHN STEARNS, b. 1797 son of Josiah Stearns; John d. at Manchester, about 1875 (probate 25 Jan 1875).

John Stearns was a farm laborer in Manchester, New Hampshire.[3333] On 25 January 1875, Thomas K. Stearns provided the following list of heirs of John Stearns of Manchester: petitioner Thomas K. Stearns, George G. Stearns, William K. Stearns, Josiah Stearns, Sarah Putnam, and Irene Green.[3334]

Zilpah Stearns and John Stearns were parents of eight children. Records of births were not found, but approximate dates of birth and birth locations were determined from census records and death records.

i   THOMAS K. STEARNS, b. 1822; d. at Manchester, NH, 1 Apr 1890; m. 1st about 1845, HANNAH F., b. at Dunbarton, 1824; Hannah d. at Manchester, 16 Feb 1867. Thomas m. 2nd at Manchester, 14 Oct 1867, ELLA S. HAMBLET, b. at Auburn, NH, 1853 daughter of Daniel and Sarah (Carr) Hamblet; Ella d. at Boston, 14 Oct 1903. Ella divorced Thomas in Mar 1888 on grounds of extreme cruelty.[3335]

ii   GEORGE G. STEARNS, b. at Cambridge, about 1823; d. after 1870 when he was living at Concord, NH; m. 1st about 1848, LOUISA DANIELS, b. at Hampton, NH, about 1825; Louisa d. at Hooksett, NH, 26 Nov 1869. George m. 2nd at Concord, 23 May 1870, SUSAN C. HILLS, b. at Williston, VT, 7 Aug 1841 daughter of Emery and Harriet (-) Hills; Susan d. at Boscawen, 23 Nov 1890.

iii   WILLIAM KIMBALL STEARNS, b. at Billerica, about 1826; d. at Lowell, 16 May 1908; m. at Lowell, 11 Jun 1860, MARTHA EASTMAN, b. at Lebanon, NH, Jul 1831 daughter of Parker and Sarah (-) Eastman; Martha d. at Lowell, 29 Sep 1914.

iv   SARAH E. STEARNS, b. at Billerica, 1828; d. at Goffstown, 5 Oct 1917; m. at Manchester, 1 Jan 1847, WILLARD A. PUTNAM, b. at Sharon, MA, 5 Nov 1827 son of William H. and Susan (Briggs) Putnam; Willard d. at Londonderry, NH, 23 Aug 1899.

v   JOHN STEARNS, b. about 1832; d. at Hooksett, NH, 5 Nov 1915; m. at Manchester, 16 Jun 1874, ANNA IZETTA MCINTIRE, b. ay Goffstown, 1853 daughter of William and Eliza (Martin) McIntire; Anna d. at Goffstown, 5 Nov 1915.

vi   JOSIAH STEARNS, b. at Holderness, 1837; d. at Epping, NH, Dec 1876; m. at Manchester, 24 Apr 1862, ELIZA JANE PIPER, b. at Meredith, NH, 1839 daughter of John and Eliza N. (Willey) Piper; Eliza d. at Auburn, NH, 21 Mar 1916. Eliza married second William S. Martin and third Abiel Cheney.

vii   IRENE A. STEARNS, b. at Manchester, 1843; d. at Manchester, 29 Apr 1912; m. at Manchester, 12 Feb 1866, as his second wife, BENJAMIN W. GREEN, b. a Burlington, VT, 1825 son of William and Mary (-) Green; Benjamin d. at Manchester, 12 Jan 1899. Benjamin was first married to Lucinda Dolby.

viii   ZOA STEARNS, b. 1846; d. at Manchester, NH, 20 Sep 1852.

1049)   MAHALA STEARNS (*Zilpah Crosby Stearns⁴, Hannah Russell Crosby³, John², Robert¹*), b. at Bedford, MA, 7 Aug 1809 daughter of Joseph and Zilpah (Crosby) Stearns; d. at Billerica, 4 Sep 1882; m. JAMES A. LOVEJOY, b. at Hebron, NH, 16 Jul 1805 son of Samuel Abbott and Elizabeth (Bowers) Lovejoy; James d. at Cambridge, Feb 1883.

James Lovejoy and Mahala Stearns were parents of three children born at Billerica.

i   ANNE FRANCES LOVEJOY, b. 9 Apr 1832; d. at Billerica, 20 Oct 1861. Anne did not marry.

ii   SARAH MELISSA LOVEJOY, b. 18 Sep 1835; d. 25 Nov 1867; m. at Billerica, 27 Feb 1862, JOSHUA BATES BRIGHAM, b. at Westborough, MA, 28 Sep 1828 son of Otis and Abigail (Bates) Brigham; Joshua died at Brookline, MA, 18 Apr 1891.

iii   JAMES ALONZO LOVEJOY, b. 5 Feb 1842; d. at Billerica, 6 Jan 1869. James did not marry.

1050)   JEROME BONAPARTE STEARNS (*Zilpah Crosby Stearns⁴, Hannah Russell Crosby³, John², Robert¹*), b. 1811 son of Joseph and Zilpah (Crosby) Stearns; d. at Billerica, 8 Apr 1895; m. at Charlestown, MA, 3 Nov 1832, ELIZABETH S. "BETSY" WHICHER, b. about 1808; Betsy d. of consumption, at Charlestown, 5 Mar 1848. Jerome was living at the almshouse in Billerica in 1880 and died as a pauper.

[3333] Year: 1850; Census Place: Manchester, Hillsborough, New Hampshire; Roll: 432; Page: 102b
[3334] New Hampshire Wills and Probate, Hillsborough County, Probate Records volume 94, p 237
[3335] New Hampshire, Marriage and Divorce Records, 1659-1947

Jerome was a morocco dresser[3336] which was a tanner of goat skin leather. Although there may have been other children, only one child of Jerome and Elizabeth lived to adulthood.

i   JAMES CHARLES STEARNS, b. at Chelmsford, about 1842; d. at Pembroke, MA, 31 Dec 1883; m. at North Bridgewater, MA, 28 Aug 1872, AROLINE AUGUSTA ESTES, b. at Hanson, MA, 7 Oct 1855 daughter of Stephen and Diana (Keene) Estes. Aroline remained widowed for 30 years and then married Arlington Cary on 19 Apr 1913.

A Few Great-Great Grandchildren of Thomas Russell

1051)   JOHN CHANDLER (*John Chandler⁵, John Chandler⁴, Mehitable Russell Chandler³, Thomas², Robert¹*), b. at Princeton, 22 May 1777 son of John and Katharine (Holman) Chandler; d. at Peru, VT, 6 Feb 1859; m. at Chelsea, MA, 8 Nov 1804, MARY WYMAN, b. at Chelsea, 15 Jul 1782; Mary d. at Peru, 23 Jan 1846.

John and Mary resided in Peru, Vermont where John was a carpenter by trade. John was known for his hand rakes.[3337]

John Chandler and Mary Wyman were parents of ten children, two of whom unnamed died as infants. The other eight children are given here.

i   MARY ADAMS CHANDLER, b. at Peru, 10 Dec 1805; d. at Peru, 29 Sep 1842; m. at Peru, 2 Dec 1830, JAMES LINCOLN, b. 1804 son of James and Lucy (Whitcomb) Lincoln; James d. at Peru, 23 Jun 1882. James married second Sybel Hale and married third Alsista Martin.

ii   JOHN C. CHANDLER, b. 29 Sep 1807; d. 23 Jul 1813.

iii   DORCAS ABBOT CHANDLER, b. (reported as at Manchester), 27 Jul 1809; d. at Landgrove, 18 Jan 1889; m. 1st 29 Sep 1836, as his second wife, LAWRENCE MCMULLEN, b. in Ireland about 1785; Lawrence d. at Peru, 12 May 1850. Lawrence was first married to Fanny Batchelder. Dorcas m. 2nd at Landgrove, 3 May 1857, JAMES JOHNSON. Dorcas m. 3rd at Landgrove, 2 Apr 1865, DAVID GARFIELD, b. at Landgrove, 1817 son of Abraham and Eunice (Thurston) Garfield; David d. at Landgrove, 10 Oct 1901. It is not known what became of James Johnson. In 1860, Dorcas had resumed using the name Dorcas McMullen and was head of household in Landgrove.

iv   MABEL COLLINS CHANDLER, b. at Peru, 11 Nov 1811; d. at Shushan, NY, 2 Oct 1890; m. at Peru, 9 Feb 1838, SIMEON LYON, b. at Peru, 15 Apr 1813 son of Freeman and Lovisa (Pease) Lyon; Simeon d. at Shushan, 17 Jun 1883.

v   EUNICE CARLTON CHANDLER, b. at Peru, 10 Oct 1815; d. at Manchester, 22 Mar 1897; m. 26 Feb 1849, BARNET RICHARDSON, b. at Manchester, 11 Apr 1805 son of Andrew and Rachel (Bowen) Richardson;[3338] Barnet d. at Manchester, 15 Jul 1893.

vi   SALLY WYMAN CHANDLER, b. 15 Aug 1820; d. 23 Mar 1836.

vii   HARRIET RITTER CHANDLER, b. at Peru, 20 Jul 1823; m. at Peru, 1 Nov 1846, AMOS R. LAWRENCE, b. at Manchester, VT, 27 Dec 1822 son of Amos and Calista (Johnson) Lawrence;[3339] Amos d. at Manchester, 24 Nov 1862.

viii   EZRA PARKER CHANDLER, b. at Peru, 5 Sep 1825; d. at Peru, 16 May 1885; m. 22 Sep 1851, ELIZABETH ENGLISH, b. at Littleton, NH, 21 Jan 1833 daughter of Eli and Emily (Stocking) English; Elizabeth d. at Peru, 28 Feb 1917.

1052)   JOSEPH CHANDLER (*John Chandler⁵, John Chandler⁴, Mehitable Russell Chandler³, Thomas², Robert¹*), b. at Princeton, 20 Mar 1780 son of John and Katharine (Holman) Chandler; d. at Hartland, VT, 7 Apr 1854; m. at Charlestown, MA, 17 Dec 1809, SARAH "SALLY" BENNETT, b. at Lunenburg, 31 May 1778 daughter of James Bennett; Sally d. at Hartland, 20 Jan 1851.

[3336] Van Wagenen, Genealogy and Memoirs of Isaac Stearns, p 365

[3337] Chandler, *Descendants of William and Annis Chandler*, p 452

[3338] The names of Barnet's parents are given as Alexander Richardson and Rachel Bowen on his death record.

[3339] Chandler, *Descendants of William and Annis Chandler*, p 815

Joseph and Sally raised their two children in Hartland, Vermont. Daughter Sarah and her husband Francis A. Kilburn were pioneers in Montezuma, Iowa, there being just six log homes when they arrived there in 1851. Sarah and Francis set up a store, Sarah serving as the shopkeeper. Francis was a successful merchant and also dealt in livestock.[3340]

i   JOSEPH CHANDLER, b. at Hartland, 4 Nov 1815; d. at Elmore, VT, 5 Oct 1873; m. 1st 1 May 1837, LYDIA CASE, b. 1815 daughter of Charles and Elizabeth (Blake) Case; Lydia d. at Hartland, 22 Sep 1855. Joseph m. 2nd 5 Nov 1856, SARAH LADD CHASE, b. at Middlesex, VT, 22 Feb 1823 daughter of Simeon B. and Susanna (Ladd) Chase; Sarah d. (buried at Middlesex), 2 May 1892. Sarah married second Hobart Crane on 6 Aug 1879.

ii   SARAH CHANDLER, b. at Hartland, 16 Oct 1818; d. at Montezuma, IA, 25 Feb 1870; m. at Hartland, 14 Jun 1841, FRANCIS ASBURY KILBURN, b. at Gilsum, NH, 21 Feb 1820 son of Iddo and Abigail (Sampson) Kilburn; Francis d. at Montezuma, 16 Jan 1896. Francis married second Mary Ferry on 2 Feb 1871.

1053)   EPHRAIM H. CHANDLER (*John Chandler⁵, John Chandler⁴, Mehitable Russell Chandler³, Thomas², Robert¹*), b. at New Braintree, 9 Jun 1783 son of John and Mary (Jackson) Chandler; d. at Princeton, MA, 30 Oct 1856; m. at Princeton, 19 Apr 1810, MARY POWERS, b. 3 Dec 1790 daughter of John Powers; Mary d. at Princeton, 16 Jun 1854.

    Ephraim and Mary resided in Princeton where Ephraim farmed on what had been his father's homestead.[3341]

    In his will written 6 June 1847 (probate 6 January 1857), Ephraim H. Chandler bequeathed three hundred dollars each to four of his children: Charles Chandler, Nancy Ann Osgood wife of Ephraim Osgood, Leonard Chandler, and Sarah Jane Chandler. The remainder of the estate goes to son Ephraim H. Chandler. This bequest to Ephraim is contingent on his well and truly maintaining in his dwelling house "my beloved wife Mary Chandler."[3342]

    Ephraim and Mary were parents of five children born at Princeton, Massachusetts.

i   CHARLES CHANDLER, b. 30 May 1811; d. at Sterling, MA, 13 Dec 1892; m. 1st 6 Dec 1840, SARAH E. NICHOLS, b. at Sturbridge, 4 Jan 1821 daughter of Jabez and Cynthia (Wilder) Nichols; Sarah d. at Princeton, 15 Jul 1845. Charles m. 2nd 21 May 1846, MARY ANN HUBBARD, b. 1824 daughter of Benjamin and Polly (Walker) Hubbard;[3343] Mary d. at Princeton, 25 Jan 1848. Charles m. 3rd 13 Apr 1848, the sister of his first wife, HANNAH NICHOLS (widow of Isaac Grover), b. at Ware, MA, 1814; Hannah d. at Sterling, 12 Nov 1882.

ii   NANCY ANN CHANDLER, b. 23 Jul 1814; d. at Princeton, 19 Mar 1890; m. at Princeton, 12 Nov 1834, EPHRAIM OSGOOD, b. at Princeton, 6 Dec 1808 son of Ephraim and Mary (Palmer) Osgood; Ephraim d. at Princeton, 13 Aug 1883.

iii   LEONARD CHANDLER, b. 3 Mar 1817; d. at Princeton, 28 Feb 1891; m. 12 Oct 1842, SARAH BLANCHARD, b. at Boxborough, MA, 10 Feb 1820 daughter of Simon and Mary (Keyes) Blanchard; Sarah d. at Princeton, 12 Mar 1903.

iv   EPHRAIM HARTWELL CHANDLER, b. 15 May 1823; d. at Westborough, MA, 17 Feb 1908; m. 19 Oct 1852, MARY KEYES SWALLOW, b. at Dunstable, 10 Feb 1831 daughter of Kendall and Martha (Keyes) Swallow; Mary d. at Sterling, 16 Sep 1895.

v   SARAH JANE CHANDLER, b. 30 Mar 1831; d. at Shrewsbury, VT, 8 Mar 1895; m. 31 Dec 1857, WILLARD SMITH, b. at Shrewsbury, VT, 8 Jun 1831 son of Nathan and Nancy (Powers) Smith; Willard d. at Shrewsbury, 17 May 1913.

1054)   MARY "POLLY" CHANDLER (*John Chandler⁵, John Chandler⁴, Mehitable Russell Chandler³, Thomas², Robert¹*), b. at Princeton, MA, 31 May 1795 daughter of John and Mary (Jackson) Chandler; d. at Salisbury, VT, 21 Dec 1842; m. at Sterling, 26 Apr 1815, SILAS HOLMAN, b. at Sterling, 17 Apr 1790 possible son of Samuel and Sarah (Davis) Holman;[3344] Silas d. at Salisbury, 17 Mar 1839.

    Silas Holman and Mary Chandler were parents of nine children.

[3340] Parker, *History of Poweshiek County, Iowa*, volume II, pp 411-412

[3341] Chandler, *The Descendants of William and Annis Chandler*, p 453

[3342] *Worcester County, MA: Probate File Papers, 1731-1881.* Online database. AmericanAncestors.org. New England Historic Genealogical Society, 2015. Case 10930

[3343] The names of Mary's parents are given and Benjamin and Polly on her death record.

[3344] Holman, *The Holmans in America*, p 58. The parentage of Silas is not certain. The Chandler genealogy reports that his father is Stephen, but he might be the grandson of Stephen.

i   CALEB FAUSON HOLMAN, b. at Princeton, 5 Apr 1816; d. at Salisbury, VT, 22 Nov 1889; m. 1ˢᵗ about 1844, ELIZA BRUSH, b. at Fairfax, VT, Dec 1824 daughter of Eperretus and Chloe (-) Brush;[3345] Eliza d. at Salisbury, 6 Oct 1866. Caleb m. 2ⁿᵈ at Middlebury, 6 Oct 1875, widow ROSENA *SHACKET* HARRINGTON, b. at Alburgh, VT, about 1824 daughter of John B. and Sarah (Bunnell) Shacket;[3346] Rosena d. at Salisbury, 21 Apr 1899.

ii   LAURA ANN HOLMAN, b. at Princeton, 13 Mar 1818; d. at Watertown, MA, 14 Dec 1904; m. 24 Nov 1844, ABIJAH LIVERMORE, b. at Waltham, 28 Aug 1812 son of Jonas and Louisa (Stearns) Livermore; Abijah d. at Waltham, 1 Aug 1860.

iii   MARILLA HOLMAN, b. at Princeton, 2 Jul 1820; d. at Williston, VT, 25 Feb 1883; m. 1ˢᵗ at Salisbury, VT, 1 Jan 1840, DANIEL H. HOWARD, b. at New Haven, VT, 3 Nov 1818 son of Daniel and Dorothy (Hickok) Howard;[3347] Daniel d. at Middlebury, VT, 21 Apr 1859. Marilla m. 2ⁿᵈ at Middlebury, 29 Mar 1864, CHARLES ELLIOT MILLER, b. 15 Jun 1808 son of Elisha and Sarah (Elliot) Miller; Charles d. at Williston, 17 Apr 1872. Charles was first married to Emily Clark.

iv   SILAS DEXTER HOLMAN, b. at Princeton, 27 Jun 1822; d. at Ewing, NJ, 13 Feb 1888; m. at Thompson, CT, 30 Sep 1846, HARRIET M. WARREN, b. at Northborough, MA, 27 Apr 1825 daughter of Timothy and Hannah (Harrington) Warren; Harriet d. at Hammonton, NJ, 2 Jun 1881. From the 1850's, Silas Dexter and Harriet lived in Hammonton, NJ until Silas was widowed in 1881, and he was in Ewing at the time of his death. They had four known children, all of whom died in early childhood. Silas was a painter and carpenter, and later listed as a farmer in New Jersey.

v   LORAIN HOLMAN, b. at Princeton, 8 Aug 1824; d. at West Salisbury, VT, 15 Dec 1881; m. at Bridport, VT, 25 Mar 1844, ANDREW JACKSON KELSEY, b. at Salisbury, VT, 1817 son of Gamaliel and Elizabeth (Soper) Kelsey; Andrew d. at Salisbury, 19 Aug 1895. Andrew married Phebe Chapman on 11 Oct 1888.

vi   MARYETTE HOLMAN, b. 1828; d. 15 Jun 1831.

vii   HENRYETTE HOLMAN, b. 1832; d. at Salisbury, VT, 28 Apr 1835.

viii HENRY HOLMAN, b. at Salisbury, VT, 1833; d. at Salisbury, 28 Jan 1848.

ix   MARY S. HOLMAN, m. at Salisbury, VT, 11 Nov 1834; d. at Ayer, MA, 7 Feb 1897; m. at Stow, MA, 24 Nov 1853, EBENEZER LAKIN BLOOD, b. at Groton, MA, 22 Jul 1832 son of Ebenezer and Tamer (Farmer) Blood; Ebenezer d. after 1865 when the family was living in Stow, MA and before 1870 when Mary was a widow.

1055)   HANNAH CHANDLER (*Joseph Chandler⁵, John Chandler⁴, Mehitable Russell Chandler³, Thomas², Robert¹*), b. at Danvers, 15 Dec 1781 daughter of John and Dorcas (Abbott) Chandler; d. at Salem, 21 Dec 1856; m. at Salem, 20 Oct 1805, JONATHAN KENNEY, b. at Middleton, 23 Aug 1771 son of Simeon and Jerusha (Johnson) Kenney; Jonathan d. at Salem, 29 Dec 1847.

Jonathan Kenney's occupation was described as a sawyer. He also served as deacon in Salem.

Jonathan Kenney did not leave a will and his estate entered probate 4 January 1848. Widow Hannah with agreement by the other heirs-at-law requested that Jonathan A. Kenney be named administrator. Those signing this request were widow Hannah Kenney, William Ramsdell and Hannah A. Ramsdell, Jonathan A. Kenney, Eliza J. Kenney, Henry P. Trask and Mary P. Trask, and George W. Kenney. Real estate was valued at $5408 and personal estate at $5810.54 and additions brough the total personal estate to $6626.47. Debts of the estate were $1569.81. The personal estate included bank shares and shares in the Naumkeag Steam Cotton Company. Real estate included three lots on South Street in Salem and a lot on Forester Street. The distribution from the personal estate included payments of $1011.33 each to the following heirs: Hannah A. Ramsdell, Mary P. Trask, Eliza J. Kenney, George W. Kenney, and Jonathan A. Kenney.[3348]

In her will written 3 August 1852 (probate 6 January 1857), Hannah Chandler Kenney bequeathed one-fifth of her estate to daughter Hannah A. Ramsdell "to be held by her as an absolute estate, without the intervention of a trustee, to her sole and separate use, free from the interference and control of her husband, if she have such." One-fifth portions go to her other four children, with the bequests to the daughters including the wording that the bequest is for their sole, separate use: Jonathan A. Kenney, Eliza J. Kenney, Mary P. Trask, and George W. Kenney. Jonathan A. Kenney was named executor. Real estate was valued at $6200 and personal estate at 176.58.[3349]

Hannah Chandler and Jonathan Kenney were parents of seven children born at Salem.

[3345] Holman, *The Holmans in America*, p 135

[3346] The names of Rosena's parents are given as John B. Shacket and Sarah Bunnel on her marriage record to Caleb Holman.

[3347] Daniel's parents are given as Daniel Howard and Dorothy Hickok on his death record.

[3348] *Essex County, MA: Probate File Papers, 1638-1881*.Online database. *AmericanAncestors.org*. New England Historic Genealogical Society, 2014. Case 44104

[3349] *Essex County, MA: Probate File Papers, 1638-1881*.Online database. *AmericanAncestors.org*. New England Historic Genealogical Society, 2014. Case 44100

i   JONATHAN A. KENNEY, b. 25 Nov 1806; d. at Salem, 1875; m. 1st at Salem, 2 Aug 1835, ELIZA B. SMOTHERS, b. 30 Jan 1814 possibly daughter of Jonathan and Elizabeth (Stone) Smothers. Jonathan m. 2nd 12 May 1845, MARY ELIZABETH EMERSON, baptized at Wenham, 20 Aug 1826 daughter of David and Pamelia Marsh (Stone) Emerson; Mary d. at Salem, 16 May 1901.

ii   HANNAH AVERY KENNEY, b. 18 Jan 1808; d. at Brockton, 8 Sep 1887; m. at Salem, 29 Jul 1835, WILLIAM RAMSDELL, b. at Marblehead, about 1810 son of James and Margaret (-) Ramsdell; William d. at Brockton, 20 Apr 1890.

iii   DORCAS KENNEY, b. 11 May 1810; d. at Salem, 19 Nov 1845.

iv   ELIZA JERUSHA KENNEY, b. about 1815. Eliza was living and unmarried in 1857.

v   MARY PEABODY KENNEY, b. 21 Feb 1818; m. at Salem, 6 Sep 1846, HENRY PAUL TRASK, b. at Cambridge, about 1821 son of William and Martha (Hoar) Trask; Henry d. at Cambridge, 8 May 1898.

vi   SALLY H. KENNEY, b. 1821; d. of consumption, at Salem, 12 Jul 1837.

vii   GEORGE W. KENNEY, b. about 1824; m. 1st at Haverhill, 14 Nov 1844, BETHIAH W. HOWE, b. at Haverhill, 1824; Bethiah d. at Salem, 8 Oct 1851. George m. 2nd at Salem, 25 Jul 1852, SARAH MACE, b. at Hampton, NH, May 1833 daughter of Henry and Elisa (Tucker) Mace; Sarah d. at Salem, 21 Oct 1859. George m. 3rd at Salem, 19 Aug 1860, ELIZA A. WOODWARD, b. in ME, about 1824. George m. 4th at Boston, 6 Aug 1872, CHARLOTTE L. AUSTIN (widow Charlotte Palmer), b. at Bethel, VT, about 1833 daughter of Charles L. and Sarah (-) Austin;[3350] Charlotte d. at Haverhill, 4 Jun 1883.

1056)   JOSEPH ABBOT CHANDLER (*Joseph Chandler⁵, John Chandler⁴, Mehitable Russell Chandler³, Thomas², Robert¹*), b. 28 Dec 1789 son of John and Dorcas (Abbott) Chandler; d. at Salem, 25 Nov 1861; m. at Salem, 24 May 1812, DEBORAH SYMONDS, b. at Salem, 1796 daughter of Thorndike and Betsey (Gurley) Symonds; Deborah d. at Salm, 3 Nov 1832.

Joseph was a saddler and a butcher, but later was rather shiftless.[3351] His sister Dorcas left money to him but held in trust to be doled out to him as needed.

Joseph Abbot Chandler and Deborah Symonds were parents of four children born at Salem.

i   JOSEPH THORNDIKE CHANDLER, b. 3 Sep 1815; d. at Everett, MA, 24 Jun 1896; m. at Salem, MA, 17 Apr 1838, ELIZABETH R. HODGKINS, b. at Bath, ME, 18 May 1816 daughter of John and Lucy (Rogers) Hodgkins; Elizabeth d. at Everett, MA, 5 Aug 1891.

ii   ELIZABETH CHANDLER, b. 5 Feb 1818; d. 4 Jul 1819.

iii   DORCAS CHANDLER, b. Sep 1820; d. Feb 1821.

iv   SUSAN ELIZABETH CHANDLER, b. 13 Jul 1832; d. at Everett, MA, 7 Oct 1895; m. at Salem, 26 Jun 1856, GEORGE B. KENISTON, b. at Danbury, NH, 1829 son of Philip and Asenath (Taylor) Keniston;[3352] George d. at Harpswell, ME, 7 Jan 1914. George was a cabinetmaker.

[3350] Names of parents as given on marriage record to George Kenney
[3351] Chandler, *The Descendants of William and Annis Chandler*, p 455
[3352] Names of George's parents are given as Philip and Asenath Keniston on his marriage record and as Philip Keniston and Asenath Taylor on his death record.

Master List of Families

The number given is the Family number.

Abbe, Elizabeth and Azariah Sanger	203
Abbott, Abigail and Theodore Russell	975
Abbott, Barachias and Sarah Holt	275
Abbott, Bridget and Phineas Ames	451
Abbott, David and Hannah Chandler	108
Abbott, Dorcas and John Holt	292
Abbott, Dorcas and Joseph Chandler	250
Abbott, Dorcas and Nicholas Holt	11
Abbott, Hannah and Abiel Holt	15
Abbott, Hannah and Benjamin Holt	255
Abbott, Hannah and Israel Towne	728
Abbott, Henry and Dorcas Holt	911
Abbott, Isaac and Mary Barker	173
Abbott, Isaac and Ruth Ames	730
Abbott, Job and Phebe Farnum	450
Abbott, Lydia and Thomas Pevey	909
Abbott, Lydia and Thomas Russell	536
Abbott, Lydia and Uriah Russell	150
Abbott, Martha and Ammi Holt	1032
Abbott, Mary and Joseph Holt	71
Abbott, Mary and Joshua Holt	95
Abbott, Mary and Lemuel Holt	389
Abbott, Mehitable and Benjamin Russell	973
Abbott, Nathan and Hannah Russell	636
Abbott, Olive and Isaac Parker	731
Abbott, Phebe and John Russell	235
Abbott, Priscilla and Zela Holt	446
Abbott, Rhoda and Jacob Holt	222
Abbott, Ruth and Thomas Williams	653
Abbott, Sally and James Brown	729
Abbott, Sarah and Abiel Holt	306
Abbott, Sarah and Abiel Russell	639
Abbott, Sarah and David Holt	930
Abbott, Sarah and James Holt	65
Abbott, Sarah and Nathan Holt	66
Abbott, Stephen and Hannah Russell	980
Abel, Anna and Abel Holt	334
Abell, Zerviah and Solomon Holt	356
Adams, Hannah and Daniel Appleton	666
Adams, Hannah and Eliphalet Farnum	471
Adams, Hephzibah and Timothy Underwood	507
Adams, Isaac and Sarah McHard	500
Adams, John and Dorcas Faulkner	499
Adams, John and Hannah Osgood	126
Adams, John and Persis Cheney	857
Adams, Lydia and Joseph Cheney	856
Adams, Mary and Elijah Holt	404
Adams, Mary and Eliphalet Farnum	118
Adams, Mary and Timothy Underwood	507
Alden, Irena and Joseph Merrick	341
Alden, Joanna and Leonard Holt	351
Alen, Asaph and Lois King	714
Alexander, Eunice and Thomas Russell	147
Allen, Anna and George W. Farnum	478
Allen, Benjamin and Hannah Case	165
Allen, Benjamin and Mehitable Ingalls	33
Allen, Betty and Nathaniel May	711
Allen, Ebenezer and Phebe Healy	709
Allen, Elizabeth and Russell Underwood	509
Allen, Hiram and Dorcas Russell	991
Allen, Isaac and Sarah French	166
Allen, Isaac and Susan Sellen	712
Allen, John and Polly McDowell	713
Allen, Joseph and Elizabeth Warner	167
Allen, Mary and Nathaniel Blood	710
Allen, Mary Jane and Ira Russell	560
Allen, Mehitable and Simeon Case	164
Allen, Sarah and James Russell	646
Allen, Sluman and Hannah Storrs	707
Allen, Zipporah and Daniel Fitch	708
Ames, Elizabeth and William Holt	252
Ames, Jonas and Jemima Stevens	248
Ames, Phineas and Bridget Abbott	451
Ames, Ruth and Isaac Abbott	730
Amidon, Jonathan and Keturah Holt	390
Amsbury, Hannah and James Underwood	511
Andrews, Daniel and Esther Holt	933
Andrews, Jacob and Mary Holt	444
Andrews, Levi and Bridget Holt	445
Andrews, Mary and Edward Herrick	1020
Andrews, Nathaniel and Mary Holt	444
Angier, Elisha and Sally Russell	622
Angier, Lucy and Joseph Russell	607
Appleton, Alice and John Swett	665
Appleton, Benjamin and Catherine Hooton	660
Appleton, Daniel and Hannah Adams	666
Appleton, Daniel and Lydia Ela	156
Appleton, George and Mary Guild	662
Appleton, Hannah and Edward Woodbury	158
Appleton, Henry and Mary Owen	661
Appleton, John and Mary Tuttle	658
Appleton, Lydia and Benjamin Wells	659
Appleton, Martha and Richard Thayer	656
Appleton, Mary and Moses Gale	155
Appleton, Samuel and Mary Russell	30
Appleton, Thomas and Anna Swett	657
Appleton, Thomas and Beulah Goodridge	667
Appleton, Thomas and Martha Barnard	154
Appleton, William and Hannah Clark	157
Armstrong, Betsey and William Barker	721
Atwood, Elizabeth and Jonathan Dwinells	564
Atwood, Mehitable and Timothy Merrick	339
Austin, Mary and Moses Holt	913
Austin, Nathan and Martha Farnum	474
Averill, Sarah and Ebenezer Chandler	441
Averill, William and Abigail Holt	402
Avery, Jonathan and Chloe Wales	823
Avery, Jonathan and Hannah Humphrey	195
Avery, Polly M. and Caleb Poor	497
Ayers, Olive and Winthrop Marcy	796
Bacon, Rebecca and Noah D. Sanger	867
Badger, Rebecca and John Peck	374

Badger, Sarah and Elisha Peck	376
Bailey, Abigail and Isaac Osgood	123
Bales, Rhoda and John Ballard	921
Ballard, Abigail and Thomas Russell	29
Ballard, Betsey and Richard Buss	918
Ballard, Frederick and Hannah Russell	985
Ballard, Hannah and David McIntire	915
Ballard, John and Rhoda Bales	921
Ballard, Mary and Amos Holt	917
Ballard, Nathan and Hannah Buss	920
Ballard, Nathan and Hannah Holt	221
Ballard, Phebe and John Gutterson	919
Ballard, Sarah and William Pettengill	916
Barker, Almira and Joseph Carr	727
Barker, Anna and Stephen Gerry	742
Barker, Deborah and Jonathan Coy	174
Barker, Ephraim and Hannah Grow	171
Barker, Ephraim and Mary Burnham	171
Barker, Ephraim and Ruth Goodnow	724
Barker, Hannah and Elijah Pitcher	722
Barker, John and Esther Richardson	723
Barker, John and Sally Guild	723
Barker, Joseph and Elizabeth Washburn	739
Barker, Lucy and Matthew Wilson	743
Barker, Lydia and Nathan Barker	725
Barker, Mary and Isaac Abbott	173
Barker, Nathan and Lydia Barker	725
Barker, Phebe and Jedediah Holt	265
Barker, Rebecca and David Lyons	740
Barker, Sally and Aaron Tufts	726
Barker, Stephen and Rebekah Gibson	175
Barker, Timothy and Betsey	741
Barker, William and Betsey Armstrong	721
Barker, William and Martha Ingalls	36
Barker, William and Sarah Foster	172
Barnard, Abigail and Samuel Downing	311
Barnard, James and Hannah Hawley	907
Barnard, James and Sarah Holt	217
Barnard, John and Alice Holt	73
Barnard, Lydia and Josiah Sawyer	312
Barnard, Martha and Thomas Appleton	154
Barnard, Mary and Jonathan Merrill	682
Barnard, Miriam and Moses Merrill	683
Barnes, Electa and William Pulsipher	631
Barnum, Zacchaeus and Sarah Cary	791
Barrett, David and Phebe Russell	539
Barrett, Nancy and Edward Herrick	1020
Barron, Rachel and Thomas Robie	518
Barron, Samuel and Sybil Cummings	526
Bartlett, Anna and Frederick Russell	534
Bartlett, James and Hannah Woodbury	669
Bartlett, Joseph and Mary Woodbury	668
Batchelder, Jonathan and Abigail Eaton	452
Batchelder, Joseph and Phebe Holt	288
Batchelder, Moses and Abigail Holt	958
Batchelder, Phebe and Nicholas Holt	269
Bean, Almira and Elijah Russell	999
Bean, Humphrey and Lydia Holt	998
Bean, Kimball and Maria Russell	1000
Bean, Timothy and Lovina Russell	1002
Beebe, Esther and Russell Hunt	575
Beebe, Lydia and Robert Russell	455
Beede, Mehitable and Ebenezer Dale	1028
Beede, Nancy and John Dale	1027
Bell, Abigail and Thomas Russell	635
Bell, Jonathan and Deborah Butterfield	516
Benjamin, Jonathan and Anness Holt	902
Benjamin, Polly and Joseph Russell	543
Bennett, Hannah and Samuel Holt	394
Bennett, Sarah and Joseph Chandler	1052
Benson, Stephen and Rebecca Cummings	531
Berry, Mary and Ebenezer Eaton	832
Berry, Nathaniel and Lydia Towne	966
Bibbens, Philatheta and Calvin Preston	366
Bibbins, Patience and Manasseh Farnum	464
Bickford, Daniel and Mehitable Russell	520
Bidwell, Polly and Sampson Hunt	576
Bigelow, Humphrey and Mary Underwood	510
Bingham, Horatio and Sarah Johnson	574
Bingham, Lucy and Jonathan Coy	734
Birchard, Phineas and Lydia Farnum	462
Bishop, Abigail and Solomon Hoar/Homer	750
Bishop, Calvin and Olive Dady	753
Bishop, Gratis and Issachar Brown	752
Bishop, Harrison and Margaret Browning	756
Bishop, John and Alfleda Blashfield	751
Bishop, Matilde and Abner Nutting	754
Bishop, Richard and Peggy Goodale	179
Bishop, Rufus and Susannah Webb	755
Bissell, Sabra and Walter Goodale	399
Black, Sarah and Ephraim Holt	227
Blaisdell, Ruth and David Stevens	937
Blaisdell, Sally and Uriah Stevens	936
Blanchard, David and Hannah Eaton	703
Blanchard, Lydia and Jonathan Holt	48
Blanchard, Susannah and Nathan Holt	254
Blanchard, Thomazin and Jeremiah Johnson	573
Blashfield, Alfleda and John Bishop	751
Blodgett, Achsa and James Sanger	870a
Blood, Nathaniel and Mary Allen	710
Bond, Elijah and Sarah Russell	986
Bottum, Asa and Elizabeth Farnum	470
Bourne, Maria and Samuel Osgood	482
Boutell, James and Chloe Preston	364
Bowers, Fanny and Stephen Holt	296
Bowers, Francis and Chloe Holt	297
Bowers, Francis and Elizabeth Holt	224
Boyd, Mary and Wesley Holt	1040
Boynton, Dorcas and Joseph Holt	71
Bradley, Jonathan and Sarah Osgood	488
Bradley, Joseph and Mary Osgood	489
Bragg, Molly and Stephen Holt	924
Bray, Diana and John Russell	978
Brevard, Prudence and Enoch Poor	496
Bridges, Chloe and Timothy Osgood	486
Briggs, Daniel and Augusta Goodale	757
Brigham, Sarah and Rachel Underwood	504
Brocklebank, John and Chloe Sanger	876
Brooks, Mary and Silas Holt	99
Brooks, Phebe and Nathan Eaton	831

Brown, Bethiah and Daniel Ingalls	760
Brown, Daniel and Betsy Russell	591
Brown, Elizabeth and Joshua Osgood	490
Brown, Ephraim and Mary Russell	1016
Brown, Hannah and Samuel Kidder	1044
Brown, Henry and Sarah Holt	1037
Brown, Issachar and Gratis Bishop	752
Brown, James and Sally Abbott	729
Brown, Lydia and James Russell	771
Brown, Miriam and Joseph Russell	144
Brown, Nathaniel and Dilly Eaton	836
Brown, Rhoda and Simeon Coye	737
Brown, Sarah and Ephraim Farnum	690
Browning, Margaret and Harrison Bishop	756
Bugby, Lucy and William Marcy	190
Burgess, Mary and Reuben Richardson	326
Burnap, Mary and Ebenezer Chandler	441
Burnham, Mary and Ephraim Barker	171
Burnham, Seymour and Dorcas Marcy	813
Burns, Eliza and Israel Herrick	1022
Burrall, Wealthy and David Hunt	582
Burrill, Nathan and Elizabeth Woodbury	670
Burt, Experience and Constant Merrick	343
Burton, John and Sarah Dale	1030
Bushnell, Lemira and Oliver Hastings	765
Buss, Hannah and Nathan Ballard	920
Buss, Richard and Betsey Ballard	918
Butterfield, Deborah and Jonathan Bell	516
Butterfield, Isaac and Ruth Spalding	439
Butterfield, John and Naomi Stevens	512
Butterfield, John and Phebe Russell	129
Butterfield, Peter and Hannah Guy	513
Butterfield, Phebe and Nathaniel Glidden	515
Butterfield, Sarah and Eliphalet Richards	514
Byles, Anna and Simeon Smith	210
Canfield, Nancy and David Coye	738
Carleton, Amos and Abiah Towne	970
Carpenter, Aaron and Hannah Holt	392
Carr, John and Lucy Sanger	877
Carr, Joseph and Almira Barker	727
Carter, Esther and Moses Farnum	677
Carter, Nathan and Sarah Farnum	676
Carter, Rhoda and Moses Farnum	677
Cary, Delight and Timothy Fuller	789
Cary, Dorcas and Rufus Palmer	790
Cary, Mary and Jedediah Kingsley	788
Cary, Nathaniel and Dorcas Marcy	189
Cary, Sarah and Zacchaeus Barnum	791
Case, Hannah and Benjamin Allen	165
Case, Samuel and Susannah Cowdrey	706
Case, Simeon and Mehitable Allen	164
Chaffee, Ebenezer and Hannah Smith	889
Chaffee, Olive and Ebenezer Sanger	871
Chaffee, Olive and Nathaniel Sanger	206
Chaffee, Rhoda and Darius Truesdell	325
Chamberlain, Asa and Sally Russell	1008
Chamberlain, Rebecca and Timothy Holt	86
Chamberlain, Samuel and Hephzibah Russell	1005
Chambers, Sarah and Reuben Coye	735
Chandler, Asa and Elinor Richardson	443

Chandler, Ebenezer and Mary Burnap	441
Chandler, Ebenezer and Sarah Averill	441
Chandler, Ephraim and Mary Powers	1053
Chandler, Hannah and David Abbott	108
Chandler, Hannah and Jonathan Kenney	1055
Chandler, Isaac and Abigail Holt	274
Chandler, Jeremiah and Judith Farnum	675
Chandler, John and Elizabeth Esty	449
Chandler, John and Hannah Phelps	58
Chandler, John and Katharine Holman	249
Chandler, John and Mary Jackson	249
Chandler, John and Mary Wyman	1051
Chandler, John and Naomi Farnum	674
Chandler, Joseph and Deborah Symonds	1056
Chandler, Joseph and Dorcas Abbott	250
Chandler, Joseph and Mehitable Russell	19
Chandler, Joseph and Sarah Bennett	1052
Chandler, Joseph and Sarah Richardson	107
Chandler, Lydia and Jonah Crosby	434
Chandler, Mary and James Holt	106
Chandler, Mary and Joseph Snow	263
Chandler, Mary and Silas Holman	1054
Chandler, Mehitable and Andrew Spalding	104
Chandler, Mehitable and Paul Holt	75
Chandler, Mehitable and Robert Crosby	104
Chandler, Peter and Mercy Ingalls	442
Chandler, Rhoda and James Russell	27
Chandler, Sarah and John Russell	8
Chandler, Stevens and Alice Snow	262
Chandler, Stevens and Mary Preston	262
Chandler, Stevens and Sarah Rogers	262
Chandler, Thomas and Elizabeth Walcott	105
Chandler, Thomas and unknown	448
Chandler, William and Mary Holt	61
Chapin, Daniel and Perthene Wheeler	421
Chapman, Jospeh and Keziah Farnum	467
Chase, Joseph and Sarah Eaton	702
Cheever, Susanna and Joseph Russell	4a
Cheney, David and Phebe Russell	111
Cheney, Ebenezer and Priscilla Lyon	202
Cheney, Ebenezer and Tabitha Whipple	855
Cheney, Joseph and Lydia Adams	856
Cheney, Joseph and Selah Tyler	852
Cheney, Persis and John Adams	857
Cheney, Ruth and Oliver Gardner	854
Cheney, William and Delia Shipman	853
Cheney, William and Mehitable Lyon	201
Chickering, Joseph and Sarah Holt	931
Chickering, Zachariah and Mary Holt	927
Child, Amity and Elijah Russell	612
Child, Ann and Willard Pearson	1043
Choate, Eliza and Martin Russell	611
Clapp, Sidney and Oliver Holt	395
Clark, Dyer and Lucinda Holt	415
Clark, Hannah and William Appleton	157
Clark, Mary and Jesse Holt	447
Clark, Samuel and Elizabeth Foster	640
Clark, Stephen and Dinah Preston	362
Clark, William and Eunice Preston	363
Clary, Joseph and Mary Holt	407

Clement, Nancy and Abel Russell — 540
Clyde, Catherine and Lester Holt — 405
Coburn, Mary and Erastus Goodell — 746
Cochran, Mary Ann and John Dale — 1027
Coffin, Moses and Susannah Farnum — 679
Coffin, Stephen and Sarah Holt — 253
Cogswell, Joshua and Thankful Eaton — 835
Colby, Archelaus and Jemima Johnson — 571
Collins, Mary and Ebenezer Holt — 317
Conant, Adelia and Abiel Farnum — 695
Conant, John and Lydia Farnum — 693
Cone, Abigail and Parley Russell — 880
Convers, Charles and Esther Sanger — 862
Convers, Molly and John Weston — 869
Convers, Roxana and Joseph Fuller — 868a
Convers, Stephen and Nellie Whipple — 870
Convers, Stephen and Zeruiah Sanger — 205
Converse, Jedediah and Priscilla Marcy — 801
Converse, Sally and Abiel Holt — 360
Cook, Asenath and Chester Goodale — 398
Coolidge, Mercy and Eliphalet Gray — 895
Coombs, James and Deborah Cummings — 525
Coon, William and Hannah Fletcher — 632
Copeland, Amasa and Tryphena Liscomb — 715
Copeland, James and Sarah Ingalls — 168
Copeland, Rebecca and Nathaniel Ford — 717
Copeland, Sarah and Richard Rindge — 716
Copeland, Willard and Alice Lyon — 718
Copeland, Willard and Rebecca White — 718
Cotton, Rowland and Keziah Holt — 403
Cowdrey, Susannah and Samuel Case — 706
Cowel, Sally and Silas Dana — 430
Coy, Jonathan and Deborah Barker — 174
Coy, Jonathan and Lucy Bingham — 734
Coy, Jonathan and Olive Pixley — 734
Coy, Patty and Peleg Janes — 733
Coy, Willis and Amy Young — 732
Coye, Beulah and Chandler Webber — 736
Coye, David and Dorcas Hannum — 738
Coye, David and Nancy Canfield — 738
Coye, Reuben and Sarah Chambers — 735
Coye, Simeon and Rhoda Brown — 737
Craft, Sarah and Lebbeus Kimball — 410
Crain, Louisa and James Dwinells — 565
Crawford, Samuel and Sarah Work — 777
Crocker, Lois and Timothy Pearl — 385
Crocker, Nathan and Lucia Rogers — 419
Crocker, Stephen and Anna Holt — 352
Crocker, Zebulon and Sarah Holt — 331
Crosby, Asa and Abigail Russell — 645
Crosby, Deborah and Peter Russell — 24
Crosby, Hannah and Phinehas Kidder — 246
Crosby, Jacob and Hannah Russell — 56
Crosby, Joel and Hannah Stevens — 436
Crosby, Jonah and Lydia Chandler — 434
Crosby, Phebe and Jabez Keep — 435
Crosby, Robert and Mehitable Chandler — 104
Crosby, Robert and Susannah Sherwin — 433
Crosby, Zilpah and Joseph Stearns — 247
Cummings, Cyrus and Abigail Davis — 529

Cummings, Deborah and James Coombs — 525
Cummings, Esther and Daniel Preston — 365
Cummings, Jonathan and Deborah Russell — 131
Cummings, Jonathan and Lydia Hill — 524
Cummings, Lucy and Peter Peavey — 908
Cummings, Mary and Solomon Holt — 294
Cummings, Rebecca and Stephen Benson — 531
Cummings, Susannah and John Stacy — 528
Cummings, Sybil and Samuel Barron — 526
Cummings, Thomas and Anna Gibson — 527
Cunnings, Sarah and Josiah Hodgman — 530
Curtis, James and Mary Marcy — 806
Curtis, Sarah and Joel Russell — 637
Curtis, William and Mary Holt — 347
Dady, Olive and Calvin Bishop — 753
Dale, Abigail and Abel Fiske — 1025
Dale, Betsey and Jesse Raymond — 1029
Dale, Ebenezer and Mehitable Beede — 1028
Dale, John and Mary Ann Cochran — 1027
Dale, John and Nancy Beede — 1027
Dale, John and Rhoda Holt — 243
Dale, Mary and Frederick Hutchinson — 1026
Dale, Rhoda and Ebenezer Hutchinson — 1024
Dale, Sarah and John Burton — 1030
Dana, Elizabeth and Amasa Owen — 429
Dana, Jedediah and Lucy Holt — 103
Dana, Mary and James Payn — 432
Dana, Sally and Thomas Payn — 431
Dana, Silas and Sally Cowel — 430
Danforth, Elizabeth and Gardner Marcy — 793
Danielson, James and Dorothy Humphrey — 196
Darby, Oliver and Lovina Stockwell — 906
Darby, Thomas and Mary Holt — 216
Darling, Benjamin and Mary Holt — 304
Darling, Elizabeth and John Merrill — 681
Darling, Jonathan and Hannah Holt — 266
Darling, Ruth and Stephen Merrill — 684
Dascomb, Elizabeth and Daniel Russell — 538
Dascomb, Hannah and Joseph Russell — 541
Davenport, Anna and Uriah Gray — 896
Davis, Abigail and Cyrus Cummings — 529
Davis, Asenath and Alvah Russell — 650
Davis, Israel and Sarah Holt — 945
Day, Hannah and Valentine Holt — 244
DeRoldos, Antoinette and Frederick Russell — 534
Derumple, Sarah and Peletiah Russell — 501
Dickey, Clement and Betsey Russell — 627
Diell, John and Mary Holt — 407
Dimock, Daniel and Hannah Marcy — 803
Dixey, Hannah and Ephraim Wilkins — 551
Dodge, Diana and Samuel Ingalls — 719
Dolliver, Margaret and Jacob Holt — 49
Dorr, Priscilla and Samuel Marcy — 786
Dow, Abel and Olive Rogers — 416
Dow, Cyrus and Abigail Rogers — 418
Downer, Clarissa and Caleb Ingalls — 761
Downer, Mary and Abiel Holt — 81
Downing, Samuel and Abigail Barnard — 311
Downing, Thomas and Catharine Williams — 652
Drake, Mary and Alvan Marcy — 809

Drew, Sally and Ephraim Merrill	686	Emery, Joseph and Dorcas Holt	261
Dunton, Samuel and Lois Pearl	382	Endicott, Robert and Mary Holt	277
Dunton, Samuel and Lovina Marcy	802	Esty, Elizabeth and John Chandler	449
Durkee, Henry and Sally Russell	774	Fairbank, Joseph and Hannah Wilbur	816
Durkee, Henry and Sarah Holt	310	Fairbank, Joshua and Zeulime Sawin	815
Durkee, John and Sarah Holt	391	Fairbank, Sibbel and Shubael Hammond	817
Durkee, Sybel and William Holt	72	Fairbank, Stephen and Martha Sabin	818
Dustin, Elizabeth and Stephen Poor	495	Fairbanks, Joseph and Tabitha Marcy	193
Dustin, Hannah and Samuel Russell	1009	FARNHAM, see Farnum	
Dustin, Sally and Harmon Holt	994	Farnsworth, Keziah and Phinehas Whitney	897
Duston, Betsey and Chandler Russell	239	Farnsworth, Submit and John Hart	768
Dutcher, Charity and Sampson Hunt	576	Farnum Ephraim and Mary Ingalls	32
Dutcher, Sylvia and William Goodell	748	Farnum, Abiel and Adelia Conant	695
Dutton, Jane and Prosper Marcy	811	Farnum, Abigail and Abiel Frye	473
Dwinell, Mehitable and Peter Russell	561	Farnum, Abigail and Eleazer Owen	473
Dwinells, Charlotte and Daniel Wiley	563	Farnum, Abigail and Issachar Kimball	697
Dwinells, James and Louisa Crain	565	Farnum, Anna and Job Wilson	696
Dwinells, Jonathan and Elizabeth Atwood	564	Farnum, Benjamin and Anna Merrill	162
Dwinells, Jonathan and Rachel Russell	137	Farnum, Benjamin and Sarah Graham	689
Dwinells, Lydia and Adam Mills	562	Farnum, Eliab and Abigail Killam	119
Eastman, Ebenezer and Esther Farnum	678	Farnum, Eliab and Hannah Osborne	479
Eastman, Ichabod and Mabel Wolf	827	Farnum, Eliphalet and Hannah Adams	471
Eastman, John and Elizabeth Stickney	826	Farnum, Eliphalet and Mary Adams	118
Eastman, Noah and Hannah Holt	260	Farnum, Eliphalet and Mary Rogers	118
Eastman, Remembrance and John Russell	619	Farnum, Elizabeth and Asa Bottum	470
Eastman, Richard and Abiah Holt	258	Farnum, Elizabeth and Daniel Knowlton	465
Eastman, Ruth and John Stearns	824	Farnum, Ephraim and Cheney White	116
Eastman, Samuel and Abigail Stowell	825	Farnum, Ephraim and Judith Hall	160
Eastman, Samuel and Dorothy Humphrey	196	Farnum, Ephraim and Sarah Brown	690
Eastman, Sarah and Thomas Russell	152	Farnum, Ephraim and Sarah Hunn	469
Eaton, Abigail and Jonathan Batchelder	452	Farnum, Esther and Ebenezer Eastman	678
Eaton, Desire and Alva Rogers	420	Farnum, Eunice and Silas Snow	468
Eaton, Diadama and Benjamin Weaver	833	Farnum, George W. and Anna Allen	478
Eaton, Dilly and Nathaniel Brown	836	Farnum, Haines and Elizabeth Whitehouse	691
Eaton, Ebenezer and Abigail Russell	109	Farnum, Hannah and Uriah Holt	926
Eaton, Ebenezer and Mary Berry	832	Farnum, Henry and Abigail Rudd	461
Eaton, Ebenezer and Mary Humphrey	198	Farnum, Henry and Phebe Russell	21
Eaton, Hannah and Abigail Sheldon	960	Farnum, Henry and Sarah Read	114
Eaton, Hannah and David Blanchard	703	Farnum, Israel and Catherine Talbert	963
Eaton, Hepsibah and Joseph Russell	25	Farnum, Israel and Phebe Sheldon	231
Eaton, Mary and David Whitcomb	704	Farnum, Jeffrey and Mercy Tracy	477
Eaton, Meriam and Elisha Whitney	834	Farnum, Jeremiah and Sally Hall	698
Eaton, Meriam and Ezra Taylor	834	Farnum, John and Polly Stone	688
Eaton, Nathan and Phebe Brooks	831	Farnum, John and Sarah Thompson	688
Eaton, Osgood and Bethiah Virgin	701	Farnum, Jonathan and Esther Perkins	694
Eaton, Phebe and Daniel Sheldon	961	Farnum, Joseph and Catherine Spring	466
Eaton, Sarah and Joseph Chase	702	Farnum, Joshua and Sarah Ford	117
Eaton, Susannah and Jeremiah Wardwell	705	Farnum, Judith and Jeremiah Chandler	675
Eaton, Thankful and Joshua Cogswell	835	Farnum, Keziah and Joseph Chapman	467
Eaton, William and Nancy Farrington	700	Farnum, Lydia and John Conant	693
Eaton, William and Sarah Farnum	163	Farnum, Lydia and Phineas Birchard	462
Edwards, Erastus and Anna Pool	378	Farnum, Lydia and Thomas Holt	279a
Ela, Lydia and Daniel Appleton	156	Farnum, Manasseh and Keziah Ford	115
Eldredge, Jemima and Philemon Holt	316	Farnum, Manasseh and Patience Bibbins	464
Eldredge, Joseph and Rhoda Goodale	397	Farnum, Martha and Nathan Austin	474
Eldridge, Solomon and Sarah Fisk	672	Farnum, Mary and Abiel Hall	687
Eldridge, Sylvanus and Allis Fisk	673	Farnum, Mary and Amos Towne	965
Eldridge, Zoeth and Elizabeth Pearl	383	Farnum, Mary and Jonathan Merrill	161
Elliot, George and Persis Kimball	411	Farnum, Mary and Stephen Holt	62
Ellis, Martin and Desire Russell	600	Farnum, Moses and Esther Carter	677

Farnum, Moses and Rhoda Carter 677
Farnum, Naomi and John Chandler 674
Farnum, Nathaniel and Hannah Sayward 692
Farnum, Phebe and Amos Parke 472
Farnum, Phebe and Daniel Frost 463
Farnum, Phebe and Ebenezer Lamson 962
Farnum, Phebe and Job Abbott 450
Farnum, Phebe and Joseph Preston 113
Farnum, Phebe and Joshua Holt 68
Farnum, Russell and Eunice Van Deuzen 475
Farnum, Sarah and Charles Griffin 699
Farnum, Sarah and Nathan Carter 676
Farnum, Sarah and Timothy Osgood 485
Farnum, Sarah and William Eaton 163
Farnum, Sarah and William MacClure 476
Farnum, Stephen and Keturah Saybott 480
Farnum, Susannah and Moses Coffin 679
Farr, Stephen and Hannah Russell 545
Farrar, Lucy and James Russell 28
Farrington, Nancy and William Eaton 700
Fasset, Pearly and Alfreada Holt 427
Faulkner, Dorcas and John Adams 499
Faulkner, Joseph and Lydia Russell 638
Feaver, Mary and Benjamin Russell 234
Fellows, Eleazer and Hannah Holt 346
Felt, Anne and Robert Russell 53
Felt, Jonathan and Martha Holt 303
Fenton, Francis and Chloe Goodale 329
Fenton, Francis and Elizabeth Holt 80
Fenton, Joseph and Alice Pool 377
Fenton, Luke and Chloe Preston 370
Fenton, Mary and Isaac Sawin 328
Fenton, Mary and James Niles 328
Fenton, Mehitable and Jedediah Sanger 861
Fisk, Allis and Sylvanus Eldridge 673
Fisk, John and Mary Ingalls 159
Fisk, Sarah and Solomon Eldridge 672
Fiske, Abel and Abigail Dale 1025
Fiske, Hannah and Darius Preston 91
Fitch, Daniel and Zipporah Allen 708
Fletcher, Adolphus and Sally Wellington 633
Fletcher, Hannah and William Coon 632
Fletcher, Luke and Hannah Russell 149
Flint, Abigail and Abner Holt 951
Flint, Abigail and Robert Russell 20
Flint, Amos and Abigail Morse 953
Flint, Asenath and Edward Pratt 950
Flint, Daniel and Lydia Shattuck 949
Flint, Ebenezer and Asenath Holt 228
Flint, Ebenezer and Dorcas Lufkin 948
Flint, Ephraim and Eleanor Holt 952
Flint, Hannah and Thomas Russell 618
Flint, John and Sarah Flint 954
Flint, Sarah and John Flint 954
Flint, Tabatha and Ezekiel Russell 110
Floyd, Hepsibah and Eli Russell 602
Ford, Dinah and Daniel Preston 90
Ford, Keziah and Manasseh Farnum 115
Ford, Nathaniel and Rebecca Copeland 717
Ford, Sarah and Joshua Farnum 117

Forrest, Anna and Uriah Russell 649
Foster, Abigail and William Shattuck 641
Foster, Davis and Amy Holt 914
Foster, Elizabeth and Samuel Clark 640
Foster, Gideon and Elizabeth Russell 151
Foster, Hannah and John Peck 374
Foster, Hannah and John Russell 51
Foster, Henry and Phylena Russell 624
Foster, Isaac and Mary Holt 290
Foster, Mary and Samuel Gale 664
Foster, Mehitable and Nathaniel Holt 892
Foster, Sarah and Jonathan Gleason 642
Foster, Sarah and William Barker 172
Fox, Lucy and Chester Kimball 412
Freeman, Jonathan and Mary Russell 648
French, Mary and James Russell 132
French, Sarah and Isaac Allen 166
Frink, Elias and Clarina Frink 414
Frink, Orlando and Eunice Russell 626
Frisbee, Ephraim and Sybil Peake 822
Frost, Daniel and Phebe Farnum 463
Frost, William and Sarah Holt 276
Frye, Abiel and Abigail Farnum 473
Frye, Isaac and Elizabeth Holt 271
Frye, Phebe and Timothy Osgood 121
Frye, Robinson and Nancy Poor 498
Frye, Sarah and Benjamin Holt 60
Fuller, Joseph and Eunice Holt 893
Fuller, Joseph and Mary Holt 387
Fuller, Joseph and Roxana Convers 868a
Fuller, Josiah and Dorcas Holt 393
Fuller, Timothy and Delight Cary 789
Gaggill, John and Dorothy Humphrey 196
Gale, Mary and Robert Treat 663
Gale, Moses and Mary Appleton 155
Gale, Samuel and Mary Foster 664
Gardner, Oliver and Ruth Cheney 854
Gaylord, Moses and Philadelphia Wheeler 423
Geer, Anne and Jonathan Kingsbury 314
Geer, Hannah and Stephen Holt 318
Gerry, Stephen and Anna Barker 742
Gibson, Anna and Thomas Cummings 527
Gibson, Rebekah and Stephen Barker 175
Gifford, William and Nancy Wilkins 553
Gilbard, Elizabeth and Isaac Russell 54
Gilbert, Daniel and Sarah Marcy 800
Gilman, John and Abigail Putnam 568
Gilman, Nathaniel and Mary Holt 259
Glazier, Abigail and Aquilla Russell 146
Glazier, Daniel and Elizabeth Holt 349
Glazier, David and Cylinda Marcy 807
Glazier, Susannah and Jeduthan Russell 145
Gleason, Jonathan and Sarah Foster 642
Glidden, Nathaniel and Phebe Butterfield 515
Gooch, Sarah and Thomas C. Russell 143
Goodale, Augusta and Daniel Briggs 757
Goodale, Benjamin and Abigail Kimball 180
Goodale, Chester and Asenath Cook 398
Goodale, Chloe and Francis Fenton 329
Goodale, Ebenezer and Phebe Holt 96

Goodale, Jacob and Martha Ingalls	36
Goodale, Lois and Nathan Holt	337
Goodale, Peggy and Richard Bishop	179
Goodale, Phebe and Gustavus Grant	401
Goodale, Rhoda and Joseph Eldredge	397
Goodale, Roxilana and Daniel Plimpton	758
Goodale, Sarah and Caleb Holt	336
Goodale, Walter and Sabra Bissell	399
Goodale, Ward and Champany	759
Goodale, Willard and Mary McLean	400
Goodell, Erastus and Mary Coburn	746
Goodell, Jerusha and Ezra Stoddard	842
Goodell, John and Betsey	745
Goodell, John and Deborah Laflin	745
Goodell, Lucy and Mr. Newbury	747
Goodell, Oliver and Paulina Salisbury	749
Goodell, Reuben and Abigail Sharpe	176
Goodell, Reuben and Sarah	744
Goodell, Silas and Sarah Marshall	178
Goodell, Simeon and Martha Williams	177
Goodell, Susanna and Joshua Holt	95
Goodell, William and Sylvia Dutcher	748
Goodnow, Ruth and Ephraim Barker	724
Goodrich, Anna and Valentine Holt	244
Goodridge, Beulah and Thomas Appleton	667
Goolden, Winsor and Mary Merrill	680
Gould, Francis and Irena Perley	460
Gould, John and Abigail Kingsbury	313
Gould, Josiah and Abigail Williams	651
Gould, Louisa and Francis Perley	458
Gould, Sally and Jesse Perley	459
Goulding, Curtis and Rachel Russell	546
Graham, Sarah and Benjamin Farnum	689
Grant, Gustavus and Phebe Goodale	401
Graves, Amos and Hannah Russell	605
Graves, John and Lucy Russell	603
Gray, Eliphalet and Mercy Coolidge	895
Gray, John and Beulah Holt	213
Gray, Uriah and Anna Davenport	896
Greeley, William and Deborah Putnam	569
Green, William and Pamelia Sanger	873
Greene, Thomas and Tabitha Holt	928
Greenslit, John and Salome Pitts	830
Griffin, Charles and Sarah Farnum	699
Griffin, Sally and Elijah Russell	612
Grow, Hannah and Ephraim Barker	171
Grow, Rebekah and Stephen Ingalls	34
Guild, Mary and George Appleton	662
Guild, Sally and John Barker	723
Gurney, Susan and Daniel Towne	968
Gurnsey, Lucy and Jeduthan Russell	606
Gustine, Theodosia and Frederick Russell	534
Gutterson, John and Phebe Ballard	919
Guy, Hannah and Peter Butterfield	513
Hall, Abiel and Mary Farnum	687
Hall, Asa and Cynthia Russell	775
Hall, Ezra and Priscilla Russell	608
Hall, Judith and Ephraim Farnum	160
Hall, Rhoda and Jeduthan Russell	606
Hall, Sally and Jeremiah Farnum	698

Hall, Tirzah and Richard Russell	620
Hammond, Shubael and Sibbel Fairbank	817
Hammond. Margaret and Asa Holt	102
Hannum, Dorcas and David Coye	738
Hardy, Wyman and Sarah Merrill	685
Harriman, Jonathan and Sarah Moulton	456
Harriman, Ruth and Thomas Russell	643
Hart, Constant and Sarah Russell	184
Hart, John and Submit Farnsworth	768
Hart, Josiah and Mehitable	767
Hart, Josiah and Susanna Putnam	767
Harvey, Lucretia and Daniel Stoddard	840
Haseltine, Phebe and Oliver Holt	894
Haskell, Mercy and Abiel Stevens	934
Haskell, Parsons and Hannah Holt	929
Hastings, Dier and Mary Ingalls	183
Hastings, Dyer and Anna Wattles	766
Hastings, Oliver and Lemira Bushnell	765
Hastings, Oliver and Philura Paine	765
Hatch, Nathan and Hannah Marcy	784
Hatch, Ruth and Samuel Marcy	814
Hawes, Sally and Simeon Smith	887
Hawes, Susannah and Solomon Preston	361
Hawley, Hannah and James Barnard	907
Hayward, King and Lucy Paine	847
Hazeltine, Sarah and John Russell	502
Healy, Phebe and Ebenezer Allen	709
Hendrick, Mary and John Stoddard	838
Herrick, Benjamin and Elcy Nugent	1017
Herrick, Betsey and Abner Russell	1013
Herrick, Edward and Mary Andrews	1020
Herrick, Edward and Mary Holt	242
Herrick, Edward and Nancy Barrett	1020
Herrick, George and Mary Holt	1019
Herrick, Israel and Eliza Burns	1022
Herrick, Larkin and Sarah Sheldon	1023
Herrick, Mary and John Putnam	1018
Herrick, Sarah and Josiah Peet	1021
Hibbard, Naomi and Darius Preston	368
Hicks, Zephaniah and Lucy Ingalls	764
Hill, Leavitt and Sarah Russell	644
Hill, Lydia and Jonathan Cummings	524
Hills, Hephzibah and Ezekiel Russell	453
Hilton, Clark and Rebecca Sheldon	972
Hinckley, David and Anne Merrick	338
Hinckley, Mercy and Oliver Pearl	330
Hoar, Benjamin and Abigail Whitney	900
Hoar/Homer. Solomon and Abigail Bishop	750
Hodgman, Abigail and Lemuel Holt	904
Hodgman, Jonathan and Mary Marcy	787
Hodgman, Josiah and Sarah Cummings	530
Holbrook, Abigail and Ephraim Houghton	938
Holbrook, Betsey and Silvanus Houghton	940
Holman, Katharine and John Chandler	249
Holman, Silas and Mary Chandler	1054
Holt, Aaron and Dorothy How	957
Holt, Abel and Anna Abel	334
Holt, Abel and Ruth King	334
Holt, Abiah and Daniel Kimball	291
Holt, Abiah and Richard Eastman	258

Holt, Abiel and Eunice Kingsbury	82
Holt, Abiel and Hannah Abbott	15
Holt, Abiel and Lydia Lovejoy	287
Holt, Abiel and Mary Downer	81
Holt, Abiel and Mary Mosher	333
Holt, Abiel and Phebe Putnam	299
Holt, Abiel and Sally Converse	360
Holt, Abiel and Sarah Abbott	306
Holt, Abigail and David Kendall	76
Holt, Abigail and Isaac Chandler	274
Holt, Abigail and Jacob Holt	922
Holt, Abigail and Jonathan Kingsbury	74
Holt, Abigail and Joseph Holt	283
Holt, Abigail and Moses Batchelder	958
Holt, Abigail and Paul Holt	13
Holt, Abigail and Richard Kimball	98
Holt, Abigail and William Averill	402
Holt, Abner and Abigail Flint	951
Holt, Adelia and Charles Mudge	409
Holt, Alfreada and Pearly Fasset	427
Holt, Alice and Daniel Holt	284
Holt, Alice and John Barnard	73
Holt, Alice and Robert Lyon	309
Holt, Ammi and Martha Abbott	1032
Holt, Amos and Mary Ballard	917
Holt, Amos and Sally Lindal	956
Holt, Amos and Sally Wooley	956
Holt, Amy and Davis Foster	914
Holt, Anna and Henry Slade	1039
Holt, Anna and Joseph Merrick	84
Holt, Anna and Stephen Crocker	352
Holt, Anness and Jonathan Benjamin	902
Holt, Asa and Dinah Holt	285
Holt, Asa and Elizabeth Woodward	426
Holt, Asa and Lydia Stevens	285
Holt, Asa and Margaret Hammond	102
Holt, Asa and Polly Rogers	426
Holt, Asenath and Ebenezer Flint	228
Holt, Asenath and Leonard Holt	350
Holt, Benjamin and Hannah Abbott	255
Holt, Benjamin and Hannah Sheldon	959
Holt, Benjamin and Lydia Holt	70
Holt, Benjamin and Sarah Frye	60
Holt, Bethiah and Solomon Wardwell	301
Holt, Bethiah and Thomas Russell	133
Holt, Beulah and John Gray	213
Holt, Bridget and Levi Andrews	445
Holt, Caleb and Sarah Goodale	336
Holt, Chloe and David Wiley	891
Holt, Chloe and Francis Bowers	297
Holt, Chloe and John Holt	891
Holt, Clarina and Elias Frink	414
Holt, Clarissa and John Holt	358
Holt, Daniel and Abigail Lovejoy	256
Holt, Daniel and Abigail Smith	18
Holt, Daniel and Alice Holt	284
Holt, Daniel and Hannah Holt	69
Holt, Daniel and Kezia Rust	97
Holt, Daniel and Mary Jones	298
Holt, David and Rebecca Osgood	219
Holt, David and Sarah Abbott	930
Holt, David and Sarah Russell	47
Holt, Deborah and Benjamin Preston	16
Holt, Deborah and Joseph White	406
Holt, Dinah and Asa Holt	285
Holt, Dinah and Timothy Pearl	94
Holt, Dorcas and Henry Abbott	911
Holt, Dorcas and Joseph Emery	261
Holt, Dorcas and Josiah Fuller	393
Holt, Dorcas and Moses Lovejoy	280
Holt, Dorcas and Thomas Holt	67
Holt, Dorcas and Thomas Peavey	218
Holt, Ebenezer and Mary Collins	317
Holt, Eleanor and Ephraim Flint	952
Holt, Elijah and Elizabeth Williams	404
Holt, Elijah and Mary Adams	404
Holt, Elijah and Molly Simmons	335
Holt, Elizabeth and Abiel Stevens	225
Holt, Elizabeth and Daniel Glazier	349
Holt, Elizabeth and Francis Bowers	224
Holt, Elizabeth and Francis Fenton	80
Holt, Elizabeth and Isaac Frye	271
Holt, Elizabeth and Timothy Holt	64
Holt, Ephraim and Hannah Holt	295
Holt, Ephraim and Jerusha Kenney	944
Holt, Ephraim and Phebe Russell	50
Holt, Ephraim and Rhoda Russell	1004
Holt, Ephraim and Sarah Black	227
Holt, Esther and Daniel Andrews	933
Holt, Esther and Daniel Parker	357
Holt, Esther and Ebenezer Pearson	245
Holt, Eunice and Joseph Fuller	893
Holt, Eunice and Josiah Wheeler	101
Holt, Frye and Mary Poor	257
Holt, Hannah and Aaron Carpenter	392
Holt, Hannah and Daniel Holt	69
Holt, Hannah and Eleazer Fellows	346
Holt, Hannah and Ephraim Holt	295
Holt, Hannah and John Sylvester	1034
Holt, Hannah and Jonathan Darling	266
Holt, Hannah and Nathan Ballard	221
Holt, Hannah and Noah Eastman	260
Holt, Hannah and Oliver Pearl	330
Holt, Hannah and Parsons Haskell	929
Holt, Hannah and Peter Holt	278
Holt, Hannah and Richard Whitney	272
Holt, Hannah and Robert Russell	20
Holt, Hannah and William Holt	72
Holt, Harmon and Sally Dustin	994
Holt, Hiram and Elohe Varril	997
Holt, Isaac and Mehitable Orcutt	345
Holt, Isaac and Sarah Orcutt	85
Holt, Jacob and Abigail Holt	922
Holt, Jacob and Anna Melvin	903
Holt, Jacob and Margaret Dolliver	49
Holt, Jacob and Mary Osgood	49
Holt, Jacob and Rhoda Abbott	222
Holt, James and Chloe Stiles	319
Holt, James and Esther Owens	88
Holt, James and Huldah Stiles	319

Holt, James and Luce Sawins	88
Holt, James and Lucy Whipple	279
Holt, James and Mary Chandler	106
Holt, James and Mary Pool	354
Holt, James and Sarah Abbott	65
Holt, Jedediah and Phebe Barker	265
Holt, Jedediah and Sarah Thorndike	268
Holt, Jesse and Mary Clark	447
Holt, John and Chloe Holt	891
Holt, John and Clarissa Holt	358
Holt, John and Dorcas Abbott	292
Holt, John and Hannah Wright	946
Holt, John and Lydia Russell	238
Holt, Jonathan and Lydia Blanchard	48
Holt, Jonathan and Ruth Kimball	220
Holt, Jonathan and Sarah Lake	905
Holt, Joseph and Abigail Holt	283
Holt, Joseph and Betsy Parker	355
Holt, Joseph and Dorcas Boynton	71
Holt, Joseph and Elizabeth Stratton	307
Holt, Joseph and Mary Abbott	71
Holt, Joseph and Mary Russell	55
Holt, Joseph and Ruth Johnson	300
Holt, Joseph and Susan Stearns	996
Holt, Joshua and Hannah Ingalls	289
Holt, Joshua and Keturah Holt	17
Holt, Joshua and Mary Abbott	95
Holt, Joshua and Phebe Farnum	68
Holt, Joshua and Susanna Goodell	95
Holt, Keturah and Jonathan Amidon	390
Holt, Keturah and Joshua Holt	17
Holt, Keziah and Rowland Cotton	403
Holt, Lemuel and Abigail Hodgman	904
Holt, Lemuel and Mary Abbott	389
Holt, Leonard and Asenath Holt	350
Holt, Leonard and Joanna Alden	351
Holt, Lester and Catherine Clyde	405
Holt, Lois and Moses Pearson	281
Holt, Lois and Moses Rogers	100
Holt, Luce and Aaron Walker	359
Holt, Lucy and Jedediah Dana	103
Holt, Lucy and William Holt	308
Holt, Lydia and Benjamin Holt	70
Holt, Lydia and Humphrey Bean	998
Holt, Lydia and Robert Parker	1033
Holt, Lydia and Samuel Towne	912
Holt, Lydia and Timothy Holt	293
Holt, Marcia and Augustus Sharp	408
Holt, Marstin and Abigail Wheeler	229
Holt, Martha and John Richardson	79
Holt, Martha and Jonathan Felt	303
Holt, Mary and Benjamin Darling	304
Holt, Mary and Daniel Needham	332
Holt, Mary and Daniel Proctor	932
Holt, Mary and Ebenezer Tarbox	302
Holt, Mary and Edward Herrick	242
Holt, Mary and George Herrick	1019
Holt, Mary and Isaac Foster	290
Holt, Mary and Jacob Andrews	444
Holt, Mary and James Larrabee	302

Holt, Mary and Jeremiah Osgood	61
Holt, Mary and John Diell	407
Holt, Mary and Joseph Clary	407
Holt, Mary and Joseph Fuller	387
Holt, Mary and Joseph Persons	87
Holt, Mary and Joseph Truesdell	78
Holt, Mary and Josiah Ingalls	10
Holt, Mary and Nathaniel Andrews	444
Holt, Mary and Nathaniel Gilman	259
Holt, Mary and Robert Endicott	277
Holt, Mary and Samuel Rich	1038
Holt, Mary and Thomas Darby	216
Holt, Mary and William Chandler	61
Holt, Mary and William Curtis	347
Holt, Mary and Zachariah Chickering	927
Holt, Mehitable and Jeremiah Phelps	320
Holt, Mehitable and Samuel Lufkin	286
Holt, Moses and Azuba Hubbard	955
Holt, Moses and Elizabeth Russell	9
Holt, Moses and Mary Austin	913
Holt, Moses and Prudence Russell	58
Holt, Nancy and James Whittier	1031
Holt, Nathan and Abigail Merrick	83
Holt, Nathan and Bathsheba Williams	83
Holt, Nathan and Lois Goodale	337
Holt, Nathan and Lydia Kingsbury	83
Holt, Nathan and Rebecca Holt	910
Holt, Nathan and Sarah Abbott	66
Holt, Nathan and Susannah Blanchard	254
Holt, Nathaniel and Elizabeth Stevens	211
Holt, Nathaniel and Mehitable Foster	892
Holt, Nehemiah and Abigail Twist	923
Holt, Nehemiah and Esther Varnum	223
Holt, Nicholas and Dorcas Abbott	11
Holt, Nicholas and Hannah Osgood	63
Holt, Nicholas and Lois Phelps	63
Holt, Nicholas and Mary Manning	11
Holt, Nicholas and Mary Russell	2
Holt, Nicholas and Molly Wormwood	269
Holt, Nicholas and Phebe Batchelder	269
Holt, Olive and Joseph White	406
Holt, Oliver and Eunice Raymond	212
Holt, Oliver and Hannah Russell	7
Holt, Oliver and Martha Sibley	348
Holt, Oliver and Phebe Haseltine	894
Holt, Oliver and Sidney Clapp	395
Holt, Oliver and Susannah Wright	45
Holt, Paul and Abigail Holt	13
Holt, Paul and Mehitable Chandler	75
Holt, Paul and Sarah Welch	315
Holt, Peter and Hannah Holt	278
Holt, Phebe and Ebenezer Goodale	96
Holt, Phebe and Israel Wood	267
Holt, Phebe and James Houghton	226
Holt, Phebe and Joseph Batchelder	288
Holt, Phebe and Zalmon How	947
Holt, Philemon and Jemima Eldredge	316
Holt, Polly and Simeon Rumrill	428
Holt, Rebecca and Nathan Holt	910
Holt, Rhoda and John Dale	243

Holt, Rhoda and John Lovejoy	925
Holt, Robert and Lucy Lakin	1035
Holt, Robert and Rebecca Preston	14
Holt, Roxanna and Ebenezer Sumner	413
Holt, Samuel and Hannah Bennett	394
Holt, Sarah and Barachias Abbott	275
Holt, Sarah and Barnabas Wood	305
Holt, Sarah and Henry Brown	1037
Holt, Sarah and Henry Durkee	310
Holt, Sarah and Israel Davis	945
Holt, Sarah and James Barnard	217
Holt, Sarah and John Durkee	391
Holt, Sarah and Jonathan Whitney	214
Holt, Sarah and Joseph Chickering	931
Holt, Sarah and Joseph Russell	541
Holt, Sarah and Joshua Preston	369
Holt, Sarah and Peletiah Lyon	77
Holt, Sarah and Stephen Coffin	253
Holt, Sarah and William Frost	276
Holt, Sarah and William Pierce	273
Holt, Sarah and Zebulon Crocker	331
Holt, Silas and Mary Brooks	99
Holt, Smith and Lydia Snow	425
Holt, Solomon and Mary Cummings	294
Holt, Solomon and Zerviah Abell	356
Holt, Stephen and Fanny Bowers	296
Holt, Stephen and Hannah Geer	318
Holt, Stephen and Mary Farnum	62
Holt, Stephen and Molly Bragg	924
Holt, Susannah and Carlton Parker	890
Holt, Tabitha and Abiel Stevens	225
Holt, Tabitha and Thomas Greene	928
Holt, Thomas and Alice Peabody	12
Holt, Thomas and Dorcas Holt	67
Holt, Thomas and Hannah Kimball	67
Holt, Thomas and Lydia Farnum	279a
Holt, Timothy and Elizabeth Holt	64
Holt, Timothy and Esther Scripture	353
Holt, Timothy and Hannah Johnson	270
Holt, Timothy and Lydia Holt	293
Holt, Timothy and Rebecca Chamberlain	86
Holt, Uriah and Anness Willard	215
Holt, Uriah and Hannah Farnum	926
Holt, Uriah and Margaret Mason	388
Holt, Uriah and Sarah Wright	46
Holt, Valentine and Anna Goodrich	244
Holt, Valentine and Hannah Day	244
Holt, Valentine and Mary Morrill	1036
Holt, Wesley and Ann Witham	1040
Holt, Wesley and Mary Boyd	1040
Holt, William and Elizabeth Ames	252
Holt, William and Elizabeth Jones	282
Holt, William and Hannah Holt	72
Holt, William and Lucy Holt	308
Holt, William and Mary Stearns	995
Holt, William and Sybel Durkee	72
Holt, Zela and Priscilla Abbott	446
Holt, Zilpha and Jonathan Whitney	396
Holt. Lucinda and Dyer Clark	415
Hood, Lydia and Asa Osgood	487
Hooton, Catherine and Benjamin Appleton	660
Hopkins, George and Rachel Russell	881
Houghton, Asenath and William Jordan	943
Houghton, Bethiah and John Mason	942
Houghton, Eliza and James Russell	613
Houghton, Ephraim and Abigail Holbrook	938
Houghton, Ephraim and Mary Nichols	938
Houghton, James and Hannah Russell	537
Houghton, James and Phebe Holt	226
Houghton, Orinda and Benjamin Learned	941
Houghton, Phebe and Ebenezer Ormsby	939
Houghton, Silvanus and Betsey Holbrook	940
How, Dorothy and Aaron Holt	957
How, Zalmon and Phebe Holt	947
Howard, David and Persis Paine	851
Howard, Hannah and Fletcher Russell	990
Howard, Manasseh and Lucy Work	781
Howe, Achsah and Stephen Marcy	785
Hubbard, Azuba and Moses Holt	955
Hudson, Rebecca and Ebenezer Russell	776
Hugg, William and Lydia Hunt	583
Humphrey, Dorothy and James Danielson	196
Humphrey, Dorothy and John Gaggill	196
Humphrey, Dorothy and Samuel Eastman	196
Humphrey, Hannah and Jonathan Avery	195
Humphrey, John and Hannah Russell	40
Humphrey, Mary and Ebenezer Eaton	198
Humphrey, Rachel and John Pitts	197
Humphrey, Sarah and Joshua Stoddard	199
Humphrey, Zerviah and Noah Paine	200
Hunn, Sarah and Ephraim Farnum	469
Hunt, Amos and Mary Lowry	584
Hunt, David and Hannah Johnson	582
Hunt, David and Wealthy Burrall	582
Hunt, Emma and Ezra Tupper	579
Hunt, Jemima and Joseph Wilcox	585
Hunt, John and Elizabeth Pulsifer	578
Hunt, Joseph and Jemima Russell	26
Hunt, Lydia and William Hugg	583
Hunt, Mary and Joseph Johnson	572
Hunt, Robert and Rebekah Peck	140
Hunt, Russell and Esther Beebe	575
Hunt, Russell and Lucy Swift	580
Hunt, Russell and Lydia Peck	141
Hunt, Salmon and Reuby Whitney	581
Hunt, Sampson and Charity Dutcher	576
Hunt, Sampson and Polly Bidwell	576
Hunt, Sarah and Josiah Johnson	139
Hunt, Sarah and Rufus Landon	577
Huntington, Andrew and Serviah Smith	884
Huntress, John and Phebe Russell	596
Hurlburt, Joseph and Phila Sanger	874
Hutchins, Eunice and Ebenezer Sanger	871
Hutchinson, Ebenezer and Rhoda Dale	1024
Hutchinson, Frederick and Mary Dale	1026
Hutchinson, Ruth and Jonathan Russell	134
Hutchinson, Sarah and Thomas Osgood	122
Ingalls, Benjamin and Eunice Woodworth	181
Ingalls, Benjamin and Mary Lyon	37
Ingalls, Caleb and Clarissa Downer	761

Ingalls, Daniel and Bethiah Brown	760
Ingalls, David and Mary May	182
Ingalls, Dorcas and Timothy Perrin	763
Ingalls, Elizabeth and John Stevens	35
Ingalls, Hannah and Joshua Holt	289
Ingalls, John and Mary Willis	31
Ingalls, John and Sarah Russell	5
Ingalls, Josiah and Mary Holt	10
Ingalls, Lemuel and Louisa Prentiss	720
Ingalls, Lucy and Zephaniah Hicks	764
Ingalls, Martha and Jacob Goodale	36
Ingalls, Martha and William Barker	36
Ingalls, Mary and Dier Hastings	183
Ingalls, Mary and Ephraim Farnum	32
Ingalls, Mary and John Fisk	159
Ingalls, Mehitable and Benjamin Allen	33
Ingalls, Mercy and Peter Chandler	442
Ingalls, Phebe and James Parker	59
Ingalls, Samuel and Deborah Meacham	170
Ingalls, Samuel and Diana Dodge	719
Ingalls, Sarah and James Copeland	168
Ingalls, Stephen and Rebekah Grow	34
Ingalls, Theda and Joshua Pratt	762
Ingalls, Thomas and Ruth Woodworth	169
Ireland, Rebecca and Ephraim Russell	542
Jackson, Mary and John Chandler	249
James, Benjamin and Cynthia Russell	879
Janes, Peleg and Patty Coy	733
Jennison, John and Elvira Russell	625
Jewett, Judith and Edward Woodbury	671
Johnson, Abel and Deborah Preston	372
Johnson, Hannah and David Hunt	582
Johnson, Hannah and Timothy Holt	270
Johnson, Jemima and Archelaus Colby	571
Johnson, Jeremiah and Sybil Kimball	573
Johnson, Jeremiah and Thomazin Blanchard	573
Johnson, Joseph and Mary Hunt	572
Johnson, Josiah and Sarah Hunt	139
Johnson, Phebe and Thomas Russell	3
Johnson, Ruth and Joseph Holt	300
Johnson, Samuel and Sarah Pearl	384
Johnson, Sarah and Horatio Bingham	574
Johnson, Sarah and Peter Osgood	120
Jones, Elizabeth and William Holt	282
Jones, Mary and Daniel Holt	298
Jordan, David and Temperance Russell	587
Jordan, Solomon and Lydia Russell	586
Jordan, William and Asenath Houghton	943
Judson, Andrew and Elizabeth Work	778
Karr, Joanna and Ebenezer Pearson	1042
Kean, Mary Ann and Robert Russell	532
Keep, Jabez and Phebe Crosby	435
Kendall, Abigail and Enos Preston	321
Kendall, David and Abigail Holt	76
Kendall, David and Mehitable Stiles	322
Kendall, Roxana and Ezra Smith	882
Kendall, William and Lydia Russell	604
Kenney, Dolly and Peabody Russell	557
Kenney, Jerusha and Ephraim Holt	944
Kenney, Jonathan and Hannah Chandler	1055

Keyes, Alvin and Amelia Russell	1015
Keyes, Edward and Mary Work	779
Keyes, Proctor and Mary Russell	1016
Kidder, Phineas and Ann Manley	1045
Kidder, Phineas and Patty Rose	1045
Kidder, Phinehas and Hannah Crosby	246
Kidder, Samuel and Hannah Brown	1044
Kilgore, Mehitable and William Russell	976
Killam, Abigail and Eliab Farnum	119
Kimball, Abigail and Benjamin Goodale	180
Kimball, Chester and Lucy Fox	412
Kimball, Daniel and Abiah Holt	291
Kimball, Hannah and Thomas Holt	67
Kimball, Issachar and Abigail Farnum	697
Kimball, Lebbeus and Sarah Craft	410
Kimball, Persis and George Elliot	411
Kimball, Richard and Abigail Holt	98
Kimball, Ruth and Jonathan Holt	220
Kimball, Sally and Peter Towne	964
Kimball, Sybil and Jeremiah Johnson	573
King, Lois and Asaph Allen	714
King, Matilda and Chester Marcy	792
King, Ruth and Abel Holt	334
Kingsbury, Abigail and John Gould	313
Kingsbury, Eunice and Abiel Holt	82
Kingsbury, Jonathan and Abigail Holt	74
Kingsbury, Jonathan and Anne Geer	314
Kingsbury, Jonathan and Lodema Ransom	314
Kingsbury, Lydia and Nathan Holt	83
Kingsley, Jedediah and Mary Cary	788
Kittredge, Stephen and Mehitable Russell	520
Kittredge, Thomas and Susanna Osgood	483
Knowlton, Chester and Priscilla Sanger	868
Knowlton, Daniel and Elizabeth Farnum	465
Knowlton, Jonathan and Zerviah Sanger	865
Knowlton, Thomas and Martha Marcy	805
Labbell, Mary Ann and Joseph Russell	607
Laflin, Deborah and John Goodell	745
Lake, Sarah and Jonathan Holt	905
Lakin, Lucy and Robert Holt	1035
Lamb, Joseph and Dorcas Marcy	804
Lamson, Ebenezer and Phebe Farnum	962
Lancaster, Thomas and Mary Moulton	457
Landon, Rufus and Sarah Hunt	577
Lane, Rebecca and David Pulsipher	629
Lane, Susan and Elias Pulsipher	630
Larrabee, James and Mary Holt	302
Lawrence, Abigail and Joshua Stoddard	839
Lawrence, Esther and Royal Stearns	1047
Lawrence, Samuel and Rhoda Russell	592
Learned, Benjamin and Orinda Houghton	941
LeBaron, James and Jane Russell	588
Lewis, Mary and Jonathan Russell	1011
Lindal, Sally and Amos Holt	956
Linkhorn, Hannah and Joseph Russell	43
Liscomb, Tryphena and Amasa Copeland	715
Locke, Reuben and Phebe Russell	547
Loring, Thomas and Sally Russell	982
Lovejoy, Abiel and Mary Poor	492
Lovejoy, Abigail and Daniel Holt	256

Lovejoy, Ebenezer and Phebe Russell	979
Lovejoy, James and Mahala Stearns	1049
Lovejoy, John and Dolly Russell	983
Lovejoy, John and Rhoda Holt	925
Lovejoy, Lydia and Abiel Holt	287
Lovejoy, Moses and Dorcas Holt	280
Lowry, Mary and Amos Hunt	584
Lufkin, Dorcas and Ebenezer Flint	948
Lufkin, Samuel and Mehitable Holt	286
Lyman, Lucy and Simeon Smith	210
Lynch, Artimesia and Ebenezer Russell	1007
Lyon, Alice and John Russell	186
Lyon, Alice and Willard Copeland	718
Lyon, Mary and Benjamin Ingalls	37
Lyon, Mehitable and William Cheney	201
Lyon, Peletiah and Sarah Holt	77
Lyon, Priscilla and Ebenezer Cheney	202
Lyon, Robert and Alice Holt	309
Lyon, Seth and Abigail Russell	41
Lyons, David and Rebecca Barker	740
MacClure, William and Sarah Farnum	476
Manley, Ann and Phineas Kidder	1045
Manning, Elizabeth and Robert Russell	20
Manning, Mary and Nicholas Holt	11
Marcy, Alvan and Mary Drake	809
Marcy, Avis and Burpee Prouty	810
Marcy, Chester and Matilda King	792
Marcy, Cylinda and David Glazier	807
Marcy, Dorcas and Joseph Lamb	804
Marcy, Dorcas and Nathaniel Cary	189
Marcy, Dorcas and Seymour Burnham	813
Marcy, Esther and Isaac Parker	808
Marcy, Gardner and Elizabeth Danforth	793
Marcy, Hannah and Daniel Dimock	803
Marcy, Hannah and Nathan Hatch	784
Marcy, John and Hannah Sharpe	188
Marcy, John and Lucy	783
Marcy, Levi and Ruth Sargent	798
Marcy, Lovina and Samuel Dunton	802
Marcy, Martha and Thomas Knowlton	805
Marcy, Mary and James Curtis	806
Marcy, Mary and Jonathan Hodgman	787
Marcy, Mary and Nathan Perkins	799
Marcy, Olive and Wilder Willard	794
Marcy, Orrin and Polly Work	812
Marcy, Priscilla and Jedediah Converse	801
Marcy, Prosper and Jane Dutton	811
Marcy, Salome and Ebenezer Pike	797
Marcy, Samuel and Lois Peake	192
Marcy, Samuel and Mary Russell	39
Marcy, Samuel and Priscilla Dorr	786
Marcy, Samuel and Ruth Hatch	814
Marcy, Sarah and Daniel Gilbert	800
Marcy, Sibbel and Moses Peake	194
Marcy, Stephen and Achsah Howe	785
Marcy, Tabitha and Joseph Fairbanks	193
Marcy, Willard and Lydia Pike	795
Marcy, William and Lucy Bugbee	190
Marcy, William and Rosanna Tucker	190
Marcy, Winthrop and Abigail Sargent	796
Marcy, Winthrop and Olive Ayers	796
Marcy, Zebadiah and Phebe Pearl	386
Marcy, Zebadiah and Priscilla Morris	191
Marshall, Deborah and Joshua Pearl	381
Marshall, Mary and Robert Russell	1
Marshall, Sarah and Silas Goodell	178
Mason, Abigail and Augustus Paine	850
Mason, Jane and Roswell Peake	820
Mason, John and Bethiah Houghton	942
Mason, Margaret and Uriah Holt	388
May, Mary and David Ingalls	182
May, Nathaniel and Betty Allen	711
McDowell, Polly and John Allen	713
McHard, Sarah and Isaac Adams	500
McIntire, David and Hannah Ballard	915
McLean, Mary and Willard Goodale	400
Meacham, Deborah and Samuel Ingalls	170
Meacham, Hannah and Ezekiel Russell	453
Mead, John and Sarah Whitney	898
Melcher, Nancy and Benjamin Putnam	570
Melross, William and Cynthia Sanger	859
Melvin, Anna and Jacob Holt	903
Merrick, Abigail and Nathan Holt	83
Merrick, Anne and David Hinckley	338
Merrick, Caleb and Charlotte Noble	342
Merrick, Constant and Experience Burt	343
Merrick, Elizabeth and Samuel Nye	344
Merrick, Joseph and Anna Holt	84
Merrick, Joseph and Irena Alden	341
Merrick, Thomas and Joanna Noble	340
Merrick, Timothy and Mehitable Atwood	339
Merrill, Anna and Benjamin Farnum	162
Merrill, Ephraim and Sally Drew	686
Merrill, John and Elizabeth Darling	681
Merrill, Jonathan and Mary Barnard	682
Merrill, Jonathan and Mary Farnum	161
Merrill, Mary and Winsor Goolden	680
Merrill, Moses and Miriam Barnard	683
Merrill, Moses and Sarah Worthing	683
Merrill, Sarah and Wyman Hardy	685
Merrill, Stephen and Ruth Darling	684
Metcalf, Asa and Sally Russell	1012
Miles, Abner and Deborah Underwood	505
Mills, Adam and Lydia Dwinells	562
Miner, Mary and Elijah Wheeler	422
Mitchell, Lydia and James Russell	142
Moore, Deborah and Samuel Robie	517
Moore, Olive and Peletiah Russell	127
Morrill, Mary and Valentine Holt	1036
Morris, Priscilla and Zebadiah Marcy	191
Morse, Abigail and Amos Flint	953
Morse, Enoch and Eunice Russell	589
Morse, Sarah and Nathaniel Russell	590
Mosher, Mary and Abiel Holt	333
Moulton, Elijah and Elizabeth Russell	112
Moulton, Mary and Thomas Lancaster	457
Moulton, Sarah and Jonathan Harriman	456
Mudge, Charles and Adelia Holt	409
Murdoch, Margaret and Charles Putnam	567
Needham, Daniel and Mary Holt	332

Needham, Sarah and Amos Sheldon	233
Newell, Olive and Ebenezer Russell	1014
Nichols, Diana and Eliab Russell	1010
Nichols, Mary and Ephraim Houghton	938
Niles, Elizabeth and Aden Sanger	864
Niles, James and Mary Fenton	328
Noble, Charlotte and Caleb Merrick	342
Noble, Joanna and Thomas Merrick	340
Norton, Dinah and Jacob Stevens	935
Noyes, Phebe and James Parker	251
Nugent, Elcy and Benjamin Herrick	1017
Nutting, Abner and Matilde Bishop	754
Nye, Elijah and Eunice Preston	371
Nye, Samuel and Elizabeth Merrick	344
Nye, Timothy and Sarah Preston	367
Oliver, John and Esther Russell	989
Orcutt, Mehitable and Isaac Holt	345
Orcutt, Sarah and Isaac Holt	85
Ordway, Olive and Ephraim Russell	1006
Ormsby, Ebenezer and Phebe Houghton	939
Osborne, Hannah and Eliab Farnum	479
Osgood, Asa and Dorcas Stevens	487
Osgood, Asa and Hannah Powers	487
Osgood, Asa and Lydia Hood	487
Osgood, Deborah and Obadiah Wood	124
Osgood, Dorcas and Benjamin Snow	264
Osgood, Elizabeth and Willard Williams	655
Osgood, Hannah and John Adams	126
Osgood, Hannah and Nicholas Holt	63
Osgood, Isaac and Abigail Bailey	123
Osgood, Isaac and Rebecca Pickman	484
Osgood, Jeremiah and Mary Holt	61
Osgood, Joshua and Elizabeth Brown	490
Osgood, Mary and Jacob Holt	49
Osgood, Mary and Joseph Bradley	489
Osgood, Peter and Hannah Porter	481
Osgood, Peter and Mary Willis	491
Osgood, Peter and Sarah Johnson	120
Osgood, Phebe and Thomas Poor	125
Osgood, Priscilla and James Russell	4
Osgood, Rebecca and David Holt	219
Osgood, Samuel and Maria Bourne	482
Osgood, Sarah and Jonathan Bradley	488
Osgood, Susanna and Thomas Kittredge	483
Osgood, Thomas and Sarah Hutchinson	122
Osgood, Timothy and Chloe Bridges	486
Osgood, Timothy and Mary Russell	22
Osgood, Timothy and Phebe Frye	121
Osgood, Timothy and Sarah Farnum	485
Owen, Amasa and Elizabeth Owen	429
Owen, Eleazer and Abigail Farnum	473
Owen, Mary and Henry Appleton	661
Owens, Esther and James Holt	88
Paine, Augustus and Abigail Mason	850
Paine, Elisha and Jerusha Welch	849
Paine, Hannah and John Work	848
Paine, Lucy and King Hayward	847
Paine, Noah and Zerviah Humphrey	200
Paine, Persis and David Howard	851
Paine, Philura and Oliver Hastings	765
Palmer, Betsey and Uriah Russell	649
Palmer, John and Mary Russell	523
Palmer, Rufus and Dorcas Cary	790
Parke, Amos and Phebe Farnum	472
Parker, Betsy and Jacob Holt	355
Parker, Carlton and Susannah Holt	890
Parker, Daniel and Esther Holt	357
Parker, Isaac and Esther Marcy	808
Parker, Isaac and Olive Abbott	731
Parker, James and Phebe Ingalls	59
Parker, James and Phebe Noyes	251
Parker, Michael and Fanny Towne	967
Parker, Robert and Lydia Holt	1033
Parmenter, Sophia and James Russell	533
Parsons, Miriam and Isaac Stoddard	844
Pattee, Benjamin and Mary Robie	519
Payn, James and Mary Dana	432
Payn, Thomas and Sally Dana	431
Peabody, Alice and Thomas Holt	12
Peabody, Francis and Mary Russell	558
Peabody, Hannah and James Russell	556
Peabody, Peggy and Jesse Wilkins	554
Peabody, Rebecca and James Russell	136
Peake, Elijah and unknown	821
Peake, Lois and Samuel Marcy	192
Peake, Moses and Sibbel Marcy	194
Peake, Oliver and Elizabeth	819
Peake, Roswell and Jane Mason	820
Peake, Sybil and Ephraim Frisbee	822
Pearl, Elizabeth and Zoeth Eldridge	383
Pearl, Joshua and Deborah Marshall	381
Pearl, Lois and Samuel Dunton	382
Pearl, Oliver and Hannah Holt	330
Pearl, Oliver and Mercy Hinckley	330
Pearl, Phebe and Zebadiah Marcy	386
Pearl, Sarah and Samuel Johnson	384
Pearl, Timothy and Dinah Holt	94
Pearl, Timothy and Lois Crocker	385
Pearl. Alice and Eleazer Scripture	380
Pearson, Ebenezer and Esther Holt	245
Pearson, Ebenezer and Joanna Karr	1042
Pearson, Esther and Ephraim Putnam	1041
Pearson, Moses and Lois Holt	281
Pearson, Willard and Ann Child	1043
Peavey, Peter and Lucy Cummings	908
Peavey, Thomas and Dorcas Holt	218
Peck, Anna and Robert Snow	375
Peck, Elisha and Sarah Badger	376
Peck, John and Hannah Foster	374
Peck, John and Jerusha Preston	92
Peck, John and Rebecca Badger	374
Peck, Levi and Hannah Stoddard	837
Peck, Lydia and Russell Hunt	141
Peck, Rebekah and Robert Hunt	140
Peet, Josiah and Sarah Herrick	1021
Perkins, Esther and Jonathan Farnum	694
Perkins, Hannah and Joseph Russell	25
Perkins, Moses and Lucy Wilkins	549
Perkins, Nathan and Mary Marcy	799
Perkins, Sophia and James Putnam	566

Perley, Francis and Louisa Gould	458
Perley, Irena and Francis Gould	460
Perley, Jesse and Elizabeth Russell	112
Perley, Jesse and Sally Gould	459
Perris, Timothy and Dorcas Ingalls	763
Perry, Sarah and Benjamin Russell	38
Persons, Joseph and Mary Holt	87
Pettengill, William and Sarah Ballard	916
Pevey, Thomas and Lydia Abbott	909
Phelps, Hannah and John Chandler	58
Phelps, Jeremiah and Mehitable Holt	320
Phelps, Lois and Nicholas Holt	63
Philbrick, Jonathan and Esther Russell	647
Phillips, Asa and Anna Work	782
Pickett, Lydia and Samuel Russell	559
Pickman, Rebecca and Isaac Osgood	484
Pierce, Marshall and Mary Stearns	1046
Pierce, William and Sarah Holt	273
Pike, Ebenezer and Salome Marcy	797
Pike, Lydia and Willard Marcy	795
Pitcher, Elijah and Hannah Barker	722
Pitts, Benjamin and Freelove Whipple	828
Pitts, Jeremiah and Irena Younglove	829
Pitts, John and Rachel Humphrey	197
Pitts, Salome and John Greenslit	830
Pixley, Olive and Jonathan Coy	734
Plant, Sarah and Gideon Russell	615
Plimpton, Daniel and Roxilana Goodale	758
Plimpton, Keziah and David Russell	769
Plummer, Mary and Stephen Poor	495
Plummer, Moses and Phebe Poor	494
Pool, Alice and Joseph Fenton	377
Pool, Amy and Elijah Sawin	379
Pool, Anna and Erastus Edwards	378
Pool, Mary and James Holt	354
Pool, Timothy and Deborah Preston	93
Poor, Caleb and Polly M. Avery	497
Poor, Enoch and Prudence Brevard	496
Poor, Hannah and William Whittier	493
Poor, Mary and Abiel Lovejoy	492
Poor, Mary and Frye Holt	257
Poor, Nancy and Robinson Frye	498
Poor, Phebe and Moses Plummer	494
Poor, Stephen and Elizabeth Dustin	495
Poor, Stephen and Mary Plummer	495
Poor, Thomas and Phebe Osgood	125
Porter, Hannah and Peter Osgood	481
Powers, Gideon and Apphia Russell	988
Powers, Hannah and Asa Osgood	487
Powers, Mary and Ephraim Chandler	1053
Pratt, David and Mary Russell	597
Pratt, Edward and Asenath Flint	950
Pratt, Joshua and Theda Ingalls	762
Pratt, Rachel and Joseph Russell	594
Pratt, Rhoda and Jedediah Russell	240
Prentiss, Louisa and Lemuel Ingalls	720
Preston, Amos and Martha Taylor	373
Preston, Benjamin and Bathsheba Snow	89
Preston, Benjamin and Deborah Holt	16
Preston, Calvin and Philatheta Bibbens	366
Preston, Chloe and James Boutell	364
Preston, Chloe and Luke Fenton	370
Preston, Daniel and Dinah Ford	90
Preston, Daniel and Esther Cummings	365
Preston, Darius and Hannah Fiske	91
Preston, Darius and Naomi Hibbard	368
Preston, Deborah and Abel Johnson	372
Preston, Deborah and Timothy Pool	93
Preston, Dinah and Stephen Clark	362
Preston, Enos and Abigail Kendall	321
Preston, Eunice and Elijah Nye	371
Preston, Eunice and William Clark	363
Preston, Jerusha and John Peck	92
Preston, Joseph and Phebe Farnum	113
Preston, Joshua and Sarah Holt	369
Preston, Mary and Benjamin Russell	6
Preston, Mary and Stevens Chandler	262
Preston, Rebecca and Robert Holt	14
Preston, Sarah and Timothy Nye	367
Preston, Solomon and Susannah Hawes	361
Proctor, Daniel and Mary Holt	932
Prouty, Burpee and Avis Marcy	810
Pulsifer, Elizabeth and John Hunt	578
Pulsipher, David and Priscilla Russell	148
Pulsipher, David and Rebecca Lane	629
Pulsipher, Elias and Susan Lane	630
Pulsipher, Samuel and Sally Weaver	628
Pulsipher, William and Electa Barnes	631
Putnam, Abigail and John Gilman	568
Putnam, Benjamin and Nancy Melcher	570
Putnam, Caleb and Hannah Russell	138
Putnam, Charles and Margaret Murdoch	567
Putnam, Deborah and William Greeley	569
Putnam, Ephraim and Esther Pearson	1041
Putnam, James and Sophia Perkins	566
Putnam, John and Mary Herrick	1018
Putnam, Phebe and Abiel Holt	299
Putnam, Susanna and Josiah Hart	767
Pynchon, Martha and David Russell	769
Ransom, Lodema and Jonathan Kingsbury	314
Raymond, Eunice and Oliver Holt	212
Raymond, Jesse and Betsey Dale	1029
Read, Sarah and Henry Farnum	114
Reed, Elizabeth and Benjamin Russell	185
Reed, Jemima and Solomon Spalding	437
Reynolds, Elizabeth and Joseph Underwood	506
Rich, Samuel and Mary Holt	1038
Richards, Eliphalet and Sarah Butterfield	514
Richardson, Elinor and Asa Chandler	443
Richardson, Esther and John Barker	723
Richardson, John and Martha Holt	79
Richardson, Reuben and Mary Burgess	326
Richardson, Sarah and Joseph Chandler	107
Richardson, Seth and Lydia Williams	654
Richardson, Stephen and Hannah Rudd	327
Richardson, Thomas and Abigail Spalding	440
Rindge, Richard and Sarah Copeland	716
Robbins, Mary and Joseph Russell	521
Robie, Mary and Benjamin Pattee	519
Robie, Samuel and Deborah Moore	517

Robie, Samuel and Phebe Russell	129
Robie, Thomas and Rachel Barron	518
Robinson, Harriet and Joseph Russell	607
Rogers, Abigail and Cyrus Dow	418
Rogers, Alva and Desire Eaton	420
Rogers, Amos and Lucy Russell	614
Rogers, Elisha and Anna Ward	417
Rogers, Lucia and Nathan Crocker	419
Rogers, Mary and Eliphalet Farnum	118
Rogers, Moses and Lois Holt	100
Rogers, Olive and Abel Dow	416
Rogers, Polly and Asa Holt	426
Rogers, Sarah and Chandler Stevens	262
Root, Desire and Azariah Sanger	863
Rose, Patty and Phineas Kidder	1045
Ross, John and Sarah Russell	23
Rudd, Abigail and Henry Farnum	461
Rudd, Hannah and Stephen Richardson	327
Rumrill, Simeon and Polly Holt	428
Russ, Priscilla and Noadiah Sanger	204
Russell, Abel and Nancy Clement	540
Russell, Abiah and Peter York	987
Russell, Abiel and Sarah Abbott	639
Russell, Abigail and Asa Crosby	645
Russell, Abigail and Ebenezer Eaton	109
Russell, Abigail and Eli Twitchell	992
Russell, Abigail and Henry Williams	153
Russell, Abigail and Nathan Stedman	454
Russell, Abigail and Seth Lyon	41
Russell, Abner and Betsey Herrick	1013
Russell, Abraham and Sarah Swan	236
Russell, Alvah and Asenath Davis	650
Russell, Amelia and Alvin Keyes	1015
Russell, Andrew and Sarah	601
Russell, Anna and Richard Ware	773
Russell, Apphia and Gideon Powers	988
Russell, Aquilla and Abigail Glazier	146
Russell, Benjamin and Elizabeth Reed	185
Russell, Benjamin and Mary Feaver	234
Russell, Benjamin and Mary Preston	6
Russell, Benjamin and Mehitable Abbott	973
Russell, Benjamin and Phebe Smith	185
Russell, Benjamin and Sarah Perry	38
Russell, Bethiah and Daniel Simonds	535
Russell, Betsey and Asa Symonds	522
Russell, Betsey and Clement Dickey	627
Russell, Betsy and Daniel Brown	591
Russell, Betsy and Jeremiah Russell	591
Russell, Betsy and Robert White	544
Russell, Betty and Thomas Smith	981
Russell, Chandler and Betsey Duston	239
Russell, Cynthia and Asa Hall	775
Russell, Cynthia and Benjamin James	879
Russell, Daniel and Elizabeth Dascomb	538
Russell, David and Keziah Plimpton	769
Russell, David and Martha Pynchon	769
Russell, David and Mary Wheeler	623
Russell, Deborah and Jonathan Cummings	131
Russell, Desire and Martin Ellis	600
Russell, Dolly and James Russell	634
Russell, Dolly and John Lovejoy	983
Russell, Dorcas and Benjamin Thomas	598
Russell, Dorcas and Hiram Allen	991
Russell, Dorcas and Samuel Woodbridge	984
Russell, Ebenezer and Artimesia Lynch	1007
Russell, Ebenezer and Olive Newell	1014
Russell, Ebenezer and Rebecca Hudson	776
Russell, Eleazer and Eunice Sykes	770
Russell, Eli and Hepsibah Floyd	602
Russell, Eliab and Diana Nichols	1010
Russell, Elijah and Almira Bean	999
Russell, Elijah and Amity Child	612
Russell, Elijah and Sally Griffin	612
Russell, Elisha and Anne Winship	209
Russell, Elizabeth and Elijah Moulton	112
Russell, Elizabeth and Gideon Foster	151
Russell, Elizabeth and Jesse Perley	112
Russell, Elizabeth and Moses Holt	9
Russell, Elvira and John Jennison	625
Russell, Ephraim and Olive Ordway	1006
Russell, Ephraim and Rebecca Ireland	542
Russell, Esther and John Oliver	989
Russell, Esther and Jonathan Philbrick	647
Russell, Eunice and Enoch Morse	589
Russell, Eunice and Orlando Frink	626
Russell, Ezekiel and Hannah Meacham	453
Russell, Ezekiel and Hannah Verder	1001
Russell, Ezekiel and Hephzibah Hills	453
Russell, Ezekiel and Tabatha Flint	110
Russell, Fletcher and Hannah Howard	990
Russell, Frederick and Anna Bartlett	534
Russell, Frederick and Antoinette DeRoldos	534
Russell, Frederick and Theodosia Gustine	534
Russell, Gideon and Sarah Plant	615
Russell, Hannah and Amos Graves	605
Russell, Hannah and Caleb Putnam	138
Russell, Hannah and Frederick Ballard	985
Russell, Hannah and Jacob Crosby	56
Russell, Hannah and James Houghton	537
Russell, Hannah and John Humphrey	40
Russell, Hannah and Joseph Williams	878
Russell, Hannah and Luke Fletcher	149
Russell, Hannah and Nathan Abbott	636
Russell, Hannah and Oliver Holt	7
Russell, Hannah and Stephen Abbott	980
Russell, Hannah and Stephen Farr	545
Russell, Hephzibah and Herman Sargent	1005
Russell, Hephzibah and Joseph Russell	52
Russell, Hephzibah and Samuel Chamberlain	1005
Russell, Ira and Mary Jane Allen	560
Russell, Isaac and Elizabeth Gilbard	54
Russell, Jacob and Dorothy Shattuck	237
Russell, Jacob and Margaret	599
Russell, Jacob and Sophia Stark	993
Russell, James and Dolly Russell	634
Russell, James and Eliza Houghton	613
Russell, James and Hannah Peabody	556
Russell, James and Joanna True	593
Russell, James and Lora	548
Russell, James and Lucy Farrar	28

Russell, James and Lydia Brown	771
Russell, James and Lydia Mitchell	142
Russell, James and Mary French	132
Russell, James and Priscilla Osgood	4
Russell, James and Rebecca Peabody	136
Russell, James and Rhoda Chandler	27
Russell, James and Sarah Allen	646
Russell, James and Sophia Parmenter	533
Russell, Jane and James LeBaron	588
Russell, Jedediah and Abigail Whiting	1003
Russell, Jedediah and Rhoda Pratt	240
Russell, Jeduthan and Lucy Gurnsey	606
Russell, Jeduthan and Rhoda Hall	606
Russell, Jeduthan and Susannah Glazier	145
Russell, Jemima and Jonathan Stevens	57
Russell, Jemima and Joseph Hunt	26
Russell, Jeremiah and Betsy Russell	591
Russell, Joanna and Asa True	595
Russell, Joel and Sarah Curtis	637
Russell, John and Alice Lyon	186
Russell, John and Diana Bray	978
Russell, John and Hannah Foster	51
Russell, John and Phebe Abbott	235
Russell, John and Rebekah Wilson	208
Russell, John and Remembrance Eastman	619
Russell, John and Sarah Chandler	8
Russell, John and Sarah Hazeltine	502
Russell, John and Susannah Twitchell	977
Russell, Jonathan and Mary Lewis	1011
Russell, Jonathan and Rachel White	241
Russell, Jonathan and Ruth Hutchinson	134
Russell, Joseph and Hannah Dascomb	541
Russell, Joseph and Hannah Linkhorn	43
Russell, Joseph and Hannah Perkins	25
Russell, Joseph and Harriet Robinson	607
Russell, Joseph and Hephzibah Russell	52
Russell, Joseph and Hepsibah Eaton	25
Russell, Joseph and Lucy Angier	607
Russell, Joseph and Mary Ann Labbell	607
Russell, Joseph and Mary Robbins	521
Russell, Joseph and Miriam Brown	144
Russell, Joseph and Naomi Wilkins	555
Russell, Joseph and Polly Benjamin	543
Russell, Joseph and Rachel Pratt	594
Russell, Joseph and Sarah Holt	541
Russell, Joseph and Susanna Cheever	4a
Russell, Levi and Elizabeth Waldo	621
Russell, Lovina and Timothy Bean	1002
Russell, Lucy and Amos Rogers	614
Russell, Lucy and John Graves	603
Russell, Lydia and John Holt	238
Russell, Lydia and Jonathan Sanger	42
Russell, Lydia and Joseph Faulkner	638
Russell, Lydia and Solomon Jordan	586
Russell, Lydia and William Kendall	604
Russell, Maria and Kimball Bean	1000
Russell, Martin and Eliza Choate	611
Russell, Mary and David Pratt	597
Russell, Mary and Ephraim Brown	1016
Russell, Mary and Francis Peabody	558
Russell, Mary and Ingoldsby Work	187
Russell, Mary and John Palmer	523
Russell, Mary and Jonathan Freeman	648
Russell, Mary and Joseph Holt	55
Russell, Mary and Nathaniel Segar	974
Russell, Mary and Nicholas Holt	2
Russell, Mary and Proctor Keyes	1016
Russell, Mary and Samuel Appleton	30
Russell, Mary and Samuel Marcy	39
Russell, Mary and Timothy Osgood	22
Russell, Mehitable and Daniel Bickford	520
Russell, Mehitable and Joseph Chandler	19
Russell, Mehitable and Stephen Kittredge	520
Russell, Moor and Elizabeth Webster	503
Russell, Nancy and Samuel Woodbridge	984
Russell, Nathaniel and Sarah Morse	590
Russell, Parley and Abigail Cone	880
Russell, Peabody and Dolly Kenney	557
Russell, Peletiah and Olive Moore	127
Russell, Peletiah and Sarah Derumple	501
Russell, Peter and Deborah Crosby	24
Russell, Peter and Mehitable Dwinell	561
Russell, Peter and Mehitable Stiles	130
Russell, Phebe and Abraham Sheldon	50
Russell, Phebe and David Barrett	539
Russell, Phebe and David Cheney	111
Russell, Phebe and Ebenezer Lovejoy	979
Russell, Phebe and Ephraim Holt	50
Russell, Phebe and Henry Farnum	21
Russell, Phebe and John Butterfield	129
Russell, Phebe and John Huntress	596
Russell, Phebe and Reuben Locke	547
Russell, Phebe and Samuel Robie	129
Russell, Phylena and Henry Foster	624
Russell, Priscilla and David Pulsipher	148
Russell, Priscilla and Ezra Hall	608
Russell, Prudence and Moses Holt	58
Russell, Rachel and Curtis Goulding	546
Russell, Rachel and George Hopkins	881
Russell, Rachel and Jonathan Dwinells	137
Russell, Rachel and Timothy Underwood	128
Russell, Rhoda and Ephraim Holt	1004
Russell, Rhoda and Samuel Lawrence	592
Russell, Richard and Tirzah Hall	620
Russell, Robert and Abigail Flint	20
Russell, Robert and Anne Felt	53
Russell, Robert and Elizabeth Manning	20
Russell, Robert and Hannah Holt	20
Russell, Robert and Lydia Beebe	455
Russell, Robert and Mary Ann Kean	532
Russell, Robert and Mary Marshall	1
Russell, Ruth and Elias Williams	616
Russell, Sally and Asa Chamberlain	1008
Russell, Sally and Asa Metcalf	1012
Russell, Sally and Elisha Angier	622
Russell, Sally and Henry Durkee	774
Russell, Sally and Thomas Loring	982
Russell, Samuel and Hannah Dustin	1009
Russell, Samuel and Lydia Pickett	559
Russell, Sarah and Constant Hart	184

Russell, Sarah and David Holt	47
Russell, Sarah and Elijah Bond	986
Russell, Sarah and John H. Thomas	617
Russell, Sarah and John Ingalls	5
Russell, Sarah and John Ross	23
Russell, Sarah and Leavitt Hill	644
Russell, Sarah and Nehemiah Wilkins	135
Russell, Stephen and Mary Sharp	772
Russell, Susanna and Erasmus Wellington	609
Russell, Temperance and David Jordan	587
Russell, Theodore and Abigail Abbott	975
Russell, Theodore and Tabitha Strickland	975
Russell, Thomas and Abigail Ballard	29
Russell, Thomas and Abigail Bell	635
Russell, Thomas and Bethiah Holt	133
Russell, Thomas and Eunice Alexander	147
Russell, Thomas and Hannah Flint	618
Russell, Thomas and Lydia Abbott	536
Russell, Thomas and Phebe Johnson	3
Russell, Thomas and Ruth Harriman	643
Russell, Thomas and Sarah Eastman	152
Russell, Thomas C. and Sarah Gooch	143
Russell, Uriah and Anna Forrest	649
Russell, Uriah and Betsey Palmer	649
Russell, Uriah and Lydia Abbott	150
Russell, William and Mehitable Kilgore	976
Russell, William and Sarah	610
Russell, Zerviah and Ezra Smith	44
Rust, Kezia and Daniel Holt	97
Sabin, Martha and Stephen Fairbank	818
Salisbury, Paulina and Oliver Goodell	749
Sanger, Aden and Elizabeth Niles	864
Sanger, Ashbel and Sarah Southworth	866
Sanger, Azariah and Desire Root	863
Sanger, Azariah and Elizabeth Abbe	203
Sanger, Benjamin and Elizabeth Woodward	872
Sanger, Chloe and John Brocklebank	876
Sanger, Cynthia and William Melross	859
Sanger, Daniel and Alice Wakefield	858
Sanger, Ebenezer and Eunice Hutchins	871
Sanger, Ebenezer and Olive Chaffee	871
Sanger, Elizabeth and Chester Wakefield	860
Sanger, Esther and Charles Convers	862
Sanger, James and Achsa Blodgett	870a
Sanger, Jedediah and Mehitable Fenton	861
Sanger, Jonathan and Lucy Sawyer	207
Sanger, Jonathan and Lydia Russell	42
Sanger, Justus and Delilah Whitmore	875
Sanger, Lucy and John Carr	877
Sanger, Nathaniel and Olive Chaffee	206
Sanger, Noadiah and Priscilla Russ	204
Sanger, Noah D. and Rebecca Bacon	867
Sanger, Pamelia and William Green	873
Sanger, Phila and Joseph Hurlburt	874
Sanger, Priscilla and Chester Knowlton	868
Sanger, Zeruiah and Stephen Convers	205
Sanger, Zerviah and Jonathan Knowlton	865
Sargent, Abigail and Winthrop Marcy	796
Sargent, Herman and Hephzibah Russell	1005
Sargent, Ruth and Levi Marcy	798
Sawin, Elijah and Amy Pool	379
Sawin, Isaac and Mary Fenton	328
Sawin, Zeulime and Joshua Fairbank	815
Sawins, Luce and James Holt	88
Sawyer, Josiah and Lydia Barnard	312
Sawyer, Lucy and Jonathan Sanger	207
Saybott, Keturah and Stephen Farnum	480
Sayward, Hannah and Nathaniel Farnum	692
Scripture, Eleazer and Alice Pearl	380
Scripture, Esther and Timothy Holt	353
Segar, Nathaniel and Mary Russell	974
Sellen, Susan and Isaac Allen	712
Sharp, Augustus and Marcia Holt	408
Sharp, Mary and Stephen Russell	772
Sharpe, Abigail and Reuben Goodell	176
Sharpe, Hannah and John Marcy	188
Shattuck, Dorothy and Jacob Russell	237
Shattuck, Lydia and Daniel Flint	949
Shattuck, William and Abigail Foster	641
Sheldon, Abraham and Hannah Eaton	960
Sheldon, Abraham and Phebe Russell	50
Sheldon, Amos and Mary Willard	971
Sheldon, Amos and Sarah Needham	233
Sheldon, Daniel and Phebe Eaton	961
Sheldon, Hannah and Benjamin Holt	959
Sheldon, Phebe and Israel Farnum	231
Sheldon, Rebecca and Clark Hilton	972
Sheldon, Rebekah and Peter Towne	232
Sheldon, Russell and Susannah Sheldon	230
Sheldon, Sarah and Larkin Herrick	1023
Sheldon, Susannah and Russell Sheldon	230
Sherwin, Susannah and Robert Crosby	433
Shipman, Delia and William Cheney	853
Sibley, Martha and Oliver Holt	348
Simmons, Molly and Elijah Holt	335
Simonds, Daniel and Bethiah Russell	535
Slade, Henry and Anna Holt	1039
Smith, Abigail and Daniel Holt	18
Smith, Abigail and Lyman Waldo	886
Smith, Anna and Sylvanus Wing	885
Smith, Dorothy and Alexander Work	780
Smith, Eleanor and Daniel Stoddard	840
Smith, Ezra and Roxana Kendall	882
Smith, Ezra and Zerviah Russell	44
Smith, Hannah and Ebenezer Chaffee	889
Smith, Mary and Perkins Woodward	883
Smith, Matilda and Elijah Whiton	888
Smith, Phebe and Benjamin Russell	185
Smith, Simeon and Anna Byles	210
Smith, Simeon and Lucy Lyman	210
Smith, Simeon and Sally Hawes	887
Smith, Thomas and Betty Russell	981
Smith, Zerviah and Andrew Huntington	884
Snow, Alice and Stevens Chandler	262
Snow, Bathsheba and Benjamin Preston	89
Snow, Benjamin and Dorcas Osgood	264
Snow, Joseph and Mary Chandler	263
Snow, Lydia and Smith Holt	425
Snow, Robert and Anna Peck	375
Snow, Silas and Eunice Farnum	468

Southworth, Sarah and Ashbel Sanger	866
Spalding, Abigail and Oliver Taylor	440
Spalding, Abigail and Thomas Richardson	440
Spalding, Andrew and Mehitable Chandler	104
Spalding, Henry and Betsey Tagart	438
Spalding, Ruth and Isaac Butterfield	439
Spalding, Solomon and Jemima Reed	437
Spring, Catherine and Joseph Farnum	466
Stacy, John and Susannah Cummings	528
Stark. Sophia and Jacob Russell	993
Stearns, Jerome and Elizabeth Whicher	1050
Stearns, John and Ruth Eastman	824
Stearns, John and Zilpah Stearns	1048
Stearns, Joseph and Zilpah Crosby	247
Stearns, Mahala and James Lovejoy	1049
Stearns, Mary and Marshall Pierce	1046
Stearns, Mary and William Holt	995
Stearns, Royal and Esther Lawrence	1047
Stearns, Susan and Joseph Holt	996
Stearns, Zilpah and John Stearns	1048
Stedman, Nathan and Abigail Russell	454
Stevens, Abiel and Elizabeth Holt	225
Stevens, Abiel and Eunice	934
Stevens, Abiel and Mercy Haskell	934
Stevens, Abiel and Tabitha Holt	225
Stevens, David and Ruth Blaisdell	937
Stevens, Dorcas and Asa Osgood	487
Stevens, Elizabeth and Nathaniel Holt	211
Stevens, Hannah and Joel Crosby	436
Stevens, Jacob and Dinah Norton	935
Stevens, Jemima and Jonas Ames	248
Stevens, John and Elizabeth Ingalls	35
Stevens, Jonathan and Jemima Russell	57
Stevens, Lydia and Asa Holt	285
Stevens, Naomi and John Butterfield	512
Stevens, Uriah and Sally Blaisdell	936
Stickney, Elizabeth and John Eastman	826
Stiles, Chloe and James Holt	319
Stiles, Huldah and James Holt	319
Stiles, Mehitable and David Kendall	322
Stiles, Mehitable and Peter Russell	130
Stockwell, Lovina and Oliver Darby	906
Stoddard, Amasa and Anna Willard	845
Stoddard, Daniel and Eleanor Smith	840
Stoddard, Daniel and Lucretia Harvey	840
Stoddard, Ebenezer and Susan	843
Stoddard, Ezra and Jerusha Goodell	842
Stoddard, Hannah and Levi Peck	837
Stoddard, Isaac and Miriam Parsons	844
Stoddard, John and Mary Hendrick	838
Stoddard, Joshua and Abigail Lawrence	839
Stoddard, Joshua and Sarah Humphrey	199
Stoddard, Rhoda and Moses Webster	846
Stoddard, Zerviah and Amasa Washburn	841
Stone, Polly and John Farnum	688
Storrs, Hannah and Sluman Allen	707
Stowell, Abigail and Samuel Eastman	825
Stratton, Elizabeth and Joseph Holt	307
Strickland, Tabitha and Theodore Russell	975
Sumner, Ebenezer and Roxanna Holt	413
Swan, Caleb and Asenath Towne	969
Swan, Sarah and Abraham Russell	236
Swett, Anna and Thomas Appleton	657
Swett, John and Alice Appleton	665
Swift, Russell and Lucy Hunt	580
Sykes, Eunice and Eleazer Russell	770
Sylvester, John and Hannah Holt	1034
Symonds, Asa and Betsey Russell	522
Symonds, Deborah and Joseph Chandler	1056
Tagart, Betsey and Henry Spalding	438
Talbert, Catherine and Israel Farnum	963
Tarbox, Ebenezer and Mary Holt	302
Taylor, Ezra and Meriam Eaton	834
Taylor, Martha and Amos Preston	373
Taylor, Oliver and Abigail Spalding	440
Thayer, Richard and Martha Appleton	656
Thomas, Benjamin and Dorcas Russell	598
Thomas, John H. and Sarah Russell	617
Thompson, Sarah and John Farnum	688
Thorndike, Sarah and Jedediah Holt	268
Towne, Abiah and Amos Carleton	970
Towne, Amos and Mary Farnum	965
Towne, Asenath and Caleb Swan	969
Towne, Daniel and Susan Gurney	968
Towne, Fanny and Michael Parker	967
Towne, Israel and Hannah Abbott	728
Towne, Lydia and Nathaniel Berry	966
Towne, Peter and Rebekah Sheldon	232
Towne, Peter and Sally Kimball	964
Towne, Samuel and Lydia Holt	912
Tracy, Mercy and Jeffrey Farnum	477
Treat, Robert and Mary Gale	663
True, Asa and Joanna Russell	595
True, Joanna and James Russell	593
Truesdell, Darius and Rhoda Chaffee	325
Truesdell, Jeduthan and Abigail White	324
Truesdell, Joseph and Mary Holt	78
Truesdell, Seth and Esther West	323
Tucker, Rosanna and William Marcy	190
Tufts, Aaron and Sally Barker	726
Tupper, Ezra and Emma Hunt	579
Tuttle, Mary and John Appleton	658
Twist, Abigail and Nehemiah Holt	923
Twitchell, Eli and Abigail Russell	992
Twitchell, Susannah and John Russell	977
Tyler, Selah and Joseph Cheney	852
Underwood, Deborah and Abner Miles	505
Underwood, James and Hannah Amsbury	511
Underwood, Joseph and Elizabeth Reynolds	506
Underwood, Mary and Humphrey Bigelow	510
Underwood, Phineas and Sarah	508
Underwood, Rachel and Sarah Brigham	504
Underwood, Russell and Elizabeth Allen	509
Underwood, Timothy and Hephzibah Adams	507
Underwood, Timothy and Mary Adams	507
Underwood, Timothy and Rachel Russell	128
Van Deuzen, Eunice and Russell Farnum	475
VanDeventer, Anna and Resolved Wheeler	424
Varnum, Esther and Nehemiah Holt	223
Varril, Elohe and Hiram Holt	997

Verder, Hannah and Ezekiel Russell	1001
Virgin, Bethiah and Osgood Eaton	701
Wakefield, Alice and Daniel Sanger	858
Wakefield, Chester and Elizabeth Sanger	860
Walcott, Elizabeth and Thomas Chandler	105
Waldo, Elizabeth and Levi Russell	621
Waldo, Lyman and Abigail Smith	886
Wales, Chloe and Jonathan Avery	823
Walker, Aaron and Luce Holt	359
Ward, Anna and Elisha Rogers	417
Wardwell, Jeremiah and Samantha Eaton	705
Wardwell, Solomon and Bethiah Holt	301
Ware, Richard and Anna Russell	773
Warner, Elizabeth and Joseph Allen	167
Washburn, Amasa and Zerviah Stoddard	841
Washburn, Elizabeth and Joseph Barker	739
Wattles, Anna and Dyer Hastings	766
Weaver, Benjamin and Diadama Eaton	833
Weaver, Sally and Samuel Pulsipher	628
Webb, Susannah and Rufus Bishop	755
Webber, Chandler and Beulah Coye	736
Webster, Elizabeth and Moor Russell	503
Webster, Moses and Rhoda Stoddard	846
Welch, Jerusha and Elisha Paine	849
Welch, Sarah and Paul Holt	315
Wellington, Erasmus and Susanna Russell	609
Wellington, Sally and Adolphus Fletcher	633
Wells, Benjamin and Lydia Appleton	659
West, Esther and Seth Truesdell	323
Weston, John and Molly Convers	869
Wheeler, Abigail and Marstin Holt	229
Wheeler, Elijah and Mary Miner	422
Wheeler, Josiah and Eunice Holt	101
Wheeler, Mary and David Russell	623
Wheeler, Perthene and Daniel Chapin	421
Wheeler, Philadelphia and Moses Gaylord	423
Wheeler, Resolved and Anna VanDeventer	424
Whicher, Elizabeth and Jerome Stearns	1050
Whipple, Freelove and Benjamin Pitts	828
Whipple, Lucy and James Holt	279
Whipple, Nellie and Stephen Convers	870
Whipple, Tabitha and Ebenezer Cheney	855
Whitcomb, David and Mary Eaton	704
White, Abigail and Jeduthan Truesdell	324
White, Cheney and Ephraim Farnum	116
White, Joseph and Deborah Holt	406
White, Joseph and Olive Holt	406
White, Rachel and Jonathan Russell	241
White, Rebecca and Willard Copeland	718
White, Robert and Betsy Russell	544
Whitehouse, Elizabeth and Haines Farnum	691
Whiting, Abigail and Jedediah Russell	1003
Whitmore, Delilah and Justus Sanger	875
Whitney, Abigail and Benjamin Hoar	900
Whitney, Elisha and Meriam Eaton	834
Whitney, Jonas and Relief Whitney	899
Whitney, Jonathan and Sarah Holt	214
Whitney, Jonathan and Zilpha Holt	396
Whitney, Phinehas and Keziah Farnsworth	897
Whitney, Rachel and Salmon Willard	901
Whitney, Relief and Jonas Whitney	899
Whitney, Reuby and Salmon Hunt	581
Whitney, Richard and Hannah Holt	272
Whitney, Sarah and John Mead	898
Whiton, Elijah and Matilda Smith	888
Whittier, James and Nancy Holt	1031
Whittier, William and Hannah Poor	493
Wilbur, Hannah and Joseph Fairbank	816
Wilcox, Joseph and Jemima Hunt	585
Wiley, Daniel and Charlotte Dwinells	563
Wiley, David and Chloe Holt	891
Wilkins, Abigail and Joseph Wright	550
Wilkins, Betsey and James Wilkins	552
Wilkins, Ephraim and Hannah Dixey	551
Wilkins, James and Betsey Wilkins	552
Wilkins, Jesse and Peggy Peabody	554
Wilkins, Lucy and Moses Perkins	549
Wilkins, Nancy and William Gifford	553
Wilkins, Naomi and Joseph Russell	555
Wilkins, Nehemiah and Sarah Russell	135
Willard, Anna and Amasa Stoddard	845
Willard, Anness and Uriah Holt	215
Willard, Mary and Amos Sheldon	971
Willard, Salmon and Rachel Whitney	901
Willard, Wilder and Olive Marcy	794
Williams, Abigail and Josiah Gould	651
Williams, Bathsheba and Nathan Holt	83
Williams, Catharine and Thomas Downing	652
Williams, Elias and Ruth Russell	616
Williams, Elizabeth and Elijah Holt	404
Williams, Henry and Abigail Russell	153
Williams, Joseph and Hannah Russell	878
Williams, Lydia and Seth Richardson	654
Williams, Martha and Simeon Goodell	177
Williams, Thomas and Ruth Abbott	653
Williams, Willard and Elizabeth Osgood	655
Willis, Mary and John Ingalls	31
Willis, Mary and Peter Osgood	491
Wilson, Job and Anna Farnum	696
Wilson, Matthew and Lucy Barker	743
Wilson, Rebekah and John Russell	208
Wing, Sylvanus and Anna Smith	885
Winship, Anne and Elisha Russell	209
Witham, Ann and Wesley Holt	1040
Wolf, Mabel and Ichabod Eastman	827
Wood, Barnabas and Sarah Holt	305
Wood, Israel and Phebe Holt	267
Wood, Obadiah and Deborah Osgood	124
Woodbridge, Samuel and Dorcas Russell	984
Woodbridge, Samuel and Nancy Russell	984
Woodbury, Edward and Hannah Appleton	158
Woodbury, Edward and Judith Jewett	671
Woodbury, Elizabeth and Nathan Burrill	670
Woodbury, Hannah and James Bartlett	669
Woodbury, Mary and Joseph Bartlett	668
Woodward, Elizabeth and Asa Holt	426
Woodward, Elizabeth and Benjamin Sanger	872
Woodward, Perkins and Mary Smith	883
Woodworth, Eunice and Benjamin Ingalls	181
Woodworth, Ruth and Thomas Ingalls	169

Wooley, Sally and Amos Holt — 956
Work, Alexander and Dorothy Smith — 780
Work, Anna and Asa Phillips — 782
Work, Elizabeth and Andrew Judson — 778
Work, Ingoldsby and Mary Russell — 187
Work, John and Hannah Paine — 848
Work, Lucy and Manasseh Howard — 781
Work, Mary and Edward Keyes — 779
Work, Polly and Orrin Marcy — 812
Work, Sarah and Samuel Crawford — 777

Wormwood, Molly and Nicholas Holt — 269
Worthing, Sarah and Moses Merrill — 683
Wright, Hannah and John Holt — 946
Wright, Joseph and Abigail Wilkins — 550
Wright, Sarah and Uriah Holt — 46
Wright, Susannah and Oliver Holt — 45
Wyman, Mary and John Chandler — 1051
York, Peter and Abiah Russell — 987
Young, Amy and Willis Coy — 732
Younglove, Irena and Jeremiah Pitts — 829

References

A. W. Bowen Company. 1898. *A Portrait and Biographical Record of Portage and Summit Counties, Ohio.* Logansport, IN: A. W. Bowen & Co.

Abbot, Abiel, and Ephraim Abbot. 1847. *Genealogical Register of the Descendants of George Abbot of Andover, George Abbot of Rowley, Thomas Abbot of Andover, Arthur Abbot of Ipswich, Robert Abbot of Branford, CT, and George Abbot of Norwalk, CT.* Boston: James Munroe and Company.

Abell, Horace Avery. 1940. *The Abell Family in America: Robert Abell of Rehoboth, Mass., his English Ancestry and his Descendants, other Abell Families and Immigrants, Abell Families in England.* Rutland, VT: Tuttle Publishing.

Adams, Andrew N. 1898. *A Genealogical History of Henry Adams, of Braintree, Mass., and His Descendants; also John Adams, of Cambridge, Mass., 1632-1897.* Rutland, VT: The Tuttle Company, printers.

—. 1900. *A Genealogical History of Robert Adams and His Descendants 1635-1900.* Rutland, VT: Published by the author.

—. 1894. *The Descendants of James and William Adams of Londonderry, now Derry, N.H.* Rutland, VT: The Tuttle Company, Printers.

Adams, William. 1893. *Historical Gazetteer and Biographical Memorial of Cattaraugus County, N.Y.* Syracuse, NY: Lyman, Horton & Co.

Aldrich, George. 1880. *Walpole As It Was and As It Is.* Claremont, NH: Claremont Manufacturing.

Aldrich, Lewis Cass, and Frank R. Holmes. 1891. *History of Windsor County, Vermont.* Syracuse, NY: D. Mason and Co.

Aldrich, Lewis Cass, and George S. Conover. 1893. *History of Ontario County, New York.* Syracuse, NY: D. Mason & Co.

Allen, Joseph. 1868. *The Worcester Association and Its Antecedents: A History of Four Ministerial Associations, the Marlborough, the Worcester (old), the Lancaster, and the Worcester (new) Associations.* Boston, MA: Nichols and Noyes.

Alvord, Samuel Morgan. 1908. *A Genealogy of the Descendants of Alexander Alvord.* Webster, NY: A. D. Andrews, Printer.

American Biographical Publishing Company. 1877. *The United States Biographical Dictionary and Portrait Gallery of Eminent and Self-Made Men, Wisconsin Volume.* Chicago, IL: American Biographical Publishing Company.

Ames, Constance Le Neve (Gilman). 1950. *The Story of the Gilmans and a Gilman Genealogy of the Descendants of Edward Gilman of Hingham, England, 1550-1950.* Yakima, WA: Printed for the author.

Ammidown, Holmes. 1877. *Historical Collections: Containing I The Reformation in France and II The Histories of Seven Towns, Second Edition.* New York, NY: Published by the author.

Appleton, W. S. 1896. *Gatherings toward a Genealogy of the Coffin Family: Five Generations of Descendants of Tristram Coffin of Newbury and Nantucket.* Boston, MA: Press of David Clapp & Son.

Appleton, William Sumner. 1874. *A Genealogy of the Appleton Family.* Boston, MA: Press of T. R. Marvin & Son.

Avery, Clara Arlette. 1914. *The Averell-Averill-Avery Family: A Record of the Descendants of William and Abigail Averell of Ipswich, Mass.* Cleveland, OH: Evangelical Publishing House.

Avery, Elroy McKendree, and Catherine Hitchcock (Tilden) Avery. 1912. *The Groton Avery Clan, Volume I.* Cleveland, OH: Privately printed. https://www.ancestry.com/imageviewer/collections/10196/images/dvm_GenMono000011-00001-0?ssrc=&backlabel=Return&rc=1771%2C4730%2C2069%2C4821%3B2120%2C4730%2C2386%2C4819%3B981%2C5243%2C1273%2C5337%3B2686%2C5244%2C2950%2C5336&pId=380.

Avery, Lillian Drake. 1926. *A Genealogy of the Ingersoll Family in America, 1629-1925: Comprising Descendants of Richard Ingersoll of Salem, Massachusetts, John Ingersoll of Westfield, Mass., and John Ingersoll of Huntington, Long Island.* Salem, MA: Higginson Book Co.

Badger, John Cogswell. 1909. *Giles Badger and His Descendants.* Manchester, NH: J.B. Clarke Printers.

Bailey, Sarah Loring. 1880. *Historical Sketches of Andover: Comprising the Present Towns of Andover and North Andover.* Boston: Houghton.

Balch, Galusha Burchard. 1897. *Genealogy of the Balch Families in America.* Salem, MA: E. Putnam.

Barber, John Warner. 1839. *Massachusetts Historical Collections: Being a General Collection of Interesting Facts, Traditions, Biographical Sketches, etc. of Every Town In Massachusetts.* Worcester, MA: Dorr, Howland & Co.

Barbour, Lucius Barnes. 1982. *Families of Early Hartford, Connecticut.* Baltimore, MD: Genealogical Publishing Company .

Barker, Elizabeth Frye. 1927. *Barker Genealogy.* New York, NY: Frye Publishing Co.

Bartlett, J. Gardner. 1918. *Gregory Stone Genealogy: Ancestry and Descendants of Dea. Gregory Stone of Cambridge, Mass., 1320-1917.* Boston, MA: Stone Family Association.

Bartlett, John Russell. 1879. *Genealogy of that Branch of the Russell Family which Comprised the Descendants of John Russell, of Woburn, Massachusetts, 1640-1878.* Providence, RI: Privately printed.

Bass, Henry Royce. 1883. *The History of Braintree, Vermont, Including a Memorial of Families that have Resided in Town.* Rutland, VT: Tuttle & Co.

Bayles, Richard Mather. 1889. *History of Windham County, Connecticut.* New York, NY: W. W. Preston.

Beard, Ruth, and John Gunn Baird. 1915. *A Genealogy of the Descendants of Widow Martha Beard of Milford, Conn.* Ansonia, CT: Emerson Publishing.

Beers, Frederick W. 1890. *Gazetteer and Biographical Record of Genesee County, N.Y., 1788-1890.* Syracuse, NY: J. W. Vose.

—. 1880. *History of Wyoming County, N.Y., with Illustrations, Biographical Sketches and Portraits of Some Pioneers and Prominent Residents.* New York, NY: F. W. Beers.

Bemis, Charles Austin. 1881. *History of the Town of Marlborough, Cheshire County, New Hampshire.* Boston, MA: Press of G. H. Ellis.

Benedict, Henry Marvin. 1870. *The Genealogy of the Benedicts in America.* Albany: J Munsell.

Best, Frank Eugene. 1899. *John Keep of Longmeadow, Massachusetts 1660-1676 and His Descendants.* Chicago, IL: Frank E. Best.

—. 1904. *The Amidon Family: A Record of the Descendants of Roger Amadowne of Rehoboth, Mass.* Chicago, IL: F. E. Best.

Bicha, Gloria Wall, and Helen Benjamin Brown. 1977. *The Benjamin Family in America.* https://archive.org/details/benjaminfamilyin00bich/mode/2up.

Biographical Publishing Company. 1885. *Portrait and Biographical Album of Henry County, Illinois.* Chicago, IL: Biographical Publishing Company.

Biographical Review. 1893. *Biographical Review of Dane County, Wisconsin.* Chicago, IL: Biographical Review Publishing Company.

—. 1896. *Biographical Review: This Volume Contains Biographical Sketches of Leading Citizens of Cumberland County, Maine.* Boston, MA: Biographical Review Publishing Company.

—. 1896. *Biographical Review: This Volume Contains Biographical Sketches of Leading Citizens of Clinton and Essex Counties, New York.* Boston, MA: Biographical Review Publishing Company.

—. 1897. *Biographical Review: This Volume Contains Biographical Sketches of Leading Citizens of Oxford and Franklin Counties, Maine.* Franklin County, ME: Biographical Review Publishing Company.

—. 1895. *Biographical Review: This Volume Contains Biographical Sketches of the Leading Citizens of Delaware County, New York.* Boston, MA: Biographical Review Publishing Company.

Birchard, Elizabeth. 1927. *The Birchard-Burchard Genealogy.* Philadelphia, PA: Elizabeth Birchard. https://www.familysearch.org/library/books/records/item/104659-the-birchard-burchard-genealogy-with-history-and-records-of-the-kindred-in-north-america-descendants-of-thomas-birchard-1635-norwich-connecticut?viewer=1&offset=0#page=1&viewer=picture&o=info&.

Blackman, Emily C. 1873. *History of Susquehanna County, Pennsylvania.* Philadelphia, PA: Claxton, Remsen & Haffelfinger.

Blake, Francis E. 1915. *History of the Town of Princeton in the County of Worcester and the Commonwealth of Massachusetts.* Princeton, MA: Published by the town.

Bliss, John Homer. 1881. *Genealogy of the Bliss Family in America, from about the Year 1550-1880.* Boston, MA: Printed by the author.

Bolton, Charles Knowles. 1932. *Nathaniel Bolton, a Forgotton New England Poet.* Worcester, MA: American Antiquarian Society.

Boltwood, Lucius Manlius. 1878. *History and Genealogy of the Family of Thomas Noble, of Westfied, Massachusetts.* Hartford, CT: Case, Lockwood & Brainard.

Bond, Henry. 1860. *Genealogies of the Families and Descendants of the Early Settlers of Watertown, Massachusetts.* Boston, MA: NEHGS.

Bouton, Nathaniel. 1856. *The History of Concord from Its First Grant in 1725 to the Organization of the City Government in 1853.* Concord, NH: Benning W. Sanborn.

Bowen, Clarence Winthrop. 1943. *The History of Woodstock, Connecticut: Genealogies of Woodstock Families.* Woodstock, CT: American Antiquarian Society.

Braiden, Clara Vaile. 1913. *Bryant Family HIstory: Ancestry and Descendants of David Bryant (1756) of Springfield, N.J.; Washington Co., Pa.; Knox Co., Ohio; and Wolf Lake, Noble Co., Ind.* Chicago, IL: Privately Printed.

Brainard, Lucy Abigail. 1908. *The Genealogy of the Brainerd-Brainard Family in America, 1649-1908.* Hartford Press.

Brewster, William. 1930. *History of the Certified Township of Kingston, Pennsylvania, 1769 to 1929: Together with a Short Account of the Fourteenth Commonwealth.* Wilkes-Barre, PA: Smith-Bennett Corporation.

Briggs, Erasmus. 1883. *History of the Original Town of Concord: Being the Present Towns of Concord, Collins, N. Collins, and Sardinia, Erie County, New York.* Rochester, NY: Union & Advertiser Co., Printers.

Brigham, Emma Elisabeth. 1927. *The History of the Brigham Family: Second Volume.* Rutland, VT: The Tuttle Company.

Brigham, Willard. 1907. *The History of the Brigham Family: A Record of Several Thousand Descendants of Thomas Brigham the Emigrant, 1603-1653.* New York: The Grafton Press.

—. 1912. *The Tyler Genealogy; the Descendants of Job Tyler, of Andover, Massachusetts, 1619-1700.* Plainfield, NJ: C. B. Tyler.

Brimfield (Town). 1879. *Historical Celebration of the Town of Brimfield, Hampden County, Mass.* Springfield, MA: C. W. Bryan.

Browne, George Waldo. 1921-22. *The History of Hillsborough, New Hampshire, 1735-1921.* Manchester, NH: John B. Clarke.

Browne, William Bradford. 1912. *The Babbitt Family History.* Taunton, MA: Babbitt Family Association.

Buck, Samuel. 1917. *Buck History and Genealogy, Embracing the Traditional and Comprehensive Genealogical History of the Buck Family in Europe and America.* Burlington, VT: Free Press Printing.

Bunker, Mary Powell. 1895. *Long Island Genealogies.* Albany, NY: J. Munsell's Sons.

Burgess, Ebenezer. 1865. *Burgess Genealogy: Memorial of the Family of Thomas and Dorothy Burgess, who Were Settled at Sandwich, in the Plymouth Colony, in 1637.* Boston, MA: Press of T. R. Marvin & Son.

Burleigh, Charles. 1887. *The Genealogy and History of the Guild, Guile and Gile Family.* Portland, ME: B. Thurston & Co.

—. 1903. *The Genealogy and History of the Ingalls Family in America.* Malden, MA: G. E. Dunbar.

—. 1880. *The Genealogy of the Burley or Burleigh Family of America.* Portland, ME: Press of B. Thurston & Company.

Butler, Francis Gould. 1885. *A History of Farmington, Franklin County, Maine, from the Earliest Explorations to the Present Time, 1776-1885.* Farmington, ME: Press of Knowlton, McLeary, and Co.

Butterfield, Consul Willshire. 1881. *History of Grant County, Wisconsin.* Chicago, IL: Western Historical Co.

Butterfield, Ernest W. 1921. *The Early History of Weathersfield, Vermont.* Weathersfield, VT: Published by the town.

Campbell, John Roy. 1876. *A History of the County of Yarmouth, Nova Scotia.* Saint John, NB: J & A McMillan.

Candage, Rufus George Frederick. 1905. *Historical Sketches of Bluehill, Maine.* Ellsworth, ME: Hancock County Publishing Company, printers.

Carpenter, Charles Carroll. 1903. *Biographical Catalogue of the Trustees, Teachers and Students of Phillips Academy 1778-1830.* Andover, MA: Andover Press.

Carpenter, Daniel Hoagland. 1891. *History and Genealogy of the Hoagland Family in America.* New York, NY: J. Polhemus Printing Co.

Carr, Edson I. 1894. *The Carr Family Records.* Rockton, IL: Herald Printing House.

Carter, Howard Williston. 1909. *Carter, a Genealogy of the Descendants of Thomas Carter of Reading and Weston, Mass., and of Hebron and Warren, Ct.* Norfolk, CT: Printed by C. B. Fiske & Co.

Carter, Nathan Franklin, and Trueworthy Ladd Fowler. 1895. *History of Pembroke, N. H. 1730-1895.* Concord, NH: Republican Press Association.

Cary, Seth Cooley. 1838. *John Cary the Plymouth Pilgrim.* Boston, MA: S. C. Cary.

Caulkins, Frances Manwaring. 1866. *History of Norwich, Connecticut: From its Possession by the Indians, to the Year 1866.* Hartford, CT: Published by the author.

Caulkins, Frances Manwaring, and Cecilia Griswold. 1895. *History of New London, Connecticut, from the First Survey of the Coast in 1612 to 1860.* New London, CT: H. D. Utley.

Caverly, Abiel Moore. 1858. *An Historical Sketch of Troy [N.H.] and Her Inhabitants, from the First Settlement of the Town, in 1764, to 1855.* Keene, NH: Sentinel Office.

Chaffee, William Henry. 1909. *The Chaffee Genealogy.* New York: Grafton Press.

Chandler, Charles Henry, and Sarah Fiske Lee. 1914. *The History of New Ipswich, New Hampshire, 1735-1914: With Genealogical Records of the Principal Families.* Fitchburg, MA: Sentinel Printing Company.

Chandler, George. 1883. *The Descendants of William and Annis Chandler who Settled in Roxbury, Mass., 1637.* Worcester: Press of C. Hamilton.

Chandler, Seth. 1883. *History of the Town of Shirley, Massachusetts, from its Early Settlement to A.D. 1882.* Shirley, MA: Published by the author.

Chapin, Charles Wells. 1893. *Sketches of the Old Inhabitants and Other Citizens of Old Springfield of the Present Century.* Springfield, MA: Springfield Printing and Binding Company.

Chapin, Gilbert Warren. 1924. *The Chapin Book of Genealogical Data.* Hartford, CT: Chapin Family Association.

Chapin, Orange. 1862. *The Chapin Genealogy: Containing a Very Large Proportion of the Descendants of Dea. Samuel Chapin.* Northapmton, MA: Printed by Metcalf and Co.

Chapman Brothers. 1894. *Midland County, Mich.: Portraits and Biographical Sketches.* Chicago, IL: Chapman Brothers.

Chapman Publishing Company. 1895. *Portrait and Biographical Record of Orange County, New York.* New York, NY: Chapman Publishing Company.

Chapman, George T. 1867. *Sketches of the Alumni of Dartmouth College, from the First Graduation in 1771 to the Present Time, with a Brief History of the Institution.* Cambridge, MA: Riverside Press.

Chapman, Jacob. 1886. *A Genealogy of the Philbrick and Philbrook Families.* Exeter Gazette Steam Printing House.

—. 1893. *Edward Chapman of Ipswich, Mass., 1642-1678, and His Descendants .* Concord, NH: Printed by Rebublican Press Association.

Charles C. Chapman Publishers. 1879. *History of Tazewell County, Illinois.* Chicago, IL: Charles C. Chapman.

Chase, George Wingate. 1861. *The History of Haverhill, Massachusetts, from its First Settlement, in 1640, to the Year 1860.* Haverhill, MA: Published by the author.

Chase, Levi B. 1884. *A Genealogy and Historical Notices of the Family of Plimpton or Plympton in America.* Hartford, CT: Plimpton Mfg. Co.

Chelsea Historical Society. 1984. *A History of Chelsea, Vermont, 1784-1984.* Chelsea, VT: Chelsea Historical Society.

Child, Elias. 1881. *Genealogy of the Child, Childs and Childe Families, of the Past and Present in the United States and the Canadas, from 1630 to 1881.* Utica, NY: Published for the author.

Child, Hamilton. 1884. *Gazetteer and Business Directory of Windham County, Vt. for 1883-1884.* Syracuse, NY: Published by Hamilton Child; Printed at the Journal Office.

—. 1887. *Gazetteer of Caledonia and Essex Counties, Vt. 1764-1887.* Syracuse, NY: The Syracuse Journal Company.

Child, William Henry. 1911. *History of the Town of Cornish, New Hampshire, with Genealogical Record, 1763-1910.* Concord, NH: Rumford Press.

Clapp, Ebenezer. 1876. *The Clapp Memorial: Record of the Clapp Family in America, Containing Sketches of the Original Six Emigrants, and a Genealogy of Their Descendants Bearing the Name.* Boston, MA: D. Clapp.

Cleaveland, Nehemiah, and Alpheus Spring Packard. 1882. *History of Bowdoin College with Biographical Sketches of Its Graduates.* Boston: James Ripley Osgood.

Cleveland, Edmund Janes. 1899. *The Genealogy of the Cleveland and Cleaveland Families.* Hartford, CT: Printed for the subscribers.

Cleveland, Stafford C. 1873. *History and Directory of Yates County.* Penn Yan, NY: S. C. Cleveland, Chronicle Office.

Cochrane, Warren Robert, and George K. Wood. 1895. *History of Francestown, N. H., from its Earliest Settlement April, 1758, to January 1, 1891: With a Brief Genealogical Record of all the Francestown Families.* Nashua, NH: Published by the town.

Coffin, Charles Carleton. 1878. *The History of Boscawen and Webster [N.H.] from 1733 to 1878.* Concord, NH: Republican Press Association.

Coffin, Selden J. 1891. *The Men of Lafayette 1826-1893.* Easton: George W. West.

Cogswell, Elliott C. 1864. *History of New Boston, New Hampshire.* Boston, MA: Pres of Geo. C. Rand & Avery.

Cogswell, Leander Winslow. 1880. *History of the Town of Henniker, Merrimack County, New Hampshire, from the Date of the Canada Grant by the Province of Massachusetts, in 1735, to 1880; with a Genealogical Register of the Families of Henniker.* Concord, NH: Republican Press Association.

Cogswell, William. 1847. *The New Hampshire Repository: Devoted to Education, Literature and Religion.* Gilmanton, NH: Printed by Alfred Prescott.

Comstock, Cyrus Ballou. 1907. *A Comstock Genealogy: Descendants of William Comstock of New London, Conn., who Died after 1662: Ten Generations.* New York, NY: The Knickerbocker Press.

Conant, Frederick Odell. 1887. *A History and Genealogy of the Conant Family in England and America, Thirteen Generations, 1520-1887.* Portland, ME: Private printing by the press of Harris & Williams.

Cone, William Whitney. 1903. *Some Account of the Cone Family in America Principally of the Descendants of Daniel Cone, Who Settled in Haddam, Connecticut, in 1662.* Topeka, KS: Crane and Company.

Connecticut General Assembly. 1889. *Record of Service of Connecticut Men in the I. War of the Revolution, II. War of 1812, III. Mexican War.* Hartford, CT: Case, Lockwood & Brainard Co.

Copeland, William Turner. 1937. *The Copeland Family: A Copeland Genealogy.* Rutland, VT: Tuttle Publishing.

Corwin, Edward Tanjore. 1872. *The Corwin Genealogy in the United States.* New York, NY: S. W. Green, printer.

Cox, Fred G. 1895. *The Illustrated Historical Souvenir History of Bethel, Vermont.* Bethel, VT.

Crandall, John Cortland. 1931. *Elder John Crandall of Rhode Island and His Descendants* . New Woodstock, NY: J. C. Crandall.

Crane, E. B. 1875. *The Rawson Family: A Revised Memoir of Edward Rawson, Secretary of the Colony of Massachusetts Bay, from 1650 to 1686.* Worcester, MA: Published by the family.

Crane, Ellery Bicknell. 1907. *Historic Homes and Institutions and Genealogical and Personal Memoirs of Worcester County, Massachusetts, with a History of Worcester Society of Antiquity.* New York: Lewis Publishing Company.

Crocker, James Russell, and William Adolph Walter. 1967. *Crocker Genealogy.* San Diego, CA: Published by the authors.

Crosby, Nathan. 1877. *A Crosby Family: Josiah Crosby, Sarah Fitch and Their Descendants.* Lowell, MA: Stone, Huse & Co.

Crozier, William Armstrong. 1907. *The Buckners of Virginia and the Allied Families of Strother and Ashby.* New York, NY: Privately published for William Dickinson Bucker by The Genealogical Association.

Cunningham, George Alfred. n.d. *Cunningham's History of the Town of Lunenburg: from the Original Grant, December 7th 1719 to January 1st, 1866.* https://dp.la/search?q=Cunningham%27s+history+of+the+town+of+Lunenburg.

Cushing, James Stevenson. 1905. *The Genealogy of the Cushing Family, an Account of the Ancestors and Descendants of Matthew Cushing, Who Came to America in 1638.* Montreal: Perrault Printing Co.

Cushing, Thomas. 1889/1975. *A Genealogical and Biographical History of Allegheny County, Pennsylvania.* Baltimore, MD: Genealogical Publishing Company.

Cutter, Daniel Bateman. 1881. *History of the Town of Jaffrey, New Hampshire, from the Date of the Masonian Charter to the Present Time, 1749-1880.* Concord, NH: Printed by the Republican Press Association.

Cutter, William Richard. 1912. *Genealogical and Family History of Central New York: A Record of the Achievements of Her People in the Making of a Commonwealth and the Building of a Nation.* New York, NY: Lewis Historical Publishing Company.

—. 1908. *Genealogical and Personal Memoirs Relating to the Families of Boston and Eastern Massachusetts.* Boston, MA: Lewis Historical Publishing Company.

—. 1910. *Genealogical and Personal Memoirs Relating to the Families of the State of Massachusetts.* New York, NY: Lewis Historical Publishing Company.

—. 1915. *New England Families, Genealogical and Memorial; a Record of the Achievements of Her People in the Making of Commonwealths and the Founding of a Nation, Volumes 1-4.* New York: Lewis Historical Publishing Co.

Darling, Nancy. 1913. "History and Anniversary of Hartland, Vermont." *The Vermonter, Volume 18.*

Davenport, A. B. 1851. *A History and Genealogy of the Davenport Family in England and America 1086-1850.* New York, NY: S. W. Benedict.

Davis, Charles Henry Stanley. 1870. *History of Wallingford, Conn., from its Settlement in 1670 to the Present Time.* Meriden, CT: Published by the author.

Davis, George L. 1884. *Samuel Davis, of Oxford, Mass., and Joseph Davis of Dudley, Mass. and Their Descendants.* North Andover, MA: George L. Davis.

Davis, Walter Alonzo, City Clerk. 1899. *The Old Records of the Town of Fitchburg, Massachusetts.* Fitchburg, MA: Published by authority of the city council.

De Wolfe, Edity. 1953. *The History of Putney, Vermont, 1753-1953.* Putney, VT: Fortnightly Club.

Dearborn, John Jacob. 1890. *The History of Salisbury, New Hampshire: From Date of Settlement to the Present Time.* Manchester, NH: Printed by W.E. Moore.

DeJulia, Henry J. 1994. "America's Citizen Soldier: Hero or Coward?" *Connecticut Nutmegger* 27: 583-584.

Dewey, Adelbert Milton, Louis Marinus Dewey, William Tarbox Dewey, and Orville C. Dewey. 1898. *Life of George Dewey, Rear Admiral, U.S.N.; and Dewey Family History: Being an Authentic Historical and Genealogical Record of More Than*

Fifteen Thousand Persons in the United States by the Name of Dewey, and Their Descendants. Westfield, MA: Dewey Publishing Company.

Dimock, Susan Whitney. 1898. *Births, Baptisms,Mmarriages and Deaths, from the Records of the Town and Churches in Mansfield, Connecticut, 1703-1850.* New York, NY: The Baker and Taylor Company.

Donaldson, Alfred Lee. 1921. *A History of the Adirondacks.* New York, NY: Century Co.

Donovan, Dennis. 1906. *The History of the Town of Lyndeborough, New Hampshire.* Tufts College Press.

Durrie, Daniel S. 1864. *A Genealogical History of the Holt Family in the United States More Particularly the Descendants of Nicholas Holt of Newbury and Andover, Mass.* Albany: Munsell.

Dwight, Benjamin Woodbridge. 1871. *The History of the Descendants of Elder John Strong.* Albany, NY: Joel Munsell.

Eastman, John Robie. 1910. *History of the Town of Andover New Hampshire, 1751-1906.* Concord, NH: Rumford Printing.

Eaton, Cyrus. 1865. *History of Thomaston, Rockland, and South Thomaston, Maine, from their First Exploration, A. D. 1605; with Family Genealogies.* Hallowell, ME: Masters, Smith & Co., Printers.

Eaton, Lilley. 1874. *Genealogical History of the Town of Reading, Mass., Including the Present Towns of Wakefield, Reading, and North Reading, with Chronological and Historical Sketches, from 1639 to 1874.* Boston, MA: A. Mudge & Son.

Edson, Carroll Andrew. 1969. *Edson Family History and Genealogy: Descendants of Samuel Edson of Salem and Bridgewater, Mass.* Ann Arbor, MI: Edwards Brothers.

Ela, David Hough. 1896. *Genealogy of the Ela Family: Descendant of Israel Ela, of Haverhill, Mass.* Manchester, CT: Elwood S. Ela, Printer.

Eldredge, Zoeth Skinner. 1896. *Eldredge Genealogy.* Boston: D. Clapp Printers.

Elliot, Hazem Tracy. 1947. *The Hazen Family in America.* Thomaston, CT: R. Hazen.

Ely, Heman. 1885. *Records of the Descendants of Nathaniel Ely, the Emigrant who Settled in Newtown, now Cambridge, Mass.* Cleveland, OH: Short & Forman.

Emery, Edwin. 1901. *The History of Sanford, Maine, 1661-1900.* Salem, MA: Salem Press Company.

Emery, Rufus. 1890. *Genealogical Records of Desendants of John and Anthony Emery, of Newbury, Mass. 1590-1890.* Salem, MA: Emery Cleaves.

Essex Institute. 1922. *Old-Time Ships of Salem, 2nd Edition.* Salem, MA: Nichols Press Printers.

Everts and Abbott. 1879. *History of Hillsdale County, Michigan with Illustrations and Biographical Sketches.* Philadelphia, PA: Press of J. B. Lippincott.

Fairbanks, Lorenzo Sayles. 1897. *Genealogy of the Fairbanks Family in America 1633-1897.* Boston, MA: Printed for the author.

Farnham, Russell Clare. 1999. *The New England Descendants of the Immigrant Ralph Farnum of Rochester, Kent County, England, and Ipswich, Massachusetts.* Peter Randall Publishing.

Field, A. D. 1896. *Worthies and Workers, both Ministers and Laymen of the Rock River Conference.* Cincinnati, OH: Printed for the author.

Fisher, Philip A. 1898. *The Fisher Genealogy: Record of the Descendants of Joshua, Anthony, and Cornelius Fisher of Dedham, Mass.* Everett, MA: Massachusetts Publishing Company.

Fitts, James Hill. 1897. *Lane Genealogies, volume II.* Exeter, NH: The News-Letter Press.

Foote, Abram William. 1907. *Foote Family: Comprising the Genealogy and History of Nathaniel Foote, of Wethersfield, Conn., and His Descendants.* Rutland, VT: Marble City Press; The Tuttle Company.

Ford, James Everett. 1936. *A History of Moniteau County, Missouri.* California, MO: H. Crawford.

Foster, E. J. 1884. "Early Settlers of Weld." *The Maine Historical and Genealogical Recorder* 1-2: 119 ff.

Freeman, Frederick. 1875. *Freeman Genealogy in Three Parts.* Boston, MA: Private Edition; Printed by Franklin Press: Rand, Avery, and Company.

French, J. H. 1860. *Gazetteer of the State of New York, Eighth Edition.* Syracuse, NY: R. P. Smith.

Frisbee, Edward S. 1919. *The Frisbee-Frisbie Genealogy: Edward Frisbye of Branford, Connecticut and His Descendants.* Rutland, VT: Printed by the Tuttle Company.

Frost, John Eldridge. 1943. *The Nicholas Frost Family.* Milford, NH: Cabinet Press.

Fuller, William Hylsop. 1914. *Genealogy of Some Descendants of Captain Matthew Fuller, John Fuller of Newton, John Fuller of Lynn, John Fuller of Ipswich, Robert Fuller of Dorchester and Dedham.* Printed for the Compiler.

Gage, George N. 1894. *A Record of Pierce Gage and His Descendants.* East Washington, NH: Printed by the author.

Gay, Frank B., and Harrie Beekman Drake. 1933. *The Descendants of John Drake of Windsor, Connecticut.* Rutland, VT: The Tuttle Company.

Gay, William Burton. 1887. *Historical Gazetteer of Tioga County, New York, 1785-1888.* Syracuse, NY: W. B. Gay & Co.

Goding, Frederic Webster. 1906. *Genealogy of the Goding Family.* Richmond, IN: Press of Nicholson Printing.

Goodspeed, Weston A., and Charles Blanchard. 1882. *Counties of Porter and Lake, Indiana. Historical and Biographical.* Chicago, IL: F. A. Battey & Co.

Gould, Isaiah. 1897. *History of Stoddard, Cheshire County, N.H.* Keene, NH: W. L. Metcalf, printer.

Gould, Sherry L, and Kathleen C. Beals. 2004. *Early Families of Bradford, NH.* Bradford, NH: Bradford Historical Society.

Grant, Arthur Hastings. 1898. *The Grant Family: A Genealogical History of the Descendants of Matthew Grant, of Windsor, Conn.1601-1898.* Poughkeepsie, NY: A. V. Haight.

Greeley, George Hiram. 1905. *Genealogy of the Greely-Greeley Family.* Boston, MA: F. Wood, printer.

Greenlee, Ralph Stebbins, and Robert Lemuel Greenlee. 1904. *The Stebbins Genealogy.* Chicago: Privately printed.

Greenwood, Frederick. 1914. *Greenwood Genealogies, 1154-1914: The Ancestry and Descendants of Thomas Greenwood, of Newton, Massachusetts.* New York, NY: Lyons Genealogical Company.

Greven, Philip. 1970. *Four Generations: Population, Land, and Family in Colonial Andover, Massachusetts.* Ithaca: Cornell University Press.

Griffin, Simon G. 1904. *A History of the Town of Keene from 1732, When the Township Was Granted by Massachusetts, to 1874, When it Became a City.* Keene, NH: Sentinel Printing Company.

H. F. Kett and Company. 1877. *The History of Winnebago County, Illinois.* Chicago, IL: H. F. Kett & Co.

Haddock, John A. 1894. *Growth of a Century: As Illustrated in the History of Jefferson County, New York, from 1793 to 1894.* Philadelphia, PA: Printed by Sherman & Co.

Hadley, George Plummer. 1924. *History of the Town of Goffstown 1733-1920.* Goffstown, NH: Published by the town.

Hagen, Louis William, and Marie Smith Hagen. 1963. *The Sanger Family: Ancestors and Descendants of Jonathan Sanger (1755-1819) Revolutionary Soldier of Pomfret, Connecticut and Canandaigua, New York.* Rochester, NY: Published by the Authors. https://www.familysearch.org/library/books/records/item/37626-the-sanger-family-ancestors-and-descendants-of-jonathan-sanger-1755-1819-revolutionary-soldier-of-pomfret-connecticut-and-canandaigua-new-york?offset=3.

Hall, David B. 1883. *The Halls of New England, Genealogical and Biographical.* Albany, NY: Joel Munsell's Sons.

Hamilton, Von Gail. 1969. *Work Family History: Twelve Generations of Works in America 1690-1969.* Park City, UT.

Hammond, Charles. 1893. *The History of Union, Conn.* New Haven: Price, Lee & Adkins.

Hammond, Frederick Stam. 1904. *Histories and Genealogies of the Hammond Families in America.* Oneida, NY: Ryan and Burkhart, Printers.

Hammond, Roland. 1894. *A History and Genealogy of the Descendants of William Hammond of London, England, and his Wife Elizabeth Penn.* Boston, MA: D. Clapp & Son, printers.

Hand, H. Wells. 1908. *1808-1908. Centennial History of the Town of Nunda.* Rochester Herald Press.

Harvard University. 1905. *Quinquennial Catalogue of the Officers and Graduates of Harvard University.* Cambridge, MA: Harvard University.

Harvey, Lanson B., and Edward P. Harvey. 1912. *Rev. Erastus Harvey and His Descendants.* East Liberty, OH: Howard H. Harvey.

Hayes, Lyman Simpson. 1907. *History of the Town of Rockingham, Vermont, Including the Villages of Bellows Falls, Saxtons River, Rockingham, Cambridgeport and Bartonsville, 1753-1907, with Family Genealogies.* Bellows Falls, VT: Published by the town.

Hayward, Paul Dillon. 1985. *William Hayward of Mendon.* Unpublished manuscript; Family Search Title Number 345296. https://www.familysearch.org/library/books/records/item/62802-william-hayward-of-mendon?offset=2.

Hayward, Silvanus. 1881. *History of the Town of Gilsum, New Hampshire from 1752 to 1879.* Manchester, NH: Printed for the author by John B. Clarke.

Hayward, William Willis. 1889. *The History of Hancock, New Hampshire, 1764-1889.* Lowell, MA: Vox Populi Press.

Hazen, Celeste Pember. 1939. *John Pember: The History of the Pember Family in America.* https://archive.org/details/johnpemberhistor00haze/mode/2up.

Hemenway, Abby Maria (Ed.). 1867. *The Vermont Historical Gazetteer: A Magazine Embracing the History of Each Town.* Burlington, VT: Miss A. M. Hemenway.

Hendrick, Charles T. 1923. *The Hendrick Genealogy: Daniel Hendrick of Haverhill, Mass. and His Descendants.* Rutland, VT: The Tuttle Company.

Hibbard, Augustine George. 1901. *Genealogy of the Hibbard Family Who are Descendants of Robert Hibbard of Salem, Massachusetts.* Hartford, CT: Case.

—. 1897. *History of the Town of Goshen, Connecticut, with Genealogies and Biographies Based upon the Records of Deacon Lewis Mills Norton, 1897.* Hartford, CT: Press of the Case, Lockwood & Brainard Co.

Hill, Henry Wayland. 1922. *Municipality of Buffalo, New York: A History 1720-1923, volume I.* New York, NY: Lewis Historical Publishing.

Hill, John Boynton. 1858. *History of the Town of Mason, N. H. from the First Grant in 1749, to the Year 1858.* Boston, MA: Lucius A. Elliot & Co.

Hill, N. N. Jr. 1881. *History of Licking County, O.: Its Past and Present.* Newark, OH: A. A. Graham & Co.

Hinds, Albert Henry. 1899. *History and Genealogy of the Hinds Family.* Portland, ME: The Thurston Print.

Historical Society of Geauga County. 1880. *Pioneer and General History of Geauga County, with Sketches of Some of the Pioneers and Prominent Men.* Burton, OH: Historical Society of Geauga County.

Hodges, Almon Danforth. 1896. *Genealogical Record of the Hodges Family of New England, Ending December 31, 1894.* Boston, MA: Published by the author.

Hodgman, Edwin Ruthven. 1883. *History of the Town of Westford, in the County of Middlesex, Massachusetts, 1659-1883.* Lowell, MA: Morning Mail Co.

Hodgman, Herbert Nelson. 1937. *Josiah Hodgman Family, 1668-1935: With Allied Families of Cummings, Fletcher, Spaulding, Foster, Scales, Jamieson.* St. Paul, MN: Unpublished manuscript. https://archive.org/details/josiahhodgmanfam00hodg/mode/2up.

Hoffman, Urias John. 1906. *History of La Salle County, Illinois.* Chicago, IL: S. J. Clarke Publishing Co.

Holcombe, Return Ira. 1914. *Compendium of History and Biography of Minneapolis and Hennepin County, Minnesota.* Chicago, IL: H. Taylor & Co.

Holman, David Emery. 1909. *The Holmans in America: Concerning the Descendants of Solaman Holman who Settled in West Newbury, Massachusetts, in 1692-3*. New York, NY: The Grafton Press.

Holt, Adoniram Judson. 1923. *Pioneering in the Southwest*. Nashville, TN: Sunday School Board of the Southern Baptist Convention.

Holton, David Parsons, and Frances K. Holton. 1877. *Winslow Memorial: Family Records of Winslows and Their Descendants in America*. New York, NY: D-P Holton.

Hopkins, Timothy. 1932. *John Hopkins of Cambridge, Massachusetts, 1634, and Some of HIs Descendants*. Printed by Stanford University Press.

Houghton, John W. 1912. *The Houghton Genealogy: The Descendants of Ralph and John Houghton of Lancaster, Massachusetts*. New York, NY: Frederick H. Hitchcok, Genealogical Publisher.

Howland, Franklyn. 1885. *A Brief Genealogical and Biographical History of Arthur, Henry, and John Howland and Their Descendants*. New Bedford, MA: Published by the author.

Hoyt, David Webster. 1857. *Hoyt Family: A Genealogical History of John Hoyt of Salisbury, and David Hoyt of Deerfield, (Massachusetts,) and Their Descendants: With Some Account of the Earlier Connecticut Hoyts*. Boston, MA: C. Benjamin Richardson.

Hubbard, Charles Horace, and Justus Dartt. 1895. *History of the Town of Springfield, Vermont*. Boston: G. H. Walker.

Humphreys, Frederick. 1883. *The Humphreys Family in America*. New York, NY: Humphreys Print.

Huntington, E. B. 1863. *Genealogical Memoir of the Huntington Family in This Country*. Stamford, CT: Published by the author.

Hurd, Duane Hamilton (Ed.). 1885. *History of Merrimack and Belknap Counties, New Hampshire*. Philadelphia: J. W. Lewis.

Hurd, Duane Hamilton. 1885. *History of Hillsborough County, New Hampshire*. Philadephia: J. W. Lewis.

—. 1878. *History of Otsego County, New York: With Illustrations and Biographical Sketches of Some of its Prominent Men and Pioneers*. Philadelphia, PA: Everts and Fariss.

Hurlbut, Henry Higgins. 1888. *The Hurlbut Genealogy: Or, Record of the Descendants of Thomas Hurlbut, of Saybrook and Wethersfield, Conn*. Albany, NY: Joel Munsell's Sons.

Hyde, William, and Howard L. Conrad. 1897. *Encyclopedia of the History of St. Louis, volume IV*. New York, NY: The Southern History Company.

Inscoe, John C. 1996. *Mountain Masters: Slavery and the Sectional Crisis in Western North Carolina*. University of Tennessee Press.

Inter-State Publishing Company. 1885. *History of McHenry County, Illinois*. Chicago, IL: Inter-State Publishing Company.

Iowa City, Iowa. 1883. *History of Johnson County, Iowa*. Iowa City, IA: Published by the town.

J. W. Lewis. 1881. *History of Litchfield County, Connecticut, with Illustrations and Biographical Sketches of Its Prominent Men and Pioneers*. Philadelphia, PA: J. W. Lewis & Co.

Jacobus, Donald Lines. 1981. *Families of Ancient New Haven*. Baltimore, MD: Genealogical Publishing Company.

Jameson, Ephraim Orcutt. 1896. *The Choates in America, 1643-1896*. Boston, MA: A. Mudge & Son, printers.

—. 1884. *The Cogswells in America*. Boston, MA: A. Mudge & Son, Printers.

Janes, Frederic. 1868. *The Janes Family: A Genealogy and Brief History*. New York, NY: John H. Dingman.

Jewell, Pliny, and Joel Jewell. 1860. *The Jewell Register: Containing a List of the Descendants of Thomas Jewell, of Braintree, Near Boston, Mass*. Hartford, CT: Case, Lockwood.

Jewett, Frederic Clarke. 1908. *History and Genealogy of the Jewetts of America: A Record of Edward Jewett, of Bradford, West Riding of Yorkshire, England, and of his two Emigrant Sons, Deacon Maximilian and Joseph Jewett, Settlers of Rowley, Massachusetts, in 1639.* New York, NY: The Grafton Press.

Johnson, Crisfield. 1877. *History of Oswego County, New York with Illustrations and Biographical Sketches of Some of Its Prominent Men and Pioneers.* Philadephia, PA: L. H. Everts & Co.

—. 1878. *History of Washington Co., New York: With Illustrations and Biographical Sketches of Some of Its Prominent Men and Pioneers.* Philadelphia, PA: Everts & Ensign.

Johnson, James Bowen. 1895. *The Johnson Memorial: Jeremiah Johnson and Thomazin Blanchard Johnson, His Wife.* Washington, DC: Howard University Print.

Johnson, William Wallace. 1892. *Johnson Genealogy: Records of the Descendants of John Johnson, of Ipswich and Andover, Mass., 1635-1892.* North Greenfield, WI: Published by the compiler.

Jones, Emma C. Brewster. 1908. *The Brewster Genealogy, 1566-1907: A Record of the Descendants of William Brewster of the "Mayflower".* New York, NY: Grafton Press.

Judd, Sylvester. 1856. *Thomas Judd and His Descendants.* Northampton: J & L Metcalf, Printers.

Kilbourne, Payn Kenyon. 1856. *The History and Antiquities of the Name and Family of Kilbourn.* New Haven, CT: Durrie & Peck.

Kimball, John. 1885. *The Joseph Kimball Family: A Genealogical Memoir of the Ascendants and Descendants of Joseph Kimball of Canterbury, N. H.* Concord, NH: Printed by the Republican Press Association.

Kingman, LeRoy Wilson. 1897. *Our County and Its People: A Memorial History of Tioga County, New York.* Elmira: NY: W. A. Fergusson & Co.

Kingsbury, Fred J. 1905. *The Genealogy of the Descendants of Henry Kingsbury.* Hartford, CT: Author.

Kingsbury, Henry D., and Simeon L. (Eds.) Deyo. 1892. *Illustrated History of Kennebec County, Maine.* New York, NY: H. W. Blake & Company.

Klumph, Richard Amidon. 1960. *Klumph Genealogy and Early Klumph History.* Kalamazoo, MI: Published by the author.

L. H. Everts. 1878. *History of Jefferson County, New York with Illustrations and Biographical Sketches.* Philadelphia, PA: L. H. Everts & Co.

Ladd, Warren. 1890. *The Ladd Family: A Genealogical and Biographical Memoir.* New Bedford, MA: Printed for the author.

Lake County Publishing Company. 1895. *Portrait and Biographical Record of Iroquois County, Illinois.* Chicago, IL: Lake County Publishing Company.

Lamson, Otis E., and Frank B. Lamson. 1908. *Memorial of Elder Ebenezer Lamson of Concord, Mass.* Buffalo, MN: Privately printed.

Lamson, William J. 1917. *Descendants of William Lamson of Ipswich, Mass. 1634-1917.* New York: T. A. Wright.

Lapham, William Berry. 1886. *Centennial History of Norway, Oxford County, Maine, 1786-1886.* Portland, ME: B. Thurston.

—. 1891. *History of Bethel, Formerly Sudbury, Canada, Oxford County, Maine, 1768-1890.* Augusta, ME: Press of the Maine Farmer.

—. 1890. *History of Rumford, Oxford County, Maine, from Its First Settlement in 1779, to the Present Time.* Augusta, ME: Press of the Maine Farmer.

Lapham, William Berry, and John Ordway Webster. 1884. *Genealogy of Some of the Descendants of John Webster of Ipswich, Mass., 1633.* Augusta, ME: Press of Charles E. Nash.

Lapham, William Berry, and Silas Packard Maxim. 1884. *History of Paris, Maine, from its Settlement to 1880, with a History of the Grants of 1736 & 1771, Together with Personal Sketches, a Copious Genealogical Register and an Appendix.* Paris, ME: Printed for the authors.

Larkin, Stillman Carter. 1908. *The Pioneer History of Meigs County.* Columbus, OH: Berlin Printing Company.

Learned, Robert C. 1861. "Congregational Churches and Ministers in Windham County, CT." *The Congregational Quarterly* III: 13-18.

Leffingwell, Albert. 1897. *Leffingwell Record: A Genealogy of the Descendants of Lieut. Thomas Leffingwell, One of the Founders of Norwich, Conn.* Aurora, NY: Leffingwell Publishing Co.

Leonard, Levi Washburn, and Josiah Lafayette Seward. 1920. *The History of Dublin, N.H.: Containing the Address by Charles Mason, and the Proceedings at the Centennial Celebration, June 17, 1852, with a Register of Families.* Dublin, NH: Published by the town.

Lewis Publishing Company. 1900. *Biographical and Genealogical Record of La Salle and Grundy Counties, Illinois.* Chicago, IL: Lewis Publishing Company.

—. 1892. *Biographical History of La Crosse, Trempealeau, and Buffalo Counties, Wisconsin.* Chicago, IL: Lewis Publishing Company.

Lincoln, Waldo. 1902. *Genealogy of the Waldo Family: A Record of the Descendants of Cornelius Waldo, of Ipswich, Mass., from 1647 to 1900.* Worcester, MA: Press of Charles Hamilton.

Littlefield, Peter F., and Karl Pfister. 2001. *Genealogies of the Early Settlers of Weston, Vermont, Second Edition.* Weston, VT: Weston Historical Society.

Littlehale, Frederick H. 1889. *A Complete History and Genealogy of the Littlehale Family in America from 1633 to 1889.* Boston, MA: A. W. and F. H. Littleehale.

Livermore, Abiel Abbot, and Putnam Sewall. 1888. *History of the Town of Wilton, Hillsborough County, New Hampshire, with a Genealogical Register.* Lowell, MA: Marden and Rowell.

Locke, John Goodwin. 1853. *Book of Lockes: A Genealogical and Historical Record of the Descendants of William Locke of Woburn.* Boston, MA: James Munroe and Company.

Lord, Henry Dutch. 1896. *Memorial of the Family of Morse: Compiled from the Original Records for Hon. Asa Porter Morse.* Cambridgeport, MA: Private distribution; printed by Harvard Printling Company.

Lord, John King. 1928. *A History of the Town of Hanover, N.H.* Hanover, NH: The Dartmouth Press.

Lovejoy, Clarence Earle. 1930. *The Lovejoy Genealogy with Biographies and History.* New York: Published by the author.

Lovejoy, Mary Elevyn Wood. 1911. *History of Royalton, Vermont, with Family Genealogies, 1769-1911.* Burlington, VT: Free Press Printing Company.

Lovelace, Jayne Pratt. 1998. *The Pratt Directory, 1998 ed.* East Haddam, CT: Ancestor House.

Lowell, Delmar Rial. 1899. *The Historic Genealogy of the Lowells of America from 1639 to 1899.* Published by the author.

Lyon(s), A. B., and G. W. A. Lyon. 1905. *Lyon Memorial: Massachusetts Families.* Detroit, MI: Press of William Graham.

Marcy, Oliver. 1875. *Record of the Marcy Family.* Evanston, IL. https://archive.org/details/recordofmarcyfam00marc/mode/2up.

Marvin, George Franklin. 1904. *Descendants of Reinold and Matthew Marvin of Hartford, Ct., 1638 and 1635, Sons of Edward Marvin, of Great Bentley, England.* Boston, MA: T. R. Marvin & Son.

Mason, Edna Warren. 1937. *Descendants of Capt. Hugh Mason in America.* New Haven, CT: Tuttle, Morehouse & Taylor.

McIntire, Robert Harry. 1940. *Descendants of Micum McIntire.* Rutland, VT: Tuttle Publishing Company.

Merrick, George Byron. 1902. *Genealogy of the Merrick--Mirick--Myrick Family of Massachusetts.* Madison, WI: Tracy, Gibbs & Company.

Merrill, Georgia Drew. 1891. *History of Androscoggin County, Maine.* Boston, MA: W. A. Ferguson & Co.

—. 1889. *History of Carroll County, New Hampshire.* Boston, MA: W. A. Ferguson.

Merrill, Samuel. 1917-1928. *A Merrill Memorial: An Account of the Descendants of Nathaniel Merrill, an Early Settler of Newbury, Massachusetts.* Cambridge, MA.

Merrimack Historical Society. 1976. *The History of Merrimack, New Hampshire: With Genealogies of Merrimack Families.* Merrimack, NH: Merrimack Historical Society.

Miles, Jonas M. 1920. *Miles Genealogy: John Miles of Concord, Massachusetts and His Descendants.* Boston, MA: C. E. Goodspeed & Company.

Miller, Edward. 1913. *History of Ryegate, Vermont, from its Settlement by the Scotch-American Company of Farmers to Present Time.* St. Johnsbury, VT: Celdonian Company.

Minard, John S., and Georgia Drew Merrill. 1896. *Allegany County and Its People: A Centennial Memorial History of Allegany County, New York. Also Histories of the Towns of the County.* Alfred, NY: W. A. Fergusson & Co.

Miner, Charles. 1845. *History of Wyoming, in a Series of Letters, from Charles Miner, to His Son William Penn Miner.* Philadelphia, PA: J Crissy.

Mitchell, S. H. 1886. *Historical Sketches of Iowa Baptists.* Burlington, IA: Burdette Company.

Molyneux, Nellie Zada Rice. 1911. *History Genealogical and Biographical of the Eaton Families.* Syracuse, NY: C. W. Bardeen.

Monroe, Ira Thompson. 1932. *History of the Town of Livermore, Androscoggin County, Maine: From its Inception in 1735 and its Grant of Land in 1772 to its Organization and Incorporation in 1795 up to the Present Time, 1928.* Lewiston, ME: Printed by the Lewiston Journal Printshop.

Mooar, George. 1903. *The Cummings Memorial: A Genealogical History of the Descendants of Isaac Cummings, an Early Settler of Topsfield, Massachusetts.* New York: B. F. Cummings.

Moran, Edward C. 1961. *Bunker Genealogy: Descendants of James Bunker of Dover, N. H.* Rockland, ME: Bunker Family Association of America.

Morgan, Nathaniel Harris. 1869. *Morgan Genealogy: A History of James Morgan, of New London, Conn., and His Descendants.* Hartford, CT: Press of Case, Lockwood & Brainard.

Morris, John E. 1893. *The Felt Genealogy: A Record of the Descendants of George Felt of Casco Bay.* Hartford, CT: Press of the Case, Lockwood & Brainard Company.

Morris, Jonathan Flynt. 1887. *A Genealogical and Historical Register of the Descendants of Edward Morris of Roxbury, Mass. and Woodstock, Conn.* Hartford, CT: Case, Lockwood & Brainard.

Morrison, Leonard Allison, and Stephen Paschall Sharples. 1897. *History of the Kimball Family in America, from 1634 to 1897: and of its Ancestors the Kemballs or Kemboldes of England; with an Account of the Kembles of Boston, Massachusetts.* Boston: Damrell & Upham.

Morse, J. Howard, and Emily W. Leavitt. 1903. *Morse Genealogy: Comprising the Descendants of Samuel, Anthony, William, and Joseph Morse and John Moss: Being a Revision of the Memorial of the Morses, Volumes 1-2.* New York, NY: Morse Society.

Mower, Anna L. 1935. *History of Morristown, Vermont.* Morrisville, VT: Messenger Sentinel Company.

Mudge, Alfred. 1868. *Memorials: Being a Genealogical, Biographical and Historical Account of the Name of Mudge in America, from 1638 to 1868.* Boston, MA: Printed by Alfred Mudge & Son, for the Family.

Musgrove, Richard W. 1904. *History of the Town of Bristol, Grafton County, New Hampshire in Two Volumes.* Bristol, NH: Printed by R. W. Musgrove.

Neill, Edward D. 1882. *History of Rice County, Including Explorers and Pioneers of Minnesota.* Minneapolis, MN: Minnesota Historical Company.

Nelson Picnic Association. 1917. *Celebration of the Town of Nelson, New Hampshire.* New York, NY: Evening Post job printing office.

Newcomb, Bethuel Merritt, and John Bearse Newcomb. 1923. *Andrew Newcomb, 1618-1686, and his Descendants.* New Haven, CT: Private printing for the author by Tuttle, Morehouse & Taylor.

Noon, Alfred. 1912. *The History of Ludlow, Massachusetts with Biographical Sketches of Leading Citizens, Reminiscences, Genealogies, Farm Histories, and an Account of the Centennial Celebration, June 17, 1874, Second Edition.* Springfield, MA: Printed by vote of the town; Springfield Printing and Binding Company.

Norton, James Edward. 1935. *Norton-Lathrop-Tolles-Doty American ancestry of Ralph Tolles Norton, James Edward Norton, Arden Lathrop Norton, Frank Porter Norton.* Privately printed. https://archive.org/details/nortonlathroptol00nort_0/mode/2up.

Nye, George Hyatt. 1907. *A Genealogy of the Nye Family.* Cleveland, OH: The Nye Family of America Association.

Olds, Edson B. 1915. *The Olds (Old, Ould) Family in England and America.* Washington, DC: Edson B. Olds.

Oliver, Rebekah Deal. 1970. *The Bottum (Longbottom) Family Album: The Descendants of Daniel (-1732) and Elizabeth (Lamb) Longbottom of Norwich, Connecticut.* Denver, CO: W. Kelly Oliver.

Orcutt, Samuel. 1878. *History of Torrington, Connecticut.* Albany, NY: J. Munsell, Printer.

Orth, Samuel P. 1910. *A History of Cleveland, Ohio.* Cleveland, OH: S. J. Clarke Publishing.

Osgood, Ira. 1894. *A Genealogy of the Descendants of John, Christopher and William Osgood, Who Came from England and Settled in New England Early in the Seventeenth Century.* Salem, MA: Salem Press.

Parker, Leonard Fletcher. 1911. *History of Poweshiek County, Iowa: A Record of Settlement, Organization, Progress and Achievement, Volume II.* Chicago, IL: S. J. Clarke Publishing.

Parks, Frank Sylvester. 1906. *Genealogy of the Parke Families of Connecticut.* Washington, DC: Privately printed.

Parshall, James C. 1897. *The Barker Genealogy: Giving the Names and Descendants of Several Ancestors, who Settled in the United States Previous to the Declaration of Independence, A.D. 1776.* Middletown, NY: Printed for the author.

Parsons, Henry. 1912. *Parsons Family: Descendants of Cornet Joseph Parsons, Springfield, 1636--Northampton,1655; Volume 2.* New York: Frank Allaben Genealogical Company.

Parsons, Usher. 1872. *A Centennial History of Alfred, York County, Maine.* Philadelphia, PA: Sanford, Everts & Co.

Peabody, Selim Hobart. 1909. *Peabody (Paybody, Pabody, Pabodie) Genealogy.* Boston, MA: Charles H. Pope.

Peck, Chauncey Edwin. 1914. *The History of Wilbraham, Massachusetts.* Town of Wilbraham.

Peck, Ira Ballou. 1868. *A Genealogical History of the Descendants of Joseph Peck.* Boston, MA: A. Mudge.

Peck, William F. 1895. *Landmarks of Monroe County, New York.* Boston, MA: The Boston History Company.

Pelton, Jeremiah M. 1892. *Genealogy of the Pelton Family in America.* Albany, NY: Joel Munsell's Sons.

Perkins, Mary Elizabeth. 1895. *Old Houses of the Antient [sic] Town of Norwich, 1660-1800.* Norwich, CT: Press of the Bulletin Company.

Perkins, Thomas A. 1913. "Biographical Sketches." *Addresses Delivered Before the California Society of the Sons of the American Revolution.* San Francisco, CA: Published by the Society. 91ff.

Perley, Sidney. 1893. *The Dwellings of Boxford, Essex County, Mass.* Salem, MA: The Essex Institute.

—. 1917. *The Plumer Genealogy: Francis Plumer, who Settled at Newbury, Massachusetts, & Some of His Descendants.* Salem, MA: Essex Institute.

Perrin, William Henry. 1881. *History of Summit County, with an Outline Sketch of Ohio.* Chicago, IL: Baskin & Battey.

Perrin, William Henry, J. H. Battle, and G. C. Kniffin. 1887. *Kentucky, A History of the State, Sixth Edition.* Louisville, KY: F. A. Battey and Company.

Phelps, Oliver Seymour, and Andrew Tinkey Servin. 1899. *The Phelps Family of America and Their English Ancestors.* Pittsfield, MA: Eagle Publishing.

Pierce, Frederic Beech. 1882. *Pierce Genealogy: Being the Record of the Posterity of Thomas Pierce, an Early Inhabitant of Charlestown, and Afterwards Charlestown Village (Woburn), in New England.* Worcester, MA: Press of C. Hamilton.

Pierce, Frederick Clifton. 1898. *Batchelder, Batcheller Genealogy. Descendants of Rev. Stephen Bachiler, of England … Who Settled the Town of New Hampton, N.H., and Joseph, Henry, Joshua and John Batcheller of Essex Co., Mass.* Chicago: W. B. Conkey.

—. 1901. *Field Genealogy: Being the Record of all the Field Family in America, Whose Ancestors Were in this Country Prior to 170.* Chicago: IL: W. B. Conkey.

—. 1896. *Fiske and Fisk Family: Being the Record of the Descendants of Symond Fiske, Lord of the Manor of Stadhaugh, Suffolk County, England, from the Time of Henry IV to Date, Including all the American Members of the Family.* Chicago, IL: The author.

Pierce, Richard Donald. 1946. "A History of Temple, Maine: Its Rise and Decline." *Boston Univeristy Graduate School, Dissertation.* https://archive.org/details/historyoftemplem00pier/mode/2up.

Piscataquis County Historical Society. 1910. *Historical Collections of Piscataquis County, Maine.* Dover, ME: Observer Press.

Plumb, Henry Blackman. 1885. *History of Hanover Township: Including Sugar Notch, Ashley, and Nanticoke Boroughs.* Wilkes-Barre, PA: R. Baur. Printer.

Pollard, Annie M. 1954. *The History of the Town of Baltimore, Vermont.* Montpelier, VT: Vermont Historical Society.

Poor, Henry V. 1904. "History of Andover, Maine: Purchase of the Township and Distribution of the Land." *The Rumford Falls Times*, Aug 13: 1-16.

Pope, Charles Henry. 1897. *The Cheney Genealogy.* Boston, MA: Charles H. Pope.

Pope, Charles, Henry, and Thomas Hooper. 1908. *Hooper Genealogy.* Boston, MA: C. H. Pope.

Porter, Joseph W. (Ed.). 1885. "The Carr Family." *Maine Historical Magazine (Bangor Historical Magazine)* I (1): 9-12.

Pratt, Francis G. Salem, MA. *The Pratt Family: A Genealogical Record of Mathew Pratt of Weymouth, Mass., and his American Descendants, 1623-1889.* 1890: Higginson Genealogical Books.

Preston, Charles Henry. 1931. *Descendants of Roger Preston of Ipswich and Salem Village.* Salem, MA: The Essex Institute.

Quick, Arthur Craig. 1942. *A Genealogy of the Quick Family in America 1625-1942.* South Haven, MI: Privately published by Arthur C. Quick. Ancestry.com. A genealogy of the Quick family in America (1625-1942), 317 years [database on-line].

Ramsdell, George Allen, and William P. Colburn. 1901. *The History of Milford, Volume 1.* Milford, NH: Rumford Press.

Randall, Oran Edmund. 1882. *History of Chesterfield, Cheshire County, N.H., from the Incorporation of "Township Number One," by Massachusetts, in 1736, to the Year 1881.* Brattleboro, VT: D. Leonard.

Rann, William S. 1886. *History of Chittenden County, Vermont.* Syracuse, NY: D. Mason & Co.

Raymond, Samuel. 1886. *Genealogies of the Raymond Families of New England 1630-1 to 1886.* New York, NY: Press of J. J. Little & Co.

Read, Benjamin. 1892. *The History of Swanzey, New Hampshire, from 1734 to 1890.* Salem, MA: Salem Press.

Redington, Edward Dana, William H. Hodgkins, and Charles Theodore Gallagher. 1907. *Military Record of the Sons of Dartmouth in the Union Army and Navy, 1861-1865.* Boston, MA: Trustees of Dartmouth College.

Richmond, Joshua Bailey. 1897. *The Richmond Family, 1594-1896, and Pre-American Ancestors, 1040-1594.* Boston, MA: Published by the compiler.

Rildon, Gideon Tibbetts. 1884. *History of the Ancient Ryedales, and Their Descendants in Normandy, Great Britain, Ireland, and America, from 860 to 1884.* Manchester, NH: Published by the author.

Rix, Guy Scoby. 1901. *History and Genealogy of the Eastman Family of America: Containing Biographical Sketches and Genealogies of both Males and Females.* Concord, NH: I. C. Evans.

Robinson, Reuel. 1907. *History of Camden and Rockport, Maine.* Camden, ME: Camden Publishing Company.

Rogers, James Swift. 1902. *James Rogers of New London, Ct: And His Descendants.* Boston, MA: Published by the compiler.

Rollins, John R. 1874. *Records of Families of the Name of Rawlins or Rollins in the United States.* Lawrence, MA: George S. Merrill & Crocker, Printers.

Roscoe, William E. 1882. *History of Schoharie County, New York, with Illustrations and Biographical Sketches of Some of its Prominent Men and Pioneers.* Syracuse, NY: D. Mason & Co.

Roser, Susan E. 1992. *Mayflower Births and Deaths.* Baltimore, MD: Genealogical Publishing Company.

Runnels, Moses Thurston. 1873. *A Genealogy of Runnels and Reynolds Families in America.* Boston, MA: Alfred Mudge & Son.

—. 1882. *History of Sanbornton, New Hampshire, Volume II.* Boston, MA: Mudge.

Russell, George Ely. 1955. *Russell Families of Seventeenth Century New England.* Unpublished manuscript. https://www.ancestry.com/imageviewer/collections/61157/images/46155_b290263-00000?pId=2842078.

Russell, Gurdon Wadsworth. 1910. *An Account of Some of the Descendants of John Russell, the Immigrant from Ipswich, England.* Hartford, CT: Case, Lockwood & Brainard Co.

Russell, Patrick. 1977. *The Moore Scott Family.* Columbus, OH: Privately printed. https://www.ancestry.com/imageviewer/collections/12595/images/dvm_GenMono001817-00001-0?pId=106.

Sargent, Edwin Everett. 1899. *Sargent Record: William Sargent of Ipswich, Newbury, Hampton, Salisbury, and Amesbury, New England.* St. Johnsbury, VT: The Caledonian Company, Printers and Publishers.

Saunderson, Henry Hamilton. 1876. *History of Charlestown, New-Hampshire, the Old No. 4.* Claremont, NH: Printed for the town by the Claremont Manufacturing Company.

Sawin, Thomas E. 1866. *Sawin: Summary Notes Concerning John Sawin, and His Posterity.* Wendell, MA: T. E. Sawin.

Sawyer, John. 1898. *History of Cherry Valley [N.Y.] from 1740 to 1898.* Cherry Valley, NY: Gazette Print.

Sayward, Charles Augustus. 1890. *The Sayward Family: Being the History and Genealogy of Henry Sayward of York, and His Descendants.* Ipswich, MA: Independent Press, E. G. Hull.

Schenck, J. S. 1887. *History of Warren County, Pennsylvania.* Syracuse, NY: D. Mason & Co.

Sedgwick, Hubert M. 1961. *A Sedgwick Genealogy: Descendants of Deacon Benjamin Sedgwick.* New Haven, CT: New Haven Historical Society.

Selkreg, John H. 1894. *Landmarks of Tompkins County, New York Including a History of Cornell University by Prof. W. T. Hewitt.* Syracuse, NY: D. Mason & Company.

Sewall, Samuel. 1868. *The History of Woburn, Middlesex County, Mass.* Boston, MA: Wiggin and Lunt.

Seward, Josiah Lafayette. 1921. *A History of the Town of Sullivan, New Hampshire, 1777-1917.* Keene, NH: J. L. Seward.

Shattuck, L'emuel. 1855. *Memorials of the Descendants of William Shattuck, the Progenitor of the Families in America that Have Borne His Name.* Boston: Dutton and Wentworth, printed for the family.

Shepley, David. 1854. *Memoir, with Sermons, of Rev. Josiah Peet.* New York, NY: John F. Trow, Printer.

Slafter, Carlos. 1905. *A Record of Education: The Schools and Teachers of Dedham, Massachusetts, 1644-1904.* Dedham, MA: Dedham Transcript Press.

Smith, Albert, and John Hopkins Morison. 1876. *History of the Town of Peterborough, Hillsborough County, New Hampshire.* Boston: Press of G.H. Ellis.

Smith, Charles James. 1907. *History of the Town of Mont Vernon, New Hampshire.* Boston, MA: Blanchard Printing Co.

Smith, Etta Marinda, and George Abbot Morison. 1954. *History of Peterborough, New Hampshire: Genealogies, by E. M. Smith.* Peterborough, NH: R. R. Smith.

Smith, H. Allen. 1889. *A Genealogical History of the Descendants of the Rev. Nehemiah Smith of New London County, Conn.* Albany, NY: Joel Munsells Sons.

Smith, Henry Perry. 1885. *History of Cortland County, with Illustrations and Biographical Sketches of some of its Prominent Men and Pioneers.* Syracuse, NY: D. Mason & Co.

Smith, Henry Perry, and William S. Rann. 1886. *History of Rutland County, Vermont, with Illustrations and Biographical Sketches of Some of its Prominent Men and Pioneers.* Syracuse, NY: D. Mason & Co.

Smith, James Hadden. 1881. *History of Livingston County, New York, with Illustrations and Biographical Sketches of Some of Its Prominent Men and Pioneers.* Syracuse, NY: D, Mason & Co.

Smith, John E. 1899. *Our County and Its People: A Descriptive and Biographical Record of Madison County, New York.* Boston: Boston History Company.

South Church of Andover. 1859. *Historical Manual of the South Church in Andover, Mass.* Edited by George Mooar. Andover, MA: Printed by Warren F. Draper.

Spalding, Charles Warren. 1897. *The Spalding Memorial: A Genealogical History of Edward Spalding of Virginia and Massachusetts Bay and His Descendants.* Chicago, IL: American Publishers Association.

Spaulding, Charles S. 1915. *An Account of Some of the Early Settlers of West Dunstable, Monson and Hollis, N. H.* Nashua, NH: Telegraph Press.

Spofford, Jeremiah, and Aphia Tenney Spofford. 1888. *A Genealogical Record: Including Two Generations in Female Lines of Families, Spelling Their Name Spofford, Spafford, Spafard, and Spaford, Descendants of John Spofford and Elizabeth Scott.* Boston, MA: A. Mudge & Son.

Spurr, William Samuel. 1953. *A History of Otisfield, Cumberland County, Maine from the Original Grant ot the Close of the Year 1944.* Otisfield, ME: Printed for the author.

Stackpole, Everett Schemerhorn. 1925. *History of Winthrop, Maine with Genealogical Notes.* Auburn, ME: Press of Merrill and Webber.

—. n.d. *Swett Genealogy: Descendants of John Swett of Newbury.* Lewiston, ME: The Journal Printshop. https://www.familysearch.org/library/books/records/item/45271-swett-genealogy-descendants-of-john-swett-of-newbury-mass?offset=1.

Stafford, Morgan Hewitt. 1941. *A Genealogy of the Kidder Family Comprising the Descendants in the Male Line of Ensign James Kidder, 1626-1676, of Cambridge and Billerica in the Colony of Massachusetts Bay.* Rutland, VT: Tuttle Publishing.

Stark, Caleb. 1860. *History of the Town of Dunbarton, Merrimack County, New-Hampshire, from the Grant by Mason's Assigns, in 1751, to the Year 1860.* Concrd: G. Parker Lyon.

Stay, Elizabeth Wardwell. 1905. *Wardwell: A Brief Sketch of the Antecedents of Solomon Wardwell, with the Descendants of his Two Sons, Ezra and Amos, who Died in Sullivan, N.H.* Greenfield, MA: Press of E. A. Hall & Co.

Stearns, Ezra Scollay. 1887. *History of Ashburnham, Massachusetts, from the Grant of Dorchester Canada to the Present Time, 1734-1886; with a Genealogical Register of Ashburnham Families.* Ashburnham, MA: Published by the town.

—. 1875. *History of the Town of Rindge, New Hampshire, from the Date of the Rowley Canada or Massachusetts Charter, to the Present Time, 1736-1874, with a Genealogical Register of the Rindge Families.* Boston: G. H. Ellis.

Stearns, Ezra Scollay, and Moses Thurston Runnels. 1906. *History of Plymouth, New Hampshire: Vol. I. Narrative--vol. II. Genealogies.* Printed for the Town by University Press.

Stearns, Ezra Scollay, William F. Witcher, and Edward E. Parker. 1908. *Genealogical and Family History of the State of New Hampshire: A Record of the Achievements of Her People in the Making of a Commonwealth and the Founding of a Nation.* New York: Lewis Publishing.

Stevens, W. W. 1907. *Past and Present of Will County, Illinois.* Chicago, IL: S. J. Clarke Publishing Company.

Stewart, James Harvey. 1872. *Recollections of the Early Settlement of Carroll County, Indiana.* Cincinnati, OH: Printed for the author by Hitchcock and Walden.

Stickney, Charles Perham, John B. Stebbins, and Abby Maria Hemenway. 1886. *The Local History of Brookline, Vt.: The General History of the Town.* Chicago, IL: Written for Volume V of the Vermont Historical Magazine.

Stickney, Matthew Adams. 1867. *The Stickney Family: A Genealogical Memoir.* Salem, MA: Printed for the Author, Essex Institute Press.

Stiles, Henry R. 1999/1892. *Families of Ancient Windsor, Connecticut: Consisting of Volume II of the History and Genealogies of Ancient Windsor, Connecticut, Including East Windsor, South Windsor, Bloomfield.* Clearfield Company; Reprinted by Genealogical Publishing Company.

Stocking, Charles Henry Wright. 1897. *The History and Genealogy of the Knowltons of England and America.* New York, NY: Kinckerbocker Press.

Storke, Elliot G. 1879. *Histroy of Cayuga County, New York with Illustrations and Biographical Sketches of Some of Its Prominent Men and Pioneers.* Syracuse, NY: D. Mason & Co.

Stowe, J. M. 1881. *History of the Town of Hubbardston, Worcester County, Mass.* Hubbardston, MA: Published by the committee.

Stowell, William Henry Harrison. 1922. *The Stowell Genealogy: A Record of the Descendants of Samuel Stowell of Hingham, Mass.* Rutland, VT: Tuttle Company.

Struthers, Parke hardy. 1968. *A History of Nelson, New Hampshire, 1767-1967.* Nelson, NH: Sentinel Print.

Talcott, Alvan. 1882. *Chittenden Family: William Chittenden of Guilford, Conn., and His Descendants.* New Haven, CT: Morehouse & Taylor.

Tarrant, Susan Frances Hale. 1904. *Hon. Daniel Pratt: A Biography, with Eulogies on his Life and Character.* Richmond, VA: Whittet & Shepperson.

Taylor, Charles James. 1882. *History of Great Barrington, Berkshire County, Massachusetts.* Great Barrington, MA: C. W. Bryan.

Temple, Josiah Howard. 1889. *History of the Town of Palmer, Massachusetts, Early Known as the Elbow Tract: Including Records of the Plantation, District and Town. 1716-1889. With a Genealogical Register.* Springfield, MA: Published by the town of Palmer.

—. 1872. *History of the Town of Whately, Mass.* Pinted for the town by T. R. Marvin & Son.

Thayer, Bazaleel. 1874. *Memorial of the Thayer Name.* Oswego: R. J. Oliphant, Steam Book and Job Printer.

Thayer, Elisha. 1835. *Family Memorial: Part I, Genealogy of Fourteen Families of the Early Settlers of New England.* Hingham, MA: J. Farmer.

Thummel, Claude E. 1965. *Descendants of John FInch of Connecticut.* Unpublished manuscript. Family Search Title 141845.

Tiffany, Nelson Otis. 1901. *The Tiffanys in America: History and Genealogy.* Buffalo, NY: N. O. Tiffany.

Tilden, William Smith. 1887. *History of the Town of Medfield, Massachusetts, 1650-1886.* Boston, MA: G. H. Ellis.

Tilson, Mercer Vernon. 1911. *The Tilson Genealogy from Edmond Tilson at Plymouth, N.E., 1638 to 1911.* Plymouth, MA: Memorial Press.

Torrey, Clarence Almon, and Charles Harvey Roe. 1958. *David Roe of Flushing, New York and Some of His Descendants, Second Edition.* Unpublished manuscript. https://archive.org/details/davidroeofflushi00torr_0/page/n3/mode/2up.

Torrey, Frederic Crosby. 1924. *The Torrey Families and Their Children in America.* Lakehurst, NJ.

Towne, Edwin Eugene. 1901. *The Descendants of William Towne.* Newtonville, MA: Published by the author.

Towne, Philip William, and Roderick Bissell Jones. 1743. "Seth Payn of Lebanon, Conn., and Paines Hollow, N.Y., and Some of His Descendants." *The New England Historical and Genealogical Register* 134.

Trask, Gwen Guiou. 1982. *Early Vital Records of the Township of Yarmouth, Nova Scotia, 1762-1811.* Yarmouth County Historical Society.

Trowbridge, Francis Bacon. 1908. *The Trowbridge Genealogy: History of the Trowbridge Family in America.* New Haven, CT: Printed for the compiler.

Tucker, William Howard. 1889. *History of Hartford, Vermont, July 4, 1761-April 4, 1889.* Burlington, VT: The Free Press Association.

Twitchell, Ralph Emerson. 1929. *Genealogy of the Twitchell Family: Record of the Descendants of the Puritan Benjamin Twitchell.* New York, NY: Privately printed for Herbert K. Twitchell.

Underwood, Lucien Marcus, and Howard James Banker. 1913. *The Underwood Families of America.* Lancaster, PA: New Era Printing.

Union Publishing Company. 1883. *History of Butler County, Iowa.* Union Publishing Company.

Upton, William Henry. 1893. *Upton Family Records: Being Genealogical Collections for an Upton Family History.* London: Mitchell and Hughes, privately printed.

Van Wagenen, Avis Stearns. 1901. *Genealogy and Memoirs of Isaac Stearns and His Descendants.* Syracuse, NY: Currier Printing.

Vinton, John Adams. 1876. *The Richardson Memorial, Comprising a Full History and Genealogy of the Posterity of the Three Brothers, Ezekiel, Samuel, and Thomas Richardson.* Portland, ME: Printed for the subscribers.

—. 1858. *The Vinton Memorial: Comprising a Genealogy of the Descendants of John Vinton of Lynn, 1648: Also, Genealogical Sketches of Several Allied Families.* S. K. Whipple, Published for the Author.

W. W. Munsell. 1880. *History of Delaware County, N.Y.* New York, NY: W. W. Munsell.

Walworth, Reuben Hyde. 1864. *Hyde Genealogy; or, The Descendants, in the Female as well as in the Male Lines, from William Hyde, of Norwich.* Albany, NY: J. Munsell.

Ware, Emma Forbes. 1901. *Ware Genealogy: Robert Ware, of Dedham, Massachusetts, 1642-1699, and His Lineal Descendants.* Boston, MA: C. H. Pope.

Warner, Lucien C., and Josephine Genung Nichols. 1919. *The Descendants of Andrew Warner.* New Haven, CT: Tuttle, Morehouse & Taylor.

Warren, Henry Pelt. 1879. *The History of Waterford: Oxford County, Maine, Comprising Historical Address, by Henry P. Warren; Record of Families, by Rev. William Warren, D.D.; Centennial Proceedings, by Samuel Warren, Esq.* Waterford, ME: Hoyt, Fogg & Donham.

Washburn, Israel. 1874. *Notes, Historical, Descriptive, and Personal, of Livermore, in Androscoggin (Formerly in Oxford) County, Maine.* Portland, ME: Bailey & Noyes.

Weaver, Lucius E. 1923. *History and Genealogy of a Branch of the Weaver Family.* Rochester, NY.

Weaver, William L. 1867. *A Genealogy of the Fenton Family : Descendants of Robert Fenton, an Early Settler of Ancient Windham, Conn. (Now Mansfield).* Willimantic, CT.

Weeks, Frank Edgar. 1908. *Pioneer History of Clarksfield.* Clarksfield, OH: Published by the author.

Weeks, Lyman Horace. 1913. *The Darling Family in America: Being an Account of the Founders and First Colonial Families, an Official List of the Heads of Families of the Name Darling, Resident in the United States in 1790, and a Bibliography.* New York, NY: W. W. Clemens.

Wellman, Joshua Wyman, George Walter Chamberlain, and Arthur Holbrook Wellman. 1918. *Descendants of Thomas Wellman of Lynn, Massachusetts.* Boston, MA: A. H. Wellman.

Western Historical Company. 1881. *History of Northern Wisconsin.* Chicago, IL: Western Historical Company.

Westmoreland History Committee. 1976. *History of Westmoreland (Great Meadow) New Hampshire: 1741-1970, and Genealogical Data.* Westmoreland, NH: Westmoreland History Committee.

Weygant, Charles H. Newburgh, NY. *The Sacketts of America, Their Ancestors and Descendants, 1630-1907.* 1907.

Wheat, Silas C. 1903. *Wheat Genealogy: A History of the Wheat Family in America*. Brooklyn, NY: Published by Silas C. Wheat.

Whitcomb, Charlotte. 1904. *The Whitcomb Family in America: A Biographical Genealogy with a Chapter on Our English Forbears "by the name of Whetcombe"*. Minneapolis, MN.

Whitman, Charles Foster. 1924. *A History of Norway, Maine: From its Earliest Settlement to the Close of the Year 1922*. Lewiston, ME: Published by the town of Norway.

Whitney, William A., and R. I. Bonner. 1879/1880. *History and Biographical Record of Lewanee County, Michigan*. Adrian, MI: Willard Stearns.

Wickham, Gertrude Van Rensselaer. 1896. *Memorial to the Pioneer Women of the Western Reserve, Volume 1*. Jefferson, OH: Ashtabula County Genealogical Society.

Willard, Joseph, Charles Wilkes Walker, and Charles Henry Pope. 1915. *Willard Genealogy: Sequel to Willard Memoir*. Boston, MA: Printed for the Willard Family Association.

Williams Brothers. 1890. *History of Franklin and Pickaway Counties, Ohio, with Illustrations and Biographical Sketches of Some of the Prominent Men and Pioneers*. Cleveland, OH: Williams Brothers.

—. 1879. *History of Lorain County, Ohio with Illustrations & Biographical Sketches*. Philadelphia, PA: Williams Brothers.

Williams, C. S. 1907. *Descendants of Thomas White of Weymouth*. New York, NY: Privately printed.

Williams, George Ebenezer. 1984. *A Genealogy of the Descendants of Robert Goodale/Goodell of Salem, Mass.* Hartford, CT: G. E. Williams.

Wing, Conway P. 1881. *A Historical and Genealogical Register of John Wing of Sandwich, Mass. and His Descendants 1662-1881*. Carlisle, PA.

Wisconsin State Old Cemetery Society. 1975. *Pvt. John Greenslit, Revolutionary War Soldier, Connecticut State Troop*. Sauk County, WI: Wisconsin State Old Cemetery Society; Familysearch Title Number 1972749. https://www.familysearch.org/library/books/records/item/41248-the-greenslit-family-much-of-the-genealogical-data-centers-around-a-six-generation-greenslit-in-america-john-1767-1856?offset=1.

Worcester, J. F. 1856. *The Worcester Family, Or the Descendants of Rev. William Worcester, with a Brief Notice of the Connecticut Wooster Family*. Lynn, MA: W. W. Kellogg, Printer.

Wyman, Thomas Bellows, and Wellington, L. G. Huntinglton. 1863. *Genealogy of the Name and Family of Hunt*. Boston, MA: Printed by J. Wilson and Son.

Wynkoop, Richard. 1904. *Wynkoop Genealogy in the United States of America, Third Edition*. New York, NY: Knickerbocker Press.

Young, Andrew W. 1875. *History of Chautauqua County, New York*. Buffalo, NY: Printing House of Matthews & Warren.

—. 1869. *History of the Town of Warsaw, New York*. Buffalo, NY: Press of the Sage, Sons & Co.

Zea, Philip, and Donald Dunlap. 2007. *The Dunlap Cabinetmakers: A Tradition in Craftmanship*. Stackpole Books.

Name Index

ABBE
Elizabeth 1734- 30, 131
Frances 1815-1841 517
Nancy A. 1830-1917 221

ABBOTT/ABBOT
Abigail 1770-1810 150, 595
Abigail B. 1819-1834 557
Abner 1761-1833 .. 194
Alice 1811-1880 333
Anna 1821- 318
Annie M. 1857-1917 610
Barachias 1739-1812 .... 45, 178
Barachias 1771-1855 178
Betsey 1773-1860. 313
Bridget 1761-1787. 71, 276
Chloe 1760-1835 ... 112
Daniel 1805-1891. 223
David 1716-1777 ... 17, 70
Deborah 1774-1806 113
Deborah 1805-1872 449
Dorcas 1698-1758 4, 11
Dorcas 1755-1821.. 39, 161
Dorcas 1766-1841.. 47, 188
Dorcas 1820-1822. 598
Dorcas S. 1813-1845 557
Dorothy 1774-1802 113
Dorothy 1816-1843 449
Elizabeth 1784-1854 178
Elizabeth H. 1804-1892 557
Encoh E. 1785-1862 431
Esther 1768- 113
Eunice 1797-1828. 400
Fanny D. 1817-1848 590
Fidelia 1770- 113
Franklin 1807-1889 449
George 1804-1868 561
Hannah 1701-1752.. 4, 13
Hannah 1743- 70

Hannah 1743-1813 42, 165
Hannah 1758-1847 .... 112, 448
Hannah 1773- 276
Hannah 1802-1870 598
Hannah 1807-1889 391
Hannah 1820-1897 562
Harriet 1819-1873 450
Harvey 1801-1864 449
Henry 1778-1845. 141, 557
Henry R. 1815-1896 391
Isaac 1732-1800 .... 27, 112
Isaac 1766-1831 .. 113, 449
James 1780-1858 178, 187
Janet 1789- 276
Jeremiah 1792- 366
Jerome J. 1785-1802 276
Job 1742-1815 70, 275
Job 1788- 276
Joel 1775-1775 178
Joel 1776-1863 178
John 1752- 71
John 1780-1854 276
John 1818-1900 600
John B. 1818-1900 598
John I. 1810-1857 597
Jonathan 1808-1837 598
Laura 1827-1899 .. 613
Louisa P. 1819-1890 590
Lydia 1745-1829 ... 23, 98
Lydia 1768-1832 . 140, 556
Lydia 1771-1855 ... 86, 332
Martha 1800-1850 .... 157, 625
Martha L. 1804-1856 598
Mary 1728-1769 15, 61
Mary 1757-1849 .... 61, 112, 240
Mary 1782-1864 ... 276
Mary 1794-1884 ... 449
Mary 1798-1879 ... 212
Mary 1805- 334
Mary E.P. 1807-1878 598

Mary F. 1791-1828 187
Mehitable 1762- 71
Mehitable 1764-1858 .... 150, 592
Metylda 1764- 112
Nathan 1778-1837 98, 391
Nathan 1799-1872 600
Nathan 1809-1863 391
Obed 1789-1855 ... 362
Olive 1772- ... 113, 450
Orinda 1803-1880 212
Paschal 1788-1859 187
Paschal 1812-1874 .... 391, 599
Phebe 1749-1809... 35, 150
Phebe 1775-1873.. 276
Phebe 1798-1872.. 190
Phebe H. 1813-1884 598
Priscilla 1743- 69, 274
Priscilla 1786- 276
Rachel 1812-1872. 632
Rebecca 1799-1860 449
Rebecca H. 1809-1871 557
Rhoda 1741-1821 .. 34, 142
Robert B. 1814-1881 449
Ruth 1785- ... 100, 401
Samuel 1743-1825 129
Samuel 1811-1834 598
Sarah 1718-1778... 12, 44
Sarah 1730-1797... 12, 45
Sarah 1751-1854... 49, 198
Sarah 1762-1846. 112, 448
Sarah 1772-1851.. 276
Sarah 1779-1858.. 178
Sarah 1787-1874. 143, 567
Sarah 1792-1846... 99, 393
Sarah 1814-1857.. 190
Sarah A. 1815-1905 557
Sewell 1795-1874 . 356
Stephen 1778-1792 113
Stephen 1779-1835 .... 151, 598
Stephen 1794-1869 362
Stephen 1797-1876 449

Stephen 1802-1822 598
Stephen D. 1817-1885 598
Susanna 1778-1862 276
Timothy 1773-1837 178
Walter 1796-1879 241
Walter 1803-1877 449
William B. 1811-1851 449

ABEL
Anna 1771-1798.... 54, 212

ABELL
Zerviah 1780-1845 57, 223

ADAM
John 1785-1871.... 359

ADAMS
Abigail H. 1810-1883 401
Adin 1800-1879 522
Asahel L. 1792-1870 396
Augustin W. 1820- 310
Charles S. 1813-1859 310
Charlotte 1796-1871 .... 298, 309
Dolly 1804-1841 ... 522
Ebenezer 1814-1888 522
Eliza 1812-1861 ... 522
Emeline O. 1808-1810 309
Fanny 1808-1850 . 531
George K. 1815- ... 310
George W. 1816-1897 281
Hannah 1760-1763 81
Hannah 1762-1844 75, 288
Hannah 1764- 81
Hannah 1791-1859 ....103, 309, 409
Hephzibah 1768-1814 .... 82, 314
Isaac 1767- 81, 310
Isaac 1798-1801 .. 309
Isaac O. 1810-1894 310
James 1802- 465
John 46, 67
John 1735-1813 19, 43, 81
John 1766-1839..... 81, 308

John 1776-1843 ...131, 522
John 1808-1885 522
John O. 1811-1832 309
Joseph H. 1790-1861 309
Keziah 1747-1811 .. 52
Louisa 1803-1842..309
Louisa 1804-1839..302
Lydia 1782-1866 ..131, 520
Martha 1801-1875 309
Mary...................... 18
Mary 1761-1805.... 82, 314
Mary 1771-1820.... 63, 249
Mary H. 1793-1869 309
Mary M. 1818- 310
Mary P. 1817-1898 401
Nancy 1802-1877..522
Nancy 1806-1849..263
Persis 1810-1852 ..522
Phebe 1787-1876...288
Priscilla 1806-1894 522
Samuel 1820-1898 522
Sarah 1762-1763.... 81
Sarah A. 1806-1882 309
Sarah M. 1808- 310
Susanna 1798-1877 575
Susannah 1818-1819 522
Walter 1816-1897 .522
William 1806-1869 522
William 1820-1893 442
William H. 1811- ..310
ADDITON
 Orintha 1822-1889 364
ADROSS
 Hannah..............4, 13
AGARD
 Isaac 1812-1848....495
AIKEN
 Mary 1800-1889....551
AINSWORTH
 Abiel 1777-1866 204
ALBEE
 Persis L. 1825-1895 376
ALDEN
 Abigail 1809-1854.398
 Irena 1772-1858.... 55, 216
 Joanna 1782-1849. 56, 214, 220
ALEXANDER
 Electa 465
 Eunice 1769-1859 . 23, 96
 Margery 277
ALLARD

Welcome 1806-1877 511
ALLEN
 Abigail 1789-1820.433
 Abigail L. 1832-1904 605
 Adeline 1802-1876 438
 Alfred 1818- 364
 Alvira 1810-1883 ..435
 Amanda 1816-1889 437
 Andrew 1798-1801 437
 Anna 1780- 76, 293
 Arathusa 1795-1821 433
 Asaph 1778-1814 .110, 437
 Asaph 1801-1871 ..438
 Benjamin 1708-1783 7, 25
 Benjamin 1734- 25, 108
 Benjamin 1773- 109
 Betsey 1817-1849 .370
 Betty 1768-1810 ..109, 436
 Caroline 1806-1832 264
 Charles 1807-1882 435
 Chloe 1769-1771 ...109
 Chloe 1776- 109
 Daniel 1788-1788..433
 David 1772-...........109
 Ebenezer 1762-1824 ....109, 434
 Ebenezer 1788-1859 435
 Edith 1782-...........110
 Edward 1805-1844 364
 Eliza 1804-1884 435
 Elizabeth 1765-1854 ....82, 316
 Elizabeth W. 1839-1923 605
 Elvira P. 1811-1893 568
 Emeline 1813-1887 437
 Ethan 1793-1822 ..435
 Hannah 1742-.........25
 Hannah 1764-1783 109
 Hannah 1794-.......433
 Hannah 1797-1864 433
 Harriet 1803-1804 434
 Harriet 1814-1883 438
 Henry 1810-1881 ..438
 Hephzibah 1789-...507
 Hiram 1795-1873.152, 605
 Hiram S. 1806-1886 434
 Horace W. 1835-1882 605

Isaac 1735-1765.....25, 109
Isaac 1774-1825...109, 436
Isaac 1797-1801....437
Isaac 1804-1883....438
James N. 1829-1842 605
Jerusha 1767-1783 109
John 1776-1859 ...109, 437
John 1801-1864 434
Joseph 1738-1815 ..25, 109
Joseph 1770- 109
Justus 1821-1842 .605
Lauretta 1799-1873 434
Lawson 1819-1865 605
Leonard 1795-1883 435
Louisa 1816-1816 .437
Lucretia 1836-1887 495
Lucy 1800-1874 435
Lyman 1808-1888.438
Marilla 1819-1821 437
Mary 1766-1830...109, 435
Mary 1790-1869....292
Mary 1802- 435
Mary J. 1809-1883.89, 347
Mehitable 1732-1788 ....25, 108
Napoleon W. 1823-1885 437
Oliver 1806-1866 ..438
Parsons 1802-1878 460
Perry W. 1818-1900 437
Phebe 1791-1861 ..435
Polly 1792-1826 433
Ruby 1778-1844 237
Sally.....................364
Sally 1786-1833 433
Samuel A. 1823-1857 605
Samuel R. 1810-1853 415
Sarah 1740-1761.....25
Sarah 1762- 109
Sarah 1765- 109
Sarah 1780- 110
Sarah 1788-1859..100, 397
Sarah F. 1841-1919 605
Seth 1749-.............25
Seth 1764-1765.....109
Seth 1790-.............435
Sluman 1760-1834 ....109, 433
Stephen L. 1802-1890 574

Warner 1797-1820 435
William 1812-1866 438
Zipporah 1762-1846 ....109, 434
ALVORD
 Rebekah 1768-1820 ....70, 275
 Royal 1806-1868 ...360
AMES
 Abigail 1824-1890.604
 Charles H. 1812-1864 489
 Elizabeth 42
 Elizabeth 1745-.....163
 Elizabeth 1829-.....325
 Fanny 1773-1859..198
 Harriet 1801-........160
 John V. 1821-........191
 Jonas 1771-1820....38, 160
 Miriam 209
 Phineas 1764-.71, 276
 Ruth 1776-1844 ...113, 449
AMIDON
 Alfred A. 1789-1817 241
 Dyer 1794-1853 241
 Elijah 1786-1863 ..241
 Hannah 1784-.......241
 Henry 1788-1840..540
 Jacob 1791-1866 ...241
 Jonathan 1759-1838 ....61, 240
 Lucinda 1804-1883 241
 Mary 1796-1819....241
 Sarah 1800-1873 ..241
AMMIDOWN
 Joseph 1801-1863 .495
AMSBURY
 Hannah 1775-1809 83, 316
ANDERSON
 James 1823-1884..536
ANDREWS
 Andrew 1802-1894 497
 Anna 1774-1844....273
 Betty 1767-1851 ...273
 Daniel 1779-1820.143, 568
 Dolly 1770-1811....273
 Esther 1777-1861 195, 273
 Esther V. 1812-1883 569
 Hannah 1769-1829 273
 Hannah 1780-.......274
 Jacob 1762-1811 ...273
 Jacob 1768-...........274
 Jacob -1786.....69, 272
 Joel 1764-.............274
 John 1758- 273
 John 1786-1874 193

Joshua 1775- 273
Katherine S. 1809-569
Letitia 1762- 273
Levi 1727- 69, 273
Levi 1766-1825..... 274
Lois B. 1816-1874. 569
Lydia 1758- 273
Mary 1761- 273
Mary 1764-1810 ... 273
Mary 1796- ... 156, 619
Mary E. 1813-1872
.... 569
Nathaniel -1759 69,
272
Nathaniel 1765- ... 273
Putnam 1822-1891631
Rebecca K. 1818-1891
.... 569
Thomas 1771-1847274
Warren 1804- 440
ANGEL
Elizabeth 1816-1893
.... 602
ANGEVINE
Emma 1846- 614
ANGIER
Amanda 1814-1877
.... 384
Andrew J. 1834-1862
.... 384
Elisha 1789-1835 .. 96,
383
Emily S. 1819-1900
.... 384
George H. 1831-1910
.... 384
Harriet M. 1831-1907
.... 384
John 1815-1896.... 384
Lucy 1792-1826..... 95,
374
Mary P. 1820-1891384
Sarah 1829- 384
Silas 1812-1874.... 383
Sophia 1825-1888. 384
APPLETON
Abigail 1780-1853 103
Alice 1778-1842... 103,
408
Ann 1793-1868..... 104
Ann 1800-1803..... 404
Ann J. 1820-1885. 407
Anne E. 1824-1918410
Benjamin 1777-1778
.... 101
Benjamin 1815-1878
.... 406
Benjamin B. 1781-
1844 .... 101, 405
Catherine K. 1817-
1899 404
Catherine M. 1824-
1898 406
Charles H. 1817-1866
.... 406

Charles H. 1819-1820
.... 409
Charles T.P. 1820-
1901 406
Daniel 1751-1828.. 24,
103
Daniel 1785-1849 103,
309, 409
Daniel S. 1824-1890
.... 409
Edward 1787- 104
Edward 1816-1898410
Emeline 1819-1820
.... 410
Emily 1821-1844.. 410
Frances 1811-1855404
George 1789- 104
George 1808-1882 404
George -1830 104
George S. 1821-1878
.... 409
George W. 1786-1851
.... 102, 406
George W. 1815-1895
.... 406
Hannah 1748-1750. 24
Hannah 1756-1824 24,
104
Hannah 1791-1843
.... 104
Harriet 1799-1799 404
Harriet 1815-1859 404
Henry K. 1786-1829
.... 101, 406
Henry K. 1811-1894
.... 406
James 1832-1833 . 406
James A. 1821-1823
.... 406
John 1774-1868... 101,
404
John 1807-1826.... 404
John A. 1805-1882
.... 404, 405
John A. 1817-1881409
Joseph C. 1825-1901
.... 407
Joseph W. 1786-1787
.... 101
Joseph W. 1813-1892
.... 406
Louisa 1830-1831. 406
Louisa M. 1815-1887
.... 409
Louisa M. 1836-1903
.... 406
Lydia 1779-1872 . 101,
404
Lydia 1787-1863 .. 103
Maria C. 1817-1886
.... 406
Martha 1770-1847
.... 101, 403
Martha E. 1823-1911
.... 407

Mary 1746-1830.... 24,
102
Mary 1783-1791 ... 101
Mary T. 1808-1823404
Nathan D. 1794-1861
.... 420
Samuel 1713-1780 .. 6,
23
Samuel 1768-1815 101
Samuel 1783-1787 103
Samuel F. 1826-1883
.... 409
Sarah 1803-1859.. 315
Sarah E. 1829-1861
.... 409
Sarah T. 1830-1859
.... 410
Thomas 1744-1803 24,
101
Thomas 1785-1872
.... 104, 409
Thomas H. 1803-1886
.... 404
Thomas R. 1772-1863
..........101, 102, 403
William 1754-1799 24,
103
William 1776-1841103
William 1784-1806104
William 1813-1815410
William 1826-1829410
William H. 1813-1837
.... 404
William H. 1814-1899
.... 409
ARMSTRONG
Betsey 1762-1832 111,
442
Jedediah 1798-1865
.... 439
John 1820- 331
ARNOLD
Elijah 1803-1876.. 516
Ezekiel 1797-1880 223
ARTHUR
Janet 1821-1899... 613
ASHLEY
William 1834-1919529
ATKINSON
Frances 1817-1880410
ATWATER
Lucy 1790-1817.... 288
Lydia 1792-1881 .. 253
ATWOOD
Augustus 1806-1853
.... 577
Eliphalet 1787-1851
.... 159
Elizabeth 1795-1880
.... 89, 348
Mehitable 1765-1855
.... 55, 215
AUSTIN
Abigail 1798-1847 291
Avra 1791- 506

Benjamin 1795-1871
.... 291
Charlotte L. 1833-
1883 637
Eliab 1792-1817 ... 291
Etta 1856-1936 629
Eunice 1800-1865 446
Harriet 1802-1832 539
Joseph 255
Lucy 1801-1889.... 231
Mary 1771- ... 141, 558
Mary A. 1796- 291
Nathan 1764-1847 76,
290
Sally 1798-1868 ... 182
Sophronia 1805-1831
.... 563
AVERILL
Almira 1795- 248
Andrew 1815-1889345
Arminda 1783- 248
Arzelia 1812-1882 449
Betsey.................... 248
Charles H. 1786-1858
.... 248
Elijah 1788- 248
James 1763-1835 . 200
Rebecca 1793-1870241
Sally 1786-1880 ... 271
Sarah 1751-1794... 69,
270
Sophia 248
William 1755-1829 63,
248
AVERY
Almira 1798-1890 500
Alpheus 1796-1824
.... 500
Amelia 1790- 500
Chloe 1785- 500
Daniel 1793-1808. 500
Elisha 1774- 499
Hannah 1777- 499
John 1783-1857.... 499
Jonathan 1722-1750
.... 29, 126
Jonathan 1750-1803
.... 126, 499
Jonathan 1781-1849
.... 499
Polly 1779-1830 ... 499
Polly Mira 1779-1857
.... 80, 307
Sally 1801-1802 ... 500
Sarah.................... 449
Silas 1788-1843.... 500
Wales 1791-1854.. 500
AYER
Hannah 1791-1848
.... 167
AYERS
Charles 1798-1852435
Olive............. 123, 484
BABBITT

Susanna 1807-1845
..........................316
BABCOCK
Amy 1806-1871.....570
Chester 1781-1864233
Roxana 1818-1891 373
BACKSTROM
Lewis O. 382
BACKUS
Harriet 1799-1825
..................116, 458
Isabella S. 1816- ...310
BACON
Frances 1824-1905407
Harriet 1815- 522
Lucina 1830-1870 .389
Mary 1827-1909....533
Rebecca B. 1785-1861
..................132, 528
BADGER
Rebecca 1768-1810 59,
231
Sarah 1771-1843... 60,
233
BAGLEY
Asahel 1799-1849 .483
Sophia 1799-1840 .504
BAILEY
Abigail 1730-1801. 19,
78
Abigail 1772-1849.201
Elizabeth 1768-1830
..........................201
Mary J. 1810-........307
Pamelia 1804-1895
..........................485
Persis 1783-1816 .151,
599
Rebecca 1804-1834190
Sally 1793-1892 433
Zora 1817-1864.....392
BAKER
Abigail C. 1830-1901
..........................383
Caroline 1820-1896
..........................619
David 1802-1864...576
Eliza M. 1810-1847
..........................294
Gardner 1832-.......338
Joseph 1803- 391
Leander 1814-1900
..........................543
Lucinda 1786-1878
..........................288
Lucy 1813-1888.....621
Philip S. 1799-1889
..........................210
Rhoda 1792-1847..519
Thirza 1804-1861..583
Warren 1813-1886326
Zebadiah C. 1802-
1840..................254
BALCH
Albert 1802-1879 ..240

Joseph 1787-1877 .523
Mason 1800-1873..187
Sarah 1810-1841...502
BALDWIN
Charlotte..............470
Charlotte 1807-1883
..........................471
Deborah L. 1816-1863
..........................568
Electa 1794-..........476
Hepsey 1812-1895 438
Joseph 1783-1860 .231
Mary 1819-............456
Ziba 1787-1872 189
BALES
Rhoda 1779-1839.142,
562
BALL
Joseph 1800-1877 .463
Mary 1815-1887....543
BALLARD
Abigail 1718-1802... 6,
23
Abigail 1815-1816.562
Abigail 1817-1818.562
Abraham 1814-1844
..........................601
Alpheus 1816-1907
..........................601
Betsey 1771-1856 142,
560
Charles 1810-1872562
Clara 1813-1850 ...562
Eunice 1820-1895 .562
Ezra 1780-1781.....142
Ezra 1802-1872.....561
Frederick 1762-1851
..................151, 601
Frederick 1796-1869
..........................601
Hamilton 1806-1895
..........................436
Hannah 1764-......142,
558
Hannah 1805-1881
..........................561
Hannah J. 1822-1852
..........................562
John 1778-1855 ...142,
562
John 1805- 601
John 1818-1902 562
Jonathan 1798-1820
..........................601
Joseph 1808-1905 .601
Mary 1769-....142, 559
Mary 1809-1880....562
Mary 1810-1865....562
Mary 1812-1893....601
Nathan 1744-1835.34,
142
Nathan 1775-1856
..................142, 561
Nathan 1816-1901 562

Phebe 1738-1815 ...12,
44
Phebe 1773-1840 .142,
560
Phebe 1807-1860 ..561
Putnam 1803- 601
Rhoda 1813-1864..562
Sarah 1766-1856..142,
558
Sarah 1810-1867...601
Sherebiah 1801-....601
Squire 1784-1864..491
Stephen 1815-1901
..........................394
Timothy 1782-1782
..........................142
William 1801-1819561
BALLOU
Harriet A. 1830-1905
..........................383
BANCROFT
Mary 1778-1852....178
BANISTER
Eliza 1811-1883....337
BARBER
Abigail G. 1797-1864
..........................279
BARKER
Abigail 1789-1872.593
Albemarle 1797-1848
..........................444
Almira 1780-1859112,
447
Almira 1804-1885.445
Anna 1780-1850...114,
456
Asa 1786- 443
Betsey 1795-1877 .444
Calvin 1789-1852..446
Cephas 1793-1857 444
Charlotte 1779-.....112
Charlotte 1788-1865
..........................302
Cicero 1793-1870..444
Cyrus G. 1801-1870
..........................446
Deborah 1739-182027,
113
Dolly 1790-1812....446
Elisha 1786-1870..446
Eliza C. 1813-1896307
Elizabeth 1803-1859
..........................455
Ephraim 1730- 26, 111
Ephraim 1759-.....111,
445
Ephraim 1786-1830
..........................445
Ephraim 1801-1876
..........................445
Fanny 1776-..........112
Franklin 1790-1799
..........................444
Franklin 1803-1859
..........................445

George 1788-1820.305
George W. 1794-1860
..........................446
Gilbert 1799-1833.446
Hannah 1754-1840
..................111, 443
Hannah 1783-.......442
Harriet 1819-1889 445
James 1785-1788..446
John 1748- 27
John 1755-1834 ...111,
443
John 1787-1829 444
John 1799- 443
John 1803-1891 538
Joseph 1774-. 114, 454
Joseph 1790-........443
Lewis 1788-1820...445
Loency 1799-1845.444
Louise 1799-1799..444
Lucretia 1797-1896
..........................443
Lucy 1784-1847 ...114,
456
Luman 1809- 445
Lydia 1763-1849..111,
446
Lydia 1794-...........443
Lydia 1803-1884...446
Martha 1737-1765..27
Martha L. 1841-1925
..........................281
Martin 1788-.........443
Mary 1735- 27, 112
Mary 1811- 445
Mary 1819- 456
Mary W. 1797-1889
..........................446
Nathan 1761-1849
..................111, 446
Nathan 1768-1821 172
Nathan 1792-1852 446
Nathan 1795-1865446
Nathan 1806-1806 445
Pelham 1801-1853455
Phebe 1750- 43, 172
Polly 1774-............112
Rebecca 1776-1819
..................114, 455
Roxana 1792-1884 446
Sally 1766-1842...112,
447
Sally 1782-............114
Sally 1792-1859....444
Sally 1824-............456
Samuel G. 1807-1892
..........................445
Sarah A..M. 1837-
1917..................599
Sewel 1791-...........445
Silas 1784-1868 443
Silas G. 1784-1858445
Sitnah 1797-1870 .446
Stephen 1741-183427,
114

Stephen 1772- 114
Thomas F. 1821-1909
.... 456
Timothy 1778-1869
.... 114, 455
William 1708-1741 .. 7, 26
William 1731-1804 27, 111
William 1753-1826
.... 111, 442
William 1788-1854444
William 1788-1881594
William S. 1807-1855
.... 446
BARKMAN
Henry 1789- 228
BARLOW
David 1783-1840 .. 478
BARNARD
Abigail 1744- .. 50, 200
Abigail 1767-1836 140
Alice 1742- 50
Benjamin 1777-1857
.... 267
David 1758- 140
David 1794-1817 .. 555
George 1803- 555
Jacob 1750- 50
Jacob 1769-1854 ... 199
Jacob 1791-1878 ... 433
James 1727- ... 33, 140
James 1769-1811 140, 555
James 1796-1799 . 555
James 1801-1832 . 555
John 1697-1752 12, 50
Joseph 1798- 555
Lydia 1746-1829 .... 50, 201
Martha 1746-1829. 24, 101
Mary 1748-1748 50
Mary 1779-1875 .. 106, 417
Mehitable 1740-1824
.... 50
Miriam 1783-1815106, 417
Rebecca 1748- 50
Rhoda 1827-1852 . 427
Sarah 1761- 140
Sarah 1764-1774 .. 140
Sarah 1792- 555
Stephen 1794-1881
.... 321
BARNES
Adam G. 1820-1868
.... 583
Amos 1757-1840 ... 168
Catherine 1810-1893
.... 333
Daniel 1779-1838 . 275
Electa 1807-1891 ... 97, 388

Frances E. 1857-1901
.... 376
Gillum 1800-1884 551
John B. 1795-1856411
Lydia 1786-1865 .. 318
Phila 1815-1867 ... 539
Philomela 515
Phineas 1822-1900347
BARNUM
Erastus 1793-1875481
Jasper 1797-1859. 481
Loyal 1805-1863... 481
Oliver 1800-1869 .. 481
Zacchaeus 1763-1840
.... 122, 481
BARRETT
Alonso 1812-1862. 334
Butler 1801-1885 . 531
David 1782-1864 ... 86, 334
Dorcas 1801-1872. 365
Emma 1818-1891 . 334
James 1817-1872 . 371
Nancy 1790-1824 155, 619
Rimmon 1815-1895
.... 334
Sarah 1780-1850 .. 272
BARRON
Dolly 1785-1827 ... 318
Hannah 1781-1849
.... 319
Jonathan 1785-1860
.... 326, 327
Mary 1791-1847 ... 327
Moses L. 1824-1856
.... 327
Rachel 1776-1839 .. 83, 322
Samuel 1757-1836 84, 327
Samuel 1784-1855 327
Sibyl 1787-1841 327
Solomon 1789-1798
.... 327
BARROWS
Stephen 1789-1878
.... 214
BARRY
William 1818-1854632
BARTHOLOMEW
Isaac 1819-1863 ... 383
Jane E. 1840-1910 393
BARTLETT
Anna -1814 ..... 85, 331
Arethusa 1794-1868
.... 176
Asa 1795-1866 602
Betsey 1808-1845. 575
Betsey 1808-1900. 511
Betsey J 419
Caroline 1830-1903
.... 390
Daniel 1812-1898. 518
Hannah W. 1819- . 410

James 1785-1809 104, 410
Joseph 1776- 104, 410
Lydia L. 1821-1858
.... 371
Mary O. 1808-1888
.... 410
Miriam 1804-1898 583
Polly H. 1802-1868593
Richard 1743-1805 . 42
Sarah 1819-1893 .. 405
William 1794- 596
BARTON
Eliza 1832-1896 ... 456
Fidelia 1809-1894 348
Flint 1749-1833 266
BASCOM
John 1783-1819 357
BASS
Mary 1822-1908 ... 428
Samuel 1790-1873 333
Seth 1803-1883 335
Simeon 201
BASSETT
Mary 288
Sophia 1817-1892. 496
BATCHELDER
Abigail 1756- 277
Abigail 1828-1887 584
Anna C. 1781- 186
Betsey 1789-1856. 186
Chloe 1788- 186
Daniel 1806-1858. 603
Ebenzer 1758- 277
Elizabeth M. 1813-1848 333
Fanny 1784- 186
Hannah 1754- 277
John 1759- 277
John 1762-1840 277
John 1791-1792 186
Jonathan 1730-1817
.... 71, 277
Jonathan 1752-1838
.... 277
Joseph 1748-1826 . 47, 186
Joseph 1786-1849 186
Josiah W. 1821-1902
.... 376
Judith 1795- 186
Judith Ray 1779- . 178
Lucy 1797- 186
Lydia 1766- 277
Margaret 1784-1867
.... 47, 191
Matilda 1816-1890366
Moses -1843 . 147, 584
Persis 1793- 186
Phebe 1754-1790 ... 44, 174, 277
Phebe 1782-1866 .. 186
Rebecca 1827-1906585
Sarah 1764- 277

Sylvania 1820-1863
.... 585
BATES
Alson 1802-1882 ... 478
Pamela 1823-1842 360
Stephen 1784-1872
.... 170
BATSON
Mary 582
BAUM
Amos 1826-1902 ... 339
BAYLEY
Abigail 1772-1849 201
John 1783-1847 553
BAYLIS
Sophia 1784-1833 208
BEAL
Sue 1839-1917 347
BEAN
Adesta F. 1848-1928
.... 609, 610
Alfonso W. 1852-1934
.... 609
Almira 1802-1880 153, 609
Catherine M. 1844-1907 .... *608*
Christopher C. 1833-1900 609
Ebenezer 1781-1839
.... 563
Eliza P. 1837-1903609
Elohe V. 1835-1918
.... 609
Elsie 1812-1870 602
Farman L. 1844-1862
.... 609
Hiram H. 1838-1921
.... 609
Humphrey 1802-1884
.... 153, 608
John 1839-1918 610
John E. 1843-1927610
John M. 1805-1875
.... 575
Kimball 1796-1864
.... 153, 609
Sally 1780- 169
Timothy 1813-1899
.... 153, 610
Timothy 1839-1915
.... 610
BEARD
David 1770-1838 .. 258
Ruth 1789-1858 ... 185
BECKER
Ann 1807-1841 250
BECKETT
John I. 1819-1887 569
BEEBE
Esther 1763-1850 .. 91, 355
Henry S. 1811-1893
.... 361
Lucy 1813-1839 360

Lydia 1761-1837 ... 72, 279

BEEDE
Mehitable 1800-1861 ....157, 623

BEELS
Sally 299

BELCHER
Abigail 1807-1889.247

BELKNAP
Elizabeth 1709-1772 6

BELL
Abigail 1786-1833. 98, 390
Alford C. 1808-1851 246
Deborah 1789- 321
Elizabeth 1784-1867 194
James 1782-1859 ..321
John 1786-1851 321
Jonathan 1755-1844 ....83, 321
Jonathan 1784-1858 321
Joseph 1805-1883 .322
Peter 1800- 321
Phebe 1797-1869...321
Rodney 1802-1892 321
Roxana 1803-1877 321
Sally 1792-1868 321
Samuel 1795- 321
William 1796-1877579

BEMIS
Charlotte F. 1798-1878................115
James...................353

BEMUS
Mary 1789-1865....249

BENEDICT
James Knapp 1790-1864..................217
Rufus 1816-1897...512

BENJAMIN
Abigail 1797-1852.553
Anise 1783-1846 ...553
Daniel 1786-1818..553
Frederick 1803-1855 553
Jonathan 1760-1834 ....139, 552
Jonathan 1782-1845 553
Lemuel 1784-1853 553
Mary 1795-1874....553
Polly W. 1775-.87, 336
Rhoda 1794- 553
Rosina 1841- 486
Sarah 1790-1855...553
Sarah 1809-1897...465

BENNETT
Abraham 1793-1857 574
Ada 1838-1924......370

Amanda 1809-1882 337
Catharine 1828-....458
Elisha 1802-..........243
Hannah 1775-1862 62, 243
Nehemiah 1791-1872 271
Oliver F. 1837-......243
Sally 1811-1881 417
Sarah 1778-1851..161, 634
Sarah 1806- 364
Sarah 1820-1901...526
Susannah 1812-1857 436

BENSON
Albert 1817-1847 ..330
Benjamin 1809-1894 330
George 1824-1900.330
Mary 1816-1816....330
Rebecca 1803-1894330
Russell 1811-1887.330
Seth E. 1801-1870 330
Sewell 1806-1868..330
Stephen 1777-1852 85, 330

BENT
William 1798-1878595

BERRY
Amos 1805-1890 ...589
Clarissa 1797-1878 506
Hannah 1812-1812 589
Hannah 1813-1908 589
Harriet 1806-1878 589
Hermon 1804-1863 589
Jonathan 1803-1880 341
Lucy D. 1837-1914592
Lydia A. 1801-1878 589
Maria F. 1810-1891 589
Mary 1763-1849...128, 506
Mary A. 1823-1913 589
Nathaniel 1776-1862 ....149, 589
Rebecca 1808-1882589
William 345
William 1817-1851589

BETTEY
Lucy 1825-1847 533

BEVERSTOCK
Sibyl 1810-1892 611

BEVINS
Polly 1762-1840 184

BIBBENS

Philatheta 1766-....59, 228

BIBBINS
Bela.....................284
Laura 1823-1875 ..452
Patience 1733- 74, 283

BICKFORD
Calvin 1813-1883..324
Daniel 1765-1834...84, 323
Josiah.....................84
Martin 1814-1876.324

BICKNELL
Erastus 1804-1870517

BIDWELL
Cordelia 1807-1853 545
Laurinda 1799-1881 292
Mary 1798-1863....357
Polly 1785- 91, 355
Susan 1801-1868 ..291

BIGELOW
Charlotte 1798-1844 443
Humphrey 1761-1842 ....83, 316
John 1787-1808 316
Sanuel 1789-1789.316
Sarah 1797- 563
Susan 1792-1860 ..444

BILLINGHURST
Martha 1837-1912 343

BILLINGS
Anna 1806- 531
Elizabeth 1819-1853 461
Lydia.....................171
Willard 1782-1855 488

BINGHAM
Betsey 1789-1870 .451
Betsey 1811- 354
Caroline 1793- 354
Caroline 1810-1853 359
Erastus 1800-1883354
Harriet 1809-1892 354
Horatio 1765-..90, 354
James 1798-1879 ..354
Lucy 1770-1852 ...113, 451
Mary 1803-1863....354
Nancy 1791-..........354
Ralph 1788-1814...354
Reuben 1795-1797 354

BIRCHARD
Amasa 1765- 283
Betsey 1768- .283, 284
Gurdon 1773-........283
Lois 1776-1799......283
Phebe 1783- ..283, 486
Phineas 1738-1811 73, 282
Phineas 1771-1817283
Polly 1777-1804 283

BIRD
Frances A. 1846-1915 608
Mary Ann 1792-1859 239
Roena 1843-1895 ..608

BISBEE
Asaph 1788-1825 ..196
Noah 1803-1880....196

BISHOP
Abigail 1774-1833116, 459
Alonzo 1811-1868 .461
Calvin 1782-1846.116, 461
Charles 1820-1879462
Davis 1824-1884...463
Elizabeth 1823-1900 462
Emelia 1835-.........461
George 1814-1893.461
Gratis 1777-1862.116, 460
Gurdon 1789-1865 254
Gurdon T. 1804-1877 254
Harrison 1789-1856 ....117, 462
Henry 1828-1874..462
Hiram 1799- 460
Jacob 1773-1847 ...116
Jacob 1806-1866 ...460
John 1776-1850 ...116, 459
John 1815- 460
Lewis 1825-1901...462
Lucia.....................463
Lucy 1782-1824 116
Lucy 1817- 461
Margaret 1815-1841 463
Maria 1812-1850 ..460
Mary 1814-1892....462
Mary 1818-1898....463
Matilde 1785-1815 ....117, 461
Oscar 1824-1884...461
Peggy 1803-1809...460
Richard 1732-1806 27, 116
Richard 1780- 116
Rufus 1787-1851..117, 462
Samuel 1811-1882 462
Sophia 1820-1850.463
Sophia 1853-1908.610
Thomas 1810-1867460
Wilbur L. 1845-1877 377
William 1819-1875461
William 1822-1910463

BISSELL
Sabra 1763-1834....63, 246

BIXBY

Mary 1805-1881 ... 516
Nancy 1795-1860 . 420
Ruth 1797-1819.... 420
Solomon E. 1821-1900
.... 620
BLACK
Sarah 1743-.... 35, 146
Sarah 1762-1854.. 165
BLACKMORE
Ann E. 1832-1904. 418
BLACKWELL
Parthana 1812-1878
.... 483
BLAIR
Shepard 1800-1883
.... 463
Walter 1796-1849. 423
BLAISDELL
George 1839-1873 382
Mary 1813-1891 ... 307
Ruth 1785-1837... 145,
571
Sally E. 1785-144, 570
Sarah 1812-1862.. 438
BLAKE
Eliphalet 1794-1877
.... 324
Leonard W. 1807-1848
.... 374
BLAKENEY
Christiana 1822-1898
.... 515
BLANCHARD
Aaron.................... 177
Abigail 1777-1843 176
Abner 1787-1855.. 157
Benjamin 1721-1791 9
Benjamin 1781-1855
.... 176
Catherine 1793-1871
.... 560
Cynthia 1797-1832483
David 1771-1810 . 108,
431
Herman 1797-1882
.... 431
Lucy 1808-1880.... 516
Lydia 1714-1788. 8, 33
Matilda 1781-1852431
Rebecca 1801-1875560
Rhoda 1812-1896 . 500
Sarah 1820-1903.. 635
Susannah 1742-1837
.... 42, 164
Susannah 1804-1892
.... 431
Thomazin 1765-1824
.... 90, 353
William 1801-....... 431
BLANDIN
Betsey 1794-......... 228
BLANDING
Harvey 1809-1859 577
BLASHFIELD
Alfleda 1774-1855116,
459

BLISS
Elam C. 1802-1882
.... 250
George 434
Joel 1816-............. 458
Lucy 1803-1888.... 446
Porter 1795-1873 . 488
Ruth 1802-1889.... 459
BLODGETT
Achsa 1789-1872. 134,
532
Eunice 1793-1854. 225
Nathaniel 1778-1824
.... 270
BLOOD
Betsey 1808-1894. 445
Charlotte 1811-1870
.... 436
Daniel 1793-......... 435
Ebenezer L. 1832- 636
Herva 1794-.......... 435
John 1802-1880.... 436
Joseph 1787-1840. 212
Lawson 1808-1881436
Nathaniel 1754-1838
.... 109, 435
Nathaniel 1799-1873
.... 435
Otis 1807-1875..... 436
Polly 1797-1880.... 435
BLOOMFIELD
Eunice 1820-1913. 228
BLOSS
Benjamin 1784-1862
.... 242
Harriet G. 1827-1914
.... 472
Polly 1789- 275
BLUNT
Anna 1763-1840 ... 194
Mary 1787-1875 ... 179
Mehitable 1769-1802
.... 194
BOARDMAN
Charles 1812-1885503
Ezra H. 1791-1831229
William E. 310
BODWELL
Mary 1795-1863 ... 321
BOGART
Harriet A. 1833-... 260
BOLLES
Louisa.................... 507
Marcia 1800-1856 286
BOLSTER
Chapin 1784-1866 271
BOLTON
Daniel 1783-1853. 255
BOND
1817-1884............. 602
Dennis 1812-1834 602
Elijah 1767-1835. 151,
602
Elijah 1807-1851.. 602
Hannah 1801-1881
.... 602

Henry 1817-1896 . 604
Jonas 1805-1857 .. 602
Leonard 1809-1859
.... 602
Sarah 1803-1881.. 602
BOOTH
Mary 1829-1894... 331
BORTON
Joshua 1812-1874 512
BOSSANGE
Leopold 1821-....... 409
BOSTON
Susan M. 1810-1875
.... 398
BOSWORTH
Abigail 1818-1903 387
Amasa 1821-1875. 349
Josephus P. 1815-
1893 419
BOTTOM
Harriet 1817-1880 527
BOTTOM/BOTTUM
Asa 1748-1812 75, 288
Asa 1791-1831...... 288
Charles 1775-1813288
David 1784-1829.. 288
Elizabeth 1788-.... 288
Jairus 1779-1828 . 288
Joshua 1786-1855 288
Sarah 1776-.......... 288
Septa 1795-1873 .. 288
Walter 1781-1857. 288
BOUGHTON
Theodocia 1806-1880
.... 292
BOURNE
Maria 1754-1814... 77,
296
BOUTELL
Ira 1785-1861....... 227
Jacob 1791-1886... 227
James 1760-1822 .. 58,
226
James 1800-1879 . 227
John 1789-........... 227
Lucius 1805-1817. 227
Lusha 1797-1800.. 227
Marcia 1797-1869 227
Sally 1807- 227
Willard 1794-1850 227
BOWEN
Augusta 1828-1899
.... 463
Candace 1836-...... 505
Jerusha 1815-1866538
Mary 1815-1852... 479
Sarah 1749-1777... 26,
110
Susannah 1799-1879
.... 353
BOWERS
Amanda 1819-1869
.... 329
Benjamin 1783-.... 144
Benjamin 1807-1811
.... 192

Betsey H. 1820-1861
.... 192
Chloe 1799-1844 .. 192
David 1777-.......... 144
Fanny 1773-1828 .. 47,
144, 191
Francis 1744- . 34, 144
Francis 1775-1835 47,
144, 192
Francis H. 1811-1864
.... 192
Hannah 1812-1886
.... 192
Luke 1792-1834 ... 188
Phebe F. 1809-1811
.... 192
Phebe F. 1823-1910
.... 192
Ruth D. 1803-1883192
Tabitha 1780-1781144
BOYD
Lucy 1802-1879.... 188
Mary L. 1838-1907
.... 158, 629
BOYNTON
Betsey 1819-1886. 603
Dorcas 1715-1775 . 12,
48
John 1797-1858.... 449
Lydia 1802-1891 .. 449
Mary 1781-.......... 268
BRACKETT
Elizabeth 1811-1891
.... 560
Sarah 1822-1895.. 575
BRADDOCK
Elizabeth 1792-1875
.... 183
BRADFORD
Stephen M. 1798-1870
.... 286
BRADLEY
Clarissa 1806-1875
.... 358
Eliza A.................. 182
Elizabeth 1784-.... 302
George 1800-1872 302
John 1789-1830.... 302
Jonathan 1745-1791
.... 78, 301
Jonathan 1786-1867
.... 302
Joseph 1745-1802 . 78,
302
Joseph 1782-1782 302
Joseph 1784-1842 302
Mary 1779-1859... 302
Mary 1786-1829... 302
Mary 1801-1885... 218
Polly O. 1783-1783302
Sally 547
Sarah 1776-1807.. 301
Thomas O. 1774-1821
.... 301

Thomas O. 1792-1798 302
Thomas O. 1798-1859 302
William 1782-1784 302
William 1789- 302
William 1795-1838 302

BRADSTREET
Eliza 1807-1881 482
Mehitable 1820-1849 343

BRAGG
John 41
Lucy 1814-1901.....595
Molly 1779-1823 ..142, 564
Pamela 1791-1878 304
William 1810-1868 525

BRAINARD
Allen 1798- 542

BRANDON
Charles W. -1832 ..285
Martha 1752-1778 77, 296

BRAY
Diana 1775-1858..150, 596

BRAZIER
Sarah L. 1796-1874 448

BREED
Amos A. 1809-1892 564

BREVARD
Prudence 1772-1850 ....80, 306

BREWER
Dorcas 1818- 293

BRIDGE
Hiram 1803- 586
William 1783-1857 553

BRIDGES
Anna 1765-1809....299
Charles D. 1831-1865 605
Chloe 1743-1798 ... 78, 299
Elizabeth 1800-1886 574

BRIGGS
Augusta 1804-1877 463
Cynthia 1783-1867 311
Daniel 1769-1840.117, 463
Daniel 1806-1863..463
George 1820-1885.463
James 1812-1893..463
Martha 1803-1872 463
Mary 1811-1848....463

BRIGHAM
Betsey 1805-1872..217
Frances 1798- 193
Hiram 1800-1836..242
John 1788-1853 313

Joshua B. 1828-1891 633
Mary 1820-1882....580
Samuel 1741-1836 .82, 313
Spafford 1782-1866 216
Uriah 1793-1860...217

BRITT
Mary 1780-1846...124, 238

BRITTON
Electa 1816-1866 ..587
Surranus 1806-1898 375

BROCK
Anna 1780-1870....276
James 1783-1847..276
John 1768-1852 276

BROCKLEBANK
Benjamin 1835-1912 536
Electa 1821-1905 ..536
Emily C. 1825-1905 536
John 1830-1904 536
John B. 1797-1874 ....135, 535
Levi 1837-1864 536
Samuel S. 1820-1888 536
Walter 1827-1899 .536

BROCKWAY
Louisa M. 1838-1933 386

BRONSON
Hosea 1786-1827 ..519

BROOKS
Jane W. 1832-1881 406
John 1797-1874 368
Mary 1735- 16, 64
Nancy 1816-1902..516
Nancy 1828-1898..527
Phebe 1757-1836 .128, 505
Thomas 1780-1835 475

BROWN
Augustus 1853- 627
Bethiah 1769-1816 ....118, 464
Betsey 1798-1878 .460
Calvin 1814-1883..461
Charles 1848-1918 627
Chloe 1798-1876 ...449
Clarence 1855- 628
Daniel 1756-1797...93, 364
Daniel N. 1810- 244
Dauphin 1791-1871 459
Dauphin 1808-1889 462
David 125
David 1813-1815...508

Desire 1786-1822..443
Dilla 1816-1864 508
Electa 1800-1859 ..508
Eliphalet 1801-1834 225
Eliza 1811-1883....460
Eliza C. 1802- 244
Elizabeth 1757-1790 ....79, 303
Elizabeth 1785-1828 227
Ephraim 1790-1871 ....155, 617
Eunice 1799-1852 .226
Eunice 1802-1871 .460
Ezra 1798-1874.....508
Flora C. 1824-1909 ....*607*
Florence 1845- 617
George 1845-1910 .627
Hammon 1793-1864 574
Hannah.................283
Hannah 1786-1864 ....159, 631
Harvey 1802-1883 508
Henry D. 1818-1864 ....158, 627
Isaac A. 1802-1878 449
Issachar 1770-1855 ....116, 460
James...................112
James 1807-1872..335
John 1806-1828 460
Jonathan.................18
Julia 1818-1845 534
Loey 1803-1884.....276
Lucy 1800-1871 460
Lydia.............119, 470
Lydia 1859- 628
Maria 1810-1900 ..622
Maria 1862- 628
Martha 1800-1883 449
Martha 1857- 628
Mary -1822 310
Mary P. 1780-1853 184
Miriam 1746- 22, 94
Nancy 1799-1865 ..401
Nathaniel B. 1772-1852 ....129, 507
Rhoda 1775-1846 .113, 453
Russell 1788-1869 365
Sally 1796-1831 449
Sarah 1774-1851..107, 422
Sarah 1807-1887...508
Sarah 1808-1855...438
Titus 1808- 508
Valentine 1849 627

BROWNING
Margaret 1793-1845 ....117, 462

BROWNSON
Thomas 1780-1824 311

BRUCE
Samuel 1770- 241

BRUNDAGE
James 1805-1888 ..294

BRUSH
Eliza 1824-1866 636

BRYANT
Chauncey 1795-1863 317
Evalina 1833-1911 536
Mary E. 1825-1905 544
Nathaniel 1807-1883 618
Richard 1766-1815 549
Sally J. 1805-1881 292
Sarah 1798-1831 ..484
Sarah 1820-1855 ..527

BUCK
Alfred I. 1817-1890 383
Asahel 1792-1863 .290
Dexter...................399
Margaret 1779-1843 290
Matilda -1846 290

BUCKINGHAM
Otis 247

BUCKMAN
Maria E. 1821-1898 401

BUCKNAM
Mary 1816-1892....369

BUCKNER
Miriam 1831-1918 584

BUFFINGTON
William 1789-1814 210

BUFFUM
Mary C. 1824-1865 442

BUGBEE
Lois 1802-1871 492
Lucy 1740-1792 .....29, 122

BUGBY
George 1839- 382

BULLARD
Abigail 1818-1858 .624
John 1800- 501

BUNKER
Sally W. 1795-1882 421

BURBANK
Catherine..............301

BURCHARD
Marionette 1820-1877 459
Martha M. -1897...217

BURGES
Mary 1810-1887....354

BURGESS
Emery 1796-1872 .557
Mary 53, 208
Ruth 1805-1869 317
Sarah 1827-1899 ..365

BURKE

Catherine 1827- ... 371
BURLEIGH
 Rhoda G. 1802-1881
 430
BURNAP
 Mary 1744-1778 69,
 270
 Nathan 1798-1886 230
BURNET
 Katherine 1762-1833
 200
BURNHAM
 Abby L. 1814-1847 517
 Alfred 1836-1897 .. 521
 Betsey 1808-1895 . 320
 Chester 1788-1857 213
 Eleanor 1804-1852 332
 Emeline R. 1813-1864
 543
 Esther C. 1816-1905
 215
 Eunice 1777- 171
 Francis 1784-1870 189
 Harriet 1806-1888 229
 Hiram 1812-1884 . 493
 Jeanette 1810-1886
 432
 Jennet 1810-1886 . 422
 Julia 1819- 493
 Mary 26, 111
 Minerva 1813-1873
 493
 Nancy 1825-1860 . 384
 Phebe 1788-1820 .. 239
 Ruth 1818-1893 618
 Seymour 1777-1832
 .... 125, 493
BURNS
 Eliza H. 1802-1848
 .... 156, 620
 Mary 1801-1831 ... 561
 Moses 1796-1864 .. 561
BURNUM
 Orson 209
BURR
 Alanson 1794-1823
 446
 Elisha 1782-1863 . 446
 Nancy Madison 1809-
 1890 510
BURRALL
 Edward 1786-1872 359
 Wealthy A. 1775-1840
 .... 92, 358
BURRELL
 Elizabeth -1856 350
BURRILL
 Elizabeth 1817-1886
 410
 Nathan 1787-1866
 .... 104, 410
BURT
 Alonzo 1829-1907 . 515
 Ann 1806-1853 477
 Experience 1776-1833
 .... 56, 216

Matilda 171
BURTON
 Abraham 1822-1870
 624
 Betsey 1824-1886 . 624
 Caroline 1826-1911
 624
 John 1796-1873 ... 157,
 624
 John 1818- 624
 Louisa P. 1821-1903
 397
 Lydia 1773-1806 .. 285
 Lydia 1793-1869 .. 272
 Sarah 1820- 624
 Warren 1800-1866 581
BUSH
 Ebenezer 122, 481
BUSHNELL
 Asa 1764-1856 282
 Ezra W. 1800-1842 467
 Horace 1802-1883 467
 Lemira 1789-1852 118,
 466
 Sophia 1800-1871 . 245
 Stephen 1781-1862
 239
BUSS
 Abel 1802-1838 560
 Achsah 1797-1869 560
 Betsey 1795-1889 . 560
 Clarissa 1805-1887
 500
 Eunice 1809-1897 560,
 561
 Hannah 1774-1857
 .... 142, 561
 John 1790-1828 170
 Julia 1811-1861 560
 Marianne 1807-1826
 560
 Nathan 1804-1893 560
 Richard 1799-1885 560
 Richard T. 1772-1862
 .... 142, 560
 Sybil 1787-1866 202
BUSWELL
 Joshua 1804-1846 307
BUTLER
 Edmond 1840-1931
 457
BUTMAN
 Stepehn W. 1810-1885
 306
BUTRICK
 Anna 1787- 228
BUTTERFIELD
 Abraham 1780- 269
 Benjamin 1782-1871
 318
 Betsey 1790-1860 . 319
 Daniel 1784-1816 . 269
 Daniel 1785-1877 . 318
 Deborah 1762-1840 83,
 321

George W. 1809-1887
 336
 Hannah 269
 Hannah 1783- 319
 Harriet 1837-1930 591
 Isaac 1750-1812 68,
 269
 Isaac 1773-1816 ... 269
 James 1788-1840 . 318
 John 1731-1765 20, 83
 John 1753-1828 83,
 317
 John 1772- 317
 John 1781-1857 319
 Jonathan 1779-1839
 318
 Jonathan 1785-1871
 319
 Joseph 1782- 269
 Joseph 1792-1855 319
 Lydia 1774-1795 .. 317
 Lydia 1797- 319
 Mary 1791-1856 ... 318
 Mary 1831-1923 ... 293
 Mehitable 1788-1867
 269
 Naomi 1778-1841 . 318
 Olive 1783-1871 ... 318
 Peter 1755-1838 83,
 318
 Peter 1777-1844 ... 319
 Phebe 1760-1839 ... 83,
 320
 Phebe 1776-1854 .. 318
 Prudence 1781-1818
 318
 Rebecca 1775-1833 318
 Relief 1798-1853 .. 319
 Ruth 1779- 269
 Sally 1779-1852 ... 319
 Samuel 1793-1860 318
 Sarah 1758-1850 ... 83,
 319
 Solomon 1776- 269
 Stephen 1794- 319
 Sybil 1792-1830 ... 183
 William 1787- 318
BUXTON
 Mary 1791-1865 ... 546
 Rodney Randal 1805-
 1880 510
 Timothy R. 1773-1847
 270
BYAM
 Ezekiel G. 1828-1896
 600
BYLES
 Anna 1749-1791 32,
 136
 Elisha 1788-1869 . 541
BYRNE
 Hannah 100
CADY
 George 255

Mary A.H. 1832-1916
 545
 Phebe W. 1754-1800
 .... 51, 203
CAIN
 John 1790- 505
CALDWELL
 Hannah 1787-1855
 326
 Jacob 1782-1863 .. 320
 Jannet 1779-1856 326
 Rufus 1808-1890 .. 599
CALKINS
 Penia 1817-1906 .. 463
CALL
 Marshall 1800-1873
 223
CALLAHAN
 Robert 1809-1889 . 599
CAMMETT
 Joseph 1774-1829 266
CAMPBELL
 Betsey A. 1812-1886
 261
 Clarissa 1807- 507
 Hannah E. 1828-1868
 607
 James 176
 Lucinda 1814-1894
 261
 Sarah A. 1835- 277
 Susan 1805-1838 .. 555
 William 1811-1859 177
CANER
 Peter 1800-1854 ... 250
CANFIELD
 Nancy 1791-1867 113,
 453
CANOUTS
 Eliza 1818-1906 ... 339
CAPEN
 Thomas 1815-1880 405
CARBY
 Dean 1807-1882 ... 170
CARD
 Elizabeth 1774-1821
 285
 Lucy 1846-1902 349
 Stephen 235
CARLE
 Jonathan 1787- 268
CARLETON/CARLTON
 Abiah A. 1829-1849
 591
 Amos 1802-1837 .. 149,
 591
 Amos P. 1831-1906
 591
 Frederick O. 1834-
 1892 591
 Lucy 1805-1886 553
 Mehitable 1775-1849
 301
 Moses 1792- 186
 Osgood L. 1836-1915
 592

CARPENTER
Aaron 1763-1836... 62, 242
Abigail 1802-1889.233
Abigail 1807-1866.242
Alfred 1801-1863 ..242
Carolina 233
Caroline D. 1811-1864 221
Charity 1783- 171
Chester 1780-1868213
Dorcas 1810-1892 .242
Electa 1811-1897 ..438
Eliza A. 1823-1880221
Ephraim 1799-1845 537
Hannah 1799-1859 242
Harvey 1804-1856 242
Lucien H. 1817-1889 221
Lucy 1804-1875.....227
Pattie 1788-1864...242
Polly 1797-1863 242
Sally 1793-1885 242
Samuel H. 1788-1850 256
Sarah 1787-1857.208
Simon 1783-1862 .. 56, 221
Sylvia L. 1821-1904 572
CARR
Ann E. 1822- 257
Ann F. 1805-1847 .447
Charlotte 1804-1807 447
Charlotte 1809-1848 448
Edward 1827-1882537
Elizabeth 1802-.....288
George 1820-1877.537
John 1796-1861 ...135, 536
Joseph 1773-1849 112, 447
Joseph 1807-1889 .447
Mary 1818-1823....448
Mary P. 1819-1864537
Sarah F. 1812-1880 448
William 1811-1813448
William 1814-1850448
CARRIER
Mary 1827-1897....531
CARRINGTON
Sybil 52
CARTER
Deborah 1793-1877 520
Esther 1778-1857 105, 414
Hannah 1809-1894 602

Henry A. 1806-1883 585
Jeremiah 1803-1871 414
John 1797-1871 414
Judith 1787-1871..413
Levi 1817-1880 630
Mary T. 1841-1932602
Moses 1790-1851 ..413
Nancy 1797-1832..317
Nathan 1761-1840 ....105, 413
Nathan 1807-1875 414
Nathaniel 1800-....329
Philip 1813-1876...603
Rhoda 1771-1808.105, 414
Timothy 1768-1845 595
William F. 1811-1888 602
CARVER
Chester 1803-1827412
Derrick 1804-1850 441
CARY
Delight 1754- 122, 481
Dorcas 1756-.122, 481
Lucretia 1760- 122
Mary 1752-1839...122, 480
Nathaniel 1729-1818 ....29, 122
Nathaniel 1758-1778 122
Sarah 1764- ..122, 481
Sibbel 1762- 122
CASE
Anthony 1803- 456
Atalanta 1833-1905 322
Daniel 1766-1766..108
Elizabeth 1769-1769 108
Esther 1800-1878 .360
Hannah 1737-1780 25, 108
John 1760-1761 108
John 1764-1788 108
John 1788-1849 433
Lydia 1815-1855 ...635
Mary 1769-1769....108
Mehitable 1767-1811 108
Reuben 1802-1882 360
Samuel 1762-1791 ....108, 433
Samuel 1791-1884 433
Simeon 1733-1785 .25, 108
Simeon 1761-1816 108
Susannah 1786-1820 433
William 1769-1769108
CASS

Clarissa 1827-1870 419
CASWELL
Mariva 1812-1847.489
CENTER
Candace 1796-1883 319
Electa 1818-1905 ..560
CHADBOURNE
Joel W. 1819- 590
Martha L. 1793-1879 170
CHADWICK
Caleb 1801-...........497
John 1793-1858 443
Joseph 1787-1868 .417
CHAFFEE
Alfred 1811-1866 ..225
David 1772-1847...287
Ebenezer 1796-1875 ....137, 545
Frederick 1767-1837 285
Jonathan 1765-1848 285
Joseph 1795-1883 .287
Maryette 1822-1891 545
Olive 1756-......31, 134
Olive 1782-1821...134, 532
Philo 1826-1880....545
Rhoda 1751-1834...53, 208
CHAMBERLAIN
Ann 1832-1895......613
Asa 1793-1858 .....154, 613
Asa 1823-1896 613
Augusta 1838-1918 614
Austin 1841-1914 .614
Benjamin 1787-1864 474
Catherine 1835-1868 614
Eliza 1829-1907....613
Ephraim 1789-1845 580
Herman 1820-1909 612
Jedediah 1820-1896 613
John 1825- 613
Rebecca 1730-1809 14, 57
Rhoda 1819-..........613
Samuel 1779- 154, 612
Samuel 1826-1911 612
Sarah 1821-1897...613
William 1827-1880613
CHAMBERS
Sarah 1780-1865..113, 452
CHANDLER

Abigail 1778-1866.275
Abigail 1781-1788.177
Abigail 1794-1866.178
Achsah 1794- 272
Alice 1791-1833 ...171
Amy 1787-1823.....271
Asa 1759-1822 69, 272
Asa 1782-1833 272
Benjamin 1785-1813 171
Betsy 1771-1822 ...270
Bridget 1719-1736..17
Bridget 1744-1761..69
Charles 1811-1892635
Chloe 1771-1859...166
Clementine E. 1805-1860.................163
David 1797- 275
Dorcas 1785-1843 .161
Dorcas 1820-1821.637
Dorcas A. 1809-1889 634
Ebenezer 1749-1823 ....69, 270
Ebenezer 1780-1781 271
Ebenezer 1781-1859 271
Edna 1790-1790....271
Elijah 1753-1775 69
Elijah 1790-1860 ..272
Elinor 1785-1851 ..272
Elizabeth 1739-1740 69
Elizabeth 1742-.......69
Elizabeth 1774-.....171
Elizabeth 1777-1816 ....194, 579
Elizabeth 1818-1819 637
Emily 1811-1874...434
Ephraim 1784-1837 413
Ephraim H. 1783-1856...........161, 635
Ephraim H. 1823-1908...................635
Eunice 1746-1749...69
Eunice 1773-1840.270
Eunice 1797-1845.363
Eunice C. 1815-1897 634
Ezra P. 1825-1885 634
Hannah 1724-...17, 70
Hannah 1754-1755 .70
Hannah 1778- 270
Hannah 1781-1856 ....161, 636
Hannah 1788-1863 275
Hannah 1792- 272
Hannah 1798-1807 178
Harriet R. 1823- ...634
Henry 1790- 275

Isaac 1754-1832 .... 45, 177
Isaac 1784-1813 ... 177
Isaac 1793- 275
James 1735- 43
James 1763- 171
Jeremiah 1763-1828 .... 105, 413
Jermiah 1794-1864 170
Joel 1765- 171
Joel 1794-1860 271
Joel 1799-1863 275
John 1722-1759. 9, 17, 38
John 1748-1749...... 39
John 1749-1824..... 70, 275
John 1750-1832..... 39, 160
John 1752-1825... 105, 412
John 1777-1859... 160, 634
John 1780-1859.... 412
John 1783-1871.... 275
John 1795-1803.... 161
John 1812-1897.... 392
John C. 1794-1866 413
John C. 1807-1813 634
Joseph 1682-1734.... 5, 16
Joseph 1717- 70
Joseph 1741- 17
Joseph 1743- 70
Joseph 1753-1827.. 39, 161
Joseph 1756- 69, 70
Joseph 1780-1854 161, 634
Joseph 1789-1837 271, 579
Joseph 1815-1873. 635
Joseph A. 1789-1861 .... 161, 637
Joseph T. 1815-1896 637
Josephus 1796-1859 413
Joshua 1763-1834 .. 74
Josiah 1763- 166
Judith H. 1793-1843 413
Leonard 1817-1891 635
Lois 1797-1811 171
Luke 1787-1804.... 272
Lydia 1735-1814.... 68, 265
Mabel C. 1811-1890 634
Mary 1713-1751 16, 69
Mary 1741-1787 .... 43, 171
Mary 1767- 171

Mary 1769-1845 ... 270
Mary 1774-1828 ... 275
Mary 1786-1855 ... 177
Mary 1786-1872 ... 413
Mary 1795-1842 .. 161, 635
Mary A. 1805-1842 634
Mary K. 1796-1855 413
Mehitable 1709-1768 .... 16, 67
Mehitable 1719-1773 .... 13, 51
Moses 1788-1850.. 272
Nancy A. 1814-1890 635
Nathan 1782-1835 412
Nathaniel 1794-1795 272
Nathaniel 1802- ... 272
Norman 1790- 275
Peter 1755-1819.... 69, 271
Phebe 1717-1737.... 16
Priscilla 1796-1830 272
Ralph H. 1791-1861 188
Reuben 1744- 70
Reuben 1791-1875 275
Rhoda 1705- 5, 22
Rhoda C. 1799-1881 413
Ruth 1775-1849.... 270
Ruth 1798-1800.... 272
Sally 1800-1813.... 272
Sally W. 1820-1836 634
Salmon 1758- 70
Sarah 1693- 3, 8
Sarah 1750- 70
Sarah 1785-1861 .. 271
Sarah 1795- 275
Sarah 1818-1870.. 635
Sarah J. 1831-1895 635
Stevens 1738-1814 43, 170
Stevens 1781-1850 171
Susan E. 1832-1895 637
Susanna F. 1788-1870 413
Thomas 1711-1761 16, 68
Thomas 1746-. 70, 275
Thomas 1751-1767. 69
Thomas 1783-1856 271
William 1704-1741 11, 42
William 1771-1800 171
William 1785-1813 275
CHANLDER
Edna 1791-1871 ... 271

CHAPEL
Affia 1797-1871.... 523
Harlow 1801-1864 523
CHAPIN
Caleb 1807-1865 .. 442
Clarissa 1806-1867 258
Daniel 1761-1821.. 65, 257
Eliza 1790-1852 ... 258
Eunice 1769-1843 239
James 1793-1825 . 258
Sophia 1795-1860. 258
Thomas 1788- 258
William W. 1785-1857 258
CHAPMAN
Elijah 1783-1872.. 235
Eunice 1780-1831 287
Hannah 1791-1835 287
Henry 1794-1873 . 602
Joseph 1747-1796 286
Joseph 1747-1796,,. 74
Joseph 1771-1847 286, 287
Keziah 1774- 286
Olive 1790-1870 ... 475
Reuben 512
Sarah 1776-1814.. 287
CHAREVOY
Jane 1805-1871.... 541
CHASE
Amy 1816- 497
Ann S. 1804-1865. 431
Catherine E. 1831-1919 372
Elizabeth B. 1806-1879 431
Joseph F. 1770-1823 431
Joseph F. 1770-1823, b. at, ... 108
Joseph F. 1808-1858 431
Judith A. 1796-1864 547
Lucinda 1791-1871 205
Lucy M. 1831-1919 502
Maria 1819-1906.. 260
Mary 1819-1880... 497
Samuel H. 1804-1890 259
Sarah E. 1814-1852 .... 430, 431
Sarah L. 1823-1879 635
William E. 1812-1895 431
CHEEVER
Daniel 1802-1877. 407
Frances 1830-1916 585

Susanna 1660-1744 3, 6
CHENEY
Albert 1826-1909 . 613
Alva 1790-1851 520
Benjamin J. 1803-1882 232
Calvin 1798-1878. 519
Celia 1803-1877 ... 521
Chester 1789-1868 519
David 1750- 18, 72
Ebenezer 1740-1800 .... 30, 131
Ebenezer 1769-1803 .... 131, 520
Ebenezer 1803-1874 520
Ebenezer 1805-1893 521
Eliza 1822-1866 ... 521
Elizabeth 1802-1820 519
Emeline 1810-1847 519
Hannah 1812-1886 520
Isaac 1819-1839 ... 521
Jervis 1804-1863.. 519
John 1772- 131
John 1782- 501
Joseph 1759-1831 131, 518
Joseph 1774-1852 131, 520
Joseph 1788-1865 519
Joseph 1805-1848 520
Joseph 1807-1884 521
Lucy 1802-1872.... 520
Luther 1775-1851 270
Mary 1762- 131
Mary 1791-1858... 519
Mary 1816-1912... 521
Mitta 1811-1897... 521
Paschal 1797-1859 519
Patience 1799- 520
Percy 1795-1875... 520
Persis 1778-1853. 131, 522
Phebe R. 1782-1860 72
Rocksana 1793-.... 519
Ruby 1810- 519
Ruth 1767- ... 131, 520
Ruth 1807-1885 ... 520
Samuel 1801-1870 521
Silence 1760-1760 131
Stephen 1814-1900 521
Warren 1801-1877 519
William 1717-. 30, 130
William 1765-1851 .... 131, 519
William 1795- 519
William 1801-1889 520
CHICKERING
Abbot 1821-1842 .. 568

Benjamin 1824-1889 568
Betsey 1818-1899..568
Ceres 1815-1817 ...566
Daniel O. 1811-1874 589
Hannah M. 1819-1870 566
Henry 1819-1881 ..568
Jacob 1806-1887 ...565
Joseph 1780-1844 143, 567
Mary 1813-1880....597
Mary O. 1804-1888 565
Sarah A. 1808-1891 565
William 1811-1890566
Zachariah 1764-1841 ....143, 565
CHILD
Amity 1801-1871 .. 95, 378
Ann P. 1810-1886 158, 631
Hiram 1835-1915..371
Lucy 1815-1902.....539
Martha 1841-1909 371
CHILDS
Ann 1816-1861......549
Charles 1802-1869286
Ephraim 1802-1847 577
Mary Ann 1807-1883 234
Stephen 1820-1887 374
CHILSON
Chloe 1839-1923 ...388
CHITTENDEN
Mary 1819-1895....457
CHOATE
Eliza 1801-1877 .... 95, 377
CHOLLAR
Samuel 1793- 439
CHUBB
Ann 1756- 284
Joseph 1719-1755 . 30, 130
CHURCH
Anna 1800- 229
Susan 1811-1856 ..286
CILLEY
Nancy J. 1823- 624
Rhoda P. 1803-1885 417
CLANCY
John 1793-1876 309
CLAPP
Billings 1790-1873551
Sidney B. 1784-1837 ....62, 244
CLARK
Abel 1779-1790 225

Alfred 1784-1787 ..226
Alfred 1789-1880 ..226
Andrew J. 1809-....255
Arastus 1783-1857225
Artemisia 1794-1887 203
Asa B. 1814-1901..577
Augustus 1788-1790 226
Caroline 1826-1911 428
Clarissa................355
David 1800-1873...217
Dolly 1779-1854....288
Dyer 1772-1846 .....65, 255
Dyer H. 1817-1897255
Eli 1799-1868........226
Elijah 1788-1873...530
Elizabeth A. 1814- 381
Enos 1820- 349
Eunice 1786- 226
Ezra 271
Fielder 1792-1875.226
Francis P. 1798-1870 541
Gideon 1797-1831.394
Hannah 1763- .24, 103
Hosea 1801-1874 ..226
Jacob......................271
Laura 1830-1869 ..458
Lucinda H. 1802-1860 255
Mariah 1811-1896 525
Mary 1745-......69, 274
Nehemiah H. 1805-1812 255
Orilla 1799-1881...226
Permelia 1781-1866 225
Phebe 1786-1854 ..226
Sabrina H. 1799-1839 255
Sally M. 1814-1899 219
Samuel............99, 394
Samuel 1773-1830 499
Sophia 1797-1843 .226
Stephen 1752-182058, 225
Warner 1812-1896 632
Willard 1790-1790 226
William 1751- 27
William 1754-1840 58, 226
William 1818-1889262
CLARKE
Esther 1786-1819 .283
Louisa 1790-1833 .283
Sarah 1815-1858...346
Sarah A. 1815-1861 469
CLARY
Betsey 1796- 252
Joseph 1792-1842 .252

Joseph -1800...64, 252
Selena 1794- 252
CLAUDE
Catherine 1820-....361
CLAY
Mehitable 1823-1907 430
CLEERE
Mary E. 250
CLEMENT
Charlotte E. 1828-1908...................437
Katherine 1838-1921 486
Margaret 1844-1917 350
Nancy 1780-1862...86, 334
CLEVELAND
Clarissa 1810-1865 527
Ephraim 1805-1845 527
Martha B. 1813-1880 527
Plinny 1801-1867..261
Thomas C. 1811-1874 244
CLIFFORD
Eunice 1800-1881.325
CLINTON
Margaret 1839-1904 371
CLOGSTON
Mary 1796-1855....319
CLOUGH
Chester 1797-1878525
CLYDE
Catherine 1769-1848 ....63, 250
COBB
Albion P. 1815-1863 430
George 1838-.........617
Laura 1797-1888 ..552
COBURN
Betsey 1812-1884 .329
Fanny 1823-1901..348
Letitia 1843-1913 .610
Mary C. 1785-1856 ....115, 457
Matilda 1815-1903322
Sally 1804-1827 552
COBURN/COLBURN
Anna 1777-1856....178
Thomas 1753-1836171
COCHRAN
Abigail 1812-1892.190
George 1805-1887.412
Mary A. 1805-1876 ....157, 623
CODMAN
Sarah 1765-1838.....79
CODY
Elijah 1775-1828 ..287
COFFIN

Abiah 1764- 164
Achsah 1793-1818 563
Benjamin 164
E. Farnum 1813-1856 416
Esther E. 1821-1843 416
Judith H. 1810-1852 416
Lucy J. 1805-1879 415
Lydia 1768-...........164
Mary 1763-1842....164
Moses 1779-1854 .105, 415
Nehemiah C. 1815-1868...................416
Nicholas 1765-1850 164
Peter 1758-1843....164
Peter 1808-1892....416
Rebecca 1804-1870415
Sarah 1756-1836 ..164
Stephen 1729-.42, 164
Susannah C. 1818-1880...................416
COGGIN
Jacob 1812-1890 ...342
COGSWELL
Clarissa 1775-1841 285
Ebenezer 1798-1799 507
Hendrick 1796-1797 507
Ira 1793-1879 507
Joshua 1772-.128, 507
COIT
Lucy 1792-1843 254
COLBURN
Celia 1819-1856....324
Naomi 1812-1879..396
COLBY
Archelaus 1762-1827 ....90, 352
Betsey 1768- 274
Betsey 1800-1856 .480
Johnson 1791-1856 352
Martha 1786-1861 352
Mary Ann 1806-1872 547
Nathaniel 1798-1872 352
Sally 1784-...........352
Sarah 1802-1828 ..413
Sarah 1820-1891 ..426
COLE
Amos 1806-1897 ...463
Erastus 253
Henry 1818-1900..340
Ira 1792-1871 481
John 1797-1880 484
Joseph 1805-1859.596
Mary 1833-1903....301
Philena 1795-1835480

COLEMAN
  Almira 1811-1892 467
COLLINS
  Nathan 1792-1887 242
  Susan 1826-1885.. 518
COLLIS
  Luther 1811-1896. 532
COMSTOCK
  Henry 1794-1879.. 257
  William 1824-1851457
CONANT
  Adelia 1793-1846 107,
    426
  Alvah 1800-1876 .. 425
  Caroline 1809-1883
    425
  Cyrus 1799-1803.. 425
  Cyrus K. 1803-1871
    425
  George D. 1811-1880
    425
  Harriet 1812-1892 527
  John 1771-1850 ... 107,
    424
  Laura 1820-1895.. 250
  Lucinda 1804-1808
    425
  Lucy M. 1812-1883
    425
  Lydia H. 1816-1854
    425
  Martha 1804-1884 507
  Nancy M. 1796-1865
    .... 420, 425
CONDON
  Samuel 1795-1881 418
CONE
  Abigail 1778-1820135,
    538
CONGDON
  Diana 1793-1841 .. 433
CONNER
  Mary 1802-1878 ... 575
CONNOR
  Jennie................... 604
  Wealthy 1841-1872
    244
CONVERS/CONVERSE
  Adin 1779-1816 486
  Adin M. 1779-1816283
  Almira 1808-1858 532
  Charles 1771-1854
    ....132, 133, 525
  Charles 1798- 525
  Clarissa 1804-1880
    525
  Cyrel................... 525
  Deborah 1795-1842
    486
  Delina 1811-1860. 532
  Edward 1788-1879486
  Eleanor 1806-1853459
  Esther 1802-1870. 525
  Jedediah 1754-1818
    .... 124, 486
  Juliana 1817-1887532

Leonard 1805-1888
    531
  Molly 1773-1856.. 133,
    530
  Nancy 1793-1877 . 486
  Orrin -1810 486
  Polly 1802-1856.... 531
  Rodolphus 1807-1868
    525
  Roxana 1769-1842
    .... 133, 529
  Roxana 1810-1896 525
  Rufus 1777-1777 .. 133
  Sally 1781- 58, 224
  Stephen 1745-1823 31,
    132
  Stephen 1775-1854
    .... 133, 531
  Stephen 1799- 531
COOK
  Asenath 1769-185862,
    245
  Chloe S. 1817-1847
    224
  Diantha 1831- 586
  Elinora 1794-1872 416
  Marietta 1802-1870
    412
  Peter 1802-1870 ... 528
COOLEY
  Aaron 1800-1866.. 525
  James E. 1802-1882
    409
  Martha 1832-1869 380
COOLIDGE
  Mary 1767- ... 138, 548
COOMBS
  Charlotte 1790-1829
    .... 326, 327
  Clarissa 1806-1865
    435
  David 1793- 326
  Elizabeth 1802-1874
    326
  Herbert 1797- 326
  James 1760-1827 .. 84,
    326
  James 1781-1782 . 326
  James 1782- 326
  Jane 1774-1843.... 443
  Jonathan 1786-1844
    326
  Mary 1805-1880 ... 326
  Rachel 1795-1867. 326
  Rebecca 1792-1866326
  Simeon 1784-1855 326
  Solomon 1799- 326
  Susanna 1788-1814
    326
COON
  Hester A. 1828-1894
    388
  William........... 98, 388
COOPER
  Mary 1830-1860 ... 604

COPELAND
  Abel W. 1809-1867441
  Amasa 1758-1852 110,
    438
  Asa 1787-1869 448
  Clarissa A. 1802-1888
    441
  Eliza 1792-1854 ... 439
  James 1724- ... 26, 110
  James 1799-1893 . 441
  John 1778- 110
  Joseph 1764- 110
  Joseph 1804-1808 439
  Lora 1797-1891 439
  Lucy 1795-1888.... 439
  Lydia 1771- 110
  Molly 1773- 110
  Phebe 1756-.......... 110
  Phebe 1790-1888.. 438
  Rebecca 1766-1844
    .... 110, 440
  Sarah 1760-.. 110, 439
  Sarah 1789-1880. 438,
    440
  Sophia 1800-1883. 439
  Stephen 1776- 110
  Thomas 1801-1882439
  Willard 1768-1852
    ....110, 200, 441
  Wyllys 1768- 110
CORBETT
  Mary 1831-1916 ... 605
CORBIN
  Caroline 1806-1893
    234
  Joseph P. 1773-1848
    473
  Luther 1775-1848 204
  Nancy P. 1807-1887
    575
COREY
  Elizabeth 1781-1826
    475
  Tryphena 1800-1863
    448
CORLISS
  Lodice 1781-1807 . 195
CORNFORTH
  Elvira 1826-1915.. 330
CORSE
  William 1806-1887402
CORSER
  Lucy A. 1817-1907 611
  Ruth K. 1817-1901566
CORTTIS
  William 1798-1823436
CORWIN
  Archibald 1809-1878
    294
COTTING
  James S. 1817-1843
    632
COTTON
  Daniel H. 1794-1881
    249

Elijah H. 1800-1882
    249
  Eliza M. 1828- 383
  Elmina 1815-1883 534
  Lester H. 1804-1878
    249
  Mary 1753-1808 34
  Mary 1790-1858 ... 249
  Rowland 1759-1847
    .... 63, 248
  Samuel 1788-1866 249
COUCH
  Eunice T. 1810-1888
    416
COUSENS
  Sally 426
COUTHOUY
  John P. 1811-1852 406
COVELL
  Elizabeth C. 1808-
    1893 417
COVENHOVEN
  Maria 1820-1895.. 522
COWDREY
  Susannah 1762-1848
    .... 108, 433
COWEL
  Sally 1782-1831 67,
    263
COWLES
  Francis 1804-1880 542
  Israel 1788-1857 .. 236
  Lucy 1815-1843.... 541
COY/COYE
  Adaline 1811-1898453
  Almira 1804- 452
  Benjamin 1776-.... 113
  Benjamin 1806-1897
    452
  Beulah 1770-1831113,
    452
  Caroline 1821-1910
    454
  Chandler 1814-1849
    452
  David 1781-1860. 113,
    453
  Deborah 1792-1862
    450
  Delila 1802-.......... 452
  Dorcas 1818-1847 454
  Emily 1816-1860.. 452
  Erastus 1801-1867451
  George 1828- 454
  Hiram 1829-......... 454
  Horace 1810-1887 452
  John 1773- 113
  John 1794-1870.... 452
  John 1832- 454
  Jonathan 1730-1815
    .... 27, 113
  Jonathan 1768-1841
    .... 113, 451
  Ladotia 1800-....... 452
  Lewis 1814-.......... 454

Loren 1812-1882...452
Martha 1799-1840 450
Mary 1809-1848....453
Mary 1835-1913....454
Oscar 1824-1825...454
Patty 1766-1861...113, 451
Reuben 1770-1843 ....113, 452
Royal 1808- 452
Samuel 1808-1874 453
Schuyler 1825-1885 454
Simeon 1774-1857113, 453
Simon B. 1807-1814 452
Sophia 1798-1886 .450
William 1817-1847453
Willis 1764-1848..113, 450

COZZENS
Eliza 1819-1895 244

CRAFT
Sarah 1756-1831... 64, 253

CRAIN
Louisa R. 1806-1857 ....89, 349

CRAM
Humphrey 1772-1813 168
Mary 1803-1886....559
Sarah 1806-1875...448

CRANDALL
Bailey 1784-1861 ..411

CRANE
Almina 1819-1883 461
Aurelia 1806-1874 505
Charles 1793-1824560
Hannah -1835 366

CRANSON
Samuel 1797-1859 530

CRAWFORD
Albert 1814-1853 ..295
Anna 1791-1820....474
Benjamin 1781-1789 474
Calvin 1773-1776..473
Ingoldsby W. 1786-1867..................474
John 1777-1863 474
Joseph 463
Lavina 1775-1796.473
Luther 1772-1853.473
Samuel 1748-1824 ....120, 473
Samuel 1779-1858 474
Sarah 1788-1826...474
Walter 1784-1785 .474

CRITTENDEN
Reuben H. 1823-1898 261

CROCKER

Alpheus 1783-1784 211
Alpheus 1787-1873 ....211, 238
Beriah 1785-1874 .221
Bethiah 1791-1860211
Candace 1785-1849 211
Charlotte 1791-1860 443
Clarissa 1802-1865 257
Crocker 1779-1863236
Edey 1794-1876 221
Edwin 1812-..........257
Eliza 1812-...........257
Experience 1794-1851 562
Fanny 1800-..........257
Hannah 1786-.......221
Hannah 1794-1881 203
Hannah 1796-.......211
Lois 1763-185061, 237
Lucy 1798-1888 257
Mary 1814-...........257
Nathan 1772-1817 .65, 257
Nathan F. 1807-1890 257
Stephen 1760-.57, 221
William D. 1805-...257
Zebulon 1757- .54, 211
Zebulon 1802-1847211

CROCKETT
Abigail D. 1824-1895 590

CROKER
Harvey 1808-1829 257

CROMWELL
Philipenia 1805-1845 520

CROSBY
Abigail 1770-1844265, 266
Alpheus 1810-1874 397
Ann E. 1812-1887 .571
Asa 1765-1836 99, 397
Asa 1766- 265
Charles 1815-1815397
Charles L. 1813-1814 397
David L. 1807-1894 571
Deborah 1709- 5, 20
Ebenezer 1772- 265
Ebenezer 1772-1863 208
Ella 1855-1900.......629
Ezra 1765-1814.....266
Hannah 1761-1850 38, 159
Hannah 1767-1842 267

Jacob 1729-1776 .9, 37
Jacob 1769- 38
Jesse 1782- 265
Joanna 1770-1815 267
Joel 1740-1775 68, 267
Jonah 1736-1814 ...68, 265
Jonah 1762-1814 ..266
Jonathan 1762-1840 265
Josiah 1741-............68
Lydia 1758-1821 ...266
Marah -1743 68
Mariah 1763- 266
Mehitable 1767-1842 266
Patty 1770-1833 ...265
Phebe 1738-1826 ...68, 266
Priscilla 1807-1808 397
Rebecca 1772-1843267
Reuben 1764-..........38
Rhoda 1772-1854...266
Robert 1711-1743 ..16, 67
Robert 1732- ...68, 265
Robert 1761-1763 .265
Robert 1764-1823 .265
Robert 1764-1832 .266
Russell 1808-1816 397
Ruth W. 1764-1843 267
Samuel 1773-..........38
Samuel 1774-1775 267
Sarah 1840-1905...626
Stephen 1774-1834 266
Stephen M. 1818-1826 397
Susanna 1778-1861 266
Susannah 1768-1805 265
Thomas R. 1816-1872 397
Zilpah 1767-1825...38, 159

CROSS
David 1795-1833...305
Jareb P. 1817-1858 343

CROSSMAN
Robert 1778-1859 .205

CROW
Maria 1834-1878 ..537

CROWELL
Robert 1787-1855 .179

CROWFOOT
Lydia 1799-1878...528

CRUTCHLY
Matilda T. 1805-1889 232

CULLY

Sarah L. 1822-1880 249

CULVER
Abigail 1795-1853.519
Sarah 1824-1910 ..503

CUMMINGS/CUMMINS
Abigail 1801-1866.328
Abigail 1818-1895.563
Achsah 1793-1863 326
Anderson 1801-.....328
Benjamin 1774-1774 85
Benjamin 1816- 329
Cyrus 1777-1858....85, 328
Cyrus 1803- 328
Daniel G. 1812-1889 328
David 1785-1855...297
Deborah 1761- 84, 326
Ebenezer...............273
Elizabeth 1772-1858 85
Elizabeth 1786-.....326
Elizabeth 1797-1890 328
Esther 1771-1862 ..58, 227
George W. 1788-1872 432
Hannah 1789-1885 240
Hiram 1810-1887..328
Irene 1831-1870....567
Jenne 1770-1775.....85
Jonathan 1729-1787 ....20, 84
Jonathan 1759-......84, 326
Jonathan 1790-1794 326
Jonathan 1794-1879 328
Jonathan 1817-.....329
Joseph 1774-1774...85
Joseph 1792-1860.188
Leonard 1802-1859 328
Lorenzo 1811-1899329
Lovisa 1822-1865..329
Lucy 1767-1854 ...140, 555
Lydia 1788-...........326
Martha 1793-........328
Mary 1775-1852.....47, 190
Mary 1779-1830......85
Mary 1808-1850....601
Mary E. 1814-1872 391
Mary J. 1819- 329
Moses 1806-1880 ..329
Olive 1813-1899....329
Pelatiah 1809-1888 328

Rachel 1775-........... 85
Rebecca 1767-1782. 84
Rebecca 1783-1857 85, 330
Rebecca 1796-1869 328
Russell 1804-........ 328
Russell 1809-1871 329
Ruth W. 1785-........ 85
Sarah 1781-.... 85, 329
Simeon 1806-........ 328
Susannah 1768- 85, 328
Sybil 1763-1811..... 84, 327
Thomas 1764-1838 84, 327
CUNNINGHAM
Marion 1842-1930 614
CURRIER
Anthony D. 1812-1838 599
John 1789-1862.... 317
Tabitha 1793-1877 413
CURTIS
Abigail 368
Alfred 1809-1878.. 219
Asa 1785-............. 214
Henry 1818-1846.. 219
Horace 1804-1887 219
James 1779-1863 124, 489
Nancy M.1808-1852 489
Oliver H. 1811-1899 219
Origen D. 1818-.... 489
Sanford 1800-1807 219
Sarah 1782-1857 ... 98, 392
Sarah H. 1805-1874 219
Selden 1815-1902. 219
William 1774-1860 56, 218
William 1802-1879 .... 216, 219
William T. 1811-1882 489
Wilson W. 1813-1890 219
Zebadiah 1806-1840 489
CURTISS
Julia 1816- 225
CUSHING
Joseph 1785-1868. 313
Lydia 1807-1862... 330
CUSHMAN
Atholinda 1809-1883 595
Betsey M. 1813-1856 424
Cynthia S. 1797-1892 237

Hannah 1813-1899 230
Julia 1817-1892.... 223
CUTLER
Abigail G.J. 1809-1837 397
Attossa 1817-1882 461
CUTTER
Nancy W. 1830-1918 565
DADY
Olive 1789-1873 .. 116, 461
DALE
Abigail 1781-1852 156, 621
Anna 1789-1862... 157
Betsey 1793-1852 157, 624
Eben 1839-1864 ... 623
Ebenezer 1788-1862 .... 157, 623
Ekiza 1828-1893 .. 623
John 1748-1809..... 37, 156
John 1779-1779.... 156
John 1785-1843... 156, 623
John 1833-1887.... 623
John F. 1835-1854 623
Martha 1817-1888 408
Mary 1783-... 156, 622
Mary 1799-1863 ... 560
Mary 1842-1917 ... 623
Mercia 1833-1916. 623
Nancy B. 1825-1844 623
Rhoda 1780-1852 156, 621
Sally 1791-1796.... 157
Sarah 1797-1862. 157, 624
Sarah 1837-1891.. 623
Serena P. 1825-1902 409
Sumner 1795-1796 157
DAME
Charles 1828-1899 352
DAMON
Ingalls 1795-1867. 585
Jerusha 1804-1884 182
DANA
Anna 1783-............ 67
Clarissa 1773- 67
Clarissa 1808- 264
Daniel 1785-.......... 67
Eliza 1803- 264
Elizabeth 1771-1840 .... 67, 263
Hiram 504
Jedediah 1739-....... 67
Jedediah 1739-1809 16
Jedediah 1778-....... 67
Lester H. 1805- 264
Lucy 1772-............. 67

Lucy 1801-1841.... 264
Mary 1781-1850.... 67, 264
Mary A. 1808- 264
Mary E. 1829-1900 588
Sally 1777-1856 .... 67, 264
Silas 1774-1846..... 67, 263
Sophia 1777-1861. 235
Wealthy 1822-1892 264
DANE
Ezra 1802-........... 192
John 1786-1850.... 192
Lydia 1817-1854 .. 562
Mary 1810-1843... 420
Moses 1800-1888.. 192
DANFORTH
Elizabeth 1763-1857 .... 123, 482
Jacob 1766-1851... 185
Thomas P. 1781-1865 251
DANIELS
James 1796-1877 . 256
Louisa 1825-1869. 633
DANIELSON
James 29, 127
DARBEE
Azariah 1762-1851 166
DARBY
Asa 1782- 140
Edward.................. 97
Ezra 1798-1835.... 582
Lovina 1810-1888. 554
Lucy 1769-1813.... 443
Lydia 1776- 140
Molly 1765- 140
Oliver 1767- . 140, 554
Thomas 1739-1833 33, 140
DARLING
Aaron B. 1819-1867 615
Adeline 1822-1912 436
Benjamin 1728-1783 .... 49, 197
Benjamin 1775-1840 198
Edah 1792-1864 ... 193
Elizabeth 1771-1834 .... 106, 416
Eunice 1774-1834 198
Hannah 1767-1767 172
Hannah 1768-1768 172
James 1779-1811 . 198
Jason 1796-1864 .. 485
Jedediah 1784-1862 173
John 1759-........... 198
Jonathan 1742- 44

Jonathan 1742-1828 172
Jonathan 1763-1765 172
Jonathan 1765-1848 172
Jonathan 1767-1820 276
Levi 1782- 198
Lois 1771-............. 198
Mary 1774-1849.... 173
Mary 1812-1887... 324
Molly 1769- 198
Patience 1767- 198
Phebe 1776-1851.. 173
Roxanna 1795-1880 505
Ruth 1774-1835 .. 106, 418
Sabrina 1799-....... 512
Samuel 1781-1859 173
Sarah 1770-1836.. 172
DARROW
Cornelia 1825-1901 293
DART
Albert 1810-1889 . 498
Henry 1807-1889 . 497
Laura 1838-1921.. 625
Sally 1789-1813 ... 214
Sybil 1787-1822 ... 214
DASCOMB
Elizabeth 1771-1852 .... 86, 334
George 1764-1842 185
Hannah 1779-1806 86, 335
Hannah 1809-1874 335
Joseph 1810-1890 334
Luther 1801-1885 334
DAVENPORT
Anna 1786-1866.. 138, 548
Anna 1815-1902... 548
Emily B. 1812-1885 577
Mary 1835-1912... 549
Mary B. 1814-1896 259
Theodosia M. 1810-1883 258
Trissia 1841-1926 614
DAVIDSON
Abigail 1786-1861 321
Jane.................... 185
DAVIS
Abigail 1780-1854. 85, 328
Asenath 1812-1893 .... 100, 399
Benjamin F. 1831-1900 .... *607*
Chauncey 1797-1854 524

Clarissa A. 1833-1869
...........................608
David 1788-1871...500
Edmund 1786-1833
...........................353
Elijah 1803- 312
Elizabeth 1804-1844
...........................439
Ellen M. 1841-1873
...........................609
Francis 627
Henrietta 1843-1911
...........................400
Herschel 1798-1886
...........................315
Ida M. 1856-..........380
Israel 1766-1848..146,
576
Israel 1803-1872...576
Israel H. 1801-1801
...........................576
Joseph H. 1797-1799
...........................576
Lydia 1806-1849 ...421
Lydia 1823-1885 ...462
Maria 1794- 210
Martha 1804-1885 502
Martha 1836-1897 463
Mary 1818-1891....464
Mary A. 1824-1904
...........................587
Richard 615
Sally 1794-1800 576
Sarah 1814-1890...368
Susanna 1782-1873
...........................215

DAVISON
Celanira 1858-1933
...........................627
Paul 1765-1805.....202
DAWLEY
Alvina 1816-1880..391
Carey 1799-1847...520
DAY
Betsey 1809-1835..522
Hannah 1792-.37, 157
John E. 1800-1836 573
William 1786-1860 538
DE MARIE
Mary 1822-1894....434
DE WOLF
Rosina 1827-1909 .262
DEAN
Hannah 1766-1848
.................121, 285
Sarah 1807-1894...337
DEANE
Eleanor 1804-1889 330
DECAMP
Martha M. 1829-1855
...........................375
DECKER
Sarah 1790- 288
DEERING

Betsey B. 1811-1852
...........................396
DELAND
William A. 1820-1857
...........................543
DELANO
Harriet 1797-1836 553
DELONG
Francis 1808-1885 454
DEMING
Herbert 1796-1871 513
Timothy 1788-1879
...........................542
DENISON
Lydia 1789-1838 ...239
Nathan 1809-1854 511
DENNIS
Rhoda 505
Sarah 1812-1890...496
DERBY
Albert 1830-1914 ..385
DEROLODS
Antoinette 1827-1898
...................85, 331
DERUMPLE
Sarah 1753-1795....82,
310
DEVAN
Abigail 1802-1838.223
DEVER
Jane 1804-1883.....263
DEWEY
John W. 1762-1839 91,
357
DEWING
Eunice C. 1808-1892
...........................286
DIBBLE
Orrin 1795-1860 ...260
DICKEY
Albert C. 1849-1941
...........................386
Clara 1826-1915 ...348
Clement S. 1806-1892
...................97, 386
Josephine H. 1842-
1877 386
Maria 1820-1903...603
DICKINSON
Sarah 1841-1912...380
DIELL
Celinda 1811-1890 252
John 1769-1813 64,
252
John 1808-1841 252
Mary A. 1804- 252
DIER
Rachel 477
DILWORTH
John 1798-1838 499
DIMICK
Nathan..................494
DIMOCK
Daniel 1750-1823.124,
487

Olivia A. 1815-1888
...........................231
Origen 1796-1871 .487
DIMOND
Charles 1835-1914 629
DINSMOOR
Sally 240
DINSMORE
Fanny 1794-1860..431
John 1792-1879 170
Stephen 1806-1852
...........................597
DIX
Betty 1769-1838 ...277
Mary 1758- 277
Nancy 1811-1881..556
DIXEY
Hannah 1787-1831 88,
341
DIXON
Abram 1787-1875 .249
Catherine 1811-1906
...........................425
Leonora 1801-1875
...........................477
DOANE
Lucinda 1829-1882
...........................371
DODGE
Cemantha 1804-1861
...........................249
Diana 1778-1833 .111,
441
Hannah 1802-.......167
Sarah 1831-1850...464
Thomas 1798- 611
Wilson 1829-1897 .624
DOHERTY
Agnes C. 1835-1912
...........................600
DOLAN
Sarah 377
DOLE
Abigail 1790-.........172
DOLLIVER
Margaret -1760...8, 34
DOLLOFF
Sally 1781-1855 169
DOMETT
Matilda 1822-1903 597
DOOLITTLE
Charles 1813-1889 528
Cyrus 1797-1856...292
Eleanor -1889 356
Relief 1806-1889...471
DORAN
James T. 1828-1900
...........................399
DORMAN
Cyrus 1799-1871...279
John 1763-1857 273
DORNBURG
Rachel 1824-1901 .490
DORR
Priscilla 1764-1846
..................122, 479

DORRANCE
Elisha 1775-1846..242
Trumbull 1774-1824
...........................239
DOUGLAS
Mary 1811- 508
Phebe 183
DOUGLASS
Samuel 1767-1841 270
DOW
Abel 1757-1826......65,
255
Almira 1798-1875.256
Cyrus 1764-1842....65,
256
Cyrus M. 1809-1873
...........................256
Enoch 1773-..........318
Job 1770- 317
Laura 1796-1875 ..256
Lois 1790-1882 256
Lydia 1794-1852...321
Lydia 1821-1892...325
Sally 1785-1809....255
William 1788-1816 256
DOWD
Flavia 1814-1886..611
DOWINING
Henry W. 1819-1837
...........................401
DOWNER
Clarissa Ann.118, 465
Mary -1766 ....14, 53
Sarah 1699-1784 4, 14
DOWNING
Abigail 1768-1814 201
Alice 1778-1820 201
Amos 1783-1856 ...201
Catherine 1804-1812
...........................401
Catherine 1814-....401
Hannah 1780-1867
...........................201
John 1766-1852 201
John W. 1808-1858
...........................401
Molly 1774-...........201
Nancy 1821-..........401
Palfrey 1761-1835.140
Richard D. 1785-1875
...........................201
Russell 1796-1881 215
Sally 1772-1854 201
Samuel 1742-1812.50,
200
Samuel 1765-1847 201
Thomas 1770-1852 201
Thomas 1772-1835
...................100, 401
Thomas 1800-1859 401
Willard W. 1811-1812
...........................401
Willard W. 1816-1880
...........................401
DRAKE

Amelia 1841-1896 630
Mary 1764-1841 .. 124,
490
Samuel 1775-1845 179
DRAPER
Mary L. 1821-1892 576
DRESBACH
Charles F. 1806-1847
.... 331
DRESSER
Aaron 1801-1890 .. 332
Caroline 590
George W. 1806- ... 531
John M. 1807-1879
.... 466
DREW
Charles 1800-1890 429
Elijah C. 1818-1877
.... 425
Sally 1791-1855 ... 106,
419
DUDBRIDGE
Loretta 1813-1881 260
DUDLEY
Caroline 1832- 616
Jason 94
Nancy 1809-1857 . 580
DUNBAR
Abigail 1814-1888 330
DUNCAN
James 328
DUNCKLEE
Francis 1791-1859 189
DUNHAM
Chauncey 1798-1850
.... 219
Eber 1798-1878 219
Lydia -1849 322
Orson 1818-1902 .. 534
Sebre 1796-1876 ... 595
Thankful 1799-1831
.... 288
DUNKLE/DUNKLEE
Hezekiah 1784-1863
.... 186
Nancy 1806-1845 . 441
Phebe E. 1832-1917
.... 223
DUNLAP
Melinda J. 1830-1883
.... 280
Robert 1779-1865. 318
DUNN
Berry W. 1823-1898
.... 382
Ferline 1812-1863 611
DUNSHEE
Emily 1809-1867 .. 376
DUNTON
Amasa 1772-1836. 236
Eliza 1801-1850 .. 222,
487
Josiah 1777-1866 . 236
Leonard 1774-1775
.... 236

Leonard 1782-1832
.... 236
Levinia 54, 213
Lodicia 1794-1857 215,
487
Lois 1784- 236
Ralph 1792-1793 .. 487
Samuel 1748-1813
.... 124, 486
Samuel 1749-1813 61,
236
Samuel 1787-1798 236
Sarah 1779- 236
DUPREE
Mary 1813- 607
DURANT
Benjamin 1800-1875
.... 361
Caroline 1813-1862
.... 341
Mary 1794-1870 ... 322
DURGIN
Lydia 1785-1841 .. 169
DURKEE
Abiel 1774-1778 ... 200
Abigail 1756- 50
Amasa 1798- 472
Elizabeth 1794-1872
.... 242
Fisk 1803-1885 242
Harvey 1797-1826 242
Henry 1749-1820 ... 49,
200
Henry 1770- 120, 200,
472
Henry 1795-1838 .. 472
John 1762-1838 62,
241
John 1784-1836 241
Lucy 1728-1747 13
Mary 1791-1873 ... 242
Oren 1786-1862 241
Robert 1779-1867. 203
Sally 1789-1879 241
Sarah 1777-1806 .. 200
Sybil 1731-1794 12, 49
DURYEA
Catherine A. 1830-
1903 375
DUSTIN
Elizabeth 1773- 80,
305
Hannah 1801- 154,
614
John R. 1784- 169
Sally 1790- ... 152, 607
DUSTON
Betsey 1782- ... 36, 153
DUTCHER
Charity 1764-1807 91,
355
Cornelia 1816- 243
Sylvia 1789-1865. 115,
458
DUTTON

Alva 1798-1878 212
Amarilla 1799-1888
.... 483
Jane 1771-1849 ... 124,
492
Sarah 1822- 618
DWIGHT
Abigail A. 1841-1926
.... 606
Emily 1832- 517
DWINELL/DWINELLS
Caroline 1824-1891
.... 349
Catherine 1786- 89
Chandler 1840-1904
.... 349
Charles W. 1834-1912
.... 349
Charlotte 1789- 89,
348
Charlotte 1836-1860
.... 349
Charlotte 1839-1841
.... 349
Elijah 88
Emma 1822- 349
George 1835-1841 349
James 1800-1859 .. 89,
349
Jonathan 1759- 21, 89
Jonathan 1795-1881
.... 89, 348
Julianna 1833-1913
.... 349
Kate 1829-1860 349
Lydia S. 1787-1874 89,
348
Mehitable P. 1805-
1880 .... 89, 347
Parker 1827-1854 349
Ruth 1751-1833 34
Sally 1830- 349
Sarah 1837-1868 .. 349
DYER
Patience -1811 202
Susie M. 1845-1941
.... 389
Waty 284
DYKE
Mary M. 1810-1905
.... 187
EAGER
Charles H. 1821-1891
.... 616
EAMES
Anna 1823-1913 ... 580
James 1789-1855 . 593
Mary 1765-1845 ... 277
EAMS
Elcy Parks 1820-1902
.... 449
EASTMAN
Abiah 1776-1776 .. 168
Abiah 1782-1840 .. 168
Abigail 1764- 127

Abigail 1794- 501
Amos 1790-1845 ... 505
Asa P. 1810-1869 . 414
Benjamin 1775-1846
.... 169
Benjamin F. 1802-
1878 415
Betsey 1800-1886. 502
Caroline 1796- 501
Charles 1802-1844 501
Charlotte 1798-1826
.... 415
Daniel 1792-1885. 170
Dorcas 1786-1873 168
Dorothy 1761- 127
Dorothy 1812-1852
.... 503
Ebenezer 1765-1833
.... 105, 415
Eleanor 1819-1907 427
Electa 1807-1881 . 503
Elizabeth 1795-1891
.... 396
Emily W. 1820-1887
.... 431
Esther 1788-1876. 169
Fry H. 1790-1874. 169
Hannah 1778-1876
.... 168
Hannah 1796-1887
.... 170
Henry 1786-1838 . 169
Horace 1798-1839 502
Hubbard 1809-1891
.... 502
Hyman 1811-1814 502
Hyman 1815-1855 503
Ichabod 1773-1841
.... 127, 503
Isaac 1808-1829 ... 502
Isaiah F. 1794-1866
.... 450
James 1820-1822 . 503
Jarvis 1810-1844 .. 501
Jeremiah L. 1795-
1854 398
Job 1782-1869 169
John 1770-1827 ... 127,
502
John 1794-1854 170
John 1797-1885 502
Jonathan 1770-1868
.... 168
Jonathan 1781-1867
.... 413
Judith 1793-1848 . 415
Laura 1800- 501
Lucy 1795-1861 477
Lucy 1805-1822 503
Lydia 1779-1872 .. 165
Mabel 1816-1906 .. 503
Martha 1788-1887 168
Martha 1831-1914 633
Mary 1806-1841 ... 242

Mary A. 1809-1834 415
Nancy 1806- 501
Noah 1753-1829.... 42, 169
Noah 1780- 169
Noah 1784-1857....169
Phebe 1773-1866...168
Phebe 1800-1877...429
Phebe B. 1799-1893 170
Philura 1815- 501
Polly 1772-1859 168
Polly C. 1801-1855 170
Remembrance 1802- 96, 381
Richard 1747-1826 42, 168
Richard 1778-1852 169
Richard 1780-1876 168
Rispah 1790-1790.501
Ruth 1766-1829 ...127, 500
Sally 1766-1801 168
Samuel 1716-1789 29, 127
Samuel 1768- 127, 500
Samuel 1792-1858 501
Sarah 1749-1836... 23, 99
Seba 1798-1850.....501
Solomon 1792-1866 431
Susanna 1786-1844 169
Thomas 1788-1846 396
Thomas 1805-1893 427
Umphira 1791-1792 501
Walter 1804- 501
Willard 1823-1912 503
William 1784-1872 168
EASTON
Edwin N. 1821-1913 340
EATMAN
Nancy 1803-1893 ..502
EATON
Abial 1803-1873....430
Abigail 1736-1817.. 71
Abigail 1756-1817.277
Abigail 1803-1899.548
Alfred 1820-1903 ..430
Amelia 1797-1823.505
Berry 1785-1867 ...506
Betsey P. 1815-1879 430
Betsy 1796-1876 ...430
Clara 1785- 505
Climena 1800-1800 430
Desire 1778-1859.. 65, 129, 257
D'Estaing 1782-1847 505

Diadama 1763-1788 ....128, 506
Dilla 1776-1855 ...129, 507
Dorothy G. 1823-1824 430
Ebenezer 1734-1815 ....29, 128
Ebenezer -1738.17, 71
Ebenezer 1760-1839 ....128, 506
Elizabeth 1767-.....128
Elsy 1793- 506
Eunice 1765- 128
Freelove 1778- 129
Gurden 1793-1868 505
Hannah 1771- 128
Hannah 1772- 108, 431
Hannah 1811-1821 430
Hannah C. 1792-1854 ....148, 585
Hepsibah -1743...5, 20
Horace 1790-1861.506
James F. 1808-1841 ....430, 431
Jeremiah 1774-.....108
Jeremiah 1794-.....430
Jeremiah 1805-1882 430
Joseph 1817-1886 .430
Lorinda 1787- 505
Malinda 1780-1865 505
Mariah 1800-1872 508
Marson 1806-1873 582
Mary 1759-............128
Mary 1776-1849...108, 432
Mary 1800-1883....430
Mehitable 1773-....274
Mehitable S. 1798-1869 430
Meriam 1769-128, 507
Nancy 1809-1902 ..430
Nathan 1755-1840 ....128, 505
Orville 1801-1885 .505
Osgood 1768-1836 108, 430
Osgood 1810-1863.430
Phebe 1737- 71
Phebe 1787-1868 .148, 586
Philip F. 1796-1877 429
Roswell 1773-1829 481
Sabrina 1795- 505
Samuel 1782-1871 181
Sarah 1769-1854..108, 430
Sarah 1798-1889...429
Sarah 1809- 561

Susannah 1778-...108, 432
Susannah 1803-1849 506
Sylvester 430
Thankful 1773-1799 ....128, 507
Thomas 1775-1812 .86
Timothy 1767- 277
William 533
William 1743-1780 25, 107
William 1766-1852 ....108, 429
William 1802- 430
William 1802-1880 430
EAYRS
Hannah 1809-1891 327
Rebekah 1806-1863 327
EDDY
Polly 1796- 435
EDES
Hannah B. 1813-1888 332
Samuel 1753-1846..86
EDGECOMB
Mary 1819-1907....369
EDGERLY
Samuel 1823- 419
EDICK
Roxana 1803-1893 468
EDMONDS
Benjamin 1794-1875 312
EDSON
Abigail 176
Isaiah -1798..........198
Keziah 1801-1877.501
Othniel W. 1818-1861 388
EDWARDS
Amos P. 1804-1843 234
Anna 1798- 234
Deborah 1807-1887 234
Erastus 1770-1850.60, 234
Erastus 1801-1880 234
Jerusha 1796-1829 234
Louisa 1826-1924 .379
EGGLESTON
Sarah 1801-1877...229
ELA
Lydia 1747-1826 ....24, 103
ELDREDGE/ELDRIDGE
Abigail 1786-.........245
Amelia 1802-.........411
Anna 1759-1833....284
Anna 1802-1891....412
Betsey 1796-1881 .412
Calista 1788-.........245

Caroline 1805-1885 412
Caroline 1816-1882 231
Celestia 1805-1829 412
Chester 1790- 245
Daniel D. 1801-1878 412
Eli 1803-1864........222
Elijah 1778-1799 ..237
Elizabeth 1781-.....245
Erastus 1775-1820 237
Evander 1798-1827 411
Freeman 1792-1861 245
Harvey 1792-1865 411
Hezekiah 1796-1881 234
Jemima 1755-1821 51, 204
John I. 1797-1866.412
Joseph 1759-... 62, 245
Mary 1792- 411
Philander 1809-1881 452
Polly 1786-1874 237
Rhoda 1780-1782 ..245
Rhoda 1784-..........245
Rosena 1786-1812.411
Sarah 1787-1857 ..411
Sarah 1813-1887 ..219
Solomon 105, 411
Sophronia 1799-1882 238
Sylvanus -1812 ....105, 412
Timothy 1773-1775 237
Timothy 1777- 237
Willis 1790-1854...411
Zoeth 61
Zoeth 1772-1780 ...236
Zoeth 1782-1844 ...236
ELKINS
Ruth B. 1801-1880 168
ELLEDGE
Hannah 1779-1805 195
ELLINGWOOD
John 1783-1816 180
ELLIOT
Elijah 1797-1873 ..254
Ethelwina 1804-1887 254
George 1757-1817..64, 253
Relecty 1795-1875 254
Sarah E. 1782-1861 253
ELLIOTT
Nancy 1821-1890 ..618
ELLIS
Bethiah 1790-1863 443

Betsey 1785-1874. 443
David 1798-1846. 540, 541
David H. 1820-1918 371
Deziah 1830-1907 371
Elisha 551
Elizabeth W. 1825-1862 371
Hannah 1840-1881 371
Isaac 1806-1858 ... 603
Jacob M. 1834-1908 371
Martin 1791-1871 . 94, 370
Martin 1818-1895 371
Mary J. 1820-1863 371
Perez R. 1814-1882 370
Reuben 1790-1869 540
Sarah G. 1816-1863 371
Thomas 1827-1838 371
Walter 1836-1911. 371

ELLISON
Alzina 1820- 378

ELMORE
Melinda 1805-1830 438

ELWELL
Frederick 1807-1892 522

ELY
Marcia 1812-1860 490

EMERICK
Christopher T. 1838-1867 382

EMERSON
Albert 1819-1864.. 581
Caroline F. 1820-1858 383
Mary E. 1826-1901 637
Stephen 1811-1885 344
Susan 1824- 429

EMERY
Abigail 1797-1859 170
Charles 1827-1900 388
Cynthia 174
David 1792-1875 .. 578
Dorcas 1791-1852. 170
Fanny 1801-1802 . 170
Hannah 1795-1883 170
Isabel 1820-1848.. 392
Joseph 1764-1830.. 42, 170
Joseph 1793-1796. 170
Joseph 1799-1886. 170
Melinda 1805-1827 170
Phebe 1788-1818.. 170
Ruth 1769-1864.... 201

Sarah 1790- 170

ENDICOTT
Mary 1782-1813 ... 180
Nathan Holt 1788-1816 180
Robert 1756-1819.. 45, 179
Robert 1785-1813. 180
Samuel 1793-1872 180
William 1799-1899 180

ENGLISH
Elizabeth 1833-1917 634
Levi 1784- 359

ENSWORTH
Thomas 1806-1868 493

EPPS
John 1809- 512

ESTERBROOK
Sophia 1821-1898. 374

ESTES
Aroline A. 1855- ... 634
Daniel 1801-1867. 594
Sumner 1827-1903 608

ESTEY
John 274

ESTY
Elizabeth 1755-1812 .... 70, 275

EVANS
Betsey 164
Thomas 1725-1802. 50

EVERDEN
Eunice 1803-1886. 262

EVERETT
Abby S. 1820-1896 242
Phineas 1776-1830 201
Samuel -1844 512

EVERTON
Emeline 1812-1857 458

EWELL
William 1804-1887 522

EWER
Anna 1816- 354

EWING
Ruth 1810-1892.... 548

FAIRBANK/FAIRBANKS
Daniel 1781- 126
Daniel 1806-1878. 494
Eunice 1821-1859. 495
Joseph 1741-1817.. 29, 125
Joseph 1773-1859 125, 494
Joseph 1796- 494
Joseph 1826-1916. 495
Joshua 1764-1812 125, 494
Martha 1839-1851 495
Mary 1817-1900 ... 494
Molly 1767-1823... 125
Molly 1794- 494
Oren 1798- 494
Orin 1829-1913 495
Orrin 1783- 126

Oshea 1802- 494
Peter 1824-1845... 495
Sabin 1822-1902 .. 495
Sally 1792- 494
Sarah 1816-1897.. 495
Sibbel 1779-1807. 125, 495
Stephen 1763-1783 125
Stephen 1787-1847 .... 126, 495
Sybil 1800- 494
Tabitha 1770-1846 125
Tabitha 1789- 494
Tabitha 1818-1899 495
Zeulime 1788- 494

FAIRMAN
Nancy 1786-1863 . 507

FALES
Azubah 1795-1835 447

FANNING
Maria 1832-1910.. 251

FARLEY
Benjamin 466

FARMER
Asa W. 1823-1886 613
Rosannah 1804-1875 210
Sybil 1774- 274
William 1720- 33

FARNHAM/FARNUM
1791- 289
1823- 428
Aaron 1814-1839.. 423
Abiel 1780-1864 .. 107, 426
Abiel 1808-1836 ... 422
Abiel 1808-1876 ... 424
Abigail 1760-.. 76, 289
Abigail 1763-1847 284
Abigail 1783-1855 107, 427
Abigail 1799-1827 292
Abigail 1801-1890 294
Abigail 1815-1894 294
Abigial 1807- 421
Adelia 1823-1858 . 426
Alfred 1817-1848.. 428
Alfred T. 1808-1886 293
Allan 1811- 293
Ame 1776-1813 284
Amos 1792-1812... 148
Amos 1816- 587
Amsa 1789-1839 .. 289
Anna 1767-1778... 107
Anna 1783-1854.. 107, 426
Arthur B. 1759-1807 284
Avery T. 1811-1889 293
Azubah 1797-1873 421
Benjamin 1739-1812 .... 25, 106

Benjamin 1768-1850 .... 107, 421
Benjamin 1804-1892 .... 414, 422
Benjamin 1820-.... 426
Benjamin F. 1801-1885 292
Betsey 1796- 421
Calvin 1819-1819. 428
Charles 1803-1888 423
Charles 1810-1887 293
Charles 1814- 426
Clarissa 1766- 282
Clement M. 1822-1843 426
Cornelia 1799- 421
Daniel 1770-1847. 184
Daniel 1777-1814. 282
Daniel O. 1807-1886 294
Deborah 1830-1833 428
Ebenezer 1747- 74
Eliab 1731-1806 19, 75
Eliab 1775-1855 .... 76, 293
Eliab 1796-1873 ... 292
Elijah 1768-1837.. 284
Eliphalet 1725- 18, 75
Eliphalet 1751-1754 75
Eliphalet 1759-1833 .... 75, 288
Eliphalet 1794-1870 289
Elisha P. 1797-1871 294
Eliza 1809-1880 ... 423
Elizabeth 1742-1786 .... 74, 284
Elizabeth 1752-1832 .... 75, 288
Elizabeth 1773-.... 284
Elizabeth 1822-1875 424
Emily 1802-1888. 414, 422
Emily 1814-1856.. 428
Emily 1828-1861.. 295
Enoch 1776-1815.. 300
Ephraim 1700-1775 7, 24
Ephraim 1721-1750 .... 18, 74
Ephraim 1733-1827 .... 24, 105
Ephraim 1745- 74, 287
Ephraim 1760-1776 284
Ephraim 1769- 288
Ephraim 1770-1836 .... 107, 422
Ephraim 1777- 76
Erastus 1770-1813 282
Esther 1772-1854 105, 415

Eunice 1757- ...74, 287
Fanny 1808- 293
Frances 1819-1904425
George -1812.........422
George 1812-1890.423
George 1813- 421
George 1825-1891.295
George B. 1818-1896
..........................426
George W. 1772- ... 76,
293
George W. 1801-1881
..........................292
George W. 1815-1852
..........................293
Haines 1771-1824107,
423
Hannah 1762-1841 74
Hannah 1789-1835
..................143, 564
Hannah 1797- 289
Hannah 1799-1800
..........................421
Hannah C. 1793-...414
Harriet 1811-1815 422
Harriet 1820-1907 295
Harriet 1828-..........426
Henry 1687-1732 5, 18
Henry 1715-1799 .. 18,
73
Henry 1742-1824 .. 73,
282
Henry 1773-1852 ..288
Henry 1803-1883 ..293
Henry 1820-1893 ..424
Henry 1826-1906 ..293
Hiram 1807-1872..423
Isaac 1766-1813 284
Isaac 1804-1877 565
Israel 1758-1842 ... 35,
148
Israel 1790-1861 ..148,
587
Ivory 1813-1828 428
James D. 1819-1892
..........................425
Jared 1783-1835 ...282
Jeffrey A. 1772-1841
....................76, 292
Jeffrey A. 1817-1883
..........................293
Jemima 1719- 18
Jemima 1754- 74
Jemima 1773- 285
Jemima 1773-1859285
Jennet W. 1816-....414
Jeremiah 1785-1869
..................107, 428
John 1743-1746 25
John 1762-1763 105
John 1766- 107, 420
John 1780-1781 282
John 1794-1840 420
John 1820-1892 428
John C. 1815-1877557

John S. 1806-1884 424
Jonathan 1773-1778
..........................107
Jonathan 1778-1831
..................107, 425
Jonathan 1798-.....289
Joseph 1748- 121
Joseph 1748-1777 ..74,
285
Joseph B. 1797-1887
..........................422
Joshua 1723-1797 ..18,
75
Joshua 1758-1781 ...75
Joshua 1771-1846.284
Joshua 1781-..........76
Joshua 1793-.........289
Judith 1764-1851.105,
413
Julia 1819-1881 294
Keziah 1741-1741 ...74
Keziah 1751-...74, 286
Lavina 1813-.........414
Lorenzo E. 1826-1832
..........................426
Lucinda 1795-1856
..........................292
Lucretia H. 1824-1899
..........................426
Lucy 1826-1888 346
Lucy 1832- 426
Luther 1809-1813 .422
Luther 1816-1897.422
Lydia 1744-1785 73,
282
Lydia 1756-.....46, 181
Lydia 1768-1858 ...282
Lydia 1776-1842 ..107,
424
Lydia 1780-...........172
Lydia 1803-1864 ...594
Lydia 1806-1834 ...422
Mahala 1803-........422
Mahala 1816-1861 294
Malinda 1814-.......294
Manassah 1717-1768
..........................73
Manassah 1739-1808
....................74, 283
Manasseh 1717-1768
..........................18
Mariah 1799-1814 294
Martha 1762-1843 .76,
290
Mary 1714-180211, 43
Mary 1729-1736......24
Mary 1737-1805.....25,
105
Mary 1762-1838......76
Mary 1764-1816...107,
419
Mary 1780-1847...149,
588
Mary 1787-...........289
Mary 1803-...........421

Mary 1812-1864....298
Mary 1816-1877....295
Mary S. 1810-1892424
Mary W. 1802-1831
..........................423
Matilda 1822-1901295
Mercy 1764- 76
Merrill 1794-1871.421
Milton 1812- 428
Moses 1769-1840 .105,
414
Moses 1814-1847 ..423
Moses H. 1797-1869
..........................291
Moses H. 1811-1908
..........................414
Nancy 1793-1800..421
Nancy 1795-1871 ..422
Naomi 1760-1832.105,
412
Nathaniel 1775-1861
..................107, 423
Nathaniel 1813-1905
..................424, 427
Oliver 1828- 426
Phebe 70
Phebe 1713-1750 ...18,
73
Phebe 1731-1806 ...12,
46
Phebe 1746-1808 ...73,
283
Phebe 1750- 70, 275
Phebe 1756- 75, 289
Phebe 1774- 282
Phebe 1788-1863 .148,
586
Phebe 1795-1868 ..291
Phebe 1809-1888 ..294
Phebe 1814-1894 ..293
Polly 1791-1862 421
Rebecca 1827- 428
Roswell 1792-1860420
Roswell 1803-1883424
Roxy 1803-1876 294
Ruby 1772-1840....282
Rufus 1801-...........421
Rufus 1816-1886...424
Russell 1764-1820 .76,
291
Sally 1771-1848 285
Sally 1796-1800 421
Sally 1801-............421
Sally A. 1812-1897294
Samuel 1805-1893 414
Sarah 1747-1829....25,
107
Sarah 1749-1758.....75
Sarah 1767- ..105, 413
Sarah 1769-1807....76,
291
Sarah 1771- 77, 298
Sarah 1787-1864..107,
428
Sarah 1804- 293

Sarah 1825-1826 ..428
Sarah 1830-1844 ..295
Sarah J. 1818-1879
..........................587
Solomon 1805-1826
..........................423
Stephen 1728-.........18
Stephen 1765-1839
..........................284
Stephen 1779-186876,
294
Stephen 1805-1889
..........................293
Stephen N. 1805-1879
..........................294
Susan D. 1801-1880
..........................422
Susannah 1781-1843
..................105, 415
Thomas P. 1814-1898
..........................425
Thompson 1805- ...421
William 1825-1892426
FARNSWORTH
Hannah 1777-1828
..........................311
Ira 1799-1860 212
Keziah 1742-1827 138,
549
Submit 1750- 119, 468
FARR
Freeman 1810-1891
..........................338
James 1816-1859..338
Joel 1821-1864......338
Jonathan D. 1830-
1903..................338
Lucinda 1818-1848
..........................338
Nancy 1822-.........338
Sally 1808-1889 338
Stephen 1781-187287,
337
FARRAR
Lucy 1714-1791 ..5, 22
Samuel 1805-1862 617
FARRINGTON
Lois 1783-1815 175
Lucy 1787-1835 176
Nancy 1779-1858.108,
429
FARWELL
Adaline 1833-1909623
FASSET/FASSETT
Abel H. 1806-1886 262
Alfreada 1803- 262
Amos T. 1809-........262
Anna 1804-1873....262
Pearly 1769-1826...66,
261
Pearly 1800-1884..262
Sarah 1813-1886 ..337
FAULKNER
Dorcas 1766-1837 ..81,
308

John 1785-1823.... 195
Joseph 1783-1831.. 99, 393
Joseph W. 1812-1871 393
Lydia A. 1810-1881 393
Mary P. 1817-1892 393
Persis 1775-1872.. 169

FAVOR
Reuben 1806-1862 588

FAY
Abigail 1806-1871 471
Caroline 1827-1901 612
Eugenia 1817-1892 422
Sarah 1786-1869.. 313
Stephen 1809-1862 384

FEARN
Sophronia 1827-1922 350

FEAVER
Mary 1739-..... 35, 150

FELLOWS
Betsey P. 1806- 218
Eleazer 1772- . 56, 218
James 328
Leonard 1800-1849 218
Lothrop 1803-1845 218

FELT
Amos 1799-1812... 197
Anne 1723-1816 . 9, 36
Benjamin 1780-1827 197
Betsy 1797-1798... 197
Henry 1791-1872.. 197
Jonathan 1753-1807 .... 48, 197
Jonathan 1776-1862 197
Joseph 1787-1874. 197
Lydia 1778-1827... 197
Marcy 1793-1873.. 197
Martha 1783-1863 197
Milly 1795-1814 ... 197
Polly 1785-1855.... 197
Solomon 1789-1801 197

FENN
Sina 1805-1885 232

FENTON
Abiel 1767-1822 ... 205
Achsah 1773-1863 235
Albray 1803-......... 233
Almira 1818- 229
Alva 1806-1891 233
Amy 1792-1867 233
Chester 1782-1783 210
Chloe 1780-1823... 210
Chloe 1790-1790... 229
Darius 1801-1885. 229

Deborah 1769-1771 233
Elijah 1778-.......... 233
Elizabeth 1777-.... 210
Eunice 1799- 229
Experience 1784-1846 233
Francis 1718-.... 14, 53
Francis 1751- .. 53, 62, 210
Horace 1812-1850 229
Joseph 1760-1814.. 60, 233
Joseph 1801- 233
Julia 1795-1850.... 233
Leister 1786-........ 210
Lewis 1806-.......... 229
Lois 1783-............. 233
Louisa 1809-......... 229
Luke 1769- 59, 229
Luke 1792-1848 ... 229
Lyman 1804-1884 229
Mary 1748-1822 .... 53, 209
Mary 1790-1814 ... 233
Mehitable 1767-1847 .... 132, 524
Miner 1808-1870.. 233
Nathan 1797-1873 233
Oliver 1778-1781.. 210
Orrin 1791-1791... 229
Phebe 1783-.......... 210
Welthy 1795-1887 229
Zilpha 1813-1880 . 224

FENTON,
Orrin 1797- 229

FERGUSON
James 1810-1867 . 401
John..................... 405

FERRY
Elijah 1790-1856.. 459
Laura 1816-1874.. 453

FERSON
David 1793-1847.. 321

FIELD
Moses 1779-1833.. 296
Samuel 1793-1843 435

FIELDS
Charlotte 1793-1878 563

FIFE
James 1742- 165
Mary 1809-1842 ... 602
Robert 1766-1854. 165
Sarah 1785-1865.. 165

FIFIELD
Alonzo 1821-1892. 593
Charles F. 1826-1863 397

FILER
Delos L. 1817-1879 264

FILKINS
Sally 1817-1887.... 264

FINCH

James M. 1811-1844 295

FISH
Elizabeth 1782-.... 239
Levi 1811-1876..... 344
Nathan 174
Sarah 1836-1913.. 620

FISHBECK
Martha 1820-1870 585

FISHER
Betsey -1814......... 237
Daniel 1796-1844. 509
Horace 1819-1885 407
Joel E. 1815-1854. 573
Otis 1811-1878..... 622
Weston A. 1806-1887 573

FISK/FISKE
Aaron 1777-1822.. 275
Abba 1815-1900 ... 622
Abel 1784-1877 ... 156, 621
Abel 1804-1873 622
Achsah 1812-1847 622
Allethenia 1819-... 622
Allis 1763-1850 ... 105, 412
Ann 1808-1878..... 622
Charles 1782-1868 225
Daniel 1766-......... 105
Delphine 1808-1839 311
Hannah 1740-1813 14, 59
Harriet 1817-1905 622
John 1731-1790..... 24, 104
John 1809-1892.... 622
John W. 1758-1776 105
Maria 1821-1888.. 622
Molly 1755- 105
Rufus 1773-1848.. 235
Sarah 1761-.. 105, 411
Sarah 1806-1879.. 622

FITCH
Calvin A. 1799- 434
Catherine L. 1802-1881 434
Charles 1804-1844 434
Daniel 1762-1855 109, 434
Daniel A. 1796-1886 434
Lot 1795-1795 434
Louisa 1801-1878. 556
Nancy 1809-1888 . 434

FITTS
Mary 1797-1882... 597

FITZGERALD
Abigail A. 1815-1888 294

FLACK
Mary 1828-1856... 337

FLANDERS

Mary 1803-1871 ... 561
Samuel 421

FLETCHER
Adolphus 1795-1851 .... 98, 389
Almira M. 1826-1892 389
Charles E. 1820-1893 389
Ebenezer E. 1837-1923 389
Eliza 1803-1882 ... 314
George W. 1832-1912 389
Gilbert M. L. 1830-1910 389
Hannah 1792-1880 98, 388
Ira J. 1834-1915... 389
Jesse L. 1822-1900 389
John 1748-1828...... 22
John 1819-1911.... 630
Lucinda 1789-1875 98
Lucy 274
Luke 1759-1841 23, 97
Mary 1813-1849... 423
Mary 1820-1892... 620
Mary 1839-1861... 389
Nathaniel 1822-1900 624
Rachel 240
Rebecca 1829-1908 389
Remembrance 1752-1833 .... 69, 270
Sabina 1798- 98
Sarah 1841-1916.. 389
William W. 1818-1877 389

FLING
Lester 468

FLINT
Abiel 1809-1889 ... 581
Abigail -1723...... 5, 17
Abigail 1771-1798 146, 194, 579
Abigail 1814-1888 578
Abigail 1816-1834 581
Amos 1778-1873.. 147, 580
Amos 1801-1870... 578
Amos 1803-1895... 581
Amos 1811-1883... 580
Asenath 1769-1817 .... 146, 579
Asenath 1806-1879 581
Charles J. 1810-1841 578
Daniel 1767-1853 146, 578
Daniel 1799-1814. 578
Daniel 1805-1870. 580
Dorcas 1797-1880 578
Ebenezer 1742-1829 .... 35, 146

Ebenezer 1765-1833 .... 146, 185, 578
Ebenezer 1793-1870 578
Ebenezer 1804-1820 580
Eleanor 1808-1875580
Eleanor 1812-1836581
Ephraim 1773-1859 .... 146, 194, 580
Ephraim 1800-1865 ....557, 580
Hannah 1782-1866 96, 381
Henry 1801-1847 ..578
Isaac 1803-1804 578
Isaac 1805-1832 578
John 1776-1778 147
John 1780-1847 ...147, 581
John 1795- 578
John 1805-1831 581
Joseph H. 1802-1871 580
Leander 1816-1820 580
Lizzy 1812-1815....578
Luther 1807-1890 .579
Lydia 1797-1880 ...578
Mahala 1814-1908 581
Mary 1793-1876....312
Mary L. 1808-1891578
Miriam 1798-1856 448
Phebe 1782-1797...147
Phebe 1810-1903...581
Ruth 1814-1906 580
Samuel 1817-1838 581
Sarah 1783-1863 ..147, 581
Sarah 1804-1836...581
Sarah 1812-1817...578
Sophronia 1808-1883 581
Tabatha 1721-1808 17, 71
William 1803-1804579
FLOWERS
Elizabeth 1810-.....395
FLOYD
Hepsibah 1779-1840 ....94, 372
Joanna 1780-1845 .546
FOLLANSBEE
Arminda 1812-1888 563
Sarah 1792-1855...552
FOLSOM
Mary 1794-1891....601
FOOT
Mary A. 1828- 310
FOOTE
Isaac 1817-1893....217
Newell 1784-1871 .416
Olivia 1814-1887...416
FORBES

Amelia A. 1803-1891 476
Maria 1818-1846...328
Wells 1812-1880 ...608
FORD
Amos 1808- 440
Asena 1804- 440
Betsey 1797-1880 .440
Dinah 1735- 14, 58
Ebenezer 1789- 440
Keziah 1721-.....18, 73
Lydia 1804- 440
Nathaniel 1765-1849 ....110, 440
Nathaniel 1795-...438, 440
Sarah 1714-1789....18, 75
Silas 1802-1855 440
Stephen 1799-1873 440
William 1790- 440
William C. 1776-...168
FORMAN
Marvin 1829-1870 485
FORREST
Anna C. 1790-1823 ....100, 399
FORSAITH
Jane 1782-1871.....318
Jonathan 1772-1821 318
Peggy 1797- 321
FOSS
Augusta 1879-.......630
James 1820-1860...368
Ruth 268
Sarah 1795-1886...324
FOSTER
Abigail 1771-1846 ..99, 394
Abigail 1789-1876.510
Abigail 1799-1853.187
Amos 1794-1882 ...187
Amy 1799-1823.....558
Ann 1805-1869......188
Ann M. 1815- 363
Anna 1781-1858....201
Caleb 1825-1901 ...385
Chloe 1799-1886 ...240
Davis 1771-1855 ..141, 558
Dorcas 1787-1879 .187
Elizabeth P. 1828- 1891 385
Elizabeth R. 1769- .99, 394
Gideon 1739-1817 ..23, 99
Hannah 1716- 9, 35
Hannah 1754-1794 .44
Hannah 1771-1848 59, 231
Hannah 1796-1885 187

Harriet 1810-1886 545
Harriet 1823-1889 346
Henry P. 1796-1861 ....96, 385
Henry T. 1826-1879 385
Isaac 1751-......47, 187
Isaac H. 1789-1882 187
Joshua 1766-1795143, 568
Leonard 1805-1874 570
Lucy 1800-1838 179
Mary 1784-1862....178
Mary 1785-1862....187
Mary 1816-1910....561
Mary A. 1780-1822 ....102, 407
Mehitable 1772-1859 ....137, 547
Nancy 1801-..........558
Nathan 1798-1877 589
Phebe 1802-1886 ..188
Priscilla 1778-1848.99
Sarah 1745- 27, 111
Sarah 1775-1847....99, 395
Sarah 1790-1853...182
Sylvia T. 1821-1861 607
Tamisen 1773-1776 99
Timothy 1790-1863 187
Timothy 1821-1902 419
Tirzah 1802- 558
William 1772-1833172
FOUTZ
Charlotte..............368
FOX
Eliphalet 1802-1862 445
Harriet 1836-1873 591
Joel 1784-1861......212
Lucia 1766-1855 ....64, 254
Prudence 1813-1896 479
Willis 1800-1852...261
FRANCIS
Abigail A. 1800-1891 444
Harriet 1821-1855 533
Maria 1794-1834 ..203
FRANKLIN
Dianah 1818-1874 505
Mary 1810-1837....531
Samuel 1815-1897 352
FRARY
Isabel 1811-1850...438
FRAZER
James...................547
FRAZIER

Theodore 1799-1884 339
FREDERICK
Rhoda 1799-1880 ..268
FREEMAN
Charles W. 1812-1813 398
Eliza R. 1819-1877398
Jonathan 1783-1871 ....100, 398
Martha 1823-1914 399
Mary E. 1831-1927 418
Mary R. 1814-1891 398
Otis R. 1809-1902 .398
Ruth 1816-1901 398
Sarah E. 1821-......398
Susan 1826-1826 ..399
FRENCH
Diana 1813-1891 ..417
Elizabeth 1815-.....421
George 1809-1883 .564
James 1785-..........550
John 1783-1861 413
Lydia 1784-1852 ...240
Mary 1755-179020, 85
Phineas C. 1805-1870 322
Reuben 1819-1890 621
Sarah 1728- 25, 109
Sarah D. 1812-1840 395
FRINK
Clarina 1809-........255
Elias 1770-1854.....65, 255
Henry O. 1836-1915 386
Lucia 1795-...........255
Mary E. 1831-1897 386
Mary T. 1801-1865255
Orlando 1810-1877 97, 386
Sarah E. 1846-1909 386
Silas H. 1797-1876255
FRISBEE
Amos 1803-1857 ...499
Anna 1806-1869....499
Elizabeth 1810-1886 499
Ephraim 1778-1862 ....126, 498
Jane 1808- 499
Mary 1815-1905....499
Roswell 1802-1880 499
Susan 499
Sybil......................499
FROST
Benjamin P. 1800- 1827 179
Betsey 1781-1819 .179

Daniel 1748-1839 .. 73, 283
Daniel 1787-1863 . 283
Dorothy C. 1785-1822 179
Elizabeth 1795-1863 420
Emma J. 1834-1920 565
Harriet H. 1791-1818 179
Hezekiah 1778-1827 283
Jane 1810-1850 562
Lardana 1802-1830 602
Lewis 1819-1886 .. 590
Lucy 1798-1842 179
Mary 1787-1846 ... 179
Nathan H. 1778-1784 179
Nathan H. 1789-1866 179
Ruth 1796-1873 581
Sally 1779-1863 179
Samuel A. 1795-1848 179
William 1754-1836 45, 178
William 1783-1784 179
William 1793-1866 179
FRY/FRYE
Abigail 1790- 290
Alfred 1788-1848 .. 290
Charles F. 1784-1845 290
Clarissa 1799-1842 290
Henry L. 1786-1860 290
Phebe R. 1792-1838 290
Sarah 1797-1866 .. 290
FRYE
Abiel 1734-1806 .... 76, 289
Abiel 1774-1820 ... 175
Alfred 1787-1867 .. 176
Betsy 1781-1862 ... 175
Caleb 1813-1819 ... 308
Daniel 1773-1837 ... 81
Daniel 1807-1864 . 308
Hannah 1785-1863 176
Hannah 1802-1850 559
Isaac 1748-1791 .... 44, 175
Isaac 1769-1814 ... 175
James 1810-1859 . 308
John 1754-1843 ... 137, 546
John 1775-1851 175
John 1798-1878 308
John 1805-1883 546

Joshua 1779-1864 175
Nancy 1799-1809 . 308
Nathan 1808-1884 395
Phebe 1721- 19, 77
Robinson 1771-1816 .... 80, 308
Robinson 1805-1818 308
Sarah 1717-1804 ... 11, 41
Sarah 1790-1835 .. 176
Sarah W. 1797-1873 566
Susannah 1803-1868 308
Timothy 1773-1776 175
Timothy H. 1777-1830 175
William 1801-1844 547
FULLER
Adelphia 1811-1881 451
Andrew H. 1811-1891 231
Chloe 1774-1854 .. 239
Clarissa 1775-1834 481
Daniel 1789-1856 . 239
David 1799-1882 .. 537
Dean 1791-1864 ... 589
Dorcas 1777-1869 . 481
Elijah 1777-1864 .. 239
Elisha 1782-1837 . 239
Elizabeth 1775-1837 300
Eunice 1796-1868 . 547
George W. 1804-1877 531
Hannah M. 1834-1897 385
Harvey 1784-1860 239
Jerusha H. 1815-1881 545
John 1787-1850 467
John 1803-1871 231
Joseph 1739-1805 .. 61, 239
Joseph 1760- 138, 547
Joseph 1760-1837 133, 529
Joseph 1779- 239
Joseph 1792- 530
Josiah 1764-1835 .. 62, 243
Lewis 1797-1883 .. 243
Loren 210
Ludophicus 1797-1802 243
Mary 1772-1851 ... 239
Mary 1798- 530
Mary 1822-1904 ... 324
Mary E. 379
Mertia 1799- 243
Moses 1794- 530

Persis 1796-1876 .. 530
Rhoda 1808- 530
Roxana 1804- 530
Sarah 1768- 200
Sarah 1802- 530
Susanna 1795- 547
Thomas 1765-1837 239
Timothy 122
FULLERTON
Beulah 1790-1861 553
FULLINGTON
Hannah 1802-1866 242
FULMER
Mary 1790-1875 ... 481
FURBUSH
Charles 1709-1756 3, 9
GAGE
Charlotte 1806-1846 190
Eunice 1786-1872 182
Moses 1791-1877 .. 327
Pierce 1813-1891 .. 619
Richard 1776-1855 413
Sally 299
GAGER
Angeline 1805-1891 238
GAGGILL
Hannah 1753- 127
John 29, 127
GAINES
Anna E. 1806-1860 206
GALE
Eliza 1815- 408
Hannah 1774-1775 102
Hannah 1779-1868 ....101, 102, 403
Harriet N. 1821-1856 408
John 1784-1787 102
Maria L. -1842 430
Mary 1772-1842 .. 102, 407
Mary A. 1808-1879 408
Moses 1746-1827 ... 24, 102
Moses 1771-1851 .. 102
Moses 1818-1821 .. 408
Nancy 1816-1908 . 408
Nathaniel 1777-1800 102
Samuel A. 1781-1829 .... 102, 407
Samuel A. 1814- ... 408
Sarah R. 1812-1892 408
Seneca 1791-1877 480
GALEUCIA
Daniel 1740-1825 . 196
GARDNER
Oliver 1760-1812 . 131, 520

William 1790-1877 520
GARFIELD
David 1817-1901 .. 634
Maria R. 1824-1848 372
GARRETSON
Nathan 1811-1896 518
GARRISON
Sarah 1795-1868 .. 221
GARVIN
Samuel 1777-1837 165
GARY
Sarah B. 1834-1878 592
GATES
Abiathar 1769- 184
James 1803-1888 . 485
Mary E. 1775-1857 549
GAY
Hannah -1803 83, 318
Harriet 1804-1835 242
Nathaniel 1814-1889 192
GAYLORD
George 1803- 259
Hector 1798-1848. 259
John 1790-1866 292
Moses 1768-1812 ... 66, 259
Sarah E. 1800-1843 259
Wells M. 1804-1846 259
GEE
Thomas 1821-1897 391
GEER
Anne 1745-1773 .... 51, 202
Electa 1815-1875 . 213
Hannah 1755-1858 51, 205
GENET
Edmond C. 1763-1834 296
GEORGE
Austin 1798-1863. 319
Eliza M. 1814-1905 396
Franklin A. 1835-1922 386
GERE
Joseph 1798-1865 523
GEROULD
Clarissa 1788-1816 448
GERRISH
Caroline 1803-1882 596
Elizabeth 1820-1882 427
Judith 1824-1913 . 416
Lydia -1788 6
GERRY
Anna 1811-1865 ... 456
Edson 1816-1904 .. 456

Elbridge 1818- 456
James 1820-1832..456
Rebecca 1813- 456
Sarah 1821-1863...456
Stephen 1784-1867
.................114, 456
Stephen 1814-1856
.....................456
GETCHELL
Dennis 1771-1852.266
GEYER
Augusta 1841-1918
.....................390
GIBBONS
Mary 1781-1834....443
GIBBS
Ann 1821-1867......325
Lucinda 1807-1889
.....................246
GIBSON
Anna 1769-1845.... 84,
327
Arrington 1812-1862
.....................528
Hannah P. 1803-1892
.....................581
Rebekah 1754-1824
.................27, 114
GIDDINGS
John H. 1832-1868613
Luke 1779-1826 159
GIFFORD
Franklin W. 1831-
1905 343
James E. 1821-1892
.....................343
Jesse W. 1827-1889
.....................343
Malantha W. 1829-
1897 343
Nancy P. 1818-1899
.....................343
Sarah J. 1825-1852
.....................343
Thomas S. 1823-1858
.....................343
William 1784-1849 88,
343
William R. 1816-...343
GILBARD
Elizabeth................. 9
GILBERT
Daniel 1796-1874.123,
486
Daniel 1825- 486
Daniel 1829-1890..486
Israel 1801-1868...483
Levi J. 1817-1879 .419
Nathaniel 1832-1842
.....................486
Sarah 1821-1907...486
William 1838-1841486
GILCHRIST
Martha 1794-1850 320
GILCREASE

John 1770-1826 201
GILE
Abigail 1803-1887.425
Jeremiah R. 1817-
1893 428
GILES
Orson S. 1803-1880
.....................442
GILL
Lydia 1800-1890 ...414
GILLILAND
Ann 1815- 492
GILMAN
Abby 1820-1829....351
Abigail 1777-1851.169
Ezekiel 1771-1804 169
John 1782- 169
John K. 1787-...90, 350
Martha 1815-........351
Martha 1817-1889
.................346, 351
Nathaniel 1748-.....42,
168
Nicholas 1773-1817
.................167, 169
Phebe 1783-1868 ..169
Sally 1779-............169
Samuel 1818-1884 351
GILMORE
Robert 1780- 319
GILPATRICK
Thomas 1767-1845267
GIPSON
John 238
GIRDLER
John 1814-1915 342
GIVENS
Maria E. 1793-1829
.....................541
GLASS
Sally A. 1818-1848571
GLAZIER
Abigail 1762-1835..22,
95
Carlos 1811-1885..489
Caroline F. 1811-1868
.....................489
Celinda 1818-1896230
Daniel 1776-1852...56,
220
David 1771-1858..124,
489
Eliza 1814-1815 220
Fear 1813-1891....231,
489
Isaac 1803-1835 220
Jasper M. 1809-1875
.....................489
Orlan 1805-1857..220,
230
Sarah 1800-1850...220
Susannah 1756-1799
.................22, 94
GLEASON

Amanda 1807-1892
.....................395
Foster 1816-1819..395
Gordon 1818-1819 396
Horatio 1810-........395
John 1785-1849 395
Jonathan 1771-1846
.................99, 395
Justin 1812-1887..395
Mary 1805-1866....453
Sarah 1805-1893...395
GLENNE
Joseph...................313
GLIDDEN
John L. 1782-1837 321
Nathaniel 1747-1814
.................83, 320
GLINES
Albert 1803-1878..428
GODDARD
Emily 1830-1906...562
Samuel 1782-1851 562
GODING
Thomas 1813-1876370
GODSHALL
Mary G. 1797-1880
.....................196
GODWIN
James 1791-1860..594
GOING
Charles 1819-1879345
GOLDEN
Mary 1810-1892....264
GOLDSMITH
Joseph 1803-1854.596
GOOCH
Sarah 1751- 22, 93
GOODALE/GOODELL
Abigail 1806-.........457
Alice 1820-1901 457
Anne 1787-1874....116
Asenath 1795-.......246
Augusta 1779-1857
.................117, 463
Austin 1815- 457
Benjamin 1753-1801
.................27, 117
Benjamin 1791-1791
.....................117
Charles 1785-1867115
Charles 1812-1887457
Charles 1821-1901464
Chester 1762-1835.62,
245
Chester 1791-1884245
Chester K. 1794-...117
Chloe 1755-1833....53,
62, 210
Clement 1779-1853
.....................115
Clement 1812- 457
Ebenezer............7, 26
Ebenezer 1729-1794
.................15, 62
Elijah 1828-1901 ..458

Ellen 1837-1895....457
Erastus 1785-1868
.................115, 457
Erastus 1824-1901458
Esther 1756-1764 ...27
Frederick 1832-1874
.....................457
George W. 1808-1890
.....................247
Harriet 1784-1842 117
Harriet 1829-1894 459
Hector M. 1801-1850
.....................246
Henry 1810-1890..457
Horace 1800-1837.246
Jacob 1708-1756.7, 26
Jerusha 1813-1882458
John 1782- 115, 457
John 1815-1898 458
John L. 1788-.......246
Jonathan 1814-.....457
Joseph 1802-1854.457
Joshua 1776-1851.115
Keziah 1822-.........458
Laura 1793-1855 ..246
Laura 1804-1868 ..246
Lemuel 1800-1897 244
Lois 1764-1842 55, 62,
214
Lorenzo 1817-1875458
Louisa 1792-1794 .117
Lucretia 1789-1879
.....................116
Lucy 1778- 115, 458
Luther 1770-1816...63
Margaret 1780-.....115
Maria 1822- 458
Mary 1817-1892....458
Mary 1828-1910....458
Nancy 1790-1880..246
Oliver 1771-1773 63
Oliver 1774-..........207
Oliver 1797-..116, 458
Parcefor 1826-1901
.....................458
Peggy 1749-1826....27,
116
Phebe 1773-1774 63
Phebe 1775-1856 ...63,
247
Phebe 1804-1860 ..246
Phila 1843-1924....459
Polly 1775-............115
Ralph 1788- 117
Ralph T. 1802-1834
.....................246
Rebecca 1818-1895457
Reuben 1744-1822.27,
114
Reuben 1775-1851
.................114, 456
Rhoda 1758-1841...62,
245
Roxilana 1781-1860
.................117, 464

Samuel 1813-1898 246
Sarah 1751- 27
Sarah 1759-1759 62
Sarah 1760-1831 ... 55,
62, 213
Sarah 1793-1879 .. 116
Silas 1747-1825 27,
115
Silas 1790-1790 117
Silas 1817-1913 457
Simeon 1746-1837. 27,
115
Simeon 1812-1813 458
Susanna 1728-1812
.... 15, 61
Walter 1766-1820 .. 63,
246
Walter 1794-1835. 246
Ward 1786- ... 117, 464
Willard 1768-1858. 63,
246
William 1779-1867
.... 115, 458
William 1786-1790116
William 1795-1871116
William 1806-1843246
William 1808-1890457
William 1831-1915459
GOODELL
Henry 1821-1894 .. 516
Jerusha 1776-1849
.... 129, 513
GOODENOUGH
Cynthia 1813-1879470
GOODHUE
Ebenezer 1783-1843
.... 88
Priscilla 1809-1839
.... 325
William 1797-1882341
GOODNOW
Ruth 1757-1843 ... 111,
445
GOODRICH
Abel 1761-1841 85
Anna 37, 157
Catherine 1786-1841
.... 199
Sarah 1806-1856 .. 337
GOODRIDGE
Beulah 1790-1830104,
410
Sarah 33, 139
GOODWIN
Azel 1769-1829 200
George 1807-1893 335
James 1784- 165
John 1827-1860 346
Mary M. 1821-1854
.... 339
GOODYEAR
Theoline M. 1827-
1907 424
GOOLDEN

Farnum 1794-1883
.... 416
Jonathan S. 1785-
1835 416
Mary 1788-1857 ... 416
Thomas 1791-1817416
Winsor 1761-1840106,
416
GORDON
James R. 1829-1897
.... 380
GORHAM
Jason 1822-1897 .. 613
Lydia 1822-1897 .. 534
GOSS
William E.S. 1839-
1878 378
GOSSOM
Sarah M. 1839-1906
.... 609
GOULD
Abigail 1760-1852 202
Annie F. 1838-1920
.... 606
Asahel 1831- 626
Caroline E. 1825-1906
.... 342
Catherine 1803- ... 401
Catherine 1827-1833
.... 282
Clarissa 1798-1883
.... 328
Edward 1799-1803400
Eliza 1831-1886 ... 619
Francis 1798-1870 73,
281
Henry 1797-1823 .. 400
Hephzibah 1808-1896
.... 564
Irene B. 1823-1892282
James 1795-1874 . 400
Jane 1746-1837 273
Jeremiah 1801-1842
.... 603
Jesse P. 1833-1857282
John 1731-1764 51,
202
John 1761- 202
Jonathan 1763-1816
.... 202
Josiah 1765-1822 100,
400
Josiah 1793-1836 . 400
Julie A. 1823-1904342
Louisa 1790-1843 .. 73,
280
Louisa 1808-1820. 401
Lydia 1805-1888 .. 401
Mary Ann 1802-1877
.... 450
Moses 1800-1843 .. 390
Nathaniel 1753-1842
.... 273
Nathaniel F. 1824-
1857 282

Phineas F. 1778-1857
.... 310
Sally 1765-1844 ... 202
Sally 1792-1809 ... 400
Sally 1800-1857 73,
281
Warren 1801-1845 400
GOULDING
Amos 1816-1891 ... 339
Curtis 1776-1857 .. 87,
338
Curtis 1820-1902 . 339
Cynthia 1806-1871339
Madison 1826-1896
.... 339
Mary 1829-1905 ... 339
Orvis 1810-1858 ... 339
Russell 1809-1866 339
GOWELL
Mary 1828- 370
GOWING
Daniel 1764-1819 . 277
GRAHAM
Sarah 1770- .. 107, 421
GRANDY
Calvin 1792-1859 . 353
Fidelia L. 1826-1880
.... 389
Levi B. 1828-1887 389
GRANGE
Ellen L. 1819-1905469
GRANT
Clark 1793-1826 .. 255
Electa 1800-1839 . 247
Elisha 1757-1788 . 267
Elizabeth 1770- 63
Elliot 1762-1846 ... 210
Frank 1804-1880 .. 247
Gustavus 1759-1841
.... 63, 247
Gustavus 1805-1867
.... 247
Horace 1807-1851 247
Lucina 1813-1884 247
Lucius 1810-1846. 247
Marilda 1801-1882247
Marvin 1802-1867 247
Mary E. 399
Nancy 1811-1886 . 247
Phebe 1814- 247
Randolph 1808-1885
.... 247
Roxy 1807-1869 247
Sarah 1785-1851 .. 282
Wealthy 1816-1899
.... 248
GRAVES
Amos 1779- 95, 373
George W. 1811-1892
.... 373
Harriet 1804-1889 372
John 1775- 94, 372
John H. 1808-1894373
Lewis 1801-1891 .. 261
Martha 1806-1894 372

Martin A. 1814-1874
.... 373
Mary L. 1820-1883373
William E. 1814-1879
.... 373
GRAY
Aaron 1801- 548
Ann 1823-1871 549
Charles 1826-1892549
Charlotte 1813- 549
Daniel 1820-1895. 549
Edward 1790- 276
Elias 1815-1882 ... 549
Elijah 1808-1831 .. 548
Eliphalet 1771- ... 138,
548
Emeline 1811-1891
.... 156, 620
Frederick 138
George W. 1825-1893
.... 340
Henry 1772-1810 . 274
Henry 1810-1887 . 548
James 1797-1867 . 561
John 138
John 1745- 32, 138
John 1775-1837 274
John 1803-1882 548
Lucy B. 1795-1871 271
Mary 1828-1896 ... 549
Matilda 1807-1835561
Miriam 1777-1858 172
Moses 1747-1775 ... 69,
274
Moses 1770-1847 .. 274
Nathan 1817-1872 549
Olive 138
Olive 1796-1848 ... 548
Oliver 1797- 548
Phebe 1799-1853 .. 548
Samuel 1803-1880 598
Samuel 1806- 548
Susanna W. 138
Uriah H. 1784- 138,
548
Vesta 1831-1870 .. 549
GRAYSON
Richard 438
GREELEY
George 1828-1909 351
James 1832-1909 . 351
Phebe 1801-1886 .. 537
William 90, 351
GREEN
Benjamin 1825-1899
.... 633
Hannah 284
Jonas 1784-1860 .. 238
Nancy 1825-1856 . 624
Phineas 1803-1833586
Reuben 1798-1860 545
Samantha D. 1812-
1842 256
Sarah 1794-1848 .. 574

Susan L. 1816-1871
.................262
Timothy 1791- 248
William 1785-1860
.................135, 534
William S. 1807-1877
.................534
GREENBANK
Thomas 1809-1885589
GREENE
Daniel 1801-1837..434
Henry S. 1807-1880
.................598
Jacob H. 1802-1874
.................566
John 1818-1901 564
Sarah A. 1800-1823
.................566
Tabitha 1801-1864
.................390, 566
Thomas 1775-1809
.................143, 566
Thomas 1803-1805566
Thomas 1808-1865566
William W. 1805-1863
.................566
GREENLEAF
Joseph P. 1815-1893
.................397
GREENOUGH
Betsey 1804- .100, 399
GREENSLIT
Augustine 1792-1820
.................504
Betsey 1796- 504
Chester 1794-........504
Henry 1804-1892 ..505
John 1767-1856 ...128,
504
John R. 1798-........505
Marcena 1798-1873
.................504
Pamelia 1790-1791
.................504
Stephen 1800-1880
.................505
GREENWOOD
Esther 1845- 265
George 1822-1889.623
GREGG
Caroline 1814-1845
.................578
GRIFFIN
Abigail 1764-1859.184
Betsey 1798-1866..206
Charles 1823-1824429
Charles P. 1786-1825
.................107, 428
Henry...................429
Isabella 1824-1825429
Jasper 1806-1844..261
Lovina M. 1815-1898
.................537
Mary 1818-1835....429

Sally 1787-1832 95,
378
Sarah 243
Sarah 1821- 429
William 1767-1830141
William 1814-1816429
William 1817-1875429
GRIFFITH
Cynthia 1826-1886493
Thomas 1803-1883402
GRIGGS
Lyman 1797-1842.460
Orlando 1789-1869
.................451
Ralph R. 1798-1874
.................215
Seth D. 1809-1890 230
GRIMES
Catherine 1803-1879
.................264
GRISWOLD
Mary A. -1874.......536
GROUT
Daniel 1777- 151
Mary E. 1834-1918
.................386
Ruth.............119, 468
GROVER
Leonard 1799-1884
.................390, 566
Silas 1801-1855 431
GROW
Anna 1808-1896....460
Elijah 1796-1863...484
Hannah 1723-1765 26,
111
Rebekah 1712-1762 7,
25
GRUBB
Rebecca 1822-1884583
GRUDY
George 1831-1892.623
GUILD
Mary 1798-1859...102,
406
Sally 1775-1843 ...111,
444
GUNN
Carver 1799-1885 .263
Jessie M. 1827-1888
.................208
GUPTILL
Elisha 1791-1867..173
GURNEY
Eliza L. 1817-1855370
Susan 1791-1864 .149,
590
Thomas C. 1813-1894
.................371
GURNSEY
Lucy 1791-1845 95,
374
GUSTIN
Adoniram 1818-1890
.................591
GUSTINE

Theodosia 1792-1828
.................85, 331
GUTTERSON
Adeline 1813-1886561
Amos 1797- 560
Amos 1797-1859 ...561
Eliza 1809-1819....561
John 1766-1841 ...142,
560
John 1795-1873 561
Martha 1805-1861 449
Mary 1816-1869....561
Nathan 1811-1883 561
Nyrha 1802-1877..561
Phebe 1799-1840 ..561
Rodney 1806-1836 561
Samuel 1804-1845 561
William 1809-1838450
HACKETT
Martha 1824- 562
HADLEY
Mark 1793-1858 ...158
Mary 1834-1880....592
Stephen 1785-1869
.................246
Stephen 1835-1912
.................349
HADLOCK
Mary 1797-1834....483
Samuel H. 1801-1886
.................263
HAGAMAN
John I. 1792-1853.290
HAGAR
Lucia 1823-1884 ...424
HAGER
Catherine 1844-1925
.................495
John 1811-1876 495
HAINES
Abraham...............499
HALE
Ann 1829-1902......414
John S. 1779-1852 197
Mary 1783-1851....185
Sarah 1791-1864...595
HALFYARD
Elizabeth C. 1809-
1849..................371
HALL
Abiel 1761-1829...107,
419
Abiel 1787-1869....420
Abigail 1788-1845.235
Almira 1808-1813.376
Almira M. 1823-1905
.................376
Amos 1790-1863 ...216
Andrew T. 1798-1875
.................405
Armstrong 1820-...376
Asa 120, 473
David 1791-1863..420,
425

David H. 1791-1875
.................511
Eliza L. 1805-1877299
Ezra 1787-1863......95,
376
Gardner E. 1810-1878
.................376
Harriet 1784-........443
Isaac H. 1826-1827
.................376
Ivory 1796-1873....420
Jane R. 1803-1841 299
John 1771- 473
John 1789- 420
Judith 1739-1809...24,
105
Julia 1804-1880....420
Julia -1846............331
Lovice...................489
Lucy 1786- 480
Lyman 1813-1877.462
Martin G. 1818-1892
.................376
Mary 1793-1838....365
Mary 1798-1872....420
Origen B. 1806-1888
.................231
Orin R. 1813-1882 376
Porter 1807-1853..420
Rebecca 1788-1863 95,
374
Rhoda 1781-1822...95,
374
Sally 1788-1859 ...107,
428
Samuel R. 1795-1877
.................190
Sarah 1823- 522
Stella 1825-1853...515
Tirzah 1795-1887...96,
382
William 1802-1858588
HALLETT
Martha 1784-1871 356
HAM
Robert 1829- 604
HAMANT
Martha 1797-1871 436
HAMBLET
Ella 1853-1903......633
HAMILTON
Elizabeth 504
Laura H. 1810-1840
.................217
Matilda 1840- 340
Sarah 1817- 408
HAMMATT
Esther 1816-1885 .447
HAMMOND
Caroline D. 1819-1853
.................229
Eleanor 1806-1887234
Ezra 1796-1863.....557
Holmes 1807-1874 492
Lemuel 1766-1805 203

Margaret 1744-1834
...... 16, 66
Mary 1807-1885 ... 495
Shubael 1776-1857
...... 125, 495
Susan 1780- 195
HANCOCK
Elizabeth 256
HAND
Sarah 1786-1855 .. 481
HANNUM
Dorcas 1786-1818 113, 453
HARDING
John 1804-1893 598
HARDY
Abner 1804-1887 .. 408
Eliza 1815- 419
Emily 1817-1881 .. 419
Emily 1822-1899 .. 632
Emma 1814-1882 . 423
Farnum 1805- 418
Merrill C. 1808-1877
...... 419
Otis 1810-1889 419
Polly 1804- 418
Russell 1808-1894 419
Thirza 1807- 419
William 1820-1889 345
Wyman 1777- 106, 418
HARMON
Elias 1820-1881 368
HARRIMAN
Elizabeth R. 1801-1880 279
George 1805- 279
George W. 1803-1875
...... 277
Ira 1795-1857 276
Irene P. 1812-1905 279
Jesse P. 1803-1889 279
Jonathan 1776-1824
...... 72, 279
Lydia M. 1820-1915
...... 279
Martha H. 1815-1855
...... 279
Mary 1809-1887 ... 279
Ruth 1774-1850 ..... 99, 396
Sarah 1807-1889 .. 279
Sophronia 1800- ... 276
Stephen 1757-1828 71, 276
Thomas J. 1801- ... 277
HARRINGTON
Amelia B. 1839-1904
...... 250
Edward 1781-1855 326
Nathan 313
HARRIS
Betsey 1825-1873 . 611
Caroline 1819-1847
...... 337
Margram 440

Mary 440
Phebe J. 1827-1877
...... 611
Rebecca 1782-1825 443
Rhoda 1797-1829 . 305
Samuel 1799-1877 181
Sarah 1821-1918 .. 456
Violetta 1825- 457
HARRISON
Louisa B. 1785-1841
...... 205
HART
Benjamin 1752- 119
Benjamin 1778- 469
Benjamin 1790- 469
Constant 1728-1792
...... 28, 119
Cynthia 1773-1849 468
Eli 1807-1891 611
Esther 1791- 468
Eunice 1776-1777 . 468
Hastings 1776-1777
...... 468
John 1750- 119, 468
Josiah 1748-1830 119, 468
Josiah 1799- 468
Lucy 1805-1876 323
Naomi 1775- 468
Polly 1798-1880 468
Seth 1793-1866 468
Susan 1795-1881 .. 468
Thomas 1773- 468
HARTLEY
James 1810-1871 . 294
HARTSHORN
Catherine 1792-1860
...... 237
Hephzibah 1771-1816
...... 201
HARTWELL
Mary 1821-1891 ... 617
HARVEY
Ellen 1839-1904 ... 531
Lucretia 1787-1857
...... 129, 511
Thomas 1828-1904 583
William 1819- 583
HARWOOD
Joel 1786-1849 176
HASELTINE
Phebe 1786- .. 138, 547
HASKELL
David H. 1812-1871
...... 567
Hannah 1805-1821
...... 566
Hannah 1823-1844
...... 567
Lydia P. 1817-1859
...... 567
Marcy 1777-1837. 144, 569
Mary A. 1820- 567

Parsons 1777-1829
...... 143, 566
Parsons 1802-1857 566
Samuel P. 1809-1881
...... 567
Sarah A.H. 1814-1890
...... 567
Sarah W. 1820-1880
...... 342
Uriah H. 1807-1808
...... 566
HASKINS
Demilah 1810-1883
...... 294
HASTINGS
Caroline 1802-1887
...... 467
Caroline 1803-1803
...... 467
Caroline 1811-1886
...... 467
Caroline F. 1818-1898
...... 589
Charles 1777- 119
Dier 28, 118
Dyer 1771-1843 ... 118, 467
Edmon 1806- 467
Eliza A. 1812-1844 467
George 1812-1873 279
George T. 1804-1825
...... 467
George W. 1817-1855
...... 467
George W. 1827-1916
...... 467
Harriet B. 1812-1881
...... 467
Henry E. 1816-1900
...... 467
John 1828-1830 467
Joseph 1808-1876 467
Juliana M. 1800-1886
...... 467
Lemira L. 1824-1855
...... 467
Lydia 1775-1776 .. 119
Lydia 1779- 119
Mary 1828-1921 ... 335
Mary A. 1811-1880
...... 587
Mary M. 1823-1883
...... 577
Mary S. 1818-1857 467
Molly 1773- 118
Oliver 1769-1848. 118, 466
Oliver W. 1804-1843
...... 467
Paine 1797-1847 .. 467
Sally S. 1810- 467
William 1794-1859 357
HATCH
Alvin 1786-1873 ... 478

Aroet M. 1792-1876
...... 304
Ballard 1803-1866 593
Betsey B. 1796- 173
Fanny 1782-1861 . 478
Hannah 1793-1869
...... 478
Hart 1795-1875 478
Joseph 1780- 478
Justus 1751-1790 ... 31
Nathan 1757-1841
...... 121, 478
Phinehas 1790-1838
...... 478
Polly 1799-1875 ... 478
Reuben 1788-1877 478
Ruth 1785-1846 .. 125, 493
Sarah 1784-1840 .. 478
HATFIELD
Lowell 1824- 442
William 1806-1880 551
HAVENS
Lovina 1774-1869 207
HAWES
Betsey 1800-1881. 354
Sally 1781-1845 .. 137, 544
Susannah 1779-1860
...... 58, 225
Wilson 627
HAWKS
Silvia 1801-1889 .. 249
HAWLEY
Hannah 1772- 140, 555
Henry A. 1815-1881
...... 466
Joanna 1810-1871 360
HAY
Samuel 1809-1864 403
HAYDEN
Eliza 234
Milton 1798-1862. 294
Phebe 1805-1875 .. 531
HAYES
Edward 1847-1908 459
Lydia 1854-1929 .. 629
Nancy J. 1831-1898
...... 590
HAYS
Edward 1782-1813 553
HAYWARD
Almira 1805-1897 516
Andrew 1810-1872 517
Augustus 1803-1859
...... 516
Ephraim 1759-1831
...... 284
George 1799-1849 516
King 1768-1829 ... 130, 516
Lucy 1800-1884 516
Lydia 1781-1851 .. 474
Mary A. 1818-1877
...... 391

Micajah 1818-1897534
Nancy 1806-1844 ..516
Noah 1801-1875....516
Pliny 1808-1879....516
Stephen 1815-1861
..........................533
Susannah 1778-1854
..........................474
HAZELTINE
Mehitable 1795-1846
..........................413
Sarah 1760-1848... 82,
311
HAZEN
Clarissa 1784-1857
..........................237
Martha 1834-1915 458
HEALY
Phebe 1765-1828..109,
434
HEATH
Fielder 1816-1895.531
Galutia 1818-1900 418
Ira 1793- 211
John 1789-1857 196
Polly 164
Truman L. 1830-1892
..........................380
HEATON
David 1785-1846...155
Nancy 1823-1890 ..615
HECOX
Olive 1798-1830....227
HEMPSTEAD
Nicholas 1809-1863
..........................292
Thomas 1805- 542
HENDRICK
Mary 1765-1849...129,
509
Mary 1815-1887....515
HENLEY
Hannah U. 1795-1878
..........................169
HENRY
Robert 248
Robert W. 1835-1899
..........................535
Ziba 1791-1859 197
HERENDEEN
Arvilla 1839-1931 .495
HERRICK
Alonzo 1827-1854 .619
Amos 1810-1863 ...618
Andrew 1834-1862619
Anna 1790-1873....156
Benjamin 1780- ...155,
617
Benjamin 1812-1892
..........................617
Benjamin 1836-1911
..........................620
Betsey 1794-1875.155,
615
Betsey 1831- 619

Charles 1818-1890619
Climena 1838-1893
..........................619
Daniel 1818- 618
Diadamia 1797-1797
..........................156
Edward 1754-1811.37,
155
Edward 1785-1873
..................155, 619
Edward 1812-1878619
Edward 1828-1873620
Eliza 1816-1872 619
Eliza 1823-1825 620
Emeline 1832-1866
..........................462
George 1784-.155, 618
George 1814-1814.617
George 1829-1907.618
Harriet 617
Harriet 1840-1927 621
Helena M. 1829-1919
..........................621
Israel 1794-1866..156,
620
Israel 1821-1877...618
John 1829-1902 619
Lafayette 1825-1888
..........................620
Larkin 1799-1866 156,
620
Larkin 1812-1831 .618
Mary 1782-1882...155,
617
Mary 1814-1878....619
Mary 1816-1832....618
Mary P. 1808-1874218
Nancy 1820-1894 ..619
Permelia 1798-1880
..........................476
Sarah 1788-1866..156,
619
Sarah 1815-1896...617
William 1827-1893620
HERRING
Daniel 1802-1877..558
HERSEY
Levi 1780- 208
Lydia 1819-1894 ...308
HESSELTINE
Cyrus 1804-1888...548
HESSELTON
John 1809-1893 619
Nathaniel 1811-1881
..........................622
HEWITT
Charles 1807-1868292
Eunice 1794-1867 ..97,
387
HIBBARD
Asa 1792-1821 290
Naomi 1770- ...59, 228
William M. 1795-1861
..........................233
HICKS

Abra 1800-1887 256
Eliza M. 1814-1846
..........................466
Lucy A. 1818-1853 466
Maggie 377
Marshall Z. 1816-1882
..........................466
Zephaniah 1773-1864
.................118, 466
HICKSON
Nancy 1842-1924 ..371
HIDDEN
David 1784-1861...177
HIGGINS
Eben P. 1811-1879557
Hannah 1798-1872
..........................177
James H. 1816-1847
..........................557
HILDRETH
Sarah 1829-1905...461
HILL
Abigail R. 1795-1837
..........................396
Amos A. 1804-1818
..........................396
Asa 1787-1827 506
Charles 1807-1877396
Ebenezer 1797-1847
..........................506
Elizabeth M. 1800-
1871 395
Eunice 1797-1862 .396
John 1791-1870 396
John B. 1796-1886450
Leavitt 1770-1843..99,
396
Leavitt 1813-1846396,
399
Mary R. 1805-1889
..........................396
Sally E. 1793- 396
Selinda 1809-1891 191
Thomas R. 1799-1878
..........................396
HILLMAN
Elmira 1816-1851.366
HILLS
Emily 1811-1888...219
Hephzibah 1749-1778
....................71, 278
Joanna 1786- 326
Lydia 1761-.....84, 326
Susan 1841-1890 ..633
Sylvester 1800-1830
..........................446
HILTON
Almer C. 1823-1872
..........................592
Amos S. 1829-1898
..........................592
Arianna 1835-1873
..........................592
Clark 1798-1834 ..150,
592

Julina R. 1831-1908
..........................592
Mary 1803-1839....268
Roswell 1870-1957629
Sarah E. 1825-1884
..........................592
HINCKLEY
Benjamin 1782-1835
..........................215
Betsey 1796-1879 .215
Caleb 1790-1790 ...215
David 1754-1835....55,
214
Eber 1791-1796 215
Hannah 1786- 215
Joanna 1792-1846 173
Joanna 1799-1857 215
Mercy -1781....61, 210
HINDS
Asher 1759-1814...267
HINKLEY
Porter 1781-1849 ..235
HINKSON
Rebecca E. 1820-1899
..........................323
HINMAN
Laura 1789-1858 ..435
HIRKCUM
Edward 1700-1781 ...6
HISCOCK
Samuel 1801-1883 574
HITCHCOCK
Eaton 1795-1837...460
Marshall 1813-1899
..........................532
HITCHINGS
Lucy 1815-1879 330
HOADLEY
Elias 1770-1843....483
HOAGLAND
George 1814-1903.408
HOAR
Abigail 1812-1888.459
Alured 1796-1870 .459
Amanda 1792-1855
..........................459
Benjamin 1757- ...139,
551
Betsey 1799-1816 .459
Jacob 1808-1809 ...459
Lucia 1794-1882 ...459
Solomon 1771-1844
..................116, 459
Solomon 1804-1879
..........................459
HOBART
Uretta 1816-1843 .457
HOBBS
Betsey E. 1833-1908
..........................565
Julia A. 1811-1883588
HODGE
Harriet 1798-1825 216
HODGES
Hannah 193-1877.297
Henry 1787-1876 ..311

HODGKINS
Elizabeth R. 1816-1891 637
Roswell F. 1823-1889 374
HODGMAN
Abigail 1774-1839 139, 553
Benjamin 1790- 480
Benjamin 1805-1875 329
Jonathan 1753-1847 .... 122, 480
Joseph 1805-1815. 329
Josiah 1778- ... 85, 329
Josiah 1799-1852 . 329
Marshall 1790- 480
Mary 1788- 480
Oliver 1782- 448
Oswyn 1800-1817. 329
Sarah 1803-1831 .. 329
Stephen 1808-1884 329
HOISINGTON
Elijah 1783-1847 .. 484
Emily 1808- 484
HOLABIRD
Amos 1787-1852 ... 358
Harlow 1798-1859 360
HOLBROOK
Abigail 1770-1815 145, 571
Betsey 1774-1820 145, 573
Honora 1857-1939 629
HOLDEN
Nathan 1786-1829 199
HOLFORD
Frederick 1813-1890 467
HOLLIDAY
George 1815- 277
HOLLISTER
Egbert 1818-1889. 361
HOLMAN
Abner 1801-1865 .. 621
Amasa 1803-1892. 603
Caleb F. 1816-1889 636
Henry 1833-1848 .. 636
Henryette 1832-1835 636
Katharine 1753-1781 .... 39, 160
Laura A. 1818-1904 636
Lorain 1824-1881. 636
Marilla 1820-1883 636
Mary S. 1834-1897 636
Maryette 1828-1831 636
Silas 1790-1839 ... 161, 635
Silas D. 1822-1888 636
William 1811-1887 218
HOLMES

Amos 1815-1892 ... 374
Dennison 1817-1893 329
George 1805-1898 383
Harriet 1802-1850 514
Henry 1806-1871 .. 510
Hiram 1800-1867 . 514
Mary 1826- 498
Persis 1819-1897 .. 560
Warren 1810-1884 242
HOLT
Aaron 1776-1826. 147, 583
Aaron 1801-1818 .. 583
Aaron 1821-1890 .. 584
Aaron P. 1808-1876 582
Abbie 1843- 627
Abbot 1796- 563
Abel 1770- 54, 212
Abiah 1747-1790 ... 42, 168
Abiah 1761-1841 ... 47, 188
Abiah 1765-1835 .. 165
Abiather 1813-1846 190
Abiel 1698-1772 . 4, 13
Abiel 1718-1744 12
Abiel 1727-1785 14, 53
Abiel 1746-1824 .... 46, 185
Abiel 1748-1811 .... 49, 198
Abiel 1755- 50
Abiel 1762-1829 .... 54, 212
Abiel 1765-1825 .... 48, 193
Abiel 1770-1834 ... 185
Abiel 1773-1801 ... 184
Abiel 1774-1839 ... 199
Abiel 1780-1826 .... 58, 224
Abiel 1781- 199
Abiel 1791-1864 ... 193
Abiel 1791-1869 ... 212
Abiel 1805-1850 ... 621
Abigail 1688-1742 ... 4, 13
Abigail 1716-1749 . 13, 50
Abigail 1719- 13
Abigail 1722- 13, 52
Abigail 1732-1774 . 16, 64
Abigail 1758-1824 . 45, 177
Abigail 1761- .. 63, 248
Abigail 1765-1851 142, 562
Abigail 1767- 55
Abigail 1767-1821 . 46, 183
Abigail 1771- 167

Abigail 1774- 200
Abigail 1779-1806 199
Abigail 1782- 147, 584
Abigail 1784- 204
Abigail 1797-1842 563
Abigail 1797-1857 554
Abigail 1799-1843 582
Abigail 1804-1871 554
Abigail 1805-1877 580
Abigail 1808-1888 618
Abigail B. 1809-1862 582
Abner 1771-1854. 146, 194, 579
Abner 1803-1807 .. 580
Abner 1807-1839 .. 580
Ada 1858- 627
Adelia 1778- ... 64, 252
Albert 1813-1889 . 244
Albert 1817-1893 . 612
Albert H. 1820-1890 585
Alfreada 1779-1814 66, 261
Alfred Converse 1806-1852 224
Alice 1722-1762 12, 50
Alice 1742-1826 46, 48, 183
Alice 1747-1814 49, 52, 200
Almira 1790-1874 .. 67
Almira 1810-1813 222
Alona 1812-1886 .. 577
Alva S. 1793-1879 260
Alvah 1763- 64
Alvah 1801-1876 .. 222
Amasa 1759-1847 ... 50
Amasa 1781-1850. 205
Ammi R. 1789-1827 .... 157, 625
Amos 1768-1826 .. 142, 559
Amos 1795-1796 ... 206
Amos 1799-1874 ... 206
Amos 1814-1895 ... 583
Amos J. 1801-1851 582
Amos S. 1774-1855 .... 147, 582
Amos T. 1811-1887 565
Amy 1776-1803 ... 141, 558
Amy 1827-1855 625
Andrew 1768-1853. 54
Anna 1735-1806 14, 55
Anna 1762- 57, 221
Anna 1781-1865 ... 553
Anna 1798- 213
Anna 1803-1897 ... 243
Anna 1845-1902 ... 627
Anna D. 1812-1895 192
Anna T. 1819-1873 .... 158, 628

Anne 1784-1855 .... 56, 221
Anness 1757- 139, 552
Annis 1808-1882 .. 554
Arnold 1794-1869. 212
Arnold 1816-1862. 225
Arthur D. 1830-1893 .... 608, 610
Asa 1736-1738 32
Asa 1742-1793 46, 184
Asa 1745-1813 .. 16, 66
Asa 1768- 184
Asa 1777-1852 66, 261
Asa 1794-1825 183
Asenath 1743-1785 35, 146
Asenath 1786-1813 56, 214, 220
Asenath F. 1820-1904 221
Austin 1807-1839. 223
Bathsheba 1770-1790 55
Bathsheba 1791-1880 214
Benjamin 1704-1779 .... 12, 48
Benjamin 1709-1774 .... 11, 41
Benjamin 1737-1741 48
Benjamin 1741- 70
Benjamin 1741-1826 .... 42, 165
Benjamin 1746-1748 48
Benjamin 1749-1822 48
Benjamin 1776-1867 167
Benjamin 1781-1847 .... 148, 584
Benjamin 1783- 164
Benjamin 1805-1856 585
Benjamin 1816-1827 192
Benjamin G. 1827-1903 565
Bethiah 1740-1817. 35
Bethiah 1743-1817 21, 85
Bethiah 1744-1812 48, 195
Bethiah 1754-1754. 49
Bethiah 1764-1833. 54
Betsey 1777-1844. 199
Betsey 1781-1801. 164
Betsey 1786- 239
Betsey 1790-1808. 562
Betsey 1802-1816. 191
Betsey C. 1805-1857 576
Betsey F. 1819-1847 584

Betty 1767-1827....141
Beulah 1744-...32, 138
Boanerges R. 1810-
1886.................548
Bridget 1737-..69, 273
Bridget 1777-........274
Caleb 1729-1810 ... 14,
31, 54
Caleb 1759-1826 ... 55,
62, 213
Caleb 1791-1880 ...218
Caleb 1798-1811 ...213
Calvin 1763-1795..274
Calvin 1801-1863..560
Calvin 1854-..........627
Catherine 1805-1834
........................251
Celinda 1796-1823
.................214, 222
Chandler 1777-1797
.........................204
Charles 1802-1824251
Charles 1803-1888261
Charles 1805-1874244
Charles 1806-........547
Charles 1810-........213
Charles 1811-1884585
Charles 1841-........627
Chloe 1755-........... 63
Chloe 1766-1855 ..137,
546
Chloe 1768-1849 ...185
Chloe 1775-1776 ...205
Chloe 1775-1849 ... 47,
144, 192
Chloe 1788-1819 ...213
Chloe 1797-..........240
Chloe 1797-1876 ...189
Choe 1777-............205
Clara F. 1851-1918
.........................609
Clarina 1769-1845 65,
255
Clarissa 1775-184058,
205, 224
Clarissa 1784-1813
.........................239
Clarissa 1789-1822
.........................206
Clarissa 1791-1872 67
Clarissa 1818-1895
.........................261
Constant 1787-1835
.........................214
Cynthia 1801-1858554
Daniel 1705-17734, 15
Daniel 1723- 13
Daniel 1731-1796.. 16,
63
Daniel 1733-1796.. 12,
46, 47
Daniel 1740- 46, 48,
183
Daniel 1744-1813.. 42,
166

Daniel 1761-1830...48,
192
Daniel 1774-1774..146
Daniel 1775- 146
Daniel 1775-1847....66
Daniel 1781-1851..185
Daniel 1792-1866..250
Daniel 1795-1866..193
Daniel 1803-1870..579
Daniel 1805-1871..611
Daniel C. 1815-1888
.........................243
Daniel G. 1814-1895
.........................563
Daniel L. 1791- 167
Darius 1765-1854 .185
David 1708-1747..8, 9,
33
David 1740-.....33, 141
David 1749-1749.....34
David 1751-1835.....34
David 1774-1859...166
David 1783-1836..143,
567
David 1806-1891...563
David 1807-1877...611
David A. 1800-1839
.........................249
David G. 1820-1821
.........................567
David O. 1814-1879
.........................565
Deborah 1700-1784. 4,
14
Deborah 1775-182764,
251
Deborah 1781-1866
.........................240
Deborah 1801-1860
.........................546
Delia 1757-1775......63
Delilah 1821-1821.580
Diah 1812-1818 611
Dinah 1726-1805 ...15,
60
Dinah 1744-1780 ...46,
184
Dinah 1750-1826 ...51,
61, 203
Diodate 1809-........223
Dolly 1785-1851....166
Dolly 1787-............199
Dolly F. 1808-1887565
Dorcas 1727-.....12, 45
Dorcas 1736-1736 ...33
Dorcas 1737-...33, 140
Dorcas 1753-...46, 181
Dorcas 1756-1778 ...45
Dorcas 1764-1850 ..42,
170
Dorcas 1767-1800 ..62,
243
Dorcas 1775-.........184
Dorcas 1776-1853 .163

Dorcas 1781-1842 141,
557
Dorcas 1783-1810 .166
Dorcas 1791-1868 .199
Dorcas 1793-1856 189,
555
Dorinda 1804-1888
.........................577
Dorothy 1776-1827
.........................271
Dorothy 1781-1861
.........................240
Dorothy 1807-1812
.........................583
Dorothy 1817-1840
.........................584
Dudley F. 1791-1856
.........................547
Ebenezer 1746-......51,
205
Ebenezer 1772-.....205
Ebenezer G. 1798-
1835...................214
Edah P. 1804-1861193
Eleanor 1777-1858
.... 146, 194, 580
Eli H. 1798-1860...582
Elias 1796-1851 581
Elijah 1757-1817 ...54,
124, 213, 487
Elijah 1762-1826 ...63,
249
Elijah 1792-1809 ..213
Elijah 1817-1888 ..250
Elijah 1823-1863 ..612
Eliphalet M. 1797-
1868...................547
Elisha............66
Elisha 1778-1857 ..205
Elisha 1811-.........243
Eliud 1822-1863 ...612
Eliza 1800-1860 243
Eliza 1803-1880 563
Eliza 1804-1892 596
Eliza 1821-1870 220
Eliza B. 1821-1860583
Eliza W. 1804-1858
.........................249
Elizabeth 1718-1776
.....................12, 44
Elizabeth 1720-1744.9
Elizabeth 1725-1753
...................14, 53
Elizabeth 1748-....44,
175
Elizabeth 1748-1794
...................34, 144
Elizabeth 1751-1777
.........................45
Elizabeth 1752-......34,
137, 144
Elizabeth 1756-.......54
Elizabeth 1772-1854
.........................185

Elizabeth 1775-1874
.................175, 176
Elizabeth 1777-......56,
220
Elizabeth 1780-.....166
Elizabeth 1782-.....167
Elizabeth 1790-1797
.........................183
Elizabeth 1792-.....249
Elizabeth 1798-1867
.................183, 333
Elizabeth 1800-1872
.........................580
Elizabeth 1801-1848
.........................212
Elizabeth 1804-1832
.........................547
Elizabeth 1810-1875
.........................261
Elizabeth 1811-1830
.........................189
Ellen 1839-1854....626
Emelia 1784-1834.199
Emily 1818-1883...213
Emma 1850- 627
Emma 1852- 627
Emma D. 1825-1900
.........................372
Enoch 1770-..........184
Enoch 1780-1873 ..164
Ephraim 1713-1749.9,
34
Ephraim 1737-1816
.................35, 146
Ephraim 1762-1844
.................146, 576
Ephraim 1769-1836
.... 47, 142, 191
Ephraim 1799-1801
.........................191
Ephraim 1803-1867
.........................191
Ephraim 1811-1841
.........................563
Ephraim A. 1778-1857
.................154, 611
Erasmus 1805-......582
Erastus 66
Erastus 1778-1875204
Esther 1760- 37
Esther 1766-1824 .165
Esther 1766-1839 ..37,
158
Esther 1774- ...58, 223
Esther 1775-1777 .143
Esther 1781-1874 143,
568
Esther 1787- 167
Esther 1794- 562
Esther 1797- 222
Esther 1804-1882 .223
Eunice 1741-.....16, 65
Eunice 1747-1774 ...33
Eunice 1764-1798 138,
547

Eunice 1772- 54
Eunice 1804-1819. 213
Eunice H. 1816-1869 223
Ezekiel 1727-1807.. 13
Fanny 1782- 164
Fanny 1800-1834 . 191
Farnum 1791-1865 .... 187, 555
Fidelia 1812- 243
Florence 1872-1955 629
Fred 1879- 630
Freeman 1790-1865 218
Frye 1746- 42, 167
Frye 1779-1850 165
Frye 1788- 167
Galen C. 1821-1876 607
George W. 1811-1877 244
George W. 1813-1889 250
Hannah 1702-1749.. 5, 17
Hannah 1707-1708... 8
Hannah 1723-1751 12, 14, 49
Hannah 1728-1756. 32
Hannah 1735- 33
Hannah 1739-1831 12, 46, 47
Hannah 1741- 44
Hannah 1741-1826 172
Hannah 1745-1754. 49
Hannah 1745-1818 34, 142
Hannah 1754- 44
Hannah 1754-1833 176
Hannah 1756-1774. 50
Hannah 1756-1832 53, 61, 210
Hannah 1758-1820 42, 169
Hannah 1763- 184
Hannah 1764-1855 62, 242
Hannah 1766-1852 184
Hannah 1768-1831 166
Hannah 1769-1857 45, 47, 180
Hannah 1771- 56, 218
Hannah 1771-1842 47, 142, 191
Hannah 1772-1775 185
Hannah 1773- 143, 175
Hannah 1775-1778 194

Hannah 1780-1868 205
Hannah 1781-1856 .... 143, 566
Hannah 1787-1873 195
Hannah 1793- 218
Hannah 1794-1825 180
Hannah 1795- 222
Hannah 1795-1879 191
Hannah 1796-1856 187
Hannah 1797-1821 189
Hannah 1798- 174
Hannah 1801- 547
Hannah 1806-1881 560
Hannah 1807-1833 585
Hannah 1810-1850 577
Hannah 1814-1892 243
Hannah 1857-1907 629
Hannah F. 1822-1897 565
Hannah G. 1795-1858 .... 158, 625
Hannah K. 1792-1842 185
Harmon 1789-1861 .... 152, 607
Harriet 1808- 250
Harriet 1823-1885 261
Harriet 1861-1928 629
Harriet B. 1816-1826 547
Harvey.................. 223
Harvey 1785-1842 240
Harvey 1808-1893 260
Harvey 1828-........ 223
Haskell 1801-1802153
Henry 1763-1821.. 194
Henry 1802-1803.. 611
Henry 1810- 251
Herman 1793- 187
Hiram 1803-. 153, 608
Hiram 1806-1886. 554
Hiram 1808-1856. 244
Hiram H. 1818-1895 607
Horace 1784-1863213, 222
Horace 1808-........ 213
Horace R. 1807-1897 582
Horatio 1803-1859 251
Horatio N. 1811-1894 250
Huldah 1772-1775 206

Humphrey B. 1835-1898 608
Isaac 1738-1822 14, 56
Isaac 1763-1813 .... 56, 218
Isaac 1792-1851 ... 240
Isaiah 1794- 560
Isaiah 1812-1878.. 560
Israel 1799- 158
Israel 1806-1869 .. 548
Jacob 1714-1760. 8, 34
Jacob 1739-1816.... 34, 142
Jacob 1759- .. 139, 553
Jacob 1765-1800.. 142, 562
Jacob 1783-1784... 143
Jacob 1783-1844... 553
Jacob 1784-1817... 183
Jacob 1797-1825... 562
Jacob 1801-1811... 191
Jacob 1807-1865... 563
Jacob 1851-1926... 629
Jacob F. 1817-1890 565
Jacob I. 1815-1815564
James 1693-1722 4
James 1707-1751 .. 16, 69
James 1723-1812 .. 12, 44
James 1746-1818 .. 14, 57
James 1749-1800 ... 44
James 1750-1826 .. 51, 206
James 1764-1766 ... 55
James 1765- 274
James 1770-1856 .. 57, 60, 222
James 1797-1856 . 181
James 1801-1890 . 206
James 1804-1851 . 222
James 1816-1897 . 554
James 1875-1954 . 630
James E. 1801-..... 582
James S. 1804-1878 260
James T. 1822-1901 223
Jane C. 1790-1835 250
Jason 1805-1893 .. 260
Jedediah 1740-174043
Jedediah 1744-1790 .... 43, 172
Jedediah 1754-1847 .... 44, 174
Jedediah 1774-1850 167
Jedediah 1779-1842 174
Jedediah R. 1826-1903 612
Jeremiah 1803-1817 180

Jeremiah T. 1781-1832 174
Jerome................. 204
Jerusha 1804-1877548
Jerusha W. 1791-1834 249
Jesse 1739-1817.... 69, 274
Joel 1753-1755 45
Joel 1803-1873 583
John 1764-1820..... 36, 152
John 1765-1835..... 47, 188
John 1769-1815... 137, 546
John 1774-1776...... 55
John 1776-1841..... 58, 205, 224
John 1777-1836... 146, 576
John 1784-1856... 167
John 1788-1789... 152
John 1792-1825.... 240
John 1799-1869... 189, 191
John 1809-1851.... 224
John 1812-1864.... 607
John 1816-1842.... 564
John 1831-1892.... 626
John 1847-1897.... 627
John 1859-1862.... 629
John 1866-1942.... 629
John J. 1787-........ 186
Johnson C. 1811-1889 580
Jonah 1783-1860.. 174
Jonathan 1711-17918, 33
Jonathan 1726-1726 13
Jonathan 1738-1810 .... 33, 141
Jonathan 1763-1764 141
Jonathan 1764-.... 139
Jonathan 1772-1843 .... 139, 554
Jonathan 1787-1818 174
Jonathan L. 1784-1848 185
Joseph 1713-1714 8
Joseph 1716-1754 . 12, 48
Joseph 1718-1789 ... 9, 37
Joseph 1740-1801 . 48, 193
Joseph 1744- 49
Joseph 1752-1803 . 49, 199
Joseph 1766-1791 . 46, 183
Joseph 1769-1775 194

Joseph 1770-1816 . 57, 222
Joseph 1771-1773 .. 64
Joseph 1779-1832 .199
Joseph 1780-1860 .194
Joseph 1782-1835 .199
Joseph 1790-1866 .183
Joseph 1792-1864 .183
Joseph 1801-1885 .175
Joseph 1804-1861 .189
Joseph 1823-1910 .608
Joseph A. 1823- 583
Joseph E. 1828-1882 585
Joseph P. 1806-1886 223
Joseph R. 1795-1878 ....153, 608
Joseph W. 1813-1897 585
Joseph W. 1819-1887 244
Joshua 1703-1787... 4, 15
Joshua 1728-1791. 15, 61
Joshua 1730-1810. 12, 46
Joshua 1733- 33
Joshua 1753- 139
Joshua 1758-1835. 47, 186
Joshua 1763-1790.. 55
Joshua 1765- 37
Joshua 1782-1834.214
Joshua 1788-1848.187
Joshua 1804-1886.190
Joshua 1805- 180
Joshua 1807-1811.189
Josiah 1754-1810... 52
Josiah 1786-1871 ..205
Jotham H. 1805-1881 583
Julianna 1796-1862 214
Justin 1781- 205
Justus W. 1825-1863 607
Keturah 1690-1781. 4, 15
Keturah 1729-1805 15
Keturah 1758-1839 61, 240
Kezia 1793-1854 ...250
Keziah 1761-1820. 63, 248
Launda 1813- 224
Laura A. 1816-1903 261
Leander 1825-1891 625
Lemuel 1737- 33
Lemuel 1748- 70
Lemuel 1756-1836 61, 112, 240

Lemuel 1787-1848 ....139, 553
Lemuel 1804-1858 554
Lemuel 1817- 244
Leonard 1782-1857 56, 214, 220
Lester 1759-1764 63
Lester 1766-1841 ...63, 250
Lester 1779-1869 ..240
Lester 1797-1840 ..250
Lester 1804-1830 ..243
Levi 1779-1814 205
Levi 1785-1879 174
Lewis M. 1808-1850 261
Liberty 1813-1887 193
Lodisa 1801-1887..260
Lois 1739-1792..16, 65
Lois 1743-1812........33
Lois 1760- 46, 182
Lois 1772-1826......184
Lois 1784-1821......214
Lois C. 1797-1876 .260
Louisa 1801-1882 .261
Louisa 1806-1871 .244
Louisa 1820-1872 .625
Louisa 1821-1879 .243
Luce 1778-1847......58, 224
Lucia L. 1813-1880 251
Lucinda 1773-1847 65, 255
Lucinda 1775-1816 205
Lucinda 1789-1849 212
Lucy 1747- 16, 67
Lucy 1804-1868 222
Lucy 1808- 554
Lucy 1833-1887 626
Lucy A. 1801-1829 181
Lucy A. 1825-1911 612
Lucy W. 1793-1865 254
Luther 1797-1861 .560
Luther P. 1827-1892 608
Lydia 1714- 12, 48
Lydia 1735-1765 48
Lydia 1736- 33
Lydia 1740-1758 33
Lydia 1767- 184
Lydia 1767-1825 ....47, 189, 194
Lydia 1770- 206
Lydia 1770-1834 ..141, 557
Lydia 1778-1869 ...181
Lydia 1780- 204
Lydia 1795-1867 ...189
Lydia 1803-1889 ...582
Lydia 1804-1889 ...181

Lydia 1805-1891 ..153, 608
Lydia 1813-1841 ...260
Lydia 1825-1883 ...584
Lydia M. 1818-1906 608
Lydia P. 1791-1792 157
Lydia P. 1793-1868 ....158, 625
Lydia S. 1823-1852 392
Lyman 1818-1849.585
Marcia 1773- ...64, 252
Marcia 1800-1831.219
Marcia C. 1833-1869 ....*607*
Maria P. 1824-1842 565
Mariah 1806-1867 219
Marilda 1802-1868 214
Marstin 1747- .35, 147
Martha 1725-1759.13, 53
Martha 1754-1829 .48, 197
Martha 1808-1895 189
Martha S. 1810-1864 220
Mary 249
Mary 1681-1715..4, 11
Mary 1711- 11, 42
Mary 1722- 10
Mary 1725- ...13, 52
Mary 1735- 69, 272
Mary 1740- 33, 140
Mary 1741- 43
Mary 1741-1829 19, 81
Mary 1742-1823 14, 57
Mary 1744- 34
Mary 1745-34, 49, 197
Mary 1751- 196
Mary 1751-1819......48
Mary 1752- 42, 168
Mary 1752-1824.....61, 239
Mary 1755-1844.....37, 155
Mary 1758- 46
Mary 1759-1760......54
Mary 1759-1819.....47, 187
Mary 1760- 54, 211
Mary 1761-1850.....45, 179
Mary 1771-1819.....64, 252
Mary 1773-1861.....56, 218
Mary 1775-1790....274
Mary 1777-1856...143, 568
Mary 1780- 165
Mary 1782-1842....239
Mary 1787- ...155, 618

Mary 1790-1851....213
Mary 1791- 559
Mary 1792-1818....193
Mary 1795-1884....240
Mary 1797-1802....153
Mary 1798-1856....187
Mary 1800-1868....563
Mary 1801-1803....190
Mary 1806-1879....243
Mary 1806-1900....190
Mary 1808- 223
Mary 1809-1880....577
Mary 1810-1872....554
Mary 1812- 554
Mary 1820- 585
Mary 1826-1914....261
Mary 1837-1918....627
Mary A. 1811-1817 564
Mary A. 1815-1889 ....*607*
Mary B. 1805-1870 191
Mary C. 1820- 223
Mary E. 1811-1883 582
Mary E.W. 1812-1887 180
Mary H. 1818-1906 ....158, 628
Mary O. 1777-1856 ....143, 565
Mary R. 1823-1868 189
Matilda 1773- 205
Matilda 1805-1834 224
Mehitable 1743-1816 ....46, 184
Mehitable 1757-1819 ....52, 206
Mehitable 1773-1848 204
Mehitable 1776-1778 166
Mehitable 1778-1855 166
Melvina 1863- 629
Mercy 1741-1799 ...49, 199
Mercy 1766-1834 ..200
Mercy H. 1803-1855 582
Molly 1765- 64
Molly 1770- 166
Molly 1773- 205
Molly 1773-1784 ...172
Molly 1784- 275
Morgianna 1800-1873 251
Morris L. 1808-1871 261
Moses 1686-1730 ..3, 9
Moses 1716-1743 9, 17, 38
Moses 1744-1772 34

Moses 1765-1819.... 56
Moses 1772-1823. 147, 581
Moses 1773-.. 141, 558
Moses 1796-1889.. 558
Moses E. 1816- 607
Moses W. 1801-1842 582
Moses W. 1810-1813 583
Nancy 1779- 141
Nancy 1788- . 157, 624
Nancy 1800-1801 . 582
Nancy 1817-1836 . 577
Nancy 1825-1859 . 626
Nathan 1725-1792 12, 45
Nathan 1733-1800 14, 55
Nathan 1735-1785 . 46
Nathan 1740-1818 42, 164
Nathan 1761-1820 55, 62, 214
Nathan 1762-1841 165
Nathan 1767-1778 . 48
Nathan 1787-1878 553
Nathan 1792-1792 187
Nathan 1795-1807 180
Nathan 1798-1827 193
Nathan 1799-1802 153
Nathan 1801- 183
Nathan 1808-1891 190
Nathan A. 1790-1839 199
Nathan K. 1778-1836 ....141, 185, 557
Nathan W. 1827-1891 607
Nathaniel 1725-1806 .... 32, 137
Nathaniel 1759-1761 137
Nathaniel 1769-1829 .... 137, 547
Nathaniel 1793-1813 547
Nehemiah 1740-1786 .... 34, 143
Nehemiah 1767-1846 .... 142, 563
Nehemiah 1772-1798 143
Nehemiah 1802-1844 563
Nelson 1816-1900. 220
Newman 1811-1812 260
Nicholas 42
Nicholas 1683-1756. 4, 11
Nicholas 1716-179811, 43
Nicholas 1745-1715.. 3

Nicholas 1756-1833 174
Nicholas 1756-183844, 277
Nicholas 1766-1816 166
Nicholas M. 1801-1866 212
Norman 1791-1792 222
Obed 1773-1775 ... 194
Olive 1768-1792 .... 64, 251
Olive 1777- 164
Olive 1785-1818 ... 165
Olive 1787-1837 ... 249
Olive 1813-1848 ... 583
Oliver 1672-1747.. 3, 8
Oliver 1698-1760 8, 32
Oliver 1723-1738.... 32
Oliver 1740- ... 32, 138
Oliver 1773-1821... 62, 244
Oliver 1775-1779.. 139
Oliver 1775-1869... 56, 219
Oliver 1776-1837. 138, 547
Oliver 1784- 553
Oliver 1809-1883.. 244
Oliver A. 1817-1876 221
Oramel 1813-1893 213
Orrin 1793-1855.. 222, 487
Orrin 1796-1887... 260
Orville 1801-1849. 560
Osgood 1794-1882 563
Paul 1684-1742 .. 4, 13
Paul 1720-1804 13, 51
Paul 1743-182751, 61, 203
Paul 1783-1868 194
Percy 1767- 64
Perley 1795- 240
Permelia 1806-1892 261
Peter 1750-1750 43
Peter 1763-1851 .... 45, 47, 180
Peter 1802-1817 ... 180
Phebe 1731-1754.. 277
Phebe 1734-1808... 15, 62
Phebe 1735-.... 35, 145
Phebe 1750-1823.... 42
Phebe 1752-1831 ... 44, 173
Phebe 1756-1849... 47, 186
Phebe 1770-1773.. 146
Phebe 1771-1844.. 172
Phebe 1772-1850.. 166
Phebe 1778-.......... 165

Phebe 1779-1867. 146, 577
Phebe 1780-.......... 181
Phebe 1785-.......... 147
Phebe 1787-1851.. 212
Phebe 1795-1844.. 214
Phebe 1795-1870.. 546
Phebe 1797-1862. 189, 191
Phebe B. 1796- 174
Phebe C. 1810-1858 190
Phebe F. 1795-1870 547
Phebe F. 1806-1880 189
Phebe S. 1825-1874 583
Philemon 1744-1818 .... 51, 204
Phineas 1742-1761. 39
Polly 1782-1852..... 67, 262
Polly 1797-1800.... 582
Polly 1798-1853... 213, 222
Polly 1799-1826.... 547
Polly 1799-1881.... 260
Priscilla 1709- 8
Priscilla 1768-1848 274
Rachel 1783- 175
Rachel P. 1803-1891 611
Ralph 1794-1973.. 214
Rebecca 1770-1774141
Rebecca 1776- 185
Rebecca 1797-1857222
Rebecca 1799- 563
Rebecca 1813-1886547
Rebecca O. 1776-1805 .... 141, 556
Rebecca O. 1802-1826 557
Recta 1815-1889... 612
Rena 1817-1840 ... 612
Rhoda 1757-1799 .. 37, 156
Rhoda 1772-1773 . 143
Rhoda 1773-1850 143, 564
Rhoda 1807-1846 . 192
Rhoda 1808-1838 . 611
Rhoda 1809-1811 . 191
Rhoda 1815-1849 . 191
Rhoda A. 1810-1878 565
Rhoda A. 1813-1864 564
Richard 1782-1836167
Robert 1696-17684, 13
Robert G. 1802- ... 158, 626
Rodney 1788-1862 240
Rose 1742-1784 33

Roxlana 1760-178764, 254
Royal 1786-1864 . 214, 488
Rufus 1783-1852.. 204
Ruth 1765-1806 ... 194
Ruth 1801-1820 ... 213
Ruth 1809-1811 ... 189
Ruth 1812-1874 ... 189
Ruth K. 1782-1799142
Sabra 1768-.......... 171
Sally 1773- 167
Sally 1780-1848 ... 239
Sally 1785-1847 ... 199
Sally 1789-1841 ... 167
Sally 1795-1828 ... 582
Sally D. 1802-1880576
Sally P. 1793-1803174
Samuel 1767- 146
Samuel 1771-1846 62, 243
Samuel 1778-1819 172
Samuel 1791-1802 183
Samuel 1807-1893 577
Samuel B. 1807-1844 243
Samuel G. 1797-... 158
Samuel K. 1806-... 213
Samuel P. 1785-1827 174
Sanford 1815-1886225
Sarah.............. 59, 229
Sarah 1691-1761 4
Sarah 1721-............ 13
Sarah 1722-1743... 13, 52
Sarah 1724-1738.... 10
Sarah 1727-1769... 32, 138
Sarah 1733-1769... 33, 140
Sarah 1738-.... 42, 164
Sarah 1746-.... 49, 198
Sarah 1747-1808... 45, 178
Sarah 1748-1777... 49, 200
Sarah 1757-..... 44, 54, 176, 211
Sarah 1758-1841... 45, 178
Sarah 1761-.......... 139
Sarah 1761-1813... 62, 241
Sarah 1764-.......... 166
Sarah 1764-1859. 146, 576
Sarah 1768-1843.. 172
Sarah 1769-1836.... 56
Sarah 1770-.......... 139
Sarah 1773-1774.. 141
Sarah 1775-1833.. 204
Sarah 1779-.......... 141
Sarah 1780-.......... 165

Sarah 1780-1857... 86, 335
Sarah 1795-1885...189
Sarah 1801-1861...243
Sarah 1802-1843...554
Sarah 1806-1874...577
Sarah 1808-1874...563
Sarah 1811-1813...611
Sarah 1813-1865...554
Sarah 1814- 607
Sarah A. 1786-1845 ....143, 567
Sarah A. 1816-1906 565
Sarah A. 1824-1851 567
Sarah B. 1825-1859 585
Sarah D. 1818-1874 ....158, 627
Sarah F. 1809-1847 180
Sarah Farnum 1809-1847...................180
Sarah G. 1819-1890 230
Sarah M. 1825- 608
Silas 1735-1773 16, 64
Silas 1757-1784 64
Simeon K. 1774-1775 185
Simeon K. 1797-1833 576
Smith 1769-1814... 66, 172, 260
Solomon 1768-183047, 190
Solomon 1772-183857, 223
Solomon 1799-1883 190
Stephen 1713-179811, 43
Stephen 1744-1771 43
Stephen 1748-183851, 205
Stephen 1771-1817 ....142, 564
Stephen 1773-1856 165
Stephen 1773-186847, 144, 191
Stephen 1775-1779 205
Stephen 1777- 181
Stephen 1779-1839 167
Stephen 1782-1852 184
Stephen 1783-1856 205
Stephen 1786- 172
Stephen 1786-1855 ....182, 183

Stephen 1788-1830 174
Stephen 1799-1800 181
Stephen 1804-1804 191
Stephen 1805-1875 563
Stephen 1810-1879 192
Stephen 1820-1887 577
Stephen A. 1820-1895 565
Stephen M. 1807-1833 564
Stephen P. 1816-1860 190
Susan 1792-1876 ..553
Susan 1807-1835 ..554
Susan 1809-1851 ..585
Susan 1815-1892 ..244
Susan 1839- 627
Susanna 1760-1760 45
Susanna 1808- 547
Susannah 1731-1748 32
Susannah 1755- ...137, 546
Susannah 1800-1856 243
Susannah 1802-1874 219
Susannah B. 1771-1843 165
Sylvanus H. 1819- 583
Sylvanus W. 1820- 607
Tabitha 1753-1778.34, 144
Tabitha 1779-143, 566
Tabitha 1785-1789194
Tabitha 1796-1872579
Tabitha 1799-1855189
Tabitha D. 1827-1890 583
Tamesin 1803-1896 ....189, 555
Thomas 1686-1767 . 4, 12
Thomas 1712-1776 12, 45
Thomas 1750- .46, 181
Thomas 1752-1754 .51
Thomas 1764-1847184
Thomas 1768-1831203
Thomas 1790- 185
Thomas 1799-1814222
Thomas 1827-1889626
Thomas A. 1796-1815 212
Thomas A. 1815-...213
Timothy 1721-180112, 44
Timothy 1739-180714, 57

Timothy 1746- 44, 175
Timothy 1765-185057, 221
Timothy 1767-185647, 189, 194
Timothy 1777-1860 175
Timothy 1801-1864 222
Timothy 1802-1867 189
Timothy A. 1773-1856 274
Timothy C. 1815-1882 580
Timothy P. 1811-1892 547
Uriah 1701-1741.8, 32
Uriah 1726- 32
Uriah 1729-1812....33, 139
Uriah 1733- 32
Uriah 1754-1828....61, 239
Uriah 1755- 139
Uriah 1757-1761...137
Uriah 1775-1849..143, 564
Uriah 1810-1871...563
Valentine 1763-1840 ....37, 157
Valentine 1812-1899 ....158, 626
Valentine 1853-1927 629
Varnum 1779-1783 143
Varnum 1788-1818 562
Varnum 1815-1863 585
Vine 1770-1828.....203
Wesley 1856-1923.629
Wesley R. 1829-1902 ....158, 629
Willard 1803-1863 554
William 1720-1793 12, 14, 49
William 1737- 42
William 1737-1816163
William 1743-1815 49, 199
William 1763- .46, 183
William 1764-1793200
William 1775-1801163
William 1776-1843165
William 1788-1820183
William 1792-1868 ....153, 607
William 1811-1878221
William 1812-1877583
William C. 1820- ...583
William C. 1828-1888 607
William C. 1830-...583

William O. 1830-1893 ....*607*
William W. 1812-1885 251
Williams 1795-1876 249
Worster 1799-1881212
Zebadiah 1702-1704 .8
Zebina 1797-1871 .212
Zela 1738- 69, 274
Ziba 1771-1860 204
Zilpha 1776-1830...62, 244
Zilphia 1776-...........62
HOLTON
  Ann J. 1820-1899..514
  Mary 1806-1859....514
HOMAN
  Nancy 1814-1902..403
HOMER
  Abigail 1812-1888.459
  Alured 1796-1870.459
  Amanda 1792-1855 459
  Lucia 1794-1882 ...459
  Margaret 1822-1894 597
  Solomon 1771-1844 ....116, 459
  Solomon 1804-1879 459
HOOD
  Allen G. 1816-1878 282
  George W. 1808-1892 281
  Lydia -1807.....78, 300
HOOPER
  Levi 1801-1876 372
  Lucy 1820-1891 385
  Martha 1815-1909 367
  William 1812-1903387
HOOTON
  Catherine 1790-1875 ....101, 405
HOPKINS
  Angelia 1811-1897419
  David 499
  Emeline 1811-1889 264
  Frederick 1806-1866 539
  George 1758-1842 136, 539
  George 1793-1821.539
  Grove 1799-1879...539
  Harriet 1830-1903 612
  Henrietta 1802-1880 539
  John 1797-1838 539
  Lyman 1817-1888.381
  Mark 1795-1873 ...539
  Zenas 1790-1875...482
HORN
  Arvesta 1845-1923627

Otis 151
HORR
   Isaac 1802-1861 ... 580
HORTON
   Betsey 1785- 204
   Eliza 1799-1890 ... 256
   Harvey 1799-1886 243
   Lucius 1804-1884. 225
   Polly 1783- 211
HOSINGTON
   Sarepta 1783-1812 205
HOSMER
   Amos 1775- 366
   Bethiah 1792-1857 365
   Horace 1794-1860 247
   Sabra 1732- 25, 109
HOTCHKISS
   Hiram 1815-1848. 234
HOUGH
   Asahel 1792-1874. 336
HOUGHTON
   Abel 1796-1890 333
   Asenath 1775-1860
   .... 145, 575
   Benjamin 1789-1882
   333
   Benjamin 1790-1882
   183
   Bethiah 1771-1846
   .... 145, 574
   Bethiah 1807-1887 333
   Betsey C. 1806-1848
   573
   Catherine 1766-1854
   265
   Daniel 1775-1855. 468
   Daniel 1812-1856. 333
   Dorcas 1820-1892. 335
   Eliza P. 1788-1830 95,
   378
   Ephraim 1759-1840
   .... 145, 571
   Ephraim 1787-1867
   333
   Ephraim 1790- 572
   Experience 1777-. 145,
   572
   Hannah 1794-1853
   333
   Harvey 1804-1893 333
   Hosea 1802- 573
   Irena 1813-1815... 573
   Irena 1815-1849... 573
   James 1728- ... 35, 145
   James 1756-1835 .. 86,
   145, 333
   James 1791-1846 . 333
   John S. 1819-1845 572
   Joseph (James 1801-
   1869 574
   Joseph 1801-1869. 333
   Lucy 1789-1833.... 572
   Lucy 1790- 204
   Mary 1805-1847 ... 552

   Mary H. 1824-1855
   335
   Nabby C. 1800- 573
   Nathan 1769-1853 265
   Orinda 1768-1843 145,
   573
   Phebe 1762-1800. 145,
   572
   Phebe 1796........... 572
   Phebe 1799-1868.. 333
   Samantha A. 1809-
   1838 573
   Sewell 1809-1889 . 333
   Silva 1796- 573
   Silvanus 1765-1816
   .... 145, 573
   Silvanus 1799- 573
   Thomas 1763-1840 265
   Thomas 1791-1827 572
HOUSER
   Mary E. 1847-1904
   389
HOVEY
   Sarah 1814-1879.. 632
   Timothy L. 1813-1887
   189
HOW/HOWE
   Achsah 1769-1836 121,
   478
   Almira 1781-1846 474
   Asenath 1804-1886
   577
   Bethiah W. 1824-1851
   637
   Demaries 1781-1861
   271
   Dorothy 1780-1873
   .... 147, 583
   Elizabeth 1797-1870
   352
   Harriet N. 1816-... 577
   Isaac 1781-1858 ... 448
   Joel 1819-1867 577
   Louisa 1805-1862. 421
   Lydia A. 182
   Mark 1803-1861 ... 341
   Martha 1808- 366
   Martha 1814-1870 577
   Mary 1811-1879 ... 577
   Moses 1819-1896.. 408
   Nelson 1807-1881. 577
   Rosilla H. 1849-1925
   609
   Sarah 1810-1847.. 577
   Zalmon 1775-1855
   .... 146, 577
HOWARD
   Achsah 1800-1872 594
   Ann M. 1820-1890 551
   Anna 1801-1876 ... 477
   Artemus 1799-1866
   579
   Daniel H. 1818-1859
   636

   David 1780-1848. 130,
   518
   Edward................. 572
   Eleazer 1793-1872 477
   Elizabeth 1776-1847
   199
   Elizabeth 1800-1826
   594
   Esther 1790-1849. 476
   Ezra 1789-1864 476
   Hannah 1796-1879
   .... 152, 604
   Jane 1818-1903.... 518
   Lewis 1804-1889 .. 563
   Lucy 1795-1878.... 477
   Lucy 1815-1897.... 518
   Manasseh 1763-1836
   .... 121, 476
   Martha 1811- 518
   Olive 1823-1875 ... 346
   Permelia 1799-1849
   551
   Polly 1798-1831... 477,
   492
   Sarah 1801-1888.. 477
   Thomas 1742-1805. 27
HOWELL
   Arthur O. 1818-1856
   467
HOWLAND
   Angelo 1829-1911. 459
HOWLETT
   Sarah 1795-1839.. 578
HOYT
   Adelaide 1852-1908
   628
   Charlotte 1805-1864
   356
   Elizabeth A. 1802-
   1852 292
   Georgianna 1850-1919
   629
   Jonathan 1775-1867
   356
   Mary 1814- 367
   Nancy 1813-1851 . 367
   William 1799-1888 367
HUABBRD
   Lucy 1788-1839.... 490
HUBBARD
   Adolphus 1838-1913
   626
   Azuba 1776-1857 147,
   581
   Lucy 1786-1849.... 314
   Mary A. 1824-1848
   635
   Priscilla 1821-1862
   457
   Sally -1826 314
HUDSON
   Rebecca 1775-1850
   .... 120, 473
HUEY

   Lydia A. 1848-1906
   381
HUFFMAN
   William 1798- 264
HUGG
   Achsah 1815-1891 360
   Daniel 1801-1861. 360
   Jemima 1813-1902 360
   Lydia 1800- 360
   Milton 1790-1878. 360
   Nancy 1788- 359
   Russell 1804- 360
   Statira 1802-1896 360
   William 1764-1826 92,
   359
HUGGINS
   Caroline 1810-1850
   569
   Charles 1808-1893 325
HUGHES
   Lucinda 1798-1870
   233
   Mary 1802-1890... 475
   Sibyl 1795-1873 ... 210
HULIT
   James 1810-1887 . 364
HULL
   Joseph 1788-1871 211
   Mary R. 1826- 418
HULSE
   Lester 1813-1893 . 520
HUMPHREY
   Abigail 1749-1749 .. 30
   Benjamin 1746-1748
   30
   Dolly 1800-1836... 366
   Dorothy 1730- 29, 127
   Hannah 1728-1752 29,
   126
   John 1702-1784.. 7, 29
   John -1748 30
   Marriam 1749- 127
   Mary 1734-1816.... 29,
   128
   Mary 1785-1812.. 125,
   494
   Mary T. 1795-1825 186
   Nathan 1739-1740 . 29
   Rachel 1732- .. 29, 128
   Sarah 1737-1812... 29,
   129
   Zerviah 1743-1827 29,
   130
HUMPHREYS
   Cornelius 1775-1853
   362
HUNN
   Sarah 1736-1805... 74,
   287
HUNT
   Abigail 1798-1838 560
   Amos 1729- 21
   Amos 1754-1768..... 91
   Amos 1774-1851.... 92,
   360
   Amos 1780- 92

Anne E. 1823- 607
Betsey 1791- 358
Caroline 1801-1849
...................360
Catharine 1810-1891
...................359
Charity 1799-1824355
Charles 1803-1869360
Chauncey 1808-1881
...................360
Chloe 1759-1822 91
Clementina 1788-1821
...................355
Cyrus 1769- 92
Cyrus 1787- 358
David 1767-1834... 92,
358
David 1812-1814...359
David 1816-1864...359
Edward 1804-1875359
Elizabeth 1774- 91
Elizabeth 1791-1835
...................357
Emeline 1800-1883
...................358, 360
Emma 1769-1862.. 91,
357
Emma 1798- 357
Frederick 1772- 91
George 1785-1825.355
Hannah 1797-1891
...................359
Harriet 1805-1895 357
Harriet 1814-1879 359
Henry 468
Henry 1808- 355
Hiram 1795- 358
Horace 1810- 356
Horace 1819-1899.515
Isaac 1759- 92
Isaac 1811-1838....360
Jane 1806-1814.....355
Jemima 1777-1832 92,
361
John 1767-1831 91,
357
John 1796-1886 355
John 1800- 357
John 1802- 564
Joseph 1694-1743 ... 5,
21
Joseph 1728- 21
Julia 1802-1890 355
Junius 1815-1838 .361
Leonard 1807-1884
...................357
Louise 1783- 355
Lucius 1815-1896..361
Lucy 1794-1861.....359
Lydia 1772-1826 ... 92,
359
Maria 1813- 356
Mary -1796......90, 352
Mary 1810-1898....357

Mary A. 1809-1841
...................470
Mary L. 1800-1869358
Milo 1765-1815 91
Minerva 1793-1879
...................357
Minerva 1803- 358
Nelson 1802-1849.357
Norman 1794- 355
Polly 1799- 358
Rebecca 1778- 91
Rebecca 1813-1897357
Reuben 1788-1872
...................358, 360
Robert 1732- 21, 91
Robert 1795-1870 .357
Rodney 1797-1854 355
Russell 1733-1806...92
Russell 1738-1806...22
Russell 1756-1831..91,
355
Russell 1762-1839..92,
358
Salmon 1765-1839 .92,
358
Salmon 1796-1873 358
Sampson R. 1761-
1826.............91, 355
Sarah 1725- 21, 90
Sarah 1763-1832....91,
356
Walter 1792- 355
Wealthy 1808-1868
...................359
Whiting 1782-1782
...................355
William 1802-1846355
William 1806-1883360
HUNTING
Abigail 1780-1836.197
HUNTINGTON
Amelia 1811-1847.541
Andrew 1766-1837
...................136, 541
Andrew 1795-1800541
Andrew 1813-1827542
Anna 1792-1795....541
Asahel 1795-1822 .259
Dan 1806-1843......541
Elisha 1793-1853...541
Eliza 1829-1907 339
Enoch 1804-1862 ..541
Horatio 1797-1800 541
Lucy 1800-1804 541
Matilda 1806-1879541
Nathan B. 1810-1885
...................541, 545
Sophia 1791-1849.541
Zeruiah 1803-1804541
HUNTOON
Andrew J. 1832-1902
...................385
HUNTRESS
Eliza 1825-1885 368

Frederick 1805-1839
...................368
James 1806-1858..368
James 1818-1883..632
John 1803- 368
John F. 1775-1852.93,
368
Mary 1822-1887....368
Nathan 1808-1839 368
Robert 1802-1872 .368
Sarah 1816-1880...368
Silas 1813-1874 368
Thomas 1811-1901368
HURD
Andrew J. 1815-1892
...................605
Marshall 1794- 292
HURLBURT
Charlotte 1805-1874
...................483
Innocent 1820-1910
...................534
John 1810- 534
Joseph...................534
Joseph 1787-.135, 534
Lucy 534
Mary 534
Mary 1794-1859....443
HURLBUT
Adeline L. 1810-1887
...................224
HURLEY
William 1809- 479
HURN
Annie 1822-1889...368
HUSE
Agnes 1834-1913 ..619
Clarissa 1808-1854
...................582
Mary 1691- 3, 8
HUSTED
John A. 1823-1881512
HUTCHINS
David 1769- 167
Dorcas 1807-1845 .365
Eunice 1796-1857 134,
532
Sally 1797-1898 197
HUTCHINSON
Abel 1818-1875 622
Achsah 1808-1878 621
Alvin E. 1826-1883
...................343
Anna 1808-1881....621
Arnold B. 1808-1888
...................189
Belinda 1821- 621
Charles 1812-1876622
Ebenezer 1780-1845
...................156, 621
Ebenezer 1806-1894
...................621
Eliza 1825-1833 621
Franklin 1796-1878
...................561

Frederick 1783-1850
...................156, 622
Joanna 1836-1881 623
John 1810-1887 621
Louisa M. 1808-1895
...................488
Luther 1819-1814.621
Lydia 1812- 621
Lydia 1816-1818 ...622
Lydia 1823- 623
Lyman 1820-1822.622
Lyman 1827-1888.623
Mary 1813-1880....622
Nathaniel 1786-1826
...................362
Nizaula 1801-1855557
Olive 1838-1916....337
Phebe 1816-1866 ..621
Reuben 1814-1904 621
Rhoda 1804- 621
Roxana 1815-1854 624
Ruth 1750- 21, 86
Sarah 1719-1798 ...19,
78
HYDE
Gordon 1801-1885 217
Mary 1811-1892....484
Thomas 401
HYNE
Ellen 1828-1875....381
IDE
Truman 1802-1830
...................491
INGALLS
Abigail 1710- 11
Abigail 1822-1904.442
Alice 1775- 111
Allis 1742-1744.......27
Allis 1756-1758.......28
Anna 1701- 7
Ardella 1809-1893 465
Asa 1772-1776 118
Augustus 1805-1889
...................441
Benjamin 1716-18007,
27
Benjamin 1746-1825
...................28, 117
Benjamin 1774-1778
...................118
Betsey 1780- .118, 207
Betsey 1815-1890 .442
Caleb 1777-...118, 465
Chester 1803-1871442
Clarissa 1802-1885
...................441
Daniel 1751-1755....28
Daniel 1770- .118, 464
David 1747-1814....28,
118
Dorcas 1774-1814 118,
466
Eliza 1806-1829....465
Elizabeth 1710-...7, 26
Esther 1782- 118

Hannah 1759-1838 47, 186
Hannah 1784-1816 118
Hannah 1815- 465
Harriott 1806-1818 464
John 1661-1743... 3, 6
John 1697-1783.. 6, 24
John 1737-1818...... 24
John 1784-............ 272
Josiah 1676-1755 4, 11
Judey 1808-1848.. 328
Justus 1805-1859. 441
Lemuel 1770- 111, 441
Lemuel P. 1805- ... 442
Louisa A. 1812-1837 442
Lucretia 1811-1883 465
Lucy 1777-1849 ... 118, 466
Marietta 1812-1890 438
Martha 1713- 7, 26
Mary 1705-......... 7, 24
Mary 1735-..... 24, 104
Mary 1743-1744 28
Mary 1749-..... 28, 118
Mary 1779-1856 ... 118
Mary 1809-.......... 465
Mehitable 1708-1756 .... 7, 25
Mercy 1761-1842... 69, 271
Molly 1774-1776... 118
Moses 1820-1881.. 442
Nancy 1790-1847 . 111
Nancy 1796-1840 . 244
Oliver 1806-1862.. 465
Oscar 1816-1899 .. 619
Peletiah 1753-1776 28
Phebe 1708-...... 11, 41
Rachel 1713-........... 11
Roxy 1788-1857.... 110
Rua D. 1818-1902. 442
Ruth 1740-1819...... 26
Samuel 1746- . 26, 111
Samuel 1770-1839 .... 111, 441
Sarah 1698-1764...... 6
Sarah 1735-.... 26, 110
Sarah 1782-1871.. 201
Sarah 1809-.......... 465
Sarah 1810-1895.. 442
Solomon 1807-...... 442
Sophronia 1810-1898 438
Stephen 1710-1771 . 7, 25
Stephen 1737-1771 26
Stephen 1772- 111
Theda 1773- . 118, 465
Thomas 1742-1816 26, 110

INGERSOLL
Eliza 1820-1905 ... 460
Joseph 1796-1861. 230
IRELAND
Rebecca 1789-1883 86, 336
IRWIN
Delia 1836-1915 ... 614
JACKMAN
Mary 1802-1884 ... 189
JACKSON
Mary 1755-1836 .... 39, 160
JACOBS
Martha 1828-1860 599
JACOY
John 1806-1876.... 465
JAMES
Aaron 1811-1896.. 538
Benjamin 1771-1848 .... 135, 537
Benjamin 1796-1819 537
Betsey 1807-1859. 538
Cyrel 1791-.......... 215
Diana 1794-1796.. 537
Elisha 1814-1876 . 538
Hannah 1801-1845 537
Jonathan 1799-1825 537
Josiah 1809-1900 . 538
Rebecca 1805-1844 538
Rhoda 1803-1875 . 537
Richard H. 1827-1904 377
JANES
Adotia 1795-1797. 451
Augustus 1787-1846 451
Clementine 1802-1892 451
Cynthia 1789-1822 451
Flavilla 1793-1885 451
Peleg C. 1760-1834 .... 113, 451
Timothy 1791-1877 451
William C. 1805-1873 451
JAQUITH
Ambrose 1810-1864 192
Benjamin 1798-1881 191
Josiah 1777-1868 . 553
Josiah 1778-1843 . 483
JELLISON
Mary 1792-1871 ... 173
JENKINS
Ebenezer 1807-1883 392
JENKS
Henry P. 1812-1850 526
JENNINGS

Eliza 1812-1887 ... 419
Lurana 1812-1888 292
JENNISON
Charles H. 1839-1910 386
David A. 1838-1913 386
Frank R. 1847-1917 386
George R. 1834-1901 385
John 1807-1880..... 96, 385
John 1837-1875.... 386
Mary E. 1842-1918 386
Warren H. 1848-1912 386
William W. 1835- . 385
JEWELL
Nathan 1809-1876 407
Nathaniel 1811-1883 438
JEWETT
Augustus 539
Isaac 1763-1852 ... 270
Judith M. 1781-1849 .... 104, 411
Mary 1802-1864 ... 444
Milo 1808-1882 312
Susan 1799-1880.. 566
JOHNSON
Abel 1781- 59, 230
Abel 1819-1861 230
Anna 1796-........... 353
Arminda 1807-1893 218
Bulkley 1788-....... 352
Catherine 1816-1895 479
Clarissa 1806-1880 243
Cynthia 1808-1876 423
Daniel 1788-......... 237
David 1779-1785... 237
David 1786-........... 237
Dinah 1777- 237
Eleanor 1811-1856 499
Elisha 1805-1873 . 230
Eliza 1816-1818 ... 230
Eliza 1818-1894 ... 230
Ellen 1800-1886 ... 279
Emma 1793-......... 352
Erastus 1786-1837 249
Eunice 1804-1805 230
Eunice 1812-1890 230
Hannah 1753- 44, 175
Hannah 1754- 90
Hannah 1768-1806 92, 358
Hannah 1787-1817 173
Henry 1791-1878 . 247
Henry J. 1810-1850 526

Ira 1794-1878....... 237
Ira 1796-1878....... 557
James................. 634
Jemima 1757- 90, 352
Jeremiah 1763-1847 .... 90, 353
John 253
John 1782- 237
John 1786- 167
John 1818-1902.... 346
Joseph 292
Joseph 1761- .. 90, 352
Joseph 1791-......... 352
Josiah 1726-..... 21, 90
Josiah 1752-.......... 90
Josiah 1789-......... 352
Keturah 1781-...... 237
Lorenzo 1805-1867 354
Lydia 43
Marcus 1811-1852 230
Martha H. 1791-1873 179
Mary 1789-.......... 353
Mary 1795-.......... 352
Mary H. 1826-1885 533
Merrick 1809-1895 230
Moses 314
Nathaniel 18
Otis....................... 530
Peter.................... 140
Philip C. 1795-1859 413
Polly 1797- 353
Ralph 1798-1826 .. 237
Reuben 1792-1852 413
Robert A. 1766-1855 285
Ruth 1744-1827 .... 48, 193
Samuel 61
Samuel 1784-1840 237
Sarah 1719-1804... 19, 76
Sarah 1766-.... 90, 354
Sarah 1791-.......... 237
Sarah 1794-1820.. 353
Seth 1786-1856 352
Solon 1828-1889... 354
Sophronia 1814-1898 .... 220, 230
Susan 1803-1862.. 354
Thomas 1756-......... 90
Thomas 1807-....... 354
Thomasin 1790-1795 353
Thomasin 1797-1871 353
Truman 1822-1851 230
JOHNSTON
Elizabeth 1803-1898 305
JOHSNON
James 1799-1872 . 353

JONES
Adeline 1803-1877 481
Betsey 318
Catherine 1813-1884
................499
Chloe 1831-876 620
Eliab 1809- 335
Elizabeth.............. 46
Ellen 1838-1891....536
Frank 1847-1920 ..628
Ira 1815-1891.......386
John 1808- 492
John 1812-1889 622
Lucinda 1787-1815
................205
Lucy 1787-1875.....175
Lydia 1780-1858 ...194
Maria 1811-1886...333
Mary..............48, 192
Mary 1780-1831....316
Phebe 1774-1798...184
Sarah 1827-1854...620
Sylvester 1835-1913
................345
William 590
JORDAN
Amanda 1846-1872
................618
Amanda M. 1811-1882
................576
Calvin 1786-1859..362
David 1759-1847... 92, 362
David 1784-..........362
Elijah 1793-1865...362
Eliza 1803-1855 580
Elsie 1848-1871 609
Hiram 1804-1857..575
James 1800-1882 ..363
Joanna 1801-1856.363
Lorenzo 1808-1894576
Lydia 1798-1855 ...363
Pearley 1799-1873 575
Phebe 1795-1854...362
Phebe 1809-1876...363
Russell 1806-1875.363
Ruth 1793-1865 362
Samuel 1797-1875 363
Solomon 1756-184692, 362
Solomon 1784-1854
................362
Temperance 1794-1842................362
Thomas 1803-1881363
Wales 1795-1877...362
Wilbur 1864-1943 .629
William 1774-1849
................145, 575
William A. 1802-1872
................575
JOSSELYN
Freeman 1778-1868
................240
JOURDAN

David 1797-1883...575
JOY
Deborah 1778-1850
................176
JUDD
Edwin 1805-1873..252
Elizabeth 1813-1842
................517
JUDKINS
Hannah 1813-1853
................621
Mary 1809-1876....621
Nathan 1805-1892 621
Perry 1811-1867 ...590
JUDSON
Andrew 1749-1804
................121, 474
Andrew T. 1784-1853
................474
John W. 1782-1811
................474
Jose 1780-1806 474
KARR
Joanna 1803-1874158, 630
KAY
Mary A. 1842-1900
................378
KEAN
Mary Ann 1792-1850
................85, 330
KEENE
Eliza 1825-1897 426
KEENEY
Marvin 1798-1834 542
Theodosia 1811-1856
................534
KEEP
Elizabeth 1769-1796
................267
Jabez 1736-1821 ....68, 266
Jabez 1759-1820 ...267
Mehitable 1773-1822
................267
Rebecca 1782-1807267
Ruth 1771-1794 267
Sarah 1763-1809...267
KELLOGG
Lorena 1792-1858.256
Lorraine 1805-1885
................257
KELLY
James 1831-1861 ..346
KELSEY
Andrew J. 1817-1895
................636
Benjamin F. 1809-1874................512
Betsey 1794-1869 .222
KEMP
Julia 1820-1852 563
KENDALL
Abigail 1742-1781..52, 206

Alice 1746-1798 52
Alpheus 1788- 97
Amanda 1810-1857
................324
Amanda 1830-1901
................361
Atlantee 1808-1828
................373
Betsey 1795-1879 .483
Charles 569
Daniel 1785- 207
David 1744- 52, 207
David -1777 ......13, 52
Edna 1824-...........569
Ervilla 1806-.........373
Eunice 1784-1856 .207
Ezekiel 1751- 52
Isaac 1787-1848....516
Jane H. 1830-1918260
Lucy H. 1779-1786207
Martin R. 1810-1811
................373
Mary 1811-1892....484
Mary A. 1804-1895
................259
Mary N. 1812-.......373
Rebecca 1749- 52
Roxana 1771-1830
................136, 539
Sarah 1776- 207
Susanna 1804-1886
................373
William 1777-1828 94, 373
William 1804-1875563
William M. 1815-1904
................373
KENISTON
George B. 1829-1914
................637
KENNEDY
Avery 1800-1870...360
Clarissa 1805-1886
................249
James W. 1796-1885
................322
Noah 1806-1881....261
KENNETT
William 1837-1902400
KENNEY
Dolly 1785-1845.....89, 345
Dorcas 1810-1845 .637
Eliza J. 1815-........637
George W. 1824- ...637
Hannah 1816-1867
................603
Hannah A. 1808-1887
................637
Jerusha 1769-1857
................146, 576
Jonathan A. 1806-1875................637
Mary P. 1818- 637
Sally H. 1821-1837637

KENNEY/see also
KINNEY
Jonathan 1771-1847
................161, 636
Ruth 1783-1877 448
KENT
Charlotte A. 1800-1885................420
Cyrel W. 1815-1900
................233
Elizabeth 1812-.....472
Irena C. 1823-1892
................282
Richard 1832-1873630
KETCHAM
Harriet J. 1793-1858
................227
KETCHUM
Sophronia 1833-1910
................381
KETTLER
Marcia 1828-1900.462
KEYES
Alvin G. 1808-1872
................155, 616
Anna 1798-1828....475
Danforth 1787-1849
................475
Edward 1759-1827
................121, 475
Edward 1793-1835475
Elias 1781-1801 475
Elizabeth 1785-1803
................475
Ellen 1838- 617
Esther 1781-1816 .475
Justus 1780-1835 .475
Mark R. 1834-1898
................616
Mary 1788-1869....475
Mary 1840- 617
Mary A. 1836-1874
................616
Proctor H. 1810-1840
................155, 617
Rebecca................333
Roxana 1779-1842 475
Sampson 1777-1861
................269
Sarah 1795-1856 ..475
Sophia 1789-1876 123, 484
KIBBE
Amelia 1805-1866.238
KIDDER
Ann 1791-1863 159
Ann 1815-1815 632
Anna 1819-1899....631
Betsey 1815-1897 .631
Catherine 1813-1848
................632
David 1797- 176
Eliza 1814-1894....344
Hannah 1793-.......159

Hannah 1821-1840 631
John 1811-1892.... 344
John 1822-1911.... 631
Levi 1827-1913..... 631
Manley 1810-1877 632
Martha 1826-1903 631
Phineas 1789-1864 .... 159, 631
Phineas 1817-1892 632
Phinehas 1756-1846 .... 38, 159
Samuel 1787-1866 .... 159, 631
Sarah D. 1825-1855 418

KILBOURN
Abigail -1844 558

KILBURN
Francis A. 1820-1896 635
Judith A. 1815-1868 414

KILE
Ephraim 1789-1872 231

KILGORE
Abigail 1806- 593
Ira 1808-1877 593
Mehitable 1773- .. 150, 595

KILLAM
Abigail 1736-1782 . 19, 75
Mary 1809-1886 ... 585

KILPATRICK
Daniel 363

KIMBALL
Abigail 1754- 64
Abigail 1761- .. 27, 117
Abigail F. 1820-1883 428
Abigail H. 1803-1835 254
Addie 1869-1955 .. 630
Alden B. 1817-1893 428
Anna 1798-1800 ... 188
Benjamin 1803-1877 188
Betsey 1785- 149
Betsey 1793-1872. 188
Betty 1767- 64
Charlotte E. 1810-1901 254
Chester 1763-1824 64, 254
Chester 1790-1823 254
Crafts P. 1788-1872 253
Daniel 1755-1843 .. 47, 188
Edwin 1808-1827 . 254
Elijah 1794-1877 .. 560
Eliza 1810-1880 ... 566

Flavel 1765- 64
Francis 1777-1843 163
Frederick 1840-1908 399
Gurdon 1788-1871 254
Hannah 1712-1748 12, 45
Hannah 1796-1881 188
Harriet 1805-1834 254
Issachar 1784-1860 .... 107, 427
Jane 1789-1861.... 185
Joanna D. 1804-1879 308
John 1785- 177
John 1792-1793.... 254
John 1800-1816.... 254
Jonathan 1773- 199
Joseph 1799-1800. 188
Joseph 1801-1864. 188
Lebbeus 1751-1839 64
Libbeus 1751-1839 253
Lucy 1796-1882.... 254
Martha A. 1816-1858 .... 424, 427
Mary 1805-1891 ... 188
Mary H. 1822-1882 428
Mary W. 1798-1828 254
Matilda 1780-1848 253
Miriam B. 1797- ... 420
Persis 1760-1845... 64, 253
Phebe 1795-1836.. 188
Phebe 1804-1887.. 596
Priscilla 1781-1868 412
Rebecca 1827-1850 246
Richard 1722-1810 16, 64
Richard 1794-1818 254
Ruth 1739-1823..... 33, 141
Sally 1786-1845... 149, 587
Sarah W. 1824-1894 .... *607*
Seth 1807-1872 590
Sylvester 1783-1830 253
Tameyson G. 1814-1907 404

KINCAIDE
Jane 1818-1866.... 455

KING
Alva 1793-1852 233
Delia A. 1845-1895 608
Eliza 1802-1887 ... 446
Lois 1777-1847.... 110, 437
Matilda 1761- 123, 481
Penelope 1778-1811 204

Persis 1805-1887.. 446
Ruth 1779- 54, 212

KINGLSEY
Eleazer 1785- 480

KINGMAN
Martha 1833-1915 397

KINGSBURY
Abigail 1742-1791 . 51, 202
Amy 1783- 203
Anna 1768-1857 ... 202
Artimissa 1776-1835 203
Eunice 1733-1784 . 14, 53
Jonathan 1712-1770 .... 13, 50
Jonathan 1745-1802 .... 51, 202
Jonathan 1794-1869 203
Lester 1787-1837 . 203
Lewis 1785-1846 .. 203
Lodema 1780- 203
Lora 1771-1810 203
Lydia 1737-1776 ... 14, 55
Mercy 1773-1774.. 203
Ransom 1789- 203
Rhoda 1778-1852 . 203

KINGSLEY
1781- 480
Hannah 1796- 481
Horace 1786- 480
Ira 1788-1866...... 480
Jedediah 1753-1832 .... 122, 480
Mary 1782- 480
Sarah 1792-1877.. 481

KIRBY
Katherine 1802-1882 469

KIRTLAND
Lucy 1817-1879.... 293

KITTREDGE
Betsey 1802-1823. 323
Catherine 1788-1824 297
Charles 1798- 323
Gratia 1790-1869 . 323
Helen L. 1837-1921 385
James 1807-1855 . 324
John 1775-1822.... 297
Joseph 1783-1847 297
Loammi 1785- 275
Marcus 1796-1869 323
Maria F. 1792-1873 297
Martha O. 1778-1839 297
Prentice 1794-1820 323
Rodney 1804-1832 324
Russell 1792-1799 323

Russell 1801-1875 323
Sarah 1781-1796.. 297
Stephen 1765-1806 84, 323
Stephen 1789- 323
Susanna 1772-1829 297
Thomas 1746-1818 77, 297

KLINE
William 1816- 350

KNIGHT
Addison 1803-1847 436
Adonijah 1764-1807 282
Benjamin 1757-1843 164
Emily 1811-1854.. 325
James 449
Jonathan 1762-1848 164
William 1816-1887 363
Zeruiah 1768- 282

KNOWLES
Susan 203

KNOWLTON
Adelia 1826- 529
Almena 1811-1895 527
Alvina 1815- 529
Arminda 1805-1886 527
Chester 1787-1871 .... 132, 529
Daniel 1738-1825.. 74, 284
Daniel 1765-1834 283, 284
Daniel 1781-1852. 285
Elizabeth 1768-1806 285
Elizabeth 1829-1914 529
Ephraim 1773- 285
Eunice 1800-1886 435
Hannah 1783-1854 285
Helen 1832-1925 .. 616
Hersey 1804-1867 446
James 1821-1878 . 529
Jane 1821-1892.... 529
Jonathan 1779-1848 .... 132, 527
Jonathan 1803-1805 527
Jonathan 1817-1898 527
Keziah 1781-1852 285
Manasseh 1770-1841 285
Martha 1777-1855 285
Martha E. 1811-1884 488
Minerva 1811- 529

Nathaniel 1770-1850
............285
Orissa 1818-1889..529
Palmer 1807-1844.527
Philena 1808-1886 529
Sophronia 1813-1871
............529
Thomas 1765-1858
............124, 488
Thomas M. 1808-1810
............488
KNOX
Anna 1782-1867....167
Mary Ann 1796-1865
............167
Polly 1792-1849 167
Sarah 1744-1802...123
KREIDLER
Rachel 1810-1875 .229
LABBELL
Mary Ann 1815-.... 95,
374
LADD
Dudley 1789-1875.415
Harriet 1809- 339
Jabez 1777-1814 ...282
Mary J. 1818-1901 503
Samuel 1768-1841 282
LAFLIN
Deborah 1780-1823
............115, 457
LAKE
Abigail 1781-1809.553
Ann Marie 1818-1875
............280
Mary 1816-1899....457
Sarah 1777-1857..139,
554
LAKIN
Betsey 1810-1878..618
Lucy 1802-1850....158,
626
Maria E. 1828-1903
............613
LAMB
Charles M. 1803-1891
............488
Dorcas M. 1787-1825
............488
Ebenezer 1801-1802
............488
Joseph 1763-1848 124,
487
Joseph 1795-1875 .488
Josiah Q. 1803-1850
............577
Lovina 1791-1856 214,
488
Lucinda 1798-1864
............488
Lydia 1792-1884 ...488
Mary 1797-1807....488
Samuel 1789-1854 486
Selinda 1788-1865 488
Thomas 1794-1803 488

LAMBERSON
John 1812- 529
LAMPSON
Ebenezer H. 1784-
1855...........148, 586
LAMSON
Goodpell 1817-1896
............379
Hannah 1824-1903
............587
Israel 1820-1902 ...587
Jane 587
Levi 1826-1901 587
Lucinda 1801- 570
Lucy P. 1817-1893 587
Mary 1805-1834....328
Rebecca 1811-1885 586
Reuben 1816-1888 586
LANCASTER
Almira J. 1810-1861
............449
Benjamin F. 1818-
1906 280
Charles 1808-1903 280
Elijah M. 1800-1891
............280
George W. 1815-1887
............280
Joseph F. 1818-1898
............280
Mary 1812-1844....280
Sewall 1805-1885..280
Thomas 1773-1864 72,
280
Thomas G. 1803-1852
............280
LANDERS
Daniel 1799-1873..520
LANDON
Catherine 1795-1885
............356
Chloe 1782-1857 ...356
Elisha 1800-1890..356
John 1798-1874 356
John M. 1789-1851
............496
Lucretia 1780-1829
............356
Luther 1787-1862 .356
Milo 1785- 356
Milo 1793-1869 356
Nelson 1810-1884.356
Robert 1802-1874 .356
Rufus 1759-1848....91,
356
Sarah 1791-1877...356
LANE
Benjamin 1789-1879
............468
Benjamin F. 1777-
1846 201
Jotham S. 1831-1903
............609
Lewis 1813-1886...384

Mary D. 1808-1898
............370
Rebecca 1794-1847 97,
387
Susan 1796-1880 ...97,
388
LANG
Mary A. -1888.......169
LANGDON
George 1804- 337
Martin 1792-1880.525
LARRABEE
James............48, 196
LASH
Joseph 1832-1903 .619
LASKY
John 276
LATHROP
Dyce 1789-1872 282
Hannah 1772-1813
............443
LAW
Abigail 1840- 497
Harriet 1856- 497
Mariah 1796-1861 519
Martha J. 1826-1896
............387
LAWRENCE
Abigail 1776-1859 129,
510
Abigail 1795-1821.366
Amos R. 1822-1862
............634
Benjamin 1813-1883
............366
Betsey 1796- 366
Esther 1801- .160, 632
Esther P. 1815-1885
............299
James 1811-1846..366
John 1804-1883 366
Joseph 1788-1854.365
Margery A. 1826-1891
............389
Nancy 1799-1877..366
Rhoda 1815-1856..366
Sally 1792-1822 365
Samuel 1766-1824 .93,
365
Samuel 1800-1862 366
Senah 1802-1874 ..366
Sophronia 1808-....366
Thomas 1789-1877 365
William 1806-1812 366
LAWSON
Emma J. 1834-......372
LAZELL
Mary 1829-1902....494
LE BOSQUET
Caleb B. 1808-1880
............279
LE BRETON
Rosetta 1795-1828 313
LEACH

Lucinda 1818-1883
............564
Sarah -1844 285
Susan 1801-1844 ..365
Wilbur 1802-1858.365
LEAKE
Ruth 1827-1860 571
LEARNED
Abigail 1779-1850.266
Asa 1791-1867 574
Asenath 1795-1882
............574
Benjamin 1767-1853
............145, 573
Benjamin 1793-1879
............574
Betsey 1808-1877 .574
Gilman 1801-1827 574
Joseph 1799-1829.574
Orinda 1806-.333, 574
Phebe 1797-1856 ..574
Polly 1803-1876 574
LEARY
James 1793-1834..453
LEATHERBEE
James H. 1772-1821
............196
LEAVITT
Almon C. 1831-1913
............400
Dudley 1772-1838.179
Jonathan 1772-1844
............166
Jonathan 1797-1852
............309
LEBARON
Elizabeth 1806-.....363
James 1759-1836...92,
363
Nathaniel 1793-1816
............363
Russell 1797-1873 363
Sarah 1808-1894 ..363
Sylvester 1815-1854
............363
William 1795-1863 363
LEBARRON
Lemuel 1780-1843 297
LECLAIR
Joseph 1800-1871.554
LEE
Elijah 1806-1835 ..503
Emily Jane 1843-1925
............588
Eunice J. 1836-1928
............396
Harriet 1786-1862 208
LEECH
Mary Thorndike 1803-
1881 180
LEIGHTON
Elizabeth 1793-1879
............362
Robert 1808-1861 .364
Sarah 1789-1882 ..362

Timothy 1846-...... 627
LELAND
  Jasper 1792-......... 354
LEMP
  John 1820-1905.... 585
LEMTON
  Lucy S. 1837-1932 280
LENOX
  Elizabeth 1820-1892
  378
LEONARD
  Adeline 1823-1865 244
  Daluka 1806-1885 214
  Electa 1818-1903.. 378
  Pamelia K. 1819-1902
  382
  Tamar 1795-1825. 240
LESTER
  Marianna 1798-1837
  472
LEWIS
  Daniel 1803-1868. 425
  Mary 1786-... 154, 614
  Nancy 1814-......... 212
  Sarah 1796-1868.. 354
LILLIE
  Levina 1816-1890. 570
LINCOLN
  James 1804-1882 . 634
  Sophia W. 1838-1889
  409
LINDAL
  Sally 1794-1838... 147,
  582
LINELL
  William B. 1802-1867
  512
LING
  Thomas 1797-....... 588
LINKHORN
  Hannah 1716-1801.. 7,
  31
LINSLEY
  Lydia 1804-.......... 537
LISCOMB
  Tryphena 1759-1834
  .... 110, 438
LITTLE
  Eliza 1787-1875 ... 304
  Eliza O. 1795-1862 251
  George 1762-1850 319
  Ira 1802-.............. 320
  Lucinda 1814-1847
  556
LITTLEFIELD
  Letitia 1796-......... 420
  Roxana 1822-1894 346
LITTLEHALE
  Isaac 1801-1865 ... 601
LIVERMORE
  Abijah 1812-1860. 636
LIVINGSTON
  Jacob 1780-1865... 251
  Sarah 1766-1849.. 185
LIVINGSTONE
  Sarah.................... 377

LOCKE
  Alfred 1823-1896.. 339
  Bezeleel 1814-1892
  339
  Clarissa 1805-1890
  339
  David 1806-1874.. 339
  Hannah M. 1819-1878
  600
  Henry 1802-1883.. 529
  J. Russell 1810-1894
  339
  James L. 1819-..... 379
  John 1843-1910.... 346
  Lydia 339
  Mary 1827-........... 340
  Philander 1826-1899
  340
  Reuben 1783-1855 87,
  339
  Reuben 1812-1845 339
  Wilber 1820-1900. 339
  William 1810-....... 529
LOCKWOOD
  Ann 1811-1896..... 493
  Charles 1780-....... 177
LONG
  John 1843-1897.... 332
  Samuel 1803-1857 313
LOOMIS
  Alma 1793-1824 ... 468
  Confucius 1809-1885
  455
  Hannah 1800-1867
  246
  Mary 1803-1845 ... 492
LORD
  Lydia K. 1813-1898
  431
  Nathaniel 1780-1852
  309
LORING
  Bailey 1786-1860 . 298
  John R. 1817-1818 599
  John R. 1821-1891 599
  Mary A. 1813-1907
  599
  Sarah 1809-.......... 599
  Thomas 1780-1826
  .... 151, 599
  Thomas F. 1807- .. 599
LORKIN
  Emeline 1812-1901
  406
LOUGEE
  James W. 1817-.... 414
LOVEJOY
  Abiel 1749-1820 80,
  304
  Abiel 1763-1837 ... 168
  Abiel 1784-1858 ... 304
  Abigail 1750-1833 . 42,
  166
  Aladen 1815-1884 587
  Anna 1785-1827 ... 168

Anne F. 1832-1861 633
Benjamin 1776-1842
  304
Dolly 1809-1889 ... 600
Dorcas 1780-1858. 182
Ebenezer 1773-1834
  .... 151, 597
Ebenezer 1795-1873
  597
Enoch 1781-1848... 304
Ezekiel 1784-1840 182
George 1798-1856 597
Hannah 1787-1843
  .... 182, 183
Hannah 1808-1808
  564
Henry 1782-1848 . 182
Isaac 1793-........... 395
Jacob 1812-1893... 564
James A. 1805-1883
  .... 160, 633
James A. 1842-1869
  633
Jeremiah 1801-1814
  597
John 1773-1832... 143,
  564
John 1779-1843.... 304
John 1780-1817... 151,
  599
John 1810-1899.... 597
John 1828-1907.... 621
Joseph 1805-1883 564
Joseph 1816-1874 597
Joshua 1818-1860 597
Josiah 1805-......... 597
Levi 1805-1882..... 588
Louisa 1809-1869. 564
Lydia 1747-1838 ... 46,
  185
Mary H. 1811-1888
  547
Mehitable 1742-1782
  70
Mehitable 1781-1804
  165
Moses 1751-1807... 46,
  181
Moses 1778-1846.. 182
Phebe 1774-1852.. 168
Phebe 1812-1896.. 597
Polly 1791-1816.... 304
Rhoda 1803-1857 . 564
Sally K. 1810-1849 590
Sarah 1808-1886.. 597
Sarah 1815-1849.. 564
Sarah M. 1835-1867
  633
Stephen 1787-...... 304
William 1796-1870 597
LOVELL
  Hannah 1793-1853
  198
LOWE

Henry S. 1818-1895
  613
Nehemiah 1805-1891
  556
LOWELL
  Lydia 1789-1857 .. 174
  Sidney 1810-1877. 507
  William B. 1813-1850
  582
LOWREY
  Jerusha 1774- 91
LOWRY
  Mary 1779-1863.... 92,
  360
LUCE
  Elizabeth A. 386
LUDDEN
  Flora 1823-1908... 549
LUFKIN
  Dorcas 1776-1848 146,
  185, 578
  Elizabeth 1825-.... 369
  Jonathan 1774-.... 185
  Mehitable 1767-1804
  185
  Samuel 1762-1838 185
  Samuel -1777. 46, 184
  Samuel 1788-1845 594
  Sarah 1769-1848.. 185
LUMMAS
  Martha 302
LUNT
  Almira 1832-1917 336
LUSCOMB
  Elizabeth 1819-1891
  292
  Lydia 1821-1853 .. 391
LYMAN
  James B. 1799-1865
  254
  Lucy 1756-1826..... 32,
  136
  Rebecca 1798-1892 446
LYNCH
  Artimesia -1860 .. 154,
  612
  Delina 1799-1856. 597
LYNDE
  Lucy 1786-1863.... 553
  Stephen 1825-1899
  344
LYON
  Esther 1819-1904. 541
  Warren W. 1817-1864
  545
LYON/LYONS
  Abigail -1760.......... 30
  Abigail D. 1802-1820
  455
  Alice 1731-1794 28, 30,
  120
  Alice 1769- 200
  Alice 1769-1804... 110,
  441
  Amasa 1771-1843 285
  Anna 1808-1812... 455

Benjamin T. 1796-1864..................257
Betsey 1815-1891..455
Chester 1772-1812200
Daniel 1778-1850.114, 455
Daniel 1817-1817..455
David 1804-1894...455
Eliza 1798-1875 487
Harriet 1817- 357
Jesse 1814-1866....455
John 1810-1905 455
Mary 1717-1784..7, 27
Mary 1728-............ 30
Mehitable 1727-.... 30, 130
Nathaniel 1800-1816 455
Peletiah 1711-...13, 52
Priscilla 1741-181330, 131
Robert 1743-1809.. 49, 52, 200
Robert 1765-1844..200
Roswell 1770-1814200
Rufus 1767-1841...200
Samuel 1806-1806 455
Sarah A. 1818-1894 238
Seth 1704-...........7, 30
Seth 1734-............. 30
Simeon 1813-1883 634
Sophia 1814-1889 .339
Sophronia 1807-1807 455

MACCLURE
Alexander H. 1805-1887..................292
David C. 1793-1870 292
Frances 1803-1846292
Henry 1794-1870 ..292
Prudence 1807-1876 292
Sally 1800-1882 292
Thomas 1802-1855292
Walter 1798-1866 .292
William 1726-1826 76, 291
William 1791-1874292

MACE
Sarah 1833-1859...637
MACK
David 1784-1847...553
MACKIE
John 1796-1872 569
MAGHER
Peter 1777-1854....250
MAGOON
Benjamin 547
MAIN
Avery 1808-1899...452
MANLEY
Ann -1810 .....159, 631
MANN

Charlotte 1797-1888 519
Michael D..............248
MANNING
Elizabeth.............5, 17
Mary -1716..........4, 11
Mary 1817-1902....615
MANSFIELD
Nathaniel B. 1796-1863 410
MARBLE
March 1793-1822..314
Phebe 1829-1914 ..626
MARCY
Abiel 1802-1887....485
Adin 1758- 123
Adolphus 1793-1814 483
Alanson 1807-1895 479
Almira 1816-1889.494
Alvan 1765-1834..124, 490
Avis 1769-1820 ....124, 491
Betsey 1797-1877 .482
Buckley 1796-1876483
Chester 1759-1845 ....123, 481
Chester 1799- 482
Clinton 1791-1859 483
Cylinda 1780-1816 ....124, 489
Danforth 1816-1884 492
Dorcas 1727-1766 ..29, 122
Dorcas 1768-1803 124, 487
Dorcas 1779-1838 125, 493
Edward 1825-1892494
Elizabeth 1788-.....238
Emily 1810- 479
Esther 1763-1839 124, 489
Esther 1826-1829 .493
Frances 1804-1835491
Gardner 1762-1837 ....123, 482
Gardner 1794-1848 482
George 1790-1862.479
George 1801-.........484
Hannah 1755-1841 ....121, 478
Hannah 1766-1828 ....124, 487
Hannah 1795-.......238
Hannah 1807-1887 485
Hannah 1821-1898 493
Harriet 1804-1879 483
Henry 1802-..........482

Hiram 1794-1856..483
Isaac.....................484
Ithamar 1809-1887 484
James 1808-1876..483
John 1724-1797 .....29, 121
John 1753- 121, 477
John 1799-1882 491
John 1800-1856 492
John 1810-1865 493
John S. 1776-.......125
John S. 1798-1838 492
John W. 1805-1888 479
Joseph 1765-.........122
Joseph 1797-1842 .492
Joseph W. 1797-1842 477
Leonard 1820-1848 494
Levi 1773-1838 ....123, 484
Levi 1803-1862 484
Lois 1781- 125
Lois 1791-1860......238
Louisa M. 1825-1851 238
Lovina 1763-1840 124, 486
Lucinda 1800-1812 482
Lucinda 1801-1843 483
Lucinda 1808-1881 238
Lucy 1793-1859 238
Lucy 1807-1887 485
Manning 1803-1806 482
Martha 1764-1831 122
Martha 1769-1853 ....124, 488
Martha 1800-1885 491
Mary 1757-1776....123
Mary 1761-1797...122, 480
Mary 1779- ...124, 489
Mary 1797-1877...123, 485
Mary 1806-1850....492
Mary 1807-1844....483
Mary 1821-1839....238
Mehitable 1790-1864 483
Nahum S. 1800-....479
Nancy 1800-1862..485
Newman S. 1817-1904 238
Olive 1763-....123, 482
Olive 1794-1877....484
Olive 1808-...........492
Orrin 1774-1828 ..125, 492

Phebe 1789-1871 .211, 238
Priscilla 1760-1834 ....124, 486
Priscilla 1786-1874 238
Prosper 1767-1770124
Prosper 1772-1855 ....124, 492
Rebecca 1789- 125
Reuben 1798-1843 477
Rufus 1797-1814...482
Ruth 1796-1878 484
Sally.....................482
Salome 1771-1809123, 484
Salome 1798-1885 485
Samuel 1704-1783...7, 28
Samuel 1739-1820.29, 124
Samuel 1759-1838 ....122, 479
Samuel 1783-1846 ....125, 493
Sarah 1792-1876 ..480
Sarah 1797- 238
Sarah 1799-1880 .123, 486
Sarah 1805-1873 ..492
Sibbel 1745- 29, 126
Squire 1803-1881..482
Stephen 1752-1753 121
Stephen 1757-1836 ....121, 478
Stephen 1785-1806 125
Stephen 1806-1865 493
Stephen 1813-.......492
Stephen 1813-1899 479
Sullivan 1792-1871 482
Tabitha 1742-1807 29, 125
Thomas 1770-1772124
Thomas 1802-1877491
Thomas J. 1780-1866 238
Timothy 1803-1858 238
Willard 1764-1849 ....123, 483
Willard 1788-1872 483
William 1730-1813 29, 122
William 1800- 482
William W. 1805-1854 488
Winthrop 1767-1841 ....123, 483
Winthrop 1806-1880 484

Zebadiah 1732-1806
.... 29, 123
Zebadiah 1761-1851
.... 61, 124, 238
Zebadiah 1806-1878
.... 238
Zerviah 1747- 29
MARDEN
Nathan 1812-1904 622
MARKHAM
Mary 1827- 463
MARSH
Agnes B. 1781-1858
.... 248
Isabella E. 1826-1892
.... 385
Nancy -1882 356
Sarah 1802-1884 .. 555
MARSHALL
Abigail 1794-1873 365
Deborah 1755- 61, 235
Hannah 1774-1800
.... 274
John 1814-1879 567
Mary 1642-1716 1
Mary J. 1829-1886 383
Melvina W. 1831-1873
.... 409
Polly 1781-1856 445
Sally P. 1780-1817 299
Sarah 1757-1822 ... 27,
115
MARSTON
Simeon 1802-1847 364
MARTIN
Asa U. 1792- 206
Bethia B. 1812-1875
.... 230
Ede 1766-1844 203
Jonathan 1796-1881
.... 546
William H. 1809-1869
.... 375
MARVIN
Dan 1808-1884 251
William 1824-1858 374
MASCRAFT
Matilda D. 1800-1852
.... 286
MASON
Abigail 1787-1823 130,
518
Almira 1823-1895 615
Anna P. 1822-1892 615
Artemas 1809-1893
.... 575
Bethiah 1793-1865 574
Betsey 1797-1869 . 575
Eunice 1793-1868 . 593
Ira 1800- 575
Jane 1782-1849 ... 126,
497
John 1769-1844 ... 145,
574
John 1789-1877 574

Lorenzo 1804-1884 575
Lydia 1791-1872 .. 574
Malinda 1809-1866
.... 493
Margaret 1754-1817
.... 61, 239
Maria 1822-1866 .. 624
Mary Ann 1811-1896
.... 412
Mary C. 1807-1895
.... 575
Merrill 1816-1897 615
Moses 1815-1897 .. 575
Orinda L. 1812-1894
.... 575
Phebe 1802-1836 .. 575
Salome C. 1805-1849
.... 575
Sophia 1807-1895 . 500
Sylvanus 1795-1875
.... 574
Ursula 1820-1904. 615
MASTERMAN
Anna 1824-1910 ... 336
Armina 1819-1883 336
Sarah 1792-1851 .. 333
MATHENA
Mary 1831-1909 ... 620
MATHEWS
Lavina 1794- 490
MATHEWSON
Charles 1812-1880 517
MATTHEWS
Sally 1804-1887 188
MAY
Allen 1788- 436
Angeline 1807- 436
Barris 1795- 436
Betsey 1792- 436
Burnice 1795-1873 436
Holloway 1786- 436
Lucinda 1805-1866
.... 521
Marinda 1811-1870
.... 521
Mary 28, 118
Nathaniel 1762-1837
.... 109, 436
Phebe H. 1803-1866
.... 436
Pruda 1790- 436
Ruth 1810-1855 436
MAYBERRY
Andrew 1807-1861 432
Anna 301
MAYNARD
Charles B. 1846-1914
.... 386
Henry 1813-1882 .. 584
Minerva 1819-1856
.... 457
Reuben 1818-1873 426
Stephen 1825-1908
.... 462
William 1781-1852 315

MAYO
Erastus 1808-1901 489
Hannah 1795-1857
.... 440
Lucy 1815- 489
Nathaniel 1803- ... 440
Roxanna 1797-1855
.... 283
MCCARSON
Elizabeth E. 1811-
1850 308
MCCLAIN
John 1792-1879 308
MCCOLLISTER
Lucy 379
MCCOMBS
George 1812-1868 338
MCCOY
Stiles 1820-1897 ... 544
MCDONALD
Betsey 1799-1862 . 301
MCDOWELL
Polly 1776-1851 ... 109,
437
William -1839 462
MCELWAIN
Nancy 1825- 390
MCENTEE
Mary S. 1821-1891 543
MCFARLAND
Moses 1775-1854 .. 301
MCFARLIN
Hephzibah 1801-1850
.... 575
MCGAW
Thornton 1799-1855
.... 447
MCGRATH
Lucy J. 1822-1864 407
MCHARD
Sarah 1777- 81, 310
MCINTIRE
Abigail 1814-1892 363
Anna 1853-1915 ... 633
Charles 1806-1882 585
David 1762- .. 142, 558
Edward 1825- 346
Ezra 1793- 558
Hannah 1797-1875
.... 558
Jacob 1791-1863 ... 336
Melinda 1804-1881
.... 558
Timothy 1773-1844
.... 352
MCKENNEY
Jane 1765-1799 266
MCKENZIE
Louisa 1837-1900 . 610
Susan 554
MCKINNEY
Daniel 319
Julia A. 1817-1896 230
MCKINSTRY
Rosina 1783-1847 . 236
MCKNIGHT

Olivia 1820-1897 .. 476
Sheldon 1810-1860 310
MCLAUGHLIN
Amos 1804-1874 ... 554
Benjamin 1801-1858
.... 366
James 1805-1884 . 366
MCLEAN
Electa 1816-1885 . 247
Mary Ann 1772-1852
.... 63, 246
MCMILLEN
Susanna 396
MCMULLEN
Lawrence 1785-1850
.... 634
MCMURPHY
Sarah J. 1810-1893
.... 565
MCNAUGHTON
Elizabeth 1831-1917
.... 395
Margaret 1830-1900
.... 391
MCNEIL
Elizabeth 1822-1882
.... 597
MCPHERSON
Hugh 1787-1875 ... 319
MCQUEEN
Grace 1809-1871 .. 469
MCQUESTEN
Sarah 1792-1858 .. 320
MEACHAM
Deborah 1749- 26, 111
Hannah -1822 71, 278
Mary E. 1845-1938
.... 389
MEAD
John 1749- ... 139, 550
John 1775- 550
Jonathan 1771- 550
Mary W. 1804-1866
.... 179
Sarah 1773-1859 .. 550
MEANS
Harriet 1842-1892 352
MEARS
Timothy V. 1812-1892
.... 242
MELCHER
Nancy 1799-1856 .. 90,
351
MELENDY
Ebenezer 1781-1871
.... 483
Joseph 1772-1863 270
MELROSS
Alena 1780- 523
Cynthia 1783- 524
George 1785- 524
Hannah 1787- 524
Jane 1804-1888 524
William -1815 132, 523
MELVIN
Anna 1760- ... 139, 553

MERRICK
Abigail 1737-1765. 14, 55
Anna 1810-1886....217
Anne 1756-1809.... 55, 214
Anne 1791-1817....215
Austin 1801-1876..216
Caleb 1767-1822 ... 56, 216
Charlotte 1802-1818 216
Constant 1772-1830 ....56, 216
Constant 1804-1805 217
Constant 1808-1834 217
Elisha A. 1800-1839 216
Eliza 1797-1815 217
Elizabeth 1774-1824 ....56, 217
Emily F. 1824-1895 230
Experience 1801-1801 217
Experience 1806-1870 217
Gideon N. 1793-1862 215
Hannah 1769-1842 56
Harriet 1795-1860 215
Harvey 1808-1887 215
Irene 1797-1814....216
Jerusha 1819-1874 217
Joseph 1733-1787 . 14, 55
Joseph 1764-1814 . 55, 216
Joseph 1789-1854 215, 487
Laura 1799-1875...217
Laura 1803-1885..216, 219
Leander 1799-1856 216
Lodica 1798-1863..216
Lovisa 1791-1863..215
Marilda 1801-1872 215
Mark 1794-1853....216
Mary 1726-1790 14, 54
Nathaniel Burt 1802-1877 217
Roxanna S. 1826-1918 246
Sophronia 1797-1843 216
Thomas 1763-1840 55, 215
Timothy 1760-1810 55, 215
Wealthy 1792-1861 216
MERRILL

Abigail 1782- 106
Abigail 1811-1900.418
Almira E. 1827-1859 419
Amos A. 1826-1898 371
Anna 1743-1803.....25, 106
Anna S. 1804-1862 ....417, 418
Betsey 1794-1873 .422
Caleb 1795-1863 ...415
Calvin C. 1814-1861 419
Catherine 1819-1901 313
Chastina 1827-1900 418
Chauncey 1816-1818 417
Clark 1804-1887 ...417
David M. 1819-1901 419
Eliza 1809-1893 432
Eliza W. 1816-1896 419
Ephraim 1779-1844 ....106, 419
Farnham 1806-1871 418
Harum 1811-1890.417
Henry A. 1795-1872 396
Isaac 1775-1843....168
Joanna 1809-1857.364
John 1760- 106
John 1769-1831 ...106, 416
John 1802-1892 417
John F. 1829-1844 419
Jonathan 1733-1795 ....25, 105
Jonathan 1761-1763 106
Jonathan 1772-1820 ....106, 417
Jonathan 1795-1868 ....417, 418
Jonathan 1820-1826 418
Judith C. 1823-1864 419
Lucy 1771- 106
Lucy 1785-1862 201
Lydia 1767- 106
Mariam 1820-1822 418
Martha S. 1829-1905 605
Mary 1763-1800...106, 416
Mary 1800-1874....417
Mary A. 1814-1871 418
Mary F. 1811-1851 307
Mary L. 1825-1892 419

Moses 1774-1841 .106, 417
Moses 1807-1868 ..417
Moses W. 1829-1919 418
Narcissa R. 1822-1900 418
Rosanna 1812-1834 417
Rufus 1809-1850...419
Sally 1802-1892 329
Samuel 1780- 168
Sarah 1766- 106
Sarah 1778-1831..106, 418
Sarah H. 1821-1874 419
Sarah J. 1821-1898 406
Sherburn S. 1818-1885 418
Stephen 1776-1860 ....106, 418
Stephen 1817-1900 418
Stephen M. 1831-1836 419
Susan 1797-1869 ..417
Sylvester 1812-1885 600
MERROW
Reuben 1776-1864 201
MERWIN
Dinah 1806-1887 ..496
MESSER
Stephen 1773-1833 173
METCALF
Asa 1787-1821 .....155, 615
Calvin 1817-1904..615
Elcena 1821-1903 .615
Elizabeth 1814-1872 492
Roxana 1815-1896 615
MIELS
Hannah 1833-1903 464
MILES
Abner 1745-1803 ...82, 313
Clarissa 1777-1830 283
Deborah 1781-1854 313
Ezekiel 1791-1844 313
Isaac 1805-1897....554
Jemima 1779- 313
Joel 1774-1814......313
Rachel 1777- 313
Sally 1775- 313
MILLER
Charles E. 1808-1872 636

Elizabeth 1832-1909 335
Luke 1815-1881....192
Martha 1834- 343
Mary Jane 1806-1870 189
Samuel 1796-1872 192
Sarah 1811-1849 ..262
Stephen 1787-1852 488
MILLETT
Hiram 1805-1862..565
MILLINGTON
Hannah 1819-1906 212
MILLS
Aaron 1754-1835 91
Adam D. 1790-1866 ....89, 348
Gawn 1826-1899...348
Lydia 1847-1930...386
Robert 1829-1903 .348
Sarah 1801-1876 ..324
MINARD
George 1802-1853.500
MINER
Mary M. 1773-1812 65, 258
Susan 1791-1862 ..226
MINOR
Mildred 1830-1895 618
MISNER
Rachel 1818-1898 .337
MITCHELL
Cleora -1838 539
Lydia 22, 92
Mary 1832-1908....570
Phebe 1784-1815 ..509
Rosetta 1835-1910 582
MOAR/MOOAR
Isaac 1759-1832......81
John 1796-1869 449
MONCRIEF
Mary 1786-1847....177
MONTGOMERY
John P. 1812-1861 589
Sarah 1838-1897 ..295
MOOAR
Eliza 1807-1892.....99, 393
MOODY
Harriet.................588
Oliver 1786- 511
Sarah A. 1826-1876 392
William 1821-1899 626
MOOR/MOORE
Abby S. 1844- 605
Ann 1785-1841 327
Asa B. 1801-1870..329
Bathsheba 1807-1893 583
Deborah 1776-1868 83, 322
Henry 1799-1853 ..485

Henry E. 1803-1841
.... 422
John..................... 319
John -1814............ 317
Margaret 1783-1848
.... 319
Margaret 1835-1910
.... 350
Mariah................. 355
Mary Ann 1829-1857
.... 281
Olive 1729-1807 20, 81
Parmela 1797-...... 537
Robert 1787-1858. 327
Waid 1787-1878 ... 430
Waity 1812-1868.. 224
MOORS
Ruth E. 1811-1845 525
MOREHOUSE
Thomas 1801-1825 213
MORGAN
Asaph W. 1809-1898
.... 261
James H. 1816-1871
.... 405
Justin 1786-1853 . 241
Mariam 1785-1853 278
Mary R. 1820-1911
.... 514
Sally 1781-1848.... 164
Samuel 1810-1847 261
MORLEY
Lucinda 1793-1854
.... 500
MORRELL
Isaac 1808-1887 ... 477
MORRILL
Enoch L. 1820-1874
.... 416
Hannah 1809-1859
.... 170
Harriet 1827-1905 336
John 1823-1895.... 450
Julia 1837-1902.... 349
Louisa 1798-1874. 168
Mary Ann 1814- .. 158,
626
Samuel 1804-1878 391
Smith 1816-1900.. 578
MORRIS
Charles 1762-1838 253
Elizabeth 1815-.... 277
Joseph 1782-1847. 279
Priscilla 1737-1785 29,
123
Rufus 1772-1848 .. 253
MORRISON
Charles F. 1815-1882
.... 231
Isaac 1760-1846 ... 166
Mary 1798-1861 ... 415
MORSE
Abigail 1787-1885 147,
580

Benjamin 1809-1890
.... 364
Charles W. 1805-1888
.... 335
Cynthia 1811-1878 364
David 1800-1851 .. 224
Drury 1757-1820... 86,
332
Ella S. 1843-1924. 616
Enoch 1772-1852... 92,
364
Enoch 1799-1862.. 364
Hannah 1815-1892
.... 364
Happiah 1808-1853
.... 364
John 1806-1892.... 581
Malinda 1799-1888
.... 197
Margaret 1799-1869
.... 175
Margaret 1820- 364
Mark 1795-........... 364
Mary 1806-........... 364
Mary B. 1846-1929
.... 342
Nathan 1816-1892 238
Rebecca 1805-1880 275
Samuel P. 1806-1864
.... 425
Sarah 1774-1861 ... 93,
364
Stephen 1803-1886
.... 364
Susan 1804-.......... 364
William B. 1818-1886
.... 391
MORTON
Abigail 1818-1890 598
Harriet Elvira 1808-
1882 216
Martha 1819-1890 528
Mary L. 1822-....... 406
MOSHER
Mary 1762-1827.... 54,
212
MOULTON
Elijah 1748-1782... 18,
72
Freeman 1828-1913
.... 400
Mary 1780-1839.... 72,
280
Sarah 1777-1852... 72,
279
MOWER
Ira 1800-1869....... 485
MOWRY
Mary 1818-.......... 622
MUDGE
Albert 1841-1911.. 348
Charles 1770-1814 64,
252
Deborah 1803-1849
.... 253

Hiram................... 253
Mary.................... 253
MULLEN
Mary 1828-1903... 351
MULVEY
Booth C. 1800-1858
.... 425
MUMFORD
Betsey 1794-1872. 286
MUNDELL
Sophia 1802-1868. 576
MURDOCH
Margaret 1805-1886
.... 90, 350
MURPHY
Ella A. 1830-1920. 381
Harriet 1823-1861 531
MURRAY
Hiram 1807-1864 . 260
Kezia 1811- 599
MUSSER
Catharine............. 331
MUZZY
John J. -1833........ 577
MYER
Ann 1823-1877..... 532
MYERS
Phebe 1812-1882.. 445
Ruth A. 1816-1894 262
NASON
Hannah A. 1831-1905
.... 409
NAY
Arvilla 1804-1844 560
Betsey 1796-1852. 197
William 1763-1813 201
NEALLEY
Margaret 1824-1910
.... 402
NEEDHAM
Daniel -1801... 54, 211
Jeremiah K. 1792-
1862 450
John 211
John 1786-............ 211
John 1792-1871.... 563
Joseph P. 1788-.... 212
Laurena 1811-1893
.... 563
Mary 1784-........... 211
Melinda L. 1839-1917
.... 609
Rachel 1791-1887. 212
Sarah 1762-1816... 35,
149
Sarah 1798-1880.. 212
NEGUS
Charles 1819-1908 536
NESMITH
Isabella R. 1784- .. 187
NEVINS
Mary 1814-1886... 598
NEWBERRY
Harriet 1812-1857 542
NEWBURY
Dorothy 1820- 458

NEWCOMB
Isaac 1818-1863 ... 624
Sarah M. 1819-1851
.... 322
NEWELL
Charles................. 141
Nancy 1781-1840 . 288
Olive 1801-1891 .. 155,
616
NEWHALL
Mary 1803-1887 ... 323
NEWSOM
Mary 1839-........... 457
NEWTON
Eunice 1806-1846 366
Eunice 1809-1879 561
Lucretia 1811-1903
.... 366
Martha 1823-1843 568
Ogden B. 1791-1836
.... 275
NICHOLS
Amy A. 1821- 376
Cyrus 1798-1872.. 500
Diana 1804-1867. 154,
614
Eunice 1739- 19, 75
Hannah 1814-1882
.... 635
Harriet 1820-1904 342
Harriet 1827-1848 624
Maria 1815-1899.. 376
Mary 1773-1855.. 145,
572
Moses 1799-1893.. 304
Nancy 1782-1851 . 207
Newton 1806-1889 581
Rebecca 1813-1871 342
Sarah E. 1821-1845
.... 635
NICHOLSON
William 1789-....... 226
NILES
Elizabeth 1774-1855
.... 132, 526
Isaac 1786-1858 .. 210,
235
James 1747-1822 .. 53,
209
John 1779-1803.... 209
Joshua Holt 1790-
1850 210
Molly 1782- 209
Nathaniel S. 1759-
1832 206
Polly 1798-1869 ... 215
NIXON
Mary..................... 491
NOBLE
Charlotte 1771-1805
.... 56, 216
Emerline 1824-1879
.... 580
Jeremiah 1794-1887
.... 361

Joanna 1769-1860. 55, 215

Mary 1785-1862....258

William 1804-1868247

NORCROSS

Aurora D. 1826-1867 280

NORRIS

Joanna 1801-1866.570

NORTH

Mary J. 1810-1843280

NORTON

Betsey 1805-1892..569

Dinah 1773-1803 .144, 570

Elvira 1823-1880 ..570

Harriet S. 1831-....343

Mary 1802-1875....414

Peter 1794-1868....594

Seymour 1802-1869 569

Sheldon 411

Walter 1786-1849 .258

NOTT

Hiram....................356

NOWELL

Henry 1797-1869 ..449

NOYES

Almira 1810-1867 .321

Frances 1814-1887566

Gilman 1804-1863 460

Martha 1787- 167

Phebe 1763-1848... 41, 163

William 1819-1907625

NUGENT

Elcy 1781- 155, 617

NUTTING

Abby 1810-1888 462

Abner 1783-1810..117, 461

Elvira 1808-1852 ..462

Judith 1795-..........504

Margaret 1809-1846 462

Sarah M. 1837-1907 ....604, 605

NYE

Anna 1810-1870....218

Buell 1790-1833....216

Chloe 1792-..........228

Elijah 1777-1844... 59, 229

Elijah C. 1805-1848 230

Harriet 1801-1879 217

Horace 1803-.........217

Jerusha 1808-1877230

Phebe 1807-1879...230

Polly 1801-1875 230

Samuel 1773-1837 56, 217

Susanna 1805-1828 217

Timothy 1765-.59, 228

O'NEAL

Judah 20, 85

OAKES

David 1790-1861...365

Edward 1792-1863366

OAKLEY

Jesse 238

OBER

Rebecca 1824-1908374

ODELL

Almira 1803-1841 .425

William 1833- 377

OLCOTT

Martha 1798-1842 500

OLDS

Anna E. 1816-1884 537

Lucy S. 1814-1847 537

OLIVER

Austin 1834-1912 .604

Elizabeth 1829-....604

John 1795-1875 ...152, 604

John 1821-1823 604

John 1823-1833 604

John R. 1825-1912 604

Mary 1826-1909....604

William 1832-1848604

OLNEY

Dorcas 1789- 354

Jeremiah C. 1792-1860 208

Thomas 1804-1854492

ORCUTT

Mehitable 1769-1851 ....56, 218

Sarah 1740-1816....14, 56

ORDWAY

Jane 1770-1854.....164

Olive 1787-....154, 612

ORMSBEE

Augustus 1810-1859 576

ORMSBY

Daniel 1789-1858..573

Ebenezer 1764-1806 ....145, 572

Ebenezer 1792-.....573

James 1799-1871..573

Thomas 1796-1832573

ORNE

Burley E. 1825-1855 281

ORTON

Esther R. 1796-1881 444

ORVIS

Josephus 1780-1855 176

OSBORN

Betsey 1779-1838 .199

Miles 1795-1873....306

Rebecca 1785-1862115

OSBORNE

Hannah 1778-1835 76, 293

Judith 1801-1857..425

OSGOOD

Abiah 1747-1825.....78

Abiah 1817-1880...301

Abigail B. 1798-1884 304

Ann 1794-1821......303

Ann 1802-1895......304

Asa 1744-1753 78

Asa 1753-1833 78, 300

Asa 1780- 300

Asa 1787-1822 300

Caroline 1801-1886 304

Caroline A. 1827-1893 409

Caroline M. 1799-1800...................296

Charles G. 1785-1868 295

Charlotte F. 1809-1838...................299

Chloe 1766-1846 ...299

Daniel 1693-1754......6

Deborah 1730-179319, 79

Dorcas 1746- 43

Dorcas 1748-1811 ..43, 171

Eliza 1793-1800 296

Eliza L.B. 1789-1837 303

Elizabeth 1789-1835 ....101, 402

Elizabeth 1789-1858 174

Ephraim 1808-1883 635

Gayton P. 1797-1861 298

Hannah 1718-1744 11, 43

Hannah 1735-1771 19, 81

Hannah 1781-1855 300

Hannah 1786-1806 173

Hannah P. 1794-1888 296

Harriet M. 1804-1860 304

Harriot 1791-1832 296

Henry 1791-1865 ..298

Henry Y.B. 1784-1831 303

Isaac 1724-1791 19, 78

Isaac 1744-1753......77

Isaac 1754-1799......79

Isaac 1755-1847.....77, 297

Isaac 1771-1796....300

Isaac 1788-............301

Isaac 1790-1824....301

Isaac 1793-1873....299

Isaac 1799-1834....298, 309

Isaac 1799-1850....304

James 1749-1753....78

James 1768-1809..299

James 1788-1856..303

James 1800-1879..301

Jeremiah 1702-.11, 42

John 1773-1828 300

Joseph 1751-1753 ...77

Joseph 1758-1862 ...77

Joseph 1767-1767 ...79

Joseph 1820-.........301

Joseph G. 1811-1878 299

Joshua B. 1753-1791 ....79, 303

Joshua B. 1782-1861 303

Josiah 1801-1868..308

Julia A. 1788-1871 ....295, 296

Lydia 1760-1763 77

Martha B. 1787-1853 296

Mary 1706-1745..8, 34

Mary 1726- 19

Mary 1752-1753......78

Mary 1755-1840.....78, 302

Mary 1756-1758......79

Mary 1776-1848....300

Mary L. 1804-1879299

Mary S. 1786-1871303

Mary W. 1797-1857 303

Peter 1717-180119, 76

Peter 1745-1801.....77, 295

Peter 1764-1856.....79, 303

Peter 1793-1865....296

Peter 1802-1849....299

Phebe 1733-1797 ...19, 79

Phebe 1746-1783 78

Phebe 1811-1813 ..301

Phebe F.................301

Phebe F. 1814-1885 301

Priscilla 1681-........3, 5

Rebecca 1740-1790 33, 141

Rebecca P. 1801-...298

Samuel 1748-1813..77, 296

Samuel 1779-1859 300

Samuel 1784-1863 303

Samuel W. 1789-1832 ....295, 296

Sarah 1749-1790 ...78, 301

Sarah 1750-1762 77

Sarah 1789-1867. 195, 298
Sarah P. 1796-1835 298
Stephen 1809-1835 301
Stephen 1830-1904 626
Susan 1790-1832.. 303
Susan 1795-1878.. 299
Susanna 1754-1840 .... 77, 297
Susanna K. 1795-1834 296
Thomas 1721-1798 19, 78
Thomas 1751-......... 78
Timothy 1693-1772 . 5, 19
Timothy 1719-1753 19, 77
Timothy 1743-1816 78, 299
Timothy 1758-1759 79
Timothy 1759-1839 79
Timothy 1763-1842 77, 298
Timothy 1767-1824 299
Timothy 1798-1847 301
Timothy 1800-1823 299
Walter F. 1791-1836 296
William 1761-1792. 79
William 1798-....... 299
William A. 1806-1885 304
Willis 1808-1887 .. 304
OSGOODBY
Jacob H. 1812-1883 375
OTIS
Abijah 1815-1883. 537
OWEN
Amasa 1766-1842.. 67, 263
Anna A. 1843-1910 386
Eleazer 1755-1779 76, 289
Eleazer 1780-1859 290
Hiram 1801-......... 263
Jedediah 1805-1881 263
Levi B. 1826-........ 419
Lucy 1796-............ 263
Lucy 1812-1884.... 263
Lydia E. 1798-...... 240
Mary 1786-1861 .. 101, 406
Miriam E. 1808-1873 263

Roderick 1803-1861 263
Timothy 1799-1886 263
William D. 1795-.. 263
OWENS
Esther 1747-1774.. 14, 57
Mary 272
Nancy 1816-1890 . 522
OZMUN
Malinda 1810-1884 488
POOL
Deborah 1769-1771 60
PACKARD
Ann 1809-1889..... 513
Betsey J. 1831-1861 371
Charles 1818-1881 565
PACKER
Henry 1798-1885.. 492
PADDLEFORD
Susan 1815-1864.. 531
PAGE
Ansel 1808-1882... 431
Francis 1820-1893 515
Lucretia 1790-...... 440
Lucy 1797-1859.... 218
Phebe.................... 240
PAINE
Albert 1809-1889.. 518
Augustine 1782-1814 .... 130, 517
Ebenezer 1811- 518
Elias 1777-1780 ... 130
Elisha 1780-1817 130, 517
Francis 1809-1856 517
Hannah 1773-1855 .... 130, 517
Lucy 1771-1814... 130, 516
Noah 1742-1826 .... 29, 130
Noah 1778-1817 ... 130
Noah 1778-1847 ... 130
Olive 1814-1835 ... 517
Persis 1785-1848. 130, 518
Sarah 1775-1780 .. 130
PAINE/PAYN
Carlos G. 1811-1882 264
Earl J. 1807-1881. 264
James 1783-1861 .. 67, 264
James A. 1819-1899 265
Lucius F. 1810-1883 264
Mary A. 1819-1857 265
Philander A. 1814-1884 264

Philura 1772-1822 .... 118, 466
Robert S. 1812-1893 280
Sally A. 1817-1839 264
Thomas 1778-1856 67, 264
Thomas A. 1805-1867 264
William D. 1809-1873 264
PALFREY
Amelia 1838-1907 350
PALMER
Asher 1779-1826.. 481
Betsey 1797-1844 100, 399
Dudley 1809-1887 325
John 84, 325
John P. 1817-1883 326
Louisa 1812-1880. 325
Mary 1815-1888... 326
Rufus 1756-.. 122, 481
Simeon 1763-1829 282
PARDEE
Czarina 1819-1908 538
PARISH
Minerva 1810-1897 582
PARK/PARKE
Amos 1749-1825.... 75, 289
Elisha 289
Erastus 1779-1861 289
Joshua.................. 289
Phebe................... 289
Shubael 1777-1826 289
PARKER
Achsah 1799-1831 450
Alfred 1788-1876.. 163
Alvan 1792-1843 .. 490
Anna 1784-1799... 546
Anne 1736-............ 41
Armela A. 1809-1891 511
Benjamin 1800-.... 163
Betsey 1800-1862. 261
Betsy 1775-1814.... 57, 222
Betsy 1812-.......... 224
Carlotn 1791-....... 546
Carlton 1750-1809 .... 137, 546
Carlton 1782-1788 546
Charles 1800-1827 546
Clarissa 1797-1852 218
Clarissa 1826-1895 538
Daniel 1777-... 58, 223
Daniel 1805-1805. 223
Daniel W. 1803-1878 410
Dexter 1799-1853. 490

Edith 1795- 174
Ednah 1828-1830. 625
Elbridge 1812-1812 590
Eliza B. 1821-1868 419
Elizabeth 1773-1862 235
Elizabeth 1789-.... 546
Elizabeth 1797-.... 163
Ellen 1844-1918... 631
Esther 1810-1883. 224
Ezra 1767-1818.... 173
Fanny T. 1806-..... 590
Gilman 1802-1866 181
Hannah 1797-1816 450
Hannah 1806-1883 223
Ira 1792-1794....... 490
Irene 1815-1878... 328
Isaac 1755-1821 .. 124, 489
Isaac 1769-1857 ... 450
Isaac 1801-1813 ... 450
James 1696-1782 .. 11, 41
James 1746-1815 .. 41, 163
James 1784- 163
Jesse 1738-............ 41
Jesse 1800-1885... 163
Joanna 1784-1820 173
John 1783-1862.... 170
John 1788- 490
John 1803- 450
Jonathan 1801-.... 223
Joseph 1793-1812 546
Kendall 1776-1855 546
Keziah 1802-1833 223
Martha 5, 17
Mary 1751-1752..... 41
Mary 1815-1897... 625
Mary 1817-.......... 590
Mary B. 1822-1900 221
Michael 1773-149, 589
Nancy 1790- 163
Nancy 1821-1919 . 625
Nathan 1810-1848 590
Nathaniel 1788-... 546
Nehemiah 1808-1871 224
Olive 1795-1825 ... 450
Oren 1797- 490
Otis 1795-1795..... 490
Peter 1769-1855... 172
Peter 1807-1832... 590
Phebe 1734-1737.... 41
Phebe 1748-............ 41
Phebe 1786-.......... 163
Priscilla 1797-1835 546
Rebecca 1823-1912 625
Reuben 1816-1881 493

Robert 1789-1831.158, 625
Rosina 1809-1898 .590
Ruth 1809-1904 344
Ruth -1849 232
Samuel 1802-1882 490
Sarah 1794- 163
Sarah B. 1806-1876 476
Simon 1792- 163
Timothy 1779-1806 546
Weltha 1790-1867.490
Zenos 1805-1896 ...490

PARKHILL
Maria 1816-1845...515

PARKHURST
Betsy 1788-1875 ...199
Henry 1793-1865 ..270
Hiram 1807-1885..492
Lydia 1762-1843 ...267
Rachel 1826-1871 .624
Rhoda 1783-1866 ..270

PARKS
Philo 1812-1862 293

PARLIN
Elizabeth 1803-1881 333
Ira 1790-1846........333
Sophia E. 1830-1909 333

PARMELEE
Edward 1807-1860521

PARMENTER
Rebecca 1783-1856205
Sarah 1782-1863...204
Sophia 1793-1845 . 85, 331

PARSONS
Edmund 1811-1842 624
Edward 1797-1874451
Harvey 1795-1861 524
Mary E. 1821-1852 219
Melinda F. 1809-1891 218
Miriam 1785-1855129, 514
Rufus 1794-1874...530
Sophia 1826-1914 .243
William 249

PARTRIDGE
Austin 1800-1889..603

PATCH
Aaron 1768-1859...199
Mary 1834-1908....449

PATRICK
William 1820-1892463

PATRON
Thomas 1798-1862196

PATTEE
Benjamin F. 1809-1861 323

Benjamin W. 1781-1849.............83, 323
David 1803-1816...323

PATTERSON
Daniel 497
Mary B. 1801-1886 556

PAUL
James 1742- 29

PAULSON
John 1820-1893 404

PAXTON
Mary M. 1851- 206

PAYSON
Eliphalet 1776-1807 302

PEABODY
Alice 1685-1726 ..4, 12
Bethiah 1681-1742 . 4, 13
Carrie 1842-1898..351
Daniel 1817-1903.346, 351
Francis 1793-1866 .89, 346
Francis 1814-1905 346
Hannah 1793-1881 88, 345
James 1815-1891.346, 586
Jane 1836-1845.....346
Jeremiah F. 1812-1887 342
Mary 1821-1866....346
Mary A. 1813-1834 589
Oren 1824-1897 346
Osgood 1819-1880.346
Peggy 1791-1840....88, 343
Rebecca 1763-1844 21, 88
Rebecca 1830-1832346
Rebecca 1832-1914346
Sarah 1827-1921...346

PEACH
Henry G. 1816-1858 416

PEAK/PEAKE
Alanson 1808-1873 498
Augustus 1813-1847 497
Caroline 1813-1883 496
Catharine 1805-....496
Charles 1818-1849497
Cyrus 1811-1889...497
Dorcas 1763- 126
Ebenezer 1768- 126
Eleazer 1770- 126
Eleazer 1821-1873 498
Elijah 1775-1858..126, 498
Elijah 1795- 496

Eliza 1808-............497
Emeline 1809-1868 497
Frederick 1809-1846 496
Homer 1815- 496
Ira 1806-1885 497
Jane 1793- 496
Julia 1818-1891 498
Lois 1743- 29, 124
Lucinda 1799-1875 496
Marcus 1805-1866 496
Maria 1804-1859 ..497
Matilda 1799-1827497
Moses 1736- 29, 126
Oliver 1772-1859 .126, 495
Oliver 1800- 496
Perlina 1807- 498
Polly 1812- 498
Roswell 1774-1824 ....126, 497
Sybil 1780- 126, 498
Sybil 1819-1899 498
Uriah 1804-..........498
Walter 1803-1866 .497
Warren 1816- 497
William 1797-1856496

PEAKE
Sarissa 1801- 497

PEARL
Achsah 1795-1857 236
Alice 1747-1747 60
Alice 1748- 61, 234
Alice 1772-1773 210
Anna 1794-1800....238
Austin 1798-1863 .238
Chloe 1792-1835 ...238
Cyrel 1797-1837....210
Cyril 1790-1797 235
Daniel 1779-1779..211
Daniel 1780-1806..211
Elijah C. 1783-1864 237
Elizabeth 1756-1779 ....61, 236
Elizabeth 1780-.....235
Eunice 1786-1797 .235
Eunice 1798-1873 .236
Hannah 1783-1786 210
Hannah 1794-1849 210
John 1726- 15
John M. 1774-1853 235
Joshua 1752-1837..61, 235
Joshua 1778-1817.235
Lois 1753-178861, 236
Lois 1785-1807......238
Lydia 1783-1841 ...235
Marcy 1785- 210

Norman 1824-1896 603
Oliver 1749-1831 ...53, 61, 210
Oliver 1774-1775 ..210
Oliver 1776-1786 ..211
Oliver 1788-1835 ..210
Phebe 1765-1816 ...61, 124, 238
Polly 1792-1857 236
Sarah 1758-1826 ...61, 237
Timothy 1723-178915, 60
Timothy 1760-183461, 237
Timothy 1776-1837 235
Walter 1788-1789 .235
Walter 1791-1814 .210

PEARS
Thomas 1837-1911586

PEARSON
Abbie 1838-1891 ...631
Abiel 1795-1851 182
Abigail 1800-1879.158
Adeline 1829-1891 630
Alva 1837-.............631
Amos 1797-1851 ...326
Amos 1802-1866 ...182
Ebenezer 1768-1852 ....37, 158
Ebenezer 1797-1864 ....158, 630
Ebenezer 1827-1893 630
Esther 1792-1856 158, 630
Eunice 1784-1866 .505
Hephzibah 1790-1880 182
Jabez 1797-1850 ...182
James 1799-..........182
James 1834-1894 ..630
Joseph J. 1792-1841 182
Julia 1835-1902 631
Kendall 1805-1824182
Mary 1841-1883 631
Mary A. 1809-1884 414
Moses 46
Moses 1750-1836 ..182
Nathan 1787-1855 182
Paul 1814-1880.....596
Sarah 1832-1894 ..630
Thomas 1785-1863182
Willard 1806-1841 ....158, 631

PEASE
Betsey 1788-1819 .182
David 228
Edwin 1812-1886..379
Horace 1799-1862.491
Josiah 1783-1860..524

Margaret 1794-1875
.... 228
Mary 1795-1872 ... 260
Peter 1803-1872 ... 544
Polly 1776-1829.... 269
PEAVEY/PEVEY
Abiel 1799-1799 ... 555
Abiel 1807-1886 ... 556
Benjamin A. 1794-
1864 555
Chloe 1806-1838... 556
Dorcas 1774-1855. 141
Dorcas 1801-1884 555,
579
Elizabeth 1803-1803
.... 556
Elizabeth 1804-1882
.... 556
Ezra 1797-1800 556
Ezra 1809-1891 556
George 1800-1800 556
Hannah 1773- 140
Jacob S. 1797-1872
.... 555
Jeremiah 1793- 556
John M. 1809-1809
.... 556
Lucy C. 1792-1874
.... 187, 555
Lydia 1803-1856... 556
Merrill C. 1812-1873
.... 556
Peter 1762-1836 .. 140,
555
Peter 1788-1879 .. 189,
555
Peter 1800-1837 ... 556
Sally 1790-1874.... 555
Thomas 1736-. 33, 140
Thomas 1765-140, 556
Thomas 1791-1814556
Zebadiah 1795-1885
.... 556
PECK
Alanson 1805-1886
.... 233
Anna 1769-1855 60,
232
Ara 1787-1862 509
Daniel D. 1817-1852
.... 232
Dolly 1794-1870 ... 231
Elisha 1777-1866 .. 60,
233
Eunice 1770- 60
Ezekiel 1801-1891 232
James F. 1812-1880
.... 232
John 1726-1805 15, 59
John 1768-1849 59,
231
Levi 1757-1835.... 129,
509
Lydia 1738-1818.... 22,
92

Minerva 1809- 233
Mira 1801-1879.... 509
Nathan 1774-1862358
Olive 1791-1840 ... 231
Oliver 1772- 60
Oliver 1789- 231
Oliver 1797-1878.. 231
Oren A. 1799-1880231
Palmer 1793-1816 231
Phila 1787-1873 ... 486
Polly 1803-1805.... 233
Rebekah 1736-1812
.... 21, 91
Rhoda 1798-1874 . 509
Rhoda 1804-1808 . 232
Rutheda 1823-1913
.... 360
Sally 1799-1873.... 292
Shubael 1794-1872
.... 509
Uri 1789-1864 509
PEET
Edward J. 1816-1885
.... 620
Josiah 1780-1852 156,
619
Mary 1818-1876 ... 359
Mary H. 1823-1889
.... 620
Sarah E. 1815-1815
.... 620
Sarah H. 1818-1892
.... 620
William H. 1824-.. 620
PELTON
Homer 1793-1868. 519
Lucy 1804-1891.... 519
PEMBER
Jabez 1780-1832 .. 291
PEMBERTON
Mary 1815-1901 ... 354
PENDEXTER
John 1784-1840.... 169
Susan 1816-1892.. 424
PERHAM
Sylvanus 1807-1874
.... 577
PERKINS
Almira A. 1809-1874
.... 222
Amelia 1816-1856 341
Ann......................... 88
Ann 1845-1921 346
Anna M. 1821-1898
.... 280
Charles 1822-1899485
Cynthia 1804-1830340
Esther 1787-1885 107,
425
George 1836-1914 486
Hannah 1720-1775.. 5,
20
Harriet E. 1830-1922
.... 607
Jesse 1808-1843 ... 340

Laura 1829-1831.. 485
Lois L. 1809-1875. 340
Maria 1825-1894.. 420
Mary 1804-1886... 597
Mary 1824-1896... 485
Moses 1775-1858... 88,
340
Nathan 1793-1865
.... 123, 485
Nathan 1831- 485
Sarah 1826-1880.. 485
Sarah A. 1821-1894
.... 402
Sophia A. 1802-1851
.... 90, 350
Susanna 1831-1866
.... 351
Warren B. 1817-1900
.... 600
PERLEY
Ancil 1796-1831 73
Caroline A. 1822-1870
.... 281
Charlotte 1820-1843
.... 281
Dean A. 1830-1911281
Edward P. 1836-1913
.... 281
Elizabeth W. 1825-
1905 281
Francis 1792-1836 73,
280
Irena 1801-1837.... 73,
281
Jesse 1761-184618, 72
Jesse 1795-1851.... 73,
281
John F. 1824-1893 281
John L. 1805-1888415
Louisa 1818-1902. 281
Nathaniel 1827-1864
.... 281
Osgood 1815-1886 280
Sarah J. 1829-1909
.... 281
PERRIN
Almond 1806- 466
Timothy 1767-1814
.... 118, 466
Zeruiah 1808-1874472
PERRY
Amos 1795-1885... 520
Anthony 1774-1854
.... 276
Demas 1784-1880. 435
Isaac 1775- 173
Sally 1774-1837 ... 235
Sarah 1708-1786 7, 28
PERSONS
Joseph -1812 .... 14, 57
PETERSON
Polly 1783-1814.... 267
Sally 1795-1825 ... 268
PETRIE

Dewitt C. 1808-1851
.... 379
PETTENGILL
Ballard 1799-1888 559
Ezra 1810-1813.... 559
Hermon 1798-1883
.... 559
Isaac 1808-1826 ... 559
Leonard 1806-1868
.... 559
Lydia A. 1828-1903
.... 343
Rhoda 1803-1893 . 559
Sally 1801-1875 ... 559
William 1759-1844
.... 142, 559
William 1785-1865202
PETTS
Nancy -1821 197
PHELON
Mary 1815-1878... 251
PHELPS
Asenath 1789-1871
.... 483
Edward 1787- 582
Fidelia 1803-1881 573
Hannah 1709-1781 . 9,
17, 38
Hannah 1774-1861
.... 175
Henry 1821-1857 . 352
James H. 1822-1878
.... 381
Jeremiah 1729- 52,
206
John 1797-1847.... 206
Josiah H. 1795-1885
.... 206
Lois 1720-1814. 11, 43
Lorenzo 1816-1901632
Lucy 1790-1871.... 206
Phebe 1814-1869.. 356
Sophia 1796-1885 575
William B. 1811-1882
.... 193
Ziba H. 1793-1878 206
PHILBRICK
Esther 1801-1876. 398
Jonathan 1775- ... 100,
398
Thomas 1804-1886398
PHILLIPS
Andrew 1847- 628
Annie 1845- 350
Asa 1769-1813..... 121,
477
Asa 1794-1865...... 477
Cyrus 1807-1879.. 477
Elijah 1795-1874.. 477
Esther O. 1826-1894
.... 467
George 1801-1873 477
John 1796-1852.... 477
John 1827-1885.... 549
Joseph 1816-1895 503

Joshua 1812-1895.625
Lovina 1795-1863 .500
Martha 1822-1883 326
Mary 1804-1877....477
Mary N. 1814-1898
..........................286
Mercy P. 1841-1925
..........................340
Michael C. 1792-...477
Nelson 1805-1881 .294
Rhoda S. 1813-1893
..........................477
Riley E. 1810-1882294
Wheeler 1783-1863
..........................474
PHINNEY
Daniel 1793-1880..440
Martha 1834-1900 621
PHIPPEN
Lucy 1786-1828.....198
PHIPPS
Mary A. G. 1799-1840
..........................573
PICKETT
Benjamin F. 1812-
1897..................279
Lydia P. 1798-184189,
347
PICKMAN
Mary 1765-1856.... 77,
297
Rebecca T. 1772-1801
..................77, 297
Sally 1771-1791 77,
297
PIERCE
Alexander C. 1796-
..........................337
Asa 1788-1874 177
Calvin 1797-..........177
Edward 1809-1894519
Elijah 1802-1875...333
Eliza 1830-1849 632
Elizabeth 1790-.....177
Hannah 1783-1820
..........................177
Hannah L. 1815-1884
..........................373
Hiram 1796-1862..469
Lucinda 1820-1826
..........................632
Lucinda 1826-1847
..........................632
Lydia....................177
Marshall 1793-1839
..................160, 632
Mary 1816-1843....632
Mary F. 1788-1854509
Phebe 1793-1834...177
Polly 1795-..........177
Roxana 1801-1874 177
Sanborn 1818-1874
..........................632
Sarah 1782-1857...177
Sarah 1800- 510

Susanna 1822-1875
..........................632
Uretta V. 1827-1916
..........................382
William 1759- .44, 176
William 1785-1867177
PIKE
Chester 484
Ebenezer 1764-1819
..................123, 484
Ebenezer 1789-1861
..........................484
Laura 1805- 525
Lucy 1799-1868 484
Lydia 1767-1839 ..123,
483
Merrill 1798-1855.328
Pliny 1793-1872....484
PILLSBURY
Phineas 1767-1859173
PILSBURY
William H. 1806-1888
..........................424
PINKHAM
Abigail 1799-1890.324
Margery 1796-1825
..........................324
Pamelia 1805-1877
..........................324
PINNEY
Abigail Z. 1847-1920
..........................382
PIPER
Eliza 1839-1916....633
Esther 1797-1888 .490
Joseph R. 1837-1902
..........................383
Lavinia..................432
PIPIN
Delilah -1821 194, 579
PITCHER
Asher 1788-1870...443
Daniel 1782-1822..443
David 1777-1857...443
Elijah 1752-1839...111,
443
Elijah 1771-1843...443
Elisha 1773-1850..443
Ephraim 1780-1858
..........................443
Gurdon 1785-1843 443
Hannah 1791-1796
..........................443
Jerusha 1797-1884443
William 1775-1835443
PITMAN
Mary A. 1811-1891
..........................405
PITTS
Benjamin 1754-1794
..................128, 503
Elizabeth 1770-.....128
James 1780-1801 ..503
Jeremiah 1758-....128,
504

John 1733- 29, 128
John 1756-1758 128
John 1768- 128
Lois 1760- 128
Marcy 1783-..........504
Perley 1791-..........504
Persis 1787- 504
Rachel 1783- 504
Sally 1781-............504
Salome 1766-1860128,
504
Samuel 1762-........128
Samuel 1785-........504
PIXLEY
Olive 1768-1795...113,
451
PLACE
Darius 1806-1871 .465
Permelia 1793-1855
..........................268
PLAISTED
Maria 392
PLANT
Sarah 1798-1874....95,
379
PLATT
Caroline A. 1807-1901
..........................252
James H. 1799-1876
..........................471
Mary A. 1831-1879
..........................577
PLIMPTON
Daniel 1781-1851.117,
464
Daniel 1815-1816..464
Joseph C. 1783-1831
..........................117
Keziah 1770-1847 119,
469
Lauretta 1806-......464
Luman 1809-1869.464
Otis 1804-1806......464
PLUMB
Leander 1796-1876
..........................227
PLUMMER
David 1798- 305
Enoch 1801-1880 ..305
Mary 1782-1845.....80,
306
Mary 1783-1865....297
Moses 1745- 80, 305
Phebe O. 1799-1873
..........................305
PLUNKETT
Elizabeth 1814-1887
..........................190
POLLARD
Lydia 1850-1895...610
Ruth B. 1833-1899388
Sarah A. 1828-1915
..........................577
POMROY

Sarah R. 1814-1882
..........................401
POOL
Alice 1765- 60, 233
Amy 1775-1817......60,
209, 234
Anna 1767-1831.....60,
234
Deborah 1781-1823 60
Lois 1772- 60
Mary 1770-1853.....57,
60, 222
Sarah 1777-1777 60
Susan 1820-1858 ..514
Timothy 1739-182115,
60
Timothy 1774- 60
POOLE
John W. 1812-1875
..........................584
POOLER
Thirza 1772-1843..200
POOR/POORE
Abigail 1680-1766....4,
12
Adeline 1812-1870307
Alfred J. 1804-1864
..........................307
Caleb 1767-.....80, 307
Caleb F. 1802-1880
..........................307
Caroline B. 1817-1850
..........................307
Edward L. 1795-1870
..........................421
Edwin 1797-1830..308
Elizabeth 1798-1835
..........................306
Enoch 1765-1834 ...80,
306
Enoch A. 1799-1847
..........................307
George 1789-1870.320
George 1796-1825.306
Hannah 1759-1835 80,
304
Harriet 1810-1901 307
Isaac T. 1808-1842308
Joel W. 1808-1885 307
John 1777-1844 302
Joseph 1776-1842.302
Leah C. 1800- 308
Mary 42, 167
Mary 1757- 80, 304
Mary 1807-1888...306,
392
Milton 1812-1828..308
Nancy 1771-1855...80,
308
Phebe 1761- 80, 305
Phebe 1803-1833 ..308
Polly O. 1799-1881308
Prudence C. 1806-
1868..................307

Robert B. 1798-1820
.... 307
Sarah 1772-1837 81
Sarah B. 1810-1902
.... 306
Stephen 1763-1812 80,
305
Stephen 1803- 306
Susannah 1778-1834
.... 81
Theodore 1766-1851
.... 201
Thomas 1732-1804 19,
79
Thomas 1774-1815. 81
Thomas O. 1795-1856
.... 307
William P. 1806-1889
.... 308
PORTER
Betsey E. 1798-1882
.... 275
Edward W. 1827-1904
.... 605
Elizabeth 1799-1877
.... 211
Elizabeth B. 1809- 233
Hannah 1762-1854 77,
295
Juliana 1796-1868 253
Lydia 1800- 516
Matilda 1797-1851 523
Sarah 1801-1852 .. 364
William 1761-1847 112
PORTERFIELD
Margaret 304
POST
John R. 1801- 257
POTTER
Susan 1842-1879 .. 424
POWELL
Ann 1818-1904 588
Stephen 1813-1881
.... 533
POWERS
Abraham 1822-1885
.... 603
Addison 1810-1897
.... 603
Anna 1806-1885 ... 603
Apphia 1815-1905 603
Asenath 1793-1869
.... 509
Betsey 1798-1841. 574
Betsey 1804-1888. 594
Eliza 1831-1902 ... 604
Gideon 1790-1879 151,
603
Hannah 1825-1852
.... 603
Hannah -1853 78, 300
Isaac 1807- 498
Lois 1828-1847 604
Lucy 1809-1890 602

Lucy M. 1824-1824
.... 603
Lydia 1774-1843 .. 207
Mary 1790-1854 .. 161,
635
Mary Ann 1821- ... 445
Mary E. 1809-1878
.... 471
Mehitable 1803-1882
.... 494
Rachel 1820-1855. 603
Ruth 1813-1832 603
Sarah 1808-1885 .. 603
Susan 1817-1877 .. 603
Zeruiah 1793-1885 573
PRATT
Abigail 1804-1842 579
Asa 1807- 369
Asenath 1793-1836
.... 271, 579
Benjamin.............. 438
Betsey 1799-1875. 597
Betsey 1800-1853. 187
Betsey 1815- 369
Charlotte 1810-1832
.... 452
Chester 1803- 466
Daniel 1799-1873. 579
David 1776-1850 ... 93,
368
David 1796- 465
David 1824- 369
Dorcas 1795-1872 271,
579
Ebenezer 1805- 369
Edward 1765-1829
.... 146, 579
Edward 1797-1838
.... 555, 579
Eliza 1808-1889 ... 579
Eunice 1813-1876. 369
George E. 1827-1894
.... 342
Hannah 1823-1884
.... 369
Isabel 1820-1901 .. 621
Jacob 1817- 369
Joanna 1806-1824 369
John...................... 366
Joseph W. 1821-1898
.... 230
Joshua 1770-1834 118,
465
Levi 1811-1883 369
Mary 1825-1836 ... 369
Otis 1821- 369
Rachel 1778- ... 93, 367
Rhoda 1762- ... 36, 153
Ruth A. 1808-1843 328
Sarah 1819- 369
Stephen 1803- 369
Susan 1826-1866 .. 367
Theda 1806-1846 .. 466
Thomas 1809-1877 369

Thomas O. 1792-1870
.... 188
Walter 1801-1862. 466
William 1794- 465
PRAY
Josiah 1819-1973 . 626
Ruth 1796- 163
PRENTISS
Louisa........... 111, 441
PRESBY
Elsa 1820-1894..... 344
PRESCOTT
Stephen 1806- 587
PRESTON
Abigail 1798-1871 227
Abraham 1771-1860
.... 207
Allis 1773- 207
Almira 1805-1869 231
Alson 1803-1877... 227
Alvah 1779-1852 ... 207
Amelia 1788- 228
Amos 1738-1756..... 15
Amos 1765-1776..... 58
Amos 1782-1864.... 59,
230
Asenath 1801-1875
.... 228
Austin 1803-1886. 229
Benjamin 1705-1784 4,
14
Benjamin 1727-1798
.... 14, 58
Benjamin 1773-...... 58
Calvin 1766-... 59, 228
Charles 1789-1872 228
Charles 1822-1829 231
Chloe 1761-1839 ... 58,
226
Chloe 1772-1841 ... 59,
229
Clarissa 1800-1853
.... 225
Cyprian 1814-1877
.... 229
Daniel 1729-..... 14, 58
Daniel 1763-1849 .. 58,
227
Daniel 1810-1885. 228
Darius 1732-1821 .. 14,
59
Darius 1766-1845 .. 59,
228
Deborah 1740-1822 15,
60
Deborah 1780-1857 59,
230
Dinah 1756-1836... 58,
225
Edward 1796- 227
Eliza J. 1810-1867 423
Enos 1737- 52, 206
Ermina 1801-1886 225
Eunice 1777-1807 . 59,
229

Eunice F. 1759-1856
.... 58, 226
Fidelia 1786-1872 228
Florinda 1799-1869
.... 229
Florinda 1810-1880
.... 231
Hannah 1760-1837 59
Hannah 1792- 228
Harriet 1815-1884 231
Henry 1736- 73
Hibbard 1790-1870
.... 228
Isabella 1798-....... 228
Jerusha 1736- .. 15, 59
Jerusha 1770-1792. 59
Jerusha 1796-1870 228
Joseph 1713-1738 . 18,
73
Joshua 1768-1810 . 59,
229
Joshua 1813-1900 231
Julia A. 1797-1878 227
Juliann 1805- 228
Lavina 1815- 228
Leander 1818-1901
.... 228
Louisa 1819-1896. 231
Lucius 1816-1899. 231
Marcia 1795- 227
Mary 1679-1753... 3, 7
Mary 1734-1742..... 15
Mary -1787..... 43, 170
Minerva 1807-1848
.... 225
Nancy 366
Oliver 1768- 58
Olivia 1811-1865 .. 231
Orren 1821-1821 .. 231
Rebecca 1689-1727 .. 4,
13
Reuben 1792-1884 477
Rufus 1794-1837 .. 227
Salina 1806-1861 . 231
Sarah 1764-.... 59, 228
Solomon 1770-1851 58,
225
Sylvester T. 1808-
1887 .... 231, 489
Truman 1807-1822
.... 230
Williston 1803-..... 229
Zalmon 1785- 228
PRICE
Allen 1820-1894 ... 494
James M............... 223
PRIM
Otis...................... 125
PRIME
Lamson 311
PRINCE
Alvira 1816-1882 .. 390
Eunice 1808-1877 564
John 1745-1811 270
PROCTOR

Adaline 1806-1888493
Charles 1804-1836493
Daniel 1769- 143
Daniel L. 1802-1877
............................568
Indianna 1803-1879
............................449
Isaac............125, 493
Lydia 1800-1893 ...363
Mary 1792-1874....362
Nehemiah H. 1806-
1808 568
Sally 1800- 311
Sarah 1799-1893...363
PROUTY
Amarillis 1792-1867
............................491
Avis 1794-1823 491
Burpee 1763-1849124,
491
Chloe 1806-1830 ...328
Esther 1803- 492
Ira 1798- 491
Lucy 1796-1863.....491
Luke 1811-............492
Lydia 1809- 492
Marcia 1801-.........491
Mary 1800-............491
Sophia 1807-1840 .492
PUGLSEY
Ivory 1822-1882....512
PULSIFER/PULSIPHER
Charles W. 1808-1888
............................387
Dana 1818-1878....387
David 1757-1835... 23,
97
David 1791-1865... 97,
387
Eli P. B. 1839-1918
............................388
Elias 1794-1858.... 97,
388
Elizabeth 1773-1820
....................91, 357
Elizabeth 1816-1875
............................387
Elizabeth 1826-1874
............................387
Elizabeth S. 1779-
1811 97
Elizabeth S. 1813-.387
Elvira 1816-1881 ..387
George 1824-.........387
George F. 1821-1821
............................388
George H. 1806-1861
............................387
Ira A. 1826-1865 ...388
Irena 1786-1809..... 97
Irena K. 1810-.......387
Laura 1815-1887...387
Lewis 1817-1825...387
Lewis 1828-1875 ...388
Lucy 1784-1830...... 97

Lucy A. 1824-1893 388
Martha A. 1823-1859
............................388
Mary 1820-1821....387
Mary 1821-1822....387
Patty 1796-1798 97
Philena 1789-1860..97
Samuel 1817-1897 387
Samuel W. 1782-1817
....................97, 386
Sarah R. 1848-1916
............................388
Sophia 1823-1876.387
William W. 1800-1870
....................97, 388
Zada P. 1831-1833 388
PURRINGTON
Rebecca 1811-1889601
PUSHEE
Nathan 1784-1810 240
PUTNAM
Abby 1813-............618
Abby 1829-1860 352
Abel 1806-1892 625
Abigail 1793-...90, 350
Abram 1802-1876 .334
Adaline 1815-1908618
Ann 1811-1888......618
Ann 1827-1831......352
Ann 1836-1861......352
Benjamin 1839-1858
............................352
Benjamin F. 1800-
1845.............90, 351
Betsey 1816-1907 .430
Bruce 1834-...........350
Caleb 1763-1826 21,
89
Charles 1826-1873618
Charles C. 1790-1862
....................90, 350
David 1790-1870...187
Deborah 1797-187790,
351
Ebenezer 1826-1826
............................630
Eliphalet 1799-1862
............................334
Emmett 1834-1871
............................350
Ephraim 1785-1862
....................158, 630
Ephraim 1809-1871
............................618
Ephraim 1815-1834
............................630
Esther 1818-1901 .630
Franklin 1823-1876
............................618
George 1820-1820.618
George 1821-1895.618
Hannah 1823-1922
............................350
Hannah 1832-1900
............................352

Hannah R. 1795-1874
............................90
Israel W. 1786-1868
............................296
Israel W. 1787-1868
............................296
James 1823-1887..350
James 1825-1864..350
James 1825-1905..351
James R. 1789-1843
....................90, 350
John 1774-1835 ...155,
617
John 1796-1877 315
John 1802-1805 90
John 1807-1867 618
John 1821-1908 350
Lyman 1818-1881.618
Mary 1814-1877....518
Mary 1823-1853....630
Mary 1834-1886....352
Mary F. 1803-1836617
Mary F. 1838-1926342
Nathaniel 1841-1891
............................352
Oscar 1827-1865 ...350
Phebe 1770-1827 ...48,
193
Samuel 1831-1920 350
Sarah 1805- 617
Sumner 1833- 631
Susanna 1756-1808
....................119, 468
Willard 1820-1856 630
Willard 1827-1899 633
William 1836-1880350
William H.H. 1840-
1923 388
PYNCHON
Martha 1755-1805
....................119, 469
QUICK
Catherine A. 1788-
1881 294
QUIMBY
Abigail 1818-1895.329
Dorothy 1824-1906
............................511
RALPH
Eunice 1809- 494
RAMSDELL
Mary 1805-1891....334
William 1810-1890637
RAND
Nathaniel..............363
Wareham 1796-1837
............................315
RANDOLPH
Wareham 1816-1887
............................534
RANGER
Olive 1826-1863....463
RANNEY
Eunice 1784-.........241
RANSOM

Lodema 1752-1814 51,
202
RANTOUL
Joanna Lovett 1803-
1863..................180
RAPPELE
Henry 1808-..........338
RATHBONE
Seldon 411
RATHBUN
Maria T. 1801-1875
............................252
Nancy 1826-1905..512
RAWSON
Catherine 1763-1837
....................123, 484
RAY
David 1806-1881...560
Minerva 1805-1875
............................291
RAYMOND
David G. 1819-1843
............................624
Eunice 1744-...32, 138
Fitch 1795-1852....508
Hannah 1781-.......183
Jesse 1792-1864...157,
624
John 1848- 627
John G. 1816-1885624
Stephen 1792-1868
............................554
REA
Albert G. 1802-1873
............................565
READ
Adoniram J. 1827-
1856..................386
Caleb 1775-1838...270
Daniel B. 1801-1882
............................527
Edward 1813-1891617
Olive 1781-............198
Sarah 1711-1781 ...18,
73
REDDING
Stevens 1780-1868169
REED
Betsy S. 1812-1884
............................571
Caroline 1811-1899
............................452
Clara P. 1804-1875
............................479
Elizabeth -1756......28,
119
Elizabeth 1825-1865
............................406
Fanny 1800-1862..440
Fanny 1801-1846..314
Huldah 1807-1848 548
Isaac 1797-1864....574
Jemima 1761-1845 68,
267
Mary 1795- 268

REEVES
    Louisa 1819-1904 . 338
REID
    Adam C. 1847-1926
    382
    Araminta 1801-1832
    .... 135, 534
REMINGTON
    Elizabeth W. 1814-
    1862 418
    Lucinda 1802-1843
    507
RENO
    Lewis 1798-1877 .. 499
REYNOLDS
    Ann 1804- 212
    Elizabeth 1758-1817
    .... 82, 313
    Lois E. 1823-1901. 466
RHOADES
    Fordyce 1811-1888 462
RHODES
    Fanny 1817-1861 . 346
    Lydia 1786- 196
    Phebe 1817-1856.. 232
RIANT
    Sarah 1786- 265
RICE
    Baxter 1772-1851. 275
    Elizabeth 1787-1838
    201
    Horace 1796-1877 444
    Horatio 1787-1871 236
    Minnie 1867-1928 628
    Moses 1787- 206
    Nancy 1788-1843 . 478
    Samantha 1815-1903
    264
RICH
    Charles 1860- 628
    Eliza 1825-1856 ... 471
    George E. 1849-.... 628
    Harris 1845-1915 . 628
    Isadore 1854- 628
    John 1852-1928.... 628
    Mary 1827-1916 ... 544
    Mary 1857-1877 ... 628
    Philena 1791-1849 241
    Samuel A. 1812-1890
    .... 158, 628
    William H. 1843-1914
    628
RICHARDS
    Benaiah 1798-1840
    320
    Benjamin 1794-1844
    318
    Calvin 1802-1836. 320
    Dexter N. 1822-1900
    406
    Eliphalet 1761-1846
    .... 83, 319
    Eliphalet 1790-1859
    320
    Ellen 1836- 354
    Isaiah 1796-1862.. 320

    James 1785-1855 . 320
    John 1800-1848.... 320
    Letitia 1804-1882. 321
    Lois F. 1777-1832. 207
    Luther 1804-1872 320
    Mary 1785-1823 ... 196
    Mitchell 1759-1845
    198
    Perry 1794-1875... 320
    Phebe 1787-1864.. 320
    Rachel 1767-1851.. 83,
    318
    Sally 1792-1862.... 320
    Sarah A. 1820-1895
    372
    Syrene 1806- 320
RICHARDSON
    Abiel 1783-1864 ... 270
    Abigail 1775-1796 270
    Albina 1844-1874. 349
    Amos 1812-1882... 398
    Angelina 1814-1895
    586
    Ann 1820-1870..... 549
    Anna 1777-1846 ... 270
    Barnet 1805-1893 634
    Clarissa 1795- 209
    Edee 1786-1871.... 270
    Elinor 1753-1834... 69,
    272
    Eliza 1808-1857 ... 402
    Elvira 1808-1857.. 244
    Esther 1767-1806 111,
    443
    Ezra 1795-1873 341
    Hannah 1813-1908
    543
    Harvey 1801-1885 209
    Herbert 1810-1883 543
    Jesse 1840-1922 ... 631
    John................... 13, 53
    John 1784- 208
    John 1789-1841.... 179
    John D. 1821-1874 382
    Leonora 1850-1873
    629
    Luther 1808-1884 611
    Mary 1778- 208
    Nancy 1829-1912 . 577
    Nancy L. 1806-1891
    579
    Olivia 1802-1882.. 568
    Reuben 1754- . 53, 208
    Reuben 1782- 208
    Samuel 1781-1869 305
    Sarah 1719- 17, 70
    Sarah 1758- 53
    Sarah 1776-1823.. 208
    Sarah 1779-1805.. 270
    Sarah 1816-1884.. 579
    Sarah P. 1814-1848
    333
    Seth 1786-1809 ... 100,
    402

    Stephen 1759-1834 53,
    209
    Stephen 1780- 208
    Thomas 1751-1786 68,
    269
    Thomas 1781- 270
    William 1778-1863 186
    William 1794-1836 305
RICHMOND
    Armenia 1807-1887
    241
    Oliver 1765- 204
    Wellington 1817-.. 584
RIDDLE
    Elijah 1772-1842.. 481
RIDEOUT
    Amos 1793- 547
RIDER
    Eunice 1812-1892 219
    Hiram 1790-1851 . 220
    Sally 1796-1868 ... 214
RIGNE
    Evelyn I. 1884-1975
    630
RINAKER
    Margaret 1822-1914
    512
RINDGE
    Anna 1788- 439
    John 1784- 439
    Joseph 1792- 439
    Lucy 1790- 439
    Nathan 1795-1795 439
    Nathan 1796- 439
    Polly 1799- 439
    Richard 1760-1843
    .... 110, 439
    Royal 1795-1878 .. 446
    Sarah 1785- 439
    Thomas 1763-1819 202
RIPLEY
    Joseph W. 1806-1891
    401
RISLEY
    Whiting 1786-1853
    246
ROATH
    Zerviah 1805-1875 434
ROBBINS
    Mary 1770-1844 84,
    324
    Melissa 1805-1862 514
    Nathaniel -1753 . 5, 18
    Noah 1771-1841 ... 197
ROBERTS
    Fanny 1810-1877 . 229
    Lydia 1778-1859 .. 200
    Reuben 1792-1865 540
ROBERTSON
    Sally 1793-1880 ... 319
ROBIE
    Albert G. 1806-1886
    322
    James C. 1815-1905
    322
    John A. 1810- 323

    Lewis H. 1818-1869
    322
    Mary 1782-1829 83,
    323
    Moores 1798-1859 322
    Phebe 1802-1855.. 322
    Phebe R. 1803-1876
    323
    Samantha 1812-1900
    322
    Samuel 1717-1793 20,
    83
    Samuel 1777-1865 83,
    322
    Samuel 1804-1807 323
    Sophronia 1810-1884
    322
    Thomas 1779-1811 83,
    322
    Thomas R. 1796- .. 322
ROBINSON
    Amasa 1764-1843 227
    Anna 1788- 171
    Betsey 1793-1832. 206
    Harriet 1807-1850 95,
    374
    Mary A. 1805- 434
    Mary R. 1818-1894
    375
    Ruth 1781-1849 ... 239
    Thankful 1762-1846
    284
ROBISNON
    Cephronia 1818-1901
    522
ROCKAFELLOW
    Mary 1819-1892 ... 384
ROCKWELL
    Frederick 1814-1874
    473
ROE
    Admiral 1800- 246
    Amanda 1800-1870
    481
    Harriet 1812-1883 462
ROGERS
    Abigail 1769-1849 . 65,
    256
    Alva 1776- 65, 129,
    257
    Alva 1820-1880 257
    Amos 1783- 95, 379
    Amos 1815-1879... 213
    Anson 1790-1872 . 236
    Chester 1760- 65
    Daniel 1769-1769 ... 65
    Elisha 1766-1807 .. 65,
    256
    George 1794-1844 256
    Harlow 1816-1908 257
    Hiram P. 1820-1864
    591
    Jarvis 1805-1857.. 257
    John 1790-1864.... 312
    John 1790-1875.... 414

John 1804-1873 301
Jonas S. 1823-1898
.........................582
Leiscter H. 1804-1827
.........................257
Lois 1762- 65
Lucia 1771-1823 ... 65,
257
Lucy J. 1830-1910.379
Martha 1823-1832 533
Martha S. 1824-1906
.........................379
Mary 1727-175318, 75
Mary H. 1807-1865
.........................257
Mary M. 1827- 379
Moses 1731-1797 .. 16,
65
Moses A. 1833-......379
Namah 1790- 256
Olive 1759-1855.... 65,
255
Polly 1784-1874 66,
261
Ralph H. 1792-1866
.........................256
Riley 1788-1874....256
Sarah 43, 170
William E. 1829-1901
.........................379
Zebediah 1796-1857
.........................407
ROICE
Joseph 1792-1827 .212
ROLFE
Jane 1783-1863.....412
ROLLINS
Charles P. 1809-1891
.........................408
Ephraim 1800-1889
.........................603
John 1837- 627
Julia 1868-1962 629
Lucy 1817-1915.....441
Susannah..............269
ROMERIL
Sophia J. 1848-1906
.........................616
ROMNEY
Samuel 1835-1878 605
ROOT
Desire 1774-1871.132,
526
Eleazer 1790-1837 215
Thankful 72
ROOTS
Benajah G. 1811-1888
.........................220
ROSE
Cyrus 1807-1898...375
Nelson 1812-1896 .349
Patty 1794-1882...159,
631
Phebe 1797-1819...444
ROSS

Elizabeth M. 1816-565
Jane 1804-1888.....524
John 1687- 5, 20
John 1716- 20
Josiah 1820-1882..346
Sarah 1720- 20
Thomas 1718-1719 .20
ROUSE
Lucy A. 1819-1875 196
ROWE
Harriet 1799-........508
Lydia 1770-1818.....91
Stephen G. 1802- ..508
ROWLEY
Leander 1822-1887
.........................527
ROY
Edith M. 1877-1960
.........................386
ROYAL
Emilie 1834-1864..604
RUDD
Abigail 1746-1824..73,
282
Hannah 1767-1848 53,
209
RUDOLPH
Jacob 228
RUGAN
James 1841-..........370
RUGGLES
Ephraim 1815-1903
.........................511
RUMRILL
Almira 1808-1894 232,
262
Alva H. 1810-1823 262
Clarissa 1811-1828
.........................262
Harriet 1813-1837 262
Harvey H. 1806-1883
.........................262
Mary H. 1822-1904
.........................263
Sarina 1815-1888 .262
Simeon 1769-1822 .67,
262
Solon B. 1817-1878
.........................262
RUNNELS
Susannah 1765-1849
.........................168
RURMRILL
Eliza M. 1820-1884
.........................262
RUSHING
Joel 1810-1892......458
RUSS
Priscilla 1743-1807 30,
132
Sarah M. 1843-1916
.........................545
RUSSELL
Aaron 1815-1883 ..344
Abby H. 1816- 539

Abel 1778-1859......86,
334
Abel 1807-1811.....335
Abel 1815-1890.....335
Abiah 1781-1831..151,
602
Abiah 1813-1847...335
Abiel 1789-1881.....99,
393
Abiel 1808-1885....390
Abiel E. 1821-1861394
Abigail 1710-.......7, 30
Abigail 1717-1746..17,
71
Abigail 1750-1822..23,
100
Abigail 1753-.........120
Abigail 1755-1812..72,
278
Abigail 1776-1856..99,
397
Abigail 1786-1859152,
605
Abigail 1792-1792.595
Abigail 1805-1825.593
Abigail 1824-1907.374
Abigail B. 1812-1879
.........................391
Abigail C. 1815-1898
.................396, 399
Abilene 1764-........120
Abner 1782- 95
Abner 1791-1855 .155,
615
Abraham 1750-1839
.....................36, 151
Achsah 1758-1851 166
Addie R. 1827-1901
.........................399
Adelia 1830-1907..614
Adoniram 1817-1839
.........................367
Adoniram 1822-1891
.........................613
Albert 1839-..........614
Albert W. 1817-1892
.........................374
Alden 1802-1857...337
Alfred 1809-..........331
Alfred 1836-1919 ..614
Alfred W. 1818-1881
.........................337
Allen K. 1833-1861
.........................616
Almina 1815- 383
Almira 1834-.........614
Almira H. 1813-1836
.........................375
Almoody 1794-........89
Alonzo 1835-1862 .605
Alonzo W. 1814-1848
.........................378
Alpheus 1829-1832
.........................399

Alvah 1796-1856..100,
399
Alvah 1821-1885...397
Amanda M. 1828-1832
.........................390
Amanda M. 1829-1912
.........................613
Amelia 1800-1873155,
616
Amelia 1832-1837.616
Amelia 1841-1926.382
Ammon 1810-1894392
Amos 1818-1882 ...381
Amos 1824-1912 ...392
Amos E. 1831-1910
.........................382
Amzi 1810-1878....396
Andrew 1768- .94, 371
Andrew 1803-1887365
Andrew J. 1829-1902
.........................375
Andrew W. 1817-1871
.........................378
Anna 1756- 31
Anna 1770-1813...120,
472
Anna 1781- 136
Apphia 1787-1858151,
603
Aquilla 1712-1718 6
Aquilla 1748-1823 .22,
95
Asa 1744- 18
Asa 1761- 72
Asa 1808-1876 538
Asenath 1786-1868.86
Asenath 1836-1892
.........................345
Augusta E. 1839-1888
.........................399
Benjamin 1677-17543,
7
Benjamin 1698-1760.6
Benjamin 1702-17547,
28
Benjamin 1728-1808
.....................28, 119
Benjamin 1735- 17
Benjamin 1739-1802
.....................35, 150
Benjamin 1753- 31
Benjamin 1755- 119
Benjamin 1759- 72
Benjamin 1763-1842
.................150, 592
Benjamin 1795-1795
.........................595
Benjamin 1796-1840
.........................595
Benjamin 1803-1871
.........................593
Benjamin 1810-1874
.........................367
Benjamin 1835- 370

Benjamin F. 1802-1877 470
Benjamin H. 1780-1848 278
Benjamin W. 1807-1883 332
Bethiah 1761-1761. 86
Bethiah 1763-1821 86, 332
Betsey 1776-1843 .. 84, 325
Betsey 1793-1815. 311
Betsey 1797-1844. 334
Betsey 1813-1859. 336
Betsey P. 1812-1903 .... 97, 386
Betsy 1768-1857.... 93, 94, 364
Betsy 1773- 87, 337
Betty 1780-1866 .. 151, 598
Brooks 1822-1905. 335
Burnam 1805-1874 344
Caleb B. 1807-1886 611
Caroline P. 1807-1809 469
Catherine 1797-1880 312
Chandler 1775-1846 .... 36, 153
Charles 1793- 152
Charles 1798-1851 557
Charles 1809-1816 378
Charles 1809-1855 335
Charles 1813-1893 313
Charles 1820-1888 390
Charles F. 1830-1906 606
Charles J. 1836-1905 616
Charles P. 1816-1889 375
Charles S. 1805-1807 471
Charles S. 1808-1808 471
Charlotte 1829-1896 360
Chloe 1789-1808... 154
Chloe 1810-1900... 611
Clara 1822-1824... 344
Clara T. 1842-1919 377
Cynthia 1771- 120, 473
Cynthia 1772-1833 .... 135, 537
Cynthia 1793-....... 595
Cynthia 1822-1884 340
Cyril 1799-1857.... 471
Daniel 1742-1743... 21
Daniel 1754-.......... 21
Daniel 1769-1841 .. 86, 334

Daniel 1795-1873. 334
Daniel 1796-1819... 89
Daniel 1803-1856. 445
Daniel 1820-1878. 346
Daniel 1821-1870. 331
Daniel G. 1813-1845 390
David 1748-1776.... 36
David 1758-1843. 119, 469
David 1794-1794 .. 469
David 1795-1863 .. 312
David 1796-1875 ... 96, 384
David 1818-1820 .. 378
David 1830-.......... 614
David A. 1818-1888 384
David S. 1795-1827 469
Davis S. 1802-1874 471
Deborah 1740-1820 20, 84
Desire 1794-1882 .. 94, 370
Desire 1839-1969 . 370
Dolly 1784-1863 .... 98, 152, 390
Dolly 1788-1809 .. 151, 599
Dolly 1804-........... 390
Dolly 1811-........... 390
Dorcas 1789-1860 .. 93, 369
Dorcas 1796-1877 151, 593, 600
Dorcas 1800-1860 152, 605
Dorcas 1808-1862. 365
Duane 1845-1882. 614
Dwight P. 1810-1879 469
Ebenezer 1773- ... 120, 473
Ebenezer 1794-1883 .... 154, 612
Ebenezer 1797-1859 .... 155, 616
Ebenezer 1817-1886 615
Edgar 1839-1920 .. 614
Edward 1804-1874 596
Eleazer 1761- 119, 470
Eleazer 1806-1875 470
Electa 1788-1863 .. 470
Eli 1775-1841. 94, 372
Eli B. 1816-1885... 372
Eliab 1804-1874 .. 154, 614
Elias 1787- 154
Elijah 1756-............ 21
Elijah 1768-.... 36, 120
Elijah 1781-1844... 95, 378

Elijah 1804-1888. 153, 609
Elisha 1746-1791 .. 31, 136
Elisha 1777-......... 136
Elisha 1780- 135
Elisha 1824-1884 . 382
Eliza 1799-1899 ... 312
Eliza 1826-1854 ... 345
Eliza E. 1827-1832 383
Eliza F. 1837-1839 377
Eliza J. 1822-1849 375
Eliza M. 1828-1899 374
Elizabeth 1687-1772 3, 9
Elizabeth 1745-1820 .... 23, 99
Elizabeth 1751-1754 119
Elizabeth 1752-1840 .... 18, 72
Elizabeth 1760-.... 120
Elizabeth 1786-1865 100
Elizabeth 1817-1890 345
Elizabeth 1818-1818 391
Elizabeth 1820-1851 379
Elizabeth 1843-1847 348
Elizabeth 1844-1861 400
Elizabeth K. 1819-1914 391
Elizabeth P. 1815-1865 392
Elmira 1812-........ 596
Elsie 1796- 595
Elsie 1800- 596
Elvira 1804-1894... 96, 385
Emily 1824-1869 .. 377
Emily 1832-1837.. 616
Emily 1842-1857.. 614
Emily A. 1814-1885 334
Emily W. 1830-1851 609
Ephraim 1783-1875 .... 86, 336
Ephraim 1811-1885 336
Ephraim P. 1785- 154, 612
Esther 1780-1807 100, 398
Esther 1792-1876 152, 604
Eunice 1746- 18
Eunice 1772-1825 . 92, 364
Eunice 1801- 367

Eunice 1808-1852 . 97, 386
Eunice 1833-1903 382
Ezekiel 1694-1708.... 6
Ezekiel 1722-1802. 17, 71
Ezekiel 1724-1724.. 28
Ezekiel 1751-1798. 71, 278
Ezekiel D. 1811-1883 .... 153, 610
Ezra 1832-1867.... 375
Ezra T. 1803-1839 596
Farnum D. 1820-.. 153
Fidelia 1836-........ 382
Fisk 1810-1892..... 333
Fletcher 1795-1853 .... 152, 604
Francis M. 1836-1863 609
Frank J. 1847-1939 .... 609, 610
Franklin F. 1820-1890 381
Frederick 1818-1818 331
Frederick A. 1787-1866 .... 85, 331
Galon 1824-.......... 614
Gardner S. 1815-.. 391
George 1834-1839 377
George 1835-1838 347
George 1837-1837 348
George 1844-1846 347
George D. 1822-1910 372
George H. 1824-1828 385
George H. 1830-1874 375
George T. 1812-.... 471
George W. 1802-1886 324
Georgianna 1835-1915 351
Gideon 1816-1862 378
Gideon 1825-1865 604
Gideon G. 1791-1833 .... 95, 379
Gilbert 1819-1880 615
Hannah 1679-1715 . 3, 8
Hannah 1707-.... 7, 29
Hannah 1726-1726 28
Hannah 1730- ... 9, 17, 37
Hannah 1740- 21
Hannah 1742- 20
Hannah 1749- 31
Hannah 1754- 36
Hannah 1754-1840 23, 97
Hannah 1760-1840 21, 89
Hannah 1761- 36

Hannah 1767-1850 86, 145, 333
Hannah 1768-1841 ....135, 537
Hannah 1775-1776 98
Hannah 1776-1848 ....151, 601
Hannah 1778-1840 ....151, 598
Hannah 1780-1832 98, 391
Hannah 1782- .95, 373
Hannah 1782-1824 87, 337
Hannah 1786- 93
Hannah 1798-1886 311
Hannah 1800-1857 334
Hannah 1813-1832 367
Hannah 1823-1883 345
Hannah A. 1794-1838 332
Hannah D. 1806-1860 335
Hannah H. 1784- ..136
Hannah H. 1823-1906 397
Harriet 1811-1887 334
Harriet 1826-1861 374
Harriet 1826-1908 347
Harriet 1832-1879 345
Harriet 1836- 375
Harriet 1847-1893 536
Harriet A. 1834-1855 377
Harriet M. 1819-1888 340
Harrison E. 1811- .469
Helen E. 1842-1861 ....608, 610
Heman 1805-1831 .311
Henry 1804- 596
Henry 1810- 378
Henry 1830-1912 ..383
Henry J. 1818-1898 390
Henry R. -1828......392
Henry W. 1829-1891 393
Hephzibah 1734-.... 21
Hephzibah 1734-1783 ....9, 36
Hephzibah 1755-.... 37
Hephzibah 1756-.... 36
Hephzibah 1783-..154, 612
Hephzibah 1783-1834 154
Hephzibah 1783-1873 279
Hiram K. 1812-1848 374

Horace 1825-1889 .378
Horace 1830-1927 .605
Hosea 1811- 378
Huldah 1795-1865 155
Huldah 1804-1872 367
Ira 1802-1859 .89, 347
Ira 1834-1837 347
Ira 1840-1878 347
Ira O. 1804-1888 ...396
Ira W. 1825-1910 ..383
Irena A. 1819-1908 374
Isaac 1724-..........9, 37
Isaac 1752-1754 36
Isaac 1759-........36, 37
Isabella 1849-1946 332
Israel 1837-1862 ...370
Israel C. 1814-1850 392
Jacob 1761-1799 ....36, 152
Jacob 1788-1873 ..152, 606
Jacob 1816- 390
Jacob 1817-1854 ...335
Jacob A. 1795-1866 332
Jacob M. 1792- 93, 370
Jacob M. 1832.......377
James 1667-1717 ..3, 5
James 1706-........5, 22
James 1710-1784 5, 22
James 1737-......22, 92
James 1742-1752 22
James 1746-1821 ...20, 85
James 1749-1749 23
James 1753-1830 ...21, 88
James 1757-1759 23
James 1763-..119, 470
James 1771-1859 ...93, 366
James 1772-............99
James 1777-1861 ...98, 152, 390
James 1778-1861 .100, 397
James 1785-1819 ...85, 331
James 1785-1858 ...95, 378
James 1787-..........154
James 1787-1849 ...88, 345
James 1793-....87, 340
James 1796-1868 ..471
James 1798-1826 ..334
James 1806-1872 ..344
James 1807-..........390
James 1822-..........379
James 1822-1845 ..392
James 1828-1902 ..336
James 1829-1862 ..345

Jane 1770-1856......92, 363
Jane 1807-1836.....367
Jane 1808-1889.....312
Jane 1830-1922.....340
Jedediah 1752-1848 ....36, 153
Jedediah 1780-1863 ....154, 610
Jedediah 1812-1888 611
Jeduthan 1745-1813 ....22, 94
Jeduthan 1785-1857 ....95, 374
Jemima 1704-1790 ..5, 21
Jemima 1733-1813 ..9, 38
Jeremiah 1772-1843 ....93, 94, 364
Jeremiah 1810-.....365
Jesse D. 1829-1902 609
Joanna 1779-1848 .93, 368
Job A. 1830-1830 ..394
Joel 1783-1871 98, 392
Joel 1808-1883.....306, 392
Joel 1822-1888......390
John 1682-1778 ....3, 8
John 1717-1788 ..9, 35
John 1730- 28, 30, 120
John 1742-1811 .....31, 135
John 1746-1830 .....35, 150
John 1753-1814 .....82, 311
John 1758- 120
John 1767- 166
John 1774-1818 ...150, 596
John 1775-1850 ...150, 596
John 1779- 136
John 1781- 93
John 1787-1845 .....96, 381
John 1793- 310
John 1794- 311
John 1798-1820 593
John 1800-1854 596
John 1801-1851 332
John 1804-1873 ...361, 538
John 1805-1889 365
John 1806-1807 367
John 1807-1886 596
John 1809-1866 367
John B. 1820-1892 385
John D. 1822-1882 377
John F. 1802-1878 334
John F. 1838-1912 382

John M. 1800-1874 324
Jonathan 1749-.21, 86
Jonathan 1758-1834 ....37, 154
Jonathan 1770-.....135
Jonathan 1785-1848 ....154, 614
Jonathan 1786-1808 87
Jonathan 1793-1859 595
Jonathan 1821-.....615
Jonathan 1832-.....340
Jonathan E. 1793- 100
Jonathan E. 1818-1856 399
Jonathan L. 1814-1859 615
Jonathan M. 1830-1900 616
Jonathan R. 1808-1899 325
Joseph 1671-1702 .3, 6
Joseph 1695-1767 6
Joseph 1702-........5, 20
Joseph 1717-........7, 31
Joseph 1720-1783 ....9, 21, 36
Joseph 1742-1775 ..22, 94
Joseph 1744-1762 ...20
Joseph 1758-...........36
Joseph 1770-...........94
Joseph 1770-1826 ..84, 324
Joseph 1771-1853 ..87, 336
Joseph 1775-...93, 367
Joseph 1780-1858 ..86, 335
Joseph 1783-1827 ..88, 344
Joseph 1786-1853 .278
Joseph 1787-1867 ..95, 374
Joseph 1794-.........371
Joseph 1796-1876 .324
Joseph 1803-1804 .332
Joseph 1809-. 333, 597
Joseph 1811-1887 .335
Joseph 1834-1893 .616
Joseph E. 1832-1906 609
Joseph H. 1800-1871 337
Joseph H. 1814-....153
Joseph M. 1819-1893 372
Joseph P. 1790-1849 469
Joshua R. 1824-...153, 603
Josiah 1756-1820....31
Josiah 1775-..........136

Josiah Q. 1830-1889 381
Julia 1810-1815.... 312
Julia 1815-1850.... 313
Julia 1827-1901.... 331
Julia F. 1843- 378
Laura 1825-1905.. 372
Laura 1831-1918.. 599
Leander 1816- 596
Leonicy 1809-1893 364
Levi 1776- 120
Levi 1795-1831 96, 383
Levi 1812- 392
Levi 1838- 378
Levi A. 1823-1894 381
Levi F. 1823- 383
Lewis 1814-1903 .. 473
Lodema D. 1828-1912 382
Lois 1829-1829 377
Lorenzo D. 1837-1901 610
Lovina A. 1818-1899 379
Lovina D. 1816-1844 .... 153, 610
Lucinda 1804-1852 324
Lucinda 1815-1882 331
Lucy 1746- 22
Lucy 1777-1854 ..... 94, 372
Lucy F. 1783- . 95, 379
Lucy F. 1819-1901 379
Luke R. 1801-1832 593
Lydia 1713- 7, 30
Lydia 1762- 92, 362
Lydia 1764-1847.... 36, 152
Lydia 1779-1866.... 94, 373
Lydia 1782-1782..... 98
Lydia 1785-1855... 279
Lydia 1785-1865.... 99, 393
Lydia 1790-1844... 595
Lydia 1796-1862... 470
Lydia 1797-1874... 332
Lydia 1812-1875... 593
Lydia A. 1808-1893 .... 390, 566
Lydia A. 1818-1878 394
Lydia A. 1821-1899 391
Lydia H. 1820-1898 383
Lydia P. 1833-1921 606
Lyman 1808- 615
Lyman K. 1801-1824 311
Lyman R. 1842-1864 609

Margaret 1843- 370
Maria E. 1844-1864 609
Maria H. 1809-1855 .... 153, 609
Martha 1773- 94
Martha A. 1810-1894 593
Martha J. 1826-1891 377
Martha M. 1791-1874 469
Martha P. 1831-1891 385
Martin 1799-1878 . 95, 377
Martin 1819- 595
Martin 1831- 377
Mary 1661-1717 3
Mary 1693-1778 . 5, 19
Mary 1705- 7, 28
Mary 1716-1803 . 6, 23
Mary 1729- 9, 37
Mary 1731- 17
Mary 1733-1771 .... 28, 120
Mary 1740- 18
Mary 1744- 31
Mary 1764- ... 150, 593
Mary 1780-1835 .... 84, 325
Mary 1782-1859 .. 100, 398
Mary 1784-1856 ... 151
Mary 1784-1857 .... 93, 368
Mary 1792-1884 .... 89, 346
Mary 1794- 593
Mary 1804-1832 ... 312
Mary 1806-1874 ... 596
Mary 1807-1835 ... 334
Mary 1807-1879 ... 344
Mary 1811-1823 ... 331
Mary 1816-1855 ... 345
Mary 1823-1849 ... 615
Mary 1828-1829 ... 331
Mary 1839-1901 ... 347
Mary 1841-1909 ... 348
Mary 1846- 614
Mary 1849- 370
Mary A. 1813-1903 335
Mary E. 1807- 471
Mary E. 1822- 377
Mary E. 1828-1904 385
Mary F. 1799-1881 324
Mary F. 1834-1915 400
Mary F. W. 1831-1832 383
Mary H. 1809-1839 335
Mary J. 1836-1923 383

Mary W. 1806-1878 .... 155, 617
Mehitable 1688-1733 .... 5, 16
Mehitable 1751- ... 120
Mehitable 1768-1848 .... 84, 323
Mehitable 1792-1854 595
Mehitable 1807-1880 593
Mehitable 1810-1817 325
Merab 1829- 374
Merriam 1834-1903 345
Miriam 1777- 93
Molly 1775-1864..... 86
Moor 1757-1851 .... 82, 311
Moor 1788-1868 ... 311
Moses 1811-1871.. 367
Moses A. 1824-1834 394
Nabby 1812- 595
Nancy 1790-1818 151, 593, 600
Nancy 1793- 155
Nancy 1793-1876 . 312
Nancy 1811-1883 . 335
Nancy 1812-1866 . 336
Nancy 1815- 367
Nancy 1816-1817 . 331
Nancy 1819-1908 . 613
Nancy A. 1836-1863 400
Nancy D. 1803-1860 396
Nancy H. 1826- 380
Nathan 1751- 31
Nathaniel 1751- 36
Nathaniel 1774-1842 .... 93, 364
Nathaniel 1841-1895 400
Obadiah 1804-1877 471
Olive 1751- 82
Olive M. 1849-1883 610
Olivia 1800-1886.. 470
Orlando P. 1840-1906 610
Orrin 1810-1880... 344
Osgood N. 1827-1882 616
Palmer 1813- 596
Parley 1777-1841 135, 538
Peabody 1789-1846 89, 345
Pelatiah 1813-1892 325
Peletiah 1727-1757 20, 81

Peletiah 1753-1831 82, 310
Peletiah 1781-1839 311
Peregrine 1813-1837 153
Perkins 1748-1765 . 21
Perkins 1789-1857 . 88
Perkins 1819-1895 336
Persis 1799-1881.. 596
Peter 1700-1759 . 5, 20
Peter 1738-1815 20, 83
Peter 1805-1843 .... 89, 347
Peter 1806-1880 ... 324
Phebe 1690- 5, 18
Phebe 1716- 9, 34
Phebe 1736-1836 ... 20, 83
Phebe 1751- 18, 72
Phebe 1760- 92
Phebe 1766- 120
Phebe 1772-1852 ... 86, 334
Phebe 1776-1858. 151, 597
Phebe 1783-1858 ... 93, 368
Phebe 1785-1856 ... 87, 339
Phebe 1786- 99
Phebe 1796-1888.. 311
Phebe 1807-1896.. 596
Phebe 1818-1905.. 392
Philancy 1801-1863 538
Phylena 1803-1839 96, 385
Polly -1793 468
Polly 1797-1868 ... 336
Polly 1799-1894 ... 332
Priscilla 1712-1732 .. 6
Priscilla 1743-1752 22
Priscilla 1753-1816 23, 97
Priscilla 1753-1842 23
Priscilla 1790- 95, 376
Priscilla J. 1824-1899 391
Priscilla P. 1810-1884 375
Prissilla 1787- 100
Prudence 1720-1745 9, 17, 38
Prudence 1748- 36
Prudence 1760- 37
Rachel 1730-1802.. 20, 82
Rachel 1757- 21, 89
Rachel 1773-1850 136, 539
Rachel 1783-1871.. 87, 338
Rachel 1790- 93
Rachel 1815-1863. 367

Rachel 1817-1858 .473
Rachel D. 1797-1837 616
Ralph 1801- 367
Ralph 1813-1843...539
Ralph 1821- 367
Rebecca 1734- 20
Rebecca 1785-1811 88
Rebecca 1810-1880538
Rebecca M. 1809-1893 299
Rebekah 1809-1897 336
Rebuen 1749-1753 . 82
Reuben 1817-1910 336
Rhoda 1755- 37
Rhoda 1766- 94
Rhoda 1770-1852 .. 93, 365
Rhoda 1782-1867 .154, 611
Rhoda 1810-1902 ..374
Rhoda 1825- 383
Richard 1774- 99
Richard 1790-1866 96, 382
Richard 1823-1824604
Riley 1795- 473
Robert 1630-1710..... 1
Robert 1669-1689..... 3
Robert 1690-17595, 17
Robert 1722-17949, 36
Robert 1757-1836.. 72, 279
Robert 1782-1860.. 85, 330
Robert 1784-1863..311
Robert 1787-1788..279
Robert 1789-1825..279
Robert 1819-1895..331
Roscoe F. 1847-1849 610
Roxana 1808- 337
Ruth 1773-1790 87
Ruth 1793-1870 .... 96, 380
Ruth 1818-1820 345
Ruth 1821-1911 345
Ruth A. 1821-1890337
Ruth A. 1842-1894382
Sally 1774-1833 ...120, 200, 472
Sally 1783-1848 ...151, 599
Sally 1785-1868 311
Sally 1788-1843 ...155, 615
Sally 1796-1859 .... 96, 383
Sally 1805- 337
Sally 1806-1896 392
Sally P. 1796-154, 613
Sally W. 1787-.......136
Salome 1803-1869.367
Samuel 1790-1874 593

Samuel 1798-1800 154
Samuel 1799-1831 .89, 347
Samuel 1801- 154, 614
Samuel 1802- 596
Samuel 1805- 367
Samuel 1812-1862 331
Samuel 1820-1893 392
Samuel 1822-1879 347
Samuel 1836-1911 370
Samuel P. 1805-1880 332
Sarah 1674-1764...3, 6
Sarah 1695- 5, 20
Sarah 1713-1781..8, 9, 33
Sarah 1726-1752....28, 119
Sarah 1742-1743.....35
Sarah 1743- 20
Sarah 1746- 36
Sarah 1750-1844....21, 87
Sarah 1753-1754...119
Sarah 1756- 120
Sarah 1763- 84
Sarah 1770-1852....99, 396
Sarah 1773- 93, 94
Sarah 1776-1849...102
Sarah 1779-1846..151, 602
Sarah 1780- 87
Sarah 1787-1877...310
Sarah 1799...........366
Sarah 1816- 472
Sarah 1829- 370
Sarah 1839-1855...348
Sarah A. 1823-1888 381
Sarah A. 1825-1896 381
Sarah A. 1826-1898 613
Sarah B. 1816-1851 394
Sarah D. 1816-1843 334
Sarah E. 1835-1893 378
Sarah E. 1837-1872 400
Sarah G. 1799-1869 ....96, 380
Sarah L. 1820-1896 375
Sarah M. 1811-1811 471
Sarah M. 1831-1909 377
Simeon 1761- 36
Smith 1786- 470
Solomon 551
Sophia 1799-1876 .471
Sophia 1811-1894 .596

Sophia 1815-1894 .374
Sophia 1817- 383
Stephen 1765-1847 ....119, 471
Stephen 1819-1902 367
Stephen A. 1788-1860 593
Stephen H. 1820-1876 472
Submit 1784- 278
Susan 1789-1862 ..151
Susan 1817-1904 ..397
Susan 1835-1922 ..605
Susan J. 1840-1938 377
Susanna 1757- 37
Susanna 1786-1824 278
Susanna 1793-1887 ....95, 376
Susanna 1808- 367
Susanna C. 1795-1854 336
Susannah 1810-....596
Sylvanus 1802-1887 365
Tabitha 1749-1776..71
Temperance 1764-1831.............92, 362
Theodore 1765-1821 ....150, 595
Theodore 1808-1884 596
Theodore 1816-1882 595
Theodosia 1825-1895 331
Theron 1804-1806.334
Theron 1809-1875.334
Thomas 1663-17313, 4
Thomas 1687- 5
Thomas 1714-1753 ..6, 23
Thomas 1732-1818 21, 35, 85
Thomas 1747-1823 23, 99
Thomas 1751-1845 23, 96
Thomas 1761- 120
Thomas 1765-1863 86, 332
Thomas 1768-1853 99, 396
Thomas 1775-1775 .98
Thomas 1777-1849 98, 390
Thomas 1785-1872 96, 381
Thomas 1786- 95
Thomas 1790-.........95
Thomas 1791-1791332
Thomas 1792-1840332
Thomas 1801-1884365

Thomas 1802-1867367
Thomas 1806- 390
Thomas 1812- 396
Thomas 1813-1900382
Thomas 1824-1826399
Thomas 1846- 370
Thomas C. 1740-....22, 93
Timothy 1733-1818.17
True 1813-1888.....367
Trueman 1837-1864 340
Truman P. 1822-1850 379
Trumbull 1823-1901 331
Uriah 1743-1822....23, 98
Uriah 1773-1799.....98
Uriah 1805-1830...392
Uriah 1831-1891...393
Uriah B. 1791-.....100, 399
Uriah B. 1821-......399
Walter 1806-1878.312
Warren E. 1814-1874 372
Warren E. 1854- ...376
Warren F. 1825- ...390
Watson G. 1799-1869 371
Wilbur 1836-1920.614
Willard 1814-1900 391
William 1744- 35
William 1770-150, 595
William 1785-1788151
William 1792-1814154
William 1797-1877366
William 1798- 595
William 1801-1872312
William 1802- 596
William 1815-1887611
William 1825-1878616
William 1828-1877605
William B. 1838-1904 609
William E. 1810-1898 612
William G. 1795-1850 ....95, 377
William G. 1817-1873 375
William H. 1829-1891 606
William W. 1828-..377
Willibe 1791-1832.593
Zada A. 1827-1828380
Zada I. 1829-1861.380
Zerviah 1719-1743...8, 31
Zilpha 1814-..........595
RUST
  Kezia 1735-182516, 63
  Susan J. 1825-1893 416

RUTENBER
William 1804-1870522
RUTHERFORD
Sidney 1824-1880. 486
SABIN
Henry W. 1818-1904
.... 515
Martha 1792-1877
.... 126, 495
SABINE
Charles W. 1811-1842
.... 512
SACKETT
George 1800- 497
SAGE
Mariah 1825-1870 536
SALE
Richard 1800-1856214
SALISBURY
Paulina 1804-116, 459
SALTMARSH
Seth 1778-1836 273
SAMPSON
Lucinda 1817-1874
.... 612
Mary 1813-1882 ... 369
SAMUELS
Rebecca 1818-1889406
SANBORN
Emily 1826-1881 .. 293
John A. 1799-1887415
Nancy 1809-1892 . 547
Thornton 1826-1892
.... 626
SANDERSON
Abel 1781-1814 353
SANFORD
Caroline 1811-1870
.... 611
SANGER
Achsah 1766-........ 132
Aden 1770-1828 .. 132,
526
Adin 1806-1837.... 527
Adna 1776-1778 ... 132
Adna 1796-1818 ... 526
Alice 1785-1860.... 523
Almira 1801-1872 527
Amanda 1835-1908
.... 535
Amarilla 1837-1917
.... 535
Amasa 1794-1857. 525
Amelia 1809- 533
Arthur 1791- 523
Arthur 1793-1855. 523
Asenath 1774-1778
.... 132
Asenath 1782- 132
Ashbel 1772-1778. 132
Ashbel 1780-1831 132,
527
Azariah 1732-1801 30,
131
Azariah 1772-132, 526
Azariah 1803-1853523

Barton 1812-1889 532
Benjamin 1782-1849
.... 135, 533
Celia 1815-1888 ... 528
Chester 1795-1852523
Chloe 1748-1815 31
Chloe 1796-1852 . 135,
535
Cynthia 1761-1842
.... 132, 523
Daniel 1760-1844 131,
522
Daniel 1787-1813. 523
Dinah 1734-............ 30
Ebenezer 1790-1863
.... 134, 532
Ebenezer C. 1816-
1877 533
Elam 1823-1823 ... 529
Eliza C. 1814-1878533
Elizabeth 1763- ... 132,
524
Elizabeth 1799-1890
.... 527
Elizabeth 1801-.... 526
Esther 1770-1851 132,
133, 525
Ethel 1799-1800... 526
George 1825-1886 533
Gilbert 1832-1846 529
Hannah 1750- 31
Hannah 1768- 132
Hannah 1795- 526
Hannah 1814-1903
.... 526
Hannah 1829-1858
.... 533
Harvey C. 1815-1889
.... 527
Henrietta 1820-1859
.... 534
Henry 1820-1876.. 534
Horatio 1809-1880526
Ira 1797-............... 134
Ira 1826-1828....... 532
James 1786-1832 134,
532
James 1810-1849 . 532
James H. 1808-1882
.... 527
Jedediah 1741-176230
Jedediah 1765-.... 132,
524
John N. 1804-1895527
Jonathan 1695-17677,
30
Jonathan 1755-1819
.... 31, 134
Jonathan 1818-1892
.... 533
Justus 1838-1863. 535
Justus H. 1791-1874
.... 135, 534
Laura 1797-.......... 526

Leander 1810-1881
.... 527
Lois R. 1810-1876 526
Lucas 1809-1895 .. 528
Lucia 1817-1896... 528
Lucien 1810-1811. 528
Lucy 1799-1844... 135,
536
Lucy 1850-1911.... 535
Lura 1797-............. 526
Luther 1818- 533
Lydia 1737- 30
Lydia 1768- 132
Marcus 1808-1886 528
Maria 1798-1844.. 525
Marvin H. 1827-1898
.... 533
Mary 1745-............. 31
Mary A. 1808-1853
.... 528
Matilda 1797-1860523
Mercy 1824-1888.. 529
Nathaniel 1754-1803
.... 31, 134
Noadiah 1738-180830,
132
Noah D. 1785-1842
.... 132, 528
Olive 1808-1855 ... 532
Olive 1833-1852 ... 533
Oliver W. 1817-1904
.... 532
Olivia 1811-1892.. 528
Pamelia 1784- 135,
534
Phebe 1796-1888.. 525
Phila 1790-1822 .. 135,
534
Phila 1822-1890 ... 534
Prescott S. 1786-1824
.... 135
Priscilla 1787-1877
.... 132, 529
Ralph 1824-1829 .. 532
Rhoda 1812-1879 . 533
Riley 1820-1890 ... 529
Russell 1834-1852 535
Sally 1799- 134
Sarah 1816-1892.. 533
Sarah 1821-1891.. 532
Selinda 1789-1851 523
Zebina 1799-1866. 523
Zeruiah 1744-1777 31,
132
Zerviah 1778-1848
.... 132, 527
SARGENT
Abigail.......... 123, 483
Daniel 1808-......... 612
Gilman 1815-1882 354
Herman L. 1782-1816
.... 154, 612
John 1810-............ 612
Louisa 1803-......... 369

Lucinda 1806-1871
.... 612
Mary 1810-1897... 367
Mary A. 1811-1891
.... 190
Oliver 323
Rebecca 1821-1891589
Ruth 1773-1847 .. 123,
484
SATTERLY
Mary 1790-1881 ... 444
SAUNDERS
Augusta A. 1820-1884
.... 255
David 1766-1847.... 72
Joshua 1791-1856 580
Stephen 1793-1875
.... 544
SAVAGE
Charity 1779-1846189
James 1781-1847 . 173
John 1771-1850.... 181
SAVORY
William 1785-1826559
SAWIN/SAWINS
Elijah 1774-1814... 60,
209, 234
Elizabeth 1770-1771
.... 209
Elizabeth 1797-.... 234
Ephraim 1806-1835
.... 234
Isaac 1748-1776 53,
209
Isaac 1804-1898 ... 234
Jeroham 1763-1859
.... 125
Luce 1740-1824 14, 57
Lucy 1812-1849.... 234
Manerva 1808- 234
Roena 1800-1801.. 234
Zeulime 1766-125, 494
SAWTELL
Polly 328
SAWTELLE
George 1815-1893 620
Martha 1797-1873 561
SAWYER
Abial 1784-1870 ... 202
Alice 1781-1849.... 201
Amanda 1809-1882
.... 427
Asaph 1793-1875 . 334
Ellen 1834-1909... 343
Ellen 1835-1912... 427
Hannah 1772-1860
.... 201
Jacob 1779-1841 .. 201
Josiah 1744-1829 .. 50,
201
Josiah 1770-1800 . 201
Lucy 1759-1846..... 31,
134
Lydia 1768-1850 .. 201
Moses 1774-1851.. 201

Rebecca 1783-1869202
Rufus 1760-1845...198
SAYBOTT
Keturah 1787-187276, 294
SAYERS
Julia 1840-1896 536
SAYRE
Ezra 1800-1864.....551
SAYWARD
Belinda 1808-1873367
Betsey 1806- 368
Hannah 1780-1846
...................107, 423
Rufus 1789-1839...420
SCAIFE
William 1812-1876499
SCARBOROUGH
Perrin 1808-1874..243
SCARLETT
Mary 1767-1832....274
SCHAEFFER
John 1833- 626
SCHOULER
Mary F. 1836-1888600
SCHREIBER
Lana 1800-1881 245
SCOTT
Mary 1795-1816....506
SCRIBNER
Lydia 1798-1884 ...574
Rebecca 1801- 575
SCRIPTURE
Allice 1790-1863 ..210, 235
Alpheus 1777-1846
...........................235
Cyrrel 1785-1853..235
Eleazer 1783-........235
Elizabeth 1781-1864
...........................235
Esther 1765-1841 . 57, 221
Hiram 1772-1849..235
Irene 1779-1861....235
Lois 1788-1846......235
Roswell 1768-1839235
Zevinah 1774- 235
SEAMON
Harriet 1807-1874 260
SEARLES
Adoniram J. 1830-1895 374
SEARS
Stephen G. 1798-1868
...........................412
SEAVER
Samuel 1795-1874 478
SEAVEY
Charles 1837-1911623
Lucretia 1793-1883
...........................304
SEBASTIAN
Eunice 316
SEDGWICK
Albert 1801-1878 ..358

Otis 1803-1893......532
SEGAR
Abigail 1791-1888.594
Allan 1793-1872....594
Apphia 1794-1861.594
Edmund 1790-1797
...........................594
Edmund 1798- 594
John E. 1803-1882594
Lucy 1796-1886 594
Mary 1797-............594
Nathan 1801-........594
Nathaniel 1755-1847
...................150, 593
Nathaniel 1804-....594
Pamelia 1798-1855
...........................594
Russell 1800- 594
Submit 1806-1824.594
SELF
William 1805-1881461
SELLEN
Susan F. 1794-1881
...................109, 436
SESSIONS
Abiah -1811.............13
SEVERENS
Franklin 1811-1897
...........................387
SEVERY
Phebe 1803-1884 ..183
SEXTON
Mary 1795-1884....210
SEYMOUR
Abby G. 1815-1865250
SHACKET
Rosena 1824-1899.636
SHANNON
John 1769-1840 166
Samuel 1774-1849 166
SHARP
Augustus.........64, 252
Mary 1776-1844...119, 471
Robert 1791-1874 214, 222
SHARPE
Abigail 1744-1819..27, 114
Hannah 1724-1801 29, 121
SHARRATT
Frederick 432
SHATTUCK
Abigail 1794-1868.395
Almira 1813-1892 .622
Anna 1800-1869....395
Arabella 1828-1900
...........................376
Brooks 1805-1872 .556
Dorothy 1764-1852 36, 152
Elizabeth 1802-1875
...........................395

Hannah C. 1810-1879
...........................581
Harriet 1805-1880 302
Joseph 1804-1831 .395
Lydia 1765-1843..146, 578
Mary 1806-1875....395
Miranda N. 1818-1909
...........................585
Pamelia 1806-1836
...........................395
Sarah 1798-1894...395
Sarah 1799-1884...231
Susan 1803-1884 ..302
Tamison 1796-1831
...........................395
Thorza 1804-1893.622
William 1769-1806 99, 394
William 1792-1878395
SHAW
Phebe 1833-1909 ..459
Sarepta 1816- 505
Zuriah 1800-1888 .505
SHEA
Abigail 1782-1856194, 579
SHED
Ebenezer 1777-1860
...........................198
SHEDD
George 1778-1855.201
SHELDON
Abraham 1717-1790 9, 34
Abraham 1789-1858
...................148, 585
Amos 148
Amos 1759-1828 ....35, 149
Amos 1796-1841 ..150, 592
Asenath 1792-1837
...........................150
Benjamin 1822- 586
Daniel 1791-1843.148, 586
Ezra R. 1813-1868 477
Hannah 1786-1836
...................148, 584
Hannah 1812-1892
...........................585
Harmon 1814-1897
...........................586
Harriet 1818-1860 586
Henrietta 1824-1892
...........................586
Mary 1818-1908....586
Mary E. 1825-1895
...........................592
Mary J. 148
Phebe 1754-1824 ...35, 148
Rebecca 1799-1871
...................150, 592

Rebekah 1757-1813
...................35, 148
Russell 1752-1816 .35, 147
Russell -1843 148
Sally 1790-1866 150
Sarah 1804-1891 .156, 620
Susan 1820-1894 ..346
Susan A. 1820-1894
...........................586
Susannah..............148
Susannah 1756-.....35, 147
Thomas 1827-1900592
William 1768- 239
William 1810-1891
...................334, 556
SHEPHARD
John 248
SHERBURN
Martha A. 1825-1904
...........................192
SHERLOCK
Josephine 1816-1904
...........................418
SHERMAN
Anner 1813-1878 ..483
Caleb 1817-1904...454
Elizabeth 1804-1886
...........................293
SHERWIN
Caroline 1828-1870
...........................322
Stillman 1807-1869
...........................554
Susannah 1734-1807
...................68, 265
Teresa 1768- 266
SHERWOOD
Henry L. 1810-1886
...........................295
Matilda C. 1826-1911
...........................375
SHIPMAN
Delia 1770-1830...131, 519
Julia 1795-1890 357
Keturah 1785-1858
...........................357
Mary 1830-1895....495
SHOREY
Eben 1819-............627
SHROPSHIRE
Nancy 1824-..........331
SHULTS
Erskine C. 1845-...378
SIAS
John 1814-1880 322
SIBLEY
Abijah 1788-1856..238
George V. 1817-1891
...........................598
Martha 1776-1846 .56, 219

Mary 1820-1852 ... 310
Polly 1781-1858.... 214
SILVER
Eliza 1803-1877 ... 246
Sally 1816-1897.... 247
SIMMONS/SIMONS
Clarissa 1807-1900
.... 320
Horace 1817-1896 404
Joseph B. 1801-1835
.... 255
Molly 1754-1814.... 54,
213
Sophia 1813- 498
William S. 1813-1867
.... 248
SIMONDS/see also
SYMONDS
Asa 1809-1888 325
Betsy 1806-1825... 325
Daniel 1782-1859. 332
Daniel -1805... 86, 332
John B. 1804-1887577
Mariah 1819-1840 325
Mary 1780-1863 ... 321
Pamelia 1813-1828
.... 325
Richard 1816-1869325
SIMPSON
Benjamin D. 1821-426
SIMS
Moses 1825-1865.. 371
SINCLAIR
Amelia N. 1825-1889
.... 616
SISSON
Francis 1812-1870 625
SIZER
Rachel 1772-1853. 208
SKIDMORE
Mary A. 1823-1903
.... 611
SKINNER
Huldah 1782-1864 289
Martha A. 1822-1892
.... 219
Mary E. 1806-1836
.... 246
SLADE
Harriet 1842-1891 629
Henry C........ 158, 628
John 1849-1850.... 629
William 1844-....... 629
SLATER
Emily E. 1839-1897
.... 606
SLAYTON
Desire 1785-1856. 553
Hannah S. 1813-1913
.... 554
Jerome C. 1796-1872
.... 553
Susan 1789-......... 248
SLOAT
Alexander C. 1822-
1900 295

SMALL
Arria 1823-1910 ... 554
Charles 1815-1875367
Eliza 1834-1864 ... 351
Jonathan 1805-1854
.... 565
SMALLEY
Emma 1844-1885. 388
SMILEY
Benjamin F. 1819-
1876 631
Thomas 1755-1816267
SMITH
Aaron 1798-1875.. 601
Abigail 1706-1752 ... 4,
15
Abigail 1777-1862137,
543
Abram 1796-1869. 311
Adeline 1837-1889 384
Alva 1798-1800 540
Alvan 1807-1882 .. 459
Amanda 1804-1872
.... 455
Ann 1800-1828 254
Anna 1774-1854.. 136,
542
Anna 1806-1871 ... 544
Apphia 1807-........ 602
Asa D. 1809-1877. 309
Barak 1791-1874.. 475
Benjamin F. 1821-
1910 264
Betsey 226
Betsey 1791-1869. 183
Clarissa 1793-1878
.... 540
Clymena 1812-1856
.... 619
Cornelia 1806-1882
.... 543
Dorothy 1769-1828
.... 121, 475
Eleanor 1775-1805
.... 129, 511
Elia 1816-1844 368
Elisha 1783- 137
Elizabeth 1815-1881
.... 599
Elizabeth 1816-1853
.... 419
Ephraim 1789-1862
.... 188
Ezra 1739-1758 31
Ezra 1767-1852 ... 136,
539
Ezra 1795-1800 540
Ezra -1798 .... 8, 31
Ezra E. 1820-1894 544
Fielding 1807-1879
.... 354
Franklin 1807-1869
.... 405
George 1758-1843 141
Hannah 1775-1855. 54

Hannah 1789-1873
.... 137, 545
Hannah 1804- 259
Hannah 1805-1889
.... 452
Henry 1830-1890 . 345
Jacob 290
Jane 1834- 370
Jeanette M. 1824-
1872 190
Jesse 1784-1867 ... 197
John 1796-1886.... 395
John R. 1807-1870598
Joseph 269
Julia A. 1821-1884537
Lucy 1794-............ 137
Lydia A. 1816-1906
.... 373
Margaret 1757-1817
.... 31
Margaret 1817-1897
.... 599
Mary 1770-... 136, 540
Mary 1819-1901 ... 484
Mary A.F. 1818-1891
.... 405
Mary H. 1809-1879
.... 599
Mary S. 1836-1914568
Matilda 1781-1861
.... 137, 544
Matilda 1828-....... 367
Mercy 1796-1856.. 181
Moses H. 1833-1902
.... 384
Nancy 1811-1909 . 455
Phebe 1735-1823... 28,
119
Phebe 1811-1866.. 599
Phebe A. 1811-1866
.... 391
Reuben 1761-1838 122
Sabra M. 1795-1872
.... 241
Sarah 1806-1888.. 519
Sarah 1809-1878.. 544
Simeon 1741-1799. 32,
136
Simeon 1779-1853137,
544
Smith 1819-.......... 585
Susan 1804- 544
Susan D. 1810-1867
.... 257
Thomas 1781-1832
.... 151, 598
Thomas 1805-....... 598
Thomas 1820-1877599
Willard 1831-1913 635
William 1813-....... 460
William B. 1814-1886
.... 544
Zerviah 1772-1837
.... 136, 541
SMOTHERS

Eliza B. 1814-....... 637
SNELL
Lydia 1789-1841 . 135,
538
SNODGRASS
Mary J. 1833-1853380
SNOW
Alden 1793-1880 .. 232
Alice 1741-1782..... 43,
170
Amos 1765-1805... 171
Bathsheba 1732-1813
.... 14, 58
Benjamin 1744-..... 43,
171
Chloe 1780- 171
Diedamia 1787-.... 287
Eli 1789-............... 287
Elias H. 1797- 238
Eliphalet 1784- 171
Elsie 1790-1868... 286,
287
Eunice 1784- 287
Hannah 1793- 287
Jefferson 1801-..... 232
Jesse 1765-........... 171
Joseph 1738- .. 43, 171
Joseph 1772- 171
Justus 1769-......... 171
Lemuel 1777- 171
Lucena 1783-........ 287
Lucia 1804-1849... 220
Lydia 1769- 66
Lydia 1769-1853 . 172,
260
Mary 1768-........... 171
Mehitable 1767-1854
.... 284
Nancy 1803-1891 . 232
Percy 1798-1875... 232
Robert 1763-1806.. 60,
232
Silas 1761-1835..... 74,
287
Silas 1791- 287
Simeon 1763-........ 171
Sybil 1795-1876 ... 227
Sybil 1806- 232
Sylvanus 1817-1860
.... 631
Warner 262
Warner 1795-1840 232
SNUFFIN
William 1797-....... 512
SNYDER
Catherine 1817-1887
.... 532
SOULE
Lavina 1809-1889 328
SOUTHWORTH
Sarah 1778-.. 132, 527
SOWARD
Elizabeth 263
SPAFFORD

William H. 1812-1893
...........................262
SPALDING/SPAULDING
Abigail 1754-1830. 68,
269
Andrew 1701-....16, 68
Andrew 1786-1857268
Andrew 1788-1862268
Anna 1790-1790....268
Eli 1799-1825........268
Eliza 1805-...........268
Elizabeth 1795-.....269
Elizabeth 1827-1895
...........................419
Eri J. 1821-1886 ...584
George W. 1796-1868
...........................268
Harriet 1800-1881 269
Henry 1750-....68, 268
Henry 1784-1811 ..268
James...................268
James 1785-1870 ..268
Jemima 1782-1861268
John 1804-1842 622
John T. 268
Josiah...................268
Lucy 1792-1874.....329
Martha 1793-........268
Mehitable 1793-1857
...........................268
Mehitable C. 1797-269
Philemon 1833-1896
...........................631
Ruth 1746- 68
Ruth 1752-1790 68,
269
Ruth 1806-1875 482
Samuel 1790-1822 268
Sarah A. 1820-1890
...........................192
Solomon 1748-182668,
267
Solomon 1780- 267
Susanna 1797-1821
...........................268
Thomas 1791-1844268
SPANN
John 1797- 308
SPARHAWK
Emily Augusta 1830-
1917..................385
SPARKS
Hannah 1794- 216
SPARROW
Clarinda 1820- 369
SPEAR
Abigail 1813-1883.392
Elias 1795-............226
Mary 1790-1876....226
SPEARING
Mary 1824-1908....350
SPENCER
Anne 1796-1877....203
Mary.................13, 51
Mary 1780-1857....499

Oliver 1801-1891 ..412
Ruby 1787-............499
SPONKNABLE
Sarah 1822-1908...501
SPRAGUE
Betsey E. 1799-1887
...........................523
SPRAKER
Margaret 1820-1907
...........................317
SPRING
Catherine 1750-.....74,
285
Catherine 1750-1786
...........................121
SPRINGER
Novvissa 590
SPRINGSTEEN
Hannah 1790-.......292
SQUIERS
Solomon 1797-1876
...........................528
STACY
John 85, 328
John 1794- 328
Susannah 1796-....328
STANDISH
Eunice 1810-1882 .365
STANLEY
Polly A. 1830-........280
Silas 1797-1879 503
STANNARD
Mary 1805-1831....257
STAPLES
Aphia 1803-1839...332
Samuel 1795-1840 332
STARBIRD
Charles H. 1829-1882
...........................605
STARK
Louisa B. 1809-1906
...........................322
Sophia 1794-1847 152,
606
STEARNS
Alvin 1819-1900....498
Betsey 1825-1884 .461
Elizabeth 1790-1871
...........................500
George 1823-.........633
George W. 1818-1878
...........................606
Harriet 1801-1878 160
Hiram...................160
Irene 1843-1912....633
Jabez 1796-1854 ...500
James C. 1842-1883
...........................634
Jerome B. 1811-1895
...................160, 633
John 1762-1826 274
John 1797- 160, 633
John 1832-1915 633
John B. 1764-1845
...................127, 500

John E. 1792-........500
Joseph 1763-1834 ..38,
159
Joseph 1796-1883 .160
Joseph W. 1808-1888
...........................437
Josiah 1837-1876 ..633
Mahala 1809-1882
...................160, 633
Maria 1801-1875 ..500
Mary 1791- ...160, 632
Mary 1795-1875...153,
607
Mary 1825- 485
Nancy 1830-1898 ..461
Otis 1794-1860......500
Royal 1794-1825 ..160,
632
Ruby 1802-1875....337
Samuel 1789-........159
Samuel E. 1806- ...500
Sarah 1828-1917...633
Susan 1797-1873 .153,
608
Susannah H. 1825-
1849..................632
Thomas 1822-1890633
William 1826-1908633
William B. 1803-1865
...........................500
Zilpah 1803-..160, 633
Zoa 1846-1852 633
STEBBINS
Alpheus 1780-1857
...........................239
Austin 1802-1852 .544
Belinda 1786-1869278
Samuel Colton 1796-
1873..................217
STEDMAN
Abigail 1794-1812.279
Achsah 1791-1833 278
Althine 1810-1868 514
Beulah 1784-1812.278
Erastus 1786-1841278
Eunice..................235
Nathan 1751-1794.72,
278
Nathan 1783-1832 278
Sofia 1788-1811 278
STEEL
Adelia 1826-1898 ..537
Hannah 1804-1882
...........................559
STEELE
Ebenezer 1814-1899
...........................625
Israel 1806-1871...373
STEPHENSON
Eleazer W. 1798-1867
...........................258
Jotham 1805-1883 612
STERLING
James 1767-..........164
STETSON

Jetson 1789-..........439
Solomon 1817-1890
...........................370
STEVENS
Abiel 1750-..............34
Abiel 1750-1806...137,
144
Abiel 1770-1853...144,
569
Abiel 1799-1881....569
Abiel H. 1806-1864
...........................571
Aden 1824-1897....571
Alma 1808-1891...569,
570
Amos 1806-1843 ...570
Anna 1744- 26
Anna 1774-1861....274
Apphia 1786- 169
Bertha 1792-1837.241
Betsey 1782- 174
Betsey 1803- 569
Charles G. 1821-1897
...........................372
David 1781-1842..145,
571
David 1808-1889...571
Dorcas 1755-1780 ..78,
300
Ebenezer 1737-.......26
Elhanan W. 1822-
1885..................571
Elizabeth 1730-1807
.....................32, 137
Elizabeth 1811-1895
...........................571
Elizabeth 1814-....154,
612
Elizabeth S. 1793-
1847..................174
Elmira 1794-1863.170
Esther L. 1799-1856
...........................572
Eunice 1796-.........569
Ezra 1810-1890.....570
Fanny 1804-1868..569
George 1812-1885.569
George W. 1814-1891
...........................571
Grove 1813-1905...427
Hannah 1737-1828 68,
267
Harriet 1814-1881 514
Jacob 1776-1856 ..144,
570
Jacob 1797-..........569
Jacob B. 1816-1896
...........................570
Jane 1826-1896 232
Jedediah 1815- 570
Jemima 1770- .38, 160
John....................7, 26
John 1733-.............26
John 1764-.............38
John 1794-............569

John 1817-1823.... 571
Jonathan 1726-1771 9,
38
Joseph 1801-1849. 547
Joshua 1798-1885 556
Julia 1809-1888.... 570
Laura 1823-1901.. 427
Leonard 1785- 145
Leonard 1820- 571
Luman 1800-1873 569,
570
Lydia 1753- 46, 184
Maria 1809-1895.. 363
Mary 1747-............ 26
Mary 1750-............ 26
Mary B. 1829- 571
Munroe 1822-1884 571
Naomi 1751-1816.. 83,
317
Nehemiah 1778-... 144
Nehemiah 1810-1897
.... 569
Peabody 1818-1871
.... 570
Polly 1801-1816.... 569
Rebecca 1825-....... 586
Sally 1800- 570
Sally 1818-1847.... 570
Samuel 1740- 26
Sarah 1742-............ 26
Sylvester 1817-1880
.... 570
Tabitha 1774-1775 144
Theodore 1814-..... 570
Theodore 1814-1876
.... 570
Uriah H. 1779-1845
.... 144, 570
Ursula 1812- 570
William 1734-......... 26
William 1767-......... 38
STEWART
Alvan 1790-1850 .. 250
Joseph 1778- 236
Mary 1820-1909 ... 339
William P. 1814-1893
.... 260
STICKNEY
Elizabeth 1772-1857
.... 127, 502
Jacob 1806-1850... 599
Jonathan 1784-1832
.... 168
Mary 1802-1850 ... 578
Mercy 1808-1868.. 597
Relief 1775-1842 .. 198
Sally W. 1788-1882
.... 303
Sarah 1829-1908.. 618
Sarah P. 1800-...... 313
William 1817-1871 566
STILES
Abigail 1795- 238
Chloe 1781- 51, 206

Elbridge 1806-1872
.... 586
Hannah 1792-1882
.... 574
Hiram 1822-1907 . 345
Huldah 1736-1799 51,
206
John 1725-.............. 32
Mehitable 1739-1811
.... 20, 83
Mehitable 1740-1827
.... 52, 207
Nathan 1787-1878 575
STILSON
Lois 1831-1916..... 587
Lyman 1805-1886 265
STINSON
Lydia 1788-1881 .. 173
STOCKER
William 1812-1887 588
STOCKWELL
Elijah 1784-1852.. 156
Lovina 140, 554
STODDARD
Abiel 1802-1895 ... 514
Abigail 1805-1889 514
Abishai 1811-1893 514
Adelia 1811-1897 . 514
Amasa 1779-1846 130,
515
Carlos 1823-1908 . 512
Casendana 1823-1890
.... 512
Cassandra 1823-1892
.... 512
Cecilia 1816-1881. 511
Celecta 1796-1865 512
Charles 1814-1819 514
Clarissa 1800- 512
Cyrus 1794-1841.. 512
Daniel 1768-1854 129,
511
Daniel 1799-1865 . 512
Diana 1813-1891.. 512
Ebenezer 1774-1847
.... 129, 514
Ebenezer 1815-1874
.... 514
Eleanor 1806-1871 512
Emily 1824-1858.. 515
Ezra 1772-1811 ... 129,
513
Ezra 1808-1821 514
Ezra 1814-1890 515
Frederick 1814-1892
.... 511
Gratia 1796-1888 . 510
Hannah 1759-1842
.... 129, 509
Harvey 1800-1873 514
Huldah 1798-1864 512
Isaac 1776-1842 .. 129,
514
James 1818- 515
Jane 1821-1906.... 515

Jerusha 1794-1868 510
John 1761-1831... 129,
509
John 1816-1844.... 515
John Humphrey 1796-
1881 510
Joseph 1800-1892 511
Joshua 1732-1816 . 29,
129
Joshua 1764-1854 129,
510
Joshua 1801-1802 511
Joshua 1812-1844 511
Joshua -1816......... 29
Julia 1810-1885 ... 511
Lydia 1757-1843 .. 129
Lydia 1790-1832 .. 510
Marilla 1798-1867 513
Martha 1809- 512
Melinda 1794-1877
.... 510
Nancy M. 1815-1898
.... 512
Persis 1826-1897.. 515
Phineas 1803-1874 511
Priscilla 1807-1893
.... 511
Prosper Franklin
1806-1852 510
Reuben 1788-1872 510
Reuben 1818-1898 512
Rhoda 1781-1867 130,
515
Romanzo 1828-..... 515
Rufus 1818-1840 .. 512
Ruth 1813-1814.... 514
Salina 1802-1849 . 510
Sarah 1791-1853.. 511
Sarepta 1800-1855 510
Sarepta 1819-1879 515
Simon 1823-1853 . 515
Sophia 1792-1856. 511
Susan 1820-1906.. 511
Sylvanus 1803-1864
.... 512
Sylvester 1804-1882
.... 514
William 1828-1837 512
Zerviah 1770-1856
.... 129, 513
STOKES
Dudley L. 1812-1863
.... 419
STOLP
Peter 1791-1853... 238
STONE
Chester H. 1822-1907
.... 263
Clarissa 1794- 483
Elizabeth 1817-1890
.... 556
Lois 1819-1875..... 576
Louisa 1813-1904. 556
Luther 1816-1884 532
Nancy 1791-1840 . 332

Philynia 1816-1895
.... 484
Phinehas 1769-1841
.... 550
Polly 107, 420
Rachel 1796-1842. 186
Samuel 1798-1869 603
Timothy D.P. 1811-
1887 190
STORRS
Hannah 1765- 109,
433
William R. 1824-1905
.... 545
STORY
Laura 1819-.......... 244
Sarah 1781-1867.. 320
STOUGH
Priscilla 1821-1905
.... 541
STOUTENBURG
William 1811-1901 496
STOVER
Ann M. 1831-1867 295
STOWELL
Abigail 1770- 127, 500
Artemesia 1784-1853
.... 204
Kezia 1781- 204
Lewis 1797-1841 .. 491
Marvin C. 1789-1813
.... 204
Olive 1779-1829 ... 204
Oliver 1792-1836.. 490
Rowena 1791-....... 453
Seth 1742-1798 61,
203
STRATTON
Daty 1826-1867.... 397
Elizabeth........ 49, 199
STRAW
Hannah C. 1816-1848
.... 423
STRAY
Phebe 1835-1921.. 495
STRICKLAND
Bathany 1780-1855
.... 304
Sarah 1824-.......... 457
Tabitha 1783-1855
.... 150, 595
STRONG
Kezia 1709-1796 4, 15
Miranda 1806-1841
.... 496
STROUD
Emily.................... 233
STUART
Alexander 1768-1840
.... 276
Eleazer 1786-1849 547
STUDLEY
Fidelia 1816-1882 225
STUNBERG
Henry 377
STURTEVANT

Amanda 1818- 325
James.................... 70
SUMNER
  Cheney 1795-1867 453
  Ebenezer 1757-1806
    ....64, 254
  Hiram F. 1800-1874
   425
  Mary 1816-1883....425
  Myra 1783- 254
  Roxalana 1785-1873
   255
SUTHERLAND
  Mary 1804-1888....344
SUTTON
  Lucy A. 1804-1888 302
SWALLOW
  Mary K. 1831-1895
   635
SWAN
  Caleb 1790-1863 ..149,
  590
  Charles 1815-1823 591
  Charles 1821-1821 591
  Fanny 1792-1862 ..302
  Horace 1828- 591
  Isadore 1830- 591
  James R. 1825-1848
   591
  Leverett 1827-1905
   591
  Mariah 1822-1890 591
  Mary A. 1812-1871
   432
  Nathaniel 1834-1913
   609
  Oren B. 1817-1873 *607*
  Rebeckah 1817-1885
   591
  Rush 1820-1870....591
  Sarah 1756-1802... 36,
  151
  Ward 1818-1824 ...591
SWEET
  Alanson 1788- 316
  Nancy 1817-1901 ..264
SWEETSER
  Caroline 428
  Eliza 1815-1850 577
  Thomas 1808-1850 577
SWETT
  Anna 1765-1826...101,
  403
  Catherine 1810-1856
   461
  Charles J. 1813-....408
  John -1834 ....103, 408
  John A. 1808-1854 408
  Mary 1808-1853....368
SWIFT
  Charles 1807-1885 514
  Jerusha 1812-1855 264
  Lucy 92, 358
  Newton 1823-1865 588
  Rebecca 1809-1845 512

Samuel 1791-1870 364
SWINERTON
  Hannah 1785-1866
   553
SWINNINGTON
  Josiah 1819-1902 ..587
SYKES
  Eunice 1770-1835 119,
  470
SYLVESTER
  Caroline 1819-1907
   625
  Francis 1831-1908 626
  Helen 1825-1826...625
  Helen 1828-1894...626
  Henchman 1788-1865
   617
  John 1788-1848 ...158,
  625
  John 1837-1858 626
  Sarah 1834-1918...626
  Seraphina 1816-1876
   329
SYMONDS/see also
SIMONDS
  Adeline E. 1810-1843
   280
  Asa 1776-1845 84, 325
  Deborah 1796-1832
    ....161, 637
  Rebecca K. 1803-1886
   280
  Willard 1818-1887 586
TAFT
  Louisa H. 1826-1905
   425
  Rhoda 1793-1864 ..474
  William N. 1835-1923
   382
TAGART
  Betsey 68, 268
TAGGERT
  Sally 1784-1847 327
TALBERT
  Catherine 1788-1875
    ....148, 587
TALCOTT
  Roswell 1798-1893 260
TANNER
  Elizabeth 1800-1826
   501
TARBELL
  Jane 1792- 500
  Joel 1816-1891......630
  John 1827- 522
  Nancy 1786-1851 ..182
TARBOX
  Banjamin 1787- 196
  Ebenezer 1763-1827
    ....48, 196
  Ebenezer 1773-1855
   611
  Ebenezer 1785-1877
   196

Elizabeth 1789-1871
   196
John 1791-1861 196
Lucinda 1799-1871
   196
Lydia 1795-1861 ...196
Mary M. 1820-1872
   612
Susan 1796-1848 ..196
TASKER
  Emily Z. 1815-1896
   396
TAY
  Mary 1805- 163
TAYLOR
  Abigail 1798-1868 .270
  Arthur....................67
  Betsey M. 1803-1838
   431
  Cyrus 1797-1872...446
  Elory 1808-1898....357
  George 1835-1915 627
  Hezekiah 1813-1879
   621
  Horace 1790-1885 357
  John 1807-1878 578
  Josiah 1778-1850 ..187
  Leonard................357
  Martha 1779-1860 .59,
  230
  Martin 1786-1825 507
  Mercy 1777-1848 ..236
  Olive 1822-1900....529
  Oliver 1746-1823 ...68,
  269
  Sarah E. 1835-1903
   591
  William R. 1796-1797
   270
TEAGUE
  Isaac 1802-1883....330
TEEPLE
  Jacob 1791-1866 ...221
TEMPLE
  Christopher 1690-
  1782.................5, 21
  Timothy 1810-1880
   581
TENANT
  Jerusha 1807-1904 216
TENNEY
  Anna 1787-1869....268
  Orlando B. 1816-1909
   279
TERRELL
  Nancy 1828-1889 ..442
TERRY
  Anson 1805-1855 ..477
  Elisha 1786-...........218
THATCHER
  Amos 1771-1869 ...283
THAYER
  Albert 1809-1834 ..618
  Charles 1812-1875 403
  George 1807- 403

Harriet M. 1818-1885
   257
Linas 1805-1858 ...354
Lydia 1809- 403
Martha 1801-1838 403
Mary 1805- 403
Mary 1808-1836....451
Richard 1803-1890 403
Richard F. 1769-1845
    ....101, 403
Thomas A. 1799-1870
   403
THISSELL
  Charles 1825-1883 603
THOMAS
  Abigail 1809- 430
  Althea 1810-1891 .242
  Anson H. 1823-1901
   380
  Benjamin 1785-1867
    ....93, 369
  Benjamin 1819-1864
   370
  Betsey 1816-1893 .370
  Charles R. 1838-1923
   381
  Esther M. 1819-1911
   527
  Freeman 1803-1884
   336
  Ichabod 1758-1845 266
  Jesse 1810-1896....430
  John H. 1795-1885 96,
  380
  John L. 1806- 430
  John N. 1834-1917 380
  Joseph -1812.........196
  Josephine L. 1829-
  1909..................380
  Lovina 1818-1856 .370
  Mary 491
  Mary 1814-1878....538
  Perez 1810-1886 ...369
  Sarah 1813-1894 ..370
  Warren C. 1836-1887
   380
  William 1821- 370
THOMPSON
  Ann 1793-1826 352
  Daniel .,................422
  Electa 1827-1909 ..631
  Emily 1834-1904...605
  Jonathan R. 1799-
  1869..................396
  Katherine 1815-1863
   406
  Mary 1790-1835....289
  Mary 1800-1853....320
  Matilda 1804-1867 452
  Sally 1789-1853.....177
  Sarah 107, 420
  Thomas 1768- 93
  William 1785-1870 510
THOMSON
  Bethia 1775- 499

THORNDIKE
Ebenezer 1785-1877
.... 196
Sarah 1751-1836... 44, 174
THORNGATE
George 1798-1881 431
THURSTON
Eunice 1826- 163
Hannah 1743-1774. 81
TIBBETS
Sarah 1798-1835.. 299
TIBBETTS
Frederick 1819-1900
.... 604
John 1825-1895.... 369
TICKNOR
Esther 1803-1875. 579
TIFFANY
Celinda 1807-1866497
Hannah 1804-1860
.... 497
TILDEN
Lydia 1780-1847... 278
William 1786- 278
TILESTON
Mary 1705-1748 6
TILLOTSON
Permelia 1806-1866
.... 455
TILLSON
Martha 1792-1834 304
TILTON
David 1834-1914 .. 347
Ellen 1839-1914 ... 351
Nancy -1886 323
TIMMERMAN
Martha 1826-1905 339
TINKER
Almerin 1799-1880
.... 485
TITUS
Asa 1810-1874...... 374
Sylvanus 1809-1873
.... 384
TOBEY
Christopher 1784-1867 228
TORREY
Charles 1818-1885529
David B. 1784-1863
.... 215
Derastus 1820-1896
.... 529
Isaac 529
TOWER
Abraham 1781-1857
.... 67
TOWN
Sophia A. 1824- 567
TOWNE
Abiah 1800-1874 . 149, 591
Abiah 1818-1916 .. 590
Albert 1804-1855.. 587

Amos 1779-1837.. 149, 588
Amos 1821-1898... 588
Andrew 1832-1842590
Ansel 1808-1893... 588
Archelaus 1782-1875
.... 448
Asenath 1789-1831
.... 149, 590
Benjamin 1818-.... 589
Betsey 1824-1906. 588
Betsey G. 1804-1873
.... 557
Charlotte 1819-1898
.... 340
Cyrene 1827-1854 630
Daniel 1787-1855 149, 590
Daniel G. 1814-1868
.... 590
Ebenzer 1795-1892
.... 448
Eshban 1825- 590
Esther 1788-1871. 448
Fanny 1785-1812 149, 589
Fanny P. 1816-1903
.... 590
Gardner 1792-1872
.... 448
Grace 1790- 448
Hannah 1786-1864
.... 448
Hannah 1792-1875
.... 149
Harmon 1797-1799
.... 149
Harmon 1817-1872
.... 589
Harriet 1816-1857 588
Herman 1799- 557
Honor P. 1820- 590
Israel 1761-1848 . 112, 448
Israel 1784-1858 .. 448
Joel 1783-1841 149
Jonathan 1822-1848
.... 590
Kendall 1810- 588
Lorenzo 1811-1877340
Lucy 1797-1888.... 448
Lydia 1781-1868 . 149, 589
Lydia 1781-1878 .. 448
Lydia 1803-1857 .. 580
Lydia P. C. 1803-1857
.... 557
Marcia 1827-1903 337
Mary 1809-1898 ... 557
Mary F. 1812-1892588
Moses 1792-1886.. 149
Myranda 1806-1847
.... 588
Nancy A. 1833-1915
.... 281

Peter 1749-1830 .... 35, 148
Peter 1777-1854 .. 149, 587
Peter 1814-1814 ... 588
Peter 1831-1909 ... 588
Peter F. 1816-1849588
Rebecca C. 1810-1859
.... 589
Rebecca S. 1814-1882
.... 588
Rollin 1829-1906 .. 590
Sally 1816-1837 ... 436
Samuel 1769-1850
.... 141, 557
Sarah 1803-1864 .. 445
Sarah 1812-1877 .. 588
Susannah 1817-1845
.... 580
TOWNSEND
Betsey B. 1805-1887
.... 574
Hannah W. 1793-1881
.... 446
TOY
Elizabeth O. 1811- 223
TRACY
Harry 433
Mercy 1775-1873... 76, 292
Thomas 1832-1913370
TRAFTON
Ebenezer 1803-1875
.... 301
TRASK
Henry P. 1821-1898
.... 637
Joseph 1858-1917 627
TREAT
Amanda E. 1844-1915
.... 393
Betsey 1798-1824. 246
Elizabeth 1813-1860
.... 407
Mary H. 1809-1844
.... 407
Nathaniel 1807-1880
.... 407
Robert 1752-1824 102, 407
TRESCOTT
Mary 7, 25
TRICKEY
Mary H. 1818-1880
.... 565
TROW
Annis 1800-1873 .. 182
Fidelia 1801-1868 404
Lucy 1786-1863.... 182
TROWBRIDGE
Amos 1790-1822... 256
Daniel 1794-1863. 455
Ephraim 1788-1852
.... 517
John 1790-1885.... 470
TRUE

Asa S. 1780-1848 .. 93, 368
Joanna 1777-1863. 93, 366
Martha 1799-1873 332
Pearson 1793-1861510
Sarah 1820- 368
William 1789-1865332
TRUESDELL
Anne 1829-1903 ... 457
Asa 1744-1796........ 52
Asa 1773- 208
Cyrus 1785-1815 .. 208
Darius 1752-1808.. 53, 208
Darius 1775-1814. 208
Elisha 1782-1849 . 208
Harvey 1783-1789 208
Jeduthan 1748-1801
.... 52, 207
Jeduthun 1789-.... 208
Jerusha 1743- 52
Jerusha 1776- 207
John 1786-1860.... 208
Joseph 1719-1762 . 13, 52
Joseph 1772-1777 207
Joseph 1779- 118, 207
Molly 1756- 53
Polly 1794- 208
Rachel 1750-1767... 52
Rhoda 1778-1795 . 208
Ruth 1771- 207
Samuel 1774-1842 207
Sarah 1753-1787.... 53
Sarah 1787-1789.. 208
Sarah 1791-1815.. 208
Seth 1746-1776 ..... 52, 207
Silas 1774-1774.... 207
Silas 1777-1787.... 207
Silas C. 1784- 208
Thomas 1789-1874208
TRYON
Matilda 1806-1841272
Rodolphus 1809-1894
.... 554
TUBBS
Solomon 1800-1865
.... 241
TUCK
Hannah D. 1820-1867
.... 394
TUCKER
James 1809- 452
Lorenzo -1839 558
Louisa 1811-1866. 453
Melinda 1812-1848
.... 547
Olive P. 182
Pascal 1794-1848 . 439
Rosanna 1754-183029, 122
Sarah J. 1811- 251
William 1761-1848184

William 1789-1861182
TUFTS
George A. 1797-1835
..........................447
Mary 1819-............332
Sarah 1796-1847...476
TUPPER
Ezra 1766-.......91, 357
Frederick 1805-1880
..........................358
Minerva 1796-1874
..........................358
TURNER
Eldridge 1809-1881
..........................583
Jane 1823-1905.....533
Lewis 1807-1841...516
Miller 1801-1876...361
TURNEY
Olive A. 1827-1920571
TUTTLE
Elsie 601
Mary 1778-1866...101,
404
Peter 1782-1828....323
Stephen 1801-1856
..........................586
Susan 1799-1895 ..365
TWEEDY
John 1774-1852 203
TWISS
Mary B. 1815- 589
TWIST
Abigail 1771-1853142,
563
TWITCHELL
Betsey 1826-1826..606
Caroline E. 1831-1862
..........................606
Cynthia 1809-1893596
Eli 1786-1869152, 605
George W. 1828-1909
..........................606
Joseph A. 1817-1890
..........................575
Martha 1830-1893 606
Philomela 1823-1837
..........................606
Susannah 1777-1856
..................150, 596
Viola J. 1851-1939 609
William L. 1825-1886
..........................606
TYLER
Addison 1813-1884
..........................344
Charles 1816-1894379
Hannah 1786-1874
..........................175
John 1803-1886 453
Levi 1800-1870 559
Lydia 1799-1875 ...451
Moody 1789-1870..444
Selah 1766-1823 ..131,
518

UNDERHILL
Betsey 1796- 546
UNDERWOOD
Anna 1793-1874....317
Betsey 1792-1840 .315
Betsey 1793-1856 .291
Deborah 1754-184082,
313
Elizabeth 1792-1825
..........................314
Elizabeth 1795-1860
..........................316
Eunice 1810- 315
Hannah 1797-1798
..........................315
Hannah 1799-1836
..........................315
Harriet 1798-1836 317
Harriet 1810- 315
Hiram 1805-1876..317
Israel 1794-...........317
James 1771-1832 ...83,
316
James 1796-1828 ..314
James 1807-1819 ..317
Joseph 1751-..........82
Joseph 1757-1818 ..82,
313
Joseph 1786- 314
Joseph 1788-1854 .314
Luther 1802-1839 .316
Mary 1768-1789.....83,
316
Mary 1793-1866....314
Mary 1795-1837....315
Persis 1793-1825 ..314
Phineas 1764-1843 82,
315
Phineas 1790-1856314
Phineas 1801-1884315
Rachel 1747-1810 ..82,
313
Rachel 1792- 315
Rachel 1801- 317
Russell 1766-1821..82,
316
Russell 1797-1828.316
Sally 1784-1853 314
Sally 1801-1871 315
Susanna 1762- 82
Timothy 1725-180420,
82
Timothy 1749-1759.82
Timothy 1759-182482,
314
Timothy 1782-1849
..........................314
Timothy 1803-1863
..........................317
UPHAM
Elihu 1783-1868 ...435
Eunice 1815-1899 .543
Gardner 1798-1899
..........................513
William 1792-1853475

UPPERMAN
Margaret 1823-1908
..........................390
UPTON
Francis 1814-1876 448
Mary 1825-1887....479
Samuel 1793-1862 448
Sarah 1820-1908...585
William -1849 613
UTLEY
Stephen 1762-1841
..........................204
VAIL
Harvey 1800-1885 294
VAN BUSKIRK
Joseph 1793-1866 .527
VAN DEUZEN
Eunice 1773-1834 ..76,
291
VAN FOSSEN
John 1808-1904 532
VAN HOOSER
Amanda 1821-1895
..........................338
VAN PATTEN
Gertrude 358
VAN VLECK
Lucretia 1788-1858
..........................289
VAN WINKLE
Mary 1816-1881....583
VANDEVENTER
N. Anna 1785-186366,
259
VARNUM
Esther 1747-1822 ..34,
143
Parker 1746-1824 ...78
VARRIL
Elohe 1801- ...153, 608
VAUGHN
John 1800-1886 483
VERDER
Hannah E. 1810-1889
..................153, 610
VEREIN
Abigail 1697-1743.....6
VERMEULE
Mary L. 1841- 280
VIBBARD
Louisa 1809-1875 .249
VILES
Mary 1782-1843....174
VINTON
Augustus 1829-1897
..........................378
Lucy 1795- 594
Lydia 1804-1871 ...445
VIRGIN
Aaron 1787-1869 ..421
Bethiah 1775-1857
..................108, 430
Ebenezer 1793-1876
..........................421
Jeremiah...............596
Sarah 1796-1824...421

VOORHIS
Mary 126
VOSE
Nancy 1793-..........318
Rebecca 1804-1866491
WADSWORTH
Waty 1827-1905....458
WAGER
Anna 1813-1872....293
WAITE
Betsey 1817-1858 .366
Chloe W. 1804-1842
..........................576
Ella 1826-1870......260
WAITT
William 1811-1888281
WAKEFIELD
Alice 1765-1842 ...131,
522
Chester 1760-132, 524
Chester 1800- 524
Elizabeth 1787-....524
Esther 1789-1875 .524
Huldah M. 1817-1873
..........................376
Relief 1790-1866...524
WAKELY
Helen 1837- 616
WALCOTT
Andrew P. 1802-1878
..........................373
Elizabeth 68
Elizabeth 1718-......16
Experience 1751-....70
WALDO
Abigail 1820-1911.543
Cecil 1804-1891 543
Elizabeth 1801-......96,
383
Emeline 1809-1813
..........................543
Esther 1812-1902 .543
George 1817-1891.543
Horatio N. 1806-1895
..........................543
John L. 1811-1894 543
Lydia 1802-1883...543
Lyman 1774-1865 137,
543
Lyman B. 1815-1879
..........................543
Orson 1800-1800 ..543
Orson 1802-1871 ..543
Ruth 1814-1814...543
Simeon 1807-1832 543
WALDRON
Martha..................553
Sarah 1793-1876 ..482
WALES
Ann 1814-1862 406
Chloe 1758-...126, 499
Elizabeth 1795-1869
..........................403
WALKER

Aaron 1776-1815... 58, 224
Angeline E. 1825-1889 387
Anna.................... 283
Bradley 1821-1857 418
James 364
Jonathan C. 1799-1863 215
Joseph 1803-1868. 538
Lucy Main 1813-1881 224
Maria 1816-1900.. 473
Maria Trumbull 1810-1812 224
Martha 1816-1886 575
Matilda 1798-1856 482
Parley 1796-1871. 477
Phebe E. 1813-1903 489
Samuel 1824-1879 549
Sarah 1758-1803.. 164
Stephen 1832-1871 549
Tristram 1828-1861 592

WALLACE
Amelia 1820-1868 328

WALRATH
Irene 1829-1862 ... 340

WALTS
Richard 1823-....... 340

WARD
Anna 1767-1872.... 65, 256
Charlotte 1810-1874 260
Emily 1816-1893.. 428
Jennison 1805-..... 496
Joseph 1814-1888. 406
Julius 1788-1828.. 451
Maria 1803-1888.. 477
Mary.................... 339

WARDWELL
Abiel 1771-1821 .. 195, 273
Amos 1779-1843... 195
Amos 1796-........... 395
Benjamin 1769-1832 195
Bethiah 1782-1855 195
Betsey 1808-1884. 580
Daniel 1784-1851 195, 298
Ezekiel 1777-1803 195
Ezra 1773-1845 195
Jeremiah 1771- ... 108, 432
Jeremiah 1810-1887 432
Joel 1787-1813 196
Louisa 1813-......... 497
Sarah 1803-1884.. 597
Solomon 1743-1825 48, 195

Solomon 1768-1789 195
Susan O. 1814-1896 433
Thomas J. 1804-1862 432

WARE
Clarissa 1800- 472
Harriet P. 1811-1887 472
Harvey 1794-........ 472
Mary 1800-1849 ... 318
Nancy D. 1797-1882 472
Oliver 1802-1886.. 472
Olivia 1802-1870.. 472
Richard 1766-120, 472

WARNER
Elizabeth 1739-1815 .... 25, 109
Joanna.................... 18
Maria 1820-1893.. 472

WARREN
Harriet M. 1825-1881 636
James V. 1812-1896 437
Rebecca 1795-1861 474
Robert 1772-1857. 318
Sarah 1787-1846.. 318

WARWIC
Susannah 1810- ... 223

WASHBURN
Abel 1817-1892 261
Amasa 1768-1857 129, 513
Amasa 1807-1890. 513
Elizabeth............. 114
Minerva 1795-1876 513
Ruth 1791-1813.... 513
Sarah S. 1802-1882 513
Thirza 1799-1878. 513

WASON
Sally 1803-1883.... 559

WATERHOUSE
Harley 1801- 501

WATERMAN
Lucy S. 1788-1877 445

WATERS
Erastus 1798-1848 443

WATKINS
Estella 1822-1887 373
Jedediah 1739-1832 202
Sarah A. 1820- 263
Stephen 1806-1882 511
Thaddeus 1729-...... 30

WATSON
Eliza 1819-1910 ... 580
Hannah 1794-1892 563
Lewis 1819-1890 .. 462
Lucretia 1817-...... 538

Mary 1803-1874... 578
Pliny 1794-1832 ... 553

WATTLES
Anna 1782-1838.. 118, 467

WAY
Betsey O. 1801-1829 411

WEAVER
Benjamin 1755-... 128, 506
Emily 1811-1902.. 259
Eunice 1781- 507
Greenbury 1823-1858 562
Humphrey 1784-1823 507
Sally 1787-1863 .... 97, 386

WEBB
Lucy 1780-1863.... 116
Peter L. 315
Sala P. 1825-1861 384
Susannah 1785-1863 .... 117, 462

WEBBER
Chandler 1763-1837 .... 113, 452
Chandler 1810- 453
Constant 1791-1873 501
Erastus 1794-1876 453
Ezra 1805-1887 453
Hudson 1811-1856 453
Lillian 1848-......... 627
Semira 1799-1859 453
Winthrop 1814-1891 453

WEBSTER
Betsey 1811-1891. 531
Charles 1811-1902 516
Elizabeth 1773-1839 .... 82, 311
Joseph 269
Mary 1799-1825... 305
Moses 1783-1872. 130, 515
Peter 1834-1909... 614
Rosamond 1820-1891 516
Sally 1791-1861 ... 302
Samuel 1788-1835 312
Sarah 1813-1846.. 516
Sarah 1819-1885.. 371
Simeon 1815-1898 516
Susan 1804-1875.. 312

WEED
Laura 1810-1886.. 431

WEEKS
Brainard 1801-1875 613
Elizabeth 1787-1871 362
Joseph 1771-1809 221

WELCH

Anna 1798-1872... 520
Jerusha 1787-1835 .... 130, 517
Lucinda 1833-1912 521
Lydia 1779-1846 .. 506
Sarah 1742-1784... 51, 203

WELD
Clarissa 1795-1815 448
George 1800-1875 401

WELLES
Alsop 1806-1898... 442

WELLINGTON
Eli R. 1819-1887 .. 376
Eliza J. 1823-1887 377
Emily H. 1815-1889 376
Erasmus 1785-1854 .... 95, 376
Isabelle 1819-1891 516
Sally 1799-1872 .... 98, 389

WELLMAN
Lucy 1782-1867.... 175

WELLS
Benjamin T. 1775-1822 .... 101, 404
Benjamin T. 1806-1834 405
Caroline A. 1810-1889 405
Charles G. 1818-1887 405
Cordelia 1817-1864 405
Elizabeth 1792-1883 290
Elizabeth 1825-1849 347
Emily F. 1820-1855 405
Francis P. 1815-1873 405
George F. 1803-1883 324
Joanna 1809-1864 405
John T. 1812-1904 405
Lydia 1800-1880 .. 405
Martha A. 1804-1894 .... 404, 405
Mary A. 1802-1885 405
Sarah 1796-1821.. 569
William 486

WENTWORTH
Edmund 549
Evelyn 1827-1910 430
Hannah 1802- 300
Paul 1759-1833 164

WEST
Elizabeth 1815-.... 244
Esther 52, 207
James 1804-1890 . 558

WESTFALL
Rachel 1808-1899 .551
WESTON
Anna 1801- 530
Elmina 1810-1871 531
James 1797-1865..530
John 1768-1820 ...133, 530
John 1803-1845 531
Louisa 1816-1852..531
Origin 1813-1859..531
Polly 1795- 530
Rozilla 1808-1851 .531
Rufus 1815-1883...531
Samuel 1805-1871 321
Stephen 1805- 531
Zurviah 1793-1847530
WHARFF
Bennett 1789-1878432
WHEAT
Clarinda 1824- 529
James 1806-1854 ..357
James 1838-1912 ..349
WHEATON
Benjamin 1775-1852 207
WHEELER
Abigail 1746-...35, 147
Abigail 1777-.......... 66
Alexander H. 1810-1877 376
Almon 1813-1892..377
Amanda E. 1805-1886 259
Anna 1777- 66
Benjamin 1756-1800 267
Betsey 1841-1900..609
Christopher V. 1807-1882 259
Elijah 1767-1827... 65, 258
Elijah G. 1812-1880 260
Emerline 1813-1866 521
Esther 1763- 65
John G. 1822-1913260
Jonas 1772-...........165
Josiah 1738-......16, 65
Josiah 1779- 66
Josiah W. 1807-1882 259
Lucy 1812-1863.....193
Mary 1804-1819....259
Mary A. 1796-1887 96, 384
Percey 1764- 65
Perthene 1762-65, 257
Peter V. 1820-1903 260
Philadelphia 1769- 66, 259
Resolved G. 1772-1839 ....66, 259

Russell C. 1795-1847 258
Sarah 1774- 66
Sarah 1813-1899...193
Sarah A. 1818-......260
Stephen 1814-.......522
Thirza 1799-1867..509
William H. 1826-1892 260
WHICHER
Elizabeth S. 1808-1848 ....160, 633
WHIPPLE
Fanny 1795-1866..275
Freelove 1747-1805 ....128, 503
Nancy 1797-1853..275
Nellie 1773-1856..133, 531
Samuel A. 1813-1886 286
Sarah 1783-1822...275
Tabitha 1768-1848 ....131, 520
WHITAKER
Margaret 1801-1869 292
WHITCOMB
David 1800-1857..432
David 1764-1835..108, 432
David 1795-1876...491
Elizabeth 1795-.....432
Elizabeth 1798-1874 432
Ephraim 1803-1854 432
James 1781-1844 ..242
Levi 1816-1817 432
Lowell 1816-1879..622
Mary 1822-1893....463
Mary A. 1797-1883 432
Mercy 1806-1898 ..432
Rebecca 1812-1882432
Sarah 1795-1820...432
William 1810-1903432
WHITE
Abigail............52, 207
Ann L. 1824-1911 .330
Apollos 1794-1868.412
Barton 1814-1870 .337
Candace L. 1827-1915 467
Delos 1790-1835 ...251
Elijah 1799- 264
Francis F. 1800-1882 472
George W. 1809-1867 251
Jeremiah 1780-.....288
John 1786- 254
Joseph 1762-1832 ..64, 251
Joseph 1801-1840 .251

Joseph 1801-1851 .337
Justus 1800-1874 .337
Levantia 1795-1889 251
Lydia 1808-1873...341
Lyman 1798-1894.337
Mary Anna 1814-1849 249
Menzo 1793-1858..251
Nancy 1844-1918..388
Olive.....................378
Oliver 1758- 273
Prudence H. 1803-1852 286
Rachel 1758-1821 ..37, 154
Rebecca 1766-1856 ....110, 441
Robert 1774-1851 ..87, 337
Robert 1795-1870 .353
Rosilla D. 1838-1919 616
Ruth 1799-1816 337
Samuel 1795-1874 232
Sarah B. 1793-1859 309
Stephen 1792-1851 520
William 1813-1845337
WHITE/see also WIGHT
Abel P. 1804-1893.262
Anna F. 1805- 214
Cheney Anne 1722-18, 74
WHITEHOUSE
Eizabeth 1777-1834 ....107, 423
WHITFORD
Electa A. 1827-1916 260
WHITING
Abigail 268
Abigail 1780-1832154, 610
Elizabeth 1773-1848 ....66, 258
Sarah L. 1799-1886 268
WHITMAN
Anne S. 1816-1904293
Mary 1790-1860.....60, 233
WHITMORE
Abigail 1815-1907.243
Delilah 1812-1885135, 534
WHITNEY
Abel 1793-1880.....551
Abigail 1763-.139, 551
Abigail 1786-.........551
Abigail 1804-1870.551
Abram 1780-1860..176
Albert G. 1817-1901 244

Annas 1761-1761..139
Annas 1765-1768..139
Annis 1785-1846...550
Arvy 1802-1884 507
Benjamin 1757- ...139, 551
Chloe 1795-...........176
Ebenezer 1778-1869 176
Elisha 1767-.. 128, 507
Emily 1797-1861...551
Esther 1768- 549
Hannah 1785-1871 176
Isaac 1782-1860....176
Israel 1774-1850..175, 176
Jacob 1784-1785 ...176
Jacob 1802-1852...621
James M. 1820-1905 244
John O. 1818-1892377
Jonas 1756-1803..139, 550
Jonas 1784-1807...550
Jonathan 1724-1770 ....32, 138
Jonathan 1749-1756 138
Jonathan 1766-1853 ....62, 244
Jonathan 1774-1846 549
Laura F. 1813-......244
Levi 1793-1876 551
Lois 1781-1859 195
Martha 1836-1905 367
Mary 1766-1841....549
Mary 1801-1865...551
Mary A. 1812-1898 507
Oliver 1763-1763 ..139
Oliver 1781-..........550
Oliver W.F. 1799-1877 551
Phinehas 1747-1830 ....138, 549
Rachel 1767-1825 139, 551
Rachel 1788- 551
Rebecca 1811- 244
Relief 1754-1756...139
Relief 1758-1818..139, 550
Relief 1780-...........549
Relief 1799-1870...551
Reuby 1765-1837...92, 358
Richard 1743- 44
Richard 1743-1816176
Roswell 1815- 244
Sally 1789-............551
Sarah 1751- ..139, 550
Sarah 1770- 549

Sarah B. 1787-1873
.... 176
Silence 1795- 551
Solomon 1790-1862
.... 176
Sophornia 1802-1824
.... 551
Theophilus 1780- . 551
Timothy H. 1776-1859
.... 176
Zachariah 1781-1812
.... 199
Zebudah 1782- 550
WHITON
Augustus 1807-1885
.... 545
Calista 1806-1808 545
Elijah 1778-1854 . 137,
544
Elijah 1814-1815 .. 545
George 1816-1887 224
Harriet 1826-1893 545
Henry 1817-1839 .. 545
Maria 1812-1898 .. 545
Matilda 1810-1841
.... 541, 545
Simeon 1804-1871 545
Sophronia 1803-1887
.... 544
WHITTAKER
Louisa A. 1823-1881
.... 281
WHITTEMORE
Clarissa 1799-1871
.... 555
WHITTEN
Mercy C. 1794-1833
.... 241
WHITTIER
Abiah 1798-1878 .. 305
Adeline 1815-1888 625
Daniel B. 1797-1797
.... 305
Emily 1813-1897 .. 624
Hannah P. 1791-1824
.... 305
James 157, 624
Mehitable 1802-1850
.... 305
Nancy 1793-1856 . 305
Susan F. 1803-1857
.... 305
William 1752-1812 80,
304
William 1795-1836 305
WHITTUM
Deborah 1808-1885
.... 601
WHITWELL
Prudence 1815-1895
.... 367
WICKHAM
Lewis 1815-1862 .. 508
WIGHT
Sarah 1816-1883 .. 596

Seth 1783-1863 574
William 1799-1870 575
WIGHT/see also WHITE
Joanna 1794- 212
WILBUR
Elizabeth 1773-1855
.... 473
Hannah 125, 494
WILCOX
Almira 1821- 174
Amanda 1797-1881
.... 361
Carolina 1815-1880
.... 361
Elizabeth 1803-1852
.... 541
Fanny 1810-1872 . 361
Helen 1821-1854 .. 361
Jeanette 1803-1867
.... 361
Jennette 1803-1867
.... 538
Joseph 1769-1852 .. 92,
361
Joseph 1806- 361
Lucy 1808-1881 361
Lydia 1813-1881 .. 361
Phebe 1799-1881 .. 361
Rhoda 1816-1867 . 361
Russell 1800- 361
WILDER
Alamander 1806-1875
.... 458
Betsey 1777-1859 . 195
Caroline 1805-1870
.... 332
Clara 1814-1888 ... 491
George S. 1826-1897
.... 385
Ira 1811-1883 458
WILDES
Abigail 1774-1848 552
WILEY
Christiana 1820-1881
.... 229
Daniel 89, 348
David 1791-1864 .. 546
David -1799 .. 137, 546
Hiram 1809-1878 . 348
James 226
James 1790-1850 546,
547
Jonathan 1796- 226
Robert W. 1825-1897
.... 387
Rodney 1815-1904 387
WILKINS
Abigail 1777-1806 . 88,
341
Abigail 1818-1891 344
Abner 1743-1820 ... 46,
184
Adrian W. 1832-1896
.... 342

Betsey 1793-1872 .. 88,
342
Betsey 1818-1898 . 342
Caroline 1822-1855
.... 344
Charles A. 1838-1844
.... 343
Cyrus K. 1821-1892
.... 342
Darius 1774-1858 . 432
Edward W. 1839-1922
.... 343
Eliza A. 1806-1846 341
Ephraim 1781-1827
.... 88, 341
Ephraim 1816-1817
.... 342
Esther 1830-1842 . 342
Franklin 1824-1828
.... 344
Harriet A. 1834-1913
.... 343
Ira 1793-1858 578
James 1785-1875 .. 88,
342
James 1808-1880 . 342
James W. 1819-1897
.... 342
Jesse 1792-1827 88,
343
Jesse 1826-1826 ... 344
Jesse A. 1828-1902
.... 342
Joseph 1769-1846 504
Lucy 1775-1868 88,
340
Lucy J. 1825-1922 342
Martha 1819-1839 342
Mary 1783-1861 88
Mary -1830 ..... 36, 150
Mary A. 1827-1867
.... 342
Nancy 1790-1874 .. 88,
343
Nancy 1816-1819 . 344
Nancy 1820-1903 . 344
Naomi 1753-1863 .. 88,
344
Nehemiah 1752-1811
.... 21, 87
Nehemiah 1779-1803
.... 88
Nehemiah 1810-1842
.... 344
Polly 1814-1814 342
Polly 1817-1842 342
Richard D. 1811-1884
.... 342
Robert C. 1788-1827
.... 88
Sarah 1774-1816 88
Sarah R. 1813-1887
.... 344
Sarah S. 1823-1882
.... 342

William 1824-1910 342
WILKINSON
Louisa 452
WILLARD
Abram 1796-1863 . 552
Anna 1786-1858 .. 130,
515
Anness 1730-1779 . 33,
139
Benjamin 1794-1866
.... 552
Catherine 1811-1856
.... 580
Henry 1810-1847 . 552
John O. 1789-1832 488
Lovina 1775-1852 200
Lucy 1783- 483
Mary E. 1801-1879
.... 150, 592
Rachel 1804- 552
Rebecca 1809-1849 541
Salmon 1770-1860
.... 139, 551
Salmon 1802-1887 552
Samuel 1800-1837 552
Sarah 1810-1810 .. 552
Schuyler 1789-1850
.... 483
Sybil 1785-1837 ... 483
Wilder 1760-1791 123,
482
WILLIAMS
Abigail 1771-1828 100,
400
Abigail O. 1823-1913
.... 402
Allen 1803- 242
Angeline 1810-1885
.... 489
Bathsheba 1737-1769
.... 14, 55
Caleb D. 1802-1878
.... 231
Catharine 1780- .. 100,
401
Catharine D. 1817-
.... 402
Charles K. 1780-1861
.... 170
Charles R. 1814-1874
.... 380
Charlotte M. 1817-
1844 489
Elias B. 1791-1826 96,
380
Elijah 1797-1872 .. 537
Eliza P. 1821-1873 402
Elizabeth 1768-1796
.... 63, 249
Esther 1828-1916 . 329
George G. 1823-1889
.... 402
Gideon 1824- 485
Henry 1744-1814 .. 23,
100

Descendants of Robert Russell and Mary Marshall

Henry R. 1773- 100
Henry R. 1806-1840
..........................401
Henry W. 1821-1895
..........................402
Jacob 1791-1856 ...548
John 1792- 101
John 1851-1917 629
Joseph 1765-1841 135, 537
Joseph W. 1777-1814
..........................100
Josephus 1807-1878
..........................537
Justin 1804-1883 ..438
Lucy A. 1816-1893 380
Lydia 1785-1861 ..100, 402
Martha 1755-1786 27, 115
Mary 1778- 550
Mary 1806-1890....355
Mary E. 1825-1902
..........................402
Mary P. 1819-1819402
Orestes H. 1808-1885
..........................383
Orrin 1804-1882 ...537
Rachel 1766-1823 .196
Russell 1814-1887.537
Ruth A. 1811-1868401
Sally 1802-1869 522
Sarah A. 1815-1822
..........................402
Susan B. 1827-1828
..........................402
Thomas A. 1809-1869
..........................401
Thomas R. 1783-1827
..................100, 401
Willard 1788-1834
..................101, 402
Willard 1813-1881 402
William 1777-1830356
WILLIAMSON
Adeline 1832- 408
WILLIS
Asenath H. 1825-1906
..........................390
Gideon G. 1812-1869
..........................577
Mary...................6, 24
Mary 1774-1825.... 79, 303
WILLY
Sarah 1822- 501
WILSON
Abigail 1812-.........427
Benjamin 1804- 427
Caroline 1820-1863
..........................451
David 1768-1818...318
Elizabeth 1813-1903
..........................334

Ephraim 1817-1883
..........................427
George 1824-1897.427
Hannah 1794-1846
..........................337
Hiram 1824-1904..604
Indiana 1838-1910620
Jeremiah 1816-1896
..........................427
Job 1776-1851......107, 426
Job 1810-...............427
John 499
Lucinda 1808-.......427
Lucy 1817-1905 351
Lucy 1819-1907 387
Lydia 1814-1872...427
Mary 1811-1886....320
Matthew 1794-1877
..................114, 456
Philea 1803-1858..222
Rebecca 1802-1860320
Rebecca 1823-1906456
Rebekah 1740-1824
..................31, 135
Sarah 1822-1879...438
Sarah A. 1832-1909
..........................308
Sophronia 1808-1890
..........................255
Thankful 1801-1835
..........................222
Thomas 1806-1861427
WINCHESTER
Polly 1779-1844 171
WING
Almira 1801-1834.542
Andrew H. 1813-1873
..........................543
Anna 1811-1812....542
Clarinda 1800-1892
..........................280
Eliza 1802-1886....542
Elizabeth 1803-1880
..........................440
Harriet 1809-1859 542
Martha 1815-1895 543
Mary A. 1806-1855
..........................542
Sabrina 1799-1832542
Sylvanus 1770-1839
..................136, 542
Sylvanus 1805-1846
..........................542
WINN
Silas 1818-1844 619
WINSHIP
Anne 1746-......31, 136
Mary B. 1828-1895
..........................232
WINSLOW
Harriet 1820-1910 498
WINTER
Benjamin 1792-1844
..........................548

Jospeh 1794-1845 .548
Luther 1799-1847.582
Waldo 1802-1887 ..582
William 1802-1883621
WITCHER
Sylvia 1808-1849 ..216
WITHAM
Ann 1830-1869.....158, 629
WITHINGTON
Moses 1828-1900 ..349
WITTER
Orrin 1797-1869 ...229
WOLCOTT
Abigail C. 1830-....489
Perez 1814-1906 ...495
Ruth 1780-1856 201
WOLF
Mabel 1783-1841 .127, 503
WOOD
Anna 1771-1776....173
Anna 1776-1841....173
Asa 1785- 480
Barnabas 1746-1822
..................49, 198
Bazaleel 1780-1849
..........................198
Benjamin 1817-1910
..........................625
Deborah 1772-1852.79
Elijah 1787-1853 ..476
Frederick 1780-1828
..........................470
George 1822-1903.632
Hannah 1788-1846
..........................173
Israel 1744-1800.....44
Israel 1782-1831...173
John 1788-1861 198
Jonathan B. 1771-1805...................198
Joseph 1785-1834.173
Katie 1864- 350
Lois 1774-1861.....173
Lucinda 1793-1825
..........................204
Lucy S. 1808-1883 329
Matilda 1792- 477
Obadiah 1734-181019, 79
Olive 1769-1815....198
Phebe 1769-1801 ..173
Ruth 1779-1865 173
Samuel H. 1791-1826
..........................173
Susanna 1759-1824 79
WOODARD
Nathaniel 1820-1866
..........................587
WOODBRIDGE
Abigail L. 1824-1901
..........................600
Albert 1835-1859 ..600

Caroline 1822-1898
..................598, 600
George 1840-1859.600
Henry W. 1833-1873
..........................600
John R. 1829-1879600
Lydia J. 1827-1898
..........................600
Nancy B. 1814-1880
..........................600
Phebe R. 1816-1848
..........................600
Samuel 1788-1867
..........151, 593, 600
Samuel F. 1818-1906
..........................600
Stephen A. 1831- ..600
WOODBURY
Edward 1761-1793 24, 104
Edward 1791-1834
..................104, 411
Edward N. -1817 ..411
Elizabeth 1789-1868
..................104, 410
Hannah 1788-......104, 410
Hephzibah 1804-1874
..........................352
Lucy 1789-1870 183
Mary 1786-1844...104, 410
Samuel A. 1793-1850
..........................104
WOODCOCK
Dennison 1817-1912
..........................456
WOODMAN
Amos 1794-1859 ...269
Mary 1816-1908....325
Sarah 1803-1838 ..414
Sarah 1814-1875 ..596
WOODRUFF
Caroline C. 1830-1906
..........................244
WOODS
George 1823-1898.281
WOODSIDE
Jane C. 1828-1895 405
WOODWARD
Anna 1794-1858....540
Christina 1810-.....541
Ebenezer 1811-1893
..........................493
Eliza 1801-1835....540
Eliza A. 1824- 637
Elizabeth 1782-1814
..................66, 261
Elizabeth 1788-1830
..................135, 533
Elizabeth 1799-1800
..........................540
Ezra S. 1805-1893 541
Horatio 1785-1856 475

Lucinda 1812-1887 187
Miranda 1822-1863 586
Parker 1803- 268
Perkins B. 1770-1860 .... 136, 540
Perkins B. 1803-1888 541
Phinehas 1797-1800 540
Polly 1795-1800.... 540
Polly 1807- 541
Theodore 1794-1874 268
Washburn 1801-1833 446

WOODWORTH
Eunice 1748-1819.. 28, 117
Ruth -1827 ..... 26, 110

WOOLEY
Emeline 1827-1854 517
Sally 1774-1814... 147, 582
Susan A. 1835-1888 392

WOOSTER
Eleazer 1811-1879 417

WORCESTER
Abigail S. 1821-1899 378
Charles 1813-1903 445
William 1780-1857 268

WORK
Alanson 1799-1879 476
Alexander 1763-1822 .... 121, 475
Alonzo 1810-1878. 286
Anna 1771-1848 .. 121, 477
Ariel 1767-1788.... 121
Ariel 1792-1874.... 476

Asa S. 1795-1803.. 476
Benjamin 1754-1777 121
Benjamin 1807-1880 286
Catherine 1804-1892 517
Elias 1797-1846 ... 476
Elizabeth 1757-1785 .... 121, 474
Emily 1805-1884 .. 286
Ezra D. 1801-1842 286
Hannah 1799-1884 517
Hannah 1804-1840 476
Hannah D. 1814-1896 286
Henry 1752-1832... 74, 121, 285
Henry 1791-1877.. 286
Ingoldsby 1726-1813 .... 28, 120
Ingoldsby 1788-1872 286
John 1796-1862.... 286
John 1802-1862.... 476
Jose J. 1807-1822. 476
Lucy 1765-1801... 121, 476
Lyman 1797-1803 476
Mary 1759-1798.. 121, 475
Mary 1810- 476
Perley 1813- 476
Polly 1779-1816... 125, 492
Polly 1799-1863.... 286
Sarah 1751-1793. 120, 473

WORMWOOD
Mary 1765-1831 ... 277
Molly 44, 174

WORTHEN

Mary M. 1824-1884 409

WORTHING
Sarah 1785-1863. 106, 417

WORTHINGTON
Huldah 1801-1874 226

WORTHLEY
Daniel M. 1798-1878 323

WRAY
David 1815-1872.. 223

WRIGHT
Franklin 1803-1889 341
Hannah 1781-1857 .... 146, 576
Hannah 1810-1857 348
Hiram 1801-1871. 341
John 1797-1881.... 260
Joseph 1770-1836 . 88, 341
Mahala 1805-1871 593
Marilla 1807-1845 317
Mary M. 1819-1900 341
Melantha 1798-1826 341
Neri 1785-1864 242
Sally R. 1800-1874 341
Sarah 1696-1779 8, 32
Solomon 1779-1843 279
Susannah 1700-1760 .... 8, 32
William................. 257
William 1790-328, 555
William 1800-1843 317
William 1804-....... 341

WRIGLEY
Abram 1787-1862. 294

WYETH
Joseph 1797-1872 339

WYMAN

Frank L. 1848-1933 382
James 1788-1847 . 513
John 1804-1883.... 502
Martha 201
Mary 1782-1846 .. 160, 634
William 1765-1842 505

WYNKOOP
Harriet 1797- 290

YALE
Henry 1821-1900 . 361

YENDES
Laurain 1830- 338

YORK
Aaron 1807-1881.. 602
Abraham 1805-1878 602
Albian 1817-1817. 603
Charlotte 1819-1900 603
Daniel 1810-1882. 602
Hester 1823-1920. 603
Martha 1814-1897 603
Mary 1801-1836... 602
Melissa 1821-1881 .... 153, 603
Peter 1779-1862.. 151, 602
Sally 1812-1888 ... 602
Thatcher 1803-1873 602

YOUNG
Amy 1765-1823 ... 113, 450
Benjamin 1785-1857 558
Deborah B. 1832-1917 .... *607*
Winthrop G. 1810-1877 262
Zachariah............. 204

YOUNGLOVE
Irena 1758-... 128, 504

www.ingramcontent.com/pod-product-compliance
Lightning Source LLC
Chambersburg PA
CBHW051426290326
41932CB00049B/3254